9th International Workshop on Semantic Evaluation

(SemEval 2015)

Held with *SEM 2015

Denver, Colorado, USA
4 – 5 June 2015

ISBN: 978-1-5108-0443-2

Printed from e-media with permission by:

Curran Associates, Inc.
57 Morehouse Lane
Red Hook, NY 12571

Some format issues inherent in the e-media version may also appear in this print version.

Printed by Curran Associates, Inc. (2015)

Association for Computational Linguistics
209 N. Eighth Street
Stroudsburg, Pennsylvania 18360

Phone: 1-570-476-8006
Fax: 1-570-476-0860

acl@aclweb.org

Additional copies of this publication are available from:

Curran Associates, Inc.
57 Morehouse Lane
Red Hook, NY 12571 USA
Phone: 845-758-0400
Fax: 845-758-2634
Email: curran@proceedings.com
Web: www.proceedings.com

Welcome to SemEval-2015

The Semantic Evaluation (SemEval) series of workshops focuses on the evaluation and comparison of systems that can analyse diverse semantic phenomena in text with the aim of extending the current state of the art in semantic analysis and creating high quality annotated datasets in a range of increasingly challenging problems in natural language semantics. SemEval provides an exciting forum for researchers to propose challenging research problems in semantics and to build systems/techniques to address such research problems.

SemEval-2015 is the ninth workshop in the series of International Workshops on Semantic Evaluation Exercises. The first three workshops, SensEval-1 (1998), SensEval-2 (2001), and SensEval-3 (2004), focused on word sense disambiguation, each time growing in the number of languages offered, in the number of tasks, and also in the number of participating teams. In 2007, the workshop was renamed to SemEval, and in the following five SemEval workshops (2007–2014) the nature of the tasks evolved to include semantic analysis tasks beyond word sense disambiguation. In 2012, SemEval turned into a yearly event. It currently runs every year, but on a two-year cycle, i.e., the tasks for SemEval-2015 were proposed in 2014.

SemEval-2015 was co-located with the 2015 Conference of the North American Chapter of the Association for Computational Linguistics: Human Language Technologies (NAACL-HLT'2015) in Denver, Colorado. It included the following 17 shared tasks[1] organized in five tracks:

- *Text Similarity and Question Answering* TRACK
  - Task 1: Paraphrase and Semantic Similarity in Twitter
  - Task 2: Semantic Textual Similarity
  - Task 3: Answer Selection in Community Question Answering
- *Time and Space* TRACK
  - Task 4: TimeLine: Cross-Document Event Ordering
  - Task 5: QA TempEval
  - Task 6: Clinical TempEval
  - Task 7: Diachronic Text Evaluation
  - Task 8: SpaceEval
- *Sentiment* TRACK
  - Task 9: CLIPEval Implicit Polarity of Events
  - Task 10: Sentiment Analysis in Twitter
  - Task 11: Sentiment Analysis of Figurative Language in Twitter
  - Task 12: Aspect Based Sentiment Analysis

[1]Task 16 was cancelled after acceptance, but we kept the original numbering

- *Word Sense Disambiguation and Induction* TRACK
  - Task 13: Multilingual All-Words Sense Disambiguation and Entity Linking
  - Task 14: Analysis of Clinical Text
  - Task 15: A CPA Dictionary-Entry-Building Task
- *Learning Semantic Relations* TRACK
  - Task 17: Taxonomy Extraction Evaluation
  - Task 18: Semantic Dependency Parsing

This volume contains both Task Description papers that describe each of the above tasks and System Description papers that describe the systems that participated in the above tasks. A total of 17 task description papers and 145 system description papers are included in this volume.

We are grateful to all task organisers (who organised 17 tasks!) and especially to the task participants whose massive participation (there were about 200 teams who submitted about 600 runs!) has made SemEval once again a successful event. We are thankful to those task organisers who also served as area chairs, and to those task organisers and task participants who helped with reviewing papers by their peers submitted to SemEval-2015: thanks for all the efforts, and for the high-quality, elaborate and thoughtful reviews! The papers in this proceedings have surely benefited from this feedback. We also thank the NAACL'2015 conference organizers for the local organization and the forum. Finally, we most gratefully acknowledge the support of our sponsor, the ACL Special Interest Group on the Lexicon (SIGLEX).

The SemEval-2015 organizers,
Daniel Cer, David Jurgens, Preslav Nakov and Torsten Zesch

SemEval-2015 Chairs:

Daniel Cer, Google
David Jurgens, McGill University
Preslav Nakov, Qatar Computing Research Institute
Torsten Zesch, University of Duisburg-Essen

Area Chairs:

(Some of the task organisers served as area chairs for the system description papers submitted to their tasks; the SemEval chairs also served as area chairs for the task description papers.)

Carmen Banea, University of Michigan
Steven Bethard, University of Alabama at Birmingham
Georgeta Bordea, Insight, NUI Galway
Tommaso Caselli, VU Amsterdam
Daniel Cer, Google
Nathanael Chambers, US Naval Academy
Leon Derczynski, University of Sheffield
Ismail El Maarouf, RIILP, University of Wolverhampton
Noémie Elhadad, Columbia University
Stefano Faralli, Sapienza University of Rome
Dimitris Galanis, Institute for Language and Speech Processing, Athena Research Center
David Jurgens, McGill University
Parisa Kordjamshidi, UIUC
Marco Kuhlmann, Linköping University
Hector Llorens, Nuance Communications
Andrea Moro, Sapienza University of Rome
Nasrin Mostafazadeh, University of Rochester
Lluís Màrquez, Qatar Computing Research Institute
Preslav Nakov, Qatar Computing Research Institute
Stephan Oepen, Universitetet i Oslo
Maria Pontiki, Institute for Language and Speech Processing (ILSP), Athena R.C.
Octavian Popescu, IBM Research
James Pustejovsky, Brandeis University
Paolo Rosso, Universitat Politècnica de València
Irene Russo, ILC CNR
Guergana Savova, Harvard University
Ekaterina Shutova, University of California at Berkeley
Carlo Strapparava, FBK-irst
Naushad UzZaman, Nuance Communications
Marieke van Erp, VU University Amsterdam
Tony Veale, UCD and KAIST
Wei Xu, University of Pennsylvania
Torsten Zesch, Language Technology Lab, University of Duisburg-Essen

Reviewers:

(Most task organisers and task participants also served as reviewers for the workshop.)

Samir Abdelrahman, University of Utah
Rodrigo Agerri, IXA NLP Group, University of the Basque Country (UPV/EHU)
Eneko Agirre, University of the Basque Country (UPV/EHU)
Mariana S. C. Almeida, Priberam / Instituto de Telecomunicações
Ana Alves, CISUC - University of Coimbra and Polythecnic Institute of Coimbra
Silvio Amir, INESC-ID, IST
Marianna Apidianaki, LIMSI-CNRS
Piyush Arora, Dublin City University
Eniafe Festus Ayetiran, CIRSFID, University of Bologna
Vít Baisa, Masaryk University
Niranjan Balasubramanian, University of Washington
Timothy Baldwin, The University of Melbourne
Carmen Banea, University of Michigan
Rajendra Banjade, The University of Memphis
Francesco Barbieri, Pompeu Fabra University, Barcelona
John Barnden, University of Birmingham
Alberto Barrón-Cedeño, Qatar Computing Research Institute
Guntis Barzdins, University of Latvia
Pierpaolo Basile, University of Bari Aldo Moro
Yonatan Belinkov, MIT CSAIL
Patrice Bellot, Aix-Marseille Université (AMU-LSIS)
Sabine Bergler, Concordia University
Dario Bertero, Human Language Technology Center, The Hong Kong University of Science and Technology
Steven Bethard, University of Alabama at Birmingham
Ergun Bicici, ADAPT CNGL Centre for Global Intelligent Content, Dublin City University
William Boag, University of Massachusetts, Lowell
Georgeta Bordea, Insight, NUI Galway
Svetla Boytcheva, Bulgarian Academy of Sciences, IICT
Davide Buscaldi, LIPN, Université Paris 13
Hanna Béchara, RIILP, University of Wolverhampton
Annalina Caputo, University of Bari Aldo Moro
Tommaso Caselli, VU Amsterdam
Esteban Castillo, Universidad de las Américas Puebla
Bamfa Ceesay, National Taiwan Normal University
Daniel Cer, Google
Nathanael Chambers, US Naval Academy
Maryna Chernyshevich, IHS / IHS Global Belarus
Prerna Chikersal, Nanyang Technological University
Guillaume Cleuziou, LIFO - University of Orléans
Kevin Cohen, U. Colorado School of Medicine
Hernani Costa, LEXYTRAD, University of Malaga
Montse Cuadros, Vicomtech-IK4

Jennifer D'Souza, University of Texas at Dallas
Giovanni Da San Martino, Qatar Computing Research Institute
Ayushi Dalmia, International Institute of Information Technology, Hyderabad
Orphee De Clercq, LT3, Ghent University
Gerard de Melo, Tsinghua University
Marcos Didonet Del Fabro, Universidade Federal do Paraná
Leon Derczynski, University of Sheffield
Mona Diab, The George Washington University
Anna Divoli, Pingar Research
Kristina Doing-Harris, University of Utah
Li Dong, Beihang University
Christos Doulkeridis, University of Piraeus
Nadir Durrani, Qatar Computing Research Institute
Sebastian Ebert, Center for Information and Language Processing, University of Munich
Judith Eckle-Kohler, Technische Universität Darmstadt
Asif Ekbal, IIT Patna
Ismail El Maarouf, RIILP, University of Wolverhampton
Noémie Elhadad, Columbia University
Luis Espinosa Anke, Universitat Pompeu Fabra
Asli Eyecioglu, University of Sussex
Stefano Faralli, Sapienza University of Rome
Milagros Fernández-Gavilanes, AtlantTIC Centre - University of Vigo
Simone Filice, University of Roma Tor Vergata
Dimitris Galanis, Institute for Language and Speech Processing, Athena Research Center
Wei Gao, Qatar Computing Research Institute
Jorge Garcia Flores, LIPN - Université Paris 13
Aitor García Pablos, Vicomtech-IK4
Omid Ghiasvand, University of Wisconsin-Milwaukee
Mayte Giménez, UPV
Jim Glass, Massachusetts Institute of Technology
Goran Glavaš, University of Zagreb
Helena Gomez, Center for Computing Reseach - Instituto Politecnico Nacional
Aitor Gonzalez-Agirre, University of the Basque Country (UPV/EHU)
Hugo Gonçalo Oliveira, CISUC, University of Coimbra
Genevieve Gorrell, University of Sheffield
Gregory Grefenstette, INRIA
Tudor Groza, The University of Queensland
Satarupa Guha, International Institute of Information Technology, Hyderabad
Weiwei Guo, Columbia University
Rohit Gupta, University of Wolverhampton
Francisco Guzmán, Qatar Computing Research Institute
Jon Ander Gómez, Universitat Politècnica de València
Nizar Habash, New York University Abu Dhabi
Christian Haenig, ExB Group
Matthias Hagen, Bauhaus-Universität Weimar
Kai Hakala, University of Turku

Hussam Hamdan, AMU
Lushan Han, Samsung Research America
Kazuma Hashimoto, University of Tokyo
Basma Hassan, Fayoum University
Hamed Hassanzadeh, The University of Queensland
Nelly Hateva, Sofia University
Hua He, University of Maryland, College Park
Delia Irazú Hernández Farías, Universitat Politècnica de València
Amin Heydari Alashty, Shiraz University
Chris Hokamp, Dublin City University - CNGL
Veronique Hoste, Ghent University
Yongshuai Hou, Harbin Institute of Technology Shenzhen
Nghia Huynh, University of Science, HoChiMinh City, VietNam
Aminul Islam, Dalhousie University
Angelina Ivanova, University of Oslo
Evan Jaffe, The Ohio State University
Salud M. Jiménez-Zafra, University of Jaén
Lifeng Jin, The Ohio State University
Jitendra Jonnagaddala, UNSW Australia
Shafiq Joty, Qatar Computing Research Institute
Dame Jovanoski, University American College Skopje
Jonathan Juncal-Martínez, AtlantTIC Centre - University of Vigo
David Jurgens, McGill University
Timo Järvinen, Lionbridge Technologies
Jenna Kanerva, University of Turku
Borislav Kapukaranov, Sofia University
Rafael - Michael Karampatsis, University of Edinburgh
Mladen Karan, University of Zagreb
Anderson Kauer, Institute of Informatics - UFRGS
Parisa Kordjamshidi, UIUC
Valia Kordoni, Humboldt University Berlin
Zornitsa Kozareva, Yahoo!
Marina Kraeva, Sofia University
Marco Kuhlmann, Linköping University
Man Lan, East China Normal University
Gabriella Lapesa, Universität Stuttgart, Institut für Maschinelle Sprachverarbeitung - Universität Osnabrück, Institut für Kognitionswissenschaft
André Leal, Faculdade de Ciências da Universidade de Lisboa
Els Lefever, LT3, Ghent University
Aaron Levine, Brandeis University
Binyang Li, University of International Relations
Peijia Li, Institute of Acoustics, Chinese Academy of Sciences
Maria Liakata, University of Warwick
Huizhi Liang, The University of Melbourne
Yang Liu, Harbin Institute of Technology
Hector Llorens, Nuance Communications

Adam Lopez, University of Edinburgh
Wei Lu, Singapore University of Technology and Design
Walid Magdy, Qatar Computing Research Institute
Simone Magnolini, Fondazione Bruno Kessler
Steve L. Manion, University of Canterbury
Justin Martineau, Samsung Research America, Silicon Valley
André F. T. Martins, Priberam, Instituto de Telecomunicacoes
Eugenio Martínez-Cámara, University of Jaén
Sérgio Matos, DETI/IEETA, University of Aveiro, Portugal
Juan Miguel Cejuela, Rostlab, Technical University of Munich
Todor Mihaylov, Sofia University
Chad Mills, University of Washington
Anne-Lyse Minard, FBK
Naoko Miura, Meiji University
Marie-Francine Moens, KU Leuven
Reham Mohamed, Alexandria University
Mitra Mohtarami, MIT Computer Science and Artificial Intelligence Lab
Viviane Moreira, Institute of Informatics - UFRGS
Andrea Moro, Sapienza University of Rome
Alessandro Moschitti, Qatar Computing Research Institute
Nasrin Mostafazadeh, University of Rochester
Danielle L Mowery, University of Utah at Salt Lake City
Hamdy Mubarak, Qatar Computing Research Institute
Lluís Màrquez, Qatar Computing Research Institute
Preslav Nakov, Qatar Computing Research Institute
Vivi Nastase, FBK
Borja Navarro, University of Alicante
Ani Nenkova, University of Pennsylvania
Hoang Long Nguyen, Yeungnam University
Eric Nichols, Honda Research Institute Japan
Massimo Nicosia, Qatar Computing Research Institute, Qatar - University of Trento
Jian-Yun NIE, University of Montreal
Ivelina Nikolova, Bulgarian Academy of Sciences
Nobal Bikram Niraula, The University of Memphis
Nicole Novielli, University of Bari Aldo Moro
Stephan Oepen, Universitetet i Oslo
John Osborne, University of Alabama at Birmingham
Sebastian Padó, Stuttgart University
Haris Papageorgiou, Institute for Language and Speech Processing ILSP/ ATHENA R.C.
Marius Pasca, Google
Parth Pathak, ezDI
Ted Pedersen, University of Minnesota, Duluth
Marco Pennacchiotti, eBay
Mohammad Taher Pilehvar, Sapienza University of Rome
Barbara Plank, University of Copenhagen
Nataliia Plotnikova, FAU Erlangen-Nürnberg

Maria Pontiki, Institute for Language and Speech Processing (ILSP), Athena R.C.
Octavian Popescu, IBM Research
Matt Post, Johns Hopkins University
Marten Postma, VU University Amsterdam
Sameer Pradhan, cemantix.org
Thomas Proisl, FAU Erlangen-Nürnberg
James Pustejovsky, Brandeis University
Md Rashadul Hasan Rakib, Dalhousie University
Carlos Ramisch, LIF, Aix-Marseille Université
Gábor Recski, Research Institute for Linguistics, Hungarian Academy of Sciences
Robert Remus, University of Leipzig
Ravikanth Repaka, University of Minnesota Duluth
Antonio Reyes, Laboratorio de Tecnologías Lingüísticas, Instituto Superior de Intérpretes y Traductores
Alan Ritter, The Ohio State University
Angus Roberts, University of Sheffield
Sara Rosenthal, Columbia University
Paolo Rosso, Universitat Politècnica de València
Pablo Ruiz, LATTICE Lab, ENS
Irene Russo, ILC CNR
Derek Ruths, McGill University
José Saias, Universidade de Evora
Hassan Sajjad, Qatar Computing Research Institute
Haritz Salaberri, University of the Basque Country (UPV/EHU)
Iman Saleh, Cairo University
Iñaki San Vicente, Elhuyar Foundation / IXA - UPV-EHU
Xabier Saralegi, Elhuyar Foundation
Abeed Sarker, Arizona State University
Taneeya Satyapanich, UBMC
Guergana Savova, Harvard University
Carolina Scarton, University of Sheffield
Kim Schouten, Erasmus University Rotterdam
Fabrizio Sebastiani, Qatar Computing Research Institute
Aliaksei Severyn, University of Trento
Ekaterina Shutova, University of California at Berkeley
Veselin Stoyanov, Facebook
Carlo Strapparava, FBK-irst
Jannik Strötgen, Heidelberg University
Roman Sudarikov, Charles University in Prague
Md Arafat Sultan, University of Colorado Boulder
Chengjie SUN, Harbin Institute of Technology
Weiwei Sun, Peking University
Mihai Surdeanu, University of Arizona
Stan Szpakowicz, EECS, University of Ottawa
Terrence Szymanski, University College Dublin
Liling Tan, Universität des Saarlandes

Irina Temnikova, Qatar Computing Research Institute
Hegler Tissot, Federal University of Parana
Zhiqiang Toh, Institute for Infocomm Research
Richard Townsend, University of Warwick
Quan Hung Tran, Japan Advance Institute of Science and Technology
Rocco Tripodi, Ca' Foscari University of Venice
L. Alfonso Urena Lopez, University of Jaen
Fatih Uzdilli, ZHAW Zurich University of Applied Sciences
Naushad UzZaman, Nuance Communications
Rob van der Goot, University of Groningen
Marieke van Erp, VU University Amsterdam
Cynthia Van Hee, LT3, Ghent University
Tony Veale, UCD and KAIST
Sumithra Velupillai, Stockholm University
Ngoc Phuoc An Vo, HLT-FBK, Trento
Tu Thanh Vu, University of Engineering and Technology, Vietnam National University, Hanoi
Viswanadh Kumar Reddy Vuggumudi, University of Minnesota Duluth
Marilyn Walker, University of California Santa Cruz
Dirk Weissenborn, German Research Center for Artificial Intelligence (DFKI)
Richard Wicentowski, Swarthmore College
Wei Xu, University of Pennsylvania
Jun Xu, The University of Texas Health Science Center at Houston
Hongzhi Xu, The Hong Kong Polytechnic University
Zachary Yocum, Brandeis University
Ivana Yovcheva, Sofia University
Dong YU, Beijing Language and Cultrual University
Ivan Zamanov, Sofia University
Marcos Zampieri, University of Cologne
Guido Zarrella, The MITRE Corporation
Torsten Zesch, Language Technology Lab, University of Duisburg-Essen
Zhifei Zhang, University of Montreal
Xiaoqiang Zhou, Harbin Institute of Technology Shenzhen
Judit Ács, Budapest University of Technology and Economics, Hungarian Academy of Sciences
Tamara Álvarez-López, AtlantTIC Centre - University of Vigo
Diarmuid Ó Séaghdha, VocalIQ Ltd/University of Cambridge

Shepherds:

Daniel Cer, Google
Preslav Nakov, Qatar Computing Research Institute

Joint *SEM / SemEval keynote speaker:

Marco Baroni, University of Trento

Table of Contents

This page intentionally left blank.

Conference Program

Thursday, June 4, 2015

08:00–08:30 ***Registration***

08:30–09:00 ***Opening remarks***

09:00–10:00 ***Joint *SEM and SemEval keynote talk by Marco Baroni, "Playing ficles and running with the corbons: What (multimodal) distributional semantic models learn during their childhood"***

Session SE1: Track I - Text Similarity and Question Answering (Session 1)

10:00–10:15 *SemEval-2015 Task 1: Paraphrase and Semantic Similarity in Twitter (PIT)*
Wei Xu, Chris Callison-Burch and Bill Dolan

10:15–10:25 *MITRE: Seven Systems for Semantic Similarity in Tweets*
Guido Zarrella, John Henderson, Elizabeth M. Merkhofer and Laura Strickhart

10:25–11:00 ***Poster Session: Tasks 1, 2, and 3 (Part 1)***

CICBUAPnlp: Graph-Based Approach for Answer Selection in Community Question Answering Task
Helena Gomez, Darnes Vilariño, David Pinto and Grigori Sidorov

HLTC-HKUST: A Neural Network Paraphrase Classifier using Translation Metrics, Semantic Roles and Lexical Similarity Features
Dario Bertero and Pascale Fung

FBK-HLT: An Effective System for Paraphrase Identification and Semantic Similarity in Twitter
Ngoc Phuoc An Vo, Simone Magnolini and Octavian Popescu

ECNU: Leveraging Word Embeddings to Boost Performance for Paraphrase in Twitter
Jiang Zhao and Man Lan

ROB: Using Semantic Meaning to Recognize Paraphrases
Rob van der Goot and Gertjan van Noord

Thursday, June 4, 2015 (continued)

AMRITA_CEN@SemEval-2015: Paraphrase Detection for Twitter using Unsupervised Feature Learning with Recursive Autoencoders
Mahalakshmi Shanumuga Sundaram, Anand Kumar Madasamy and Soman Kotti Padannayil

Ebiquity: Paraphrase and Semantic Similarity in Twitter using Skipgrams
Taneeya Satyapanich, Hang Gao and Tim Finin

RTM-DCU: Predicting Semantic Similarity with Referential Translation Machines
Ergun Bicici

Twitter Paraphrase Identification with Simple Overlap Features and SVMs
Asli Eyecioglu and Bill Keller

TKLBLIIR: Detecting Twitter Paraphrases with TweetingJay
Mladen Karan, Goran Glavaš, Jan Šnajder, Bojana Dalbelo Bašić, Ivan Vulić and Marie-Francine Moens

CDTDS: Predicting Paraphrases in Twitter via Support Vector Regression
Rafael - Michael Karampatsis

yiGou: A Semantic Text Similarity Computing System Based on SVM
Yang Liu, Chengjie Sun, Lei Lin and Xiaolong Wang

USAAR-SHEFFIELD: Semantic Textual Similarity with Deep Regression and Machine Translation Evaluation Metrics
Liling Tan, Carolina Scarton, Lucia Specia and Josef van Genabith

TrWP: Text Relatedness using Word and Phrase Relatedness
Md Rashadul Hasan Rakib, Aminul Islam and Evangelos Milios

MiniExperts: An SVM Approach for Measuring Semantic Textual Similarity
Hanna Béchara, Hernani Costa, Shiva Taslimipoor, Rohit Gupta, Constantin Orasan, Gloria Corpas Pastor and Ruslan Mitkov

FBK-HLT: A New Framework for Semantic Textual Similarity
Ngoc Phuoc An Vo, Simone Magnolini and Octavian Popescu

UMDuluth-BlueTeam: SVCSTS - A Multilingual and Chunk Level Semantic Similarity System
Sakethram Karumuri, Viswanadh Kumar Reddy Vuggumudi and Sai Charan Raj Chitirala

SemantiKLUE: Semantic Textual Similarity with Maximum Weight Matching
Nataliia Plotnikova, Gabriella Lapesa, Thomas Proisl and Stefan Evert

ECNU: Using Traditional Similarity Measurements and Word Embedding for Semantic Textual Similarity Estimation
Jiang Zhao, Man Lan and Jun Feng Tian

UQeResearch: Semantic Textual Similarity Quantification
Hamed Hassanzadeh, Tudor Groza, Anthony Nguyen and Jane Hunter

WSL: Sentence Similarity Using Semantic Distance Between Words
Naoko Miura and Tomohiro Takagi

SOPA: Random Forests Regression for the Semantic Textual Similarity task
Davide Buscaldi, Jorge Garcia Flores, Ivan V. Meza and Isaac Rodriguez

MathLingBudapest: Concept Networks for Semantic Similarity
Gábor Recski and Judit Ács

DCU: Using Distributional Semantics and Domain Adaptation for the Semantic Textual Similarity SemEval-2015 Task 2
Piyush Arora, Chris Hokamp, Jennifer Foster and Gareth Jones

DLS@CU: Sentence Similarity from Word Alignment and Semantic Vector Composition
Md Arafat Sultan, Steven Bethard and Tamara Sumner

FCICU: The Integration between Sense-Based Kernel and Surface-Based Methods to Measure Semantic Textual Similarity
Basma Hassan, Samir AbdelRahman and Reem Bahgat

AZMAT: Sentence Similarity Using Associative Matrices
Evan Jaffe, Lifeng Jin, David King and Marten van Schijndel

NeRoSim: A System for Measuring and Interpreting Semantic Textual Similarity
Rajendra Banjade, Nobal Bikram Niraula, Nabin Maharjan, Vasile Rus, Dan Stefanescu, Mihai Lintean and Dipesh Gautam

Samsung: Align-and-Differentiate Approach to Semantic Textual Similarity
Lushan Han, Justin Martineau, Doreen Cheng and Christopher Thomas

UBC: Cubes for English Semantic Textual Similarity and Supervised Approaches for Interpretable STS
Eneko Agirre, Aitor Gonzalez-Agirre, Inigo Lopez-Gazpio, Montse Maritxalar, German Rigau and Larraitz Uria

ASAP-II: From the Alignment of Phrases to Textual Similarity
Ana Alves, David Simões, Hugo Gonçalo Oliveira and Adriana Ferrugento

Thursday, June 4, 2015 (continued)

TATO: Leveraging on Multiple Strategies for Semantic Textual Similarity
Tu Thanh Vu, Quan Hung Tran and Son Bao Pham

HITSZ-ICRC: Exploiting Classification Approach for Answer Selection in Community Question Answering
Yongshuai Hou, Cong Tan, Xiaolong Wang, Yaoyun Zhang, Jun Xu and Qingcai Chen

QCRI: Answer Selection for Community Question Answering - Experiments for Arabic and English
Massimo Nicosia, Simone Filice, Alberto Barrón-Cedeño, Iman Saleh, Hamdy Mubarak, Wei Gao, Preslav Nakov, Giovanni Da San Martino, Alessandro Moschitti, Kareem Darwish, Lluís Màrquez, Shafiq Joty and Walid Magdy

ICRC-HIT: A Deep Learning based Comment Sequence Labeling System for Answer Selection Challenge
Xiaoqiang Zhou, Baotian Hu, Jiaxin Lin, Yang xiang and Xiaolong Wang

JAIST: Combining multiple features for Answer Selection in Community Question Answering
Quan Hung Tran, Vu Tran, Tu Vu, Minh Nguyen and Son Bao Pham

Shiraz: A Proposed List Wise Approach to Answer Validation
Amin Heydari Alashty, Saeed Rahmani, Meysam Roostaee and Mostafa Fakhrahmad

Al-Bayan: A Knowledge-based System for Arabic Answer Selection
Reham Mohamed, Maha Ragab, Heba Abdelnasser, Nagwa M. El-Makky and Marwan Torki

FBK-HLT: An Application of Semantic Textual Similarity for Answer Selection in Community Question Answering
Ngoc Phuoc An Vo, Simone Magnolini and Octavian Popescu

ECNU: Using Multiple Sources of CQA-based Information for Answers Selection and YES/NO Response Inference
Liang Yi, JianXiang Wang and Man Lan

Voltron: A Hybrid System For Answer Validation Based On Lexical And Distance Features
Ivan Zamanov, Marina Kraeva, Nelly Hateva, Ivana Yovcheva, Ivelina Nikolova and Galia Angelova

CoMiC: Adapting a Short Answer Assessment System for Answer Selection
Björn Rudzewitz and Ramon Ziai

MITRE: Seven Systems for Semantic Similarity in Tweets
Guido Zarrella, John Henderson, Elizabeth M. Merkhofer and Laura Strickhart

ExB Themis: Extensive Feature Extraction from Word Alignments for Semantic Textual Similarity
Christian Hänig, Robert Remus and Xose de la Puente

VectorSLU: A Continuous Word Vector Approach to Answer Selection in Community Question Answering Systems
Yonatan Belinkov, Mitra Mohtarami, Scott Cyphers and James Glass

10:30–11:00 ***Coffee Break and Poster Session***

Session SE2: Track I - Text Similarity and Question Answering (Session 2)

11:00–11:15 *SemEval-2015 Task 2: Semantic Textual Similarity, English, Spanish and Pilot on Interpretability*
Eneko Agirre, Carmen Banea, Claire Cardie, Daniel Cer, Mona Diab, Aitor Gonzalez-Agirre, Weiwei Guo, Inigo Lopez-Gazpio, Montse Maritxalar, Rada Mihalcea, German Rigau, Larraitz Uria and Janyce Wiebe

11:15–11:25 *ExB Themis: Extensive Feature Extraction from Word Alignments for Semantic Textual Similarity*
Christian Hänig, Robert Remus and Xose de la Puente

11:25–11:40 *SemEval-2015 Task 3: Answer Selection in Community Question Answering*
Preslav Nakov, Lluís Màrquez, Walid Magdy, Alessandro Moschitti, Jim Glass and Bilal Randeree

11:40–11:50 *VectorSLU: A Continuous Word Vector Approach to Answer Selection in Community Question Answering Systems*
Yonatan Belinkov, Mitra Mohtarami, Scott Cyphers and James Glass

11:50–12:30 ***Poster Session: Tasks 1, 2, and 3 (Part 2)***

12:30–13:30 ***Lunch Break***

Session SE3: Track IV - Word Sense Disambiguation and Induction

13:30–13:45 *SemEval-2015 Task 13: Multilingual All-Words Sense Disambiguation and Entity Linking*
Andrea Moro and Roberto Navigli

13:45–13:55 *LIMSI: Translations as Source of Indirect Supervision for Multilingual All-Words Sense Disambiguation and Entity Linking*
Marianna Apidianaki and Li Gong

13:55–14:10 *SemEval-2015 Task 14: Analysis of Clinical Text*
Noémie Elhadad, Sameer Pradhan, Sharon Gorman, Suresh Manandhar, Wendy Chapman and Guergana Savova

14:10–14:20 *UTH-CCB: The Participation of the SemEval 2015 Challenge – Task 14*
Jun Xu, Yaoyun Zhang, Jingqi Wang, Yonghui Wu, Min Jiang, Ergin Soysal and Hua Xu

14:20–14:35 *SemEval-2015 Task 15: A CPA dictionary-entry-building task*
Vít Baisa, Jane Bradbury, Silvie Cinkova, Ismail El Maarouf, Adam Kilgarriff and Octavian Popescu

14:35–14:45 *BLCUNLP: Corpus Pattern Analysis for Verbs Based on Dependency Chain*
Yukun Feng, Qiao Deng and Dong Yu

14:45–16:00 ***Poster Session: Tasks 13, 14, and 15***

WSD-games: a Game-Theoretic Algorithm for Unsupervised Word Sense Disambiguation
Rocco Tripodi and Marcello Pelillo

DFKI: Multi-objective Optimization for the Joint Disambiguation of Entities and Nouns & Deep Verb Sense Disambiguation
Dirk Weissenborn, Feiyu Xu and Hans Uszkoreit

EBL-Hope: Multilingual Word Sense Disambiguation Using a Hybrid Knowledge-Based Technique
Eniafe Festus Ayetiran and Guido Boella

VUA-background : When to Use Background Information to Perform Word Sense Disambiguation
Marten Postma, Ruben Izquierdo and Piek Vossen

TeamUFAL: WSD+EL as Document Retrieval
Petr Fanta, Roman Sudarikov and Ondrej Bojar

EL92: Entity Linking Combining Open Source Annotators via Weighted Voting
Pablo Ruiz and Thierry Poibeau

UNIBA: Combining Distributional Semantic Models and Sense Distribution for Multilingual All-Words Sense Disambiguation and Entity Linking
Pierpaolo Basile, Annalina Caputo and Giovanni Semeraro

SUDOKU: Treating Word Sense Disambiguation & Entitiy Linking as a Deterministic Problem - via an Unsupervised & Iterative Approach
Steve L. Manion

TeamHCMUS: Analysis of Clinical Text
Nghia Huynh and Quoc Ho

UTU: Adapting Biomedical Event Extraction System to Disorder Attribute Detection
Kai Hakala

IHS-RD-Belarus: Identification and Normalization of Disorder Concepts in Clinical Notes
Maryna Chernyshevich and Vadim Stankevitch

UWM: A Simple Baseline Method for Identifying Attributes of Disease and Disorder Mentions in Clinical Text
Omid Ghiasvand and Rohit Kate

TAKELAB: Medical Information Extraction and Linking with MINERAL
Goran Glavaš

TMUNSW: Identification of Disorders and Normalization to SNOMED-CT Terminology in Unstructured Clinical Notes
Jitendra Jonnagaddala, Siaw-Teng Liaw, Pradeep Ray, Manish Kumar and Hong-Jie Dai

UtahPOET: Disorder Mention Identification and Context Slot Filling with Cognitive Inspiration
Kristina Doing-Harris, Sean Igo, Jianlin Shi and John Hurdle

ULisboa: Recognition and Normalization of Medical Concepts
André Leal, Bruno Martins and Francisco Couto

Thursday, June 4, 2015 (continued)

ezDI: A Supervised NLP System for Clinical Narrative Analysis
Parth Pathak, Pinal Patel, Vishal Panchal, Sagar Soni, Kinjal Dani, Amrish Patel and Narayan Choudhary

CUAB: Supervised Learning of Disorders and their Attributes using Relations
James Gung, John Osborne and Steven Bethard

BioinformaticsUA: Machine Learning and Rule-Based Recognition of Disorders and Clinical Attributes from Patient Notes
Sérgio Matos, José Sequeira and José Luís Oliveira

LIST-LUX: Disorder Identification from Clinical Texts
Asma Ben Abacha, Aikaterini Karanasiou, Yassine Mrabet and Julio Cesar Dos Reis

CMILLS: Adapting Semantic Role Labeling Features to Dependency Parsing
Chad Mills and Gina-Anne Levow

Duluth: Word Sense Discrimination in the Service of Lexicography
Ted Pedersen

LIMSI: Translations as Source of Indirect Supervision for Multilingual All-Words Sense Disambiguation and Entity Linking
Marianna Apidianaki and Li Gong

UTH-CCB: The Participation of the SemEval 2015 Challenge – Task 14
Jun Xu, Yaoyun Zhang, Jingqi Wang, Yonghui Wu, Min Jiang, Ergin Soysal and Hua Xu

BLCUNLP: Corpus Pattern Analysis for Verbs Based on Dependency Chain
Yukun Feng, Qiao Deng and Dong Yu

15:30–16:00 ***Coffee Break and Poster Session***

Thursday, June 4, 2015 (continued)

Session SE3: Track III - Sentiment

16:00–16:15 *SemEval-2015 Task 9: CLIPEval Implicit Polarity of Events*
Irene Russo, Tommaso Caselli and Carlo Strapparava

16:15–16:30 *SemEval-2015 Task 10: Sentiment Analysis in Twitter*
Sara Rosenthal, Preslav Nakov, Svetlana Kiritchenko, Saif Mohammad, Alan Ritter and Veselin Stoyanov

16:30–16:40 *UNITN: Training Deep Convolutional Neural Network for Twitter Sentiment Classification*
Aliaksei Severyn and Alessandro Moschitti

16:40–16:55 *SemEval-2015 Task 11: Sentiment Analysis of Figurative Language in Twitter*
Aniruddha Ghosh, Guofu Li, Tony Veale, Paolo Rosso, Ekaterina Shutova, John Barnden and Antonio Reyes

16:55–17:05 *CLaC-SentiPipe: SemEval2015 Subtasks 10 B,E, and Task 11*
Canberk Özdemir and Sabine Bergler

17:05–17:20 *SemEval-2015 Task 12: Aspect Based Sentiment Analysis*
Maria Pontiki, Dimitris Galanis, Haris Papageorgiou, Suresh Manandhar and Ion Androutsopoulos

17:20–17:30 *NLANGP: Supervised Machine Learning System for Aspect Category Classification and Opinion Target Extraction*
Zhiqiang Toh and Jian Su

17:30–18:30 ***Poster Session: Tasks 9, 10, 11, and 12***

SHELLFBK: An Information Retrieval-based System For Multi-Domain Sentiment Analysis
Mauro Dragoni

DIEGOLab: An Approach for Message-level Sentiment Classification in Twitter
Abeed Sarker, Azadeh Nikfarjam, Davy Weissenbacher and Graciela Gonzalez

Splusplus: A Feature-Rich Two-stage Classifier for Sentiment Analysis of Tweets
Li Dong, Furu Wei, Yichun Yin, Ming Zhou and Ke Xu

IIIT-H at SemEval 2015: Twitter Sentiment Analysis – The Good, the Bad and the Neutral!
Ayushi Dalmia, Manish Gupta and Vasudeva Varma

Thursday, June 4, 2015 (continued)

CIS-positive: A Combination of Convolutional Neural Networks and Support Vector Machines for Sentiment Analysis in Twitter
Sebastian Ebert, Ngoc Thang Vu and Hinrich Schütze

GTI: An Unsupervised Approach for Sentiment Analysis in Twitter
Milagros Fernández-Gavilanes, Tamara Álvarez-López, Jonathan Juncal-Martínez, Enrique Costa-Montenegro and Francisco Javier González-Castaño

Gradiant-Analytics: Training Polarity Shifters with CRFs for Message Level Polarity Detection
Héctor Cerezo-Costas and Diego Celix-Salgado

IOA: Improving SVM Based Sentiment Classification Through Post Processing
Peijia Li, Weiqun Xu, Chenglong Ma, Jia Sun and Yonghong Yan

RoseMerry: A Baseline Message-level Sentiment Classification System
Huizhi Liang, Richard Fothergill and Timothy Baldwin

UDLAP: Sentiment Analysis Using a Graph-Based Representation
Esteban Castillo, Ofelia Cervantes, Darnes Vilariño, David Báez and Alfredo Sánchez

ECNU: Multi-level Sentiment Analysis on Twitter Using Traditional Linguistic Features and Word Embedding Features
Zhihua Zhang, Guoshun Wu and Man Lan

Lsislif: Feature Extraction and Label Weighting for Sentiment Analysis in Twitter
Hussam Hamdan, Patrice Bellot and Frederic Bechet

ELiRF: A SVM Approach for SA tasks in Twitter at SemEval-2015
Mayte Giménez, Ferran Pla and Lluís-F. Hurtado

Webis: An Ensemble for Twitter Sentiment Detection
Matthias Hagen, Martin Potthast, Michel Büchner and Benno Stein

Sentibase: Sentiment Analysis in Twitter on a Budget
Satarupa Guha, Aditya Joshi and Vasudeva Varma

UNIBA: Sentiment Analysis of English Tweets Combining Micro-blogging, Lexicon and Semantic Features
Pierpaolo Basile and Nicole Novielli

IITPSemEval: Sentiment Discovery from 140 Characters
Ayush Kumar, Vamsi Krishna and Asif Ekbal

Thursday, June 4, 2015 (continued)

Swiss-Chocolate: Combining Flipout Regularization and Random Forests with Artificially Built Subsystems to Boost Text-Classification for Sentiment
Fatih Uzdilli, Martin Jaggi, Dominic Egger, Pascal Julmy, Leon Derczynski and Mark Cieliebak

INESC-ID: A Regression Model for Large Scale Twitter Sentiment Lexicon Induction
Silvio Amir, Wang Ling, Ramón Astudillo, Bruno Martins, Mario J. Silva and Isabel Trancoso

KLUEless: Polarity Classification and Association
Nataliia Plotnikova, Micha Kohl, Kevin Volkert, Stefan Evert, Andreas Lerner, Natalie Dykes and Heiko Ermer

SWASH: A Naive Bayes Classifier for Tweet Sentiment Identification
Ruth Talbot, Chloe Acheampong and Richard Wicentowski

SWATCS65: Sentiment Classification Using an Ensemble of Class Projects
Richard Wicentowski

SWATAC: A Sentiment Analyzer using One-Vs-Rest Logistic Regression
Yousef Alhessi and Richard Wicentowski

TwitterHawk: A Feature Bucket Based Approach to Sentiment Analysis
William Boag, Peter Potash and Anna Rumshisky

SeNTU: Sentiment Analysis of Tweets by Combining a Rule-based Classifier with Supervised Learning
Prerna Chikersal, Soujanya Poria and Erik Cambria

INESC-ID: Sentiment Analysis without Hand-Coded Features or Linguistic Resources using Embedding Subspaces
Ramón Astudillo, Silvio Amir, Wang Ling, Bruno Martins, Mario J. Silva and Isabel Trancoso

WarwickDCS: From Phrase-Based to Target-Specific Sentiment Recognition
Richard Townsend, Adam Tsakalidis, Yiwei Zhou, Bo Wang, Maria Liakata, Arkaitz Zubiaga, Alexandra Cristea and Rob Procter

UIR-PKU: Twitter-OpinMiner System for Sentiment Analysis in Twitter at SemEval 2015
Xu Han, Binyang Li, Jing Ma, Yuxiao Zhang, Gaoyan Ou, Tengjiao Wang and Kam-fai Wong

Thursday, June 4, 2015 (continued)

Friday, June 5, 2015

Session SE5: Track II - Time and Space (Part 1)

09:00–09:15 *SemEval-2015 Task 4: TimeLine: Cross-Document Event Ordering*
Anne-Lyse Minard, Manuela Speranza, Eneko Agirre, Itziar Aldabe, Marieke van Erp, Bernardo Magnini, German Rigau and Ruben Urizar

09:15–09:25 *SPINOZA_VU: An NLP Pipeline for Cross Document TimeLines*
Tommaso Caselli, Antske Fokkens, Roser Morante and Piek Vossen

09:25–09:40 *SemEval-2015 Task 5: QA TempEval - Evaluating Temporal Information Understanding with Question Answering*
Hector Llorens, Nathanael Chambers, Naushad UzZaman, Nasrin Mostafazadeh, James Allen and James Pustejovsky

09:40–09:50 *HLT-FBK: a Complete Temporal Processing System for QA TempEval*
Paramita Mirza and Anne-Lyse Minard

09:50–10:05 *SemEval-2015 Task 6: Clinical TempEval*
Steven Bethard, Leon Derczynski, Guergana Savova, James Pustejovsky and Marc Verhagen

10:05–10:15 *BluLab: Temporal Information Extraction for the 2015 Clinical TempEval Challenge*
Sumithra Velupillai, Danielle L Mowery, Samir Abdelrahman, Lee Christensen and Wendy Chapman

10:15–11:00 ***Poster Session: Tasks 4, 5, 6, 7, and 8 (Part 1)***

GPLSIUA: Combining Temporal Information and Topic Modeling for Cross-Document Event Ordering
Borja Navarro and Estela Saquete

HeidelToul: A Baseline Approach for Cross-document Event Ordering
Bilel Moulahi, Jannik Strötgen, Michael Gertz and Lynda Tamine

HITSZ-ICRC: An Integration Approach for QA TempEval Challenge
Yongshuai Hou, Cong Tan, Qingcai Chen and Xiaolong Wang

Friday, June 5, 2015 (continued)

UFPRSheffield: Contrasting Rule-based and Support Vector Machine Approaches to Time Expression Identification in Clinical TempEval
Hegler Tissot, Genevieve Gorrell, Angus Roberts, Leon Derczynski and Marcos Didonet Del Fabro

IXAGroupEHUDiac: A Multiple Approach System towards the Diachronic Evaluation of Texts
Haritz Salaberri, Iker Salaberri, Olatz Arregi and Beñat Zapirain

USAAR-CHRONOS: Crawling the Web for Temporal Annotations
Liling Tan and Noam Ordan

AMBRA: A Ranking Approach to Temporal Text Classification
Marcos Zampieri, Alina Maria Ciobanu, Vlad Niculae and Liviu P. Dinu

IXAGroupEHUSpaceEval: (X-Space) A WordNet-based approach towards the Automatic Recognition of Spatial Information following the ISO-Space Annotation Scheme
Haritz Salaberri, Olatz Arregi and Beñat Zapirain

UTD: Ensemble-Based Spatial Relation Extraction
Jennifer D'Souza and Vincent Ng

SPINOZA_VU: An NLP Pipeline for Cross Document TimeLines
Tommaso Caselli, Antske Fokkens, Roser Morante and Piek Vossen

HLT-FBK: a Complete Temporal Processing System for QA TempEval
Paramita Mirza and Anne-Lyse Minard

BluLab: Temporal Information Extraction for the 2015 Clinical TempEval Challenge
Sumithra Velupillai, Danielle L Mowery, Samir Abdelrahman, Lee Christensen and Wendy Chapman

UCD : Diachronic Text Classification with Character, Word, and Syntactic N-grams
Terrence Szymanski and Gerard Lynch

SpRL-CWW: Spatial Relation Classification with Independent Multi-class Models
Eric Nichols and Fadi Botros

10:30–11:00 ***Coffee Break and Poster Session***

Friday, June 5, 2015 (continued)

Session SE6: Track II - Time and Space (Part 2)

11:00–11:15 *SemEval 2015, Task 7: Diachronic Text Evaluation*
Octavian Popescu and Carlo Strapparava

11:15–11:25 *UCD : Diachronic Text Classification with Character, Word, and Syntactic N-grams*
Terrence Szymanski and Gerard Lynch

11:25–11:40 *SemEval-2015 Task 8: SpaceEval*
James Pustejovsky, Parisa Kordjamshidi, Marie-Francine Moens, Aaron Levine, Seth Dworman and Zachary Yocum

11:40–11:50 *SpRL-CWW: Spatial Relation Classification with Independent Multi-class Models*
Eric Nichols and Fadi Botros

11:50–12:30 ***Poster Session: Tasks 4, 5, 6, 7, and 8 (Part 2)***

12:30–14:00 ***Lunch Break***

Session SE6: Track V - Learning Semantic Relations

14:00–14:15 *SemEval-2015 Task 17: Taxonomy Extraction Evaluation (TExEval)*
Georgeta Bordea, Paul Buitelaar, Stefano Faralli and Roberto Navigli

14:15–14:25 *INRIASAC: Simple Hypernym Extraction Methods*
Gregory Grefenstette

14:25–14:40 *SemEval 2015 Task 18: Broad-Coverage Semantic Dependency Parsing*
Stephan Oepen, Marco Kuhlmann, Yusuke Miyao, Daniel Zeman, Silvie Cinkova, Dan Flickinger, Jan Hajic and Zdenka Uresova

14:40–14:50 *Peking: Building Semantic Dependency Graphs with a Hybrid Parser*
Yantao Du, Fan Zhang, Xun Zhang, Weiwei Sun and Xiaojun Wan

14:50–16:00 ***Poster Session: Tasks 17 and 18***

Friday, June 5, 2015 (continued)

USAAR-WLV: Hypernym Generation with Deep Neural Nets
Liling Tan, Rohit Gupta and Josef van Genabith

NTNU: An Unsupervised Knowledge Approach for Taxonomy Extraction
Bamfa Ceesay and Wen Juan Hou

LT3: A Multi-modular Approach to Automatic Taxonomy Construction
Els Lefever

TALN-UPF: Taxonomy Learning Exploiting CRF-Based Hypernym Extraction on Encyclopedic Definitions
Luis Espinosa Anke, Horacio Saggion and Francesco Ronzano

QASSIT: A Pretopological Framework for the Automatic Construction of Lexical Taxonomies from Raw Texts
Guillaume Cleuziou, Davide Buscaldi, Gaël Dias, Vincent Levorato and Christine Largeron

Riga: from FrameNet to Semantic Frames with C6.0 Rules
Guntis Barzdins, Peteris Paikens and Didzis Gosko

Turku: Semantic Dependency Parsing as a Sequence Classification
Jenna Kanerva, Juhani Luotolahti and Filip Ginter

Lisbon: Evaluating TurboSemanticParser on Multiple Languages and Out-of-Domain Data
Mariana S. C. Almeida and André F. T. Martins

INRIASAC: Simple Hypernym Extraction Methods
Gregory Grefenstette

Peking: Building Semantic Dependency Graphs with a Hybrid Parser
Yantao Du, Fan Zhang, Xun Zhang, Weiwei Sun and Xiaojun Wan

15:30–16:00 ***Coffee Break and Poster Session***

16:00–16:40 ***SemEval-2016 Task Announcements***

16:40–17:40 ***Closing Session (statistics, polls, questions)***

SemEval-2015 Task 1: Paraphrase and Semantic Similarity in Twitter (PIT)

Wei Xu and Chris Callison-Burch
University of Pennsylvania
Philadelphia, PA, USA
xwe, ccb@cis.upenn.edu

William B. Dolan
Microsoft Research
Redmond, WA, USA
billdol@microsoft.com

Abstract

In this shared task, we present evaluations on two related tasks Paraphrase Identification (PI) and Semantic Textual Similarity (SS) systems for the Twitter data. Given a pair of sentences, participants are asked to produce a binary yes/no judgement or a graded score to measure their semantic equivalence. The task features a newly constructed Twitter Paraphrase Corpus that contains 18,762 sentence pairs. A total of 19 teams participated, submitting 36 runs to the PI task and 26 runs to the SS task. The evaluation shows encouraging results and open challenges for future research. The best systems scored a F1-measure of 0.674 for the PI task and a Pearson correlation of 0.619 for the SS task respectively, comparing to a strong baseline using logistic regression model of 0.589 F1 and 0.511 Pearson; while the best SS systems can often reach >0.80 Pearson on well-formed text. This shared task also provides insights into the relation between the PI and SS tasks and suggests the importance to bringing these two research areas together. We make all the data, baseline systems and evaluation scripts publicly available.[1]

1 Introduction

The ability to identify paraphrases, i.e. alternative expressions of the same (or similar) meaning, and the degree of their semantic similarity has proven useful for a wide variety of natural language processing applications (Madnani and Dorr, 2010). It is particularly useful to overcome the challenge of high redundancy in Twitter and the sparsity inherent in their short texts (e.g. *oscar nom'd doc* ↔ *Oscar-nominated documentary*; *some1 shot a cop* ↔ *someone shot a police*). Emerging research shows paraphrasing techniques applied to Twitter data can improve tasks like first story detection (Petrović et al., 2012), information retrieval (Zanzotto et al., 2011) and text normalization (Xu et al., 2013; Wang et al., 2013).

Previously, many researchers have investigated ways of automatically detecting paraphrases on more formal texts, like newswire text. The ACL Wiki[2] gives an excellent summary of the state-of-the-art paraphrase identification techniques. These can be categorized into supervised methods (Qiu et al., 2006; Wan et al., 2006; Das and Smith, 2009; Socher et al., 2011; Blacoe and Lapata, 2012; Madnani et al., 2012; Ji and Eisenstein, 2013) and unsupervised methods (Mihalcea et al., 2006; Rus et al., 2008; Fernando and Stevenson, 2008; Islam and Inkpen, 2007; Hassan and Mihalcea, 2011). A few recent studies have highlighted the potential and importance of developing paraphrase identification (Zanzotto et al., 2011; Xu et al., 2013) and semantic similarity techniques (Guo and Diab, 2012) specifically for tweets. They also indicated that the very informal language, especially the high degree of lexical variation, used in social media has posed serious challenges to both tasks.

[1] http://www.cis.upenn.edu/~xwe/semeval2015pit/

[2] http://aclweb.org/aclwiki/index.php?title=Paraphrase_Identification_(State_of_the_art)

Paraphrase?	Sentence 1	Sentence 2
yes	Ezekiel Ansah wearing 3D glasses wout the lens	Wait Ezekiel ansah is wearing 3d movie glasses with the lenses knocked out
yes	Marriage equality law passed in Rhode Island	Congrats to Rhode Island becoming the 10th state to enact marriage equality
yes	Aaaaaaaaand stephen curry is on fire	What a incredible performance from Stephen Curry
no	Finally saw the Ciara body party video	ciara s Body Party video is on point
no	Now lazy to watch Manchester united vs arsenal	Early lead for Arsenal against Manchester United
debatable	That s the new Ciroc flavor	Need a little taste of that new Ciroc
debatable	sarah Palin at the IndyMia game	Sarah Palin is at the game are you pumped

Table 1: Representative examples from PIT-2015 Twitter Paraphrase Corpus

	# Unique Sent	# Sent Pair	# Paraphrase	# Non-Paraphrase	# Debatable
Train	13231	13063	3996 (30.6%)	7534 (57.7%)	1533 (11.7%)
Dev	4772	4727	1470 (31.1%)	2672 (56.5%)	585 (12.4%)
Test	1295	972	175 (18.0%)	663 (68.2%)	134 (13.8%)

Table 2: Statistics of PIT-2015 Twitter Paraphrase Corpus. Debatable cases are those received a medium-score from annotators. The percentage of paraphrases is lower in the test set because it was constructed without topic selection.

The SemEval-2015 shared task on **P**araphrase and Semantic Similarity **I**n **T**witter (PIT) uses a training and development set of 17,790 sentence pairs and a test set of 972 sentence pairs with paraphrase annotations (see examples in Table 1) that is the same as the Twitter Paraphrase Corpus we developed earlier in (Xu, 2014) and (Xu et al., 2014). This PIT-2015 paraphrase dataset is distinct from the data used in previous studies in many aspects: (i) it contains sentences that are opinionated and colloquial, representing realistic informal language usage; (ii) it contains paraphrases that are lexically diverse; and (iii) it contains sentences that are lexically similar but semantically dissimilar. It raises many interesting research questions and could lead to a better understanding of our daily used language and how semantics can be captured in such language. We believe that such a common testbed will facilitate docking of the different approaches for purposes of comparison, lead to a better understanding of how semantics are conveyed in natural language, and help advance other NLP techniques for noisy user-generated text in the long run.

2 Task Description and Evaluation Metrics

The task has two sentence-level sub-tasks: a paraphrase identification task and an optional semantic textual similarity task. The two sub-tasks share the same data but differ in annotation and evaluation.

Task A – Paraphrase Identification (PI)
Given two sentences, determine whether they express the same or very similar meaning. Following the literature on paraphrase identification, we evaluate system performance by the F-1 score (harmonic mean of precision and recall) against human judgements.

Task B – Semantic Textual Similarity (SS)
Given two sentences, determine a numerical score between 0 (no relation) and 1 (semantic equivalence) to indicate their semantic similarity. Following the literature, the system outputs are compared by Pearson correlation with human scores. We also compute the maximum F-1 score over the precision-recall curve as an additional data point.

3 Corpus

In this shared task, we use the Twitter Paraphrase Corpus that we first presented in (Xu, 2014) and (Xu et al., 2014). Table 2 shows the basic statistics of the corpus. The sentences are preprocessed with tokenization,[3] POS and named entity tags.[4] The training and development set consists of 17,790 sentence pairs posted between April 24th and May 3rd, 2013 from 500+ trending topics featured on Twitter (excluding hashtags). The training and development set is a random split. Each sentence pair is annotated by 5 different crowdsourcing workers. For the test set, we obtain both crowdsourced and expert labels on 972 sentence pairs from 20 randomly sampled Twitter trending topics between May 13th and June 10th, 2013. We use expert labels in this SemEval evaluation. Our dataset is more realistic and balanced, containing about 70% non-paraphrases vs. the 34% non-paraphrases in the benchmark Microsoft Paraphrase Corpus derived from news articles by Dolan et al. (2004). As noted in (Das and Smith, 2009), the lack of natural non-paraphrases in the MSR corpus creates bias towards certain models.

4 Annotation

In this section, we describe our data collection and annotation methodology. Since Twitter users are free to talk about anything regarding any topic, a random pair of sentences about the same topic has a low chance of expressing the same meaning (empirically, this is less than 8%). This causes two problems: a) it is expensive to obtain paraphrases via manual annotation; b) non-expert annotators tend to loosen the criteria and are more likely to make false positive errors. To address these challenges, we design a simple annotation task and introduce two selection mechanisms to select sentences which are more likely to be paraphrases, while preserving diversity and representativeness.

[3]The tokenizer was developed by O'Connor et al. (2010): https://github.com/brendano/tweetmotif

[4]The POS tagger was developed by Derczynski et al. (2013) and the NER tagger was developed by Ritter et al. (2011): https://github.com/aritter/twitter_nlp

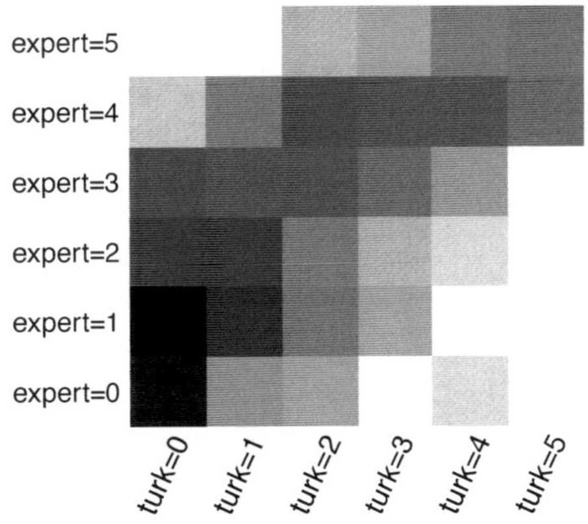

Figure 1: A heat-map showing overlap between expert and crowdsourcing annotation. The intensity along the diagonal indicates good reliability of crowdsourcing workers for this particular task; and the shift above the diagonal reflects the difference between the two annotation schemas. For crowdsourcing (turk), the numbers indicate how many annotators out of 5 picked the sentence pair as paraphrases; 0,1 are considered non-paraphrases; 3,4,5 are paraphrases. For expert annotation, all 0,1,2 are non-paraphrases; 4,5 are paraphrases. Medium-scored cases (2 for crowdsourcing; 3 for expert annotation) are discarded in the system evaluation of the PI sub-task.

4.1 Raw Data from Twitter

We crawl Twitter's trending topics and their associated tweets using public APIs.[5] According to Twitter, trends are determined by an algorithm which identifies topics that are immediately popular, rather than those that have been popular for longer periods of time or which trend on a daily basis. We tokenize, remove emoticons[6] and split tweet into sentences.

4.2 Task Design on Mechanical Turk

We show the annotator an **original** sentence, then ask them to pick sentences with the same meaning from 10 **candidate** sentences. The original and candidate sentences are randomly sampled from the same topic. For each such 1 vs. 10 question, we obtain binary judgements from 5 different annotators, paying each annotator $0.02 per question. On average, each question takes one annotator about 30 $\sim$ 45 seconds to answer.

[5]More information about Twitter's APIs: https://dev.twitter.com/docs/api/1.1/overview

[6]We use the toolkit developed by O'Connor et al. (2010): https://github.com/brendano/tweetmotif

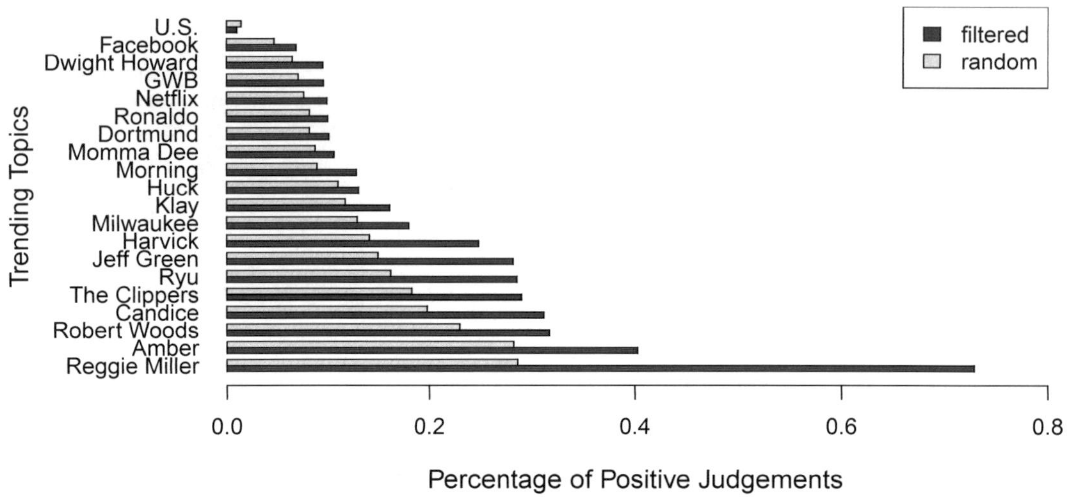

Figure 2: The proportion of paraphrases (percentage of positive votes from annotators) vary greatly across different topics. Automatic filtering in Section 4.4 roughly doubles the paraphrase yield.

4.3 Annotation Quality

We remove problematic annotators by checking their Cohen's Kappa agreement (Artstein and Poesio, 2008) with other annotators. We also compute inter-annotator agreement with an expert annotator on the test dataset of 972 sentence pairs. In the expert annotation, we adopt a 5-point Likert scale to measure the degree of semantic similarity between sentences, which is defined by Agirre et al. (2012) as follows:

5: Completely equivalent, as they mean the same thing;
4: Mostly equivalent, but some unimportant details differ;
3: Roughly equivalent, but some important information differs/missing.
2: Not equivalent, but share some details;
1: Not equivalent, but are on the same topic;
0: On different topics.

Although the two scales of expert and crowdsourcing annotation are defined differently, their Pearson correlation coefficient reaches 0.735 (two-tailed significance 0.001). Figure 1 shows a heatmap representing the detailed overlap between the two annotations. It suggests that the graded similarity annotation task could be reduced to a binary choice in a crowdsourcing setup. As for the binary paraphrase judgements, the integrated judgement of five crowdsourcing workers achieve a F1-score of 0.823, precision of 0.752 and recall of 0.908 against expert annotations.

4.4 Automatic Summarization Inspired Sentence Filtering

We filter the sentences within each topic to select more probable paraphrases for annotation. Our method is inspired by a typical problem in extractive summarization, that the salient sentences are likely redundant (paraphrases) and need to be removed in the output summaries. We employ the scoring method used in SumBasic (Nenkova and Vanderwende, 2005; Vanderwende et al., 2007), a simple but powerful summarization system, to find salient sentences. For each topic, we compute the probability of each word $P(w_i)$ by simply dividing its frequency by the total number of all words in all sentences. Each sentence s is scored as the average of the probabilities of the words in it, i.e.

$$Salience(s) = \sum_{w_i \in s} \frac{P(w_i)}{|\{w_i | w_i \in s\}|} \quad (1)$$

We then rank the sentences and pick the **original** sentence randomly from top 10% salient sentences and **candidate** sentences from top 50% to present to the annotators.

In a trial experiment of 20 topics, the filtering technique double the yield of paraphrases from 152 to 329 out of 2000 sentence pairs over naïve random sampling (Figure 2 and Figure 3). We also use PINC (Chen and Dolan, 2011) to measure the quality of paraphrases collected (Figure 4). PINC was designed to measure n-gram dissimilarity between two sentences, and in essence it is the inverse of BLEU. In general, the cases with high PINC scores include more complex and interesting rephrasings.

4.5 Topic Selection using Multi-Armed Bandits (MAB) Algorithm

Another approach to increasing paraphrase yield is to choose more appropriate topics. This is particularly important because the number of paraphrases varies greatly from topic to topic and thus the chance to encounter paraphrases during annotation (Figure 2). We treat this topic selection problem as a variation of the Multi-Armed Bandit (MAB) problem (Robbins, 1985) and adapt a greedy algorithm, the bounded ϵ-first algorithm, of Tran-Thanh et al. (2012) to accelerate our corpus construction.

Our strategy consists of two phases. In the first exploration phase, we dedicate a fraction of the total budget, ϵ, to explore randomly chosen arms of each slot machine (trending topic on Twitter), each m times. In the second exploitation phase, we sort all topics according to their estimated proportion of paraphrases, and sequentially annotate $\lceil \frac{(1-\epsilon)B}{l-m} \rceil$ arms that have the highest estimated reward until reaching the maximum $l = 10$ annotations for any topic to insure data diversity.

We tune the parameters m to be 1 and ϵ to be between 0.35 $\sim$ 0.55 through simulation experiments, by artificially duplicating a small amount of real annotation data. We then apply this MAB algorithm in the real-world. We explore 500 random topics and then exploited 100 of them. The yield of paraphrases rises to 688 out of 2000 sentence pairs by using MAB and sentence filtering, a 4-fold increase compared to only using random selection (Figure 3).

5 Baselines

We provide three baselines, including a random baseline, a strong supervised baseline and a state-of-the-art unsupervised system:

Random:
This baseline provides a randomized real number between [0, 1] for each test sentence pair as semantic similarity score, and uses 0.5 as cutoff for binary paraphrase identification output.

Logistic Regression:
This is a supervised logistic regression (LR) baseline used by Das and Smith (2009). It uses simple n-gram (also in stemmed form) overlapping features but shows very competitive performance on the MSR news paraphrase corpus. It uses 0.5 as cutoff to create binary outputs for the paraphrase identification task.

Weighted Matrix Factorization (WTMF):[7]
The third baseline is a state-of-the-art unsupervised method developed by Guo and Diab (2012). It is specially developed for short sentences by modeling the semantic space of both words that are present in and absent from the sentences (Guo and Diab, 2012). The model was learned from WordNet (Fellbaum, 2010), OntoNotes (Hovy et al., 2006), Wiktionary, the Brown corpus (Francis and Kucera, 1979). It uses 0.5 as cutoff in the binary paraphrase identification task.

6 Systems and Results

A total of 18 teams participated in the PI task (required), 13 of which also submitted to the SS task (optional). Every team submitted 2 runs except one (up to 2 were are allowed).

6.1 Evaluation Results

Table 3 shows the evaluation results. We use the F1-score and Pearson correlation as the primary evaluation metric for the PI and SS task respectively. The results are very exciting that most systems outperformed the two strong baselines we chose, while still showing room for improvement towards the human upper-bound estimated by the crowdsourcing worker's performance.

6.2 Discussion

Most participants choose supervised methods, except for MathLingBp who uses semi-supervised,

[7]The source code and data for WTMF is available at: `http://www.cs.columbia.edu/~weiwei/code.html`

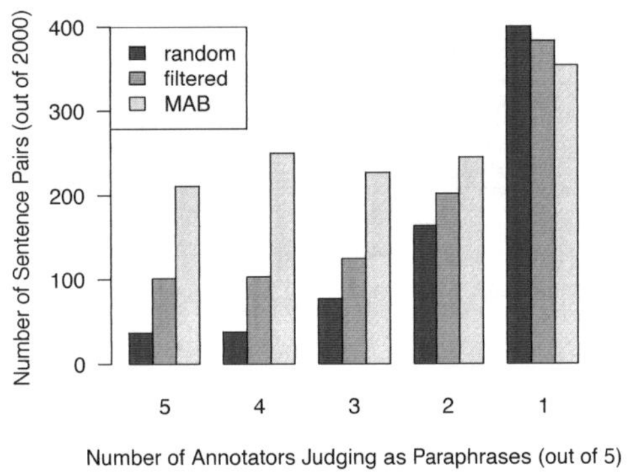

Figure 3: Numbers of paraphrases collected by different methods. The annotation efficiency (3,4,5 are regarded as paraphrases) is significantly improved by the sentence filtering and Multi-Armed Bandits (MAB) based topic selection.

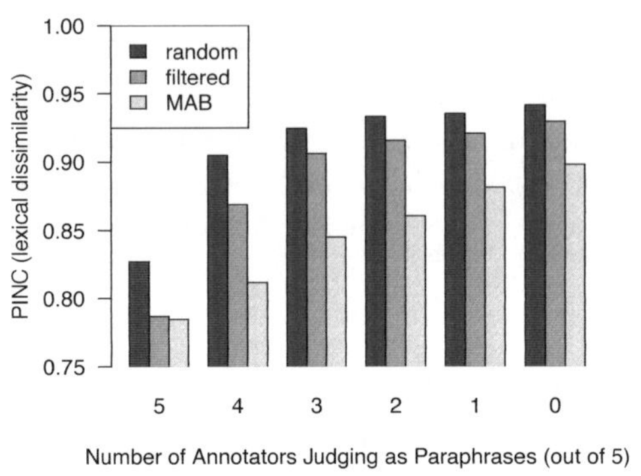

Figure 4: PINC scores of paraphrases collected. The higher the PINC, the more significant the rewording. Our proposed annotation strategy quadruples paraphrase yield, while not greatly reducing diversity as measured by PINC.

Columbia and Yamraj who use unsupervised methods. While the best performed systems are supervised, the best unsupervised system still outperforms some supervised systems and the state-of-the-art unsupervised baseline. About half of systems use word embeddings and many use neural networks.

To out best knowledge, this is the first time to have a large number of systems in an evaluation that has the two related tasks — paraphrase identification and semantic similarity, side by side for comparison. One interesting observation that comes out is the performance of the same system on the two tasks ("F1 vs. Pearson") are not necessarily related. For example, ASOBEK ranked 1st (out of 35 runs) and 18th (out of 25 runs) in the PI and SS tasks respectively, RTM-DCU ranked 27th and 3rd, while the MITRE system ranked 3nd and 1st place. Neither "F1 vs. max-F1" nor "Pearson vs. maxF1" nor "F1 vs. Pearson" show a strong correlation. It implies that (i) high-performance PI systems can be developed focusing on the binary classification problem without focusing on the degree of similarity; (ii) it is crucial to select the threshold to balance precision and recall for the PI binary classification problem; (iii) it is important for SS system to handle the debatable cases proporiately.

6.3 Participants' Systems

There are in total 19 teams participated:

AJ: This team utilizes TERp and BLEU – automatic evaluation metrics for Machine Translation. The system uses a logistic regression model and performs threshold selection.

AMRITACEN: This team uses Recursive Auto Encoders (RAEs). The matrix generated for the given input sentences is of variable size, then converted to equal sized matrix using repeat matrix concept.

ASOBEK (Eyecioglu and Keller, 2015): This team uses SVM classifier with simple lexical word overlap and character n-grams features.

CDTDS (Karampatsis, 2015): This team uses support vector regression trained only on the training set using the numbers of positive votes out of the 5 crowdsourcing annotations.

Columbia: This system maps each original sentence to a low dimensional vector as Orthogonal Matrix Factorization (Guo et al., 2014), and then computes similarity score based on the low dimensional vectors.

Depth: This team uses neural network that learns representation of sentences, then compute similarity scores based on hidden vector representations between two sentences.

EBIQUITY (Satyapanich et al., 2015): This team trains supervised SVM and logistic re-

Rank				Paraphrase Identification (PI)			Semantic Similarity (SS)			
PI	SS	Team	Run	F1	Precision	Recall	Pearson	maxF1	mPrec	mRecall
		Human Upperbound		**0.823**	**0.752**	**0.908**	**0.735**	—	—	—
1		ASOBEK	01_svckernel	0.674^{1}	0.680	0.669	0.475^{18}	0.616	0.732	0.531
	8	ASOBEK	02_linearsvm	0.672^{2}	0.682	0.663	0.504^{14}	0.663	0.723	0.611
2	1	MITRE	01_ikr	0.667^{3}	0.569	0.806	0.619^{1}	0.716	0.750	0.686
3		ECNU	02_nnfeats	0.662^{4}	0.767	0.583	—	—	—	—
4		FBK-HLT	01_voted	0.659^{5}	0.685	0.634	0.462^{19}	0.607	0.551	0.674
5		TKLBLIIR	02_gs0105	0.659^{5}	0.645	0.674	—	—	—	—
		MITRE	02_bieber	0.652^{7}	0.559	0.783	0.612^{2}	0.724	0.753	0.697
6		HLTC-HKUST	02_run2	0.652^{7}	0.574	0.754	0.545^{6}	0.669	0.738	0.611
	3	HLTC-HKUST	01_run1	0.651^{9}	0.594	0.720	0.563^{5}	0.676	0.697	0.657
		ECNU	01_mlfeats	0.643^{10}	0.754	0.560	—	—	—	—
7	4	AJ	01_first	0.622^{11}	0.523	0.766	0.527^{7}	0.642	0.571	0.731
8	5	DEPTH	02_modelx23	0.619^{12}	0.652	0.589	0.518^{8}	0.636	0.602	0.674
9	9	CDTDS	01_simple	0.613^{13}	0.547	0.697	0.494^{15}	0.626	0.675	0.583
		CDTDS	02_simplews	0.612^{14}	0.542	0.703	0.491^{16}	0.624	0.589	0.663
		DEPTH	01_modelh22	0.610^{15}	0.647	0.577	0.505^{13}	0.638	0.642	0.634
	10	FBK-HLT	02_multilayer	0.606^{16}	0.676	0.549	0.480^{17}	0.604	0.504	0.754
10		ROB	01_all	0.601^{17}	0.519	0.714	0.513^{10}	0.612	0.721	0.531
11		EBIQUITY	01_run	0.599^{18}	0.651	0.554	—	—	—	—
		TKLBLIIR	01_gsc054	0.590^{19}	0.461	0.817	—	—	—	—
		EBIQUITY	02_run	0.590^{19}	0.646	0.543	—	—	—	—
		BASELINE	**logistic reg.**	$\mathbf{0.589^{21}}$	**0.679**	**0.520**	$\mathbf{0.511^{11}}$	**0.601**	**0.674**	**0.543**
12	11	COLUMBIA	02_ormf ◇	0.588^{22}	0.593	0.583	0.425^{20}	0.599	0.623	0.577
13	12	HASSY	01_train	0.571^{23}	0.449	0.783	0.405^{22}	0.645	0.657	0.634
14		RTM-DCU	01_PLSSVR	0.562^{24}	0.859	0.417	0.564^{4}	0.678	0.649	0.709
		COLUMBIA	01_ormf ◇	0.561^{25}	0.831	0.423	0.425^{20}	0.599	0.623	0.577
		HASSY	02_traindev	0.551^{25}	0.423	0.789	0.405^{22}	0.629	0.648	0.611
	2	RTM-DCU	02_SVR	0.540^{27}	0.883	0.389	0.570^{3}	0.693	0.695	0.691
		BASELINE	**WTMF ◇**	$\mathbf{0.536^{28}}$	**0.450**	**0.663**	$\mathbf{0.350^{26}}$	**0.587**	**0.570**	**0.606**
	6	ROB	02_all	0.532^{29}	0.388	0.846	0.515^{9}	0.616	0.685	0.560
	7	MATHLING	02_twimash ◇	0.515^{30}	0.364	0.880	0.511^{11}	0.650	0.648	0.651
15		MATHLING	01_twiemb ◇	0.515^{30}	0.454	0.594	0.229^{27}	0.562	0.638	0.503
16		YAMRAJ	01_google ◇	0.496^{32}	0.725	0.377	0.360^{25}	0.542	0.502	0.589
17		STANFORD	01_vs	0.480^{33}	0.800	0.343	—	—	—	—
		AJ	02_second	0.477^{34}	0.618	0.389	—	—	—	—
	13	YAMRAJ	02_lexical ◇	0.470^{35}	0.677	0.360	0.363^{24}	0.511	0.508	0.514
late	late	AMRITACEN	01_RAE	0.457	0.543	0.394	0.303	0.457	0.543	0.394
18		WHUHJP	02_whuhjp	0.425^{36}	0.299	0.731	—	—	—	—
		WHUHJP	01_whuhjp	0.387^{37}	0.275	0.651	—	—	—	—
		BASELINE	**random ◇**	$\mathbf{0.266^{38}}$	**0.192**	**0.434**	$\mathbf{0.017^{28}}$	**0.350**	**0.215**	**0.949**

Table 3: Evaluation results. The first column presents the rank of each team in the two tasks based on each team's best system. The superscripts are the ranks of systems, ordered by F1 for Paraphrase Identification (PI) task and Pearson for Semantic Similarity (SS) task. ◇ indicates unsupervised or semi-supervised system. In total, 19 teams participated in the PI task, of which 14 teams also participated in the SS task. Note that although the two sub-tasks share the same test set of 972 sentence pairs, the PI task ignores 134 debatable cases (received a medium-score from expert annotator) and uses only 838 pairs (663 paraphrases and 175 non-paraphrases) in evaluation, while SS task uses all 972 pairs. This causes that the F1-score in the PI task can be higher than the maximum F1-score in the SS task. Also note that the F1-scores of the baselines in the PI task are higher than reported in the Table 2 of (Xu et al., 2014), because the later reported maximum F1-scores on the PI task, ignoring the debatable cases.

gression models using features of semantic similarities between sentence pairs.

ECNU (Zhao and Lan, 2015): This team adopts typical machine learning classifiers and uses a variety of features, such as surface text, semantic level, textual entailment, word distributional representations by deep learning methods.

FBK-HLT (Ngoc Phuoc An Vo and Popescu, 2015): This team uses supervised learning model with different features for the 2 runs, such as n-gram overlap, word alignment and edit distance.

Hassy: This team uses a bag-of-embeddings approach via supervised learning. Two sentences are first embedded into a vector space, and then the system computes the dot-product of the two sentence embeddings.

HLTC-HKUST (Bertero and Fung, 2015): This team uses supervised classification with a standard two-layer neural network classifier. The features used include translation metrics, lexical, syntactic and semantic similarity scores, the latter with an emphasis on aligned semantic roles comparison.

MathLingBp: This team implements the align-and-penalize architecture described by Han et al. (2013) with slight modifications and makes use of several word similarity metrics. One metric relies on a mapping of words to vectors built from the Rovereto Twitter N-Gram corpus, another on a synonym list built from Wiktionary's translations, while a third approach derives word similarity from concept graphs built using the 4lang lexicon and the Longman Dictionary of Contemporary English (Kornai et al., 2015).

MITRE (Zarrella et al., 2015): A recurrent neural network models semantic similarity between sentences using the sequence of symmetric word alignments that maximize cosine similarity between word embeddings. We include features from local similarity of characters, random projection, matching word sequences, pooling of word embeddings, and alignment quality metrics. The resulting ensemble uses both semantic and string matching at many levels of granularity.

RTM-DCU (Bicici, 2015): This team uses referential translation machines (RTM) and machine translation performance prediction system (MTPP) for predicting semantic similarity where indicators of translatability are used as features (Biçici and Way, 2014) and instance selection for RTM is performed with FDA5 (Biçici and Yuret, 2014). RTM works as follows: FDA5 $\rightarrow$ MTPP $\rightarrow$ ML training $\rightarrow$ predict.

Rob (van der Goot and van Noord, 2015): This system is inspired by a state-of-the-art semantic relatedness prediction system by Bjerva et al. (2014). It combines features from different parses with lexical and compositional distributional feature using a logistic regression model.

STANFORD: This team uses a supervised system with sentiment, phrase similarity matrix, and alignment features. Similarity metrics are based on vector space representation of phrases which was trained on a large corpus.

TkLbLiiR (Glavaš et al., 2015): This team uses a supervised model with about 15 comparison-based numeric features. The most important features are the distributional features weighted by the topic-specific information.

WHUHJP: This team uses the word2vec tool to train a vector model on the training data, then computes distributed representations of sentences in the test set and their cosine similarity.

Yamraj: This team uses pre-trained word and phrase vectors on Google News data set (about 100 billion words) and Wikipeida articles. The system relies on the cosine distance between vectors representing the sentences computed using open-source toolkit Gensim.

7 Conclusions and Future Work

We have presented the task definition, data annotation and evaluation results to the first Paraphrase and Semantic Similarity In Twitter (PIT) shared task.

Our analysis provides some initial insights into the relation and the difference between paraphrase identification and semantic similarity problems. We make all the data, baseline systems and evaluation scripts publicly available.[8]

In the future, we plan to extend the task to allow leverage of more information from social networks, for example, by providing the full tweets (and their ids) that are associated with each sentence and with each topic.

Acknowledgments

We would like to thank all participants, reviewers and SemEval organizers Preslav Nakov, Torsten Zesch, Daniel Cer, David Jurgens. This material is based in part on research sponsored by the NSF under grant IIS-1430651, DARPA under agreement number FA8750-13-2-0017 (the DEFT program) and through a Google Faculty Research Award to Chris Callison-Burch. The U.S. Government is authorized to reproduce and distribute reprints for governmental purposes. The views and conclusions contained in this publication are those of the authors and should not be interpreted as representing official policies or endorsements of DARPA or the U.S. Government.

References

Agirre, E., Diab, M., Cer, D., and Gonzalez-Agirre, A. (2012). Semeval-2012 task 6: A pilot on semantic textual similarity. In *Proceedings of SemEval*.

Artstein, R. and Poesio, M. (2008). Inter-coder agreement for computational linguistics. *Computational Linguistics*, 34(4).

Bertero, D. and Fung, P. (2015). HLTC-HKUST: A neural network paraphrase classifier using translation metrics, semantic roles and lexical similarity features. In *Proceedings of SemEval*.

Biçici, E. and Way, A. (2014). RTM-DCU: Referential translation machines for semantic similarity. In *Proceedings of SemEval*.

Biçici, E. and Yuret, D. (2014). Optimizing instance selection for statistical machine translation with feature decay algorithms. *IEEE/ACM Transactions On Audio, Speech, and Language Processing (TASLP)*.

Bicici, E. (2015). RTM-DCU: Predicting semantic similarity with referential translation machines. In *Proceedings of SemEval*.

Bjerva, J., Bos, J., van der Goot, R., and Nissim, M. (2014). The meaning factory: Formal semantics for recognizing textual entailment and determining semantic similarity. In *Proceedings of SemEval*.

Blacoe, W. and Lapata, M. (2012). A comparison of vector-based representations for semantic composition. In *Proceedings of EMNLP-CoNLL*.

Chen, D. L. and Dolan, W. B. (2011). Collecting highly parallel data for paraphrase evaluation. In *Proceedings of ACL*.

Das, D. and Smith, N. A. (2009). Paraphrase identification as probabilistic quasi-synchronous recognition. In *Proceedings of ACL-IJCNLP*.

Derczynski, L., Ritter, A., Clark, S., and Bontcheva, K. (2013). Twitter part-of-speech tagging for all: Overcoming sparse and noisy data. In *Proceedings of RANLP*.

Dolan, B., Quirk, C., and Brockett, C. (2004). Unsupervised construction of large paraphrase corpora: Exploiting massively parallel news sources. In *Proceedings of COLING*.

Eyecioglu, A. and Keller, B. (2015). ASOBEK: Twitter paraphrase identification with simple overlap features and SVMs. In *Proceedings of SemEval*.

Fellbaum, C. (2010). WordNet. In *Theory and Applications of Ontology: Computer Applications*. Springer.

Fernando, S. and Stevenson, M. (2008). A semantic similarity approach to paraphrase detection. *Computational Linguistics UK (CLUK) 11th Annual Research Colloquium*.

Francis, W. N. and Kucera, H. (1979). Brown corpus manual. Technical report, Brown University. Department of Linguistics.

Glavaš, G., Karan, M., Šnajder, J., Bašić, B. D., Vulić, I., and Moens, M.-F. (2015). TKLBLIIR:

[8] https://github.com/cocoxu/SemEval-PIT2015

Detecting Twitter paraphrases with TweetingJay. In *Proceedings of SemEval*.

Guo, W. and Diab, M. (2012). Modeling sentences in the latent space. In *Proceedings of ACL*.

Guo, W., Liu, W., and Diab, M. (2014). Fast tweet retrieval with compact binary codes. In *Proceedings of COLING*.

Han, L., Kashyap, A., Finin, T., Mayfield, J., and Weese, J. (2013). UMBC EBIQUITY-CORE: Semantic textual similarity systems. In *Proceedings of *SEM*.

Hassan, S. and Mihalcea, R. (2011). Semantic relatedness using salient semantic analysis. In *Proceedings of AAAI*.

Hovy, E., Marcus, M., Palmer, M., Ramshaw, L., and Weischedel, R. (2006). OntoNotes: the 90% solution. In *Proceedings of HLT-NAACL*.

Islam, A. and Inkpen, D. (2007). Semantic similarity of short texts. In *Proceedings of RANLP*.

Ji, Y. and Eisenstein, J. (2013). Discriminative improvements to distributional sentence similarity. In *Proceedings of EMNLP*.

Karampatsis, R.-M. (2015). CDTDS: Predicting paraphrases in Twitter via support vector regression. In *Proceedings of SemEval*.

Kornai, A., Makrai, M., Nemeskey, D., and Recski, G. (2015). Extending 4lang using monolingual dictionaries. Unpublished manuscript.

Madnani, N. and Dorr, B. J. (2010). Generating phrasal and sentential paraphrases: A survey of data-driven methods. *Computational Linguistics*.

Madnani, N., Tetreault, J., and Chodorow, M. (2012). Re-examining machine translation metrics for paraphrase identification. In *Proceedings of NAACL-HLT*.

Mihalcea, R., Corley, C., and Strapparava, C. (2006). Corpus-based and knowledge-based measures of text semantic similarity. In *Proceedings of AAAI*.

Nenkova, A. and Vanderwende, L. (2005). The impact of frequency on summarization. Technical report, Microsoft Research. MSR-TR-2005-101.

Ngoc Phuoc An Vo, S. M. and Popescu, O. (2015). FBK-HLT: An application of semantic textual similarity for paraphrase and semantic similarity in Twitter. In *Proceedings of SemEval*.

O'Connor, B., Krieger, M., and Ahn, D. (2010). Tweetmotif: Exploratory search and topic summarization for Twitter. In *Proceedings of ICWSM*.

Petrović, S., Osborne, M., and Lavrenko, V. (2012). Using paraphrases for improving first story detection in news and twitter. In *Proceedings of NAACL-HLT*.

Qiu, L., Kan, M.-Y., and Chua, T.-S. (2006). Paraphrase recognition via dissimilarity significance classification. In *Proceedings of EMNLP*.

Ritter, A., Clark, S., and Etzioni, O. (2011). Named entity recognition in tweets: an experimental study. In *Proceedings of EMNLP*.

Robbins, H. (1985). Some aspects of the sequential design of experiments. In *Herbert Robbins Selected Papers*. Springer.

Rus, V., McCarthy, P. M., Lintean, M. C., McNamara, D. S., and Graesser, A. C. (2008). Paraphrase identification with lexico-syntactic graph subsumption. In *Proceedings of FLAIRS*.

Satyapanich, T., Gao, H., and Finin, T. (2015). Ebiquity: Paraphrase and semantic similarity in Twitter using skipgrams. In *Proceedings of SemEval*.

Socher, R., Huang, E. H., Pennin, J., Manning, C. D., and Ng, A. (2011). Dynamic pooling and unfolding recursive autoencoders for paraphrase detection. In *Proceedings of NIPS*.

Tran-Thanh, L., Stein, S., Rogers, A., and Jennings, N. R. (2012). Efficient crowdsourcing of unknown experts using multi-armed bandits. In *Proceedings of ECAI*.

van der Goot, R. and van Noord, G. (2015). ROB: Using semantic meaning to recognize paraphrases. In *Proceedings of SemEval*.

Vanderwende, L., Suzuki, H., Brockett, C., and Nenkova, A. (2007). Beyond SumBasic: Task-focused summarization with sentence simplification and lexical expansion. *Information Processing & Management*, 43.

Wan, S., Dras, M., Dale, R., and Paris, C. (2006). Using dependency-based features to take the parafarce out of paraphrase. In *Proceedings of the Australasian Language Technology Workshop*.

Wang, L., Dyer, C., Black, A. W., and Trancoso, I. (2013). Paraphrasing 4 microblog normalization. In *Proceedings of EMNLP*.

Xu, W. (2014). *Data-Drive Approaches for Paraphrasing Across Language Variations*. PhD thesis, Department of Computer Science, New York University.

Xu, W., Ritter, A., Callison-Burch, C., Dolan, W. B., and Ji, Y. (2014). Extracting lexically divergent paraphrases from Twitter. *Transactions of the Association for Computational Linguistics (TACL)*, 2(1).

Xu, W., Ritter, A., and Grishman, R. (2013). Gathering and generating paraphrases from twitter with application to normalization. In *Proceedings of the Sixth Workshop on Building and Using Comparable Corpora*.

Zanzotto, F. M., Pennacchiotti, M., and Tsioutsiouliklis, K. (2011). Linguistic redundancy in twitter. In *Proceedings of EMNLP*.

Zarrella, G., Henderson, J., Merkhofer, E. M., and Strickhart, L. (2015). MITRE: Seven systems for semantic similarity in tweets. In *Proceedings of SemEval*.

Zhao, J. and Lan, M. (2015). ECNU: Boosting performance for paraphrase and semantic similarity in Twitter by leveraging word embeddings. In *Proceedings of SemEval*.

MITRE: Seven Systems for Semantic Similarity in Tweets

Guido Zarrella, John Henderson, Elizabeth M. Merkhofer and **Laura Strickhart**
The MITRE Corporation
202 Burlington Road
Bedford, MA 01730-1420, USA
{jzarrella,jhndrsn,emerkhofer,lstrickhart}@mitre.org

Abstract

This paper describes MITRE's participation in the Paraphrase and Semantic Similarity in Twitter task (SemEval-2015 Task 1). This effort placed first in Semantic Similarity and second in Paraphrase Identification with scores of Pearson's r of 61.9%, F1 of 66.7%, and maxF1 of 72.4%. We detail the approaches we explored including mixtures of string matching metrics, alignments using tweet-specific distributed word representations, recurrent neural networks for modeling similarity with those alignments, and distance measurements on pooled latent semantic features. Logistic regression is used to tie the systems together into the ensembles submitted for evaluation.

1 Introduction

Paraphrase identification is the task of judging if two texts express the same or very similar meaning. Automatic identification of paraphrases has practical applications for a range of domains, including news summarization, information retrieval, essay grading, and evaluation of machine translation outputs. Furthermore, work on paraphrase detection tends to advance the state of art in modeling semantics and semantic similarity in natural language in general.

Current approaches to paraphrase detection vary widely. The Microsoft Research Paraphrase Corpus, with pairs of sentences from newswire text, serves as a benchmark for the task (Dolan et al., 2004). One top result on this dataset uses features from surface characteristics of text (Madnani et al., 2012). Another system with comparable results models sentences as hierarchical compositions of distributed word embeddings (Socher et al., 2011). SemEval-2015 Task 1 (Xu et al., 2015), with a corpus drawn from Twitter, offers an opportunity to test paraphrase systems in a domain with an expanded vocabulary and informal grammar.

Our contribution builds upon the recent success of distributed representations of language (Mikolov et al., 2013a; Pennington et al., 2014). We further aim to minimize reliance on language- and domain-dependent tools. However we do not possess enough labeled paraphrase data to train a generalized model of word composition. Instead we explore models that examine low-dimensional relationships between individual pairs of aligned words, and combine the above with string similarity features that generalize well to out-of-vocabulary terms.

In the remainder of this paper, we describe our high-performing system for modeling semantic similarity between two tweets. In Section 2 we describe the data, task, and evaluation. In Section 3 we discuss details of systems we built to solve the semantic similarity task. We describe our experiments on different parameterizations in Section 4. In Section 5 we present performance results for our ensembles and all subsystems, and in Section 6 we summarize our findings.

2 Task, data and evaluation

Paraphrase and Semantic Similarity in Twitter was a shared task organized within SemEval-2015.

The task organizers released 18,762 pairs of English-language tweets with a 70/25/5 split for train, development, and test sets. The organizers removed URLs, deleted non-alphanumeric characters, and provided part of speech tags. Tweet pairs were judged by five human annotators to be a paraphrase (e.g. *Amber alert gave me a damn heart attack* and *That Amber alert scared the crap out of me*) or not (e.g. *My phone is annoying me with these amber alert* and *Am I the only one who dont get Amber alert*). Approximately 35% of provided pairs are paraphrases. For each pair, task participants predict a binary label and optionally provide a confidence score. Systems were evaluated by F1 measure, F1 at the best confidence threshold, and Pearson correlation with expert annotation.

3 System overview

We created an ensemble of seven systems which each independently predicted a semantic similarity score. Some features were reused among the components, including word embeddings and alignments.

3.1 Twitter Word Embeddings

We used word2vec to learn distributed representations of words and phrases from an unlabeled corpus of 330.3 million tweets sampled in 2013 from Twitter's public streaming API. Retweets and non-English messages were not included in the sample. Text was lowercased and processed to mimic the style of the task data. We applied word2phrase (Mikolov et al., 2013b) twice consecutively to identify phrases comprised of up to four words. We then trained a skip-gram model of size 256 for the 1.87 million vocabulary items which appeared at least 25 times, using a context window of 10 words and 15 negative samples per positive example. These hyperparameters were selected based on our prior experience in training embeddings for identification of word analogies.

3.2 Alignment

Comparing semantics in two tweets can be imagined as a tallying process. One finds some semantic atom on the left hand side and searches for it in the right hand side. If found, it gets crossed off. Otherwise, that atom contributes to a difference. Repeat on the other side. This idealized process is reminiscent of finding translation equivalences for training machine translation systems (Al-Onaizan et al., 1999).

To this end, we built an alignment system on top of word embeddings. Each tweet was converted into a bag of words, and two different alignments were created. The *min alignment* maximized the cosine similarity of aligned pairs under the constraint that no word could be aligned more than once. The *max alignment* was constrained such that each word must be paired with at least one other, and the total number of edges in the alignment can be no more than word count of the longer string. `LPSOLVE` was employed to find the assignment maximizing these criteria (Berkelaar et al., 2004).

3.3 Seven Systems

Random Projection The random projection family of Locality Sensitive Hashing algorithms is a probabilistic technique for reducing high dimensional inputs to a fixed-length low dimensional sketch (Charikar, 2002), in which similar inputs yield similar hashes. This characteristic is useful for approximate nearest neighbor search and online clustering (Petrović et al., 2010), but we use it here to obtain an unsupervised similarity metric that identifies string overlap at many levels of granularity. Concretely, we extract the set of all word unigrams, word bigrams, and character n-grams of lengths 2 through 5. These features are input to 2048 independent binary classifiers with random weights, and each classifier contributes a single bit to the resulting hash. We assess similarity of two tweets by measuring the Hamming distance between their bit vectors.

Recurrent Neural Network One common approach to paraphrase detection is to construct a model of each sentence before learning a distance function over these representations. We chose to sidestep this global semantics modeling problem and instead directly measured the relationships between embedded lexical items.

In particular, we used a Recurrent Neural Network to examine the sequence of aligned word pairs obtained from the min alignment process described in section 3.2. For each aligned pair, we computed descriptive statistics that were used as input to the network: cosine similarity and Euclidean distance of the aligned word embeddings, the magnitudes of each word's vector, and the relative position of each word in the sentence. These features enabled the network to consider the quality of the alignment without introducing sparsity by including the word vectors themselves. The RNN also received two global features at each time step: the ratio of sentence lengths and the normalized Hamming distance computed via random projection as described above.

The RNN contained 8 input features, 16 hidden units, and a single output, composed as an Elman network (Elman, 1990) with tied weights.

We unfolded it using backpropagation through time (Williams and Zipser, 1990) to create a deep network with as many hidden layers as there were lexical units in the shorter sentence. We trained the RNN with stochastic gradient descent and a formulation of dropout (Hinton et al., 2012) that randomly removed a single word pair from each training sequence. Parameters were tuned on the development set, including a minibatch of 20, a learning rate of 0.05 or 0.06, hyperbolic tangent activation functions, and early stopping after about 2000 iterations. Two RNNs were used in the final ensemble, each trained with different learning rates.

Paris: String Similarity MITRE entered a system based on string similarity metrics in the 2004 Pascal RTE competition (Bayer et al., 2005). We revivified the code base (called `libparis`) and updated it for this evaluation. Eight different string similarity and machine translation evaluation approaches are implemented in this package; measures include an implementation of the MT evaluation BLEU (Papineni et al., 2002); WER, a common speech recognition word error rate based on Levenshtein distance (Levenshtein, 1966); WER-g, an error rate similar to WER, but with denominator based on the min edit traceback (Foster et al., 2003); the MT evaluation ROUGE (Lin and Och, 2004); a simple position-independent error rate similar to PER as described in Leusch et al. (2003); both global and local similarity metrics often used for biological string comparison as described in Gusfield (1997). Finally, there are precision and recall measures based on bags of *all* substrings (or n-grams in word tokenization).

In total we computed 22 metrics for a pair of strings. The metrics were run on both lowercased and original versions as well as on word tokens and characters, yielding 88 string similarity features. Some of the metrics are not symmetric, so they were run both forward and reversed based on presentation in the dataset yielding 176 features. Finally, for each feature value x, $\log(x)$ was added as a feature, producing a final count of 352 string similarity features. We used `LIBLINEAR` with these features to build a L1-regularized logistic regression model.

Simple Alignment Measures Section 3.2 describes methods we used for aligning two strings. We built one component that computed similarity between tweets using simple metrics applied only to the aligned word pairs. Mean vectors and pooled component-wise min and max vectors were computed for both sides of the two different types of alignments. Those six pairs of vectors were compared using cosine distance, Manhattan distance, and Euclidean distance, resulting in eighteen features. Separately, the alignments were traversed and pairs of word vectors were compared using the three distance functions. The means of those comparisons produced six more features. L2-regularized logistic regression combined these 24 features into a single measure of semantic similarity.

Similarity Matrices, Averaged and Min/Max Two subsystems drew upon a similarity matrix and dynamic pooling technique presented in Socher et al. (2011). This method considers distance between all syntactically meaningful subunits of two sentences. First, a representation is induced for each node of the parse tree of two sentences, starting from word embeddings at leaf nodes. Then a similarity matrix is created from measurements of Euclidean distance between every pair of nodes. Finally, a dynamic pooling scheme reduces this to a fixed-size representation that is used as input to a logistic regression classifier. For one subsystem in MITRE's contribution, nodes were represented as averages of their child nodes; for another, nodes were represented as the concatenation of the minimum and maximum of the child nodes.

Normalized Averages This subsystem computed an unsupervised distance metric based on semantic features. We first replaced each word in the tweet with its synonym from the Twitter normalization lexicon (Han and Baldwin, 2011), for example converting *tv* to *television*. The embeddings of these words were used in experiments on weighted averaging and pooling, folding of part-of-speech tags, and various distance and similarity metrics. The best F1 score on the development set was achieved by averaging the word vectors and computing Euclidean distance between the two tweets' resulting vectors.

3.4 Ensembles

The predictors described above were selected for inclusion in a larger ensemble on the basis of their

Name	Factored	Ablated
BLEU	61.5	64.6
ROUGE	60.2	63.8
PER	60.0	64.4
substring bags	58.7	63.5
WER	58.0	63.9
WER-g	57.9	63.9
global sim	57.7	64.1
local sim	55.9	63.1
none	–	63.9

Table 1: Dev set F1 scores for string similarities.

performance on the development set. Each component's semantic similarity score contributed to the final prediction with a weighting determined by L2-regularized logistic regression. Binary paraphrase labels were assigned by choosing an ensemble score threshold that optimized development set F1.

The ensemble described in this paper was submitted for scoring under the name MITRE IKR. A second submission was identical with one exception: its supervised subsystems were retrained on the concatenation of the train and development data.

4 Experiments

In all experiments, systems were trained while omitting debatable examples with scores of 2 as suggested by the task organizers. The development set was used both to fit the hyperparameters (ablations, lambdas) and the eventual ensemble.

String Similarity Ablations The MT evaluation metrics and string similarities contributed varying amounts to that system. In Table 1 we show the score achieved by the logistic regression system built using just that one measure (in the *Factored* column) as well as the F1 achieved by the logistic regression when only that one measure is left out (*Ablated* column). BLEU was omitted from the subsystem as a result of this analysis.

Ensemble Construction We focused our ensembles only on the output of our individual components, ignoring the features from the original data they attempt to model. Table 3 shows the weights of these components. Note that NormalizedAvg produced larger outputs than the rest; as a result its coefficient is about 10 times smaller than its effect.

System	Pearson	F1	maxF1
MITRE	**61.9**	66.7	**71.6**
RTM-DCU	57.0	54.0	69.1
HLTC-UST	56.3	65.1	67.6
ASOBEK	50.4	**67.2**	66.3
MITRE components			
RNN	**60.8**		**71.8**
Paris	58.7		68.2
RandProj	54.9		64.6
SimMat_avg	54.6		64.7
SimMat_minmax	53.5		62.8
Aligner	51.8		61.9
NormalizedAvg	45.8		61.1

Table 2: Test scores of Semantic Similarity Systems (%).

5 Results

The evaluation of our components on the competition test set is shown in Table 2, along with a sample of top-scoring competitors. Our best ensemble achieves 0.619 Pearson correlation with expert judgments, a state-of-the-art result. In contrast, the correlation of crowdsourced annotations with expert ratings is 0.735 (Xu et al., 2015). Our system's F1 on the binary paraphrase judgment task was 0.667, with a maximum F1 of 0.716 using an optimal threshold. Additionally several individual components performed well in isolation. The recurrent neural network alone achieved Pearson of 0.608 and a max F1 of 0.718.

6 Conclusion

Seven models of semantic similarity were combined for paraphrase detection in Twitter. This ensemble placed first in the Semantic Similarity competition organized within SemEval-2015 Task 1. The similarity judgments showed 0.619 correlation with expert judgment, a relative improvement of 8.6% over other published results (Xu et al., 2015).

Our best performing single system represents a novel departure from existing paraphrase detection approaches. The recurrent neural network makes use of the relationships between aligned word pairs, an approach which we feel is well-suited to informal contexts where explicit models of syntax face additional challenges.

Component	Φ	Component	Φ
RNN1	-1.89	SimMat_minmax	0.84
RNN2	-1.11	Aligner	0.28
Paris	-1.81	NormalizedAvg	-0.034
SimMat_avg	-1.28	bias	0.91
RandProj	1.11		

Table 3: Final MITRE component coefficients in the ensemble logistic regression.

Acknowledgments

This work was funded under the MITRE Innovation Program. Many thanks to John Burger for his comments on machine translation alignments. Approved for Public Release; Distribution Unlimited: Case Number 15-0811.

References

Yaser Al-Onaizan, Jan Curin, Michael Jahr, Kevin Knight, John Lafferty, I. Dan Melamed, Franz-Josef Och, David Purdy, Noah A. Smith, and David Yarowsky. 1999. Statistical machine translation: Final report. Technical report, JHU Center for Language and Speech Processing.

Samuel Bayer, John Burger, Lisa Ferro, John Henderson, and Alexander Yeh. 2005. MITRE's submissions to the EU Pascal RTE challenge. In *Proceedings of the Pattern Analysis, Statistical Modelling, and Computational Learning (PASCAL) Challenges Workshop on Recognising Textual Entailment.*

Michel Berkelaar, Kjell Eikland, and Peter Notebaert. 2004. lp_solve 5.5, open source (mixed-integer) linear programming system. Software. Available at http://lpsolve.sourceforge.net/5.5/.

Moses S. Charikar. 2002. Similarity estimation techniques from rounding algorithms. In *Proceedings of the Thirty-fourth Annual ACM Symposium on Theory of Computing*, STOC '02, pages 380–388.

Bill Dolan, Chris Quirk, and Chris Brockett. 2004. Unsupervised construction of large paraphrase corpora: Exploiting massively parallel news sources. In *Proceedings of the 20th International Conference on Computational Linguistics*, COLING '04.

Jeffrey L. Elman. 1990. Finding structure in time. *COGNITIVE SCIENCE*, 14(2):179–211.

George Foster, Simona Gandrabur, Cyril Goutte, Erin Fitzgerald, Alberto Sanchis, Nicola Ueffing, John Blatz, and Alex Kulesza. 2003. Confidence estimation for machine translation. Technical report, JHU Center for Language and Speech Processing.

Dan Gusfield. 1997. *Algorithms on Strings, Trees, and Sequences: Computer Science and Computational Biology.*

Bo Han and Timothy Baldwin. 2011. Lexical normalisation of short text messages: Makn sens a #twitter. In *Proceedings of the 49th Annual Meeting of the Association for Computational Linguistics: Human Language Technologies - Volume 1*, HLT '11, pages 368–378.

Geoffrey E. Hinton, Nitish Srivastava, Alex Krizhevsky, Ilya Sutskever, and Ruslan Salakhutdinov. 2012. Improving neural networks by preventing co-adaptation of feature detectors. *CoRR*, http://arxiv.org/abs/1207.0580.

Gregor Leusch, Nicola Ueffing, and Hermann Ney. 2003. A novel string-to-string distance measure with applications to machine translation evaluation. In *Proc. of the Ninth MT Summit*, pages 240–247.

Vladimir Iosifovich Levenshtein. 1966. Binary codes capable of correcting deletions, insertions and reversals. *Soviet Physics Doklady*, 10(8):707–710.

Chin-Yew Lin and Franz Josef Och. 2004. ORANGE: a method for evaluating automatic evaluation metrics for machine translation. In *Proceedings of the 20th International Conference on Computational Linguistics (COLING 2004)*, August.

Nitin Madnani, Joel Tetreault, and Martin Chodorow. 2012. Re-examining machine translation metrics for paraphrase identification. In *Proceedings of the 2012 Conference of the North American Chapter of the Association for Computational Linguistics: Human Language Technologies*, pages 182–190.

Tomas Mikolov, Kai Chen, Greg Corrado, and Jeffrey Dean. 2013a. Efficient estimation of word representations in vector space. In *International Conference on Learning Representations Workshop*.

Tomas Mikolov, Ilya Sutskever, Kai Chen, Greg S Corrado, and Jeff Dean. 2013b. Distributed representations of words and phrases and their compositionality. In *Advances in Neural Information Processing Systems*, pages 3111–3119.

Kishore Papineni, Salim Roukos, Todd Ward, and Wei-Jing Zhu. 2002. BLEU: A method for automatic evaluation of machine translation. In *Proceedings of the 40th Annual Meeting on Association for Computational Linguistics*, ACL '02, pages 311–318.

Jeffrey Pennington, Richard Socher, and Christopher D Manning. 2014. GloVe: Global vectors for word representation. *Proceedings of the Empiricial Methods in Natural Language Processing (EMNLP 2014)*, 12.

Saša Petrović, Miles Osborne, and Victor Lavrenko. 2010. Streaming first story detection with application to Twitter. In *Human Language Technologies: The*

2010 Annual Conference of the North American Chapter of the Association for Computational Linguistics, pages 181–189.

Richard Socher, Eric H. Huang, Jeffrey Pennin, Christopher D. Manning, and Andrew Y. Ng. 2011. Dynamic pooling and unfolding recursive autoencoders for paraphrase detection. In *Advances in Neural Information Processing Systems*, pages 801–809.

Ronald J. Williams and David Zipser. 1990. Gradient-based learning algorithms for recurrent connectionist networks. pages 433–486.

Wei Xu, Chris Callison-Burch, and Bill Dolan. 2015. Semeval-2015 task 1: Paraphrase and semantic similarity in twitter. In *Proceedings of the 9th International Workshop on Semantic Evaluation (SemEval 2015)*.

CICBUAPnlp: Graph-Based Approach for Answer Selection in Community Question Answering Task

Helena Gómez-Adorno, Grigori Sidorov
Center for Computing Research
Instituto Politécnico Nacional
Av. Juan de Dios Bátiz
C.P. 07738, Mexico City, Mexico
helena.adorno@gmail.com
sidorov@cic.ipn.mx

Darnes Vilariño, David Pinto
Faculty of Computer Science
Benemérita Universidad Autónoma de Puebla
Av. San Claudio y 14 sur
C.P. 72570, Puebla, Mexico
darnes@cs.buap.mx
dpinto@cs.buap.mx

Abstract

This paper describes our approach for the Community Question Answering Task, which was presented at the SemEval 2015. The system should read a given question and identify good, potentially relevant, and bad answers for that question. Our approach transforms the answers of the training set into a graph based representation for each answer class, which contains lexical, morphological, and syntactic features. The answers in the test set are also transformed into the graph based representation individually. After this, different paths are traversed in the training and test sets in order to find relevant features of the graphs. As a result of this procedure, the system constructs several vectors of features: one for each traversed graph. Finally, a cosine similarity is calculated between the vectors in order to find the class that best matches a given answer. Our system was developed for the English language only, and it obtained an accuracy of 53.74 for subtask A and 44.0 for subtask B.

1 Introduction

In this paper we present the experiments carried out as part of our participation in the SemEval-2015 Task 3 (Answer Selection in Community Question Answering). The Answer Selection in Community Question Answering task is proposed for the first time this year in the International Workshop on Semantic Evaluation (SemEval-2015). The task is based on an application scenario, which is related to textual entailment, semantic similarity and NL inference.

Community question answering (CQA) websites enable people to post questions and answers in various domains. In this way, users can obtain specific answers to their questions, instead of searching in the large volume of information available in the web. However, it takes effort to go through all possible answers and select which one is the most accurate one for a specific question. The task proposes to automate this process by predicting the quality of existing answers with respect to a question.

There are few works in the literature on evaluating the quality of answers provided in CQA sites. Most of such works employ non-textual and temporal features in order to built classification models for predicting the best answer for a given question. In (Jeon et al., 2006), the authors extract 13 non-textual features from the Naver data set and build a maximum entropy classification model to predict the quality (three classes: Bad, Medium and Good) of a given answer. A similar approach is used in (Shah and Pomerantz, 2010), but extracting 21 features (mainly non-textual) from *Yahoo! Answers*; the authors employ a logistic regression and classification model to predict the best answer. Besides, a set of temporal features is proposed in (Cai and Chakravarthy, 2011) in order to predict the best answer for a given question. In this work the authors argue that the traditional classification approaches are not well suited for this problem because of the highly imbalanced ratio of the best answer and the non-best answers in their data set, so they propose to use learning to rank approaches.

Unlike these approaches, we use only textual information for predicting the quality of the answers.

Our approach is based on our previous research (Pinto et al., 2014) and (Sidorov et al., 2014), where we propose the graph-based representation model (Integrated Syntactic Graph) and the soft similarity measure (soft cosine measure). Our experimental results are promising, they overcome the baseline system for this challenge.

The rest of the paper is organized as follows. Section 2 describes our approach. Section 3 presents the configuration of the submitted runs and the evaluation results. Finally, Section 4 presents the conclusions and outlines some directions of future work.

2 Approach

For many problems in natural language processing, graph structure is an intuitive, natural and direct way to represent data. There exist several research works that have employed graphs for text representation in order to solve some particular problem (Mihalcea and Radev, 2011). We propose an approach based on a graph methodology, which was described in detail in (Pinto et al., 2014), for building the corresponding system of the two subtasks. These subtasks are described as follows:

Subtask A Given a question (short title + extended description) and a list of community answers, classify each of the answers as: Good, Potential or Bad (bad, dialog, non-English, other).

Subtask B Given a YES/NO question (short title + extended description) and a list of community answers, decide whether the global answer to the question should be yes, no or unsure, based on the individual good answers.

The proposed system consists of the following submodules: document preprocessing, graph generation, and answer quality classification.

2.1 Document Preprocessing

An XML parser receives as input a structured corpus in XML format. This XML file contains all the questions, along with their respective answers. An XML interpreter extracts the questions and associated answers.

Thereafter, we process the answers for both subtasks separately. All the answers belonging to the same class are grouped together, and the result is passed to the next module. This means that at the end of this module, we will have all the good answers in one document, the bad ones in another document and so on for all classes. In the same way, for the task B, the yes/no answers are grouped together in different documents.

2.2 Graph Generation

In the graph generation module, all sentences of each class are parsed to produce what we call their Integrated Syntactic Graph (ISG) representation (see (Pinto et al., 2014)). For the graph representation we took into account various linguistic levels (lexical, syntactic, morphological, and semantic) in order to capture the majority of the features present in the text.

The process of the graph generation is performed by the following submodules:

The Syntactic Parser is the base of the graph structure. We use the Stanford Dependency Parser[1] for producing the parsed tree for each sentence of the documents. In this type of parsing, we detect grammatical relation.

The Morphological Tagger obtains PoS tags of words. For this purpose we used the Stanford Log linear Part-Of-Speech Tagger[2] for English. The Lancaster stemmer algorithm was used in order to obtain word stems.

As a result of this process, each class is represented as a graph rooted in a $ROOT - 0$ node. The vertices to sub-trees represent all sentences in the class document. The nodes of the trees represent words or lemmas of the sentences along with their part-of-speech tags. The vertices between nodes represent the dependency tags between these connected nodes along with a frequency label, for example: *nsubj-5*, that shows the number of occurrences of the pair (initial_node, final_node) in the graph plus the frequency of the dependency tag of the same pair of nodes. In the same way, the answers to be classified in one of the quality classes are represented in an ISG with the same characteristics.

In order to fully understand the process of construction of the ISG and the collapse of nodes in the

[1] http://nlp.stanford.edu/software/lex-parser.shtml

[2] http://nlp.stanford.edu/software/tagger.shtml

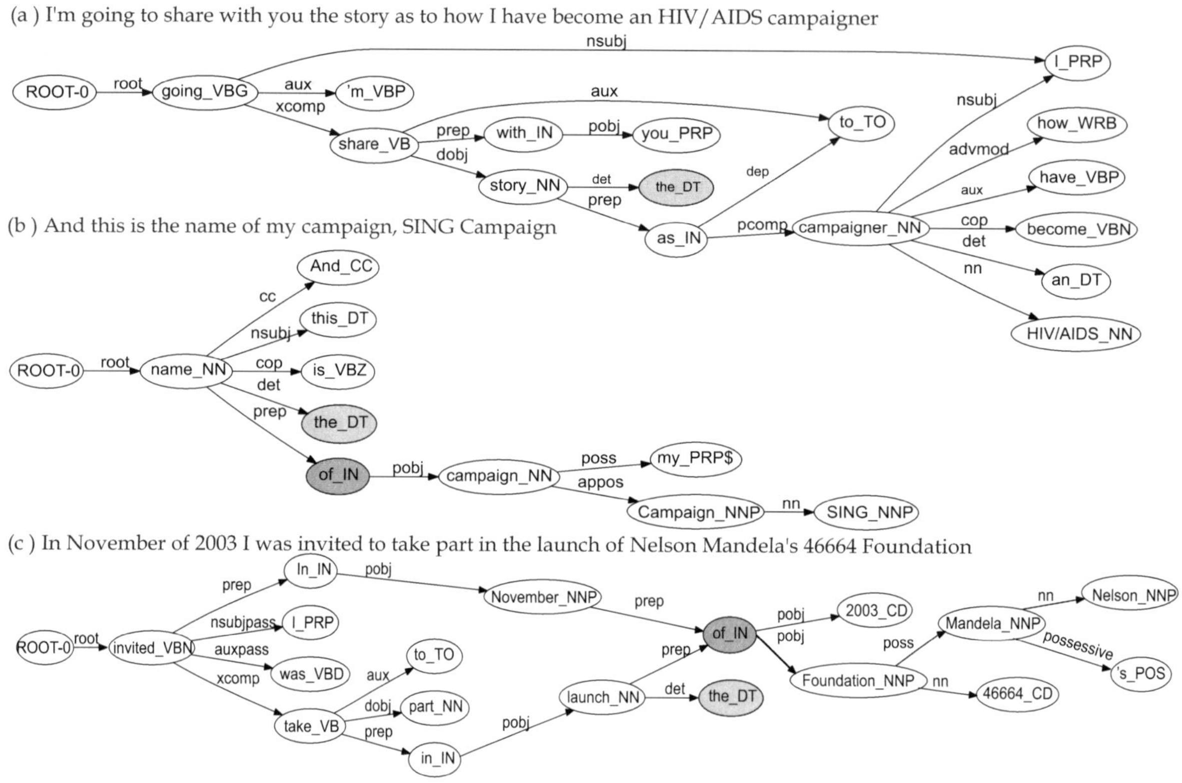

Figure 1: Dependency trees of three sentences of a target text using word POS combination for the nodes and dependency labels for the edges

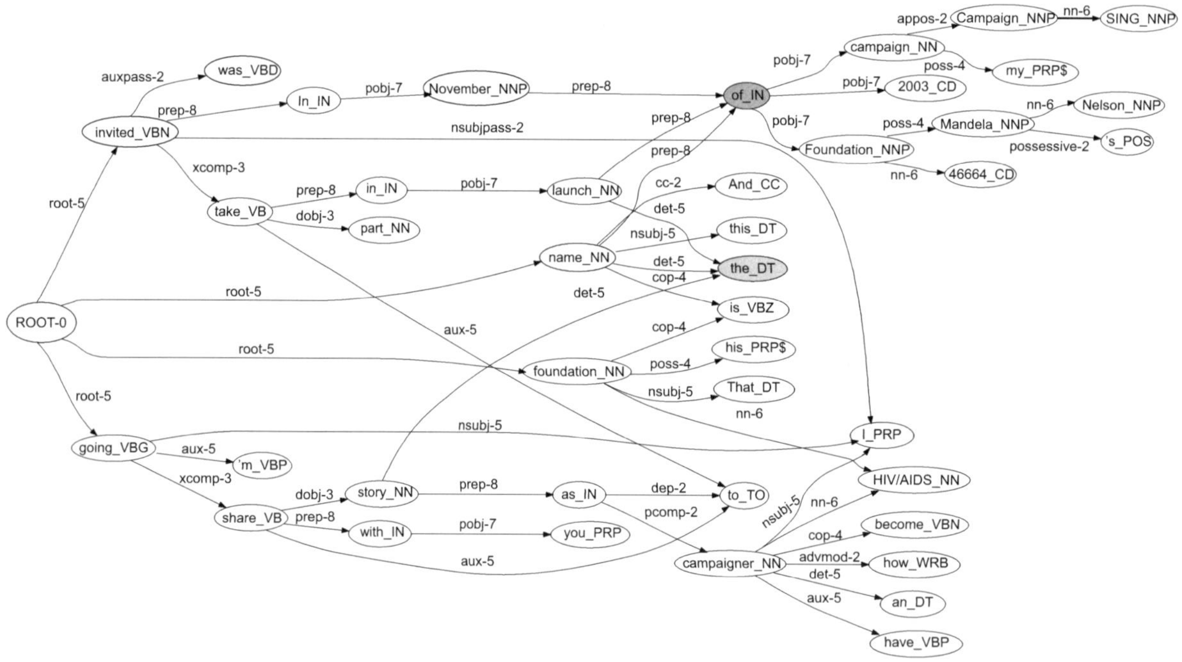

Figure 2: The Integrated Syntactic Graph for the three sentences considered as example

graph, in Figure 1, we show the dependency trees of three sentences; each node of the graph is augmented with other annotations, such as the combination of lemma (or word) and POS tags: (lemma POS).

The collapsed graph of the three sentences is shown in Figure 2. Each edge of this graph contains the dependency tag together with a number that indicates the frequency of the dependency tag plus the frequency of the pair of nodes, both calculated using the occurrences of the dependency trees associated to each sentence.

The feature extraction process starts by fixing the root node of the answer graph as the initial node, whereas the selected final nodes correspond to the remaining nodes of the answer graph. We use the $Dijkstra's\ Algorithm$ (Dijkstra, 1959) for finding the shortest paths between the initial and each final node. After this, we count the occurrences of all the multi-level linguistic features considered in the text representation such as POS tags and dependency tags found in the path. The same procedure is performed with the class document graph, using the pair of nodes identified in the answer graph as the initial and final node. As a result of this procedure, we obtain two feature vectors: one for the answer and another one for the class document. This module was implemented in Python, using the NetworkX[3] package for creation and manipulation of graphs.

2.3 Classification based on Quality of Answers

This module receives several feature vectors $(\overrightarrow{f_{t,i}})$ for each class document. Thus, the class document d is now represented by m features $(d^* = \{\overrightarrow{f_{d,1}}, \overrightarrow{f_{d,2}}, ..., \overrightarrow{f_{d,m}}\})$, as well as the different answers a, $(a^* = \{\overrightarrow{f_{a,1}}, \overrightarrow{f_{a,2}}, ..., \overrightarrow{f_{a,m}}\})$, being m the number of different paths that can be traversed in both graphs.

We use the cosine similarity measure from the equation below for calculating the degree of similarity among each traversed path.

$$Similarity(a^*, d^*) = \sum_{i=1}^{m} Cosine(\overrightarrow{f_{a,i}}, \overrightarrow{f_{d,i}})$$

$$= \sum_{i=1}^{m} \frac{\overrightarrow{f_{a,i}} \cdot \overrightarrow{f_{d,i}}}{||\overrightarrow{f_{a,i}}|| \cdot ||\overrightarrow{f_{d,i}}||}$$

[3]https://networkx.github.io/

After obtaining all similarity scores between the answers with each of the class documents, the class (to which the document belongs) achieving the highest score is selected as the correct class for each answer.

3 Results

The acronym of our system is CICBUAPnlp. Tables 1 and 2 show the scores for the English subtasks A and B on the test data, respectively. Although, our results did not overcome the general average, it is worth noting that our methodology is quite simple and straightforward. We only used syntactic and morphological features, thus comparing the structures of the answers against the structure of the labeled sets. Instead of training a classifier, we built a Syntactic Integrated Graph for each class and then try to match the answers in the test set against them, calculating in this way the similarity between the graphs.

Table 1: Results of the subtask A, English

TeamId	Macro F1	Accuracy	Rank
JAIS	57.19	72.52	1
HITSZ-ICRC	56.41	68.67	2
QCRI	53.74	70.50	3
ECNU	53.47	70.55	4
ICRC-HIT	49.60	67.68	5
VectorSlu	49.10	66.45	5
Shiraz	47.34	56.83	7
FBK-HLT	47.32	69.13	8
Voltron	46.07	62.35	9
CICBUAPnlp	**40.40**	**53.74**	**10**
Yamraj	37.65	45.50	11
CoMiC	30.63	54.20	12

4 Conclusion and Future Work

We described the approach and the system developed as a part of our participation in the Answer Selection in Community Question Answering task. The approach uses a graph structure for representing the classes and the answers. It extracts linguistic features from both graphs—classes and answers—by traversing shortest paths. The features

Table 2: Results of the subtask B, English

TeamId	Macro F1	Accuracy	Rank
VectorSlu	63.7	72.0	1
ECNU	55.8	68.0	2
QCRI	53.6	64.0	3=4
HITSZ-ICRC	53.6	64.0	3=4
CICBUAPnlp	**38.8**	**44.0**	**5**
ICRC-HIT	30.9	52.0	6
Yamraj	29.8	28.0	7
FBK-HLT	27.8	40.0	8

are further used for computing the similarity between the classes and the answers.

We sent two runs (primary and contrastive) for each English subtask to the evaluation forum. The best run in both cases was the primary run.

In future work, we are planning to use the soft cosine measure to compare the similarity between the answers and the quality classes, thus evaluating the feasibility of this kind of structures for this task.

Acknowledgments

This work was done under partial support of the Mexican Government (CONACYT, SNI, COFAA-IPN, SIP-IPN 20144534, 20144274) and FP7 -PEOPLE-2010-IRSES: "Web Information Quality Evaluation Initiative (WIQ-EI)" European Commission project 269180.

References

Yuanzhe Cai and Sharma Chakravarthy. 2011. Predicting answer quality in q/a social networks: Using temporal features. Technical report, University of Texas at Arlington.

Edsger. W. Dijkstra. 1959. A note on two problems in connexion with graphs. *Numerische Mathematik*, 1:269–271.

Jiwoon Jeon, W. Bruce Croft, Joon Ho Lee, and Soyeon Park. 2006. A framework to predict the quality of answers with non-textual features. In *Proceedings of the 29th Annual International ACM SIGIR Conference on Research and Development in Information Retrieval*, SIGIR '06, pages 228–235, New York, NY, USA. ACM.

Rada Mihalcea and Dragomir Radev. 2011. *Graph-based natural language processing and information retrieval*. Cambridge; New York.

David Pinto, Helena Gómez-Adorno, Darnes Vilariño, and Vivek Kumar Singh. 2014. A graph-based multi-level linguistic representation for document understanding. *Pattern Recognition Letters*, 41(0):93 – 102. Supervised and Unsupervised Classification Techniques and their Applications.

Chirag Shah and Jefferey Pomerantz. 2010. Evaluating and predicting answer quality in community qa. In *Proceedings of the 33rd International ACM SIGIR Conference on Research and Development in Information Retrieval*, SIGIR '10, pages 411–418, New York, NY, USA. ACM.

Grigori Sidorov, Alexander F. Gelbukh, Helena Gmez-Adorno, and David Pinto. 2014. Soft similarity and soft cosine measure: Similarity of features in vector space model. *Computación y Sistemas*, 18(3):491 – 504.

HLTC-HKUST: A Neural Network Paraphrase Classifier using Translation Metrics, Semantic Roles and Lexical Similarity Features

Dario Bertero, Pascale Fung
Human Language Technology Center
Department of Electronic and Computer Engineering
The Hong Kong University of Science and Technology, Clear Water Bay, Hong Kong
dbertero@ust.hk, pascale@ece.ust.hk

Abstract

This paper describes the system developed by our team (HLTC-HKUST) for task 1 of SemEval 2015 workshop about paraphrase classification and semantic similarity in Twitter. We trained a neural network classifier over a range of features that includes translation metrics, lexical and syntactic similarity score and semantic features based on semantic roles. The neural network was trained taking into consideration in the objective function the six different similarity levels provided in the corpus, in order to give as output a more fine-grained estimation of the similarity level of the two sentences, as required by subtask 2. With an F-score of 0.651 in the binary paraphrase classification subtask 1, and a Pearson coefficient of 0.697 for the sentence similarity subtask 2, we achieved respectively the 6th place and the 3rd place, above the average of what obtained by the other contestants.

1 Introduction

Paraphrase identification is the problem to determine whether two sentences have the same meaning, and is the objective of the task 1 of SemEval 2015 workshop (Xu et al., 2015).

Conventionally this task has been mainly evaluated on the Microsoft Research Paraphrase corpus (Dolan and Brockett, 2005), which consists of pairs of sentences taken out from news headlines and articles. News domain sentences are usually grammatically correct and of average to long length. The current state-of-the-art method to our knowledge on this corpus (Ji and Eisenstein, 2013) trains an SVM over latent semantic vectors, lexical and syntactic similarity features. Although their main objective was to show the effectiveness of a method based on latent semantic analysis, it is also evident that other features pertinent to different aspects of sentence similarity are able to boost the results. Previously Socher et al. (2011) used a recursive autoencoder to similarly obtain a vector representation of each sentence, again combining other lexical similarity features to improve the results. Other methods, such as Madnani et al. (2012) or Wan et al. (2006) used instead a more traditional supervised classification approach over different sets of features and different classifiers, most of which improved previous results.

Task 1 of SemEval 2015 workshop required to evaluate paraphrases on a new corpus, consisting of sentences taken from Twitter posts (Xu et al., 2014). Twitter sentences notoriously differ from those taken from news articles: the 140 characters limit makes the sentences short, with few words, lots of different abbreviations; they also include many misspelled and invented words, and often lack a correct grammatical structure. Another important difference is the six-level classification labels provided, compared to the binary labels of MSRP corpus, which allows a fine-grained evaluation of the similarity level between the sentences.

The task was divided into two subtasks. Subtask 1 was the classical binary paraphrase classification task, where given a pair of sentences the system had to identify if it is a paraphrase or not. Subtask 2 instead required the system to provide a score in the range $[0, 1]$ that measures the actual similarity level of the two sentences.

2 System Description

We chose a supervised machine learning strategy based on a multi-view set of features. Our first goal was to select the features in order to get a complete estimation of lexical, syntactic and semantic similarity between any given pair of sentences. In particular we were interested in what roles semantic features can play in this task. The second goal was to make use of a classifier which can take full advantage of the six level labeling provided in order to have good performance in both subtasks, identified in an artificial neural network.

2.1 Lexical and Syntactic Similarity Features

The first set of lexical features includes three binary indexes obtained from the analysis of the numerical tokens: the first of them is 1 if they are the same in both sentences or there are not any, the second is 1 only if they are the same, and the third is 1 if the tokens representing numbers of one sentences are the subset of the other (Socher et al., 2011). Two other features include the percentage of overlapping tokens, and the difference in sentence length. Another feature considers the word order: starting from one sentence we align the tokens that matches with the other sentence, and for each aligned pair we take the average of the differences of the absolute positions of the two elements, normalized by the length of the first sentence, and we do the same switching the order of the two sentences. Another group of features involves WordNet word synonym sets (Miller, 1995). We take from them, separately for nouns and verbs, the average of the path similarity scores obtained, among all word alignments, from the one which gives the maximum score. When the two words in the pair to be scored have multiple synonym sets we select the two sets that again are giving the highest score. Finally, in order to include an estimation of the level of similarity in the syntax parse tree of the sentences, we use the parse tree edit distance from the Zhang-Shasha algorithm (Zhang and Shasha, 1989; Wan et al., 2006).

2.2 Semantic Similarity Features

The way we evaluate the semantic similarity of each pair of sentences is through the analysis of the semantic roles. The first feature we choose in this sense is the semantic role based MEANT machine translation score (Lo et al., 2012), effective to provide, as shown by various experiments, a translation evaluation closer to human judges. This metric first annotates each sentence with semantic roles (Pradhan et al., 2004), then aligns them and computes a similarity score only within the aligned frames (Fung et al., 2007) using the Jaccard coefficient (Tumuluru et al., 2012). Another set of features is obtained by looking at the semantic roles themselves and their alignment without looking at the content: these include the percentage of semantic roles of one sentence that are also present in the other, the percentage of correct pairs of semantic roles after the alignment operated for MEANT, and a binary feature equal to 1 in case the semantic parser fails to give any output for at least one of the sentences. In this last case all the other features based on semantic roles are 0 except the MEANT score which is set to the value of the Jaccard coefficient between the whole sentences (Lo and Wu, 2013).

2.3 Translation Metrics

Previous work (Finch et al., 2005; Madnani et al., 2012) have shown that machine translation evaluation metrics are useful for the paraphrase recognition task, due to their ability to capture useful similarity information to correctly classify the sentence pairs.

The various translation metrics all take into account different aspects of sentence similarities. BLEU (Papineni et al., 2002) and the subsequent evaluation metrics such as NIST (Goutte, 2006) and SEPIA (Habash and Elkholy, 2008) look at n-gram overlaps between the source and the target sentences. While the most basic BLEU takes into consideration only n-gram overlap, the other metrics also consider synonyms, stemming, simple paraphrase patterns and the syntactic structure of the n-grams. Yet another set of metrics are based instead on different principles: TER (Snover et al., 2006) and TERp (Snover et al., 2009) count the number of edits needed to transform a sentence into the other, MAXSIM (Chan and Ng, 2008) evaluates lexical similarity performing a word-by-word matching and finding out how much the aligned words are similar in each meaning, BADGER (Parker, 2008) the distance between the compression of each sentence obtained from the Burrows-Wheeler transform algorithm (Burrows and

Wheeler, 1994), and MEANT which, as discussed in the previous section, scores the similarity of aligned semantic frames.

For each pair of sentences the scores are calculated first taking one of the sentences as the reference and the other as the sample and then vice-versa. Both scores are included as distinct features except in the case of BADGER, as it computes a distance between two objects without taking into account the direction. In case of BLEU and NIST we use the scores from unigrams up to 4-grams for BLEU (Madnani et al., 2012) and up to the maximum order which gives at least one result different than zero for NIST.

2.4 Classifier

To classify the sentence pairs we design a feedforward neural network. One of the main properties of the neural network is its ability to learn complex functions of the input values (Hornik et al., 1989). It follows that in our task, given the combination of features, the network would learn how to combine them effectively and take advantage of their mutual interaction. The neural network can also be trained using an objective function that takes into consideration a label not just binary but which can take multiple values in a given range. Therefore it has a good ability to determine as output a precise estimation of the similarity level of the sentence pair, particularly useful in subtask 2. During our experiments the results we obtained in the binary classification task over the development set with the neural network were always at least slightly higher than those obtained with an SVM we used as a comparison system, further justifying our neural network choice.

We choose a two layer standard configuration (hidden and output layer), where we fix the size of the hidden layer large enough at three times the size of the input layer; the hyperbolic tangent ($\tanh$) and the sigmoid are used respectively as the non-linear activation functions of the hidden layer and the output layer. Due to this choice the output assumes values in the interval $[0, 1]$, which is also exactly the output range required in subtask 2. The network weights, with the exception of the ones associated to the bias terms set at zero, are initialized (Glorot and Bengio, 2010) with uniform values in the range:

$$w_{t=0} \in \left[-\alpha \left(\frac{6}{n_{in} + n_{out}} \right)^{\frac{1}{2}}, \alpha \left(\frac{6}{n_{in} + n_{out}} \right)^{\frac{1}{2}} \right] \quad (1)$$

Where $\alpha = 1$ in case the activation function is the hyperbolic tangent, and $\alpha = 4$ with the sigmoid. We train the model using standard backpropagation algorithm, taking the cross-entropy as the cost objective function:

$$E = -l \, \log(y) - (1 - l) \log(1 - y) + R \quad (2)$$

where y is the network output, l the objective value (both in the range $[0, 1]$), and R is an L2 regularization term.

3 Experiments

3.1 Corpus

We made use of the corpus provided for the contest (Xu et al., 2014), made of a training set of 13063 sentence pairs, a development set of 4727 pairs, and a test set of 972 pairs released a few days before the deadline without the labels. Each pair of sentences was labeled by five users via Amazon Mechanical Turk, hence providing a six-level classification label (from $(5, 0)$ when all the five user classify the pair as a paraphrase, to $(0, 5)$ when none of them identifies the pair to be a paraphrase).

3.2 Experimental Setup

The neural network was setup with a hidden layer dimension of three times the input. The development set was used to tune the L2 regularization coefficient, set at $\gamma = 0.01$, as well as the learning rate and the other hyperparameters, and to have a measure of improvement against the official thresholding baseline provided for the task (Das and Smith, 2009). To implement the neural network we used THEANO Python toolkit (Bergstra et al., 2010).

We train the network with all the sentences provided in the training set. The objective label of the cross-entropy objective function was set to 1.0 for pairs labeled $(5, 0)$ and $(4, 1)$, 0.75 for pairs labeled $(3, 2)$, 0.5 for pairs labeled $(2, 3)$ and 0.0 for pairs labeled $(0, 5)$. This choice allowed a more fine training for task 2, where a continuous similarity value must be estimated, without altering too much the behavior in the binary estimation task 1.

The training procedure was repeated several times, each time with a different random initialization of the weights and with a different random pair order. In order to avoid overfitting, in each run the training was

Description	Subtask 1 Precision	Subtask 1 Recall	Subtask 1 F-score	Subtask 2 Precision	Subtask 2 Recall	Subtask 2 F-score	Subtask 2 Pearson
Subtask 1 best (ASOBEK)	0.680	0.669	0.674	0.732	0.531	0.616	0.475
Subtask 2 best (MITRE)	0.569	0.806	0.667	0.750	0.686	0.716	0.619
Our method, run 2	0.574	0.754	0.652	0.738	0.611	0.669	0.545
Our method, run 1	0.594	0.720	0.651	0.697	0.657	0.676	0.563
Baseline (Das and Smith, 2009)	0.679	0.520	0.589	0.674	0.543	0.601	0.511
Contest average result	0.600	0.626	0.581	0.645	0.626	0.631	0.483

Table 1: Result comparison between our method and the winners of subtask 1 and subtask 2.

stopped when the best results on the development set were obtained. The final results were taken from the run that yielded the best accuracy, and in case of tie the best F1 score, on the development set for subtask 1.

Run 2 instead was an attempt to include latent semantic vectors obtained through the procedure described in Ji and Eisenstein (2013) and added to the network from an extra layer whose output was concatenated to the features input vector.

3.3 Results and Discussion

F-measure and Pearson coefficient were the official evaluation metrics used to rank respectively subtask 1 and subtask 2. In subtask 1 – binary evaluation of the sentence pairs – we achieved an F-score of 0.651 and ranked 6th over 18 methods, the best method (ASOBEK) achieved an F-score of 0.674. In subtask 2, which was aimed at finding a similarity score in the range $[0, 1]$, with a Pearson coefficient of 0.563 we reached the 3rd place among 13 methods (the other five provided only a binary output), with the winner (MITRE) obtaining a Pearson score of 0.619. A summary and comparison of our results with the winners of the two subtasks, with the average results and with the supervised official baseline (n-gram overlapping features with logistic regression from Das and Smith (2009)) is shown in table 1. For both tasks our results are above the average both in term of ranking and average results.

Semantic features were useful to identify paraphrases, as they improved the accuracy and F-score on the development set by 0.6%. But often the shallow semantic parser failed to give an output for many sentences, limiting their potential contribution. This is due to two main reasons. The first one is the imperfect accuracy of the semantic parser itself, also observed in previous experiments where we employed it, which fails to analyze sentences containing certain patterns and predicates. The second reason, more specific to Twitter domain, is that some sentences lack a valid predicate or a proper grammatical structure. This prevents the semantic parser from giving an accurate output.

The inclusion on latent semantic features in run 2 proved to be ineffective, as it improved subtask 1 F-score by less than 0.001, and gave a worse performance in subtask 2. During the evaluation phase other experiments were tried as using the latent semantic vectors of Guo and Diab (2012), or using the vectors as described in Ji and Eisenstein (2013) instead of the extra layer, and other modifications, all without obtaining any perceptible improvement when the system was tested on the development set. The non-perfect implementation and usage of these features, together with the fact they might not be suitable to be applied to Twitter domain, may explain this lack of improvement.

4 Conclusions

We have used a neural network classifier, with a combination of multiple views of lexical, syntactic and semantic information, as the system which participated in SemEval 2015 task 1, whose goal was to classify paraphrases in Twitter. The inaccurate semantic parsing is the main reason which prevented us from obtain higher results. A possible future directions that can improve the quality of the semantic roles annotations, apart from improving the semantic parser, is to apply an effective lexical normalization method (such as Han and Baldwin (2011)), and eventually find ways to reconstruct the predicate in case it is missing.

Acknowledgments

This work is partially funded by the Hong Kong PhD Fellowship Scheme and by grant number 1314159-0PAFT20F003 of the Ping An Research Institute.

References

James Bergstra, Olivier Breuleux, Frédéric Bastien, Pascal Lamblin, Razvan Pascanu, Guillaume Desjardins, Joseph Turian, David Warde-Farley, and Yoshua Bengio. Theano: a CPU and GPU Math Expression Compiler. In *Proceedings of the Python for Scientific Computing Conference (SciPy)*, June 2010.

Michael Burrows and David J. Wheeler. A Block-sorting Lossless Data Compression Algorithm. Technical report, 1994.

Yee Seng Chan and Hwee Tou Ng. Maxsim: A Maximum Similarity Metric for Machine Translation Evaluation. In *ACL*, pages 55–62, 2008.

Dipanjan Das and Noah A. Smith. Paraphrase Identification as Probabilistic Quasi-Synchronous Recognition. In *Proceedings of the Joint Conference of the 47th Annual Meeting of the ACL and the 4th International Joint Conference on Natural Language Processing of the AFNLP: Volume 1*, pages 468–476, 2009.

William B. Dolan and Chris Brockett. Automatically Constructing a Corpus of Sentential Paraphrases. In *Proc. of IWP*, 2005.

Andrew Finch, Young-Sook Hwang, and Eiichiro Sumita. Using Machine Translation Evaluation Techniques to Determine Sentence-level Semantic Equivalence. In *Proceedings of the Third International Workshop on Paraphrasing (IWP2005)*, pages 17–24, 2005.

Pascale Fung, Zhaojun Wu, Yongsheng Yang, and Dekai Wu. Learning Bilingual Semantic Frames: Shallow Semantic Parsing vs. Semantic Role Projection. In *11th Conference on Theoretical and Methodological Issues in Machine Translation (TMI 2007)*, pages 75–84, 2007.

Xavier Glorot and Yoshua Bengio. Understanding the difficulty of training deep feedforward neural networks. In *International Conference on Artificial Intelligence and Statistics*, pages 249–256, 2010.

Cyril Goutte. Automatic Evaluation of Machine Translation Quality. *Presentation at the European Community, Xerox Research Centre Europe, on January*, 2006.

Weiwei Guo and Mona Diab. Modeling Sentences in the Latent Space. In *Proceedings of the 50th Annual Meeting of the Association for Computational Linguistics: Long Papers-Volume 1*, pages 864–872, 2012.

Nizar Habash and Ahmed Elkholy. Sepia: Surface Span Extension to Syntactic Dependency Precision-based mt Evaluation. In *Proceedings of the NIST metrics for machine translation workshop at the association for machine translation in the Americas conference, AMTA-2008. Waikiki, HI*, 2008.

Bo Han and Timothy Baldwin. Lexical Normalisation of Short Text Messages: Makn Sens a #Twitter. In *Proceedings of the 49th Annual Meeting of the Association for Computational Linguistics: Human Language Technologies - Volume 1*, HLT '11, pages 368–378, 2011.

Kurt Hornik, Maxwell Stinchcombe, and Halbert White. Multilayer feedforward networks are universal approximators. *Neural networks*, 2(5):359–366, 1989.

Yangfeng Ji and Jacob Eisenstein. Discriminative Improvements to Distributional Sentence Similarity. In *EMNLP*, pages 891–896, 2013.

Chi-kiu Lo and Dekai Wu. Meant at wmt 2013: A tunable, accurate yet inexpensive semantic frame based mt evaluation metric. In *8th Workshop on Statistical Machine Translation*, page 422, 2013.

Chi-kiu Lo, Anand Karthik Tumuluru, and Dekai Wu. Fully Automatic Semantic mt Evaluation. In *Proceedings of the Seventh Workshop on Statistical Machine Translation*, pages 243–252, 2012.

Nitin Madnani, Joel Tetreault, and Martin Chodorow. Re-examining Machine Translation Metrics for Paraphrase Identification. In *Proceedings of the 2012 Conference of the North American Chapter of the Association for Computational Linguistics: Human Language Technologies*, pages 182–190, 2012.

George A. Miller. Wordnet: A Lexical Database for English. *Communications of the ACM*, 38(11): 39–41, 1995.

Kishore Papineni, Salim Roukos, Todd Ward, and Wei-Jing Zhu. Bleu: a Method for Automatic

Evaluation of Machine Translation. In *Proceedings of the 40th annual meeting on association for computational linguistics*, pages 311–318, 2002.

Steven Parker. Badger: A New Machine Translation Metric. *Metrics for Machine Translation Challenge*, 2008.

Sameer S. Pradhan, Wayne Ward, Kadri Hacioglu, James H. Martin, and Daniel Jurafsky. Shallow Semantic Parsing using Support Vector Machines. In *HLT-NAACL*, pages 233–240, 2004.

Matthew Snover, Bonnie Dorr, Richard Schwartz, Linnea Micciulla, and John Makhoul. A Study of Translation Edit Rate with Targeted Human Annotation. In *Proceedings of association for machine translation in the Americas*, pages 223–231, 2006.

Matthew G. Snover, Nitin Madnani, Bonnie Dorr, and Richard Schwartz. Ter-Plus: paraphrase, semantic, and alignment enhancements to Translation Edit Rate. *Machine Translation*, 23(2-3):117–127, 2009.

Richard Socher, Eric H. Huang, Jeffrey Pennin, Christopher D. Manning, and Andrew Y. Ng. Dynamic Pooling and Unfolding Recursive Autoencoders for Paraphrase Detection. In *Advances in Neural Information Processing Systems*, pages 801–809, 2011.

Anand Karthik Tumuluru, Chi-kiu Lo, and Dekai Wu. Accuracy and robustness in measuring the lexical similarity of semantic role fillers for automatic semantic mt evaluation. In *Proceedings of the 26th Pacific Asia Conference on Language, Information, and Computation*, 2012.

Stephen Wan, Mark Dras, Robert Dale, and Cécile Paris. Using Dependency-Based Features to Take the Para-farce out of Paraphrase. In *Proceedings of the Australasian Language Technology Workshop*, 2006.

Wei Xu, Alan Ritter, Chris Callison-Burch, William B. Dolan, and Yangfeng Ji. Extracting Lexically Divergent Paraphrases from Twitter. *Transactions Of The Association For Computational Linguistics*, 2:435–448, 2014.

Wei Xu, Chris Callison-Burch, and William B. Dolan. SemEval-2015 Task 1: Paraphrase and semantic similarity in Twitter (PIT). In *Proceedings of the 9th International Workshop on Semantic Evaluation (SemEval)*, 2015.

Kaizhong Zhang and Dennis Shasha. Simple fast algorithms for the editing distance between trees and related problems. *SIAM journal on computing*, 18(6):1245–1262, 1989.

FBK-HLT: An Effective System for Paraphrase Identification and Semantic Similarity in Twitter

Ngoc Phuoc An Vo
University of Trento,
Fondazione Bruno Kessler
Trento, Italy
ngoc@fbk.eu

Simone Magnolini
University of Brescia,
Fondazione Bruno Kessler
Trento, Italy
magnolini@fbk.eu

Octavian Popescu
IBM Research, T.J. Watson
Yorktown, US
o.popescu@us.ibm.com

Abstract

This paper reports the description and performance of our system, FBK-HLT, participating in the SemEval 2015, Task #1 "Paraphrase and Semantic Similarity in Twitter", for both subtasks. We submitted two runs with different classifiers in combining typical features (lexical similarity, string similarity, word n-grams, etc) with machine translation metrics and edit distance features. We outperform the baseline system and achieve a very competitive result to the best system on the first subtask. Eventually, we are ranked 4th out of 18 teams participating in subtask "Paraphrase Identification".

1 Introduction

Paraphrase identification/recognition is an important task that can be used as a feature to improve many other NLP tasks as Information Retrieval, Machine Translation Evaluation, Text Summarization, Question and Answering, and others. Besides this, analyzing social data like tweets of social network Twitter is a field of growing interest for different purposes. The interesting combination of these two tasks was brought forward as Shared Task #1 in the SemEval 2015 campaign for "Paraphrase and Semantic Similarity in Twitter" (Xu et al., 2015). In this task, given a set of sentence pairs, which are not necessarily full tweets, their topic and the same sentences with part-of-speech and named entity tags; participating system is required to predict for each pair of sentences is a paraphrase (Subtask 1) and optionally compute a graded score between 0 and 1 for their semantic equivalence (Subtask 2). We participate in this shared task with a system combining different features using a binary classifier. We are interested in finding out whether semantic similarity, textual entailment and machine translation evaluation techniques could increase the accuracy of our system. This paper is organized as follows: Section 2 presents the System Description, Section 3 describes the Experiment Settings, Section 4 reports the Evaluations, Section 5 shows the Error Analysis, and finally Section 6 is the Conclusions and Future Work.

2 System Description

In order to build our system, we extract and select several different linguistic features ranging from simple (word/string similarity, edit distance) to more complex ones (machine translation evaluation metrics), then we consolidate them by a binary classifier. Moreover, different features can be used independently or together with others to measure the semantic similarity and recognize the paraphrase of given sentence pair as well as to evaluate the significance of each feature to the accuracy of system's predictions. On top of this, the system is expandable and scalable for adopting more useful features aiming for improving the accuracy.

2.1 Data Preprocessing

In order to optimizing the system performance, we carefully analyze the given data and notice that Tweets' topic is a sentence part that is always present in both sentences; this redundant similarity in the pairs does not give any information about paraphrase as two sentences can always have a same topic, yet they are may be paraphrase or not. Hence, we remove the topic from the sentences, and we did the same in the pairs with Part-of-Speech (POS) and named entity tags. We have not try our system with the topic inside tweets. As being suggested by the guideline of the task, we remove all the pairs with uncertain judgment, such as "debatable" (2, 3). After this data processing, we obtain two smaller datasets with very short texts, sometime reduced to a single word and with very poor syntactic structure. We split the original dataset into two subsets, in which one is composed by sentence pairs and the other one is composed by pairs with POS and named entity tags. Because of the simple structure of given datasets, after undergoing the preprocessing, we decide to focus on exploiting the lexical and string similarity information, rather than syntactic information.

2.2 Lexical and String Similarity

Firstly, for computing the lexical and string similarity between two sentences, we take advantage from the task baseline (Das and Smith, 2009) which is a system using a logistic regression model with eighteen features based on n-grams. This baseline system uses precision, recall and F1-score of 1-gram, 2-grams and 3-grams of tokens and stems from sentence pair to build a binary classification model for identifying paraphrase. We extract these eighteen features from baseline system, without modifications, to use in our classification model.

2.3 Machine Translation Evaluation Metrics

Other than similarity features, we also use evaluation metrics for machine translation as suggested in (Madnani et al., 2012) for paraphrase recognition on Microsoft Research paraphrase corpus (MSRP) (Dolan et al., 2004). In machine translation, the evaluation metric scores the hypotheses by aligning them to one or more reference translations. We take into consideration to use all the eight metrics proposed, but we find that adding some of them without a careful process of training on the dataset may decrease the performance of the system. Thus, we use two metrics for word alignment in our system, the METEOR and BLEU. We actually also take into consideration the metric TERp (Snover et al., 2009), but it does not make any improvement on system performance, hence, we exclude it.

2.3.1 METEOR (Metric for Evaluation of Translation with Explicit ORdering)

We use the latest version of METEOR (Denkowski and Lavie, 2014) that find alignments between sentences based on exact, stem, synonym and paraphrase matches between words and phrases. We used the system as distributed on its website, using only the "norm" option that tokenizes and normalizes punctuation and lowercase as suggested by documentation.[1] We compute the word alignment scores on sentences and on sentences with part-of-speech and named entity tags, as our idea is that if two sentences are similar, their tagged version also should be similar.

2.3.2 BLEU (Bilingual Evaluation Understudy)

We use another metric for machine translation BLEU (Papineni et al., 2002) that is one of the most commonly used and because of that has an high reliability. It is computed as the amount of n-gram overlap, for different values of n=1,2,3, and 4, between the system output and the reference translation, in our case between sentence pairs. The score is tempered by a penalty for translations that might be too short. BLEU relies on exact matching and has no concept of synonymy or paraphrasing.

2.4 Edit Distance

We use the edit distance between sentences as a feature; for that we used the Excitement Open Platform (EOP) (Magnini et al., 2014). To obtain the edit distance, we use EDITS Entailment Decision Algorithm (EDITS EDA), this algorithm classifies the pairs on the base of their edit distance, we take only this one without considering the entailment or not entailment decision. We configure the system to use lemmas and synonyms as identical words to compute sentence distance, the system normalizes the score on the number of token of the shortest sentence. We choose this configuration because it returns the best performance evaluated on training and development data.

2.5 Classification Algorithms

We build two systems for the task with different classifiers, to optimize the Accuracy and F1-score. We use WEKA (Hall et al., 2009) to obtain robust and efficient implementation of the classifiers. We try several classification algorithms in WEKA, among

[1]http://www.cs.cmu.edu/ alavie/METEOR/index.html

Classifier / Features	Baseline features (n-grams)	Baseline +METEOR	Baseline +METEOR +TERp	Baseline +METEOR +BLEU	Baseline +METEOR +BLEU +EditDistance
Baseline (Das and Smith, 2009)	72.4				
EOP EditDistance	73.3				
VotedPerceptron	73.7	75.6	75.5	75.8	**76.2**
MultiLayerPerceptron	73.9	75.6	75.3	75.4	**76.1**

Table 1: Accuracy obtained on development dataset using different classifiers with different features.

others, we find that the VotedPerceptron (with exponent 0.8) and MultilayerPerceptron (with learn rate 0.1; momentum 0.3 and N 10000) return the best performance for the evaluation on training and development data.

3 Experiment Settings

For Subtask 1, we train two models with different feature settings using the VotedPerceptron and MultilayerPerception classification algorithms on the training dataset and we evaluate these models on the development dataset. Finally, we use the same models for the evaluation on the test dataset. In table 1, we report the Accuracy results obtained by using different classifiers with different features. Our chosen classification algorithms outperform the baseline and EOP EditDistance (standalone setting). Table 2 shows F1-score obtained with different classifiers on our best set of features, and our classification algorithms again perform much better the baseline and EOP EditDistance.

For Subtask 2, due to no training data is given for computing the semantic similarity, a different approach is needed. We do not use a classifier, our similarity score is simply the average between METEOR score and edit distance score.

Classifier	F1
Baseline (Das and Smith, 2009)	.502
EOP EditDistance	.609
VotedPerceptron	**.746**
MultiLayerPerceptron	**.741**

Table 2: F1-score obtained using different classifiers on the best set of features (baseline + METEOR + BLEU + EditDistance).

	Subtask1			Subtask2
Team	Prec	Rec	F1	Pearson
Baseline$^{(\text{logistic reg})}$	.679	.520	.589	.511
Baseline$^{(\text{WTMF})}$	.450	.663	.536	.350
Baseline$^{(\text{random})}$	.192	.434	.266	.017
ASOBEK$^{(1^{st}\ \text{Subtask1})}$	.680	.669	.674	.475
MITRE$^{(1^{st}\ \text{Subtask2})}$	.569	.806	.667	.619
FBK-HLT$^{(\text{voted})}$	**.685**	.634	.659	.462
FBK-HLT$^{(\text{multilayer})}$	.676	.549	.606	.480

Table 3: Paraphrase and Semantic Similarity Results.

4 Evaluations

We submit two runs using two models described in the Section 3 for both subtasks. In the Table 3, we report the performance of our two runs against the baselines and best systems in each subtask. In Subtask 1, our runs outperform all three baselines and achieve very competitive results to the best system ASOBEK. In the run FBK-HLT$^{(\text{voted})}$, we even achieve a better Precision than the best system. In Subtask 2, though we apply a simple computation method for semantic similarity by averaging the word alignment score and EditDistance, we still have better results than two our of three baselines.

5 Error Analysis

In this section, we conduct an analysis of the misclassifications that our best system, FBK-HLT$^{(\text{voted})}$, makes on test dataset. We extract and show some randomly selected examples in which our system classifies incorrectly, both false positive or false negative; and then we analyze the possible causes for the misclassification. This inspection yields not only the top sources of error for our approach but also uncovers sources of unclear annotations in dataset.

True Positive	True Negative	False Positive	False Negative
111	612	51	64

Table 4: Error Analysis.

5.1 False positive

[1357] *omg Family Guy is killing me right now - OMG we were quoting family guy*
[1357] *family guy is trending in the US - Family guy is so racist or maybe they just point out the racism in America*
[4135] *hahaha that sounds like me - That sounds totally reasonable to me*
[5211] *The world of jenks is such a real show - Jenks from the World of Jenks is such a good person*
[128] *Anyone trying to see After Earth sometime soon - Me and my son went to see After Earth last night*

Though all these sentence pairs share many word similarity/matching and alignments, they are annotated as non-paraphrase. For example, the sentence pair **[4135]** has very high word matching and alignment after removing the common topic "sounds", but the important words "like" and "reasonable" which differ the meaning between two sentences, are not really semantically captured and distinguished by our system. As our system does not use any semantic feature, this kind of semantic difference is difficult to distinguish,leading to false positive case.

5.2 False negative

[4220] *Hell yeah Star Wars is on - Star Wars and lord of the rings on tv*
[785] *Chris Davis is putting the team on his back - Chris Davis doing what he does*
[400] *Rafa Benitez deserves a hell of a thank you - Any praise for Benitez from my Chelsea followers*
[2832] *Classy gesture by the Mets for Mariano - real class shown by The Mets Mo Rivera is a legend*
[4062] *Shonda is a freaking genius - THAT LADY IS AMAZING I LOVE SHONDA*

This case is opposite to the previous case, even though these sentence pairs do not share many word similarity and alignment, they are annotated as paraphrase. We can possibly propose some hypothesis as follows:

Extra information Though the pairs **[4220]** and **[400]** may not be paraphrase according to the paraphrase definition in the literature (Bhagat and Hovy, 2013), they are annotated as paraphrase in the gold-standard labels. We notice that as one sentence contains more extra information than the other one, it leads to low word similarity and alignment, which makes our system make wrong classification.
Specific knowledge-base In this case, the pairs **[785]** and **[2832]** require a specific knowledge-base, which is about baseball, to recognize the paraphrase; hence, even for human without any related knowledge, it might be difficult detect the paraphrase.
Common sense Though both sentences of the pair **[4062]** do not share any word similarity/alignment, they have a positive polarity that may allow identifying the paraphrase. This case may be easy for human to identify the paraphrase, yet it is difficult for machine to capture the same perception.

Table 4 shows that we can improve our system performance by reducing the false positive and false negative. In other word, we need to exploit more semantic features to make correct classification. However, according to our analysis for the false negative, it is difficult to cover these cases.

6 Conclusions and Future Work

In this paper, we describe a system participating in the SemEval 2015, Task #1 "Paraphrase and Semantic Similarity in Twitter", for both subtasks. We present a supervised system which considers multiple features at low level, such as lexical, string similarities, word alignment and edit distance. The performance of our runs is much better than the baselines and very competitive to the best system; we are ranked 4th of total 18 teams in Subtask 1.
A lower result was obtained in Subtask 2, as the chosen features have not really acquired the semantic similarity judgment. Hence, we expect to study more useful features (e.g the POS information, semantic word similarity) to improve our system performance on both identifying paraphrase and computing semantic similarity scores.

References

Rahul Bhagat and Eduard Hovy. 2013. What is a paraphrase? *Computational Linguistics*, 39(3):463–472.

Dipanjan Das and Noah A Smith. 2009. Paraphrase identification as probabilistic quasi-synchronous recognition. In *Proceedings of the Joint Conference of the 47th Annual Meeting of the ACL and the 4th International Joint Conference on Natural Language Processing of the AFNLP: Volume 1-Volume 1*, pages 468–476.

Michael Denkowski and Alon Lavie. 2014. Meteor universal: Language specific translation evaluation for any target language. In *Proceedings of the EACL 2014 Workshop on Statistical Machine Translation*.

Bill Dolan, Chris Quirk, and Chris Brockett. 2004. Unsupervised construction of large paraphrase corpora: Exploiting massively parallel news sources. In *Proceedings of the 20th international conference on Computational Linguistics*, page 350.

Mark Hall, Eibe Frank, Geoffrey Holmes, Bernhard Pfahringer, Peter Reutemann, and Ian H Witten. 2009. The WEKA data mining software: an update. *ACM SIGKDD explorations newsletter*, 11(1):10–18.

Nitin Madnani, Joel Tetreault, and Martin Chodorow. 2012. Re-examining machine translation metrics for paraphrase identification. In *Proceedings of the 2012 Conference of the North American Chapter of the Association for Computational Linguistics: Human Language Technologies*, pages 182–190.

Bernardo Magnini, Roberto Zanoli, Ido Dagan, Kathrin Eichler, Günter Neumann, Tae-Gil Noh, Sebastian Pado, Asher Stern, and Omer Levy. 2014. The excitement open platform for textual inferences. In *Proceedings of the 52nd Annual Meeting of the Association for Computational Linguistics (ACL 2014)*.

Kishore Papineni, Salim Roukos, Todd Ward, and Wei-Jing Zhu. 2002. Bleu: a method for automatic evaluation of machine translation. In *Proceedings of the 40th annual meeting on association for computational linguistics*, pages 311–318.

Matthew G Snover, Nitin Madnani, Bonnie Dorr, and Richard Schwartz. 2009. TER-Plus: paraphrase, semantic, and alignment enhancements to translation edit rate. *Machine Translation*, 23(2-3):117–127.

Wei Xu, Chris Callison-Burch, and William B. Dolan. 2015. SemEval-2015 Task 1: Paraphrase and semantic similarity in Twitter (PIT). In *Proceedings of the 9th International Workshop on Semantic Evaluation (SemEval)*.

ECNU: Leveraging Word Embeddings to Boost Performance for Paraphrase in Twitter

Jiang Zhao, Man Lan*
Shanghai Key Laboratory of Multidimensional Information Processing
Department of Computer Science and Technology,
East China Normal University Shanghai 200241, P. R. China
`51121201042@ecnu.cn; mlan@cs.ecnu.edu.cn*`

Abstract

This paper describes our approaches to paraphrase recognition in Twitter organized as task 1 in Semantic Evaluation 2015. Lots of approaches have been proposed to address the paraphrasing task on conventional texts (surveyed in (Madnani and Dorr, 2010)). In this work we examined the effectiveness of various linguistic features proposed in traditional paraphrasing task on informal texts, (i.e., Twitter), for example, string based, corpus based, and syntactic features, which served as input of a classification algorithm. Besides, we also proposed novel features based on distributed word representations, which were learned using deep learning paradigms. Results on test dataset show that our proposed features improve the performance by a margin of 1.9% in terms of F1-score and our team ranks third among 10 teams with 38 systems.

1 Introduction

Generally, a **paraphrase** is an alternative surface form in the same language expressing the same semantic content as the original form and it can appear at different levels, e.g., lexical, phrasal, sentential (Madnani and Dorr, 2010). Identifying paraphrase can improve the performance of several natural language processing (NLP) applications, such as query and pattern expansion (Metzler et al., 2007), machine translation (Mirkin et al., 2009), question answering (Duboue and Chu-Carroll, 2006), see survey (Androutsopoulos and Malakasiotis, 2010) for completion. Most of previous work of paraphrase are on formal text. Recently with the rapidly growth of microblogs and social media services, the computational linguistic community is moving its attention to informal genre of text (Java et al., 2007; Ritter et al., 2010). For example, (Zanzotto et al., 2011) defined the problem of redundancy detection in Twitter and proposed SVM models based on bag-of-word, syntactic content features to detect paraphrase.

To provide a benchmark so as to compare and develop different paraphrasing techniques in Twitter, the paraphrase and semantic similarity task in *SemEval* 2015 (Xu et al., 2015) requires the participants to determine whether two tweets express the same meaning or not and optionally a degree score between 0 and 1, which can be regarded as a binary classification problem. Paraphrasing task is very close to semantic textual similarity and textual entailment task (Marelli et al., 2014) since substantially these tasks all concentrated on modeling the underlying similarity between two sentences. The commonly-used features in these tasks can be categorized into several following groups: (1) string based which measures the sequence similarities of original strings with others, e.g., *n*-gram `Overlap`, cosine similarity; (2) corpus based which measures word or sentence similarities using word distributional vectors learned from large corpora using distributional models, like *Latent Semantic Analysis* (LSA), etc. (3) knowledge based which estimates similarities with the aid of external resources, such as WordNet; (4) syntactic based which utilizes syntax information to measure similarities; (5) other features such as using Named Entity similarity.

In this work, we built a supervised binary classifier for paraphrase judgment and adopted multiple features used in conventional texts to recognize paraphrase in Twitter, which includes string based features, corpus based features, etc. Besides, we also proposed a novel feature based on distributed word representations (i.e., word embeddings) learned over a large raw corpus using neural language models. The results on test dataset demonstrate that linguistic features are effective for paraphrase in Twitter task and proposed word embedding features further improve the performance.

The rest of this paper is organized as follows. Section 2 describes the features used in our systems. System setups and experimental results on training and test datasets are presented in Section 3. Finally, conclusions and future work are given in Section 4.

2 Feature Engineering

In this section, we describe the our preprocessing step and the traditional NLP linguistic features, as well as the word embedding features used in our systems.

2.1 Preprocessing

We conducted following text preprocessing operations before we extracted features: (1) we recovered the elongated words to their normal forms, e.g., "*goooooood*" to "*good*"; (2) about 5,000 slangs or abbreviations collected from Internet were used to convert these informal texts into their complete forms, e.g., "*1dering*" to "*wondering*", "*2g2b4g*" to "*to good to be forgotten*"; (3) the WordNet-based Lemmatizer implemented in Natural Language Toolkit[1] was used to lemmatize all words to their nearest base forms in WordNet, for example, *was* is lemmatized to *be*. (4) we replaced a word from one sentence with another word from the other sentence if the two words share the same meaning, where WordNet was used to look up synonyms. No word sense disambiguation was performed and all synsets for a particular lemma were considered.

2.2 String Based Features

We firstly recorded length information of given sentences pairs using following eight measure functions: $|A|, |B|, |A-B|, |B-A|, |A \cup B|, |A \cap B|, \frac{(|A|-|B|)}{|B|}, \frac{(|B|-|A|)}{|A|}$ where $|A|$ stands for the number of non-repeated words in sentence A, $|A-B|$ means the number of unmatched words found in A but not in B, $|A \cup B|$ stands for the set size of non-repeated words found in either A or B and $|A \cap B|$ means the set size of shared words found in both A and B.

Motivated by the hypothesis that two texts are considered to be more similar if they share more strings, we adopted the following five types of measurements: (1) longest common sequence similarity on the original and lemmatized sentences; (2) `Jaccard`, `Dice`, `Overlap` coefficient on original word sequences; (3) `Jaccard` similarity using n-grams, where n-grams were obtained at three different levels, i.e., the original word level (n=1,2,3), the lemmatized word level (n=1,2,3) and the character level (n=2,3,4); (4) weighted word overlap feature (Šarić et al., 2012) that takes the importance of words into consideration, where Web 1T 5-gram Corpus[2] was used to estimate the importance of words. (5) sentences were represented as vectors in *tf*idf* schema based on their lemmatized forms and then these vectors were used to calculate `cosine`, `Manhattan`, `Euclidean` distance and `Pearson`, `Spearmanr`, `Kendalltau` correlation coefficients based on different perspectives. Totally, we got thirty-one string based features.

2.3 Corpus Based Features

Corpus based features aim to capture the semantic similarities using distributional meanings of words and *Latent Semantic Analysis* (LSA) (Landauer and Dumais, 1997) is widely used to estimate the distributional vectors of words. Hence, we adopted two distributional sets released in TakeLab (Šarić et al., 2012), where LSA is performed over the New York Times Annotated Corpus (NYT)[3] and Wikipedia. Then two strategies were used to convert the distributional meanings of words to sentence level: (i) simply summing up the distributional vectors of words in the sentence, (ii) using the information content (Šarić et al., 2012) to weigh the LSA vector of each word w and summing them up. At last we used cosine similarity to measure the similarity of two sentences based on these vectors. Besides, we used the Co-occurrence Retrieval Model (CRM) (Weeds,

[1] http://nltk.org/

[2] https://catalog.ldc.upenn.edu/LDC2006T13

[3] https://catalog.ldc.upenn.edu/LDC2008T19

2003) as another type of corpus based feature. The CRM was calculated based on a notion of substitutability, that is, the more appropriate it was to substitute word w_1 in place of word w_2 in a suitable natural language task, the more semantically similar they were.

Besides, the extraction of aforementioned features rely on large external corpora, while (Guo and Diab, 2012) proposed a novel latent model, i.e., weighted textual matrix factorization (WTMF), to capture the contextual meanings of words in sentences based on internal term-sentence matrix. WTMF factorizes the original term-sentence matrix X into two matrices such that $X_{i,j} \approx P^T_{*,i} Q_{*,j}$, where $P_{*,i}$ is a latent semantics vector profile for word w_i and $Q_{*,j}$ is the vector profile that represents the sentence s_j. The weight matrix W is introduced in the optimization process in order to model the missing words at the right level of emphasis. Then, we used `cosine`, `Manhattan`, `Euclidean` functions and `Pearson`, `Spearmanr`, `Kendalltau` correlation coefficients to calculate the similarities based on sentence representations. At last, we obtained twelve corpus based features.

2.4 Syntactic Features

We estimated the similarities of sentence pairs at syntactic level. Stanford CoreNLP toolkit (Manning and Surdeanu, 2014) was used to obtain POS tag sequences. Afterwards, we performed eight measure functions described in Section 2.2 over these sequences, which resulted in eight syntactic based features.

2.5 Other Features

We built a binary feature to indicate whether two sentences in a pair have the same polarity (*affirmative* or *negative*) by looking up a manually-collected negation list with 29 negation words (e.g., *scarcely*, *no*, *little*). Also, we checked whether one sentence entails the other only using the named entity information which was provided in the dataset. Finally, we obtained nineteen other features.

2.6 Word Embedding Features

Recently, deep learning has achieved a great success in the fields of computer vision, automatic speech recognition and natural language processing. As a consequence of its application in NLP, word embeddings have been building blocks in many tasks, e.g., named entity recognition and chunking (Turian et al., 2010), semantic word similarities (Mikolov et al., 2013a), etc. Being distributed representation of words, word embeddings usually are learned using neural networks over a large raw corpus and has outperformed LSA for preserving linear regularities among words (Mikolov et al., 2013a). Due to its superior performance, we adopted word embeddings to estimate the similarities of sentence pairs. In our experiments, we used seven different word embeddings with different dimensions: *word2vec* (Mikolov et al., 2013b), *Collobert and Weston* embeddings (Collobert and Weston, 2008) and *HLBL* embeddings (Mnih and Hinton, 2007). Word2vec embeddings are distributed within the word2vec toolkit[4] and they are 300-dimensional vectors learned from Google News Corpus which consists of over a 100 billion words. *Collobert and Weston* and *HLBL* embeddings are learned over a part of RCV1 corpus which consists of 63 millions words, with 25, 50, 100, or 200 dimensions and 50, 100 dimensions over 5-gram windows respectively. To obtain sentence representations, we simply summed up embedding vectors corresponding to the non-stopwords tokens in bag of words (BOW) of sentences. After that, we used `cosine`, `Manhattan`, `Euclidean` functions and `Pearson`, `Spearmanr`, `Kendalltau` correlation coefficients to calculate the similarities based on these synthetic sentence representations. We got ninety word embedding features.

3 Experiments and Results

3.1 System Setups

The organizers provided 13,063 training pairs together with 4,727 development pairs in development phase and 972 test pairs in test phase. We removed the debatable instances (i.e., two annotators vote for *yes* and the other three for *no*) existing in the dataset, which resulted in 11,530 training pairs and 4,142 development pairs. We built two supervised classification systems over these datasets. One is `mlfeats` which only uses the traditional linguistic features

[4] https://code.google.com/p/word2vec

Algorithm	mlfeats			nnfeats		
	Precision	*Recall*	*F1*	*Precision*	*Recall*	*F1*
SVC(0.1)	0.756	0.942	0.839	0.756	0.942	0.839
GB(140)	0.756	0.939	0.838	0.754	0.940	0.837
GB(150)	0.755	0.939	0.837	0.753	0.939	0.836
RF(45)	0.754	0.937	0.835	0.749	0.936	0.832

Table 1: Top results of different classification algorithms in systems `mlfeats` and `nnfeats` on development dataset together with parameter values in brackets.

System	F1-Rank	*Precision*	*Recall*	*F1*
ECNU_nnfeats	4	0.767	0.583	0.662
ECNU_mlfeats	10	0.754	0.560	0.643
BASELINE_logistic	21	0.679	0.520	0.589
BASELINE_WTMF	28	0.450	0.663	0.536
BASELINE_random	38	0.192	0.434	0.266
ASOBEK_svckernel	1	0.680	0.669	0.674
ASOBEK_linearsvm	2	0.682	0.663	0.672
MITRE_ikr	3	0.569	0.806	0.667

Table 2: Performance and rankings of systems `mlfeats`, `nnfeats` and baseline systems on test dataset officially released by the organizers, as well as top ranking systems.

(i.e., features described in Section 2.2-2.5, 64 features in total) and the other is `nnfeats` which combines the traditional linguistic features with the word embedding features (148 features in total). Several classification algorithms were explored on development dataset including Support Vector Classification (SVC, *linear*), Random Forest (RF), Gradient Boosting (GB) implemented in the scikit-learn toolkit (Pedregosa et al., 2011) and a large scale of parameter values in these algorithms were tuned, i.e., the trade-off parameter c in SVR, the number of trees n in RF, the number of boosting stages n in GB. F-score was used to evaluate the performance of systems.

3.2 Results and Discussion

Table 1 presents the best four F1 results achieved by different algorithms together with their parameters in system `mlfeats` and `nnfeats` on development dataset. The results show that these two systems consistently yield comparable performance, which means that our proposed features based on word embeddings have little help to detect paraphrase on development set. And we also find that SVC performs slightly better than GB and RF algorithm. Therefore, we adopted a major voting schema based on SVC (c=0.1) and GB (n=140,150) in test period.

Table 2 summarizes the performance and ranks of our systems on test dataset, along with the baseline systems provided by the organizers and the top three systems. From this table, we observe following findings. Firstly, `nnfeats` using word embedding features outperforms the system `mlfeats` only using traditional linguistic features by 1.9%, which is inconsistent with the findings on development set. The possible reason may be that test data is collected from a different time period while train and development data is from the same time period while the word embedding features might more or less capture this differences. Secondly, our results are significantly better than the three baseline systems since our systems incorporate the features used in baseline systems and other effective features. Thirdly, the top 1 system (i.e., ASOBEK_svckernel) yields 3.1% and 1.2% improvement over our system `mlfeats` and `nnfeats` respectively, which indicates that word embedding features and traditional linguistic features are effective in resolving Twitter paraphrase problem.

To explore the influence of different feature types, we conducted feature ablation experiments where we removed one feature group from all feature set every time and then executed the same classification procedure. Table 3 shows the results of feature ablation experiments. From this table, we can see that the most influential features for recognizing tweet paraphrase is corpus based features and the second most important feature group is word embedding features, which are within our expectation since these two kinds of feature take advantage of the semantic meaning of words.

Feature	*Precision*	*Recall*	*F1*
All	0.767	0.583	0.662
-string	0.717	0.594	0.650 (-0.012)
-corpus	0.772	0.543	0.638 (-0.024)
-syntactic	0.797	0.560	0.658 (-0.004)
-other	0.784	0.560	0.653 (-0.009)
-embedding	0.823	0.531	0.646 (-0.016)

Table 3: The results of feature ablation experiments.

4 Conclusion

In this paper we address paraphrase in Twitter task by building a supervised classification model. Many linguistic features used in traditional paraphrase task and newly proposed features based on word embeddings were extracted. The results on test dataset demonstrate that (1) our proposed word embedding features improve the performance by a value of 1.9%; (2) the linguistic features used in paraphrase on conventional texts task are also useful and effective in Twitter domain.

Acknowledgements

This research is supported by grants from Science and Technology Commission of Shanghai Municipality under research grant no. (14DZ2260800 and 15ZR1410700) and Shanghai Collaborative Innovation Center of Trustworthy Software for Internet of Things (ZF1213).

References

Ion Androutsopoulos and Prodromos Malakasiotis. 2010. A survey of paraphrasing and textual entailment methods. *J. Artif. Int. Res.*, pages 135–187.

Ronan Collobert and Jason Weston. 2008. A unified architecture for natural language processing: Deep neural networks with multitask learning. In *Proceedings of the 25th international conference on Machine learning*, pages 160–167.

Pablo Ariel Duboue and Jennifer Chu-Carroll. 2006. Answering the question you wish they had asked: The impact of paraphrasing for question answering. In *NAACL, Companion Volume: Short Papers*, pages 33–36.

Weiwei Guo and Mona Diab. 2012. Modeling sentences in the latent space. In *ACL*, pages 864–872.

Akshay Java, Xiaodan Song, Tim Finin, and Belle Tseng. 2007. Why we Twitter: understanding microblogging usage and communities. In *Proceedings of the 9th WebKDD and 1st SNA-KDD 2007 workshop on Web mining and social network analysis*, pages 56–65.

Thomas K Landauer and Susan T Dumais. 1997. A solution to Plato's problem: The latent semantic analysis theory of acquisition, induction, and representation of knowledge. *Psychological review*, page 211.

Nitin Madnani and Bonnie J Dorr. 2010. Generating phrasal and sentential paraphrases: A survey of data-driven methods. *Computational Linguistics*, 36(3):341–387.

Christopher D. Manning and Mihai et al. Surdeanu. 2014. The Stanford CoreNLP natural language processing toolkit. In *52nd ACL : System Demonstrations*.

Marco Marelli, Luisa Bentivogli, Marco Baroni, Raffaella Bernardi, Stefano Menini, and Roberto Zamparelli. 2014. Semeval-2014 task 1: Evaluation of compositional distributional semantic models on full sentences through semantic relatedness and textual entailment. In *SemEval*, pages 1–8.

Donald Metzler, Susan Dumais, and Christopher Meek. 2007. *Similarity measures for short segments of text.*

Tomas Mikolov, Kai Chen, Greg Corrado, and Jeffrey Dean. 2013a. Efficient estimation of word representations in vector space. *arXiv preprint arXiv:1301.3781*.

Tomas Mikolov, Ilya Sutskever, Kai Chen, Greg S Corrado, and Jeff Dean. 2013b. Distributed representations of words and phrases and their compositionality. In *Advances in Neural Information Processing Systems*, pages 3111–3119.

Shachar Mirkin, Lucia Specia, Nicola Cancedda, Ido Dagan, Marc Dymetman, and Idan Szpektor. 2009. Source-language entailment modeling for translating unknown terms. In *ACL*, pages 791–799.

Andriy Mnih and Geoffrey Hinton. 2007. Three new graphical models for statistical language modelling. In *Proceedings of the 24th international conference on Machine learning*, pages 641–648.

Fabian Pedregosa, Gaël Varoquaux, Alexandre Gramfort, et al. 2011. Scikit-learn: Machine learning in Python. *The Journal of Machine Learning Research*, 12:2825–2830.

Alan Ritter, Colin Cherry, and Bill Dolan. 2010. Unsupervised modeling of Twitter conversations. pages 172–180.

Joseph Turian, Lev Ratinov, and Yoshua Bengio. 2010. Word representations: a simple and general method for semi-supervised learning. In *the 48th ACL*, pages 384–394.

Frane Šarić, Goran Glavaš, Mladen Karan, Jan Šnajder, and Bojana Dalbelo Bašić. 2012. TakeLab: Systems for measuring semantic text similarity. In **SEM 2012 and (SemEval 2012)*, pages 441–448, Montréal, Canada.

Julie Elizabeth Weeds. 2003. *Measures and applications of lexical distributional similarity*. Ph.D. thesis, University of Sussex.

Wei Xu, Chris Callison-Burch, and William B. Dolan. 2015. SemEval-2015 Task 1: Paraphrase and semantic similarity in Twitter (PIT). In *Proceedings of the 9th International Workshop on Semantic Evaluation (SemEval)*, Denver, CO.

Fabio Massimo Zanzotto, Marco Pennacchiotti, and Kostas Tsioutsiouliklis. 2011. Linguistic redundancy in Twitter. In *EMNLP*, pages 659–669.

ROB: Using Semantic Meaning to Recognize Paraphrases

Rob van der Goot
University of Groningen
r.van.der.goot@rug.nl

Gertjan van Noord
University of Groningen
g.j.m.van.noord@rug.nl

Abstract

Paraphrase recognition is the task of identifying whether two pieces of natural language represent similar meanings. This paper describes a system participating in the shared task 1 of SemEval 2015, which is about paraphrase detection and semantic similarity in twitter. Our approach is to exploit semantically meaningful features to detect paraphrases. An existing state-of-the-art model for predicting semantic similarity is adapted to this task.

A wide variety of features is used, ranging from different types of models, to lexical overlap and synset overlap. A maximum entropy classifier is then trained on these features. In addition to the detection of paraphrases, a similarity score is also predicted, using the probabilities of the classifier. To improve the results, normalization is used as preprocessing step.

Our final system achieves a F1 score of 0.620 (10th out of 18 teams), and a Pearson correlation of 0.515 (6th out of 13 teams).

1 Introduction

A good paraphrase detection system can be useful in many natural language processing tasks, like searching, translating or summarization. For clean texts, F1 scores as high as 0.84 have been reported on paraphrase detection (Madnani et al., 2012).

However, previous research focused almost solely on clean text. Thanks to the Twitter Paraphrase Corpus (Xu et al., 2014), this has now changed. Carrying out this task on noisy texts is a new challenge. The abundant availability of social media data and the high redundancy that naturally exists in this data makes this task highly relevant (Zanzotto et al., 2011).

Our approach is based on the model described by Bjerva et al. (2014). This model has proved to achieve state-of-the-art results at predicting semantic similarity (Marelli et al., 2014). It is based on overlaps of semantically meaningful properties of sentences. A random forest regression model (Breiman, 2001) combines these features to predict a semantic similarity score. We rely heavily on the assumption that semantically meaningful features can also be used to identify paraphrases.

The features of the existing system are also used in the new system. However, the old system used a regression model, while the new task demands class-based output. Hence, the machine learning model model is changed to a maximum entropy model.

2 Data

The Twitter Paraphrase Corpus consists of two distinct parts, the training data differs significantly from the test data.

The 17,790 tweet pairs for training are collected between April 24th and May 3rd, 2014. These tweets are selected based on the trending topics of that period. Annotation of the training data is done by human annotators from Amazon Mechanical Turk. Every sentence pair is annotated by 5 different annotators, resulting in a score of 0-5. Based on this score we create a binary paraphrase judgement. If 0, 1 or 2 annotators judged positively, we treat the sentence pair as not being a paraphrase, for 3, 4 or 5 positive judgements we treat the sentence pair as a paraphrase.

The test data is collected between May 13th and June 10th, and is thus based on different trending topics. This assures the integrity of the evaluation. In contrast to the training data, this data is annotated by an expert similarity rating on a 5-point Likert scale (Likert, 1932), to mimic the training data. Sentence pairs with a similarity score of 0, 1 and 2 are considered non-paraphrases, and sentence pairs with scores of 4 and 5 are considered paraphrases. The one uncertain category (similarity score of 3) is discarded in the evaluation.

Using this data, we end up with two different types of gold data per sentence pair. Firstly, we have the binary gold data that indicates if a sentence pair is a paraphrase. Secondly, we have the raw annotations that can be used as a similarity score. These annotations are normalized by dividing them by their maximum score (5), so we end up with $\langle 0.0, 0.2, 0.4, 0.6, 0.8, 1.0\rangle$ as possible similarity scores.

The tweets in the corpus are already tokenized using TweetMotif (O'Connor et al., 2010). Additionally, Part Of Speech (POS) tags are provided by a tagger that is adapted to twitter (Derczynski et al., 2013). Named entity tags are also obtained from an adapted tagger (Ritter et al., 2011).

3 Method

The model is based on a state-of-the-art semantic similarity prediction model (Bjerva et al., 2014). It is mainly based on overlap features extracted from different parsers, but also includes synset overlap, and a Compositional Distributional Semantic Model (CDSM). The parsers used in this model are a constituency parser (Steedman, 2001), logical parser Paradox (Claessen and Sörensson, 2003) and the DRS parser Boxer (Bos, 2008).

3.1 Features

Our model uses 25 features in total. Due to space constraints we cannot describe them all in detail here. Instead we group the features as follows:

- Lexical features: word overlap, proportional sentence length difference.
- POS: noun overlap, verb overlap.
- Logical model: instance overlap, relation overlap.
- DRS: agent overlap, patient overlap, DRS complexity.
- Entailments: binary features for: neutral, entailment and contradiction predictions.
- CDSM: The cosine distance between the element wise addition of the vectors in each sentence is used.
- Synsets (WordNet): The distance of the closest synsets of each word in both sentences, and the distance between the noun synsets.
- Named entity: overlap between named entities[1].

For a complete detailed overview we refer to the paper describing the semantic similarity system (Bjerva et al., 2014), or for even more detail (van der Goot, 2014).

3.2 Maximum Entropy Models

We will compare two different maximum entropy models. The maximum entropy implementation of Scikit-Learn (Pedregosa et al., 2011) is used.

The first maximum entropy model is a **binary** model that also outputs a probability. From this model, the normal binary output is not used, instead we use the estimated probability that something is a paraphrase. Using this value, we can set our own threshold to have more control on the final output.

The second maximum entropy model is a **multi-class** model. This classifier is based on the 6 different classes in our data, and thus outputs 6 probabilities. We use the similarity score of each class as weight to convert all probabilities to one probability. For each class we multiply the similarity score with the probability that our model predicts for this class. The results of the 6 classes are then summed to get a single probability. This classification model uses more specific training data, thus it should have a more precise output.

3.3 Normalization

A normalization approach very similar to that described by Han et al. (2013) is used to try to improve the parses. This normalization consists of three steps.

[1]This is the only feature not present in the original semantic similarity system

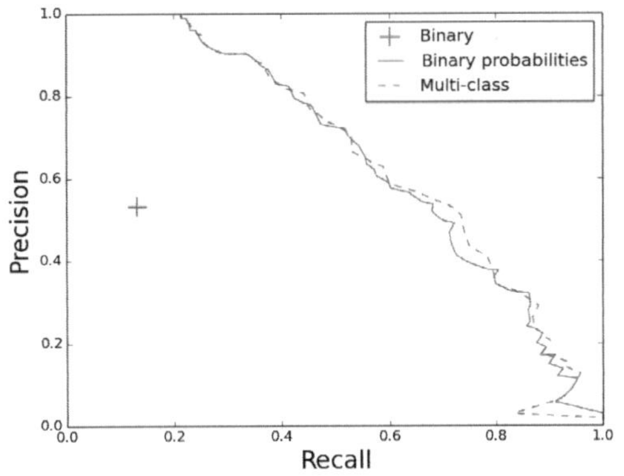

Figure 1: Precision and recall for the different classifiers.

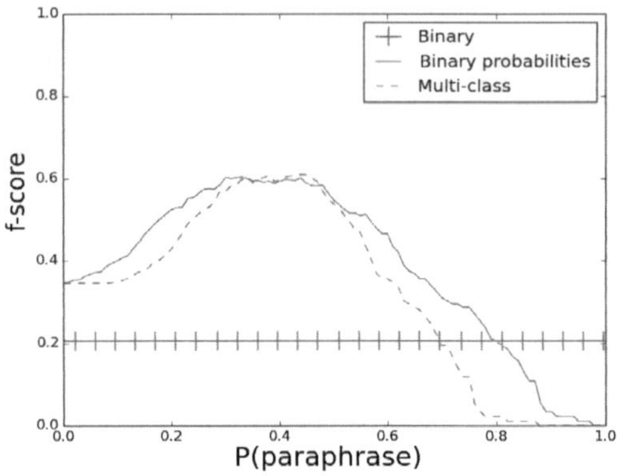

Figure 2: F-Score for the different classifiers. P is the threshold that decides if a sentence pair is a paraphrase.

The first step is to decide which tokens might need a correction, this is decided by a dictionary lookup in the Aspell dictionary[2].

The second step is the generation of possible corrections for every misspelled word. For this, the Aspell source code is adapted to lower the costs of deletion in its algorithm, because we assume words are often typed in an abbreviated form in this domain.

The last step is the ranking of the candidates. Here we use a different approach than the traditional approach. Instead of using a static formula to predict the probability of each candidate, we want to use a more flexible approach. Google N-gram probabilities (Brants and Franz, 2006), Aspell scores and dictionary lookups are combined using logistic regression. To adjusts the weights of the regression model, 200 sentences are normalized manually. The resulting model is then applied to all the other sentences.

This normalization approach does not reach a perfect accuracy, and normalizing a sentence might remove meaningful information. So instead of using the normalization as straightforward pre processing of the data, we use the raw and the normalized sentence in the model. For each feature, scores are calculated for both versions of the sentence. The highest of these scores be used as input for our maximum entropy model.

4 Evaluation

This chapter is divided in the two sub tasks of paraphrase detection and similarity prediction. A strong baseline is used, namely a state-of-the art model for clean text: a logistic regression model that uses simple lexical overlap features (Das and Smith, 2009).

[2]www.aspell.net

4.1 Paraphrase Detection

The evaluation is done on expert annotations, which are only available for the test set. The binary and multi-class classifiers are evaluated separately. Additionally, we also tried to improve the system by using normalization.

The precision and recall of both classifiers is plotted in Figure 1. In this graph the differences are barely visible, therefore it looks like both models are approximately equal.

If we look at the F-scores of Figure 2, the differences are bigger. The highest F-scores of both classifiers are 0.604 and 0.610 for respectively the binary and the multi-class classifier. Both classifiers outperform the baseline F-score of 0.583.

These graphs also show that the default output of the binary deos not perform well, so it is really necessary to use the probabilities.

4.1.1 Feature Comparisons

We use the same grouping for features as in 3.1. The absolute weights of all features within each group are summed. For the multi-class classifier the weights are averaged over all 6 classes. Also an ablation experiment is done. An overview this evaluation is shown in Table 1.

In the ablation experiments we see that it is not always better to use more features. Especially the

	Weights		Ablation	
Feat. group	**Binary**	**Multi**	**Binary**	**Multi**
Lexical	2.43	1.65	**0.601**	0.598
POS	0.79	0.71	0.600	0.600
Log. model	0.74	1.61	0.573	**0.606**
DRS	3.57	1.88	0.551	0.553
Entailments	0.51	2.79	0.584	0.589
CDSM	5.29	3.63	0.538	0.523
Synsets	0.49	0.63	0.588	0.584
NE	0.06	0.09	0.597	0.599
All	-	-	0.600	0.604

Table 1: Absolute weights of the feature groups and feature group ablation F1-Scores.

logical model should be left out in the multi-class entropy model. The models differ in some aspects, whereas some features are important for both. More specifically, we can see that the parsers outputs and lexical features are more important for the multi-class model, while the other features are more important for the binary model.

4.1.2 Normalization

After the normalization of the sentences, we run the systems again. These runs are not plotted in the graphs, because the differences are small. Despite the small differences, there is one little performance boost on the top-runs of the multi-class classifiers, resulting in the highest F-score of 0.62.

4.2 Semantic Similarity Prediction

Even though we do not have real semantic similarity training data, we simulate semantic similarity using the amount of the positive judgements per sentence pair. Our system is evolved from a semantic similarity prediction system, so this model should work well for this task. The Pearson correlation between the different annotations of experts (test) and crowd-sourcing (training) is 0.735.

For this sub task we will also try different heuristics using both our classifiers. We start with the multi-class classifier, because it is trained to give back a similarity score. The model produces probabilities for each class, the class with the highest probability is used as output. We call this the `Highest P` method.

Another model can be built using the predicted weights, similar to section 3.2. We refer to this as the `Weighted` method.

	Baseline	Highest P	Binary P	Weighted
R	0.511	0.416	0.508	0.515

Table 2: Pearson correlation (R) for the different similarity prediction approaches.

Besides the multi-class classifier, we also trained a binary classifier. The only way for this classifier to output a degree score, is using the probability. This is called `Binary P`.

Only the weighted method beats the baseline. Results of all three approaches and the baseline can be found in Table 2.

5 Conclusion

The main conclusion to draw from these experiments is that by using deep semantic features, we can achieve a maximum F-score of 0.61 on the paraphrase detection task. By using normalization we can improve this F-score to 0.62.

Following from this, it is safe to conclude that a semantic similarity prediction system can be used in paraphrase detection reasonably well. Our system had an average result on this shared task (10th out of 18 teams)[3]. The advantage of this system is that it can be created easily from existing tools.

Unsurprisingly, the results on the semantic similarity task were better (6th out of 13 teams). Even though the gold data does not represent a real semantic similarity, but a scale of positive annotations of the paraphrase detection task.

The source code of our system has been made publicly available[4].

Acknowledgements

This paper is part of the 'Parsing Algorithms for Uncertain Input' project, supported by the Nuance Foundation.

We would like to thank the organizers of the shared task (Xu et al., 2015). Additionally, we would also like to thank the anonymous reviewers and Johannes Bjerva for the valuable feedback on this paper.

[3] http://alt.qcri.org/semeval2015/task1

[4] https://bitbucket.org/robvanderg/sem15

References

Johannes Bjerva, Johan Bos, Rob van der Goot, and Malvina Nissim. 2014. The Meaning Factory: Formal semantics for recognizing textual entailment and determining semantic similarity. *SemEval 2014: International Workshop on Semantic Evaluation*, pages 642–646.

Johan Bos. 2008. Wide-coverage semantic analysis with Boxer. In *Proceedings of the 2008 Conference on Semantics in Text Processing*, pages 277–286.

Thorsten Brants and Alex Franz. 2006. Web 1T5-gram corpus version 1.1.

Leo Breiman. 2001. Random forests. *Machine learning*, 45(1):5–32.

Koen Claessen and Niklas Sörensson. 2003. New techniques that improve MACE-style finite model finding. In *Proceedings of the CADE-19 Workshop: Model Computation-Principles, Algorithms, Applications*, pages 11–27.

Dipanjan Das and Noah A Smith. 2009. Paraphrase identification as probabilistic quasi-synchronous recognition. In *Proceedings of the Joint Conference of the 47th Annual Meeting of the ACL and the 4th International Joint Conference on Natural Language Processing of the AFNLP: Volume 1-Volume 1*, pages 468–476.

Leon Derczynski, Alan Ritter, Sam Clark, and Kalina Bontcheva. 2013. Twitter part-of-speech tagging for all: Overcoming sparse and noisy data. In *RANLP*, pages 198–206.

Bo Han, Paul Cook, and Timothy Baldwin. 2013. Lexical normalization for social media text. *ACM Transactions on Intelligent Systems and Technology (TIST)*, 4(1):5.

Rensis Likert. 1932. A technique for the measurement of attitudes. *Archives of psychology*.

Nitin Madnani, Joel Tetreault, and Martin Chodorow. 2012. Re-examining machine translation metrics for paraphrase identification. In *Proceedings of the 2012 Conference of the North American Chapter of the Association for Computational Linguistics: Human Language Technologies*, pages 182–190.

Marco Marelli, Luisa Bentivogli, Marco Baroni, Raffaella Bernardi, Stefano Menini, and Roberto Zamparelli. 2014. Semeval-2014 task 1: Evaluation of compositional distributional semantic models on full sentences through semantic relatedness and textual entailment. *SemEval-2014*.

Brendan O'Connor, Michel Krieger, and David Ahn. 2010. Tweetmotif: Exploratory search and topic summarization for Twitter.

Fabian Pedregosa, Gaël Varoquaux, Alexandre Gramfort, Vincent Michel, Bertrand Thirion, Olivier Grisel, Mathieu Blondel, Peter Prettenhofer, Ron Weiss, Vincent Dubourg, et al. 2011. Scikit-learn: Machine learning in Python. *The Journal of Machine Learning Research*, 12:2825–2830.

Alan Ritter, Sam Clark, Oren Etzioni, et al. 2011. Named entity recognition in tweets: an experimental study. In *Proceedings of the Conference on Empirical Methods in Natural Language Processing*, pages 1524–1534.

Mark Steedman. 2001. *The Syntactic Process*.

Rob van der Goot. 2014. Automatic estimation of semantic relatedness for sentences using machine learning. Master's thesis, University of Groningen.

Wei Xu, Alan Ritter, Chris Callison-Burch, William B Dolan, and Yangfeng Ji. 2014. Extracting lexically divergent paraphrases from Twitter. *Transactions of the Association for Computational Linguistics*, 2:435–448.

Wei Xu, Chris Callison-Burch, and William B. Dolan. 2015. SemEval-2015 Task 1: Paraphrase and semantic similarity in Twitter (PIT). In *Proceedings of the 9th International Workshop on Semantic Evaluation (SemEval)*.

Fabio Massimo Zanzotto, Marco Pennacchiotti, and Kostas Tsioutsiouliklis. 2011. Linguistic redundancy in Twitter. In *Proceedings of the Conference on Empirical Methods in Natural Language Processing*, pages 659–669.

AMRITA_CEN@SemEval-2015: Paraphrase Detection for Twitter using Unsupervised Feature Learning with Recursive Autoencoders

Mahalakshmi Shanmuga Sundaram, Anand Kumar Madasamy and Soman Kotti Padannayil
Center for Excellence in Computational Engineering and Networking
Amrita Vishwa Vidyapeetham
Coimbatore, India
mahalakshmisklu@gmail.com
m_anandkumar@cb.amrita.edu
kp_soman@amrita.edu

Abstract

We explore using recursive autoencoders for SemEval 2015 Task 1: Paraphrase and Semantic Similarity in Twitter. Our paraphrase detection system makes use of phrase-structure parse tree embeddings that are then provided as input to a conventional supervised classification model. We achieve an F1 score of 0.45 on paraphrase identification and a Pearson correlation of 0.303 on computing semantic similarity.

1 Introduction

The process of rewriting text with a different choice of words or using a different sentence structure while preserving meaning is called paraphrasing. Identifying paraphrases can be a difficult task owing to the fact that evaluating surface level similarity is often not enough, but rather systems must take into account the underlying semantics of the content being assessed.

Paraphrasing and paraphrase detection are important and challenging tasks, which find their application in various subfields of Natural Language Processing (NLP) such as information retrieval, question answering (Erwin and Emiel, 2005), plagiarism detection (Paul Clough et al., 2002), text summarization and evaluation of machine translation (Chris Callison Burch, 2008).

We explore using recursive autoencoders for paraphrase detection and similarity scoring as a part of SemEval 2015 Task 1: Paraphrase and Semantic Similarity in Twitter. Twitter is an online social networking service with millions of users who casually converse about diverse topics in a continuous and contemporaneous manner (Wei Xu et al., 2014; Wei Xu et al., 2015). Table 1 gives an example of real tweets, some of which are paraphrases of each other. The very casual style of the Twitter corpus makes it more challenging to work with for many NLP tools. We use vector space embeddings, in part, since they are relatively good at dealing with noisy data.

2 Related Work

Socher et al. (2011) explored using recursive autoencoders (RAEs) and dynamic pooling for paraphrase detection. They parse each sentence within a pair, compute embeddings for each node in the parse trees, and then construct a similarity matrix comparing the embedding vectors for all nodes within the two parse trees. Using dynamic pooling, they convert the variable size similarity matrix for each sentence pair to a matrix of fixed size. The resulting fixed size matrix is then given to a softmax classifier to detect whether the sentences are paraphrases.

3 A Deep Learning System

The architecture of our system is depicted in Figure 1. The raw Twitter corpus is preprocessed using a phrase-structure parser. The resulting parse trees are then used to train an unfolding RAE model. This model provides us with embedding vectors that are then used to compute the similarity between every node in the parse trees associated with a sentence pair. A similarity matrix is populated with the node-to-node similarity scores as measured by the Euclidean distance beween the node embedding vectors. The size of the similarity matrix depends on

Sentence 1	Sentence 2	Paraphrase or Not
AAP is in the Adidas commercial	AAP in that Adidas Commercial lol	Paraphrase
That amber alert was getting annoying	Why do I get amber alerts tho	Not paraphrase
I am so watching Cinderella right now	Im so watching Cinderella right now	Paraphrase
That shot counted by Bayless	Bayless just RAN for it	Not Paraphrase
Damon EJ 1st Qb off the board	if EJ is the 1st QB off the board	Paraphrase

Table 1: Sample tweets from SemEval 2015 Twitter Paraphrase Corpus.

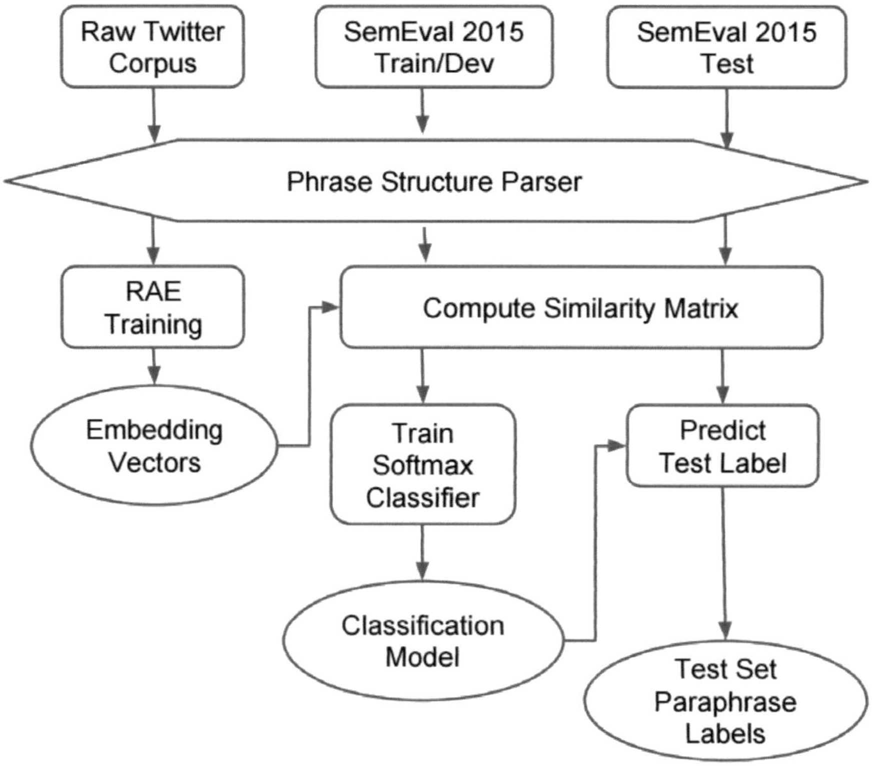

Figure 1: System architecture: The unfolding recursive autoencoder computes phrase embedding vectors for each node in a parse tree. For a pair of sentences being evaluated, the distances between all the nodes in the paired parse trees are computed and fill a variable sized similarity matrix. Dynamic pooling is used to convert the variable size similarity matrix to fixed size matrix. The fixed size similarity matrix is given to a softmax classifier to detect both whether the paired sentences are paraphrases and for paraphrase similarity scoring.

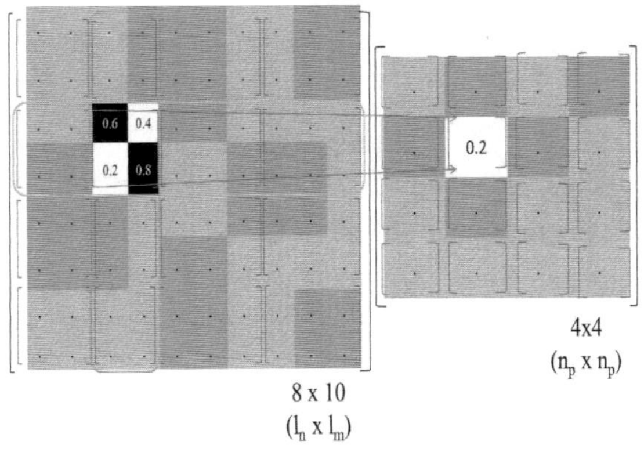

Figure 2: Dynamic pooling: The original variable sized matrix is partitioned into an $n_p \times n_p$ grid of blocks of approximately equivalent size. We use *min-pooling* as the aggregation operation, whereby the values of the cells in the fixed size $n_p \times n_p$ matrix are assigned to the minimum value of the corresponding partition in the original matrix.

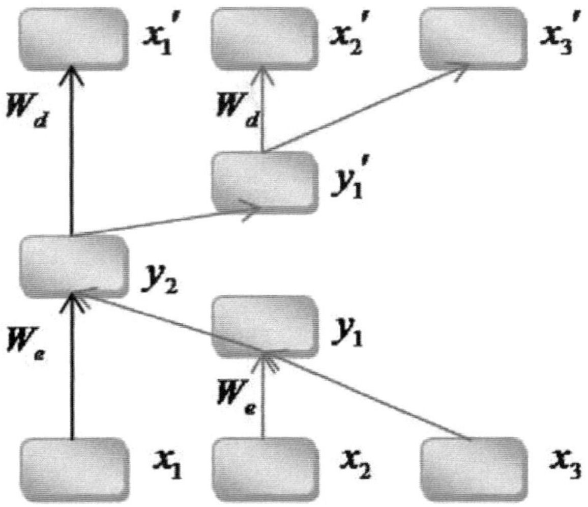

Figure 3: Architecture of unfolding RAEs. Using unfolding RAEs, the embedding vector associated with each node in a parse tree is trained to reconstruct the whole parse tree fragment rooted at the current node.

the number of nodes in the parse trees being compared. This variable size similarity matrix is converted to a fixed size matrix using Dynamic Pooling (Socher et.al, 2011). Dynamic pooling partitions the rows and columns of similarity matrix into n_p approximately equivalent segments which creates an $n_p \times n_p$ grid. As depicted in Figure 2, the individual cells in the fixed size $n_p \times n_p$ matrix are assign to the minimum values of their corresponding partitions in the original matrix. The resulting fixed size matrix is then used to train a softmax classifier to perform the actual paraphrase detection and pairwise similarity scoring tasks. To classify a pair of new sentences, the sentences are first parsed. Using the parse trees, the embedding vectors for each sentence are constructed and used to populate a node-to-node similarity matrix. This matrix is converted to a fixed size using dynamic pooling and passed to the softmax classification model.

3.1 Unfolding Recursive Autoencoders (RAEs)

The architecture of our unfolding RAEs is illustrated in Figure 2. The main difference between standard RAEs and unfolding RAEs is that standard RAEs are only directly trained to have each node reconstruct its immediate children. Unfolding RAEs differ in that the training objective assess not only how well the representation of each node reconstructs it's immediate children, but rather how well the node's representation reconstructs the entire parse tree fragment rooted at the current node.

4 Experimental Results

We use a general domain parsing model distributed with the Stanford Parser, englishPCFG v1.6.9 (Klein and Manning, 2003). Prior to training the RAE vectors, we pre-trained word embedding vectors for use as the word level representations (Ronan and Jason, 2008). The hyperparameter values used for our system are as follows: (1) the size of the pooling matrix n_p = 13; (2) the regularization for the softmax classifier c = 0.05; (3) Both the RAE and word embeddings are 100-dimensional vectors.

4.1 Data Set Details

Our SemEval task provided the PIT-2015 Twitter Paraphrase corpus for training and system development (Wei Xu, 2014; Wei Xu et al., 2014; Wei Xu et al., 2015). The corpus contains a training set with 13,063 sentence pairs, a development set with 4,727 sentence pairs, and a test set with 972 sentence pairs. Table 2 shows the label distribution statistics for this corpus. This data set is distinct from the data used

Category	Paraphrase Sentence pair	Non-Paraphrase Sentence pair	Debatable Sentence pair	Total
Training	3,996	7,534	1,533	13,063
Development	1,470	2,672	585	4,727
Testing	175	663	134	972

Table 2: Statistics of PIT-2015 Twitter Paraphrase Corpus.

Twitter Corpus	Training	Testing/ Development	Precision	Recall	F1 Measure
50,000	13,063	4,727	0.51	0.48	0.49
80,000	13,063	4,727	0.65	0.37	0.51
95,000	13,063	4,727	0.77	0.35	0.56

Table 3: PIT-2015 dev set performance using varying amounts of training data.

in other work on paraphrasing in the following ways: (1) it contains sentences that are colloquial and opinionated; (2) it contains paraphrases that are lexically diverse; and (3) it contains many sentences that are lexically similar but semantically dissimilar (Wei Xu et al., 2015).

The training and development data was jointly collected from 500+ trending topics and then randomly split into the final training and development sets. The test data was drawn from 20 randomly sampled Twitter trending topics. Labels were collected by having each sentence pair annotated by 5 different crowdsourced workers.

4.2 Evaluation and Discussion

For the unsupervised unfolding RAE training, we experimented with using subsets of different sized Twitter corpora of 50,000, 80,000 and 95,000 sentences to evaluate the proposed system. Using PIT-2015, we trained using tweets from the training set and evaluated the resulting series of systems on the dev set (Wei Xu et al., 2015). For supervised training, we used the training set from PIT-2015. For training the unsupervised unfolding RAE vectors, we collected additional data using the Twitter Developer API. As shown in Table 3, we found that increasing the size of the data set used to train the RAE embeddings leads to strong gains in system performance.[1] Notice that as the amount of data used to train the RAE vectors increases, the precision value for paraphrase detection increases significantly while the recall value is actually falling.

[1]Due to time constraints we did not explore using more than 95,000 sentences to train our embedding model.

Metrics Type	Accuracy
maxF1	0.457
mPrecision	0.543
mRecall	0.394
Pearson	0.303

Table 4: Results from the SemEval-2015.

The official evaluation metrics for SemEval-2015 Task 1 are F1-score for paraphrase identification and Pearson correlation for the semantic similarity scores. The performance of our system on the shared task evaluation data using these metrics is presented in Table 4.

5 Conclusion and Future Work

We participated in SemEval 2015 Task 1: Paraphrase and Semantic Similarity in Twitter using a system architecture motivated by the success of prior work on using RAE for paraphrase detection (Socher et al. 2011). We find that the performance of the system receives a sizable boost with the addition of a moderate amount of unsupervised RAE training data.

In future work, we plan to try to improve performance by first normalizing the Twitter data prior to parsing. Given the mismatch between general domain English data and tweets, parse accuracy would have likely been improved by performing a preprocessing step that normalized the tweets prior to giving them to the parser (Juri Ganitkevitch et al., 2013; Brendan O Connor et al., 2010). This could lead to improved downstream paraphrase detection and similarity scoring. We would also like to explore using new learning algorithms for the final paraphrase classification as well as alternative mechanisms of constructing the sentence level embedding vectors.

Acknowledgments

In this work, we would like to convey our sincere gratitude and special thanks towards Wei Xu, organizer of SemEval PIT 2015, who helped us in the training and development data set and to evaluate our system results. We would like again to convey our sincere gratitude towards Daniel Cer, who encouraged and motivated us throughout the final submission. And we would convey our sincere thanks to all the organizers of SemEval 2015.

References

Bill Dolan., Chris Quirk and Chris Brockett. 2004. *Unsupervised construction of large paraphrase corpora: Exploiting massively parallel news sources.* Proceedings of the 20th international conference on Computational Linguistics (pp. 350).

Brendan O Connor., Michel Krieger and David Ahn. 2010. *TweetMotif: Exploratory Search and Topic Summarization for Twitter.*

Chris Callison Burch. 2008. *Syntactic constraints on paraphrases extracted from parallel corpora.* Proceedings of the Conference on Empirical Methods in Natural Language Processing (pp. 196-205).

Dan Klein and Christopher D. Manning. 2003. *Accurate unlexicalized parsing.* Proceedings of the 41st Annual Meeting on Association for Computational Linguistics-Volume 1, pp. 423-430.

Duyu Tang., Furu Wei., Bing Qin., Ting Liu and Ming Zhou. 2014. *Coooolll: A Deep Learning System for Twitter Sentiment Classification.* Proceedings of the 8th International Workshop on Semantic Evaluation (SemEval-2014). (pp. 208-212).

Eric Huang 2011. *Paraphrase Detection Using Recursive Autoencoder.*

Erwin Marsi and Emiel Krahmer 2005. *Explorations in sentence fusion.* Proceedings of the European Workshop on Natural Language Generation (pp. 109-117).

Fabio Massimo Zanzotto., Marco Pennacchiotti and Kostas Tsioutsiouliklis. 2011. *Linguistic redundancy in twitter.* In Proceedings of the Conference on Empirical Methods in Natural Language Processing (pp. 659-669).

Juri Ganitkevitch., Benjamin Van Durme and Chris Callison-Burch. 2013. *PPDB: The Paraphrase Database.* In HLT-NAACL (pp. 758-764).

Leon Derczynski., Alan Ritter., Sam Clark and Kalina Bontcheva. 2013. *Twitter Part-of-Speech Tagging for All: Overcoming Sparse and Noisy Data.* In RANLP (pp. 198-206).

Microsoft research paraphrase corpus. Accessed on September-2014. *http://research.microsoft.com/en-us/.*

Nitin Madnan and Bonnie J. Dorr. 2010. *Generating phrasal and sentential paraphrases: A survey of data-driven methods.* Computational Linguistics, 36(3), (pp. 341-387).

Paul Clough., Robert Gaizauskas., Scott SL Piao and Yorick Wilks. 2002. *Meter: Measuring text reuse.* Proceedings of the 40th Annual Meeting on Association for Computational Linguistics (pp. 152-159).

Qayyum Ul Zia and Altaf Wasif. 2012. *Paraphrase Identification using Semantic Heuristic Features.* Research Journal of Applied Sciences, Engineering and Technology 4(22): 4894-4904.

Richard Socher., Eric H. Huang., Jeffrey Pennin., Christopher D. Manning and Andrew Y. Ng. 2011. *Dynamic pooling and unfolding recursive autoencoders for paraphrase detection.* Advances in Neural Information Processing Systems (pp. 801-809).

Ronan Collobert and Jason Weston. 2008. *A unified architecture for natural language processing: Deep neural networks with multitask learning.* Proceedings of the 25th international conference on Machine learning (pp. 160-167).

Samuel Fernando and Mark Stevenson. 2008. *A semantic similarity approach to paraphrase detection.* Computational Linguistics UK (CLUK 2008) 11th Annual Research Colloquium (pp. 45-52).

Sasa Petrovic., Miles Osborne and Victor Lavrenko. 2012. *Using paraphrases for improving first story detection in news and Twitter.* Proceedings of the 2012 Conference of the North American Chapter of the Association for Computational Linguistics: Human Language Technologies (pp. 338-346).

Wang Ling., Chris Dyer., Alan W. Black and Isabel Trancoso. 2013. *Paraphrasing 4 Microblog Normalization.* In EMNLP (pp. 73-84).

Wei Wu., Yun-Cheng Ju., Xiao Li and Ye-Yi Wang. 2010. *Paraphrase detection on SMS messages in automobiles.* In Acoustics Speech and Signal Processing (ICASSP), 2010 IEEE International Conference on (pp. 5326-5329).

Wei Xu., Alan Ritter., Bill Dolan., Ralph Grishman and Colin Cherry. 2012. *Paraphrasing for Style.* Proceedings of COLING 2012:Technical paper, pages 2899-2914, Coling 2012, Mumbai, December 2012.

Wei Xu., Alan Ritter and Ralph Grishmann. 2013. *Gathering and generating paraphrases from twitter with application to normalization.* Proceedings of the Sixth Workshop on Building and Using Comparable Corpora (pp. 121-128).

Wei Xu., Ralph Grishman., Adam Meyers and Alan Ritter. 2013. *A Preliminary Study of Tweet Summarization using Information Extraction.*

Wei Xu 2014. *Data-driven approaches for paraphrasing across language variations (Doctoral dissertation, New York University).*

Wei Xu., Alan Ritter., Chris Callison Burch., William B. Dolan and Yangfeng Ji. 2014. *Extracting Lexically Divergent Paraphrases from Twitter.* Transactions Of The Association For Computational Linguistics, 2, 435-448.

Wei Xu., Chris Callison Burch and William B. Dolan. 2015. *Paraphrase and Semantic Similarity in Twitter (PIT2015).* International Workshop on Semantic Evaluation (SemEval 2015).

Ebiquity: Paraphrase and Semantic Similarity in Twitter using Skipgram

Taneeya Satyapanich, Hang Gao and Tim Finin
University of Maryland, Baltimore County
Baltimore, MD, 21250, USA
taneeya1@umbc.edu, hanggao1@umbc.edu, finin@umbc.edu

Abstract

We describe the system we developed to participate in *SemEval 2015 Task 1, Paraphrase and Semantic Similarity in Twitter*. We create similarity vectors from two-skip trigrams of preprocessed tweets and measure their semantic similarity using our UMBC-STS system. We submit two runs. The best result is ranked eleventh out of eighteen teams with F1 score of 0.599.

1. Introduction

In this task (Wei, et al., 2015), participants were given pairs of text sequences from Twitter trends and produced a binary judgment for each stating whether or not they are paraphrases (e.g., semantically the same) and optionally a graded score (0.0 to 1.0) measuring their degree of semantic equivalence. For example, for the trending topic "*A Walk to Remember*" (a film released in 2002), the pair *A Walk to Remember is the definition of true love*" and "*A Walk to Remember is on and Im in town and Im upset*" might be judged as not paraphrases with score 0.2 whereas the pair "*A Walk to Remember is the definition of true love*" and "*A Walk to Remember is the cutest thing*" could be judged as paraphrases with a score of 0.6.

Many methods have been proposed to solve the paraphrase detection problem. Early approaches were often based on lexical matching techniques, e.g., word n-gram overlap (Barzilay and Lee, 2003) or predicate argument tuple matching (Qiu, et al., 2006). Some other approaches that go beyond simple lexical matching have also been developed. For example, (Mihalcea, et al., 2006) estimated semantic similarity of sentence pairs with word-to-word similarity measures and a word specificity measure. (Zhang and Patrick, 2005) uses text canonicalization to transfer texts of similar meaning into the same surface text with a higher probability than those with different meaning.

Many of these approaches adopt distributional semantic models, but limited to a word level. To extend distributional semantic models beyond words, several researchers have learned phrase or sentence representation by composing the representation of individual words (Mitchell and Lapata, 2010; Baroni and Zamparelli, 2010). An alternative approach by (Socher et al., 2011) represents phrases and sentences with fixed matrices consisting of pooled word and phrase pairwise similarities. (Le and Mikolov, 2014) learns representation of sentences directly by predicting context without composition of words.

In our work, we judge that two sentences are paraphrases if they have high degree of semantic similarity. We use the UMBC-Semantic Textual Similarity system (Lushan Han et al., 2013), which provides high accurate semantic similarity measurement. The remainder of this paper is organized as follows. Section 2 describes the task and the details of our method. Section 3 presents our results and a brief discussion. The last section offers conclusions.

2. Our Method

To decide whether two tweets are paraphrases or not, we use a measurement based on semantic similarity values. If two tweets are semantically similar, they are judged as paraphrases, otherwise they are not. We described steps of our method as follows.

1.1. Preprocessing

Generally, tweets are informal text sequences that include abbreviations, neologisms, emoticons and slang terms as well genre-specific elements such as hashtags, URLs and @mentions of other Twitter accounts. This is due to both the informal nature of the medium and the requirement to limit content to at most 140 characters. Thus, before measuring the semantic similarity, we replace abbreviation and slang to the readable version. We collected about 685 popular abbreviations and slang terms from several Web resources[1] and combined these with the provided twitter normalization lexicon developed by Han Bo and Timothy Baldwin (2011).

After replacing abbreviations and slang terms, we remove all stop words to get our final desired processed tweets. Then we produce a set of two-skip trigrams for each tweet and name these sets as *trigram sets*. We adapted the skip-gram technique from (Guthrie, et al., 2006).

Take the tweet "*Google Now for iOS simply beautiful*" as an example, after removing stop word s, we get *'Google Now iOS simply beautiful'*. Then a two-skip trigram set is produced: {*'Google Now iOS', 'Now iOS simply', 'iOS simply beautiful', 'Google iOS simply', 'Google simply beautiful', 'Now simply beautiful', 'Google Now beautiful', 'Google Now simply', 'Now iOS beautiful'*}, which is referred as trigram set. We transform every raw tweet into its processed version and then corresponding trigram set.

[1] These included http://webopedia.com, http://blog.-mltcreative.com and http://internetslang.com and others.

1.2. LSA Word Similarity Model

Our LSA word similarity model is a revised version of the one we used in the 2013 and 2014 SemEval semantic text similarity tasks (Han, et al., 2013, Kashyap et al., 2014). LSA relies on the fact that semantically similar words (e.g., cat and feline or nurse and doctor) are more likely to occur near one another in text. Thus evidence for word similarity can be computed from a statistical analysis of a large text corpus. We extract raw word co-occurrence statistics from a portion of a 2007 Stanford WebBase dataset (Stanford, 2001).

We performed part of speech tagging and lemmatization on the corpus using the Stanford POS tagger (Toutanova et al., 2000). Word/term co-occurrences were counted with a sliding window of fixed size over the entire corpus. We generate two co-occurrence models using window sizes ±1 and ±4. The smaller window provides more precise context which is better for comparing words of the same part of speech while the larger one is more suitable for computing the semantic similarity between words of different syntactic categories.

Our word co-occurrence models are based on a predefined vocabulary of 22,000 common English open-class words and noun phrases, extended with about 2,000 verb phrases from WordNet. The final dimensions of our word/phrase co-occurrence matrices are 29,000×29,000 when words/phrases are POS tagged. We apply singular value decomposition on the word/phrase co-occurrence matrices (Burgess 1998) after transforming the raw word/phrase co-occurrence counts into their log frequencies, and select the 300 largest singular values. The LSA similarity between two words/phrases is then defined as the cosine similarity of their corresponding LSA vectors generated by the SVD transformation.

To compute the semantic similarity of two text sequences, we use the simple *align-and-penalize* algorithm described in (Han et al., 2013) with a few improvements. These improvements include some sets of common disjoint concepts and an enhanced stop word list.

1.3. Features

For two trigram sets, we compute the semantic similarity of every possible pair of trigrams in these two sets using the UMBC Semantic Textual

Similarity system. For each pair of tweet (T1 and T2), six features are produced as:

- Feature1 = semantic similarity value between each pair of tweets (whole sentence with abbreviation and slangs replaced, and stop words removed)
- Feature2 = $Max(Max(sim(T1,T2)))$
- Feature3 = $Max(Max(sim(T2,T1)))$
- Feature4 = $Avg(Max(sim(T1,T2)))$
- Feature5 = $Avg(Max(sim(T2,T1)))$
- Feature6 = the weighted average on length of tweets of two averages above.

1.5. Training

We used the LIBSVM system (Chang and Lin, 2011) for training a *logistic regression* model and a *support vector regression* model. We run a grid search to find the best parameters for both models. All training data (13,063 pairs of tweets) were used to train the models without discarding any debatable data. We tested the contribution for of each of the features through ablation experiments on the development data in which each feature was deleted in each experimental run. Table 1 shows the statistical results for each feature ablation run.

Feature deleted	F1	Precision	Recall
Feature 1	0.7	0.709	0.728
Feature 2	0.697	0.706	0.726
Feature 3	0.697	0.706	0.726
Feature 4	0.691	0.700	0.722
Feature 5	0.696	0.706	0.726
Feature 6	0.695	0.705	0.725

Table 1. Performance of our system on runs against the development data in which each feature was removed.

From Table 1, we can see that the feature of lowest performance is Feature 1, the semantic similarity computed with entire tweets without using the skip-gram technique. But we still keep Feature 1 since performance of these six features is not significantly different. We show the performance of each model on development data in Table 2.

Model	F1	Precision	Recall
Logistic Regression	0.697	0.706	0.726
Support Vector Regression	0.691	0.707	0.726

Table 2. Performance of system on development data.

Since the performance of both systems is almost the same, we decide to submit one run of each system.

3. Results and Discussions

We submit two runs: Run_1 (Logistic Regression) obtained an F1 score of 0.599, precision score of 0.651 and recall score of 0.554, and Run_2 (Support Vector Regression), which received an F1 of 0.590, precision of 0.646, and recall of 0.543. When ranked, we are in the eighteenth (Run_1) and the nineteenth (Run_2) out of the 38 runs. The first rank has F1 score of 0.674. The full distribution of F1 score is shown in Figure 1. The relatively low ranking of our system might be the result of several factors.

First factor is the prevalence of neologisms, misspellings, informal slang and abbreviations in tweets. Better preprocessing to make the tweets closer to normal text might improve our results.

Another factor is the UMBC STS system. Examples of input on which UMBC STS system perform poorly are shown in Table 3. We can group these into two sets, each associated with problem in performing the paraphrase task.

The first problem is that a slang word may have different meanings when it is used in different genres. As we can see in the first example in Table 3, *'bombs'* does not mean *'a container filled with explosive'* but is a synonym of *'home runs'* when mentioned in a sports or baseball context. We can recognize this meaning by reading sport articles but it is not included in any dictionaries or WordNet. Thus our system predicts that the two tweets, each containing either 'bombs' or 'home runs', have low semantic similarity and thus are not paraphrases.

The second problem involves out-of-vocabulary words, such as the named entities found in the examples in Table 3. Tweet 2 of the second example

'NOW YOU SEE ME and AFTER EARTH Cant Outpace FAST FURIOUS 6' is full of movie names whose meanings our STS system cannot recognize. We can solve this problem by adding name entity recognition to the system. Another potential solution would be to adopt a simple string-matching component. With string matching, we may handle those out-of-vocabulary words situations similar to the third and fourth example. We can match *'orr'* and *'chara'* between two tweets of the third example and *'new ciroc'* in the fourth example.

To improve our STS performance, which is trained on a corpus that mostly consisted of reasonably well-written narrative text, we need to expand training corpus. Training a LSA model on a collection of tweets or a mixture of tweets and narrative text, and adding name entity recognition process may lead to better results.

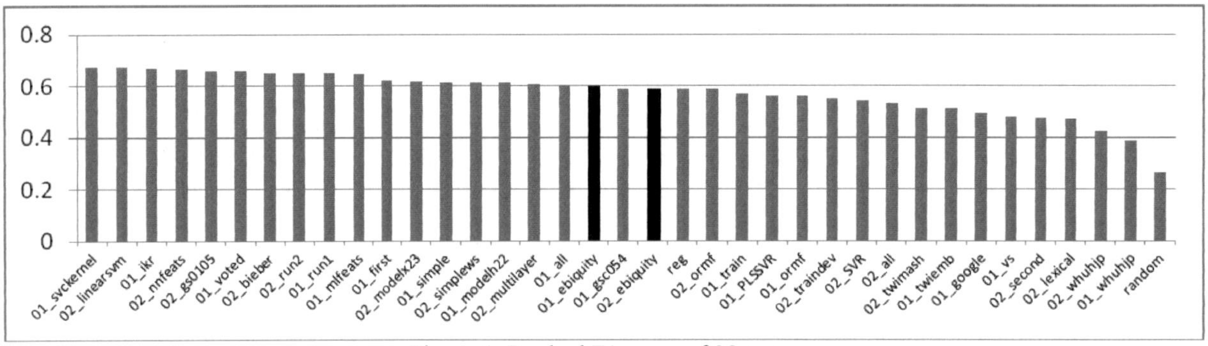

Figure 1. Ranked F1 score of 38 runs

#	Tweet 1	Tweet 2	System	Gold
1	chris davis is 44 with two bombs	Chris Davis has 2 home runs tonight	False	True
2	I wanna see the movie after earth	NOW YOU SEE ME and AFTER EARTH Cant Outpace FAST FURIOUS 6	True	False
3	Orr with a big hit on Chara	I keep waiting for the chara vs orr fight	False	True
4	New Ciroc Amaretto I NEED THAT	Oh shit I gotta try that new ciroc flavor	False	True

Table 3. Examples of input pairs on which our system performed poorly

4. Conclusion

We describe our system submitted in participating the *SemEval 2015 Task 1 Paraphrase and Semantic Similarity in Twitter*. We preprocess tweets using two-skip trigrams to produce sets of possible trigrams and measure their semantic similarity using the UMBC-STS system. We computed the statistical value as maximum and average of each pair and use two regression models; logistic regression and support vector regression. Our best performing run achieved an F1 score of 0.599 and was ranked eleventh out of eighteen teams.

Acknowledgments

Partial support for this research was provided by grants from the National Science Foundation (1228198 and 1250627) and a grant from the Maryland Industrial Partnerships program.

References

Marco Baroni and Roberto Zamparelli. 2010. Nouns are vectors, adjectives are matrices: Representing adjective-noun constructions in semantic space. In Proceedings of the 2010 Conference on Empirical Methods in Natural Language Processing (EMNLP 2010).

Regina Barzilay and Lillian Lee. 2003. Learning to paraphrase: An unsupervised approach using multiple-sequence alignment. In Proceedings of Conference of the North American Chapter of the Association for Computational Linguistics – Human Language Technologies(HLT-NAACL)

William Blacoe. and Mirella Lapata 2012. A comparison of vector-based representations for semantic composition, Proceedings of EMNLP, Jeju Island, Korea, pp. 546-556.

Han, Bo, and Timothy Baldwin. 2011. Lexical normalisation of short text messages: Makn sens a# twitter. Proceedings of the 49th Annual Meeting of the Association for Computational Linguistics: Human Language Technologies-Volume 1. Association for Computational Linguistics, 2011.

Curt Burgessa, Kay Livesayb and Kevin Lundb 1998. Explorations in context space: Words, sentences, discourse. Discourse Processes, 25:211–257.

Chih-Chung Chang and Chih-Jen Lin. 2011. LIBSVM : a library for support vector machines. ACM Transactions on Intelligent Systems and Technology, 2:27:1--27:27, 2011.

David Guthrie, Ben Allison, Wei Liu, Louise Guthrie, Yorick Wilks. 2006. "A closer look at skip-gram modelling." In Proceedings of the 5th international Conference on Language Resources and Evaluation (LREC-2006), pp. 1-4. 2006.

Lushan Han, Tim Finin, Paul McNamee, Anupam Joshi and Yelena Yesha, Improving Word Similarity by Augmenting PMI with Estimates of Word Polysemy, IEEE Transactions on Knowledge and Data Engineering, IEEE Computer Society, v25n6, pp. 1307-1322, 2013.

Lushan Han, Abhay L. Kashyap, Tim Finin, James Mayfield, and Johnathan Weese. 2013. UMBC EBIQUITY-CORE: Semantic Textual Similarity Systems, In Second Joint Conf. on Lexical and Computational Semantics. Association for Computational Linguistics , June.

Lushan Han, Schema Free Querying of Semantic Data, Ph.D. Dissertation, University of Maryland, Baltimore County, August 2014.

Abhay Kashyap, Lushan Han, Roberto Yus, Jennifer Sleeman, Taneeya Satyapanich, Sunil Gandhi and Tim Finin. 2014. Meerkat Mafia: Multilingual and Cross-Level Semantic Textual Similarity Systems, Int. Workshop on Semantic Evaluation, Association for Computational Linguistics.

Rada Mihalcea, Courtney Corley and Carlo Strapparava. 2006. Corpus-based and knowledge-based measures of text semantic similarity, Proceedings of the National Conference on Artificial Intelligence (AAAI 2006), Boston, Massachusetts, pp. 775-780

Jeff Mitchell and Mirella Lapata. 2010. Composition in distributional models of semantics. Cognitive Science, 34(8).

Long Qiu, Min-Yen Kan, and Tat-Seng Chua. 2006. Paraphrase recognition via dissimilarity significance classification. In Proceedings of the 2006 Conference on Empirical Methods in Natural Language Processing, pages 18–26, Sydney, Australia, July. Association for Computational Linguistics.

Le, Quoc V., and Tomas Mikolov. "Distributed representations of sentences and documents." arXiv preprint arXiv:1405.4053 (2014).

Richard Socher, Eric H. Huang, Jeffrey Pennington, Andrew Y. Ng, and Christopher D. Manning. 2011. Dynamic pooling and unfolding recursive autoencoders for paraphrase detection. In Advances in Neural Information Processing Systems (NIPS 2011).

Stanford. 2001. Stanford WebBase project. http://bit.ly/WebBase.

Kristina Toutanova, Dan Klein, Christopher Manning, William Morgan, Anna Rafferty, and Michel Galley. 2000. Stanford log-linear part-of-speech tagger. http://nlp.stanford.edu/software/tagger.shtml.

Wei Xu, Chris Callison-Burch and William B. Dolan. 2015. SemEval-2015 Task 1: Paraphrase and Semantic Similarity in Twitter ,Proceedings of the 9th International Workshop on Semantic Evaluation (SemEval),2015.

Yitao Zhang and Jon Patrick. 2005. Paraphrase identification by text canonicalization. In Proceedings of the Australasian Language Technology Workshop 2005, pages 160–166, Sydney, Australia, December.

RTM-DCU: Predicting Semantic Similarity with Referential Translation Machines

Ergun Biçici
ADAPT CNGL Centre for Global Intelligent Content
School of Computing
Dublin City University, Dublin, Ireland.
ergun.bicici@computing.dcu.ie

Abstract

We use referential translation machines (RTMs) for predicting the semantic similarity of text. RTMs are a computational model effectively judging monolingual and bilingual similarity while identifying translation acts between any two data sets with respect to interpretants. RTMs pioneer a language independent approach to all similarity tasks and remove the need to access any task or domain specific information or resource. RTMs become the 2nd system out of 13 systems participating in Paraphrase and Semantic Similarity in Twitter, 6th out of 16 submissions in Semantic Textual Similarity Spanish, and 50th out of 73 submissions in Semantic Textual Similarity English.

1 Referential Translation Machine (RTM)

We present positive results from a fully automated judge for semantic similarity based on Referential Translation Machines (Biçici and Way, 2014b) in two semantic similarity tasks at SemEval-2015, Semantic Evaluation Exercises - International Workshop on Semantic Evaluation (Nakov et al., 2015). Referential translation machine (RTM) is a computational model for identifying the acts of translation for translating between any given two data sets with respect to a reference corpus selected in the same domain. An RTM model is based on the selection of interpretants, training data close to both the training set and the test set, which allow shared semantics by providing context for similarity judgments. Each RTM model is a data translation and translation prediction model between the instances in the training set and the test set and translation acts are indicators of the data transformation and translation. RTMs present an accurate and language independent solution for making semantic similarity judgments.

RTMs pioneer a computational model for quality and semantic similarity judgments in monolingual and bilingual settings using retrieval of relevant training data (Biçici and Yuret, 2015) as interpretants for reaching shared semantics. RTMs achieve (i) top performance when predicting the quality of translations (Biçici, 2013; Biçici and Way, 2014a); (ii) top performance when predicting monolingual cross-level semantic similarity; (iii) second performance when predicting paraphrase and semantic similarity in Twitter (iv) good performance when judging the semantic similarity of sentences; (iv) good performance when evaluating the semantic relatedness of sentences and their entailment (Biçici and Way, 2014b).

RTMs use Machine Translation Performance Prediction (MTPP) System (Biçici et al., 2013; Biçici and Way, 2014b), which is a state-of-the-art (SoA) performance predictor of translation even without using the translation. MTPP system measures the coverage of individual test sentence features found in the training set and derives indicators of the closeness of test sentences to the available training data, the difficulty of translating the sentence, and the presence of acts of translation for data transformation. MTPP features for translation acts are provided in (Biçici and Way, 2014b). RTMs become the 2nd system out of 13 systems participating in Paraphrase and Semantic Similarity in Twitter (Task 1) (Xu et al., 2015) and achieve good results in Semantic Tex-

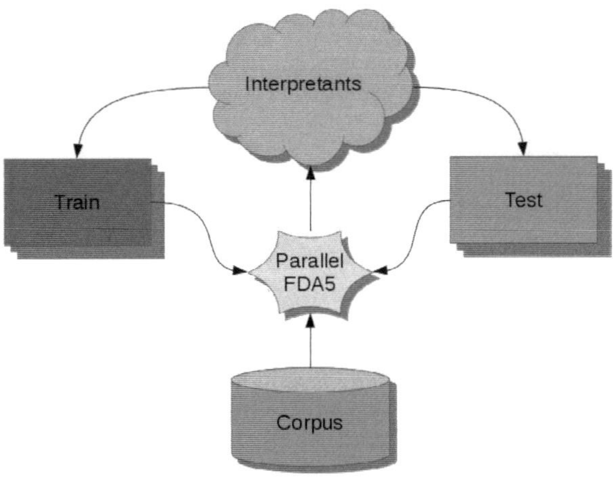

Figure 1: RTM depiction.

Algorithm 1: Referential Translation Machine

Input: Training set `train`, test set `test`, corpus $\mathcal{C}$, and learning model M.
Data: Features of `train` and `test`, $\mathcal{F}_{\texttt{train}}$ and $\mathcal{F}_{\texttt{test}}$.
Output: Predictions of similarity scores on the test $\hat{q}$.

FDA5($\texttt{train}, \texttt{test}, \mathcal{C}$) $\rightarrow \mathcal{I}$
MTPPSystem($\mathcal{I}, \texttt{train}$) $\rightarrow \mathcal{F}_{\texttt{train}}$
MTPPSystem($\mathcal{I}, \texttt{test}$) $\rightarrow \mathcal{F}_{\texttt{test}}$
learn($M, \mathcal{F}_{\texttt{train}}$) $\rightarrow \mathcal{M}$
predict($\mathcal{M}, \mathcal{F}_{\texttt{test}}$) $\rightarrow \hat{y}$

tual Similarity (Task 2) (Agirre et al., 2015) becoming 6th out of 16 submissions in Spanish.

We use the Parallel FDA5 instance selection model for selecting the interpretants (Biçici et al., 2014; Biçici and Yuret, 2015), which allows efficient parameterization, optimization, and implementation of Feature Decay Algorithms (FDA), and build an MTPP model. We view that acts of translation are ubiquitously used during communication:

Every act of communication is an act of translation (Bliss, 2012).

Translation need not be between different languages and paraphrasing or communication also contain acts of translation. When creating sentences, we use our background knowledge and translate information content according to the current context.

Figure 1 depicts RTM and Algorithm 1 describes the RTM algorithm. Our encouraging results in the semantic similarity tasks increase our understanding of the acts of translation we ubiquitously use when communicating and how they can be used to predict semantic similarity. RTMs are powerful enough to be applicable in different domains and tasks with good performance. We describe the tasks we participated as follows:

Task	Setting	Train	LM
Task 1, ParSS	English	313	7813
Task 2, STS	English	441	6441
Task 2, STS	English headlines	531	8031
Task 2, STS	English images	411	6411
Task 2, STS	Spanish	409	6409

Table 1: Number of sentences in $\mathcal{I}$ (in thousands) selected for each task.

ParSS Paraphrase and Semantic Similarity in Twitter (ParSS) (Xu et al., 2015):

Given two sentences S_1 and S_2 in the same language, produce a similarity score indicating whether they express a similar meaning: a discrete real number in $[0, 1]$.

We model as sentence MTPP between S_1 to S_2.

STS Semantic Textual Similarity (STS) (Agirre et al., 2015):

Given two sentences S_1 and S_2 in the same language, quantify the degree of similarity: a real number in $[0, 5]$.

STS is in English and Spanish (a real number in $[0, 4]$). We model as sentence MTPP of S_1 and S_2.

2 SemEval-15 Results

We develop individual RTM models for each task and subtask that we participate at SemEval-2015 with the RTM-DCU team name. Interpretants are selected from the LM corpora distributed by the translation task of WMT14 (Bojar et al., 2014) and LDC for English (Parker et al., 2011) and Spanish (Ângelo Mendonça et al., 2011) [1]. We use the Stanford POS tagger (Toutanova et al., 2003) to obtain the lemmatized corpora for the ParSS task. The number of instances we select for the interpretants

[1] English Gigaword 5th, Spanish Gigaword 3rd edition.

RTM-DCU results

Data	Model	F_1	Precision	Recall	maxF_1	mPrecision	mRecall	r_P	MAE	RAE	MAER	MRAER	Rank
R	SVR	0.54	0.883	0.389	0.693	0.695	0.691	0.5697	0.1953	0.7918	0.4278	0.8694	3
R	PLS-SVR	0.562	0.859	0.417	0.678	0.649	0.709	0.564	0.2001	0.8109	0.4442	0.9105	4

RTM results with further optimization

Data	Model	F_1	Precision	Recall	maxF_1	mPrecision	mRecall	r_P	MAE	RAE	MAER	MRAER
R	PLS-SVR	0.502	0.938	0.343	0.674	0.686	0.663	0.5798	0.1912	0.775	0.6901	0.838
R	RR	0.521	0.94	0.36	0.681	0.735	0.634	0.5777	0.1866	0.7564	0.7438	0.7944
R+L	SVR	0.53	0.892	0.377	0.669	0.652	0.686	0.5719	0.1944	0.7879	0.6788	0.8615
R+L	PLS-SVR	0.5	0.884	0.349	0.642	0.649	0.634	0.5245	0.2028	0.8218	0.7425	0.8864

Table 2: ParSS test results.

in each task is given in Table 1.

We use ridge regression (RR), support vector regression (SVR), and extremely randomized trees (TREE) (Geurts et al., 2006) as the learning models. These models learn a regression function using the features to estimate a numerical target value. We also use them after a dimensionality reduction and mapping step with partial least squares (PLS) (Specia et al., 2009). We optimize the learning parameters, the number of dimensions used for PLS, and the parameters for parallel FDA5. More details about the optimization processes are in (Biçici and Way, 2014b; Biçici et al., 2014). We optimize the learning parameters by selecting ε close to the standard deviation of the noise in the training set (Biçici, 2013) since the optimal value for ε is shown to have linear dependence to the noise level for different noise models (Smola et al., 1998). At testing time, the predictions are bounded to obtain scores in the corresponding ranges.

We use Pearson's correlation (r_P), mean absolute error (MAE), and relative absolute error (RAE) for evaluation:

$$\text{MAE}(\hat{\mathbf{y}}, \mathbf{y}) = \frac{\sum_{i=1}^{n} |\hat{y}_i - y_i|}{n} \quad \text{RAE}(\hat{\mathbf{y}}, \mathbf{y}) = \frac{\sum_{i=1}^{n} |\hat{y}_i - y_i|}{\sum_{i=1}^{n} |\bar{y} - y_i|} \tag{1}$$

We define MAER and MRAER for easier replication and comparability with relative errors for each instance:

$$\text{MAER}(\hat{\mathbf{y}}, \mathbf{y}) = \frac{\sum_{i=1}^{n} \frac{|\hat{y}_i - y_i|}{\lfloor |y_i| \rfloor_\epsilon}}{n}$$
$$\text{MRAER}(\hat{\mathbf{y}}, \mathbf{y}) = \frac{\sum_{i=1}^{n} \frac{|\hat{y}_i - y_i|}{\lfloor |\bar{y} - y_i| \rfloor_\epsilon}}{n} \tag{2}$$

MAER is the mean absolute error relative to the magnitude of the target and MRAER is the mean absolute error relative to the absolute error of a predictor always predicting the target mean assuming that target mean is known. MAER and MRAER are capped from below[2] with $\epsilon = \text{MAE}(\hat{\mathbf{y}}, \mathbf{y})/2$, which is the measurement error and it is estimated as half of the mean absolute error or deviation of the predictions from target mean. ϵ represents half of the score step with which a decision about a change in measurement's value can be made. ϵ is similar to half of the standard deviation, σ, of the data but over absolute differences. For discrete target scores, $\epsilon = \frac{\textit{step size}}{2}$. A method for learning decision thresholds for mimicking the human decision process when determining whether two translations are equivalent is described in (Biçici, 2013).

MAER and MRAER are able to capture averaged fluctuations at the instance level and they may evaluate the performance of a predictor at performance prediction tasks at the instance level (e.g. performance of the similarity of sentences, performance of translation of different translation instances) better. RAE compares sums of prediction errors and MRAER averages instance prediction error comparisons.

[2] We use $\lfloor \, . \, \rfloor_\epsilon$ to cap the argument from below to ϵ.

RTM-DCU r_P results

Model	answers-forums	answers-students	belief	headlines	images	Weighted r_P	Rank
PLS-TREE	0.5484	0.5549	0.6223	0.7281	0.7189	0.6468	50

RTM top result r_P selected according to Weighted r_P among top 3 results with further optimization

Model	answers-forums	answers-students	belief	headlines	images	Weighted r_P
TREE	0.5517	0.6729	0.6750	0.7812	0.7830	0.7126
Rank	48	38	39	29	49	38

Table 4: STS English test r_P results for each domain.

Data	Model	F_1	r_P	MAE	RAE	MAER	MRAER
R	PLS-SVR	.4740	.6183	.2106	.6963	1.5408	.9223
R	RR	.4920	.6165	.2174	.7188	1.8609	.9132
R	PLS-TREE	.5330	.6156	.2201	.7276	1.939	.9144
R	SVR	.4800	.6152	.2107	.6965	1.5012	.9306
R	PLS RR	.5110	.6140	.2170	.7175	1.8443.	.9240
R+L	SVR	.5040	.6216	.2085	.6893	1.4723	.9344
R+L	PLS-SVR	.4970	.6209	.2093	.6919	1.5402	.9226
R+L	PLS-TREE	.5410	.6205	.2177	.7196	1.8834	.9161
R+L	RR	.4970	.6194	.2164	.7154	1.8448	.9096
R	PLS-SVR	.4740	.6183	.2106	.6963	1.5408	.9223

Table 3: ParSS training results of top 5 RTM systems with further optimization.

RTM-DCU r_P results

Model	Wikipedia	News	Weighted r_P	Rank
TREE	0.5823	0.5251	0.5443	6

RTM top result r_P selected according to Weighted r_P among top 3 results with further optimization

Model	Wikipedia	News	Weighted r_P	Rank
TREE	0.6622	0.5833	0.6096	5
Rank	4	5		

Table 5: STS Spanish test results.

2.1 Task 1: Paraphrase and Semantic Similarity in Twitter (ParSS)

ParSS contains sentences provided by Twitter [3] (Xu et al., 2015). Official evaluation metric is Pearson's correlation score, which we use to select the top systems on the training set. RTM-DCU results on the ParSS test set are given in Table 2. The setting R using SVR becomes 2nd out of 13 systems and 3rd out of 25 submissions. Looking at MAE and MAER allows us to obtain explanations to train and test performance differences for example without knowing their target distribution. Even though MAE of PLS-SVR is about $\%5$ smaller on the ParSS test set, MAER is $\%55$ smaller due to test set containing fewer zero entries ($\%16$ vs. $\%39$ on the train set). Lower test MAE than training MAE may be attributed to RTMs.

We obtained results with lemmatized datasets and further optimized the learning model parameters after the challenge. We present the performance of the top 5 individual RTM models on the training set in Table 3. R uses the regular truecase (Koehn et al., 2007; Koehn, 2010) corpora and L uses the lemmatized truecased corpora. R+L correspond to using the features from both R and L, which doubles the number of features.

[3]www.twitter.com

2.2 Task 2: Semantic Textual Similarity (STS)

STS contains sentence pairs from different domains: answers-forums, answers-students, belief, headlines, and images for English and wikipedia and newswire for Spanish. Official evaluation metric in STS is the Pearson's correlation score. We build separate RTM models for headlines and images domains for STS English. Domain specific RTM models obtain improved performance in those domains (Biçici and Way, 2014b). STS English test set contains 2000, 1500, 2000, 1500, and 1500 sentences respectively from the specified domains however for evaluation, STS use a subset of the test set, 375, 750, 375, 750, and 750 instances respectively from the corresponding domains. This may lower the performance of RTMs by causing FDA5 to select more domain specific data and less task specific since RTMs use the test set to select interpretants and build a task specific RTM prediction model.

Table 4 and Table 5 list the results on the test set

along with their ranks out of 73 and 16 submissions respectively for English STS and Spanish STS.

RTM top test results selected according to Weighted r_P among top 3 results on STS for each subtask as well as top RTM-DCU results in STS 2014 (Biçici and Way, 2014b) are presented in Table 6, where we have used the top results from domain specific RTM models for headlines and images domains in the overall model results. Top 3 individual RTM model performance on the training set with further optimized learning model parameters after the challenge are presented in Table 7. Better r_P, RAE, and MRAER on the test set than on the training set in STS 2015 English may be attributed to RTMs.

2.3 RTMs Across Tasks and Years

We compare the difficulty of tasks according to MRAER where the correlation of RAE and MRAER is 0.89. In Table 8, we list the RAE, MAER, and MRAER obtained for different tasks and subtasks, also listing RTM results from SemEval-2013 (Biçici and van Genabith, 2013), from SemEval-2014 (Biçici and Way, 2014b), and and from quality estimation task (QET) (Biçici and Way, 2014a) of machine translation (Bojar et al., 2014). RTMs at SemEval-2013 contain results from STS. RTMs at SemEval-2014 contain results from STS, semantic relatedness and entailment (SRE) (Marelli et al., 2014), and cross-level semantic similarity (CLSS) tasks (Jurgens et al., 2014). RTMs at WMT2014 QET contain tasks involving the prediction of an integer in $[1, 3]$ representing post-editing effort (PEE), a real number in $[0, 1]$ representing human-targeted translation edit rate (HTER), or an integer representing post-editing time (PET) of translations.

The best results are obtained for the CLSS paragraph to sentence subtask, which may be due to the larger contextual information that paragraphs can provide for the RTM models. For the ParSS task, we can only reduce the error with respect to knowing and predicting the mean by about 22.5%. Prediction of bilingual similarity as in quality estimation of translation can be expected to be harder and RTMs achieve SoA performance in this task as well (Biçici and Way, 2014a). Table 8 can be used to evaluate the difficulty of various tasks and domains based on our SoA predictor RTM. MRAER considers both the predictor's error and the target scores' fluctuations at the instance level. We separated the results having MRAER greater than 1 as in these tasks and subtasks RTM does not perform significantly better than mean predictor and fluctuations render these as tasks that may require more work.

3 Conclusion

Referential translation machines pioneer a clean and intuitive computational model for automatically measuring semantic similarity by measuring the acts of translation involved and achieve to become the 2nd system out of 13 systems participating in Paraphrase and Semantic Similarity in Twitter, 6th out of 16 submissions in Semantic Textual Similarity Spanish, and 50th out of 73 submissions in Semantic Textual Similarity English. RTMs make quality and semantic similarity judgments possible based on the retrieval of relevant training data as interpretants for reaching shared semantics. We define MAER, mean absolute error relative to the magnitude of the target, and MRAER, mean absolute error relative to the absolute error of a predictor always predicting the target mean assuming that target mean is known. RTM test performance on various tasks sorted according to MRAER can identify which tasks and subtasks may require more work.

Acknowledgments

This work is supported in part by SFI (13/TIDA/I2740) for the project "Monolingual and Bilingual Text Quality Judgments with Translation Performance Prediction" (`www.computing.dcu.ie/~ebicici/Projects/TIDA_RTM.html`) and in part by SFI (12/CE/I2267) as part of the ADAPT CNGL Centre for Global Intelligent Content (`www.adaptcentre.ie`) at Dublin City University. We also thank the SFI/HEA Irish Centre for High-End Computing (ICHEC) for the provision of computational facilities and support.

References

Eneko Agirre, Carmen Banea, Claire Cardie, Daniel Cer, Mona Diab, Aitor Gonzalez-Agirre, Weiwei Guo, Rada Mihalcea, German Rigau, and Janyce Wiebe.

		Domain	Model	r_P	MAE	RAE	MAER	MRAER
STS 2015	English	answers-forums	PLS-SVR	0.6215	1.2239	1.1675	1.5369	1.3449
		answers-students	PLS-SVR	0.6125	0.9635	0.7819	0.5542	0.8404
		belief	PLS-SVR	0.5879	1.3625	1.1825	1.5749	1.4119
		headlines	RR	0.7812	0.8318	0.5894	0.4844	0.6380
		images	TREE	0.7830	0.8502	0.5885	0.5424	0.6229
		ALL	PLS-SVR	0.6739	0.9847	0.7224	0.7379	0.7883
	Spanish	News	TREE	0.5303	0.6315	0.9426	0.4096	1.1052
		Wikipedia	TREE	0.5867	0.6448	0.9499	0.4844	1.2062
		ALL	TREE	0.5618	0.6360	0.9459	0.4348	1.1344
STS 2014	English	deft-forum	TREE	0.4341	1.1609	1.0908	0.7724	1.216
		deft-news	TREE	0.6974	0.9032	0.8716	0.6271	0.881
		headlines	TREE	0.6199	0.9254	0.7845	0.6711	0.7854
		images	TREE	0.6995	0.9499	0.7395	0.8338	0.7246
		OnWN	TREE	0.8058	1.0028	0.5585	0.7975	0.546
		tweet-news	TREE	0.6882	0.831	0.8093	0.4601	0.875
		ALL	TREE	0.6473	0.9534	0.7449	0.7274	0.7566
	Spanish	News	TREE	0.7	1.351	1.4141	0.5994	1.8053
		Wikipedia	TREE	0.4216	1.298	1.3579	0.65	1.6612
		ALL	TREE	0.62	1.3296	1.3823	0.6191	1.7719
STS 2013	English	headlines	L+S SVR	0.6552	1.2763	1.0231	1.0456	1.1444
		OnWN		0.6943	1.3545	0.8255	1.2875	0.8605
		SMT		0.3005	0.6886	1.6132	0.1669	2.0718
		FNWN		0.2016	1.0604	1.2633	1.5087	1.4048
		ALL	L+S SVR	0.5844	1.0818	0.7791	0.8494	0.77

Table 6: RTM top test results selected according to Weighted r_P among top 3 results on STS as well as top RTM-DCU results in STS 2013 and STS 2014 (Biçici and Way, 2014b). ALL presents results over all of the test set.

Lang		Model	r_P	MAE	RAE	MAER	MRAER
English		PLS-SVR	0.7477	0.7679	0.6050	0.4444	0.6947
		SVR	0.7452	0.7688	0.6058	0.4504	0.686
		TREE	0.7265	0.8093	0.6377	0.504	0.6812
	headlines	RR	0.7453	0.7559	0.6215	0.4389	0.6835
		PLS-SVR	0.7411	0.7619	0.6265	0.4298	0.7087
		TREE	0.7386	0.7710	0.6340	0.4726	0.6686
	images	TREE	0.7600	0.8020	0.6248	0.5308	0.7013
		PLS-SVR	0.7574	0.7839	0.6106	0.4898	0.724
		RR	0.7564	0.7945	0.6189	0.5025	0.7161
Spanish		TREE	0.8390	0.5154	0.5115	0.4145	0.5931
		RR	0.8260	0.5473	0.5431	0.4571	0.6208
		PLS-SVR	0.8218	0.5363	0.5322	0.4171	0.635

Table 7: RTM training results of top 3 systems on STS English, English images, English headlines, and Spanish tasks.

2015. SemEval-2015 Task 2: Semantic textual similarity. In *Proc. of the 9th International Workshop on Semantic Evaluation (SemEval 2015)*, Denver, Colorado, USA, June.

Ângelo Mendonça, Daniel Jaquette, David Graff, and Denise DiPersio. 2011. Spanish Gigaword third edition, Linguistic Data Consortium.

Ergun Biçici and Josef van Genabith. 2013. CNGL-CORE: Referential translation machines for measuring semantic similarity. In **SEM 2013: The Second Joint Conference on Lexical and Computational Semantics*, pages 234–240, Atlanta, Georgia, USA, 13-14 June.

Ergun Biçici and Andy Way. 2014a. Referential translation machines for predicting translation quality. In *Proc. of the Ninth Workshop on Statistical Machine Translation*, pages 313–321, Baltimore, Maryland, USA, June.

Ergun Biçici and Andy Way. 2014b. RTM-DCU: Referential translation machines for semantic similarity. In *Proceedings of the 8th International Workshop on Semantic Evaluation (SemEval-2014)*, pages 487–496, Dublin, Ireland, 23-24 August.

Ergun Biçici and Deniz Yuret. 2015. Optimizing instance selection for statistical machine translation with feature decay algorithms. *IEEE/ACM Transactions On Audio, Speech, and Language Processing (TASLP)*, 23:339–350.

Ergun Biçici, Declan Groves, and Josef van Genabith. 2013. Predicting sentence translation quality using extrinsic and language independent features. *Machine Translation*, 27:171–192, December.

Ergun Biçici, Qun Liu, and Andy Way. 2014. Parallel FDA5 for fast deployment of accurate statistical machine translation systems. In *Proc. of the Ninth Workshop on Statistical Machine Translation*, pages 59–65, Baltimore, USA, June.

Ergun Biçici. 2013. Referential translation machines for quality estimation. In *Proc. of the Eighth Workshop on Statistical Machine Translation*, pages 343–351, Sofia, Bulgaria, August.

Chris Bliss. 2012. Comedy is translation, February. http://www.ted.com/talks/chris_bliss_comedy_is_translation.html.

Ondrej Bojar, Christian Buck, Christian Federmann, Barry Haddow, Philipp Koehn, Johannes Leveling, Christof Monz, Pavel Pecina, Matt Post, Herve Saint-Amand, Radu Soricut, Lucia Specia, and Aleš Tamchyna. 2014. Findings of the 2014 workshop on statistical machine translation. In *Proceedings of the Ninth Workshop on Statistical Machine Translation*, pages 12–58, Baltimore, Maryland, USA, June.

Pierre Geurts, Damien Ernst, and Louis Wehenkel. 2006. Extremely randomized trees. *Machine Learning*, 63(1):3–42.

David Jurgens, Mohammad Taher Pilehvar, and Roberto Navigli. 2014. SemEval-2014 Task 3: Cross-level semantic similarity. In *Proc. of the 8th International Workshop on Semantic Evaluation (SemEval 2014)*, pages 17–26, Dublin, Ireland, August.

Philipp Koehn, Hieu Hoang, Alexandra Birch, Chris Callison-Burch, Marcello Federico, Nicola Bertoldi, Brooke Cowan, Wade Shen, Christine Moran, Richard Zens, Chris Dyer, Ondrej Bojar, Alexandra Constantin, and Evan Herbst. 2007. Moses: Open source toolkit for statistical machine translation. In *ACL*, pages 177–180, Prague, Czech Republic, June.

Philipp Koehn. 2010. An experimental management system. *The Prague Bulletin of Mathematical Linguistics*, 94:87–96.

Marco Marelli, Luisa Bentivogli, Marco Baroni, Raffaella Bernardi, Stefano Menini, and Roberto Zamparelli. 2014. SemEval-2014 Task 1: Evaluation of compositional distributional semantic models on full sentences through semantic relatedness and textual entailment. In *Proc. of the 8th International Workshop on Semantic Evaluation (SemEval 2014)*, pages 1–8, Dublin, Ireland, August.

Preslav Nakov, Torsten Zesch, Daniel Cer, and David Jurgens, editors. 2015. *Proc. of the 9th International Workshop on Semantic Evaluation (SemEval 2015)*. Denver, Colorado, USA, 4-5 June.

Robert Parker, David Graff, Junbo Kong, Ke Chen, and Kazuaki Maeda. 2011. English Gigaword fifth edition, Linguistic Data Consortium.

A. J. Smola, N. Murata, B. Schölkopf, and K.-R. Müller. 1998. Asymptotically optimal choice of ε-loss for support vector machines. In L. Niklasson, M. Boden, and T. Ziemke, editors, *Proc. of the International Conference on Artificial Neural Networks*, Perspectives in Neural Computing, pages 105–110, Berlin.

Lucia Specia, Nicola Cancedda, Marc Dymetman, Marco Turchi, and Nello Cristianini. 2009. Estimating the sentence-level quality of machine translation systems. In *Proc. of the 13th Annual Conference of the European Association for Machine Translation (EAMT)*, pages 28–35, Barcelona, Spain, May.

Kristina Toutanova, Dan Klein, Christopher D. Manning, and Yoram Singer. 2003. Feature-rich part-of-speech tagging with a cyclic dependency network. In *Proc. of the 2003 Conference of the North American Chapter of the Association for Computational Linguistics on Human Language Technology - Volume 1*, NAACL '03, pages 173–180, Stroudsburg, PA, USA.

Wei Xu, Chris Callison-Burch, and William B. Dolan. 2015. SemEval-2015 Task 1: Paraphrase and semantic similarity in Twitter (PIT). In *Proc. of the 9th International Workshop on Semantic Evaluation (SemEval)*, Denver, Colorado, USA, June.

Task	Subtask	Domain	Model	RAE	MAER	MRAER
CLSS 2014	Paragraph to Sentence	Mixed	TREE	0.4579	0.5112	0.5037
STS 2014	English	OnWN	TREE	0.5585	0.7975	0.546
QET 2014	English-Spanish PEE	Europarl	PLS-TREE	1.0794	0.304	0.614
STS 2015	English	Images	TREE	0.5885	0.5424	0.6229
STS 2015	English	Headlines	RR	0.5894	0.4844	0.6380
CLSS 2014	Sentence to Phrase	Mixed	TREE	0.6255	0.6857	0.6444
QET 2014	German-English PEE	Europarl	RR	0.8204	0.3575	0.679
QET 2014	English-German PEE	Europarl	TREE	0.8602	0.3692	0.6985
STS 2014	English	Images	TREE	0.7395	0.8338	0.7246
QET 2014	Spanish-English PEE	Europarl	FS-RR	0.9	0.3798	0.7491
QET 2014	English-Spanish PET	Europarl	SVR	0.7223	0.4651	0.7786
STS 2014	English	Headlines	TREE	0.7845	0.6711	0.7854
SRE 2014	English	SICK	R+L PLS-SVR	0.6645	0.1827	0.8177
ParSS 2015	English	Tweets	SVR	0.775	0.6901	0.838
STS 2015	English	Answers-students	PLS-SVR	0.7819	0.5542	0.8404
CLSS 2014	Phrase to Word	Mixed	TREE	0.9488	1.1454	0.8483
STS 2013	English	OnWN	L+S SVR	0.8255	1.2875	0.8605
STS 2014	English	Tweet-news	TREE	0.8093	0.4601	0.875
QET 2014	English-Spanish HTER	Europarl	SVR	0.8532	0.7727	0.8758
STS 2014	English	Deft-news	TREE	0.8716	0.6271	0.881
STS 2015	Spanish	News	TREE	0.9426	0.4096	1.1052
STS 2013	English	Headlines	L+S SVR	1.0231	1.0456	1.1444
STS 2015	Spanish	Wikipedia	TREE	0.9499	0.4844	1.2062
STS 2014	English	Deft-forum	TREE	1.0908	0.7724	1.216
STS 2015	English	Answers-forums	PLS-SVR	1.1675	1.5369	1.3449
STS 2013	English	FNWN	L+S SVR	1.2633	1.5087	1.4048
STS 2015	English	Belief	PLS-SVR	1.1825	1.5749	1.4119
STS 2014	Spanish	Wikipedia	TREE	1.3579	0.65	1.6612
STS 2014	Spanish	News	TREE	1.4141	0.5994	1.8053
STS 2013	English	SMT	L+S SVR	1.6132	0.1669	2.0718

Table 8: Best RTM test results for different tasks and subtasks sorted according to MRAER.

ASOBEK: Twitter Paraphrase Identification with Simple Overlap Features and SVMs

Asli Eyecioglu and **Bill Keller**
Department of Informatics
The University of Sussex
Brighton, UK
A.Eyecioglu@sussex.ac.uk,
billk@sussex.ac.uk

Abstract

We present an approach to identifying Twitter paraphrases using simple lexical overlap features. The work is part of ongoing research into the applicability of *knowledge-lean* techniques to paraphrase identification. We utilize features based on overlap of word and character n-grams and train support vector machine (SVM). Our results demonstrate that character and word level overlap features in combination can give performance comparable to methods employing more sophisticated NLP processing tools and external resources. We achieve the highest F-score for identifying paraphrases on the Twitter Paraphrase Corpus as part of the SemEval-2015 Task1.

1 Introduction

This paper presents an approach to identifying Twitter paraphrase pairs using lexical overlap features. Paraphrase identification (PI) may be defined as "the task of deciding whether two given text fragments have the same meaning" (Lintean & Rus 2011). Methods for identifying paraphrases thus take a pair of texts and make a binary judgment. The PI task has practical importance in the Natural Language Processing (NLP) community because of the pervasive problem of linguistic variation. Accurate methods for PI should help improve the performance of NLP systems that would seem to require language understanding. This includes key applications such as question answering, information retrieval and machine translation, amongst others. Acquired paraphrases have been shown to improve the performance of Statistical Machine Translation (SMT) systems, for example (Callison-Burch et al. 2006, Owczarzak et al., 2006; Madnani et al., 2007)

Many researchers on PI make use of existing NLP tools and other resources to identify paraphrases. For example, Duclaye et al., (2002) exploits the NLP tools of a question answering system for reformulating rules to identify paraphrases. Other researchers (Finch et al 2005, Mihalcea et al 2006, Fernando & Stevenson 2008, Malakasiotis 2009, Das & Smith 2009) have employed lexical semantic similarity information based on resources such as WordNet (Miller, 1995).

Although the PI task aims to identify sentences that are semantically equivalent, a number of researchers have shown that classifiers trained on lexical overlap features may achieve relatively high accuracy. Good performance is achieved without the use of knowledge-based semantic features or other external knowledge sources such as parallel corpora (Lintean & Rus 2011, Blacoe & Lapata, 2012). We consider methods as *knowledge-lean* if they make use of just the text at hand and avoid the use of external processing tools and other resources. Knowledge-lean PI methods may thus employ shallow overlap measures based on lexical items or n-grams, but they might also make use of distributional techniques where these are based on simple text statistics.

The work described here is part of ongoing research that is investigating the extent to which knowledge-lean techniques may help to identify paraphrases. Preliminary work has been conducted using the Microsoft Research Paraphrase Corpus

(MSRPC) (Dolan & Brockett, 2005). However, the approach may be of particular value where knowledge-based language resources are not readily available or applicable. In this context, Twitter presents interesting challenges. Its short texts (tweets), widespread use of non-standard grammar, spelling and punctuation, as well as slang, abbreviations and neologisms, etc. make syntactic and semantic analysis difficult.

We apply a supervised learning approach using SVMs and learn classifiers based on simple lexical and character n-gram overlap features. SVM classifiers benefit from features that are interdependent and informative, so good choice of feature combinations is crucial. We also experimented with different kernels to find out whether a non-linear kernel works well for this task.

2 Related Work

A number of researchers have investigated whether near state-of-the-art PI results can be obtained without use of external sources. Blacoe & Lapata (2012) use distributional methods to find compositional meaning of phrases and sentences. They find that performance of shallow approaches is comparable to methods that are computationally intensive or that use very large corpora. Lintean & Rus (2011) apply word unigrams and bigrams. Bigrams capture word order information, which can in turn capture syntactic similarities between two text fragments. Finch et al. (2005) combines several MT metrics and uses them as features. Madnani et al. (2012) also shows that good results are obtained by combining different MT metrics. Ji & Eisenstein (2013) attains state-of-the-art results based on latent semantic analysis and a new term-weighting metric, TF-KLD.[1]

A variety of classifiers has been employed for the purpose of identifying paraphrases. Kozarova & Montoyo (2006) measures lexical and semantic similarity with the combination of different classifiers: k-Nearest Neighbours, Support Vector Machines, and Maximum Entropy. The SVM Classifiers remains the most applicable in recent research whether applied solely (Finch et al., 2005; Wan et al., 2006) or part of combined classifiers (Kozoreva & Montotyo, 2006; Lintean & Rus, 2011; Madnani et al, 2012).

[1] State-of-the-art results are shown in Section 5.

3 The Task

The Semeval-2015 task “Paraphrase and Semantic Similarity in Twitter” involves predicting whether two tweets have the same meaning. Training and test data are provided in the form of a Twitter Paraphrase Corpus (TPC) (Xu, 2014). The TPC is constructed semi-randomly and annotated via Amazon Mechanical Turk by 5 annotators. It consists of around 35% paraphrases and 65% non-paraphrases. Training and development data consists of 18K tweet pairs and 1K test data. Test data is drawn from a different time period and annotated by an expert.

4 Approach

4.1 Text Preprocessing

Text preprocessing is essential to many NLP applications. It may involve tokenizing, removal of punctuation, PoS-tagging, and so on. For identifying paraphrases, this may not always be appropriate. Removing punctuation and stop words, as commonly done for many NLP applications, arguably results in the loss of information that may be critical in terms of PI. We therefor keep text preprocessing to a minimum.

The TPC is already tokenized (O’Connor et al., 2010), part-of-speech tagged (Derczynski et al., 2013), and named entity tagged (Ritter et al., 2011). Here we only experiment on tokenized data, ignoring part-of-speech and named entity tagged data. In the next section we also report results for the MSR Paraphrase Corpus. We used the Rasp Toolkit (Briscoe et al., 2006) to perform tokenization in this case.

A particular issue in dealing with Twitter is the use of capitalization. Variability in the use of capitals (some tweets may be uncapitalised, others written in all uppercase) presents a problem for simple lexical overlap measures between candidate paraphrase pairs. To help overcome this, tokenized tweets are lowercased. Although this potentially causes confusion between proper nouns and common nouns (e.g. *apple* the fruit v. *Apple* the company) our experimental work shows that it most likely increases the quantity of identified paraphrase pairs.

Tweets tend to have a higher proportion of out-of-vocabulary (OOV) words than other texts.

Due to the character limit, words are often shortened or abbreviated and standard spelling rules ignored. In addition, characters may be added for emphasis. Nevertheless, we have not normalized the original texts to compensate for this.

A novel aspect of the TPC compared to other paraphrase corpora is the inclusion of topic information, which is also used during the construction process. Despite the possibility that topic features might be utilized, we have not made use of this information in our approach.

4.2 Features and Instances

As the basis for deriving a number of overlap features, we consider different representations of a text as a set of tokens, where a token may be either a word or character n-gram. For the work described here we restrict attention to word and character unigrams and bigrams. Use of a variety of machine translation techniques (Madnani et al., 2012) that utilise word n-grams motivated their use in representing texts for this task. In particular, word bigrams may provide potentially useful syntactic information about a text. Character bigrams, on the other hand, allow us to capture similarity between related word forms. Possible overlap features are constructed using basic set operations:

Size of union: the size of the union of the tokens in the two texts of a candidate paraphrase pair.

Size of intersection: the number of tokens common to the texts of a candidate paraphrase pair.

Text Size: the size of the set of tokens representing a given text.

This yields a total of eight possible overlap features for a pair of texts, plus four ways of measuring text size. Each data instance is a vector of features representing a pair of tweets. In order to select an optimal set of features we ran a number of preliminary experiments. Table 1 presents the results for different features and combinations of features on the development data. We present results obtained for a linear kernel. The general pattern for an RBF kernel is similar.

Intuitively, knowing about the union, intersection or size of a text in isolation may not be very informative. However, for a given token type, these four features in combination provide potentially useful information about similarity of texts. In the following, C1 and C2 each denote four features (union, intersection, sizes of tweet 1 and tweet 2) produced by character unigrams and bigrams, respectively. Similarly, W1 and W2 denote the four features generated by word unigrams and bigrams, respectively. Combinations (e.g. C1W2) represent eight features: those for C1 plus those for W2.

Features	**Acc**	**Pre.**	**Rec.**	**F-sc.**
C1	64.5	0.0	0.0	0.0
C2	74.5	70.2	48.4	57.7
C1C2	74.5	70.3	48.5	57.4
W1	74.1	70.5	46.5	56.0
W2	70.5	63.9	38.8	48.3
W1W2	74.0	69.9	46.9	56.2
C1W1	74.2	70.4	47.2	56.5
C2W2	74.9	71.1	49.1	58.1
C1W2	71.4	72.0	31.9	44.2
C2W1	75.6	72.4	50.6	59.6
Baseline	72.6	70.4	38.9	50.1

Table 1: Individual and Combined Results by Linear SVM

It is clear that features based on character bigrams are more informative than character unigrams (for C1, all instances are classified negative). For words, on the other hand, use of bigrams did not improve performance over unigrams. However, combining features for words and characters proved beneficial. Although, the combination of character and word bigrams increases performance, combining word unigrams and character bigrams is more informative. We therefore chose to represent instances using a combination of character bigrams and word unigrams. [2]

An important step in SVM classification is rescaling of the features. Apart from a simple scaling mechanism, which is applied during the classification process, features are kept as they are.

4.3 SVM Classifiers

An SVM classifier maps the feature vectors into high dimensional vector space and computes the dot product of the two vectors inside the kernel. Its applicability to both linear and non-linear systems has been proven for different NLP applications. We used SVM implementations from scikit-learn (Pedregosa et al., 2011) and experimented with a number of classifiers. We report here on results obtained using SVC adapted from libsvm (Chang & Lin, 2011) by embedding different kernels. We

[2] The submitted system used just six features: four character bigram features together with just the union and intersection of word unigrams. This had no impact on performance.

experimented with linear and Radial Basis Function (RBF) kernels. Linear kernels are known to work well with large datasets and RBF kernels are the first choice if small number of features are applied (Hsu et al., 2003), which both cases to apply our datasets. Classifiers are used with their default parameters and trained on the data provided.

5 Results

Table 2 shows that SVC with a linear kernel achieved an F-score of 67.4. This represent the highest score amongst those systems participating in Task 1, though still some way below Xu et al (2014) and the human upper-bound. Xu et al. (2014)'s approach constructs a joint word-sentence paraphrase model (MULTIP) and utilizes topic information, which outperforms other features individually. Table 2 also shows the result for the RBF kernel, which was not submitted for the task. For this task the non-linear kernel does not provide any performance gain over the linear SVM.

Model	Acc.	Pre.	Rec.	F-sc.
Human Upperbound	--	75.2	90.8	82.3
Xu et al. (2014)	--	72.2	72.6	72.4
SVC (linear kernel)	86.5	68.0	66.9	67.4
SVC (rbf kernel)	85.7	64.9	68.6	66.7
Baseline	--	67.9	52.0	58.9

Table 2: TPC Results

For comparison, Table 3 shows state-of-the-art results for the PI task on the MSRPC, together with our classifiers trained using of same set of features as for the TPC. Our method performs well above baseline, but with relatively lower precision than other systems. In contrast to Table 2, our highest result is obtained using the RBF kernel.

Model	Acc.	Pre.	Rec.	F-sc.
Ji&Eisenstein(2013)	80.4			85.96
Madnani et al (2012)	77.4	-	-	84.1
Socher et al. (2011)	76.8	-	-	83.6
Wan et al. (2006)	75.6	77.0	90.0	83.0
SVC(rbf kernel)	**74.4**	**74.8**	**92.9**	**82.8**
Das & Smith (2009)	76.1	79.6	86.1	82.7
Finch et al. (2005)	75.0	76.6	89.8	82.7
Fernando&Stevenson (2008)	74.1	75.2	91.3	82.4
SVC (linear kernel)	**73.7**	**75.0**	**90.1**	**82.1**
Qiu et al. (2006)	72.0	72.5	93.4	81.6
Zhang and Patrick (2005)	71.9	74.3	88.2	80.7
BASELINE	**65.4**	**71.6**	**79.5**	**75.3**

Table 3: Paraphrase Identification State-of-the-art Results on MSRPC

We note that the features that we adopt as informative for the Twitter PI task outperform some recent approaches to PI on the MSRPC. This is encouraging and indicates applicability of knowledge-lean approaches to other data sets.

6 Conclusions

Our results demonstrate that knowledge-lean methods based on character and word level overlap features in combination can give good results in terms of the identification of Twitter paraphrases. SVM classifiers were successfully used to identify paraphrase pairs given just a few simple features. Our approach performed as well as and generally much better (in terms of F-score) than other, more sophisticated participating systems.

Overlap of character bigrams was more informative than that of character unigrams. We hypothesize that measuring overlap of character bigrams provides a way of detecting similarity of related word-forms. It thus performs a similar function to stemming or lemmatization in other domains, whilst retaining some information about difference. This may be especially helpful with Twitter, where a variety of idiosyncratic spellings and short forms may be observed alongside the usual morphological variants.

A strength of our approach is that pre-processing is kept to a minimum. This may explain why our system outperforms other approaches that use a similar set of overlap features. Methods that require the removal of stop words, punctuation, OOV words etc., lose potentially useful information. On the other hand, we found that normalizing tweets with regard to capitalization enhanced performance of the classifier.

The current work on paraphrase identification is ongoing. There is clearly room for reaching to human upper bound shown in Table 2. Our latest work shows that extending character and word n-grams to up to 4 is promising and gives performance that is close to the state–of-the-art results on TPC obtained by Xu et al. (2014). We intend to report on these results in a future paper.

References

Blacoe, W., & Lapata, M. (2012). A Comparison of Vector-based Representations for Semantic Composition. *Proceedings of the 2012 Joint Confer-*

ence on Empirical Methods in Natural Language Processing and Computational Natural Language Learning (EMNLP-CoNLL '12), (July), 546–556.

Briscoe, E., J. Carroll and R. Watson (2006) The Second Release of the RASP System. *In Proceedings of the COLING/ACL 2006 Interactive Presentation Sessions.* Sydney, Australia, 77-80.

Callison-burch, C., Koehn, P., & Osborne, M. (2006). Improved Statistical Machine Translation Using Paraphrases. *In Proceedings of the main conference on Human Language Technology Conference of the North American Chapter of the Association of Computational Linguistics (HLT-NAACL '06). Association for Computational Linguistics* (pp. 17-24). Stroudsburg, PA, USA

Chang, C.C. & Lin, C.J. (2011). LIBSVM: a library for support vector machines. *ACM Transactions on Intelligent Systems and Technology, 2:27:1--27:27.* Software available at http://www.csie.ntu.edu.tw/~cjlin/libsvm

Das, D., & Smith, N. A. (2009). Paraphrase Identification as Probabilistic Quasi-Synchronous Recognition. *In Proceedings of the Joint Conference of the 47th Annual Meeting of the ACL and the 4th International Joint Conference on Natural Language Processing of the AFNLP: Volume 1 - Volume 1 (ACL '09), Vol. 1. Association for Computational Linguistics* (pp. 468-476). Stroudsburg, PA, USA.

Derczynski, L., Ritter, A., Clark, S., & Bontcheva, K. (2013). Twitter Part-of-Speech Tagging for All: Overcoming Sparse and Noisy Data. *In Proceedings of the International Conference on Recent Advances in Natural Language Processing.*

Dolan, W. B. & Brockett, C. (2005). Automatically Constructing a Corpus of Sentential Paraphrases, 9-16. *In Proceedings of The Third International Workshop on Paraphrasing (IWP2005), Jeju, Republic of Korea.*

Duclaye, F., Yvon, F., Collin, O., R, F. T., Marzin, P., & Cedex, L. (2002). Using the Web as a Linguistic Resource for Learning Reformulations Automatically. *In Proceedings of the Third International Conference on Language Resources and Evaluation. (pp. 390-396).*

Fernando, S., & Stevenson, M. (2008). A Semantic Similarity Approach to Paraphrase Detection. In *In Proceedings of the 11th Annual Research Colloquium of the UK Special Interest Group for Computational Linguistics* (pp. 45–52).

Finch, A., Hwang, Y.-S., & Sumita, E. (2005). Using Machine Translation Evaluation Techniques to Determine Sentence-level Semantic Equivalence. In *Proceedings of the Third International Workshop on Paraphrasing (IWP2005)* (pp. 17–24).

C.-W. Hsu, C.-C. Chang, C.-J. Lin. (2003) A practical guide to support vector classification. *Technical report, Department of Computer Science, National Taiwan University. July.*

Ji, Y., & Eisenstein, J. (2013). Discriminative Improvements to Distributional Sentence Similarity. In *Proceedings of the 2013 Conference on Empirical Methods in Natural Language Processing* (pp. 891–896). Seattle, Washington, USA: Association for Computational Linguistics.

Kozareva, Z., & Montoyo, A. (2006). Paraphrase Identification on the Basis of Supervised Machine Learning Techniques. *in Proceedings of the 5th International Conference on Natural Language Processing (FinTAL 2006),Lecture Notes in Artificial Intelligence* (pp. 524-533). Turku, Finland.

Lintean, M., & Rus, V. (2011). Dissimilarity Kernels for Paraphrase Identification. *Proceedings of the 24th International Florida Artificial Intelligence Research Society Conference.* (pp. 263-268). Palm Beach, FL.

Madnani, N., Ayan, N. F., Resnik, P., Dorr, B. J., & Park, C. (2007). Using Paraphrases for Parameter Tuning in Statistical Machine Translation. *Proceedings of the Second Workshop on Statistical Machine Translation (WMT'07).* (Vol. 20742). Prague, Czech Republic: Association for Computational Linguistics.

Madnani, N., Tetreault, J., & Chodorow, M. (2012). Re-examining Machine Translation Metrics for Paraphrase Identification. *In Proceedings of the 2012 Conference of the North American Chapter of the Association for Computational Linguistics: Human Language Technologies (NAACL HLT '12) (pp. 182–190).* Stroudsburg, PA, USA

Malakasiotis, P. (2009). Paraphrase Recognition Using Machine Learning to Combine Similarity Measures. *Proceedings of the ACL-IJCNLP 2009 Student Research Workshop* (pp. 27-35). Suntec, Singapore.

Mihalcea, R., Corley, C., & Strapparava, C. (2006). Corpus-based and Knowledge-based Measures of Text Semantic Similarity. In A. Cohn (Ed.), *Proceedings of the 21st national conference on Artificial intelligence- Volume 1* (pp. 775–780). AAAI Press.

Miller, G.A. (1995). WordNet: A Lexical Database for English. *Communications of the ACM Vol. 38, No. 11: 39:41.*

O'Connor, B., Krieger, M., & Ahn, D. (2010). TweetMotif : Exploratory Search and Topic Summarization for Twitter. In *Proceedings of the Fourth International AAAI Conference on Weblogs and Social Media* (pp. 384–385). Association for the Advancement of Artificial Intelligence.

Owczarzak, K., Gorves, D., Genabith, J. V., & Way, A. (2006). Contextual Bitext-Derived Paraphrases in Automatic MT Evaluation. *In Proceedings of the Workshop on Statistical Machine Translation (StatMT '06). Association for Computational Linguistics* (pp. 86-93). Stroudsburg, PA, USA.

Pedregosa, F., Varoquaux, G., Gramfort, A. , Michel, V.,Thirion, B.,Grisel, O., Blondel, M., Prettenhofer, P., Weiss, R., Dubourg, V., Vanderplas, J., Passos, A., Cournapeau, D., Brucher, M., Perrot, M., Duchesnay, É. (2011). Scikit-learn: Machine Learning in Python. *Journal of Machine Learning Research,* 12, *2825-2830*

Qiu, L., Kan, M.-Y., & Chua, T.-S. (2006). Paraphrase Recognition via Dissimilarity Significance Classification. *Proceedings of the 2006 Conference on Empirical Methods in Natural Language Processing (EMNLP '06)*, (July), 18–26. doi:10.3115/1610075.1610079

Ritter, A., Clark, S., Mausam & Etzioni, O. (2011). Named entity recognition in tweets: an experimental study. *In Proceedings of the Conference on Empirical Methods in Natural Language Processing (EMNLP'11). Association for Computitional Linguistics.* Stroudsburg, PA, USA, 1524-1534.

Socher, R., Huang, E. H., Pennington, J., Ng, A. Y., & Manning, C. D. (2011) *Dynamic Pooling and Unfolding Recursive Autoencoders for Paraphrase Detection. Science*, 1-9.

Wan, S., Dras, M., & Dale, R. (2006). Using Dependency-Based Features to Take the " Para-farce " out of Paraphrase. *In proceedings of the Australasian Language Technology Workshop* (pp. 131-138). Sydney, Australia.

Xu, W. (2014). Data-Drive Aprroches for Paraphrasing Across Language Variations. *PhD Thesis.* Department of Computer Science, New York University.

Xu, W., Ritter, A., Callison-Burch, C., Dolan, W., & Ji, Y. (2014). Extracting Lexically Divergent Paraphrases from Twitter. Transactions Of The Association For Computational Linguistics, 2, 435-448. Retrieved fromhttps://tacl2013.cs.columbia.edu/ojs/index.php/tacl/article/view/498

Zhang, Y., & Patrick, J. (2005). Paraphrase Identification by Text Canonicalization. *In proceedings of the Australasian Language Technology Workshop* (pp. 160-166). Sydney, Australia.

TKLBLIIR: Detecting Twitter Paraphrases with TweetingJay

Mladen Karan[1], Goran Glavaš[1], Jan Šnajder[1], Bojana Dalbelo Bašić[1], Ivan Vulić[2], and Marie-Francine Moens[2]

[1]University of Zagreb, Faculty of Electrical Engineering and Computing
Text Analysis and Knowledge Engineering Lab, Unska 3, 10000 Zagreb, Croatia
{goran.glavas, mladen.karan, jan.snajder, bojana.dalbelo}@fer.hr

[2]KU Leuven, Department of Computer Science
Language Intelligence & Information Retrieval Group, Celestijnenlaan 200A, Leuven, Belgium
{ivan.vulic, sien.moens}@cs.kuleuven.be

Abstract

When tweeting on a topic, Twitter users often post messages that convey the same or similar meaning. We describe *TweetingJay*, a system for detecting paraphrases and semantic similarity of tweets, with which we participated in Task 1 of SemEval 2015. TweetingJay uses a supervised model that combines semantic overlap and word alignment features, previously shown to be effective for detecting semantic textual similarity. TweetingJay reaches 65.9% F1-score and ranked fourth among the 18 participating systems. We additionally provide an analysis of the dataset and point to some peculiarities of the evaluation setup.

1 Introduction

Recognizing tweets that convey the same meaning (paraphrases) or similar meaning is useful in applications such as event detection (Petrović et al., 2012), tweet summarization (Yang et al., 2011), and tweet retrieval (Naveed et al., 2011). Paraphrase detection in tweets is a more challenging task than paraphrase detection in other domains such as news (Xu et al., 2013). Besides brevity (max. 140 characters), tweets exhibit all the irregularities typical of social media text (Baldwin et al., 2013), such as informality, ungrammaticality, disfluency, and excessive use of jargon.

In this paper we present the *TweetingJay* system for detecting paraphrases in tweets, with which we participated in Task 1 of SemEval 2015 evaluation exercise (Xu et al., 2015). Our system builds on findings from a large body of work on semantic textual similarity (STS) (Šarić et al., 2012; Sultan et al., 2014) and recent breakthroughs in distributed word representations (Mikolov et al., 2013a). We design a set of measures that capture the semantic similarity of tweets and train a support vector machine (SVM) using these measures as features. Positioning of our system at rank four among 18 teams, with only point and a half lower performance compared to the the best-performing system, suggests that STS measures are useful for detecting paraphrases in Twitter. We make our system freely available.[1]

Besides providing the description of the TweetingJay system, in this paper we analyze the evaluation setup, with special focus on the provided dataset and its subsets (train, validation, and test), and discuss the stability of the evaluation results.

2 Related Work

There is a large body of work on automated paraphrase detection; see (Madnani and Dorr, 2010) for a comprehensive overview. The majority of research efforts focus on detecting paraphrases in standard texts such as news (Das and Smith, 2009; Madnani et al., 2012) or artificially generated text (Madnani et al., 2012). State-of-the-art approaches typically combine several measures of semantic similarity between text fragments. For instance, Madnani et al. (2012) achieve state-of-the-art performance by combining eight different machine translation metrics in a supervised fashion.

A task closely related to paraphrase detection is semantic textual similarity (STS), introduced at SemEval 2012 (Agirre et al., 2012). There is now a

[1]http://takelab.fer.hr/tweetingjay

significant amount of work on this task. The best performing STS systems employ various methods for aligning semantically corresponding words or otherwise quantifying the amount of semantically congruent content between two sentences (Sultan et al., 2014; Šarić et al., 2012).

In contrast, STS research on Twitter data has been scarce. Zanzotto et al. (2011) detect content redundancy between tweets, where redundant means paraphrased or entailed content. They achieve reasonable performance with SVM using vector-comparison and syntactic tree kernels. Xu et al. (2014) propose MULTIP, a latent variable model for joint inference of correspondence of words and sentences. An unsupervised model based on representing sentences in latent space is presented by Guo and Diab (2012).

3 TweetingJay

TweetingJay is essentially a supervised machine learning model, which employs a number of semantic similarity features (18 features in total). Because the number of features is relatively small, we use SVM with a non-linear (RBF) kernel. Our features can be divided into (1) semantic overlap features, most of which are adaptations of STS features proposed by Šarić et al. (2012), and (2) word alignment features, based on (a) the output of the word alignment model by Sultan et al. (2014) and (b) a re-implementation of the MULTIP model by Xu et al. (2014).

In the dataset provided by the organizers, each tweet is associated with a topic, with 10 to 100 tweet pairs per topic. An important preprocessing step is to remove tokens that can be found in the name of a topic. For example, for the topic *"Roberto Mancini"*, we trim the tweets *"Roberto Mancini gets the boot from the Man City"* and *"City sacked Mancini"* to *"gets the boot from the Man City"* and *"City sacked"*, respectively, and then compute the features on the trimmed tweets. The rationale is that, given a topic, there is an overlap in topic words between both paraphrase and non-paraphrase tweet pairs, which diminishes the discriminative power of the model's comparison features.

3.1 Semantic Overlap Features

Semantic overlap features compare the content words (nouns, verbs, adjectives, adverbs, and numbers).

Ngram overlap. We compute the number of matching n-grams between two tweets. This number is normalized by the length of the first and the second tweet, respectively, and the harmonic mean of these two measures is taken as the similarity score. These features are computed separately for unigrams and bigrams. We also compute a weighted version by weighting the matched words w with their information content:

$$ic(w) = -\log \frac{\mathit{freq}(w) + 1}{\sum_{w' \in C} \mathit{freq}(w') + 1}$$

where C is the set of all words in the corpus and $\mathit{freq}(w)$ is the word's frequency. We obtained the frequencies from the Google Books Ngrams (GBN) (Michel et al., 2011). In the weighted version of the ngram overlap, the overlap is normalized by the sum of information contents of all words in the first and second tweet, respectively, and the resulting similarity score is the harmonic mean of these two scores.

Greedy word alignment overlap (GWAO). To compute this feature, we iteratively pair the words – one word from each tweet – according to their semantic similarity. In each iteration we greedily select the pair of words with the largest semantic similarity, and remove the words from their corresponding tweets, until no words are left in shorter of the two tweets. The similarity between words is computed as the cosine between their corresponding 300-dimension embedding vectors obtained using `word2vec` tool (Mikolov et al., 2013b) on a 100 billion words portion of the Google News dataset. Let $P(t_1, t_2)$ be the set of word pairs obtained through the alignment on a pair of tweets (t_1, t_2) and let $vec(w)$ be the embedding vector of the word w. The GWAO score is computed as:

$$gwao(t_1, t_2) = \sum_{\substack{(w_1, w_2) \\ \in P(t_1, t_2)}} \alpha \cdot \cos\left(vec(w_1), vec(w_2)\right)$$

where α is the larger of the information contents of the two words, $\alpha = \max\left(ic(w_1), ic(w_1)\right)$. The $gwao(t_1, t_2)$ score is normalized with the sum of information contents of words from t_1 and t_2, respectively, and the harmonic mean of the two normalized scores is taken as the feature value.

Tweet embedding similarity. Linear combinations of word embedding vectors have been shown to correspond well to the semantic composition of the individual words (Mikolov et al., 2013a; Mikolov et al., 2013b). Building on this finding, we embed a tweet as a weighted sum of the embeddings of its content words, where we use information content of words as their weights:

$$vec(t) = \sum_{w \in t} ic(w) \cdot vec(w).$$

As the tweet embedding similarity, we simply compute the cosine between the corresponding tweet embeddings, i.e., $\cos(vec(t_1), vec(t_2))$.

Topic-specific information content. While information content computed on a general corpus such as GBN indicates how informative the word is in general, we also wanted to have a measure of how informative each word is within a tweet's topic. To this end we also compute topic-specific versions of all the above features using topic-specific instead of GBN information contents.

3.2 Word Alignment Features

We adopt the word alignment features from two alignment-based systems: (1) the DLS@CU system of Sultan et al. (2014), which achieved the best performance on the STS task at SemEval 2014 (Agirre et al., 2014), and (2) our implementation of the MULTIP latent variables model (Xu et al., 2014), which utilizes the concept of an *anchor*: a pair of semantically aligned words from a paraphrased pair of tweets.

Aligned word pairs (AWP). A state-of-the art monolingual word alignment model by Sultan et al. (2014) outputs pairs of semantically aligned words between two given sentences.[2] We used the output of the DLS@CU model to generate two features: (1) the raw count of the aligned word pairs, and (2) the normalized count, which is the harmonic mean of the scores obtained by normalizing the raw count with the length of the first and second tweet, respectively. We computed two versions for both of these features, one considering all the tokens in tweets, and the other taking into account only content words.

Anchor count (ANC). We re-implemented the MULTIP model of Xu et al. (2014).[3] As anchor candidates we consider all pairs of content words from the two tweets. We use a minimalistic set of features including (1) Levenshtein distance between candidate words, (2) several binary features indicating relatedness of words (e.g., lowercased tokens match, POS-tags match), and (3) semantic similarity obtained as the cosine of word embeddings, obtained with the GloVe model (Pennington et al., 2014) trained on Twitter data.[4] To account for feature interactions, following (Xu et al., 2014), we also use conjunction features. We use the number of anchors identified by this method for a pair of tweets as a feature for our SVM model.

4 Evaluation

Each team was allowed to submit two runs on the test set provided by the task organizers (Xu et al., 2015). Participants were provided with a training set (13,063 pairs) and a development set (4,727 pairs). We used the train and development set to optimize the hyperparameters C and γ of our SVM model with the RBF kernel. For the final evaluation, the organizers used a test set of 972 tweet pairs.

Feature sets. We divided the features in three groups: (1) semantic overlap features (SO) from Section 3.1, (2) aligned word pairs (AWP) features, and (3) the anchor count feature (ANC) from Section 3.2.

Model optimization. There are three ways how the optimization of the SVM model (hyperparameters C and γ) could have been carried out: (1) training and optimization on the train set using 10-folded cross-validation, with no use of the development set (model M1); (2) training on the train set and optimization on the development set (model M2), and (3) training on the union of the train and development set using 10-folded cross-validation (model M3). Following the advice of the task organizers, we removed debatable cases from both the train and dev sets. We submitted models M1 and M2 for the official evaluation (our team name was TKLBLIIR).

[2] `https://github.com/ma-sultan/monolingual-word-aligner`

[3] We obtain lower results on the test set (61.3% F_1 vs. 69.6%). This is likely caused by the use of slightly different features and perhaps by differences in implementation.

[4] `http://nlp.stanford.edu/projects/glove/`

Team	P	R	F_1	Rank
ASOBEK	68.0	66.9	**67.4**	1
MITRE	80.6	56.9	66.7	2
ECNU	76.7	58.3	66.2	3
FBK-HLT	68.5	63.4	65.9	4
TKLBLIIR M1	64.5	67.4	**65.9**	5
TKLBLIIR M2	46.1	81.7	59.0	19
MULTIP	71.9	67.4	**69.6**	–
Baseline (log.reg.)	67.9	52.0	58.9	21
Baseline (WTMF)	45.0	66.3	53.6	28

Table 1: Official SemEval Task 1 evaluation.

	M1		M2		M3	
Features	dev	test	dev	test	dev	test
SO	63.3	63.4	**64.9**	59.0	63.3	61.5
SO+AWP	64.0	61.6	64.7	60.4	64.0	61.6
SO+ANC	60.8	**65.9**	64.6	60.8	64.5	62.5
SO+AWP+ANC	64.1	63.2	**64.9**	59.0	64.4	61.2

Table 2: Model optimization using different datasets.

4.1 Official Results

A subset of the official ranking is shown in Table 4.1. Our model M1 ranked fourth (sharing that place with FBK-HLT) in the official evaluation with a 1.5% lower F_1 score than the best-performing system. Our model M2 outperforms both baselines. The state-of-the-art model MULTIP outperforms all participating systems. There is a notable performance gap between our two runs. We believe this comes from the high sensitivity of the performance on the test set to small changes in hyperparameter values. We elaborate more on this in the next section.

4.2 Dataset Analysis

In Table 4.2 we show the performance of the models M1, M2, and M3 on the development and test set. We observe an unusual behavior for all three models: a model that performs good on the development set typically performs bad on the test set, and vice versa. Furthermore, optimal cross-validated F_1 performance on the train set is 72%, which is 7 points above the best performance on the validation set. We believe this may be indicative of significant differences in the distributions underlying the datasets.

To investigate this further, we applied the Kolmogorov-Smirnov two-sample goodness-of-fit test (K-S test) (Daniel, 1990) for each of the used features to determine whether the train set is drawn from the same distribution as the development and test set. The K-S test is a nonparametric test that determines whether two independent samples differ in some respect, both in the measure of locations (means, median) and the shapes of the distributions (skewness, dispersion, kurtosis). The assumptions for the K-S test (independence of random samples and continuous variables) are met for all our features. We tested all features at the level of significance of 0.05 and rejected the null hypothesis for all features but one (bigram overlap). This confirms our initial assumption that the features in the train set are not identically distributed to those in the test set, bringing into question the representativeness of the test set. Reasons for this may include different annotation sources (crowdsourcing vs experts) and differences in time periods of tweets. Moreover, due to differences in the datasets, the performance is very much affected by the choice of the model optimization setup.

4.3 Feature Analysis

Due to volatile performance, it is difficult to say much about which features are most useful. However, we have observed consistent performance boosts in all settings when introducing topic-specific versions of features.

5 Conclusion

We described TweetingJay, a supervised model for detecting Twitter paraphrases with which we participated in Task 1 of SemEval 2015. TweetingJay relies on features capturing semantic similarity and word alignments between tweets and achieves performance comparable to best-performing models on the task.

On the methodological side, we investigated the cause for unusual behavior of our models on the different datasets. Our preliminary statistical analysis of the datasets seems to suggest that the underlying distributions datasets are significantly different. We believe this makes the performance estimates less reliable and suggest that the results should be taken with caution.

References

Eneko Agirre, Mona Diab, Daniel Cer, and Aitor Gonzalez-Agirre. 2012. SemEval-2012 task 6: A pilot on semantic textual similarity. In *Proceedings of SemEval 2012*, pages 385–393.

Eneko Agirre, Carmen Banea, Claire Cardie, Daniel Cer, Mona Diab, Aitor Gonzalez-Agirre, Weiwei Guo, Rada Mihalcea, German Rigau, and Janyce Wiebe. 2014. SemEval-2014 task 10: Multilingual semantic textual similarity. pages 81–91.

Timothy Baldwin, Paul Cook, Marco Lui, Andrew MacKinlay, and Li Wang. 2013. How noisy social media text, how diffrnt social media sources. In *Proceedings of IJCNLP 2013*, pages 356–364.

Wayne W. Daniel. 1990. *Applied nonparametric statistics*. The Duxbury advanced series in statistics and decision sciences.

Dipanjan Das and Noah A Smith. 2009. Paraphrase identification as probabilistic quasi-synchronous recognition. In *Proceedings of ACL 2009*, pages 468–476.

Weiwei Guo and Mona Diab. 2012. Modeling sentences in the latent space. In *Proceedings of ACL 2012*, pages 864–872.

Nitin Madnani and Bonnie J Dorr. 2010. Generating phrasal and sentential paraphrases: A survey of data-driven methods. *Computational Linguistics*, 36(3):341–387.

Nitin Madnani, Joel Tetreault, and Martin Chodorow. 2012. Re-examining machine translation metrics for paraphrase identification. In *Proceedings of NAACL 2012*, pages 182–190.

Jean-Baptiste Michel, Yuan Kui Shen, Aviva Presser Aiden, Adrian Veres, Matthew K Gray, Joseph P Pickett, Dale Hoiberg, Dan Clancy, Peter Norvig, Jon Orwant, et al. 2011. Quantitative analysis of culture using millions of digitized books. *Science*, 331(6014):176–182.

Tomas Mikolov, Kai Chen, Greg Corrado, and Jeffrey Dean. 2013a. Efficient estimation of word representations in vector space. *arXiv preprint arXiv:1301.3781*.

Tomas Mikolov, Ilya Sutskever, Kai Chen, Greg S Corrado, and Jeff Dean. 2013b. Distributed representations of words and phrases and their compositionality. In *Proceedings of NIPS 2013*, pages 3111–3119.

Nasir Naveed, Thomas Gottron, Jérôme Kunegis, and Arifah Che Alhadi. 2011. Searching microblogs: coping with sparsity and document quality. In *Proceedings of CIKM 2011*, pages 183–188.

Jeffrey Pennington, Richard Socher, and Christopher D Manning. 2014. Glove: Global vectors for word representation. In *Proceedings of EMNLP 2014*, pages 1532–1541.

Saša Petrović, Miles Osborne, and Victor Lavrenko. 2012. Using paraphrases for improving first story detection in news and twitter. In *Proceedings of NAACL 2012*, pages 338–346.

Frane Šarić, Goran Glavaš, Mladen Karan, Jan Šnajder, and Bojana Dalbelo Bašić. 2012. TakeLab: systems for measuring semantic text similarity. In *Proceedings of SemEval 2012*, pages 441–448.

Md Arafat Sultan, Steven Bethard, and Tamara Sumner. 2014. DLS@CU: Sentence similarity from word alignment. In *Proceedings of SemEval 2014*, pages 241–245.

Wei Xu, Alan Ritter, and Ralph Grishman. 2013. Gathering and generating paraphrases from twitter with application to normalization. In *Proceedings of the Sixth Workshop on Building and Using Comparable Corpora*, pages 121–128.

Wei Xu, Alan Ritter, Chris Callison-Burch, William B. Dolan, and Yangfeng Ji. 2014. Extracting lexically divergent paraphrases from Twitter. *Transactions of the Association for Computational Linguistics (TACL)*, 2(1).

Wei Xu, Chris Callison-Burch, and William B. Dolan. 2015. SemEval-2015 Task 1: Paraphrase and semantic similarity in Twitter (PIT). In *Proceedings of SemEval 2015*.

Zi Yang, Keke Cai, Jie Tang, Li Zhang, Zhong Su, and Juanzi Li. 2011. Social context summarization. In *Proceedings of ACM SIGIR 2011*, pages 255–264.

Fabio Massimo Zanzotto, Marco Pennacchiotti, and Kostas Tsioutsiouliklis. 2011. Linguistic redundancy in twitter. In *Proceedings of EMNLP 2011*, pages 659–669.

CDTDS: Predicting Paraphrases in Twitter via Support Vector Regression

Rafael Michael Karampatsis
Department of Informatics
University of Edinburgh
10 Crichton Street, EH8 9AB Edinburgh, United Kingdom
mpatsis13@gmail.com

Abstract

In this paper we describe a system that recognizes paraphrases in Twitter for tweets that refer to the same topic. The system participated in Task1 of SEMEVAL-2015 and uses a support vector regression machine to predict the degree of similarity. The similarity is then thresholded to create a binary prediction. The model and experimental results are discussed along with future work that could improve the method.

1 Introduction

Recently, Twitter has gained significant popularity among the social network services. Lots of users often use Twitter to express feelings or opinions about a variety of subjects. Analysing this kind of content can lead to useful information for fields such as personalized marketing or social profiling. However, such a task is not trivial, because the language used on Twitter is often informal, presenting new challenges to text analysis.

Task1 of SEMEVAL-2015 (Xu et al., 2015) focuses on recognition of paraphrases and semantic similarity in Twitter i.e., recognizing if two tweets are alternative linguistic expressions of the same, or similar, meaning (Bhagat and Hovy, 2013). The task is based on a crowdsourced corpus of 18000 pairs of paraphrases and non-paraphrased sentences from Twitter (Xu et al., 2014) and each pair consists of two tweets from the same topic. A label is provided with each pair, which is the number of yes votes from 5 crowdsourced annotators when asked if the second tweet is a paraphrase of the first one.

Paraphrase Example:

Roberto Mancini gets the boot from Man City

Roberto Mancini has been sacked by Manchester City with the Blues saying

Non-Paraphrase Example:

WORLD OF JENKS IS ON AT 11

World of Jenks is my favorite show on tv

Figure 1: Examples of both a paraphrase and a non-paraphrase pair of the data.

The method utilizes a support vector regression machine (SVR). The regression model tries to predict the degree of semantic similarity between two tweets, by assuming that it can be represented by the probability that random human annotators would annotate the pair as a paraphrase. The predicted value is transformed into a binary decision via a threshold.

Section 2 describes the data provided by the organizers. Sections 4 and 5 present the system and its performance respectively. Finally, Section 6 provides ideas for future work and Section 7 concludes.

2 Data

The objective of this task is to predict whether two sentences from Twitter sharing the same topic, imply the same or very similar meaning and optionally a degree score between 0 and 1. In Figure 1, a paraphrase and a non-paraphrase example taken from the task website are illustrated.

The organizers released a training (Train) and a development set (Dev), both labeled and they also provided a test set (Test) for the task. To collect

Set	Size	Paraphrase	Non-Paraphrase	Debatable
Train	13693	3996	7534	1533
Dev	724	948	2672	585
Test	972	175	663	134

Table 1: Class distribution of the train, development and test sets.

the data they used Twitter's public API[1] to crawl trending topics and their associated tweets (Xu et al., 2014). Annotation of the collected tweets was performed via crowdsourcing (*Amazon Mechanical Turk*). From each topic, 11 random tweets were selected and 5 different annotators were used. One of the 11 tweets was randomly selected as the original sentence. The annotators were asked to select which of the remaining 10 tweets have the same meaning as the original one. Each topic's pairs are annotated with the number of annotators that voted for them. Problematic annotators were removed by checking their Cohen's Kappa agreement (Artstein and Poesio, 2008) with other annotators. Agreement with an expert annotator on 972 sentence pairs (test set) was also measured and the Pearson correlation coefficient was 0.735 although the expert annotator had actually used a different scale for the annotation. Both Train and Dev were collected from the same time period while Test was collected from a different time period.

Table 1 illustrates the class distribution of the data. The task organizers have stated that when a pair has either 1 or 0 votes it should be considered a non-paraphrase, while pairs that have 3, 4, and 5 votes should be considered as paraphrases. Pairs that have exactly 2 votes are assumed debatable and the organizers suggest that they should be discarded. We can observe that all the data sets have a very similar distribution and that the majority class is in all cases the non-paraphrase one with about 60% of the data (debatable instances included).

3 Previous Work

Measuring semantic text similarity has been a research subject in natural language processing, information retrieval and artificial intelligence for many years. Most works have focused on the document level (i.e., comparing two long texts or comparing a small text with a long one). Recently, there has been growing interest at the sentence level, specifically on computing the similarity of two sentences. The most related task to computing tweets similarity is the computation of sentence similarity.

According to (Han et al., 2012), there are three main approaches for sentence similarity. The first is based on a vector space model (Meadow, 1992) that models the text as a "bag of words" and represents it using a vector, and the similarity between the two texts is computed as the cosine similarity of their vectors. The second approach relies on the assumption that the words or expressions of two semantically equivalent sentences should be able to be aligned. The quality of this alignment can then be used as a similarity measure. When this approach is utilized, words from the two sentences are paired (Mihalcea et al., 2006) by maximizing the summation of the word similarity of the resulting pairs. Finally, the third and final approach utilizes machine learning and combines different measures and features (such as lexical, semantic and syntactic features) which are supplied to a classifier that learns a model on the training data.

The unique characteristics of Twitter present new challenges and opportunities for paraphrase research (Xu et al., 2013; Ling et al., 2013). Most of the work has focused on paraphrase generation (Xu et al., 2013; Ling et al., 2013) in order to use it for text normalization. However, the task organizers (Xu et al., 2014) created a dataset, implemented a system and reimplemented several baselines and state-of-the-art systems for sentence paraphrase recognition. They showed that their method, which combines a previous system with latent space achieves at least as good results as state-of-the-art systems.

4 System Overview

The main objective of the implemented system is to classify pairs of tweets from the same topic as semantically similar or not. The approach used differs from previous works because it models the problem as a regression task first and then as a classification task, while typical approaches treat the problem as a classification task (usually binary since debatable pairs are discarded). The main inspiration for this

[1] https://dev.twitter.com/docs/api/1.1/overview

Number of Votes	0	1	2	3	4	5
Label Value	0	0.2	0.4	0.6	0.8	1

Table 2: Mapping of the number of positive votes from the annotators to real valued labels.

approach comes from the observation that for example, pairs that got voted from 3 of the annotators will not be as similar as pairs that got voted from 5. Treating these instances in the same way is very likely to confuse the model. The regression approach is a possible way to avoid this effect since instances with different number of votes will not just use different values but will have a relation between their values. For example, instances that got 5 votes will use a better score as their label than instances that got 4 or 3.

To extract this relation from Train data, the ratio of positive votes against the total number of annotators (5) for each pair was used to create the labels. The debatable instances correspond to exactly 2 votes from the human annotators, which maps to 0.4. These instances were discarded as the organizers suggested. This resulted in the use of the values shown in Table 2 as labels.

An SVR with a linear kernel function[2] was used to predict the degree of similarity between the tweet pairs. For each training instance (i.e. a tweet pair) a feature vector is supplied to the regression model[3] along with the corresponding label. The output of the SVR can be used for classification by using a threshold. 0.35 was chosen as the classification threshold as it belongs to the debatable space and it is slightly less than 0.4, in order to increase the recall of the minority class (Paraphrases). However, the threshold could be tuned using cross validation on the training data or by testing on the development set for better results.

4.1 Data Preprocessing

Preprocessing can greatly affect the performance of a system. The tweets were passed through a Twitter specific tokenizer and part-of-speech (POS) tagger (Ritter et al., 2011) by the organizers. We converted all the tweets to lower case and stopwords were removed using the NLTK (Loper and Bird, 2002) stopwords list. Moreover, we removed the tokens of the topic since they always exist in both tweets. Finally, we applied stemming to each one of the remaining tokens and the stemmed representations are stored.

4.2 Feature Engineering

In this section the features used in the model will be described in detail. We made two submissions. Both share the same features except for the sentiment matching feature.

4.2.1 Lexical Overlap Features

A very popular and competitive baseline is to use lexical overlap features (Das and Smith, 2009). These features use the unigrams, bigrams and trigrams of the sentences, both with and without stemming. The cardinality of the intersection of the n-grams between each pair of tweets as a proportion of the length of each tweet is used as a feature. The harmonic mean of these two values is also calculated and used as a feature. These three types of features for each n-gram size were named precision, recall and F1 (harmonic mean of precision and recall) by Das and Smith (2009).

4.2.2 Ratio of the Tweets Length in Tokens

The ratio of the length of the shortest tweet in the pair divided by the length of the longer tweet is used as a feature. This feature is used because if the tweets differ a lot in length then they will probably not have similar meaning.

4.2.3 Overlap of POS Tags

Similar to the lexical overlap features the overlap of POS tags of unigrams, bigrams and trigrams is checked and a total of 9 features is created. For example the tweet "Wow EJ Manuel" contains the following two POS bigrams: UH NNP and NNP NNP.

4.2.4 Overlap of Named Entities Tags (NE)

Similar to the lexical overlap features the overlap of NE is checked and three features are created.

4.2.5 GloVe Word Vectors Similarity

Vector space representations of words have succeeded in capturing semantic and syntactic regularities using vector arithmetic (Pennington et al., 2014;

[2]The LIBLINEAR distribution (Fan et al., 2008)

[3]The regression model uses L2-regularized regression with the default parameter C=1.

Mikolov et al., 2013). The word vectors from GloVe (Pennington et al., 2014) were used to calculate the semantic similarity between tokens of the two sentences by measuring their cosine similarity. The word vectors utilized were created from a corpus of 2B tweets which contains 27B tokens. Experiments on the development set were also done with vectors from Wikipedia2014 + Gigawords5 (about 6B tokens) but were not used for submission since they performed worse than the Twitter ones.

The calculation of these features is based on the alignment algorithm described by (Han et al., 2013). For each of the two tweets we iterate over its tokens. For each token the similarity to all the tokens of the other tweet that exist in the model is calculated and the maximum is returned. When the algorithm finishes, the maximum, minimum and average values of the matched similarities for each tweet are returned as features. This makes a total of 6 features. An additional feature is calculated by finding the similarity of the centroids of the two tweets.

4.2.6 Sentiment Matching

A Twitter sentiment classifier was used to predict the sentiment of the tweets (Karampatsis et al., 2014). The feature has a value of 1 if both tweets of the pair have the same sentiment and 0 otherwise.

5 Experimental Results

Each system had to submit for each test set instance its prediction (paraphrase or not) (subtask1) and optionally a degree of semantic similarity (subtask2). To evaluate system performance for subtask1 the organizers used F_1 against human judgements on the predictions. While for subtask2 they used the Pearson correlation of the predicted similarity scores with the human scores. Our team was ranked 9th on both subtasks[4] and our systems were ranked 13th and 14th on subtask1 and 15th and 16th on subtask2. Table 3 illustrates the results and rankings of our systems and the baselines. The results indicate that the sentiment feature decreases performance and should be removed from our system.

We used the official evaluation script to assess the performance of our systems on the test set for different threshold values. The results are illustrated in Figure 2. We used thresholds from 0 to 1 with a step of 0.05 except for the space $[0.3, 0.4]$ where we used a step of 0.01. The two systems behave similarly and the best performance (0.622) was achieved from the All-Sentiment system using a threshold of 0.36.

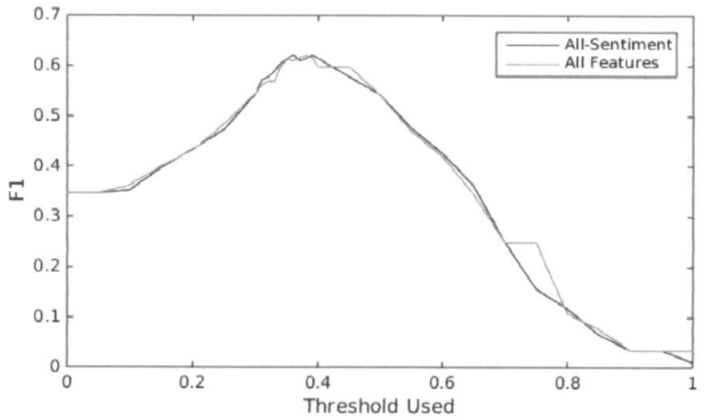

Figure 2: F1 for subtask1 on the test set for our systems using different threshold values.

6 Future Work

A possible direction would be to use locality sensitive hashing on the tweets (Petrovic et al., 2012) to create more features. Moreover, ordinal regression could be used to train the model (Hardin and Hilbe, 2001). The addition of a text normalization algorithm in the preprocessing step could enhance the performance of lexical overlap features and that of other methods such as wordnet, LDA (Blei et al., 2003) or LSA (Deerwester et al., 1990). Finally, the overlap of character n-grams could also be used as features.

7 Conclusion

We described a system that predicts semantic similarity between tweets from the same topic. The system's aim is to identify paraphrases of a tweet on a specific topic, which is really useful in event recognition systems. It employs a support vector regression to predict the probability that human annotators would annotate a pair of tweets as a paraphrase. The predicted value is then used for binary classification by using a threshold. The system's performance was measured on SemEval-2015 Task1 and it achieves better results than the task baselines.

[4] 6 teams did not participate in subtask2

System	F1	F1 Rank	Precision	Recall	Pearson	Pearson Rank	maxF1	mPrecision	mRecall
All Features	0.613	13/38	0.547	0.697	0.494	15/28	0.626	0.675	0.583
All-Sentiment	0.612	14/38	0.542	0.703	0.491	16/28	0.624	0.589	0.663
LR Baseline	0.589	21/38	0.679	0.520	0.511	11/28	0.601	0.674	0.543
WTMF Baseline	0.536	28/38	0.450	0.663	0.350	26/28	0.587	0.570	0.606
Random	0.266	38/38	0.192	0.434	0.350	28/28	0.350	0.215	0.949
Human Bound	0.823	-	0.752	0.908	0.017	-	-	-	-

Table 3: Results of our systems, baselines and human annotators on the test set.

References

Ron Artstein and Massimo Poesio. 2008. Inter-coder agreement for computational linguistics. *Comput. Linguist.*, 34(4):555–596, December.

Rahul Bhagat and Eduard H. Hovy. 2013. What is a paraphrase? *Computational Linguistics*, 39(3):463–472.

David M. Blei, Andrew Y. Ng, and Michael I. Jordan. 2003. Latent dirichlet allocation. *J. Mach. Learn. Res.*, 3:993–1022, March.

Dipanjan Das and Noah A. Smith. 2009. Paraphrase identification as probabilistic quasi-synchronous recognition. In *In Proc. of ACL-IJCNLP*.

Scott Deerwester, Susan T. Dumais, George W. Furnas, Thomas K. Landauer, and Richard Harshman. 1990. Indexing by latent semantic analysis. *JASIS*, 41(6):391–407.

Rong-En Fan, Kai-Wei Chang, Cho-Jui Hsieh, Xiang-Rui Wang, and Chih-Jen Lin. 2008. Liblinear: A library for large linear classification. *The Journal of Machine Learning Research*, 9:1871–1874.

Bo Han, Paul Cook, and Timothy Baldwin. 2012. Automatically constructing a normalisation dictionary for microblogs. In *Proceedings of the 2012 Joint Conference on Empirical Methods in Natural Language Processing and Computational Natural Language Learning (EMNLP-CoNLL 2012)*, pages 421–432, Jeju Island, Korea.

Lushan Han, Abhay Kashyap, Tim Finin, James Mayfield, and Jonathan Weese. 2013. Umbc ebiquity-core: Semantic textual similarity systems.

James W. Hardin and Joseph Hilbe. 2001. *Generalized Linear Models and Extensions*. College Station, Texas: Stata Press.

Rafael Michael Karampatsis, John Pavlopoulos, and Prodromos Malakasiotis. 2014. Aueb: Two stage sentiment analysis of social network messages. In *Proceedings of the 8th International Workshop on Semantic Evaluation (SemEval 2014)*, pages 114–118, Dublin, Ireland, August. Association for Computational Linguistics and Dublin City University.

Wang Ling, Chris Dyer, Alan W. Black, and Isabel Trancoso. 2013. Paraphrasing 4 microblog normalization. In *EMNLP*, pages 73–84. ACL.

Edward Loper and Steven Bird. 2002. NLTK: The Natural Language Toolkit. ETMTNLP '02, pages 63–70, Stroudsburg, PA, USA. Association for Computational Linguistics.

Charles T. Meadow. 1992. *Text Information Retrieval Systems*. Academic Press, Inc.

Rada Mihalcea, Courtney Corley, and Carlo Strapparava. 2006. Corpus-based and knowledge-based measures of text semantic similarity. In *AAAI06*, pages 775–780.

Tomas Mikolov, Wen tau Yih, and Geoffrey Zweig. 2013. Linguistic regularities in continuous space word representations. In *HLT-NAACL*, pages 746–751.

Jeffrey Pennington, Richard Socher, and Christopher D. Manning. 2014. Glove: Global vectors for word representation. In *Proceedings of EMNLP*.

Sasa Petrovic, Miles Osborne, and Victor Lavrenko. 2012. Using paraphrases for improving first story detection in news and twitter. In *HLT-NAACL*, pages 338–346. The Association for Computational Linguistics.

Alan Ritter, Sam Clark, Mausam, and Oren Etzioni. 2011. Named entity recognition in tweets: An experimental study. In *EMNLP*, pages 1524–1534.

Wei Xu, Alan Ritter, and Ralph Grishman. 2013. Gathering and generating paraphrases from twitter with application to normalization.

Wei Xu, Alan Ritter, Chris Callison-Burch, William Dolan, and Yangfeng Ji. 2014. Extracting lexically divergent paraphrases from twitter. *Transactions of the Association for Computational Linguistics*, 2:435–448.

Wei Xu, Chris Callison-Burch, and William B. Dolan. 2015. SemEval-2015 Task 1: Paraphrase and semantic similarity in Twitter (PIT). In *Proceedings of the 9th International Workshop on Semantic Evaluation (SemEval)*.

yiGou: A Semantic Text Similarity Computing System Based on SVM

Yang Liu, Chengjie Sun, Lei Lin, and Xiaolong Wang
School of Computer Science and Technology
Harbin Institute of Technology, China
{yliu,cjsun,linl,wangxl}@insun.hit.edu.cn

Abstract

This paper describes the yiGou system we developed to compute the semantic similarity of two English sentences, which we submitted to the SemEval 2015 Task 2 (English subtask). The system uses a support vector machine model with literal similarity, shallow syntactic similarity, WordNet-based similarity and latent semantic similarity to predict the semantic similarity score of two short texts. In our experiments, WordNet-based and LSA-based features performed better than other features. Out of the 73 submitted runs, our two runs ranked 38th and 42th, with mean Pearson correlation 0.7114 and 0.6964 respectively.

1 Introduction

Semantic Text Similarity (STS) plays an important role in many Natural language processing tasks, such as Question Answering (Narayanan and Harabagiu, 2004), Machine Translation (Beale et al., 1995), Automatic Summarization (Wang et al., 2008) and Word Sense Disambiguation (Navigli and Velardi, 2005). Since STS is an essential challenge in NLP, that has attracted a significant amount of attention by the research community. SemEval has held tasks about STS for four years in a row, from which we can see the importance and difficulty of this challenge. Particularly, SemEval focuses on semantic similarity of short texts as a lot of researches about long texts have been done in past years and the demand of finding new methods to measure short texts similarity has become stronger in many new applications.

In this paper, we proposed a SVM-based solution to compute the semantic similarity between two sentences which is the goal of SemEval 2015 Task 2. Knowledge-based and corpus-based features were involved in our solution. We used the combination of the word similarity to estimate sentence similarity. And the training data of SemEval 2012 (Agirre et al., 2012) was used to train our model. In our experiments, WordNet-based and LSA-based features performed better than other features. Out of the 73 submitted runs, our two runs ranked 38th and 42th, with mean Pearson correlation 0.7114 and 0.6964 respectively. The evaluation results showed that our solution has good generalization ability on the test dataset of SemEval 2015 which is very different from our training set in terms of the sources of the sentences. Some of the relatively new technologies such as Word2Vec (Mikolov et al., 2013) and Sentence2Vec (Le and Mikolov, 2014) are potential methods to represent sentences and will be included in our further works.

2 Data and Metrics

In SemEval 2015, the trial dataset comprises the 2012, 2013 and 2014 datasets, which can be used to develop and train models. Because of the limitation of the time, we only used the training data of SemEval 2012 as our training set. The training data of SemEval 2012 contained 2000 sentence pairs from existing paraphrase datasets and machine translation evaluation resources, while the test set of SemEval 2015 coming from image description, news headlines, student answers paired with reference answer, answers to questions posted in stack exchange forums and English discussion forum data exhibiting committed belief. The evaluation metric of SemEval 2015 task 2 is mean Pearson correlation, which is calculated by averaging the Pearson correlations of each subset in the test set.

3 Feature engineering

Considering the training set used in our system, we were trying to generate features which have little relation with the sources where the sentences came from. Four kinds of features are included in our model. They are literal similarity, shallow syntactic similarity, WordNet-based similarity and latent semantic similarity.

3.1 Literal Similarity

Intuitively, a pair of sentences that look similar to each other may be similar semantically. For example:
S1: A boy is playing a guitar.
S2: A man is playing a guitar.
S3: Someone is drawing.
Apparently, S1 and S2 look more similar and they are closer in semantics than S1 and S3. We chose the *Edit Distance* (also known as *Levenshtein Distance*) over characters to measure the similarity between two sentences. The higher the value is, the less similar the two sentences are. As this measure is case sensitive, we lowercase all letters in the sentences before computing the similarity. Although this method may draw opposite conclusions to our expectations in some specific occasions (For example, *I hate it* VS *I have it*, the Edit Distance of this pair of sentences is two, but they express very different meaning), the feature was still kept as we observed that it contributed to the overall performance in our experiments.

3.2 Shallow Syntactic Similarity

It is quite a common phenomenon that two sentences only differ in one or two syntactic constituents and have very similar syntactic structures. For example (example comes from training set):
S1: A man is peeling a potato.
S2: A man is slicing a potato.
This pair of sentences got very high score in golden standard file. As we can see, only the predicates of the two sentences are different, and the rest of the sentences are the same. This gives us a clue that using syntactic similarity to build the feature could be feasible. Moreover, two sentences may express exactly the same meaning, but use different English voices. This situation was also considered in our model. *Jaccard Distance* was chosen to compute this feature, which is defined as follows:

$$J(S_1, S_2) = \frac{|S_1 \cap S_2|}{|S_1 \cup S_2|}$$

Where S_1 and S_2 are the collections of Part-Of-Speech tags of each sentence. We used the NLTK toolkit (Bird, 2006) to tag each sentence. Since *Jaccard distance* measure only cares about the appearance of the tags, and ignores the order of them, it can reduce the impact of the tense change.

3.3 WordNet-based Similarity

WordNet (Miller, 1995) is a widely used lexical database for English, and it's a convenient tool to find synonyms of nouns, verbs, adjectives and adverbs. WordNet supports numerous lexical similarity measures (Pedersen et al., 2004). In this work, we explore using two of these similarity measures: *res_similarity* and *path_similarity*. The core idea behind the *path_similarity* measure is that the similarity between two concepts can be derived from the length of the path linking the concepts and the position of the concepts in the WordNet taxonomy. (Meng et al., 2013). While *res_similarity* (Resnik, 2011) is a similarity measure based on information content. The result of *res_similarity* is dependent on the corpus that generates the information content.

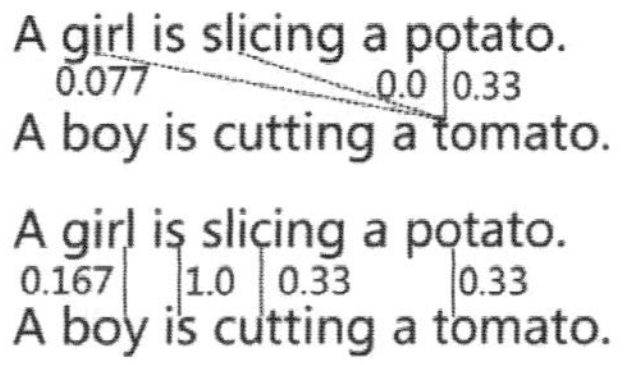

Figure 1 An example of word alignment using maximum *path_similarity*. The upper part of the figure is showing the alignment candidates for *tomato* scored with *path_similarity* and the lower part of the figure is showing the max *path_similarity* alignment for the content words in the sentence pair.

In our system, we used the NLTK WordNet API to compute WordNet-based similarity. Based on WordNet and *Brown corpus,* the computing of *res_similarity* and *path_similarity* involve following steps:

- Partition a pair of sentences into two lists of tokens.
- Part-of-speech tagging.
- Find out the most appropriate sense for every word according to the tagging results; put the

Features	MSRpar	MSRvid	SMTeuroparl	Sur.OnWN	Sur.SMTnews	Mean
All	0.51237	0.83766	0.48213	0.67070	0.47941	**0.596454**
w/o *res_similarity*	0.50939	0.83920	0.47976	0.66406	0.47976	**0.594434**
w/o *path_similarity*	0.37667	0.78555	0.38714	0.64145	0.45963	**0.530088**
w/o *WN-based sim*	0.37583	0.79046	0.38930	0.64348	0.45767	**0.531348**

Table 1 Results of comparing the importance of *res_similarity* and *path_similarity* on test set of SemEval 2012. The *WN-based sim* included both *res_similarity* and *path_similarity*.

Corpus	MSRpar	MSRvid	SMTeuroparl	Sur.OnWN	Sur.SMTnews	Mean
Brown	0.51237	0.83766	0.48213	0.67070	0.47941	**0.596454**
Bnc	0.51199	0.83770	0.48157	0.66719	0.48050	**0.595790**
Treebank	0.51199	0.83781	0.48181	0.66689	0.48066	**0.595832**
Semcor	0.51269	0.83768	0.48017	0.66763	0.48017	**0.595668**
Semcorraw	0.51274	0.83792	0.48138	0.66691	0.47997	**0.595784**
Shaks	0.51120	0.83746	0.48229	0.66665	0.48105	**0.595730**

Table 2 Results of using different corpus in res_similarity on test set of SemEval 2012.

results into two lists *S1* and *S2*.

- For every word *w* in *S1*, find out the word in *S2* that has the maximum *res_similarity/ path_similarity* with *w*. Adding all of the similarity values together, and then average this value with the length of *S1*.
- For every word *w* in *S2*, find out the word in *S1* that has the maximum *res_similarity/ path_similarity* with *w*. Adding all of the similarity values together, and then average this value with the length of *S2*.
- Computing the harmonic mean of the two average values, and the result is the value of this feature.

Figure 1 is an example shows how we find the corresponding word which has the maximum *res_similarity/path_similarity* with the words in the second sentence. In this example, *potato* has the maximum *path_similarity* score with *tomato*, compared to *girl* and *slicing* (0.33 vs. 0.0077 and 0.0). In the bottom part of the figure, each word in the first sentence would find one word which has the maximum similarity score in the second sentence, these scores would then be used to compute this feature.

To compare the importance of the two measures, we separately exclude one of the two features from all the features used in our solution to train two models and compare their performance. The results are shown in Table 1. As we can see from the table, *path_similarity* contributes more to our overall performance than *res_similarity*. According to the definition of *res_similarity*, we changed the corpus to find out the influence of the corpus on our overall performance. The results are showed in Table 2, from which we can see that the results varied very little with different corpora. In our submitted model, Brown corpus (Francis and Kucera, 1979) was used to compute information content.

3.4 Latent Semantic Similarity

All of the features generated above contained little semantic information. While sentences from some sources such as headlines and image descriptions are always have various forms which may not be easily compared through some string match measures or shallow syntactic oriented measures. So, a new feature that measures similarity in semantic space is necessary. Latent semantic analysis (Landauer et al., 1998) is a very popular technique to convert the term-document matrix which describes the occurrences of terms in document into three smaller matrixes like follows:

$$X = U\Sigma V^T$$

Where U could be preserved as the semantic space of words. Each word could be represented as a row vector in U. When measuring semantic similarity of two sentences, all word vectors appeared in the sentence were summed and then averaged with the length of the sentences. Thus we can get vector representations of the two sentences V1 and V2. With *V1* and *V2*, the similarity of the two sentences can be measured with cosine similarity. Cosine similarity defined as follows:

$$Cos(V1, V2) = \frac{V1 \cdot V2}{||V1||||V2||}$$

Features	MSRpar	MSRvid	SMTeuroparl	Sur.OnWN	Sur.SMTnews	Mean
1 *to* 2	-0.05064	0.23562	-0.13259	0.07697	-0.03636	**0.018600**
1 *to* 3	0.50225	0.82813	0.41859	0.57242	0.35525	**0.535328**
1 *to* 4	0.50593	0.82628	0.41881	0.57676	0.35390	**0.536336**
1 *to* 5	0.51120	0.83746	0.48229	0.66665	0.48105	**0.595730**
1 *to* 7	0.51237	0.83766	0.48213	0.67070	0.47941	**0.596454**

Table 4 Results of SVR on SemEval 2012 test set with different feature combinations.

Feature_ID	Feature_Name
1	*Edit Distance*
2	*Jaccard Distance*
3	*path_similarity*
4	*res_similarity*
5	*Latent Semantic Similarity*
6	*IDF-weighted-LSA*
7	*Freq-weighted-LSA*

Table 3 All features we used in our submitted model.

In our experiment, we directly used the LSA model provided by SEMILAR[1]. A word is represented as a row vector in the LSA model (Niraula et al., 2014), and the model was decomposed from the whole Wikipedia articles.

We also developed two weighted LSA features to further use semantic information, they are *IDF-weighted-LSA* and *Freq-weighted-LSA*. *IDF-weighted-LSA* weighted the words (one word is represented as a 200-dimension vector generated from LSA) using inverse document frequency and then summed up all the weighted vectors of words which appeared in the sentence to be the representation of the sentence. The cosine distance of two sentence representations is the value of this feature. *Freq-weighted-LSA* used word frequency to weight the words and following the same steps mentioned above. In our experiment, the IDF and Word-Frequency values were calculated on Wikipedia corpus dumped in December of 2012 (Jin et al., 2014). These features were only included in our second run *yiGou-midbaitu*. Unfortunately, this system got worse performance than the first run in official estimation. This may be caused by the overfitting of our model on the training data.

4 Experiments and Results

Due to the limitation of the time, in our submitted system, we trained Support Vector Regression (SVR) models using Scikit-learn toolkit (Pedregosa et al., 2011). Table 3 shows the features used in our submitted models. The results with different feature combinations on the test set of SemEval 2012 are shown in Table 4. Table 5 is our parameter settings.

parameter	*kernel*	*gamma*	*C*	*epsilon*
value	rbf	0.0	1.0	0.1

Table 5 Parameter setting in our models.

The performance of the best system in SemEval 2012 is 0.67 (*Mean*) with 19 features, and our best performance is 0.596 (*Mean*) with 7 features. In SemEval 2015, out of the 73 submitted runs, our two runs ranked 38th and 42th (with mean Pearson correlation 0.7114 and 0.6964 respectively). And the best performance in 2015 is 0.8015.

5 Conclusions and Future Work

In this paper, we presented our system that participated in the Semantic Text Similarity task in SemEval 2015. We proposed a method using SVR to combine various features to evaluate the similarity between two sentences. We found that WordNet based and LSA-based features are very useful for semantic similarity computing. For future work, we would like to further explore features about semantic representations of words, generate more features related to sentence structures and try to employ some new technologies such as Word2Vec and Sentence2Vec in our model. Besides, using a single model is not adequate to get a better accuracy, other models will be tried and compared in our further work.

Acknowledgments

The authors would like to thank the SemEval-2015 Task 2 organizers for their hard work. We also thank Daniel Cer and the anonymous reviewers for their helpful suggestions and comments. This work is supported by the National Natural Science Foundation of China (61100094 & 61300114).

[1] http://www.semanticsimilarity.org/

References

Eneko Agirre, Mona Diab, Daniel Cer, & Aitor Gonzalez-Agirre. (2012). *Semeval-2012 task 6: A pilot on semantic textual similarity.* In Proceedings of the First Joint Conference on Lexical and Computational Semantics-Volume 1: Proceedings of the main conference and the shared task, and Volume 2: Proceedings of the Sixth International Workshop on Semantic Evaluation.

Stephen Beale, Sergei Nirenburg, & Kavi Mahesh. (1995). *Semantic analysis in the Mikrokosmos machine translation project.* In Proceedings of the 2nd Symposium on Natural Language Processing.

Steven Bird. (2006). *NLTK: the natural language toolkit.* In Proceedings of the COLING/ACL on Interactive presentation sessions.

W Nelson Francis, & Henry Kucera. (1979). Brown corpus manual. *Brown University Department of Linguistics.*

Pedregosa, F., Varoquaux, G., Gramfort, A., Michel, V., Thirion, B., Grisel, O., ... & Duchesnay, É. (2011). Scikit-learn: Machine learning in Python. *The Journal of Machine Learning Research, 12*, 2825-2830.

Meng, L., Huang, R., & Gu, J. (2013). A review of semantic similarity measures in wordnet. *International Journal of Hybrid Information Technology, 6*(1), 1-12.

Xiaoqiang Jin, Chengjie Sun, Lei Lin, & Xiaolong Wang. (2014). Exploiting Multiple Resources for Word-Phrase Semantic Similarity Evaluation *Chinese Computational Linguistics and Natural Language Processing Based on Naturally Annotated Big Data* (pp. 46-57): Springer.

Thomas K Landauer, Peter W Foltz, & Darrell Laham. (1998). An introduction to latent semantic analysis. *Discourse processes, 25*(2-3), 259-284.

Quoc V Le, & Tomas Mikolov. (2014). Distributed Representations of Sentences and Documents. *arXiv preprint arXiv:1405.4053.*

Tomas Mikolov, Kai Chen, Greg Corrado, & Jeffrey Dean. (2013). Efficient estimation of word representations in vector space. *arXiv preprint arXiv:1301.3781.*

George A Miller. (1995). WordNet: a lexical database for English. *Communications of the ACM, 38*(11), 39-41.

Srini Narayanan, & Sanda Harabagiu. (2004). *Question answering based on semantic structures.* In Proceedings of the 20th international conference on Computational Linguistics.

Roberto Navigli, & Paola Velardi. (2005). Structural semantic interconnections: a knowledge-based approach to word sense disambiguation. *Pattern Analysis and Machine Intelligence, IEEE Transactions on, 27*(7), 1075-1086.

Nobal B Niraula, Vasile Rus, Rajendra Banjade, Dan Stefanescu, William Baggett, & Brent Morgan. (2014). The dare corpus: A resource for anaphora resolution in dialogue based intelligent tutoring systems. *Proceedings of Language Resources and Evaluation, LREC.*

Ted Pedersen, Siddharth Patwardhan, & Jason Michelizzi. (2004). *WordNet:: Similarity: measuring the relatedness of concepts.* In Proceedings of the Demonstration Papers at HLT-NAACL 2004.

Philip Resnik. (2011). Semantic similarity in a taxonomy: An information-based measure and its application to problems of ambiguity in natural language. *arXiv preprint arXiv:1105.5444.*

Sheldon Ross. (2009). *A First Course in Probability 8th Edition*: Pearson.

Frane Šarić, Goran Glavaš, Mladen Karan, Jan Šnajder, & Bojana Dalbelo Bašić. (2012). *Takelab: Systems for measuring semantic text similarity.* In Proceedings of the First Joint Conference on Lexical and Computational Semantics-Volume 1: Proceedings of the main conference and the shared task, and Volume 2: Proceedings of the Sixth International Workshop on Semantic Evaluation.

Dingding Wang, Tao Li, Shenghuo Zhu, & Chris Ding. (2008). *Multi-document summarization via sentence-level semantic analysis and symmetric matrix factorization.* In Proceedings of the 31st annual international ACM SIGIR conference on Research and development in information retrieval.

USAAR-SHEFFIELD: Semantic Textual Similarity with Deep Regression and Machine Translation Evaluation Metrics

Liling Tan[α], **Carolina Scarton**[β], **Lucia Specia**[β] **and Josef van Genabith**[γ]
[α]Universität des Saarlandes / Campus A2.2, Saarbrücken, Germany
[β]University of Sheffield / Regent Court, 211 Portobello, Sheffield, UK
[γ]Deutsches Forschungszentrum für Künstliche Intelligenz / Saarbrücken, Germany
`alvations@gmail.com`, `c.scarton@sheffield.ac.uk`,
`l.specia@sheffield.ac.uk`, `josef.van_genabith@dfki.de`

Abstract

This paper describes the USAAR-SHEFFIELD systems that participated in the Semantic Textual Similarity (STS) English task of SemEval-2015. We extend the work on using machine translation evaluation metrics in the STS task. Different from previous approaches, we regard the metrics' robustness across different text types and conflate the training data across different subcorpora. In addition, we introduce a novel deep regressor architecture and evaluated its efficiency in the STS task.

1 Introduction

Semantic Textual Similarity (STS) is the task of measuring the degree to which two text snippets have the same meaning (Agirre et al., 2014). For instance, given the two texts, "*a dog sprints across the water*" and "*a dog jumps through water*", participating systems are required to predict a real number similarity score on a scale of 0 (no relation) to 5 (semantic equivalence).

This paper presents a collaborative submission between Saarland University and University of Sheffield to the STS English shared task at SemEval-2015. We have submitted three models that use Machine Translation (MT) evaluation metrics as features to build supervised regressors that predict the similarity scores for the STS task. We introduce two variants of a novel deep regressor architecture and a classical baseline regression system that uses MT evaluation metrics as input features.

2 Related Work

Previously, research teams have applied MT evaluation metrics for the STS task with increasingly better results (Agirre et al., 2012; Agirre et al., 2013; Agirre et al., 2014). Rios et al. (2012) trained a Support Vector Regressor scoring a Pearson correlation mean of 0.3825 (Baseline[1]: 0.4356). Barrón-Cedeño et al. (2013) also used a Support Vector Regressor and did better than the baseline at 0.4037 mean score (Baseline: 0.3639). Huang and Chang (2014) used a linear regressor and scored 0.792 beating the baseline system (Baseline: 0.613).

Another notable mention of MT technology in the STS task is the use of referential translation machines to predict and derive features instead of using MT evaluation metrics (Biçici and van Genabith, 2013; Biçici and Way, 2014).

These previous approaches have trained a different system for each subcorpus provided by the task organizers. We have chosen to combine the different subcorpora since MT evaluation metrics are expected to be robust against text types and domains (Han et al., 2012; Padó et al., 2009).

Much of the previous work on using MT evaluation metrics is based on improving the regressors through algorithm choice, feature selection and parameters tuning. We introduce a novel architecture of hybrid supervised machine learning, *Deep Regression*, which attempts to combine different regressors and automating feature selection by means of dimensionality reduction.

[1]Refers to the token cosine baseline system (`baseline-tokencos`) from the task organizers.

3 Deep Regression Architecture

Ensemble learning constructs a set of models based on different algorithms and then labels new data points by taking a (weighted) vote from the algorithms' predictions (Dietterich, 2000). A typical single layer feed-forward neural network creates a layer of perceptrons that receives inputs and predicts a series of outputs converted by means of an activation function and then the outputs will enter a final layer of a single classifier to provide a final prediction (Auer et al., 2008). We propose a deep regression architecture that is a unique way to combine a single-layer feed-forward neural net architecture with ensemble-like supervised learning.

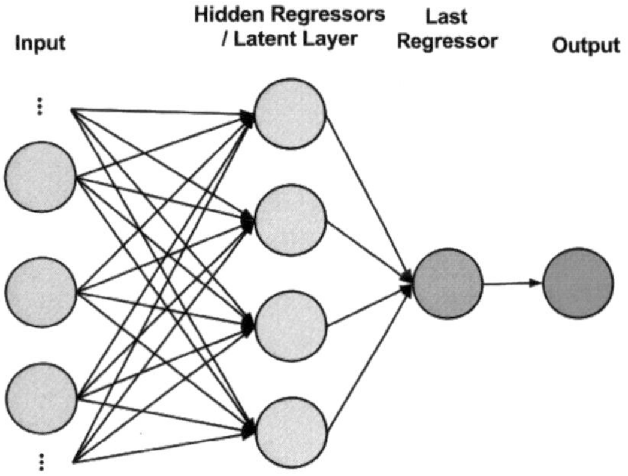

Figure 1: Deep Regression Architecture.

Figure 1 presents the Deep Regression architecture where the inputs are fed into the different hidden regressors and unlike traditional neural network, each regressor produces a discrete output with a different cost function unlike the consistent activation function in neural nets. Different from ensemble learning, the voting/selection determinant has been replaced by a last layer of a single regressor that takes latent layer as input to produce the final output STS score.

By designing the architecture in this way, the feature space from the input is reduced to the number of hidden regressors and the input for the last layer regressors is a latent layer in the higher dimensional space. Within a standard neural net, every node in the latent layer is influenced by all the perceptrons in the previous layer. In contrast, each latent dimension is only dependent on one regressor; in this respect it resembles ensemble learning where the regressors/classifiers are trained independently.

4 Feature Matrix

Machine Translation evaluation metrics consider varying degrees of information at the lexical, syntactic and semantic levels. Each metric comprises several features that compute the translation quality by comparing every translation against one or several reference translations. We consider three sets of features: n-gram overlaps, Shallow Parsing metrics and METEOR. These metrics correspond to the lexical, syntactic and semantic levels respectively.

4.1 N-gram Overlaps

Gonzàlez et al. (2014) reintroduces the notion of language independent metrics relying on n-gram overlaps. This is similar to the BLEU metric that calculates the geometric mean of n-gram precision by comparing the translation against its reference(s) (Papineni et al., 2002) without the brevity penalty.

Different from BLEU, the n-gram overlaps are computed as similarity coefficients instead of taking the crude proportion of overlap n-gram.

$$n\text{-gram}_{overlap} = sim\left(n\text{-gram}_{trans} \cap n\text{-gram}_{ref}\right)$$

We use 16 features of n-gram overlap by considering both the cosine similarity and Jaccard Index in calculating the n-gram overlaps for character and token n-gram from the order of bigrams to 5-grams. In addition, we use the ratio of n-gram lengths and the Jaccard similarity of pseudo-cognates (Simard et al., 1992) as the 17th and 18th n-gram overlap features.

4.2 Shallow Parsing

The Shallow Parsing (SP) metric measures the syntactic similarities by computing the overlaps between the translation and the reference translation at the Parts-Of-Speech (POS), word lemmas and base phrase chunks level. The purpose of the SP metric is to capture the proportion of lexical items correctly translated according to their shallow syntactic realization.

The base phrase chunks are tagged using the BIOS toolkit (Surdeanu et al., 2005) and POS tagging and lemmatization are achieved using SVMTool (Giménez and Màrquez, 2004). For instance, given a pair of sentences in the format (word/POS/lemma/chunk):

- ***NP***(*a*/DT/*a*/B-NP *dog*/NN/*dog*/I-NP) *sprints*/VBZ/*sprint*/B-VP *across*/IN/*across*/O ***NP***(*the*/DET/*the*/B-NP *water*/NN/*water*/I-NP)

- ***NP***(*a*/DT/*a*/B-NP *dog*/NN/*dog*/I-NP) *jumps*/VBZ/*jump*/B-VP *through*/IN/*through*/O *water*/NN/*water*/B-NP

We consider the overlap proportions for the POS features, lemma, IOB features, shallow chunks. The Inside, Outside, Begin (IOB) features refer to the shallow parsing tags at the lexical level, e.g. `B-NP` represents the beginning of a noun phrase (Sang et al., 2000). The IOB features are measured lexically by considering each IOB tag while the shallow chunk features only consider the number of bracketed chunks.

For instance, the POS tag DT occurs twice in first sentence one and once in second sentence, thus we extract the feature `SP-POS`(DT) = 1/2 = 0.5.

- `SP-POS(`DT,NN,VBZ,IN`)` = [0.5,1,1,1]
- `SP-LEMMA(`*a,dog,jump,through,water*`)` = [1,1,0,0,1]
- `SP-IOB(`B-NP,I-NP,B-VP,O`)` = [1,1,-0.5,1,1]
- `SP-CHUNK(`NP`)` = [0.5]

For `SP-POS`, `SP-LEMMA` and `SP-IOB`, we use the NIST-like measure where we not only consider the individual POS, LEMMA or IOB tags but an accumulated score over a sequence of 1-5 n-grams, e.g. `SP-POS(`DT+NN,DT+NN+VBZ, ...`)` or `SP-LEMMA(`*a+dog,a+dog+jump, ...*`)`.

5 METEOR

METEOR aligns the translation to a reference translation first then it uses unigram mapping to match words at their surface forms, word stems, synonym matches and paraphrase matches (Banerjee and Lavie, 2005; Denkowski and Lavie, 2010).

Different from the n-gram and shallow parsing features, METEOR makes a distinction between content words and function words and the precision and recall is measured by weighing them differently. It also accounts for word order differences by penalizing chunks from the translation that do not appear in the translation.

We use the METEOR 1.5 system with tuned weights and penalty using the WMT12 data. For the STS experiment, we use all four variants of METEOR: exact matches, stem matches, synonym matches and paraphrase matches.

6 Experiments and Results

6.1 Training Data

We conflated all training and test data of various text types from previous SemEval STS shared tasks into a single training set with 10597 paragraph/sentence/caption pairs. The MT metrics for each text pair were computed with the Asiya toolkit (Giménez and Màrquez, 2010). Tokenization and preprocessing operations, such as lemmatization, POS tagging, parsing and n-gram extraction, are performed by the Asiya toolkit.

6.2 Models

We submitted three models to the SemEval-2015 STS English Task:

- `ModelX`: Deep Regression framework with the full feature set from n-gram overlaps, Shallow Parsing and METEOR.

- `ModelY`: Bayesian Ridge Regressor with the full feature set

- `ModelZ`: Deep Regression framework with only METEOR features

For the hidden regressors layer of the deep regression models, we have used the multivariate linear, logistic, Bayesian ridge, elastic net, random sample consensus and support vector (radial basis function kernel) regressors.[2] The final layer regressor is a Bayesian ridge regressor. These supervised regressors are implemented in `scikit-learn` (Pedregosa et al., 2011).

[2] No comprehensive parameter tuning was attempted on the models and the default parameters for each regressor can be found on our code repository, https://github.com/alvations/USAAR-SemEval-2015.

	Ans-Forums	Ans-Student	Belief	Headlines	Images	Mean	Rank
ModelX	0.3706	0.3609	0.4767	0.5183	0.5436	0.4616	68
ModelY	0.6264	0.7386	0.705	0.7927	0.8162	**0.7275**	**21**
ModelZ	0.4237	0.6757	0.6994	0.5239	0.6833	0.6111	58

Table 1: Spearman's Results for STS English Task @ SemEval-2015.

6.3 Results

Table 1 presents the official results for the English STS task where our baseline model (ModelY) strikingly outperforms the deep regressor models (ModelX and ModelZ).

Our baseline model achieved modest results ranking 24 out of 73 submissions, however our deep regressors have failed to function on par with a simple baseline regressor. We note that the deep regressor with the full feature set (ModelX) scored lower than the deep regressor with only the METEOR features (ModelZ). This reiterates the effectiveness of semantically motivated METEOR features in determining similarity as previously indicated by Huang and Chang (2014).

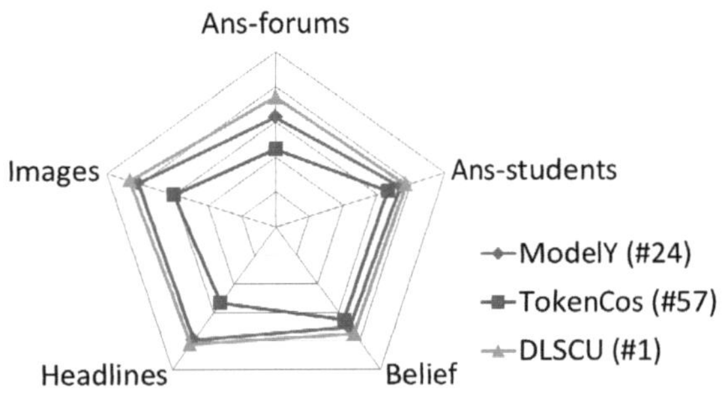

Figure 2: Comparison of Results with Best and Baseline Systems

Interestingly, the conflation of datasets has no obvious detrimental effects on the performance for any specific domains. Figure 2 presents a comparison of results between ModelY, the top system from DLSU and the organizers' baseline system (TokenCos). It shows that the distribution of Spearman's correlation for our model is as well-balanced as the best system.

7 Conclusion

In this paper, we have described our submissions to the STS English task for SemEval-2015. We have introduced a novel deep regression infrastructure with MT evaluation metrics to measure semantic similarity. Although our deep regressors performed poorly, our baseline system have achieved promising results amongst the participating systems and we showed that conflating datasets of different genres has negligible effects on a semantic similarity system based on MT evaluation metrics.

The results also confirm the good performance of METEOR, a traditional MT evaluation metric, for the STS task.

Acknowledgements

The research leading to these results has received funding from the People Programme (Marie Curie Actions) of the European Union's Seventh Framework Programme FP7/2007-2013/ under REA grant agreement n ° 317471.

References

Eneko Agirre, Daniel Cer, Mona Diab, and Aitor Gonzalez-Agirre. 2012. SemEval-2012 Task 6: A Pilot on Semantic Textual Similarity. In *First Joint Conference on Lexical and Computational Semantics (*SEM): Proceedings of the Main Conference and the Shared Task*, pages 385–393, Montréal, Canada.

Eneko Agirre, Daniel Cer, Mona Diab, Aitor Gonzalez-Agirre, and Weiwei Guo. 2013. SEM 2013 shared task: Semantic Textual Similarity. In *Second Joint Conference on Lexical and Computational Semantics (*SEM), Volume 1: Proceedings of the Main Conference and the Shared Task*, pages 32–43, Atlanta, Georgia.

Eneko Agirre, Carmen Banea, Claire Cardic, Daniel Cer, Mona Diab, Aitor Gonzalez-Agirre, Weiwei Guo, Rada Mihalcea, German Rigau, and Janyce Wiebe. 2014. SemEval-2014 Task 10: Multilingual Semantic Textual Similarity. In *Proceedings of the 8th Inter-*

national Workshop on Semantic Evaluation (SemEval 2014), pages 81–91, Dublin, Ireland.

Peter Auer, Harald Burgsteiner, and Wolfgang Maass. 2008. A learning rule for very simple universal approximators consisting of a single layer of perceptrons. *Neural Networks*, 21(5):786–795.

Satanjeev Banerjee and Alon Lavie. 2005. METEOR: An Automatic Metric for MT Evaluation with Improved Correlation with Human Judgments. In *Proceedings of the ACL 2005 Workshop on Intrinsic and Extrinsic Evaluation Measures for MT and/or Summarization*, pages 65–72, Ann Arbor, Michigan.

Alberto Barrón-Cedeño, Lluís Màrquez, Maria Fuentes, Horacio Rodríguez, and Jordi Turmo. 2013. UPC-CORE: What Can Machine Translation Evaluation Metrics and Wikipedia Do for Estimating Semantic Textual Similarity? In *Second Joint Conference on Lexical and Computational Semantics (*SEM), Volume 1: Proceedings of the Main Conference and the Shared Task*, pages 143–147, Atlanta, Georgia.

Ergun Biçici and Josef van Genabith. 2013. CNGL-CORE: Referential Translation Machines for Measuring Semantic Similarity. In *Second Joint Conference on Lexical and Computational Semantics (*SEM), Volume 1: Proceedings of the Main Conference and the Shared Task*, pages 234–240, Atlanta, Georgia.

Ergun Biçici and Andy Way. 2014. RTM-DCU: Referential Translation Machines for Semantic Similarity. In *Proceedings of the 8th International Workshop on Semantic Evaluation (SemEval 2014)*, pages 487–496, Dublin, Ireland.

Michael Denkowski and Alon Lavie. 2010. Extending the METEOR Machine Translation Evaluation Metric to the Phrase Level. In *Proceedings of the HLT: The 2010 Annual Conference of the North American Chapter of the Association for Computational Linguistics*, pages 250–253, Los Angeles, California.

Thomas G. Dietterich. 2000. Ensemble Methods in Machine Learning. In *Proceedings of the First International Workshop on Multiple Classifier Systems*, MCS '00, pages 1–15.

Jesús Giménez and Lluís Màrquez. 2004. Fast and Accurate Part-of-Speech Tagging: The SVM Approach Revisited. *Recent Advances in Natural Language Processing III*, pages 153–162.

Jesús Giménez and Lluís Màrquez. 2010. Asiya: An Open Toolkit for Automatic Machine Translation (Meta-)Evaluation. *The Prague Bulletin of Mathematical Linguistics*, (94):77–86.

Meritxell Gonzàlez, , Alberto Barrón-Cedeo, and Llus Màrquez. 2014. Ipa and stout: Leveraging linguistic and source-based features for machine translation evaluation. In *Ninth Workshop on Statistical Machine Translation*, page 8.

Aaron L.F. Han, Derek F. Wong, and Lidia S. Chao. 2012. Lepor: A robust evaluation metric for machine translation with augmented factors. In *24th International Conference on Computational Linguistics*, page 441. Citeseer.

Pingping Huang and Baobao Chang. 2014. SSMT:A Machine Translation Evaluation View To Paragraph-to-Sentence Semantic Similarity. In *Proceedings of the 8th International Workshop on Semantic Evaluation (SemEval 2014)*, pages 585–589, Dublin, Ireland.

Sebastian Padó, Michel Galley, Dan Jurafsky, and Chris Manning. 2009. Robust machine translation evaluation with entailment features. In *Proceedings of the Joint Conference of the 47th Annual Meeting of the ACL and the 4th International Joint Conference on Natural Language Processing of the AFNLP: Volume 1*, pages 297–305.

Kishore Papineni, Salim Roukos, Todd Ward, and Wei jing Zhu. 2002. BLEU: A Method for Automatic Evaluation of Machine Translation. In *Proceedings of the 40th Annual Meeting of the Association for Computational Linguistics*, pages 311–318, Philadelphia, Pennsylvania.

Fabian Pedregosa, Gaël Varoquaux, Alexandre Gramfort, Vincent Michel, Bertrand Thirion, Olivier Grisel, Mathieu Blondel, Peter Prettenhofer, Ron Weiss, Vincent Dubourg, Jake Vanderplas, Alexandre Passos, David Cournapeau, Matthieu Brucher, Matthieu Perrot, and Édouard Duchesnay. 2011. Scikit-learn: Machine Learning in Python. *Journal of Machine Learning Research*, 12:2825–2830.

Miguel Rios, Wilker Aziz, and Lucia Specia. 2012. UOW: Semantically Informed Text Similarity. In *First Joint Conference on Lexical and Computational Semantics (*SEM): Proceedings of the Main Conference and the Shared Task*, pages 673–678, Montréal, Canada.

Tjong Kim Sang, Erik F., and Sabine Buchholz. 2000. Introduction to the conll-2000 shared task: Chunking. In *Proceedings of the 2Nd Workshop on Learning Language in Logic and the 4th Conference on Computational Natural Language Learning - Volume 7*, ConLL '00, pages 127–132, Stroudsburg, PA, USA.

Michel Simard, George F. Foster, and Pierre Isabelle. 1992. Using Cognates to Align Sentences in Bilingual Corpora. In *Proceedings of the Forth International Conference on Theoretical and Methodological Issues in Machine Translation*, Montréal, Canada.

Mihai Surdeanu, Jordi Turmo, and Eli Comelles. 2005. Named Entity Recognition from Spontaneous Open-Domain Speech. In *Proceedings of the 9th International Conference on Speech Communication and Technology (Interspeech)*, Lisbon, Portugal.

$TrWP$: Text Relatedness using Word and Phrase Relatedness

Md Rashadul Hasan Rakib **Aminul Islam** **Evangelos Milios**
Faculty of Computer Science
Dalhousie University, Canada
{rakib,islam,eem}@cs.dal.ca

Abstract

Text is composed of words and phrases. In bag-of-word model, phrases in texts are split into words. This may discard the inner semantics of phrases which in turn may give inconsistent relatedness score between two texts. $TrWP$, the unsupervised text relatedness approach combines both word and phrase relatedness. The word relatedness is computed using an existing unsupervised co-occurrence based method. The phrase relatedness is computed using an unsupervised phrase relatedness function f that adopts Sum-Ratio technique based on the statistics in the Google n-gram corpus of overlapping n-grams associated with the two input phrases. The second run of $TrWP$ ranked 30th out of 73 runs in SemEval-2015 task2a (English STS).

1 Introduction

Generally, a phrase is an ordered sequence of multiple words that all together refer to a particular meaning (Zamir and Etzioni, 1999). Phrase relatedness quantifies how two phrases relate to each other. It plays an important role in different Text Mining tasks; for instance, document similarity [1], classification and clustering are performed on the documents composed of phrases. Several document clustering methods use phrase similarity to determine the similarity between documents so as to improve the clustering result (Chim and Deng, 2008; Shrivastava et al., 2013). SpamED (Pera and Ng, 2009) uses the bi-gram and tri-gram phrase similarity between an incoming e-mail message and a previously marked spam to enhance the accuracy of spam detection.

Most works on text relatedness can be abstracted as a function of word relatedness (Ho et al., 2010). The classical Bag-of-Word (BoW) text relatedness methods split phrases into words; then compute text-pair relatedness by word-pair relatedness (Islam and Inkpen, 2008; Islam et al., 2012; Tsatsaronis et al., 2010). $TrWP$ considers text as Bag-of-Word-and-Phrase (BoWP). It considers a (word, bi-gram) or (bi-gram, bi-gram) pair as a phrase-pair [2] and computes text relatedness using both word and phrase relatedness.

There are phrase relatedness tasks that use compositional distributional semantic (CDS) model (Annesi et al., 2012; Hartung and Frank, 2011). Some use different tools and knowledge-based resources (Han et al., 2013; Tsatsaronis et al., 2010). These methods split phrases into words without considering the word order that might change the meaning of phrases leading to inconsistent phrase relatedness score (Turney and Pantel, 2010). For example, if we split the phrases "boat house" and "house boat" into words, we get the relatedness score one, nonetheless as a whole unit, these two phrases do not refer to exactly the same meaning (Turney and Pantel, 2010). To preserve the phrase meaning, $TrWP$ uses the phrase relatedness function f that considers a phrase as a single unit.

[1]We use 'relatedness' and 'similarity' interchangeably in our paper, albeit 'similarity' is a special case of 'relatedness'.

[2]We consider the bi-grams as phrases. A word is also considered as a phrase when relatedness is computed between word and bi-gram.

2 Terminology used in Phrase Relatedness

The terminologies used in measuring phrase relatedness are described below.

2.1 Bi-gram Context

Bi-gram context is a bi-gram, extracted by placing a phrase in the left most, middle and right position within the Google n(=3,4)-grams. Sample bi-gram contexts for the bi-gram phrase "large number" are shown in Table 1.

Phrase position	Google 4-grams
Left most	large number **of files**
Middle	**very** large number **generator**
Right most	**multiply a** large number

Table 1: Positions of the bi-gram phrase ("large number") in Google 4-grams and corresponding bi-gram contexts marked bold.

2.2 Overlapping Bi-gram Context

The overlapping bi-gram context is a bi-gram which is overlapped between two Google n(=3,4)-grams that contain two target phrases at the same position. Consider two Google 4-grams "large number of death" and "vast amount of death" where "large number" and "vast amount" are the target phrases and "of death" is an overlapping bi-gram context.

2.3 Sum-Ratio (SR)

Sum-Ratio refers to the product of sum and ratio between the minimum (min) and maximum (max) of two numbers. The Sum-Ratio of two numbers indicates the strength of association between them by maximizing the sum of two numbers with respect to their ratio. The objective of Sum-Ratio is to capture the strength of association between two overlapping Google n(=3,4)-grams. Given two numbers a and b, the Sum-Ratio of a and b is defined as follows.

$$Sum(a,b) = a + b$$
$$Ratio(a,b) = min(a,b)/max(a,b)$$
$$Sum\text{-}Ratio(a,b) = Sum \times Ratio$$

2.4 Relatedness Strength

Relatedness strength is the strength of association between two phrases P_1 and P_2, computed using the Sum-Ratio values between the counts of any two Google n(=3,4)-grams that contain P_1 and P_2, respectively and an overlapping bi-gram context.

3 Phrase Detection

Given a specific text, we elicit bi-grams of interest as candidate phrases if they are highly frequent in the Google bi-gram corpus, asserted in the Google Book-Ngram-Viewer (books.google.com/ngrams/info). We adopt a naive approach to detect the bi-gram phrases using the mean (u_{bg}) and standard deviation (sd_{bg}) of all Google bi-gram frequencies which are computed once. At first, the whole text is split by stop-words producing a list of c-grams [3]. Then for each c-gram, the following two steps are executed.

Step 1: If the c-gram is a bi-gram and its frequency is greater than $u_{bg} + sd_{bg}$, then we add it to the list of bi-gram phrases.

Step 2: If the length of c-gram is greater than two, we generate an array of bi-grams from the c-gram and find the most frequent bi-gram ($mfbg$) among them; If the frequency of $mfbg$ is greater than $u_{bg} + sd_{bg}$, then we add $mfbg$ to the list of bi-gram phrases and split the c-gram into two parts (e.g., left, right) by $mfbg$. After splitting, for each of the left and right parts, we examine the **Step 1** and **Step 2** recursively.

4 Computing Phrase Relatedness

The phrase relatedness function f, computes relatedness strength between two phrases P_1 and P_2 using the Google n-gram corpus (Brants and Franz, 2006) which is then normalized between 0 and 1 using NGD (Cilibrasi and Vitanyi, 2007) in conjunction with NGD´ (Gracia et al., 2006).

4.1 Lexical Pruning on the Bi-gram Contexts

At first the bi-gram contexts of phrases are extracted. However some phrases along with their bi-gram contexts do not convey meaningful insight due to the improper positioning of stop-words within bi-gram contexts. Therefore lexical pruning [4] is performed

[3]c-gram: A chunk of uni-grams with no stop-word.

[4]Perform pruning on the bi-gram contexts implies to the pruning of the Google n(=3,4)-grams from which those contexts are extracted.

based on the position of stop-words inside the bi-gram contexts. When the target phrase is placed at the left or right most positions respectively, then the Google n(=3,4)-gram is pruned if the right or left most word is a stop-word. When the phrase is in the middle surrounded by two context words, then the Google n(=3,4)-gram is pruned if both the surrounding context words are stop-words. After performing lexical pruning, we have two sets of non-pruned Google n(=3,4)-grams containing the bi-gram contexts of two phrases, respectively.

4.2 Finding Overlapping Bi-gram Contexts

We find the overlapping bi-gram contexts between two sets of non-pruned Google n(=3,4)-grams. The Google n(=3,4)-grams having overlapping bi-gram contexts are separated from the Google n(=3,4)-grams that have no overlapping contexts.

4.3 Statistical Pruning on the Overlapping Bi-gram Contexts

Each Google n(=3,4)-gram pair with overlapping bi-gram context possesses a strength of association. We presume that if most of the Google n(=3,4)-gram pairs have higher strengths of association, the relatedness score between two phrases tends to be higher and vice versa. However some strengths of association do not lie within the group of maximum number of strengths of association called outliers and because of the outliers the relatedness score between two phrases becomes inconsistent. Hence we apply statistical pruning on the strengths of association to prune the outliers. To find the group of maximum number of strengths of association and prune the outliers, we adopt the Normal Distribution (Bohm and Zech, 2010) for statistical pruning. It has been shown that in Normal Distribution most of the samples exist within the mean $\pm$ standard deviation.

We divide each Google n(=3,4)-gram count (frequency) within a pair by the count of its corresponding n(=1,2)-gram phrase, resulting a normalized count. For each Google n(=3,4)-gram pair, the minimum and maximum among the two normalized counts are determined. After that we calculate the ratio (e.g., minimum/maximum) between them. Following that, for each Google n(=3,4)-gram pair, we multiply the ratio with the sum of two Google n(=3,4)-gram counts, producing a resultant product (e.g., strength of association). Later on we compute the mean (u_{sr}) and standard deviation (sd_{sr}) from the strengths of association of the Google n(=3,4)-gram pairs. If the strength of association is within the $u_{sr} \pm sd_{sr}$, it is kept otherwise pruned.

4.4 Computing Relatedness Strength

Relatedness strength between P_1 and P_2 is computed by multiplying the relatedness strengths from overlapping and all bi-gram contexts.

4.4.1 Relatedness Strength using Overlapping Bi-gram Contexts

For each non-pruned Google n(=3,4)-gram pair having overlapping bi-gram context, the strength of association is calculated following the Sum-Ratio technique. We sum the two Google n(=3,4)-gram counts and find the minimum and maximum among them. After that we calculate the ratio (e.g., minimum/maximum) between them. Then the Sum-Ratio value is calculated by multiplying the sum with ratio which signifies the strength of association for a Google n(=3,4)-gram pair. By summing up the strength of association of each Google n(=3,4)-gram pair, we get the relatedness strength between the phrases P_1 and P_2 denoted by $RSOB(P_1, P_2)$ as shown in Eq. 1. GP_1 and GP_2 are the Google n(=3,4)-grams that contain P_1 and P_2, respectively and an overlapping bi-gram context. $C(GP_1)$ and $C(GP_2)$ are the counts of GP_1 and GP_2, respectively. k is the number of non-pruned Google n(=3,4)-gram pairs.

$$RSOB(P_1, P_2) = \sum^{n} \frac{min(C(GP_1), C(GP_2))}{max(C(GP_1), C(GP_2))} \times sum(C(GP_1), C(GP_2)) \quad (1)$$

4.4.2 Relatedness Strength using all Bi-gram Contexts

All bi-gram contexts of a phrase P_1 include both non-pruned overlapping and non-overlapping bi-gram contexts, extracted from the Google n(=3,4)-grams where P_1 appears. Two vectors V_1 and V_2 in Vector Space Model are constructed for P_1 and P_2, respectively using their corresponding all bi-gram Contexts. The elements of V_1 and V_2 are binary and reflect the presence or absence of a bi-gram context belonging to the phrases P_1 and P_2, correspondingly. The relatedness strength between P_1 and P_2 using all bi-gram contexts is designated as $cosSim(V_1, V_2)$, and computed by the cosine similarity between V_1 and V_2, defined in Eq. 2.

$$cosSim(V_1, V_2) = \frac{V_1.V_2}{||V_1||\ ||V_2||} \quad (2)$$

4.4.3 Multiplying Relatedness Strengths from Overlapping and all Bi-gram Contexts

We multiply the relatedness strengths $RSOB(P_1, P_2)$ and $cosSim(V_1, V_2)$ obtained from overlapping and all bi-gram contexts, respectively to compute the overall relatedness strength $f(P_1, P_2)$ between the phrases P_1 and P_2, defined in Eq. 3. The purpose of multiplying these two strengths is to quantify $RSOB(P_1, P_2)$ with respect to $cosSim(V_1, V_2)$.

$$f(P_1, P_2) = RSOB(P_1, P_2) \times cosSim(V_1, V_2) \quad (3)$$

4.5 Normalizing Overall Relatedness Strength

The relatedness between phrases P_1 and P_2 is computed by normalizing the overall relatedness strength between 0 and 1 using NGD in conjunction with NGD′ as defined in Eq. 4. $C(P)$ is the count of phrase P where P is a Google n(=1,2)-gram. N = total number of web documents used in the Google n-gram corpus.

$$NGDf(P_1, P_2) = e^{-2\times\frac{max(log\ C(P_1), log\ C(P_2)) - log\ f(P_1,P_2)}{log\ N - min(log\ C(P_1), log\ C(P_2))}} \quad (4)$$

5 Computing Text Relatedness

At first punctuations are removed from texts. The phrases are extracted using phrase detection algorithm. Other than phrases the rest of the text is split into non stop-words. The relatedness between two texts is calculated by the word-pair and phrase-pair relatedness following the notion of text relatedness in (Islam et al., 2012). Word-pair relatedness is computed by the word relatedness method in (Islam et al., 2012).

Step 1: We assume that the two texts $A = \{a_1, a_2, ..., a_p\}$ and $B = \{b_1, b_2, ..., b_q\}$ have p and q tokens, respectively and $p \leq q$. Otherwise we switch A and B. A token is a word or bi-gram phrase.

Step 2: We count the number of common tokens (δ) in both A and B where $\delta \leq p$. Common tokens are determined by applying PorterStemmer (Porter, 1980) on each token pair. Common tokens are removed from A and B. So, $A = \{a_1, a_2, ..., a_{p-\delta}\}$ and $B = \{b_1, b_2, ..., b_{q-\delta}\}$. If all tokens match e.g., $p - \delta = 0$, go to step **Step 5**.

Step 3: We construct a $(p - \delta) \times (q - \delta)$ 'semantic relatedness matrix' (Say, $M = (\alpha_{ij})_{(p-\delta)\times(q-\delta)}$) using the following process. We set $\alpha_{ij} \leftarrow relatedness(a_i, b_j) \times w^2$ where $i = 1...p - \delta$, $j = 1...q - \delta$, w = weighting factor to boost the relatedness score. The value of w is the average number of words within a word or phrase-pair. The reason for boosting is that same relatedness score of a phrase-pair is more weighted than that of a word-pair. If (a_i, b_j) is a word-pair, $relatedness(a_i, b_j)$ = word-pair relatedness (Islam et al., 2012); otherwise $relatedness(a_i, b_j)$ = phrase-pair relatedness from Eq. 4.

$$M = \begin{pmatrix} \alpha_{1,1} & \cdots & \alpha_{1,j} & \cdots & \alpha_{1,q-\delta} \\ \alpha_{2,1} & \cdots & \alpha_{2,j} & \cdots & \alpha_{2,q-\delta} \\ \vdots & \ddots & \vdots & \ddots & \vdots \\ \alpha_{i,1} & \cdots & \alpha_{i,j} & \cdots & \alpha_{i,q-\delta} \\ \vdots & \ddots & \vdots & \ddots & \vdots \\ \alpha_{p-\delta,1} & \cdots & \alpha_{p-\delta,j} & \cdots & \alpha_{p-\delta,q-\delta} \end{pmatrix}$$

Step 4: For each row we compute the mean (u) and standard deviation (sd) of the relatedness scores and select the scores which are larger than $u+sd$. The idea is to find more related tokens among $(q - \delta)$, for each $(p - \delta)$ tokens. The average of the selected scores is computed for a row and for $(p-\delta)$ rows we get $(p - \delta)$ averages. We sum the $(p - \delta)$ average values denoted by $SAvg$.

Step 5: To compute relatedness between the texts A and B, we use the normalization in (Islam et al., 2012) with minor modification, given in Eq. 5.

$$rel.(A, B) = \frac{(2|\delta| + SAvg) \times (2|A| + 2|B|)}{2 \cdot 2|A| \cdot 2|B|} \quad (5)$$

Number of words in A, B and δ are denoted by $|A|$, $|B|$, $|\delta|$, respectively. Since we multiply w with relatedness score while constructing the matrix M; $|A|$, $|B|$ and $|\delta|$ are multiplied by 2.

6 Experiments

We submit three runs of $TrWP$ on 5 datasets of SemEval-2015 task2a (English STS) (Agirre et al., 2015).

6.1 Run1

In the first run we consider words, phrases and numbers as tokens. After removing punctuations and stop-words, if any sentence within a pair has no tokens, then the relatedness of that sentence pair is 0.

6.2 Run2

The tokens are same as in the first run. After removing punctuations and stop-words, if any sentence within a pair has no tokens, then we keep the stop-words.

6.3 Run3

We consider words and phrases as tokens. The following steps are same as in the first run.

7 Result

The result from three different runs of $TrWP$ are shown in Table 2.

SemEval-2015 task2a Dataset (English STS)	Run1 (r)	Run2 (r)	Run3 (r)
answers-forums	0.6857	0.6857	0.6857
answers-students	0.6618	0.6618	0.6612
belief	0.6769	0.7245	0.6772
headlines	0.7709	0.7709	0.7710
images	0.7865	0.7865	0.7865
Weighted mean	0.7251	0.7311	0.7250
Ranking out of 73 runs	31	30	32

Table 2: Pearson's r on five datasets, obtained from three different runs of $TrWP$.

8 Conclusion

$TrWP$ is an unsupervised text relatedness method that combines both word and phrase relatedness. Both the word and phrase relatedness are computed in unsupervised manner. The word relatedness is computed using the co-occurrences of two words in the Google 3-gram corpus. To compute phrase relatedness, $TrWP$ uses an unsupervised function f based on the Sum-Ratio technique along with the statistical pruning. Unlike other phrase relatedness methods based on word relatedness, f considers the whole phrase as a single unit without losing inner semantic meaning within a phrase.

References

Eneko Agirre, Carmen Banea, Claire Cardie, Daniel Cer, Mona Diab, Aitor Gonzalez-Agirre, Weiwei Guo, Iigo Lopez-Gazpio, Montse Maritxalar, Rada Mihalcea, German Rigau, Larraitz Uria, and Janyce Wiebe. 2015. SemEval-2015 Task 2: Semantic Textual Similarity, English, Spanish and Pilot on Interpretability. In *Proceedings of the 9th International Workshop on Semantic Evaluation (SemEval 2015)*, Denver, CO, June.

Paolo Annesi, Valerio Storch, and Roberto Basili. 2012. Space projections as distributional models for semantic composition. In *Proceedings of the 13th International Conference on Computational Linguistics and Intelligent Text Processing - Volume Part I*, CICLing'12, pages 323–335, Berlin, Heidelberg.

Gerhard Bohm and Gnter Zech. 2010. *Introduction to statistics and data analysis for physicists*.

Thorsten Brants and Alex Franz. 2006. Web 1T 5-gram corpus version 1.1. *Linguistic Data Consortium*.

Hung Chim and Xiaotie Deng. 2008. Efficient phrase-based document similarity for clustering. *IEEE Trans. on Knowl. and Data Eng.*, 20(9):1217–1229, September.

Rudi L. Cilibrasi and Paul M. B. Vitanyi. 2007. The google similarity distance. *IEEE Trans. on Knowl. and Data Eng.*, 19(3):370–383, March.

Jorge Gracia, Raquel Trillo, Mauricio Espinoza, and Eduardo Mena. 2006. Querying the web: A multiontology disambiguation method. In *Proceedings of the 6th International Conference on Web Engineering*, ICWE '06, pages 241–248, New York, NY, USA.

Lushan Han, Abhay L. Kashyap, Tim Finin, James Mayfield, and Johnathan Weese. 2013. UMBC_EBIQUITY-CORE: Semantic Textual Similarity Systems. In *Proceedings of the Second Joint Conference on Lexical and Computational Semantics*, June.

Matthias Hartung and Anette Frank. 2011. Assessing interpretable, attribute-related meaning representations for adjective-noun phrases in a similarity prediction task. In *Proceedings of the GEMS 2011 Workshop on GEometrical Models of Natural Language Semantics*, GEMS '11, pages 52–61, Stroudsburg, PA, USA.

Chukfong Ho, Masrah Azrifah Azmi Murad, Rabiah Abdul Kadir, and Shyamala C. Doraisamy. 2010. Word sense disambiguation-based sentence similarity. In *Proceedings of the 23rd International Conference on*

Computational Linguistics: Posters, COLING '10, pages 418–426, Stroudsburg, PA, USA.

Aminul Islam and Diana Inkpen. 2008. Semantic text similarity using corpus-based word similarity and string similarity. *ACM Trans. Knowl. Discov. Data*, 2(2):10:1–10:25, July.

Aminul Islam, Evangelos Milios, and Vlado Kešelj. 2012. Text similarity using google tri-grams. In *Proceedings of the 25th Canadian conference on Advances in Artificial Intelligence*, Canadian AI'12, pages 312–317, Berlin, Heidelberg.

Maria Soledad Pera and Yiu-Kai Ng. 2009. Spamed: A spam e-mail detection approach based on phrase similarity. *J. Am. Soc. Inf. Sci. Technol.*, 60(2):393–409, February.

Martin Porter. 1980. An algorithm for suffix stripping. *Program*, 14(3):130–137, July.

Shailendra Kumar Shrivastava, J. L. Rana, and R. C. Jain. 2013. Article: Text document clustering based on phrase similarity using affinity propagation. *International Journal of Computer Applications*, 61(18):38–44, January. Published by Foundation of Computer Science, New York, USA.

George Tsatsaronis, Iraklis Varlamis, and Michalis Vazirgiannis. 2010. Text relatedness based on a word thesaurus. *J. Artif. Int. Res.*, 37(1):1–40, January.

Peter D. Turney and Patrick Pantel. 2010. From frequency to meaning: Vector space models of semantics. *J. Artif. Int. Res.*, 37(1):141–188, January.

Oren Zamir and Oren Etzioni. 1999. Grouper: A dynamic clustering interface to web search results. In *Proceedings of the Eighth International Conference on World Wide Web*, WWW '99, pages 1361–1374, New York, NY, USA.

MiniExperts: An SVM Approach for Measuring Semantic Textual Similarity

Hanna Béchara*[a], Hernani Costa*[b], Shiva Taslimipoor[a], Rohit Gupta[a], Constantin Orăsan[a], Gloria Corpas Pastor[b] and Ruslan Mitkov[a]
[a]RIILP, University of Wolverhampton, UK
[b]LEXYTRAD, University of Malaga, Spain
{hanna.bechara,hercos,shiva.taslimi,r.gupta, c.orasan,gcorpas,r.mitkov}@{[a]wlv.ac.uk,[b]uma.es}
*These two authors contributed equally to this work.

Abstract

This paper describes the system submitted by the University of Wolverhampton and the University of Malaga for SemEval-2015 Task 2: *Semantic Textual Similarity*. The system uses a Supported Vector Machine approach based on a number of linguistically motivated features. Our system performed satisfactorily for English and obtained a mean 0.7216 Pearson correlation. However, it performed less adequately for Spanish, obtaining only a mean 0.5158.

1 Introduction

Similarity measures play an important role in a wide variety of Natural Language Processing (NLP) applications. Information Retrieval (IR), for example, relies on semantic similarity in order to determine the best result for a related query. Semantic similarity also plays a crucial role in other applications such as Paraphrasing and Translation Memory (TM). However, computing semantic similarity between sentences remains a complex and difficult task. Over the years, SemEval's shared tasks worked to fine-tune and perfect these similarity measures, and explore the nature of meaning in language.

SemEval2015's Task 2 involves computing how similar two sentences are in both English (Subtask 2a) and Spanish (Subtask 2b). In this paper we detail our submission to SemEval Task 2. We use an improved and revised version of the system presented in our SemEval 2014 submission (Gupta et al., 2014). As in Gupta et al., 2014, we employ a Machine Learning (ML) method which exploits available NLP technology, adding features inspired by deep semantics (such as parsing and paraphrasing) with distributional Similarity Measures, Conceptual Similarity Measures, Semantic Similarity Measures and Corpus Pattern Analysis[1] (CPA).

The remainder of the paper is structured as follows. Section 2 describes our approach, i.e. explains how the data was preprocessed and what features were extracted. Section 3 is divided in two section, the first one describes the ML algorithm and how it was tuned for this task (section 3.1) and the second one shows the obtained results along with a descriptive analysis of the runs based on the test and training data provided by the SemEval-2015 Task 2 (section 3.2). Finally, section 4 presents the final remarks and highlights our future plans for improving the system.

2 Approach

This section describes our approach to calculating semantic relatedness. It covers all the required preprocessing steps to extract the features themselves.

2.1 Data Preprocessing

This section presents all the tools, libraries and frameworks used to preprocess not only the test datasets but also the training datasets.

2.1.1 POS-Tagger, Lemmatiser, Stemmer

The software we used for these specific NLP tasks were: the Stanford CoreNLP[2] (Toutanova et al.,

[1] http://pdev.org.uk
[2] http://nlp.stanford.edu/software/corenlp.shtml

2003) toolkit, which provides a lemmatiser, POS-Tagger, NER, parsing, and coreference; the TT4J[3] library, which is a Java wrapper around the popular TreeTagger (Schmid, 1995); and the Porter stemmer algorithm provided by the Snowball[4] library.

2.1.2 Named Entity Recogniser (NER)

The library used to identify named entities in English and Spanish was the Apache OpenNLP library[5]. For English, all the pre-trained NER models made available by the Apache OpenNLP library were used (i.e. we used models to identify dates, locations, money, organisations, percentages, persons and time). We also used all the pre-trained NER models for Spanish (in this case, we used models to identify persons, organisations, locations and miscellanea).

2.1.3 Translation Model

Since one of the features we implemented was available only for English (i.e. the Semantic Similarity Measures), we trained a Statistical Machine Translation (SMT) system to translate our Spanish dataset into English. For this purpose, we used the PB-SMT system Moses (Koehn et al., 2007), 5-gram language models with Kneser-Ney smoothing trained with SRILM (Stolcke, 2002), the GIZA++ implementation of IBM word alignment model 4 (Och and Ney, 2003), with refinement and phrase-extraction heuristics as described in Koehn et al., 2003. We trained this system on the Europarl Corpus (Koehn, 2005) and used Minimum Error Rate Training (MERT) (Och, 2003) for tuning on the development set.

2.1.4 Resources

Given that a number of our features depends on stopwords (see section 2.2), we compiled two lists of stopwords, one for English and another one for Spanish. Both are freely available to download[6].

We also used two lists (English and Spanish) of candidates for Multiword Expressions (MWEs) as a resource for one of the features (see section 2.2.5). These lists were extracted from the Europarl Corpus (Koehn, 2005) using the collocation modules of the NLTK package (Loper and Bird, 2002), and sorted by the degree of likelihood association between their components.

2.2 Extracted Features

This section details the features that our system uses to measure the semantic textual similarity between two sentences. The system uses the same features for both Subtask 2a and Subtask 2b. In addition to the baseline features used in Gupta et al., 2014, we introduced a set of Distributional, Semantic and Conceptual Similarity Measures, as well as a feature reflecting MWEs across sentences.

2.2.1 Baseline Features

The system is built on the baseline system developed for SemEval2014, which consists of 13 features explained in detail in Gupta et al., 2014. The code which implements these features can be found on GitHub[7].

2.2.2 Distributional Similarity Measures

Information Retrieval (IR) (Singhal, 2001) is the task of locating specific information within a collection of documents or other natural language resources according to some request (Salton and Buckley, 1988; Costa et al., 2010; Costa et al., 2011). Among IR methods, we can find a large number of statistical approaches based on the occurrence of words in documents or sentences. Following Harris' distributional hypothesis (Harris, 1970), which assumes that similar words tend to occur in similar contexts, these methods are suitable, for instance, to find similar sentences based on the words they contain or to compute the similarity of words based on their co-occurrence. To that end, we can assume that the amount of information contained in a sentence could be evaluated by summing the amount of information contained in the sentence words. Moreover, the amount of information conveyed by a word can be represented by means of the weight assigned to it (Salton and Buckley, 1988). Bearing this in mind, we used two independent IR measures, the Spearman's Rank Correlation Coefficient (SCC) and the χ^2 to compute the similarity between two sentences

[3] `https://code.google.com/p/tt4j`
[4] `http://snowball.tartarus.org`
[5] `http://opennlp.apache.org`
[6] `https://github.com/hpcosta/stopwords`
[7] `https://github.com/rohitguptacs/wlvsimilarity`

written in the same language (cf. Kilgarriff, 2001). Both measures are particularly useful for this task because they are independent of text size (mostly because both measures use a list of the common entities), and they are language-independent. In detail, for every pair of sentence (English and Spanish), we used the lemmas to extract the list of common terms to compute both measures.

2.2.3 Conceptual Similarity Measures

This feature aims to find the conceptual similarity between two sentences written in the same language. In order to calculate the conceptual similarity, we took advantage of the BabelNet[8] (Navigli and Paolo Ponzetto, 2012) multilingual semantic network. As BabelNet organises lexical information in a semantic conceptual way, we created a conceptual sentence for all input pair of sentences (English and Spanish). More precisely, for every pair of sentence we only extracted lemmatised nouns, verbs, adjectives and adverbs. Then, a conceptual term list was built by extracting all the occurrences of the term in the conceptual network (i.e. BabelNet). As a result, we got a "conceptual representation" of both sentences, each of them containing a set of conceptual term lists. Next, for every term in the "conceptual_sentence_1", we counted the number of co-occurrences in the conceptual term lists in the "conceptual_sentence_2". In other words, we intersected the terms in sentence 1 with all the conceptual term lists in sentence 2. After computing all the co-occurrences, we used these values to calculate the Jaccard' (Jaccard, 1901), Lin' (Lin, 1998) and PMI' (Turney, 2001) scores.

2.2.4 Semantic Similarity Measures

This feature takes advantage of the Align, Disambiguate and Walk (ADW)[9] library (Pilehvar et al., 2013), a WordNet-based approach for measuring semantic similarity of arbitrary pairs of lexical items. It is important to mention that this feature is the only one that only works for English, which explains why we have a translation model (see section 2.1.3). In other words, when we are dealing with Spanish text, we use the trained model to translate from Spanish to English.

As the ADW library permits us to measure the semantic similarity between two raw English sentences, either by using disambiguation or not, we used both options to calculate all the comparison methods made available by the library, i.e. WeightedOverlap, Cosine, Jaccard, KLDivergence and JensenShannon divergence.

2.2.5 Multiword Expressions

Multiword Expressions (MWEs) are meaningful lexical units whose distinct idiosyncratic properties call for special treatment within a computational system. Non-compositionality is one of the properties of MWEs. The degree of association between the components of a MWE has been proved to be a promising approach to find out how much they are non-compostional and therefore how probable they are acceptable MWEs (Ramisch et al., 2010). The more non-compositional a MWE is, the more important is not to treat its components separately for NLP purposes, including processing semantic similarities.

For the purpose of our experiments, we focused on two more common types of MWEs in English and Spanish: `verb noun` combinations and `verb particle` constructions. Whenever a `verb+noun` or a `verb+particle` combination occurs in our sentence pair, we search a prepared list MWEs, sorted according to their likelihood measures of association. The degree of association of these combinations served as a feature in our ML system.

3 Predicting Through Machine Learning

In this section, we outline the ML model trained on the extracted features to compute a relatedness score between two sentences. It details the tools and parameters used to build a support vector regressor, which we used to predict a number between 0 and 5, denoting a degree of semantic similarity.

3.1 Model Description

We used a Support Vector Machine (SVM) in order to compute semantic relatedness for both subtasks.

[8] `http://babelnet.org`

[9] `http://lcl.uniroma1.it/adw`

We used LibSVM[10], a library for SVMs developed by Chang and Lin, 2011.

We built a regression model which estimates a continuous score between 0 and 5 for each sentence pair. The values of C and γ have been optimised through a grid-search which uses a 5-fold cross-validation method, and all systems use an RBF kernel.

The system for Subtask 2a (English) is trained on a combination of training and trial data provided by the 2012, 2013 and 2014 SemEval tasks. We used these datasets to form a training set of 9750 sentence pairs combining the different domains covered by the STS task: image description (image), news headlines (headlines), student answers paired with reference answers (answers-students), answers to questions posted in stach exchange forums (answers-forum), English discussion forum data exhibiting committed belief (belief). However, the training set for Subtask 2b (Spanish) was much smaller, at only 804 sentence pairs collected by combining previous datasets from the Newswire and Wikipedia domains.

3.2 Results and Analysis

The task required the submission of 3 different runs for each task. The runs for the Subtask 2a (English) were identical except for some parameter differences for the SVM training. Our system performed adequately, with our primary run achieving a mean Pearson Correlation of 0.7216.

However, the runs for Subtask 2b (Spanish) were trained on different training sets. Run-1 and Run-2 are trained on the 804 Spanish sentence-pairs. The Spanish set's Run-3, however, is trained on the much larger English training set. For this purpose, we needed to translate the Spanish test set into English in order to use the Semantic Similarity language-dependent features (see sections 2.1.3 and 2.2.4). This system did not outperform the basic Spanish model used in Run-1 and Run-2, despite the much larger training set. Our Spanish system did not yield a satisfactory performance, achieving a Pearson Correlation score of only 0.5158. This could be part due to the smaller training set in Spanish, and the imperfect translations into English which consequently influenced the performance of the language-dependent features. The detailed results for both tasks are given in Table 1 and 2.

[10] `http://www.csie.ntu.edu.tw/~cjlin/libsvm/`

	Run-1	**Run-2**	**Run-3**
answers-forums	0.6781	0.6454	0.6179
answers-students	0.7304	0.7093	0.6977
belief	0.6294	0.5165	0.3236
headlines	0.6912	0.6084	0.5775
images	0.8109	0.7999	0.7954
mean	***0.7216***	***0.6746***	***0.6353***
rank (out of 74)	***33***	***45***	***55***

Table 1: Task 2a – Pearson Correlation for English.

	Run-1	**Run-2**	**Run-3**
wikipedia	0.5239	0.4671	0.4402
newswire	0.5076	0.5437	0.5524
mean	***0.5158***	***0.5054***	***0.4963***
rank (out of 17)	***9***	***10***	***11***

Table 2: Task 2b – Pearson Correlation for Spanish.

4 Conclusion and Future Work

We have presented an efficient approach to calculate semantic relatedness for both English and Spanish sentence pairs. We used the same feature set for both tasks, even though it meant translating the Spanish sentences into English before extracting one of the features (i.e. the Semantic Similarity). The system did not performed well for Spanish as it ranked 9 out of 17, with a 0.5158 average Person correlation over two test sets (0.1747 correlation points less than the best submitted run). On the other hand, it performed reasonably well for English, where the system's best result ranked 33 among 74 submitted runs with 0.7216 Pearson correlation over five test sets (only 0.0799 correlation points less than the best submitted run).

In the future we plan to extract the conceptual description provided by the BabelNet network in order to match it with the conceptual terms. We have not done that for now because we need to treat these descriptions as sentences, which requires filtering out the noise produced by them.

Acknowledgements

Hanna Béchara, Hernani Costa and Rohit Gupta are supported by the People Programme (Marie Curie Actions) of the European Union's Framework Programme (FP7/2007-2013) under REA grant agreement n° 317471. Also, the research reported in this work has been partially carried out in the framework of the Educational Innovation Project TRADICOR (PIE 13-054, 2014-2015); the R&D project INTELITERM (ref. n° FFI2012-38881, 2012-2015); and the R&D Project for Excellence TERMITUR (ref. n° HUM2754, 2014-2017).

References

Chih-Chung Chang and Chih-Jen Lin. 2011. LIBSVM: A library for support vector machines. *ACM Transactions on Intelligent Systems and Technology*, 2:27.

Hernani Costa, Hugo Gonçalo Oliveira, and Paulo Gomes. 2010. The Impact of Distributional Metrics in the Quality of Relational Triples. In *19th European Conf. on Artificial Intelligence, Workshop on Language Technology for Cultural Heritage, Social Sciences, and Humanities*, ECAI'10, pages 23–29, Lisbon, Portugal.

Hernani Costa, Hugo Gonçalo Oliveira, and Paulo Gomes. 2011. Using the Web to Validate Lexico-Semantic Relations. In *15th Portuguese Conf. on Artificial Intelligence*, volume 7026 of *EPIA'11*, pages 597–609, Lisbon, Portugal. Springer.

Rohit Gupta, Hanna Bechara, Ismail El Maarouf, and Constantin Orasan. 2014. UoW: NLP techniques developed at the University of Wolverhampton for Semantic Similarity and Textual Entailment. In *8th Int. Workshop on Semantic Evaluation (SemEval'14)*, pages 785–789, Dublin, Ireland. ACL and Dublin City University.

Zelig Harris. 1970. Distributional Structure. In *Papers in Structural and Transformational Linguistics*, pages 775–794. D. Reidel Publishing Company, Dordrecht, Holland.

Paul Jaccard. 1901. Étude comparative de la distribution florale dans une portion des alpes et des jura. *Bulletin del la Société Vaudoise des Sciences Naturelles*, 37:547–579.

Adam Kilgarriff. 2001. Comparing Corpora. *Int. Journal of Corpus Linguistics*, 6(1):97–133.

Philipp Koehn, Franz Och, and Daniel Marcu. 2003. Statistical Phrase-Based Translation. In *Conf. of the North American Chapter of the ACL on Human Language Technology - Volume 1*, NAACL'03, pages 48–54. ACL.

Philipp Koehn, Hieu Hoang, Alexandra Birch, Chris Callison-Burch, Marcello Federico, Nicola Bertoldi, Brooke Cowan, Wade Shen, Christine Moran, Richard Zens, Chris Dyer, Ondřej Bojar, Alexandra Constantin, and Evan Herbst. 2007. Moses: Open Source Toolkit for Statistical Machine Translation. In *45th Annual Meeting of the ACL on Interactive Poster and Demonstration Sessions*, pages 177–180.

Philipp Koehn. 2005. Europarl: A Parallel Corpus for Statistical Machine Translation. In *MT Summit*.

Dekang Lin. 1998. An Information-Theoretic Definition of Similarity. In *15th Int. Conf. on Machine Learning*, ICML'98, pages 296–304, San Francisco, CA, USA. Morgan Kaufmann.

Edward Loper and Steven Bird. 2002. NLTK: The Natural Language Toolkit. In *ACL-02 Workshop on Effective Tools and Methodologies for Teaching Natural Language Processing and Computational Linguistics - Volume 1*, ETMTNLP'02, pages 62–69. ACL.

Roberto Navigli and Simone Paolo Ponzetto. 2012. BabelNet: The Automatic Construction, Evaluation and Application of a Wide-Coverage Multilingual Semantic Network. *Artificial Intelligence*, 193:217–250.

Franz Och and Hermann Ney. 2003. A Systematic Comparison of Various Statistical Alignment Models. *Computational Linguistics*, 29(1):19–51.

Franz Och. 2003. Minimum Error Rate Training in Statistical Machine Translation. In *41st Annual Meeting on ACL - Volume 1*, ACL'03, pages 160–167. ACL.

Mohammad Taher Pilehvar, David Jurgens, and Roberto Navigli. 2013. Align, Disambiguate and Walk: A Unified Approach for Measuring Semantic Similarity. In *51st Annual Meeting of the ACL - Volume 1*, pages 1341–1351, Sofia, Bulgaria. ACL.

Carlos Ramisch, Aline Villavicencio, and Christian Boitet. 2010. Multiword Expressions in the Wild?: The Mwetoolkit Comes in Handy. In *23rd Int. Conf. on Computational Linguistics: Demonstrations*, COLING'10, pages 57–60. ACL.

Gerard Salton and Christopher Buckley. 1988. Term-Weighting Approaches in Automatic Text Retrieval. *Information Processing & Management*, 24(5):513–523.

Helmut Schmid. 1995. Improvements In Part-of-Speech Tagging With an Application To German. In *ACL SIGDAT-Workshop*, pages 47–50, Dublin, Ireland.

Amit Singhal. 2001. Modern Information Retrieval: A Brief Overview. *Bulletin of the IEEE Computer*

Society Technical Committee on Data Engineering, 24(4):35–42.

Andreas Stolcke. 2002. SRILM - an Extensible Language Modeling Toolkit. In *7th Int. Conf. on Spoken Language Processing*, ICSLP'02, pages 901–904.

Kristina Toutanova, Dan Klein, Christopher Manning, and Yoram Singer. 2003. Feature-Rich Part-of-Speech Tagging with a Cyclic Dependency Network. In *HLT-NAAC 2003*, pages 252–259, Edmonton, Canada. ACL.

Peter D. Turney. 2001. Mining the Web for Synonyms: PMI-IR Versus LSA on TOEFL. In *12th European Conf. on Machine Learning*, EMCL'01, pages 491–502, London, UK. Springer.

FBK-HLT: A New Framework for Semantic Textual Similarity

Ngoc Phuoc An Vo
Fondazione Bruno Kessler,
University of Trento
Trento, Italy
ngoc@fbk.eu

Simone Magnolini
University of Brescia,
Fondazione Bruno Kessler
Trento, Italy
magnolini@fbk.eu

Octavian Popescu
IBM Research, T.J. Watson
Yorktown, US
o.popescu@us.ibm.com

Abstract

This paper reports the description and performance of our system, FBK-HLT, participating in the SemEval 2015, Task #2 "Semantic Textual Similarity", English subtask. We submitted three runs with different hypothesis in combining typical features (lexical similarity, string similarity, word n-grams, etc) with syntactic structure features, resulting in different sets of features. The results evaluated on both STS 2014 and 2015 datasets prove our hypothesis of building a STS system taking into consideration of syntactic information. We outperform the best system on STS 2014 datasets and achieve a very competitive result to the best system on STS 2015 datasets.

1 Introduction

Semantic related tasks have been a noticed trend in Natural Language Processing (NLP) community. Particularly, the task Semantic Textual Similarity (STS) has captured a huge attention in the NLP community despite being recently introduced since SemEval 2012 (Agirre et al., 2012). Basically, the task requires to build systems which can compute the similarity degree between two given sentences. The similarity degree is scaled as a real score from 0 (no relevance) to 5 (semantic equivalence). The evaluation is done by computing the correlation between human judgment scores and system scores by the mean of Pearson correlation method.

At SemEval 2015, Task #2 "Semantic Textual Similarity (STS)", English STS subtask (Agirre et al., 2015) evaluates participating systems on five test datasets: image description (*image*), news headlines (*headlines*), student answers paired with reference answers (*answers-students*), answers to questions posted in stach exchange forums (*answers-forum*), and English discussion forum data exhibiting commited belief (*belief*). As being inspired by the UKP system (Bär et al., 2012), which was the best system in STS 2012, we build a supervised system on top of it. Our system adopts some word and string similarity features in UKP, such as string similarity, character/word n-grams, and pairwise similarity; however, we also add other distinguished features, like syntactic structure information, word alignment and semantic word similarity. As a result, our team, FBK-HLT, submitted three runs and achieve very competitive results in the top-tier systems of the task.

The remainder of this paper is organized as follows: Section 2 presents the System Description, Section 3 describes our Experiment Settings, Section 4 reports the Evaluations of our system. Finally, Section 5 is Conclusions and Future Work.

2 System Description

We describe our system, which is built from different linguistic features. We construct a pipeline system, in which each component produces different features independently and at the end, all features are consolidated by a machine learning tool, which learns a regression model for predicting the similarity scores from given sentence-pairs. On top of this, the system is expandable and scalable for adopting more useful features aiming for improving the accuracy. The System Overview in Figure 1 shows the logic and design processes in which different com-

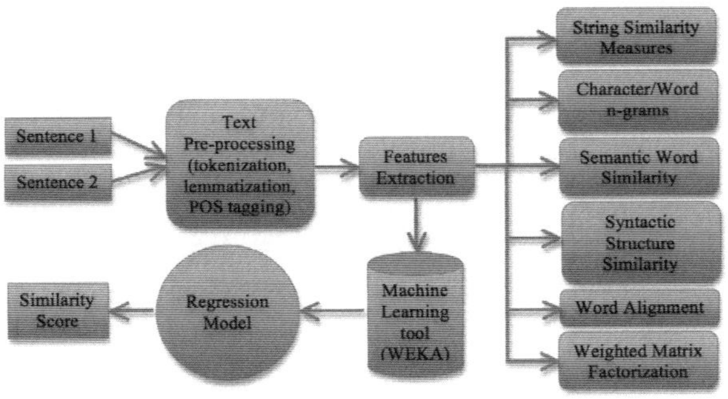

Figure 1: System Overview.

ponents connect and work together.

2.1 Data Preprocessing

The input data undergoes the data preprocessing in which we use Tree Tagger (Schmid, 1994) to perform tokenization, lemmatization, and Part-of-Speech (POS) tagging. On the other hand, we use Stanford Parser (Klein and Manning, 2003) to obtain the dependency parsing from given sentences.

2.2 Word and String Similarity Features

We adopt some word and string similarity features from the UKP system (Bär et al., 2012), which are briefly described as follows:

- String Similarity: we use Longest Common Substring (Gusfield, 1997), Longest Common Subsequence (Allison and Dix, 1986) and Greedy String Tiling (Wise, 1996) measures.

- Character/Word n-grams: we compare character n-grams (Barrón-Cedeno et al., 2010) with the variance n=2, 3, ..., 15. In contrast, we compare the word n-grams using Jaccard coefficient done by Lyon (Lyon et al., 2001) and containment measure (Broder, 1997) with the variance of n=1, 2, 3, and 4.

- Semantic Word Similarity: we use the pairwise similarity algorithm by Resnik (Resnik, 1995) on WordNet (Fellbaum, 1998), and the vector space model Explicit Semantic Analysis (ESA) (Gabrilovich and Markovitch, 2007) which is constructed by two lexical semantic resources Wikipedia [1] and Wiktionary [2].

2.3 Syntactic Structure Features

We exploit the syntactic structure information by the mean of three different toolkits: Syntactic Tree Kernel, Distributed Tree Kernel and Syntactic Generalization. We describe how each toolkit is used to learn and extract the syntactic structure information from texts to be used in our STS system.

2.3.1 Syntactic Tree Kernel

Syntactic Tree Kernel (Moschitti, 2006) is a tree kernels approach to learn the syntactic structure from syntactic parsing information, particularly, the Partial Tree (PT) kernel is proposed as a new convolution kernel to fully exploit dependency trees. We use the open-source toolkit "Tree Kernel in SVM-Light[3]" to learn this syntactic information.

Having assumed that paraphrased pairs would share the same content and similar syntactic structures, we decide to choose the Microsoft Research Paraphrasing Corpus (Dolan et al., 2005) which contains 5,800 sentence pairs extracted from news sources on the web, along with human annotations indicating whether each pair captures a paraphrase/semantic equivalence relationship. This corpus is split into Training set (4,076 pairs) and Testing set (1,725 pairs).

We use Stanford Parser (Klein and Manning, 2003) to obtain the dependency parsing from sentence pairs. Then we use the machine learning tool svm-light-tk 1.2 which uses Tree Kernel approach to learn the similarity of syntactic structure to build a binary classifying model on the Train dataset. The output predictions are probability confidence scores in [-1,1], corresponds to the probability of the label to be positive. According to the assumption above, we label paraphrased pairs as 1, -1 otherwise. We obtain the Accuracy of 69.16% on the Test set.

2.3.2 Distributed Tree Kernel

Distributed Tree Kernel (DTK) (Zanzotto and Dell'Arciprete, 2012) is a tree kernels method using a linear complexity algorithm to compute vectors for trees by embedding feature spaces of tree fragments

[1] http://en.wikipedia.org/wiki/Main_Page
[2] http://en.wiktionary.org
[3] http://disi.unitn.it/moschitti/Tree-Kernel.htm

Settings	deft-forum	deft-news	headlines	images	OnWN	tweet-news	Mean
Baseline	0.353	0.596	0.510	0.513	0.406	0.654	0.507
DLS@CU (ranked 1st)	0.4828	0.7657	0.7646	0.8214	0.8589	0.7639	0.761
Word/String Sim (1)	0.4314	0.7089	0.6887	0.7671	0.8125	0.6932	0.7008
Syntactic Features (2)	0.2402	0.3886	0.3233	0.2419	0.4066	0.4489	0.3441
(1) & (2)	0.4495	0.7032	0.6902	0.7627	0.8115	0.6974	0.7026
All Features	**0.5076**	0.7616	**0.7647**	0.8182	**0.8953**	0.7485	**0.7672**

Table 1: Evaluation Results on STS 2014 datasets.

System	ans-forums	ans-students	belief	headlines	images	Mean
Baseline	0.4453	0.6647	0.6517	0.5312	0.6039	0.5871
DLS@CU-S1 (ranked 1st)	0.739	0.7725	0.7491	0.825	0.8644	**0.8015**
FBK-HLT Run1	0.7131	0.7442	0.7327	0.8079	0.8574	**0.7831**
FBK-HLT Run2	0.7101	0.7410	0.7377	0.8008	0.8545	0.7801
FBK-HLT Run3	0.6555	0.7362	0.7460	0.7083	0.8389	0.7461

Table 2: Evaluation Results on STS 2015 datasets.

in low-dimensional spaces. Then a recursive algorithm is proposed with linear complexity to compute reduced vectors for trees. The dot product among reduced vectors is used to approximate the original tree kernel when a vector composition function with specific ideal properties is used.

Firstly, we use Stanford Parser (PCFG Parser) trained on Penn TreeBank (Klein and Manning, 2003) to obtain the dependency parsing of sentences, and feed them to the software "distributed-tree-kernels" to produce the distributed trees.[4] Then, we compute the Cosine similarity between the vectors of distributed trees of each sentence pair. This cosine similarity score is converted to the scale of STS and SR for evaluation.

2.3.3 Syntactic Generalization

Given a pair of parse trees, the Syntactic Generalization (SG) (Galitsky, 2013) finds a set of maximal common subtrees. The toolkit "relevance-based-on-parse-trees" is an open-source project which evaluates text relevance by using syntactic parse tree-based similarity measure.[5] Given a pair of parse trees, it measures the similarity between two sentences by finding a set of maximal common subtrees, using representation of constituency parse trees via chunking. Each type of phrases (NP, VP, PRP etc.) will be aligned and subject to generalization. It uses the OpenNLP system to derive dependency trees for generalization (chunker and parser).[6] This tool is made to give as a tool for text relevance which can be used as a black box, no understanding of computational linguistics or machine learning is required. We apply the tool on the STS datasets to compute the similarity of syntactic structure of sentence pairs.

2.4 Further Features

We also deploy other features which also may help in identifying the semantic similarity degree between two given sentences, such as word alignment in machine translation evaluation metric and the vector space model Weighted Matrix Factorization (WMF) for pairwise similarity.

2.4.1 Machine Translation Evaluation Metric - METEOR

METEOR (Metric for Evaluation of Translation with Explicit ORdering) (Banerjee and Lavie, 2005) is an automatic metric for machine translation evaluation, which consists of two major components: a flexible monolingual word aligner and a scorer. For machine translation evaluation, hypothesis sentences are aligned to reference sentences. Alignments are then scored to produce sentence and corpus level scores. We use this word alignment feature

[4]https://code.google.com/p/distributed-tree-kernels

[5]https://code.google.com/p/relevance-based-on-parse-trees

[6]https://opennlp.apache.org

to learn the similarity between words, phrases in two given texts in case of different orders.

2.4.2 Weighted Matrix Factorization (WMF)

WMF (Guo and Diab, 2012) is a dimension reduction model to extract nuanced and robust latent vectors for short texts/sentences. To overcome the sparsity problem in short texts/sentences (e.g. 10 words on average), the missing words, a feature that LSA/LDA typically overlooks, is explicitly modeled. We use the pipeline to compute the similarity score between texts.

3 Experiment Settings

We generate and select 25 optimal features, ranging from lexical level to string level and syntactic level. We deploy the machine learning toolkit WEKA (Hall et al., 2009) for learning a regression model (*GaussianProcesses*) to predict the similarity scores. We build three models based on three sets of features to verify our hypothesis in which we augment that computing semantic similarity degree is not only about lexical similarity and string similarity, but also taking into consideration a deeper level at syntactic structure where more semantic information is embedded.

In the system development process, we train our system on the given datasets of STS 2012, 2013 and use the STS 2014 datasets for evaluating the system. In Table 1, we also examine the contribution of different features to the overall accuracy of system, and prove that syntactic structure information also has some impact to the performance of our system. Our model using all features described above outperform the best system DLS@CU in STS 2014 evaluation.

We submitted three runs with different sets of features as below:

- **Run1**: All features described in Section 2 used.

- **Run2**: The feature obtained by Distributed Tree Kernel approach is excluded as sometimes it returns negative correlation.

- **Run3**: No syntactic features are included.

4 Evaluations

In Table 2 we report the performance of our three runs achieved on the STS 2015 test datasets. Among three submitted runs, Run1 has the best score, which confirm that exploiting the syntactic structure information benefits the overall performance of our system. Besides, although occasionally the features extracted by Distributed Tree Kernel approach returns negative result, it still contributes a small positive portion in the final result, which is shown in the Run2. In contrast, the Run3 which excludes all syntactic structure features, eventually, returns 4% lower than the other two runs.

In overall, our system achieves a very competitive result compared to the best ranked system, DLS@CU-S1. Specifically, the difference between our Run1 and the DLS@CU-S1 on each test dataset of STS 2015 varies slightly 1%-2%. However, this difference is not statistically significant, as we can understand that each system may perform slightly different on different evaluation datasets. Generally, by taking into account the results of our system and DLS@CU on both STS 2014 and 2015 evaluation datasets, we can consider that we are almost equivalent in performance.

5 Conclusions and Future Work

In this paper, we describe the pipeline system FBK-HLT participating in the SemEval 2015, Task #2 "Semantic Textual Similarity", English subtask. We present a supervised system which considers multiple linguistic features from low to high language level, such as lexical, string and syntactic. We also augment that looking into the syntactic structure of text will more or less benefit the capability of predicting the semantic similarity. Among our three submitted runs, our performance is much above the baseline and very competitive to the best system; we are ranked in the top-tier (12th, 13th, and 23nd) out of total 73 systems.

For the time being, we can see that the contribution of syntactic features is still limited (about 4%) to the overall performance. However, it does not deny the significance of syntactic information in semantic related tasks, especially, this STS task. Hence, we expect to study to exploit more useful features from the syntactic information, which intuitively, is supposed to play a significant role in semantic reasoning.

References

Eneko Agirre, Mona Diab, Daniel Cer, and Aitor Gonzalez-Agirre. 2012. Semeval-2012 task 6: A pilot on semantic textual similarity. In *Proceedings of the First Joint Conference on Lexical and Computational Semantics-Volume 1: Proceedings of the main conference and the shared task, and Volume 2: Proceedings of the Sixth International Workshop on Semantic Evaluation*, pages 385–393.

Eneko Agirre, Carmen Banea, Claire Cardie, Daniel Cer, Mona Diab, Aitor Gonzalez-Agirre, Weiwei Guo, Inigo Lopez-Gazpio, Montse Maritxalar, Rada Mihalcea, German Rigau, Larraitz Uria, and Janyce Wiebe. 2015. SemEval-2015 Task 2: Semantic Textual Similarity, English, Spanish and Pilot on Interpretability. In *Proceedings of the 9th International Workshop on Semantic Evaluation (SemEval 2015)*, Denver, CO, June.

Lloyd Allison and Trevor I Dix. 1986. A bit-string longest-common-subsequence algorithm. *Information Processing Letters*, 23(5):305–310.

Satanjeev Banerjee and Alon Lavie. 2005. METEOR: An automatic metric for mt evaluation with improved correlation with human judgments. In *Proceedings of the ACL Workshop on Intrinsic and Extrinsic Evaluation Measures for Machine Translation and/or Summarization*, pages 65–72.

Daniel Bär, Chris Biemann, Iryna Gurevych, and Torsten Zesch. 2012. Ukp: Computing semantic textual similarity by combining multiple content similarity measures. In *Proceedings of the First Joint Conference on Lexical and Computational Semantics-Volume 1: Proceedings of the main conference and the shared task, and Volume 2: Proceedings of the Sixth International Workshop on Semantic Evaluation*, pages 435–440.

Alberto Barrón-Cedeno, Paolo Rosso, Eneko Agirre, and Gorka Labaka. 2010. Plagiarism detection across distant language pairs. In *Proceedings of the 23rd International Conference on Computational Linguistics*, pages 37–45.

Andrei Z Broder. 1997. On the resemblance and containment of documents. In *Compression and Complexity of Sequences 1997*, pages 21–29. IEEE.

Bill Dolan, Chris Brockett, and Chris Quirk. 2005. Microsoft research paraphrase corpus. *Retrieved March*, 29:2008.

Christiane Fellbaum. 1998. *WordNet*. Wiley Online Library.

Evgeniy Gabrilovich and Shaul Markovitch. 2007. Computing semantic relatedness using wikipedia-based explicit semantic analysis. In *IJCAI*, volume 7, pages 1606–1611.

Boris Galitsky. 2013. Machine learning of syntactic parse trees for search and classification of text. *Engineering Applications of Artificial Intelligence*, 26(3):1072–1091.

Weiwei Guo and Mona Diab. 2012. Modeling sentences in the latent space. In *Proceedings of the 50th Annual Meeting of the Association for Computational Linguistics: Long Papers-Volume 1*, pages 864–872.

Dan Gusfield. 1997. *Algorithms on strings, trees and sequences: computer science and computational biology*. Cambridge University Press.

Mark Hall, Eibe Frank, Geoffrey Holmes, Bernhard Pfahringer, Peter Reutemann, and Ian H Witten. 2009. The WEKA data mining software: an update. *ACM SIGKDD explorations newsletter*, 11(1):10–18.

Dan Klein and Christopher D Manning. 2003. Accurate unlexicalized parsing. In *Proceedings of the 41st Annual Meeting on Association for Computational Linguistics-Volume 1*, pages 423–430.

Caroline Lyon, James Malcolm, and Bob Dickerson. 2001. Detecting short passages of similar text in large document collections. In *Proceedings of the 2001 Conference on Empirical Methods in Natural Language Processing*, pages 118–125.

Alessandro Moschitti. 2006. Efficient convolution kernels for dependency and constituent syntactic trees. In *Machine Learning: ECML 2006*, pages 318–329.

Philip Resnik. 1995. Using information content to evaluate semantic similarity in a taxonomy. In *Proceedings of the 14th International Joint Conference on Artificial Intelligence - Volume 1*, IJCAI'95, pages 448–453.

Helmut Schmid. 1994. Probabilistic part-of-speech tagging using decision trees. In *Proceedings of international conference on new methods in language processing*, volume 12, pages 44–49. Manchester, UK.

Michael J Wise. 1996. Yap3: Improved detection of similarities in computer program and other texts. In *ACM SIGCSE Bulletin*, volume 28, pages 130–134. ACM.

Fabio Massimo Zanzotto and Lorenzo Dell'Arciprete. 2012. Distributed tree kernels. In *Proceedings of the 29th International Conference on Machine Learning*.

UMDuluth-BlueTeam : SVCSTS - A Multilingual and Chunk Level Semantic Similarity System

Sakethram Karumuri
Viswanadh Kumar Reddy Vuggumudi
Sai Charan Raj Chitirala
Department of Computer Science
University of Minnesota Duluth
{karum006, vuggu001, chiti001}@d.umn.edu

Abstract

This paper describes SVCSTS, a system that was submitted in SemEval-2015 Task 2: Semantic Textual Similarity(STS)(Agirre et al., 2015). The task has 3 subtasks viz., English STS, Spanish STS and Interpretable STS. SVCSTS uses Monolingual word aligner (Sultan et al., May 2014), supervised machine learning, Google and Bing translator API's. Various runs of the system outperformed all other participating systems in Interpretable STS for non-chunked sentence input.

1 Introduction

Semantic Textual Similarity gives a quantifier to evaluate semantic equivalence between two sentences. Earlier SemEval tasks (Agirre et al., 2012), (Agirre et al., 2013), (Agirre et al., 2014) focused on finding the semantic equivalence between sentences in English and Spanish. A new pilot task was introduced this year to find which parts (chunks) of the sentences are equivalent in meaning.

SVCSTS is an extension to (Sultan et al., 2014) and it handles both Spanish STS and Interpretable STS. SVCSTS uses Monolingual word aligner (Sultan et al., May 2014), supervised machine learning techniques, Google and Bing translator API's.

Section 2 describes a brief overview of SVCSTS's approach for various subtasks. Section 3 outlines the performance of SVCSTS in various subtasks of SemEval 2015 Task-2.

2 System Description

Following 3 sub sections describe SVCSTS's approach for the 3 subtasks.

2.1 English STS

This task was about finding the semantic similarity between English sentences. (Sultan et al., 2014) system was used to find the semantic equivalence between two sentences and a score on a scale of 0-5 was given.

2.2 Spanish STS

Spanish STS is built upon English STS to calculate similarity scores for a given pair of Spanish sentences on a scale of 0 to 4. Spanish sentences were translated to English, fed to English STS system and the scores are scaled accordingly. Translations were done using Bing Translator API (Bing Translator API) and Google Translate API. Two translators were used to improve the accuracy of the translations.

Google Translate API was obtained from (Kashyap et al., 2014). We used this system to get multiple translations of each chunk in a sentence. Multiple sentences are generated by combining the top two translations of each chunk. We then randomly pick a maximum of ten sentences for each Spanish sentence. Translation pairs are formed by choosing corresponding numbered sentences from sentence 1 and sentence 2 translations. We limited the number of translations to 10 to reduce the overall computation time.

Translation pairs were then passed to English STS system. Final score was obtained as the average taken from all translation pairs for a given Spanish sentence pair and the score is scaled accordingly.

2.3 Interpretable STS

Existing STS systems report similarity for a pair of sentences.

This is a pilot task where the challenge is to find the semantic relationships between the chunks of sentence 1 and sentence 2. Chunks from the input sentence pair are to be aligned, labeled with the type (described here) of alignment and are to be scored on a scale of 0-5 based on their semantic similarity.

The type of alignments defined in the task description are:

1. EQUI : both chunks are semantically similar.
2. OPPO : both chunks are semantically opposite.
3. SPE1 : both chunks are semantically similar but chunk1 has more information.
4. SPE2 : both chunks are semantically similar but chunk2 has more information.
5. SIMI : similar chunks but no EQUI, OPPO, SPE1 or SPE2.
6. REL : related chunks but no SIMI, EQUI, OPPO, SPE1, SPE2.
7. ALIC : when 1:1 alignment of chunks is not possible extra chunks are given ALIC
8. NOALI: a chunk has no corresponding semantically similar chunk

There are two variations in the input for this subtask:

1. Raw input - Plain sentences are provided and the system has to identify the chunks
2. Chunked input - Chunked sentences are provided by the task organizers

2.3.1 Identifying Chunks

OpenNLP chunker was used to chunk the input sentences and some post processing was done. For the post processing we observed a few rules from gold standard chunks. Those rules include combining chunks of specific chunk tags given by OpenNLP chunker. A large number of rules were discovered but the following were the rules, which maximized accuracy.

- PP + NP + PP + NP
- PP + NP
- VP + PRT
- NP + O + NP
- VP + ADVP
- VP + PP + NP + O
- NP + O

Applying these rules we have increased accuracy from 86.58% to 90.16% against the gold standard chunks.

2.3.2 Aligning Chunks

Monolingual word aligner (Sultan et al., May 2014) was used to find word alignments in the two input sentences. For chunked input, sentences are generated from the chunks prior to running the word aligner. For words aligned their corresponding chunks are aligned.

2.3.3 Labeling Aligned Chunks

Supervised machine learning was performed using Scikit-Learn (scikit-learn). We used the following features for each chunk alignment to assign a type for the alignment.

1. Length of sentence 1 chunk
2. Length of sentence 2 chunk
3. Number of nouns in sentence 1 chunk
4. Number of nouns in sentence 2 chunk
5. Number of verbs in sentence 1 chunk
6. Number of verbs in sentence 2 chunk
7. Number of adjectives in sentence 1 chunk
8. Number of adjectives in sentence 2 chunk
9. Number of prepositions in sentence 1 chunk
10. Number of prepositions in sentence 2 chunk

Type of Alignment	Score
EQUI	5
SPE1	3.75
SPE2	3.55
ALIC	NIL
NOALI	0
SIMI	2.94
REL	2.82
OPPO	4

Table 1: Avg. alignment type scores

Runs	Features Used
Run - 1	3,4,5,6,7,8,9,10,11,12
Run - 2	3,4,5,6,7,8,9,10,11,12,13
Run - 3	1,2,3,4,5,6,7,8,9,10,11,12,13

Table 2: Features used in various runs

11. The path similarity between words of sentence 1 and sentence 2 chunks
12. Unigram overlap between sentence 1 and sentence 2 chunks
13. Bigram overlap between sentence 1 and sentence 2 chunks

We experimented the classification of labels using 3 classifiers LinearSVC, SVC with RBF (Radial Basis Function) Kernel and SVC with Polynomial Kernel. But the classifier SVC with RBF (with parameters C = 1.0, gamma=0.7) proved to give better results.

2.3.4 Scoring Aligned Chunks

Average score for each alignment type was calculated from the gold standard data. The average scores that were used to score chunk alignment are described in Table 1.

2.3.5 Multiple Runs

We tried various combination of features (described in Section 2.3.3) for training the classifier. The details of three runs that resulted in better accuracy on training data are described in Table 2.

3 Results

The results of all the subtracks were very encouraging. For English STS, the results are outlined in Table 3. SVCSTS was ranked 14th among 73 runs. The results of Spanish STS are shown in Table 4. We were ranked 4th among 16 runs. Table 5 and Table 6 summarize the results of Interpretable STS for chunked and non-chunked input respectively. Runs 2 and 3 seemed to outperform many other participating systems for non-chunked sentence input.

Inputs	Baseline	SVCSTS
answers-forums	0.4453	0.6561
answers-students	0.6647	0.7816
belief	0.6517	0.7363
headlines	0.5312	0.8085
images	0.6039	0.8236
Mean	0.5871	0.7775
Rank	59	14

Table 3: Scores for English STS

Inputs	SVCSTS
Wikipedia	0.59364
Newswire	0.65471
Mean	0.63430
Rank	4

Table 4: Scores for Spanish STS

Acknowledgments

We thank Dr. Ted Pedersen for introducing us to SemEval shared tasks.

Inputs	Baseline	SVCSTS
For Headlines - Run 2		
F1 Ali	0.6701	0.7820
F1 Type	0.4571	0.5154
F1 Score	0.6066	0.7024
F1 Type+Score	0.4571	0.5098
For Images - Run 3		
F1 Ali	0.7060	0.8336
F1 Type	0.3696	0.5759
F1 Score	0.6092	0.7511
F1 Type+Score	0.3693	0.5634

Table 5: Scores for Interpretable STS (Chunked Input)

Inputs	Baseline	SVCSTS
For Headlines - Run 1		
F1 Ali	0.8448	0.8861
F1 Type	0.5556	0.5962
F1 Score	0.7551	0.7960
F1 Type+Score	0.5556	0.5887
For Images - Run 2		
F1 Ali	0.8388	0.8853
F1 Type	0.4328	0.6095
F1 Score	0.7210	0.7968
F1 Type+Score	0.4326	0.5964

Table 6: Scores for Interpretable STS (Raw Input)

References

Eneko Agirre, Carmen Banea, Claire Cardie, Daniel Cer, Mona Diab, Aitor Gonzalez-Agirre, Weiwei Guo, Iigo Lopez-Gazpio, Montse Maritxalar, Rada Mihalcea, German Rigau, Larraitz Uria, and Janyce Wiebe. SemEval-2015 Task 2: Semantic Textual Similarity, English, Spanish and Pilot on Interpretability. In *Proceedings of the 9th International Workshop on Semantic Evaluation (SemEval 2015)*, Denver, CO, June 2015. Association for Computational Linguistics.

Eneko Agirre, Daniel Cer, Mona Diab, and Aitor Gonzalez-Agirre. Semeval-2012 task 6: A pilot on semantic textual similarity. In **SEM 2012: The First Joint Conference on Lexical and Computational Semantics – Volume 1: Proceedings of the main conference and the shared task, and Volume 2: Proceedings of the Sixth International Workshop on Semantic Evaluation (SemEval 2012)*, pages 385–393, Montréal, Canada, 7-8 June 2012. Association for Computational Linguistics.

Eneko Agirre, Daniel Cer, Mona Diab, Aitor Gonzalez-Agirre, and Weiwei Guo. *sem 2013 shared task: Semantic textual similarity. In *Second Joint Conference on Lexical and Computational Semantics (*SEM), Volume 1: Proceedings of the Main Conference and the Shared Task: Semantic Textual Similarity*, pages 32–43, Atlanta, Georgia, USA, June 2013. Association for Computational Linguistics.

Eneko Agirre, Carmen Banea, Claire Cardie, Daniel Cer, Mona Diab, Aitor Gonzalez-Agirre, Weiwei Guo, Rada Mihalcea, German Rigau, and Janyce Wiebe. Semeval-2014 task 10: Multilingual semantic textual similarity. In *Proceedings of the 8th International Workshop on Semantic Evaluation (SemEval 2014)*, pages 81–91, Dublin, Ireland, August 2014. Association for Computational Linguistics and Dublin City University.

Abhay Kashyap, Lushan Han, Roberto Yus, Jennifer Sleeman, Taneeya Satyapanich, Sunil Gandhi, and Tim Finin. Meerkat mafia: Multilingual and cross-level semantic textual similarity systems. In *Proceedings of the 8th International Workshop on Semantic Evaluation (SemEval 2014)*, pages 416–423, Dublin, Ireland, August 2014. Association for Computational Linguistics and Dublin City University.

Md. Arafat Sultan, Steven Bethard, and Tamara Sumner. Dls@cu: Sentence similarity from word alignment. In *Proceedings of the 8th International Workshop on Semantic Evaluation (SemEval 2014)*, pages 241–246, Dublin, Ireland, 2014. Association for Computational Linguistics and Dublin City University. Winner of the shared task.

Md. Arafat Sultan and Steven Bethard and Tamara Sumner Back to Basics for Monolingual Alignment: Exploiting Word Similarity and Contextual Evidence *Transactions of the Association for Computational Linguistics*, Vol. 2, (May), pages 219–230.

Pedregosa, F. and Varoquaux, G. and Gramfort, A. and Michel, V. and Thirion, B. and Grisel, O. and Blondel, M. and Prettenhofer, P. and Weiss, R. and Dubourg, V. and Vanderplas, J. and Passos, A. and Cournapeau, D. and Brucher, M. and Perrot, M. and Duchesnay, E. Scikit-learn: Machine Learning in Python *Journal of Machine Learning Research*, Vol 12, pages 2825–2830 2011

https://github.com/openlabs/Microsoft-Translator-Python-API

SemantiKLUE: Semantic Textual Similarity with Maximum Weight Matching

Nataliia Plotnikova and **Gabriella Lapesa** and **Thomas Proisl** and **Stefan Evert**
Friedrich-Alexander-Universität Erlangen-Nürnberg (FAU)
Professur für Korpuslinguistik
Bismarckstr. 6, 91054 Erlangen, Germany
{nataliia.plotnikova,gabriella.lapesa,thomas.proisl,stefan.evert}@fau.de

Abstract

This paper describes the SemantiKLUE system (Proisl et al., 2014) used for the SemEval-2015 shared task on Semantic Textual Similarity (STS) for English. The system was developed for SemEval-2013 and extended for SemEval-2014, where it participated in three tasks and ranked 13th out of 38 submissions for the English STS task. While this year's submission ranks 46th out of 73, further experiments on the selection of training data led to notable improvements showing that the system could have achieved rank 22 out of 73. We report a detailed analysis of those training selection experiments in which we tested different combinations of all the available STS datasets, as well as results of a qualitative analysis conducted on a sample of the sentence pairs for which SemantiKLUE gave wrong STS predictions.

1 Introduction

The SemEval-2015 task on "Semantic Textual Similarity for English" (Agirre et al., 2015) is a rerun of the corresponding task from SemEval-2014 with new test data and updated categories. The predictions of participating systems were evaluated against manually annotated and subsequently filtered data. STS was measured on a scale ranging from 0 (no similarity at all) to 5 (total equivalence). SemantiKLUE, developed in 2014, uses a distributional bag-of-words model as well as a word-to-word alignment for each pair of sentences based on a maximum weight matching algorithm.

Our SemEval-2015 submission for all 5 test categories (headlines, images, belief, answers-forums, answers-students) was based on the training data set from 2014 with 2234 sentence pairs from 3 categories, namely paraphrase sentence pairs (MSRpar), sentence pairs from video descriptions (MSRvid) and MT evaluation sentence pairs (SMTeuroparl). Follow up experiments conducted after the submission deadline showed us that this training configuration was far from optimal, and that our system would have benefited a lot from a better training, as we managed to significantly improve the overall scores. With the best training configuration, SemantiKLUE would have ranked 22nd out of 73 submissions (11th out of 28 teams), with a weighted mean of Pearson correlation coefficients over all test categories of 0.7508 (best system: 0.8015)

In the following sections, we first give a short overview of the system (Section 2), and then we describe the follow-up experiments that allowed us to define the best training data set in terms of its subsets (Section 3); finally, we present the results of a qualitative analysis of the performance of our system (Section 4).

2 System Description

SemantiKLUE combines supervised and unsupervised approaches for the computation of textual similarity: a number of similarity measures are computed and passed to a support vector regression learner, which is trained on the available training data and test sets of previous years. The learnt weights are then used to generate semantic similarity scores for the test data in the desired range.

2.1 Training Data and Preprocessing

The system was trained on manually annotated sentence pairs from the STS task at SemEval 2014. All sentence pairs were preprocessed with Stanford CoreNLP[1] for part-of-speech annotation and lemmatization. Each sentence was represented as a graph using the CCprocessed variant of the Stanford Dependencies (collapsed dependencies with propagation of conjunct dependencies) implemented with the NetworkX[2] module. This graph representation was involved in the computation of all 39 similarity measures for words and tokens in each sentence. Prepositions, articles, conjunctions as well as auxiliary verbs like *be* and *have* were ignored in the computation of token-based measures.

2.2 Similarity Measures: Overview

A detailed description of all 39 similarity measures used as features in SemantiKLUE is provided in Proisl et al., 2014 (Sections 2.2 - 2.7). Similarity measures used by our system include:

- **Heuristic similarity measures**: word form overlap and lemma overlap between two texts computed with Jaccard coefficient; difference in text length used by Gale and Church (1993); a binary feature to treat negation in each sentence pair.
- **Document similarity measures** based on two distributional models: a model based on non-lemmatized information, built from the second release of the Google Books N-Grams database (Lin et al., 2012); a lemmatized model, built from a 10-billion word Web corpus[3].
- **Alignment-based measures**: one-to-one alignment and one-to-many alignment for both words and lemmata, computed via maximum weight matching, based on cosine similarity between two words in paired sentences as edge weight. Figure 1 visualizes a one-to-many alignment based on lemmatized data. The colors of the connections correspond to different cosine ranges, reported in the legend to the right of the plot.
- **WordNet-based similarity measures**: Leacock and Chodorow's (1998) normalized path length and Lin's (1998) universal similarity measure. Using these similarity measures, the best one-to-one and the best one-to-many alignment are computed. After that, the arithmetic mean of the similarities between the aligned words from text A and text B with and without identical word pairs is calculated. An additional WordNet-based feature is the number of unknown words in both texts.
- **Dependency-based heuristic measures**: overlap of dependency relation labels between the two texts; arithmetic mean of the similarities between the best aligned one-to-one dependency relations based on Leacock and Chodorow's normalized path lengths; average overlap of neighbors for all aligned word pairs based on one-to-one alignment created with similarity scores from the lemma-based DSM.
- **Experimental features**: cosine similarities for each pair of sentences; average neighbor rank based on the rank of text A among the nearest neighbors from text B and vice versa.

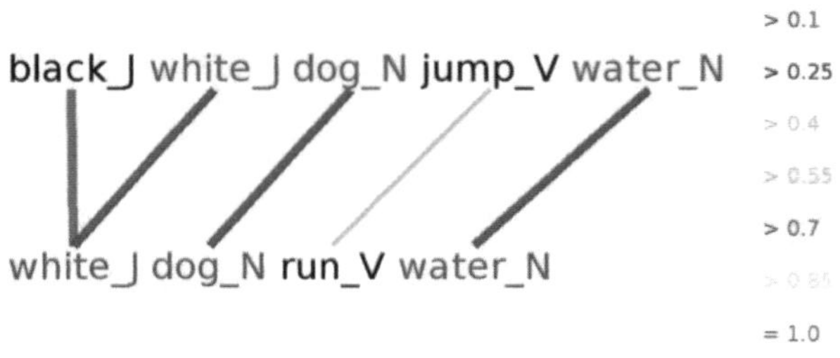

Figure 1: One-to-many alignment plot. Sentences: "A black and white dog is jumping into the water" , "A white dog runs across the water"; Subset: Images; Gold Score: 2.8; SemantiKLUE score: 2.93.

The feature set described above was processed by the support vector regressor implemented in the scikit-learn[4] (Pedregosa et al., 2011) library. All the experiments presented in this paper rely on the best support vector setting identified by Proisl et al. (2014), namely: RBF kernel of degree 2 and penalty C = 0.7. In what follows, we describe the procedures adopted to adjust training data and find the best training configurations.

3 Experiments

This section describes all post-hoc experiments on the STS 2015 test data performed to improve the

[1] http://nlp.stanford.edu/software/corenlp.shtml

[2] http://networkx.github.com

[3] Wackypedia and UkWaC (Baroni et al., 2009), UMBC WebBase (Han et al., 2013), and UKCOW 2012 (Schäfer and Bildhauer, 2012).

[4] http://scikit-learn.org/

predictions of the system. The abbreviations used in the following tables reporting experiment results are listed in Table 1.

short	full name	source
mp	MSRpar[5]	train 2014
mv	MSRvid[6]	train 2014
smt	SMTeuroparl[7]	train 2014
img	images[8]	test 2014
hl	headlines[9]	test 2014
ow	OnWN[10]	test 2014
df	deft-forum[11]	test 2014
dn	deft-news[12]	test 2014
tn	tweet-news	test 2014
fn	FNWN [13]	test 2013
ans-f	answers-forums	test 2015
ans-s	answers-students	test 2015
head	headlines	test 2015

Table 1: Training set categories: abbreviations.

All 39 similarity measures were used by the regression learner to train the system. SemantiKLUE was tested on different training data with various combinations of training and test sets from 2013 and 2014. Results for the submitted system are typeset in italics in Table 2, the best results in each column are typeset in bold font.

The best results would have been obtained by training on the MSR data from SemEval 2014 for all test sets. Considerable improvements can be achieved removing the SMTeuroparl category from the training set. This category consists of MT pairs of sentences whose exclusion would have given the system rank 37 (weighted mean of .7148) instead of 46 (.6717) out of 73 submissions.

We turned the test data from SemEval 2014 into a training set for the 2015 test data (see Table 3). The figures in Table 3 show that training sets for images and headlines perform best with the corresponding categories of the test set (images and headlines) from SemEval 2014.

STS results appear to be extremely sensitive to the choice of the training dataset. For this reason, we conducted more fine-grained experiments to look for the best combination of training data for the 2015 test sets. We combined training and test data of SemEval 2014 with the best training categories of SemEval 2013 (see Table 4) to test the performance of the system on the optimal training subset defined for SemEval 2014[14]. That optimal training configuration consists of the FNWN, headlines, MSR and OnWN data sets: the corresponding performance is typeset in italics. Comparable or even better results can be achieved with a combination of test and train categories of SemEval 2014 only. Thus, combining the training category MSR (*mp + mv*) with another test category of 2014 (such as tweets or headlines) results in about 1.5%-2% improvement. A more precise investigation helped us to find the best test combination with MSR, headlines, images, and tweet-news categories. This brought our system to the weighted mean of .7508, corresponding to the 11th place out of 28 teams. We tried to further improve these results, by adding the optimal categories for training found in 2014 and extended the best training set defined for 2015 with FNWN (*mp+mv+hl+img+tn+fn*), but this led to slightly worse results in all test categories.

A further set of experiments was aimed at testing different subsets of similarity measures used at the

	ans-f	ans-s	head	belief	images	mean
mp	-.2533	.5944	.4515	.3102	.6497	.4310
mv	.3262	.5990	.6044	.5021	.7879	.6014
smt	.2603	.5263	.4073	.3177	.4715	.4235
mp + mv	**.5509**	**.7259**	**.7009**	**.6961**	**.8088**	**.7148**
mv + smt	.4891	.6849	.6822	.5658	.7991	.6734
smt + mp	-.0893	.4989	.2947	.1296	.3781	.2980
mp + mv + smt	*.4913*	*.7005*	*.6681*	*.5617*	*.7915*	*.6717*

Table 2: Evaluation results for different training sets from 2014.

	ans-f	ans-s	head	belief	images	mean
img	.2673	.6549	.6574	.5669	**.8180**	.6367
hl	.5760	**.6760**	**.7734**	.6439	.7249	**.6960**
ow	.3446	.6661	.5960	.5386	.7334	.6093
df	.3743	.5884	.5618	.6023	.5818	.5551
dn	.2620	.6746	.5765	.5804	.7246	.5992
tn	**.6484**	.6134	.6968	**.6858**	.7018	.6698

Table 3: Evaluation results for different training sets based on the 2014 test categories.

[5]Microsoft Research Paraphrase Corpus.
[6]Microsoft Research Video Description Corpus.
[7]WMT2008 development dataset.
[8]Image descriptions from the Flickr dataset.
[9]Headlines mined from news sources.
[10]Sense definitions from OntoNotes and WordNet .
[11]Forum posts.
[12]News summaries.
[13]Sense definitions from FrameNet and WordNet

[14]For space reasons we list only the combinations resulting in the best scores. Combinations with SMTeuroparl, for example, led to consistently worse results and are therefore left out.

	answers-forums	answers-students	headlines	belief	images	mean
img+hl	.5119	.6995	.7663	.6296	.8262	.7157
tn+img	.6158	.6949	.7354	.6982	.8187	.7265
tn+hl	.6313	.6625	.7736	.6887	.7350	.7078
tn+mp+mv	**.6460**	.7213	.7462	**.7118**	.8136	.7400
tn+hl+img	.6223	.7028	.7682	.7004	.8247	.7392
mp+mv+img	.4853	.7297	.7110	.6596	.8302	.7108
mp+mv+hl	.6246	**.7336**	.7766	.7057	.8210	.7491
mp+mv+hl+fn	.5426	.7335	**.7775**	.6664	.8147	.7326
mp+mv+tn+hl	.6458	.6961	.7734	.7106	.8180	.7414
mp+mv+tn+img	.6319	.7292	.7434	.7076	.8269	.7423
mp+mv+tn+fn	.5891	.7212	.7459	.6895	.8087	.7288
mp+mv+img+fn	.3337	.6693	.4005	.5791	.7756	.5755
mp+mv+ow+fn+hl	*.5906*	*.7225*	*.7600*	*.6762*	*.8135*	*.7324*
mp+mv+hl+img+tn	.6341	.7325	.7686	.7067	**.8315**	**.7508**
mp+mv+hl+img+tn+fn	.5931	.7313	.7684	.6869	.8291	.7422

Table 4: Evaluation results for different training sets based on train and test categories of 2014 and 2013.

	answers-forums	answers-students	headlines	belief	images	mean
token (one to one)	.5377	.6483	.6393	.6663	.6608	.6375
token (one to many)	.3930	.6566	.5744	.5449	.5901	.5725
lemma (one to one)	**.6423**	.6484	**.6610**	**.7075**	**.7774**	**.6904**
lemma (one to many)	.6043	**.6749**	.6082	.6777	.7469	.6677

Table 5: Single-feature experiments with different alignments: correlation based on cosine similarity.

	img	hl	ow	df	dn	tn
img	*.8689*	.6141	.6767	.3363	.4479	.5183
hl	.7249	*.8173*	.6754	.4179	.6028	.6763
ow	.7039	.5707	*.8926*	.3790	.5666	.5760
df	.5497	.4931	.5969	*.7818*	.5193	.4836
dn	.6957	.5582	.6428	.4008	*.8588*	.3935
tn	.6823	.6453	.6321	.3816	.5222	*.8697*

Table 6: Test data categories of 2014 against each other (columns = training sets, lines = test sets).

machine learning stage. Results showed that the use of fewer similarity features (exclusion of all identical words in each pair of sentences from the calculation of similarity scores) resulted in worse performance of the whole system.

Our system is based on a relatively large feature set, but we were also interested in discovering how well SemantiKLUE would have performed if trained on a single feature. We tested a feature based on cosine similarity between the two centroid vectors as a measure of semantic similarity for each sentence pair as suggested by Schütze (1998) using either tokens or lemmas (see Table 5). We selected cosine between centroid vectors as a candidate feature, because it is most intuitive and naturally connects to the representation of topical information, crucial in capturing textual similarity.

We found that regardless of the alignment (one to one or one to many both for lemma and tokens), the weighted mean of Pearson correlation coefficients is low (.6904 for the one-to-one alignment) for the cosine similarity value calculated with lemma based centroid vectors, but still higher than what is achieved by the more complex system with a large set of features with a poor training set (.6717) in the submission with *mp+mv+smt* used for the training set (see Table 4 for comparison).

As we were interested in identifying the most balanced training sets in the test categories of 2014, we tested all categories against each other. Results are shown in Table 6: the rows of the table correspond to test subsets, while columns represent training sets. The results typeset in italics show that there is a high level of overtraining for the cases in which training and test data are identical. The most balanced and robust test data are those of the image and OnWN categories: they can be used as training data for future experiments.

To sum up, our results show that the best training configuration for SemEval 2015 involves **MSR, headlines, images, and tweet-news categories** (see Table 4). The scatter plots in Figures 2 to 4 relate the similarity score in the gold standard (*x-axis*) to the relatedness score produced by SemantiKLUE (*y-axis*) in its best training configuration, for three of

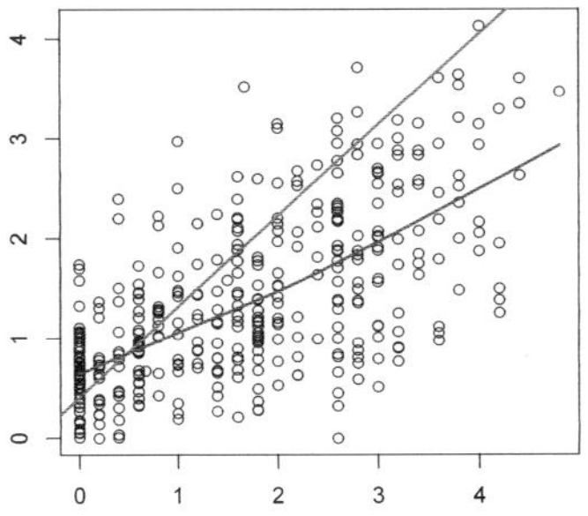

Figure 2: Answers Forums.

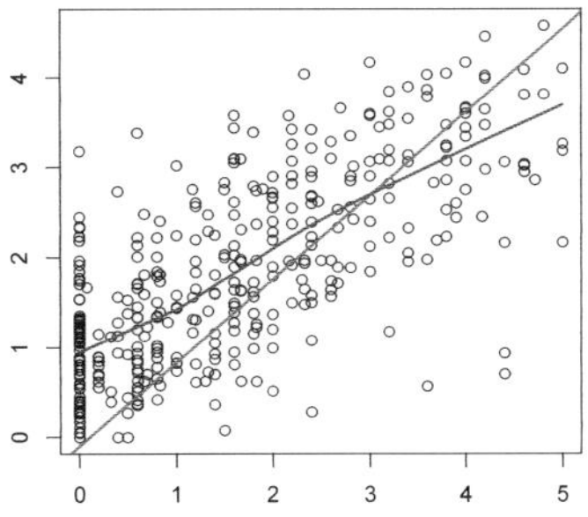

Figure 3: Belief.

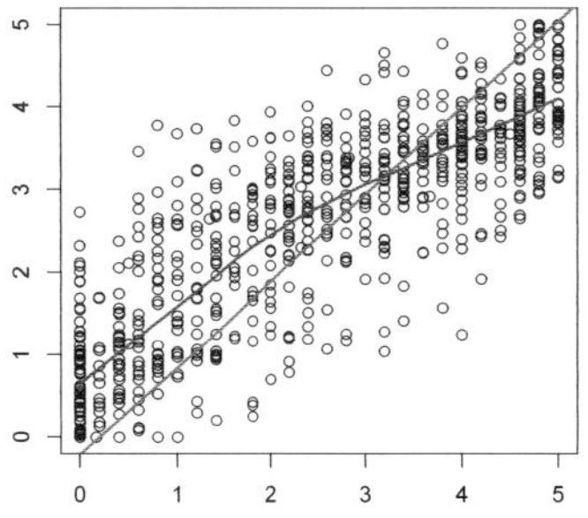

Figure 4: Images.

the five Semeval 2015 test sets. For each plot we show the regression line (drawn in red) as well as a smoother, drawn (in blue) with the LOWESS function from R[15]. Smoothed lines show different non-linear patterns for the different subsets.

4 Qualitative Analysis

In this section, we report the results of a qualitative analysis conducted on sentence pairs for which SemantiKLUE, in the optimal training configuration identified in Section 2.2, made wrong predictions.

Our goal was to identify a taxonomy of SemantiKLUE's problems. Broadly speaking, there are two possibilities for SemantiKLUE to make a wrong similarity guess: the system can **overestimate** the similarity between the two sentences - thus generating a relatedness score higher than the speakers' judgments - or it can **underestimate** similarity - generating a score lower than the gold standard. In the process of interpretation/classification, we relied on the inspection of alignment plots (cf. Figure 1) and on our knowledge of the dynamics of the features within SemantiKLUE.

The analysis was conducted manually on a selected sample of sentence pairs from the test data. We selected sentences for which the absolute difference between the similarity score in the gold standard and the relatedness score produced by SemantiKLUE was between 1.5 and 2.5 points. That range was identified by inspecting the distribution of gold standard/relatedness score differences in the five subsets (corresponding plots are not shown here for reasons of space). Within this range, we randomly picked 40 items (sentence pairs) per subset, 20 with positive difference (underestimation), 20 with negative difference (overestimation)[16].

Let us start with the cases in which SemantiKLUE overestimated STS. We list the identified mistake categories, providing a short description for the cases in which the label is not self-explanatory, and report the percentage of affected sentences. Each item can be affected by more than one mistake type.

- **One or two words** (often very frequent and with generic meaning) **dominate the alignment**, or one sentence is practically a subset of the other: **56%** of the items.
- **Wrong alignments**: **25%** of the items.
- **Modification**: presence of identical modifiers with different heads boosts overall similarity. This mistake type affects **7%** of the cases.
- **Same frame, different participants**: the sentences depict the same event, but the participants (or the background) determine a significant difference in meaning that our system fails to capture. This problem affects **8%** of the items.
- **Same participants, different frames**: **11%** of the items.
- **Negation**: **10%** of the items.
- **(Near) Antonyms**: **8%** of the items.
- **Proper Names**: **18%** of the items.
- **Amounts**: when building the alignment, SemantiKLUE ignores numerical values, which are in some cases crucial in determining (dis)similarities between sentences otherwise near identical (e.g., "2 people killed.." vs. "100 people killed"). This problem affects **18%** of the items.

We now proceed to cases of underestimation, for which we identified the following mistake types:

[15] http://www.r-project.org/

[16] In two cases, we had to enlarge the range to ensure that at least 20 items would have been selected: belief/positive, between 1.4 and 3.5; answers-forums/negative, between 1 and 2.5.

- **Collocations** (e.g, "heads up", "make sense") negatively affect the alignment process: SemantiKLUE would have performed better if multiwords had entered the alignment process as a whole, and not as individual edges. This mistake type affects **10%** of the items.
- **Crucial alignments missing or weaker than expected**: **17%** of the items.
- **The similarity between the sentences is due to logical form, compositionality or world knowledge**. This problem affects **16%** of the items.
- **Different register** makes alignment problematic, even if the sentences are content-wise similar: **12%** of the items.
- **Displacement of different pieces of information between two sentences otherwise centered on the same topic** makes them less similar for SemantiKLUE then for the raters: **28%** of the items.
- **Spelling mistakes** prevent otherwise straightforward alignments: **10%** of the items.
- **Difficult cases**, for which the alignment would simply suggest a score higher than the one predicted by the regressor. Such cases, (**15%**), require further investigation.

5 Conclusion

In this paper, we presented the results of our evaluation experiments on the performance of the SemantiKLUE system (Proisl et al., 2014) on the SemEval-2015 STS task. Our experiments showed that the performance of our system is heavily dependent on the choice of the training set, as we managed to significantly improve the performance of our system with respect to the original submission. The qualitative evaluation sketched in Section 4 provided interesting insights into specific features of the STS data and it allowed us to identify some idiosyncracies (e.g., the behavior of the system in case of alignment of identical words) and weaknesses (e.g., the treatment of multiwords in the process of alignment) that we are already working on improving.

References

Eneko Agirre, Carmen Banea, Claire Cardie, Daniel Cer, Mona Diab, Aitor Gonzalez-Agirre, Weiwei Guo, Iñigo Lopez-Gazpio, Montse Maritxalar, Rada Mihalcea, German Rigau, Larraitz Uria, Janyce Wiebe. 2015. SemEval-2015 Task 2: Semantic Textual Similarity, English, Spanish and Pilot on Interpretability. In *Proceedings of the 9th International Workshop on Semantic Evaluation (SemEval 2015)*. Denver, CO.

Marco Baroni, Silvia Bernardini, Adriano Ferraresi, and Eros Zanchetta. 2009. The WaCky Wide Web: A collection of very large linguistically processed Web-crawled corpora. *Language Resources and Evaluation*, 43(3):209–226.

William A. Gale and Kenneth W. Church. 1993. A program for aligning sentences in bilingual corpora. *Computational Linguistics*, 19(1):75–102.

Lushan Han, Abhay L. Kashyap, Tim Finin, James Mayfield, and Johnathan Weese. 2013. UMBC_EBIQUITY-CORE: Semantic textual similarity systems. In *Proceedings of the 2nd Joint Conference on Lexical and Computational Semantics*. Atlanta, GA.

Claudia Leacock and Martin Chodorow. 1998. Combining local context and WordNet similarity for word sense identification. In Christiane Fellbaum, editor, *WordNet: An Electronic Lexical Database*, pages 265–283. MIT Press, Cambridge, MA.

Dekang Lin. 1998. An information-theoretic definition of similarity. In *Proceedings of the Fifteenth International Conference on Machine Learning*, pages 296–304. San Francisco, CA.

Yuri Lin, Jean-Baptiste Michel, Erez Lieberman Aiden, Jon Orwant, Will Brockman, and Slav Petrov. 2012. Syntactic annotations for the Google Books Ngram Corpus. In *Proceedings of the ACL 2012 Syst. Demonstrations*, pages 169–174, Jeju Island, Korea.

Fabian Pedregosa, Gaël Varoquaux, Alexandre Gramfort, Vincent Michel, Bertrand Thirion, Olivier Grisel, Mathieu Blondel, Peter Prettenhofer, Ron Weiss, Vincent Dubourg, Jake Vanderplas, Alexandre Passos, David Cournapeau, Matthieu Brucher, Matthieu Perrot, and Douard Duchesnay. 2011. Scikit-learn: Machine learning in Python. *Journal of Machine Learning Research*, 12:2825–2830.

Thomas Proisl, Stefan Evert, Paul Greiner, and Besim Kabashi. 2014. SemantiKLUE: Robust semantic similarity at multiple levels using maximum weight matching. In *Proceedings of the 8th International Workshop on Semantic Evaluation (SemEval 2014)*, pages 532–540. Dublin, Ireland.

Roland Schäfer and Felix Bildhauer. 2012. Building large corpora from the web using a new efficient tool chain. In *Proceedings of the Eighth International Conference on Language Resources and Evaluation (LREC '12)*, pages 486–493. Istanbul, Turkey.

Hinrich Schütze. 1998. Automatic word sense discrimination. *Computational Linguistics*, 24(1):97–123.

ECNU: Using Traditional Similarity Measurements and Word Embedding for Semantic Textual Similarity Estimation

Jiang Zhao, Man Lan*, Jun Feng Tian
Shanghai Key Laboratory of Multidimensional Information Processing
Department of Computer Science and Technology,
East China Normal University, Shanghai 200241, P. R. China
51121201042,10112130275@ecnu.cn; mlan@cs.ecnu.edu.cn*

Abstract

This paper reports our submissions to semantic textual similarity task, i.e., task 2 in Semantic Evaluation 2015. We built our systems using various traditional features, such as string-based, corpus-based and syntactic similarity metrics, as well as novel similarity measures based on distributed word representations, which were trained using deep learning paradigms. Since the training and test datasets consist of instances collected from various domains, three different strategies of the usage of training datasets were explored: (1) use all available training datasets and build a unified supervised model for all test datasets; (2) select the most similar training dataset and separately construct a individual model for each test set; (3) adopt multi-task learning framework to make full use of available training sets. Results on the test datasets show that using all datasets as training set achieves the best averaged performance and our best system ranks 15 out of 73.

1 Introduction

Estimating the degree of semantic similarity between two sentences is the building block of many natural language processing (NLP) applications, such as textual entailment (Zhao et al., 2014a), text summarization (Lloret et al., 2008), question answering (Celikyilmaz et al., 2010), etc. Therefore, semantic textual similarity (STS) has been received an increasing amount of attention in recent years, e.g., the Semantic Textual Similarity competitions in Semantic Evaluation Exercises have been held from 2012 to 2014. This year the participants in the STS task in *SemEval* 2015 (Agirre et al., 2015) are required to rate the similar degree of a pair of sentences by a value from 0 (no relation) to 5 (semantic equivalence) with an optional confidence score.

To identify semantic textual similarity of text pairs, most existing works adopt at least one of the following feature types: (1) string based similarity (Bär et al., 2012; Jimenez et al., 2012) which employs common functions to calculate similarities over string sequences extracted from original strings, e.g., lemma, stem, or *n*-gram sequences; (2) corpus based similarity (Šarić et al., 2012; Han et al., 2013) where distributional models such as *Latent Semantic Analysis* (LSA) (Landauer and Dumais, 1997), are used to derive the distributional vectors of words from a large corpus according to their occurrence patterns, afterwards, similarities of sentence pairs are calculated using these vectors; (3) knowledge based method (Shareghi and Bergler, 2013; Mihalcea et al., 2006) which estimates the similarities with the aid of external resources, such as WordNet[1]. Among them, lots of researchers (Sultan et al., 2014; Han et al., 2013) leverage different word alignment strategies to bring word-level similarity to sentence-level similarity.

In this work, we first borrow aforementioned effective types of similarity measurements including string-based, corpus-based, syntactic features and so on, to capture the semantic similarity between two sentences. Beside, we also present a novel feature type based on *word embeddings* that are induced using neural language models over a large raw cor-

[1] http://wordnet.princeton.edu/

pus (Mikolov et al., 2013b). Then these features are served as input of a regression model. Notice that, the organizers provide us seventeen training datasets and five test datasets, which are drawn from different but related domains. Accordingly, we build three different systems in terms of the usage of training datasets: (1) exploit all the training datasets and train a single model for all test datasets; (2) choose one domain-dependent training dataset for each test dataset using *cosine* distance selection criterion and train models individually for each test dataset; (3) to overcome overuse or underuse of training datasets, we adopt multi-task learning (MTL) framework to make full use of available training datasets, that is, for each test set the main task is built upon designated training datasets and the rest training datasets are used in the auxiliary tasks.

The rest of this paper is organized as follows. Section 2 describes various similarity measurements used in our systems. System setups and experimental results on training and test datasets are presented in Section 3. Finally, conclusions and future work are given in Section 4.

2 Semantic Similarity Measurements

Following our previous work (Zhao et al., 2014b), we adopted the traditional widely-used features (i.e., string, corpus, syntactic features) for semantic similarity measurements. In this work, we also proposed several novel features using word embeddings.

2.1 Preprocessing

Several text preprocessing operations were performed before we extracted features. We first converted the contractions to their formal writings, for example, *doesn't* is rewritten as *does not*. Then the WordNet-based Lemmatizer implemented in Natural Language Toolkit[2] was used to lemmatize all words to their nearest base forms in WordNet, for example, *was* is lemmatized to *be*. After that, We replaced a word from one sentence with another word from the other sentence if these two words share the same meaning, where WordNet was used to look up synonyms. No word sense disambiguation was performed and all synsets in WordNet for a particular lemma were considered.

[2]http://nltk.org/

2.2 String Based Features

We firstly recorded length information of given sentences pairs using the following eight measure functions: $|A|, |B|, |A - B|, |B - A|, |A \cup B|, |A \cap B|, \frac{(|A|-|B|)}{|B|}, \frac{(|B|-|A|)}{|A|}$, where $|A|$ stands for the number of non-repeated words in sentence A , $|A - B|$ means the number of unmatched words found in A but not in B , $|A \cup B|$ stands for the set size of non-repeated words found in either A or B and $|A \cap B|$ means the set size of shared words found in both A and B .

Motivated by the hypothesis that two texts are considered to be semantic similar if they share more common strings, we adopted the following five types of measurements: (1) longest common sequence similarity on the original and lemmatized sentences; (2) `Jaccard`, `Dice`, `Overlap` coefficient on original word sequences; (3) `Jaccard` similarity using *n*-grams, where *n*-grams were obtained at three different levels, i.e., the original word level (*n*=1,2,3), the lemmatized word level (*n*=1,2,3) and the character level (n=2,3,4); (4) weighted word overlap feature (Šarić et al., 2012) that takes the importance of words into consideration, where Web 1T 5-gram Corpus[3] was used to estimate the importance of words; (5) sentences were represented as vectors in *tf*idf* schema based on their lemmatized forms and then these vectors were used to calculate `cosine`, `Manhattan`, `Euclidean` distance and `Pearson`, `Spearmanr`, `Kendalltau` correlation coefficients.

Totally, we got thirty-one string based features.

2.3 Corpus Based Features

The distributional meanings of words own good semantic properties and *Latent Semantic Analysis* (LSA) (Landauer and Dumais, 1997) is widely used to estimate the distributional vectors of words. Hence, we adopted two distributional word sets released by TakeLab (Šarić et al., 2012), where LSA was performed on the New York Times Annotated Corpus (NYT)[4] and Wikipedia. Then two strategies were used to convert the distributional meanings of words to sentence level: (i) simply summing up the distributional vector of each word w in the sentence, (ii)

[3]https://catalog.ldc.upenn.edu/LDC2006T13
[4]https://catalog.ldc.upenn.edu/LDC2008T19

using the information content (Šarić et al., 2012) to weigh the LSA vector of each word w and then summing them up. After that we used *cosine* similarity to measure the similarity of two sentences based on these vectors. Besides, we used the Co-occurrence Retrieval Model (CRM) (Weeds, 2003) as another type of corpus based feature. The CRM was calculated based on a notion of substitutability, that is, the more appropriate it was to substitute word w_1 in place of word w_2 in a suitable natural language task, the more semantically similar they were.

At last, we obtained six corpus based features.

2.4 Syntactic Features

Besides semantic similarity, we also estimated the similarities of sentence pairs at syntactic level. Stanford CoreNLP toolkit (Manning et al., 2014) was used to obtain the POS tag sequences for each sentence. Afterwards, we performed eight measure functions described above in Section 2.2 over these sequences, resulting in eight syntactic features.

2.5 Word Embedding Features

Recently, deep learning has archived a great success in the fields of computer vision, automatic speech recognition and natural language processing. One result of its application in NLP, i.e., word embeddings, has been successfully explored in named entity recognition, chunking (Turian et al., 2010) and semantic word similarities(Mikolov et al., 2013a), etc. The distributed representations of words (i.e., word embeddings) learned using neural networks over a large raw corpus have been shown that they performed significantly better than LSA for preserving linear regularities among words (Mikolov et al., 2013a). Due to its superior performance, we adopted word embeddings to estimate the similarities of sentence pairs. In our experiments, we used two different word embeddings: *word2vec* (Mikolov et al., 2013b) and *Collobert and Weston* embeddings (Turian et al., 2010). The word embeddings from Word2vec are distributed within the word2vec toolkit[5] and they are 300-dimensional vectors learned from Google News Corpus which consists of over a 100 billion words. The Collobert and Weston embeddings are learned over a part of RCV1 corpus which consists of 63 millions words, resulting in 100-dimensional continuous vectors. To obtain the sentence representations from word representations, we used *idf* to weigh the embedding vectors of words and simply summed them up. Although the word embedding is obtained from large corpus in consideration of its context, using this bag of words (BOW) representation of sentences, the current word sequence in sentence is neglected. After that, we used `cosine`, `Manhattan`, `Euclidean` functions and `Pearson`, `Spearmanr`, `Kendalltau` correlation coefficients to calculate the similarities based on these synthetic sentence representations.

[5]https://code.google.com/p/word2vec

2.6 Other Features

Besides the shallow semantic similarities between words and strings, we also calculated the similarities of named entities in two sentences using longest common sequence function. Seven types of named entities, i.e., *location*, *organization*, *date*, *money*, *person*, *time* and *percent*, recognized by Stanford CoreNLP toolkit (Manning et al., 2014) were considered. We designed a binary feature to indicate whether two sentences in a given pair have the same polarity (i.e., *affirmative* or *negative*) by looking up a manually-collected negation list with 29 negation words (e.g., *scarcely*, *no*, *little*). Finally, we obtained in eight features.

3 Experiments and Results

3.1 Datasets

Participants built their systems on seventeen datasets in development period and evaluated their systems on five test datasets in test period. Each dataset consists of a number of sentence pairs and each pair has a human-assigned similarity score in the range [0, 5] which increases with similarity. The datasets were collected from different but related domains. Due to limitation of page length, we only provide a brief description of test sets in Table 1. Refer (Agirre et al., 2014) for more details. As we can see from this table, datasets from different domains have distinct average lengths of sentence `A` and `B`.

Dataset	# of pairs	average length
answers-forums	2000	(17.56,17.37)
answers-students	1500	(10.49,11.17)
belief	2000	(15.16,14.56)
headlines	1500	(7.86,7.91)
images	1500	(10.59,10.58)

Table 1: The statistics of test datasets for STS task in *SemEval* 2015.

3.2 Experimental Setups

We built three different systems according to the usage of training datasets as follows.

allData: We used all the training datasets and built a single global regression model regardless of domain information of different test datasets.

DesignatedData: For each test dataset, we calculated the cosine distance with every candidate training dataset. Then the training dataset with the lowest distance score was chose as the training dataset to fit a regression model for specific test dataset.

$$\texttt{Dist}(X_{tst}, X_c) = 1 - \sum_{x_i \in X_{tst}} \sum_{x_j \in X_c} \frac{\text{cosine}(x_i, x_j)}{|X_{tst}||X_c|}$$

MTL: On one hand, taking all the training datasets into consideration may hurt the performance since training and test datasets are from different domains. On the other hand, using the most related datasets leads to insufficient usage of available datasets. Therefore, we considered to adopt multi-task learning framework to take full advantage of available training sets. Under multi-task learning framework, a main task learns together with other related auxiliary tasks at the same time, using a shared representation. This often leads to a better model for the main task, because it allows the learner to use the commonality among the tasks. Hence, for each test dataset we selected the datasets whose *cosine* distances are less than 0.1 (at least one training set) as training set to construct the main task, and then used the remaining training sets to construct auxiliary tasks. In this work, we adopted the robust multi-task feature learning (rMTFL) (Gong et al., 2012), which assumes that the model W can be decomposed into two components: a shared feature structure P that captures task relatedness and a group-sparse structure Q that detects outlier tasks. Specifically, it solves following formulation:

$$\min_{W} \sum_{i=1}^{t} \|W_i^F X_i - Y_i\|_F^2 + \rho_1 \|P\|_{2,1} + \rho_2 \|Q^T\|_{2,1}$$

$$\text{subject to} : W = P + Q$$

where X_i denotes the input matrix of the i-th task, Y_i denotes its corresponding label, W_i is the model for task i, the regularization parameter ρ_1 controls the joint feature learning, and the regularization parameter ρ_2 controls the columnwise group sparsity on Q that detects outliers.

In our preliminary experiments, several regression algorithms were examined, including Support Vector Regression (SVR, *linear*), Random Forest (RF) and Gradient Boosting (GB) implemented in the scikit-learn toolkit (Pedregosa et al., 2011). The system performance is evaluated using Pearson correlation (r).

3.3 Results on Training Data

To configure the parameters in the three systems, i.e., the trade-off parameter c in SVR, the number of trees n in RF, the number of boosting stages n in GB in **allData** and **DesignatedData**, $\rho_{1,2}$ in **MTL**, we conducted a series of experiments on STS 2014 datasets (eleven datasets for training, six datasets for development). Table 2 shows the Pearson performance of our systems on development datasets. We explored a large scale of parameter values and only the best result for each algorithm was listed due to the limitation of page length. The numbers in the brackets in algorithms column indicate the parameter values and those in bold font represent the best performance for each dataset and system. From the table we find that (1) GB and SVR obtain the best averaged results in system **allData** and **DesignatedData** respectively; (2) although **DesignatedData** uses only one most-closely dataset for training for each test set, it achieves comparable or even better performance on some datasets when compared with **allData**; (3) our multi-task learning framework can indeed boost the performance.

3.4 Results on Test Data

According to the results on training datasets, we configured three submitted runs as following:

Algorithms	deft-forum	deft-news	headlines	images	OnWN	tweet-news	Mean
SVR (0.01)	0.458	**0.761**	**0.728**	**0.813**	0.836	0.727	0.721
RF (65)	0.491	0.751	0.718	0.789	**0.873**	**0.741**	0.727
GB (50)	**0.499**	0.760	0.725	0.805	0.863	0.739	**0.732**
SVR (0.1)	**0.549**	**0.725**	**0.765**	**0.790**	0.810	0.740	**0.730**
RF (75)	0.513	0.709	0.741	0.768	**0.814**	**0.767**	0.719
GB (50)	0.504	0.694	0.738	0.790	0.809	0.751	0.714
MTL (0.1, 0.1)	0.556	0.772	0.738	0.808	0.819	0.745	0.740

Table 2: Pearson of **allData, DesignatedData** using different algorithms and **MTL** on STS 2014 datasets.

RUN	answers-forums	answers-students	belief	headlines	images	Mean	Rank
ECNU-1stSVMALL	**0.715**	0.712	**0.728**	0.798	0.847	**0.755**	15
ECNU-2ndSVMONE	0.687	0.733	0.698	**0.820**	0.836	0.747	19
ECNU-3rdMTL	0.692	**0.752**	0.695	0.805	**0.858**	0.752	18
DLSCU-S1	0.739	0.773	0.749	0.825	0.864	0.785	1
ExBThemis-themisexp	0.695	0.778	0.748	0.825	0.853	0.773	2

Table 3: Results of our three runs on STS 2015 test datasets, as well as top rank runs.

ECNU-1stSVMALL which builds a global model on all datasets using SVR with parameter c=0.1; **ECNU-2ndSVMONE** which fits individual model for each test set on a designated training set using GB with parameter n=50; **ECNU-3rdMTL** which employs robust multi-task feature learning with parameter $\rho_1 = \rho_2 = 0.1$.

Table 3 summarizes the results of our submitted runs on test datasets officially released by the organizers, as well as the top rank runs. In terms of mean Pearson measurement, system **ECNU-1stSVMALL** performs the best, which is comparable to **ECNU-3rdMTL**. However, the **ECNU-2ndSVMONE** performs the worst. This is inconsistent with the results on training datasets wherein **ECNU-3rdMTL** yields the best performance. On test dataset, we find that **ECNU-3rdMTL** has much worse performances than **ECNU-1stSVMALL** on answers-forums and belief while it achieves much better results on answers-students, headlines and images datasets. The possible reason may be that the training dataset selected from the candidate datasets in main task are ill-suited for answers-forums and belief test datasets, which is also verified by the results of system **ECNU-2ndSVMONE**. It is noteworthy that on answers-students and headlines **ECNU-2ndSVMONE** achieves much better results than **ECNU-1stSVMALL** although the former system only uses much less training instances (750,750 vs. 10592). In addition, the difference between top system **DLSCU-S1** and our systems is about 3%, which means our systems are promising.

4 Conclusion

We used traditional NLP features including string-based, corpus-based and syntacitc features, for textual semantic similarity estimation, as well as novel word embedding features. We also presented three different systems to compare the strategies of different usage of training data, i.e., single supervised learning with all training datasets and individual training dataset for each test dataset, and multi-task learning framework. Our best system achieves 15th place out of 73 systems on test datasets. Noticeably each system achieves the best performance on different test datasets, which indicates the usage of training datasets is important, we will explore more sophisticated way to utilize these training datasets in future work.

Acknowledgements

This research is supported by grants from Science and Technology Commission of Shanghai Municipality under research grant no. (14DZ2260800 and 15ZR1410700) and Shanghai Collaborative Innovation Center of Trustworthy Software for Internet of

Things (ZF1213).

References

Eneko Agirre, Carmen Banea, and et al. 2014. SemEval-2014 task 10: Multilingual semantic textual similarity. In *Proceedings of the 8th International Workshop on Semantic Evaluation (SemEval 2014)*, pages 81–91.

Eneko Agirre, Carmen Banea, and et al. 2015. SemEval-2015 task 2: Semantic textual similarity, English, Spanish and pilot on interpretability. In *Proceedings of the 9th International Workshop on Semantic Evaluation (SemEval 2015)*, June.

Daniel Bär, Chris Biemann, Iryna Gurevych, and Torsten Zesch. 2012. Ukp: Computing semantic textual similarity by combining multiple content similarity measures. In *Proceedings of the First Joint Conference on Lexical and Computational Semantics*, pages 435–440.

Asli Celikyilmaz, Dilek Hakkani-Tur, and Gokhan Tur. 2010. LDA based similarity modeling for question answering. In *Proceedings of the NAACL HLT 2010 Workshop on Semantic Search*, pages 1–9.

Pinghua Gong, Jieping Ye, and Changshui Zhang. 2012. Robust multi-task feature learning. In *Proceedings of the 18th ACM SIGKDD international conference on Knowledge discovery and data mining*, pages 895–903.

Lushan Han, Abhay L. Kashyap, Tim Finin, James Mayfield, and Jonathan Weese. 2013. UMBC_EBIQUITY-CORE: Semantic textual similarity systems. In *Second *SEM*, pages 44–52.

Sergio Jimenez, Claudia Becerra, and Alexander Gelbukh. 2012. Soft cardinality: A parameterized similarity function for text comparison. In **SEM 2012 and (SemEval 2012)*, pages 449–453.

Thomas K Landauer and Susan T Dumais. 1997. A solution to Plato's problem: The latent semantic analysis theory of acquisition, induction, and representation of knowledge. *Psychological review*.

Elena Lloret, Oscar Ferrández, Rafael Munoz, and Manuel Palomar. 2008. A text summarization approach under the influence of textual entailment. In *Proceedings of NLPCS 2008*, pages 22–31.

Christopher D. Manning, Mihai Surdeanu, John Bauer, Jenny Finkel, Steven J. Bethard, and David McClosky. 2014. The Stanford CoreNLP natural language processing toolkit. In *Proceedings of 52nd ACL: System Demonstrations*, pages 55–60.

Rada Mihalcea, Courtney Corley, and Carlo Strapparava. 2006. Corpus-based and knowledge-based measures of text semantic similarity. In *AAAI*, volume 6, pages 775–780.

Tomas Mikolov, Kai Chen, Greg Corrado, and Jeffrey Dean. 2013a. Efficient estimation of word representations in vector space. *arXiv preprint arXiv:1301.3781*.

Tomas Mikolov, Ilya Sutskever, Kai Chen, Greg S Corrado, and Jeff Dean. 2013b. Distributed representations of words and phrases and their compositionality. In *Advances in Neural Information Processing Systems*, pages 3111–3119.

Fabian Pedregosa, Gaël Varoquaux, Alexandre Gramfort, et al. 2011. Scikit-learn: Machine learning in Python. *The Journal of Machine Learning Research*, 12:2825–2830.

Ehsan Shareghi and Sabine Bergler. 2013. CLaC-CORE: Exhaustive feature combination for measuring textual similarity. In *Second Joint Conference on Lexical and Computational Semantics (*SEM)*.

Md Arafat Sultan, Steven Bethard, and Tamara Sumner. 2014. DLS@CU: sentence similarity from word alignment. In *SemEval 2014*, pages 241–246.

Joseph Turian, Lev Ratinov, and Yoshua Bengio. 2010. Word representations: a simple and general method for semi-supervised learning. In *Proceedings of the 48th Annual Meeting of the Association for Computational Linguistics*, pages 384–394.

Frane Šarić, Goran Glavaš, Mladen Karan, Jan Šnajder, and Bojana Dalbelo Bašić. 2012. TakeLab: Systems for measuring semantic text similarity. In **SEM 2012 and (SemEval 2012)*, pages 441–448.

Julie Elizabeth Weeds. 2003. *Measures and applications of lexical distributional similarity*. Ph.D. thesis, University of Sussex.

Jiang Zhao, Man Lan, Zheng-Yu Niu, and Dong-Hong Ji. 2014a. Recognizing cross-lingual textual entailment with co-training using similarity and difference views. In *IJCNN 2014, Beijing, China, 2014*, pages 3705–3712.

Jiang Zhao, Tiantian Zhu, and Man Lan. 2014b. Ecnu: One stone two birds: Ensemble of heterogenous measures for semantic relatedness and textual entailment. In *Proceedings of the SemEval 2014*, pages 271–277, Dublin, Ireland, August.

UQeResearch: Semantic Textual Similarity Quantification

Hamed Hassanzadeh[1], Tudor Groza[1,2], Anthony Nguyen[3], Jane Hunter[1]
[1]School of ITEE, The University of Queensland, St Lucia, QLD, Australia
[2]Garvan Institute of Medical Research, Darlinghurst, NSW, Australia
[3]Australian e-Health Research Centre, CSIRO, Brisbane, QLD, Australia
h.hassanzadeh@uq.edu.au, t.groza@garvan.org.au,
anthony.nguyen@csiro.au, jane@itee.uq.edu.au

Abstract

This paper presents an approach for estimating the Semantic Textual Similarity of full English sentences as specified in Shared Task 2 of SemEval-2015. The semantic similarity of sentence pairs is quantified from three perspectives - structural, syntactical, and semantic. The numerical representations of the derived similarity measures are then applied to train a regression ensemble. Although none of these three sets of measures is able to represent the semantic similarity of two sentences individually, our experimental results show that the combination of these features can precisely assess the semantic similarity of the sentences. In the English subtask our system's best result ranked 35 among 73 system runs with 0.7189 average Pearson correlation over five test sets. This was 0.08 correlation points less than the best submitted run.

1 Introduction

Semantic textual similarity (STS) aims to automatically estimate the relatedness of the meaning of sentences (Agirre et al., 2015). The literature consists of a series of well-established frameworks to explore a deeper understanding of the semantic relationship between entities, ranging from ontological reasoning to compositional as well as distributional semantics (Cohen et al., 2009). However, automatically estimating the semantic similarity of full sentences is still a challenging task.

Our system aims to quantify the similarity of pairs of sentences by encoding a variety of relatedness features in a vector of attributes and then predicting their similarity scores by employing machine-learning algorithms. Different syntactic, semantic, and structural similarity measures have been applied to quantify the similarity of texts. We have chosen to approach the estimation of similarity as a regression problem. Hence, we use the quantified similarity of sentence pairs to train a regressor that can then be applied to predict similarity scores for the unseen pairs. The paper is structured as follows: Section 2 presents the proposed similarity measures. In Section 3, the regression models are introduced and the experimental results are discussed in detail. The conclusions are summarized in Section 4.

2 Similarity Measures

In this section we describe the similarity measures we have employed to calculate semantic relatedness of pairs of sentences.

2.1 Syntactic Similarity Measures

Bags of words overlap: A simple measure for computing the similarity of a sentence pair is the number of words they have in common. Although a pair of sentences with the same bag of words (i.e. unordered list of all words of a sentence) can convey completely different meanings, this measure along with some structural measures can form an effective criterion for semantic comparison.

Bags of lemmatised/stemmed words overlap: The value of this feature is computed using the same method as above, however, instead of using bags of words, it uses bags of lemmas / stems.

Set similarity of lemmatised effective words: There are a number of words in a sentence that do not play effective roles in modelling the meaning of that sentence, such as determiners (*the, a, an*) and preposition or subordinating conjunctions (*in, on, at*). We remove these terms from the bag of words of a sentence and we call the remaining words the set of effective words. In this measure we lemmatise the effective words and compare the resulting sets of lemmas for a pair of sentences.

Jaccard similarity of sets of words/lemmas: A sentence can be considered as a set of words. To incorporate this perspective, we calculate the Jaccard similarity coefficient of a pair of sentences.

Windows of words overlap: We perform a sliding window of different sizes (from window of two words up to the size of the smaller sentence in a pair) over a pair of sentences. Afterwards we compute the total number of equal windows of words of two sentences. Also, we keep the size of the longest equal window of words that two sentences share together. Due to varying sizes of sentences and therefore varying sizes and number of windows, we normalise each of these measures to reach a comparable value between zero and one. The same window-based measures can be alternatively be calculated by only considering effective words in sentences and also, from a grammatical perspective, by only considering Part of Speech (POS) tags of the constituent words of sentences.

Ratio of shared skipped bigrams: Skipped bigrams are the pairs of words which are created by combining two words of a sentence that are located in arbitrary positions. The set of these bigrams can then be used as a basis for similarity comparison. We create the skipped bigrams of participating verbs, nouns, adjectives, and adverbs of a sentence (we ignore other unimportant terms) and then calculate the intersection of each set of these bigrams with the corresponding set from the other sentence in a pair.

Pairwise Sentence Polarity: We investigate the presence of some lexical elements that act as negation agent, e.g., *not, neither, no*, etc. We apply the NegEx algorithm (Chapmana et al., 2001) to find the negation in sentences and then we perform pairwise comparison of the polarity of sentences.

Ratio of Sentence Lengths: The relative length of two sentences (length of smaller sentence over the longer one) provides a simple measure of similarity. However, this naïve attribute of a pair can be useful when combined with other more conceptual measures.

2.2 Structural Similarity Measures

Ratio of number of clauses: The meaning of a sentence can be inferred from the meaning of its clause(s). Consequently, the equality of the clauses of a pair of sentences provides another measure for assessing the relatedness of those sentences. In this case, the level of equality is calculated by analysing the parse tree of each sentence and finding the number of clauses that each sentence is composed of. The ratio of this clause-level equality is then obtained by dividing the smaller number of clauses by the larger number of clauses for each pair. Parse trees were produced with the Stanford Parser (Klein et al., 2003).

Reduced parse tree overlap: While the previous measure only considered the shallow size-based comparison, this measure provides a more in-depth analysis of the structural similarity. More concretely, it quantifies the overlap of the parsed trees for each sentence, composed of only the POS tags of the effective words.

2.3 Semantic Similarity Measures

Role-based word-by-word similarity: In order to compute this measure, we first split the sentences into clauses and determine the subject, predicate and object within each clause. Each of these roles is then transformed into a bag of lemmatised words, which is then compared to corresponding bags of lemmatised words denoting the same role in the other sentence. The similarity between the two bags of words is calculated using a mixture of two well-known semantic similarity measures – i.e., Lin (1998) and Wu & Palmer (1994), both having WordNet (Miller, 1995) as background knowledge. Due to WordNet's lower coverage of verbs, for the words in the predicate bags we compute the similarity between words using FrameNet (Fillmore et al., 2003) and by comparing sets of corresponding frames of words in each bag.

Semantic similarity of effective words: Given the sets of effective words of a pair of sentences, we compute their similarity using the same method as above, however, without taking into account the underlying roles – i.e., it is computed in a sentence-wide manner.

Cosine similarity of Information Content (IC) vectors: We map the sequence of words in a sentence to a vector of corresponding numeric values. In order to create this vector we use the notion of Information Content (IC) (Resnik, 1995). The relatedness of a given pair can then be estimated by employing a distance measure between the two vectors, such as the cosine similarity.

Role-based POS tags alignment: For this similarity measure we get the POS tags of each word in the subject and object phrases of a sentence and form a sequence of these tags. We then employ Needleman-Wunsch algorithm (Needleman et al., 1970) for aligning these sequences of POS tags to find their similarity ratio.

WordNet/FrameNet based synonym similarity: Other sets of vocabulary-based similarity measures can be devised by getting all the synonyms of each word of sentences and considering them in the comparison process. One of these measures can be calculated by applying WordNet for obtaining synonyms of words. For this WordNet synonymy measure, the corresponding synsets of all the lemmas of the effective words in sentences are retrieved from WordNet. The sets of synsets of a pair of sentences are then compared to each other and the ratio of their similarity is calculated. Another similar measure can be calculated using FrameNet as the background knowledge instead of WordNet.

Cosine similarity of the best senses: This measure uses a WordNet-based word sense disambiguation approach to find the best senses of effective words of a pair. These senses are then used to form vectors of best senses, which can then be compared using cosine similarity.

Normalised set similarity for best senses synsets: Similar to the previous measure, we apply word sense disambiguation to retrieve the best senses for all words of the sentence, and subsequently create a set of synsets which can be compared to the corresponding set of synsets extracted from the other sentence.

Normalised set similarity of the best senses skipped bigrams: We create a set of skipped bigrams of best senses of words instead of the skipped bigrams of words of a sentence and then calculate each pair's sets similarity.

Similarity of sets of associated terms: Our last two sets of features make use of vector space models, using Wikipedia English articles as the background corpus and Hyperspace Analogue to Language (HAL) model to produce term vectors (Lund et al., 1996) by employing the SemanticVector library (Widdows et al., 2008). The associated terms for words of a sentence form a set that can be compared with a corresponding set of another sentence – for example, by calculating their intersection. The resulting value is normalised by size of the smallest set.

Cosine similarity of matrices of associated terms vectors: For this last feature, we use the numerical representation (vector) of each term, retrieved from the distributional model, to form a matrix of associated terms vectors for a sentence. To enhance the effectiveness of this similarity measure, only vectors of effective words of a sentence are used to build the matrix.

3 Results

In this section, the results from applying our system to STS 2015 (Task 2) are presented. Before discussing the results, we firstly describe the experimental setup and training process.

3.1 Experimental Setup

All the data released in STS 2012, 2013, and 2014 was permitted to be used to develop and train the systems. All the data sets consist of pairs of sentences along with their human annotated similarity scores. The similarity scores ranged from 0 to 5, with 0 representing completely dissimilar pairs and 5 representing perfect similarity (or equality). In order to evaluate the English STS systems, five test sets were provided. Although the test data in total consists of 8500 pairs, a subset of the instances of each test set was sampled and used for the final official evaluations by the organizers. The official measurement criterion for evaluation is the Pearson correlation. It should be mentioned that prior to computing the measures the punctuations were removed from sentences to avoid naïve token-level matching of them in some similarity measures.

3.2 Experiments Over Training Data

We first performed a number of experiments over the training data in order to prepare the final regression system. The training set consists of 10592 annotated pairs, achieved by merging previous SemEval STS data sets. We approached the semantic similarity estimation as a regression problem. Hence, we investigated different regression algorithms and Table 1 lists their evaluation results. The WEKA implementations of these algorithms have been used in our system (Hall et al., 2009).

Algorithm	Pearson Correlation	Root mean squared error
Regression Algorithms		
RepTree	0.6747	1.1207
K*	0.6968	1.1497
Linear Regression	0.6809	1.1088
Regression By Classification		
Regression by Random Forest	0.7745	0.964
Regression by KNN	0.7139	1.0651
Regression Ensemble		
Ensemble	**0.7813**	**0.9484**

Table 1: Experiments on training data (5-fold cross validation).

The first part of Table 1 shows the results achieved by selected regression approaches. Among these algorithms, K* achieved the best Pearson correlation. In regression by classification, the continuous similarity scores are discretised to nominal values. Then, a classifier was used to categorize instances into the resultant nominal classes. In our experiments, the continuous range of 0 to 5 scores is discretised into 10 bins. The best results have been achieved by applying Random Forest as the base classifier. Finally, the ensemble of regressors is composed of three meta-regressors: bagging, random SubSpace, and regression by discretisation. Regression by discretisation follows precisely the same methodology as above. The bagging strategy uses RepTree as its first level regressor, while the random SubSpace employs the K* algorithm. The final outputs of the ensemble are the average of the prediction values from all of the regressors. This ensemble gained the best correlation amongst all of the models.

3.3 Results Over Test Data and Discussions

We submitted three different runs to the English STS 2015 Task 2. The same regression ensemble has been applied to all three runs. The main difference between them is related to the data that was used for training. The data used to train the *run1* system were STS 2012 train and test sets, STS 2013 test set, and STS 2014 test set. In the second system (*run2)*, we used all the run1 data as well as one additional data set which was the training set of the SICK corpus (Marelli et al., 2014). It was introduced in SemEval-2014 Task 1. Contrary to STS corpora, the similarity scores from the SICK corpus ranged from 1 to 5 (instead of 0 to 5). We gave a unique numerical ID to each pair in the data sets, which were then kept in the feature vectors as well. In *run3,* exactly the same data was used as *run1* but without the IDs in the feature vectors.

	run1	run2	run3
answers-forums	0.5923	0.6132	**0.6188**
answers-students	0.6876	**0.6882**	0.6757
belief	0.5904	0.6229	**0.7178**
headlines	0.7521	**0.7602**	0.7549
images	0.7817	**0.7855**	0.7769
Means	0.7032	0.7130	**0.7189**
Rank	40	37	**35**

Table 2: Our systems' results over test sets.

Table 2 lists the results of our system runs. It can be observed that the third run achieved better overall correlations compared with the other two. By applying the additional data set (i.e. training set of the SICK corpus) the average correlation slightly improved (i.e. in run2). However, as previously mentioned, the difference in scoring the semantic similarities (0-5 vs. 1-5) caused the regressor model to fail to encode the scores properly (especially for lower similarity scores). In addition, as a side experiment, but contrary to the positive experience gained from SemEval-2014 semantic relatedness Task, the unique numerical ID had a negative impact over the outcome of the system (comparing run1's results – with IDs, to run3's – without IDs).

4 Conclusions

This paper describes the system we submitted to SemEval-2015 Task 2: STS in order to estimate semantic similarity of full English sentences. We approached the task as a regression problem. An ensemble of regressors as well as a variety of similarity measures was proposed. These measures (that compared syntactic, semantic, and structural aspects) were extracted from pairs of sentences. Our system's best result ranked 35 among 73 submitted runs with 0.7189 average Pearson correlations over five test sets. This was 0.08 correlation points less than the best submitted run.

Acknowledgments

This research is funded by the Australian Research Council (ARC) Discovery Early Career Researcher Award (DECRA) -- DE120100508. It is also partially supported by CSIRO Postgraduate Studentship.

References

Eneko Agirre, Carmen Banea, Claire Cardie, Daniel Cer, Mona Diab, Aitor Gonzalez-Agirre, Weiwei Guo, Iñigo Lopez-Gazpio, Montse Maritxalar, Rada Mihalcea, German Rigau, Larraitz Uria, and Janyce Wiebe. 2015. SemEval-2015 Task 2: Semantic Textual Similarity, English, Spanish and Pilot on Interpretability. In *Proceedings of the 9th International Workshop on Semantic Evaluation (SemEval 2015)*, Denver, CO.

Wendy W. Chapmana, Will Bridewellb, Paul Hanburya, Gregory F. Coopera, and Bruce G. Buchanan. 2001. A simple algorithm for identifying negated findings and diseases in discharge summaries. *Journal of Biomedical Informatics, 34*(5), 301-310.

Trevor Cohen and Dominic Widdows. 2009. Empirical distributional semantics: Methods and biomedical applications. *Journal of Biomedical Informatics, 42*(2), 390-405.

Charles J. Fillmore, Christopher R. Johnson, and Miriam R.L. Petruck. 2003. Background to FrameNet. *International Journal of Lexicography, 16*(3), 235-250.

Mark Hall, Eibe Frank, Geoffrey Holmes, Bernhard Pfahringer, Peter Reutemann, and Ian H. Witten. 2009. The WEKA Data Mining Software: An Update. *SIGKDD Explorations, 11*(1).

Dan Klein and Christopher D. Manning. 2003. Accurate unlexicalized parsing. In *Proceedings of the Conference 41st Annual Meeting of the Association for Computational Linguistics*, pages 423-430.

Dekang Lin. 1998. An Information-Theoretic Definition of Similarity. In *Proceedings of the 15th International Conference on Machine Learning*, pages 296-304.

Kevin Lund and Curt Burgess. 1996. Producing high-dimensional semantic spaces from lexical co-occurrence. *Behavior Research Methods Instruments & Computers, 28*(2), 203-208.

Marco Marelli, Stefano Menini, Marco Baroni, Luisa Bentivogli, Raffaella Bernardi, and Roberto Zamparelli. 2014. A SICK cure for the evaluation of compositional distributional semantic models. In *Proceedings of the Ninth International Conference on Language Re-sources and Evaluation (LREC-2014)*, Reykjavik, Iceland.

George A. Miller. 1995. Wordnet - a Lexical Database for English. *Communications of the ACM, 38*(11), 39-41.

Saul B. Needleman and Christian D. Wunsch. 1970. A general method applicable to the search for similarities in the amino acid sequence of two proteins *Journal of Molecular Biology, 48*(3), 443 - 453.

Philip Resnik. 1995. Using information content to evaluate semantic similarity in a taxonomy. In *Proceedings of the Fourteenth International Joint Conference on Artificial Intelligence*, pages 448-453.

Dominic Widdows and Kathleen Ferraro. 2008. Semantic Vectors: A Scalable Open Source Package and Online Technology Management Application. In *Sixth International Conference on Language Resources and Evaluation, Lrec 2008*, pages 1183-1190.

Zhibiao Wu and Martha Palmer. 1994. Verbs Semantics and Lexical Selection. In *Proceedings of the 32nd Annual Meeting on Association for Computational Linguistics*, pages 133-138, Las Cruces, New Mexico.

WSL: Sentence Similarity Using Semantic Distance Between Words

Naoko Miura Tomohiro Takagi
Meiji University, Japan
1-1-1 Higashi-Mita, Tama-ku, Kawasaki-shi,Kanagawa 214–8571
E-mail:{n_miura,takagi}@cs.meiji.ac.jp

Abstract

A typical social networking service contains huge amounts of data, and analyzing this data at the level of the sentence is important. In this paper, we describe our system for a SemEval2015 semantic textual similarity task (task2). We present our approach, which uses edit distance to consider word order, and introduce word appearance in context. We report the results from SemEval2015.

1 Introduction

The Internet, particularly sites related to social networking services (SNS), contains a vast array of information used for a variety of purposes. The vector space model is conventionally used for natural language processing. This model creates vectors on the basis of frequency of word appearance and co-occurring words, without taking word order into account. When it comes to short texts, word co-occurrence is rare (or even non-existent), and the number of words is often less than in a typical newspaper article. Because the average SNS contains data consisting mostly of short sentences, the vector space model is not the best choice.

In this work, we describe a system we developed and submitted to SemEval2015. In the proposed system, we compute sentence similarity using edit distance to consider word order along with the semantic distance between words. We also introduce word appearance in context.

The rest of this paper is organized as follows. Section 2 reviews related work and in Section 3 we present the three systems we submitted for SemEval2015. In Section 4, we discuss the results of our evaluation at SemEval2015.We conclude in Section 5 with a brief summary.

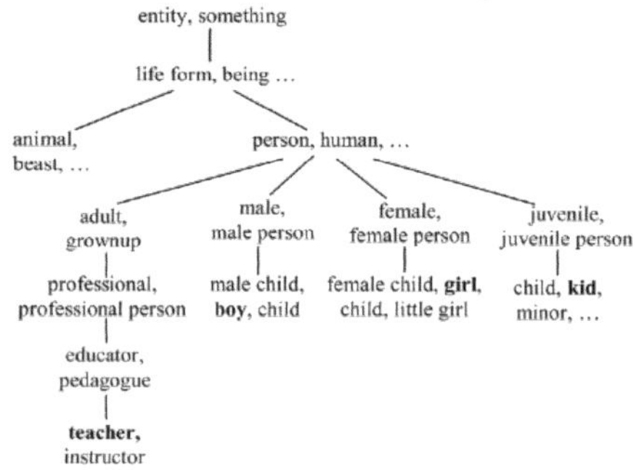

Fig. 1. Hierarchical semantic knowledge base (Li et al., 2006).

2 Related Work

Recent research has introduced the lexical database as a dictionary to analyze short texts(Aziz et al.,2010). Aziz uses a set of similar noun phrases and similar verb phrases and common words to compute sentence similarity. Li combines semantic similarity between words into a hierarchical semantic knowledge base and word order(Li et al.,2006). There are currently a few hierarchical semantic knowledge bases available, one of which is WordNet(Miller,1995). WordNet contains 155,287 words and 117,659 synsets that were stored in 2012 into the lexical categories of nouns, verbs, adjectives, and adverbs(WordNet Statistics, 2014). All synsets have semantic relation to other synsets. An example in the case of using nouns is shown in Fig.1. Li proposed a formula to measure the similarity $s(w_1,w_2)$ between words w_1 and w_2 as

$$s(w_1,w_2)=e^{-\alpha l}\cdot\frac{e^{\beta h}-e^{-\beta h}}{e^{\beta h}+e^{-\beta h}} \quad , \qquad (1)$$

where l is the shortest path length between w_1 and w_2 and h is the depth of the subsumer of w_1 and w_2 in WordNet. For example, we describe the path between "boy" and "girl" in Fig. 1. The shortest path is *boy-male-person-female-girl*, which is 4, so $l = 4$. The subsumer of "boy" and "girl" is "person, human...", so the depth of this synset is h. In hierarchical semantic nets, words at the upper layers have a general meaning and less similarity than words at the lower layers. Li sets $\alpha = 0.2$ and $\beta = 0.45$.

Not only the similarity between words but also word order is important. For example, the two sentences "a dog bites Mike" and "Mike bites a dog" consist of the same words, but the meanings are very different. In this case, we use vectors such that when each vector completely matches, the sentence similarity is high. Our approach is based on edit distance to take into account word order and combined semantic similarity between words.

3 System Details

The proposed system uses edit distance to take word order into account. It also uses the impact of word appearance in each context.

In this paper, we describe sentence S_1 as $S_1=\{a_1,a_2,\cdots,a_n\}$ and sentence S_2 as $S_2=\{b_1,b_2,\cdots,b_m\}$. S_1 consists of n words and S_2 consists of m words. a_i is the i th word of S_1 and b_j is the j th word of S_2. We describe the similarity $Sim(S_1,S_2)$ between S_1 and S_2 within the range of 0 (no relation) to 1 (semantic equivalence).

3.1 Edit Distance

Edit distance is a way of computing the dissimilarity between two strings. Conventionally, the distance is computed for a set of characters with three kinds of operations (substitution, insertion, deletion). However, our approaches are for word sets. Here, we describe the two kinds of edit distance extended in our system.

3.1.1 Levenshtein Distance

The Levenshtein distance between S_1 and S_2 ($|S_1|=n,|S_2|=m$) is $L(n,m)$, where

$0 \leqq i \leqq n,\ 0 \leqq j \leqq m$

$$L(i,j) = \max(i,j) \qquad \text{if } \min(i,j)=0,$$

$$L(i,j) = \min\begin{cases} L(i-1,j-1)+c_1(a_i,b_j) \\ L(i,j-1)+1 \\ L(i-1,j)+1 \end{cases} \quad \text{otherwise.} \tag{2}$$

The indicator function $c_1(a_i,b_j)$ is defined as

$$c_1(a_i,b_j) = \begin{cases} 0 & (a_i = b_j) \\ 1 & (a_i \neq b_j) \end{cases} \tag{3}$$

3.1.2 Jaro-Winkler Distance

The Jaro distance between S_1 and S_2 ($|S_1|=n,|S_2|=m$) is d_j:

$$d_j = \begin{cases} 0 & (q=0) \\ \frac{1}{3}\left(\frac{q}{n}+\frac{q}{m}+\frac{q-t}{q}\right) & (q \neq 0) \end{cases}, \tag{4}$$

where q is the number of matching words between S_1 and S_2. We consider two words as matching when they are the same and not father than

$$\left\lfloor \frac{\max(n,m)}{2} \right\rfloor - 1$$

t is half the number of transpositions.

The Jaro-Winkler distance is d_w:

$$d_w = \begin{cases} d_j & \text{if } d_j < 0.7 \\ d_j + (k * p * (1-d_j)) & \text{otherwise.} \end{cases}, \tag{5}$$

where k is the length of common words at the start of the sentence. p is constant and usually set to $p = 0.1$.

3.2 Semantic Distance

We borrow our approach to compute similarity between words from Li (Li et al.,2006)(Eq. (1)). It can be used for both nouns and verbs because both are organized into hierarchies. However, it is not available for adjectives and adverbs, which are not organized into hierarchies. Therefore, in addition to Eq. (1), when $w_1 \in synsetA$, $w_2 \in synsetB$, we define semantic similarity between words if they are adverbs and adjectives as

$$s(w_1,w_2) = \begin{cases} 1 & (synsetA = synsetB) \\ 0 & (synsetA \neq synsetB) \end{cases} \tag{6}$$

$s(w_1,w_2)$ is 1 if w_1 and w_2 are in the same synset.

Conventionally, we calculated edit distance on the basis of match or mismatch between words and ignored how similar two words are. However, with this approach, if two words have the same meaning although they are different words (e.g., "fall" and "autumn"), edit distance defines them as a mismatch. We address this issue by introducing semantic similarity between words as distance.

(a) Levenshtein distance
We rewrite Eq. (3) as

$$c_1(a_i,b_j)=1-s(a_i,b_j) \tag{7}$$

We propose a measure for the sentence similarity of S_1 and S_2 $Sim(S_1,S_2)$ as

$$Sim(S_1,S_2)=1.0-\frac{L(n,m)}{\max(n,m)} \tag{8}$$

(b) Jaro-Winkler distance
We rewrite Jaro-distance d_j defined by Eq. (4) as

$$d_j=\begin{cases}0 & (q'=0)\\ \frac{1}{3}\left(\frac{q'}{n}+\frac{q'}{m}+\frac{q'-t}{q'}\right) & (q'\neq 0)\end{cases} \tag{9}$$

We define q' in Eq. (10). q' indicates the sum of all semantic similarity between words in S_1 and S_2 ($1\leqq i\leqq n, 1\leqq j\leqq m$, $SUM(c_2(a_i,b_j))$). Further, originally, we calculated t only if two words are matching ($a_i=b_j$); however, in our proposed methods we change to $s(a_i,b_j)>0.5$ to take into account of the semantic similarity of words.

$$1\leqq i\leqq n,\ 1\leqq j\leqq m$$
$$q'=q+SUM(c_2(a_i,b_j)) \tag{10}$$

C_2 in Eq. (10) is defined by Eq. (11). It means the semantic similarity of words.

$$c_2(a_i,b_j)=\begin{cases}0 & (a_i=b_j)\\ s(a_i,b_j) & (a_i\neq b_j)\end{cases} \tag{11}$$

We propose a measure for the sentence similarity of S_1 and S_2 $Sim(S_1, S_2)$ as

$$Sim(S_1,S_2)=d_w \tag{12}$$

3.3 The Impact of Word Appearance in Context

There is one issue when we compute $Sim(S_1,S_2)$, as follows. Let us consider two sentences: "I ate an apple" and "I hate an apple". These sentences indicate opposite meanings. However, except for "ate" and "hate", both sentences consist of the same words and have the same word order. Therefore, the method we mentioned above (Eq. (8)) computes the $Sim(S_1,S_2)$ as high. However, we decide that the similarity between these sentences have opposite meanings because of "ate" and "hate". For this reason, we introduce conditional probability to estimate word appearance for each context and extract the probabilities from a corpus as training data. Further, we give this word appearance for semantic similarity (Eq. (1)) as a weight.

Let us show an example. P(I | S_2), P(ate| S_2), P(an| S_2), and P(apple|S_2) are words of S_1 appearance in context S_2. We define S^* as the set of nouns, verbs, adjectives, and adverbs (e.g., when sentence S is "It is a dog", S^* is {"is", "dog"}).
We measure each word appearance $weight(w)$ in context S as:

$$P(w\mid S)=\frac{doc_{w,S^*}}{doc_{S^*}} \tag{13}$$

$$weight(w)=\frac{1}{(1+e^{-\gamma*P(w|S)})}, \tag{14}$$

where $doc_{w,S*}$ is the number of documents that contains both w and S^* and doc_{S*} is the number of documents that contains S^*. We set $\gamma=5.0$.

We take into account the impact of words in context and apply it to Levenshtein distance, rewriting Eq. (7) as

$$c_1(a_i,b_j)=(1-s(a_i,b_j))*weight(a_i)^{-1}*weight(b_j)^{-1} \tag{15}$$

When a word in one sentence co-occurs with words in the other sentence frequently, the impact is low, and when it co-occurs less frequently, the impact is high. We use Eq.(15) when a_i and b_j are nouns or verbs and $s(a_i,b_j)<0.7$.

4 Results

STS systems at SemEval 2015 were evaluated on five data sets. Each data set contained a number of sentence pairs that have a gold-standard score in the range of 0–5 as correct answers. The STS systems were evaluated by Pearson correlation between the system output and the gold-standard score. We used the Reuters Corpus as training data.

4.1 Submissions

We submitted the outputs of three of our system runs. In the STS task, the similarity between the *score*(S_1,S_2) of two sentences needed to be in the range of 0–5. Accordingly, we set *score*(S_1,S_2) as *score*(S_1,S_2) =5* *Sim*(S_1,S_2). For pre-processing, we use Stanford-NLP tools for tokenization and POS-tagging. We also remove punctuation marks.
And we use JWNL to measure the similarity between words. (Eq.(1))

-run1
Levenshtein distance approach (Eq. (8))

-run2
Jaro-Winkler distance approach (Eq. (12))

-run3
Using run1 (Eq. (8)) in conjunction with word appearance in context (Eq. (15))

4.2 Evaluation on STS 2015 Data

Table 1 shows the results (Pearson correlation) of each of our three runs evaluated on five data sets. Our best system was **run3**. It was ranked 64 out of 74 systems.

The weighted-mean scores of **run1** and **run2** were almost the same. When we compare the scores of **run1** and **run3**, **run3** performed better on four datasets (the exception was "answers-forums"). Overall, the best performance in terms of weighted-mean score was by **run3**.

Data Set	run1	run2	run3
answers-forums	0.3759	0.4287	0.3709
answers-students	0.5269	0.6028	0.5437
belief	0.6387	0.5231	0.6478
headlines	0.5462	0.6029	0.5752
images	0.5710	0.4879	0.6407
Weighted-Mean	0.5379	0.5424	0.5672

Table 1 . Results of evaluation on SemEval2015 STS task.

5 Conclusion

In this paper, we proposed methods for determining sentence similarity. We adopted the semantic distance of word on edit distance along with word appearance in context. Evaluation results suggest that using word appearance in context is an effective element for determining sentence similarity.

References

Eneko Agirre, Carmen Banea, Claire Cardie, Daniel Cer, Mona Diab, Aitor Gonzalez-Agirre, Weiwei Guo, Iñigo Lopez-Gazpio, Montse Maritxalar, Rada Mihalcea, German Rigau, Larraitz Uria, Janyce Wiebe. SemEval-2015 Task 2: Semantic Textual Similarity, English, Spanish and Pilot on Interpretability. In *Proceedings of the 9th International Workshop on Semantic Evaluation (SemEval 2015)* June,2015, Denver,CO, Association for Computational Linguistics.

Yuhua Li, David McLean, Zuhair A. Bander, James D. O'Shea, and Keeley Crockett (2006). Sentence Similarity Based on Semantic Nets and Corpus Statistics. *IEEE Transactions on Knowledge and Data Engineering Vol. 18 No. 8 August 2006.*

Mehwish Aziz and Muhammad Rafi (2010). Sentence based semantic similarity measure for blog-posts. *Digital Content, Multimedia Technology and its Applications (IDC). 2010 6th International Conference.*

G.A. Miller, "WordNet: A Lexical Database for English". (1995) *Communications of the ACM, Vol. 38, Issue 11 Nov. 1995.*

WordNet Statistics WordNet.princeton.edu. Retrieved2014-03-11 http://wordnet.princeton.edu/wordnet/man/wnstats.7WN.html

Reuters Corpus English Language, 1996/08/20-1997/08/19. http://about.reuters.com/researchandstandards/corpus/

JWNL (Java WordNet Library) http://sourceforge.net/projects/jwordnet/

SOPA: Random Forests Regression for the Semantic Textual Similarity task

Davide Buscaldi, Jorge J. García Flores,
Laboratoire d'Informatique de Paris Nord, CNRS (UMR 7030)
Université Paris 13, Sorbonne Paris Cité, Villetaneuse, France
{buscaldi,jgflores}@lipn.univ-paris13.fr

Ivan V. Meza and Isaac Rodríguez
Instituto de Investigaciones en Matemticas Aplicadas y en Sistemas (IIMAS)
Universidad Nacional Autnoma de México (UNAM)
Ciudad Universitaria, DF, Mexico
ivanvladimir,isaac@turing.iimas.unam.mx

Abstract

This paper describes the system used by the LIPN-IIMAS team in the Task 2, Semantic Textual Similarity, at SemEval 2015, in both the English and Spanish sub-tasks. We included some features based on alignment measures and we tested different learning models, in particular Random Forests, which proved the best among those used in our participation.

1 Introduction

Our participation in SemEval 2015 was focused on solving the technical problems that afflicted our previous participation (Buscaldi et al., 2014) and including additional features based on alignments, such as the Sultan similarity (Sultan et al., 2014b) and the measure available in CMU Sphinx-4 (Lamere et al., 2003) for speech recognition. We baptised the new system SOPA from the Spanish word for "soup", since it uses a heterogeneous mix of features. Well aware of the importance that the training corpus and the regression algorithms have for the STS task, we used language models to select the most appropriate training corpus for a given text, and we explored some alternatives to the ν-Support Vector Regression (ν-SVR) (Schölkopf et al., 1999) used in our previous participations, specifically the Multi-Layer Perceptron (Bishop and others, 1995) and Random Forest (Breiman, 2001) regression algorithms. The obtained results show that Random Forests outperforms the other algorithms on every test set. We describe all the features in Section 2; the details on the learning algorithms and the training corpus selection process are described in Section 3, and the results obtained by the system are detailed in Section 4.

2 Similarity Measures

In this section we describe the measures used as features in our system. The total number of features used was 16 in English and 14 in Spanish. Since most measures have already been used in our previous participation, we provide only basic overview, referring the reader to the complete description in (Buscaldi et al., 2013) for further details. When POS tagging and NE recognition were required, we used the Stanford CoreNLP for English and Spanish (Manning et al., 2014).

2.1 WordNet-based Conceptual Similarity

This measure has been introduced in order to measure similarities between concepts with respect to an ontology. The similarity is calculated as follows: first of all, words in sentences p and q are lemmatised and mapped to the related WordNet synsets. All noun synsets are put into the set of synsets associated to the sentence, C_p and C_q, respectively. If the synsets are in one of the other POS categories (verb, adjective, adverb) we look for their derivationally related forms in order to find a related noun synset: if there exists one, we put this synset in C_p (or C_q). No disambiguation process is carried out, so we take all possible meanings into account.

Given C_p and C_q as the sets of concepts contained in sentences p and q, respectively, with $|C_p| \geq |C_q|$, the conceptual similarity between p and q is calculated as:

$$ss(p,q) = \frac{\sum_{c_1 \in C_p} \max_{c_2 \in C_q} s(c_1, c_2)}{|C_p|}$$

where $s(c_1, c_2)$ is a conceptual similarity measure. Concept similarity can be calculated in different ways. We used a variation of the Wu-Palmer formula (Wu and Palmer, 1994) named "ProxiGenea3", introduced by (Dudognon et al., 2010), which is inspired by the analogy between a family tree and the concept hierarchy in WordNet. The ProxiGenea3 measure is defined as:

$$s(c_1, c_2) = \frac{1}{1 + d(c_1) + d(c_2) - 2 \cdot d(c_0)}$$

where c_0 is the most specific concept that is present both in the synset path of c_1 and c_2 (that is, the Least Common Subsumer or LCS). The function returning the depth of a concept is noted with d.

2.2 IC-based Similarity

This measure has been proposed by (Mihalcea et al., 2006) as a corpus-based measure which uses Resnik's Information Content (IC) and the Jiang-Conrath (Jiang and Conrath, 1997) similarity metric. This measure is more precise than the one introduced in the previous subsection because it takes into account also the importance of concepts and not only their relative position in the hierarchy. We refer to (Buscaldi et al., 2013) and (Mihalcea et al., 2006) for a detailed description of the measure. The idf weights for the words were calculated using the Google Web 1T (Brants and Franz, 2006) frequency counts, while the IC values used are those calculated by Ted Pedersen (Pedersen et al., 2004) on the British National Corpus[1].

2.3 Syntactic Dependencies

This measure tries to capture the syntactic similarity between two sentences using dependencies. Previous experiments showed that converting constituents to dependencies still achieved best results on out-of-domain texts (Le Roux et al., 2012), so we decided to use a 2-step architecture to obtain syntactic dependencies. First we parsed pairs of sentences with the LORG parser[2]. Second we converted the resulting parse trees to Stanford dependencies.

Given the sets of parsed dependencies D_p and D_q, for sentence p and q, a dependency $d \in D_x$ is a triple (l, h, t) where l is the dependency label (for instance, *dobj* or *prep*), h the governor and t the dependant. The similarity measure between two syntactic dependencies $d_1 = (l_1, h_1, t_1)$ and $d_2 = (l_2, h_2, t_2)$ is the levenshtein distance between the labels l_1 and l_2 multiplied by the average of $idf_h * s(h_1, h_2)$ and $idf_t * s(t_1, t_2)$, where idf_h and idf_t are the inverse document frequencies calculated on Google Web 1T for the governors and the dependants (we retain the maximum for each pair), respectively, and s is the ProxiGenea3 measure. NOTE: This measure was used only in the English sub-task.

2.4 Information Retrieval-based Similarity

Let us consider two texts p and q, an IR system S and a document collection D indexed by S. This measure is based on the assumption that p and q are similar if the documents retrieved by S for the two texts, used as input queries, are ranked similarly.

Let be $L_p = \{d_{p_1}, \ldots, d_{p_K}\}$ and $L_q = \{d_{q_1}, \ldots, d_{q_K}\}$, $d_{x_i} \in D$ the sets of the top K documents retrieved by S for texts p and q, respectively. Let us define $s_p(d)$ and $s_q(d)$ the scores assigned by S to a document d for the query p and q, respectively. Then, the similarity score is calculated as:

$$sim_{IR}(p,q) = 1 - \frac{\sum_{d \in L_p \cap L_q} \frac{\sqrt{(s_p(d) - s_q(d))^2}}{\max(s_p(d), s_q(d))}}{|L_p \cap L_q|}$$

if $|L_p \cap L_q| \neq \emptyset$, 0 otherwise.

For the participation in the English sub-task we indexed a collection composed by the AQUAINT-2[3] and the English NTCIR-8[4] document collections, using the Lucene[5] 4.2 search engine with BM25 similarity. We indexed also DBPedia[6] abstracts and the UkWaC (Ferraresi et al., 2008), but they were used to produce two additional features (separate

[1] http://www.d.umn.edu/ tpederse/similarity.html

[2] https://github.com/CNGLdlab/LORG-Release

[3] http://www.nist.gov/tac/data/data_desc.html#AQUAINT-2

[4] http://metadata.berkeley.edu/NTCIR-GeoTime/ntcir-8-databases.php

[5] http://lucene.apache.org/core

[6] http://www.dbpedia.org/

from the basic IR one). The Spanish index was created using the Spanish QA@CLEF 2005 (agencia EFE1994-95, El Mundo 1994-95) and multiUN (Eisele and Chen, 2010) collections. The K value was set to 70 after a study detailed in (Buscaldi, 2013). Another IR-based feature was derived by the rank-biased overlap measure introduced by (Webber et al., 2010) which compares rankings without the need of weights. In total, we had 4 IR-based measures for English and 2 for Spanish.

2.5 N-gram Based Similarity

This measure tries to capture the fact that similar sentences have similar n-grams, even if they are not placed in the same positions. The measure is based on the Clustered Keywords Positional Distance (CKPD) model proposed in (Buscaldi et al., 2009) for the passage retrieval task.

The similarity between a text fragment p and another text fragment q is calculated as:

$$sim_{ngrams}(p,q) = \sum_{\forall x \in Q} \frac{h(x,P)}{\sum_{i=1}^{n} w_i d(x, x_{max})}$$

Where P is the set of the heaviest n-grams in p where all terms are also contained in q; Q is the set of all the possible n-grams in q, and n is the total number of terms in the longest sentence. The weights for each term w_i are calculated as $w_i = 1 - \frac{log(n_i)}{1+log(N)}$ where n_i is the frequency of term t_i in the Google Web 1T collection, and N is the frequency of the most frequent term in the Google Web 1T collection. The weight for each n-gram ($h(x,P)$), with $|P| = j$ is calculated as:

$$h(x,P) = \begin{cases} \sum_{k=1}^{j} w_k & \text{if } x \in P \\ 0 & \text{otherwise} \end{cases}$$

The function $d(x, x_{max})$ determines the minimum distance between a n-gram x and the heaviest one x_{max} as the number of words between them.

2.6 Geographical Context Similarity

This measure tries to measure if the two sentences refer to events that took place in the same geographical area. It is based on the observation that the compatibility of the geographic context between the sentences is an important clue to determine whether the sentences are related or not, especially in news. We built a database of geographically-related entities, using geo-WordNet (Buscaldi and Rosso, 2008) and expanding it with all the synsets that are related to a geographically grounded synset. This implies that also adjectives and verbs may be used as clues for the identification of the geographical context of a sentence. For instance, "Afghan" is associated to "Afghanistan", "Sovietize" to "Soviet Union", etc. The Named Entities of type PER (Person) are also used as clues: we use Yago[7] to check whether the NE corresponds to a famous leader or not, and in the affirmative case we include the related nation to the geographical context of the sentence. For instance, "Merkel" is mapped to "Germany". Given G_p and G_q the sets of places found in sentences p and q, respectively, the geographical context similarity is calculated as follows:

$$sim_{geo}(p,q) = 1 - \log_K \left(1 + \frac{\sum_{x \in G_p} \min_{y \in G_q} d(x,y)}{\max(|G_p|, |G_q|)} \right)$$

Where $d(x,y)$ is the spherical distance in Km. between x and y, and K is a normalization factor set to 10000 Km. to obtain similarity values between 1 and 0. If no toponyms or geographically groundable entities are found in either sentences, then the geographic context similarity is set to 1.

2.7 Word Alignment Similarity

This similarity metric is based on the work of (Sultan et al., 2014b; Sultan et al., 2014a). The metric calculates a similarity score based on an alignment between two texts. It starts with an alignment between similar words, it proceeds to align similar name entities, to continue with words with similar content, to finally align stop words. In the case of content words, it proposes to use the syntactic context to identify similar words. At the end, the similarity is calculated as a harmonic mean between the ratios of align words from sentence one to sentence two, and from sentence two to sentence one.

CMU Sphinx-4 (Lamere et al., 2003) is a speech recognition system that includes an alignment function that is used to align speech transcriptions with

[7] http://www.mpi-inf.mpg.de/yago-naga/yago/

text. We took one of the sentence as a reference and the other one as a transcription and we used the output of the Sphinx alignment measure as a feature.

2.8 Other Measures

In addition to the above text similarity measures, we used also the difference in size between sentences and the following measures:

Cosine

Cosine distance calculated between $\mathbf{p} = (w_{p_1}, \ldots, w_{p_n})$ and $\mathbf{q} = (w_{q_1}, \ldots, w_{q_n})$, the vectors of $tf.idf$ weights associated to sentences p and q, with idf values calculated on Google Web 1T.

Edit Distance

This similarity measure is calculated using the Levenshtein distance on characters between the two sentences.

Named Entity Overlap

This is a per-class overlap measure (in this way, "France" as an Organization does not match "France" as a Location) calculated using the Dice coefficient between the sets of NEs found, respectively, in sentences p and q.

Skip-gram Similarity

This measure is obtained as the dice coefficient calculated between the set of skip-grams contained in the two sentences.

3 Learning Models

Besides the ν-Support Vector Regression (ν-SVR) (Schölkopf et al., 1999) used in previous participation, we used Multilayer Perceptron and Random Forests. The Multilayer perceptron (Bishop and others, 1995) is a neural network model which has several interesting properties, such as robustness and nonlinearity. Our implementation uses a simple gradient descent learning algorithm with backpropagation and one hidden layer with 5 units. Random Forests (Breiman, 2001) are an ensemble learning method based on boosting and bagging of classification trees. In our experiments, we used Random Forests with 10 bootstrap samples.

In our runs, we selected a subset of the training set according to a similarity measure between the test and the training set based on a 1- to 3-grams language model and average sentence length. The idea behind this selection process is that learning sentence similarities on a specific type of text will increase the accuracy of predictions on text with similar characteristics: image descriptions are usually written in a very different form than word definitions or forum answers. For each coherent subset of the training set, we built a language model $L_m = (G_1, G_2, G_3)$ where G_n is the distribution frequency of n-grams in the subset. We obtained the same for the input dataset (L_i) and we calculated $S(L_m, L_i) = (b(L_{m1}, L_{i1}) + 2 * b(L_{m2}, L_{i2}) + 3 * b(L_{m3}, L_{i3}))/6$ where $b(F_1, F_2)$ is the Bhatthacharyya distance between the distributions F_1 and F_2. We selected only those training dataset where $S(L_m, L_i) > 0.2$. In Table 3 we show the comparison of the results obtained with such selection (the official ones) and those obtained using the complete training set (not submitted). The complete English training set was composed by the data from SemEval STS 2012, 2013 and 2014. In Spanish, we used our 2014 training set, which included the automatically translated English 2012-2013 pairs from STS and a corpus we made from RAE[8] definitions, and the 2014 Spanish test set.

4 Results

Table 1 and 2 presents our results our runs in SemEval 2015 (Agirre et al., 2015). Our participation consisted on three runs for three different machine learning approaches to regressions: Support Vector Regression (*LIPN-SVM*), Multi Layer Perceptron (*LIPN-MLP*) and Random Forest (*LIPN-RF*). The *LIPN-RF* configuration was our best one and was ranked 25th run-wise and 14th system wise for the English corpora; 5th run-wise and 3rd system-wise for Spanish. Our English system had better overall performance than Spanish. The best performance was reached for the *Believe* dataset in English and *News* dataset in Spanish.

Part of our proposal uses a language model to select a subset of the corpus used to train the regression. Table 3 shows performance with the full dataset and the selected training corpus for the En-

[8] "Real Academia Española de la lengua" Spanish dictionary: `http://www.rae.es`

	Answer-forums	Answer-students	Headlines	Believe	Images	Overall
LIPN-RF	**0,6709**	**0,5914**	**0,7243**	**0,8123**	**0,8414**	**0,7356**
LIPN-MLP	0,6178	0,5864	0,6886	0,8121	0,8184	0,7175
LIPN-SVM	0,5918	0,5718	0,7028	0,7985	0,8104	0,7070

Table 1: English results (Official runs).

	Wikipedia	News	Overall
LIPN-RF	**0,5637**	**0,5655**	**0,5649**
LIPN-MLP	0,25257	0,5342	0,4401
LIPN-SVM	0,4194	0,4007	0,4069

Table 2: Spanish results (Official runs).

glish dataset with the three regression approaches. The overall score points that the corpus selection was not beneficial. The most significant improvement was concentrated on the *Answer-students* dataset, in this case the performance felt 0,0588 points.

We checked the contribution of each feature using the relief attribute selection measure (Kononenko, 1994) over the English training set. The best feature was the WordNet one, followed by Sultan and IC-based similarity. The worst features were Rank-biased Overlap followed by NE Overlap and the Geographic context similarity (however, apart from RBO, the other ones don't have complete coverage). The other features have a statistically similar contribution.

5 Conclusions and Future Work

The new learning models adopted were particularly effective, outperforming the Support Vector Regression algorithm that we used in our previous participation. The alignment measure based on Sultan was also very effective, as indicated by feature selection. On the other hand, our corpus selection strategy did not prove useful in general, although it provided slight improvements on specific corpora. We will need to further analyse these results to understand how SOPA can still be improved.

Acknowledgements

This work is supported/ partially supported by a public grant overseen by the French National Research Agency (ANR) as part of the progam "Investissements d'Avenir" (reference: ANR-10-LABX-0083).

References

Eneko Agirre, Carmen Banea, Claire Cardie, Daniel Cer, Mona Diab, Aitor Gonzalez-Agirre, Weiwei Guo, Iigo Lopez-Gazpio, Montse Maritxalar, Rada Mihalcea, German Rigau, Larraitz Uria, and Janyce Wiebe. 2015. SemEval-2015 Task 2: Semantic Textual Similarity, English, Spanish and Pilot on Interpretability. In *Proceedings of the 9th International Workshop on Semantic Evaluation (SemEval 2015)*, Denver, CO, June.

Christopher M Bishop et al. 1995. Neural networks for pattern recognition.

Thorsten Brants and Alex Franz. 2006. Web 1t 5-gram corpus version 1.1.

Leo Breiman. 2001. Random forests. *Machine learning*, 45(1):5–32.

Davide Buscaldi and Paolo Rosso. 2008. Geo-WordNet: Automatic Georeferencing of WordNet. In *Proceedings of the International Conference on Language Resources and Evaluation, LREC 2008*, Marrakech, Morocco.

Davide Buscaldi, Paolo Rosso, José Manuel Gómez, and Emilio Sanchis. 2009. Answering questions with an n-gram based passage retrieval engine. *Journal of Intelligent Information Systems (JIIS)*, 34(2):113–134.

Davide Buscaldi, Joseph Le Roux, Jorge J. Garcia Flores, and Adrian Popescu. 2013. LIPN-CORE: Semantic Text Similarity using n-grams, WordNet, Syntactic Analysis, ESA and Information Retrieval based Features. In *Second Joint Conference on Lexical and Computational Semantics (*SEM), Volume 1: Proceedings of the Main Conference and the Shared Task: Semantic Textual Similarity*, pages 162–168, Atlanta, Georgia, USA, June.

Davide Buscaldi, Jorge J García Flores, Joseph Le Roux, Nadi Tomeh, and Belem Priego-Sanchez. 2014. LIPN: Introducing a new Geographical Context Similarity Measure and a Statistical Similarity Measure based on the Bhattacharyya coefficient. In *SemEval 2014*, pages 400–405.

Davide Buscaldi. 2013. Une mesure de similarité sémantique basée sur la Recherche d'Information. In

	Answer-forums	Answer-students	Headlines	Believe	Images	Overall
			Selected			
LIPN-RF	**0,6709**	0,5914	0,7243	0,8123	**0,8414**	0,7244
LIPN-MLP	0,6178	0,5864	0,6886	0,8121	0,8184	0,6986
LIPN-SVM	0,5918	0,5718	0,7028	0,7985	0,8104	0,6894
			Full			
LIPN-RF	0,6418	**0,6502**	**0,7320**	**0,8155**	**0,8301**	**0,7339**
LIPN-MLP	0,6252	0,6213	0,8047	0,6856	0,8047	0,7120
LIPN-SVM	0,5701	0,6177	0,7939	0,7003	0,7939	0,7001

Table 3: Comparison of the results obtained with corpus selection and using the full corpus.

5ème Atelier Recherche d'Information SEmantique - RISE 2013, pages 81–91, Lille, France, July.

Damien Dudognon, Gilles Hubert, and Bachelin Jhonn Victorino Ralalason. 2010. Proxigénéa : Une mesure de similarité conceptuelle. In *Proceedings of the Colloque Veille Stratégique Scientifique et Technologique (VSST 2010)*.

Andreas Eisele and Yu Chen. 2010. MultiUN: A Multilingual Corpus from United Nation Documents. In Daniel Tapias, Mike Rosner, Stelios Piperidis, Jan Odjik, Joseph Mariani, Bente Maegaard, Khalid Choukri, and Nicoletta Calzolari (Conference Chair), editors, *Proceedings of the Seventh conference on International Language Resources and Evaluation*, pages 2868–2872, 5.

Adriano Ferraresi, Eros Zanchetta, Marco Baroni, and Silvia Bernardini. 2008. Introducing and evaluating UkWaC, a very large web-derived corpus of English. In *Proceedings of the 4th Web as Corpus Workshop (WAC-4) Can we beat Google*, pages 47–54.

Jay J. Jiang and David W. Conrath. 1997. Semantic similarity based on corpus statistics and lexical taxonomy. In *Proc. of the Int'l. Conf. on Research in Computational Linguistics*, pages 19–33.

Igor Kononenko. 1994. Estimating attributes: analysis and extensions of RELIEF. In *Machine Learning: ECML-94*, pages 171–182.

Paul Lamere, Philip Kwok, Evandro Gouvea, Bhiksha Raj, Rita Singh, William Walker, Manfred Warmuth, and Peter Wolf. 2003. The cmu sphinx-4 speech recognition system. In *IEEE Intl. Conf. on Acoustics, Speech and Signal Processing (ICASSP 2003), Hong Kong*, pages 2–5. Citeseer.

Joseph Le Roux, Jennifer Foster, Joachim Wagner, Rasul Samad Zadeh Kaljahi, and Anton Bryl. 2012. DCU-Paris13 Systems for the SANCL 2012 Shared Task. In *The NAACL 2012 First Workshop on Syntactic Analysis of Non-Canonical Language (SANCL)*, pages 1–4, Montréal, Canada.

Christopher D. Manning, Mihai Surdeanu, John Bauer, Jenny Finkel, Steven J. Bethard, and David McClosky. 2014. The Stanford CoreNLP Natural Language Processing Toolkit. In *Proceedings of 52nd Annual Meeting of the Association for Computational Linguistics: System Demonstrations*, pages 55–60.

Rada Mihalcea, Courtney Corley, and Carlo Strapparava. 2006. Corpus-based and knowledge-based measures of text semantic similarity. In *Proceedings of the 21st national conference on Artificial intelligence - Volume 1*, AAAI'06, pages 775–780.

Ted Pedersen, Siddharth Patwardhan, and Jason Michelizzi. 2004. Wordnet::similarity: measuring the relatedness of concepts. In *Demonstration Papers at HLT-NAACL 2004*, HLT-NAACL–Demonstrations '04, pages 38–41, Stroudsburg, PA, USA.

Bernhard Schölkopf, Peter Bartlett, Alex Smola, and Robert Williamson. 1999. Shrinking the tube: a new support vector regression algorithm. In *Proceedings of the 1998 conference on Advances in neural information processing systems II*, pages 330–336, Cambridge, MA, USA.

Md Arafat Sultan, Steven Bethard, and Tamara Sumner. 2014a. Back to Basics for Monolingual Alignment: Exploiting Word Similarity and Contextual Evidence.

Md Arafat Sultan, Steven Bethard, and Tamara Sumner. 2014b. DLS@ CU: Sentence Similarity from Word Alignment. *SemEval 2014*, page 241.

William Webber, Alistair Moffat, and Justin Zobel. 2010. A similarity measure for indefinite rankings. *ACM Transactions on Information Systems (TOIS)*, 28(4):20.

Zhibiao Wu and Martha Palmer. 1994. Verbs semantics and lexical selection. In *Proceedings of the 32nd annual meeting on Association for Computational Linguistics*, ACL '94, pages 133–138, Stroudsburg, PA, USA.

MathLingBudapest: Concept Networks for Semantic Similarity

Gábor Recski
Research Institute for Linguistics
Hungarian Academy of Sciences
Benczúr u. 33
1068 Budapest, Hungary
recski@mokk.bme.hu

Judit Ács
HAS Research Institute for Linguistics and
Dept. of Automation and Applied Informatics
Budapest U of Technology and Economics
Magyar tudósok krt. 2 (Bldg. Q.)
1117 Budapest, Hungary
judit@mokk.bme.hu

Abstract

We present our approach to measuring semantic similarity of sentence pairs used in Semeval 2015 tasks 1 and 2. We adopt the sentence alignment framework of (Han et al., 2013) and experiment with several measures of word similarity. We hybridize the common vector-based models with definition graphs from the `4lang` concept dictionary and devise a measure of graph similarity that yields good results on training data. We did not address the specific challenges posed by Twitter data, and this is reflected in placing 11th from 30 in Task 1, but our systems perform fairly well on the generic datasets of Task 2, with the hybrid approach placing 11th among 78 runs.

1 Introduction

This paper describes the systems participating in Semeval-2015 Task 1 (Xu et al., 2015) and Task 2 (Agirre et al., 2015). To compute the semantic similarity of two sentences we use the architecture presented in (Han et al., 2013) to find, for each word, its counterpart in the other sentence that is semantically most similar to it. We implemented several methods for measuring word similarity, among them (i) a word embedding created by the method presented in (Mikolov et al., 2013) and (ii) a metric based on networks of concepts derived from the `4lang` concept lexicon (Kornai and Makrai, 2013; Kornai et al., 2015) and definitions from the Longman Dictionary of Contemporary English (Bullon, 2003). A hybrid system exploiting both of these metrics yields the best results and placed 11th among 73 systems on Semeval Task 2a (Semantic Textual Similarity for English). All components of our system are available for download under an MIT license from GitHub[1][2]. Section 2 describes the system architecture and points out the main differences between our system and that in (Han et al., 2013), section 3 outlines our word similarity metric derived from the `4lang` concept lexicon. We present the evaluation of our systems on both tasks in section 4, and section 5 provides a brief conclusion.

2 Architecture

Our framework for determining the semantic similarity of two sentences is based on the system presented in (Han et al., 2013). Their architecture, *Align and Penalize*, involves computing an alignment score between two sentences based on some measure of word similarity. We've chosen to reimplement this system so that we can experiment with various notions of word similarity, including the one based on `4lang` and presented in section 3. Although we reimplemented virtually all rules and components described by (Han et al., 2013) for experimentation, we shall only describe those that ended up in at least one of the five configurations submitted to Semeval.

The core idea behind the *Align and Penalize* architecture is, given two senteces S_1 and S_2 and some measure of word similarity, to align each word of one sentence with some word of the other sentence so that the similarity of word pairs is maximized.

[1] http://github.com/juditacs/semeval
[2] http://github.com/kornai/pymachine

The mapping need not be one-to-one and is calculated independently for words of S_1 (aligning them with words from S_2) and words of S_2 (aligning them with words from S_1). The score of an alignment is the sum of the similarities of each word pair in the alignment, normalized by sentence length. The final score assigned to a pair of sentences is the average of the alignment scores for each sentence. For out-of-vocabulary (OOV) words, i.e. those that are not covered by the component used for measuring word similarity, we use the Dice-similarity over the sets of character 4-grams in each word. Additionally, we use simple rules to detect acronyms and compounds: if a word of one sentence that is a sequence of 2-5 characters (e.g. *ABC*) has a matching sequence of words in the other sentence (e.g. *American Broadcasting Company*), all words of the phrase are aligned with this word and recieve an alignment score of 1. If a sentence contains a sequence of two words (e.g. *long term* or *can not*) that appear in the other sentence without a space and with or without a hyphen (e.g. *long-term* or *cannot*), these are also aligned with a score of 1. The score returned by the word similarity component can be boosted based on WordNet (Miller, 1995), e.g. if one is a hypernym of the other, if one appears frequently in glosses of the other, or if they are derivationally related. For the exact cases covered and a description of how the boost is calculated, the reader is referred to (Han et al., 2013). In our submissions we only used this boost on word similarity scores obtained from word embeddings.

The similarity score may be reduced by a variety of penalties, which we only enabled for Task 1 runs – they haven't brought any improvement on Task 2 datasets in any of our early experiments. Of the penalties described in (Han et al., 2013) we only used the one which decreases alignment scores if the word similarity score for some word pair is very small (< 0.05). We also introduced two new types of penalties based on our observations of error types in Twitter data: if one sentence starts with a question word and the other one does not or if one sentence contains a past-tense verb and the other does not, we reduce the overall score by $1/(L(S_1) + L(S_2))$, where $L(S_1)$ and $L(S_2)$ are the numbers of words in each sentence.

3 Similarity from Concept Networks

This section will present the word similarity measure based on principles of lexical semantics presented in (Kornai, 2010). The `4lang` concept dictionary (Kornai and Makrai, 2013) contains 3500 definitions created manually. Because the Longman Defining Vocabulary (LDV) (Boguraev and Briscoe, 1989) is a subset of `4lang`, we could automatically extend this manually created seed to every headword of the Longman Dictionary of Contemporary English (LDOCE) by processing their definitions with the Stanford Dependency Parser (Klein and Manning, 2003), and mapping dependency relations to sets of edges in the `4lang`-style concept graph. Details of the mapping will be described elsewhere (Recski, 2015).

Since these definitions are essentially graphs of concepts, we have experimented with similarity functions over pairs of such graphs that capture semantic similarity of the concepts defined by each of them. There are two fundamentally different configurations present in `4lang` graphs:

1. two nodes may be connected via a 0-edge, which is a generalization over unary predication (`dog` $\xrightarrow{0}$ `bark`), attribution (`dog` $\xrightarrow{0}$ `faithful`), and hypernymy, or the `IS_A` relation (`dog` $\xrightarrow{0}$ `mammal`).
2. two nodes can be connected, via a 1-edge and a 2-edge respectively, to a third one representing a binary relation. Binaries include all transitive verbs (e.g. `cat` $\xleftarrow{1}$ `CATCH` $\xrightarrow{2}$ `branch`). and a handful of binary primitives (e.g. `tree` $\xleftarrow{1}$ `HAS` $\xrightarrow{2}$ `branch`).

We start by the intuition that similar concepts will overlap in the elementary configurations they take part in: they might share a 0-neighbor, e.g. `train` $\xrightarrow{0}$ `vehicle` $\xleftarrow{0}$ `car`, or they might be on the same path of 1- and 2-edges, e.g. `park` $\xleftarrow{1}$ `IN` $\xrightarrow{2}$ `town` and `street` $\xleftarrow{1}$ `IN` $\xrightarrow{2}$ `town`.

We'll define the *predicates* of a node as the set of such configurations it takes part in. For example, based on the definition graph in Figure 1, the predicates of the concept

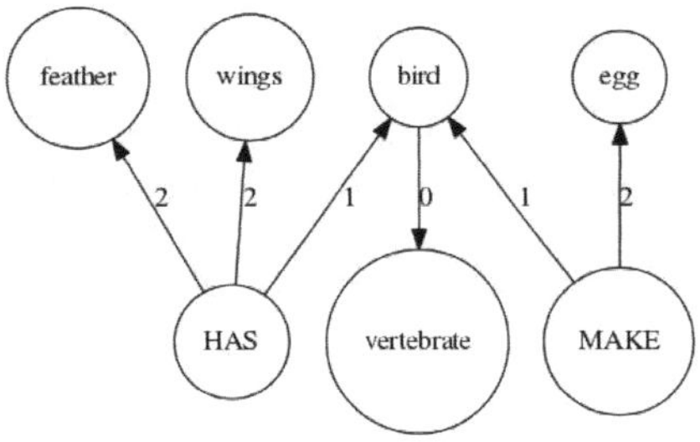

Figure 1: 4lang definition of `bird`.

`bird` are {`vertebrate; (HAS, feather); (HAS, wing); (MAKE, egg)`}.

Our initial version of graph similarity is the Jaccard similarity of the sets of predicates of each concept, i.e.

$$S(w_1, w_2) = \frac{|P(w_1) \cap P(w_2)|}{|P(w_1) \cup P(w_2)|}$$

For all words that are not among the 3500 defined in `4lang` we obtain definition graphs by automated parsing of Longman definitions and the application of a simple mapping from dependency relations to graph edges (Recski, 2015). By far the largest source of noise in these graphs is that currently there is no postprocessor component that recognizes common structures of dictionary definitions like appositive relative clauses. For example the word `casualty` is defined by LDOCE as *someone who is hurt or killed in an accident or war* and we currently build the graph in Figure 2 instead of that in Figure 3. To mitigate the effects of these anomalities, we updated our definition of predicates: we let them be "inherited" via paths of 0-edges encoding the `IS_A`-relationship.

We've also experimented with similarity measures that take into account the sets of all nodes accessible from each concept in their respective definition graphs. This proved useful in establishing that two concepts which would otherwise be treated as entirely dissimilar are in fact somewhat related. For example, given the definitions of the concepts `casualty` and `army` in Figures 2 and 4, the node `war` will allow us to assign nonzero similarity to the pair `(army, casualty)`. We found it most effective to use the maximum of these two types of similarity.

Testing several versions of graph similarity on

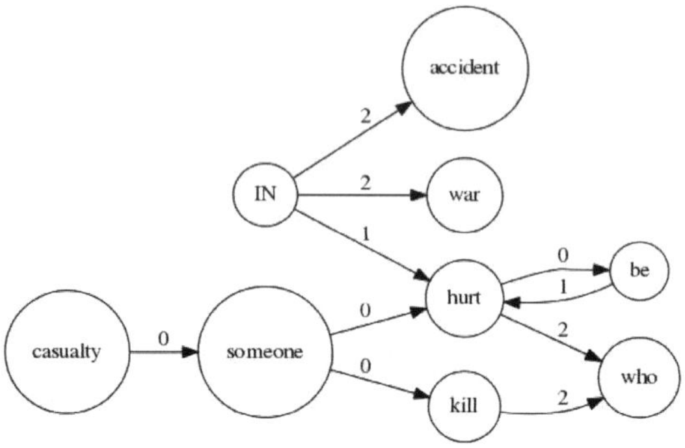

Figure 2: Definition of `casualty` built from LDOCE.

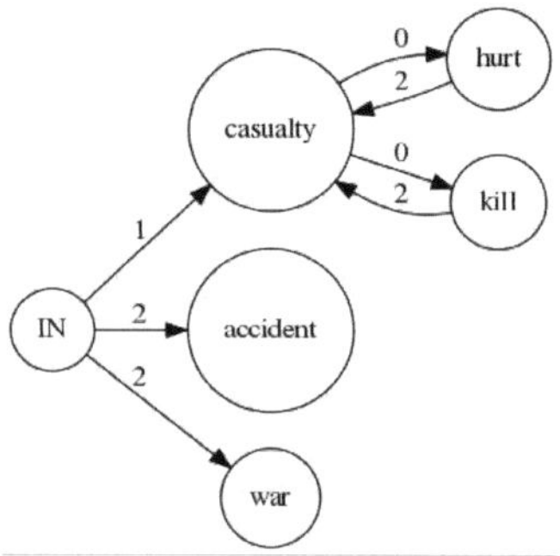

Figure 3: Expected definition of `casualty`.

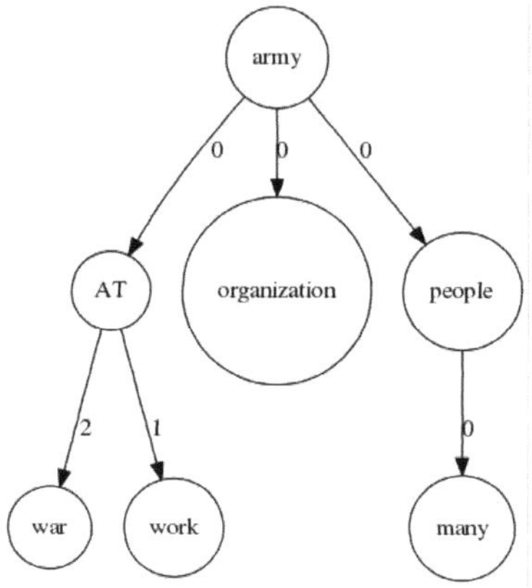

Figure 4: Definition of `army` in `4lang`.

past years' STS data, we found that if two words w_1 and w_2 are connected by a path of 0-edges, it is best to treat them as synonymous, i.e. assign to them a similarity of 1. This proved very efficient for determining semantic similarity of the most common types of sentence pairs in the Semeval datasets. Two descriptions of the same event (common in the *headlines* dataset) or the same picture (in *images*) will often only differ in their choice of words or choice of concreteness. In a dataset from 2014, for example, two descriptions, likely of the same picture, are *A bird holding on to a metal gate* and *A multi-colored bird clings to a wire fence*. Similarly, a pair of news headlines are *Piers Morgan questioned by police* and *Piers Morgan Interviewed by Police*. Although *wire* is by no means a synonym for *metal*, nor does being *questioned* mean exactly the same as being *interviewed*, treating them as perfect synonyms proved to be an efficient strategy when trying to assign sentence similarity scores that correlate highly with human annotators' judgements.

4 Submissions

We shall now describe the particular configurations used for each submission in Semeval. For Task 1 (Paraphrase and Semantic Similarity in Twitter) we ran two systems: `twitter-embed` uses a single source of word similarity, a word embedding built from a corpus of word 6-grams from the Rovereto Twitter N-Gram Corpus[3] using the `gensim`[4] package's implementation of the method presented in (Mikolov et al., 2013). Our second submission, `twitter-mash` combines several sources of word similarity by averaging the output of various systems using weights that have been learned using plain least squares regression on the training data available. The systems participating in the vote differ in the word similarity measure they use: one subset uses the character ngram baseline described in section 2 with various parameters ($n = 2, 3, 4$, each with Jaccard- and Dice-similarity), two systems use word embeddings (built from 5-grams and 6-grams of the Rovereto corpus, respectively) and one uses the `4lang`-based word similarity described in section 3.

	`embedding`	`hybrid`
Task 1a: *Paraphrase Identification*		
Precision	0.454	0.364
Recall	0.594	0.880
F-score	**0.515**	**0.515**
Task 1b: *Semantic Similarity*		
Pearson	0.229	**0.511**

Table 1: Performance of submitted systems on Task 1.

	`embedding`	`machine`	`hybrid`
Task 2a: *Semantic Similarity*			
answers-forums	0.704	0.698	0.723
answers-students	0.700	0.746	0.751
belief	0.733	0.736	0.747
headlines	0.769	0.805	0.804
images	0.804	0.841	0.844
mean Pearson	0.748	0.777	**0.784**

Table 2: Performance of submitted systems on Task 2.

For Task 2 (Semantic Textual Similarity) we were allowed three submissions. The `embedding` system uses a word embedding built from the first 1 billion words of the English Wikipedia using the `word2vec`[5] tool (Mikolov et al., 2013). The `machine` system uses the word similarity measure described in section 3 (both systems use the character ngram baseline as a fallback for OOVs). Finally, for the `hybrid` submission we used a weighted sum of these two systems and the character ngram baseline (weights were once again obtained using simple least square regression on the available training data). In both hybrid submissions we trained on a single dataset consisting of all training data available, we haven't experimented with genre-specific models.

Our results on each task are presented in Tables 1 and 2. In case of Task 1a (Paraphrase Identification) our two systems performed equally in terms of F-score and ranked 30th among 38 systems. On Task 1b the hybrid system performed considerably better than the purely vector-based run, placing 11th out of 28 runs. On Task 2 our hybrid system ranked 11th among 78 systems, the systems using the word embedding and the `4lang`-based similarity alone (with string similarity as a fallback for OOVs in each case) ranked 22nd and 15th, respectively.

[3]http://clic.cimec.unitn.it/amac/twitter_ngram/

[4]http://radimrehurek.com/gensim

[5]https://code.google.com/p/word2vec/

5 Conclusion

In a framework like (Han et al., 2013) which approximates sentence similarity by word similarity, the first order of business is to get the word similarity right. Character ngrams are quite useful for this, and remain an invaluable fallback even when more complex measures of word similarity, such as embeddings, are used. Dictionary-based methods, such as the `4lang`-based system presented here, are slightly better, and require only a one-time investment of manual labor to generate the seed. Critically, the error characteristics of the context-based (embedding) and the dictionary-based systems are quite different, so hybridizing the two provides a real boost over both.

Acknowledgments

Recski designed and implemented the machine-based similarity, Ács reimplemented the align-and-penalize architecture and created the word embedding. We thank András Kornai (HAS Institute for Computer Science) and Márton Sipos (Budapest U of Technology) for useful comments and discussions.

References

Eneko Agirre, Carmen Banea, Claire Cardie, Daniel Cer, Mona Diab, Aitor Gonzalez-Agirre, Weiwei Guo, Iigo Lopez-Gazpio, Montse Maritxalar, Rada Mihalcea, German Rigau, Larraitz Uria, and Janyce Wiebe. 2015. SemEval-2015 Task 2: Semantic Textual Similarity, English, Spanish and Pilot on Interpretability. In *Proceedings of the 9th International Workshop on Semantic Evaluation (SemEval 2015)*, Denver, CO, U.S.A.

Branimir K. Boguraev and Edward J. Briscoe. 1989. *Computational Lexicography for Natural Language Processing*. Longman.

Stephen Bullon. 2003. *Longman Dictionary of Contemporary English 4*. Longman.

Lushan Han, Abhay Kashyap, Tim Finin, James Mayfield, and Jonathan Weese. 2013. UMBC_EBIQUITY-CORE: Semantic textual similarity systems. In *Proceedings of the 2nd Joint Conf. on Lexical and Computational Semantics*, pages 44–52.

Dan Klein and Christopher D Manning. 2003. Accurate unlexicalized parsing. In *Proceedings of the 41st Annual Meeting on Association for Computational Linguistics-Volume 1*, pages 423–430.

András Kornai and Márton Makrai. 2013. A 4lang fogalmi szótár. In Attila Tanács and Veronika Vincze, editors, *IX. Magyar Számitógépes Nyelvészeti Konferencia*, pages 62–70.

András Kornai, Judit Ács, Márton Makrai, Dávid Nemeskey, Katalin Pajkossy, and Gábor Recski. 2015. Competence in lexical semantics. To appear in Proc. *SEM-2015.

András Kornai. 2010. The algebra of lexical semantics. In Christian Ebert, Gerhard Jäger, and Jens Michaelis, editors, *Proceedings of the 11th Mathematics of Language Workshop*, LNAI 6149, pages 174–199. Springer.

Tomas Mikolov, Kai Chen, Greg Corrado, and Jeffrey Dean. 2013. Efficient estimation of word representations in vector space. In Y. Bengio and Y. LeCun, editors, *Proc. ICLR 2013*.

George A. Miller. 1995. Wordnet: a lexical database for English. *Communications of the ACM*, 38(11):39–41.

Gábor Recski. 2015. Building concept graphs from monolingual dictionary entries. Unpublished manuscript.

Wei Xu, Chris Callison-Burch, and William B. Dolan. 2015. SemEval-2015 Task 1: Paraphrase and semantic similarity in Twitter (PIT). In *Proceedings of the 9th International Workshop on Semantic Evaluation (SemEval)*.

DCU: Using Distributional Semantics and Domain Adaptation for the Semantic Textual Similarity SemEval-2015 Task 2

Piyush Arora, Chris Hokamp, Jennifer Foster, Gareth J.F.Jones
ADAPT Centre
School of Computing
Dublin City University
Dublin, Ireland
{parora,chokamp,jfoster,gjones}@computing.dcu.ie

Abstract

We describe the work carried out by the DCU team on the Semantic Textual Similarity task at SemEval-2015. We learn a regression model to predict a semantic similarity score between a sentence pair. Our system exploits distributional semantics in combination with tried-and-tested features from previous tasks in order to compute sentence similarity. Our team submitted 3 runs for each of the five English test sets. For two of the test sets, *belief* and *headlines*, our best system ranked second and fourth out of the 73 submitted systems. Our best submission averaged over all test sets ranked 26 out of the 73 systems.

1 Introduction

This paper describes DCU's participation in the SemEval 2015 English Semantic Textual Similarity (STS) task, whose goal is to predict how similar in meaning two sentences are (Agirre et al., 2014). The semantic similarity between two sentences is defined on a scale from 0 (no relation) to 5 (semantic equivalence). Thus, given a sentence pair, our aim is to learn a model which outputs a score between 0 and 5 reflecting the semantic similarity between the two sentences.

We explore distributional representations of words computed using neural networks – specifically Word2Vec vectors (Mikolov et al., 2013) – and we design features which attempt to encode semantic similarity at the sentence level. We also experiment with several methods of data selection, both for training word embeddings, and for selecting training data for our regression models. We submitted three runs for this task: for all three runs, the features used are identical, and the only difference between them is the training instance selection method used.

2 Data and Resources

The training data for the task is comprised of all the corpora from previous years STS tasks: STS-2012, STS-2013 and STS-2014 (Agirre et al., 2012; Agirre et al., 2013; Agirre et al., 2014). The test data is taken from five domains: *answers-forums*, *answers-students*, *belief*, *headlines* and *images*. Two domains (*headlines* and *images*) have some training data available from the previous STS tasks[1] – the other three have been introduced for the first time.

We use the Word2Vec (W2V) representation for computing semantic similarity between two words. We then expand to incorporate the similarity between two sentences. Using W2V, a word can be represented as a vector of D dimensions, with each dimension capturing some aspect of the word's meaning in the form of different concepts learnt from the trained model. We use the `gensim` W2V implementation (Řehůřek and Sojka, 2010).

We use the *text8* Wikipedia corpus to train our general W2V model. This corpus is comprised of 100MB of compressed Wikipedia data.[2] We use the *UMBC* corpus (Han et al., 2013) for building domain-specific W2V models.

[1] http://ixa2.si.ehu.es/stswiki/index.php/Main_Page
[2] http://mattmahoney.net/dc/textdata.html

3 Methodology

3.1 Pre-processing

We perform minimal pre-processing, replacing all hyphens and apostrophes with spaces, and removing all non-alphanumeric symbols from the data. Our general domain model uses the NLTK[3] stop word list for stop word removal and the Porter stemming algorithm (Porter, 1980). Word2Vec handles the stem variations to some extent when it learns the vector representation from the raw input data. Thus for the domain-specific models, we only remove stopwords and do not stem.

3.2 Feature Design

To predict a semantic similarity score, we learn a regression model using the M5P algorithm.[4] We represent a sentence pair using the features described in the folowing subsections.

3.2.1 Cosine Similarity

We have two features representing the cosine similarity between two sentences, $s1$ and $s2$, where the sentences are represented as binary vectors with each dimension indicating the presence of a word. The first feature is the basic cosine similarity between the two sentence vectors and the second is the weighted cosine similarity between the two vectors, where each word is weighted by its inverse collection frequency (ICF).[5]

3.2.2 Word2Vec

Sum W2V: For a given sentence we represent each word by its W2V representation and then sum each word vector in a sentence to find the centroid of the word vectors representing the entire sentence. The cosine of the centroids of the two sentences indicates the similarity between them. Using the sum approach, two features, *sum* and *sum_icf*, are calculated, one corresponding to the basic cosine similarity between the vectors, and the other representing the weighted cosine similarity where, before calculating the centroid, each word vector is multiplied by its ICF weight.

$$sim(\mathbf{s1},\mathbf{s2}) = \frac{\frac{\sum_{i=1}^{n}\vec{s1}_i}{n} \cdot \frac{\sum_{j=1}^{m}\vec{s2}_j}{m}}{\sqrt{(\frac{\sum_{i=1}^{n}\vec{s1}_i}{n})^2}\sqrt{(\frac{\sum_{j=1}^{m}\vec{s2}_j}{m})^2}} \quad (1)$$

Product W2V: Given $s1$ and $s2$, we take the element-wise product of each word vector in $s1$ and $s2$ and store the maximum product value for each word in $s1$ and similarly for $s2$. The Product W2V feature is the average of the maximum weights between each word of $s1$ with $s2$ and vice versa:

$$sim(\mathbf{s1},\mathbf{s2}) = \frac{\sum_{i=1}^{n}(max\sum_{j=1}^{m}\frac{(\vec{s1}_i.\vec{s2}_j)}{\sqrt{(\vec{s1}_i)^2}\sqrt{(\vec{s2}_j)^2}})}{n} + \frac{\sum_{j=1}^{m}(max\sum_{i=1}^{n}\frac{(\vec{s1}_i.\vec{s2}_j)}{\sqrt{(\vec{s1}_i)^2}\sqrt{(\vec{s2}_j)^2}})}{m} \quad (2)$$

The sum and product W2V models are inspired by the composition models of Mitchell and Lapata (2008) and semantic similarity measures of Mihalcea et al. (2006).

Domain-specific Cosine Similarity: Good coverage is obtained using the *text8* corpus to train the W2V model. However, we also want to explore the performance with respect to an *in-domain* W2V model. So, for each of the test corpora, we first extract a corpus of similar sentences from the *UMBC* corpus by selecting up to 500 sentences for each content word in the test corpus and then use the extracted dataset to train a W2V model that has better coverage of the test domain. Using the domain-specific W2V corpus, we compute the feature *domain_w2v_cosine_similarity* in a similar fashion to the Sum W2V feature – we compute the centroid vector of the content words in each sentence and then compute the cosine between the two centroids.

Syntax: We also hypothesize that two semantically similar sentences should have high overlap between their nouns, verbs, adjectives and adverbs. For each coarse-grained POS tag (`NN*`, `VB*`, `JJ*` and `RB*`) we calculate the W2V cosine similarity between all words from $s1$ and $s2$ which have the same POS tag (using the Sum W2V combination method). For each coarse-grained POS tag, we also calculate the number of lexical matches with that particular POS tag.

[3]http://www.nltk.org/

[4]We used the weka implementation: http://www.cs.waikato.ac.nz/ml/weka/ without performing any extra hyper-parameter optimization.

[5]ICF is calculated using word frequency from the *wikipedia* 2011 dump.

We also parse each sentence using the Stanford parser (Manning et al., 2014) and look for dependency relation overlap between $s1$ and $s2$.[6] We concentrate on six dependency relations – `nsubj`, `dobj`, `det`, `prep`, `amod` and `aux`. For each relation we calculate the degree of overlap between the occurrences of this relation in the two sentences. We have two notions of relation overlap: a non-lexicalized version which just counts the relation itself (e.g. `nsubj`) and a lexicalized version which counts the relation and the two tokens it connects (e.g. `nsubj_word1_word2`).

3.2.3 Monolingual Alignment

We compute the monolingual alignment between the two sentences using the word aligner introduced in (Sultan et al., 2014). Their system aligns related words in a sentence pair by exploiting semantic and contextual similarities of the words. From the aligned sentences, we then extract two features: *percent_aligned_source* and *percent_aligned_target*, which represent the fraction of tokens in each sentence which have an alignment in the other sentence. The intuition behind these features is that sentences which are semantically similar should have a higher fraction of aligned tokens, since alignments constitute either identical strings or paraphrases.

3.2.4 TakeLab

The Takelab system (Šarić et al., 2012) was the top performing system in STS-2012 task. Their system used support vector regression models with multiple features measuring word overlap similarity and syntactic similarity. We find that adding the Takelab features provides additional knowledge to our system and improves performance for the training datasets. We add the 21 features of the Takelab system to our feature set.

3.3 Training instance selection

After designing features to model semantic similarity between two sentences, the next important task is to select the training corpus for learning the weights for these features. Out of the five test sets for STS-2015, we only have in-domain training corpora for the *headlines* and *images* data sets. We hypothesize that finding vocabulary similarity between the entire training and test corpus could be used to select more similar corpus for training of the system. We calculate the similarity between each of the corpora we have from previous STS tasks and each of the test corpora. Using the entire corpus vocabulary as a vector we find the cosine similarity between different corpora using the TFIDF (Manning et al., 2008), LSI (Hofmann, 1999), LDA (Blei et al., 2003b) and HLDA (Blei et al., 2003a) measures.

Next, we describe the mechanism we used for training data selection for each run:

1. *Run-1*: For the two corpora for which we have prior training data we took the previous years' training data. For the other test corpora we select the most similar corpus from the previous years' training data based on the corpus vector cosine similarity, where each word in a vector is replaced by its TFIDF weight. The training corpora we selected are as follows:
   Images: Images_2014, *Headlines*: Headlines-_2014, *Belief*: Deft_Forum_2014, *Answers-students*: MSRVid_2012_train, *Answers-forums*: Deft_Forum_2014
2. *Run-2*: We want to make sure that the training data has instances similar to the test samples. To capture diversity in our training corpus we compute corpus vector cosine similarity where each word is replaced by its TFIDF weight, then we merge the top three most similar training corpora for each test set as shown below:
   Images: Images_2014 + MSRVid_2012_train + MSRVid_2012_test
   Headlines: Headlines_2013 + Headlines_2014 + MSRPar_2012_train
   Belief: Deft_Forum_2014 + Headlines_2014 + Headlines_2013
   Answers-students: OnWn_2012_test + MSR-Vid_2012_train + MSRPar_2012_test
   Answers-forums: Deft_forum_2014 + SMT-_2012_train + MSRPar_2012_train

   For each test set instance, we find the five[7] most similar instances from the merged training

[6] Parsing is carried out on the raw sentences.

[7] Five was empirically chosen by experimenting with different values on the training data.

Test Set	Baseline	Run-1	Run-2	Run-3	Top System	Our Rank
Images	0.6039	0.8394	0.835	**0.8434**	0.8713	19
Headlines	0.5312	**0.8284**	0.8187	0.8181	0.8417	4
Belief	0.6517	0.5464	**0.7549**	0.6977	0.7717	2
Answers-students	0.6647	**0.6582**	0.6233	0.6108	0.7879	47
Answers-forum	0.4453	0.5556	0.5628	**0.653**	0.739	30
Mean		0.7192	0.734	**0.7369**		26

Table 1: Results of our final runs compared to the baseline and the best system for each test set.

corpus (similar instances are computed using cosine similarity between the feature vectors). By combining these five training instances for all test instances and removing duplicates, we form a more focused training set which is expected to capture the test set diversity more effectively.

3. *Run-3*: In this variant, we do not want to limit ourselves to just the top three corpora, so we merge all the training data and then look for the five most similar training instances for each test instance to form a focused training set.

4 Results

Table 1 shows the results of our systems on the five test sets. For the test sets *answers-forum* and *belief* there was a considerable difference in the results across the three runs, indicating that selecting training instances has a significant effect on performance. For these two datasets across two runs the absolute difference in the Pearson coefficient is about 10% for *answers-forum* and about 20% for the *belief* dataset. Overall, our best system rank is 26 out of 73. If we look at the results for individual test sets, it seems our approach works well for the *belief*, *headlines* and *image* test set but performs poorly for the *answer-student* and *answer-forum* test sets. For the *belief* test set our Run-2 was ranked 2nd overall and for the *headlines* test set our Run-1 was ranked 4th overall. For the *images* test set, the results are competitive – the absolute difference in the Pearson value between our best run and the best system is only 0.03. Thus, apart from two corpora, *answers-students* and *answer-forums*, our approach performed quite well.

We analyzed the features using GradientBoostingRegressor[8] for all the training sets. The feature importance varies slightly across different domains. For all datasets, we remove features with gini importance[9] < 0.01, then we look for the features which are present in at least three of the different domain for this year's test set. The features that performed well are shown in Table 2.

Our Features
sum_icf, sum, product, domain_w2v_cosine, percent_aligned_target, percent_source_target, nn_w2v, vb_w2v, jj_w2v, nsub_1, cosine, cosine_icf
TakeLab Features
wn_sim_match, weighted_word_match, weighted_word_match, dist_sim, weighted_dist_sim, weighted_dist_sim, relative_len_difference, relative_ic_difference

Table 2: Important features.

5 Conclusions

All of our runs have the same features, but use different training corpora to learn the weights. We thus show that training data selection can have an impact on the performance of a model, especially for a novel genre. Using Word2Vec to find semantic similarity between a sentence pair proved to be effective. Furthermore, composing W2V features in different ways can help to reveal new information about semantic similarity.

Investigating the test sets where we failed to perform well, *answer-forums* and *answer-students*, reveals that we need to handle phrasal information more effectively by, for example, handling negation,

[8] http://scikit-learn.org/stable/modules/generated/sklearn.ensemble.GradientBoostingRegressor.html

[9] http://www.stat.berkeley.edu/~breiman/RandomForests/cc_home.htm

devising measures to compare the sentences at the entity level and making better use of parser output.

Acknowledgments

We would like to thank Rasoul Kaljahi for helping with running some of the preliminary experiments using tree kernels and Debasis Ganguly for his suggestions and guidance. This research is supported by Science Foundation Ireland (SFI) as a part of the CNGL Centre for Global Intelligent Content at DCU (Grant No: 12/CE/I2267).

References

Eneko Agirre, Mona Diab, Daniel Cer, and Aitor Gonzalez-Agirre. 2012. SemEval-2012 Task 6: A Pilot on Semantic Textual Similarity. In *Proceedings of the First Joint Conference on Lexical and Computational Semantics - Volume 1: Proceedings of the Main Conference and the Shared Task, and Volume 2: Proceedings of the Sixth International Workshop on Semantic Evaluation*, pages 385–393, Montréal, Canada.

Eneko Agirre, Daniel Cer, Mona Diab, Aitor Gonzalez-Agirre, and Weiwei Guo. 2013. *SEM 2013 shared task: Semantic Textual Similarity. In *Second Joint Conference on Lexical and Computational Semantics (*SEM), Volume 1: Proceedings of the Main Conference and the Shared Task: Semantic Textual Similarity*, pages 32–43, Atlanta, Georgia, USA.

Eneko Agirre, Carmen Banea, Claire Cardie, Daniel Cer, Mona Diab, Aitor Gonzalez-Agirre, Weiwei Guo, Rada Mihalcea, German Rigau, and Janyce Wiebe. 2014. SemEval-2014 Task 10: Multilingual Semantic Textual Similarity. In *Proceedings of the 8th International Workshop on Semantic Evaluation (SemEval 2014)*, pages 81–91, Dublin, Ireland.

David M. Blei, Thomas L. Griffiths, Michael I. Jordan, and Joshua B. Tenenbaum. 2003a. Hierarchical Topic Models and the Nested Chinese Restaurant Process. In *Advances in Neural Information Processing Systems 16 [Neural Information Processing Systems, NIPS 2003]*, pages 17–24, Vancouver and Whistler, British Columbia, Canada.

David M. Blei, Andrew Y. Ng, and Michael I. Jordan. 2003b. Latent Dirichlet Allocation. *Journal of Machine Learning Research - Volume 3*, pages 993–1022.

Lushan Han, Abhay L. Kashyap, Tim Finin, James Mayfield, and Johnathan Weese. 2013. UMBC_EBIQUITY-CORE: Semantic Textual Similarity Systems. In *Proceedings of the Second Joint Conference on Lexical and Computational Semantics*, pages 42–54, Atlanta, Georgia, USA.

Thomas Hofmann. 1999. Probabilistic Latent Semantic Indexing. In *Proceedings of the 22nd Annual International ACM SIGIR Conference on Research and Development in Information Retrieval*, pages 50–57, Berkeley, California, USA.

Christopher D Manning, Prabhakar Raghavan, and Hinrich Schütze. 2008. Scoring, term weighting and the vector space model. *Introduction to Information Retrieval*, pages 118–120.

Christopher D. Manning, Mihai Surdeanu, John Bauer, Jenny Finkel, Steven J. Bethard, and David McClosky. 2014. The Stanford CoreNLP Natural Language Processing Toolkit. In *Proceedings of 52nd Annual Meeting of the Association for Computational Linguistics: System Demonstrations*, pages 55–60, Baltimore, Maryland.

Rada Mihalcea, Courtney Corley, and Carlo Strapparava. 2006. Corpus-based and knowledge-based measures of text semantic similarity. In *Proceedings of the 21st National Conference on Artificial Intelligence - Volume 1*, pages 775–780, Boston, Massachusetts.

Tomas Mikolov, Quoc V. Le, and Ilya Sutskever. 2013. Exploiting Similarities among Languages for Machine Translation. *CoRR*, abs/1309.4168.

Jeff Mitchell and Mirella Lapata. 2008. Vector-based Models of Semantic Composition. In *Proceedings of ACL-08: HLT*, pages 236–244, Columbus, Ohio.

Martin F Porter. 1980. An algorithm for suffix stripping. *Program - Volume 14*, pages 130–137.

Radim Řehůřek and Petr Sojka. 2010. Software Framework for Topic Modelling with Large Corpora. In *Proceedings of the LREC 2010 Workshop on New Challenges for NLP Frameworks*, pages 45–50, Valletta, Malta.

Arafat Md Sultan, Steven Bethard, and Tamara Sumner. 2014. Back to Basics for Monolingual Alignment: Exploiting Word Similarity and Contextual Evidence. *Transactions of the Association of Computational Linguistics – Volume 2, Issue 1*, pages 219–230.

Frane Šarić, Goran Glavaš, Mladen Karan, Jan Šnajder, and Bojana Dalbelo Bašić. 2012. TakeLab: Systems for Measuring Semantic Text Similarity. In *Proceedings of the First Joint Conference on Lexical and Computational Semantics - Volume 1: Proceedings of the Main Conference and the Shared Task, and Volume 2: Proceedings of the Sixth International Workshop on Semantic Evaluation*, SemEval '12, pages 441–448, Montréal, Canada.

DLS@CU: Sentence Similarity from Word Alignment and Semantic Vector Composition

Md Arafat Sultan[†], **Steven Bethard**[‡], **Tamara Sumner**[†]
[†]Institute of Cognitive Science and Department of Computer Science
University of Colorado Boulder
[‡]Department of Computer and Information Sciences
University of Alabama at Birmingham
arafat.sultan@colorado.edu, bethard@cis.uab.edu, sumner@colorado.edu

Abstract

We describe a set of top-performing systems at the SemEval 2015 English Semantic Textual Similarity (STS) task. Given two English sentences, each system outputs the degree of their semantic similarity. Our unsupervised system, which is based on word alignments across the two input sentences, ranked 5th among 73 submitted system runs with a mean correlation of 79.19% with human annotations. We also submitted two runs of a supervised system which uses word alignments and similarities between compositional sentence vectors as its features. Our best supervised run ranked 1st with a mean correlation of 80.15%.

1 Introduction

Identification of short text similarity is an important research problem with application in a multitude of areas: natural language processing (machine translation, text summarization), information retrieval (question answering), education (short answer scoring), and so on. The SemEval Semantic Textual Similarity (STS) task series (Agirre et al., 2012; Agirre et al., 2013; Agirre et al., 2014; Agirre et al., 2015) has become a central platform for the task: a publicly available corpus of more than 14,000 sentence pairs have been developed over the past four years with human annotations of similarity for each pair; and a total of 290 system runs have been evaluated.

In this article, we describe a set of systems that were submitted at the SemEval 2015 English STS task (Agirre et al., 2015). Given two English sentences, the objective is to compute their semantic similarity in the range [0, 5], where the score increases with similarity (i.e., 0 indicates no similarity and 5 indicates identicality). The official evaluation metric was the Pearson correlation coefficient with human annotations. The best of our three system runs achieved the highest mean correlation (80.15%) with human annotations among all submitted systems on five test sets (containing a total of 3000 test pairs).

Early work on sentence similarity (Corley and Mihalcea, 2005; Mihalcea et al., 2006; Li et al., 2006; Islam and Inkpen, 2008) established the basic procedural framework under which most modern algorithms operate: computing sentence similarity as a mean of word similarities across the two input sentences. With no human annotated STS data set available, these algorithms were unsupervised and were evaluated extrinsically on tasks like paraphrase detection and textual entailment recognition. The SemEval STS task series has made an important contribution through the large annotated data set, enabling intrinsic evaluation of STS systems and making supervised STS systems a reality.

At SemEval 2012, domain-specific training data was provided for most of the test pairs (Agirre et al., 2012) and consequently, supervised systems were the most successful (Bär et al., 2012; Šarić et al., 2012). These systems combined different similarity measures, e.g., lexico-semantic, syntactic and string similarity, using regression models. However, at the 2013 and 2014 STS events, no such training data was provided; instead, the systems were allowed to use all past data to train their systems. Interestingly, the best systems at these two events were unsupervised (Han et al., 2013; Sultan et al., 2014b); some super-

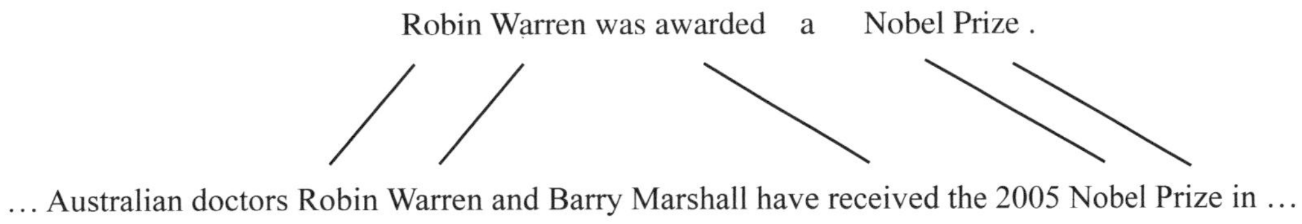

Figure 1: Words aligned by our aligner across two sentences taken from the MSR alignment corpus (Brockett, 2007). (We show only part of the second sentence.) Besides exact word/lemma matches, it identifies and aligns semantically similar word pairs using PPDB (*awarded* – *received* in this example).

vised systems did well, too (Wu et al., 2013; Lynum et al., 2014). The core component of a typical unsupervised system is term alignment: semantically related terms across the two sentences are aligned at first and then their semantic similarity is computed as a monotonically increasing function of the degree of alignment.

At SemEval 2015, we submitted an unsupervised system based on word alignments which is almost identical to our winning system at SemEval 2014 (Sultan et al., 2014b). We also submitted a supervised ridge regression model that uses (1) the output of our unsupervised system, and (2) the cosine similarity between the vector representations of the two sentences (derived from neural word embeddings of their content words (Baroni et al., 2014)) as its features. Our unsupervised system ranked 5th and the two supervised runs ranked 1st and 3rd. Evaluation also shows that our best run outperforms the winning systems at all past SemEval STS events.

2 System Overview

We describe our three system runs in this section in order of their complexity – new capabilities and/or features are added with each run.

2.1 Run 1: U

This is an unsupervised system that first aligns related words across the two input sentences and then outputs the proportion of aligned content words as their semantic similarity. It is similar to our last year's system (Sultan et al., 2014b) based on the word aligner described in (Sultan et al., 2014a). However, where last year's system computed a separate proportion for each sentence and then took their harmonic mean, this year's system computes a single proportion over all words in the two sentences. In other words, given sentences $S^{(1)}$ and $S^{(2)}$,

$$sts(S^{(1)}, S^{(2)}) = \frac{n_c^a(S^{(1)}) + n_c^a(S^{(2)})}{n_c(S^{(1)}) + n_c(S^{(2)})}$$

where $n_c(S^{(i)})$ and $n_c^a(S^{(i)})$ are the number of content words and the number of aligned content words in $S^{(i)}$, respectively. This is a conceptually simpler step and yielded better experimental results on data from past STS events.

The aligner aligns words based on their semantic similarity and the similarity between their local semantic contexts in the two sentences. It uses the Paraphrase Database (PPDB) (Ganitkevitch et al., 2013) to identify semantically similar words, and relies on dependencies and surface-form neighbors of the two words to determine their contextual similarity. Word pairs are aligned in decreasing order of a weighted sum of their semantic and contextual similarity. Figure 1 shows an example set of alignments. For more details, see (Sultan et al., 2014a).

We also consider a levenshtein distance[1] of 1 between a misspelled word and a correctly spelled word (of length > 2) to be a match. In all runs, we truncate at the extremes to keep the score in [0, 5].

2.2 Run 2: S_1

A fundamental limitation of our unsupervised system is that it only relies on PPDB to identify semantically similar words; consequently, similar word pairs are limited to only lexical paraphrases. Hence it fails to utilize semantic similarity or relatedness between non-paraphrase word pairs (e.g., 'sister' and

[1]the minimum number of single-character edits needed to change one word into the other, where an edit is an insertion, a deletion or a substitution.

'related'). In this run, we leverage neural word embeddings to overcome this limitation. We use the 400-dimensional vectors[2] developed by Baroni et al. (2014). They used the word2vec toolkit[3] to extract these vectors from a corpus of about 2.8 billion tokens. These vectors performed exceedingly well across different word similarity data sets in their experiments. Details on their approach and findings can be found in (Baroni et al., 2014).

Instead of comparing word vectors across the two input sentences, we adopt a simple vector composition scheme to construct a vector representation of each input sentence and then take the cosine similarity between the two sentence vectors as our second feature for this run. The vector representing a sentence is the centroid (i.e., the componentwise average) of its content lemma vectors.

Finally, we combine the two features – output of our unsupervised run ($\boldsymbol{U}$) and the sentence vectors' cosine similarity – using a ridge regression model (implemented in scikit-learn (Pedregosa et al., 2011), with $\alpha = 1.0$ and the 'auto' solver that automatically selects a feature weight learning algorithm from a pool depending on the type of the data). The model is trained using annotations from SemEval 2012–2014 (details in Section 3).

2.3 Run 3: S_2

The aligner used in our previous two runs aligns content words even if there are no similarities between their contexts in the two sentences. In this run, we use an alignment-based feature (in addition to our two features in $\boldsymbol{S_1}$) where content words are aligned only if they have some contextual similarity – a common word either in their dependencies or in a neighborhood of 3 words to the left and 3 words to the right (considering only content words for the latter).

3 Data

The 3000 test sentence pairs at SemEval 2015 were divided into five sets, each consisting of pairs from a different domain. Each pair was assigned similarity scores in the range [0, 5] by multiple human annotators (0: no similarity, 5: identicality) and the average of the annotations was taken as their final similarity score. We describe each data set briefly in Table 1.

Data Set	Source of Text	# of Pairs
answers-forums	forum answers	375
answers-students	student short answers	750
belief	belief annotations	375
headlines	news headlines	750
images	image descriptions	750

Table 1: Test sets at SemEval STS 2015.

We trained our supervised systems using data from the past three years of SemEval STS (Agirre et al., 2012; Agirre et al., 2013; Agirre et al., 2014). For *answers-forums*, *answers-students* and *belief*, we used all past annotations. For *headlines*, we used all *headlines* (2013), *headlines* (2014), *deft-news* (2014) and *smtnews* (2012) pairs. For *images*, we used all *msrpar* (2012; train and test), *msrvid* (2012; train and test) and *images* (2014) pairs. The specific training corpus selections for the two latter data sets were based on our experiments with past *headlines* and *images* data, where these subsets yielded better results than an all-inclusive training set (seemingly due to the fact that they were drawn from similar domains and were still large-enough to provide the model with effective supervision).

4 Evaluation

In addition to the official evaluation at SemEval 2015, we report evaluation results on past STS (2012–2014) test data. For all these evaluations, the performance metric is the Pearson correlation coefficient between system output and average human annotations. Correlation is computed for each individual test set, and a weighted sum of all correlations (i.e. over all test sets) is used as the final evaluation metric. The weight of a test set is proportional to the number of sentence pairs it contains.

Before presenting the results, we describe a preprocessing step for one of the 2015 test sets. Identifying the right stop words (some of which can be domain-specific) proved key in our past investigation of STS (Sultan et al., 2014b); therefore we consider it very important to manually examine individual domains to ensure proper categorization of words. An inspection of the trial data for the *answers-students* set indicated that the expressions in the

[2] http://clic.cimec.unitn.it/composes/semantic-vectors.html

[3] https://code.google.com/p/word2vec/

Data Set	Runs			Best
	U	S_1	S_2	Score
answers-forums	0.6821	***0.7390***	0.7241	**0.7390**
answers-students	***0.7879***	0.7725	0.7569	**0.7879**
belief	0.7325	*0.7491*	0.7223	**0.7717**
headlines	0.8238	*0.8250*	*0.8250*	**0.8417**
images	0.8485	*0.8644*	0.8631	**0.8713**
Weighted Mean	0.7919	***0.8015***	0.7921	-
Rank	5	***1***	3	-

Table 2: Performance on STS 2015 data. Each number in rows 1–5 is the correlation between system output and human annotations for the corresponding data set. The rightmost column shows the best score by any system. The last two rows show the value of the final evaluation metric and the system rank, respectively, for each run.

following pairs are semantically equivalent for the given domain: {'battery terminal', 'terminal'} and {'electrical state', 'state'}. Therefore, we treated the two words 'battery' and 'electrical' as special stop words during occurrences of these pairs across the input sentences.

4.1 STS 2015 Results

Performances of our three runs on each of the STS 2015 test sets are shown in Table 2. Each bold number represents the best score by any system on the corresponding test set and each italic number shows the best score among our runs. The weighted mean of correlations and rank for each run is also shown.

Our best run (S_1) did not perform the best on all test sets (in fact it does so on only one test set), but it maintained the best balance across all test sets. The second best overall system run (ExBThemis-themisexp) had a mean correlation of 79.42%. We found the difference of 0.73% between this system and S_1 to be statistically significant at $p < 0.0001$ in a two-sample one-tailed z-test[4] (unlike last year's 0.05% (Agirre et al., 2014)).

The third feature in S_2 did not prove useful as S_2 performed worse than S_1 on almost all test sets. This result falls in line with our observation reported in (Sultan et al., 2014a): "more often than not content words are inherently sufficiently meaningful to be aligned even in the absence of contextual evidence when there are no competing pairs."

[4]Standard deviation was computed from the frequency distribution of correlations across the five test sets.

Year	S_1	Winning System
2014	**0.779**	0.761
2013	**0.6542**	0.6181
2012	**0.6803**	0.6773

Table 3: Performance of our top system (S_1) on past STS test sets (mean correlation with human annotations). The score of the winning system at each event is shown on column 3. S_1 outperforms all past winning systems.

Contrary to our findings from past years' data, the special stop words for the *answers-students* test set (discussed in the previous section) did not improve performance – considering these words as content words, we observed a slightly higher correlation of 0.7895 for our unsupervised system U.

4.2 Results on Past Test Sets

Table 3 shows the performance of our best system S_1 on test data from SemEval 2012–2014. To ensure fair comparison with other systems, for years 2013 and 2014, we used only past data to train our model. For year 2012, we used the designated training data for test sets *msrpar*, *msrvid* and *smteuroparl*, and all 2012 training pairs for the other two test sets.

S_1 outperformed all winning systems from 2012 through 2014. Without any domain-specific training data, the top systems at SemEval 2013 and 2014 were unsupervised. S_1 achieved the best performance on both despite its supervised nature.

4.3 Ablation Study

We performed a feature ablation study for S_1 on STS 2015 data to determine the relative importances of its two features. Table 4 shows the results. Columns 2 and 4 show performances of our U and S_1 systems. (Remember that the former is used as a feature by the latter.) Column 3 shows the performance of the second feature of S_1 (i.e. cosine similarity between the sentence vectors) as a measure of STS.

On four of the five test sets, U outperformed sentence vector similarity. However, combining the two features improved system performance on four out of five test sets, and overall. These results indicate that each feature captures aspects of STS that the other does not and consequently the two complement each other when used together.

Data Set	U	Vector Sim	S_1
answers-forums	0.6821	0.7330	**0.7390**
answers-students	**0.7879**	0.6899	0.7725
belief	0.7325	0.6981	**0.7491**
headlines	0.8238	0.7511	**0.8250**
images	0.8485	0.8411	**0.8644**
Weighted Mean	0.7919	0.7494	**0.8015**

Table 4: Performance of each individual feature of our best run (S_1) on STS 2015 test sets. Combining the two features improves performance on all but one test set.

5 Conclusions and Future Work

At SemEval 2014, we reported a top-performing unsupervised STS system (Sultan et al., 2014b) that relied only on word alignment. This year, we present a supervised system that is statistically significantly better than our last year's system. Combining a vector similarity feature derived from word embeddings with alignment-based similarity, it outperforms all past and current STS systems. Since it makes use of only off-the-shelf software[5] and data, it is easily replicable as well.

The primary limitation of our system is the inability to model semantics of units larger than words (phrasal verbs, idioms, and so on). This is an important future direction not only for our system but also for STS and text comparison tasks in general. Incorporation of stop word semantics is key to identifying similarities and differences in subtle aspects of sentential semantics like polarity and modality. Finally, rather than studying STS as a standalone problem, the time has come to develop algorithms that can adapt to requirements posed by different data domains and applications.

Acknowledgments

This material is based in part upon work supported by the National Science Foundation under Grant Numbers EHR/0835393 and EHR/0835381. Any opinions, findings, and conclusions or recommendations expressed in this material are those of the author(s) and do not necessarily reflect the views of the National Science Foundation.

[5]Our aligner is also available at: `https://github.com/ma-sultan/monolingual-word-aligner`

References

Eneko Agirre, Daniel Cer, Mona Diab, and Aitor Gonzalez-Agirre. 2012. SemEval-2012 task 6: A Pilot on Semantic Textual Similarity. In *Proceedings of the First Joint Conference on Lexical and Computational Semantics, Volume 2: Proceedings of the Sixth International Workshop on Semantic Evaluation*, SemEval '12, pages 385-393, Montreal, Canada.

Eneko Agirre, Daniel Cer, Mona Diab, Aitor Gonzalez-Agirre, and Weiwei Guo. 2013. *SEM 2013 Shared Task: Semantic Textual Similarity. In *Proceedings of the Second Joint Conference on Lexical and Computational Semantics*, *SEM '13, pages 32-43, Atlanta, Georgia, USA.

Eneko Agirre, Carmen Banea, Claire Cardie, Daniel Cer, Mona Diab, Aitor Gonzalez-Agirre, Weiwei Guo, Rada Mihalcea, German Rigau, and Janyce Wiebe. 2014. SemEval-2014 Task 10: Multilingual Semantic Textual Similarity. In *Proceedings of the 8th International Workshop on Semantic Evaluation*, SemEval '14, pages 81-91, Dublin, Ireland.

Eneko Agirre, Carmen Banea, Claire Cardie, Daniel Cer, Mona Diab, Aitor Gonzalez-Agirre, Weiwei Guo, Iñigo Lopez-Gazpio, Montse Maritxalar, Rada Mihalcea, German Rigau, Larraitz Uria, and Janyce Wiebe. 2015. SemEval-2015 Task 2: Semantic Textual Similarity, English, Spanish and Pilot on Interpretability. In *Proceedings of the 9th International Workshop on Semantic Evaluation*, SemEval '15, Denver, Colorado, USA.

Daniel Bär, Chris Biemann, Iryna Gurevych, and Torsten Zesch. 2012. UKP: Computing Semantic Textual Similarity by Combining Multiple Content Similarity Measures. In *Proceedings of the 6th International Workshop on Semantic Evaluation, held in conjunction with the 1st Joint Conference on Lexical and Computational Semantics*, SemEval '12, pages 435-440, Montreal, Canada.

Marco Baroni, Georgiana Dinu, and Germán Kruszewski 2014. Dont Count, Predict! A Systematic Comparison of Context-Counting vs. Context-Predicting Semantic Vectors. In *Proceedings of the 52nd Annual Meeting of the Association for Computational Linguistics*, ACL '14, pages 238-247, Baltimore, Maryland, USA.

Chris Brockett. 2007. Aligning the RTE 2006 Corpus. Technical Report MSR-TR-2007-77, Microsoft Research.

Courtney Corley and Rada Mihalcea. 2005. Measuring the Semantic Similarity of Texts. In *Proceedings of the ACL Workshop on Empirical Modeling of Semantic Equivalence and Entailment*, pages 13-18, Ann Arbor, Michigan, USA.

Juri Ganitkevitch, Benjamin Van Durme, and Chris Callison-Burch. 2013. PPDB: The Paraphrase

Database. In *Proceedings of the 2013 Conference of the North American Chapter of the Association for Computational Linguistics*. Association for Computational Linguistics, 758-764.

Lushan Han, Abhay Kashyap, Tim Finin, James Mayfield, and Jonathan Weese. 2013. UMBC EBIQUITY-CORE: Semantic Textual Similarity Systems. In *Proceedings of the Second Joint Conference on Lexical and Computational Semantics*, *SEM '13, pages 44-52, Atlanta, Georgia, USA.

Aminul Islam and Diana Inkpen. 2008. Semantic Text Similarity using Corpus-Based Word Similarity and String Similarity. *ACM Transactions on Knowledge Discovery from Data (TKDD)*, 2(2):10:1-10:25.

Yuhua Li, David McLean, Zuhair A. Bandar, James D. OShea, and Keeley Crockett. 2006. Sentence Similarity Based on Semantic Nets and Corpus Statistics. *IEEE Transactions on Knowledge and Data Engineering*, 18(8):1138-1150.

André Lynum, Partha Pakray, Björn Gambäck 2014. NTNU: Measuring Semantic Similarity with Sublexical Feature Representations and Soft Cardinality. In *Proceedings of the 8th International Workshop on Semantic Evaluation*, SemEval '14, pages 448-453, Dublin, Ireland.

Rada Mihalcea, Courtney Corley, and Carlo Strapparava. 2006. Corpus-Based and Knowledge-Based Measures of Text Semantic Similarity. In *Proceedings of the 21st National Conference on Artificial Intelligence*, pages 775-780, Boston, Massachusetts, USA.

Fabian Pedregosa, Gaël Varoquaux, Alexandre Gramfort, Vincent Michel, Bertrand Thirion, Olivier Grisel, Mathieu Blondel, Peter Prettenhofer, Ron Weiss, Vincent Dubourg, Jake Vanderplas, Alexandre Passos, David Cournapeau, Matthieu Brucher, Matthieu Perrot, and Édouard Duchesnay 2011. Scikit-learn: Machine Learning in Python. *Journal of Machine Learning Research*, vol. 12, pages 2825-2830.

Frane Šarić, Goran Glavaš, Mladen Karan, Jan Šnajder, and Bojana Dalbelo Bašić. 2012. TakeLab: Systems for Measuring Semantic Text Similarity. In *Proceedings of the 6th International Workshop on Semantic Evaluation, held in conjunction with the 1st Joint Conference on Lexical and Computational Semantics*, SemEval '12, pages 441-448, Montreal, Canada.

Md Arafat Sultan, Steven Bethard, and Tamara Sumner. 2014a. Back to Basics for Monolingual Alignment: Exploiting Word Similarity and Contextual Evidence. *Transactions of the Association for Computational Linguistics*, 2 (May), pages 219-230.

Md Arafat Sultan, Steven Bethard, and Tamara Sumner. 2014b. DLS@CU: Sentence Similarity from Word Alignment. In *Proceedings of the 8th International Workshop on Semantic Evaluation*, SemEval '14, pages 241-246, Dublin, Ireland.

Stephen Wu, Dongqing Zhu, Ben Carterette, and Hongfang Liu. 2013. MayoClinicNLP-CORE: Semantic Representations for Textual Similarity. In *Proceedings of the Second Joint Conference on Lexical and Computational Semantics*, *SEM '13, pages 148-154, Atlanta, Georgia, USA.

FCICU: The Integration between Sense-Based Kernel and Surface-Based Methods to Measure Semantic Textual Similarity

Basma Hassan
Computer Science Department, Faculty of Computers and Information
Fayoum University
Fayoum, Egypt
bhassan@fayoum.edu.eg

Samir AbdelRahman
Computer Science Department, Faculty of Computers and Information
Cairo University
Giza, Egypt
s.abdelrahman@fci-cu.edu.eg

Reem Bahgat
Computer Science Department, Faculty of Computers and Information
Cairo University
Giza, Egypt
r.bahgat@fci-cu.edu.eg

Abstract

This paper describes FCICU team participation in SemEval 2015 for Semantic Textual Similarity challenge. Our main contribution is to propose a word-sense similarity method using BabelNet relationships. In the English subtask challenge, we submitted three systems (runs) to assess the proposed method. In Run1, we used our proposed method coupled with a string kernel mapping function to calculate the textual similarity. In Run2, we used the method with a tree kernel function. In Run3, we averaged Run1 with a previously proposed surface-based approach as a kind of integration. The three runs are ranked 41st, 57th, and 20th of 73 systems, with mean correlation 0.702, 0.597, and 0.759 respectively. For the interpretable task, we submitted a modified version of Run1 achieving mean F1 0.846, 0.461, 0.722, and 0.44 for alignment, type, score, and score with type respectively.

1 Introduction

Semantic Textual Similarity (STS) is the task of measuring the similarity between two text snippets according to their meaning. Human has an intrinsic ability to recognize the degree of similarity and difference between texts. Simulating the process of human judgment in computers is still an extremely difficult task and has recently drawn much attention. STS is very important because a wide range of NLP applications such as information retrieval, question answering, machine translation, etc. rely heavily on this task.

This paper describes our proposed STS systems by which we participated in two subtasks of STS task (Task2) at SemEval 2015, namely English STS and Interpretable STS. The former calculates a graded similarity score from 0 to 5 between two sentences (with 5 being the most similar), while the latter is a pilot subtask that requires aligning chunks of two sentences, describing what kind of relation exists between each pair of chunks, and a score for the similarity between the pair of chunks (Agirre et al., 2015).

Sense or meaning of natural language text can be inferred from several linguistic concepts, including lexical, syntactic, and semantic knowledge of the language. Our approach employs those aspects to calculate the similarity between senses of text constituents, phrases or words, relying mainly on BabelNet senses. The similarity between two text snippets is firstly calculated using kernel functions, which map a text snippet to the feature space based on a proposed word sense similarity method. Besides, the sense-based similarity score obtained is combined with a surface-based similarity score to study the consolidation impact in the STS task.

The paper is organized as follows. Section 2 explains our proposed word sense similarity method. Section 3 describes the proposed systems. Section 4 presents the experiments conducted and analyzes the results achieved. Section 5 concludes the paper and suggests some future directions.

2 The proposed Word-Sense Similarity (WSS) Method

Several semantic textual similarity (STS) methods have been proposed in literature. Sense-based methods are qualified when different words are used to convey the same meaning in different texts (Pilehvar et al., 2013). Surface-based methods, mostly fail in identifying similarity between texts with maximal semantic overlap but minimal lexical overlap. We present a sense-based STS approach that produces similarity score between texts by means of a kernel function (Shawe-Taylor and Cristianini, 2004). Then, we integrate the sense-based approach with the surface-based soft cardinality approach presented in (Jimenez et al., 2012) to demonstrate that both sense-based and surface-based similarity methods are complementary to each other.

The design of our kernel function relies on the hypothesis that the greater the similarity of word senses between two texts, the higher their semantic equivalence will be. Accordingly, our kernel maps a text to feature space using a similarity measure between word senses. We proposed a WSS measure that computes the similarity score between two word senses (ws_i, ws_j) using the arithmetic mean of two measures: *Semantic Distance* (sim_D) and *Contextual Similarity* (sim_C). That is:

$$WSS(ws_i, ws_j) = \frac{sim_D(ws_i, ws_j) + sim_C(ws_i, ws_j)}{2} \quad (1)$$

2.1 Semantic Distance

This measure computes the similarity between word senses based on the distance between them in a multilingual semantic network, named BabelNet (Navigli and Ponzetto, 2010). BabelNet[1] is a rich semantic knowledge resource that covers a wide range of concepts and named entities connected with large numbers of semantic relations. Concepts and relations are gathered from *WordNet* (Miller, 1995); and *Wikipedia*[2]. The semantic knowledge is encoded as a labeled directed graph, where vertices are BabelNet senses (concepts), and edges connect pairs of senses with a label indicating the type of the semantic relation between them. Our semantic distance measure is a function of two similarity scores: $\boldsymbol{sim_{Bn}}$ and $\boldsymbol{sim_{NBn}}$.

The first score (sim_{Bn}) is based on the distance between two word-senses, ws_i and ws_j; where, the shorter the distance between them, the more semantically related they are. That is:

$$sim_{Bn}(ws_i, ws_j) = 1 - \frac{len(ws_i, ws_j)}{Maxlen} \quad (2)$$

where $Maxlen$[3] is the maximum path length connecting two senses in BabelNet, and $len(ws_i,ws_j)$ is the length of the shortest path between two senses, ws_i and ws_j, in BabelNet in both directions; i.e $ws_i \rightarrow ws_j$, and $ws_j \rightarrow ws_i$. The shortest path is calculated using Dijkstra's algorithm.

The second score (sim_{NBn}) represents the degree of similarity between the neighbors of ws_i and the neighbors of ws_j, which influences the degree of similarity between the two senses. Hence, sim_{NBn} is calculated by taking the arithmetic mean of all neighbor-pairs similarity. That is:

$$sim_{NBn}(ws_i, ws_j) = \frac{1}{n_i \times n_j} \sum_{ws_k \in NS_i} \sum_{ws_l \in NS_j} sim_{WuP}(ws_k, ws_l) \quad (3)$$

where NS_i and NS_j are the sets of the most semantically related senses directly connected to ws_i and ws_j respectively in BabelNet; $n_i = | NS_i |$, and $n_j = | NS_j |$; and $sim_{WuP}(ws_k, ws_l)$ is Wu and Palmer similarity measure (Wu and Palmer, 1994).

The values of the two scores presented above determine the way of calculating the semantic distance measure (sim_D) for word senses' pair (ws_i, ws_j). For zero similarity of both scores, sim_D is simply equals to Wu and Palmer similarity measure; i.e. $sim_D(ws_i,ws_j) = sim_{WuP}(ws_i,ws_j)$. Generally, for non-zero similarity scores, sim_D is calculated using the arithmetic mean of the two scores.

2.2 Contextual Similarity

This measure calculates the similarity between the word senses pair (ws_i, ws_j) based on the overlap between their contexts derived from a corpus. The overlap coefficient used is *Jaccard Coefficient*. That is:

$$sim_C(ws_i, ws_j) = \frac{|C_i \cap C_j|}{|C_i \cup C_j|} \quad (4)$$

where C_i is the set of: 1) all the word senses that co-occur with ws_i in the corpus, and 2) all senses directly connected to ws_i in BabelNet; C_j is similar.

[1] http://babelnet.org/
[2] http://en.wikipedia.org/

[3] We tried different values in experiments and the best was 7.

3 Systems Description

3.1 Text Preprocessing

The given input sentences are first preprocessed to map the raw natural language text into structured or annotated representation. This process includes different tasks: tokenization, lemmatization, Part-of-Speech tagging, and word-sense tagging. All tasks except word-sense tagging are carried out using Stanford CoreNLP (Manning et al., 2014). Sense tagging is the task of attaching a sense to a word or a token. It is performed by selecting the most commonly used BabelNet sense that matches the part of speech (POS) of the word. Accordingly, we restricted sense tagging to: nouns, verbs, adjectives, and adverbs.

3.2 English STS Subtask

We submitted three systems in this subtask, named Run1, Run2, and Run3.

3.2.1 Sense-based String Kernel (Run1)

Given two sentences, s_1 and s_2, the similarity score between s_1 and s_2 resulted by this system is the value of a designed string kernel function between the two sentences. This kernel is defined by an embedded mapping from the space of sentences possibly to a vector space F, whose coordinates are indexed by a set I of word senses contained in s_1 and s_2; i.e. $\phi : s \rightarrow (\phi_{ws}(s))_{ws\in I} \in F$. Thus, given a sentence s, it can be represented by a row vector as: ϕ (s) = ($\phi_{ws1}(s)$, $\phi_{ws2}(s)$ … $\phi_{wsN}(s)$), in which each entry records how similar a particular word sense ($ws\in I$) is to the sentence s. The mapping is given by:

$$\phi_{ws}(s) = \max_{1\le i\le n} \{ \ WSS(ws, ws_i) \ \}, \tag{5}$$

where $WSS(ws, ws_i)$ is our defined word sense similarity method (Eq. (1)), and n is the number of word senses contained in sentence s.

The string kernel between two sentences s_1 and s_2 is calculated as (Shawe-Taylor and Cristianini, 2004):

$$\kappa_S(s_1,s_2) = \langle \phi(s_1), \phi(s_2) \rangle = \sum_{ws\in I} \phi_{ws}(s_1)\cdot \phi_{ws}(s_2) \tag{6}$$

The last step remaining is normalizing the kernel (i.e. range = [0,1]) to avoid any biasness to sentence length. The normalized string kernel $\kappa_{NS}(s_1,s_2)$ is calculated by (Shawe-Taylor and Cristianini, 2004):

$$\kappa_{NS}(s_1,s_2) = \frac{\kappa_S(s_1,s_2)}{\sqrt{\kappa_S(s_1,s_1)\kappa_S(s_2,s_2)}} \tag{7}$$

Hence, $sim_{Run1}(s_1,s_2) = \kappa_{NS}(s_1,s_2)$.

3.2.2 Sense-based Tree Kernel (Run2)

This system applies tree kernel instead of string kernel. Tree kernels generally map a tree to the feature space of subtrees. There are various types of tree kernel designed in literature, among them is the *all-subtree kernel* presented in (Shawe-Taylor and Cristianini, 2004). The all-subtree kernel is defined by an embedded mapping from the space of all finite syntactic trees to a vector space F, whose coordinates are indexed by a subset T of syntactic subtrees; i.e. $\phi : t \rightarrow (\phi_{st}(t))_{st\in T} \in F$. The mapping $\phi_{st}(t)$ is a simple exact matching function that returns 1 if st is a subtree in t, and returns 0 otherwise. We modified the mapping of all-subtree kernel to capture the semantic similarity between subtrees instead of the structural similarity. The semantic similarity between subtrees is calculated recursively bottom-up from leaves to the root, in which the similarity between leaves is calculated using our defined word sense similarity method.

From this point, the remaining steps are typical to the string kernel steps followed in the first system. Hence, given two sentences s_1 and s_2, their similarity score is the normalized kernel value between their syntactic parse trees t_1 and t_2; i.e. $sim_{Run2}(s_1,s_2) = \kappa_{NT}(t_1,t_2)$.

3.2.3 Sense-based with Surface-based (Run3)

This system provides the results of taking the arithmetic mean of: 1) our sense-based string kernel (Run1); and 2) the surface-based similarity function proposed by Jimenez et al. (2012). The approach presented in (Jimenez et al., 2012) represents sentence words as sets of *q-grams* on which the notion of Soft Cardinality is applied. In this system, all the calculations in the approach are used unchanged with the following parameters setup: p=2, bias=0, and α=0.5. Accordingly, the similarity function is the Dice overlap coefficient on q-grams; i.e. $sim_{SC}(A,B) = 2|A\cap B|'/(|A|'+|B|')$.

Hence,

$$sim_{Run3}(s_1,s_2) = \frac{(\kappa_{NS}(s_1,s_2) + sim_{SC}(s_1,s_2))}{2} \tag{8}$$

3.3 Interpretable STS Subtask

The interpretable STS is a pilot subtask, which aims to determine the parts of sentences, chunks, that are equivalent in meaning and the parts that are not. This is twofold: (a) aligning corresponding chunks, and (b) assigning a *similarity score*, and a *type* to each alignment. Given two sentences splitted into gold standard chunks, our system carries out the task requirements using our sense-based string kernel by considering each chunk as a text snippet. Firstly, the similarity between chunks of all possible chunk-pairs is calculated, upon which chunks are aligned. Where, chunk pairs with a high similarity score are aligned first, followed by pairs with lower similarity. Thereafter, for each alignment of chunks c_1 and c_2, the alignment type is determined according to the following rules:

- If the similarity score between c_1 and c_2 is 5, the type is EQUI.
- If all word senses of c_1 matched the word senses in c_2, the type is SPEC2; similarly for SPEC1.
- If both c_1 and c_2 contain a single word sense, and are directly connected by an antonym relation in BabelNet, then the type is OPPO.
- If the similarity score between c_1 and c_2 is in range [3,5[, the type is SIM; while if it is in range]0,3[, the type is REL.
- If any chunk has no corresponding chunk in the other sentence, then the type is either NOALI or ALIC based on the alignment restriction in the subtask.

4 Experimental Results

4.1 English STS

The main evaluation measure selected by the task organizers was the mean Pearson correlation between the system scores and the gold standard scores calculated on the test set (3000 sentence pairs from five datasets). Table 1 presents the official results of our submissions in this subtask on SemEval-2015 test set. It also includes the results of the Soft Cardinality STS approach (SC) on the same test set for analysis. Our best system (Run3) achieved 0.7595 and ranked the 20th out of 73 systems.

We conducted preliminary experiments on the training dataset of SemEval-2015 for evaluating our sense-based string and tree kernel similarity methods, and the integration between each of them with the SC approach. The results of those experiments led to the final submission of the two kernels separately (Run1 and Run2) and integrating the string kernel method with SC (Run3). Table 2 focuses on the results obtained from our integrated system (Run3) and SC approach in training, but includes also the recent SC approach (SC-ML) proposed in (Jimenez et al., 2014).

It is noteworthy from the tables that Run3 improved the SC system results on both the training and testing sets for all the different settings for alpha value in the SC approach. The possible reason based on our observation on the training datasets is that the two systems have opposite strength and weakness points. Figure 1 depicts the similarity scores resulted from Run1, Run3, and SC systems along with the gold standard scores (GS) on some sentence pairs from images dataset. It is shown from the figure that Run1 outperforms SC for semantically equivalent sentence pairs (i.e. scores > 3.5), while SC outperforms Run1 for less-related sentence pairs (i.e. score < 2). Hence, their integration by taking their average (Run3) improves the performance of their individual use and did not reduce the SC results. Also, though this integration is simple, it outperformed SC-ML that applies machine learning on some extracted text features.

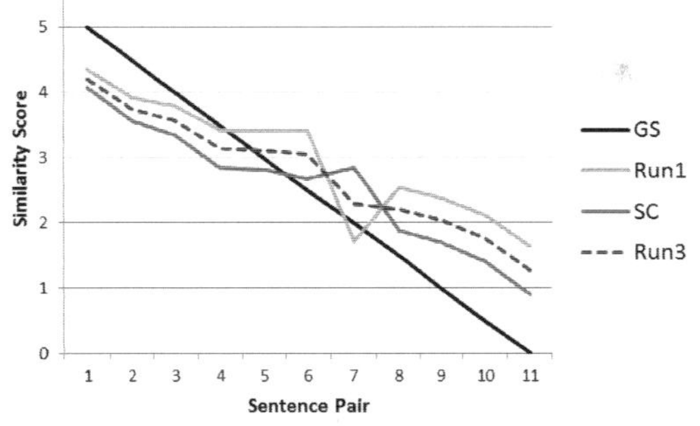

Figure 1. Sample Results of Run1, Run3, and SC on 'images' Dataset of SemEval Training data.

4.2 Interpretable STS

There were two datasets only in the test set, namely images and headlines. The results in this subtask are evaluated by four F1 measures for alignment, score, alignment type, and both score with alignment. The results of our submitted run (average of the two datasets) were 0.846, 0.461, 0.722, and 0.44 for F1-Ali, F1-type, F1-score, and F1-score+type respectively.

System	answers-forums	answers-students	belief	headlines	images	Mean	Rank
Run1	0.6152	0.6686	0.6109	0.7418	0.7853	0.7022	41st/73
Run2	0.3659	0.6460	0.5896	0.6448	0.6194	0.5970	57th/73
Run3	0.7091	0.7096	0.7184	0.7922	0.8223	**0.7595**	20th/73
SC	0.7078	0.7020	0.7232	0.7966	0.8120	0.7565	-

Table 1. Our Results on SemEval-2015 Test Datasets.

αα	System	deft-forum	deft-news	headlines	images	OnWN	tweet-news	Mean
-	**Run1**	0.4259	0.7271	0.6914	0.7576	0.7597	0.7227	0.6955
-	**SC-ML**	0.4607	0.7216	0.7605	0.7782	0.8426	0.6583	0.7209
0.25	**Run3**	0.5092	0.7479	0.7383	0.7902	0.7857	0.7744	**0.7387**
	SC	0.5047	0.7311	0.7362	0.7785	0.7727	0.7709	0.7307
0.5	**Run3**	0.4937	0.7531	0.7377	0.7887	0.7834	0.7723	**0.7359**
	SC	0.4789	0.7407	0.7374	0.7763	0.7671	0.7641	0.7257
0.7	**Run3**	0.4816	0.7541	0.7356	0.7862	0.7806	0.7681	**0.7322**
	SC	0.4558	0.7396	0.7321	0.7694	0.7586	0.7496	0.7158

Table 2. Results of Run3 vs. SC on SemEval-2014 Test Datasets (SemEval-2015 Training dataset).

5 Conclusions and Future work

Our experiments proved that sense-based and surface-based similarity methods are complementary to each other in STS. We also realized that string kernel is more beneficial than tree kernel. Our potential future work includes: 1) enhancing our sense-based kernel approach, and 2) further enhancement in the integration between SC and our sense-based approach.

References

Eneko Agirre, Carmen Banea, Claire Cardie, Daniel Cer, Mona Diab, Aitor Gonzalez-Agirrea, Weiwei Guo, Iñigo Lopez-Gazpio, Montse Maritxalar, Rada Mihalcea, German Rigau, Larraitz Uria, and Janyce Wiebe. 2015. SemEval-2015 Task 2: Semantic Textual Similarity, English, Spanish and Pilot on Interpretability. In *Proceedings of the 9th International Workshop on Semantic Evaluation (SemEval 2015)*, Denver, CO, USA.

Sergio Jimenez, Claudia Becerra, and Alexander Gelbukh. 2012. Soft Cardinality: A Parameterized Similarity Function for Text Comparison. In *Proceedings of the First Joint Conference on Lexical and Computational Semantics (*SEM)*, pages 449–453, Montreal, Canada.

Sergio Jimenez, George Dueñas, Julia Baquero, and Alexander Gelbukh. 2014. UNAL-NLP: Combining Soft Cardinality Features for Semantic Textual Similarity, Relatedness and Entailment. In *Proceedings of the 8th International Workshop on Semantic Evaluation (SemEval 2014)*, pages 732–742, Duplin, Ireland.

Christopher D. Manning, Mihai Surdeanu, John Bauer, Jenny Finkel, Steven J. Bethard, and David McClosky. 2014. The Stanford CoreNLP Natural Language Processing Toolkit. In *Proceedings of the 52nd Annual Meeting of the Association for Computational Linguistics: System Demonstrations*, pages 55–60, Baltimore, Maryland.

George A. Miller. 1995. WordNet: A Lexical Database for English. *Communications of the ACM*, 38(11): 39–41.

Roberto Navigli and Simone Paolo Ponzetto. 2010. BabelNet: Building a Very Large Multilingual Semantic Network. In *Proceedings of the 48th Annual Meeting of the Association for Computational Linguistics,* pages 216–225, Uppsala, Sweden.

Mohammad Taher Pilehvar, David Jurgens, and Roberto Navigli. 2013. Align, Disambiguate and Walk: A Unified Approach for Measuring. In *Proceedings of the 51st Annual Meeting of the Association for Computational Linguistics (ACL 2013)*, pages 1341–1351, Sofia, Bulgaria.

John Shawe-Taylor and Nello Cristianini. 2004. *Kernel Methods for Pattern Analysis.* Cambridge University Press.

Zhibiao Wu and Martha Palmer. 1994. Verbs Semantics and Lexical Selection. In *Proceedings of the 32nd annual meeting on Association for Computational Linguistics (ACL'94)*, pages 133–138, Stroudsburg, PA, USA.

Azmat: Sentence Similarity using Associative Matrices

Evan Jaffe **Lifeng Jin** **David King** **Marten van Schijndel**
Department of Linguistics
The Ohio State University
{jaffe.59, jin.544, king.2138}@osu.edu, vanschm@ling.osu.edu

Abstract

This work uses recursive autoencoders (Socher et al., 2011), word embeddings (Pennington et al., 2014), associative matrices (Schuler, 2014) and lexical overlap features to model human judgments of sentential similarity on SemEval-2015 Task 2: English STS (Agirre et al., 2015). Results show a modest positive correlation between system predictions and human similarity scores, ranking 69th out of 74 submitted systems.

1 Introduction

This work uses a support vector machine (SVM) to determine the similarity of sentence pairs, taking as input the similarity judgments of four subsystems: a set of surface features, unfolding recursive autoencoders (URAE; Socher et al., 2011), Global Vector word embeddings (GloVe; Pennington et al., 2014), and the Schuler (2014) associative matrix approach using the Nguyen et al. (2012) Generalized Categorial Grammar (GCG). Evaluation is run on SemEval 2015 task 2, Semantic Textual Similarity (STS), which includes a corpus of human similarity judgments. The test set consists of 3000 randomly chosen sentence pairs from a corpus of 8500 pairs, which spans five domains (news headlines, image captions, student answers, forum responses, and sentences about belief). Similarity scores range from 0 (no similarity) to 5 (complete semantic equivalence).

2 System Overview

All subsystems in Azmat are trained with sentences from previous SemEval tasks 2012 - 2014 (Agirre et al., 2012; Agirre et al., 2013; Agirre et al., 2014). In total, 15,406 sentences were selected from the Microsoft video, news headlines, images, and paraphrase datasets. The main purpose of the subsystems (excluding surface features) is to generate binarized phrase-structure trees, which are used to create cosine similarity features between multiple levels of paired sentences. The URAE subsystem preprocesses training sentences by parsing them with the Stanford Parser (Klein and Manning, 2003) and then binarizing. The associative matrix and GloVe subsystems use GCG parses of the training sentences, obtained by training the Berkeley parser (Petrov and Klein, 2007) with the Nguyen et al. (2012) GCG reannotated Penn Treebank. GCG parse trees are converted into typed dependency graphs and binarized. Around 2% of the sentences fail to parse; these are omitted from the training set.

2.1 Subsystem Combination

Because vector composition methods vary across subsystems, this work incorporates multiple subsystems to give insight on which composition methods perform better at finding semantic textual similarity. For each sentence, each subsystem generates a single binarized phrase-structure tree with a single embedding labeled at each node. Cosine similarity scores are calculated between each node in one tree and each node in the other tree, allowing comparison between input sentences at and across leaf, phrasal and sentential levels. These similarity scores are used to generate a feature vector for training an SVM regressor with a linear kernel.[1]

[1] http://scikit-learn.org/stable/modules/svm.html

In order to generalize findings across sentence pairs with varying lengths and tree structures, however, similarity scores must be consistently ordered for the SVM and must generate a feature vector of consistent length. To accomodate these constraints, each output node (n) in a tree is assigned a *composition depth* (d_n) based on the depth of its child nodes (a and b):

$$d_n = \begin{cases} 0 & \text{if } n \text{ is a leaf} \\ \max(d_a, d_b) + 1 & \text{otherwise} \end{cases} \quad (1)$$

Similarity between two nodes are grouped with similarities of similar depth (x and y) into a vector (v_{xy}), which is sorted before being concatenated with other depth similarities[2] to form the actual feature vector which will be input to the SVM:

$$| \underbrace{0.8\ 0.7\ 0.3 \ldots}_{(d{=}0\ d{=}0)} | \underbrace{0.9\ 0.4\ 0.2 \ldots}_{(d{=}0\ d{=}1)} | \ldots \quad (2)$$

The actual ordering of the concatenated depth groups within the vector does not matter to the downstream SVM classifier so long as the ordering is consistent. Each v_{xy} is given a constant length to losslessly capture the similarity of balanced trees up to 50 words in length:[3]

$$|v_{xy}| = \frac{50}{2^{d_x}} \cdot \frac{50}{2^{d_y}} \quad (3)$$

Each depth-pair subvector is duplicated up to the needed length before being re-sorted. This approach is analogous to a lossless version of the dynamic pooling used by Socher et al. (2011).

Using the above approach, each subsystem generates its own version of the vector in (2). Then each of those vectors is concatenated together to form the entire SVM input vector.

2.2 Surface Features

Surface features include n-gram overlap measures of precision, recall, and F-score, where precision and recall are defined as overlap from sentence A to sentence B, and from sentence B to sentence A, respectively. 1- through 3-grams are measured using stemmed[4] and unstemmed lexical items for each of the 3 overlaps, resulting in a total of 18 surface features. These features are based on those used by Das and Smith (2009) for paraphrase detection.

2.3 Unfolding Recursive Autoencoders

Socher et al. (2011) show good results for paraphrase detection by using recursive autoencoders (RAEs) to compose word embeddings into phrasal and sentential embeddings, allowing similarity metrics at various structural levels. Their method uses word embeddings from Turian et al. (2010) as input, along with a binarized phrase-structure parse from the Stanford Parser (Klein and Manning, 2003). Given a binarized parse tree and leaf node embeddings, weight matrices are learned to both encode and decode nodes above the leaves by minimizing reconstruction error. 'Unfolding' refers to a learning objective that reconstructs the entire subtree below each node, not just the immediate children. Once a model is trained, the learned encoding matrix can generate embeddings at each node for novel sentences. The current work uses the pre-trained model and code from Socher et al. (2011) to generate features from the previous SemEval task sentences.

2.4 Associative Matrices

The associative matrix subsystem (AM) is inspired by a cognitively-grounded parsing model that stores associations between words as dependency relations (Nguyen et al., 2012; Wu and Schuler, 2011). Dependency-like associations are learned from typed dependency graphs generated from gold Nguyen et al. (2012) GCG annotations of Simple Wikipedia. Dependency-based skip-grams are used to build a co-occurrence matrix for all words, and single value decomposition (SVD; Landauer and Dumais, 1997) generates word embeddings with reduced dimensionality.

Each labeled dependency in the training data is recorded in associative matrices by adding the outer product of the governor and the dependent to the matrix corresponding to the dependency label, creating

[2] Remember that similarities are computed between all nodes in one tree and all nodes in the other tree, which results in some similarities being computed between nodes of different depths.

[3] Consistent lengths permit each v_{xy} to be at a consistent position within the overall feature vector.

[4] NLTK Lancaster Stemmer (Bird et al., 2009; Paice, 1990)

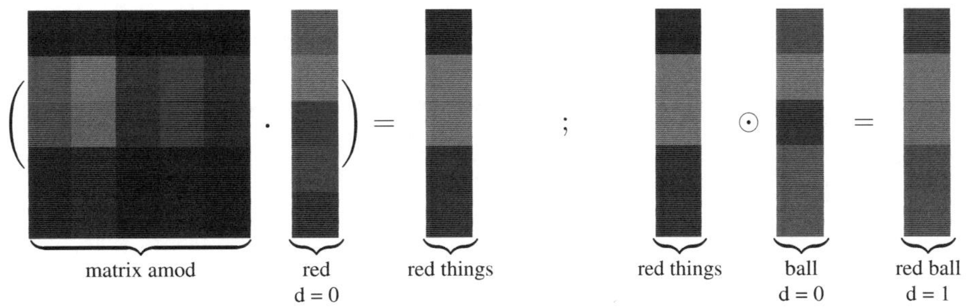

Figure 1: Example vector composition using learned associative matrices. The dependency triple (*red*, *ball*, *amod*) can be composed by first cueing *red* off of the *amod* matrix. The resulting target vector represents a superposition of all governors *red* stands in an *amod* relation to. The target is then pointwise multiplied with the embedding for *ball* to get a final phrasal representation. Note that words are depth 0, and the composition results in an embedding at depth 1.

an associative matrix for each dependency type:

$$M_{deplabel} = \sum_{D} (\bar{u} \otimes \bar{v}) \quad (4)$$

where (*u*, *v*, *deplabel*) is a labeled dependency.

To compose a phrasal embedding, the dependent word embedding is first inner multiplied with the association matrix for the dependency type, a process called cueing, which returns a target vector. Cueing converts the dependent word embedding into the space of its governor, essentially representing the superposed vectors of all governors that the dependent co-occurs with. Finally, the target is pointwise multiplied with the governor embedding, reinforcing the influence of the observed governor and specifying the meaning of the phrase as a combination of the meaning of the dependent and of its governor. See Table 1 for an example. All unknown (OOV) word vectors are filled with ones to avoid contaminating products during composition. As with all subsystems, a single binarized parse tree with an embedding at each node is the result.

2.5 Global Vectors

Due to the success of word embeddings in word similarity judgment tasks (Mikolov et al., 2013), this work also makes use of Global Vector word embeddings (GloVe; Pennington et al., 2014). 300-dimensional GloVe embeddings are trained on 42 billion lower-cased tokens from the Stanford tokenized Common Crawl. These word embeddings are combined using the same GCG structure as the AM subsystem. Each node in the GCG tree is assigned the embedding of that subtree's head word, so the 'red ball' node is assigned the embedding for 'ball'. All OOV word vectors are drawn from a uniform distribution between 0 and 1.

Model	Unk ρ	Known ρ	Test ρ
SUGA	0.5370	0.6118	0.4512
UGA	0.4620	0.5493	
SUA	0.5547	0.6233	
SGA	0.5650	0.6299	
SUG	0.5897	0.6566	

Table 1: Model correlation with human judgments on unknown and known domains in development as each subsystem is omitted (included subsystems are noted: **S** for surface, **U** for URAE, **G** for GloVe, and **A** for AM). Final system performance on test data for the task is also shown at right.

3 Experiments and Error Analysis

For development, 1000 pairs are held out of the training data in jack-knifed batches. Table 1 shows how the system performs when each subsystem is omitted. Each model is designated using the first letter of each subsystem, so the full model is named *SUGA*. Table 1 (left) shows the performance of the system when all of the held-out pairs are from a single domain (e.g., news headlines) and thus approximates the system's performance on unknown domains. Table 1 (middle) shows the performance when the held-out pairs are distributed evenly across

Dataset	Leaf	Comp	Cross	Full
Belief	0.5435	0.4966	0.4338	0.3587
Forums	0.4871	0.4114	0.4535	0.2933
Headlines	0.6583	0.6389	0.5826	0.5264
Images	0.6276	0.5587	0.5369	0.5145
Students	0.6399	0.5454	0.5222	0.4293
Mean	0.5913	0.5302	0.5058	0.4244
Wt. Mean	0.6103	0.5493	0.5213	0.4491

Table 2: Correlations with human judgments when only certain similarity relations are used: only word-level similarity (leaf), only compositional non-leaf similarity (comp), only similarity between leaf and non-leaf nodes (cross), and permitting all similarities (full). The weighted mean accounts for the proportion of test cases in each dataset.

all domains and so estimates the system's performance on domains that are familiar. SemEval-2015 Task 2 test results are shown in Table 1 (right).[5]

Omission of the surface features results in a sharp performance decrease, showing they capture complementary information to other features. See *UGA* model as compared to the *SUGA* model in Table 1. Also observable in the table is that excluding any one of the three main subsystems (URAE, GloVe, AM) improves performance, which implies the full system overfits to the training data.[6] Since the composition method differs between all three subsystems, and since URAE even uses a different underlying dependency structure, the overfit likely stems from the fact that all three systems are computing leaf/leaf similarity. Overfitting might be reduced by either only using the leaf/leaf similarity from a single system or by tuning the tolerance of the SVM.[7]

Since the development results suggest that the full system overfits, it may be informative to test how the different parts of the compositional framework behave. To test this, the full SUGA system is retrained with some similarity relations removed (see Table 2). When only leaf/leaf similarities are used during training, the system performs the best. This finding is likely due to the ubiquity of word-level similarity/analogy as a task, for which word embeddings such as GloVe were designed. System performance declines when trained only on similarities between non-leaf nodes, suggesting the compositions are less good at reflecting phrasal- and sentence-level similarity. The system becomes even less accurate when only using similarities between leaf nodes and non-leaf nodes, which were hoped to enable the system to capture similarities between more and less general phrases (e.g., between 'red ball' and 'ball'). This finding is somewhat surprising since URAE is thought to capture these types of similarities.

Although leaf/leaf similarities are useful, overreliance on non-compositional nodes causes problems when comparing pairs with more abstract differences. For example, the system rates the following unrelated pair as very similar despite completely different subject-predicate and modifier compositions:

Zoo worker dies after tiger attack
Teacher dies after attack in New Zealand

Further, while coarse feature selection (e.g., removing all non-leaf features) improves performance, it is not a foregone conclusion that composition features are completely uninformative. For example, comparisons between nodes of similar depths (e.g., 0-1, 4-3) might be more informative than node comparisons of dissimilar depths (e.g., 1-7, 6-2), so future work should determine whether there is an information gradient when comparing compositional nodes. Additionally, the fixed length chosen in this work for each depth-paired subvector guarantees a lossless representation of similarities between balanced trees up to 50 words long, but the similarity vectors involving non-leaf nodes become increasingly lossy as the input trees become less balanced. Therefore, the current system possibly underestimates the informativity of non-leaf features.

4 Conclusion

The current work combined surface lexical features with lexical and phrasal tree node similarity features using URAE, GLoVe, and an associative matrix composition system to model sentential similarity. Since phrasal similarity is likely extremely useful in determining sentence similarity, this work provides insight into the use and combination of multiple phrasal similarity systems.

[5] *SUGA* ranked 69th of 74 systems. For full results, see http://alt.qcri.org/semeval2015/task2/index.php?id=results

[6] One example of overfitting is that the larger *SUGA* model performs worse than the smaller *SUG* model for the same *known* dataset (0.6118<0.6566).

[7] The current work uses an untuned tolerance of 0.001.

Acknowledgements

This material is based upon work supported by the National Science Foundation Graduate Research Fellowship under Grant No. DGE-1343012. Any opinion, findings, and conclusions or recommendations expressed in this material are those of the authors and do not necessarily reflect the views of the National Science Foundation. We would also like to thank the anonymous reviewers for their helpful suggestions and comments.

References

Eneko Agirre, Mona Diab, Daniel Cer, and Aitor Gonzalez-Agirre. 2012. Semeval-2012 task 6: A pilot on semantic textual similarity. In *Proceedings of the First Joint Conference on Lexical and Computational Semantics-Volume 1: Proceedings of the main conference and the shared task, and Volume 2: Proceedings of the Sixth International Workshop on Semantic Evaluation*, pages 385–393. Association for Computational Linguistics.

Eneko Agirre, Daniel Cer, Mona Diab, Aitor Gonzalez-Agirre, and Guo WeiWei. 2013. sem-2013 shared task: Semantic textual similarity, including a pilot on typed-similarity. In *In *SEM 2013: The Second Joint Conference on Lexical and Computational Semantics, Association for Computational Linguistics*.

Eneko Agirre, Carmen Banea, Claire Cardie, Daniel Cer, Mona Diab, Aitor Gonzalez-Agirre, Weiwei Guo, Rada Mihalcea, German Rigau, and Janyce Wiebe. 2014. Semeval-2014 task 10: Multilingual semantic textual similarity. In *Proceedings of the 8th International Workshop on Semantic Evaluation (SemEval 2014)*, pages 81–91, Dublin, Ireland, August. Association for Computational Linguistics and Dublin City University.

Eneko Agirre, Carmen Banea, Claire Cardie, Daniel Cer, Mona Diab, Aitor Gonzalez-Agirre, Guo WeiWei, Iigo Lopez-Gazpio, Montse Maritxalar, Rada Mihalcea, German Rigau, Larraitz Uria, and Janyce Wiebe. 2015. SemEval-2015 Task 2: Semantic Textual Similarity, English, Spanish and Pilot on Interpretability. In *Proceedings of the 9th International Workshop on Semantic Evaluation (SemEval 2015)*, Denver, CO, June. Association for Computational Linguistics.

Steven Bird, Ewan Klein, and Edward Loper. 2009. *Natural Language Processing with Python: Analyzing Text with the Natural Language Toolkit*. O'Reilly, Beijing.

Dipanjan Das and Noah A. Smith. 2009. Paraphrase identification as probablistic quasi-synchronous recognition. In *Proc. of ACL-IJCNLP*.

Dan Klein and Christopher D. Manning. 2003. Accurate unlexicalized parsing. In *Proceedings of the 41st Annual Meeting of the Association for Computational Linguistics*, pages 423–430, Sapporo, Japan.

T.K. Landauer and S.T. Dumais. 1997. A solution to Plato's problem: The latent semantic analysis theory of acquisition, induction, and representation of knowledge. *Psychological Review*, 104(2):211–240.

Tomas Mikolov, Kai Chen, Greg Corrado, and Jeffrey Dean. 2013. Efficient estimation of word representations in vector space. *CoRR*, abs/1301.3781:1–12.

Luan Nguyen, Marten van Schijndel, and William Schuler. 2012. Accurate unbounded dependency recovery using generalized categorial grammars. In *Proceedings of the 24th International Conference on Computational Linguistics (COLING '12)*, pages 2125–2140, Mumbai, India.

Chris D. Paice. 1990. Another stemmer. *SIGIR Forum*, 24:56–61.

Jeffrey Pennington, Richard Socher, and Christopher D. Manning. 2014. Glove: Global vectors for word representation. In *Proceedings of EMNLP*.

Slav Petrov and Dan Klein. 2007. Improved inference for unlexicalized parsing. In *Proceedings of NAACL HLT 2007*, pages 404–411, Rochester, New York, April. Association for Computational Linguistics.

William Schuler. 2014. Sentence processing in a vectorial model of working memory. In *Fifth Annual Workshop on Cognitive Modeling and Computational Linguistics (CMCL 2014)*.

Richard Socher, Eric Huang, Jeffrey Pennington, Andrew Ng, and Christopher Manning. 2011. Dynamic pooling and unfolding recursive autoencoders for paraphrase detection. In *Neural Information Processing Systems (NIPS)*.

Joseph Turian, Lev Ratinov, and Yoshua Bengio. 2010. Word representations: A simple and general method for semi-supervised learning. In *Proc. of ACL 2010*.

Stephen Wu and William Schuler. 2011. Structured composition of semantic vectors. In *Proceedings of the International Workshop on Semantic Computing*.

NeRoSim: A System for Measuring and Interpreting Semantic Textual Similarity

Rajendra Banjade*, **Nobal B. Niraula***, **Nabin Maharjan***, **Vasile Rus**, **Dan Stefanescu**†
Mihai Lintean†, **Dipesh Gautam**
Department of Computer Science
The University of Memphis
Memphis, TN
{rbanjade,nbnraula,nmharjan,vrus,dstfnscu,mclinten,dgautam}@memphis.edu

Abstract

We present in this paper our system developed for SemEval 2015 Shared Task 2 (2a - English Semantic Textual Similarity, STS, and 2c - Interpretable Similarity) and the results of the submitted runs. For the English STS subtask, we used regression models combining a wide array of features including semantic similarity scores obtained from various methods. One of our runs achieved weighted mean correlation score of 0.784 for sentence similarity subtask (i.e., English STS) and was ranked tenth among 74 runs submitted by 29 teams. For the interpretable similarity pilot task, we employed a rule-based approach blended with chunk alignment labeling and scoring based on semantic similarity features. Our system for interpretable text similarity was among the top three best performing systems.

1 Introduction

Semantic Textual Similarity (STS) is the task of measuring the degree of semantic equivalence for a given pair of texts. The importance of semantic similarity in Natural Language Processing is highlighted by the diversity of datasets and shared task evaluation campaigns over the last decade (Dolan et al., 2004; Agirre et al., 2012; Agirre et al., 2013; Agirre et al., 2014; Rus et al., 2014) and by many uses such as in text summarization (Aliguliyev, 2009) and student answer assessment (Rus and Lintean, 2012; Niraula et al., 2013).

This year's SemEval shared task on semantic textual similarity focused on English STS, Spanish STS, and Interpretable Similarity (Agirre et al., 2015). We participated in the English STS and Interpretable Similarity subtasks. We describe in this paper our systems participated in these two subtasks.

The English STS subtask was about assigning a similarity score between 0 and 5 to pairs of sentences; a score of 0 meaning the sentences are unrelated and 5 indicating they are equivalent. Our three runs for this subtask combined a wide array of features including similarity scores calculated using knowledge based and corpus based methods in a regression model (cf. Section 2). One of our systems achieved mean correlation score of 0.784 with human judgment on the test data.

Although STS systems measure the degree of semantic equivalence in terms of a score which is useful in many tasks, they stop short of explaining why the texts are similar, related, or unrelated. They do not indicate what kind of semantic relations exist among the constituents (words or chunks) of the target texts. Finding explicit relations between constituents in the paired texts would enable a meaningful interpretation of the similarity scores. To this end, Brockett (2007) and Rus et al. (2012) produced datasets where corresponding words (or multiword expressions) were aligned and in the later case their semantic relations were explicitly labeled. Similarly, this year's pilot subtask called Interpretable Similarity required systems to align the segments (chunks) either using the chunked texts given by the organizers or chunking the given texts and indicating the type of semantic relations (such as EQUI for

* These authors contributed equally to this work
†Work done while at University of Memphis

equivalent, OPPO for opposite) between each pair of aligned chunks. Moreover, a similarity score for each alignment (0 – unrelated, 5 – equivalent) had to be assigned. We applied a set of rules blended with similarity features in order to assign the labels and scores for the chunk-level relations (cf. Section 3). Our system was among the top performing systems in this subtask.

2 System for English STS

We used regression models to compute final sentence-to-sentence similarity scores using various features such as different sentence-to-sentence similarity scores, presence of negation cues, lexical overlap measures etc. The sentence-to-sentence similarity scores were calculated using word-to-word similarity methods and optimal word and chunk alignments.

2.1 Word-to-Word Similarity

We used knowledge based, corpus based, and hybrid methods to compute word-to-word similarity. From the knowledge based category, we used WordNet (Fellbaum, 1998) based similarity methods from SEMILAR Toolkit (Rus et al., 2013) which include Lin (Lin, 1998), Lesk (Banerjee and Pedersen, 2003), Hso (Hirst and St-Onge, 1998), Jcn (Jiang and Conrath, 1997), Res (Resnik, 1995), Path, Lch (Leacock and Chodorow, 1998), and Wup (Wu and Palmer, 1994).

In corpus based category, we developed Latent Semantic Analysis (LSA) (Landauer et al., 2007) models[1] from the whole Wikipedia articles as described in Stefanescu et al. (2014a). We also used pre-trained Mikolov word representations (Mikolov et al., 2013)[2] and GloVe word vectors (Pennington et al., 2014)[3]. In these cases, each word was represented as a vector encoding and the similarity between words were computed as cosine similarity between corresponding vectors. We exploited the lexical relations between words, i.e. synonymy and antonymy, from WordNet 3.0. As such we computed similarity scores between two words a and b as:

$$sim(a,b) = \begin{cases} 1, \text{ if a and b are synonyms} \\ 0, \text{ if a and b are antonyms} \\ \dfrac{\mathbf{A}.\mathbf{B}}{|\mathbf{A}||\mathbf{B}|}, \text{ otherwise} \end{cases}$$

where $\mathbf{A}$ and $\mathbf{B}$ are vector representations of words a and b respectively.

In hybrid approach, we developed a new word-to-word similarity measure (hereafter referred as Combined-Word-Measure) by combining the WordNet-based similarity methods with corpus based methods (using Mikolov's word embeddings and GloVe vectors) by applying Support Vector Regression (Banjade et al., 2015).

2.2 Sentence-to-Sentence Similarity

We applied three different approaches to compute sentence-to-sentence similarity.

2.2.1 Optimal Word Alignment Method

Our alignment step was based on the optimal assignment problem, a fundamental combinatorial optimization problem which consists of finding a maximum weight matching in a weighted bipartite graph. An algorithm, the Kuhn-Munkres method (Kuhn, 1955), can find solutions to the optimum assignment problem in polynomial time.

In our case, we first computed the similarity of word pairs (all possible combinations) using all similarity methods described in Section 2.1. The similarity score less than 0.3 (empirically set threshold), was reset to 0 in order to avoid noisy alignments. Then the words were aligned so that the overall alignment score between the full sentences was maximum. Once the words were aligned optimally, we calculated the sentence similarity score as the sum of the word alignment scores normalized by the average length of the sentence pair.

2.2.2 Optimal Chunk Alignment Method

We created chunks and aligned them to calculate sentence similarity as in Stefanescu et al. (2014b) and applied optimal alignment twice. First, we applied optimal alignment of words in two chunks to measure the similarity of the chunks. As before, word similarity threshold was set to 0.3. We then

[1]Models available at http://semanticsimilarity.org
[2]Downloaded from http://code.google.com/p/word2vec/
[3]Downloaded from http://nlp.stanford.edu/projects/glove/

normalized chunk similarity by the number of tokens in the shorter chunk such that it assigned higher scores to pairs of chunks such as *physician* and *general physician*. Second, we applied optimal alignment at chunk level in order to calculate the sentence level similarity. We used chunk-to-chunk similarity threshold 0.4 to prevent noisy alignments. In this case, however, the similarity score was normalized by the average number of chunks in the given texts pair. All threshold values were set empirically based on the performance on the training set.

2.2.3 Resultant Vector Based Method

In this approach, we combined vector based word representations to obtain sentence level representations through vector algebra. We added the vectors corresponding to content words in each sentence to create a resultant vector for each sentence and the cosine similarity was calculated between the resultant vectors. We used word vector representations from Wiki LSA, Mikolov and GloVe models.

For a missing word, we used vector representation of one of its synonyms obtained from the WordNet. To compute the synonym list, we considered all senses of the missing word given its POS category.

2.3 Features for Regression

We summarize the features used for regression next.

1. Similarity scores using optimal alignment of words where word-to-word similarity was calculated using vector based methods using word representations from Mikolov, GloVe, LSA Wiki models and Combined-Word-Measure which combines knowledge based methods and corpus based methods.

2. Similarity score using optimal alignment of chunks where word-to-word similarity scores were calculated using Mikolov's word representations.

3. Similarity scores based on the resultant vector method using word representations from Mikolov, GloVe, and LSA Wiki models.

4. Noun-Noun, Adjective-Adjective, Adverb-Adverb, and Verb-Verb similarity scores and similarity score for other words using optimal word alignment and Mikolov's word representations.

Data set	Count	Release time
SMTnews	351	STS2012-Test
Headlines	1500	STS2013-Test
Deft-forum	423	STS2014-Test
Deft-news	299	STS2014-Test
Images	749	STS2014-Test

Table 1: Summary of training data

5. Multiplication of noun-noun similarity score and verb-verb similarity score (scores calculated as described in 4).

6. Whether there was any antonym pair present.

7. $\frac{|C_{i1} - C_{i2}|}{C_{i1} + C_{i2}}$ where C_{i1} and C_{i2} are the counts of $i \in \{$all tokens, adjectives, adverbs, nouns, and verbs$\}$ for sentence 1 and 2 respectively.

8. Presence of adjectives and adverbs in first sentence, and in the second sentence.

9. Unigram overlap with synonym check, bigram overlap and BLEU score (Papineni et al., 2002).

10. Presence of negation cue (e.g. no, not, never) in either of sentences.

11. Whether one sentence was a question while the other was not.

12. Total number of words in each sentence. Similarly, the number of adjectives, nouns, verbs, adverbs, and others, in each sentence.

2.4 Experiments and Results

Data: For training, we used data released in previous shared tasks (summarized in Table 1). We selected datasets that included texts from different genres. However, some others, such as Tweet-news and MSRPar were not included. Tweet-news data were quite different from most other texts. MSRPar, being more biased towards overlapping text (Rus et al., 2014), was also a concern.

The test set included data (sentence pairs) from Answers-forums (375), Answers-students (750), Belief (375), Headlines (750), and Images (750).

Preprocessing: We removed stop words, labeled each word with Part-of-Speech (POS) tag and lemmatized them using Stanford CoreNLP Toolkit (Manning et al., 2014). We did spelling corrections in student answers and forum data using Jazzy tool (Idzelis, 2005) with WordNet dictionary. Moreover, in student answers data, we found that the symbol A (such as in bulb A and node A) typed in lowercase was incorrectly labeled as a determiner 'a' by the POS tagger. We applied a rule to correct it. If the token after 'a' is not an adjective, adverb, or noun, or the token is the last token in the sentence, we changed its type to noun (NN). We then created chunks as described by Stefuanescu et al. (2014b).

Regression: We generated various features as described in Section 2.3 and applied regression methods in three different settings. In the first run (R1), all features were used in Support Vector Regression (SVR) with Radial Basis Function kernel. The second run (R2) was same as R1 except that the features in R2 did not include the count features (i.e., features in 12). In the third run (R3), we used features same as R2 but applied linear regression instead.

For SVR, we used LibSVM library (Chang and Lin, 2011) in Weka (Holmes et al., 1994) and for the linear regression we used Weka's implementation. The 10-fold cross validation results (*r*) of three different runs with the training data were 0.7734 (R1), 0.7662 (R2), and 0.7654 (R3).

Data set	Baseline	R1	R2	R3
Ans-forums	0.445	0.526	0.694	0.677
Ans-students	0.664	0.725	0.744	0.735
Belief	0.651	0.631	0.751	0.722
Headlines	0.531	0.813	0.807	0.812
Images	0.603	0.858	0.864	0.857
Mean	0.587	0.743	**0.784**	0.776

Table 2: Results of our submitted runs on test data.

The results on the test set have been presented in Table 2. Though R1 had the highest correlation score in a 10-fold cross validation process using the training data, the results of R2 and R3 on the test data were consistently better than the results of R1. It suggests that absolute count features used in R1 tend to overfit the model. The weighted mean correlation of R2 was 0.784 - the best among our three runs and ranked 10th among 74 runs submitted by 29

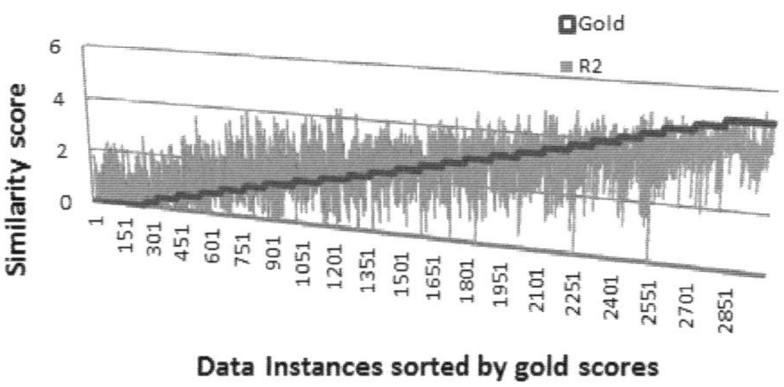

Figure 1: A graph showing similarity scores predicted by our system (R2) and corresponding human judgment in test data (sorted by gold score).

participating teams. The correlation score was very close to the results of other best performing systems. Moreover, we observed from Figure 1 that our system worked fairly well at all range of scores. The actual variation of scores at extreme (very low and very high) points is not very high though the regression line seems to be more skewed. However, the correlation scores of answer-forum, answer-students, and belief data were found to be lower than those of headlines and images data. The reason might be the texts in the former data being not well-written as compared to the latter. Also, more contextual information is required to fully understand them.

3 Interpretable STS

For each sentence pair, participating systems had to identify the chunks in each sentence or use the given gold chunks, align corresponding chunks and assign a similarity/relatedness score and type of the alignment for each alignment. The alignment types were EQUI (semantically equivalent), OPPO (opposite in meaning), SPE (one chunk is more specific than other), SIM (similar meanings, but no EQUI, OPPO, SPE), REL (related meanings, but no SIM, EQUI, OPPO, SPE), ALIC (does not have any corresponding chunk in the other sentence because of the 1:1 alignment restriction), and NOALI (has no corresponding chunk in the other sentence). Further details about the task including type of relations and evaluation criteria can be found in Agirre et al. (2015).

Our system uses gold chunks of a given sentence pair and maps chunks of the first sentence to those from the second by assigning different relations and scores based on a set of rules. The system performs stop word marking, POS tagging, lemmatization, and named-entity recognition in the preprocessing steps. It also uses lookups for synonym, antonym and hypernym relations.

For synonym lookup, we created a strict synonym lookup file using WordNet. Similarly, an antonym lookup file was created by building an antonym set for a given word from its direct antonyms and their synsets. We further constructed another lookup file for strict hypernyms.

3.1 Rules

In this section, we describe the rules used for chunk alignments and scoring. The scores given by each rule are highlighted.

Conditions: We define below a number of conditions for a given chunk pair that might be checked before applying a rule.

C_1: One chunk has a conjunction and other does not
C_2: A content word in a chunk has an antonym in the other chunk
C_3: A word in either chunk is a NUMERIC entity
C_4: Both chunks have LOCATION entities
C_5: Any of the chunks has a DATE/TIME entity
C_6: Both chunks share at least one content word other than noun
C_7: Any of the chunks has a conjunction

Next, we define a set of rules for each relation type. For aligning a chunk pair (A, B), these rules are applied in order of precedence as NOALIC, EQUI, OPPO, SPE, SIMI, REL, and ALIC. Once a chunk is aligned, it would not be considered for further alignments. Moreover, there is a precedence of rules within each relation type e.g. EQ_2 is applied only if EQ_1 fails and EQ_3 is applied if both EQ_1 and EQ_2 fail and so on. If a chunk does not get any relation after applying all the rules, a NOALIC relation is assigned. Note that we frequently use $sim\text{-}Mikolov(A, B)$ to refer to the similarity score between the chunks A and B using Mikolov word vectors as described in Section 2.2.2.

3.1.1 NOALIC Rules

NO_1: If a chunk to be mapped is a single token and is a punctuation, assign NOALIC.

3.1.2 EQUI Rules

EQUI Rules $EQ_1 - EQ_3$ are applied unconditionally. The rest rules ($EQ_4 - EQ_5$) are applied only if none of conditions C_1 - C_5 are satisfied.

EQ_1 - Both chunks have same tokens (**5**) - e.g. to compete ⇔ To Compete

EQ_2 - Both chunks have same content words (**5**) - e.g. in Olympics ⇔ At Olympics

EQ_3 - All content words match using synonym lookup (**5**) - e.g. to permit ⇔ Allowed

EQ_4 : All content words of a chunk match and unmatched content word(s) of the other chunk are all of proper noun type (**5**) - e.g. Boeing 787 Dreamliner ⇔ on 787 Dreamliner

EQ_5 : Both chunks have equal number of content words and $sim - Mikolov(A, B) > 0.6$ (**5**) - e.g. in Indonesia boat sinking ⇔ in Indonesia boat capsize

3.1.3 OPPO Rules

OPPO rules are applied only when none of C_3 and C_7 are satisfied.

OP_1: A content word in a chunk has an antonym in the other chunk (**4**) - e.g. in southern Iraq ⇔ in northern Iraq

3.1.4 SPE Rules

SP_1: If chunk A but B has a conjunction and A contains all the content words of B then A is SPE of B (**4**) - e.g. Angelina Jolie ⇔ Angelina Jolie and the complex truth.

SP_2: If chunk A contains all content words of chunk B plus some extra content words that are not verbs, A is a SPE of B or vice-versa. If chunk B has multiple SPEs, then the chunk with the maximum token overlap with B is selected as the SPE of B. (**4**) - e.g. Blade Runner Pistorius ⇔ Pistorius.

SP_3: If chunks A and B contain only one noun each say n_1 and n_2 and n_1 is hypernym of n_2, B is SPE of A or vice versa (**4**) - e.g. by a shop ⇔ outside a bookstore.

3.1.5 SIMI Rules

SI_1: Only the unmatched content word in each chunk is a CD type(**3**)-e.g. 6.9 magnitude earthquake ⇔ 5.6 magnitude earthquake

SI_2: Each chunk has a token of DATE/TIME type (**3**)- e.g. on Friday ⇔ on Wednesday

	Run	A	T	S	T+S
Headlines	Baseline	0.844	0.555	0.755	0.555
	R_1	**0.898**	0.654	0.826	0.638
	R_2	0.897	0.655	**0.826**	0.640
	R_3	0.897	**0.666**	0.815	**0.642**
Images	Baseline	0.838	0.432	0.721	0.432
	R_1	**0.887**	**0.614**	**0.787**	**0.584**
	R_2	0.880	0.585	0.781	0.561
	R_3	0.883	0.603	0.783	0.575

Table 3: F_1 scores for Images and Headlines. A, T and S refer to Alignment, Type, and Score respectively. The highlighted scores are the best results produced by our system.

SI_3: Each chunk has a token of LOCATION type (**3**) - e.g. Syria ⇔ Iraq
SI_4: When both chunks share at least one noun then assign **3** if $sim\text{-}Mikolov(A,B) >= 0.4$ and **2** otherwise. - e.g. Nato troops ⇔ NATO strike
SI_5: This rule is applied only if C_6 is not satisfied. Scores are assigned as : (i) **4** if $sim\text{-}Mikolov(A,B) \in [0.7, 1.0]$ (ii) **3** if $sim\text{-}Mikolov(A,B) \in [0.65, 0.7)$ (iii) **2** if $sim\text{-}Mikolov(A,B) \in [0.60, 0.65)$

3.1.6 REL Rules

RE_1: If both chunks share at least one content word other than noun then assign REL relation. Scores are assigned as follows : (i) **4** if $sim\text{-}Mikolov(A,B) \in [0.5, 1.0]$ (ii) **3** if $sim\text{-}Mikolov(A,B) \in [0.4, 0.5)$ (iii) **2** otherwise. e.g. to Central African Republic ⇔ in Central African capital

3.1.7 ALIC Rules

AL_1: If a chunk in a sentence X (C_x) is not aligned yet but has a chunk in another pair-sentence Y (C_y) that is already aligned and has $sim\text{-}Mikolov(C_x, C_y) >= 0.6$, assign ALIC relation to C_x with a score of (**0**).

3.2 Experiments and Results

We applied above mentioned rules in the training data set by varying thresholds for $sim\text{-}Mikolov$ scores and selected the thresholds that produced the best results in the training data set. Since three runs were allowed to submit, we defined them as follows:
$Run1(R_1)$: We applied our full set of rules with limited stop words (375 words). However EQ_4 was modified such that it would apply when unmatched content words of the bigger chunk were of noun rather than proper noun type.
$Run2(R_2)$: Same as R_1 but with extended stop words (686 words).
$Run3(R_3)$: Applied full set of rules with extended stop words.

The results corresponding to our three runs and that of the baseline are presented in Table 3. In Headlines test data, our system outperformed the rest competing submissions in all evaluation metrics (except when alignment type and score were ignored). In Images test data, R_1 was the best in alignment and type metrics. Our submissions were among the top performing submissions for score and type+score metrics.

R_3 performed better among all runs in case of Headlines data in overall. This was chiefly due to modified EQ_4 rule which reduced the number of incorrect EQUI alignments. We also observed that performance of our system was least affected by size of stopword list for Headlines data as both R_1 and R_2 recorded similar F_1-measures for all evaluation metrics. However, R_1 performed relatively better than R_2 in Images data-particularly in correctly aligning chunk relations. It could be that images are described mostly using common words and thus were filtered by R_2 as stop words.

4 Conclusion

In this paper we described our submissions to the Semantic Text Similarity Task in SemEval Shared Task 2015. Our system for the English STS subtask used regression models that combined a wide array of features including semantic similarity scores obtained with various methods. For the Interpretable Similarity subtask, we employed a rule-based approach for aligning chunks in sentence pairs and assigning relations and scores for the alignments. Our systems were among the top performing systems in both subtasks. We intend to publish our systems at http://semanticsimilarity.org.

Acknowledgments

This research was partially sponsored by University of Memphis and the Institute for Education Sciences under award R305A100875 to Dr. Vasile Rus.

References

Eneko Agirre, Mona Diab, Daniel Cer, and Aitor Gonzalez-Agirre. 2012. Semeval-2012 task 6: A pilot on semantic textual similarity. In *Proceedings of the First Joint Conference on Lexical and Computational Semantics-Volume 1: Proceedings of the main conference and the shared task, and Volume 2: Proceedings of the Sixth International Workshop on Semantic Evaluation*, pages 385–393. Association for Computational Linguistics.

Eneko Agirre, Daniel Cer, Mona Diab, Aitor Gonzalez-Agirre, and Weiwei Guo. 2013. sem 2013 shared task: Semantic textual similarity, including a pilot on typed-similarity. In *In* SEM 2013: The Second Joint Conference on Lexical and Computational Semantics. Association for Computational Linguistics*. Citeseer.

Eneko Agirre, Carmen Baneab, Claire Cardiec, Daniel Cerd, Mona Diabe, Aitor Gonzalez-Agirrea, Weiwei Guof, Rada Mihalceab, German Rigaua, and Janyce Wiebeg. 2014. Semeval-2014 task 10: Multilingual semantic textual similarity. *SemEval 2014*, page 81.

Eneko Agirre, Carmen Banea, Claire Cardie, Daniel Cer, Mona Diab, Aitor Gonzalez-Agirre, Weiwei Guo, Iigo Lopez-Gazpio, Montse Maritxalar, Rada Mihalcea, German Rigau, Larraitz Uria, and Janyce Wiebe. 2015. SemEval-2015 Task 2: Semantic Textual Similarity, English, Spanish and Pilot on Interpretability. In *Proceedings of the 9th International Workshop on Semantic Evaluation (SemEval 2015)*, Denver, CO, June. Association for Computational Linguistics.

Ramiz M Aliguliyev. 2009. A new sentence similarity measure and sentence based extractive technique for automatic text summarization. *Expert Systems with Applications*, 36(4):7764–7772.

Satanjeev Banerjee and Ted Pedersen. 2003. Extended gloss overlaps as a measure of semantic relatedness. In *IJCAI*, volume 3, pages 805–810.

Rajendra Banjade, Nabin Maharjan, Nobal B. Niraula, Vasile Rus, and Dipesh Gautam. 2015. Lemon and tea are not similar: Measuring word-to-word similarity combining different methods. In *Proceedings of the 16th International Conference on Intelligent Text Processing and Computational Linguistics*, pages 335–346.

Chris Brockett. 2007. Aligning the rte 2006 corpus. *Microsoft Research.*

Chih-Chung Chang and Chih-Jen Lin. 2011. Libsvm: a library for support vector machines. *ACM Transactions on Intelligent Systems and Technology (TIST)*, 2(3):27.

Bill Dolan, Chris Quirk, and Chris Brockett. 2004. Unsupervised construction of large paraphrase corpora: Exploiting massively parallel news sources. In *Proceedings of the 20th international conference on Computational Linguistics*, page 350. Association for Computational Linguistics.

Christiane Fellbaum. 1998. *WordNet*. Wiley Online Library.

Graeme Hirst and David St-Onge. 1998. Lexical chains as representations of context for the detection and correction of malapropisms. *WordNet: An electronic lexical database*, 305:305–332.

Geoffrey Holmes, Andrew Donkin, and Ian H Witten. 1994. Weka: A machine learning workbench. In *Intelligent Information Systems, 1994. Proceedings of the 1994 Second Australian and New Zealand Conference on*, pages 357–361. IEEE.

Mindaugas Idzelis. 2005. Jazzy: The java open source spell checker.

Jay J Jiang and David W Conrath. 1997. Semantic similarity based on corpus statistics and lexical taxonomy. *arXiv preprint cmp-lg/9709008.*

Harold W Kuhn. 1955. The hungarian method for the assignment problem. *Naval research logistics quarterly*, 2(1-2):83–97.

Thomas K Landauer, Danielle S McNamara, Simon Dennis, and Walter Kintsch. 2007. *Handbook of latent semantic analysis*. Psychology Press.

Claudia Leacock and Martin Chodorow. 1998. Combining local context and wordnet similarity for word sense identification. *WordNet: An electronic lexical database*, 49(2):265–283.

Dekang Lin. 1998. An information-theoretic definition of similarity. In *ICML*, volume 98, pages 296–304.

Christopher D Manning, Mihai Surdeanu, John Bauer, Jenny Finkel, Steven J Bethard, and David McClosky. 2014. The stanford corenlp natural language processing toolkit. In *Proceedings of 52nd Annual Meeting of the Association for Computational Linguistics: System Demonstrations*, pages 55–60.

Tomas Mikolov, Ilya Sutskever, Kai Chen, Greg S Corrado, and Jeff Dean. 2013. Distributed representations of words and phrases and their compositionality. In *Advances in Neural Information Processing Systems*, pages 3111–3119.

Nobal B. Niraula, Rajendra Banjade, Dan Ştefănescu, and Vasile Rus. 2013. Experiments with semantic similarity measures based on lda and lsa. In *Statistical Language and Speech Processing*, pages 188–199. Springer.

Kishore Papineni, Salim Roukos, Todd Ward, and Wei-Jing Zhu. 2002. Bleu: a method for automatic evaluation of machine translation. In *Proceedings of the 40th annual meeting on association for computational linguistics*, pages 311–318. Association for Computational Linguistics.

Jeffrey Pennington, Richard Socher, and Christopher D Manning. 2014. Glove: Global vectors for word representation. *Proceedings of the Empiricial Methods in Natural Language Processing (EMNLP 2014)*, 12.

Philip Resnik. 1995. Using information content to evaluate semantic similarity in a taxonomy. *arXiv preprint cmp-lg/9511007*.

Vasile Rus and Mihai Lintean. 2012. A comparison of greedy and optimal assessment of natural language student input using word-to-word similarity metrics. In *Proceedings of the Seventh Workshop on Building Educational Applications Using NLP*, pages 157–162. Association for Computational Linguistics.

Vasile Rus, Mihai Lintean, Cristian Moldovan, William Baggett, Nobal Niraula, and Brent Morgan. 2012. The similar corpus: A resource to foster the qualitative understanding of semantic similarity of texts. In *Semantic Relations II: Enhancing Resources and Applications, The 8th Language Resources and Evaluation Conference (LREC 2012), May*, pages 23–25.

Vasile Rus, Mihai Lintean, Rajendra Banjade, Nobal Niraula, and Dan Stefanescu. 2013. Semilar: The semantic similarity toolkit. In *Proceedings of the 51st Annual Meeting of the Association for Computational Linguistics*. Association for Computational Linguistics.

Vasile Rus, Rajendra Banjade, and Mihai Lintean. 2014. On paraphrase identification corpora. In *Proceeding on the International Conference on Language Resources and Evaluation (LREC 2014)*.

Dan Stefanescu, Rajendra Banjade, and Vasile Rus. 2014a. Latent semantic analysis models on wikipedia and tasa.

Dan Ştefănescu, Rajendra Banjade, and Vasile Rus. 2014b. A sentence similarity method based on chunking and information content. In *Computational Linguistics and Intelligent Text Processing*, pages 442–453. Springer.

Zhibiao Wu and Martha Palmer. 1994. Verbs semantics and lexical selection. In *Proceedings of the 32nd annual meeting on Association for Computational Linguistics*, pages 133–138. Association for Computational Linguistics.

Samsung: Align-and-Differentiate Approach to Semantic Textual Similarity

Lushan Han, Justin Martineau, Doreen Cheng and Christopher Thomas
Samsung Research America
665 Clyde Avenue
Mountain View, CA 94043, USA
{lushan.han, justin.m, doreen.c, c2.thomas}@samsung.com

Abstract

This paper describes our Align-and-Differentiate approach to the SemEval 2015 Task 2 competition for English Semantic Textual Similarity (STS) systems. Our submission achieved the top place on two of the five evaluation datasets. Our team placed 3rd among 28 participating teams, and our three runs ranked 4th, 6th and 7th among the 73 runs submitted by the 28 teams. Our approach improves upon the UMBC *PairingWords* system by semantically differentiating distributionally similar terms. This novel addition improves results by 2.5 points on the Pearson correlation measure.

1 Introduction

Since its inception in 2012, the annual Semantic Textual Similarity (STS) task has attracted and increasing amount of interest in the NLP community. The task is to measure the semantic similarity between two sentences using a scale ranging from 0 to 5 (Agirre et al., 2012; Agirre et al., 2013; Agirrea et al., 2014). In this task, 0 means *unrelated* and 5 means *complete semantic equivalence*. For example, the sentence "China's new PM rejects US hacking claims" is semantically equivalent to the sentence "China Premier Li rejects 'groundless' US hacking accusations" even though there are many word level differences between the two sentences.

Improvements in the STS task can advance or benefit many research areas, such as paraphrase recognition (Dolan et al., 2004), automatic machine translation evaluation (Kauchak and Barzilay, 2006), ontology mapping and schema matching (Han, 2014), Twitter search (Sriram et al., 2010), image retrieval by captions (Coelho et al., 2004) and information retrieval in general.

Measuring semantic similarity is difficult because it is relatively easy to express the same idea in very different ways. Both word choice and word order can have a great impact on the semantics of a sentence, or not at all. For example, the sentences "A woman is playing piano on the street" and "A lady is playing violin on the street" have a semantic similarity score of only 2, because pianos are not violins so the two events in the sentences must be different. This is problematic because common solutions, such as bag-of-words representations, parse trees, and word alignments measure word choice and word order. We improve upon existing word choice approaches with better measures to semantically differentiate distributionally similar terms, and by using these measures to also improve the word alignment.

Our solution is an *Align-and-Differentiate* approach, in which we greedily align words between sentences, before penalizing non-matching words in the differentiate-phase. Our system improves upon the successful UMBC *PairingWords* system by about 2 points of Pearson's Correlation measure. The success of the *PairingWords* system is largely due to their high-quality distributional word similarity model[1] described in (Han et al., 2013). The distributional similarity model can tell that "woman" and "lady" in the above example are highly similar, which is usually correct, but it also says that "pi-

[1] See `http://swoogle.umbc.edu/SimService/` for a demo.

ano" and "violin" are very similar, which in many contexts is incorrect. While distributional similarity measures can be criticized for producing high similarity scores for antonyms and contrasting words, we find that this property is actually advantageous when performing word alignment between two sentences. We take advantage of this property by first aligning with distributional similarity, and then differentiate by penalizing alignments of words that are semantically disjoint (Ex: antonyms). This technique to first align and then differentiate is our key improvement.

The remainder of the paper proceeds as follows. Section 2 briefly revisits the UMBC *PairingWords* system. Section 3 presents our new *Align-and-Differentiate* approach. Section 4 presents and discusses our results.

2 UMBC PairingWords System

The *PairingWords* system (Han et al., 2013) uses a state-of-the-art word similarity measure to align words in the sentence pair and computes the STS score using a simple metric that combines individual term alignment scores.

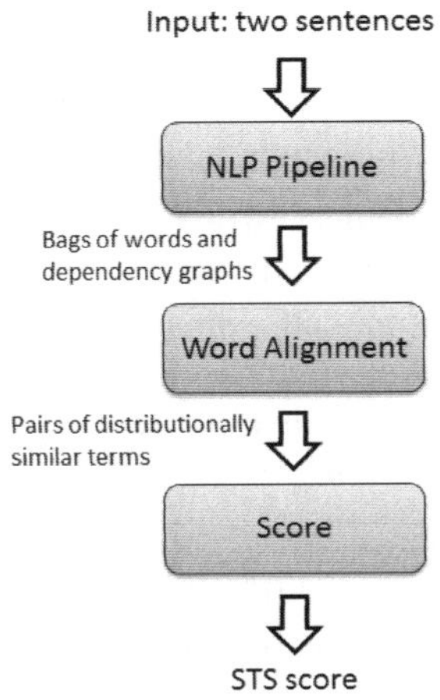

Figure 1: Overview of UMBC PairingWords system.

2.1 Precompute Word Similarities

First, a distributional model was built on an English corpus[2] of three-billion words and separated into paragraphs. Words are POS tagged and lemmatized. A small context window of ± 4 words is used to count word co-occurrences. The vocabulary has a size of 29,000 terms, which includes primarily open-class words (i.e. nouns, verbs, adjectives and adverbs). Singular Value Decomposition (SVD) (Landauer and Dumais, 1997; Burgess et al., 1998) has been used to reduce the 29K word vectors to 300 dimensions. The distributional similarity between two words is measured by the cosine similarity of their corresponding reduced word vectors. The distributional similarity is then enhanced with WordNet (Fellbaum, 1998) relations in eight categories (See (Han et al., 2013)). Finally it is wrapped with surface similarity modules to handle the matching of out-of-vocabulary words.

[2]The UMBC WebBase corpus is available for download at `http://ebiq.org/r/351`

2.2 NLP Pipeline

The Stanford POS tagger is applied to tag and lemmatize the input sentences. A predefined vocabulary, POS tags, and regular expressions are used to recognize multi-word terms including noun and verb phrases, proper nouns, numbers and time. Stop words are ignored. The stop word list was augmented with adverbs that occurred more than $500,000$ times in the corpus.

2.3 Word Alignment Between Two Sentences

The alignment function g for a target word w in one sentence S is simply defined as its most similar word w' in the other sentence S' with respect to the aforementioned word similarity measure. See Equation 1.

$$g(w) = \underset{w' \in S'}{argmax}\ sim(w, w') \tag{1}$$

2.4 Score

The *PairingWords* systems yield an STS score in the range [0, 1] with a linearly scaled definition corresponding to the standard STS score. This score is computed using the word level semantic similarity of the aligned words. The *PairingWords* system uses a similarity threshold to decide whether a term can be aligned. If a term cannot be aligned then a penalty is imposed. Therefore, the *PairingWords* STS score is the result of subtracting the penalty score P from the overall term alignment score T, which is defined in Equation 2.

$$T = \frac{\sum_{t \in S_1} sim(t, g(t))}{2 \cdot |S_1|} + \frac{\sum_{t \in S_2} sim(t, g(t))}{2 \cdot |S_2|} \quad (2)$$

where S_1 and S_2 are the sets of words/terms in two input sentences.

3 Align-and-Differentiate Approach

Our system extends the UMBC *PairingWords* system by differentiating distributionally similar terms, resulting in a conceptually new framework to tackle the STS challenge. Figure 2 illustrates our system. After preprocessing there are four main algorithms: align, differentiate, score, and rescore.

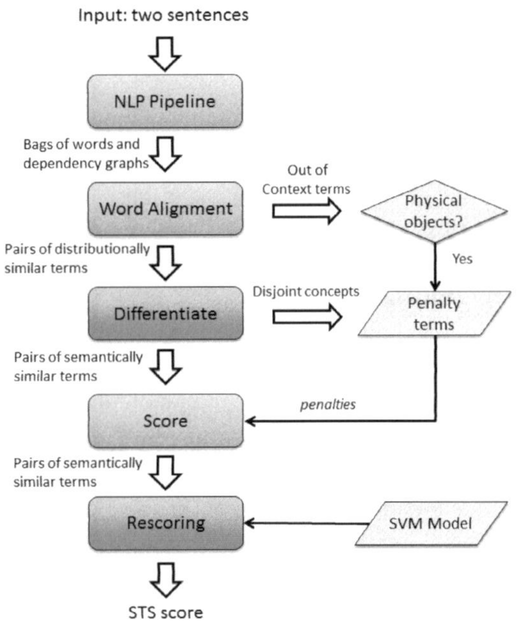

Figure 2: Our system overview. Blue components (Differentiate and Rescore) mark the most novel additions to the PairingWords system.

3.1 Precompute Word Similarities

We reused the distributional model built for the UMBC PairingWords system.

3.2 NLP Pipeline

In addition to the basic NLP techniques used by the *PairingWords* in Section 2.2 we use the Stanford dependency parser to translate the input sentences into their dependency graph representation.

3.3 Word Alignment Between Two Sentences

For alignment we upgraded the *PairingWords* approach (see Equation 1) with candidate disambiguation. If multiple candidates (ambiguity) exist, we use their neighboring words in the sentences and dependency graphs to carry out disambiguation. For two mapping candidates, we found their neighboring words in terms of dependency relations. Then we choose the candidate with the highest neighbor similarity. This alignment method is directional. In domains for which we have high confidence that the dependency parser will correctly parse both sentences, we require mutual agreement in both directions. Mutual alignment is computed by finding g such that $g(w) = w'$ and $g(w') = w$.

The similarity function $sim(w, w')$ is the word similarity function described in Section 2.1.

Following the *PairingWords* system, we use a similarity threshold of .05 to determine whether a vocabulary word[3] has at least some minimum similarity with any of the words in the other sentence. We call a word *Out Of Context (OOC)* if the threshold is not satisfied. The appearance of OOC words could be an indicator of different sentence semantics, as illustrated in the example "A beautiful red car" vs. "A beautiful red rose" where "car" is an OOC word with respect to the other sentence. The impact of OOC words to semantic equivalence is disproportionately high. Therefore, we penalize semantic similarity scores in proportion to the number of OOC words.

However, we observed that if OOC words occur because there are additional details, then these words should not be penalized. For example, in the two sentences "Matt Smith to leave Doctor Who after 4 years" and "Matt Smith quits Doctor Who", the word 'year' is an OOC word that does not significantly reduce the semantic equivalence. We found that many of these extraneous and benign OOC words do not represent physical objects, i.e. something that can be touched. Hence, we chose to only penalize OOC words that are physical objects.

[3]A vocabulary word means a word in our vocabulary of 29k words

WordNet has a synset *physical objects* and we use its descendants to collect the set of physical objects.

3.4 Differentiate

This subsection defines and then describes how we identify *Disjoint Similar Concepts*.

The *semantic similarity* of two words is the degree of semantic equivalence between the two words. We may also say, it is the ability to substitute one term for the other without changing the meaning of a sentence.

Many distributionally similar terms are not semantically similar. Examples include "good" vs "bad", "cat" vs "dog", "Thuesday" vs "Monday", "France" vs "England" and etc. Existing research on distributional models has mainly been focused on studying antonyms or contrasting words (Mohammad et al., 2008; Scheible et al., 2013; Mohammad et al., 2013). However, as shown by the above examples, the scope of distributionally similar but not semantically similar terms goes far beyond antonyms. Hereafter, we refer to this new category of terms as *Disjoint Similar Concepts (DSCs)*.

To the best of our knowledge, collecting *Disjoint Similar Concepts* is a novel research problem. General statistical methods are not easily available, but we can extract such information from human-crafted ontologies, such as WordNet. For this work, we identify *Disjoint Similar Concepts* as siblings under a common parent in an ontology, such as WordNet. For example, in the electronics domain, we can assert that *smart phone* and *tablet* are *DSCs* if they are siblings with the same parent *electronics* in the ontology.

We use a semi-automatic method to produce several sets of potential *DSCs* for our STS system. The sets include animals, countries, vehicles, weekdays, colors and etc. First, we decide what types of *DSCs* are likely to appear in a dataset. For example, animals and vehicles will likely appear in the *images* training dataset.

We penalize each aligned word pair that has *Disjoint Similar Concepts*. If both words are antonyms then they are *DSCs*. If both words share the same hypernym in WordNet, and that hypernym is a potential *DSC*, then they are *DSCs*. Otherwise, the concepts are considered semantically similar.

3.5 Score

We create a base similarity score E_i, and then apply penalties for OOC words O_i and *Disjoint Similar Concepts* D_i.

$$T_i = \frac{E_i - O_i - D_i}{2 \cdot |S_i|} \qquad i \in \{1,2\} \quad (3)$$

$$E_i = \sum_{\langle t,g(t)\rangle \in SS_i} sim(t, g(t)) \qquad i \in \{1,2\} \quad (4)$$

$$O_i = \sum_{t \in OOC_i} \alpha(t) \qquad i \in \{1,2\} \quad (5)$$

$$D_i = \sum_{\langle t,g(t)\rangle \in DSC_i} \beta(\langle t, g(t)\rangle) \qquad i \in \{1,2\} \quad (6)$$

$$STS = T_1 + T_2 \quad (7)$$

Our primary method of producing the STS score is shown in Equations 3 to 7. The method is based on the directional alignment function described in Section 3.3. E_i is the base score where i indicates the alignment direction and SS_i represents the collection of pairs of semantically similar terms for direction i. O_i is the sum of penalties applied to OOC terms for direction i. In our current system, the function $\alpha(t)$ has a constant value 1.0. D_i is the sum of penalties applied to *Disjoint Similar Concepts* for direction i. We normally set $\beta(\langle t, g(t)\rangle)$ to 0.5 but we can also tune β coefficient depending on different types of *Disjoint Similar Concepts* (e.g.*animal* and *color*), if a training dataset is available.

3.6 Rescore by Learning STS Offset Scores

We learn an offset score to account for and correct systemic biases in the Align and Differentiate algorithm using supervised machine learning. For domains with labeled data we used bag-of-words Support Vector Machines (SVMs) in regression mode, with a linear kernel, to compute an offset score measuring the difference between our Equation 7 STS score and the gold standard training STS score. We add this offset score to the Equation 7 STS score. This process improved our Pearson Correlation scores from .7936 to .8162 on the 2014 STS data in a ten fold cross-validation setting.

The SVM was trained on a length normalized bag-of-words with additional non-normalized meta

Dataset	alpha	beta	delta
headlines (750 pairs)	0.8342 (2)	0.8342	**0.8417 (1)**
images (750 pairs)	0.8701 (2)	**0.8713 (1)**	0.8634
students (750 pairs)	0.7827 (2)	0.7819	0.7825
forums (375 pairs)	0.6589	0.6586	0.6639
belief (375 pairs)	0.7029	0.6995	0.6952
weighted mean	0.7920 (4)	0.7916 (7)	0.7918 (6)

Table 1: Pearson correlation and STS 2015 Competition Rank of our three runs on test sets.

features for (1) the length difference between sentence pairs, (2) the percentage of exact word to word matches between both sentences, and (3) the STS score produced in Equation 7. The bag-of-words feature values were calculated by taking the absolute value of the difference between the number of times a word occurred in the first sentence versus the number of occurrences in the paired sentence. The bag-of-words was created with both words and bi-gram word sequences.

4 Results and Discussion

Table 1 shows the official results of our three runs, alpha, beta and delta, in the 2015 STS task. Each entry supplies a run's Pearson correlation on a dataset and the rank of the run among all 73 runs submitted by the 28 teams. The last row shows the weighted mean and the overall ranks of our three runs.

The alpha run was produced by applying the align-and-differentiate algorithm to the five datasets with the same parameter settings. The beta run was produced without penalizing OOC terms, except for the *images* dataset. The result for penalizing OOC terms are slightly better, but are just shy of a 95% confidence interval (using paired T-tests). On the *images* dataset, we exploited dependency structure in the align and differentiate algorithm. We use the supervised ML model to rescuer our STS scores only for the delta run on the *Headlines* and *Images* datasets.

Our results on the *forums* and *beliefs* datasets were surprisingly much lower than other datasets due to the *PairingWords* system's poor baseline performance on these datasets as shown in Table 2. We speculate that this drop in performance is caused by the *PairingWords* system ignoring words that are not nouns, verbs, adjectives and limited adverbs. These include common meaningful words such as "how" and "why" in both datasets.

System	headline	image	student	forum	belief	*mean*
UMBC	.8059	.8431	.7588	.6646	.6996	.7725
alpha	.8342	.8701	.7827	.6589	.7029	.7920

Table 2: Our approach improves results by 2.5% in Pearson's correlation.

Our approach of semantically differentiating distributionally similar terms, as shown in Table 2 is a statistically significant improvement at the 95% confidence interval.

Acknowledgments

We thank Ebiquity lab, CSEE department, University of Maryland, Baltimore County for providing their 2013 STS code.

References

Eneko Agirre, Mona Diab, Daniel Cer, and Aitor Gonzalez-Agirre. 2012. Semeval-2012 task 6: a pilot on semantic textual similarity. In *Proceedings of the First Joint Conference on Lexical and Computational Semantics*, pages 385–393.

Eneko Agirre, Daniel Cer, Mona Diab, Aitor Gonzalez-Agirre, and Weiwei Guo. 2013. *sem 2013 shared task: Semantic textual similarity, including a pilot on typed-similarity. In **SEM 2013: The Second Joint Conference on Lexical and Computational Semantics*.

Eneko Agirrea, Carmen Baneab, Claire Cardiec, Daniel Cerd, Mona Diabe, Aitor Gonzalez-Agirrea, Weiwei Guof, Rada Mihalceab, German Rigaua, and Janyce Wiebeg. 2014. Semeval-2014 task 10: Multilingual semantic textual similarity. *SemEval 2014*, page 81.

C. Burgess, K. Livesay, and K. Lund. 1998. Explorations in context space: Words, sentences, discourse. *Discourse Processes*, 25:211–257.

T.A.S. Coelho, Pável Pereira Calado, Lamarque Vieira Souza, Berthier Ribeiro-Neto, and Richard Muntz. 2004. Image retrieval using multiple evidence ranking. *IEEE Trans. on Knowl. and Data Eng.*, 16(4):408–417.

Bill Dolan, Chris Quirk, and Chris Brockett. 2004. Unsupervised construction of large paraphrase corpora: exploiting massively parallel news sources. In *Proceedings of the 20th international conference on Computational Linguistics*, COLING '04.

Christiane Fellbaum. 1998. *WordNet: An Electronic Lexical Database*. The MIT Press, May.

Lushan Han, Abhay L. Kashyap, Tim Finin, James Mayfield, and Johnathan Weese. 2013.

UMBC_EBIQUITY-CORE: Semantic Textual Similarity Systems. In *Proceedings of the Second Joint Conference on Lexical and Computational Semantics*. Association for Computational Linguistics, June.

Lushan Han. 2014. *Schema Free Querying of Semantic Data*. Ph.D. thesis, University of Maryland, Baltimore County, August.

David Kauchak and Regina Barzilay. 2006. Paraphrasing for automatic evaluation. In *HLT-NAACL '06*, pages 455–462.

T. Landauer and S. Dumais. 1997. A solution to plato's problem: The latent semantic analysis theory of the acquisition, induction, and representation of knowledge. In *Psychological Review, 104*, pages 211–240.

Saif Mohammad, Bonnie Dorr, and Graeme Hirst. 2008. Computing word-pair antonymy. In *Proc. Conf. on Empirical Methods in Natural Language Processing and Computational Natural Language Learning (EMNLP-2008)*, October.

Saif M. Mohammad, Bonnie J. Dorr, Graeme Hirst, and Peter D. Turney. 2013. Computing Lexical Contrast. *Computational Linguistics*, 39(July 2012):555–590.

S. Scheible, S. Schulte im Walde, and S. Springorum. 2013. Uncovering distributional differences between synonyms and antonyms in a word space model. In *Proceedings of the Sixth International Joint Conference on Natural Language Processing*, pages 489–497.

Bharath Sriram, Dave Fuhry, Engin Demir, Hakan Ferhatosmanoglu, and Murat Demirbas. 2010. Short text classification in twitter to improve information filtering. In *Proceedings of the 33rd international ACM SIGIR conference on Research and development in information retrieval*, pages 841–842.

UBC: Cubes for English Semantic Textual Similarity and Supervised Approaches for Interpretable STS

Eneko Agirre, Aitor Gonzalez-Agirre, Iñigo Lopez-Gazpio, Montse Maritxalar, German Rigau, Larraitz Uria
University of the Basque Country
Donostia, 20018, Basque Country
{e.agirre, aitor.gonzalez-agirre, inigo.lopez, montse.maritxalar, german.rigau, larraitz.uria}@ehu.eus

Abstract

In Semantic Textual Similarity, systems rate the degree of semantic equivalence on a graded scale from 0 to 5, with 5 being the most similar. For the English subtask, we present a system which relies on several resources for token-to-token and phrase-to-phrase similarity to build a data-structure which holds all the information, and then combine the information to get a similarity score. We also participated in the pilot on Interpretable STS, where we apply a pipeline which first aligns tokens, then chunks, and finally uses supervised systems to label and score each chunk alignment.

1 Introduction

In Semantic Textual Similarity (STS), systems rate the degree of semantic equivalence on a graded scale from 0 to 5, with 5 being the most similar. We participated in two of the subtask for STS in 2015 (Agirre et al., 2015). For the English subtask, we present a system which relies on several resources for token-to-token and phrase-to-phrase similarity to build a data-structure which holds all the information, and then combine the information to get a similarity score. We also participated in the pilot on Interpretable STS, where we apply a pipeline which first aligns tokens, then chunks, and finally uses supervised systems to label and score each chunk alignment.

Note that some of the authors participated in the organization of the task. We scrupulously separated the tasks in such a way that the developers of the systems did not have access to the test sets, and that they only had access to the same training data as the rest of the participants.

2 Cubes for English STS

In this section we describe a novel approach to compute similarity scores between two sentences using a cube where each layer contains token-to-token and phrase-to-phrase similarity scores from a different method and/or resource. Our assumption is that we can obtain better results using this similarity scores together than independently.

2.1 Building Cubes

The first step is to produce parse trees for the sentences using the Stanford Parser (Toutanova et al., 2003). After parsing the sentences each pair of sentences can be represented by a NxM matrix, being N is the number of nodes of the parse tree of the first sentence, and M the number of nodes of the parse tree of the second sentence. Note that some nodes (terminals) correspond to words, while others (non-terminals) represent phrases. We can have as many matrices as we wish, and fill them with different similarity scores, forming a cube.

In this first attempt we used three layers:

1. Euclidean distance between Collobert and Weston Word Vector (Collobert and Weston, 2008). The vector representations for each non-terminal node in the tree were learnt using Recursive Autoencoder (RAE) (Socher et al., 2011).

2. Euclidean distance between Mikolov Word Vectors (Mikolov et al., 2013a; Mikolov et al., 2013b). To compute the vector representations for each non-terminal node in the tree, we summed the vectors and normalize them dividing by the number of words in the phrase.

3. PPDB Paraphrase database values (Ganitkevitch et al., 2013). We used the XXXL version. In this case both words and some phrases

are contained in the resource. This resource yields conditional probabilities. As our scores are undirected, in case the database contains values for both directions, we average.

The first two produce a dense layer, where most of the cells have a value. The third one produces a sparse layer, where only the pairs occurring in the resource have a value. Note that some of the phrases in PPDB do not correspond to a node in the tree. In this case, we add extra columns and rows.

2.2 Producing STS Score

Before computing a similarity score we flatten our cube into a single layer, where each of the element in the new NxM matrix is the maximum between the values for that position across all the layers. We do that because we studied the different resources and we think that these resources have less False Positives (FP) than False Negatives (FN). In other words, if one of the resources says that something is very similar we trust on it and take that similarity score instead of the other (even if they are very low). Moreover, our assumption is that the final similarity score is specially based in similarities between tokens/phrases in the sentences, and not on dissimilarities.

Once we have this matrix, we compute the final STS score using the scoring function seen in (Mihalcea et al., 2006).

$$sim(S_1, S_2) = \frac{1}{2}\left(\frac{\sum_{w \in S_1}(maxSim(w_{\in} S_2) * idf(w))}{\sum_{w \in S_1} idf(w)}\right.$$
$$\left. + \left(\frac{\sum_{w \in S_2}(maxSim(w_{\in} S_1) * idf(w))}{\sum_{w \in S_2} idf(w)}\right)\right)$$

2.3 Results

Due to time constraints we submitted a single run, which ranked 54 among 74 runs. We expect to improve this results adding more layers and combining them using more sophisticated aggregation methods.

3 Participating on the Interpretable STS Pilot Subtask

The SemEval 2015 STS task offered a new *pilot subtask on interpretable STS*[1]. Given a sentence pair, the objective of the subtask is to align segments pertaining to one sentence with the segments pertaining to the other sentence. The whole subtask is in deep described in (Agirre et al., 2015).

In sum, every alignment may consist of a **similarity score** and a **relatedness tag**. The similarity score is a real number bounded by [0,5] where 0 means no relation at all and 5 means complete equivalence. As regards the relatedness tag, there exists a set of categorical values to choose on, such as: *equivalence*, *opposition*, *specialization* (direction is relevant), *similarity* and one more tag for *other kind of relatedness*.

For the case of unaligned segments there are another two possible categorical values. The one for declaring segments unaligned (*not aligned*); and the other to declare that the segment related to the current segment has already been aligned (*context alignment*). Notice that due to the limitations of the current pilot the only way to align segments is making 1:1 alignments. Thus, 1:N alignments are simulated making an 1:1 alignment and several *context alignments*. This concept is relevant to the work done in section 3.1.2 when we extend the *Hungarian-Munkres* (Clapper, 2009) algorithm to identify *already aligned chunks*.

In addition, *factuality* or *polarity* connotations can be added as requested to the previously mentioned tags. Two different scenarios are provided in the pilot subtask, the first one makes gold standard segments available for participants (***Gold Chunks** or GS scenario*); and, the second one, only provides sentence raw text (***System Chunks** or SYS scenario*).

In conclusion, the first pilot on interpretable STS seems challenging because participating systems must not only discover and score the relatedness between segments, but also identify the inner relation between them.

3.1 System Description

This section describes the principal algorithm and the distinct modules it uses, modules are further described in the following subsections (3.1.1, 3.1.2, 3.1.3 and 3.1.4). System configurations (***runs***) used to submit results are described in section 3.1.5.

The system makes use of **several modules** to identify segments over sentence pairs, and then, make alignments between them. First of all, the *input handling and chunking module* is responsible

[1] http://alt.qcri.org/semeval2015/task2/index.php?id=proba

for linguistically processing the given input, and for creating the internal representation of the sentences. Once the input is processed the *alignment module* identifies related and unrelated segments among sentences. Finally, by using segment pair based features the *classification module* and the *scoring module* produce respectively the final relatedness tag and the similarity score.

3.1.1 Input Handling and Chunking Module

We use the **Stanford NLP parser** (Klein and Manning, 2003) to linguistically process input sentences and register lowercased token information (lemma, part of speech analysis and dependency structure is also needed for the following module). The next step consists of determining segments or token regions. This information is gathered according to the specified scenario (GS or SYS). In the case of the GS scenario the baseline obviously uses gold standard input; and, in the SYS scenario the baseline uses the *ixa-pipes-chunker* (Agerri et al., 2014).

Ixa-pipes-chunk has been trained using the Apache OpenNLP API (OpenNLP, 2011), which is a maximum entropy chunker. Nevertheless, the chunker's output has been improved using simple regular expressions to fit to our task proposal. Actually, we developed four rules to optimize how conjunctions, punctuations and prepositions are handled. In brief, the developed rules try to join consequent chunks forming new chunks consisting of the previous ones, for instance, we found significant improvement if prepositional phrases followed by a nominal phrase were unified as a single chunk. We also developed some rules to unify nominal phrases separated by punctuations or conjunctions, or a combination of those.

3.1.2 Alignment Module

The alignment module mainly focuses on the work done by the monolingual word aligner described in (Sultan et al., 2014), and *Hungarian-Munkres* algorithm.

The **monolingual word aligner** is a simple and ready-to-use system that has demonstrated state-of-the-art performance. To begin with we start by constructing the *token to token link matrix* in which each element at position (i,j) determines that there exists a link between token i (from sentence 1) and token j (from sentence 2). A link exists in the matrix if and only if the monolingual word aligner has determined that both tokens are related.

Then, the system uses token regions to group individual tokens into segments, and calculates the weight between every segment in the sentence pair. The weight among two segments is proportional to the number of links that interconnect tokens inside those segments. In other words, by summing regions we collapse the token to token link matrix onto a *chunk to chunk link matrix*. After that, we use the mentioned **Hungarian-Munkres** algorithm to discover which are the segments (x,y) which score the highest weight (link ratio); but also, we extend it to discover which are the segments that are linked to either segment x or segment y, but not with a maximum alignment ratio. This processing to find not-maximal weights is essential to effectively assign the *context alignment* tag for 1:N relations. In addition, the system is also aware of chunks that have been left unaligned.

3.1.3 Classification Module

The system can use one of the following approaches to assign relatedness tags to segment pairs: the *naive approach* and the *machine learning approach*. The **naive approach** directly assigns the tag as a majority classifier would do, that is: for the segments with highest weight it always assigns the equivalence tag, for the segments that are linked with lower weights it always assigns the *context alignment* tag, and for the not aligned segments it always assigns the not aligned tag.

The **machine learning approach** makes use of the segment-pair to calculate a total of 21 features to improve the tag assignment. The objective of the induced model is to refine the output given by the naive approach only for segment pairs tagged as equivalent. The features used to induce the model can be classified in the following groups: Jaccard overlap related features, segment length related features, WordNet similarity related features among segment heads, WordNet depth related features, and other kind of features obtained by means of the cube described in section 2.

To induce the model we use the *Support Vector Machine* (SVM) implementation described in (Chang and Lin, 2011) under the latest experimental version of *Weka* (Hall et al., 2009) using randomly shuffled 5-fold cross validation. We indistinctly join the available datasets and grid search to optimize the cost and gamma parameters.

3.1.4 Scoring Module

To assign segment pair similarity scores the system can also use two distinct approaches: the *naive approach* and the *cube based regression approach*. The **naive scorer** directly assigns a certain score to each one of the tags, which has been previously assigned using the naive tagger: for equivalence tags it assigns a score of 5 and for not aligned and context aligned tags it assigns 'NIL'. (as requested by the guidelines). The **regression approach** uses the cube described in section 2 to improve the score given to segment pairs tagged by the machine learning tagger. Its returning value is used directly as the value for the pair similarity score.

3.1.5 Submitted Runs

Even the subtask allows the submission of up to three runs, we only submitted two distinct configurations, named *run1* and *run2*. run1 and run2 are mainly the same system, but **run1** makes use of the naive approaches for both classification and scoring tasks; whereas **run2** makes use of the machine learning approach for the tag assignment and the cube based regression approach for the scoring assignment.

3.2 Result Analysis

Participating runs were evaluated using the official scorer provided by task organizers, which computes four distinct metrics: *F1 ALI* (segment pair alignment correctness regardless of the tag), *F1 Type* (segment pair alignment correctness taking tag into account), *F1 Score* (segment pair alignment correctness taking score into account) and *F1 Type + Score* (segment pair alignment correctness taking tag and score into account).

3.2.1 Development

We developed two runs as above described using the training data provided by task organizers. Training data consists of two datasets (images dataset and headlines dataset) with 750 sentence pairs each. We built and evaluated our system using 5-fold cross validation and using a grid search optimization to tune the SVM parameters. Results for both runs are shown in table 1.

I GS	Ali	Type	Score	Type + Score
Run1	0.8942	0.5115	0.7776	0.5115
Run2	0.8942	0.7408	0.8175	0.6934
I SYS	**Ali**	**Type**	**Score**	**Type + Score**
Run1	0.8379	0.4734	0.7271	0.4734
Run2	0.8379	0.6499	0.7627	0.6106
H GS	**Ali**	**Type**	**Score**	**Type + Score**
Run1	0.8920	0.5740	0.7869	0.5738
Run2	0.8920	0.6908	0.8133	0.6544
H SYS	**Ali**	**Type**	**Score**	**Type + Score**
Run1	0.7650	0.4808	0.6707	0.4808
Run2	0.7650	0.5210	0.6862	0.4902

Table 1: Development results for both datasets in the two scenarios. 'I' stands for the images dataset, and 'H' stands for the headlines dataset.

The table shows that run2 outperforms run1 in all of the scenarios, which was expected as run1 is using the naive approach for both: the relatedness tag and the similarity score assignment. Notice that both runs obtain the same F1 Alignment score as both runs are using the same input handling and chunking module. Without the shadow of a doubt, we can observe that for both datasets the **F1 alignment is noticeable higher** in the *GS scenario* than in the *SYS scenario*. Moreover, as evaluation measures are incremental, F1 Type, F1 Score and F1 Type + Score are also lower for the SYS scenario.

It is also important to mention that the difference in performance (F Type+Score) between run1 and run2 is **more noticeable in the images dataset**, actually, for the headlines dataset in the SYS scenario, the difference between both runs is under 0.01. This difference increases up to 0.08 for the headlines dataset in the GS scenario.

3.2.2 Test

The test dataset was composed of 378 sentence pairs for the headlines dataset and of 375 sentence pairs for the images dataset. Table 2 illustrates the results obtained by run1 and run2. The results obtained for the test datasets follow in general the same tendency as the one seen for the development. In fact, **run2 most of the times outperforms run1**; being this difference in performance more noticeable in the images dataset than in the headlines dataset. It might be necessary to further analyze the

I GS	Ali	Type	Score	Type + Score
Baseline	0.8388	0.4328	0.721	0.4326
Run1	0.8846	0.4749	0.7709	0.4746
Run2	0.8846	0.6557	0.8085	0.6159
MAX Par	0.887	0.6143	0.7968	0.5964
AVG Par	0.8193	0.5004	0.7197	0.4748
I SYS	**Ali**	**Type**	**Score**	**Type + Score**
Baseline	0.706	0.3696	0.6092	0.3693
Run1	0.8388	0.445	0.728	0.4447
Run2	0.8388	0.6019	0.7634	0.5643
MAX Par	0.8336	0.5759	0.7511	0.5634
AVG Par	0.67	0.4086	0.5892	0.3912
H GS	**Ali**	**Type**	**Score**	**Type + Score**
Baseline	0.8448	0.5556	0.7551	0.5556
Run1	0.8991	0.5882	0.8031	0.5882
Run2	0.8991	0.6402	0.8211	0.6185
MAX Par	0.8984	0.6666	0.8263	0.6426
AVG Par	0.8365	0.5576	0.7468	0.5381
H SYS	**Ali**	**Type**	**Score**	**Type + Score**
Baseline	0.6701	0.4571	0.6066	0.4571
Run1	0.7709	0.5019	0.6892	0.5019
Run2	0.7709	0.4865	0.7014	0.4705
MAX Par	0.782	0.5154	0.7024	0.5098
AVG Par	0.6870	0.4498	0.6094	0.4335

Table 2: Test results for both datasets in the two scenarios. 'I' stands for the images dataset, 'H' stands for the headlines dataset and 'Par' stands for participants.

unique scenario in which run1 obtains higher accuracy than run2 (Headlines SYS), but actually, results have been also very close at development in this context.

The baseline seems to be not that trivial as it sometimes outperforms participants average performance; but as we can see both of our runs obtain higher accuracy than the baseline, in both cases by large margin. For example, in the images dataset the difference between the baseline and the second run is 0.18 and 0.19 respectively for the GS and the SYS scenario. Regarding other participants, we can conclude that our runs obtain quite good results, specially for the images dataset where run2 obtains the highest score.

4 Conclusions and Future Work

Through this paper we have described the systems that participated in the Semantic Textual Similarity task 2A (English STS) and 2C (Interpretable STS). Our main focus in the English subtask was on deploying our idea of building a cube with similarity information from several sources. We are currently working on more layers, including Random Walks over WordNet and Wikipedia, string similarity (Ferrone and Zanzotto, 2014), and also a special layer to deal with numbers. Additionally, we are considering the idea of dissimilarity layers, for instance, adding information about negation and antonymy. We are also developing new methods to combine these knowledge to generate the final STS score.

Regarding the interpretable STS system, this was the first time a pilot was put in place. We obtained excellent results, even if we had very little time to develop the system. Future work will focus on further improvements. For instance, our experiments showed that grouping chunks lead to a considerable improvement for the F1 Type evaluation score. We would also like to incorparate factuality or polarity information.

Although our original idea was to combine the cube and the interpretable system, we did not have time for that. In one direction, we would like to incorparate some of the semantic similarity information in the cube into our system, including similarity between chunks. On the other direction, the information from the similarity module might be a good feature to improve the overall STS score.

Acknowledgements

This work was partially funded by MINECO (CHIST-ERA READERS project – PCIN-2013-002-C02-01, SKaTeR project – TIN2012-38584-C06-02), and the European Commission (QTLEAP – FP7-ICT-2013.4.1-610516). Aitor Gonzalez-Agirre and Iñigo Lopez-Gazpio are supported by doctoral grants from MINECO. The IXA group is funded by the Basque Government (A type Research Group).

References

Rodrigo Agerri, Josu Bermudez, and German Rigau. 2014. Ixa pipeline: Efficient and ready to use multilingual nlp tools. In *Proceedings of the 9th Language Resources and Evaluation Conference (LREC2014), Reykjavik, Iceland, May*, pages 26–31.

Eneko Agirre, Carmen Banea, Claire Cardie, Daniel Cer, Mona Diab, Aitor Gonzalez-Agirre, Weiwei Guo, Iñigo Lopez-Gazpio, Montse Maritxalar, Rada Mihalcea, German Rigau, Larraitz Uria, and Janyce Wiebe. 2015. SemEval-2015 Task 2: Semantic Textual Similarity, English, Spanish and Pilot on Interpretability. In *Proceedings of the 9th International Workshop on Semantic Evaluation (SemEval 2015)*, Denver, CO, June.

Chih-Chung Chang and Chih-Jen Lin. 2011. Libsvm: a library for support vector machines. *ACM Transactions on Intelligent Systems and Technology (TIST)*, 2(3):27.

BM Clapper. 2009. munkres: a python module implementing the "hungarian method" described by munkres (1957). version 1.0. 5.3.

Ronan Collobert and Jason Weston. 2008. A unified architecture for natural language processing: Deep neural networks with multitask learning. In *Proceedings of the 25th International Conference on Machine Learning*, ICML '08, pages 160–167, New York, NY, USA.

Lorenzo Ferrone and Massimo Fabio Zanzotto. 2014. Towards syntax-aware compositional distributional semantic models. In *Proceedings of COLING 2014, the 25th International Conference on Computational Linguistics: Technical Papers*, pages 721–730.

Juri Ganitkevitch, Benjamin Van Durme, and Chris Callison-Burch. 2013. PPDB: The paraphrase database. In *Proceedings of NAACL-HLT*, pages 758–764, Atlanta, Georgia, June.

Mark Hall, Eibe Frank, Geoffrey Holmes, Bernhard Pfahringer, Peter Reutemann, and Ian H Witten. 2009. The weka data mining software: an update. *ACM SIGKDD explorations newsletter*, 11(1):10–18.

Dan Klein and Christopher D Manning. 2003. Accurate unlexicalized parsing. In *Proceedings of the 41st Annual Meeting on Association for Computational Linguistics-Volume 1*, pages 423–430. Association for Computational Linguistics.

Rada Mihalcea, Courtney Corley, and Carlo Strapparava. 2006. Corpus-based and knowledge-based measures of text semantic similarity. In *Proceedings of the American Association for Artificial Intelligence (AAAI 2006)*, Boston, Massachusetts, July.

Tomas Mikolov, Kai Chen, Greg Corrado, and Jeffrey Dean. 2013a. Efficient estimation of word representations in vector space. *CoRR*, abs/1301.3781.

Tomas Mikolov, Ilya Sutskever, Kai Chen, Greg Corrado, and Jeffrey Dean. 2013b. Distributed representations of words and phrases and their compositionality. *CoRR*, abs/1310.4546.

Apache OpenNLP. 2011. Apache software foundation. *URL http://opennlp. apache. org.*

Richard Socher, Eric H. Huang, Jeffrey Pennington, Andrew Y. Ng, and Christopher D. Manning. 2011. Dynamic pooling and unfolding recursive autoencoders for paraphrase detection. In *Advances in Neural Information Processing Systems 24.*

Md Arafat Sultan, Steven Bethard, and Tamara Sumner. 2014. Back to basics for monolingual alignment: Exploiting word similarity and contextual evidence. *Transactions of the Association for Computational Linguistics*, pages 219–230.

Kristina Toutanova, Dan Klein, Christopher D. Manning, and Yoram Singer. 2003. Feature-rich part-of-speech tagging with a cyclic dependency network. In *Proceedings of HLT-NAACL 2003*, pages 252–259.

ASAP-II: From the Alignment of Phrases to Text Similarity

Ana O. Alves[1,2]
David Simões[1]
[1]Polytechnic Institute of Coimbra
Portugal
aalves@isec.pt
a21210644@alunos.isec.pt

Hugo Gonçalo Oliveira[2]
Adriana Ferrugento[2]
[2]CISUC, University of Coimbra
Portugal
hroliv@dei.uc.pt
aferr@student.dei.uc.pt

Abstract

ThisThis work is licensed under a Creative Commons Attribution 4.0 International Licence. Page numbers and proceedings footer are added by the organisers. Licence details: http://creativecommons.org/licenses/by/4.0/ paper describes the second version of the ASAP system[1] and its participation in the SemEval-2015, task 2a on Semantic Textual Similarity (STS). Our approach is based on computing the WordNet semantic relatedness and similarity of phrases from distinct sentences. We also apply topic modeling to get topic distributions over a set of sentences as well as some linguistic heuristics. In a special addition for this task, we retrieve named entities and compound nouns from DBPedia. All these features are used to feed a regression algorithm that learns the STS function.

1 Introduction

Semantic Textual Similarity (STS), which is the task of computing the similarity between two sentences, has received an increasing amount of attention in recent years (Agirre et al., 2012; Agirre et al., 2013; Marelli et al., 2014a; Agirre et al., 2014; Agirre et al., 2015). Our contribution to this challenge is to learn the STS function for English texts. ASAP-II is an evolution of the ASAP system (Alves et al., 2014), which participated in *SemEval 2014 - Task 1: Evaluation of compositional distributional semantic models on full sentences through semantic relatedness and textual entailment*. Although with a different goal from STS, which goes beyond relatedness and entailment, and different datasets, which include pairs of short texts instead of controlled sentences, we believe that, rather than specifying rules, constraints and lexicons manually, it is possible to adapt a system from one to the other task, by automatically acquiring linguistic knowledge through machine learning (ML) methods. For this purpose, we apply some pre-processing techniques to the training set in order to extract different types of features. On the semantic aspect, we compute the similarity/relatedness between phrases using known measures over WordNet (Miller, 1995).

Considering the problem of modeling a text corpus to find short descriptions of documents, we aim at an efficient processing of large collections, while preserving the essential statistical relationships that are useful for similarity judgment. Therefore, we also apply topic modeling, in order to get topic distribution over each sentence set. These features are then used to feed an ensemble ML algorithm for learning the STS function. Our system is entirely developed as a Java independent software package, publicly available[2] for training and testing on given and new datasets containing pairs of texts.

The remainder of this paper comprises 4 sections. In section 2, fundamental concepts are introduced in order to understand the proposed approach delineated in section 3. Section 4 presents some results of our approach, using not only the SemEval-2015's dataset, but also datasets from previous tasks. Finally, section 5 presents some conclusions and complementary work to be done in a near future.

[1]This work was supported by the InfoCrowds project - FCT-PTDC/ECM-TRA/1898/2012

[2]See https://github.com/examinus-/ASAP

2 Background

2.1 Knowledge Bases

WordNet (Miller, 1995) is a lexical knowledge base structured in synsets – groups of synonymous words that may be seen as possible lexicalizations of a concept – and relations between them, including hypernymy or part-of. DBpedia (Auer et al., 2007) is an effort for extracting structured information from Wikipedia, a well-known collaborative encyclopedia. DBPedia is a central part of the Linked Data initiative and consequently, it is linked to many other resources, including a RDF version of WordNet. In fact, some DBPedia entities are connected to their abstract category in WordNet, through the `wordnet_type` property. For instance, *CNN* is connected to the synset {*channel, transmission channel*} and *Berlusconi* to {*chancellor, premier, prime minister*}.

2.2 Semantic Similarity

There are two main approaches to semantic similarity: (i) semantic relatedness is based on co-occurrence statistics, typically over a large corpus; (ii) classic semantic similarity exploits semantic relations in a lexical knowledge base, such as WordNet. Semantic similarity differs from semantic relatedness because it computes proximity between concepts in a given concept hierarchy (see (Resnik, 1995) and (Jiang and Conrath, 1997)), while the former computes the usage of common concepts together (see (Lesk, 1986), in this case on dictionary definitions/glosses).

2.3 Topic Modeling

Topic modeling relies on the assumption that documents are mixtures of topics, which, in turn, are probability distributions over words. Latent Dirichlet Allocation (LDA) is a generative probabilistic topic model (Blei et al., 2003) where documents are represented as random mixtures over latent topics, characterized by a distribution over words. Assumptions are not made on the word order, only their frequency is relevant. In LDA, main variables are the topic-word distribution Φ and topic distributions θ for each document.

3 Proposed Approach

Our approach to STS is based on a regression function, learned automatically to compute the similarity between sentences, using their components as features. Sentence features are obtained after a preprocessing stage, where sentences are lexically, syntactically and semantically decomposed to obtain different partial similarities. Clustering is applied by LDA in order to obtain the difference of topic distribution between pairs of sentences, which can be considered a composed partial similarity on each topic distribution. Partial similarities are used as features in the supervised learning process. In the following section, complementary stages of our system are explained in detail.

3.1 Natural Language Preprocessing

Sentences are decomposed after applying well-known Natural Language Processing subtasks, namely tokenization, part-of-speech tagging and chunking. For this purpose, we use OpenNLP[3], a tool for processing natural language text out-of-the-box, based on a maximum entropy (ME) approach (Berger et al., 1996). Although OpenNLP offers an English stemmer, this is not sufficient for our approach. Instead, we rely on the lemmatization performed by the WS4J library[4], with some additional heuristics (see section 3.2.3).

3.2 Feature Engineering

Features encode information from raw data that allows machine learning algorithms to estimate an unknown value. We focus on, what we call, *light* features since they are computed automatically, not requiring a specific labeled dataset and we are using already trained models. Each feature is computed as a partial similarity metric, which will later feed the posterior regression analysis. This process is fully automatized, as all features are extracted using OpenNLP and other tools that will be introduced later. For convenience, we set an id for each feature, which has the form $f\#n, n \in \{1..\}$.

[3]See `http://opennlp.sourceforge.net`

[4]A thread-safe, self-contained, Java implementation of some of useful functions over WordNet.See `https://code.google.com/p/ws4j/`

3.2.1 Lexical Features

Some basic similarity metrics are used as features related exclusively with word forms. In this set, we include for each text: the number of stop words, from the Snowball list (Porter, 2001) ($f1$ and $f2$ respectively) and the absolute difference of those counts ($f3 = |f1 - f2|$); the number of those words expressing negation ($f4$ and $f5$ respectively) and the absolute difference of those counts ($f6 = |f4 - f5|$). In addition, we used the absolute difference of overlapping words for each text pair ($f7..10$)[5].

3.2.2 Syntactic Features

The Max Entropy models of OpenNLP were used for tokenization, part-of-speech tagging and text chunking, applied in a pipeline for identifying Noun Phrases (NPs), Verbal Phrases (VPs) and Prepositional Phrases (PPs) of each sentence. Heuristically, these NPs are further identified as subjects if they are in the beginning of sentences. This kind of shallow parser is useful for identifying the syntactic structure of texts. Considering only this property, different features were computed as the absolute value of the difference of the number of NPs ($f11$), VPs ($f12$) and PPs($f13$) for each text pair.

3.2.3 Semantic Features

When possible, suitable WordNet synsets are retrieved for NPs, VPs and PPs of each sentence. These will enable the computation of similarity measures to be used as semantic features. These phrases might be simple words or compounds, language words or named entities, and they might be inflected (e.g. nouns as *electrics* or *economic electric cars* are in the plural form). In order to increase the coverage of named entities, when a word is not in WordNet, we look it up in DBPedia to identify WordNet synset corresponding to its category. Inflected words can also be problematic because WordNet synsets are retrieved by the lemma of their words. Although some WordNet APIs already perform some kind of lemmatization, many situations are not covered. Therefore, to increase the number of words with a suitable synset, the leftmost word of a compound phrase, generally a modifier, is removed until the phrase is empty or a synset is retrieved. If still unsuccessful and the last word ends with an 's', the last character is removed and the word is looked up again.

After retrieving a WordNet sense for each phrase, semantic similarity is computed for each pair, using Resnik (1995) ($f14$), Jiang & Conrath (1997) ($f15$) and the Adapted Lesk metrics (Banerjee and Pedersen, 2003) ($f16$) using WS4j tool, where algorithms in the WordNet::Similarity (Pedersen et al., 2004) Perl package are implemented. For part-of-speech tagged words with multiple senses, the one maximizing partial similarity is selected.

3.3 Distributional Features

The distribution of topics over documents (in our case, short texts) may contribute to model Semantic Similarity since there is no notion of mutual exclusivity that restricts words to be part of one topic only. This allows topic models to capture polysemy. We may thus see topics as natural word sense contexts, as words occur in different topics with distinct "senses".

Gensim (Řehůřek and Sojka, 2010) is a machine learning framework for topic modeling. It includes several pre-processing techniques, such as stop-word removal and TF-IDF, a standard statistical method that combines the frequency of a term in a particular document with its inverse document frequency in general use (Salton and Buckley, 1988). This score is high for rare terms that occur frequently in a document and are therefore more likely to be significant.

Gensim computes a distribution of 25 topics over texts with or without using TF-IDF ($f17...41$). Each feature is the absolute difference of topic$_i$ (i.e. $topic[i] = |topic[i]_{s1} - topic[i]_{s2}|$). The euclidean distance over the difference of topic distribution between text pairs was used as another feature ($f42$).

3.4 Supervised Learning

WEKA (Hall et al., 2009) is a large collection of machine learning algorithms, written in Java, used for learning our STS function from aforementioned features.

[5]We thank the *SemEval 2014 - Task 1* organizers for providing a Python script for computing baselines available at `http://alt.qcri.org/semeval2014/task1/data/uploads/sick_baseline.zip`, which we used as a different setting for stop word removal (from 0 to 3, 4 different combinations)

One of four approaches is commonly adopted for building classifier ensembles, each focused on a different level of action. Approach A concerns the different ways of combining the results from the classifiers. Approach B uses different models.At feature level (Approach C), different feature subsets can be used for the classifiers, either if they use the same classification model or not. Finally, datasets can be modified so that each classifier in the ensemble is trained on its own dataset (Approach D) (Kuncheva and Whitaker, 2003).

Different methods where applied such as *Voting* (Franke and Mandler, 1992) (Approach A), *Stacking* (Seewald, 2002) (Approach B), and variation of the feature subset used (Approach C). Voting is perhaps a simpler approach, as it selects the class with the largest number of votes. Stacking is used to combine different types of classifiers and demands the use of another learning algorithm to predict which of the models would be the most reliable for each case. This is done with a meta-learner, another learning scheme that combines the output of the base learners. The predictions of base learners are used as input to the meta-learner.

We used WEKA's "Stacking" (Wolpert, 1992) meta-classifier in our *first run*, combining the following base models: three K-Nearest Neighbour (KNN) classifiers ($K = 1$, $K = 3$, $K = 5$) (Aha et al., 1991); a Linear Regression model without an attribute selection method ($-S1$) and default ridge parameter (1.0^{-8}); three M5P classifiers which implement base routines for generating M5 Model trees and rules with a different minimum number of instances ($M = 4$, $M = 10$, $M = 20$) (Quinlan, 1992; Wang and Witten, 1997). The meta-classifier was a M5P classifier with $M = 4$. Other ensembles were added for the *second* and *third runs*:

1. Stacking combining *three* base models: KNN classifier ($K = 1$); Linear Regression model without an attribute selection method ($-S1$) and default ridge parameter (1.0^{-8}); M5P, with $M = 4$, being the meta-classifier[6].

2. Stacking combining *four* base models: KNN classifier ($K = 1$); Linear Regression model without an attribute selection method ($-S1$) and default ridge parameter (1.0^{-8}); ZeroR, a simple rule-based classifier which determines the median similarity score; and Isotonic Regression model. M5P, with $M = 4$, as the meta-classifier.

3. Voting model of the seven classifiers of the *first run*.

Specifically, the *second* and *third run* consisted in the average similarity score produced by the three models presented above, plus the model considered in the *first run*. The only difference between the two runs was that distributional features were not considered in the third run (Approach C).

4 Some Results and Discussion

Although, STS might look similar to *SemEval 2014 - Task 1*, available datasets showed that they are very different from each other. Therefore, we made individual sets of data for training models and for extracting distributional features to evaluate with each target dataset. In *SemEval 2014 - Task 1*, there was only one homogeneous dataset, SICK (Marelli et al., 2014b), with a relatively big amount of entries (5000 for training, 5000 for evaluation) which generally results in better ML outcome. Since answers-forums, answers-students and belief were from new sources, we opted to target these with the same systems, built with most of the available data from previous STS tasks.Table 1 shows that ASAP-II performed better in the SICK dataset, followed by the two datasets that are recurring (images and headlines). Unexpectedly though, the configuration targeting answers-students performed well with only a little difference to the best performance on the headlines, especially if compared to the very low correlation achieved on both answers-forums and belief. Finally, weighted average pearson coefficient was computed considering the size of each evaluation dataset.

5 Conclusions and Future Work

We used complementary features for learning the STS function, which is also part of the challenge of building Compositional Distributional Semantic Models. For this purpose, for each sentence, we extracted lexical, syntactic, semantic and distributional features. On the semantic aspect, we computed the

[6]A Regression Tree using the M5 algorithm (Quinlan, 1992)

	First-run	Second-run	Third-run
answers-forums	0.2304	0.2374	0.2302
answers-students	0.6503	0.7095	0.6719
belief	0.3928	0.3986	0.4342
headlines	0.6614	0.7039	0.7156
images	0.6548	0.7294	0.7250
SICK	0.7200	0.7013	0.7735
Weighted Average	0.57 ± 0.07	0.62 ± 0.08	0.61 ± 0.07

Table 1: Pearson's correlation coefficient for ASAP-II in *SemEval2015-STS*, by dataset, and a simulation of *SemEval2014 - Task 1*, with the same configuration.

semantic similarity and relatedness between phrases using known measures on WordNet, whose "coverage" was increased with the help of DBPedia. We also applied topic modeling to get topic distributions over sets of sentences. All these features were used to feed an ensemble algorithm for learning the STS function. This resulted in a Pearson's r of 0.62 ± 0.08 in our best performance over different datasets.

We are motivated by this participation in STS and intend to participate in further editions, while improving ASAP. To this end, we should: make a deeper analysis of the ensemble, to identify where it can be improved; try to complement the feature set with additional relevant features; explore different topic distributions while varying the number of topics and hopefully maximizing the log likelihood; and assess the impact of each feature.

References

Eneko Agirre, Mona Diab, Daniel Cer, and Aitor Gonzalez-Agirre. 2012. Semeval-2012 task 6: A pilot on semantic textual similarity. In *Proceedings of the First Joint Conference on Lexical and Computational Semantics - Volume 1: Proceedings of the Main Conference and the Shared Task, and Volume 2: Proceedings of the Sixth International Workshop on Semantic Evaluation*, SemEval'12, pages 385–393, Stroudsburg, PA, USA.

Eneko Agirre, Daniel Cer, Mona Diab, Aitor Gonzalez-agirre, and Weiwei Guo. 2013. sem 2013 shared task: Semantic textual similarity, including a pilot on typed-similarity. In *In *SEM 2013: The Second Joint Conference on Lexical and Computational Semantics*.

Eneko Agirre, Carmen Banea, Claire Cardie, Daniel Cer, Mona Diab, Aitor Gonzalez-Agirre, Weiwei Guo, Rada Mihalcea, German Rigau, and Janyce Wiebe. 2014. Semeval-2014 task 10: Multilingual semantic textual similarity. SemEval-2014.

Eneko Agirre, Carmen Banea, Claire Cardie, Daniel Cer, Mona Diab, Aitor Gonzalez-Agirre, Weiwei Guo, Iigo Lopez-Gazpio, Montse Maritxalar, Rada Mihalcea, German Rigau, Larraitz Uria, and Janyce Wiebe. 2015. SemEval-2015 Task 2: Semantic Textual Similarity, English, Spanish and Pilot on Interpretability. In *Proceedings of the 9th International Workshop on Semantic Evaluation (SemEval 2015)*, Denver, CO, June.

David W. Aha, Dennis Kibler, and Marc K. Albert. 1991. Instance-based learning algorithms. *Mach. Learn.*, 6(1):37–66.

Ana Alves, Adriana Ferrugento, Mariana Loureno, and Filipe Rodrigues. 2014. Asap: Automatic semantic alignment for phrases. In *SemEval Workshop, COLING 2014, Ireland*, n/a.

Sören Auer, Christian Bizer, Georgi Kobilarov, Jens Lehmann, Richard Cyganiak, and Zachary Ives. 2007. Dbpedia: A nucleus for a web of open data. In *Proceedings of the 6th International The Semantic Web and 2Nd Asian Conference on Asian Semantic Web Conference*, ISWC'07/ASWC'07, pages 722–735, Berlin, Heidelberg.

Satanjeev Banerjee and Ted Pedersen. 2003. Extended gloss overlaps as a measure of semantic relatedness. In *Proceedings of the 18th International Joint Conference on Artificial Intelligence (IJCAI'03)*, pages 805–810, CA, USA.

Adam L. Berger, Vincent J. Della Pietra, and Stephen A. Della Pietra. 1996. A maximum entropy approach to natural language processing. *Comput. Linguist.*, 22(1):39–71.

David M. Blei, Andrew Y. Ng, and Michael I. Jordan. 2003. Latent dirichlet allocation. *Journal of Machine Learning Research*, 3:993–1022.

Jürgen Franke and Eberhard Mandler. 1992. A comparison of two approaches for combining the votes of cooperating classifiers. In *Pattern Recognition, 1992. Vol.II. Conference B: Pattern Recognition Methodology and Systems, Proceedings., 11th IAPR International Conference on*, pages 611–614, Aug.

Mark Hall, Eibe Frank, Geoffrey Holmes, Bernhard Pfahringer, Peter Reutemann, and Ian H. Witten. 2009. The weka data mining software: An update. *SIGKDD Explor. Newsl.*, 11(1):10–18.

Jay J. Jiang and David W. Conrath. 1997. Semantic similarity based on corpus statistics and lexical taxonomy. In *Proc. of the Int'l. Conf. on Research in Computational Linguistics*, pages 19–33.

Ludmila I. Kuncheva and Christopher J. Whitaker. 2003. Measures of diversity in classifier ensembles and their relationship with the ensemble accuracy. *Mach. Learn.*, 51(2):181–207, May.

Michael Lesk. 1986. Automatic sense disambiguation using machine readable dictionaries: How to tell a pine cone from an ice cream cone. In *Proceedings of the 5th Annual International Conference on Systems Documentation (SIGDOC '86)*, pages 24–26, NY, USA.

Marco Marelli, Luisa Bentivogli, Marco Baroni, Raffaella Bernardi, Stefano Menini, and Roberto Zamparelli. 2014a. Semeval-2014 task 1: Evaluation of compositional distributional semantic models on full sentences through semantic relatedness and textual entailment. SemEval-2014.

Marco Marelli, Stefano Menini, Marco Baroni, Luisa Bentivogli, Raffaella Bernardi, and Robertomode Zamparelli. 2014b. A sick cure for the evaluation of compositional distributional semantic models. In *Proceedings of LREC 2014*.

George A. Miller. 1995. Wordnet: A lexical database for english. *Commun. ACM*, 38(11):39–41, November.

Ted Pedersen, Siddharth Patwardhan, and Jason Michelizzi. 2004. Wordnet::similarity: Measuring the relatedness of concepts. In *Demonstration Papers at HLT-NAACL 2004*, HLT-NAACL–Demonstrations '04, pages 38–41, PA, USA.

Martin F. Porter. 2001. Snowball: A language for stemming algorithms. Published online.

Ross J. Quinlan. 1992. Learning with continuous classes. In *5th Australian Joint Conference on Artificial Intelligence*, pages 343–348, Singapore.

Radim Řehůřek and Petr Sojka. 2010. Software Framework for Topic Modelling with Large Corpora. In *Proceedings of the Workshop on New Challenges for NLP Frameworks (LREC 2010)*, pages 45–50, Valletta, Malta.

Philip Resnik. 1995. Using information content to evaluate semantic similarity in a taxonomy. In *Proceedings of the 14th International Joint Conference on Artificial Intelligence - Volume 1*, IJCAI'95, pages 448–453, San Francisco, CA, USA.

Gerard Salton and Christopher Buckley. 1988. Term-weighting approaches in automatic text retrieval. *Inf. Process. Manage.*, 24(5):513–523.

Alexander K. Seewald. 2002. How to make stacking better and faster while also taking care of an unknown weakness. In C. Sammut and A. Hoffmann, editors, *Nineteenth International Conference on Machine Learning*, pages 554–561.

Yong Wang and Ian H. Witten. 1997. Induction of model trees for predicting continuous classes. In *Poster papers of the 9th European Conference on Machine Learning*.

David H. Wolpert. 1992. Stacked generalization. *Neural Networks*, 5:241–259.

TATO: Leveraging on Multiple Strategies for Semantic Textual Similarity

Tu Thanh Vu[†], **Quan Hung Tran**[††], **Son Bao Pham**[†]
[†]University of Engineering and Technology, Vietnam National University, Hanoi, Vietnam
[††]Japan Advanced Institute of Science and Technology, Japan
[†] {tuvt,sonpb}@vnu.edu.vn
[††] quanth@jaist.ac.jp

Abstract

In this paper, we describe the TATO system which participated in the SemEval-2015 Task 2a: "Semantic Textual Similarity (STS) for English". Our system is trained on published datasets from the previous competitions. Based on some machine learning techniques, it combines multiple similarity measures of varying complexity ranging from simple lexical and syntactic similarity measures to complex semantic similarity ones to compute semantic textual similarity. Our final model consists of a simple linear combination of about 30 main features out of a numerous number of features experimented. The results are promising, with Pearson's coefficients on each individual dataset ranging from 0.6796 to 0.8167 and an overall weighted mean score of 0.7422, well above the task baseline system.

1 Introduction

Measuring semantic textual similarity (STS) can be defined as the task of computing the degree of semantic equivalence between pairs of texts. It has drawn an increasing amount of attention from the NLP community, especially at level of short text fragments, as partly reflected in the SemEval tasks in recent years. In the SemEval-2015 Task 2, the degree of semantic equivalence for each sentence pair is represented by a similarity score between 0 (no relation) and 5 (semantic equivalence). STS has a wide range of applications which includes applications for machine translation evaluation, information extraction, question answering, and summarization.

STS is related to, but different from textual entailment (TE) (Dagan et al., 2006) and paraphrase recognition (PARA) (Dolan et al., 2004) as it aims to render a graded notion of semantic equivalence between two textual snippets, rather than a binary yes/no decision. STS requires a bidirectional similarity relation between sentences, while TE annotates them with an unidirectional entailment relation.

The literature of STS is rife with attempts to compute similarity between texts using a multitude of measures at different levels of depth: lexical (Malakasiotis and Androutsopoulos, 2007), syntactic (Malakasiotis, 2009; Zanzotto et al., 2009), and semantic (Rinaldi et al., 2003; Bos and Markert, 2005). (Gomaa and Fahmy, 2013) discusses existing works on STS and partitions them into three categories based on the similarity measures used: *(i)* string-based approaches (Bär et al., 2012; Malakasiotis and Androutsopoulos, 2007) which operate on string sequences and character composition to compute similarities and can be categorized into two groups: character-based and term-based approaches; *(ii)* corpus-based approaches (Li et al., 2006) which gain statistics information about words from large corpora and reflect their semantics in distributional high semantic space to determine the similarity, such as Latent Semantic Analysis (LSA) (Landauer et al., 1998; Foltz et al., 1998) and Explicit Semantic Analysis (ESA) (Gabrilovich and Markovitch, 2007); *(iii)* knowledge-based approaches (Mihalcea et al., 2006) which determine the degree of similarity between texts using information derived from semantic networks, such as WordNet (Miller, 1995).

Though each of these existing measures has its own advantages, they are typically used in separation. In our work, we integrate multiple similarity measures of varying complexity ranging from simple lexical and syntactic similarity measures to complex semantic similarity ones and rely on supervised machine learning to take advantage of the different contributions of different features.

We organize the remainder of the paper as follows: Section 2 describes the features in detail. Section 3 presents the machine learning setup and our submitted system. Sections 4 discusses the results. The conclusions follow in the final section.

2 Text Similarity Measures

In this section, we describe the various features we experimented and selected for our final model.

2.1 Lexical Similarity Measures

2.1.1 Word/Phrase Alignment Measures

When two sentences are related semantically, they tend to be similar in appearance. Hence, we develop an automatic word/phrase alignment module based on the METEOR metric (Denkowski and Lavie, 2010) to align corresponding words and phrases between each pair of sentences. Alignments here are based on exact, stem, synonym (via WordNet), and paraphrase (via a lookup table) matches between words and phrases. Given two sentences of text, s_1 and s_2 (stop-words are removed from each sentence), we define the following metrics:

$$\mathscr{S}(s_1,s_2) = \left| numOfMatches(s_1,s_2) - \frac{min\{len(s_1),len(s_2)\}}{2} \right|$$

and

$$\mathscr{D}(s_1, s_2) = \frac{2 \times numOfMatches(s_1,s_2)}{min\{len(s_1),len(s_2)\}},$$

where $numOfMatches(s_1, s_2)$ and $len(s)$ are the number of aligned word/phrase pairs between s_1 and s_2, and the number of words in s, respectively.

2.1.2 Machine Translation Measures

We treat the task as a monolingual machine translation (MT) task (the source and target languages are the same, and the input and output should be similar in meaning), and take advantage of a variety of MT measures. At the lexical level, we experiment different n-gram and edit-distance-based metrics.

BLEU (Papineni et al., 2002), NIST (Doddington, 2002), and METEOR (Denkowski and Lavie, 2010) are n-gram-based metrics commonly used for MT evaluation. BLEU scores the target output by counting n-gram matches with the reference, relying on exact matching and has no concept of synonymy or paraphrasing. NIST is similar to BLEU, however, it uses the arithmetic mean of n-gram overlaps, rather than the geometric mean. Unlike BLEU which focuses on precision, METEOR uses a combination of both precision and recall. Moreover, it incorporates stemming, synonymy and paraphrase. MAXSIM (Chan and Ng, 2008) models the MT problem as a maximum bipartite matching one and maps each word in one sentence to at most one word in the other sentence. We also experiment with TESLA (Liu et al., 2010) - a variant of MAXSIM.

Besides those, we also use edit-distance-based metrics. TER (Snover et al., 2006) and TERp (Snover et al., 2009) measure the number of edit operations (e.g. insertions, deletions, and substitutions) necessary to transform one text into the other.

2.2 Syntactic Similarity Measures

2.2.1 Content Word Match and Mismatch

Given a sentence pair, we extract corresponding content words (nouns, verbs, adjectives, and adverbs) between the sentences. This syntactic information is obtained from the Stanford parser (Klein and Manning, 2003). We have both the proportions of aligned words and the proportions of unaligned words in the two sentences (by normalizing with the harmonic mean of their number of content words) for each lexical category of content word.

2.2.2 Subject-Verb-Object Comparison

We also employ dependency parsing in measuring semantic similarity. Specifically, some attributes like subjects, verbs, objects are identified for each pair of sentences. These attributes are used for our matching procedure which is based on the following comparisons between each pair of sentences:

- Subject-Subject Comparison
- Verb-Verb Comparison
- Object-Object Comparison
- Subject-Verb Comparison
- Verb-Object Comparison
- Cross Subject-Object Comparison

For each of these comparisons, we assign a matching score of 1.0 (match) or 0.0 (mismatch).

2.3 Semantic Similarity Measures

2.3.1 Named Entity, Number, Time Expression Match and Mismatch

Careful observation of the development dataset revealed that mismatch of named entities, numbers or time expressions might cause semantic dissimilarity, for example, when s_1 consists of a named entity that does not appear in s_2. Based on this, we detect both match and mismatch of named entities, numbers and time expressions between each pair of sentences (similar to that of content words). We use the Stanford Named Entity Recognizer (Finkel et al., 2005) to detect named entities in sentences.

2.3.2 LDA-based measures

We build two Latent Dirichilet Allocation (LDA) models (Blei et al., 2003) from Wikipedia and the training dataset separately, using the Gensim (Řehůřek and Sojka, 2010) and Mallet (McCallum, 2002) software with 100 requested latent topics. Each sentence is represented by a vector using topics estimated by LDA. The similarity between two sentences is calculated as the cosine similarity between their corresponding vectors.

2.3.3 Word-representation-based measures

Word representation computes vector representations of each word based on its context from very large datasets, usually capturing both syntactic and semantic information of words. Given two sentences s_1 and s_2 (stop-words are removed), each word of the sentences is represented as a single vector. We develop two different strategies as follows:

Strategy 1 For each word w_i in s_1, we identify a word w_j most similar to w_i in s_2 by using cosine similarity measure. We define a measure $\mathscr{W2V}(s_1, s_2)$ as follows:

$$\mathscr{W2V}(s_1, s_2) = \frac{\sum_{w_i \in s_1} \max_{w_j \in s_2} cos(w_i, w_j)}{len(s_1)},$$

where $cos(w_i, w_j)$ is the cosine similarity between the word vectors of w_i and w_j. We also apply this strategy for each category of content words (noun, verb, adjective, and adverb) separately.

Strategy 2 We sum up all of the vectors of words that occur in each sentence and define a sentence similarity measure $\mathscr{S2V}(s_1, s_2)$ as follows:

$$\mathscr{S2V}(s_1, s_2) = cos(\sum_{w_i \in s_1} w_i, \sum_{w_j \in s_2} w_j),$$

For word representation, we use both the Word2vec model (Mikolov et al., 2013) trained on Google News and the GloVe model (Pennington et al., 2014) trained on Common Crawl data.

2.3.4 WordNet-based measures

WordNet (Miller, 1995) is a commonly used lexical database of English where words of the same meaning are grouped into synonym sets (synsets). By using information derived from WordNet, we construct some similarity measures as follows:

Strategy 1 This is similar to **Strategy 1** for word-representation-based measures, however, instead of using cosine similarity, we use the Wordnet path similarity (the shortest path that connects the senses in the is-a (hypernym/hypnoym) taxonomy).

Strategy 2 We determine some semantic relationships, e.g, synonym, antonym, and hypernym between sentences. The proportions of synonym word pairs, antonym word pairs, hypernym word pairs in two sentences (by normalizing with the harmonic mean of their number of content words) are taken as proxies of their semantic similarity.

3 System Description

3.1 Machine Learning Setup

The machine learning setup is described as follows:

Pre-processing The pre-processing phase includes tokenization, POS tagging, lemmatization, NER, syntactic parsing with the Stanford CoreNLP Toolkit (Manning et al., 2014). For some measures, we filter out punctuations and stop-words by using a pre-compiled stop-words list.

Feature Generation We run each of the similarity measures separately and use the resulting scores as features for a machine learning classifier. A feature is selected for our final model if it proves useful in improving the performance of the system.

Feature Combination The pre-computed similarity score vectors serve as features for this step. Our system utilizes a classifier combination approach, using a simple linear regression model to combine all the similarity measures. We use the trial dataset that comprises the 2012, 2013 and 2014 datasets to develop and train our model. In the development cycle, we used a training dataset consisting of 6842 sentence pairs and a test dataset consisting of 3750 sentence pairs, with gold standard scores. We use the WEKA machine learning toolkit (Hall et al., 2009) to perform our experiments.

Post-processing If the pre-processed sentences match, we set their similarity score to 5 regardless of the output of our classifier. If the classifier outputs an invalid similarity score s which is not in the score range [0-5], we set the similarity score to $f(s)$ defined as follows: $f(s) = \begin{cases} 0 + \alpha & \texttt{if } s < 0 \\ 5 - \alpha & \texttt{if } s > 5 \end{cases}$

In our experiments, the best value for α is 0.5.

3.2 Submitted System

TATO-1stWTW Because of our limited time, we submitted only one run to the SemEval-2015 Task 2a. After the development cycle, we identified about 30 main features out of a numerous number of features experimented. These features achieved the best performance on the training dataset. For our final system, we trained the classifier on a joint dataset of all known training datasets, instead of training a separate classifier for each individual dataset.

4 Results

4.1 Results on the 2014 Test Data

We evaluated our model on the 2014 test data comprising pairs of news headlines (headlines), pairs of glosses (OnWN), image descriptions (images), DEFT-related discussion forums (deft-forum) and news (deft-news), and tweet comments and newswire headline mappings (tweet-news). We used the 2012, 2013 datasets consisting of 6842 sentence pairs to train our model. The test dataset contains 3750 sentence pairs excluded from training. Our model was compared against the best performing system on the SemEval-2014 English STS sub-task (DLS@CU-run2) using the official scorer. The results are summarized in Table 1. With regard to Deft-forum and Tweets, our system outperformed the DLS@CU's system, we also achieved a higher score in the weighted mean across all datasets.

4.2 Results on the 2015 Test Data

The official score is based on the average of Pearson correlation. Besides Pearson correlations computed for individual datasets, including answers-forums, answers-students, belief, headlines, and images, Mean scores are provided to show the weighted means across all datasets (the weight is based on the number of sentence pairs in each dataset).

Run	DF	DN	H	I	OWN	TN	Mean
TATO1	.550	.748	.755	.807	.817	.777	.764
DLS@CU2	.483	.766	.765	.821	.859	.764	.761

Table 1: Results on the 2014 test datasets: deft-forum (DF), deft-news (DN), headlines (H), images (I), OnWN (OWN), tweet-news (TN).

Table 2 reports our official results achieved on the test data (**TATO-1stWTW**), besides the highest-performance and lowest-performance systems (according to Mean), and also the task baseline system. Our system was ranked among the most robust systems out of more than 70 participating systems and achieved good performance on answers-forums and belief datasets.

#	Run	AF	AS	B	H	I	Mean
1	DLS@CU1	.739	.773	.749	.825	.864	.802
⋮	⋮	⋮	⋮	⋮	⋮	⋮	⋮
25	TATO1	.680	.685	.721	.767	.817	.742
⋮	⋮	⋮	⋮	⋮	⋮	⋮	⋮
59	baseline1	.445	.665	.652	.531	.604	.587
⋮	⋮	⋮	⋮	⋮	⋮	⋮	⋮
73	DalGTM1	.290	-.053	.063	.060	.066	.062

Table 2: Official results on the test datasets: answers-forums (AF), answers-students (AS), belief (B), headlines (H), and images (I).

5 Conclusions and Future Work

This paper describes the TATO team's submission to the SemEval-2015 Task 2a: "Semantic Textual Similarity for English". Our system uses a simple linear regression model to combine multiple text similarity measures at different levels of depth: lexical, syntactic, and semantic. While we did not achieve the highest ranks on any of the particular datasets, our system was ranked among the most robust systems out of more than 70 participating systems.

For the future work, we will explore other evaluation measures for STS and try to train a separate classifier for each type of the existing datasets. We also suggest that we should work on some other types of data, such as legal or medical data.

References

Daniel Bär, Chris Biemann, Iryna Gurevych, and Torsten Zesch. 2012. UKP: Computing Semantic Textual Similarity by Combining Multiple Content Similarity Measures. In *Proceedings of the First Joint Conference on Lexical and Computational Semantics*, pages 435–440.

David M. Blei, Andrew Y. Ng, and Michael I. Jordan. 2003. Latent Dirichlet Allocation. *Journal of Machine Learning Research*, 3:993–1022.

Johan Bos and Katja Markert. 2005. Recognising Textual Entailment with Logical Inference. In *Proceedings of the Human Language Technology Conference and Conference on Empirical Methods in Natural Language Processing*, pages 628–635.

Yee Seng Chan and Hwee Tou Ng. 2008. MAXSIM: A Maximum Similarity Metric for Machine Translation Evaluation. In *Proceedings of the 46th Annual Meeting of the Association for Computational Linguistics: Human Language Technologies*, pages 55–62.

Ido Dagan, Oren Glickman, and Bernardo Magnini. 2006. The PASCAL Recognising Textual Entailment Challenge. In *Machine Learning Challenges*, Lecture Notes in Computer Science, pages 177–190.

Michael Denkowski and Alon Lavie. 2010. Extending the METEOR Machine Translation Evaluation Metric to the Phrase Level. In *Human Language Technologies: The 2010 Annual Conference of the North American Chapter of the Association for Computational Linguistics*, pages 250–253.

George Doddington. 2002. Automatic Evaluation of Machine Translation Quality Using N-gram Cooccurrence Statistics. In *Proceedings of the Second International Conference on Human Language Technology Research*, pages 138–145.

Bill Dolan, Chris Quirk, and Chris Brockett. 2004. Unsupervised Construction of Large Paraphrase Corpora: Exploiting Massively Parallel News Sources. In *Proceedings of the 20th International Conference on Computational Linguistics*, pages 350–356.

Jenny Rose Finkel, Trond Grenager, and Christopher Manning. 2005. Incorporating Non-local Information into Information Extraction Systems by Gibbs Sampling. In *Proceedings of the 43rd Annual Meeting on Association for Computational Linguistics*, pages 363–370.

P. Foltz, W. Kintsch, and T. Landauer. 1998. The Measurement of Textual Coherence with Latent Semantic Analysis. In *Journal of the Discourse Processes*, 25(2&3):285–307.

Evgeniy Gabrilovich and Shaul Markovitch. 2007. Computing Semantic Relatedness Using Wikipedia-based Explicit Semantic Analysis. In *Proceedings of the 20th International Joint Conference on Artifical Intelligence*, pages 1606–1611.

Wael H. Gomaa and Aly A. Fahmy. 2013. Article: A Survey of Text Similarity Approaches. *International Journal of Computer Applications*, 68(13):13–18.

Mark Hall, Eibe Frank, Geoffrey Holmes, Bernhard Pfahringer, Peter Reutemann, and Ian H. Witten. 2009. The WEKA Data Mining Software: An Update. *SIGKDD Explorations*, 11(1):10–18.

Dan Klein and Christopher D. Manning. 2003. Accurate Unlexicalized Parsing. In *Proceedings of the 41st Annual Meeting on Association for Computational Linguistics*, pages 423–430.

T. K. Landauer, P. W. Foltz, and D. Laham. 1998. An Introduction to Latent Semantic Analysis. In *Journal of the Discourse Processes*, 25:259–284.

Yuhua Li, David McLean, Zuhair A. Bandar, James D. O'Shea, and Keeley Crockett. 2006. Sentence Similarity Based on Semantic Nets and Corpus Statistics. *IEEE Transactions on Knowledge and Data Engineering*, 18(8):1138–1150.

Chang Liu, Daniel Dahlmeier, and Hwee Tou Ng. 2010. Tesla: Translation Evaluation of Sentences with Linear-programming-based Analysis. In *Proceedings of the Joint Fifth Workshop on Statistical Machine Translation and MetricsMATR*, pages 354–359.

Prodromos Malakasiotis and Ion Androutsopoulos. 2007. Learning Textual Entailment Using SVMs and String Similarity measures. In *Proceedings of of the ACL-PASCAL Workshop on Textual Entailment and Paraphrasing*, pages 42–47.

Prodromos Malakasiotis. 2009. Paraphrase Recognition Using Machine Learning to Combine Similarity measures. In *Proceedings of the 47th Annual Meeting of ACL and the 4th Int. Joint Conference on Natural Language Processing of AFNLP*, pages 27–35.

Christopher Manning, Mihai Surdeanu, John Bauer, Jenny Finkel, Steven Bethard, and David McClosky. 2014. The stanford corenlp natural language processing toolkit. In *Proceedings of 52nd Annual Meeting of the Association for Computational Linguistics: System Demonstrations*, pages 55–60.

Andrew Kachites McCallum. 2002. MALLET: A Machine Learning for Language Toolkit. http://mallet.cs.umass.edu.

Rada Mihalcea, Courtney Corley, and Carlo Strapparava. 2006. Corpus-based and Knowledge-based Measures of Text Semantic Similarity. In *Proceedings of the 21st National Conference on Artificial Intelligence*, pages 775–780.

Tomas Mikolov, Kai Chen, Greg Corrado, and Jeffrey Dean. 2013. Efficient Estimation of Word Representations in Vector Space. *arXiv preprint arXiv:1310.4546*.

George A. Miller. 1995. Wordnet: A Lexical Database for English. *Communications of the Association for Computing Machinery*, 38(11):39–41.

Kishore Papineni, Salim Roukos, Todd Ward, and Wei-Jing Zhu. 2002. Bleu: A Method for Automatic Evaluation of Machine Translation. In *Proceedings of the 40th Annual Meeting on Association for Computational Linguistics*, pages 311–318.

Jeffrey Pennington, Richard Socher, and Christopher Manning. 2014. Glove: Global Vectors for Word Representation. In *Proceedings of the 2014 Conference on Empirical Methods in Natural Language Processing*, pages 1532–1543.

Radim Řehůřek and Petr Sojka. 2010. Software Framework for Topic Modelling with Large Corpora. In *Proceedings of the LREC 2010 Workshop on New Challenges for NLP Frameworks*, pages 45–50.

Fabio Rinaldi, James Dowdall, Kaarel Kaljurand, Michael Hess, and Diego Mollá. 2003. Exploiting Paraphrases in a Question Answering System. In *Proceedings of the 2nd International Workshop on Paraphrasing*, pages 25–32.

Matthew Snover, Bonnie Dorr, Richard Schwartz, Linnea Micciulla, and John Makhoul. 2006. A Study of Translation Edit Rate with Targeted Human Annotation. In *Proceedings of Association for Machine Translation in the Americas*.

Matthew G. Snover, Nitin Madnani, Bonnie Dorr, and Richard Schwartz. 2009. TER-Plus: Paraphrase, Semantic, and Alignment Enhancements to Translation Edit Rate. *Machine Translation*, 23(2-3):117–127.

Fabio massimo Zanzotto, Marco Pennacchiotti, and Alessandro Moschitti. 2009. A Machine Learning Approach to Textual Entailment Recognition. *Natural Language Engineering*, 15(4):551–582.

HITSZ-ICRC: Exploiting Classification Approach for Answer Selection in Community Question Answering

Yongshuai Hou, Cong Tan, Xiaolong Wang
Yaoyun Zhang, Jun Xu and Qingcai Chen
Key Laboratory of Network Oriented Intelligent Computation
Department of Computer Science and Technology
Harbin Institute of Technology Shenzhen Graduate School
HIT Campus, The University Town of Shenzhen, Shenzhen, 518055, China
{yongshuai.hou, viptancong}@gmail.com, wangxl@insun.hit.edu.cn
{xiaoni5122, hit.xujun,qingcai.chen}@gmail.com

Abstract

This paper describes the participation of the HITSZ-ICRC team on the Answer Selection Challenge in SemEval-2015. Our team participated in English subtask A, English subtask B and Arabic task. Two approaches, ensemble learning and hierarchical classification were proposed for answer selection in each task. Bag-of-words features, lexical features and non-textual features were employed. For the Arabic task, features were extracted from both Arabic data and English data that translated from the Arabic data. Evaluation demonstrated that the proposed methods were effective, achieving a macro-averaged F1 of 56.41% (rank 2nd) in English subtask A, 53.60 % (rank 3rd) in English subtask B and 67.70% (rank 3rd) in Arabic task, respectively.

1 Introduction

In recent years, community question answering (CQA) systems are becoming more and more popular on the Internet. By using CQA system, a user can post his/her question on CQA portal and receive answers from other users. All users can post questions and answers on CQA portal freely. Although it makes CQA users to get answers easily, the answer quality evaluation becomes a challenge for questions with multiple answers. To reduce the inconvenient in going through plenty of candidate answers, it makes sense to evaluate the quality of answers and select high-quality answers automatically for CQA systems. As a consequently, the task of answer quality evaluation and answer selection in CQA have attracted more and more attention in recent years (Arai and Handayani, 2013; Shah and Pomerantz, 2010; Agichtein et al., 2008).

The Answer Selection in CQA challenge was opened as one new task in SemEval-2015: SemEval-2015 Task 3 (Màrquez et al., 2015). It created a venue and provided annotated datasets for researchers to compare their methods for answer selection in CQA. This challenge consisted of Subtask A and Subtask B. Subtask A required participant system to classify answers as *relevant*, *potentially useful* and *bad* for each question. Subtask B required participant system to decide whether the answer to a *YES_NO* question should be *Yes*, *No* or *Unsure* based on the answer list. Subtask A was offered for two languages: English and Arabic. Data for the two languages was in different data set format. In remainder of this paper, Subtask A in English is abbreviated to English subtask A, Subtask A in Arabic is abbreviated to Arabic task and Subtask B in English is abbreviated to English subtask B.

HITSZ-ICRC team participated in English subtask A, English subtask B and Arabic task. This paper describes the ensemble learning method and hierarchical classification method proposed for each subtask in SemEval-2015 Task 3.

2 Methods for Answer Classification

Different classification methods were tried by previous researchers for answer evaluation, prediction and selection in CQA. Jeon et al. (2006) designed a framework using non-textual features, most of which were user profile features, to predict the document quality and tried the framework on CQA.

Shah and Pomerantz (2010) used text, user information and answer rank features to evaluate and predict answer quality. Arai and Handayani (2013) tried non-textual features mainly include no-content features of text to train models to predict answer quality in CQA. For SemEval-2015 Task 3, we proposed ensemble learning method and hierarchical classification method to classify answers for each task.

2.1 English subtask A

English subtask A required participant system to classify each answer of test questions as definitely relevant (*good*), potentially useful (*potential)* or bad (*bad*, *dialog*, *non-English* and *other*).

Features employed to train classifiers for English subtask A include:

Word length features: length of the max length word, average word length.

Word number features: word number, capital word number, polite word number, word "yes" number, word "no" number, word "thank" number.

Punctuation features: question mark number, exclamation mark number.

Sentence features: average sentence length, sentence number.

Part-of-speech features: noun word number and ratio, verb word number and ratio, pronoun word number and ratio, WH word number and ratio.

Name entity feature: number of name entity.

Content tag features: number of web link and number of image link contained in content.

The 7 groups features in the upper list were extracted separately on questions and answers.

Answer position in Answer list: whether the answer is first, whether the answer is last.

User id features: whether user id of answer is the question user id, whether the user id of previous answer is question user id, whether the user id of next answer is question user id.

Answer and question correlative features: number and ratio of same n-gram terms between answer and question, cosine similarity between answer body and question body, KL distance between answer body and question body.

Class tag features: QCATEGORY tag of question, QTYPE tag of question.

Frequent n-gram term features: frequent unigram terms, bigram terms and trigram terms.

Two methods were proposed to classify answers for English subtask A: (1) two-level hierarchical classification: classifying answers as *good_potential* and *bad_dialog* in the first level; classifying *good_potential* answers as *good* and *potential,* classifying *bad_dialog* answers as *bad* and *dialog* separately in the second level; (2) ensemble learning: training and choosing top N best classifiers based on cross validation on training data, then using the N classifiers to vote final result.

2.2 English subtask B

The English subtask B required participant system to give "*Yes*", "*No*" or "*Unsure*" answer directly to a *YES_NO* question based on its candidate answers.

Evidence to answer *YES_NO* question is the *yes/no* opinion of each *good* answer in answer list. *YES_NO* question answering can be split into three steps: first, finding out *good* answers from candidate answers; second, classifying each *good* answer into *yes*, *no* or *unsure* based on its opinion; third, summarizing final answer for *YES_NO* question according to opinions of all *good* answers.

Given a *YES_NO* question, recognizing *good* answers can be achieved with the classifiers trained in English subtask A; final answer is predicted based on the comparison between the number of *yes* class answers and the number of *no* class answers in answer list of the question. So the remaining task for *YES_NO* question answering is *good* answer classification according to the opinion.

Two methods were proposed for answer opinion classification: (1) piping the best performance classifier for answer selection and the best classifier for answer opinion classification; (2) classifying answers of *YES_NO* question into 5 classes with single classifier: *yes*, *no*, *unsure*, *bad* and *dialogue*.

Feature extraction for English subtask A was same as English subtask A. Features employed were selected according to gain ratio. We proposed ensemble learning method for the answer classification in English subtask B.

2.3 Arabic task

Dataset for Arabic task is in Arabic. The task required participant system to classify answers of question into definitely relevant (*direct*), potentially useful (*related)* and bad (*irrelevant*).

Features extracted for Arabic task are similar to English subtask A. But some features were not extracted for Arabic task, such as "answer position" was ineffective for Arabic task; "WH word number" cannot be extracted on Arabic data. To get more effective features, the dataset for Arabic task was translated to English by Google Translate[1], and feature extraction was done on both original Arabic data and English data translated from original Arabic data.

Features extracted for answer classification in Arabic task include:

Word length features: length of the max length word, average word length.

Word number feature: number of words.

Punctuation features: question mark number, exclamation mark number.

Sentence features: average sentence length, sentence number.

The features in the upper list were extracted separately on answers and questions.

Answer and question correlative features: number and ratio of same n-gram terms, cosine similarity between answer and question body, KL distance between answer and question body.

Name entity feature: number of name entity in answer.

Frequent n-gram term features: frequent unigram, bigram terms and trigram terms in Arabic data and English data.

Features were extracted only on translated English data in the following 2 groups:

Word number features in English: all capital word number, polite word number, word "yes" number, word "no" number.

Part-of-speech features: noun word number and ratio, verb word number and ratio, pronoun word number and ratio, WH word number and ratio.

Methods proposed for Arabic task include: (1) two-level hierarchical classification method: classifying answers as *irrelevant* and *not irrelevant* in the first level and classifying *not irrelevant* answers as *direct* and *related* in the second level; (2) ensemble learning method: training and choosing top N best classifiers and using the results of those classifiers to vote final result.

3 Data Sets

Data sets used for classifiers training includes the training and development data provided. No external data was used for classifiers training.

[1] http://translate.google.com

For English task, CQA-QL corpus (Màrquez et al., 2015) was provided. This corpus was gotten from the Qatar Living Forum[2] and was filtered and annotated manually. Questions in the corpus were labeled into *GENERAL* and *YES_NO* class in *QTYPE* dimension, and *yes*, *no*, *unsure* and *Not Applicable* class in *QGOLD_YN* dimension. Answers were labeled into *Good*, *Potential*, *Bad*, *Dialogue*, *Not English* and *Other* class in *CGOLD* dimension, and *Yes*, *No*, *Unsure* and *Not Applicable* class in *CGOLD_YN* dimension.

For Arabic task, Fatwa corpus (Màrquez et al., 2015) was provided, which was manually processed and annotated on source data from the Fatwa website[3]. Answers in this corpus were labeled into *direct*, *related*, and *irrelevant* class. The *irrelevant* class answers for each question were random selected from answers of other questions.

4 Results Evaluation

Some toolkits were employed to extract features and train classifiers. NLTK (Bird et al., 2009) was used to extract features, include part-of-speech of question and answer, frequent n-gram terms, cosine similarity and so on. WEKA (Hall et al., 2009) toolkit was used to do feature selection and classifier training and choosing. LIBSVM (Chang and Lin, 2011) and LIBLINEAR (Fan et al., 2008) were used to train SVM classifier. Scikit-learn toolkit (Pedregosa et al., 2011) was used to train classifiers.

We submitted 3 formal results for each subtask including English subtask A, English subtask B and Arabic task following task result submission requests: 1 primary result as team official result, 2 contrastive results to compare effects of different methods.

4.1 Measures

The official metric to evaluate results is the macro-averaged *F1-score* (Màrquez et al., 2015), which is calculated as:

$$macro-F1 = \frac{\sum_{i=1}^{NumC} F1_i}{NumC} \quad (1)$$

where $NumC$ is the number of class in test set, $F1_i$ is the $F1$ value for class i in test set. $F1$ value is calculated as:

[2] http://www.qatarliving.com/forum

[3] http://fatwa.islamweb.net

$$F1 = \frac{2 \times P \times R}{P + R} \quad (2)$$

where P and R is the precision and recall of test results for a class in test set.

The total *accuracy* for test result is used as secondary metric for results comparison, which is calculated as:

$$Accuracy = \frac{totalRighNum}{totalTestCaseNum} \quad (3)$$

4.2 Results of English subtask A

Official evaluation on English subtask A was different to other task. In CQA-QL corpus, all answers were labeled in fine-grained labels which include 6 classes: *good*, *bad*, *potential*, *dialogue*, "*not English*" and *other*. But in official evaluation, the *macro-F1* score was calculated based on the coarse-grained labels which include 3 classes: *good*, *bad*, *potential*. The class *dialogue*, "*not English*" and *other* were merged with class *bad*.

We considered English subtask A as a 5-class (*good*, *potential*, *bad*, *dialogue*, and "*not English*") classification problem. The answers in "not English" class were firstly recognized by toolkit Language Detection (Shuyo, 2010). Other answers were classified with methods we proposed.

The evaluation results for English subtask A submissions are shown in table 1.

Submission	Macro F1	Accuracy
primary	56.41	68.67
contrastive1	**56.44**	**69.43**
contrastive2	55.22	67.91

Table 1. Macro F1 and accuracy of English subtask A.

The primary submission was gotten by two-level hierarchical classification method: in the first level, answers were classified into *good_potential* and *bad_dialogue*. In the second level, *good_potential* answers and *bad_dialogue* answers were classified separately: *good_potential* answers were classified into *good* and *potential*, *bad_dialogue* answers were classified into *bad* and *dialogue*. The classifiers used here were SVM which were trained using toolkit LIBLINEAR.

In contrastive1 submission, two-level hierarchical classification method was used, and a special ensemble learning method was designed for *potential* answers classifying. The *potential* class answers were classified using ensemble learning method in the first level. The other 3 classes answers were classified in the second level. The ensemble learning method for *potential* answers classification using 5 binary classifiers: 3 *good-potential* classifiers trained using different training data; 1 *bad-potential* classifier and 1 *dialogue-potential* classifier. The training data for *good-potential* classifiers was gotten by random splitting *good* answers into 3 parts. Classifiers used for the contrastive1 submission were SVM trained with toolkit LIBLINEAR.

Steps for getting the contrastive2 submission were similar to the primary submission. The difference was that the first level classifier was trained using Random Forest algorithm (Breiman, 2001). The training data *good-potential* classifier was resampled to balance the instance distribution between *good* and *potential* class.

Features employed for English subtask A includes 4044 features: the top 4000 frequent n-gram terms and the top 44 maximum gain ratio features of all the features described in section 2.1 except the "Frequent n-gram term features".

4.3 Results of English subtask B

Three submissions were submitted for English subtask B including primary submission, contrastive1 submission and contrastive2 submission. The evaluation results are presented in table 2.

Submission	Macro F1	Accuracy
primary	**53.60**	**64.00**
contrastive1	42.50	60.00
contrastive2	42.40	60.00

Table 2. Macro F1 and accuracy of English subtask B.

For the primary submission, answers in *YES_NO* question answer list were classified into 5 classes. Steps to classify answers in *CGOLD_YN* dimension were: first, a rule based method was used to classify answers; second, ensemble learning method was used to classify the answers that cannot be classified by rule based method. Classifiers used in ensemble learning method include: SMO (sequential minimal optimization algorithm for SVM) (Keerthi et al., 2001), Random Forest, DMNBtext (Discriminative Multinomial Naïve Bayes) (Su et al., 2008), Logistic Regression (Le Cessie and Van Houwelingen, 1992) and RBFNetwork (normalized Gaussian radial basis function network). Those classifiers were the top 5 best of all classifiers have been tried based on 10 folds cross validation on training data. Features employed for the primary submission include 187 features, which were the top 187 maximum gain ratio features of the 4400 features used in English task A.

The contrastive1 submission and contrastive2 submission were based on the *good* answers in English subtask A primary submission. Only *good* answers of *YES_NO* question in subtask A primary submission were classified in *CGOLD_YN* dimension. *Good* answers of *YES_NO* question were classified into: *yes*, *no* and *unsure*.

For the contrastive1 submission, *good* class answers were classified with ensemble learning method. Classifiers used for the ensemble learning method included the top 5 best classifiers for answer classification in *CGOLD_YN* dimension: SMO, Random Forest, DMNBtext, Logistic Regression and LMT (logistic model tree) (Sumner et al., 2005).

For the contrastive2 submission, only classifier LMT, which was the best classifier of all classifiers tried based on 10 folds cross validation results on training data, was used to classify *good* answers.

Features employed for the contrastive1 and contrastive2 submission include 110 features, which were the top 110 maximum gain ratio features of the 4400 features used in English task A.

4.4 Results of Arabic task

Answers were classified into 3 classes in Arabic task: *direct*, *related*, and *irrelevant*. Evaluation results for Arabic task are presented in table 3.

The primary submission was gotten by ensemble learning method using 3 classifiers. The classifiers were top 3 classifiers chosen based on 10 folds cross validation results on training data: SMO, REPTree (decision/regression tree) and J48graft (grafted C4.5 decision tree) (Webb, 1999).

Submission	Macro F1	Accuracy
primary	67.70	74.53
contrastive1	**68.36**	**73.93**
contrastive2	67.98	73.23

Table 3. Macro F1 and accuracy of Arabic task.

The contrastive1 submission was gotten by two-level hierarchical classification method: in the first level, answers were classified into *irrelevant* and *not irrelevant*; in the second level, *not irrelevant* answers were classified into *direct* and *related*. All classifiers were trained using SMO algorithm.

The contrastive2 submission was gotten only by SMO classifier. The SMO classifier was trained as multi-class classifier to classify answers into *direct*, *related* and *irrelevant*.

Features employed for Arabic task include 5049 features: the top 5000 frequent n-gram terms and the top 49 maximum gain ratio features of all the features described in section 2.3 except "Frequent n-gram term features".

5 Discussion

In English subtask A, performance of the submission contrastive1, the hierarchical classification method result, was better than other submissions. The performance of hierarchical classification method was also better than other submission in Arabic task. This shows that the hierarchical classification method is effective for answer selection task.

The performances on different class varied from each other remarkable for English subtask A and Arabic task as shown in table 4. It is difficult to distinguish the potentially useful class answers for all classification methods that have been tried. Analysis on feature extraction showed that, most features were extracted to judge whether the answer was *good* or *bad*, but few features were extracted to judge whether the answer was potentially useful.

Submission	Class	P	R	F1
English subtask A contrastive1	*Good*	78.02	79.74	78.87
	Bad	80.6	66.01	72.58
	Pot.	14.04	24.55	17.86
English subtask B primary	*Yes*	80	80	80
	No	28.57	50	36.36
	Unsure	66.67	33.33	44.44
Arabic task contrastive1	*direct*	62.4	74.88	68.08
	Irrel.	85.14	83.33	84.23
	related	57.07	49.1	52.78

Table 4. Detailed evaluation results (P, R and F1) of the best performance result for each task.

In English subtask B, performance on primary submission, which was result of one-step classification method on all answers of YES_NO question, was much better than other submissions which were results of two-step classification method. The results showed that cascade error of piping classifiers for answer classification in *CGOLD* and answer classification in *CGOLD_YN* had great impact on final answer accuracy for *YES_NO* question. The one-step classification method can avoid the cascade error for *Yes_NO* questions answering.

We compared performance of SVM classifier using bag-of-word features, non-bag-of-word features and all features for English subtask A, subtask B and Arabic task on *macro-F1* scores. The results are shown in table 5.

Task	*bow*	*non_bow*	*bow+non_bow*
Subtask A	0.39	0.48	0.50
Subtask B	0.42	0.64	0.68
Arabic Task	0.36	0.35	0.42

Table 5. Macro F1 of SVM classifier using bag-of-word features, non-bag-of-word features and all features.

Feature set bag-of-words (*bow*) includes **Frequent n-gram term features** described in section 2.1 and 2.3. Feature set non-bag-of-words (*non_bow*) includes other features described in section 2.1 and 2.3 which were specially designed for answer selection task. Set *bow+non_bow* includes all features in set *bow* and *non_bow*.

The performance of the classifier using *bow+non_bow* features is better than using the other two sets features in isolation, which means *bow* set features and *non_bow* set features are effective to improve performance of answer classifier if used both. The contribution of different sets is different on different tasks. Performance of *non_bow* (44 features for English data and 49 features for Arabic data) is better than *bow* (4000 for English and 5000 for Arabic) on Answer Selection task. It shows the features specially extracted for answer selection are more effective. But performance of *non_bow* (22 features) is worse than *bow* (165 features) on *YES_NO* questions answering. The reason is that the *non_bow* features are not designed for opinion recognition. It shows that designing special features for opinion recognition for task B is necessary.

6 Conclusions and Future Work

In this paper, we presented multi-classifier ensemble method and hierarchical classification method proposed for each subtask in SemEval-2015 Task 3. Experimental results demonstrated that the proposed classification methods were effective in both English and Arabic subtasks.

In the next stage, syntax feature and deep semantic feature will be exploited to further improve the performance of our approaches. Besides, more effective features for *potential* answers classification will also be explored.

Acknowledgments

The authors thank Daniel Cer and all the anonymous reviewers for their insightful comments for this paper.

This work was supported in part by the National Natural Science Foundation of China (61272383, 61173075 and 61203378), the Strategic Emerging Industry Development Special Funds of Shenzhen (ZDSY20120613125401420 and JCYJ20120613151940045) and the Key Basic Research Foundation of Shenzhen (JC201005260118A).

References

Chih-Chung Chang and Chih-Jen Lin. 2011. LIBSVM: A library for support vector machines. *ACM Transactions on Intelligent Systems and Technology*, 2(3):1-27.

Chirag Shah and Jefferey Pomerantz. 2010. Evaluating and Predicting Answer Quality in Community QA. In *Proceedings of the 33rd International ACM SIGIR Conference on Research and Development in Information Retrieval*, 411-418, Geneva, Switzerland, 19-23 July.

Eugene Agichtein, Carlos Castillo, Debora Donato, Aristides Gionis, and Gilad Mishne. 2008. Finding High-quality Content in Social Media. In *Proceedings of the 2008 International Conference on Web Search and Data Mining*, 183-194, Palo Alto, California, USA, 11-12 February.

Fabian Pedregosa, Gaël Varoquaux, Alexandre Gramfort, Vincent Michel, Bertrand Thirion, Olivier Grisel, Mathieu Blondel, Peter Prettenhofer, Ron Weiss, Vincent Dubourg, Jake Vanderplas, Alexandre Passos, David Cournapeau, Matthieu Brucher, Matthieu Perrot, and Édouard Duchesnay. 2011. Scikit-learn: Machine Learning in Python. *The Journal of Machine Learning Research*, 12:2825-2830.

Geoffrey I Webb. 1999. Decision tree grafting from the all-tests-but-one partition. In *Proceedings of the Sixteenth International Joint Conference on Artificial Intelligence*, 2:702-707, San Francisco, California, USA.

Jiang Su, Harry Zhang, Charles X Ling, and Stan Matwin. 2008. Discriminative parameter learning for Bayesian networks. In *Proceedings of the 25th international conference on Machine learning*, 1016-1023, Helsinki, Finland.

Jiwoon Jeon, W. Bruce Croft, Joon Ho Lee, and Soyeon Park. 2006. A Framework to Predict the Quality of Answers with Non-textual Features. In *Proceedings of the 29th Annual International ACM SIGIR Conference on Research and Development in Information Retrieval*, 228-235, Seattle, Washington, USA, 6-11 August.

Kohei Arai and Anik Nur Handayani. 2013. Predicting quality of answer in collaborative Q/A community. *Society and culture*, 2(3):21-25.

Leo Breiman. 2001. Random forests. *Machine learning*, 45(1):5-32.

Lluís Màrquez, James Glass, Walid Magdy, Alessandro Moschitti, Preslav Nakov, and Bilal Randeree. 2015. SemEval-2015 Task 3: Answer Selection in Community Question Answering. In *Proceedings of the 9th International Workshop on Semantic Evaluation (SemEval 2015),* Denver, Colorado, USA.

Marc Sumner, Eibe Frank, and Mark Hall. 2005. Speeding up logistic model tree induction. In *Knowledge Discovery in Databases: PKDD 2005*, 3721:675-683.

Mark Hall, Eibe Frank, Geoffrey Holmes, Bernhard Pfahringer, Peter Reutemann, and Ian H. Witten. 2009. The WEKA Data Mining Software: An Update. *ACM SIGKDD Explorations Newsletter*, 11(1):10-18.

Nakatani Shuyo. 2010. *Language Detection Library for Java.*

Rong-En Fan, Kai-Wei Chang, Cho-Jui Hsieh, Xiang-Rui Wang, and Chih-Jen Lin. 2008. LIBLINEAR: A Library for Large Linear Classification. *The Journal of Machine Learning Research*, 9:1871-1874.

Sathiya Sathiya Keerthi, Shirish Krishnaj Shevade, Chiru Bhattacharyya, and K. R. K. Murthy. 2001. Improvements to Platt's SMO Algorithm for SVM Classifier Design. *Neural Computation*, 13(3):637-649.

Saskia Le Cessie and Johannes C Van Houwelingen. 1992. Ridge estimators in logistic regression. *Applied statistics*, 191-201.

Steven Bird, Ewan Klein, and Edward Loper. 2009. *Natural language processing with Python.* O'Reilly Media, Inc. .

QCRI: Answer Selection for Community Question Answering – Experiments for Arabic and English

Massimo Nicosia[1], **Simone Filice**[2], **Alberto Barrón-Cedeño**[2], **Iman Saleh**[3], **Hamdy Mubarak**[2], **Wei Gao**[2], **Preslav Nakov**[2], **Giovanni Da San Martino**[2], **Alessandro Moschitti**[2], **Kareem Darwish**[2], **Lluís Màrquez**[2], **Shafiq Joty**[2] and **Walid Magdy**[2]

[1] University of Trento [2] Qatar Computing Research Institute [3] Cairo University

massimo.nicosia@unitn.it

{sfilice,albarron,hmubarak,wgao,pnakov,gmartino}@qf.org.qa

{amoschitti,kdarwish,lmarquez,sjoty,wmagdy}@qf.org.qa

iman.saleh@fci-cu.edu.eg

Abstract

This paper describes QCRI's participation in SemEval-2015 Task 3 "Answer Selection in Community Question Answering", which targeted real-life Web forums, and was offered in both Arabic and English. We apply a supervised machine learning approach considering a manifold of features including among others word n-grams, text similarity, sentiment analysis, the presence of specific words, and the context of a comment. Our approach was the best performing one in the Arabic subtask and the third best in the two English subtasks.

1 Introduction

SemEval-2015 Task 3 "Answer Selection in Community Question Answering" challenged the participants to automatically predict the appropriateness of the answers in a community question answering setting (Màrquez et al., 2015). Given a question $q \in Q$ asked by user u_q and a set of comments C, the main task was to determine whether a comment $c \in C$ offered a suitable answer to q or not.

In the case of Arabic, the questions were extracted from *Fatwa*, a community question answering website about Islam.[1] Each question includes five comments, provided by scholars on the topic, each of which has to be automatically labeled as (*i*) `DIRECT`: a direct answer to the question; (*ii*) `RELATED`: not a direct answer to the question but with information related to the topic; and (*iii*) `IRRELEVANT`: an answer to another question, not related to the topic. This is subtask A, Arabic.

In the case of English, the dataset was extracted from *Qatar Living*, a forum for people to pose questions on multiple aspects of daily life in Qatar.[2] Unlike *Fatwa*, the questions and comments in this dataset come from regular users, making them significantly more varied, informal, open, and noisy. In this case, the input to the system consists of a question and a variable number of comments, each of which is to be labeled as (*i*) `GOOD`: the comment is definitively relevant; (*ii*) `POTENTIAL`: the comment is potentially useful; and (*iii*) `BAD`: the comment is irrelevant (e.g., it is part of a dialogue, unrelated to the topic, or it is written in a language other than English). This is subtask A, English.

Additionally, a subset of the questions required a `YES`/`NO` answer, and there was another subtask for them, which asked to determine whether the overall answer to the question, according to the evidence provided by the comments, is (*i*) `YES`, (*ii*) `NO`, or (*iii*) `UNSURE`. This is subtask B, English.

Details about the subtasks and the experimental settings can be found in (Màrquez et al., 2015).

Below we describe the supervised learning approach of QCRI, which considers different kinds of features: lexical, syntactic and semantic similarities; the context in which a comment appears; n-grams occurrence; and some heuristics. We ranked first in the Arabic, and third in the two English subtasks.

The rest of the paper is organized as follows: Section 2 describes the features used, Section 3 discusses our models and our official results, and Section 4 presents post-competition experiments and offers some final remarks.

[1] http://fatwa.islamweb.net

[2] http://www.qatarliving.com/forum

2 Features

In this section, we describe the different features we considered including similarity measures (Section 2.1), the context in which a comment appears (Section 2.2), and the occurrence of certain vocabulary and phrase triggers (Sections 2.3 and 2.4). How and where we apply them is discussed in Section 3. Note that while our general approach is based on supervised machine learning, some of our contrastive submissions are rule-based.

2.1 Similarity Measures

The similarity features measure the similarity $sim(q, c)$ between the question and a target comment, assuming that high similarity signals a GOOD answer. We consider three kinds of similarity measures, which we describe below.

2.1.1 Lexical Similarity

We compute the similarity between word n-gram representations ($n = [1, \ldots, 4]$) of q and c, using the following lexical similarity measures (after stopword removal): greedy string tiling (Wise, 1996), longest common subsequences (Allison and Dix, 1986), Jaccard coefficient (Jaccard, 1901), word containment (Lyon et al., 2001), and cosine similarity. We further compute cosine on lemmata and POS tags, either including stopwords or not.

We also use similarity measures, which weigh the terms using the following three formulæ:

$$sim(q, c) = \sum_{t \in q \cap c} idf(t) \quad (1)$$

$$sim(q, c) = \sum_{t \in q \cap c} log(idf(t)) \quad (2)$$

$$sim(q, c) = \sum_{t \in q \cap c} log\left(1 + \frac{|C|}{tf(t)}\right) \quad (3)$$

where $idf(t)$ is the inverse document frequency (Sparck Jones, 1972) of term t in the entire Qatar Living dataset, C is the number of comments in this collection, and $tf(t)$ is the term frequency of the term in the comment. Equations 2 and 3 are variations of idf; cf. Nallapati (2004).

For subtask B, we further considered the cosine similarity between the tf-idf-weighted intersection of the words in q and c.

2.1.2 Syntactic Similarity

We further use a partial tree kernel (Moschitti, 2006) to calculate the similarity between the question and the comment based on their corresponding shallow syntactic trees. These trees have word lemmata as leaves, then there is a POS tag node parent for each lemma leaf, and POS tag nodes are in turn grouped under shallow parsing chunks, which are linked to a root sentence node; finally, all root sentence nodes are linked to a super root for all sentences in the question/comment.

2.1.3 Semantic Similarity

We apply three approaches to build word-embedding vector representations, using *(i)* latent semantic analysis (Croce and Previtali, 2010), trained on the Qatar Living corpus with a word co-occurrence window of size ± 3 and producing a vector of 250 dimensions with SVD (we produced a vector for each noun in the vocabulary); *(ii)* GloVe (Pennington et al., 2014), using a model pre-trained on *Common Crawl (42B tokens)*, with 300 dimensions; and *(iii)* COMPOSES (Baroni et al., 2014), using previously-estimated predict vectors of 400 dimensions.[3] We represent both q and c as a sum of the vectors corresponding to the words within them (neglecting the subject of c). We compute the cosine similarity to estimate $sim(q, c)$.

We also experimented with *word2vec* (Mikolov et al., 2013) vectors pre-trained with both *cbow* and *skipgram* on news data, and also with both word2vec and GloVe vectors trained on Qatar Living data, but we discarded them as they did not help us on top of all other features we had.

2.2 Context

Comments are organized sequentially according to the time line of the comment thread. Whether a question includes further comments by the person who asked the original question or just several comments by the same user, or whether it belongs to a category in which a given kind of answer is expected, are all important factors. Therefore, we consider a set of features that try to describe a comment in the context of the entire comment thread.

[3]They are available at `http://nlp.stanford.edu/projects/glove/` and `http://clic.cimec.unitn.it/composes/semantic-vectors.html`

We have boolean context features that explore the following situations:

- c is written by u_q (i.e., the same user behind q),
- c is written by u_q and contains an acknowledgment (e.g., *thank**, *appreciat**),
- c is written by u_q and includes further question(s), and
- c is written by u_q and includes no acknowledgments nor further questions.

We further have numerical features exploring whether comment c appears in the proximity of a comment by u_q; the assumption is that an acknowledgment or further questions by u_q could signal a bad answer:

- among the comments following c there is one by u_q containing an acknowledgment,
- among the comments following c there is one by u_q not containing an acknowledgment,
- among the comments following c there is one by u_q containing a question, and
- among the comments preceding c there is one by u_q containing a question.

The numerical value of these last four features is determined by the distance k, in number of comments, between c and the closest comment by u_q ($k = \infty$ if no comments by u_q exist):

$$f(c) = \max(0,\ 1.1 - (k \cdot 0.1)) \tag{4}$$

We also tried to model potential dialogues by identifying interlacing comments between two users. Our dialogue features rely on identifying conversation chains between two users:

$$u_i \rightarrow \ldots \rightarrow u_j \rightarrow \ldots \rightarrow u_i \rightarrow \ldots \rightarrow [u_j]$$

Note that comments by other users can appear in between the nodes of this "pseudo-conversation" chain. We consider three features: whether a comment is at the beginning, in the middle, or at the end of such a chain. We have copies of these three features for the special case when $u_q = u_j$.

We are also interested in modeling whether a user u_i has been particularly active in a question thread. Thus, we add one boolean feature: whether u_i wrote more than one comment in the current thread.

Three more features identify the first, the middle and the last comments by u_i. One extra feature counts the total number of comments written by u_i. Moreover, we empirically observed that the likelihood of a comment being GOOD decreases with its position in the thread. Therefore, we also include another real-valued feature: $\max(20, i)/20$, where i represents the position of the comment in the thread.

Finally, Qatar Living includes twenty-six different categories in which one could request information and advice. Some of them tend to include more open-ended questions and even invite discussion on ambiguous topics, e.g., *Socialising*, *Life in Qatar*, *Qatari Culture*. Some other require more precise answers and allow for less discussion, e.g., *Visas and Permits*. Therefore, we include one boolean feature per category to consider this information.

2.3 Word n-Grams

Our features include n-grams, independently obtained from both the question and the comment: $[1, 2]$-grams for Arabic, and stopworded $[1, 2, 3]$-grams for English. That is, each n-gram appearing in the texts becomes a member of the feature vector. The value for such features is tf-idf, with idf computed on the entire Qatar Living dataset.

Our aim is to capture the words that are associated with questions and comments in the different classes. We assume that objective and clear questions would tend to produce objective and GOOD comments. On the other hand, subjective or badly formulated questions would call for BAD comments or discussion, i.e., dialogues, among the users. This can be reflected by the vocabulary used, regardless of the topic of the formulated question. This is also true for comments: the occurrence of particular words could make a comment more likely to be GOOD or BAD , regardless of what question was asked.

2.4 Heuristics

Exploring the training data, we noticed that many GOOD comments suggested visiting a Web site or contained an email address. Therefore, we included two boolean features to verify the presence of URLs or emails in c. Another feature captures the length of c, as longer (GOOD) comments usually contain detailed information to answer a question.

2.5 Polarity

These features, which we used for subtask B only, try to determine whether a comment is positive or negative, which could be associated with `YES` or `NO` answers. The polarity of a comment c is

$$pol(c) = \sum_{w \in c} pol(w) \tag{5}$$

where $pol(w)$ is the polarity of word w in the NRC Hashtag Sentiment Lexicon v0.1 (Mohammad et al., 2013). We disregarded $pol(w)$ if its absolute value was less than 1.

We further use boolean features that check the existence of some keywords in the comment. Their values are set to true if c contains words like (*i*) *yes, can, sure, wish, would*, or (*ii*) *no, not, neither*.

2.6 User Profile

With this set of features, we aim to model the behavior of the different participants in previous queries. Given comment c by user u, we consider the number of `GOOD`, `BAD`, `POTENTIAL`, and `DIALOGUE` comments u has produced before.[4] We also consider the average word length of `GOOD`, `BAD`, `POTENTIAL`, and `DIALOGUE` comments. These features are computed both considering all questions and taking into account only those from the target category. [5]

3 Submissions and Results

Below we describe our primary submissions for the three subtasks; then we discuss our contrastive submissions. Our classifications for subtask A, for both Arabic and English, are at the comment level. Table 1 shows our official results at the competition; all reported F_1 values are macro-averaged.

3.1 Primary Submissions

Arabic. We used logistic regression. The features are lexical similarities (Section 2.1) and n-grams (Section 2.3). In a sort of stacking, the output of our cont$_1$ submission is included as another feature (cf. Section 3.2).

This submission achieved the first position in the competition ($F_1 = 78.55$, compared to 70.99 for the second one). It showed a particularly high performance when labeling `RELATED` comments.

English, subtask A. Here we used a linear SVM, and a one-vs.-rest approach as we have a multiclass problem. The features for this submission consist of lexical, syntactic, and semantic similarities (Section 2.1), context information (Section 2.2), n-grams (Section 2.3), and heuristics (Section 2.4). Similarly to Arabic, the output of our rule-based system from the cont$_2$ submission is another feature.

This submission achieved the third position in the competition ($F_1 = 53.74$, compared to 57.19 for the top one). `POTENTIAL` comments proved to be the hardest, as the border with respect to the rest of the comments is very fuzzy. Indeed, a manual inspection on some random comments has shown that distinguishing between `GOOD` and `POTENTIAL` comments is often impossible.

English, subtask B. Following the organizers' manual labeling strategy for the `YES`/`NO` questions (Màrquez et al., 2015), we used three steps: (*i*) identifying the `GOOD` comments for q; (*ii*) classifying each of them as `YES`, `NO`, or `UNSURE`; and (*iii*) aggregating these predictions to the question level (majority). In case of a draw, we labeled the question as `UNSURE`.[6]

Step (*i*) is subtask A. For step (*ii*), we train a classifier as for subtask A, including the polarity and the user profile features (cf. Sections 2.5 and 2.6).[7]

This submission achieved the third position in the competition: $F_1 = 53.60$, compared to 63.70 for the top one. Unlike the other subtasks, for which we trained on both the training and the testing datasets, here we used the training data only, which was due to instability of the results when adding the development data. Post-submission experiments revealed this was due to some bugs as well as to unreliability of some of the statistics. Further discussion on this can be found in Section 4.3.

[4] About 72% of the comments in the test set were written by users who had been seen in the training/development set.

[5] In Section 4.3, we will observe that computing these category-level features was not a good idea.

[6] The majority class in the training and dev. sets (`YES`) could be the default answer. Still, we opted for a conservative decision: choosing `UNSURE` if no enough evidence was found.

[7] Even if the user profile information seems to fit for subtask A rather than B, at development time it was effective for B only.

ar	DIRECT	IRREL	RELATED	F_1
primary	77.31	91.21	67.13	78.55
$cont_1$	74.89	91.23	63.68	76.60
$cont_2$	76.63	90.30	63.98	76.97
en A	GOOD	BAD	POT	F_1
primary	78.45	72.39	10.40	53.74
$cont_1$	76.08	75.68	17.44	56.40
$cont_2$	75.46	72.48	7.97	51.97
en B	YES	NO	UNSURE	F_1
primary	80.00	44.44	36.36	53.60
$cont_1$	75.68	0.00	0.00	25.23
$cont_2$	66.67	33.33	47.06	49.02

Table 1: Per-class and macro-averaged F_1 scores for our official primary and contrastive submissions to SemEval-2015 Task 3 for Arabic (ar) and English (en), subtasks A and B.

3.2 Contrastive Submissions

Arabic. We approach our contrastive submission 1 as a ranking problem. After stopword removal and stemming, we compute $sim(q, c)$ as follows:

$$sim(q,c) = \frac{1}{|q|} \sum_{t \in q \cap c} \omega(t) \qquad (6)$$

where we empirically set $\omega(t) = 1$ if t is a 1-gram, and $\omega(t) = 4$ if t is a 2-gram. Given the 5 comments $c_1, \ldots, c_5 \in C$ associated with q, we map the maximum similarity $\max_C sim(q, c)$ to a maximum 100% similarity and we map the rest of the scores proportionally. Each comment is assigned a class according to the following ranges: [80, 100]% for DIRECT, (20,80)% for RELATED, and [0,20]% for IRRELEVANT. We manually tuned these threshold values on the training data.

As for the contrastive submission 2, we built a binary classifier DIRECT vs. NO-DIRECT using logistic regression. We then sorted the comments according to the classifier's prediction confidence and we assigned labels as follows: DIRECT for the top ranked, RELATED for the second ranked, and IRRELEVANT for the rest. We only included lexical similarities as features, discarding those weighted with idf variants.

The performance of these two contrastive submissions was below but close to that of our primary submission (F_1 of 76.60 and 76.97, vs. 78.55 for primary), particularly for IRRELEVANT comments.

English, subtask A. Our contrastive submission 1, uses the same features and schema as our primary submission, but with SVM^{light} (Joachims, 1999), which allows us to deal with the class imbalance by tuning the j parameter, i.e., the cost of making mistakes on positive examples. This time, we set the C hyper-parameter to the default value. As we focused on improving the performance on POTENTIAL instances, we obtained better results for this category (F_1 of 17.44 vs. 10.40 for POTENTIAL), surpassing the overall performance for our primary submission (F_1 of 56.40 vs. 53.74).

Our contrastive submission 2 is similar to our Arabic contrastive submission 1, using the same ranges, but now for GOOD, POTENTIAL, and BAD. We also have post-processing heuristics: c is classified as GOOD if it includes a URL, starts with an imperative verb (e.g., *try*, *view*, *contact*, *check*), or contains *yes words* (e.g., *yes*, *yep*, *yup*) or *no words* (e.g., *no*, *nooo*, *nope*). Moreover, comments written by the author of the question or including acknowledgments are considered dialogues, and thus classified as BAD. The result of this submission is slightly lower than for primary and contrastive 1: F_1=51.97.

English, subtask B. Our contrastive submission 1 is like our primary, but is trained on both the training and the development data. The reason for the low results (an F_1 of 25.23, compared to 53.60 for the primary) were bugs in the polarity features (cf. Section 2.5) and lack of statistics for properly estimating the category-level user profiles (cf. Section 2.6).

The contrastive submission 2 is a rule-based system. A question is answered as YES if it starts with affirmative words: *yes*, *yep*, *yeah*, etc. It is labeled as NO if it starts with negative words: *no*, *nop*, *nope*, etc. The answer to q becomes that of the majority of the comments: UNSURE in case of tie. It is worth noting the comparably high performance when dealing with UNSURE questions: F_1=47.06, compared to 36.36 for our primary submission.

4 Post-Submission Experiments

We carried out post-submission experiments in order to understand how different feature families contributed to the performance of our classifiers; the results are shown in Table 2. We also managed to improve our performance for all three subtasks.

ar (only)	DIR	IRREL	REL	F_1
n-grams	30.40	41.07	72.27	47.91
$cont_1$	74.89	63.68	91.23	76.60
similarities	61.83	25.63	82.55	56.67
ar (without)	DIR	REL	IRREL	F_1
n-grams	75.51	91.31	63.85	76.89
$cont_1$	69.50	82.85	50.87	67.74
similarities	77.24	91.07	67.76	**78.69**
en A (only)	GOOD	BAD	POT	F_1
context	67.65	45.03	11.51	47.90
n-grams	71.22	40.12	5.99	44.86
heuristics	76.46	41.94	7.11	52.57
similarities	62.93	44.58	9.62	46.16
lexical	62.25	41.46	8.66	44.82
syntactic	59.18	36.20	0.00	36.47
semantic	55.56	40.42	9.92	42.16
en A (without)	GOOD	BAD	POT	F_1
context	76.05	41.53	8.98	51.50
n-grams	77.25	45.56	12.23	**55.17**
heuristics	73.84	65.33	6.81	48.66
similarities	78.02	71.82	9.88	53.24
lexical	78.23	72.81	9.91	53.65
syntactic	78.81	43.89	9.91	53.73
semantic	78.41	71.82	10.30	53.51
en B	YES	NO	UNS	F_1
$post_1$	78.79	57.14	20.00	51.98
$post_2$	85.71	57.14	25.00	**55.95**
primary	D/G/Y	I/B/N	R/P/U	F_1
ar	77.31	91.21	67.13	78.55
en A	78.45	72.39	10.40	53.74
en B	80.00	44.44	36.36	53.60

Table 2: Post-submission results for Arabic (ar) and English (en), for subtasks A and B. The lines marked with *only* show results using a particular type of features only, while those marked as *without* show results when using all features but those of a particular type. The best results for each subtask are marked in bold; the results for our official primary submissions are included for comparison.

4.1 Arabic

We ran experiments with the same framework as in our primary submission by considering the subsets of features in isolation (*only*) or all features except for a subset (*without*). The n-gram features together with our $cont_1$ submission (recall that we also use $cont_1$ as a feature in our primary submission) allow for a slightly better performance than our —already winning— primary submission ($F_1 = 78.69$, compared to $F_1 = 78.55$). The $cont_1$ feature turns out to be the most important one, and, as it already contains similarity, combining it with other similarity features does not yield any further improvements.

4.2 English, Subtask A

We performed experiments similar to those we did for Arabic. According to the *only* figures, the heuristic features seem to be the most useful ones, followed by the context-based ones. The latter explore a dimension ignored by the rest: these features are completely uncorrelated and provide a good performance boost (as the *without* experiments show). On the other hand, using all features but the n-grams improves over the performance of our primary run ($F_1 = 55.17$ compared to $F_1 = 53.74$). This is an interesting but not very significant result as these features had already boosted our performance at development time. Further research is necessary.

4.3 English, Subtask B

Our post-submission efforts focused on investigating why learning from the training data only was considerably better than learning from training+dev. The output labels on the test set in the two learning scenarios showed considerable differences: when learning from training+dev, the predicted labels were YES for all but three cases. After correcting a bug in our implementation of the polarity-related features, the result when learning on training+dev became F_1=51.98 (Table 2, $post_1$). Further analysis showed that the features counting the number of GOOD , BAD , and POTENTIAL comments within categories by the same user (cf. Section 2.6) varied greatly when computed on training and on training+dev, as the number of comments by a user in a category was, in most cases, too small to yield very reliable statistics. After discarding these three features, the F_1 raised to 55.95 (Table 2, $post_2$), which is higher than what we obtained at submission time. Note that, once again, the UNSURE class is by far the hardest to identify properly.

Surprisingly, learning with the bug-free implementation from the training set yielded a much higher F_1 of 69.35 on the test dataset (not shown in the table). Analysis revealed that the difference in performance was due to misclassifying just four questions. Indeed, the differences seem to occur due to the natural randomness of the classifier on a small test dataset and they cannot be considered statistically significant (Màrquez et al., 2015).

5 Conclusions and Future Work

We have presented the system developed by the team of the Qatar Computing Research Institute (QCRI) for participating in SemEval-2015 Task 3 on Answer Selection in Community Question Answering. We used a supervised machine learning approach and a manifold of features including word n-grams, text similarity, sentiment dictionaries, the presence of specific words, the context of a comment, some heuristics, etc. Our approach was the best performing one in the Arabic task, and the third best in the two English tasks.

We further presented a detailed study of which kinds of features helped most for each language and for each subtask, which should help researchers focus their efforts in the future.

In future work, we plan to use richer linguistic annotations, more complex kernels, and large semantic resources.

Acknowledgments

This research is developed by the Arabic Language Technologies (ALT) group at the Qatar Computing Research Institute (QCRI), Qatar Foundation in collaboration with MIT. It is part of the Interactive sYstems for Answer Search (Iyas) project.

References

Lloyd Allison and Trevor Dix. 1986. A bit-string longest-common-subsequence algorithm. *Inf. Process. Lett.*, 23(6):305–310, December.

Marco Baroni, Georgiana Dinu, and Germán Kruszewski. 2014. Don't count, predict! A systematic comparison of context-counting vs. context-predicting semantic vectors. In *Proceedings of the 52nd Annual Meeting of the Association for Computational Linguistics (Volume 1: Long Papers)*, ACL '14, pages 238–247, Baltimore, MD, USA.

Danilo Croce and Daniele Previtali. 2010. Manifold Learning for the Semi-Supervised Induction of FrameNet Predicates: An Empirical Investigation. In *Proceedings of the 2010 Workshop on GEometrical Models of Natural Language Semantics*, GEMS '10, pages 7–16, Uppsala, Sweden.

Paul Jaccard. 1901. Étude comparative de la distribution florale dans une portion des Alpes et des Jura. *Bulletin del la Société Vaudoise des Sciences Naturelles*, 37:547–579.

Thorsten Joachims. 1999. Making Large-scale Support Vector Machine Learning Practical. In Bernhard Schölkopf, Christopher J. C. Burges, and Alexander J. Smola, editors, *Advances in Kernel Methods*, pages 169–184. MIT Press, Cambridge, MA, USA.

Caroline Lyon, James Malcolm, and Bob Dickerson. 2001. Detecting short passages of similar text in large document collections. In *Proceedings of the 2001 Conference on Empirical Methods in Natural Language Processing*, EMNLP '01, pages 118–125, Pittsburgh, PA, USA.

Lluís Màrquez, James Glass, Walid Magdy, Alessandro Moschitti, Preslav Nakov, and Bilal Randeree. 2015. SemEval-2015 Task 3: Answer Selection in Community Question Answering. In *Proceedings of the 9th International Workshop on Semantic Evaluation*, SemEval '15, Denver, CO, USA.

Tomas Mikolov, Wen-tau Yih, and Geoffrey Zweig. 2013. Linguistic Regularities in Continuous Space Word Representations. In *Proceedings of the 2013 Conference of the North American Chapter of the Association for Computational Linguistics: Human Language Technologies*, NAACL-HLT '13, pages 746–751, Atlanta, GA, USA.

Saif Mohammad, Svetlana Kiritchenko, and Xiaodan Zhu. 2013. NRC-Canada: Building the state-of-the-art in sentiment analysis of tweets. In *Proceedings of the Second Joint Conference on Lexical and Computational Semantics (*SEM), Volume 2: Proceedings of the Seventh International Workshop on Semantic Evaluation*, SemEval '13, pages 321–327, Atlanta, GA, USA.

Alessandro Moschitti. 2006. Efficient Convolution Kernels for Dependency and Constituent Syntactic Trees. In Johannes Fürnkranz, Tobias Scheffer, and Myra Spiliopoulou, editors, *Machine Learning: ECML 2006*, volume 4212 of *Lecture Notes in Computer Science*, pages 318–329. Springer Berlin Heidelberg.

Ramesh Nallapati. 2004. Discriminative models for information retrieval. In *Proceedings of the 27th Annual International ACM SIGIR Conference on Research and Development in Information Retrieval*, SIGIR '04, pages 64–71, Sheffield, United Kingdom.

Jeffrey Pennington, Richard Socher, and Christopher Manning. 2014. Glove: Global vectors for word representation. In *Proceedings of the 2014 Conference on Empirical Methods in Natural Language Processing*, EMNLP '14, pages 1532–1543, Doha, Qatar.

Karen Sparck Jones. 1972. A statistical interpretation of term specificity and its application in retrieval. *Journal of Documentation*, 28:11–21.

Michael Wise. 1996. Yap3: Improved detection of similarities in computer program and other texts. In *Proceedings of the Twenty-seventh SIGCSE Technical Symposium on Computer Science Education*, SIGCSE '96, pages 130–134, New York, NY, USA.

ICRC-HIT: A Deep Learning based Comment Sequence Labeling System for Answer Selection Challenge

Xiaoqiang Zhou **Baotian Hu** **Jiaxin Lin** **Yang Xiang** **Xiaolong Wang**
Intelligence Computing Research Center
Department of Computer Science &Technology
Harbin Institute of Technology, Shenzhen Graduate School
{xiaoqiang.jeseph,baotianchina,dongshanjx,xiangyang.hitsz}@gmail.com
wangxl@insun.hit.edu.cn

Abstract

In this paper, we present a comment labeling system based on a deep learning strategy. We treat the answer selection task as a sequence labeling problem and propose recurrent convolution neural networks to recognize good comments. In the recurrent architecture of our system, our approach uses 2-dimensional convolutional neural networks to learn the distributed representation for question-comment pair, and assigns the labels to the comment sequence with a recurrent neural network over CNN. Compared with the conditional random fields based method, our approach performs better performance on Macro-F1 (53.82%), and achieves the highest accuracy (73.18%), F1-value (79.76%) on predicting the *Good* class in this answer selection challenge.

1 Introduction

The community question answering site or system (CQA) is one kind of common platforms where people can freely ask questions, deliver comments and participate in discussions. The high-quality comments given a question are the important resources to generate useful question-answer pairs, which are of great value for knowledge base construction and information retrieval (IR). However, due to the unrestricted expressions in CQA, it still one problem to recognize the high-quality comments from the open domain data, which are involve in a large of noise information. Nevertheless, the semantic relevance between question and comment makes sense to predict the quality of comment by modeling the semantic matching for question-comment pair.

Prior work on predicting the class of comment (or answer) mainly attempted to measure the semantic similarity between question and comment with typical classification approaches, such as LR and SVM. To achieve the semantic relevance matching for question-comment pair, a large number of works focus on constructing feature-engineering to extract the features of question and comment as the input of models. Beyond typical textual feature, some works integrate the structural information (Wang et al., 2009; Huang et al., 2007) into the discrete representations of question-comment pairs to improve the performances of comment classifiers. Another option is extracting user metadata (Chen and Nayak, 2008; Shah and Pomerantz, 2010) from the question answering portal for enriching the feature-engineering. Empirically the approaches above have been shown to improve performances on recognizing positive answers, but they rely on large numbers of hand-crafted features, and require various external resources which may be difficult to obtain. Furthermore, they suffer from the limitation of requiring task-specific feature extraction for new domain.

Recently the works about neural network-based distributed sentence models (Socher et al., 2012; Kalchbrenner et al., 2014) have achieved successes in natural language processing (NLP). As a consequence of this success, it appears natural to attempt to solve question answering using similar techniques. To recognize the high-quality answers, Hu et al. (2013) learned the joint representation for each question-answer pair

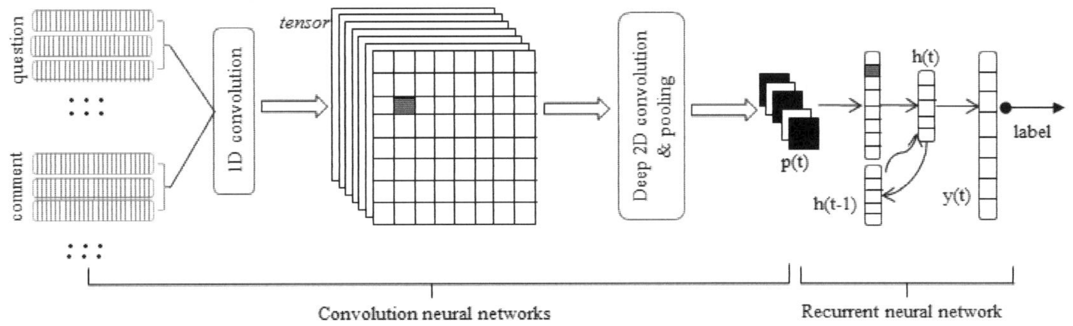

Figure 1. The architecture of comment labeling system based on deep learning

by taking both of the textual and non-textual features as the input of multi-DBN model. To achieve the answer sentence selection, Yu et al. (2014) proposed convolution neural networks based models to represent the question and answer sentences. For the semantic matching between question and answer, the methods based on deep learning generally exploit to learn the distributed representation of question-answer pair as the input. Instead of extracting a variety of features, these approaches learn the semantic features to represent question and answer. However, these approaches only focus on modeling the semantic relevance between question and answer, ignoring the semantic correlations in answer sequence.

In this work, we present a novel comment labeling system based on deep learning. We propose the recurrent convolutional neural networks (R&CNN) approach to assign the labels to comments given a question. Based on the distributed representations learned form 2-dimensional CNN (2D-CNN) matching, our approach achieves to comment sequence learning and predict the classes of comments. Using the word embedding trained by provided Qatar Living data, R&CNN not only models the semantic relevance for question and comment, but also captures the correlative context in comment sequence for predicting the class of comment. The experimental results show that our system performs better performances than the CRF based method (Ding et al., 2008) on recognizing good comments, and performs more adaptive on the development and test dataset.

2 System Description

The architecture of our comment labeling system is a recurrent architecture (shown in Figure 1) with a recurrent neural network over the convolutional neural networks. Given a question, our approach achieves to learn the semantic relevance between question and comment by 2D-CNN matching and generate the distributed representation of each question-comment pair. After that, our approach uses the RNN to model the semantic correlations in comment sequence, and makes the quality predictions for the comment sequence with the captured context.

2.1 Convolutional Neural Networks for question-comment matching

Convolutional neural networks are a natural extension of neural networks for treating image. Hu et al. (2014) proposed the 2D-CNN model to do semantic matching between two sentences. In our work, we use 2D-CNN to learn the distributed representations for question-comment pairs. Unlike 1D-CNN, executing the interaction between question and answer in final multi-layer perception (MLP) with their individual representations, 2D-CNN maps question and comment into a common space for learning the representation of question-comment pair and captures the rich matching patterns between question and answer by layer-by-layer convolution and pooling.

The first layer is 1D-convolution layer, whose role is converting word embedding of question and comment into one common space with the sliding window, whose size k is (3×3). For the word i on question q and word j on comment c, 1D-convolution can formulated as:

$$\hat{z}_{i,j}^{(0)} = \left[q_{i:i+k-1}^{T}, c_{i:i+k-1}^{T}\right] \quad (1)$$

where $\hat{z}_{i,j}^{(0)}$ simply concatenates the vectors of sentence segments in question q and comment c;

The 1D-convolution converts the concatenated matrix H_0 of question and comment into the real-value matrix H_1 . After that, 2D-CNN executes deep 2D-convolution and pooling, similar to that of traditional image input. The output of the mth hidden layer is computed as:

$$H_m = \sigma\big(pool(w_m H_{m-1} + b_m)\big) \quad (2)$$

Here, w_m is the parameter matrix for the feature maps on m^{th} hidden layer and b_m is the bias vector. $\sigma(.)$ is the sigmoid activation function. The final distributed representation p_t of question-comment pair learned from 2D-CNN represents the semantic relevance between question and comment, and provides the reliable evidences to make a quality prediction for the corresponding comment.

2.2 Recurrent Neural Network for comment sequence labeling

Recurrent neural network is a straightforward adaptation of the standard feed-forward neural network (Bengio et al., 2012) to allow it to model sequential data. The recurrent neural network in our work has one input layer *X*, one hidden layer *H* for updating the hidden state, and the output layer Y. For the time step t, the input to RNN includes the learned representation $p(t)$ and the previous hidden state $h(t-1)$. The output is denoted as $y(t)$. The output of input, hidden and output layers are computed as:

$$x(t) = w_i p(t) + w_h h(t-1) + b_h \quad (3)$$

$$h(t) = \sigma\big(x(t)\big) \quad (4)$$

$$y(t) = g\big(w_y h(t) + b_y\big) \quad (5)$$

where w_i is the matrix of connection between CNN and the input layer of RNN; w_h plays role in updating network state or context; and w_y is the matrix of connection between hidden layer and output layer. Both of b_h and b_y are bias vectors. Here, $\sigma(.)$ is the sigmoid activation function; $g(.)$ is the softmax function. $x(t)$ is the joint representation of current pair and context. Our approach is able to capture the context by updating the hidden state $h(t)$.

To train the networks proposed here, we use the backpropagation through time with stochastic gradient descent (SGD) algorithm. At each training step, error vector is computed according to cross entropy criterion, weights are updated as:

$$Error(t;\theta) = R(t) - y(t) \quad (6)$$

where $y(t)$ is the result from our system, and $R(t)$ is the true class; and θ includes all the parameters of CNN and RNN.

3 Experiments

3.1 Experimental setup

We evaluate our approach (R&CNN) on both the development and test data of this answer selection challenge. The statistics of experimental dataset are summarized in Table 1. In this dataset, there are 3,229 questions and 21,062 answers, and the percentage of good comments is about 50%. The average length of comment sequence is 6.

data	#question	#comment	#average	% good
Train	2600	16541	6.36	48.78
Devel	300	1645	5.48	53.19
Test	329	1976	6.00	50.46

Table 1. Statistics of experimental dataset

In our approach, we use 100-dimensional word embedding trained on the provided Qatar Living data with Word2vec (Mikolov et al., 2013). The maximum size of coding the sentences with word embedding is set to be 100, and we use 3-words sliding window for 1D-convolution. The learning rate is initialized to be 0.01 and adapted dynamically using *ADADELTA* Method (Matthew, 2012). Based on the results on development set, all the hyperparameters of our approach are optimized on train set.

Table 2 lists the experimental methods and the corresponding official results. The baselines of comment sequence labeling include the method based on CRF and the approach CRF+V, which integrates distributed representation learnt from our approach (R&CNN). In addition, we illustrate the best result achieved by the supervised feature-rich approach *SFR*[1].

Results	Methods
ICRC-HIT-primary	CRF+V
ICRC-HIT-contrastive1	R&CNN
ICRC-HIT-contrastive2	CRF
JAIST-contrasive1	SFR

Table 2. The official results and experimental methods

[1]It is the approach of JAIST team in subtask-A English.

3.2 Results and analysis

Table 3 and Table 4 illustrate the results in development and test dataset respectively. As can be seen, our proposed R&CNN outperforms CRF and CRF+V on whole performances. Specifically, R&CNN achieves the state-of-the-art with the accuracy 73.18%, and 79.76% in F1-value of predicting *Good* class while performs 53.82% in Macro-F1 on the test dataset.

Methods	Macro.	Acc.	P	R	F1
CRF	50.56	59.82	72.41	**77.37**	74.81
CRF+V	**52.14**	**61.03**	74.80	76.00	**75.40**
R&CNN	52.10	60.85	**75.09**	75.09	75.09

Table 3. Performances on development dataset (%)

Methods	Macro.	Acc.	P	R	F1
CRF	40.54	60.12	57.90	**95.89**	72.21
CRF+V	49.50	67.86	65.99	91.68	76.74
R&CNN	53.82	**73.18**	74.39	85.96	**79.76**
SFR	**57.29**	72.67	**80.51**	78.03	79.11

Table 4. Performances on test dataset (%)

Compared to CRF and CRF+V, our approach outperforms them in evolution metrics. There are several reasons for the unsatisfying performances of CRF and CRF+V. First, it is sparse to extract semantic features of question-comment pairs from short contents in baselines. In contrast, the distributed representation learned from our model is able to capture semantic relationship between words of question-comment pairs based on deep convolution and pooling. Secondly, there are large amount of noise information involved in CQA, such as various emotional symbols and the abbreviated words. The feature-engineering of CRF based method generally suffers from the quality of dataset. Besides of that, the divergences of class distribution between the development and test influence the effectiveness directly. Hence, our approach performs more powerful and adaptive to different dataset or new domain. We also can demonstrate this point by comparing the experimental results of CRF and CRF+V on the test (shown in Table 4). By integrating the distributed representation from our R&CNN, CRF+V improves 9% on Macro-F1, 7.74% on accuracy over CRF, and 4.53% in F1-value of predicting *Good* class.

Taking only word embedding as the original features, our approach has achieved 53.82% in Macro-F1. In contrast, the supervised feature-rich (SFR) approach performs 57.29% in Macro-F1 by integrating multi-type features, such as word embedding, features from topic models and user metadata etc. The main reason for that is the low performance of our approach on predicting the answers of *Potential* class, which has a major import on Macro-F1 due to the effect of marcoaveraging. There are several factors for that result. The first is the imbalance distribution in training data, which is lacking of the train samples of *Potential* class. So the distributed models based purely on word embedding are not very well equipped to learn the meaningful representations for question and potential comments. Secondly, *Potential* class is an intermediate category (Màrquez et al., 2015) that was quite hard to human annotators. Hence, surface-form matching between the words of question-comment pair is hard to identify its correct class merely using word embedding.

In addition, when considering the heavy reliance of feature-engineer of SFR in comparison to the simplicity of our approach, the Macro-F1 our approach obtained is highly encouraging. What's more, our model achieves the start-of-the-art in accuracy and F1-value of *Good* class. These promising results indicate the effectiveness of our approach in predicting the high-quality comments in CQA.

4 Conclusion

In this paper, we present a comment labeling system based on the deep learning architecture. Without the complicated feature-engineering and external semantic resources, the recurrent convolutional neural networks (R&CNN) approach proposed by us not only is able to capture semantic matching patterns between question and comments, but also learn the meaningful context in the comment sequence. In this answer selection task, our approach achieves the state-of-the-art on recognizing good comments, and performs better accuracy than baselines while obtains powerful results in Macro-F1.

In the future, we would like to investigate the methods of training the imbalance data (e.g. the *Potential* class) to improve the performances of our approach, such as the typical oversampling and undersampling methods.

Acknowledgments

This work was supported in part by the National N atural Science Foundation of China (61272383, 61 173075 and 61203378), the Strategic Emerging In dustry Development Special Funds of Shenzhen (J CYJ20120613151940045).

References

Baotian Hu, Zhengdong Lu, Hang Li, Qingcai Chen. 2014. Convolutional neural network architectures for matching natural language sentences. In Proceedings of Neural Information Processing Systems (NIPS), Montreal, Quebec, Canada. 2014.

Baoxun Wang, Bingquan Liu, Chengjie Sun, Xiaolong Wang, and Lin Sun. 2009. Extracting Chinese Question-Answer Pairs from Online Forums. IEEE International Conference on Systems, Man, and Cybernetics (SMC), pages 1159-1164. 2009.

Haifeng Hu, Bingquan Liu, Baoxun Wang, Ming Liu, Xiaolong Wang. 2013. Multimodal DBN for predicting high-quality answers in cQA portals. In Proceedings of Association for Computational Linguistics (ACL), pages 843–847, Sofia, *Bulgaria.* 2013.

Jizhou Huang, Ming Zhou, and Dan Yang. 2007. Extracting chatbot knowledge from online discussion forums. In Proceedings of International Joint Conference on Artificial Intelligence (IJCAI), pages 423–428, Hyderabad, India. 2007.

Lei Yu, Karl Moritz Hermann, Phil Blunsom, Stephen Pulman. 2014. Deep learning for answer sentence selection. In Proceeding of Neural Information Processing Systems (NIPS): Deep Learning and Representation Learning Workshop, Montreal, Quebec, Canada. 2014.

Lin Chen, Richi Nayak. 2008. Expertise Analysis in a Question Answer Portal for Author Ranking. IEEE/WIC/ACM International Conference on Web Intelligence and Intelligent Agent Technology (WI-IAT), pages 134-140. 2008.

Lluís Màrquez, James Glass, Walid Magdy, Alessandro Moschitti, Preslav Nakov, and Bilal Randeree. 2015. SemEval-2015 Task 3: Answer Selection in Community Question Answering. In Proceedings of the 9th International Workshop on Semantic Evaluation (SemEval-2015). 2015

Matthew D. Zeiler. 2012. ADADELTA: An Adaptive Learning Rate Method. CoRR abs/1212.5701. 2012

Nai Kalchbrenner, Edward Grefenstette, and Phil Blunsom. A convolutional neural network for modelling sentences. In Proceedings of the Association for Computational Linguistics (ACL), pages 655-665, Baltimore, USA. 2014.

Richard Socher, Brody Huval, Christopher D. Manning, and Andrew Y. Ng. 2012. Semantic compositionality through recursive matrix-vector spaces. In Proceedings of Empirical Methods on Natural Language Processing and Computational Natural Language Learning (EMNLP), pages 1201-1211, Jeju Island, Korea. 2012.

Chirag Shah and Jefferey Pomerantz. 2010. Evaluating and predicting answer quality in community QA. In the 33rd International Conference on Research and development information retrieval on Research and Development in Information Retrieval (SIGIR'10), pages 411-418, NewYork, USA. 2010.

Shilin Ding, Gao Cong, Chin-Yew Lin, and Xiaoyan Zhu. 2008. Using conditional random fields to extract contexts and answers of questions from online forums. In Proceedings of Association for Computational Linguistics (ACL), pages 710-718, Columbus, Ohis, USA. 2008.

Tom Mikolov, Kai Chen, Greg Corrado, and Jeffrey Dean. 2013. Efficient estimation of word representations in vector space. CoRR, abs/1301.3781. 2013

Nicolas Boulanger-Lewandowski, Yoshua Bengio, and Pascal Vincent. 2012. Modeling temporal dependencies in high-dimensional sequences: Application to polyphonic music generation and transcription. In Proceedings of the 29th International Conference on Machine Learning (ICML), Edinburgh, Scotland, UK. 2012.

JAIST: Combining multiple features for Answer Selection in Community Question Answering

Quan Hung Tran[1], **Vu Duc Tran**[1], **Tu Thanh Vu**[2], **Minh Le Nguyen**[1], **Son Bao Pham**[2]
[1]Japan Advanced Institute of Science and Technology
[2]University of Engineering and Technology, Vietnam National University, Hanoi
[1]{quanth,vu.tran,nguyenml}@jaist.ac.jp
[2]{tuvt,sonpb}@vnu.edu.vn

Abstract

In this paper, we describe our system for SemEval-2015 Task 3: Answer Selection in Community Question Answering. In this task, the systems are required to identify the good or potentially good answers from the answer thread in Community Question Answering collections. Our system combines 16 features belong to 5 groups to predict answer quality. Our final model achieves the best result in subtask A for English, both in accuracy and F1-score.

1 Introduction

Nowadays, community question answering (cQA) websites like Yahoo! Answers play a crucial role in supporting people to seek desired information. Users can post their questions on these sites for finding help as well as personal advice. However, the quality of these answers varies greatly. Typically, only a few of the answers in an answer thread are useful to the users and it may take a lot of efforts to identify them manually. Thus, a system that automatically identifies answer quality is much needed.

The task of identifying answer quality has been studied by many researchers in the field of Question Answering. Many methods have been proposed: web redundancy information (Magnini et al., 2002), non-textual features (Jeon et al., 2006), textual entailment (Wang and Neumann, 2007), syntactic features (Grundström and Nugues, 2014). However, most of these works used independent dataset and evaluation metrics; thus it is difficult to compare the results of these methods. The SEMEVAL task 3 (Màrquez et al., 2015) addresses this problem by providing a common framework to compare different methods in multiple languages.

Our system incorporates a range of features: word-matching features, special component features, topic-modeling-based features, translation-based features and non-textual features to achieve the best performance in subtask A (Màrquez et al., 2015). In the remainder of the paper, we will describe our system with the focus on the features.

2 System Description

For extracting the features, we first preprocess the questions and the answers then build a number of models based on training data or other sources (Figure 1).

2.1 Preprocessing

All the questions and the answers are preprocessed through the following steps: Tokenization, POS-tagging, Syntactic parsing, Dependency parsing, Lemmatization, Stopword removal, Name-Entity recognition. These preprocessing steps are completed using The Stanford CoreNLP Natural Language Processing Toolkit (Manning et al., 2014). Because of the noisy nature of community data, the syntactic parsing, dependency parsing and Name-Entity recognition steps do not produce highly accurate results. Thus, we rely mainly on the bag-of-word representation of text. Removing stopwords or lemmatization can alter the meaning of the text, so in the system, we keep both the original version and the processed version of the text. The choice between using the two versions is made using experiments in

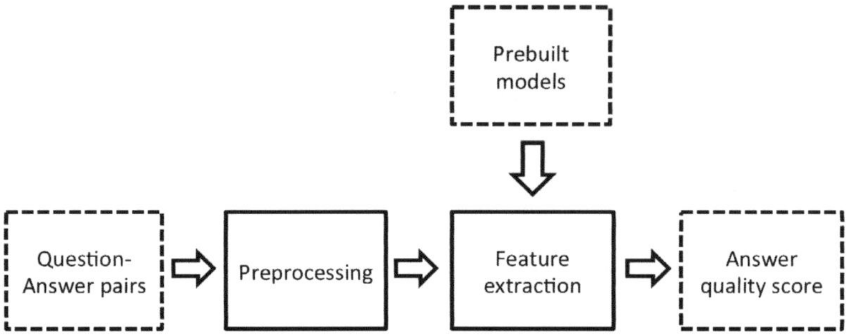

Figure 1: *System components*

development set.

2.2 Building models from data

In this section, we describe the resources we use, or build for extracting features, these resources are: Translation models, LDA models, Word vector representation models, Word Lists. The translation models are built to bridge the lexical chasm between the questions and the answers (Surdeanu et al., 2008). In previous works (Jeon et al., 2005; Zhou et al., 2011), monolingual translation models between questions have been successfully used in finding similar questions in Question Answering archive. We adapt the idea and build translation models between the questions and their answers using the training data and the Qatar Living forum data. We treat the question-answer pairs similar to dual language sentence pairs in machine translation. First, each question-answer pair is tokenized and all special characters are removed. In the process, if any answer has too few tokens (less than two tokens), it is removed from the training data. Then the translation probabilities are calculated by IBM Model 1 (Brown et al., 1993) and Hidden Markov Model. Each model is trained with 200 iterations. The calculated translation probabilities help us to calculate the probability that an answer is the translation of the question. The translation feature will be detailed in Section 2.3.

We build two topic models, the first one is trained in the training data, the second one is trained in Wikipedia data[1] using Gensim toolkit (Řehůřek and Sojka, 2010) and Mallet toolkit (McCallum, 2002). These LDA models have 100 topics. The choice between which model will be used is based on experiments in the development set.

We experiment with two word vector representation models built using Word2Vec tool (Mikolov et al., 2013), the first one is pre-trained word2vec model provided by the authors, and the second one is trained from the Qatar Living forum data. Our Word2Vec model was built with word vector size of 300, window size of 3 (n-skip-gram, n=3) and minimum word frequency of 1. In Section 2.3, we detail how to extract feature using these models.

We also build several word lists from the training set to extract features:

- The words that usually appear on each type of answers (Good, Bad, Potential).
- The words pairs (one from the question, one from the good answers) that have high frequency in the training set. We aim to extract the information about word collocations through this list.

2.3 Features

Word-matching feature group: This feature group exploits the surface word-based similarity between the Question and the Answer to assign score:

- Cosine similarity:

$$cosine\_sim = \frac{\sum_{i=1}^{n} u_i \times v_i}{\sqrt{\sum_{i=1}^{n} (u_i)^2} \times \sqrt{\sum_{i=1}^{n} (v_i)^2}} \quad (1)$$

With *u* and *v* are binary bag of words vectors (with stopwords are removed), u_i is the i-th dimension of vector *u* and *n* is vector size. This

[1]The compressed version of all article from Wikipedia downloaded at http://dumps.wikimedia.org/enwiki/

feature returns the cosine similarity between question vector and answer vector.

- Dependency cosine similarity: We represent the questions and the answers as bag of word-dependency, with words are associated with their dependency label in the dependency tree. For example: a dependency arc in the dependency tree: prep(buy-4, for-7) will generate the following word-dependency: prep-by-for. We consider the sentence to be the collection of these word-dependencies. The cosine similarity score is calculated similar to bag-of-word cosine similarity.

- Word alignment: We also use the Meteor toolkit (Denkowski and Lavie, 2014) to align the words from the question and the answers, and use the alignment score returned as a feature in the feature space

- Noun match: This feature is similar to Cosine similarity feature, however; only nouns are retained in the bag-of-word.

Special-component feature group: This feature group identifies the special characteristics of the answers that show the answer quality:

- Special words feature: This feature identifies if an answer contains some of the special tokens (question marks, laugh symbols). Typically, the posts that contains this type of tokens are not a serious answer (laugh symbols), or a further question (question marks). The laugh symbols are identified using a regular expression.

- Typical words feature: This feature identifies if an answer contains some specific words that are typical for an answer quality class (good, bad, potential). The typical word lists are built using training data and described in the previous section. After the experiment step, however, only the typical word list for bad answers was found to be effective and was used in the final version of the system.

Non-textual feature group: This feature group exploits some non-textual information of the posts in the answer thread to assign answer quality:

- Question author feature: This feature identifies if an answer in the answer thread belongs to the author of the question. If a post belongs to the author of the question, it is very unlikely to be an answer.

- Question category: We also include the question category (27 categories) in the feature space because we found out that the quality distribution of different types of question are very different.

- The number of posts from the same user: We include the number of posts from the same user as a feature because we observe that if a user has a large number of posts, most of them will be non-informative, irrelevant to the original question.

Topic model based feature: We use the previously mentioned LDA models to transform questions and answers to topic vectors and calculate the cosine similarity between the topic vectors of the question and its answers. We use this feature because a question and its correct answer should be about similar topics. After experimenting on the development set, only the LDA model built from training data is effective and thus, it is used in the final system.

Word Vector representation based feature: We use the word vector representation to model the relevance between the question and the answer. All the questions and answers are tokenized and the words are transformed to vector using the pre-trained word2vec model. Each word in the question will then be aligned to the word in the answer that has the highest vector cosine similarity. The returned value will be the sum of the scores of these alignments normalized by the question's length:

$$align(w_i) = \max_{0<j\leq m}(cosine(w_i, w'_j)) \quad (2)$$

$$word2vec\_sim = \frac{\sum_{i=1}^{n} align(w_i)}{n} \quad (3)$$

With $cosine(w_i, w'_j)$ is the cosine similarity of two vector representations of i-th word in the question with the j-th word in the answer. n and m are the length (in number of words) of the question and the answer respectively.

Translation based feature: We use the previously mentioned translation models to find the word to word alignments between the question and the answer. This feature is calculated similar to the Word Vector representation based feature. Each word in the question will be aligned with the word in the answer with the highest translation score. The feature value will be the sum of translation scores normalized by question' length.

2.4 System run configuration

The straightforward way to identify the quality classes for answers is using a classification model. However, the classification model has problem in identifying the Potential class. In our experiments, the classification model ignores the Potential class entirely. This problem may be caused by our feature design as the features actually aim to identify either good or bad answers.

To solve this problem, we use another approach. As we observe the data, most of the Potential answers can be considered "Not good enough" and "Not bad enough". An answer which is not quite good nor quite bad can be considered "Potential", thus using a regression model[2] to score the quality of the answer would probably be better. In our experiment with the development data, the regression model outperforms the classification model by 3.4 F-measure score.

Features are extracted from the answers (with their questions treated as the context), and then the feature values are passed through a regression model. However, the provided data only has quality classes but not regression value, thus we need to assign the regression value for each answer quality class: 1.0 for Good answers, 0.5 for Potential answers, and 0.0 for Bad answers.

Our system runs are different in the feature space. Our best run (JAIST-contrastive1) uses all the features described above. Our main run (JAIST-primary) excludes the topic-modeling based feature while the third run (JAIST-contrastive2) includes several other experimental features that did not have contribution when tested on the development set.

[2]We use SVM-regression model in WEKA toolkit (Hall et al., 2009)

Table 1: System performance

Runs	F1-score	Accuracy	Rank
primary	57.19 (%)	72.52 (%)	2
contrastive1	57.29 (%)	72.67 (%)	1
contrastive2	46.96 (%)	57.74 (%)	18

Table 2: Detail Class F1-score

Runs	F1-score
Good	78.96 (%)
Bad	78.24 (%)
Potential	14.36 (%)

3 Result and Discussion

We only take part in subtask A for English. Our system has the best accuracy and F1-score in subtask A (primary runs) shown in Table 1. Classifying the Potential class is quite difficult (Màrquez et al., 2015) and our system only achieve 14.36 % F1 score on this class. Although the use of regression model partly solves this problem, our feature space is not adequate for identifying this class reliably (Table 2)

4 Conclusion

In this paper, we present our approach for the subtask A - English of the SEMEVAL 2015 task 3 - Answer Selection in Community Question Answering. We propose an Answer quality scoring based approach for classifying answers in Community Question Answering. Our system achieves high results in the task, however, does not handle the Potential class well. A possible explanation is that we still rely heavily on the bag-of-word representation of text. In the future, other semantically rich representations of text would be employed to improve performance.

References

Peter F. Brown, Vincent J. Della Pietra, Stephen A. Della Pietra, and Robert L. Mercer. The Mathematics of Statistical Machine Translation: Parameter Estimation. *Computational Linguistics*, 19(2):263–311, June 1993.

Jakob Grundström and Pierre Nugues. Using Syntactic Features in Answer Reranking. In *AAAI 2014 Workshop on Cognitive Computing for Augmented Human Intelligence*, pages 13–19, 2014.

Mark Hall, Eibe Frank, Geoffrey Holmes, Bernhard Pfahringer, Peter Reutemann, and Ian H. Witten. The WEKA Data Mining Software: An Update. *SIGKDD Explor. Newsl.*, 11(1):10–18, November 2009.

Jiwoon Jeon, W. Bruce Croft, and Joon Ho Lee. Finding Similar Questions in Large Question and Answer Archives. In *Proceedings of the 14th ACM International Conference on Information and Knowledge Management*, CIKM '05, pages 84–90, New York, NY, USA, 2005.

Jiwoon Jeon, W. Bruce Croft, Joon Ho Lee, and Soyeon Park. A Framework to Predict the Quality of Answers with Non-textual Features. In *Proceedings of the 29th Annual International ACM SIGIR Conference on Research and Development in Information Retrieval*, SIGIR '06, pages 228–235, New York, NY, USA, 2006.

Michael Denkowski Alon Lavie. Meteor Universal: Language Specific Translation Evaluation for Any Target Language. *ACL 2014*, page 376, 2014.

Bernardo Magnini, Matteo Negri, Roberto Prevete, and Hristo Tanev. Is it the right answer?: exploiting web redundancy for Answer Validation. In *Proceedings of the 40th Annual Meeting on Association for Computational Linguistics*, pages 425–432, 2002.

Christopher D Manning, Mihai Surdeanu, John Bauer, Jenny Finkel, Steven J Bethard, and David McClosky. The Stanford CoreNLP natural language processing toolkit. In *Proceedings of 52nd Annual Meeting of the Association for Computational Linguistics: System Demonstrations*, pages 55–60, 2014.

Andrew Kachites McCallum. MALLET: A Machine Learning for Language Toolkit. http://mallet.cs.umass.edu, 2002.

Tomas Mikolov, Kai Chen, Greg Corrado, and Jeffrey Dean. Efficient Estimation of Word Representations in Vector Space. *CoRR*, abs/1301.3781, 2013.

Lluís Màrquez, James Glass, Walid Magdy, Alessandro Moschitti, Preslav Nakov, and Bilal Randeree. SemEval-2015 Task 3: Answer Selection in Community Question Answering. In *Proceedings of the 9th International Workshop on Semantic Evaluation (SemEval 2015)*.

Radim Řehůřek and Petr Sojka. Software Framework for Topic Modelling with Large Corpora. In *Proceedings of the LREC 2010 Workshop on New Challenges for NLP Frameworks*, pages 45–50, Valletta, Malta, May 2010.

Mihai Surdeanu, Massimiliano Ciaramita, and Hugo Zaragoza. Learning to rank answers on large online QA collections. In *In Proceedings of the 46th Annual Meeting for the Association for Computational Linguistics: Human Language Technologies (ACL-08: HLT*, pages 719–727, 2008.

Rui Wang and Günter Neumann. DFKILT at AVE 2007: Using Recognizing Textual Entailment for Answer Validation. In *In online proceedings of CLEF 2007 Working Notes, ISBN*, pages 2–912335, 2007.

Guangyou Zhou, Li Cai, Jun Zhao, and Kang Liu. Phrase-based Translation Model for Question Retrieval in Community Question Answer Archives. In *Proceedings of the 49th Annual Meeting of the Association for Computational Linguistics: Human Language Technologies - Volume 1*, HLT '11, pages 653–662, Stroudsburg, PA, USA, 2011.

Shiraz: A Proposed List Wise Approach to Answer Validation

Amin Heydari Alashty **Saeed Rahmani** **Meysam Roostaee** **Mostafa Fakhrahmad**
Shiraz University
Eram Street
Shiraz, Iran
heidari@cse.shirazu.ac.ir
{srahmani,mroostaee,mfakhrahmad}@shirazu.ac.ir

Abstract

Answer Validation is an important step in Automatic Question Answering systems and nowadays by spreading Community Question Answering systems it is known as an important task by itself. Previous works just considered it as a binary classification problem in which they try to find the best answer among all the candidate answers for a question. Accordingly, they do not consider the possible unique information which may have been included other answers. This can be considered by having a multiclass label classification problem, it is not only able to find the best answer but also can find "potentially good", "bad", and etc. answers too. By doing so, it is fully expected to extract and rate all the necessary information from existing candidates to help questioner to find the best and general answer for his question. This work tries to consider some features which are gained from importance of comments of the questioner. Finally, by using a good classifier, we try to overcome this problem. The designed system participated in subtask A of the Semeval-2015 Task 3. The primary submission ranked at the 5th and 7th places in four class label and three class label evaluation, accordingly.

1 Introduction

By spreading Community Question Answering (CQA) systems, there have been created a new taxonomy for Question Answering (QA) systems: Regular QAs, and CQAs. A regular QA, accepts a natural language input and after searching into it's available resources, returns the best shortest answer, it could find. In these systems, answering to factoid questions may be an easier challenge than the other question types. One of the features of CQA systems is its users. Once one asks a question, others try to answer that question. Then these kinds of systems just try to use users knowledge to answer users questions. Of course instead of finding the correct answer of an asked question from some candidate answers which must be done by questioner, system tries to tell the questioner which answer is helpful and which one is not. Then discussing about factoid questions is maybe so hard and it could not be handled just by using the answers and questions body, rather, it should have access to a great knowledge source to check if an answer is correct or not.

Community Question Answering systems' spreaded over the internet, and accordingly, it made researchers to be interested in getting involved to the challenges related to these systems. One of the main challenges which may be so important in the aspect of all the people who are using these systems is Answer Validation. More researches has been done as CQA systems are getting more and more popular. This challenge is a kind of classification problem which classifies comments of a question and by doing so, it can help questioner to find the correct answer, sooner, and without spending so much time to read all the comments. Alternately, it can help other web users who had searched for the similar question in a search engine and redirected to our website, to find the answer they are looking for. Next it can help us to find the questions without any proper answer, and in addition it can be used for question routing challenge (Gkotsis et al., 2014).

Eventually its important to CQA systems owners to attract more users and accordingly, attracting more users means earning more money.

In this work a new type of features will be discussed which could be gained by considering the information of questioner comments. Experiments shows, this kind of features are more valuable in contrast of the most valuable features of previous works.

Some previous works focused on the deep textual features such as syntactic, lexical, and discourse features to find the best answer. And some others tried to overcome this problem using shallow features such as word count in an answer, answer count for a question, (Gkotsis et al., 2014; Toba et al., 2014). Some others, tried to propose a solution by using reputational features of such a system like user rating (a high ranked user may produce a more reliable answer), Answer rating (an answer with more ratings from other users may be more reliable), (Anderson et al., 2012).

Of course previous works, mostly have just tried to find the best answer (designed a binary classifier) but present work classifies answers into six classes: *Good*, *Potential*, *Bad*, *Dialogue*, *Not English*, and *Other*. *Good* is a comment with a complete bunch of relevant information. *Potential* is a comment with some helpful information but is not a complete answer. *Bad* is a comment with no helpful information to answer the question. *Dialogue* is a comment which shows a kind of discussion between users and obviously contains no useful information. *Not English* is a comment in other languages. *Other* is a comment which is not a kind of above mentioned classes. Samples of *English*, and *Other* classes have no valuable information as samples related to *Bad* and *Dialogue* classes.

The remainder of the paper is organized as follows: related works are presented at section 2. There is an introduction to the used dataset at section 3. At section 4 the Features will be introduced. At section 5 experiments are discussed. Finally, Section 6 would have a conclusion.

2 Related Works

In (Jeon et al., 2006) there was an attempt to overcome this challenge using non-textual features. Non-textual features are acclaimed to have lots of information which can be helpful for finding class label of an answer. Its pointed that a not properly usage of these features is the cause to not have good results. For feature selection they had estimated the correlation between the feature values and the manually judged quality scores. Higher correlation means the feature is a better indicator to predict the quality of answers. Then because Maximum Entropy models need monotonic features a feature converter was used. KDE (Kernel Density Estimation) is the one which is used in this work. At last they could get a better performance than the random ranker.

In (Shah and Pomerantz, 2010) the goal is to predict if an answer was chosen by the questioner as the best answer. They have just used features related to answers, because question's features were not that much effective. Experiments were done twice: first by estimating features' values using Amazon Turk, and second by using values automatically generated from source of questions and answers and users profiles. The results show that using second approach is more useful. First approachs features are so correlated and cannot model the variability in the data but the second approachs model is quite good in terms of its power to explain the variability in the data.

(Wang et al., 2009) proposed an analogical reasoning-based approach to measure the analogy between the new question-answer linkages and those of previous relevant knowledge which only contains positive links. And the most analogous link was assumed to be the best answer. There is an assumption that provides each answer is connected to its question with various types of latent links. Positive links indicating high-quality answers and Negative links indicating incorrect answers or user-generated spam. This work tried to solve problem of lexical gap between questions and answers. To do so, similar question and answer pairs from available questions and their correct answers in the system were utilized.

In (Surdeanu et al., 2011) linguistic features were used to represent content. The proposed method is called FMIX (feature mix), that is a mixture of four types of features: Similarity Features, Translation Features, Density/Frequency Features, and Web Correlation Features. Value of these set of features estimated using a generative model but a discriminative model (SVM, Perceptron are used) was used to combine them.

In (Gkotsis et al., 2014) some shallow textual features (like answer count, longest sentence length and any other feature which does not need that much effort to retrieve from text like semantic or syntactic features) had been mainly considered. Experimental results for different mixtures of mentioned features and some other types like reputational features (e.g. answer rating, question rating) had been estimated to confirm a suitable usage of shallow features can result a prosper approach. This work's main contribution is proposing a discretization method to solve language evolution, generality problems, and accuracy. The discretization method is consists of three steps: grouping (group answers related to a question), sorting (sort answers according to their value for that feature), and discretization (assign a rank for each answer, starting from 1 and incrementing this rank by one).

In (Toba et al., 2014) a 2-layer classification method has been proposed. The first layer just tries to find the type of the question and the second layer uses the result of the first layer to find the best answer of the question. For each question type there is a specific classifier at the second layer, and furthermore a feature set which consists of a mixture of shallow and deep textual features and reputational features.

3 Dataset

The source of the corpus is the Qatar Living Forum data[1]. Details of the method of extracting and labeling its content are described at (Màrquez et al., 2015). This corpus was provided into three parts: train set, development set, and test set. And for two sub-tasks. Each of the mentioned sets is consists of a number of questions and for each question, there is some comments.

4 Features

In this section, features used for training and testing the classifier are introduced. Some shallow textual features are considered. Alternatively, we tried to extract and use reputational features as well. Some of the shallow features used, are the same as shallow features in (Gkotsis et al., 2014; Toba et al., 2014) and some other features are from the available information in the corpus like: Creation Date, Category, and Question Type. It was assumed Questioners comments can be so informative, experiments show that, features which are using this fact can be so effective.

4.1 Reputational Features

An important part of CQA systems is users reputational information. There are some previous works used the authority of the users like Anderson (2012). There is somehow no explicit information in our train set to have features of this type. But by knowing that there is an overlap between user set whose questions or comments are presented in train set and in test set two features were added to cover this type:

- **Which User Group**: gives to all comments of a certain user a unique identifier.
- **Which User Category**: gives to each comment of a certain user in each category a unique identifier.

4.2 List Wise Features

Some approaches tried to use some kinds of prior knowledge like previous available questions and their comments in system. Some others without caring about that knowledge just tried to overcome this problem using the information exists in domain of a question. In this work the most important extracted feature is presented in this type. Its according to the fact that, valuable information can be gained from differentiating questioner and commenters comments. At first we used 2 features to use this information and we were hopeful that our machine learning method can detect the relationship between these two features:

- **Questioner Id**: questioner identifier which is represented by QUSERID in dataset.
- **Commenter Id**: commenter identifier which is represented by CUSERID in dataset.

But disappointingly, those methods could not detect relationships. Then one aspect of their relationships is used and ids eliminated:

[1] http://www.qatarLiving.com/forum

- **Is Commenter Asker**: its a binary feature. *Zero* would be assigned to a comment if its CUSERID is different from QUSERID of the corresponding question. Then one would be assigned to a comment which its CUSERID is the same as the QUSERID.

Emperical results show that, this feature can seperate samples of "Dialogue" class in an acceptable rate. When a questioner make a comment, this comment can be classified into different classes as below:

- **Dialogue**: If questioner just wants to express his opinion about previous comments to his question or may be in another case, if questioner is comminicating with other users about his question using comments, and may be some other cases this comments can be classified as Dialogue class.
- **Good, Potential**: If questioner himself had found the correct answer or at least the his expected answer, he can make a comment to share the answer to other and again in this case and may be some other cases this kind of comment can be classified into Good or Potential classes.
- **Bad**: Questioner even can make a bad comment. It can has some reasons like: if he had been hopeless of receiving any response from other users then this situation can make him to post a irrelevant comment which can not help to find the answer of question.

Of course, its believed that this feature is not the true complete potentiality of the mentioned fact. There is a ranking between all the above discussed features in Table 1 according to their Gain Ratio. Answer Count is the feature with the best Information Gain (IG) in Gkotsis (2014). But it's obvious that the "Is Commenter Asker" which is a List Wise feature has gained a much better Gain Ratio from other features.

5 Experiments

5.1 Learning Method

Different kinds of learning methods had been tested to find the best method. At last, J48 method could result better than the others. Then it used in a bagging method. Weka (Hall et al., 2009) was used to apply learning methods to extracted features. The overall configurations in Weka are:

Bagging -P 100 -S 1 -I 10 -W weka.classifiers.trees.J48 – -C 0.25 -M 10

Before test set release time, 10-Fold cross validation was used for system evaluation. (-I 10) Experiments shown that the best minNumObj option in J48 method is 10 for this problem. (-M 10)

Feature	Gain Ratio
Is Commenter Asker	0.18002
Answer Count	0.0431
Type	0.03762
Category	0.01835
Length	0.01678
Avg Word Per Sentence	0.01671
Avg Char Per Sentence	0.01503
Longest Sentence	0.01296
Which User Group	0.00847
Creation Date	0.00817
Which User Category	0.0042

Table 1: General Features Gain Ration.

5.2 Discussion

As previously mentioned, CQA systems dataset are unbalanced. According to this fact, two types of train data has been generated from questions and comments. First one has the same number of comments and Second one is generated from the first set, of course with additionally redundant smaples. For each class, redundant samples have been added till its samples number get equal to the majority class. The first model was submitted as contrastive1 and the second model was the primary submission.

There was two ways of evaluation in this task. First one maps "Dialogue", "Not English", "Other" class labels to "Bad" class label, and this was called "COARSE EVALUATION" and official ranking of teams was done according to this measurement. And the second one maps just "Not English", and "Other" class labels to "Bad" class label, and it was called "FINE-GRAINED EVALUATION".

Shiraz group's primary submission has gained two different ranking according to each of the evaluation methods. According to fine-grained evaluation, we were ranked as the 5th, and according to coarse evaluation, were ranked as the 7th team, and the latter ranking is our official ranking for subtask A. For each of the groups two measure were estimated: F1-Score and Accuracy. Groups were ranked according to F1-Score. Shiraz's two most important submissions for each of the evaluation methods measurements are shown in Table 2.

Most of previous works had just tried to improve accuracy of their system, but using macro-F1 as the measurement of official ranking has shown that considering accuracy in this problem which has multi class labels, and data is imbalance can not be a good idea. For example, there may be a system which just tries to cover classes with majority samples in data set then it is expected to improve accuracy but it can not ensure that it could gain a suitable macro-F1. It's because that system may not be able to classify correctly samples of other classes. It means, the best system is the one which could has the best behaviour in all the classes not just some of them.

At last, it needs to be mentioned that the list wise approach is not limited to a special kind of features like textual or non-textual features. Of course, it can help to extract some new features which are so helpful to improve the classifier.

	F1-Score	Accuracy
Prm[2]_Coarse	47.34	56.83
Contr[3]_Coarse	45.03	62.55
Prm_Fine	40.06	48.53
Contrl_Fine	37.77	55.16

Table 2: System Evaluation Measure values.

The most important point in Gkotsis (2014) is discretization method. That method had been used for some continuous shallow features, but as can be seen in Table 3 F1-Score is not improved. Then the discretization method described in Gkotsis (2014) is not useful for this problem on this dataset.

[2]Primary

[3]Contrastive

	F1-Score	Accuracy
UnBalanced_Coarse	42.85	61.74
Balanced_Coarse	25.89	36.84
UnBalanced_Fine	36.61	52.83
Balanced_Fine	21.09	23.48

Table 3: System evaluation measure value for discretized Feature values.

6 Conclusion

By widely spreading of Community Question Answering systems, solving challenges of these systems is essential. The proposed system aims to improve previous solutions for Answer Validation using some new valuable features. Moreover, questioners comments have been introduced as a source of feature which can be used for extracting more powerful features from it. Only one feature was extracted using this source in this work, but it was the most valuable one. Using just a few number of features Shiraz system could gain an acceptable ranking.

As mentioned before in this kind of problems F1-score is the main measurement which should be improved in designig a system, but empirically it was shown that discretization is not helpful to achieve this goal.

Acknowledgments

We thank Living Qatar for providing data and Semeval task organizers for organizing this problem.

It is essential to thank Dr. Hooman Tahayori, Abolfazl Moridi, and all other people help us in this work with their comments.

References

Anderson, Ashton and Huttenlocher, Daniel and Kleinberg, Jon and Leskovec, Jure (2012). Discovering value from community activity on focused question answering sites: a case study of stack overflow. In Proceedings of the 18th ACM SIGKDD International Conference on Knowledge Discovery and Data Mining (pp. 850-858).

Gkotsis, George and Stepanyan, Karen and Pedrinaci, Carlos and Domingue, John and Liakata, Maria (2014). It's all in the content: state of the art best answer prediction based on discretisation of shallow linguistic features. In Proceedings of the 2014 ACM conference on Web science (pp. 202-210).

Hall, Mark and Frank, Eibe and Holmes, Geoffrey and Pfahringer, Bernhard and Reutemann, Peter and Witten, Ian H. (2009). The WEKA data mining software: an update. ACM SIGKDD Explorations Newsletter, 11(1), (pp. 10-18).

Jeon, Jiwoon and Croft, William Bruce and Lee, Joon Ho and Park, Soyeon (2006). A framework to predict the quality of answers with non-textual features. In Proceedings of the 29th annual international ACM SIGIR conference on Research and development in information retrieval (pp. 228-235).

Màrquez, Lluís and Glass, James and Magdy, Walid and Moschitti, Alessandro and Nakov, Preslav and Randeree, Bilal (2015). SemEval-2015 Task 3: Answer Selection in Community Question Answering. In Proceedings of the 9th International Workshop on Semantic Evaluation (SemEval 2015).

Shah, Chirag and Pomerantz, Jefferey (2010). Evaluating and predicting answer quality in community QA. In Proceedings of the 33rd international ACM SIGIR conference on Research and development in information retrieval (pp. 411-418).

Surdeanu, Mihai and Ciaramita, Massimiliano and Zaragoza, Hugo (2011). Learning to rank answers to non-factoid questions from web collections. Computational Linguistics, 37(2), (pp. 351-383).

Toba, Hapnes and Ming, Zhao-Yan and Adriani, Mirna and Chua, Tat-Seng (2014). Discovering high quality answers in community question answering archives using a hierarchy of classifiers. Information Sciences, 261, (pp. 101-115).

Wang, Xin-Jing and Tu, Xudong and Feng, Dan and Zhang, Lei (2009). Ranking community answers by modeling question-answer relationships via analogical reasoning. In Proceedings of the 32nd international ACM SIGIR conference on Research and development in information retrieval (pp. 179-186).

Al-Bayan: A Knowledge-based System for Arabic Answer Selection

Reham Mohamed
reham.mohmd@alexu.edu.eg
Maha Ragab
maha.ragab@alexu.edu.eg
Heba Abdelnasser
heba.abdelnasser@alexu.edu.eg
Nagwa M. El-Makky
nagwamakky@alexu.edu.eg
Marwan Torki
mtorki@alexu.edu.eg
Computer and Systems Engineering Department
Alexandria University, Egypt

Abstract

This paper describes Al-Bayan team participation in SemEval-2015 Task 3, Subtask A. Task 3 targets semantic solutions for answer selection in community question answering systems. We propose a knowledge-based solution for answer selection of Arabic questions, specialized for Islamic sciences. We build a Semantic Interpreter to evaluate the semantic similarity between Arabic question and answers using our Quranic ontology of concepts. Using supervised learning, we classify the candidate answers according to their relevance to the users questions. Results show that our system achieves 74.53% accuracy which is comparable to the other participating systems.

1 Introduction

With the increase of the popularity of community question answering (CQA) systems, answer selection became more challenging. CQA systems are often open for public to answer any questions with no restriction or review from field experts. This highlights the importance of developing systems that automatically detects the most relevant answers from the irrelevant ones. These systems might be open-domain or closed-domain, causing a tradeoff between accuracy and generality.

SemEval-2015 task 3 targets semantically oriented solutions for answer selection in community question answering data. We focus on Subtask A for the Arabic language which provides questions and several community answers from the Fatwa website[1]. The goal is to classify each answer as: Direct, Related or Irrelevant.

[1]Fatwa is a question about the Islamic religion.

In this paper, we propose a knowledge-based answer selection system for Arabic. We use our Quranic ontology, enriched with Quran verses and Tafseer books, to convert each question and its candidate answers into weighted vectors of ontology concepts. We use these vectors to compute a semantic similarity score between the question and each candidate answer. We also compute a keyword matching score and feed the two scores into a decision tree classifier which predicts how much the answer is related to the question.

The rest of the paper is organized as follows: Section 2 shows some of the related work to the system. Section 3 shows the details of the system architecture. In Section 4, we show the results of the task evaluation. Finally, we conclude the paper in Section 5.

2 Related Work

Our work is related to prior work in both Quranic research and Question Answer Selection systems.

(a) Quranic Research: Several studies have been made to understand the Quranic text and extract knowledge from it using computational linguistics. Saad et al. (2009) proposed a simple methodology for automatic extraction of concepts based on the Quran in order to build an ontology. In (Saad et al., 2010), they developed a framework for automated generation of Islamic knowledge concrete concepts that exist in the holy Quran. Qurany (Abbas, 2009) builds a Quran corpus augmented with a conceptual ontology, taken from a recognized expert source 'Mushaf Al Tajweed'. Quranic Arabic Corpus (Atwell et al., 2011) also builds a Quranic ontology of concepts based on the knowledge contained in traditional sources of Quranic analysis, including the sayings of the prophet Muhammad (PBUH), and the *Tafseer* books. Khan et al. (2013) developed a simple ontology for the Quran based on living creatures including animals and birds that are mentioned in the Quran in order to provide Quranic semantic search. AlMaayah et al. (2014) proposed to develop a WordNet for the Quran by building semantic connections between words in order to achieve a better understanding of the meanings of the Quranic words using traditional Arabic dictionaries and a Quran ontology.

Other attempts for text-mining the Quran were proposed such as: QurAna (Sharaf and Atwell, 2012) which is a corpus of the Quran annotated with pronominal anaphora and QurSim (Sharaf and Atwell, 2012) which is another corpus for extracting the relations between Quran verses.

b) Question Answer Selection Systems: Few attempts have been proposed for Arabic Answer Selection. In CLEF 2012, the Arabic language was introduced for the first time for selecting answers to questions from multiple answer choices of short Arabic texts. Abouenour et al. (2012) proposed a system based on distance density N-gram model and Arabic WordNet expansion. Trigui et al. (2012) proposed another system that used inference rules on the CLEF background collection. However, those systems have low accuracy, 0.21 and 0.19 respectively. In CLEF 2013, Al-QASIM system (Ezzeldin et al., 2013) was proposed which focused on answer selection and validation. This approach divided the task into 3 phases: (i) Document analysis, (ii) locating questions and answers and (iii) answer selection. The overall accuracy of the system is 0.36.

3 System Architecture

3.1 System Overview

The system architecture is shown in Figure 1. The dataset consists of Arabic questions and their candidate answers. The goal is to classify each candidate answer into: (Direct, Related or Irrelevant).

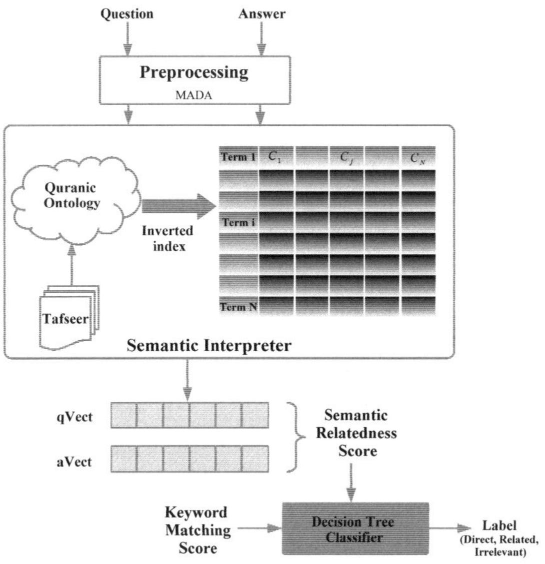

Figure 1: System Architecture.

The question and the answers are preprocessed and fed into the Semantic Interpreter. The Semantic Interpreter uses a Quranic ontology of concepts enriched with Quran interpretation *(Tafseer)* books to build an inverted index. The question is converted into a weighted vector of concepts (qVect) and similarly the candidate answer (aVect). A semantic relatedness score and a keyword matching score are computed and fed into a decision tree classifier which outputs the label of the answer.

3.2 Preprocessing

First, we apply morphological analysis on the Arabic text to identify its structure and remove the unwanted words (stopwords). For this purpose, we use MADA (Morphological Analysis and Disambiguation for Arabic) (Habash et al., 2009) which is one of the most accurate Arabic preprocessing toolkits. MADA can derive extensive morphological and contextual information from raw Arabic text, and then use this information for high-accuracy part-of-speech tagging, diacritization, lemmatization, disambiguation, stemming, and glossing in one step.

Each term in the input text is represented by its stem and POS tag using Buckwalter transliteration (Buckwalter, 2002). We identify the stopwords according to their POS tags. Pronouns, prepositions, conjunctions and other POS types are all removed.

3.3 Building the Ontology

We integrated the Quranic Corpus Ontology (Atwell et al., 2011) and the Qurany Ontology (Abbas, 2009), to form our Quranic conceptual ontology proposed in (Abdelnasser et al., 2014). The **Quranic Corpus Ontology** uses knowledge representation to define the key concepts in the Quran, and shows the relationships between these concepts using predicate logic. The **Qurany Ontology** is a tree of concepts that includes all the abstract concepts covered in the Quran. It is imported from 'Mushaf Al Tajweed' list of topics. This integration was difficult since we had to resolve the overlapping between the two ontologies. There were also some mistakes in the Qurany Concept Tree. So, we had to manually revise the 1200 concepts and their verses.

The Holy Quran consists of 6236 verses. Each verse has to be under at least one concept in our Quranic ontology. After the previous integration process, there were 621 verses without concepts, so we added them under their most suitable concepts to complete the ontology using a similarity measure module. This module measures the similarity between classified and unclassified verses to determine the concepts of unclassified verses. Now, our final ontology contains 1217 leaf concepts and all verses of the Quran. Under each concept in our ontology, we save the related verses with their *Tafseer*, that is used to build the inverted index. We use two *Tafseer*[2] books: (Ibn-Kathir, 1370) and (Al-Jaza'iri, 1986), which are two of the most traditional books used by Islamic scholars. It is possible to add other books to enrich our corpus data.

3.4 Building the Semantic Interpreter

We use machine-learning techniques to build a Semantic Interpreter using the Explicit Semantic Analysis (Gabrilovich and Markovitch, 2007) approach. The Semantic Interpreter maps the input Arabic text into a weighted vector of Quranic concepts.

For each leaf concept C_i, we construct a document D_i such that D_i contains all the verses related to this concept and their Tafseer. We used Lucene Indexer[3] to build an inverted index on the constructed documents where each term T_j is represented as a weighted vector of concepts. Entries of this vector are assigned weights using the TFIDF scheme which quantifies the strength of association between terms and concepts.

Any input query to the system can be represented as a weighted vector of concepts by calculating the mean of concept vectors of the query terms.

3.5 Semantic Relatedness Score

In order to evaluate the semantic relatedness between two Arabic texts, we enter each text into the Semantic Interpreter as a query. The Semantic Interpreter represents each text as a weighted vector of concepts. We compute the Cosine similarity between the two weighted vectors which represents the semantic relatedness score. Therefore, if two texts are semantically related, they will have similar weights for the same concepts and consequently a high Cosine similarity score, and vice versa.

3.6 Keyword Matching Score

In this mechanism, the answers of a question are weighted based on the matched words between the answers and the question. For answer k and question term j, $Score_{k_j}$ is the number of j repetitions in k normalized by the maximum number of repetitions of j in all answers. $Score_k$ is the summation of $Score_{k_j}$, $(j = 1, .., n)$ where n is the number of the question terms. Finally, we normalize all answers by the maximum $Score_k$.

3.7 Answer Classification

We compute the semantic relatedness score and the keyword matching score for each combination of question and answer in the training data. The two scores are normalized for each question. Now to classify the answers as (Direct, Related, Irrelevant), we train a decision tree classifier using the two normalized scores with the gold-standard labels supplied with the training data. The normalized scores are also computed for the test data and the classifier predicts the label of each answers. Results are shown in the next section.

[2]Tafseer is the interpretation of the Quran.

[3]http://lucene.apache.org/

Class	Direct	Related	Irrelevant	Precision	Recall	F-measure
Direct	150	40	25	0.721	0.698	0.709
Related	43	94	85	0.519	0.423	0.467
Irrelevant	15	47	502	0.820	0.890	0.854
Macro	-	-	-	0.687	0.6704	0.6765
Overall	-	-	-	0.732	0.745	0.737

Table 1: The confusion matrix, and precision,recall and F-measure of the SemEval 2015 testset.

	Training	Testing
Questions	1300	200
Answers	6500	1001
Direct	1300	215
Related	1469	222
Irrelevant	3731	564

Table 2: Statistics of the training and testing data.

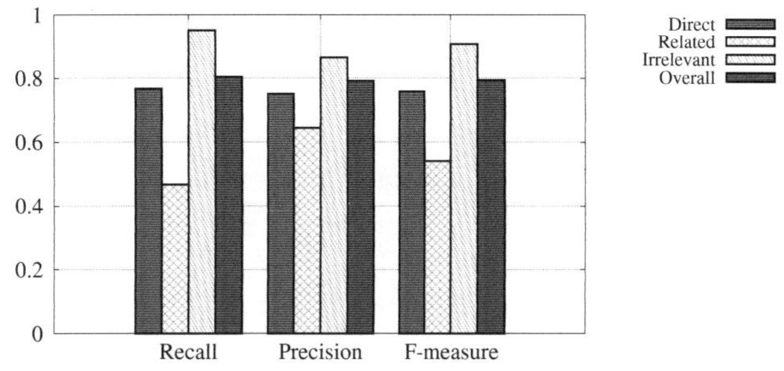

Figure 2: The training data cross validation results.

4 Evaluation

We evaluate our learning linguistic system by applying it on Fatwa questions/answers selection with a supervised learning framework.

4.1 Dataset Description

We train our classifier on the provided benchmark dataset in SemEval2015 (Màrquez et al., 2015). The used data is from Fatwa website [4]. Each question in the dataset is provided with five different answers. Each answer is labeled as Direct, Related, or Irrelevant. The distribution of the dataset we use is given in Table 2.

4.2 Results

In this section, we provide the experimental results of the training data and the SemEval 2015 test set.

Figure 2 shows the 10-folds cross validation results of the system training data using the two scores (the semantic relatedness and keyword matching scores). From the figure, the Direct and Irrelevant classes have better accuracies than the Related class. This is intuitive as the Related class is more general than the others (with few special marks), so it is more difficult to be classified.

Table 1 shows the confusion matrix of the SemEval 2015 test set results. The results also show that the Related class has lower accuracy than the Direct and Irrelevant. The overall system accuracy is 74.53% and the system Macro-F1 is 67.65%

5 Conclusion

In this paper, we proposed our system to automate the process of Arabic answer selection in Community Question Answering systems where candidate answers are classified into answers that directly answer the question vs. those that can be helpful vs. those that are irrelevant. We constructed our knowledge-based system using a Quranic semantic ontology and the provided dataset in (Màrquez et al., 2015). The system first applies some preprocessing tasks over the question and answers, then a Semantic Interpreter converts the preprocessed sentences into weighted vectors of concepts. Using those vectors the system calculates a semantic score for each answer, which is fed, with an additional keyword matching score, into a decision tree classifier. The system has an overall accuracy of 74.53%.

[4] http://fatwa.islamweb.net/

References

Abdul-Baquee M. Sharaf and Eric Atwell. 2012. *QurAna: Corpus of the Quran annotated with Pronominal Anaphora*. LREC.

Abdul-Baquee M. Sharaf and Eric Atwell. 2012. *QurSim: A corpus for evaluation of relatedness in short texts*. LREC.

Abu Bakr Al-Jaza'iri. 1986. *Aysar al-Tafasir li Kalaam il 'Aliyy il Kabir*.

Ahmed Magdy Ezzeldin, Mohamed Hamed Kholief, and Yasser El-Sonbaty. 2013. *ALQASIM: Arabic language question answer selection in machines*. In Information Access Evaluation. Multilinguality, Multimodality, and Visualization, Springer, Berlin Heidelberg.

Eric Atwell, Claire Brierley, Kais Dukes, Majdi Sawalha and Abdul-Baquee Sharaf. 2011. *A An Artificial Intelligence Approach to Arabic and Islamic Content on the Internet*. Proceedings of NITS 3rd National Information Technology Symposium.

Evgeniy Gabrilovich and Shaul Markovitch. 2007. *Computing Semantic Relatedness Using Wikipedia-based Explicit Semantic Analysis*, volume 7. Proceedings of the 20th international joint conference on artificial intelligence.

Heba Abdelnasser, Reham Mohamed, Maha Ragab, Alaa Mohamed, Bassant Farouk, Nagwa El-Makky, and Marwan Torki. 2014. *Al-Bayan: An Arabic Question Answering System for the Holy Quran*. Proceedings of the EMNLP 2014 Workshop on Arabic Natural Language Processing (ANLP).

Hikmat Ullah Khan and Syed Muhammad Saqlain and Muhammad Shoaib and Muhammad Sher. 2013. *Ontology Based Semantic Search in Holy Quran.*, volume 2. International Journal of Future Computer and Communication, 570-575.

Ismail Ibn-Kathir. 1370. *Tafsir al-Qur'an al-Azim*.

Lahsen Abouenour, Karim Bouzoubaa, and Paolo Rosso. 2012. *IDRAAQ: New Arabic Question Answering System Based on Query Expansion and Passage Retrieval*. In CLEF.

Lluìs Màrquez and James Glass and Walid Magdy and Alessandro Moschitti and Preslav Nakov and Bilal Randeree. 2015. *SemEval-2015 Task 3: Answer Selection in Community Question Answering*. Proceedings of the 9th International Workshop on Semantic Evaluation.

Manal AlMaayah, Majdi Sawalha, and Mohammad AM Abushariah. 2014. *A Proposed Model for Quranic Arabic WordNet*. LRE-REL2, 9.

Nizar Habash, Owen Rambow and Ryan Roth. 2009. *MADA+ TOKAN: A toolkit for Arabic tokenization, diacritization, morphological disambiguation, POS tagging, stemming and lemmatization*. Proceedings of the 2nd International Conference on Arabic Language Resources and Tools (MEDAR), Cairo, Egypt.

Noorhan Hassan Abbas. 2009. *Quran'search for a Concept'Tool and Website*. M. Sc. thesis, University of Leeds (School of Computing).

Omar Trigui, Lamia Hadrich Belguith, Paolo Rosso, Hichem Ben Amor and Bilel Gafsaoui. 2012. *Arabic QA4MRE at CLEF 2012: Arabic Question Answering for Machine Reading Evaluation*. CLEF (Online Working Notes/Labs/Workshop).

Saidah Saad, Naomie Salim, and Hakim Zainal. 2009. *Pattern extraction for Islamic concept.*, volume 2. Proceedings of IEEE 2nd. International Conference on Electrical Engineering & Informatics (ICEEI).

Saidah Saad, Naomie Salim, Hakim Zainal and S. Azman M. Noah. 2010. *A framework for Islamic knowledge via ontology representation.*. International Conference on Information Retrieval and Knowledge Management (CAMP).

Tim Buckwalter. 2002. *Arabic transliteration*. URL http://www.qamus.org/transliteration.htm.

FBK-HLT: An Application of Semantic Textual Similarity for Answer Selection in Community Question Answering

Ngoc Phuoc An Vo
University of Trento,
Fondazione Bruno Kessler
Trento, Italy
ngoc@fbk.eu

Simone Magnolini
University of Brescia,
Fondazione Bruno Kessler
Trento, Italy
magnolini@fbk.eu

Octavian Popescu
IBM Research, T.J. Watson
Yorktown, US
o.popescu@us.ibm.com

Abstract

This paper reports the description and performance of our system, FBK-HLT, participating in the SemEval 2015, Task #3 "Answer Selection in Community Question Answering" for English, for both subtasks. We submit two runs with different classifiers in combining typical features (lexical similarity, string similarity, word n-grams, etc.) with machine translation evaluation metrics and with some ad hoc features (e.g user overlapping, spam filtering). We outperform the baseline system and achieve interesting results on both subtasks.

1 Introduction

Answer selection is an important task inside the wider task of question answering that represents at the moment a topic of great interest for research and business as well. Analyzing social data like answers given inside a forum is a way to maximize the value of this type of knowledge source that is usually affected by a very noisy information due to out of topic spam, double posting, cross posting or other issues. Recognizing useful posts from bad ones, and automatically detecting the main polarity of answers to a given question is a way to treat an amount of data that otherwise might be difficult to handle.

A promising way to provide insight into these questions was brought forward as Shared Task #3 in the SemEval-2015 campaign for "Answer Selection in Community Question Answering" (Màrquez et al., 2015) for English and Arabic languages. In the Subtask A, each system is given a set of questions in which each one contains some data like posting date, author's Id, a set of comments, at least one, but usually more; then the participating the system has to classify comments as *good*, *bad* or *potential* according to their relevance with the question. In Subtask B, a subset of these questions are predefined as *yes/no questions*, system has to classify them into *yes*, *no* or *unsure* classes based on the individual good answers. We participate in this shared task (only in English) with a system composing several different features using a multiclass classifier. We are interested in finding out whether similarity, machine translation evaluation metrics and task specific techniques could increase the accuracy of our system. In this paper, we outline our method and present the results for the answer selection task; the paper is organized as follows: Section 2 presents the System Description, Section 3 describes the Experiment Settings, Section 4 reports the Evaluations, Section 5 is the Error Analysis and finally, Section 6 presents the Conclusions and Future Work.

2 System Description

In order to build our system, we extract and adopt several different linguistic features from a Semantic Textual Similarity (STS) system (Vo et al., 2015) and then consolidate them by a multiclass classifier. Different features can be used independently or together with others to measure the semantic similarity and recognize the paraphrase of a given sentence pair as well as to evaluate the significance of each feature to the accuracy of system's predictions. Hence, the system is expandable and scalable for adopting more useful features aiming for improving the accuracy.

2.1 Data Preprocessing

As data preprocessing is a crucial step for preparing useful information to be learned by the system, we focus the beginning of our work trying to simplify data without losing information. Our system is based on semantic similarity, so it needs pairs of sentences to compare; we pair-up every question with all of its comments, one by one, e.g. a question with five comments becomes five pairs of sentences composed by the question and five different comments. Questions and comments are composed by subject and body, so for questions, we merge the subject and body together if the subject does not occur inside the body; and for comments, we also check if the comment's subject is not identical to question's subject with the prefix *RE:*. As the forum data also contains lot of informal writing, we normalize them by applying a simple filter that substitutes common abbreviation: *"u - you", "r - are", "ur - your", "Iam - I am", "any1 - anyone"*.

2.2 Syntactic Generalization

Given a pair of parse trees, the Syntactic Generalization (SG) (Galitsky, 2013) finds a set of maximal common subtrees. The toolkit "relevance-based-on-parse-trees" is an open-source project, which evaluates text relevance by using syntactic, parse-tree-based similarity measure.[1] It measures the similarity between two sentences by finding a set of maximal common subtree for a pair of parse trees, using representation of constituency parse trees via chunking. Each type of phrases (NP, VP, PRP etc.) will be aligned and subject to generalization. It uses the OpenNLP system to derive constituent trees for generalization (chunker and parser).[2] As it is an unsupervised approach, we apply the tool directly to the preprocessed texts to compute the similarity of syntactic structure of sentence pairs.

2.3 Machine Learning Evaluation Metric - METEOR

We also use evaluation metrics for machine translation as suggested in (Madnani et al., 2012) for paraphrase recognition on Microsoft Research paraphrase corpus (MSRP) (Dolan et al., 2004). In machine translation, the evaluation metric scores the hypotheses by aligning them to one or more reference translations. We take into consideration to use all the eight metrics proposed, but we find that adding some of them without a careful process of training on the dataset may decrease the performance of the system.

We use the latest version of METEOR (Denkowski and Lavie, 2014) that finds alignments between sentences based on exact, stem, synonym and paraphrase matches between words and phrases. We used the system as distributed on its website, using only the "norm" option that tokenizes and normalizes punctuation and lowercase as suggested by documentation.[3] We compute the word alignment scores between questions and comments.

2.4 Weighted Matrix Factorization (WMF)

WMF (Guo and Diab, 2012) is a dimension reduction model to extract nuanced and robust latent vectors for short texts/sentences. To overcome the sparsity problem in short texts/sentences (e.g. 10 words on average), the missing words, a feature that Latent Semantic Analysis (LSA) and Latent Dirichlet Allocation (LDA) typically overlook, is explicitly modeled. We use the pipeline to compute the similarity scores for question-comment pairs.[4]

2.5 User Overlapping

We extract a simple binary feature focused on comment's author. We suppose that question's author is not usually as same as comment's author, so if a question has one or more comments associated with the same question's author, these comments are probably descriptions or explanations about the question. We label 1 for comments made by the same question's author and 0 otherwise.

2.6 Spam Filtering - JFilter

Recognizing good comments from bad comment is a task somehow similar to spam filtering, to capture this feature, we use a Java implementation, Jfilter (Francesco Saverio Profiti, 2007), based on a fuzzy version of the Rocchio algorithm (Rocchio, 1971). This system uses a classifier that needs training, so to avoid overfitting, from the training and development datasets, we randomly choose a subset of *good*

[1] https://code.google.com/p/relevance-based-on-parse-trees/
[2] https://opennlp.apache.org

[3] http://www.cs.cmu.edu/%7Ealavie/METEOR/index.html
[4] http://www.cs.columbia.edu/%7Eweiwei/code.html

	Accuracy	F1 (G)	F1 (B)	F1 (D)	F1 (P)	F1 (NE)	F1 (O)	F1 WM
Baseline	53.19	0.694	0	0	0	0	0	0.369
1-against-all	**60.06**	0.731	0.189	0.545	0	0	0	0.523
Random Correction Code	59.02	0.722	0.319	0.540	0	0	0	**0.539**
Exhausted Correction Code	60.00	0.731	0.18	0.545	0	0	0	0.521

Table 1: Result obtained using different classification algorithms for Subtask A (G good; B bad; D dialog; P potential; NE not-English; O other; WM Weighted Mean) on Development dataset.

	Accuracy	F1 (Yes)	F1 (No)	F1 (Unsure)	F1 (Not-Applicable)	F1 WM
Standard Features	44.4444	0.316	0	0.077	0.593	0.355
Standard Features + Subtask A output	45.4444	0.327	0	0.08	0.589	0.358
Standard Features + Subtask A gold-standard labels	70.7071	0.667	0	0.069	1	0.635

Table 2: Subtask B system performances on Development dataset.

comments to use as non-spam dataset; in contrast, we select a subset of *bad* and *potential* to use as spam dataset to train JFilter. This configuration was used to train our system during development; for the final run with test dataset, we train JFilter with both development and training datasets. JFilter gives a binary judgment (HAM or SPAM) which is used as a feature for our system in Subtask A.

3 Experiment Settings

We use the machine learning toolkit WEKA (Hall et al., 2009) to obtain robust and efficient implementation of different classifiers, as well as to reduce develop time of the system. For Subtask A, we build one model using all the features described in Section 2. Table 1 reports some experiments in which we select a good classifier to optimize both the Accuracy and F1-score of the system. During the development, we select the default implementation "1-against-all" classification algorithm (with logistic regression) for both subtasks.

For Subtask B, we make some modifications to the system due to some important differences between two subtasks. As the question classification depends on the quality of its comments, we substitute the spam filtering feature by the comments' labels from Subtask A system's output. In order to examine this hypothesis, we firstly use the gold-standard labels of comments from Subtask A as a feature for the question classification in Subtask B. The high Accuracy and F1-score from this setting proves our hypothesis correct. To avoid the overfitting, we again use only the label predictions from Subtask A as a feature for our Subtask B system. Table 2 shows that a precise output from Subtask A can significantly benefit the performance of Subtask B system.

As Subtask B does not focus on comment labeling, but question labeling, to achieve this purpose after classifying all comments as *yes*, *no*, *unsure* or *Not Applicable*, we simply aggregate comments of every question with a majority vote. We label a question as *yes* if the majority of its comments are classified as *yes*, the same for *no*; if there no major judgment of either *yes* or *no*, the question is classified as *unsure*.

	Subtask A		Subtask B	
Team	Mac F1	Acc	Mac F1	Acc
JAIST	57.19	72.52		
VectorSlu			63.7	72.0
FBK-HLT	47.32	69.13	27.8	40.0

Table 3: Evaluation Results on Subtasks A and B.

Team	Accuracy	F1 (G)	F1 (B)	F1 (D)	F1 (P)	Macro F1
JAIST (3-classes)	72.67	79.11	78.29	0	14.48	57.29
HLT-FBK (3-classes)	69.13	75.80	66.15	0	0	47.32
JAIST (4-classes)	59.62	76.52	40.38	57.21	18.41	48.13
HLT-FBK (4-classes)	62.40	75.80	43.42	51.23	0	42.61

Table 4: Subtask A - Comparison with best system for 3-classes and 4-classes evaluation (G good; B bad; D dialog; P potential; Macro F1).

Team	Accuracy	F1 (Yes)	F1 (No)	F1 (Unsure)	Macro F1
VectorSlu	72.0	83.87	57.14	50.0	63.67
FBK-HLT	40.0	50.0	0.0	33.33	27.78

Table 5: Subtask B - Comparison with best system.

4 Evaluations

We submit only one run for both subtasks (English language) using the "1-against-all" classification algorithms. In Subtask A, we achieve good results, especially, we are ranked 4th out of 12 teams in Accuracy. In Subtask B, as we only apply the simple approach "majority vote", the result is reasonable as expected. Table 3 shows our performance in both subtasks in regard to the best systems, both in Macro F1 and Accuracy measures.

5 Error Analysis

In this section, we conduct an analysis of our system's performance on test dataset. In Subtask A, our analysis consists of some comparison between our system and the best system, JAIST. According to results in Table 4, for the evaluation on 3-classes (*good*, *bad*, and *potential*), our system is dramatically penalized by low performance on detecting *bad* comments, besides, it is not able to classify the *potential* ones. This particular class of comments is very small in training dataset. There are 50.45% for *good* comments, 41.09% for *bad* and only 8.25% for *potential*. During the development, as we decide to optimize the Accuracy and F1 weighted on the number of comments, this decision misleads our system to ignore this small class. Hence, in order to improve the system performance, we may need to search for a specific feature for *potential* comments like what we did with user overlapping for *dialog* ones. For the evaluation on 4-classes (*good*, *bad*, *dialog* and *potential*), our system performance rises significantly, our system shows a good capability to distinguish between *dialog* and other comments.

In Subtask B, the performance comparison in Table 5 shows that our system achieves reasonable performance on the *Yes* and *Unsure* classes, but has no capability to capture the *No* class. Moreover, most of the instances of *No* class have been misclassified as *Unsure* class. This shows an unclear separation between these two classes which confuses the system. Thus, to fix this issue, we need to find more specific features which may help to distinguish the *No* class and others.

6 Conclusions and Future Work

In this paper, we describe our system participating in the SemEval 2015, Task #3 "Answer Selection in Community Question Answering" in English, for both subtasks. We present a supervised system which considers multiple linguistic features such as lexical, string and some task-specific features. Our performance is much above the baseline and shows some interesting properties in specific scenarios. We also show some error analysis in which we investigate the limit and drawback of our system on specific comment and question classes.

For future work, we expect to study to exploit more useful features, especially, task-related features, to improve the classification performance on *potential* labeled comments and *No* labeled questions, which will lead to a significant improvement of the overall performance.

References

Michael Denkowski and Alon Lavie. 2014. Meteor universal: Language specific translation evaluation for any target language. In *Proceedings of the EACL 2014 Workshop on Statistical Machine Translation*.

Bill Dolan, Chris Quirk, and Chris Brockett. 2004. Unsupervised construction of large paraphrase corpora: Exploiting massively parallel news sources. In *Proceedings of the 20th international conference on Computational Linguistics*, page 350.

Claudio Biancalana Francesco Saverio Profiti. 2007. Jfilter: un filtro antispam intelligente in java. *Mokabyte*, (124). in Italian.

Boris Galitsky. 2013. Machine learning of syntactic parse trees for search and classification of text. *Engineering Applications of Artificial Intelligence*, 26(3):1072–1091.

Weiwei Guo and Mona Diab. 2012. Modeling sentences in the latent space. In *Proceedings of the 50th Annual Meeting of the Association for Computational Linguistics: Long Papers-Volume 1*, pages 864–872.

Mark Hall, Eibe Frank, Geoffrey Holmes, Bernhard Pfahringer, Peter Reutemann, and Ian H Witten. 2009. The weka data mining software: an update. *ACM SIGKDD explorations newsletter*, 11(1):10–18.

Nitin Madnani, Joel Tetreault, and Martin Chodorow. 2012. Re-examining machine translation metrics for paraphrase identification. In *Proceedings of the 2012 Conference of the North American Chapter of the Association for Computational Linguistics: Human Language Technologies*, pages 182–190.

Lluís Màrquez, James Glass, Walid Magdy, Alessandro Moschitti, Preslav Nakov, and Bilal Randeree. 2015. Semeval-2015 task 3: Answer selection in community question answering. In *Proceedings of the 9th International Workshop on Semantic Evaluation (SemEval 2015)*.

Joseph John Rocchio. 1971. Relevance feedback in information retrieval.

Ngoc Phuoc An Vo, Simone Magnolini, and Octavian Popescu. 2015. FBK-HLT: A new framework for semantic textual similarity. *In Proceedings of the 9th International Workshop on Semantic Evaluation (SemEval-2015), Denver, US.*

ECNU: Using Multiple Sources of CQA-based Information for Answer Selection and YES/NO Response Inference

Liang Yi, Jianxiang Wang, Man Lan*
Shanghai Key Laboratory of Multidimensional Information Processing
Department of Computer Science and Technology,
East China Normal University, Shanghai 200241, China
{51121201035, 51141201062}@ecnu.cn; mlan@cs.ecnu.edu.cn*

Abstract

This paper reports our submissions to community question answering task in SemEval-2015, which consists of two subtasks: (1) predict the quality of answers to given question as *good*, *bad*, or *potentially relevant* and (2) identify *yes*, *no* or *unsure* response to a given YES/NO question based on the *good* answers identified by subtask 1. For both subtasks, we adopted supervised classification method and examined the effects of heterogeneous features generated from community question answering data, such as bag-of-words, string matching, semantic similarity, answerer information, answer-specific features, question-specific features, etc. Our submitted primary systems ranked the forth and the second for the two subtasks of English data respectively.

1 Introduction

Community Question Answering (CQA) systems such as *Yahoo!Answers* rely on users to provide answers (i.e., user generated content) for questions posted. Generally such systems are quite open and the answers provided by users are not always of high quality. For example, a bad answer may present irrelevant opinions or issues, contain only URL links without direct answer, or even be written informally. Therefore, in order to achieve high-quality user experience and maintain high levels of adherence, it is critical to present high-quality answers and provide direct responses for users.

The CQA task in SemEval-2015 (Màrquez et al., 2015) provides such a universal platform for researchers to make a comparison between different approaches. This task consists of two subtasks: (1) subtask A is to classify the quality of answers as *good*, *potential* or *bad*, which also refers to the task of answer quality prediction (Jeon et al., 2006; Agichtein et al., 2008); (2) subtask B is to infer the global answer of a YES/NO question to be *yes*, *no* or *unsure* based on individual *good* answers.

Most of the previous research on answer quality prediction has focused on extracting various features to employ ranking or classification methods (Surdeanu et al., 2011; Shah and Pomerantz, 2010), such as textual features (Agichtein et al., 2008; Blooma et al., 2010) including the length of an answer, overlapped words between a question-answer (QA) pair, etc. Another kind of widely used feature is extracted from answerer profile information (Shah and Pomerantz, 2010), such as the number of best answers, the achieved levels and the earned points. However, such information is not often available in real world. Moreover, a recent study (Toba et al., 2014) has taken question type into consideration to make the answers quality prediction.

In this paper, we built two classification systems for the two tasks respectively. For Task A, we extracted six types of features from multiple sources of CQA-based information to predict the answer quality, such as answer-, question-, answerer-specific information, surface word similarity and semantic similarity between question-answer pair, ect. For Task B, the global answer of a YES/NO question is summarized just from the individual *good* answers identified by Task A. Specifically, we first built a classifier to predict *Yes/No/Unsure* labels for each predicted *good* answer, then we performed a majority voting to summarize the global answer for each question.

The rest of this paper is structured as follows. Section 2 describes our systems, including features, algorithms, etc. Section 3 shows experiments on training data and results on test data. Finally, conclusions and future work are given in Section 4.

2 Our Systems

For both tasks we adopted supervised classification methods and extracted various features from multiple sources to predict answer quality and infer YES/NO response.

2.1 Data Extraction

English data is extracted from Qatar Living Forum[1] and provided with XML-format. Each data file consists of a list of question tags, where each question is followed by a list of answer tags to this question. Each question or answer has a subject, a body, and a list of attributes from which we can extract significant features. For example, a question has attributes of question category (overall 27 categories, e.g., Education, Cars, etc.), identifier of asker, question type (GENERAL or YES/NO) and an answer also has answerer identifier.

To obtain complete contents of a question or an answer, we merged the contents extracted from subject and body. Exceptionally, if subject is substring of body or subject of an answer starts with "RE:", we just extracted the contents from body.

Moreover, to reduce the influence of *Not English* answers to the subsequent classification, we filtered out the *Not English* answers from data. To discover such answers we found out unusual words for each answer by comparing word set of this answer with an English vocabulary with $235,887$ words from NLTK[2] *words* corpus, if the number of unusual words is over 10 and the ratio over answer length is above 60% we then regarded it as *Not English.*

2.2 Pre-processing

After data extraction we performed the following preprocessing operations. Firstly, HTML character encodings are substituted by the actual characters (e.g., "&" is converted into whitespace). Then HTML tags, URLs, emoticons, ending signatures and repeating punctuation are removed from data. After that, we collected a slang list from Internet and replaced the informal words with formal words (e.g., "*u r*" is converted into "*you are*"). For the processed data, we performed tokenization and POS tagging using Penn Treebank tokenizer and POS tagger in NLTK. The words are lemmatized using WordNet-based lemmatizer implemented in NLTK.

2.3 Features of Task A

We extracted six types of features from multiple sources of CQA-based information, i.e., bag-of-words (BoW) and answer-specific features (AS) from answer, string matching (SM) and semantic similarity (SS) from QA pair, answerer information features (AI) from answerer profile, question-specific features (QS) from question.

2.3.1 Bag-of-Words for Answer (BoW)

We collected words from training and development answer set and adopted binary BoW representation. To reduce the problem of data sparse, we selected the words with frequency higher than four, resulting in $5,730$ words.

2.3.2 Answer-Specific Features (AS)

For each question, we extracted three answer-specific features. The first is answer length, which is computed at three levels, i.e., word, sentence and paragraph. We used L_1 normalization on the global answer set. To gain insight on the effect of answer length for each individual question, we also designed a length ratio feature to record the ratio of the length of each answer to the maximal answer length for the same question.

A good answer is generally supposed to answer a question explicitly instead of starting a new question or suggesting other consulting approaches. Therefore, the second binary feature is to represent whether an answer contains a question mark or not. In addition, we manually collected eight words and phrases from training set, which contains the meaning of suggestion (i.e., "*suggest*", "*recommend*", "*advise*", "*try*", "*call*", "*you may*", "*may be*", "*you could*"). Thus the third binary feature is to

[1] http://www.qatarliving.com/forum

[2] http://www.nltk.org/

represent if there is at least one of above suggestion words in a given answer.

2.3.3 String Matching between QA (SM)

The above two types of features are both extracted from answer regardless of the question asked. However, the string matching features are to consider the overlapped words from a given QA pair.

Word: This feature group records the proportions of co-occurred words between a QA pair, which are calculated using six measures: $|A \cap B|/|A|$, $|A \cap B|/|B|$, $|A - B|/|A|$, $|B - A|/|B|$, $|A \cap B|/|A \cup B|$, $2 * |A \cap B|/(|A| + |B|)$, where $|A|$ and $|B|$ denote the number of non-repeated words of question A and answer B. However, the same word appearing in different context could vary in word forms and normalizing words may obtain more accurate overlapped proportions, so we computed each measure at three word forms: original, lemmatized and stem form.

POS: This POS feature is similar to the above word feature. We use three measures: $|A \cap B|/|A|$, $|A \cap B|/|B|$, $|A \cap B|/|A \cup B|$ to compute overlapped proportion of POS tags for nouns, verbs, adjectives and adverbs.

n-gram: Unlike the above two features measuring the overlap of single words or POS without considering multiple continuous words, the n-gram feature is to calculate the Jaccard similarity of overlapped n-grams between each QA pair. The n-grams are obtained at word level ($n = 2, 3$) and character level ($n = 2, 3, 4$). In addition, the n-grams at word level are obtained from original form and lemmatized form respectively.

Longest Common Sequence (LCS): The LCS feature is to measure the LCS similarity for a QA pair on the original and lemmatized form. It is calculated as the length of the LCS between each QA pair at word level divided by the length of question.

2.3.4 Semantic Similarity between QA (SS)

The previous string matching feature only considers the overlapped surface words or substrings in a QA pair and it may not capture the semantic information between a QA pair. Therefore, we presented the following semantic similarity features, which are borrowed from previous work.

Determining semantic similarity of sentences commonly uses measures of semantic similarity between individual words. We used knowledge-based and corpus-based word similarity features. The knowledge-based similarity estimation relies on a semantic network of words such as WordNet. In this work, we employed four WordNet-based word similarity metrics: *Path* (Banea et al., 2012), *WUP* (Wu and Palmer, 1994), *LCH* (Leacock and Chodorow, 1998) and *Lin* (Lin, 1998) similarity. Following (Zhu and Man, 2013), the best alignment strategy and the aggregation strategy are employed to propagate the word similarity to the text similarity. Moreover, Latent Semantic analysis (LSA) (Landauer et al., 1997) is a widely used corpus-based measure when evaluating textual similarity. We used the vector space sentence similarity proposed by (Šarić et al., 2012), which represents each sentence as a single distributional vector by summing up the LSA vector of each word in the sentence. In this work, two corpora are used to compute the LSA vector of words: New York Times Annotated Corpus (NYT) and Wikipedia.

Besides, following (Zhao et al., 2014), we adopted the weighted textual matrix factorization (WTMF) (Guo and Diab, 2012) to model the semantics representations of sentences and then employed the new representations to calculate the semantic similarity between QA pairs using Cosine, Manhattan, Euclidean, Person, Spearmanr, Kendalltau measures respectively.

2.3.5 Answerer Information (AI)

Previous work (Zhou et al., 2012) showed that information about answerer has great impact on answer ranking in CQA. Inspired by this work, we designed two answerer-specific features to represent answerer level and answerer expert domain information. To calculate the answerer level feature, we used the number of answers and the percentage of *good* answers for each answerer. For expert domain feature, we employed the question categories where the answerer is an expert. Specifically, for each answerer, let G be the number of *good* answers the answerer responses and G_i be the number of *good* answers to the i-th question category ($i <= 27$). Then we used G_i/G to measure the answerer's expert domain. Besides, for each of the 27 question categories (e.g., Education, Cars), we recorded the maximal value M_i over all values of G_i from each answerer and then calculated the G_i/M_i score to measure expert level of an answerer in current domain among all answerers. Totally, we adopted 54 features to indicate expert domain for each answerer.

2.3.6 Question-Specific Features (QS)

Since the domain of questions may also affect the performance of answer selection, we considered to use 27 binary features to indicate the question category. In addition, we manually collected 9 question words (i.e., *where*, *what*, *when*, *which*, *who*, *whom*, *whose*, *why* and *how*) and used 9 binary features to indicate if one of these question words occurs in the question.

2.4 Features of Task B

To address task B, we performed two steps. Firstly, we extracted features from *good* answers identified from task A and trained a classifier to predict the *Yes*, *No* or *Unsure* label for each *good* answer. Secondly, for each given YES/NO question, we counted the answer labels of *Yes*, *No* or *Unsure* and used majority voting to obtain the global answer.

We used three types of features for this task, which are all extracted from answer: (1) Bag-of-Words from answer (BoW), the same as in Task A; (2) Semantic Word2Vec (W2V): this feature indicates a vector representation of answer. We used word2vec tool[3] to get word vectors with dimension $d = 300$ and then summed up all the word vectors to obtain the answer vector. (3) Yes/No Word List (YN): we manually collected 50 affirmative words and 45 negation words by starting from several seed words (e.g., "*yes*", "*sure*", "*definitely*", "*no*", "*seldom*", "*never*", etc) and then expanding the list using snowball with the aid of WordNet synset. Besides, several phrases are manually added in the list (e.g., "*beyond a doubt*", "*beyond question*", "*not at all*", "*only just*", etc). We utilized 2 binary features to indicate whether an answer contains at least one of these affirmative and negation words or not.

2.5 Classification Algorithms

We explored several widely-used supervised classification algorithms including Support Vector Machine (SVM), Random Forest (RF), and Gradient Boosting(GB), which are implemented in scikit-learn toolkit (Pedregosa et al., 2011).

[3]https://code.google.com/p/word2vec/

Algorithm	macro-F_1(Task A)	macro-F_1(Task B)
SVM (linear)	**54.25**	**58.60**
SVM (rbf)	29.44	25.05
GB	49.70	39.05
RF	45.40	27.14

Table 1: Results on training data for different algorithms.

2.6 Evaluation Measures

The official evaluation measures for both tasks is macro-averaged F_1. For Task A the official score is calculated on three labels: *Good*, *Bad*, *Potential* (where *Bad* includes *Dialogue*, *Not English* and *Other*).

3 Experiments and Results

3.1 English Data Set

The English training and development set contain $2,900$ questions with $18,186$ answers and the test set contains 329 questions with $1,976$ answers, consisting of around 50% *good*, 40% *bad* and 10% *potential* answers. The YES/NO questions are about 10% of all the questions, which indicates that the data for Task B is much less than Task A.

For both tasks we used training set with $2,600$ questions to build classifiers and validated the performance on development set with 300 questions for algorithms comparison and features choosing.

3.2 Algorithm Choosing Experiments

We performed algorithm choosing experiments using all designed features. All the parameters of algorithms are set to be default values from scikit-learn (Pedregosa et al., 2011). Table 1 lists the preliminary algorithm comparison experimental results. We found SVM with linear kernel outperforms other algorithm choices for both tasks. Moreover, we tuned the trade-off parameter c of SVM and when set c to 0.8 we obtained a better score 54.78% and 58.82% for Task A and B respectively. Therefore, in the following experiments on training and test data, we set the algorithm to SVM with linear kernel.

3.3 Feature Comparison Experiments

We performed a series of experiments for both tasks to explore the effects of various feature types using

SVM (linear). In Task B we always chose the predicted *good* answers from the system with the best macro-F_1 in Task A. Table 2 shows the results of different feature combinations where for each time we selected and added one best feature type. From this table we found the following interesting observations.

	BoW	AS	SM	SS	AI	QS	macro-F_1(%)
Task A	+						48.91
	+	+					49.73(+0.82)
	+	+			+		51.85(+2.12)
	+	+	+		+		52.03(+0.18)
	+	+	+	+	+		53.22(+1.19)
	+	+	+	+	+	+	**54.25**(+1.03)

	BoW	W2V	YN	macro-F_1(%)
Task B	+			47.82
	+	+		49.54(+1.72)
	+	+	+	**58.60**(+9.06)

Table 2: Results of feature combinations for Task A and B, the numbers in the bracket are the performance increments compared with previous result.

First, for both tasks the most effective feature type is bag-of-words from answer and this feature alone achieves 48.91% for Task A and 47.82% for Task B, which both outperforms the baseline system provided by organizers respectively. The baseline of Task A which predicts all answers as *good* just achieves 22.36% and for Task B it achieves 25.0% which predict all answers as *yes*. Moreover, in Task A the performance of other five feature types alone is far lower than bag-of-words, ranging from 23% to 38% approximately.

Second, for Task A, when combining all the features together the system achieves the best performance, which indicates that all types of features make contribution more or less. Specially, among the six types of features, answerer information and semantic similarity between QA pairs make more contribution than others. This indicates that answerer profile information is important, which is consistent with the findings in (Zhou et al., 2012). Besides, the semantic similarity captures deep relationship between Q-A pair than the surface word, which is helpful for performance improvement. In Task B, we also observed the similar findings, i.e., the system using all types of features achieves the best performance. Moreover, the YES/NO word list feature makes great contribution to the performance improvement. This is consistent with our expectation. Besides, although in this work the word vector feature improves the performance, this improvements is not as much as our expectation. The possible reason may be the simple way of using the vector by only summing up.

3.4 Results on Test Data

According to the above experiments on training data, we configured one primary and two contrastive systems for both tasks. The only difference between these systems lies in the features and parameters in SVM. Table 3 lists the configuration of three systems and their corresponding results on test data. Besides, we also list the top three results officially released by organizers.

Systems	Task A			Task B		
	features	para.	result	features	para.	result
primary	all	c=0.8	**53.47**(9)	all	c=0.8	**55.8**(3)
contrastive1	all	c=1.0	52.55(10)	all	c=1.0	50.6(4)
contrastive2	all-SS	c=0.8	52.27(11)	all-W2V	c=0.8	53.9(6)

Top Systems	Task A Result	Task B Result
rank 1st	**57.19**	**63.7**
rank 2nd	56.41	55.8
rank 3rd	53.74	53.6

Table 3: Configurations and results of our three submitted systems and top three results, the numbers in bracket are the official ranking out of all submitted systems.

Our primary system ranked the 4th out of 12 participants in Task A and the 2nd out of 7 participants in Task B. For both tasks the performance of the primary system is higher than the two contrastive systems, which is consistent with the results on training data.

4 Conclusion

We build two supervised classification systems for answer selection and YES/NO response inference in CQA. Specially, we extract heterogeneous features from various information sources, i.e., answer, question, answer-question pair and answerer. Our experiments reveal that our designed features are all effective and when we combine all types of features together the system achieves the best performance.

Although multiple features extracted from CQA, the way of using these features are quite simple. Besides, due to the huge number of bag-of-word feature, the effects of other specific features are impaired. For future work, we may explore other underlying useful features and the advanced way of integrating these features to further improve the performance, such as the fine-grained semantic relationship between question and answer, etc.

Acknowledgments

This research is supported by grants from Science and Technology Commission of Shanghai Municipality under research grant no. (14DZ2260800 and 15ZR1410700) and Shanghai Collaborative Innovation Center of Trustworthy Software for Internet of Things (ZF1213).

References

Eugene Agichtein, Carlos Castillo, Debora Donato, Aristides Gionis, and Gilad Mishne. 2008. Finding high-quality content in social media. In *Proceedings of the 2008 International Conference on Web Search and Data Mining*, pages 183–194.

Carmen Banea, Samer Hassan, Michael Mohler, and Rada Mihalcea. 2012. Unt: A supervised synergistic approach to semantic text similarity. In *Proceedings of the First Joint Conference on Lexical and Computational Semantics-Volume 1: Proceedings of the main conference and the shared task, and Volume 2: Proceedings of the Sixth International Workshop on Semantic Evaluation*, pages 635–642.

Mohan John Blooma, Alton Yeow-Kuan Chua, and Dion Hoe-Lian Goh. 2010. Selection of the best answer in cqa services. In *Information Technology: New Generations (ITNG), 2010 Seventh International Conference on*, pages 534–539.

Weiwei Guo and Mona Diab. 2012. Modeling sentences in the latent space. In *Proceedings of the 50th Annual Meeting of the Association for Computational Linguistics: Long Papers-Volume 1*, pages 864–872.

Jiwoon Jeon, William Bruce Croft, Joon Ho Lee, and Soyeon Park. 2006. A framework to predict the quality of answers with non-textual features. In *Proceedings of the 29th annual international ACM SIGIR conference on Research and development in information retrieval*, pages 228–235.

Thomas K Landauer, Darrell Laham, Bob Rehder, and Missy E Schreiner. 1997. How well can passage meaning be derived without using word order? a comparison of latent semantic analysis and humans. In *Proceedings of the 19th annual meeting of the Cognitive Science Society*, pages 412–417.

Claudia Leacock and Martin Chodorow. 1998. Combining local context and wordnet similarity for word sense identification. *WordNet: An electronic lexical database*, 49(2):265–283.

Dekang Lin. 1998. An information-theoretic definition of similarity. In *ICML*, volume 98, pages 296–304.

Lluís Màrquez, James Glass, Walid Magdy, Alessandro Moschitti, Preslav Nakov, and Bilal Randeree. 2015. Semeval-2015 task 3: Answer selection in community question answering. In *SemEval 2015*.

Fabian Pedregosa, Gaël Varoquaux, Alexandre Gramfort, Vincent Michel, Bertrand Thirion, Olivier Grisel, Mathieu Blondel, Peter Prettenhofer, Ron Weiss, Vincent Dubourg, et al. 2011. Scikit-learn: Machine learning in python. *The Journal of Machine Learning Research*, 12:2825–2830.

Frane Šarić, Goran Glavaš, Mladen Karan, Jan Šnajder, and Bojana Dalbelo Bašić. 2012. Takelab: Systems for measuring semantic text similarity. In *Proceedings of the First Joint Conference on Lexical and Computational Semantics-Volume 1: Proceedings of the main conference and the shared task, and Volume 2: Proceedings of the Sixth International Workshop on Semantic Evaluation*, pages 441–448.

Chirag Shah and Jefferey Pomerantz. 2010. Evaluating and predicting answer quality in community qa. In *Proceedings of the 33rd international ACM SIGIR conference on Research and development in information retrieval*, pages 411–418.

Mihai Surdeanu, Massimiliano Ciaramita, and Hugo Zaragoza. 2011. Learning to rank answers to non-factoid questions from web collections. *Computational Linguistics*, 37(2):351–383.

Hapnes Toba, Zhao-Yan Ming, Mirna Adriani, and Tat-Seng Chua. 2014. Discovering high quality answers in community question answering archives using a hierarchy of classifiers. *Information Sciences*, 261:101–115.

Zhibiao Wu and Martha Palmer. 1994. Verbs semantics and lexical selection. In *Proceedings of the 32nd annual meeting on Association for Computational Linguistics*, pages 133–138.

Jiang Zhao, Tian Tian Zhu, and Man Lan. 2014. Ecnu: One stone two birds: Ensemble of heterogenous measures for semantic relatedness and textual entailment. *SemEval 2014*, page 271.

Zhi-Min Zhou, Man Lan, Zheng-Yu Niu, and Yue Lu. 2012. Exploiting user profile information for answer ranking in cqa. In *Proceedings of the 21st international conference companion on World Wide Web*, pages 767–774.

Tian Tian Zhu and LAN Man. 2013. Ecnucs: Measuring short text semantic equivalence using multiple similarity measurements. *Atlanta, Georgia, USA*, page 124.

Voltron: A Hybrid System For Answer Validation Based On Lexical And Distance Features

Ivan Zamanov[1], Nelly Hateva[1], Marina Kraeva[1], Ivana Yovcheva[1], Ivelina Nikolova[2], Galia Angelova[2]

[1] FMI, Sofia University, Sofia, Bulgaria
[2] IICT, Bulgarian Academy of Sciences, Sofia, Bulgaria

ivo.zamanov@gmail.com, nelly.hateva@gmail.com, mvkraeva@gmail.com, ivana.yovcheva@gmail.com, iva@lml.bas.bg, galia@lml.bas.bg

Abstract

The purpose of this paper is to describe our submission to the SemEval-2015 Task 3 on Answer Selection in Community Question Answering. We participated in subtask A, where the systems had to classify community answers for a given question as definitely relevant, potentially useful, or irrelevant. For every question-answer pair in the training data we extract a vector with a variety of features. These vectors are then fed to a MaxEnt classifier for training. Given a question and an answer the trained classifier outputs class probabilities for each of the three desired categories. The one with the highest probability is chosen. Our system scores better than the average score in subtask A of Task 3.

1 Introduction

Nowadays, text analysis and semantic similarity are subject to a lot of research and experiments due to the growth of social media influence, the increasing usage of forums for finding a solution of common known problems and the Web upgrowth. As beginners in the computational linguistics field, we were very interested in dealing with these topics and have found Answer Validation as a good start. Our team chose to focus on subtask A of Task 3 in the SemEval-2015 workshop, namely *Answer selection in community question answering data*. In order to achieve good results, we combined most of the techniques familiar to us. We process the data as question-answer pairs. The framework GATE (Cunningham et al., 2002) was used for the preprocessing in the system because it offers convenient natural language processing pipelines and has an API allowing for system integration. For classification we used the Maximum Entropy classifier provided by MALLET (McCallum and Kachites, 2002). We use a combination of surface, morphological, syntactic, and contextual features as well as distance metrics between the question and answer. Distance metrics are based on word2vec (Mikolov et al., 2013a) and DKPro Similarity (Bär, et al.), (de Castilho, 2014).

2 Related work

Several recent systems were created and used for similar analysis. Although their applications have some differences from the system described in this paper, we consider them relevant because they deal with semantic similarity.

(Başkaya, 2014) uses Vector Space Models which have some similarity to our usage of word2vec centroid metrics with the difference that we do not organize the whole text according to the structure of the result matrix, as the VSMs do. The cosine similarity is common for both systems. The big difference is that we use only the input words while in his system the words' likely synonyms according to a language model are also used. We believe this contributes to the consistently higher scores of his system.

Another work of (Vilariño et al., 2014) also uses n-grams, cosine similarity and that is a common feature with our system. Some differing features are Jaccard coefficient, Latent Semantic Analysis, Pointwise Mutual Information. Their results are very close to ours.

Most of the works dealing with semantic similarity use n-grams, metadata features and stop words as we do. Our scores are not among the highest in subtask A of Task 3, but they come close to and substantially differ from the average score in this field of works.

3 Resources

The datasets we use to train our system are provided from the SemEval-2015 organizers. The datasets consist of 2600 training and 300 development questions including 16,541 training and 1,645 development comments.
Also for the extraction of some features we use pre-trained word and phrase vectors. They are trained on part of Google News dataset (about 100 billion words). The model contains 300-dimensional vectors for 3 million words and phrases.

4 Method

The task at hand is to measure how appropriate and/or informative a comment is with respect to a question. Our approach is to measure the relatedness of a comment to the question or, in other words, to measure if a question-comment pair is consistent. Therefore we attempt to classify each pair as Good, Potential or Bad.

The main characteristic of a good comment is that it is related to the corresponding question. Also, we assume that when answering a question, people tend to use the same words with which the question was asked because that would make it easier for the question author to understand. Therefore, similar wording and especially similar phrases would be an indication of a more informative comment.

4.1 Features

We will call tokens that are not punctuation or stop words meaningful, as they carry some information regardless of exactly how a sentence is formulated.

4.1.1 Lexical Features

For every meaningful token, we extract its stem, lemma and orthography.

4.1.2 N-gram Features

Bigrams and trigrams of tokens (even non-meaningful ones) are also extracted since this should capture similar phrases used in the question-comment pair. We assume that n-grams of higher order could contribute as well, however we believe $n = 2$ and $n = 3$ would carry the most information and $n \geq 4$ would impact training time adversely.

4.1.3 Bad-answer-specific Features

Bad comments often include a lot of punctuation, more than one question in the answer, questions, followed by their obvious answer (when the expression or its synonyms could be directly found in the answer), more than two repeating letters next to each other (i.e. exclamations such as "ahaa"), greetings, chat abbreviations, more than one uppercase word, a lot of emoticons, exclamations and other very meaningless words. Emphasizing such tokens helps to distinguish bad comments specifically.

4.1.4 Structural Features

We include the comment's length in meaningful tokens, length in sentences and each sentence's length as features, since longer comments should include more information. Since named entities, such as locations and organizations etc. would be especially indicative of the topic similarity between question and comment, we give them greater weight by again including named entities, recognized by GATE's built-in NER tools.

4.1.5 TF Vector Space Features

Another attempt to capture similar terms in the question and comment is to convert each entry to a local term-frequency vector and compute the cosine similarity between the vectors for the question and comment rounded to 0.1 precision. Similar wording, regardless of term occurrence frequency, should lead to a higher cosine similarity. We use DKPro's implementation of cosine similarity to achieve this (Bär, et al.). The term "local" refers to the fact that TF vectors of distinct entries are not related, that is, the vector space is specific to a question-comment pair.

4.1.6 Word2vec Semantic Similarity

A good answer, however, does not necessarily use the exact same words. Therefore we need a way to capture the general "topic" of a question. We opted for the word2vec word vectors, proposed by (Mikolov et al., 2013a), (Mikolov et al.,

2013b), (Mikolov et al., 2013c). The general idea of word2vec is to represent each word as a real vector that captures the contexts of word occurrences in a corpus. For a given question-comment pair, we extract word2vec vectors from a pre-trained set for all tokens for which one is available. We compute the centroids for the question and the comment, then use the cosine between the two as a feature. The intention is to capture the similarity between different terms in the pair. The same procedure is then applied once more for only NP-S, i.e. noun phrase, tokens because they carry more information about the topic than other parts of speech.

4.2 Classifier Model

After all described features are extracted, they form a list of string values associated with each question-answer pair. As explained above, some of them are characteristic for bad answers, while others are mainly found in good ones. Therefore, it makes sense to consider the feature list for a given question-answer pair as a document itself. Classifying these documents with any standard approach will then group pairs with similar features together and will differentiate good from bad answers.

In our system, we use MALLET (McCallum and Kachites, 2002) to perform classification on the extracted feature documents. For classification we have chosen the default MALLET workflow that calculates term-frequency feature vectors from its input documents. These vectors are then fed to a MaxEnt classifier, trained and evaluated using ten-fold cross validation. For the final classification, the trained classifier outputs class probabilities for each of the three desired categories: Good, Potential or Bad (which also includes Not English/Dialogue), and the one with the highest score is chosen as the label for the question-answer pair.

5 Experiments and results

Various experiments were conducted to analyse the contribution of the chosen features. In each of them, training was performed on the combined data from the train and development datasets, provided by the organizers. Testing was done on the official test dataset used for evaluation of the task, after it was released by the organizers. The analysis will only focus on the coarse-grained evaluation in the three main classes (Good, Potential, Bad) since our system does not try to target the finer-grained classification.

We defined our baseline system as the one that uses only the lexical and structural features described in the Method section, i.e. word tokens, sentence, question and answer length, as well as the bigrams and trigrams of the question-answer pair. With only these features, the system is very weak - the accuracy as reported by the scorer script against the gold standard is 44.18% and the F1 score is 24.05%.

Next, we included the features that rely on GATE gazetteers, such as the named entities features. This improved the system's performance by more than 1%, reaching accuracy of 45.14% and F1 score of 25.33%.

Another experiment we did was to add to the baseline system only the DKPro cosine similarity. This approach yielded a significant increase in the scores on the test set over the baseline system, around 4%.

Finally, we tested the baseline system with the word2vec cosine values. This experiment was not as successful as the others, offering no improvement. The result may be attributed to the fact that we use a set of vectors trained on generic Web data instead of vectors specifically trained for the SemEval task. However, the community generated datasets are not sufficiently large and cannot be used for adequate word2vec training.

When all features were combined, the scores were boosted to 50% accuracy and 32.02% F1. The improvement from the baseline system is greater than the accumulated improvement from adding the single features because those features influence each other.

All of the described experiments were done on the data from the train and development sets. However, when preparing our final submission for the competition, we trained our system on a training set that included the development data twice. This way more weight was given to those question-answer pairs. The result was an impressive 14% increase in our F1 score.

In order to further analyse this surprising result, we did train a MaxEnt classifier using only the smaller development dataset. All described features were combined here as well. The experiment showed that indeed the larger train dataset provided for the competition has less effect on the performance of our system than the smaller development dataset. We suspect that the contents of the test dataset are closer to the development dataset because that would mean more common n-gram features are detected. This would explain the boost in the F1 score and the accuracy.

A summary of the results obtained in the experiments can be seen in Tables 1 and 2

	Accuracy	**F1 score**
baseline	44.18%	24.05%
+ gazetteers	45.14%	25.33%
+ cosine similarity	47.87%	28.98%
+ word2vec	44.13%	24.03%
all combined	50.00%	32.02%
final system	62.35%	46.07%

Table 1: Accuracy and F1 score achieved using various combinations of features

Training Data	**Accuracy**	**F1 score**
Train + Devel	50.00%	32.02%
Devel Only	57.74%	44.37%
Final System (Train + 2*Devel)	62.35%	46.07%

Table 2: Accuracy and F1 score achieved using all features, but extracted from different training datasets

It should be noted that the results are greatly impacted by the low score we get on the Potential answers class. The scores on this label are very close to 0 with all devised systems, which is to be expected since none of our features were specifically targeted at distinguishing Potential answers from Good and Bad ones.

In all experiments, the highest precision and recall were achieved on the Bad answers.

6 Conclusion

In this paper we introduced our system for answer classification of question answering data. We described the method of preprocessing and applying features to the tokens and also mentioned the intergrated systems used for its implementation. All the steps of the data preparation for analysis were exhaustively described in the method description. Lexical and structural features proved to be insufficient for achieving high results. The gazetteers helped increase our scores but the most important part were the vector calculations made after the preparation process. The experiments showed that examining cosine distance between question and answer can lead to much greater performance. However, the most dramatic improvement was caused by increasing the size of the training data set and giving more weight to some question-answer pairs. For future work, we would try to add more syntactic features into the preprocessing and to integrate language models for the Good and Bad comments classification. With this system, we achieved satisfactory results for the SemEval 2015 answer-validation task.

References

McCallum, Andrew Kachites. 2002. *"MALLET: A Machine Learning for Language Toolkit."* http://mallet.cs.umass.edu.

H. Cunningham, V. Tablan, A. Roberts, K. Bontcheva. 2013. *Getting More Out of Biomedical Documents with GATE's Full Lifecycle Open Source Text Analytics.* PLoS Comput Biol 9(2): e1002854. doi:10.1371/journal.pcbi.1002854 http://tinyurl.com/gate-life-sci/

H. Cunningham, et al. 2011. *Text Processing with GATE (Version 6).* University of Sheffield Department of Computer Science. 15 April 2011. ISBN 0956599311.

Tomas Mikolov, Ilya Sutskever, Kai Chen, Greg Corrado, and Jeffrey Dean. 2013. *Distributed Representations of Words and Phrases and their Compositionality.* In Proceedings of NIPS, 2013.

Tomas Mikolov, Kai Chen, Greg Corrado, and Jeffrey Dean. 2013. *Efficient Estimation of Word Representations in Vector Space.* In Proceedings of Workshop at ICLR, 2013.

Tomas , Wen-tau Yih, and Geoffrey Zweig. 2013. *Linguistic Regularities in Continuous Space Word Representations.* In Proceedings of NAACL HLT, 2013.

Daniel Bär, Torsten Zesch, and Iryna Gurevych. 2013. *DKPro Similarity: An Open Source Framework for Text Similarity.* In Proceedings of the 51st Annual Meeting of the Association for Computational Linguistics: System Demonstrations, pages 121-126, August 2013, Sofia, Bulgaria.

Eckart de Castilho, R. and Gurevych, I. 2014. *A broad-coverage collection of portable NLP components for building shareable analysis pipelines.* In Proceedings of the Workshop on Open Infrastructures and Analysis Frameworks for HLT (OIAF4HLT) at COLING 2014, Dublin, Ireland.

Osman Başkaya. 2014. *AI-KU: Using Co-Occurrence Modeling for Semantic Similarity.* Artificial Intelligence Laboratory, Koç University, Istanbul, Turkey. SemEval-2014.

Darnes Vilariño, David Pinto, Saúl León, Mireya Tovar, Beatriz Beltrán. 2014. *BUAP: Evaluating Features for Multilingual and Cross-Level Semantic Textual Similarity.* Benemérita Universidad Autónoma de Puebla Faculty of Computer Science, Puebla, México. SemEval-2014.

Magdalena Kacmajor, John D. Kelleher. 2014. *DIT: Summarisation and Semantic Expansion in Evaluating Semantic Similarity.* IBM Technology Campus, Applied Intelligence Research Centre, Dublin, Ireland. SemEval-2014.

CoMiC: Adapting a Short Answer Assessment System for Answer Selection

Björn Rudzewitz **Ramon Ziai**
Sonderforschungsbereich 833
Eberhard Karls Universität Tübingen
Nauklerstraße 35
72070 Tübingen, Germany
{brzdwtz,rziai}@sfs.uni-tuebingen.de

Abstract

Open forum threads exhibit a great variability in the quality and quantity of the answers they attract, making it difficult to manually moderate and separate relevant from irrelevant content. The goal of SemEval 2015 Task 3 (Subtask A, English) is to build systems that automatically distinguish between relevant and irrelevant content in forum threads.

We extend a short answer assessment system to build relations between forum questions and answers with respect to similarity, question type, and answer content. The features are used in a sequence classifier to account for the conversation character of threads. The performance of this approach is modest in comparison to the other task participants and also to the performance the system usually reaches in short answer assessment. However, the new features implemented for this task are a first step in developing more fine-grained question-answer features and identifying relevant answers.

1 Introduction

In this paper, we discuss the adaptation of our Short Answer Assessment (SAA) system CoMiC (Meurers et al., 2011) to Task 3, Subtask A (English) of SemEval 2015, *Answer Selection in Community Question Answering*. The aim in the task was to distinguish helpful from unhelpful answers in a community forum given a question.

We enter the QA landscape from the perspective of evaluating student answers to reading comprehension questions with respect to whether they contain the targeted content. In such settings, one generally has a reference answer to which a candidate answer can be compared, making alignment-based systems a natural solution. This is not the case for QA, where a system has to select or rank candidate answers with regard to a question posed. However, the present task is still interesting to us because it shares a central characteristic with SAA: one needs to identify the relevant part of an answer, given a question. In theoretical linguistics, that relevant part is usually called *focus* (cf., e.g., Krifka (2007)), and several research groups have made efforts to annotate it in corpus data (Hajičová and Sgall, 2001; Ritz et al., 2008; Calhoun et al., 2010; Ziai and Meurers, 2014).

Automatic approaches to identifying focus have however yet to be proposed, so for the current task, we adapted and used our SAA system to align candidate answers with the forum question, identifying whether and how question material was picked up, which in turn should indicate whether answers are on-topic. We then used a number of features to characterize the unaligned answer material, from POS classes to temporal expressions. We also encoded which question words were present in the question in the hope that the resulting classifier would pick up connections between individual question words and the different answer features in an approximation to identifying the focus of the answer.

The paper is organized as follows: Section 2 briefly discusses the data of the task before section 3 presents the details of our system architecture and the features we used. Section 4 then shows the results of our efforts and a short error analysis, and finally section 5 concludes and discusses directions for further efforts.

2 Data

The English dataset used in the task is a collection of web-crawled forum[1] texts where each item consists of a question and responses to the question. Each response has one of the six labels *Good*, *Bad*, *Potential*, *Dialogue*, *non-English*, or *Other*, describing its potential for answering the corresponding question. The correct label for every response had to be predicted by the systems at test time. The dataset is not balanced since it contains more *Good* labelled answers than answers with another label. The language used in the questions and responses exhibits strong deviations from standard English. For a detailed description, refer to (Màrquez et al., 2015).

3 System Details

In this section, we describe the CoMiC system and its extensions for Task 3 of SemEval 2015. We begin by going briefly over the baseline system and its features and continue by describing in detail the new features introduced for this task.

The baseline CoMiC system is an alignment-based short answer assessment system. Alignments between a student and a target answer are computed on different linguistic levels. The quantities of alignments of a certain quality are used as features and given to a classifier that predicts a binary correctness label for the student answer. A detailed description can be found in (Meurers et al., 2011).

For this task, we adapt the system by making it establish alignments between forum questions and the corresponding answers. Thus it is used primarily as a text similarity system extended by features to differentiate between given and new material.

3.1 Features

The system uses the standard features from the CoMiC system and a range of new features. Although the new features described here were used in the context of Question Answering, we are planning to explore to what extent the usage of these features will improve the CoMiC system in the context of short answer assessment. The following sections will start with an overview about the standard CoMiC features and will continue with a detailed description of the new features.

[1]http://www.qatarliving.com/forum

3.1.1 CoMiC

As mentioned in the introduction, the CoMiC system is designed to judge the contents of a short answer to a reading comprehension question based on alignment with a target answer (Meurers et al., 2011). The features it uses express the linguistic unit and nature of the successful alignments found between candidate and target answer. In the present setting, we used the standard CoMiC features to determine the degree of similarity between the candidate answer and the forum question, in order to find out whether the answer does indeed pick up on question topic material. These features are summarized in Table 1.

Feature	Description
1. Keyword Overlap	Percent of dependency heads aligned (relative to question)
2./3. Token Overlap	Percent of aligned question/candidate tokens
4./5. Chunk Overlap	Percent of aligned question/candidate chunks (as identified by OpenNLP[2])
6./7. Triple Overlap	Percent of aligned question/candidate dependency triples
8. Token Match	Percent of token alignments that were token-identical
9. Similarity Match	Percent of token alignments resolved using PMI-IR (Turney, 2001)
10. Type Match	Percent of token alignments resolved using WordNet hierarchy (Fellbaum, 1998)
11. Lemma Match	Percent of token alignments that were lemma-resolved
12. Synonym Match	Percent of token alignments sharing same WordNet synset
13. Variety of Match (0-5)	Number of kinds of token-level alignments (features 8–12)

Table 1: Standard features in the CoMiC system

3.1.2 POS-Specific Weighting

The system uses four features that measure how much of the material not given in the question belongs to a group of syntactically related categories. The idea is to weight new material by estimating a distribution of general syntactic classes over it. After

[2]http://opennlp.apache.org/

the alignment process, the distribution of groups of POS categories of non-aligned tokens is computed with respect to all non-aligned tokens. As a basis, the Penn Treebank POS tags from prior annotation are used. Four groups are distinguished which are composed in the following way:

- *nouns*: subsumes all nominal categories
- *verbs*: subsumes full verbs, auxiliaries, modals, and participles
- *adj/v*: subsumes all adjectival and adverbial categories
- *rest*: subsumes all categories not listed above

For every of the four groups, the frequency of each POS tag in this group in the non-aligned material is computed, normalized against the frequency of all POS tags in the non-aligned material, and summed up to get the overall proportion of this group in the non-aligned material. Previous experiments suggested to prefer this approach with coarse groups over an approach with more fine-grained POS classes due to its overall robustness needed in this context.

3.1.3 Question Words

In an approximation to identifying question types, we encoded the presence or absence of the *wh*-words *who*, *how*, *why*, *when*, *where*, *which*, *whom*, *whose* and *what* with a binary feature for each. We also encode the presence of modal and auxiliary verbs in the first three tokens of a sentence in order to detect questions such as "Can anyone help me?".

The idea behind these features was to enable associations between them and the features characterizing the new material in the answer.

3.1.4 Named Entity Recognition

We used the Stanford Named Entity Recognizer (Finkel et al., 2005) to detect named entities in new answer material. For each of the three standard NE classes PERSON, ORGANIZATION and LOCATION, we encode its presence or absence in a binary feature. Additionally, we encode the total number of syntactic chunks found in the answer, of which the named entities constitute a subset.

By detecting NEs, we wanted to enable the resulting classifier to pick up connections between the previously mentioned *wh*-features and the named entities.

3.1.5 Temporal Expressions

The system uses a binary feature indicating the presence or absence of one or more temporal expressions in every answer. In combination with the question word features, the system can build relations between questions asking for temporal content and the presence of temporal expressions in the answer. The system therefore makes use of an adapted version of the HeidelTime temporal tagger (Strötgen and Gertz, 2013) due to its ability to parse web content with a high accuracy. No distinction is made between different kinds of temporal expressions recognized by the HeidelTime module.

3.2 Adaptation to Social Media Language

Since the CoMiC system is designed for the assessment of short answers of language learners, several adaptations were needed in order for the system to be able to deal with the noisiness of social media language. These adaptations consist of multiple steps that will be described in this section.
The first step towards normalizing the language consists of the removal of HTML markup present in several answers. For this purpose, the CoMiC system was extended by adding an additional module that parses the raw input and recursively extracts the text content while removing any HTML markup. The jsoup module[3] was used to accomplish this task.
The second step in the normalization process is driven by the idea to exclude certain tokens from further processing if they are recognized as being of a category unlikely to contribute usefully in deeper analysis by the system, such as emoticons, e-mail addresses, hashtags, abbreviations, symbols, punctuation sequences, etc. Therefore we use an adapted version of the ark-tweet-nlp module (Gimpel et al., 2011) in the tokenization step which allows parallel tokenization and POS tagging with a tagset tailored to cover the specifics of social media language. The exclusion of noisy material is done after sentence segmentation, allowing to preserve sentences including all tokens from the text, at the same time excluding unwanted material from further analysis and alignment.

[3] http://jsoup.org/

3.3 Model

We trained two different models based on separate classification methods. We first experimented with memory-based learning using TiMBL (Daelemans et al., 2007), using the cosine as distance metric and $k = 5$ nearest neighbors that each instance was compared to. In order to take advantage of the fact that a forum thread is in fact a conversation and the usefulness of a given forum answer may depend on previous answers, we also employed a CRF tagger (MALLET, McCallum (2002)) to classify a sequence of forum posts instead of a single instance. We used one Markov order for the CRF. To our knowledge, this is the only model in the competition that attempted to classify answer sequences.

The CRF performed slightly better than the memory-based approach on the development set, which we attribute to its ability to take an answer's context into account. We submitted it as our primary run and the memory-based one as the contrastive run.

4 Results

Evaluation was done using two scenarios: fine-grained (*Good*, *Potential*, *Dialogue*, *Bad*) and coarse-grained (*Good*, *Potential*, *Bad*), with missing classes always collapsed into *Bad*. Table 2 shows the coarse-grained accuracies and Macro F1 scores of our system variants on development and test set for the English Subtask A. The CRF approach used in the primary system outperforms the contrastive memory-based approach on both data sets in terms of accuracy. In case of the primary system, the model seems to transfer well since the accuracy on the test set is even higher than on the development set. In case of the contrastive system, the accuracy drops when the model is applied to the test set. The table also shows the accuracy for the best-performing system, JAIST-contrastive, and the majority baseline.

System	Dev. Set		Test Set	
	Acc.	F1	Acc.	F1
Best system	–	–	73.76	57.29
CoMiC-prim.	54.89	28.41	54.20	30.63
CoMiC-contr.	53.37	24.36	50.56	23.36
Maj. baseline	53.19	23.15	50.46	22.36

Table 2: Coarse-grained accuracy and Macro F1 of systems on development and test set for Subtask A, English

These accuracies are rather modest, both in comparison to accuracy values of the CoMiC system when used for the task of short answer assessment for which the system is intended and designed, and also in comparison to other task participants.

An error analysis showed several problems that influenced the performance of the system. The noisiness of the input text on the syntactic and morphological level caused the POS tagger to assign incorrect POS tags. This led to problems for modules that make use of POS information. The noisiness is reflected also in the fact that not all lemmas are identified correctly. Another problem is that the spelling correction component struggled with certain forms and did not always find the spelling-corrected form. The main problem was that too few tokens and hardly any chunks could be aligned to the question, severely influencing the alignment-based features. The system also got mislead in cases where the person who posed the question reformulated the question for others, since the classifier failed to use the high similarity between the question and the answer as a clear indicator for an unhelpful answer.

5 Conclusion

We applied the short answer system CoMiC to the task of question selection. The standard CoMiC system was used to determine the similarity between a question and an answer. We added new features to the CoMiC system to enable the classifier to build relations between the question type and certain answer features. Extensions to the system were necessary in order to deal with the noisiness of web texts. We applied a CRF classifier that takes into account the context of answers in the forum and found a positive effect on performance. The results of the task show that our system performs rather moderately when used for this task it is not designed or intended for. However, the new features implemented for this task are a first step in developing more fine-grained question-answer features which eventually could be useful for identifying the relevant part of an answer.

Acknowledgments

We would like to thank two anonymous reviewers for their detailed and helpful comments.

References

Sasha Calhoun, Jean Carletta, Jason Brenier, Neil Mayo, Dan Jurafsky, Mark Steedman, and David Beaver. 2010. The NXT-format switchboard corpus: A rich resource for investigating the syntax, semantics, pragmatics and prosody of dialogue. *Language Resources and Evaluation*, 44:387–419.

Walter Daelemans, Jakub Zavrel, Ko van der Sloot, and Antal van den Bosch, 2007. *TiMBL: Tilburg Memory-Based Learner Reference Guide, ILK Technical Report ILK 07-03*. Induction of Linguistic Knowledge Research Group Department of Communication and Information Sciences, Tilburg University, Tilburg, The Netherlands, July 11. Version 6.0.

Christiane Fellbaum, editor. 1998. *WordNet: An Electronic Lexical Database*. MIT Press, Cambridge, Massachusetts.

Jenny Rose Finkel, Trond Grenager, and Christopher Manning. 2005. Incorporating non-local information into information extraction systems by gibbs sampling. In *Proceedings of the 43rd Annual Meeting on Association for Computational Linguistics*, pages 363–370, Stroudsburg, PA, USA. Association for Computational Linguistics.

Kevin Gimpel, Nathan Schneider, Brendan O'Connor, Dipanjan Das, Daniel Mills, Jacob Eisenstein, Michael Heilman, Dani Yogatama, Jeffrey Flanigan, and Noah A Smith. 2011. Part-of-speech tagging for twitter: Annotation, features, and experiments. In *Proceedings of the 49th Annual Meeting of the Association for Computational Linguistics: Human Language Technologies: short papers-Volume 2*, pages 42–47. Association for Computational Linguistics.

Eva Hajičová and Petr Sgall. 2001. Topic-focus and salience. In *Proceedings of the 39th Annual Meeting on Association for Computational Linguistics*, ACL '01, pages 276–281, Toulouse, France. Association for Computational Linguistics.

Manfred Krifka. 2007. Basic notions of information structure. In Caroline Fery, Gisbert Fanselow, and Manfred Krifka, editors, *The notions of information structure*, volume 6 of *Interdisciplinary Studies on Information Structure (ISIS)*, pages 13–55. Universitätsverlag Potsdam, Potsdam.

Andrew Kachites McCallum. 2002. MALLET: A machine learning for language toolkit. http://mallet.cs.umass.edu.

Detmar Meurers, Ramon Ziai, Niels Ott, and Stacey Bailey. 2011. Integrating parallel analysis modules to evaluate the meaning of answers to reading comprehension questions. *IJCEELL. Special Issue on Automatic Free-text Evaluation*, 21(4):355–369.

Lluís Màrquez, James Glass, Walid Magdy, Alessandro Moschitti, Preslav Nakov, and Bilal Randeree. 2015. Semeval-2015 task 3: Answer selection in community question answering. In *Proceedings of the 9th International Workshop on Semantic Evaluation (SemEval 2015)*. Association for Computational Linguistics.

Julia Ritz, Stefanie Dipper, and Michael Götze. 2008. Annotation of information structure: An evaluation across different types of texts. In *Proceedings of the 6th International Conference on Language Resources and Evaluation*, pages 2137–2142, Marrakech, Morocco.

Jannik Strötgen and Michael Gertz. 2013. Multilingual and cross-domain temporal tagging. *Language Resources and Evaluation*, 47(2):269–298.

Peter Turney. 2001. Mining the web for synonyms: PMI-IR versus LSA on TOEFL. In *Proceedings of the Twelfth European Conference on Machine Learning (ECML-2001)*, pages 491–502, Freiburg, Germany.

Ramon Ziai and Detmar Meurers. 2014. Focus annotation in reading comprehension data. In *Proceedings of the 8th Linguistic Annotation Workshop (LAW VIII, 2014)*, pages 159–168, Dublin, Ireland. COLING, Association for Computational Linguistics.

SemEval-2015 Task 2: Semantic Textual Similarity, English, Spanish and Pilot on Interpretability

Eneko Agirre[a]*, Carmen Banea[b]*, Claire Cardie[c], Daniel Cer[d], Mona Diab[e]*, Aitor Gonzalez-Agirre[a], Weiwei Guo[f], Iñigo Lopez-Gazpio[a], Montse Maritxalar[a]*, Rada Mihalcea[b], German Rigau[a], Larraitz Uria[a], Janyce Wiebe[g]

[a]University of the Basque Country
Donostia, Basque Country

[b]University of Michigan
Ann Arbor, MI

[c]Cornell University
Ithaca, NY

[d]Google Inc.
Mountain View, CA

[e]George Washington University
Washington, DC

[f]Columbia University
New York, NY

[g]University of Pittsburgh
Pittsburgh, PA

Abstract

In semantic textual similarity (STS), systems rate the degree of semantic equivalence between two text snippets. This year, the participants were challenged with new datasets in English and Spanish. The annotations for both subtasks leveraged crowdsourcing. The English subtask attracted 29 teams with 74 system runs, and the Spanish subtask engaged 7 teams participating with 16 system runs. In addition, this year we ran a pilot task on interpretable STS, where the systems needed to add an explanatory layer, that is, they had to align the chunks in the sentence pair, explicitly annotating the kind of relation and the score of the chunk pair. The train and test data were manually annotated by an expert, and included headline and image sentence pairs from previous years. 7 teams participated with 29 runs.

1 Introduction and Motivation

Given two snippets of text, semantic textual similarity (STS) captures the notion that some texts are more similar than others, measuring their degree of semantic equivalence. Textual similarity can range from complete unrelatedness to exact semantic equivalence, and a graded similarity score intuitively captures the notion of intermediate shades of similarity, as pairs of text may differ from some minor nuanced aspects of meaning to relatively important semantic differences, to sharing only some details, or to simply unrelated in meaning (cf. Sect. 2).

One of the goals of the STS task is to create a unified framework for combining several semantic components that otherwise have historically tended to be evaluated independently and without characterization of impact on NLP applications. By providing such a framework, STS allows for an extrinsic evaluation of these modules. Moreover, such an STS framework could itself be in turn evaluated intrinsically and extrinsically as a grey/black box within various NLP applications.

STS is related to both textual entailment (TE) and paraphrasing, but it differs in a number of ways and it is more directly applicable to a number of NLP tasks. STS is different from TE inasmuch as it assumes bidirectional graded equivalence between a pair of textual snippets. In the case of TE the equivalence is directional, e.g. *a car is a vehicle*, but *a vehicle is not necessarily a car*. STS also differs from both TE and paraphrasing (in as far as both tasks have been defined to date in the literature) in that rather than being a binary yes/no decision (e.g. *a vehicle is not a car*), we define STS to be a graded similarity notion (e.g. *a vehicle* and *a car* are more similar than *a wave* and *a car*). A quantifiable graded bidirectional notion of textual similarity is useful for many NLP tasks such as MT evaluation, information extraction, question answering, summarization.

In 2012, we held the first pilot task at SemEval 2012, as part of the *SEM 2012 conference, with great success (Agirre et al., 2012). In addition, we

*Coordinators: e.agirre@ehu.eus, carmennb@umich.edu, mtdiab@gwu.edu, montse.maritxalar@ehu.eus

held a DARPA sponsored workshop at Columbia University.[1] In 2013, STS was selected as the official shared task of the *SEM 2013 conference, with two subtasks: a core task, which was similar to the 2012 task, and a pilot task on typed-similarity between semi-structured records. In 2014, new datasets including new genres were used, and we expanded the evaluations to address sentence similarity in a new language, namely Spanish (Agirre et al., 2014).

This year we presented three subtasks: the English subtask, the Spanish subtask and the interpretable pilot subtask. The English subtask comprised pairs from headlines and image descriptions, and it also introduced new genres, including answer pairs from a tutorial dialogue system and from Q&A websites, and pairs from a dataset tagged with committed belief annotations. For the Spanish subtask, additional pairs from news and Wikipedia articles were selected. The annotations for both tasks leveraged crowdsourcing. Finally, with the interpretable STS pilot subtask, we wanted to start exploring whether participant systems are able to explain *why* two sentences are related/unrelated, adding an explanatory layer to the similarity score.

2 Task Description

In this section, we will focus on each one of the subtasks individually.

2.1 English Subtask

The English subtask dataset comprises pairs of sentences from news headlines (HDL), image descriptions (Images), answer pairs from a tutorial dialogue system (Answers-student), answer pairs from Q&A websites (Answers-forum), and pairs from a committed belief dataset (Belief).

For **HDL**, we used naturally occurring news headlines gathered by the Europe Media Monitor (EMM) engine (Best et al., 2005) from several different news sources (from April 2nd, 2013 to July 28th, 2014). EMM clusters together related news. Our goal was to generate a balanced dataset across the different similarity ranges. Therefore, we built two sets of headline pairs: a set where the pairs come from the same EMM cluster and another set where the headlines come from a different EMM cluster. Then, we computed the string similarity between those pairs. Accordingly, we sampled 1000 headline pairs of headlines that occur in the same EMM cluster, aiming for pairs equally distributed between minimal and maximal similarity using simple string similarity as a metric. We sampled another 1000 pairs from the different EMM cluster in the same manner.

[1] http://www.cs.columbia.edu/~weiwei/workshop/

year	dataset	pairs	source
2012	MSRpar	1500	newswire
2012	MSRvid	1500	videos
2012	OnWN	750	glosses
2012	SMTnews	750	MT eval.
2012	SMTeuroparl	750	MT eval.
2013	HDL	750	newswire
2013	FNWN	189	glosses
2013	OnWN	561	glosses
2013	SMT	750	MT eval.
2014	HDL	750	newswire headlines
2014	OnWN	750	glosses
2014	Deft-forum	450	forum posts
2014	Deft-news	300	news summary
2014	Images	750	image descriptions
2014	Tweet-news	750	tweet-news pairs
2015	HDL	750	newswire headlines
2015	Images	750	image descriptions
2015	Answers-student	750	student answers
2015	Answers-forum	375	Q&A forum answers
2015	Belief	375	commited belief

Table 2: English subtask: Summary of train (2012, 2013, 2014) and test (2015) datasets.

The **Images** dataset is a subset of the PASCAL VOC-2008 dataset (Rashtchian et al., 2010), which consists of 1000 images with around 10 descriptions each, and has been used by a number of image description systems. It was also sampled using string similarity, discarding those that had been used in previous years. We organized two bins with 1000 pairs each: one with pairs of descriptions from the same image, and the other one with pairs of descriptions from different images.

The source of the **Answers-student** pairs is the BEETLE corpus (Dzikovska et al., 2010), which is a question-answer dataset collected and annotated during the evaluation of the BEETLE II tutorial dialogue system. The BEETLE II system is an intelligent tutoring engine that teaches students basic electricity and electronics. The corpus was used in

Score	English (E)	Spanish (S)
5(E)/ 4(S)	*The two sentences are completely equivalent, as they mean the same thing.*	
	The bird is bathing in the sink. Birdie is washing itself in the water basin.	El pájaro se esta bañando en el lavabo. El pájaro se está lavando en el aguamanil.
4(E)/ 3(S)	*The two sentences are mostly equivalent, but some unimportant details differ.*	
	In May 2010, the troops attempted to invade Kabul. The US army invaded Kabul on May 7th last year, 2010.	
3(E)/ 3(S)	*The two sentences are roughly equivalent, but some important information differs/missing.*	
	John said he is considered a witness but not a suspect. "He is not a suspect anymore." John said.	John dijo que él es considerado como testigo, y no como sospechoso. "Él ya no es un sospechoso," John dijo.
2	*The two sentences are not equivalent, but share some details.*	
	They flew out of the nest in groups. They flew into the nest together.	Ellos volaron del nido en grupos. Volaron hacia el nido juntos.
1	*The two sentences are not equivalent, but are on the same topic.*	
	The woman is playing the violin. The young lady enjoys listening to the guitar.	La mujer está tocando el violín. La joven disfruta escuchar la guitarra.
0	*The two sentences are completely dissimilar.*	
	John went horse back riding at dawn with a whole group of friends. Sunrise at dawn is a magnificent view to take in if you wake up early enough for it.	Al amanecer, Juan se fue a montar a caballo con un grupo de amigos. La salida del sol al amanecer es una magnífica vista que puede presenciar si usted se despierta lo suficientemente temprano para verla.

Table 1: Similarity scores with explanations and examples for the English and Spanish subtasks, where the sentences in Spanish are translations of the English ones. A similarity score of 5 in English is mirrored by a maximum score of 4 in Spanish; the definitions pertaining to scores 3 and 4 in English are collapsed under a score of 3 in Spanish, with the definition "*The two sentences are mostly equivalent, but some details differ.*"

the student response analysis task of Semeval-2013. Given a question, a known correct "reference answer" and the "student answer", the goal of the task was to assess whether student answers were correct, contradictory or incorrect (partially correct, irrelevant or not in the domain). For STS, we selected pairs of answers made up of single sentences. The pairs were sampled from string similarity values between 0.6 and 1.

The **Answers-forums** dataset consists of paired answers collected from the Stack Exchange question and answer websites (http://stackexchange.com/). Some of the paired answers are responses to the same question, while others are responses to different questions. Each answer in the pair consists of a statement composed of a single sentence or sentence fragment. For multi-sentence answers, we extracted the single sentence from the larger answer that appears to best summarize the answer.

The **Belief** pairs were collected from the DEFT Committed Belief Annotation dataset (LDC2014E55). All source documents are English Discussion Forum data. We sampled 2000 pairs using string similarity values between 0.5 and 1. It is worth noting that the similarity values were skewed, with very few pairs above 0.8 similarity.

In an attempt to improve the quality of the data, we selected 2000 pairs from each dataset and annotated them. This "raw" data was automatically filtered in order to achieve the following three (partially conflicting) goals: (1) to obtain a more uniform distribution across scores; (2) to select pairs with high inter-annotator agreement; (3) to select pairs which were difficult for a string-matching baseline. The filtering process was purely automated and involved no manual selection of pairs. The raw annotations and the Perl scripts that generated the final gold standard are available at the task website. See Table 2 for the number of selected pairs per dataset.

Table 1 shows the explanations and values associated with each score between 5 and 0. As in prior years, we used Amazon Mechanical Turk (AMT)[2] to crowdsource the annotation of the English pairs. Five sentence pairs were presented to each annotator at once, per human intelligence task (HIT), at a payrate of $0.20. We collected five separate annotations per sentence pair. Annotators were only eligible to work on the task if they had the Mechanical Turk Master Qualification, a special qualification conferred by AMT (using a priority statistical model) to annotators who consistently maintain a very high level of quality across a variety of tasks from numerous requesters. Access to these skilled workers entails a 20% surcharge.

To monitor the quality of the annotations, we used a gold dataset of 105 pairs that were manually annotated by the task organizers during STS 2013. We included one of these gold pairs in each set of five sentence pairs, where the gold pairs were indistinguishable from the rest. Unlike when we ran on CrowdFlower for STS 2013, the gold pairs were not used for training purposes, neither were workers automatically banned from the task if they made too many mistakes annotating the pairs. Rather, the gold pairs were only used to help in identifying and removing the data associated with poorly performing annotators. With few exceptions, 90% of the answers from each individual annotator fell within +/-1 of the answers selected by the organizers for the gold dataset.

The distribution of scores obtained from the AMT providers in the all the datasets is roughly uniform across the different grades of similarity, although the scores are slightly lower for Belief. Compared to the other datasets, the Answer-students dataset has considerably fewer 0 scores.

In order to assess the annotation quality, we measure the correlation of each annotator with the average of the rest of the annotators, and then average the results. This approach to estimate the quality is identical to the method used for evaluations (see Section 3), and it can thus be considered as the upper bound of the systems. The pre-filtering inter-tagger correlation for each English dataset is as follows:

- Answer-forums; 64.7%
- Answer-students; 76.6%
- Belief: 73.8%
- Headlines: 82.1%
- Images: 84.6%

And post-filtering inter-tagger correlations:

- Answer-forums; 74.2%
- Answer-students; 82.2%
- Belief: 72.1%
- Headlines: 86.9%
- Images: 88.8%

The correlation figures are generally very high (over 70%). The post-filtering process helps to increase the inter-tagger correlation.

2.2 Spanish Subtask

The Spanish subtask follows a setup similar to the English subtask, except that the similarity scores were adapted to fit a range from 0 to 4 (see Table 1). We thought that the distinction between a score of 3 and 4 for the English task would pose more difficulty for us in conveying into Spanish, as the sole difference between the two lies in how the annotators perceive the importance of additional details or missing information with respect to the core semantic interpretation of the pair. As this aspect entails a subjective judgement, we casted the annotation guidelines into straightforward and unambiguous instructions, and thus opted to use a similarity range from 0 to 4.

Prior to the evaluation window, the participants had access to a trial dataset consisting of 65 sentence pairs annotated for similarity and the test data released as part of SemEval 2014 Task 10 (Agirre et al., 2014), consisting of approximately 800 sentence pairs extracted from Spanish newswire and encyclopedic content. For the evaluations, we constructed two datasets, one extracted from the Spanish Wikipedia[3] (December 2013 dump) consisting of 251 sentence pairs, and the other one from contemporary news articles collected from news media in Spanish (November 2014) of 500 pairs.

Spanish Wikipedia. The Wikipedia dump was processed using the Parse::MediaWikiDump Perl library. We removed all titles, html tags, wiki tags and

[2] www.mturk.com

[3] es.wikipedia.org

hyperlinks (keeping only the surface forms). Each article was split into paragraphs, where the first paragraph was considered to be the article's abstract, while the remaining ones were deemed to be its content. Each of these were split into sentences using the Perl library Uplug::PreProcess::SentDetect, and only the sentences longer than eight words were used. We iteratively computed the lexical similarity[4] between every sentence in the abstract and every sentence in the content, and retained those pairs whose sentence length ratio was higher than 0.5, and their similarity scored over 0.35.

The final set of sentence pairs was split into five bins, and their scores were normalized to range from 0 to 1. The more interesting and difficult pairs were found, perhaps not surprisingly, in bin 0, where synonyms/short paraphrases were more frequent, and 251 sentence pairs were manually selected from this bin in order to ensure a diverse and challenging set.

We then proceeded to annotate the sentence pairs for textual similarity by designing an AMT task, following a similar structure as in 2014, namely creating HITs consisting of seven sentence pairs, where six of them were a subset of the newly developed dataset, and one of them was reused from 2014 data with the purpose of control and to enable annotation quality comparisons.[5] As in the previous year, AMT providers were eligible to complete a task if they had more than 500 accepted HITs, with an over 90% acceptance rate. Each HIT was annotated by five AMT providers, and the remuneration was of $0.30 per HIT.[6] The final sentence pair similarity scores was computed by averaging over the judgments of the five AMT providers.

In order to assess the robustness of the AMT annotations, we computed the Pearson correlation between the similarity scores newly assigned to the control sentences, and those assigned in 2014. We obtained a measure of over 0.92, indicating a high resemblance between the two sets of judgements and highlighting the consistency of crowd wisdom, which is able to produce coherent outcomes irrespective of the individuals participating in the decision process.

[4]Algorithm based on the Linux *diff* command (Algorithm::Diff Perl module).

[5]The control pair appeared randomly within each HIT.

[6]For additional information, we refer the reader to (Agirre et al., 2014).

Spanish News. The second Spanish dataset was extracted from news articles published in Spanish language media from around the world in November 2014. The hyperlinks to the articles were obtained by parsing the "International" page of Spanish Google News,[7] which aggregates or clusters in real time articles describing a particular event from a diverse pool of news sites, where each grouping is labeled with the title of one of the predominant articles. By leveraging these clusters of links pointing to the sites where the articles were originally published, we were able to gather raw text that had a high probability to contain semantically similar sentences. We encountered several difficulties while mining the articles, ranging from each article having its own formatting depending on the source site, to advertisements, cookie requirements, to encoding for Spanish diacritics. We used the *lynx text-based browser*,[8] which was able to standardize the raw articles to a degree. The output of the browser was processed using a rule based approach taking into account continuous text span length, ratio of symbols and numbers to the text, etc., in order to determine when a paragraph is part of the article content. After that, a second pass over the predictions corrected mislabeled paragraphs if they were preceded and followed by paragraphs identified as content. All the content pertaining to articles on the same event was joined, sentence split, and *diff* pairwise similarities were computed. The set of candidate sentences followed the same constraints as those enforced for the Wikipedia dataset. From these, we manually extracted 500 sentence pairs, which were annotated in an AMT task mirroring the same setup as used for the encyclopedic data annotation. The correlation between this year's annotations and those of the 2014 STS task using the control sentence pairs remained high, at 0.886.

Since historically many of the text-to-text similarity algorithms have relied heavily on lexical matching, this year's Spanish datasets featured sentence pairs with a higher degree of difficulty. This was achieved by handpicking pairs which shared some common vocabulary, yet carried completely different meanings at the sentence level.

[7]`news.google.es`

[8]`lynx.browser.org`

2.3 Interpretable Subtask

Given the setup of STS tasks to date, this year we wanted to shift focus, and gauge the ability of participating systems to explain *why* two sentences may be related/unrelated, by supplementing the similarity score with an explanatory layer. As a first step in this direction, given a pair of sentences, systems needed to align the chunks across both sentences, and for each alignment, classify the type of relation, and provide the corresponding similarity score.

In previous work, Brockett (2007) and Rus et al. (2012) produced a dataset where corresponding words (including some multiword expressions like named-entities) were aligned. Although this alignment is useful, we wanted to move forward to the alignment of segments, and decided to align chunks (Abney, 1991). Brockett (2007) did not provide any label to alignments, while Rus et al. (2012) defined a basic typology. In our task, we provided a more detailed typology for the aligned chunks as well as a similarity/relatedness score for each alignment. Contrary to the mentioned works, we first identified the segments (chunks in our case) in each sentence separately, and then aligned them. In a different strand of work, Nielsen et al. (2009) defined a textual entailment model where the "facets" (words under some syntactic/semantic relation) in the response of a student were linked to the concepts in the reference answer. The link would signal whether each facet in the response was entailed by the reference answer or not, but would not explicitly mark which parts of the reference answer caused the entailment. This model was later followed by Levy et al. (2013). Our task was different in that we identified the corresponding chunks in both sentences. We think that, in the future, the aligned facets could provide complementary information to chunks.

For interpretable STS the similarity scores range from 0 to 5, as in the English subtask. With respect to the relation between the aligned chunks, the present pilot only allowed 1:1 alignments. As a consequence, we had to include a special alignment context tag (ALIC) to simulate those chunks which had some semantic similarity or relatedness in the other sentence, but could not have been aligned because of the 1:1 restriction. In the case of the aligned chunks, the following relatedness tags were defined:

- EQUI, for chunks which are semantically equivalent in the context.
- OPPO, for chunks which are in opposition to each other in the context.
- SPE1 and SPE2, for chunks which have similar meanings, but which include different level of detailed information, chunk in sentence1 more specific than chunk in sentence2, or vice versa.
- SIMI, for chunks with similar meanings, but no EQUI, OPPO, SPE1, or SPE2.
- REL, for chunks which have related meanings, but no EQUI, OPPO, SPE1, SPE2, or SIMI.

In addition, a pair of chunks could be annotated with factuality (FACT) and polarity (POL), if there was a phenomena associated to those which made the meaning of the two chunks different. Finally, in the case of chunks which did not have any similarity/relatedness in the other sentence, they were tagged as NOALI.

The pilot presented two scenarios: sentence raw text and gold standard chunks. In the first scenario, given a pair of sentences, participants had to identify the composing chunks, and then align them; after that they would assign a relatedness tag and a similarity score to each alignment. In the gold standard scenario, participants were provided with the gold standard chunks, which were based on those used in the CoNLL 2000 chunking task (Tjong Kim Sang and Buchholz, 2000), with some adaptations (see annotation guidelines available at the task website).

The training and test datasets consisted of 1500 and 753 sentence pairs, respectively, extracted from the HDL and Images datasets used in 2014. Listing 1 shows the annotation format for a given sentence pair from the training set (note that each alignment is reported in one line as follows: token-id-sent1 <==> token-id-sent2 // label // score // comment).

Listing 1: STS interpretable - annotation format

```
<sentence id="6" status="">
 A woman riding a brown horse
 A young girl riding a brown horse
 ...
 <alignment>
  1 2 <==> 1 2 3 // SIMI // 4 // A woman <==>
    A young girl
  4 5 6 <==> 5 6 7 // EQUI // 5 // a brown
    horse <==> a brown horse
  3 <==> 4 // EQUI // 5 // riding <==> riding
 </alignment>
</sentence>
```

3 System Evaluation for STS

This Section reports the results for the English and Spanish subtasks. Note that participants could submit a maximum of three runs per subtask.

3.1 Evaluation Metrics

As in previous exercises, we used Pearson product-moment correlation between the system scores and the GS scores. In order to compute statistical significance among system results, we use a one-tailed parametric test based on Fisher's z-transformation (Press et al., , equation 14.5.10).

3.2 Baseline System

In order to provide a simple word overlap baseline (Baseline-tokencos), we tokenized the input sentences splitting on white spaces, and then each sentence was represented as a vector in the multidimensional token space. Each dimension had 1 if the token was present in the sentence, 0 otherwise. Vector similarity was computed using cosine similarity.

We also ran the TakeLab system (Šarić et al., 2012) from STS 2012, which yielded strong results in previous years evaluations.[9]. The system was trained on all previous datasets STS12, STS13 and STS14, and tested on each subset of STS15.

3.3 Participation

29 teams participated in the English subtask, submitting 74 system runs. One team submitted fixes on one run past the deadline, as explicitly marked in Table 3. After the submission deadline expired, the organizers published the gold standard, the evaluation script, the scripts to generate the gold standard from raw annotation files, and participant submissions on the task website, in order to ensure a transparent evaluation process. As regards the Spanish STS task, it attracted 7 teams, which participated with 16 system runs.

3.4 English Subtask Results

Table 3 shows the results of the English subtask, with runs listed in alphabetical order. The correlation in each dataset is given, followed by the weighted mean correlation (the official measure) and the rank of the run. The Table also shows the results of the baseline, which would rank 61st, and TakeLab, which was trained with all datasets from previous years. TakeLab would rank 42nd, 10 absolute points below the best system, a larger difference than in 2014.

The highest results are for images (87.1%, by Samsung) and headlines (84.2%, by Samsung), followed by answers-students (78.8%, by DLS@CU), belief (77.2%, by IITNLP) and answers-forums (73.9% by DLS@CU). Note that the highest results are very close but below the inter-annotator correlation, with the exception of belief, where the systems attain a better correlation than the annotators (88.8%, 86.9%, 82.2%, 72.1% and 74.2%, respectively).

The results of the best system run were significantly different (p-value < 0.05) from the 11th top scoring system run and below. The top 10 systems did not show statistical significant variation among them. None of these runs was significantly different from any other in the top ten runs, indicating that the best systems performed very close to each other.

Regarding the relative difficulty of headlines and images in 2014 and 2015, both baseline and best system perform better this year than in 2014, but the differences between baseline and best system has increased in headlines, while it is similar in images.

3.4.1 Analysing the Full Dataset

On a separate note, we felt filtering was specifically needed for new datasets, in order to guarantee a minimum quality. For datasets like images and headlines, where the sampling strategy was already shown to work, it might not be as necessary. For completeness, we also evaluated the systems on the full set of annotations. The system scoring best was the same as in the official test set (DLS@CU-S1), with a mean correlation of 73.4%. The baseline scored 49.6%, and it would rank in position 55. The best results in each dataset decreased more or less uniformly. The filtering ensured a test set of better quality, but we interpret that the full set can also be used for development. It's available from the task website.

3.5 Tools and Resources

Given the number of participants, for the sake of space, we just give a broad overview. Aligning words between sentences has been the most popular

[9] Code is available at `http://ixa2.si.ehu.eus/stswiki`

Run Name	answers-forums	answers-students	belief	headlines	images	Mean	Rank
Baseline-tokencos	0.4453	0.6647	0.6517	0.5312	0.6039	0.5871	61
Baseline-TakeLab	0.5391	0.6176	0.6165	0.7790	0.8115	0.6965	42
A96T-RUN1	0.6686	0.7192	0.7117	0.7357	0.7896	0.7337	29
ASAP-FIRSTRUN	0.2304	0.6503	0.3928	0.6614	0.6548	0.5695	63
ASAP-SECONDRUN	0.2374	0.7095	0.3986	0.7039	0.7294	0.6152	56
*ASAP-THIRDRUN	0.2303	0.6719	0.4342	0.7156	0.7250	0.6112	57
AZMAT-RUNABS	0.3099	0.4282	0.3568	0.5280	0.5118	0.4503	70
AZMAT-RUNCAP	0.2932	0.4282	0.3526	0.5350	0.5186	0.4512	69
AZMAT-RUNSCALE	0.2933	0.4293	0.3587	0.5264	0.5145	0.4490	71
BLCUNLP-1stRUN	0.4231	0.5152	0.5510	0.5651	0.7163	0.5709	62
BLCUNLP-2ndRUN	0.5725	0.6586	0.5510	0.7238	0.8271	0.6928	44
BLCUNLP-3rdRUN	0.5725	0.5753	0.4462	0.7309	0.8070	0.6556	49
BUAP-RUN1	0.5564	0.6901	0.6473	0.7167	0.7658	0.6936	43
DalGTM-run1	0.2902	-0.0534	0.0625	0.0598	0.0663	0.0623	74
DalGTM-run2	0.3537	0.1189	0.0625	0.2354	0.2042	0.1917	72
DalGTM-run3	0.1533	0.1189	-0.1319	-0.0395	0.2021	0.0731	73
DCU-RUN1	0.5556	0.6582	0.5464	0.8284	0.8394	0.7192	34
DCU-RUN2	0.5628	0.6233	0.7549	0.8187	0.8350	0.7340	28
DCU-RUN3	0.6530	0.6108	0.6977	0.8181	0.8434	0.7369	26
DLS@CU-S1	**0.7390**	0.7725	0.7491	0.8250	0.8644	**0.8015**	1
DLS@CU-S2	0.7241	0.7569	0.7223	0.8250	0.8631	0.7921	3
DLS@CU-U	0.6821	**0.7879**	0.7325	0.8238	0.8485	0.7919	5
ECNU-1stSVMALL	0.7145	0.7122	0.7282	0.7980	0.8467	0.7696	19
ECNU-2ndSVMONE	0.6865	0.7329	0.6977	0.8196	0.8358	0.7701	18
ECNU-3rdMTL	0.6919	0.7515	0.6951	0.8049	0.8575	0.7769	16
ExBThemis-default	0.6946	0.7505	0.7521	0.8245	0.8527	0.7878	8
ExBThemis-themis	0.6946	0.7505	0.7482	0.8245	0.8527	0.7873	9
ExBThemis-themisexp	0.6946	0.7784	0.7482	0.8245	0.8527	0.7942	2
FBK-HLT-RUN1	0.7131	0.7442	0.7327	0.8079	0.8574	0.7831	12
FBK-HLT-RUN2	0.7101	0.7410	0.7377	0.8008	0.8545	0.7801	13
FBK-HLT-RUN3	0.6555	0.7362	0.7460	0.7083	0.8389	0.7461	23
FCICU-Run1	0.6152	0.6686	0.6109	0.7418	0.7853	0.7022	41
FCICU-Run2	0.3659	0.6460	0.5896	0.6448	0.6194	0.5970	59
FCICU-Run3	0.7091	0.7096	0.7184	0.7922	0.8223	0.7595	20
IITNLP-FirstRun	0.3728	0.6605	**0.7717**	0.5996	0.8523	0.6712	47
MathLingBudapest-embedding	0.7039	0.7004	0.7325	0.7690	0.8038	0.7478	22
MathLingBudapest-hybrid	0.7231	0.7513	0.7473	0.8037	0.8442	0.7836	11
MathLingBudapest-machines	0.6977	0.7455	0.7363	0.8046	0.8414	0.7771	15
MiniExperts-Run1	0.6781	0.7304	0.6294	0.6912	0.8109	0.7216	33
MiniExperts-Run2	0.6454	0.7093	0.5165	0.6084	0.7999	0.6746	45
MiniExperts-Run3	0.6179	0.6977	0.3236	0.5775	0.7954	0.6353	55
NeRoSim-R1	0.5260	0.7251	0.6311	0.8131	0.8585	0.7438	24
NeRoSim-R2	0.6940	0.7446	0.7512	0.8077	0.8647	0.7849	10
NeRoSim-R3	0.6778	0.7357	0.7220	0.8123	0.8570	0.7762	17
RTM-DCU-1stPLS.svr	0.5484	0.5549	0.6223	0.7281	0.7189	0.6468	50
RTM-DCU-2ndST.svr	0.5484	0.5549	0.6223	0.7281	0.7189	0.6468	51
RTM-DCU-3rdST.rr	0.5484	0.5549	0.6223	0.7281	0.7189	0.6468	52
Samsung-alpha	0.6589	0.7827	0.7029	0.8342	0.8701	0.7920	4
Samsung-beta	0.6586	0.7819	0.6995	0.8342	**0.8713**	0.7916	7
Samsung-delta	0.6639	0.7825	0.6952	**0.8417**	0.8634	0.7918	6
SemantiKLUE-RUN1	0.4913	0.7005	0.5617	0.6681	0.7915	0.6717	46
SopaLipnIimas-MLP	0.6178	0.5864	0.6886	0.8121	0.8184	0.7175	36
SopaLipnIimas-RF	0.6709	0.5914	0.7238	0.8123	0.8414	0.7356	27
SopaLipnIimas-SVM	0.5918	0.5718	0.7028	0.7985	0.8104	0.7070	39
T2a-TrWP-run1	0.6857	0.6618	0.6769	0.7709	0.7865	0.7251	31
T2a-TrWP-run2	0.6857	0.6618	0.7245	0.7709	0.7865	0.7311	30
T2a-TrWP-run3	0.6857	0.6612	0.6772	0.7710	0.7865	0.7250	32
TATO-1stWTW	0.6796	0.6853	0.7206	0.7667	0.8167	0.7422	25
UBC-RUN1	0.4764	0.5459	0.6788	0.6368	0.7852	0.6364	53
UMDuluth-BlueTeam-Run1	0.6561	0.7816	0.7363	0.8085	0.8236	0.7775	14
UQeResearch-AllRuns-run1	0.5923	0.6876	0.5904	0.7521	0.7817	0.7032	40
UQeResearch-AllRuns-run2	0.6132	0.6882	0.6229	0.7602	0.7855	0.7130	37
UQeResearch-AllRuns-run3	0.6188	0.6757	0.7178	0.7549	0.7769	0.7189	35
USAAR_SHEFFIELD-modelx	0.3706	0.3609	0.4767	0.5183	0.5436	0.4616	68
USAAR_SHEFFIELD-modely	0.6264	0.7386	0.7050	0.7927	0.8162	0.7533	21
USAAR_SHEFFIELD-modelz	0.4237	0.6757	0.6994	0.5239	0.6833	0.6111	58
WSL-run1	0.3759	0.5269	0.6387	0.5462	0.5710	0.5379	66
WSL-run2	0.4287	0.6028	0.5231	0.6029	0.4879	0.5424	65
WSL-run3	0.3709	0.5437	0.6478	0.5752	0.6407	0.5672	64
Yamraj-1stRUNNAME	0.5634	0.6727	0.6387	0.6067	0.7425	0.6558	48
Yamraj-2ndRUNNAME	0.4367	0.4716	0.4890	0.5533	0.4799	0.4919	67
Yamraj-3rdRUNNAME	0.5168	0.5835	0.6540	0.5861	0.6097	0.5912	60
yiGou-midbaitu	0.5797	0.6571	0.6473	0.7115	0.8036	0.6964	42
yiGou-xiaobaitu	0.6102	0.6872	0.6065	0.7369	0.8133	0.7114	38
*UBC-RUN1	0.4764	0.5459	0.6788	0.6368	0.7852	0.6364	54

Table 3: Task 2a: English evaluation results in terms of Pearson correlation.

approach for the top three participants (DLS@CU, ExBThemis, Samsung). They use WordNet (Miller, 1995), Mikolov Embeddings (Mikolov et al., 2013; Baroni et al., 2014) and PPDB (Ganitkevitch et al., 2013). In general, generic NLP tools such as lemmatization, PoS tagging, distributional word embeddings, distributional and knowledge-based similarity are widely used, and also syntactic analysis and named entity recognition. Most teams add a machine learning algorithm to learn the output scores, but note that Samsung team did not use it in their best run.

3.6 Spanish Subtask Results

The official evaluation results of the Spanish subtask are presented in Table 4. The last row, Baseline-tokencos, shows the results obtained using the same baseline as for the English STS task, which 69% of the system runs were able to surpass. Only about one fifth of the systems were unsupervised, among which, the top performing system, UMDuluth-BlueTeam-run1, was able to come within 0.1 correlation points from the top performing system on Wikipedia and within 0.03 on the Newswire dataset. This relatively narrow gap suggests that unsupervised semantic textual similarity is a viable option for languages with limited resources.

Statistical significance tests were performed across the teams, by only considering their best run. In the case of the Wikipedia dataset, all runs were significantly different (at p-value < 0.05) with respect to the other teams; the same behavior was encountered on the newswire dataset, with the exception of two pairs of system runs that were not statistically different (ExBThemis & RTM-DCU, and MiniExperts & Yamraj).

Our efforts for generating closer to real-life textual similarity scenarios, and thus more difficult cases to be discerned by automated systems, were reflected in the lower correlations obtained on this year's datasets in comparison to those of 2014. For Wikipedia, the highest ranking system, ExBThemis-trainMini, achieved a correlation of 0.70, while in 2014, the highest correlation on the same dataset type was of 0.78. This difference was even steeper for the newswire data, where the top system, ExBThemis-trainEs, scored 0.683 in comparison to 2014, where the top ranked system attained a correlation of 0.845.

4 System Evaluation for Interpretable STS

4.1 Evaluation Metrics

Participating runs were evaluated using four different metrics: F1 where alignment type and score are ignored; F1 where alignment types need to match, but scores are ignored; F1 where alignment type is ignored, but each alignment is penalized when scores do not match; and, F1 where alignment types need to match, and each alignment is penalized when scores do not match.

4.2 Baseline System

The baseline system used for the interpretable subtask consists of a cascade concatenation of several procedures. First, we undertake a brief NLP step in which input sentences are tokenized using simple regular expressions. Additionally, this step collects chunk regions coming either from gold standard or from the chunking done by *ixa-pipes-chunk* (Agerri et al., 2014). This is followed by a lower-cased token aligning phase, which consists of aligning (or linking) identical tokens across the input sentences. Then we use chunk boundaries as token regions to group individual tokens into groups, and compute all links across groups. The weight of the link across groups is proportional to the number of links counted between within-group tokens. The next phase consists of an optimization step in which groups x,y that have the highest link weight are identified, as well as the chunks that are linked to either x or y but not with a maximum alignment weight (thus enabling us to know which chunks were left unaligned). Finally, in the last phase, the baseline system uses a rule-based algorithm to directly assign labels and scores: to chunks with the highest link weight assign label = "EQUI" and score = 5, to the rest of aligned chunks (with lower weights) assign label = "ALIC" and score = NIL, and, to unaligned chunks assign label = "NOALI" and score = NIL.

4.3 Participation

The interpretable subtask allowed up to a total of three submissions for each team on each of the evaluation scenarios. As previously mentioned, the first evaluation scenario provided gold standard chunks for all input sentence pairs. This way, participating systems only had to worry about making cor-

Run Name	System Type	Wikipedia	Newswire	Weighted Mean	Rank
BUAP-run1	unknown	0.489	0.405	0.433	14
ExBThemis-trainEn	supervised	0.676	0.671	0.672	3
ExBThemis-trainEs	supervised	0.705	**0.683**	**0.690**	1
ExBThemis-trainMini	supervised	**0.706**	0.681	0.689	2
RTM-DCU-1stST.tree	supervised	0.582	0.525	0.544	8
RTM-DCU-2ndST.rr	supervised	0.582	0.525	0.544	7
RTM-DCU-3rdST.SVR	supervised	0.582	0.525	0.544	6
SopaLipnIimas-MLP	supervised	0.253	0.534	0.440	12
SopaLipnIimas-RF	supervised	0.564	0.565	0.565	5
SopaLipnIimas-SVM	supervised	0.419	0.401	0.407	15
UMDuluth-BlueTeam-run1	unsupervised	0.594	0.655	0.634	4
MiniExperts-run1	supervised	0.524	0.508	0.513	11
MiniExperts-run2	supervised	0.467	0.544	0.518	9
MiniExperts-run3	supervised	0.440	0.552	0.515	10
Yamraj-1stNoConfidence	unsupervised	0.577	0.365	0.436	13
Yamraj-1stWithConfidence	unsupervised	0.532	0.342	0.405	16
Baseline-tokencos		0.529	0.495	0.506	

Table 4: Task 2b: Spanish evaluation results in terms of Pearson correlation.

Run Name	H ALI	H TYPE	H SCORE	H T+S	Rank	I ALI	I TYPE	I SCORE	I T+S	Rank
NeRoSim_R3	0.8976	**0.6666**	0.8157	**0.6426**	1	0.8834	0.6035	0.7837	0.5759	4
NeRoSim_R2	0.8972	0.6558	**0.8263**	0.6401	2	0.8800	0.5854	0.7818	0.5619	6
NeRoSim_R1	**0.8984**	0.6543	0.8262	0.6389	3	**0.8870**	**0.6143**	0.7877	0.5841	2
UMDuluth_BlueTeam_1	0.8861	0.5962	0.7960	0.5887	4	0.8853	0.5842	0.7932	0.5729	5
UMDuluth_BlueTeam_2	0.8861	0.5962	0.7968	0.5883	5	0.8853	0.6095	**0.7968**	**0.5964**	1
UMDuluth_BlueTeam_3	0.8861	0.5900	0.7980	0.5834	6	0.8853	0.5964	0.7909	0.5822	3
SimCompass_prefix	0.8360	0.5834	0.7474	0.5338	8	0.8361	0.4708	0.7269	0.4157	12
SimCompass_word2vec	0.8716	0.5806	0.7654	0.5253	9	0.8624	0.4599	0.7405	0.4017	13
SimCompass_combined	0.8710	0.5813	0.7651	0.5239	10	0.8490	0.4555	0.7294	0.3965	14
ExBThemis_avgScorer	0.8146	0.4943	0.7171	0.4885	11	0.8057	0.4413	0.6992	0.4246	11
ExBThemis_mostFreqScorer	0.8146	0.4943	0.7140	0.4884	12	0.8057	0.4413	0.7007	0.4296	9
ExBThemis_regressionScorer	0.8146	0.4943	0.7158	0.4883	13	0.8052	0.4406	0.6989	0.4288	10
FCICU_Run1	0.8455	0.4480	0.7160	0.4325	14	0.8457	0.4740	0.7273	0.4482	7
+RTM-DCU_1stIBM2Alignment	0.4914	0.3712	0.4550	0.3712	15	0.3540	0.2283	0.3187	0.2282	15
∗UBC_RUN2	0.8991	0.6402	0.8211	0.6185	-	0.8846	0.6557	0.8085	0.6159	-
∗UBC_RUN1	0.8991	0.5882	0.8031	0.5882	-	0.8846	0.4749	0.7709	0.4746	-
BASELINE	0.8448	0.5556	0.7551	0.5556	7	0.8388	0.4328	0.7210	0.4326	8

Table 5: STS interpretable results for the gold chunks scenario. Best results have been marked in bold. 'H' stands for Headlines data set and 'I' stands for Images data set. + symbol denotes resubmissions and ∗ symbol denotes task organizers.

rect alignments and providing them with appropriate labels and scores. The second evaluation scenario consisted of using only raw text as input, and so, each system was also responsible for segmenting the input.

Seven teams participated on the gold chunks scenario, and out of them five teams also participated in the system chunks scenario as it was more challenging. The UBC system participation, marked with a ∗, corresponds to the organizer team for the interpretable STS subtask. However, it should be noted that the actual participating team was an independent subteam that was not involved in the task organization. Moreover, one more team is marked with + as their results reflect a resubmission.

4.4 Interpretable Subtask Results

Results for the gold chunks scenario and the system chunks scenario are shown in Table 5 and Table 6, respectively. Each row of the tables corresponds to a run configuration named *TeamID_RunID*, and each column corresponds to a evaluation result.

Note that task results are separately written with respect to the scenario, but distinct datasets that pertain to the same scenario have been collapsed in the corresponding table so that 'H' corresponds to the

Run Name	H ALI	H TYPE	H SCORE	H T+S	Rank	I ALI	I TYPE	I SCORE	I T+S	Rank
UMDuluth_BlueTeam_3	**0.7820**	**0.5154**	**0.7024**	**0.5098**	1	**0.8336**	0.5605	0.7456	0.5473	2
UMDuluth_BlueTeam_2	**0.7820**	0.5109	0.6986	0.5049	2	**0.8336**	**0.5759**	**0.7511**	**0.5634**	1
UMDuluth_BlueTeam_1	**0.7820**	0.5058	0.6968	0.5004	3	**0.8336**	0.5529	0.7498	0.5431	3
ExBThemis_avgScorer	0.7032	0.4331	0.6224	0.4290	5	0.6966	0.3970	0.6068	0.3806	6
ExBThemis_mostFreqScorer	0.7032	0.4331	0.6200	0.4288	6	0.6966	0.3970	0.6106	0.3870	4
ExBThemis_regressionScorer	0.7032	0.4331	0.6209	0.4284	7	0.6966	0.3970	0.6092	0.3867	5
SimCompass_word2vec	0.6461	0.4334	0.5619	0.3878	8	0.5428	0.2831	0.4561	0.2427	8
SimCompass_prefix	0.6310	0.4284	0.5526	0.3872	9	-	-	-	-	-
SimCompass_combined	0.6467	0.4333	0.5636	0.3870	10	0.5433	0.2854	0.4545	0.2421	9
+RTM-DCU_1stIBM2Alignment	0.4914	0.3712	0.4550	0.3712	11	0.3540	0.2283	0.3187	0.2282	10
∗UBC_RUN2	0.7709	0.4865	0.7014	0.4705	-	0.8388	0.6019	0.7634	0.5643	-
∗UBC_RUN1	0.7709	0.5019	0.6892	0.5019	-	0.8388	0.4450	0.7280	0.4447	-
BASELINE	0.6701	0.4571	0.6066	0.4571	4	0.7060	0.3696	0.6092	0.3693	7

Table 6: STS interpretable results for the system chunks scenario. Best results have been marked in bold. 'H' stands for Headlines data set and 'I' stands for Images data set. + symbol denotes resubmissions and ∗ symbol denotes task organizers.

Headlines dataset and 'I' corresponds to the Images dataset. A unique baseline was used for both evaluation scenarios and its performance is jointly presented with the scores obtained by participants.

Results clearly show that the system chunks scenario was considerably more challenging than the gold chunks scenario. Actually, the complexity of the evaluation was incremental for the four available metrics, and, the most challenging F Type+Score metric performance seems bounded by the performance obtained in the F alignment metric, which obviously, was lower for the system chunks.

With regard to both datasets, the Images dataset ended up being more challenging than the Headlines dataset. For instance, in the gold chunks scenario, the participant average F Type+Score metric reached 0.4748 for the Images dataset (compared to 0.5381 for Headlines).[10] The maximum value obtained by participants was also higher, as it reached 0.6426 and 0.5964 respectively for Headlines and Images. Under the system chunks scenario, the average results followed the same tendency, as the participant average F Type+Score metric reached 0.3912 for the Images dataset and 0.4335 for Headlines (both values lower than the ones obtained for the gold chunks). In contrast, the maximum metric obtained by participants was in this case greater for Images, as it reached 0.5634, attaining 0.5098 for Headlines.

4.5 Tools and Resources

The majority of the systems used the same kind of tools for both scenarios despite integrating an auxiliary chunker for system chunks runs. The most used NLP tools for preprocessing are Stanford's NLP parser and the OpenNLP framework. Actually, all of the teams confirmed that they performed some kind of input text processing such as lemmatization, part of speech tagging or syntactic parsing. Additional resources such as named-entity recognition and acronym repositories, ConceptNet, NLTK, time and date resolution or PPDB were also used by most of the participants. Participants also revealed that most of their systems were built using some kind of distributional or knowledge-based similarity metrics. We noticed, for instance, that WordNet or Mikolov embeddings were used by several teams to compute word similarity.

5 Conclusion

This year participants were challenged with new datasets for English and Spanish, including image captions, news headlines, Wikipedia articles, news, and new genres like answers from a tutorial dialogue system, answers from Q&A websites, and commited belief. The crowdsourced annotations had a high inter-tagger agreement. The English subtask attracted 29 teams, while the Spanish subtask had 7 teams.

In addition, we succesfully introduced a new subtask on interpretability, where systems add a explanatory layer, in the form of alignments between text segments, explicitly annotating the kind of relation and the score for each segment pair. The interpretable subtask attracted 7 teams.

[10] The team pertaining to the organizers (marked by the symbol ∗) is not taken into account in the ranking.

Acknowledgements

We are grateful to the reviewers for their comments. This work was partially funded by MINECO (CHIST-ERA READERS project – PCIN-2013-002-C02-01, SKaTeR project – TIN2012-38584-C06-02), the European Commission (QTLEAP – FP7-ICT-2013.4.1-610516), the National Science Foundation (CAREER award #1361274), and DARPA-BAA-12-47 (DEFT grant #12475008). Aitor Gonzalez-Agirre and Iñigo Lopez-Gazpio are supported by doctoral grants from MINECO. The IXA group is funded by the Basque Government (A type Research Group). Any opinions, findings, and conclusions or recommendations expressed in this material are those of the authors and do not necessarily reflect the views of the National Science Foundation, DARPA, or the other sources of support.

References

Steven Abney. 1991. Parsing by chunks. In *Principle-based parsing: Computation and psycholinguistics. Robert Berwick and Steven Abney and Carol Tenny(eds.)*, pages 257–278.

Rodrigo Agerri, Josu Bermudez, and German Rigau. 2014. Ixa pipeline: Efficient and ready to use multilingual NLP tools. In *Proceedings of the 9th Language Resources and Evaluation Conference (LREC 2014)*, pages 26–31.

Eneko Agirre, Daniel Cer, Mona Diab, and Aitor Gonzalez-Agirre. 2012. SemEval-2012 Task 6: A pilot on semantic textual similarity. In **SEM 2012: The First Joint Conference on Lexical and Computational Semantics – Volume 1: Proceedings of the main conference and the shared task, and Volume 2: Proceedings of the Sixth International Workshop on Semantic Evaluation (SemEval 2012)*, Montréal, Canada, 7-8 June.

Eneko Agirre, Carmen Banea, Claire Cardie, Daniel Cer, Mona Diab, Aitor Gonzalez-Agirre, Weiwei Guo, Rada Mihalcea, German Rigau, and Janyce Wiebe. 2014. SemEval-2014 Task 10: Multilingual semantic textual similarity. In *Proceedings of the 8th International Workshop on Semantic Evaluation (SemEval 2014)*, Dublin, Ireland, August.

Marco Baroni, Georgiana Dinu, and Germán Kruszewski. 2014. Don't count, predict! A systematic comparison of context-counting vs. context-predicting semantic vectors. In *Proceedings of the 52nd Annual Meeting of the Association for Computational Linguistics (Volume 1: Long Papers) (ACL 2014)*.

Clive Best, Erik van der Goot, Ken Blackler, Teófilo Garcia, and David Horby. 2005. Europe Media Monitor - System description. In *EUR Report 22173-En*, Ispra, Italy.

Chris Brockett. 2007. Aligning the RTE 2006 corpus. *Microsoft Research*.

Juri Ganitkevitch, Benjamin Van Durme, and Chris Callison-Burch. 2013. PPDB: The paraphrase database. In *Proceedings of the 2013 Conference of the North American Chapter of the Association for Computational Linguistics: Human Language Technologies (NAACL-HLT 2013)*, pages 758–764, Atlanta, Georgia, June.

Omer Levy, Torsten Zesch, Ido Dagan, and Iryna Gurevych. 2013. Recognizing partial textual entailment. In *ACL (2)*, pages 451–455.

Tomas Mikolov, Kai Chen, Greg Corrado, and Jeffrey Dean. 2013. Efficient estimation of word representations in vector space. In *Proceedings of Workshop at the International Conference on Learning Representations (ICLR 2013)*.

George A. Miller. 1995. Wordnet: A lexical database for english. *Commun. ACM*, 38(11):39–41, November.

Rodney D. Nielsen, Wayne Ward, and James H. Martin. 2009. Recognizing entailment in intelligent tutoring systems. *Natural Language Engineering*, 15(04):479–501.

William H. Press, Saul A. Teukolsky, William T. Vetterling, and Brian P. Flannery. *Numerical recipes: The art of scientific computing V 2.10 with Linux or single-screen license*.

Cyrus Rashtchian, Peter Young, Micah Hodosh, and Julia Hockenmaier. 2010. Collecting image annotations using Amazon's Mechanical Turk. In *Proceedings of the NAACL HLT 2010 Workshop on Creating Speech and Language Data with Amazon's Mechanical Turk*, CSLDAMT 2010, pages 139–147.

Vasile Rus, Mihai Lintean, Cristian Moldovan, William Baggett, Nobal Niraula, and Brent Morgan. 2012. The SIMILAR corpus: A resource to foster the qualitative understanding of semantic similarity of texts. In *Semantic Relations II: Enhancing Resources and Applications, The 8th Language Resources and Evaluation Conference (LREC 2012), May*, pages 23–25.

Erik F. Tjong Kim Sang and Sabine Buchholz. 2000. Introduction to the CoNLL-2000 shared task: Chunking. In *Proceedings of the 2nd workshop on Learning language in logic and the 4th conference on Computational natural language learning-Volume 7 (CoNLL 2000)*, pages 127–132.

Frane Šarić, Goran Glavaš, Mladen Karan, Jan Šnajder, and Bojana Dalbelo Bašić. 2012. TakeLab: Systems for measuring semantic text similarity. In *Proceedings of the 6th International Workshop on Semantic Evaluation (SemEval 2012)*, Montréal, Canada, 7-8 June.

ExB Themis: Extensive Feature Extraction from Word Alignments for Semantic Textual Similarity

Christian Hänig, Robert Remus, Xose De La Puente
ExB Research & Development GmbH
Seeburgstr. 100
04103 Leipzig, Germany
{haenig, remus, puente}@exb.de

Abstract

We present *ExB Themis* – a word alignment-based semantic textual similarity system developed for SemEval-2015 Task 2: Semantic Textual Similarity. It combines both string and semantic similarity measures as well as alignment features using Support Vector Regression. It occupies the first three places on Spanish data and additionally places second on English data. *ExB Themis* proved to be the best multilingual system among all participants.

1 Introduction

Semantic Textual Similarity (STS) is the task of measuring the degree of semantic equivalence of a sentence pair and is applicable to problems in Machine Translation and Summarization among others (Agirre et al., 2012). STS has drawn a lot of attention in the last few years leading to the availability of multilingual training and test data and to the development of a variety of approaches. These approaches fall broadly into three categories (Han et al., 2013):

Vector space approaches: Texts are represented as bag-of-words vectors and a vector similarity – e.g. cosine – is used to compute a similarity score between two texts (Meadow et al., 1992).

Alignment approaches: Words and phrases in two texts are aligned and the quality or coverage of the resulting alignments are used as similarity measure (Mihalcea et al., 2006; Sultan et al., 2014).

Machine Learning approaches: Multiple similarity measures and features are combined using supervised Machine Learning (ML). This approach relies on the availability of training data (Bär et al., 2012; Šarić et al., 2012).

ExB Themis combines advantages of all three categories: we implemented a complex alignment algorithm focusing on named entities, temporal expressions, measurement expressions and dedicated negation handling. Unlike other alignment-based approaches, we extract a variety of features to better model the properties of alignments instead of providing only one alignment feature (see Section 4.1).

Moreover, we employ a variety of similarity measures based on strings and lexical items (see Section 4.2). Our system integrates two well-known language resources – WordNet[1] and ConceptNet (Speer and Havasi, 2012). Additionally, it uses word embeddings to cope with data sparseness and the insufficiency of overlaps between sentences.

Finally, we train a Support Vector Regression (SVR) model using these features (see Section 5).

2 Preprocessing

Our text preprocessing comprises tokenization, case correction (e.g. *US Flying Surveillance Missions to Help Find Kidnapped Nigerian Girls* is corrected to *US flying surveillance missions to help find kidnapped Nigerian girls*), unsupervised part-of-speech (POS) tagging based on SVD2 (Lamar et al., 2010),

[1]English: we use the one described by Miller (1995); Spanish: we use the one presented in (González-Agirre et al., 2012).

supervised POS tagging using the Stanford Maximum Entropy tagger[2] as well as lemmatization using Stanford CoreNLP[3] for English and IXA Pipes[4] for Spanish. We also identify measurements (e. g. *55.8 g/mol*) and temporal expressions (e. g. *last week*), data set-specific stop words (e. g. *A close-up of* for *images* dataset) using in-house algorithms as well as named entities as described by Hänig et al. (2014) and their titles (e. g. *President Barack Obama*).

3 ExB Themis Alignment

Our word alignment is direction-dependent and not restricted to one-to-one alignments. Different mapping types are distinguished and handled differently during feature extraction (see Section 4.1). We use the same type labels as provided by the organizers for the third subtask (interpretable STS) of this task (Agirre et al., 2015): *EQUI* denotes semantically equivalent chunks, oppositional meaning is labeled with *OPPO*, *SPE1/2* denote similar meaning of the chunks, but the chunk in sentence 1/2 is more specific than the other one. *SIM* and *REL* denote similar and related meanings, respectively. *ALIC* is not used, because our algorithm is not restricted to one-to-one alignments. Finally, all unaligned chunks are labeled with *NOALI*.

Similar to Sultan et al. (2014), our alignment process follows a strict chronological order:

Named entities are aligned to each other. Because we did not observe text pairs with possibly ambiguous name alignments (e. g. *Michael* in one text and both *Michael Jackson* and *Michael Schumacher* in the other) in the training data, we simply aligned all name pairs that share at least one identical token.

Normalized temporal expressions are aligned iff they denote the same point in time or the same time interval (e. g. *14:03* and *2.03 pm*).

Measurement expressions are aligned iff they express the same absolute value (e. g. *$100k* and *100.000$*).

Arbitrary token sequence alignment consists of multiple steps and is very time consuming[5]. We apply a high precision test for identical sequences based on Sultan et al. (2014): Our test uses synonym-lookups and ignores case information, punctuation characters and symbols. This enables us to match expressions like *long term* and *long-term*[6]. If one of both sequences consists of exactly one all-caps-token then we test if it is the acronym of the other sequence (e. g. *US* and *United States*).

We used WordNet and ConceptNet[7] to obtain information about synonymy, antonymy and hypernymy and equip the resulting alignments with the corresponding type. We additionally created a small database containing high-frequency synonyms (e. g. *does* and *do*), antonyms (e. g. *doesn't* and *does*) and negations (e. g. *don't, never, no*).

Negations can significantly effect the semantic similarity of two sentences (e. g. *You are a Christian.* vs. *Therefore you are not a Christian.*). Therefore, we explicitly model negations in our alignment. Some negations are handled during arbitrary token sequence alignment. We resolve the scope of all remaining negations using co-occurrence analysis: if exactly one of both neighboring tokens $w_{n-1}^{1/2}$ and $w_{n+1}^{1/2}$ is already aligned then the negation $w_n^{1/2}$ is attached to it and we inverse the alignment type (e. g. *EQUI* becomes *OPPO* and vice versa). If both neighboring tokens are aligned then we pick the one contained in the co-occurence out of $\left\langle w_{n-1}^{1/2}, w_n^{1/2} \right\rangle$ and $\left\langle w_n^{1/2}, w_{n+1}^{1/2} \right\rangle$ yielding the highest co-occurrence significance score.

Remaining content words are aligned using cosine similarity on word2vec vectors (Mikolov et al., 2013). Analogously to Han et al. (2013), we align each content word to the content word of the other sentence with the same POS tag that yields the highest similarity score. To prevent weak alignments, we reject alignments with a similarity less than $1/3$.

[2] nlp.stanford.edu/software/tagger.shtml
[3] nlp.stanford.edu/software/corenlp.shtml
[4] ixa2.si.ehu.es/ixa-pipes/

[5] Therefore, we restrict ourselves to a maximum of 5 tokens.
[6] A similar method was described by Han et al. (2013).
[7] From ConceptNet we only imported synonyms.

4 Feature Extraction

Some approaches to STS relying on word alignment are unsupervised and extract a defined score based on the alignment process (e. g. proportions of aligned content words (Sultan et al., 2014)), others extract a single feature from the alignment and use it along with other features to train a regression model (e. g. align-and-penalize approach (Han et al., 2013; Kashyap et al., 2014)).

Unlike these approaches, we extract 40 features from our alignment (see Section 4.1) to (a) build a complex model that is capable of modeling phenomena like alignments of different types and negations, and (b) not be forced to combine alignment properties arbitrarily.

We additionally extract 51 non-alignment features (see Section 4.2) leading to a total of 91 features.

4.1 Alignment Features

To encode the properties of a set of alignments A of sentences s_1 and s_2 as comprehensive as possible, we extract the following features[8]:

Proportion features describe the ratio of aligned words of a specified group with respect to all words of that group (Sultan et al., 2014)[9]: $prop_{group} = \frac{2 \cdot prop^1_{group} \cdot prop^2_{group}}{prop^1_{group} + prop^2_{group}}$ with $prop^{1/2}_{group} = \frac{|\{i:[\exists j:(i,j) \in A_{group}] \text{ and } w_i^{1/2} \in C\}|}{|\{i:w_i^{1/2} \in C\}|}$ where C is the set of all content words. We extract these features for alignments of type *EQUI*, *OPPO*, *SPE1/2*, *REL*[10] and *NOALI* (5 features).

Frequency features are encoded in binary format.

We encode frequencies of alignments of type *OPPO* (3 features), *SPE1/2* (3), *REL* (3) and *NOALI* (5). We also encode the frequency of unaligned negations with 3 features.

UMBC align-and-penalize features: We also include two features[11] based on Han et al. (2013): we use their T as it is and integrated a simplified version of P' with $P_i^A = \frac{\sum_{\langle t,g(t)\rangle \in A_i}(1+w_p(t))}{2 \cdot |s_i|}$ and $P_i^B = \frac{|\langle t,g(t)\rangle \in B_i|}{2 \cdot |s_i|}$ (2 features).

All proportion features, binary frequency features of *REL*-alignments, unaligned content words and unaligned negations were additionally computed and extracted for nouns only (16 features).

[8]Type-filtered subsets of A are denoted by A_{type}.

[9]See Sultan et al. (2014) for details on the formulae.

[10]Each content word is weighted by the similarity score achieved by word2vec for this type.

[11]Splitting $STS = T - P'$ into two features T and P' achieves better results than keeping it in the original form.

4.2 Non-Alignment Features

We use a variety of non-alignment features:

UKP: We use several features described in Bär et al. (2012): longest common substring (1 feature), longest common subsequence (1), longest common subsequence with and without normalization (2), greedy string tiling (1), character n-grams for $n = 2, 3, 4$ with and without stop words (6), word n-grams Jaccard coefficient for $n = 1, 2, 3, 4$ (4), word n-grams Jaccard coefficient without stop words for $n = 2, 4$ (2), word n-grams containment measure for $n = 1, 2$ (2) as well as pairwise word similarity (1).

TakeLab: We use several features described in Šarić et al. (2012)[12]: PathLen similarity (1 feature), corpus-based word similarity (3), vector space sentence similarity (1), n-gram overlap of tokens and lemmas for $n = 1, 2, 3$ (6), weighted word overlap for lowercased tokens and lemmas (2), normalized sentence length difference (1), shallow named entity features (4) and numbers overlap (3).

UMBC: We use several features described in Han et al. (2013): word n-gram similarity for $n = 1, 2, 3, 4$ (4 features). Moreover, we used word n-gram similarity for $n = 1$ where only nouns or only verbs where taken into account (2).

Readability Indicators: We use several features that are typically used as indicators for readability (Oelke et al., 2012): relative difference in sentence length, average word length in characters, number of nouns per sentence, number of verbs per sentence and noun-verb-ratio (5).

[12]`takelab.fer.hr/sts/`

5 STS Model

We compute STS scores using ν-SVR (Schölkopf et al., 2000) as implemented by LibSVM[13]. We use LibSVM's default SVR parameter settings without further optimization.

6 Interpretable STS Model

We align chunks using our word alignment (see Section 3). Because our word alignment itself does not rely on chunks, we extend its alignments using given chunk boundaries. If alignments overlap, we choose the longest alignment and discard the others. We do not differentiate between *SIMI* and *REL* – all *REL* alignments are considered as *SIMI* alignments.

For chunking we use the OpenNLP[14] chunker with the default model trained on CoNLL-2000 shared task data (Sang and Buchholz, 2000).

7 Results

For English we train on all available data sets from STS challenges in 2012 (Agirre et al., 2012), 2013 (Agirre et al., 2013) and 2014 (Agirre et al., 2014). For Spanish, each run trains on a different setting. Mean Pearson correlation is employed as an evaluation metric.

7.1 Subtask 2a – STS English

Table 1 presents the official scores of our system. Run *default* uses our system as it is. Run *themis* only relies on alignment features in the *belief* model, all other models are the same as for *default*. Our third run – *themisexp* – is identical to run *themis* except for one improvement: it penalizes scores of the *answers-students* dataset exponentially to cope with the high ratio of common content words that lead to over-estimation of similarity scores.

7.2 Subtask 2b – STS Spanish

Table 2 presents the official scores of our system. Run *trainEs* was trained on both Spanish test sets of 2014. Run *trainEn* was trained on all available English data sets. Run *trainMini* uses different training sets for each test set: *Wikipedia* model was trained on the 2014 *Wikipedia* test set and the *Newswire* model was trained on the *News* test set of 2014.

[13]`www.csie.ntu.edu.tw/~cjlin/libsvm/`
[14]`opennlp.apache.org`

Dataset	default	themis	themisexp
forum	0.6946 (10)	0.6946 (10)	0.6946 (10)
students	0.7505 (11)	0.7505 (11)	0.7784 (6)
belief	0.7521 (3)	0.7482 (6)	0.7482 (6)
headlines	0.8245 (7)	0.8245 (7)	0.8245 (7)
images	0.8527 (12)	0.8527 (12)	0.8527 (12)
Mean	0.7878 (8)	0.7873 (9)	**0.7942 (2)**

Table 1: Results (rank) of our three runs on English data.

Dataset	trainEs	trainMini	trainEn
Wikipedia	0.7055 (2)	0.7055 (1)	0.6763 (3)
Newswire	0.6830 (1)	0.6811 (2)	0.6705 (3)
Mean	**0.6905 (1)**	0.6893 (2)	0.6725 (3)

Table 2: Results (rank) of our three runs on Spanish data.

7.3 Subtask 2c – Interpretable STS

Our three runs only differ regarding the applied alignment scorer method: we use the *average* similarity score per alignment type as observed in STSint training data, the *most frequent* similarity score per alignment type as observed in STSint training data, and an STS *regression* model per alignment type trained on all available English STS data sets.

For subtrack *gold chunks*, our runs score 0.4885 to 0.4883 (F1 TYPE + SCORE) on headlines (ranks 10 - 12 out of 14) and 0.4296 to 0.4246 on images (ranks 8 - 10). Using *system chunks* we achieve scores of 0.4290 to 0.4284 on headlines (ranks 4–6 out of 10) and 0.3870 to 0.3806 on images (ranks 4–6).

8 Conclusions & Future Work

We presented our alignment-based STS system *ExB Themis*. Our system outperformed all other participants by a large margin on Spanish data. Furthermore, our system placed second on English data. *ExB Themis* proved to be the best multilingual STS system that easily can be adapted to further languages. We conclude that extensive feature extraction from word alignments is a very robust approach – especially when being applied to languages that lack high-quality resources.

In future work, we will investigate the influence of particular features in more detail and we want to enrich our model with structural information (Severyn et al., 2013; Sultan et al., 2014) and improved phrase similarity computation.

References

Eneko Agirre, Daniel Cer, Mona Diab, and Aitor Gonzalez-Agirre. 2012. SemEval-2012 Task 6 : A Pilot on Semantic Textual Similarity. In *First Joint Conference on Lexical and Computational Semantics (*SEM)*, pages 385–393.

Eneko Agirre, Daniel Cer, Mona Diab, Aitor Gonzalez-Agirre, and Weiwei Guo. 2013. *SEM 2013 shared task: Semantic Textual Similarity. In *Second Joint Conference on Lexical and Computational Semantics (*SEM), Volume 1: Proceedings of the Main Conference and the Shared Task*, pages 32–43, Atlanta, USA.

Eneko Agirre, Carmen Banea, Claire Cardie, Daniel Cer, Mona Diab, Ann Arbor, Aitor Gonzalez-Agirre, Weiwei Guo, Rada Mihalcea, German Rigau, and Janyce Wiebe. 2014. SemEval-2014 Task 10: Multilingual Semantic Textual Similarity. In *Proceedings of the 8th International Workshop on Semantic Evaluation (SemEval 2014)*, pages 81–91, Dublin, Ireland.

Eneko Agirre, Carmen Banea, Claire Cardie, Daniel Cer, Mona Diab, Aitor Gonzalez-Agirre, Weiwei Guo, Iigo Lopez-Gazpio, Montse Maritxalar, Rada Mihalcea, German Rigau, Larraitz Uria, and Janyce Wiebe. 2015. SemEval-2015 Task 2: Semantic Textual Similarity, English, Spanish and Pilot on Interpretability. In *Proceedings of the 9th International Workshop on Semantic Evaluation (SemEval 2015)*, Denver, CO.

Daniel Bär, Chris Biemann, Iryna Gurevych, and Torsten Zesch. 2012. UKP: Computing Semantic Textual Similarity by Combining Multiple Content Similarity Measures. In *Proceedings of the First Joint Conference on Lexical and Computational Semantics Volume 2: Proceedings of the Sixth International Workshop on Semantic Evaluation*, pages 435–440.

Aitor González-Agirre, Egoitz Laparra, and German Rigau. 2012. Multilingual Central Repository version 3.0: upgrading a very large lexical knowledge base. In *Proceedings of the Sixth International Global WordNet Conference (GWC12)*, Matsue, Japan.

Lushan Han, Abhay Kashyap, Tim Finin, James Mayfield, and Jonathan Weese. 2013. UMBC EBIQUITY-CORE: Semantic Textual Similarity Systems. In *Proceedings of the Second Joint Conference on Lexical and Computational Semantics*.

Christian Hänig, Stefan Bordag, and Stefan Thomas. 2014. Modular Classifier Ensemble Architecture for Named Entity Recognition on Low Resource Systems. In *Workshop Proceedings of the 12th Edition of the KONVENS Conference*, pages 113–116, Hildesheim, Germany.

Abhay Kashyap, Lushan Han, Roberto Yus, Jennifer Sleeman, Taneeya Satyapanich, Sunil Gandhi, and Tim Finin. 2014. Meerkat Mafia: Multilingual and Cross-Level Semantic Textual Similarity Systems. In *Proceedings of the 8th International Workshop on Semantic Evaluation (SemEval 2014)*, pages 416–423, Dublin, Ireland.

Michael Lamar, Yariv Maron, Mark Johnson, and Elie Bienenstock. 2010. SVD and Clustering for Unsupervised POS Tagging. In *Proceedings of ACL 2010*, pages 215–219, Uppsala, Sweden.

Charles T. Meadow, Bert R. Boyce, and Donald H. Kraft. 1992. *Text Information Retrieval Systems*, volume 2. Academic Press San Diego.

Rada Mihalcea, Courtney Corley, and Carlo Strapparava. 2006. Corpus-based and Knowledge-based Measures of Text Semantic Similarity. In *Proceedings of the 21st national conference on Artificial intelligence*, pages 775–780.

Tomas Mikolov, Kai Chen, Greg Corrado, and Jeffrey Dean. 2013. Efficient Estimation of Word Representations in Vector Space. In *Proceedings of Workshop at ICLR*, pages 1–12, January.

George A. Miller. 1995. WordNet: a lexical database for English. *Communications of the ACM*, 38(11):39–41.

Daniela Oelke, David Spretke, Andreas Stoffel, and Daniel A Keim. 2012. Visual readability analysis: How to make your writings easier to read. *IEEE Transactions on Visualization and Computer Graphics*, 18(5):662–674.

Erik F. Tjong Kim Sang and Sabine Buchholz. 2000. Introduction to the CoNLL-2000 Shared Task: Chunking. In *Proceedings of CoNLL 2000*, pages 127–132.

Bernhard Schölkopf, Alex J Smola, Robert C Williamson, and Peter L Bartlett. 2000. New Support Vector Algorithms. *Neural Computation*, 12(5):1207–1245.

Aliaksei Severyn, Massimo Nicosia, and Alessandro Moschitti. 2013. iKernels-Core: Tree Kernel Learning for Textual Similarity. In *Second Joint Conference on Lexical and Computational Semantics (*SEM), Volume 1: Proceedings of the Main Conference and the Shared Task*, pages 53–58, Atlanta, USA.

Robert Speer and Catherine Havasi. 2012. ConceptNet 5: A Large Semantic Network for Relational Knowledge. In *The Peoples Web Meets NLP*, pages 161–176.

Md Arafat Sultan, Steven Bethard, and Tamara Sumner. 2014. DLS@CU: Sentence Similarity from Word Alignment. In *Proceedings of the 8th International Workshop on Semantic Evaluation (SemEval 2014)*, pages 241–246, Dublin, Ireland.

Frane Šarić, Goran Glavaš, Mladen Karan, Jan Šnajder, and Bojana Dalbelo Bašić. 2012. TakeLab: Systems for Measuring Semantic Text Similarity. In *First Joint Conference on Lexical and Computational Semantics*, pages 441–448, Montreal, Canada.

SemEval-2015 Task 3: Answer Selection in Community Question Answering

Preslav Nakov Lluís Màrquez Walid Magdy Alessandro Moschitti
ALT Research Group, Qatar Computing Research Institute

James Glass
MIT Computer Science and Artificial Intelligence Laboratory

Bilal Randeree
Qatar Living

Abstract

Community Question Answering (cQA) provides new interesting research directions to the traditional Question Answering (QA) field, e.g., the exploitation of the interaction between users and the structure of related posts. In this context, we organized SemEval-2015 Task 3 on *Answer Selection in cQA*, which included two subtasks: (a) classifying answers as *good*, *bad*, or *potentially relevant* with respect to the question, and (b) answering a YES/NO question with *yes*, *no*, or *unsure*, based on the list of all answers. We set subtask A for Arabic and English on two relatively different cQA domains, i.e., the Qatar Living website for English, and a Quran-related website for Arabic. We used crowdsourcing on Amazon Mechanical Turk to label a large English training dataset, which we released to the research community. Thirteen teams participated in the challenge with a total of 61 submissions: 24 primary and 37 contrastive. The best systems achieved an official score (macro-averaged F_1) of 57.19 and 63.7 for the English subtasks A and B, and 78.55 for the Arabic subtask A.

1 Introduction

Many social activities on the Web, e.g., in forums and social networks, are accomplished by means of the community Question Answering (cQA) paradigm. User interaction in this context is seldom moderated, is rather open, and thus has little restrictions, if any, on who can post and who can answer a question.

On the positive side, this means that one can freely ask a question and expect some good, honest answers. On the negative side, it takes efforts to go through all possible answers and to make sense of them. It is often the case that many answers are only loosely related to the actual question, and some even change the topic. It is also not unusual for a question to have hundreds of answers, the vast majority of which would not satisfy a user's information needs; thus, finding the desired information in a long list of answers might be very time-consuming.

In our SemEval-2015 Task 3, we proposed two subtasks. First, subtask A asks for identifying the posts in the answer thread that answer the question *well* vs. those that can be *potentially useful* to the user (e.g., because they can help educate him/her on the subject) vs. those that are just *bad or useless*. This subtask goes in the direction of automating the answer search problem that we discussed above, and we offered it in two languages: English and Arabic. Second, for the special case of YES/NO questions, we propose an extreme summarization exercise (subtask B), which aims to produce a simple YES/NO overall answer, considering all *good* answers to the questions (according to subtask A).

For English, the two subtasks are built on a particular application scenario of cQA, based on the Qatar Living forum.[1] However, we decoupled the tasks from the Information Retrieval component in order to facilitate participation, and to focus on aspects that are relevant for the SemEval community, namely on learning the relationship between two pieces of text.

[1] http://www.qatarliving.com/forum/

Subtask A goes in the direction of passage reranking, where automatic classifiers are normally applied to pairs of questions and answer passages to derive a relative order between passages, e.g., see (Radlinski and Joachims, 2005; Jeon et al., 2005; Shen and Lapata, 2007; Moschitti et al., 2007; Surdeanu et al., 2008). In recent years, many advanced models have been developed for automating answer selection, producing a large body of work.[2] For instance, Wang et al. (2007) proposed a probabilistic quasi-synchronous grammar to learn syntactic transformations from the question to the candidate answers; Heilman and Smith (2010) used an algorithm based on Tree Edit Distance (TED) to learn tree transformations in pairs; Wang and Manning (2010) developed a probabilistic model to learn tree-edit operations on dependency parse trees; and Yao et al. (2013) applied linear chain CRFs with features derived from TED to automatically learn associations between questions and candidate answers. One interesting aspect of the above research is the need for syntactic structures; this is also corroborated in (Severyn and Moschitti, 2012; Severyn and Moschitti, 2013). Note that answer selection can use models for textual entailment, semantic similarity, and for natural language inference in general.

For Arabic, we also made use of a real cQA portal, the Fatwa website,[3] where questions about Islam are posed by regular users and are answered by knowledgeable scholars. For subtask A, we used a setup similar to that for English, but this time each question had *exactly* one correct answer among the candidate answers (see Section 3 for detail); we did not offer subtask B for Arabic.

Overall for the task, we needed manual annotations in two different languages and for two domains. For English, we built the Qatar Living datasets as a joint effort between MIT and the Qatar Computing Research Institute, co-organizers of the task, using Amazon's Mechanical Turk to recruit human annotators. For Arabic, we built the dataset automatically from the data available in the Fatwa website, without the need for any manual annotation. We made all datasets publicly available, i.e., also usable beyond SemEval.

[2] aclweb.org/aclwiki/index.php?title=Question_Answering_(State_of_the_art)

[3] http://fatwa.islamweb.net/

Our SemEval task attracted 13 teams, who submitted a total of 61 runs. The participants mainly focused on defining new features that go beyond question-answer similarity, e.g., author- and user-based, and spent less time on the design of complex machine learning approaches. Indeed, most systems used multi-class classifiers such as MaxEnt and SVM, but some used regression. Overall, almost all submissions managed to outperform the baselines using the official F_1-based score. In particular, the best system can detect a correct answer with an accuracy of about 73% in the English task and 83% in the easier Arabic task. For the extreme summarization task, the best accuracy is 72%.

An interesting outcome of this task is that the Qatar Living company, a co-organizer of the challenge, is going to use the experience and the technology developed during the evaluation excercise to improve their products, e.g., the automatic search of comments useful to answer users' questions.

The remainder of the paper is organized as follows: Section 2 gives a detailed description of the task, Section 3 describes the datasets, Section 4 explains the scorer, Section 5 presents the participants and the evaluation results, Section 6 provides an overview of the various features and techniques used by the participating systems, Section 7 offers further discussion, and finally, Section 8 concludes and points to possible directions for future work.

2 Task Definition

We have two subtasks:

- **Subtask A:** Given a question (short title + extended description), and several community answers, classify each of the answers as
  - (a) definitely relevant (good),
  - (b) potentially useful (potential), or
  - (c) bad or irrelevant (bad, dialog, non-English, other).
- **Subtask B:** Given a YES/NO question (short title + extended description), and a list of community answers, decide whether the global answer to the question should be *yes*, *no*, or *unsure*, based on the individual good answers. This subtask is only available for English.

```xml
<Question QID="Q2261" QCATEGORY="Qatar Living Lounge" QDATE="2008-11-17 07:42:22" QUSERID="U4904" QTYPE="YES_NO" QGOLD_YN="Yes">
    <QSubject>MarryBrown Branch</QSubject>
    <QBody>Hi to all QL members.Good Morning to all of you. I just want to ask if theres any other branch of MarryBrown aside from Freej
    Nasser. Its difficult to fim=nd parking on that area. If theres other branch thats good.. Thanks</QBody>
    <Comment CID="Q2261_C1" CUSERID="U4904" CGOLD="Good" CGOLD_YN="Unsure">
        <CSubject>i went in najma barnch but</CSubject>
        <CBody>i went in najma barnch but the gravy is out of stock.
gggggggrrrrrrrrr</CBody>
    </Comment>
    <Comment CID="Q2261_C2" CUSERID="U37" CGOLD="Good" CGOLD_YN="Yes">
        <CSubject>they have their new branch</CSubject>
        <CBody>they have their new branch in Najma but it is smaller than in Nasser, 2 floors also near in Doha Cinema. Gravy always out
        of stock!!!! ggggrrr.....</CBody>
    </Comment>
    <Comment CID="Q2261_C3" CUSERID="U2204" CGOLD="Bad" CGOLD_YN="Not Applicable">
        <CSubject>Gravy out of stock....</CSubject>
        <CBody>Gravy out of stock.... errrr!</CBody>
    </Comment>
    <Comment CID="Q2261_C4" CUSERID="U24" CGOLD="Bad" CGOLD_YN="Not Applicable">
        <CSubject>Marrybrown chix tastes like PAPER...</CSubject>
        <CBody>(he he he as if I tastes the paper). Even the gravy it doesn't tastes that good.

I am just buying gravy in marrybrown then will buy chicken at KFC... OR I will buy chix at KFC then I'll cook gravy as i know the
simpliest recipe.


" AN END DOES NOT JUSTIFY THE MEANS"</CBody>
    </Comment>
    <Comment CID="Q2261_C5" CUSERID="U37" CGOLD="Good" CGOLD_YN="Yes">
        <CSubject>GULFLINE07 IT WILL OPEN</CSubject>
        <CBody>GULFLINE07 IT WILL OPEN WITHIN TWO WEEKS</CBody>
    </Comment>
    <Comment CID="Q2261_C6" CUSERID="U37" CGOLD="Bad" CGOLD_YN="Not Applicable">
        <CSubject>owner???</CSubject>
        <CBody>Can anyone from here knows the name of the company franchisee of Marrybrown here in Qatar?

Thanks..

&lt;a href="http://www.blinkyou.com/glitters.php" target="_blank"&gt;&lt;img src="http://image.blinkyou.
com/glitter_images/scorpiogreenlogo.gif" border="0" alt="picture hosting"&gt;&lt;/a&gt;&lt;p style="margin-top: 0; margin-bottom: 0"&gt;&
lt;a href="http://www.blinkyou.com/glitte</CBody>
    </Comment>
    <Comment CID="Q2261_C7" CUSERID="U2654" CGOLD="Bad" CGOLD_YN="Not Applicable">
        <CSubject>been in Najma branch last</CSubject>
        <CBody>been in Najma branch last night, its awful....i would rather settle for KFC even w/ out gravy.......</CBody>
    </Comment>
    <Comment CID="Q2261_C8" CUSERID="U646" CGOLD="Good" CGOLD_YN="No">
        <CSubject>yesterday i saw new branch</CSubject>
        <CBody>yesterday i saw new branch in najma, near najma signal i think it's beside another restaurant (AMWAJ) but it has not
        opened yet.</CBody>
    </Comment>
</Question>
```


Figure 1: Annotated English question from the CQA-QL corpus.

3 Datasets

We offer the task in two languages, English and Arabic, with some differences in the type of data provided. For English, there is a question (short title + extended description) and a list of several community answers to that question. For Arabic, there is a question and a set of possible answers, which include (i) a highly accurate answer, (ii) potentially useful answers from other questions, and (iii) answers to random questions. The following subsections provide all the necessary details.

3.1 English Data: CQA-QL corpus

The source of the CQA-QL corpus is the Qatar Living forum. A sample of questions and answer threads was selected and then manually filtered and annotated with the categories defined in the task.

We provided a split in three datasets: training, development, and testing. All datasets were XML-formated and the text was encoded in UTF-8.

A dataset file is a sequence of examples (questions), where each question has a subject and a body (text), as well as the following attributes:

- QID: question identifier;
- QCATEGORY: the question category, according to the Qatar Living taxonomy;
- QDATE: date of posting;
- QUSERID: identifier of the user asking the question;
- QTYPE: type of question (GENERAL or YES/NO);
- QGOLD_YN: for YES/NO questions only, an overall *Yes/No/Unsure* answer based on all comments.

Each question is followed by a list of comments (or answers). A comment has a subject and a body (text), as well as the following attributes:

- CID: comment identifier;
- CUSERID: identifier of the user posting the comment;
- CGOLD: human assessment about whether the comment is *Good*, *Bad*, *Potential*, *Dialogue*, *non-English*, or *Other*.
- CGOLD_YN: human assessment on whether the comment suggests a *Yes*, a *No*, or an *Unsure* answer.

At test time, CGOLD, CGOLD_YN, and QGOLD_YN are hidden, and systems are asked to predict CGOLD for subtask A, and QGOLD_YN for subtask B; CGOLD_YN is not to be predicted.

Figure 1 shows a fully annotated English YES/NO question from the CQA-QL corpus. We can see that it is asked and answered in a very informal way and that there are many typos, incorrect capitalization, punctuation, slang, elongations, etc. Four of the comments are good answers to the question, and four are bad. The bad answers are irrelevant with respect to the YES/NO answer to the question as a whole, and thus their CGOLD_YN label is *Not Applicable*. The remaining four good answers predict *Yes* twice, *No* once, and *Unsure* once; as there are more *Yes* answers than the two alternatives, the overall QGOLD_YN is *Yes*.

3.2 Annotating the CQA-QL corpus

The manual annotation was a joint effort between MIT and the Qatar Computing Research Institute, co-organizers of the task. After a first internal labeling of a trial dataset (50+50 questions) by several independent annotators, we defined the annotation procedure and prepared detailed annotation guidelines. We then used Amazon's Mechanical Turk to collect human annotations for a much larger dataset. This involved the setup of three HITs:

- **HIT 1:** Select appropriate example questions and classify them as GENERAL vs. YES/NO (QCATEGORY);
- **HIT 2:** For GENERAL questions, annotate each comment as *Good*, *Bad*, *Potential*, *Dialogue*, *non-English*, or *Other* (CGOLD);
- **HIT 3:** For YES/NO questions, annotate the comments as in HIT 2 (CGOLD), plus a label indicating whether the comment answers the question with a clear *Yes*, a clear *No*, or in an undefined way, i.e., as *Unsure* (CGOLD_YN).

For all HITs, we collected annotations from 3-5 annotators for each decision, and we resolved discrepancies using majority voting. Ties led to the elimination of some comments and sometimes even of entire questions.

We assigned the *Yes/No/Unsure* labels at the question level (QGOLD_YN) automatically, using the *Yes/No/Unsure* labels at the comment level (CGOLD_YN). More precisely, we labeled a YES/NO question as *Unsure*, unless there was a majority of *Yes* or *No* labels among the *Yes/No/Unsure* labels for the comments that are labeled as *Good*, in which case we assigned the majority label.

Table 1 shows some statistics about the datasets. We can see that the YES/NO questions are about 10% of the questions. This makes subtask B generally harder for machine learning, as there is much less training data. We further see that on average, there are about 6 comments per question, with the number varying widely from 1 to 143. About half of the comments are *Good*, another 10% are *Potential*, and the rest are *Bad*. Note that for the purpose of classification, *Bad* is in fact a heterogeneous class that includes about 50% *Bad*, 50% *Dialogue*, and also a tiny fraction of *non-English* and *Other* comments. We released the fine grained labels to the task participants as we thought that having information about the heterogeneous structure of *Bad* might be helpful for some systems. About 40-50% of the YES/NO annotations at the comment level (CGOLD_YN) are *Yes*, with the rest nearly equally split between *No* and *Unsure*, with *No* slightly more frequent. However, at the question level, the YES/NO annotations (QGOLD_YN) have more *Unsure* than *No*. Overall, the label distribution in development and testing is similar to that in training for the CGOLD values, but there are somewhat larger differences for QGOLD_YN.

We further released the raw text of all questions and of all comments from Qatar Living, including more than 100 million word tokens, which are useful for training word embeddings, topic models, etc.

```
<Question QID = "109486" QCATEGORY = "فقه العبادات > الجنائز" QDATE = "2008-19-06">
    <QSubject>حكم وضع الماء على القبر لسقي الطير والبهائم</QSubject>
    <QBody>بعض الناس يرش على القبر الماء ويسكب قليلا في كأس توضع على القبر من جهة الرأس بنية أنه إذا شرب منه
    الطائر أو أي بهيمة يعتبر صدقة، كما أن البعض يغرس شجرة من العطر أو الياسمين ويسقيها كل يوم جمعة عند زيارته
    للقبر، فما حكم ذلك كله في ديننا؟ وشكرا.</QBody>
    <Answer CID = "218983" CGOLD = "direct">فكل هذا من البدع أو يفضي إلى الاعتقادات الباطلة والتعبدات المحدثة،
    ومن أراد سقيا الطيور والبهائم جعلها بعيدة عن القبور حتى لا تتخذ طريقا وممرا للبهائم، وراجع الفتوى رقم: ،
    والفتوى رقم: . والله أعلم.</Answer>
    <Answer CID = "273352" CGOLD = "irrelevant">الحمد لله والصلاة والسلام على رسول الله وعلى آله وصحبه، أما بعد:
    فإذا لم يتم مس الفرج مباشرة من غير حائل فلا ينتقض الوضوء، لأن مس الفرج بحائل لا ينقض الوضوء لعدم المباشرة
    والإفضاء كما سبق بيانه في الفتوى :، علما بأن البحث والتفتيش من أجل معرفة ما إذا كان نزل شيء أم لا غير مطلوب
    شرعا ما لم يتحقق من خروجه، كما سبق بيانه في الفتوى رقم :. والله أعلم.</Answer>
    <Answer CID = "155491" CGOLD = "related">لا يجوز رش القبر بالماء إلا إذا كان من أجل تثبيت ترابه، وراجع -3
    في ذلك الفتوى رقم: 4152، والفتوى رقم: . والله أعلم.</Answer>
    <Answer CID = "130233" CGOLD = "irrelevant">الحمد لله والصلاة والسلام على رسول الله وعلى آله وصحبه أما بعد: فإن
    قوله: "مخاضها" يريد أن <REF>المخاض عند المرأة هو أن يأتيها الطلق، وهو الوجع عند الولادة، قال في المحلى:
    والطلق اسم لوجع الولادة. إذن يعرف حصول المخاض عند <NE>السرخسي</NE> وفي المبسوط </REF> يضربها الطلق.
    المرأة بحدوث وجع عند الولادة. والله أعلم.</Answer>
    <Answer CID = "154092" CGOLD = "irrelevant">فالمسكين هو الذي يجد شيئا لا يكفيه، كمن كانت كفايته عشرة ريالات
    ولا يجد إلا خمسة أو سبعة، فإذا كانت هذه صفتك فلا حرج عليك في الأخذ من الزكاة، ومن باب أولى الصدقات
    والمساعدات، التي تكون أنت أو زوجتك وكيلا على توزيعها لأهلها. ولكن إن عين صاحب المال شخصا بعينه، ووكلك أو
    وكل زوجتك في دفعه إليه، وجب عليكما أن تؤدياه إلى من عين، وراجع الفتاوى التالية أرقامها: //. والله أعلم.
    </Answer>
</Question>
```


Figure 2: Annotated Arabic question from the Fatwa corpus.

3.3 Arabic Data: Fatwa corpus

For Arabic, we used data from the Fatwa website, which deals with questions about Islam. This website contains questions by ordinary users and answers by knowledgeable scholars in Islamic studies. The user question can be general, for example "How to pray?", or it can be very personal, e.g., the user has a specific problem in his/her life and wants to find out how to deal with it according to Islam.

Each question (Fatwa) is answered carefully by a knowledgeable scholar. The answer is usually very descriptive: it contains an introduction to the topic of the question, then the general rules in Islam on the topic, and finally an actual answer to the specific question and/or guidance on how to deal with the problem. Typically, links to related questions are also provided to the user to read more about similar situations and to look at related questions.

In the Arabic version of subtask A, a question from the website is provided with a set of exactly five different answers. Each answer of the provided five ones carries one of the following labels:

- *direct:* direct answer to the question;
- *related:* not directly answering the question, but contains related information;
- *irrelevant:* answer to another question not related to the topic.

Similarly to the English corpus, a dataset file is a sequence of examples (Questions), where each question has a subject and a body (text), as well as the following attributes:

- QID: internal question identifier;
- QCATEGORY: question category;
- QDATE: date of posting.

Each question is followed by a list of possible answers. An answer has a subject and a body (text), as well as the following attributes:

- CID: answer identifier;
- CGOLD: label of the answer, which is one of three: direct, related, or irrelevant.

Moreover, the answer body text can contain tags such as the following:

- NE: named entities in the text, usually person names;
- Quran: verse from the Quran;
- Hadeeth: saying by the Islamic prophet.

Figure 2 shows some fully annotated Arabic question from the Fatwa corpus.

Category	Train	Dev	Test
Questions	**2,600**	**300**	**329**
– *GENERAL*	*2,376*	*266*	*304*
– *YES/NO*	*224*	*34*	*25*
Comments	**16,541**	**1,645**	**1,976**
– *min per question*	*1*	*1*	*1*
– *max per question*	*143*	*32*	*66*
– *avg per question*	*6.36*	*5.48*	*6.01*
CGOLD values	**16,541**	**1,645**	**1,976**
– *Good*	*8,069*	*875*	*997*
– *Potential*	*1,659*	*187*	*167*
– *Bad*	*6,813*	*583*	*812*
– *Bad*	*2,981*	*269*	*362*
– *Dialogue*	*3,755*	*312*	*435*
– *Not English*	*74*	*2*	*15*
– *Other*	*3*	*0*	*0*
CGOLD_YN values	**795**	**115**	**111**
– *Yes*	*346*	*62*	–
– *No*	*236*	*32*	–
– *Unsure*	*213*	*21*	–
QGOLD_YN values	**224**	**34**	**25**
– *Yes*	*87*	*16*	*15*
– *No*	*47*	*8*	*4*
– *Unsure*	*90*	*10*	*6*

Table 1: Statistics about the English data.

Category	Train	Dev	Test	Test30
Questions	**1,300**	**200**	**200**	**30**
Answers	**6,500**	**1,000**	**1,001**	**151**
– *Direct*	*1,300*	*200*	*215*	*45*
– *Related*	*1,469*	*222*	*222*	*33*
– *Irrelevant*	*3,731*	*578*	*564*	*73*

Table 2: Statistics about the Arabic data.

3.4 Annotating the Fatwa corpus

We selected the shortest questions and answers from IslamWeb to create our training, development and testing datasets. We avoided long questions and answers since they are likely to be harder to parse, analyse, and classify. For each question, we labeled its answer as *direct*, the answers of linked questions as *related*, and we selected some random answers as *irrelevant* to make the total number of provided answers per question equal to 5.

Table 2 shows some statistics about the resulting datasets. We can see that the number of *direct* answers is the same as the number of questions, since each question has only one direct answer.

One issue with selecting random answers as *irrelevant* is that the task is too easy; thus, we manually annotated a special *hard testset* of 30 questions (Test30), where we selected the *irrelevant* answers using information retrieval to guarantee significant term overlap with the questions. For the general testset, we used these 30 questions and 170 more where the *irrelevant* answers were chosen randomly.

4 Scoring

The official score for both subtasks is F_1, macro-averaged over the target categories:

- For English, subtask A they are *Good*, *Potential*, and *Bad*.
- For Arabic, subtask A these are *direct*, *related*, and *irrelevant*.
- For English, subtask B they are *Yes*, *No*, and *Unsure*.

We also report classification accuracy.

Team ID	Affiliation and reference
Al-Bayan	Alexandria University, Egypt (Mohamed et al., 2015)
CICBUAPnlp	Instituto Politécnico Nacional, Mexico
CoMiC	University of Tübingen, Germany (Rudzewitz and Ziai, 2015)
ECNU	East China Normal University, China (Yi et al., 2015)
FBK-HLT	Fondazione Bruno Kessler, Italy (Vo et al., 2015)
HITSZ-ICRC	Harbin Institute of Technology, China (Hou et al., 2015)
ICRC-HIT	Harbin Institute of Technology, China (Zhou et al., 2015)
JAIST	Japan Advance Institute of Science and Technology, Japan (Tran et al., 2015)
QCRI	Qatar Computing Research Institute, Qatar (Nicosia et al., 2015)
Shiraz	Shiraz University, Iran (Heydari Alashty et al., 2015)
VectorSLU	MIT Computer Science and Artificial Intelligence Lab, USA (Belinkov et al., 2015)
Voltron	Sofia University, Bulgaria (Zamanov et al., 2015)
Yamraj	Masaryk University, Czech Republic

Table 3: The participating teams.

	Submission	Macro F_1	Acc.
	JAIST-contrastive1	57.29	72.67
1	**JAIST-primary**	**57.19**	**72.52_{1}**
	HITSZ-ICRC-contrastive1	56.44	69.43
2	**HITSZ-ICRC-primary**	**56.41**	**68.67_{5}**
	*QCRI-contrastive1	56.40	68.27
	HITSZ-ICRC-contrastive2	55.22	67.91
	ICRC-HIT-contrastive1	53.82	73.18
3	***QCRI-primary**	**53.74**	**70.50_{3}**
4	**ECNU-primary**	**53.47**	**70.55_{2}**
	ECNU-contrastive1	52.55	69.48
	ECNU-contrastive2	52.27	69.38
	*QCRI-contrastive2	51.97	69.48
5	**ICRC-HIT-primary**	**49.60**	**67.86_{6}**
	*VectorSLU-contrastive1	49.54	70.45
6	***VectorSLU-primary**	**49.10**	**66.45_{7}**
7	**Shiraz-primary**	**47.34**	**56.83_{9}**
8	**FBK-HLT-primary**	**47.32**	**69.13_{4}**
	JAIST-contrastive2	46.96	57.74
9	**Voltron-primary**	**46.07**	**62.35_{8}**
	Voltron-contrastive2	45.16	61.74
	Shiraz-contrastive1	45.03	62.55
	ICRC-HIT-contrastive2	40.54	60.12
10	**CICBUAPnlp-primary**	**40.40**	**53.74_{11}**
	CICBUAPnlp-contrastive1	39.53	52.33
	Shiraz-contrastive2	38.00	60.53
11	**Yamraj-primary**	**37.65**	**45.50_{12}**
	Yamraj-contrastive2	37.60	44.79
	Yamraj-contrastive1	36.30	39.57
12	**CoMiC-primary**	**30.63**	**54.20_{10}**
	CoMiC-contrastive1	23.35	50.56
	baseline: always "Good"	22.36	50.46

Table 4: **Subtask A, English:** results for all submissions. The first column shows the rank for the primary submissions according to macro F_1, and the subindex in the last column shows the rank based on accuracy. Teams marked with a * include a task co-organizer.

5 Participants and Results

The list of all participating teams can be found in Table 3. The results for subtask A, English and Arabic, are shown in Tables 4-5 and 6-7, respectively; those for subtask B are in Table 8. The systems are ranked by their macro-averaged F_1 scores for their primary runs (shown in the first column); a ranking based on accuracy is also shown as a subindex in the last column. We mark explicitly with an asterisk the teams that had a task co-organizer as a team member. This is for information only; these teams competed in the same conditions as everybody else.

	Submission	Macro F_1	Acc.
1	HITSZ-ICRC	48.13	59.62_{4}
2	*QCRI	47.01	62.15_{2}
3	ECNU	46.57	61.34_{3}
4	FBK-HLT	42.61	62.40_{1}
5	Shiraz	40.06	48.53_{10}
6	ICRC-HIT	39.93	59.51_{5}
7	*VectorSLU	38.69	54.35_{7}
8	CICBUAPnlp	36.13	44.89_{11}
9	JAIST	35.09	54.61_{6}
10	Voltron	29.15	50.05_{9}
11	Yamraj	24.48	35.93_{12}
12	CoMiC	23.35	51.77_{8}

Table 5: **Subtask A, English with *Dialog* as a separate category:** results for the primary submissions. The first column shows the rank based on macro F_1, the subindex in the last column shows the rank based on accuracy. Teams marked with a * include a task co-organizer.

5.1 Subtask A, English

Table 4 shows the results for subtask A, English, which attracted 12 teams, which submitted 30 runs: 12 primary and 18 contrastive. We can see that all submissions outperform, in terms of macro F_1, the majority class baseline that always predicts *Good* (shown in the last line of the table); for the primary submissions, this is so by a large margin. However, in terms of accuracy, one of the primary submissions falls below the baseline; this might be due to them optimizing for macro F_1 rather than for accuracy.

The best system for this subtask is JAIST, which ranks first both in the official macro F_1 score (57.19) and in accuracy (72.52); it used a supervised feature-rich approach, which includes topic models and word vector representation, with an SVM classifier.

The second best system is HITSZ-ICRC, which used an ensemble of classifiers. While it ranked second in terms of macro F_1 (56.41), it was only fifth on accuracy (68.67); the second best in accuracy was ECNU, with 70.55.

The third best system, in both macro F_1 (53.74) and accuracy (70.50), is QCRI. In addition to the features they used for Arabic (see the next subsection), they further added cosine similarity based on word embeddings, sentiment polarity lexicons, and metadata features such as the identity of the users asking and answering the questions or the existence of acknowledgments.

Interestingly, the top two systems have contrastive runs that scored higher than their primary runs both in terms of macro F_1 and accuracy, even though these differences are small. This is also true for QCRI's contrastive run in terms of macro F_1 but not in terms of accuracy, which indicates that they optimized for macro F_1 for that contrastive run. Note that ECNU was very close behind QCRI in macro F_1 (53.47), and it slightly outperformed it in accuracy.

Note that while most systems trained a four-way classifier to distinguish *Good/Bad/Potential/Dialog*, where *Bad* includes *Bad*, *Not English* and *Other*, some systems targetted a three-way distinction *Good/Bad/Potential*, following the grouping in Table 1, as for the official scoring the scorer was merging *Dialog* with *Bad* anyway.

Table 5 shows the results with four classes. The last four systems did not predict *Dialog*, and thus are severely penalized by macro F_1. Comparing Tables 4 and 5, we can see that the scores for the 4-way classification are up to 10 points lower than for the 3-way case. Distinguishing *Dialog* from *Bad* turns out to be very hard: e.g., HITSZ-ICRC achieved an F_1 of 76.52 for *Good*, 18.41 for *Potential*, 40.38 for *Bad*, 57.21 for *Dialog*; however, merging *Bad* and *Dialog* yielded an F_1 of 74.32 for the *Bad+Dialog* category. The other systems show a similar trend.

Finally, note that *Potential* is by far the hardest class (with an F_1 lower than 20 for all teams), and it is also the smallest one, which amplifies its weight with F_1 macro; thus, two teams (CoMiC and FBK-HLT) have chosen never to predict it.

5.2 Subtask A, Arabic

Table 6 shows the results for subtask A, Arabic, which attracted four teams, which submitted a total of 11 runs: 4 primary and 7 contrastive. All teams performed well above a majority class baseline that always predicts *irrelevant*.

QCRI was a clear winner with a macro F_1 of 78.55 and accuracy of 83.02. They used a set of features composed of lexical similarities and word $[1, 2]$-grams. Most importantly, they exploited the fact that there is at most one good answer for a given question: they rank the answers by means of logistic regression, and label the top answer as *direct*, the next one as *related* and the remaining as *irrelevant* (a similar strategy is used by some other teams too).

	Submission	Macro F_1	Acc.
1	***QCRI-primary**	**78.55**	**83.02**$_1$
	*QCRI-contrastive2	76.97	81.92
	*QCRI-contrastive1	76.60	81.82
	*VectorSLU-contrastive1	73.18	78.12
2	***VectorSLU-primary**	**70.99**	**76.32**$_2$
	HITSZ-ICRC-contrastive1	68.36	73.93
	HITSZ-ICRC-contrastive2	67.98	73.23
3	**HITSZ-ICRC-primary**	**67.70**	**74.53**$_3$
4	**Al-Bayan-primary**	**67.65**	**74.53**$_3$
	Al-Bayan-contrastive2	65.70	72.53
	Al-Bayan-contrastive1	61.19	71.33
	baseline: always "irrelevant"	24.03	56.34

Table 6: **Subtask A, Arabic:** results for all submissions. The first column shows the rank for the primary submissions according to macro F_1, and the subindex in the last column shows the rank based on accuracy. Teams marked with a * include a task co-organizer.

	Submission	Macro F_1	Acc.
1	***QCRI-primary**	**46.09**	**48.34**
	*QCRI-contrastive1	43.32	46.36
	*QCRI-contrastive2	43.08	49.67
	Al-Bayan-contrastive1	42.04	47.02
	HITSZ-ICRC-contrastive1	39.61	40.40
	HITSZ-ICRC-contrastive2	39.57	40.40
2	**HITSZ-ICRC-primary**	**38.58**	**39.74**
	*VectorSLU-contrastive1	36.43	43.05
3	***VectorSLU-primary**	**36.75**	**37.09**
4	**Al-Bayan-primary**	**34.93**	**38.41**
	Al-Bayan-contrastive2	34.42	35.76
	baseline: always "irrelevant"	21.73	48.34

Table 7: **Subtask A, Arabic:** results for the 30 manually annotated Arabic questions.

Even though QCRI did not consider semantic models for this subtask, and the second best team did, the distance between them is sizeable.

The second place went to VectorSLU (F_1=70.99, Acc=76.32), whose feature vectors incorporated text-based similarities, embedded word vectors from both the question and answers, and features based on normalized ranking scores. Their word embeddings were generated with word2vec (Mikolov et al., 2013), and trained on the Arabic Gigaword corpus. Their contrastive condition labeled the top scoring response as *direct*, the second best as *related*, and the others as *irrelevant*. Their primary condition did not make use of this constraint.

Then come HITSZ-ICRC and Al-Bayan, which are tied on accuracy (74.53), and are almost tied on macro F_1: 67.70 vs. 67.65. HITSZ-ICRC translated the Arabic to English and then extracted features from both the Arabic original and from the English translation. Al-Bayan had a knowledge-rich approach that used MADA for morphological analysis, and then combined information retrieval scores with explicit semantic analysis in a decision tree.

For all submitted runs, identifying the *irrelevant* answers was easiest, with F_1 for this class ranging from 85% to 91%. This was expected, since most of these answers were randomly selected and thus the probability of finding common terms between them and the questions was low. The F_1 for detecting the *direct* answers ranged from 67% to 77%, while for the *related* answers, it was lowest: 47% to 67%.

Table 7 presents the results for the 30 manually annotated Arabic questions, for which a search engine was used to find possibly *irrelevant* answers. We can see that the results are much lower than those reported in Table 6, which shows that detecting *direct* and *related* answers is more challenging when the *irrelevant* answers contain many common terms with the question. The decrease in performance can be also explained by the different class distribution in training and testing, e.g., on the average, there are 1.5 *direct* answers in Test30 vs. just 1 in *training*, and the proportion of *irrelevant* also changed (see Table 2). The team ranking changed too. QCRI remained the best-performing team, but the worst performing group now has one of its contrastive runs doing quite well. VectorSLU, which relies heavily on word overlap and similarity between the question and the answer experienced a relatively higher drop in performance compared to the rest. In future work, we plan to study further the impact of selecting the *irrelevant* answers in various challenging ways.

5.3 Subtask B, English

Table 8 shows the results for subtask B, English, which attracted eight teams, who submitted a total of 20 runs: 8 primary and 12 contrastive. As for subtask A, all submissions outperformed the majority class baseline that always predicts *Yes* (shown in the last line of the table). However, this is so in terms of macro F_1 only; in terms of accuracy, only half of the systems managed to beat the baseline.

	Submission	Macro F_1	Acc.
1	***VectorSLU-primary**	**63.7**	**72_1**
	*VectorSLU-contrastive1	61.9	68
2	**ECNU-primary**	**55.8**	**68_2**
	ECNU-contrastive2	53.9	64
3	***QCRI-primary**	**53.6**	**64_3**
3	**$^\diamond$HITSZ-ICRC-primary**	**53.6**	**64_3**
	ECNU-contrastive1	50.6	60
	*QCRI-contrastive2	49.0	56
	HITSZ-ICRC-contrastive1	42.5	60
	HITSZ-ICRC-contrastive2	42.4	60
	ICRC-HIT-contrastive2	40.3	60
5	**CICBUAPnlp-primary**	**38.8**	**44_6**
	ICRC-HIT-contrastive1	37.6	56
6	**ICRC-HIT-primary**	**30.9**	**52_5**
7	**Yamraj-primary**	**29.8**	**28_8**
	Yamraj-contrastive1	29.8	28
	CICBUAPnlp-contrastive1	29.1	40
8	**FBK-HLT-primary**	**27.8**	**40_7**
	*QCRI-contrastive1	25.2	56
	Yamraj-contrastive2	25.1	36
	baseline: always "Yes"	25.0	60

Table 8: **Subtask B, English:** results for all submissions. The first column shows the rank for the primary submissions according to macro F_1, and the subindex in the last column shows the rank based on accuracy. Teams marked with a * include a task co-organizer. The submission marked with a $^\diamond$ was corrected after the deadline.

For most teams, the features used for subtask B were almost the same as for subtask A, with some teams adding extra features, e.g., that look for positive, negative and uncertainty words from small hand-crafted dictionaries.

Most teams designed systems that make Yes/No/Unsure decisions at the comment level, predicting CGOLD_YN labels (typically, for the comments that were predicted to be *Good* by the team's system for subtask A), and were then assigned a question-level label using majority voting.[4] This is a reasonable strategy as it mirrors the human annotation process. Some teams tried to extract features from the whole list of comments and to predict QGOLD_YN directly, but this yielded drop in performance.

[4]In fact, the authors of the third-best system HITSZ-ICRC submitted by mistake for their primary run predictions for CGOLD_YN instead of QGOLD_YN; the results reported in Table 8 for this team were obtained by converting these predictions using simple majority voting.

The top-performing system, in both macro F_1 (63.7) and accuracy (72), is VectorSLU. It is followed by ECNU with F_1=55.8, Acc=68. The third place is shared by QCRI and HITSZ-ICRC, which have exactly the same scores (F_1=53.6, Acc=64), but different errors and different confusion matrices. These four systems are much better than the rest; the next system is far behind at F_1=38.8, Acc=44.

Interestingly, once again there is a tie for the third place between the participating teams, as was the case for subtask A, Arabic and English. Note, however, that this time all top systems' primary runs performed better than their corresponding contrastive runs, which was not the case for subtask A.

6 Features and Techniques

Most systems were supervised,[5] and thus the main efforts were focused on feature engineering. We can group the features participants used into the following four categories:

- **question-specific features:** e.g., length of the question, words/stems/lemmata/n-grams in the question, etc.
- **comment-specific features:** e.g., length of the comment, words/stems/lemmata/n-grams in the question, punctuation (e.g., does the comment contain a question mark), proportion of positive/negative sentiment words, rank of the comment in the list of comments, named entities (locations, organizations), formality of the language used, surface features (e.g., phones, URLs), etc.
- **features about the question-comment pair:** various kinds of similarity between the question and the comment (e.g., lexical based on cosine, or based on WordNet, language modeling, topic models such as LDA or explicit semantic analysis), word/lemma/stem/n-gram/POS overlap between the question and the comment (e.g., greedy string tiling, longest common subsequences, Jaccard coefficient, containment, etc.), information gain from the comment with respect to the question, etc.
- **metadata features:** ID of the user who asked the question, ID of the one who posted the comment, whether they are the same, known number of *Good*/*Bad*/*Potential* comments (in the training data) written by the user who wrote the comment, timestamp, question category, etc.

Note that the metadata features overlap with the other three groups as a metadata feature is about the question, about the comment, or about the question-comment pair. Note also that the features above can be binary, integer, or real-valued, e.g., can be calculated using various weighting schemes such as TF.IDF for words/lemmata/stems.

Although most participants focused on engineering features to be used with a standard classifier such as SVM or a decision tree, some also used more advanced techniques. For example, some teams used sequence or partial tree kernels (Moschitti, 2006). Another popular technique was to use word embeddings, e.g., modeled using convolution or recurrent neural networks, or with latent semantic analysis, and also vectors trained using word2vec and GloVe (Pennington et al., 2014), as pre-trained on Google News or Wikipedia, or trained on the provided Qatar Living data. Less popular techniques included dialog modeling for the list of comments for a given question, e.g., using conditional random fields to model the sequence of comment labels (*Good*, *Bad*, *Potential*, *Dialog*), mapping the question and the comment to a graph structure and performing graph traversal, using word alignments between the question and the comment, time modeling, and sentiment analysis. Finally, for Arabic, some participants translated the Arabic data to English, and then extracted features from both the Arabic and the English version; this is helpful, as there are many more tools and resources for English than for Arabic.

When building their systems, participants used a number of tools and resources for preprocessing, feature extraction, and machine learning, including Deeplearning4J, DKPro, GATE, GloVe, Google translate, HeidelTime, LibLinear, LibSVM, MADA, Mallet, Meteor, Networkx, NLTK, NRC-Canada sentiment lexicons, PPDB, sklearn, Spam filtering corpus, Stanford NLP toolkit, TakeLab, TiMBL, UIMA, Weka, Wikipedia, Wiktionary, word2vec, WordNet, and WTMF.

[5]The only two exceptions were Yamraj (unsupervised) and CICBUAPnlp (semi-supervised).

There was also a rich variety of preprocessing techniques used, including sentence splitting, tokenization, stemming, lemmatization, morphological analysis (esp. for Arabic), dependency parsing, part of speech tagging, temporal tagging, named entity recognition, gazetteer matching, word alignment between the question and the comment, word embedding, spam filtering, removing some content (e.g., all contents enclosed in HTML tags, emoticons, repetitive punctuation, stopwords, the ending signature, URLs, etc.) substituting (e.g., HTML character encodings and some common slang words), etc.

7 Discussion

The task attracted 13 teams and 61 submissions. Naturally, the English subtasks were more popular (with 12 and 8 teams for subtasks A and B, respectively; compared to just 4 for Arabic): there are more tools and resources for English as well as more general research interest. Moreover, the English data followed the natural discussion threads in a forum, while the Arabic data was somewhat artificial.

We have seen that all submissions managed to outperform, on the official macro F_1 metric,[6] a majority class baseline for both subtasks and for both languages; this improvement is smaller for English and much larger for Arabic. However, if we consider accuracy, many systems fall below the baseline for English in both subtasks.

Overall, the results for Arabic are higher than those for English for subtask A, e.g., there is an absolute difference of over 21 points in macro F_1 (78.55 vs. 57.19) for the top systems. This suggests that the Arabic task was generally easier. Indeed, it uses very formal polished language both for the questions and the answers (as opposed to the noisy English forum data); moreover, it is known a priori that each question can have at most one *direct* answer, and the teams have exploited this information.

However, looking at accuracy, the difference between the top systems for Arabic and English is just 10 points (82.02 vs. 72.52). This suggests that part of the bigger difference for F_1 macro comes from the measure itself.

[6]Curiously, there was a close tie for the third place for all three subtask-language combinations.

Indeed, having a closer look at the distribution of the F_1 values for the different classes before the macro averaging, we can see that the results are much more balanced for Arabic (F_1 of 77.31/67.13/91.21 for *direct/related/irrelevant*; with P and R very close to F_1) than for English (F_1 of 78.96/14.36/78.24 for *Good/Potential/Bad*; with P and R very close to F_1). We can see that the *Potential* class is the hardest. This can hurt the accuracy but only slightly as this class is the smallest. However, it can still have a major impact on macro-F_1 due to the effect of macro-averaging.

Overall, for both Arabic and English, it was much easier to recognize *Good/direct* and *Bad/irrelevant* examples (P, R, F_1 about 80-90), and much harder to do so for *Potential/related* (P, R, F_1 around 67 for Arabic, and 14 for English). This should not be surprising, as this intermediate category is easily confusable with the other two: for Arabic, these are answers to related questions, while for English, this is a category that was quite hard for human annotators.

We should say that even though we had used majority voting to ensure agreement between annotators, we were still worried about the the quality of human annotations collected on Amazon's Mechanical Turk. Thus, we asked eight people to do a manual re-annotation of the QGOLD_YN labels for the test data. We found a very high degree of agreement between each of the human annotators and the Turkers. Originally, there were 29 YES/NO questions, but we found that four of them were arguably general rather than YES/NO, and thus we excluded them. For the remaining 25 questions, we had a discussion between our annotators about any potential disagreement, and finally, we arrived with a new annotation that changed the labels of three questions. This corresponds to an agreement of 22/25=0.88 between our consolidated annotation and the Turkers, which is very high. This new annotation was the one we used for the final scoring. Note that using the original Turkers' labels yielded slightly different scores but exactly the same ranking for the systems. The high agreement between our re-annotations and the Turkers and the fact that the ranking did not change makes us optimistic about the quality of the annotations for subtask A too (even though we are aware of some errors and inconsistencies in the annotations).

8 Conclusion and Future Work

We have described a new task that entered SemEval-2015: task 3 on Answer Selection in Community Question Answering. The task has attracted a reasonably high number of submissions: a total of 61 by 13 teams. The teams experimented with a large number of features, resources and approaches, and we believe that the lessons learned will be useful for the overall development of the field of community question answering. Moreover, the datasets that we have created as part of the task, and which we have released for use to the community,[7] should be useful beyond SemEval.

In our task description, we especially encouraged solutions going beyond simple keyword and bag-of-words matching, e.g., using semantic or complex linguistic information in order to reason about the relation between questions and answers. Although participants experimented with a broad variety of features (including semantic word-based representations, syntactic relations, contextual features, meta-information, and external resources), we feel that much more can be done in this direction. Ultimately, the question of whether complex linguistically-based representations and inference can be successfully applied to the very informal and ungrammatical text from cQA forums remains unanswered to a large extent.

Complementary to the research direction presented by this year's task, we plan to run a follow-up task at SemEval-2016, with a focus on answering *new* questions, i.e., that were not already answered in Qatar Living. For Arabic, we plan to use a real community question answering dataset, similar to Qatar Living for English.

Acknowledgments

This research is developed by the Arabic Language Technologies (ALT) group at Qatar Computing Research Institute (QCRI) within the Qatar Foundation in collaboration with MIT. It is part of the Interactive sYstems for Answer Search (Iyas) project.

We would like to thank Nicole Schmidt from MIT for her help with setting up and running the Amazon Mechanical Turk annotation tasks.

[7] http://alt.qcri.org/semeval2015/task3/

References

Yonatan Belinkov, Mitra Mohtarami, Scott Cyphers, and James Glass. 2015. VectorSLU: A continuous word vector approach to answer selection in community question answering systems. In *Proceedings of the 9th International Workshop on Semantic Evaluation*, SemEval '15, Denver, Colorado, USA.

Michael Heilman and Noah A. Smith. 2010. Tree edit models for recognizing textual entailments, paraphrases, and answers to questions. In *Human Language Technologies: The 2010 Annual Conference of the North American Chapter of the Association for Computational Linguistics*, HLT '10, pages 1011–1019, Los Angeles, California, USA.

Amin Heydari Alashty, Saeed Rahmani, Meysam Roostaee, and Mostafa Fakhrahmad. 2015. Shiraz: A proposed list wise approach to answer validation. In *Proceedings of the 9th International Workshop on Semantic Evaluation*, SemEval '15, Denver, Colorado, USA.

Yongshuai Hou, Cong Tan, Xiaolong Wang, Yaoyun Zhang, Jun Xu, and Qingcai Chen. 2015. HITSZ-ICRC: Exploiting classification approach for answer selection in community question answering. In *Proceedings of the 9th International Workshop on Semantic Evaluation*, SemEval '15, Denver, Colorado, USA.

Jiwoon Jeon, W. Bruce Croft, and Joon Ho Lee. 2005. Finding similar questions in large question and answer archives. In *Proceedings of the 14th ACM International Conference on Information and Knowledge Management*, CIKM '05, pages 84–90, Bremen, Germany.

Tomas Mikolov, Ilya Sutskever, Kai Chen, Greg S Corrado, and Jeff Dean. 2013. Distributed representations of words and phrases and their compositionality. In C.J.C. Burges, L. Bottou, M. Welling, Z. Ghahramani, and K.Q. Weinberger, editors, *Advances in Neural Information Processing Systems 26*, pages 3111–3119. Curran Associates, Inc.

Reham Mohamed, Maha Ragab, Heba Abdelnasser, Nagwa M. El-Makky, and Marwan Torki. 2015. Al-Bayan: A knowledge-based system for Arabic answer selection. In *Proceedings of the 9th International Workshop on Semantic Evaluation*, SemEval '15, Denver, Colorado, USA.

Alessandro Moschitti, Silvia Quarteroni, Roberto Basili, and Suresh Manandhar. 2007. Exploiting syntactic and shallow semantic kernels for question answer classification. In *Proceedings of the 45th Annual Meeting of the Association of Computational Linguistics*, ACL '07, pages 776–783, Prague, Czech Republic.

Alessandro Moschitti. 2006. Efficient Convolution Kernels for Dependency and Constituent Syntactic Trees. In Johannes Fürnkranz, Tobias Scheffer, and Myra

Spiliopoulou, editors, *Machine Learning: ECML 2006*, volume 4212 of *Lecture Notes in Computer Science*, pages 318–329. Springer Berlin Heidelberg.

Massimo Nicosia, Simone Filice, Alberto Barrón-Cedeño, Iman Saleh, Hamdy Mubarak, Wei Gao, Preslav Nakov, Giovanni Da San Martino, Alessandro Moschitti, Kareem Darwish, Lluís Màrquez, Shafiq Joty, and Walid Magdy. 2015. QCRI: Answer selection for community question answering - experiments for Arabic and English. In *Proceedings of the 9th International Workshop on Semantic Evaluation*, SemEval '15, Denver, Colorado, USA.

Jeffrey Pennington, Richard Socher, and Christopher Manning. 2014. Glove: Global vectors for word representation. In *Proceedings of the 2014 Conference on Empirical Methods in Natural Language Processing*, EMNLP '14, pages 1532–1543, Doha, Qatar.

Filip Radlinski and Thorsten Joachims. 2005. Query chains: Learning to rank from implicit feedback. In *Proceedings of the Eleventh ACM SIGKDD International Conference on Knowledge Discovery in Data Mining*, KDD '05, pages 239–248, Chicago, Illinois, USA.

Björn Rudzewitz and Ramon Ziai. 2015. CoMiC: Adapting a short answer assessment system for answer selection. In *Proceedings of the 9th International Workshop on Semantic Evaluation*, SemEval '15, Denver, Colorado, USA.

Aliaksei Severyn and Alessandro Moschitti. 2012. Structural relationships for large-scale learning of answer re-ranking. In *Proceedings of the 35th International ACM SIGIR Conference on Research and Development in Information Retrieval*, SIGIR '12, pages 741–750, Portland, Oregon, USA.

Aliaksei Severyn and Alessandro Moschitti. 2013. Automatic feature engineering for answer selection and extraction. In *Proceedings of the 2013 Conference on Empirical Methods in Natural Language Processing*, EMNLP '13, pages 458–467, Seattle, Washington, USA.

Dan Shen and Mirella Lapata. 2007. Using semantic roles to improve question answering. In *Proceedings of the 2007 Joint Conference on Empirical Methods in Natural Language Processing and Computational Natural Language Learning*, EMNLP-CoNLL '07, pages 12–21, Prague, Czech Republic.

Mihai Surdeanu, Massimiliano Ciaramita, and Hugo Zaragoza. 2008. Learning to rank answers on large online QA collections. In *Proceedings of the 46th Annual Meeting of the Association for Computational Linguistics and the Human Language Technology Conference*, ACL-HLT '08, pages 719–727, Columbus, Ohio, USA.

Quan Hung Tran, Vu Tran, Tu Vu, Minh Nguyen, and Son Bao Pham. 2015. JAIST: Combining multiple features for answer selection in community question answering. In *Proceedings of the 9th International Workshop on Semantic Evaluation*, SemEval '15, Denver, Colorado, USA.

Ngoc Phuoc An Vo, Simone Magnolini, and Octavian Popescu. 2015. FBK-HLT: An application of semantic textual similarity for answer selection in community question answering. In *Proceedings of the 9th International Workshop on Semantic Evaluation*, SemEval '15, Denver, Colorado, USA.

Mengqiu Wang and Christopher D. Manning. 2010. Probabilistic tree-edit models with structured latent variables for textual entailment and question answering. In *Proceedings of the 23rd International Conference on Computational Linguistics*, COLING '10, pages 1164–1172, Beijing, China.

Mengqiu Wang, Noah A. Smith, and Teruko Mitamura. 2007. What is the Jeopardy model? A quasi-synchronous grammar for QA. In *Proceedings of the 2007 Joint Conference on Empirical Methods in Natural Language Processing and Computational Natural Language Learning*, EMNLP-CoNLL '07, pages 22–32, Prague, Czech Republic.

Xuchen Yao, Benjamin Van Durme, Chris Callison-Burch, and Peter Clark. 2013. Answer extraction as sequence tagging with tree edit distance. In *Proceedings of the 2013 Conference of the North American Chapter of the Association for Computational Linguistics: Human Language Technologies*, NAACL-HLT '13, pages 858–867.

Liang Yi, JianXiang Wang, and Man Lan. 2015. ECNU: Using multiple sources of CQA-based information for answers selection and YES/NO response inference. In *Proceedings of the 9th International Workshop on Semantic Evaluation*, SemEval '15, Denver, Colorado, USA.

Ivan Zamanov, Marina Kraeva, Nelly Hateva, Ivana Yovcheva, Ivelina Nikolova, and Galia Angelova. 2015. Voltron: A hybrid system for answer validation based on lexical and distance features. In *Proceedings of the 9th International Workshop on Semantic Evaluation*, SemEval '15, Denver, Colorado, USA.

Xiaoqiang Zhou, Baotian Hu, Jiaxin Lin, Yang xiang, and Xiaolong Wang. 2015. ICRC-HIT: A deep learning based comment sequence labeling system for answer selection challenge. In *Proceedings of the 9th International Workshop on Semantic Evaluation*, SemEval '15, Denver, Colorado, USA.

VectorSLU: A Continuous Word Vector Approach to Answer Selection in Community Question Answering Systems

Yonatan Belinkov, Mitra Mohtarami, Scott Cyphers, James Glass
MIT Computer Science and Artificial Intelligence Laboratory, Cambridge, MA 02139, USA
{belinkov, mitra, cyphers, glass}@csail.mit.edu

Abstract

Continuous word and phrase vectors have proven useful in a number of NLP tasks. Here we describe our experience using them as a source of features for the SemEval-2015 task 3, consisting of two community question answering subtasks: *Answer Selection* for categorizing answers as *potential*, *good*, and *bad* with regards to their corresponding questions; and *YES/NO inference* for predicting a *yes*, *no*, or *unsure* response to a YES/NO question using all of its *good* answers. Our system ranked 6th and 1st in the English answer selection and YES/NO inference subtasks respectively, and 2nd in the Arabic answer selection subtask.

1 Introduction

Continuous word and phrase vectors, in which similar words and phrases are associated with similar vectors, have been useful in many NLP tasks (Al-Rfou et al., 2013; Bansal et al., 2014; Bowman et al., 2014; Boyd-Graber et al., 2012; Chen and Rudnicky, 2014; Guo et al., 2014; Iyyer et al., 2014; Levy and Goldberg, 2014; Mikolov et al., 2013c).

To evaluate the effectiveness of continuous vector representations for *Community question answering* (CQA), we focused on using simple features derived from vector similarity as input to a multi-class linear SVM classifier. Our approach is language independent and was evaluated on both English and Arabic. Most of the vectors we use are domain-independent.

CQA services provide forums for users to ask or answer questions on any topic, resulting in high variance answer quality (Màrquez et al., 2015). Searching for good answers among the many responses can be time-consuming for participants. This is illustrated by the following example of a question and subsequent answers.

Q: *Can I obtain Driving License my QID is written Employee?*

A1: *the word employee is a general term that refers to all the staff in your company ... you are all considered employees of your company*

A2: *your qid should specify what is the actual profession you have. I think for me, your chances to have a drivers license is low.*

A3: *his asking if he can obtain. means he have the driver license.*

Answer selection aims to automatically categorize answers as: *good* if they completely answer the question, *potential* if they contain useful information about the question but do not completely answer it, and *bad* if irrelevant to the question. In the example, answers **A1**, **A2**, and **A3** are respectively classified as *potential*, *good*, and *bad*. The Arabic answer selection task uses the labels *direct*, *related*, and *irrelevant*.

YES/NO inference infers a *yes*, *no*, or *unsure* response to a question through its *good* answers, which might not explicitly contain *yes* or *no* keywords. For example, the answer for **Q** is *no* with respect to **A2** that can be interpreted as a *no* answer to the question.

The remainder of this paper describes our features and our rationale for choosing them, followed by an analysis of the results, and a conclusion.

Text-based features
Text-based similarities
yes/no/probably-like words existing
Vector-based features
Q&A vectors
OOV Q&A
yes/no/probably-based cosine similarity
Metadata-based features
Q&A identical user
Rank-based features
Normalized ranking scores

Table 1: The different types of features.

2 Method

Continuous vector representations, described by Schütze (Schütze, 1992a; Schütze, 1992b), associate similar vectors with similar words and phrases. Most approaches to computing vector representations use the observation that similar words appear in similar contexts (Firth, 1957). The theses of Sahlgren (Sahlgren, 2006), Mikolov (Mikolov, 2012), and Socher (Socher, 2014) provide extensive information on vector representations.

Our system analyzes questions and answers with a `DkPro` (Eckart de Castilho and Gurevych, 2014) `uimaFIT` (Ogren and Bethard, 2009) pipeline. The `DkPro OpenNLP` (Apache Software Foundation, 2014) segmenter and chunker tokenize and find sentences and phrases in the English questions and answers, followed by lemmatization with the Stanford lemmatizer (Manning et al., 2014). In Arabic, we only apply lemmatization, with no chunking, using `MADAMIRA` (Pasha et al., 2014). Stop words are removed in both languages.

As shown in Table 1, we compute *text-based*, *vector-based*, *metadata-based* and *rank-based* features from the pre-processed data. The features are used for a linear SVM classifier for answer selection and YES/NO answer inference tasks. YES/NO answer inference is only performed on *good* YES/NO question answers, using the YES/NO majority class, and *unsure* otherwise. SVM parameters are set by grid-search and cross-validation.

Text-based features These features are mainly computed using text similarity metrics that measure the string overlap between questions and answers: The *Longest Common Substring* measure (Gusfield, 1997) identifies uninterrupted common strings, while the *Longest Common Subsequence* measure (Allison and Dix, 1986) and the *Longest Common Subsequence Norm* identify common strings with interruptions and text replacements, while *Greedy String Tiling* measure (Wise, 1996) allows reordering of the subsequences. Other measures which treat text as sequences of characters and compute similarities include the *Monge Elkan Second String* (Monge and Elkan, 1997) and *Jaro Second String* (Jaro, 1989) measures. A *Cosine Similarity-type* measure based on term frequency within the text is also used. Sets of (1-4)-grams from the question and answer are compared with *Jaccard coefficient* (Lyon et al., 2004) and *Containment* measures (Broder, 1997).[1]

Another group of text-based features identifies answers that contain *yes*-like (e.g., "yes", "oh_yes", "yeah", "yep"), *no*-like (e.g., "no", "none", "nope", "never") and *unsure*-like (e.g., "possibly", "conceivably", "perhaps", "might") words. These word groups were determined by selecting the top 20 nearest neighbor words to the words *yes*, *no* and *probably* based on the cosine similarity of their `Word2Vec` vectors. These features are particularly useful for the YES/NO answer inference task.

Vector-based features Our *vector-based* features are computed from `Word2Vec` vectors (Mikolov et al., 2013a; Mikolov et al., 2013b; Mikolov et al., 2013d). For English word vectors we use the GoogleNews vectors dataset, available on the `Word2Vec` web site,[2] which has a 3,000,000 word vocabulary of 300-dimensional word vectors trained on about 100 billion words. For Arabic word vectors we use `Word2Vec` to train 100-dimensional vectors with default settings on a lemmatized version of the Arabic Gigaword (Linguistic Data Consortium, 2011), obtaining a vocabulary of 120,000 word lemmas.

We also use `Doc2Vec`,[3] an implementation of (Le and Mikolov, 2014) in the `gensim`

[1]These features are mostly taken from the QCRI baseline system: `http://alt.qcri.org/semeval2015/task3/index.php?id=data-and-tools`.

[2]`https://code.google.com/p/word2vec`.

[3]`http://radimrehurek.com/gensim/models/`

toolkit (Řehůřek and Sojka, 2010). `Doc2Vec` provides vectors for text of arbitrary length, so it allows us to directly model answers and questions. The `Doc2Vec` vectors were trained on the CQA English data, creating a single vector for each question or answer. These are the only vectors that were trained specifically for the CQA domain.

We implemented a UIMA annotator that associates a `Word2Vec` word vector with each in-vocabulary token (or lemma). No vectors are assigned for out of vocabulary tokens. Another annotator computes the *average* of the vectors for the entire question or answer, with no vector assigned if all tokens are out of vocabulary.

We initially used the cosine similarity of the question and answer vectors as a feature for the SVM classifier, but we found that we had better results using the normalized vectors themselves. We hypothesize that the SVM was able to tune the importance of the components of the vectors, whereas cosine similarity weights each component equally. If the question or answer has no vector, we use a 0 vector. To make it easier for the classifier to ignore the vectors in these cases, we add boolean features indicating out of vocabulary, *OOV Question* and *OOV Answer*.

Even though the bag of words approach showed encouraging results, we found it to be too coarse, so we also compute average vectors for each sentence. For English, we also compute average vectors for each chunk. Then we look for the best matches between sentences (and chunks) in the question and answer in terms of cosine similarity, and use the pairs of (unnormalized) vectors as features.[4] More formally, given a question with sentence vectors $\{q_i\}$ and an answer with sentence vectors $\{a_j\}$, we take as features the values of the vector pair $(\hat{q}, \hat{a})$ defined as:

$$(\hat{q}, \hat{a}) = \arg\max_{(q_i, a_j)} \frac{q_i \cdot a_j}{\|q_i\| \, \|a_j\|}$$

We also have six features corresponding to the greatest cosine similarity between the comment word vectors and the vectors for the words *yes, Yes, no, No, probably* and *Probably*. These features are more effective for the YES/NO classification task.

`doc2vec.html`.

[4]Post-evaluation testing showed no significant difference between using normalized or unnormalized vectors.

Metadata-based features As a *metadata-based* indicator, the *Q&A identical user* identifies if the user who posted the question is the same user who wrote the answer. This indicator is useful for detecting irrelevant *dialogue* answers.

Rank-based features We employ SVM Rank[5] to compute ranking scores of answers with respect to their corresponding questions. After generating all other features, SVM Rank is run to produce ranking scores for each possible answer. For training SVM Rank, we convert answer labels to ranks according to the following heuristic: *good* answers are ranked first, *potential* ones second, and *bad* ones third. Ranking scores are then used as features for the classifier. The normalization of these scores can be used as *rank-based* features to provide more information to the classifier, although these scores are also used without any other features as explained in Section 3.

3 Evaluation and Results

We evaluate our approach on the answer selection and YES/NO answer inference tasks. We use the CQA datasets provided by the Semeval 2015 task that contain 2600 training and 300 development questions and their corresponding answers (a total number of 16,541 training and 1,645 development answers). About 10% of these questions are of the YES/NO type. We combined the training and development datasets for training purposes. The test dataset includes 329 questions and 1976 answers. About 9% of the test questions are bipolar.

We also evaluate our performance on the Arabic answer selection task. The dataset contains 1300 training questions, 200 development questions, and 200 test questions. This dataset does not include YES/NO questions.

English answer selection Our approach for the answer selection task in *English* ranked 6th out of 12 submissions and its results are shown in Table 2. *VectorSLU-Primary* shows the results when we include all the features listed in Table 1 except the rank-based features. *VectorSLU-Contrastive* shows the results when we include all the features except

[5]`http://www.cs.cornell.edu/people/tj/svm_light/svm_rank.html`.

Method	Macro-F1	Accuracy
VectorSLU-Primary	49.10	66.45
VectorSLU-Contrastive	49.54	70.45
JAIST (best)	**57.19**	**72.52**
Baseline	22.36	50.46

Table 2: Results for the English answer selection task.

Method	Macro-F1	Accuracy
VectorSLU-Primary	70.99	76.32
VectorSLU-Contrastive	73.18	78.12
QCRI (best)	**78.55**	**83.02**
Baseline	24.03	56.34

Table 3: Results for the Arabic answer selection task.

the rank-based and text-based features. Interestingly, *VectorSLU-Contrastive* leads to a better performance than *VectorSLU-Primary*. The lower performance of *VectorSLU-Primary* could be due to the high overlap between text-based features in different classes that can clearly mislead classifiers. For example, **A1**, **A2** and **A3** (see Section 1) all have a considerable word overlap with their question, while only **A2** is a *good* answer. The last two rows of the table are respectively related to the best performance among all submissions and the majority class baseline that always predicts *good*.

Arabic answer selection Our approach for answer selection in *Arabic* ranked 2nd out of 4 submissions. Table 3 shows the results. In these experiments, we employ all features listed in Table 1 except for yes/no/probably-based features, since the Arabic task does not include YES/NO answer inference. Vectors were trained from the Arabic Gigaword (Linguistic Data Consortium, 2011). We found lemma vectors to work better than token vectors.

We computed ranking scores with SVM Rank for both *VectorSLU-contrastive* and *VectorSLU-Primary*. In the case of *VectorSLU-contrastive*, we used these scores to predict labels according to the following heuristic: the top scoring answer is labeled as *direct*, the second scoring answer as *related*, and all other answers as *irrelevant*. This decision mechanism is based on the distribution in the training and development data, and proved to work well on the test data. However, for our primary submission we were interested in a more principled mechanism. Thus, in the *VectorSLU-primary* system we computed 10 extra classification features from the ranking scores. These features are used to provide prior knowledge about relative ranking of answers with respect to their corresponding questions. To compute these features, we first rank answers with respect to questions and then scale the resultant scores into the [0,1] range. We then consider 10 binary features that indicate whether the score of each input answer is the range of [0,0.1), [0.1,0.2), ..., [0.9,1), respectively. Note that each feature vector contains exactly one 1 and nine 0s.

The last two rows of the table are related to the best performance and the majority class baseline that always predicts *irrelevant*.

Method	Macro-F1	Accuracy
VectorSLU-Primary (best)	**63.70**	**72.00**
VectorSLU-Contrastive	61.90	68.00
Baseline	25.00	60.00

Table 4: Results for the English YES/NO inference task.

English YES/NO inference For the indirect YES/NO answer inference task, we achieve the best performance and ranked 1st out of 8 submissions. Table 4 shows the results. *VectorSLU-Primary* and *VectorSLU-Contrastive* have the same definition as in Table 2. Both approaches with or without the text-based features outperform the baseline that always predicts *yes* as the majority class and other submissions. This indicates the effectiveness of the vector-based features.

4 Related Work

We are not aware of any previous CQA work using continuous word vectors. Our vector features were somewhat motivated by existing text-based features, taken from the QCRI baseline system, replacing text-similarity heuristics with cosine similarity. Some of the approaches to classifying answers can be found in the general CQA literature, such as (Toba et al., 2014; Bian et al., 2008; Liu et al., 2008).

5 Conclusion

In summary, we represented words, phrases, sentences and whole questions and answers in vector space, and computed various features from them for a classifier, for both English and Arabic. We showed the utility of these vector-based features for addressing the answer selection and the YES/NO answer inference tasks in community question answering.

Acknowledgments

This research was supported by the Qatar Computing Research Institute (QCRI). We would like to thank Alessandro Moschitti, Preslav Nakov, Lluís Màrquez, Massimo Nicosia, and other members of the QCRI Arabic Language Technologies group for their collaboration on this project.

References

Rami Al-Rfou, Bryan Perozzi, and Steven Skiena. 2013. Polyglot: Distributed Word Representations for Multilingual NLP. *CoRR*, abs/1307.1662.

Lloyd Allison and Trevor I. Dix. 1986. A bit-string longest-common-subsequence algorithm. *Information Processing Letters*, 23(5):305 – 310.

Apache Software Foundation. 2014. OpenNLP.

Mohit Bansal, Kevin Gimpel, and Karen Livescu. 2014. Tailoring Continuous Word Representations for Dependency Parsing. In *Proceedings of the 52nd Annual Meeting of the Association for Computational Linguistics, ACL 2014, June 22-27, 2014, Baltimore, MD, USA, Volume 2: Short Papers*, pages 809–815.

Jiang Bian, Yandong Liu, Eugene Agichtein, and Hongyuan Zha. 2008. Finding the Right Facts in the Crowd: Factoid Question Answering over Social Media. In *Proceedings of the 17th International Conference on World Wide Web*, WWW '08, pages 467–476, New York, NY, USA.

Samuel R. Bowman, Christopher Potts, and Christopher D. Manning. 2014. Recursive Neural Networks for Learning Logical Semantics. *CoRR*, abs/1406.1827.

Jordan L. Boyd-Graber, Brianna Satinoff, He He, and Hal Daumé III. 2012. Besting the Quiz Master: Crowdsourcing Incremental Classification Games. In *Proceedings of the 2012 Joint Conference on Empirical Methods in Natural Language Processing and Computational Natural Language Learning, EMNLP-CoNLL 2012, July 12-14, 2012, Jeju Island, Korea*, pages 1290–1301.

Andrei Z. Broder. 1997. On the Resemblance and Containment of Documents. In *Proceedings of the Compression and Complexity of Sequences 1997*, SEQUENCES '97, pages 21–, Washington, DC, USA.

Yun-Nung Chen and Alexander I. Rudnicky. 2014. Dynamically Supporting Unexplored Domains in Conversational Interactions by Enriching Semantics with Neural Word Embeddings. In *Proceedings of the 2014 Spoken Language Technology Workshop, December 7-10, 2014, South Lake Tahoe, Nevada, USA*, pages 590–595.

Richard Eckart de Castilho and Iryna Gurevych. 2014. A broad-coverage collection of portable NLP components for building shareable analysis pipelines. In Nancy Ide and Jens Grivolla, editors, *Proceedings of the Workshop on Open Infrastructures and Analysis Frameworks for HLT (OIAF4HLT) at COLING 2014*, pages 1–11, Dublin, Ireland, August.

John Firth. 1957. A Synopsis of Linguistic Theory, 1930-1955. *Studies in Linguistic Analysis*, pages 1–32.

Daniel (Zhaohan) Guo, Gokhan Tur, Wen-tau Yih, and Geoffrey Zweig. 2014. Joint Semantic Utterance Classification and Slot Filling with Recursive Neural Networks. pages 554–559.

Dan Gusfield. 1997. *Algorithms on Strings, Trees, and Sequences: Computer Science and Computational Biology*. Cambridge University Press, New York, NY, USA.

Mohit Iyyer, Jordan L. Boyd-Graber, Leonardo Max Batista Claudino, Richard Socher, and Hal Daumé III. 2014. A Neural Network for Factoid Question Answering over Paragraphs. In *Proceedings of the 2014 Conference on Empirical Methods in Natural Language Processing, EMNLP 2014, October 25-29, 2014, Doha, Qatar, A meeting of SIGDAT, a Special Interest Group of the ACL*, pages 633–644.

Matthew A. Jaro. 1989. Advances in Record-Linkage Methodology as Applied to Matching the 1985 Census of Tampa, Florida. *Journal of the American Statistical Association*, 84(406):414–420.

Quoc V. Le and Tomas Mikolov. 2014. Distributed Representations of Sentences and Documents. *CoRR*, abs/1405.4053.

Omer Levy and Yoav Goldberg. 2014. Dependency-Based Word Embeddings. In *Proceedings of the 52nd Annual Meeting of the Association for Computational Linguistics, ACL 2014, June 22-27, 2014, Baltimore, MD, USA, Volume 2: Short Papers*, pages 302–308.

Linguistic Data Consortium. 2011. Arabic Gigaword Fifth Edition. `https://catalog.ldc.upenn.edu/LDC2011T11`.

Yandong Liu, Jiang Bian, and Eugene Agichtein. 2008. Predicting Information Seeker Satisfaction in Community Question Answering. In *Proceedings of the 31st Annual International ACM SIGIR Conference on Research and Development in Information Retrieval*, SIGIR '08, pages 483–490, New York, NY, USA.

Caroline Lyon, Ruth Barrett, and James Malcolm. 2004. A theoretical basis to the automated detection of copying between texts, and its practical implementation in the ferret plagiarism and collusion detector. In *Plagiarism: Prevention, Practice and Policies 2004 Conference*.

Christopher D. Manning, Mihai Surdeanu, John Bauer, Jenny Finkel, Steven J. Bethard, and David McClosky. 2014. The Stanford CoreNLP Natural Language Processing Toolkit. In *Proceedings of 52nd Annual Meeting of the Association for Computational Linguistics: System Demonstrations*, pages 55–60.

Lluís Màrquez, James Glass, Walid Magdy, Alessandro Moschitti, Preslav Nakov, and Bilal Randeree. 2015. SemEval-2015 Task 3: Answer Selection in Community Question Answering. In *Proceedings of the 9th International Workshop on Semantic Evaluation (SemEval 2015)*.

Tomas Mikolov, Kai Chen, Greg Corrado, and Jeffrey Dean. 2013a. Efficient Estimation of Word Representations in Vector Space. *CoRR*, abs/1301.3781.

Tomas Mikolov, Ilya Sutskever, Kai Chen, Greg Corrado, and Jeffrey Dean. 2013b. Distributed Representations of Words and Phrases and their Compositionality. *CoRR*, abs/1310.4546.

Tomas Mikolov, Ilya Sutskever, Kai Chen, Gregory S. Corrado, and Jeffrey Dean. 2013c. Distributed Representations of Words and Phrases and their Compositionality. In *Advances in Neural Information Processing Systems 26: 27th Annual Conference on Neural Information Processing Systems 2013. Proceedings of a meeting held December 5-8, 2013, Lake Tahoe, Nevada, United States.*, pages 3111–3119.

Tomas Mikolov, Wen-tau Yih, and Geoffrey Zweig. 2013d. Linguistic Regularities in Continuous Space Word Representations. In *Human Language Technologies: Conference of the North American Chapter of the Association of Computational Linguistics, Proceedings, June 9-14, 2013, Westin Peachtree Plaza Hotel, Atlanta, Georgia, USA*, pages 746–751.

Tomàš Mikolov. 2012. *Statistical Language Models Based on Neural Networks*. Ph.D. thesis, Brno University of Technology.

Alvaro Monge and Charles Elkan. 1997. An Efficient Domain-Independent Algorithm for Detecting Approximately Duplicate Database Records.

Philip Ogren and Steven Bethard. 2009. Building Test Suites for UIMA Components. In *Proceedings of the Workshop on Software Engineering, Testing, and Quality Assurance for Natural Language Processing (SETQA-NLP 2009)*, pages 1–4, Boulder, Colorado, June.

Arfath Pasha, Mohamed Al-Badrashiny, Mona Diab, Ahmed El Kholy, Ramy Eskander, Nizar Habash, Manoj Pooleery, Owen Rambow, and Ryan Roth. 2014. MADAMIRA: A Fast, Comprehensive Tool for Morphological Analysis and Disambiguation of Arabic. In *Proceedings of the Ninth International Conference on Language Resources and Evaluation (LREC'14)*, pages 1094–1101, Reykjavik, Iceland.

Radim Řehůřek and Petr Sojka. 2010. Software Framework for Topic Modelling with Large Corpora. In *Proceedings of the LREC 2010 Workshop on New Challenges for NLP Frameworks*, pages 45–50, Valletta, Malta, May.

Magnus Sahlgren. 2006. *The Word-Space Model*. Ph.D. thesis, Stockholm University.

Hinrich Schütze. 1992a. Dimensions of Meaning. In *Proceedings of Supercomputing '92*, pages 787–796.

Hinrich Schütze. 1992b. Word Space. In *NIPS*, pages 895–902.

Richard Socher. 2014. *Recursive Deep Learning for Natural Language Processing and Computer Vision*. Ph.D. thesis, Stanford University.

Hapnes Toba, Zhao-Yan Ming, Mirna Adriani, and Tat-Seng Chua. 2014. Discovering high quality answers in community question answering archives using a hierarchy of classifiers. *Information Sciences*, 261(0):101 – 115.

Michael J. Wise. 1996. YAP3: Improved Detection Of Similarities In Computer Program And Other Texts. In *SIGCSEB: SIGCSE Bulletin (ACM Special Interest Group on Computer Science Education)*, pages 130–134.

SemEval-2015 Task 13: Multilingual All-Words Sense Disambiguation and Entity Linking

Andrea Moro and **Roberto Navigli**
Dipartimento di Informatica,
Sapienza Università di Roma,
Viale Regina Elena 295, 00161 Roma, Italy
{moro,navigli}@di.uniroma1.it

Abstract

In this paper we present the Multilingual All-Words Sense Disambiguation and Entity Linking task. Word Sense Disambiguation (WSD) and Entity Linking (EL) are well-known problems in the Natural Language Processing field and both address the lexical ambiguity of language. Their main difference lies in the kind of meaning inventories that are used: EL uses encyclopedic knowledge, while WSD uses lexicographic information. Our aim with this task is to analyze whether, and if so, how, using a resource that integrates both kinds of inventories (i.e., BabelNet 2.5.1) might enable WSD and EL to be solved by means of similar (even, the same) methods. Moreover, we investigate this task in a multilingual setting and for some specific domains.

1 Introduction

The Senseval and SemEval evaluation series represent key moments in the community of computational linguistics and related areas. Their focus has been to provide objective evaluations of methods within the wide spectrum of semantic techniques for tasks mainly related to automatic text understanding.

Through SemEval-2015 task 13 we both continue and renew the longstanding tradition of disambiguation tasks, by addressing multilingual WSD and EL in a joint manner. WSD (Navigli, 2009; Navigli, 2012) is a historical task aimed at explicitly assigning meanings to single-word and multi-word occurrences within text, a task which today is more alive than ever in the research community. EL (Erbs et al., 2011; Cornolti et al., 2013; Rao et al., 2013) is a more recent task which aims at discovering mentions of entities within a text and linking them to the most suitable entry in a knowledge base. Both these tasks aim at handling the inherent ambiguity of natural language, however WSD tackles it from a lexicographic perspective, while EL tackles it from an encyclopedic one. Specifically, the main difference between the two tasks lies in the kind of inventory they use. For instance, WordNet (Miller et al., 1990), a manually curated semantic network for the English language, has become the main reference inventory for English WSD systems thanks to its wide coverage of verbs, adverbs, adjectives and common nouns. More recently, Wikipedia has been shown to be an optimal resource for recovering named entities, and has consequently become - together with all its semi-automatic derivations such as DBpedia (Auer et al., 2007) and Freebase (Bollacker et al., 2008) - the main reference inventory for EL systems.

Over the years, the research community has typically focused on each of these tasks separately. Recently, however, joint approaches have been proposed (Moro et al., 2014b). One of the reasons for pursuing the unification of these tasks derives from the current trend in knowledge acquisition which consists of the seamless integration of encyclopedic and lexicographic knowledge within structured language resources (Hovy et al., 2013). A case in point here is BabelNet[1], a multilingual semantic network and encyclopedic dictionary (Navigli and Ponzetto, 2012). Resources like BabelNet provide a common ground for the tasks of WSD and EL.

[1]http://babelnet.org

In this task our goal is to promote research in the direction of joint word sense and named entity disambiguation, so as to concentrate research efforts on the aspects that differentiate these two tasks without duplicating research on common problems such as identifying the right meaning in context. However, we are also interested in systems that perform only one of the two tasks, and even systems which tackle one particular setting of WSD, such as all-words sense disambiguation vs. any subset of part-of-speech tags. Moreover, given the recent upsurge of interest in multilingual approaches, we developed the task dataset in three different languages (English, Italian and Spanish) on parallel texts which have been independently and manually annotated by different native/fluent speakers. In contrast to the SemEval-2013 task 12 on Multilingual Word Sense Disambiguation (Navigli et al., 2013), our focus in task 13 is to present a dataset containing both kinds of inventories (i.e., named entities and word senses) in different specific domains (biomedical domain, maths and computer domain, and a broader domain about social issues). Our goal is to further investigate the distance between research efforts regarding the dichotomy EL vs. WSD and those regarding the dichotomy open domain vs. closed domain.

2 Task Setup

The task setup consists of annotating four tokenized and part-of-speech tagged documents for which parallel versions in three languages (English, Italian and Spanish) have been provided. Differently from previous editions (Navigli et al., 2013; Lefever and Hoste, 2013; Manandhar et al., 2010; Lefever and Hoste, 2010; Pradhan et al., 2007; Navigli et al., 2007; Snyder and Palmer, 2004; Palmer et al., 2001), in this task we do not make explicit to the participating systems which fragments of the input text should be disambiguated, so as to have, on the one hand, a more realistic scenario, and, on the other hand, to follow the recent trend in EL challenges such as TAC KBP (Ji et al., 2014), MicroPost (Basave et al., 2013) and ERD (Carmel et al., 2014).

2.1 Corpora

The documents considered in this task are taken from the OPUS project (http://opus.lingfil.uu.se/), more specifically from the EMEA (European Medicines Agency documents), KDEdoc (the KDE manual corpus) and "The EU bookshop corpus", which make available parallel and POS-tagged documents. We took four documents from these repositories. Two documents contain medical information about drugs. One document consists of the manual of a mathematical graph calculator (i.e., KAlgebra). The remaining document contains a formal discussion about social issues, like supporting elderly workers and, more in general, about issues and solutions to unemployment discussed by the members of the European Commission.

2.2 Sense Inventory

As our sense inventory we use the BabelNet 2.5.1 (http://babelnet.org) multilingual semantic network and encyclopedic dictionary (Navigli and Ponzetto, 2012), which is the result of the automatic integration of multiple language resources: Princeton WordNet, Wikipedia, Wiktionary, OmegaWiki, Wikidata, Open Multi WordNet and automatic translations. The meanings contained within this resource are organized in Babel synsets. Each of these synsets can contain Wikipedia pages, WordNet synsets and items from the other integrated resources. For instance, in BabelNet it is possible to find the concept *"medicine"* (bn:00054128n), which is represented by both the second word sense of *medicine* in WordNet and the Wikipedia page *Pharmaceutical drug*, among others, together with synonyms such as *drug* and *medication* in English and lexicalizations in other languages, such as *farmaco* in Italian and *medicamento* in Spanish.

2.3 Dataset Creation

The manual annotation of documents was performed in a language-specific manner, i.e., different taggers worked on the various translated versions of the input documents. More precisely, we had two taggers for each language, who annotated each fragment of text recognized as linkable with all the senses deemed appropriate. During the annotation procedure, for all languages, each tagger was shown an HTML page containing the sentence within which the target fragment was boldfaced. Then a table of checkable meanings identified by their glosses (in English or, if not available, in Spanish or Italian), to-

Domain	Language	Instances	Single words	Multi words	Named Entities	Mean senses per instance	Mean senses per lemma	Mean senses per POS N	V	R	A	Wikipedia pages	WordNet keys
Biomedical	EN	623	534	41	48	8.0	7.0	8.8	10.0	2.4	3.8	295	549
	ES	628	552	30	46	6.2	6.5	5.6	9.0	3.1	5.9	251	-
	IT	610	545	29	36	5.4	5.7	5.8	6.0	3.1	3.5	254	-
Maths and computer	EN	325	292	11	22	9.0	9.5	10.1	10.3	2.9	5.9	135	276
	ES	308	277	10	21	7.5	7.6	7.9	8.0	3.8	6.0	120	-
	IT	313	275	15	23	6.9	6.8	7.3	7.6	3.3	4.4	136	-
Social issues	EN	313	268	29	16	7.4	6.9	9.1	6.3	1.5	4.1	119	294
	ES	303	259	27	17	7.4	7.4	8.1	7.3	3.2	5.9	102	-
	IT	302	265	22	15	6.6	6.5	7.7	6.8	1.7	3.0	101	-
All	EN	1261	1094	81	86	8.1	7.6	9.1	9.5	2.4	4.4	549	1119
	ES	1239	1088	67	84	6.8	6.8	6.8	8.4	3.2	5.9	473	-
	IT	1225	1085	66	74	6.1	5.9	6.6	6.7	2.8	3.5	491	-

Table 1: Statistics of the datasets.

gether with the available synonyms and hypernyms (as found in WordNet and the Wikipedia Bitaxonomy (Flati et al., 2014)). The taggers agreed on at least one meaning for 68% of the instances. A third tagger acted as judge by going through all the items and discarding overly general or irrelevant annotations, especially in the case of disagreement between the two taggers. To enforce coherence and spot missing annotations, we projected the English annotations to the other two languages. Finally, the third tagger determined if the projected English annotations that were missing in one of the other two languages were either correctly not included, or if the taggers had actually missed a correct annotation.

As a result of this procedure we obtained a dataset with around 1.2k items, but with only around 80 named entity mentions per language. Please refer to Table 1 for general statistics about the dataset: we show the number of annotated instances per language and domain, together with their classification as single- or multi-word expressions and named entities. We then show the degree of ambiguity both per POS and per instance and lemma (i.e., multiple instances with the same lemma count as a single instance) and, finally, we show how many of the instances have Wikipedia pages or WordNet keys as annotations[2].

2.4 Evaluation Measures

To evaluate the performance of the participating systems we used the classical precision, recall and F1 measures:

[2]Please note that the sum of Wikipedia pages and WordNet keys does not amount to the number of instances, as BabelNet can have integrated synsets that contain both WordNet keys and Wikipedia pages.

$$Precision = \frac{TP}{TP + FP} \quad (1)$$

$$Recall = \frac{TP}{TP + FN} \quad (2)$$

$$F1 = \frac{2 \cdot Precision \cdot Recall}{Precision + Recall} \quad (3)$$

To handle systems that output multiple answers for a single instance we followed the standard scorer of previous Senseval and SemEval challenges in uniformly weighting the multiple answers when computing the TP counts. Moreover, we decided not to take into account fragments annotated by the systems which were not contained in the gold standard, similarly to the D2KB setting of the GERBIL evaluation framework for EL (Usbeck et al., 2015).

2.5 Baseline

As baseline we considered the performance of a simple heuristic (called BabelNet first sense or BFS) that exploits the default comparator integrated within the BabelNet 2.5.1 API (i.e., the BabelSynsetComparator Java class). Babel synsets in BabelNet can be viewed as nodes of a semantic network and each of them can contain Wikipedia pages, WordNet synsets and items from the other integrated resources. The comparator takes as input the lemma of the word for which we are ranking the Babel synsets. There are three main cases managed by the comparator. The first case is when both Babel synsets contain a WordNet synset for the considered word. If this is the case, then the WordNet sense numbers are used to rank the synsets. The second case is when only one of the Babel synsets contains a WordNet synset: in this case the Babel synset that contains the WordNet synset gets ranked first. The last case is when no WordNet synsets are contained within the two Babel synsets. In this case a lexicographic ordering of the Wikipedia pages contained within the Babel synsets is taken into account. As is well known, the first sense heuristic based on WordNet has always proved a really hard to beat baseline, outperforming all the developed systems for the English language over almost all settings and system combinations. In contrast, the BFS heuristic in the other languages shows itself to be weaker, achieving lower performances in almost all settings and system combinations.

3 Participating Systems

DFKI (Supervised). This system exploits BabelNet as reference inventory and a CRF-based named entity recognizer. The disambiguation system is divided in two parts: one for nouns and another for verbs. For nouns the approach is based on the idea of maximizing multiple objectives at the same time. Similarly to (Hoffart et al., 2011), the disambiguation objectives consist of a global (coherence, unsupervised) part and a local (supervised) part. The global objective makes sure that disambiguation maximizes coherence of the selected synsets and it is based on the semantic signature graph (Moro et al., 2014b). The local objective ensures that the WordNet synset type fits the local context of the noun to be disambiguated. One important aspect of this approach is that, unlike previous work (Hoffart et al., 2011; Moro et al., 2014b), it does not apply discrete optimization, but continuous optimization on the normalized sum of all objectives. The disambiguation procedure aims to optimize the objective function by iteratively updating the candidate probabilities for each fragment. As far as verbs are concerned, a feed-forward neural network is trained using local features such as arguments of the semantic roles of a verb in a sentence, context words, and the verb and its lemma.

EBL-Hope (Unsupervised + Sense relevance). This approach uses a modified version of the Lesk algorithm and the Jiang & Conrath similarity measure (Jiang and Conrath, 1997). It validates the output from both techniques for enhanced accuracy and exploits semantic relations and corpus (SemCor) information available in BabelNet and WordNet in an unsupervised manner.

el92 (Systems mix). This system is a general-domain system for entity detection and linking. It does not perform WSD. The system combines, via a weighted voting, Entity Linking outputs from four publicly available services: Tagme (Ferragina and Scaiella, 2010), DBpedia Spotlight (Mendes et al., 2011), Wikipedia Miner (Milne and Witten, 2008) and Babelfy (Moro et al., 2014b; Moro et al., 2014a). The different runs correspond to different settings in the weighting formula (De La Clergerie et al., 2008; Fiscus, 1997).

LIMSI (Unsupervised + Sense relevance). The system performs WSD by taking advantage of the parallelism of the test data, a feature that was not exploited by the systems that participated in the SemEval-2013 Multilingual Word Sense Disambiguation task 12 (Navigli et al., 2013). The system needs no training and is applied directly to the test dataset, nor does it use distributional (context) information. The texts are sentence- and word-aligned pairwise, and content words are tagged by their translations in another language. The alignments serve to retrieve the BabelNet synsets that are relevant for each instance of a word in the texts (i.e., synsets that contain both the disambiguation target and its aligned translation). If a Babel synset is retained, this is used to annotate the instance of the word in the test set. If more than one synset is retained, these are ranked using the BabelSynsetComparator Java class available in the BabelNet API (please refer to Section 2.5 for a detailed explanation). The highest ranked synset among the ones that contain the aligned translation is used to annotate the instance. The system falls back to the BabelNet first sense (BFS) provided by the BabelSynsetComparator for instances with no aligned translation, or in cases where the translation was not found in any of the synsets available for the word in BabelNet.

SUDOKU (Unsupervised). This deterministic constraint-based approach relies on a reasonable degree of "document monosemy" (percentage of unique monosemous lemmas in a document) and exploits Personalised PageRank (Agirre et al., 2014) to select the best candidate. The PPR is started with a surfing vector biased towards monosemous words (i.e., their respective sense). Each submission differs by its imposed constraints: Run1 is the plain approach (Manion and Sainudiin, 2014) applied at the document level; Run2 is the iterative version of the previous approach applied at the document level and with words disambiguated in order of increasing polysemy; Run3 is like Run2, but it is first applied to nouns and then to verbs, adjectives, and adverbs.

TeamUFAL (Unsupervised). This system exploits Apache Lucene search engine to index Wikipedia documents, Wiktionary entries and WordNet senses. Then, to perform disambiguation, the Lucene ranking method is used to query the index with multiple queries (consisting of the text fragment and context words). Finally, all query results are merged and the disambiguated meaning is selected thanks to a simple threshold heuristic.

UNIBA (Unsupervised + Sense relevance). This system[3] extends two well-known variations of the Lesk WSD method. The main contribution of the approach relies on the use of a word similarity function defined on a distributional semantic space (Word2vec tool (Mikolov et al., 2013)) to compute the gloss-context overlap. Entities are identified by exploiting a list of possible surface forms extracted from BabelNet synsets. Moreover, each synset has a prior probability computed over an annotated corpus. For WordNet synsets, SemCor is exploited, while for Wikipedia entities the number of citations in Wikipedia internal links is counted.

vua-background (Partially supervised). This approach exploits the Named Entities contained in the test data to generate a background corpus. This is done by finding similar DBpedia entities for the entities in the input documents. Using this background corpus, the system tries to find the predominant sense of the words in the test data (McCarthy et al., 2004). If a predominant sense is recognized for a specific lemma, then it is used, otherwise the system falls back to the "It Makes Sense" WSD system (Zhong and Ng, 2010).

[3]During the evaluation period the system did not return any annotation for adjectives due to a misinterpretation of the POS tag set. For full evaluations see the system paper.

WSD-games (Unsupervised). This approach is formulated in terms of Evolutionary Game Theory, where each word to be disambiguated is represented as a node in a graph and each sense as a class. The proposed algorithm performs a consistent class assignment of senses according to the similarity information of each word with the others, so that similar words are constrained to similar classes. The propagation of the information over the graph is formulated in terms of a non-cooperative multi-player game, where the players are the data points, in order to decide their class memberships, and equilibria correspond to consistent labeling of the data.

4 Results and Discussion

The results obtained by the participating systems are shown in Tables 2-6. In Table 2 we show the precision, recall and F1 scores of the participating systems that annotated all classes of items (named entities, nouns, verbs, adverbs, adjectives) over the whole dataset. Six out of the nine participating teams annotated the full set of items. We also show the F1 performance on each considered domain independently and for different kinds of subsets of the item classes (i.e., we show the F1 score over all items, then only on named entities, all open-class word senses and individually).

4.1 Overall Performance

From Table 2 we can see that the best system for English (i.e., LIMSI) is able to obtain a performance more than five percentage points higher than the second ranked system. This is due to the good-quality indirect supervision provided by the alignments combined with the use of the BabelSynsetComparator. However, on the other two languages this system obtains lower performance than the other competing systems. The performance of the SUDOKU system is of a particular interest, as it obtains the second best scores on the English part of the dataset and the top scores overall on the other two languages. It exploits monosemous words within the input documents to run Personalized PageRank. The three runs differ mainly in respect of the order in which the words get disambiguated.

In Table 3 we show the F1 scores of all the systems over the whole dataset for each class of the

	EN			ES			IT		
System	P	R	F1	P	R	F1	P	R	F1
LIMSI	**68.7**	**63.1**	**65.8**	47.9	42.4	45.0	51.3	45.7	48.4
SUDOKU-Run2	62.9	60.4	61.6	59.9	**54.6**	**57.1**	59.7	54.3	56.9
SUDOKU-Run3	61.9	59.4	60.7	59.5	54.2	56.8	59.7	54.3	56.9
vua-background	67.5	51.5	58.4	-	-	-	-	-	-
SUDOKU-Run1	60.1	52.1	55.8	**60.2**	52.3	56.0	**64.4**	**55.9**	**59.9**
WSD-games-Run2	58.8	50.0	54.1	-	-	-	-	-	-
WSD-games-Run1	57.4	48.9	52.8	-	-	-	-	-	-
WSD-games-Run3	53.5	45.4	49.1	-	-	-	-	-	-
EBL-Hope	48.4	44.4	46.3	-	-	-	-	-	-
TeamUFAL	40.4	36.5	38.3	-	-	-	-	-	-
BFS	67.9	67.2	67.5	38.9	36.2	37.5	41.7	38.8	40.2
# items	1261			1239			1225		

Table 2: Precision, Recall and F1 on all domains.

manually annotated items and for each language. In the English part of the datasets the DFKI system performs best for verb, noun and named entity disambiguation, thanks to precomputed random walks called semantic signatures, along the lines of Babelfy (Moro et al., 2014b), and supervised techniques. The UNIBA system on the English dataset obtains the best result on adverbs. Finally, in the Spanish dataset the EBL-Hope system based on a combination of a Lesk-based measure together with the Jiang & Conrath similarity measure shows the best performance for named entities.

4.2 Domain-based Evaluation

In Tables 4-6 we show the detailed performances of all the systems over different classes of items, and on different domains. One of the main goals of this task is to investigate the performance of disambiguation methods over different domains. Our documents derive from the biomedical domain, the maths and computer domain, and a broader domain (a document discussing social issues, especially for elderly workers and possible solutions).

Biomedical domain. In Table 4 we show the performance of the systems on the biomedical documents. The first thing to notice is the much higher best score of the first ranked system (i.e., LIMSI), which attains an F1 score of 71.3%. This is due to the lower ambiguity of nouns and named entities (see Table 1) resulting from the greater numbers of domain-specific concepts used within this kind of documents. This can also be seen from the higher scores obtained by the BFS. Overall, all systems obtained a better performance than in the other domains, with a gain of more than four percentage points each. The second ranked system (i.e., SUDOKU) shows its ability to exploit monosemous words obtaining a 0.1 difference from the first ranked system and a 0.9 point distance from the BFS baseline. This is of particular interest as the system does not explicitly exploit any sense relevance information. Moreover, the DFKI system obtains the best scores for nouns and verbs, and is the only system able to obtain a 100% F1 score on NE disambiguation. However, several other systems performed above 90%, showing that in this particular set of documents named entities are easy to disambiguate.

On the other two languages the performances are a little bit lower, but the SUDOKU system confirms its ability to exploit monosemous words at a quality comparable to the one obtained in the English dataset. The LIMSI system, instead, obtains a reduction of around 20% due to its exploitation of the BabelSynsetComparator, which performs badly in these languages (see the BFS scores).

Maths and computer domain. In Table 5 we show the results for the maths and computer domain. As can be seen in Table 1, this is the most ambiguous domain and the best systems obtain much lower performances than in the other domains. Interestingly, the DFKI system is not able to achieve the best performance on any of the considered item classes, while UNIBA and SUDOKU show the best results for nouns and verbs. As regards named en-

System	EN All	Named Entities	Word Senses All	N	V	R	A
LIMSI	**65.8**	82.9	**64.7**	64.8	56.0	76.5	**79.5**
SUDOKU-Run2	61.6	87.0	59.9	62.5	49.6	70.4	71.7
SUDOKU-Run3	60.7	87.0	58.9	62.7	46.0	71.7	68.1
vua-background	58.4	14.9	60.3	53.8	55.2	77.2	72.5
SUDOKU-Run1	55.8	16.8	57.5	53.4	52.2	48.9	74.4
WSD-games-Run2	54.1	12.6	55.8	51.4	43.7	75.3	69.9
WSD-games-Run1	52.8	12.6	54.5	49.6	42.5	75.3	69.9
WSD-games-Run3	49.1	12.6	50.7	47.4	35.8	74.1	64.0
EBL-Hope	46.3	84.2	43.8	45.7	30.6	76.5	57.8
TeamUFAL	38.3	79.8	35.5	46.4	18.8	45.8	28.8
DFKI	-	**88.9**	-	**70.3**	**57.7**	-	-
el92-Run1	-	86.1	-	-	-	-	-
UNIBA-Run1	-	84.4	-	63.3	57.1	**79.0**	-
UNIBA-Run2	-	82.9	-	63.2	57.1	**79.0**	-
UNIBA-Run3	-	82.9	-	63.2	57.1	**79.0**	-
el92-Run3	-	79.7	-	-	-	-	-
el92-Run2	-	79.2	-	-	-	-	-
BFS	67.5	85.7	66.3	66.7	55.1	82.1	82.5

System	ES All	Named Entities	Word Senses All	N	V	R	A
SUDOKU-Run2	**57.1**	36.9	**58.0**	**56.3**	55.6	61.9	61.1
SUDOKU-Run3	56.8	36.9	57.7	54.9	**57.9**	60.3	61.5
SUDOKU-Run1	56.0	17.4	57.6	54.0	56.4	61.4	**62.0**
LIMSI	45.0	30.8	45.6	48.3	28.6	**64.6**	49.7
EBL-Hope	-	**70.8**	-	48.2	-	-	-
BFS	37.5	37.0	37.6	40.6	19.8	55.1	46.2

System	IT All	Named Entities	Word Senses All	N	V	R	A
SUDOKU-Run1	**59.9**	21.7	**61.3**	**56.6**	**62.7**	**62.5**	68.3
SUDOKU-Run3	56.9	**54.9**	57.0	56.3	51.5	57.1	65.8
SUDOKU-Run2	56.9	**54.9**	57.0	54.1	60.9	61.2	62.0
LIMSI	48.4	46.5	48.4	43.9	44.2	56.0	**69.6**
UNIBA-Run3	-	50.0	-	53.7	61.1	60.0	-
UNIBA-Run2	-	48.5	-	53.8	61.1	60.0	-
UNIBA-Run1	-	48.5	-	53.7	61.1	60.0	-
EBL-Hope	-	48.5	-	38.8	-	-	-
BFS	40.2	50.0	39.8	35.4	38.3	48.0	61.0

Table 3: F1 performance by item class and language on all domains.

System	EN All	Named Entities	Word Senses All	N	V	R	A
LIMSI	**71.3**	98.9	**68.9**	76.5	50.6	77.5	75.0
SUDOKU-Run3	71.2	98.9	68.8	75.8	50.6	75.3	77.8
SUDOKU-Run2	68.9	98.9	66.4	71.9	47.3	77.9	**83.3**
vua-background	63.6	4.1	66.4	62.7	53.8	76.9	77.4
SUDOKU-Run1	62.4	4.1	65.0	62.8	52.5	50.7	82.3
WSD-games-Run2	58.4	4.1	60.8	55.8	45.8	**80.0**	79.2
WSD-games-Run1	56.3	4.1	58.6	52.2	45.8	**80.0**	79.2
WSD-games-Run3	54.4	4.1	56.6	54.1	35.0	72.5	77.8
EBL-Hope	52.0	98.9	48.0	54.1	28.2	**80.0**	65.3
TeamUFAL	45.6	93.5	41.6	57.2	18.6	39.7	30.9
DFKI	-	**100.0**	-	**79.1**	**58.3**	-	-
UNIBA-Run3	-	98.9	-	72.1	52.3	**80.0**	-
UNIBA-Run1	-	98.9	-	71.9	52.3	**80.0**	-
UNIBA-Run2	-	98.9	-	71.9	52.3	**80.0**	-
el92-Run1	-	90.9	-	-	-	-	-
el92-Run2	-	81.5	-	-	-	-	-
el92-Run3	-	81.5	-	-	-	-	-
BFS	72.1	98.9	69.9	75.3	52.5	82.9	81.9

System	ES All	Named Entities	Word Senses All	N	V	R	A
SUDOKU-Run1	**62.7**	8.3	**65.1**	**65.5**	54.3	**65.7**	62.1
SUDOKU-Run3	62.6	12.2	64.7	64.3	**56.7**	52.6	**71.2**
SUDOKU-Run2	60.8	12.2	62.9	64.5	51.2	52.6	63.2
LIMSI	51.0	12.2	52.7	59.6	28.3	59.7	40.7
EBL-Hope	-	**77.3**	-	59.6	-	-	-
BFS	43.7	12.2	45.1	51.7	20.5	49.4	39.0

System	IT All	Named Entities	Word Senses All	N	V	R	A
SUDOKU-Run1	**65.1**	10.5	**67.0**	**65.9**	**64.2**	48.0	64.3
SUDOKU-Run3	61.4	**28.6**	62.7	62.3	52.3	48.0	**70.6**
SUDOKU-Run2	58.8	**28.6**	60.0	56.7	61.5	**56.0**	64.7
LIMSI	53.1	24.4	54.1	54.2	42.2	38.5	63.5
UNIBA-Run3	-	**28.6**	-	62.4	63.6	46.2	-
UNIBA-Run1	-	24.4	-	62.2	63.6	46.2	-
UNIBA-Run2	-	24.4	-	62.2	63.6	46.2	-
EBL-Hope	-	24.4	-	50.5	-	-	-
BFS	44.3	28.6	44.9	43.3	38.7	38.5	56.8

Table 4: F1 performance by item class and language on biomedical domain.

tities, the system EBL-Hope obtains the best results in all languages. This system, in addition to exploiting a Lesk-based measure combined with the Jiang & Conrath similarity measure, uses the BabelNet semantic relations, which have already been shown to be useful for attaining state-of-the-art performances in EL (Moro et al., 2014b). Interestingly, in the Italian dataset the system UNIBA (which is based on an extended version of the Lesk measure and a semantic relatedness measure) obtains the same performance for NE as the EBL-Hope system.

Social issues domain. In Table 6 we show the performance on our last domain. In this social issues domain DFKI confirms its quality on disambiguating nouns and named entities, while for verbs the best system is vua-background, which is based on the predominant sense algorithm (McCarthy et al., 2004) and, as a fallback routine, on the "It Makes Sense" supervised WSD system (Zhong and Ng, 2010). For the other two languages the SUDOKU system obtains the best scores, with the exception of adverbs in the Italian dataset where the UNIBA system is able to reach an F1 score of 100%.

5 Conclusion and Future Directions

In this paper we described the organization and results obtained within the SemEval 2015 task 13: Multilingual Word Sense Disambiguation. Our analysis of the results revealed interesting aspects of the integration of WSD and EL tasks, such as the effectiveness of techniques like semantic signatures, PPR and similarity measures for noun and named entity

System	EN						
	All	Named Entities	Word Senses All	N	V	R	A
LIMSI	**54.1**	57.1	**53.9**	39.3	59.4	71.7	**90.0**
SUDOKU-Run2	53.2	56.3	53.1	**51.4**	49.1	56.6	67.5
SUDOKU-Run3	49.4	56.3	49.1	48.9	42.3	64.2	57.5
EBL-Hope	41.7	**74.3**	39.8	42.5	28.6	67.9	50.0
TeamUFAL	29.8	54.5	28.4	35.8	12.6	37.8	39.2
el92-Run1	-	70.6	-	-	-	-	-
el92-Run3	-	66.7	-	-	-	-	-
el92-Run2	-	64.7	-	-	-	-	-
DFKI	-	57.1	-	44.9	52.3	-	-
UNIBA-Run1	-	57.1	-	44.1	**60.6**	**75.5**	-
UNIBA-Run2	-	57.1	-	44.1	**60.6**	**75.5**	-
UNIBA-Run3	-	57.1	-	44.1	**60.6**	**75.5**	-
WSD-games-Run2	-	-	48.5	39.6	37.7	64.2	80.0
vua-background	-	-	47.7	30.5	49.7	70.6	73.0
WSD-games-Run1	-	-	47.4	39.6	34.3	64.2	80.0
SUDOKU-Run1	-	-	44.7	28.5	51.4	52.0	75.0
WSD-games-Run3	-	-	43.4	36.2	35.4	67.9	58.2
BFS	55.3	57.1	55.2	43.6	55.7	77.8	87.5

System	ES						
	All	Named Entities	Word Senses All	N	V	R	A
SUDOKU-Run2	**49.7**	50.0	**49.7**	42.4	**60.9**	66.7	44.1
SUDOKU-Run3	48.4	50.0	48.3	39.2	58.7	66.7	**52.9**
SUDOKU-Run1	44.2	-	45.9	32.0	58.7	56.0	**52.9**
LIMSI	34.8	56.3	33.6	32.2	27.2	**81.5**	47.1
EBL-Hope	-	**68.8**	-	**45.4**	-	-	-
BFS	28.7	62.5	26.8	27.1	16.3	74.1	50.0

System	IT						
	All	Named Entities	Word Senses All	N	V	R	A
SUDOKU-Run2	**52.1**	68.6	**51.1**	**46.6**	59.0	**66.7**	58.5
SUDOKU-Run3	49.1	68.6	47.9	43.0	53.0	**66.7**	63.4
SUDOKU-Run1	48.4	-	50.5	35.8	**60.2**	**66.7**	70.7
LIMSI	44.6	64.9	43.3	33.4	45.8	**66.7**	**85.4**
UNIBA-Run1	-	**75.7**	-	43.4	57.8	50.0	-
UNIBA-Run2	-	**75.7**	-	43.4	57.8	50.0	-
UNIBA-Run3	-	**75.7**	-	42.2	57.8	50.0	-
EBL-Hope	-	**75.7**	-	37.1	-	-	-
BFS	36.7	64.9	34.8	27.4	37.3	66.7	70.7

Table 5: F1 performance by item class and language on maths and computer domain.

System	EN						
	All	Named Entities	Word Senses All	N	V	R	A
LIMSI	**67.2**	54.5	**67.7**	63.7	63.6	82.8	**77.8**
vua-background	60.8	54.5	61.1	54.8	**70.6**	**89.7**	65.3
SUDOKU-Run1	56.4	60.9	56.2	56.4	52.9	36.4	63.6
SUDOKU-Run2	55.6	81.5	54.5	52.8	56.8	75.9	59.3
WSD-games-Run1	53.5	45.5	53.8	53.0	50.0	82.8	50.0
WSD-games-Run2	53.5	45.5	53.8	53.0	50.0	82.8	50.0
SUDOKU-Run3	51.1	81.5	49.7	48.2	40.9	75.9	63.0
WSD-games-Run3	46.7	45.5	46.7	44.2	38.6	**89.7**	50.0
EBL-Hope	39.5	36.4	39.6	31.5	40.9	82.8	53.7
TeamUFAL	32.5	64.2	31.0	33.6	31.8	72.4	18.4
DFKI	-	**90.3**	-	**73.4**	66.7	-	-
el92-Run1	-	89.7	-	-	-	-	-
el92-Run2	-	89.7	-	-	-	-	-
el92-Run3	-	89.7	-	-	-	-	-
UNIBA-Run1	-	66.7	-	63.0	63.6	82.8	-
UNIBA-Run2	-	54.5	-	62.3	63.6	82.8	-
UNIBA-Run3	-	54.5	-	61.9	63.6	82.8	-
BFS	70.8	77.4	70.5	69.2	61.4	87.5	79.6

System	ES						
	All	Named Entities	Word Senses All	N	V	R	A
SUDOKU-Run2	**57.0**	**69.2**	**56.5**	**51.6**	57.5	**87.0**	**70.0**
SUDOKU-Run1	54.2	52.2	54.3	49.7	57.5	52.6	68.0
SUDOKU-Run3	53.3	**69.2**	52.5	49.5	**59.8**	78.3	56.0
LIMSI	43.1	34.8	43.5	39.3	32.2	60.9	62.0
EBL-Hope	-	52.2	-	26.6	-	-	-
BFS	34.0	51.9	33.1	30.2	25.0	52.2	52.0

System	IT						
	All	Named Entities	Word Senses All	N	V	R	A
SUDOKU-Run1	**61.0**	63.6	**60.9**	56.0	**63.4**	90.9	**72.4**
SUDOKU-Run2	57.9	**80.0**	56.9	55.6	**63.4**	66.7	60.3
SUDOKU-Run3	55.8	**80.0**	54.7	**56.1**	46.3	66.7	60.3
LIMSI	42.9	57.1	42.4	33.1	46.3	83.3	67.2
UNIBA-Run3	-	47.6	-	47.1	61.0	**100.0**	-
UNIBA-Run2	-	47.6	-	46.7	61.0	**100.0**	-
UNIBA-Run1	-	47.6	-	46.3	61.0	**100.0**	-
EBL-Hope	-	47.6	-	16.7	-	-	-
BFS	35.7	64.0	34.5	27.0	39.0	50.0	60.3

Table 6: F1 performance by item class and language on social issues domain.

disambiguation, and Lesk-based measures for verb, adjective and adverb disambiguation. Another interesting outcome that emerges from this task is that supervised approaches are difficult to generalize in a multilingual setting. In fact, the supervised systems that participated in this task took into account only the English language. Moreover, the task confirms yet again that the WordNet first sense heuristic is a hard baseline to beat. Unfortunately, no domain-specific disambiguation system participated in the task. However, in the biomedical domain, the participating systems show higher quality performances than in the other considered domains.

As future directions, we would like to continue to investigate the nature of this novel joint task, and to concentrate on the differences between named entity disambiguation and word sense disambiguation with a special focus on non-European languages.

Acknowledgments

The authors gratefully acknowledge the support of the ERC Starting Grant MultiJEDI No. 259234.

The organization of this task could not have been possible without the help of many people. In particular, we would like to thank José Camacho Collados, Claudio Delli Bovi, Tiziano Flati, Darío Garigliotti, Ignacio Iacobacci, Luca Matteis, Mohammad Taher Pilehvar, Alessandro Raganato, Daniele Vannella for the help provided with the annotations, all the participating teams for the useful discussions and Jim McManus for his comments on the manuscript.

References

Eneko Agirre, Oier Lopez de Lacalle, and Aitor Soroa. 2014. Random Walks for Knowledge-Based Word Sense Disambiguation. *Computational Linguistics*, 40(1):57–84.

Sören Auer, Christian Bizer, Georgi Kobilarov, Jens Lehmann, Richard Cyganiak, and Zachary Ives. 2007. DBpedia: A Nucleus for a Web of Open Data. In *Proc. of ISWC/ASWC*, pages 722–735.

Amparo Elizabeth Cano Basave, Andrea Varga, Matthew Rowe, Milan Stankovic, and Aba-Sah Dadzie. 2013. Making Sense of Microposts (# MSM2013) Concept Extraction Challenge. In *Proc. of # MSM*, pages 1–15.

Kurt D. Bollacker, Colin Evans, Praveen Paritosh, Tim Sturge, and Jamie Taylor. 2008. Freebase: a collaboratively created graph database for structuring human knowledge. In *Proc. of SIGMOD*, pages 1247–1250.

David Carmel, Ming-Wei Chang, Evgeniy Gabrilovich, Bo-June (Paul) Hsu, and Kuansan Wang. 2014. ERD'14: Entity Recognition and Disambiguation Challenge. *SIGIR Forum*, 48(2):63–77.

Marco Cornolti, Paolo Ferragina, and Massimiliano Ciaramita. 2013. A framework for benchmarking entity-annotation systems. In *Proc. of WWW*, pages 249–260.

Éric Villemonte De La Clergerie, Olivier Hamon, Djamel Mostefa, Christelle Ayache, Patrick Paroubek, and Anne Vilnat. 2008. Passage: from french parser evaluation to large sized treebank. *Proc. of LREC*.

Nicolai Erbs, Torsten Zesch, and Iryna Gurevych. 2011. Link Discovery: A Comprehensive Analysis. In *Proc. of ICSC*, pages 83–86.

Paolo Ferragina and Ugo Scaiella. 2010. TAGME: on-the-fly annotation of short text fragments (by wikipedia entities). In *Proc. of CIKM*, pages 1625–1628.

Jonathan G. Fiscus. 1997. A post-processing system to yield reduced word error rates: Recognizer output voting error reduction (rover). In *Proc. of Automatic Speech Recognition and Understanding*, pages 347–354.

Tiziano Flati, Daniele Vannella, Tommaso Pasini, and Roberto Navigli. 2014. Two Is Bigger (and Better) Than One: the Wikipedia Bitaxonomy Project. In *Proc. of the 52nd Annual Meeting of the Association for Computational Linguistics*, pages 945–955.

Johannes Hoffart, Mohamed Amir Yosef, Ilaria Bordino, Hagen Fürstenau, Manfred Pinkal, Marc Spaniol, Bilyana Taneva, Stefan Thater, and Gerhard Weikum. 2011. Robust Disambiguation of Named Entities in Text. In *Proc. of EMNLP*, pages 782–792.

Eduard H. Hovy, Roberto Navigli, and Simone P. Ponzetto. 2013. Collaboratively built semi-structured content and Artificial Intelligence: The story so far. *Artificial Intelligence*, 194:2–27.

Heng Ji, Joel Nothman, and Ben Hachey. 2014. Overview of TAC-KBP2014 Entity Discovery and Linking Tasks. In *Proc. Text Analysis Conference (TAC2014)*.

Jay J. Jiang and David W. Conrath. 1997. Semantic similarity based on corpus statistics and lexical taxonomy. In *Proc. of the International Conference on Research in Computational Linguistics*, pages 19–33.

Els Lefever and Veronique Hoste. 2010. Semeval-2010 task 3: Cross-lingual word sense disambiguation. In *Proc. of SemEval*, pages 15–20.

Els Lefever and Véronique Hoste. 2013. SemEval-2013 Task 10: Cross-lingual Word Sense Disambiguation. In *Proc. of SemEval*, pages 158–166.

Suresh Manandhar, Ioannis P. Klapaftis, Dmitriy Dligach, and Sameer S. Pradhan. 2010. SemEval-2010 task 14: Word sense induction & disambiguation. In *Proc. of SemEval*, pages 63–68.

Steve L. Manion and Raazesh Sainudiin. 2014. An iterative 'sudoku style' approach to subgraph-based word sense disambiguation. In *Proceedings of the Third Joint Conference on Lexical and Computational Semantics (*SEM 2014)*, pages 40–50, Dublin, Ireland, August.

Diana McCarthy, Rob Koeling, Julie Weeds, and John Carroll. 2004. Finding predominant word senses in untagged text. In *Proceedings of the 42nd Annual Meeting on Association for Computational Linguistics*, pages 279–286.

Pablo N. Mendes, Max Jakob, Andrés García-Silva, and Christian Bizer. 2011. DBpedia spotlight: shedding light on the web of documents. In *Proc. of I-Semantics*, pages 1–8.

Tomas Mikolov, Ilya Sutskever, Kai Chen, Greg S Corrado, and Jeff Dean. 2013. Distributed representations of words and phrases and their compositionality. In *Proc. of Advances in Neural Information Processing Systems*, pages 3111–3119.

George A. Miller, Richard Beckwith, Christiane Fellbaum, Derek Gross, and Katherine Miller. 1990. Introduction to WordNet: An On-Line Lexical Database. *Int. Journal of Lexicography*, 3(4):235–244.

David Milne and Ian H. Witten. 2008. Learning to link with wikipedia. In *Proc. of CIKM*, pages 509–518.

Andrea Moro, Francesco Cecconi, and Roberto Navigli. 2014a. Multilingual word sense disambiguation and entity linking for everybody. In *Proc. of ISWC (P&D)*, pages 25–28.

Andrea Moro, Alessandro Raganato, and Roberto Navigli. 2014b. Entity Linking meets Word Sense Disambiguation: A Unified Approach. *Transactions of the Association for Computational Linguistics*, 2:231–244.

Roberto Navigli and Simone Paolo Ponzetto. 2012. BabelNet: The automatic construction, evaluation and application of a wide-coverage multilingual semantic network. *Artificial Intelligence*, 193:217–250.

Roberto Navigli, Kenneth C. Litkowski, and Orin Hargraves. 2007. SemEval-2007 Task 07: Coarse-Grained English All-Words Task. In *Proc. of SemEval-2007*, pages 30–35.

Roberto Navigli, David Jurgens, and Daniele Vannella. 2013. SemEval-2013 Task 12: Multilingual Word Sense Disambiguation. In *Second Joint Conference on Lexical and Computational Semantics (*SEM), Volume 2: Proc. of the Seventh International Workshop on Semantic Evaluation (SemEval 2013)*, pages 222–231, Atlanta, Georgia, USA.

Roberto Navigli. 2009. Word sense disambiguation: A survey. *ACM Comput. Surv.*, 41(2):1–69.

Roberto Navigli. 2012. A quick tour of word sense disambiguation, induction and related approaches. In *Proceedings of the 38th Conference on Current Trends in Theory and Practice of Computer Science (SOFSEM)*, pages 115–129.

Martha Palmer, Christiane Fellbaum, Scott Cotton, Lauren Delfs, and Hoa Trang Dang. 2001. English tasks: All-words and verb lexical sample. In *Proc. of Senseval-2*, pages 21–24.

Sameer S. Pradhan, Edward Loper, Dmitriy Dligach, and Martha Palmer. 2007. SemEval-2007 task 17: English lexical sample, SRL and all words. In *Proc. of SemEval-2007*, pages 87–92.

Delip Rao, Paul McNamee, and Mark Dredze. 2013. Entity linking: Finding extracted entities in a knowledge base. In *Multi-source, Multilingual Information Extraction and Summarization*, pages 93–115.

Benjamin Snyder and Martha Palmer. 2004. The English all-words task. In *Proc. of Senseval-3*, pages 41–43.

Ricardo Usbeck, Michael Röder, Axel-Cyrille Ngonga Ngomo, Ciro Baron, Andreas Both, Martin Brümmer, Diego Ceccarelli, Marco Cornolti, Didier Cherix, Bernd Eickmann, Paolo Ferragina, Christiane Lemke, Andrea Moro, Roberto Navigli, Francesco Piccinno, Giuseppe Rizzo, Harald Sack, René Speck, Raphaël Troncy, Jörg Waitelonis, and Lars Wesemann. 2015. GERBIL - General Entity Annotator Benchmark. In *Proc. of WWW*.

Zhi Zhong and Hwee Tou Ng. 2010. It Makes Sense: A Wide-Coverage Word Sense Disambiguation System for Free Text. In *Proc. of the ACL 2010 System Demonstrations*, pages 78–83, Uppsala, Sweden, July.

LIMSI: Translations as Source of Indirect Supervision for Multilingual All-Words Sense Disambiguation and Entity Linking

Marianna Apidianaki
LIMSI-CNRS
Rue John von Neumann
91405 Orsay Cedex, France
marianna@limsi.fr

Li Gong
IMMI-CNRS
Rue John von Neumann
91405 Orsay Cedex, France
gong@limsi.fr

Abstract

We present the LIMSI submission to the Multilingual Word Sense Disambiguation and Entity Linking task of SemEval-2015. The system exploits the parallelism of the multilingual test data and uses translations as source of indirect supervision for sense selection. The LIMSI system gets best results in English in all domains and shows that alignment information can successfully guide disambiguation. This simple but effective method can serve to generate high quality sense annotated data for WSD system training.

1 Introduction

This paper describes the LIMSI system at the Multilingual Word Sense Disambiguation (WSD) and Entity Linking (EL) task of SemEval-2015 (Moro and Navigli, 2015). The system performs sense selection by combining translation information obtained through alignment of the multilingual test set with sense ranking. It can thus be described as semi-supervised given the indirect supervision provided by the translations. The alignment correspondences serve as constraints for reducing the search space for each word to BabelNet synsets (hereafter, BabelSynsets) containing the translation and the retained synsets are sorted according to the BabelNet sense ranking. Our goal is to test the contribution of translations in multilingual WSD with no recourse to context information. The system needs no training and can be applied directly to parallel data.

The evaluation results show that the LIMSI system outperforms all systems in all domains in English and highlight the important role of translations in guiding disambiguation. This simple yet effective approach can serve to generate high quality sense annotations for WSD system training. In what follows, we provide a detailed description of the system, an analysis of the results and a discussion of the factors that determine the efficiency of the method.

2 Task Description

The SemEval-2015 Multilingual WSD and EL task (Moro and Navigli, 2015) aims to promote joint research in these two closely-related topics. WSD refers to the task of assigning meanings to occurrences of words in texts (Navigli, 2009) and its multilingual counterpart involves the identification of semantically adequate translations (Resnik and Yarowsky, 1997; Ide et al., 2002; Apidianaki, 2009). EL, on the other side, aims at linking entities in a text to the most suitable entry in a knowledge base. The systems participating in the Multilingual WSD and EL task can make a choice between different options (WSD, EL or both) and one or several WSD settings (all-words or specific part-of-speech disambiguation). Contrary to previous tasks (Navigli et al., 2013), the SemEval-2015 task addresses the disambiguation of words of all content parts of speech. No training data is provided and the test set consists of parallel texts in three languages (English, Italian and Spanish) pertaining to both open and closed domains (biomedical, math and computer, and a broader (social issues) domain). For evaluation, the data is manually annotated with senses from BabelNet (version 2.5.1), a wide-coverage multilingual semantic network.[1] Senses in BabelNet are described by synsets which contain lexicographic and encyclopedic knowledge extracted from various sources[2] in many languages, and are linked between them with different types of relations (Navigli and Ponzetto, 2012). The LIMSI system disambiguates words of all parts of speech in the three languages. No multi-word units are extracted. However, although only WSD is addressed explicitly, the system is also assigned EL scores as it manages to annotate several Named Entities with the correct synset.

3 System Description

3.1 Alignment of the Evaluation Dataset

The test data contains four parallel documents in English, Spanish and Italian. Our system exploits the parallelism of the test set, a feature overlooked by previous systems (Navigli et al., 2013). In order to avoid some discrepancies observed at the level of sentence correspondences, we first align the texts pairwise using the Hunalign sentence aligner (Varga et al., 2005). Then we run GIZA++ (Och and Ney, 2003) in both directions at the lemma level and retain only intersecting alignments to rule out spurious correspondences. For each instance of an English content word in the test set we identify its Spanish translation in context and, alternatively, the English translations of Spanish and Italian words. We use the lemma and part-of-speech information provided by the task organizers.

3.2 Sense Selection

The established alignment correspondences serve as constraints to retrieve the BabelSynsets that are relevant for words in the test set, based on the assumption of a semantic correspondence between a word and its translation in context (Diab and Resnik, 2002). BabelSynsets group synonymous English words and their translations in different languages. Polysemous words are found in different synsets, as in WordNet (Miller et al., 1990), and are associated to different translations.

The procedure for selecting the most adequate BabelSynset for an occurrence of a word (w) in context is described in Figure 1. First, we find the synsets of

Notation:
S_w: the set of BabelSynsets for w
t: a translation of w in context
S_w^t: the set of synsets in which t appears

The Sense Selection Algorithm:
$S_w^t \leftarrow \emptyset$
$S_w \leftarrow$ `getBabelSynsets`(w)
for each BabelSynset $s \in S_w$ **do**
  if $t \in s$ **then**
    add s to S_w^t
if $|S_w^t| \geq 1$ **then**
  return getBFS(S_w^t)
else
  return getBFS(S_w)

Figure 1: The `getBabelSynsets` function retrieves the synsets available for w in BabelNet. The `getBFS` function ranks synsets according to importance. If the aligned translation is contained in different synsets of w, the most frequent one among this set of synsets is returned. If no synset is retained through alignment, the system falls back to the BFS baseline.

w (S_w) in BabelNet 2.0 and filter them to keep only synsets that contain both w and its aligned translation t in this context ($S_w^t \subseteq S_w$).[3] If more than one synsets are retained, we rank them using the default sense comparator integrated within the BabelNet-API 2.5 (`BabelSynsetComparator`) and keep the highest ranked synset. Otherwise, if t is found in only one synset, this constitutes the sense tag for the word. The system falls back to the BabelNet First Sense (BFS)[4] for unaligned instances or in cases where t is not found in any synset. As the alignment constraint does not apply in this case, the BFS corresponds to the highest ranked among *all* synsets of w. Note that the sense selected by our method for a word might correspond to its BFS or not. As selection is done among the subset of senses that satisfy the alignment constraint, if this is the case for the BFS it remains among the candidate synsets and can

[1] The resource is available at `http://babelnet.org/`
[2] WordNet, wiki resources and automatic translations.

[3] In these experiments, we only use translations in one language. We would expect the use of translations in different languages to increase the accuracy of the filtering but as a downside, it could reduce the recall as synsets should contain all translations.
[4] The most frequent sense (MFS) for a word in BabelNet.

All domains			Biomedical			Math & computer			Social issues		
System	All	WSD	System	All	WSD	System	All	WSD	System	All	WSD
LIMSI	**65.8**	**64.7**	LIMSI	**71.3**	**68.9**	LIMSI	**54.1**	**53.9**	LIMSI	**67.2**	**67.7**
SUDOKU-2	61.6	59.9	SUDOKU-3	71.2	68.8	SUDOKU-2	53.2	53.1	vua-background	60.8	61.1
SUDOKU-3	60.7	58.9	SUDOKU-2	68.9	66.4	SUDOKU-3	49.4	49.1	SUDOKU-1	56.4	56.2
vua-background	58.4	60.3	vua-background	63.6	66.4	EBL-Hope	41.7	39.8	SUDOKU-2	55.6	54.5
SUDOKU-1	55.8	57.5	SUDOKU-1	62.4	65.0	TeamUFAL	29.8	28.4	WSD-games-1-2	53.5	53.8
BFS	67.5	66.3	BFS	72.1	69.9	BFS	55.3	55.2	BFS	70.8	70.5

Table 1: Best performing systems at the SemEval-2015 Multilingual WSD and Entity Linking task for English.

	All domains		Biomedical		Math & computer		Social issues	
System	ES	IT	ES	IT	ES	IT	ES	IT
LIMSI	45.0	48.4	51.0	53.1	34.8	44.6	43.1	42.9
SUDOKU 1/2	**57.1**	**59.9**	**62.7**	**65.1**	**49.7**	**52.1**	**57.0**	**61.0**
BFS	37.5	40.2	43.7	44.3	28.7	36.7	34.0	35.7

Table 2: LIMSI, best system and BFS scores in Spanish and Italian.

be selected, otherwise it is discarded. For instance, the noun *side* has 21 BabelSynsets but its Spanish translation in this context:

> *The tablets are pale-orange and have a score line on both sides so that they can be halved.*

cara, is found in only two synsets: `00032604n` and `00071434n`. These are semantically close and describe fine-grained nuances of the "outer surface of an object" meaning of *side*, also expressed by *cara*.[5] Sense ranking correctly suggests `00032604n` ("a surface forming part of the outside of an object") as the most adequate sense annotation for this instance of the word. In this case our method improves over the BFS baseline which proposes `00071431n` ("a place within a region identified relative to a center or reference location"), a synset that our system rules out from the beginning as it does not contain the translation `cara`.

4 Evaluation Results

Table 1 gives an overview of the results obtained for English.[6] The systems are evaluated using standard WSD evaluation metrics. Precision measures the percentage of the sense assignments provided by the system that are identical to the gold standard; recall measures the percentage of instances that are correctly labeled by the system. Results in the table are reported in F1 score. The five best performing systems in both tasks (WSD & EL) and WSD only are compared to the BFS baseline.

The LIMSI alignment-based system yields the top performance in English among the 17 submitted systems, in all domains. This result is very interesting given that our method is very simple: it needs no training and is very easy to compute as it only relies on alignment and sense ranking. Note that the BFS baseline for English is a very strong one that none of the systems manages to beat. As the test set is very small ($\sim$ 138 parallel sentences), we expect the method to perform even better on larger corpora where the automatic alignment will have higher accuracy and coverage.

Our system performs poorly in Spanish and Italian in comparison to English, and is ranked in the fourth position. The scores obtained in these languages are given in Table 2 and are compared to the best performing system and the baseline. A close analysis of the results reveals that the weaker system performance is due to the way the BabelNet API carries out sense ranking in these languages. In English, WordNet senses are ranked first sorted

[5] BabelSynsets often correspond to WordNet synsets describing fine-grained nuances of meaning.

[6] A full presentation of the results is available in the task description paper (Moro and Navigli, 2015).

System		EN	ES	IT
LIMSI		596	596	592
LIMSI = BFS	both ✓	396	231	236
	both ×	150	218	198
LIMSI ≠ BFS	LIMSI ✓	37	136	142
	BFS ✓	13	11	16
BFS		563	500	499
	✓	363	158	182
	×	200	342	317

Table 3: The top part of the table gives the # of correct/wrong annotations made by the LIMSI system. The lower part shows the # of correct/wrong predictions when the system falls back to the BFS.

by sense number[7] and are followed by Wikipedia senses in lexicographic order (Navigli, 2013). For languages other than English where frequency information is not available, senses are sorted in lexicographic order,[8] a criterion that often fails to reflect their relevance (i.e. rare senses might be placed higher than more frequent ones). This certainly affects our system which relies on sense ranking a) when multiple senses are retained after filtering by alignment, and b) when the BFS is needed.[9]

The low values of the Spanish and Italian BFS baseline reported by the task organizers confirm this finding. As the first sense retained by the BabelNet API in these languages often is not the most frequent sense, the baseline is outperformed by almost all participating systems. The higher scores obtained by our system compared to the baseline show that the alignment-based filtering remains beneficial in spite of the problematic sense ranking, as the aligned translation might occur in only one BabelSynset. Table 3 provides a detailed analysis of the results. The top part of the table shows the accuracy of the alignment-based predictions, which might coincide with the BFS or not. Our system improves over the BFS in 37 cases in English, 136 in Spanish and 142 in Italian. On the contrary, the BFS does better only 13, 11 and 16 times in the three languages. The system falls back to the BFS in case of unaligned words or when the translations are not found in some BabelNet synset. As shown in the lower part of Table 3, the BFS predictions are often wrong, especially in Spanish and Italian (342 and 317 wrong predictions, respectively). This analysis shows the limited impact of the BFS on the performance of the LIMSI system which manages to improve over the baseline in numerous cases.

The system fails to provide the correct sense in cases of parallel ambiguities where a word and its translation carry the same senses. For exemple, this instance of *window*:

Here's a screenshot of kalgebra main window.

is aligned to *ventana* in the Spanish text, which translates both the "opening" and the "computer" sense of the word. Although the Spanish translation helps to rule out 11 of the 15 BabelSynsets of *window*, ranking the remaining four synsets puts forward the more frequent "opening" sense (`00081285n`) which is incorrect for this instance. Using translations in multiple languages could improve accuracy in these cases.

5 Conclusion

We have described the LIMSI system submitted to the SemEval-2015 Multilingual All-Words Sense Disambiguation and Entity Linking task. The system is based on automatic translation alignment and sense ranking, it needs no training and is directly applied to the evaluation data. By exploiting the indirect supervision provided through alignment, this simple approach gives top performance in English. The high quality semantic annotations provided by our system can serve as training data for supervised WSD algorithms.

Based on these encouraging results, we see a number of research directions for future work. As the method in its current form is bound to be used on parallel data, we would like to experiment with alignments provided by Machine Translation systems and disambiguate monolingual texts. Moreover, we intend to explore alternative sense ranking solutions to improve the performance of the method in languages other than English.

[7]Sense numbers in WordNet reflect the frequency of the senses in the SemCor corpus (Miller et al., 1993).

[8]An additional criterion applies to Wikipedia senses according to which pages that contain a parenthetical explanation, as in disambiguation pages, are ranked lower than ones that do not.

[9]For exemple, in cases of unaligned words or where the aligned translation is not found in some synset.

References

Marianna Apidianaki. 2009. Data-driven Semantic Analysis for Multilingual WSD and Lexical Selection in Translation. In *Proceedings of the 12th Conference of the European Chapter of the Association for Computational Linguistics (EACL-09)*, pages 77–85, Athens, Greece.

Mona Diab and Philip Resnik. 2002. An Unsupervised Method for Word Sense Tagging using Parallel Corpora. In *Proceedings of 40th Annual Meeting of the Association for Computational Linguistics*, pages 255–262, Philadelphia, USA.

Nancy Ide, Tomaž Erjavec, and Dan Tufiş. 2002. Sense Discrimination with Parallel Corpora. In *Proceedings of the ACL Workshop on Word Sense Disambiguation: Recent Successes and Future Directions*, pages 54–60, Philadelphia, USA.

George A. Miller, Richard Beckwith, Christiane Fellbaum, Derek Gross, and Katherine Miller. 1990. Introduction to WordNet: An On-line Lexical Database. *International Journal of Lexicography*, 3:235–244.

George A. Miller, Claudia Leacock, Randee Tengi, and Ross T. Bunker. 1993. A semantic concordance. In *Proceedings of a Workshop on Human Language Technology*, pages 303–308, Plainsboro, New Jersey, USA.

Andrea Moro and Roberto Navigli. 2015. SemEval-2015 Task 13: Multilingual All-Words Sense Disambiguation and Entity Linking. In *Proceedings of the 9th International Workshop on Semantic Evaluation (SemEval 2015)*, Denver, Colorado, USA.

Roberto Navigli and Simone Paolo Ponzetto. 2012. BabelNet: The Automatic Construction, Evaluation and Application of a Wide-Coverage Multilingual Semantic Network. *Artificial Intelligence*, 193:217–250.

Roberto Navigli, David Jurgens, and Daniele Vannella. 2013. SemEval-2013 Task 12: Multilingual Word Sense Disambiguation. In *Second Joint Conference on Lexical and Computational Semantics (*SEM), Volume 2: Proceedings of the Seventh International Workshop on Semantic Evaluation (SemEval 2013)*, pages 222–231, Atlanta, Georgia, USA.

Roberto Navigli. 2009. Word Sense Disambiguation: a Survey. *ACM Computing Surveys*, 41(2):1–69.

Roberto Navigli. 2013. A Quick Tour of BabelNet 1.1. In *Computational Linguistics and Intelligent Text Processing - 14th International Conference, CICLing 2013, Part I*, pages 25–37, Samos, Greece.

Franz Josef Och and Hermann Ney. 2003. A Systematic Comparison of Various Statistical Alignment Models. *Computational Linguistics*, 29:19–51.

Philip Resnik and David Yarowsky. 1997. A Perspective on Word Sense Disambiguation Methods and Their Evaluation. In *Proceedings of the SIGLEX Workshop on Tagging Text with Lexical Semantics: Why, What and How?*, Washington, DC, USA.

Dániel Varga, Péter Halácsy, András Kornai, Viktor Nagy, László Németh, and Viktor Trón. 2005. Parallel corpora for medium density languages. In *Proceedings of Recent Advances in Natural Language Processing (RANLP 2005)*, pages 590–596, Borovets, Bulgaria.

SemEval-2015 Task 14: Analysis of Clinical Text

Noémie Elhadad♣, Sameer Pradhan†, Sharon Lipsky Gorman♣,
Suresh Manandhar◇, Wendy Chapman♠, Guergana Savova†
♣ Columbia University, USA
† Boston Children's Hospital, USA
◇ University of York, UK
♠ University of Utah, USA
noemie.elhadad@columbia.edu, guergana.savova@childrens.harvard.edu

Abstract

We describe two tasks—named entity recognition (Task 1) and template slot filling (Task 2)—for clinical texts. The tasks leverage annotations from the ShARe corpus, which consists of clinical notes with annotated mentions disorders, along with their normalization to a medical terminology and eight additional attributes. The purpose of these tasks was to identify advances in clinical named entity recognition and establish the state of the art in disorder template slot filling. Task 2 consisted of two subtasks: template slot filling given gold-standard disorder spans (Task 2a) and end-to-end disorder span identification together with template slot filling (Task 2b). For Task 1 (disorder span detection and normalization), 16 teams participated. The best system yielded a strict F1-score of 75.7, with a precision of 78.3 and recall of 73.2. For Task 2a (template slot filling given gold-standard disorder spans), six teams participated. The best system yielded a combined overall weighted accuracy for slot filling of 88.6. For Task 2b (disorder recognition and template slot filling), nine teams participated. The best system yielded a combined relaxed F (for span detection) and overall weighted accuracy of 80.8.

1 Introduction

Patient records are abundant with reports, narratives, discussions, and updates about patients. This unstructured part of the record is dense with mentions of clinical entities, such as conditions, anatomical sites, medications, and procedures. Identifying the different entities discussed in a patient record, their status towards the patient, and how they relate to each other is one of the core tasks of clinical natural language processing. Indeed, with robust systems to extract such mentions, along with their associated attributes in the text (e.g., presence of negation for a given entity mention), several high-level applications can be developed such as information extraction, question answering, and summarization.

In biomedicine, there are rich lexicons that can be leveraged for the task of named entity recognition and entity linking or normalization. The Unified Medical Language System (UMLS) represents over 130 lexicons/thesauri with terms from a variety of languages. The UMLS Metathesaurus integrates standard resources such as SNOMED-CT, ICD9, and RxNORM that are used worldwide in clinical care, public health, and epidemiology. In addition, the UMLS also provides a semantic network in which every concept in the Metathesaurus is represented by its Concept Unique Identifier (CUI) and is semantically typed (Bodenreider and McCray, 2003).

The SemEval-2015 Task 14, Analysis of Clinical Text is the newest iteration in a series of community challenges organized around the tasks of named entity recognition for clinical texts. In SemEval-2014 Task 7 (Pradhan et al., 2014) and previous challenge 2013 (Pradhan et al., 2013), we had focused on the task of named entity recognition for disorder mentions in clinical texs, along with normalization to UMLS CUIs. This year, we shift focus on the task of identifying a series of attributes describing a disorder mention. Like for previous challenges, we use the ShARe corpus[1] and introduce a new set of annotations for disorder attributes.

In the remainder of this paper, we describe the dataset and the annotations provided to the task participants, the subtasks comprising the overall task, and the results of the teams that participated along with notable approaches in their systems.

2 Dataset

	Train	**Dev**	**Test**
Notes	298	133	100
Words	182K	153K	109K

Table 1: Notes, words, and disorder distributions in the training, development, and testing sets.

The dataset used is the ShARe corpus (Pradhan et al., 2015). As a whole, it consists of 531 deidentified clinical notes (a mix of discharge summaries and radiology reports) selected from the MIMIC II clinical database version 2.5 (Saeed et al., 2002). Part of the ShARe corpus was released as part of Semeval 2014 Task 7. In fact, to enable meaningful comparisons of systems performance across years, the 2015 SemEval training set combines the 2014 training and development sets, while the 2015 SemEval development set consists of the 2014 test set. The 2015 test set is a previously unseen set of clinical notes from the ShARe corpus. Table 2 provides descriptive statistics about the different sets. In addition to the ShARe corpus annotations, task participants were provided with a large set of unlabeled deidentified clinical notes, also from MIMIC II (400,000+ notes).

The ShARe corpus contains gold-standard annotations of disorder mentions and a set of attributes, as described in Table 2. We refer to the nine attributes as a disorder template. The annotation schema for the template was derived from the established clinical element model[2]. The complete guidelines for the ShARe annotations are available on the ShARe website[3]. Here, we provide a few examples to illustrate what each attribute captures.

[1]share.healthnlp.org
[2]www.clinicalelement.com
[3]share.healthnlp.org

	Train	**Dev**
Disorder mentions	11,144	7,967
CUI=CUI-less	30%	24%
CUI	70%	76%
Unique CUIs	1,352	1,139
Negation = yes	19.6%	20.1%
Negation = no	80.4%	79.9%
Subject = patient	99.2%	98.4%
Subject = family_member	<1%	1.4%
Subject = other	<1%	<1%
Subject = donor_other	<1%	0%
Uncertainty = yes	8.9%	5.9%
Uncertainty = no	91.1%	94.1%
Course = changed	<1%	<1%
Course = resolved	<1%	<1%
Course = worsened	< 1%	<1%
Course = improved	< 1%	1%
Course = decreased	1.6%	<1%
Course = increased	2%	1.7%
Course = unmarked	94.1%	95.2%
Severity = slight	1.1%	<1%
Severity = severe	3.5%	2.6%
Severity = moderate	5.9%	2.3%
Severity = unmarked	89.49%	94.2%
Conditional = true	4.9%	6.2%
Conditional = false	95.1%	93.8%
Generic = true	<1%	1%
Generic = false	99.1	99%
Body Location = CUI	55.3%	44.7%
Body Location = null	44.4%	54.6%
Body Location = CUI-less	<1%	<1%
Unique BL CUIs	734	511

Table 3: Distribution of different attribute values in the training and testing sets.

- In the statement "patient denies numbness," the disorder numbness has an associated negation attribute set to "yes."
- In the sentence "son has schizophrenia", the disorder schizophrenia has a subject attribute set to "family_member."
- The sentence "Evaluation of MI." contains a disorder (MI) with the uncertainty attribute set to "yes".
- An example of disorder with a non-default course attribute can be found in the sentence "The cough got worse over the next two weeks.", where its value is "worsened."
- The severity attribute is set to "slight" in "He has slight bleeding."

Slot	Description	Possible Values
CUI	CUI; indicates normalized disorder	CUI, CUI-less
NEG	Negation; indicates whether disorder is negated	no*, yes
SUB	Subject; indicates who experiences the disorder	patient*, null, other, family_member, donor_family_member, donor_other
UNC	Uncertainty; indicates presence of doubt about the disorder	no*, yes
COU	Course; indicates progress or decline of the disorder	unmarked*, changed, increased, decreased, improved, worsened, resolved
SEV	Severity; indicates how severe the disorder is	unmarked*, slight, moderate, severe
CND	Conditional; indicates conditional existence of disorder under specific circumstances	false*, true
GEN	Generic; indicates a generic mention of a disorder	false*, true
BL	Body Location; represents normalized CUI of body location(s) associated with disorder	null*, CUI, CUI-less

Table 2: Disorder attributes and their possible values. Default values are indicated with an *.

- In the sentence "Pt should come back if any rash occurs," the disorder rash has a conditional attribute with value "true."
- In the sentence "Patient has a facial rash", the body location associated with the disorder "facial rash" is "face" with CUI C0015450. Note that the body location does not have to be a substring of the disorder mention, even though in this example it is.

The ShARe corpus was annotated following a rigorous process. Annotators were professional coders who trained for the specific task of ShARe annotations. The annotation process consisted of a double annotation step followed by an adjudication phase. For all annotations, in addition to all the values for the attributes, their corresponding character spans in the text were recorded and are available as part of the ShARe annotations. Table 3 shows the distribution of the different attributes in the training and development sets.

3 Tasks

The Analysis of Clinical Text Task is split into two tasks, one on named entity recognition, and one on template slot filling for the named entities. Participants were able to submit to either or both tasks.

3.1 Task 1: Disorder Identification

For task 1, disorder identification, the goal is to recognize the span of a disorder mention in input clinical text and to normalize the disorder to a unique CUI in the UMLS/SNOMED-CT terminology. The UMLS/SNOMED-CT terminology is defined as the set of CUIs in the UMLS, but restricted to concepts that are included in the SNOMED-CT terminology.

Participants were free to use any publicly available resources, such as UMLS, WordNet, and Wikipedia, as well as the large corpus of unannotated clinical notes.

The following are examples of input/output for Task 1.

1 In "The rhythm appears to be atrial fibrillation." the span "atrial fibrillation" is the gold-standard disorder, and its normalization is CUI C0004238 (preferred term atrial fibrillation). This is a
2 In "The left atrium is moderately dilated." the disorder span is discontiguous: "left atrium...dilated" and its normalization is CUI C0344720 (preferred term left atrial dilatation).
3 In "53 year old man s/p fall from ladder." the disorder is "fall from ladder" and is normalized to C0337212 (preferred term accidental fall from ladder).

Example 1 represents the easiest cases. Example 2 represents instances of disorders as listed in the UMLS that are best mapped to discontiguous mentions. In Example 3, one has to infer that the description is a synonym of the UMLS preferred term. Finally, in some cases, a disorder mention is present, but there is no good equivalent CUI in UMLS/SNOMED-CT. The disorder is then normalized to "CUI-less".

3.2 Task 2: Disorder Slot Filling

This task focuses on identifying the normalized value for the nine attributes described above: the CUI of the disorder (very much like in Task 1), negation indicator, subject, uncertainty indicator, course, severity, conditional, generic indicator, and body location.

We describe Task 2 as a slot-filling task: given a disorder mention (either provided by gold-standard or identified automatically) in a clinical note, identify the normalized value of the nine slots. Note that there are two aspects to slot filling: cues in the text and normalized value. In this task, we focus on normalized value and ignore cue detection.

To understand the state of the art for this new task, we considered two subtasks. In both cases, given a disorder span, participants are asked to identify the nine attributes related to the disorder. In Task 2a, the gold-standard disorder span(s) are provided as input. In Task 2b, no gold-standard information is provided; systems must recognize spans for disorder mentions and fill in the value of the nine attributes.

4 Evaluation Metrics

4.1 Task 1 Evaluation Metrics

Evaluation for Task 1 is reported according to a F-score, that captures both the disorder span recognition and the CUI normalization steps. We compute two versions of the F-score:

- *Strict F-score:* a predicted mention is considered a true positive if (i) the character span of the disorder is exactly the same as for the gold-standard mention; and (ii) the predicted CUI is correct. The predicted disorder is considered a false positive if the span is incorrect or the CUI is incorrect.
- *Relaxed F-score:* a predicted mention is a true positive if (i) there is any word overlap between the predicted mention span and the gold-standard span (both in the case of contiguous and discontiguous spans); and (ii) the predicted CUI is correct. The predicted mention is a false positive if the span shares no words with the gold-standard span or the CUI is incorrect.

Thus, given, D_{tp}, the number of true positives disorder mentions, D_{fp}, the number of false positive disorder mentions, and D_{fn}, the number of false negative disorder mentions

$$Precision = P = \frac{D_{tp}}{D_{tp} + D_{fp}} \quad (1)$$

$$Recall = R = \frac{D_{tp}}{D_{tp} + D_{fn}} \quad (2)$$

$$F = \frac{2 \times P \times R}{P + R} \quad (3)$$

4.2 Task 2 Evaluation Metrics

We introduce a variety of evaluation metrics, which capture different aspects of the task of disorder template slot filling. Overall, for Task 2a, we reported average unweighted accuracy, weighted accuracy, and per-slot weighted accuracy for each of the nine slots. For Task 2b, we report the same metrics, and in addition report relaxed F for span identification.

We now describe per-disorder evaluation metrics, and then describe the overall evaluation metrics which provide aggregated system assessment. Given the K slots $(s_1, ..., s_K)$ to fill (in our task the nine different slots), each slot s_k has n_k possible normalized values $(s_k^i) i \in 1..n_k$. For a given disorder, its gold-standard value for slot s_k is denoted gs_k, and its predicted value is denoted ps_k.

4.2.1 Per-Disorder Evaluation Metrics

Per-disorder unweighted accuracy The unweighted accuracy represents the ability of a system to identify all the slot values for a given disorder. The per-disorder unweighted accuracy is simply defined as:

$$\frac{\sum_{k=1}^{K} I(gs_k, ps_k)}{K}$$

where I is the identity function: $I(x, y) = 1$ if $x = y$ and 0 otherwise.

Per-disorder weighted accuracy The weighted per-disorder accuracy takes into account the prevalence of different values for each of the slots. This metric captures how good a system is at identifying rare values of different slots. The weights are thus defined as follows:

- The CUI slot's weight is set to 1, for all CUI values.
- The body location slot's weight is defined as weight(NULL) = 1-prevalence(NULL), and the weight for any non-NULL value (including CUI-less) is set to weight(CUI) = 1-prevalence(body location with a non-NULL value).

- For each other slot s_k, we define n_k weights $weight(s_k^i)$ (one for each of its possible normalized values) as follows:

$$\forall i \in 1..n_k, weight(s_k^i) = 1 - prevalence(s_k^i)$$

where $prevalence(s_k^i)$ is the prevalence of value s_k^i in the overall corpus(training, development, and testing sets). The weights are such that highly prevalent values have smaller weights and rare values have bigger weight.

Thus, weighted per-disorder accuracy is defined as

$$\frac{\sum_{k=1}^{K} weight(gs_k) * I(gs_k, ps_k)}{\sum_{k=1}^{K} weight(gs_k)} \quad (4)$$

where, like above, gs_k is the gold-standard value of slot s_k and ps_k is the predicted value of slot s_k, and I is the identity function: $I(x, y) = 1$ if $x = y$ and 0 otherwise.

4.2.2 Overall Evaluation Metrics

Weighted and Unweighted Accuracy. Armed with the per-disorder unweighted and weighted accuracy scores, we can compute an average across all true-positive disorders. For task 2a, the disorders are provided, so they are all true positive, but for task 2b, it is important to note that we only consider the true-positive disorders to compute the overall accuracy.

$$Accuracy = \frac{\sum_{i=1}^{\#tp} per\_disorder\_acc(tp_i)}{\#tp} \quad (5)$$

Per-Slot Accuracy. Per-slot accuracy are useful in assessing the ability of a system to fill in a particular slot. For each slot, an average per-slot accuracy is defined as the accuracy for each true-positive disorder to recognize the value for that particular slot across the true-positive spans. Thus, for slot s_k, the per-slot accuracy is:

$$\frac{\sum_{i=1}^{\#tp} weight(gs_{i,k}) * I(gs_{i,k}, ps_{i,k})}{\sum_{i=1}^{\#tp} weight(gs_{i,k})} \quad (6)$$

where for each true-positive span there is a gold-standard value $gs_{i,k}$ and a predicted value $ps_{i,k}$ for slot s_k.

team	run	strict_P	strict_R	strict_F	relax_P	relax_R	relax_F
ezDI	run 1	0.783	0.732	0.757	0.815	0.761	0.787
ULisboa	run 3	0.779	0.705	0.740	0.806	0.729	0.765
UTH-CCB	run 3	0.778	0.696	0.735	0.797	0.714	0.753
UWM	run 2	0.773	0.699	0.734	0.809	0.731	0.768
UTH-CCB	run 1	0.748	0.713	0.730	0.777	0.741	0.759
UTH-CCB	run 2	0.748	0.713	0.730	0.777	0.741	0.759
TAKELAB	run 1	0.761	0.696	0.727	0.794	0.727	0.759
ULisboa	run 2	0.749	0.681	0.713	0.780	0.709	0.743
Bioinformatics-UA	run 2	0.690	0.736	0.712	0.719	0.766	0.742
Bioinformatics-UA	run 3	0.691	0.735	0.712	0.720	0.765	0.742
ULisboa	run 1	0.748	0.676	0.710	0.782	0.706	0.742
CUAB	run 2	0.735	0.683	0.708	0.762	0.708	0.734
NYUClinicalML	run 3	0.741	0.676	0.707	0.775	0.707	0.740
Bioinformatics-UA	run 1	0.669	0.738	0.702	0.698	0.769	0.732
NYUClinicalML	run 1	0.722	0.662	0.691	0.763	0.699	0.729
NYUClinicalML	run 2	0.722	0.663	0.691	0.762	0.700	0.730
IHS-RD-Belarus	run 2	0.722	0.662	0.690	0.746	0.684	0.714
IHS-RD-Belarus	run 1	0.720	0.655	0.686	0.745	0.677	0.709
TeamHCMUS	run 1	0.680	0.633	0.656	0.711	0.662	0.685
TeamHCMUS	run 2	0.680	0.633	0.656	0.711	0.662	0.685
TeamHCMUS	run 3	0.680	0.633	0.656	0.711	0.662	0.685
CUAB	run 1	0.718	0.572	0.636	0.742	0.591	0.658
LIST-LUX	run 3	0.649	0.580	0.613	0.675	0.603	0.637
LIST-LUX	run 2	0.648	0.579	0.612	0.674	0.602	0.636
LIST-LUX	run 1	0.649	0.577	0.611	0.677	0.602	0.637
umlnlp2014	run 3	0.611	0.567	0.588	0.675	0.626	0.650
umlnlp2014	run 2	0.559	0.488	0.521	0.653	0.571	0.609
umlnlp2014	run 1	0.557	0.487	0.519	0.652	0.570	0.608
KPSCMI	run 1	0.429	0.565	0.488	0.472	0.620	0.536
UWM	run 1	0.760	0.258	0.385	0.813	0.276	0.412
TMUNSW	run 1	0.328	0.349	0.338	0.396	0.420	0.408
TMUNSW	run 2	0.321	0.340	0.330	0.387	0.410	0.398
TMUNSW	run 3	0.321	0.340	0.330	0.387	0.410	0.398
UtahPOET	run 2	0.295	0.315	0.305	0.352	0.376	0.364
UtahPOET	run 3	0.295	0.315	0.305	0.352	0.376	0.364
UtahPOET	run 1	0.270	0.306	0.287	0.344	0.390	0.366
Sanj-TUM	run 2	0.098	0.110	0.104	0.475	0.531	0.502
Sanj-TUM	run 3	0.098	0.110	0.104	0.444	0.496	0.469
Sanj-TUM	run 1	0.082	0.107	0.093	0.425	0.552	0.481

Figure 1: Task 1 results.

Disorder Span Identification. This overall metric is only meaningful for Task 2b, where the system has to identify disorders prior to filling in their templates. Like in Task 1, we report an F-score metric to assess how good the system is at identifying disorder span. Note that unlike in Task 1, this F score does not consider CUI normalization, as this is captured through the accuracy in the template filling task. Thus, a true disorder span is defined as any overalp with a gold-stand disorder span. In the case of several predicted spans that overlap with a gold-standard span, then only one of them is chosen to be true positive (the longest ones), and the other predicted spans are considered false positives.

5 Results

5.1 Task 1

16 teams participated in Task 1. Strict and relaxed precision, recall, and F metrics are reported in Figure 1. We relied on the strict F to rank different submissions. The best system from team ezDI reported

75.7 strict F, also reporting the highest relaxed F (78.7) (Pathak et al., 2015).

For disorder span recognition, most teams used a CRF-based approach. Features explored included traditional NER features: lexical (bag of words and bigrams, orthographic features), syntactic features derived from either part-of-speech and phrase chunking information or dependency parsing, and domain features (note type and section headers of clinical note). Lookup to dictionary (either UMLS or customized lexicon of disorders) was an essential feature for performance. To leverage further these lexicons, for instance, Xu and colleagues (Xu et al., 2015) implemented a vector-space model similarity computation to known disorders as an additional feature in their appraoch.

The best-performing teams made use of the large unannotated corpus of clinical notes provided in the challenge (Pathak et al., 2015; Leal et al., 2015; Xu et al., 2015). Teams explored the use of Brown clusters (Brown et al., 1992) and word embeddings (Collobert et al., 2011). Pathak and colleagues (Pathak et al., 2015) note that word2vec (Mikolov et al., 2013) did not yield satisfactory results. Instead, they report better results clustering sentences in the unannotated texts based on their sequence of part-of-speech tags, and using the clusters as feature in the CRF.

Teams continued to explore approaches for recognizing discontiguous entities. Pathak and colleagues (Pathak et al., 2015), for instance, built a specialized SVM-based classifier for that purpose.

For CUI normalization, the best performing teams focused on augmenting existing dictionaries with lists of unambiguous abbreviations (Leal et al., 2015) or by pre-processing UMLS and breaking down existing lexical variants to account for high paraphrasing power of disorder terms (Pathak et al., 2015).

5.2 Task 2

Six teams participated in Task 2a. Evaluation metrics are reported in Figure 2. We relied on the Weighted Accuracy (WA) to rank the teams (highlighted in the Figure is F*WA, but since in Task 2a gold-standard disorders are provided, F is 1). The best system (team UTH-CCB) yielded a WA of 88.6 (Xu et al., 2015).

For Task 2b, nine teams participated. Evaluation metrics are reported in Figure 3. We relied on the combination of F score for disorder span identification and Weighted Accuracy for template filling to rank the teams (F*WA in the figure). The best system (team UTH-CCB) yielded a F*WA of 80.8.

Approaches to template filling focused on building classifiers for each attribute. Specialized lexicons of trigger terms for each attribute (e.g., list of negation terms) along with distance to disorder spans was a helpful feature. Overall, like in Task 1, a range of feature types from lexical to syntactic proved useful in the template filling task.

The per-slot accuracies (columns BL, CUI, CND, COU, GEN, NEG, SEV, SUB, and UNC in Figures 2 and 3) indicate that overall some attributes are easier to recognize than others. Body Location, perhaps not surprisingly, was the most difficult after CUI normalization, in part because it also requires a normalization to an anatomical site.

6 Conclusion

In this task, we introduced a new version of the ShARe corpus, with annotations of disorders and a wide set of disorder attributes. The biggest improvements in the task of disorder recognition (both span identification and CUI normalization) come from leveraging large amounts of unannotated texts and using word embeddings as additional feature in the task. The detection of discontiguous disorder seems to still be an open challenge for the community, however.

The new task of template filling (identifying nine attributes for a given disorder) was met with enthusiasm by the participating teams. We introduced a variety of evaluation metrics to capture the different aspects of the task. Different approaches show that while some attributes are harder to identify than other, overall the best performing teams achieved excellent results.

Acknowledgments

This work was supported by the Shared Annotated Resources (ShARe) project NIH R01 GM090187. We greatly appreciate the hard work of our program committee members and the ShARe annotators.

Team	Run	F	A	F*A	WA	F*WA	BL	CUI	CND	COU	GEN	NEG	SEV	SUB	UNC
UTH-CCB	run 1	1.000	0.943	0.943	0.886	0.886	0.862	0.854	0.903	0.887	0.911	0.975	0.936	0.975	0.911
UTH-CCB	run 3	1.000	0.943	0.943	0.886	0.886	0.862	0.854	0.903	0.887	0.911	0.975	0.936	0.975	0.911
ezDI	run 1	1.000	0.934	0.934	0.880	0.880	0.812	0.918	0.695	0.887	0.887	0.916	0.803	0.960	0.854
UTH-CCB	run 2	1.000	0.953	0.953	0.876	0.876	0.862	0.854	0.817	0.811	0.873	0.975	0.899	0.964	0.834
UTU	run 3	1.000	0.945	0.945	0.857	0.857	0.825	0.827	0.823	0.798	0.888	0.970	0.915	0.920	0.853
UTU	run 2	1.000	0.944	0.944	0.855	0.855	0.814	0.827	0.823	0.798	0.888	0.970	0.915	0.920	0.853
UTU	run 1	1.000	0.939	0.939	0.846	0.846	0.775	0.827	0.822	0.792	0.888	0.964	0.918	0.923	0.857
UWM	run 2	1.000	0.859	0.859	0.818	0.818	0.531	0.911	0.838	0.802	0.836	0.924	0.895	0.933	0.831
TeamHCMUS	run 1	1.000	0.195	0.195	0.576	0.576	0.614	0.804	0.292	0.345	0.076	0.426	0.310	0.173	0.311
TeamHCMUS	run 2	1.000	0.195	0.195	0.576	0.576	0.614	0.804	0.292	0.345	0.076	0.426	0.310	0.173	0.311
TeamHCMUS	run 3	1.000	0.195	0.195	0.576	0.576	0.614	0.804	0.292	0.345	0.076	0.426	0.310	0.173	0.311
UtahPOET	run 3	0.936	0.795	0.744	0.476	0.446	0.457	0.234	0.483	0.814	0.838	0.845	0.759	0.908	0.660
UtahPOET	run 1	0.931	0.769	0.716	0.378	0.351	0.456	0.000	0.481	0.815	0.836	0.848	0.758	0.907	0.659
UtahPOET	run 2	0.931	0.769	0.716	0.378	0.351	0.456	0.000	0.481	0.815	0.836	0.848	0.758	0.907	0.659

Figure 2: Task 2a results.

References

Olivier Bodenreider and Alexa T McCray. 2003. Exploring semantic groups through visual approaches. *Journal of biomedical informatics*, 36(6):414–432.

Peter F Brown, Peter V Desouza, Robert L Mercer, Vincent J Della Pietra, and Jenifer C Lai. 1992. Class-based n-gram models of natural language. *Computational linguistics*, 18(4):467–479.

Ronan Collobert, Jason Weston, Léon Bottou, Michael Karlen, Koray Kavukcuoglu, and Pavel Kuksa. 2011. Natural language processing (almost) from scratch. *The Journal of Machine Learning Research*, 12:2493–2537.

André Leal, Bruno Martins, and Francisco Couto. 2015. ULisboa: Semeval 2015 - task 14 analysis of clinical text: Recognition and normalization of medical concepts. In *Proceedings of SemEval-2015*.

Tomas Mikolov, Ilya Sutskever, Kai Chen, Greg S Corrado, and Jeff Dean. 2013. Distributed representations of words and phrases and their compositionality. In *Advances in Neural Information Processing Systems*, pages 3111–3119.

Parth Pathak, Pinal Patel, Vishal Panchal, Sagar Soni, Kinjal Dani, Narayan Choudhary, and Amrish Patel. 2015. ezDI: A semi-supervised nlp system for clinical narrative analysis. In *Proceedings of SemEval-2015*.

Sameer Pradhan, Noemie Elhadad, Brett R South, David Martinez, Lee Christensen, Amy Vogel, Hanna Suominen, Wendy Chapman, and Guergana Savova. 2013. Task 1: Share/clef ehealth evaluation lab 2013. In *Online Working Notes of CLEF*, page 230.

Sameer Pradhan, Noémie Elhadad, Wendy Chapman, Suresh Manandhar, and Guergana Savova. 2014. Semeval-2014 task 7: Analysis of clinical text. In *Proceedings of the 8th International Workshop on Semantic Evaluation (SemEval 2014)*, pages 54–62.

Sameer Pradhan, Noémie Elhadad, Brett R South, David Martinez, Lee Christensen, Amy Vogel, Hanna Suominen, Wendy W Chapman, and Guergana Savova. 2015. Evaluating the state of the art in disorder recognition and normalization of the clinical narrative. *Journal of the American Medical Informatics Association*, 22(1):143–154.

Mohammed Saeed, C Lieu, G Raber, and RG Mark. 2002. Mimic II: a massive temporal ICU patient database to support research in intelligent patient monitoring. In *Computers in Cardiology, 2002*, pages 641–644. IEEE.

Jun Xu, Yaoyun Zhang, Jingqi Wang, Yonghui Wu, Min Jian, Ergin Soysal, and Hua Xu. 2015. UTH-CCB: The participation of the SemEval 2015 challenge - task 14. In *Proceedings of SemEval-2015*.

Team	run	F	A	F*A	WA	F*WA	BI	CUI	CND	COU	GEN	NEG	SEV	SUB	UNC
UTH-CCB	run 1	0.926	0.941	0.871	0.873	0.808	0.864	0.819	0.899	0.899	0.919	0.976	0.939	0.973	0.912
UTH-CCB	run 2	0.926	0.950	0.879	0.863	0.799	0.864	0.819	0.822	0.837	0.884	0.976	0.904	0.963	0.831
UTH-CCB	run 3	0.903	0.943	0.852	0.881	0.796	0.873	0.834	0.897	0.895	0.925	0.977	0.943	0.974	0.913
ezDI	run 1	0.915	0.935	0.856	0.868	0.795	0.826	0.858	0.816	0.866	0.921	0.978	0.812	0.911	0.857
UWM	run 2	0.893	0.852	0.761	0.798	0.713	0.532	0.858	0.839	0.794	0.845	0.932	0.907	0.929	0.838
CUAB	run 2	0.905	0.908	0.822	0.785	0.710	0.655	0.810	0.660	0.774	0.885	0.850	0.860	0.846	0.749
Bioinformatics-UA	run 2	0.853	0.884	0.754	0.814	0.695	0.691	0.866	0.697	0.856	0.889	0.807	0.877	0.819	0.800
Bioinformatics-UA	run 3	0.853	0.883	0.754	0.814	0.695	0.689	0.867	0.697	0.856	0.890	0.806	0.878	0.818	0.798
Bioinformatics-UA	run 1	0.843	0.883	0.745	0.813	0.686	0.692	0.864	0.697	0.857	0.887	0.807	0.878	0.811	0.799
TeamHCMUS	run 1	0.855	0.884	0.756	0.784	0.671	0.603	0.801	0.725	0.851	0.904	0.935	0.843	0.931	0.802
TeamHCMUS	run 2	0.855	0.884	0.756	0.784	0.671	0.603	0.801	0.725	0.851	0.904	0.935	0.843	0.931	0.802
TeamHCMUS	run 3	0.855	0.884	0.756	0.784	0.671	0.603	0.801	0.725	0.851	0.904	0.935	0.843	0.931	0.802
umlnlp2014	run 3	0.882	0.867	0.765	0.648	0.571	0.525	0.731	0.495	0.569	0.869	0.530	0.535	0.752	0.550
LIST-LUX	run 1	0.884	0.865	0.765	0.641	0.567	0.515	0.719	0.496	0.575	0.870	0.529	0.544	0.751	0.559
LIST-LUX	run 3	0.882	0.866	0.763	0.642	0.566	0.517	0.720	0.500	0.578	0.873	0.528	0.543	0.749	0.560
LIST-LUX	run 2	0.881	0.866	0.763	0.641	0.565	0.517	0.720	0.497	0.575	0.873	0.530	0.543	0.749	0.557
CUAB	run 1	0.839	0.873	0.732	0.669	0.561	0.523	0.784	0.490	0.564	0.855	0.543	0.522	0.736	0.539
umlnlp2014	run 2	0.820	0.864	0.708	0.641	0.526	0.511	0.732	0.482	0.547	0.882	0.516	0.521	0.761	0.544
umlnlp2014	run 1	0.820	0.864	0.708	0.640	0.525	0.511	0.730	0.482	0.547	0.882	0.516	0.521	0.761	0.544
UtahPOET	run 2	0.756	0.821	0.620	0.580	0.438	0.453	0.468	0.475	0.831	0.862	0.853	0.746	0.896	0.651
UtahPOET	run 3	0.756	0.821	0.620	0.580	0.438	0.453	0.468	0.475	0.831	0.862	0.853	0.746	0.896	0.651
UtahPOET	run 1	0.724	0.836	0.605	0.596	0.431	0.566	0.494	0.475	0.566	0.857	0.805	0.629	0.848	0.631
UWM	run 1	0.485	0.835	0.405	0.769	0.373	0.374	0.849	0.870	0.810	0.937	0.942	0.888	0.966	0.845

Figure 3: Task 2b results.

UTH-CCB: The Participation of the SemEval 2015 Challenge – Task 14

Jun Xu, Yaoyun Zhang, Jingqi Wang, Yonghui Wu, Min Jiang, Ergin Soysal, and Hua Xu
School of Biomedical Informatics, The University of Texas Health Science Center at Houston
Houston, TX, USA
{Jun.Xu, Yaoyun.Zhang, Jingqi.Wang, Yonghui.Wu, Min.Jiang, Ergin.Soysal, Hua.Xu}@uth.tmc.edu

Abstract

This paper describes the system developed by the University of Texas Health Science Center at Houston (UTHealth), for the 2015 SemEval shared task on "Analysis of Clinical Text" (Task 14). We participated in both sub-tasks: Task 1 for "Disorder Identification", which aims to detect disorder entities and encode them to UMLS (Unified Medial Language System) CUI (Concept Unique Identifier) and Task 2 for Disorder Slot Filling, where the task is to identify normalized value for modifiers of disorders. For Task 1, we developed an ensemble approach that combined machine learning based named entity recognition classifiers with MetaMap, an existing symbolic biomedical NLP system, to recognize disorder entities, and we used a general Vector Space Model-based approach for disorder encoding to UMLS CUIs. To identify modifiers of disorders (Task 2), we developed Support Vector Machines-based classifiers for each type of modifier, by exploring various types of features. Our system was ranked 3rd for Task 1 and 1st for the Task 2 (both 2A and 2B), demonstrating the effectiveness of machine learning-based approaches for extracting clinical entities and their modifiers from clinical narratives.

1 Introduction

Natural language processing (NLP) plays a critical role in unlocking important patient information from narrative clinical texts, to support various clinical applications such as decision support systems and translational research. One of the very important tasks for clinical NLP research is to extract clinical concepts such as diseases and treatments. Many clinical NLP systems such as MedLEE system (Friedman et al., 1994), MetaMAP system (Aronson and Lang, 2010) and cTAKES system (Savova et al., 2010), have been developed to extract these important clinical concepts from text.

A number of shared tasks for clinical concepts extraction have been organized by different entities, including i2b2 (The Center for Informatics for Integrating Biology and the Bedside), ShARe/CLEF eHealth Evaluation Lab, and SemEval (International Workshop on Semantic Evaluation) (Kelly et al., 2014; Pradhan et al., 2014; Suominen et al., 2013; Uzuner et al., 2011). These challenges have greatly promoted clinical NLP research by building benchmark datasets and innovative methods. The 2015 SemEval Shared Task 14, entitled "Analysis of Clinical Text", is to identify disorders and their modifiers from clinical text, which is an extension of the SemEval-2014 challenge. The 2015 SemEval challenge consists of two subtasks: Task 1 - disorder recognition, where disorder entities need to be detected and normalized to UMLS CUIs, and Task 2 - disorder slot filling, where the normalized value for nine types of modifiers of disorders are to be identified. Task 2 is further divided into two subtasks: 1) Task 2A – identifying modifiers based on gold standard disorders; and 2) Task 2B – identifying modifiers based on disorders recognized by our system, an end-to-end evaluation. In this paper, we describe our approaches and results for both tasks.

2 Methods

2.1 Datasets

For this shared task, organizers prepared three datasets: 1) training set - 298 clinical documents, 2) development set - 133 documents and 3) test set – 100 documents. We developed our models using the training set and optimized parameters using the development set. For final submissions on the test set, we combined training and development sets to build the machine learning classifiers.

2.2 Task 1 – Disorder Identification

The disorder identification consists of two subtasks: 1) recognize disorder entities, and 2) encode recognized disorder entities to concept IDs (CUIs) in UMLS (limited to SNOMED-CT). We describe our approaches for both steps below:

Disorder Entity Recognition - The disorder recognition task is a typical named entity recognition (NER) task. We developed two machine learning based NER models, including the Conditional Random Fields (CRFs) (Lafferty et al., 2001) and the Structural Support Vector Machines (SSVMs). The CRFsuite package (Okazaki, 2007) and SVM^{hmm} * are used for CRFs and SSVMs implementations, respectively. In addition, we also developed hybrid models that combine the two machine learning models with an existing symbolic biomedical NLP system – MetaMap. We developed hybrid systems for disorder recognition by adopting two previously developed ensemble learning strategies, including $ensemble^{ML}$ and $ensemble^{MV}$, which were originally developed in our participation of the SemEval-2014 (Zhang et al., 2014). The $ensemble^{MV}$ approach follows the majority voting strategy to combine the three systems. The $ensemble^{ML}$ approach trains an SVM classifier to combine the predictions from the three systems.

We adopted the features engineered in the previous participation of SemEval 2014 (Zhang et al., 2014), including: word-level features, such as bag-of-word; linguistic features; and discourse features, such as section name in the clinical notes and type of the notes (e.g. '*DISCHARGE_ SUMMARY*'). In this challenge, we further explored the deep neural network (DNN) based word embeddings. We obtained word embeddings by training a deep neural network (Collobert et al., 2011) from the unlabeled MIMIC II corpus (about 3G clinical notes) provided by the SemEval organizers.

Disorder Entity Encoding - We adopted the same Vector Space Model (VSM) approach developed for the SemEval-2014 to encode the disorder to UMLS/SNOMED-CT CUIs (Zhang et al., 2014). This is a general approach to encode clinical entities to UMLS CUIs, without utilizing training samples provided by this task.

2.3 Task 2 – Disorder Slot Filling

The task is to identify eight types of disorder modifiers, including negation indicator (NI), subject class (SC), uncertainty indicator (UI), course class (CC), severity class (SV), conditional class (CO), generic class (GC) and body location (BL). For each of the first seven types of modifiers, we built SVMs-based individual classifiers. The implementation of SVMs in LibShortText package (Yu et al., 2013) was used for this purpose. The LibShortText package is an open source library for large-scale short-text classification.

We systematically extracted the following features to train SVMs classifiers, including:

1). N-gram features. All unigrams and bigrams in the sentence were extracted as features.

2). Context words with position and direction (left or right) information. Here we describe the features using the following sentence: "*patient said he has no acute distress before*". There is one disorder ('distress') in this sentence.

Group-1 features: context words within the window size of 1 to disorder: ['acute_L1', 'before_R1']

Group-2 features: context words within the window size of 4 to disorder: ['he_L4', 'has_L4', 'no_L4', 'acute_L4', 'before_R4']

Group-3 features: context words within window size range of 5 to 8: ['patient_L8', 'said_L8']

3). Lexicon features, including word lists for negation, pseudo-negation, conjunction, condition, uncertainty, subject, severity, and course.

4). Dependency relation features. We used the Stanford Parser to generate dependency relations of a sentence. We only counted dependency relations where a target disorder is the governor or the dependent in the relation. We extracted all these syntactic relations as features.

5). Section names, e.g. '*Family History*'.

The final set of features was optimized based on the performance of cross-validation of the training set for each modifier.

* http://www.cs.cornell.edu/people/tj/svm_light/svm_hmm.html

The body location modifiers require specification of the text spans and the corresponding UMLS CUIs. Therefore, we first built a NER system for body location entities and then applied the same encoding approach, similar to the methods used in disorder identification task. We also constructed a comprehensive body location dictionary from UMLS and WordNet (Miller, 1995). The relative positions of the target disorder and the candidate body location were extracted as features (e.g., whether the body location is part of the target disorder). For body location encoding, we extended VSM-based lookup method by adding a regression-based re-ranking layer trained from the training corpus.

2.4 Submissions and Evaluation

We combined training and development datasets to build our final models for all tasks. Since each task allows for three submissions, we tried different strategies for the three runs. For Task 1, run 0 and run 1 used the ensemble^{MV} method to get better F1; while run 2 used the ensemble^{ML} method to get higher precision, in disorder entity recognition. For Task 2A and Task 2B, run 0 and run 2 used two sets of parameters optimized for better weighted performances; while run 1 used a set of parameters optimized for un-weighted performance. For body location recognition, only run 2 of Task 2A used SSVMs model, all other runs used CRFs models for better prediction.

The evaluation metrics for this task include F-1 score (strict vs. relaxed), un-weighted accuracy, and weighted accuracy etc., as defined by the organizers. For more details, please refer to the task description paper or the task website[†].

3 Results and Discussion

For Task 1, the main evaluation scores were strict F1. Table 1 shows the overall performance of three runs of our system in Task 1 as reported by the organizer, where 'P', 'R', 'F' denotes precision, recall, and F1 score respectively. Our best run of Task 1 ranked 3rd among all participants. Our disorder entity recognition step actually achieved the highest F1 of 0.927 under 'relaxed' criterion (please see Table 2). The performance of disorder encoding was not as good as other top performed teams in task 1, because we used a general encoding module that did not use the CUI annotations in the training/development set for training.

Run	Strict			Relaxed		
	P	R	F	P	R	F
0	.748	.713	.730	.777	.741	.759
1	.748	.713	.730	.777	.741	.759
2	.778	.696	.735	.797	.714	.753

Table 1. The performances of the three runs of our system on Task 1.

As reported by the organizers, our system achieved the best performance in Task 2, both for Task 2A - slot filling given gold-standard disorder spans and Task 2B - end-to-end system for disorder span identification and slot filling. Table 2 shows the overall performance of our systems in Task 2A and Task 2B. 'F,' 'A', and 'WA' denotes 'relaxed' F1 score for disorder entity recognition, overall unweighted and weighted accuracy respectively.

Task	Run	F	A	F*A	WA	F*WA
2A	0	1.00	.943	.943	**.886**	**.886**
	1	1.00	**.953**	**.953**	.876	.876
	2	1.00	.943	.943	**.886**	**.886**
2B	0	**.927**	.940	.872	.872	**.808**
	1	**.927**	**.949**	**.880**	.862	.800
	2	.907	.943	.855	**.880**	.798

Table 2. The overall performances of our system on Task 2.

4 Conclusion

In this paper, we described our participation in the SemEval-2015 challenge – Task 14 "Analysis of Clinical Text". Our system was among the top ranked systems (ranked 3rd for Task 1, 1st for Task 2A and Task 2B). These results show that machine learning based methods, integrated with medical domain specific features, could reasonably identify disorders and associated modifiers from clinical narratives.

Acknowledgments

This study is supported in part by grants from NLM 2R01LM010681-05, NIGMS 1R01GM103859 and

† http://alt.qcri.org/semeval2015/task14/index.php

1R01GM102282, and CPRIT R1307. The first author is partially supported by NSFC 61203378.

References

Aronson, A. R., and Lang, F. M. 2010. An Overview of MetaMap: Historical Perspective and Recent Advances. *Journal of the American Medical Informatics Association*, 17(3):229-236.

Collobert, R., Weston, J., et al. 2011. Natural Language Processing (Almost) from Scratch. *Journal of Machine Learning Research*, 12:2493-2537.

Friedman, C., Alderson, P. O., et al. 1994. A General Natural-Language Text Processor for Clinical Radiology. *Journal of the American Medical Informatics Association*, 1(2):161-174.

Kelly, L., Goeuriot, L., et al. (2014). Overview of the ShARe/CLEF eHealth Evaluation Lab 2014. In E. Kanoulas, M. Lupu, et al. (Eds.), *Information Access Evaluation. Multilinguality, Multimodality, and Interaction* (Vol. 8685, pp.172-191): Springer International Publishing.

Lafferty, J. D., McCallum, A., et al. 2001. Conditional Random Fields: Probabilistic Models for Segmenting and Labeling Sequence Data. In *Proceedings of the Eighteenth International Conference on Machine Learning*. pp.282-289.

Miller, G. A. 1995. WordNet: A Lexical Database for English. *Communications of the ACM*, 38(11):39-41.

Okazaki, N. 2007. *CRFsuite: a Fast Implementation of Conditional Random Fields (CRFs).* http://www.chokkan.org/software/crfsuite/

Pradhan, S., Elhadad, N., et al. 2014. SemEval-2014 Task 7: Analysis of Clinical Text. In *Proceedings of the 8th International Workshop on Semantic Evaluation (SemEval 2014)*. pp.54-62. Dublin, Ireland.

Savova, G. K., Masanz, J. J., et al. 2010. Mayo clinical Text Analysis and Knowledge Extraction System (cTAKES): Architecture, Component Evaluation and Applications. *Journal of the American Medical Informatics Association*, 17(5):507-513.

Suominen, H., Salanterä, S., et al. (2013). Overview of the ShARe/CLEF eHealth Evaluation Lab 2013. In P. Forner, H. Müller, et al. (Eds.), *Information Access Evaluation. Multilinguality, Multimodality, and Visualization* (Vol. 8138, pp.212-231): Springer Berlin Heidelberg.

Uzuner, O., South, B. R., et al. 2011. 2010 i2b2/VA Challenge on Concepts, Assertions, and Relations in Clinical Text. *Journal of the American Medical Informatics Association*, 18(5):552-556.

Yu, H.-F., Ho, C.-H., et al. 2013. *LibShortText: A Library for Short-text Classification and Analysis.* http://www.csie.ntu.edu.tw/~cjlin/libshorttext

Zhang, Y., Wang, J., et al. 2014. UTH_CCB: A Report for SemEval 2014 – Task 7 Analysis of Clinical Text. In *Proceedings of the 8th International Workshop on Semantic Evaluation (SemEval 2014).* pp.802-806. Dublin, Ireland.

SemEval-2015 Task 15: A Corpus Pattern Analysis Dictionary-Entry-Building Task

Vít Baisa
Masaryk University
xbaisa@fi.muni.cz

Jane Bradbury
University of Wolverhampton
J.Bradbury3@wlv.ac.uk

Silvie Cinková
Charles University
cinkova@ufal.mff.cuni.cz

Ismaïl El Maarouf
University of Wolverhampton
i.el-maarouf@wlv.ac.uk

Adam Kilgarriff
Lexical Computing Ltd
adam@sketchengine.co.uk

Octavian Popescu
IBM Research Center
o.popescu@us.ibm.com

Abstract

This paper describes the first SemEval task to explore the use of Natural Language Processing systems for building dictionary entries, in the framework of Corpus Pattern Analysis. CPA is a corpus-driven technique which provides tools and resources to identify and represent unambiguously the main semantic patterns in which words are used. Task 15 draws on the Pattern Dictionary of English Verbs (www.pdev.org.uk), for the targeted lexical entries, and on the British National Corpus for the input text.

Dictionary entry building is split into three subtasks which all start from the same concordance sample: 1) CPA parsing, where arguments and their syntactic and semantic categories have to be identified, 2) CPA clustering, in which sentences with similar patterns have to be clustered and 3) CPA automatic lexicography where the structure of patterns have to be constructed automatically.

Subtask 1 attracted 3 teams, though none could beat the baseline (rule-based system). Subtask 2 attracted 2 teams, one of which beat the baseline (majority-class classifier). Subtask 3 did not attract any participant.

The task has produced a major semantic multidataset resource which includes data for 121 verbs and about 17,000 annotated sentences, and which is freely accessible.

1 Introduction

It is a central vision of NLP to represent the meanings of texts in a formalised way, amenable to automated reasoning. Since its birth, SEMEVAL (or SENSEVAL as it was then; (Kilgarriff and Palmer, 2000)) has been part of the programme of enriching NLP analyses of text so they get ever closer to a 'meaning representation'. In relation to lexical information, this meant finding a lexical resource which

- identified the different meanings of words in a way that made high-quality disambiguation possible,
- represented those meanings in ways that were useful for the next steps of building meaning representations.

Most lexical resources explored to date have had only limited success, on either front. The most obvious candidates—published dictionaries and WordNets—look like they might support the first task, but are very limited in what they offer to the second.

FrameNet moved the game forward a stage. Here was a framework with a convincing account of how the lexical entry might contribute to building the meaning of the sentence, and with enough meat in the lexical entries (e.g. the verb frames) so that it might support disambiguation. Papers such as (Gildea and Jurafsky, 2002) looked promising, and in 2007 there was a SEMEVAL task on Frame Semantic Structure Extraction (Baker et al., 2007) and in 2010, one on Linking Events and Their Participants (Ruppenhofer et al., 2010).

While there has been a substantial amount of follow-up work, there are some aspects of FrameNet that make it a hard target.

- It is organised around frames, rather than words, so inevitably its priority is to give a coherent account of the different verb senses in a frame, rather than the different senses of an individual verb. This will tend to make it less good for supporting disambiguation.

- Frames are not 'data-driven': they are the work of a theorist (Fillmore) doing his best to make sense of the data for a set of verbs. The prospects of data-driven frame discovery are, correspondingly, slim.
- While FrameNet has worked hard at being systematic in its use of corpus data, FrameNetters looked only for examples showing the verb being used in the relevant sense. From the point of view of a process that could possibly be automated, this is problematic.

An approach which bears many similarities to FrameNet, but which starts from the verb rather than the frame, and is more thoroughgoing in its empiricism, is Hanks's Corpus Pattern Analysis (Hanks and Pustejovsky, 2005; Hanks, 2012; Hanks, 2013).

2 Corpus Pattern Analysis

Corpus Pattern Analysis (CPA) is a new technique of language analysis, which produces the main patterns of use of words in text. Figure 1 is a sample lexical entry from the main output of CPA, the Pattern Dictionary of English Verbs[1] (PDEV).

This tells us that, for the verb *abolish*, three patterns were found. For each pattern it tells us the percentage of the data that it accounted for, its grammatical structure and the semantic type (drawn from a shallow ontology of 225 semantic types[2]) of each of the arguments in this structure. For instance, pattern 1 means: i) that the subject is preferably a word referring to [[Human]] or [[Institution]] (semantic alternation), and ii) that the object is preferably [[Action]], [[Rule]] or [[Privilege]].

It also tells us the implicature (which is similar to a "definition" in a traditional dictionary) of a sentence exemplifying the pattern: that is, if we have a sentence of the pattern **[[Institution | Human]]** `abolish` **[[Action=Punishment | Rule | Privilege]]**, then we know that **[[Institution | Human]]** `formally declares that` **[[Action=Punishment | Rule | Privilege]]** `is no longer legal or operative.` *Abolish* has only one sense. For many verbs, there will be multiple senses, each with one or more pattern.

There are currently full CPA entries for more than 1,000 verbs with a total of over 4,000 patterns. For each verb a random sample of (by default) 250 corpus instances was examined, used to build the lexical entry, and tagged with the senses and patterns they represented. For commoner verbs, more corpus lines were examined. The corpus instances were drawn from the written part of the British National Corpus[3] (BNC).

PDEV has been studied from different NLP perspectives, all mainly involved with Word Sense Disambiguation and semantic analysis (Cinková et al., 2012a; Holub et al., 2012; El Maarouf et al., ; El Maarouf and Baisa, 2013; Kawahara et al., ; Popescu, 2013; Popescu et al., ; Pustejovsky et al., 2004; Rumshisky et al.,). For example, (Popescu, 2013) described experiments in modeling finite state automata on a set of 721 verbs taken from PDEV. The author reports an accuracy of over 70% in pattern disambiguation. (Holub et al., 2012) trained several statistical classifiers on a modified subset of 30 PDEV entries (Cinková et al., 2012c) using morpho-syntactic as well as semantic features, and obtained over 80% accuracy. On a smaller set of 20 high frequency verbs (El Maarouf and Baisa, 2013) reached a similar 0.81 overall F1 score with a supervised SVM classifier based on dependency parsing and named entity recognition features.

The goal of Task 15 at SemEval 2015 are i) to explore in more depth the mechanics of corpus-based semantic analysis and ii) to provide a high-quality standard dataset as well as baselines for the advancement of semantic processing. Given the complexity and wealth of PDEV, a major issue was to select relevant subtasks and subsets. The task was eventually split into three essential steps in building a CPA lexical entry, that systems could tackle separately:

1. *CPA parsing*: all sentences in the dataset to be syntactically and semantically parsed.
2. *CPA clustering*: all sentences in the dataset to be grouped according to their similarities.

[1] http://pdev.org.uk

[2] http://pdev.org.uk/#onto

[3] http://www.natcorp.ox.ac.uk/

1	*Pattern* *Implicature*	**Institution or Human abolishes Action or Rule or Privilege** Institution or Human formally declares that Action = Punishment or Rule or Privilege is no longer legal or operative	58.8%
2	*Pattern* *Implicature*	**Institution 1 or Human abolishes Institution 2 or Human_Role** Institution 1 or Human formally puts an end to Institution 2 or Human_Role	24.4%
3	*Pattern* *Implicature*	**Process abolishes State_of_Affairs** Process brings State_of_Affairs to an end	14.4%

Figure 1: PDEV Entry for *abolish.*

Tag	Definition
subj	Subject
obj	Object
iobj	Indirect Object
advprep	Adverbial Preposition or other Adverbial/Verbal Link
acomp	Adverbial or Verb Complement
scomp	Noun or Adjective complement

Table 1: Syntactic tagset used for subtask 1.

3. *CPA lexicography*: all verb patterns found in the dataset to be described in terms of their syntactic and semantic properties.

3 Task Description

In order to encourage participants to design systems which could successfully tackle all three subtasks, all tasks were to be evaluated on the same set of verbs. As opposed to previous experiments on PDEV, it was decided that the set of verbs from the test dataset would be different from the set of verbs given in the training set. This was meant to avoid limiting tasks to supervised approaches and to encourage innovative approaches, maybe using patterns learnt in an unsupervised manner from very large corpora and other resources. This also implied that the dataset would be constructed so as to make it possible for systems to generalize from the behaviour and description of one set of verbs to a set of unseen verbs used in similar structures, as human language learners do. Although this obviously makes the task harder, it was hoped that this would put us in a better position to evaluate current limits of automatic semantic analysis.

3.1 Subtask 1: CPA Parsing

The CPA parsing subtask focuses on the detection and classification (syntactic and semantic) of the arguments of the verb. The subtask is similar to Semantic Role Labelling (Carreras and Marquez, 2004) that arguments will be identified in the dependency parsing paradigm (Buchholz and Marsi, 2006), using head words instead of phrases.

The syntactic tagset was designed specially for this subtask and kept to a minimum, and the semantic tagset was based on the CPA Semantic Ontology.

In Example (1), this would mean identifying *government* as subject of *abolish*, from the [[Institution]] type, and *tax* as object belonging to [[Rule]]. The expected output is represented in XML format in Example (2).

(1) *In 1981 the Conservative government abolished capital transfer tax capital transfer tax and replaced it with inheritance tax.*

(2) *In 1981 the Conservative* <entity syn='subj' sem='Institution'> **government** </entity> <entity syn='v' sem='-'> **abolished** </entity> *capital transfer* <entity synt='obj' sem='Rule'> **tax** </entity> *capital transfer tax and replaced it with inheritance tax*

The only dependency relations shown are those involving the node verb. Thus, for example, the dependency relation between *Conservative* and *government* is not shown. Also only the relations in Table 1 are shown. The relation between *abolished* and *replaced* is not shown as it is not one of the targeted dependency relations. The input text consisted of individual sentences one word per line with both ID and FORM fields, and in which only the target verb token was pre-tagged.

3.2 Subtask 2: CPA Clustering

The CPA clustering subtask is similar to a Word Sense Discrimination task in which systems have to

Layer	Annotator	dataset	observations	categories	Kappa (Cohen)	F-score
Syn	Annotator 1	both	3,662	5	0.898	0.924
	Annotator 2	train	4,106	5	0.752	0.789
	Annotator 3	test	1,518	5	0.931	0.942
Sem	Annotator 1	both	3,662	108	0.649	0.693
	Annotator 2	train	4,106	113	0.444	0.498
	Annotator 3	test	1,518	75	0.765	0.782

Table 2: Inter-annotator figures where annotators are compared to the expert (annotator 4) who reviewed all the annotations (Microcheck Task 1).

predict which pattern a verb instance belongs to.

With respect to *abolish* (Figure 1), it would involve identifying all sentences containing the verb *abolish* which belonged to the same pattern (one of the patterns in Figure 1) and tagging them with the same number.

3.3 Subtask 3: CPA Automatic Lexicography

The CPA automatic lexicography subtask aims to evaluate how systems can approach the design of a lexicographical entry within CPA's framework.

The input was, as for the other tasks, plain text with node verb identified. The output format was a variant of that shown in Figure 1, simplified to a form which would be more tractable by systems while still being a relevant representation from the lexicographical perspective.

Specifically, contextual roles were discarded and semantic alternations were decomposed into semantic strings[4] so that pattern 1 in Figure 1 would give rise to six strings (with V for the verb, here *abolish*):

```
[[Human]] V [[Action]]
[[Human]] V [[Rule]]
[[Human]] V [[Privilege]]
[[Institution]] V [[Action]]
[[Institution]] V [[Rule]]
[[Institution]] V [[Privilege]]
```

This transformation from the PDEV format as in Figure 1 was done automatically and checked manually. These strings are different to (and generally more numerous than) the patterns evaluated in subtask 2. The goal of this subtask was to generalize sentence examples for each verb and create a list of possible semantic strings. This subtask was autonomous with respect to other subtasks in that participants did not have to return the set of sentences which matched their candidate patterns, patterns were evaluated independently.

[4]See (Bradbury and El Maarouf, 2013).

4 Task Data

4.1 The Microcheck and Wingspread Datasets

All subtasks (except the first) include two setups and their associated datasets: the number of patterns for each verb is disclosed in the first dataset but not in the second. This setup was created to see whether it would influence the results.

The two datasets were also created in the hope that system development would start on the first small and carefully crafted dataset (Microcheck) and only then be tested on a larger and more varied subset of verbs (Wingspread)[5].

4.2 Annotation Process

Both Microcheck and Wingspread start from data extracted from PDEV and the manually pattern-tagged BNC. We took only verbs declared as complete and started by the same lexicographer, so that each verb had been checked twice: once by the lexicographer who compiled the entry and once by the editor-in-chief. Some tagging errors may have slipped in but the tagging is generally of high quality (Cinková et al., 2012a; Cinková et al., 2012b). Additional checks have been performed on Microcheck, since this was the dataset chosen for subtask 1, for which data had to be created. This section describes the annotation process.

PDEV contains only one kind of link between a given pattern and a given corpus instance: each verb token found in the sample is tagged with a pattern identifier, and the pattern then specifies syntactic

[5]The datasets as well as the systems' outputs will soon be made publicly available on the task website.

V	P	I	IMP	%MP	V	P	I	IMP	%MP
boo	2	36	27	0.769	ascertain	2	7	4	0.676
teeter	2	28	23	0.828	totter	2	19	12	0.697
begrudge	2	19	11	0.678	tense	3	37	23	0.628
avert	2	240	230	0.958	belch	3	24	14	0.612
breeze	2	12	7	0.679	attain	3	240	200	0.833
wing	2	22	19	0.867	avoid	3	242	176	0.728
brag	2	29	18	0.692	adapt	4	182	98	0.583
sue	2	247	242	0.980	advise	8	230	84	0.391
bluff	2	25	14	0.673	ask	9	573	299	0.518
afflict	2	179	172	0.961	SUM	59	2,423	1,689	—
bludgeon	2	32	16	0.667	AVERAGE	2.95	121.15	84.45	0.721

Table 3: Statistics on the Wingspread test dataset with V standing for verb, P for patterns, I for instances, IMP for instances of majority pattern, and %MP for proportion of the majority pattern.

V	P	I	IMP	%MP	V	P	I	IMP	%MP
appreciate	2	160	215	0.765	apprehend	3	77	123	0.652
crush	5	62	170	0.413	decline	3	135	201	0.690
continue	7	71	203	0.401					
undertake	2	204	228	0.896	SUM	30	749	1,280	—
operate	8	40	140	0.300	AVERAGE	4.286	107	182.857	0.588

Table 4: Statistics on the Microcheck test dataset; abbreviations as for previous table.

roles and their semantic types. The job in subtask 1 annotation consists of tagging the arguments of each token in the sample, both syntactically and semantically (see Table 1 for tagsets of each layer). The syntactic information was the same as for subtask 3 except that category names were shortened and pairs of categories were merged in two places.[6]

The annotation was carried out by 4 annotators, with 3 for the training data and 3 for test data, and 2 annotators annotating both training and test data, one of them being an expert PDEV annotator. Annotators could ask for feedback on the task at any moment, and any doubts were cleared by the expert annotator. Each pair of annotators annotated one share of the dataset, and their annotation was double-checked by the expert annotator. The agreement was not very high (e.g. Annotator 2, see Table 2) in some cases so the double-check by the expert annotator was crucial. Table 2 reports the agreement in terms of F-score and Cohen's Kappa (Cohen, 1960) between each annotator and the expert annotator.[7]

[6]See http://alt.qcri.org/semeval2015/task15/index.php?id=appendices

[7]The expert did not start from scratch, but from other annotators' work. Since his target was the conformity of the tagging with guidelines as well as with CPA's principles, we maintain that the expert would have produced a very similar output had he not started from the product of other annotators, who themselves used the output of a system to speed up their work.

4.3 Statistics on the Data

Strict rules were implemented to develop a high-quality and consistent dataset:

1. PDEV patterns discriminate exploited[8] uses of a pattern using a different tag; these were left aside for the CPA task.
2. For the test set, when patterns contained at least one semantic type or grammatical category which was not covered in the training set, they were discarded.
3. Only patterns which contained more than 3 examples were kept in the final dataset.

Applying these filters led to the Microcheck dataset, containing 28 verbs (train: 21; test: 7), 378 patterns (train: 306; test: 72) with 4,529 annotated sentences (train: 3,249; test: 1,280) and to the Wingspread dataset set containing 93 verbs (train:

[8]An exploitation corresponds to an anomalous use of a pattern, as in a figurative use.

73; test: 20), 856 patterns (train: 652; test: 204), and 12,440 annotated sentences (train: 10,017; test: 2,423). More detailed figures for the test datasets are provided in Tables 3 and 4.

4.4 Metrics

The final score for all subtasks is the average of F-scores over all verbs (Eq. 1). What varies across subtasks is the way Precision and Recall are defined.

$$\begin{aligned} \mathrm{F1}_{\mathrm{verb}} &= \frac{2 \times \mathrm{Precision}_{\mathrm{verb}} \times \mathrm{Recall}_{\mathrm{verb}}}{\mathrm{Precision}_{\mathrm{verb}} + \mathrm{Recall}_{\mathrm{verb}}} \\ \mathrm{Score}_{\mathrm{Task}} &= \frac{\sum_{i=1}^{n_{\mathrm{verb}}} \mathrm{F1}_{\mathrm{verb}_i}}{n_{\mathrm{verb}}} \end{aligned} \quad (1)$$

Subtask 1. Equation 2 illustrates that Precision and Recall are computed on all tags, both syntactic and semantic. To count as correct, tags had to be set on the same token as in the gold standard.

$$\begin{aligned} \mathrm{Precision} &= \frac{\text{Correct tags}}{\text{Retrieved tags}} \\ \mathrm{Recall} &= \frac{\text{Correct tags}}{\text{Reference tags}} \end{aligned} \quad (2)$$

Subtask 2. Clustering is known to be difficult to evaluate. Subtask 2 used the B-cubed definition of Precision and Recall, first used for coreference (Bagga and Baldwin, 1999) and later extended to cluster evaluation (Amigó et al., 2009). Both measures are averages of the precision and recall over all instances. To calculate the precision of each instance we count all correct pairs associated with this instance and divide by the number of actual pairs in the candidate cluster that the instance belongs to. Recall is computed by interchanging Gold and Candidate clusterings (Eq. 3).

$$\begin{aligned} \mathrm{Precision_i} &= \frac{\mathrm{Pairs_i} \text{ in Candidate found in Gold}}{\mathrm{Pairs_i} \text{ in Candidate}} \\ \mathrm{Recall_i} &= \frac{\mathrm{Pairs_i} \text{ in Gold found in Candidate}}{\mathrm{Pairs_i} \text{ in Gold}} \end{aligned} \quad (3)$$

Subtask 3. This task was evaluated as a slot-filling exercise (Makhoul et al., 1999), so the scores were computed by taking into account the kinds of errors that systems make over the 9 slots: errors of Insertion, Substitution, Deletion. Equation 4 formulates how Precision and Recall are computed.

$$\begin{aligned} \mathrm{Precision} &= \frac{\text{Correct}}{\text{Correct} + \text{Subst} + \text{Ins}} \\ \mathrm{Recall} &= \frac{\text{Correct}}{\text{Correct} + \text{Subst} + \text{Del}} \end{aligned} \quad (4)$$

In order not to penalize systems, the best match was computed for each Candidate pattern, and one candidate pattern could match more than one Gold pattern. When a given slot was filled both in the Gold data and the Candidate data, this counted as a "match". When not, it was a Deletion. If a slot was filled in the run but not in the gold, it was counted as an Insertion. When a match (aligned slots) was also a semantic type match, it was Correct (1 point). When not, it was a Substitution; the CPA ontology was used to allow for partial matches, allowing hypernyms and hyponyms. For that particular task, the maximum number of Candidate patterns was limited to 150% with respect to the number in the Gold set.

5 Evaluation

The evaluation was split into 2 phases (one week for each): a feedback phase and a validation phase. The reason for this was to allow for the detection of unforeseen issues in the output of participants' systems so as to prepare for any major problem. However, this was not put to use by participants since only one team submitted their output in the first phase which also happened to be their final submission.

5 teams[9] participated in the task, but none participated in more than one subtask. Subtask 1 attracted 3 teams and subtask 2 attracted 2, while subtask 3 did not receive any submissions. Systems were allowed 3 runs on each subtask and each dataset, and were asked to indicate which would be the official one. The following subsections report in brief on the main features of their systems (for more details see relevant papers in SemEval proceedings).

5.1 Subtask 1

All systems for this subtask used syntactic dependencies and named entities as features. Since the

[9]Unfortunately, teams BOB90 and FANTASY did not submit articles, so it is difficult to analyze their results.

Category	#Gold	CMILLS	FANTASY	BLCUNLP	baseline
subj	1,008	0.564	0.694	0.739	**0.815**
obj	777	0.659	**0.792**	0.777	0.783
Human	580	0.593	**0.770**	0.691	0.724
Activity	438	0.450	**0.479**	0.393	0.408
acomp	308	0.545	0.418	0.702	**0.729**
LexicalItem	303	0.668	**0.830**	0.771	0.811
advprep	289	0.621	0.517	0.736	**0.845**
State Of Affairs	192	**0.410**	0.276	0.373	0.211
Institution	182	0.441	**0.531**	0.483	0.461
Action	115	0.421	**0.594**	0.526	0.506

Table 6: Detailed scores for subtask 1 (10 most frequent categories).

Team	Score
baseline	0.624
FANTASY	**0.589**
BLCUNLP	0.530
CMILLS	0.516

Table 5: Official scores for subtask 1.

subtask allowed it, some systems used external resources such as Wordnet or larger corpora.

BLCUNLP (Feng et al., 2015) used the Stanford CoreNLP package[10] to get POS, NE and basic dependency features. These features were used to predict both syntax and semantic information. The method did not involve the use of a statistical classifier.

CMILLS (Mills and Levow, 2015) used three models to solve the task: one for argument detection, and the other two for each layer. Argument detection and syntactic tagging were performed using a MaxEnt supervised classifier, while the last was based on heuristics. CMILLS also reported the use of an external resource, the enTentTen12 (Jakubíček et al., 2013) corpus available in Sketch Engine (Kilgarriff et al., 2014).

FANTASY approached the subtask in a supervised setting to predict first the syntactic tags, and then the semantic tags. The team used features from the MST parser[11], as well as Stanford CoreNLP for NE, Wordnet[12], they also applied word embedding representations to predict the output of each layer.

The baseline system was a rule-based system taking as input the output of the BLLIP parser (Charniak and Johnson, 2005), and mapping heads of relevant dependency relations to the most probable tags from subtask 1 tagset. The semantic tags were only then added to those headwords based on the most frequent semantic category found in the training set.

5.2 Subtask 2

As opposed to subtask 1, systems in subtask 2 used very few semantic and syntactic resources.

BOB90 used a supervised approach to tackle the clustering problem. The main features used were preposition analyses.

DULUTH (Pedersen, 2015) used an unsupervised approach and focused on lexical similarity (both first and second order representations) based on unigrams and bigrams (see SenseClusters[13]). The number of clusters was predicted on the basis of the best value for the clustering criterion function. The team also performed some corpus pre-processing, like conversion to lower case and conversion of all numeric values to a string.

The baseline system clusters everything together, so its score depends on the distribution of patterns: the more a pattern covers all instances of the data (majority class), the higher the baseline score.

6 Results

6.1 Subtask 1

As previously noted, subtask 1 provided only one dataset, Microcheck. The results on the test set are

[10] `http://nlp.stanford.edu/software/corenlp.shtml`

[11] `http://www.seas.upenn.edu/~strctlrn/MSTParser/MSTParser.html`

[12] `http://wordnet.princeton.edu/`

[13] `http://senseclusters.sourceforge.net`

described in Table 5: FANTASY is the best system with 0.589 average F1 score, but does not beat the baseline (0.624).

It is worth noting that, on the same set of verbs, BLCUNLP and FANTASY are almost on a par, but since the former did not submit one verb file, the score gap is more significant. FANTASY is a more precise system while BLCUNLP has higher recall.

To get a better picture of the results, Table 6 provides the F-scores for the ten most frequent categories in the test set. We can see that FANTASY has the best semantic model since it gets the highest scores on most semantic categories (except for *State Of Affairs*) and systematically beats the baseline, which assigns a word the most frequent semantic category in the training set. The baseline and BCUNLP however get higher scores on most syntactic relations except on *obj*, where the difference is low. The gap is much more significant on *advprep* and *acomp*, which suggests that FANTASY does not properly handle prepositional complements correctly (and/or causal complements). This could be due to the choice of parser or to model parameters. Overall, it seems that progress can still be made, since systems can benefit from one another.

6.2 Subtask 2

Subtask 2 was evaluated on both datasets. BOB90 only submitted one run while DULUTH submitted three. The results are displayed on Table 7. For this task, only BOB90 beat the baseline with a higher amplitude on Microcheck (+0.153) than on Wingspread (+0.071). This high score welcomes a more detailed evaluation of the system, since it would seem that, as also found for subtask 1, prepositions play a substantial role in CPA patterns and semantic similarity.

It can also be observed that overall results are better on Wingspread. This seems to be mainly due to the higher number of verbs with a large majority class in Wingspread (see Table 3), since the baseline system scores 0.72 on Wingspread, and 0.588 on Microcheck. This shows that when the distribution of patterns is highly skewed, the evaluation of systems is difficult, and tends to underrate potentially useful systems.

Team	Scores	
	Microcheck	Wingspread
BOB90	**0.741**	**0.791**
baseline	0.588	0.720
DULUTH-1 (off)	0.525	0.604
DULUTH-2	0.439	0.581
DULUTH-3	0.439	0.615

Table 7: Official scores for subtask 2.

7 Conclusion

This paper introduces a new SemEval task to explore the use of Natural Language Processing systems for building dictionary entries, in the framework of Corpus Pattern Analysis. Dictionary entry building is split into three subtasks: 1) CPA parsing, where arguments and their syntactic and semantic categories have to be identified, 2) CPA clustering, in which sentences with similar patterns have to be clustered and 3) CPA automatic lexicography where the structure of patterns have to be constructed automatically.

Drawing from the Pattern Dictionary of English Verbs, we have produced a high-quality resource for the advancement of semantic processing: it contains 121 verbs connected to a corpus of 17,000 sentences. This resource will be made freely accessible from the task website for more in depth future research.

Task 15 has attracted 5 participants, 3 on subtask 1 and 2 on subtask 2. Subtask 1 proved to be more difficult for participants than expected, since no system beat the baseline. We however show that the submissions possess interesting features that should be put to use in future experiments on the dataset. Subtask 2's baseline was beaten by one of the participants on a large margin, despite the fact that the baseline is very competitive.

It seems that splitting the task into 3 subtasks has had the benefit of attracting different approaches (supervised and unsupervised) towards the common target of the task, which is to build a dictionary entry. Lexicography is such a complex task that it needs major efforts from the NLP community to support it. We hope that this task will stimulate more research and the development of new approaches to the automatic creation of lexical resources.

Acknowledgments

We are very grateful for feedback on the task from Ken Litkowski as well as from participants who greatly contributed to the overall quality of the task. We would also like to thank SemEval's organizers for their support. The work was also supported by the UK's AHRC grant [DVC, AH/J005940/1, 2012-2015], by the Ministry of Education of Czech Republic within the LINDAT-Clarin project LM2010013, by the Czech-Norwegian Research Programme within the HaBiT Project 7F14047 and by the Czech Science Foundation grant [GA15-20031S].

References

Enrique Amigó, Julio Gonzalo, Javier Artiles, and Felisa Verdejo. 2009. A Comparison of Extrinsic Clustering Evaluation Metrics Based on Formal Constraints. *Information Retrieval*, 12(4):461–486.

Amit Bagga and Breck Baldwin. 1999. Cross-document event coreference: Annotations, experiments, and observations. In *Proceedings of the Workshop on Coreference and its Applications*, pages 1–8.

Collin Baker, Michael Ellsworth, and Katrin Erk. 2007. SemEval-2007 Task 19: Frame Semantic Structure Extraction. In *Proceedings of the Fourth International Workshop on Semantic Evaluations (SemEval-2007)*, pages 99–104, Prague, Czech Republic.

Jane Bradbury and Ismaïl El Maarouf. 2013. An empirical classification of verbs based on Semantic Types: the case of the 'poison' verbs. In *Proceedings of JSSP2013*, pages 70–74, Trento,Italy.

Sabine Buchholz and Erwin Marsi. 2006. CoNLL-X shared task on multilingual dependency parsing. In *Proceedings of CoNLL*, New York, USA.

Xavier Carreras and Lluis Marquez. 2004. Introduction to the CoNLL-2004 shared task: Semantic role labeling. In *Proceedings of CoNLL*, Boston, USA.

Eugene Charniak and Mark Johnson. 2005. Coarse-to-fine n-best parsing and MaxEnt discriminative reranking. In *Proceedings of the 43rd Annual Meeting on Association for Computational Linguistics*, pages 173–180.

Silvie Cinková, Martin Holub, and Vincent Kríž. 2012a. Managing Uncertainty in Semantic Tagging. In *Proceedings of 13th Conference of the European Chapter of the Association for Computational Linguistics*, pages 840–850, Avignon, France.

Silvie Cinková, Martin Holub, and Vincent Kríž. 2012b. Optimizing semantic granularity for NLP - report on a lexicographic experiment. In *Proceedings of the 15th EURALEX International Congress*, pages 523–531, Oslo, Norway.

Silvie Cinková, Martin Holub, Adam Rambousek, and Lenka Smejkalová. 2012c. A database of semantic clusters of verb usages. In *Proceedings of the 8th International Conference on Language Resources and Evaluation (LREC 2012)*, pages 3176–3183, Istanbul, Turkey.

Jacob Cohen. 1960. A Coefficient of Agreement for Nominal Scales. *Educational and Psychological Measurement*, 20(1):37–46.

Ismaïl El Maarouf and Vít Baisa. 2013. Automatic classification of semantic patterns from the Pattern Dictionary of English Verbs. In *Proceedings of JSSP2013*, pages 95–99, Trento, Italy.

Ismaïl El Maarouf, Jane Bradbury, Vít Baisa, and Patrick Hanks. Disambiguating Verbs by Collocation: Corpus Lexicography meets Natural Language Processing. In *Proceedings of LREC*, pages 1001–1006, Reykjavik, Iceland.

Yukun Feng, Qiao Deng, and Dong Yu. 2015. BLCUNLP: Corpus Pattern Analysis for Verbs Based on Dependency Chain. In *Proceedings of SemEval 2015*, Denver, USA.

Daniel Gildea and Daniel Jurafsky. 2002. Automatic Labeling of Semantic Roles. *Computational Linguistics*, 28(3):245–288, September.

Patrick Hanks and James Pustejovsky. 2005. A Pattern Dictionary for Natural Language Processing. *Revue Française de linguistique applique*, 10:2.

Patrick Hanks. 2012. How people use words to make meanings: Semantic types meet valencies. In A. Boulton and J. Thomas, editors, *Input, Process and Product: Developments in Teaching and Language Corpora*, pages 54–69. Brno.

Patrick Hanks. 2013. *Lexical Analysis: Norms and Exploitations*. MIT Press, Cambridge, MA.

Martin Holub, Vincent Kríž, Silvie Cinková, and Eckhard Bick. 2012. Tailored Feature Extraction for Lexical Disambiguation of English Verbs Based on Corpus Pattern Analysis. In *Proceedings of the 24th International Conference on Computational Linguistics (Coling 2012)*, pages 1195–1209, Mumbai, India.

Miloš Jakubíček, Adam Kilgarriff, Vojtěch Kovář, Pavel Rychlý, and Vít Suchomel. 2013. The TenTen Corpus Family. In *Proceedings of the International Conference on Corpus Linguistics.*

Daisuke Kawahara, Daniel W Peterson, Octavian Popescu, and Martha Palmer. Inducing Example-based Semantic Frames from a Massive Amount of Verb Uses. In *Proceedings of the 14th Conference of the European Chapter of the Association for Computational Linguistics*, pages 58–67.

Adam Kilgarriff and Martha Palmer. 2000. Introduction to the Special Issue on SENSEVAL. *Computers and the Humanities*, 34:1–2.

Adam Kilgarriff, Vít Baisa, Jan Bušta, Miloš Jakubíček, Vojtěch Kovář, Jan Michelfeit, Pavel Rychlý, and Vít Suchomel. 2014. The Sketch Engine: ten years on. *Lexicography*, 1(1):7–36.

John Makhoul, Francis Kubala, Richard Schwartz, and Ralph Weischedel. 1999. Performance Measures For Information Extraction. In *Proceedings of DARPA Broadcast News Workshop*, pages 249–252.

Chad Mills and Gina-Anne Levow. 2015. CMILLS: Adapting SRL Features to Dependency Parsing. In *Proceedings of SemEval 2015*, Denver, USA.

Ted Pedersen. 2015. Duluth: Word Sense Discrimination in the Service of Lexicography. In *Proceedings of SemEval 2015*, Denver, USA.

Octavian Popescu, Martha Palmer, and Patrick Hanks. Mapping CPA onto OntoNotes Senses. In *Proceedings of LREC*, pages 882–889, Reykjavik, Iceland.

Octavian Popescu. 2013. Learning corpus patterns using finite state automata. In *Proceedings of the 10th International Conference on Computational Semantics*, pages 191–203, Potsdam, Germany.

James Pustejovsky, Patrick Hanks, and Anna Rumshisky. 2004. Automated Induction of Sense in Context. In *Proceedings of COLING*, Geneva, Switzerland.

Anna Rumshisky, Patrick Hanks, Catherine Havasi, and James Pustejovsky. Constructing a corpus-based ontology using model bias. In *Proceedings of FLAIRS*, pages 327–332, Melbourne, FL.

Josef Ruppenhofer, Caroline Sporleder, Roser Morante, Collin Baker, and Martha Palmer. 2010. SemEval-2010 Task 10: Linking Events and Their Participants in Discourse. In *5th International Workshop on Semantic Evaluation*, pages 45–50, Uppsala, Sweden.

BLCUNLP: Corpus Pattern Analysis for Verbs Based on Dependency Chain

Yukun Feng, Qiao Deng and **Dong Yu**[†]
College of Information Science, Beijing Language and Culture University
No.15 Xueyuan Rd., Beijing, China, 100083. †The corresponding author.
{fengyukun,dengqiao,yudong}@blcu.edu.cn

Abstract

We implemented a syntactic and semantic tagging system for SemEval 2015 Task 15: Corpus Pattern Analysis. For syntactic tagging, we present a Dependency Chain Search Algorithm that is found to be effective at identifying structurally distant subjects and objects. Other syntactic labels are identified using rules defined over dependency parse structures and the output of a verb classification module. Semantic tagging is performed using a simple lexical mapping table combined with post-processing rules written over phrase structure constituent types and named entity information. The final score of our system is 0.530 F1, ranking second in this task.

1 Introduction

Corpus Pattern Analysis (CPA) is an important language analysis technique, which attempts to describe the patterns of word usage in text. In this paper, we present the system we developed for SemEval-2015 Task 15: CPA, Subtask1: CPA parsing. The system operates in two stages: syntactic tagging and semantic tagging. We first search for the syntactic roles of a verb's arguments in a sentence. We use the following tag set for the syntactic roles: "subj" is for subject, "obj" is for object, "iobj" is for indirect object, "advprep" is for adverbial preposition or other adverbial/verbal link, "acomp" is for adverbial or verb complement, and "scomp" is for noun or adjective complement. For example, take a sentence whose core verb is "plan": "Mr Eigen plans to wage his war diplomatically". The correct tagging of syntactic and semantic roles is: Mr [**subj/Human** Eigen] plans [**advprep/LexicalItem** to] [**acomp/Activity** wage] his war diplomatically.

Due to time constraints, we put more effort into improving the accuracy of syntactic tagging. We rely on simpler techniques for semantic tagging. For syntactic tagging, we use Stanford CoreNLP to extract linguistic attributes, deduce dependency chains through dependency relations and to classify verbs. When performing semantic tagging, we use a data driven mapping of words to their most frequent semantic tag in the task's training data in conjunction with a small number of post-processing rules.

2 Our Methods

2.1 System Framework

Our system consists of five modules (Figure 1). The first module is Preprocessing, which generates input files with the correct format for Stanford CoreNLP to extract linguistic attributes.

The second module is Linguistic Attributes. For the syntactic layer, tagged arguments must have direct or indirect dependency relations with the core verb. Dependency relations are thus a critical attribute for correctly selecting tagged units and types. We employ a number of additional linguistic attributes for our tagging rules: parts of speech (POS) provide useful information for syntactic tagging; direct dependency relations and phrase type are helpful in identifying and following a dependency chain. Last, named entity (NE) tags and phrase-structure constituent types contribute to semantic tagging. In general, we extract four categories of attributes from sentences: dependency relations, POS tags, phrase-structure parse, and NE.

The third module is Verb Classification. Even when a verb's dependency relations with related

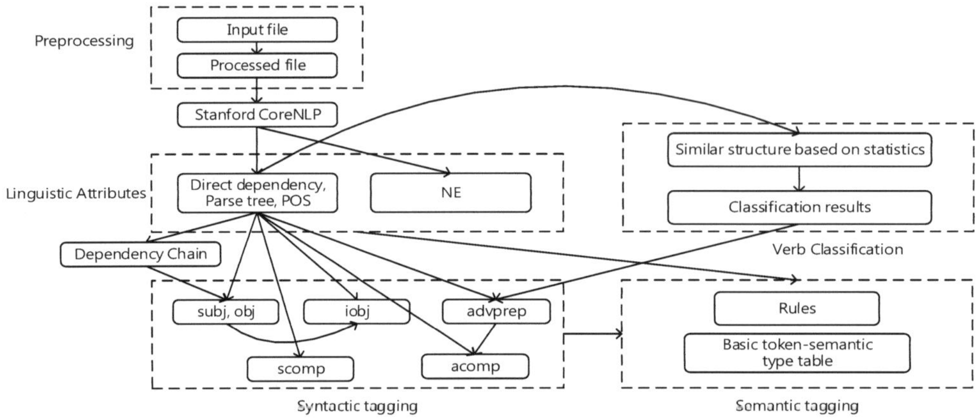

Figure 1. The system has five modules: Preprocessing, Linguistic Attributes, Verb classification, Syntactic tagging, and Semantic tagging. First, it preprocesses input files and extracts 4 attributes: direct dependency, parse tree, POS, and NE. Second, it uses the first three attributes for syntactic tagging, during which indirect dependencies are deduced for "subj" and "obj" relations, and verbs are classified as candidates for "advprep" tagging. Last, our system uses all four attributes and some post-processing rules to do semantic tagging.

prepositions are the same, we find that different verbs have varying degrees of preference for an "advprep" argument. For example, both "abandon" and "account" can be followed by "for", yet only "account" is tagged as "advprep". According to corpus statistics, "account" frequently co-occurs with prepositions. The Verb Classification module is designed to decide whether a verb is strongly related to prepositions, allowing the use of this information in our tagging rules.

The fourth module is the Syntactic Tagging. This module assigns syntactic tags using a set of rules that operate over the annotations provided by the Linguistic Attributes module. When tagging "subj" and "obj" with basic dependency relations, we observed that many of the tagged arguments have no direct dependency relation with the core verb. We handle these arguments by performing a heuristic search for the subj or obj of the nearest ancestor having the missing relation. We find that this is an effective approach.

The last module is Semantic Tagging. The training data provides us with plenty of semantically tagged words, and most of the tagged words have only one corresponding semantic type. We construct a word to semantic tag mapping heuristic based on the most frequent tag for each word in the training set. Semantic tags are related to certain NE tags and phrase-structure constituent types. For instance, person name is normally tagged as "Human", and a place is often tagged as "Location". To capture this, we augment our mapping table with a small number of semantic tagging rules.

2.2 Linguistic Attribute Extraction

We use the Stanford CoreNLP toolkit to get word-to-word dependency relations, phrase-structure parse trees, POS, and NE attributes. Our system rewrites some of the syntactic tags. For example, the CoreNLP tag "nsubj" is replaced by "subj" in train data. Table 1 shows the aggregation of all of the linguistic attributes used by the tagging modules in our system.

Attributes	Description
dependent ID	Sequence number in dependency tree
dependent	Dependent token
phrase type	Phrase type
POS	Part of speech
NE	Named entity type
governor-dependent type	Dependency relation
governor	Governor token
governor ID	Sequence number of the governor

Table 1. Attributes used for syntactic and semantic tagging.

2.3 Verb Classification

Before tagging, we divide verbs into two categories according to the relationship between the verb and its related prepositions, which leads to better "advprep" tagging. Our system gathers corpus statistics that cue the affinity of each verb for the advprep relation. Specifically, we compute how often the verb takes a direct prepositional argument and how often the direct prepositional argument is adjacent to the verb:

$$P(\text{DirectPrep} \mid V) = \frac{\text{cnt}(\text{DirectPrep and } V)}{\text{cnt}(V)}$$

$$P(\text{Adjacent}|\text{DirectPrep}, V) = \frac{\text{cnt}(\text{Adjacent}, \text{DirectPrep and } V)}{\text{cnt}(\text{DirectPrep and } V)}$$

Here, cnt(V) is the total number of sentences that contain the verb V, cnt(DirectPrep and V) is the number of sentences where the verb V has a direct prepositional argument, and cnt(Adjacent, DirectPrep and V) counts sentences where the verb not only has a direct dependency relation but is also directly adjacent to the preposition. Take the verb "account" as an example, according to our statistics, P(DirectPrep|V) of "account" is 0.9241, and P(Adjacent|DirectPrep, V) is 0.8425. Therefore, we can tell that "account" is strongly related to prepositions. Through considerable experiments, we set up two threshold values to decide whether one verb is related to certain prepositions. When P(DirectPrep|V)>=0.45 and P(Adjacent|DirectPrep, V)>=0.5, the current verb is considered to be related to prepositions.

2.4 Syntactic Tagging

2.4.1 subj and obj

For both subj and obj tagging, we first check whether the verb has any direct subj and obj dependencies. When such dependencies exist, we use them directly to assign the subj or obj tag. If a subj or obj is not contained in the direct dependency relations, we carry out our Dependency Chain Search Algorithm to attempt to find and tag a near-by possibly related subj or obj. Figure 2 illustrates this algorithm for subj relations.

```
goverWordID = GetGoverWordID(verbID);
for goverWordID != TREE_ROOT_NODE
   POS = GetPOSofID(goverWordID);
   if POS == "VP"
         subjID = GetDirectSubjID(goverWordID);
         if subjID != "null"
               Tagging(subjID, "subj");
          break;
   goverWordID = GetGoverWordID(goverWordID);
```

Figure 2. Dependency Chain Search Algorithm.

Figure 3 illustrates the operation of this algorithm. The first column of the table is the dependent word with its id, the second is POS, the third is dependency relation, and the forth is govern id.

(8) Court	NP	nsubj	16
(9) of	PP	prep	8
(10) law	NP	pobj	9
(11) in	PP	prep	10
(14) Kingdom	NP	pobj	11
(15) would	VP	aux	16
(16) need	VP	ccomp	5
(18) evidence	NP	dobj	16
(19) before	PP	prep	16
(20) becoming	VP	pcomp	19
(21) willing	ADJP	scomp	20
(23) abandon	VP	xcomp	21

Figure 3. An example of the Dependency Chain Search algorithm at work. The algorithm traverses five dependency relations to find that "court" is the subject of "abandon".

2.4.2 iobj

For tokens whose indirect dependency relation with the verb is "iobj", we tag it directly. To increase coverage, we build a table which contains common double object verbs. If the core verb belongs to this table, we replace the original tag "obj" with "iobj".

2.4.3 advprep

As for prepositions which have direct dependency relations with core verbs and their POS are "PP", we check the category of the verb generated by the Verb Classification module. We produce the "advprep" tag only if the verb is heuristically identified as a good candidate for this relation, otherwise we abandon tagging.

2.4.4 acomp

As for tokens whose dependency type with verb is ccomp" or "xcomp", and if its POS is "VP" or its governor's POS is "VP", we tag it with "acomp". For tokens whose tag is "advprep", we search downward for a near-by word whose dependency type is "pobj" and then tag it with "acomp".

2.4.5 scomp

When a token has the dependency type "acomp" within the dependency relations produced by Stanford CoreNLP, it is tagged with "scomp".

2.5 Semantic Tagging

We extract words and their semantic types from the SemEval2015 training data, and populate a word-to-semantic-type mapping table with the most frequent semantic type for each word. We then apply the following semantic tagging rules:

1) If the phrase type of the current token is "WHNP", we tag it as "Anything", or if the token itself is "who", "whom", then we tag it as "Human".
2) If the phrase type of the current token is "SBAR" or "WHADVP", then we tag its semantic type as "LexicalItem".
3) If the NE type of the current token is "NUMBER", we tag it as "Numerical Value".
4) If the NE type of the current token is "PERSON", we tag it as "Human".
5) Else, we tag it according to the word-to-semantic-type mapping table.

3 Evaluation Results

Our syntactic and semantic tagging results from the official evaluation are shown in Table 2. During the official evaluation, we failed to upload the "undertake" file, which lead to a comparatively lower score on this task.

Verbs	syntactic tagging			semantic tagging		
	P	R	F	P	R	F
operate	.462	.635	.535	.348	.278	.309
apprehend	.749	.634	.687	.669	.403	.503
appreciate	.795	.735	.764	.718	.489	.581
continue	.857	.776	.814	.701	.495	.580
crush	.788	.679	.729	.561	.296	.388
decline	.862	.862	.862	.660	.474	.552
undertake	.000	.000	.000	.000	.000	.000

Table 2. Syntactic and semantic tagging results.

The final overall F-score of our system is 0.53, ranking second on the task, with the baseline system achieving 0.624. This F-score is calculated by averaging the F-scores achieved on syntactic and semantic tagging. On the evaluation data, if we ignore the "undertake" file that we failed to upload, the average F-score of syntactic tagging increases to 0.732, and the combined overall score increases to 0.619. Similar to our work, the baseline methods are also rule based, but we observe that our rules underperform the baseline. We believe this is because we used a simpler rule set that we spent less time refining for the semantic task.

4 Conclusions

In this paper, we propose simple but reliable techniques for syntactic and semantic tagging. These techniques were shown to perform well within SemEval 2015 Task 15: Corpus Pattern Analysis. We find that an effective way to accomplish "subj" and "obj" syntactic tagging is to utilize our simple Dependency Chain Search algorithm. We also incorporated verb classification using simple rules based on corpus statistics to increase syntactic tagging accuracy.

Acknowledgments

We would like to thank the anonymous reviewers for their helpful suggestions and comments. The research work is funded by the Natural Science Foundation of China (No.61300081, 61170162), and the Fundamental Research Funds for the Central Universities in BLCU (No. 15YJ030006).

References

Patrick Hanks. 2004. *Corpus Pattern Analysis.* In EURAALEX Proceedings. Vol. I, pp. 87-98. Lorient, France: Université de Bretagne-Sud.

Marie-Catherine de Marneffe and Christopher D. *Manning, Stanford typed dependencies manual.* 2008.

Bradbury, Jane and El Maarouf, Ismail. 2013. *An empirical classification of verbs based on Semantic Types: the case of the 'poison' verbs"* . In Proceedings of JSSP.

Buchholz, Sabine and Marsi, Erwin. 2006. *CoNLL-X shared task on multilingual dependency parsing.* In Proceedings of CoNLL, New York.

Carreras, Xavier and Marquez, Lluis. 2004. *Introduction to the CoNLL-2004 shared task: Semantic role labeling.* In Proceedings of CoNLL, Boston.

Hanks, Patrick, and Pustejovsky, James. 2005. *A Pattern Dictionary for Natural Language Processing* . In Revue Française de linguistique appliquée, 10:2.

El Maarouf, Ismail and Baisa, Vít. 2013. *Automatic classification of semantic patterns from the Pattern Dictionary of English Verbs.* In Proceedings of JSSP.

Popescu, Octavian. 2012. *Building a Resource of Patterns Using Semantic Types.* In Proceedings of LREC, Istanbul.

WSD-games: a Game-Theoretic Algorithm for Unsupervised Word Sense Disambiguation

Rocco Tripodi **Marcello Pelillo**
Ca' Foscari University of Venice
Via Torino 155
30172 Venezia, Italy
{rocco.tripodi, pelillo}@unive.it

Abstract

In this paper we present an unsupervised approach to word sense disambiguation based on evolutionary game theory. In our algorithm each word to be disambiguated is represented as a node on a graph and each sense as a class. The algorithm performs a consistent class assignment of senses according to the similarity information of each word with the others, so that similar words are constrained to similar classes. The dynamics of the system are formulated in terms of a non-cooperative multi-player game, where the players are the data points to decide their class memberships and equilibria correspond to consistent labeling of the data.

1 Introduction

Word sense disambiguation (WSD) is the task to identify the intended sense of a word in a computational manner based on the context in which it appears (Navigli, 2009). It has been studied since the beginning of NLP (Weaver, 1955) and also today it is a central topic of this discipline. Many algorithms have been proposed during the years, based on supervised (Zhong and Ng, 2010; Tratz et al., 2007), semi-supervised (Pham et al., 2005) and unsupervised (Mihalcea, 2005; McCarthy et al., 2007) learning models. Nowadays, even if supervised methods perform better in general domains, unsupervised and semi-supervised models are gaining attention from the research community with performances close to the state of the art (Ponzetto and Navigli, 2010). In particular Knowledge-based and graph based algorithms are emerging as interesting ways to face the problem (Agirre et al., 2009; Sinha and Mihalcea, 2007). The peculiarities of those algorithms are that they do not require any corpus evidence and use only the structural properties of a lexical database to perform the disambiguation task.

An unsupervised algorithm which has been implemented in different ways by the community (Mihalcea et al., 2004; Haveliwala, 2002; Agirre et al., 2014; De Cao et al., 2010) is the PageRank (Page et al., 1999). This algorithm is similar in spirit to ours but we instead of using the graph to compute the most important nodes (senses) in it, we use the network to model the geometry of the data and the interactions among the data points. In our system the nodes of the graph are interpreted as players, in the game theoretic sense (see Section 2), which play a game in order to maximize their utility. The concept of utility has been used in different ways in the game theory (GT) literature and in general it refers to the satisfaction that a player derives from the outcome of a game (Szabó and Fath, 2007). From our point of view increasing the utility of a word means increasing the textual coherence, in a distributional semantics perspective (Firth, 1957). In fact, in our framework a word always tries to chose a sense close to the senses which the other words in the text are likely to choose.

The starting point of our research is based on the assumption that the meaning of a sentence emerges from the interaction of the components which are involved in it. In our study we tried to model this interaction and to develop a system in which it is possible to map lexical items onto concepts. For this reason we decided to use a powerful tool, derived from Evolutionary Game Theory (EGT): the non-cooperative games (see Section 2). EGT and GT have been used in different ways to study the language use (Pietarinen, 2007; Skyrms, 2010) and evolution (Nowak et al., 2001) but as far as we know, our is the first attempt to use it in a specific NLP task. This choice is motivated by the fact that GT models are able to perform a consistent labeling of the data (Hummel and Zucker, 1983; Pelillo, 1997), taking into account the contextual information. These features are of great importance for an unsupervised algorithm which tries to perform a WSD task, because them can be obtained without any supervision and help the system to adapt to different contextual domains.

2 Game Theory

In this section we briefly introduce some concepts of GT and EGT, for detailed analysis of these topics we refer to (Weibull, 1997; Leyton-Brown and Shoham, 2008; Sandholm, 2010).

GT provides predictive power in interactive decision situations. It has been introduced by Von Neumann and Morgenstern (1944) and in its normal form representation (which is the one we will use in our algorithm) it consists in: a finite set of players $I = (1, .., n)$, a set of pure strategies for each player $S_i = (s_1, ..., s_n)$ and an utility function $u_i : S_1 \times ... \times S_n \rightarrow \mathbb{R}$ which associates strategies to payoffs. The utility function depends on the combination of two strategies played together, not just on the strategy of a single player. An important assumption in GT is that the players are rational and try to maximize the value of u_i; furthermore in *non-cooperative games* the players choose their strategies independently. A strategy s_i^* is said to be *dominant* if and only if $u_i(s_i^*, s_{-i}) > u_i(s_i, s_{-i}), \forall s_{-i} \in S_{-i}$. As an example we can consider the famous *Prisoner's Dilemma* (in Table 1) where the strategy $confess$ is a *dominant strategy* for both players and this strategy combination is the *Nash equilibrium* of the game. Nash equilibria are those strategy profiles which are best response to the strategy of the co-player and no player has the incentive to unilaterally deviate from his strategy, because there is no way to do better.

1 \ 2	confess	don't confess
confess	-5,-5	0,-6
don't confess	-6,0	-1,-1

Table 1: The Prisoner's Dilemma.

2.1 Evolutionary Game Theory

EGT has been introduce by Smith and Price (1973) overcoming some limitations of traditional GT such as the hyper-rationality imposed on the players, in fact in real life situations the players choose a strategy according to heuristics or social norms (Szabó and Fath, 2007). Another important aspect of EGT is the introduction of an *inductive learning* process, in which the agents play the game repeatedly with their neighborhood, updating their believes on the state of the game and choosing their strategy accordingly. The strategy space of each player is defined as a probability distribution over its pure strategies. It is represented as a vector $x_i = (x_{i1}, \ldots, x_{im})$ where m is the number of pure strategies and each component x_{ih} denotes the probability that player i choose its hth pure strategy. The strategy space lies on the m-dimensional standard simplex Δ_m where: $\sum_{h=1}^{m} x_{ih} = 1$ and $x_{ih} \geq 0$ for all h. The expected payoff of a pure strategy e^h in a single game is $u(e^h, x) = e^h \cdot Ax$ where A is the $m \times m$ payoff matrix. The average payoff of all the player strategies is $u(x, x) = \sum_{h \in S} x_h u(e^h, x)$. In order to find the Nash equilibria of the game it is used the replicator dynamic equation (Taylor and Jonker, 1978)

$$\dot{x} = [u(e^h, x) - u(x, x)] \cdot x^h \; \forall h \in S \qquad (1)$$

which allows better than average strategies (best replies) to grow. As in (Erdem and Pelillo, 2012) we used the discrete time version of the replicator dynamic equation:

$$x^h(t+1) = x^h(t) \frac{u(e^h, x)}{u(x, x)} \; \forall h \in S \qquad (2)$$

where at each time step t the players update their strategies until the system converges and the Nash equilibria are found.

3 WSD Games

In this section we will show how we created the data necessary for our framework and how the games are played.

3.1 Graph Construction

We model the geometry of the data as a graph, with nodes corresponding to the words to be disambiguated, denoted by $I = \{i_j\}_{j=1}^{N}$, where i_j corresponds to the j-th word and N is the number of target words in a specific text. From I we construct a $N \times N$ similarity matrix W where each element w_{ij} is the similarity value assigned for the words i and j. W can be exploited as an useful tool for graph-based algorithms since it is treatable as weighted adjacency matrix of a weighted graph.

A crucial factor for the graph construction is the choice of the similarity measure, $sim(\cdot,\cdot) \rightarrow \mathbb{R}$ to weights the edges of the graph. For our experiments we used similarity measures which compute the strength of co-occurrence between any two words i_i and i_j

$$w_{ij} = sim(i_i, i_j)\ \forall i, j \in I : i \neq j \tag{3}$$

Specifically we used the modified Dice coheffi-cient ($mDice$) (Dice, 1945), the pointwise mutual information (PMI) (Church and Hanks, 1990) and the log likelihood ratio (D^2) (Dunning, 1993) These measure have been calculate using the Google Web1T corpus (Brants and Franz, 2006), a large collection of n-grams (with a window of max 5 words) occurring in one terabyte of Web documents as collected by Google.

At this point we have the similarity graph W, we recall that we will use this matrix in order to allow the words to play the games only with similar words. The higher the similarity among two words, the higher the reciprocal influence and the possibility that they belong to a similar class. For this reason, at first we smooth the data in W and then choose only the most significant js for each $j \in W$. The first point is solved using a gaussian kernel on W, $w_{ij} = \exp(-\frac{w_{ij}^2}{2\sigma^2})$, where σ is the kernel width parameter; the second point is solved applying a $k - nearest\ neighbor$ algorithm to W, which allows us to remove the edges which are less significant for each $i \in I$. In our experiments we used $\sigma = 0.5$ and $k = 25$. Moreover, this operation reduces the computational cost of the algorithm, which will focus only on relevant similarities.

3.2 The Strategy Space

In order to create the strategy space of the game, we first use WordNet (Mallery, 1995) to collect the sense inventories $M_i = 1, \ldots, m$ of each word, where m is the number of synsets associated to word i. Then we set all the sense inventories and obtain the list of all possible senses, $C = 1, \ldots, c$.

We can now define the strategy space S of the game in matrix form as:

$$\begin{matrix} s_{i1} & s_{i2} & \cdots & s_{ic} \\ \vdots & \vdots & \cdots & \vdots \\ s_{n1} & s_{n2} & \cdots & s_{nc} \end{matrix}$$

where each row corresponds to the strategy space of a player and each column corresponds to a sense. Formally it is a c-dimensional space Δ_c and each mixed strategy profile lives in the mixed strategy space of the game, given by the Cartesian product $\Theta = \times_{i \in I} \Delta_i$.

At this point the strategy space can be initialized with the following formula in order to follow the constraints described in Section 2.1

$$s_{ij} = \begin{cases} |M_i|^{-1}, & \text{if sense } j \text{ is in } M_i. \\ 0, & \text{otherwise.} \end{cases} \tag{4}$$

for all $i \in I$ and $j \in S$.

3.3 The Payoff Matrix

We encoded the payoff matrix of a WSD game as a sense similarity matrix among all the senses in the strategy spaces of the game. In this way the higher the similarity among two sense candidates, the higher the incentive for a player to chose that sense, and play the strategy associated to it.

The $c \times c$ sense similarity matrix Z is defined as follows:

$$z_{ij} = ssim(s_i, s_j)\ \forall i, j \in C : i \neq j \tag{5}$$

In our experiments we used the $GlossVector$ measure (Patwardhan and Pedersen, 2006) in order to compute the semantic relatedness $ssim(\cdot,\cdot)$. This measure calculates the cosine similarity among two second order context vectors. Each vector is obtained from a WordNet super-glosse, which is the gloss of a synset plus the glosses of the synsets related to it.

run	sim	P	R	F1	math	med.	gen.
1	PMI	57.4	48.9	52.8	47.4	56.3	53.5
2	$mDice$	58.8	50.0	54.1	48.5	58.4	53.5
3	D^2	53.5	45.4	49.1	43.4	54.4	46.7

Table 2: The results of the WSD-games team at SemEval-2015 task 13. Precision, Recall and F1 in all domains and F1 in specific domains.

From Z we can obtain the partial semantic similarity matrix for each pair of player, $Z_{ij} = m \times n$, where m and n are the senses of i and j in Z.

In a previous work (Tripodi et al., 2015) we did not use this information, instead we used labeled data points to propagate the class membership information over the graph. In this new version the use of the semantic information made the algorithm completely unsupervised.

3.4 System Dynamics

Now that we have the topology of the data W, the strategy space of the game S and the payoff matrix Z we can compute the Nash equilibria of the game according to equation (2). So in each iteration of the system each player gain its payoffs according to equation (6) which allows each payoff to be proportional to the similarity (w_{ij}) and to the affinity that player j has to the hs strategy of player i.

$$u_i(e^h, x) = \sum_{j \in N_i} ((w_{ij} Z_{ij}) x_j)_h \quad (6)$$

When the system converges each player chooses the strategy with the highest value.

4 Results and Analysis

The dataset proposed by the organizers of SemEval-2015 Task 13 (Moro and Navigli, 2015) consists of five texts from three different domains: math and computer, biomedical and general. The english corpus is composed of 1426 instances to disambiguate and 1262 of them have been used in the evaluation. For our experiments we used only the instances whose lemma has an entry in WordNet 3.0 without looking up multi-words or trying to link the entities to other sources such as Wikipedia or BabelNet (Navigli and Ponzetto, 2012)

We submitted three runs for our system with 1227 single words disambiguated for each run. The only difference for each run is the similarity measure that we used to construct the graph W. For run-1 we used the PMI measure, for run-2 the $mDice$ coefficient and for run-3 the D^2. As we expected from previous experiments on similar datasets, the best results have been achieved using the $mDice$ coefficient (see Table 2). We obtained low recall values for all our runs and this because we did not search multi-words and did not use other sources of information for the named entities, in fact the number of named entities is limited in WordNet.

Looking more closely at the results, we noticed that we obtained a very low precision (48.5%) in the math and computer domain and this because even if the lexical entry of certain instances (eg. in text2: *tab*, *dialog*, *script*) have an entry in WordNet, their intended meaning is not present; it can only be accessible to those systems which use BabelNet to collect the sense inventories. This unexpected problem affects the performances of the system because even if those instances will not be considered in the evaluation, they have been used by other instances in our system to play the disambiguation games, compromising the dynamics of the system.

5 Conclusions and Future Works

We have presented an unsupervised system for WSD based on EGT which takes into account contextual similarity and semantic similarity information in order to perform a consistent labeling of the data. Its performances are below those of supervised systems and are comparable with unsupervised and semi-supervised systems even if on the Semeval-2015 task 13 dataset we did not use other source of information except WordNet, did not search multi-words and did not aspect that the intended meaning of some instances is not present in WordNet.

As future work we are planning to do a detailed evaluation of the system in order to find the most appropriate measures to use and to incorporate in the framework other sources of information like BabelNet. Furthermore we are also thinking to test the system as supervised and semi-supervised, implementing a new initialization of the strategy space and to test new graph construction techniques.

References

Eneko Agirre, Oier Lopez De Lacalle, Aitor Soroa, and Informatika Fakultatea. 2009. Knowledge-based WSD and Specific Domains: Performing Better than Generic Supervised WSD. In *IJCAI*, pages 1501–1506.

Eneko Agirre, Oier Lopez de Lacalle, and Aitor Soroa. 2014. Random Walks for Knowledge-Based Word Sense Disambiguation. *Computational Linguistics*, 40(1):57–84.

Thorsten Brants and Alex Franz. 2006. {Web 1T 5-gram Version 1}.

Kenneth Ward Church and Patrick Hanks. 1990. Word Association Norms, Mutual Information, and Lexicography. *Computational linguistics*, 16(1):22–29.

Diego De Cao, Roberto Basili, Matteo Luciani, Francesco Mesiano, and Riccardo Rossi. 2010. Robust and Efficient PageRank for Word Sense Disambiguation. In *Proceedings of the 2010 Workshop on Graph-based Methods for Natural Language Processing*, pages 24–32.

Lee R. Dice. 1945. Measures of the amount of ecologic association between species. *Ecology*, 26(3):297–302.

Ted Dunning. 1993. Accurate Methods for the Statistics of Surprise and Coincidence. *Computational linguistics*, 19(1):61–74.

Aykut Erdem and Marcello Pelillo. 2012. Graph Transduction as a Noncooperative Game. *Neural Computation*, 24(3):700-723.

John R. Firth. 1957. A Synopsis of Linguistic Theory 1930-1955. *Studies in linguistic analysis. Oxford: Blackwell.*

Taher H. Haveliwala. 2002. Topic-Sensitive PageRank. In *Proceedings of the 11th international conference on World Wide Web*, pages 517–526.

Robert A. Hummel and Steven W. Zucker. 1983. On the Foundations of Relaxation Labeling Processes. *Pattern Analysis and Machine Intelligence, IEEE Transactions on*, (3):267–287.

Kevin Leyton-Brown and Yoav Shoham. 2008. Essentials of Game Theory: A Concise Multidisciplinary Introduction. *Synthesis Lectures on Artificial Intelligence and Machine Learning*, 2(1):1–88.

John C. Mallery. 1995. WordNet: a Lexical Database for English. *Communications of the ACM*, 38(11):39-41.

Diana McCarthy, Rob Koeling, Julie Weeds, and John Carroll. 2007. Unsupervised Acquisition of Predominant Word Senses. *Computational Linguistics*, 33(4):553–590.

Rada Mihalcea, Paul Tarau, and Elizabeth Figa. 2004. PageRank on Semantic Networks, with Application to Word Sense Disambiguation. In *Proceedings of the 20th international conference on Computational Linguistics*, page 1126.

Rada Mihalcea. 2005. Unsupervised Large-Vocabulary Word Sense Disambiguation with Graph-Based Algorithms for Sequence Data Labeling. In *Proceedings of the conference on Human Language Technology and Empirical Methods in Natural Language Processing*, pages 411–418.

Andrea Moro and Roberto Navigli. 2015. SemEval-2015 Task 13: Multilingual All-Words Sense Disambiguation and Entity Linking. In *Proceedings of SemEval-2015.*

Roberto Navigli and Simone Paolo Ponzetto. 2012. BabelNet: The Automatic Construction, Evaluation and Application of a Wide-Coverage Multilingual Semantic Network. *Artificial Intelligence*, 193:217–250.

Roberto Navigli. 2009. Word Sense Disambiguation: A Survey. *ACM Computing Surveys (CSUR)*, 41(2):10.

Martin A. Nowak, Natalia L. Komarova, and Partha Niyogi. 2001. Evolution of Universal Grammar. *Science*, 291(5501):114–118.

Lawrence Page, Sergey Brin, Rajeev Motwani, and Terry Winograd. 1999. The PageRank Citation Ranking: Bringing Order to the Web.

Siddharth Patwardhan and Ted Pedersen. 2006. Using WordNet-Based Context Vectors to Estimate the Semantic Relatedness of Concepts. In *Proceedings of the EACL 2006 Workshop Making Sense of Sense-Bringing Computational Linguistics and Psycholinguistics Together*, volume 1501, pages 1–8.

Marcello Pelillo. 1997. The Dynamics of Nonlinear Relaxation Labeling Processes. *Journal of Mathematical Imaging and Vision*, 7(4):309–323.

Thanh Phong Pham, Hwee Tou Ng, and Wee Sun Lee. 2005. Word Sense Disambiguation with Semi-Supervised Learning. In *Proceedings of the National Conference on Artificial Intelligence*, volume 20, page 1093.

Ahti-Veikko Pietarinen. 2007. *Game theory and linguistic meaning.*

Simone Paolo Ponzetto and Roberto Navigli. 2010. Knowledge-Rich Word Sense Disambiguation Rivaling Supervised Systems. In *Proceedings of the 48th annual meeting of the association for computational linguistics*, pages 1522–1531.

William H. Sandholm. 2010. *Population games and evolutionary dynamics.*

Ravi Som Sinha and Rada Mihalcea. 2007. Unsupervised Graph-based Word Sense Disambiguation Using Measures of Word Semantic Similarity. In *ICSC*, volume 7, pages 363–369.

Brian Skyrms. 2010. *Signals: Evolution, learning, and information.*

John M. Smith and George R. Price. 1973. The Logic of Animal Conflict. *Nature*, 246:15.

György Szabó and Gabor Fath. 2007. Evolutionary Games on Graphs. *Physics Reports*, 446(4):97-216.

Peter D. Taylor and Leo B. Jonker. 1978. Evolutionary Stable Strategies and Game Dynamics. *Mathematical biosciences*, 40(1):145–156.

Stephen Tratz, Antonio Sanfilippo, Michelle Gregory, Alan Chappell, Christian Posse, and Paul Whitney. 2007. PNNL: A Supervised Maximum Entropy Approach to Word Sense Disambiguation. In *Proceedings of the 4th International Workshop on Semantic Evaluations*, pages 264–267.

Rocco Tripodi, Marcello Pelillo, and Rodolfo Delmonte. 2015. An Evolutionary Game Theoretic Approach to Word Sense Disambiguation. In *Proceedings of NLPCS 2014.*

John Von Neumann and Oskar Morgenstern. 1944. *Theory of Games and Economic Behavior (60th Anniversary Commemorative Edition).*

Warren Weaver. 1955. Translation. *Machine translation of languages*, 14:15-23.

Jörgen W. Weibull. 1997. *Evolutionary game theory.*

Zhi Zhong and Hwee Tou Ng. 2010. It Makes Sense: A Wide-Coverage Word Sense Disambiguation System for Free Text. In *Proceedings of the ACL 2010 System Demonstrations*, pages 78–83.

DFKI: Multi-objective Optimization for the Joint Disambiguation of Entities and Nouns & Deep Verb Sense Disambiguation

Dirk Weissenborn
LT, DFKI
Alt-Moabit 91c
Berlin, Germany
dirk.weissenborn@dfki.de

Feiyu Xu
LT, DFKI
Alt-Moabit 91c
Berlin, Germany
feiyu@dfki.de

Hans Uszkoreit
LT, DFKI
Alt-Moabit 91c
Berlin, Germany
uszkoreit@dfki.de

Abstract

We introduce an approach to word sense disambiguation and entity linking that combines a set of complementary objectives in an extensible multi-objective formalism. During disambiguation the system performs continuous optimization to find optimal probability distributions over candidate senses. Verb senses are disambiguated using a separate neural network model. Our results on noun and verb sense disambiguation as well as entity linking outperform all other submissions on the SemEval 2015 Task 13 for English.

1 Introduction

The task of assigning the correct meaning to a given word or entity mention in a document is called word sense disambiguation (WSD) (Navigli, 2009) or entity linking (EL) (Bunescu and Pasca, 2006), respectively. Successful disambiguation requires not only an understanding of the topic or domain a document is dealing with (global), but also an analysis of how an individual word is used within its local context. E.g., the meanings of the word "newspaper" as the company or the physical product, often cannot be distinguished by the topic, but by recognizing which type of meaning fits best into the local context of its occurrence. On the other hand, for an ambiguous entity mention such as "Michael Jordan" it is important to recognize the topic of the wider context to distinguish, e.g., between the basketball player and the machine learning expert.

The combination of the two most commonly used reference knowledge bases for WSD and EL, e.g., WordNet (Fellbaum, 1998) and Wikipedia, by BabelNet (Navigli and Ponzetto, 2012) has enabled a new line of research towards the joint disambiguation of words and named entities. *Babelfy* (Moro et al., 2014) has shown the potential of combining these two tasks in a purely knowledge-driven approach that jointly finds connections between potential word senses in the global context. On the other hand, typical supervised methods (Zhong and Ng, 2010) trained on sense-annotated corpora are usually quite successful in dealing with individual words in a local context. Hoffart et al. (2011) recognize the importance of combining both local context and global context for robust disambiguation. However, their approach is limited to EL, where optimization is performed in a discrete setting.

We present a system that combines disambiguation objectives for both global and local contexts into a single multi-objective function. In contrast to prior work we model the problem in a continuous setting based on probability distributions over candidate meanings. Our approach exploits lexical and encyclopedic knowledge, local context information and statistics of the mapping from text to candidate meanings. Furthermore, we introduce a deep learning approach to verb sense disambiguation based on semantic role labeling.

2 Approach

The SemEval-2015 task 13 (Moro and Navigli, 2015) requires a system to jointly detect and disambiguate word and entity mentions given a reference knowledge base. The provided input to the system are tokenized, lemmatized and POS-tagged documents; the output are sense-annotated mentions.

Our system employs BabelNet 1.1.1 as reference knowledge base (KB). BabelNet is a multilingual semantic graph of concepts and named entities that are represented by synonym sets, called *Babel synsets*.

2.1 Mention Extraction & Entity Detection

We define a mention to be a sequence of tokens in a given document for which there exists at least one candidate meaning in the KB. The system considers all content words (nouns, verbs, adjectives, adverbs) as mentions including also multi-token words of up to 5 tokens that contain at least one noun. In addition, we apply a pre-trained stacked linear-chain CRF (Lafferty et al., 2001) using the FACTORIE toolkit of version 1.1 (McCallum et al., 2009) to identify named entity (NE) mentions. In our approach, we distinguish NEs from common nouns and treat them as two different classes because there are many common nouns also referring to NEs making disambiguation unnecessarily complicated.

2.2 Candidate Search

After potential mentions are extracted the system tries to identify their candidate meanings, i.e., the appropriate synsets. Mentions without such candidates are discarded. The mapping of candidate mentions to synsets is based on similarities of their surface strings or lemmas. If the surface string or lemma of a mention matches the lemma of a synonym in a synset that has the same part of speech, the synset will be considered a candidate meaning. We allow partial matches for BabelNet synonyms derived from Wikipedia titles or redirections. A partial match allows the surface string of a mention to differ by up to two tokens from the Wikipedia title (excluding everything in parentheses) if the partial string was used at least once as an anchor for the corresponding Wikipedia page. For example, for the Wikipedia title Armstrong_School_District_(Pennsylvania), the following surface strings would be considered matches: "Armstrong School District (Pennsylvania)", "Armstrong School District", "Armstrong", but not "School", since "School" was never used as an anchor. If there is no match we try the same procedure applied to the lowercased text or lemma.

Because of the distinction between nouns and named entities we treat NE as a separate POS tag. Candidate synsets for NEs are Babel synsets considered NEs in BabelNet, and additionally Babel synsets of all Wikipedia senses that are not considered NEs. Similarly, candidate synsets for nouns are noun synsets that are not considered NEs in addition to all synsets of WordNet senses in BabelNet. We add synsets of Wikipedia senses and WordNet senses, respectively, because the distinction of NEs and simple concepts is not always clear in BabelNet. For example the synset for "UN" (United Nations) is considered a concept whereas it could also be considered a NE. Finally, if there is no candidate for a potential noun mention we try to find NE candidates for it and vice versa.

2.3 Disambiguation of Nouns and Named Entities

We formulate the disambiguation problem in a continuous setting by using probability distributions over candidates. This has several advantages over a discrete setting. First, we can exploit well established continuous optimization algorithms, such as conjugate gradient or LBFGS, which guarantee to converge to a local optimum. Second, by optimizing upon probability distributions we are optimizing the actually desired result in contrast to densest subgraph algorithms where such probabilities need to be calculated artificially afterwards, e.g., Moro et al. (2014). Third, discrete optimization usually works on a single candidate per iteration whereas in a continuous setting, probabilities are adjusted for each candidate, which is computationally advantageous for highly ambiguous documents.

Given a set of objectives $\mathfrak{O}$ the overall objective function $\mathbf{O}$ is defined as the sum of all normalized objectives $O \in \mathfrak{O}$ given a set of mentions M:

$$\mathbf{O}(M) = \sum_{O \in \mathfrak{O}} \frac{O(M)}{O_{max}(M) - O_{min}(M)}. \quad (1)$$

We normalize each objective using the difference of their maximum and minimum value for the given document. For disambiguation we optimize the multi-objective function using Conjugate Gradient (Hestenes and Stiefel, 1952) with up to 1000 iterations per document.

Coherence Jointly disambiguating all mentions within a document has been shown to have a large impact on disambiguation quality. We adopt the idea of semantic signatures and the idea of maximizing the semantic agreement among selected candidate senses from Moro et al. (2014). We define the continuous objective function based on probability distributions $p_m(c)$ over the candidate set C_m of each mention $m \in M$ in a document as follows:

$$O_{\text{coh}}(M) = \sum_{\substack{m \in M \\ c \in C_m}} \sum_{\substack{m' \in M \\ m' \neq m \\ c' \in C_{m'}}} s(m, c, m', c')$$

$$s(m, c, m', c') = p_m(c) \cdot p_{m'}(c') \cdot \mathbb{1}((c, c') \in S)$$

$$p_m(c) = \frac{e^{\lambda_{m,c}}}{\sum_{c' \in C_m} e^{\lambda_{m,c'}}}, \qquad (2)$$

where S denotes the semantic interpretation graph, $\mathbb{1}$ the indicator function and $p_m(c)$ is a softmax function. The only free, optimizable parameters are the softmax weights $\lambda_{m,c}$. This objective can be interpreted as finding the densest subgraph of the semantic interpretation graph where each node is weighted by its probability and therefore each edge is weighted by the product of its adjacent vertex probabilities.

Type Classification One of the biggest problems of supervised approaches to WSD is the size and synset coverage of training corpora such as SemCor (Miller et al., 1993). One way to circumvent this problem is to use a coarser set of semantic classes that groups synsets together. Previous studies on using semantic classes for disambiguation showed promising results (Izquierdo-Beviá et al., 2006). WordNet provides a mapping, called lexnames, of synsets into 45 types based on the syntactic categories of synsets and their logical groupings[1].

A multi-class logistic (softmax) regression model was trained that calculates a probability distribution $q_m(t)$ over lexnames t given a potential WordNet mention m. The features used as input to the model are the following: embedding of the mention's text, sum of embeddings of all sentence words, embedding of the dependency parse parent, collocations of surrounding words (Zhong and Ng, 2010), surrounding POS tags and possible lexnames. We used pre-trained embeddings from Mikolov et al. (2013).

Type classification is included in the overall objective in the following form:

$$O_{\text{typ}}(M) = \sum_{\substack{m \in M \\ c \in C_m}} q_m(t_c) \cdot p_m(c) \qquad (3)$$

Priors Another advantage of working with probability distributions over candidates is the easy integration of prior information. E.g., the word "Paris" without further context has a strong prior on its meaning as a city instead of a person. Our approach utilizes prior information in form of frequency statistics over candidate synsets for a mention's surface string. These priors are derived from annotation frequencies provided by WordNet for Babelsynsets containing the respective WordNet sense and from occurrence frequencies in Wikipedia extracted by DBpedia Spotlight(Daiber et al., 2013) for synsets containing only Wikipedia senses. Laplace-smoothing is applied to all prior frequencies. This prior is used to initialize the probability distribution over candidate synsets. Note that the priors are used "naturally", i.e., as actual priors and not during context based optimization itself.

Furthermore, because candidate priors for NE mentions can be very high we add an additional L2-regularization objective for NE mentions with $\lambda = 0.001$, which we found to work best on development data. Finally, named entities were filtered out if they were included in another NE, had no connection in the semantic interpretation graph with another candidate sense of the input document or were overlapping with another NE but were connected worse.

2.4 Disambiguation of Verbs

The disambiguation of verbs requires an approach that focuses more on the local context and especially the usage of a verb within a sentence. Therefore, we train a neural network based on semantic role labeling (SRL) and sentence words. Figure 1 illustrates an example network. The input is composed of the word embeddings (Turian et al., 2010) for each feature (word itself, its lemma, SRLs and bag of sentence words). All individual input embeddings are

[1] http://wordnet.princeton.edu/man/lexnames.5WN.html

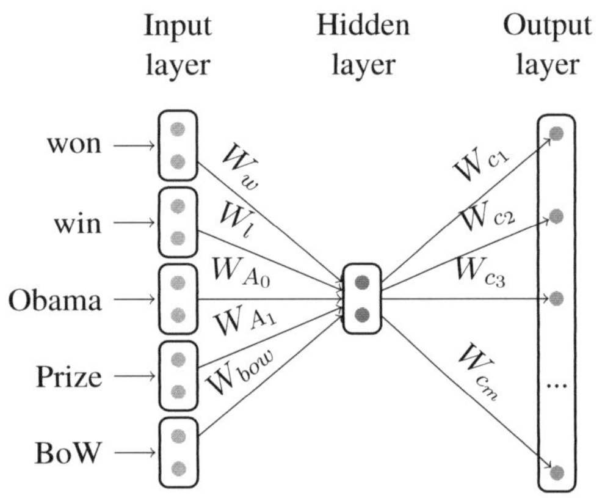

Figure 1: Disambiguation neural network for "won" in the sentence *"Obama won the Nobel Prize."*

50-dimensional and connected to a 100-dimensional hidden layer. The output layer consists of all candidate synsets of the verb. The individual output weights W_c are candidate specific. To ensure better generalization and to deal with the sparseness of training corpora, W_c is defined as the following sum:

$$W_c = W_{s(c)} + \sum_{s_p \in P_{s(c)}} W_{s_p} + \sum_{s_e \in E_{s(c)}} W_{s_e}, \quad (4)$$

where $s(c)$ is the respective synset of c, P_s is the set of all *hypernyms* of s (transitive closure) and E_s are the synsets *entailed* by s. We used ClearNLP[2](Choi, 2012) for extracting SRLs.

3 Results

The results of our system are shown in Table 1. Our approaches to the disambiguation of English nouns, named entities and verbs generally outperformed all other submissions across different domains as well as the strong baseline provided by the most-frequent-sense (MFS). This demonstrates the system's capability to adapt to different domains. However, results on the *math and computer* domain also reveal that performance strongly depends on the document topic. The results for this domain are worse compared to the other domains for almost all participating systems, which may indicate that existing resources do not cover this domain as well as the others. Another potential explanation is that enforcing only pairwise coherence does not take the hidden topics *computer* and *maths* into account that connect all concepts in the specific document. This might be an interesting point for further research.

[2]http://clearnlp.wikispaces.com

	bio	math	gen	all
MFS	75.3	43.6	69.2	66.7
best other	76.5	**51.4**	63.7	64.8
DFKI	**79.1**	44.9	**73.4**	**70.3**

(a) Nouns

	bio	math	gen	all
MFS	98.9	57.1	77.4	85.7
best other	98.9	**74.3**	89.7	87.0
DFKI	**100.0**	57.1	**90.3**	**88.9**

(b) Named Entities

	bio	math	gen	all
MFS	52.5	55.7	61.4	55.1
best other	53.8	**60.6**	**70.6**	57.1
DFKI	**58.3**	52.3	66.7	**57.7**

(c) Verb

Table 1: F1 scores of our system, the best other system and an MFS baseline on the disambiguation of English nouns, named entities and verbs for all domains of the SemEval 2015 task 13. *bio- biomedical; math- math & computer; gen- general*

4 Conclusion

We have presented a robust approach for disambiguating nouns and named entities as well as a neural network for verb sense disambiguation that we used in the SemEval 2015 task 13. Our system achieved an overall F1 score of 70.3 for nouns, 88.9 for NEs and 57.7 for verbs across different domains, outperforming all other submissions for these categories of English. The disambiguation of nouns and named entities performs especially well compared to other systems and can still be extended through the introduction of additional, complementary objectives. Disambiguating verbs remains a very challenging task and the promising results of our model still leave much room for improvement.

Acknowledgment

This research was partially supported by the German Federal Ministry of Education and Research (BMBF) through the projects Deependance (01IW11003), ALL SIDES (01IW14002) and

BBDC (01IS14013E) and by Google through a Focused Research Award granted in July 2013.

References

[Bunescu and Pasca2006] Razvan C Bunescu and Marius Pasca. 2006. Using encyclopedic knowledge for named entity disambiguation. In *EACL*, volume 6, pages 9–16.

[Choi2012] Jinho D Choi. 2012. Optimization of natural language processing components for robustness and scalability.

[Daiber et al.2013] Joachim Daiber, Max Jakob, Chris Hokamp, and Pablo N Mendes. 2013. Improving efficiency and accuracy in multilingual entity extraction.

[Fellbaum1998] Christiane Fellbaum. 1998. *WordNet*. Wiley Online Library.

[Hestenes and Stiefel1952] Magnus Rudolph Hestenes and Eduard Stiefel. 1952. *Methods of conjugate gradients for solving linear systems*, volume 49. National Bureau of Standards Washington, DC.

[Hoffart et al.2011] Johannes Hoffart, Mohamed Amir Yosef, Ilaria Bordino, Hagen Fürstenau, Manfred Pinkal, Marc Spaniol, Bilyana Taneva, Stefan Thater, and Gerhard Weikum. 2011. Robust disambiguation of named entities in text. In *Proceedings of the Conference on Empirical Methods in Natural Language Processing*, pages 782–792. Association for Computational Linguistics.

[Izquierdo-Beviá et al.2006] Rubén Izquierdo-Beviá, Lorenza Moreno-Monteagudo, Borja Navarro, and Armando Suárez. 2006. Spanish all-words semantic class disambiguation using cast3lb corpus. In *MICAI 2006: Advances in Artificial Intelligence*, pages 879–888. Springer.

[Lafferty et al.2001] John Lafferty, Andrew McCallum, and Fernando CN Pereira. 2001. Conditional random fields: Probabilistic models for segmenting and labeling sequence data.

[McCallum et al.2009] Andrew McCallum, Karl Schultz, and Sameer Singh. 2009. FACTORIE: Probabilistic programming via imperatively defined factor graphs. In *Neural Information Processing Systems (NIPS)*.

[Mikolov et al.2013] Tomas Mikolov, Ilya Sutskever, Kai Chen, Greg S Corrado, and Jeff Dean. 2013. Distributed representations of words and phrases and their compositionality. In *Advances in Neural Information Processing Systems*, pages 3111–3119.

[Miller et al.1993] George A Miller, Claudia Leacock, Randee Tengi, and Ross T Bunker. 1993. A semantic concordance. In *Proceedings of the workshop on Human Language Technology*, pages 303–308. Association for Computational Linguistics.

[Moro and Navigli2015] Andrea Moro and Roberto Navigli. 2015. SemEval-2015 Task 13: Multilingual All-Words Sense Disambiguation and Entity Linking. In *Proc. of SemEval-2015*.

[Moro et al.2014] Andrea Moro, Alessandro Raganato, and Roberto Navigli. 2014. Entity linking meets word sense disambiguation: A unified approach. *Transactions of the Association for Computational Linguistics*, 2.

[Navigli and Ponzetto2012] Roberto Navigli and Simone Paolo Ponzetto. 2012. Babelnet: The automatic construction, evaluation and application of a wide-coverage multilingual semantic network. *Artificial Intelligence*, 193:217–250.

[Navigli2009] Roberto Navigli. 2009. Word sense disambiguation: A survey. *ACM Computing Surveys (CSUR)*, 41(2):10.

[Turian et al.2010] Joseph Turian, Lev Ratinov, and Yoshua Bengio. 2010. Word representations: a simple and general method for semi-supervised learning. In *Proceedings of the 48th Annual Meeting of the Association for Computational Linguistics*, pages 384–394. Association for Computational Linguistics.

[Zhong and Ng2010] Zhi Zhong and Hwee Tou Ng. 2010. It makes sense: A wide-coverage word sense disambiguation system for free text. In *Proceedings of the ACL 2010 System Demonstrations*, pages 78–83. Association for Computational Linguistics.

EBL-Hope: Multilingual Word Sense Disambiguation Using A Hybrid Knowledge-Based Technique

Eniafe Festus Ayetiran
CIRSFID, University of Bologna
Via Galliera, 3 - 40121
Bologna, Italy
eniafe.ayetiran2@unibo.it

Guido Boella
Department of Computer Science
University of Turin
Turin, Italy
boella@di.unito.it

Abstract

We present a hybrid knowledge-based approach to multilingual word sense disambiguation using BabelNet. Our approach is based on a hybrid technique derived from the modified version of the Lesk algorithm and the Jiang & Conrath similarity measure. We present our system's runs for the word sense disambiguation subtask of the Multilingual Word Sense Disambiguation and Entity Linking task of SemEval 2015. Our system ranked 9th among the participating systems for English.

1 Introduction

The computational identification of the meaning of words in context is called Word Sense Disambiguation (WSD), also known as Lexical Disambiguation. There have been a significant amount of research on WSD over the years with numerous different approaches being explored. Multilingual word sense disambiguation aims to disambiguate the target word in different languages. This, however, involves a different scenario compared to monolingual WSD in the sense that a single word in a language might have varying number of senses in other languages with significant differences in the semantics of some of the available senses.

Approaches to word sense disambiguation may be: (1) knowledge-based which depends on some knowledge dictionary or lexicon (2) supervised machine learning techniques which train systems from labelled training sets and (3) unsupervised which is based on unlabelled corpora, and do not exploit any manually sense-tagged corpus to provide a sense choice for a word in context.

We present a hybrid knowledge-based approach based on the Modified Lesk algorithm and the Jiang & Conrath similarity measure using BabelNet (Navigli and Ponzetto, 2012). The system presented here is an adaptation of our earlier work on monolingual word sense disambiguation in English (Ayetiran et al., 2014).

2 Methodology

Figure 1 illustrates the general architecture of our hybrid disambiguation system.

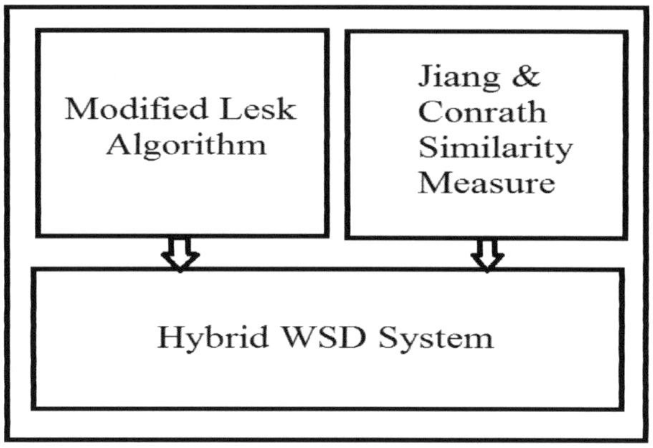

Figure 1: The Hybrid Word Sense Disambiguation System - A system that combines two distinct disambiguation submodules.

2.1 The Lesk Algorithm

Micheal Lesk (1986) invented this approach named gloss overlap or the Lesk algorithm. It is one of the first algorithms developed for the semantic disambiguation of all words in unrestricted texts. The only resource required by the algorithm is a set of dictionary entries, one for each possible word sense, and knowledge about the immediate context where the sense disambiguation is performed. The idea behind the Lesk algorithm represents the seed for today's corpus-based algorithms. Almost every supervised WSD system relies one way or the other on some form of contextual overlap, with the overlap being typically measured between the context of an ambiguous word and contexts specific to various meanings of that word, as learned from previously annotated data.

The main idea behind the original definition of the algorithm is to disambiguate words by finding the overlap among their sense definitions. Namely, given two words, W_1 and W_2, each with NW_1 and NW_2 senses defined in a dictionary, for each possible sense pair W_{1_i} and W_{2_j}, $i = 1, ..., NW_1$, $j = 1, ..., NW_2$, we first determine the overlap of the corresponding definitions by counting the number of words they have in common. Next, the sense pair with the maximum overlap is selected, and therefore the sense is assigned to each word in the text as the appropriate sense. Several variations of the algorithm have been proposed after the initial work of Lesk. Ours follow the work of Banerjee and Pedersen (2002) who adapted the algorithm using WordNet (Miller, 1990) and the semantic relations in it.

2.2 Jiang & Conrath Similarity Measure

Jiang & Conrath similarity (Jiang & Conrath, 1997) is a similarity metric derived from corpus statistics and the WordNet lexical taxonomy. The method makes use of information content (IC) scores derived from corpus statistics (Reisnik 1995) to weight edges in the taxonomy. Edge weights are set to the difference in IC of the concepts represented by the two connected notes.

For this algorithm, Reisnik (1995)'s IC measure is augmented with the notion of path length between concepts. This approach includes the information content of the concepts themselves along with the information content of their lowest common subsumer. A lowest common subsumer is a concept in a lexical taxonomy which has the shortest distance from the two concepts compared. They argue that the strength of a child link is proportional to the conditional probability of encountering an instance of the child sense s_i given an instance of its parent sense. The resulting formula can be expressed in Equation (1) below:

$$\begin{aligned} Dist(w_1, w_2) &= IC(s_1) + IC(s_2) \\ &\quad -2 \times IC(Lsuper(s_1, s_2)) \end{aligned} \tag{1}$$

Where s_1 and s_2 are the first and second senses respectively and LSuper (lowest common subsumer) is the lowest super-ordinate of s1 and s2. IC is the information content given by equation (2):

$$IC(c) = log^{-1}P(s) \tag{2}$$

P(s) is the probability of encountering an instance of sense s.

3 The Hybrid WSD System

For monosemous words, the sense is returned as disambiguated based on the part of speech. For polysemous words, we followed the Adapted Lesk approach of Banerjee and Pederson (2002) but instead of a limited window size used by Banerjee and Pederson, we used all context words as the window size.

Most prior work has not made use of the antonymy relation for WSD. But according to Ji (2010), if two context words are antonyms and belong to the same semantic cluster, they tend to represent the alternative attributes for the target word. Furthermore, if two words are antonymous, the gloss and examples of the opposing senses often contain many words that are mutually useful for disambiguating both the original sense and its opposite. Therefore, we added the glosses of antonyms in addition to hypernyms, hyponyms, meronyms etc. used by Banerjee and Pedersen (2002). Also, for verbs we have added the glosses of entailment and causes relations of each word sense to their vectors. For adjectives and adverbs, we added the morphologically related nouns to the vectors of each word sense in computing the similarity score.

The similarity score for the Modified Lesk algorithm is computed using the Cosine similarity. The vectors are composed using the glosses of the word senses, that of their hypernyms, hyponyms, and antonyms. We then compute the cosine of the angle between the two vectors. This metric is a measurement of orientation and not magnitude. The magnitude of the score for each word is normalized by the magnitude of the scores for all words within the vector. The resulting normalized scores reflect the degree the sense is characterized by each of the component words.

Cosine similarity can be trivially computed as the dot product of vectors normalized by their Euclidean length:

$$\vec{a} = (a_1, a_2, a_3, ...a_n) \quad \text{and} \quad \vec{b} = (b_1, b_2, b_3, ...b_n)$$

Here a_n and b_n are the components of vectors containing length normalized TF-IDF scores for either the words in a context window or the words within the glosses associated with a sense being scored. The dot product is then computed as follows:

$$\vec{a}.\vec{b} = \sum_{i=1}^{n} a_i b_i = a_1 b_1 + a_2 b_2 + ... + a_n b_n$$

The dot product is a simple multiplication of each component from the both vectors added together. The geometric definition of the dot product given by equation (3):

$$\vec{a}.\vec{b} = ||\vec{a}||\,||\vec{b}||cos\theta \tag{3}$$

Using the the cummutative property, we have equation (4):

$$\vec{a}.\vec{b} = ||\vec{b}||||\vec{a}||\,cos\theta \tag{4}$$

where $||\vec{a}||\,cos\theta$ is the projection of $\vec{a}$ into $\vec{b}$ in which solving the dot product equation for $cos\theta$ gives the cosine similarity in equation (5):

$$cos\theta = \frac{\vec{a}.\vec{b}}{||\vec{a}||\,||\vec{b}||} \tag{5}$$

where $a.b$ is the dot product and $||a||$ and $||b||$ are the vector lengths of a and b, respectively.

We disambiguated each target word in a sentence using the Jiang & Conrath similarity measure using all the context words as the window size. We did this by computing Jiang & Conrath similarity score for each candidate senses of the target word and select the sense that has the highest sum total similarity score to all the words in the context window.

For each context word w and candidate word senses c_{eval}, we compute individual similarity scores using equation (6):

$$sim(w, c_{eval}) = \text{max}_{c \in sen(w)}[sim(c, c_{eval})] \tag{6}$$

where $sim(w, c_{eval})$ function computes the maximum similarity score obtained by computing Jiang & Conrath similarity for all the candidate senses in a context word. The aggregate summation of the individual similarity scores is given in equation (7):

$$\text{argmax}_{c_{eval} \in sen(\text{W})} = \sum_{w \in context(\text{W})} \text{max}_{c \in sen(w)} [sim(c, c_{eval})] \tag{7}$$

An agreement between the results produced by each of the two algorithms means the word under consideration has been likely correctly disambiguated and the sense on which they agreed is returned as the correct sense. Whenever one module fails to produce any sense that can be applied to a word but the other succeeds, we just return the sense computed by the successful module. Module failures occur when all of the available senses receive a score of 0 according to the module's underlying similarity algorithm (e.g., due to lack of overlapping words for Modified Lesk).

Finally, in a situation where the two modules select different senses, we heuristically resolved the disagreement. Our heuristic first computes the derivationally related forms of all of the words in the context window and adds each of them the vector representation of the word being assessed. Then for the senses produced by the Modified Lesk and Jiang & Conrath algorithms, we obtain the similarity score between the vector representations of the two competing senses and the new expanded context vector. The algorithm returns the sense selected by the module whose winning vector is most similar to the augmented context vector.

The intuition behind this notion of validation is that the glosses of a word sense, and that of their semantically related ones in the WordNet lexical taxonomy should share words in common as much as possible with words in context with the target word. Adding the derivationally related forms of the words in the context window increases the chances of overlap when there are mismatches caused by changes in word morphology. When both modules fail to identify a sense, the Most Frequent Sense (MFS) in the Semcor corpus is used as the appropriate sense.

4 Experimental Setting

The SemEval 2015 Multilingual Word Sense Disambiguation and Entity Linking task provides datasets in English, Spanish and Italian. BabelNet (Navigli and Ponzetto, 2012) which provides automatic translation of each word sense in other languages have been employed. To enrich the glosses used by the Modified Lesk algorithm, the glosses provided by BabelNet from Wikipedia in the 3 subtask languages have been used to extend the initial glosses available in WordNet (Miller, 1990).

Furthermore, BabelNet contains some word senses which are not available in WordNet. These senses and their glosses were used directly without any reference to WordNet translation since it does not have any. For English, we disambiguate all the open target words while for Spanish and Italian, we disambiguate all noun target words. Due to some challenges we faced close to our task's evaluation deadline, we were unable to obtain BabelNet 2.5 which is the official resource for the task. Instead, we used BabelNet 1.1.1 from the SemEval 2013 Multilingual Word Sense Disambiguation Task, which we initially used to develop our system but unfortunately contains only noun words for Spanish and Italian and does not include some English words found in the test set.

5 Results and Discussion

Table 1 compares the performance of our system with other participating systems on the English subtask. Table 2 shows the result of our system for the Spanish and Italian subtask where we submitted a run for only nouns and named enitities.

System	Precision	Recall	F1
LIMSI	68.7	63.1	65.8
SUDOKU-Run2	62.9	60.4	61.6
SUDOKU-Run3	61.9	59.4	60.6
vua-background	67.5	51.4	58.4
SUDOKU-Run1	60.1	52.1	55.8
WSD-games-Run2	58.8	50.0	54.0
WSD-games-Run1	57.4	48.8	52.8
WSD-games Run3	53.5	45.4	49.1
EBL-Hope	48.4	44.4	46.3
TeamUFAL	40.4	36.5	38.3

Table 1: Performance of All Participating Systems for English Subtask. Our *EBL-Hope* System ranked 9th out of the submitted systems.

Subtask	Precision	Recall	F1
Spanish	52.5	44.6	48.2
Italian	43.1	35.3	38.8

Table 2: *EBL-Hope's* hybrid system performance on the Spanish and Italian subtasks.

Our system performs noticeably better in Spanish than Italian. Further analysis shows that the weakest area of our system for the English subtask are the verbs, which achieve 35.8 F1 score. We achieve high scores on named-entities with an F1 scores of 80.2 in English, 48.5 in Italian and the highest F1 score across all participating systems on Spanish with 70.8.

Table 3 and Table 4 give the performance obtained when using the Modified Lesk and Jiang & Conrath modules independently. Our hybrid system outperforms the individual component modules on both English and Spanish. On Italian, the Hybrid system performs comparably to Jiang & Conrath, which is the best individual module.

Subtask	Precision	Recall	F1
English	43.6	41.3	42.4
Spanish	48.1	41.2	44.3
Italian	46.3	33.5	38.9

Table 4: Performance of the Jiang & Conrath module in isolation on the 3 subtasks.

Subtask	Precision	Recall	F1
English	44.2	40.6	42.3
Spanish	47.6	40.1	43.5
Italian	40.3	31.7	35.4

Table 3: Performance of the Modified Lesk module in isolation on the 3 subtasks.

6 Conclusion

In this work, we have combined two algorithms for word sense disambiguation, Modified Lesk and an approach based on Jiang & Conrath similarity. The resulting hybrid system improves performance by heuristically resolving disagreements in the word sense assigned by the individual algorithms. We observe the results of the combined algorithm do consistently outperform each of the individual algorithms used in isolation. However, our poor performance on the official evaluation could likely have been improved by making use of the more recent 2.5 version of BabelNet as recommended by the task organizers.

Acknowledgement

This work has been supported by European Commission scholarship under the Erasmus+ doctoral scholarship programmes. We would like to thank the anonymous reviewers for their helpful suggestions and comments. Special thanks to Daniel Cer for his great and useful editorial input on the final manuscript.

References

Satanjeev Banerjee and Ted Pedersen. 2002. An adapted Lesk Algorithm for Word Sense Disambiguation using WordNet. In *Proceedings of the 3rd International Conference on Computational Linguistics and Intelligent Text Processing (CICLING)*, Mexico City, Mexico, 17 - 23 February, 2002, pp. 136 - 145.

George Miller. 1990. An Online Lexical Database. *International Journal of Lexicography*, 3(4): 235 - 244.

Jay J. Jiang and David W. Conrath. 1997. Semantic similarity Based on Corpus Statistics and Lexical Taxonomy. In *Proceedings of the 10th International Conference on Research in Computational Linguistics*, Taipei, Taiwan, 2 - 4 August 1998, pp. 19 - 33.

Michael E. Lesk. 1986. Automatic Sense Disambiguation Using Machine Readable Dictionaries: How to Tell a Pine Cone from an Ice Cream Cone. In *Proceedings of the 5th ACM-SIGDOC Conference*, Toronto, Canada, 8 - 11 June 1986, pp. 24 - 26.

Eniafe F. Ayetiran, Guido Boella, Luigi Di Caro, Livio Robaldo. 2014. Enhancing Word Sense Disambiguation Using A Hybrid Knowledge-Based Technique. In *Proceedings of 11th international workshop on natural language processing and cognitive science*, Venice, Italy 27 - 29, October, pp. 15 - 26.

Heng Ji. 2010. One Sense per Context Cluster: Improving Word Sense Disambiguation Using Web-Scale Phrase Clustering. In *Proceedings of the 4th Universal Communication Symposium (IUCS)*, Beijing, China, 18 -19 October 2010, pp. 181 -184.

Roberto Navigli and Simone P. Ponzetto. 2012. BabelNet: The automatic construction, evaluation and application of a wide-coverage multilingual semantic network. In *Artificial Intelligence*, 193(2012) 217-250.

Philip Reisnik. 1995. One Sense per Context Cluster: Using Information Content to Evaluate Semantic Similarity. In *Proceedings of the 14th International Joint Conference on Artificial Intelligence (IJCAI)*, Montreal, Canada, 20 25 August 1995, pp. 448453.

VUA-background : When to Use Background Information to Perform Word Sense Disambiguation

Marten Postma VU University Amsterdam
Ruben Izquierdo VU University Amsterdam
Piek Vossen VU University Amsterdam
{m.c.postma, ruben.izquierdobevia, p.t.j.m.vossen}@vu.nl

Abstract

We present in this paper our submission to task 13 of SemEval2015, which makes use of background information and external resources (DBpedia and Wikipedia) to automatically disambiguate texts. Our approach follows two routes for disambiguation: one route is proposed by a state–of–the–art WSD system, and the other one by the predominant sense information extracted in an unsupervised way from an automatically built background corpus. We reached 4th position in terms of F1-score in task number 13 of SemEval2015: "Multilingual All-Words Sense Disambiguation and Entity Linking" (Moro and Navigli, 2015). All the software and code created for this approach are publicly available on GitHub[1].

1 Introduction

Word Sense Disambiguation is still an unsolved problem in Natural Language Processing. Many different approaches have been proposed throughout the years to tackle this task from different perspectives. In addition, competitions have been organized to compare the performance of these approaches. Our hypothesis is that, in general, the context is not being modelled properly by the systems, which usually consider very narrow contexts and do not pay any attention to the background information or information that is not explicitly included in the text. We conducted an in-depth error analysis of previous all-words tasks (Senseval–2 : English all words (Palmer et al., 2001), Senseval–3 : English all words (Snyder and Palmer, 2004), Semeval–2007 : all words task 17 (Pradhan et al., 2007), Semeval–2010 : all words task 17 (Agirre et al., 2010), Semeval–2013 : all words task 12 (Navigli et al., 2013)) in order to gain better insight as to why some approaches perform better than others, to detect problems not properly addressed and to try to overcome them. [2]

We observed that most systems tend to rely on **local features** (words surrounding the words in question) to perform word sense disambiguation. Besides this, there is a very acute trend by all WSD systems to assign in most cases the most frequent sense, regardless the domain under consideration, as can be seen in Figure 1:

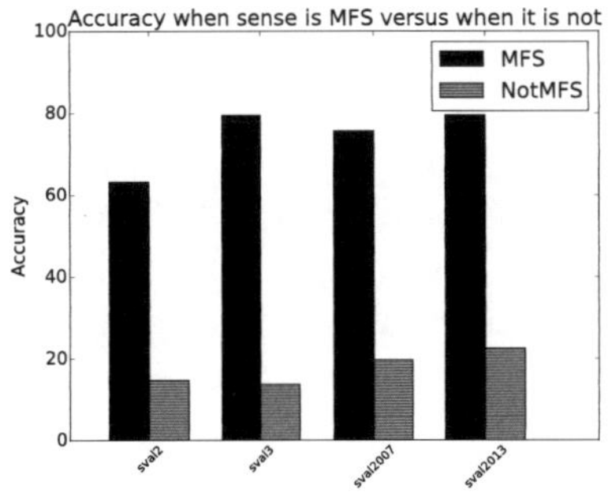

Figure 1: The average accuracy of all systems per competition is shown.

Figure 1 shows the average accuracy of all the systems per competition. We clearly observe the trend that systems perform well when the sense is the most frequent sense, but not in other cases. Furthermore, when the sense is not the most frequent one, the systems still propose the most frequent sense. For instance in Senseval–2, out of 799 tokens for which the correct sense is not the most frequent one, systems still wrongly assign the most frequent sense in 84% of the cases.

Based on these observations, we designed a system that creates background corpora starting from a set of seed documents, from now on SD (preferably from a specific and unique domain). From this

[1] https://github.com/cltl/vua-wsd-sem2015

[2] The error analysis can be found here: https://github.com/cltl/WSD_error_analysis.

corpus, we use the entities automatically detected to access DBpedia and create the first background corpus, which will be called Entity Article (EA) corpus. By applying different techniques, we expand this EA corpus with more domain related documents, which results in the Entity Expanded (EE) corpus. Once the whole background corpus (EA+EE) has been created, we use this information to automatically derive the specific predominant sense of each word in our target domain (the domain of the starting documents and also the domain of the background corpus).

The rationale behind this approach starts with the observation that the predominant sense of a lemma is very dominant in a document. Hence, by focusing on when to use or not to use this predominant sense, a high performance seems plausible. In addition, we observed that local features are not always enough to determine the correct sense of a lemma and we should only rely on these features when they are necessary.

The structure of this paper is as follows. We introduce our approach in section 2. followed by the results in section 3. Finally we discuss and conclude our results in section 4.

2 Our Approach

Figure 2 shows the overall architecture of our system, that will be explained more in detail in this section.

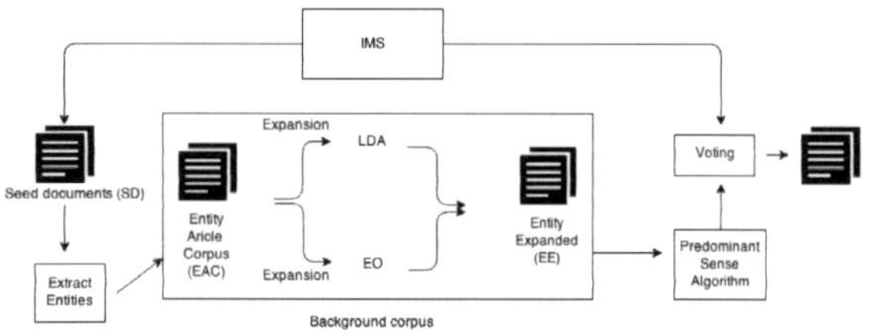

Figure 2: Overall architecture

Seed documents: We focused on the WSD part of the task. The input for our approach is a collection of seed documents, which represent the target domain that is used for calculating the predominant domain information. These documents can either be the task test documents (**online approach**) or a different set of documents that we could compile in advance if the target domain is known (**offline approach**). We first converted these documents to the NAF format (Fokkens et al., 2014).[3]. We then applied a POS–tagger to get the lemmas and part-of-speech labels for all the tokens. As explained before, two different approaches were followed: online and offline. We experimented with both approaches and finally the online approach was selected for our participation due to the mixed-domain nature of the test documents. The documents follow two different and parallel routes of analysis: one route which favors the domain predominant sense by using the **background knowledge** and one route which favors the most frequent sense (in a general domain) by using one of the state–of–the–art WSD systems that performs very well in such domains. Finally, a voting heuristic of the two routes is applied to assign the final senses.

2.1 Route 1: Background knowledge

Extract entities from collection of documents We started with one corpus of documents (the test documents in the online approach or a pre–compiled set in the offline version): the seed documents (SD). Then we applied the statistical implementation of DBPedia Spotlight (Daiber et al., 2013) in order to obtain entities and their corresponding links to DBPedia[4]. With this we compile the EA corpus, which contains all the Wikipedia texts associated to the DBpedia links extracted[5]. We experimented with some filtering techniques on the list of DBPedia links in order to keep just domain specific ones, such as considering only those DBPedia links tagged with an ontological concept which is a leaf of the ontology tree. Nevertheless, we found a better performance when using all the DBpedia links without any filtering.

[3] `http://www.newsreader-project.eu/files/2013/01/techreport.pdf`

[4] We developed our own module that calls automatically the DBPedia Spotlight end–point and allows to work with NAF files: `http://github.com/rubenIzquierdo/dbpedia_ner`

[5] We also created our own modules to query DBPpedia (`http://github.com/rubenIzquierdo/dbpediaEnquirerPy` based on SPARQL) and WikiPedia: `https://github.com/rubenIzquierdo/wikipediaEnquirerPy`

Expansion The EA corpus generated in the previous section represents the domain of our test data (online/offline), but probably suffers from a low coverage, especially for our idea of applying a predominant sense algorithm which relies on the availability of a large domain corpus. In order to expand this EA corpus, we developed two strategies to generate the EE corpus: a) Latent Dirichlet Allocation–based (LDA), targeting a high recall and low precision/quality, and b) Entity overlapping (EO), aiming a high quality and medium/low recall.

The **LDA technique** first obtains a topic model using LDA on the EA corpus[6]. This is our domain model for comparison. Moreover, we obtain the DBPedia ontology classes for all the documents in the EA corpus (one example could be *HumanGene*). For each of these labels, DBPedia is queried to get all the entities belonging to that label (following our example, all the entities that are *HumanGene*)[7]. The Wikipedia text for every of these entities is gathered and compared against the LDA model obtained previously. Only those reaching a certain similarity are selected to be part of the EE corpus. The whole process is highly time consuming and the result in terms of quality is not as good as expected, probably related to the fact that the number of documents retrieved is very high, the domains are very diverse and in many cases different to our reference domain.

The **EO expansion** follows a different approach. On the one hand, all the DBpedia entities in the EA corpus are extracted, which makes up our set of domain entities (DE). On the other hand, each of the Wikipedia pages that can be reached from these DE is processed to extract all the possible wiki–links. All these wiki–links are possible candidates for the EE corpus. To select the final set of candidates, the similarity is obtained by measuring the overlap between the wiki–links of the candidate with our initial domain set DE. Only those surpassing a certain overlapping threshold are selected.

Predominant sense algorithm Our background corpus is considered the union of the EA and the EE corpus, which usually is a large collection of NLP-processed documents. For each lemma in these documents, we extract all the sentences containing this lemma. If there are at least 100 sentences, we feed the sentences for this specific lemma into the predominant sense algorithm. The predominant sense algorithm we use is based on topic modeling (Lau et al., 2012; Lau et al., 2014). The algorithm first tries to induce senses using a Hierarchical Dirichlet Process and then tries to determine the sense ranking of all senses of a lemma according to the documents. The output of this step is a list of sense confidences for each lemma for which we had enough training data. [8]

2.2 Route 2: it–makes–sense WSD system

Our idea is to start from the output of a state-of-the-art WSD system, and combine it with the predominant sense information automatically gathered with our approach, in order to obtain an overall WSD approach specific to our target domain. We selected the it–makes–sense system (Zhong and Ng, 2010) that has proved to be one of the best performing WSD systems in general domains. Similarly, we have created our own wrapper around the it–makes–sense system that allows the use of NAF format as input/output for this tool[9]. Following our purpose, we did not only select the most likely sense in each case according to the WSD engine, but we stored all the possible senses for each lemma along with the probability returned by it–makes–sense.

2.3 Voting

For each token in the test data, we first check if we have predominant sense output for this lemma. In addition, we check if the sense ranking is skewed, which we determine by checking if the two senses with the highest confidence have a combined confidence of higher than 85%. If this is the case, we calculate the average of the sense rankings of the predominant sense output and the it-makes-sense sys-

[6]We have used the Python library GenSim for this purpose `http://radimrehurek.com/gensim/`

[7]This process can be quite time consuming (there are a total of 15 entries in DBpedia for *HumanGene*, but there are 1.65 million entries for *Person*)

[8]we created a wrapper around the GitHub repositories that were created to run the predominant sense algorithm (`https://github.com/jhlau/hdp-wsi`, `https://github.com/jhlau/predom\_sense`). This github can be found at `https://github.com/MartenPostma/predominantsense`

[9]This wrapper module can be found at `http://github.com/rubenIzquierdo/it_makes_sense_WSD`

tem and choose the sense with the highest confidence. If we do not have predominant sense output, we assign the sense with the highest confidence according to the it-makes-sense system. Finally, we did not provide answers to all instances in the test set due to the fact we used an older version of WordNet, which did not contain all the gold senses. These lemmas mainly consisted of computer related senses.

3 Results

The results can be found in Table 1:

All_domains			
Measure	**all**	**n**	**v**
Precision	67.5 (2)	64.7	56.6
Recall	51.4 (5)	42.9	53.9
F1	58.4 (4)	51.6	55.2
Social_issues_domain			
Measure	**all**	**n**	**v**
F1	61.1 (2)	54.8 (7)	70.6 (1)
Math_Computer_domain			
Measure	**all**	**n**	**v**
F1	47.7 (5)	30.5 (13)	49.7 (7)
Biomedical_domain			
Measure	**all**	**n**	**v**
F1	66.4 (4)	62.7 (9)	53.8 (2)

Table 1: Results of VUA-background are shown for the domains: 'All', 'Social_issues', 'Math_Computer, and 'Biomedical'. The results per domain are presented for all part of speeches, as well as for nouns and verbs. The numbers in parentheses are competition ranks.

As can be seen in Table 1, our system finished 4nd in terms of F1-score, 2nd in terms of precision, and 5th in terms of recall. In particular. our system performed well on the biomedical domain and the Social_Issues domain, and mainly for verbs. In addition, running the evaluation using only the predominant sense output led to an improvement in the precision for nouns (69.1% versus 64.7%) and verbs (61.6% versus 56.6%), but also a drop in recall for both nouns (20.1% versus 42.9%) and verbs (17.7% versus 53.9%).

4 Discussion and Conclusion

A number of reasons have attributed to the fact that our system performed relatively well in terms of precision, but not so well in terms of recall.

Firstly, our system, and in particular our offline approach, is built around the notion of one dominant theme or topic. The domain of this evaluation was announced to be the biomedical domain, but the test documents ended up belonging to several domains, which has hurt the performance of our algorithm. We believe that adapting our system to work with multiple domains is the next step in improving the algorithm.

In addition, our system was built around WordNet 1.7.1. This means that we did not provide answers to all instances, which has had an impact on the recall.

Finally, we claim that size is an issue in obtaining good results. Especially our online approach could have benefited from more data.

We presented a WSD framework that exploits both information available in a document or a set of documents, and background information from different external resources. We believe the results achieved in this evaluation task are promising, despite the problems and issues mentioned in the previous paragraphs. Our approach is especially suited to deal with one single domain, or with a domain that is known in advance. We will continue working on the adaptation of the whole framework to a multi–domain scenario. Furthermore, all software developed is publicly available on different GitHub repositories. Our system can be found at `https://github.com/cltl/vua-wsd-sem2015`. Scripts are included, which will run the whole process step by step starting from the official test documents and apply: linguistic processors (tokenizer, lemmatizer), entity detection, linking to DBpedia, call to it–makes–sense system, creation of the background corpus and expansion, creation of the predominant sense information and final voting heuristic.

Acknowledgments

The research for this paper was supported by the Netherlands Organisation for Scientific Research (NWO) via the Spinoza-prize Vossen projects (SPI 30-673, 2014-2019).

References

Eneko Agirre, Oier López de Lacalle, Christiane Fellbaum, Shu-Kai Hsieh, Maurizio Tesconi, Monica Monachini, Piek Vossen, and Roxanne Segers. 2010. Semeval-2010 task 17: All-words Word Sense Disambiguation on a Specific Domain. In *Proceedings of the 5th International Workshop on Semantic Evaluation*, pages 75–80, Uppsala, Sweden, July.

Joachim Daiber, Jakob Max, Chris Hokamp, and Pablo N. Mendes. 2013. Improving Efficiency and Accuracy in Multilingual Entity Extraction. In *Proceedings of the 9th International Conference on Semantic Systems*, I-SEMANTICS '13, pages 121–124, New York, NY, USA.

Antske Fokkens, Aitor Soroa, Zuhaitz Beloki, Niels Ockeloen, German Rigau, Willem Robert van Hage, and Piek Vossen. 2014. NAF and GAF: Linking linguistic annotations. In *Proceedings 10th Joint ISO-ACL SIGSEM Workshop on Interoperable Semantic Annotation*, pages 9–16, Reykjavik, Iceland.

Jey Han Lau, Paul Cook, Diana McCarthy, David Newman, and Timothy Baldwin. 2012. Word Sense Induction for Novel Sense Detection. In *Proceedings of the 13th Conference of the European Chapter of the Association for Computational Linguistics*, EACL '12, pages 591–601, Stroudsburg, PA, USA. Association for Computational Linguistics.

Jey Han Lau, Paul Cook, Diana McCarthy, David Newman, and Timothy Baldwin. 2014. Learning Word Sense Distributions, Detecting Unattested Senses and Identifying Novel Senses Using Topic Models. In *Proceedings of the 52nd Annual Meeting of the Association for Computational Linguistics (Volume 1: Long Papers)*, pages 259–270, Baltimore, Maryland, USA, June 23-25.

Andrea Moro and Roberto Navigli. 2015. SemEval-2015 Task 13: Multilingual All-Words Sense Disambiguation and Entity Linking. In *Proc. of SemEval-2015.*

Roberto Navigli, David Jurgens, and Daniele Vannella. 2013. Semeval-2013 task 12: Multilingual word sense disambiguation. In *Second Joint Conference on Lexical and Computational Semantics (*SEM), Volume 2: Proceedings of the Seventh International Workshop on Semantic Evaluation (SemEval 2013)*, pages 222–231, Atlanta, Georgia, USA, June.

Martha Palmer, Christiane Fellbaum, Scott Cotton, Lauren Delfs, and Hoa Trang Dang. 2001. English tasks: All-words and verb lexical sample. In *Proceedings of SENSEVAL-2 Second International Workshop on Evaluating Word Sense Disambiguation Systems*, pages 21–24, Toulouse, France, July.

Sameer S. Pradhan, Edward Loper, Dmitriy Dligach, and Martha Palmer. 2007. Semeval-2007 Task-17: English Lexical Sample, SRL and All Words. In *Proceedings of the Fourth International Workshop on Semantic Evaluations (SemEval-2007)*, pages 87–92, Prague, Czech Republic, June.

Benjamin Snyder and Martha Palmer. 2004. The English all-words task. In Rada Mihalcea and Phil Edmonds, editors, *Senseval-3: Third International Workshop on the Evaluation of Systems for the Semantic Analysis of Text*, pages 41–43, Barcelona, Spain, July.

Zhi Zhong and Hwee Tou Ng. 2010. H.t.: It makes sense: A wide-coverage Word Sense Disambiguation system for free text. In *Proceedings of the 48th Annual Meeting of the Association for Computational Linguistics (ACL*, pages 78–83.

TeamUFAL: WSD+EL as Document Retrieval*

Petr Fanta, Roman Sudarikov, Ondřej Bojar
Charles University in Prague
Faculty of Mathematics and Physics
Institute of Formal and Applied Linguistics
Malostranské náměstí 25, 11800 Praha 1, Czech Republic
p.fanta@seznam.cz, {sudarikov, bojar}@ufal.mff.cuni.cz

Abstract

This paper describes our system for SemEval-2015 Task 13: Multilingual All-Words Sense Disambiguation and Entity Linking. We have participated with our system in the sub-task which aims at monolingual all-words disambiguation and entity linking. Aside from system description, we pay closer attention to the evaluation of system outputs.

1 Introduction

Word sense disambiguation (WSD, i.e. picking the right sense for a given word from a fixed inventory) and entity linking (EL, i.e. identifying a particular named entity listed in a database given its mention in a text) are among the fashionable tasks in computational linguistics and natural language processing these days. WSD has been, after some debate, shown to help machine translation (Carpuat and Wu, 2007), other applications include knowledge discovery or machine reading in general (Etzioni et al., 2006; Schubert, 2006). WSD and EL are usually applied with large and rich context available (Navigli, 2009), but the arguably harder setting of short context has a wider range of applications, including text similarity measurements (Abdalgader and Skabar, 2011), Named Entities Extraction and Named Entities Disambiguation (Habib and Keulen, 2012) or handling data from social networks, such as attempts to translate tweets (Šubert and Bojar, 2014).

Our attempt at WSD and EL can be classified as unsupervised, corpus-based and our implementation relies on an information retrieval tool. We do not take longer context into account.

2 Task Description

As participants of SemEval-2015 Task 13 (Moro and Navigli, 2015), we were given only a very brief instructions, effectively just one example of a POS-tagged sentence:

The/X European/J/european Medicines/N/medicine Agency/N/agency (/X EMA/N/ema)/X is/V/be ,...

We were expected to provide such input with labels indicating that e.g. the words “European Medicines Agency” refer to the entity described in the English Wikipedia under the title European_Medicines_Agency (“wiki:European_Medicines_Agency”), the word “Medicines” refers to the BabelNet concept 00054128n etc. The repertoire of word sense and entities came from BabelNet 2.5 which included: Wikipedia page titles (2012/10 dump), WordNet 3.0 synsets, OmegaWiki senses (2013/09 dump) and Open Multilingual WordNet synsets (2013/08 dump). The output format accepted Wikipedia titles, BabelNet IDs and Wordnet sense keys.

The test set for SemEval-2015 task 13 was released for three languages: English, Italian and Spanish. We joined only the English task. All the data was gathered from 3 domains: biomedicine, mathematics and computers and general domain.

At the time of the shared task, neither a scoring

*This research was supported by the grants FP7-ICT-2013-10-610516 (QTLeap). This research was partially supported by SVV project number 260 224. This work has been using language resources developed, stored and distributed by the LINDAT/CLARIN project of the Ministry of Education, Youth and Sports of the Czech Republic (project LM2010013).

script, nor any development set with annotations was provided. It was also not very clear how the different allowed ID sources (Wikipedia, BabelNet and Wordnet) will be used concurrently.

The official scoring script and golden annotation was provided later, and we use it here to report the scores of our submission and a few variations of it.

3 Our System

Our system is unsupervised and relies on an information retrieval (IR) tool applied to a large collection of documents. We thus call it corpus-based.

Given an input sentence, we remove all stopwords (as defined by the IR tool) and punctuation, putting together even words which were originally not adjacent. For each span up to a given length in this abridged sentence, the system tries to find a document in the database. If found, this document implies the sense or entity ID for the given span.

The words in the span and (separately) other words in the sentence are used to construct the query for the IR engine. We construct multiple queries and merge their results in a candidate selection process, possibly returning no document at all.

Due to the different nature of our sources (see Section 3.1), we run sub-systems with different configurations for each of them. We return the union of responses from these sub-systems.

3.1 Data Sources

BabelNet alone is not a good resource for our approach, because it does not include textual data. We resort to the original sources of BabelNet and map them back to BabelNet. Our sources are thus the English Wikipedia, English Wiktionary and WordNet. Short of the original versions as used in BabelNet 2.5, we used Wiki dumps from November 2014 and WordNet 3.0, facing some ID mismatches.

3.2 Indexing

For each source, we create a full text index using Apache Lucene search engine which provides several ranking models. We experiment with models based on TF-IDF (Salton et al., 1975) and Okapi BM25 (Robertson et al., 1995), selecting the better one for each subsystem in our submission.

All indexes have a similar structure, they contain:

Score	Document ID (ie. Wikipedia Title)
8.201	Medical_condition → Disease
8.201	Medical_conditions → Disease
6.561	Frostbite_(medical_condition) → Frostbite

Figure 1: Query results (→ means redirection closure).

ID of the element in the given source (Wikipedia ID, Wiktionary ID or Wordnet sense key),

Title of Wikipedia or Wiktionary article or word from WordNet,

Body text of articles from Wiki sources (markup removed) or all textual data from Wordnet synset (including other words in the synset),

POS tag (only in WordNet index).

The Title and the Body field are stemmed by Porter stemmer implemented in Lucene.

3.3 Proposing Candidates

We use different sets of queries for each source. We query Wiktionary and Wordnet for single-word spans only, while Wikipedia seems suitable for both, single and multi-word spans.

The queries typically require all the words from the span to appear in the Title field of the document and the words from the context to appear in the Body field of the document. A number of slightly different queries, incl. queries that use n-grams of words or some boosting for some of the terms, is run in parallel, giving us multiple lists scored by the selected IR model (see Section 3.2). The results for a simple query *+TITLE:medical +TITLE:condition* for Wikipedia documents are shown in Figure 1.

3.4 Final Candidate Selection

Final candidates are picked from the results of the queries. Before this selection, the results for each span are grouped and scores for the same ID (coming from different lists or redirection) are summed.

For Wikipedia, we select the highest-scoring candidate and it is returned only if its score is greater than double the score of the second candidate. After this selection, the system checks if there are overlapping spans labeled with same ID and returns only the span with the best score.

For Wordnet and Wiktionary, we simply return the highest-scoring candidate for each span. Since Wiktionary IDs are not expected in the shared task,

System	Official			Offic+penalty	Our Exact			Our Partial			Bag of IDs		
	P	R	F1	P	P	R	F1	P	R	F1	P	R	F1
Submitted	40.4	36.5	38.3	30.4	25.9	48.2	33.7	26.6	49.4	34.6	24.0	50.5	32.5
Submitted-fix	41.2	37.3	39.1	30.7	25.7	49.6	33.9	26.3	50.8	34.7	23.4	52.0	32.3
DFKI	67.4	52.6	59.1	55.2	51.5	49.2	50.3	52.1	49.8	50.9	51.3	49.2	50.2
EBL-Hope	48.4	44.4	46.3	40.4	36.8	40.4	38.5	37.1	40.8	38.9	37.3	41.0	39.0
el92-Run1	69.9	21.4	32.8	62.6	59.9	20.4	30.5	61.2	20.9	31.1	62.2	21.2	31.7
el92-Run2	71.9	19.1	30.2	64.8	61.8	18.2	28.2	62.5	18.4	28.5	62.9	18.5	28.6
el92-Run3	**75.2**	18.5	29.6	**69.6**	**66.0**	17.5	27.7	**66.8**	17.7	28.0	**66.9**	17.8	28.1
LIMSI	68.7	63.1	65.8	57.3	55.4	60.9	58.0	55.6	61.2	58.3	55.6	61.2	58.2
SUDOKU-Run1	60.1	52.1	55.8	50.3	47.0	48.6	47.8	47.2	48.8	48.0	47.0	48.6	47.8
SUDOKU-Run2	62.9	60.4	61.6	53.0	49.2	56.1	52.4	49.7	56.6	52.9	49.3	56.2	52.5
SUDOKU-Run3	61.9	59.4	60.6	52.2	48.6	55.4	51.8	49.0	55.8	52.1	48.7	55.5	51.9
UNIBA-Run1	66.2	52.3	58.4	54.3	51.6	49.8	50.7	51.9	50.0	50.9	51.9	50.0	50.9
UNIBA-Run2	66.1	52.1	58.3	53.5	50.9	49.6	50.2	51.5	50.2	50.8	51.4	50.1	50.7
UNIBA-Run3	66.1	52.1	58.3	53.0	50.5	49.7	50.1	51.3	50.4	50.8	51.1	50.2	50.7
vua-background	67.5	51.4	58.4	56.3	52.1	47.5	49.7	52.3	47.8	50.0	52.3	47.7	49.9
WSD-games-Run1	57.4	48.8	52.8	47.9	44.1	45.0	44.6	44.3	45.2	44.7	44.3	45.2	44.7
WSD-games-Run2	58.8	50.0	54.0	49.0	45.3	46.2	45.7	45.5	46.4	45.9	45.5	46.4	45.9
WSD-games-Run3	53.5	45.4	49.1	44.6	40.7	41.5	41.1	41.0	41.8	41.4	41.0	41.8	41.4
MFS	67.9	**67.1**	**67.5**	67.9	65.2	**64.5**	**64.9**	65.5	**64.8**	**65.2**	65.2	**64.5**	**64.9**

Table 1: All submissions evaluated on all domains using various official and our scorings.

we map them to BabelNet IDs prior to picking the highest-scoring one. (Wiktionary IDs that cannot be mapped are discarded.)

4 Evaluation

Having thoroughly reviewed the official scoring script, we find some of its features unusual:

- The precision of a system is not penalized for spans, which don't occur in the golden set.
- The recall should consider only to what extent the expected answers are covered by the system's answers. The official scoring script reduces the recall score for any 'unexpected' answers.
- An exact match in span is needed to give any credit to the system answer.

We thus propose a slightly different evaluation procedure and apply it to all submitted systems.

4.1 Our Proposed Scoring

Our scoring is based on a credit for partially overlapping spans, similarly to Cornolti et al. (2013), who however disregard the overlap size. We call a 'label' $l = (l_1, l_2)$ the pair of a span (a range of words in the sentence; denoted l_1) and an ID attached to the span, l_2. For a label s in the system output and a label g in the golden annotation, we define their match as:

$$\text{match}(s, g) = \begin{cases} \frac{|g_1 \cap s_1|}{|g_1 \cup s_1|} & \text{if } |g_1 \cap s_1| > 0 \wedge g_2 = s_2 \\ 0 & \text{otherwise} \end{cases}$$

In other words overlapping spans labeled with the same ID get a credit proportional to the size of the overlap. We define precision and recall as follows:

$$\text{precision} = \frac{\sum_{s \in S, g \in G} \text{match}(s, g)}{|S|}$$

$$\text{recall} = \frac{\sum_{s \in S, g \in G} \text{match}(s, g)}{|G|}$$

where G and S are sets of labels from the gold standard and a system output, respectively. Our approach gives a partial credit for inexact, but overlapping, spans with correct identifiers.

Our precision and recall are only meaningful, if all IDs come from a single source. We pick BabelNet IDs for this purpose and map all system outputs as necessary. Note that the mapping from the Wikipedia IDs to the BabelNet IDs is ambiguous but not in more than 1 ‰ cases.

WSD-games and vua-background report only WordNet sense keys. We map them unambiguously to BabelNet IDs.

el92 produces lowercase Wikipedia titles so the ambiguous mapping to BabelNet IDs is slightly worse.

DFKI and our system produce both Wikipedia titles and WordNet IDs, we map both as above and union the results.

SUDOKU produces BabelNet IDs but some spans have no ID at all. We ignore these spans.

	Fix Wikt→BN mapping	Model for Wikipedia	Model for Wiktionary	Use context in Wikt. search	Precision	Recall	F1
Submitted	-	TF-IDF	BM25	no	40.4%	36.5%	36.5%
Submitted_fix	yes	TF-IDF	BM25	no	41.2%	37.3%	39.1%
Wiki_BM25	no	BM25	BM25	no	38.4%	35.0%	36.7%
Wikt+context_BM25	no	TF-IDF	BM25	yes	38.4%	35.3%	36.8%
Wikt+context_TF-IDF	no	TF-IDF	TF-IDF	yes	40.3%	37.0%	38.6%

Table 2: Our system outputs.

4.2 Results

Table 1 reports systems' scores using these evaluation metrics:

Official Precision and recall as reported by the official scoring script.

Official+penalty A modified version of the official scoring script which treats spans in system output and no counterpart in the golden set in the same way as if the golden set assigned a different ID to the span.

Our Exact Our method (Section 4.1), but rounding the 'match' down to zero, so only exactly matching spans get the credit (of 1).

Our Partial Our method (Section 4.1).

Bag of IDs disregards spans altogether, checking just the match of the BabelNet IDs needed and produced. Precision is the fraction of correct (confirmed by the golden data) IDs among all labels produced by the system. Recall is the number of correct IDs divided by the number of labels in the gold set. This scoring gives an idea of how well the system guesses the "meaning" (bag of concepts) of the whole sentence.

The Table 1 documents that the official scoring heavily boosted our precision and hurt our recall. The performances of other systems are affected as well, but fortunately, the overall impression is similar across the scoring techniques.

4.3 Variants of Our Submission

As the official scores in the overview paper (Moro and Navigli, 2015) show, our system performed acceptably on Named Entities Recognition task, but it clearly failed on word senses disambiguation.

Table 2 reports the scores (official scoring) of a few variations of our approach. The first row is the submitted system, the second row is a correction which allows Wiktionary results to map to BabelNet senses of all parts of speech, not just nouns. The remaining rows use a different IR model or include sentence context in Wiktionary search but no improvement is obtained.

4.4 Recommendations for Future Evaluation

For future shared tasks, we recommend:

- Define precision and recall to better match the common meaning, e.g. as in our proposal.
- Preserve letter case in IDs to avoid ambiguity in Wikipedia to BabelNet mapping.
- Use only one repertoire of IDs in the gold set.

4.5 Future Work

In future we want to evaluate other heuristics such as weighted words picking instead of first one, offered by search algorithms. Also we'll examine possibilities to enhance Wordnet and Wiktionary records to make search results more reliable. Another way of improvement is using Named Entities Recognition systems to define correct span boundaries and to achieve better results for Named Entities.

5 Conclusion

We described our system for SemEval Task 13 based on information retrieval. The system performs acceptably in Named Entity Linking (NEL) but fails in Word Sense Disambiguation. One of the reasons is that we used small information records for Wiktionary and especially for Wordnet and little or no sentence context in WSD queries, so the information retrieval algorithms performed poorly.

Additionally, we proposed different scoring techniques that, in our opinion, better reflect the performance of the systems. Fortunately, the overall ranking of systems ends up similar to the official scoring. We nevertheless recommend a few changes for future shared tasks.

References

Khaled Abdalgader and Andrew Skabar. Short-text similarity measurement using word sense disambiguation and synonym expansion. In *AI 2010: Advances in Artificial Intelligence*, pages 435–444. 2011.

Marine Carpuat and Dekai Wu. Improving Statistical Machine Translation Using Word Sense Disambiguation. In *EMNLP-CoNLL*, volume 7, pages 61–72, 2007.

Marco Cornolti, Paolo Ferragina, and Massimiliano Ciaramita. A framework for benchmarking entity-annotation systems. In *Proceedings of the 22nd international conference on World Wide Web*, pages 249–260, 2013.

Oren Etzioni, Michele Banko, and Michael J. Cafarella. Machine Reading. In *AAAI*, volume 6, pages 1517–1519, 2006.

Mena B. Habib and Maurice Keulen. Unsupervised improvement of named entity extraction in short informal context using disambiguation clues. 2012.

Andrea Moro and Roberto Navigli. SemEval-2015 Task 13: Multilingual All-Words Sense Disambiguation and Entity Linking. In *Proc. of SemEval-2015*, 2015.

Roberto Navigli. Word sense disambiguation: A survey. *ACM Computing Surveys (CSUR)*, 41(2):10, 2009.

Stephen E. Robertson, Steve Walker, Susan Jones, Micheline M. Hancock-Beaulieu, Mike Gatford, et al. Okapi at TREC-3. *NIST SPECIAL PUBLICATION SP*, pages 109–109, 1995.

Gerard Salton, Anita Wong, and Chung-Shu Yang. A vector space model for automatic indexing. *Communications of the ACM*, 18(11):613–620, 1975.

Lenhart Schubert. Turing's Dream and the Knowledge Challenge. In *Proc. of the national conference on artificial intelligence*, volume 21, page 1534, 2006.

Eduard Šubert and Ondřej Bojar. Twitter Crowd Translation – Design and Objectives. 2014.

EL92: Entity Linking Combining Open Source Annotators via Weighted Voting

Pablo Ruiz and **Thierry Poibeau**
Laboratoire LATTICE
CNRS, École Normale Supérieure, U. Paris 3 Sorbonne Nouvelle
1, rue Maurice Arnoux
92120 Montrouge, France
{pablo.ruiz.fabo,thierry.poibeau}@ens.fr

Abstract

Our participation at SemEval's Multilingual All-Words Sense Disambiguation and Entity Linking task is described. An English entity linking (EL) system is presented, which combines the annotations of four public open source EL services. The annotations are combined through a weighted voting scheme inspired on the ROVER method, which had not been previously tested on EL outputs. Results on the task's EL items were competitive.

1 Introduction

The paper describes our participation at SemEval 2015, Task 13 (Moro and Navigli, 2015): Multilingual all-words Sense Disambiguation (WSD) and Entity Linking (EL). Systems performing both tasks, or either one, can participate. The preferred word-sense and entity inventory is Babelnet (Navigli and Ponzetto, 2012); other inventories are allowed. Our system performs English EL to Wikipedia, combining the output of open-source, publicly available EL systems via weighted voting. The system is relevant to the task's interest in comparing the results of EL systems that apply encyclopedic knowledge only, like ours, and systems that jointly exploit encyclopedic and lexicographic resources for EL.

The paper's structure is the following: Section 2 discusses related work, and Section 3 describes the system. Sections 4 and 5 present the results and a conclusion.

2 Related Work

General surveys on EL can be found in (Cornolti et al., 2013) and (Rao et al., 2013). Work on combining NLP annotators and on evaluating EL systems is particularly relevant for our submission.

The goal of combining different NLP systems is obtaining combined results that are better than the results of each individual system. Fiscus (1997) created the ROVER method, with weighted voting to improve speech recognition outputs. A ROVER was found to improve parsing results by De la Clergerie et al. (2008). Rizzo et al. (2014) improved Named Entity Recognition results, combining systems via different machine learning algorithms. Our approach is inspired on the ROVER method, which had not been previously attempted for EL to our knowledge. Systems that combine entity linkers exist (NERD, Rizzo and Troncy, 2012). However, a difference in our system is that the set of linkers we combine is public and open-source. A second difference is the set of methods we employed to combine annotations.

EL evaluation work (Cornolti et al., 2013), (Usbeck et al., 2015) has highlighted to what an extent EL systems' performance can differ depending on characteristics of the corpus. This motivates testing whether different EL systems, properly combined, can complement each other.

3 System Description

The system performs English EL to Wikipedia, combining the outputs of the following EL systems: Tagme 2[1] (Ferragina and Scaiella, 2010), DBpedia Spotlight[2] (Mendes et al. 2011), Wikipedia Miner[3] (Milne and Witten, 2008) and Babelfy[4] (Moro et al. 2014). Babelfy outputs were only considered if they started with a *WIKI* prefix or their first character was uppercase.[5] Details about each of our workflow's steps follow.

3.1 Individual Systems' Thresholds

First of all, a client requests the annotations for a text from each linker's web-service, using the services' default settings except for the confidence threshold, which is configured in our system. Annotations whose confidence is below a threshold are eliminated.

All of the linkers used, except Babelfy, output confidence scores for their annotations. Cornolti et al., (2013) reported optimal confidence-score thresholds for all our linkers (except Babelfy). Using Cornolti's BAT Framework, we verified that the thresholds are still valid.[6] We adopted the weak-annotation match thresholds for the IITB dataset, since we consider the IITB corpus close to the task's data, in text-length and topical variety. Our thresholds were 0.102 for Tagme, 0.023 for Spotlight, and 0.219 for Wikipedia Miner. Since Babelfy does not output confidence scores, all of its annotations were accepted to the next step in the workflow.

3.2 Ranking the Systems to Combine

Our method for combining annotators' outputs requires the annotators to be previously ranked for precision on an annotated reference set. It is not viable to annotate a reference set for each new corpus. To help overcome this issue, we adopt the following heuristic: We have ranked the annotators on a series of very different reference corpora. To perform EL on a new corpus, our heuristic considers the following criteria: First, the types of EL annotations needed by the user. Second, how similar the new corpus is (along dimensions described below) to the reference corpora on which we have pre-ranked the annotators. To apply the workflow to a new corpus, the heuristic chooses the annotator-ranking obtained with the reference corpus that is most similar to that new corpus, while still respecting the annotation-types needed by the user.

The reference corpora on which we pre-ranked the annotators are AIDA/CoNLL Test B (Hoffart et al., 2011), and IITB (Kulkarni et al., 2009). These corpora are very different to each other, in terms of character length, topical variety, and regarding whether they annotate common-noun mentions or not. Moreover, some EL systems obtain opposite results when evaluated on AIDA/CoNLL B vs. IITB, as tests by Cornolti et al. (2013) and on the GERBIL platform[7] have shown.

The heuristic's first criterion is the types of annotations needed: If the user needs annotations for common-noun mentions, the IITB ranking is used, since IITB is the only one in our reference-datasets that was annotated for such mentions. If the user does not need common noun annotations, our heuristic compares the user's corpus with our two reference corpora in terms of character length and of a measure of lexical cohesion. Both factors have been argued to influence linkers' uneven results across corpora (Cornolti et al., 2013).

We accepted common-noun annotations for the task, as they were relevant for the task's domains (e.g. disease names for the biomedical texts). Accordingly, the heuristic ranked annotators as per their IITB results: 1st Wikipedia Miner (0.568 precision), 2nd Babelfy (0.493), 3rd Spotlight (0.462), 4th Tagme (0.452).[8]

3.3 Weighting and Selecting Annotations

Using the linker ranking from the previous step, the annotations are voted, and selected for final output or rejected based on the vote. We used two

[1] http://tagme.di.unipi.it/tagme_help.html
[2] https://github.com/dbpedia-spotlight/dbpedia-spotlight/wiki
[3] http://wikipedia-miner.cms.waikato.ac.nz/
[4] http://babelfy.org/download.jsp
[5] Babelfy was a late addition to our pipeline; the reader will note that we made some ad-hoc decisions to benefit from its outputs while complying with previously defined features in our workflow.
[6] https://github.com/marcocor/bat-framework
[7] See http://gerbil.aksw.org/gerbil/overview at the site for the GERBIL platform (Usbeck et al., 2015):
[8] The precision is from tests in Cornolti et al., 2013, using weak-annotation-match. Babefly was not tested. In order to be able to rank it, instead of its precision we assigned it the average of all other annotators' precisions.

voting schemes. The first one relies on each annotation's confidence score, weighted by the annotator's rank and precision on the ranking datasets from 3.2. The rationale is that a high-confidence annotation for a low-ranked annotator can be better than a low-confidence annotation for a higher-ranked annotator. The definition is in Figure 1: For each annotation *(m, e)* in the results, m is its mention,[9] e is the entity paired with m, and Ω_m is the set of annotations in the results whose mentions overlap[10] with m. If the size of Ω_m is 1, the scaled confidence[11] o_{scf} of Ω_m's unique annotation o must reach threshold t_{uniq} in order for o to be accepted. Threshold t_{uniq} is the average of the scaled confidence scores for all annotations in the corpus. If Ω_m has more than one annotation, the voting is thus: For each annotation o in Ω_m, o's vote is a product determined by several factors: o_{scf} is o's scaled confidence.[12] N is the total number of annotators we combine (i.e. 4). Operand ro_{ant} is the rank of annotator o_{ant}, which produced annotation o. Po_{ant} is that annotator's precision on the ranking reference corpus (3.2 above). For ro_{ant}, 0 is the best rank and $N - 1$ the worst. Parameter α influences the distance between the annotations' votes based on their annotators' rank, and was set at 0. The annotation with the highest vote in Ω_m is accepted; the rest are rejected.

for each set Ω_m of overlapping annotations:
  if $|\Omega_m| = 1$
    for $o \in \Omega_m$: if $o_{scf} \geq t_{uniq}$ accept o
              else reject o
  else
    select $\max_{o \in \Omega_m} \left[(o_{scf} \cdot (N - (ro_{ant} - \alpha)) \cdot Po_{ant}\right]$

Figure 1: Annotation voting scheme used in Run 1.

The second voting scheme is similar to the ROVER method in (De la Clergerie et al., 2008). The method assesses annotations based on how many linkers have produced them, using the linkers' rank, and their precision on the ranking-sets, as weights. If enough lower-ranked annotators have linked to an entity, this entity can win over an entity proposed by a higher-ranked annotator.

The voting is defined in Figure 2. For each annotation (mention m, entity e), Ω_m is the set of annotations whose mentions overlap[10] with m. Based on the different entities in Ω_m's annotations, Ω_m is divided into disjoint subsets, each of which contains annotations linking to a different entity. Each of these subsets L is voted by *vote(L)*. In *vote(L)*, for each annotation o in L, terms N, ro_{ant}, α, Po_{ant} have the same meaning as the terms bearing the same names in Figure 1, and are described above.

for each set Ω_m of overlapping annotations:
 for $L \in \Omega_m$:

$$vote(L) = \frac{\sum_{o \in L} (N - (ro_{ant} - \alpha)) \cdot Po_{ant}}{N}$$

 if $\max_{L \in \Omega_m} (vote(L)) > P_{max}$: select $\operatorname{argmax}_{L \in \Omega_m}(vote(L))$

Figure 2: Entity voting scheme used in Runs 2 and 3.

The entity for the subset L which obtains the highest vote among Ω_m's subsets is selected if its vote is higher than P_{max}, i.e. the maximum precision in the ranking dataset (0.568, see Section 3.2). After selecting the winning entity, we still need to select a mention for it. The mention is selected at random among the mentions of the annotations in the winning subset L. This implementation of mention selection is meant as a baseline that can be refined in the future. Two initial factors to consider in mention selection would be mention length and the annotators having chosen each mention.

3.4 Entity Classification

After the vote, entities in the selected annotations are classified before final output. The classification is rule-based. It exploits the category or type labels output by the EL services we combined—except Babelfy, which does not output such information.

The classification-rules are based on type labels in the NERD ontology (Rizzo and Troncy, 2012)[13]

[9] The string of characters in the text that the annotation is based on (the term *mention* is often used in EL for this notion).

[10] Assume two mentions (p1, e1) and (p2, e2), where p1 and p2 are the mentions' first character indices, and e1 and e2 are the mentions' last character indices. The mentions overlap iff $((p1 = p2) \wedge (e1 = e2)) \vee ((p1 = p2) \wedge (e1 < e2)) \vee ((p1 = p2) \wedge (e2 < e1)) \vee ((e1 = e2) \wedge (p1 < p2)) \vee ((e1 = e2) \wedge (p2 < p1)) \vee ((p1 < p2) \wedge (p2 < e1)) \vee ((p2 < p1) \wedge (p1 < e2))$.

[11] Since the range of confidence-scores output by each annotator was different, we minmax-scaled all original (*orig*) confidence scores to a 0-1 range: *scaled_confidence* = (orig_*confidence* – *corpus_min_orig_confidence) / (corpus_max_orig_confidence–corpus_min_orig_confidence)*

[12] As Babelfy does not provide confidence scores, its annotations were assigned the average over the whole result-set of the scaled confidence-scores output by the other annotators.

[13] http://nerd.eurecom.fr/ontology/nerd-v0.5.n3

and on a subset of the DBpedia ontology classes (Mendes et al. 2011)[14] relevant for the task's domains. For types *Person*, *Location*, *Organization*, Wikipedia category labels were also exploited.

Some rules involve an exact match against the annotations' categories or types, e.g. "Assign type *Location* if the annotation has type *DBpedia:Place*". Some rules involve a partial match, e.g. "Assign type *Person* if one of the Wikipedia category labels for the entity contains *births*".

For Babelfy outputs, Wikipedia category labels and DBpedia types were obtained through Wikipedia Miner's[3] and DBpedia's[15] APIs.

4 Results and Discussion

Since the task was open to systems doing either WSD or EL, or both, the corpus targeted both WSD and EL. Participant systems were evaluated on a different set of items depending on their nature (EL only, WSD only, both). The corpus contained 4 generic and domain-specific documents with 1094 single-word instances, 82 multi-words and 86 named entities (NE).

Our system was conceived and evaluated as an EL system. Table 1 shows our precision, recall and F1 for all three runs. Column *TopF1* is the maximum F1 attained by a participant on the EL items.

EL	P	R	F1	TopF1
Run1	**100**	**75.6**	**86.1**	88.9
Run2	98.3	66.3	79.2	
Run3	**100**	66.3	79.7	

Table 1: English EL results for all domains.

Run 1 results were competitive, ranking 3rd of 10, if we compare all participants' best runs. Runs 2 and 3 lag behind, due to lower recall. Run 1 employed the voting scheme in Figure 1. Runs 2 and 3 correspond to the scheme defined in Figure 2, with parameter α set to 0 in Run 2 and to 1 in Run 3. In spite of its results, the voting scheme from Figure 2 has advantages over the first one: It does not require confidence scores, so it accommodates linkers that don't score their annotations. Also, it does not need a separate threshold to decide on annotations produced by one annotator only. More work is needed to determine the reason for this difference in results, i.e. whether the second approach itself is not useful to combine EL annotations, or whether its worse results were related to our implementation.

One of the task's purposes was to compare systems' performance across domains. Table 2 shows our best run's results per domain. Column *N* reflects the number of EL items in the corpus for each domain. All other columns have the same meaning as in Table 1, but considering the per-domain results.

	N	P	R	F1	TopF1
Biomedical	48	100	83.3	90.9	100
Math & Computer	22	100	54.4	70.6	74.3
General	16	100	81.3	89.7	90.3

Table 2: English EL Run 1 results by domain.

Note that the small number of EL items available for each domain limits in our opinion the reliability of interpretations for these results.

Since our workflow combines several EL systems, it would be interesting to compare results for each individual system by itself vs. the results for the combined system. In later work (Ruiz and Poibeau, 2015), using an improved version of the system described here, and larger EL golden-sets, we performed such comparisons, finding significant improvements in the combined system vs. the individual ones.

5 Conclusion

The entity linking (EL) system presented was ranked 3rd (out of 10) on the task's EL items. The system combines the outputs of four public open source EL services. Two weighted voting methods were described to combine the outputs. The first method relies on annotations' confidence scores; the second one is a weighted majority vote. The first method obtained better results, but the second one has the advantage of being easily applicable to non-scored annotations. More work is needed to assess the reasons for the methods' differential performance. Future work also includes adding other public open source systems to the workflow.

Acknowledgments

Pablo Ruiz was supported by a PhD scholarship from Région Île-de-France.

[14] http://mappings.dbpedia.org/server/ontology/classes/

[15] http://dbpedia.org/sparql

References

Marco Cornolti, Paolo Ferragina, and Massimiliano Ciaramita. (2013). A framework for benchmarking entity-annotation systems. In *Proc. of WWW*, 249–260.

Éric Vilemonte De La Clergerie, Olivier Hamon, Djamel Mostefa, Christelle Ayache, Patrick Paroubek, and Anne Vilnat. (2008). Passage: from French parser evaluation to large sized treebank. In *Proc. of LREC 2008*, 3570–3576.

Paolo Ferragina and Ugo Scaiella. (2010). Tagme: on-the-fly annotation of short text fragments (by wikipedia entities). In *Proc. of CIKM'10*, 1625–1628.

Jonathan G Fiscus. (1997). A post-processing system to yield reduced word error rates: Recognizer output voting error reduction (ROVER). In *Proc. of the IEEE Workshop on Automatic Speech Recognition and Understanding, 1997*, 347–354.

Johannes Hoffart, Mohamed Amir Yosef, Ilaria Bordino, Hagen Fürstenau, Manfred Pinkal, Marc Spaniol, Bilyana Taneva, Stefan Thater, and Gerhard Weikum. (2011). Robust disambiguation of named entities in text. In *Proc. of EMNLP*, 782–792.

Sayali Kulkarni, Amit Singh, Ganesh Ramakrishnan, and Soumen Chakrabarti. (2009). Collective annotation of Wikipedia entities in web text. In *Proc. ACM SIGKDD*, 457–466.

Pablo N. Mendes, Max Jakob, Andrés García-Silva, and Christian Bizer. (2011). DBpedia spotlight: shedding light on the web of documents. In *Proc. of the 7th Int. Conf. on Semantic Systems, I-SEMANTICS'11*, 1–8.

David Milne and Ian H. Witten. (2008). An effective, low-cost measure of semantic relatedness obtained from Wikipedia links. In *Proc. of AAAI Workshop on Wikipedia and Artificial Intelligence: an Evolving Synergy,* 25–30

Andrea Moro and Roberto Navigli (2015) SemEval-2015 Task 13: Multilingual All-Words Sense Disambiguation and Entity Linking. In *Proc. of SemEval-2015.*

Andrea Moro, Alessandro Raganato, and Roberto Navigli. (2014). Entity Linking meets Word Sense Disambiguation: A Unified Approach. *Transactions of the ACL*, 2, 231–244.

Roberto Navigli and Simone Ponzetto. (2012). BabelNet: The automatic construction, evaluation and application of a wide-coverage multilingual semantic network. *Artificial Intelligence*, 193, 217–250.

Delip Rao, Paul McNamee, and Mark Dredze. (2013). Entity linking: Finding extracted entities in a knowledge base. In *Multi-source, Multilingual Information Extraction and Summarization*, 93–115. Springer.

Giuseppe Rizzo and Raphaël Troncy. (2012). NERD: a framework for unifying named entity recognition and disambiguation extraction tools. In *Proc. of the Demonstrations at EACL'12*, 73–76.

Giuseppe Rizzo, Marieke van Erp, and Raphaël Troncy. (2014). Benchmarking the Extraction and Disambiguation of Named Entities on the Semantic Web. In *Proc. of LREC 2014*, 4593–4600.

Pablo Ruiz and Thierry Poibeau. (2015). Combining Open Source Annotators for Entity Linking through Weighted Voting. In *Proceedings of *SEM 2015. Fourth Joint Conference on Lexical and Computational Semantics*. Denver, U.S.

Ricardo Usbeck, Michael Röder, Axel-Cyrille Ngonga, Ciro Baron, Andrea Both, Martin Brümmer, Diego Ceccarelli, Marco Cornolti, Didier Cherix, Bernd Eickmann, Paolo Ferragina, Christiane Lemke, Andrea Moro, Roberto Navigli, Francesco Piccino, Giuseppe Rizzo, Harald Sack, René Speck, Raphaël Troncy, Jörg Waitelonis, and Lars Wesemann. (2015). GERBIL–General Entity Annotator Benchmarking Framework. In *Proc. of WWW.*

UNIBA: Combining Distributional Semantic Models and Sense Distribution for Multilingual All-Words Sense Disambiguation and Entity Linking

Pierpaolo Basile and **Annalina Caputo** and **Giovanni Semeraro**
Department of Computer Science
University of Bari Aldo Moro
Via, E. Orabona, 4 - 70125 Bari (Italy)
{pierpaolo.basile,annalina.caputo,giovanni.semeraro}@uniba.it

Abstract

This paper describes the participation of the UNIBA team in the Task 13 of SemEval-2015 about Multilingual All-Words Sense Disambiguation and Entity Linking. We propose an algorithm able to disambiguate both word senses and named entities by combining the simple Lesk approach with information coming from both a distributional semantic model and usage frequency of meanings. The results for both English and Italian show satisfactory performance.

1 Introduction

SemEval-2015 Task 13 (Moro and Navigli, 2015) aims to evaluate systems that provide a comprehensive representation of text through linking of both words and entities with concepts in a knowledge base. Besides the traditional difficulties of word sense disambiguation, this task requires specific methods able to tackle the challenges posed by the named entity recognition, disambiguation and linking steps.

This paper proposes a unified strategy for word sense and named entity disambiguation which leverages BabelNet, a multilingual resource that encompasses both encyclopedic and lexicographic knowledge (Navigli and Ponzetto, 2012). Our approach relies on the Distributional Lesk (DL-WSD) algorithm (Basile et al., 2014), which is able to disambiguate a word occurrence by computing the similarity between word context and the glosses associated with all possible word meanings. Such a similarity is computed through a Distributional Semantic Model (DSM) (Sahlgren, 2006).

In this work we describe an extension of the DL-WSD algorithm that exploits a specific module for entity discovery given a list of possible surface forms. In particular, we build an index in which each surface form (i.e. candidate entity) is paired to the list of all its possible meanings in a semantic network. This index of surface forms is exploited to look up all candidate entities in a text.

The rest of this paper is structured as follows: Section 2 provides details about the adopted strategy, and describes the two main steps: 1) Entity Recognition and 2) Disambiguation. An experimental evaluation, along with details about results, is presented in Section 3, while conclusions close the paper.

2 Methodology

Our methodology is a two-step algorithm consisting in an initial identification of all possible entities mentioned in a text followed by the disambiguation of both words and named entities through the DL-WSD algorithm. The semantic network is exploited twice in order to 1) extract all the possible surface forms related to entities, and 2) retrieve glosses used in the disambiguation process.

2.1 Entity Recognition

In order to speed up the entity recognition step we build an index in which for each surface form (entity) the set of all its possible meanings in the semantic network is reported. Lucene[1] is exploited to

[1] http://lucene.apache.org/

build the index, specifically for each surface form (lexeme) occurring in BabelNet, a document composed of two fields is created. The first field stores the surface form, while the second one contains the list of all possible BabelSynsets that refer to the surface form in the first field. The index is built separately for each language, Italian and English. The entity recognition module exploits this index in order to find entities in a text. Given a text fragment, the module performs the following steps:

- Building all n-grams up to five words;
- Querying the index and retrieving the list of the top t matching surface forms for each n-gram. It is possible to enable a multi-match strategy; for example the 3-gram "European Union Commission" can match two entities: "European Union" and "European Union Commission". The multi-match strategy provides disambiguation for all the possible entities, otherwise the longest surface form is selected;
- Scoring each surface form by exploiting two different approaches:

  EXACT_MATCH computes the linear combination between the score provided by the search engine and a string similarity function based on the Levenshtein Distance between the n-gram and the candidate surface form in the index;

  PARTIAL_MATCH computes the linear combination between the two scores provided by the EXACT_MATCH and the Jaccard Index in terms of common words between the n-gram and the candidate surface form;
- Filtering the candidate entities recognized in the previous steps; entities are removed if the score computed in the previous step is below a given threshold and/or the sequence of PoS-tags related to the n-gram does not match a set of defined patterns;
- Assigning to each candidate entity two additional scores according to the percentage of: 1) stop words, and 2) words that do not contain at least one upper-case character. A threshold can be fixed for each score to filter out some entities.

Moreover, for each entity we build a set of alternatives. For example, given the candidate entity "European Union" we create the set of alternative surface forms $\{$*European, Union, EU, E.U.*$\}$. Then, we add all the BabelSynsets of "European Union" to the list of possible meanings of those words that follow the candidate entity and belong to the set of alternative forms.

The output of the entity recognition module is a list of candidate entities in which a set of possible meanings (BabelSynset) is assigned to each surface form in the list. The set of named entities extracted by this module and the list of all the words in the text are the input to the DL-WSD algorithm.

2.2 DL-WSD

We exploit the distributional Lesk algorithm proposed by Basile et al. (2014) for disambiguating words and named entities. The algorithm replaces the concept of word overlap initially introduced by (Lesk, 1986) with the broader concept of semantic similarity computed in a distributional semantic space. Let $w_1, w_2, ...w_n$ be a sequence of words/entities, the algorithm disambiguates each target word/entity w_i by computing the semantic similarity between the glosses of senses associated with the target word/entity and its context. This similarity is computed by representing in a DSM both the gloss and the context as the sum of words they are composed of; then this similarity takes into account the co-occurrence evidences previously collected through a corpus of documents. The corpus plays a key role since the richer it is the higher is the probability that each word is fully represented in all its contexts of use. We exploit the word2vec tool[2](Mikolov et al., 2013) in order to build a DSM, by analyzing all the pages in the last English/Italian Wikipedia Dump. The correct sense for a word is the one whose gloss maximizes the semantic similarity with the word/entity context. The sense description can still be too short for a meaningful comparison with the word/entity context. Following this observation, we adopted an approach inspired by the adapted Lesk (Banerjee and Pedersen, 2002), and

[2]https://code.google.com/p/word2vec/

we decided to enrich the gloss of the sense with those of related meanings, duly weighted to reflect their distances with respect to the original sense. The algorithm consists of the following steps.

Building the glosses. We retrieve the set $S_i = \{s_{i1}, s_{i2}, ..., s_{ik}\}$ of senses associated to the word/entity w_i. For named entities such a set is provided by the entity recognition module, while for words the set is obtained by firstly looking up to the WordNet portion of BabelNet, then if no sense is found we seek for senses from Wikipedia. For each sense s_{ij}, the algorithm builds the extended gloss representation g^*_{ij} by adding to the original gloss g_{ij} the glosses of related meanings retrieved through the BabelNet function *getRelatedMap*, with the exception of *antonym* senses. Each word in g^*_{ij} is weighted by a function inversely proportional to the distance d between s_{ij} and the related glosses where the word occurs. Moreover, in order to emphasize discriminative words among the different senses, in the weight we introduce a variation of the inverse document frequency (*idf*) for retrieval that we named *inverse gloss frequency* (*igf*). The *igf* for a word w_k occurring gf^*_k times in the set of extended glosses for all the senses in S_i (the sense inventory of w_i) is computed as $IGF_k = 1 + log_2 \frac{|S_i|}{gf^*_k}$. The final weight for the word w_k appearing h times in the extended gloss g^*_{ij} is given by:

$$weight(w_k, g^*_{ij}) = h \times IGF_k \times \frac{1}{1+d} \quad (1)$$

Building the context. The context C for the word w_i is represented by all the words that occur in the text.

Building the vector representations. The context C and each extended gloss g^*_{ij} are represented as vectors in the *SemanticSpace* built through the DSM.

Sense ranking. The algorithm computes the cosine similarity between the vector representation of each extended gloss g^*_{ij} and that of the context C. Then, the cosine similarity is linearly combined with a function which takes into account the usage of the meaning in the language. We analyse a function that computes the probability assigned to each synset given a word/named entity as follows:

Word. We exploit a synset-tagged corpus and we attempt to map each word occurrence to WordNet (Miller, 1995). Then, we select the WordNet sysnet with the maximum probability.

Named Entity. We retrieve from BabelNet the Wikipedia title pages related to the BabelSynset and count the number of times a Wikipedia page is linked from another page. In this way we use Wikipedia as a synset-tagged corpus.

We define the probability $p(s_{ij}|w_i)$ that takes into account the sense distribution of s_{ij} given the word/entity w_i. The sense distribution is computed as the number of times the word/entity w_i is tagged with the sense. Zero probabilities are avoided by introducing an additive (Laplace) smoothing. The probability is computed as follows:

$$p(s_{ij}|w_i) = \frac{t(w_i, s_{ij}) + 1}{\#w_i + |S_i|} \quad (2)$$

where $t(w_i, s_{ij})$ is the number of times the word/entity w_i is tagged with the sense s_{ij}.

3 Evaluation

The evaluation aims at comparing the system result against a gold standard manually annotated using synsets from BabelNet 2.5.1. Test data consists of four documents that belong to three different domains: biomedical, maths and computer science, and general. The idea is to evaluate the algorithm performance both in general and specific domains. We submitted three runs with different parameter settings that mainly affected the entity recognition module. System settings are reported in Table 1.

Run	Match	PoS-Tag	Threshold
Run1	EXACT	YES	1.0
Run2	PARTIAL	YES	0.75
Run3	PARTIAL	NO	0.75

Table 1: System settings.

The Match column indicates the type of matching used during the entity recognition step, PoS-Tag reports the usage of the filter based on PoS-Tag patterns, and finally the table reports the Threshold used by the matching filter. Moreover, we set the number

	EN							IT						
Run	all	NE	WSD	n	v	r	a	all	NE	WSD	n	v	r	a
best	65.8	88.9	64.6	70.3	57.7	79.0	79.5	59.9	54.9	61.3	56.6	62.7	62.5	69.6
Run1	58.4	84.4	56.5	63.3	57.1	79.0	-	50.8	48.5	51.0	53.7	61.1	60.0	-
Run2	58.3	82.9	56.5	63.2	57.1	79.0	-	50.9	48.5	51.0	53.8	61.1	60.0	-
Run3	58.3	82.9	56.5	63.2	57.1	79.0	-	50.9	50.0	51.0	53.7	61.1	60.0	-

Table 2: Official task results.

	EN				IT			
Run	all	NE	WSD	a	all	NE	WSD	a
Run1	**61.3**	88.1	59.5	48.2	**59.5**	51.0	59.9	77.7
Run2	61.0	85.2	59.3	47.6	59.6	51.0	60.0	77.7
Run3	60.8	84.4	59.2	47.6	**59.5**	51.0	59.9	77.7

Table 3: Task results after the adjective fix.

of entities retrieved by the search engine to 25, and the thresholds for stop-word and lower-case filters to 0.3.

Table 2 reports the official results released by the task organizers. Our best system ranks 4th among 17 submissions for English, and 4th among 8 for Italian. As reported in Table 2, our system is not scored for adjective. This issue is due to a problem with PoS-tag: in trial data adjectives are tagged with 'A', while in the test data with 'J'. Inadvertently, we did not report this modification in our system during the testing. After the release of the gold standard, we fixed that issue in our system and performed a new experiment whose results are reported in Table 3. Since results for noun, verbs and adverbs are not affected by the fix, they are not reported again in the table. Considering the new results reported in Table 3, our system is able to rank 3rd for English, and 2nd for Italian.

Another goal of the task is to evaluate system performance on different domains. In particular three domains were provided: biomedical (**bio**), maths and computer science (**math**), and general domain (**gnr**). Results for each domain and language are reported in Table 4. Our performance on each domain shows a trend very similar to the best system for each language: the math/computer science domain is the hardest to disambiguate, while the biomedical one seems to be the easiest. A deep analysis of domain results shows that our system is the best to disambiguate named entities for Italian biomedical and math/computer science domains, while it provides the lowest performance in the general domain for both Italian and English. It is important to note that the system settings seem not to affect the overall performance, while a deep analysis focused on the only named entities reveals slight differences between settings. This behaviour is due to the different methods used to recognize named entities. The task description paper reports more details about results (Moro and Navigli, 2015).

	EN			IT		
Run	bio	math	gnr	bio	math	gnr
best	71.2	54.1	67.2	65.5	52.1	61.0
Run1	66.6	50.8	62.0	64.4	51.2	58.4
Run2	66.4	50.8	60.7	64.4	51.2	58.7
Run3	66.4	50.8	60.2	64.4	51.2	58.4

Table 4: System performance for each domain.

4 Conclusions

We presented a unified approach to entity linking and word sense disambiguation which relies on a distributional extension of the simple Lesk disambiguation algorithm. This algorithm has been extended with an entity recognition module able to recognize candidate named entities. We evaluated three different configurations of such recognition module within the Task 13 of SemEval-2015. Experimental evaluation showed competitive results, with our best run ranked among the top systems.

References

Satanjeev Banerjee and Ted Pedersen. 2002. An Adapted Lesk Algorithm for Word Sense Disambiguation Using WordNet. In Alexander Gelbukh, editor, *Computational Linguistics and Intelligent Text Processing*, volume 2276 of *Lecture Notes in Computer Science*, pages 136–145.

Pierpaolo Basile, Annalina Caputo, and Giovanni Semeraro. 2014. An Enhanced Lesk Word Sense Disambiguation Algorithm through a Distributional Semantic Model. In *Proceedings of COLING 2014, the 25th International Conference on Computational Linguistics: Technical Papers*, pages 1591–1600, Dublin, Ireland.

Michael Lesk. 1986. Automatic Sense Disambiguation Using Machine Readable Dictionaries: How to Tell a Pine Cone from an Ice Cream Cone. In *Proceedings of the 5th Annual International Conference on Systems Documentation*, SIGDOC '86, pages 24–26, New York, NY, USA.

Tomas Mikolov, Kai Chen, Greg Corrado, and Jeffrey Dean. 2013. Efficient estimation of word representations in vector space. *CoRR*, abs/1301.3781.

George A Miller. 1995. WordNet: a lexical database for English. *Communications of the ACM*, 38(11):39–41.

Andrea Moro and Roberto Navigli. 2015. SemEval-2015 Task 13: Multilingual All-Words Sense Disambiguation and Entity Linking. In *Proceedings of SemEval-2015*.

Roberto Navigli and Simone Paolo Ponzetto. 2012. BabelNet: The automatic construction, evaluation and application of a wide-coverage multilingual semantic network. *Artificial Intelligence*, 193:217–250.

Magnus Sahlgren. 2006. *The Word-Space Model: Using distributional analysis to represent syntagmatic and paradigmatic relations between words in high-dimensional vector spaces*. Ph.D. thesis.

SUDOKU: Treating Word Sense Disambiguation & Entity Linking as a Deterministic Problem – via an Unsupervised & Iterative Approach

Steve L. Manion
University of Canterbury, Christchurch, New Zealand
steve.manion @pg.canterbury.ac.nz

Abstract

SUDOKU's submissions to SemEval Task 13 treats Word Sense Disambiguation and Entity Linking as a deterministic problem that exploits two key attributes of open-class words as constraints – their *degree of polysemy* and their *part of speech*. This is an extension and further validation of the results achieved by Manion and Sainudiin (2014). SUDOKU's three submissions are incremental in the use of the two aforementioned constraints. Run1 has no constraints and disambiguates all lemmas in one pass. Run2 disambiguates lemmas at increasing degrees of polysemy, leaving the most polysemous until last. Run3 is identical to Run2, with the additional constraint of disambiguating all named entities and nouns first before other types of open-class words (verbs, adjectives, and adverbs). Over all-domains, for English Run2 and Run3 were placed second and third. For Spanish Run2, Run3, and Run1 were placed first, second, and third respectively. For Italian Run1 was placed first with Run2 and Run3 placed second equal.

1 Introduction & Related Work

Almost a decade ago, Agirre and Edmonds (2007) suggested the promising potential for WSD that could exploit the interdependencies between senses in an interactive manner. In other words, this would be a WSD system which allows the disambiguation of word a to directly influence the *consecutive* disambiguation of word b. This is analogous to treating WSD as a deterministic problem, much like the Sudoku puzzle in which the final solution is reached by adhering to a set of pre-determined constraints. *Conventional* approaches to WSD often overlook the potential to exploit sense interdependencies, and simply disambiguate all senses in one pass based on a context window (e.g. a sentence or document). For this task the author proposes an *iterative* approach which makes several passes based on a set of constraints. For a more formal distinction between the *conventional* and *iterative* approach to WSD, please refer to this paper (Manion and Sainudiin, 2014).

Yr	%NE	%N	%V	%R	%A	F	ΔF
'04	-	37.7	34.0	12.6	15.6	27.1	+16.8
'10	-	73.8	26.2	-	-	26.8	+11.1
'13	17.1	82.9	-	-	-	58.3	+6.1
'15	*6.0*	*44.9*	*28.9*	*6.5*	*13.7*	*55.8*	*+5.8*

Table 1: Parts of Speech disambiguated (as percentages) for each SemEval Task (denoted by its year). In-Degree Centrality as implemented in (Manion and Sainudiin, 2014) observes F-Score improvement (F + ΔF) by applying the *iterative* approach.

The author found in the investigations of his thesis (Manion, 2014) that the iterative approach performed best on the SemEval 2013 Multilingual WSD Task (Navigli et al., 2013), as opposed to earlier tasks such as SensEval 2004 English All Words WSD Task (Snyder and Palmer, 2004) and the SemEval 2010 All Words WSD task on a Specific Domain (Agirre et al., 2010). While these earlier tasks also experienced improvement, F-Scores remained lower overall. Table 1 above and Figures 1(a) to (i) help highlight what changed between these tasks.

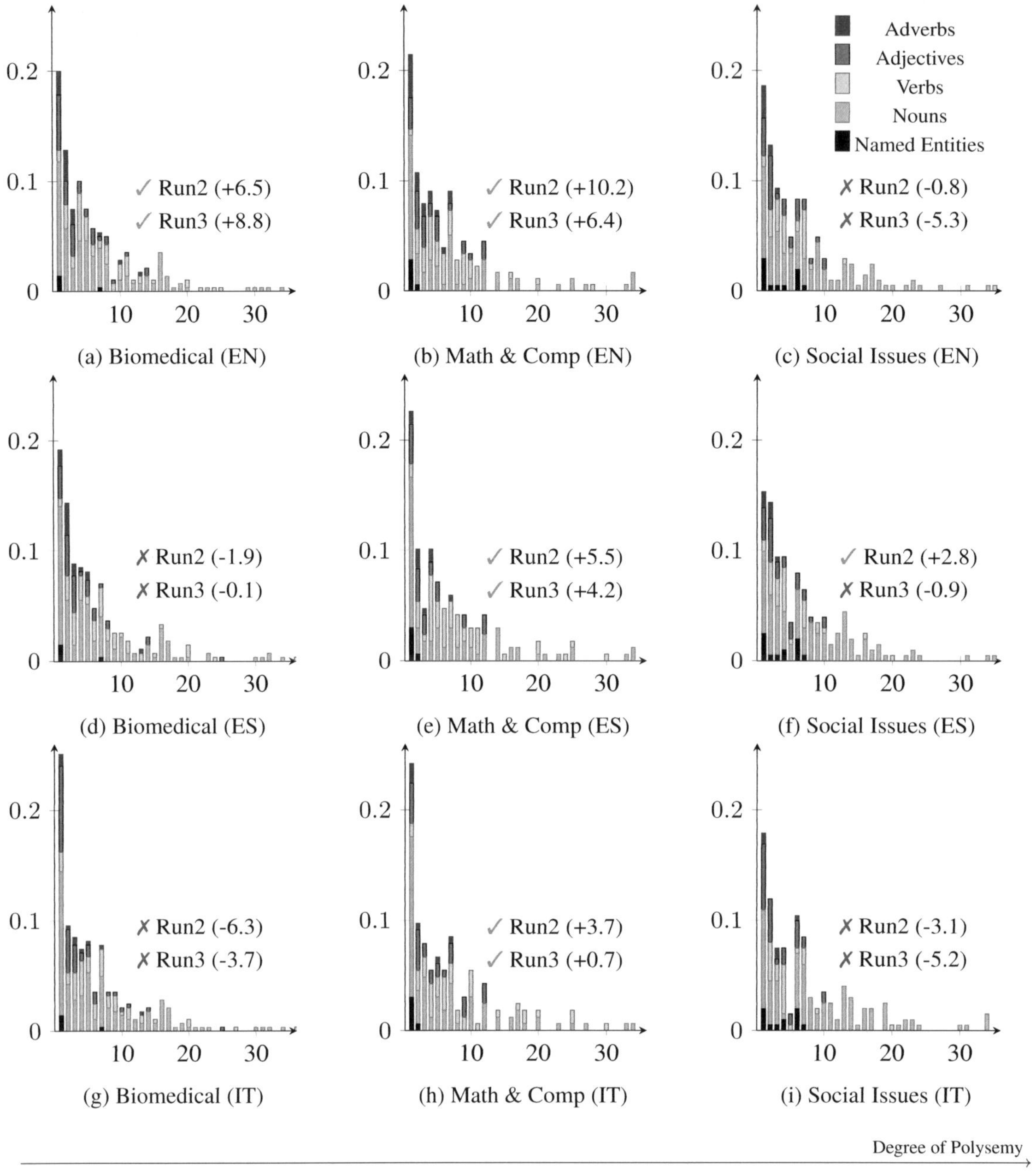

(a) Biomedical (EN) (b) Math & Comp (EN) (c) Social Issues (EN)

(d) Biomedical (ES) (e) Math & Comp (ES) (f) Social Issues (ES)

(g) Biomedical (IT) (h) Math & Comp (IT) (i) Social Issues (IT)

Figure 1: Depicted above are distributions for each domain and language, detailing the probability (y-axis) of specific parts of speech at increasing degrees of polysemy (x-axis). These distributions were produced from the gold keys (or synsets) of the test documents by querying BabelNet for the polysemy of each word. Each distribution was normalised with one sense per discourse assumed, therefore duplicate synsets were ignored. Lastly the difference in F-Score between the *conventional* Run1 and the *iterative* Run2 and Run3 is listed beside each distribution.

Firstly WSD tasks before 2013 generally relied on only a lexicon, such as WordNet (Fellbaum, 1998) or an alternative equivalent, whereas SemEval 2013 Task 12 WSD and this task (Moro and Navigli, 2015) included Entity Linking (EL) using the encyclopaedia Wikipedia via BabelNet (Navigli and Ponzetto, 2012). Secondly, as shown by Manion and Sainudiin (2014) with a simple linear regression, the iterative approach increases WSD performance for documents that have a higher degree of *document monosemy* - the percentage of unique monosemous lemmas in a document. As seen in Figures 1(a) to (i) on the previous page, named entities (or *unique* rather than *common* nouns) are more monosemous compared to other parts of speech, especially for more technical domains. Lastly, the SemEval 2013 WSD task differs in that only nouns and named entities required disambiguation. This simplifies the WSD task, as shown in the experiments on local context by Yarowsky (1993), nouns are best disambiguated by directly adjacent nouns (or modifying adjectives). Based on these observations, the author hypothesized the following implementations of the iterative approach should perform well.

2 System Description & Implementation

Run1 (SUDOKU-1) is the *conventional* approach – *no constraints* are applied. Formalised in (Manion and Sainudiin, 2014), this run can act as a baseline to gauge any improvement for Run2 and Run3 that apply the *iterative* approach. Run2 (SUDOKU-2) has the constraint of words being disambiguated in order of increasing polysemy, leaving the most polysemous to last. Run3 (SUDOKU-3) is an untested and unpublished version of the *iterative* approach. It includes Run2's constraint plus a second constraint – that all nouns and named entities must be disambiguated before other parts of speech.

For each run, a semantic subgraph is constructed from BabelNet (version 2.5.1). Then for disambiguation the graph centrality measure PageRank (Brin and Page, 1998) is used in conjunction with a surfing vector that biases probability mass to certain sense nodes in the semantic subgraph. This idea is taken from Personalised PageRank (PPR) (Agirre and Soroa, 2009), which applies the method put forward by Haveliwala (2003) to the field of WSD. In the previous SemEval WSD task (Navigli et al., 2013) team UMCC_DLSI (Gutierrez et al., 2013) implemented this method and achieved the best performance by biasing probability mass based on SemCor (Miller et al., 1993) sense frequencies. As the winning method for this task, PPR was selected to test the iterative approach on. For SUDOKU's implementation to be *unsupervised*, all runs biased probability mass towards senses from monosemous lemmas. Additionally for Run2 and Run3, once a lemma is disambiguated it is considered to be monosemous. Therefore with each iteration of Run2 and Run3, probability mass is redistributed across the surfing vector to acknowledge these *newly appointed* monosemous lemmas.

All system runs are applied at the document level, across all languages and domains, for all named entities, nouns, verbs, adverbs, and adjectives. Semantic subgraphs are constructed from BabelNet via a Depth First Search (DFS) up to 2 hops in path length. PageRank's damping factor is set to 0.85, with a maximum of 30 iterations[1]. In order to avoid masking the effect of using the iterative approach, a *back-off* strategy (see (McCarthy et al., 2004)) was *not* used. Multiword units were found by finding lemma sequences that contained at least one noun and at the same time could return a result from BabelNet. Lemma sequences beginning with definite/indefinite articles (e.g. *the*, *a*, *il*, *la*, and *el*) were removed as they induced too much noise, given they almost always returned a result from BabelNet (such as a book or movie title).

3 Results, Discussions, & Conclusions

As seen in Figures 1(a) to (i) on the previous page, the Biomedical and Math & Computers domains include a substantial degree of monosemy, no doubt increased by the monosemous technical terms and named entities present. Given the importance of document monosemy for the iterative approach, it is of no surprise that Run2 and Run3 in most cases performed much better than Run1 for these technical domains. Equally so, Run2 and Run3 were outperformed by Run1 for the less technical Social Issues

[1]PageRank iterations remain at the atomic level, i.e. they do not influence the construction of the semantic subgraph, see (Manion and Sainudiin, 2014) Section 3.1 for more details.

Part of Speech	All Domains (1)	Δ(2-1)	Δ(3-1)	Biology (1)	Δ(2-1)	Δ(3-1)	Math & Comp (1)	Δ(2-1)	Δ(3-1)	Social Issues (1)	Δ(2-1)	Δ(3-1)
Named Ents	16.8	+70.2	+70.2	4.1	+94.8	+94.8	0.0	+56.3	+56.3	60.9	+20.6	+20.6
Nouns	53.4	+9.1	+9.3	62.8	+9.1	+13.0	28.5	+22.9	+20.4	56.4	-3.6	-8.2
Verbs	52.2	-2.6	-6.2	52.5	-5.2	-1.9	51.4	-2.3	-9.1	52.9	+3.9	-12.0
Adverbs	48.9	+21.5	+22.8	50.7	+27.2	+24.6	52.0	+4.6	+12.2	36.4	+39.5	+39.5
Adjectives	74.4	-2.7	-6.3	82.3	+1.0	-4.5	75.0	-7.5	-17.5	63.6	-4.3	-0.6

Table 2: The difference in F-Scores over each Domain and Part of Speech for English SUDOKU Runs.

domain in which many of the named entities are polysemous rather than monosemous.

While the iterative approach achieved reasonably competitive results in English, this success did not translate as well to Spanish and Italian. The Italian Biomedical domain had the highest document monosemy, observable in Figure 1 (g), yet this did not help the *iterative* Run2 and Run3. Yet it is worth noting the results of the task paper (Moro and Navigli, 2015) report that SUDOKU Run2 and Run3 achieved very low F-Scores for named entity disambiguation (<28.6) in Spanish and Italian. Given that more than half of the named entities were monosemous in Figure 1(d) and (g), the WSD system either did not capture them in text or filtered them out during subgraph construction (see BabelNet API). This underscores the importance of named entities being included in disambiguation tasks. To further support this evidence, while the iterative approach is suited to domain based WSD, recall that the 2010 domain based WSD task in Table 1 also had no tagged named entities (and thus scores were lower than for successive named entity *inclusive* WSD tasks).

As seen in Table 2, the iterative approach has a varied effect on different parts of speech. Always improved is the disambiguation of named entities and adverbs. This is also the case for nouns in technical domains (e.g. Biomedical as opposed to Social Issues). On the other hand the disambiguation of verbs and adjectives suffers under the iterative approach. In hindsight, the iterative approach could be restricted to the parts of speech it is known to improve, while remaining with the conventional approach on others. To the right in Table 3 the author's SUDOKU runs are compared against the team with the most competitive results – LIMSI. The author could not improve on their superior results achieved in English, however for Spanish and Italian the BabelNet First Sense (BFS) baseline was much lower since it often resorted to lexicographic sorting in the absence of WordNet synsets – see (Navigli et al., 2013). The author's *baseline-independent* submissions were unaffected by this, which on reviewing results in (Moro and Navigli, 2015) appears to have helped SUDOKU do best for these languages.

	Team Run	All	Bio	Mat	Soc
(EN)	LIMSI	**65.8**	**71.3**	**54.1**	**67.2**
(EN)	SUDOKU-2	61.6	68.9	53.2	55.6
(EN)	SUDOKU-3	60.7	71.2	49.4	51.1
(EN)	SUDOKU-1	55.8	62.4	43.0	56.4
	BFS	67.5	72.2	55.3	70.8
(ES)	SUDOKU-2	**57.1**	60.8	**49.7**	**57.0**
(ES)	SUDOKU-3	56.8	62.6	48.4	53.3
(ES)	SUDOKU-1	56.0	**62.7**	44.2	54.2
(ES)	LIMSI	45.0	51.0	34.8	43.1
	BFS	37.5	43.7	28.7	34.0
(IT)	SUDOKU-1	**59.9**	**65.1**	48.4	**61.0**
(IT)	SUDOKU-3	56.9	64.1	49.1	55.8
(IT)	SUDOKU-2	56.9	58.8	**52.1**	57.9
(IT)	LIMSI	48.4	53.1	44.6	42.9
	BFS	40.2	44.3	36.7	35.7

Table 3: F1 scores for each domain/language for SUDOKU and LIMSI.

In summary, the inclusion of named entities in disambiguation tasks certainly improves results, as well as the effectiveness of the iterative approach. Furthermore in Table 3 above, the *iterative* Run3 for the English Biomedical domain is 0.1 short of achieving the best result of 71.3. Investigating exactly which factors contributed to the success of this *unsupervised* result is a top priority for future work.

Resources

Codebase and resources are at the author's homepage: `http://www.stevemanion.com`.

Acknowledgments

This submission is an extension of the author's PhD thesis completed under the supervision of Dr Raazesh Sainudiin and with the help of the Korean Foundation Graduate Studies Fellowship.

References

Eneko Agirre and Philip Edmonds 2007. Chapter 1: Introduction. *Word Sense Disambiguation Algorithms and Applications*, pages 1-28. Springer, New York.

Eneko Agirre, Oier Lopez De Lacalle, Christiane Fellbaum, Shu-Kai Hsieh, Maurizio Tesconi, Monica Monachini, Piek Vossen, and Roxanne Segers. 2010. SemEval-2010 Task 17: All-words Word Sense Disambiguation on a Specific Domain. *In Proceedings of the 5th International Workshop on Semantic Evaluation (SemEval-2010)*, pages 75-80. Uppsala, Sweden.

Eneko Agirre and Aitor Soroa. 2009. Personalizing PageRank for Word Sense Disambiguation. *In Proceedings of the 12th Conference of the European Chapter of the Association for Computational Linguistics (EACL'09)*, pages 33-41. Athens, Greece.

Sergey Brin and Lawrence Page. 1998. The Anatomy of a Large-scale Hypertextual Web Search Engine. *Computer Networks and ISDN Systems*, 30:107-117.

Christiane Fellbaum. 1998, ed. *WordNet: An Electronic Lexical Database.*, Cambridge, MA: MIT Press.

Yoan Gutirrez, Antonio Fernndez Orqun, Franc Camara, Yenier Castaeda, Andy Gonzlez, Andrs Montoyo, Rafael Muoz, Rainel Estrada, Dennys D. Piug, Jose I. Abreu, and Roger Prez. 2013. UMCC_DLSI: Reinforcing a Ranking Algorithm with Sense Frequencies and Multidimensional Semantic Resources to solve Multilingual Word Sense Disambiguation. *Proceedings of the 7th International Workshop on Semantic Evaluation (SemEval-2013)*, pages 241-249. Atlanta, Georgia.

Taher H. Haveliwala. 2003. A Context-Sensetive Ranking Algorithm for Web Search. *IEEE Transactions on Knowledge and Data Engineering*, 15(4):784–796.

Steve L. Manion and Raazesh Sainudiin. 2014. An Iterative Sudoku Style Approach to Subgraph-based Word Sense Disambiguation. *In Proceedings of the 3rd Joint Conference on Lexical and Computational Semantics (*SEM'14)*, pages 40-50. Dublin, Ireland.

Steve L. Manion. 2014. Unsupervised Knowledge-based Word Sense Disambiguation: Exploration & Evaluation of Semantic Subgraphs. *Doctoral Thesis*. University of Canterbury.

Diana McCarthy, Rob Koeling, Julie Weeds, and John Carroll. 2004. Finding Predominant Word Senses in Untagged Text. *In Proceedings of the 42nd Annual Meeting for the Association for Computational Linguistics (ACL'04)*, pages 280-287. Barcelona, Spain.

George A. Miller, Claudia Leacock, Randee Tengi, and Ross T. Bunker. 1993. A Semantic Concordance. *In Proceedings of the Workshop on Human Language Technology (HLT93)*, pages 303-308. Princeton, New Jersey.

Andrea Moro and Roberto Navigli. 2015. SemEval-2015 Task 13: Multilingual All-Words Sense Disambiguation and Entity Linking. *In Proceedings of the 9th International Workshop on Semantic Evaluation (SemEval-2015)*. Denver, Colorado.

Roberto Navigli, David Jurgens, and Daniele Vannella. 2013. SemEval-2013 Task 12: Multilingual-Word Sense Disambiguation. *In Proceedings of the 7th International Workshop on Semantic Evaluation (SemEval-2013)*, pages 222-231. Atlanta, Georgia.

Roberto Navigli and Simone Paolo Ponzetto. 2012. BabelNet: The automatic construction, evaluation and application of a wide-coverage multilingual semantic network. *Artificial Intelligence*, 193:217–250.

Benjamin Snyder and Martha Palmer. 2004. The English All-Words Task. *In Proceedings of the 3rd International Workshop on the Evaluation of Systems for the Semantic Analysis of Text (SENSEVAL-3)*, pages 41-43. Barcelona, Spain.

David Yarowsky. 1993. One Sense Per Collocation. *In Proceedings of the ARPA Workshop on Human Language Technology (HLT'93)*, pages 266-271. Morristown, New Jersey.

TeamHCMUS: Analysis of Clinical Text

Nghia Huynh
Faculty of Information Technology
University of Science, Ho Chi Minh City, Vietnam
huynhnghiavn@gmail.com

Quoc Ho
Faculty of Information Technology
University of Science, Ho Chi Minh City, Vienam
hbquoc@fit.hcmus.edu.vn

Abstract

We developed a system to participate in shared tasks on the analyzing clinical text. Our system approaches are both machine learning-based and rule-based. We applied the machine learning-based approach for Task 1: disorder identification, and the rule-based approach for Task 2: template slot filling for the disorder. In Task 1, we developed a supervised conditional random fields model that was based on a rich set of features, and used for predicting disorder mentions. In Task 2, we based on the dependency tree to build a rule set. This rule set was extracted from the training data and applied to fill values of disorder attribute types on the test data. The evaluation on the test data showed that our system achieved the F-score of 0.656 (0.685 in case of relaxed score) for Task 1 and the F*WA of 0.576 for Task 2A and the F*WA of 0.671 for Task 2B.

1 Introduction

SemEval-2015 Task 14 is a continuation of previous tasks such as: CLEF eHealth Evaluation Labs 2013[1] (Hanna Suominen et al., 2013), CLEF eHealth Evaluation Labs 2014[2] (Liadh Kelly et al., 2014), and SemEval-2014 task 7[3] (Sameer Pradhan et al., 2014). The aim of the tasks is to improve the methods of natural language processing (NLP) of the clinical domain and to widely introduce the clinical text processing to the community of NLP research.

The clinical narrative is abundant in mentions of clinical conditions, anatomical sites, medications and procedures. It is completely different from the newswire domain where text is dominated by mentions of countries, locations and people. Many surface forms represent the same concept. Unlike the general domain, in biomedicine which are rich lexical and ontology resources that can be leveraged when applications are built.

The SemEval-2015 Task 14 is split into two tasks: 1) Task 1 is disorder identification, and its goal is to recognize the span of disorder mentions, the named entity recognition, and the normalization to a unique CUI in a SNOMED-CT terminology in a set of clinical notes. The SNOMED-CT is a resource provided by the organizers for the normalization of Task 1; and 2) Task 2 is disorder slot filling; it focuses on identifying the normalized value for nine modifiers in a disorder mentioned in a clinical note: the CUI of the disorder (much similar to Task 1), as well as the potential attributes (e.g. negation indicator, subject, uncertainty indicator, course, severity, conditional, generic indicator, and body location). Participants can submit to either or both of the tasks. We participated in both tasks.

In this paper, we describe a combined machine learning and rule-based approach for the two tasks.

2 Our Approach

2.1 Data Analysis

[1] https://sites.google.com/site/shareclefehealth/
[2] http://clefehealth2014.dcu.ie/
[3] http://alt.qcri.org/semeval2014/task7/

The Organizing Committee provided a data set including one on-set of training data (train) and one on developing data (devel). The training data set contains 298 files, including radiology reports, discharge summaries, and ECG/ECHO reports. The developing data set contains 133 files being discharged summaries.

Processing the data shows that there are 3 forms to represent disorder mentions: 1) disorder with a continuous bundle of words (*Form 1*); 2) disorder with two separated chunks (*Form 2*); 3) disorder with three separated chunks (*Form 3*). Figure 1 illustrates the three forms. The statistics of the appearing rate of disorder representable forms on the training and the developing data sets are shown in Table 1.

	Data	Form 1	Form 2	Form 3	Totals
Train	#disorder	10077	1028	62	11167
	Percentage	*91.8%*	*7.9%*	*0.3%*	
Devel	#disorder	7374	608	16	7998
	Percentage	*92.2%*	*7.6%*	*0.2%*	

Table 1. The statistics of the number and percentage of each disorder expressed in the sets of training and developing data.

Form 1: "The rhythm appears to be *atrial fibrillation*."

Form 2: "The *left atrium* is moderately *dilated*."

Form 3: "*Heart*: VI systolic murmur, *irregular* rate and *rhythm*."

Figure 1. Examples of disorder representable forms.

The analysis results help us develop a more effective disorder extraction approach in solving problems.

2.2 Disorder Identification

In disorder identification, the system is based on the machine-learning approach, the set of training data is converted into a BIO format, in which each word is assigned into one of three labels: B means the beginning of a disorder, I means the inside of a disorder, and O means the outside of a disorder. These labels can be used for a disorder only when it has consecutive words (*Form 1*) and cannot work when the disorder has nonconsecutive words (*Form 2* or *Form 3*) as mentioned in Section 2.1. Therefore, we developed different strategies for the disorder forms with consecutive and nonconsecutive words. For the disorder with consecutive words, we labeled words using the traditional BIO. For discontinuous disorder mentions, we created two addition sets of tags: 1) {B2, I2} which is used to assign to the words of disorder with two separate chunks (*Form 2*); 2) {B3, I3} is used to label the disorder with 3 separate chunks (*Form 3*). Figure 2 shows some examples of labeling disorders with consecutive and nonconsecutive words using our new tagging sets. In this approach, we assigned one of seven tags {B, I, O, B2, I2, B3, I3} to each word. Thus, the disorder identification problem was converted into a classification problem to assign one of the seven labels to each word.

Form 1: "The/O rhythm/O appears/O to/O be/O *atrial/B fibrillation/I* ./O"

Form 2: "The/O *left/B2 atrium/I2* is/O moderately/O *dilated/I2* ./O"

Form 3: "*Heart/B3* :/O VI/O systolic/O murmur/O ,/O *irregular/I3* rate/O and/O *rhythm/I3* ./O"

Figure 2. Examples of labeling for the consecutive and nonconsecutive disorder words.

The algorithms machine learning and feature set offered by Stanford Named Entity Recognizer[4] was used. The Stanford CoreNLP[5] was used for splitting sentences and tokenizers from the training and test data. Also, some simple rules were used for labeling disorder words, i.e. {B, B2, B3) labeled to the begin-token of disorders, and {I, I2, I3} labeled to the inside-tokens of disorders as indicated in Figure 2. The Stanford-NER tool and the feature set offered by the Stanford NLP were used to build a supervised conditional random fields model on the training data. Then, this model was used to assign a label to each token in the test data. Some of our rules

[4] http://nlp.stanford.edu/software/CRF-NER.shtml
[5] http://nlp.stanford.edu/software/corenlp.shtml

were built to identify disorders. For sentences, we identified each disorder in turn based on the label sets consisting of {B, I}, {B2, I2}, and {B3, I3}.

In disorder normalization to a unique CUI in the UMLS/SNOMED-CT terminology, we extracted a list of annotated disorder from the training and developing date with disorder entities and CUI. This list was a primary search source for each of the recognized disorder entities. When a disorder was not found on the list, we used the MetaMap[6] (Willie, 2013) and UMLS[7] to continue the search. Then, when the disorder was not defined as CUI, it was defined as "CUI–less".

2.3 Disorder Slot Filling

Huu Nghia Huynh et al. (2014) developed a system to participate in Task 2 of the CLEF eHealth Evaluation Labs 2014. They used the rule-based and machine learning methods for the task of disease/disorder template filling. The result of the system achieved the accuracy of 0.827.

Our system was developed based on the rule-based approach. The rules are based on the representation of the dependency tree. One rule is established when there is a path from the node containing *disorder* to the node containing *Cue word* on the dependency tree. Each of these attributes has a rule set and a handling difference because of the data representation. For example, to fill values for the Uncertainty Indicator (UI) attribute, in the segment as illustrated in Figure 3, there are three disorders *"Congestive heart failure", "Coronary artery disease"* and *"Aortic valve disease"* whose all of the cue words are **"Indication"**. This segment are split into 3 sentences as shown in Figure 4, and *Sent 2* and *Sent 3* lost the Cue word information. Then when we based on the dependency tree, it is impossible to determine Normalized Values for an attribute.

Indication: *Congestive heart failure. Coronary artery disease. Aortic valve disease.*

Figure 3. Example of a text segment in discharge summary.

Sent 1: **Indication**: *Congestive heart failure.*
Sent 2: *Coronary artery disease.*
Sent 3: *Aortic valve disease.*

Figure 4. Example of separating the text segment result.

The attributes of Negation Indicator, Subject Class, Uncertainty Indicator, Course Class, Sever-ity Class, Conditional Class, and Generic Class are processed with the same method as follows: From the training and developing data, the system extracts lists, including a list of disorders and trigger and lists of the *Normalized Values* and the *Cue word* for each attribute. Every trigger list consists of two columns: the first column contains the *Normalized Values,* and the 2nd column contains the *Cue Word* of the respective disorder slot. The lists of disorder and trigger are the input parameters to define the sets of rules based on the dependency tree. Figure 5 is the illustration of the dependency tree in the sentence "Gastric lavage shown maroon/ black but no fresh blood" in which "blood" is a disorder, "no" is the *Cue word* of "blood" and the *Normalized Value* of "blood" to be determined is "yes".

A rule is set up to the Negation Indicator attribute type as follows: ({relation = "**neg**"} {governor = "***blood***"} {dependent = "**no**"}) → ("***blood***": yes). Each attribute has its own separated rule set.

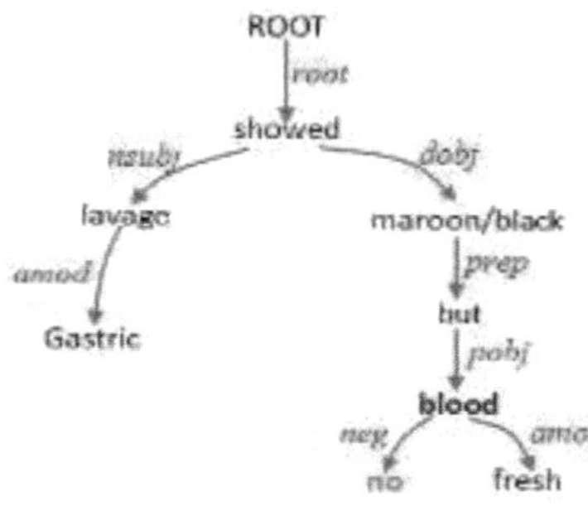

Figure 5. An example illustrates the dependency tree of the sentence *"Gastric lavage showed maroon/black but no fresh blood."*

The disorder CUI attribute type is analyzed in the method similar to that of normalization of disorders mentioned above. For the Body Loca-

[6] http://metamap.nlm.nih.gov/JavaApi.shtml
[7] https://uts.nlm.nih.gov/home.html

tion attribute type, the system determines the *Cue word* candidates by searching the list of triggers and UMLS, and then uses the rule set to identify the *Cue word* related to the disorder.

3 Results

We used data that was provided by the organizers as training data for the system including 298 files (train) and 133 files (devel). The Organizing Committee provided the test data including 100 files (text) used to run Tasks 1 and 2b, followed by 100 files (pipe) used to run Task 2a. In task 2, there are two subtasks. In Task 2a, the gold-standard spans of disorder are given, and the participant has to fill the slots (including the CUI of the disorder). In Task 2b *End-to-end*: no gold-standard information is provided, and the participant has to (i) identify disorders (i.e. span recognition), and (ii) fill the slots for the disorders (including normalized disorders).

	Strict score	Relaxed score
Precision	0.680	0.711
Recall	0.633	0.662
F-score	0.656	0.685

Table 2. The system results of Task 1.

Accuracy	0.195
F*Accuracy	0.195
Wt_Accuracy	0.576
F*Wt_Accuracy	0.576

Table 3. The system results of Task 2a.

Accuracy	0.884
F*Accuracy	0.756
Wt_Accuracy	0.784
F*Wt_Accuracy	0.671

Table 4. The system results of Task 2b.

Attribute types	Weighted Accuracy
Body Location	0.603
Disorder CUI	0.801
Conditional Class	0.725
Course Class	0.851
Generic Class	0.904
Negation Indicator	0.935
Severity Class	0.843
Subject Class	0.931
Uncertainty Indicator	0.802

Table 5. The results of the attribute types in Task 2b.

Assessing the results in Task 2a, we made a mistake in filling out the default values for the slots of the disorders in the results submitted to the Organizing Committee. Therefore, the results are very low (see Table 3) and cannot reflect the effectiveness of our system.

The following metrics are computed with the F-measure for span identification: A true positive disorder span is defined as any overlap with a gold-standard span. If there are several predicted spans overlapping with a gold-standard one, then only one of them is chosen to be a true positive (the longest span), and the other predicted spans are considered as false positives.

#TP	5078
#FP	644
#FN	1070
Precision	88.7%
Recall	82.6%
F-score	85.6%

Table 6. The F-measure for span identification.

Table 6 illustrates the results obtained on the F-measure for span identification. On observing the results, a lot of predicted spans contain several tokens that were not part of disorders. If these tokens are removed, the results of span identification will be more accurate.

4 Discussion

The disorder identification task has a lot of challenges in the clinical domain. It was shown through the results in CLEF 2013 (Souminen,

H., et al., 2013), SemEval 2014 (Sameer Pradhan et al., 2014), and SemEval 2015.

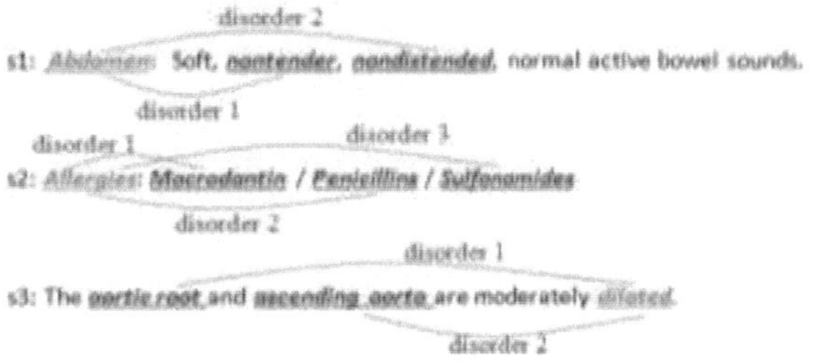

Figure 6. Different representable forms of Disorders

In Section 2.1 we presented three representable forms of disorder in the clinical text. In addition, it shows the other representable forms as illustrated in Figure 6, and the different disorders sharing a word in the sentence. For example, the sentence 2 has 3 disorders containing the same word "***Allergies***".

The diversity and complexity of representation of disorders in clinical documents lead to a major challenge in the problem of extracting concepts in the clinical domain.

5 Conclusion

We described the system which realized the recognition, normalization and template filling of disorders in clinical docments. The system used the rule-based and machine learning-based approaches. The results of system will be able to serve a good foundation for our further research and propose enhancements to improve the efficiency for conceptual extraction problems. Specifically, we will study the proposal of more appropriate label sets for different representable forms of disorders as we presented in Sections 2.1 and 4, and conduct more pieces of research to supplement new features for disorder identification. In addition, we will propose a solution to remove several tokens which are not parts of disorder in the future.

References

Hanna Suominen, Sanna Salanterä, Sumithra Velupillai, Wendy W. Chapman, Guergana Savova, Noemie Elhadad, Sameer Pradhan, Brett R. South, Danielle L. Mowery, Gareth J. F. Jones, Johannes Leveling9, Liadh Kelly, Lorraine Goeuriot, David Martinez, and Guido Zuccon. *Overview of the shARe/CLEF eHealth evaluation lab 2013*. In: Proceedings of ShARe/CLEF eHealth Evaluation Labs. (2013).

Huu Nghia Huynh and Bao Quoc Ho (2014). *A Rule-based Approach for Relation Extraction from Clinical Documents.* In Proceedings of Asian Conference 2014 on Information Systems, pp. 314-317.

Huu Nghia Huynh, Son Lam Vu, and Bao Quoc Ho (2014). *ShARe/CLEFeHealth: A Hybrid Approach for Task 2.* In Working Notes for CLEF 2014 Conference Sheffield, UK, pp. 103-110.

Liadh Kelly, Lorraine Goeuriot, Hanna Suominen, Tobias Schreck, Gondy Leroy, Danielle L. Mowery, Sumithra Velupillai, Wendy W. Chapman, David Martinez, Guido Zuccon, João Palotti (2014). *Overview of the ShARe/CLEF eHealth Evaluation Lab 2014.* In Information Access Evaluation. Multilinguality, Multimodality, and Interaction Lecture Notes in Computer Science Volume 8685, pp. 172-191.

Olivier Bodenreider and Alexa T. McCray (2003). *Exploring Semantic Groups through Visual Approaches.* Journal of Biomedical Informatics 36 (2003), pp. 414-432.

Sameer Pradhan, Noémie Elhadad, Wendy Chapman, Suresh Manandhar and Guergana Savova (2014). *SemEval-2014 Task 7: Analysis of Clinical Text.* In Proceedings of the 8th International Workshop on Semantic Evaluation (SemEval 2014), pp.54-62.

Willie Rogers (2013). *Installing and Running the Public Version of MetaMap.*

UTU: Adapting Biomedical Event Extraction System to Disorder Attribute Detection

Kai Hakala
University of Turku Graduate School (UTUGS), University of Turku, Finland
Dept. of Information Technology, University of Turku, Finland
kahaka@utu.fi

Abstract

In this paper we describe our entry to the SemEval 2015 clinical text analysis task. We participated only in the disorder attribute detection task 2a. Our main goal was to assess how well an information extraction system originally developed for a different task and domain can be utilized in this task. Our system, based on SVM and CRF classifiers, showed promising results, placing 3rd out of 6 participants in this task with performance of 0.857 measured in weighted accuracy, the official evaluation metric.

1 Introduction

SemEval 2015 introduced a new subtask for the clinical text analysis track focusing on disorder mention attribute detection. These attributes describe the relevant information extracted from the textual context of the given disease mention, such as the severity or body location of the disease. The attributes were grouped into 9 separate categories, each with a predefined set of valid attribute classes. The task was defined as a template filling task where the textual cue words for the attributes have to be first identified and then normalized to the correct class. Similar task with slightly different definition has previously been organized as part of the ShARe/CLEF eHealth shared task (Mowery et al., 2014).

Due to time limitations we participated only in the task 2a in which the gold standard disorder mentions were given and only the attribute values had to be predicted. Our main motivation for this years entry was to evaluate the performance of an existing information extraction system, TEES (Björne and Salakoski, 2013), previously developed for a different domain and to assess how easily it can be adapted to a new task.

2 System Description

Turku Event Extraction System (TEES) was originally developed in 2009 for the BioNLP Shared Task on Event Extraction (Kim et al., 2009). This task focused on the extraction of biological processes and interactions between genes and proteins (GGPs) described in biomedical literature. In this task each *event*, i.e. biological process or interaction, is represented by a *trigger* word, which also describes the type of the event, and a set of argument GGP mentions. The argument GGPs may also act in various roles, i.e. each argument is also typed. The participants were thus required to detect these trigger words, their types from a predefined set and the arguments, i.e. the relations between the trigger words and GGPs. Gold standard gene and protein mentions were provided by the organizers and consequently TEES does not include tools for named entity recognition, but presumes these to be given as input data. An example sentence along with the extracted event is illustrated in figure 1.

TEES was the best performing system in the 2009 BioNLP Shared Task as well as in various subtasks in subsequent years (Björne and Salakoski, 2011; Nédellec et al., 2013) showing state-of-the-art performance in biomedical event extraction. Whereas the event extraction task requires the detection of trigger words and argument relations, the disorder attribute detection can be solved by first finding the

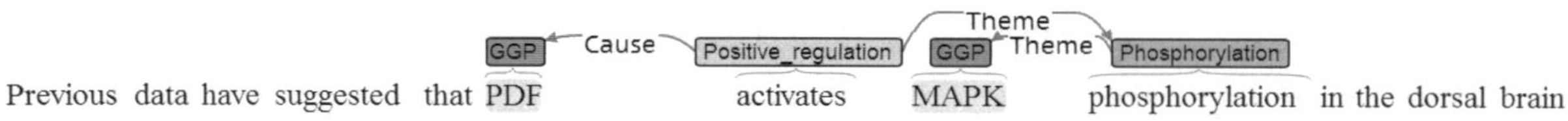

Figure 1: Visualization of an extracted event. In BioNLP Shared Task on Event Extraction the GGP mentions are given and the participants are asked to detect the trigger words, here *activates* and *phosphorylation*, as well as the relation between these entities.

cue words and then relating them to the correct disease mentions, making TEES applicable also for this task.

2.1 Cue Word and Relation Detection

TEES consists of two main processing stages. The first step, called trigger detection, resembles common NER classification task, and classifies each token in the text to either negative class or one of the positive classes, i.e. the predefined trigger types. In this task the trigger detector is used to detect the attribute cue words and their classes.

The second step detects relations between the known named entities and trigger words. This is implemented by generating all plausible entity pairs in a sentence in which case the task becomes a simple classification problem: each pair is classified to either negative class or a positive class resembling the type of the relation.

As trigger and relation detection tasks are both multiclass classification problems, they have been implemented with a multiclass SVM (Tsochantaridis et al., 2004) using the SVM^{multiclass} software, bundled with TEES. TEES generates a vast amount of classification features from the examined words as well as their context. The relation detection, in particular, relies heavily on syntactic dependencies.

The optimal value for C-parameter is selected independently for each step. However, the independently optimized trigger detection model may not result in the optimal overall system. This is due to the fact that the relation detector is able to discard unwanted triggers, but cannot recover from low trigger detection recall. To overcome this issue, the recall of the trigger detector is artificially increased and the final verdict is made by the relation detector. The amount of overgeneration is selected by evaluating the overall performance of the system.

Whereas TEES relies on graph based data representation with textual entities and the relations between them, the disorder attribute detection task in SemEval 2015 is defined as a slot filling problem. The main issue in the conversion between these two formats is that the default normalization slot values with the corresponding cue defined as *null* cannot be represented in TEES format. Due to this, the default value was decided to be the negative class. In this definition, our system is only aiming to predict the non-default values and if no cue word and a relation between the cue word and disorder entity can be found the default value is preserved. As the slot filling format defines different categories and predefined normalization classes inside these categories, whereas TEES uses a single class for each trigger, the category and normalization classes are concatenated into a single class. E.g. our system is not aware that cue word classes *SV_slight* and *SV_severe* are both normalization values of the severity category, but sees them as independent classes. The relations between cue words and disorder mentions are predicted to only exist or not, i.e. the relations are not typed.

2.2 Body Location Detection

In our evaluation on the development set, the performance of the TEES trigger detector was extremely poor for the body location attributes. This might be due to various reasons. Firstly, whereas the other attribute categories are rather closed sets of expressions, the body locations are named entities. Secondly, TEES does not use any features tailored for the clinical domain and thus generalizes poorly to body location mentions not seen on the training data, resulting in a high precision and low recall system.

As the first attempt to adapt TEES to this task and generalize better for the body locations, we included dictionary features for the trigger detection stage. The used dictionary was composed of the UMLS concepts included in the semantic categories "Body Part, Organ, or Organ Component", "Body Location or Region", "Body System", "Body Space or Junction", "Body Substance", "Tissue", "Cell" and "Embryonic Structure". These semantic types cover 98.9% of the body locations seen in the training data. For each concept, the preferred term as well as the synonyms were included in the dictionary.

The addition of these features did not improve our performance significantly and thus in the final system, the TEES trigger detector was replaced with a CRF classifier for the body locations. In this approach we used the NERsuite software based on the CRFsuite implementation (Okazaki, 2007). In addition to the standard features such as the word form, lemma, part-of-speech tag and text chunk we incorporated the same dictionary features used in the TEES trigger detector. Moreover, we trained another CRF using the AnatomyTagger software and AnatEM corpus (Pyysalo and Ananiadou, 2013). These two models were stacked, i.e. the predictions from the AnatEM model were given as features for the other classifier.

As the gold standard data includes only attributes related to a disease mention, the annotation is incomplete for NER purposes, and thus using the whole data resulted in poor performance. To prevent this, we trained the body location NER system with only the sentences including at least one annotated body location mention. The development set was filtered in similar fashion for evaluation purposes. The feature set which resulted in the best performance in this evaluation set was used in the final system. This approach boosted the performance on sentences which included at least one annotated body location mention, but the impact on other sentences is hard to assess without complete evaluation data. However, this approach leads to a similar outcome as the aforementioned trigger word overgeneration and shifts the responsibility of removing the excessive body location mentions to the relation detector.

2.3 Disorder and Body Location Normalization

The body location attribute differs from the other categories in that the cue spans were required to be normalized into the corresponding UMLS concepts. As TEES does not include tools for this type of normalization and the normalization was not our main focus in this year's entry, we used a simple tfidf-weighted vector space model. As the first attempt the model was created from the same UMLS concepts used in the body location NER features, but due to high amount of ambiguity this led to poor results. Consequently, we naively generated the model from the gold standard body location annotations and a given entity was then mapped to the UMLS identifier of the most similar entity seen on the training set. If an entity was annotated with various identifiers in different contexts, we used the most frequently occurring identifier.

The entities were predicted to be "CUI-less" if the most similar gold standard entity was annotated as such or if the maximum cosine similarity was zero. Thus in this naive approach there was no need for more complex "CUI-less" value identification as is necessary in our previously suggested normalization method (Kaewphan et al., 2014).

The disorder mention normalization was not part of the original slot filling task, but was later on added to the task definition. For simplicity we used the same naive method as with the body location entities.

3 Results

We submitted three separate runs to the final evaluation. Runs 1 and 2 used the same approach, but run 2 includes a last-minute bug fix which we were not able to thoroughly test. This bug caused some of the attribute mentions to be duplicated during the conversion between SemEval and TEES data formats, misleading the system. These runs use the method described in this paper, but the system was only allowed to predict one value for each slot. This was forced by only selecting the value with highest classification confidence for the relation detection; the confidence of the trigger word detection was ignored. In run 3 we allowed the system to predict multiple body location values for each disorder mention. This is beneficial in statements such as *"Osteophytes are seen along the medial tibial plateau as well as the superior aspect of the patella"* where both body locations *tibial plateau* and *patella* are related to the same disorder mention *Osteophytes*. The results for these runs are shown in table 1 along with the best runs from the other participated groups.

Our best performance was obtained from the run

Team	WA	A
UTH-CCB	0.886	0.943
ezDI	0.880	0.934
UTU run3	0.857	0.945
UTU run2	0.855	0.944
UTU run1	0.846	0.939
UWM	0.818	0.859
TeamHCMUS	0.576	0.195
UtahPOET	0.446	0.744

Table 1: Official test set results for our 3 submissions and the other 5 participating teams. Only the best runs measured in weighted accuracy are shown for other teams. WA = weighted accuracy, A = non-weighted accuracy.

3 with weighted accuracy of 0.857, resulting in the third best performing system in the task. Measured on the non-weighted accuracy which was not the main evaluation metric, but still included in the official results, we achieved score 0.945, the second best performance in the task.

Runs 1 and 2 which did not allow multiple body locations to be predicted performed slightly worse, run 2 achieving weighted accuracy of 0.855. This difference between runs 2 and 3 is solely caused by the body location category in which the difference between these two runs is 1.1pp. The category-wise performance is shown in table 2.

The comparison of our results to the best performing system by team UTH-CCB reveals that our system performs consistently weaker in every category. Worth noticing is that our naive normalization approach is not affecting our performance dramatically, showing weighted accuracy of 0.827 in disorder normalization category (CUI), where as UTH-CCB system achieved score of 0.854. As the gold standard disorder mentions were given in this task, this score is only measuring the normalization performance.

Our submitted runs were all trained with the combination of training and development data sets. The overall results on development and test sets are fairly similar showing that the system is not overfitting to the development data. On the other hand it seems that combining the training and development sets for the final models does not improve the performance significantly, although we cannot confirm this speculation before the gold standard annotation for the test data is released. As an exception to this is our normalization method, which greatly benefits from the added training data as can be seen from the +5.5pp improvement in the CUI category. This shows that the naive approach does not generalize well and is applicable only when the training data covers most of the disorder mentions seen in the test data.

4 Discussion and Future Work

The current implementation of TEES induces some limitations for this task. Firstly, the current data format used in TEES does not allow the representation of discontiguous entities, which are not common in various other tasks. In this submission we thus represented the discontiguous disorder entities with a single span during the cue word and relation detection. As the discontiguous entities are much less frequent in the attribute entities, we discarded them completely. As a future work we would like to allow TEES to support this type of entities. This will require not only altering the used data format, but also modifying the feature extraction process to be able to fully express the characteristics of these entities.

Secondly, TEES uses micro-averaged F-score of positive classes as the internal evaluation metric for parameter optimization, which may be suboptimal for tasks evaluated in different metrics. Due to this, we plan to modify TEES to accept various user-defined evaluation metrics.

To improve our performance in this task specifically, we need to first perform a detailed error analysis. This might reveal for instance whether some domain specific features could improve the accuracy of our system.

5 Conclusions

We have demonstrated that an information extraction system originally developed for scientific literature can be easily adapted to the clinical domain. The described system shows competitive performance being the third best system in the disorder attribute slot filling task. We have also discussed some of the limitations of the system and suggested multiple future improvements for better suitability to new task definitions and domains.

Team	WA	A	BL	CUI	CND	COU	GEN	NEG	SEV	SUB	UNC
UTH-CCB	0.886	0.943	0.862	0.854	0.903	0.887	0.911	0.975	0.936	0.975	0.911
Run3	0.857	0.945	0.825	0.827	0.823	0.798	0.888	0.970	0.915	0.920	0.853
Run2	0.855	0.944	0.814	0.827	0.823	0.798	0.888	0.970	0.915	0.920	0.853
Run3 devel	0.830	0.933	0.798	0.772	0.862	0.848	0.864	0.941	0.940	0.920	0.872

Table 2: Performance of our system in each attribute category compared to the best performing system. *Run 3 devel* shows our best results for the development set evaluated with the evaluation tool provided by the organizers.

Acknowledgements

Computational resources were provided by CSC — IT Center for Science Ltd, Espoo, Finland.

References

Jari Björne and Tapio Salakoski. 2011. Generalizing biomedical event extraction. In *Proceedings of BioNLP Shared Task 2011 Workshop*, pages 183–191, June.

Jari Björne and Tapio Salakoski. 2013. TEES 2.1: Automated annotation scheme learning in the BioNLP 2013 Shared Task. In *Proceedings of BioNLP Shared Task 2013 Workshop*, pages 16–25.

Suwisa Kaewphan, Kai Hakala, and Filip Ginter. 2014. UTU: Disease mention recognition and normalization with CRFs and vector space representations. In *Proceedings of the 8th International Workshop on Semantic Evaluation (SemEval 2014)*, pages 807–811, August.

Jin-Dong Kim, Tomoko Ohta, Sampo Pyysalo, Yoshinobu Kano, and Jun'ichi Tsujii. 2009. Overview of BioNLP'09 Shared Task on Event Extraction. In *Proceedings of the BioNLP 2009 Workshop Companion Volume for Shared Task*, pages 1–9, June.

Danielle L. Mowery, Sumithra Velupillai, Brett R. South, Lee Christensen, David Martinez, Liadh Kelly, Lorraine Goeuriot, Noemie Elhadad, Sameer Pradhan, Guergana Savova, and Wendy Chapman. 2014. Task 2: ShARe/CLEF eHealth Evaluation Lab 2014. In *Proceedings of CLEF 2014*, September.

Claire Nédellec, Robert Bossy, Jin-Dong Kim, Jung-Jae Kim, Tomoko Ohta, Sampo Pyysalo, and Pierre Zweigenbaum. 2013. Overview of BioNLP Shared Task 2013. In *Proceedings of the BioNLP Shared Task 2013 Workshop*, pages 1–7, August.

Naoaki Okazaki. 2007. CRFsuite: a fast implementation of conditional random fields (CRFs). http://www.chokkan.org/software/crfsuite/.

Sampo Pyysalo and Sophia Ananiadou. 2013. Anatomical entity mention recognition at literature scale. *Bioinformatics*.

Ioannis Tsochantaridis, Thomas Hofmann, Thorsten Joachims, and Yasemin Altun. 2004. Support vector machine learning for interdependent and structured output spaces. In *International Conference on Machine Learning (ICML)*, page 104.

IHS-RD-Belarus: Identification and Normalization of Disorder Concepts in Clinical Notes

Maryna Chernyshevich
IHS Inc. / IHS Global Belarus
131 Starovilenskaya St
220123, Minsk, Belarus
{Marina.Chernyshevich}@ihs.com

Vadim Stankevitch
IHS Inc. / IHS Global Belarus
131 Starovilenskaya St
220123, Minsk, Belarus
{Vadim.Stankevitch}@ihs.com

Abstract

This paper describes clinical disorder recognition and encoding system submitted by IHS R&D Belarus team at the SemEval-2015 shared task related to analysis of clinical texts. Our system is based on IHS Goldfire Linguistic Processor and uses a rich set of lexical, syntactic and semantic features. The proposed system consists of two components: a CRF-based approach to recognize disorder entities and empirical ranking to encode disorders to UMLS CUIs. Evaluation on the test data set showed that our system achieved the F-measure of 0.898 for entity recognition and the F-measure of 0.794 for UMLS CUI. The combined score for whole task is 0.690 (rank 17 out of 40 submissions).

1 Introduction

Named entity recognition (NER) is an information extraction task where the aim is to identify mentions of specific types of entities in text. This task has been one of the main focuses in the biomedical text mining research field, especially when applied to the scientific literature. Such efforts have led to the development of various tools for the recognition of diverse entities, including species names, genes and proteins, chemicals and drugs, anatomical concepts and diseases. These tools use methods based on dictionaries, rules, and machine learning, or a combination of those depending on the specificities and requirements of each concept type (Campos et al., 2013). After identifying entities occurring in texts, it is also relevant to disambiguate those entities and associate each occurrence with a specific concept, using a univocal identifier from a reference database such as Uniprot1 for proteins, or OMIM2 for genetic disorders. This is usually performed by matching the identified entities against a knowledge-base, possibly evaluating the textual context in which the entity occurred to identify the best matching concept.

In this paper, we describe a system (IHS_RD_Belarus in official results) developed to participate in the international shared task organized by the Conference on Semantic Evaluation Exercises (SemEval-2015) and focused on the analysis of clinical notes. This task is the repetition of task 7 at SemEval-2014 (Pradhan, et al., 2014) and aims at the recognition of entities belonging to the 'disorders' semantic group of the Unified Medical Language System (UMLS) (Bodenreider, 2004) and normalization of these entities to a specific UMLS Concept Unique Identifier (CUI). Specifically, the task definition required that concepts should only be normalized to CUIs that could be mapped to the SNOMED CT3 terminology.

2 System description

2.1 Dataset

The dataset for Tasks 1 consists of de-identified clinical notes of 4 different types (Discharge summary, ECG, Echo, Radiology) from MIMIC corpus (Lee et al., 2011). The organizer annotated 298 clinical notes with disorder entities on a predefined guideline and then mapped them to SNOMED-CT concepts represented by the UMLS CUIs. If a disorder entity cannot be found in SNOMED-CT, it was marked as "CUI-less". These notes were used as training dataset. The unlabelled notes are provided for exploring semi-supervised and unsupervised methods.

Two types of disorder mentions are annotated: consecutive and discontiguous. The discontiguous dirorder mentions consist of multiple tokens with some distance between each other, for example, "*The left atrium is moderately dilated*".

Table 1 shows the counts of words, annotated disorders and unique CUIs in the training dataset.

	Train data
Documents	298
Words count	162,511
Disorder mentions	11,141
consecutive	10,050
discontiguous	1,091
Unique UMLS CUI	1,355
CUI-less entities	3,471

Table 1. Distribution of the training data.

2.2 Lexicon

The disorder lexicon was created using the UMLS Metathesaurus, where each disorder concept is represented by set of synonymous terms.

To satisfy the annotation guidelines, the concept identifiers (CUIs) were restricted to the 11 recommended disorder semantic types:

- Congenital Abnormality
- Acquired Abnormality
- Injury or Poisoning
- Pathologic Function
- Disease or Syndrome
- Mental or Behavioural Dysfunction
- Cell or Molecular Dysfunction
- Experimental Model of Disease
- Anatomical Abnormality
- Neoplastic Process
- Signs and Symptoms

The disorder lexicon was enriched using automatically generated lists of synonymous words. For this purpose we used 3 techniques:

- lexical derivations, for example, *"optical, optically"*;
- synonymous words based on the Levenstein distance within a set of synonymous terms representing one UMLS disorder concept, for example, *"hyperchromasia, hyperchromatism, hyperchromia"*;
- similar noun phrases suggested by our inhouse autocorrection and autocompletion module that indexed UMLS terms, including correction of typing errors (*"carotic artery" = "carotid artery"*) and similar terms (*"tick disease" = "tick-borne disease"*).

2.3 Evaluation

Evaluation was to be carried out according to the following F-scores:

- *Strict F-score*: a predicted mention is considered a true positive if:
  1. its predicted span is exactly the same as for the gold-standard mention;
  2. the predicted CUI is correct.

The predicted disorder is considered a false positive if the span is incorrect or the CUI is incorrect.

- *Relaxed F-score:* a predicted mention is a true positive if:
  1. there is any word overlap between the predicted mention span and the gold-standard span (both in the case of contiguous and discontinuous spans);
  2. the predicted CUI is correct.

The predicted mention is a false positive if the span shares no words with the gold-standard span or the CUI is incorrect.

2.4 Disorder identification

We formulated disorder mention identification as a sequence labeling problem at token level and used Conditional Random Fields (CRF) (Lafferty, 2001). CRFs have shown empirical successes recently in named entity recognition (McCallum and Li, 2003), opinion target extraction (Chernyshevich, 2014), noun phrase segmentation (Sha and Pereira, 2003).

To facilitate feature generation for supervised CRF learning, sentences were pre-processed with IHS Goldfire Linguistic Processor that performs the following operations: word splitting, part-of-speech tagging, parsing, noun phrase extraction, semantic role labeling within expanded Subject-Action-Object (eSAO) relations (Todhunter et al., 2010). We removed all footers and headers, which are associated with the whole document and are irrelevant for the task. The notes are de-identified: the private data, e.g. names, data and places, are replaced by placeholders, for example, "`[**Location**]`". We replaced these placeholders with natural language expressions to assure correct POS-tagging and parsing.

Two separate CRF models were trained to identify consecutive and discontiguous disorder mentions with the same tagging scheme and same set of features.

2.4.1 CRF labels

We conducted several experiments with different tagging conventions and decided to use the ILO (Inside-Last-Outside) tagging scheme, where tag I represents the beginning and the inside token of an entity, L represents the last word of entity and O not a member of a disorder structure. The following is an example of our tagging for consecutive and discontiguous disorder mentions:

*The/**O** rhythm/**O** appears/**O** to/**O** be/**O** atrial/**I** fibrillation/**L***

*The/**O** left/**I** atrium/**I** is/**O** moderately/**O** dilated/**L***

The BIO (Begin-Inside-Outside) tagging scheme showed the classification accuracy lower by 5.5%.

2.4.2 Features

Given a sentence *s* and a token under consideration w_k, we define features over w_k and window of 5 tokens: w_{k-2}, w_{k-1}, w_k, w_{k+1}, w_{k+2}.

Token: This feature represents the string of the token w_k.

Context features: This feature has been used with a window of five tokens (the 2 tokens before and the 2 tokens after the target token). The surrounding words usually convey useful information about a token which help in predicting the correct tag for each token.

Part of speech: This feature represents the POS tag of the token w_k. It can provide some means of lexical disambiguation and help in determining the boundaries of instances.

Word letter case feature: This feature includes one of the three case tags for lowercase, uppercase and capitalized words correspondingly.

Letter n-grams: 3- and 4-letter n-grams starting and ending the token w_k.

Word frequency in out-of-domain corpus: we used social media texts as an out-of-domain corpus.

Part of a longer noun phrase: whether the word belongs to the same noun group as the next word.

Semantic category: This feature represents the semantic class to which the token w_k belongs, for example, body part, process, units of measure, drug, and animal being. We used two sources of semantic information: WordNet and the UMLS. The UMLS provides a set of semantic groups like anatomic terms, chemical substances and drugs, devices, disorders, etc. The WordNet was used to define semantic category of words not found in the UMLS. We selected the most representative nodes, for example, physical property, human, process etc. and all subordinate terms were assumed to belong to the appropriate category.

Document section: This unigram feature assigns the id of the section in which the token w_k belongs. Many clinical notes are divided into sections. These section headers provide very useful information, for example, the section "Past Medical History" or "Diagnosis" contains a lot of disorder mentions, while "Medications" do not. We created list of section headers, mapped to about 80 different unified names.

UMLS Features: We performed lookup in the disorder lexicon at two levels: word level and phrase level.

- The word-level feature represents the probability of a separate word to occur in a disorder mention. For this purpose, we collected all words contained in the UMLS disorders and calculated their probabilities of being a part of a disorder mention using the TF-IDF weighting. The TF of each word in the training set is calculated as the number of times the corresponding token appears in the UMLS disorder terminology. The IDF for each word is calculated from the number of unlabelled notes, which contain the word. These weighted metrics show how important the word is for disorder identification and help to exclude a lot of common words like frequent adjectives or conjunctions that often appear both in disorder terms and other terms.
- The phrase-level feature marks all phrases (with more than 2 words) that match a disorder term.

2.5 Disorder normalization

We propose a simple sieve-based algorithm that applies tiers of string matching for selecting the candidates with further candidates ranking.

2.5.1 Candidates selection

We applied following string matching rules to select candidate UMLS concepts for a disorder entity identified on the previous stage. Each rule assigns the score of confidence.

- **Exact match**: disorder and UMLS concept contain exactly the same extent text, excluding modifiers and determiners, with the same word order.

- **Relaxed match**: all informative words (excluding preposition, conjunctions, stop words etc.) from disorder are included in the UMLS concept.
- **Partial match**: at least one informative word from disorder is included in the UMLS concept.
- **Variants match**: all possible variants are generated for the disorder entity using synonyms, corrections and suggestions from our in-house autocorrection and autocompletion module and selected candidate UMLS concepts by relaxed matching rule.

2.5.2 Candidates ranking

All found candidate UMLS concepts were ranked on basis of a set of empirical parameters:

- score of match confidence;
- TF-IDF of the intersecting words;
- total number of disorder variants in the UMLS presenting the same CUI;
- number of times the UMLS concepts was already mentioned in this document;
- number of occurrences of the UMLS concept in the unlabelled corpus.

The top ranked UMLS concepts were selected as the system's output. If some concepts have the same ranking score, the first one by CUI number was selected.

2.6 Results and error analysis

The Table 2 summarizes the results separated by subtasks, disorder identification and disorder normalization, where the first column contains results obtained on development corpus and the second column shows the results on test corpus.

	Dev corpus	*Test corpus*
Disorder identification		
precision:	0.904	0.940
recall:	0.868	0.859
F1 measure:	0.886	0.898
Disorder normalization:		
accuracy:	0.794	0.794

Table 2: Separated results of disorder identification and normalization.

Our best performance on task 1 combining the disorder identification and normalization subtasks is shown in Table 3.

	Precision	*Recall*	*F1 measure*
Strict	0.722	0.662	0.690
Relaxed	0.746	0.684	0.714

Table 3: Combined result of disorder identification and normalization.

In this work we did not address the problem of discontiguous disorder mentions and correctly identified only about 10% of all discontiguous disorder mentions. Another source of errors are the one-, two-letters disorder acronyms, for example, "N", "V", "BM", etc. They remain untagged as diseases, as they may also refer to other entities, for example, chemicals.

As for disorder normalization task, the most challenging problem is the abbreviation disambiguation. The primary reason is a lack of abbreviations in UMLS terminology and their high ambiguity, for example, "AS" can refer to "Angelman Syndrome", "Aortic Stenosis", "Alzheimer Sclerosis" etc.

3 Conclusion

In this paper, we presented a clinical analysis system designed for participation in Task 1a of the SemEval 2015 Task 14 challenge. Our system performance was at 0.69 F-measure in the strict evaluation context and 0.714 F-measure in the relaxed evaluation context, obtaining a mid-range position. Our disorder recognition system presents good precision but performs worse in terms of recall, especially in discontiguous mentions identification. In order to improve our disorder normalization we plan to develop context similarity measures and improve the abbreviation disambiguation.

References

Andrew McCallum, Wei Li. Early Results for Named Entity Recognition with Conditional Random Fields, Feature Induction and Web-Enhanced Lexicons. In the Proceedings of the Seventh Conference on Natural Language Learning at HLT-NAACL 2003.

Campos G., Vazquez A. I., Fernando R. L., K. Y. C., and S. Daniel, 2013. Prediction of complex human traits using the genomic best linear unbiased predictor. PLoS Genet. 7.

James Todhunter, Igor Sovpel and Dzianis Pastanohau. System and method for automatic semantic labeling of natural language texts. U.S. Patent 8 583 422, November 12, 2013.

John Lafferty, Andrew McCallum, and Fernando Pereira. 2001. Conditional Random Fields: Probabilistic Models for Segmenting and Labeling Sequence Data. In Proceedings of the Eighteenth International Conference on Machine Learning, (ICML-2001).

Joon Lee, Daniel J. Scott, Mauricio Villarroel, Gari D. Clifford, Mohammed Saeed and Roger G. Mark. Open-Access MIMIC-II Database for Intensive Care Research. In the Proceedings of the 33rd Annual International Conference of the IEEE EMBS, 2011.

F. Sha and F. Pereira. Shallow parsing with conditional random fields. In the proceedings of Human Language Technology/North American chapter of the Association for Computational Linguistics annual meeting (HLT/NAACL), 2003.

Maryna Chernyshevich. IHS R&D Belarus: Cross-domain extraction of product features using CRF. In the Proceedings of the International Workshop on Semantic Evaluation (SemEval), 2014.

Olivier Bodenreider. 2004. The Unified Medical Language System (UMLS): Integrating Biomedical Terminology. Nucleic Acids Research, 32:267–270.

Sameer Pradhan, Noemie Elhadad, Wendy Chapman, Suresh Manandhar and Guergana Savova. SemEval-2014 Task 4: Aspect Based Sentiment Analysis. In *Proceedings of the 8th International Workshop on Semantic Evaluation* (SemEval 2014), Dublin, Ireland.

UWM: A Simple Baseline Method for Identifying Attributes of Disease and Disorder Mentions in Clinical Text

Omid Ghiasvand
University of Wisconsin-Milwaukee
Milwaukee, Wisconsin
ghiasva2@uwm.edu

Rohit J. Kate
University of Wisconsin-Milwaukee
Milwaukee, Wisconsin
katerj@uwm.edu

Abstract

In this paper the system that was developed by Team UWM for the Task 14 of SemEval 2015 competition is described. Task 14 included two tasks: Task 1 was identification of disorder mentions and their normalization, and Task 2 was identification of the following attributes for disorder mentions: the CUI of the disorder, negation indicator, subject, uncertainty indicator, course, severity, conditional, generic indicator, and body location. For Task 1, an earlier system was applied that uses Conditional Random Fields (CRFs) for disorder recognition and learned edit distance patterns for normalization. Task 2 was implemented by a simple method that finds the attribute terms around the disease mentions by matching them in the training data. Among all participants Team UWM was ranked fourth in Task 1, fourth in Task 2A (over gold-standard mentions) and third in Task 2B (over extracted mentions).

1 Introduction

Automated extraction tools are crucial for managing huge amount of clinical texts. These tools have the potential to enable many automated applications in healthcare. The Task 14 of SemEval 2015 was designed to serve as a platform for evaluating one such extraction tool. Its Task 1 involved extracting and normalizing disorder mentions from clinical text and its Task 2 involved assertion identification for the mentions.

Task 1 is challenging because there is a lot of variability in which diseases and disorders are mentioned in clinical text and hence a pre-defined list of mentions is not sufficient to extract them. The task also required normalizing the extracted mentions by mapping them to UMLS CUIs if they exist in the SNOMED-CT part of UMLS and are marked as disease/disorder, otherwise they were to be declared as "CUI-less." This normalization process is also challenging because disorder names are frequently mentioned in modified forms which prevents them from exactly matching the concepts in UMLS. Task 2 required finding certain attributes for the mentions and finding the spans of these attributes in text. This task is also challenging due to the variability in which attributes are attributed to disease and disorder mentions in clinical text.

Our team, UWM, participated in both Task 1 and Task 2. For Task 1, we used the same system that we had previously developed for the Task 7 of SemEval 2014 (Ghiasvand and Kate 2014). For Task 2, we used a simple method that finds attributes of mentions by first collecting lists of attribute terms from the training data and then matching in this list. The nearest attribute terms to a mention are assigned to that mention. The attribute terms are normalized by finding their normalized values in the training data. Despite being simple, this method gave competitive results. The methods used in this paper are described in more details in the next section.

2 Methods

2.1 Task 1

We briefly describe the system we had developed for Task 7 of SemEval 2014 (Ghiasvand and Kate 2014) which we used for Task 1. We treated disorder mention extraction as a standard sequence labeling task with "BIO" (Begin, Inside, Outside) labeling scheme. The model was trained using Conditional Random Fields (Lafferty et al., 2001) with various types of lexical and semantic features that included MetaMap (Aronson and Lang 2010) matches. These features are fully described in (Ghiasvand, 2014). This model was also inherently capable of extracting discontinuous disorder mentions. To normalize disorder mentions, our system first looked for exact matches with disorder mentions in the training data and then in the UMLS. If no exact match was found, then suitable variations of the disorder mentions were generated based on possible variations of disorder mentions learned from UMLS synonyms. These variations were learned in the form of edit distance patterns (Levenshtein 1966) using a novel method described in (Ghiasvand and Kate 2014).

2.2 Task 2

In this task, attributes related to disease or disorder mentions were to be identified along with their normalized values and spans in the text (Bodenreider, 2003). There were nine attributes related to each disorder mention for this task which were: the CUI of the disorder (same as Task 1), negation indicator, subject, uncertainty indicator, course, severity, conditional, generic indicator, and body location.

For identifying CUI attribute, we used the same normalization method that we had used for Task 1. For identifying the rest of the attributes, we used a simple matching method based on the training data for Task 2. The method first collects a list of attribute terms from the training data for each attribute type. For example, if "likely arising from", "lower suspicion of", and "possibly secondary" are marked as uncertainty terms in the training data then they will be included in our list of attribute terms for uncertainty. Table 1 lists the number of attribute terms thus collected from the training data for each of the attribute type. The only attribute that has many more values than other attributes is body location. For this attribute we used not only training data but also UMLS matches of body locations. Our training dataset consisted of combined training and development dataset parts, but when we collected these terms from only the training part, we found that a majority of these match in the development part. Thus we determined that only a small list of terms are frequently used to indicate most of the attributes of disease and disorder mentions and decided to use the simple matching method.

Our method identifies attributes of disease and disorder mentions as follows. Using the list of attribute terms, it first identifies attribute terms in the same sentence in which the mention is included. For each attribute type, the nearest attribute term (if present) is associated with the mention. The normalized value of the attribute is then simply obtained from the training data. For example the term "increasingly" in the course attribute type has normalized value "increased" in the training data, and the term "maternal aunt" in the subject attribute type has the normalized value "family_member". Hence if "increasingly" is the course attribute term found nearest to a disease mention in the test data then its course attribute will be assigned the value "increased". Similarly if "maternal aunt" is found as the nearest subject attribute term then its value will be assigned as "family_member".

Task 2 had two subtasks. In Subtask 2A, gold-standard disease and disorder mentions were provided and in Subtask 2B the mentions were to be first extracted by the system, hence it combined Task 1 and Subtask 2A.

Attribute	**Number of attribute terms in training data**
Conditional (CND)	154
Course (COU)	168
Generic (GEN)	45
Negation (NEG)	139
Severity (SEV)	92
Subject (SUB)	33
Uncertainty (UNC)	295
Body Location (BL)	1108

Table 1: Number of attribute terms for each attribute type in the training data.

3 Results

The training, development and test datasets of SemEval 2015 Task 14 had 298, 133 and 100 clinical notes respectively. We formed our training dataset by combining training and development datasets. The clinical notes contained different types of notes including de-identified discharge summaries, electrocardiogram, echocardiogram and radiology reports (Pradhan et al., 2013). The extraction and normalization performance in Task 1 was evaluated in terms of precision, recall and F-measure for strict (exact boundaries) and relaxed (overlapping boundaries) settings. Table 2 shows the results of this task. In this task, based on relaxed F-score, we got second rank, and based on strict F-score we got fourth rank considering only the best run of each participating team.

	Precision	Recall	F-score
Strict	0.773	0.699	0.734
Relaxed	0.809	0.731	0.768

Table 2: Results of Task1 (mention extraction and normalization).

For the Task 2A, unweighted and weighted accuracies were used as evaluation measures. For each disorder, a per-disorder, unweighted accuracy is computed, which represents the ability to identify all the slots for that disorder. The unweighted accuracy is the average of the per-disorder unweighted accuracy over all the disorders in the test set. For each disorder, a weighted per-disorder accuracy is computed, which represents the ability to identify all the slots for that disorder.

For Task 2B, the following evaluation measures were used: F-score for span identification, unweighted accuracy (which is same as the unweighted accuracy described in Task 2A computed over the true-positive identified disorders), and weighted accuracy (which is same as the weighted accuracy described in Task 2A computed over the true-positive identified disorders).

In Table 3 and 4, the results of these two subtasks are shown. Table 5 shows the results separately for each attribute type for both the subtasks. In Task 2A, except for the body location attribute our method got above eighty percent accuracy on all other attributes and above ninety percent on three of them. We also want point out that for the attribute type CUI we got 0.911 accuracy in Task 2A which is only slightly behind the best accuracy of 0.918 got by another team.

The reason our system got a very low accuracy for the body location attribute is because we forgot to include the CUI values for this attribute during the competition. This then also adversely affected our overall performance scores. Overall, in Task 2A our team ranked fourth and in Task 2B our team ranked third considering the best run of each participating team.

Our method for Task 2 was found to be competitive despite being very simple. For example, this simple matching scheme got 92.4% accuracy for negation attribute while the best team got 97.5% accuracy in Task 2A. Hence this method forms a very good baseline for comparing more sophisticated methods. It can also serve as a method that provides potential attributes which then can be tested and filtered by machine learning methods.

F-Score	Accuracy	F*A	Weighted-Accuracy	F*WA
1.00	0.859	0.859	0818	0.818

Table 3: Results of Task 2A.

F-Score	Accuracy	F*A	Weighted-Accuracy	F*WA
0.893	0.852	0.761	0.798	0.713

Table 4: Results of Task 2B.

Attribute	Accuracy (Task 2A)	Accuracy (Task 2B)
BL	0.531	0.551
CUI	0.911	0.858
CND	0838	0.839
COU	0.802	0.793
GEN	0.836	0.845
NEG	0.924	0.931
SEV	0.895	0.905
SUB	0.933	0.929
UNC	0.831	0.837

Table 5: Accuracy for each attribute type in Task 2A and Task 2B.

4 Conclusion and future work

We participated in Task 14 of SemEval 2015 which involved disorder mention extraction, normalization, and attribute identification. Our system used conditional random fields to extract disorder mentions and edit distance patterns for normalization of the extracted mentions. For identifying attributes, we used a simple matching based method using the training data. Our team preformed competitively on all the subtasks. In future, we plan to combine machine learning methods with our simple matching method for attribute identification.

Acknowledgment

This work was supported by grant UL1RR031973 from the Clinical and Translational Science Award (CTSA) program of the National Center for Research Resources and the National Center for Advancing Translational Sciences.

References

Aronson A. R., and Lang F. M. An overview of MetaMap: historical perspectives and recent advances. *Journal of American Medical Informatics Association*. 2010;17(3):229–36.

Bodenreider, O. and McCray, A. 2003. *Exploring semantic groups through visual approaches*. Journal of Biomedical Informatics, 36(2203): pp. 414-432.

Omid Ghiasvand, 2014. *Disease Name Extraction from Clinical Text Using Conditional Random Fields*, Thesis and Dissertation, University of Wisconsin-Milwaukee, Milwaukee, USA.

Omid Ghiasvand and Rohit J. Kate, 2014. *UWM: Disorder Mention Extraction from Clinical Text Using CRFs and Normalization Using Learned Edit Distance Patterns*, in Proceeding of the Eight International Workshop on Semantic Evaluations (SemEval 2014), pages 828-832, Dublin, Ireland.

John Lafferty, Andrew McCallum, and Fernando Pereira. 2001. *Conditional Random Fields: Probabilistic models for segmenting and labeling sequence data*. In Proceedings of 18th International Conference on Machine Learning (ICML-2001), pages 282–289, Williamstown, MA.

Vladimir I Levenshtein. 1966. *Binary codes capable of correcting deletions, insertions and reversals*. In Soviet physics doklady, volume 10, page 707.

Sameer Pradhan, Noemie Elhadad, B South, David Martinez, Lee Christensen, Amy Vogel, Hanna Suominen, W Chapman, and Guergana Savova. 2013. *Task 1: ShARe/CLEF eHealth Evaluation Lab 2013*. Online Working Notes of CLEF, CLEF, 230.

TAKELAB: Medical Information Extraction and Linking with MINERAL

Goran Glavaš
University of Zagreb
Faculty of Electrical Engineering and Computing
Text Analysis and Knowledge Engineering Lab
Unska 3, 10000 Zagreb, Croatia
goran.glavas@fer.hr

Abstract

Medical texts are filled with mentions of diseases, disorders, and other clinical conditions, with many different surface forms relating to the same condition. We describe *MINERAL*, a system for extraction and normalization of disease mentions in clinical text, with which we participated in the Task 14 of SemEval 2015 evaluation campaign. MINERAL relies on a conditional random fields-based model with a rich set of features for mention detection, and a semantic textual similarity measure for entity linking. MINERAL reaches joint extraction and linking performance of 75.9% relaxed F_1-score (strict score of 72.7%) and ranks fourth among 16 participating teams.

1 Introduction

Clinical narratives contain numerous mentions of diseases and disorders. Recognizing these mentions in text and normalizing the different superficial forms of a disorder to the same canonical form could enable new types of analyses that would be beneficial for both medical professionals and patients.

Detection and normalization of various concepts such as named entities (McCallum and Li, 2003; Krishnan and Manning, 2006) or events (Bethard, 2013; Glavaš and Šnajder, 2014) has long been in the focus of the NLP community. Disorder mentions in clinical text, however, have some peculiarities not typical for traditional information extraction tasks such as discontinuity or distributivity of a single token to multiple disorder mentions. For example, the snippet

> *"Patient's extremities were turned in and clinched together as a consequence of... "*

contains two mentions of medical conditions, *"extremities turned in"* and *"extremities clinched together"*, which share the token *"extremities"*, with the latter mention being discontinuous.

In this paper we present the *MINERAL* (Medical INformation ExtRAction and Linking) system for recognizing and normalizing mentions of clinical conditions, with which we participated in Task 14 of SemEval 2015 evaluation campaign. The system recognizes disorder mentions via the supervised conditional random fields (CRF) model with a rich set of lexical, gazetteer-based, and informativeness-based features. We apply a set of post-processing rules to construct disorder mentions from token-level annotations which follow the BEGIN-INSIDE-OUTSIDE scheme. We utilize a measure of semantic textual similarity to link recognized disorder mentions to entries in the SNOMED-CT medical database. Our approach is resource light in the sense that, except for SNOMED-CT which is necessary for normalization, it does not rely on medical NLP resources.

We ranked fourth (relaxed evaluation setting) among 16 teams in the official evaluation, with 3% lower performance than the best-performing system. Such a result suggests that coupling sequence labelling for mention recognition with an STS measure for concept normalization poses a viable solution for entity recognition in the clinical domain. We make the MINERAL system freely available.[1]

[1] http://takelab.fer.hr/mineral

2 Clinical Information Extraction

Clinical concept extraction is an essential task in medical natural language processing. While early approaches heavily relied on domain-specific vocabularies (Friedman et al., 1994; Aronson, 2001; Zeng et al., 2006), more recent efforts leverage the human-annotated corpora to develop machine learning models for the extraction of medical concepts (Tang et al., 2013; Uzuner et al., 2010). The rise in the number of data-driven efforts in the medical domain was particularly motivated by the shared tasks such as i2b2 challenges (Uzuner et al., 2010) and ShARe/CLEF eHealth Evaluation Lab (Suominen et al., 2013).

The first subtask of the SemEval Task 14, in which we participated, was essentially the same as the first task in the ShARe/CLEF eHealth campaign. We did not participate in the second subtask on extracting arguments of disorder mentions. The best performing system of the ShARe/CLEF eHealth task on disorder extraction and normalization (Tang et al., 2013) employed CRF and structured SVM models for mention extraction and the traditional vector-space model from information retrieval (Salton et al., 1975) for disorder normalization.

Similar to (Tang et al., 2013), we employ the CRF model for extraction of disorder mentions, but we leverage recent findings in word vector representations (Mikolov et al., 2013) for feature computation. We make use of the state-of-the-art measure of semantic similarity of short texts (Šarić et al., 2012) for concept normalization.

3 MINERAL

MINERAL consists of two subsystems: one for extracting disorder mentions and the other for normalizing extracted mentions by assigning them a Concept Unique Identifier (CUI) from the SNOMED-CT database (Stearns et al., 2001).

3.1 Disorder Mention Extraction

At the core of the extraction subsystem is the CRF model with lexical, gazetteer-based, and informativeness-based features. We decided to use the BEGIN-INSIDE-OUTSIDE annotation scheme for the CRF model, although this scheme does not account for token-sharing disorder mentions. Thus, we apply a set of postprocessing rules to derive disorder mentions from token-level outputs produced by the CRF model and to handle most frequent cases of token-sharing mentions (e.g., *"abdomen non-disturbed and non-distended"*).

3.1.1 Features

We feed the CRF model with a rich set of features that can be divided into (1) token-based features, (2) gazetteer-based features, and (3) information content-based features. All of the features are templated on the symmetric window of size two, i.e., computed for two preceding tokens, current token, and two subsequent tokens.

Token-based features (TK). Token-based features group all features which can be computed just from the token at hand. These include the surface form, lemma, stem, POS-tag, and shape (encoding of the capitalization of the word, e.g., "UL" for "Atrial") of the word. We also encode the first and the last character bigram and trigram of the word as features.

Gazetter-based features (GZ). Features in this group rely on comparison of tokens in text with entries in the SNOMED-CT database and with disease annoations on the training set. For each token we compute: the maximum similarity with any of the words (1) *starting* a SNOMED-CT entry, (2) *inside* a SNOMED-CT entry, and (3) *ending* a SNOMED-CT entry. We compute the same three features only considering gold annotations in the training set as gazetteer entries. We compute the semantic similarity between two words as the cosine between their corresponding word embedding vectors. We trained the embedding vectors with the word2vec tool (Mikolov et al., 2013) on the large unlabeled corpus of clinical texts (with over 400K documents) provided by the task organizers. We also counted the number of gazetteer entries that start with, contain, and end with the token at hand.

Information content-based features (IC). These features compute the informativeness of ngrams within the clinical domain and compare it their general informativeness. We use *information content* as a measure of the informativeness of the word w within a corpus C:

$$ic(w) = -\log \frac{freq(w) + 1}{\sum_{w' \in C} freq(w') + 1}$$

where $\mathit{freq}(w)$ is the frequency of the word w in corpus C. We compute three different information content-based features. First, we compute the information content of the word within a large corpus of clinical narratives. Secondly, we compute the ratio of the information content of the word computed on the clinical corpus and the information content of the same word computed on a large general corpus. We used Google Books ngrams (Michel et al., 2011) as the general corpus. The rationale here is that the clinical concepts such as diseases and disorders will have a higher relative frequency and, consequently, lower information content in the clinical corpus than in the general corpus. Finally, the third feature we compute is the mutual information of the bigrams in the clinical corpus, which we define via the information content:

$$mi(w_1, w_2) = \frac{ic(w_1 w_2)}{ic(w_1) \cdot ic(w_2)}$$

where $ic(w_1 w_2)$ is the information content of the bigram $w_1 w_2$. Mutual information score indicates pairs of words that often appear together (e.g., *"atrial dilatation"*). For each word w_i we compute the mutual information of the bigrams it constitues with the previous word (i.e., $w_{i-1}w_i$) and the subsequent word (i.e., $w_i w_{i+1}$).

3.1.2 Postprocessing

The only reasonable postprocessing strategy with the B-I-O scheme is to join each INSIDE token with the closest preceding BEGIN token. However, this strategy requires rule-based fixes for common situations in which two disorder mentions share a token. We designed postprocessing rules by observing the most frequent mistakes our CRF model made on the development set provided by the organizers. This led to three particular fixes: (1) mentions of *abdomen condition* typically correspond to two disorder mentions sharing the token *"abdomen"* (e.g., processing *"abdomen non-tender and non-distended"* results with two disorder mentions – *"abdomen non-tender"* and *"abdomen non-distended"*); (2) mentions of *allergies* typically share the token *"allergies"* (e.g., processing *"Allergies: Roxicet / Penicillins / Aspirin"* produces three mentions – *"Allergies Roxicet"*, *"Allergies Penicillins"*, and *"Allergies Aspirin"*); and (3) the CRF model rather frequently fails to recognize the type of the *hepatitis*. We associate the type of the *hepatitis* (e.g., *"B"*) found in the proximity of the token *"hepatitis"* when CRF fails to do so.

3.2 Mention Normalization

The normalization subsystem assigns a CUI to each extracted disorder mention by comparing the semantic similarity of the mention with the SNOMED-CT entries. Given that SNOMED-CT has over 650K entries, it is infeasible to compute the similarity of the disorder mentions with all database entries. Therefore, we first filtered out only the entries which contain at least one lemma from the extracted mention. E.g., for the mention *"melena due to gastrointestinal haemorrhage"* we would consider only the SNOMED-CT entries containing either *"melena"*, *"gastrointestinal"*, or *"haemorrhage"*.

We compute the similarity as the modified variant of the *greedy weighted alignment overlap* (GWAO) measure from (Šarić et al., 2012). To compute this score, we iteratively pair the words – one from extracted mention and the other from the database entry – according to their semantic similarity. In each iteration we greedily select the pair of words with the largest semantic similarity, and remove these words from their corresponding text snippets. The similarity between words is computed as the cosine between their embedding vectors obtained with `word2vec` (Mikolov et al., 2013) on the large unlabeled corpus of clinical narratives. Let $P(m, s)$ be the set of word pairs obtained through the alignment between the extracted mention m and the SNOMED-CT entry s and let $vec(w)$ be the embedding vector of the word w. The GWAO score is then computed as follows:

$$gwao(m, s) = \sum_{\substack{(w_m, w_s) \\ \in P(m,s)}} \alpha \cdot \cos\left(vec(w_m), vec(w_s)\right)$$

where α is the larger of the information contents of the two words, $\alpha = \max\left(ic(w_m), ic(w_s)\right)$. The $gwao(m, s)$ score is normalized with the sum of information contents of words from m and s, respectively, and the harmonic mean of the two normalized scores is the final similarity score. We assign to the extracted mention the CUI of the most similar SNOMED-CT entry, assuming the similarity is above some treshold λ (otherwise, the label "CUI-less" is assigned to the mention). The optimal value of λ is

Model	Strict			Relaxed		
	P	R	F_1	P	R	F_1
TK	75.6	65.6	70.2	90.0	80.4	84.9
TK + GZ	75.1	66.1	70.3	89.6	80.9	85.0
TK + IC	76.4	66.3	71.0	90.2	80.4	85.1
All feat.	76.3	66.9	71.3	90.1	81.1	85.4
All + PPR	77.4	69.1	73.0	90.1	82.2	86.0

Table 1: Model selection results.

Team	Strict			Relaxed		
	P	R	F_1	P	R	F_1
ezDI	78.3	73.2	75.7	81.5	76.1	78.7
ULisboa	77.9	70.5	74.0	80.6	72.9	76.5
UTH-CCB	77.8	69.6	73.5	79.7	71.4	75.3
UWM	77.3	69.9	73.4	80.9	73.1	76.8
TakeLab	**76.1**	**69.6**	**72.7**	**79.4**	**72.7**	**75.9**
Bioinf.-UA	69.0	73.6	71.2	71.9	76.6	74.2

Table 2: Official SemEval Task 14 (subtask 1) evaluation.

determined by maximizing the CUI prediction accuracy on the training and development set. A useful add-on to the normalization step is the memorization of CUIs for all disorder mentions observed in the training set. In other words, a memorized mention observed in the test set will be assigned the CUI it had in the training set.

4 Evaluation

Participants were provided with a training set consisting of 298 clinical documents and a development set with 133 documents. We used the training and development set to optimize the model (features, postprocessing rules, and the similarity treshold λ). A test set of 100 clinical documents was used for official evaluation.

4.1 Model Optimization

We trained the CRF model with different combinations of feature groups (TK, GZ, and IC) and evaluated the performance of these models on the development set. We also evaluated the contribution of the postprocessing rules (PPR) on the development set. The extraction performance of the different models is shown in Table 4.1. The model using only token-based features alone (model TK) achieves solid performance. Information content-based features (model TK + IC) seem to have a more positive impact on the performance than the gazetteer-based features (model TK + GZ). Still, the model with all features displays the best performance. Applying postprocessing rules further boosts the performance on the development set, which is expected, because the rules were designed precisely to fix the most frequent errors on that dataset. We submitted the model *All + PPR* for official evaluation. We also optimized the similarity treshold λ to maximize the normalization accuracy on the development set, selecting the optimal value of $\lambda = 0.83$.

4.2 Official Results

A subset of the official ranking on the test set is shown in Table 4.2. MINERAL ranks fourth among 16 teams in relaxed evaluation and fifth in strict evaluation, with only 3% lower F_1 performance than the best performing system.

Like most other systems, MINERAL displays higher precision than recall. This would suggest a non-negligible amount of obdurate disorder mentions which appear rarely in clinical documents and which are not semantically similar with more frequent disorders.

5 Conclusion

We described MINERAL, a system for extraction and normalization of disorder mentions in clinical text, with which we participated in Task 14 of SemEval 2015. At the core of the mention extraction approach is the CRF model built on B-I-O annotation scheme and a rich set of lexical, gazetteer-based, and informativeness-based features. We link the disease mentions to the SNOMED-CT entries using a measure of semantic textual similarity of short texts.

MINERAL achieved performance of almost 76% F_1 (relaxed evaluation setting), ranking us fourth out of 16 teams participating in the task, with 3% lower performance than the best-performing team. Such a result suggests that a resource light approach with sequence labeling (with semantic features) for mention extraction and STS measures for concept normalization offers competitive performance in the clinical domain.

References

Alan R. Aronson. 2001. Effective mapping of biomedical text to the UMLS metathesaurus: the MetaMap program. In *Proceedings of the AMIA Symposium*, page 17.

Steven Bethard. 2013. ClearTK-TimeML: A minimalist approach to TempEval 2013. In *Second Joint Conference on Lexical and Computational Semantics (StarSEM)*, volume 2, pages 10–14.

Carol Friedman, Philip O. Alderson, John H.M. Austin, James J. Cimino, and Stephen B. Johnson. 1994. A general natural-language text processor for clinical radiology. *Journal of the American Medical Informatics Association*, 1(2):161–174.

Goran Glavaš and Jan Šnajder. 2014. Construction and evaluation of event graphs. *Natural Language Engineering*, pages 1–46.

Vijay Krishnan and Christopher D. Manning. 2006. An effective two-stage model for exploiting non-local dependencies in named entity recognition. In *Proceedings of the 21st International Conference on Computational Linguistics and the 44th Annual Meeting of the Association for Computational Linguistics*, pages 1121–1128.

Andrew McCallum and Wei Li. 2003. Early results for named entity recognition with conditional random fields, feature induction and web-enhanced lexicons. In *Proceedings of the Seventh Conference on Natural Language Learning at HLT-NAACL 2003*, pages 188–191.

Jean-Baptiste Michel, Yuan Kui Shen, Aviva Presser Aiden, Adrian Veres, Matthew K. Gray, Joseph P. Pickett, Dale Hoiberg, Dan Clancy, Peter Norvig, and Jon Orwant. 2011. Quantitative analysis of culture using millions of digitized books. *Science*, 331(6014):176–182.

Tomas Mikolov, Ilya Sutskever, Kai Chen, Greg S. Corrado, and Jeff Dean. 2013. Distributed representations of words and phrases and their compositionality. In *Advances in Neural Information Processing Systems*, pages 3111–3119.

Gerard Salton, Anita Wong, and Chung-Shu Yang. 1975. A vector space model for automatic indexing. *Communications of the ACM*, 18(11):613–620.

Frane Šarić, Goran Glavaš, Mladen Karan, Jan Šnajder, and Bojana Dalbelo Bašić. 2012. TakeLab: Systems for measuring semantic text similarity. In *Proceedings of the Sixth International Workshop on Semantic Evaluation (SemEval)*, pages 441–448.

Michael Q. Stearns, Colin Price, Kent A. Spackman, and Amy Y. Wang. 2001. SNOMED Clinical Terms: Overview of the development process and project status. In *Proceedings of the AMIA Symposium*, page 662.

Hanna Suominen, Sanna Salanterä, Sumithra Velupillai, Wendy W. Chapman, Guergana Savova, Noemie Elhadad, Sameer Pradhan, Brett R. South, Danielle L. Mowery, and Gareth J.F. Jones. 2013. Overview of the ShARe/CLEF eHealth Evaluation Lab 2013. In *Information Access Evaluation: Multilinguality, Multimodality, and Visualization*, pages 212–231.

Buzhou Tang, Yonghui Wu, Min Jiang, Joshua C. Denny, and Hua Xu. 2013. Recognizing and encoding discorder concepts in clinical text using machine learning and vector space model. In *Workshop of ShARe/CLEF eHealth Evaluation Lab 2013*.

Özlem Uzuner, Imre Solti, and Eithon Cadag. 2010. Extracting medication information from clinical text. *Journal of the American Medical Informatics Association*, 17(5):514–518.

Qing T. Zeng, Sergey Goryachev, Scott Weiss, Margarita Sordo, Shawn N. Murphy, and Ross Lazarus. 2006. Extracting principal diagnosis, co-morbidity and smoking status for asthma research: Evaluation of a natural language processing system. *BMC Medical Informatics and Decision Making*, 6(1):30.

TMUNSW: Identification of disorders and normalization to SNOMED-CT terminology in unstructured clinical notes

Jitendra Jonnagaddala[a,b,c] **Siaw-Teng Liaw**[*,a] **Pradeep Ray**[b]
Manish Kumar[c]
School of Public Health and Community Medicine [a],
Asia-Pacific Ubiquitous Healthcare Research Centre [b],
Prince of Wales Clinical School [c]
University of New South Wales
Sydney 2031, Australia
{Z3339253, siaw, p.ray, manish.kumar}@unsw.edu.au

Hong-Jie Dai*
Graduate Institute of Biomedical Informatics, College of Medical Science and Technology
Taipei Medical University
Taipei City 110, Taiwan
hjdai@tmu.edu.tw

Abstract

Unstructured clinical notes are rich sources for valuable patient information. Information extraction techniques can be employed to extract this valuable information, which in turn can be used to discover new knowledge. Named entity recognition and normalization are the basic tasks involved in information extraction. In this paper, identification of disorder named entities and the mapping of identified disorder entities to SNOMED-CT terminology using UMLS Metathesaurus is presented. A supervised linear chain conditional random field model based on sets of features to predict disorder mentions is used in conjunction with MetaMap to identify and normalize disorders. Error analysis conclude that recall of the developed system can be significantly increased by adding more features during model development and also by using a frame based approach for handling disjoint entities.

1 Introduction

Electronic health record (EHR) also referred to as electronic medical record (EMR), electronic patient record (EPR), or personal health record (PHR) store or capture patients' medical history. EHR data typically contains demographics, medications, administrative and billing data. The contents of EHR can be either in structured, semi-structured or unstructured. Clinical notes contribute to majority of the unstructured data in EHR.

Clinical notes in EHR are often plain text records and valuable resources to obtain patient information (Denny, 2012). Clinical notes are rich in content and may include information on a patient's demographics, medical history, family history, medications prescribed and lab test results. Information extraction tools can be used to extract the aforementioned unstructured data to discover new knowledge (Jensen, Jensen, & Brunak, 2012).

Named entity recognition (NER) is an important subtask of information extraction to identify the boundaries of named entities. Clinical notes often include a wide variety of entities like diseases, disorders, anatomical sites, symptoms and procedures. However, often these entities are expressed in various forms and formats. Normalization is another sub-task of information extraction where the entities identified during NER are accurately mapped to concepts of standard terminologies or ontologies. Rich tools and resources are available to access various

* Corresponding author

standard terminologies and ontologies. Unified Medical Language System (UMLS) Metathesaurus and National Center for Biomedical Ontology (NCBO) BioPortal are two resources that are very useful for normalization in the biomedicine domain. The UMLS Metathesaurus provides access to medical standard terminologies such as SNOMED-CT, ICD9, and RxNorm (Bodenreider, 2004). In this paper, the authors presented an information extraction system to i) identify the disorders in clinical notes using conditional random fields (CRFs) (Lafferty, McCallum, & Pereira, 2001), and ii) normalize the identified disorders to SNOMED-CT terminology concepts (Spackman, Campbell, & CÃ, 1997) using MetaMap (Aronson & Lang, 2010).

2 Materials and Methods

2.1 Dataset

The authors used SemEval 2015 ShARe corpus to develop a CRF based information extraction system (Suominen et al., 2013). The ShARe corpus included training, development and test sets which were prepared using clinical notes from the MIMICII database (Saeed, Lieu, Raber, & Mark, 2002). The clinical notes were manually annotated by the annotators for disorder mentions and were normalized to SNOMED-CT concepts using UMLS concept unique identifiers (CUIs). Details on the corpus development are available in the annotation guideline[1]. Table 1 summarizes the details of training, development and test sets. In this paper, disorder refers to SNOMED-CT concepts that belong to the eleven UMLS semantic types: Congenital Abnormality; Acquired Abnormality; Injury or Poisoning; Pathologic Function; Disease or Syndrome; Mental or Behavioral Dysfunction; Cell or Molecular Dysfunction; Experimental Model of Disease; Anatomical Abnormality; Neoplastic Process; and Signs and Symptoms. In other words, an entity which is not part of these eleven UMLS semantic types or is not possible to map to a SNOMED-CT is not a disorder. These kinds of disorders are annotated as CUI-less in the corpus.

Type of clinical notes	Trai-ning	Develo-pment	Test
Discharge	136	133	100
Electro Cardiogram	54	0	0
Echo Cardiogram	54	0	0
Radiology	54	0	0

Table 1: Summary of SemEval 2015 ShARe Corpus

2.2 System Design

The authors developed a CRF-based classifier to identify disorder concepts and normalize the identified concepts to UMLS CUIs using MetaMap (Aronson & Lang, 2010). The pre-processing involves sentence detection,

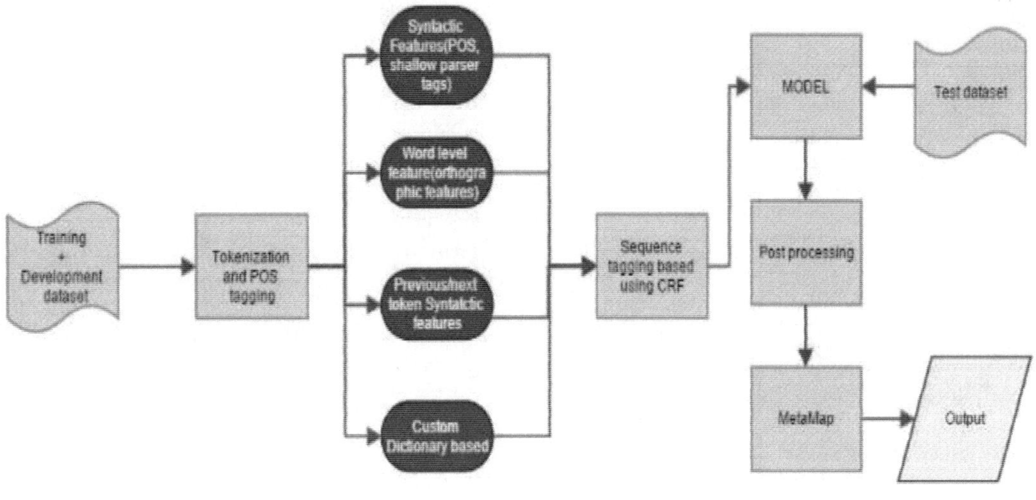

Figure 1: TMUNSW system design for SemEval-2014 Task 7

[1]http://alt.qcri.org/semeval2015/task14/data/uploads/share_annotation_guidelines.pdf

tokenization, part of speech tagging and shallow parsing. For pre-processing, the authors used apache OpenNLP[2] library which is a machine learning based toolkit. The output from preprocessing was used to extract several features which were used to train a Conditional Random Field based model. An overview of the developed system is schematized in figure 1.

2.3 Disorder Identification

The authors used discharge summaries from both training and development sets to develop the CRF model. Mallet implementation of CRF was used for disorder recognition using BIO tagging method (McCallum, 2002). The authors developed the CRF-model using BIO tagging method where each word token is assigned one of three tags "B","I","O". The "B" tag corresponds to beginning of a disorder entity, "I" tag corresponds to Inside disorder entity and "O" tag corresponds to outside (not a disorder entity). For example, let us consider this sentence - "*The patient had headache with neck stiffness and was unable to walk for minutes.*" The classifier will produce the following token annotation "*The/O patient/O had/O headache/B with/O neck/B stiffness/I and/O was/O unable/B to/I walk/I for/O minutes/O. /O*". The disorder identification CRF classifier uses word, syntactic features like POS tags and shallow parser tags. Authors also used previous word, its POS tags and next word and its POS tags as feature. Also, the authors developed a custom dictionary by extracting all disorder mentions in the training set, tokenized them and labelled each tokens as B-dict and I-dict. The developed custom dictionary was also used as features to build the classifier.

2.4 Disorder Normalization

Each disorder recognized by the CRF model was passed through MetaMap to find normalized concepts. For normalization of disorder concepts to UMLS SNOMED-CT CUIs, MetaMap 2013 version with UMLS 2013AB as data source was used. MetaMap server (also known as mmserver) is configured to process the output from the CRF model using Java API. MetaMap was configured to normalize entities that can be mapped to SNOMED-CT terminology only. No additional rules or logic is used to handle one entity mapped to multiple UMLS CUIs from different UMLS semantic types. Entity with the highest MetaMap score is considered. In situations where MetaMap failed to assign a CUI, they are automatically annotated as CUI-less.

[2] https://opennlp.apache.org/

2.5 Evaluation Metrics

The system developed (disorder identification and normalization) was evaluated using the test set. The official evaluation script provided by the SemEval 2015 Task 14 organizers was used to evaluate performance of the developed system using precision (P), recall (R) and F score (F). Evaluation was carried using strict (St) and relaxed (Re) F-scores. In strict setting, the official evaluation script identified the predicted disorder mention as a true positive if the spans (start and end offsets) are exactly the same as in the gold standard and the predicted CUI is correct. The predicted disorder is evaluated as false positive if spans are incorrect or the identified CUI is incorrect. In relaxed setting, the official evaluation script identified the predicted disorder mention as a true positive if there is any overlap between the predicted (start and end offsets) and gold standard spans. The predicted disorder is evaluated as false positive if spans are incorrect or identified CUI is incorrect. It is important to note that the evaluation metrics for both NER and normalization are calculated together.

3 Results

3.1 Individual Runs

The performance of the developed system using different configurations is presented in table 2. Run1 (r1) is the output from the CRF model with markov order as 1, Run2 (r2) is the output from the CRF model with markov order 2 and custom dictionary for disjoint annotation, Run3 (r3) is the output from the CRF model with markov order as 1 with custom dictionary for disjoint annotation. In terms of normalization, Run1 and Run2 had default MetaMap configuration and Run3 included Word sense disambiguation (WSD). The results displayed for training set are based on 10 fold cross validation.

	Training			Development		
St	P	R	F	P	R	F
r1	0.42	0.46	0.44	0.41	0.38	0.39
r2	0.44	0.47	0.45	0.40	0.39	0.39
r3	0.43	0.42	0.42	0.41	0.42	0.41

Re	Training			Development		
	P	R	F	P	R	F
r1	0.48	0.46	0.47	0.46	0.44	0.45
r2	0.51	0.48	0.49	0.49	0.47	0.48
r3	0.49	0.46	0.47	0.48	0.42	0.45

Table 2: Performance of system with different configurations on training and development sets

3.2 Official Evaluation

Table 3 presents the official evaluation results of the three different runs on the test set. The official evaluation results are provided by the SemEval 2015 shared task 14 organizers. Under both strict and relaxed setting, Run1 performed better than the other two runs. Run1 achieved an overall F-measure of 0.338 under strict settings, while under relaxed settings it achieved an F-measure of 0.408. Run2 and Run3 under both relaxed and strict settings had similar F-scores. The performance of the system on the test set is not so different from its performance on the training and the development sets. The gold set used to calculate the performance of the system by the organizers is not accessible to the authors.

	St			Re		
	r1	r2	r3	r1	r2	r3
P	0.32	0.32	0.32	0.39	0.38	0.38
R	0.34	0.34	0.34	0.42	0.41	0.41
F	0.33	0.33	0.33	0.40	0.39	0.39

Table 3: Official evaluation results on SemEval 2015 ShARe corpus test set

4 Discussion

The authors developed the current system based on their previous work (Jonnagaddala, Kumar, Dai, Rachmani, & Hsu, 2014). A custom built dictionary to handle disjoint disorders is integrated into the current system. With this addition, the system was able to find most of the disjoint mentions in the development set. The official evaluation results of the performance of the developed system on NER and normalization was not reported independently. A thorough error analysis was performed on the output generated by the developed system. Unfortunately, it is found that the authors misinterpreted the UMLS semantic types covered in the training, development and test sets. The authors used the default disease disorder semantic group which consists of twelve semantic types including "Findings" type. However, in the ShARe corpus "Findings" semantic type was ignored. The concepts related to this type should have been normalized as CUI-less. This significantly made an impact on the overall system performance. Implementing additional rules to filter out CUIs belonging to "Findings" semantic type and labelling them as CUI-less have significantly improved the system performance. During CRF model development, the authors experimented with various n-grams on the training set and found that trigrams performed best, so trigram of word and trigram of word POS tags as a feature. The identification of disorder might have been improved further with post processing if custom dictionaries to handle abbreviations, acronyms and misspelled entities were employed (Jonnagaddala, Liaw, Ray, Kumar, & Dai, 2014).

5 Conclusion

In conclusion, the authors presented an information extraction system based on CRF and MetaMap to identify disorder mentions in clinical notes and normalize the identified entities to SNOMED CT terminology using UMLS CUIs. The performance of the developed system was not as expected mainly due to the fact that system included "findings" semantic type in the normalized entities, when they were supposed to be normalized as CUI-less. In future, the authors would like to improve the performance of the system by employing semi-supervised techniques and custom dictionaries for abbreviations, acronyms and misspellings.

Acknowledgments

The authors would like to thank the organizers of 2015 SemEval Task 14 shared task. This study was conducted as part of the electronic Practice Based Research Network (ePBRN) and Translational Cancer research network (TCRN) research programs. ePBRN was/is funded in part by the School of Public Health & Community Medicine, Ingham Institute for Applied Medical Research, UNSW Medicine and South West Sydney Local Health District. TCRN is funded by Cancer Institute of New South Wales and Prince of Wales Clinical School, UNSW Medicine. The content is solely the responsibility of the authors and does not necessarily reflect the official views of funding bodies.

References

Aronson, A. R., & Lang, F. M. (2010). An overview of MetaMap: historical perspective and recent advances. *J Am Med Inform Assoc, 17*(3), 229-236. doi: 10.1136/jamia.2009.002733

Bodenreider, O. (2004). The unified medical language system (UMLS): integrating biomedical terminology. *Nucleic acids research, 32*(suppl 1), D267-D270.

Denny, J. C. (2012). Mining electronic health records in the genomics era. *PLoS computational biology, 8*(12), e1002823.

Jensen, P. B., Jensen, L. J., & Brunak, S. (2012). Mining electronic health records: towards better research applications and clinical care. *Nat Rev Genet, 13*(6), 395-405.

Jonnagaddala, J., Kumar, M., Dai, H.-J., Rachmani, E., & Hsu, C.-Y. (2014). *TMUNSW: Disorder Concept Recognition and Normalization in Clinical Notes for SemEval-2014 Task 7.* Paper presented at the 8th International Workshop on Semantic Evaluation (SemEval 2014), Dublin, Ireland, August 23-24, 2014.

Jonnagaddala, J., Liaw, S.-T., Ray, P., Kumar, M., & Dai, H.-J. (2014). HTNSystem: Hypertension Information Extraction System for Unstructured Clinical Notes. In S.-M. Cheng & M.-Y. Day (Eds.), *Technologies and Applications of Artificial Intelligence* (Vol. 8916, pp. 219-227): Springer International Publishing.

Lafferty, J. D., McCallum, A., & Pereira, F. C. N. (2001). *Conditional Random Fields: Probabilistic Models for Segmenting and Labeling Sequence Data.* Paper presented at the Proceedings of the Eighteenth International Conference on Machine Learning.

McCallum, A. K. (2002). Mallet: A machine learning for language toolkit.

Saeed, M., Lieu, C., Raber, G., & Mark, R. (2002). *MIMIC II: a massive temporal ICU patient database to support research in intelligent patient monitoring.* Paper presented at the Computers in Cardiology, 2002.

Spackman, K. A., Campbell, K. E., & CÃ, R. (1997). *SNOMED RT: a reference terminology for health care.* Paper presented at the Proceedings of the AMIA annual fall symposium.

Suominen, H., Salanterä, S., Velupillai, S., Chapman, W. W., Savova, G., Elhadad, N., . . . Jones, G. J. (2013). Overview of the ShARe/CLEF eHealth Evaluation Lab 2013 *Information Access Evaluation. Multilinguality, Multimodality, and Visualization* (pp. 212-231): Springer.

UtahPOET: Disorder mention identification and context slot filling with cognitive inspiration

Kristina Doing-Harris
Department of Biomedical Informatics
University of Utah Health Sciences Center
421 Wakara Way, Ste 140
Salt Lake City, UT 84108 USA
kristina.doing-harris@utah.edu

Sean Igo
Department of Biomedical Informatics
University of Utah Health Sciences Center
421 Wakara Way, Ste 140
Salt Lake City, UT 84108 USA
Sean.igo@utah.edu

Jianlin Shi
Department of Biomedical Informatics
University of Utah Health Sciences Center
421 Wakara Way, Ste 140
Salt Lake City, UT 84108 USA
Jianlin.shi@utah.edu

John Hurdle
Department of Biomedical Informatics
University of Utah Health Sciences Center
421 Wakara Way, Ste 140
Salt Lake City, UT 84108 USA
John.hurdel@utah.edu

Abstract

We describe the performance of UtahPOET on SemEval 2015 Task 14. UtahPOET is a cognitively inspired system designed to extract semantic content from general clinical texts. We find that our system performs much better on the context slot-filling aspects of Tasks 2A and 2B than the disorder CUI mapping of Tasks 1 and 2B or the body location CUI mapping of Task 2B. Our problems with CUI mapping suggested several possible system improvements. An alteration in the correspondence between the system architecture and psycholinguistic findings is also indicated.

1 Introduction

We note at the outset that our team approaches clinical NLP using a new, cognitively inspired architecture. We value dataset independence, so our design priorities do not completely overlap those encompassed by the goals of Task 14. We share the SemEval vision of extracting the full semantic content of clinical text. Our short-term goal, however, was to field test an early prototype of our new architecture and Task 14 provided a convenient and well-designed use case.

1.1 Cognitive inspirations

Only the human brain is currently able to extract full semantic content from text. We propose an intermediate step between artificial neurons (Merolla et al., 2014; Sowa, 2010) and statistical machine learning (ML). We use ML and rule-based NLP components with demonstrated success in clinical information extraction arranged in an architecture inspired by well-documented findings with respect to cortical processing.

Briefly, UtahPOET is inspired by findings related to: layered cognitive processes, the distinction between the dorsal and ventral language processing streams, and the phenomenon of iterative refinement. The type of layered (i.e., staged or hierarchical) processing we use shares much in common with traditional NLP and biologically inspired cognitive architectures (Chella, Cossentino, Gaglio, & Seidita, 2012; Indurkhya & Damerau, 2010; Sowa, 2010). We will discuss our system's layering in the system description below.

Our distinctive model of dorsal-ventral processing streams comes from psycholinguistic findings. The interpretation of unfamiliar or ungrammatical constructions, rule-based processing, and learning have been linked to dorsal processing streams in the brain. Ventral processing streams handle familiar, expected, regular constructions as well as heuristic-type processing (Dominey & Inui, 2009; Hickok & Poeppel, 2004; Kellmeyer et al., 2013; Levy et al., 2009; Price, 2013; Yeatman, Rauschecker, & Wandell, 2013). Iterative refinement is the repeated application of top-down processing during bottom-up processing. In Cognitive Science top-down and bottom-up refer, in essence, to processes that rely on previous knowledge and those that do not, respectively (Traxler, 2012).

Top-down processing is evident in each stage of an NLP pipeline, e.g., "knowing" how the end of a sentence is marked. We see combining world knowledge with the outcome of one processing stage and then using that to update the outcome of a previous stage as iterative refinement. This resembles how humans 're-parse' garden path sentences (McKoon & Ratcliff, 2007).

The UtahPOET approaches solving semantic extraction problems by enabling dependency parsing. However, ungrammatical text is common in clinical notes (Fan et al., 2013; Meystre, Savova, Kipper-Schuler, & Hurdle, 2008). This text often "breaks" dependency parsers, so we process grammatical and ungrammatical text separately. Dependency parsing is useful because it exploits world knowledge about the structure of English sentences. As such, it simplifies the processing of conjunctions and the aggregation of words and relationships, particularly those separated in the text, without supervised training. Retaining sentence structure allows dataset independence and latitude in future relationship finding.

1.2 Considerations for evaluation

We propose a couple of considerations useful for evaluating NLP systems' results under Task 14. The current evaluation includes strict matching to a Gold Standard set of Unified Medical Library System (UMLS) Metathesaurus (Browne, Divita, Aronson, & McCray, 2003) CUIs. We think this standard leads to over-fitting the data, which leads to less generally useful systems. Clinical terms do not guarantee a one-to-one correspondence between term and referent. A point demonstrated by inter-annotator agreement of anything less than 100%.

The redundancy of the UMLS Methathesaurus further undermines strict CUI mapping. Redundancy is best illustrated by body location mapping. Within the UMLS semantic types relevant to body location are T023 (Body part, organ or organ component) and T029 (Body location or region). We notice inconsistency in the Gold Standard in the use of these semantic types. For one document annotators chose 'Pericardial sac structure (T023)' over "Pericardial body location (T029)', while in another annotators preferred 'Neck (T029)' over 'Entire neck (T023).'

Partial matches create problems as well. The Task evaluation only considers partial span matches correct if the CUI for the full match is reported. However, if the span is only partially matched the correct CUI should change. For example, the mapping 'Left ventricular hypertrophy' to C0149721, when partially matched with 'Ventricular hypertrophy' would seem to be more correctly mapped to C0340279.

2 System description

The UtahPOET system is built in Apache UIMA (Ferrucci & Lally, 1999). It has the layered structure common to NLP pipelines (see Figure 1). The pre-processing stage finds sentence boundaries (stages A), breaks the sentence into tokens (stage B), and assigns each token a part-of-speech (POS) tag (stage B).

2.1 Dorsal-ventral stream separation and iterative refinement

After preprocessing, we add stages to begin dorsal and ventral separation and iterative refinement. In stage C, we divide dorsal and ventral streams by separating ungrammatical and grammatical text. We refer to ungrammatical text as *nonprose qs_segments*. Nonprose is differentiated from prose (well-formed sentences) by two rules. First, well-formed sentences contain at least one verb. Second, well-formed sentences do not contain more than four numbers (e.g., labs) per verb.

Iterative refinement occurs in Stage D. Realizing that standard sentence segmentation may not perform well with nonprose (e.g., consider common lists like medications with no periods), we then re-segment the text breaking each nonprose qs_segment at the next carriage return, line break, or end-of-line character. The dotted line in Figure 1 signifies that it is a repeated process.

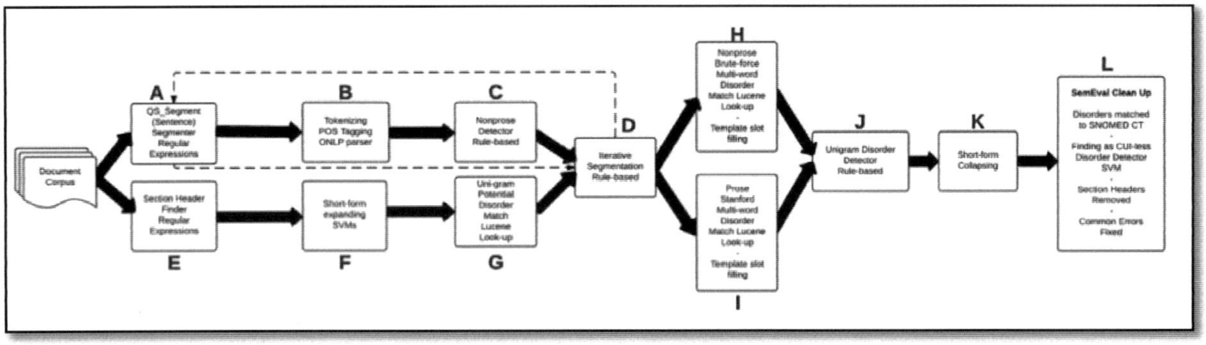

Figure 1. The overall UIMA pipeline for UtahPOET (please zoom for readability).

2.2 UtahPOET specific parallel 'pre-processing'

UtahPOET has section header identification and short-form expansion processes that run parallel to the 'pre-processing' stages. These stages are E and F in Figure 1.

In stage E regular expressions are used to identify section headers. The regular expression rules are found using automatic regular expression extraction (Bui & Zeng-Treitler, 2014).

In stage F, a series of SVMs are used to expand short forms. The feature vectors for these SVMs include context vectors as bags-of-words and section headers. The short form-long form pairs are extracted from the ADAM dataset (Zhou, Torvik, & Smalheiser, 2006) but limited to clinical terms. One classifier is trained for each ambiguous normalized short form that has multiple corresponding long forms. Classifiers are trained using the UMN clinical abbreviation and acronym sense inventory (Moon, Pahkhomov, Liu, Ryan, & Melton, 2014) and context information retrieved from PubMed case reports. The features are built on LVG (Browne et al., 2003) normalized bag of word, section header and short form string. The expanded short forms are inserted into the original text, preserving the original span information in UIMA annotations for span matching back to original text in the final stage.

2.3 Disorder detection in dorsal and ventral streams

Stage G has two purposes: to identify single-word disorder terms and to limit the number of words that will be looked up in later stages. After stop-words are removed, each word in the document is stemmed using LVG (Browne et al., 2003) and fetched from a Lucene index made from the UMLS Metathesaurus restricted to the clinical sources indicated in (Wu et al., 2012), including SNOMEDCT, MSH, NCI, RDC, MTH, SNMI, MDR, SCTSPA, CHV, CCPS. The sematic types included reflect disorders, body locations, and modifiers. Modifiers include qualitative, quantitative and spatial concepts.

For the identification of multi-word terms and context slot filling in stages H and I, we split the text segments based on the previously described nonprose (stage H) prose (stage I) distinction. The dorsal stream is associated with rule-based processing. In this case the rule associated with nonprose qs_segments, is that adjacent unigram disorder terms are likely to be part of a multi-word term. Equivalently, the body location and severity relevant to a disorder will be adjacent to the disorder mention. The ventral processing stream exploits world knowledge about regularity of construction by dependency parsing. Unigram matches that share dependencies are likely to be part of a multi-word term and reflect relevant body locations and severities.

In both stages (H and I), we build as long a multi-word term as possible then attempt to match the term to a Lucene index into the UMLS Metathesaurus restricted to the clinical sources listed above and only the disorder semantic types. If the term does not match, it is incrementally reduced token-by-token, with all combinations of words checked for a match at each step.

Context slots are filled by overwriting entries in a default template: the mention is not negated, the subject is the patient, the mention is not uncertain, severity and course are unmarked, the mention is not conditional or generic, and there is no body location given.

Negation, uncertainty, subject, and generic mention are found at the sentence level in nonprose and the dependency level in prose by looking for specific text. The remaining slot values were located by adjacency (nonprose) or dependency (prose).

2.4 Post-processing

Stage K takes place outside of UIMA. It collapses expanded short-forms back to their original spans and updates spans of all the other annotations in the file so our output spans reflect those from the SemEval gold standard. Stage L (SemEval clean up) is the final stage of the pipeline in Figure 1. Here we map, where possible, disorder CUIs from SNOMED CT. This stage also incorporates a process for identifying terms matched to the UMLS Metathesaurus semantic type finding (T033) that are considered CUI-less disorders in the SemEval gold standard. We use a structured SVM to classify the spans of *findings* to CUI-less disorder or not. We used the Cornell SVM^{struct} SVM^{hmm} model. (Joachims, n.d.) Feature vectors are 4-word context-window (2 before and 2 after), bag-of-words stemmed with stopwords removed using NLTK (Bird, Loper, & Klein, 2009). The SVM parameters were slack vs. weight vector magnitude (-c) of 25000 and epsilon (-e) of 0.5.

This stage also removes all disorders found within section headers as well as annotations that reflect either spurious UMLS Metathesaurus mappings or problems with short-form expansion.

3 Results

UtahPOET was not expected to perform well on either Task 1 or Task 2A. In both cases, our unwillingness to adhere to the gold standard CUIs caused us to score at the bottom of the pack. Sixteen teams competed in Task 1. We were 15th. Only 6 teams competed in Task 2A, we were last. Considering the context slot filling, apart from CUI and body location, in Task 2A would have moved us up one rank.

We were mainly focused on Task 2B where we scored in the middle of the pack until many of the teams withdrew. Nine teams remain in the Task 2B competition. Our three runs come second to the last. Again looking at only slot filling, we would have moved up three ranks.

Our results for the development set closely mirrored those on the test set; so will not be described.

3.1 Difference between runs

We were unsure whether scoring favored F-scores or accuracy so we submitted runs favoring one or the other. For both tasks, we submitted 2 copies of our best run in case there was a problem creating one of the submissions. If one failed, there would still be one left. In tasks 1 and 2A runs 1 and 2 were the same. Run 3 had a stricter Lucene match leading to higher accuracy and lower F-score (i.e., reduced numbers of true positive, false positive and false negative concepts). The stricter match required that only the words found in the document appear in the matched term, no extra words were allowed. Thus, "hypertension" would not match the UMLS Metathesaurus entry "hypertensive disease." In task 2B, runs 2 and 3 are the same. This time run 1 has a slightly higher accuracy, but lower F-score due to change in Lucene matching.

For task 2A, we also realized that we could use the gold standard spans to match the context found by UtahPOET without finding an associated concept, if we reported the span as a CUI-less disorder.

Count	Error type
Errors from system problems	
1265	CUI-less disorders (False Positive)
131	CT to 'carpal tunnel (C0007286)'
98	missed mappings of SOB to 'dyspnea (C0013404)'
98	'Chest Pain (C0008031)' mapped to 'Pain (CUI-less).'
Errors from UMLS diffuseness	
45	'he' to 'ideopathic hypereosinophillic syndrome (C0206141).'
58	'secondary' to 'neoplasm metastasis (C0027617)' from the phrase 'secondary to'
Errors from disagreement with Gold Standard	
'no apparent distress' to the negated disorder 'distress (C0700361)' gold standard is CUI-less	

Table 2. Examples of CUI mapping error for disorders (please zoom for readability).

3.2 CUI and body location error analysis

Tables 2 and 3 list examples of the CUI mapping errors made by UtahPOET. For disorders, they fall into three increasingly large groups, system problems, UMLS diffuseness, and disagreement with the gold standard.

CUI-mapping errors in body location assignment were, in increasing order of size, due to system problems, disagreement with the gold standard and near misses or equivalences.

Count	Error type
Errors from system problems	
125	'CT' to 'carpal tunnel (C0007286)' with the Body Location 'entire carpal tunnel (C1269543)'
71	missed 'chest (C0817096)' from 'chest pain (C0008031)'
66	body location 'breath (C0225386)' should be null
Errors from disagreement with Gold Standard	
61	'vomiting (C0042963)' to body location 'vomitus (C0042965),'
27	'drainage (CUI-less),' to body location 'body fluid discharge (C0012621)'
Errors from Near Misses or Equivalences	
'coronary artery part (C1268112)' for 'coronary artery (C0205042),'	
'other part of heart (C0446988)' for 'heart (C0019787),'	
'surface region of back of chest (C0565929)' for 'chest (C0817096),'	
'lower respiratory system (C1302847)' for 'respiratory system (C0035237)'	

Table 3. Examples of CUI mapping error for body locations.

4 Discussion

The UtahPOET system can successfully extract semantic information from clinical text. The system construction has slightly different priorities than the Task organizers. Our priority of creating a dataset agnostic solution for semantic extraction problems prompted us to offer considerations for the evaluation and to look to cognitive findings for system design inspiration.

4.1 Implications for system improvement

Necessary system alterations are revealed by disorder CUI mapping error analysis in Table 3. CUI-less disorders are the most error prone. We will be adding features to the CUI-less disorder SVM to improve performance. Two mapping mistakes 'CT' and 'he' that may be fixed by a walk back to the most common form. We will investigate a method to implement a walk back. Standardizing the expanded long-forms would catch the missed 'SOB' mappings. Checking for phrase 'secondary to' would also be helpful.

We find support for our evaluation considerations above in CUI and body location mappings, which disagree with the gold standard. For example, if 'shortness of breath' is given the body location 'breath,' giving 'vomiting' to body location 'vomitus' and 'drainage' to location 'body fluid discharge' should be acceptable.

UtahPOET is prone to near misses. We see these near misses as a type of graceful degradation, which is a hallmark of cognitive systems. Graceful degradation is the ability to function despite making errors. Ferreira and Patson call this "good enough" processing (Ferreira & Patson, 2007).

4.2 Implications for cognitive architecture

The hierarchical layers from psycholinguistics are lexical, syntactic and semantic processing, which proceed in that order. We do not adhere strictly to this hierarchy. Many cognitive scientists think a proper hierarchy is unlikely (Frank, Bod, & Christiansen, 2012).

We were inspired to separate prose and nonprose based on the ventral-dorsal distinction between grammatical and ungrammatical text. It is tempting to equate heuristics with ML and rules with specific if...then statements. The cognitive science literature indicates that this is a mistake (Hahn & Chater, 1998). All heuristics are thought to start as rule-based. The rule-based decision is overlearned to the point of automaticity and called a heuristic. Therefore we do not use ML components in only one path.

Currently, UtahPOET leverages iterative refinement for sentence segmentation only. Once we implement greater integration with long-term memory (LTM) representation, we will have the facility to recognize clashes and implement more extensive iterative refinement. With our ML components, we can clearly see how learning requires its own pathway. Each of these systems is trained outside the UtahPOET pipeline and would require retraining, if new information were introduced.

Acknowledgments

We are grateful for the support of the National Library of Medicine grant R01LM010981. The support and resources from the Center for High Performance Computing at the University of Utah are gratefully acknowledged. We would like to thank Duy Duc An Bui for building the Section Header component and Sarathkrishna Swaminathan for building the CUI-less disorder structure SVM.

References

Bird, Steven, Loper, Edward, & Klein, Edward. (2009). *Natural Language Processing with Python*. O'Reilly Media Inc.
Browne, Allen C., Divita, Guy, Aronson, Alan R., & McCray, Alexa T. (2003). UMLS Language and Vocabulary Tools: AMIA 2003 Open Source Expo, *2003*, 798.
Bui, Duy D. A., & Zeng-Treitler, Qing. (2014). Learning regular expressions for clinical text classification. *Journal of the American Medical Informatics Association*, *21*(5), 850–857.
Chella, Antonio, Cossentino, Massimo, Gaglio, Salvatore, & Seidita, Valeria. (2012). A general theoretical framework for designing cognitive architectures: Hybrid and meta-level architectures for BICA. *Biologically Inspired Cognitive Architectures*, *2*(C), 100–108.
Doing-Harris, K.ristina Patterson, Olga, Igo, Sean, & Hurdle, John. (2013). Document sublanguage clustering to detect medical specialty in cross-institutional clinical texts. Proceedings of the 7th international workshop on Data and text mining in biomedical informatics, ACM, 9-12.
Dominey, Peter F., & Inui, Toshio. (2009). Cortico-striatal function in sentence comprehension: Insights from neurophysiology and modeling. *Cortex*, *45*(8), 1012–1018.
Fan, Jung-wei, Yang, Elly W., Jiang, Min, Prasad, Rashmi, Loomis, Richard M., Zisook, Daniel S., et al. (2013). Syntactic parsing of clinical text: guideline and corpus development with handling ill-formed sentences. *Journal of the American Medical Informatics Association*, *20*(6), 1168-1177.
Ferreira, Fernanda, & Patson, Nikole D. (2007). The "good enough" approach to language comprehension. *Language and Linguistics Compass*, *1*(1-2), 71–83.
Ferrucci, David, & Lally, Adam. (1999). UIMA: an architectural approach to unstructured information processing in the corporate research environment. *Natural Language Engineering*, *10*(3-4), 327–348.
Frank, Stefan L., Bod, Rens, & Christiansen, Morten H. (2012). How hierarchical is language use? *Proceedings of the Royal Society B: Biological Sciences*, *279*(1747), 4522-4531.
Hahn, Ulrike, & Chater, Nick. (1998). Similarity and rules: distinct? Exhaustive? Empirically distinguishable? *Cognition*, *65*(2-3), 197–230.
Hickok, Gregory, & Poeppel, David. (2004). Dorsal and ventral streams: a framework for understanding aspects of the functional anatomy of language. *Cognition*, *92*(1-2), 67–99.
Indurkhya, Nitin, & Damerau, Fred J. (Eds.). (2010). *Handbook of Natural Language Processing* (Second.). Chapman and Hall. p. 168.
Joachims, Thorston. (Ed.). *Cornell SVM^{struct}*. Retrieved January 30, 2015, from http://www.cs.cornell.edu/people/tj/svm_light/svm_hmm.html
Kellmeyer, Phillipp, Ziegler, Wolfram, Peschke, Claudia, Juliane, Eisenberger, Schnell, Susanne, Baumgaertner, Annette, et al. (2013). Fronto-parietal dorsal and ventral pathways in the context of different linguistic manipulations. *Brain and Language*, *127*(2), 241–250.
Levy, Jonathan, Pernet, Cyril, Treserras, Sébastien, Boulanouar, Kader, Aubry, Florent, Démonet, Jean-Fronçois, & Celsis, Pierre. (2009). Testing for the dual-route cascade reading model in the brain: An fMRI Effective Connectivity Account of an Efficient Reading Style. *PLoS ONE*, *4*(8), e6675.
McKoon, Gail, & Ratcliff, Roger. (2007). Interactions of meaning and syntax: Implications for models of sentence comprehension. *Journal of Memory and Language*, *56*(2), 270–290.
Merolla, Paul A., Arthur, John V., Alvarez-Icaza, Rodrigo, Cassidy, Andrew S., Sawada, Jun, Akopyan, Filipp, et al. (2014). A million spiking-neuron integrated circuit with a scalable communication network and interface. *Science*, *345*(6197), 668–673.
Meystre, Stéphane M., Savova, Guergana K., Kipper-Schuler, Karin C., & Hurdle, John F. (2008). Extracting information from textual documents in the electronic health record: a review of recent research. *Yearb Med Inform*, *35*, 128–144.
Moon, Sungrim, Pahkhomov, Serguei, Liu, Nathan, Ryan, James O., & Melton, Genevieve B. (2014). A sense inventory for clinical abbreviations and acronyms created using clinical notes and medical dictionary resources. *Journal of the American Medical Informatics Association*, *21*(2), 299–307.
Price, Cathy J. (2013). Current themes in neuroimaging studies of reading. *Brain and Language*, *125*(2), 131–133.
Sowa, John F. (2010). Biological and psycholinguistic influences on architectures for natural language processing. Proceedings of the First Annual Meeting of the BICA Society, IOS Press, Incorporated, 221, 131.

Traxler, Matthew. (2012). Introduction to Psycholinguistics. Wiley-Blackwell.
Wu, Stephen T., Liu, Hongfang, Li, DDingcheng, Tao, Cui, Musen, Mark A., Chute, Christopher G., & Shah, Nigam H. (2012). Unified Medical Language System term occurrences in clinical notes: a large-scale corpus analysis. *Journal of the American Medical Informatics Association*, *19*(e1), e149–56.
Yeatman, Jason D., Rauschecker, Andreas M., & Wandell, Brian A. (2013). Anatomy of the visual word form area: adjacent cortical circuits and long-range white matter connections. *Brain and Language*, *125*(2), 146–155.
Zhou, Wei, Torvik, Vetle I., & Smalheiser, Neil R. (2006). ADAM: another database of abbreviations in MEDLINE. *Bioinformatics*, *22*(22), 2813–2818.

ULisboa: Recognition and Normalization of Medical Concepts

André Leal+, Bruno Martins*, and Francisco M. Couto+
+LASIGE, Faculdade de Ciências, Universidade de Lisboa, 1749-016 Lisboa, Portugal.
*INESC-ID, Instituto Superior Técnico, Universidade de Lisboa, Portugal
aleal@lasige.di.fc.ul.pt, bruno.g.martins@ist.ul.pt, fcouto@di.fc.ul.pt

Abstract

This paper describes a system developed for the disorder identification subtask within task 14 of SemEval 2015. The developed system is based on a chain of two modules, one for recognition and another for normalization. The recognition module is based on an adapted version of the Stanford NER system to train CRF models in order to recognize disorder mentions. CRF models were build based on a novel encoding of entity spans as token classifications to also consider non-continuous entities, along with a rich set of features based on (i) domain lexicons and (ii) Brown clusters inferred from a large collection of clinical texts. For disorder normalization, we (i) generated a non ambiguous dictionary of abbreviations from the labelled files, using it together with (ii) an heuristic method based on similarity search and (iii) a comparison method based on the information content of each disorder. The system achieved an F-measure of 0.740 (the second best), with a precision of 0.779, a recall of 0.705.

1 Introduction

Clinical notes are an important source of information recorded by medical professionals. However, this information, when available, is not easily accessible within automated procedures. Clinical notes are inherently complex, due to their lack of structure (i.e., narrative language) and due to the need for contextual interpretation. To address this complexity, text mining approaches represent an effective solution to assist the users in retrieving and extracting the required information.

This paper presents a text mining system for processing clinical text, that we developed for SemEval based on a pipeline with two modules, one for entity recognition and another for normalization.

The entity recognition module is based on the Stanford NER tool (Finkel et al., 2005), and it uses CRF models trained on annotated biomedical notes. The module tags the text according to an SBIEON encoding of entities as token classes, supporting the recognition of non-continuous entities (Leal et al., 2014). We relied on features based on Brown clusters and domain specific lexicons. Thus, this approach combines both supervised (Stanford NER) and unsupervised methods (Brown Clusters).

For practical applications, entity recognition is incomplete without performing normalization, i.e. without mapping each entity to an identifier (CUI) in a controlled vocabulary like SNOMED CT (Cornet and Keizer, 2008), that defines its semantic meaning. One of the main challenges in this task consists in resolving the ambiguous cases, where the same entity can have distinct semantic meanings (i.e., mapped to distinct CUIs) depending on the context.

Our normalization module relies on the following components: (i) a procedure for the automatic generation of auxiliary dictionaries from the labelled training data (e.g, abbreviations) and from SNOMED CT, to be used as mapping dictionaries, (ii) an heuristic for similarity search, and (iii) an information content measure for each concept.

Our system is an extension of the one used in the 2014 edition of SemEval (Leal et al., 2014). Both systems used the same approach for entity recognition but, in terms of the normalization component, the system from 2014 was entirely based on a lexical similarity approach using NGram, Levenstein and JaroWinkler distances. The current system is instead based on a pipeline were the information content was also incorporated. Besides SNOMED CT, the current system also integrated dictionaries automatically generated from the training data.

2 The SemEval Task

Task 14 of SemEval 2015 was composed of two subtasks: recognition and normalization of medical concepts (subtask 1) and disorder slot filling (subtask 2). We only participated in subtask 1.

The recognition part of subtask 1 consisted on performing the recognition of medical concepts, who belong to the UMLS semantic group *disorders*, within unstructured clinical notes. The disorders group of UMLS corresponds to concepts defined within SNOMED CT (Cornet and Keizer, 2008). Recognized entities can be continuous, non-continuous or even overlapped in the text.

The normalization part consisted on the mapping of an unique UMLS CUI (Concept Unique Identifier) to each previously recognized entity, or none at all (CUI-Less) for the cases where there is no suitable CUI for the recognized entity within the SNOMED CT database. Ambiguous entities represent the main challenge of this task, since identifying the correct CUI depends on their context.

Task 14 evaluated the recognition and normalization parts as one single task, by measuring the final system's precision, recall and F-measure. The evaluation could also be performed in a strict or relaxed way. In strict evaluation, a predicted mention is considered a true positive if the predicted span is exactly the same as the gold-standard. On the relaxed evaluation, the predicted spans only need to overlap the gold-standard spans to be considered a true positive. On both evaluation methods the CUI must be correctly identified to be considered a true positive. Thus, even with a perfect recognition system, it is possible to achieve low results on the task, depending on the normalization performance

3 Datasets

Similarly to the last edition of the competition (Zhang et al., 2014), two sets of labelled data were given to the participants, which were separated into two categories (training and development). They were used for training and testing of our system, respectively. Unlabelled clinical notes from the MIMIC corpus were also provided. Later, an unlabelled test set was released to evaluate the final system. Unlabelled clinical notes consisted on plain text without any additional information, while labelled clinical notes consist on plain text together with a list of disorder mentions contained on them. Table 1 summarizes each dataset.

	Train	Devel	Test	Unlabelled
Notes	298	133	100	404k
Words	182k	154k	8k	123M
Disorder Mentions	11.5k	8k	-	-
CUI-ied	8k (88%)	6k (76%)	-	-
CUI-less	3.5k (12%)	2k (24%)	-	-

Table 1: Statistical characterization of the datasets.

4 Entity Recognition

We applied the same type of approach used in our system from last year (Leal et al., 2014) for entity recognition. The Stanford NER software (Finkel et al., 2005) was used to train Conditional Random Fields (CRF) models using labelled data as input.

All input text had to be tokenized and encoded according to a named entity recognition scheme that encodes entities as token classifications. To be able to recognize non-continuous entities, an SBIEON (Leal et al., 2014) encoding was used. Besides the tags defined in the SBIEO encoding (Ratinov and Roth, 2009), a new tag **N** was added to identify words that do not belong to the entity but are inside the continuous span that contains the recognized entity. The remain tags are used to identify **S**ingle entities, the **B**egin, **I**nside and **E**nd token of a non-single token entity, and the **O**ther tag for words which are neither entities nor related to them. For overlapped entities we did not develop any approach, i.e. we only recognize the first entity in an overlapping group of entities. Thus, handling overlapping entities remains an open issue in our system.

4.1 Recognition Features

We generated 2nd-order CRF models by using, as training data, the labelled notes together with a rich set of features. In 2nd-order models, the features

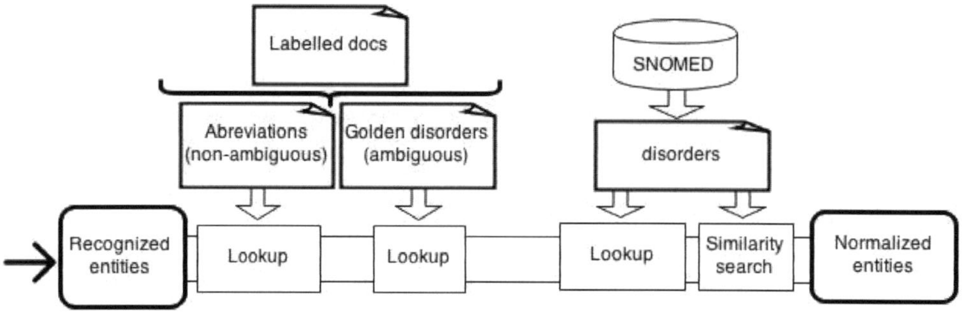

Figure 1: Overview on the normalization approach.

are computed from representations composed by the current class and the two previous/next classes.

Training Data: Two different sets of data were employed: one with notes belonging to the training set only, and another with notes from both the training and devel sets.

Brown Clusters: We inferred word representations in the form of Brown clusters (Brown et al., 1992) from all data that was made available, i.e. from MIMIC, train and devel. According to (Turian et al., 2009), this technique reduces the data sparsity, generating lower-dimensional representations of the word vocabulary, and therefore increasing the accuracy. Each word cluster contains a group of words, and clusters are formed by maximizing the mutual information of bi-grams, according to a class-based language model. We used a total of 404k documents, containing an approximate total of 123M tokens, to infer 100 different clusters using the implementation provided by (Turian et al., 2010). The number of clusters was chosen through a separate set of experiments as the one that maximized the F-measure.

Encoding: The aforementioned SBIEON encoding was employed in all recognition models.

Features: The CRF models rely on a set of features that includes (i) word tokens within a window of size 2, (ii) token shape (upper-cased, numeric, etc), (iii) token position in a sentence and (iv) token prefixes and suffixes. This basic set of features was also extended with features based on Brown clusters, and domain-specific lexicons.

Domain-specific lexicon: We built lexicons for the medical domain that include (i) SNOMED CT disorders, (ii) drugs and diseases from DBPedia and (iii) a list of disorders from the labelled data.

5 Normalization

Each recognized entity needs to be normalized, if possible, with a unique identifier (CUI) from an existing controlled vocabulary. This way, a semantic meaning is associated to each entity. Since ambiguous entities can have multiple identifiers depending on the context, one of the main challenges in this task consists in the disambiguation of these cases.

To address this challenge, we developed a pipeline framework (Figure 1) composed of several modules. First, a recognized entity will be looked up in an abbreviation dictionary. If it is unambiguously present there, then the associated CUI is assigned, otherwise the entity moves on to the next module (i.e. lookup on the golden dictionary). The CUI-less tag is assigned to the entity if no suitable CUI is found at the end of this process, or if the most similar SNOMED CT candidate found is not a disorder.

5.1 Resources

Abbreviation dictionary: This dictionary contains the small (up to 4 letters) upper-cased non-ambiguous concept descriptors found in the labelled data. For instance, the entity *ASD* is an abbreviation of *atrial septal defect* with the CUI *C0018817*. Since this descriptor is unique in SNOMED CT, it is considered non-ambiguous.

Golden disorders dictionary: All entity spans (ambiguous included) retrieved from the labelled notes are used to form this dictionary. This dictionary is thus composed by all concept descriptors which were dropped by the abbreviation dictionary, for their length or because they were ambiguous.

SNOMED CT dictionary: All concepts from SNOMED CT are included.

5.2 Methods

Similarity Search: This module was implemented using a Lucene index (MacCandless et al., 2010). NGram (Kondrak, 2005) and Levenshtein distances were used to retrieve the best SNOMED CT candidates. An extended Levenshtein distance, based on a best-token-match approach, was developed. This distance gives the similarity between a *target* (recognized entity descriptor) and a *candidate* descriptor (SNOMED CT concept), regardless of their token's orders. First, both *target* and *candidate* descriptors are split into tokens. For each *target*'s token, we compute the Levenshtein distance with all *candidate* tokens, and we finally pick the token corresponding to the minimum value. Each token in the candidate can only be compared to a single token in the target. The distance is represented by the following formula:

$$S_{dt} = \mathrm{SplitTokens}(d_t)$$
$$S_{dc} = \mathrm{SplitTokens}(d_c)$$

$$\mathrm{Sim}(d_t, d_c) = \begin{cases} -1, & \text{if} |S_{dt}| > |S_{dc}| \\ \dfrac{\sum_{w_{dt} \in S_{dt}} \mathrm{BestMatch}(w_{dt}, S_{dc})}{|S_{dt}|}, & \text{otherwise} \end{cases}$$

In the formula, we have that

$$\mathrm{BestMatch}(w_{dt}, S_{dc}) = \mathrm{Min}\{\mathrm{LevDist}(w_{dt}, w_{dc}) : w_{dc} \in S_{d}c\}$$

In the previous expressions, d_t is the *target* and d_c the *candidate* descriptor. SplitTokens is the function responsible for splitting the descriptor into tokens. BestMatch returns the minimum Levenshtein distance between the token w_{dt} and all available tokens in S_{dc}. The token in S_{dc} which minimizes the Levenshtein distance is removed from the list for posterior iterations against the remain tokens in S_t.

Information Content (IC): The Information Content (IC) was calculated for each disorder entity using the UMLS-Similarity (McInnes et al., 2009) software implementation. This measure enabled us to disambiguate entities by choosing, from the list of candidates, the ones with the lowest IC. This assumes that more general concepts have a higher probability to appear on a text. The intrinsic method by (Sánchez et al., 2012) was chosen to calculate the IC of each concept, using the following formula where $\mathrm{leaves(c)}$ represents the number of leaves of c, $\mathrm{subsumers(c)}$ represents the number of parents of c, and $\mathrm{max.leaves}$ is the number of nodes which are leaves in the SNOMED CT taxonomy:

$$\mathrm{IC}(c) = -\log\left(\frac{\frac{|\mathrm{leaves}(c)|}{|\mathrm{subsumers}(c)|} - 1}{\mathrm{max.leaves} + 1}\right)$$

5.3 Approach

We implemented a lookup method in each dictionary. If the entity was found, then the associated identifier was immediately assigned. Ambiguous cases were resolved using the information content, choosing the concept with the lowest IC value. For descriptions not found in the considered dictionaries, we used Lucene to retrieve the top 300 most similar candidates from SNOMED CT and, for each candidate, we applied the following formula to obtain the final similarity measure:

$$\mathrm{Sim}(d_c, d_t) = 0.15 * \mathrm{Lev}(d_c, d_t) + 0.15 * \mathrm{NGram}(d_c, d_t) + 0.7 * \mathrm{LevExt}(d_c, d_t)$$

In the previous expression, Sim represents the similarity between the target d_t and candidate d_c descriptor. Lev, NGram and LevExt represent the Levenshtein, NGram5 and Extended Levenshtein distance, respectively. The constant values were chosen according to a separate empirical evaluation using the devel dataset, although in future work we intent to use systematic approaches based on learning to rank. For each CUI associated to the chosen candidate descriptor (higher similarity with target descriptor), the one with the lowest IC was chosen.

6 Evaluation Experiments

Three runs were submitted to the SemEval 2015 competition:

Run 1: A 2nd-order CRF model was trained using the SBIEON encoding, and a rich set of features that includes the domain lexicons and 100 Brown clusters. For training, we only used notes from the training set. For assigning a UMLS identifier to each entity, we used the framework that was previously described.

Run	Strict Evaluation			Relaxed Evaluation		
	Precision	Recall	F-measure	Precision	Recall	F-measure
1	0.748	0.676	0.710	0.782	0.706	0.742
2	0.749	0.681	0.713	0.780	0.709	0.743
3	**0.779**	**0.705**	**0.740**	**0.806**	**0.729**	**0.765**
Best System SemEval 2015	0.783	0.732	0.757	0.815	0.762	0.788

Table 2: The official results for Task 1 of the SemEval 2015 challenge on clinical NLP.

Run 2: This run is identical to **Run 1** with the exception of the domain lexicon features that were not included. Normalization followed the same strategy as in **Run 1**.

Run 3: Identical to **Run 1**, with the exception that both train and devel documents were used as training data, resulting in the addition of 133 notes to the training set.

7 Results and Discussion

We present our official results in Table 2, highlighting our best results in comparison to those of the best participating system in the competition.

Our best run achieved the second best F-measure in the competition, with an F-measure of 0.740 in the strict evaluation and 0.765 in the relaxed evaluation. As previously said, the predicted mention can only be correct if and only if the mapped CUI is correct.

One of the first things to notice when comparing the runs is the difference on the results between the third run and the others. As expected, the addition of 133 notes (devel set) to the training data produced a better recognition model, thus improving the global performance of the system.

The addition of domain lexicon features to the recognition model resulted in a lower precision on the strict evaluation. On the relaxed evaluation a small improvement was achieved.

The small difference between the strict and relaxed evaluation modes can be associated to a really precise recognition model or, more likely, with the normalization pipeline having trouble in normalizing the concepts when they are not fully recognized. For example, if an entity E was only partially recognized, then it will be harder to normalize it.

In what concerns normalization, all runs were produced using the same pipeline and with the same features. Since our approach for the recognition task is similar to the one used in the SemEval 2014 edition, and since a significant improvement in the overall performance was obtained, we can conclude that our recent developments in the normalization part of the system were particularly effective.

8 Conclusions and Future Work

This paper describes our participation in Task 14 of the SemEval 2015 competition. Although this task was divided into two subtasks, our work only addressed on the recognition and normalization of entity disorders on clinical notes.

For the recognition part, we used a similar approach to the one followed in the 2014 edition of SemEval. Specifically, a 2nd-order CRF model was generated using the Stanford NER software, considering different sets of features. All models used the SBIEON encoding (Leal et al., 2014) to support the recognition of non-continuous entities. Overlapped entities continue to be an open issue.

For the normalization part, we developed a pipeline that takes advantage of the existing labelled data to generate and explore auxiliary dictionaries (e.g., an abbreviation dictionary). For the recognized entities that do not match to any dictionary, we employ a similarity search based on Lucene's implementation of Levenshtein and NGram distances. An extension of the Levenshtein distance was developed to compare descriptors independently of the order of their words. Ambiguous cases were resolved by choosing the concepts with the lowest information content, which was calculated using the approach proposed by (Sánchez et al., 2012);

As expected, results show that a more comprehensive training set enables the generation of better recognition models, maintaining the same set of features. We also saw that the addition of a domain lexicon increased the precision, although not significantly and with almost no impact on the F-measure. Our normalization framework was likely the main reason for the large improvement in our results, when comparing to the results from SemEval 2014.

In our opinion, the evaluation method followed in this year's competition is good for evaluating the system as a whole, but on the other hand it also limits the evaluation of the two tasks separately, which we believe would bring some advantages while developing the system and when comparing results.

For future work, we intend to evaluate both tasks individually, to better understand which components are performing well, and which ones need to be improved. In the normalization task, we intend to improve the framework that was presented, exploring semantic similarity based on ontology relations (Couto et al., 2006). By assuming that concepts within the same text are semantically related to each other, we intend also to disambiguate entities based on their semantic similarity towards all other previously normalized entities (Lamurias et al., 2015).

To improve the module related to similarity search for disambiguation, we also intend to develop a learning to rank approach similar to the one presented by (Leaman et al., 2013).

Acknowledgments

The authors would like to thank Fundação para a Ciência e Tecnologia (FCT) for the financial support of LASIGE (UID/CEC/00408/2013) and INESC-ID (UID/CEC/50021/2013).

References

Peter F. Brown, Peter V. deSouza, Robert L. Mercer, Vincent J. Della Pietra, and Jenifer C. Lai. 1992. Class-based N-gram Models of Natural Language. *Computational linguistics*, 18(4):467–479.

Ronald Cornet and Nicolette de Keizer. 2008. Forty years of SNOMED: A literature review. *BMC Medical Informatics and Decision Making*, 8(Suppl 1:S2):1–6.

Francisco M Couto, Mário J Silva, and Pedro M Coutinho. 2006. Validating associations in biological databases. In *Proceedings of the 15th ACM international conference on Information and knowledge management*, pages 142–151. ACM.

Jenny Rose Finkel, Trond Grenager, and Christopher Manning. 2005. Incorporating Non-local Information into Information Extraction Systems by Gibbs Sampling. In *Proceedings of the 43rd Annual Meeting on Association for Computational Linguistics*, pages 363–370.

Grzegorz Kondrak. 2005. N-gram similarity and distance. In *Proceedings of the 12th International Conference String Processing and Information Retrieval*, pages 115–126.

Andre Lamurias, João D Ferreira, and Francisco M Couto. 2015. Improving chemical entity recognition through h-index based semantic similarity. *Journal of Cheminformatics*, 7(Suppl 1):S13.

André Leal, Diogo Gonçalves, Bruno Martins, and Francisco M Couto. 2014. Ulisboa: Identification and Classification of Medical Concepts. In *Proceedings of the 8th International Workshop on Semantic Evaluation*, pages 711–715.

Robert Leaman, Rezarta Islamaj Doğan, and Zhiyong Lu. 2013. DNorm: disease name normalization with pairwise learning to rank. *Bioinformatics*, 29(22):2909–2917.

Michael MacCandless, Erik Hatcher, and Otis Gospodnetić. 2010. *Lucene in Action*. Manning Publications Company.

Bridget T McInnes, Ted Pedersen, and Serguei VS Pakhomov. 2009. UMLS-Interface and UMLS-Similarity: open source software for measuring paths and semantic similarity. In *Proceedings of the 2009 Annual Symposium of the American Medical Association*, pages 431–435.

Lev Ratinov and Dan Roth. 2009. Design challenges and misconceptions in named entity recognition. In *Proceedings of the 13th Conference on Computational Natural Language Learning*, pages 147–155.

David Sánchez, Montserrat Batet, David Isern, and Aida Valls. 2012. Ontology-based semantic similarity: A new feature-based approach. *Expert Systems with Applications*, 39(9):7718 – 7728.

Joseph Turian, Lev Ratinov, Yoshua Bengio, and Dan Roth. 2009. A preliminary evaluation of word representations for named-entity recognition. In *Proceedings of the NIPS-09 Workshop on Grammar Induction, Representation of Language and Language Learning*, pages 1–8.

Joseph Turian, Lev Ratinov, and Yoshua Bengio. 2010. Word representations: A Simple and General Method for Semi-supervised Learning. In *Proceedings of the 48th Annual Meeting of the Association for Computational Linguistics*, pages 384–394.

Yaoyun Zhang, Jingqi Wang, Buzhou Tang, Yonghui Wu, Min Jiang, Yukun Chen, and Hua Xu. 2014. Uth_ccb: A Report for Semeval 2014 - Task 7 Analysis of Clinical Text. In *Proceedings of the 8th International Workshop on Semantic Evaluation*, pages 802–806.

ezDI: A Supervised NLP System for Clinical Narrative Analysis

Parth Pathak, Pinal Patel, Vishal Panchal, Sagar Soni,
Kinjal Dani, Narayan Choudhary, Amrish Patel
ezDI, LLC.
{parth.p, pinal.p, vishal.p, sagar.s,
kinjal.d, narayan.c, amrish.p} @ezdi.us

Abstract

This paper describes the approach used by ezDI at the SemEval 2015 Task-14: "Analysis of Clinical Text". The task was divided into two embedded tasks. Task-1 required determining disorder boundaries (including the discontiguous ones) from a given set of clinical notes and normalizing the disorders by assigning a unique CUI from the UMLS/SNOMEDCT[1]. Task-2 was about finding different type of modifiers for given disorder mention. Task-2 was divided further into two subtasks. In subtask-2a, gold set of disorder was already provided and system needed to just fill modifier types into the pre-specified slots. Subtask 2b did not provide any gold set of disorders and both the disorders and its related modifiers are to be identified by the system itself. In Task-1 our system was ranked first with F-score of 0.757 for strict evaluation and 0.788 for relaxed evaluation. In both Task-2a and 2b our system was placed second with weighted F-score of 0.88 and 0.795 respectively.

1 Introduction

Extracting medical information from clinical natural text has gained a lot of attraction over the past few years. Approximately 80% of patient related information resides under unstructured transcribed text. Amount of this unstructured text is increasing constantly and automated methods of extracting crucial information is of paramount interest to health care informatics industry. Task-14 of SemEval 2015 on "analysis of clinical text" addresses the same concern.

Task-14 of SemEval-2015 was in continuation of the 2013 ShaRe/CLEF Task-1 (Suominen, H. et al., 2013) and task-7 of SemEval 2014. The task was divided into two parts. In continuation of last year, task-1 was about finding disorder mentions from the clinical text and associating them with their related CUIs (concept unique identifiers) as given in the UMLS (Unified Medical Language System). This year one additional task (Task-2) of disorder modifier slot filing was added. Task-2 was further subdivided into two parts. In subtask-2a, a gold set of disorder mentions was provided and the participants had to only fill the pre-specified slots with the normalized modifiers. In task 2b, no gold set of disorder mentions was provided. Figure1 provides detailed overview about task 1 and 2.

Clinical NLP has evolved a lot in the tasks related to medical entity detection. NLP systems like cTAKES (Savova, Guergana K., et al., 2010), MetaMap (A. Aronson, 2001) and MedLEE (C. Friedman et al., 1994) have focused on rule based and dictionary look-up approaches for thid task. Recently a few attempts have been made to use supervised and semi-supervised learning models. In 2009, Yefang Wang (Wang et al., 2009) used cascading classifiers on manually annotated data and achieved around 83.2% accuracy. In 2010, i2b2 shared task challenge focused on finding test, treatment and problem mentions from clinical document. From 2013 on-words, entity detection task is regularly featuring in Share/CLEF and SemEval tasks.

Tasks related to modifier slot filling are relatively

[1] http://www.nlm.nih.gov/research/umls/

new and no extensive research has been done yet. However for negation modifier, negEx (Chapman et al., 2011) or various other variants of negEx have been used in the last 10 years. These are keyword based dictionary look-up algorithms, but still gives around 92% of accuracy. However, these algorithms are not scalable because there is no proper mechanism defined to detect boundary for given negated keyword. In 2010 i2b2 challenge, there was a separate task for detecting 5 categories of negation. Systems used in this task showcase various statistical approaches and the accuracy numbers were in the range of 90 to 93%.

In this paper we have proposed a hybrid supervised learning approach based on CRF and SVM to find out disorder mentions from clinical documents, a dictionary look-up approach on a customized UMLS meta-thesaurus to find corresponding CUIs and a SVM based generic approach to find out all different disorder modifiers.

Disease/Disorder (DD) Attribute Types	**Definitions from ShARe guidelines** A span of text that …	**Normalized Values**	**Cue word** span offset of lexical cue
Disorder CUI	indicates a disease/disorder	*null	span offset of lexical cue
Negation (NI)	*indicates a disease/disorder was negated*	*no, yes	span offset of lexical cue
Subject (SC)	*indicates who experienced the disease/disorder*	*patient, family_member, donor_family_member, donor_other, null, and other	span offset of lexical cue
Uncertainty Indicator (UI)	*indicates a measure of doubt into a statement about a disease/disorder*	*no, yes	span offset of lexical cue
Course Class (CC)	indicates progress or decline of a disease/disorder	*unmarked, changed, increased, decreased, improved, worsened, and resolved	span offset of lexical cue
Severity Class (SV)	indicates how severe a disease/disorder is	*unmarked, slight, moderate, and severe	span offset of lexical cue
Conditional Class (CO)	indicates conditional existence of disease/disorders under certain circumstances	true, *false	span offset of lexical cue
Generic Class (GC)	indicates a generic mention of a disease/disorder	true, *false	span offset of lexical cue
Body Location (BL)	represents an anatomical location of these UMLS semantic types: Anatomical structure; Body location or region; Body part; organ or organ component; Body space or junction; Body substance; Body system; Cell; Cell component; Embryonic structure; Fully formed anatomical structure; Tissue	*null	span offset of lexical cue

Default values indicated with *

Figure 1: Task-2 with Examples.

2 Data Set

The SemEval-2015 corpus comprises of de-identified plain text from MIMIC[2] version 2.5 database. A disorder mention was defined as any span of text which can be mapped to a concept in UMLS and which belongs to the disorder semantic group. Some other disorders which were not present in the UMLS were marked as CUI-less. The training and development data sets of the previous year's task were combined to be used as training set (298 documents) while the test data set of the previous year was used as development set. There were 100 documents used as test data set. Same set of 4 hundred thousand unlabelled documents were added to encourage use of unsupervised learning methods.

3 Disorder Detection and Normalization

For Task-1 our system was very similar to the system we developed last year (Pathak, et al, 2014). Entity detection task was converted into sequence labelling task using BIO format. A Conditional Random Fields (CRF) was used to detect continuous entity using CRF++[3] toolkit. To detect discontiguous entities, a binary SVM classifier was used to detect whether relationship existed between two disorder mentions or not. For contiguous entity detection task, our feature set was very similar to the one we used last year:

- Standard features like bag of words (for window +2 to -2), word stemmer (snowball stemmer) [4], prefix and suffix of length 1 to 5.
- Orthographic features like word contains digit, contains slash, contains special character and word shape (ezDI becomes aA).
- Grammatical features like parts of speech (PoS) tags for which we used an internally developed PoS tagger (Choudhary et al. , 2014), chunk (using Charniak's parser (Charniak and Johnson , 2005)) and head of noun and verb phrases.
- Dictionary look-up matches for window +2 to -2, stop words
- Section header and document type information and sentence cluster id

Support Vector Machine (LibSVM[5]) was used to identify disjoint entities. For all the possible combination of entities within a sentence, we ran a binary SVM classifier to find whether a relationship existed between those two entities or not. Feature set consisted of following features:

[2]http://mimic.physionet.org/database/releases/70-version-25.html

[3]http://crfpp.googlecode.com/

[4]http://snowball.tartarus.org/

[5]http://www.csie.ntu.edu.tw/\~cjlin/libsvm/

- Bag of words, PoS tags and chunk labels for all the tokens appearing in between two entities.

- Few simple rules were implemented on Charniak parse output to find relationship between two entities. A binary feature was used stating whether relationship was found using rules or not.

- Position of preposition, conjunction, main verb and special characters like colon (:), hyphen (-) and semi colon (;) in the context of the first entity.

- Binary feature stating whether any of the detected entity contained head of a noun phrase.

This hybrid approach was very helpful in detecting disjoint entities. We got around 70% accuracy in detecting disjoint entities using this approach.

3.1 CUI Detection

CUI detection task was divided into three separate steps:

1) Direct dictionary search: In the first step, for each word found in an entity we found all of its lexical variants using LVG [6]. After that, for all the possible permutations we tried searching the string in the UMLS. If the string matched any UMLS entry, we associated the corresponding CUI with that entity.

2) Dictionary search on modified entities: For a better mapping of the entities detected by NLP inside the given input text, we found it to be a better approach to divide the UMLS entities into various phrases. This was done semi-automatically by splitting the strings based on function words such as prepositions, particles and non-nominal word classes such as verbs, adjectives and adverbs. While most of the disorder entities in UMLS can be contained into a single noun phrase (NP) there are also quite a few that contain multiple NPs related with prepositional phrases (PPs), verb phrases (VPs) and adjectival phrases (ADJPs).

This exercise gave us a modified version of the UMLS disorder entities along with their CUIs. Table 4 gives a snapshot of what this customized UMLS dictionary looked like.

[6] http://lexsrv2.nlm.nih.gov/

CUI	Text	P1	P2	P3
C001 3132	Dribbling from mouth	Dribbling	from	mouth
C001 4591	Bleeding from nose	Bleeding	from	nose
C002 9163	Hemorr-hage from mouth	Hemo-rrhage	from	mouth
C039 2685	Chest pain at rest	Chest pain	at	rest
C026 9678	Fatigue during pregnancy	Fatigue	during	pregn ancy

Table 1: An example of the modified UMLS disorder entities split as per their linguistic phrase types.

3) String similarity algorithm: If an entity was not found even after the first two steps, then we generated a list of possible text span from UMLS which can possibly match with the given entity. After that, Levenshtein edit distance algorithm was used to find best string match. If the best string match was greater than a certain threshold value, the corresponding CUI was associated with the entity otherwise the entity was marked as "CUI-less".

4 Modifier Detection:

For this task we tried to develop a generic approach so that it can be applied to any type of modifier. We divided the task of modifier detection into two parts: 1) Modifier keywords detection 2) Relating detected keywords with entity.

1) Modifier keywords detection: For each modifier type, an extensive dictionary was prepared having different possible keywords with its normalized values. A simple dictionary look-up algorithm was used to calculate a baseline accuracy. On training data set, accuracy ranged from 60% to 85% for different modifier types. This baseline algorithm achieved great recall but much less precision. To counter this, we used CRF algorithm with common features like bag of words, stem value and other orthographic features. CRF helped significantly in improving precision for modifier keyword detection.

2) Relating detected modifier with entities: We

treated this task similar to the task of finding relationship between two entities. So a binary classifier was used to check if relationship existed between a modifier keyword and an entity or not. Feature set consisted of: Bag of Words between entity and modifier keyword, PoS tags, a binary flag stating whether the modifier keyword and the entity appeared in the same chunk or not, relative position of entity and modifier, special characters appearing in the sentence, section header (for subject modifier type).

5 System Accuracy

For Task-1, the accuracy was defined as the number of pre-annotated spans with correctly generated code divided by the total number of pre-annotated spans.

$$\text{Strict Accuracy} = \frac{\#of\ CUIs\ with\ Exact\ span\ match}{Total\ annotation\ in\ gold\ standard}$$

$$\text{Relaxed Accuracy} = \frac{\#of\ CUIswithpartialspanmatch}{Total\ annotation\ in\ gold\ standard}$$

Both training and development data sets were used for training purpose. We used only 1 run with above mentioned system set up. We were ranked first for this task with results shown in Table 3.

	Precision	Recall	Accuracy
Strict	0.783	0.732	0.757
Relaxed	0.815	0.761	0.787

Table 2: Task-1 Results.

For Task 2, weighted and unweighted accuracies were calculated. The unweighted accuracy is the average of the per-disorder unweighted accuracy over all the disorders in the test set. Each gold-standard slot value is pre-assigned a weight based on its prevalence in the training set. The weighted accuracy is the average of the per-disorder weighted accuracy over all the disorders in the test set.

Ranks for task-2 were given based on weighted accuracy. ezDI was ranked second in both Task-2a and Task-2b. The results were as given below:

	F	A	F*A	WA	F*WA
Task-2A	1	0.934	0.934	0.880	0.880
Task-2B	0.915	0.935	0.856	0.868	0.795

Table 3: Task-2 Results.

6 Error Analysis

Abbreviations and disjoint entities still cause a lot of error in CUI normalization task. Dictionary related features are still not very helpful. Accuracy decreases significantly if medical domain is changed. Probably more sophisticated approach will be required to fully utilize UMLS dictionary. There is still a lot to explore in modifier detection. Statistical approaches are still not out-performing baseline dictionary based approaches. Modifier boundary detection is still a bigger challenge to be solved.

7 Conclusion

In this paper we have proposed a CRF and SVM based hybrid approach to find disorder mentions from a given clinical text, a novel dictionary look-up approach for discovering CUIs from UMLS metathesaurus and a generic statistical approach for modifier slot filling. Our system did produce competitive results and was best among all the participants for task 1. In future, we would like to explore semi-supervised learning approaches to take advantage of large amount of available un-annotated free clinical text.

References

Aronson, Alan R. 2001. *Effective mapping of biomedical text to the UMLS Metathesaurus: the MetaMap program.*

Chapman W, Bridewell W, Hanbury P, Cooper G, Buchanan B. 2001. *A simple algorithm for identifying negated findings and diseases in discharge summaries.*

Charniak, Eugene and Mark Johnson. 2005. *Coarse-to-Fine n-best Parsing and MaxEnt Discriminative Reranking.*

Choudhary, Narayan, Parth Pathak, Pinal Patel, Vishal Panchal. 2014. *Annotating a Large Representative Corpus of Clinical Notes for Parts of Speech.*

Friedman C, Alderson PO, Austin JH, Cimino JJ, Johnson SB. 1994. *A general natural-language text processor for clinical radiology.*

Pathak, Parth, Pinal Patel, Vishal Panchal, Narayan Choudhary, Amrish Patel, Gautam Joshi. 2014. *ezDI: A Hybrid CRF and SVM based Model for Detecting and Encoding Disorder Mentions in Clinical Notes.*

Savova, Guergana K., James J. Masanz, Philip V. Ogren, Jiaping Zheng, Sunghwan Sohn, Karin C. Kipper-Schuler, and Christopher G. Chute. 2010. *Mayo clinical Text Analysis and Knowledge Extraction System (cTAKES): architecture, component evaluation and applications.*

Suominen, Hanna, Sanna Salanter, Sumithra Velupillai, Wendy W. Chapman, Guergana Savova, Noemie Elhadad, Sameer Pradhan. 2013. *Overview of the ShARe/CLEF eHealth evaluation lab 2013.*

Wang, Yefeng and Jon Patrick. 2009. *Cascading classifiers for named entity recognition in clinical notes.*

CUAB: Supervised Learning of Disorders and their Attributes Using Relations

James Gung
University of Colorado
1111 Engineering Drive
Boulder, Colorado 80309, USA
james.gung@colorado.edu

John David Osborne, Steven Bethard
University of Alabama at Birmingham
1720 2nd Ave South
Birmingham, AL, USA 35294
{ozborn,bethard}@cis.uab.edu

Abstract

We implemented an end-to-end system for disorder identification and slot filling. For identifying spans for both disorders and their attributes, we used a linear chain conditional random field (CRF) approach coupled with cTAKES for pre-processing. For combining disjoint disorder spans, finding relations between attributes and disorders, and attribute normalization, we used l2-regularized l2-loss linear support vector machine (SVM) classification. Disorder CUIs were identified using a back-off approach to YTEX lookup (CUAB1) or NLM UTS API (CUAB2) if the target text was not found in the training data. Our best system utilized UMLS semantic type features for disorder/attribute span identification and the NLM UTS API for normalization. It was ranked 12th in Task 1 (disorder identification) and 6th in Task 2b (disorder identification and slot filling) with a weighted F Measure of 0.711.

1 Introduction

One of the core problems in the field of clinical text processing is the identification and normalization of medical disorders (Pradhan et al., 2014). A secondary problem is the identification of attributes for the identified disorders such as their severity or body location. Attribute identification and normalization helps to better describe the disorder context, allowing for a better determination of the appropriateness of the discovered disorder for the task at hand.

SemEval-2015 Task 14 addresses these problems as separate tasks, assessing end to end systems capable of identifying both disorders and attributes from unlabeled clinical text. The first task requires participants to identify discontinuous disorder spans in clinical text and normalize them to a UMLS Concept Unique Identifier (CUI) that is both within the disorder Semantic Group and present in SNOMED CT. The second task requires identification of disorder CUIs as well as 8 additional attributes associated with each disorder as shown in Table 1 on the shared task page[1]. For each attribute, the span offset of the lexical cue must also be identified, which may be discontinuous.

2 Approach

We combined and extended our previous work (Gung, 2014; Osborne et al., 2014) for the ShARe/CLEF 2013 eHealth Evaluation Lab (Suominen et al., 2013). Both previous systems and our base system for this task are based on the clinical Text Analysis and Knowledge Extraction System (cTAKES) (Savova et al., 2010), an open source pipeline for the natural language processing (NLP) of clinical text that utilizes the Unstructured Information Management Architecture (UIMA) (Ferrucci and Lally, 2004) framework. Our combined system is available for download at https://github.com/jgung/ClearClinical.

We developed two systems for this task that differed in their method of CUI lookup and the presence of UMLS semantic type features. The first system (CUAB1) uses YTEX (Garla et al., 2011) to disambiguate CUIs returned from the cTAKES dictionary

[1] http://alt.qcri.org/semeval2015/task14/index.php?id=task-description

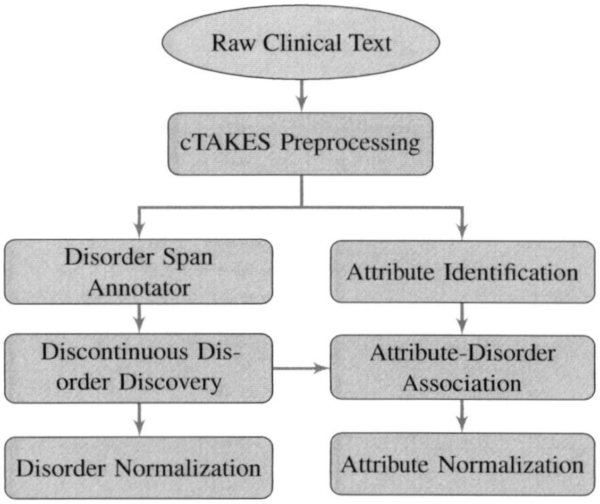

Figure 1: Pipeline of the system components

annotator. The second system (CUAB2) uses UMLS Terminology Services (UTS) for the same task and additional UMLS features for disorder/attribute span annotation. For both of these systems, we relied on cTAKES for pre-processing, using the default pipeline from the cTAKES ClinicalPipelineFactory class to perform tokenization, sentence segmentation, part of speech (POS) tagging and chunking.

2.1 Task 1 - Disorder Identification and Normalization

We broke down Task 1 into 3 different tasks as shown in Figure 1: identification of disorder spans, linking of disjoint disorder spans into single discontinuous disorders, and association of the final (dis)continuous disorder spans with CUIs.

2.1.1 Disorder Span Annotation

Span identification in Task 1 was accomplished with the same begin-inside-outside (BIO) token classification methodology as in previous work (Gung, 2014) but using the updated training data. Spans of putative disorders were labeled using a linear chain CRF with features identical to those used in previous work. Examples of these features are shown in Table 1. The disorder span tagger was implemented using the ClearTK machine learning framework (Bethard et al., 2014) which presents a UIMA interface for machine learning models and wraps classifiers such as CRFSuite (Okazaki, 2007).

Feature Type	Example Feature
Token	First token of each of the two annotations
POS	Part-of-speech tags (e.g, NN) of each of the two annotations
Phrase-chunk	Phrase chunks (e.g., NP, VP) between the two annotations
Dependency path	Max distance to common ancestor of the two annotations
Dependency tree	Concatenation of head word and governing word for each of the two annotations
Named entity	Number of named entity mentions between the two annotations

Table 1: Feature types and examples for features used to associated disjoint spans into a discontinuous disorder and to associate attributes with a candidate disorder

2.1.2 Discontinuous Disorder Discovery

In a departure from previous work (Gung, 2014), we trained our own relation extractor for the discovery of discontinuous spans, rather than relying on existing models used by ClearNLP's SRL system and the cTAKES relation extractor. We used a l2-regularized l2-loss linear SVM classifier (via the ClearTK wrapper to LibLinear) to predict when two disorder spans identified in the previous step should be combined into a single disorder. We used a subset of features from the cTAKES relation extractor including token features (e.g., last word in disjoint span), POS features, phrase chunks (e.g., phrase chunk between first head), dependency tree information (e.g., dependencies on POS tags, words), dependency path information (e.g., mean distance to common ancestor) and the number of named entities between the disjoint spans. A list of these features with examples is shown in Table 1 and more interested readers can review the source code made available.

We explored some additional features to improve span detection including pointwise mutual information from the provided unlabeled MIMIC notes and CUI-normalized segment header information. Neither feature provided a performance improvement on the training data and thus they were excluded from our final systems.

System	Rank	TP	FP	FN	P	R	F
Strict Results							
CUAB1	23	3514	1381	2634	0.718	0.572	0.636
CUAB2	12	4202	1516	1946	0.735	0.683	0.708
ezDI	1	-	-	-	0.783	0.732	0.757
Relaxed Results							
CUAB1	-	3632	1263	2516	0.742	0.591	0.658
CUAB2	-	4357	1361	1791	0.762	0.709	0.734
ezDI	-	-	-	-	0.815	0.761	0.787

Table 2: Performance on disorder identification and normalization (Task 1), including rank among the 39 competing systems (Rank), true positives (TP), false positives (FP), false negatives (FN), precision (P), recall (R) and F-measure (F). Task ranking was only given for strict scoring.

2.1.3 Disorder Normalization

Disorder normalization in both systems used a dictionary of text-to-CUI mappings from the training data as the primary attempt to normalize the disorders. In CUAB2, any text not normalized by this training dictionary was assigned a CUI using UMLS UTS web services whereas in CUAB1 the assignment was made using the cTAKES dictionary annotator with YTEX to resolve ambiguous terms. In both systems text that failed all of these methods was designated as CUI-less.

2.2 Task 2 - Attribute Identification and Normalization

We broke this task down into 3 different steps as shown in Figure 1: detection of attribute spans, association of those spans to the disorders already identified, and the normalization of the attribute spans (slot filling).

2.2.1 Attribute Identification

To detect attribute spans we used the same linear chain CRF model with the same features that we used to detect disorder spans in Task 1.

As in disorder identification, we labeled tokens as either the beginning, inside, or outside (BIO) of an attribute. Contiguous non-outside chunks were assembled and marked as possible candidate attributes.

2.2.2 Associating Attributes with Disorders

We again used a l2-regularized l2-loss linear SVM classifier model to link our candidate attributes to the disorders discovered by our system in Task 1. This classifier used the same feature set as was used for merging disorder spans (see Table 1).

System	Accuracy
YTEX	0.650
UTS	0.644

Table 3: Accuracy of Disorder Normalization on Training Data

2.2.3 Attribute Normalization

Attributes for disorders were normalized using a l2-regularized l2-loss linear SVM classifier using as features the full text of the attribute, the text of the tokens within the attribute annotation, and the text of the tokens appended with the attribute type.

3 Results

3.1 Task 1

Table 2 shows the performance of the CUAB systems on disorder identification and normalization (Task 1), as well as the performance of the top system in the shared task. The best CUAB system (CUAB2) used UMLS semantic type features for disorder span identification and UMLS Terminology Services (UTS) for CUI lookup and ranked 12th out of 39 systems, achieving precision and recall that were both about 0.05 below the top system. CUAB1 was ranked 23rd but not because the system was less able to normalize disorder CUIs. As shown by the training data in Table 3, both UTS and YTEX had similar accuracy in predicting CUIs. A more plausible explanation for the relatively higher performance of CUAB2 is a result of more accurate span detection due to its

System	Rank	TP	FP	FN	P	R	F	A	WA	F*A	F*WA
CUAB1	17	4627	258	1521	0.947	0.753	0.839	0.873	0.669	0.732	0.561
CUAB2	6	5376	328	772	0.942	0.874	0.907	0.908	0.784	0.824	0.711
UTH-CCB	1	-	-	-	-	-	0.926	0.941	0.873	0.871	0.808

Table 4: Performance on disorder identification, normalization and slot-filling (Task 2b), including rank among the 23 competing systems (Rank), true positives (TP), false positives (FP), false negatives (FN), precision (P), recall (R), F-measure (F), accuracy (A), weighted accuracy (WA).

Slot	CUAB1	CUAB2
BodyLoc	-	0.656
Disorder CUI	0.783	0.808
Conditional	-	0.661
Course	-	0.773
Generic	-	0.885
Negation	-	0.850
Severity	-	0.861
Subject	-	0.846
Uncertainty	-	0.750

Table 5: Weighted accuracy by attribute type on slot-filling

incorporation of additional UMLS lookup features for span detection that were unintentionally left absent in CUAB1. Given the nearly identical results in training between UTS and YTEX, the much better performance of CUAB2 in Task 1 is best explained by the importance of vocabulary features in disorder normalization. Unfortunately the test dataset is not available for us to re-run and confirm this.

Table 4 shows the performance of the CUAB systems on the combined task of disorder identification, normalization and slot-filling (Task 2b). The best CUAB system (CUAB2) again used UMLS features for disorder span and attribute annotation and UTS for CUI lookup and ranked 6th out of 23 systems, achieving an F-measure, accuracy and weighted accuracy about 0.02, 0.03 and 0.09, respectively, below the top system.

Table 5 shows the performance of the CUAB systems broken down by attribute type. The CUAB1 system made only disorder predictions for Task 2b, hence all other results are omitted.

4 Discussion

One strength of our system is that it took exactly the same approach (classifier and feature set) to the problem of merging disjoint disorder spans and the problem of associating attributes with disorder mentions. Our CUAB2 system ranked well and was close to the top systems, which suggests that treating these two problems in the same way was a reasonable approach. This lends credence to the notion that deriving new features for either the merging of disjoint disorder spans or the association of attributes with disorders could be useful for either problem.

One issue of concern is that the accuracy of CUI prediction is still very dependent on training data. Our submitted systems used a direct string lookup from a dictionary built on the training data, before falling back to UTS or YTEX if the example was not found in the training data. This approach achieved a disorder CUI accuracy of up to nearly 81%. But when the training data isn't used for CUI identification, as shown in an experiment on the task training data (Table 3), we only achieve about 65% accuracy. This suggests that approximately 15%+ additional accuracy is entirely a result of having already seen the concept in the training data and that our system (and others relying on the training data) would likely see close to a 15% drop off in disorder CUI prediction accuracy when applied to a new medical sub-domain.

Our scheme uses two classifiers, one to detect and another to merge entities. Future work may include investigating the possibility of employing a single classifier with a more complex tagging schema than BIO to perform these tasks jointly.

Acknowledgments

This work was supported by the National Center for Advancing Translational Sciences of the National Institutes of Health under award number UL1TR00165. The content is solely the responsibility of the authors and does not necessarily represent the official views of the National Institutes of Health.

References

Steven Bethard, Philip Ogren, and Lee Becker. 2014. Cleartk 2.0: Design patterns for machine learning in uima. In *Proceedings of the Ninth International Conference on Language Resources and Evaluation (LREC'14)*, pages 3289–3293, Reykjavik, Iceland, 5. European Language Resources Association (ELRA). (Acceptance rate 61%).

David Ferrucci and Adam Lally. 2004. Uima: an architectural approach to unstructured information processing in the corporate research environment. *Nat. Lang. Eng.*, 10(3-4):327–348.

V. Garla, V.L. Re III, Z. Dorey-Stein, F. Kidwai, M. Scotch, J. Womack, A. Justice, and C. Brandt. 2011. The yale ctakes extensions for document classification: architecture and application. *Journal of the American Medical Informatics Association*, 18(5):614–620.

James Gung. 2014. Using relations for identification and normalization of disorders: Team clear in the share/clef 2013 ehealth evaluation lab.

Naoaki Okazaki. 2007. Crfsuite: a fast implementation of conditional random fields (crfs). *URL http://www. chokkan. org/software/crfsuite*.

John David Osborne, Binod Gyawali, and Thamar Solorio. 2014. Evaluation of ytex and metamap for clinical concept recognition. *arXiv preprint arXiv:1402.1668*.

Sameer Pradhan, Noémie Elhadad, Wendy Chapman, Suresh Manandhar, and Guergana Savova. 2014. Semeval-2014 task 7: Analysis of clinical text. *SemEval 2014*, 199(99):54.

G.K. Savova, J.J. Masanz, P.V. Ogren, J. Zheng, S. Sohn, K.C. Kipper-Schuler, and C.G. Chute. 2010. Mayo clinical text analysis and knowledge extraction system (ctakes): architecture, component evaluation and applications. *Journal of the American Medical Informatics Association*, 17(5):507–513.

H Suominen, S Salantera, S Velupillai, et al. 2013. Three shared tasks on clinical natural language processing. In *Proceedings of the Conference and Labs of the Evaluation Forum*.

BioinformaticsUA: Machine Learning and Rule-Based Recognition of Disorders and Clinical Attributes from Patient Notes

Sérgio Matos
DETI/IEETA
University of Aveiro
3810-193 Aveiro, Portugal
aleixomatos@ua.pt

José Sequeira
DETI/IEETA
University of Aveiro
3810-193 Aveiro, Portugal
sequeira@ua.pt

José Luís Oliveira
DETI/IEETA
University of Aveiro
3810-193 Aveiro, Portugal
jlo@ua.pt

Abstract

Natural language processing and text analysis methods offer the potential of uncovering hidden associations from large amounts of unprocessed texts. The SemEval-2015 Analysis of Clinical Text task aimed at fostering research on the application of these methods in the clinical domain. The proposed task consisted of disorder identification with normalization to SNOMED-CT concepts, and disorder attribute identification, or template filling.

We participated in both sub-tasks, using a combination of machine-learning and rules for recognizing and normalizing disease mentions, and rule-based methods for template filling. We achieved an F-score of 71.2% in the entity recognition and normalization task, and a slot weighted accuracy of 69.5% in the template filling task.

1 Introduction

Biomedical text mining offers the promise of leveraging the huge amounts of information available on scientific documents to help raise new hypotheses and uncover hidden knowledge. Biomedical text mining (TM) has been an important focus of research during the last years, sustained by the high volumes of data, the diverse computational and multi-disciplinary challenges posed, and by the potential impact of new discoveries (Simpson and Demner-Fushman, 2012). These benefits have been demonstrated in recent studies in which text mining methods were used to suggest biomarkers for diagnosis and for measuring disease progression, targets for new drugs, or new uses for existing drugs (Frijters et al., 2010). Likewise, clinical information stored as natural language text in discharge notes and reports could be exploited to identify important associations, and this has led to an increased interest in applying text mining techniques to such texts, in order to extract information related to diseases, medications, and adverse drug events, for example (Zhu et al., 2013).

Research efforts in biomedical text mining have led to the development of various methods and tools for the recognition of diverse entities, including species names, genes and proteins, chemicals and drugs, anatomical concepts and diseases. These methods are based on dictionaries, rules, and machine learning, or a combination of those depending on the specificities and requirements of each concept type. After identifying entity mentions in text, it becomes necessary to perform entity normalization, which consists in assigning a specific concept identifier to each entity. This is usually performed by matching the identified entities against a knowledge-base, possibly evaluating the textual context in which the entity occurred to identify the best matching concept.

Following up on the 2014 task, in which the objective was the identification and normalization of disease concepts in clinical texts (Pradhan et al., 2014), two subtasks were defined for the SemEval-2015 Analysis of Clinical Text task. Task 1 consisted of recognizing concepts belonging to the 'disorders' semantic group of the Unified Medical Language System (UMLS) and normalizing to the

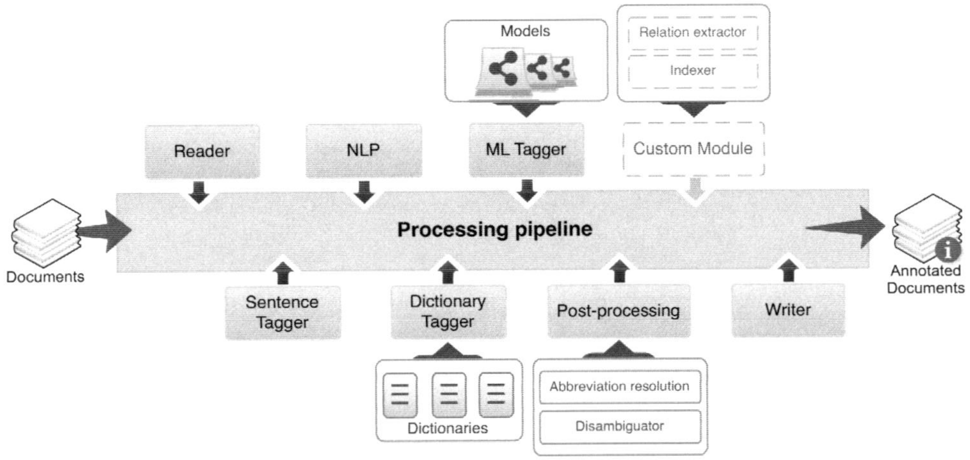

Figure 1: Neji's processing pipeline used for annotating the documents. Dashed boxes indicate optional modules.

SNOMED CT[1] terminology, and Task 2 consisted of identifying and normalizing specific attributes for each disorder mention, including negation, severity, and body location, for example. The task made use of the ShARe corpus (Pradhan et al., 2013), which contains manually annotated clinical notes from the MIMIC II database[2] (Saeed et al., 2011). The task corpus comprised 531 documents, divided into a training portion with 298 documents, a development portion with 133 documents, and a test portion with 100 documents.

In this paper, we present a combined machine-learning and rule-based approach for these tasks, supported by a modular text analysis and annotation pipeline.

2 Methods

Our approach consists of three sequential steps, namely: entity recognition, rule-based span adjustment and normalization, and rule-based template filling. For entity recognition we used Gimli (Campos et al., 2013b), an open-source tool for training machine learning (ML) models that includes simple configuration of the feature extraction process, and Neji, a framework for biomedical concept recognition, integrating modules for natural language processing (NLP) and information extraction (IE), specially tuned for the biomedical domain (Campos et al., 2013a). Figure 1 shows the complete processing pipeline.

2.1 Entity Recognition

We applied a supervised machine-learning approach, based on Conditional Random Fields (CRFs) (Lafferty et al., 2001; McCallum, 2002). The BIO (Beginning, Inside, Outside) scheme was used to encode the entity annotations. To select the best combination of features, we performed backward feature elimination using the supplied training and development data to create and evaluate the models. We then used all the data to train a first-order CRF model with the final feature set, which consisted of the following features:

- NLP features:
  - Token and lemma
- Orthographic features:
  - Capitalization (e.g., "StartCap" and "AllCaps");
  - Digits and capitalized characters counting (e.g., "TwoDigit" and "TwoCap");
  - Symbols (e.g., "Dash", "Dot" and "Comma");
- Morphological features:

[1] http://www.ihtsdo.org/snomed-ct/
[2] http://mimic.physionet.org/database.html

- Suffixes and char n-grams of 2, 3 and 4 characters;

- Local context:
  - Conjunctions of lemma and POS features, built from the windows {-1, 0}, {-2, -1}, {0, 1}, {-1, 1} and {-3, -1} around the current token.

Apart from the ML model, documents were also annotated with dictionaries for the UMLS 'Disorders' semantic group and a specially compiled acronyms dictionary, as used in the 2014 edition of the task (Matos et al., 2014). In total, these dictionaries contain almost 1.5 million terms, of which 525 thousand (36%) are distinct terms, for nearly 293 thousand distinct concept identifiers. Including this dictionary-matching step produced a small improvement in terms of F-score.

2.2 Normalization

According to the task description, only those UMLS concepts that could be mapped to a SNOMED-CT identifier should be considered in the normalization step, while all other entities should be added to the results without a concept identifier. To achieve this step, we indexed the terms of the UMLS concepts that included a SNOMED-CT identifier in a Solr [3] instance. Additionally, we also indexed each term that occurred in the training and development data, together with the corresponding identifier.

To perform normalization of an identified entity mention, we follow a series of steps. First we search the index for the exact term and, if it is found as a gold-standard annotation on the training data, we assign the same identifier to the new mention. If multiple identifiers were used on the training data for the same term, we keep the most commonly assigned one. If the exact mention is not found on the training data, we try to remove a set of 162 prefix (e.g. 'chronic', 'acute', 'large') and 48 suffix terms (e.g. 'changes', 'episodes') obtained from an error analysis on the development data. We then look for this adjusted term on the gold standard annotations and on the UMLS concept synonyms, and use the corresponding identifier and the adjusted mention span. Finally, we try to expand the term to include anatomical regions occurring before or after the identified disorder mention, in order to identify more specific concepts. If such a concept is found on the index, the corrected span is used, together with the corresponding identifier.

[3] http://lucene.apache.org/solr/

2.3 Template Filling

This subtask consists of identifying various attributes of the disorders, such as negation or uncertainty, and normalizing their values according to the nomenclature specified by the task. To address this task, we followed a rule-based approach. For each type of attribute, or slot, we compiled the cue words and the corresponding normalized value from the training and development data. We then created patterns, implemented through regular expressions, to locate these possible cues in the vicinity of each disorder term. To apply the regular expressions, we replace each entity mention in the texts by a generic placeholder, adjusting the cue word spans accordingly when a match is found. For example, to fill the 'Severity' attribute we look for the occurrence of a cue word, associated to this attribute in the training data, that occurs up to n[4] characters before or after a disorder mention. This can be expressed by the following regular expression, in which only two alternative cue words are shown for brevity:

```
(mild|sharp|...)\s.{0,15}?__DISO__ |
__DISO__\s.{0,15}?(mild|sharp|...)
```

3 Results and Discussion

3.1 Evaluation Metrics

Task 1 was evaluated by strict and relaxed F-scores. In the first case, the identified text span has to be exactly the same as the gold-standard annotation, and the predicted concept identifier has to match the gold annotation. In the second case, a prediction is considered a true-positive is there is any word overlap between the predicted span and the gold-standard, as long as the identified is correctly predicted.

Task 2 was evaluated in terms of weighted accuracy, which is calculated using a pre-assigned weight for each slot based on its prevalence in the training set.

[4] n was empirically set as 5 for the body location attribute, and 15 for all other attributes

	Task 1 performance (P / R / F)			
	Development		Test	
Run	Strict	Relaxed	Strict	Relaxed
1	48.1 / 54.4 / 51.0	51.8 / 58.0 / 54.7	0.669 / 0.738 / 0.702	0.698 / 0.769 / 0.732
2	62.3 / 70.6 / **66.2**	67.5 / 74.7 / **70.9**	0.690 / 0.736 / **0.712**	0.719 / 0.766 / **0.742**
3	62.3 / 70.5 / 66.1	67.4 / 74.5 / 70.8	0.691 / 0.735 / **0.712**	0.720 / 0.765 / **0.742**

Table 1: Development results and official results on the test dataset, for Task 1. P: Precision; R: Recall; F: F-score.

3.2 Test Results

We submitted three runs of annotations for the documents in the test set, as described below:

- Run 1: In this run, the identified disorder mentions were not first checked against the training data annotations;
- Run 2: The identified disorder mentions were first checked against the training data annotations and the corresponding identifier was used;
- Run 3: Same as Run 2, but the machine learning model was trained only on discharge documents, that is, other document types were not used in the training.

Table 1 shows the results obtained on the development set, and the official results obtained on the test set for each submitted run in Task 1.

As can be observed from the results, using the identifiers assigned in the training data for disease mentions that re-occur in the test data has a very positive impact on the results, increasing precision by 2%. Although this approach may be considered to artificially improve the results, the rationale for using it is that human annotators tend to re-use the same identifier in the case of a ambiguous term. The same might also be true for clinical coders when processing the patient notes.

Comparing our results to the best submitted runs, we verify that we obtain the best recall rates when considering both strict and relaxed scores, but with a significant drop in precision when compared to those results.

Figure 2 illustrates the results obtained on the template filling task. We achieved a slot weighted accuracy of 69.5%. Comparing the results, we achieved the best accuracy for the disease CUI slot. On the other hand, we achieved considerable lower accuracies on the body location and conditional slots, when compared to the top performing runs.

4 Conclusions

We present results for the recognition, normalization and template filling of disorder concepts in clinical texts, using a machine-learning and rule-based approach. We achieved a strict F-score of 71.2% and a relaxed F-score of 74.2%, and obtained the best recall under both evaluation modes. One of the reasons for the lower precision is related to the normalization method. As future work, we will continue developing this step.

We applied a simple rule-based approach for the template filling task, and achieved a weighted accuracy of 69.5%. We aim to continue improving this information extraction step, by acquiring a larger set of possible cue words and revising some of the extraction rules.

Acknowledgements

This work was supported by National Funds through FCT - Foundation for Science and Technology, in the context of the project PEst-OE/EEI/UI0127/2014. S. Matos is funded by FCT under the FCT Investigator programme.

References

David Campos, Sérgio Matos, and José L. Oliveira. 2013a. A modular framework for biomedical concept recognition. *BMC Bioinformatics*, 14:281.

David Campos, Sérgio Matos, and José L. Oliveira. 2013b. Gimli: open source and high-performance biomedical name recognition. *BMC bioinformatics*, 14:54.

Raoul Frijters, Marianne van Vugt, Ruben Smeets, Ren C. van Schaik, Jacob de Vlieg, and Wynand

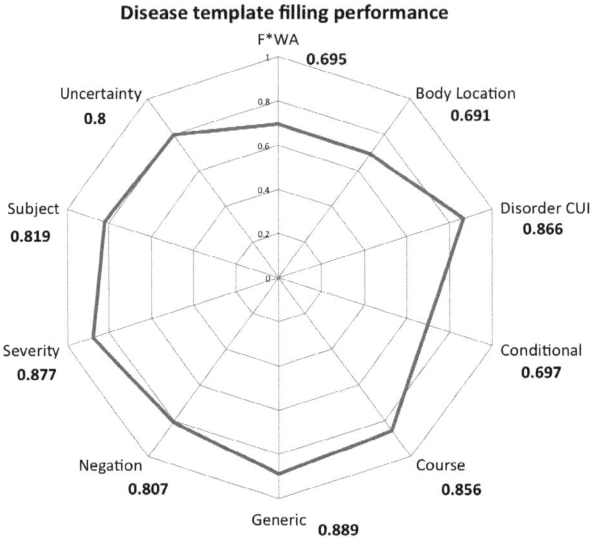

Figure 2: Official results for disease template filling (Task 2).

Alkema. 2010. Literature mining for the discovery of hidden connections between drugs, genes and diseases. *PLoS Computational Biology*, 6(9):e1000943.

John D. Lafferty, Andrew McCallum, and Fernando C. N. Pereira. 2001. Conditional random fields: Probabilistic models for segmenting and labeling sequence data. In *Proceedings of the Eighteenth International Conference on Machine Learning*, ICML '01, pages 282–289, San Francisco, CA, USA.

Sérgio Matos, Tiago Nunes, and José L. Oliveira. 2014. BioinformaticsUA: Concept recognition in clinical narratives using a modular and highly efficient text processing framework. In *Proceedings of the 8th International Workshop on Semantic Evaluation (SemEval 2014)*, pages 135–139.

Andrew K. McCallum. 2002. MALLET: A Machine Learning for Language Toolkit.

Sameer Pradhan, Noemie Elhadad, Brett South, David Martinez, Lee Christensen, Amy Vogel, Hanna Suominen, Wendy Chapman, and Guergana Savova. 2013. Task 1: ShARe/CLEF eHealth Evaluation Lab 2013. *Online Working Notes of the CLEF 2013 Evaluation Labs and Workshop*.

Sameer Pradhan, Noémie Elhadad, Wendy Chapman, Suresh Manandhar, and Guergana Savova. 2014. SemEval-2014 Task 7: Analysis of clinical text. In *Proceedings of the 8th International Workshop on Semantic Evaluation (SemEval 2014)*, pages 54–62, Dublin, Ireland, August.

Mohammed Saeed, Mauricio Villarroel, Andrew Reisner, Gari Clifford, Li-Wei Lehman, George Moody, Thomas Heldt, Tin Kyaw, Benjamin Moody, and Roger Mark. 2011. Multiparameter Intelligent Monitoring in Intensive Care II (MIMIC-II): a public-access intensive care unit database. *Critical Care Medicine*, 39(5):952.

Matthew S. Simpson and Dina Demner-Fushman. 2012. Biomedical text mining: A survey of recent progress. In Charu C. Aggarwal and ChengXiang Zhai, editors, *Mining Text Data*, pages 465–517.

Fei Zhu, Preecha Patumcharoenpol, Cheng Zhang, Yang Yang, Jonathan Chan, Asawin Meechai, Wanwipa Vongsangnak, and Bairong Shen. 2013. Biomedical text mining and its applications in cancer research. *Journal of Biomedical Informatics*, 46(2):200–211.

LIST-LUX: Disorder Identification from Clinical Texts

Asma Ben Abacha, Aikaterini Karanasiou, Yassine Mrabet, and Julio Cesar Dos Reis*
Luxembourg Institute of Science and Technology (LIST)
29, avenue John F. Kennedy, L-1855 Kirchberg, Luxembourg
[asma.benabacha, aikaterini.karanasiou, yassine.mrabet]@list.lu
* Institute of Computing, University of Campinas
Av. Albert Einstein, 1251, Cidade Universitária Zeferino Vaz, 13083-852, Campinas, SP Brazil
julio.dosreis@ic.unicamp.br

Abstract

This paper describes our participation in task 14 of SemEval 2015. This task focuses on the analysis of clinical texts and includes: (i) the recognition of the span of a disorder mention and (ii) its normalization to a unique concept identifier in the UMLS/SNOMED-CT terminology. We propose a two-step approach which relies first on Conditional Random Fields to detect textual mentions of disorders using different lexical, syntactic, orthographic and semantic features such as ontologies and, second, on a similarity measure and SNOMED to determine the relevant CUI. We present and discuss the obtained results on the development corpus and the official test corpus.

1 Introduction

With the exponential growth of clinical texts, recognizing named entities becomes more and more important for several applications such as information retrieval, question answering or scientific analysis. The task of identifying mentions to medical concepts in free text and mapping these mentions to a knowledge base was recently proposed in ShARe/CLEF eHealth Evaluation Lab 2013 (Suominen et al., 2013).

The task 7 in SemEval 2014 (Pradhan et al., 2014) elaborates in that previous effort focusing on the recognition and normalization of named entity mentions belonging to the UMLS semantic group "Disorders". Similarly, task 14-1 of SemEval 2015[1] targets the identification of disorder mentions and their association to the relevant concept identifiers (CUI) in the UMLS/SNOMED_CT terminology. A disorder is normalized to "CUI-less" if the disorder mention is present, but there is no good equivalent CUI in UMLS/SNOMED-CT. Task 14-2b of SemEval 2015 specifically addresses *Disorder Slot Filling*. The aim is to identify the values of nine slots (negation indicator, subject, uncertainty indicator, course, severity, conditional, generic indicator and body location), given the span of disorder mentions from task 14-1.

In this paper we focus on task 1, *i.e.* disorder identification. In the following section we describe our approach to the detection of disorder mentions in clinical texts and their categorization with the relevant UMLS/SNOMED-CT CUI. In section 3 we present and discuss the obtained results on the development corpus and the official results before giving our concluding remarks in section 4.

2 Two-Step Approach for Disorder Identification

Our method includes two main steps: (1) the detection of disorder mentions using Conditional Random Fields (CRFs) and (2) the extraction of the associated CUI from SNOMED based on similarity measures. These two steps are described in more details in the following sections.

2.1 Step I - Disorder Mention Detection

The goal in this first step is to recognize the span of disorder mentions in a target clinical text. A mention can be a set of consecutive words, *e.g.* "***atrial***

[1] http://alt.qcri.org/semeval2015/task14/

fibrillation", or disjoint, *e.g.* "***left atrium** is moderately **dilated***". In order to tackle the disjoint-mention problem, we annotated the data with the BIESTO format that is introduced by (Cogley et al., 2013).

2.1.1 BIESTO Labels

According to BIESTO format, the first word of a mention is tagged with B (beginning), the following words with I (inside), the last word with E (end) and the words between mention's words with T (beTween). The mentions that have one word are annotated as S (single) and the words that are not related to disorder mentions are annotated as O (outside). Furthermore, in the training and test corpus there are disorder mentions that end or start with the same word. In such case, when two serial B labels are followed by one E label, we consider two disorder mentions that start with different words and end with the same word. Similarly, if there is one B label followed by two different E labels, we consider two disorder terms that start with the same word and end with different words.

It is also observed that there is collision of BIESTO labels when one word exists into multiple disorder mentions and is annotated with different labels. In this case, we gather all the mentions which contain the common word and select the longest disorder mention (has the most words). If two mentions have the maximum length, the common word is annotated with two labels such as I/E.

Some examples of BIESTO labels are the following:

1. Disorder mentions that start with the same word, *e.g.*:
   - "The nasal septum deviates to the left with a rather large spur."
   - The nasal/B septum/I deviates/E to/T the/T left/T with/T a/T rather/T large/T spur/E.
   - "nasal septum deviates" and "nasal septum spur" are two disorder mentions with the same start word.
2. Collision between BIESTO labels, *e.g.*:
   - "osteophytes at C3/4 resulting in compression of the spinal cord with associated cord edema;"
   - Osteophytes/S at/O C3/O //O 4/O resulting/O in/O compression/B of/T the/T spinal/I/B cord/E/I with/T associated/T cord/T edema/E.
   - There are three disorder mentions: "Osteophytes" , "compression spinal cord" and "spinal cord edema".

2.1.2 CRF Algorithm

We use the Conditional Random Fields (CRFs) learning algorithm (Lafferty et al., 2001) in order to annotate the words with BIESTO labels. According to (McCallum and Li, 2003), suppose $x = \{x_1, x_2, x_3, ..., x_T\}$ is a set of input values (*e.g.* a sequence of words) and $s = \{s_1, s_2, s_3, ..., s_T\}$ is a set of states that are assigned to named entity labels, CRF estimates the conditional probability of a state sequence given an input sequence as follows:

$$P(s|x) = \frac{1}{Z} exp \left(\sum_{t=1}^{T} \sum_{k=1}^{K} \lambda_k f_k(s_{t-1}, s_t, x, t) \right)$$

where $1, ..., T$ represent the word positions, $1, ..., K$ represent the positions of the weighted features, the f_k represents the feature function and the λ_k is the weight of each feature function.

Using the CRF algorithm, the decision on a word's label can be influenced by the decision on the label of the preceding word. This dependency is taken into account in sequential models such as Hidden Markov Models (HMMs). However, the CRF model maximizes the conditional probability, unlike the HMM model which maximizes the joint probability. Therefore, the CRF model can use a number of features that are related to other words of the target texts in order to achieve better accuracy in its predictions. In our implementation we used the CRF++ tool[2].

2.1.3 Feature Set

In each experiment, we discard all the predicted disorder-mentions beyond 50 characters. In the last

[2]http://crfpp.googlecode.com/svn/trunk/doc/index.html

run, the "[**.......**]" and ":[** .... **]" expressions as well as their lemmas and pos-tags were replaced by a sequence of "$".

We define a set of token and semantic features to train the CRF model.

Token features: The word, the part-of-speech tag (pos-tags) and the lemma; two tokens after and two tokens before the word, their lemmas and their pos-tags. We used StanfordTagger[3] to obtain the words of clinical texts as well as their lemmas and their part-of-speech tags.

StanfordTagger recognizes the word_1/word_2 token as one word. Since, many UMLS terms contain either the word_1 or the word_2, we separate the word_1/word_2 phrase into three words: word_1, / and word_2. For instance, given the following sentence: *"There is left lower lobe consolidation/volume loss."*, the system recognizes two disorder mentions that are: *"consolidation"* and *"volume loss"*.

Linguistic and orthographic features: Indicating whether a word (i) is capitalized, (ii) contains digits, (iii) contains only lowercase characters without digits, the word length, suffixes and prefixes up to 4 characters.

2.2 Semantic Features

We use regular expressions to find the phrases which represent dates or time values (such as "2014-09-26", "4:07", "TUE", "Jan") and annotate them with the keyword DATE.

Stopwords (such as prepositions, conjunctions, articles) are annotated using a binary feature (yes/no). Precisely, if a word exists in the stopwords list[4], it is tagged with "YES", otherwise it is tagged with "NO".

Two features are derived from the Symptom Ontology[5] in order to annotate the words as SYMPTOM. We constructed a list of symptoms that contains the names of the ontology classes. If a word/phrase exists in the list of symptoms, then it is annotated as SYMPTOM. Since the names of ontology classes describe either a symptom or a group of symptoms, it is important to annotate only the names of symptoms. Consequently we added another feature which is the number of descendants for each class. The classes with no descendants (leaves) are likely to be symptoms and not a group of symptoms.

Following this same method, we annotate the words as DISEASES if they correspond to classes in the Human Disease Ontology[6].

One feature is derived from Human Development Anatomy Ontology[7] to annotate the words as anatomical_structure. We create a list of anatomical structures that contain the names of the ontology classes. If a word/phrase is in the list, it is tagged as Anatomical_Structure. We did not consider the number of descendants in this case because most of the names of ontology classes describe specific parts of the human body (anatomical structures).

Many phrases are frequent in clinical texts (*e.g.* headlines) and are not related to UMLS/SNOMED_CT terms. In order to improve the performance of the CRF algorithm, we gather and annotate them as OUTLINE. First, we extract all the phrases that end with colon and are located in the beginning of each sentence (such as "date of birth:", "review of symptoms:", "family history:") and we remove the phrases that contain digits (such as "Calcium 500 500 mg Tablet Sig:" and "[**2017-05-23**] 2:48 pm SWAB").

2.3 Step II - CUI Identification

In a second step we tackle the categorization of the detected disorder mentions with UMLS concept identifiers (CUI). The UMLS-Metathesaurus concept structure includes concept names, their identifiers, and some key characteristics of these concept names such as language and vocabulary source. In the *Rich Release Format* of the UMLS Metathesaurus, the important tables for this step are MRCONSO and MRSTY, which contain information about concepts and semantic types. The entire concept structure appears in MRCONSO while semantic types are obtained from the MRSTY.

A disorder mention is defined as any span of text that can be mapped to a concept in the SNOMED-

[3]http://nlp.stanford.edu/software/tagger.shtm

[4]http://www.ranks.nl/stopwords

[5]http://bioportal.bioontology.org/ontologies/SYMP

[6]http://www.obofoundry.org/cgi-bin/detail.cgi?id=disease_ontology

[7]http://www.obofoundry.org/cgi-bin/detail.cgi?id=human-dev-anat-abstract2

CT terminology, which belongs to the **Disorder semantic group**. A concept is in the Disorder semantic group if it belongs to one of 11 specific UMLS semantic types (87,412 concepts associated to disorders from 1,190,741 concepts of UMLS-2012AB) :

1. Congenital Abnormality (6130 concepts)
2. Acquired Abnormality (1746 concepts)
3. Injury or Poisoning (26607 concepts)
4. Pathologic Function (5115 concepts)
5. Disease or Syndrome (34213 concepts)
6. Mental or Behavioral Dysfunction (2710)
7. Cell or Molecular Dysfunction (383 concepts)
8. Experimental Model of Disease (3 concepts)
9. Anatomical Abnormality (1455 concepts)
10. Neoplastic Process (9050 concepts)
11. Sign or Symptom (2708 concepts)

We use SQL queries to construct our own table containing only disorders from the source "SNOMED" and related to the 11 semantic types (for a total of 348,760 rows). The proposed method then identifies the associated CUI for each disorder mention detected in step 1.

We start by performing an exact string comparison between the recognized disorder and the preferred terms and synonyms from the concepts of our table. If no exact match exists, we explore a similarity measure to calculate the relatedness between the detected mention and the available concepts. We use the *bigram* similarity measure following the observations of Cheatham and Hitzler (2013) on its suitability for ontology matching tasks. The selected CUI is the one with the highest similarity value. We fixed the word-based similarity threshold to 0.8 which led to the best results in our experiments (among different tested threshold values). If no exact match exists and all compared concepts have a similarity value under the threshold, the CUI-less class is associated to the detected mention.

3 Runs and Results

3.1 Evaluation Metrics

The results of our systems for task 14-1 are compared with the annotations of the gold-standard dataset using the F-measure, Precision and Recall metrics which are measured under strict and relaxed settings. In the strict setting, a disorder mention is correctly recognized, if its span and CUI code match exactly with a mention in the gold-standard dataset. In the relaxed setting, a disorder mention is correctly recognized if (i) there is an overlap with only one gold-standard mention from the same sentence, and (ii) the assigned CUI is correct.

In the following we present our results on the DEVelopment corpus (DEV) and the results on the official TEST corpus.

3.2 Experiments on the DEV Corpus

Table 1 presents the recall, precision and F-measure values for the strict and relaxed settings when different sets of features are used. More precisely, we consider the following sets:

- S1: Only Lexical features.
- S2: S1 + prefixes and suffixes.
- S3: S2 + labels of Symptoms ontology.
- S4: S3 + number of descendants for each symptom.
- S5: S4 + labels of Human Anatomy ontology.
- S6: S5 + number of descendants for each disease.

3.3 Configuration of the Submitted Runs

For the final evaluation we considered the two following sets of features: $Set_1 = \{$current word, 2 next words, 2 previous words lemmas, pos-tags, capital letters without digits, lower letters without digits, length of words, stop words, suffixes & prefixes [1,4], Dates/Time format $\}$ and $Set_2 = Set_1 \cup \{$labels from Symptom Ontology, number of descendants for each symptom, labels of Human Anatomy Ontology, labels from Human Disease Ontology, number of descendants for each disease $\}$ and we submitted 3 runs:

LIST-LUX, TASK1	strict_P	strict_R	**strict_F**	relax_P	relax_R	relax_F
S1	0.607	0.492	**0.543**	0.641	0.515	0.571
S2	0.601	0.544	**0.571**	0.633	0.568	0.599
S3	0.604	0.544	**0.572**	0.637	0.569	0.601
S4	0.604	0.544	**0.572**	0.638	0.570	0.602
S5	0.606	0.546	**0.575**	0.638	0.570	0.602
S6	0.609	0.547	**0.576**	0.641	0.572	0.604

Table 1: Results on the DEV corpus.

- Run 1: Feature Set_1, similarity threshold fixed to 0.8 for the CUI identification.
- Run 2: Feature Set_1, similarity threshold fixed to 0.83.
- Run 3: Feature Set_2, similarity threshold fixed to 0.8.

3.4 Official Results

Table 2 presents the final results on the TEST corpus[8]. When comparing the 3 runs we observe that increasing the similarity threshold had a slight negative impact on precision and a slight positive impact on recall. In a second observation, semantic features have a slight positive impact on both precision and recall which suggests their relevance, but also the need for larger ontologies and vocabularies.

Matching	Run	Precision	Recall	F-measure
Strict	1	0.649	0.577	0.611
	2	0.648	0.579	0.612
	3	0.649	0.580	0.613
Relaxed	1	0.677	0.602	0.637
	2	0.674	0.602	0.636
	3	0.675	0.603	0.637

Table 2: Task1: Official Results on the TEST corpus.

In order to evaluate the results in the second subtask, the metrics of F-measure, Precision, Recall, unweighted accuracy, weighted accuracy and per-slot weighted accuracy are estimated (*c.f.* table 3). Both unweighted and weighted accuracy are measures that show how well our system identifies all the slots for each disorder. The difference between them is that before estimating the weighted accuracy, each gold-standard slot value is assigned a weight based on its prevalence in the training corpus. The last metric is the Per-slot weighted accuracy that shows how well our system identifies the different values of each slot for all the disorders.

TASK2b	Run 1	Run 2	Run 3
F	0.884	0.882	0.881
A	0.865	0.866	0.866
F*A	0.765	0.763	0.763
WA	0.641	0.642	0.641
F*WA	**0.567**	**0.566**	**0.565**
BL	0.515	0.517	0.517
CUI	0.719	0.720	0.720
CND	0.496	0.500	0.497
COU	0.575	0.578	0.575
GEN	0.870	0.873	0.873
NEG	0.529	0.528	0.530
SEV	0.544	0.543	0.543
SUB	0.751	0.749	0.749
UNC	0.559	0.560	0.557

Table 3: Task 2b: Official Results on the TEST corpus.

3.5 Discussion

Table 4 presents the results of the first step (disorder detection) on the DEV corpus. It shows that F-measure decreased, in run 3, from 75,3% to 57,6% between mention detection (step 1) and CUI detection (step 2) in strict matching. Precision and Recall decreased with approximately the same factor. F-measure decreased, with a slightly higher factor in relaxed matching, from 86,1% to 60,4% between step 1 and step 2 (on the DEV corpus). Each matching setting shows a different estimation of the limitation related to similarity-based detection of CUI. This may be due to the additional noise when comparing partially-detected mentions with SNOMED

[8]http://alt.qcri.org/semeval2015/task14/index.php?id=results

labels and synonyms. Our similarity-based detection of CUI allowed reaching 57,6% F-measure on the DEV corpus and 61,3% F-measure on the TEST corpus (in strict matching, run 3), but it can still be enhanced further by taking into account additional features from the words surrounding the mentions and the concepts related to the candidate concepts in SNOMED (e.g. in the scope of global coherence maximization).

Matching	Run (Set)	P	R	F
Strict	R2 (S2)	0.792	0.717	0.752
	R3 (S6)	0.795	0.715	0.753
Relaxed	R2 (S2)	0.910	0.818	0.861
	R3 (S6)	0.913	0.814	0.861

Table 4: Task1: Results of the step 1 on the DEV corpus (disorder mention detection without CUI identification). P: Precision, R: Recall, F: F-measure.

4 Conclusion

In this article, we described our participation on two subtasks of the SemEval 2015 focused on disorder mention identification. We proposed a two-step approach suited to recognize spans of disorder mentions as a first step using a CRF learning algorithm with a set of features representing relevant aspects selected for the task. The method included a second step which accounted for the detection of adequate CUI from UMLS/SNOMEDCT concepts that might correspond to the recognized disorders from the target clinical texts. This research investigated the use of word-based similarity measures in the detection of CUI. The experiments running the method on two distinct corpora examined the influence of the defined features and configurations. Our approach based on CRF and similarity measures achieved 61.3% F-measure on the official TEST corpus. Using labels from ontology classes as semantic features was relevant for this task. In future work, we are planning to improve our CUI identification method. We are particularly considering the combination of supervised detection and categorization methods with semantic annotations obtained from unsupervised tools such as KODA(Mrabet et al., 2015) which allows annotating texts with both open-domain and domain-specific ontologies.

Acknowledgments

The last author was funded by São Paulo Research Foundation (FAPESP) (grant #2014/14890-0). We also want to acknowledge the efforts of the task organizers.

References

Michelle Cheatham and Pascal Hitzler. 2013. String similarity metrics for ontology alignment. In Harith Alani, Lalana Kagal, and *et. al.*, editors, *ISWC 2013*, volume 8219 of *LNCS*, pages 294–309.

James Cogley, Nicola Stokes, and Joe Carthy. 2013. Medical disorder recognition with structural support vector machines. In *Working Notes for CLEF 2013 Conference , Valencia, Spain, September 23-26, 2013.*

John D. Lafferty, Andrew McCallum, and Fernando C. N. Pereira. 2001. Conditional random fields: Probabilistic models for segmenting and labeling sequence data. In *Proceedings of the Eighteenth International Conference on Machine Learning (ICML 2001), Williams College, Williamstown, MA, USA, June 28 - July 1, 2001*, pages 282–289.

Andrew McCallum and Wei Li. 2003. Early results for named entity recognition with conditional random fields, feature induction and web-enhanced lexicons. In *Proceedings of the Seventh Conference on Natural Language Learning, CoNLL 2003, Held in cooperation with HLT-NAACL 2003, Edmonton, Canada, May 31 - June 1, 2003*, pages 188–191.

Yassine Mrabet, Claire Gardent, Muriel Foulonneau, Elena Simperl, and Eric Ras. 2015. Towards Knowledge Driven Annotation. In *Twenty-Ninth AAAI Conference on Artificial Intelligence*, AAAI'15, Austin, Texas, USA.

Sameer Pradhan, Noémie Elhadad, Wendy Chapman, Suresh Manandhar, and Guergana Savova. 2014. Semeval-2014 task 7: Analysis of clinical text. *SemEval 2014*, 199(99):54.

Hanna Suominen, Sanna Salanterä, Sumithra Velupillai, Wendy W Chapman, Guergana Savova, Noemie Elhadad, Sameer Pradhan, Brett R South, Danielle L Mowery, Gareth JF Jones, et al. 2013. Overview of the share/clef ehealth evaluation lab 2013. In *Information Access Evaluation. Multilinguality, Multimodality, and Visualization*, pages 212–231.

CMILLS: Adapting Semantic Role Labeling Features to Dependency Parsing

Chad Mills
University of Washington
Guggenheim Hall, 4th Floor
Seattle, WA 98195, USA
chills@uw.edu

Gina-Anne Levow
University of Washington
Guggenheim Hall, 4th Floor
Seattle, WA 98195, USA
levow@uw.edu

Abstract

We describe a system for semantic role labeling adapted to a dependency parsing framework. Verb arguments are predicted over nodes in a dependency parse tree instead of nodes in a phrase-structure parse tree. Our system participated in SemEval-2015 shared Task 15, Subtask 1: CPA parsing and achieved an F-score of 0.516. We adapted features from prior semantic role labeling work to the dependency parsing paradigm, using a series of supervised classifiers to identify arguments of a verb and then assigning syntactic and semantic labels. We found that careful feature selection had a major impact on system performance. However, sparse training data still led rule-based systems like the baseline to be more effective than learning-based approaches.

1 Introduction

We describe our submission to the SemEval-2015 Task 15, Subtask 1 on Corpus Pattern Analysis (Baisa et al. 2015). This task is similar to semantic role labeling but with arguments based on nodes in dependency parses instead of a syntactic parse tree. The verb's arguments are identified and labeled with both their syntactic and semantic roles.

For example, consider the sentence "But he said Labour did not agree that Britain could or should abandon development, either for itself or for the developing world." This subtask involves taking that sentence and making the following determinations relative to the given verb "abandon":

- "Britain" is the syntactic subject of "abandon" and falls under the "Institution" semantic type
- "development" is the syntactic object of "abandon" and is of semantic type "Activity"

We organize the remainder of our paper as follows: Section 2 describes our system, Section 3 presents experiments, and Section 4 concludes.

2 System Description

Our system consists of a pipelined five-component system plus source data and resources. A system diagram is shown in Figure 1. A cascading series of MaxEnt classifiers are used to identify arguments, their syntactic labels, and then their semantic labels. Each token in an input sentence was a training example.

Sketch Engine (Kilgarriff 2014) was used to help with featurization. All sentences in the training data were parsed and POS tagged using the Stanford CoreNLP tools (Manning et al. 2014). This data was used to generate features which are then supplied to an Argument Identification Classifier (AIC) that identifies whether or not a particular token is one of the relevant verb's arguments.

For the tokens identified as arguments to the verb, a Syntax Classifier identifies the syntactic role of the token. This is done using a multi-class MaxEnt model with the same features as the AIC plus features derived from the AIC's predictions. A similar Semantics Classifier follows, taking the Syntax

Classifier's features and output. Finally, a Semantics Consistency Heuristic Filter is applied to clean up some of the predictions using a series of heuristics to ensure the system is outputting semantic predictions that are consistent with the syntax predictions for the same token.

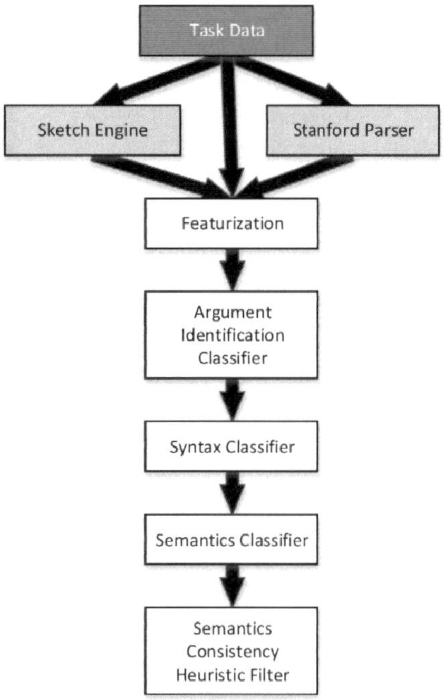

Figure 1: System Architecture Diagram. The input data is parsed by the Stanford Parser and the argument heads are expanded using the Sketch Engine thesaurus. This data is then featurized and passed through three successive classifiers: the Argument Identification Classifier identifies verb arguments, the Syntax Classifier assigns syntax labels to the arguments, and the Semantics Classifier assigns semantic labels to the arguments. Finally, the Semantics Consistency Heuristic Filter eliminates some systematic errors in the Semantics Classifier.

2.1 Featurization

Many of the features used in our system were inspired by the system produced by Toutanova et al. (2008), which used many features from prior work. This was a top-performing system and we incorporated each of the features that applied to the dependency parsing framework adopted in this task. We then augmented this feature set with a number of novel additional features. Many of these were adaptations of Semantic Role Labeling (SRL) features from the phrase-structure to dependency parsing paradigm (Gildea and Jurafsky 2002, Surdeanu et al. 2003, Pradhan et al. 2004). Others were added to generalize better to unseen verbs, which is critical for our task.

Some of our features depend on having a phrase-structure parse node corresponding to the candidate dependency parse node. Since dependency parse nodes each correspond to a token in the sentence, the tokens corresponding to the candidate node and its descendants in the dependency parse tree were identified. Then, in the phrase-structure parse tree, the lowest ancestor to all of these tokens was taken to be the phrase-structure parse node best corresponding to the candidate dependency parse node.

The baseline features included some inspired by Gildea and Jurafsky (2002):

- *Phrase Type*: the syntactic label of the corresponding node in the parse tree
- *Predicate Lemma*: lemma of the verb
- *Path*: the path in the parse tree between the candidate syntax node and the verb including the vertical direction and syntactic parse label of each node (e.g. "--up-->S--down-->NP")
- *Position*: whether the candidate is before or after the verb in the sentence
- *Voice*: whether the sentence is active or passive voice; due to sparse details in Gildea and Jurafsky this was based on tgrep search pattern heuristics found in Roland and Jurafsky (2001)
- *Head Word of Phrase*: the highest token in the dependency parse under the syntax parse tree node corresponding to the candidate token
- *Sub-Cat CFG*: the CFG rule corresponding to the parent of the verb, defined by the syntactic node labels of the parent and its children

Additional baseline features were obtained from Surdeanu et al. (2003) and Pradhan et al. (2004):

- *First/Last Word/POS*: For the syntactic parse node corresponding to the candidate node, this includes four separate features: the first word in the linear sentence order, its part of speech, the last word, and its part of speech
- *Left/Right Sister Phrase-Type*: The *Phrase Type* of each of the left and right sisters
- *Left/Right Sister Head Word/POS*: The word and POS of the head of the left and right sisters
- *Parent Phrase-Type*: The *Phrase Type* of the parent of the candidate parse node
- *Parent POS/Head-Word*: The word and part of speech of the parent of the parse node corresponding to the candidate node

- *Node-LCA Partial Path*: The *Path* between the candidate node and the lowest common ancestor between the candidate node and the verb
- *PP Parent Head Word*: The head word of the parent node in the syntax tree, if that parent is a prepositional phrase.
- *PP NP Head Word/POS*: If the syntax parse node representing the candidate node is a PP, the head word and POS of the rightmost NP directly under the PP.

Finally, baseline features that consisted entirely of pairs of already-mentioned features were also taken from Xue and Palmer (2004):

- *Predicate Lemma & Path*
- *Predicate Lemma & Head Word of Phrase*
- *Predicate Lemma & Phrase Type*
- *Voice & Position*
- *Predicate Lemma & PP Parent Head Word*

We added additional features adapted from the aforementioned features to generalize better given the sparse training data relative to other SRL tasks:

- *Head POS of Phrase*: the tagged POS of the *Head Word of Phrase*
- *Head Lemma of Phrase*: the lemma of the *Head Word of Phrase*
- *First/Last Lemma*: the lemma of the first and last word under the candidate parse node
- *Left/Right Sister Head Lemma*: the lemmas of the *Left/Right Sister Head Words*
- *Parent Head Lemma*: the lemma of the *Parent Head Word*
- *PP Parent Head Lemma/POS*: the lemma and part of speech of the *PP Parent Head Word*
- *PP NP Head Lemma*: the lemma of the *PP NP Head Word*
- *Candidate CFG*: the context-free grammar rule rooted at the syntax parse node corresponding to the candidate node (one step down from *Sub-Cat CFG*)

Additional features were added to extend these features or to adapt them to dependency parsing:

- *Candidate DP CFG:* a CFG-like expansion of the dependency parse of the candidate node plus children, each represented by its POS (e.g. "NNS->PRP$" or "NNS->DT JJ NNS")
- *Sub-Cat DP CFG:* a similar CFG expansion of the dependency parse of the parent of the verb
- *First/Last DP Word/Lemma/POS* – of all of the descendants of the candidate node in the dependency parse, inclusive, the first/last word/lemma/POS from the linear sentence
- *Dependency Path*: the path in the dependency parse from the candidate node to the verb
- *Dependency Node-LCA Partial Path*: path in the dependency parse from the candidate node to its lowest common ancestor with the verb
- *Dependency Depth*: the depth in the dependency parse of the candidate node
- *Dependency Descendant Coverage*: of all of the tokens under the candidate syntax parse node, the percentage of those also under the candidate node in the dependency parse tree. This measures the candidate syntax and dependency parse node alignment.

Additionally, due to the importance of the *Predicate Lemma* feature in prior SRL work and the need to generalize entirely to unseen verbs for evaluation in this task, we used Sketch Engine (Kilgarriff 2014) word sketches for each verb. A word sketch is obtained for each unseen test verb and the most similar verb from the training data is used as the *Similar Predicate Lemma* feature.

We use a novel similarity function to identify similar verbs. A word sketch for each verb v_i identifies an ordered set of n grammatical relations r_{1i}, r_{2i}, r_{3i}, ..., r_{ni} that tend to co-occur with v_i. These are relations like "object", "subject", prepositional phrases head by "of", etc. The word sketch for each relation r_{ji} associated with v_i also includes a significance value $s_i(r_{ji})$. For a given verb v_i we calculate a directional similarity d_{ik} with verb v_k as:

$$d_{ik} = \sum_{j=1}^{n} (0.8)^{j-1} \left| s_i(r_{ji}) - s_k(r_{ji}) \right|$$

$\left| s_i(r_{ji}) - s_k(r_{ji}) \right|$ is defined as zero if the relation r_{ji} doesn't appear in both word sketches. The final similarity score u_{ik} between v_i and v_k is then:

$$u_{ik} = u_{ki} = \frac{d_{ik} + d_{ki}}{2}$$

2.2 Classifiers

We used a series of three classifiers with similar features, each trained using the mallet implementation of MaxEnt (McCallum 2002).

First, the AIC is a binary model predicting if a given candidate token is an argument of the verb. In the dependency parsing framework used for this task, a single token in the dependency parse would represent a verbal argument. This was different from previous SRL tasks where a node in the parse tree was taken as the argument; this is more similar to identifying the headword of the phrase that's an argument rather than identifying the full phrase. Each token was treated as one example, with all of the features described in Section 2.1 calculated for each example. We filtered out features that did not appear at least five times in the training data, and trained with the default learning parameters.

Next, the multi-class Syntax Classifier uses the same features as the AIC plus a binary feature of AIC's score rounded to the nearest tenth, the AIC's predicted class, and these last two combined. The labels predicted were the syntactic label associated with the argument in the train data.

Finally, the multi-class Semantics Classifier predicts the semantic label of the argument using the features from the Syntax Classifier plus its output score rounded to the nearest tenth as a binary feature, its output label, and these last two combined.

2.3 Semantics Consistency Heuristic Filter

After running the classifiers, overgeneration by the semantic component was cleaned up using heuristics. Semantic predictions for tokens without a syntactic prediction were removed. For tokens with a syntactic but not semantic label prediction, if the token appeared in the train data with a semantic label the most common one was taken; if not, the most prominent distributional synonym (determined by the Sketch Engine thesaurus) found in the training data that has a semantic label was used.

3 Experiments

The system was evaluated using leave-one-out cross-validation on each verb in the train data. For the initial baseline configuration, only the features present in prior work were included, with a total of 31 feature classes. This configuration achieved an f-score of 0.238. The system was then run with our new features added, which outperformed the baseline by a relative 4% with an f-score of 0.248. In these cross-validation experiments, for each training example we used its *Similar Predicate Lemma* in place of its *Predicate Lemma* feature. This was a pessimistic assumption that we did not apply to the final system submitted for evaluation.[1] We suspect this explains why the final f-score on the test data was twice as good as that of the cross-validation experiments. The argument identification module performed well on its own with an f-score of 0.627, which is an upper bound on our overall system performance.

We used a hill climbing heuristic search for the best possible subset of the available features. This was a time-consuming process that involved running cross-validation for each feature class being evaluated with our three-stage classifier resulting in 63 classifiers being trained per iteration. All the feature removals or additions that improved performance were greedily accepted, yielding 22% feature churn. The best individual feature changes predicted 0.5% improvements to overall performance, but together they produced only a 0.9% improvement.

We repeated this a second time but only made the five most valuable changes, yielding a 0.8% point improvement. We did not have time to continue this greedy search, leaving further performance gains from searching for the best collection of features unrealized. We ended our search with 39 feature classes included, with only 21 of these from the original set. Through the course of these experiments, 10 of the original feature classes were removed while 18 new feature classes were added in our best model.

A final series of experiments were used to heuristically improve the semantic component which was significantly overgenerating. This yielded the Semantics Consistency Heuristics Filter which results in a 5% improvement to the overall system performance.

The final results on the test data are shown in Table 1. The baseline system still outperformed all teams including ours. The baseline was a heuristic system that used two dependency parsers to be more robust to parsing errors. It mapped dependency parse relations to syntax output directly, with logic to handle conjunctions, passives, and other phenomena. Semantic labels were a mixture of hard-coded

[1] *Predicate Lemma* is a critical feature in prior SRL work. In the test data, which only included unseen verbs, we used Sketch Engine data to identify the verb in the train data most similar to the verb in the test sentence, the *Similar Predicate Lemma* feature. In an attempt to mirror the features and avoid the possibility of cheating during our experiments, we repeated the same process during the cross-validation experiments, treating the other most similar verb in the training data as the *Similar Predicate Lemma*.

values for particular syntactic predictions and the most common value in the train data for the corresponding word or syntactic label.

Team	F-score
Baseline	0.624
FANTASY	0.589
BLCUNLP	0.530
CMILLS (our system)	**0.516**

Table 1: Performance on Test Data. Systems were evaluated on predicting the syntactic and semantic labels for the arguments of seven test verbs not present in the train data. Each system was evaluated by independently measuring the f-scores of its syntactic and semantic label predictions on each verb, averaged together by verb and then across verbs to arrive at the final f-score.

4 Conclusion

The experiments suggest that more iterations of the search for the best possible collection of features could yield significant additional improvements in system performance. However, we ran out of time before being able to complete more iterations of the search. While we trailed the second-place system by only 1.4% in overall f-score, the first-place system was ahead by 7.3% indicating significant improvements are still possible.

Additionally, the heuristic baseline outperformed all systems including ours, indicating that important patterns and intuitions were not encoded into features effectively. Given the sparsity of training data, it is possible that having more data could have also helped our approach based on pipelined classifiers.

In the future, we will evaluate using a single dev set instead of using cross-validation to reduce the computational cost of experiments. We were concerned about the sparse training data, but given the missed opportunity to further optimize the feature sets used by our models due to computational resource constraints, a single dev set could have been a much better approach. We would also like to use features from the semantic ontology rather than treating the semantic labels as unrelated tokens.

With our precision and recall within 2% of one another and relatively low, it would be challenging to reliably generate real-world lexical entries using this system, even with a delimited scope. However, approaches like this could be valuable at giving lexicographers a starting point to verify or modify, rather than starting from scratch.

This was a valuable learning experience, and while our efforts improved performance over our own baseline by nearly 12%, there is still plenty of room to improve and we have a clear path to do so by incorporating more features and improving experimental design.

Acknowledgments

Thank you to the anonymous reviewers, Ismail El Maarouf, and Daniel Cer for their helpful comments. Any mistakes that remain are our own.

References

Baisa, Vit, et al. (2015). SemEval-2015 Task 15: A CPA dictionary-entry-building task. *Proceedings of the 9th International Workshop on Semantic Evaluation (SemEval 2015)*. Denver, Co, USA, Association for Computational Linguistics.

Gildea, Daniel; Jurafsky, Daniel. (2002). "Automatic Labeling of Semantic Roles." *Computational Linguistics* 28(3): 245-288.

Kilgarriff, Adam, et al. The Sketch Engine: ten years on. In *Lexicography* (2014): 1-30.

Manning, Christopher; Surdeanu, Mihai; Bauer, John; Finkel, Jenny; Bethard, Steven; and McClosky, David. 2014. The Stanford CoreNLP Natural Language Processing Toolkit. In *Proceedings of 52nd Annual Meeting of the Association for Computational Linguistics: System Demonstrations*, pp. 55-60.

McCallum, Andrew Kachites. "MALLET: A Machine Learning for Language Toolkit." http://mallet.cs.umass.edu. 2002.

Pradhan, Sameer, et al. (2004). Shallow Semantic Parsing using Support Vector Machines. HLT-NAACL.

Roland, Douglas and Jurafsky, Daniel (2002). "Verb sense and verb subcategorization probabilities." The lexical basis of sentence processing: Formal, computational, and experimental issues 4: 325-45.

Surdeanu, Mihai, et al. (2003). Using predicate-argument structures for information extraction. *Proceedings of the 41st Annual Meeting of the Association for Computational Linguistics-Volume 1*, Association for Computational Linguistics.

Toutanova, Kristina, et al. (2008). "A Global Joint Model for Semantic Role Labeling." *Computational Linguistics* 34(2): 161-191.

Xue, Nianwen and Palmer, Martha (2004). Calibrating Features for Semantic Role Labeling. *EMNLP*.

Duluth: Word Sense Discrimination in the Service of Lexicography

Ted Pedersen
Department of Computer Science
University of Minnesota
Duluth, MN, 55812, USA
tpederse@d.umn.edu

Abstract

This paper describes the Duluth systems that participated in Task 15 of SemEval 2015. The goal of the task was to automatically construct dictionary entries (via a series of three subtasks). Our systems participated in subtask 2, which involved automatically clustering the contexts in which a target word occurs into its different senses. Our results are consistent with previous word sense induction and discrimination findings, where it proves difficult to beat a baseline algorithm that assigns all instances of a target word to a single sense. However, our method of predicting the number of senses automatically fared quite well.

1 Introduction

A Corpus Pattern Analysis (CPA) dictionary entry building task (SemEval 2015 Task 15) included three subtasks, the combination of which creates a dictionary entry based on CPA (Hanks, 2013). The Duluth systems participated in the second subtask, which sought to cluster the contexts in which target words occur based on their underlying sense or meaning. Note that for this task all of the target words are verbs. This is unusual for a word sense shared task, since nouns are much more commonly studied.

The task input includes two sets of words : the Microcheck includes 8 target verbs, where the number of senses for each are given to task participants, while the Wingspread includes 20 target verbs where the number of senses are withheld. Both sets of target verbs and their frequencies are shown in Tables 3.2 and 3.2.

The CPA method is based on finding patterns of use in corpora, and definitions of word senses refer explicitly to these patterns. For example, the verb *totter* has three senses, where a person (sense 1), building (sense 2), or institution (sense 3) may be what totters. The verb *undertake* has two senses, where a person or institution embarks on an activity (sense 1) or promises to do so (sense 2).

There is certainly a role for syntactic information in defining such senses – direct and indirect objects are clearly important, and chunking would in general be quite useful. It also seems that incorporating semantic features, for example, those based on selectional restrictions or constraints, might be fruitful. In fact, subtask 1 focuses on shallow parsing and is said to be similar to semantic role labeling. Given different syntactic and semantic features discovered in subtask 1, it would be possible to pursue subtask 2 using a more rule based approach.

However, the Duluth systems do not explicitly account for syntax or semantics and do not try to identify these kinds of patterns. While we believe such approaches are extremely useful, we are primarily interested in exploring the limits of methods that depend on purely lexical features.

As a result, the Duluth systems rely on clustering target verbs based on the context in which they occur (e.g., (Schütze, 1998), (Purandare and Pedersen, 2004), (Pedersen, 2007)). This follows from the distributional hypothesis (Harris, 1954). Simply put, words that are used in similar contexts may often have similar meanings. However, words with different meanings can also be used in similar contexts (e.g., antonyms) so results are often noisy.

The Duluth systems take a knowledge-lean approach (Pedersen, 1997), and treat this task as an unsupervised word sense discrimination or induction problem, and use the freely available open-source software package SenseClusters[1].

2 Systems

We submitted three runs for subtask 2 : run1, run2, and run3. These three systems share a few basic characteristics, but differ in important respects. All use SenseClusters, and all utilize the same relatively simple pre–processing. Text was converted to lower case, and numeric values were all converted to a single string. Also, all three runs automatically determined the number of clusters (senses) using the PK2 measure (Pedersen and Kulkarni, 2006). This measure looks at the degree of change in the clustering criterion function, and stops the clustering process when the criterion function begins to plateau. This indicates that additional clustering of the data is not improving the quality of the clusters, and that further divisions will break apart relatively homogeneous senses.

There are however important differences between the systems. Runs run1 and run2 rely on second–order co–occurrences, run1 uses words that co–occur near the target verb as features, and run2 uses words that occur anywhere in the contexts to be clustered. Both run1 and run2 represent these features using second–order co–occurrences, where run1 derives these from the contexts to be clustered, and run2 uses the WordNet 3.0 glosses[2] as a 1.46 million word corpus for building these features. run3 use first–order unigrams found in the contexts to be clustered as features.

While the Microcheck data provided the number of senses, the Duluth systems elected not to use this. We felt that in most realistic use cases the number of senses is not known, and we were curious to see how well our systems could perform at identifying the number of senses automatically.

2.1 First and Second–Order Co–Occurrences

A first–order representation simply looks for features that directly occur in the contexts to be clustered and uses their occurrence (or not) as the basis for making clustering decisions. First–order unigrams depend on having multiple occurrences of the same words in various different contexts, and as such often do not perform well with smaller numbers of contexts. Among our systems, run3 is the only to take a first order unigram approach.

A second–order representation takes a somewhat fuzzier approach, and allows for a more flexible sort of feature matching. Rather than looking for the same features in multiple contexts, this representation seeks features that co–occur with the same words in different contexts. This can be thought of as a kind of a *friend of a friend* approach to feature matching.

For example, suppose that *car* and *auto* occur in two different contexts. They do not match (as first–order features) but if both are known to occur with *repairs* then that second–order co–occurrence can be the basis for considering them as matching features that could then be used to cluster the contexts in which *car* and *auto* occur in together.

This is operationalized by replacing words in the context to be clustered with a co–occurrence vector. For run1, the only word that is replaced is the target verb, which is instead represented by a vector of words that occur within 8 positions of that target in that particular context.

For run2, all the words in the contexts to be clustered that are used in a WordNet gloss (version 3.0) are replaced by a vector representing all the words in WordNet glosses that immediately follow that word in a definition.

As a simple example, imagine a gloss corpus with two definitions : *a vehicle powered by an internal combustion engine* and *a medication used to speed up the internal clock*. If the word *internal* occurs in a context, it would be replaced by a vector consisting of *combustion* and *clock*.

Then, all the vectors associated with the words in a context are averaged together (although in the case of run1 this might just be a single vector). Each context is represented now by its averaged vector, and the closeness or distance of contexts to or from each other is based on the number of second–order feature matches.

[1] http://senseclusters.sourceforge.net

[2] http://www.d.umn.edu/˜tpederse/Code/glossExtract-v0.03.tar.gz

	Microcheck	Wingspread
run1	0.525	0.604
run2	0.440	0.581
run3	0.439	0.615
baseline	0.588	0.720

Table 1: B–Cubed F–Scores.

2.2 Lexical Feature Selection

run1 finds what are known in SenseClusters as target co–occurrences (tco) in the contexts to be clustered, and run2 finds bigrams in the WordNet 3.0 gloss corpus. While there are many methods for identifying statistically significant or associated pairs of words in corpora, the number of contexts in the Wingspread data is relatively small – 12 of 20 target verbs have fewer than 40 contexts, so we simply relied on frequency counts when selecting features. Given this, run1 used a long distance definition of co–occurrence to help overcome the smaller numbers of contexts, and so any word that occurs anywhere within 8 positions of the target word 2 or more times is considered a target co–occurrence. In run2 any bigram that occurred 5 or more times in the WordNet 3.0 gloss corpus was used as a feature. In run3 any unigram that occurred 2 or more times in the contexts to be clustered was used as a feature.

We used the nearly 400 word stoplist from the Ngram Statistics Package[3] (Banerjee and Pedersen, 2003) for all three of our runs. Any bigram or co–occurrence where both words are stop words was not used as a feature, and any unigram in the stoplist was likewise discarded.

3 Results and Analysis

Official results from task 15 are based on the B–cubed F–score (Bagga and Baldwin, 1998). In addition to reporting those values, we also carried out our own analysis using the SenseClusters F–measure.

3.1 B–cubed F–score

Table 3.1 shows the B–Cubed F–scores as reported by the task organizers. Note that the baseline system assigns all contexts to a single cluster or sense.

Prior to the evaluation we designated run1 as our official submission, since we felt that this system was likely to be most successful with this task. This was based on our pre–evaluation tuning with the training data which had been made available by the task organizers. This prediction was largely confirmed – run1 was easily our most accurate system with the Microcheck data, and was only narrowly exceeded by run3 for the Wingspread data.

There were several hundred contexts available for each target verb in the Microcheck data. This is large enough to generate a rich second–order representation of context. Given that we focused on somewhat localized target co–occurrences in run1, the number of spurious features will be somewhat less than if we had looked more generally at features that occur anywhere in a context (as is the case with run2 and run3). This is why we believe that run1 had a fairly significant advantage in the Microcheck data.

However, in the Wingspread data run3 slightly outperformed run1, although not to a significant degree. We believe this occurred because the Wingspread data has a majority of target verbs with less than 40 contexts. This small amount of data will result in very sparse second–order co–occurrences. Given that run1 seeks target co–occurrences, when these are very sparse they essentially reduce to first–order co–occurrences, leading to very similar performance between run1 and run3.

3.2 SenseClusters F–Measure

Tables 3.2 and 3.2 provide results for run1 using the SenseClusters F-Measure (F) (Pedersen, 2007). This measure first assigns the discovered clusters to gold standard senses in whatever way optimizes the agreement between them using the (Munkres, 1957) algorithm. Then any senses or clusters that are not aligned are discarded, and precision and recall are computed in the usual way. In these experiments all contexts are assigned to clusters, so recall and precision are the same, and the F-measure can be viewed as accuracy. In this case the F-measure is the percentage of contexts that were assigned to the correct cluster.

These tables also show the most frequent sense baseline (M). This is the percentage of contexts that belong to the most frequent sense. This is a well known baseline in supervised approaches to word sense disambiguation, and also proves to be the same for unsupervised approaches. Given the defini-

[3] http://ngram.sourceforge.net

	N	C	D	M	F
appreciate	215	2	2	.744	.693
apprehend	123	3	5	.626	.435
continue	203	7	4	.350	.291
crush	170	5	5	.365	.324
decline	201	3	4	.672	.439
operate	140	8	4	.286	.250
undertake	228	2	2	.895	.750
total (w)		4.1	3.5	.585	.478
total	1,280	4.3	3.7	.562	.455

Table 2: Microcheck run1, N is number of instances, C is number of actual clusters, D is number of discovered clusters, M is majority sense baseline, F is SenseClusters F-Measure, total (w) are weighted averages.

tion of the SenseClusters F-Measure, if all contexts are assigned to a single cluster, then the F-Measure will be equal to the most frequent sense percentage. As can be seen in Tables 2 and 3, in general this baseline outperformed the Duluth systems for nearly every target verb.

We were pleased that in general the PK2 method of identifying the number of clusters was reasonably successful. While it did not always predict exactly the same number of clusters as found in the gold standard data, in general there were no cases where it differed radically. On average the Microcheck data had 4.3 senses, while run1 discovered 3.7. For the Wingspread data there were 3.0 senses, while run1 discovered 2.7. While the results show that the clusters themselves are noisy, in general we are pleased that our ability to predict the number of clusters is reasonably accurate.

4 Conclusions

SenseClusters has participated in numerous SensEval and SemEval shared tasks that have included word sense discrimination and induction (Pedersen, 2007; Pedersen, 2010; Pedersen, 2013). In all of these prior events, the most frequent sense baseline has proven hard to beat. In general assigning all instances of a target verb to a single cluster replicates most frequent sense performance. The results in this subtask are similar, and suggest that for the moment, automatic word sense discrimination is still not a viable replacement for human lexicographic expertise.

	N	C	D	M	F
adapt	182	4	1	.539	.539
advise	230	8	2	.365	.365
afflict	179	2	2	.961	.687
ascertain	7	2	1	.571	.571
ask	573	9	2	.522	.470
attain	240	3	4	.833	.627
avert	240	2	7	.958	.374
avoid	242	3	2	.727	.566
begrudge	19	2	4	.579	.581
belch	24	3	4	.583	.468
bludgeon	32	2	2	.500	.500
bluff	25	2	2	.560	.520
boo	36	2	2	.750	.640
brag	29	2	2	.621	.586
breeze	12	2	1	.583	.583
sue	247	2	2	.980	.846
teeter	28	2	2	.821	.750
tense	37	3	2	.622	.432
totter	19	2	5	.632	.533
wing	22	2	4	.474	.864
total (w)		4.6	2.7	.694	.548
total	2,421	3.0	2.7	.659	.575

Table 3: Wingspread run1, N is number of instances, C is number of actual clusters, D is number of discovered clusters, M is majority sense baseline, F is SenseClusters F-Measure, total (w) are weighted averages.

However, we are encouraged by the accurate results from the PK2 method in identifying the number of senses automatically. If the discovered clusters themselves can be made less noisy (through improved feature selection), our overall results could improve significantly since we are already able to identify the number of distinct senses accurately. We believe that the incorporation of more grammatical and semantic features will certainly help improve the quality of the clustering, and so plan to pursue that in future work.

Acknowledgments

I would like to thank Bridget McInnes for her help in understanding the task, and for very useful brainstorming discussions.

References

Amit Bagga and Breck Baldwin. 1998. Entity–based cross–document co–referencing using the vector space model. In *Proceedings of the 17th International Conference on Computational Linguistics*, pages 79–85.

Satanjeev Banerjee and Ted Pedersen. 2003. Extended gloss overlaps as a measure of semantic relatedness. In *Proceedings of the Eighteenth International Joint Conference on Artificial Intelligence*, pages 805–810, Acapulco, August.

Patrick Hanks. 2013. *Lexical Analysis : Norms and Exploitations*. The MIT Press, Cambridge, MA.

Zellig Harris. 1954. Distributional structure. *Word*, 10(23):146–162.

James Munkres. 1957. Algorithms for the assignment and transportation problems. *Journal of the Society of Industrial and Applied Mathematics*, 5(1):32–38, March.

Ted Pedersen and Anagha Kulkarni. 2006. Selecting the right number of senses based on clustering criterion functions. In *Proceedings of the Posters and Demo Program of the Eleventh Conference of the European Chapter of the Association for Computational Linguistics*, pages 111–114, Trento, Italy, April.

Ted Pedersen. 1997. Knowledge lean word sense disambiguation. In *Proceedings of the Fourteenth National Conference on Artificial Intelligence*, page 814, Providence, RI, July.

Ted Pedersen. 2007. UMND2 : SenseClusters applied to the sense induction task of Senseval-4. In *Proceedings of the Fourth International Workshop on Semantic Evaluations (SemEval-2007)*, pages 394–397, Prague, Czech Republic, June.

Ted Pedersen. 2010. Duluth-WSI: SenseClusters applied to the sense induction task of semEval-2. In *Proceedings of the SemEval 2010 Workshop : the 5th International Workshop on Semantic Evaluations*, pages 363–366, Uppsala, July.

Ted Pedersen. 2013. Duluth : Word sense induction applied to web page clustering. In *Second Joint Conference on Lexical and Computational Semantics (*SEM), Volume 2: Proceedings of the Seventh International Workshop on Semantic Evaluation (SemEval 2013)*, pages 202–206, Atlanta, Georgia, USA, June. Association for Computational Linguistics.

Amruta Purandare and Ted Pedersen. 2004. Word sense discrimination by clustering contexts in vector and similarity spaces. In *Proceedings of the Conference on Computational Natural Language Learning*, pages 41–48, Boston, MA.

Hinrich Schütze. 1998. Automatic word sense discrimination. *Computational Linguistics*, 24(1):97–123.

SemEval-2015 Task 9: CLIPEval Implicit Polarity of Events

Irene Russo
ILC-CNR "A. Zampolli"
Via G. Moruzzi, 1
56124 Pisa
irene.russo@ilc.cnr.it

Tommaso Caselli
Vrije Universiteit Amsterdam
De Boelelaan 1105
1081 HV Amsterdam
t.caselli@gmail.com

Carlo Strapparava
Fondazione Bruno Kessler
Via Sommarive, 18
38123 Povo (TN)
strappa@fbk.eu

Abstract

Sentiment analysis tends to focus on the polarity of words, combining their values to detect which portion of a text is opinionated. CLIPEval wants to promote a more holistic approach, looking at psychological researches that frame the connotations of words as the emotional values activated by them. The implicit polarity of events is just one aspect of connotative meaning and we address it with a task that is based on a dataset of sentences annotated as instantiations of *pleasant* and *unpleasant* events previously collected in psychological research as the ones on which human judgments converge.

1 Introduction

Current research in sentiment analysis (SA, henceforth) is mostly focused on lexical resources that store polarity values. For bag-of-words approaches the polarity of a text depends on the presence/absence of a set of lexical items. This methodology is successful to detect opinions about entities (such as reviews) but it shows mixed results when complex opinions about events - involving perspectives and points of view - are expressed.

In terms of parts of speech involved, SA approaches tend to focus on lexical items that explicitly convey opinions - mainly adjectives, adverbs and several nouns - leaving verbs on the foreground. Improvements have been proposed by taking into account syntax (Greene and Resnik 2009) and by investigating the connotative polarity of words (Cambria et al., 2009; Akkaya et al., 2009, Balhaur et al., 2011; Russo et al. 2011; Cambria et al., 2012, Deng et al., 2013 among others). One of the key aspects of sentiment analysis, which has been only marginally tackled so far, is the identification of implicit polarity. By implicit polarity we refer to the recognition of subjective textual units where no polarity markers are present but still people are able to state whether the text portion under analysis expresses a positive or negative sentiment. Recently, methodologies trying to address this aspect have been developed, incorporating ideas from linguistic and psychological studies on the subjective aspects of linguistic expressions.

Aiming at promoting a more holistic approach to sentiment analysis, combining the detection of implicit polarity with the expression of opinions on events, we propose CLIPEval, a task based on a dataset of events annotated as instantiations of *pleasant* and *unpleasant* events (PE/UPEs henceforth) previously collected in psychological research as the ones that correlate with mood (both good and bad feelings) (Lewinsohn and Amenson, 1978; MacPhillamy and Lewinsohn, 1982).

2 Measuring Emotional Connotations: Psychological Studies

For a long time research in psychology has been interested in a subjective cultural and/or emotional coloration in addition to the explicit or denotative meaning of any specific word or phrase. Starting with the work of Charles E. Osgood, who in the 50s developed a technique for measuring the connotative meaning of concepts and analyzed human attitudes (Osgood et al., 1957), psychologists have experimented with emotional values activated by words, often through the evaluation of their pleasantness. Osgood and his colleagues proposed a factor analysis based on semantic differential scales measuring three basic attitudes that people display cross-culturally: evaluation (along the scale of adjectives "good-bad"), potency (along "strong-weak") and activity ("active-passive").

This line of research continued with studies evaluating Osgood's findings with different population and the pleasantness of words became also a dimension to correlate with other dimensions reported in semantic norms studies, such as familiarity and imagery. We know today that pleasantness is a semantic factor influencing short and long term memory (Monnier et al., 2008); similarly, (Hadley and MacKay, 2006) showed that STM for certain unpleasant emotional words (i.e., taboo words) was better than that for neutral words. Emotional words are better recalled because they are related to long-term representations of autobiographical and self-reference units (Ochsner, 2000). Other factors have a role: depressed subjects, for example, recalled more unpleasant words than pleasant words.

Osgood's studies were revised for the production of the Affective Norms for English Words (ANEW) (Bradley et al, 1999), a set of normative emotional ratings for 1034 words in American English. This set of verbal materials have been rated in terms of *pleasure*, *arousal*, and *dominance* in order to create a standard for use in studies of emotion and attention (the same three basic dimensions used by Osgood). Affective valence (or pleasure, ranging from pleasant to unpleasant) and arousal (ranging from calm to excited) were the two primary dimensions. A third, less strongly-related dimension, was called "dominance" or "control".

Connotative meaning emerges as a complex and stratified concept and only psychological studies can guide in this maze, especially when they are supported by significant experimental outputs such as list of words evaluated by human subjects.

All these studies are relevant for NLP because connotative meanings of words can help to refine automatic sentiment analysis on social media, where shared contents are often just short reports on pleasant or unpleasant events and activities. For example, (Fenf et al., 2013) report that connotation lexicon guarantees better performance than other sentiment analysis lexicons that do not encode connotations on Twitter data.

That said, when psychological experiments ask for judgments about single words they oversimplify: we experience the meanings of single words as arising from compositionality, in expressions and sentences. Even neutral words in specific contexts can acquire a polarity as effect of semantic prosody (Louw 1993).

When subjects are asked for the pleasantness of an event they need to evaluate not just single words but complete sentences; for this reason (Lewinsohn and Amenson, 1978; MacPhillamy and Lewinsohn, 1982) developed two psychometric instruments, the Pleasant Events Schedule and the Unpleasant Events Schedule, by sampling events that were reported to be source of pleasure or distress by highly diverse samples of people that rated the frequency of event's occurrence during past month plus a complete mood ratings.

3 CLIPEval Annotation

The CLIPEval exercise provides the NLP community with a newly developed dataset grounded on psychological studies about the pleasantness of events. Dedicated annotation specifications and guidelines for the release of the dataset have been developed.

The starting point for the development of the annotation guidelines was the PE/UPEs lists, the set of 640 pleasant and unpleasant events (320 pleasant events and 320 unpleasant events, respectively) collected by (Lewinsohn and Amenson, 1978) and (MacPhillamy and Lewinsohn, 1982). The dataset could not be used as it is since it is a list of generic sentences describing either states or actions which are labeled as pleasant or unpleasant events. To clarify this, we report two examples extracted from the original dataset. Example 1.) is a pleasant event while example 2.) is an an unpleasant event. The numbers in brackets at the beginning of the sentence refer to the PE/UPEs number in the original dataset.

1.) *(9) Planning trips or vacations.*

2.) *(10) Getting separated or divorced from my spouse.*

Furthermore, a closer examination of PE/UPEs has shown that ambiguity occurs, with the same events considered both as a pleasant and an unpleasant one (e.g. *Being alone*), since this is plausible from a psychological point of view. To overcome these issues and to make the task relevant for sentences from news articles, we have applied the following strategies:

- all ambiguous PE/UPEs have been removed from the original dataset;
- PE/UPEs have been grouped into classes whose labels describe and aggregate different PE/UPEs, referring often to a more general event class with respect to the one the single instance of a PE/UPE event describes. This choice has been necessary because the event instances in the original psychological dataset are conceptually similar but using the original descriptions would result either in too generic cases (e.g. *Being with children*) or too simple (e.g. *Washing my hair*).

The grouping of PE/UPEs in classes has been conducted in two phases by two annotators. In the first phase, both annotators have worked independently: for each PE/UPE the annotators had to decide which of them could be clustered in a more generic class and which were to be excluded, either because it describes a too specific (or a too generic) event or because it explicitly express the pleasanteness of the event (e.g. *(25) Driving skillfully*). As a measure of agreement for this task, we preferred not to use kappa score, because it's not a standard classification task, but we computed the percentage of agreement. The first evaluation shown a relatively low agreement, only 59.06% of the 640 events were considered as belonging to a cluster. An analysis on the cases of disagreement has highlighted some inconsistencies. Thus, a second clusterization task has been performed by asking to the same annotators to go over the same data following new additional rules that were developed during the analysis. The evaluation of this second phase shown a clear improvement with a percentage agreement of 68.25%. As a result of these annotation phases, we had a set of clusters that the annotators were allowed to discuss, finding a joint solution in cases of disagreements and identifying the best labels for the PE/UPEs clusters. The final output of these two phases resulted in 8 classes of PE/UPEs (see Table 1 column "Event Class"). It is important to point out that most of these classes contain PE/UPEs both from the 320 pleasant events and the 320 unpleasant events and as a consequence the polarities of their occurrences in the training data are mixed(see Table 1). Due to the novelty of the task, we could not re-use available datasets for SA. For this reason, the second step concerns the identification and manual annotation of real sentences from the Annotated English Gigaword corpus (Napoles et al., 2012), an automatically-generated syntactic and discourse structure annotated version of the English Gigaword corpus Fifth Edition, which contains a large English corpus of newspaper articles (four billion words ca.). To facilitate the sentence extraction phase, we manually identified the verbal and the nominal keywords from the event mentions composing the classes. We used WN30 and the Oxford Dictionary to extract all verb and noun synonyms of the PE/UPEs in each class. We then queried the Gigaword corpus with this extended set of keywords to extract sentences which contain self-reported events by means of following patterns:

- "I|we + [verbal_keyword]"
- "I|we + [nominal_keyword]"
- "I|we + [verbal_keyword] + [nominal_keyword]".

The sentences thus extracted were manually filtered and annotated with respect to the 8 classes and to their polarity. The annotation has been conducted at sentence level. To provide homogeneous data and annotations, the following guidelines have been developed for the assignment of the class label:

- the class label and the polarity value must be assigned on the basis of the event that correspond syntactically to the main verb in the sentence;
- in case of coordinated main clauses, only the first main clause is taken into account to assign the class label and the polarity value;

Table 1: CLIPEval corpus: Training data.

Event Class	POSITIVE	NEGATIVE	NEUTRAL	Tot. Instances
(FEAR_OF)_PHYSICAL_PAIN	19	131	10	160
ATTENDING_EVENT	83	35	42	160
COMMUNICATION_ISSUE	21	120	19	160
GOING_TO_PLACES	55	72	33	160
LEGAL_ISSUE	24	115	21	160
MONEY_ISSUE	20	109	31	160
OUTDOOR_ACTIVITY	125	18	17	160
PERSONAL_CARE	88	40	32	160

Table 2: CLIPEval corpus: Test data.

Event Class	POSITIVE	NEGATIVE	NEUTRAL	Tot. Instances
(FEAR_OF)_PHYSICAL_PAIN	10	30	5	45
ATTENDING_EVENT	29	5	11	45
COMMUNICATION_ISSUE	8	29	7	44
GOING_TO_PLACES	22	23	3	48
LEGAL_ISSUE	5	27	13	45
MONEY_ISSUE	12	27	12	51
OUTDOOR_ACTIVITY	34	4	8	46
PERSONAL_CARE	24	10	13	43

- subordinated clauses are not annotated with class labels and polarity values.

Although all event mentions in the selected clusters have either a positive (pleasant events) or negative (unpleasant events) polarity that could be reversed by negation, during the annotation phase a third value, namely neutral, has been introduced to cope with those sentences containing self-reporting events whose occurrence is uncertain

We are referring here to the notion of event factuality (Sauríand Pustejovsky, 2009), i.e. the degrees of certainty (e.g. possible, probable, certain) associated to an event description along the category of epistemic modality. In the annotation we focused on the syntactic information between target events instances and factuality markers, such as modal auxiliaries and negation cues (including adverbs, adjectives, prepositions, pronouns and determiners). Events which are in the scope of factuality markers signaling uncertainty or improbability have been marked as neutral.

4 CLIPEval Tasks

The CLIPEval evaluation exercise is composed of two tasks described as follows:

- Task A: identification of the polarity value associated to the event instance. Participants are required to associate each sentence with a polarity value (POSITIVE, NEGATIVE or NEUTRAL);
- Task B: identification of the event mentions with respect to one of the 8 event class labels plus identification of the polarity value. The class labels used are: ATTENDING_EVENT, COMMUNICATION_ISSUE, GOING_TO_PLACES; LEGAL_ISSUE, MONEY_ISSUE, OUTDOOR_ACTIVITIES, PERSONAL_CARE, (FEAR_OF)_PHYSICAL_PAIN. As in Task A the polarity values are (POSITIVE, NEGATIVE or NEUTRAL).

5 Dataset Description

The CLIPEval evaluation exercise is based on the CLIPEval dataset, which consists of two parts: a training set and a test set. The final size of the dataset is 1,651 sentences, divided in 1,280 sentences for the training and 371 for the test. Each event class in the training data contains 160 sentences.

Each class in the training set is available in a separate file composed of four tab separated fields: a sentence id, the sentence extracted from the Gigaword corpus, the polarity value and the class label. Each file is named with the class label. Some examples of the training data are provided in the examples below (examples from 3.) to 5.)):

3.) 8 *I had just gone to a concert with my parents and I identified with the conductor a lot Dudamel said in Spanish during a recent interview in Caracas.* POSITIVE ATTENDING_EVENT

4.) 14 *"It's too cold and I can't ride my bike" he lamented.* NEGATIVE OUTDOOR_ACTIVITY

5.) 4 *"I could take the boys to the sports museum' says James.* NEUTRAL GOING_TO_PLACES

The test data has been provided in a single file with only two fields: the sentence id and the sentence extracted from the Gigaword corpus:

6.) 12 *After having given a friend a lift home I was stopped by police.*

7.) 23 *And then we went to a library.*

Table 1 and Table 2 report the figures for polarity values per class in the training and in the test set, respectively.

The division of the training data for the three polarity values is not balanced due to the event mentions composing the clusters. Only three clusters, namely GOING_TO_PLACES, PERSONAL_CARE and ATTENDING_EVENT, present a relatively balanced distribution for the polarity values. This lack of balance reflects real language data: the prevalence of positive or negative values is due to the classes which may have more PEs or UPEs (e.g. OUTDOOR_ACTIVITY and COMMUNICATION_ISSUE, respectively). Including more sentences which reverse the polarity of the PEs or UPEs to balance the occurrences per polarity value would mean to force the data from real language toward an artificial equilibrium.

6 Evaluation

Since both Task A and Task B of CLIPEval are essentially classification tasks (classification of the polarity value for Task A and classification of the event instance and the polarity value for Task B), we have used Precision, Recall and F1-measure to evaluate the system results against the test set. Furthermore, since this is a multi-classification task (3 possible values for Task A and 24 possible values for Task B), we have computed micro average Precision, Recall and F1-measure per class. This latter measure has been used for the final ranking of the systems. We have adopted standard definitions for these measures, namely:

- Precision: the number of correctly classified positive examples, tp_i per class C_i, divided by number of examples labeled by the system as positive (tp_i plus false positive fp_i): $\frac{\sum_{i=1}^{l} tp_i}{tp_i+fp_i}$
- Recall: the number of correctly classified positive examples tp_i per class C_i divided by the number of positive examples in the data (tp_i plus false negatives fn_i) : $\frac{\sum_{i=1}^{l} tp_i}{tp_i+fn_i}$
- F-measure: the mean of Precision and Recall calculated as follows: $\frac{(\beta^2+1)PrecisionRecall}{\beta^2 Precision+Recall}$

To better evaluate systems' performances, we have developed three baselines, one per Task A and two per Task B. In particular:

- Task A baseline has been obtained by assigning to each sentence in the test set the most frequent polarity value on the basis of the data in the training set. This resulted in marking all 371 sentences in the test set with NEGATIVE polarity;
- Task B baseline_1 has been obtained in two steps: first, for each class in the training data we have selected the most frequent nouns and verbs lemmas. This has provided us with a list of keywords representing each class. We have then compared each sentence in the test set with each group of keywords and assigned as correct the class which scored the higher number of matches. In case of a draw, a random class between the classes with the highest scores is assigned. If no match is found, a random class is assigned. As for the polarity, we have used the absolute most frequent polarity values, like in task A (i.e. all test set entries have been assigned to NEGATIVE value).

- Task B baseline_2 has been obtained following the approach in Task B baseline_1 for the class assignment and we have assigned the most frequent polarity value per class according to training data (e.g. for items classified as ATTENDING_EVENTS the assigned polarity value is POSITIVE).

6.1 Participant Systems

Overall 26 different teams registered for the task, only two submitted the output of their system for a total of 3 runs: SHELLFBK (Fondazione Bruno Kessler) and SIGMA2320 (Peking Univeristy). Only SHELLFBK submitted results for both tasks. Furthermore, we can provide a short description just for SHELLFBK since the SIGMA2320 team has not submitted a system description paper.

SHELLFBK system implements a supervised approach based on information retrieval techniques for representing polarized information. During the training phase, each sentence is analyzed by applying the parser contained in the Stanford NLP Library. From the results of the parsing activity, both the list of the dependency relations and the parsed trees are used for populating an inverted index data structure containing the relationships between each relation extracted from the sentences and the corresponding information about its polarization. The result of the training phase is a set of three indexes containing, respectively, the positive, negative, and neutral information analyzed in the training set. When the polarity of a new sentence has to be computed, the new sentence is given as input to the Stanford NLP Library by obtaining the list of its dependency relations, as well as, the corresponding parsed tree. Such information are built together for composing a query that is afterwards performed on the indexes built during the training phase. For each of the built indexes, a retrieval score value is retrieved by the system and, based on this, the polarity of the new sentence is assigned.

6.2 Evaluation Results

We report in Table 3 the results of both systems for Task A and the Task A baseline. In Table 4 we report the results for Task B and both baseline for Task B (baseline_1 and baseline_2, respectively).

Table 3: Evaluation for Task A : polarity identification.

System	Precision	Recall	F1-measure
SIGMA2320	0.41	0.42	0.38
SHELLFBK	0.56	0.56	**0.54**
baseline	0.17	0.42	0.25

Table 4: Evaluation for Task B : event instance and polarity identification.

System	Precision	Recall	F1-measure
SHELLFBK	0.36	0.27	**0.29**
baseline_1	0.02	0.04	0.02
baseline_2	0.03	0.05	0.04

SHELLFBK outperforms SIGMA2320 for the Task A; both systems improve the baseline. The results are not as good as in classification tasks concerning the polarities of tweets (Rosental et al., 2014) or reviews (Pontiki et al., 2014) but since this is a novel task about implicit polarity we think they are promising.

For task B SHELLFBK has a better performance both in terms of precision and recall if compared with the two baselines. At the moment we do not know if the results are due to SHELLFBK methodology or if data sparseness in the classes has an influence on the classification task: maybe classes more cohesive from conceptual and lexical point of view could be easier to detect.

7 Conclusions and Future Work

The implicit polarity of words concerns the arising of occasional polarized meanings in specific expressions/linguistic contexts. Labeled as semantic prosody in corpus studies and part of what psychologists call connotative meanings, the implicit polarity is a quite marginal concept in sentiment analysis. It requires a dynamic representation for the polarity of words (i.e. a verb can be neutral in the vast majority of case but can be clearly positive in some contexts) and a compositional approach to sentiment values that goes beyond the oversimplifying assumptions of bag-of-words approaches.

With the CLIPEval task we asked the NLP community to look at these complexities, considering the detection of a set of events as relevant for SA analyses because they have been judged as pleasant or unpleasant by subjects in psychological experiments conducted by (Lewinsohn and Amenson, 1978; MacPhillamy and Lewinsohn, 1982). As future work we plan to extend the dataset, including new classes of events and annotating instances from blogs and tweets. Also, we want to integrate the detection of polarized events with the work on stance and perspectives in news, going toward a theoretical model for SA that takes into account the interplay of linguistic means used by humans to express opinions and feelings.

Acknowledgments

One of the author wants to thanks the NWO Spinoza Prize project Understanding Language by Machines (sub-track 3) for partially supporting this work.

References

Cem Akkaya, Janyce Wiebe and Mihalcea Rada. 2010. Subjectivity Word Sense Disambiguation. *Proceedings of the 2009 Conference on Empirical Methods in Natural Language Processing*, pages 190 - 199.

Alexandra Balahur, Jesús M. Hermida and Andrés Montoyo. 2011. Detecting implicit expressions of sentiment in text based on commonsense knowledge. *Proceedings of the 2nd Workshop on Computational Approaches to Subjectivity and Sentiment Analysis.*, pages 53 - 60.

Margaret M. Bradley and Peter J. Lang. 1999. Affective norms for English words (ANEW): Stimuli, instruction manual and affective ratings. *Tech. Rep. No. C-1*

Erik Cambria, Robert Speer, Catherine Havasi and Amir Hussain. 2010. SenticNet: A Publicly Available Semantic Resource for Opinion Mining. *AAAI fall symposium: commonsense knowledge*, pages 14 - 18.

Erik Cambria, Catherine Havasi and Amir Hussain. 2012. SenticNet 2: A Semantic and Affective Resource for Opinion Mining and Sentiment Analysis. *FLAIRS Conference*, pages 202 - 207.

Ling Deng, Yoonjung Choi and Janyce Wiebe. 2012. Benefactive/Malefactive Event and Writer Attitude Annotation. *Proceedings of the 51st Annual Meeting of the Association for Computational Linguistics (Volume 2: Short Papers)*, pages 120 - 125.

Song Feng, Jun Seok Kang, Polina Kuznetsova, and Yejin Choi. 2013. Connotation lexicon: A dash of sentiment beneath the surface meaning. *Proceedings of the 51st Annual Meeting of the Association for Computational Linguistics (Volume 1: Long Papers)*, pages 1774 - 1784.

Stephan Greene and Philip Resnik. 2009. More than words: Syntactic packaging and implicit sentiment. *Proceedings of human language technologies: The 2009 Annual Conference of the North American Chapter of the Association for Computational Linguistics*, pages 503 - 511.

Christopher B. Hadley and Donald G. MacKay. 2006. Does emotion help or hinder immediate memory? Arousal versus priority-binding mechanism. *Journal of Abnormal Psychology*, 87(6), pages 644 - 654.

Peter M. Lewinsohn and Christopher S Amenson. 1978. Some Relations between Pleasant and Unpleasant Events and Depression. *Journal of Experimental Psychology: Learning, Memory, and Cognition*, 32, pages 79 - 88.

Douglas J. MacPhillamy and Peter M. Lewinsohn. 1982. The Pleasant Event Schedule: Studies on Reliability, Validity, and Scale Intercorrelation. *Journal of Counseling and Clinical Psychology*, 50(3), pages 363 - 380.

Catherine Monnier and Arielle SyssauMonnier. 2008. Semantic contribution to verbal short-term memory: Are pleasant words easier to remember than neutral words in serial recall and serial recognition? *Memory and Cognition*, 36, pages 35 - 42.

Courtney Napoles, Matthew Gormley and Benjamin Van Durme. 2012. Annotated gigaword. *Proceedings of the Joint Workshop on Automatic Knowledge Base Construction and Web-scale Knowledge Extraction*, pages 95 - 100.

Kevin N. Ochsner. 2000. Are affective events richly recollected or simply familiar? The experience and process of recognizing feelings past. *Journal of Experimental Psychology. General*, 129 (2), pages 242 261.

Charles E. Osgood, George Suci and Percy Tannenbaum. 1957. *The Measurement of Meaning.* University of Illinois Press,

Roser Saurí and James Pustejovsky. 2009. FactBank: A corpus annotated with event factuality. *Language resources and evaluation*, 3, pages 227 - 268.

Maria Pontiki, Dimitris Galanis, Pavlopoulos Ioannis, Harris Papageorgiou, Androutsopoulos Ion and Manandhar Suresh. 2014. SemEval 2014 Task 4: Aspect Based Sentiment Analysis. *Proceedings of the 8th International Workshop on Semantic Evaluation (SemEval 2014)*, pages 27 - 35.

Sara Rosenthal, Alan Ritter, Preslav Nakov and Veselin Stoyanov. 2014. SemEval-2014 Task 9: Sentiment Analysis in Twitter. *Proceedings of the 8th International Workshop on Semantic Evaluation (SemEval 2014)*

Irene Russo, Tommaso Caselli, Francesco Rubino, Ester Boldrini and Patricio Barco Martínez. 2011. EMO-Cause: An Easy-adaptable Approach to Extract Emotion Cause Contexts. *Proceedings of the 2nd Workshop on Computational Approaches to Subjectivity and Sentiment Analysis (WASSA 2.011)*, pages 152 - 160.

SemEval-2015 Task 10: Sentiment Analysis in Twitter

Sara Rosenthal
Columbia University
sara@cs.columbia.edu

Preslav Nakov
Qatar Computing Research Institute
pnakov@qf.org.qa

Svetlana Kiritchenko
National Research Council Canada
Svetlana.Kiritchenko@nrc-cnrc.gc.ca

Saif M Mohammad
National Research Council Canada
saif.mohammad@nrc-cnrc.gc.ca

Alan Ritter
The Ohio State University
aritter@cs.washington.edu

Veselin Stoyanov
Facebook
vesko.st@gmail.com

Abstract

In this paper, we describe the 2015 iteration of the SemEval shared task on Sentiment Analysis in Twitter. This was the most popular sentiment analysis shared task to date with more than 40 teams participating in each of the last three years. This year's shared task competition consisted of five sentiment prediction subtasks. Two were reruns from previous years: (A) sentiment expressed by a phrase in the context of a tweet, and (B) overall sentiment of a tweet. We further included three new subtasks asking to predict (C) the sentiment towards a topic in a single tweet, (D) the overall sentiment towards a topic in a set of tweets, and (E) the degree of prior polarity of a phrase.

1 Introduction

Social media such as Weblogs, microblogs, and discussion forums are used daily to express personal thoughts, which allows researchers to gain valuable insight into the opinions of a very large number of individuals, i.e., at a scale that was simply not possible a few years ago. As a result, nowadays, sentiment analysis is commonly used to study the public opinion towards persons, objects, and events. In particular, opinion mining and opinion detection are applied to product reviews (Hu and Liu, 2004), for agreement detection (Hillard et al., 2003), and even for sarcasm identification (González-Ibáñez et al., 2011; Liebrecht et al., 2013).

Early work on detecting sentiment focused on newswire text (Wiebe et al., 2005; Baccianella et al., 2010; Pang et al., 2002; Hu and Liu, 2004). As later research turned towards social media, people realized this presented a number of new challenges.

Misspellings, poor grammatical structure, emoticons, acronyms, and slang were common in these new media, and were explored by a number of researchers (Barbosa and Feng, 2010; Bifet et al., 2011; Davidov et al., 2010; Jansen et al., 2009; Kouloumpis et al., 2011; O'Connor et al., 2010; Pak and Paroubek, 2010). Later, specialized shared tasks emerged, e.g., at SemEval (Nakov et al., 2013; Rosenthal et al., 2014), which compared teams against each other in a controlled environment using the same training and testing datasets. These shared tasks had the side effect to foster the emergence of a number of new resources, which eventually spread well beyond SemEval, e.g., NRC's Hashtag Sentiment lexicon and the Sentiment140 lexicon (Mohammad et al., 2013).[1]

Below, we discuss the public evaluation done as part of SemEval-2015 Task 10. In its third year, the SemEval task on Sentiment Analysis in Twitter has once again attracted a large number of participants: 41 teams across five subtasks, with most teams participating in more than one subtask.

This year the task included reruns of two legacy subtasks, which asked to detect the sentiment expressed in a tweet or by a particular phrase in a tweet. The task further added three new subtasks. The first two focused on the sentiment towards a given topic in a single tweet or in a set of tweets, respectively. The third new subtask focused on determining the strength of prior association of Twitter terms with positive sentiment; this acts as an intrinsic evaluation of automatic methods that build Twitter-specific sentiment lexicons with real-valued sentiment association scores.

[1] http://www.purl.com/net/lexicons

In the remainder of this paper, we first introduce the problem of sentiment polarity classification and our subtasks. We then describe the process of creating the training, development, and testing datasets. We list and briefly describe the participating systems, the results, and the lessons learned. Finally, we compare the task to other related efforts and we point to possible directions for future research.

2 Task Description

Below, we describe the five subtasks of SemEval-2015 Task 10 on Sentiment Analysis in Twitter.

- **Subtask A. Contextual Polarity Disambiguation:** Given an instance of a word/phrase in the context of a message, determine whether it expresses a positive, a negative or a neutral sentiment in that context.

- **Subtask B. Message Polarity Classification:** Given a message, determine whether it expresses a positive, a negative, or a neutral/objective sentiment. If both positive and negative sentiment are expressed, the stronger one should be chosen.

- **Subtask C. Topic-Based Message Polarity Classification:** Given a message and a topic, decide whether the message expresses a positive, a negative, or a neutral sentiment towards the topic. If both positive and negative sentiment are expressed, the stronger one should be chosen.

- **Subtask D. Detecting Trend Towards a Topic:** Given a set of messages on a given topic from the same period of time, classify the overall sentiment towards the topic in these messages as (a) strongly positive, (b) weakly positive, (c) neutral, (d) weakly negative, or (e) strongly negative.

- **Subtask E. Determining Strength of Association of Twitter Terms with Positive Sentiment (Degree of Prior Polarity):** Given a word/phrase, propose a score between 0 (lowest) and 1 (highest) that is indicative of the strength of association of that word/phrase with positive sentiment. If a word/phrase is more positive than another one, it should be assigned a relatively higher score.

3 Datasets

In this section, we describe the process of collecting and annotating our datasets of short social media text messages. We focus our discussion on the 2015 datasets; more detail about the 2013 and the 2014 datasets can be found in (Nakov et al., 2013) and (Rosenthal et al., 2014).

3.1 Data Collection

3.1.1 Subtasks A–D

First, we gathered tweets that express sentiment about popular topics. For this purpose, we extracted named entities from millions of tweets, using a Twitter-tuned NER system (Ritter et al., 2011). Our initial training set was collected over a one-year period spanning from January 2012 to January 2013. Each subsequent Twitter test set was collected a few months prior to the corresponding evaluation. We used the public streaming Twitter API to download the tweets.

We then identified popular topics as those named entities that are frequently mentioned in association with a specific date (Ritter et al., 2012). Given this set of automatically identified topics, we gathered tweets from the same time period which mentioned the named entities. The testing messages had different topics from training and spanned later periods.

The collected tweets were greatly skewed towards the neutral class. In order to reduce the class imbalance, we removed messages that contained no sentiment-bearing words using SentiWordNet as a repository of sentiment words. Any word listed in SentiWordNet 3.0 with at least one sense having a positive or a negative sentiment score greater than 0.3 was considered a sentiment-bearing word.[2]

For subtasks C and D, we did some manual pruning based on the topics. First, we excluded topics that were incomprehensible, ambiguous (e.g., *Barcelona*, which is a name of a sports team and also of a place), or were too general (e.g., *Paris*, which is a name of a big city). Second, we discarded tweets that were just mentioning the topic, but were not really about the topic. Finally, we discarded topics with too few tweets, namely less than 10.

[2]Filtering based on an existing lexicon does bias the dataset to some degree; however, note that the text still contains sentiment expressions outside those in the lexicon.

Instructions: Subjective words are ones which convey an opinion or sentiment. Given a Twitter message, identify whether it is objective, positive, negative, or neutral. Then, identify each subjective word or phrase in the context of the sentence and mark the position of its start and end in the text boxes below. The number above each word indicates its position. The word/phrase will be generated in the adjacent textbox so that you can confirm that you chose the correct range. Choose the polarity of the word or phrase by selecting one of the radio buttons: positive, negative, or neutral. If a sentence is not subjective please select the checkbox indicating that "There are no subjective words/phrases". If a tweet is sarcastic, please select the checkbox indicating that "The tweet is sarcastic". Please read the examples and invalid responses before beginning if this is your first time answering this hit.

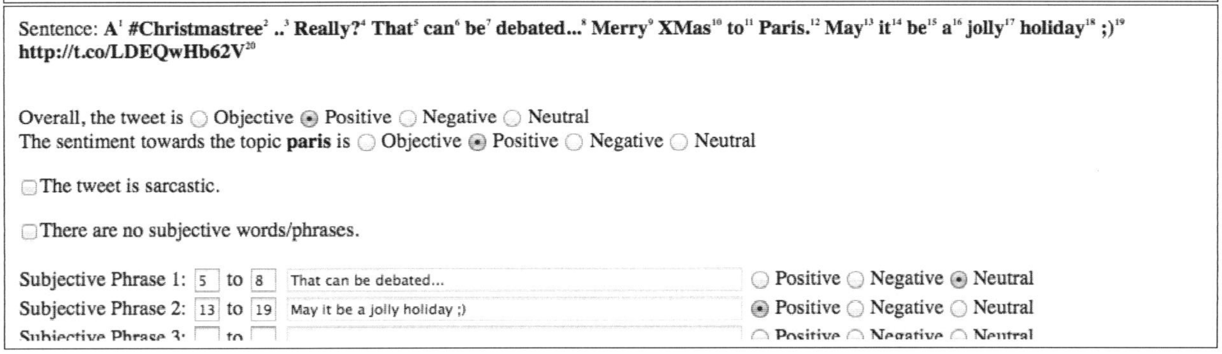

Figure 1: The instructions we gave to the workers on Mechanical Turk, followed by a screenshot.

3.1.2 Subtask E

We selected high-frequency target terms from the Sentiment140 and the Hashtag Sentiment tweet corpora (Kiritchenko et al., 2014). In order to reduce the skewness towards the neutral class, we selected terms from different ranges of automatically determined sentiment values as provided by the corresponding Sentiment140 and Hashtag Sentiment lexicons. The term set comprised regular English words, hashtagged words (e.g., *#loveumom*), misspelled or creatively spelled words (e.g., *parlament* or *happeeee*), abbreviations, shortenings, and slang. Some terms were negated expressions such as *no fun*. (It is known that negation impacts the sentiment of its scope in complex ways (Zhu et al., 2014).) We annotated these terms for degree of sentiment manually. Further details about the data collection and the annotation process can be found in Section 3.2.2 as well as in (Kiritchenko et al., 2014).

The trial dataset consisted of 200 instances, and no training dataset was provided. Note, however, that the trial data was large enough to be used as a development set, or even as a training set. Moreover, the participants were free to use any additional manually or automatically generated resources when building their systems for subtask E. The testset included 1,315 instances.

3.2 Annotation

Below we describe the data annotation process.

3.2.1 Subtasks A–D

We used Amazon's Mechanical Turk for the annotations of subtasks A–D. Each tweet message was annotated by five Mechanical Turk workers, also known as Turkers. The annotations for subtasks A–D were done concurrently, in a single task. A Turker had to mark all the subjective words/phrases in the tweet message by indicating their start and end positions and to say whether each subjective word/phrase was positive, negative, or neutral (subtask A). He/she also had to indicate the overall polarity of the tweet message in general (subtask B) as well as the overall polarity of the message towards the given target topic (subtasks C and D). The instructions we gave to the Turkers, along with an example, are shown in Figure 1. We further made available to the Turkers several additional examples, which we show in Table 1.

Providing all the required annotations for a given tweet message constituted a Human Intelligence Task, or a HIT. In order to qualify to work on our HITs, a Turker had to have an approval rate greater than 95% and should have completed at least 50 approved HITs.

Authorities are *only too aware* that Kashgar is 4,000 kilometres (2,500 miles) from Beijing but *only* a tenth of the distance from the Pakistani border, and are *desperate* to *ensure instability or militancy* does not leak over the frontiers.

Taiwan-made products *stood a good chance* of becoming *even more competitive thanks to* wider access to overseas markets and lower costs for material imports, he said.

"March *appears* to be a *more reasonable* estimate while earlier admission *cannot be entirely ruled out*," according to Chen, also Taiwan's chief WTO negotiator.

friday evening plans were great, but saturday's plans *didnt go as expected* – i went dancing & it was an *ok* club, but *terribly crowded :-(*

WHY THE *HELL* DO YOU GUYS ALL HAVE MRS. KENNEDY! SHES A FUCKING DOUCHE

AT&T was *okay* but whenever they do something *nice* in the name of customer service it seems like a favor, while T-Mobile makes that a *normal everyday thin*

obama should be *impeached* on *TREASON* charges. Our Nuclear arsenal was TOP Secret. Till HE told our enemies what we had. *#Coward #Traitor*

My graduation speech: "I'd like to *thanks* Google, Wikipedia and my computer!" *:D* #iThingteens

Table 1: List of example sentences and annotations we provided to the Turkers. All subjective phrases are italicized and color-coded: positive phrases are in green, negative ones are in red, and neutral ones are in blue.

I would love to watch Vampire Diaries ***:)*** and some Heroes! ***Great combination***	9/13
I would love to watch Vampire Diaries :) and some ***Heroes! Great*** combination	11/13
I ***would love*** to watch Vampire Diaries ***:)*** and some Heroes! ***Great*** combination	10/13
I would ***love*** to watch Vampire Diaries :) and some Heroes! ***Great*** combination	13/13
I would love to watch Vampire Diaries :) and some Heroes! ***Great*** combination	12/13
I would ***love*** to watch Vampire Diaries :) and some Heroes! ***Great*** combination	

Table 2: Example of a sentence annotated for subjectivity on Mechanical Turk. Words and phrases that were marked as subjective are in bold italic. The first five rows are annotations provided by Turkers, and the final row shows their intersection. The last column shows the token-level accuracy for each annotation compared to the intersection.

We further discarded the following types of message annotations:

- containing overlapping subjective phrases;
- marked as subjective but having no annotated subjective phrases;
- with every single word marked as subjective;
- with no overall sentiment marked;
- with no topic sentiment marked.

Recall that each tweet message was annotated by five different Turkers. We consolidated these annotations for subtask A using intersection as shown in the last row of Table 2. A word had to appear in 3/5 of the annotations in order to be considered subjective. It further had to be labeled with a particular polarity (positive, negative, or neutral) by three of the five Turkers in order to receive that polarity label. As the example shows, this effectively shortens the spans of the annotated phrases, often to single words, as it is hard to agree on long phrases.

Corpus	Pos.	Neg.	Obj. / Neu.	Total
Twitter2013-train	5,895	3,131	471	9,497
Twitter2013-dev	648	430	57	1,135
Twitter2013-test	2,734	1,541	160	4,435
SMS2013-test	1,071	1,104	159	2,334
Twitter2014-test	1,807	578	88	2,473
Twitter2014-sarcasm	82	37	5	124
LiveJournal2014-test	660	511	144	1,315
Twitter2015-test	1899	1008	190	3097

Table 3: Dataset statistics for subtask A.

We also experimented with two alternative methods for combining annotations: (*i*) by computing the union of the annotations for the sentence, and (*ii*) by taking the annotations by the Turker who has annotated the highest number of HITs. However, our manual analysis has shown that both alternatives performed worse than using the intersection.

Corpus	Pos.	Neg.	Obj. / Neu.	Total
Twitter2013-train	3,662	1,466	4,600	9,728
Twitter2013-dev	575	340	739	1,654
Twitter2013-test	1,572	601	1,640	3,813
SMS2013-test	492	394	1,207	2,093
Twitter2014-test	982	202	669	1,853
Twitter2014-sarcasm	33	40	13	86
LiveJournal2014-test	427	304	411	1,142
Twitter2015-test	1040	365	987	2392

Table 4: Dataset statistics for subtask B.

Corpus	Topics	Pos.	Neg.	Obj. / Neu.	Total
Train	44	142	56	288	530
Test	137	870	260	1256	2386

Table 5: Twitter-2015 statistics for subtasks C & D.

For subtasks B and C, we consolidated the tweet-level annotations using majority voting, requiring that the winning label be proposed by at least three of the five Turkers; we discarded all tweets for which 3/5 majority could not be achieved. As in previous years, we combined the objective and the neutral labels, which Turkers tended to mix up.

We used these consolidated annotations as gold labels for subtasks A, B, C & D. The statistics for all datasets for these subtasks are shown in Tables 3, 4, and 5, respectively. Each dataset is marked with the year of the SemEval edition it was produced for. An annotated example from each source (Twitter, SMS, LiveJournal) is shown in Table 6; examples for sentiment towards a topic can be seen in Table 7.

3.2.2 Subtask E

Subtask E asks systems to propose a numerical score for the positiveness of a given word or phrase. Many studies have shown that people are actually quite bad at assigning such absolute scores: inter-annotator agreement is low, and annotators struggle even to remain self-consistent. In contrast, it is much easier to make relative judgments, e.g., to say whether one word is more positive than another. Moreover, it is possible to derive an absolute score from pairwise judgments, but this requires a much larger number of annotations. Fortunately, there are schemes that allow to infer more pairwise annotations from less judgments.

One such annotation scheme is MaxDiff (Louviere, 1991), which is widely used in market surveys (Almquist and Lee, 2009); it was also used in a previous SemEval task (Jurgens et al., 2012).

In MaxDiff, the annotator is presented with four terms and asked which term is most positive and which is least positive. By answering just these two questions, five out of six pairwise rankings become known. Consider a set in which a judge evaluates A, B, C, and D. If she says that A and D are the most and the least positive, we can infer the following: $A > B, A > C, A > D, B > D, C > D$. The responses to the MaxDiff questions can then be easily translated into a ranking for all the terms and also into a real-valued score for each term. We crowdsourced the MaxDiff questions on CrowdFlower, recruiting ten annotators per MaxDiff example. Further details can be found in Section 6.1.2. of (Kiritchenko et al., 2014).

3.3 Lower & Upper Bounds

When building a system to solve a task, it is good to know how well we should expect it to perform. One good reference point is agreement between annotators. Unfortunately, as we derive annotations by agreement, we cannot calculate standard statistics such as Kappa. Instead, we decided to measure the agreement between our gold standard annotations (derived by agreement) and the annotations proposed by the best Turker, the worst Turker, and the average Turker (with respect to the gold/consensus annotation for a particular message). Given a HIT, we just calculate the overlaps as shown in the last column in Table 2, and then we calculate the best, the worst, and the average, which are respectively 13/13, 9/13 and 11/13, in the example. Finally, we average these statistics over all HITs that contributed to a given dataset, to produce lower, average, and upper averages for that dataset. The accuracy (with respect to the gold/consensus annotation) for different averages is shown in Table 8. Since the overall polarity of a message is chosen based on majority, the upper bound for subtask B is 100%. These averages give a good indication about how well we can expect the systems to perform. We can see that even if we used the best annotator for each HIT, it would still not be possible to get perfect accuracy, and thus we should also not expect it from a system.

Source	Message	Message-Level Polarity
Twitter	Why would you [still]- wear shorts when it's this cold?! I [love]+ how Britain see's a bit of sun and they're [like 'OOOH]+ LET'S STRIP!'	positive
SMS	[Sorry]- I think tonight [cannot]- and I [not feeling well]- after my rest.	negative
LiveJournal	[Cool]+ posts , dude ; very [colorful]+ , and [artsy]+ .	positive
Twitter Sarcasm	[Thanks]+ manager for putting me on the schedule for Sunday	negative

Table 6: Example annotations for each source of messages. The subjective phrases are marked in [...], and are followed by their polarity (subtask A); the message-level polarity is shown in the last column (subtask B).

Topic	Message	Message-Level Polarity	Topic-Level Polarity
leeds united	Saturday without Leeds United is like Sunday dinner it doesn't feel normal at all (Ryan)	negative	positive
demi lovato	Who are you tomorrow? Will you make me smile or just bring me sorrow? #HottieOfTheWeek Demi Lovato	neutral	positive

Table 7: Example of annotations in Twitter showing differences between topic- and message-level polarity.

Corpus	Subtask A			Subtask B
	Low	Avg	Up	Avg
Twitter2013-train	75.1	89.7	97.9	77.6
Twitter2013-dev	66.6	85.3	97.1	86.4
Twitter2013-test	76.8	90.3	98.0	75.9
SMS2013-test	75.9	97.5	89.6	77.5
Livejournal2014-test	61.7	82.3	94.5	76.2
Twitter2014-test	75.3	88.9	97.5	74.7
Sarcasm2014-test	62.6	83.1	95.6	71.2
Twitter2015-test	73.2	87.6	96.8	75.7

Table 8: Average (over all HITs) overlap of the gold annotations with the worst, average, and the worst Turker for each HIT, for subtasks A and B.

3.4 Tweets Delivery

Due to restrictions in the Twitter's terms of service, we could not deliver the annotated tweets to the participants directly. Instead, we released annotation indexes and labels, a list of corresponding Twitter IDs, and a download script that extracts the corresponding tweets via the Twitter API.[3]

As a result, different teams had access to different number of training tweets depending on when they did the downloading. However, our analysis has shown that this did not have a major impact and many high-scoring teams had less training data compared to some lower-scoring ones.

[3]https://dev.twitter.com

4 Scoring

4.1 Subtasks A-C: Phrase-Level, Message-Level, and Topic-Level Polarity

The participating systems were required to perform a three-way classification, i.e., to assign one of the folowing three labels: *positive*, *negative* or *objective/neutral*. We evaluated the systems in terms of a macro-averaged F_1 score for predicting positive and negative phrases/messages.

We first computed positive precision, P_{pos} as follows: we found the number of phrases/messages that a system correctly predicted to be positive, and we divided that number by the total number of examples it predicted to be positive. To compute positive recall, R_{pos}, we found the number of phrases/messages correctly predicted to be positive and we divided that number by the total number of positives in the gold standard. We then calculated an F_1 score for the positive class as follows $F_{pos} = \frac{2P_{pos}R_{pos}}{P_{pos}+R_{pos}}$. We carried out similar computations for the negative phrases/messages, F_{neg}. The overall score was then computed as the average of the F_1scores for the positive and for the negative classes: $F = (F_{pos} + F_{neg})/2$.

We provided the participants with a scorer that outputs the overall score F, as well as P, R, and F_1 scores for each class (positive, negative, neutral) and for each test set.

4.2 Subtask D: Overall Polarity Towards a Topic

This subtask asks to predict the overall sentiment of a set of tweets towards a given topic. In other words, to predict the ratio r_i of positive (pos_i) tweets to the number of positive and negative sentiment tweets in the set of tweets about the i-th topic:

$$r_i = Pos_i/(Pos_i + Neg_i)$$

Note, that neutral tweets do not participate in the above formula; they have only an indirect impact on the calculation, similarly to subtasks A–C.

We use the following two evaluation measures for subtask D:

- **AvgDiff** (official score): Calculates the absolute difference betweeen the predicted r'_i and the gold r_i for each i, and then averages this difference over all topics.

- **AvgLevelDiff** (unofficial score): This calculation is the same as AvgDiff, but with r'_i and r_i first remapped to five coarse numerical categories: 5 (strongly positive), 4 (weakly positive), 3 (mixed), 2 (weakly negative), and 1 (strongly negative). We define this remapping based on intervals as follows:
  - 5: $0.8 < x \leq 1.0$
  - 4: $0.6 < x \leq 0.8$
  - 3: $0.4 < x \leq 0.6$
  - 2: $0.2 < x \leq 0.4$
  - 1: $0.0 \leq x \leq 0.2$

4.3 Subtask E: Degree of Prior Polarity

The scores proposed by the participating systems were evaluated by first ranking the terms according to the proposed sentiment score and then comparing this ranked list to a ranked list obtained from aggregating the human ranking annotations. We used Kendall's rank correlation (Kendall's τ) as the official evaluation metric to compare the ranked lists (Kendall, 1938). We also calculated scores for Spearman's rank correlation (Lehmann and D'Abrera, 2006), as an unofficial score.

Team ID	Affiliation
CIS-positiv	University of Munich
CLaC-SentiPipe	CLaC Labs, Concordia University
DIEGOLab	Arizona State University
ECNU	East China Normal University
elirf	Universitat Politècnica de València
Frisbee	Frisbee
Gradiant-Analytics	Gradiant
GTI	AtlantTIC Center, University of Vigo
IHS-RD	IHS inc
iitpsemeval	Indian Institute of Technology, Patna
IIIT-H	IIIT, Hyderabad
INESC-ID	IST, INESC-ID
IOA	Institute of Acoustics, Chinese Academy of Sciences
KLUEless	FAU Erlangen-Nürnberg
lsislif	Aix-Marseille University
NLP	NLP
RGUSentimentMiners123	Robert Gordon University
RoseMerry	The University of Melbourne
Sentibase	IIIT, Hyderabad
SeNTU	Nanyang Technological University, Singapore
SHELLFBK	Fondazione Bruno Kessler
sigma2320	Peking University
Splusplus	Beihang University
SWASH	Swarthmore College
SWATAC	Swarthmore College
SWATCMW	Swarthmore College
SWATCS65	Swarthmore College
Swiss-Chocolate	Zurich University of Applied Sciences
TwitterHawk	University of Massachusetts, Lowell
UDLAP2014	Universidad de las Américas Puebla, Mexico
UIR-PKU	University of International Relations
UMDuluth-CS8761	University of Minnesota, Duluth
UNIBA	University of Bari Aldo Moro
unitn	University of Trento
UPF-taln	Universitat Pompeu Fabra
WarwickDCS	University of Warwick
Webis	Bauhaus-Universität Weimar
whu-iss	International Software School, Wuhan University
Whu-Nlp	Computer School, Wuhan University
wxiaoac	Hong Kong University of Science and Technology
ZWJYYC	Peking University

Table 9: The participating teams and their affiliations.

5 Participants and Results

The task attracted 41 teams: 11 teams participated in subtask A, 40 in subtask B, 7 in subtask C, 6 in subtask D, and 10 in subtask E. The IDs and affiliations of the participating teams are shown in Table 9.

5.1 Subtask A: Phrase-Level Polarity

The results (macro-averaged F_1 score) for subtask A are shown in Table 10. The official results on the new Twitter2015-test dataset are shown in the last column, while the first five columns show F_1 on the 2013 and on the 2014 progress test datasets:[4] Twitter2013-test, SMS2013-test, Twitter2014-test, Twitter2014-sarcasm, and LiveJournal2014-test. There is an index for each result showing the relative rank of that result within the respective column. The participating systems are ranked by their score on the Twitter2015-test dataset, which is the official ranking for subtask A; all remaining rankings are secondary.

[4]Note that the 2013 and the 2014 test datasets were made available for development, but it was explicitly forbidden to use them for training.

#	System	2013: Progress Tweet	2013: Progress SMS	2014: Progress Tweet	2014: Progress Tweet sarcasm	2014: Progress Live-Journal	2015: Official Tweet
1	unitn	90.10_{1}	88.60_{2}	87.12_{1}	73.65_{5}	84.46_{2}	**84.79_{1}**
2	KLUEless	88.56_{2}	88.62_{1}	84.99_{3}	75.59_{4}	83.94_{4}	**84.51_{2}**
3	IOA	83.90_{7}	84.18_{7}	85.37_{2}	71.58_{6}	85.61_{1}	**82.76_{3}**
4	WarwickDCS	84.08_{6}	84.40_{5}	83.89_{5}	78.03_{2}	83.18_{5}	**82.46_{4}**
5	TwitterHawk	82.87_{8}	83.64_{8}	84.05_{4}	75.62_{3}	83.97_{3}	**82.32_{5}**
6	iitpsemeval	85.81_{3}	85.86_{3}	82.73_{6}	65.71_{9}	81.76_{7}	**81.31_{6}**
7	ECNU	85.28_{4}	84.70_{4}	82.09_{7}	70.96_{7}	82.49_{6}	**81.08_{7}**
8	Whu-Nlp	79.76_{9}	81.78_{9}	81.69_{8}	63.14_{11}	80.87_{9}	**78.84_{8}**
9	GTI	84.64_{5}	84.37_{6}	79.48_{9}	81.53_{1}	81.61_{8}	**77.27_{9}**
10	whu-iss	74.02_{10}	70.26_{11}	72.20_{10}	69.33_{8}	73.57_{10}	**71.35_{10}**
11	UMDuluth-CS8761	72.71_{11}	71.80_{10}	69.84_{11}	64.53_{10}	71.53_{11}	**66.21_{11}**
	baseline	38.1	31.5	42.2	39.8	33.4	**38.0**

Table 10: **Results for subtask A: Phrase-Level Polarity.** The systems are ordered by their score on the Twitter2015 test dataset; the rankings on the individual datasets are indicated with a subscript.

There were less participants this year, probably due to having a new similar subtask: C. Notably, many of the participating teams were newcomers.

We can see that all systems beat the majority class baseline by 25-40 F_1 points absolute on all datasets. The winning team unitn (using deep convolutional neural networks) achieved an F_1 of 84.79 on Twitter2015-test, followed closely by KLUEless (using logistic regression) with F_1=84.51.

Looking at the progress datasets, we can see that unitn was also first on both progress Tweet datasets, and second on SMS and on LiveJournal. KLUEless won SMS and was second on Twitter2013-test. The best result on LiveJournal was achieved by IOA, who were also second on Twitter2014-test and third on the official Twitter2015-test. None of these teams was ranked in top-3 on Twitter2014-sarcasm, where the best team was GTI, followed by WarwickDCS.

Compared to 2014, there is an improvement on Twitter2014-test from 86.63 in 2014 (NRC-Canada) to 87.12 in 2015 (unitn). The best result on Twitter2013-test of 90.10 (unitn) this year is very close to the best in 2014 (90.14 by NRC-Canada). Similarly, the best result on LiveJournal stays exactly the same, i.e., F_1=85.61 (SentiKLUE in 2014 and IOA in 2015). However, there is slight degradation for SMS2013-test from 89.31 (ECNU) in 2014 to 88.62 (KLUEless) in 2015. The results also degraded for Twitter2014-sarcasm from 82.75 (senti.ue) to 81.53 (GTI).

5.2 Subtask B: Message-Level Polarity

The results for subtask B are shown in Table 11. Again, we show results on the five progress test datasets from 2013 and 2014, in addition to those for the official Twitter2015-test datasets.

Subtask B attracted 40 teams, both newcomers and returning, similarly to 2013 and 2014. All managed to beat the baseline with the exception of one system for Twitter2015-test, and one for Twitter2014-test. There is a cluster of four teams at the top: Webis (ensemble combining four Twitter sentiment classification approaches that participated in previous editions) with an F_1 of 64.84, unitn with 64.59, lsislif (logistic regression with special weighting for positives and negatives) with 64.27, and INESC-ID (word embeddings) with 64.17.

The last column in the table shows the results for the 2015 sarcastic tweets. Note that, unlike in 2014, this time they were not collected separately and did not have a special #sarcasm tag; instead, they are a subset of 75 tweets from Twitter2015-test that were flagged as sarcastic by the human annotators. The top system is IOA with an F_1 of 65.77, followed by INESC-ID with 64.91, and NLP with 63.62.

Looking at the progress datasets, we can see that the second ranked unitn is also second on SMS and on Twitter2014-test, and third on Twitter2013-test. INESC-ID in turn is third on Twitter2014-test and also third on Twitter2014-sarcasm. Webis and lsislif were less strong on the progress datasets.

#	System	2013: Progress Tweet	2013: Progress SMS	2014: Progress Tweet	2014: Progress Tweet sarcasm	2014: Progress Live-Journal	2015: Official Tweet	2015: Official Tweet sarcasm
1	Webis	68.49$_{10}$	63.92$_{14}$	70.86$_{7}$	49.33$_{12}$	71.64$_{14}$	**64.84**$_{1}$	53.59$_{22}$
2	unitn	72.79$_{2}$	68.37$_{2}$	73.60$_{2}$	55.44$_{5}$	72.48$_{12}$	**64.59**$_{2}$	55.01$_{19}$
3	lsislif	71.34$_{4}$	63.42$_{17}$	71.54$_{5}$	46.57$_{22}$	73.01$_{10}$	**64.27**$_{3}$	46.00$_{33}$
4	INESC-ID*	71.97$_{3}$	63.78$_{15}$	72.52$_{3}$	56.23$_{3}$	69.78$_{22}$	**64.17**$_{4}$	64.91$_{2}$
5	Splusplus	72.80$_{1}$	67.16$_{5}$	74.42$_{1}$	42.86$_{31}$	75.34$_{1}$	**63.73**$_{5}$	60.99$_{7}$
6	wxiaoac	66.43$_{16}$	64.04$_{13}$	68.96$_{11}$	54.38$_{7}$	73.36$_{9}$	**63.00**$_{6}$	52.22$_{26}$
7	IOA	71.32$_{5}$	68.14$_{3}$	71.86$_{4}$	51.48$_{9}$	74.52$_{2}$	**62.62**$_{7}$	65.77$_{1}$
8	Swiss-Chocolate	68.80$_{9}$	65.56$_{6}$	68.74$_{12}$	48.22$_{16}$	73.95$_{4}$	**62.61**$_{8}$	54.66$_{20}$
9	CLaC-SentiPipe	70.42$_{7}$	63.05$_{18}$	70.16$_{10}$	51.43$_{10}$	73.59$_{6}$	**62.00**$_{9}$	58.55$_{9}$
10	TwitterHawk	68.44$_{11}$	62.12$_{20}$	70.64$_{9}$	56.02$_{4}$	70.17$_{19}$	**61.99**$_{10}$	61.24$_{6}$
11	SWATCS65	68.21$_{12}$	65.49$_{8}$	67.23$_{14}$	37.23$_{39}$	73.37$_{8}$	**61.89**$_{11}$	52.64$_{24}$
12	UNIBA	61.66$_{29}$	65.50$_{7}$	65.11$_{25}$	37.30$_{38}$	70.05$_{20}$	**61.55**$_{12}$	48.16$_{32}$
13	KLUEless	70.64$_{6}$	67.66$_{4}$	70.89$_{6}$	45.36$_{26}$	73.50$_{7}$	**61.20**$_{13}$	56.19$_{17}$
14	NLP	66.96$_{14}$	61.05$_{25}$	67.45$_{13}$	39.87$_{34}$	66.12$_{31}$	**60.93**$_{14}$	63.62$_{3}$
15	ZWJYYC	69.56$_{8}$	64.72$_{11}$	70.77$_{8}$	46.34$_{23}$	71.60$_{15}$	**60.77**$_{15}$	52.40$_{25}$
16	Gradiant-Analytics	65.29$_{22}$	61.97$_{21}$	66.87$_{17}$	59.11$_{1}$	72.63$_{11}$	**60.62**$_{16}$	56.45$_{16}$
17	IIIT-H	65.68$_{20}$	62.25$_{19}$	67.04$_{16}$	57.50$_{2}$	69.91$_{21}$	**59.83**$_{17}$	62.75$_{5}$
18	ECNU	65.25$_{23}$	68.49$_{1}$	66.37$_{20}$	45.87$_{25}$	74.40$_{3}$	**59.72**$_{18}$	52.67$_{23}$
19	CIS-positiv	64.82$_{24}$	65.14$_{10}$	66.05$_{21}$	49.23$_{14}$	71.47$_{16}$	**59.57**$_{19}$	57.74$_{11}$
20	SWASH	63.07$_{27}$	56.49$_{34}$	62.93$_{31}$	48.42$_{15}$	69.43$_{24}$	**59.26**$_{20}$	54.30$_{21}$
21	GTI	64.03$_{25}$	63.50$_{16}$	65.65$_{22}$	55.38$_{6}$	70.50$_{17}$	**58.95**$_{21}$	57.02$_{13}$
22	iitpsemeval	60.78$_{31}$	60.56$_{26}$	65.09$_{26}$	47.32$_{19}$	73.70$_{5}$	**58.80**$_{22}$	58.18$_{10}$
23	elirf	57.05$_{32}$	60.20$_{28}$	61.17$_{35}$	45.98$_{24}$	68.33$_{28}$	**58.58**$_{23}$	43.91$_{34}$
24	SWATAC	65.86$_{19}$	61.30$_{24}$	66.64$_{19}$	39.45$_{35}$	68.67$_{27}$	**58.43**$_{24}$	50.66$_{27}$
25	UIR-PKU*	67.41$_{13}$	64.67$_{12}$	67.18$_{15}$	52.58$_{8}$	70.44$_{18}$	**57.65**$_{25}$	59.43$_{8}$
26	SWATCMW	65.67$_{21}$	65.43$_{9}$	65.62$_{23}$	37.48$_{36}$	69.52$_{23}$	**57.60**$_{26}$	56.69$_{14}$
27	WarwickDCS	66.57$_{15}$	61.92$_{22}$	65.47$_{24}$	45.03$_{28}$	68.98$_{25}$	**57.32**$_{27}$	56.58$_{15}$
28	SeNTU	63.50$_{26}$	60.53$_{27}$	66.85$_{18}$	45.18$_{27}$	68.70$_{26}$	**57.06**$_{28}$	49.53$_{29}$
29	DIEGOLab	62.49$_{28}$	58.60$_{30}$	63.99$_{28}$	47.62$_{18}$	63.74$_{34}$	**56.72**$_{29}$	55.56$_{18}$
30	Sentibase	61.56$_{30}$	59.26$_{29}$	63.29$_{30}$	47.07$_{20}$	67.55$_{29}$	**56.67**$_{30}$	62.96$_{4}$
31	Whu-Nlp	65.97$_{18}$	61.31$_{23}$	63.93$_{29}$	46.93$_{21}$	71.83$_{13}$	**56.39**$_{31}$	22.25$_{40}$
32	UPF-taln	66.15$_{17}$	57.84$_{31}$	65.05$_{27}$	50.93$_{11}$	64.50$_{32}$	**55.59**$_{32}$	41.63$_{35}$
33	RGUSentimentMiners123	56.41$_{34}$	57.14$_{32}$	59.44$_{36}$	44.72$_{29}$	64.39$_{33}$	**53.73**$_{33}$	48.21$_{31}$
34	IHS-RD*	55.06$_{35}$	57.08$_{33}$	61.39$_{32}$	37.32$_{37}$	66.99$_{30}$	**52.65**$_{34}$	36.02$_{37}$
35	RoseMerry	52.33$_{37}$	53.00$_{36}$	61.27$_{34}$	49.25$_{13}$	62.54$_{35}$	**51.18**$_{35}$	49.62$_{28}$
36	Frisbee	49.37$_{38}$	46.59$_{38}$	53.92$_{38}$	42.07$_{32}$	57.94$_{38}$	**49.19**$_{36}$	48.26$_{30}$
37	UMDuluth-CS8761	54.17$_{36}$	50.64$_{37}$	55.82$_{37}$	43.74$_{30}$	60.23$_{37}$	**47.77**$_{37}$	34.40$_{38}$
38	UDLAP2014	41.93$_{39}$	39.35$_{39}$	45.93$_{39}$	41.04$_{33}$	50.11$_{39}$	**42.10**$_{38}$	40.59$_{36}$
39	SHELLFBK	32.14$_{40}$	26.14$_{40}$	32.20$_{40}$	35.58$_{40}$	34.06$_{40}$	**32.45**$_{39}$	25.73$_{39}$
40	whu-iss	56.51$_{33}$	54.28$_{35}$	61.31$_{33}$	47.78$_{17}$	61.98$_{36}$	**24.80**$_{40}$	57.73$_{12}$
	baseline	29.2	19.0	34.6	27.7	27.2	**30.3**	30.2

Table 11: **Results for subtask B: Message-Level Polarity.** The systems are ordered by their score on the Twitter2015 test dataset; the rankings on the individual datasets are indicated with a subscript. Systems with late submissions for the *progress* test datasets (but with timely submissions for the official 2015 test dataset) are marked with a *.

Compared to 2014, there is improvement on Twitter2013-test from 72.12 (TeamX) to 72.80 (Splusplus), on Twitter2014-test from 70.96 (TeamX) to 74.42 (Spluplus), on Twitter2014-sarcasm from 58.16 (NRC-Canada) to 59.11 (Gradiant-Analytics), and on LiveJournal from 74.84 (NRC-Canada) to 75.34 (Splusplus), but not on SMS: 70.28 (NRC-Canada) vs. 68.49 (ECNU).

#	System	Tweet	Tweet sarcasm
1	TwitterHawk	**50.51**$_1$	31.30$_2$
2	KLUEless	**45.48**$_2$	39.26$_1$
3	Whu-Nlp	**40.70**$_3$	23.37$_5$
4	whu-iss	**25.62**$_4$	28.90$_4$
5	ECNU	**25.38**$_5$	16.20$_6$
6	WarwickDCS	**22.79**$_6$	13.57$_7$
7	UMDuluth-CS8761	**18.99**$_7$	29.91$_3$
	baseline	**26.7**	26.4

Table 12: **Results for Subtask C: Topic-Level Polarity.** The systems are ordered by the official 2015 score.

#	Team	avgDiff	avgLevelDiff
1	KLUEless	**0.202**	0.810
2	Whu-Nlp	**0.210**	0.869
3	TwitterHawk	**0.214**	0.978
4	whu-iss	**0.256**	1.007
5	ECNU	**0.300**	1.190
6	UMDuluth-CS8761	**0.309**	1.314
	baseline	**0.277**	0.985

Table 13: **Results for Subtask D: Trend Towards a Topic.** The systems are sorted by the official 2015 score.

5.3 Subtask C: Topic-Level Polarity

The results for subtask C are shown in Table 12. This proved to be a hard subtask, and only three of the seven teams that participated in it managed to improve over a majority vote baseline. These three teams, TwitterHawk (using subtask B data to help with subtask C) with F_1=50.51, KLUEless (which ignored the topics as if it was subtask B) with F_1=45.48, and Whu-Nlp with F_1=40.70, achieved scores that outperform the rest by a sizable margin: 15-25 points absolute more than the fourth team.

Note that, despite the apparent similarity, subtask C is much harder than subtask B: the top-3 teams achieved an F_1 of 64-65 for subtask B vs. an F_1 of 41-51 for subtask C. This cannot be blamed on the class distribution, as the difference in performance of the majority class baseline is much smaller: 30.3 for B vs. 26.7 for C.

Finally, the last column in the table reports the results for the 75 sarcastic 2015 tweets. The winner here is KLUEless with an F_1 of 39.26, followed by TwitterHawk with F_1=31.30, and then by UMDuluth-CS8761 with F_1=29.91.

5.4 Subtask D: Trend Towards a Topic

The results for subtask D are shown in Table 13. This subtask is closely related to subtask C (in fact, one obvious way to solve D is to solve C and then to calculate the proportion), and thus it has attracted the same teams, except for one. Again, only three of the participating teams managed to improve over the baseline; not suprisingly, those were the same three teams that were in top-3 for subtask C. However, the ranking is different from that in subtask C, e.g., TwitterHawk has dropped to third position, while KLUEless and Why-Nlp have each climbed one position up to positions 1 and 2, respectively.

Finally, note that avgDiff and avgLevelDiff yielded the same rankings.

5.5 Subtask E: Degree of Prior Polarity

Ten teams participated in subtask E. Many chose an unsupervised approach and leveraged newly-created and pre-existing sentiment lexicons such as the Hashtag Sentiment Lexicon, the Sentiment140 Lexicon (Kiritchenko et al., 2014), the MPQA Subjectivity Lexicon (Wilson et al., 2005), and SentiWordNet (Baccianella et al., 2010), among others. Several participants further automatically created their own sentiment lexicons from large collections of tweets. Three teams, including the winner INESC-ID, adopted a supervised approach and used word embeddings (supplemented with lexicon features) to train a regression model.

The results are presented in Table 14. The last row shows the performance of a lexicon-based baseline. For this baseline, we chose the two most frequently used existing, publicly available, and automatically generated sentiment lexicons: Hashtag Sentiment Lexicon and Sentiment140 Lexicon (Kiritchenko et al., 2014).[5] These lexicons have real-valued sentiment scores for most of the terms in the test set. For negated phrases, we use the scores of the corresponding negated entries in the lexicons. For each term, we take its score from the Sentiment140 Lexicon if present; otherwise, we take the term's score from the Hashtag Sentiment Lexicon. For terms not found in any lexicon, we use the score of 0, which indicates a neutral term in these lexicons. The top three teams were able to improve over the baseline.

[5] `http://www.purl.com/net/lexicons`

Team	Kendall's τ coefficient	Spearman's ρ coefficient
INESC-ID	**0.6251**	0.8172
lsislif	**0.6211**	0.8202
ECNU	**0.5907**	0.7861
CLaC-SentiPipe	**0.5836**	0.7771
KLUEless	**0.5771**	0.7662
UMDuluth-CS8761-10	**0.5733**	0.7618
IHS-RD-Belarus	**0.5143**	0.7121
sigma2320	**0.5132**	0.7086
iitpsemeval	**0.4131**	0.5859
RGUSentminers123	**0.2537**	0.3728
Baseline	**0.5842**	0.7843

Table 14: **Results for Subtask E: Degree of Prior Polarity.** The systems are ordered by their Kendall's τ score, which was the official score.

6 Discussion

As in the previous two years, almost all systems used supervised learning. Popular machine learning approaches included SVM, maximum entropy, CRFs, and linear regression. In several of the subtasks, the top system used deep neural networks and word embeddings, and some systems benefited from special weighting of the positive and negative examples.

Once again, the most important features were those derived from sentiment lexicons. Other important features included bag-of-words features, hashtags, handling of negation, word shape and punctuation features, elongated words, etc. Moreover, tweet pre-processing and normalization were an important part of the processing pipeline.

Note that this year we did not make a distinction between constrained and unconstrained systems, and participants were free to use any additional data, resources and tools they wished to.

Overall, the task has attracted a total of 41 teams, which is comparable to previous editions: there were 46 teams in 2014, and 44 in 2013. As in previous years, subtask B was most popular, attracting almost all teams (40 out of 41). However, subtask A attracted just a quarter of the participants (11 out of 41), compared to about half in previous years, most likely due to the introduction of two new, very related subtasks C and D (with 6 and 7 participants, respectively). There was also a fifth subtask (E, with 10 participants), which further contributed to the participant split.

We should further note that our task was part of a larger Sentiment Track, together with three other closely-related tasks, which were also interested in sentiment analysis: Task 9 on CLIPEval Implicit Polarity of Events, Task 11 on Sentiment Analysis of Figurative Language in Twitter, and Task 12 on Aspect Based Sentiment Analysis. Another related task was Task 1 on Paraphrase and Semantic Similarity in Twitter, from the Text Similarity and Question Answering track, which also focused on tweets.

7 Conclusion

We have described the five subtasks organized as part of SemEval-2015 Task 10 on Sentiment Analysis in Twitter: detecting sentiment of terms in context (subtask A), classifiying the sentiment of an entire tweet, SMS message or blog post (subtask B), predicting polarity towards a topic (subtask C), quantifying polarity towards a topic (subtask D), and proposing real-valued prior sentiment scores for Twitter terms (subtask E). Over 40 teams participated in these subtasks, using various techniques.

We plan a new edition of the task as part of SemEval-2016, where we will focus on sentiment with respect to a topic, but this time on a five-point scale, which is used for human review ratings on popular websites such as Amazon, TripAdvisor, Yelp, etc. From a research perspective, moving to an ordered five-point scale means moving from binary classification to *ordinal regression*.

We further plan to continue the trend detection subtask, which represents a move from classification to *quantification*, and is on par with what applications need. They are not interested in the sentiment of a particular tweet but rather in the percentage of tweets that are positive/negative.

Finally, we plan a new subtask on trend detection, but using a five-point scale, which would get us even closer to what business (e.g. marketing studies), and researchers, (e.g. in political science or public policy), want nowadays. From a research perspective, this is a problem of *ordinal quantification*.

Acknowledgements

The authors would like to thank SIGLEX for supporting subtasks A–D, and the National Research Council Canada for funding subtask E.

References

Eric Almquist and Jason Lee. 2009. What do customers really want? *Harvard Business Review*.

Stefano Baccianella, Andrea Esuli, and Fabrizio Sebastiani. 2010. SentiWordNet 3.0: An enhanced lexical resource for sentiment analysis and opinion mining. In *Proceedings of the Seventh International Conference on Language Resources and Evaluation*, LREC '10, pages 2200–2204, Valletta, Malta.

Luciano Barbosa and Junlan Feng. 2010. Robust sentiment detection on Twitter from biased and noisy data. In *Proceedings of the 23rd International Conference on Computational Linguistics: Posters*, COLING '10, pages 36–44, Beijing, China.

Albert Bifet, Geoffrey Holmes, Bernhard Pfahringer, and Ricard Gavaldà. 2011. Detecting sentiment change in Twitter streaming data. *Journal of Machine Learning Research, Proceedings Track*, 17:5–11.

Dmitry Davidov, Oren Tsur, and Ari Rappoport. 2010. Semi-supervised recognition of sarcasm in Twitter and Amazon. In *Proceedings of the Fourteenth Conference on Computational Natural Language Learning*, CoNLL '10, pages 107–116, Uppsala, Sweden.

Roberto González-Ibáñez, Smaranda Muresan, and Nina Wacholder. 2011. Identifying sarcasm in Twitter: a closer look. In *Proceedings of the 49th Annual Meeting of the Association for Computational Linguistics: Human Language Technologies - Short Papers*, ACL-HLT '11, pages 581–586, Portland, Oregon, USA.

Dustin Hillard, Mari Ostendorf, and Elizabeth Shriberg. 2003. Detection of agreement vs. disagreement in meetings: Training with unlabeled data. In *Proceedings of the 2003 Conference of the North American Chapter of the Association for Computational Linguistics on Human Language Technology: Volume 2*, NAACL '03, pages 34–36, Edmonton, Canada.

Minqing Hu and Bing Liu. 2004. Mining and summarizing customer reviews. In *Proceedings of the 10th ACM SIGKDD International Conference on Knowledge Discovery and Data Mining*, KDD '04, pages 168–177, New York, NY, USA.

Bernard Jansen, Mimi Zhang, Kate Sobel, and Abdur Chowdury. 2009. Twitter power: Tweets as electronic word of mouth. *J. Am. Soc. Inf. Sci. Technol.*, 60(11):2169–2188.

David Jurgens, Saif Mohammad, Peter Turney, and Keith Holyoak. 2012. SemEval-2012 Task 2: Measuring degrees of relational similarity. In *Proceedings of the Sixth International Workshop on Semantic Evaluation*, SemEval '12, pages 356–364, Montréal, Canada.

Maurice G Kendall. 1938. A new measure of rank correlation. *Biometrika*, pages 81–93.

Svetlana Kiritchenko, Xiaodan Zhu, and Saif M. Mohammad. 2014. Sentiment analysis of short informal texts. *Journal of Artificial Intelligence Research (JAIR)*, 50:723–762.

Efthymios Kouloumpis, Theresa Wilson, and Johanna Moore. 2011. Twitter sentiment analysis: The good the bad and the OMG! In *Proceedings of the Fifth International Conference on Weblogs and Social Media*, ICWSM '11, pages 538–541, Barcelona, Catalonia, Spain.

Erich Leo Lehmann and Howard JM D'Abrera. 2006. *Nonparametrics: statistical methods based on ranks*. Springer New York.

Christine Liebrecht, Florian Kunneman, and Antal Van den Bosch. 2013. The perfect solution for detecting sarcasm in tweets #not. In *Proceedings of the 4th Workshop on Computational Approaches to Subjectivity, Sentiment and Social Media Analysis*, pages 29–37, Atlanta, Georgia, USA.

Jordan J. Louviere. 1991. Best-worst scaling: A model for the largest difference judgments. Technical report, University of Alberta.

Saif Mohammad, Svetlana Kiritchenko, and Xiaodan Zhu. 2013. NRC-Canada: Building the state-of-the-art in sentiment analysis of tweets. In *Proceedings of the Seventh International Workshop on Semantic Evaluation*, SemEval '13, pages 321–327, Atlanta, Georgia, USA.

Preslav Nakov, Sara Rosenthal, Zornitsa Kozareva, Veselin Stoyanov, Alan Ritter, and Theresa Wilson. 2013. SemEval-2013 Task 2: Sentiment analysis in Twitter. In *Proceedings of the Seventh International Workshop on Semantic Evaluation*, SemEval '13, pages 312–320, Atlanta, Georgia, USA.

Brendan O'Connor, Ramnath Balasubramanyan, Bryan Routledge, and Noah Smith. 2010. From tweets to polls: Linking text sentiment to public opinion time series. In *Proceedings of the Fourth International Conference on Weblogs and Social Media*, ICWSM '10, pages 122–129, Washington, DC, USA.

Alexander Pak and Patrick Paroubek. 2010. Twitter based system: Using Twitter for disambiguating sentiment ambiguous adjectives. In *Proceedings of the 5th International Workshop on Semantic Evaluation*, SemEval '10, pages 436–439, Uppsala, Sweden.

Bo Pang, Lillian Lee, and Shivakumar Vaithyanathan. 2002. Thumbs up?: Sentiment classification using machine learning techniques. In *Proceedings of the Conference on Empirical Methods in Natural Language Processing - Volume 10*, EMNLP '02, pages 79–86, Philadephia, Pennsylvania, USA.

Alan Ritter, Sam Clark, and Oren Etzioni. 2011. Named entity recognition in tweets: An experimental study. In

Proceedings of the Conference on Empirical Methods in Natural Language Processing, EMNLP '11, pages 1524–1534, Edinburgh, Scotland, UK.

Alan Ritter, Oren Etzioni, Sam Clark, et al. 2012. Open domain event extraction from Twitter. In *Proceedings of the 18th ACM SIGKDD International Conference on Knowledge Discovery and Data Mining*, KDD '12, pages 1104–1112, Beijing, China.

Sara Rosenthal, Alan Ritter, Preslav Nakov, and Veselin Stoyanov. 2014. SemEval-2014 Task 9: Sentiment analysis in Twitter. In *Proceedings of the 8th International Workshop on Semantic Evaluation*, SemEval '14, pages 73–80, Dublin, Ireland.

Janyce Wiebe, Theresa Wilson, and Claire Cardie. 2005. Annotating expressions of opinions and emotions in language. *Language Resources and Evaluation*, 39(2-3):165–210.

Theresa Wilson, Janyce Wiebe, and Paul Hoffmann. 2005. Recognizing contextual polarity in phrase-level sentiment analysis. In *Proceedings of the Conference on Human Language Technology and Empirical Methods in Natural Language Processing*, HLT-EMNLP '05, pages 347–354, Vancouver, British Columbia, Canada.

Xiaodan Zhu, Hongyu Guo, Saif Mohammad, and Svetlana Kiritchenko. 2014. An empirical study on the effect of negation words on sentiment. In *Proceedings of the 52nd Annual Meeting of the Association for Computational Linguistics (Volume 1: Long Papers)*, ACL '14, pages 304–313, Baltimore, Maryland, USA.

UNITN: Training Deep Convolutional Neural Network for Twitter Sentiment Classification

Aliaksei Severyn
DISI, University of Trento
38123 Povo (TN), Italy
severyn@disi.unitn.it

Alessandro Moschitti
Qatar Computing Research Institue
5825 Doha, Qatar
amoschitti@qf.org.qa

Abstract

This paper describes our deep learning system for sentiment analysis of tweets. The main contribution of this work is a process to initialize the parameter weights of the convolutional neural network, which is crucial to train an accurate model while avoiding the need to inject any additional features. Briefly, we use an unsupervised neural language model to initialize word embeddings that are further tuned by our deep learning model on a distant supervised corpus. At a final stage, the pre-trained parameters of the network are used to initialize the model which is then trained on the supervised training data from Semeval-2015. According to results on the official test sets, our model ranks 1st in the phrase-level subtask A (among 11 teams) and 2nd on the message-level subtask B (among 40 teams). Interestingly, computing an average rank over all six test sets (official and five progress test sets) puts our system 1st in both subtasks A and B.

1 Introduction

In this work we describe our deep convolutional neural network for sentiment analysis of tweets. Its architecture is most similar to the deep learning systems presented in (Kalchbrenner et al., 2014; Kim, 2014) that have recently established new state-of-the-art results on various NLP sentence classification tasks also including sentiment analysis. While already demonstrating excellent results, training a convolutional neural network that would beat hand-engineered approaches that also rely on multiple manual and automatically constructed lexicons, e.g. (Mohammad et al., 2013; Xiaodan Zhu, 2014; Severyn and Moschitti, 2015), requires careful attention. This becomes an even harder problem especially in cases when the amount of labelled data is relatively small, e.g., thousands of examples.

Turns out, providing the network with good initialisation parameters makes all the difference in training an accurate model. We propose a three-step process we follow to train our deep learning model for sentiment classification. It can be summarized as follows: (i) word embeddings are initialized using a neural language model (Ronan Collobert, 2008; Mikolov et al., 2013) which is trained on a large unsupervised collection of tweets; (ii) we use our convolutional neural network to further refine the embeddings on a large distant supervised corpus (Go et al., 2009); (iii) the word embeddings and other parameters of the network obtained at the previous stage are used to initialize the network that is then trained on a supervised corpus from Semeval-2015.

We apply our deep learning model on two subtasks of Semeval-2015 Twitter Sentiment Analysis (Task 10) challenge (Rosenthal et al., 2015): phrase-level (subtask A) and message-level (subtask B). Our system ranks 1st on the official test set of the phrase-level and 2nd on the message-level subtask. In addition to the test set used to establish the final ranking in Semeval-2015, all systems were also evaluated on the progress test set which consists of five test sets, where our system also shows strong results. In particular, we rank all systems according to their performance on each test set and compute their average ranks. Interestingly, our model appears to be the most robust across all six test sets ranking 1st according to the average rank in both subtasks A and B.

In the following, we describe the architecture of our convolutional neural network and the parameter initialization process process we follow to train it.

2 Our Deep Learning model for sentiment classification

The architecture of our convolutional neural network for sentiment classification is shown on Fig. 1. It is mainly inspired by the architectures used in (Kalchbrenner et al., 2014; Kim, 2014) for performing various sentence classification tasks. Given that our training process (described in Sec. 3.3) requires to run the network on a rather large corpus, our design choices are mainly driven by the computational efficiency of our network. Hence, different from (Kalchbrenner et al., 2014) that presents an architecture with several layers of convolutional feature maps, we adopt a single level architecture, which has been shown in (Kim, 2014) to perform equally well.

Our network is composed of a single convolutional layer followed by a non-linearity, *max* pooling and a soft-max classification layer.

In the following we give a brief explanation of the main components of our network architecture: sentence matrix, activations, convolutional, pooling and softmax layers. We also describe how to adapt the network for predicting sentiment of phrases inside the tweets.

2.1 Sentence matrix

The input to our model are tweets each treated as a sequence of words: $[w_i, .., w_{|s|}]$, where each word is drawn from a vocabulary V. Words are represented by distributional vectors $\mathbf{w} \in \mathbb{R}^d$ looked up in a word embeddings matrix $\mathbf{W} \in \mathbb{R}^{d \times |V|}$. This matrix is formed by concatentating embeddings of all words in V. For convenience and ease of lookup operations in $\mathbf{W}$, words are mapped to indices $1, \ldots, |V|$.

For each input tweet $\mathbf{s}$ we build a sentence matrix $\mathbf{S} \in \mathbb{R}^{d \times |s|}$, where each column i represents a word embedding $\mathbf{w}_i$ at the corresponding position i in a sentence (see Fig. 1):

$$\mathbf{S} = \begin{bmatrix} | & & | \\ \mathbf{w}_1 & \ldots & \mathbf{w}_{|s|} \\ | & & | \end{bmatrix}$$

To learn to capture and compose features of individual words in a given sentence from low-level word embeddings into higher level semantic concepts, the neural network applies a series of transformations to the input sentence matrix $\mathbf{S}$ using convolution, non-linearity and pooling operations, which we describe next.

2.2 Convolutional feature maps

The aim of the convolutional layer is to extract patterns, i.e., discriminative word sequences found within the input tweets that are common throughout the training instances.

More formally, the convolution operation $*$ between an input matrix $\mathbf{s} \in \mathbb{R}^{d \times |s|}$ and a filter $\mathbf{F} \in \mathbb{R}^{d \times m}$ of width m results in a vector $\mathbf{c} \in \mathbb{R}^{|s|+m-1}$ where each component is computed as follows:

$$\mathbf{c}_i = (\mathbf{S} * \mathbf{F})_i = \sum_{k,j} (\mathbf{S}_{[:,i-m+1:i]} \otimes \mathbf{F})_{kj} \quad (1)$$

where $\otimes$ is the element-wise multiplication and $\mathbf{S}_{[:,i-m+1:i]}$ is a matrix slice of size m along the columns. Note that the convolution filter is of the same dimensionality d as the input sentence matrix. As shown in Fig. 1, it slides along the column dimension of $\mathbf{S}$ producing a vector $\mathbf{c} \in \mathbb{R}^{1 \times (|s|-m+1)}$ in output. Each component c_i is the result of computing an element-wise product between a column slice of $\mathbf{S}$ and a filter matrix $\mathbf{F}$, which is then summed to a single value.

So far we have described a way to compute a convolution between the input sentence matrix and a single filter. To form a richer representation of the data, deep learning models apply a set of filters that work in parallel generating multiple feature maps (also shown on Fig. 1). A set of filters form a filter bank $\mathbf{F} \in \mathbb{R}^{n \times d \times m}$ sequentially convolved with the sentence matrix $\mathbf{S}$ and producing a feature map matrix $\mathbf{C} \in \mathbb{R}^{n \times (|s|-m+1)}$.

In practice, we also need to add a bias vector $\mathbf{b} \in \mathbb{R}^n$ to the result of a convolution – a single b_i value for each feature map $\mathbf{c}_i$. This allows the network to learn an appropriate threshold.

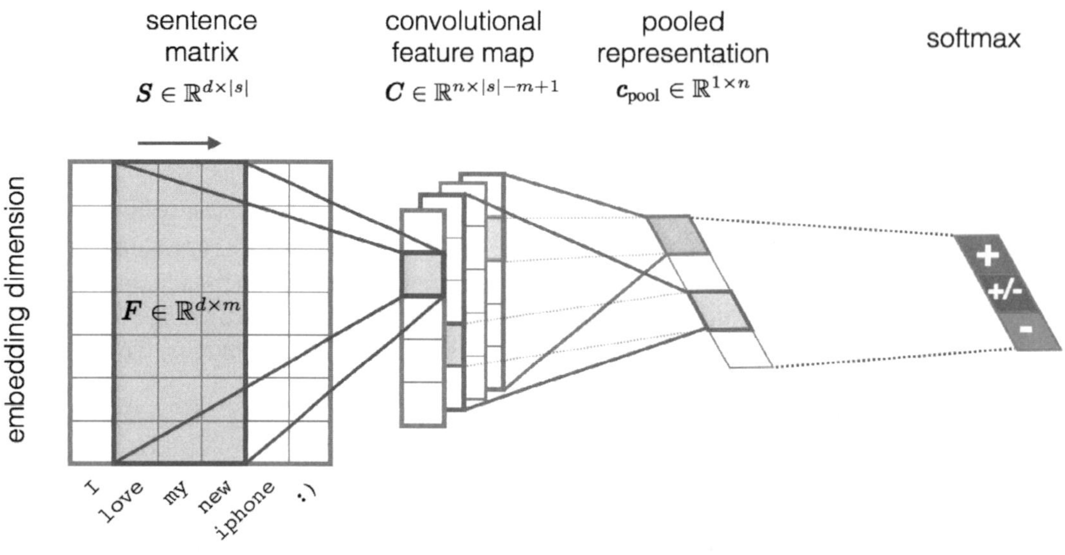

Figure 1: The architecture of our deep learning model for sentiment classification.

2.3 Activation units

To allow the network learn non-linear decision boundaries, each convolutional layer is typically followed by a non-linear activation function $\alpha()$ applied element-wise. Among the most common choices of activation functions are: sigmoid (or logistic), hyperbolic tangent *tanh*, and a rectified linear (ReLU) function defined as simply $max(0, \mathbf{x})$ to ensure that feature maps are always positive.

We use ReLU in our model since, as shown in (Nair and Hinton, 2010), it speeds up the training and sometimes produces more accurate results.

2.4 Pooling

The output from the convolutional layer (passed through the activation function) are then passed to the pooling layer, whose goal is to aggregate the information and reduce the representation. The result of the pooling operation is:

$$\mathbf{c}_{\text{pooled}} = \begin{bmatrix} \text{pool}(\alpha(\mathbf{c}_1 + b_1 * \mathbf{e})) \\ \cdots \\ \text{pool}(\alpha(\mathbf{c}_n + b_n * \mathbf{e})) \end{bmatrix}$$

where $\mathbf{c}_i$ is the ith convolutional feature map with added bias (the bias is added to each element of $\mathbf{c}_i$ and $\mathbf{e}$ is a unit vector of the same size as $\mathbf{c}_i$) and passed through the activation function $\alpha()$.

Among the most popular choices for pooling operation are: max and average pooling. Recently, *max* pooling has been generalized to k-max pooling (Kalchbrenner et al., 2014), where instead of a single max value, k values are extracted in their original order. We use *max* pooling in our model which simply returns the maximum value. It operates on columns of the feature map matrix $\mathbf{C}$ returning the largest value: $\text{pool}(\mathbf{c}_i) : \mathbb{R}^{1\times(|s|+m-1)} \rightarrow \mathbb{R}$ (also shown schematically in Fig. 1).

Convolutional layer passed through the activation function together with pooling layer acts as a non-linear feature extractor. Given that multiple feature maps are used in parallel to process the input, deep learning networks are able to build rich feature representations of the input.

2.5 Softmax

The output of the penultimate convolutional and pooling layers $\mathbf{x}$ is passed to a fully connected softmax layer. It computes the probability distribution over the labels:

$$\begin{aligned} P(y = j|\mathbf{x}, \mathbf{s}, \mathbf{b}) &= \text{softmax}_j(\mathbf{x}^T\mathbf{w} + \mathbf{b}) \\ &= \frac{e^{\mathbf{x}^T\mathbf{w}_j + b_j}}{\sum_{k=1}^{K} e^{\mathbf{x}^T\mathbf{w}_k + b_k}}, \end{aligned}$$

where $\mathbf{w}_k$ and b_k are the weight vector and bias of the k-th class.

2.6 Phrase-level sentiment analysis

To perform phrase-level sentiment analysis, we feed the network with an additional input sequence indicating the location of the target phrase in a tweet. The elements are encoded using only two word types: tokens spanning the phrase to be predicted are encoded with 1s and all the other with 0s. Each word type is associated with its own embedding. So, when tackling the phrase-level sentiment classification, we form a sentence matrix $\mathbf{S}$ as follows: for each token in a tweet we have to look up its corresponding word embedding in the word matrix $\mathbf{W}$, and the embedding for one of the two word types. Hence, the input sentence matrix is augmented with an additional set of rows from the word type embeddings. Other than that, the architecture of our network remains unchanged.

This ends the description of our convolutional neural network for sentiment classification of tweets.

3 Our approach to train the network

Convolutional neural networks can be tricky to train often severely overfitting on small datasets. In the following we describe our approach to train our deep learning model.

3.1 Network Parameters and Training

We use stochastic gradient descent (SGD) to train the network and use backpropogation algorithm to compute the gradients. We opt for the *Adadelta* (Zeiler, 2012) update rule to automatically tune the learning rate.

The following parameters are optimized by our network:

$$\theta = \{\mathbf{W}; \mathbf{F}; \mathbf{b}; \mathbf{w}_s; \mathbf{b}_s\},$$

namely the word embeddings matrix $\mathbf{W}$, filter weights and biases of the convolutional layer, the weight and bias of the softmax layers.

3.2 Regularization

While neural networks have a large capacity to learn complex decision functions they tend to easily overfit especially on small and medium sized datasets. To mitigate the overfitting issue we augment the cost function with l_2-norm regularization terms for the parameters of the network.

We also adopt another popular and effective technique to improve regularization of the NNs — dropout (Srivastava et al., 2014). Dropout prevents feature co-adaptation by setting to zero (dropping out) a portion of hidden units during the forward phase when computing the activations at the softmax output layer. As suggested in (Goodfellow et al., 2013) dropout acts as an approximate model averaging.

3.3 Initializing the model parameters

Convolutional neural networks live in the world of non-convex function optimization leading to locally optimal solutions. Hence, starting the optimization from a good point can be crucial to train an accurate model. We propose the following 3-step process to initialize the parameter weights of the network:

1. Given that the largest parameter of the network is the word matrix $\mathbf{W}$, it is crucial to feed the network with the high quality embeddings. We use a popular `word2vec` neural language model (Mikolov et al., 2013) to learn the word embeddings on an unsupervised tweet corpus. For this purpose, we collect 50M tweets over the two-month period. We perform minimal preprocessing tokenizing the tweets, normalizing the URLs and author ids. To train the embeddings we use a skipgram model with window size 5 and filtering words with frequency less than 5.

2. When dealing with small amounts of labelled data, starting from pre-trained word embeddings is a large step towards successfully training an accurate deep learning system. However, while the word embeddings obtained at the previous step should already capture important syntactic and semantic aspects of the words they represent, they are completely clueless about their sentiment behaviour. Hence, we use a distant supervision approach (Go et al., 2009) using our convolutional neural network to further refine the embeddings.

3. Finally, we take the the parameters θ of the network obtained at the previous step and use it to

Table 1: Semeval-2015 data.

Dataset	Subtask A	Subtask B
Twitter'13-train	5,895	9,728
Twitter'13-dev	648	1,654
Twitter'13-test	2,734	3,813
LiveJournal'14	660	1,142
SMS'13	1,071	2,093
Twitter'14	1,807	1,853
Sarcasm'14	82	86
Twitter'15	3,092	2,390
# Teams	11	40

Table 2: Testing the model on the progress test sets from Semeval-2015 with different parameter initializion schemes: `Random` (random word embeddings); `Unsup` (word2vec embeddings); `Distant` (all parameters from a network trained on a distant supervised dataset).

Dataset	Random	Unsup	Distant
LiveJournal'14	63.58	73.09	72.48
SMS'13	58.41	65.21	68.37
Twitter'13	64.51	72.35	72.79
Twitter'14	63.69	71.07	73.60
Sarcasm'14	46.10	52.56	55.44

initialize the network which is trained on a supervised training corpus from Semeval-2015.

4 Experiments and evaluation

Data and setup. We test our model on two subtasks from Semeval-2015 Task 10: phrase-level (subtask A) and message-level (subtask B). The datasets use in Semeval-2015 are summarized in Table 1. We use train and dev from Twitter'13 for training and Twitter'13-test as a validation set. The other datasets are used for testing, whereas Twitter'15 is used to establish the official ranking of the systems.

Additionally, to pre-train the weights of our network, we use a large unsupervised corpus containing 50M tweets for training the word embeddings and a 10M tweet corpus for distant supervision. The latter corpus was built similarly to (Go et al., 2009), where tweets with positive emoticons, like ':)', are assumed to be positive, and tweets with negative emoticons, like ':(', are labeled as negative. The dataset contains equal number of positive and negative tweets.

The parameters of our model were (chosen on the validation set) as follows: the width m of the convolution filters is set to 5 and the number of convolutional feature maps is 300. We use ReLU activation function and a simple max-pooling. The L2 regularization term is set to $1e-4$, dropout is applied to the penultimate level with $p = 0.5$. The dimensionality of the word embeddings d is set to 100. For the phrase-level subtask the size of the word type embeddings, which encode tokens that span the target phrase or not, is set to 10.

Pre-training the network. To train our deep learning model we follow our 3-step process as described in Sec. 3.3. We report the results for training the network on the official supervised dataset from Semeval'15 using parameters that were initialized: (i) completely at random (`Random`); (ii) using word embeddings from the neural language model trained on a large unsupervised dataset (`Unsup`) with the `word2vec` tool and (iii) initializing all the parameters of our model with the parameters of the network which uses the word embeddings from the previous step and are further tuned on a distant supervised dataset (`Distant`).

Table 2 summarizes the performance of our model on five test sets using three parameter initialization schemas. First, we observe that training the network with all parameters initialized completely at random results in a rather mediocre performance. This is due to a small size of the training set. Secondly, using embeddings pre-trained by a neural language model considerably boosts the performance. Finally, using a large distant supervised corpus to further tune the word embeddings to also capture the sentiment aspect of the words they represent results in a further improvement across all test sets (except for a small drop on LiveJournal'14).

Official rankings. The results from the official rankings for both subtasks A and B are summarized in Table 3. As we can see our system performs particularly well on subtask A ranking 1st on the official Twitter'15 set, while also showing excellent performance on all other test sets.

On subtask B our system ranks 2nd also showing high rankings on the other test sets (apart from the LiveJournal'14). In fact, no single system at Semeval-2015 performed equally well across all test

Table 3: Results on Semeval-2015 for phrase and tweet-level subtasks. Rank shows the absolute position of our system on each test set. AveRank is the averaged rank across all test sets.

Dataset	Score	Rank
Phrase-level subtask A		
LJournal'14	84.46	2
SMS'13	88.60	2
Twitter'13	90.10	1
Twitter'14	87.12	1
Sarcasm'14	73.65	5
Twitter'15	**84.79**	**1**
AveRank	2.0	1
Message-level subtask B		
LJournal'14	72.48	12
SMS'13	68.37	2
Twitter'13	72.79	3
Twitter'14	73.60	2
Sarcasm'14	55.44	5
Twitter'15	**64.59**	**2**
AveRank	4.3	1

sets. For example, a system that ranked 1st on the official Twitter'15 dataset performs much worse on the progress test sets ranking $\{14, 14, 11, 7, 12\}$ on {`LiveJournal'14`, `SMS'13`, `Twitter'13`, `Twitter'14`, and `Sarcasm'14`} correspondingly. It has an AveRank of 9.8, which is only 6th best result if systems were ranked according to this metric. In contrast, our system shows robust results across all tests having the best AveRank of 4.3 among all 40 systems.

5 Conclusions

We described our deep learning approach to Twitter sentiment analysis on both message and phrase levels. We gave a detailed description of our 3-step process to train the parameters of the network that is the key to our success. The resulting model demonstrates state-of-the-art performance on both the phrase-level and message-level subtasks. Considering the average rank across all test sets (including progress test sets) our system is 1st on both subtasks.

References

Alex Go, Richa Bhayani, and Lei Huang. 2009. Twitter sentiment classification using distant supervision. In *CS224N Project Report, Stanford*.

Ian J. Goodfellow, David Warde-Farley, Mehdi Mirza, Aaron C. Courville, and Yoshua Bengio. 2013. Maxout networks. In *ICML*, pages 1319–1327.

Nal Kalchbrenner, Edward Grefenstette, and Phil Blunsom. 2014. A convolutional neural network for modelling sentences. *Proceedings of the 52nd Annual Meeting of the Association for Computational Linguistics*.

Yoon Kim. 2014. Convolutional neural networks for sentence classification. In *EMNLP*, pages 1746–1751, Doha, Qatar.

Tomas Mikolov, Ilya Sutskever, Kai Chen, Greg S Corrado, and Jeff Dean. 2013. Distributed representations of words and phrases and their compositionality. In *Advances in Neural Information Processing Systems 26*, pages 3111–3119.

Saif M. Mohammad, Svetlana Kiritchenko, and Xiaodan Zhu. 2013. Nrc-canada: Building the state-of-the-art in sentiment analysis of tweets. In *7th International Workshop on Semantic Evaluation (Semeval'13)*.

Vinod Nair and Geoffrey E. Hinton. 2010. Rectified linear units improve restricted boltzmann machines. In *ICML*, pages 807–814.

Jason Weston Ronan Collobert. 2008. A unified architecture for natural language processing: deep neural networks with multitask learning. In *ICML*.

Sara Rosenthal, Preslav Nakov, Svetlana Kiritchenko, Saif M Mohammad, Alan Ritter, and Veselin Stoyanov. 2015. Semeval-2015 task 10: Sentiment analysis in twitter. In *Proceedings of the 9th International Workshop on Semantic Evaluation*, SemEval '2015, Denver, Colorado.

Aliaksei Severyn and Alessandro Moschitti. 2015. On the automatic learning of sentiment lexicons. In *Proceedings of the Conference of the North American Chapter of the Association for Computational Linguistics (NAACL HLT 2015)*.

Nitish Srivastava, Geoffrey Hinton, Alex Krizhevsky, Ilya Sutskever, and Ruslan Salakhutdinov. 2014. Dropout: A simple way to prevent neural networks from overfitting. *Journal of Machine Learning Research*, 15:1929–1958.

Saif M. Mohammad Xiaodan Zhu, Svetlana Kiritchenko. 2014. Nrc-canada-2014: Recent improvements in sentiment analysis of tweets, and the Voted Perceptron. In *Eighth International Workshop on Semantic Evaluation Exercises (SemEval-2014)*.

Matthew D. Zeiler. 2012. Adadelta: An adaptive learning rate method. *CoRR*.

SemEval-2015 Task 11: Sentiment Analysis of Figurative Language in Twitter

Aniruddha Ghosh
University College Dublin, Ireland.
arghyaonline@gmail.com

Tony Veale
University College Dublin, Ireland.
Tony.Veale@UCD.ie

Ekaterina Shutova
University of Cambridge.
Ekaterina.Shutova@cl.cam.ac.uk

John Barnden
University of Birmingham, UK
J.A.Barnden@cs.bham.ac.uk

Guofu Li
University College Dublin, Ireland.
li.guofu.l@gmail.com

Paolo Rosso
Universitat Politècnica de València, Spain.
prosso@dsic.upv.es

Antonio Reyes
Instituto Superior de Intérpretes y Traductores
Mexico
antonioreyes@isit.edu.mx

Abstract

This report summarizes the objectives and evaluation of the SemEval 2015 task on the sentiment analysis of figurative language on Twitter (Task 11). This is the first sentiment analysis task wholly dedicated to analyzing figurative language on Twitter. Specifically, three broad classes of figurative language are considered: *irony*, *sarcasm* and *metaphor*. Gold standard sets of 8000 training tweets and 4000 test tweets were annotated using workers on the crowdsourcing platform *CrowdFlower*. Participating systems were required to provide a fine-grained sentiment score on an 11-point scale (-5 to +5, including 0 for neutral intent) for each tweet, and systems were evaluated against the gold standard using both a Cosine-similarity and a Mean-Squared-Error measure.

1 Introduction

The limitations on text length imposed by micro-blogging services such as Twitter do nothing to dampen our willingness to use language creatively. Indeed, such limitations further incentivize the use of creative devices such as metaphor and irony, as such devices allow strongly-felt sentiments to be expressed effectively, memorably and concisely. Nonetheless, creative language can pose certain challenges for NLP tools that do not take account of how words can be used playfully and in original ways. In the case of language using figurative devices such as irony, sarcasm or metaphor – when literal meanings are discounted and secondary or extended meanings are intentionally profiled – the affective polarity of the literal meaning may differ significantly from that of the intended figurative meaning. Nowhere is this effect more pronounced than in ironical language, which delights in using affirmative language to convey critical meanings. Metaphor, irony and sarcasm can each sculpt the affect of an utterance in complex ways, and each tests the limits of conventional techniques for the sentiment analysis of supposedly literal texts.

Figurative language thus poses an especially significant challenge to sentiment analysis systems, as standard approaches anchored in the dictionary-defined affect of individual words and phrases are often shown to be inadequate in the face of indirect figurative meanings. It would be convenient if such language were rare and confined to specific genres of text, such as poetry and literature. Yet the reality is that figurative language is pervasive in almost any genre of text, and is especially commonplace on the texts of the Web and on social media platforms such as Twitter. Figurative language often draws attention to itself as a creative artifact, but is just as likely to be viewed as part of the general fabric of human communication. In any case, Web users widely employ figures of speech (both old and new) to project their personality through a text, especially when their texts are limited to the 140 characters of a tweet.

Natural language researchers have attacked the problems associated with figurative interpretations at multiple levels of linguistic representation. Some have focused on the conceptual level, of which the text is a surface instantiation, to identify the schemas and mappings that are implied by a figure of speech (see e.g. Veale and Keane (1992); Barnden (2008); Veale (2012)). These approaches yield a depth of insight but not a robustness of analysis in the face of textual diversity. More robust approaches focus on the surface level of a text, to consider word choice, syntactic order, lexical properties and affective profiles of the elements that make up a text (e.g. Reyes and Rosso (2012, 2014)). Surface analysis yields a range of discriminatory features that can be efficiently extracted and fed into machine-learning algorithms.

When it comes to analyzing the texts of the Web, the Web can also be used as a convenient source of ancillary knowledge and features. Veale and Hao (2007) describe a means of harvesting a common-sense knowledge-base of stereotypes from the Web, by directly targeting simile constructions of the form "*as X as Y*" (e.g. "*as hot as an oven*", "*as humid as a jungle*", "*as big as a mountain*", etc.). Though largely successful in their efforts, Veale and Hao were surprised to discover that up to 20% of Web-harvested similes are ironic (examples include "*as subtle as a freight train*", "*as tanned as an Irishman*", "*as sober as a Kennedy*", "*as private as a park bench*"). Initially filtering ironic similes manually – as irony is the worst kind of noise when acquiring knowledge from the Web – Hao & Veale (2010) report good results for an automatic, Web-based approach to distinguishing ironic from non-ironic similes. Their approach exploits specific properties of similes and is thus not directly transferrable to the detection of irony in general. Reyes, Rosso and Veale (2013) and Reyes, Rosso and Buscaldi (2012) thus employ a more general approach that applies machine learning algorithms to a range of structural and lexical features to learn a robust basis for detecting humor and irony in text.

The current task is one that calls for such a general approach. Note that the goal of Task 11 is not to detect irony, sarcasm or metaphor in a text, but to perform robust sentiment analysis on a fine-grained 11-point scale over texts in which these kinds of linguistic usages are pervasive. A system may find detection to be a useful precursor to analysis, or it may not. We present a description of Task 11 in section 2, before presenting our dataset in section 3 and the scoring functions in section 4. Descriptions of each participating system are then presented in section 5, before an overall evaluation in reported in section 6. The report then concludes with some general observations in section 7.

2 Task Description

The task concerns itself with the classification of overall sentiment in micro-texts drawn from the micro-blogging service Twitter. These texts, called tweets, are chosen so that the set as a whole contains a great deal of irony, sarcasm or metaphor, so no particular tweet is guaranteed to manifest a specific figurative phenomenon. Since irony and sarcasm are typically used to criticize or to mock, and thus skew the perception of sentiment toward the negative, it is not enough for a system to simply determine whether the sentiment of a given tweet is positive or negative. We thus use an 11-point scale, ranging from –5 (very negative, for tweets with highly critical meanings) to +5 (very positive, for tweets with flattering or very upbeat meanings). The point 0 on this scale is used for neutral tweets, or those whose positivity and negativity cancel each other out. While the majority of tweets will have sentiments in the negative part of the scale, the challenge for participating systems is to decide just how negative or positive a tweet seems to be.

So, given a set of tweets that are rich in metaphor, sarcasm and irony, the goal is to determine whether a user has expressed a positive, negative or neutral sentiment in each, and the degree to which this sentiment has been communicated.

3 Dataset Design and Collection

Even humans have difficulty in deciding whether a given text is ironic or metaphorical. Irony can be remarkably subtle, while metaphor takes many forms, ranging the dead to the conventional to the novel. Sarcasm is easier for humans to detect, and is perhaps the least sophisticated form of non-literal language. We sidestep problems of detection by harvesting tweets from Twitter that are *likely* to contain figurative language, either because they have been explicitly tagged as such (using e.g. the hashtags *#irony*, *#sarcasm*, *#not*, *#yeahright*) or because they use words commonly associated with the use of metaphor (ironically, the words "*literally*" and "*virtually*" are reliable markers of metaphorical intent, as in "*I literally want to die* ").

Datasets were collected using the Twitter4j API (*http://twitter4j.org/en/index.html*), which supports the harvesting of tweets in real-time using search queries. Queries for hashtags such as *#sarcasm*, *#sarcastic* and *#irony*, and for words such as "*figuratively*", yielded our initial corpora of candidate tweets to annotate. We then developed a Latent Semantic Analysis (LSA) model to extend this seed set of hashtags so as to harvest a wider range of figurative tweets (see Li. *et. al.*, 2014). This tweet dataset was collected over a period of 4 weeks, from June 1st to June 30th, 2014. Though URLs have been removed from tweets, all other content, including hashtags – even those used to retrieve each tweet – has been left in place. Tweets must contain at least 30 characters when hashtags are *not* counted, or 40 characters when hashtags *are* counted. All others are eliminated as too short.

3.1 Dataset Annotation on an 11-point scale

A trial dataset, consisting of 1025 tweets, was first prepared by harvesting tweets from Twitter users that are known for their use of figurative language (e.g. comedians). Each trial tweet was annotated by seven annotators from an internal team, three of whom are native English speakers, the other four of whom are competent non-native speakers. Each annotator was asked to assign a score ranging from -5 (for any tweets conveying disgust or extreme discontent) to +5 (for tweets conveying obvious joy and approval or extreme pleasure), where 0 is reserved for tweets in which positive and negative sentiment is balanced. Annotators were asked to use ±5, ±3 and ±1 as scores for tweets calling for strong, moderate or weak sentiment, and to use ±4 and ±2 for tweets with nuanced sentiments that fall between these gross scores. An overall sentiment score for each tweet was calculated as a weighted average of all 7 annotators, where a double weighting was given to native English speakers.

Sentiment was assigned on the basis of the perceived meaning of each tweet – the meaning an author presumably intends a reader to unpack from the text – and not the superficial language of the tweet. Thus, a sarcastic tweet that expresses a negative message in language that feigns approval or delight should be marked with a negative score (as in "*I just love it when my friends throw me under the bus.*"). Annotators were explicitly asked to consider *all* of a tweet's content when assigning a score, including any hashtags (such as *#sarcasm*, *#irony*, etc.), as participating systems are expected to use all of the tweet's content, including hashtags.

Tweets of the training and test datasets – comprising 8000 and 4000 tweets respectively – were each annotated on a crowd-sourcing platform, *CrowdFlower.com,* following the same annotation scheme as for the trial dataset. Some examples of tweets and their ideal scores, given as guidelines to *CrowdFlower* annotators, are shown in Table 1.

Tweet Content	Score
@ThisIsDeep_ you are about as deep as a turd in a toilet bowl. Internet culture is #garbage and you are bladder cancer.	-4
A paperless office has about as much chance as a paperless bathroom	-3
Today will be about as close as you'll ever get to a "PERFECT 10" in the weather world! Happy Mother's Day! Sunny and pleasant! High 80.	3
I missed voting due to work. But I was behind the Austrian entry all the way, so to speak. I might enter next year. Who knows?	1

Table 1: Annotation examples, given to Annotators

Scammers tend to give identical or random scores for all units in a task. To prevent scammers from abusing the task, trial tweets were thus interwoven as test questions for annotators on training and test tweets. Each annotator was expected to provide judgments for test questions that fall within the range of scores given by the original members of the internal team. Annotators are dismissed if their overall accuracy on these questions is below 70%. The standard deviation $std_u(u_i)$ of all judgments provided by annotator u_i also indicates that u_i is likely to be a scammer when $std_u(u_i)=0$. Likewise, the standard deviation $std_t(t_j)$ of all judgments given for a tweet t_j allows us to judge that annotation $A_{i,j}$ as given by u_i for t_j is an outlier if:

$$\left| A_{i,j} - \operatorname*{avg}_{i'}(A_{i',j}) \right| > std_t(t_j)$$

If 60% or more of an annotator's judgements are judged to be outliers in this way then the annotator is deemed a scammer and dismissed from the task.

Each tweet-set was cleaned of all annotations provided by those deemed to be scammers. After cleaning, each tweet has 5 to 7 annotations. The ratio of in-range judgments on trial tweets, which was used to detect scammers on the annotation of training and test data, can also be used to assign a reliability score to each annotator. The reliability of an annotator u_i is given by $R(u_i)=m_i/n_i$, where n_i is the number of judgments contributed by u_i on trial tweets, and m_i is the number of these judgments that fall within the range of scores provided by the original annotators of the trial data. The final sentiment score for tweet $S(t_j)$ is the weighted average of scores given for it, where the reliability of each annotator is used as a weight.

$$S(t_j) = \frac{\sum_i R(u_i) \times A_{i,j}}{\sum_i R(u_i)}$$

The weighted sentiment score is a real number in the range [-5 … +5], where the most reliable annotators contribute most to each score. These scores were provided to task participants in two CSV formats: tweet-ids mapped to real number scores, and tweet-ids to rounded integer scores.

3.2 Tweet Delivery

The actual text of each tweet was not included in the released datasets due to copyright and privacy concerns that are standard for use of Twitter data. Instead, a script was provided for retrieving the text of each tweet given its released tweet-id.

Tweets are a perishable commodity and may be deleted, archived or otherwise made inaccessible over time by their original creators. To ensure that tweets did not perish in the interval between their first release and final submission, all training and test tweets were re-tweeted via a dedicated account to give them new, non-perishable tweet-ids. The distributed tweet-ids refer to this dedicated account.

Type	# Tweets	Mean Sentiment
Sarcasm	746	-1.94
Irony	81	-1.35
Metaphor	198	-0.34
Overall	1025	-1.78

Table 2: Overview of the Trial Dataset

3.3 Dataset Statistics

The trial dataset contains a mix of figurative tweets chosen manually from Twitter. It consists of 1025 tweets annotated by an internal team of seven members. Table 2 shows the number of tweets in each category. The trial dataset is small enough to allow these category labels to be applied manually.

The training and test datasets were annotated by CrowdFlower users from countries where English is spoken as a native language. The 8,000 tweets of the training set were allocated as in Table 3. As the datasets are simply too large for the category labels *Sarcasm*, *Irony* and *Metaphor* to be assigned manually, the labels here refer to our expectations of the kind of tweets in each segment of the dataset, which were each collated using harvesting criteria specific to different kinds of figurative language.

Type	# Tweets	Mean Sentiment
Sarcasm	5000	-2.25
Irony	1000	-1.70
Metaphor	2000	-0.54
Overall	8000	-1.99

Table 3: Overview of the Training Dataset

To provide balance, an additional category *Other* was also added to the Test dataset. Tweets in this category were drawn from general Twitter content, and so were not chosen to capture any specific figurative quality. Rather, the category was added to ensure the ecological validity of the task, as sentiment analysis is never performed on texts that are wholly figurative. The 4000 tweets of the Test set were drawn from four categories as in Figure 4.

Type	# Tweets	Mean Sentiment
Sarcasm	1200	-2.02
Irony	800	-1.87
Metaphor	800	-0.77
Other	1200	-0.26
Overall	4000	-0.50

Table 4: Overview of the Test Dataset

4 Scoring Functions

The Cosine-similarity scoring function represents the gold-standard annotations for the Test dataset as a vector of the corresponding sentiment scores. The scores provided by each participating system are represented in a comparable vector format, so that the cosine of the angle between these vectors captures the overall similarity of both score sets. A score of 1 is achieved only when a system provides all the same scores as the human gold-standard. A script implementing this scoring function was released to all registered participants, who were required in turn to submit the outputs of their systems as a tab-separated file of tweet-ids and integer sentiment scores (as systems may be based either on a regression or a classification model).

A multiplier p_{cos} is applied to all submissions, to penalize any that do not give scores for *all* tweets.

Thus, $$p_{\cos} = \frac{\text{\#submitted-entries}}{\text{\#all-entries}}$$

E.g., a cherry-picking system that scores just 75% of the test tweets is hit with a 25% penalty.

Mean-Squared-Error (MSE) offers a standard basis for measuring the performance of predictive systems, and is favored by some developers as a basis for optimization. When calculating MSE, in which lower measures indicate better performance, the penalty-coefficient p_{MSE} is instead given by:

$$p_{MSE} = \frac{\text{\#all-entries}}{\text{\#submitted-entries}}$$

5 Overview of Participating Systems

A total of 15 teams participated in Task 11, submitting results from 29 distinct runs. A clear preference for supervised learning methods can be observed, with two types of approach – SVMs and regression models over carefully engineered features – making up the bulk of approaches.

Team ***UPF*** used regression with a Random-Sub-Space using M5P as a base algorithm. They exploited additional external resources such as SentiWordnet, Depeche Mood, and the American National Corpus. Team ***ValenTo*** used a regression model combined with affective resources such as *SenticNet* (see Poria *et al.*, 2014) to assign polarity scores. Team ***Elirf*** used an SVM-based approach, with features drawn from character N-grams ($2 < N < 10$) and a bag-of-words model of the tf-idf coefficient of each N-gram feature. Team ***BUAP*** also used an SVM approach, taking features from dictionaries, POS tags and character n-grams. Team ***CLaC*** used four lexica, one that was automatically generated and three than were manually crafted. Term frequencies, POS tags and emoticons were also used as features. Team ***LLT_PolyU*** used a semi-supervised approach with a Decision Tree Regression Learner, using word-level sentiment scores and dependency labels as features. Team ***CPH*** used ensemble methods and ridge regression (without stopwords), and is notable for its specific avoidance of sentiment lexicons. Team ***DsUniPi*** combined POS tags and regular expressions to identify useful syntactic structures, and brought sentiment lexicons and WordNet-based similarity measures to bear on their supervised approach. Team ***RGU***'s system learnt a sentiment model from the training data, and used a linear Support Vector Classifier to generate integer sentiment labels. Team ***ShellFBK*** also used a supervised approach, extracting grammatical relations for use as features from dependency tree parses.

Team ***HLT*** also used an SVM-based approach, using lexical features such as negation, intensifiers and other markers of amusement and irony. Team ***KElab*** constructed a supervised model based on term co-occurrence scores and the distribution of emotion-bearing terms in training tweets. Team ***LT3*** employed a combined, semi-supervised SVM- and regression-based approach, exploiting a range of lexical features, a terminology extraction system and and both WordNet and DBpedia. Team ***PRHLT*** used a deep auto-encoder to extract features, employing both words and character 3-grams as tokens for the autoencoder. Their best results were obtained with ensembles of Extremely Random Trees with character n-grams as features.

6 Results and Discussions

For comparison purposes, we constructed three baseline systems, each implemented as a naïve classifier with shallow bag-of-word features. The results of these baseline systems for both the MSE and Cosine metrics are shown in Table 5.

Baseline	Cosine	MSE
Naïve Bayes	0.390	5.672
MaxEnt	0.426	5.450
Decision Tree	0.547	4.065

Table 5: Performance of Three Baseline approaches

Table 6 shows the results for each participating system using these metrics. Team ***CLaC*** achieves the best overall performance on both, achieving **0.758** on the Cosine metric and 2.117 on the MSE metric. Most of the other systems also show a clear advantage over the baselines reported in Table 5.

Team	Cosine	MSE
CLaC	**0.758**	**2.117**
UPF	0.711	2.458
LLT_PolyU	0.687	2.6
elirf	0.658	3.096
LT3	0.658	2.913
ValenTo	0.634	2.999
HLT	0.63	4.088
CPH	0.625	3.078
PRHLT	0.623	3.023
DsUniPi	0.602	3.925
PKU	0.574	3.746
KELabTeam	0.552	4.177
RGU	0.523	5.143
SHELLFBK	0.431	7.701
BUAP	0.059	6.785

Table 6: Overall results, sorted by cosine metric. Scores are for last run submitted for each system.

The best performance on *sarcasm* and *irony* tweets was achieved by teams ***LLT_PolyU*** and ***elirf***, who ranked 3rd and 4th respectively. Team ***ClaC*** came first on tweets in the *Metaphor* category. One run of team ***CPH*** excelled on the *Other* (non-figurative) category, but scored poorly on figurative tweets. Most teams performed well on *sarcasm* and *irony* tweets, but the *Metaphor* and *Other* categories prove more of a challenge. Table 7 presents the Spearman's rank correlation between the ranking of a system overall, on all tweet categories, and its ranking of different categories of tweets. The right column limits this analysis to the top 10 systems.

	Spearman Correl – All	Spearman Correl – Top10
Sarcasm	0.854	0.539
Irony	0.721	0.382
Metaphor	0.864	0.939
Other	0.857	0.624

Table 7. How well does overall performance correlate with performance on different kinds of tweets?

When we consider all systems, their performance on each category of tweet is strongly correlated to their overall performance. However, looking only at the top 10 performing systems, we see a strikingly strong correlation between performance overall and performance on the category *Metaphor*. Performance on *Metaphor* tweets is a bellwether for performance on figurative language overall. Then category *Other* also plays an important role here. Both the trail data and the training datasets are heavily biased to negative sentiment, given their concentration of ironic and sarcastic tweets. In contrast, the distribution of sentiment scores in the test data is more balanced due to the larger proportion of Metaphor tweets and the addition of non-figurative *Other* tweets. To excel at this task, systems must not treat all tweets as figurative, but learn to spot the features that cause figurative devices to influence the sentiment of a tweet.

7 Summary and Conclusions

This paper has described the design and evaluation of Task 11, which concerns the determination of sentiment in tweets which are likely to employ figurative devices such as irony, sarcasm and metaphor. The task was constructed so as to avoid questions of what specific device is used in which tweet: a glance at Twitter, and the use of the *#irony* hashtag in particular, indicates that there are as many folk theories of irony as there are users of the hashtag *#irony*. Instead, we have operationalized the task to put it on a sound and more ecologically valid footing. The effect of figurativity in tweets is instead measured via an extrinsic task: measuring the polarity of tweets that use figurative language.

The task is noteworthy in its use of an 11-point sentiment scoring scheme, ranging from -5 to +5. The use of 11 fine-grained categories precludes the measurement of inter-annotator agreement as a reliable guide to annotator/annotation quality, but it allows us to measure system performance on a task and a language type in which negativity dominates. We expect the trial, training and test datasets will prove useful to future researchers who wish to explore the complex relation between figurativity and sentiment. To this end, we have taken steps to preserve the tweets used in this task, to ensure that they do not perish through the actions of their original creators. Detailed results of the evaluation of all systems and runs are shown in Tables 9 and 10, or can be found online here:

http://alt.qcri.org/semeval2015/task11/

Team Name	Name of Run	Rank	Overall	Sarcasm	Irony	Metaphor	Other
ClaC		1	**0.758**	0.892	0.904	**0.655**	0.584
UPF		2	0.711	0.903	0.873	0.520	0.486
LLT_PolyU		3	0.687	0.896	**0.918**	0.535	0.290
LT3	*run 1*	4	0.6581	0.891	0.897	0.443	0.346
	run 2		0.648	0.872	0.861	0.355	0.357
elirf		5	0.6579	**0.904**	0.905	0.411	0.247
ValenTo		6	0.634	0.895	0.901	0.393	0.202
HLT		7	0.630	0.887	0.907	0.379	0.365
CPH	*ridge*	8	0.625	0.897	0.886	0.325	0.218
	ensemble		0.623	0.900	0.903	0.308	0.226
	special-ensemble		0.298	-0.148	0.281	0.535	**0.612**
PRHLT	*ETR-ngram*	9	0.623	0.891	0.901	0.167	0.218
	ETR-word		0.611	0.890	0.901	0.294	0.129
	RFR-word		0.613	0.888	0.898	0.282	0.170
	RFR-ngram		0.597	0.888	0.898	0.135	0.192
	BRR-word		0.592	0.883	0.880	0.280	0.110
	BRR-ngram		0.593	0.886	0.879	0.119	0.186
DsUniPi		10	0.601	0.87	0.839	0.359	0.271
PKU		11	0.574	0.883	0.877	0.350	0.137
KELabTeam			0.531	0.883	0.895	0.341	0.117
	content based	12	0.552	0.896	0.915	0.341	0.115
	emotional pattern based		0.533	0.874	0.900	0.289	0.135
RGU	*test-sent-final*	13	0.523	0.829	0.832	0.291	0.165
	test-sent-warppred		0.509	0.842	0.861	0.280	0.090
	test-sent-predictions		0.509	0.842	0.861	0.280	0.090
SHELLFBK	*run3*	14	0.431	0.669	0.625	0.35	0.167
	run2		0.427	0.681	0.652	0.346	0.146
	run1		0.145	0.013	0.104	0.167	0.308
BUAP		15	0.058	0.412	-0.209	-0.023	-0.025

Table 9. Detailed evaluation of each submitted run of each system (using the **Cosine similarity** metric).

Key: ***CLaC****= Concordia University;* ***UPF****= Universitat Pompeu Fabra;* ***LLT_PolyU****=Hong Kong Polytechnic University;* ***LT3****= Ghent University;* ***elirf****= Universitat Politècnica de València;* ***ValenTo****= Universitat Politècnica de València;* ***HLT****= FBK-Irst, University of Trento;* ***CPH****= Københavns Universitet;* ***PRHLT****= PRHLT Research Center;* ***DsUniPi****= University of Piraeus;* ***PKU****= Peking University;* ***KELabTeam****= Yeungnam University;* ***RGU****= Robert Gordon University;* ***SHELLFBK****= Fondazione Bruno Kessler;* ***BUAP****= Benemérita Universidad Autónoma de Puebla*

Team Name	Name of Run	Rank	Overall	Sarcasm	Irony	Metaphor	Other
ClaC		1	**2.117**	1.023	0.779	**3.155**	**3.411**
UPF		2	2.458	**0.934**	1.041	4.186	3.772
LLT_PolyU		3	2.600	1.018	**0.673**	3.917	4.587
LT3	run1		3.398	1.287	1.224	5.670	5.444
	run2	4	2.912	1.286	1.083	4.793	4.503
elirf		8	3.096	1.349	1.034	4.565	5.235
ValenTo		5	2.999	1.004	0.777	4.730	5.315
HLT		11	4.088	1.327	1.184	6.589	7.119
CPH	ridge		3.079	1.041	0.904	4.916	5.343
	ensemble	7	3.078	0.971	0.774	5.014	5.429
	special-ensemble		11.274	19.267	9.124	7.806	7.027
PRHLT	ETR-ngram	6	3.023	1.028	0.784	5.446	4.888
	ETR-word		3.112	1.041	0.791	5.031	5.448
	RFR-word		3.107	1.060	0.809	5.115	5.345
	RFR-ngram		3.229	1.059	0.811	5.878	5.243
	BRR-word		3.299	1.146	0.934	5.178	5.773
	BRR-ngram		3.266	1.100	0.941	5.925	5.205
DsUniPi		10	3.925	1.499	1.656	7.106	5.744
PKU		9	3.746	1.148	1.015	5.876	6.743
KELabTeam			5.552	1.198	1.255	7.264	9.905
	content based		6.090	1.756	1.811	8.707	11.526
	emotional pattern	12	4.177	1.189	0.809	6.829	7.628
RGU	test-sentfinal	13	5.143	1.954	1.867	8.015	8.602
	test-sent-warppred		5.323	1.855	1.541	8.033	9.505
	test-sent-predictions		5.323	1.855	1.541	8.033	9.505
SHELLFBK	run3	15	7.701	4.375	4.516	9.219	12.16
	run2		9.265	5.183	5.047	11.058	15.055
	run1		10.486	12.326	9.853	10.649	8.957
BUAP		14	6.785	4.339	7.609	8.93	7.253

Table 10. Detailed evaluation of each submitted run of each system (using the **Mean-Squared-Error** metric).

Key: ***CLaC****= Concordia University;* ***UPF****= Universitat Pompeu Fabra;* ***LLT_PolyU****=Hong Kong Polytechnic University;* ***LT3****= Ghent University;* ***elirf****= Universitat Politècnica de València;* ***ValenTo****= Universitat Politècnica de València;* ***HLT****= FBK-Irst, University of Trento;* ***CPH****= Københavns Universitet;* ***PRHLT****= PRHLT Research Center;* ***DsUniPi****= University of Piraeus;* ***PKU****= Peking University;* ***KELabTeam****= Yeungnam University;* ***RGU****= Robert Gordon University;* ***SHELLFBK****= Fondazione Bruno Kessler;* ***BUAP****= Benemérita Universidad Autónoma de Puebla*

Acknowledgements

The authors gratefully acknowledge the support of the following projects funded by the European Commission: *PROSECCO* (Grant No. 600653), *WIQ-EI IRSES* (Grant No. 269180) and *MICINN DIANA-Applications* (TIN2012-38603-C02-01). We are also grateful for the support of the *CNGL Centre for Global Intelligent Content*, funded by Science Foundation Ireland (SFI).

References

Barnden, J.A. (2008). Metaphor and artificial intelligence: Why they matter to each other. In R.W. Gibbs, Jr. (Ed.), The Cambridge Handbook of Metaphor and Thought, 311-338. Cambridge, U.K.: Cambridge University Press.

Hao, Y., Veale, T. (2010). An Ironic Fist in a Velvet Glove: Creative Mis-Representation in the Construction of Ironic Similes. Minds and Machines 20(4):635–650.

Li G., Ghosh A., Veale T. (2014). Constructing A corpus of Figurative Language for a Tweet Classification and Retrieval Task. In the preceedings of FIRE 2014, the 6th Forum for Information Retrieval Evaluatio. Bengaluru, India.

Poria, S., Cambria, E., Winterstein, G. and Huang, G.B. (2014). Sentic patterns Dependency-based rules for concept-level sentiment analysis. *Knowledge-Based Systems* 69, pp. 45-63.

Reyes A., Rosso P. (2014). On the Difficulty of Automatically Detecting Irony: Beyond a Simple Case of Negation. Knowledge and Information Systems. 40(3): 595-614. DOI: 10.1007/s10115-013-0652-8.

Reyes A., Rosso P., Veale T. (2013). A Multidimensional Approach for Detecting Irony in Twitter. Languages Resources and Evaluation 47(1): 239-268.

Reyes A., Rosso P. (2012). Making Objective Decisions from Subjective Data: Detecting Irony in Customers Reviews. Journal on Decision Support Systems 53(4): 754–760.

Reyes A., Rosso P., Buscaldi D. (2012). From Humor Recognition to Irony Detection: The Figurative Language of Social Media. Data & Knowledge Engineering 74:1-12.

Shutova, E., L. Sun, A. Korhonen. (2010). Metaphor identification using verb and noun clustering. Proceedings of the 23rd International Conference on Computational Linguistics.

Veale, T., Keane, M. T. (1992). Conceptual Scaffolding: A spatially founded meaning representation for metaphor comprehension. Computational Intelligence 8(3): 494-519.

Veale, T. (2012). Detecting and Generating Ironic Comparisons: An Application of Creative Information Retrieval. AAAI Fall Symposium Series 2012, Artificial Intelligence of Humor. Arlington, Virginia.

Veale, T., Hao, Y. (2007). Comprehending and Generating Apt Metaphors: A Web-driven, Case-based Approach to Figurative Language. In proceedings of AAAI 2007, the 22nd AAAI Conference on Artificial Intelligence. Vancouver, Canada.

CLaC-SentiPipe: SemEval2015 Subtasks 10 B,E, and Task 11

Canberk Özdemir and Sabine Bergler
CLaC Labs, Concordia University
1455 de Maisonneuve Blvd West
Montreal, Quebec, Canada, H3G 1M8
ozdemir.berkin@gmail.com, bergler@cse.concordia.ca

Abstract

CLaC Labs participated in two shared tasks for SemEval2015, Task 10 (subtasks B and E) and Task 11. The underlying system configuration is nearly identical and consists of two major components: a large Twitter lexicon compiled from tweets that carry certain selected hashtags (assumed to guarantee a sentiment polarity) and then inducing that same polarity for the words that occur in the tweets. We also use standard sentiment lexica and combine the results. The lexical sentiment features are further differentiated according to some linguistic contexts in which their triggers occur, including bigrams, negation, modality, and dependency triples. We studied feature combinations comprehensively for their interoperability and effectiveness on different datasets using the exhaustive feature combination technique of (Shareghi and Bergler, 2013a; Shareghi and Bergler, 2013b). For Subtask 10B we used a SVM, and a decision tree regressor for Task 11. The resulting systems ranked ninth for Subtask 10B, fourth for Subtask 10E, and first for Task 11.

1 Introduction

The field of Sentiment Analysis is in its second phase: initially, the task was defined, annotation standards, corpora, and feature resources were identified and provided to the research community (see (Pang and Lee, 2008)). Now, we have regular community challenges such as the SemEval Twitter Sentiment shared tasks which allow us to compare different feature choice and combination across research labs and across successive data sets. We describe here the systems we submitted to SemEval15 for Twitter Sentiment Analysis at the tweet level (Task 10B) and Figurative Language in Twitter (Task 11). The tasks and the design of the datasets is described in detail in (Rosenthal et al., 2015) for Task 10 and in (Ghosh et al., 2015) for Task 11. We also submitted a sentiment lexicon transformed from our in-house lexical resource for Task 10E.

Our system is based on a pipeline design in 5 major phases, described below. Following standard text preprocessing, we use Stanford dependencies (De Marneffe et al., 2006) and linguistic features negation, modality and their scope in connection with standard sentiment lexica from the literature and an in-house lexical resource compiled with the technique used for the NRC lexicon (Mohammad et al., 2013). These features were successful in both Task 10B (rank 9 on 40 for Twitter 2015 data, seventh on 40 for Twitter 2015 sarcasm data) and Task 11 (rank 1 of 35 runs by 15 teams). Our sentiment lexicon submitted to Task 10E ranked fourth of ten.

2 Pipeline Design

CLaCSentiPipe is a pipeline system that attempts to test the interoperability of different sentiment lexica and a selected set of linguistic annotations.

The lexical resources used are aFinn (Nielsen, 2011), MPQA (Wilson et al., 2005), BingLiu (Hu and Liu, 2004), and Gezi, our own lexical resource described below.

Third party processing resources in our GATE environment (Cunningham et al., 2013) include a hybrid of Annie and CMU tokenizers (Cunningham et al., 2002; Gimpel et al., 2011), named entity recognition (Ritter et al.,), Stanford Parser Version 3.4.1 (Socher et al., 2013) and dependency module (De Marneffe et al., 2006).

Linguistic notions used are negation and modality triggers (Kilicoglu, 2012; Rosenberg, 2013) and scope (Rosenberg, 2013) as well as dependency relations (De Marneffe et al., 2006).

Phase 1 Following tokenization, sentence splitting, POS tagging, and named entity recognition (Ritter et al.,) (to fuse multi-word names into a single token) and lookup in the sentiment lexica used, we ignore Twitter-specific items (*@name*, URLs ...) when parsing with the Stanford parser.

Phase 2 Using POS tags information for disambiguation, the prior polarity (value *positive, negative, neutral* and score where available) is determined for each token from each of the lexical resources.

Phase 3 Based on the Stanford dependencies produced in Phase 1, we identify negation and modality triggers and their scope (Rosenberg, 2013) and look up PMI scores (Church and Hanks, 1990) for dependency triples in the Gezi dependency resource.

Phase 4 The resulting features are the polarity class according to each lexical resource, embeddedness in modality or negation, as well as sentiment scores for each lexical token according to appropriate lexical resources; dependency score features using PMI scores of dependency triples and their types; dependency count features mapping PMI scores into discrete polarity classes; ad hoc features from specific annotations observed on training data.

Phase 5 The resulting feature space is grouped into subsets of features in order to create feature combinations (Shareghi and Bergler, 2013a; Shareghi and Bergler, 2013b) and processed with Weka (Witten and Frank, 2011) libSVM (Chang and Lin, 2011) with RBF kernel and parameters of cost=5, gamma=0.001 and weights=[neutral=1; positive=2; negative=2.9] for Subtask 10B and M5P (Wang and Witten, 1997), a decision tree regressor, to predict continuos values[1] for Task 11.

[1] http://www.opentox.org/dev/documentation/components/m5p

3 Lexica

In the past two years, the team that developed the NRC lexicon (Mohammad et al., 2013) dominated the Twitter sentiment task and our first question was: is the NRC lexicon itself the ultimate resource, or is the technique that derived it the essential lesson, and can that technique be reused to similar effect. We compiled a similar resource, Gezi, and compared it with the NRC lexicon, but also much smaller traditional resources, namely Bing Liu's dictionary (Hu and Liu, 2004), MPQA (Wiebe et al., 2006), and aFinn (Nielsen, 2011), a manually compiled dictionary. Extensive ablation studies showed that all the resulting dictionaries contributed to the best performing feature combination, but that the contribution of the lexica was not proportional to size (suggesting significant overlap). Surprisingly, aFinn, the smallest lexicon, by itself performs better than any of the other dictionaries by themselves and it is the one stable component in all our top performing feature combinations. In our competition system, we did not use the NRC lexicon, in order to assess whether Gezi, derived in a similar manner, was performing as well.

4 Gezi Lexical Resources

Gezi corpus To assess whether the strong performance of the NRC lexicon can be replicated and enhanced, we used their technique to compile a new resource, Gezi, by selecting positive and negative hashtags from the Twitter API from December 2013 to May 2014. The set of 35 positive and 34 negative seed hashtags were obtained from the Oxford American Writer's Thesaurus (Moody and Lindberg, 2012) by expanding the adjectives *good* and *bad*, resulting in nearly 20 million tweets, from which unigram, bigram, and dependency triple information was collected.

After removing retweets, tweets with conflicting hashtags, and tweets with little or no content words, as well as all URLs in tweets, we annotate the remaining tweets with the polarity class of their seed hashtag for our Gezi tweet corpus and project the tweet polarity onto each token inside the tweet for our unigram and bigram features.

Data processing After applying Phase 1 to the Gezi corpus the same way we use it in our main pipeline, we also parse tweets and identify negation triggers and their scopes. Then we record counts of unigrams, bigrams and dependency triples (type-head-modifier) in the context they occurred by also taking negation scope into consideration. For instance; if a term occurs in a positive-annotated tweet where it is not in the scope of a negation, its *positive* count is incremented; if it is in a positive-annotated tweet and in the scope of negation, then its *negated-positive* count is incremented. This reflects the different contexts in which the terms of the lexicon were found and associates them with the resulting sentiment. In addition, we keep terms with different POS tags separate in the resources. The counts of the terms in the *positive*, *negative*, *negated-positive* and *negated-negative* categories for the entire collection are then transformed into association scores using pointwise mutual information.

NRC and Gezi A quick comparison of Gezi and NRC unigrams and bigrams on three years of SemEval data in Table 1 shows their performance is close, with a small advantage for the much larger Gezi lexicon. Analyzing overlap of NRC (25721 unigrams) and Gezi (220399 unigrams), we find they agree only on 13957 of 16868 shared entries (both have higher agreement rates with aFinn!)

We interpret these findings as confirmation that the NRC technique can profitably be replicated and thus be used to create sentiment lexica that are bigger or smaller, that span a relevant period or contain relevant topics. We also conclude that size alone does not change results proportionally, as these large lexica clearly expand into the long tail of infrequently used words.

	SemEval Test data		
	2015	2014	2013
NRC unigrams	49.83	52.39	50.9
NRC bigrams	51.31	53.48	52.31
Gezi unigrams	54.65	60.81	57.86
Gezi bigrams	51.14	56.40	50.45
all four combined	56.07	64.26	59.60

Table 1: Comparison NRC and Gezi.

5 Features and Feature Space

Primary Features Lexicon features (*aFinn*, *NRC*, ...) encode the prior polarity of the terms in a lexicon.

Recent work in our lab on embedding predication (Kilicoglu, 2012), negation (Rosenberg, 2013), and modality (Rosenberg et al., 2012) highlighted that syntactically embedding constructions exert an influence over the meaning of constituents, so we applied this insight to sentiment values. On the 2013 dataset, most (of the 6822) tweets contained named entities (6286), as expected, but surprisingly the second most frequent feature was modality (1785), followed by negation (1356). Thus these features have the potential to influence the results to a measurable degree.

These linguistic context features were encoded as occurrences. The general schema of this integration for our system can be formulated as `polarityClass,lexicalResource,linguisticScope`, where `polarityClass` is one of *positive, negative, neutral, strong positive, strong negative*, `lexicalResource` represents a lexical resource and `linguisticScope` is one of *none, negation, modality, negation+modality*. For each tweet token, its prior polarity and any scope annotation is checked (a score feature is created if a lexicon provides score information for its terms).

The features for each feature type are aggregated into tweet-level aggregates, creating a compact feature space (94 features for Subtask 10B, 90 for Task 11).

Table 2 shows the primary features created from the aFinn lexical resource for Example 1.

(1) El Classico on a Sunday Night isn't perfect for the Monday Morning !!

This particular example has only one sentiment trigger in aFinn, *perfect*, with *aFinn score*=3 and *positive-aFinn*=1 (it is a strong positive sentiment trigger in the lexicon). In the context of Example 1, however, it occurs in the scope of a negation, thus the score is multiplied by -0.5 and the count feature *positive-aFinn-negated*=1 is activated instead, resulting in the feature assignment of Table 2.

Secondary Features The contrastive conjunction *but* and a list of contrastive adverbs (*although*, etc)

feature	value
positive-aFinn	0
positive-aFinn-negated	1
positive-aFinn-mod	0
positive-aFinn-mod-negated	0
negative-aFinn	0
negative-aFinn-negated	0
negative-aFinn-mod	0
negative-aFinn-mod-negated	0
aFinn-score	-1.5

Table 2: aFinn features for Example 1.

each constitute a feature, as do named entities. Additional ad hoc features are some special Twitter-specific POS tags (i.e. emphasis from *!!!!!*), special phrases indicative of sentiment (*can't wait*). We also found the first and last token in a tweet to carry potentially special meaning, as well as the association scores between the highest and lowest sentiment carriers in a tweet.

Feature Combinations We create feature spaces for each combination of feature subsets described above and we experiment on each combination. The submitted feature combinations for Subtask 10B and Task 11 were selected using the exhaustive feature combination technique of (Shareghi and Bergler, 2013a; Shareghi and Bergler, 2013b).

	# feat's
Primary Feature Subsets	
aFinn	9
MPQA	12
BingLiu	8
NRC unigrams	17
NRC bigrams	17
Gezi unigrams	17
Gezi bigrams	17
dependency scores	13
dependency counts	8
Secondary Feature Subsets	
pos tag based scores and counts	9
frequencies of specific annotations	12
position and top-lowest scores	6

Table 3: Feature subset bundles.

Table 3 lists the feature bundles used in our ablation studies.

6 Subtask 10B: Polarity Classification of Tweets

The task is a 3-way classification problem of labelling a tweet as *positive*, *neutral*, or *negative*, see (Rosenthal et al., 2015) for a detailed description.

We trained an SVM classifier for our experiments using last year's test sets for development. Performing manual feature selection, we selected not the feature combination that performed best on the training data but instead one that was close to the top on 2015 training data and both, 2014 and 2013 test data (for robustness) but that did not include NRC data (to better assess Gezi). The competition system included aFinn, MPQA, Bing Liu, Gezi unigrams and dependency based features in addition to all secondary features listed above.

Results The task of assigning sentiment to a tweet attracted the most participants. CLaC-SentiPipe ranked 9 of 40, a very strong placement considering less than 3% separated our results from the top ranking one. A comparison of the competing systems on the past two years' data shows that our system ranked 7 on 2013 Twitter data, 10 on 2014 Twitter data, 6 on 2014 Live Journal data, 18 on SMS messages from 2013, and 10 on Twitter 2014 Sarcasm data. This demonstrates robustness in performance. The detailed official results are shown in Table 4.

The best performing system dips to rank 12 and 13 for the LiveJournal and Sarcasm tasks of the previous years, which indicates that the different datasets compared show a certain difference, but not a big one. The very close performance of the systems in the top quarter on this task (less than 3% difference) suggests that the different approaches are drowned out by the constancy in the datasets: we may have reached the beginning of the long tail at this margin, where improvements contribute only small amounts and are not individually measurable in the general task.

7 Subtask 10E: Determining Strength of Association of Terms

SemEval 2015 Subtask 10E was a pilot task requesting association scores of terms extracted from tweets. The test set consisted of words or phrases that had to be associated with scores between 0 and

dataset	positive P	R	F1	negative P	R	F1	neutral P	R	F1	overall F1
Twitter2015	75.58	63.20	68.84	43.51	75.34	55.17	66.63	60.08	63.19	62.00
Twitter2015-sarcasm	55.56	55.56	55.56	61.54	61.54	61.54	43.75	43.75	43.75	58.55
LiveJournal2014	79.33	66.51	72.36	68.39	82.57	74.81	67.87	68.86	68.36	73.59
SMS2013	59.26	68.29	63.46	54.39	73.86	62.65	83.55	68.60	75.34	63.05
Twitter2013	73.45	75.13	74.28	59.50	75.54	66.57	75.66	66.52	70.80	70.42
Twitter2014	78.76	70.98	74.67	58.53	74.75	65.65	63.10	66.97	64.97	70.16
Twitter2014Sarcasm	50.91	84.85	63.64	90.91	25.00	39.22	40.00	61.54	48.48	51.43

Table 4: Official CLaC-SentiPipe results for Task 10B: rank 9.

1 where 1 stands for maximum association with positive sentiment and 0 does for maximum association with negative sentiment.

We followed a simple, rule-based approach:

1. aFinn sentiment scores and Gezi (unigrams and bigrams) PMI values are used

2. if a term is part of a bigram, the unigram sentiment trigger and negation annotations are removed, if they exist

3. if a trigger is in negation scope, its prior sentiment score is multiplied with -0.5

4. if there is more than one sentiment trigger per term, the triggers' scores are summed up

5. each prior sentiment score is scaled to [0,1]

6. if there is no trigger for a term, score is 0.5

Results The evaluation metrics are Kendall and Spearman rank correlation coefficients (Nelson, 2001) for subtask 10E between gold values of words or phrases and predicted values. Gold values are human judgements from the compilation of the NRC lexicon (Kiritchenko et al., 2014).

Our simple rule-based and lexica-driven system submitted for Task 10E ranked 4th among 10 submitted systems in both correlation coefficient evaluations. Our Kendall rank correlation coefficient result is 0.584 where all results range between 0.625 and 0.254, and our Spearman rank correlation coefficient result is 0.777 where results range between 0.817 and 0.373.

8 Task 11: Figurative Language

Figurative language permeates daily life and social media, conveying non-explicit meanings using tropes such as irony, sarcasm, or metaphor. However, understanding these phenomena is not trivial for sentiment analysis systems, that usually assume that each word has only one (literal) meaning and an a priori sentiment value.

SemEval 2015 Subtask 11 Sentiment Analysis of Figurative Language in Twitter was organized for the first time this year (Ghosh et al., 2015). The challenge dataset contains tweets that contain at least one instance of figurative language and non-figurative tweets (labelled *other*). The labels are in form of sentiment scores obtained from human judgements. The dataset distinguished 3 types of figurative language, *Sarcasm, Irony* and *Metaphor*. The organizers made the tweet data available with both integer-based and float-based scores.

We tested the robustness of our linguistic embedding features by submitting the same pipeline for text processing, feature creation and the exhaustive feature combination evaluation technique of (Shareghi and Bergler, 2013a; Shareghi and Bergler, 2013b) via 10-fold cross validation on the training set with M5P (Wang and Witten, 1997), a decision tree regressor. We evaluated 10-fold cross validation predictions by calculating correlation coefficients (Nelson, 2001).

The extracted features are the same as the features we extracted for Subtask 10B. The only difference is the gold labels since Task 11 requires continuous classes while these are discrete in Subtask 10B.

We used float-based gold labels for training data and treat the problem as a regression problem. The output of our system's predictions were then

MSE				
Overall	Sarcasm	Irony	Metaphor	Other
2.117	1.023	0.779	3.155	3.411
Cosine				
Overall	Sarcasm	Irony	Metaphor	Other
0.758	0.892	0.904	0.655	0.584

Table 5: CLaC-SentiPipe in Task 11: rank 1.

rounded to integer values, as required.

Results The single submission from CLaC ranked first in both, cosine and mean squared error measures. There were wide margins between the first three systems.

The different types of figurative language were scored individually, see Table 5. In mean square error, CLaC ranked first in the *overall* score, the *metaphor*, and *other* categories. For the cosine measure, the third system of a competitor obtained best performance in the *other* category, but with a high mean squared error.

The second best system, interestingly, does not hold best performance in a single category, which demonstrates the good performance of a steady approach. The third ranked team obtained best performance for irony both in cosine similarity and least squared error, but not in their best performing (ranked) submission.

Our system has shown robustness across tasks and the linguistic features encoded have been validated for their adaptability to figurative language.

Further analysis We compared our technique with automatic forward feature selection, which interestingly selected the following six features: Gezi strong negative unigram, Gezi strong negative bigram, NRC strong positive unigram, NRC strong positive bigram: all four under scopes of both negation and modality; average scores of hashtag sentiment; counts of named entities. The results for this feature set would have been 66.41, which places it between the third and fourth-ranked systems in the competition.

This reinforces the observation that negation and modality contexts interoperate well with strong lexicon scores and are essential.

9 Conclusion

CLaCSentiPipe showed a strong top quarter performance in sentiment annotation of tweets and in its submitted lexicon, but it excelled at figurative language. We claim that the use of linguistic features negation, modality, embedding and dependency triples provides a wider context to the a priori sentiment values found in a lexicon. We combined our own large Twitter derived lexicon (Gezi) with standard resources for a range of a priori values. Gezi used the technique of extracting tweets with hashtags that are believed to guarantee sentiment polarity and inducing sentiment values for the words contained accordingly. This technique has been used for the NRC lexicon and here we showed that it can be reimplemented with good success. Our lexicon was derived from a Twitter stream of two years ago. The drastically lower performance of all systems on 2015 test data as compared to 2014 or 2013 data suggests that some events or story lines in the 2015 data use sentiment triggers differently.

Closeness of results suggest that the systems largely cover common ground, and that their specializations now fall in the area of the long tail, where incremental improvements become small and are hard to detect and measure. This confirms the observation that sentiment carrying words form a fuzzy set as demonstrated by (Andreevskaia and Bergler, 2006).

It is thus especially pleasing that the same system performed best on Task 11, sentiment annotation of tweets containing figurative language of various forms: *irony, sarcasm, metaphor*, or *other*. Here, we feel the explicit annotation of the embedding constructs has given the system the required degree of freedom to adapt to the non-literal usage. We interpret the fact that our features had not been designed specifically for this task (but were repurposed from Task 10 and merely retrained) as an indicator of robustness and a strong endorsement of our linguistically inspired features.

Acknowledgments

This work has been funded by a grant from Canada's Natural Science and Engineering Research Council (NSERC) and has benefitted from collaboration with Marc-André Faucher and Nasrin Baratalipour.

References

Alina Andreevskaia and Sabine Bergler. 2006. Mining WordNet for a fuzzy sentiment: Sentiment tag extraction from WordNet glosses. In *Proceedings of the 11th Conference of the European Chapter of the Association for Computational Linguistics (EACL-06)*.

Chih-Chung Chang and Chih-Jen Lin. 2011. LIBSVM: A library for support vector machines. *Transactions on Intelligent Systems and Technology (TIST)*, 2(3).

Kenneth Ward Church and Patrick Hanks. 1990. Word association norms, mutual information, and lexicography. *Computational linguistics*, 16(1).

Hamish Cunningham, Diana Maynard, Kalina Bontcheva, and Valentin Tablan. 2002. GATE: A framework and graphical development environment for robust NLP tools and applications. In *Proceedings of the 40th Anniversary Meeting of the Association for Computational Linguistics (ACL'02)*.

Hamish Cunningham, Valentin Tablan, Angus Roberts, and Kalina Bontcheva. 2013. Getting more out of biomedical documents with GATE's full lifecycle open source text analytics. *PLoS Computational Biology*, 9(2).

Marie-Catherine De Marneffe, Bill MacCartney, and Christopher D. Manning. 2006. Generating typed dependency parses from phrase structure parses. In *Proceedings of the 5th International Conference on Language Resources and Evaluation (LREC 2006)*.

Aniruddha Ghosh, Guofu Li, Tony Veale, Paolo Rosso, Ekaterina Shutova, Antonio Reyes, and John Barnden. 2015. SemEval-2015 task 11: Sentiment analysis of figurative language in Twitter. In *Proceedings of the International Workshop on Semantic Evaluation (SemEval-2015)*.

Kevin Gimpel, Nathan Schneider, Brendan O'Connor, Dipanjan Das, Daniel Mills, Jacob Eisenstein, Michael Heilman, Dani Yogatama, Jeffrey Flanigan, and Noah A. Smith. 2011. Part-of-speech tagging for Twitter: Annotation, features, and experiments. In *Proceedings of the 49th Annual Meeting of the Association for Computational Linguistics: Human Language Technologies (ACL/HLT 2011)*.

Minqing Hu and Bing Liu. 2004. Mining and summarizing customer reviews. In *Proceedings of the International Conference on Knowledge Discovery & Data Mining (KDD-2004)*.

Halil Kilicoglu. 2012. *Embedding Predications*. Ph.D. thesis, Concordia University.

Svetlana Kiritchenko, Xiaodan Zhu, and Saif M. Mohammad. 2014. Sentiment analysis of short informal texts. *Journal of Artificial Intelligence Research*, 50.

Saif M. Mohammad, Svetlana Kiritchenko, and Xiaodan Zhu. 2013. NRC-Canada: Building the state-of-the-art in sentiment analysis of tweets. In *Proceedings of the Seventh International Workshop on Semantic Evaluation (SemEval-2013)*.

Rick Moody and Christine A Lindberg. 2012. *Oxford American Writer's Thesaurus*. OUP.

Roger B. Nelson. 2001. Kendall tau metric. *Encyclopaedia of Mathematics*, 3.

Finn A. Nielsen. 2011. A new ANEW: Evaluation of a word list for sentiment analysis in microblogs. In *Proceedings of ESWC2011 Workshop on 'Making Sense of Microposts': Big Things Come in Small Packages*.

Bo Pang and Lillian Lee. 2008. Opinion mining and sentiment analysis. *Foundations and Trends in Information Retrieval*, 2(1-2).

Alan Ritter, Sam Clark, and Oren Etzion. Named entity recognition in Tweets: an experimental study.

Sabine Rosenberg, Halil Kilicoglu, and Sabine Bergler. 2012. CLaC Labs: Processing modality and negation. In *Working Notes for QA4MRE Pilot Task at CLEF 2012*.

Sabine Rosenberg. 2013. Negation triggers and their scope. Master's thesis, Concordia University.

Sara Rosenthal, Preslav Nakov, Svetlana Kiritchenko, Saif M. Mohammad, Alan Ritter, and Veselin Stoyanov. 2015. SemEval-2015 Task 10: Sentiment analysis in Twitter. In *Proceedings of the 9th International Workshop on Semantic Evaluation (SemEval2015)*.

Ehsan Shareghi and Sabine Bergler. 2013a. CLaC-CORE: Exhaustive feature combination for measuring textual similarity. In *Proceedings of *SEM 2013 Shared Task STS*.

Ehsan Shareghi and Sabine Bergler. 2013b. Feature combination for sentence similarity. In *Proceedings of the 26th Canadian Conference on Artificial Intelligence (AI 2013)*. Springer Berlin. LNAI 7884.

Richard Socher, John Bauer, Christopher D. Manning, and Andrew Y. Ng. 2013. Parsing with compositional vector grammars. In *Proceedings of the 51st Meeting of the Association for Computational Linguistics (ACL 2013)*.

Yong Wang and Ian H. Witten. 1997. Induction of model trees for predicting continuous classes. In *Poster in Proceedings of the 9th European Conference on Machine Learning*. Faculty of Informatics and Statistics, Prague.

Janyce Wiebe, Theresa Wilson, and Claire Cardie. 2006. Annotating expressions of opinions and emotions in language. *Language Resources and Evaluation*, 39(2-3).

Theresa Wilson, Janyce Wiebe, and Paul Hoffmann. 2005. Recognizing contextual polarity in phrase-level sentiment analysis. In *Proceedings of HLT-EMNLP*.

Ian H. Witten and Eibe Frank. 2011. *Data Mining: Practical Machine Learning Tools and Techniques*. Morgan Kaufmann Publishers, 3rd edition.

SemEval-2015 Task 12: Aspect Based Sentiment Analysis

Maria Pontiki*, Dimitrios Galanis*, Haris Papageorgiou*,
Suresh Manandhar±, Ion Androutsopoulos◊*

*Institute for Language and Speech Processing, Athena R.C., Athens, Greece
± Dept. of Computer Science, University of York, UK
◊ Dept. of Informatics, Athens University of Economics and Business, Greece
{mpontiki, galanisd, xaris} @ilsp.gr
suresh@cs.york.ac.uk
ion@aueb.gr

Abstract

SemEval-2015 Task 12, a continuation of SemEval-2014 Task 4, aimed to foster research beyond sentence- or text-level sentiment classification towards Aspect Based Sentiment Analysis. The goal is to identify opinions expressed about specific entities (e.g., laptops) and their aspects (e.g., price). The task provided manually annotated reviews in three domains (restaurants, laptops and hotels), and a common evaluation procedure. It attracted 93 submissions from 16 teams.

1 Introduction and Related Work

The rise of e-commerce, as a new shopping and marketing channel, has led to an upsurge of review sites for a variety of services and products. In this context, Aspect Based Sentiment Analysis (ABSA) -i.e., mining opinions from text about specific entities and their aspects- can help consumers decide what to purchase and businesses to better monitor their reputation and understand the needs of the market (Pavlopoulos 2014). Given a target of interest (e.g., Apple Mac mini), an ABSA method can summarize the content of the respective reviews in an aspect-sentiment table like the one in Fig 1. Some review sites also generate such tables based on customer ratings, but usually only for a limited set of predefined aspects and not from free-text reviews.

Several ABSA methods have been proposed for various domains, like consumer electronics (Hu and Liu {2004a, 2004b}), restaurants (Ganu et al., 2009) and movies (Thet et al., 2010). The available methods can be divided into those that adopt domain-independent solutions (Lin and He, 2009), and those that use domain-specific knowledge to improve their results (Thet et al., 2010). Typically, most methods treat aspect extraction and sentiment classification separately (Brody and Elhadad, 2010), but there are also approaches that model the two problems jointly (Jo and Oh, 2011).

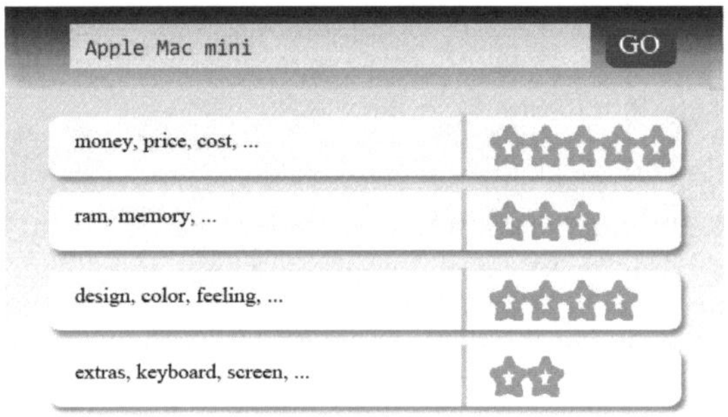

Figure 1. Table summarizing the average sentiment for each aspect of an entity.

Publicly available ABSA datasets adopt different annotation schemes for different subtasks and languages (Pavlopoulos 2014). For example, the datasets of McAuley et al. (2012) provide aspects and respective ratings at the review level (i.e., aspects and ratings associated with entire reviews, not particular sentences)[1] about Beers, Pubs, Toys and Games, and Audiobooks. The reviews are obtained from sites that allow users to evaluate a product not only in terms of its overall quality, but also focusing on specific predefined aspects (e.g. "smell" and "taste" for Beers, "fun" and "educational value" for Toys and Games). The IGGSA Shared Tasks on German Sentiment Analysis (Ruppenhofer et al., 2014) provided human annotated datasets of political speeches (STEPS task)

[1] A subset of the datasets has been annotated with aspects at the sentence level.

and reviews about products (StAR task) like coffee machines and washers. The StAR task focused on the extraction of evaluative phrases (e.g., "*bad*") and aspect expressions (e.g., "*washer*"). The STEPS dataset includes annotations for evaluative phrases, opinion targets, and the corresponding sources (opinion holders). The extraction of opinion targets and holders has also been addressed in the context of the Multilingual Opinion Analysis Task (Seki et al., 2007; Seki et al., 2008; Seki et al., 2010) and the Sentiment Slot Filling[2] Task of the Knowledge Base Population Track (Mitchell, 2013). However, these tasks deal with the identification of opinion targets in general, not in the context of ABSA.

SemEval-2014 Task 4 (SE-ABSA14) provided datasets annotated with aspect terms (e.g., "hard disk", "pizza") and their polarity for laptop and restaurant reviews, as well as coarser aspect categories (e.g., PRICE) and their polarity only for restaurants[3] (Pontiki et al., 2014). The task attracted 165 submissions from 32 teams that experimented with a variety of features (e.g., based on n-grams, parse trees, named entities, word clusters), techniques (e.g., rule-based, supervised and unsupervised learning), and resources (e.g., sentiment lexica, Wikipedia, WordNet). The participants obtained higher scores in the restaurants domain. The laptops domain proved to be harder involving more entities (e.g., hardware and software components) and complex concepts (e.g., usability, portability) that are often discussed implicitly in the text. The SE-ABSA14 task set-up has been adopted for the creation of aspect-level sentiment datasets in other languages, like Czech (Steinberger et al., 2014).

SemEval-2015 Task 12 (SE-ABSA15) built upon SE-ABSA14 and consolidated its subtasks (aspect category extraction, aspect term extraction, polarity classification) into a principled unified framework (described in Section 2). In addition, SE-ABSA15 included an aspect level polarity classification subtask for the hotels domain in which no training data were provided (out-of-domain ABSA). The annotation schema and the provided datasets are described in Section 3. The evaluation measures and the baseline methods are described in Section 4, while the evaluation scores and the main characteristics of the developed systems are presented in Section 5. The paper concludes with a general assessment of the task.

2 Task Set-Up

2.1 ABSA Framework: From SE-ABSA14 to SE-ABSA15

In SE-ABSA14, given a sentence from a user review about a target entity *e* (e.g., a laptop), the goal was to identify all aspects (explicit terms or categories) and the corresponding polarities. Following Liu (2006) & Zhang and Liu (2014), an aspect (term or category) indicated: (a) a part/component of *e* (e.g., battery), (b) an attribute of *e* (e.g., price), or (c) an attribute of a part/component of *e* (e.g., battery life). In SE-ABSA15, an aspect category is defined as a combination of an entity type E and an attribute type A. This definition of aspect makes more explicit the difference between entities and the particular facets that are being evaluated. E can be the reviewed entity *e* itself (e.g., laptop), a part/component of it (e.g., battery or customer support), or another relevant entity (e.g., the manufacturer of *e*), while A is a particular attribute (e.g., durability, quality) of E. E and A are concept names (classes) from a given domain ontology and do not necessarily occur as terms in a sentence. For example, in "*They sent it back with a huge crack in it and it still didn't work; and that was the fourth time I've sent it to them to get fixed*" the reviewer is evaluating the *quality* (A) of the *customer support* (E) without explicitly mentioning it.

In contrast to SE-ABSA14, in the current framework aspect terms correspond to explicit mentions of the entities E (e.g., service, pizza) or attributes A (e.g., price, quality). However, only the extraction of the explicit mentions of E is required (see Section 2.2). Another difference is that the datasets of SE-ABSA15 consist of whole reviews, not isolated sentences. Correctly identifying the E, A pairs of a sentence and their polarities often requires examining a wider part or the whole review.

In this setting, the ABSA problem has been formalized into a principled unified framework in which all the identified constituents of the expressed opinions (i.e., opinion target expressions, aspects and sentiment polarities) meet a set of guidelines/specifications and are linked to each other within tuples. The extracted tuples directly

[2] http://www.nist.gov/tac/2014/KBP/Sentiment/index.html

[3] The SE-ABSA14 inventory of categories for the restaurants domain is similar to the one of Ganu et al. (2009).

reflect the intended meaning of the texts and, thus, can be used to generate structured aspect-based opinion summaries from user reviews in realistic applications (e.g., review sites).

2.2 Task Description

SE-ABSA15 consisted of the following subtasks. Participants were free to choose the subtasks, slots and domains they wished to participate in.

Subtask 1: In-domain ABSA. Given a review text about a laptop or restaurant, identify all the opinion tuples with the following types (tuple slots) of information:

Slot 1: **Aspect Category**. The goal is to identify every entity E and attribute A pair towards which an opinion is expressed in the given text. E and A should be chosen from predefined inventories of entity types (e.g., LAPTOP, MOUSE, RESTAURANT, FOOD) and attribute labels (e.g., DESIGN, PRICE, QUALITY). The E, A inventories for each domain are described in section 3.

Slot 2: Opinion Target Expression (OTE). The task is to extract the OTE, i.e., the linguistic expression used in the given text to refer to the reviewed entity E of each E#A pair. The OTE is defined by its starting and ending offsets. When there is no explicit mention of the entity, the slot takes the value "NULL". The identification of Slot 2 values was required only in the restaurants domain.

Slot 3: Sentiment Polarity. Each identified E#A pair has to be assigned one of the following polarity labels: positive, negative, neutral (mildly positive or mildly negative sentiment).

Two examples of opinion tuples with Slot 1-3 values from the restaurants domain are shown below. Such tuples can be used to generate aspect-sentiment tables like the one of Fig 1.

a. *The food was delicious but do not come here on an empty stomach.* →
{category= "FOOD#QUALITY", target= "food", from: "4", to: "8", polarity= "positive"},
{category= "FOOD#STYLE_OPTIONS"[4], target = "food", from: "4", to: "8", polarity= "negative"}

b. *Prices are in line.* →
{category: "RESTAURANT#PRICES", target= "NULL", from: "-", to: "-", polarity: "neutral"}

[4] Opinions evaluating the food quantity (e.g. portions size) are assigned the label "FOOD#STYLE_OPTIONS".

Subtask 2: Out-of-domain ABSA. In this subtask, participants had the opportunity to test their systems in a previously unseen domain (hotel reviews) for which no training data was made available. The gold annotations for Slots 1 and 2 were provided and the teams had to return the sentiment polarity values (Slot 3).

3 Datasets and Annotation

3.1 Data Collection

Datasets for three domains (laptops, restaurants, hotels) were provided; consult Table 1 for more information.

	Laptops	Restaurants	Hotels
	Training data		
Review texts	277	254	-
Sentences	1739	1315	-
	Test data		
Review texts	173	96	30
Sentences	761	685	266

Table 1. Datasets provided for ABSA.

Note that in the domain of hotels no training data were provided (Out-of-Domain ABSA).

3.2 Annotation Schema and Guidelines

Given a review text about a laptop, a restaurant or a hotel, the task of the annotators was to identify opinions expressed towards specific entities and their attributes and to assign the respective aspect category (Slot 1) and polarity (Slot 3) labels. The category (E#A) values had to be chosen from predefined inventories of entities and attributes for each domain; the inventories were described in detail in the respective annotation guidelines[5]. In particular, the entity E could be assigned 22 possible labels for the laptops domain (e.g., LAPTOP, SOFTWARE, SUPPORT), 6 labels for the restaurants domain (e.g., RESTAURANT, FOOD), and 7 labels for the hotels domain (e.g., HOTEL, ROOMS). The attribute A could be assigned 9 possible labels for the laptops domain (e.g., USABILITY), 5 labels for the restaurants domain (e.g., QUALITY), and 8 labels for the hotels domain (e.g., COMFORT). The

[5] The detailed annotation guidelines are available at: http://alt.qcri.org/semeval2015/task12/index.php?id=data-and-tools

full inventories of the aspect category labels for each domain are provided below in appendices A-C. Quite often reviews contain opinions towards entities that are not directly related to the entity being reviewed, for example, restaurants/hotels that the reviewer has visited in the past, other laptops or products (and their components) of the same or a competitive brand. Such entities as well as comparative opinions are considered to be out of the scope of SE-ABSA15. In these cases, no opinion annotations were provided.

The {E#A, polarity} annotations had to be assigned at the sentence level taking into account the context of the whole review. For example, "*Laptop still did not work, blue screen within a week...*" (Previous sentence: "*Horrible customer support-they lost my laptop for a month-got it back 3 months later*") had to be assigned a negative opinion about the customer support, not about the operation of the laptop, as implied by the previous sentence. Similarly, in "*I was so happy with my new Mac.*" (Next sentences: "*For two months... Then the hard drive failed.*"), even though the reviewer says how happy he/she was with the laptop, he/she is expressing a negative opinion.

For the polarity slot the possible values were: positive, negative, and neutral. Contrary to SE-ABSA14, the "neutral" label applies only to mildly positive or mildly negative sentiment, thus it does not indicate objectivity (e.g., "*Food was okay, nothing great.*" → {FOOD#QUALITY, "*Food*", neutral}). Another difference is that this year the "conflict" label was not used, since –due to the adopted fine-grained aspect classification schema– it is very rare to encounter (in a sentence) both a positive and a negative opinion about the same attribute A of an entity E. In the few cases where this happened, the dominant sentiment was chosen (e.g., "*The OS takes some getting used to but the learning curve is so worth it!*" → {OS#USABILITY, positive}).

For the restaurants and the hotels domain the annotators also had to tag the OTE (explicit mention) for each identified entity E (Slot 2). Such mentions can be named entities (e.g., "The Four Seasons"), common nouns (e.g., "place", "steak", "bed") or multi-word terms (e.g., "vitello alla marsala", "conference/banquet room"). Similarly to SE-ABSA14, the identified OTEs were annotated as they appeared, even if misspelled. When an evaluated entity E was only implicitly inferred or referred to (e.g., through pronouns), the OTE slot was assigned the value "NULL" (e.g. "*Everything was wonderful.*" → {RESTAURANT#GENERAL, NULL, positive}).

In the laptops domain we did not provide OTE annotations, since most entities are instantiated through a limited set of expressions (e.g., MEMORY: "memory", "ram", CPU: "processing power", "processor", "cpu") as opposed to the restaurants domain, where for example, the entity "FOOD" is instantiated through a variety of food types and dishes (e.g. "pizza", "Lobster Cobb Salad"). Furthermore, LAPTOP, which is the majority category label in laptops (see Section 3.3), is instantiated mostly through pronominal mentions, while the explicit mentions are limited to nouns like laptop, computer, product, etc.

3.3 Annotation Process and Statistics

Each dataset was annotated by a linguist (annotator A) using BRAT (Stenetorp et al., 2012), a web-based annotation tool, which was configured appropriately for the needs of the task. Then, one of the organizers (annotator B) validated/inspected the resulting annotations. When B was not confident or disagreed with A, a decision was made collaboratively between them and a third annotator. The main disagreements encountered during the annotation process are summarized below:

Slot 1. In the laptops domain the main difficulty was that in some negative evaluations the annotators were unsure about the actual problem/target. For example, in "*Sometimes the screen even goes black on this computer*", the black screen may be related to the graphics, the laptop operation (e.g., motherboard issue) or the screen itself. The decision for such cases was to assign the E#A pair that reflected what the reviewer is saying and not the possible interpretations that a technician would give. So, if someone reports screen issues without providing further details, then the opinion is considered to be about the screen[6]. Another issue was when an attribute could be inferred from an explicitly evaluated attribute. For example, DESIGN affects USABILITY (e.g., "*With the switch being at the top you need to memorize the key combination*

[6] "Blue screen" is an exception since it is well-known that it refers to the laptop operation.

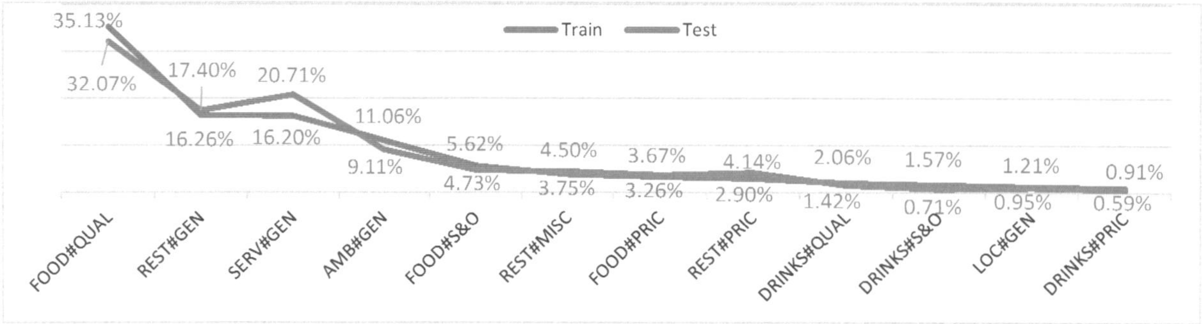

Figure 2. Aspect category (E#A) distribution in the restaurants domain. REST = restaurant, SERV = service, AMB = ambience, LOC = location, GEN=general, PRIC = price, S&O = style&options, MISC= miscellaneous

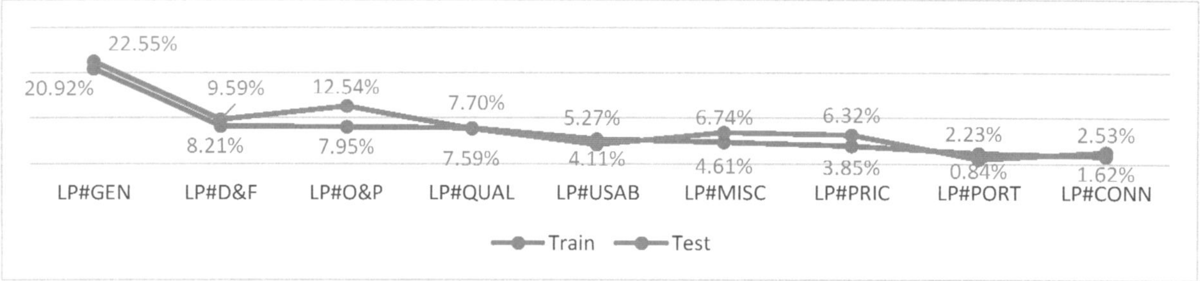

Figure 3. LAPTOP#ATTRIBUTE categories distribution in the laptops domain. LP= laptop, O&P= operation &performance, QUAL= quality, D&F= design &features, USAB=usability, CONN=connectivity, PORT=portability.

rather than just flicking a switch"). In such cases annotators assigned both attribute labels. The annotation in the restaurants domain was easier, due to the less fine-grained schema. A common problem was that (as in SE-ABSA14) the distinction between the GENERAL and MISCELLANEOUS and between the RESTAURANT and AMBIENCE labels was not always clear.

Slot 2. The annotators found it easier to identify explicit references to the target entities as opposed to the more general aspect terms of SE-ABSA14. However, the problem of distinguishing aspect terms when they appear in conjunctions or disjunctions remains. In this case the maximal phrase (e.g. the entire conjunction or disjunction) is annotated (e.g. *"Greek or Cypriot dishes"* instead of *"Greek dishes"*, *"Cypriot dishes"*).

Slot 3. Most cases in which the annotators had difficulty deciding the correct polarity label fall into one of the following categories: (a) *Change of sentiment over time*. Some reviewers tend to start their review by saying how excited they were at first (e.g., with the laptop) and continue by reporting problems or negative evaluations. (b) *Negative fact vs. positive opinion*. Some reviewers do mention particular deficiencies of a laptop or a restaurant saying, however, at the same time that they do not bother (e.g., *"Overheats but put a pillow and problem solved!"*). (c) *Mildly positive and negative sentiments are both denoted by the "neutral" label*. In some cases the annotators reported that it would be helpful to have a more fine-grained schema (e.g., "negative", "somewhat negative", "neutral", "somewhat positive", "positive"). Finally, in some cases it is difficult to decide a polarity label without knowing the reviewer's intention (e.g., *"50% of the food was very good"*).

The annotation process resulted in 5,761 opinion tuples in total that correspond to more than 15,000 label assignments (E, A, OTE, polarity); consult Table 2 for more information.

Laptops			
	training	test	total
{E#A, polarity}	1974	949	2923
Restaurants			
	training	test	total
{E#A, OTE, polarity}	1654	845	2499
Hotels			
	training	test	total
{E#A, OTE, polarity}	-	339	339

Table 2. Number of tuples annotated per dataset.

The distribution of the category annotations in the restaurants domain (Fig. 2) is similar across the training and test set. In the laptops domain, 81 E,A combinations (different pairs) were annotated in the training set and 58 in the test set. LAPTOP is the majority entity class in both sets; 62.36% in training, 72.81% in test data. Figure 3 presents the distribution for all the attributes of the LAPTOP entity in the training and test sets. Again, the category distributions are similar. The remaining 37.64% of the annotations in the laptops training data correspond to 72 categories with frequencies ranging from 6.53% to 0.05%. In the test set, the remaining 27.19% of the annotations correspond to 49 categories with frequencies from 2.32 % to 0.11%.

Regarding polarity, positive is the majority class in all domains (Table 3). The polarity distribution is balanced in the laptops domain, while in the restaurants domain there is a significant imbalance between the positive and negative classes across the training and the test sets.

	positive	negative	neutral
RS-TR	72.43%	24.36%	3.20%
RS-TE	53.72%	40.96%	5.32%
LP-TR	55.87%	38.75%	5.36%
LP-TE	57%	34.66%	8.32%
HT-TE	71.68%	24.77%	3.53%

Table 3. Polarity distribution per domain (RS-restaurants, LP-laptops, HT-hotels). TR and TE indicate the training and test sets.

3.4 Datasets Format and Availability

The datasets[7] of the SE-ABSA15 task were provided in an XML format. They are available under a non-commercial, no redistribution license through META-SHARE[8], a repository devoted to the sharing and dissemination of language resources (Piperidis, 2012).

4 Evaluation Measures and Baselines

Similarly to SE-ABSA14, the evaluation ran in two phases. In Phase A, the participants were asked to return the {category, OTE} tuples for the restaurants domain and only the category slot (Slot1) for the laptops domain. Subsequently, in Phase B, the participants were given the gold annotations for the reviews of Phase A and they were asked to return the polarity (Slot3). Each participating team was allowed to submit up to two runs per slot and domain in each phase; one constrained (C), where only the provided training data could be used, and one unconstrained (U), where other resources (e.g., publicly available lexica) and additional data of any kind could be used for training. In the latter case, the teams had to report the resources they used. To evaluate aspect category (Slot1) and OTE extraction (Slot2) in Phase A, we used the F-1 measure. To evaluate sentiment polarity (Slot 3) in Phase B, we used accuracy. Furthermore, we implemented and provided three baselines (see below) for the respective slots.

4.1 Evaluation Measures

Slot 1: F-1 scores are calculated by comparing the category annotations that a system returned (for all the sentences) to the gold category annotations (using micro-averaging). These category annotations are extracted from the values of Slot 1 (category). Duplicate occurrences of categories (for the same sentence) are ignored.

Slot 2: F-1 scores are calculated by comparing the targets that a system returned (for all the sentences) to the corresponding gold targets (using micro-averaging). The targets are extracted using their starting and ending offsets. The calculation for each sentence considers only distinct targets and discards NULL targets, since they do not correspond to explicit mentions.

Slot 1&2 (jointly): Again F-1 scores are calculated by comparing the {category, OTE} tuples of a system to the gold ones (using micro-averaging).

Slot 3: To evaluate sentiment polarity detection in Phase B, we calculated the accuracy of each system, defined as the number of correctly predicted polarity labels of aspect categories, divided by the total number of aspect categories. Recall that we use the gold aspect categories in Phase B.

4.2 Baselines

Slot 1: For category (E#A) extraction, a Support Vector Machine (SVM) with a linear kernel was trained. In particular, *n* unigram features are extracted from the respective sentence of each tuple that is encountered in the training data. The category value (e.g., SERVICE#GENERAL) of the tuple is

[7] The data are available at http://metashare.ilsp.gr:8080/.

[8] META-SHARE (http: //www.metashare.org/) was implemented in the framework of the META-NET Network of Excellence (http://www.meta-net.eu/).

used as the correct label of the feature vector. Similarly, for each test sentence *s*, a feature vector is built and the trained SVM is used to predict the probabilities of assigning each possible category to *s* (e.g., {SERVICE#GENERAL, 0.2}, {RESTAURANT# GENERAL, 0.4}. Then, a threshold[9] t is used to decide which of the categories will be assigned[10] to *s*. As features, we use the 1,000 most frequent unigrams of the training data excluding stop-words.

Slot 2: The baseline uses the training reviews to create for each category *c* (e.g., SERVICE# GENERAL) a list of OTEs (e.g., SERVICE#GENERAL → {"staff", "waiter"}). These are extracted from the (training) opinion tuples whose category value is *c*. Then, given a test sentence *s* and an assigned category *c*, the baseline finds in *s* the first occurrence of each OTE of *c*'s list. The OTE slot is filled with the first of the target occurrences found in *s*. If no target occurrences are found, the slot is assigned the value NULL.

Slot 3: For polarity prediction we trained a SVM classifier with a linear kernel. Again, as in Slot 1, *n* unigram features are extracted from the respective sentence of each tuple of the training data. In addition, an integer-valued feature[11] that indicates the category of the tuple is used. The correct label for the extracted training feature vector is the corresponding polarity value (e.g., positive). Then, for each tuple {category, OTE} of a test sentence *s*, a feature vector is built and it is classified using the trained SVM. Furthermore, for Slot 3 we also used a majority baseline that assigns the most frequent polarity (in the training data) to all test tuples.

The baseline systems and evaluation scripts are available for download as a single zip from the SE-ABSA15 website[12]. They are implemented in Java and can be used via a Linux shell script. The baselines use the LibSVM package[13] (Chang and Lin, 2011) for SVM training and prediction. The scores of the baselines in the test datasets are presented in Tables 4–8 along with the system scores.

[9] The threshold *t* was tuned on a subset of the training data (for each domain) using a trial and error approach.
[10] We use the –b 1 option of LibSVM to obtain probabilities.
[11] Each category (E#A pair) has been assigned a distinct integer value.
[12] http://alt.qcri.org/semeval2015/task12/index.php?id=data-and-tools
[13] http://www.csie.ntu.edu.tw/~cjlin/libsvm/

5 Evaluation Results

In total, the task attracted 92 submissions from 16 teams. The evaluation results per phase and slot are presented below. For the teams that submitted more than one unconstrained runs per slot and domain, we included in the tables only the run with the highest score.

5.1 Results of Phase A

The aspect category identification slot attracted 6 teams for the laptops dataset and 9 teams for the restaurants dataset (consult Table 4). As expected, the systems achieved significantly higher scores (+12%) in the restaurants domain since in this domain the classification schema is less fine-grained; it contains 6 entity types and 5 attribute classes that result in 12 possible combinations, as opposed to the laptops domain where the 22 entities and 9 attribute labels give rise to more than 80 combinations. The best F-1 scores in both domains, 50.86% for laptops and 62.68% for restaurants, were achieved by the unconstrained submission of the NLANGP team, which modeled aspect category extraction as a multiclass classification problem with features based on n-grams, parsing, and word clusters learnt from Amazon and Yelp data (for laptops and restaurants, respectively). The system of Sentiue (scores: 50% on laptops, 54.10% on restaurants) used a separate MaxEnt classifier with bag-of-word-like features (e.g. words, lemmas) for each entity and for each attribute. Subsequently, heuristics are applied to the output of the classifiers to determine which categories will be assigned to each sentence.

Laptops		Restaurants	
Team	F1	Team	F1
NLANGP	50.86*	NLANGP	62.68*
Sentiue	50.00*	NLANGP	61.94
IHS-RD.	49.59	UMDuluthC	57.19
NLANGP	49.06	UMDuluthT	57.19
TJUdeM	46.49	SIEL	57.14*
UFRGS	44.95	Sentiue	54.10*
UFRGS	44.73*	LT3	53.67*
V3	24.94*	TJUdeM	52.44*
		UFRGS	52.09*
		UFRGS	51.88
		IHS-RD.	49.87
		IHS-RD.	49.16
		V3	41.85*

Baseline	**48.06**	Baseline	**51.32**

Table 4. F-1 scores for aspect category extraction (slot 1). * indicate unconstrained systems.

The OTE slot, which was used only in the restaurants domain, attracted 14 teams; consult Table 5. The best F1 score (70.05%) was achieved by the unconstrained submission of EliXa that addressed the problem using an averaged perceptron with a BIO tagging scheme. The features EliXa used included n-grams, token classes, n-gram prefixes and suffixes, and word clusters learnt from additional data (Yelp for Brown and Clark clusters; Wikipedia for word2vec clusters). Similarly, NLANGP (67.11%) was based on a Conditional Random Fields (CRF) model with features based on word strings, head words (obtained from parse trees), name lists (e.g. extracted using frequency), and Brown clusters.

Restaurants			
Team	F1	Team	F1
EliXa	70.05*	UMDuluthC	50.36
NLANGP	67.11*	UMDuluthT	50.36
IHS-RD.	63.12	LT3	49.97*
Lsislif	62.22	UFRGS	49.32*
NLANGP	61.49	V3	45.67*
wnlp	57.63	Sentiue	39.82*
SIEL	53.38*	CU-BDDA	36.01
TJUdeM	52.44*	CU-BDDA	33.86*
Baseline		**48.06**	

Table 5. Results for OTE extraction (slot 2). * indicate unconstrained systems.

Finally, as expected, the scores are significantly lower when systems have to link the extracted OTEs to the relevant aspect categories (Slot1&2 jointly). As shown in Table 6, the best F-1 score (42.90%) was achieved by the NLANGP team that simply combined the output for each slot to construct the corresponding tuples.

Restaurants			
Team	F1	Team	F1
NLANGP	42.90*	LT3	35.50*
IHS-RD.	42.72	UFRGS	34.87*
IHS-RD.	41.96	UMDuluthC	32.59
NLANGP	39.81	UMDuluthT	32.59
TJUdeM	37.15*	Sentiue	31.20*
Baseline		**34.44**	

Table 6. Results for Slot1&2. * indicate unconstrained systems.

5.2 Results of Phase B

The sentiment polarity slot attracted 10 teams for the laptops and 12 teams for the restaurants domain (see Table 7). The best accuracy scores in both domains, 79.34% for laptops and 78.69% for restaurants, were achieved by Sentiue with a MaxEnt classifier along with features based on n-grams, POS tagging, lemmatization, negation words and publicly available sentiment lexica (MPQA, Bing Liu's lexicon, AFINN). The system of ECNU (scores: 78.29% laptops, 78.10% restaurants) used features based on n-grams, PMI scores, POS tags, parse trees, negation words and scores based on 7 sentiment lexica. The lsislif team (77.87% laptops, 75.50% restaurants) relied on a logistic regression model (Liblinear) with various features: syntactic (e.g., unigrams, negation), semantic (Brown dictionary), sentiment (e.g., MPQA, SentiWordnet).

Laptops		Restaurants	
Team	Acc.	Team	Acc.
Sentiue	79.34*	Sentiue	78.69*
ECNU	78.29	ECNU	78.10*
Lsislif	77.87	Lsislif	75.50
ECNU	74.49*	LT3	75.02*
LT3	73.76*	UFRGS	71.71
TJUdeM	73.23*	Wnlp	71.36
EliXa	72.91*	UMDuluthC	71.12
Wnlp	72.07	EliXa	70.05*
EliXa	71.54	ECNU	69.82
V3	68.38*	V3	69.46*
UFRGS	67.33	TJUdeM	68.87*
SINAI	65.85	EliXa	67.33
SINAI	51.84*	SINAI	60.71*
		SIEL	70.76*
SVM+ BOW Baseline	**69.96**	SVM+ BOW Baseline	**63.55**
Majority Baseline	**57.00**	Majority Baseline	**53.72**

Table 7. Accuracy scores for slot 3 (polarity extraction). * indicate unconstrained systems. The evaluated run of SIEL team was submitted after the deadline had expired, but before the release of the gold polarity labels.

Most teams performed (slightly) better in the laptops domain. This is probably due to the fact that in the restaurants domain the positive polarity is significantly more frequent in the training than in the test data, which may have led to biased models. Nevertheless, most system scores indicate robustness across the two domains, with Sentiue achieving the most stable performance: 79.34% in laptops and 78.69% in restaurants.

A similar score was obtained also by Sentiue in the hidden domain (78.76%). The (hidden) hotels domain (subtask 2) attracted 9 teams. Lsislif achieved the best score based on a Liblinear model developed for the restaurants domain. LT3 achieved the second best score (80.53%) with an SVM model trained on the restaurants training data. The model used features based on unigrams, sentiment lexica (by Bing Liu, General Inquirer) and PMI scores learnt from TripAdvisor data. The team of EliXa (79.64%) used a multiclass SVM and features based on word clusters, lemmas, n-grams, POS tagging, and well known sentiment lexica. The system of Sentiue (78.76%) is somewhat similar; it uses BOW, POS tags, lemmas, and sentiment lexica. The results of some systems (LT3, EliXa, V3) suggest that the hidden domain was easier, but other systems (e.g., ECNU, wnlp) achieved significantly lower scores in the hidden domain, compared to the in-domain ABSA scores.

Hotels			
Team	Acc.	Team	Acc.
lsislif	85.84	V3	71.09*
LT3	80.53*	UFRGS	65.78
EliXa	79.64*	SINAI	63.71*
sentiue	78.76*	Wnlp	55.45
EliXa	74.92	UMDuluthC	71.38
Majority Baseline		**71.68**	

Table 8. Accuracy scores for slot 3 (polarity extraction). * indicate unconstrained systems. The evaluated run of UMDuluthC team was submitted after the deadline had expired but before the release of the gold polarity labels.

6 Conclusions

The SE-ABSA15 task is a continuation of SE-ABSA14 task. The SE-ABSA15 task provided a new definition of aspect –that makes explicit the difference between entities and the particular facets that are being evaluated- within a new principled, unified ABSA framework and output representation, which may be used in realistic applications (e.g., review sites). We also provided benchmark datasets containing manually annotated reviews from three domains (restaurants, laptops, hotels) and baselines for the respective SE-ABSA15 slots. The task attracted 93 submissions from 16 teams that were evaluated in three slots: aspect categories, opinion target expressions, and polarity classification. Future work includes applying the new framework and annotation schema to other languages (e.g., Spanish, Greek) and enhancing it with information about topics or events, opinion holders, and annotations for linguistic phenomena like metaphor and irony.

Acknowledgments

We thank Konstantina Papanikolaou, who carried out a critical part of the annotation process, Thomas Keefe for his help during the initial phases of the annotation process, Juli Bakagianni for her support on the META-SHARE platform and John Pavlopoulos for his valuable contribution in shaping the SE-ABSA tasks. Maria Pontiki & Haris Papageorgiou were supported by the POLYTROPON (KRIPIS-GSRT, MIS: 448306) project.

References

Bing Liu. 2006. Web Data Mining: Exploring Hyperlinks, Contents, and Usage Data, 2006 and 2011: Springer.

Samuel Brody and Noemie Elhadad. 2010. An unsupervised aspect-sentiment model for online reviews. In Proceedings of NAACL, pages 804–812, Los Angeles, California.

Chih-Chung Chang and Chih-Jen Lin. 2011. LIBSVM: a library for support vector machines. ACM Transactions on Intelligent Systems and Technology, 2:27:1--27:27.

Gayatree Ganu, Noemie Elhadad, and Amelie Marian. 2009. Beyond the stars: Improving rating predictions using review text content. In Proceedings of WebDB, Providence, Rhode Island, USA.

Minqing Hu and Bing Liu. 2004a. Mining and summarizing customer reviews. In Proceedings of KDD, pages 168–177, Seattle, WA, USA.

Minqing Hu and Bing Liu. 2004b. Mining opinion features in customer reviews. In Proceedings of AAAI, pages 755–760, San Jose, California.

Yohan Jo, and Alice H Oh. 2011. Aspect and sentiment unification model for online review analysis. In Proceedings of the fourth ACM international conference on Web search and data mining, pages 815-824.

Chenghua Lin and Yulan He. 2009. Joint sentiment/topic model for sentiment analysis. In Proceedings of the 18th ACM Conference on Information and Knowledge Management, pages 375–384.

Julian McAuley, Jure Leskovec, and Dan Jurafsky. 2012. Learning attitudes and attributes from multi-aspect reviews. In Proceedings of the 12th IEEE International Conference on Data Mining, ICDM '12, pages 1020–1025, Brussels, Belgium.

Margaret Mitchell. 2013. Overview of the TAC2013 Knowledge Base Population Evaluation: English Sentiment Slot Filling. In Proceedings of the Text Analysis Conference (TAC), Gaithersburg, MD, USA.

John Pavlopoulos. 2014. *Aspect based sentiment analysis*. PhD thesis, Dept. of Informatics, Athens University of Economics and Business, Greece.

Stelios Piperidis. 2012. The META-SHARE language resources sharing infrastructure: Principles, challenges, solutions. In Proceedings of LREC-2012, pages 36–42, Istanbul, Turkey.

Maria Pontiki, Dimitrios Galanis, John Pavlopoulos, Harris Papageorgiou, Ion Androutsopoulos, and Suresh Manandhar. 2014. Semeval-2014 task 4: Aspect based sentiment analysis. In Proceedings of the 8th International Workshop on Semantic Evaluation (SemEval 2014), pages 27–35, Dublin, Ireland.

Josef Ruppenhofer, Roman Klinger, Julia Maria Struß, Jonathan Sonntag, and Michael Wiegand. 2014. IGGSA Shared Tasks on German Sentiment Analysis (GESTALT). In Workshop Proceedings of the 12th Edition of the KONVENS Conference, pages 164-173.

Yohei Seki, David Kirk Evans, Lun-Wei Ku, Hsin-Hsi. Chen, Noriko Kando, and Chin-Yew Lin. 2007. Overview of opinion analysis pilot task at ntcir-6. In Proceedings of NTCIR-6 Workshop Meeting, pages 265–278.

Yohei Seki, David Kirk Evans, Lun-Wei Ku, Le Sun, Hsin-Hsi Chen, and Noriko Kando. 2008. Overview of multilingual opinion analysis task at NTCIR-7. In Proceedings of the 7th NTCIR Workshop Meeting on Evaluation of Information Access Technologies: Information Retrieval, Question Answering, and Cross-Lingual Information Access, pages 185–203.

Yohei Seki, Lun-Wei Ku, Le Sun, Hsin-Hsi Chen, and Noriko Kando. 2010. Overview of Multilingual Opinion Analysis Task at NTCIR-8: A Step Toward Cross Lingual Opinion Analysis. In Proceedings of the 8th NTCIR Workshop Meeting on Evaluation of Information Access Technologies: Information Retrieval, Question Answering and Cross-Lingual Information Access, pages 209–220.

Josef Steinberger, Tomáš Brychcín and Michal Konkol. 2014. Aspect-Level Sentiment Analysis in Czech. In *Proceedings of the 5th workshop on computational approaches to subjectivity, sentiment and social media analysis*, Association for Computational Linguistics, pages 24–30, Baltimore, Maryland.

Pontus Stenetorp, Sampo Pyysalo, Goran Topi´c, Tomoko Ohta, Sophia Ananiadou, and Jun'ichi Tsujii. 2012. BRAT: a web-based tool for NLP-assisted text annotation. In Proceedings of EACL, pages 102–107, Avignon, France.

Tun Thura Thet, Jin-Cheon Na, and Christopher S. G. Khoo. 2010. Aspect-based sentiment analysis of movie reviews on discussion boards. J. Information Science, 36(6):823–848.

Lei Zhang and Bing Liu. 2014. Aspect and Entity Extraction for Opinion Mining", book chapter in Data Mining and Knowledge Discovery for Big Data: Methodologies, Challenges, and Opportunities, Springer, 2014.

Appendix A. Laptop Aspect Categories

Entity Labels	
1. LAPTOP	13. BATTERY
2. DISPLAY	14. GRAPHICS
3. KEYBOARD	15. HARD DISK
4. MOUSE	16. MULTIMEDIA DEVICES
5. MOTHERBOARD	17. HARDWARE
6. CPU	18. SOFTWARE
7. FANS& COOLING	19. OS
8. PORTS	20. WARRANTY
9. MEMORY	21. SHIPPING
10. POWER SUPPLY	22. SUPPORT
11. OPTICAL DRIVES	23. COMPANY
Attribute Labels	
A. GENERAL	E. USABILITY
B. PRICE	F. DESIGN& FEATURES
C. QUALITY	G. PORTABILITY
D. OPERATION& PERFORMANCE	H. CONNECTIVITY
	I. MISCELLANEOUS

Appendix B. Restaurant Aspect Categories

Entity Labels	Attribute Labels
1. RESTAURANT	A. GENERAL
2. FOOD	B. PRICES
3. DRINKS	C. QUALITY
4. AMBIENCE	D. STYLE & OPTIONS
5. SERVICE	E. MISCELLANEOUS
6. LOCATION	

Appendix C. Hotel Aspect Categories

Entity Labels	Attribute Labels
1. HOTEL	A. GENERAL
2. ROOMS	B. PRICE
3. FACILITIES	C. COMFORT
4. ROOM AMENITIES	D. CLEANLINESS
5. SERVICE	E. QUALITY
6. LOCATION	F. DESIGN & FEATURES
7. FOOD & DRINKS	G. STYLE & OPTIONS
	H. MISCELLANEOUS

NLANGP: Supervised Machine Learning System for Aspect Category Classification and Opinion Target Extraction

Zhiqiang Toh
Institute for Infocomm Research
1 Fusionopolis Way
Singapore 138632
ztoh@i2r.a-star.edu.sg

Jian Su
Institute for Infocomm Research
1 Fusionopolis Way
Singapore 138632
sujian@i2r.a-star.edu.sg

Abstract

This paper describes our system used in the Aspect Based Sentiment Analysis Task 12 of SemEval-2015. Our system is based on two supervised machine learning algorithms: sigmoidal feedforward network to train binary classifiers for aspect category classification (Slot 1), and Conditional Random Fields to train classifiers for opinion target extraction (Slot 2). We extract a variety of lexicon and syntactic features, as well as cluster features induced from unlabeled data. Our system achieves state-of-the-art performances, ranking 1st for three of the evaluations (Slot 1 for both restaurant and laptop domains, and Slot 1 & 2) and 2nd for Slot 2 evaluation.

1 Introduction

The amount of user-generated content on the web has grown rapidly in recent years, prompting increasing interests in the research area of sentiment analysis and opinion mining. Most previous work is concerned with detecting the overall polarity of a sentence or paragraph, regardless of the target entities (e.g. restaurants) and their aspects (e.g. food). By contrast, the Aspect Based Sentiment Analysis task of SemEval 2014 (SE-ABSA14) is concerned with identifying the aspects of given target entities and the sentiment expressed towards each aspect (Pontiki et al., 2014).

The SemEval-2015 Aspect Based Sentiment Analysis (SE-ABSA15) task is a continuation of SE-ABSA14 (Pontiki et al., 2015). The SE-ABSA15 task features a number of changes that address issues raised in SE-ABSA14 and also encourage further in-depth research. For example, (1) instead of isolated (potentially out of context) sentences, the input datasets will contain entire reviews; (2) information linking aspect terms and aspect categories are now provided; (3) besides in-domain ABSA (Subtask 1), SE-ABSA15 will include an out-of-domain ABSA subtask (Subtask 2).

We participate in Subtask 1 of SE-ABSA15, namely aspect category classification (Slot 1) and opinion target extraction (Slot 2). We also participate in the evaluation which assesses whether a system identifies both the aspect categories and opinion targets correctly (Slot 1 & 2).

For Slot 1, we model the problem as a multi-class classification problem where binary classifiers are trained to predict the aspect categories. We follow the one-vs-all strategy and train a binary classifier for each category in the training set. Each classifier is trained using sigmoidal feedforward network with 1 hidden layer. For Slot 2, we follow the approach of Toh and Wang (2014) by modeling the problem as a sequential labeling task, using Conditional Random Fields (CRF) as the training algorithm. For Slot 1 & 2, we perform a simple combination of Slot 1 predictions and Slot 2 predictions.

The remainder of this paper is structured as follows. In Section 2, we describe our system in detail, including the feature description and approaches. In Section 3, the official results are presented. Feature ablation results are shown in Section 4. Finally, Section 5 summarizes our work.

2 System Description

In this section, we present the details of our sentiment analysis system. The training set consists of 254 English review documents containing 1315 sentences for the restaurant domain and 277 English review documents containing 1739 sentences for the laptop domain.

As a first step of our system, we perform basic data preprocessing. All sentences are tokenized and parsed using the Stanford Parser[1].

2.1 Features

This section briefly describes the features used in our system, where some of the features are useful across different slots. The features used are a subset of the features described in Toh and Wang (2014), which also provides a more detailed description of the features.

2.1.1 Word

The current word is used as a feature. For opinion target extraction, the previous word and next word are also used as features.

2.1.2 Bigram

All word bigrams found in a sentence are used as features.

2.1.3 Name List

For the restaurant domain, we extract two high precision name lists from the training set and use them for membership testing. For the first list, we collect and keep only high frequent opinion targets. For the second list, we consider the counts of individual words in the opinion targets and keep those words that frequently occur as part of an opinion target in the training set.

2.1.4 Head Word

From the sentence parse tree, we extract the head word of each word and use it as a feature.

2.1.5 Word Cluster

We induce Brown clusters and K-means clusters from two different sources of unlabeled dataset: the Multi-Domain Sentiment Dataset that contains Amazon product reviews (Blitzer et al., 2007)[2], and the Yelp Phoenix Academic Dataset that contains user reviews[3]. We also experiment using a third dataset that is created by combining the initial two datasets into one.

For Brown clusters[4], we experiment with different datasets, cluster sizes ($\{100, 200, 500, 1000\}$), minimum occurrences ($\{1, 2, 3\}$) and binary prefix lengths. The best settings to use are determined using 5-fold cross validation.

K-means clusters are induced using the `word2vec` tool (Mikolov et al., 2013)[5]. Similarly, among different datasets, word vector sizes ($\{50, 100, 200, 500, 1000\}$), cluster sizes ($\{50, 100, 200, 500, 1000\}$), and sub-sampling thresholds ($\{0.00001, 0.001\}$), we use 5-fold cross validation to select the best settings.

2.1.6 Name List Generated using Double Propagation

For the restaurant domain, we generate a name list of possible opinion targets using the Double Propagation (DP) algorithm (Qiu et al., 2011). The propagation rules are modified from the logic rules presented in Liu et al. (2013), where we write our rules in Prolog and use SWI-Prolog[6] as the solver. As the rules can only identify single-word targets, to consider multi-word targets, we extend the left boundary of the identified target to include any consective noun words right before the target.

2.2 Approaches

We developed our system to return results for Slot 1 (restaurant and laptop domains), Slot 2 (restaurant domain) and Slot 1 & 2 (restaurant domain). This section describes our machine learning approaches used to generate the predictions for each slot.

2.2.1 Aspect Category Classification (Slot 1)

Aspect category classification is based on a set of one-vs-all binary classifiers, one classifier for each

[1] http://nlp.stanford.edu/software/lex-parser.shtml

[2] We used the unprocessed.tar.gz archive found at http://www.cs.jhu.edu/ mdredze/datasets/sentiment/

[3] http://www.yelp.com/dataset_challenge/

[4] Brown clusters are induced using the implementation by Percy Liang found at https://github.com/percyliang/brown-cluster/

[5] https://code.google.com/p/word2vec/

[6] http://www.swi-prolog.org/

Parameter	Restaurant	Laptop
learning rate	0.9	0.7
hidden units	4	4
threshold	0.2	0.2

Table 1: Tuned parameter values for Slot 1 on the restaurant and laptop domain.

category found in the training set. For each sentence in the training set, we extract features from all words in the sentence to create a training example. The label of the example depends on which category *C* we are training: 1 if the sentence contains *C* as one of its categories, −1 otherwise. The number of binary classifiers is 13 for the restaurant domain and 79 for the laptop domain, which equals to the number of categories annotated in the training set for the respective domain.

We use the Vowpal Wabbit tool[7] to train the binary classifiers. Each classifier is trained using sigmoidal feedforward network with 1 hidden layer (`--nn`), with `--ngram` enabled to generate word bigrams. The learning rate (`-l`) and number of hidden units are tuned using 5-fold cross validation.

We also tuned the probability threshold where we regard the classifier output as positive outcome. Any classifier that returns a probability score greater than the threshold will be added to the output set of categories. The tuned parameter values used are shown in Table 1.

Table 2 shows the features used for the restaurant and laptop domain, as well as the 5-fold cross-validation performances after adding each feature group.

2.2.2 Opinion Target Extraction (Slot 2)

Opinion target extraction is modeled as a sequential labeling task, where each word in the sentence is assigned a label using the IOB2 scheme (Sang and Veenstra, 1999). The classifier is trained using Conditional Random Fields (CRF), which has shown to achieve state-of-the-art performances in previous work (Toh and Wang, 2014; Chernyshevich, 2014). We use the CRFsuite tool (Okazaki, 2007) for CRF training and enable negative state and transition features (`-p feature.possible_states=1` `-p feature.possible_transitions=1`).

[7] https://github.com/JohnLangford/vowpal_wabbit/wiki

Restaurant	
Feature	F1
Word	0.6245
+ Bigram	0.6423
+ Name List	0.6608
+ Head Word	0.6660
+ Word Cluster	0.7038
Laptop	
Feature	F1
Word	0.4520
+ Bigram	0.4611
+ Head Word	0.4721
+ Word Cluster	0.4841

Table 2: 5-fold cross-validation performances for Slot 1 on the restaurant and laptop domain. Each row uses all features added in the previous rows.

We experiment with two different methods of returning predicted opinion targets, one suitable for Slot 1 & 2 evaluation (Method-1), the other suitable for Slot 2 evaluation (Method-2).

For Slot 1 & 2 evaluation, the explicit opinion targets may have more than one categories. Thus, we use the following method (Method-1): we train a separate CRF model for each category found in the training set. That is, for each category *C*, we assign the label "B-*C*" to indicate the start of an opinion target, "I-*C*" to indicate the continuation of an opinion target, and "O" if the opinion target does not have *C* as one of its categories.

Using FOOD#PRICES category as an example, for the training set that is used to train the FOOD#PRICES CRF model, we assign the label "B-FOOD#PRICES" to indicate the start of a FOOD#PRICES opinion target, "I-FOOD#PRICES" to indicate the continuation of a FOOD#PRICES opinion target, and "O" if the opinion target does not have FOOD#PRICES as one of its categories.

However, our initial experiments suggest that Method-1 does not achieve optimum performance for Slot 2 evaluation. The reason is that the number of positive training examples for most of the categories is small.

	Slot 1									
	Restaurant					Laptop				
System	Type	Rank	P	R	F1	Type	Rank	P	R	F1
NLANGP (U)	U	1	0.6386	**0.6155**	**0.6268**	U	1	**0.6425**	0.4209	**0.5086**
NLANGP (C)	C	2	**0.6637**	0.5806	0.6194	C	4	0.5743	0.4283	0.4906
1st	U	1	0.6386	**0.6155**	**0.6268**	U	1	**0.6425**	0.4209	**0.5086**
2nd	C	2	**0.6637**	0.5806	0.6194	U	2	0.5773	0.4409	0.5000
3rd	C	3	0.5698	0.5742	0.5720	C	3	0.5548	**0.4483**	0.4959
Baseline	–	–	–	–	0.5133	–	–	–	–	0.4631

	Slot 2					Slot 1 & 2				
	Restaurant									
System	Type	Rank	P	R	F1	Type	Rank	P	R	F1
NLANGP (U)	U	2	0.7053	0.6402	0.6712	U	1	0.4463	**0.4130**	**0.4290**
NLANGP (C)	C	7	**0.7129**	0.5406	0.6149	C	4	0.4387	0.3645	0.3982
1st	U	1	0.6893	**0.7122**	**0.7005**	U	1	0.4463	**0.4130**	**0.4290**
2nd	U	2	0.7053	0.6402	0.6712	C	2	**0.5937**	0.3337	0.4273
3rd	C	3	0.6723	0.6661	0.6691	U	3	0.5832	0.3278	0.4197
Baseline	–	–	–	–	0.4807	–	–	–	–	0.3444

Table 4: Comparison of our unconstrained (U) and constrained (C) systems with the top three participating systems and official baselines for Slot 1, Slot 2 and Slot 1 & 2. P, R, and F1 denote the precision, recall and F1 measure respectively.

Restaurant	
Feature	F1
Word	0.6225
+ Name List	0.6796
+ Head Word	0.6840
+ Word Cluster	0.7224
+ DP Name List	0.7237

Table 3: 5-fold cross-validation performances of Slot 2 on the restaurant domain. Each row uses all features added in the previous rows. The cross-validation experiments use Method-1 to train the models.

Since Slot 2 evaluation only requires the identified text span to be returned and does not require any category information, we can increase the number of positive training examples by collapsing all categories into a single category (e.g. "TERM"). Thus, for Slot 2 evaluation, the following method (Method-2) is used: we train a single CRF model where all opinion targets in the training set are assigned the labels "B-TERM", "I-TERM" and "O" accordingly.

Table 3 shows the features used for the restaurant domain as well as the 5-fold cross-validation performances after adding each feature group.

Due to time constraints, all cross-validation experiments for Slot 2 use Method-1 to train the models. The same settings will then be used to train the final models using both Method-1 (for Slot 1 & 2 evaluation) and Method-2 (for Slot 2 evaluation).

2.2.3 Slot 1 & 2

To create the predictions for Slot 1 & 2 evaluation, we perform a simple combination of Slot 1 predictions and Slot 2 predictions. First, we use all Slot 2 predictions. Next, for each sentence, we add categories that are found in Slot 1 predictions but not Slot 2 predictions of the same sentence. Those additional categories are assumed to be NULL targets.

3 Results

We have submitted results for unconstrained and constrained (using only the provided training set of the corresponding domain) systems. The constrained system only uses Word, Bigram (for Slot 1) and Name List (for the restaurant domain) features. Table 4 presents the official results of our submissions. We also include the results of the top three

Restaurant		
System	Method-1	Method-2
NLANGP (U)	0.6099	0.6712
NLANGP (C)	0.5489	0.6149

Table 5: Comparison of F1 performances for Slot 2 evaluation. Our official submissions for Slot 2 evaluation use Method-2, which is better than Method-1 used for Slot 1 & 2 evaluation.

participating systems and official baselines for comparison (Pontiki et al., 2015).

As shown from the table, our system performed well for all four evaluations. Our system is ranked 1st for three of the evaluations (Slot 1 for both restaurant and laptop domains, and Slot 1 & 2) and 2nd for Slot 2 evaluation. In addition, our constrained system also achieves competitive results, ranking 2nd in Slot 1 Restaurant and 4th in Slot 1 Laptop and Slot 1 & 2. Another observation is that our unconstrained systems achieved better performances than the corresponding constrained systems for all evaluations, indicating the use of external resources are beneficial.

We are interested to know whether the Slot 2 predictions that help to achieve best results in Slot 1 & 2 evaluation are also useful for Slot 2 evaluation. Table 5 shows the F1 performances of Slot 2 evaluation if we have used Method-1 (Section 2.2.2) to generate the Slot 2 predictions. As shown from the table, using the same Slot 2 predictions for both Slot 2 evaluation and Slot 1 & 2 evaluation are detrimental to Slot 2 performances, with performance difference greater than 6.0%. Our approach of using a different method to generate Slot 2 predictions for Slot 2 evaluation helps to overcome the data sparseness problem and improves the performances of target extraction.

4 Feature Ablation

Table 6 and Table 7 show the (unconstrained) F1 measure and loss on the test set resulting from training with each group of feature removed for Slot 1 and Slot 2 respectively. The ablation experiments indicate that each feature is helpful in improving the performance, with performance gains in the range of $1.0\% - 6.0\%$. The only exception is the use of bigram feature in Slot 1 evaluation on the laptop domain, where a slight decrease of 0.27% is observed. Among the external resources used, the Word Cluster feature consistently provides the most gain: an increase in F1 measure greater than 3.0% for both slots on the restaurant domain.

Restaurant		
Feature	F1	Loss
Word	0.5914	0.0354
Bigram	0.6031	0.0237
Name List	0.6123	0.0145
Head Word	0.6136	0.0132
Word Cluster	0.5910	0.0358
Laptop		
Feature	F1	Loss
Word	0.4483	0.0603
Bigram	0.5114	-0.0027
Head Word	0.4978	0.0108
Word Cluster	0.4940	0.0146

Table 6: Test set ablation experiments for Slot 1 on the restaurant and laptop domain. The quantity is the (unconstrained) F1 measure and loss resulted from the removal of a single feature group.

Restaurant		
Feature	F1	Loss
Word	0.6280	0.0432
Name List	0.6540	0.0172
Head Word	0.6602	0.0110
Word Cluster	0.6387	0.0325
DP Name List	0.6608	0.0104

Table 7: Test set ablation experiments for Slot 2 on the restaurant domain. The quantity is the (unconstrained) F1 measure and loss resulted from the removal of a single feature group.

5 Conclusion

In this paper, we report our work on aspect category classification and opinion target extraction using supervised machine learning approaches. By leveraging on external resources, careful feature selection and performance tuning, our system achieves top performances in all four evaluations, ranking 1st for three of the evaluations, and second for the remaining evaluation. In future, we hope to improve our opinion target extraction system by taking into account surrounding sentence context and incorporating sentiment lexicon features to better classify aspect categories and detect opinion expressions.

Acknowledgments

This work is a study conducted at Baidu-I^{2}R Research Centre.

We thank the anonymous reviewers for their helpful comments and suggestions.

References

John Blitzer, Mark Dredze, and Fernando Pereira. 2007. Biographies, Bollywood, Boom-boxes and Blenders: Domain Adaptation for Sentiment Classification. In *Proceedings of the 45th Annual Meeting of the Association of Computational Linguistics*, pages 440–447, Prague, Czech Republic, June.

Maryna Chernyshevich. 2014. IHS R&D Belarus: Cross-domain Extraction of Product Features using Conditional Random Fields. In *Proceedings of the 8th International Workshop on Semantic Evaluation (SemEval 2014)*, pages 309–313.

Qian Liu, Zhiqiang Gao, Bing Liu, and Yuanlin Zhang. 2013. A Logic Programming Approach to Aspect Extraction in Opinion Mining. In *Proceedings of the 2013 IEEE/WIC/ACM International Joint Conferences on Web Intelligence (WI) and Intelligent Agent Technologies (IAT) - Volume 01*, WI-IAT '13, pages 276–283, Washington, DC, USA, November.

Tomas Mikolov, Wen-tau Yih, and Geoffrey Zweig. 2013. Linguistic Regularities in Continuous Space Word Representations. In *Proceedings of the 2013 Conference of the North American Chapter of the Association for Computational Linguistics: Human Language Technologies*, pages 746–751, Atlanta, Georgia, June.

Naoaki Okazaki. 2007. CRFsuite: a fast implementation of Conditional Random Fields (CRFs).

Maria Pontiki, Dimitris Galanis, John Pavlopoulos, Harris Papageorgiou, Ion Androutsopoulos, and Suresh Manandhar. 2014. SemEval-2014 Task 4: Aspect Based Sentiment Analysis. In *Proceedings of the 8th International Workshop on Semantic Evaluation (SemEval 2014)*, pages 27–35.

Maria Pontiki, Dimitris Galanis, Harris Papageorgiou, Suresh Manandhar, and Ion Androutsopoulos. 2015. SemEval-2015 Task 12: Aspect Based Sentiment Analysis. In *Proceedings of the 9th International Workshop on Semantic Evaluation (SemEval 2015)*.

Guang Qiu, Bing Liu, Jiajun Bu, and Chun Chen. 2011. Opinion Word Expansion and Target Extraction through Double Propagation. *Computational Linguistics*, 37(1):9–27.

Erik F. Tjong Kim Sang and Jorn Veenstra. 1999. Representing Text Chunks. In *Proceedings of the Ninth Conference on European Chapter of the Association for Computational Linguistics*, EACL '99, pages 173–179, Stroudsburg, PA, USA.

Zhiqiang Toh and Wenting Wang. 2014. DLIREC: Aspect Term Extraction and Term Polarity Classification System. In *Proceedings of the 8th International Workshop on Semantic Evaluation (SemEval 2014)*, pages 235–240.

SHELLFBK: An Information Retrieval-based System For Multi-Domain Sentiment Analysis

Mauro Dragoni
Fondazione Bruno Kessler
Via Sommarive 18
Povo, Trento
dragoni@fbk.eu

Abstract

This paper describes the SHELLFBK system that participated in SemEval 2015 Tasks 9, 10, and 11. Our system takes a supervised approach that builds on techniques from information retrieval. The algorithm populates an inverted index with pseudo-documents that encode dependency parse relationships extracted from the sentences in the training set. Each record stored in the index is annotated with the polarity and domain of the sentence it represents. When the polarity or domain of a new sentence has to be computed, the new sentence is converted to a query that is used to retrieve the most similar sentences from the training set. The retrieved instances are scored for relevance to the query. The most relevant training instant is used to assign a polarity and domain label to the new sentence. While the results on well-formed sentences are encouraging, the performance obtained on short texts like tweets demonstrate that more work is needed in this area.

1 Introduction

Sentiment analysis is a natural language processing task whose aim is to classify documents according to the opinion (polarity) they express on a given subject (Pang et al., 2002). Generally speaking, sentiment analysis aims at determining the attitude of a speaker or a writer with respect to a topic or the overall tonality of a document. This task has created a considerable interest due to its wide applications. In recent years, the exponential increase of the Web for exchanging public opinions about events, facts, products, etc., has led to an extensive usage of sentiment analysis approaches, especially for marketing purposes.

By formalizing the sentiment analysis problem, a "sentiment" or "opinion" has been defined by (Liu and Zhang, 2012) as a quintuple:

$$\langle o_j, f_{jk}, so_{ijkl}, h_i, t_l \rangle, \tag{1}$$

where o_j is a target object, f_{jk} is a feature of the object o_j, so_{ijkl} is the sentiment value of the opinion of the opinion holder h_i on feature f_{jk} of object o_j at time t_l. The value of so_{ijkl} can be positive (by denoting a state of happiness, bliss, or satisfaction), negative (by denoting a state of sorrow, dejection, or disappointment), or neutral (it is not possible to denote any particular sentiment), or a more granular rating. The term h_i encodes the opinion holder, and t_l is the time when the opinion is expressed.

Such an analysis, may be *document-based*, where the positive, negative, or neutral sentiment is assigned to the entire document content; or it may be *sentence-based* where individual sentences are analyzed separately and classified according to the different polarity values. In the latter case, it is often desirable to find with a high precision the entity attributes towards which the detected sentiment is directed.

In the classic sentiment analysis problem, the polarity of each term within the document is computed independently of the domain which the document's domain. However, conditioning term polarity by domain has been found to improve performance (Blitzer et al., 2007). We illustrate the intuition behind domain specific term polarity. Let us consider the following example concerning the adjective "small":

1. The sideboard is **small** and it is not able to contain a lot of stuff.

2. The **small** dimensions of this decoder allow to move it easily.

In the first sentence, we considered the Furnishings domain and, within it, the polarity of the adjective "small" is, for sure, "negative" because it highlights an issue of the described item. On the other hand, in the second sentence, where we considered the Electronics domain, the polarity of such an adjective may be considered "positive".

Unlike the approaches already discussed in the literature (and presented in Section 2), we address the multi-domain sentiment analysis problem by applying Information Retrieval (IR) techniques for representing information about the linguistic structure of sentences and by taking into account both their polarity and the domain.

The rest of the work is structured as follows. Section 2 presents a survey on works about sentiment analysis. Section 3 provides a description of the SHELLFBK system by described how information are stored during the training phase and exploited during the test one. Section 4 reports the system evaluation performed on the Tasks 9, 10, and 11 proposed at SemEval 2015 and, finally, Section 5 concludes the paper.

2 Related Work

The topic of sentiment analysis has been studied extensively in the literature (Pang and Lee, 2008; Liu and Zhang, 2012), where several techniques have been proposed and validated.

Machine learning techniques are the most common approaches used for addressing this problem, given that any existing supervised methods can be applied to sentiment classification. For instance, in (Pang et al., 2002) and (Pang and Lee, 2004), the authors compared the performance of Naive-Bayes, Maximum Entropy, and Support Vector Machines in sentiment analysis on different features like considering only unigrams, bigrams, combination of both, incorporating parts of speech and position information or by taking only adjectives. Moreover, beside the use of standard machine learning method, researchers have also proposed several custom techniques specifically for sentiment classification, like the use of adapted score function based on the evaluation of positive or negative words in product reviews (Dave et al., 2003), as well as by defining weighting schemata for enhancing classification accuracy (Paltoglou and Thelwall, 2010).

An obstacle to research in this direction is the need of labeled training data, whose preparation is a time-consuming activity. Therefore, in order to reduce the labeling effort, opinion words have been used for training procedures. In (Tan et al., 2008) and (Qiu et al., 2009b), the authors used opinion words to label portions of informative examples for training the classifiers. Opinion words have been exploited also for improving the accuracy of sentiment classification, as presented in (Melville et al., 2009), where a framework incorporating lexical knowledge in supervised learning to enhance accuracy has been proposed. Opinion words have been used also for unsupervised learning approaches like the ones presented in (Taboada et al., 2011) and (Turney, 2002).

Another research direction concerns the exploitation of discourse-analysis techniques. (Somasundaran, 2010) and (Asher et al., 2008) discuss some discourse-based supervised and unsupervised approaches for opinion analysis; while in (Wang and Zhou, 2010), the authors present an approach to identify discourse relations.

The approaches presented above are applied at the document-level, i.e., the polarity value is assigned to the entire document content. However, for improving the accuracy of the sentiment classification, a more fine-grained analysis of the text, i.e., the sentiment classification of the single sentences, has to be performed. In the case of sentence-level sentiment classification, two different sub-tasks have to be addressed: (i) to determine if the sentence is subjective or objective, and (ii) in the case that the sentence is subjective, to determine if the opinion expressed in the sentence is positive, negative, or neutral. The task of classifying a sentence as subjective or objective, called "subjectivity classification", has been widely discussed in the literature (Riloff et al., 2006; Wiebe et al., 2004; Wilson et al., 2004; Wilson et al., 2006; Yu and Hatzivassiloglou, 2003). Once subjective sentences are identified, the same methods as for sentiment classification may be applied. For example, in (Hatzivassiloglou and Wiebe, 2000) the authors consider gradable adjectives for sentiment spotting; while in (Kim and Hovy, 2007) and (Kim et al., 2006) the authors built models to identify some specific types of opinions.

The growth of product reviews was the perfect floor for using sentiment analysis techniques in marketing activities. However, the issue of improving the ability of detecting the different opinions concerning the same product expressed in the same review became a challenging problem. Such a task has been faced by introducing "aspect" extraction approaches that were able to extract, from each sentence, which is the aspect the opinion refers to. In the literature, many approaches have been proposed: conditional random fields (CRF) (Jakob and Gurevych, 2010; Lafferty et al., 2001), hidden Markov models (HMM) (Freitag and McCallum, 2000; Jin and Ho, 2009; Jin et al., 2009), sequential rule mining (Liu et al., 2005), dependency tree kernels (Wu et al., 2009), and clustering (Su et al., 2008). In (Qiu et al., 2009a; Qiu et al., 2011), a method was proposed to extract both opinion words and aspects simultaneously by exploiting some syntactic relations of opinion words and aspects.

A particular attention should be given also to the application of sentiment analysis in social networks. More and more often, people use social networks for expressing their moods concerning their last purchase or, in general, about new products. Such a social network environment opened up new challenges due to the different ways people express their opinions, as described by (Barbosa and Feng, 2010) and (Bermingham and Smeaton, 2010), who mention "noisy data" as one of the biggest hurdles in analyzing social network texts.

One of the first studies on sentiment analysis on micro-blogging websites has been discussed in (Go et al., 2009), where the authors present a distant supervision-based approach for sentiment classification.

At the same time, the social dimension of the Web opens up the opportunity to combine computer science and social sciences to better recognize, interpret, and process opinions and sentiments expressed over it. Such multi-disciplinary approach has been called *sentic computing* (Cambria and Hussain, 2012b). Application domains where sentic computing has already shown its potential are the cognitive-inspired classification of images (Cambria and Hussain, 2012a), of texts in natural language, and of handwritten text (Wang et al., 2013).

Finally, an interesting recent research direction is domain adaptation, as it has been shown that sentiment classification is highly sensitive to the domain from which the training data is extracted. A classifier trained using opinionated documents from one domain often performs poorly when it is applied or tested on opinionated documents from another domain, as we demonstrated through the example presented in Section 1. The reason is that words and even language constructs used in different domains for expressing opinions can be quite different. To make matters worse, the same word in one domain may have positive connotations, but in another domain may have negative connotations; therefore, domain adaptation is needed. In the literature, different approaches related to the Multi-Domain sentiment analysis have been proposed. Briefly, two main categories may be identified: (i) the transfer of learned classifiers across different domains (Yang et al., 2006; Blitzer et al., 2007; Pan et al., 2010; Bollegala et al., 2013; Xia et al., 2013; Yoshida et al., 2011), and (ii) the use of propagation of labels through graph structures (Ponomareva and Thelwall, 2013; Tsai et al., 2013; Tai and Kao, 2013; Huang et al., 2014). Independently of the kind of approach, works using concepts rather than terms for representing different sentiments have been proposed.

3 The SHELLFBK System

The proposed system is based on the implementation of an IR approach for inferring both the polarity of a sentence and, if requested, the domain to which the sentence belongs to. The rational behind the usage of such an approach is that by using indexes, the computation of the Retrieval Status Value (RSV) (da Costa Pereira et al., 2012) of a term or expression, automatically takes into account which are the elements that are more significant in each index with respect to the ones that, instead, are not important with respect to the index content. In this section, we present the steps we carried out to implement our IR based sentiment and theme classification system.

3.1 Indexes Construction

The proposed approach, with respect to a classic IR system, does not use a single index for containing all information, but a set of indexes are created in order to facilitate the identification of the correct polarity and domain, of a sentence during the validation phase. In particular, we built the following set of indexes:

- **Polarity Indexes:** from the training set, the positive, negative, and neutral sentences have been indexed separately.
- **Domain Indexes:**: a different index has been built for each domain identified in the training set. This way, it is possible to store information about which terms, or expression, are relevant for each domain.
- **Mixed Indexes:** by considering the multi-domain nature of the system, this further set of indexes allows to have, for each domain, information about the correlation between the domain and the polarities. This way, we are able to know if the same term, or expression, has the same polarity in different domains or not.

For each sentence of the training set, we exploited the Stanford NLP Library for extracting the dependencies between the terms. Such dependencies are then used as input for the indexing procedure.

As example, let's consider the following sentence extracted from the training set of the Task 9:

"*I came here to reflect my happiness by fishing.*"

This sentence has a positive polarity and belongs to the "outdoor_activity" domain. By applying the Stanford parser, the dependencies that are extracted are the following ones:

```
nsubj(came-2, I-1)
nsubj(reflect-5, I-1)
root(ROOT-0, came-2)
advmod(came-2, here-3)
aux(reflect-5, to-4)
xcomp(came-2, reflect-5)
poss(happiness-7, my-6)
dobj(reflect-5, happiness-7)
prep_by(reflect-5, fishing-9)
```

Each dependency is composed by three elements: the name of the "relation" (R), the "governor" (G) that is the first term of the dependency, and the "dependent" (D) that is the second one. We extract, from each dependency, the structure "field - content" shown in Table 1 by using as example the dependency "dobj(reflect-5, happiness-7)". Such a structure is then given as input to the index.

Field Name	Content
RGD	"dobj-reflect-happiness"
RDG	"dobj-happiness-reflect"
GD	"reflect-happiness"
DG	"happiness-reflect"
G	"reflect"
D	"happiness"

Table 1: Field structure and corresponding content stored in the index.

The structure shown in Table 1 is created for each dependency extracted from the sentence and the aggregation of all structures are stored as final record in the index.

3.2 Polarity and Domain Computation

Once the indexes are built, both the polarity and the domain of each sentence that need to be evaluated, are computed by performing a set of queries on the indexes. In our approach, we implemented a variation of classic IR scoring formula for our purposes. In the classical TF-IDF IR model (van Rijsbergen, 1979), the *inverse document frequency* value is used for identifying which are the most significant documents with respect to a particular query. This value is useful when we want to identify the uniqueness of a document with respect to a term contained in a query, with respect to the other documents stored into the index. In our case, the scenario is different because if a term, or expression, occurs often in the index, this aspect has to be emphasized instead of being discriminated. Therefore, in our scoring formula we consider, as final score of a term or an expression, the document frequency (DF) value (i.e., the inverse of the IDF). This way, we are able to infer if a particular term or expression is significant or not for a given polarity value or domain.

The queries are built with the same procedure used for creating the records stored in the indexes. For each sentence to evaluate, a set of queries, one for each dependency extracted from the sentence is performed on the indexes and the results are aggregated for inferring both the polarity and domain of the sentence.

As example of how the system works, let's consider the following sentence:

"I feel good and I feel healthy."

For simplicity, we only consider the following two extracted dependencies:

```
acomp(feel-2, good-3)
acomp(feel-6, healthy-7)
```

From these two dependencies, we generate the following two queries:

```
Q1: "RGD:"acomp-feel-good"
     OR RDG:"acomp-good-feel"
     OR GD:"feel-good" OR DG:"good-feel"
     OR G:"feel" OR D:"good"
Q2: "RGD:"acomp-feel-healthy"
     OR RDG:"acomp-healthy-feel"
     OR GD:"feel-healthy" OR DG:"healthy-feel"
     OR G:"feel" OR D:"healthy"
```

For computing the polarity of the sentence, the queries are performed on the three indexes containing polarized records: positive (POS), negative (NEG), and neutral (NEU). From the computed ranks, we extract only the DF associated to each field F contained in the query:

$$DF(F) = 1/IDF(F) \tag{2}$$

where DF is the value extracted.

As a direct consequence, for each index I, the value representing the RSV of a sentence is:

$$\begin{aligned} RSV(I) = DF(RGD_{Q1}) + DF(RDG_{Q1}) + \\ DF(GD_{Q1}) + DF(DG_{Q1}) + DF(G_{Q1}) + \\ DF(D_{Q1}) + DF(RGD_{Q2}) + DF(RDG_{Q2}) + \\ DF(GD_{Q2}) + DF(DG_{Q2}) + DF(G_{Q2}) + \\ DF(D_{Q2}) \end{aligned} \tag{3}$$

Finally, the polarity of the sentence S is inferred by considering the maximum RSV computed over the three indexes:

$$\begin{aligned} \text{Polarity}(S) = \\ \text{argmax}_{P \in \text{POS,NEU,NEG}} \text{RSV}(S, P) \end{aligned} \tag{4}$$

In case of domain assignment, given a set D of k domains, the domain is computed by:

$$\text{Domain}(S) = \text{argmax}_{\ i \in 1 \ldots k} \text{RSV}(S, D_i) \tag{5}$$

4 Results

The SHELLFBK system participated in three SemEval 2015 tasks: 9, 10, and 11. All three tasks were about the sentiment analysis topic with the following differences:

- Task 9 (Russo et al., 2015): this task is based on a dataset of events annotated as instantiations of pleasant and unpleasant events previously collected in psychological researches as the ones on which human judgments converge (Lewinsohn and Amenson, 1978),(MacPhillamy. and Lewinsohn, 1982). Task 9 concerns classification of the events that are pleasant or unpleasant for a person writing in first person. This task was organized around two subtasks: (A) identification of the polarity value associated to an event instance, and (B) identification of both the event instantiations and the associated polarity values. The SHELLFBK system has been tested on both tasks.

- Task 10 (Rosenthal et al., 2015): this task aims to identify sentiment polarities in short text messages contained in the Twitter microblog. This task contains five subtasks: (A) expression-level, (B) message-level, (C) topic-related, (D) trend, and (E) a task on prior polarity of terms. The SHELLFBK has been tested only on the subtask (B).

- Task 11 (Ghosh et al., 2015): this task consists in the classification of tweets containing irony and metaphors. Given a set of tweets that are rich in metaphor and irony, the goal is to determine whether the user has expressed a positive, negative, or neutral sentiment in each, and the degree to which this sentiment has been communicated. With respect to the other tasks, here the polarity is expressed through a fine-grained scale in the interval [-5, 5].

In the following subsections, we will briefly report the performance obtained on each task.

4.1 Task 9

Table 2 reports the results obtained in Task 9. This task consisted in the identification of the polarity of a sentence written in first person (subtask A) and in

Task	Precision	Recall	F-Measure
Subtask A	0.555	0.384	0.454
Subtask B	0.261	0.155	0.197

Table 2: Results obtained by the SHELLFBK system on Task 9.

the identification of both the polarity and the domain of the sentence (subtask B). Precision, recall and F-Measure have been computed. As expected, the accuracy obtained on the sole prediction of the sentence polarity is higher with respect to the one obtained on the subtask combining the inference of both the domain and the polarity itself. Unfortunately, the recall values obtained on both subtasks are quite low, especially for the subtask B.

4.2 Task 10

Performance obtained by the SHELLFBK system on Task 10 have been reported in Table 3. For this task, the SHELLFBK system has been tested only on the message-level polarity subtask (B). By observing either the overall f-measure and the ones obtained on the different portions of the dataset, the performance of the system are too low for considering it a reliable solution for being used in contexts where short texts are taken into account.

4.3 Task 11

Results of the proposed system concerning Task 11 are shown in Table 4. In this task, due to the fine-grained nature of the polarity predictions, the cosine similarity and the mean square error with respect to the gold standard have been computed. In the first result-line, the values obtained on the four figurative categories are reported, while in the second one, the overall results. By observing the results, for the "Sarcasm" and "Irony" topics the obtained results are acceptable; while, for the "Metaphor" and for the "Other" category, both the cosine similarity and the MSE are significantly worse with respect to the first two. These results, either with the ones obtained on Task 10, confirm that the analysis of short texts is the first issue to address for improving the general quality of the system.

5 Conclusion

In this paper, we described the SHELLFBK system presented at SemEval 2015 that participated in SemEval 2015 Tasks 9, 10, and 11. Our system makes use of IR techniques to classify sentences by polarity, domain and the joint prediction of polarity and domain, effectively providing domain specific sentiment analysis. The results demonstrated that, while on well-formed sentences the system obtained good performance, the method performs less well on short texts like tweets. Therefore, future work will focus on the improvement of the system in this direction. In future work, we intend to explore the integration of sentiment knowledge bases (Dragoni et al., 2014) in order to move toward a more cognitive approach.

Acknowledgments

We would like to thank the anonymous reviewers for their helpful suggestions and comments.

References

Nicholas Asher, Farah Benamara, and Yvette Yannick Mathieu. 2008. Distilling opinion in discourse: A preliminary study. In *COLING (Posters)*, pages 7–10.

Luciano Barbosa and Junlan Feng. 2010. Robust sentiment detection on twitter from biased and noisy data. In *COLING (Posters)*, pages 36–44.

Adam Bermingham and Alan F. Smeaton. 2010. Classifying sentiment in microblogs: is brevity an advantage? In *CIKM*, pages 1833–1836.

John Blitzer, Mark Dredze, and Fernando Pereira. 2007. Biographies, bollywood, boom-boxes and blenders: Domain adaptation for sentiment classification. In *ACL*, pages 187–205.

Danushka Bollegala, David J. Weir, and John A. Carroll. 2013. Cross-domain sentiment classification using a sentiment sensitive thesaurus. *IEEE Trans. Knowl. Data Eng.*, 25(8):1719–1731.

Erik Cambria and Amir Hussain. 2012a. Sentic album: Content-, concept-, and context-based online personal photo management system. *Cognitive Computation*, 4(4):477–496.

Erik Cambria and Amir Hussain. 2012b. *Sentic Computing: Techniques, Tools, and Applications*, volume 2 of *SpringerBriefs in Cognitive Computation*. Springer, Dordrecht, Netherlands.

Kushal Dave, Steve Lawrence, and David M. Pennock. 2003. Mining the peanut gallery: opinion extraction

Task	Live Journal 2014	SMS 2013	Twitter 2013	Twitter 2014	Twitter 2014 Sarcasm
Progress Test	0.3406	0.2614	0.3214	0.3220	0.3558
Task	F-Measure	-	-	-	-
Overall	0.3245	-	-	-	-

Table 3: Results obtained by the SHELLFBK on Task 10.

	Mean Square Error				Cosine Similarity			
	Sarcasm	Irony	Metaphor	Other	Sarcasm	Irony	Metaphor	Other
Detailed Results	4.375	4.516	9.219	12.16	0.669	0.625	0.35	0.167
	MSE	Cosine	-	-	-	-	-	-
General Result	7.701	0.431	-	-	-	-	-	-

Table 4: Results obtained by the SHELLFBK on Task 11.

and semantic classification of product reviews. In *WWW*, pages 519–528.

Mauro Dragoni, Andrea G.B.Tettamanzi, and Célia da Costa Pereira. 2014. Propagating and aggregating fuzzy polarities for concept-level sentiment analysis. *Cognitive Computation*, pages 1–12.

Dayne Freitag and Andrew McCallum. 2000. Information extraction with hmm structures learned by stochastic optimization. In *AAAI/IAAI*, pages 584–589.

Aniruddha Ghosh, Guofu Li, Tony Veale, Paolo Rosso, Ekaterina Shutova, Antonio Reyes, and John Barnden. 2015. SemEval-2015 task 11: Sentiment analysis of figurative language in twitter. In *Proceedings of the 9th International Workshop on Semantic Evaluation*, SemEval '2015, Denver, Colorado, June.

Alec Go, Richa Bhayani, and Lei Huang. 2009. Twitter sentiment classification using distant supervision. CS224N Project Report, Standford University.

Vasileios Hatzivassiloglou and Janyce Wiebe. 2000. Effects of adjective orientation and gradability on sentence subjectivity. In *COLING*, pages 299–305.

Sheng Huang, Zhendong Niu, and Chongyang Shi. 2014. Automatic construction of domain-specific sentiment lexicon based on constrained label propagation. *Knowl.-Based Syst.*, 56:191–200.

Niklas Jakob and Iryna Gurevych. 2010. Extracting opinion targets in a single and cross-domain setting with conditional random fields. In *EMNLP*, pages 1035–1045.

Wei Jin and Hung Hay Ho. 2009. A novel lexicalized HMM-based learning framework for web opinion mining. In *Proceedings of the 26th Annual International Conference on Machine Learning*, ICML '09, pages 465–472, New York, NY, USA. ACM.

Wei Jin, Hung Hay Ho, and Rohini K. Srihari. 2009. Opinionminer: a novel machine learning system for web opinion mining and extraction. In *KDD*, pages 1195–1204.

Soo-Min Kim and Eduard H. Hovy. 2007. Crystal: Analyzing predictive opinions on the web. In *EMNLP-CoNLL*, pages 1056–1064.

Soo-Min Kim, Patrick Pantel, Timothy Chklovski, and Marco Pennacchiotti. 2006. Automatically assessing review helpfulness. In *EMNLP*, pages 423–430.

John D. Lafferty, Andrew McCallum, and Fernando C. N. Pereira. 2001. Conditional random fields: Probabilistic models for segmenting and labeling sequence data. In *ICML*, pages 282–289.

Peter M. Lewinsohn and Christopher S. Amenson. 1978. Some relations between pleasant and unpleasant events and depression. *Journal of Abnormal Psychology*, 87:644–654.

Bing Liu and Lei Zhang. 2012. A survey of opinion mining and sentiment analysis. In C. C. Aggarwal and C. X. Zhai, editors, *Mining Text Data*, pages 415–463. Springer.

Bing Liu, Minqing Hu, and Junsheng Cheng. 2005. Opinion observer: analyzing and comparing opinions on the web. In *WWW*, pages 342–351.

Douglas MacPhillamy, and Peter M. Lewinsohn. 1982. The pleasant event schedule: Studies on reliability, validity, and scale intercorrelation. *Journal of Counseling and Clinical Psychology*, 50:363–380.

Prem Melville, Wojciech Gryc, and Richard D. Lawrence. 2009. Sentiment analysis of blogs by combining lexical knowledge with text classification. In *KDD*, pages 1275–1284.

Georgios Paltoglou and Mike Thelwall. 2010. A study of information retrieval weighting schemes for sentiment analysis. In *ACL*, pages 1386–1395.

Sinno Jialin Pan, Xiaochuan Ni, Jian-Tao Sun, Qiang Yang, and Zheng Chen. 2010. Cross-domain sentiment classification via spectral feature alignment. In *WWW*, pages 751–760.

Bo Pang and Lillian Lee. 2004. A sentimental education: Sentiment analysis using subjectivity summarization based on minimum cuts. In *ACL*, pages 271–278.

Bo Pang and Lillian Lee. 2008. Opinion mining and sentiment analysis. *Foundations and Trends in Information Retrieval*, 2(1-2):1–135.

Bo Pang, Lillian Lee, and Shivakumar Vaithyanathan. 2002. Thumbs up? sentiment classification using machine learning techniques. In *Proceedings of EMNLP 2002*, pages 79–86, Philadelphia, July.

Natalia Ponomareva and Mike Thelwall. 2013. Semi-supervised vs. cross-domain graphs for sentiment analysis. In *RANLP*, pages 571–578.

Guang Qiu, Bing Liu, Jiajun Bu, and Chun Chen. 2009a. Expanding domain sentiment lexicon through double propagation. In *IJCAI*, pages 1199–1204.

Likun Qiu, Weishi Zhang, Changjian Hu, and Kai Zhao. 2009b. Selc: a self-supervised model for sentiment classification. In *CIKM*, pages 929–936.

Guang Qiu, Bing Liu, Jiajun Bu, and Chun Chen. 2011. Opinion word expansion and target extraction through double propagation. *Computational Linguistics*, 37(1):9–27.

Ellen Riloff, Siddharth Patwardhan, and Janyce Wiebe. 2006. Feature subsumption for opinion analysis. In *EMNLP*, pages 440–448.

Sara Rosenthal, Preslav Nakov, Svetlana Kiritchenko, Saif M Mohammad, Alan Ritter, and Veselin Stoyanov. 2015. SemEval-2015 task 10: Sentiment analysis in twitter. In *Proceedings of the 9th International Workshop on Semantic Evaluation*, SemEval '2015, Denver, Colorado, June.

Irene Russo, Tommaso Caselli, and Carlo Strapparava. 2015. SemEval-2015 Task 9: CLIPEval Implicit Polarity of Events. In *Proceedings of the 9th International Workshop on Semantic Evaluation*, SemEval '2015, Denver, Colorado, June.

Swapna Somasundaran. 2010. *Discourse-level relations for Opinion Analysis*. Ph.D. thesis, University of Pittsburgh.

Qi Su, Xinying Xu, Honglei Guo, Zhili Guo, Xian Wu, Xiaoxun Zhang, Bin Swen, and Zhong Su. 2008. Hidden sentiment association in chinese web opinion mining. In *WWW*, pages 959–968.

Maite Taboada, Julian Brooke, Milan Tofiloski, Kimberly D. Voll, and Manfred Stede. 2011. Lexicon-based methods for sentiment analysis. *Computational Linguistics*, 37(2):267–307.

Yen-Jen Tai and Hung-Yu Kao. 2013. Automatic domain-specific sentiment lexicon generation with label propagation. In *iiWAS*, pages 53:53–53:62. ACM.

Songbo Tan, Yuefen Wang, and Xueqi Cheng. 2008. Combining learn-based and lexicon-based techniques for sentiment detection without using labeled examples. In *SIGIR*, pages 743–744.

Angela Charng-Rurng Tsai, Chi-En Wu, Richard Tzong-Han Tsai, and Jane Yung jen Hsu. 2013. Building a concept-level sentiment dictionary based on common-sense knowledge. *IEEE Int. Systems*, 28(2):22–30.

Célia da Costa Pereira, Mauro Dragoni, and Gabriella Pasi 2012. Multidimensional relevance: Prioritized aggregation in a personalized Information Retrieval setting. *Inf. Process. Manage.*, 48(2):340–357.

Peter D. Turney. 2002. Thumbs up or thumbs down? semantic orientation applied to unsupervised classification of reviews. In *ACL*, pages 417–424.

Cornelis Joost van Rijsbergen. 1979. *Information Retrieval*. Butterworth.

Hongling Wang and Guodong Zhou. 2010. Topic-driven multi-document summarization. In *IALP*, pages 195–198.

Qiu Feng Wang, Erik Cambria, Cheng Lin Liu, and Amir Hussain. 2013. Common sense knowledge for handwritten chinese recognition. *Cognitive Computation*, 5(2):234–242.

Janyce Wiebe, Theresa Wilson, Rebecca F. Bruce, Matthew Bell, and Melanie Martin. 2004. Learning subjective language. *Computational Linguistics*, 30(3):277–308.

Theresa Wilson, Janyce Wiebe, and Rebecca Hwa. 2004. Just how mad are you? finding strong and weak opinion clauses. In *AAAI*, pages 761–769.

Theresa Wilson, Janyce Wiebe, and Rebecca Hwa. 2006. Recognizing strong and weak opinion clauses. *Computational Intelligence*, 22(2):73–99.

Yuanbin Wu, Qi Zhang, Xuanjing Huang, and Lide Wu. 2009. Phrase dependency parsing for opinion mining. In *EMNLP*, pages 1533–1541.

Rui Xia, Chengqing Zong, Xuelei Hu, and Erik Cambria. 2013. Feature ensemble plus sample selection: Domain adaptation for sentiment classification. *IEEE Int. Systems*, 28(3):10–18.

Hui Yang, Jamie Callan, and Luo Si. 2006. Knowledge transfer and opinion detection in the TREC 2006 blog track. In *TREC*.

Yasuhisa Yoshida, Tsutomu Hirao, Tomoharu Iwata, Masaaki Nagata, and Yuji Matsumoto. 2011. Transfer learning for multiple-domain sentiment analysis—identifying domain dependent/independent word polarity. In *AAAI*, pages 1286–1291.

Hong Yu and Vasileios Hatzivassiloglou. 2003. Towards answering opinion questions: Separating facts from opinions and identifying the polarity of opinion sentences. In *Proceedings of EMNLP 2003*, pages 129–136, Stroudsburg, PA, USA.

DIEGOLab: An Approach for Message-level Sentiment Classification in Twitter

Abeed Sarker, Azadeh Nikfarjam, Davy Weissenbacher, Graciela Gonzalez
Department of Biomedical Informatics
Arizona State University
Scottsdale, AZ 85281, USA
{abeed.sarker,anikfarj,dweissen,graciela.gonzalez}@asu.edu

Abstract

We present our supervised sentiment classification system which competed in SemEval-2015 Task 10B: Sentiment Classification in Twitter— Message Polarity Classification. Our system employs a Support Vector Machine classifier trained using a number of features including n-grams, dependency parses, synset expansions, word prior polarities, and embedding clusters. Using weighted Support Vector Machines, to address the issue of class imbalance, our system obtains positive class F-scores of 0.701 and 0.656, and negative class F-scores of 0.515 and 0.478 over the training and test sets, respectively.

1 Introduction

Social media has seen unprecedented growth in recent years. Twitter, for example, has over 645,750,000 users and grows by an estimated 135,000 users every day, generating 9,100 tweets per second[1]). Users often express their views and emotions regarding a range of topics on social media platforms. As such, social media has become a crucial resource for obtaining information directly from end-users, and data from social media has been utilized for a variety of tasks ranging from personalized marketing to public health monitoring. While the benefits of using a resource such as Twitter include large volumes of data and direct access to end-user sentiments, there are several obstacles associated with the use of social media data. These include the use of non-standard terminologies, misspellings, short and ambiguous posts, and data imbalance, to name a few.

In this paper, we present a supervised learning approach, using Support Vector Machines (SVMs) for the task of automatic sentiment classification of Twitter posts. Our system participated in the SemEval-2015 task *Sentiment Classification in Twitter— Message Polarity Classification*. The goal of the task was to automatically classify the polarity of a Twitter post into one of three predefined categories— positive, negative and neutral. In our approach, we apply a small set of carefully extracted lexical, semantic, and distributional features. The features are used to train a SVM learner, and the issue of data imbalance is addressed by using distinct weights for each of the three classes. The results of our system are promising, with positive class F-scores of 0.701 and 0.656, and negative class F-scores of 0.515 and 0.478 over the training and test sets, respectively.

2 Related Work

Following the pioneering work on sentiment analysis by Pang *et. al.* (2002), similar research has been carried out under various umbrella terms such as: semantic orientation (Turney, 2002), opinion mining (Pang and Lee, 2008), polarity classification (Sarker et al., 2013), and many more. Pang *et al.* (2002) utilized machine learning models to predict sentiments in text, and their approach showed that SVM classifiers trained using bag-of-words features produced promising results. Similar approaches have been applied to texts of various granularities— documents,

[1] `http://www.statisticbrain.com/twitter-statistics/`. Accessed on: 26th August, 2014.

sentences, and phrases.

Due to the availability of vast amounts of data, there has been growing interest in utilizing social media mining for obtaining information directly from users (Liu and Zhang, 2012). However, social media sources, such as Twitter posts, present various natural language processing (NLP) and machine learning challenges. The NLP challenges arise from factors, such as, the use of informal language, frequent misspellings, creative phrases and words, abbreviations, short text lengths and others. From the perspective of machine learning, some of the key challenges include data imbalance, noise, and feature sparseness. In recent research, these challenges have received significant attention (Jansen et al., 2009; Barbosa and Feng, 2010; Davidov et al., 2010; Kouloumpis et al., 2011; Sarker and Gonzalez, 2014).

3 Methods

3.1 Data

Our training and test data consists of the data made available for SemEval 2015 task 10 (A–D). Each instance of the data set made available consisted of a tweet ID, a user ID, and a sentiment category for the tweet. For training, we downloaded all the annotated tweets that were publicly available at the time of development of the system. We were able to obtain, from the training and development sets released by the organizers, a total of 9,289 tweets for which the annotations were available. Of these, 4,445 (48%) were annotated as neutral, 1,416 (15%) as negative, and 3,428 (37%) as positive. The data is heavily imbalanced with particularly small number of negative instances.

3.2 Features

We derive a set of lexical, semantic, and distributional features from the training data. A brief description of each feature and preprocessing technique is described below.

3.2.1 Preprocessing

We perform standard preprocessing such as tokenization, lowercasing and stemming of all the terms using the Porter stemmer[2] (Porter, 1980). Our preliminary investigations suggested that stop words can play a positive effect on classifier performances by their presence in word 2-grams and 3-grams; so, we do not remove stop words from the texts.

3.2.2 N-grams

Our first feature set consists of word n-grams of the tweets. A word n-gram is a sequence of contiguous n words in a text segment, and this feature enables us to represent a document using the union of its terms. We use 1-, 2-, and 3-grams as features.

3.2.3 Synset

It has been shown in past research that certain terms, because of their prior polarities, play important roles in determining the polarities of sentences (Sarker et al., 2013). Certain adjectives, and sometimes nouns and verbs, or their synonyms, are almost invariably associated with positive or non-positive polarities. For each adjective, noun or verb in a tweet, we use WordNet[3] to identify the synonyms of that term and add the synonymous terms as features.

3.2.4 Average Sentiment Score

For this feature, we incorporate a score that attempts to represent the general sentiment of a tweet using the prior polarities of its terms. Each word-POS pair in a comment is assigned a score and the overall score assigned to the comment is equal to the sum of all the individual term-POS sentiment scores divided by the length of the sentence in words. For term-POS pairs with multiple senses, the score for the most common sense is chosen. To obtain a score for each term, we use the lexicon proposed by Guerini *et al.* . The lexicon contains approximately 155,000 English words associated with a sentiment score between -1 and 1. The overall score a sentence receives is therefore a floating point number with the range [-1:1]. One problem faced, when using such a lexicon on tweets, is words are frequently misspelled and, thus, missed by the lexicon matching process. We, therefore, used a fast, moderately accurate, and publicly available spelling correction sys-

[2]We use the implementation provided by the NLTK toolkit `http://www.nltk.org/`.

[3]`http://wordnet.princeton.edu/`. Accessed on October 13, 2014.

tem[4] to process each tweet before performing lexicon matches.

3.2.5 Grammatical Dependencies

Stanford grammatical dependencies have been designed with a view to provide a simple and usable analysis of the grammatical structure of a sentence by people who are not (computational) linguists (de Marneffe et al., 2006). In this schema, each relation between words of a sentence are encoded as binary predicates between two words. A semantic interpretation which uses the notions of traditional grammar are attached to the relations to facilitate their comprehension. For example, from the sentence *I love the banner*, we expect in the analysis the relations *nsubj(love, I), det(banner, the), dobj(love, banner)* denoting subject, determinant and direct object roles, respectively. Based on previous research (Nikfarjam et al., 2012), our intuition is that dependency relationships maybe useful for polarity classification. We used the Stanford parser integrated in the Stanford CoreNLP 3.4 suite,[5] and computed collapsed and propagated dependency trees for each tweet.

3.2.6 Embedding Cluster Features

Considering the nature of the user posts in Twitter, it is common to observe rarely occurring or unseen tokens in the test data. In order to address this issue, we use embedding cluster features introduced in (Nikfarjam et al., 2014). We categorize the similar tokens into clusters, and as a result, each token in the corpus has an associated cluster number. Therefore, every tweet is represented with a set of cluster numbers, with similar tokens having the same cluster number. The word clusters are generated based on K-means clustering of the token representative vectors (known as embeddings). The embeddings are meaningful real-valued vectors of configurable dimensions (usually, 150 to 500 dimensions) learned from large volumes of unlabeled sentences. We generate 150-dimensional vectors using the word2vec tool.[6]. Our corpus includes a large number of unlabeled sentences from the provided train/test tweets plus an additional 860,000 in-house set of collected tweets about user opinions on medications. The vector and cluster dimensions are selected based on extrinsic evaluation of different configurations for the embedding clusters, generated from the same in-house Twitter corpus in our previous study. Word2vec learns the embeddings by training a neural network-based language model, and mapping tokens from similar contexts into vectors that can then be clustered using vector similarity techniques. More information about generating the embeddings can be found in the related papers (Bengio et al., 2003; Turian et al., 2010; Mikolov et al., 2013).

3.2.7 Other Features

In addition to the abovementioned features, we used the post lengths, in number of characters, as a feature.

3.3 Classification

Using the abovementioned features, we trained SVM classifiers for the classification task. The performance of SVMs can vary significantly based on the kernel and specific parameter values. For our work, based on some preliminary experimentation on the training set, we used the RBF kernel. We computed optimal values for the *cost* and γ parameters via grid-search and 10-fold cross validation over the training set. To address the problem of data imbalance, we utilized the weighted SVM feature of the LibSVM library (Chang and Lin, 2011), and we attempted to find optimal values for the weights in the same way using 10-fold cross validation over the training set. We found that $cost = 8.0$, $\gamma = 0.0$, $\omega_1 = 3.5$, and $\omega_2 = 2.2$ to produce the best results, where ω_1 and ω_2 are the weights for the positive and negative classes, respectively.

4 Results

Table 1 presents the performance of our system on the training and test data sets. The table presents the positive and negative class F-scores for the system, and the average of the two scores— the metric that is used for ranking systems in the SemEval evaluations for this task. For the training set, the results are those obtained via 10-fold cross validation. The test set

[4] `http://norvig.com/spell-correct.html`. Accessed on January 7, 2015.

[5] `http://nlp.stanford.edu/software/corenlp.shtml`. Accessed on January 8, 2015

[6] Available at: `https://code.google.com/p/word2vec/`. Accessed on 13 January, 2015

consists of 2,390 instances and the full training set is used when performing classification on this set.

Data set	Positive F-score (P)	Negative F-score (N)	$\frac{P+N}{2}$
Training	0.701	0.515	0.608
Test	0.656	0.478	0.567

Table 1: Classification results for the DIEGOLab system over the training and test sets.

4.1 Feature Analysis

To assess the contribution of each feature towards the final score, we performed leave-one-out feature and single feature experiments. Tables 3 and 2 show the $\frac{P+N}{2}$ values for the training and the test sets for the two set of experiments. The first row of the tables present the results when all the features are used, and the following rows show the results when a specific feature is removed or when a single feature is used. The tables illustrate that the most important feature set is n-grams, and there is a large drop in the evaluation score when that feature is removed (in Table 2). For all the other feature sets, the drops in the evaluation scores shown in Table 3 are very low, meaning that their contribution to the final evaluation score is quite limited. Table 3 suggests that the sentiment score feature is the second most useful feature after n-grams. The experiments suggest that the classifier settings (*i.e.*, the parameter values and the class weights) play a more important role in our final approach, as greater deviations from the scores presented can be achieved by fine tuning the parameter values than by adding, removing, or modifying the feature sets. Further experimentation is required to identify useful features and to configure existing features to be more effective.

5 Conclusions and Future Work

Our system achieved moderate performance on the SemEval sentiment analysis task utilizing very basic settings. The F-scores were particularly low for the negative class, which can be attributed to the class imbalance. Considering that the performance of our system was achieved by very basic settings, there is promise of better performance via the utilization of various feature generation and engineering techniques.

Feature removed	Training set average	Test set average
None	0.608	0.567
N-grams	0.575	0.527
Synset	0.606	0.565
Sentiment Score	0.608	0.561
Grammatical Dependencies	0.601	0.562
Embedding Clusters	0.602	0.566
Other	0.608	0.565

Table 2: Leave-one-out $\frac{P+N}{2}$ feature scores for the training and test sets.

Feature	Training set average	Test set average
All	0.608	0.567
N-grams	0.587	0.560
Synset	0.507	0.478
Sentiment Score	0.561	0.489
Grammatical Dependencies	0.435	0.436
Embedding Clusters	0.482	0.461
Other	0.303	0.272

Table 3: Single feature $\frac{P+N}{2}$ scores for the training and test sets.

We have several planned future tasks to improve the classification performance on this data set, and for social media based sentiment analysis in general. Following on from our past work on social media data (Patki et al., 2014; Sarker and Gonzalez, 2014), a significant portion of our future work will focus on the application of more informative features for automatic classification of social media text, including sentiment analysis. We are also keen to explore the use of text normalization techniques, at various granularities, to improve classification performance over social media data.

Acknowledgments

This work was supported by NIH National Library of Medicine under grant number NIH NLM 1R01LM011176. The content is solely the responsibility of the authors and does not necessarily represent the official views of the NLM or NIH.

References

Luciano Barbosa and Junlan Feng. 2010. Robust Sentiment Detection on Twitter from Biased and Noisy Data. In *Proceedings of COLING*, pages 36–44.

Yoshua Bengio, Réjean Ducharme, Pascal Vincent, and Christian Jauvin. 2003. A Neural Probabilistic Language Model. *Journal of Machine Learning Research*, 3:1137–1155.

Chih-Chung Chang and Chih-Jen Lin. 2011. LIBSVM: A library for support vector machines. *ACM Transactions on Intelligent Systems and Technology*, 2:27:1–27:27. Software available at `http://www.csie.ntu.edu.tw/~cjlin/libsvm`.

Dmitry Davidov, Oren Tsur, and Ari Rappoport. 2010. Enhanced Sentiment Learning Using Twitter Hashtags and Smileys. In *Proceedings of COLING*, pages 241–249.

Marie-Catherine de Marneffe, Bill MacCartney, and Christopher D Manning. 2006. Generating Typed Dependency Parsers from Phrase Structure Parses. In *Proceedings of the Fifth International Conference on Language Resources and Evaluation*, pages 449–454.

Marco Guerini, Lorenzo Gatti, and Marco Turchi. 2013. Sentiment Analysis: How to Derive Prior Polarities from SentiWordNet. In *Proceedings of Empirical Methods in Natural Language Processing (EMNLP)*, pages 1259–1269.

Bernard J Jansen, Mimi Zhang, Kate Sobel, and Abdur Chowdury. 2009. Twitter Power: Tweets as Electronic Word of Mouth. *Journal of the American Society for Information Science and Technology*, 60(11):2169–2188.

Efthymios Kouloumpis, Theresa Wilson, and Johanna Moore. 2011. Twitter Sentiment Analysis: The Good the Bad and the OMG! In *Proceedings of the Fifth International AAAI Conference on Weblogs and Social Media*.

Bing Liu and Lei Zhang. 2012. A survey of opinion mining and sentiment analysis. In Charu C. Aggarwal and ChengXiang Zhai, editors, *Mining Text Data*, pages 415–463.

Tomas Mikolov, Kai Chen, Greg Corrado, and Jeffrey Dean. 2013. Efficient Estimation of Word Representations in Vector Space. arXiv:1301.3781v3.

Azadeh Nikfarjam, Ehsan Emadzadeh, and Graciela Gonzalez. 2012. A Hybrid System for Emotion Extraction from Suicide Notes. *Biomedical Informatics Insights*, 5. Suppl 1:165–174.

Azadeh Nikfarjam, Abeed Sarker, Karen O'Connor, Rachel Ginn, and Graciela Gonzalez. 2014. Pharmacovigilance from social media: mining adverse drug reaction mentions using sequence labeling with word embedding cluster features. *Journal of the American Medical Informatics Association (JAMIA)*.

Bo Pang and Lillian Lee. 2008. Opinion Mining and Sentiment Analysis. *Foundations and Trends in Information Retrieval*, 2(1):1–135.

Bo Pang, Lillian Lee, and Shivakumar Vaithyanathan. 2002. Thumbs up? Sentiment Classification using Machine Learning Techniques. In *Proceedings of the ACL conference on Empirical Methods in Natural Language Processing (EMNLP)*, pages 79–86.

Apurv Patki, Abeed Sarker, Pranoti Pimpalkhute, Azadeh Nikfarjam, Rachel Ginn, Karen O'Connor, Karen Smith, and Graciela Gonzalez. 2014. Mining Adverse Drug Reaction Signals from Social Media: Going Beyond Extraction. In *Proceedings of BioLinkSig 2014*.

Martin F. Porter. 1980. An algorithm for suffix stripping. *Program*, 14(3):130–137.

Abeed Sarker and Graciela Gonzalez. 2014. Portable Automatic Text Classification for Adverse Drug Reaction Detection via Multi-corpus Training. *Journal of Biomedical Informatics*.

Abeed Sarker, Diego Molla, and Cecile Paris. 2013. Automatic Prediction of Evidence-based Recommendations via Sentence-level Polarity Classification. In *Proceedings of the International Joint Conference on Natural Language Processing (IJCNLP)*, pages 712–718.

Joseph Turian, Lev Ratinov, and Yoshua Bengio. 2010. Word representations: A simple and general method for semi-supervised learning. In *Proceedings of the 48th Annual Meeting of the Association for Computational Linguistics*, pages 384–394.

Peter Turney. 2002. Thumbs up or thumbs down? Semantic orientation applied to unsupervised classification of reviews. In *Proceedings of ACL-02, 40th Annual Meeting of the Association for Computational Linguistics*, pages 417–424.

Splusplus: A Feature-Rich Two-stage Classifier for Sentiment Analysis of Tweets

Li Dong[†]*, **Furu Wei**[‡], **Yichun Yin**[§*], **Ming Zhou**[‡], **and Ke Xu**[†]
[†]Beihang University, Beijing, 100191, China
[‡]Microsoft Research, Beijing, 100080, China
[§]Peking University, Beijing, 100871, China
dl@cse.buaa.edu.cn {fuwei,mingzhou}@microsoft.com
yichunyin@pku.edu.cn kexu@nlsde.buaa.edu.cn

Abstract

This paper describes our sentiment classification system submitted to SemEval-2015 Task 10. In the message-level polarity classification subtask, we obtain the highest macro-averaged F1-scores on three out of six testing sets. Specifically, we build a two-stage classifier to predict the sentiment labels for tweets, which enables us to design different features for subjective/objective classification and positive/negative classification. In addition to n-grams, lexicons, word clusters, and twitter-specific features, we develop several deep learning methods to automatically extract features for the message-level sentiment classification task. Moreover, we propose a polarity boosting trick which improves the performance of our system.

1 Introduction

In the task 10 of SemEval-2015, submitted systems are required to categorize tweets to positive, negative, and neutral classes (Rosenthal et al., 2015). There are six testing sets in SemEval-2015. Four of them are tweets: Twitter13, Twitter14, Twitter14Sarcasm, and Twitter15. The TwitterSarcasm14 consists of the tweets which express sarcasm. In order to evaluate the performance on out-of-domain data, the other two datasets are LiveJournal14 and SMS13 that are from web blogs and SMS messages respectively. The details of these datasets are described in (Nakov et al., 2013; Rosenthal et al., 2014; Rosenthal et al., 2015).

*Contribution during internship at Microsoft Research.

We utilize both basic features and deep learning features in our system. Deep learning is used to automatically learn representations, which has achieved some promising results on sentiment analysis (Kim, 2014; Socher et al., 2013; Dong et al., 2014). In order to design more flexible features, we use a two-stage classification framework which conducts subjective/objective (sub/obj) classification and positive/negative (pos/neg) classification. In addition, we introduce a polarity boosting trick that can utilize pos/neg training data to improve classifying tweets to sub/obj. With the help of these features and methods, our system achieves the best results on three out of six datasets among 40 teams in SemEval-2015. We describe the basic features and deep learning features used in our system, and compare their contributions. Moreover, we make the word2vec clustering results on Twitter data publicly available for research purpose.

2 System Description

2.1 Overview

As shown in Figure 1, our sentiment analysis system is a two-stage sentiment classifier which consists of a subjective/objective (sub/obj) classifier and a positive/negative (pos/neg) classifier. By using this artitacture, we can design different feature sets for the two classification steps. Notably, the predicted values of pos/neg classifier is employed to help classify tweets to sub/obj classes. We employ the LIBLINEAR (Fan et al., 2008) with option "*-s 1*" as our classifier. All the input tweets are normalized by replacing the @ mentions and URLs. Moreover, the

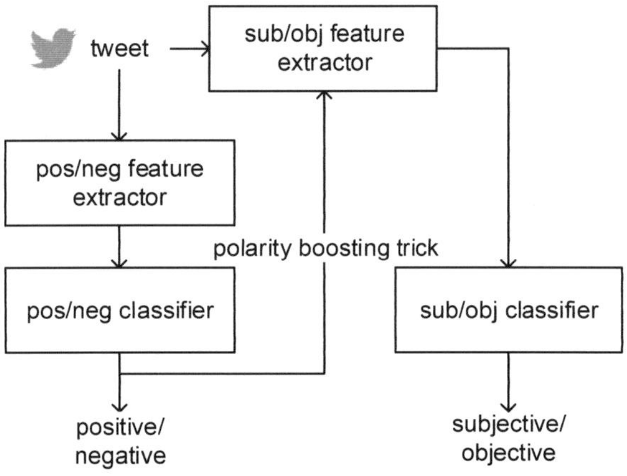

Figure 1: The overview of our two-stage sentiment analysis system. We use two classifiers to predict labels for tweets. Different features are extracted for sub/obj and pos/neg classification steps. The predicted value of pos/neg classifier is used to extract features for sub/obj step, which is called as polarity boosting trick.

elongated words are normalized by shortening them to three contiguous letters.

2.2 Basic Features

We briefly describe the basic features used in our system as follows. The features are used in both pos/neg and sub/obj classifiers unless noted otherwise. The features which appear less than two times are pruned to reduce the model size.

Word ngrams We use unigrams and bigrams for words.

Character ngrams For each word, character ngrams are extracted. We use four-grams and five-grams in our system.

Word skip-grams For all the trigrams and four-grams, one of the words is replaced by $*$ to indicate the presence of non-contiguous words. This feature template is used in sub/obj classification.

Brown cluster ngrams We use Brown clusters[1] to represent words, and extract unigrams and bigrams as features.

POS The presence or absence of part-of-speech tags are used as binary features. We use the CMU ARK Twitter Part-of-Speech Tagger (Owoputi et al., 2013) in our implementation.

Lexicons The NRC Hashtag Sentiment Lexicon and Sentiment140 Lexicon[2] are used. These two lexicons are automatically generated by calculating pointwise mutual information (PMI) scores between the words and positive or negative labels (Kiritchenko et al., 2014). The hashtags and emoticons are used to assign noisy polarity labels for tweets. For both positive and negative lexicons, we extract the following features: (1) the number of occurrences; (2) the maximal PMI score; (3) the score of last term; (4) the total PMI score of terms.

Twitter-specific features The number of hashtags, emoticons, elongated words, and puncuations are used as features.

2.3 Deep Learning Features

In order to automatically extract features, we explore using some deep learning techniques in our system. These features and the basic features described in Section 2.2 are used together to learn classifiers.

Word2vec cluster ngrams We use the word2vec tool (Mikolov et al., 2013) to learn 40-dimensional word embeddings from a twitter dataset. Then, we employ K-means algorithm and L2 distance of word vectors to cluster the $255,657$ words to 4960 classes. The clusters are used to represent words. We extract unigrams and bigrams as features, and use them in sub/obj classifier. The word2vec clustering results are publicly available[3] for research purposes. As shown in Table 1, similar words are clustered into the same clusters. This feature template is used in sub/obj classification.

CNN predicted distribution The convolutional neural networks (dos Santos, 2014) are used to predict the probabilities of three sentiment classes, and the predicted distribution is used as a three-dimension feature template. As illustrated in Figure 2, we use the network architecture proposed by Collobert et al. (2011). The dimension of word vectors is 50, and the window size is 5. Then the concatenated word vectors are fed into a convolutional layer. The vector representation of a sentence is obtained by a max pooling layer, and is used to predict the probabilities of three classes by the softmax layer. We employ stochastic gradient descent to minimize the cross-entropy loss. In order to pre-

[1] http://www.ark.cs.cmu.edu/TweetNLP/clusters/50mpaths2

[2] http://goo.gl/ee2CVo

[3] http://goo.gl/forms/8pLMMClzxB

Cluster	Words
4493	good, hope, great, nice, lovely, special, gr8, enjoying, goood, enjoyed, fabulous, magical, beaut, fab, g8, spectacular, pleasant, spoilt, swell, brill, greaaat, amazin, terrific, kickass, gr9, grrreat, greatt, fabbb, lush, marvellous, frantastic, greeeat, amzing, badasss, greaat, beauitful, pawsome
2123	love, miss, luv, loveee, looove, luh, lovee, misss, ilove, luvvv, lub, wuv, luhhh, luhh, imiss, thnk, loove, loooveee, iove, luuuv, luvv, lovvve, looovvveee, luff, mish, lobe, lovveee, wuvvv, lurv, mith, lovve, love/miss, luuuvvv, lubb, lurve

Table 1: Examples of word2vec clusters. Similar words are clustered to the same cluster.

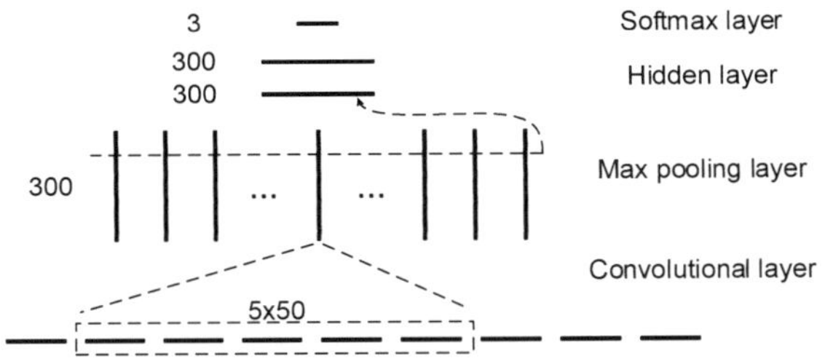

Figure 2: Architecture of convolutional neural network used in our system. The lines represent vectors, and the numbers indicate the vector dimensions.

vent overfitting, a L2-norm constraint for the column vectors of weight matrices is used. The back-propagation algorithm (Rumelhart et al., 1986) is employed to compute the gradients for parameters. The word vectors provided by Tang et al. (2014) are used for initialization.

Sentiment-specific embedding Tang et al. (2014) improve the word2vec model to learn sentiment-specific word embeddings from tweets annotated by emoticons. We use element-wise max, min, and avg operations for the word vectors to extract features.

2.4 Polarity Boosting Trick

Predicted scores indicate the confidence of classifier. If the pos/neg classifier has a high confidence to classify a tweet to positive or negative, it is less likely that this tweet is objective. Consequently, the absolute value of output of pos/neg classifier is used as a feature in sub/obj classification step, which is called as *polarity boosting trick*. This method better utilizes the pos/neg training data to help sub/obj step instead of only using the sub/obj training data. Moreover, this approach is based on the fact that classifying pos/neg is much easier than categorizing sub/obj (Pang and Lee, 2008).

Unlike most of previous work, we perform the pos/neg classification for every message to extract the polarity boosting feature, even if it is classified as an objective message.

3 Experimental Results

The macro-averaged F1-score of positive and negative classes is used as the evaluation metric (Rosenthal et al., 2015). Notably, this evaluation metric also takes the neutral class into consideration. We train the model on TRAIN/DEV (7,072/1,120) provided in SemEval-2013.

3.1 Overall Results

As shown in Table 2, we compare our system with the best results of other teams on six datasets. Our system ranks first on three out of six datasets, namely, Twitter13 (Twt13), Twitter14 (Twt14), and LiveJournal14 (LvJn14). The results indicate that our system performs well for short texts in online social networks. Furthermore, we find that the performance drops for the tweets which are sarcastic. Another model is needed to better address the sarcasm problem in Twitter. In addition, the performance on SMS13 is worse than on Twitter data. This suggests that the mismatch of domains between training data and testing data harms the results.

3.2 Contribution of Features

We conduct ablation experiments on six testing sets to show effectiveness of features. As presented in Table 3, the overall conclusion is that both basic features and deep learning features contribute to the performance. In addition, the polarity boosting trick improves the performance.

Specifically, after removing the ngrams features, our system still performs well, and the results on

Feature	Twt13	Twt14	Twt15	LvJn14	SMS13	Sarc14
all	72.80	74.42	63.73	75.34	67.16	42.86
- basic features	69.80	70.35	59.48	72.74	63.32	47.90
- word/char ngrams & skip-grams	72.70	73.14	62.99	75.43	66.32	44.41
- Brown cluster ngrams	72.03	73.62	63.85	74.75	67.75	42.75
- lexicons	72.48	72.40	62.84	74.78	66.76	44.18
- deep learning features	70.13	70.46	62.23	72.25	66.91	51.47
- word2vec cluster ngrams	72.71	74.14	62.66	74.99	67.11	43.35
- CNN predicted distribution	71.83	70.60	62.81	74.81	68.08	45.87
- sentiment-specific embedding	72.78	74.29	63.69	74.70	67.31	44.10
- polarity boosting trick	72.42	72.20	62.91	75.10	65.74	41.46

Table 3: Results of ablation experiments.

Dataset	Best of Others	Spp (Ours)
Twt13	72.79	**72.80**
Twt14	73.60	**74.42**
Twt15	64.84	63.73
LvJn14	74.52	**75.34**
SMS13	68.37	67.16
Sarc14	59.11	42.86

Table 2: We compare the macro-averaged F1-scores of our system (Spp) with the best results of other teams in SemEval-2015. Our system achieves the highest F1-scores on three out of six datasets.

LvJn14 and Sarc14 become better. Moreover, the automatically learned lexicons play a positive role in our system. We also try some manually annotated lexicons (such as MPQA Lexicon (Wilson et al., 2005), and Bing Liu Lexicon (Hu and Liu, 2004)), but the performance drops on the dev data. It illustrates the coverage of lexicons is important for the informal text data. The cluster features are also useful in this task, because the clusters reduce the feature sparsity and have the ability to deal with out-of-vocabulary words.

The deep learning significantly improves test results on all the datasets except on the sarcastic tweets. Using the clustering results of word2vec performs better and more stable than directly using the vectors as features. This feature template contributes more than other features on Twitter-15 (Twt15). The CNN predicted probabilities also increase the F1-scores. It is the most useful feature template on Twitter-13 (Twt13) and Twitter-14 (Twt14). Additionally, the sentiment-specific embeddings which is learned on emoticon annotated tweets contributes to the performances. It provides more explicit sentiment information than word2vec vectors.

As shown in Table 2, the polarity boosting trick also contributes to the performance of our system on all the six datasets.

4 Conclusions

We describe our message-level sentiment classification system submitted in SemEval-2015. Our system ranks first on three out of six testing sets in the message-level polarity classification task. It employs various basic features and modern deep learning techniques. The deep learning methods help us get rid of feature engineering and improve the results significantly. Furthermore, the polarity boosting trick which is easy to implement is a good way to utilize positive/negative data to improve the subjective/objective classification. There are several interesting directions to further improve the results. First, more recently proposed deep learning models can be used to automatically learn features. Second, we can utilize the noisy data annotated by hashtags or emoticons to learn lexicons of higher quality. Third, making the classifier robust for out-of-domain test data is crucial in practice.

Acknowledgments

We thank Dr. Nan Yang for sharing his K-means clustering code. This research was partly supported by NSFC (Grant No. 61421003).

References

Ronan Collobert, Jason Weston, Léon Bottou, Michael Karlen, Koray Kavukcuoglu, and Pavel Kuksa. 2011. Natural language processing (almost) from scratch. *J. Mach. Learn. Res.*, 12:2493–2537, November.

Li Dong, Furu Wei, Ming Zhou, and Ke Xu. 2014. Adaptive multi-compositionality for recursive neural models with applications to sentiment analysis. In *AAAI Conference on Artificial Intelligence*, pages 1537–1543.

Cicero dos Santos. 2014. Think positive: Towards Twitter sentiment analysis from scratch. In *Proceedings of the 8th International Workshop on Semantic Evaluation (SemEval 2014)*, pages 647–651, Dublin, Ireland, August.

Rong-En Fan, Kai-Wei Chang, Cho-Jui Hsieh, Xiang-Rui Wang, and Chih-Jen Lin. 2008. Liblinear: A library for large linear classification. *JMLR*, 9:1871–1874, June.

Minqing Hu and Bing Liu. 2004. Mining and summarizing customer reviews. In *Proceedings of the tenth ACM SIGKDD international conference on Knowledge discovery and data mining*, pages 168–177.

Yoon Kim. 2014. Convolutional neural networks for sentence classification. Proceedings of the 2014 Conference on Empirical Methods in Natural Language Processing (EMNLP), pages 1746–1751.

Svetlana Kiritchenko, Xiaodan Zhu, and Saif M Mohammad. 2014. Sentiment analysis of short informal texts. *Journal of Artificial Intelligence Research*, pages 723–762.

Tomas Mikolov, Ilya Sutskever, Kai Chen, Greg S Corrado, and Jeff Dean. 2013. Distributed representations of words and phrases and their compositionality. In *Advances in Neural Information Processing Systems*, pages 3111–3119.

Preslav Nakov, Sara Rosenthal, Zornitsa Kozareva, Veselin Stoyanov, Alan Ritter, and Theresa Wilson. 2013. Semeval-2013 task 2: Sentiment analysis in Twitter. In *Second Joint Conference on Lexical and Computational Semantics (*SEM), Volume 2: Proceedings of the Seventh International Workshop on Semantic Evaluation (SemEval 2013)*, pages 312–320, Atlanta, Georgia, USA, June.

Olutobi Owoputi, Brendan OConnor, Chris Dyer, Kevin Gimpel, Nathan Schneider, and Noah A Smith. 2013. Improved part-of-speech tagging for online conversational text with word clusters. In *Proceedings of NAACL-HLT*, pages 380–390.

Bo Pang and Lillian Lee. 2008. Opinion mining and sentiment analysis. *Foundations and trends in information retrieval*, 2(1-2):1–135.

Sara Rosenthal, Alan Ritter, Preslav Nakov, and Veselin Stoyanov. 2014. Semeval-2014 task 9: Sentiment analysis in Twitter. In *Proceedings of the 8th International Workshop on Semantic Evaluation (SemEval 2014)*, pages 73–80, Dublin, Ireland, August.

Sara Rosenthal, Preslav Nakov, Svetlana Kiritchenko, Saif M Mohammad, Alan Ritter, and Veselin Stoyanov. 2015. Semeval-2015 task 10: Sentiment analysis in Twitter. In *Proceedings of the 9th International Workshop on Semantic Evaluation*, SemEval '2015, Denver, Colorado, June.

David E. Rumelhart, Geoffrey E. Hinton, and Ronald J. Williams. 1986. Learning representations by back-propagating errors. *Nature*, 323(6088):533–536.

Richard Socher, Alex Perelygin, Jean Y Wu, Jason Chuang, Christopher D Manning, Andrew Y Ng, and Christopher Potts. 2013. Recursive deep models for semantic compositionality over a sentiment treebank. In *Proceedings of the conference on empirical methods in natural language processing (EMNLP)*, volume 1631, page 1642.

Duyu Tang, Furu Wei, Nan Yang, Ming Zhou, Ting Liu, and Bing Qin. 2014. Learning sentiment-specific word embedding for Twitter sentiment classification. In *Proceedings of the 52nd Annual Meeting of the Association for Computational Linguistics*, pages 1555–1565.

Theresa Wilson, Janyce Wiebe, and Paul Hoffmann. 2005. Recognizing contextual polarity in phrase-level sentiment analysis. In *Proceedings of the conference on human language technology and empirical methods in natural language processing*, pages 347–354.

IIIT-H at SemEval 2015: Twitter Sentiment Analysis The good, the bad and the neutral!

Ayushi Dalmia, Manish Gupta*, Vasudeva Varma
Search and Information Extraction Lab
International Institute of Information Technology, Hyderabad
{ayushi.dalmia@research.iiit.ac.in, manish.gupta@iiit.ac.in, vv@iiit.ac.in }

Abstract

This paper describes the system that was submitted to SemEval2015 Task 10: Sentiment Analysis in Twitter. We participated in Subtask B: Message Polarity Classification. The task is a message level classification of tweets into positive, negative and neutral sentiments. Our model is primarily a supervised one which consists of well designed features fed into an SVM classifier. In previous runs of this task, it was found that lexicons played an important role in determining the sentiment of a tweet. We use existing lexicons to extract lexicon specific features. The lexicon based features are further augmented by tweet specific features. We also improve our system by using acronym and emoticon dictionaries. The proposed system achieves an F1 score of 59.83 and 67.04 on the Test Data and Progress Data respectively. This placed us at the 18th position for the Test Dataset and the 16th position for the Progress Test Dataset.

1 Introduction

Micro-blogging has become a very popular communication tool among Internet users. Millions of users share opinions on different aspects of life, everyday on popular websites such as Twitter, Tumblr and Facebook. Spurred by this growth, companies and media organizations are increasingly seeking ways to mine these social media for information about what people think about their companies and products. Political parties may be interested to know if people support their program or not. Social organizations may need to know people's opinion on current debates. All this information can be obtained from micro-blogging services, as their users post their opinions on many aspects of their life regularly.
Twitter contains an enormous number of text posts and the rate of posts is increasing every day. Its audience varies from regular users to celebrities, company representatives, politicians, and even country presidents. Therefore, it is possible to collect text posts of users from different social and interest groups. However, analyzing Twitter data comes with its own bag of difficulties. Tweets are small in length, thus ambiguous. The informal style of writing, a distinct usage of orthography, acronymization and a different set of elements like hashtags, user mentions demand a different approach to solve this problem.
In this work we present the description of the supervised machine learning system developed while participating in the shared task of message based sentiment analysis in SemEval 2015 (Rosenthal et al., 2015). The system takes as input a tweet message, pre-processes it, extracts features and finally classifies it as either positive, negative or neutral. Tweets in the positive and negative classes are subjective in nature. However, the neutral class consists of both subjective tweets which do not have any polarity as well as objective tweets.
Our paper is organized as follows. We discuss related work in Section 2. In Section 3, we discuss the existing resources which we use in our system. In Section 4 we present the proposed system and give a detailed description for the same. We present experimental results and the ranking of our system for different datasets in Section 5. The paper is summarized in Section 6.

2 Related Work

Sentiment analysis has been an active area of research since a long time. A number of surveys (Pang and Lee, 2008; Liu and Zhang, 2012) and books (Liu, 2010) give a thorough analysis of the existing techniques in sentiment analysis. Attempts have been made to analyze sentiments at different levels starting from document (Pang and Lee, 2004),

*The author is also a researcher at Microsoft (gmanish@microsoft.com)

sentences (Hu and Liu, 2004) to phrases (Wilson et al., 2009; Agarwal et al., 2009). However, micro-blogging data is different from regular text as it is extremely noisy in nature. A lot of interesting work has been done in order to identify sentiments from Twitter micro-blogging data also. (Go et al., 2009) used emoticons as noisy labels and distant supervision to classify tweets into positive or negative class. (Agarwal et al., 2011) introduced POS-specific prior polarity features along with using a tree kernel for tweet classification. Besides these two major papers, a lot of work from the previous runs of the SemEval is available (Rosenthal et al., 2014; Nakov et al., 2013).

3 Resources

3.1 Annotated Data

Tweet IDs labeled as positive, negative or neutral were given by the task organizers. In order to build the system we first downloaded these tweets. The task organizers provided us with a certain number of tweet IDs. However, it was not possible to retrieve the content of all the tweet IDs due to changes in the privacy settings. Some of the tweets were probably deleted or may not be public at the time of download. Thus we were not able to download the tweet content of all the tweets IDs provided by the organizers. For the training and the dev-test datasets, while the organizers provided us with 9684 and 1654 tweet IDs respectively, we were able to retrieve only 7966 and 1368 tweets, respectively.

3.2 Sentiment Lexicons

It has been found that lexicons play an important role in determining the polarity of a message. Several lexicons have been proposed in the past which are used popularly in the field of sentiment analysis. We use the following lexicons to generate our lexicon based features: (1) Bing Liu's Opinion Lexicon[1], (2) MPQA Subjectivity Lexicon (Wilson et al., 2005), (3) NRC Hashtag Sentiment Lexicon (Mohammad et al., 2013), and (4) Sentiment140 Lexicon (Mohammad et al., 2013).

3.3 Dictionary

Besides the above sentiment lexicons, we used two other dictionaries described as follows.

- **Emoticon Dictionary:** We use the emoticons list [2] and manually annotate the related sentiment. We categorize the emoticons into four classes as follows: (1) Extremely- Positive, (2) Positive, (3) Extremely- Negative, and (4) Negative.

- **Acronym Dictionary:** We crawl the noslang.com website [3] in order to obtain the acronym expansion of the most commonly used acronyms on the web. The acronym dictionary helps in expanding the tweet text and thereby improves the overall sentiment score. The acronym dictionary has 5297 entries. For example, *asap* has the translation *As soon as possible*.

Other than this we also use Tweet NLP (Owoputi et al., 2013), a Twitter specific tweet tokenizer and tagger which provides a fast and robust Java-based tokenizer and part-of-speech tagger for Twitter.

4 System Overview

Figure 1 gives a brief overview of our system. In the offline stage, the system takes the tweet IDs and the N-Gram model as inputs (shown in red) to learn a classifier. The classifier is then used online to process a test tweet and output (shown in green) its sentiment. The basic building blocks of the system include Pre-processing, Feature Extraction and Classification. We first build a baseline model based on unigram, bigrams and trigrams and later add more features to it. In this section we discuss each module in detail.

4.1 Pre-processing

Since the tweets are very noisy, they need a lot of pre-processing. Table 1 lists the various steps of pre-processing applied on the tweets. They are discussed as follows.

- *Tokenization*
  After downloading the tweets using the tweet IDs provided in the dataset, we first tokenize them. This is done using the Tweet-NLP tool (Gimpel et al., 2011) developed by ARK Social Media Search. This tool tokenizes the

[1] http://www.cs.uic.edu/~liub/FBS/opinion-lexicon-English.rar

[2] http://en.wikipedia.org/wiki/List_of_emoticons

[3] http://www.noslang.com/dictionary/

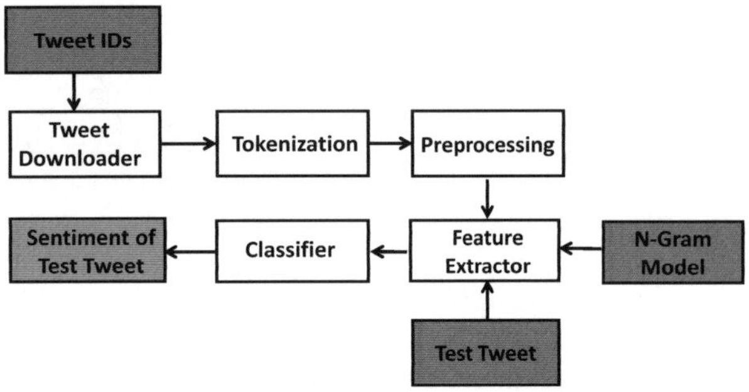

Figure 1: System Architecture (Red: Inputs, Green: Outputs).

Table 1: List of Pre-processing Steps.

Tokenisation
Remove Non-English Tweets
Replace Emoticons
Remove Urls
Remove Target Mentions
Remove Punctuations from Hashtags
Handle Sequences of Repeated Characters
Remove Numbers
Remove Nouns and Prepositions
Remove Stop Words
Handle Negative Mentions
Expand Acronyms

tweet and returns the POS tags of the tweet along with the confidence score. It is important to note that this is a Twitter specific tagger and tags the Twitter specific entries like emoticons, hashtags and mentions along with the regular parts of speech. After obtaining the tokenized and tagged tweets, we move to the next step of preprocessing.

- *Remove Non-English Tweets*
  Twitter allows more than 60 languages. However, this work currently focuses on English tokens only. We remove the tweets with non-English tokens.

- *Replace Emoticons*
  Emoticons play an important role in determining the sentiment of the tweet. Hence we replace the emoticons by their sentiment polarity by looking up in the Emoticon Dictionary generated using the dictionary mentioned in Section 3.

- *Remove Urls*
  The urls which are present in the tweet are shortened due to the limitation on the length of the tweet text. These shortened urls do not carry much information regarding the sentiment of the tweet. Thus these are removed.

- *Remove Target Mentions*
  The target mentions in a tweet done using '@' are usually the twitter handle of people or organizations. This information is also not needed to determine the sentiment of the tweet. Hence they are removed.

- *Remove Punctuations from Hashtags*
  Hashtags represent a concise summary of the tweet, and hence are very critical. In order to capture the relevant information from hashtags, all special characters and punctuations are removed before using them as a feature.

- *Handle Sequences of Repeated Characters*
  Twitter provides a platform for users to express their opinion in an informal way. Tweets are written in a noisy form, without any focus on correct structure and spelling. Spell correction is an important part in sentiment analysis of user-generated content. People use words like 'coooool' and 'hunnnnngry' in order to emphasize the emotion. In order to capture such expressions, we replace the sequence of more than three similar characters by three characters. For example, 'woooow' is replaced by 'wooow'. We replace by three characters so as to distinguish words like 'wow' and 'wooooow'.

- *Remove Numbers*
  Numbers are of no use when measuring sentiment. Thus, numbers which are obtained as tokenized units from the tokenizer are removed in order to refine the tweet content.

- *Remove Nouns and Prepositions*
  Given a tweet token, we identify the word as a noun word by looking at its part-of-speech

tag assigned by the tokenizer. If the majority sense (most commonly used sense) of that word is noun, we discard the word. Noun words do not carry sentiment and thus are of no use in our experiment. Similarly we remove prepositions too.

- *Remove Stop Words*
  Stop words play a negative role in the task of sentiment classification. Stop words occur in both positive and negative training set, thus adding more ambiguity in the model formation. Also, stop words do not carry any sentiment information and thus are of no use.

- *Handle Negative Mentions*
  Negation plays a very important role in determining the sentiment of the tweet. Tweets consist of various notions of negation. Words which are either 'no', 'not' or ending with 'n't' are replaced by a common word indicating negation.

- *Expand Acronyms*
  As described in Section 3 we use an acronym expansion list. In the pre-processing step we expand the acronyms if they are present in the tweet.

4.2 Baseline Model

We first generate a baseline model as discussed in (Bakliwal et al., 2012). We perform the pre-processing steps listed in Section 4.1 and learn the positive, negative and neutral frequencies of unigrams, bigrams and trigrams in our training data. Every token is given three probability scores: Positive Probability (P_p), Negative Probability (N_p) and Neutral Probability (NE_p). Given a token, let P_f denote the frequency in positive training set, N_f denote the frequency in negative training set and NE_f denote the frequency in neutral training set. The probability scores are then computed as follows.

$$P_p = \frac{P_f}{P_f + N_f + NE_f} \tag{1}$$

$$N_p = \frac{N_f}{P_f + N_f + NE_f} \tag{2}$$

$$NE_p = \frac{NE_f}{P_f + N_f + NE_f} \tag{3}$$

Next we create a feature vector of tokens which can distinguish the sentiment of the tweet with high confidence. For example, presence of tokens like *am happy!*, *love love* , *bullsh*t !* helps in determining that the tweet carries positive, negative or neutral sentiment with high confidence. We call such words, **Emotion Determiner**. A token is considered to be an Emotion Determiner if the probability of the emotion for any one sentiment is greater than or equal to the probability of the other two sentiments by a certain threshold. It is found that we need different thresholds for unigrams, bigrams and trigrams. The threshold parameters are tuned and the optimal threshold values are found to be 0.7, 0.8 and 0.9 for the unigram, bigram and trigram tokens, respectively. Note that before calculating the probability values, we filter out those tokens which are infrequent (appear in less than 10 tweets). This serves as a baseline model. Thus, our baseline model is learned using a training dataset which contains for every given tweet, a binary vector of length equal to the set of Emotion Determiners with 1 indicating its presence and 0 indicating its absence in the tweet. After building this model we will append the features discussed in Section 4.3. After appending the features to the baseline model, we get enhanced richer vectors containing Emotion Determiners along with the new feature values.

4.3 Feature Extraction

We propose a set of features listed in Table 2 for our experiments. There are a total of 34 features. We calculate these features for the whole tweet in case of message based sentiment analysis. We can divide the features into two classes: a) Tweet Based Features, and b) Lexicon Based Features. Table 2 summarizes the features used in our experiment. Here features $f_1 - f_{22}$ are tweet based features while features $f_{23} - f_{34}$ are lexicon based features.

A number of our features are based on prior polarity score of the tweet. For obtaining the prior polarity of words, we use AFINN dictionary [4] and extend it using SENTIWORDNET (Esuli and Sebastiani, 2006). We first look up the tokens in the tweet in the AFINN lexicon. This dictionary of about 2490 English language words assigns every word a pleasantness score between -5 (Negative) and +5 (Posi-

[4] http://www2.imm.dtu.dk/pubdb/views/publication_details.php?id=6010

Table 2: Description of the Features used in the Model.

Feature Description	Feature ID
Prior Polarity Score of the Tweet	f_0
Brown Clusters	f_1
Percentage of Capitalised Words	f_2
# of Positive Capitalised Words	f_3
# of Negative Capitalised Words	f_4
Presence of Capitalised Words	f_5
# of Positive Hashtags	f_6
# of Negative Hashtags	f_7
# of Positive Emoticons	f_8
# of Extremely Positive Emoticons	f_9
# of Negative Emoticons	f_{10}
# of Extremely Negative Emoticons	f_{11}
# of Negation	f_{12}
# Positive POS Tags	f_{13}
# Negative POS Tags	f_{14}
Total POS Tags Score	f_{15}
# of special characters like ? ! and *	$f_{16}.f_{17}, f_{18}$
# of POS (Noun, Verb, Adverb, Adjective)	$f_{19}, f_{20}, f_{21}, f_{22}$
# of words with nonzero score using Bing Liu's Opinion Lexicon	f_{23}
# of words with nonzero score using MPQA Subjectivity Lexicon	f_{24}
# of words with nonzero score using NRC Hashtag Sentiment Lexicon	f_{25}
# of words with nonzero score using Sentiment140 Lexicon	f_{26}
Maximum positive score for a token in the message using Bing Liu's Opinion Lexicon	f_{27}
Maximum positive score for a token in the message using MPQA Subjectivity Lexicon	f_{28}
Maximum positive score for a token in the message using NRC Hashtag Sentiment Lexicon	f_{29}
Maximum positive score for a token in the message using Sentiment140 Lexicon	f_{30}
Total score of the message using Bing Liu's Opinion Lexicon	f_{31}
Total score of the message using MPQA Subjectivity Lexicon	f_{32}
Total score of the message using NRC Hashtag Sentiment Lexicon	f_{33}
Total score of the message using Sentiment140 Lexicon	f_{34}

tive). We normalize the scores by diving each score by the scale (which is equal to 5) to obtain a score between -1 and +1. If a word is not directly found in the dictionary we retrieve all its synonyms from SENTIWORDNET. We then look for each of the synonyms in AFINN. If any synonym is found in AFINN, we assign the original word the same pleasantness score as its synonym. If none of the synonyms is present in AFINN, we perform a second level look up in the SENTIWORDNET dictionary to find synonyms of synonyms. If the word is present in SENTIWORDNET, we assign the score retrieved from SENTIWORDNET (between -1 and +1).

Table 3: Accuracy on 3-way classification task extending the baseline with additional features. All f_i refer to Table 2.

Model	F Measure			
	Positive Class	Negative Class	Neutral Class	Macro-Average
Baseline Model	36.93	30.66	15.38	33.79
$+f_0$	37.14	36.48	59.02	36.81
$+ f_0$ - f_1	63.73	47.19	66.24	55.46
$+ f_0$ - f_5	63.66	47.50	66.08	55.58
$+ f_0$ - f_7	63.58	47.55	66.08	55.56
$+ f_0$ - f_{11}	63.18	46.98	66.06	55.08
$+ f_0$ - f_{12}	63.14	48.52	65.75	55.83
$+ f_0$ - f_{15}	63.84	48.40	66.11	56.12
$+ f_0 + f_{18}$	64.42	48.57	66.30	56.50
$+ f_0$ - f_{22}	64.00	48.09	66.48	56.04
$+ f_0$ - f_{22} + Lexicon Based Features (f_{23} - f_{34})	67.50	52.26	66.57	59.83

4.4 Classification

After pre-processing and feature extraction we feed the features into a classifier. We tried various classifiers using the Scikit library [5]. After extensive experimentation it was found that SVM gave the best performance. The parameters of the model were computed using grid search. It was found that the model performed best with radial basis function kernel and 0.75 as the penalty parameter C of the error term. All the experimental are performed using these parameters for the model.

5 Results

In this section we present the experimental results for the classification task. We first present the score and rank obtained by the system on various test dataset followed by a discussion on the feature analysis for our system.

5.1 Overall Performance

The evaluation metric used in the competition is the macro-averaged F measure calculated over the positive and negative classes. Table 4 presents the overall performance of our system for different datasets.

5.2 Feature Analysis

Table 3 represents the results of the ablation experiment on the Twitter Test Data 2015. Using this ablation experiment, one can understand which features play an important role in identifying the sentiment of the tweet. It can be observed that the brown clusters plays an important role in determining the class of the tweet and improves the F-measure by around 20. Also, lexicon based features play a significant role by improving the F-measure by 3.

6 Conclusion

We presented results for sentiment analysis on Twitter by building a supervised system which combines lexicon based features with tweet specific features. We reported the overall accuracy for 3-way classification tasks: positive, negative and neutral. For our feature based approach, we perform feature analysis which reveals that the most important features are

Table 4: Overall Performance of the System.

Dataset	Our Score	Best Score	Rank
Twitter 2015	59.83	64.84	18
Twitter Sarcasm 2015	52.67	65.77	23
Twitter 2014	67.04	74.42	16
Twitter 2013	65.68	72.80	20
Twitter Sarcasm 2014	57.50	59.11	2
Live Journal 2014	69.91	75.34	21
SMS 2013	62.25	68.49	19

[5] http://scikit-learn.org/stable/modules/svm.html

those that combine the prior polarity of words and the lexicon based features. In the future, we will explore even richer linguistic analysis, for example, parsing, semantic analysis and topic modeling to improve our feature extraction component.

Acknowledgement

We thank Mayank Gupta and Arpit Jaiswal, International Institute of Information Technology, Hyderabad, India for assisting with the experiments as well as for interesting discussions on the subject. We would like to thank the SemEval 2015 shared task organizers for their support throughout this work. We would also like to thank the anonymous reviewers for their valuable comments.

References

Apoorv Agarwal, Fadi Biadsy, and Kathleen R. Mckeown. 2009. Contextual Phrase-level Polarity Analysis Using Lexical Affect Scoring and Syntactic N-grams. In *Proceedings of the 12th Conference of the European Chapter of the ACL (EACL)*, pages 24–32.

Apoorv Agarwal, Boyi Xie, Ilia Vovsha, Owen Rambow, and Rebecca Passonneau. 2011. Sentiment Analysis of Twitter Data. In *Proceedings of the Workshop on Languages in Social Media (LSM)*, pages 30–38.

Akshat Bakliwal, Piyush Arora, Senthil Madhappan, Nikhil Kapre, Mukesh Singh, and Vasudeva Varma. 2012. Mining Sentiments from Tweets. In *Proceedings of the 3rd Workshop in Computational Approaches to Subjectivity and Sentiment Analysis (WASSA)*, pages 11–18.

Andrea Esuli and Fabrizio Sebastiani. 2006. SENTIWORDNET: A Publicly Available Lexical Resource for Opinion Mining. In *Proceedings of the 5th Conference on Language Resources and Evaluation (LREC*, pages 417–422.

Kevin Gimpel, Nathan Schneider, Brendan O'Connor, Dipanjan Das, Daniel Mills, Jacob Eisenstein, Michael Heilman, Dani Yogatama, Jeffrey Flanigan, and Noah A Smith. 2011. Part-of-speech Tagging for Twitter: Annotation, Features, and Experiments. In *Proc. of the 49th Annual Meeting of the ACL: Human Language Technologies (HLT)*, pages 42–47.

Alec Go, Richa Bhayani, and Lei Huang. 2009. Twitter Sentiment Classification using Distant Supervision. *CS224N Project Report, Stanford*, pages 1–12.

Minqing Hu and Bing Liu. 2004. Mining and Summarizing Customer Reviews. In *Proceedings of the 10th ACM SIGKDD International Conference on Knowledge Discovery and Data Mining (KDD)*, pages 168–177.

Bing Liu and Lei Zhang. 2012. A Survey of Opinion Mining and Sentiment Analysis. In Charu C. Aggarwal and ChengXiang Zhai, editors, *Mining Text Data*, pages 415–463.

Bing Liu. 2010. Sentiment Analysis and Subjectivity. In *Handbook of Natural Language Processing, Second Edition. Taylor and Francis Group, Boca.*

Saif M. Mohammad, Svetlana Kiritchenko, and Xiaodan Zhu. 2013. NRC-Canada: Building the State-of-the-Art in Sentiment Analysis of Tweets. In *Proceedings of the 7th International Workshop on Semantic Evaluation Exercises*, Atlanta, Georgia, USA.

Preslav Nakov, Sara Rosenthal, Zornitsa Kozareva, Veselin Stoyanov, Alan Ritter, and Theresa Wilson. 2013. SemEval-2013 Task 2: Sentiment Analysis in Twitter. In *The 2nd Joint Conference on Lexical and Computational Semantics (*SEM), Volume 2: Proceedings of the 7th International Workshop on Semantic Evaluation*, pages 312–320.

Olutobi Owoputi, Brendan O'Connor, Chris Dyer, Kevin Gimpel, Nathan Schneider, and A. Noah Smith. 2013. Improved Part-of-Speech Tagging for Online Conversational Text with Word Clusters. In *Proceedings of the 2013 Conference of the North American Chapter of the ACL: Human Language Technologies*, pages 380–390.

Bo Pang and Lillian Lee. 2004. A Sentimental Education: Sentiment Analysis Using Subjectivity Summarization Based on Minimum Cuts. In *Proceedings of the 42nd Meeting of the ACL*, pages 271–278.

Bo Pang and Lillian Lee. 2008. Opinion Mining and Sentiment Analysis. *Foundations and Trends in Information Retrieval*, 2(1-2):1–135.

Sara Rosenthal, Alan Ritter, Preslav Nakov, and Veselin Stoyanov. 2014. SemEval-2014 Task 9: Sentiment Analysis in Twitter. In *Proceedings of the 8th International Workshop on Semantic Evaluation*, pages 73–80.

Sara Rosenthal, Preslav Nakov, Svetlana Kiritchenko, Saif M Mohammad, Alan Ritter, and Veselin Stoyanov. 2015. SemEval-2015 Task 10: Sentiment Analysis in Twitter. In *Proceedings of the 9th International Workshop on Semantic Evaluation.*

Theresa Wilson, Janyce Wiebe, and Paul Hoffmann. 2005. Recognizing Contextual Polarity in Phrase-level Sentiment Analysis. In *Proceedings of the Conference on Human Language Technology and Empirical Methods in Natural Language Processing (HLT)*, pages 347–354.

Theresa Wilson, Janyce Wiebe, and Paul Hoffmann. 2009. Recognizing Contextual Polarity: An Exploration of Features for Phrase-level Sentiment Analysis. *Computational Linguistics*, 35(3):399–433.

CIS-positive: Combining Convolutional Neural Networks and SVMs for Sentiment Analysis in Twitter

Sebastian Ebert and **Ngoc Thang Vu** and **Hinrich Schütze**
Center for Information and Language Processing
University of Munich, Germany
{ebert|thangvu}@cis.lmu.de, inquiries@cislmu.org

Abstract

This paper describes our automatic sentiment analysis system – CIS-positive – for SemEval 2015 Task 10 "Sentiment Analysis in Twitter", subtask B "Message Polarity Classification". In this system, we propose to normalize the Twitter data in a way that maximizes the coverage of sentiment lexicons and minimizes distracting elements. Furthermore, we integrate the output of Convolutional Neural Networks into Support Vector Machines for the polarity classification. Our system achieves a macro F_1 score of the positive and negative class of 59.57 on the SemEval 2015 test data.

1 Introduction

On the Internet, text containing different forms of sentiment appears everywhere. Mining this information supports many types of interest groups. Companies, for instance, are interested in user feedback about the advantages and drawbacks of their products. Users want to read short reviews or ratings of hotels they want to book for their next vacation. Politicians try to predict the outcome of the next presidential election. An automatic sentiment analysis system can support all these different requirements. One source of these types of information covering many domains and topics is the social networking service Twitter. Its popularity and the users' productivity in creating new text makes it an interesting research topic. However, Twitter introduces specific challenges as we will see next.

In general, automatic sentiment analysis is challenging due to many different factors, such as ambiguous word senses, context dependency, sarcasm, etc. Specific properties of Twitter text make this task even more challenging. The limit of 140 character per message leads to countless acronyms and abbreviations. Moreover, the vast majority of tweets is of informal character and contains intentional miss-spellings and wrong use of grammar. Hence, the out-of-vocabulary (OOV) rate of Twitter text is rather high, which leads to information loss.

One of the SemEval 2015 shared tasks – Task 10: Sentiment Analysis in Twitter – addresses these challenges (Rosenthal et al., 2015). We participated in Subtask B the "Message Polarity Classification" task. The goal is to predict the polarity of a given tweet into *positive*, *negative*, or *neutral*. The task organizers provided tweet IDs and corresponding labels to have a common ground for training polarity classification systems. More information about the task, its other subtasks as well as information about how the data was selected can be found in (Rosenthal et al., 2015).

In this paper, we present our sentiment analysis system for SemEval 2015 - Task 10. Our system addresses the above mentioned challenges in two ways. First, we normalize the text to maximize the coverage of sentiment lexicons and minimize distracting elements such as user names or URLs. Second, we combine deep Convolutional Neural Networks (CNN) and support vector machines (SVM) for a better overall classification. The motivation of using CNNs is to extract not only local features but also context to predict sentiment. Integrating CNN output into an SVM improves classification.

2 Data Preprocessing

Twitter texts are challenging and differ from other domains in some specific properties. Due to the 140 characters limit of tweet length, users make heavy use of abbreviations and acronyms. This leads to a high OOV rate and makes tasks like tokenizing, part-of-speech (POS) tagging, and lexicon search more difficult. Furthermore, special tokens such as user mentions (e.g., "@isar"), urls, hashtags (e.g., "#happy"), and punctuation sequences like "!?!?" are often utilized. Therefore, normalization of all tweets is necessary to facilitate later polarity classification. Our text preprocessing pipeline can be described as follows: Tweets are first tokenized and POS tagged with the CMU tokenizer and tagger (Owoputi et al., 2013). This tagger is specialized for Twitter and therefore superior to other general domain taggers. Afterwards, all user mentions are replaced by "<user>" and all urls by "<web>", because they do not provide any cues of polarity. We do not replace hashtags, because they often contain valuable information such as topics or even sentiment.

Punctuation sequences like "!?!?" can act as exaggeration or other polarity modifier. However, the sheer amount of possible sequences increases the OOV rate dramatically. Therefore, all sequences of punctuations are replaced by a list of distinct punctuations in this sequence (e.g., "!?!?" is replaced by "[!?]"). That reduces the OOV rate and still keeps most of the information.

Mohammad et al. (2013) showed that sentiment lexicons are crucial for achieving good polarity classification. Unfortunately, miss-spellings and elongated surface forms of sentiment-bearing tokens, such as "coooooollllll", lead to lower coverage of all sentiment lexicons. Since elongated words often convey sentiment (Brody and Diakopoulos, 2011), we carefully normalize them in the following way. First, all elongated words are identified by searching for tokens that contain a sequence of at least three equal characters. Afterwards, for each elongated word a candidate set is created by removing the repeated character one by one until only one occurrence is left. If a word contains several repeated character sequences, all combinations are taken as candidates. For instance, the candidate set of the word "cooolll" will be {coolll, colll, cooll, coll, cool, col}. We then search every candidate in a sentiment lexicon to find the correct canonical form of the elongated word. If there is more than one match,

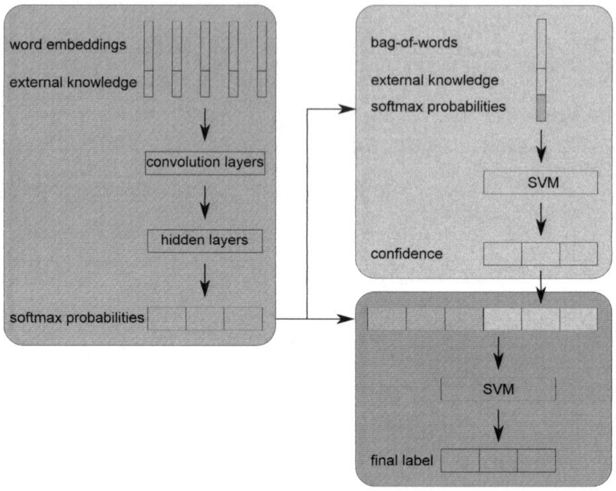

Figure 1: System architecture

the shortest match is taken. Since several sentiment lexicons with different qualities exist, we apply a sequential approach. We search the canonical form of the elongated word in one lexicon. If it does not exist, the next lexicon in the sequence is searched. The sequence of sentiment lexicons is sorted based on the reliability of the lexicon. Manually created lexicons precede automatically created lexicons. In this paper, the ordering is as follows: MPQA subjectivity cues lexicon (Wilson et al., 2005), Opinion lexicon (Hu and Liu, 2004), NRCC Emotion lexicon (Mohammad and Turney, 2013), sentiment 140, and Hashtag lexicon (both in (Mohammad et al., 2013)). As a result, a mapping from elongated words to their canonical form is found and used to normalize the corpus. Lowercasing finalizes the preprocessing step.

3 Model

The system architecture consists of three main components and is depicted in Figure 1. The first component is a CNN (left part in the figure), which makes use of the sequence of all words in a tweet. The second component is an SVM classifier which uses several linguistic features and the CNN's output as input (top right part in Figure 1). Finally, to combine the polarity prediction of the CNN and the SVM we use another SVM on top to receive the final polarity label (bottom right part in Figure 1). In this section all components are described in detail.

3.1 CNN

The intuition of using a CNN for sentence modeling is to have a model that is able to capture sequential phenomenon and considers words in their contexts. In a bag-of-words approach the word *not*, indicating negation, is not set into relation to the words it negates. An n-gram approach might tackle this problem to some extent, but long distance effects are still not captured. Furthermore, a bag-of-words model suffers from sparsity. A CNN is a neural network that can handle sequences by performing a mathematical convolution operation with a filter matrix and the input. The goal is to conflate the input sequence into a meaningful representation by finding salient features that indicate polarity. More formally, the words in the model are represented by two matrices. First, $P \in \mathbb{R}^{d_p \times V}$ denotes a matrix of low dimensional word representations, so called *word embeddings*. d_p, the size of the embeddings, is usually set to 50-300, depending on the task. V denotes the size of the vocabulary. The matrix P is learned during model training. It is initialized either randomly or with a pretrained matrix, as we will describe later. In addition to P, we introduce another matrix $Q \in \mathbb{R}^{d_q \times V}$ which contains external word features. In this case, d_q is the number of features per word. This approach allows us to add as much external knowledge into the training process as needed. The features are precomputed and not embedded into any embeddings space, i.e. Q is fixed during training. A description of all features is given later in this section.

Both components are concatenated into a lookup table $LT = \begin{bmatrix} P \\ Q \end{bmatrix}$, where each column corresponds to the entire representation of a certain word in the vocabulary. Given a sentence of n words w_1 to w_n, the model concatenates all n word representation to the input of the CNN

$$S = \begin{bmatrix} | & & | \\ LT_{:,w_1} & \cdots & LT_{:,w_n} \\ | & & | \end{bmatrix}.$$

A one dimensional convolution is a mathematical operation that slides a filter $\mathbf{m} \in \mathbb{R}^{1 \times m}$ over a vector and computes a dot product at every position. The length of the filter m specifies how many elements the filter spans. Applying this concept to a two dimensional input leads to a convolution matrix where the elements are computed by

$$C_{i,j} = \mathbf{m}^T S_{i,j:j+m-1},$$

where i is the ith row in S and j is the start index of the convolution.

A, the output of the convolution layer is computed by an element-wise addition of a bias term (one bias per row) and an element-wise non-linearity: $A = f(C + \mathbf{b})$. As non-linear function we use a rectified linear unit: $f(x) = max(0, x)$. This non-linearity proved to be a crucial part in object recognition (Jarrett et al., 2009), machine translation (Vaswani et al., 2013), and speech recognition (Zeiler et al., 2013).

Our model uses two layers of convolution. The concatenation of all rows of the second convolution layer output is the input to a sequence of three fully connected hidden layers. A hidden layer transforms the input vector $\mathbf{x}$ into $\mathbf{z} = f(W\mathbf{x} + b)$, where W is a weight matrix that is learned during training and b is a bias. In order to convert the final hidden layer output $\mathbf{z}$ into a probability distribution over polarity labels $\mathbf{o} \in \mathbb{R}^3$, the softmax function is used: $\mathbf{o}_i = \frac{\exp(\mathbf{z}_i)}{\sum_j \exp(\mathbf{z}_j)}$.

Pretraining of Word Embeddings The standard way of initializing the word embeddings matrix P is by sampling from a uniform distribution. Since there is only a small amount of training data available, word representations cannot be learned from scratch before the model would overfit. Therefore, instead of initializing the word embeddings matrix randomly, we precompute word embeddings with the word2vec toolkit on a large amount of Twitter text data.[1] We first downloaded about 60 million tweets from the unlabeled Twitter Events data set (McMinn et al., 2013). This corpus is normalized as described in Section 2. We then select V words, comprising all the words of the SemEval training data, words from the sentiment lexicons, and the most frequent words of the Twitter Events data set. Finally a continuous bag-of-words model (Mikolov et al., 2013) with 50 dimensional vectors is trained and used to initialize P.

[1] `https://code.google.com/p/word2vec/`

Word Features In addition to the word embeddings the CNN receives additional external features (matrix Q). These features are the following:

binary sentiment indicators binary features that indicate the polarity of a token in a sentiment lexicon. The lexicons for this feature are MPQA (Wilson et al., 2005), Opinion lexicon (Hu and Liu, 2004) and NRCC Emotion lexicon (Mohammad and Turney, 2013).

sentiment scores the sentiment 140 lexicon and the Hashtag lexicon (Mohammad et al., 2013) both provide a score for each token instead of just a label. We directly use these scores. Both lexicons also contain scores for bigrams and skip ngrams. In such a case each word of an ngram receives the score of the entire ngram.

binary negation following the procedure of Christopher Potts' Sentiment Symposium tutorial[2] we mark each token between a negation word and the next punctuation as negated.

3.2 SVM 1

Since training the CNN for many epochs (entire runs over the whole dataset) always led to overfitting, we decided to use a second classifier, an SVM. Following Mohammad et al. (2013) we use the following features:

binary bag-of-words binary bag-of-words features of uni- and bigrams, as well as character trigrams. In contrast to (Mohammad et al., 2013) our system does not use trigrams or character ngrams of higher order, because it degraded the performance on the validation set.

sentiment features for every tweet and every lexicon we add the following features: number of tokens in the tweet that occur in the lexicon, sum of all sentiment scores in the tweet, maximum sentiment score, and the sentiment score of the last token in the tweet.

CNN output to inform the SVM about the CNN's classification decision and certainty, we add the softmax output of the CNN as an additional feature.

[2] `http://sentiment.christopherpotts.net/lingstruc.html`

As linear SVM implementation we use LIBLINEAR (Fan et al., 2008).

3.3 SVM 2

Analyzing the CNN and SVM 1 predictions we found that both classifiers learn orthogonal features. Therefore, we introduce a second linear SVM into the classification pipeline, which combines the softmax probabilities of the CNN and the confidence scores of the first SVM. The output is the final predicted polarity label of our system.

4 Experiments

Twitter's terms of service do not allow to provide tweets as text. Instead, the participants of the SemEval 2015 task had to download the tweets using a list of user and tweet IDs. However, not all tweets are still available. After downloading, our training data comprises a total of 8394 tweets, 3133 of which are positive, 1237 negative, and 4023 neutral. The evaluation is done on two separate test sets. The first test set, the progress test set, was used as test set in previous years of SemEval 2013 (Nakov et al., 2013) and SemEval 2014 (Rosenthal et al., 2014). It consists of 3506 positive, 1541 negative, and 3940 neutral short text (a total of 8987). This set contains not only Twitter texts, but also SMS text messages, blog posts (LiveJournal), and tweets that are marked as sarcastic. The second test set, the SemEval 2015 test set, contains 2390 Twitter tweets, 1038 positive, 365 negative, and 987 neutral. Table 1 lists all test set sizes in detail. As evaluation measure the organizers chose to report the macro F_1 score of positive and negative examples, i.e., $F_{1,macro} = (F_{1,positive} + F_{1,negative})/2$.

The CNN is trained using minibatch stochastic gradient descent with a batch size of 200 examples. For learning rate adaptation we use AdaGrad (Duchi et al., 2011) with an initial learning rate of 0.001. ℓ_2 with $\lambda = 0.001$ is utilized to avoid overfitting as much as possible. The embeddings size is set to 50. In the first convolution layer, we use 30 filters with a $m = 5$, which means it spans 5 words. The second convolution layer uses 10 filters with $m = 3$. The three hidden layers have sizes 200, 40, and 200. This choice of layer sizes with a bottleneck layer between two larger layers is frequently

Table 1: Test set sizes and results

	#pos	#neg	#neu	$F_{1,positive}$	$F_{1,negative}$	$F_{1,neutral}$	$F_{1,macro}$
SemEval 2013 Twitter	1572	601	1640	71.32	58.31	72.53	64.82
SemEval 2013 SMS	492	394	1207	66.94	63.34	80.33	65.14
SemEval 2014 LiveJournal	427	304	411	71.09	71.84	69.04	71.47
SemEval 2014 Twitter	982	202	669	73.63	58.47	67.14	66.05
SemEval 2014 Twitter sarcasm	33	40	13	60.00	38.46	53.33	49.23
SemEval 2015 Twitter	1038	365	987	65.32	53.82	68.06	59.57

used in automated speech recognition systems. For example Grézl et al. (2007) showed that using the bottleneck layer's output leads to lower word error rates than using hidden layer outputs. However, our experimental results show that using the output of the CNN softmax layer as input for the first SVM achieves slightly better performance than using the output of the bottle-neck layer.

For both linear SVMs we tune the C parameter on the validation data.

Results The last line in Table 1 lists the F_1 performances of our system on the SemEval 2015 test set. The performance on negative examples is much worse than on positive or neutral examples. This is due to the small number of negative training examples. The macro F_1 score of 59.57 leads to rank 20 out of 40 participants in this year's SemEval. The fact that our system scores much better on LifeJournal and the SMS data in terms of $F_{1,negative}$ suggests that Twitter is an especially difficult medium for automated analysis.

The performance difference on Twitter from 2013 and 2014 compared to Twitter 2015 suggests that this year's Twitter data was different than in the years before. Our system scored similarly on Twitter from 2013 and 2014, but worse on 2015. Even worse results are achieved on the sarcasm data. However, the results should be taken with care, because this sub set is very small.

5 Related Work

One early work that used CNNs to model sentences was published by Collobert et al. (2011). They used one convolution layer followed by a max pooling layer to create a sentence representation. We extend their method by incorporating additional features focused on the polarity classification task. In contrast to their approach, we do not embed our external features, but make direct use of them.

Kalchbrenner et al. (2014) show that a CNN for modeling sentences can achieve competitive results in polarity classification. Among others, they introduce dynamic k-max pooling, a method that adapts max pooling to the length of an input sentence. Compared to their work we use a simpler architecture of the CNN without max-pooling, because this technique did not show any improvements in our experiments. Furthermore, we use the same filter for each dimension to reduce the number of parameters, whereas their model uses a different filter per dimension. Finally, our CNN model is combined with another classifier to produce the final polarity label.

Using an SVM for polarity classification is a common approach. One of the first polarity classification systems used bag-of-words features and an SVM to classify the polarity of movie reviews (Pang et al., 2002). The winning system of SemEval 2013 and SemEval 2014 also used an SVM with many different features (Mohammad et al., 2013). We implemented their most helpful features, which is bag-of-words and lexicon features and added the CNN output as an additional feature to improve the final performance.

6 Conclusion

This paper summarizes the features of our automatic sentiment analysis system – CIS-positive – for the SemEval 2015 shared task - Task 10, subtask B. We carefully normalize the Twitter data and integrate the output of convolutional neural networks into support vector machines for the polarity classification. Our system achieves a macro F-score of 59.57 on the SemEval 2015 test data. Among the 40 participants in this subtask our system reached rank 20 with a distance of 5.0 F_1 points to the winning system.

Acknowledgments

This work was supported by DFG (grant SCHU 2246/10).

References

Samuel Brody and Nicholas Diakopoulos. 2011. Cooooooooooooooollllllllllllll!!!!!!!!!!!!!! Using Word Lengthening to Detect Sentiment in Microblogs. In *EMNLP*.

Ronan Collobert, Jason Weston, Léon Bottou, Michael Karlen, Koray Kavukcuoglu, and Pavel Kuksa. 2011. Natural Language Processing (almost) from Scratch. *JMLR*, 12.

John C. Duchi, Elad Hazan, and Yoram Singer. 2011. Adaptive Subgradient Methods for Online Learning and Stochastic Optimization. *JMLR*, 12.

Rong-En Fan, Kai-Wei Chang, Cho-Jui Hsieh, Xiang-Rui Wang, and Chih-Jen Lin. 2008. LIBLINEAR: A Library for Large Linear Classification. *JMLR*, 9.

Frantisek Grézl, Martin Karafiát, Stanislav Kontar, and Jan Cernocký. 2007. Probabilistic and Bottle-Neck Features for LVCSR of Meetings. In *ICASSP*.

Minqing Hu and Bing Liu. 2004. Mining and Summarizing Customer Reviews. In *KDD*.

Kevin Jarrett, Koray Kavukcuoglu, Marc'Aurelio Ranzato, and Yann LeCun. 2009. What is the Best Multi-Stage Architecture for Object Recognition? In *ICCV*.

Nal Kalchbrenner, Edward Grefenstette, and Phil Blunsom. 2014. A Convolutional Neural Network for Modelling Sentences. In *ACL*.

Andrew J. McMinn, Yashar Moshfeghi, and Joemon M. Jose. 2013. Building a large-scale corpus for evaluating event detection on twitter. In *CIKM*.

Tomas Mikolov, Kai Chen, Gregory S. Corrado, and Jeffrey Dean. 2013. Efficient Estimation of Word Representations in Vector Space. In *ICLR*.

Saif M. Mohammad and Peter D. Turney. 2013. Crowdsourcing a Word-Emotion Association Lexicon. *Computational Intelligence*, 29(3).

Saif M. Mohammad, Svetlana Kiritchenko, and Xiaodan Zhu. 2013. NRC-Canada: Building the State-of-the-Art in Sentiment Analysis of Tweets. In *SemEval*.

Preslav Nakov, Sara Rosenthal, Zornitsa Kozareva, Veselin Stoyanov, Alan Ritter, and Theresa Wilson. 2013. SemEval-2013 Task 2: Sentiment Analysis in Twitter. In *SemEval*.

Olutobi Owoputi, Brendan O'Connor, Chris Dyer, Kevin Gimpel, Nathan Schneider, and Noah A. Smith. 2013. Improved Part-of-Speech Tagging for Online Conversational Text with Word Clusters. In *NAACL HLT*.

Bo Pang, Lillian Lee, and Shivakumar Vaithyanathan. 2002. Thumbs Up?: Sentiment Classification Using Machine Learning Techniques. In *EMNLP*.

Sara Rosenthal, Alan Ritter, Preslav Nakov, and Veselin Stoyanov. 2014. SemEval-2014 Task 9: Sentiment Analysis in Twitter. In *SemEval*.

Sara Rosenthal, Preslav Nakov, Svetlana Kiritchenko, Saif M. Mohammad, Alan Ritter, and Veselin Stoyanov. 2015. SemEval-2015 Task 10: Sentiment Analysis in Twitter. In *SemEval*.

Ashish Vaswani, Yinggong Zhao, Victoria Fossum, and David Chiang. 2013. Decoding with Large-Scale Neural Language Models Improves Translation. In *EMNLP*.

Theresa Ann Wilson, Janyce Wiebe, and Paul Hoffmann. 2005. Recognizing Contextual Polarity in Phrase-Level Sentiment Analysis. In *HLT/EMNLP*.

Matthew D. Zeiler, Marc'Aurelio Ranzato, Rajat Monga, Mark Z. Mao, K. Yang, Quoc Le Viet, Patrick Nguyen, Andrew W. Senior, Vincent Vanhoucke, Jeffrey Dean, and Geoffrey E. Hinton. 2013. On rectified linear units for speech processing. In *ICASSP*.

GTI: An Unsupervised Approach for Sentiment Analysis in Twitter

Milagros Fernández-Gavilanes, Tamara Álvarez-López, Jonathan Juncal-Martínez, Enrique Costa-Montenegro, Francisco Javier González-Castaño
GTI Research Group
AtlantTIC Centre, School of Telecommunication Engineering, University of Vigo
36310 Vigo, Spain
{milagros.fernandez, talvarez, jonijm, kike}@gti.uvigo.es, javier@det.uvigo.es

Abstract

This paper presents the approach of the GTI Research Group to SemEval-2015 task 10 on Sentiment Analysis in Twitter, or more specifically, subtasks A (Contextual Polarity Disambiguation) and B (Message Polarity Classification). We followed an unsupervised dependency parsing-based approach using a sentiment lexicon, created by means of an automatic polarity expansion algorithm and *Natural Language Processing* techniques. These techniques involve the use of linguistic peculiarities, such as the detection of polarity conflicts or adversative/concessive subordinate clauses. The results obtained confirm the competitive and robust performance of the system.

1 Introduction

The domain of sentiment analysis has received increasing attention in recent years (Liu, 2012), particularly due to the growth of the Internet and content generated by users of social networks and other platforms. Some of these, such as Twitter, allow people to express their opinions using colloquial, compact language. The result is a new form of expression that may in the long term become a source of extremely valuable information. An increasing number of companies are now focusing their marketing campaigns on online comments, sentiments, and opinions of brands from clients or potential clients, and some are even trying to predict the acceptance and rejection of certain products using this information (Jansen et al., 2009).

Even though the approaches used for this purpose are numerous and varied, they can be broadly divided into two categories: supervised machine-learning and unsupervised semantic-based approaches. The former are often classifiers built from features of a "*bag of words*" representation (Hu and Liu, 2004; Pak et al., 2010). In other words, they consist of automatically analyzing n-grams in search of recurrent combinations of opinion words. The latter aim at capturing and modeling linguistic knowledge through the use of dictionaries (Taboada et al., 2011) containing words that are tagged with their semantic orientation. These methods detect the words present in a text using different strategies involving lexics, syntax or semantics (Quinn et al., 2010) and then aggregate their values. Such methods usually combine two or more levels of analysis.

In recent years, work on sentiment classification using different types of texts has shown that specialized methods are required. For example, emotions are not conveyed in the same manner in newspaper articles as in blogs, reviews, forums or other types of user-generated content (Balahur, 2013). Dealing with sentiment in Twitter, thus, requires an analysis of the characteristics of tweets and the design of adapted methods.

This paper presents a method for sentiment analysis in English that uses dependency parsing to determine the polarity of tweets, using a previously created sentiment lexicon and considering the special structure and linguistic content of these postings.

The remainder of this article is structured as follows: Section 2 provides a brief description of the task and some of its subtasks. Section 3 presents in detail the system proposed for the performance of these tasks, and Section 4 shows the results obtained and discusses them. Finally, Section 5 summarizes the main findings and conclusions.

2 Task Description

This paper describes our contribution to the SemEval-2015 Task 10: Sentiment Analysis in Twitter. Of the five subtasks established, we participated in two:

- **Contextual Polarity Disambiguation (A)**, on determining the polarity of a marked instance of a word or phrase in the context of a given message.

- **Message Polarity Classification (B)**, on classifying the content of a whole message.

This year there were two datasets for testing candidate systems for substasks A and B: The Official 2015 Test and a Progress Test. The first test consisted of a set of Twitter messages (Rosenthal et al., 2015) whilst the second test was a rerun of SemEval-2014 Task 9 (Rosenthal et al., 2014), which includes Twitter messages and other kinds of texts from different domains. Datasets formed by the datasets given in SemEval-2013 Task 2 (Nakov et al., 2013) were also provided for training and development. In our case, the approach does not involve any training, and all the datasets were used to test the behavior of our system.

3 System Overview

The main objective of the tasks was to detect whether a marked instance of word/phrase in a given context (A) or message (B) expresses *positive*, *negative* or *neutral* sentiment. Most learning- or lexicon-based systems do not usually take into account relations between words, although they try to simulate comprehension of some linguistic constructions, such as negation, but this does not always work correctly due to the complexity of human language. For this reason, in this paper, we propose an alternative system to exploit the information present in dependencies obtained from a parsing analysis, *without the need for any kind of training*. The research we describe in this section has several linguistic peculiarities that were used to improve sentiment detection performance. Our method, which was fully unsupervised, consisted of four stages, which are each explained in detail below.

3.1 Preprocessing

Working with tweets presents several challenges for natural language processing. The language used on social media sites is quite different from that used in other forums because it often contains words that are not found in a dictionary. One reason is that tweets have particular orthographic and typographical characteristics, such as letter or word duplication. Hence, before applying our approach, it was necessary to start with a data preprocessing stage to normalize the language used, remove noisy elements and generalize the vocabulary used to express sentiment. The aim of the preprocessing module is to bring tweets as close as possible to natural language by eliminating expressions that are not considered part of current usage, in order to minimize the noise in later stages. There are four main steps involved:

- URL links (such as "*http://url*"), hashtags links (such as "*#hashtag*") and username links (such as "*@username*") are replaced with "URL", "HASHTAG" and "USERNAME" placeholders respectively.

- Replicated characters are removed to return the word to its normal form, such as *sweeeeet* → *sweet*.

- Emoticons[1] are replaced by one of nine labels: `e_laugh`, `e_happy`, `e_surprise`, `e_positive_state`, `e_neutral_state`, `e_inexpressive`, `e_negative_state`, `e_sad` and `e_sick`. For instance, :-(is replaced with `e_sad`.

- Abbreviations[2] are replaced with their respective full written forms, such as *h8* → *hate*.

[1]taken from the list available at http://www.datagenetics.com/blog/october52012/index.html

[2]taken from the lists available at http://chatslang.com/terms/abbreviations.

3.2 Lexical and syntactic analysis

In order to derive the syntactic context, each preprocessed social media message must first be broken into tokens and then into sentences. To then ensure that all inflected forms of a word are covered, lemmatization and *part-of-speech* (POS) tagging are performed using the *Freeling Tagger* (Atserias et al., 2006; Padró et al., 2012), or more specifically, its tagger implementation based on HMM (Brants, 2000). *Freeling* is a library that provides multiple language analysis services, including probabilistic prediction of categories of unknown words. POS tagging allows the identification of lexical items that can contribute to the correct recognition of sentiment in message. These items are namely adjectives, adverbs, verbs and nouns.

The resulting lemmatized and POS-annotated messages are fed to a parser that transforms the output of the tagger into a full parse tree. Finally, the tree is converted to dependencies, and the functions are annotated. The entire process is performed with *Freeling Parser* (Padró et al., 2012).

3.3 Sentiment lexicons

Sentiment lexicons, such as SOCAL (Taboada et al., 2011), AFINN (Nielsen et al., 2011) and *NRC Emotion and Hashtag Sentiment Lexicon* (Mohammad et al., 2013; Mohammad et al., 2013b), have been used in many systems for determining the semantic orientation of a phrase within a tweet or sentence. These lexicons contain English word lists sorted by lexical category, i.e. adjectives, verbs, nouns and adverbs. Each word is assigned a score of between -5 and 5.

However, these lexical resources are intrinsically non-contextual, so it is necessary to improve their coverage. To do this, we need to acquire new polarities of subjective words that are not present in generic dictionaries and adapt the scores of the other words using the data available. Consequently, we apply an automatic polarity expansion algorithm based on graphs (Cruz et al., 2011). The graph is generated from the syntactic dependencies provided by the *Freeling Parser*, considering only those involving verbs, nouns and adjectives. The starting point of the algorithm is a subset of negative and positive words, that are fed into the system as seed words. In this regard, we chose the most negative and positive words in the SOCAL and AFINN lexicons, as they resulted to work quite well for the datasets provided, after carrying out different experiments through the training datasets. Then, we apply the iterative polarity expansion through the created graph, and the result is merged with the unique word list of SOCAL/AFINN lexicons, incorporating 5982 of new words. The next step is to include emoticon labels, together with their polarities, in the resulting sentiment lexicon.

3.4 Sentiment Detection

Once the lexical and syntactic analyses are complete, it is possible to estimate the polarity resulting from a message. In other words, its sentiment can be expressed by a real number, which can be later interpreted as positive, negative or neutral. This value is computed by using the lexical polarities of the words included in the text (provided by the sentiment lexicon we have generated), and subjecting the special parsing structure and its content to linguistic processing which is described below. Once these have been applied, the resulting sentiment is a propagation of the values of linguistic elements within the dependencies, from the leaves to the upper levels until the root is achieved (Caro, 2013). Then, it is classified according to defined interval.

3.4.1 Intensification treatment

Intensifiers and diminishers, such as "*very*" or "*a little*", are usually adverbs that emphasize or attenuate the semantic orientation of the words or expressions they precede. Intensification is achieved by associating a positive or negative percentage, which implies a graduation depending on its type (Zhang et al., 2012). For instance, in "*very good*", "*very*" enhances the positivity of "*good*". Our system detects these structures and uses the parsing to identify the exact scope of the intensification whose semantic orientation will be altered. Superlative adjectives are also taken into account by asuming that they behave like a word accompanied by an intensifier. An example is "*greatest*", where the superlative implies an intensification of the word "*great*".

3.4.2 Negation treatment

Negation can be used to deny or reject statements. It is expressed grammatically through a variety of negator words, such as "*no*", "*not*", "*never*" or "*neither*" (Zhang et al., 2012). In our case, it is first necessary to identify the dependencies in which any of the above negator forms are present to estimate the negation scope. Later, the semantic polarities of the words involved in the affected dependencies are modified using a negative factor.

3.4.3 Polarity conflict treatment

The mere application of polar lexicons, intensifiers, diminishers and negators on a syntactic structure is insufficient. That is, words cannot be considered individually (Moilanen et al., 2007). The meaning and polarity of "*unpleasant dream*" differs for example from those of "*wonderful dream*". The first statement has a negative connotation while the second has a positive one. In both cases, the word "*dream*" is involved, and we could expect that, regardless of its accompanying terms, it should behave in a specific way, with certain polarity effects or expectations. However, the meaning changes significantly with the addition of "*unpleasant*" or "*wonderful*". In these cases, our system is able to detect *polarity conflicts*, i.e., it recognizes when a positive adjective modifies a negative noun, or vice-versa, and subsequently reduces the polarity of the elements that cause the conflict.

3.4.4 Adversative/concessive clause treatment

There is a point in common between adversative and concessive subordinate clauses. While the former express an objection in compliance with what is said in the main clause, the latter express a difficulty in fulfilling the main clause, although it is not impossible. In both cases, one part of the sentence is in contrast with the other part. For this reason, in a context of sentiment analysis, we can assume that both constructions will restrict, exclude, amplify or diminish the sentiment reflected in the clauses. In this regard, it is necessary to clearly distinguish them. In an adversative structure, the argument introduced by items such as "*but*" or "*however*" is usually more important (Winterstein, 2012; Poria et al., 2014), while in a concessive structure, that introduced by items such as "*despite*" or "*in spite of*" is the least important (Rudolph, 1996).

Our approach is able to coherently estimate the sentiment of sentences that involve not only adversative clauses, such as "*Bill Maher may be a little out there, but he does make some points*" (where the speaker is backing the view of Bill in general), but also concessive clauses such as "*Despite going off on Saturday, it looks like Ian Bennett could be fine for Wembley*" (where what appears to be really important is that Ian could go to Wembley).

4 Experimental Results

In this section we describe the experiments we conducted for both subtasks. These experiments were carried out using the datasets provided by the SemEval-2015 task organizers. These datasets are composed of texts extracted from Twitter (including sarcastic tweets), LiveJournal and phone text messages. The performance of each system is measured by means of the *F-score*, calculated as shown in Equation 1,

$$F\text{-}score = (F_P + F_N)/2 \quad (1)$$

where F_P stands for the *F-score* estimated only for positive results. In this case, this value is computed as shown in Equation 2, where P_P represents the precision and R_P the recall, both for positive results. The same is calculated for negative results, denominated F_N.

$$F_P = (2 * P_P * R_P)/(P_P + R_P) \quad (2)$$

Table 1 presents the overall score for subtasks A and B, in *Twitter2015 Test*, as well as *precision*, *recall* and *F-measure* values for positive (**P**), negative (**N**) and neutral (**NEU**) results.

Twitter 2015

		Precision	**Recall**	**F-score**
Task A	P	87.33%	71.26%	78.48%
	N	80.02%	72.47%	76.06%
	NEU	10.25%	34.21%	15.78%
	Overall score: 77.27%			
Task B	P	72.13%	66.09%	68.98%
	N	41.57%	59.45%	48.93%
	NEU	61.72%	57.35%	59.45%
	Overall score: 58.95%			

Table 1: Results of our approach for subtasks A and B.

The approach previously described was applied on both datasets (A and B) in the same way using the

		TASK A					TASK B				
		LJ'14	SMS'13	T'13	T'14	TS'14	LJ'14	SMS'13	T'13	T'14	TS'14
Precision	P	84.65%	82.16%	91.41%	93.23%	88.75%	73.53%	56.57%	68.54%	76.27%	52.17%
	N	85.04%	92.64%	87.53%	78.86%	95.83%	74.52%	58.47%	54.56%	51.94%	87.50%
	NEU	31.62%	16.55%	7.76%	9.79%	10.00%	62.00%	81.64%	67.69%	60.03%	37.50%
Recall	P	76.06%	83.85%	81.38%	76.26%	86.59%	70.26%	71.75%	73.73%	70.06%	72.73%
	N	81.21%	79.80%	79.23%	71.63%	62.16%	64.47%	70.05%	59.73%	63.34%	35.00%
	NEU	51.39%	30.19%	29.38%	52.27%	40.00%	71.05%	67.44%	60.43%	62.18%	69.23%
F-score	P	80.13%	82.99%	86.11%	83.90%	87.65%	71.86%	63.26%	71.04%	73.04%	60.76%
	N	83.08%	85.74%	83.17%	75.07%	75.41%	69.14%	63.74%	57.03%	58.26%	50.00%
	NEU	39.15%	21.38%	12.27%	16.49%	16.00%	66.21%	73.87%	63.85%	61.09%	48.65%
Overall		81.61%	84.37%	84.64%	79.48%	81.53%	70.50%	63.50%	64.03%	65.65%	55.38%

Table 2: Performance of our approach on the progress test A and B.

generated sentiment lexicon and applying the propagation of the sentiment values within the dependencies. After performing several tests on the training datasets provided by organizers, we set the neutral sentiment intervals to $[-0.05, 0.05]$ for subtask A and $[-1.0, 1.0]$ for subtask B.

As can be seen, all our results are adjusted, so we can state that our system has no bias for one particular result, but performs quite well for all three types of answers. However, as can be seen in subtask A, the performance measures for neutral tweets are notably lower than those obtained for positive and negative tweets. This can be explained by the content of the dataset provided, which contained 1006 negative and 1896 positive tweets, but just 190 neutral tweets, which is an insufficient sample for producing reliable estimates on precision. The same problem happened for progress test A, where the proportions of tweets are similarly unbalanced.

Detailed scores for progress tests of subtasks A and B are shown in Table 2. In general, we can say that our system is quite stable, as it generates similar results for the different kinds of texts under evaluation. Also of note are the high percentages obtained for sarcastic tweets, which ranked in the first position in subtask A and in the tenth (test dataset) and sixth positions (progress dataset) in subtask B (as shown in Table 3).

5 Conclusions

This paper describes the participation of the GTI Research Group, AtlantTIC Centre, University of Vigo, in SemEval-2015 task 10: Sentiment Analysis in Twitter. We achieved our results using a *fully* unsupervised approach for message-level and phrase-level sentiment analysis of tweets. Table 3 shows our position in the ranking published for both subtasks A and B for all the different datasets evaluated.

Test sets	Task A	Task B
Twitter2015	9/11	22/40
Twitter2015Sarcasm	-	10/40
LiveJournal2014	8/11	18/40
SMS2013	6/11	16/40
Twitter2013	5/11	25/40
Twitter2014	9/11	22/40
Twitter2014Sarcasm	1/11	6/40

Table 3: Position of our approach for each test and task, according to results provided on January 1, 2015.

Our approach comprises different processing stages, including the generation of sentiment lexicons, test preprocessing and the application of different methods for determining contextual polarity based on syntactical structure. This makes our approach robust in diverse contexts without the need for previous manual tagging of datasets. To the best of our knowledge, it is the only system presented in this competition whose sentiment analysis method does not require any supervision.

Acknowledgments

This work was supported by the Spanish Government, co-financed by the European Regional Development Fund (ERDF) under project TACTICA, and REdTEIC (R2014/037).

References

Atserias Jordi, Casas Bernardino, Comelles Elisabeth, González Meritxell, Padró Luis and Padró Muntsa.

2006. *FreeLing 1.3: Syntactic and semantic services in an open-source NLP library*. In *Proc. of the 5th International Conference on Language Resources and Evaluation*, p. 48–55. Genoa, Italy.

Balahur Alexandra. 2013. *Sentiment Analysis in Social Media Texts*. In *Proc. of the 4th Workshop on Computational Approaches to Subjectivity, Sentiment and Social Media Analysis*, p. 120–128, ACL. Atlanta, Georgia.

Brants Thorsten. 2000. *TnT: A Statistical Part-of-speech Tagger*. In *Proc. of the 6th Conference on Applied Natural Language Processing*, p. 224–231. Seattle, Washington.

Caro Luigi and Grella Matteo. 2013. *Sentiment analysis via dependency parsing*. In *Computer Standards & Interfaces Journal*, p. 442–453, volume 35 (5), New York.

Cruz Fermín L., Troyano José A., Ortega F. Javier and Enríquez Fernando. 2011. *Automatic Expansion of Feature-level Opinion Lexicons*. In *Proc. of the 2nd Workshop on Computational Approaches to Subjectivity and Sentiment Analysis*, p. 125–131. ACL. Portland.

Jansen Bernard J., Zhang Mimi, Sobel Kate and Chowdury Abdur. 2009. *Twitter power: Tweets as electronic word of mouth. Journal of the American Society for Information Science and Technology*, p.2169–2188, volume 60 (1), New York.

Hu Minqing and Liu Bing. 2004. *Mining and summarizing customer reviews*. In *Proc. of the 10th ACM SIGKDD International Conference on Knowledge Discovery and Data Mining*, p. 168–177. ACM Press.

Liu Bing. 2012. *Sentiment Analysis and Opinion Mining*. In *Synthesis Digital Library of Engineering and Computer Science*, Morgan & Claypool Publisher.

Mohammad Saif M. and Turney Peter D. 2013. *Crowdsourcing a Word-Emotion Association Lexicon. Journal of Computational Intelligence*, p. 436–465, volume 29 (3).

Mohammad Saif M., Kiritchenko Svetlana and Zhu Xiaodan 2013. *NRC-Canada: Building the State-of-the-Art in Sentiment Analysis of Tweets*. In *Proc. of the 7th International workshop on Semantic Evaluation Exercises (SemEval-2013)*, p. 282–290. Vienna, Austria.

Moilanen Karo and Pulman Stephen. 2007. *Sentiment Composition*. In *Proc. of Recent Advances in Natural Language Processing (RANLP)*, p.378–382, Borovets, Bulgaria.

Nakov Preslav, Rosenthal Sara, Kozareva Zornitsa, Stoyanov Veselin, Ritter Alan and Wilson Theresa. 2013. *SemEval-2013 Task 2: Sentiment Analysis in Twitter*. In *Proc. of the 7th International Workshop on Semantic Evaluation*, p. 312–320. ACL. Atlanta, Georgia, USA.

Nielsen Finn Årup. 2011. *A new ANEW: Evaluation of a word list for sentiment analysis in microblogs*. In *Proc. of the ESWC2011 Workshop on Making Sense of Microposts*, p. 93–98.

Padró Lluís and Stanilovsky Evgeny. 2012. *FreeLing 3.0: Towards Wider Multilinguality*. In *Proc. of the 8th International Conference on Language Resources and Evaluation*, p.23–25, Istanbul, Turkey.

Pak Alexander and Paroubek Patrick. 2010. *Twitter as a Corpus for Sentiment Analysis and Opinion Mining*. In *Proc. of the 7th International Conference on Language Resources and Evaluation (LREC'10)*, p.19–21, Valleta, Malta.

Poria Soujanya, Cambria Erik, Winterstein Grégoire and Huang Guang-Bin. 2014. *Sentic patterns: Dependency-based rules for concept-level sentiment analysis. Journal of Knowledge-Based Systems*, p.45–63, volume 69 (1).

Quinn Kevin M., Monroe Burt L., Colaresi Michael, Crespin Michael H. and Radev Dragomir R. 2010. *How to Analyze Political Attention with Minimal Assumptions and Costs. American Journal of Political Science*, p.209–228, volume 54 (1).

Rosenthal Sara, Nakov Preslav, Kiritchenko Svetlana, Mohammad Saif M., Ritter Alan and Stoyanov Veselin. 2015. *SemEval-2015 Task 10: Sentiment Analysis in Twitter*. In *Proc. of the 9th International Workshop on Semantic Evaluation*, ACL. Denver, Colorado.

Rosenthal Sara, Ritter Alan, Nakov Preslav and Stoyanov Veselin. 2014. *SemEval-2014 Task 9: Sentiment Analysis in Twitter*. In *Proc. of the 8th International Workshop on Semantic Evaluation*, p.73–80. ACL. Dublin, Ireland.

Rudolph Elisabeth. 1996. *Contrast: Adversative and Concessive Relations and Their Expressions in English, German, Spanish, Portuguese on Sentence and Text Level. Research in text theory*, Walter de Gruyter. Berlin.

Taboada Maite, Brooke Julian, Tofiloski Milan, Voll Kimberly and Stede Manfred. 2011. *Lexicon-based Methods for Sentiment Analysis. Journal of the Computational Linguistics*, p.267–307, volume 35 (2), MIT Press. Cambridge, MA, USA.

Winterstein Grégoire. 2012. *What but-sentences argue for: a modern argumentative analysis of but. Lingua 122 (15)*, p. 1864–1885.

Zhang Lei, Ferrari Silvia and Enjalbert Patrice. 2012. *Opinion Analysis: the Effect of Negation on Polarity and Intensity*. In *Proc. of KONVENS 2012 (PATHOS 2012 Workshop)*, p. 282–290. Vienna, Austria.

Gradiant-Analytics: Training Polarity Shifters with CRFs for Message Level Polarity Detection

Héctor Cerezo-Costas, Diego Celix-Salgado
Gradiant - Galician Research and Development Center in Advanced Telecommunications
Edificio CITEXVI, local 14
Vigo, Pontevedra 36310, SPA
{hcerezo, dcelix}@gradiant.org

Abstract

In this paper we present our solution for obtaining sentiment at message-level of short sentences. The system combines the use of polarity dictionaries and *Conditional Random Fields* to obtain syntactic and semantic features, which are afterwards fed to a statistical classifier in order to obtain the sentence polarity. To improve results, an ensemble of classifiers was employed by combining the individual outputs with majority voting strategy. Our solution was evaluated in the SemEval 2015 Task 10, subtask B: Sentiment Analysis in Twitter, achieving competitive performance in all testsets.

1 Introduction

Sentiment Analysis (SA) is a hot-topic in the academic world, and also in the industry. In SA, a label is automatically assigned to a piece of content carrying the polarity of the composition. The relevance for the web industry is clear, as new services promote content sharing among users. The number of registers generated by these services is paramount, discouraging manual analysis. Hence, automatic systems capable of processing this information have great value for the industry. Many services, such as web advertisement, recommendation, and mail campaigns (to name a few) could benefit from the information gathered with polarity analysis of user content.

This work is focused on message-level sentiment analysis, that is, the objective is the assignment of polarity to a small piece a text, typically one or two sentences with less than 140 characters. This restriction is motivated by the popularity of microblogging services such as Twitter. Here, users write messages of up to 140 characters to share information, their opinions or their feelings with other users. Those messages are shared in real time, and are a sample of the public opinion. Therefore, these small compositions published in microblogging sites can be analyzed to deduce the opinions about any topic of interest.

Nevertheless, automatic systems are not perfect. The results of the sentiment analysis in short sentences is not completely reliable. State of the art solutions are still far from being comparable to human performance, though very promising results were obtained recently using deep learning systems (Socher et al., 2013; Tang et al., 2014), and a careful selection of features with *Support Vector Machines* (SVM) (Zhu et al., 2014) or other statistical classifiers (Go et al., 2009).

This paper describes our sentiment classifier for short sentences and the results in our participation in the SemEval 2015 competition. We have implemented a supervised solution for learning the polarity of short messages. We made extensive use of sequential *Conditional Random Fields* (CRFs) in order to obtain the scope of polarity modifiers and shifters (e.g. negation, intensification). Although a complete explanation of CRFs is out of scope of this paper, the reader can obtain comprehensive information about it in the literature (Lafferty et al., 2001; Sutton and McCallum, 2011).

2 The SA System

This section presents a detailed overview of our system for sentiment tagging of short sentences. Our system performs several steps over each register to determine the polarity of the sentence. Initially, each register is preprocessed to obtain a normalized representation of the data. Next, syntactic information is extracted generating high-level features. As a final step, the features extracted in previous analysis are fed to a statistical classifier, obtaining the polarity of the register.

This is a supervised system, and therefore it needs a learning phase where data are tagged manually. The supervised models are trained only with the data provided by the organization, and therefore it can be considered a constraint solution.

2.1 Preprocessing

The sort of language used in microblogging services is colloquial style, with misspelled words and grammatical and syntactic errors. In order to solve this problem, basic normalization is performed as the first step. The actions executed in this stage are the substitution of emoticons for equivalent words and the substitution of frequent abbreviations. By lack of space, a complete Lookup Table of emoticons cannot be displayed in this paper but a sample of relevant transformations are in Table 1. We divided the emoticons in twelve categories: angry, bad, boring, complicity, happy, laugh, love, neutral, sad shy, surprise and worried.

<table>
<tr><th>Emoticons</th><th>Replacement</th></tr>
<tr><td>:), :-), :o), etc</td><td>happy</td></tr>
<tr><td>XD, x-D, xD, etc</td><td>laugh</td></tr>
<tr><td>:*, :^ *, etc</td><td>love</td></tr>
<tr><td>;), ;-), ;D, etc</td><td>complicity</td></tr>
<tr><td>:(, :'-(, :-[, etc</td><td>sad</td></tr>
<tr><td>D;, DX, D:, etc</td><td>worried</td></tr>
<tr><td>:@, :-||, etc</td><td>angry</td></tr>
<tr><td>o_O, o.O, o_0, etc</td><td>surprise</td></tr>
<tr><td>:O, >:O, :-O, etc</td><td>boring</td></tr>
<tr><td>:-###.., etc</td><td>bad</td></tr>
<tr><td>:$, ^^;, etc</td><td>shy</td></tr>
<tr><td>:#, :-#, :X, etc</td><td>neutral</td></tr>
</table>

Table 1: Sample of Emoticon Transformations.

Input Hashtags	Output Words
#classicmovielotto	classic movie lotto
#notupinhere	not up in here
#Thatisall	That is all
#shoptilwedrop	shop til we drop
#whatabadass	what a bad ass
#wordtomymuva	word to my muva

Table 2: Inputs and Outputs of the Hashtag Splitter.

One kind of specific language artefacts appearing in Twitter are hashtags. Hashtags are small pieces of text which usually contain valuable information to extract the sense of a whole sentence. Users use those chunks to voice those parts more relevant of the message and, very frequently, they are opinionated. Nevertheless, hashtags do not follow the grammar rules (e.g. no case used, words are stuck together, incomplete sentences without subject, verb, etc). To deal with the multiword problem of hashtags, we developed a module that uses CRFs with character-level features to find word terminations in hashtags. If more than one word is found, the system handles them as separated words in following steps.

Table 2 contains different multi-word hashtags that appear in the testsets provided in the SemEval competition and the corresponding output of the hashtag splitter. One of the hashtags, #whatabadass, is wrongly processed but with no significant change in meaning. In internal tests, 93% of words are correctly extracted by this approach.

2.2 Word Features

Our system uses several dictionaries as an input for different steps of the feature extraction process. These dictionaries are used to extract labels that get combined with features in the learning steps.

- Polar Dictionary: contains polar words, positive and negative, in English. This is a general purpose dictionary and no adaptation to the context of analysis was performed. If a word is registered as a positive/negative word, it is labelled with the corresponding polar tag. In case of ambiguity (the word appears in both dictionaries) the polarity label is not used for this word. The baseline for this dictionary was SentiWordNet (Baccianella et al., 2010), augmented after observation of training records.

- Denier particles: this dictionary contains particles that reverse the polarity of the words affected by them (e.g. not, no, etc). Detecting the scope of negation plays an important role in detecting the polarity of a sentence. The academic literature follows different approaches, such as hand-crafted rules (Sidorov et al., 2013; Pang et al., 2002; Athar, 2011), or CRFs (Lapponi et al., 2012b; Nakagawa et al., 2010; Councill et al., 2010).

- Reversal verbs: their behaviour is similar to denier particles. Some verbs reverse the polarity of the content under their scope of influence (e.g. *avoid*, *prevent*, *solve*, etc). In order to obtain the list of reversal verbs, basic syntactic rules and a manual supervision was applied afterwards. A similar approach can be found in (Choi and Cardie, 2008).

- Comparators and Superlatives: a dictionary with comparatives and superlatives was built in a similar way as the polar dictionary. There is a bit of redundancy with this feature as the morphological tagger used by the system gives the same information. However, the syntactic parser is not very reliable for informal style, unless it is specifically trained, which is not the case of our system. This information is needed to track intensification and comparisons within a sentence.

2.3 Syntactic Features

Several language constructions can act like polarity shifters with those parts influenced by them. This is the case of negation particles and some specific verbs. Detecting the scope of this modifiers is a hard task. Our system employs CRFs to obtain labels of those part of sentences that can act as polarity shifters, or that are influenced by polarity shifters. In this sense, we consider the detection of these scopes as an special case of a sequential labelling problem. CRFs are supervised techniques and they learnt the parameters of the system using manually labelled examples. We have built training records using a subset of the data available in the task.

Input Features
words, word bigrams, word trigrams, stems, stem bigrams, stem trigrams, PoS, PoS bigrams, PoS trigrams, distance to denier particle, distance to denier verb, distance to advers. particles

Table 3: Input Features of CRFs.

Our system follows a similar approach to (Lapponi et al., 2012a) but it was enhanced to track intensification, comparisons within a sentence, and the effect of adversative clauses (e.g. sentences with *but* particles). Figure 1 shows an example of the labels assigned by the system to each word of a sentence. Table 3 show the inputs and the combination of features included in the CRFs. The particles of negation (e.g. *none*, *not*), denier verbs (e.g. *prevent*, *avoid*) and others present in internal dictionaries such as *more*, *very*, *less* or *but* are marked as CUEs of negation, intensification and adversarial scopes respectively.

Sentences are tagged to obtain morphosyntactic data to use this information as input to the polarity shifter modules. In our case, we use the Freeling tool (Padró and Stanilovsky, 2012) for this stage. Freeling is an open source suite with tools to analyse textual data. It contains parsers with different degree of complexity but to the purpose of our system, only the *Part of Speech (PoS)* information was needed. We do not use dependence parsing as input feature in contrast to previous state of the art. The approach followed could experience problems with discontinuous scopes (e.g. when subordinate or participle clauses are intermingled within a sentence), but this problem is negligible due to the typically direct and colloquial style of short sentences.

The labels gathered with the CRF modules are used in conjunction with the Word, Stem, PoS and polar dictionaries to generate high-level features which serve as input to the classifier and thus to assign the polarity to the message in the final step.

2.4 Classification Algorithm

All the characteristics from previous steps are included as input features of a statistical classifier. The lexical features (word, stem, word and stem bigrams and flags extracted from the polar dictionaries) with

	Joachim	Rodriguez	may	have	missed	out	on	the	pink	jersey	but	he	is	top	ranking
CRF-INT	O	O	O	O	O	O	O	O	O	O	O	I	I	CUE_I	I
CRF-NEG	N	N	N	N	CUE_N	N	N	N	N	N	O	O	O	O	O
CRF-ADV	O	O	O	O	O	O	O	O	O	O	CUE_A	A	A	A	A

Figure 1: Example sentence with the CRF label notation.

Polarity	Positives	Neutral	Negatives
N. Samples	3456	4468	1432

Table 4: Training vector.

PoS and the labels from the CRFs. The algorithm employed for learning was a logistic regressor. Due to the size of the feature space and their sparsity, l1 (0.000001) and l2 (0.000001) regularization was applied to learn the important features and discard those with low relevance to the task.

2.5 Ensemble of classifiers

It could be possible to use the whole training vector available in one unique classifier, but we chose a different strategy that provided better results.

The ensemble was obtained by replicating the individual schema but using a small subset of the data available for training. The final decision combines the outputs of the classifiers using majority voting. Despite the time complexity of the ensemble and the lower precision of the individual classifiers, this strategy yielded better results than the one-classifier approach (between 1% and 3%) though it depended on the individual execution. An ensemble of 15 to 30 classifiers performed reasonably well in the evaluation tests.

3 Evaluation

3.1 Dataset

To train and validate the system during development, the SemEval organization provides the team competitors with a) an index set of tweets (that should be downloaded by teams), and b) a progress and input test for fair comparison of the different approaches. All the records that can be used as training vector are labelled with a tag (positive, negative and neutral). Due to cancellations of tweets that were not available, our system employed a subset of training of those provided by the organization. Table 4 shows the distribution of the training vector used by our system. A subset of those records are employed to train the CRF models.

Test	**F-score**
LiveJournal 2014	72.63
SMS 2013	61.97
Twitter 2013	65.29
Twitter 2014	66.87
Twitter 2014 sarcasm	59.11
Twitter 2015	60.62
Twitter 2015 sarcasm	56.45

Table 5: Performance in progress and input test.

Finally, the performance of our system is evaluated using a F-score that combines the F-score of positive and negative tweet, whilst neutral records are used to reckon the precision and recall of the positive/negative classes. We refer the reader to (Rosenthal et al., 2015) for a complete description of the task and the evaluation process.

3.2 Results

Table 5 shows the results of our system in the progress test of 2014 and the new input tests of 2015. The system shows a distinguished performance in nearly all the progress tests of 2014. It achieved 17th position in Twitter 2014 sentences, 1st in Twitter Sarcasm and 11th in LiveJournal2014. In SMS 2013 and in Twitter 2013 datasets we achieved also a good result (21th and 22th respectively). Regarding sarcasm detection in 2014 dataset, our system had good results in tweets with hashtags (25 right answers out of 35) whereas it was more prone to fail when users expressed positive opinions over negative events. Paying more attention to these specific constructions would lead to better results in the future.

In the new tests of Twitter 2015, our system performed in the 16th position of all competitors in both sarcasm and normal datasets. There is a clear gap of 6 points between the 2014 and 2015 Twitter F-score and the new testset. Our system is supervised and was only trained with the vector provided by the SemEval community which could mean the gap between the training and test vectors has increased this year. In this sense, it would be interesting to train with external records to see if the performance over the 2015 tests could be improved.

4 Conclusions

This paper shows the solution developed by Gradiant (http://www.gradiant.org) for the Sentiment Analysis Task 10 (subtask B) of SemEval 2015. The system finished in a notable 16th position out of 40 participants. In general terms, our system exhibits stability in all the different subtasks, achieving the 1st position in one of them, 2014 Tweet Sarcasm. We emphasize the modularity of our solution as one of the advantages of our approach. New functionality could be easily added to the current configuration, tracking new aspects of polarity detection that was left unattended in the current state of development.

Despite the overall goodness of the system, there is a generalized degradation in the evaluation results between 2014 and 2015 Twitter datasets. This result is very interesting and encouraging for future lines of work, as there exists a clear need in research of new models which provide better abstraction of the data and improve the adaptation to new contexts that differ substantially the training vectors.

References

Awais Athar. 2011. Sentiment Analysis of Citations using Sentence Structure-Based Features. In *Proceedings of the ACL 2011 student session*, pages 81–87.

Stefano Baccianella, Andrea Esuli, and Fabrizio Sebastiani. 2010. Sentiwordnet 3.0: An Enhanced Lexical Resource for Sentiment Analysis and Opinion Mining. In *LREC*, volume 10, pages 2200–2204.

Yejin Choi and Claire Cardie. 2008. Learning with Compositional Semantics as Structural Inference for Subsentential Sentiment Analysis. In *Proceedings of the Conference on Empirical Methods in Natural Language Processing*, pages 793–801.

Isaac G Councill, Ryan McDonald, and Leonid Velikovich. 2010. What's Great and What's Not: Learning to Classify the Scope of Negation for Improved Sentiment Analysis. In *Proceedings of the Workshop on Negation and Speculation in Natural Language Processing*, pages 51–59.

Alec Go, Richa Bhayani, and Lei Huang. 2009. Twitter Sentiment Classification using Distant Supervision. *CS224N Project Report, Stanford*, pages 1–12.

John Lafferty, Andrew McCallum, and Fernando CN Pereira. 2001. Conditional random fields: Probabilistic models for Segmenting and Labeling Sequence Data.

Emanuele Lapponi, Jonathon Read, and Lilja Ovrelid. 2012a. Representing and Resolving Negation for Sentiment Analysis. In *Data Mining Workshops (ICDMW), 2012 IEEE 12th International Conference on*, pages 687–692.

Emanuele Lapponi, Erik Velldal, Lilja Øvrelid, and Jonathon Read. 2012b. Uio 2: Sequence-Labeling Negation Using Dependency Features. In *Proceedings of the First Joint Conference on Lexical and Computational Semantics-Volume 1: Proceedings of the main conference and the shared task, and Volume 2: Proceedings of the Sixth International Workshop on Semantic Evaluation*, pages 319–327.

Tetsuji Nakagawa, Kentaro Inui, and Sadao Kurohashi. 2010. Dependency Tree-Based Sentiment Classification using crfs with Hidden Variables. In *Human Language Technologies: The 2010 Annual Conference of the North American Chapter of the Association for Computational Linguistics*, pages 786–794.

Lluís Padró and Evgeny Stanilovsky. 2012. Freeling 3.0: Towards Wider Multilinguality. In *Proceedings of the Language Resources and Evaluation Conference (LREC 2012)*, Istanbul, Turkey, May.

Bo Pang, Lillian Lee, and Shivakumar Vaithyanathan. 2002. Thumbs up?: Sentiment Classification using Machine Learning Techniques. In *Proceedings of the*

ACL-02 Conference on Empirical methods in Natural Language Processing-Volume 10, pages 79–86.

Sara Rosenthal, Preslav Nakov, Svetlana Kiritchenko, Saif M Mohammad, Alan Ritter, and Veselin Stoyanov. 2015. Semeval-2015 Task 10: Sentiment Analysis in Twitter. In *Proceedings of the 9th International Workshop on Semantic Evaluation*, SemEval '2015, Denver, Colorado, June.

Grigori Sidorov, Sabino Miranda-Jiménez, Francisco Viveros-Jiménez, Alexander Gelbukh, Noé Castro-Sánchez, Francisco Velásquez, Ismael Díaz-Rangel, Sergio Suárez-Guerra, Alejandro Treviño, and Juan Gordon. 2013. Empirical Study of Machine Learning Based Approach for Opinion Mining in Tweets. In *Advances in Artificial Intelligence*, pages 1–14.

Richard Socher, Alex Perelygin, Jean Y Wu, Jason Chuang, Christopher D Manning, Andrew Y Ng, and Christopher Potts. 2013. Recursive Deep Models for Semantic Compositionality over a Sentiment Treebank. In *Proceedings of the Conference on Empirical Methods in Natural Language Processing (EMNLP)*, pages 1631–1642.

Charles Sutton and Andrew McCallum. 2011. An Introduction to Conditional Random Fields. *Machine Learning*, 4(4):267–373.

Duyu Tang, Furu Wei, Bing Qin, Ting Liu, and Ming Zhou. 2014. Coooolll: A Deep Learning System for Twitter Sentiment Classification. *SemEval 2014*, page 208.

Xiaodan Zhu, Svetlana Kiritchenko, and Saif M Mohammad. 2014. Nrc-canada-2014: Recent Improvements in the Sentiment Analysis of Tweets. *SemEval 2014*, page 443.

IOA: Improving SVM Based Sentiment Classification Through Post Processing

Peijia Li, Weiqun Xu, Chenglong Ma, Jia Sun, Yonghong Yan
The Key Laboratory of Speech Acoustics and Content Understanding
Institute of Acoustics, Chinese Academy of Sciences
No. 21 North 4th Ring West Road, Haidian District, 100190 Beijing, China
{lipeijia,xuweiqun,machenglong,sunjia,yanyonghong}@hccl.ioa.ac.cn

Abstract

This paper describes our systems for expression-level and message-level sentiment analysis – two subtasks of SemEval-2015 Task 10 on *sentiment analysis in Twitter*. First we built two baseline systems for the two subtasks using SVM with a variety of features. Then we improved the systems through model iteration and probability-output weighting respectively. Our submissions are ranked the 3rd and 2nd among eleven teams on the 2015 test set and progress test set in subtask A and the 7th and 4th among 40 teams on the two test sets respectively in subtask B.

1 Introduction

Recently sentiment analysis has become one of the most popular research topics in the natural language processing community, mainly due to the exponential growth of social media data replete with subjective information. The once neglected topic has spurred immense interests from both academia and industry. Many approaches have been proposed for sentiment analysis in customer reviews, blogs and microblogs (for good reviews, see (Pang and Lee, 2008; Liu, 2012; Kiritchenko et al., 2014)). These approaches can be roughly divided into two categories. One is knowledge intensive or rule-based approaches, e.g., (Taboada et al., 2011; Reckman et al., 2013). Such approaches can achieve reasonably good results when tailored for a specific domain but their maintainability and cross domain portability is usually weak. The other is data intensive or machine learning-based, which learns to analyse sentiment from data. It is currently the most predominant approach, including supervised learning, deep learning etc. Sentiment analysis is often taken as a classification task. Widely used classifiers include Support Vector Machines (SVM), Maximum Entropy Models (MaxEnt), and naive Bayes classifiers. Common features include word/character n-grams and sentiment lexicons, among others. Key research issues for learning approaches include feature engineering, model selection, ensemble learning, etc.

SemEval 2015 task10 (Rosenthal et al., 2015) is a sequel to the two tasks on *sentiment analysis in Twitter* in the past two years (Nakov et al., 2013; Rosenthal et al., 2014). They have provided freely available, annotated corpus as a common testbed and significantly promoted sentiment analysis in tweet-like short and informal texts. The same metric, i.e., the average F_1 score of positive and negative classes, is used for measuring performances. But this year there are some changes. Besides the classical expression-level (A) and message-level (B) subtasks, another three subtasks are added, i.e., subtask C – topic-based message polarity classification, subtask D – detecting trends towards a topic, and subtask E – determining strength of association of twitter terms with positive sentiment. The organisers make no distinction between constrained and unconstrained systems, which means participants could utilise any other data. But it has to be described in the submission form.

We submitted systems only for the expression-level and message-level subtasks. In this paper, we provide some details behind the systems.

Data	TaskA	TaskB
Twittter2013-train	7,639	7,972
Twittter2013-dev	929	1,372
Twittter2013-test	3,625	3,198
SMS2013-test	2,334	2,093
Twittter2014-test	2,028	1,561
LiveJournal2014-test	1,315	1,142
Sarcasm2014-test	124	86
Twitter2015-test	3,092	2,390
Progress2015-test	10,681	8,987

Table 1: Statistics of all the datasets. The last row of Progress2015-test data is composed of all the previous test data sets.

Feature	subtask A	subtask B
word ngrams	✓	✓
POS		✓
clusters		✓
word vector	✓	✓
negation	✓	✓
lexicons	✓	✓
characters	✓	

Table 2: Features extracted for each subtask.

2 Our System

Our systems are built with an SVM classifier using various features and resources, including sentiment lexicons and word vectors. To further improve the performance, we use model iteration and probability-output weighting.

2.1 Resources

The resources used in our system are as follows:

Labeled training and test data: Although the organisers make no difference between constrained and unconstrained systems, it is not easy to make additional data effective (Rosenthal et al., 2014). So we just use the provided labeled data. However, since we did not participate in the past two evaluations, we are unable to get the full labeled data because some tweets are unavailable. But we crawled as much data as possible using the provided script. Table 1 shows the size of the labeled data and test data we get. The 2015 test data is released directly and the results are required to be submitted in one week. We take the training data and development data as our training data. The test data from the previous years can be used for tuning parameters (but NOT for training).

Sentiment Lexicons and Word Embedding: As many researchers have showed, e.g., (Mohammad et al., 2013), sentiment lexicons play an important role in sentiment analysis. In our system, seven sentiment lexicons are used: the Hashtag Sentiment lexicon, the Sentiment140 lexicon (Mohammad and Turney, 2010), the MPQA lexicon (Wilson et al., 2005), the Bing Liu lexicon (Hu and Liu, 2004), the AFINN-111 (Nielsen, 2011), the SentiWordNet (Baccianella et al., 2010) and the Hedonometer lexicon[1]. In addition, as word embeddings have been utilised to produce promising results in various NLP applications, we use sentiment-specific word embedding (Tang et al., 2014) in our system.

LibSVM: We used the package LibSVM (Chang and Lin, 2011) to construct the classification model for both subtasks.

CMU Tweet NLP: It is an open resource (Owoputi et al., 2013) for analysing tweets and was used to extract features for tokenising, POS tagging and clustering.

2.2 Preprocessing

The main preprocessing steps are the following:

- All upper case letters are converted to lower case ones
- URLs and user names are replaced with strings 'http://someurl' and '@someuser' respectively
- Tokenise and label the tweets with part-of-speech using Carnegie Mellon University (CMU) tool (Owoputi et al., 2013)

2.3 Features

After preprocessing, each tweet is represented as a feature vector made up of part of the following features, the features used in each subtask are shown in Table 2.

- **Word N-grams:** A binary value of contiguous n-grams of 1, 2, 3, and 4 tokens and non-contiguous n-grams (n=3, 4). Non-contiguous

[1]http://hedonometer.org/words.html

n-grams are those intermediate grams that are replaced with a special symbol like '*'. For example, a 4-gram "I * * guys" is the corresponding non-contiguous gram of contiguous gram "I love you guys".

- **Character N-grams:** Although character n-grams have been used in sentiment analysis by many researchers, we find that the features are not effective for subtask B, so they are only used for subtask A. This feature is the binary value of the two and three prefix and suffix letters.

- **POS:** Ten features are added by pos tagging. They are respectively the count of interjection, adverb, preposition, article, verb, punctuation, noun, pronoun, adjective and hashtag in a tweet.

- **Clusters:** Every token in a tweet is mapped to one of Twitter Word Clusters by CMU tool (Owoputi et al., 2013). The features extracted are a boolean vector showing the presence or absence of the tweet in the 1000 clusters which are generated from about 56 million tweets.

- **Word Vector:** Words are represented as a vector of 50 dimensions. Then we use min, average and max functions to convert the embeddings into fixed-length features, in a way similar to the pooling technique used in CNN to get a tweet vector representation. So another three features are added.

- **Negation:** A binary value indicating the negated contexts. The "_NEG" suffix is appended to grams if they are in a negation scope which starts with a negation word and ends with certain punctuation marks[2].

- **Lexicons:** For each token in one tweet, if it appears in sentiment lexicons in section 2.1, it is mapped to the corresponding score. In the lexicons which have no sentiment score we set the positive +1 and the negative -1. Other tokens are set to zero. Then a tweet would be represented with its total score, maximal score, minimal score, negative score, last word score which does not equal zero, and the count of tokens with non-negative score.

[2]http://sentiment.christopherpotts.net/lingstruc.html#negation

2.4 Training

SVM is used as the classifier in our systems with the features described in section 2.3. We trained SVM on the labeled tweets with the RBF kernel and tuned the parameters on the dev dataset. For both subtasks, we tuned the parameters for Twitter2015 test data using the Twitter2013, Twitter2014 test data as dev dataset and tuned the parameters for the progress2015 test data using all the previous test data as dev dataset. The parameters were tuned to maximise the average F_1 score of positive and negative classes using brute-force grid search.

2.5 Post-processing

We tried different strategies for the different subtasks. For subtask A, we adopted a model iteration approach described in Algorithm 1. For subtask B, we used probability-output weighting to adapt SVM model with RBF kernel to the data set, similar to (Miura et al., 2014).

2.5.1 Model iteration for expression-level subtask

It was found that utilising more external data did not improve the performance as expected because of the different data resource and annotation method (Rosenthal et al., 2014). So we tried a model iteration approach.[3] We added the test data labeled with high confidence into the training data and then retrained a new model. The algorithm for subtask A is given in Algorithm 1 and the experiment results are given in section 3.1.

[3]NB: Our approach is different from the semi-supervised learning in that we use limited test data while semi-supervised learning usually uses a large number of external data.

Data	c	g	I	p	w_{pos}	w_{neg}
A-Twitter15	1100	0.00287	2	0.8	-	-
A-Progress15	1100	0.00287	2	0.8	-	-
B-Twitter15	1200	0.00267	-	-	3.2	2.2
B-Progress15	1200	0.00267	-	-	2.1	1.4

Table 3: The parameters for different test data. I is the maximum number of iteration. w_{pos} and w_{neg} are weight parameters.

Data: Train data D; Test data T; Polarity $C = \{pos, neg, neu\}$; Threshold p; The maximum number of iteration I;
Result: The probability-output $p(c|x)$ for each instance $x \in T$; The label $l^{(x)}$ for each instance $x \in T$, $l^{(x)} \in C$

begin
  $i := 0$;
  do
    Train a sentiment model M with D;
    Compute $p(c|x)$ for each instance $x \in T$;
    $\Delta D := \emptyset$;
    for x *in* T **do**
      $p^{(x)}_{max} := \max_{c \in C} p(c|x)$;
      $l^{(x)} := \arg\max_{c \in C} p(c|x)$;
      if $p^{(x)}_{max} \geq p$ **then**
        remove x from T;
        add $(x, l^{(x)})$ to ΔD ;
      end
    end
    $D \leftarrow D \bigcup \Delta D$;
    i++
  while $(\Delta D \neq \emptyset$ *and* $i \leq I)$;
end

Algorithm 1: Model iteration for subtask A.

2.5.2 Probability output weighting for message-level subtask

We applied probability-output weighting (Miura et al., 2014) into SVM and adapted it to subtask B. For a tweet x, the base model output probability $p(c|x)$ for each polarity c ($c \in \{pos, neg, neu\}$). A weighting factor w_c that adjusted the probability-output $p(c|x)$ was introduced. The system labeled the tweet with polarity c which maximises the product of w_c and $p(c|x)$, namely $\arg\max_c w_c \times p(c|x)$. The weighting parameters w_c for each polarity was tuned by maximising the accuracy using grid-search in the corresponding dev data. The results can be seen in section 3.2.

Data	subtask A		subtask B	
	baseline	submitted	baseline	submitted
Twtitter15	82.31	82.76	60.02	62.62
Twitter13	83.86	83.90	68.79	71.32
SMS	84.38	84.18	68.03	68.14
Twitter14	85.09	85.37	68.70	71.86
LiveJounal	85.47	85.62	71.68	74.52
Sarcasm	71.81	71.81	53.70	51.48

Table 4: The overall results.

3 Experiments and Results

The official evaluation metric of the task is the average F_1 score of the positive and the negative classes. After the base training (Section 2.4), we got the base results in Table 4, "baseline" columns. Then we focused on improving systems for both subtasks. And the improved (or not) results are shown in the "submitted" columns.

3.1 Subtask A: expression-level sentiment analysis

We built the system using 8,568 tweets, including 7,639 training tweets and 929 development tweets described in section 2.1 using the features in section 2.3. After the release of the labeled test data, we compared the performance using the same model to rerun the test data. We set different threshold parameters p referred in section 2.5 to compare the results. The experiment results are given in Table 5.

Threshold p	0.70	0.75	**0.80**	0.85	0.90	0.95	1.00
Twitter2015	82.42	82.56	**82.76**	82.76	82.70	82.53	82.31
Twitter2013	83.95	84.00	**83.90**	84.62	84.49	84.38	83.86
SMS	84.02	84.09	**84.18**	84.41	84.43	84.48	84.38
Twitter2014	84.96	85.44	**85.37**	85.13	84.81	85.17	85.09
LiveJounal	85.58	85.31	**85.62**	85.61	85.58	85.58	85.47
Sarcasm	71.81	71.58	**71.81**	73.07	71.81	71.58	71.81

Table 5: The results for subtask A under different threshold p . Numbers in bold are the submitted results.

3.2 Subtask B: message-level sentiment analysis

We adapted the probability-output weighting approach to subtask B. The experiment result shows that weighting is effective for this subtask. The improvement using the parameters in Table 3 can be seen from Table 4.

The approach is effective for improving the twitter F_1 score but degrades the performance on the Sarcasm data, maybe because it depends too much on the data.

3.3 Experiment analysis

For subtask A, we made iteration stop at $i = 2$. The reason why there is little improvement is: (1) After each iteration, the number of new data added to the training data for retraining a new model is rather small. (2) Once the classifier puts a high confidence on a label, this instance is very likely to be similar to existing instances, which means the added instances would not contribute very much to classification.

In the experiments after submission, we tried to interchange the improvement method between the subtasks, but they showed a little decrease on both subtasks. When the model iteration approach was used in subtask B, we did not receive expected improvement. This may be because that the performance for subtask B is lower than that for subtask A, which may result in the wrong samples added into the training data. When the probability-output weighting approach was used on subtask A, we only got limited improvement in the F_1 score.

4 Conclusion

We described our system for two subtasks of SemEval 2015 task 10 – *Sentiment Analysis in Twitter*. Our systems are built by integrating a variety of features into SVM as baselines and then improved by model iteration and probability-output weighting for expression-level and message-level subtasks respectively. We compared the results and analyse the reason of the improvement. Our submissions are ranked the 3rd and 2nd among eleven teams on the 2015 test set and progress test set in subtask A and the 7th and 4th among 40 teams on the two test sets respectively in subtask B.

Acknowledgments

We would like to thank the shared task organisers for their support throughout this work. This work is partially supported by the National Natural Science Foundation of China (Nos. 11161140319, 91120001, 61271426), the Strategic Priority Research Program of the Chinese Academy of Sciences (Grant Nos. XDA06030100, XDA06030500), the National 863 Program (No. 2012AA012503) and the CAS Priority Deployment Project (No. KGZD-EW-103-2).

References

Stefano Baccianella, Andrea Esuli, and Fabrizio Sebastiani. 2010. SentiWordNet 3.0: An enhanced lexical resource for sentiment analysis and opinion mining. In *LREC*, volume 10, pages 2200–2204.

Chih-Chung Chang and Chih-Jen Lin. 2011. LIBSVM: a library for support vector machines. *ACM Transactions on Intelligent Systems and Technology (TIST)*, 2(3):27.

Minqing Hu and Bing Liu. 2004. Mining and summarizing customer reviews. In *Proceedings of the tenth ACM SIGKDD international conference on Knowledge discovery and data mining*, pages 168–177.

Svetlana Kiritchenko, Xiaodan Zhu, and Saif M. Mohammad. 2014. Sentiment analysis of short informal texts. *Journal of Artificial Intelligence Research (JAIR)*, 50:723–762.

Bing Liu. 2012. Sentiment analysis and opinion mining. *Synthesis Lectures on Human Language Technologies*, 5(1):1–167.

Yasuhide Miura, Shigeyuki Sakaki, Keigo Hattori, and Tomoko Ohkuma. 2014. Teamx: A sentiment analyzer with enhanced lexicon mapping and weighting scheme for unbalanced data. In *Proceedings of the 8th International Workshop on Semantic Evaluation (SemEval 2014)*, pages 628–632, Dublin, Ireland, August.

Saif M Mohammad and Peter D Turney. 2010. Emotions evoked by common words and phrases: Using mechanical turk to create an emotion lexicon. In *Proceedings of the NAACL HLT 2010 Workshop on Computational Approaches to Analysis and Generation of Emotion in Text*, pages 26–34.

Saif Mohammad, Svetlana Kiritchenko, and Xiaodan Zhu. 2013. Nrc-canada: Building the state-of-the-art in sentiment analysis of tweets. In *Second Joint Conference on Lexical and Computational Semantics (*SEM), Volume 2: Proceedings of the Seventh International Workshop on Semantic Evaluation (SemEval 2013)*, pages 321–327, Atlanta, Georgia, USA, June.

Preslav Nakov, Sara Rosenthal, Zornitsa Kozareva, Veselin Stoyanov, Alan Ritter, and Theresa Wilson. 2013. Semeval-2013 task 2: Sentiment analysis in Twitter. In *Second Joint Conference on Lexical and Computational Semantics (*SEM), Volume 2: Proceedings of the Seventh International Workshop on Semantic Evaluation (SemEval 2013)*, pages 312–320, Atlanta, Georgia, USA, June.

Finn Årup Nielsen. 2011. A new ANEW: evaluation of a word list for sentiment analysis in microblogs. In *Proceedings of the ESWC2011 Workshop on 'Making Sense of Microposts': Big things come in small packages, Heraklion, Crete, Greece, May 30, 2011*, pages 93–98.

Olutobi Owoputi, Brendan O'Connor, Chris Dyer, Kevin Gimpel, Nathan Schneider, and Noah A. Smith. 2013. Improved part-of-speech tagging for online conversational text with word clusters. In *HLT-NAACL*, pages 380–390.

Bo Pang and Lillian Lee. 2008. Opinion mining and sentiment analysis. *Foundations and trends in information retrieval*, 2(1-2):1–135.

Hilke Reckman, Cheyanne Baird, Jean Crawford, Richard Crowell, Linnea Micciulla, Saratendu Sethi, and Fruzsina Veress. 2013. teragram: Rule-based detection of sentiment phrases using sas sentiment analysis. In *Second Joint Conference on Lexical and Computational Semantics (*SEM), Volume 2: Proceedings of the Seventh International Workshop on Semantic Evaluation (SemEval 2013)*, pages 513–519, Atlanta, Georgia, USA, June.

Sara Rosenthal, Alan Ritter, Preslav Nakov, and Veselin Stoyanov. 2014. Semeval-2014 task 9: Sentiment analysis in Twitter. In *Proceedings of the 8th International Workshop on Semantic Evaluation (SemEval 2014)*, pages 73–80, Dublin, Ireland, August.

Sara Rosenthal, Preslav Nakov, Svetlana Kiritchenko, Saif M Mohammad, Alan Ritter, and Veselin Stoyanov. 2015. Semeval-2015 task 10: Sentiment analysis in Twitter. In *Proceedings of the 9th International Workshop on Semantic Evaluation*, SemEval '2015, Denver, Colorado, June.

Maite Taboada, Julian Brooke, Milan Tofiloski, Kimberly D. Voll, and Manfred Stede. 2011. Lexicon-based methods for sentiment analysis. *Computational Linguistics*, 37(2):267–307.

Duyu Tang, Furu Wei, Bing Qin, Ming Zhou, and Ting Liu. 2014. Building large-scale Twitter-specific sentiment lexicon : A representation learning approach. In *COLING 2014, 25th International Conference on Computational Linguistics, Proceedings of the Conference: Technical Papers, August 23-29, 2014, Dublin, Ireland*, pages 172–182.

Theresa Wilson, Janyce Wiebe, and Paul Hoffmann. 2005. Recognizing contextual polarity in phrase-level sentiment analysis. In *Proceedings of the conference on human language technology and empirical methods in natural language processing*, pages 347–354.

RoseMerry: A Baseline Message-level Sentiment Classification System

Huizhi Liang, Richard Fothergill and Timothy Baldwin
The University of Melbourne
VIC 3010, Melbourne
oklianghuizi@gmail.com, r.fothergill@student.unimelb.edu.au, tb@ldwin.net

Abstract

In this paper, we propose a baseline message-level sentiment classification method, as developed for SemEval-2015 Task 10, Subtask B. This system leverages both hand-crafted features and message-level embedding features, and uses an SVM classifier for message-level sentiment classification. In pre-training the embedding features, we use one million randomly-selected tweets. We present results over SemEval-2015 Task 10, Subtask B, as well as the Stanford Sentiment Treebank. Our experiments show the effectiveness of our method over both datasets.

1 Introduction

The rise of social media such as blogs and micro-blogs (e.g., Twitter) has fueled interest in sentiment analysis (Liu, 2012; Pang and Lee, 2008). One of the most popular settings for carrying out sentiment analysis is at the sentence level or over individual micro-blog posts, using the simple three-label class set of POSITIVE, NEGATIVE and NEUTRAL (Liu, 2012; Pang and Lee, 2008; Rosenthal et al., 2014). Sentiment classification has been shown to have utility in various business intelligence applications, including product marketing, identifying new business opportunities, and managing a company's reputation (Liu, 2012; Pang and Lee, 2008).

Learning effective features plays an important role in building sentiment classification systems (Liu, 2012; Pang and Lee, 2008). For example, the winning system in the SemEval-2013 message polarity classification task (Nakov et al., 2013) was based on a rich set of hand-tuned features such as word-sentiment association lexicon features, word n-grams, punctuation, and emoticons, which were combined using a simple SVM-based classifier (Mohammad et al., 2013). Recently, there has been a surge of interest in representation learning — automatically learning word and document representations, often in the form of continuous-valued vectors or "embeddings" — using auto-encoders or neural network language models (Mikolov et al., 2013; Le and Mikolov, 2014). Of particular relevance to message-level sentiment analysis, Tang et al. (2014) proposed a deep learning approach to learn sentiment-specific word representation features, and Le and Mikolov (2014) proposed a neural network auto-encoder to learn message-level vectors.

In this paper, we detail RoseMerry, a (strong) baseline sentiment analysis method that combines hand-crafted features with message-level[1] embeddings generated by `doc2vec` (Le and Mikolov, 2014), using a linear-kernel SVM.

2 The Proposed Method

The proposed method combines a set of hand-crafted features with automatically-generated message-level representation features. The features are concatenated into a combined feature representation, and fed into a linear-kernel SVM learner using `LibSVM` (Chang and Lin, 2011). The

[1]Throughout the paper, we will use "message" as a generic term to refer to both tweets and also sentences in the case of the Stanford Sentiment Treebank. Note that the method could potentially be applied to any granularity of document.

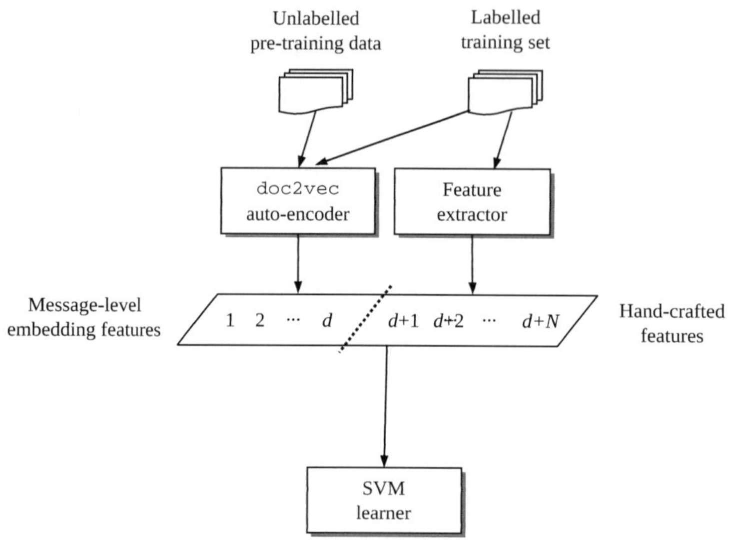

Figure 1: System architecture

architecture of the method is shown in Figure 1.

Our interest in sentiment analysis stems from a desire to use it as part of a commercial text analytics system. As such, there is an overarching constraint associated with the system and all third-party components must be licensed in a manner which is compatible with commercial use. In our description below, we point out places where we were unable to use notable resources because of this constraint.

The message-level embeddings are pre-trained using `doc2vec` over the combination of the training data and a random sample of 1M English tweets, as detailed in Section 2.1. The hand-crafted features are based heavily off the work of Mohammad et al. (2013), and are detailed in Section 2.2. Finally, the d-dimensional message-level embedding is concatenated with the N-dimensional hand-crafted features to form a $d+N$-dimensional combined feature vector. We experiment with each of the two feature subsets, in addition to the combined feature set.

One significant divergence from Mohammad et al. (2013) is that we do not use many of the sentiment lexicons, due to non-commercial licensing. Given that one of the key findings in that work was that lexicons are one of the most reliable features, we expect that this will have a large impact on our results.

2.1 Message-level embeddings

The message-level embeddings are generated using `doc2vec` (Le and Mikolov, 2014). In this framework, words and documents are represented in a common d-dimensional space, using real-valued vectors. The embeddings are learned by prediction of each word in a given document based on the document embedding and word embeddings of its surrounding context. The document vector acts as another word which captures the larger context of a word that is missing from its immediate word context.

The word and document vectors are trained using stochastic gradient descent, based on back propagation.

After pre-training, the document vector of each training document is used as its representation, and test documents are fed through the pre-trained autoencoder to generate a message-level embedding.

2.2 Hand-crafted features

The hand-crafted features are largely lexical:

- word n-grams: binary features capturing the presence or absence of word n-grams observed in the training data, i.e. contiguous sequences of n words ($n \in \{1, 2, 3, 4\}$); we also included binary features for non-contiguous 3- and 4-grams included in the training data (n-grams with one non-final word removed)

- character n-grams: continuous features capturing the proportion of contiguous character n-grams ($n \in \{3, 4, 5\}$) of each type observed in the training data, which make up a given message
- proportion of words in all caps: the proportion of words which are in all caps (e.g. *YAY*)
- punctuation features: the proportion of tokens which are made up of multiple exclamation marks, question marks, or a combination of the two (e.g. *??!*)
- elongated words: the proportion of words which have "elongated" vowels, i.e. a given vowel repeated more than twice (e.g. *coool*)
- proportion of emoticons: the proportion of tokens which are (a) positive- and (b) negative-polarity emoticons, as identified by Chris Potts' scripts[2]
- polarity of message-final emoticon: if the last token is a polarised emoticon, its polarity (NEGATIVE, POSITIVE or None)
- negated words: the presence or absence of words in "negated contexts", where a negated context is defined as span from a negation word[3] to a punctuation mark (matching the regular expression `[,.:;!?]`)

3 Experiments

In this section, we will detail the experimental setup and the results of our experiments.

3.1 Datasets

We evaluate our method over two labelled datasets, and also two unlabelled datasets to pre-train `doc2vec`, as detailed below.

[2]`http://sentiment.christopherpotts.net/tokenizing.html`

[3]Defined based on Chris Potts' word list: `http://sentiment.christopherpotts.net/lingstruc.html`.

	Training Set	Development Set	Test Set
POSITIVE	3043	438	1038
NEGATIVE	1177	212	365
NEUTRAL	4082	542	987

Table 1: The number of POSITIVE, NEGATIVE, NEUTRAL documents in the SemEval-2015 dataset

	Training Set	Test Set
POSITIVE	3606	444
NEGATIVE	3304	428
NEUTRAL	1623	226

Table 2: The number of POSITIVE, NEGATIVE and NEUTRAL sentences in the Stanford Sentiment Treebank dataset

3.1.1 Labelled Datasets

SemEval-2015 Dataset: the official SemEval-2015 Task 10, subtask B dataset, comprised of tweets which have been hand-labelled for sentiment at the message-level (in terms of POSITIVE, NEGATIVE and NEUTRAL sentiment). The dataset is partitioned into three components, as detailed in Table 1:[4] (1) training set, (2) development set, and (3) test set.

Stanford Sentiment Treebank Dataset: a collection of movie review documents from `www.rottentomatoes.com`, which have been sentence tokenised and annotated for sentiment at the sentence level (Maas et al., 2011) and pre-partitioned into training and test data, as detailed in Table 2. Socher et al. (2013) additionally annotated the data at the phrase and lexical levels, but we use only the sentence-level annotations in this paper.

3.1.2 Unlabelled Datasets

Twitter Dataset: a random sample of 10M English tweets from a 5.3TB Twitter dataset crawled from 18 June to 4 Dec, 2014 using the Twitter Trending API. This is used as additional data to pre-train the message-level embeddings for the SemEval-2015 Dataset.

IMDB Dataset: a 100K sentence movie review dataset from `www.imdb.com`, collected by Maas

[4]As the labels have not been released for the progress test set, we omit this from the table.

et al. (2011). This is used as additional data to pre-train the message-level embeddings for the Stanford Sentiment Treebank dataset.

3.2 Experimental setup

To evaluate the effectiveness of the different feature sets, we report on results as follows:

- **RM-manual**: only hand-crafted features
- **RM-doc2vec**: only message-level embeddings
- **RM-all**: both hand-crafted features and message-level embeddings

As our primary evaluation metric, we use $F1_{PN}$, which is the average $F1_{PN}$ for the POSITIVE (i.e., $F1_{pos}$) and NEGATIVE classes (i.e., $F1_{neg}$):

$$F1_{PN} = \frac{F1_{pos} + F1_{neg}}{2}$$

We also report the overall classification accuracy (Acc) across the three classes, and the $F1_{PN}$ score of each class (i.e., $F1_{pos}$, $F1_{neg}$ and $F1_{neu}$).

For the message-level embeddings, we used $d = 100$ and a context window size of 10. We used `LibSVM` with a linear-kernel and default parameter settings.

3.3 Experimental results

In this section, we present the results first over the SemEval-2015 datasets, and then over the Stanford Sentiment Treebank.

3.3.1 Results for SemEval-2015

The results for the SemEval-2015 test set and progress test set are shown in Table 3. Figure 2a is a learning curve of RM-`doc2vec`, pre-trained over varying numbers of documents. We can see that the results plateau at 1M tweets; this is the document collection size we used for pre-training RM-`doc2vec` and RM-all in our official runs. The overall Acc and F1 of each class for the three feature sets are shown in Figure 2b. RM-`doc2vec` is marginally better than RM-manual overall, and for the NEGATIVE class in particular. When combined, RM-all outperforms the two component feature sets across all classes, pointing to (weak) complementarity between the two feature sets.

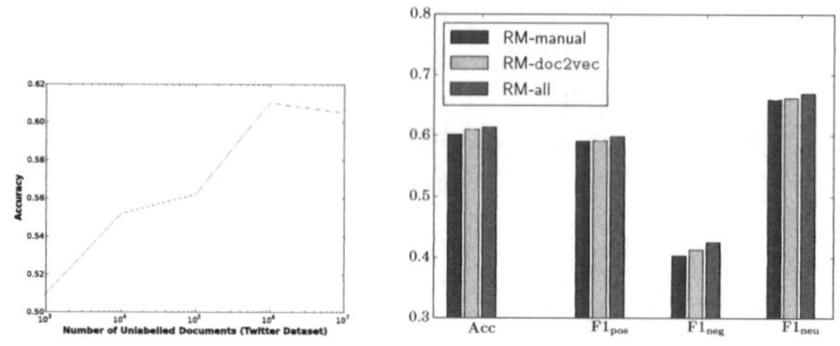

(a) Learning curve (b) Acc and per-class F1 score

Figure 2: The learning curve for RM-`doc2vec`, and the Acc, $F1_{pos}$, $F1_{neg}$, and $F1_{neu}$ results for SemEval-2015

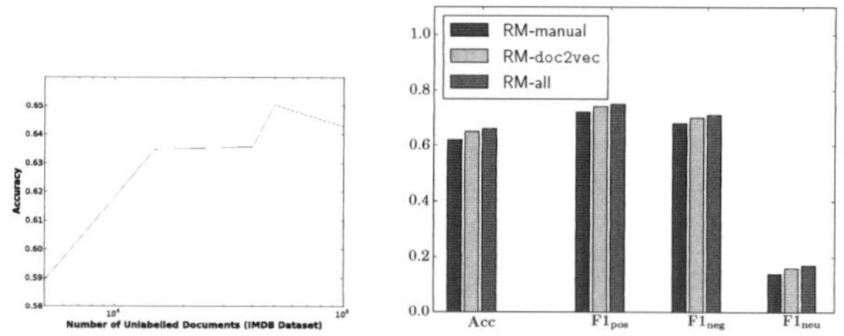

(a) Learning curve (b) Acc and per-class F1 score

Figure 3: The learning curve for RM-`doc2vec`, and the Acc, $F1_{pos}$, $F1_{neg}$, and $F1_{neu}$ results for the Stanford Sentiment Treebank

3.3.2 Results for the Stanford Sentiment Treebank

The learning curve for RM-`doc2vec` over the Stanford Sentiment Treebank with varying numbers of unlabelled (IMDB) documents is given in Figure 3a. RM-`doc2vec` performed best when pre-trained over 50K documents (plus the Stanford Sentiment Treebank data), and this is the model we include in the remainder of our results over this dataset. Figure 3b shows the Acc, in addition to the per-class F1 over the Stanford Sentiment Treebank for the three feature sets. The overall trend is strikingly similar to that for SemEval-2015, with the combined feature set performing marginally better than the two component feature sets in all cases.

4 Conclusion

In this paper, we described the method used in our official submission to the SemEval-2015 message polarity classification task, which combines message-level embeddings with hand-crafted features using a simple linear-kernel SVM. We pre-

Test Set		Progress Test Set				
Twitter 2015	Twitter 2015 Sarcasm	LiveJournal 2014	SMS 2013	Twitter 2013	Twitter 2014	Twitter 2014 Sarcasm
0.5118	0.4962	0.6254	0.5300	0.5233	0.6127	0.4925

Table 3: The official evaluation results for the SemEval-2015 Test and Progress Test set ($F1_{PN}$)

sented results over the SemEval-2015 dataset and Stanford Sentiment Treebank, and showed that the combined feature achieved the best results. The difference between the combined feature set and the two component feature sets is not statistically significant (based on randomised estimation, $p > 0.05$). While we were not able to achieve state-of-the-art results, we commend the proposed approach as a strong baseline method.

Acknowledgements

This research was supported by the Australian Research Council. The authors would like to acknowledge the support of Pitchwise (`www.pitchwi.se`), and also the coding assistance of Fei Liu.

References

Chih-Chung Chang and Chih-Jen Lin. 2011. LIBSVM: A library for support vector machines. *ACM Transactions on Intelligent Systems and Technology*, 2:27:1–27:27.

Quoc V. Le and Tomas Mikolov. 2014. Distributed representations of sentences and documents. *CoRR*, abs/1405.4053.

Bing Liu. 2012. *Sentiment Analysis and Opinion Mining*. Synthesis Lectures on Human Language Technologies. Morgan & Claypool Publishers.

Andrew L. Maas, Raymond E. Daly, Peter T. Pham, Dan Huang, Andrew Y. Ng, and Christopher Potts. 2011. Learning word vectors for sentiment analysis. In *Proceedings of the 49th Annual Meeting of the Association for Computational Linguistics: Human Language Technologies*, pages 142–150, USA.

Tomas Mikolov, Kai Chen, Greg Corrado, and Jeffrey Dean. 2013. Efficient estimation of word representations in vector space. *CoRR*, abs/1301.3781.

Saif M. Mohammad, Svetlana Kiritchenko, and Xiaodan Zhu. 2013. NRC-Canada: Building the state-of-the-art in sentiment analysis of tweets. *CoRR*, abs/1308.6242.

Preslav Nakov, Sara Rosenthal, Zornitsa Kozareva, Veselin Stoyanov, Alan Ritter, and Theresa Wilson. 2013. Semeval-2013 task 2: Sentiment analysis in Twitter. In *Second Joint Conference on Lexical and Computational Semantics (*SEM), Volume 2: Proceedings of the Seventh International Workshop on Semantic Evaluation (SemEval 2013)*, pages 312–320, USA.

Bo Pang and Lillian Lee. 2008. Opinion mining and sentiment analysis. *Foundations and Trends in Information Retrieval*, 2(12):1–135.

Sara Rosenthal, Alan Ritter, Preslav Nakov, and Veselin Stoyanov. 2014. Semeval-2014 task 9: Sentiment analysis in Twitter. In *Proceedings of the 8th International Workshop on Semantic Evaluation (SemEval 2014)*, pages 73–80, Ireland.

Richard Socher, Alex Perelygin, Jean Wu, Jason Chuang, Christopher D. Manning, Andrew Y. Ng, and Christopher Potts. 2013. Recursive deep models for semantic compositionality over a sentiment treebank. In *Proceedings of the 2013 Conference on Empirical Methods in Natural Language Processing*, pages 1631–1642, USA.

Duyu Tang, Furu Wei, Bing Qin, Ting Liu, and Ming Zhou. 2014. Coooolll: A deep learning system for Twitter sentiment classification. In *Proceedings of the 8th International Workshop on Semantic Evaluation (SemEval 2014)*, pages 208–212, Ireland.

UDLAP: Sentiment Analysis Using a Graph Based Representation

Esteban Castillo[1], **Ofelia Cervantes**[1], **Darnes Vilariño**[2], **David Báez**[1] and **Alfredo Sánchez**[1]

[1]Universidad de las Américas Puebla
Department of Computer Science, Electronics and Mechatronics, Mexico
{esteban.castillojz, ofelia.cervantes}@udlap.mx
{david.baez, alfredo.sanchez}@udlap.mx

[2]Benemérita Universidad Autónoma de Puebla
Faculty of Computer Science, Mexico
darnes@cs.buap.mx

Abstract

We present an approach for tackling the Sentiment Analysis problem in SemEval 2015. The approach is based on the use of a co-occurrence graph to represent existing relationships among terms in a document with the aim of using centrality measures to extract the most representative words that express the sentiment. These words are then used in a supervised learning algorithm as features to obtain the polarity of unknown documents. The best results obtained for the different datasets are: 77.76% for positive, 100% for negative and 68.04% for neutral, showing that the proposed graph-based representation could be a way of extracting terms that are relevant to detect a sentiment.

1 Introduction

In the past decade, new forms of communication, such as microblogging and text messaging have emerged and become ubiquitous. While there is no limit to the range of information conveyed by tweets and texts, often these short messages are used to **share opinions and sentiments** that people have about what is going on in the world around them. Working with these informal text genres presents challenges for natural language processing (NLP) beyond those encountered when working with more traditional text genres. Typically this kind of texts are short and the language used is very informal. We can find creative spelling and punctuation, slang, new words, URLs, and genre-specific terminology and abbreviations that make their manipulation more challenging.

Representing that kind of text for automatically mining and understanding the opinions and sentiments that people communicate inside them has very recently become an attractive research topic (Pang, 2008). In this sense, the experiments reported in this paper were carried out in the framework of the SemEval 2015[1] (**Sem**antic **Eval**uation) which has created a series of tasks for Sentiment Analysis on Twitter (Rosenthal, 2015). Among the proposed tasks we find Task 10, subtask B which was named **Message Polarity Classification** and was defined as follows: "Given a message, classify whether the message is of positive, negative, or neutral sentiment. For messages conveying both a positive and a negative sentiment, whichever is the stronger sentiment should be chosen". In order to solve this task we create an approach that uses a graph based representation to extract relevant words that are used in a supervised learning method to classify a set of unknown documents in different topics and genres provided by the SemEval team. The methodology for our approach is discussed in detail in the next sections.

The rest of the paper is structured as follows. In Section 2 we present some related work found in the literature with respect to the identification of sentiments in text documents. In Section 3 a graph based representation is proposed. In Section 4 the methodology and the tools used to detect the sentiments of a set of unknown documents are explained. In Section 5, the experimental results are presented and discussed. Finally, in Section 6 the conclusions as well as further work are described.

[1]http://alt.qcri.org/semeval2015/

2 Related Work

There exist a number of works in literature associated to the automatic identification of sentiments in documents. Some of these works have focused on the contribution of particular features, such as the use of the vocabulary to extract lexical elements associated to the documents (Kim, 2006), the use of bigrams and trigrams (Dave, 2008) to capture syntactic features of texts associated with a sentiment, the use of dictionaries and emoticons of positive and negative words (Agarwal, 2011) as well as lexical-syntactic features or the use of Part of Speech tags (PoS) (Wilks, 1999; Whitelaw, 2005) as syntactic features that can help to disambiguate the polarity of the words in a context.

In the other hand, many contributions focused on the use of structures to represent the features associated to a document like the frequency of occurrence vector (Wrobel, 2002; Aizawa, 2003; Serrano, 2006). Finally, linear representation of documents features combined with the use of a Support Vector Machine (SVM) has shown great performance in the tasks associated with the classification of texts (Vapnik, 1995; Joachims, 1998).

Research works that use graph representations for texts in the context of Sentiment Analysis barely appear in the literature (Pinto, 2014; Poria, 2014). It usually has been proposed the concept of n-grams with a frequency of occurrence vector to solved it (Pang, 2008). However, there is still an enormous gap between this approach and the use of more detailed graph structures that represent in a natural way the lexical, semantic and stylistic features.

3 Graph-Based Representation

Among different proposals for mapping texts to graphs, the co-occurrence of words (Sonawane, 2014) has become a simple but effective way to represent the relationship of one term over another one in texts where there is no syntactic order (usually social media texts like Twitter or SMS). Formally the proposed co-ocurrence graph is represented by $G = (V, E, L, \alpha)$, where:

- $V = \{v_i | i = 1, ..., n\}$ is a finite set of vertices that consists of the words contained in one or several texts.
- $E \subseteq V \times V$ is the finite set of edges which represents that two vertices are connected by means of the co- occurrence, where:
  - **Two vertices are connected if their corresponding lexical units co-occur within a window of maximum N words**, where N can be set to any value (typically between two and ten words).
- L is the edges tag set which consists of the number of times that two vertices co-occur in a text window.
- $\alpha : E \rightarrow L$ is a function that assigns a tag to a pair of associated vertices.

As an example, consider the following sentence ζ extracted from a text T in the dataset: "They may have a SuperBowl in Dallas, but Dallas ain't winning a SuperBowl. Not with that quarterback and owner, they are really bad.", which after the preprocessing stage (see Section 4) would be as follows: "may have SuperBowl Dallas Dallas ain't winning SuperBowl quarterback owner are bad". Based on the proposed representation, preprocessed sentence ζ can be mapped to the proposed co-ocurrence graph shown in Figure 1.

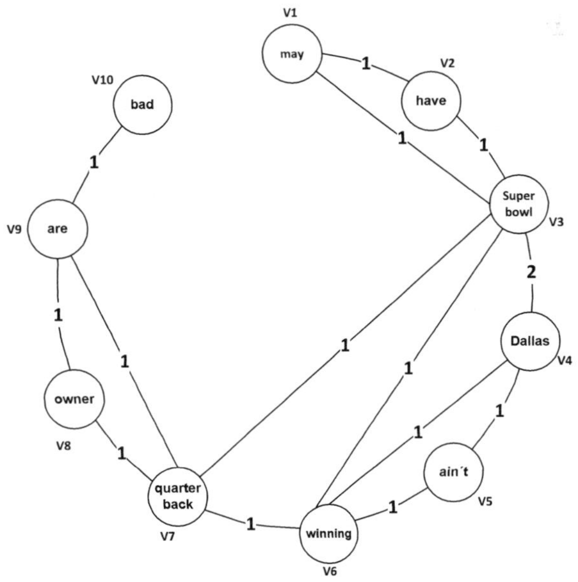

Figure 1: co-ocurrence graph example

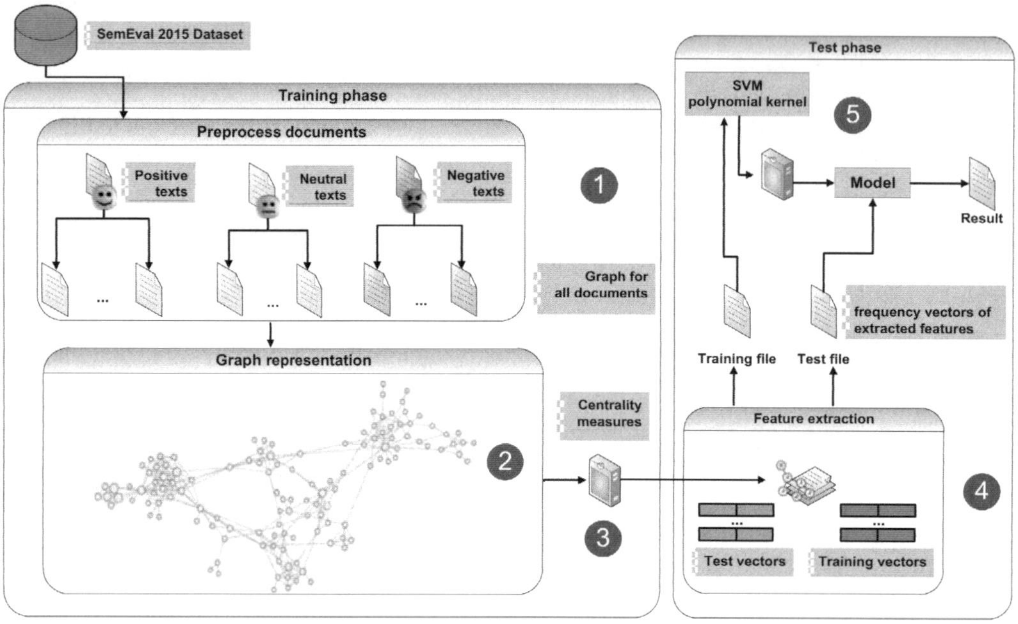

Figure 2: Sentiment Analysis Process

The co-occurrence graph shown in figure 1 has the following features:

- Terms co-occur within a window of 3 words.
- The set of vertices consists of the preprocessed words in sentence ζ.
- An edge between two vertices represent that both words appear in the same co-occurrence window (at least once).
- The label edge between two vertices represents the number of times that two words appear in a co-occurrence window in sentence ζ.

4 Sentiment Analysis Process Using A Graph Representation

Figure 2 shows the methodology used to detect the sentiments associated to a set of unknown documents, considering the use of graphs to extract the most relevant words associated to the documents. The methodology consists of five steps:

1. Preprocess all documents associated with the SemEval 2015 dataset. This task includes elimination of punctuation symbols and all the elements that are not part of the ASCII encoding. Then, each preprocessed sentence in a text is tagged with its corresponding PoS tags, for this step, the TreeTagger tool[2] was used.
2. Map only the nouns, verbs and adjectives of all documents in the training set to a graph representation (see section 3).
3. Apply the Degree and Closeness centrality measures (Freeman, 1979) which are indicators that identify the most important vertices within a graph, where:
   - The Degree centrality is defined as the number of links incident upon a vertex in the graph and is used to find the topologically representative words.
   - The Closeness centrality is defined as the average sum of the shortest paths from one vertex to the others in the graph and is used to find the most accessible words in the graph which consequently are syntactically relevant.
4. For each document in the training and test collection extract the **top 100 ranked vertices** (the

[2]www.ims.uni-stuttgart.de/projekte/corplex/TreeTagger/

Table 2: Evaluation of the graph model approach using the test dataset

Test Dataset	Methodology Runtime	% Correct Positive	% Correct Negative	% Correct Neutral	% Overall score	Baseline
Official 2015 Test	00:04:56	70.90	43.23	52.06	42.10	30.28
LiveJournal 2014	00:05:14	63.95	59.57	48.82	50.11	29.2
SMS 2013	00:05:14	52.16	42.56	68.04	39.35	19.0
Twitter 2013	00:05:14	70.44	44.49	54.69	41.93	34.6
Twitter 2014	00:05:14	77.76	45.00	49.50	45.93	27.7
Twitter Sarcasm	00:05:14	50.00	100.00	26.32	41.04	27.2

most important words in the graph) from both centrality measures in the graph without repetition and use them to build a frequency of occurrence vector (Manning, 2008).

5. Apply a SVM classifier (Harrington, 2012) with a polynomial kernel implemented in the scikit-learn[3] platform (Pedregosa, 2011), in order to construct a classification model which is used for determining the sentiment of a given anonymous document.

5 Experimental results

The results obtained with the proposed approach are discussed in this section. First, we describe the dataset used in the experiments and, thereafter, the results obtained.

5.1 Dataset

The description of the three text collections used in the experiments for the SemEval 2015 is shown in the next table:

Table 1: Datasets used in the Sentiment Analysis problems

Dataset	Name	# Documents
Training	Development	7493
Test	Official 2015 Test	2390
Test	Progress Test	8987

The test corpus was made up of short texts (messages) categorized as: "Progress Test" and Official 2015 Test. The Progress Test includes the following datasets: LiveJournal2014, SMS2013, Twitter2013, Twitter2014 and Twitter2014Sarcasm. A complete description of the training and test datasets can be found at the task description paper (Rosenthal, 2015).

5.2 Obtained results

In Table 2 we present results obtained with each dataset considered in the SemEval 2015 competition. The results were evaluated according to the $(F1_{pos} + F1_{neg})/2$ measure (Rosenthal, 2014) for the overall score and the precision measure (Manning, 2008) for each one of the sentiments. Our approach performed in all cases above the baseline. We consider that these results were obtained even though the training corpus was very unbalanced (there were more positive texts than others) and there was a high difference between the vocabulary of the training and test datasets. Further analysis on the use of centrality measures and on the methodology for constructing the graph will allow us to find more accurate features that can be used in a supervised learning method for the Sentiment Analysis problem.

6 Conclusions

We have presented an approach that uses a supervised learning method with a graph based representation. The results obtained show a competitive performance that is above the baseline score. The model presents a good performance on the Twitter dataset. However, there is still a great deal to improve on the LiveJournal and SMS datasets where the text could be smaller and the use of slang and genre-specific terminology is usual. One of the contributions of this paper is that we use a graph based representation (with an excellent runtime) with centrality measures to discover words related to each

[3]http://scikit-learn.org/stable/

sentiment instead of using traditional features like n-grams and vocabulary. As further work we propose the following:

- Experiment with other graph representations for texts that include alternative levels of language descriptions such as the use of sentence chunks, pragmatic sentences, etc.
- Apply the graph representation described in this paper to the Authorship Attribution problem (Holmes, 1994), where training and test data sets are balanced and belong to the same linguistic domain.
- Explore different supervised/unsupervised classification algorithms.

Acknowledgements

This work was partially supported by the REAU-MOBILE Proyect: CONACYT-OSEO no. 192321

References

Agarwal A., Xie B., Vovsha I., Rambow O., Passonneau R. 2011. *Sentiment Analysis of Twitter Data.* Proceedings of the Workshop on Languages in Social Media. Stroudsburg, PA, USA, 30-38.

Aizawa, A. 2003. *An information-theoretic perspective of tf-idf measures.* Journal of Information Processing and Management, 39, 45–65.

Dave, S. L. K. and Pennock, D. M. 2003. *Mining the Peanut Gallery: Opinion Extraction and Semantic Classification of Product Reviews,* Proceedings of the 12th International Conference on World Wide Web. New York, NY, USA, 519-528.

Freeman, L.C. 1979. *Centrality in Social Networks: Conceptual Clarification.* Journal of Social Networks, 1, 215–239.

Harrington, P. 2012. *Machine Learning in Action.* Manning Publications Co., Greenwich, CT, USA.

Holmes, D. 1999. *Authorship Attribution.* Journal of Computers and the Humanities, 28, 87–106.

Joachims, T. 1998. *Text Categorization with Suport Vector Machines: Learning with Many Relevant Features,* Proceedings of the 10th European Conference on Machine Learning, London, UK, 137–142.

Kim, S.-M. and Hovy, E. 2006. *Automatic Identification of Pro and Con Reasons in Online Reviews.* Proceedings of the COLING/ACL Main Conference Poster Sessions, Stroudsburg, PA, USA, 483–490.

Manning, C. D., Raghavan, P. and Schütze, H. 2008. *Introduction to Information Retrieval.* Cambridge University Press, New York, NY, USA.

Pang, Bo and Lee, Lillian. 2008. *Analysis mining opinion sentiment.* Journal of Foundations and Trends in Information Retrieval, 2, 1–135.

Pedregosa, F. 2011. *Scikit-learn: Machine Learning in Python,* Journal of Machine Learning Research, 12, 2825–2830.

Pinto, D., Vilariño D., Leon S., Jasso M., and Lucero C. 2014. *BUAP: Polarity Classification of Short Texts,* Proceedings of the 8th International Workshop on Semantic Evaluation (SemEval 2014), Dublin, Ireland, 154–159.

Poria S., Cambria E., Winterstein G., Huang H. 2014. *Sentic patterns: Dependency-based rules for concept-level sentiment analysis,* Journal of Knowledge-Based Systems USA.

Rosenthal S., Nakov P., Kiritchenko S., Mohammad S., Ritter A., Stoyanov V. 2014. *SemEval-2014 Task 9: Sentiment Analysis in Twitter,* Proceedings of the 8th International Workshop on Semantic Evaluation, Dublin, Ireland, 73–80.

Rosenthal S., Nakov P., Kiritchenko S., Mohammad S., Ritter A., Stoyanov V. 2015. *SemEval-2015 Task 10: Sentiment Analysis in Twitter,* Proceedings of the 9th International Workshop on Semantic Evaluation, Denver, Colorado, USA.

Serrano, J. and del Castillo, M. 2006. *Text Representation by a Computational Model of Reading.* Journal of Neural Information Processing, 237–246.

Sonawane S and Kulkarni P. 2014. *Graph based Representation and Analysis of Text Document: A Survey of Techniques.* Journal of Computer Applications, 96(19):1-8.

Vapnik, V. N. 1995. *The Nature of Statistical Learning Theory.* Springer. New York, NY, USA.

Whitelaw, C., Garg, N. and Argamon, S. 2005. *Using appraisal groups for sentiment analysis.* Proceedings of the ACM SIGIR Conference on Information and Knowledge, New York, NY, USA, 625–631.

Wilks, Y. and Stevenson, M. 1999. *The Grammar of Sense: Using part-of-speech tags as a first step in semantic disambiguation.* Journal of Natural Language Engineering, 4(3), 4.

Wrobel, S. and Scheffer, T. 2002. *Text Classication Beyond the Bag-of-Words Representation.*

ECNU: Multi-level Sentiment Analysis on Twitter Using Traditional Linguistic Features and Word Embedding Features

Zhihua Zhang, Guoshun Wu, Man Lan*
Shanghai Key Laboratory of Multidimensional Information Processing
Department of Computer Science and Technology,
East China Normal University Shanghai 200241, P. R. China
{51131201039, 51141201064}@ecnu.cn, mlan@cs.ecnu.edu.cn*

Abstract

This paper reports our submission to task 10 (Sentiment Analysis on Tweet, SAT) (Rosenthal et al., 2015) in SemEval 2015 , which contains five subtasks, i.e., contextual polarity disambiguation (subtask A: expression-level), message polarity classification (subtask B: message-level), topic-based message polarity classification and detecting trends towards a topic (subtask C and D: topic-level), and determining sentiment strength of twitter terms (subtask E: term-level). For the first four subtasks, we built supervised models using traditional features and word embedding features to perform sentiment polarity classification. For subtask E, we first expanded the training data with the aid of external sentiment lexicons and then built a regression model to estimate the sentiment strength. Despite the simplicity of features, our systems rank above the average.

1 Introduction

In the past few years, hundreds of millions of people shared and expressed their opinions through microblogging websites, such as Twitter. The study on this platform is increasingly drawing attention of many researchers and organizations. Given the character limitations on tweets, the sentiment orientation classification on tweets is usually analogous to the sentence-level sentiment analysis (Kouloumpis et al., 2011; Kim and Hovy, 2004; Yu and Hatzivassiloglou, 2003). However, considering opinions adhering on different topics and expressed by various expression words in tweets, (Wang et al., 2011; Jiang et al., 2011; Chen et al., 2012) have investigated various ways to settle these target dependent issues. Recently, inspired by (Mikolov et al., 2013a) using neural network to construct distributed word representation (word embedding), several researchers employed neural network to perform sentiment analysis. For example, (Kim, 2014; dos Santos and Gatti, 2014) adopted convolutional neural networks to learn sentiment-bearing sentence vectors, and (Mikolov et al., 2013b) proposed *Paragraph vector* which outperformed bag-of-words model for sentiment analysis.

The task of Sentiment Analysis in Twitter (SAT) in SemEval 2015 consists of five subtasks. The first three subtasks focus on determining the polarity of the given tweet, phrase or topic (i.e., subtask A aims at classifying the sentiment of a marked instance in a given message, subtask B is to determine the polarity of the whole message and subtask C focuses on identifying the sentiment of the message towards the given topic). The fourth subtask D is to detect the sentiment trends of a given set of messages towards a topic from the same period of time. The last subtask E is to predict a score between 0 and 1, which is indicative of the strength of association of twitter terms with positive sentiment.

Following previous works (Rosenthal et al., 2014; Zhao et al., 2014; Mohammad et al., 2013; Evert et al., 2014; Mohammad et al., 2013; Wasi et al., 2014), we adopted a rich set of traditional features, e.g., linguistic features (e.g., *n-gram* at word level, part-of-speech (POS) tags, negations, etc), sentiment lexicon features (e.g., MPQA, Bing Liu opinion lexicon, SentiWordNet, etc) and twitter specifical features (e.g., the number of *URL*, emoticons, capital words, elongated words, hashtags, etc). Besides, inspired by (Kim, 2014; Mikolov et al., 2013b), we also employed novel word embedding features in these tasks.

The remainder of this paper is organized as follows. Section 2 reports our systems including preprocessing, feature engineering, evaluation metrics, etc. The data sets and experiments descriptions are shown in Section 3. Finally, we conclude this paper in Section 4.

2 System Description

For subtask A and B, we compared two classifiers built on traditional NLP features (linguistic and Sentiment Lexicon) and word embedding features respectively. We also combined the results of the above two classifiers by summing up the predicted probability score. Due to time limitation, for subtask C and D, we only used the traditional feature sets to build a classifier. Unlike the above four subtasks, for subtask E we built a regression model to calculate a sentimental strength score for each target term with the aid of sentiment lexicon score features and word embedding features.

2.1 Data Preprocessing

Firstly, we collected about $5,000$ slangs or abbreviations from Internet to convert the irregular writing to formal forms. By doing this, we also recovered the elongated words to its initial forms, e.g., *"goooooood"* to *"good"*, *"asap"* to *"as soon as possible"*, *"3q"* to *"thank you"*, etc. Then the processed data was performed for tokenization, POS tagging and parsing by using *CMU Parsing tools* (Owoputi et al., 2013).

2.2 Feature Engineering

Although the first four subtasks all focus on sentiment polarity classification, they have very different definitions. For example, since subtask B focuses on sentiment classification on whole tweet, we extract features from all words in tweet. However, the other three subtasks, i.e, A, C, and D, perform sentiment polarity classification only on a certain piece of tweet, i.e., expression words or topic in tweet. Since organizers have provided the annotated target words (for A) and topics (for C and D) for each tweet, we only chose related words rather than all words in whole tweet as pending words for consequential feature extraction. To pick out related words from whole tweet, following (Kiritchenko et al., 2014), for each annotated target word we only treated the surrounding words from parse tree with distance $d \leq 2$ as its relevant words.

In this task, we used four types of features: sentiment lexicon features (the score calculated from seven sentiment lexicons), linguistic features (*n-grams*, POS tagger, negations, etc), tweet-specific features (emoticons, all-caps, hashtag, etc) and word embedding features.

Sentiment Lexicon Features (SentiLexi):

We employed the following seven sentiment lexicons to extract sentimental lexicon features: *Bing Liu lexicon*[1], *General Inquirer lexicon*[2], *IMDB*[3], *MPQA*[4], *SentiWordNet*[5], *NRC Hashtag Sentiment Lexicon*[6], and *NRC Sentiment140 Lexicon*[7]. Generally, we transformed the scores of all words in all sentiment lexicons to the range of -1 to 1, where the minus sign denotes negative sentiment and the positive number indicates positive sentiment.

Given extracted pending words, we first converted them to lowercase. Then for each sentiment lexicon, we calculated the following five sentimental scores on the processed pending words: (1) the ratio of positive words to pending words, (2) the ratio of negative words to pending words, (3) the maximum sentiment score, (4) the minimum sentiment score, (5) the sum of sentiment scores. If the pending word does not exist in one sentiment lexicon, its corresponding score is set to zero. Specifically, before locating the corresponding term in *SentiWordNet* lexicon, we conducted lemmatization for words and selected its first item in searched results according to its POS tag.

Linguistic Features:

- *Word n-grams:* We first converted all pending

[1] http://www.cs.uic.edu/liub/FBS/sentiment-analysis.html#lexicon

[2] http://www.wjh.harvard.edu/inquirer/homecat.htm

[3] http://anthology.aclweb.org//S/S13/S13-2.pdf#page=444

[4] http://mpqa.cs.pitt.edu/

[5] http://sentiwordnet.isti.cnr.it/

[6] http://www.umiacs.umd.edu/saif/WebDocs/NRC-Hashtag-Sentiment-Lexicon-v0.1.zip

[7] http://help.sentiment140.com/for-students/

words to lowercase and removed URLs, mentions, hashtags, and low frequency (threshold value is 10) words. Then we extracted **unigram** and **bigram** features. Besides, inspired by (Kiritchenko et al., 2014), the words connected on parse tree are extracted as **pairgram**.

- *POS Features:* We recorded the number of nouns (the corresponding POS tags in *CMU parser* are $N, O, \hat{}, S, Z$), verbs (i.e., V, L, M), adjectives (i.e., A), and adverbs (i.e., R) in pending words.

- *Negation Features:* Usually, the sentiment orientation of a message or phrase can be reversed by a modified negation. Thus, we collected 29 negations[8] from Internet and this binary feature is set as 1 or 0 if corresponding negation is present or absent in pending words.

Tweet Specific Features (PAHE):

- *Emoticon:* We gathered 69 emoticons from Internet and this binary feature records whether the corresponding emoticon is present or absent in pending words.

- *Punctuation:* The numbers of exclamations (!) and questions (?) are also noted.

- *All-caps:* It indicates the number of words with uppercase letters.

- *Hashtag:* It is the number of hashtags in the sentence or phrase.

- *Elongated:* It represents the number of words with one character repeated more than two times, e.g., *"gooooood"*.

Word Embedding Features: Word embedding is a continuous-valued representation of the word which usually carries syntactic and semantic information (Zeng et al., 2014). Since a phrase or sentence contains more than one word, usually there are two strategies to convert the words vectors into a sentence vector: (1) summing up all words vectors; (2) rolling up the sequential words to obtain a vector that contains context information (i.e., convolution neutral network). The convolution neural network (*CNN*) is usually employed in image recognition, while many researchers have adopted it in Natural Language Processing (Kim, 2014; dos Santos and Gatti, 2014) and achieved good performance. For subtask A and B, we adopted the *CNN tools* in (Kim, 2014) and extracted the penultimate hidden layer content as the sentence word embedding features to perform classification. For subtask E, we simply adopted the first strategy to sum up the word vectors in the given phrase.

Specifically, in this work we used the publicly available *word2vec* vectors to get the word embedding with dimensionality of 300, which is trained on 100 billion words from Google News (Mikolov et al., 2013b). If a word is not in *word2vec* list, we initialize its vector values to random values.

2.3 Evaluation Metrics

For subtask A, B and C, we used the macro-averaged F score of positive and negative classes (i.e., $F_{macro} = \frac{F_{pos}+F_{neg}}{2}$) to evaluate the performance, which considers a sense of effectiveness on small classes. For subtask D, the averaged absolute difference (i.e., $avgAbsDiff = \frac{1}{n}\sum_{i=1}^{n}|x_i - \bar{x}|$) is employed, which is a common measure of how much a set of observations differ from the average. Since the subtask E aims at predicting the sentiment score for target term, in order to make the comparison of predicted strength of different terms reasonable, the Kendall rank correlation coefficient (usually measures the association between two measured quantities) and Spearman rank correlation (a nonparametric measure of statistical dependence between two variables) are adopted in this subtask, where the Kendall rank correlation coefficient is the official evaluation criteria.

3 Experiments

3.1 Datasets

The organizers provided tweet ids and a script for all participants to collect data. Table 1 shows the statistics of the data sets we used in our experiments.

For subtask A and B, the training data set is composed of SemEval 2013 Task 2 training and development data (Nakov et al., 2013) and the development

[8]The 29 negations and other following manually collected data are available upon request.

data set is made up of the test sets from the same tasks in previous two years. For subtask C and D, this data is divided into many topic sets.

With regard to subtask E, the organizers provided 200 terms labeled with a decimal in the range of 0 to 1. We observed that among these 200 given terms, 22% are hashtags and 15% contain negator. In consideration of the lack of training data, we expanded it with $1,346$ terms collected from following sources: 916 terms which are present in all above mentioned 7 sentiment lexicons, 230 terms with hashtag and 200 terms with negator extracted from *NRC Hashtag sentiment lexicon* randomly. The provided 200 terms were used as development data. To predict the strength values of the extended data, we used the M-PQA sentiment lexicon label as reference. There are 6 polarity types in MPQA, i.e., strong positive, weak positive, both strong, both weak, weak negative and strong negative. We converted them to numeric score as $1, 0.75, 0.5, 0.5, 0.25, 0$ respectively. By doing so, if a target term is present in this expanded lexicon, the output is its corresponding score. Otherwise we split the term to several words and calculated their averaged sentiment score as output.

dataset	Positive	Negative	Neutral	Total
subtask A:				
train	5,738(62%)	3,097(33%)	456(5%)	9,291
dev	10,159(58%)	6,416(37%)	875(5%)	17,450
test				
LiveJournal	660(50%)	511(39%)	144(11%)	1,315
SMS2013	1,071(46%)	1,104(47%)	159(7%)	2,334
Twitter2013	2,734(62%)	1,541(35%)	160(3%)	4,435
Twitter2014	1,807(73%)	578(23%)	88(4%)	2,473
Twitter2014S	82(66%)	37(30%)	5(4%)	124
offical2015	1,896(61%)	1,006(33%)	190(6%)	3,092
all	8,250(60%)	4,777(35%)	746(6%)	13,773
subtask B:				
train	3,774(37%)	1,598(16%)	4,842(47%)	10,214
dev	5,570(37%)	2,536(17%)	6,788(46%)	14,894
test				
LiveJournal	427(37%)	304(27%)	411(36%)	1,142
SMS2013	492(24%)	394(19%)	1,207(57%)	2,093
Twitter2013	1,572(41%)	601(16%)	1,640(43%)	3,813
Twitter2014	982(53%)	202(11%)	669(36%)	1,853
Twitter2014S	33(38%)	40(47%)	13(15%)	86
offical2015	1,038(43%)	365(15%)	987(41%)	2,390
all	5,411(39%)	2,166(16%)	6,183(45%)	13,760
subtask C and D:				
train	142(29%)	56(11%)	288(59%)	489
dev	65(35%)	34(18%)	85(46.%)	184
test	867(36%)	260(11%)	1256(53%)	2383

Table 1: Statistics of data sets in training (train), development (dev), test (test) set for subtask A, B, C and D. Twitter2014S stands for Twitter2014Sarcasm.

3.2 Experiments on Training Data

3.2.1 Subtask A and B

To address subtask A and B, we conducted a series of experiments to examine the effects of different traditional features. Table 2 describes the experiments of various traditional features on subtask A and B. From Table 2, it is interesting to find that: (1) SentiLexi and unigram are the most effective feature types to detect the polarities; (2) POS feature makes contribution to improve the performance for subtask B but no improvement for A. It may be because the neutral instances in subtask B (i.e., 45.58%) are much more than that in subtask A (i.e., 5.01%); (3) The emoticons features are not as effective as expected since most emoticons are already present in unigram.

Besides, following (Kim, 2014) we adopted sentence modeling and extracted the penultimate hidden layer content as novel word embedding feature to build another classifier. Furthermore, we combined the intermediate results (i.e., the distances between point to multiple hyperplanes returned from SVM) of two classifiers. The experimental results of using word embedding features in isolation and in combination are shown in Table 3. From Table 3, we find that the word embedding alone performs a bit worse than the traditional features. This may be because the traditional features are dozens of times more than word embedding features and as a result the effectiveness of word embeddings is impaired. However, when we combined the two experimental results, we find that the combination result of two classifiers achieves the best performances in both subtasks. This indicates that although the size of word embeddings is small, it still makes contribution to performance improvement.

Features	Subtask A	Subtask B
Traditional	86.65%	66.81%
Word embedding	83.80%	64.85%
Combination	87.68%	67.80%

Table 3: Results of subtask A and B using traditional features, word embedding features and their combination in terms of F_{macro} on training data.

Besides, in our preliminary experiments, we examined several supervised machine learning classification algorithms with different parameters imple-

Features	Subtask A	Features	Subtask B	Features	Subtask C
SentiLexi	81.83	SentiLexi	60.99	unigram	32.87
.+unigram	85.32(+3.49)	.+unigram	64.60(+3.61)	.+PAHE	33.51(+0.64)
.+Negation	86.20(+0.88)	.+pairgram	65.76(+1.16)	.+SentiLexi	34.37(+0.86)
.+pairgram	86.52(+0.32)	.+POS	66.19(+0.43)	.+POS	35.45(+1.03)
.+PAHE	86.57(+0.05)	.+Negation	66.68(+0.49)	.+Emoticon	**36.03**(+0.58)
.+bigram	**86.65**(+0.08)	.+PAHE	**66.81**(+0.13)	.+Negation	34.94(-1.09)
.+POS	86.53(-0.12)	.+Emoticon	66.76(-0.05)	-	-
.+Emoticon	86.50(-0.03)	.+bigram	66.21(-0.55)	-	-

Table 2: Results of feature selection experiments for subtask A, B and C in terms of F_{macro} on the training data. The numbers in the brackets are the performance increments compared with the previous results. *PAHE* stands for Punctuation&All-caps&Hashtag&Enlongated features. ".+" means to add current feature to the previous feature set.

mented in *scikit-learn* tools (Pedregosa et al., 2011) (e.g., SVM with *kernel*={*linear, rbf*}, *c=0.1 ,1 ,10*, SGD with *loss*={*hinge, log*}, RandomForestClassifier with *n*={*10, 50, 100*}, etc). Table 4 shows the configuration of classifiers with best performance. Thus, in subsequential experiments, we adopted the configurations listed in Table 4.

Task	Features	Configuration
Subtask A	traditional	SVM, kernel=linear,c=0.1
	word embedding	SVM, kernel=rbf,c=0.1
Subtask B	traditional	SVM, kernel=linear,c=0.1
	word embedding	SVM, kernel=rbf,c=0.1

Table 4: System configurations for subtask A and B.

3.2.2 Subtask C and D

Table 2 lists the experimental results using several traditional features on subtask C. Since the sentiment trend of given topic in subtask D is calculated from the results of subtask C (i.e., $sentiment\ trend = positive/(positive + negative)$), we have not conducted additional experiments for subtask D.

Similar with the first two subtasks, we adopted the SVM classification algorithm with *kernel=linear, c=0.1* as system configurations for follow-up experiments.

3.2.3 Subtask E

We transformed the informal terms to their normal forms and used the sentiment lexicons mentioned in Section 2.2 except *MPQA* to extract sentiment lexicon feature. If the target term contained more than one word, we averaged their scores as its final sentiment lexicon feature. Besides, the word embedding features were also adopted in this subtask.

To explore the effectiveness of different feature types, we conducted several feature combination experiments shown in Table 5.

Features	Kendall Rank	Spearman Rank
SentiLexi	48.24%	66.17%
Word embedding	52.97%	70.90%
SentiLexi + Word embedding	56.73%	75.56%

Table 5: Results of feature section experiments for subtask E on training data.

From Table 5, we find that: (1) The combination of SentiLexi and word embedding is the most effective feature type for sentiment score prediction; (2) The word embedding features achieved better result than SentiLexi features about 4.7% improvement in terms of Kendall measure, which indicates that word embedding feature preserves the sentiment information and semantic relationship between words.

We also performed a series of experiments to optimize the parameters of SVM classifiers. Similarly, we found that SVM classifier with *kernel=linear* and *c=1* obtained the best performance. Thus, in following experiments on test data, we adopted this configuration with SentiLexi and word embedding features together.

3.3 Results on Test Data

Using the optimum feature set and configurations described in Section 3.2, we trained separate models for each subtasks and evaluated them against the SemEval-2015 Task 10 test set.

Table 6 shows the results of our systems and the top-ranked systems on subtask A, B, C and D. From

Subtask	Systems	LiveJournal	SMS2013	Twitter2013	Twitter2014	Twitter2014S	Offical2015	Twitter2015
	ECNU	82.49(6)	84.70(4)	85.28(4)	82.09(7)	70.96(7)	81.08(7)	-
A	unitn	84.46(2)	88.60(2)	90.10(1)	87.12(1)	73.65(3)	84.79(1)	-
	KLUEless	83.94(4)	88.62(2)	88.56(2)	84.99(3)	75.59(3)	84.51(2)	-
	ECNU	74.40(3)	68.49(1)	65.25(22)	66.37(20)	45.87(24)	59.72(19)	-
B	Webis	71.64(14)	63.92(14)	68.49(10)	70.86(6)	49.33(11)	64.84(1)	-
	unitn	72.48(12)	68.37(2)	72.79(3)	73.60(2)	55.44(4)	64.59(2)	-
	ECNU	-	-	-	-	-	-	25.38(5)/0.300(5)
C/D	TwitterHawk	-	-	-	-	-	-	50.51(1)/0.214(3)
	KLUEless	-	-	-	-	-	-	45.48(2)/0.202(1)

Table 6: Performances of our systems and top-ranked systems for subtask A, B, C ($F_{macro}(\%)$) and D (*avgAbsDiff*) on test data. The numbers in the brackets are the rankings on corresponding data set.

the Table 6, we observe the following findings.

Firstly, in accordance with previous work (Rosenthal et al., 2014), the results of subtask B is much worse than those of subtask A. On one hand, the text in message-level task is long and contains multiple/mixed sentiments with different strength and the text in expression-level usually contain a single sentiment orientation. On the other hand, the polarity distributions of subtask A and B are significantly different (i.e., about 6.14% instances in expression-level are neutral while 41.30% in message-level).

Secondly, the performances on LiveJournal and SMS are comparable to the results on Twitter2013 and Twitter2014 in both subtasks, which means the Twitter, SMS and LiveJournal have similar characteristics and then we may consider to use SMS as training data when the available tweet data is insufficient.

Thirdly, the submissions of subtask C and D only adopted traditional linguistic features rather than the combination of word embeddings, which may result in the poor performance in subtask C and D.

Our systems ranked $7th$ out of 11 submissions for subtask A, $19th$ out of 40 submissions for subtask B and performed well on LiveJournal and SMS2013 data sets. For subtask C and D, our systems ranked $5th$ out of 7 submissions and $5th$ out of 6 submissions respectively.

Team ID	Kendall Rank	Spearman Rank
ECNU	59.07%(3)	78.61%(3)
INESC-ID	62.51%(1)	81.72%(2)
lsislif	62.11%(2)	82.02%(1)

Table 7: Performances of our systems and the top-ranked systems for subtask E. The numbers in the brackets are the official ranking.

Table 7 shows the results of our system and the top ranked system provided by organizer for subtask E. Our system ranked 3rd out of 10 submissions. Although the word embedding features obtained from large amount of contexts are believed to contain semantic information, they contain sentiment information more or less induced from context. As a consequence, with the aid of sentiment lexicon and word embedding, our system is promising.

4 Conclusion

In this paper, we combined the results of two classifiers (adopting traditional features and word embedding features respectively) to detect the sentiment polarity towards expression-level and message-level (i.e., subtask A, B), adopted several basic feature types to settle topic-level task (i.e., subtask C, D) and built regression model with the aid of sentiment lexicon features and word embedding features to predict degree of polarity strength on term-level (i.e., subtask E). Using word embedding features alone may not perform good results, but it makes contribution to performance improvement in combination with traditional linguistic features. In future work, we consider to construct the word representations bearing sentiment information to address sentiment analysis.

5 Acknowledgements

This research is supported by grants from Science and Technology Commission of Shanghai Municipality under research grant no. (14DZ2260800 and 15ZR1410700) and Shanghai Collaborative Innovation Center of Trustworthy Software for Internet of Things (ZF1213).

References

Lu Chen, Wenbo Wang, Meenakshi Nagarajan, Shaojun Wang, and Amit P Sheth. 2012. Extracting diverse sentiment expressions with target-dependent polarity from Twitter. In *ICWSM*.

Cícero Nogueira dos Santos and Maíra Gatti. 2014. Deep convolutional neural networks for sentiment analysis of short texts. In *Proceedings of the 25th International Conference on Computational Linguistics (COLING), Dublin, Ireland*.

Stefan Evert, Thomas Proisl, Paul Greiner, and Besim K-abashi. 2014. SentiKLUE: Updating a polarity classifier in 48 hours. *SemEval 2014*, page 551.

Long Jiang, Mo Yu, Ming Zhou, Xiaohua Liu, and Tiejun Zhao. 2011. Target-dependent Twitter sentiment classification. In *Proceedings of the 49th Annual Meeting of the Association for Computational Linguistics: Human Language Technologies-Volume 1*, pages 151–160.

Soo-Min Kim and Eduard Hovy. 2004. Determining the sentiment of opinions. In *Proceedings of the 20th international conference on Computational Linguistics*, page 1367.

Yoon Kim. 2014. Convolutional neural networks for sentence classification. *arXiv preprint arXiv:1408.5882*.

Svetlana Kiritchenko, Xiaodan Zhu, Colin Cherry, and Saif Mohammad. 2014. NRC-Canada-2014: Detecting aspects and sentiment in customer reviews. pages 437–442, August.

Efthymios Kouloumpis, Theresa Wilson, and Johanna Moore. 2011. Twitter sentiment analysis: The good the bad and the omg! *ICWSM*, 11:538–541.

Tomas Mikolov, Kai Chen, Greg Corrado, and Jeffrey Dean. 2013a. Efficient estimation of word representations in vector space. *arXiv preprint arXiv:1301.3781*.

Tomas Mikolov, Ilya Sutskever, Kai Chen, Greg S Corrado, and Jeff Dean. 2013b. Distributed representations of words and phrases and their compositionality. In *Advances in Neural Information Processing Systems*, pages 3111–3119.

Saif Mohammad, Svetlana Kiritchenko, and Xiaodan Zhu. 2013. NRC-Canada: Building the state-of-the-art in sentiment analysis of tweets. In *Second Joint Conference on Lexical and Computational Semantics (*SEM), Volume 2: Proceedings of the Seventh International Workshop on Semantic Evaluation (SemEval 2013)*, pages 321–327, Atlanta, Georgia, USA, June.

Preslav Nakov, Sara Rosenthal, Zornitsa Kozareva, Veselin Stoyanov, Alan Ritter, and Theresa Wilson. 2013. SemEval-2013 Task 2: Sentiment analysis in Twitter. In *Second Joint Conference on Lexical and Computational Semantics (*SEM), Volume 2: Proceedings of the Seventh International Workshop on Semantic Evaluation (SemEval 2013)*, pages 312–320, Atlanta, Georgia, USA, June.

Olutobi Owoputi, Brendan O'Connor, Chris Dyer, Kevin Gimpel, Nathan Schneider, and Noah A Smith. 2013. Improved part-of-speech tagging for online conversational text with word clusters. In *HLT-NAACL*, pages 380–390.

Fabian Pedregosa, Gaël Varoquaux, Alexandre Gramfort, Vincent Michel, Bertrand Thirion, Olivier Grisel, Mathieu Blondel, Peter Prettenhofer, Ron Weiss, Vincent Dubourg, et al. 2011. Scikit-learn: Machine learning in Python. *The Journal of Machine Learning Research*, 12:2825–2830.

Sara Rosenthal, Preslav Nakov, Alan Ritter, and Veselin Stoyanov. 2014. Semeval-2014 task 9: Sentiment analysis in Twitter. *Proc. SemEval*, pages 73–80.

Sara Rosenthal, Preslav Nakov, Svetlana Kiritchenko, Saif M Mohammad, Alan Ritter, and Veselin Stoyanov. 2015. SemEval-2015 Task 10: Sentiment analysis in Twitter. In *Proceedings of the 9th International Workshop on Semantic Evaluation*, SemEval '2015, Denver, Colorado, June.

Xiaolong Wang, Furu Wei, Xiaohua Liu, Ming Zhou, and Ming Zhang. 2011. Topic sentiment analysis in Twitter: a graph-based hashtag sentiment classification approach. In *Proceedings of the 20th ACM international conference on Information and knowledge management*, pages 1031–1040.

Sabih Bin Wasi, Rukhsar Neyaz, Houda Bouamor, and Behrang Mohit. 2014. CMUQ@ Qatar: Using rich lexical features for sentiment analysis on Twitter. *SemEval 2014*, page 186.

Hong Yu and Vasileios Hatzivassiloglou. 2003. Towards answering opinion questions: Separating facts from opinions and identifying the polarity of opinion sentences. In *Proceedings of the 2003 conference on Empirical methods in natural language processing*, pages 129–136.

Daojian Zeng, Kang Liu, Siwei Lai, Guangyou Zhou, and Jun Zhao. 2014. Relation classification via convolutional deep neural network. In *Proceedings of COLING*, pages 2335–2344.

Jiang Zhao, Man Lan, and Tian Tian Zhu. 2014. ECNU: Expression-and message-level sentiment orientation classification in Twitter using multiple effective features. *SemEval 2014*, page 259.

Lsislif: Feature Extraction and Label Weighting for Sentiment Analysis in Twitter

Hussam Hamdan
Aix-Marseille University
hussam.hamdan@lsis.org

Patrice Bellot
Aix-Marseille University
patrice.bellot@lsis.org

Frederic Bechet
Aix-Marseille University
frederic.bechet@lif.univ-mrs.fr

Abstract

This paper describes our sentiment analysis systems which have been built for SemEval-2015 Task 10 Subtask B and E. For subtask B, a Logistic Regression classifier has been trained after extracting several groups of features including lexical, syntactic, lexicon-based, Z score and semantic features. A weighting schema has been adapted for positive and negative labels in order to take into account the unbalanced distribution of tweets between the positive and negative classes. This system is ranked third over 40 participants, it achieves average F1 64.27 on Twitter data set 2015 just 0.57% less than the first system. We also present our participation in Subtask E in which our system has got the second rank with Kendall metric but the first one with Spearman for ranking twitter terms according to their association with the positive sentiment.

1 Introduction

Twitter is one of the most social media platforms which allows the users to express their opinions and feelings towards different issues. The users have become an important source of content. This content may be interesting to analyze for those who are interested in understanding user's interests such as buyers, sellers and producers.

Sentiment Analysis can be done in different levels; Document level; Sentence level; Clause level or Aspect-Based level. SA in Twitter can be seen as sentence level task, but some limitations should be considered in such sentences. The size of tweet is limited to 140 characters, informal language, emotion icons and non-standard expressions are very used, and many spelling errors can be find due to the absence of correctness verification.
Three different approaches can be identified in the literature of Sentiment Analysis in Twitter, the first approach is a lexicon based which uses specific types of lexicons to derive the polarity of a text, this approach suffers from the limited size of lexicon and requires human expertise to build manual lexicons, in the other hand the automatic lexicons needs labeled data. The second approach is machine learning one which uses annotated texts with given labels to learn a classifying model. Both lexicon and machine learning approaches can be combined to achieve a better performance. These two approaches are used for SA task but the third one is specific for Twitter or social content, the social approach exploits social network properties and data for enhancing the accuracy of the classification.

In this paper, we present our supervised system which adapts a logistic regression classifier with several groups of features and weighting schema for positive and negative labels. The features are grouped into 5 groups: word n-gram, lexicon-based, negation, Z score and semantic features. We also describe our system used for ranking terms according to their positivity, in which we derive the term polarity score from different lexicons.

The rest of this paper is organized as follows. Section 2 outlines existing work of sentiment analysis in Twitter. Section 3 describes the data and resources. The features we used for training the classifier presented in Section 4. Our experiments are described in section 5, our participation in subtask E is described in section 6 and future work is presented in section 7.

2 Related Work

Three main approaches for sentiment analysis can be identified in Twitter. The lexicon based approach which depends on sentiment lexicons containing positive, negative and neutral words or expressions; the polarity is computed according to the number of common opinionated words between the lexicons and the text. Many dictionaries have been created manually such as MPQA Lexicon (Wilson et al., 2005) or automatically such as SentiWordNet (Baccianella et al., 2010).

Machine learning approach adapts different classifiers and features. Naive Bayes, Maximum Entropy MaxEnt and Support Vector Machines (SVM) were adapted in (Go et al., 2009) in which the authors reported that SVM outperforms other classifiers. They tried a unigram and a bi-gram model in conjunction with parts-of-speech (POS) features; they noted that the unigram model outperforms all other models when using SVM and that POS features decrease the results. Authors in (Hamdan et al., 4 29) used the concepts extracted from DBPedia and the adjectives from WordNet, they reported that the DBpedia concepts are useful with Nave-Bayes classifier but less useful with SVM. Many features were used with SVM including the lexicon-based features in (Mohammad et al., 2013) which seem to get the most gain in performance. Another work has also proved the importance of lexicon-based features with logistic regression classifier (Miura et al., 4 08; Hamdan et al., 2015a; Hamdan et al., 2015b).

The third main approach takes into account the influence of users on their followers and the relation between the users and the tweets they wrote. It assumes that using the Twitter follower graph might improve the polarity classification. In (Speriosu et al., 2011) authors demonstrated that using label propagation with Twitter follower graph improves the polarity classification. In (Tan et al., 2011) authors employed social relation for user-level sentiment analysis. In (Hu et al., 2013) a Sociological Approach to handling the Noisy and short Text (SANT) for supervised sentiment classification is used; they reported that social theories such as Sentiment Consistency and Emotional Contagion could be helpful for sentiment analysis.

3 Data and Resources

3.1 Labeled Data

We used the data set provided in SemEval 2013 for subtask B of sentiment analysis in Twitter (Nakov et al., 2013). The participants have been provided with training tweets annotated positive, negative or neutral. We downloaded these tweets using the given script. We obtained 9646 tweets, the whole training data set is used for training, the provided development set containing 1654 tweets is used for tuning the machine learner. The test data set 2015 contains about 2390 tweets (Rosenthal et al., 5 06). Table 1 shows the distribution of each label in each data set.

Twitter	all	neg.	pos.	neut.
train	9684	1458	3640	4586
dev	1654	340	739	575
test-2015	2390	365	1038	987

Table1. Sentiment labels distribution in the training and development, test data sets.

3.2 Sentiment Lexicons

The system exploits two types of sentiment lexicons: manual constructed lexicons and automatic ones. The manual ones are the Bing Lius Opinion Lexicon which is created in (Hu and Liu, 2004) and augmented in many research papers; and MPQA subjectivity lexicons (Wilson et al., 2005). Both lexicons contain English words annotated positive and negative. While the automatic lexicons are NRC Hashtag Sentiment Lexicon (Mohammad, 6 07), Sentiment140 Lexicon (Mohammad et al., 2013), and SentiWordNet (Baccianella et al., 2010). NRC Hashtag Sentiment Lexicon and Sentiment140 Lexicon contain tweet terms with scores, positive score indicates association with positive sentiment, whereas negative score indicates association with negative sentiment. NRC has entries for 54,129 unigrams and 316,531 bigrams; Sentiment140 has entries for 62,468 unigrams, 677,698 bigrams. SentiWordNet is the result of automatically annotating all WORDNET synsets according to their degrees of positivity, negativity, and neutrality.

3.3 Twitter Dictionary

We constructed a dictionary for the abbreviations and the slang words used in Twitter in order to overcome the ambiguity of the these terms. This dictionary maps certain twitter expressions and emotion icons by their meaning or their corresponding sentiment (e.g. gr8 replaced by great, :) replaced by very-happy).

4 Feature Extraction

4.1 Word ngrams

unigram and bigram are extracted for each word in text without any stemming or stop-word removing, all terms with occurrence less than 3 are removed from the feature space.

4.2 Negation Features

The rule-based algorithm presented in Christopher Potts Sentiment Symposium Tutorial is implemented. This algorithm appends a negation suffix to all words that appear within a negation scope which is determined by the negation key and a punctuation. All these words have been added to the feature space.

4.3 Twitter dictionary

All terms presented in a text and in the twitter dictionary presented in 3.3 are mapped to their corresponding terms in the dictionary and added to the feature space.

4.4 Sentiment Lexicons

The system extracts four features from the manual constructed lexicons and six features from the automatic ones. For each sentence the number of positive words, the number of negative ones, the number of positive words divided by the number of negative ones and the polarity of the last word are extracted from manual constructed lexicons. In addition to the sum of the positive scores and the sum of the negative scores from the automatic constructed lexicons.

4.5 Z score

Z score can distinguish the importance of each term in each class, their performances have been proved in (Hamdan et al., 2014). We assume as in the mentioned work that the term frequencies are following a multi-nomial distribution. Thus, Z score can be seen as a standardization of the term frequency using multi-nomial distribution. We compute the Z score for each term ti in a class C_j (t_{ij}) by calculating its term relative frequency tfr_{ij} in a particular class C_j, as well as the mean ($mean_i$) which is the term probability over the whole corpus multiplied by the number of terms in the class C_j, and standard deviation (sd_i) of term ti according to the underlying corpus. Like in (Hamdan et al., 4 29) we tested different thresholds for choosing the words which have higher Z score.

$$Zscore(ti) = \frac{tfr_{ij} - mean_i}{sd_i} \quad (1)$$

Thus, we added the number of words having Z score higher than the threshold in each class positive,negative and neutral, the two classes which have the maximum number and minimum number of words having Z score higher than the threshold. These 5 features have been added to the feature space.

4.6 Semantic Features

The semantic representation of a text may bring some important hidden information, which may result in a better text representation and a better classification system.

4.6.1 Brown Dictionary Features

Each word in the text is mapped to its cluster in Brown, 1000 features are added to feature space where each feature represents the number of words in the text mapped to each cluster. The 1000 clusters is provided in Twitter Word Clusters of CMU ARK group. 1000 clusters were constructed from approximately 56 million tweets.

4.6.2 Topic features

Latent dirichlet association or topic modeling is used to extract 10 features. Lda-c is configured with 10 topics and the training data is used for training the model, then for each sentence in the test set, the trained model estimates the number of words assigned to each topic.

4.6.3 Semantic Role Labeling Features

Authors in (Ruppenhofer and Rehbein, 2012) encode semantic role labeling features in SVM classifier. Our system also extract two types of features, the names: the whole term which represents an argument of the predicate and the tags: the type of each argument in the text (A0 represents the subject of predicate, A1 the object, AM-TMP the time, AM-ADV the situation, AM-loc the location). These encodings are defined by the tool which we used (Senna). We think that the predicate arguments can constitute a multi-word expression which may be helpful in Sentiment Classification.

5 Experiments

5.1 Experiment Setup

We trained the L1-regularized Logistic regression classifier implemented in LIBLINEAR (Fan et al., 2008). The classifier is trained on the training data set using the features of Section 4 with the three polarities (positive, negative, and neutral) as labels. A weighting schema is adapted for each class, we use the weighting option $-w_i$ which enables a use of different cost parameter C for different classes. Since the training data is unbalanced, this weighting schema adjusts the probability of each label. Thus, we tuned the classifier in adjusting the cost parameter C of Logistic Regression, weight wpos of positive class and weight Wneg of negative class. We used the development set for tuning the three parameters, all combinations of C in range 0.1 to to 4 by step 0.1, w_{pos} in range 1 to 8 by step 0.1, w_{neg} in range 1 to 8 by step 0.1 are tested. The combination C=0.2, w_{pos}=5.2, w_{neg}=4.2 have given the best F1 score for the development set and therefore it was selected for our submission.

5.2 Results

The evaluation score used by the task organizers was the averaged F1-score of the positive and negative classes. In the SemEval-2015 competition, our submission is ranked third (64.27) over 40 submissions, just 0.57% less than the first system.

Table 2 shows the results of our experiments after removing a feature group at each run for the three test sets 2013, 2014, and 2015. For the test set 2015, we note that using Z score feature provides a gain of 0.45%, n-gram provides a gain of 0.28%, lexicon features gain is about 3.31%, LDA gain is 0.8%, Brown clusters 0.44%, semantic role labeling decreases the F1 score by 0.83%. The most influential features is the sentiment lexicon features; they provided gains of 3.31%.

Because of negative effect of semantic role labeling features, we have done another analysis in order to estimate if these features are useful or not, the fact that the combination of features makes some of them not influential are not sufficient to consider the features not useful. Thus, we repeat the same classification process but add one feature group at a time (Tabel 3). Z score seems to give gain of 1.91%, LDA topics gain is 0.66%, semantic role labeling 0.64%, brown clusters 3.38% and sentiment lexicons 6.58%. The most influential features is also the sentiment lexicon features. Brown cluster features obtains an interesting gain of 3.38%. From the previous two analysis, we find that sentiment lexicon features are the most influential ones as concluded by (S. M. Mohammad et al., 2013). Some features have improved the performance in test set 2015 but not in the other test sets such as Z score, Semantic Role Labeling.

Run	Test-2015	Test-2014	Test-2013
All features	64.27	71.54	71.34
all-zscore	63.82	73.05	69.99
all-lexicons	60.96	67.6	66.63
all-ngram	63.99	69.06	69.67
all-srl	65.1	71.81	70.41
all-topics	63.47	71.49	71
all-brown	63.82	70.74	69.9

Table2. The F1 score for each run, All features run exploits all features while the others remove a feature group at each run Zscore, lexicons, n-gram, srl, topics and brown cluster, respectively.

Run	Test-2015	Test-2014	Test-2013
bl	57.47	66.71	66.25
bl+lexicon	64.05	70.57	69.31
bl+zscore	59.38	63.47	65.28
bl+brown	60.85	66.71	66.25
bl+topics	58.13	-	-
bl+srl	58.13	66.69	63.35

Table3. The F1 score for each run, bl run exploits the n-gram, negation, twitter dictionary features

while the other runs add to bl one feature group at each run, lexicon, Zscore, brown, topics, slr features have been respectively added.

6 SubTask E: determining strength of association of Twitter terms with positive sentiment

This subtask is new in SemEval-2015, the objective is to provide for each Twitter term a score between 0 and 1 that is indicative of its strength of association with positive sentiment. If a word is more positive than another, then it should have a higher score than the other. Participants are provided with 200 terms with their scores as a trail data. The test data includes 1315 terms to rank. The organizers have chosen Kendall's Tau correlation coefficient to compare the ranked lists, they have also provided the scores of Spearman's Rank Correlation, but participating teams will be ranked according to Kendall's Tau.

To rank these terms, we have used six different sentiment lexicons for computing the score for each twitter term. Four of them are described in section 3.2 (manaul lexicons: Bing Liu and MPQA Subjectivity Lexicon , automatic constructed lexicons: NRC Hashtag and Sentiment140) and we have built two other automatic construction lexicons: the first named PMi-Sem from the training tweets provided by SemEval-2013 sub-task B Table 1, the second named PMI-sentiment140 from the sentiment140 corpus (Go et al., 2009), we calculated PMI from the labeled tweets for the two corpus using the following equation:

$$PMI(word, positive) = log\frac{p(positive, word)}{p(positive).p(word)} \quad (2)$$

where p(positive,word): The joint probability of the positive class and the word. p(positive): the probability of positive class. p(word): the probability of the word in whole corpus.

6.1 Score computing

If the word exists in a manual constructed lexicon (two lexicons), a score of 1 is assigned if the word is positive else -1 if negative. If the word exists in an automatic constructed lexicon (four lexicons), the lexicon score of the word is used. For each lexicon which does not have the word a default score is assigned, this default score is chosen to be 1/(number of the words in the test set). the final score is the average score of the previous six scores.

Run	Kendall	Spearman
all	0.621	0.820
all-BingLiu	0.616	0.816
all-MPQA	0.616	0.815
all-NRC Hashtag	0.510	0.689
all-Sentiment140	0.617	0.813
all-PMI-Sem	0.620	0.822
all-PMI-sentiment140	0.621	0.821

Table4. The results of Twitter term ranking, the first run *all* exploits all six lexicons, one lexicon is removed in the following runs.

The test data set contains 1315 twitter terms. Our system is ranked second with Kendall 0.004% less than the first ranked system, but first with Spearman. Table 4 shows our results with the two evaluation metrics. We repeat the experiment after removing one lexicon at each run, we can note that NRC Hashtag is the most influential lexicon.

7 Conclusion and Future Work

In this paper, we tested the impact of combining several groups of features on the sentiment classification of tweets. A logistic regression classifier with weighting schema is used, the sentiment lexicon-based features seem to get the most influential effect with the combination.
We have also exploited four existing lexicons and constructed two other lexicons using PMI metric in order to rank the twitter terms according to their association with positive sentiment.
As the sentiment lexicon-based features have proved their performance, future work will focus on the automatic lexicon construction on testing several metrics like Z score which we think promising in measuring the association between each term and sentiment labels.

References

Baccianella, S., Esuli, A., and Sebastiani, F. (2010). SentiWordNet 3.0: An enhanced lexical resource for sentiment analysis and opinion mining. In *in Proc. of LREC*.

Fan, R.-E., Chang, K.-W., Hsieh, C.-J., Wang, X.-R., and Lin, C.-J. (2008). LIBLINEAR: A library for large linear classification. 9:1871–1874.

Go, A., Bhayani, R., and Huang, L. (2009). Twitter sentiment classification using distant supervision. pages 1–6.

Hamdan, H., Bechet, F., and Bellot, P. (2013-04-29). Experiments with DBpedia, WordNet and SentiWordNet as resources for sentiment analysis in micro-blogging. In *International Workshop on Semantic Evaluation SemEval-2013 (NAACL Workshop)*.

Hamdan, H., Bellot, P., and Bechet, F. (2014). The impact of z_score on twitter sentiment analysis. In *In Proceedings of the Eighth International Workshop on Semantic Evaluation (SemEval 2014)*, page 636.

Hamdan, H., Bellot, P., and Bechet, F. (2015a). lsislif: Feature extraction and label weighting for sentiment analysis in twitter. In *In Proceedings of the 9th International Workshop on Semantic Evaluation (SemEval 2015)*.

Hamdan, H., Bellot, P., and Bechet, F. (2015b). Sentiment lexicon-based features for sentiment analysis in short text. In *In Proceeding of the 16th International Conference on Intelligent Text Processing and Computational Linguistics*.

Hu, M. and Liu, B. (2004). Mining and summarizing customer reviews. In *Proceedings of the Tenth ACM SIGKDD International Conference on Knowledge Discovery and Data Mining*, KDD '04, pages 168–177. ACM.

Hu, X., Tang, L., Tang, J., and Liu, H. (2013). Exploiting social relations for sentiment analysis in microblogging. In *Proceedings of the Sixth ACM International Conference on Web Search and Data Mining*, WSDM '13, pages 537–546. ACM.

Miura, Y., Sakaki, S., Hattori, K., and Ohkuma, T. (2014-08). TeamX: A sentiment analyzer with enhanced lexicon mapping and weighting scheme for unbalanced data. In *Proceedings of the 8th International Workshop on Semantic Evaluation (SemEval 2014)*, pages 628–632. Association for Computational Linguistics and Dublin City University.

Mohammad, S. (2012-06-07). #emotional tweets. In **SEM 2012: The First Joint Conference on Lexical and Computational Semantics Volume 1: Proceedings of the main conference and the shared task, and Volume 2: Proceedings of the Sixth International Workshop on Semantic Evaluation (SemEval 2012)*, pages 246–255. Association for Computational Linguistics.

Mohammad, S. M., Kiritchenko, S., and Zhu, X. (2013). NRCCanada: Building the state-of-the-art in sentiment analysis of tweets. In *In Proceedings of the International Workshop on Semantic Evaluation, SemEval 13*.

Nakov, P., Rosenthal, S., Kozareva, Z., Stoyanov, V., Ritter, A., and Wilson, T. (2013). SemEval-2013 task 2: Sentiment analysis in twitter. In *Second Joint Conference on Lexical and Computational Semantics (*SEM), Volume 2: Proceedings of the Seventh International Workshop on Semantic Evaluation (SemEval 2013)*, pages 312–320. Association for Computational Linguistics.

Rosenthal, S., Nakov, P., Kiritchenko, S., Mohammad, S. M., Ritter, A., and Stoyanov, V. (2015-06). SemEval-2015 task 10: Sentiment analysis in twitter. In *Proceedings of the 9th International Workshop on Semantic Evaluation*, SemEval '2015. Association for Computational Linguistics.

Ruppenhofer, J. and Rehbein, I. (2012). Semantic frames as an anchor representation for sentiment analysis. In *Proceedings of the 3rd Workshop in Computational Approaches to Subjectivity and Sentiment Analysis*, pages 104–109. Association for Computational Linguistics.

Speriosu, M., Sudan, N., Upadhyay, S., and Baldridge, J. (2011). Twitter polarity classification with label propagation over lexical links and the follower graph. In *Proceedings of the First Workshop on Unsupervised Learning in NLP*, EMNLP '11, pages 53–63. Association for Computational Linguistics.

Tan, C., Lee, L., Tang, J., Jiang, L., Zhou, M., and Li, P. (2011). User-level sentiment analysis incorporating social networks. In *Proceedings of the 17th ACM SIGKDD International Conference on Knowledge Discovery and Data Mining*, KDD '11, pages 1397–1405. ACM.

Wilson, T., Hoffmann, P., Somasundaran, S., Kessler, J., Wiebe, J., Choi, Y., Cardie, C., Riloff, E., and Patwardhan, S. (2005). OpinionFinder: A system for subjectivity analysis. In *Proceedings of HLT/EMNLP on Interactive Demonstrations*, HLT-Demo '05, pages 34–35. Association for Computational Linguistics.

ELiRF: A Support Vector Machine Approach for Sentiment Analysis Tasks in Twitter at SemEval-2015

Mayte Giménez Ferran Pla Lluís-F. Hurtado
Universitat Politècnica de València
Camí de Vera s/n, 46022 València
{mgimenez, fpla, lhurtado}@dsic.upv.es

Abstract

This paper describes our participation at tasks 10 (sub-task B, Message Polarity Classification) and 11 task (Sentiment Analysis of Figurative Language in Twitter) of Semeval2015. We describe the Support Vector Machine system we used in this competition. We also present the relevant feature set that we take into account in our models. Finally, we show the results we obtained in this competition and some conclusions.

1 Introduction

Nowadays social media, such as Twitter, produce a vast amount of information that lead us to new challenges in Machine Learning (ML) and in Natural Language Processing (NLP) fields.
Twitter [1] is a micro-blogging service, which according to latest statistics, has 284 million active users, 77 % outside the US that generate 500 million tweets a day in 35 different languages. That means 5,700 tweets per second and they had peaks of activity of 43,000 per second. This numbers justify the great interest in the automatic processing of this information.
The study (Analytics, 2009) estimates that 50.9% of tweets have some useful information that are capable of mobilize opinions in Internet and also in the real world. Therefore, social media users opinions have great strategic value for different organizations.

Our work is focused on automatically identify the prevailing sentiment in a tweet using ML and NLP techniques. We developed a system for determining the tweets polarity for 10B and 11 tasks at the SemEval-2015 competition.
The aim of task 10 (subtask B) (Rosenthal et al., 2015) is to classify tweets among positive, negative, and neutral polarity. In task 11 (Ghosh et al., 2015) we had to deal with figurative language, and we should assign a polarity to each tweet with a score that vary in the range [-5..5], this score represents the degree of the sentiment. Due to this last requirement, we formalized this task as a regression problem.
Our approach shared some points for solving both tasks. Preprocessing and feature extraction processes from the corpora were similar. We considered some common problems when we are dealing with text from social media and in particular from Twitter: short texts, slang, peculiarities of the language (*hashtags*, *retweets*, *user mentions*, etc.). We represented features extracted using a bag of n-grams. We used Support Vector Machine (SVM) formalism due to the fact to its ability to handle large feature space and to determine the relevant features.
Task 10B has been considered as a classification problem and it has been modeled by means of SVM classifiers. For Task 11 we used regression SVM, due to the granularity of the scores.
Both tasks were solved using a supervised technique. Our systems learned from the training set supplied by the Semeval organization. We also used external resources such as polarity dictionaries.
The rest of this paper is organized as follows. In section 2, we briefly present some relevant works related to these tasks. In section 3, we describe

[1] About twitter,inc. https://about.twitter.com/company. Accessed: 30-12-2014.

the main features of the used corpora. In section 4, we present the system we developed to solve these tasks. Section 5 is dedicated to show the results of our experimental work and the results we obtained for the SemEval tasks. Finally, in section 6, we will share some conclusions from our work and possible future directions.

2 Related Work

Sentiment Analysis has been widely studied in the last decade in multiple domains. Most work focuses on classifying the polarity of the texts as positive, negative, mixed, or neutral. The pioneering works in this field used supervised (Pang et al., 2002) or unsupervised (knowledge-based) (Turney, 2002) approaches. In (Pang et al., 2002), the performance of different classifiers on movie reviews was evaluated. In (Turney, 2002), some patterns containing POS information were used to identify subjective sentences in reviews to then estimate their semantic orientation.

In (Pang and Lee, 2008) we can find a comprehensive study of the different techniques used to identify the polarity of a text.

Many efforts have been made to transfer this knowledge to language extracted from social media. In the literature we can find recent attempts to solve this problem using different machine learning approaches such as, SVM, Maximum Entropy, Naive Bayes, etc, (Barbosa and Feng, 2010; O'Connor et al., 2010a; Zhu et al., 2014). At best, these works achieve F1-score close to 70%, therefore we still could improve these proposed systems.

The construction of polarity lexicons is another widely explored field of research. Opinion lexicons have been obtained for English (Liu et al., 2005; Wilson et al., 2005) and also for Spanish (Perez-Rosas et al., 2012). A good presentation of the SA problem and a description of the state-of-the-art of the more relevant approaches to SA can be found in (Liu, 2012).

Research works about SA on Twitter are much more recent. Twitter appeared in the year 2006 and the early works in this field are from 2009 when Twitter started to achieve popularity. Some of the most significant works are (Barbosa and Feng, 2010), (Jansen et al., 2009), and (O'Connor et al., 2010b). A survey of the most relevant approaches to SA on Twitter can be see in (Vinodhini and Chandrasekaran, 2012). The SemEval competition has also dedicated specific tasks for SA on Twitter (Wilson et al., 2013; Rosenthal et al., 2014a,b) which shows the great interest of the scientific community in this field.

TASS workshop has proposed different tasks for SA focused on the Spanish language (Villena-Román and García-Morera, 2013) and (Villena-Román et al., 2014). In this paper, we have included some ideas that we have used in previous works in the context of some SA tasks at TASS competition for Spanish (Pla and Hurtado, 2013, 2014b,a)

3 Corpus Description

In the following section, we describe the main features of SemEval2015 corpora used in 10B and 11 tasks, respectively.

3.1 Task 10 B

The corpora supplied by the Semeval2015 organization is composed by 7,236 tweets for training, 1,242 tweets for tuning (development set) and 2,880 tweets for test-time development composed by part of the Semeval2013 corpora used in that edition (Nakov et al., 2013). The test corpora has an official test with 2,390 tweets and a progress test with 8,987 tweets.

Figure 1 plots the polarity distribution over these train, tuning and test-time development corpora. On average, 16.53% of the tweets are negatives, 45.75% are neutrals and 37.72% are positives. Vocabulary from training corpus has 25,973 words, development corpus has 6,700 words and test-time development corpus has 13,672 words after we deleted the *stop-words*. We found that 57.57% of the words from test-time development were never seen in training.

We studied the Zipf's distribution of the words from train, tune and test-time development corpora and we find out that words with less number of synsets, less ambiguity, appear with more frequency. We used this information in the normalization of the SentiWordNet Lexicon.

Since we used lexicons as a features for training our systems, it is important to know the percentage of words from corpus which appear in these lexicons.

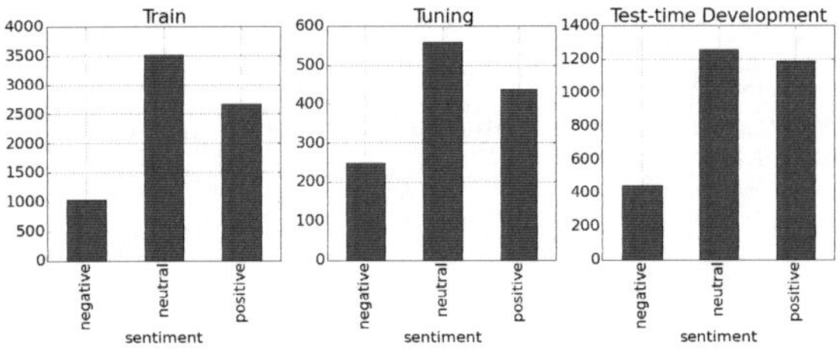

Figure 1: Polarity distribution studied over train, tune (dev) and test-time development corpora in Task 10.

Table 1 highlights how less than 10 % of the vocabulary from the corpus can be found in the lexicons; with the exception of the lexicons *NRC* and *SentiWordNet* (Baccianella et al., 2010) but in this lexicon we have to deal with the semantic ambiguity of the words.

Lexicon	Train	Test
Afinn	3.14 %	3.85 %
Pattern	4.28 %	5.21 %
SentiWordNet	45.21 %	51.26 %
Jeffrey	4.01 %	4.56 %
NRC	29.42 %	33.26 %

Table 1: Percentage of words from task 10's corpora with polarity using different lexicons in Task 10.

It is noteworthy that only 19.98% of training tweets and 20.31% of tweets from the test-time development set have *hashtags*. Users tag the content of their tweets with *hashtags*, consequently its meaning may be relevant when we try to classify a tweet. However *hashtags* often have multiple words together and segmentation of these words it is a problem in itself.

3.2 Task 11

The Task 11 corpus is similar to previous one, but its main feature is that it contains figurative language such as irony and affective metaphor. This kind of language will increase the complexity of the task. Also this task requires a much more fine grained polarity identification. Two corpora were provided to address this task.

- A trial corpus with 1,000 figurative tweets annotated. We were able to retrieve 925 tweets –86.6 % from total–.
- A train corpus with 8,000 tweets, of these we recover 6,928 tweets – 92.5 % from total–.

Trial and a train corpus share some tweets. We had 7,135 unique tweets to train and tune our systems. The corpus has 22,227 words without *stop words*.

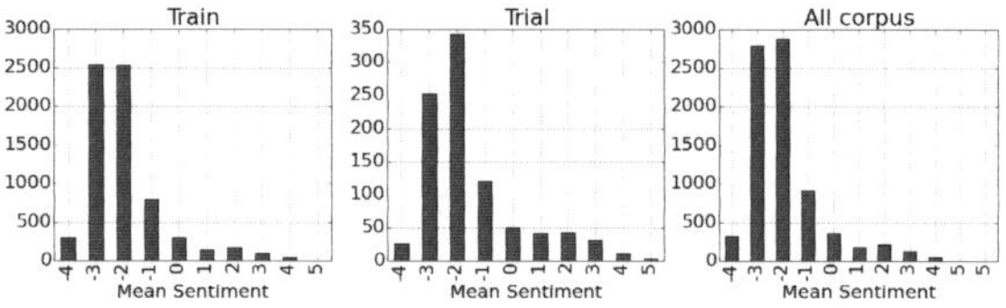

Figure 2: Polarity distribution in the development corpora in Task 11.

Table 2 shows the percentage of words from task 11 corpus we could find in the lexicons. Just like vocabulary from task 10, a small percentage of the vocabulary will have a polarity score.

Lexicon	Corpus
Afinn	5.75 %
Pattern	5.69 %
SentiWordNet	43.23 %
Jeffrey	5.64 %
NRC	38.09 %

Table 2: Percentage of words from task 11's corpora with polarity using different lexicons in Task 11.

As expected, the corpora for this task has a lot of figurative language. If we assume that Twitter's users tag semantically its tweets using *hashtags* and tags as #irony or #sarcasm indicates the presence of figurative text then at least 46.22 % of the corpus has figurative text. This was the only knowledge we add to deal with task 11 differently from the knowledge used in task 10. Finally, a remarkable 85.58% of tweets have at least one *hashtag*. Therefore these features will be relevant in our classification system.

4 Our System

In this section we describe the main features of the system developed for SemEval tasks We determined

the baseline for both tasks by selecting the most probable class in the training set. In task 10B we got a 26.49% of F1-score, a 43.61% of precision, and a 43.61 % of recall. In task 11 we got a 19.53% of F1-score, a 36.51 % of precision and a 36.51% of recall.
After studying the corpus, we train and tune different classifiers using features extracted from the text and from the lexicons. We did a 10-cross validation to tune the SVM models.

4.1 Feature Extraction

We selected the best set of features in order to solve each task. The best features considered were:

N-grams We used a *bag-of-words* approach to represent each tweet as a feature vector that contains the tf-idf factors of the selected features of the training set. After tokenizing the tweet and deleting its *stop words* we extract n-grams of characters. We have two approaches: we got all n-grams joining words or just n-grams within words. In task 10 we used 1-grams to 6-grams and we vectorized them using tf-idf coefficients. In task 11 we used the same approach but we used 3-grams to 9-grams.

Negation We need to deal with negation to predict polarity correctly. Thus, we label every word in a negation context. We assume that a *negation context* begins with a negation word as: "never", "no", "nothing", "none", ..., and ends with a punctuation mark, following the approach of (Pang et al., 2002). We used this strategy only in task 10. After labeling negation context, our system extracted the n-grams from labeled tweets.

Lexicons In order to use lexicons, tweets are tokenized, cleaned the *stop words* and all the tokens are converted to lowercase. We applied five lexicons.

1. *Pattern* (De Smedt and Daelemans, 2012): Given a tweet this lexicon will return a score with the polarity and another one with the objectivity.

2. *Afinn-111* (Hansen et al., 2011): This lexicon has a set of words tagged with a score. We sum the polarity of every word in a tweet to get a score for the whole tweet. $\sum_{w \in W} Afinn(w)$

3. *Jeffrey* (Hu and Liu, 2004): This lexicon has two sets of words: a positive and a negative word set. We got two scores from this lexicon. First score is the count of positive words and the second one is the count of negative words. $\sum_{w \in W} Jeffrey(w)$

4. *NRC* (Mohammad et al., 2013): Likewise, we obtain a score for each tweet adding the polarity of each word from this lexicon. Also we return a score normalized by the length of the tweet. $\frac{1}{|W|} \sum_{w \in W} NRC(w)$

5. *SentiWordNet* (Baccianella et al., 2010): In this lexicon each word could belong to multiple sets of meaning (*Synsets* S), therefore we normalize the score of a word by its number of meanings. This lexicon provides three scores for: positive, negative and objective words, and we used these three scores. $\sum_{w \in W} \frac{1}{|S|} \sum_{s \in S} SentiWordNet(w, s)$

Features from Twitter: We count the number of *hashtags*, *retweets*, mentions and URLs for each tweet.
Some *hashtags* like: #irony, #sarcasm o #not,... are useful in order to identify the presence of figurative text in a tweet. We count the number of these *hashtags* as a feature.

Encoding We consider number of capitalized words and the number of words with elongated characters.

Obviously we tried different set of features like: POS tags, word n-grams, binary bag of words, ...also we tried different combinations of features in order to optimize the system.

4.2 Clasification

We classified tweets using a SVM approach. In task 10B we used a linear kernel for classification and in task 11 we also used a linear kernel for regression.
Feature selection process was performed in task 10 using the development corpus and in task 11 using a cross-validation technique (10-fold cross validation) on training set. We selected the set of features that optimized the accuracy of the system

on the development set.
We used *scikit-lean toolkit* (Pedregosa et al., 2011), and we developed a framework to define functional classification models. These models included: preprocess, mining, vectorization features, and classification functions. This framework receive 1 to N models. A tweet is classified using the most voted category or using the mean of predictions if we are doing regression.

5 Experiments

We tested a set of configurations in order to obtain a competitive classifier. In this section, we present only the systems which achieved best performance in development time. We submitted only the best system to the SemEval 2015 competition.

5.1 Task 10B

1. **Model 1**: We used a linear SVM. The set of features considered were:
    - 1-gram to 6-grams of characters from tweet.
    - 1-gram to 6-grams of characters from negation labelled tweet.
    - Lexicons 1, 2, and 5.
    - Features extracted from Twitter
2. **Model 2**: A linear SVM trained using these features:
    - 1-gram to 6-grams of characters from negation labelled tweet.
    - All lexicons described in section 4.1.
    - Features extracted from Twitter
3. **Model 3**: A linear SVM trained using these set of features:
    - 1-gram to 6-grams of characters from tweet.
    - Lexicons 1, 2, and 5.
    - Features extracted from Twitter
4. **Model 4**: We created three SVMs classifiers. Each one of them were trained with this set of features:
    - 1-gram to 6-grams of characters from tweet.
    - A lexicon. Each SVM has its own lexicon. We used lexicons 1, 2, and 5.

    Then we used a majority voting system to combine these classifiers.

Table 3 shows the best systems in development phase. The accuracy is computed globally. Precision and recall are the average of these metrics for each class.

	$accuracy$	$\overline{precision}$	$\overline{recall}$
Model 1	0.6899	0.7035	0.6942
Model 2	0.7073	0.7201	0.7024
Model 3	0.6989	0.7146	0.7026
Model 4	0.6920	0.7074	0.6190

	F1	$F1_{neg}$	$F1_{neu}$	$F1_{pos}$
Model 1	0.6826	0.5014	0.7303	0.6994
Model 2	0.7013	0.5365	0.7407	0.7209
Model 3	0.6901	0.4802	0.7391	0.7162
Model 4	0.6816	0.4759	0.7307	0.7060

Table 3: Performance in development phase from our best systems in Task 10B.

For the competition we submitted the model 2 which achieved the best performance in the development phase. Table 4 shows evaluation performance. Forty teams participated in this task. In the official rank our system achieved the 24th position and the 35th position in the progress test.

5.2 Task 11

Our best model for this task was trained using these features:

- 3-grams to 9-grams of characters from tweet.
- Lexicons 1, 2, and 5.
- Features extracted from Twitter including the number of figurative *hashtags*.

We selected this set of features by cross validation. We tuned our system using the official measure, the cosine distance.

		F1	Rank	Best	Worst
Official Test	Twitter 2015	58.58	**24**	64.84	24.80
Progress Test	LiveJournal 2014	68.33	28	75.34	34.06
	SMS 2013	60.20	28	68.49	26.14
	Twitter 2013	57.05	32	93.62	32.14
	Twitter 2014	61.17	**35**	74.42	32.2
	Twitter 2014 sarcasm	45.98	24	59.11	35.58

Table 4: Evaluation results in Task 10B.

	Cosine	Rank	Best	Worst
Overall	0.6579	**5**	0.758	0.059
Sarcasm	0.904	1	0.904	0.412
Irony	0.905	4	0.918	-0.209
Metaphor	0.411	5	0.655	-0.023
Other	0.247	8	0.584	-0.025

Table 5: Official evaluation results in Task 11.

	MSE	Rank	Best	Worst
Overall	3.096	**8**	2.117	6.785
Sarcasm	1.349	9	0.934	4.375
Irony	1.034	8	0.671	7.609
Metaphor	4.565	4	3.155	9.219
Other	5.235	5	3.411	12.16

Table 6: MSE evaluation results in Task 11.

Table 5 shows the official results of our system in task 11. We achieved the 5th position in the rank. Our system obtained the first position in detecting sarcasm. We achieved a 0.918 of cosine similarity measure. For non figurative language, our system performed worse, obtaining the 8th position in the rank. We think this is due to the fact that training corpus lacks of non-figurative tweets, therefore our system was not able to learn this class properly.

Mean square error metric (MSE) was also considered by Task 11 organizers. Table 6 shows the results achieved using this metric. We obtained worse results because we didn't tune the system for this metric.

6 Conclusions

We have presented a system for 10B and 11 tasks at SemEval 2015. We used a machine learning approach based on SVM formalism for both tasks. We handled both tasks uniformly with regard to the preprocesing, feature extraction and feature representation. We have not included any knowledge about the tasks, except from resources used, that is, corpora and dictionaries. In this respect, our system will be easy to adapt to other SA tasks and other languages with this kinds of resources.

Even we did not include any external knowledge we plan to study the impact of including external resources to improve our system. Moreover, we also find interesting to extend existing corpora based on Twitter in order to increase the accuracy of the machine learning system.

Acknowledgments

This work has been partially funded by the projects, DIANA: DIscourse ANAlysis for knowledge understanding (MEC TIN2012-38603-C02-01) and Tímpano: Technology for complex Human-Machine conversational interaction with dynamic learning (MEC TIN2011-28169-C05-01).

References

Pear Analytics. Twitter study–august 2009. 2009.

Stefano Baccianella, Andrea Esuli, and Fabrizio Sebastiani. Sentiwordnet 3.0: An enhanced lexical resource for sentiment analysis and opinion mining. In *in Proc. of LREC*, 2010.

Luciano Barbosa and Junlan Feng. Robust sentiment detection on Twitter from biased and noisy data. In *Proceedings of the 23rd International Conference on Computational Linguistics: Posters*, pages 36–44. Association for Computational Linguistics, 2010.

Tom De Smedt and Walter Daelemans. "vreselijk mooi!"(terribly beautiful): A subjectivity lexicon for dutch adjectives. In *LREC*, pages 3568–3572, 2012.

A. Ghosh, G. Li, Tony Veale, Paolo Rosso, Ekaterina Shutova, Antonio Reyes, and John Barnden. Semeval-2015 task 11: Sentiment analysis of figurative language in Twitter. *Proc. Int. Workshop on Semantic Evaluation (SemEval-2015)*, June 2015.

Lars Kai Hansen, Adam Arvidsson, Finn Årup Nielsen, Elanor Colleoni, and Michael Etter. Good friends, bad news-affect and virality in Twitter. In *Future information technology*, pages 34–43. 2011.

Minqing Hu and Bing Liu. Mining and summarizing customer reviews. In *Proceedings of the tenth ACM SIGKDD international conference on Knowledge discovery and data mining*, pages 168–177. ACM, 2004.

Bernard J Jansen, Mimi Zhang, Kate Sobel, and Abdur Chowdury. Twitter power: Tweets as electronic word of mouth. *Journal of the American society for information science and technology*, 60(11):2169–2188, 2009.

Bing Liu. *Sentiment Analysis and Opinion Mining. A Comprehensive Introduction and Survey.* 2012.

Bing Liu, Minqing Hu, and Junsheng Cheng. Opinion observer: Analyzing and comparing opinions on the web. In *Proceedings of the 14th International Conference on World Wide Web*, WWW '05, pages 342–351, New York, NY, USA, 2005. ISBN 1-59593-046-9.

Saif M. Mohammad, Svetlana Kiritchenko, and Xiaodan Zhu. Nrc-canada: Building the state-of-the-art in sentiment analysis of tweets. In *Proceedings of the seventh international workshop on Semantic Evaluation Exercises (SemEval-2013)*, Atlanta, Georgia, USA, June 2013.

Preslav Nakov, Sara Rosenthal, Zornitsa Kozareva, Veselin Stoyanov, Alan Ritter, and Theresa Wilson. Semeval-2013 task 2: Sentiment analysis in Twitter. In *Second Joint Conference on Lexical and Computational Semantics (*SEM), Volume 2: Proceedings of the Seventh International Workshop on Semantic Evaluation (SemEval 2013)*, pages 312–320, Atlanta, Georgia, USA, June 2013.

Brendan O'Connor, Ramnath Balasubramanyan, Bryan R Routledge, and Noah A Smith. From tweets to polls: Linking text sentiment to public opinion time series. *ICWSM*, 11:122–129, 2010a.

Brendan O'Connor, Michel Krieger, and David Ahn. Tweetmotif: Exploratory search and topic summarization for Twitter. In William W. Cohen and Samuel Gosling, editors, *Proceedings of the Fourth International Conference on Weblogs and Social Media, ICWSM 2010, Washington, DC, USA, May 23-26, 2010*, 2010b.

Bo Pang and Lillian Lee. Opinion mining and sentiment analysis. *Foundations and trends in information retrieval*, 2(1-2):1–135, 2008.

Bo Pang, Lillian Lee, and Shivakumar Vaithyanathan. Thumbs up?: sentiment classification using machine learning techniques. In *Proceedings of the ACL-02 conference on Empirical methods in natural language processing-Volume 10*, pages 79–86. Association for Computational Linguistics, 2002.

Fabian Pedregosa, Gaël Varoquaux, Alexandre Gramfort, Vincent Michel, Bertrand Thirion, Olivier Grisel, Mathieu Blondel, Peter Prettenhofer, Ron Weiss, Vincent Dubourg, Jake Vanderplas, Alexandre Passos, David Cournapeau, Matthieu Brucher, Matthieu Perrot, and Edouard Duchesnay. Scikit-learn: Machine learning in Python. *Journal of Machine Learning Research*, 12:2825–2830, 2011.

Veronica Perez-Rosas, Carmen Banea, and Rada Mihalcea. Learning sentiment lexicons in spanish. In Nicoletta Calzolari (Conference Chair), Khalid Choukri, Thierry Declerck, Mehmet Uğur Doğan, Bente Maegaard, Joseph Mariani, Jan Odijk, and Stelios Piperidis, editors, *Proceedings of the Eight International Conference on Language Resources and Evaluation (LREC'12)*, Istanbul, Turkey, may 2012. ISBN 978-2-9517408-7-7.

Ferran Pla and Lluıs-F Hurtado. ELiRF-UPV en TASS-2013: Análisis de sentimientos en Twitter. In *XXIX Congreso de la Sociedad Española para el Procesamiento del Lenguaje Natural (SEPLN 2013). TASS*, pages 220–227, 2013.

Ferran Pla and Lluís-F. Hurtado. Political tendency identification in Twitter using sentiment analysis techniques. In *Proceedings of COLING 2014, the 25th International Conference on Computational Linguistics: Technical Papers*, pages 183–192, Dublin, Ireland, August 2014a.

Ferran Pla and Lluís-F. Hurtado. Sentiment analysis in Twitter for spanish. In *Natural Language Processing and Information Systems*, volume 8455 of *Lecture Notes in Computer Science*, pages 208–213. 2014b. ISBN 978-3-319-07982-0.

Sara Rosenthal, Preslav Nakov, Alan Ritter, and Veselin Stoyanov. Semeval-2014 task 9: Sentiment analysis in Twitter. *Proc. SemEval*, 2014a.

Sara Rosenthal, Alan Ritter, Preslav Nakov, and Veselin Stoyanov. Semeval-2014 task 9: Sentiment analysis in Twitter. In *Proceedings of the 8th International Workshop on Semantic Evaluation (SemEval 2014)*, pages 73–80, Dublin, Ireland, August 2014b.

Sara Rosenthal, Preslav Nakov, Svetlana Kiritchenko, Saif M Mohammad, Alan Ritter, and Veselin Stoyanov. Semeval-2015 task 10: Sentiment analysis in Twitter. In *Proceedings of the 9th International Workshop on Semantic Evaluation*, SemEval '2015, Denver, Colorado, June 2015.

Peter D. Turney. Thumbs up or thumbs down? semantic orientation applied to unsupervised classification of reviews. In *ACL*, pages 417–424, 2002.

Julio Villena-Román and Janine García-Morera. Workshop on sentiment analysis at sepln 2013: An over view. In *Proceedings of the TASS workshop at SEPLN 2013*. IV Congreso Español de Informática, 2013.

Julio Villena-Román, Miguel Angel Garcia Cumbreras, Janine García-Morera, Eugenio Martínez Cámara, César de Pablo Sánchez, Alfonso Ureña López, and Maria Teresa Martín Valdivia. Tass2014-workshop on sentiment analysis at sepln-overview. In *Proceedings of the TASS workshop at SEPLN 2014*. IV Congreso Español de Informática, 2014.

G Vinodhini and RM Chandrasekaran. Sentiment analysis and opinion mining: A survey. *International Journal*, 2(6), 2012.

Theresa Wilson, Paul Hoffmann, Swapna Somasundaran, Jason Kessler, Janyce Wiebe, Yejin Choi, Claire Cardie, Ellen Riloff, and Siddharth Patwardhan. Opinionfinder: A system for subjectivity analysis. In *Proceedings of HLT/EMNLP on Interactive Demonstrations*, pages 34–35. Association for Computational Linguistics, 2005.

Theresa Wilson, Zornitsa Kozareva, Preslav Nakov, Sara Rosenthal, Veselin Stoyanov, and Alan Ritter. Semeval-2013 task 2: Sentiment analysis in Twitter. *Proceedings of the International Workshop on Semantic Evaluation, SemEval*, 13, 2013.

Xiaodan Zhu, Svetlana Kiritchenko, and Saif M Mohammad. Nrc-canada-2014: Recent improvements in the sentiment analysis of tweets. *SemEval 2014*, page 443, 2014.

Webis: An Ensemble for Twitter Sentiment Detection

Matthias Hagen **Martin Potthast** **Michel Büchner** **Benno Stein**
Bauhaus-Universität Weimar
`<first name>.<last name>@uni-weimar.de`

Abstract

We reproduce four Twitter sentiment classification approaches that participated in previous SemEval editions with diverse feature sets. The reproduced approaches are combined in an ensemble, averaging the individual classifiers' confidence scores for the three classes (positive, neutral, negative) and deciding sentiment polarity based on these averages. The experimental evaluation on SemEval data shows our re-implementations to slightly outperform their respective originals. Moreover, not too surprisingly, the ensemble of the reproduced approaches serves as a strong baseline in the current edition where it is top-ranked on the 2015 test set.

1 Introduction

We reproduce four state-of-the-art approaches to classifying the sentiment expressed in a given tweet, and combine the four approaches to an ensemble based on the individual classifiers' confidence scores. In particular, we focus on subtask B of SemEval 2015's task 10 "Sentiment Analysis in Twitter," where the goal is to classify the whole tweet as either positive, neutral, or negative. Since the notebook descriptions accompanying submissions to shared tasks are understandably very terse, it is often a challenge to reproduce the results reported. Therefore, we attempt to reproduce the state-of-the-art Twitter sentiment detection algorithms that have been submitted to the aforementioned task in its previous two editions. Furthermore, we combine the reproduced classifiers in an ensemble. Since the individual approaches employ diverse feature sets, the goal of the ensemble is to combine their individual strengths. The paper at hand is a slight extension of the approach from our ECIR 2015 reproducibility track paper (Hagen et al., 2015) such that also text passages are reused. In our ECIR paper, we showed that three selected approaches participating in the SemEval 2013 Twitter sentiment task 2 could be reproduced from the papers accompanying the individual approaches. Adding the best participant of the respective SemEval 2014 task 9 is shown to form a very strong baseline that was not outperformed by the SemEval 2015 participants on the 2015 test data and that also places in the top-10 in the progress test.

In Section 2 we briefly describe some related work while in Section 3 we provide more details on the four individual approaches as well as our ensemble scheme. Some concluding remarks and an outlook on future work close the paper in Section 4. An experimental evaluation of our approach and an in-depth comparison to the other participants is not included in this paper since it can be found in the task overview (Rosenthal et al., 2015).

2 Related Work

Sentiment detection is a classic problem of text classification. Unlike other text classification tasks, the goal is not to identify topics, entities, or authors of a text but to rate the expressed sentiment as positive, negative, or neutral. Most approaches used for sentiment detection usually involve methods from machine learning, computational linguistics, and statistics. Typically, several approaches from these fields are combined for sentiment detection (Pang et al., 2002; Turney, 2002; Feldman, 2013).

Since Twitter is one of the richest sources of opinion, a lot of different approaches to sentiment detection in tweets have been proposed. Different approaches use different feature sets ranging from standard word polarity expressions or unigram features also applied in general sentiment detection (Go et al., 2009; Kouloumpis et al., 2011), to the usage of emoticons and uppercases (Barbosa and Feng, 2010), word lengthening (Brody and Diakopoulos, 2011), phonetic features (Ermakov and Ermakova, 2013), multi-lingual machine translation (Balahur and Turchi, 2013), or word embeddings (Tang et al., 2014). The task usually is to detect the sentiment expressed in a tweet as a whole (also focus of this paper). But it can also be used to identify the sentiment in a tweet with respect to a given target concept expressed in a query (Jiang et al., 2011). The difference is that a generally negative tweet might not say anything about the target concept and must thus be considered neutral with respect to the target concept.

Both tasks, namely sentiment detection in a tweet, and sentiment detection with respect to a specific target concept, are part of the SemEval sentiment analysis tasks since 2013 (Nakov et al., 2013; Rosenthal et al., 2014). SemEval fosters research on sentiment detection for short texts in particular, and gathers the best-performing approaches in a friendly competition. The problem we are dealing with is formulated as subtask B: given a tweet, decide whether its message is positive, negative, or neutral.

State-of-the-art approaches have been submitted to the SemEval tasks. However, up to now, no one had trained a meta-classifier based on the submitted approaches to determine what can be achieved when combining them, whereas each participating team only trains their individual classifier using respective individual feature sets. Our idea is to combine four of the best-performing approaches from the last years with different feature sets, and to form an ensemble classifier that leverages the individual classifiers' strengths forming a strong baseline.

Ensemble learning is a classic approach of combining several classifiers to a more powerful ensemble (Opitz and Maclin, 1999; Polikar, 2006; Rokach, 2010). The classic approaches of Bagging (Breiman, 1996) and Boosting (Schapire, 1990; Freund and Schapire, 1996) try to either combine the outputs of different classifiers trained on different random instances of the training set or on training the classifiers on instances that were misclassified by the other classifiers. Both rather work on the final predictions of the classifiers just as for instance averaging or majority voting on the predictions (Asker and Maclin, 1997) would do. In our case, we employ the confidence scores of the participating classifiers. Several papers describe different ways of working with the classifiers' confidence scores, such as learning a dynamic confidence weighting scheme (Fung et al., 2006), or deriving a set cover with averaging confidences (Rokach et al., 2014). Instead, we simply average the three confidence scores of the three classifiers for each individual class. This straightforward approach performs superior to its individual parts and performs competitive in the SemEval competitions. Thus, its sentiment detection results can be directly used in any of the above use cases for Twitter sentiment detection.

3 Individual Approaches and Ensemble

For our ECIR 2015 reproducibility paper (Hagen et al., 2015), we originally selected three state-of-the-art approaches for Twitter sentiment detection among the 38 participants of SemEval 2013. To identify worthy candidates—and to satisfy the claim "state of the art"—we picked the top-ranked approach by team NRC-Canada (Mohammad et al., 2013). However, instead of simply picking the approaches on ranks two and three to complete our set, we first analyzed the notebooks of the top-ranked teams in order to identify approaches that are significantly dissimilar from NRC-Canada. We decided to handpick approaches this way so they complement each other in an ensemble. As a second candidate, we picked team GU-MLT-LT (Günther and Furrer, 2013) since it uses some other features and a different sentiment lexicon. As a third candidate, we picked team KLUE (Proisl et al., 2013), which was ranked fifth. We discarded the third-ranked approach as it is using a large set of not publicly available rules probably hindering reproducibility, whereas the fourth-ranked system seemed too similar to NRC and GU-MLT-LT to add something new to the planned ensemble. Finally, for participation in SemEval 2015, we also included TeamX (Miura et al., 2014) as the 2014 top-performing approach resulting in an ensemble of four.

Note that due to the selection process, reproducing the four approaches does not deteriorate into reimplementing the feature set of one approach and reusing it for the other two. Moreover, combining the four approaches into an ensemble classifier actually makes sense, since, due to the feature set diversity, they tap sufficiently different information sources. In what follows, we first briefly recap the features used by the individual classifiers and then explain our ensemble strategy.

3.1 NRC-Canada

Team NRC-Canada (Mohammad et al., 2013) used a classifier with a wide range of features. A tweet is first preprocessed by replacing URLs and user names by some placeholder. The tweets are then tokenized and POS-tagged. An SVM with linear kernel is trained using the following feature set.

N-grams The occurrence of word 1- to 4-grams as well as occurrences of pairs of non-consecutive words where the intermediate words are replaced by a placeholder. No term-weighting like $tf{\cdot}idf$ is used. Similarly for occurrence of character 3- to 5-grams.

ALLCAPS Number of all-capitalized words.

Parts of speech Occurrence of part-of-speech tags.

Polarity dictionaries In total, five polarity dictionaries are used. Three of these were manually created: the NRC Emotion Lexicon (Mohammad and Turney, 2010; Mohammad and Turney, 2013) with 14,000 words, the MPQA Lexicon (Wilson et al., 2005) with 8,000 words, and the Bing Liu Lexicon (Hu and Liu, 2004) with 6,800 words. Two other dictionaries were created automatically. For the first one, the idea is that several hash tags can express sentiment (e.g., #good). Team NRC crawled 775,000 tweets from April to December 2012 that contain at least one of 32 positive or 38 negative hash tags that were manually created (e.g., #good and #bad). For word 1-grams and word 2-grams in the tweets, PMI-scores were calculated for each of the 70 hash tags to yield a score for the n-grams (i.e., the ones with higher positive hash tag PMI are positive, the others negative). The resulting dictionary contains 54,129 unigrams, 316,531 bigrams, and 308,808 pairs of non-consecutive words. The second automatically created dictionary is not based on PMI for hash tags but for emoticons. It was created in a similar way as the hash tag dictionary and contains 62,468 unigrams, 677,698 bigrams, and 480,010 pairs of non-consecutive words.

For each entry of the five dictionaries, the dictionary score is either positive, negative, or zero. For a tweet and each individual dictionary, several features are computed: the number of dictionary entries with a positive score and the number of entries with a negative score, the sum of the positive scores and the sum of the negative scores of the tweet's dictionary entries, the maximum positive score and minimum negative score of the tweet's dictionary entries, and the last positive score and negative score.

Punctuation marks The number of non-single punctuation marks (e.g., !! or ?!) is used as a feature and whether the last one is an exclamation or a question mark.

Emoticons The emoticons contained in a tweet, their polarity, and whether the last token of a tweet is an emoticon are employed features.

Word lengthening The number of words that are lengthened by repeating a letter more than twice (e.g., cooooolll) is a feature.

Clustering Via unsupervised Brown clustering (Brown et al., 1992) a set of 56,345,753 tweets by Owoputi (Owoputi et al., 2013) clustered into 1,000 clusters. The IDs of the clusters in which the terms of a tweet occur are also used as features.

Negation The number of negated segments is a feature. A negated segment starts with a negation (e.g., shouldn't) and ends with a punctuation mark (Pang et al., 2002). Every token in a negated segment (words, emoticons) gets a suffix NEG attached (e.g., perfect_NEG).

3.2 GU-MLT-LT

Team GU-MLT-LT (Günther and Furrer, 2013) was ranked second in SemEval 2013. They train a stochastic gradient decent classifier on a much smaller feature set compared to NRC. The following feature set is computed for tokenized versions of the original raw tweet, a lowercased normalized version of the tweet, and a version of the lowercased tweet where consecutive identical letters are collapsed (e.g., helllo gets hello).

Normalized unigrams The occurrence of the normalized word unigrams is one feature set. No term weighting like for instance $tf \cdot idf$ is used.

Stems Porter stemming (Porter, 1980) is used to identify the occurrence of the stems of the collapsed word unigrams as another feature set. Again, no term weighting is applied.

Clustering Similar to NRC, the cluster IDs of the raw, normalized, and collapsed tokens are features.

Polarity dictionary The SentiWordNet assessments (Baccianella et al., 2010) of the individual collapsed tokens and the sum of all tokens' scores in a tweet are further features.

Negation Normalized tokens and stems are added as negated features similar to NRC.

3.3 KLUE

Team KLUE (Proisl et al., 2013) was ranked fifth in the SemEval 2013 ranking. Similarly to NRC, team KLUE first replaces URLs and user names by some placeholder and tokenizes the lowercased tweets. A maximum entropy-based classifier is trained on the following features.

N-grams Word unigrams and bigrams are used as features but in contrast to NRC and GU-MLT-LT not just by occurrence but frequency-weighted. Due to the short tweet length this however often boils down to a simple occurrence feature. To be part of the feature set, an n-gram has to be contained in at least five tweets. This excludes some rather obscure and rare terms or misspellings.

Length The number of tokens in a tweet (i.e., its length) is used as a feature. Interestingly, NRC and GU-MLT-LT do not explicitly use this feature.

Polarity dictionary The employed dictionary is the AFINN-111 lexicon (Nielsen, 2011) containing 2,447 words with assessments from -5 (very negative) to $+5$ (very positive). Team KLUE added another 343 words. Employed features are the number of positive tokens in a tweet, the number of negative tokens, the number of tokens with a dictionary score, and the arithmetic mean of the scores in a tweet.

Emoticons and abbreviations A list of 212 emoticons and 95 colloquial abbreviations from Wikipedia was manually scored as positive, negative, or neutral. For a tweet, again the number of positive and negative tokens from this list, the total number of scored tokens, and the arithmetic mean are used as features.

Negation Negation is not treated for the whole segment as NRC and GU-MLT-LT do but only on the next three tokens except the case that the punctuation comes earlier. Only negated word unigrams are used as an additional feature set. The polarity scores from the above dictionary are multiplied by -1 for terms up to 4 tokens after the negation.

3.4 TeamX

TeamX (Miura et al., 2014) was ranked first in the SemEval 2014 ranking. The approach was inspired by NRC Canada's 2013 method but uses fewer features and more polarity dictionaries—some differences are outlined below. Although it is very close to NRC Canada, some differences exist that justify TeamX's selection for our ensemble—besides its good performance in SemEval 2014.

Parts of speech Two different POS taggers are used: the Stanford POS tagger's tags are used for the polarity dictionaries based on formal language and for word sense disambiguation while the CMU ARK POS tagger is used for the polarity dictionaries containing more informal expressions, n-grams and the cluster features. Since the CMU ARK tagger was explicitly developed for handling tweets, it is better suited for the informal language often used in tweets while the Stanford tagger better addresses the needs of the formal dictionaries.

N-grams Word uni- up to 4-grams (consecutive words but also with gaps) and consecutive character 3- up to 5-grams are used as features similar to NRC.

Polarity dictionaries TeamX uses all the dictionaries of NRC, GU-ML-LT, and KLUE except for the NRC emoticon dictionary. Additionally, also SentiWordNet is used.

3.5 Remarks on Reimplementing

As was to be expected, it turned out to be impossible to re-implement all features precisely as the original authors did. Either not all data were publicly available, or the features themselves were not sufficiently explained in the notebooks. We deliberated to contact the original authors to give them a chance to supply missing data as well as to elaborate on missing information. However, we ultimately opted against doing so for the following reason: our goal was to reproduce their results, not to repeat them. The difference between reproducibility and repeatability is subtle, yet important. If an approach can be re-implemented with incomplete information and if it then achieves a performance within the ballpark of the original, it can be considered much more robust than an approach that must be precisely the same as the original to achieve its expected performance. The former hints reproducibility, the latter only repeatability. This is why we have partly re-invented the approaches on our own, wherever information or data were missing. In doing so, we sometimes found ourselves in a situation where departing from the original approach would yield better performance. In such cases, we decided to maximize performance rather than sticking to the original, since in an evaluation setting, it is unfair to not maximize performance wherever one can.

In particular, the emoticons and abbreviations added by the KLUE team were not available, such that we only choose the AFINN-111 polarity dictionary and re-implemented an emoticon detection and manual polarity scoring ourselves. We also chose not to use the frequency information in the KLUE system but only Boolean occurrence like NRC and GU-MLT-LT, since pilot studies on the SemEval 2013 training and development sets showed that to perform much better. For all three approaches, we unified tweet normalization regarding lowercasing and completely removing URLs and user names instead of adding a placeholder. As for the classifier itself, we did not use the learning algorithms used originally but L2-regularized logistic regression from the LIBLINEAR SVM library for all three approaches. In our pilot experiments on the SemEval 2013 training and development set this showed a very good trade-off between training time and accuracy. We set the cost parameter to 0.5 for NRC, to 0.15 for GU-MLT-LT, and to 0.05 for TeamX and KLUE.

Note that most of our design decisions do not hurt the individual performances but instead improve the accuracy for GU-MLT-LT and KLUE on the SemEval 2013 test set. Table 1 shows the performance of the original SemEval 2013 and 2014

Table 1: F1-scores of the original and reimplemented classifiers on the SemEval 2013 and 2014 test data and performance of the final system on the 2015 test data.

Classifier	Original SemEval 2013	Reimplemented
NRC	69.02	69.44
GU-MLT-LT	65.27	67.27
KLUE	63.06	67.05
	Original SemEval 2014	**Reimplemented**
TeamX	72.12	70.09
	SemEval 2015 result	
Ensemble	64.84	(rank 1 among 40 systems)

rankings and that of our re-implementations based on the averaged F1-score for the positive and negative class only (as is done at SemEval). While the reimplemented NRC performance is slightly better, GU-MLT-LT and KLUE are substantially improved. That TeamX lost performance is probably due to a fact that we only recognized after the competition: The word sense feature was unintentionally not switched on in the re-implementation of TeamX. Since for this "handicapped" version of TeamX (again, we just noticed the reason for the handicap after the SemEval 2015 deadline) the weighting scheme of the classification probabilities proposed for the original approach (Miura et al., 2014) did decrease the performance, we also did not use these weights. If we would have noticed our mistake before, the performance of the TeamX classifier would probably have been better.

Altogether, we conclude that reproducing the SemEval approaches was generally possible but involved some subtleties that sometimes lead to difficult design decisions. Our resolution is to maximize performance rather than to dogmatically stick to the original approach; even though this includes the error in the TeamX re-implementation that went through unnoticed until after the deadline.

3.6 Ensemble Combination

In our pilot studies on the SemEval 2013 training and development sets, we tested several ways of combining the classifiers to an ensemble method. One of the main observations was that each individual approach classifies some tweets correctly that others fail for. This is not too surprising given the different feature sets but also supports the idea of using an ensemble to combine the individual strengths. Although we briefly tried different ways of bagging and boosting the three classifiers, it soon turned out that some simpler combination performs better. A problem, for instance, was that some misclassified tweets are very difficult (e.g., the positive `Cant wait for the UCLA midnight madness tomorrow night`). Since often at least two classifiers fail on a hard tweet, this rules out some basic combination schemes, such as the majority vote which turned out to perform worse on the SemEval 2013 development set than NRC alone.

The solution that we finally came up with is motivated by observing how the classifiers trained on the SemEval 2013 training set behave for tweets in the development set. Typically, not the four final decisions but the respective confidences or probabilities of the individual classifiers give a good hint on uncertainties. If two are not really sure about the final classification, sometimes the remaining ones favor another class with high confidence. Thus, instead of looking at the classifications, we decided to use the confidence scores or probabilities to build the ensemble. This approach is also motivated by old and also more recent research on ensemble learning (Asker and Maclin, 1997; Fung et al., 2006; Rokach et al., 2014). But instead of learning a weighting scheme for the different individual classifiers, we decided to simply compute the average probability of the four classifiers for each of the three classes (positive, negative, neutral).

Our ensemble thus works as follows. The four individual re-implementations of the TeamX, the NRC, the GU-MLT-LT, and the KLUE classifier are individually trained on the SemEval 2013 training and development set as if being applied individually—without boosting or bagging. As for the classification of a tweet, the ensemble ignores the individual classifiers' classification decisions but requests the classifiers' probabilities (or confidences) for each class. The ensemble decision then chooses the class with the highest average probability—again, no sophisticated techniques like dynamic confidence weighting (Fung et al., 2006) or set covering schemes (Rokach et al., 2014) are involved. Thus, our final ensemble method is a rather straightforward system based on averaging confidences instead of voting schemes on the actual classifications of the individual classifiers. It can be easily implemented on top of the four classifiers and thus incurs no additional overhead. It also proves a very strong baseline in the SemEval 2015 evaluation. This is not really surprising since typically ensembles of good and diverse approaches should achieve better performances. Our code for the four reproduced approaches as well as that of the ensemble is publicly available.[1]

4 Conclusion and Outlook

We have reproduced four state-of-the-art approaches to sentiment detection for Twitter tweets. Our findings include that not all aspects of the approaches could be reproduced precisely, but that missing data, missing information, as well as opportunities to improve the approaches' performances lead us to re-invent them and to depart to some extent from the original descriptions. Most of our changes have improved the performances of the original approaches (except the erroneously and unintentionally switched off word sense feature of TeamX). Moreover, we have demonstrated that the approaches can be reproduced even with incomplete information about them, which is a much stronger property than being merely repeatable.

In addition, we investigated a combination of confidence scores of the four approaches within an ensemble that altogether yields a top-performing Twitter sentiment detection system forming a very strong baseline. The ensemble computation is as efficient as its components, and its effectiveness can be seen from the top rank on the SemEval 2015 test set and the top-10 ranking in the progress test involving the previous years' test data.

Promising directions for future research are an extensive error analysis and the identification of further classifiers potentially strengthening the ensemble. Following our philosophy of selecting approaches that are significantly different from each other, it will be interesting to observe how much new approaches can improve the existing ensemble.

[1] `http://www.uni-weimar.de/medien/webis/publications/by-year/#stein_2015d`

References

Lars Asker and Richard Maclin. 1997. Ensembles as a sequence of classifiers. In *Proceedings of the Fifteenth International Joint Conference on Artificial Intelligence, IJCAI 97, Nagoya, Japan, August 23-29, 1997, 2 Volumes*, pages 860–865.

Stefano Baccianella, Andrea Esuli, and Fabrizio Sebastiani. 2010. SentiWordNet 3.0: An enhanced lexical resource for sentiment analysis and opinion mining. In *Proceedings of the International Conference on Language Resources and Evaluation, LREC 2010, 17-23 May 2010, Valletta, Malta.*

Alexandra Balahur and Marco Turchi. 2013. Improving sentiment analysis in twitter using multilingual machine translated data. In *Proceedings of the International Conference Recent Advances in Natural Language Processing, RANLP 2013*, pages 49–55.

Luciano Barbosa and Junlan Feng. 2010. Robust sentiment detection on twitter from biased and noisy data. In *COLING 2010, 23rd International Conference on Computational Linguistics, Posters Volume, 23-27 August 2010, Beijing, China*, pages 36–44.

Leo Breiman. 1996. Bagging predictors. *Machine Learning*, 24(2):123–140.

Samuel Brody and Nicholas Diakopoulos. 2011. Cooooooooooooooollllllllllllll!!!!!!!!!!!!!! using word lengthening to detect sentiment in microblogs. In *Proceedings of the 2011 Conference on Empirical Methods in Natural Language Processing, EMNLP 2011, 27-31 July 2011, John McIntyre Conference Centre, Edinburgh, UK, A meeting of SIGDAT, a Special Interest Group of the ACL*, pages 562–570.

Peter F. Brown, Vincent J. Della Pietra, Peter V. de Souza, Jennifer C. Lai, and Robert L. Mercer. 1992. Class-based n-gram models of natural language. *Computational Linguistics*, 18(4):467–479.

Sergei Ermakov and Liana Ermakova. 2013. Sentiment classification based on phonetic characteristics. In *Advances in Information Retrieval - 35th European Conference on IR Research, ECIR 2013, Moscow, Russia, March 24-27, 2013. Proceedings*, pages 706–709.

Ronen Feldman. 2013. Techniques and applications for sentiment analysis. *Communications of the ACM*, 56(4):82–89.

Yoav Freund and Robert E. Schapire. 1996. Experiments with a new boosting algorithm. In *Machine Learning, Proceedings of the Thirteenth International Conference (ICML '96), Bari, Italy, July 3-6, 1996*, pages 148–156.

Gabriel Pui Cheong Fung, Jeffrey Xu Yu, Haixun Wang, David W. Cheung, and Huan Liu. 2006. A balanced ensemble approach to weighting classifiers for text classification. In *Proceedings of the 6th IEEE International Conference on Data Mining (ICDM 2006), 18-22 December 2006, Hong Kong, China*, pages 869–873.

Alec Go, Richa Bhayani, and Lei Huang. 2009. Twitter sentiment classification using distant supervision. Technical Report CS224N Project Report, Stanford University.

Tobias Günther and Lenz Furrer. 2013. GU-MLT-LT: Sentiment analysis of short messages using linguistic features and stochastic gradient descent. In *Second Joint Conference on Lexical and Computational Semantics (*SEM), Volume 2: Proceedings of the Seventh International Workshop on Semantic Evaluation (SemEval 2013)*, pages 328–332.

Matthias Hagen, Martin Potthast, Michel Büchner, and Benno Stein. 2015. Twitter sentiment detection via ensemble classification using averaged confidence scores. In *Proceedings of ECIR 2015 (to appear).*

Minqing Hu and Bing Liu. 2004. Mining and summarizing customer reviews. In *Proceedings of the Tenth ACM SIGKDD International Conference on Knowledge Discovery and Data Mining, Seattle, Washington, USA, August 22-25, 2004*, pages 168–177.

Long Jiang, Mo Yu, Ming Zhou, Xiaohua Liu, and Tiejun Zhao. 2011. Target-dependent twitter sentiment classification. In *The 49th Annual Meeting of the Association for Computational Linguistics: Human Language Technologies, Proceedings of the Conference, 19-24 June, 2011, Portland, Oregon, USA*, pages 151–160.

Efthymios Kouloumpis, Theresa Wilson, and Johanna D. Moore. 2011. Twitter sentiment analysis: The good the bad and the OMG! In *Proceedings of the Fifth International Conference on Weblogs and Social Media, Barcelona, Catalonia, Spain, July 17-21, 2011.*

Yasuhide Miura, Shigeyuki Sakaki, Keigo Hattori, and Tomoko Ohkuma. 2014. Teamx: A sentiment analyzer with enhanced lexicon mapping and weighting scheme for unbalanced data. In *Proceedings of the 8th International Workshop on Semantic Evaluation (SemEval 2014)*, pages 628–632, Dublin, Ireland, August. Association for Computational Linguistics and Dublin City University.

Saif M. Mohammad and Peter D. Turney. 2010. Emotions evoked by common words and phrases: Using mechanical turk to create an emotion lexicon. In *Proceedings of the NAACL HLT 2010 Workshop on Computational Approaches to Analysis and Generation of Emotion in Text, CAAGET 2010*, pages 26–34.

Saif M. Mohammad and Peter D. Turney. 2013. Crowdsourcing a word-emotion association lexicon. *Computational Intelligence*, 29(3):436–465.

Saif M. Mohammad, Svetlana Kiritchenko, and Xiaodan Zhu. 2013. NRC-Canada: Building the state-of-the-art in sentiment analysis of tweets. In *Second Joint Conference on Lexical and Computational Semantics (*SEM), Volume 2: Proceedings of the Seventh International Workshop on Semantic Evaluation (SemEval 2013)*, pages 321–327.

Preslav Nakov, Zornitsa Kozareva, Alan Ritter, Sara Rosenthal, Veselin Stoyanov, and Theresa Wilson. 2013. Semeval-2013 task 2: Sentiment analysis in twitter. In *Second Joint Conference on Lexical and Computational Semantics (*SEM), Volume 2: Proceedings of the Seventh International Workshop on Semantic Evaluation (SemEval 2013)*, pages 312–320.

Finn Årup Nielsen. 2011. A new ANEW: evaluation of a word list for sentiment analysis in microblogs. In *Proceedings of the ESWC2011 Workshop on 'Making Sense of Microposts': Big things come in small packages, Heraklion, Crete, Greece, May 30, 2011*, pages 93–98.

David W. Opitz and Richard Maclin. 1999. Popular ensemble methods: An empirical study. *Journal of Artificial Intelligence Research*, 11:169–198.

Olutobi Owoputi, Brendan O'Connor, Chris Dyer, Kevin Gimpel, Nathan Schneider, and Noah A. Smith. 2013. Improved part-of-speech tagging for online conversational text with word clusters. In *Human Language Technologies: Conference of the North American Chapter of the Association of Computational Linguistics, Proceedings, June 9-14, 2013, Westin Peachtree Plaza Hotel, Atlanta, Georgia, USA*, pages 380–390.

Bo Pang, Lillian Lee, and Shiuvakumar Vaithyanathan. 2002. Thumbs up?: Sentiment classification using machine learning techniques. In *Proceedings of the Conference on Empirical Methods in Natural Language Processing, EMNLP 2002*, pages 79–86.

Robi Polikar. 2006. Ensemble based systems in decision making. *IEEE Circuits and Systems Magazine*, 6(3):21–45.

Martin Porter. 1980. An algorithm for suffix stripping. *Program: electronic library and information systems*, 14(3):130–137.

Thomas Proisl, Paul Greiner, Stefan Evert, and Besim Kabashi. 2013. Klue: Simple and robust methods for polarity classification. In *Second Joint Conference on Lexical and Computational Semantics (*SEM), Volume 2: Proceedings of the Seventh International Workshop on Semantic Evaluation (SemEval 2013)*, pages 395–401.

Lior Rokach, Alon Schclar, and Ehud Itach. 2014. Ensemble methods for multi-label classification. *Expert Systems with Applications*, 41(16):7507–7523.

Lior Rokach. 2010. Ensemble-based classifiers. *Artificial Intelligence Review*, 33(1-2):1–39.

Sara Rosenthal, Alan Ritter, Preslav Nakov, and Veselin Stoyanov. 2014. Semeval-2014 task 9: Sentiment analysis in twitter. In *Proceedings of the 8th International Workshop on Semantic Evaluation (SemEval 2014)*, pages 73–80.

Sara Rosenthal, Preslav Nakov, Svetlana Kiritchenko, Saif M Mohammad, Alan Ritter, and Veselin Stoyanov. 2015. Semeval-2015 task 10: Sentiment analysis in twitter. In *Proceedings of the 9th International Workshop on Semantic Evaluation, SemEval 2015*, SemEval 2015, Denver, Colorado, June. Association for Computational Linguistics.

Robert E. Schapire. 1990. The strength of weak learnability. *Machine Learning*, 5:197–227.

Duyu Tang, Furu Wei, Nan Yang, Ming Zhou, Ting Liu, and Bing Qin. 2014. Learning sentiment-specific word embedding for twitter sentiment classification. In *Proceedings of the 52nd Annual Meeting of the Association for Computational Linguistics, ACL 2014, June 22-27, 2014, Baltimore, MD, USA, Volume 1: Long Papers*, pages 1555–1565.

Peter D. Turney. 2002. Thumbs up or thumbs down? Semantic orientation applied to unsupervised classification of reviews. In *Proceedings of the 40th Annual Meeting of the Association for Computational Linguistics, ACL 2002,J uly 6-12, 2002, Philadelphia, PA, USA.*, pages 417–424.

Theresa Wilson, Janyce Wiebe, and Paul Hoffmann. 2005. Recognizing contextual polarity in phrase-level sentiment analysis. In *HLT/EMNLP 2005, Human Language Technology Conference and Conference on Empirical Methods in Natural Language Processing, Proceedings of the Conference, 6-8 October 2005, Vancouver, British Columbia, Canada*, pages 347–354.

Sentibase: Sentiment Analysis in Twitter on a Budget

Satarupa Guha *, Aditya Joshi *, Vasudeva Varma
Search and Information Extraction Lab
International Institute of Information Technology, Hyderabad
Gachibowli, Hyderabad, Telengana, India
{satarupa.guha,aditya.joshi}@research.iiit.ac.in
vv@iiit.ac.in

Abstract

Like SemEval 2013 and 2014, the task Sentiment Analysis in Twitter found a place in this year's SemEval too and attracted an unprecedented number of participations. This task comprises of four sub-tasks. We participated in subtask 2 — Message polarity classification. Although we lie a few notches down from the top system, we present a very simple yet effective approach to handle this problem that can be implemented in a single day!

1 Introduction

Social media not only acts as a proxy for the real world society, it also offers a treasure trove of data for different types of analyses like Trend Analysis, Event Detection and Sentiment Analysis, to name a few. SemEval 2015 Task 10 subtask B (Rosenthal et al., 2015) specifically deals with the task of Sentiment Analysis in Twitter. Sentiment Analysis in social media in general and Twitter in particular has a wide range of applications — Companies/services can gauge the public sentiment towards the new product or service they launched, political parties can estimate their chances of winning the upcoming elections by monitoring what people are saying on Twitter about them, and so on. In spite of the availability of huge amount of data and the huge promises they entail, working with social media data is far more challenging than regular text data. Being user-generated, the data is noisy; there are misspellings, unreliable capitalization, widespread use of creative acronyms, lack of grammar, and a style of writing that is very typical of its own which makes the problem of Sentiment Analysis on Twitter more challenging. Also, the cues for positive or negative sentiment in social media text are starkly different, thereby generating a whole new domain for exploration.

The first two authors made equal contribution to this work

2 Related Work

SemEval 2013 (Nakov et al., 2013) and 2014 tasks (Rosenthal et al., 2014) on Sentiment Analysis in Twitter not only contributed to this field by making huge amounts of annotated datasets available for research, but also encouraged researchers to come up with better solutions for this challenging problem. There has been numerous initiatives outside SemEval too. (Pak and Paroubek, 2010) is one of the early attempts at using Twitter as a corpus for Sentiment Analysis, which shows how to automatically collect a corpus for the same and performs linguistic analysis of the collected corpus. (Bakliwal et al., 2012) presents a simple sentiment scoring function which uses prior information to classify and weight various sentiment bearing words/phrases in tweets. (Wilson et al., 2005) demontrates an efficient technique for automatically identifying the contextual polarity for a large subset of sentiment expressions. (Mohammad et al., 2013) and (Kiritchenko et al., 2014) establishes benchmark in Sentiment Analyis in Twitter as well as in the field of Aspect Based Sentiment Analysis by incorporating various innovative linguistic features. (Agarwal et al., 2011) introduced POS-specific prior polarity features and (Kouloumpis et al., 2011) explored the use of a tree kernel to obviate the need for tedious feature engineering. (Kouloumpis et al., 2011) evaluate the usefulness of existing lexical resources as well as features that capture information about the informal and creative language used in microblogging. Recent publication from (Socher et al., 2013) has further raised the bar for Sentiment Analysis in general, but it is not specifically designed to tackle tweets data.

3 Approach

3.1 Preprocessing

We acquire a list of acronyms and their expanded forms [1]. We use this list as a look-up table and replace all occurrences of acronyms in our data by their expanded forms. We normalize all numbers that find a place in our data by replacing them with the string '0'. We do not remove stop words because they often contribute heavily towards expressing sentiment/emotion. We do not also stem the words because stemming leads to the loss of the parts of speech information of the word and makes the use of lexicons unnecessarily complicated.

3.2 Vocabulary Generation

We assign a unique ID to all words occurring in our data. All the hashtags we encounter in the data are hashed to a single string place holder and a single unique ID is assigned to it, as opposed to different Ids for different hashtags. Hashtags are mostly formed by concatenation of multiple words without any space in between, and therefore, unless hashtags are segmented into meaningful chunks, raw hashtags seldom add any semantics to the sentence. Hence, we do not distinguish between the different hashtags and consider them as a single unit. Similarly, we hash all mentions of the kind @user1 and @user2 to a single string placeholder and assign a single ID to it. This is because these words prefixed by '@' are all named entities and do not contribute anything to the semantic meaning or towards the polarity of a tweet.

[1] Dowloaded from `https://github.com/TaikerLiang/Twitter/blob/master/Data/Knowledge\_Database/Slang\%20Dictionary/a.`

3.3 Feature Engineering

The task required us to classify a tweet into positive, negative and neutral polarity categories. This can essentially be treated as a 2-step process

- Classify each tweet into subjective (positive/negative) and objective(neutral) classes.
- Classify subjective tweets into positive and negative ones.

We keep this philosophy in mind, but do not explicitly model the problem as two sub-problems. We treat them as a single step, but we select features such that some of the features are best suited for distinguishing between subjective and objective classes, while some others are engineered to be able to tell a positive tweet from a negative one. The problem with treating the problem as a pipeline of two steps is that we would have to deal with the propagation of errors from one step to the other. If a subjective tweet is mis-classified as an objective one, we rob that tweet of its opportunity of being classified any further in the next step and immediately label them as neutral. This might be detrimental in cases where certain features lead us to believe a tweet is objective, while a combination of all features might rightly lean them towards positive or negative polarities. We take aid from both extrinsic features like emoticons and grapheme stretching as well as intrinsic ones like unigrams and so on. Following is the list of features we employ and also their underlying motivation:

- *Unigrams* — For each word in a tweet, we look up the vocabulary we generated in the previous step. If the word is present in the vocabulary, we determine its position in the feature vector from the unique ID assigned to it and put 1 in its position. All other positions are 0 by default. Unigram features contribute to understanding both the distinction between subjective and objective tweets as well as between positive and negative tweets.
- *Number of hashtags* — Inspection of the data lead us to believe that the more the number of hashtags in the tweets, the more the author's involvement with it and hence more the subjectivity.

- *Presence of URLs* — A factual tweet is often accompanied by a URL as a proof of its validity or for more enthusiastic of the author's followers to go and explore the news/fact further. Hence, presence of URLs is likely to indicate that the sentence is objective/neutral.

  For example- "Jose Iglesias / Igleisas started at shortstop Wednesday night for the second http://t.co/Gkpx9Blu" and "Today In History November 02, 1958 Elvis gave a party at his hotel before going out on maneuvers. He sang and... http://t.co/Za9bLTcE"

- *Presence of exclamation marks* — From our observation, a subjective tweet is much more likely to be ended by exclamation marks than a purely factual or objective tweet. Further, positive tweets are more prone to contain exclamation than negative ones.

- *Presence of question marks and wh-words* — Tweets containing question marks or wh-words like "why" and "where" are seldom objective. Statistics tells us that this feature can act as a strong cue for not only subjectivity, but also of negativity.

- *Number of positive/negative emoticons* — An emoticon is a representation of a facial expression such as a smile or frown, formed by various combinations of keyboard characters and used heavily in tweets to convey the writer's feelings or intended tone. Quite intuitively, positive emoticons accompany positive tweets and negative emotions juxtapose negative tweets. More the number of emoticons, it leans with more confidence towards the corresponding polarity. However, a lot of sarcastic tweets also contain positive emoticons, but we do not explicitly handle sarcasm and hence ignore such possibility.

- *Number of named entities* — Just like URLs, named entities act as another indication for factual and hence neutral sentences. For example, "Remember this? Santorum: Romney, Obama healthcare mandates one and the same http://t.co/sIoG48TO #TheRealRomney @userX @userY". We extract named entities using a python wrapper for the Stanford NER tool (Finkel et al., 2005). However, ablation experiments done after the submission of system in the competition revealed that this feature actually ended up degrading performance by more than 2% of F1 score.

- *Grapheme Stretching* — Words with characters repeated multiple times (at least twice) herald strong subjectivity, most often positive. For example, "Not only is @userZ home from China, she's in LA...I called her and screamed Mandyyyyyyyyyyyyy...I'm gonna hug her for 2 hrs tomorrow!" and "daniel radcliffe was sooo attractive in the 3rd and 5th films omg im in love". We used the number of grapheme stretched words as a feature for our sentiment classifier.

- *Number of words with unusual capitalization* — Words with characters made upper-case or lower-case out of turn might potentially convey subjectivity. This feature also proved to slightly degrade performance, during post-competition ablation experiments.

- *Number of words with all the characters capitalized* — Strongly positive or strongly negative tweets often have words in all caps in order to convey the excitement that normally the loudness of a voice intones.

- *Presence of numbers* — Numbers are used profusely in factual tweets. For example- "13:58 Steven Pourier, Jr. (OLC) MADE the 2nd of the 2 shot Free Throw. DaSU leads 90 - 36 in the 2nd Half. #NAIAMBB". Hence the presence of numbers can be used as an useful feature to distinguish between subjective and objective tweets.

- *Lexicon features*- We use 15 lexicon features extracted from publicly available lexicons, which prove to be one of the most powerful features in our features list. Social media data, specially tweets, have a style of language use that is quite different from other text data. We included lexicons which are specially tailored to handle social media data, like Sentiment140 and NRC Hashtag Lexicon. We elaborate on the lexicon features as the following:

From Sentiwordnet (Baccianella et al., 2010), we extract

- Number of positive tokens
- Number of negative tokens
- Total positive sentiment score
- Total negative sentiment score
- Maximum sentiment score

From Bing Liu's opinion lexicon (Hu and Liu, 2004), we extract

- Number of positive tokens
- Number of negative tokens

From MPQA subjectivity lexicon (Wilson et al., 2005), we extract

- Number of positive tokens
- Number of negative tokens

From NRC Emotion Association lexicon (Mohammad and Turney, 2013), we extract

- Number of positive tokens
- Number of negative tokens

From Sentiment140 lexicon (Go et al., 2009), we extract

- Sum of sentiment score
- Maximum sentiment score

From NRC Hashtag Lexicon (Mohammad and Kiritchenko, 2014), we extract

- Sum of sentiment score
- Maximum sentiment score

3.4 Training Classifier

Once we have extracted all the features, we train a linear SVM using Python based Scikit Learn library (Pedregosa et al., 2011) for the purpose of classification. We experimentally ascertained the optimal value of the parameter C to be 0.025. In order to cope with the slight class imbalance in the data, we automatically adjust weights inversely proportional to class frequencies.

Feature	F1
all	56.67
all - number of entities	58.68 [2]
all - grapheme	56.52
all - exclamation	55.91
all - emoticons	56.61
all - number of hastags	56.69
all - unigrams	53.52
all - lexicons	48.40
all - wh words	56.62
all - illegal capitalization	56.90 [2]

Table 1: Ablation Experiment on Twitter 2015 dataset.

Dataset	Our Score	Best Score
Twitter 2015	56.67	64.84
Twitter 2015 Sarcasm	62.96	65.77
Twitter 2014	63.29	74.42
Twitter 2014 Sarcasm	47.07	59.11
Twitter 2013	61.56	72.80
Live Journal 2014	67.55	75.34
SMS 2013	59.26	68.49

Table 2: Official Results for SemEval 2015.

4 Experiments and Results

We used the official training and test sets provided for the SemEval 2015 task to train and evaluate our system. Tweets in the training data that were not available any more through the Twitter API were removed from the training set. For the evaluation, we compute precision, recall and F1 measures as computed by the scorer package provided for the task. Table 1 shows the ablation experiment we carried out, thereby highlighting the usefulness of the various features used. Table 2 records the F1 score obtained by our submission on different datasets. Our performance on Twitter 2015 Sarcasm data set is encouraging - we stand 4th on the data set.

5 Conclusion

This papers details the description of the system submitted by team Sentibase for SemEval 2015 Task 10. As the title of the paper suggests, the goal

[2]The fact that this feature degrades performance became clear during post-competition experiments

of this work was more to, put together a complete Sentiment Analyzer for Twitter in a day's time that achieves competitive performance without going through complex modeling techniques, than to up the ante in the state-of-the-work picture of Sentiment Analysis.

References

Apoorv Agarwal, Boyi Xie, Ilia Vovsha, Owen Rambow, and Rebecca Passonneau. 2011. Sentiment analysis of twitter data. In *Proceedings of the Workshop on Languages in Social Media*, LSM '11, pages 30–38, Stroudsburg, PA, USA.

Stefano Baccianella, Andrea Esuli, and Fabrizio Sebastiani. 2010. Sentiwordnet 3.0: An enhanced lexical resource for sentiment analysis and opinion mining. In *in Proc. of LREC*.

Akshat Bakliwal, Piyush Arora, Senthil Madhappan, Nikhil Kapre, Mukesh Singh, and Vasudeva Varma. 2012. Mining sentiments from tweets. In *Proceedings of the 3rd Workshop in Computational Approaches to Subjectivity and Sentiment Analysis*, WASSA '12, pages 11–18, Stroudsburg, PA, USA.

Jenny Rose Finkel, Trond Grenager, and Christopher Manning. 2005. Incorporating non-local information into information extraction systems by gibbs sampling. In *In ACL*, pages 363–370.

Alec Go, Richa Bhayani, and Lei Huang. 2009. Twitter sentiment classification using distant supervision. *Processing*, pages 1–6.

Minqing Hu and Bing Liu. 2004. Mining and summarizing customer reviews. In *Proceedings of the Tenth ACM SIGKDD International Conference on Knowledge Discovery and Data Mining*, KDD '04, pages 168–177, New York, NY, USA.

Svetlana Kiritchenko, Xiaodan Zhu, Colin Cherry, and Saif Mohammad. 2014. Nrc-canada-2014: Detecting aspects and sentiment in customer reviews. In *Proceedings of the 8th International Workshop on Semantic Evaluation (SemEval 2014)*, pages 437–442.

Efthymios Kouloumpis, Theresa Wilson, and Johanna Moore. 2011. Twitter sentiment analysis: The good the bad and the omg!

Edward Loper and Steven Bird. 2002. Nltk: The natural language toolkit. In *In Proceedings of the ACL Workshop on Effective Tools and Methodologies for Teaching Natural Language Processing and Computational Linguistics. Philadelphia: Association for Computational Linguistics*.

Saif M. Mohammad and Svetlana Kiritchenko. 2014. Using hashtags to capture fine emotion categories from tweets. *Computational Intelligence*, pages n/a–n/a.

Saif M. Mohammad and Peter D. Turney. 2013. Crowdsourcing a word-emotion association lexicon. 29(3):436–465.

Saif M. Mohammad, Svetlana Kiritchenko, and Xiaodan Zhu. 2013. Nrc-canada: Building the state-of-the-art in sentiment analysis of tweets. *CoRR*, abs/1308.6242.

Preslav Nakov, Sara Rosenthal, Zornitsa Kozareva, Veselin Stoyanov, Alan Ritter, and Theresa Wilson. 2013. Semeval-2013 task 2: Sentiment analysis in twitter. In *Second Joint Conference on Lexical and Computational Semantics (*SEM), Volume 2: Proceedings of the Seventh International Workshop on Semantic Evaluation (SemEval 2013)*, pages 312–320, Atlanta, Georgia, USA, June.

Alexander Pak and Patrick Paroubek. 2010. Twitter as a corpus for sentiment analysis and opinion mining. In *Proceedings of the Seventh conference on International Language Resources and Evaluation (LREC'10)*.

Fabian Pedregosa, Gal Varoquaux, Alexandre Gramfort, Vincent Michel, Bertrand Thirion, Olivier Grisel, Mathieu Blondel, Peter Prettenhofer, Ron Weiss, Vincent Dubourg, Jake Vanderplas, Alexandre Passos, David Cournapeau, Matthieu Brucher, Matthieu Perrot, and douard Duchesnay. 2011. Scikit-learn: Machine learning in Python. *Journal of Machine Learning Research*, 12:2825–2830.

Maria Pontiki, Dimitris Galanis, John Pavlopoulos, Harris Papageorgiou, Ion Androutsopoulos, and Suresh Manandhar. 2014. Semeval-2014 task 4: Aspect based sentiment analysis. In *Proceedings of the 8th International Workshop on Semantic Evaluation (SemEval 2014)*, pages 27–35, Dublin, Ireland, August.

Sara Rosenthal, Alan Ritter, Preslav Nakov, and Veselin Stoyanov. 2014. Semeval-2014 task 9: Sentiment analysis in twitter. In *Proceedings of the 8th International Workshop on Semantic Evaluation (SemEval 2014)*, pages 73–80, Dublin, Ireland, August.

Sara Rosenthal, Preslav Nakov, Svetlana Kiritchenko, Saif M Mohammad, Alan Ritter, and Veselin Stoyanov. 2015. Semeval-2015 task 10: Sentiment analysis in twitter. In *Proceedings of the 9th International Workshop on Semantic Evaluation*, SemEval '2015, Denver, Colorado, June.

Richard Socher, Alex Perelygin, Jean Y. Wu, Jason Chuang, Christopher D. Manning, Andrew Y. Ng, and Christopher Potts. 2013. Recursive deep models for semantic compositionality over a sentiment treebank.

Theresa Wilson, Janyce Wiebe, and Paul Hoffmann. 2005. Recognizing contextual polarity in phrase-level sentiment analysis. In *Proceedings of the Conference on Human Language Technology and Empirical Methods in Natural Language Processing*, HLT '05, pages 347–354, Stroudsburg, PA, USA.

UNIBA: Sentiment Analysis of English Tweets Combining Micro-blogging, Lexicon and Semantic Features

Pierpaolo Basile and **Nicole Novielli**
Department of Computer Science, University of Bari Aldo Moro
Via, E. Orabona, 4 - 70125 Bari (Italy)
{pierpaolo.basile,nicole.novielli}@uniba.it

Abstract

This paper describes the UNIBA team participation in the Sentiment Analysis in Twitter task (Task 10) at SemEval-2015. We propose a supervised approach relying on keyword, lexicon and micro-blogging features as well as representation of tweets in a word space.

1 Introduction

Sentiment analysis is the study of the subjectivity and polarity (positive vs. negative) of a text (Pang and Lee, 2008). With the worldwide diffusion of social media, a huge amount of textual data has been made available, thus attracting the interest of researchers in this domain (Rosenthal et al., 2014). Sentiment analysis on such informal texts poses new challenges due to the presence of slang, misspelled words and micro-blogging features such as hashtags or links and traditional approaches may not be successfully exploited in this domain. Previous research has successfully exploited approaches based on lexical and micro-blogging features (Mohammad et al., 2013). In this study, we investigate a supervised approach including three kinds of features based on keywords and micro-blogging properties of tweets, sentiment lexicons and semantics. Rather than using word-sense disambiguation (Miura et al., 2014), we represent tweets in a distributional semantic model (DSM) (Vanzo et al., 2014), which is able to learn the context of usage of words analysing co-occurrences in large corpora.

This paper describes our participation at the SemEval 2015 Sentiment Analysis in Twitter task (Rosenthal et al., 2015). We discuss methods and results of our experimental study for the overall polarity classification of tweets (*message level* subtask B). The Sentiment Analysis task focuses on English tweets. Data provided for training are annotated according to the overall polarity of each tweet (i.e., 'negative', 'positive' or 'neutral'). The system evaluation is performed on different test sets. In particular, the rank of the systems is calculated on the offical Twitter 2015 test set. Further evaluation is performed on a progress set including test instances from the previous edition of the task, to allow comparision with previous studies (Rosenthal et al., 2014). We build a supervised system based on our sentiment classifier for Italian tweets, which ranked 1st in both the polarity and subjectivity tasks at Evalita 2014 (Basile and Novielli, 2014).

The paper is structured as follows: we introduce our system and report the details about features in Section 2. We describe the evaluation and the system setup in Section 3. We conclude by reporting results and discussion in Section 4.

2 System Description

Our system is built upon our classifier for sentiment analysis of Italian tweets (Basile and Novielli, 2014). We adopt a supervised approach using Support Vector Machine as a classification algorithm. We investigate three groups of features based on: (i) keyword and micro-blogging characteristics, (ii) sentiment lexicons, and (iii) a Distributional Semantic Model (DSM).

Keywords and micro-blogging features. Keyword-based features exploit tokens occurring in the tweets (Table 1). During the tokenization we replace the user mentions, URLs and hashtags with three metatokens, "_USER_", "_URL_" and "_TAG_", for which we also count the total occurrences. As for keywords, we consider unigrams and bigrams. To deal with negations, all the n-grams occurring in a negated context receive the *neg* suffix. A negated context is a tweet fragment starting with a negation word[1] and ending with a punctuation mark (Pang et al., 2002). Moreover, we create features capturing typical aspects of micro-blogging, such as the use of upper case ratio and character repetitions[2], positive and negative emoticons, informal expressions of laughters[3], as well as the presence of exclamation and interrogative marks, negations, intensifiers [4]. Finally we include features based on word count for 1000 large-scale word clusters built on English tweets[5].

Lexicon-based Features. The second group contains features calculated for each of the eight lexicons we consider in this study. These lexicons can be differentiated based on how they represent the information about prior polarity of words.

The NRC Emotion Lexicon (Mohammad and Turney, 2010), the MPQA Lexicon (Wilson et al., 2005) and the Bing Liu Lexicon (Hu and Liu, 2004) provide lists of positive and negative words. We assign a positive score equal to 1 to the positive sentiment terms, and a negative score equal to 1 to the negative ones. Similarly, the NRC Hashtag Sentiment Lexicon and the Sentiment140 Lexicon provide a list of words with their sentiment association score, calculated as pointwise mutual information with respect to collections of positive and negative tweets (Mohammad et al., 2013). Positive and negative scores are associated, respectively, to positive and negative sentiment, while the magnitude indicates the degree of association. We consider also the lexicon used by SentiStrength[6], a state-of-the-art tool for extracting sentiment strength from informal English text on social media (Thelwall et al., 2010). The SentiStrength lexicon is structured as a list of words with scores ranging in $[-5, +5]$. A set of booster words is also provided, to increase or decrease the strength of the prior polarity of terms. Finally, we use a list of emoticons as taken from Wikipedia[7]: we assign +1 and -1 as a score for positive and negative emoticons, respectively. In all the lexicons mentioned so far either a positive or negative score is associated to each term. Using these lexicons, we extract a set of features based on prior polarity of words occuring in the tweets, as reported in Table 2. The features are computed separately for terms in affirmative contexts and terms in negated contexts.

In addition, we use SentiWordNet 3.0 (Esuli and Sebastiani, 2006). SentiWordNet extends WordNet by associating positive, negative and objective scores to each synset, where the three scores sum up to 1. A lemma can receive multiple polarity scores if it occurs in more than one synset. In such cases, we select the most frequent sense for the lemma, with respect to its part-of-speech. Thanks to the availability of the objective scores, additional features can be computed to model the presence of neutral terms, as reported in (Basile and Novielli, 2014). Also the features based on SentiWordNet are calculated separately for affirmative and negated contexts.

Finally, we consider the word classes defined in the Linguistic Inquiry and Word Count (LIWC) taxonomy, developed in the scope of psycholinguistic research (Pennebaker and Francis, 2001). LIWC organizes words into psychologically meaningful categories based on the assumption that words and language reflect most part of cognitive and emotional phenomena involved in communication. Previous research has shown how the language use varies with respect to the communicative intention, thus making possible to distinguish between objective and subjective statements as well as between agreement and disagreement expressions (Novielli and Strapparava, 2013). Therefore, we include word count features

[1]The complete list of negation words provided by Christopher Potts in his tutorial on sentiment `http://sentiment.christopherpotts.net/`.

[2]These features usually plays the same role of intensifiers in informal writing contexts.

[3]i.e., sequences of "ah".

[4]The list of booster words is the same used by Sentistrength: `http://sentistrength.wlv.ac.uk/`

[5]Twitter Word Clusters: `http://www.ark.cs.cmu.edu/TweetNLP/#resources`

[6]`http://sentistrength.wlv.ac.uk/`

[7]`http://it.wikipedia.org/wiki/Emoticon`

for each word class in LIWC. Similarly, we include word count features for the emotion word classes in the NRC Emotion Lexicon.

Semantic Features. Finally, we calculate features based on the Distributional Semantic Model (DSM). Given a set of 15M unlabelled downloaded tweets, we build a geometric space in which each word is represented as a mathematical point (Sahlgren, 2006). The similarity between words is computed as their closeness in the space. To represent a tweet in the geometric space, we adopt the superposition operator (Smolensky, 1990), that is the vector sum of all the vectors of words occurring in the tweet. We use the tweet vector $\overrightarrow{t}$ as a semantic feature in training our classifier.

In the same fashion, we build prototype vectors for each class based on the sentiment lexicons that provide prior polarity scores for words (i.e. SentiWordNet, SentiStrength, and the merge of NRC Hashtag and the Sentiment140). For example, the prototype vector for the positive class $\overrightarrow{p_{pos}}$ based on SentiStrength is obtained by summing up all the vectors of words with positive prior polarity in the SentiStrength lexicon. We use three prototype vectors to represent, for each lexicon, the positive $\overrightarrow{p_{pos}}$, negative $\overrightarrow{p_{neg}}$, and subjective $\overrightarrow{p_s}$ class (defined by considering both positive and negative words). In the case of SentiWordNet, objectivity scores are also available and allow us to build a prototype for objectivity $\overrightarrow{p_o}$. To capture the subjectivity and the polarity of a tweet $\overrightarrow{t}$, we compute the cosine similarity between $\overrightarrow{t}$ and each prototype vector.

3 Evaluation

The message level subtask (subtask B) is designed for evaluating systems on their ability to predict the overall polarity of a given tweet, with respect to three classes: positive, negative, and neutral.

Organizers provided 8,006 manually annotated tweets as training data. We use the training set[8] to extract the features described in Section 2. Details on our system setup are reported in Section 3.1. As test set, organizers provided a collection of 2,390 manually annotated tweets (Official 2015 test set). Further data from different sources (8,987 tweets overall) are included in the progress test set and are provided to allow comparison with systems participating in previous editions. Systems are compared against the gold standard of the official test set in terms of macro average F measure calculated over the positive and negative classes. For the sake of completeness, we report also weighted F measure considering all the three categories in the classification task (see Section 4).

3.1 System Setup

The system is completely developed in JAVA. We used the Liblinear[9] implementation of L_2-loss support vector classifier. Tweets are tokenized using the Twitter NLP and Part-of-Speech Tagging API[10]. We use both the tokenizer and the part-of-speech tagger to preprocess the data.

Regarding the DSM, we download 15 million tweets using the Twitter Streaming API. Tweets are downloaded by querying the API using three lexicons extracted from the training data for each class, based on Kullback-Leibler divergence (KLD) as described in (Basile and Novielli, 2014).

We download the same number of tweets for each lexicon. We exploit these unlabeled tweets to build a DSM, using the "word2vec"[11] tool based on a revised implementation of the Recurrent Neural Net Language Model (Mikolov et al., 2013) using a log-linear approach. We use the skipgram model, which is more accurate in presence of infrequent words, with 300 vector dimensions and remove the terms with less than ten occurrences, obtaining 308,493 terms overall.

In training our classifier, we set the C parameter to 0.01. We select this value after a 10-fold validation on training data to select the best combination. The total number of features exploited is 145,967.

4 Results and Discussion

The final ranking issued by the organizers considers the system performance in terms of average between F measures for the positive and negative classes only. Table 3 reports the system performance and

[8]Further development data provided by the organizers are not used for training

[9]`http://www.csie.ntu.edu.tw/~cjlin/liblinear/`

[10]`http://www.ark.cs.cmu.edu/TweetNLP/`

[11]`https://code.google.com/p/word2vec/`

Keyword and micro-blogging features	
$n-grams$	uni- and bi-grams are considered. User mentions, URLs and hashtag are replaced with metatokens
$count_{USER}$	total occurrences of user mentions
$count_{URL}$	total occurrences of URLs
$count_{TAG}$	total occurrences of hashtags
$uppercase_{ratio}$	the ratio between the number of upper case characters and the total number of characters
emo_{pos}	the number of positive emoticons
emo_{neg}	the number of negative emoticons
$count_{Laugh}$	the count of sequences of 'ah' as slang expression of laughters
$count_{Intensif}$	the ratio between the number of tokens with repeated characters and the total number of tokens
$count_{QMark}$	the total occurrences of question marks
$count_{ExMark}$	the total occurrences of exclamation marks
$count_{Negation}$	the total occurrences of negation words
$count_{cluster_i}$	the total occurrences of words belonging to the *i*-th cluster

Table 1: Description of keyword and micro-blogging features.

Sentiment lexicon based features	
o_{pos}	the number of tokens with positive score
o_{neg}	the number of tokens with negative score
o_{subj}	the number of tokens with either positive or negative score
$last_{pos}$	the score of the last positive token in the tweet
$last_{neg}$	the score of the last negative token in the tweet
$last_{emo}$	the score of the last emoticon in the tweet
sum_{pos}	the sum of positive scores for the tokens in the tweet
sum_{neg}	the sum of negative scores for the tokens in the tweet
sum_{subj}	the subjectivity polarity, it is the sum of the positive and negative scores
$sum_{Max_{pos}}$	the maximum positive score observed for tokens in the tweet
$sum_{Max_{neg}}$	the maximum negative score observed for tokens in the tweet
$count_{C_i}$	the total occurrences of words belonging to the i-th word class C_i, where word classes are defined by the LIWC and NRC Emotion Lexicon taxonomies

Table 2: Description of sentiment lexicon features.

its rank. The system rank on the progress set is calculated on the performance on the Twitter 2014 subset. For completeness, we report also the F measure calculated considering all the three classes in our model, including the neutral category 4.

The results are very encouraging: even if far from optimum, the system differs for only 3.29 points from the first ranked one (F=64.84). Furthermore, we observe that even if our system is trained only on tweets it is able to generalize on datasets from other domains, such as SMS and other microblogging services (i.e., LiveJournal). Conversely, the system performance drops on the Twitter 2014 Sarcasm set. This is consistent with results observed in our previous study (Basile and Novielli, 2014) on Italian tweets (Basile et al., 2014), where the 43% of misclassified negative cases were mostly ironic and would require common sense reasoning to detect the negative opinion expressed. Moreover a drop in perfomance on the sarcasm test set had been already

System	Positive			Negative			Neutral			F	
	P	R	F	P	R	F	P	R	F		
All features	85.42	55.30	67.13	60.51	52.05	55.96	61.11	86.93	71.77	64.95	
w/o keyword	88.23	49.81	63.67	59.62	51.78	55.43	59.18	89.16	71.14	63.41	(-2.37%)
w/o semantic	84.12	54.62	66.24	58.16	53.70	55.84	61,.28	85.61	71.43	64.50	(-0.69%)
w/o lexicons	83.31	52.89	64.70	60.92	39.73	48.09	58.14	58.14	70.00	60.93	(-6.19%)

Table 4: System results for all feature settings and all classes on the official test set Twitter 2015.

Test set	AVG (Fpos,Fneg)	Rank
Official 2015	61.55	12/40
Twitter 2014	65.11	25/40
LiveJournal 2014	70.05	-
SMS 2013	65.50	-
Twitter 2013	61.66	-
Twitter 2014 Sarcasm	37.30	-

Table 3: Task results.

observed for systems participating in the previous edition of the task (Rosenthal et al., 2014) and can be observed for all systems in the current edition. However, our system had a greater than average performance drop and we are currently studying this issue.

Observing the detailed scores for each class (first row of Table 4) we discover that the system performs better in the recognition of positive and neutral cases, in contrast with previous evidence from the experiment on the Italian corpus.

To further investigate the predictive power of the features in our model, we perform an ablation test on the Twitter 2015 test set, for which organizers provided the gold standard. We remove each group of features to assess the decrease of F measure on test data with respect to the setting including all features. Results are reported in Table 4 and demonstrate the importance of all feature groups.

Removing the sentiment lexicon group of features causes the highest decrease in performance. This is in contrast with previous evidence of our experiment on the Italian dataset of tweets, where a drop of performance of only 1% was observed. We provide a possible explanation to this by observing that only one sentiment lexicon was adopted in the study on the Italian dataset. On the contrary, in the current experiment on English tweets we can rely on a richer set of features due to the avaliablity of numerous lexicons, as explained in Section 2. Moreover, the Sentiment140 Lexicon and the Hashtag Sentiment Lexicon are both developed specifically to address sentiment analysis of tweets, thus providing higher coverage of lexical cues that are typical of microblogging.

Keyword and microblogging features are the second most useful group. This is consistent with evidence from the Italian experiment, for which we observe a comparable drop in performance on the polarity detection task. However, in the current experiment we also consider n-grams, which are not included in the feature set of the system for Italian. This consideration suggest that n-grams might contribute differently to the performance of sentiment classifiers depending on the language being used, thus suggesting directions for further investigation.

Finally, semantic features lead to the smaller drop in F measure when removed (-0.69%). This is in contrast with our previous findings in the Italian setting, where the semantic features plays a key role. This might be due to the prevalence of political topics in the Italian dataset, possibly causing a bias in our classifier due to the domain-specific lexicon about politics. This discrepancy indicates further directions for future investigation on the ability of semantic features in disambiguating polarity in microblogging, with respect to the topic being discussed and the language being used.

Future replications of this study will involve further data to validate and generalize our findings.

References

Pierpaolo Basile and Nicole Novielli. 2014. UNIBA at EVALITA 2014-SENTIPOLC Task: Predicting tweet sentiment polarity combining micro-blogging, lexicon and semantic features. In *Proceedings of EVALITA 2014*, pages 58–63.

Valerio Basile, Andrea Bolioli, Malvina Nissim, Viviana Patti, and Paolo Rosso. 2014. Overview of the Evalita 2014 SENTIment POLarity Classification Task. In *Proc. of EVALITA 2014*, Pisa, Italy.

Andrea Esuli and Fabrizio Sebastiani. 2006. Sentiwordnet: A publicly available lexical resource for opinion mining. In *Proceedings of LREC*, volume 6, pages 417–422.

Minqing Hu and Bing Liu. 2004. Mining and Summarizing Customer Reviews. In *Proceedings of the Tenth ACM SIGKDD International Conference on Knowledge Discovery and Data Mining*, pages 168–177.

Tomas Mikolov, Kai Chen, Greg Corrado, and Jeffrey Dean. 2013. Efficient Estimation of Word Representations in Vector Space. *CoRR*, abs/1301.3781.

Yasuhide Miura, Shigeyuki Sakaki, Keigo Hattori, and Tomoko Ohkuma. 2014. TeamX: A Sentiment Analyzer with Enhanced Lexicon Mapping and Weighting Scheme for Unbalanced Data. In *Proceedings of the 8th International Workshop on Semantic Evaluation (SemEval 2014)*, pages 628–632, Dublin, Ireland, August.

Saif M. Mohammad and Peter D. Turney. 2010. Emotions Evoked by Common Words and Phrases: Using Mechanical Turk to Create an Emotion Lexicon. In *Proceedings of the NAACL HLT 2010 Workshop on Computational Approaches to Analysis and Generation of Emotion in Text*, CAAGET '10, pages 26–34.

Saif Mohammad, Svetlana Kiritchenko, and Xiaodan Zhu. 2013. Nrc-canada: Building the state-of-the-art in sentiment analysis of tweets. In *Second Joint Conference on Lexical and Computational Semantics (*SEM), Volume 2: Proceedings of the Seventh International Workshop on Semantic Evaluation (SemEval 2013)*, pages 321–327, Atlanta, Georgia, USA, June.

Nicole Novielli and Carlo Strapparava. 2013. The Role of Affect Analysis in Dialogue Act Identification. *IEEE Transactions on Affective Computing*, 4:439–451.

Bo Pang and Lillian Lee. 2008. Opinion Mining and Sentiment Analysis. *Foundations and trends in information retrieval*, 2(1-2):1–135, January.

Bo Pang, Lillian Lee, and Shivakumar Vaithyanathan. 2002. Thumbs up? Sentiment Classification using Machine Learning Techniques. In *Proceedings of the 2002 Conference on Empirical Methods in Natural Language Processing*, pages 79–86, July.

J. Pennebaker and M. Francis. 2001. Linguistic Inquiry and Word Count: LIWC. Erlbaum Publishers.

Sara Rosenthal, Alan Ritter, Preslav Nakov, and Veselin Stoyanov. 2014. SemEval-2014 Task 9: Sentiment Analysis in Twitter. In *Proceedings of the 8th International Workshop on Semantic Evaluation (SemEval 2014)*, pages 73–80, Dublin, Ireland, August.

Sara Rosenthal, Preslav Nakov, Svetlana Kiritchenko, Saif M Mohammad, Alan Ritter, and Veselin Stoyanov. 2015. SemEval-2015 Task 10: Sentiment Analysis in Twitter. In *Proceedings of the 9th International Workshop on Semantic Evaluation*, SemEval '2015, Denver, Colorado, June.

Magnus Sahlgren. 2006. *The Word-Space Model: Using distributional analysis to represent syntagmatic and paradigmatic relations between words in high-dimensional vector spaces*. Ph.D. thesis.

Paul Smolensky. 1990. Tensor product variable binding and the representation of symbolic structures in connectionist systems. *Artificial Intelligence*, 46(1-2):159–216, November.

Mike Thelwall, Kevan Buckley, Georgios Paltoglou, Di Cai, and Arvid Kappas. 2010. Sentiment in Short Strength Detection Informal Text. *Journal of the American Society for Information Science and Technology*, 61(12):2544–2558, December.

Andrea Vanzo, Danilo Croce, and Roberto Basili. 2014. A context-based model for Sentiment Analysis in Twitter. In *Proceedings of COLING 2014, the 25th International Conference on Computational Linguistics: Technical Papers*, pages 2345–2354, Dublin, Ireland, August.

Theresa Wilson, Janyce Wiebe, and Paul Hoffmann. 2005. Recognizing Contextual Polarity in Phrase-level Sentiment Analysis. In *Proceedings of the Conference on Human Language Technology and Empirical Methods in Natural Language Processing*, HLT '05, pages 347–354.

IITPSemEval: Sentiment Discovery from 140 Characters

Ayush Kumar, Vamsi Krishna Akella and Asif Ekbal
Department of Computer Science and Engineering
Indian Institute of Technology, Patna
Patna, 800013
Email: ayush.cs12@iitp.ac.in, vamsi.cs11@iitp.ac.in, asif@iitp.ac.in

Abstract

This paper presents an overview of the system developed and submitted as a part of our participation to the SemEval-2015 Task 10 that deals with Sentiment Analysis in Twitter. We build a Support Vector Machine (SVM) based supervised learning model for Subtask A (term level task) and Subtask B (message level task). We also participate in Subtask E viz., determining degree of polarity, and build a very simple system by employing the available lexical resources. Experiments with the 2015 official datasets show F1 scores of 81.31% and 58.80% for Task A and Task B, respectively. For Subtask E, our model achieves a score of 0.413 on Kendal's Tau metric.

1 Introduction

The use of social media platforms has become central to many teenager's and adult's lives. With the emerging forms of communication, much of the freely available texts in the opinionated texts are linguistically unstructured. People have adopted creative spellings and abbreviations, and are excessively using more intelligent forms of messages that involves typos, hash-tags and emoticons to convey their messages. The huge abundance of inexpensive data, rich in applications, can prove handy for public and corporate institutions. This has urged the scientific community to extract the substantive information from these texts. The proliferation of microblogging sites like Twitter which boasts of user's comments on everything trending in real time opens up an unprecedented opportunity to explore and develop techniques to mine the information.

Task 10 in Semantic Evaluation 2015 provides a research platform promoting the knowledge discovery in Twitter. Task 10 consists of five different subtasks: Contextual Polarity Disambiguation (A), Message Polarity Classification (B), Topic-Based Message Polarity Classification (C), Detecting Trends Towards a Topic (D) and Determining degree of polarity of Twitter terms with the sentiment (E). Complete details of the task can be found at (Rosenthal et al., 2015). We participated in Subtasks A, B and E, the first two of which require the sentiments to be classified into positive, negative and neutral classes for a given segment of the tweet (for A) or the entire message (for B), while the Task E needs to compute the strength of association of the given terms to the sentiment on a scale of 0 to 1 with 1 denoting the maximum strength.

The technical study of public sentiment has been a subject of trending research and a significant amount of extensive work is being carried out in the domain. Sentiment Analysis has been handled at the various levels of granularity. Early research works (Pang and Lee, 2004) focussed on the document level classification with further studies at message and term level (Rosenthal et al., 2014). Twitter has also been investigated for its possible applications in the fields of commerce (Jansen et al., 2009; Bollen et al., 2011), elections (O'Connor et al., 2010; Tumasjan et al., 2010), disaster management (Nagy and Stamberger, 2012; Terpstra et al., 2012) etc. using varied approaches and different experimental setups. Semantic Evaluation tasks (Nakov et al., 2013; Rosenthal et al., 2014) continue to pitch in with the newer systems for the sentiment classification of tweets.

2 Proposed Approach

In this section, we describe the supervised learning system that we develop for the first two subtasks, namely A and B. The first section would focus on Tasks A and B and later section would describe the method that was adopted for Task E.

2.1 Preprocessing

We normalize all URLs to http://someurl and all usernames to @someuser. We also pre-process the dataset to convert character encodings like \u2019('), \u002c(,) &(&), <(<), >(>), (whitespace), <3(love) etc. to their usual text so as to reduce the noise.

2.2 Methods for Contextual Disambiguation and Message Classification

We develop the methods for the first two tasks based on supervised Support Vector Machine (Cortes and Vapnik , 1995).

Consider $\{(\mathbf{x}_1, y_1), \ldots, (\mathbf{x}_N, y_N)\}$, which represents the training data for the two-class problem, where $y_k \in \{+1, -1\}$ represents the class associated with $\mathbf{x}_k$ and $\mathbf{x}_k \in R^D$ is the feature vector corresponding to the k-th sample in the training set. The aim of the SVM is to learn a linear hyperplane that divides the negative examples from the positive examples such that the separation between the two classes is maximal. The equation of this hyperplane may be obtained as follows: $(\mathbf{w}.\mathbf{x}) + b = 0 \quad \mathbf{w} \in \mathbf{R}^D, b \in \mathbf{R}$.

In our work we make use of the SVM implementation as available with the LibLinear [1] model (Fan et al., 2008). LibLinear has been optimized for data with millions of instances with very large feature spaces. To develop the feature-based learning model, we categorize the features into three groups: Token-level Features (Group-I), Semantic Features (Group-II) and Encoding Features (Group-III).

The set of features that we implement for the target tasks are described as follows.

[1]www.csie.ntu.edu.tw/cjlin/liblinear

1. **Group-1: Token-level Features**: These correspond to the features like n-grams and Part-of-Speech (PoS).

   - **Word n-grams**: All n-grams of sizes 1 and 2 are extracted for Task A using Ngram Statistics Package (Banerjee and Pedersen, 2003). This binary valued feature is implemented as contextual feature for Task A. Based on the results obtained on the development set, two words on each side of the targeted segment are taken into consideration. For Task B, all n-grams of size upto three are extracted.
   - **Character n-Grams**: For each token in the target text in the tweet, all the character n-grams of prefix and suffix of lengths of two and three characters are extracted. This feature is implemented only for the term level task.
   - **Part of Speech (PoS) Information**: For both the subtasks, we label each token in the tweet with CMU ARK PoS tagger (Gimpel et al., 2011). The number of each of the PoS tags is kept as feature.

2. **Group-II: Semantic Features**: To take into account the semantics of the text present in the tweet/targeted segment, we use Lexicon and SentiWordNet based features.

   - **Lexicon Features**: We use lexicons such as NRC Hashtag [2], Sentiment 140 [3], Bing Liu (Liu et al., 2005) and NRC Emotion Lexicons (Mohammad and Turney, 2013) to implement various features. The implementation of features for these tasks is based on the number of tokens associated with positive and negative sentiment using NRC Hashtag, Sentiment 140 and Bing Liu lexicon. For NRC Hashtag and Sentiment 140 lexicon, the sentiment scores of the tokens are used to implement total score of the message as another feature.

[2]http://www.umiacs.umd.edu/saif/WebDocs/NRC-Hashtag-Sentiment-Lexicon-v0.1.zip

[3]http://www.umiacs.umd.edu/saif/WebDocs/Sentiment140-Lexicon-v0.1.zip

The NRC emotion lexicon is a list of words and their associations with eight emotions (anger, fear, anticipation, trust, surprise, sadness, joy and disgust) and two sentiments (negative and positive). We categorize joy, surprise, trust and anticipation as positive emotions and the rest as negative emotions. Based on the categorization, we compute the number of tokens with positive score, number of tokens with negative score and number of tokens with neutral score as the features.

- **SentiWordNet Feature**: We compute the average positive score (posScore) and negative score (negScore) for each word in the tweet using SentiWordNet3.0 (Baccianella et al., 2010). For a given tweet we define two features that denote the number of words which have posScore greater than negScore, and number of word with negScore greater than posScore.
- **Inverted Segment**: An inverted segment is defined as the part of the tweet which occurs after an inverting word (i.e. the tokens that denote the negative context) such as doesn't, isn't, can't, etc. until a punctuation. The polarity of the words occurring in the inverted segment is reversed, i.e. a token with positive or negative sentiment is converted to the token bearing negative or positive sentiment, respectively. The intensity values of the tokens are adopted from the NRC Hashtag lexicon (Mohammad et al., 2013) and Sentiment140 lexicon (Mohammad et al., 2013) which are used to construct the feature vector. The feature vector contains several pieces of information that denote the number of inverted segments in the tweet, sum of intensities of all the words that appear in the inverted segments in the tweet, etc.
- **Tweet Clusters**: We use the CMU Twitter Word Clusters (Owoputi et al., 2013) to generate the clusters of words that appear either in the context of positive or negative sentiment. All the tokens which belong to the positive sub-cluster occur more in positive context than in negative context. Similarly all the tokens which belong to the negative sub-cluster occur more in negative context than in the positive context. The categorization of positive and negative sub-cluster is done based on the number of times the token occurs in positive and negative contexts. A feature vector of length 2000 is defined, each bit of which takes a value denoting the number of times the token appears in the tweet.

3. **Group-III: Encoding Features**: The text of the tweet is normally different from the general English text. It contains emoticons, hashtags, repetitive characters and irregular punctuations. To incorporate these encodings, we implement the following features.
   - **Intensifiers**: There are several words that denote the intensity of sentiment, and these can be used as the features of the model. We use the number of hashtags, number of words in uppercase (e.g. BIG loser) and number of elongated words (e.g. yummmmmy) in the tweet as the features. These features were used for both the tasks.
   - **Emoticon Features**: This is a binary valued feature that denotes the presence or absence of the positive and negative emoticon.
   - **Punctuation**: The number of occurrences of contiguous sequences of question marks (????), exclamation marks (!!!) and question-exclamation marks (?!!?) are extracted from the tweet. This feature is not used for subtask A as we observe lower performance of the system on the development set.
   - **URL and Username**: This feature takes into account the number of occurrences of the username and URLs. The feature is defined for the term level task.

2.3 Method for Determining the Strength

Our approach for determining the strength of sentiment bearing words is based on the rule-based ap-

Set	Positive	Negative	Neutral
Training	5480	2967	434+434
Development	648	430	57
2015 Test	1896	1006	190
Progress Test	6354	3771	556

Table 1: Dataset for Task A.

Set	Positive	Negative	Neutral
Training	3064	1204	3942
Development	575	340	739
2015 Test	1038	365	987
Progress Test	3506	1541	3940

Table 2: Dataset for Task B.

proach that is developed using various available resources. We use the sentiment scores of terms extracted from SentiWordNet, Sentiment140 bigram lexicon and NRC Hashtag unigram lexicon. In these lexicons, terms have been assigned scores based on their association to the positive or negative sentiment in some contexts. We also observe that out of the 200 words present in the trial data, 167 words are present at least in one of these three lexicons, which is more than 83%. This is why we use these resources for subtask E.

At first we extract the scores of the given term from the SentiWordNet. The scores denote the associativity of the word towards the positive and negative sentiment in various contexts. Let us assume that posScore and negScore denote the positive and negative scores of the target word, respectively. We compute the average positive and negative scores of all the terms, and the final score is set as Score = Avg posScore - Avg negScore.

If the word or term is not available in the SentiWordNet, we look at the Sentiment140 or NRC Hashtag lexicon. The score of each term in these lexicons corresponds to the number of times the term co-occurs with the positive and negative sentiment. For unigram we search in the NRC Hashtag lexicon, and for the others we look at Sentiment140 lexicon. The score of each term is set as: Score = (no. of positive occurrences - no. of negative occurrences)/(no. of positive occurrences + no. of negative occurrences). For the word that does not appear in any of these lexicons, we assign the default score of 0.5. If the range of the scores is between -1 to 1, we normalize the values between 0 and 1.

3 Datasets and Experimental Results

To train and tune our system, we use the training and development datasets that were employed for Task 2 in SemEval 2013 (Nakov et al., 2013). The system is tested on two datasets for this year's tasks, one is the progress set and the other one is the 2015 official test set. The datasets are annotated with three classes, namely positive, negative and neutral. The training sets consist of 9,315 and 8,210 annotated tweets for subtask A and B, respectively. The progress set contains tweets from five different categories: LiveJournal 2014, SMS 2013, Twitter 2013, Twitter 2014 and Twitter 2014 Sarcasm. The datasets used for the Tasks A and B are summarized in Table 1 and Table 2, respectively. The metric used for evaluating the system is average F1-score (averaged F1-positive and averaged F1-negative, and ignoring the F1-neutral) for 2015 test set, while the ranking for progress set is done on the F1 score of the Twitter 2014 subset.

For Task E, the trial dataset comprise of 200 unique words/phrases with the corresponding scores denoting the strength of the terms with positive or negative sentiment. The test set contains 1,315 words/phrases which has to be scored in between 0 to 1 indicating their association with the positive or negative sentiment.

We observe that proportion of neutral tweets in the training set of Task A is quite less (4.88%). In order to create a balanced dataset, we perform oversampling to increase the number of neutral tweets in the training data. Experiments are carried out with various oversampling rates. Based on the evaluation on the development data, we observe that oversampling the neutral tweets by increasing its number twice lead to better scores while constructing the dataset with thrice the number of neutral tweets results in over-fitting, and hence, lowers the F1-score value. For the second task, we also perform this oversampling technique for the better representations of negative tweet instances. However we notice a reduction in the overall F1-score compared to the performance that we achieved with our original

Features	F1-Score: Task A	F1-Score: Task B
All	81.31	58.80
All-Token	80.04 (-1.27)	54.51 (-4.29)
All-Semantic	76.09 (-5.22)	48.29 (-10.51)
All-Encoding	81.18 (-0.13)	58.24 (-0.56)
All-WordNgram	80.75 (-0.56)	54.92 (-3.88)
All-CharNgram	81.25 (-0.06)	-
All-Ngram	80.30 (-1.01)	54.92 (-3.88)
All-POS	81.23 (-0.08)	59.10 (+0.30)
All-NRCHashtag	81.23 (-0.08)	57.31 (-1.49)
All-Senti140	81.93 (+0.62)	56.73 (-2.07)
All-Bing	80.91 (-0.40)	56.16 (-2.64)
All-Emotion	81.01 (-0.30)	57.68 (-1.12)
All-Lexicon	80.19 (-1.12)	43.23 (-15.57)
All-Cluster	81.24 (0.07)	55.62 (-3.18)
All-Inverted	81.37 (+0.06)	58.73 (-0.07)
All-SentiWord	81.14 (-0.17)	58.44 (-0.36)
All-Intensifiers	81.22 (-0.09)	58.49 (-0.31)
All-Emoticon	81.25 (-0.06)	58.33 (-0.47)
All-URL/Username	81.31 (0.0)	-
All-Punctuation	-	58.64 (-0.16)

Table 3: Experimental results for feature-ablation experiment for Task A and B. The values in the parenthesis denotes the deviation from the score when all the features were taken into consideration.

setup.

For subtask A, our system achieves a F1-score of 81.31% for 2015 test set and 82.73% for Twitter 2014 subset of progress set. For the message level task, i.e. for subtask B, our system obtains the F1-scores of 58.80% for the 2015 test set and 65.09% for the progress test set. The best ranked team for the term level task shows the F1-score of 84.79% for the 2015 test set and 87.12% for the progress test. For Subtask B, the best performing system produces the F1-scores of 64.84% for the 2015 test set and 74.42% for the progress set.

For Task E, we have to provide a score between 0 and 1 for a word or phrase denoting the associativity of the phrase with the positive sentiment. The evaluation metric used for this task is based on Kendall's Tau rank correlation coefficient. Our model obtains a score of 0.413 with respect to the best team's score of 0.625.

3.1 Feature Engineering and Analysis of Results

We observe that our system performs much better for the term level task than the message level task. This can be contributed to the fact that the contextual polarity disambiguation is, in general, single sentiment oriented whereas a message level sentiment classification is ambiguous because of the tweet containing mixed sentiments. To get an insight to the contribution of each feature in development of the system, we perform feature engineering. Experiments of the detailed feature ablation study are shown in Table 3.

From the feature ablation experiment, we observe that in both the tasks, semantic features (i.e. sentiment lexicons) contribute significantly. Among semantic features, both Task A and B rely heavily on lexicon features. It can also be noted that the encoding features which are characteristics of twitter text also help in marginal improvement.

However, the inverted segment feature does not result in the expected performance gain. This can be explained in light of the following two aspects. Let us consider the two statements as: (a) *The coffee tastes bad.* and (b) *The book is not bad.*, the first statement signifies negative sentiment while the second statement is neutral. However, if we take into account the method that we adopted, in sentence (b) according to our approach a negative word (*bad*) becomes positive with the same intensity as we only invert the polarity without changing the intensity of the word, but in this sentence *bad* actually becomes neutral when it occurs in an inverted segment (i.e. after 'not'). Another reason might be the possible conflict between the lexicon and inverted segment features. In lexicon feature, we consider the scores of each token for generating the feature vector where the word '*bad*' is taken into negative sense for both the cases.

3.2 Conclusions and Future Work

In this paper we describe our systems that we developed as part of our participation to the SemEval shared task on Sentiment Analysis on Twitter. Out of the five defined tasks, we participated in three tasks. We have developed a supervised SVM model for the contextual polarity disambiguation (Task A) and message level sentiment classification (Task B). Our system showed promising results for the Task A and satisfactory performance for Task B. However, when we did feature ablation experiment, we found that certain features (like inverted segment) did not contribute substantially as expected. In our future work, we will try to address this issue. The n-grams feature that we have used, generates sparse feature vector. Proper smoothing techniques might be helpful to reduce the noise in the feature vector due to the sparsity in the n-grams feature. Apart from this, we also plan to develop a method in order to automatically identify the most relevant set of features for the individual tasks.

Our approach for the Task E was purely based on the rules that we derived from the various available resources. The lexicons that we used have different ranking schemes, i.e. the same term can have different ranks based on its sentiment intensity as present in the different lexicons. We are exploring to come up with the appropriate method to merge the different ranks obtained from the different lexicons. Some other resources like NRC Emotion lexicon and MPQA Subjectivity lexicon can also be used. Other future works include developing methods for tasks C and D.

References

Corinna Cortes and Vladimir Vapnik. 1995. Support-vector Networks. Machine Learning. Volume 20, pages. 273–297.

Olutobi Owoputi, Brendan O'Connor, Chris Dyer, Kevin Gimpel, Nathan Schneider and Noah A Smith. 2013. Improved Part-of-Speech Tagging for Online Conversational Text with Word Clusters. HLT-NAACL. pages. 380–390.

Stefano Baccianella, Andrea Esuli and Fabrizio Sebastiani. 2010. SentiWordNet 3.0: An Enhanced Lexical Resource for Sentiment Analysis and Opinion Mining. LREC. pages. 2200–2204.

Bing Liu, Minqing Hu and Junsheng Cheng. 2005. Opinion Observer: Analyzing and Comparing Opinions on the Web. In *Proceedings of the 14th International World Wide Web conference*. Journal of Machine Learning Research. May 10-14. Chiba, Japan

Saif M Mohammad and Peter D Turney. 2013. Crowdsourcing a Word-Emotion Association Lexicon. Book-title: Computational Intelligence. Volume 29, pages. 436–465.

Rong-En Fan, Kai-Wei Chang, Cho-Jui Hsieh, Xiang-Rui Wang, and Chih-Jen Lin. 2008. Liblinear: A Library for Large Linear Classification. Journal of Machine Learning Research. Volume 9, pages. 1871-1874.

Sara Rosenthal, Alan Ritter, Preslav Nakov, Svetlana Kiritchenko, Saif M Mohammad, Alan Ritter and Veselin Stoyanov. 2015. SemEval-2015 Task 10: Sentiment Analysis in Twitter. In *Proceedings of the 9th International Workshop on Semantic Evaluation* Denver, Colorado, June 2015.

Sara Rosenthal, Alan Ritter, Preslav Nakov and Veselin Stoyanov. 2014. SemEval-2014 Task 9: Sentiment Analysis in Twitter. In *Proceedings of the 8th International Workshop on Semantic Evaluation (SemEval 2014)* pages 73–80, Dublin, Ireland, August 2014.

Preslav Nakov, Zornitsa Kozareva, Alan Ritter, Sara Rosenthal, Veselin Stoyanov and Theresa Wilson. 2013. Semeval-2013 Task 2: Sentiment Analysis in Twitter. In *Proceedings of the Seventh International Workshop on Semantic Evaluation (SemEval 2013).* pages 312–320, Atlanta, Georgia, USA, June 2013.

Bernard J Jansen, Mimi Zhang, Kate Sobel and Abdur Chowdury. 2009. Twitter Power: Tweets as Electronic Word of Mouth. In *Journal of the American Society for Information Science and Technology*. Volume 60, Number 11, pages 2169–2188.

Johan Bollen, Huina Mao and Xiaojun Zeng. 2011. Twitter Mood Predicts The Stock Market. In *Journal of Computational Science*. Volume 10, Number 1 pages 1–8.

Teun Terpstra, A de Vries, R Stronkman and GL Paradies. 2012. Towards a Realtime Twitter Analysis during Crises for Operational Crisis Management. In *Proceedings of the 9th International ISCRAM Conference*.

Kevin Gimpel, Nathan Schneider, Brendan OConnor, Dipanjan Das, Daniel Mills, Jacob Eisenstein, Michael Heilman, Dani Yogatama, Jeffrey Flanigan and Noah A Smith. 2011. Part-of-Speech Tagging for Twitter: Annotation, Features, and Experiments.. In *Proceedings of the 49th Annual Meeting of the Association for Computational Linguistics*. pages 42–47.

Satanjeev Banerjee and Ted Pedersen. 2003. The Design, Implementation, and Use of the Ngram Statistic Package. In *Proceedings of the Fourth International Conference on Intelligent Text Processing and Computational Linguistics*. pages 370–381, February 2003, Mexico City.

Ahmed Nagy and Jeannie Stamberger. 2012. Crowd Sentiment Detection During Disasters and Crises. In *Proceedings of the 9th International ISCRAM Conference*. pages 1–9.

Saif M Mohammad, Svetlana Kiritchenko and Xiaodan Zhu. 2013. NRC-Canada: Building the state-of-the-art in sentiment analysis of tweets. In *Proceedings of the Seventh International Workshop on Semantic Evaluation Exercises*. 2013.

Andranik Tumasjan, Timm Oliver Sprenger, Philipp G Sandner, and Isabell M Welpe. 2010. Predicting Elections with Twitter: What 140 Characters Reveal about Political Sentiment. In *ICWSM*. Volume 10, pages 178–185.

Bo Pang and Lillian Lee. 2004. A Sentimental Education: Sentiment Analysis Using Subjectivity Summarization Based on Minimum Cuts. In *Proceedings of the 42nd Annual Meeting on Association for Computational Linguistics*. page 271.

Brendan O'Connor, Ramnath Balasubramanyanand, Bryan R Routledge and Noah A Smith. 2010. From Tweets to Polls: Linking Text Sentiment to Public Opinion Time Series. In *ICWSM*. Volume 11, pages 122–129.

Swiss-Chocolate: Combining Flipout Regularization and Random Forests with Artificially Built Subsystems to Boost Text-Classification for Sentiment

Fatih Uzdilli
Zurich University of Applied Sciences
Switzerland
uzdi@zhaw.ch

Martin Jaggi
ETH Zurich
Switzerland
jaggi@inf.ethz.ch

Dominic Egger
Zurich University of Applied Sciences
Switzerland
dominicegger@bluewin.ch

Pascal Julmy
Zurich University of Applied Sciences
Switzerland
pascal.julmy@gmail.com

Leon Derczynski
University of Sheffield
UK
leon@dcs.shef.ac.uk

Mark Cieliebak
Zurich University of Applied Sciences
Switzerland
ciel@zhaw.ch

Abstract

We describe a classifier for predicting message-level sentiment of English micro-blog messages from Twitter. This paper describes our submission to the SemEval-2015 competition (Task 10). Our approach is to combine several variants of our previous year's SVM system into one meta-classifier, which was then trained using a random forest. The main idea is that the meta-classifier allows the combination of the strengths and overcome some of the weaknesses of the artificially-built individual classifiers, and adds additional non-linearity. We were also able to improve the linear classifiers by using a new regularization technique we call flipout.

1 Introduction

With the availability of huge amounts of user generated text online, the interest in automatic sentiment analysis of text has greatly increased recently in both academia and industry.

The goal is to classify a tweet (on the full message level) into the three classes positive, negative, and neutral. In this paper, we describe our approach using a modified SVM based classifier on short text as in Twitter messages. Our system has participated in the SemEval-2015 Task 10 competition, "Sentiment Analysis in Twitter, Subtask–B Message Polarity Classification" (Rosenthal et al., 2015). Previous iterations of the evaluation were run in 2013 and 2014.

Our Results in the Competition. Our system was ranked 8th out of 40 participants, with an F1-score of 62.61 on the Twitter-2015 test set. The 2015 winning team obtained an average F1-score of 64.84.

The detailed rankings of our approach were: 4th rank on the LiveJournal data; 6th on the SMS data (2013); 10th on Twitter-2013; 12th on Twitter-2014; and 25th on Twitter Sarcasm. See (Rosenthal et al., 2015) for full details and all results.

Data. In the competition, tweets for training and development were provided as tweet IDs. A fraction (10-15%) of the tweets were no longer available on Twitter, which made results of the competition not fully comparable. For testing, in addition to last year's data (tweets, SMS, LiveJournal), new tweets were provided. An overview of the data that we were able to download is given in Table 1.

Our Approach. Our system is based on two main ideas. First, we propose a new regularization technique called *flipout*, which post-processes a trained classifier model for better generalization performance. Details of this are given in Section 2. Second, we combine multiple classifiers with a meta-classifier, to yield better performance than each single sub-classifier (Dürr et al., 2014; Cieliebak et al., 2014). To achieve this, we extended our existing system (Jaggi et al., 2014). The result is simple: a large collection of features used in a linear SVM classifier. We replicated that system with several different choices of features and parameters. The output of all those artificially built classifiers is then feed as input to a random forest classifier, which generated final classification results, and gave our system additional non-linear output capabilities.

Table 1: Overview of the data we found available for training, development and testing.

Dataset	Total	Posit.	Negat.	Neutr.
Train (Tweets)	8224	3058	1210	3956
Dev (Tweets)	1417	494	286	637
Test: Twitter2015	2390	1038	365	987
Test: Twitter2014	1853	982	202	669
Test: Twitter2013	3813	1572	601	1640
Test: SMS2013	2093	492	394	1207
Test: Tw2014Sarcasm	86	33	40	13
Test: LiveJournal2014	1142	427	304	411

2 Flipout Regularization

We propose a new kind of post-processing/regularization technique to improve classification accuracy in a setting with several different available datasets. The intuition comes from the setting of transfer learning. Many words in the training data do not occur in the same context as in the target data (as for example caused by topic shifts, such as in the evaluation task's scenario here). By finding suitable replacements for some input words, the generalization performance of a pre-trained linear classifier can be improved. Since this post-processing of a pre-trained classifier overrides potentially many of its weights, the post-processing has an additional regularizing effect with respect to the original training set, in addition to the transfer effect towards the target dataset.

We follow a greedy approach to find the best word-replacements which is as follows:

1. Split the dataset into 4 parts, here called fliptrain, flipdev1, flipdev2 and fliptest.
2. Train a classifier (e.g. SVM) on the set fliptrain, using the original full set of features.
3. Calculate prediction score on datasets flipdev1 and flipdev2.
4. Pick a subset S of words from the vocabulary of fliptrain. This is the *word-pool* for the flipout trick.
5. For each word $w_1 \in S$:
   - For each word $w_2 \in S$:
     Consider the modified classifier using the replacement (flip) of input words $w_1 \mapsto w_2$. Compute its prediction score on the validation datasets flipdev1 and flipdev2.
   - Keep the replacement $w_1 \mapsto w_2^*$ which resulted in the maximum improvement for the word w_1, in the sense of min(improvement on flipdev1, improvement on flipdev2),

One would expect that this approach would replace words of the original set (fliptrain) with words having a better discriminative power on the new set (flipdev). In reality, it turned out that words without an obvious relation to each other were replaced such as: *2nd* $\mapsto$ *may*, *about* $\mapsto$ *I'm*, *we* $\mapsto$ *day*, etc. The reason we have separated the development sets (flipdev1 and flipdev2) is to better avoid potential overfitting.

3 System Description

For our system, we preprocessed the tweets and extracted textual features. Using different subsets of these features and flipout, we train different linear classifiers resulting in sentiment classification systems which are intrinsically different from each other. These "subsystems" were then combined into a meta-classifier using a random forest (Breiman, 2001). The random forest uses the outputs of individual classifiers as features and the labels on the training data as input for training. Afterwards, in the test phase, the random forest makes predictions using the outputs of the same individual classifiers.

3.1 Preprocessing

The tweets were preprocessed with standard methods before extracting the features.

- URLs and usernames are each normalized to a replacement token
- Tokenizer: We used ArkTweetNLP (Owoputi et al., 2013) which is suitable for tweets. All text was transformed to lowercase (except for special features relying on case information).
- Negation encoding: The negated context of a sentence is marked as in (Pang et al., 2002), us-

ing the list of negation words from Christopher Potts' sentiment tutorial[1].

3.2 Features for the Subsystems

The subsystems use different subsets of the features we introduce here. Most of them are the same as in our last years submission (Jaggi et al., 2014). New additions are marked with a + sign.

Features:

- **n-grams**: presence of word n-grams (n = 1...4)
- **POS-n-grams**: presence of word n-grams with one or more words replaced by the POS-Tag (Jaggi et al., 2014). The ArkTweetNLP structured prediction POS tagger provided by (Owoputi et al., 2013) together with their provided standard model (model.20120919) suitable for Twitter data was used ($n = 3...5$)
- **non-contiguous n-gram**: presence of word n-grams with one or more words replaced by a wildcard ($n = 3...5$)
- **character n-grams**: presence of character n-grams (n = 3...6) weighted increasingly by their length (weights $0.7 \cdot \{1.0, 1.1, 1.2, 1.4, 1.6, 1.9\}$ for length $3, 4, \ldots$)
- **# upper cased**: number of tokens written with all characters in upper case
- **# of hashtags**
- **# of POS tags**: for each POS-tag the number of occurrences
- **continuous punctuation**: number of continuous exclamation marks, number of continuous question marks (max)
- **last token punctuation**: whether the last token contains an exclamation mark or question mark or a period
- **# elongated words** number of words which repeat the same character more than two times
- **# negated tokens** the number of words occurring in a negation context
- **Lexicons**: For each lexicon (NRC-emotion, BingLiu, MQA, NRC-HashtagSentiment, Sentiment140, Sentiment140-3-class, RottenTomatoes-3-class):

  - total tokens for each class (positive, negative and neutral for 3-class lexicons)
  - score of last token for each class
  - maximum score over all tokens for each class
  - total score over all tokens for each class
  - +score of last token regardless of the class
  - +maximum score over all tokens for all classes together
  - +total score over all tokens

  For the 2-class lexicons, we flip the score of tokens occurring in the negation scope. The 3-class lexicons are already trained with marked negations (Jaggi et al., 2014).
- **+lemma n-grams**: presence of lemma n-grams (n = 1...4), by using the Standford Core NLP lemmatizer.
- **+cluster unigram**: whether a word from each cluster in the CMU tweet clusters occurs or not
- **+GloVe**: GloVe word embeddings (Pennington et al., 2014) are a newer version of the word2vec embedding by (Mikolov et al., 2013), using a matrix factorization instead of deep learning. We used the sum, minimum and maximum of the GloVe-vectors for the tokens occuring in the tweet.

3.3 Subsystems

For the subsystems we used different linear classifier variants trained using the LibLinear package (Fan et al., 2008), all being multi-class classifiers for the three classes in a one-against-all setting.

Subsystem 1. We combined all features to a single feature vector using an ℓ_1-regularized squared loss SVM classifer and flipout regularization as described in Section 2. We trained the SVM and optimized the regularization parameter using 10-fold cross-validation on the training set. The remaining sets were used for flipout: dev as flipdev1 and twitter-test13 as flipdev2 and twitter-test14 for testing. We chose the word pool S for flipout as the most frequent 50 words in fliptrain.

Subsystem 2. The same as subsystem 1 but without flipout. The system was trained on train+dev and the SVM regularization parameter C was optimized against the test sets.

[1]`http://sentiment.christopherpotts.net/lingstruc.html`

Subsystem 3. The same as subsystem 2 but using Logistic Regression instead of SVM.

Subsystem 4. The same as subsystem 2 but without any lexicon features.

Subsystem 5. The same as subsystem 2 but using only the GloVe word-embedding features.

3.4 Meta-Classifier

Each subsystem outputs three real values corresponding to the three sentiment classes. In addition, it outputs the categorical value for the predicted sentiment class. Our meta-classifier used these 4 values as input features. We trained a random forest using the Weka Java-library on the train data, although the subsystems are trained on the same data. To avoid overfitting, we regularized the random forest against the test sets by trying different values for number of trees, maximum depth of the forest and the number of features used per random selection.

4 Results

	Subsystem 1	Subsystem 2	Subsystem 3	Subsystem 4	Subsystem 5	**Final System**
Twitter15	62.70	62.07	62.41	53.72	58.11	62.73
Twitter14	69.44	69.07	69.34	61.60	63.42	70.19
Twitter13	69.64	69.05	69.49	61.73	61.84	69.70
LiveJournal14	73.54	74.14	74.29	62.32	62.67	74.48
Sarcarsm14	52.94	52.15	50.69	56.15	56.17	49.83

Table 2: Results of our subsystems and final system.

Overall Performance. Looking at the overall performance, we managed to increase the scores on every test set compared to our previous year's submission. Table 2 shows the scores of our individual subsystems as well as the final system on each test set. Note that our results in the official submission are slightly different from Table 2, because of a mistake we made in the class assignments in our random forest input, which is fixed here.

Classifiers. Subsystems 2 and 3 only differ in the choice of the linear classifier. Our results here show that logistic regression slightly outperforms SVM.

Flipout Regularization. Flipout proved very useful. Subsystem 1 (with flipout) reached from 0.37 to 0.79 higher F1 than Subsystem 2 (without flipout).

Features from Unsupervised Learning: Lexicons and Word-Embeddings. Subsystem 4 does not use any of the lexicon features which were constructed on a separate unlabeled large corpus. The large decrease in performance shows the importance of the lexicons. Also we can see that Subsystem 5 (which only uses the GloVe word-embedding features) results in a very small variation of its scores on the different test sets, compared to the other systems. This confirms our expectation that features generated from unsupervised training on a large data set will generalize better, i.e. are more robust to topic and domain changes.

Meta-Classifier. The final system compared with Subsystem 1 shows the gain from performing meta-classification. On last year's Twitter test set, we obtain an improvement of 0.75 F1-Score. On this year's test set (which was hidden), we achieved an improvement of 0.03, which was low. However, we are encouraged by the large improvement of 0.94 F1-Score on out-of-domain data (Live Journal) – which was not seen during training.

5 Conclusion

We have described a classifier to predict the sentiment of short texts such as tweets. Our system is built upon the approach of our previous systems (Jaggi et al., 2014) and (Dürr et al., 2014), with several modifications and extensions in features and regularization. We have seen that our system significantly improves upon last year's approach, achieving a gain of 2.65 points in F1 score on last year's test data.

We showed that our newly introduced flipout regularization technique improved the score on our system. To be able to make general statements we need to further investigate its behavior on different data sets. We also showed that artificially-built subsystems can be used to improve upon the best classifier using meta-classification. A question which remains is how one could automatize the meta-classification approach to built the most beneficial subsystems.

References

Leo Breiman. (2001). Random Forests. *Machine Learning*, 45(1):5–32.

Mark Cieliebak, Oliver Dürr, and Fatih Uzdilli (2014). Meta-Classifiers Easily Improve Commercial Sentiment Detection Tools. In *LREC 2014 - Proceedings of the 9th International Conference on Language Resources and Evaluation.*

Oliver Dürr, Fatih Uzdilli, and Mark Cieliebak (2014). JOINT FORCES: Unite Competing Sentiment Classifiers with Random Forest. In *SemEval 2014 - Proceedings of the 8th International Workshop on Semantic Evaluation*, pages 366–369, Dublin, Ireland.

Rong-En Fan, Kai-Wei Chang, Cho-Jui Hsieh, Xiang-Rui Wang, and Chih-Jen Lin (2008). LIBLINEAR: A Library for Large Linear Classification. *JMLR*, 9:1871–1874.

Martin Jaggi, Fatih Uzdilli, and Mark Cieliebak (2014). Swiss-Chocolate: Sentiment Detection using Sparse SVMs and Part-Of-Speech n-Grams. In *SemEval 2014 - Proceedings of the 8th International Workshop on Semantic Evaluation*, pages 601–604, Dublin, Ireland.

Tomas Mikolov, Quoc V Le, and Ilya Sutskever (2013). Exploiting Similarities among Languages for Machine Translation. *arXiv.org*.

Olutobi Owoputi, Brendan O'Connor, Chris Dyer, Kevin Gimpel, Nathan Schneider, and Noah A Smith (2013). Improved Part-Of-Speech Tagging for Online Conversational Text with Word Clusters. In *Proceedings of NAACL-HLT*, pages 380–390.

Bo Pang, Lillian Lee and Shivakumar Vaithyanathan (2002). Thumbs up? Sentiment Classification using Machine Learning Techniques. In *ACL 2002 - Conference of the Association for Computational Linguistics*, pages 79–86, Morristown, NJ, USA.

Jeffrey Pennington, Richard Socher and Christopher D Manning (2014). GloVe: Global Vectors for Word Representation, EMNLP 2014 - Conference on Empirical Methods in Natural Language Processing.

Sara Rosenthal, Preslav Nakov, Svetlana Kiritchenko, Saif M Mohammad, Alan Ritter and Veselin Stoyanov (2015). SemEval-2015 Task 10: Sentiment Analysis in Twitter. In *Proceedings of the 9th International Workshop on Semantic Evaluation*, Denver, Colorado.

INESC-ID: A Regression Model for Large Scale Twitter Sentiment Lexicon Induction

Ramon F. Astudillo, Silvio Amir, Wang Ling, Bruno Martins[†], Mário Silva, Isabel Trancoso
Instituto de Engenharia de Sistemas e Computadores Investigação e Desenvolvimento
Rua Alves Redol 9
Lisbon, Portugal
{ramon.astudillo, samir, wlin, mjs, isabel.trancoso}@inesc-id.pt
[†]bruno.g.martins@tecnico.ulisboa.pt

Abstract

We present the approach followed by INESC-ID in the SemEval 2015 Twitter Sentiment Analysis challenge, subtask E. The goal was to determine the strength of the association of Twitter terms with positive sentiment. Using two labeled lexicons, we trained a regression model to predict the sentiment polarity and intensity of words and phrases. Terms were represented as word embeddings induced in an unsupervised fashion from a corpus of tweets. Our system attained the top ranking submission, attesting the general adequacy of the proposed approach.

1 Introduction

Sentiment lexicons are one of the key resources for the automatic analysis of opinions, emotive and subjective text (Liu, 2012). They compile words annotated with their *prior polarity* of sentiment, regardless of the context. For instance, words such as *beautiful* or *amazing* tend to express a positive sentiment, whereas words like *boring* or *ugly* are considered negative. Most sentiment analysis systems use either *word count* methods, based on sentiment lexicons, or rely on text classifiers. In the former, the polarity of a message is estimated by computing the ratio of (positive and negative) sentiment bearing words. Despite its simplicity, this method has been widely used (O'Connor et al., 2010; Bollen and Mao, 2011; Mitchell et al., 2013). Even more sophisticated systems, based on supervised classification, can be greatly improved with features derived from lexicons (Kiritchenko et al., 2014). However, manually created sentiment lexicons consist of few carefully selected words. Consequently, they fail to capture the use of non-conventional word spelling and slang, commonly found in social media.

This problem motivated the creation of a task in the SemEval 2015 Twitter Sentiment Analysis challenge. This task (subtask E), intended to evaluate automatic methods of generating Twitter specific sentiment lexicons. Given a set of words or phrases, the goal was to assign a score between 0 and 1, reflecting the intensity and polarity of sentiment these terms express. Participants were asked to submit a list, with the candidate terms ranked according to sentiment score. This list was then compared to a ranked list obtained from human annotations and the submissions were evaluated using the Kendall (1938) Tau rank correlation metric.

In this paper, we describe a system developed for this challenge, based on a novel method to create large scale, domain-specific sentiment lexicons. The task is addressed as a regression problem, in which terms are represented as word embeddings, induced from a corpus of 52 million *tweets*. Then, using manually annotated lexicons, a regression model was trained to predict the polarity and intensity of sentiment of any word or phrase from that corpus. We found this approach to be effective for the proposed problem.

The rest of the paper proceeds as follows: we review the work related to lexicon expansion in Section 2 and describe the methods used to derive word embeddings in Section 3. Our approach and the experimental results are presented in Sections 5 and 6, respectively. We conclude in Section 7.

2 Related Work

Most of the literature on automatic lexicon expansion consists of dictionary-based or corpora-based approaches. In the former, the main idea is to use a dictionary, such as *WordNet*, to extract semantic relations between words. Kim and Hovy (2006) simply assign the same polarity to synonyms and the opposite polarity to antonyms, of known words. Others, create a graph from the semantic relationships, to find new sentiment words and their polarity. Using the seed words, new terms are classified using a distance measure (Kamps et al., 2004), or propagating the labels along the edges of the graph (Rao and Ravichandran, 2009). However, given that dictionaries mostly describe conventional language, these methods are unsuited for social media.

Corpora based approaches follow the assumption that the polarity of new words can be inferred from co-occurrence patterns with known words. Hatzivassiloglou and McKeown (1997) discovered new polar adjectives by looking at conjunctions found in a corpus. The adjectives connected with *and* got the same polarity, whereas adjectives connected with *but* were assigned opposing polarities. Turney and Littman (2003) created two small sets of prototypical polar words, one containing positive and another containing negative examples. The polarity of a new term was computed using the point-wise mutual information between that word and each of the prototypical sets (Lin, 1998). The same method was used by Kiritchenko et al. (2014), to create large scale sentiment lexicons for Twitter.

A recently proposed alternative is to learn word embeddings specific for Twitter sentiment analysis, using distant supervision (Tang et al., 2014). The resulting features are then used in a supervised classifier to predict the polarity of phrases. This work is the most related to our approach, but it differs in the sense that we use general word embeddings, learned from unlabeled data, and predict both polarity and intensity of sentiment.

3 Unsupervised Word Embeddings

In recent years, several models have been proposed, to derive *word embeddings* from large corpora. These are essentially, dense vector representations that implicitly capture syntactic and semantic properties of words (Collobert et al., 2011; Mikolov et al., 2013a; Pennington et al., 2014). Moreover, a notion of *semantic similarity*, as well as other linguistic regularities seem to be encoded in the embedding space (Mikolov et al., 2013b). In `word2vec`, Mikolov et al. (2013a) induce word vectors with two simple neural network architectures, CBOW and skip-gram. These models estimate the optimal word embeddings by maximizing the probability that, words within a given window size are predicted correctly.

Skip-gram and Structured Skip-gram

Central to the **skip-gram** is a log-linear model of word prediction. Given the i-th word from a sentence w_i, the skip-gram estimates the probability of each word at a distance p from w_i as:

$$p(w_{i+p}|w_i; \mathbf{C}_p, \mathbf{E}) \propto \exp\left(\mathbf{C}_p \cdot \mathbf{E} \cdot \mathbf{w}_i\right) \quad (1)$$

Here, $\mathbf{w}_i \in \{1, 0\}^{v \times 1}$ is a one-hot representation of the word, i.e., a sparse column vector of the size of the vocabulary v with a 1 on the position corresponding to that word. The model is parametrized by two matrices: $\mathbf{E} \in \mathbb{R}^{e \times v}$ is the embedding matrix, transforming the one-hot sparse representation into a compact real valued space of size e; $\mathbf{C}_p \in \mathbb{R}^{v \times e}$ is a matrix mapping the real-valued representation to a vector with the size of the vocabulary v. A distribution over all possible words is then attained by exponentiating and normalizing over the v possible options. In practice, due to the large value of v, various techniques are used to avoid having to normalize over the whole vocabulary (Mikolov et al., 2013a). In the particular case of the **structured skip-gram** model, the matrix $\mathbf{C}_p$ depends only of the relative position between words p (Ling et al., 2015).

After training, the low dimensional embedding $\mathbf{E} \cdot \mathbf{w}_i \in \mathbb{R}^{e \times 1}$ encapsulates the information about each word and its surrounding contexts.

CBOW

The CBOW model defines a different objective function, that predicts a word at position i given the window of context $i - d$, where d is the size of the context window. The probability of the word w_i is

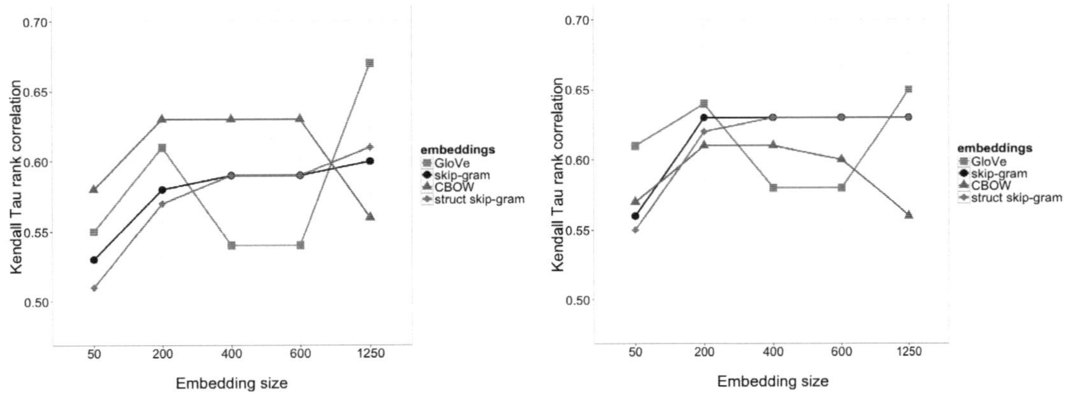

(a) Phrases as the **sum** of embeddings

(b) Phrases as the **mean** of embeddings

Figure 1: Performance of the different embeddings and phrase representations, as function of vector size.

defined as:

$$p(w_i|w_{i-d}, ..., w_{i+d}; \mathbf{C}, \mathbf{E}) \propto \exp(\mathbf{C} \cdot \mathbf{S}_{i-d}^{i+d}) \quad (2)$$

where $\mathbf{S}_{i-d}^{i+d}$ is the point wise sum of the embeddings of all context words starting at $\mathbf{E} \cdot w_{i-d}$ to $\mathbf{E} \cdot w_{i+d}$, excluding the index w_i, and once again $\mathbf{C} \in \mathbb{R}^{e \times v}$ is a matrix mapping the embedding space into the output vocabulary space v.

GloVe

The models discussed above rely on different assumptions about the relations between words within a context window. The Global Vector model, referred as GloVe (Pennington et al., 2014), combines this approach with ideas drawn from matrix factorization methods, such as LSA (Deerwester et al., 1990). The embeddings are derived with an objective function that combines context window information, with corpus statistics computed efficiently from a global term co-occurrence matrix.

4 Labeled Data

The evaluation of the shared task was performed on a labeled test set, consisting of 1315 words and phrases. To support the development of the systems, the organizers released a *trial* set with 200 examples. The terms are representative of the informal style of Twitter text, containing hashtags, slang, abbreviations and misspelled words. Negated expressions were also included. We show a sample of the words and phrases in Table 1. For more details on these datasets, see (Kiritchenko et al., 2014).

Given the small size of the trial set, we used an additional labeled lexicon: the Language Assessment by Mechanical Turk (LabMT) lexicon (Dodds et al., 2011). It consists of 10,000 words collected from different sources. Words were rated on a scale of 1 (sad) to 9 (happy), by users of Amazon's Mechanical Turk service, resulting in a measure of average happiness for each given word. Note that LabMT contains annotations for *happiness* but our goal is to label words in terms of *sentiment polarity*. We rely on the fact that some emotions are correlated with sentiment, namely, joy/happiness are associated with positivity, while sadness/disgust relate to negativity (Liu, 2012).

This complementary dataset was used for two purposes: first, as the development set to evaluate and tune our system, and second, as additional training data for the candidate submission.

Type	Sample words
words	*sweetest, giggle, sleazy, broken*
slang	*bday, lmao, kewl, pics*
negations	*can't cope, don't think, no probs*
interjections	*weee, yays, woooo, eww*
emphasized	*gooooood, loveeee, cuteeee, excitedddd*
hashtags	*#gorgeous, #smelly, #fake, #classless*
multiword hashtag	*#goodvibes, #everyonelikesitbutme*
emoticons	*:o): -.- :') <33*

Table 1: A sample of the different types of terms.

5 Proposed Approach

We addressed the task of inducing large scale sentiment lexicons for Twitter as a regression problem. Each term $\mathbf{w}_i$ was represented with an embedding $\mathbf{E} \cdot \mathbf{w}_i \in \mathbb{R}^{e \times 1}$, with $e \in \{50, 200, 400, 600, 1250^1\}$ as discussed in Section 3. Then, the manually annotated lexicons were used to train a model that, given a new term $\mathbf{w}_j$, predicts a score $y \in [0, 1]$ reflecting the polarity and intensity of sentiment it conveys.

Note that the embeddings represent words, so to deal with phrases we leveraged on the compositional properties of word vectors (Mikolov et al., 2013b). Given that algebraic operations in the embedding space preserve meaning, we represented phrases as the sum or mean of individual word vectors.

5.1 Learning the Word Embeddings

The first step of our approach, requires a corpus of tweets to support the unsupervised learning of the embedding matrix $\mathbf{E}$. We resorted to the corpus of 52 million tweets used by Owoputi et al. (2013) and the tokenizer described in the same work.

The CBOW and skip-gram embeddings were induced using the `word2vec`[2] tool, while we used our own implementation of the structured skip-gram. The default values in `word2vec` were employed for most of the parameters, but we set the negative sampling rate to 25 words (Goldberg and Levy, 2014). For the GloVe model, we used the available implementation[3] with the default parameters. In all the models, words occurring less than 100 times in the corpus were discarded, resulting in a vocabulary of around 210,000 tokens.

Finally, embeddings of different sizes were built, with 50, 200, 400 and 600 dimensions.

Hyperparameter Optimization and Model Selection

Regarding the choice of learning algorithm, several linear regression models were considered: least squares and regularized variants, namely, the *lasso*, *ridge* and *elastic net* regressors. We also experimented with *Support Vectors Regression (SVR)* using non-linear kernels, namely, polynomial, sigmoid and Radial Basis Function (RBF). Most of these models have hyperparameters, thus the combination of possible algorithms and parameters represents a huge configuration space. A brute force approach to find the optimal model would be cumbersome and time consuming. Instead, for each parameter, we defined meaningful distributions and ranges of values. Then, a hyperparameter optimization algorithm was used to find the best combination of model and parameters, by sampling from the specified configuration pool. The *Tree of Parzen Estimators* algorithm, as implemented in `HyperOpt`[4], was used (Bergstra et al., 2013).

6 Experiments

Learning word embeddings from large corpora allowed us to derive representations for a considerable number of words. Thus, we were able to find embeddings for 94% of the candidate terms. Using simple normalization steps, we could find embeddings for the remaining terms. However, we found that this improvement in recall had almost no impact in the performance of the system.

After mapping terms to their respective embeddings, we performed experiments to find the best regression model and respective hyperparameters. For this purpose, the LabMT lexicon was employed as the development set and the trial data as a validation set, against which different configurations were evaluated. After 1000 trials, the SVR model with RBF kernel was selected. Finally, we performed detailed experiments to compare word embedding models and vectors of different dimensions.

6.1 Submitted System

The evaluation on the trial data indicated that several configurations of embedding model and size could achieve the optimal results. Therefore, our candidate system was based on structured skip-gram embeddings with 600 dimensions, and SVR with RBF kernel. The hyperparameters were set to $C = 50$, $\epsilon = 0.05$ and $\gamma = 0.01$ and the system was trained using the trial data and the LabMT lexicon.

[1]corresponds to the concatenation of all the embeddings

[2]`https://code.google.com/p/word2vec/`

[3]`http://nlp.stanford.edu/projects/GloVe/`

[4]`http://hyperopt.github.io/hyperopt/`

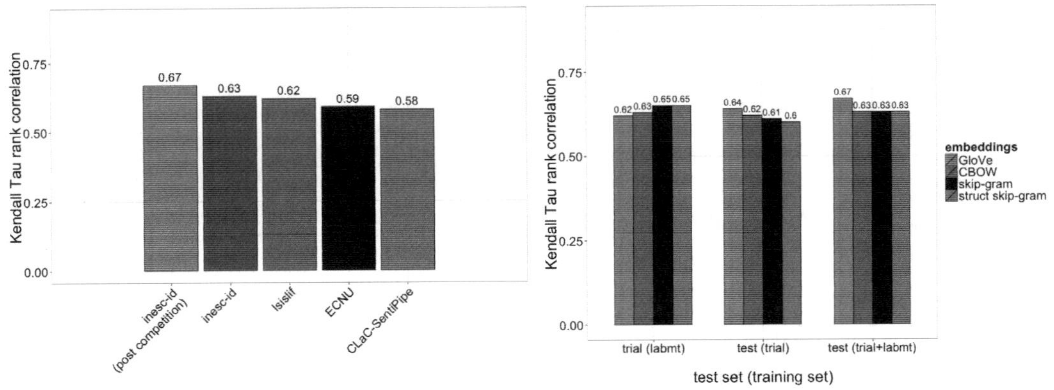

(a) Results of the top 4 ranking systems

(b) Comparing word embedding models under various training and test data regimes

Figure 2: Evaluation of the INESC-ID system.

6.2 Results

The experiments showed that all the word embeddings have comparable capabilities. In Figure 1, we compare the results of different embeddings with the same regression model. Regarding the representation of phrases, the skip-gram and structured skip-gram embeddings performed better when averaged. However, the GloVe and CBOW seemed to be more effective when summing the individual word vectors. These results were consistent across all the experiments. In terms of embedding size, we observed that smaller vectors tend to perform worse and, in general, concatenating vectors of different dimensionality improved performance. The CBOW representations were the only exception. This suggests that embeddings of different size capture different aspects of words.

Our final method, attained the highest ranking result of the competition, with 0.63 rank correlation. Figure 2a shows the results of the top 4 submissions to SemEval. Further experiments were conducted after the release of the test set labels. We found that the concatenation of GloVe embeddings outperforms our previous choice of features on the test set. Surprisingly, these embeddings obtained the worst results on the trial data, but are much better than the others in the test set, achieving a rank correlation of 0.67. At this point, it is still not clear why this is the case.

Figure 2b shows the performance of each embedding model, under different combinations of training and test data. We can see that the proposed approach is effective, and our models outperform the other systems with as few as 200 training examples.

7 Conclusions

We described the approach followed by INESC-ID for subtask E of SemEval 2015 Twitter Sentiment Analysis challenge. This work presents the first steps towards a general method to extract large-scale lexicons with fine-grained annotations from Twitter data. Although the results are encouraging, further investigation is required to shed light on some unexpected outcomes (e.g., the inconsistent behavior of the GloVe features on the trial and test sets). It should nonetheless be noted that, given the small size of the labeled sets, it is hard to draw definitive conclusions about the soundness of any method. Furthermore, the merit of a sentiment lexicon should be assessed in terms of its impact on the performance of concrete sentiment analysis applications.

Acknowledgements

This work was partially supported by Fundação para a Ciência e Tecnologia (FCT), through contracts Pest-OE/EEI/LA0021/2013, EXCL/EEI-ESS/0257/2012 (DataStorm), grant number SFRH/BPD/68428/2010 and Ph.D. scholarship SFRH/BD/89020/2012.

References

James Bergstra, Daniel Yamins, and David Cox. 2013. Making a science of model search: Hyperparameter optimization in hundreds of dimensions for vision architectures. In *Proceedings of the 30th International Conference on Machine Learning*, pages 115–123.

Johan Bollen and Huina Mao. 2011. Twitter mood as a stock market predictor. *Computer*, 44:91–94.

Ronan Collobert, Jason Weston, Léon Bottou, Michael Karlen, Koray Kavukcuoglu, and Pavel Kuksa. 2011. Natural language processing (almost) from scratch. *The Journal of Machine Learning Research*, 12:2493–2537.

Scott C. Deerwester, Susan T Dumais, Thomas K. Landauer, George W. Furnas, and Richard A. Harshman. 1990. Indexing by latent semantic analysis. *JAsIs*, 41:391–407.

Peter Sheridan Dodds, Kameron Decker Harris, Isabel M Kloumann, Catherine A Bliss, and Christopher M Danforth. 2011. Temporal patterns of happiness and information in a global social network: Hedonometrics and twitter. *PloS one*, 6(12):e26752.

Yoav Goldberg and Omer Levy. 2014. word2vec explained: deriving mikolov et al.'s negative-sampling word-embedding method. *arXiv preprint arXiv:1402.3722*.

Vasileios Hatzivassiloglou and Kathleen R McKeown. 1997. Predicting the semantic orientation of adjectives. In *Proceedings of the 8th Conference of the European Chapter of the Association for Computational Linguistics*, pages 174–181.

Jaap Kamps, Maarten Marx, Robert J. Mokken, and Maarten de Rijke. 2004. Using wordnet to measure semantic orientations of adjectives. In *Proceedings of 4th International Conference on Language Resources and Evaluation, Vol IV,*, pages 1115–1118.

Maurice G Kendall. 1938. A new measure of rank correlation. *Biometrika*, pages 81–93.

Soo-Min Kim and Eduard Hovy. 2006. Identifying and analyzing judgment opinions. In *Proceedings of the Human Language Technology Conference of the NAACL, Main Conference*, pages 200–207.

Svetlana Kiritchenko, Xiaodan Zhu, and Saif M Mohammad. 2014. Sentiment analysis of short informal texts. *Journal of Artificial Intelligence Research*, pages 723–762.

Dekang Lin. 1998. An information-theoretic definition of similarity. In *Proceedings of the 15th International Conference on Machine Learning*, volume 98, pages 296–304.

Wang Ling, Chris Dyer, Alan Black, and Isabel Trancoso. 2015. Two/too simple adaptations of word2vec for syntax problems. In *Proceedings of the 2015 Conference of the North American Chapter of the Association for Computational Linguistics: Human Language Technologies*.

Bing Liu. 2012. Sentiment analysis and opinion mining. *Synthesis Lectures on Human Language Technologies*, 5(1):1–167.

Tomas Mikolov, Kai Chen, Greg Corrado, and Jeffrey Dean. 2013a. Efficient estimation of word representations in vector space. In *Workshop at the International Conference on Learning Representations*.

Tomas Mikolov, Ilya Sutskever, Kai Chen, Greg Corrado, and Jeffrey Dean. 2013b. Distributed representations of words and phrases and their compositionality. In *Proceedings of the 27th Annual Conference on Neural Information Processing Systems*.

Lewis Mitchell, Kameron Decker Harris, Morgan R Frank, Peter Sheridan Dodds, and Christopher M Danforth. 2013. The geography of happiness: connecting twitter sentiment and expression, demographics, and objective characteristics of place. *PLoS ONE*, 8(5).

Brendan O'Connor, Ramnath Balasubramanyan, Bryan R Routledge, and Noah A Smith. 2010. From tweets to polls: Linking text sentiment to public opinion time series. In *Proceedings of the 4th International AAAI Conference on Weblogs and Social Media*.

Olutobi Owoputi, Brendan O'Connor, Chris Dyer, Kevin Gimpel, Nathan Schneider, and Noah A Smith. 2013. Improved part-of-speech tagging for online conversational text with word clusters. In *Proceedings of the 2013 Conference of the North American Chapter of the Association for Computational Linguistics: Human Language Technologies*, pages 380–390.

Jeffrey Pennington, Richard Socher, and Christopher D Manning. 2014. Glove: Global vectors for word representation. *Proceedings of the 2014 Empiricial Methods in Natural Language Processing*, 12.

Delip Rao and Deepak Ravichandran. 2009. Semi-supervised polarity lexicon induction. In *Proceedings of the 12th Conference of the European Chapter of the Association for Computational Linguistics*, pages 675–682.

Duyu Tang, Furu Wei, Bing Qin, Ming Zhou, and Ting Liu. 2014. Building large-scale twitter-specific sentiment lexicon : A representation learning approach. In *Proceedings of the 25th International Conference on Computational Linguistics*, pages 172–182.

Peter D Turney and Michael L Littman. 2003. Measuring praise and criticism: Inference of semantic orientation from association. *ACM Transactions on Information Systems (TOIS)*, 21(4):315–346.

KLUEless: Polarity Classification and Association

Nataliia Plotnikova and **Micha Kohl** and **Kevin Volkert** and **Andreas Lerner** and **Natalie Dykes** and **Heiko Ermer** and **Stefan Evert**
Professur für Korpuslinguistik
Friedrich-Alexander-Universität Erlangen-Nürnberg
Bismarckstr. 6, 91054 Erlangen, Germany
{nataliia.plotnikova, micha.kohl, kevin.volkert, andreas.lerner, natalie.dykes, heiko.ermer, stefan.evert}@fau.de

Abstract

This paper describes the KLUEless system which participated in the SemEval-2015 task on "Sentiment Analysis in Twitter". This year the updated system based on the developments for the same task in 2014 (Evert et al., 2014) and 2013 (Proisl et al., 2013) participated in all five subtasks. The paper gives an overview of the core features extended by different additional features and parameters required for individual subtasks. Experiments carried out after the evaluation period on the test dataset 2015 with the gold standard available are integrated into each subtask to explain the submitted feature selection.

1 Introduction

The SemEval-2015 shared task on "Sentiment Analysis in Twitter" (Rosenthal et al., 2015) is a rerun of the shared task from SemEval-2014 (Rosenthal et al., 2014) with three new subtasks. While subtasks A and B were identical to the tasks of SemEval-2014 and dealt with the identification of polarity in a given message, subtask C, D and E were new. In subtask C a topic was given, towards which the sentiment in a message had to be identified. Subtask D was similar to subtask C, as the sentiment towards a given topic had to be identified, but in this subtask several messages were given from which the sentiment had to be drawn. Ultimately in subtask E, the sentiment of a given word or phrase had to be measured on a score ranging [0, 1], indicating its association with positive sentiment.

The training data for subtasks A and B are the same as in SemEval-2014 (Rosenthal et al., 2014) and SemEval-2013 (Nakov et al., 2013). For subtask A, there are 9,505 training items with 6,769 items in development set and 3,912 items in the test set. For subtask B, there are 10,239 training items, 5,907 items in the development set and 3,861 in the test set. For subtasks C and D the same training sets as for subtasks A and B were used by our team. A pilot task E aimed at evaluation of automatic methods of generating sentiment lexicons had no training set, a detailed approach used for this subtask will be given in Section 3.

This paper describes the updated system with our efforts to improve it after the evaluation period. The KLUEless system was ranked within the top 3 participants to subtasks A (rank 2 out of 11), C (rank 2 out of 7) and D (best result out of 6 teams). It scored 5th place in subtask E, but only 13th place in subtask B (rank 13 out of 40 teams). In the following chapters, we will describe the way KLUEless dealt with the tasks stated and our results for these tasks.

2 The KLUEless Approach

The KLUEless polarity classifier is an updated version of the SentiKLUE system used for the SemEval-2014 shared task on "Sentiment Analysis in Twitter" (Evert et al., 2014) which in its turn was based on the KLUE system that participated in the SemEval-2013 task for sentiment analysis of tweets (Proisl et al., 2013). Maximum Entropy (known as Logistic Regression in the implementations of the Python library scikit-learn[1] (Pedregosa et al., 2011))

[1] http://scikit-learn.org

is a machine learning algorithm in the submission for all subtasks (A-D). The detailed overview of all features used by the system is given in the previous papers. This section is a brief summary of the old features extended by the new set of features that the system extracted from the training data for subtasks A,B,C, and D. The old feature vectors taken by the system as input are:

1) the sum of positive and negative scores over all words of each message as well as an average polarity score per tweet. The scores are taken from 8 different sentiment lexicons (AFINN [2], MPQA[3], SentiWords[4], Sentiment140 (both bigrams and unigrams) [5], NRC Hashtag Sentiment Lexicon (both bigrams and unigrams) with numeric polarity scores extended with lists of distributionally similar words based on the AFINN sentiment lexicon (Proisl et al., 2013, Sec. 2.2).

2) counts of positive and negative emoticons based on the list of 212 emoticons and 95 internet slag abbreviations from Wikipedia classified manually as negative (-1), neutral (0) or positive (1) (Proisl et al., 2013, Sec. 2.3).

3) a bag-of-words model with word ngrams (unigrams and bigrams) occurring in at least 2 different messages for subtask A and in 3 different messages for subtask B, C and D.

4) a negation heuristic inverting the polarity score of the first sentiment word within 4 tokens after a negation marker. In the bag-of-words representation the following 4 tokens after a negation are prefixed with not_.

The new feature set added to the old one encompasses the following new features:

5) a number of question marks in a message,

6) a number of exclamation marks,

7) a number of combinations of "!?",

8) a number of letters in upper case,

9) presence or absence of elongated vowels occurring more than twice,

10) automatically generated lexicons described in Section 3 which were left out in the submission, though used in the development phase.

These features form the core system. The features specific to subtasks A and B are described in their corresponding subsections below.

3 Creating Sentiment Lexica

3.1 Subtask E

For Subtask E, we collected Twitter data for automatic annotation and subsequent score computation for individual target terms. A similar approach was suggested last year (Kiritchenko et al., 2014). Our tweet collection was built mostly by filtering the English Twitter Streaming API for target terms provided in the test data using a Python script based on code from Russell (2014). The downloaded tweet texts were stripped of retweet boilerplate and usernames and URLs were replaced with anonymous placeholders. Redundant tweets and tweets containing no useful information (e.g. no English words) were discarded, resulting in a total of about 6.5 million.

We used three sources to annotate our tweet data. One was our main KLUEless system, assigning either positive, negative or neutral sentiment to a tweet. The other two were manually annotated lists of 328 hashtags (manually selected and reannotated from a lexicon generated by Mohammad et al. (2013)) and 67 emoticons (manually selected from a list generated from wikipedia articles[6,7]). Tweets were tagged positive when they contained at least one positive and no negative hashtag or emoticon respectively and vice versa.

Because annotation based on hashtags and emoticons showed promising results on the test data and because we wanted to rely as little as possible on existing sentiment lexica that greatly influence the annotations provided by our KLUEless system, we gave priority to hashtag and emoticon based sentiments in this order and fell back to KLUEless annotations if either no other information was available or the available information was conflicting. This overall sentiment annotation also allowed for tweets to be tagged as neutral as this was a possible output from the KLUEless annotation.

To counter data sparsity, a back-off approach relying on large scale word clusters based on twitter

[2] http://www2.imm.dtu.dk/pubdb/p.php?6010

[3] http://mpqa.cs.pitt.edu/lexicons/subj_lexicon/

[4] https://hlt.fbk.eu/technologies/sentiwords

[5] http://www.umiacs.umd.edu/ saif/WebPages/Abstracts/NRC-SentimentAnalysis.htm

[6] http://de.wikipedia.org/wiki/Emoticon

[7] http://en.wikipedia.org/wiki/Emoticons_(Unicode_block)

data (Owoputi et al., 2012) was introduced. The frequency information of any target term occurring below a set frequency threshold t_f was replaced by combined frequency information from cluster members. In order to exclude marginal cluster members, only those members that together made up a set proportion t_c of the original cluster data were used. So, if back-off was applied for the term *okayyy* for example, and t_c was set to 0.8, the combined frequency information of the terms *ok*, *okay* and *alright*, which are the three most frequent cluster members that make up 80% of all tokens in this cluster, would be used. We disabled back-off for hashtags as the cluster data contained a considerably big cluster with arbitrary hashtags that would disrupt any positive effect of cluster based back-off for these cases. The final scores for the target terms

$$score = \frac{f_{pos}}{f_{pos} + f_{neg}} \quad (1)$$

Figure 1: Maximum likelihood scoring equation.

were computed using a simplistic maximum likelihood estimate based on their occurrences in positive and negative contexts (see Figure 1), ignoring information from tweets tagged as neutral. Multiple occurrences of the same term within one tweet were counted as one. Any terms that after cluster back-off still had no frequency information available were assigned a default score of 0.5. More sophisticated scoring systems based on extensions to this approach will be discussed in Section 8.

3.2 Lexica for Use with the KLUEless System

We applied a similar method for creating our own sentiment lexica for use with our main system. We used the same procedure described above for counting frequencies of uni- and bigrams in all data that was collected for subtask E trial and test runs (approximately 13 million tweets). Since there were no target terms for which cluster based back-off could be applied we implemented a workaround in order to still be able to remedy data sparseness.

By creating separate lexica for every application of our KLUEless system, we were able to use the trial and test data of any specific run as a target for back-off, effectively using all words found in the data of a given run as a list of target terms. This also enabled us to filter out any terms that weren't useful for the specific run and create lexica that only contained relevant information. For missing unigrams, we tried to find the most frequent term in its cluster that also occurred in our tweet data and adopted its frequency data. For missing bigrams, we applied a more complex approach as the cluster data didn't contain information about bigrams. We set an arbitrary threshold of 10, assuming that any bigram occurring at least this frequently in the target data would probably not be a spelling error. For bigrams that occurred less often in the target data and not at all in the data used for collecting our frequency information we applied cluster-back off on a unigram level and tried to find a combination that also occurred in our tweet data.

After this process of filtering and back-off, we used the same simplistic scoring approach as before to generate separate uni- and bigram lexica for each submission run of our KLUEless system.

4 Task A: Contextual Polarity Disambiguation

Using the core system described in Section 2, we computed the features for the whole message and received three features with probabilities of being positive, negative and neutral for each complete tweet. In order to adjust the classifier to message parts, we added an additional feature to the core system, character ngrams. 1 to 5 characters were taken within word boundaries of a marked part of a message if it occurred at least 20 times. Using the extended classifier we computed the new set of features for marked parts of each message and added previously assigned class probabilities to feature vectors generated from corresponding full messages. The KLUEless system received its core feature vectors extended by ngrams and three class probabilities as input and generated final polarity labels to all marked parts of each message.

The specific features used improved the performance (see Table 1). Results for the submitted version is typeset in italics, the best result is typeset in bold.

The character ngrams improved the overall classifier performance for subtask A. The system achieved rank 2 out of 11 systems (with F-score 84.51). Inter-

features	F_{pos}	F_{neg}	F_{neut}	F_w	$F_{pos+neg}$	Acc
SentiKLUE	.8740	.7874	.0303	.7939	.8307	.8186
KLUEless						
+ ngrams$_{1..5}$	.8814	.8080	.1513	.8126	*.8451*	.8289
+ lexicon$_{2014B}$	.8829	.8155	.1513	.8160	**.8492**	.8321

Table 1: Evaluation results for subtask A on the test set 2015.

estingly, using automatically generated lexicon with tools developed for Task E for the training data of SemEval 2014 (Task B) could have improved the results bringing our system to the first place with F-score of 84.92 (best system: 84.79). As it was not evident on the development data, we have not included this lexicon when submitting the results. Trying to use this lexicon for other subtasks after the evaluation stage did not improve the scores. Therefore, it might be a coincidence.

5 Task B: Message Polarity Classification

The system scored 13th place out of 40 on subtask B with F-score 61.20 (best system: 64.84). As in subtask A, we used the basic feature set described in Section 2 extended by task specific features. We extended the initial bag-of-words model with trigrams occurring in at least 3 different messages. The large character ngrams generated from characters inside word boundaries only (padded with space on each side) were added to the feature vectors. Using the extended set of features KLUEless generated final polarity labels for test messages.

Results for the submitted version is typeset in italics, the best result is typeset in bold (see Table 2).

features	F_{pos}	F_{neg}	F_{neut}	F_w	$F_{pos+neg}$	Acc
SentiKLUE	.6618	.5348	.6731	.6471	.5983	.6448
KLUEless						
+ ngram$_{8..9}$	.6644	.5533	.6777	.6529	.6089	.6506
+ ngram$_{8..9}$ +						
+ trigrams	.6674	.5566	.6792	.6554	***.6120***	.6531

Table 2: Evaluation results for subtask B on the test set 2015.

8 and 9 characters inside word boundaries improved the overall total score both on the development set and on the test set 2015. The same positive influence was noticed for trigrams added to the bag-of-words model.

6 Task C: Topic-Based Polarity Classification

For the subtask C we used exactly the same approach used for subtask B. Therefore, we have ignored topics towards which sentiments were to be identified and assigned polarity labels generated by KLUEless to the full messages. Nevertheless, the system ranked 2 out of 7 teams with F-score 45.48 (best system: 50.51). The assigned labels were projected onto the list of test topics. The feature set for this subtask was extended as described in Section 5 since it is the best found configuration. For messages where both a positive and negative sentiment towards the topic are expressed, the stronger sentiment is chosen by the classifier.

7 Task D: Detecting Trends on a Topic

The task was in determining a dominant sentiment towards a target topic. Feature vectors based on the values listed in Section 2 were extracted from the 2,383 test sentences and processed by KLUEless. The classifier assigned numeric values in the range from 0 to 1, which corresponds to the probability of being positive, negative and neutral to each tweet. For each tweet the highest score was selected and its value was added to the total score of positive, negative or neutral values assigned to the tweets of the same topic. These triples were used to calculate the correlation between positive scores and the sum of positive and negative ones for each topic.

In the submitted version we made use of neutral values as well and ended up with the following formula for the sentiment score of a topic:

$$score = \frac{topic_{pos} + topic_{neut} * A/2}{topic_{pos} + topic_{neut} * A + topic_{neg}} \quad (2)$$

Figure 2: Sentiment score calculation.

where $topic_{pos}$ is a sum of all positive values of tweets on the same topic for which the highest value was positive. The same idea was used for $topic_{neut}$ and $topic_{neg}$. The factor A is a numeric value added to incorporate neutral tweets into the ratio of positive values to [positive + negative] values of tweets. This is the system we submitted with factor A set to 0.2 defined on experiments for the training data. The system performed best of all and achieved the

1st place out of 6 on the task.

After the evaluation stage, we tried to improve the performance and test the same approach with different parameters for factor A as well as without a factor at all using the test data with their gold standard set. The result for the submitted system is typeset in italics, the best result is in bold font in Table 3.

A = 0.0	A = 0.01	A = 0.1	A = 0.2	A = 0.8
0.1926	**0.1924**	0.1954	*0.2017*	0.2320

Table 3: Average absolute difference depending on factor A on the test set 2015.

8 Task E: Association of Terms with Positive Sentiment

For our submission, we set t_c to 0.8 and t_f to 0, effectively applying back-off only for terms that didn't occur in our data at all. We did not disable back-off for hash-tag terms as has been noted in section 3, a change which should have had little impact on the resulting score, as our submission relied on cluster information for only seven items in the target terms, only one of which was a hashtag. Our results were ranked 5th out of 10 participants for task 10 subtask E with a Spearman rank correlation coefficient of 0.766, which was to be expected on the basis of very similar results on the trial data with the same setup.

In the following, the effect of the applied back-off method based on clustering, the individual effects of its two parameters t_c and t_f as well as some experimental extensions for improving our score shall be discussed. Back-off for hashtag terms was disabled for all subsequent experiments.

	Spearman Correlation		
t_f	$t_c = 0.8$	$t_c = 0.6$	$t_c = 0.4$
-	0.767	0.767	0.767
0	0.766	0.767	0.767
20	0.765	0.765	0.766
100	0.751	0.751	0.752
200	0.742	0.742	0.742
500	0.722	0.722	0.720

Table 4: Results for different settings for frequency and cluster threshold parameters (t_f: frequency threshold for back-off, t_c: cluster proportion threshold).

8.1 Cluster Parameters

The first set of experiments was conducted to evaluate the effect of the two clustering parameters, the cluster proportion threshold t_c, which determines the proportion of cluster members that is used for collecting cluster information during frequency counting, and the frequency threshold t_f, which determines the maximum frequency of terms in our data to be affected by back-off.

The results in Table 4 show that, first of all, t_c seems to have only minimal effect on the final correlation score. This suggests that either a very small number of cluster members make up most of each cluster, minimizing the effect of different cut-off points, or that the clusters are in fact very homogeneous in their structure, at least for the majority of each cluster's members, resulting in similar frequency proportions for most of their members.

The second finding was that as more terms are affected by back-off with higher values for t_f, the score seems to get progressively worse. This is a somewhat unexpected result, as we were able to achieve some gains by using a frequency threshold of 100 on the trial data (after the deadline for subtask E), but is most likely due to the fact that our two tweet corpora are approximately the same size for both trial and test data, albeit the considerable difference in the number of target terms. The obvious consequence is data sparsity, resulting in much more terms being affected by back-off using the same threshold in the test run as compared to the trial run.

8.2 Extensions

A second set of experiments was based on three extensions to our basic approach. The first consists of add-λ smoothing, which adds a given number λ to all frequency counts, eliminating zero frequencies and generally smoothing frequency counts. Another extension was the inclusion of a method for bias correction. This means we assumed that the population contains a certain proportion b of positive tweets and adjusted the frequency counts obtained through our balanced sample to those expected under this bias assumption (the default assumption, where no correction is applied being of course 50%). The last extension was to adjust our frequency proportions by computing binomial confidence intervals for a set confidence level c and replacing the actual proportions by conservative estimates (the lower end of the confidence interval for proportions over 50% and the upper end for those below). This results in an overall correction towards a balanced proportion and consequently in scores closer to the neutral 50% mark.

As general experiments with these extensions confirmed our findings of higher frequency thresholds for clustering worsening results, and cluster thresholds being of small importance, the systematic experiments discussed in the following were conducted with t_f set to zero, effectively applying back-off only for terms that didn't occur at all in our data and t_c set to 0.8, which is a configuration consistent with the settings used for submission. Experimenting with the proposed extensions led to rather discouraging results and a maximum improvement of 1.0% for the Spearman correlation score.

	Spearman Correlation	
b	$\lambda = 0$	$\lambda = 1$
0.6	0.763	0.768
0.5	0.766	0.768
0.4	0.768	0.768
0.3	0.767	0.768
0.2	0.762	0.768

Table 5: Results for different bias correction settings (b: assumed proportion of positive tweets in population).

Applying bias correction only led to a marginal improvement of 0,2% when b was set to 40%, add-one smoothing seemed to offset the negative effect of different proportion assumptions (see Table 5). Keeping bias correction at this setting and including conservative estimates based on confidence intervals had consistently negative effects, which were increased by add-one smoothing and minimized by a very low confidence level c of 0.1 (see Table 6). Surprisingly, another experiment including conservative estimates for this confidence level and different bias correction settings achieved an optimal result of 77.6% correlation with add-one smoothing and an assumed population proportion b of 0.1 positive tweets (see Table 7), which is of course a highly unlikely assumption.

		Spearman Correlation	
b	c	$\lambda = 0$	$\lambda = 1$
0.4	-	0.768	0.768
0.4	0.1	0.768	0.758
0.4	0.2	0.766	0.756
0.4	0.3	0.763	0.753

Table 6: Results for conservative estimates using different confidence levels (b: assumed proportion of positive tweets in population, c: confidence level for conservative estimates).

		Spearman Correlation	
b	c	$\lambda = 0$	$\lambda = 1$
0.4	-	0.768	0.768
0.6	0.1	0.752	0.743
0.3	0.1	0.775	0.767
0.2	0.1	0.773	0.773
0.1	0.1	0.760	0.776

Table 7: Results for conservative estimates using different bias correction settings (b: assumed proportion of positive tweets in population, c: confidence level for conservative estimates).

The results of all performed experiments seem to indicate that, while add-one smoothing and the proposed method of bias correction may provide opportunity for optimization, adjusting proportions with regard to conservative estimates using binomial confidence intervals seems to only show positive effects in combination with the other extensions. Intuition and the fact that these effects proved to be rather arbitrary suggest that no predictable effects seem possible and this third extension could only lead to a score improvement because of strong overtraining. The proposed back-off approach using cluster information has been shown to have exclusively negative effects, even when applied only to terms that didn't occur in our data at all. This can of course be said to be a matter of luck, depending on how close the gold standard labels for such terms are to a given default score that is assigned instead of the result of cluster based back-off. Further experiments should be conducted to evaluate whether this approach can be beneficial when applied to scores that are based on a larger data set.

9 Conclusion

The methods discussed in this paper are suited to the polarity classification in Twitter, our system ranking among the top systems for 3 out of 5 subtasks. In future, we would like to experiment with new features for message polarity classification that can improve the prediction quality. We would also like to experiment with automatically generated lexica for new domains. Overall it can be assumed that our approach to determining association of terms with positive sentiment was most likely limited by data sparsity due to insufficient tweet data for our frequency counts. Collecting more tweet data, we will experiment with different methods involving add-λ smoothing and bias correction.

References

Stefan Evert, Thomas Proisl, Paul Greiner, and Besim Kabashi. 2014. SentiKLUE: Updating a polarity classifier in 48 hours. In *Proceedings of the 8th International Workshop on Semantic Evaluation (SemEval 2014)*, pages 551–555, Dublin, Ireland, August.

Svetlana Kiritchenko, Xiaodan Zhu, and Saif M. Mohammad. 2014. Sentiment analysis of short informal texts. *Journal of Artificial Intelligence Research (JAIR)*, 50:723–762.

Saif Mohammad, Svetlana Kiritchenko, and Xiaodan Zhu. 2013. NRC-Canada: Building the state-of-the-art in sentiment analysis of tweets. In *Proceedings of the seventh international workshop on Semantic Evaluation Exercises (SemEval-2013)*, Atlanta, Georgia, USA, June.

Preslav Nakov, Sara Rosenthal, Zornitsa Kozareva, Veselin Stoyanov, Alan Ritter, and Theresa Wilson. 2013. Semeval-2013 task 2: Sentiment analysis in Twitter. In *Second Joint Conference on Lexical and Computational Semantics (*SEM), Volume 2: Proceedings of the Seventh International Workshop on Semantic Evaluation (SemEval 2013)*, pages 312–320, Atlanta, Georgia, USA, June.

Olutobi Owoputi, Brendan O'Connor, Chris Dyer, Kevin Gimpel, and Nathan Schneider. 2012. Part-of-speech tagging for twitter: Word clusters and other advances. *School of Computer Science*.

Fabian Pedregosa, Gaël Varoquaux, Alexandre Gramfort, Vincent Michel, Bertrand Thirion, Olivier Grisel, Mathieu Blondel, Peter Prettenhofer, Ron Weiss, Vincent Dubourg, Jake Vanderplas, Alexandre Passos, David Cournapeau, Matthieu Brucher, Matthieu Perrot, and Edouard Duchesnay. 2011. Scikit-learn: Machine learning in Python. In *Journal of Machine Learning Research*, volume 12, pages 2825–2830.

Thomas Proisl, Paul Greiner, Stefan Evert, and Besim Kabashi. 2013. KLUE: Simple and robust methods for polarity classification. In *Second Joint Conference on Lexical and Computational Semantics (*SEM), Volume 2: Proceedings of the Seventh International Workshop on Semantic Evaluation (SemEval 2013)*, pages 395–401, Atlanta, Georgia, USA, June.

Sara Rosenthal, Alan Ritter, Preslav Nakov, and Veselin Stoyanov. 2014. Semeval-2014 task 9: Sentiment analysis in Twitter. In *Proceedings of the 8th International Workshop on Semantic Evaluation (SemEval 2014)*, pages 73–80, Dublin, Ireland, August. Association for Computational Linguistics and Dublin City University.

Sara Rosenthal, Preslav Nakov, Svetlana Kiritchenko, Saif M Mohammad, Alan Ritter, and Veselin Stoyanov. 2015. Semeval-2015 task 10: Sentiment analysis in Twitter. In *Proceedings of the 9th International Workshop on Semantic Evaluation*, SemEval '2015, Denver, Colorado, June.

Matthew A. Russell, 2014. *Mining the Social Web: Data Mining Facebook, Twitter, LinkedIn, Google+, GitHub, and More*, chapter 9.8. Sampling the Twitter Firehose with the Streaming API. O'Reilly, 2 edition.

SWASH: A Naive Bayes Classifier for Tweet Sentiment Identification

Ruth Talbot[1], **Chloe Acheampong**[2] **and Richard Wicentowski**[1]
[1]Swarthmore College, Swarthmore, PA USA
[2]Ashesi University, Accra, Ghana
{rtalbot1, richardw}@cs.swarthmore.edu
chloeacheampong@gmail.com

Abstract

This paper describes a sentiment classification system designed for SemEval-2015, Task 10, Subtask B. The system employs a constrained, supervised text categorization approach. Firstly, since thorough preprocessing of tweet data was shown to be effective in previous SemEval sentiment classification tasks, various preprocessessing steps were introduced to enhance the quality of lexical information. Secondly, a Naive Bayes classifier is used to detect tweet sentiment. The classifier is trained only on the training data provided by the task organizers. The system makes use of external human-generated lists of positive and negative words at several steps throughout classification. The system produced an overall F-score of 59.26 on the official test set.

1 Introduction

Over the past few years, an increasing number of people have begun to express their opinion through social networks and microblogging services. Twitter, as one of the most popular of these social networks, has become a major platform for social communication, allowing its users to send and read short messages called 'tweets'. Tweets have become important in a variety of tasks, including the prediction of election results (O'Connor et al., 2010). The emergence of online expressions of opinion has attracted interest in sentiment analysis of tweets in both academia and industry. Sentiment analysis, also known as opinion mining, focuses on computational treatments of sentiments (emotions, attitudes, opinions) in natural language text. In this paper we describe our submission to Task 10, subtask B: Message Polarity Classification. The task is defined as: 'Given a message, classify whether the message is of positive, negative, or neutral sentiment. For a message conveying both a positive and negative sentiment, whichever is the stronger sentiment should be chosen' (Rosenthal et al., 2015).

This paper describes a system which utilizes a Naive Bayes classifier to determine the sentiment of tweets. This paper describes the resources used, the system details, including preprocessing steps taken, feature extraction and classifier implemented, and the test runs and end results.

2 Resources

2.1 Labeled Tweets

This system is constrained, and the only training data used is the sentiment labeled training data provided by the task organizers. The training data we used includes 8142 tweets, each labeled as positive, negative or neutral.

2.2 Sentiment Lexicon

Our system relies on an external lexicon of approximately 6800 tokens labeled as either positive or negative (Liu et al., 2005). The lexicon consists of words that humans have tagged as having either strongly negative or strongly positive sentiment. If a word in a tweet is preidentified as highly positive or negative, we add a special feature to the tweet's features to indicate that the tweet included a highly positive word or a highly negative word (Kiritchenko et al., 2014). Although multiple lexicons exist, e.g.

Preprocessing Step	F1 score change
jazzy	−5.67
stopwords	−.56
negation	1.74
username normalization	0.34
url normalization	0.40
overriding	1.74
lowercasing	2.21
tokenization	4.00
sentiment lexicon	5.81

Table 1: Changes in F1-score obtained by each preprocessing step (taken individually, not cumulatively) using 5-fold cross validation on the provided training set.

(Wilson et al., 2005) and (Mohammad et al., 2013), we were unable to include them due to time constraints.

3 System Details

The system consists of several preprocessing steps, feature extraction, a Naive Bayes classifier and a secondary classifier that makes use of tokens that are strongly correlating with either a positive or negative sentiment. Improvements that were attempted but were unsuccessful in improving the system are also described.

3.1 Preprocessing Steps

3.1.1 Tokenization

All tweets are tokenized using Twokenizer, a Twitter-specific tokenizer (Owoputi et al., 2013). The tokenizer can detect and handle conditions unlikely to occur in more formal writing, such as mentions, hashtags and retweet tokens.

3.1.2 Normalization

During preprocessing, all tweets are normalized. This included several steps:

- Lowercasing all words (e.g. 'Hello' to 'hello' or 'heRe' to 'here')
- Converting all URLs (identified as strings containing '.com', 'http', 'www' and '.co') to the string 'URL'
- Converting all mentions (identified as strings beginning with '@') to 'username'

3.1.3 Negation

The system implements a basic version of negation to improve the accuracy of the classifier. When processing the data, any words in between a negative adverb or verb, a 'negation key' (e.g. never, not, can't) and the next end of sentence indicator, in this case, any punctuation symbol, are negated. Negation was implemented to avoid misclassification of tweets due to a word of one sentiment following a negation key and therefore being of the opposite sentiment. For instance, a sentence could state: "That movie was not the best thing I've ever seen." Clearly, this sentence is negative, but without negation, the presence of the word 'best,' a typically positive word, might lead this tweet to be classified as positive, not negative. If however, a tag is added (in this case 'NOT_') to any words following a negation key, those words will be more likely to be classified appropriately, as 'NOT_best' will more often be seen in negative contexts (Kiritchenko et al., 2014).

3.1.4 Other Preprocessing Considered

Several other preprocessing steps were considered. In particular, a spell corrector, Jazzy[1], was used as it had previously been shown to be effective (Miura et al., 2014). This step was taken to reduce dimensionality and provide better matches with the sentiment lexicon, e.g. converting 'luve' into 'love', so instead of seeing 'love' once in a positive context and 'luve' once in a positive context, we would see 'love' twice in a positive context, giving it more weight as a positive feature and finding a match in the sentiment lexicon. However, Jazzy actually reduced accuracy and F-score of our system. One potential explanation for this finding is that tweets may contain significant amounts of abbreviations, slang and misspellings that are too far removed from the original spelling for a spell checker to identify and adjust to its correct spelling.

Additionally, removing stopwords was attempted. A list of the 25 most common words in the English language was acquired using the Brown Corpus. This list provided the system with common words unlikely to be strongly associated with any sense. These words were then removed before feature selection. In our final implementation of the

[1]http://jazzy.sourceforge.net/

Sentiment	Precision	Recall	F-score
Negative	61.72	50.45	55.52
Positive	73.98	66.17	69.86
Neutral	64.09	76.21	69.63
F1 score:	62.69	Accuracy:	67.42

Table 2: F-scores for individual sentiments and overall score, produced using 5-fold cross validation on SemEval-2015 training data.

classifier, removing stopwords has a small negative effect on performance.

3.2 Feature Extraction

The features used in our classifier are unigrams, negated unigrams, and two special tags indicating the presence or absence of words in the tweet being found in the sentiment lexicon. During preprocessing, negated unigrams are created by prepending 'NOT_' to a unigram if it follows a negation key, described above. If the unigram follows a negation key, only the negated unigram, not its original form, is included as a feature. In addition, a 'positive' or 'negative' feature (represented by 'POSW' or 'NEGW') is added for each positive or negative word a tweet contained, as identified by inclusion in the sentiment lexicon.

3.3 Classifiers

3.3.1 Naive Bayes Classifier

We used a Naive Bayes classifier to classify the tweets. Naive Bayes relies on the assumption of conditional independence among the features, something that is clearly not true here. While Naive Bayes classifiers manage to perform well despite this assumption, a classifier not reliant on this assumption might outperform a Naive Bayes classifier (Gamallo and Garcia, 2014).

The Naive Bayes classifier employed Laplace smoothing. More advanced smoothing techniques were attempted, but actually reduced both the accuracy and F1 score of the system. The additive smoothing constant was empirically chosen to be 0.4. The Naive Bayes classifier was trained solely on the training data from SemEval-2015.

3.3.2 Other Classifiers Attempted

In addition to Naive Bayes, several other classifiers were tried, and an attempt was made to employ a combination of multiple classifiers to predict sentiment. These classifiers included a typical decision list (which defaults to most frequent sense classification), and a number of classifiers included in scikit-learn (Pedregosa et al., 2011): LinearSVC, GaussianNB, NearestCentroid, MultinomialNB, and BernoulliNB. Each classifier used the same preprocessing and feature selection employed by the Naive Bayes classifier. However, after implementing all of these classifiers and attempting to use a combination of their sense decisions to make a more accurate prediction, none of the classifiers, nor any combination of their decisions, outperformed the Naive Bayes classifier, and therefore none were used in our submission.

3.3.3 Post-Processing

Several features were identified that, when present, were strongly indicative of a positive or negative sense (e.g. ':)', ':(', 'awful', 'love'). If one of those features was present in a tweet, a rule-based system overrode the decision of the Naive Bayes classifier, labeling the tweet as either positive or negative. This step was conducted after negation so that no unnegated words would be used to classify a tweet incorrectly. Suprisingly, this 'overriding' step improved our F1 score by several points, indicating that there are several features that when present are strongly indicative of a tweet's sense.

These strongly positive or negative overriding features were determined by inspection of training data and using our own knowledge to come up with symbols and words which were highly polar in sentiment. The positive word list contained 4 emoticons[2] and 7 overly positive words: 'love', 'great', 'happy', 'wonderful', 'good', 'perfect', and 'beautiful'. The negative list contained 6 emoticons[3], 4 curse words and 5 negative words: 'fuck', 'shit', 'ass', 'crap', 'hate', 'awful', 'stupid', 'horrible', and 'ugh'. Future work could include automatically inducing such a list from training data.

[2]Positive :) :D :-) ;)

[3]Negative :(:-(:/ :'(:.(>:(

Laplace λ	F-score	sentiment weight	F-score
.3	62.40	1	59.25
.4	**62.69**	**5**	**62.69**
.5	62.39	6	62.39

Table 3: Two parameters empirically determined using crossvalidation. In Laplace smoothing, λ is the additive constant for unknown words. The 'positive' and 'negative' features introduced by the sentiment lexicon were given five times the weight of the token unigrams.

Dataset	Rank	F1
Twitter 2015	21	59.26
Live Journal 2014	24	69.43
SMS 2013	34	56.49
Twitter 2013	27	63.07
Twitter 2014	31	62.93
Twitter 2014 Sarcasm	15	48.42

Table 4: Performance on the official 2015 test data as well as on the progress data sets.

4 Test Runs

In addition to attempting additional classifiers, several parameter values were experimented with using 5-fold cross validation to determine which produced the best F-scores.

4.1 Parameter Selection

As mentioned earlier, the constant used for additive Laplace smoothing was determined empirically. Values between 0 and 1 were tested, and it was determined that the ideal value was 0.4. Table 3 shows the change in score for 3 different values close to 0.4.

The second parameter tuned empirically was the weight given to the 'positive' and 'negative' features added if a tweet contained a positive or negative word listed in the sentiment lexicon. After experimenting with various ways of oversampling this feature, we determined that giving these words five times the weight of other unigrams was the optimal number under crossvalidation. (see Table 3).

5 Conclusion

This paper describes the implementation of a sentiment classification system that uses extensive preprocessing and a Naive Bayes sentiment classifier. Using only a Naive Bayes classifier the system achieved a 59.26 F1 score, placing 21st out of 40 overall in Task 10, subtask B. Interestingly, our system overperformed in the sarcasm progress data set, requiring some further investigation.

While our attempt at weighting the decision of multiple classifiers was unsuccessful, we believe this was due to using the same features for each classifier, and that these features may have been overfitted to those found effective in a Naive Bayes classifier.

Additionally, our human-generated list of positive and negative words and symbols, whose presence automatically overrode the classifier's decision, should be further explored. It is highly likely that more words and symbols exist whose presence is highly indicative of a negative or positive tweet sentiment. Automatic creation of these lists would likely improve performance and be more experimentally justified.

References

Pablo Gamallo and Marcos Garcia. 2014. Citius: A naive-bayes strategy for sentiment analysis on english tweets. In *Proceedings of SemEval-2014*, pages 171–175.

Svetlana Kiritchenko, Xiaodan Zhu, Colin Cherry, and Saif Mohammad. 2014. NRC-Canada-2014: Detecting aspects and sentiment in customer reviews. In *Proceedings of SemEval-2014*, pages 437–442.

Bing Liu, Minqing Hu, and Junsheng Cheng. 2005. Opinion observer: analyzing and comparing opinions on the Web. In *Proceedings of WWW'05*, pages 342–351.

Yasuhide Miura, Shigeyuki Sakaki, Keigo Hattori, and Tomoko Ohkuma. 2014. TeamX: A sentiment analyzer with enhanced lexicon mapping and weighting scheme for unbalanced data. In *Proceedings of SemEval-2014*, pages 628–632.

Saif Mohammad, Svetlana Kiritchenko, and Xiaodan Zhu. 2013. NRC-Canada: Building the state-of-the-art in sentiment analysis of tweets. In *Proceedings of SemEval-2013*, pages 321–327.

Brendan O'Connor, Ramnath Balasubramanyan, Bryan Routledge, and Noah Smith. 2010. From tweets to polls: Linking test sentiment to public opinion time series. In *Proceedings of the International AAAI Conference on Weblogs and Social Media*, pages 122–129.

Olutobi Owoputi, Brendan O'Connor, Chris Dyer, Kevin Gimpel, Nathan Schneider, and Noah A. Smith. 2013. Improved part-of-speech tagging for online conversational text with word clusters. In *Proceedings of NAACL-2013*, pages 380–390.

Fabian Pedregosa, Gael Varoquaux, Alexandre Gramfort, Vincent Michel, Bertrand Thirion, Olivier Grisel, Mathieu Blondel, Peter Prettenhofer, Ron Weiss, Vincent Dubourg, Jake Vanderplas, Alexandre Passos, David Cournapeau, Matthieu Brucher, Matthieu Perrot, and Edouard Duchesnay. 2011. Scikit-learn: Machine learning in Python. *Journal of Machine Learning Research*, 12:2825–2830.

Sara Rosenthal, Preslav Nakov, Svetlana Kiritchenko, Saif M Mohammad, Alan Ritter, and Veselin Stoyanov. 2015. Semeval-2015 task 10: Sentiment analysis in Twitter. In *Proceedings of SemEval-2015*.

Theresa Wilson, Janyce Wiebe, and Paul Hoffmann. 2005. Recognizing contextual polarity in phrase-level sentiment analysis. In *Proceedings HLT '05*, pages 347–354.

SWATCS65: Sentiment Classification Using an Ensemble of Class Projects

Richard Wicentowski
Swarthmore College
500 College Avenue
Swarthmore, PA 19081
richardw@cs.swarthmore.edu

Abstract

This paper presents the SWATCS65 ensemble classifier used to identify the sentiment of tweets. The classifier was trained and tested using data provided by Semeval-2015, Task 10, subtask B with the goal to label the sentiment of an entire tweet. The ensemble was constructed from 26 classifiers, each written by a group of one to three undergraduate students in the Fall 2014 offering of a natural language processing course at Swarthmore College. Each of the classifiers was designed independently, though much of the early structure was provided by in-class lab assignments. There was high variability in the final performance of each of these classifiers, which were combined using a weighted voting scheme with weights correlated with performance using 5-fold cross-validation on the provided training data. The system performed very well, achieving an F1 score of 61.89.

1 Introduction

Workshops designed around competitions such as Semeval-2015 provide an excellent entry-point for undergraduate students to work on real-world problems in the field by providing both the training and test data as well as a framework for comparing their work to the state-of-the-art. These competitions have a low barrier to entry while also providing students with an external motivation to continually improve their systems.

As part of the Fall 2015 offering of CPSC 065 at Swarthmore College[1], undergraduate students enrolled in the class were required to build a classifier for Semeval-2015 Task 10, subtask B (Rosenthal et al., 2015). The goal of this task was to provide a labeling of the sentiment expressed in a tweet: either negative, neutral or positive.

Fifty-one students were enrolled in the class and each student worked in a small group. Of the 26 groups, 23 were comprised of two students, one group had three students, and two had only one student. Approximately 35% of the students in the class (18 of 51) took this class as their first upper-level course in the discipline, having completed only the equivalents of CS1 and CS2 prior to this class.

The classifiers were developed over a seven week period beginning in the eighth week of the course.

2 Required Components

Each group was provided with boilerplate code to read in the tweets and were tasked with writing a Naive Bayes classifier to label each of the tweets. In the first two weeks, groups were required to first evaluate their system using five-fold cross-validation without any preprocessing of the tweets using only unigrams. Then they compared those results to those obtained after performing a few basic preprocessing steps (removal of stopwords, case-folding, and simple handling of negation) and

[1] http://goo.gl/ydgE5r

tokenization using Twokenizer (Owoputi et al., 2013).

In the third week, students read three papers from Semeval-2014 Task 9 subtask B, a similar task held in the previous year. Students were not told which papers they had to read. Each group wrote a short literature review based on their reading and implemented something they read about that sounded interesting. There was no requirement that the new piece they implemented would improve their performance, but many groups continued to add to their systems until they had made at least a minor improvement over their previous baseline.

After the third week, students were provided guidance as needed, but there were no additional requirements aside from writing a four-page system description paper using the conference's style files.

3 Features

At its most basic, this sentiment classification task can be performed somewhat effectively without preprocessing the tweets, using only unigrams as features input to a supervised classifier. What sets each of the better performing classifiers apart is how the data is preprocessed, which features are extracted, whether or not external tweets or other sources (e.g. sentiment lexicons) are included, and the specifics of the classifier and its parameter settings. Many of the early modifications parroted the choices of the most successful past participants (Miura et al., 2014; Tang et al., 2014; Günther et al., 2014; Zhu et al., 2014).

Although there was no single modification that all teams implemented, many teams ended up with somewhat similar systems. Most teams case-folded the tweets, tokenized them using Twokenizer, then extracted only the unigrams as features. Most of the teams also included Twitter-specific preprocessing such as normalizing URLs and mentions to reduce dimensionality (e.g. nytimes.com → someurl.net, @fmanjoo → @someone), which has previously been shown to be effective (Amir et al., 2014).

Nearly all of the teams that attempted to handle negation followed the lead of (Pang et al., 2002), modifying the token in the tweet with some uniquely occurring affix such as "_NEG" to every word following a negation word (e.g. "not", "never") until reaching a punctuation mark.

n-gram features	
Unigrams only	18
Unigrams and bigrams	5
Unigrams, bigrams and trigrams	3
pre-processing	
Case folding	24
URL normalization	22
Negation handling	22
Tokenization	21
@mention normalization	18
Stemming/lemmatization	7
Repeated character handling	7
Spell checking	6
Part-of-speech tags	3
external lexicons	
Opinion lexicon (Liu et al., 2005)	14
Emoticon lists	13
Sentiment140 (Mohammad et al., 2013)	7
MPQA Subjectivity (Wilson et al., 2005)	4
classifiers	
Naive Bayes	20
Support Vector Machines	10
Logistic Regression	8
Decision Lists	6
Random Forests/Boosting	2
k-Nearest Neighbors	2
Deep belief networks	1

Table 1: Common features and classifiers used by the 26 systems built in the class.

Although not well represented in the final systems, many teams tried to use a spell checker to reduce dimensionality. After experimenting with a few options, students often chose the Jazzy[2] spell checker used by (Miura et al., 2014), though this option was largely abandoned because it produced inferior results. In particular, the dictionaries used by the spell checkers were not tailored for the colloquial, abbreviated and slangy language found

[2] http://jazzy.sourceforge.net/

Classifier	F1 score
Logistic Regression	59.6
Support Vector Machines	57.4
Naive Bayes	56.5
Decision Lists	53.5

Table 2: Average F1 score for systems based on the classifier used. F1 score is reported for performance on cross-validation on the training data. Note that a majority of the systems (16/26) used more than one classifier so the same system may be represented in multiple rows.

in many of the tweets, yielding high rates of false positives: words marked as incorrectly spelled that were actually spelled correctly, for example "LOL". As an alternative to spell checking, a few teams tried to identify and correct words where the author had repeated characters for the purposes of emphasis, e.g. "sweeeeeet" or "nooooooo!", similar to (Günther et al., 2014). When this occurred, teams often gave extra weight to these unigrams as a way to carry the author's intended emphasis into the feature set.

A few students made use of a part-of-speech tagger (Owoputi et al., 2013) to include tag n-grams in the feature set, but no groups used the tags as a way to disambiguate unigram features.

Table 1 contains a summary of the most common features and classifiers used. Nine of the groups only used the Naive Bayes and decision list classifiers that they had written for class assignments. The majority of the students also made extensive use of scikit-learn (Pedregosa et al., 2011), which provides access to many more standard classifiers such as support vector machines, logistic regression, and k-nearest neighbors.

4 Classifiers

Students were required to implement a Naive Bayes classifier as part of the initial specification of the assignment. In a previous assignment, students had written a decision list classifier. About half of the groups (12 of 26) only used these two classifiers, either on their own or in some combination. Although a few of the better systems in the class used only a Naive Bayes classifier, the majority of the class, and most of the best systems in the class (7 of the top 10) made use of scikit-learn (Pedregosa et al., 2011). Overall, more students tried to use SVM than Logistic Regression, perhaps because this had been talked about in class or referenced more in previous system description papers. However, similar to most of the best results from Semeval-2014, students who used the Logistic Regression classifiers tended to outperform those who used SVMs.

The large majority of the classifiers were able to read in raw tweets and produce a labeling of the test data in minutes. The small number of students who used Jazzy needed to cache the spell-checked versions of the tweets because of the very slow runtime. The deep belief network classifier was very slow, taking several hours to run.

It is difficult to make strong claims about the effectiveness of each classifier given the differences in implementation between each of the systems. However, as shown in Table 2, the average F1 score of systems that used Logistic Regression was higher than the average F1 score for any other classifier.

5 System Results and Combination

In consultation with the task organizers, it was agreed that rather than submitting each of the 26 systems individually, only the best-performing individual systems and a single system combining all of the systems would be submitted. As a proxy to determine how well each of the systems would do on the 2015 task, each of the 26 systems was evaluated using five-fold cross-validation on the 2015 training data and on the test data from 2014. The three top-performing systems were submitted individually to the workshop: SWATCMW, SWATAC, and SWASH. It is likely that one or more of the next-best systems could have outperformed the systems that were submitted on the 2015 test data, but this evaluation has not been conducted. The results of each of the systems using cross-validation and on the 2014 test data are included in Table 3.

As can be seen in Table 3, most of the groups in the class did well. Some groups had last-minute

rank	xvalid	2014	rank	xvalid	2014
1	**62.93**	**66.06**	14	58.11	58.40
2	**64.20**	**64.67**	15	57.31	57.18
3	**62.69**	**62.84**	16	55.89	56.49
4	61.60	61.63	17	55.37	56.14
5	58.97	61.51	18	55.73	55.54
6	59.97	61.19	19	53.80	54.94
7	60.56	60.28	20	54.10	54.91
8	58.44	60.23	21	53.37	54.52
9	57.28	60.21	22	54.53	53.52
10	60.19	60.00	23	51.60	47.76
11	60.81	59.92	24	36.22	27.63
12	57.84	59.84	25	55.08	24.53
13	62.01	59.62	26	52.94	21.80

Table 3: Performance of each of the 26 systems, evaluated using 5-fold cross-validation on the 2015 training data and sorted by their F1 score on the 2014 test data. The top three systems were submitted individually as SWATCMW, SWATAC and SWASH, respectively.

bugs in their system that caused precipitous drop-offs in performance between the cross-validation and the 2014 test data. Comparing individual system performances to those of in the 2014 task (Rosenthal et al., 2014), all of the students' systems were in the third quartile, though some of the best of student systems were in the middle of the pack.

To obtain the final classifier, a simple weighted voting scheme was used. Each classifier was run on the test data from Semeval-2014 Task 9 subtask B. The F1 score obtained on the test data set was used as the weight for each classifier. This gave the better performing classifiers more votes in the final outcome and gave each of the students in the class a way to participate in this year's task. Systems that had major flaws (shown as systems 24, 25 and 26 in Table 3) were omitted from the final system.

As can be seen in Table 4, the combined system did very well on the 2015 test data. On that test set, the system ranked 11th out of 40, performing quite similarly to systems ranked approximately 7 through 15.

However, looking more deeply into the progress data sets, it becomes clear that this system strug-

Dataset	Rank	F1
Twitter 2015	11	61.89
Live Journal 2014	8	73.37
SMS 2013	8	65.49
Twitter 2013	13	68.21
Twitter 2014	15	67.23
Twitter 2014 Sarcasm	39	37.23

Table 4: Performance of combination system compared to the 40 participants in Semeval-2015.

gled with detecting sarcasm, finishing nearly at the bottom of all the systems submitted. It is unclear why this subtlety was missed, but this was not only a problem for the combined system. Two of the three individual systems that contributed to this ensemble but were submitted separately to the workshop (SWATAC and SWATCMW) also did very poorly on the sarcasm subset, finishing 35th and 36th. Further analysis is warranted to see if the problem with sarcasm was widespread across all of the systems or if it was particular to the highest scoring systems whose vote was over-weighted in the final system.

6 Conclusion

We present an ensemble classifier created from 26 class projects completed during an undergraduate class in natural language processing. These projects were completed over a seven week period beginning midway through the semester. Many of the students had never taken an advanced computer science class before, but the availability of the Twitter data, preprocessing tools and machine learning toolkits made participation in this task possible even for inexperienced young researchers. The contributions of all of the systems yielded a highly effective sentiment classifier on all of the tweets excluding the sarcastic dataset.

7 Acknowledgements

The author acknowledges all of the students whose hard work is represented here: Jocelyn, Yousef, Pravin, Izzi, Lihu, Amanda, Sara, Bradley, Rex, Ying Yu, Yenny, Jacob, Riley, Raymond, Daniel F., Molly, Andrew, Samantha, Nora, Klarissa, Terry, Ryerson, Richard, Mike L, Uriel, Ben M., Dan M., Mike M., Chris M., Gautam, Chris N., Winnie,

Flore, Shawn, Alec, Cappy, Razi, Alex, Mike S., Ruth, Lee, Elyse, A.J., Aly, Noah, Anastaisa, Ben X., David, Rita, Andrew, Peng and Chloe. Thanks!

References

Silvio Amir, Miguel B. Almeida, Bruno Martins, João Filgueiras, and Mario J. Silva. 2014. Tugas: Exploiting unlabelled data for Twitter sentiment analysis. In *Proceedings of SemEval-2014*, pages 673–677.

Tobias Günther, Jean Vancoppenolle, and Richard Johansson. 2014. RTRGO: Enhancing the GU-MLT-LT system for sentiment analysis of short messages. In *Proceedings of SemEval-2014*, pages 497–502.

Bing Liu, Minqing Hu, and Junsheng Cheng. 2005. Opinion observer: analyzing and comparing opinions on the Web. In *WWW'05*, pages 342–351.

Yasuhide Miura, Shigeyuki Sakaki, Keigo Hattori, and Tomoko Ohkuma. 2014. TeamX: A sentiment analyzer with enhanced lexicon mapping and weighting scheme for unbalanced data. In *Proceedings of SemEval-2014*, pages 628–632.

Saif Mohammad, Svetlana Kiritchenko, and Xiaodan Zhu. 2013. NRC-Canada: Building the state-of-the-art in sentiment analysis of tweets. In *Proceedings of SemEval-2013*, pages 321–327.

Olutobi Owoputi, Brendan O'Connor, Chris Dyer, Kevin Gimpel, Nathan Schneider, and Noah A. Smith. 2013. Improved part-of-speech tagging for online conversational text with word clusters. In *Proceedings of NAACL-2013*, pages 380–390.

Bo Pang, Lillian Lee, and Shivakumar Vaithyanathan. 2002. Thumbs up? sentiment classification using machine learning techniques. In *Proceedings of EMNLP*, pages 79–86.

Fabian Pedregosa, Gael Varoquaux, Alexandre Gramfort, Vincent Michel, Bertrand Thirion, Olivier Grisel, Mathieu Blondel, Peter Prettenhofer, Ron Weiss, Vincent Dubourg, Jake Vanderplas, Alexandre Passos, David Cournapeau, Matthieu Brucher, Matthieu Perrot, and Edouard Duchesnay. 2011. Scikit-learn: Machine learning in Python. *Journal of Machine Learning Research*, 12:2825–2830.

Sara Rosenthal, Alan Ritter, Preslav Nakov, and Veselin Stoyanov. 2014. Semeval-2014 task 9: Sentiment analysis in Twitter. In *Proceedings of SemEval-2014*, pages 73–80.

Sara Rosenthal, Preslav Nakov, Svetlana Kiritchenko, Saif M Mohammad, Alan Ritter, and Veselin Stoyanov. 2015. Semeval-2015 task 10: Sentiment analysis in Twitter. In *Proceedings Semeval-2015*.

Duyu Tang, Furu Wei, Bing Qin, Ting Liu, and Ming Zhou. 2014. Coooolll: A deep learning system for Twitter sentiment classification. In *Proceedings of SemEval-2014*, pages 208–212.

Theresa Wilson, Janyce Wiebe, and Paul Hoffmann. 2005. Recognizing contextual polarity in phrase-level sentiment analysis. In *Proceedings of HLT/EMNLP*, pages 347–354.

Xiaodan Zhu, Svetlana Kiritchenko, and Saif Mohammad. 2014. NRC-Canada-2014: Recent improvements in the sentiment analysis of tweets. In *Proceedings of SemEval-2014*, pages 443–447.

SWATAC: A Sentiment Analyzer using One-Vs-Rest Logistic Regression

Yousef Alhessi and Richard Wicentowski
Swarthmore College
Swarthmore, PA 19081 USA
{yalhess1, richardw}@cs.swarthmore.edu

Abstract

This paper describes SWATAC, a system built for SemEval-2015's Task 10 Subtask B, namely the Message Polarity Classification Task. Given a tweet, the system classifies the sentiment as either positive, negative, or neutral. Several preprocessing tasks such as negation detection, spell checking, and tokenization are performed to enhance lexical information. The features are then augmented with external sentiment lexicons. Classification is done with Logistic Regression using a one-vs-rest configuration. For the test runs, the system was trained using only the provided training tweets. The classifier was successful, with an F1 score of 58.43 on the official 2015 test data, and an F1 score of 66.64 on the Twitter 2014 progress data.

1 Introduction

Since 2006, Twitter has grown into a ubiquitous global social platform. Millions of users compose Twitter messages, which are known as "tweets", to express their opinions and sentiments about the world around them. These tweets turn into valuable resources for sentiment analysis, a field that focuses on analyzing the attitude of speakers or writers towards a certain topic. Working with this informal text genre opens up a new realm of challenges in the natural language processing world. This paper describes a tweet sentiment classifier which has been applied to Subtask B of SemEval-2015 Task 10 (Rosenthal et al., 2015). The tweets generated by users contain Internet slang, unconventional punctuation and spelling, and typos, which require a different set of preprocessing tools than traditional genres like newswire text.

After preprocessing the tweets, classifying them into categories of positive, negative, and neutral presents another challenge. Many sentiment applications make use of lexicons to supply features to the system, populating a list of positive and negative types. Some publicly available sources include the MPQA Subjectivity Lexicon (Wilson et al., 2005), the Opinion Lexicon (Liu et al., 2005), and the Sentiment140 Lexicon (Mohammad et al., 2013). While some of these lexicons do not target tweets as their analysis subject, they each provide a mapping from n-grams to sentiment labels, which proves to be helpful in building our tweet sentiment analyzer.

After preprocessing, the system performs the classification task. The classifier we use is a one-vs-rest logistic regression classifier, so the system uses three binary classifiers: positive/not-positive, negative/not-negative, and neutral/not-neutral. The classifier also over-samples the low-frequency classes, learning from the same number of examples of each class overall.

The accompanying sections of the papers are organized as follows: Section 2 describes resources such as the lexicons used in the system. It also outlines the system design and the APIs that the system adopts. Section 3 describes the test runs and evaluates the system. Section 4 concludes the paper.

2 System Details

The main objective of our system is to determine if a tweet conveys a positive, negative, or neutral sentiment. To achieve this goal, the system first employs some preprocessing tools to enhance the lexical information. Then it relies on various sentiment lexicons to help with the classification of sentiments. For preprocessing, the system performs case-folding, detects negation, optionally uses a spell checker, performs tokenization, and makes use of unigrams, bigrams, and pairs of n-grams.

In addition to features extracted from the tweets, the system relies on four external sentiment lexicons. Three of them are pre-existing resources: the MPQA Subjectivity Lexicon (Wilson et al., 2005), the Opinion Lexicon (Liu et al., 2005), and the Sentiment140 Lexicon (Mohammad et al., 2013). The final lexicon is a manually created Emoji lexicon compiled by the authors.

After extracting features, a Logistics Regression classifier using a one-vs-rest setup is used to label each of the tweets.

2.1 Preprocessing

2.1.1 Case Folding

We use case folding to make every letter of every word in both the training and the test data lowercase. This helps in dimensionality reduction.

2.1.2 Negation Detector

The system includes a negation detector. Similar to (Pang et al., 2002), in this detector, we append a negation suffix to words that occur within a negation window between a negation key word and some punctuation. For example, the word "great", which is considered a positive word, is treated and learned as a different token if it is preceded by "not" as in "this pasta is not very great". This sentence would become "this pasta is not NOT_very NOT_great".

2.1.3 Jazzy

Jazzy is the Java Open Source Spell Checker[1]. Previous work had shown Jazzy to be effective (Miura et al., 2014). Though this was used during the development of the system, time constraints didn't allow its use in the final submission. Using five-fold crossvalidation, including Jazzy improved performance slightly, from an F1 score of 63.8 to 64.75.

[1] http://jazzy.sourceforge.net/

2.1.4 Twokenizer

Twokenizer is a tokenizer designed specifically for tweets (Gimpel et al., 2011). Twokenizer properly handles the tokenization of tweets without mangling URLs, mentions, or hashtags.

2.2 Sentiment Lexicons

2.2.1 MPQA

We make use of the MPQA Subjectivity Lexicon (Wilson et al., 2005). The lexicon is generated from the MPQA Opinion Corpus, which incorporates a wide range of news articles manually annotated for opinions and other private states. Although the MPQA lexicon list mainly targets news articles, it improved our system's classifications. The MPQA subjectivity lexicon provides a list of words with both their polarity (positive, negative, and neutral) and their strength (strong subjective, weak subjective). Our system made use of the polarity, but not the strength.

2.2.2 Opinion Lexicon

The Opinion Lexicon provided by Liu et al. (2005) consists of a list of positive words and a list of negative words. Because the lexicon is automatically generated from social media content, it contains misspelled lemmas, which could be beneficial to tweet analysis as tweets tend to include erroneous spellings and Internet slang (Liu, 2010). For example, we can find both words "awesome" and "awsome" in the list of positive words. In the negative list, we find "awful" as well as "aweful".

2.2.3 Sentiment140 Lexicon

The Sentiment140-Lexicon is a list of features with associations to positive and negative sentiments (Mohammad et al., 2013). The lexicon was created from the automatically-labeled sentiment140 corpus of 1.6 million tweets. The labeled features are unigrams, bigrams, and pairs of n-grams (unigrams-unigrams, unigrams-bigrams, bigrams-unigrams, and bigrams-bigrams). For example, some of the features we could see in the list are: the unigrams "@jeffery_donovan" and "xoxoxo", the bigrams "yeh yeh" and "praise !", and the pairs "done—had", "i—, drinking", "thank you—lovely", and "good morning—can be". Each feature has a score that reflects how positive or negative the feature is. If the word was seen in more positive contexts than negative contexts, it's score is positive. The magnitude of the score is highest when the distribution is overwhelmingly positive, and the magnitude is closest to zero when the word appears equally in both positive and negative contexts. Negative words are scored similarly using negative values instead of positive values.

2.2.4 Emoji Lexicon

Our system uses a hand-created Emoji dictionary comprised of 16 positive[2] and 7 negative[3] emoticons. Only the most common Emoji in the training set were added to the lexicon. However, we chose to some exclude some emoticons because they portray a wide range of sentiments. For example, emoticons like ":-|" and ":|" were seen in both neutral and negative tweets. Using this specific set of emoticons improved the results when using cross-validation from an F1 score of around 62.5 to 64.8. A more extensive list might improve results, but given the time constraints, these 23 emoticons covered the test set adequately.

2.3 Classifier

Our system uses a one-vs-rest logistic regression classifier to analyze the sentiment of each tweet. Before the tweets get passed to the classifier, an oversampling process takes place to ensure equal numbers of each sentiment class during training. The classifier uses a one-vs-rest scheme, breaking down the classification process into three tasks: positive, negative, and neutral. Our classification task assumes that each sample is assigned to one and only one label.

2.3.1 One-Vs-Rest

We use a one-vs-rest strategy, building a classifier for each sentiment label (Hong and Cho, 2008). This means our system is comprised of three classifiers: positive/not-positive, negative/not-negative, and neutral/not-neutral. For each classifier, the class is compared against all the other classes. In other words, the features are screened to determine if they are positive, negative, or neutral in three separate stages: positive vs. non-positive, negative vs. non-negative, and neutral vs. non-neutral.

During testing, each instance is labeled by each of the three classifiers. When determining the label for a test instance, we would ideally like to have only one of the binary classifiers find a match. This usually happens when a tweet has many features expressing the same sentiment. However, when a tweet has contradicting features, the classifiers may contradict each either, either finding no matching class, or having multiple classifiers match a class. In cases of uncertainty, we use the labeling returned by the classifier with the highest confidence. Removing the one-vs-rest strategy decreases the score on cross-validation from 64.8 to 64.0.

2.3.2 Oversampling

In our classifier, we over-sample classes according to the number of examples we have in the training data. This means no matter what the distribution of our underlying training data is, the system learns from an equal number of examples of each class label. For example, if we have 100 negative instances in the training data and 200 non-negative instances, the negative instances would be sampled twice, whereas every non-negative example would be sampled only once. This way, a negative feature that is seen once is twice as strong or informative to our system as a non-negative feature that is seen once, and it would have the same weight as a non-negative feature that had been seen twice. This method decreased the system's bias towards positive features. Removing oversampling decreases the score on cross-validation from 64.8 to 62.3.

2.3.3 Logistic Regression Model

The system uses the scikit-learn (Pedregosa et al., 2011) implementation of a Logistic Regression classifier. In this system, we use a simple logistic regression, where the model has one nominal variable (a class or non-class), and the features are used as measurement variables.

3 Test Runs

The final classifier included in the submitted system is an L2 regularized logistic regression algo-

[2]Positive :) :D :-) :-D :] :-] :') :'-) ;) =) (: ;-) XD =D =] ;D
[3]Negative :(:-(:[:-[=(=/ :/

System	Live Journal 2014	SMS 2013	Twitter 2013	Twitter 2014	Twitter 2014 Sarcasm	Twitter 2015
SWATAC	68.67	61.30	65.86	66.64	39.45	58.43
Webis	71.64	63.92	68.49	70.86	49.33	64.84
Splusplus	75.34	67.16	72.80	74.42	42.86	63.73
Average	68.13	60.21	63.88	64.90	47.06	57.13

Table 1: Official results comparing the SWATAC system to the best performing systems on the Twitter 2015 and Twitter 2014 datasets, as well as the average performance on each dataset.

rithm, with a C value (the inverse of regularization strength) set to 1, and the tolerance for stopping criteria set to 0.0001, which are the default values provided by the scikit-learn library (Pedregosa et al., 2011). This system is stochastic and returns slightly different labellings on each run. Using five-fold cross-validation, the final classifier had an F1 score between 64.0 and 65.0.

The official results for our system are in Table 1. Our system has successfully scored a better than average F1 in all of the test sets, except for Twitter 2014 Sarcasm dataset. The table compares our system to two other submitted systems: Webis, the best scoring system on the Twitter 2015 dataset, Splusplus, the best scoring system on the Twitter 2014 progress test data, as well as the average scores of all submitted systems in each test data set.

4 Conclusion

This paper describes our submission to SemEval-2015's Task 10 subtask B. Our system uses several preprocessing tools, which includes case folding, negation, and tokenization. Several sentiment lexicons and a manually created Emoji lexicon are employed to help with classifying message polarities. The system uses a logistic regression classifier along with a one-vs-rest scheme to perform a three-stage classification. The results indicate that our system generally performs well, with an F1 score of 58.43 on the 2015 test data.

References

Kevin Gimpel, Nathan Schneider, Brendan O'Connor, Dipanjan Das, Daniel Mills, Jacob Eisenstein, Michael Heilman, Dani Yogatama, Jeffrey Flanigan, and Noah A. Smith. 2011. Part-of-speech tagging for Twitter: Annotation, features, and experiments. In *Proceedings of HLT '11: Short Papers*, volume 2, pages 42–47.

Jin-Hyuk Hong and Sung-Bae Cho. 2008. A probabilistic multi-class strategy of one-vs.-rest support vector machines for cancer classification. *Neurocomputing*, 71(16-18):3275–3281.

Bing Liu, Minqing Hu, and Junsheng Cheng. 2005. Opinion observer: analyzing and comparing opinions on the Web. In *WWW '05*, pages 342–351.

Bing Liu. 2010. Sentiment analysis and subjectivity. *Handbook of natural language processing*, 2:627–666.

Yasuhide Miura, Shigeyuki Sakaki, Keigo Hattori, and Tomoko Ohkuma. 2014. TeamX: A sentiment analyzer with enhanced lexicon mapping and weighting scheme for unbalanced data. In *Proceedings of SemEval-2014*, pages 628–632.

Saif Mohammad, Svetlana Kiritchenko, and Xiaodan Zhu. 2013. NRC-Canada: Building the state-of-the-art in sentiment analysis of tweets. In *Proceedings of SemEval-2013*, pages 321–327.

Bo Pang, Lillian Lee, and Shivakumar Vaithyanathan. 2002. Thumbs up? Sentiment classification using machine learning techniques. In *Proceedings of EMNLP '02*, pages 79–86.

Fabian Pedregosa, Gael Varoquaux, Alexandre Gramfort, Vincent Michel, Bertrand Thirion, Olivier Grisel, Mathieu Blondel, Peter Prettenhofer, Ron Weiss, Vincent Dubourg, Jake Vanderplas, Alexandre Passos, David Cournapeau, Matthieu Brucher, Matthieu Perrot, and Edouard Duchesnay. 2011. Scikit-learn: Machine learning in Python. *Journal of Machine Learning Research*, 12:2825–2830.

Sara Rosenthal, Preslav Nakov, Svetlana Kiritchenko, Saif M Mohammad, Alan Ritter, and Veselin Stoyanov. 2015. Semeval-2015 task 10: Sentiment analysis in Twitter. In *Proceedings of SemEval-2015*.

Theresa Wilson, Janyce Wiebe, and Paul Hoffmann. 2005. Recognizing contextual polarity in phrase-level sentiment analysis. In *Proceedings of HTL-EMNLP '05*, pages 347–354.

TwitterHawk: A Feature Bucket Approach to Sentiment Analysis

William Boag, Peter Potash, Anna Rumshisky
Dept. of Computer Science
University of Massachusetts Lowell
198 Riverside St, Lowell, MA 01854, USA
{wboag,ppotash,arum}@cs.uml.edu

Abstract

This paper describes TwitterHawk, a system for sentiment analysis of tweets which participated in the SemEval-2015 Task 10, Subtasks A through D. The system performed competitively, most notably placing 1st in topic-based sentiment classification (Subtask C) and ranking 4th out of 40 in identifying the sentiment of sarcastic tweets. Our submissions in all four subtasks used a supervised learning approach to perform three-way classification to assign positive, negative, or neutral labels. Our system development efforts focused on text pre-processing and feature engineering, with a particular focus on handling negation, integrating sentiment lexicons, parsing hashtags, and handling expressive word modifications and emoticons. Two separate classifiers were developed for phrase-level and tweet-level sentiment classification. Our success in aforementioned tasks came in part from leveraging the Subtask B data and building a single tweet-level classifier for Subtasks B, C and D.

1 Introduction

In recent years, microblogging has developed into a resource for quickly and easily gathering data about how people feel about different topics. Sites such as Twitter allow for real-time communication of sentiment, thus providing unprecedented insight into how well-received products, events, and people are in the public's eye. But working with this new genre is challenging. Twitter imposes a 140-character limit on messages, which causes users to use novel abbreviations and often disregard standard sentence structures.

For the past three years, the International Workshop on Semantic Evaluation (SemEval) has been hosting a task dedicated to sentiment analysis of Twitter data. This year, our team participated in four subtasks of the challenge: Contextual Polarity Disambiguation (phrase-level), B: Message Polarity Classification (tweet-level), C: Topic-Based Message Polarity Classification (topic-based), and D: Detecting Trends Towards a Topic (trending sentiment). For a more thorough description of the tasks, see Rosenthal et al. (2015). Our system placed 1st out of 7 submissions for topic-based sentiment prediction (Subtask C), 3rd out of 6 submissions for detecting trends toward a topic (Subtask D), 10th out of 40 submissions for tweet-level sentiment prediction (Subtask B), and 5th out of 11 for phrase-level prediction (Subtask A). Our system also ranked 4th out of 40 submissions in identifying the sentiment of sarcastic tweets.

Most systems that participated in this task over the past two years have relied on basic machine learning classifiers with a strong focus on developing robust and comprehensive feature set. The top system for Subtask A in both 2013 and 2014 from NRC Canada (Mohammad et al., 2013; Zhu et al., 2014) used a simple linear SVM while putting great effort into creating and incorporating sentiment lexicons as well as carefully handling negation contexts. Other teams addressed imbalances in data distributions, but still mainly focused on feature engineering, including an improved spelling correction, POS tagging, and word sense disambiguation (Miura et al., 2014). The second place submission for the 2014 Task B competition also used a neural network setup to learn sentiment-specific word embedding features along with state-of-the-art hand-crafted features (Tang et al., 2014).

Our goal in developing TwitterHawk was to build on the success of feature-driven approaches established as state-of-the-art in the two previous years of SemEval Twitter Sentiment Analysis competitions. We therefore focused on identifying and incorporating the strongest features used by the best systems, most notably, sentiment lexicons that showed good performance in ablation studies. We also performed multiple rounds of pre-processing which included tokenization, spelling correction, hashtag segmentation, wordshape replacement of URLs, as well as handling negated contexts. Our main insight for Task C involved leveraging additional training data, since the provided training data was quite small (489 examples between training and dev). Although not annotated with respect to a particular topic, we found that message-level sentiment data (Subtask B) generalized better to topic-level sentiment tracking than span-level data (Subtask A). We therefore used Subtask B data to train a more robust model for topic-level sentiment detection.

The rest of this paper is organized as follows. In Section 2, we discuss text preprocessing and normalization, describe the two classifiers we created for different subtasks, and present the features used by each model. We report system results in Section 3, and discuss system performance and future directions in Section 4.

2 System Description

We built a system to compete in four subtasks of SemEval Task 10 (Rosenthal et al., 2015). Subtasks A-C were concerned with classification of Twitter data as either positive, negative, or neutral. Subtask A involved phrase-level (usually 1-4 tokens) sentiment analysis. Subtask B dealt with classification of the entire tweet. Subtask C involved classifying a tweet's sentiment towards a given topic. Subtask D summarized the results of Subtask C by analyzing the sentiment expressed towards a topic by a group of tweets (as opposed to the single tweet classification for Subtask C).

We trained two classifiers one for phrase-level classification and one for tweet-level sentiment classification. We use the phrase-level classifier for Subtask A and we use the tweet-level classifier for Subtasks B and C. Subtask D did not require a separate classifier since it effectively just summarized the output of Subtask C. We experimented to determine whether data from Subtasks A or B generalized for C, and we found that the Subtask B model performed best at predicting for Subtask C.

2.1 Preprocessing and Normalization

Prior to feature extraction, we perform several preprocessing steps, including tokenization, spell correction, hashtag segmentation, and normalization.

Tokenization and POS-tagging Standard word tokenizers are trained on datasets from the Wall Street Journal, and consequently do not perform well on Twitter data. Some of these issues come from shorter and ill-formed sentences, unintentional misspellings, creative use of language, and abbreviations. We use ARK Tweet NLP toolkit for natural language processing in social media (Owoputi et al., 2013; Gimpel et al., 2011) for tokenization and part-of-speech tagging. An additional tokenization pass is used to split compound words that may have been mis-tokenized. This includes splitting hyphenated phrases such as 'first-place' or punctuation that was not detached from its leading text such as 'horay!!!'.

Spell Correction Twitter's informal nature and limited character space often cause tweets to contain spelling errors and abbreviations. To address this issue, we developed a spell correction module that corrects errors and expands abbreviations. Spell correction is performed in two passes. The first pass identifies the words with alternative spellings common in social media text. The second pass uses a general-purpose spell correction package from PyEnchant library.[1]

If a word w is misspelled, we check if it is one of four special forms we define:

1. **non-prose** - w is hashtag, URL, user mention, number, emoticon, or proper noun.
2. **abbreviation** - w is in our custom hand-built list that contains abbreviations as well as some common misspellings.
3. **elongated word** - w is an elongated word, such as 'heyyyy'. We define 'elongated' as repeating the same character 3 or more times in a row.

[1] http://pythonhosted.org/pyenchant/

4. **colloquial** - w matches a regex for identifying common online phrases such as 'haha' or 'lol'. We use a regex rather than a closed list for elongated phrases where more than one character is repeated in order. This allows, for 'haha' and 'hahaha', for example, to be normalized to the the same form.

Non-prose forms are handled in the tweet normalization phase (see sec 2.1). For abbreviations, we look up the expanded form in our hand-crafted list. For elongated words, we reduce all elongated substrings so that the substring's characters only occur twice. For example, this cuts both 'heeeeyyyy' and 'heeeyyyyyyyyy' down to 'heeyy'. Finally, colloquials are normalized to the shortened form (e.g., 'hahaha' becomes 'haha'). If w is not a special form, we feed it into PyEnchant library's candidate generation tool. We then filter out all candidates whose edit distance is greater than 2, and select the top candidate from PyEnchant.

Hashtag Segmentation Hashtags are often used in tweets to summarize the key ideas of the message. For instance, consider the text: We're going bowling #WeLoveBowling. Although the text "We're going bowling" does not carry any sentiment on its own, the positive sentiment of the message is expressed by the hashtag.

Similarly to spell correction, we define a general algorithm for hashtag segmentation, as well as several special cases. If hashtag h is not a special form, we reduce all characters to lowercase and then use a greedy segmentation algorithm which scans the hashtag from left to right, identifying the longest matching dictionary word. We split off the first word and repeat the process until the entire string is scanned. The algorithm does not backtrack at a dead end, but rather removes the leading character and continues. We use a trie structure to insure the efficiency of longest-prefix queries.

We identify three special cases for a hashtag h:

1. **manually segmented** - h is in our custom hand-built list of hashtags not handled correctly by the general algorithm;
2. **acronym** - h is all capitals;
3. **camel case** - h is written in CamelCase, checked with a regex.

For hashtags that are in the manually segmented list, we use the segmentation that we identified as correct. If h is an acronym, we do not segment it. Finally, for CamelCase, we treat the capitalization as indicating the segment boundaries.

Normalization and Negation During the normalization phrase, all tokens are lowercased. Next, we replace URLs, user mentions, and numbers with generic URL, USER, and NUMBER tokens, respectively. The remaining tokens are stemmed using NLTKs Snowball stemmer (Bird et al., 2009).

We also process negation contexts following the strategy used by Pang et al. (2002). We define a negation context to be a text span that begins with a negation word (such as 'no') and ends with a punctuation mark, hashtag, user mention, or URL. The suffix _neg is appended to all words inside of a negation context. We use the list of negation words from Potts (2011).

2.2 Machine Learning

For the phrase-level sentiment classification, we trained a linear Support Vector Machine (SVM) using scikit-learn's LinearSVC (Pedregosa et al., 2011) on the Subtask A training data, which contained 4832 positive examples, 2549 negative, and 384 neutral. The regularization parameter was set to C=0.05, using a grid search over the development data (648 positive, 430 negative, 57 neutral). To account for the imbalance of label distributions, we used sklearn's 'auto' class weight adjustment which applies a weight inversely proportional to a given class's frequency in the training data to the numeric prediction of each class label.

The tweet-level model was trained using scikit-learn's SGDClassifier with the hinge loss function and a learning rate of 0.001. The main difference between the learning algorithms of our classifiers was the regularization term of the loss function. While the phrase-level classifier uses the default SVM regularization, the tweet-level classifier uses an 'elasticnet' penalty with l1 ratio of .85. These parameter values were chosen following Gunther (2014) from last year's SemEval and verified in cross validation. We also used the 'auto' class weight for this task because the training label distribution was 3640 positive, 1458 negative, and 4586 neutral. We used scikit-learn's *norm_mat* function to normalize the data matrix so that each column vector is normalized to unit length.

2.3 Features

Our system used two kinds of features: *basic text features* and *lexicon features*. We describe the two feature classes below. There was a substantial overlap between the features used for the phrase-level classifier and those used for the tweet-level classifier, with some additional features used at the phrase level.

Basic Text Features Basic text features include the features derived from the text representation, including token-level unigram features, hashtag segmentation, character-level analysis, and wordshape normalization. For a given text span, basic text features included

- presence or absence of: raw bag-of-words (BOW) unigrams, normalized/stemmed BOW unigrams, stemmed segmented hashtag BOW, user mentions, URLs, hashtags;
- number of question marks and number of exclamation points;
- number of positive, negative, and neutral emoticons; emoticons were extracted from the training data and manually tagged as positive, negative or neutral; [2]
- whether the text span contained an elongated word (see Section 2.1, special form 3).

The above features were derived from the annotated text span in both phrase-level and tweet-level analysis. For the phrase-level analysis, these were supplemented with the following:

- normalized BOW unigram features derived from 3 tokens preceding the target phrase;
- normalized BOW unigram features derived from 3 tokens following the target phrase;
- length 2, 3, and 4 character prefixes and suffixes for each token in the target phrase;
- whether the phrase was in all caps;
- whether phrase contained only stop words;
- whether a phrase contained only punctuation;
- whether the phrase contained a word whose length is eight or more;
- whether the phrase contained an elongated word (cf. Section 2.1).

There were a few other differences in the way each classifier handled some of the features. The phrase-level classifier changed the feature value from 1 to 2 for elongated unigrams. In the tweet-level classifier, we ignored unigrams with proper noun and preposition part-of-speech tags. Negation contexts were also handled differently. For the phrase-level classifier, a negated word was treated as a separate feature, whereas for the tweet-level classifier, negation changed the feature value from 1 to -1.

Lexicon Features We used several Twitter-specific and general-purpose lexicons. The lexicons fell into one of two categories: those that provided a numeric score (usually, -5 to 5) score and those that sorted phrases into categories. For a given lexicon, categories could correspond to a particular emotion, to a strong or weak positive or negative sentiment, or to automatically derived word clusters.

We used the features derived from the following lexicons: AFINN (Nielsen, 2011), Opinion Lexicon (Hu and Liu, 2004), Brown Clusters (Gimpel et al., 2011), Hashtag Emotion (Mohammad, 2012), Sentiment140 (Mohammad et al., 2013), Hashtag Sentiment (Mohammad et al., 2013), Subjectivity (Wilson et al., 2005), and General Inquirer (Stone et al., 1966). Features are derived separately for each lexicon. General Inquirer and Hashtag Emotion were excluded from the tweet-level analysis since they did not improve system performance in cross-validation. We also experimented with features derived from WordNet (Fellbaum, 1998), but these failed to improve performance for either task in ablation studies. See Section 3.1 for ablation results.

The features for the lexicons that provided a numeric score included:

- the average sentiment score for the text span;
- the total number of positively scored words in the span;
- the maximum score (or zero if no words had a sentiment score);
- the score of the last positively scored word;

[2] http://text-machine.cs.uml.edu/twitterhawk/emoticons.txt

	Opinion	Hashtag Sentiment	Sentiment140	Subjectivity	AFINN	Hashtag Emotion	Brown Clusters	General Inquirer
Phrase-level	✓	✓	✓	✓	✓		✓	
Tweet-level	✓	✓	✓	✓	✓	✓		✓

Table 1: Which lexicons we used for each classifier.

Withholding	**F-score**
– (Full System)	63.76
Opinion Lexicon	63.70
Hashtag Sentiment	63.49
Sentiment140	63.22
Hashtag Emotion (HE)	**63.77**
Brown Clusters	63.01
Subjectivity Lexicon	63.49
AFINN Lexicon	63.43
General Inquirer (GI)	**63.94**
WordNet (WN)	**65.49**
WN, GI, HE	**66.38**

Table 2: Ablation results for lexicons features in tweet-level classification.

- three most influential (most positive or most negative) scores for the text span; this was only used by the phrase-level system.

The features derived from lexicons that provided categories for words and phrases included the number of words that belonged to each category.

For phrase-level analysis, the text span used for these features was the target phrase itself. For the tweet-level analysis, the text span covered the whole tweet. Table 1 shows which lexicons we used when building each classifier.

3 Results

In this section, we describe the experiments we conducted during system development, as well as the official SemEval Task 10 results.

The scores reported throughout this section are calculated as the average of the positive and negative class F-measure (Nakov et al., 2013); the neutral label classification does not directly affect the score.

3.1 System Development Experiments

Both phrase-level and tweet-level systems were tuned in 10-fold cross-validation using the 2013 training, dev, and test data (Nakov et al., 2013). We used fixed data folds in order to compare different runs. Feature ablation studies, parameter tuning, and comparison of different pre-processing steps were performed using this setup.

We conducted ablation studies for lexicon features using tweet-level evaluation. Table 2 shows ablation results obtained in 10-fold cross-validation. The figures are bolded if withholding the features derived from a given lexicon produced a higher score. Note that these experiments were conducted using a Linear SVM classifier with a limited subset of basic text features.

Our best cross-validation results using the configuration described in sections 2.2 and 2.3 above were 87.12 average F-measure for phrase-level analysis (Subtask A), and 68.50 for tweet-level analysis (Subtask B).

For topic-level sentiment detection in Subtask C, we investigated three different approaches: (1) using our phrase-level classifier "as is", (2) training our phrase level classifier only on phrases that resembled topics[3], and (3) using our tweet-level classifier "as is". We found that our phrase-level classifiers did not perform well (F-scores in the 35-38 range), which could be explained by the fact that the Subtask A data was annotated so that the target phrases actually carried sentiment (e.g., the phrase "good luck"), whereas the Subtask C assumption was that the topic itself had no sentiment and that the topics context determined the expressed sentiment. For example, in the tweet "Gotta go see Flight tomorrow Denzel is the greatest actor ever", positive sentiment is carried by the phrase "the greatest actor ever", rather than the token "Denzel" (corresponding to the topic). It is therefore not surprising that our tweet-level classifier achieved an F-score of 54.90, since tweet-level analysis is better able to capture long-range dependencies between sentiment-carrying expressions and the target topic. Consequently, we

[3]We kept the phrases comprised by 0-or-1-determiner followed by 0-or-more-adjectives, followed by a noun.

	Phrase-level	Tweet-level
Live Journal 2014	83.97	70.17
SMS 2013	86.64	62.12
Twitter 2013	82.87	68.44
Twitter 2014	84.05	70.64
Twitter 2014 Sarcasm	85.62	56.02
Twitter 2015	**82.32**	**61.99**

Table 3: Official results

used the tweet-level classifier in our submission for Subtask C.

3.2 Official Results

Our official results for phrase-level and tweet-level tasks on the *2014 progress tests* are given in Table 3. The models were trained on the 2013 training data.

In the *official 2015 ranking*, our system performed competitively in each task. For subtask A (phrase-level), we placed 5th with an F-score of 82.32, compared to the winning teams F-score of 84.79. For subtask B, we placed 10th out of 40 submissions, with an F-score of 61.99, compared to the top team's 64.84. Our classifier for Subtask C won 1st place with an F-score of 50.51, leading the second place entry of 45.48 by over 5 points. Finally, for Subtask D, we came in 3rd place, with an average absolute difference of .214 on a 0 to 1 regression, as compared to the gold standard (Rosenthal et al., 2015).

Our system also ranked 4th out of 40 submissions in identifying the message-level sentiment of sarcastic tweets in 2014 data, with an F-score of 56.02, as compared to the winning team's F-score of 59.11.

4 Discussion

Consistent with previous years' results, our system performed better on phrase-level data than on tweet-level data. We believe this is largely due to the skewed class distributions, as the majority baselines for Subtask A are much higher, and there are very few neutral labels. This is not the case for Subtask B, where the neutral labels outnumber positive labels. Also, the phrase-level text likely carries clearer sentiment, while the tweet-level analysis has to deal with conflicting sentiments across a message.

Note that hashtag segmentation strategy can be improved by using a language model to predict which segmentations are more likely, as well as evaluating the hashtag's distributional similarity to the rest of the tweet. A language model could also be used to improve the spell correction.

	Live Journal 2014	SMS 2013	Twitter 2013	Twitter 2014	Twitter Sarcasm 2014
nBow -spell	58.64	56.55	58.38	59.18	44.67
nBOW	58.87	57.22	59.19	60.27	46.76
nBOW +hashtag	58.94	57.81	60.09	61.38	53.00
nBOW +lexicon	70.65	62.08	68.46	67.86	52.89
nBOW +hashtag +lexicon	70.59	62.23	68.78	68.22	54.27

Table 4: Contribution of different features in tweet-level classification. *nBOW* stands for normalized bag-of-words features.

Our system's large margin of success at detecting topic-directed sentiment in Subtask C (over 5 points in F-score better than the 2nd place team) likely comes from the fact that we leverage the large training data of Subtask B and the tweet-level model is able to capture long-range dependencies between sentiment-carrying expressions and the target topic.

We found that the most influential features for detecting sarcasm were normalized BOW unigrams, lexicon-based features, and unigrams from hashtag segmentation. Not surprisingly, lexicon features improved performance for all genres, including SMS, LiveJournal, and non-sarcastic tweets (see rows 2 and 4 in Table 4). The same was true of spelling correction (as shown in Table 4, row 1). Hashtag-based features, on the other hand, only yielded large improvements for the sarcastic tweets, as shown in the gain achieved by adding hashtag features to the normalized BOW unigrams (see rows 2 and 3 in Table 4). Note that the 6.24 point gain is only observed for sarcasm data; other genres showed the average improvement of about 0.67. We believe that hashtags were so effective at predicting sentiment for sarcasm, because sarcastic tweets facetiously emulate literal tweets at first but then express their true sentiment at the end by using a hashtag, e.g. "On the bright side we have school today... Tomorrow and the day after ! #killmenow".

Acknowledgments

@JonMadden @TaskOrganizers #thanks

References

Steven Bird, Ewan Klein, and Edward Loper. 2009. *Natural language processing with Python*. O'Reilly Media, Inc.

Christiane Fellbaum. 1998. *WordNet*. Wiley Online Library.

Kevin Gimpel, Nathan Schneider, Brendan O'Connor, Dipanjan Das, Daniel Mills, Jacob Eisenstein, Michael Heilman, Dani Yogatama, Jeffrey Flanigan, and Noah A Smith. 2011. Part-of-speech tagging for twitter: Annotation, features, and experiments. In *Proceedings of the 49th Annual Meeting of the Association for Computational Linguistics: Human Language Technologies: short papers-Volume 2*, pages 42–47. Association for Computational Linguistics.

Tobias Günther, Jean Vancoppenolle, and Richard Johansson. 2014. Rtrgo: Enhancing the gu-mlt-lt system for sentiment analysis of short messages. In *Proceedings of the 8th International Workshop on Semantic Evaluation (SemEval 2014) August 23-24, 2014 Dublin, Ireland*.

Minqing Hu and Bing Liu. 2004. Mining and summarizing customer reviews. In *Proceedings of the tenth ACM SIGKDD international conference on Knowledge discovery and data mining*, pages 168–177. ACM.

Yasuhide Miura, Shigeyuki Sakaki, Keigo Hattori, and Tomoko Ohkuma. 2014. Teamx: A sentiment analyzer with enhanced lexicon mapping and weighting scheme for unbalanced data. *SemEval 2014*, page 628.

Saif M Mohammad, Svetlana Kiritchenko, and Xiaodan Zhu. 2013. Nrc-canada: Building the state-of-the-art in sentiment analysis of tweets. *arXiv preprint arXiv:1308.6242*.

Saif M Mohammad. 2012. # emotional tweets. In *Proceedings of the First Joint Conference on Lexical and Computational Semantics-Volume 1: Proceedings of the main conference and the shared task, and Volume 2: Proceedings of the Sixth International Workshop on Semantic Evaluation*, pages 246–255. Association for Computational Linguistics.

Preslav Nakov, Sara Rosenthal, Zornitsa Kozareva, Veselin Stoyanov, Alan Ritter, and Theresa Wilson. 2013. Semeval-2013 task 2: Sentiment analysis in twitter. In *Second Joint Conference on Lexical and Computational Semantics (*SEM), Volume 2: Proceedings of the Seventh International Workshop on Semantic Evaluation (SemEval 2013)*, pages 312–320, Atlanta, Georgia, USA, June. Association for Computational Linguistics.

Finn Årup Nielsen. 2011. A new anew: Evaluation of a word list for sentiment analysis in microblogs. *arXiv preprint arXiv:1103.2903*.

Olutobi Owoputi, Brendan O'Connor, Chris Dyer, Kevin Gimpel, Nathan Schneider, and Noah A Smith. 2013. Improved part-of-speech tagging for online conversational text with word clusters. In *HLT-NAACL*, pages 380–390.

Bo Pang, Lillian Lee, and Shivakumar Vaithyanathan. 2002. Thumbs up?: sentiment classification using machine learning techniques. In *Proceedings of the ACL-02 conference on Empirical methods in natural language processing-Volume 10*, pages 79–86. Association for Computational Linguistics.

Fabian Pedregosa, Gaël Varoquaux, Alexandre Gramfort, Vincent Michel, Bertrand Thirion, Olivier Grisel, Mathieu Blondel, Peter Prettenhofer, Ron Weiss, Vincent Dubourg, et al. 2011. Scikit-learn: Machine learning in python. *The Journal of Machine Learning Research*, 12:2825–2830.

Christopher Potts. 2011. Sentiment symposium tutorial. In *Sentiment Symposium Tutorial. Acknowledgments*.

Sara Rosenthal, Preslav Nakov, Svetlana Kiritchenko, Saif M Mohammad, Alan Ritter, and Veselin Stoyanov. 2015. Semeval-2015 task 10: Sentiment analysis in twitter. In *Proceedings of the 9th International Workshop on Semantic Evaluation*, SemEval '2015, Denver, Colorado, June. Association for Computational Linguistics.

Philip J Stone, Dexter C Dunphy, and Marshall S Smith. 1966. The general inquirer: A computer approach to content analysis.

Duyu Tang, Furu Wei, Bing Qin, Ting Liu, and Ming Zhou. 2014. Coooolll: A deep learning system for twitter sentiment classification. *SemEval 2014*, page 208.

Theresa Wilson, Janyce Wiebe, and Paul Hoffmann. 2005. Recognizing contextual polarity in phrase-level sentiment analysis. In *Proceedings of the conference on human language technology and empirical methods in natural language processing*, pages 347–354. Association for Computational Linguistics.

Xiaodan Zhu, Svetlana Kiritchenko, and Saif Mohammad. 2014. Nrc-canada-2014: Recent improvements in the sentiment analysis of tweets. In *Proceedings of the 8th International Workshop on Semantic Evaluation (SemEval 2014)*, pages 443–447, Dublin, Ireland, August. Association for Computational Linguistics and Dublin City University.

SeNTU: Sentiment Analysis of Tweets by Combining a Rule-based Classifier with Supervised Learning

Prerna Chikersal, Soujanya Poria, and Erik Cambria
School of Computer Engineering
Nanyang Technological University
Singapore - 639798
{prernal,sporia,cambria}@ntu.edu.sg

Abstract

We describe a Twitter sentiment analysis system developed by combining a rule-based classifier with supervised learning. We submitted our results for the message-level subtask in SemEval 2015 Task 10, and achieved a F[1]-score of 57.06%. The rule-based classifier is based on rules that are dependent on the occurrences of emoticons and opinion words in tweets. Whereas, the Support Vector Machine (SVM) is trained on semantic, dependency, and sentiment lexicon based features. The tweets are classified as *positive*, *negative* or *unknown* by the rule-based classifier, and as *positive*, *negative* or *neutral* by the SVM. The results we obtained show that rules can help refine the SVM's predictions.

1 Introduction

Our opinions and the opinions of others play a very important role in our decision-making process and even influence our behaviour. In recent times, an increasing number of people have taken to expressing their opinions on a wide variety of topics on microblogging websites such as Twitter. Being able to analyse this data and extract opinions about a number of topics, can help us make informed choices and predictions regarding those topics. Due to this, sentiment analysis of tweets is gaining importance across a number of domains such as e-commerce (Wang and Cardie, 2014), politics (Tumasjan et al., 2010; Johnson et al., 2012; Wang et al., 2012), health and psychology (Cambria et al., 2010; Harman, ; Harman,), multimodality (Poria et al., 2015), crowd validation (Cambria et al., 2010), and even intelligence and surveillance (Jansen et al., 2009).

SemEval 2015 Task 10 (Rosenthal et al., 2015) is an international shared-task competition that aims to promote research in sentiment analysis of tweets by providing annotated tweets for training, development and testing. We created a sentiment analysis system to participate in the message-level task of this competition. The objective of the system is to label the sentiment of each tweet as "positive", "negative" or "neutral".

In this paper, we describe our sentiment analysis system, which is a combined classifier created by integrating a rule-based classification layer with a support vector machine.

2 System Description

Our Sentiment Analysis System consists of two classifiers – (i) Rule-based and (ii) Supervised, integrated together. This section describes both these classifiers and how we combine them.

During pre-processing, all the @*<username>* references are changes to @*USER* and all the *URLs* are changed to *http://URL.com*. Then, we use the CMU Twitter Tokeniser and POS Tagger (Gimpel et al., 2011) to tokenise the tweets and give a parts-of-speech tag to each token. We use the POS tags to remove all emoticons from the pre-processed tweets. Pre-processed tweets **with emoticons** are given as input to the rule-based classifier, whereas the support vector machine takes pre-

[1]We average the positive and negative F-measures to get the F-score, which is the evaluation metric for this task.

processed tweets **without emoticons** as an input.

2.1 Supervised Learning

For the supervised classifier, we cast the sentiment analysis problem as a multi-class classification problem, where each tweet has to be labeled as "positive", "negative" or "neutral". We train a Support Vector Machine (SVM) (Cortes and Vapnik, 1995) on the tweets provided for training. For all our experiments, we use a linear kernel and L1-regularisation. The C parameter is chosen by cross-validation. As mentioned above, emoticons have already been removed from tweets given as input to the SVM.

Each tweet is represented as a feature vector, containing the following features:

- **Word N-grams:** Frequencies of contiguous sequences of 1, 2 or 3 tokens. The TF-IDF weighting scheme is applied.
- **Character N-grams:** Frequencies of contiguous sequences of 1, 2 or 3 characters inside each word's boundary. The TF-IDF weighting scheme is applied.
- **POS Tags:** Using CMU Twitter Tagger (Gimpel et al., 2011) output, for each tweet we compute – (i) *countAdj* (number of adjectives), (ii) *countAdv* (number of adverbs), (iii) *countNoun* (number of nouns, proper nouns, and proper nouns+possessives), (iv) *countVerb* (number of verbs), and (v) *countIntj* (number of interjections). The sum of these five counts, gives us the *totalPos*. The POS features are: $[\frac{countAdj}{totalPos}, \frac{countAdv}{totalPos}, \frac{countNoun}{totalPos}, \frac{countVerb}{totalPos}, \frac{countIntj}{totalPos}]$.
- **@USER:** A boolean feature that is set to 1 if the tweet contains a @<*username*> reference.
- **Hashtag:** A boolean feature that is set to 1 if the tweet contains a hashtag.
- **URL:** A boolean feature that is set to 1 if the tweet contains a URL.
- **Discourse:** A boolean feature that is set to 1 if the tweet contains a "discourse marker". Examples of discourse markers would be a "RT" followed by a username to indicate that the tweet is a re-tweet, news article headline followed by "..." followed by a URL to the news article, etc. Basically, this feature indicates whether or not the tweet is a part of a discourse.
- **Sentiment140 Lexicon:** The Sentiment140 Lexicon (Mohammad et al., 2013) contains unigrams and bigrams along with their polarity scores in the range of -5.00 to $+5.00$. Considering all uni/bi-grams with polarity less than -1.0 to be negative and with polarity greater than $+1.0$ to be positive, we count the number of negative (*negativesCount*) and the number of positive (*positivesCount*) uni/bi-gram occurrences in every tweet. For each tweet,
  - the *polarityMeasure* is based on the *positivesCount* and *negativesCount*, and calculated using Algorithm 1.
  - the maximum polarity value (*maxPolarityValue*) is the most positive or most negative polarity value of all polar uni/bi-gram occurrences in the tweet.

  Both these features are normalised to values between -1 and $+1$.

Algorithm 1 Calculating *polarityMeasure* based on *positivesCount* and *negativesCount*

```
if positivesCount > negativesCount then
    if negativesCount != 0 then
        polarityMeasure = positivesCount / negativesCount
    else
        polarityMeasure = positivesCount
    end if
else if negativesCount > positivesCount then
    if positivesCount != 0 then
        polarityMeasure = -1 × negativesCount / positivesCount
    else
        polarityMeasure = -1× negativesCount
    end if
end if
```

- **Bing Liu Lexicon:** The Bing Liu lexicon (Liu et al., 2005) is a list of positive and negative words. We count the number of positive (*positivesCount*) and negative words (*negativesCount*) in each tweet, and calculate *polarityMeasure* using Algorithm 1. The *polarityMeasure* is appended to the feature vector.

- **NRC Emotion Lexicon:** The NRC Emotion Lexicon (Mohammad and Turney, 2013) contains a list of positive and negative words. The *polarityMeasure* is calculated using the method used for the Bing Liu Lexicon.

- **NRC Hashtag Lexicon:** The NRC Hashtag Lexicon (Mohammad et al., 2013) contains unigrams and bigrams along with their polarity scores in the range of -5.00 to $+5.00$. Using the method used for the Sentiment140 Lexicon, we calculate *polarityMeasure* and *maxPolarityValue*, and append them to the feature vector.

- **SentiWordNet:** SentiWordNet (Esuli and Sebastiani, 2006) assigns to each synset of WordNet (Fellbaum, 2010) 3 scores: positivity, negativity, objectivity. A word whose positivity score is greater than negativity and objectivity is positive, while a word whose negativity score is greater than positivity and objectivity is negative. For each tweet, we calculate *polarityMeasure* and *maxPolarityValue* using the method used for the Bing Liu Lexicon.

- **SenticNet:** SenticNet (Cambria et al., 2014) contains polarity scores of single and multi-word phrases. We count the number of positive and negative words/phrases in each tweet, and calculate *polarityMeasure* using the method used for the Sentiment140 Lexicon.

- **Negation:** The Stanford Dependency Parser (De Marneffe et al., 2006) is used to find negation in tweets. Negation is not a feature on its own. Rather, it affects the word n-grams and the lexicons related features. The negated word is appended with a "_NEG" in all n-grams, while the polarity of all negated words is inverted in the lexicon features.

2.2 Rule-based Classifier

For the rule-based classifier, we cast the problem as a multi-class classification problem, where each tweet is to be labeled as "positive", "negative" or "unknown". This is an unsupervised classifier, which applies the following rules for predictions:

- **Emoticon-related Rules:** If a tweet contains only positive emoticons and no negative emoticons, it is classified as positive. If a tweet contains only negative emoticons and no positive emoticons, it is classified as negative. If a tweet contains no emoticons, we apply the sentiment lexicon-related rules. The following emoticons are considered to be positive: :) , (: , ;) , :-) , (-: , :D , :-D , :P , :-P . While, the following emoticons are considered to be negative: :(,): , ;(, :-(,)-: , D: , D-: , :'(, :'-(,)': ,)-': .

- **Sentiment Lexicon-related Rules:** The Bing Liu lexicon, the NRC Emotion lexicon, and SentiWordNet are used as resources for positive and negative opinion words. If a tweet contains **more than two** positive words, and no negation or negative words from either of the lexicons, it is classified as positive. If a tweet contains **more than two** negative words, and no negation or positive words from either of the lexicons, it is classified as negative. If none of the above rules apply, the tweet is classified as unknown.

2.3 Combining the Classifiers

After developing the rule-based classifier and training the SVM, we combine the them to refine the SVM's predictions. Since, our goal is to maximise positive and negative precision and recall, we use the rule-based classifier to correct or verify the "neutral" SVM predictions. So, for every tweet labeled as neutral by the SVM, we consider the predictions of the rule-based layer as the final labels.

3 Experiments and Results

We trained a Support Vector Machine (SVM) on 9418 tweets allowed to be used for training purposes. The results we submitted to SemEval 2015 were yielded by using all SVM features and emoticon-related rules. The sentiment lexicon-related rules were implemented later, and thus could not be used for the official submission. Table 2 shows the official test results for SemEval 2015.

Features	Positive			Negative			Neutral			F_{pn}
	P	R	F	P	R	F	P	R	F	
All Features	0.824	0.629	0.713	0.612	0.607	0.610	0.679	0.831	0.748	0.662
w/o N-grams	0.671	0.597	0.632	0.430	0.574	0.491	0.645	0.637	0.641	0.562
w/o POS Tags	0.814	0.611	0.698	0.633	0.589	0.610	0.669	0.839	0.744	0.654
w/o @User, Hashtag, URL, Discourse	0.821	0.616	0.704	0.602	0.607	0.605	0.672	0.826	0.741	0.654
w/o Sentiment140	0.814	0.616	0.701	0.602	0.599	0.600	0.676	0.830	0.745	0.651
w/o Bing Liu	0.821	0.621	0.707	0.616	0.603	0.610	0.676	0.833	0.746	0.658
w/o NRC Emotion + Hashtag	0.816	0.619	0.705	0.609	0.597	0.603	0.676	0.832	0.746	0.654
w/o SentiWordNet	0.821	0.624	0.709	0.610	0.597	0.603	0.674	0.830	0.744	0.656
w/o SenticNet	0.820	0.615	0.703	0.610	0.597	0.603	0.674	0.837	0.747	0.653
w/o Negation	0.811	0.610	0.701	0.598	0.601	0.593	0.674	0.824	0.744	0.647

Table 1: Feature ablation study for the SVM classifier. Each row shows the precision, recall, and F-score for the positive, negative, and neutral classes respectively, followed by the average positive and negative F-score, which is the chosen evaluation metric. All values in the table are between 0 and 1, and are rounded off to 3 decimal places.

Dataset	Our Score	Best Score
Twitter 2015	57.06	64.84
LiveJournal 2014	68.70	75.34
Twitter 2014	66.85	74.42
Twitter 2013	63.50	72.80
SMS 2013	60.53	68.49
Twitter 2014 Sarcasm	45.18	57.50

Table 2: Average positive and negative F-scores for system with all SVM features and only emoticon rules.

Table 1 reports the results of a feature ablation study carried out by testing the SVM classifier on 3204 development tweets (from SemEval 2013) not included in the training data. These are cross-validation results obtained using the hold-out method.This study helps us understand the importance of different features. From the table, we can see that the word and character n-grams features are the most useful, followed by negation and then the rest. All sentiment lexicon related features appear to have similar importance, but we get the best F-score when we append them all to the feature vector.

Features	F_{pn}	Classification Rate (%)
All Features	66.2	71.5
All Features and Rules	66.7	72.3

Table 3: Comparison between the results obtained using SVM alone, and using SVM with a rule-based layer.

Since, using all the previously described features gives the best SVM predictions, we add the rule-based classification layer to a SVM trained on all features. Table 3 compares the results obtained using the SVM alone with the results obtained using SVM along with all the rules (emoticon and lexicon-based) specified in section 2.2. We observe that the F-score further increases by around half a unit and the classification rate[2] increases by around 0.8.

4 Conclusion

In this paper, we described a sentiment analysis system developed by combining a SVM with a rule-based classification layer. Even though we do not get the best scores, we find that a rule-based classification layer can indeed refine the SVM's predictions. We also devise creative twitter-specific, negation and lexicon-related features for the SVM, and demonstrate how they improve the sentiment analysis system. In future, we aim to use enriched sentiment and emotion lists like the ones used by (Poria et al., 2012). We would also like to experiment with refining the SVM's predictions using more rules based on complex semantics.

Acknowledgments

We wish to acknowledge the funding for this project from Nanyang Technological University under the Undergraduate Research Experience on CAmpus (URECA) programme.

[2]Classification rate $= \frac{number\ of\ tweets\ classified\ correctly}{total\ number\ of\ tweets}$

References

Erik Cambria, Amir Hussain, Catherine Havasi, Chris Eckl, and James Munro. 2010. Towards crowd validation of the uk national health service. *WebSci10*, pages 1–5.

Erik Cambria, Daniel Olsher, and Dheeraj Rajagopal. 2014. Senticnet 3: a common and common-sense knowledge base for cognition-driven sentiment analysis. In *Twenty-eighth AAAI conference on artificial intelligence*, pages 1515–1521.

Corinna Cortes and Vladimir Vapnik. 1995. Support-vector networks. *Machine learning*, 20(3):273–297.

Marie-Catherine De Marneffe, Bill MacCartney, Christopher D Manning, et al. 2006. Generating typed dependency parses from phrase structure parses. In *Proceedings of LREC*, volume 6, pages 449–454.

Andrea Esuli and Fabrizio Sebastiani. 2006. Sentiwordnet: A publicly available lexical resource for opinion mining. In *Proceedings of LREC*, volume 6, pages 417–422.

Christiane Fellbaum. 2010. Wordnet: An electronic lexical database. 1998. *WordNet is available from http://www. cogsci. princeton. edu/wn.*

Kevin Gimpel, Nathan Schneider, Brendan O'Connor, Dipanjan Das, Daniel Mills, Jacob Eisenstein, Michael Heilman, Dani Yogatama, Jeffrey Flanigan, and Noah A Smith. 2011. Part-of-speech tagging for twitter: Annotation, features, and experiments. In *Proceedings of the 49th Annual Meeting of the Association for Computational Linguistics: Human Language Technologies: short papers-Volume 2*, pages 42–47.

Glen Coppersmith Mark Dredze Craig Harman. Quantifying mental health signals in twitter.

Bernard J Jansen, Mimi Zhang, Kate Sobel, and Abdur Chowdury. 2009. Twitter power: Tweets as electronic word of mouth. *Journal of the American society for information science and technology*, 60(11):2169–2188.

Christopher Johnson, Parul Shukla, and Shilpa Shukla. 2012. On classifying the political sentiment of tweets. *cs. utexas. edu.*

Bing Liu, Minqing Hu, and Junsheng Cheng. 2005. Opinion observer: analyzing and comparing opinions on the web. In *Proceedings of the 14th international conference on World Wide Web*, pages 342–351.

Saif M Mohammad and Peter D Turney. 2013. Crowdsourcing a word–emotion association lexicon. *Computational Intelligence*, 29(3):436–465.

Saif Mohammad, Svetlana Kiritchenko, and Xiaodan Zhu. 2013. Nrc-canada: Building the state-of-the-art in sentiment analysis of tweets. In *Proceedings of the seventh international workshop on Semantic Evaluation Exercises (SemEval-2013)*, Atlanta, Georgia, USA, June.

Soujanya Poria, Alexander Gelbukh, Erik Cambria, Peipei Yang, Amir Hussain, and Tariq Durrani. 2012. Merging senticnet and wordnet-affect emotion lists for sentiment analysis. In *Signal Processing (ICSP), 2012 IEEE 11th International Conference on*, volume 2, pages 1251–1255.

Soujanya Poria, Erik Cambria, Amir Hussain, and Guang-Bin Huang. 2015. Towards an intelligent framework for multimodal affective data analysis. *Neural Networks*, 63:104–116.

Sara Rosenthal, Preslav Nakov, Svetlana Kiritchenko, Saif M Mohammad, Alan Ritter, and Veselin Stoyanov. 2015. Semeval-2015 task 10: Sentiment analysis in twitter. In *Proceedings of the 9th International Workshop on Semantic Evaluation*, SemEval '2015, Denver, Colorado, June.

Andranik Tumasjan, Timm Oliver Sprenger, Philipp G Sandner, and Isabell M Welpe. 2010. Predicting elections with twitter: What 140 characters reveal about political sentiment. *ICWSM*, 10:178–185.

Lu Wang and Claire Cardie. 2014. A piece of my mind: A sentiment analysis approach for online dispute detection. In *Proceedings of the 52nd Annual Meeting of the Association for Computational Linguistics*, volume 2, pages 693–699.

Hao Wang, Dogan Can, Abe Kazemzadeh, François Bar, and Shrikanth Narayanan. 2012. A system for real-time twitter sentiment analysis of 2012 us presidential election cycle. In *Proceedings of the ACL 2012 System Demonstrations*, pages 115–120.

INESC-ID: Sentiment Analysis without hand-coded Features or Liguistic Resources using Embedding Subspaces

Ramon F. Astudillo, Silvio Amir, Wang Ling, Bruno Martins[†], Mário Silva, Isabel Trancoso
Instituto de Engenharia de Sistemas e Computadores Investigação e Desenvolvimento
Rua Alves Redol 9
Lisbon, Portugal
{ramon.astudillo, samir, wlin, mjs, isabel.trancoso}@inesc-id.pt
[†]bruno.g.martins@tecnico.ulisboa.pt

Abstract

We present the INESC-ID system for the message polarity classification task of SemEval 2015. The proposed system does not make use of any hand-coded features or linguistic resources. It relies on projecting pre-trained structured skip-gram word embeddings into a small subspace. The word embeddings can be obtained from large amounts of Twitter data in unsupervised form. The sentiment analysis supervised training is thus reduced to finding the optimal projection which can be carried out efficiently despite the little data available. We analyze in detail the proposed approach and show that a competitive system can be attained with only a few configuration parameters.

1 Introduction

Web-based social networks are a rich data source for both businesses and academia. However, the sheer volume, diversity and rate of creation of social media, imposes the need for automated analysis tools. The growing interest in this problem motivated the creation of a shared task for Twitter Sentiment Analysis (Nakov et al., 2013). The Message Polarity Classification task consists in classifying a message as positive, negative, or neutral in sentiment.

A great deal of research has been done on methods for sentiment analysis on user generated content. However, state-of-the-art systems still largely depend on linguistic resources, extensive feature engineering and tuning. Indeed, if we look at the best performing systems from SemEval 2014 (Zhu et al., 2014), (Malandrakis et al., 2014), both make extensive use of these resources, including hundreds of thousands of features, special treatment for negation, multi-word expressions or special strings like emoticons.

In this paper we present the INESC-ID system for the 2015 SemEval message polarity classification task (Rosenthal et al., 2015). The system is able to learn good message representations for message polarity classification directly from raw text with a simple tokenization scheme. Our approach is based on using large amounts of unlabeled data to induce *word embeddings*, that is, continuous word representations containing contextual information. Instead of using these word embeddings directly with, for instance, a logistic regression classifier, we estimate a *sentiment subspace* of the embeddings. The idea is to find a projection of the embedding space that is meaningful for the supervised task. In the proposed model, we jointly learn the sentiment subspace projection and the classifier using the SemEval training data. The resulting system attains state-of-the-art performance without hand-coded features or linguistic resources and only a few configuration parameters.

2 Unsupervised Learning of Word Embeddings

Unsupervised word embeddings trained from large amounts of unlabeled data have been shown to improve many NLP tasks (Turian et al., 2010; Collobert et al., 2011). Embeddings capture generic regularities about the data and can be trained with virtually an infinite amount of data in unsupervised fashion. Once trained, they can be used as features for supervised tasks or to initialize more complex models (Collobert et al., 2011; Chen and Manning, 2014; Bansal et al., 2014). Other unsupervised approaches that can also be used for feature extraction include brown clustering (Brown et al., 1992) and LDA (Blei et al., 2003),

One popular objective function for embeddings is to maximize the prediction of contextual words. In the work described in (Mikolov et al., 2013), commonly referred as word2vec, the models defined estimate the optimal word embeddings by maximizing the probability that the words within a given window size are predicted correctly. In the work presented here, a structured skip-gram (Ling et al., 2015) was used to generate the embeddings. Central to the skip-gram (Mikolov et al., 2013) is a log linear model of word prediction. Let $w = i$ denote that a word at a given position of a sentence is the i-th word on a vocabulary of size v. Let $w^p = j$ denote that the word p positions further in the sentence is the j-th word on the vocabulary. The skip-gram models the following probability:

$$p(w^p = j | w = i; \mathbf{C}, \mathbf{E}) \propto \exp\left(\mathbf{C}_j \cdot \mathbf{E} \cdot \mathbf{w}^i\right). \quad (1)$$

Here, $\mathbf{w}^i \in \{1, 0\}^{v \times 1}$ is a one-hot representation of $w = i$. That is, a vector of zeros of the size of the vocabulary v with a 1 on the i-th entry of the vector. The symbol $\cdot$ denotes internal product and $\exp()$ acts element-wise. The log-linear model is parametrized by two matrices. $\mathbf{E} \in \mathbb{R}^{e \times v}$ is the embedding matrix, transforming the one-hot sparse representation into a compact real valued embedding vector of size $e \times 1$. The matrix $\mathbf{C} \in \mathbb{R}^{v \times e}$ maps the embedding to a vector with the size of the vocabulary v. In the particular case of the structured skip-gram, here used, a different prediction matrix is trained for each relative position between words $\mathbf{C}_p$. After exponentiating and normalizing over the v possible options, the j-th element of the resulting vector corresponds thus to the probability of $w^p = j$.

In practice, due to the large value of v, various techniques are used to avoid having to normalize over the whole vocabulary.

After the embeddings are trained, the low dimensional embedding of each word $\mathbf{E} \cdot \mathbf{w}^i \in \mathbb{R}^{e \times 1}$ encapsulates the information about each word and its surrounding contexts. This embedding can thus be used as input to other learning algorithms to further enhance performance.

3 Using Embeddings for Sentiment Prediction

3.1 Sentiment Embedding Subspace

There are multiple ways in which embeddings could be incorporated as a pre-training step into a supervised task. The initial attempts for the proposed system included log-linear classifiers using the embeddings as initialization values or features, but these led to poor results. Ideally, embeddings should be adapted to the supervised task. However, this faces an additional difficulty: only a small subset of the words will actually be present in the training set of the supervised task. Words not present in the supervised training set will never get their embeddings updated.

To avoid this, here we employ a simple projection scheme. We consider the adapted embeddings $\mathbf{S} \cdot \mathbf{E}$, where $\mathbf{E} \in \mathbb{R}^{e \times v}$ is the original unadapted embedding matrix and $\mathbf{S} \in \mathbb{R}^{s \times e}$, with $s \ll e$, is a projection matrix trained on the supervised data. The idea is that, by only training $\mathbf{S}$ on the supervised data, we determine a sub-space of the embeddings which is optimal for the supervised task. An additional advantage is that, unlike with a direct re-estimation of $\mathbf{E}$, all embeddings are updated based on the supervised task data. This simple approach proved very useful and it accounts for most of the performance attained in our system.

3.2 Non-linear Sub-space Model

Based on the sub-space concept, various log-linear and non-linear models were explored. Most of the models attempted were prone to get trapped in poor local minima or showed stability problems during training. The only exception identified is the non-linear model here presented, which showed both fast convergence and high performance.

In what follows, we will denote a message, e.g. a tweet, of n words as a matrix $\mathbf{m} \in \{0, 1\}^{v \times n}$, where each column is a one-hot representation of each word. The vocabulary v is equal to that of the unsupervised pre-training. Words of the SemEval task not appearing in that vocabulary are represented as a vector of zeros, equivalent to an embedding of e zeros. In the SemEval task, each message has to be classified as neutral, negative or positive. Let y denote a categorical random variable over those three classes. The sub-space non-linear model estimates thus the probability of each possible category $y = k$ given a message $\mathbf{m}$ as

$$p(y = k|\mathbf{m}; \mathbf{C},\mathbf{S}) \propto \exp\left(\mathbf{C}_k \cdot \sigma\left(\mathbf{S} \cdot \mathbf{E} \cdot \mathbf{m}\right) \cdot \mathbf{B}\right), \quad (2)$$

where $\sigma()$ is a sigmoid function acting on each element of the matrix. The matrix $\mathbf{C} \in \mathbb{R}^{3\times s}$ maps the embedding sub-space to the classification space and $\mathbf{B} \in 1^{n\times 1}$ is a matrix of ones that sums the scores for all words up prior to normalization. This simplification, equivalent to a bag of words assumption, outperformed other approaches like convolution.

The model is thus equivalent to a multi-layer perceptron (MLP) (Rumelhart et al., 1985) with one hidden sigmoid layer and a soft-max output layer. The input to the MLP would be the fixed word embeddings attained by applying $\mathbf{E}$. The input layer $\mathbf{S}$ learns a projection of $\mathbf{E}$ into a small sub-space of size $s \ll e$.

4 Proposed System

4.1 Unsupervised Word Embeddings Learning

The embedding matrix $\mathbf{E}$ was trained in unsupervised fashion using the structured skip-gram model, described in Section 2.

We used the corpus of 52 million tweets used in (Owoputi et al., 2013) with the tokenizer described in the same work. The words that occurred less than 40 times in the data were discarded from the vocabulary. To train the model, we used a negative sampling rate of 25 words, sampled from a multinomial of unigram word probabilities over all the vocabulary (Goldberg and Levy, 2014). Embeddings of 50, 200, 400 and 600 dimensions were trained.

It should be noted that the training configuration is generic and was not adapted to the SemEval task. One consequence of this is a relatively strong pruning of the vocabulary. Around 23% of words in the SemEval tasks did not have an embedding and thus were set to have an embedding of e zeros.

4.2 Supervised Embedding Sub-space Learning

Text normalization for the supervised task employed the CMU tokenizer plus the following additional steps: messages were lower-cased, Twitter user mentions and URLs were replaced with special tokens and any character repetition above 3 was mapped to 3 characters.

The small amount of supervised data available was the main driving factor behind the design and optimization of the supervised training component. In order to maintain the number of free parameters low, small sizes of the subspace were selected with values ranging from 5 to 30. Training was also kept as simple as possible. The training set of SemEval was split into 80% for parameter learning and 20% for hyper-parameter selection, maintaining the original sentiment relative frequencies in each set. The 2013 and 2014 SemEval sentiment analysis test sets were used to validate the different candidate models. The most probable class was selected as the model prediction.

The parameters of subspace model in Equation 2, $\mathbf{S}$ and $\mathbf{C}$ were estimated to minimize the negative log-likelihood of the correct class. Training employed conventional Stochastic Gradient Descent (Rumelhart et al., 1985) with mini-batch size 1 and random uniform initialization similar to (Glorot and Bengio, 2010). After some initial experiments, it was determined that a learning rate of 0.01 and selecting the model with the best accuracy on the 20% set after 8 iterations led to the best results.

5 Experiments and Results

5.1 Sensibility Analysis

This section analyzes the performance of the proposed system on the message polarity classification task of SemEval 2015. In general, the sentiment subspace model showed consistent and fast convergence towards the optimum in very few iterations. Despite using class log-likelihood as training criterion and accuracy as stopping criterion, the model showed good performance in terms of average F-measure for positive and negative sentiments. This was not always the case for other tested models.

Regarding the two main parameters, embedding size e and sub-space size s, sensibility analysis were carried out and are shown in Tables 1 and 2. For these experiments learning rate and stopping condition were left fixed to the previously indicated values. Variations of learning rate to smaller values e.g. 0.005 were explored but did not lead to a clear pattern.

Table 1 shows the effect of embedding size on the system's performance. Very small embeddings lead clearly to worse results. Larger embeddings not always provide the best performance. However, they provide more consistent results across test sets. It was also inferred from other tasks that using larger embeddings had in general a positive effect.

Emb Size (e)	Dev	2013	2014
50	65.96	68.35	70.54
200	**70.65**	70.28	72.80
400	70.19	71.54	72.24
600	70.08	**72.16**	**72.72**

Table 1: Avg. F-measure on SemEval development and test sets varying with embedding size e. Sub-space size $s = 10$. Best model per column in bold.

Table 2 shows the variation of system performance with sub-space size. The optimal value was consistently found to be at $s = 10$ regardless of embedding size.

Subsp. Size (s)	Dev	2013	2014
5	69.78	71.82	72.17
10	**70.08**	**72.16**	**72.72**
20	69.18	71.97	72.52
30	67.81	70.97	72.45

Table 2: Avg. F-measure on SemEval test sets varying with embedding sub-space size s. Embedding size $e = 600$. Best model per column in bold.

5.2 Submitted System and Revised Candidates

Due to time constraints, not all planned configurations could be tested prior to system submission. Consequently, some of the experiments shown in the previous section were carried out after submission. Based on these results, two new candidates were selected and then tested on the 2015 dataset. These were a system that showed a very stable performance using $e = 600$ and $s = 10$ and a good system with a smaller embedding size using $e = 200$, $s = 10$. The same configuration, learning rate and number of iterations, as in the submitted model were used for these experiments.

The results for the submitted system and the a posteriori selected ones are displayed in Table 3. The results on 2015, confirm the sensibility analysis of e and s. The high performance of the $e = 600$, $s = 10$ model on the 2015 dataset was however unexpected, since it tops the submitted system by more than a 1% absolute. The second model selected, using a smaller e size displayed a performance comparable to that of the submitted system thus showing the overall robustness of the approach.

e	s	Dev	2013	2014	2015
600	20	69.18	71.97	72.52	64.12
600	10	70.08	**72.16**	72.72	**65.19**
200	10	**70.65**	70.28	**72.80**	64.09

Table 3: Avg. F-measure of the submitted system (top) and posteriorly selected candidates (bottom). Best model per column in bold.

It should be noted as well that there is small difference between the result attained in the submitted predictions (64.17) and the ones reported here for the submitted system (64.12). Upon revision of the code we could determine that this was due to a minor bug affecting how the embeddings of the $\mathbf{E}$ matrix were constructed.

6 Conclusions

We have presented the INESC-ID system for the SemEval 2015 message classification task. The system does not make use of any hand-coded features or linguistic resources and employs a simple tokenization scheme. The system is however able to attain state-of-the-art performance with few configuration parameters and a small number of iterations. The results are also consistent across sets and configuration settings.

Acknowledgments

This work has been partially supported by the FCT through national funds with reference UID/CEC/50021/2013 and grant number SFRH/BPD/68428/2010.

References

Mohit Bansal, Kevin Gimpel, and Karen Livescu. 2014. Tailoring continuous word representations for dependency parsing. In *Proceedings of the Annual Meeting of the Association for Computational Linguistics*.

David M Blei, Andrew Y Ng, and Michael I Jordan. 2003. Latent dirichlet allocation. *the Journal of machine Learning research*, 3:993–1022.

Peter F. Brown, Peter V. deSouza, Robert L. Mercer, Vincent J. Della Pietra, and Jenifer C. Lai. 1992. Class-based n-gram models of natural language. *Comput. Linguist.*, 18(4):467–479, December.

Danqi Chen and Christopher D Manning. 2014. A fast and accurate dependency parser using neural networks. In *Proceedings of the 2014 Conference on Empirical Methods in Natural Language Processing (EMNLP)*, pages 740–750.

Ronan Collobert, Jason Weston, Léon Bottou, Michael Karlen, Koray Kavukcuoglu, and Pavel Kuksa. 2011. Natural language processing (almost) from scratch. *The Journal of Machine Learning Research*, 12:2493–2537.

Xavier Glorot and Yoshua Bengio. 2010. Understanding the difficulty of training deep feedforward neural networks. In *In Proceedings of the International Conference on Artificial Intelligence and Statistics*, pages 249–256.

Yoav Goldberg and Omer Levy. 2014. word2vec explained: deriving mikolov et al.'s negative-sampling word-embedding method. *arXiv preprint arXiv:1402.3722*.

Wang Ling, Chris Dyer, Alan Black, and Isabel Trancoso. 2015. Two/too simple adaptations of word2vec for syntax problems. In *Proceedings of the 2015 Conference of the North American Chapter of the Association for Computational Linguistics: Human Language Technologies*.

Nikolaos Malandrakis, Michael Falcone, Colin Vaz, Jesse Bisogni, Alexandros Potamianos, and Shrikanth Narayanan. 2014. Sail: Sentiment analysis using semantic similarity and contrast. In *Proceedings of the 8th International Workshop on Semantic Evaluation (SemEval 2014)*.

Tomas Mikolov, Ilya Sutskever, Kai Chen, Greg S Corrado, and Jeff Dean. 2013. Distributed representations of words and phrases and their compositionality. In *Advances in Neural Information Processing Systems*, pages 3111–3119.

Preslav Nakov, Sara Rosenthal, Zornitsa Kozareva, Veselin Stoyanov, Alan Ritter, and Theresa Wilson. 2013. SemEval-2013 task 2: Sentiment analysis in Twitter. In *Proceedings of the 7th International Workshop on Semantic Evaluation*.

Olutobi Owoputi, Brendan O'Connor, Chris Dyer, Kevin Gimpel, Nathan Schneider, and Noah A Smith. 2013. Improved part-of-speech tagging for online conversational text with word clusters. In *Proceedings of the 2013 Conference of the North American Chapter of the Association for Computational Linguistics: Human Language Technologies*, pages 380–390.

Sara Rosenthal, Preslav Nakov, Svetlana Kiritchenko, Saif M Mohammad, Alan Ritter, and Veselin Stoyanov. 2015. Semeval-2015 task 10: Sentiment analysis in twitter. In *Proceedings of the 9th International Workshop on Semantic Evaluation*, SemEval '2015, Denver, Colorado, June.

David E Rumelhart, Geoffrey E Hinton, and Ronald J Williams. 1985. Learning internal representations by error propagation. Technical report, DTIC Document.

Joseph Turian, Lev Ratinov, and Yoshua Bengio. 2010. Word representations: a simple and general method for semi-supervised learning. In *Proceedings of the 48th annual meeting of the association for computational linguistics*, pages 384–394. Association for Computational Linguistics.

Xiaodan Zhu, Svetlana Kiritchenko, and Saif Mohammad. 2014. NRC-Canada-2014:: Recent improvements in the sentiment analysis of tweets. In *Proceedings of the 8th International Workshop on Semantic Evaluation (SemEval 2014)*.

WarwickDCS: From Phrase-Based to Target-Specific Sentiment Recognition

Richard Townsend University of Warwick richard@sentimentron.co.uk
Adam Tsakalidis University of Warwick A.Tsakalidis@warwick.ac.uk
Yiwei Zhou University of Warwick Yiwei.Zhou@warwick.ac.uk
Bo Wang University of Warwick Bo.Wang@warwick.ac.uk
Maria Liakata University of Warwick M.Liakata@warwick.ac.uk
Arkaitz Zubiaga University of Warwick A.Zubiaga@warwick.ac.uk
Alexandra Cristea University of Warwick acristea@dcs.warwick.ac.uk
Rob Procter University of Warwick rob.procter@warwick.ac.uk

Abstract

We present and evaluate several hybrid systems for sentiment identification for Twitter, both at the phrase and document (tweet) level. Our approach has been to use a novel combination of lexica, traditional NLP and deep learning features. We also analyse techniques based on syntactic parsing and token-based association to handle topic specific sentiment in subtask C. Our strategy has been to identify subphrases relevant to the designated topic/target and assign sentiment according to our subtask A classifier. Our submitted subtask A classifier ranked fourth in the SemEval official results while our BASELINE and μPARSE classifiers for subtask C would have ranked second.

1 Introduction

Twitter holds great potential for analyses in the social sciences both due to its explosive popularity, increasing accessibility to large amounts of data and its dynamic nature. For sentiment analysis on twitter the best performing approaches (Mohammad et al., 2013; Zhu et al., 2014) have used a set of rich lexical features. However, the development of lexica can be time consuming and is not always suitable when shifting between domains, which examine new topics and user populations (Thelwall and Buckley, 2013). Excitingly, the state of the art has recently shifted toward novel semi-supervised techniques such as the incorporation of word embeddings to represent the context of words and concepts (Tang et al., 2014b). Moreover, it is important to be able to identify sentiment in relation to particular entities, topics or events (aspect-based sentiment).

We have followed a hybrid approach which incorporates traditional lexica, unigrams and bigrams as well as word embeddings using word2vec (Mikolov et al., 2013) to train classifiers for subtasks A and B. For subtask C, sentiment targeted towards a particular topic, we have developed a set of different strategies which use either syntactic dependencies or token-level associations with the topic word in combination with our A classifier to produce sentiment annotations.

2 Phrase-Based Sentiment Analysis (Subtask A) as a Means to an End (subtask C)

Phrase-based sentiment analysis (subtask A) in tweets is a long standing task where the goal is to classify the sentiment of a designated expression within the tweet as either positive, negative or neutral. The state of the art for subtask A achieves high performance usually based on methodologies employing features obtained from either manually or automatically generated lexica (Mohammad et al., 2013; Zhu et al., 2014). However, lexica by definition lack contextual information and are oftain domain dependent. Recent work (Tang et al., 2014a) has successfully used sentiment-specific word embeddings, vector representations of the n-gram context of positive, negative and neutral sentiment in tweets to obtain performance which approaches that of lexicon-based approaches.

Here we employ a combination of lexical features and word embeddings to maximise our performance in task A. We build phrase-based classifiers both with an emphasis on the distinction between positive and negative sentiment, which conforms to the distribution of training data in task A, as well as phrase-based classifiers trained on a balanced set of positive, negative and neutral tweets. We use the latter to identify sentiment in the vicinity of topic words in task C, for targeted sentiment assignment. In previous work (Tang et al., 2014a; Tang et al., 2014b) sentiment-specific word embeddings have been used as features for identification of tweet-level sentiment but not phrase-level sentiment. Other work which considered word embeddings for phrase level sentiment (dos Santos, 2014) did not focus on producing sentiment-specific representations and the embeddings learnt were a combination of character and word embeddings, where the relative contribution of the word embeddings is not clear. In this work we present two different strategies for learning phrase level sentiment specific word embeddings.

2.1 Feature Extraction for Task A

Here we provide a detailed description of data preprocessing and feature extraction for phrase-level sentiment. Working on the training set (7,643 tweets), we replaced URLs with "URLINK", converted everything to lower case, removed special characters and tokenised on whitespace, as in (Brody and Diakopoulos, 2011). We decided to keep user mentions, as potentially sentiment-revealing features. We then extracted features both for the *target* (the designated highlighted phrase) and its *context* (the whole tweet):

Ngrams: For a target at the position n in a tweet, we created binary unigram and bigram features of the sequence between $\{n-4, n+4\}$, as suggested by Saif et al. (Mohammad et al., 2013).

Lexicons: We used four different lexica: Bing Liu's lexicon (Hu and Liu, 2004) (about 6,800 polarised terms), NRC's Emotion Lexicon (Mohammad and Turney, 2010) (about 14,000 words annotated based on 10 emotional dimensions), the Sentiment140 Lexicon (62,468 unigrams, 677,968 bigrams and 480,010 non-contiguous pairs) and NRC's Hashtag Sentiment Lexicon (Mohammad et al., 2013) (54,129 unigrams, 316,531 bigrams and 308,808 non-contiguous pairs). We extracted the number of words in the text that appear in every dimension of the Bing Liu and NRC Emotion Lexica. For every lexicon, we extracted features indicating the number of positive unigrams, bigrams and pairs, their maximum sentimental value as indicated by each lexicon, the sum of their sentiment values and the value of the last non-zero (non-neutral) token. All features were extracted both from the tweet as well as the target.

Word Embeddings: We used the tweets collected by (Purver and Battersby, 2012) as training data for sentiment-specific word embeddings. These tweets contain emoticons and hashtags for six different emotions, which we group together to compile positive and negative subsets. To create phrase-level word embeddings, we applied two strategies: *(i)* we searched for positive and negative words (as defined in Bing Liu's lexicon) in the corpus; *(ii)* we performed chi-squared feature selection and extracted the *5,000* most important tokens to be used as our index; for both strategies, we extracted the phrase included in the 2-token-length, two-sided window. The embeddings were learnt by using Gensim (Řehůřek and Sojka, 2010), a Python package that integrates word2vec[1]. In both cases, we created representations of length equal to 100[2]. For each strategy, class and dimension, we used the functions suggested by (Tang et al., 2014b) (average, maximum and minimum), resulting in 2,400 features.

Extra Features: We used several features, potentially indicative of sentiment, a subset of those in (Mohammad et al., 2013). These include: the total number of words of the target phrase, its position within the tweet ("start", "end", or "other"), the average word length of the target/context and the presence of elongated words, URLs and user mentions. We manually labelled various emoticons as positive (strong/weak), negative (strong/weak) and "other" and counted how many times each label appeared in the target and its context.

2.2 Experiments and Results

We experimented with Random Forests and LibSVM with a linear kernel on the training set (4,769 positive, 2,493 negative and 381 neutral tweets) using 10-fold cross-validation and selected LibSVM as the algorithm which achieved the best average F1 score on the positive and negative classes. We then

[1] https://code.google.com/p/word2vec/

[2] The generated, phrase-level Word Embeddings are available at https://zenodo.org/record/14732

used the development set (387 positive, 229 negative and 25 neutral tweets) to fine-tune the value of parameter C, achieving an F1 score of 86.40. The final model was applied on the two test sets provided to us; the "Official 2015 Test" ("OT") included 3,092 instances and the "Progress Test" ("PT"), including 10,681.

Our results are summarised in Table 1. Our algorithm was ranked fourth in OT and fifth in PT out of 11 competitors, achieving F1 scores of 82.46 and 83.89 respectively. It is clear from the table that lexicon-based features have the most important impact on the results. Interestingly, without ngram features, our results would have been better in both sets; however, there was a 0.8 gain in F1 score with the development set (F1 score 85.60) when these were incorporated in our model. The comparison between all the different pairwise sets of features illustrates that lexica together with word embeddings contribute the most (the results are most affected when they are removed), whereas from the individual feature sets (not presented due to space limitations), lexicon-based features outperform the rest (79.96, 82.18), followed by word embeddings (77.75, 79.92 in OT and PT respectively).

Features Used	OT	PT
All features	82.46	83.89
– lexica	79.31	80.45
– embeddings	82.01	84.58
– ngrams	**82.72**	**84.63**
– extra	82.37	84.46
– lexica, embeddings	73.11	72.60
– lexica, ngrams	77.70	79.88
– lexica, extra	78.91	80.49
– embeddings, ngrams	79.83	82.66
– embeddings, extra	81.71	84.09
– ngrams, extra	82.64	84.36

Table 1: Average F1 scores of positive/negative classes on the test set with different features.

3 Tweet-Level Sentiment Analysis (Subtask B) Using Multiple Word Embeddings

Our approach to subtask B follows the same logic as for subtask A, feeding a combination of hybrid features (lexical features, n-grams and word embeddings) to an SVM classifier to determine tweet-level polarity. Our approach integrates rich lexicon-based resources and semantic features of tweets, which enables us to achieve an average F1-score of 65.78 on positive tweets and negative tweets in the development dataset. In the final evaluation for subtask B, we got a rank of 27 out of 40 teams for the test dataset and a rank of 24 out of 40 teams for the test progress dataset. The results are discussed in more detail in subsection 3.2.

The features we used are presented below:

3.1 Features

N-grams: We extract unigrams, bigrams and trigrams from the tweets.

Twitter syntax features: These include the number of tokens that are all in uppercase; the numbers of special marks (?, !, #, @); the numbers of positive emoticons (<3, :DD, ;), :D, 8), :-), :), (-:) and the number of negative emoticons (:(, :'(, :/, :-(, :<).

Lexicon-based features: For lexica that only provided the polarities of sentiment bearing words, we used the numbers of matched positive words and negative words in a tweet as features; for lexica that provided sentiment scores for words or ngrams, we included the sum of positive scores of matched words and the sum of negative scores of matched words as two separate features. The lexica we utilised fell into two categories: manually generated sentiment lexica like the AFINN (Nielsen, 2011), MPQA (Wilson et al., 2005), and Bing Liu's lexica (Liu, 2010); and automatically generated sentiment lexica like the Sentiment140 (Mohammad et al., 2013) and NRC Hashtag Sentiment lexica (Mohammad et al., 2013).

Word embeddings representations features: We learned positive and negative word embeddings separately by training on the HAPPY and NON-HAPPY tweets from Purver & Battersby's multi-class Twitter emoticon and hashtag corpus (Purver and Battersby, 2012), as with subtask A. The difference with subtask A is that here we used the whole tweet as our input (compared to the two-sided window around a polarised word in subtask A) in order to create tweet-level representations. We set the word embeddings dimension to 100 in order to gain enough semantic information whilst reducing training time.

We also employed the word embeddings encoding sentiment information generated through the unified models in (Tang et al., 2014b). Similar to Tang, we represent each tweet by the min, average, max and sum on each dimension of the word embeddings of all the words in the tweet. In the end, the number of our word embeddings features is $4 \times 100 = 400$. A tweet's representations of word embeddings generated from the HAPPY and non-HAPPY subset of tweets and the embeddings generated by Tang et al. were incorporated into the feature set. Their word embeddings have 50 dimensions, so another $4 \times 50 = 200$ features are added to our feature set.

3.2 Experiments

For our SemEval submission we trained an SVM classifier on 9684 tweets (37.59% positive, 47.36% neutral, 15.05% negative) from the training data set, and used the classifier to classify the 2390 tweets (43.43% positive, 41.30% neutral, 15.27% negative) in the test data set. After the training process, we tested the performance of classifiers with different feature sets (shown in the first column in Table 2) on the development data set (1654 tweets with 34.76% positive, 44.68% neutral, 20.56% negative), and used the average F1 scores of positive and negative tweets as performance measurement. The classifier had the best performance on the development data set, achieving a score of 65.78, compared with 57.32 and 65.47 on the test and test progress datasets. We hypothesize that these differences are caused by differences in the proportions of positive and negative tweets in these datasets.

Experiment	Score
All features	58.53
– positive and negative embeddings	57.32
– n-grams	58.63
– Tang's embeddings	58.83
– Twitter-specific features	58.38
– Manual lexica	57.58
– Automatic lexica	58.39
– All embeddings	56.54

Table 2: The scores obtained on the test set with different features.

In Table 2 we list the average F1 scores of positive and negative tweets in the test data set when removing certain features. The results we submitted were generated by the second classifier. Table 2 demonstrates that representing the tweet with positive and negative word embeddings is the most effective feature (performance is affected the most when we remove these) followed by the manually generated lexicon-based features. This combined with a 2% reduction in F1 score when the embeddings are removed, indicates that the embeddings improve sentiment analysis performance. Contrary to the approach by (Tang et al., 2014b), we didn't integrate the sentiment information in the word embeddings training process, but rather the sentiment-specific nature of the embeddings was reflected in the choice of different training datasets, yielding different word embedding features for positive and negative tweets. To measure the contributions of our word embeddings and Tang's sentiment-specific word embeddings separately in the F1 score, we performed a further test. When we only removed Tang's word embeddings features, the F1 score dropped by 0.15%; when we only removed our word embedding features, the F1 score dropped by 1.21%. This illustrates that for our approach, our word embedding features contribute more. However, it is the combination of the two types of word embeddings that boosts our classifier's performance.

4 Target-Specific Sentiment: Subtask C

Experiment	Score
SUBMISSION	22.79
SUBMISSION-SENTIMENT	29.37
SUBMISSION-RETOKENIZED	27.88
CONLL-PROPAGATION	31.84
BASELINE	46.59
μPARSE	46.87

Table 3: Summary of the performance of our subtask C classifiers.

In subtask C the goal is to identify the sentiment targeted towards a particular topic or entity. This is closely linked to aspect-based sentiment (Pontiki et al., 2014) and is very important for understanding the reasons behind the manifestation of different reactions. We develop several strategies for selecting a topic-relevant portion of a tweet and use it to produce a sentiment annotation. A driving force of our approach has been to use phrase-based sentiment identification from subtask A to annotate the topic-relevant selections.

4.1 Topic Relevance Through Syntactic Relations

A syntactic parser generates possible grammatical relations between words in unstructured text, which are potentially useful for capturing the context around a target topic. We experimented with the Stanford parser (Klein and Manning, 2003) and the recently released TweeboParser (Kong et al., 2014). TweeboParser is explicitly designed to parse tweets – supporting multi-word annotations and multiple roots – but instead of the popular Penn Treebank annotation it uses a simpler annotation scheme and outputs much less dependency type information and was therefore not deemed suitable for our purpose. We used the Stanford parser with a caseless parsing model, expected to work better for short documents. We define the topic-relevant portion of a tweet as the weakly connected components of the dependency graph containing a given topic word.

4.2 Generating Per-Token Annotations

Our four different systems BASELINE, SUBMISSION-SENTIMENT, CONLL-PROPAGATION and μPARSE all use per-token sentiment annotations generated in advance by the linear SVM- and random forest-based classifiers discussed in subtask A, using balanced and imbalanced versions of subtask A's training data. Because the classifier can perform better with additional context, we generated two versions of each annotation set – one token at a time (1-WINDOW), and three at a time (3-WINDOW). 3-WINDOW annotations undergo a further majority pre-processing operation to generate a per-token annotation, since adjacent windows overlap. We found again that the SVM classifier outperformed the random forest classifer, with SUBMISSION-RETOKENIZED and CONLL-PROPAGATION performing best with the balanced version, and μPARSE and BASELINE performing best using the imbalanced training data. In the following we explain each of the above mentioned Task C strategies.

4.3 Using Dependency Relations

CONLL-PROPAGATION builds a dependency graph from a supplied parse, trims some of the relations[3], attaches a 1-WINDOW sentiment to each node using our subtask A classifier, and then propagates those values along variably weighted edges to the target. To help the algorithm propagate successfully, the graph is undirected. We opted to train the edge weights using a simple genetic algorithm. Whilst its performance is modestly better than our submission, the approach is constrained by its inefficiency.

SUBMISSION builds a directed co-dependency graph from the supplied parse, and then attempts to match it against parse trees seen previously, to capture syntactic features that may be relevant to the topic's sentiment. Because subgraph isomorphism is a computationally difficult problem, we use a diffusion kernel (as in (Fouss et al., 2006)) to normalise the adjacency matrix for SVM classification. We also add unigrams within the same window used for BASELINE as an additional feature. SUBMISSION-RETOKENIZED updates the result and replaces whitespace tokenization with that used by (Gimpel et al., 2011), more aggressively trims the adjacency matrix, and improves the pre-processing pipeline, improving performance a little. SUBMISSION-SENTIMENT changes the structure of the dependency graph by connecting tokens to their 1-WINDOW sentiment derived from task A, improving performance further still.

4.4 Classification Without Dependency Relations

The simplest classification method (BASELINE) identifies the topic and then only considers those tokens around it. Despite being rudimentary, we found BASELINE difficult to beat when teamed with the sentiment analyser developed for part A, producing an F1-score of 46.59 with a window of 8 tokens. BASELINE is also useful because it doesn't require the use of the training data for task C, leaving it free for validation.

μPARSE is an approach offering a compromise between potentially noisy dependency parsing and the

[3]We select 9 dependency relations – 'amod', 'nsubj', 'advmod', 'dobj', 'xcomp', 'ccomp', 'rcmod', 'cop' and 'acomp' which feasibly impact sentiment (Li et al., 2011).

model-free baseline. It feeds a buffer of word2vec-derived word representations into *min-max-average* feature map (similar to (Tang et al., 2014a)), which is then classified with a linear SVM to decide whether to segment the tweet at the position of an incoming token, or to add the current token to the existing segment. The aim is to extract the neighbourhood around the root words that would have been identified by a perfect syntactic parser, making it conceptually similar to chunking. μPARSE then seeks out a cluster containing the target concept and then uses 1-WINDOW or 3-WINDOW to obtain a consensus annotation. When trained and evaluated on TweeboParser's dataset, it incorrectly groups root words together at a rate of 16%, but this is sufficient to slightly outperform BASELINE.

4.5 Discussion

We found it surprising that our task C submission did not need to be very complex, since we could determine phrase-level sentiment accurately. Whilst we decided not to submit BASELINE as our official entry – owing to uncertainty about the best subtask A parameters and its lack of technical sophistication – our results in Table 3 clearly demonstrate that we should have done so. Syntactic information does seem effective on its own in combination with phrase-level sentiment data, but its real utility might be to guide a more advanced approach that detects syntactically complex structures, and cedes the rest to BASELINE.

5 Conclusions

We have presented our system's components for phrase-, tweet- and topic-based sentiment classification. While lexica remain a critical aspect of our system, we have found that word embeddings are highly important and have great potential for future research in this domain. For both subtasks A and B we generated sentiment-specific word embeddings which yield a performance comparable to that of our lexicon-based approach and further enhance performance. Furthermore, we have found that syntactic features can be useful for topic-based sentiment classification, achieving good results when combined with phrase-based sentiment labels. However, our findings also indicate that simpler approaches can perform better (perhaps due to the need for improvements in dependency parsing for Twitter), and further investigation will be required to determine how to exploit the relationship between topic-specific and phrase-level sentiment.

Acknowledgements

This work was partially funded by the Engineering and Physical Sciences Research Council (grant EP/L016400/1) through the University of Warwick's Centre for Doctoral Training in Urban Science and Progress.

References

Samuel Brody and Nicholas Diakopoulos. 2011. Cooooooooooooooollllllllllllll!!!!!!!!!!!!!!: using word lengthening to detect sentiment in microblogs. In *Proceedings of the conference on empirical methods in natural language processing*, pages 562–570. Association for Computational Linguistics.

Cicero dos Santos. 2014. Think positive: Towards Twitter sentiment analysis from scratch. In *Proceedings of the 8th International Workshop on Semantic Evaluation (SemEval 2014)*, pages 647–651, Dublin, Ireland, August.

Francois Fouss, Luh Yen, Alain Pirotte, and Marco Saerens. 2006. An experimental investigation of graph kernels on a collaborative recommendation task. In *Data Mining, 2006. ICDM'06. Sixth International Conference on*, pages 863–868. IEEE.

Kevin Gimpel, Nathan Schneider, Brendan O'Connor, Dipanjan Das, Daniel Mills, Jacob Eisenstein, Michael Heilman, Dani Yogatama, Jeffrey Flanigan, and Noah A. Smith. 2011. Part-of-speech tagging for Twitter: Annotation, features, and experiments. In *Proceedings of the 49th Annual Meeting of the Association for Computational Linguistics: Human Language Technologies: Short Papers - Volume 2*, HLT '11, pages 42–47, Stroudsburg, PA, USA.

Minqing Hu and Bing Liu. 2004. Mining and summarizing customer reviews. In *Proceedings of the tenth ACM SIGKDD international conference on Knowledge discovery and data mining*, pages 168–177.

Dan Klein and Christopher D. Manning. 2003. Accurate unlexicalized parsing. In *Proceedings of the 41st Annual Meeting on Association for Computational Linguistics - Volume 1*, ACL '03, pages 423–430, Stroudsburg, PA, USA.

Lingpeng Kong, Nathan Schneider, Swabha Swayamdipta, Archna Bhatia, Chris Dyer, and

Noah A Smith. 2014. A dependency parser for tweets. In *Proceedings of the Conference on Empirical Methods in Natural Language Processing, Doha, Qatar, to appear*.

Peifeng Li, Qiaoming Zhu, and Wei Zhang. 2011. A dependency tree based approach for sentence-level sentiment classification. In *Software Engineering, Artificial Intelligence, Networking and Parallel/Distributed Computing (SNPD), 2011 12th ACIS International Conference on*, pages 166–171. IEEE.

Bing Liu. 2010. Sentiment analysis: a multifaceted problem. *IEEE Intelligent Systems*, 25(3):76–80.

Tomas Mikolov, Ilya Sutskever, Kai Chen, Greg S Corrado, and Jeff Dean. 2013. Distributed representations of words and phrases and their compositionality. In *Advances in Neural Information Processing Systems*, pages 3111–3119.

Saif M Mohammad and Peter D Turney. 2010. Emotions evoked by common words and phrases: Using mechanical turk to create an emotion lexicon. In *Proceedings of the NAACL HLT 2010 Workshop on Computational Approaches to Analysis and Generation of Emotion in Text*, pages 26–34. Association for Computational Linguistics.

Saif Mohammad, Svetlana Kiritchenko, and Xiaodan Zhu. 2013. Nrc-canada: Building the state-of-the-art in sentiment analysis of tweets. In *Proceedings of the seventh international workshop on Semantic Evaluation Exercises (SemEval-2013)*, Atlanta, Georgia, USA, June.

Finn Årup Nielsen. 2011. A new anew: Evaluation of a word list for sentiment analysis in microblogs. *arXiv preprint*.

Maria Pontiki, Haris Papageorgiou, Dimitrios Galanis, Ion Androutsopoulos, John Pavlopoulos, and Suresh Manandhar. 2014. Semeval-2014 task 4: Aspect based sentiment analysis. In *Proceedings of the 8th International Workshop on Semantic Evaluation (SemEval 2014)*, pages 27–35.

Matthew Purver and Stuart Battersby. 2012. Experimenting with distant supervision for emotion classification. In *Proceedings of the 13th Conference of the European Chapter of the Association for Computational Linguistics*, pages 482–491. Association for Computational Linguistics.

Radim Řehůřek and Petr Sojka. 2010. Software Framework for Topic Modelling with Large Corpora. In *Proceedings of the LREC 2010 Workshop on New Challenges for NLP Frameworks*, pages 45–50, Valletta, Malta, May.

Duyu Tang, Furu Wei, Bing Qin, Ting Liu, and Ming Zhou. 2014a. Coooolll: A deep learning system for Twitter sentiment classification. *SemEval 2014*, page 208.

Duyu Tang, Furu Wei, Nan Yang, Ming Zhou, Ting Liu, and Bing Qin. 2014b. Learning sentiment-specific word embedding for Twitter sentiment classification. In *Proceedings of the 52nd Annual Meeting of the Association for Computational Linguistics*, pages 1555–1565.

Mike Thelwall and Kevan Buckley. 2013. Topic-based sentiment analysis for the social web: The role of mood and issue-related words. *Journal of the American Society for Information Science and Technology*, 64(8):1608–1617.

Theresa Wilson, Janyce Wiebe, and Paul Hoffmann. 2005. Recognizing contextual polarity in phrase-level sentiment analysis. In *Proceedings of the Conference on Human Language Technology and Empirical Methods in Natural Language Processing*, HLT '05, pages 347–354, Stroudsburg, PA, USA.

Xiaodan Zhu, Svetlana Kiritchenko, and Saif Mohammad. 2014. Nrc-canada-2014: Recent improvements in the sentiment analysis of tweets. In *Proceedings of the 8th International Workshop on Semantic Evaluation (SemEval 2014)*, pages 443–447, Dublin, Ireland, August.

UIR-PKU: Twitter-OpinMiner System for Sentiment Analysis in Twitter at SemEval 2015

Xu Han[2,4], Binyang Li[1*], Jing Ma[2], Yuxiao Zhang[3], Gaoyan Ou[3], Tengjiao Wang[3], Kam-fai Wong[2,4,5]

[1]School of Information and Technology, University of Information Relations, Beijing
[2]Dept. of Sys. Engineering&Engineering Management, The Chinese University of Hong Kong
[3]School of Information Science, Peking University, Beijing
[4]Shenzhen Research Institute, The Chinese University of Hong Kong
[5]MoE Key Laboratory of High Confidence Software Technologies, China
{xhan, jma, kfwong}@cuhk.edu.hk; byli@uir.cn; {yxzhang, gyou, tjwang}@pku.edu.cn

Abstract

Microblogs are considered as We-Media information with many real-time opinions. This paper presents a Twitter-OpinMiner system for Twitter sentiment analysis evaluation at SemEval 2015. Our approach stems from two different angles: topic detection for discovering the sentiment distribution on different topics and sentiment analysis based on a variety of features. Moreover, we also implemented intra-sentence discourse relations for polarity identification. We divided the discourse relations into 4 predefined categories, including *continuation, contrast, condition,* and *cause*. These relations could facilitate us to eliminate polarity ambiguities in compound sentences where both positive and negative sentiments are appearing. Based on the SemEval 2014 and SemEval 2015 Twitter sentiment analysis task datasets, the experimental results show that the performance of Twitter-OpinMiner could effectively recognize opinionated messages and identify the polarities.

1 Introduction

This year comes the third edition of SemEval Twitter sentiment analysis task consisting of new genres, including topic-based polarity classification, trends detection towards a topic, and the sentimental strength of association of terms (Nakov et al., 2013).

We only participated in the subtask of message sentiment analysis and built up a system, named Twitter-OpinMiner for the task. Twitter-OpinMiner stems from two different angles: LDA-based topic detection for discovering the opinionated features of trending tweets' topics and sentiment analysis based on a variety of features.

- **Topic detection**

Recent studies show that people often search Twitter to find temporally relevant information (Teevan et al., 2011), such as emergent events, trending topics. In fact, similar opinions were likely to express on the same topic/event in Twitter. For example, there are 20 tweets expressing similar opinions on "Blood moon" in SemEval 2015 dataset. Therefore, it can facilitate us to discover the sentiment distribution on different topics.

- **Sentiment analysis**

Unlike traditional news content, tweets are specialists in short texts with long compound sentences, and a number of irregular expressions, including emoticon, hashtag, and special punctuations. In order to better support tweets analysis, we extract features from following aspects: textual content, irregular expression, discourse relations, and word embedding. Then we introduce above features into a SVM classifier for sentiment analysis.

This paper is organized as follows. Section 2 describes the framework of our system. Section 3 introduces the details of our feature extraction. We

*Corresponding author

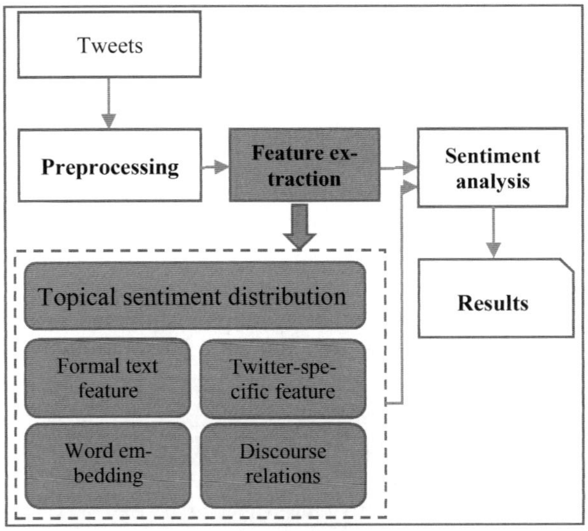

Figure 1. System architecture.

present the evaluation results in Section 4. Finally, Section 5 concludes the paper.

2 System Overview

2.1 Architecture

The architecture of Twitter-OpinMiner is described in Figure 1. Twitter-OpinMiner system is comprised of three modules:

(1) Pre-processing module: reads all data of training data and test data. It performs, POS tagging, named entity recognition, and semantic role labeling.

(2) Feature extraction module: extracts the features including formal text features, tweet-specific features, discourse features, sentiment distribution among topics, and word embedding.

(3) Sentiment analysis module: creates a SVM classifier that incorporates the above features classify the polarity of each tweet.

Finally, Twitter-OpinMiner outputs the polarity of each tweet.

2.2 Development Data and Lexicon

The development data are necessary in our system. We fully utilize the training tweets provided by SemEval 2013. The dataset consists of 9,912 annotated tweets.

Besides, for sentiment analysis, we also utilize several sentiment lexicons, including Liu's sentiment lexicon (Liu, 2012), MPQA subjectivity lexicon (Wilson et al., 2005), and the sentiment lexicon generated from tweets (Mohammad et al., 2013).

Table 1. Features of text in our system.

Word-Level and entity-level features
The presence of sentiment word
The ratio of sentiment word in a sentence
The total number of positive words
The total number of negative words
The presence of negation words
The total number of the word in all-caps
Bi-gram features
Named entities + opinion operators
Pronouns + opinion operators
Nouns or named entities + opinion words
Pronouns + opinion words
Opinion words (adjective) + (noun)

3 Feature Extraction

The objective of this task is to determine whether a given message is positive, negative, or neutral. We train sentiment classifiers with LibLinear (Fan et al., 2008) on the training set and dev set, and tune parameter $-c$, $-w_i$ of SVM on the test set of SemEval 2013. SVM is a popular machine learning algorithm, the effectiveness of which has been proved in sentiment analysis on formal texts in related work (Pang and Lee, 2002; Liu, 2012). Since the performance of SVM classifier will be greatly influenced by the features selection, we explore a variety of features in the evaluation.

3.1 Features of topical sentiment distribution

The advancement of Twitter is fast response to the real world, so people often search Twitter to find temporally relevant information, such as emergent events, trending topics. In fact, tweets are likely to converge on some opinions for a specific topic, which will lead to different sentiment distributions among topics.

In our system, we adopt LDA-based approach for representing the typical sentiment distribution features. We use the Mallet toolkit, set the topic number as 50, and map each tweet into 50 dimensions to extract those features.

3.2 Features of formal text

Although the task is to analyze sentiment in Twitter, much research proved the effectiveness of the classic features of formal texts on tweets. The features we adopted in this task are partly the same with (Zhou et al., 2010) and listed in Table 1, and two types of features are incorporated in the classifier.

These features are also integrated into our SVM classifier for training and treated as the baseline in our experiment.

3.3 Twitter specific feature

Unlike formal texts, tweet has its own characteristics, including irregular expressions, emoticon, hashtag, ill format, and special punctuations. In our system, we combine the features proposed by Mohammad et al. (2013) with some new features as Twitter-specific features for supplementary to the forma text.

- Hashtags: the number of hashtags in one tweet;
- Ill format: the presence of ill format with some characters replacing by *, for example, f**k;
- Punctuation: the number of contiguous sequences of exclamation marks, question marks, and both exclamation and question marks; whether the last token contains an exclamation or question mark;
- Emoticons: the presence of positive and negative emoticons at any position in the tweet; whether the last token is an emoticon;
- OOV: the ratio of words out of vocabulary;
- Elongated words: the presence of sentiment words with one character repeated more than two times, for example, 'cooool';
- URL: whether the tweet contains a URL.
- Reply or Retweet: Is the current tweet a reply/retweet tweet

3.4 Word embedding

We also utilize word embedding technique for feature extraction. We adopt sentiment-specific word embedding method (Tang et al., 2014) that could encode sentiment information in the continuous representation of words. In our approach, each term is extended into a 150 dimensional vector.

3.5 Discourse specific feature

Since tweets are usually expressed informally, there are many compound sentences in a tweet, which always contain positive sentiment and negative sentiment with ambiguity. For example,

It may not be the biggest squad in the last 10yrs, but Ancelotti is working for quality over quantity. Everyone... http://t.co/oCdPXQWggT.

Table 2. Examples of cue-phrases.

Relation	Cue Phrases
Contrast	*although, but, however, though*
Condition	*if, despite, in case of*
Continuation	*and, moreover, not only but also*
Cause	*because, so that, due to, in order that*

In this case, there are two segments in the tweet that holds a Contrast discourse relation, and the polarity is determined by "but" segment. In our system, we also take into consideration of intra-sentence discourse relation features for processing compound sentences.

Mann and Thompson (1988) defined a complete discourse scheme Rhetorical Structure Theory (RST). Since not all of the discourse relations in RST would help eliminate polarity ambiguities, the discourse relations were implemented in our system was on a subset (Zhou et al., 2011).

In our system, we use cue-phrase based method for discourse relation identification. We maintain a cue phrase lexicon and the examples of the cue phrases were shown in Table 2.

4 Experiment

We trained a SVM classifier on 9,912 annotated tweets (8,258 in the training set and 1,654 in the development set). We used the same evaluation metrics with SemEval 2013, including the macro-averaged F-score of the positive and negative classes. The experimental results obtained by our system on the training set (ten-fold cross validation), development set, and test sets on Twitter 2013 were shown in Table 3 where the baseline was achieved by using the formal text features as well as twitter-specific features. Since the effectiveness of these two types of features were analyzed in (Mohammad et al., 2013), we mainly evaluated the effectiveness of other features.

Table 3 showed that the most effective feature on Twitter 2013 dataset turned out to be the word embedding features: they provided gains of about 7%. For LDA, we set the numbers of topic from 10 to 100, and found it could achieve best performance when equaling 50. We then constructed the sentiment distribution among 50 topics for the further evaluation.

Besides, we also investigated the effectiveness of discourse features on compound sentences, and the statistics were shown in Table 6.

Table 3. Experimental results on Twitter 2013 dataset.

Approaches	Metrics						
	pos-P	pos-R	pos-F	neg-P	neg-R	neg-F	ave-F
Baseline (BL)	0.743	0.673	0.706	0.451	0.679	0.542	0.624
BL+LDA	0.752	0.679	0.714	0.465	0.707	0.561	0.634
BL+Word Embedding	0.772	0.685	0.724	0.561	0.798	0.659	0.692
BL+Discourse Relation	0.756	0.680	0.716	0.467	0.705	0.562	0.635
BL+All	**0.791**	**0.704**	**0.745**	**0.563**	**0.809**	**0.664**	**0.704**

Table 4. Experimental results of 2015 test.

Method	Metrics						
	pos-P	pos-R	pos-F	neg-P	neg-R	neg-F	ave-F
UIR-PKU	0.7518	0.6098	0.6734	0.4636	0.6110	0.5272	0.6003
Best run	**0.7702**	**0.6975**	**0.7321**	**0.5171**	**0.6219**	**0.5647**	**0.6484**

Table 5. Experimental results of progress test on Average F-value.

Approaches	Corpus			
	Live Journal 2014	SMS 2013	Twitter 2014	Twitter 2014 Sarcasm
UIR-PKU	0.7044	0.6741	0.6718	**0.5258**
Best run	**0.7534**	**0.6716**	**0.7448**	0.4286

Table 6. Distribution of discourse relations and the contribution in the evaluation.

Discourse Relation	Occurrence	Contribution
Cause	26.9%	33.9%
Condition	12.6%	22.1%
Contrast	18.2%	10.1%
Continuation	42.3%	33.9%

By adopting discourse features, around 59% sentences with discourse relations were identified. Among these four types of relations, better performance were achieved on *cause* and *condition* relations. Especially for the sentences with *condition* relation, they were all classified correctly. It is because that more cue-phrase of *cause* and *condition* relations were used to explicitly denote the discourse relations in tweets, but more likely use context to imply *contrast* and *continuation* relations.

Table 4 and Table 5 showed the evaluation results in SemEval 2015 Task 10. Compared with the best run in Table 5, our system achieved comparable results on Twitter sentiment analysis and better performance on the evaluation of *sarcasm*. In fact, many sarcasm are likely expressed in ironic, hence most feature types are ineffective for this case. In our system, we also used the features of topical sentiment distribution, which assumed the polarity of *sarcasm* tweet the same with *non-sarcasm* tweets.

5 Conclusion

We describe our Twitter-OpinMiner systems for participating in SemEval 2015 sentiment analysis in Twitter. Our approach stems the features from two different aspects: topical sentiment distribution and a variety of short text based features. In our paper, we also implemented intra-sentence discourse relations for polarity identification in compound sentences where both positive and negative sentiments are appearing. In this way, the polarity ambiguities will be eliminated. Based on SemEval 2015 and SemEval 2014 datasets for Twitter sentiment analysis task, we examined the performance of Twitter-OpinMiner, which could achieved comparable results on recognizing opinionated messages and identifying the polarities.

Acknowledgments

This research is partially supported by Fundamental Research Funds for the Central Universities (3262014T75, 3262015T20), Shenzhen Fundamental Research Program (JCYJ20130401172046450), General Research Fund of Hong Kong (417112). We also thank Liyu Chen, Jianxiong Wu, and anonymous reviewers for their helpful comments.

References

Rong-En Fan, Kai-Wei Chang, Cho-Jui Hsieh, Xiang-Rui Wang, and Chih-Jen Lin. 2008. LIBLINEAR: A Library for Large Linear Classification. *Journal of Machine Learning Research*, 9: 1871-1874.

Bing Liu, Mingqing Hu, and Junsheng Cheng. 2005. Opinion Observer: Analyzing and Comparing Opinions on the Web. In *Proceedings of the 14th international conference on World Wide Web*, pages 342-351, Chiba, Japan, ACM.

Bing Liu. 2012. Sentiment analysis and opinion mining. *Synthesis Lectures on Human Lcanguage Tehnologies*, 5(1): 1-167.

William C. Mann and Sandra A. Thompson. 1988. Rhetorical structure theory: Toward a functional theory of text organization. *Text-Interdisciplinary Journal for the Study of Discourse*, 8(3): 243-281.

Saif M. Mohammad, Svetlana Kiritchenko, and Xiaodan Zhu. 2013. NRC-Canada: Building the state-of-the-art in sentiment analysis of tweets. In *Proceedings of the 2nd Joint Conference on Lexical and Computational Semantics*.

Preslav Nakov, Sara Rosenthal, Zornitsa Kozareva, Veselin Stoyanov, Alan Ritter, and Theresa Wilson. 2013. SemEval-2013 task 2: Sentiment analysis in twitter. In Proceedings of the International Workshop on Semantic Evaluation, volume 13.

Bo Pang, Lillian Lee, and Shivakumar Vaithyanathan. 2002. Thumbs up? Sentiment Classification Using Machine Learning Techniques. In Proceedings of the Conference on Empirical Methods in Natural Language Processing, pages 79-86.

Duyu Tang, Furu Wei, Nan Yang, Ming Zhou, Ting Liu, and Bing Qin. 2014. Learning sentiment-specific word embedding for twitter sentiment classification. In Proceedings of the 52nd Annual Meeting of the Association for Computational Linguistics, pages 1555-1565.

Jaime Teevan, Daniel Ramage, and Merredith R. Morris. 2011. #TwitteSearch： A Comparison of Microblog Search and Web Search. In Proceedings of the 4th ACM International Conference on Web Search and Data Mining, pages 35-44.

Theresa Wilson, Janyce Wiebe, and Paul Hoffmann. 2005. Recognizing contextual polarity in phrase-level sentiment analysis. In Proceedings of the International Conference on Human Language Technology and Empirical Methods in Natural Language Processing, pages 347-354.

Lanjun Zhou, Yunqing Xia, Binyang Li, and Kam-fai Wong. 2010. WIA-Opinmine System in NTCIR-8 MOAT Evaluation. In the 8th NTCIR Workshop Meeting, pages 286-292.

Lanjun Zhou, Binyang Li, Wei Gao, Zhongyu Wei, and Kam-fai Wong. 2011. Unsupervised discovery of discourse relations for eliminating intra-sentence polarity ambiguities. In Proceedings of the Conference on Empirical Methods in Natural Language Processing, pages 162-171.

SWAT-CMW: Classification of Twitter Emotional Polarity using a Multiple-Classifier Decision Schema and Enhanced Emotion Tagging

Riley Collins, Daniel May, Noah Weinthal, and Richard Wicentowski
Swarthmore College
Swarthmore, PA 19081
{rcollin4, dmay1, nweinth1, richardw}@cs.swarthmore.edu

Abstract

In this paper, we describe our approach to Semeval 2015 task 10 subtask B, message level sentiment detection. Our system implements a variety of classifiers and data preparation techniques from previous work. The set of features and classifiers used in the final system produced consistently strong results using cross-validation on the provided training data. Our final system achieved an F-score of 57.60 on the provided test data. The overall best performing system had an F-score of 64.84.

1 Introduction

With the unprecedented growth of social media in the past decade, more individuals than ever before have a means to share their opinions and broadcast their voice. As the number of readily available opinions grows, a challenge of academic and commercial importance emerges. Namely, if the sentiment of social media communications can be reliably determined algorithmically, a deeply informative dataset can be developed. Such data can be used in a variety of applications, from predicting election results to seeing how well a new product is received. However, this task is greatly complicated by inconsistencies in spelling, grammar, lexicon, and other linguistic phenomena found in online communications. The SemEval 2015 Task 10 Subtask B (Rosenthal et al., 2015) challenges participants to determine the sentiment polarity of posts on the social media site Twitter. Specifically, the task is to decide whether the sentiment of a given tweet is positive, negative, or neutral. In this paper we present an approach to this task which synthesizes a number of different preprocessing techniques and classification methods, which we use to classify the tweets.

Our approach was inspired by several approaches to previous iterations of this task. The winning team in 2014, TeamX, used several preprocessors including text normalization, lexical sense mapping, clustering, and word sense disambiguation to train a machine learner to determine emotion (Miura et al., 2014). Ultimately, we hypothesized that a successful approach relies not only on the choice of a good classifier, but also in large part upon the preparation of data for that classifier. This hypothesis led us to place high value on our prepocessing, and as such we focused our energy on implementing strategies that would lead to improvements within existing classifiers, a decision which ultimately led to the creation of our decision schema.

2 System Description

2.1 Preprocessing

Our system makes use of various preprocessing steps in order to reduce the dimensionality of the data set and improve overall performance. These steps included:

- Tokenization using Twokenizer (Gimpel et al., 2011), a tokenizer designed specifically for Tweets.
- Case-folding so that all text is lower-cased.
- All unique URLs were conflated to a single token in both the training and test data.

Each of these preprocessing steps improved performance regardless of which features we later extracted and which classifier we tried.

2.2 External Lexicons

As part of feature extraction, our system makes use of two external lexicons. We used a manually created list of definitively positive and negative words (Hu and Liu, 2004) and an automatically generated list of words and their associated sentiment polarities in the Sentiment140 lexicon (Mohammad et al., 2013). The polarities associated with the words in the Sentiment140 lexicon are determined based on how often the word appears in automatically labeled positive or negative Tweets.

Our system searches through each token in the Tweet for matches against the two sentiment lexicons. When a match was found in the Sentiment140 lexicon, a special positive (or negative) feature was added to the feature set with a magnitude correlated to the polarity listed in the lexicon. When a match was found only in the Hu and Liu lexicon, a special positive (or negative) feature was added to the feature set but with a fixed magnitude because this lexicon did not provide strength of the sentiment along with each word.

2.3 Features

Our system finds tokens indicating negation, such as "no", "never", and "not" plus any contractions containing "not". Unlike many other implementations, which prefixes negation words with a single identifying term, our implementation prefixes each negation token with either "NO", "NEVER", or "NOT" until the next punctuation mark, similar to (Zhu et al., 2014). This strategy performed better than one which used a single negation prefix.

Features in our system included unigrams and bigrams of tokens in the Tweet (modified as necessary by negation as described above) and the positive and negative features added by finding matches in the external lexicons.

2.4 Classifiers

The system uses an SVM and Naive Bayes classifier from SciKit Learn (Pedregosa et al., 2011), and a simple classifier that counts occurrences of tokens in the Tweet that match words in the sentiment lexicon (Hu and Liu, 2004). Our experience with the SVM was that while it was our best preforming classifier overall, it had a tendency to mislabel both positive and negative Tweets as neutral. Therefore, once the SVM has performed its classification, our system uses a secondary classifier before providing its final sentiment labeling. Figure 1 gives an overview of the classification system.

SVM + Neutralizer The initial classifier involves using the default SVM classifier found in SciKit. This produces a three-way labeling of either positive, negative or neutral. After the initial SVM classification, we use a rule-based classifier to reduce the number of tweets that are incorrectly labeled as negative. This classifier counts the number of positive and negative words in the tweet according to the sentiment lexicon. If the number of positive words is greater than the number of negative words and the tweet was labeled negative, we change the label to neutral; otherwise the label is unchanged.

Naive Bayes We used the default implementation of the Naive Bayes classifier from SciKit.

Sentiment Lexicon We use the sentiment lexicon to count the number of tokens in the tweet that have positive or negative sentiment. If there are more negative words in the tweet than positive words, we label the tweet negative; otherwise, positive.

2.5 The Decision Schema

The SVM classifier had two large sources of error. First, it incorrectly labeled many neutral tweets as positive. Second, it labeled many positive and negative tweets as neutral. In order to address this, we implemented a decision schema to correct for these errors in the SVM, as shown in Figure 1.

To correct for errors where the SVM incorrectly labeled neutral tweets as positive, we used a secondary Naive Bayes classifier. This secondary classifier was trained only on positive and neutral tweets, and provides a final classification as either positive or neutral.

To correct for errors where the SVM incorrectly over-labeled tweets as neutral, we also used a secondary Naive Bayes classifier. However, this classifier was trained on all tweets in a binary fashion, where the tweets were labeled as either neutral or non-neutral. If this Naive Bayes classifier provided

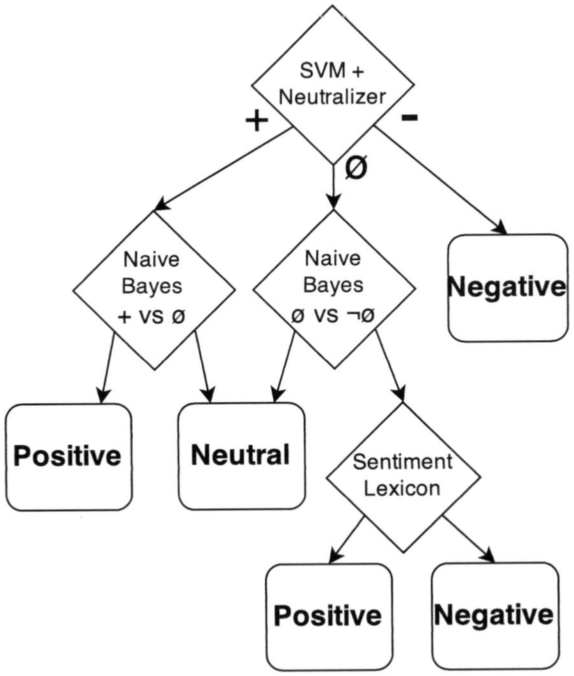

Figure 1: The System's Decision Schema.

a neutral labeling, that became the final label. In the case where a non-neutral label was predicted, we used the sentiment lexicon classifier to provide the final labeling.

3 Results

3.1 Decision Schema Performance

During development, the performance of our Decision Schema was evaluated in two ways. First, we performed a cross-evaluation, where we split the training test into a number of 'chunks', reserved one chunk for testing and trained on the others, then swapped which chunk was reserved and repeated until all 'folds' had been tested and reported an average of the results. Then, we tested against a small development Tweet corpus. Results for each can be seen in Tables 1 and 2, respectively. Against the 2015 test data, we achieved an overall score of 57.60.

3.2 Conclusions

As can be seen from Table 1 and Table 2, our classifier performs quite well in assigning tags to positive and neutral Tweets. Our system tends not to perform as well in our tests at tagging negative Tweets. This potentially implies that we may not be providing enough weight to negative-polarity Tweet features throughout our preprocessing and feature extraction processes, that our decision schema logic unfairly discourages negative tags, or simply that more training data is needed due to the comparatively small number of negative Tweets in the corpus.

Sentiment	Prec	Recall	F1
Negative	51.52	57.48	54.34
Neutral	77.16	71.98	74.78
Positive	69.66	73.51	71.53
Overall Score	62.93		

Table 1: Performance of the system cross-validated on the 2015 training set.

Sentiment	Prec	Recall	F1
Negative	54.77	60.55	57.51
Neutral	72.96	68.06	70.42
Positive	68.26	70.91	69.56
Overall Score	63.53		

Table 2: Performance of the system trained on the 2015 training set and evaluated on the 2015 development set.

4 Future Work

With every new preprocessing and classification system that we added, numerous potential improvements presented themselves. While time constraints prohibited implementing these improvements, we briefly mention them here.

4.1 Preprocessing

We experimented with using case (e.g. HAPPY vs happy) as a feature and expected that all-caps would serve as an indicator of stronger emotional content. In evaluation, this was not the case, but we would like to explore this further.

We would like to incorporate a dependency parser, such as (Kong et al., 2014), which might enable more accurate negation by better revealing where the negating word stops modifying the words in the Tweet. We would also like to include the part-of-speech tagger in Twokenizer (Gimpel et al., 2011) and incorporate word-sense disambiguation, both of which might allow us to better determine emotional polarities for homographs.

4.2 Classification

We would like to experiment with more classifiers. In particular, we would like to investigate SciKit's AdaBoost and Decision Tree modules, both of which promise better performance but are computationally expensive. We would also like to further develop our approach of dividing the task into a series of binary classifications rather than a ternary classification. Additionally, we would like to explore dimensionality-reduction methods like Spectral Clustering on the feature matrices, in order to address some of the failings we observed in our decision schema.

References

Kevin Gimpel, Nathan Schneider, Brendan O'Connor, Dipanjan Das, Daniel Mills, Jacob Eisenstein, Michael Heilman, Dani Yogatama, Jeffrey Flanigan, and Noah A. Smith. 2011. Part-of-speech tagging for Twitter: Annotation, features, and experiments. In *Proceedings of the 49th Annual Meeting of the Association for Computational Linguistics: Human Language Technologies: Short Papers - Volume 2*, pages 42–47.

Minqing Hu and Bing Liu. 2004. Mining and summarizing customer reviews. In *Proceedings of the Tenth ACM SIGKDD International Conference on Knowledge Discovery and Data Mining*, pages 168–177.

Lingpeng Kong, Nathan Schneider, Swabha Swayamdipta, Archna Bhatia, Chris Dyer, and Noah A. Smith. 2014. A dependency parser for tweets. In *Proceedings of the 2014 Conference on Empirical Methods in Natural Language Processing (EMNLP)*, pages 1001–1012.

Yasuhide Miura, Shigeyuki Sakaki, Keigo Hattori, and Tomoko Ohkuma. 2014. TeamX: A sentiment analyzer with enhanced lexicon mapping and weighting scheme for unbalanced data. In *Proceedings of the 8th International Workshop on Semantic Evaluation (SemEval 2014)*, pages 628–632.

Saif Mohammad, Svetlana Kiritchenko, and Xiaodan Zhu. 2013. NRC-Canada: Building the state-of-the-art in sentiment analysis of tweets. In *Proceedings of SemEval-2013*, pages 321–327.

Fabian Pedregosa, Gael Varoquaux, Alexandre Gramfort, Vincent Michel, Bertrand Thirion, Olivier Grisel, Mathieu Blondel, Peter Prettenhofer, Ron Weiss, Vincent Dubourg, Jake Vanderplas, Alexandre Passos, David Cournapeau, Matthieu Brucher, Matthieu Perrot, and Edouard Duchesnay. 2011. Scikit-learn: Machine learning in Python. *Journal of Machine Learning Research*, 12:2825–2830.

Sara Rosenthal, Preslav Nakov, Svetlana Kiritchenko, Saif M Mohammad, Alan Ritter, and Veselin Stoyanov. 2015. Semeval-2015 task 10: Sentiment analysis in Twitter. In *Proceedings of the 9th International Workshop on Semantic Evaluation*, SemEval '2015.

Xiaodan Zhu, Svetlana Kiritchenko, and Saif Mohammad. 2014. NRC-Canada-2014: Recent improvements in the sentiment analysis of tweets. In *Proceedings of the 8th International Workshop on Semantic Evaluation (SemEval 2014)*, pages 443–447.

LLT-PolyU: Identifying Sentiment Intensity in Ironic Tweets

Hongzhi Xu, Enrico Santus, Anna Laszlo and Chu-Ren Huang
The Department of Chinese and Bilingual Studies
The Hong Kong Polytechnic University
{hongz.xu, esantus}@gmail.com
mandarin1985@yahoo.de
churenhuang@gmail.com

Abstract

In this paper, we describe the system we built for Task 11 of SemEval2015, which aims at identifying the sentiment intensity of figurative language in tweets. We use various features, including those specially concerned with the identification of irony and sarcasm. The features are evaluated through a decision tree regression model and a support vector regression model. The experiment result of the five-cross validation on the training data shows that the tree regression model outperforms the support vector regression model. The former is therefore used for the final evaluation of the task. The results show that our model performs especially well in predicting the sentiment intensity of tweets involving irony and sarcasm.

1 Introduction

Sentiment analysis aims to identify the polarity and intensity of certain texts in order to shed light on people's sentiments, perceptions, opinions, and beliefs about a particular product, service, scheme, etc. Knowing what people think can, in fact, help companies, political parties, and other public entities in strategizing and decision making.

While impressive results have been achieved in analysing literal texts (Abbasi et al., 2008; Yan et al., 2014), the study of polarity shifting in sentiment analysis still requires much research. For example, Li, et.al. (2010), explores the polarity shifters in English which significantly improve the performance of sentiment analysis. Besides, figurative uses of language, such as irony or sarcasm, are also able to invert the polarity of the surface text. Theoretical research in irony and sarcasm often emphasize that humans have difficulties in deciphering messages with underlying meaning (Hay, 2001; Kotthoff, 2003; Kreuz and Caucci, 2007). Factors that can facilitate the understanding of these messages include prosody (e.g. stress or intonation), kinesics (e.g. facial gestures), co-text (i.e. immediate textual environment) and context (i.e. wider environment), as well as cultural background. Computers, however, cannot always rely on this kind of information.

Currently, there is no method that can guarantee the unequivocal recognition of irony or sarcasm. Training a computer to perform such a highly pragmatic task does indeed pose a challenge to computational linguists. A good number of studies have been recently devoted to finding a solution to the problem. Most of them have focused on tweets (González-Ibáñez et al., 2011; Reyes et al., 2013; Liebrecht et al., 2013; Riloff et al., 2013; Barbieri et al., 2014; Vanzo et al., 2014).

Identifying figurative language in short messages (generally consisting of no more than 140 characters) that do not make use of conventional language, but employ "little space-consuming" elements, such as emoticons (":D"), abbreviations ("abbr.") and slang ("slng") is not a self-evident task. The reason why none of these studies has proved to be the representative method that could widely be adopted and applied by other researchers is that they have not yet reached optimal results. Thus, the devising of a computational model able to accurately detect polarity is very much on-going.

This paper describes the model we developed for Task 11 of SemEval-2015 (Ghosh et al., 2015), which is concerned with the Sentiment Analysis of Figurative Language in Twitter. Our model came first in the SemEval-2015 task for irony and third in the overall ranking, showing that the features we proposed produce more reliable results in sentiment analysis of ironic tweets.

2 Related Work

Irony is defined by Quintilian in the first century CE as "saying the opposite of what you mean" (Quintilian, 1922). It violates the expectations of the listener by flouting the maxim of quality (Grice, 1975; Stringfellow Jr, 1994; Gibbs and Colston, 2007; Tungthamthiti et al., 2014). In the same fashion, sarcasm is generally understood as the use of irony "to mock or convey contempt" (Stevenson, 2010).

While irony and sarcasm are well studied in linguistics and psychology, their automatic identification through Natural Language Processing methods is a relatively novel task (Pang and Lee, 2008). Not to mention that irony and sarcasm pose a difficult problem in Sentiment Analysis of micro blogging and social media (Barbieri et al., 2014).

Up to this date, several approaches have been proposed to automatically identify irony and sarcasm in tweets and comments. Carvalho et al. (2009), for example, proposed to identify irony in comments to newspaper articles by relying on the presence of emoticons, onomatopoeic expressions, and heavy punctuation in the text surface. Hao and Veale (2010) have investigated similes of the form "x as y" in a large corpus, proposing a method to automatically discriminate ironic from non-ironic similes. Tsur et al. (2010) proposed a semi-supervised approach for the automatic recognition of sarcasm in Amazon product reviews, exploiting some features that were specific to Amazon. Their method employed two modules: a semi-supervised acquisition of sarcastic patterns and a classifier. This method was then applied to tweets by Davidov et al. (2010), achieving even better results. González-Ibáñez et al. (2011) constructed a corpus of sarcastic tweets and used it to compare judgements made by humans and machine learning algorithms, concluding that none of them performed well.

More recently, Reyes et al. (2013) defined a complex model for identifying sarcasm which goes far behind the surface of the text and takes into account features on four levels: signatures, degree of unexpectedness, style, and emotional scenarios. They have demonstrated that these features do not help the identification in isolation. However, they do if they are combined in a complex framework. Barbieri and Saggion (2014) focused their approach on the use of lexical and semantic features, such as the frequency of the words in different reference corpora, the length of the words, and the number of related synsets in WordNet (Miller and Fellbaum, 1998).

Finally, Buschmeier et al. (2014) assessed the impact of features used in previous studies, and they provide an important baseline for irony detection in English.

Many datasets for the study of irony and sarcasm in Twitter are nowadays available. Thanks to the use of hashtags, it is easier to collect data with specific characteristics in Twitter. Reyes et al. (2013), for example, created a corpus of 40.000 tweets with four categories: Irony, Education, Humour, and Politics. Among the other resources, it is worth mentioning the sarcastic Amazon product reviews collected by Filatova (2012) and the Italian examples collected and annotated by Gianti et al. (2012), later used in Bosco et al. (2013).

3 Methodology

3.1 Data Pre-processing

Considering the unregulated and arbitrary nature of the texts we are working with, we use some heuristic rules to pre-process them. These rules help us get more reliable syntactic structures when calling the syntactic parser.

Twitter users often use repeated vowels (e.g. "*loooove*") or capitalization (e.g. "*LOVE*") to emphasize certain sentiments or emotions. The normalization consists of removing the repeated vowels (e.g. from "*loooove*" to "*love*") and the capitalization (e.g. from "*LOVE*" to "*love*"). The normalized forms can help improve the parsing accuracy. Moreover, they are saved in a special feature bag as they are important indicators of sentiments, especially when they are in sentiment lexicons. Other special uses of language in tweets include the so-called heavy punctuation and emoticons. In our system, we substitute every combination of exclamation and question marks (e.g. "*?!?!!*") with the form "*?!*". We also compiled an emoticon dictionary based on training data and internet resources.

Another step that we considered relevant at this point is the maximal matching segmentation. The segmentation is, in fact, often lost in tweets, as white spaces and punctuation are not always used in their customary format (e.g. "*yeahright*"). In order to get rid of this problem, we tried to segment all the out of vocabulary tokens through a maximal matching algorithm according to an English dictionary (e.g. the token "*yeahright*" would be segmented as "*yeah right*").

Finally, we use Stanford parser (Klein and Manning, 2003) to get the POS tags and dependency structures of the normalized tweets.

3.2 Feature Set

After the pre-processing, we then extract features of the following kinds.

UniToken Token uni-grams are the basic features in our approach. The normalized forms of the emphasized tokens are put in a special bag with tags describing their emphasis types {duplicate_vowel, capitalized, heavy_punctuation, emoticon}

BiToken Bi-grams of the normalized tokens are also used as features.

DepTokenPair The "parent-child" pairs based on dependency structures are also used as features.

PolarityWin In order to identify the polarity values of tokens, we used four sentiment dictionaries: Opinion Lexicon (Hu and Liu, 2004), Afinn (Nielsen, 2011), MPQA (Wiebe et al., 2005), and SentiWordnet (Baccianella et al., 2010). Their union and their intersection are also used as two additional dictionaries. A window size of five is used to verify whether negations are present. If a negation is present the resulting value is set to zero. Six features are used to save the sum polarity values of a tweet based on the six dictionaries respectively. Besides, we also use features recording the polarity contribution of different POS tags. For example, one possible feature-value pair can be (*adj-mpqa*, 1.0) meaning that according to the dictionary $MPQA$, the sum of the polarity contributed by adjectives in the current tweet is 1.0.

PolarityDep This feature set is similar to $PolarityWin$, but it differs in that the negation is checked in the dependency structure.

PolarShiftWin This feature set is designed for irony which has been discussed in (Riloff et al., 2013). Let us consider the tweets (1) "I love working for eight hours without any break" and (2) "I hate people giving me such a big surprise". In these tweets the verbs "love" (positive) and "hate" (negative) are used with reference to a negative and a positive clause ("working for eight hours without any break" and "people giving me such a big surprise") respectively. Based on a 5-window we check whether a shift of polarity is present.

PolarShiftDep This feature set is similar to $PolarShiftWin$, but it differs in that the shift is checked in the dependency structure.

3.3 Feature Normalization and Evaluation

In order to avoid noise and sparseness, only features that occur at least 3 times are kept. All the feature values are normalized into the range [-1, 1] according to the formula shown in Equation 1, where $f_{i,j}$ is the value of feature j in the ith example, and N is the sample size.

$$norm(f_{i,j}) = \frac{f_{i,j}}{\max\limits_{1 \le k \le N} |f_{k,j}|} \quad (1)$$

We use the correlative coefficient (Pearson's r) measure to rank all the features. Then, we can use the threshold value of r to rule out less important features. The calculation of r is described in Equation 2, where X and Y are the two variables that are evaluated, X_i is the ith sample value of X, Y_i is the ith sample value of Y and N is the sample size.

$$r(X,Y) = \frac{\sum_{i=1}^{N}(X_i - \bar{X})(Y_i - \bar{Y})}{\sqrt{\sum_{i=1}^{N}(X_i - \bar{X})^2}\sqrt{\sum_{i=1}^{N}(Y_i - \bar{Y})^2}} \quad (2)$$

The goal of the first experiment is to find the optimal threshold value of r with all the features as listed in 3.2. Two different models are used: Decision Tree

Feature Set	Features	mse	cosine
Baseline	N/A	1.9847	0.8184
UniToken	136	1.6821	0.8507
+BiToken	410	1.7007	0.8485
+DepTokenPair	409	1.6733	0.8514
+PolarityWin	582	1.6573	0.8524
+PolarityDep	748	1.6436	0.8536
+PolarShiftWin	825	1.6403	0.8542
+PolarShiftDep	841	1.6393	0.8543

Table 1: Experiment result of the 5-fold cross validation by RegTree and SVR on the training data.

Regression model (RepTree) implemented in Weka (Hall et al., 2009) and Support Vector Regression model (SVR) implemented in LibSVM (Chang and Lin, 2011). The result is shown in Figure 1. The best performance is obtained with the value of r between 0.03 and 0.04 with the RepTree model. The experiment also shows that RepTree always outperforms SVR (i.e. higher $cosine$ value and lower $rmse$ value). Therefore, in the following experiments and in the evaluation the RepTree model is adopted.

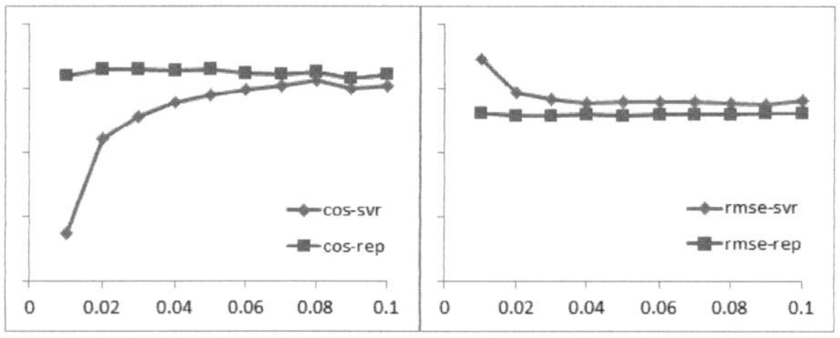

Figure 1: Effect of Pearson value threshold on the overall performance in cosine (left) and root mean squared error (right).

In the second experiment, we use $r = 0.035$ as threshold for feature selection by testing how different kinds of features contribute to the overall performance. The features listed in Section 3.2 are gradually added and their contribution is assessed. If the new feature does not improve the performance, it is removed in the next running. The results of the second experiment are shown in Table 1. The baseline is obtained with a naive prediction using the average polarity value of the training data. As can be seen, only $BiToken$ harms the performance, while all other features contribute to its improvement.

category	mse	cosine
Sarcasm	0.997	0.896
Irony	0.671	0.918
Metaphor	3.917	0.535
Other	4.617	0.290
Overall	2.602	0.687

Table 2: Test result of SemEval Task 11.

3.4 Evaluation Result

Based on the described analysis, for the final test we used RepTree and all the feature sets, except for $BiToken$. The threshold for feature frequency is set to 3 and the r value for feature selection is set to 0.035. Finally, the trained model on the 8,000 tweets is used to predict the sentiment intensity of the evaluation dataset which includes 4,000 tweets. The results are shown in Table 2. Among the fifteen participants in the SemEval task on *Sentiment Analysis of Figurative Language in Twitter*, our model achieves the best performance in the identification of irony, and ranks third in the overall performance.

4 Conclusions

In this paper, we introduced our model for the *Sentiment Analysis of Figurative Language in Twitter* following the track of Task 11 of SemEval 2015. We first used heuristic rules to pre-process the tweets by identifying and normalizing the emphasized tokens. Then, features were extracted based on both window and dependency structures. We adopted polarity shift features with special consideration on the identification of irony. As expected, our system performed best in predicting the sentiment intensity of tweets containing irony according to the evaluation. This confirms the robustness of our design and points to promising development of automatic processing of irony in the future.

Acknowledgments

The work is supported by a General Research Fund (GRF) sponsored by the Research Grants Council (Project no. 543512 & 543810). This work is partially supported by HK PhD Fellowship Scheme, under PF11-00122 and PF12-13656.

References

Ahmed Abbasi, Hsinchun Chen, and Arab Salem. 2008. Sentiment analysis in multiple languages: Feature selection for opinion classification in web forums. *ACM Transactions on Information Systems (TOIS)*, 26(3):12:1–12:34.

Stefano Baccianella, Andrea Esuli, and Fabrizio Sebastiani. 2010. Sentiwordnet 3.0: An enhanced lexical resource for sentiment analysis and opinion mining. In *LREC*, volume 10, pages 2200–2204.

Francesco Barbieri and Horacio Saggion. 2014. Modelling irony in twitter. In *Proceedings of the Student Research Workshop at the 14th Conference of the European Chapter of the Association for Computational Linguistics*, pages 56–64.

Francesco Barbieri, Francesco Ronzano, and Horacio Saggion. 2014. Italian irony detection in twitter: a first approach. In *The First Italian Conference on Computational Linguistics CLiC-it 2014 & the Fourth International Workshop EVALITA 2014*, pages 28–32.

Cristina Bosco, Viviana Patti, and Andrea Bolioli. 2013. Developing corpora for sentiment analysis and opinion mining: the case of irony and senti-tut. *IEEE Intelligent Systems*, 28(2):55–63.

Konstantin Buschmeier, Philipp Cimiano, and Roman Klinger. 2014. An impact analysis of features in a classification approach to irony detection in product reviews.

Paula Carvalho, Luís Sarmento, Mário J Silva, and Eugénio de Oliveira. 2009. Clues for detecting irony in user-generated contents: oh...!! it's so easy;-). In *Proceedings of the 1st international CIKM workshop on Topic-sentiment analysis for mass opinion*, pages 53–56. ACM.

Chih-Chung Chang and Chih-Jen Lin. 2011. Libsvm: A library for support vector machines. *ACM Transactions on Intelligent Systems and Technology*, 2:1–27.

Dmitry Davidov, Oren Tsur, and Ari Rappoport. 2010. Semi-supervised recognition of sarcastic sentences in twitter and amazon. In *Proceedings of the Fourteenth Conference on Computational Natural Language Learning*, pages 107–116.

Elena Filatova. 2012. Irony and sarcasm: Corpus generation and analysis using crowdsourcing. In *Proceedings of Language Resources and Evaluation Conference*, pages 392–398.

Aniruddha Ghosh, Guofu Li, Tony Veale, Paolo Rosso, Ekaterina Shutova, Antonio Reyes, and John Barnden. 2015. Semeval-2015 task 11: Sentiment analysis of figurative language in twitter. In *Proceedings of the International Workshop on Semantic Evaluation (SemEval-2015), Co-located with NAACL and *SEM*, Denver, Colorado, US, June 4-5.

Andrea Gianti, Cristina Bosco, Viviana Patti, Andrea Bolioli, and Luigi Di Caro. 2012. Annotating irony in a novel italian corpus for sentiment analysis. In *Proceedings of the 4th Workshop on Corpora for Research on Emotion Sentiment and Social Signals*, pages 1–7.

Raymond W Gibbs and Herbert L Colston. 2007. *Irony in language and thought: A cognitive science reader*. Psychology Press.

Roberto González-Ibáñez, Smaranda Muresan, and Nina Wacholder. 2011. Identifying sarcasm in twitter: a closer look. In *Proceedings of the 49th Annual Meeting of the Association for Computational Linguistics: Human Language Technologies: short papers*, volume 2, pages 581–586.

H Paul Grice, 1975. *Logic and conversation*, volume 3 of *Syntax and Semantics*, pages 41–58. Academic Press, New York.

Mark Hall, Eibe Frank, Geoffrey Holmes, Bernhard Pfahringer, Peter Reutemann, and Ian H. Witten. 2009. The weka data mining software: An update. *SIGKDD Explorations*, 11.

Yanfen Hao and Tony Veale. 2010. An ironic fist in a velvet glove: Creative mis-representation in the construction of ironic similes. *Minds and Machines*, 20(4):635–650.

Jennifer Hay. 2001. The pragmatics of humor support. *International Journal of Humor Research*, 14:1–27.

Minqing Hu and Bing Liu. 2004. Mining and summarizing customer reviews. In *Proceedings of the tenth ACM SIGKDD international conference on Knowledge discovery and data mining*, pages 168–177. ACM.

Dan Klein and Christopher D. Manning. 2003. Accurate unlexicalized parsing. In *Proceedings of the 41st Annual Meeting on Association for Computational Linguistics-Volume 1*, pages 423–430.

Helga Kotthoff. 2003. Responding to irony in different contexts: On cognition in conversation. *Journal of pragmatics*, 35(9):1387–1411.

Roger J Kreuz and Gina M Caucci. 2007. Lexical influences on the perception of sarcasm. In *Proceedings of the Workshop on computational approaches to Figurative Language*, pages 1–4.

Shoushan Li, Sophia Yat Mei Lee, Ying Chen, Chu-Ren Huang, and Guodong Zhou. 2010. Sentiment classification and polarity shifting. In *Proceedings of the 23rd International Conference on Computational Linguistics*, pages 635–643.

Christine Liebrecht, Florian Kunneman, and Antal van den Bosch. 2013. The perfect solution for detecting sarcasm in tweets# not. In *Proceedings of the 4th Workshop on Computational Approaches to Subjectivity, Sentiment and Social Media Analysis*. New Brunswick, NJ: ACL.

George Miller and Christiane Fellbaum. 1998. Wordnet: An electronic lexical database.

Finn Årup Nielsen. 2011. A new anew: Evaluation of a word list for sentiment analysis in microblogs. In *Proceedings of the ESWC2011 Workshop on 'Making Sense of Microposts': Big things come in small packages.*

Bo Pang and Lillian Lee. 2008. Opinion mining and sentiment analysis. *Foundations and trends in information retrieval*, 2(1-2):1–135.

Quintilian. 1922. *With An English Translation. Harold Edgeworth Butler.* Cambridge, Mass., Harvard University Press; London, William Heinemann, Ltd.

Antonio Reyes, Paolo Rosso, and Tony Veale. 2013. A multidimensional approach for detecting irony in twitter. *Language Resources and Evaluation*, 47(1):239–268.

Ellen Riloff, Ashequl Qadir, Prafulla Surve, Lalindra De Silva, Nathan Gilbert, and Ruihong Huang. 2013. Sarcasm as contrast between a positive sentiment and negative situation. In *Proceedings of Conference on Emperical Methods for Natural Language Processing (EMNLP)*, pages 704–714.

Angus Stevenson. 2010. *Oxford dictionary of English.* Oxford University Press.

Frank Stringfellow Jr. 1994. *The meaning of irony: A psychoanalytic investigation.* SUNY Press.

Oren Tsur, Dmitry Davidov, and Ari Rappoport. 2010. Icwsm-a great catchy name: Semi-supervised recognition of sarcastic sentences in online product reviews. In *In International AAAI Conference on Web and Social Media.*

Piyoros Tungthamthiti, Shirai Kiyoaki, and Masnizah Mohd. 2014. Recognition of sarcasms in tweets based on concept level sentiment analysis and supervised learning approaches. In *Proceedings of Pacific Asia Conference on Language, Information and Computing*, Phuket, Thailand.

Andrea Vanzo, Giuseppe Castellucci, Danilo Croce, and Roberto Basili. 2014. A context based model for sentiment analysis in twitter for the italian language. In R. Basili, A. Lenci, and B. Magnini, editors, *Proceedings of the First Italian Conference on Computational Linguistics CLiC-it & the Fourth International Workshop EVALITA*, pages 379–383, Pisa. Pisa University Press.

Janyce Wiebe, Theresa Wilson, and Claire Cardie. 2005. Annotating expressions of opinions and emotions in language. *Language resources and evaluation*, 39(2-3):165–210.

Gongjun Yan, Wu He, Jiancheng Shen, and Chuanyi Tang. 2014. A bilingual approach for conducting chinese and english social media sentiment analysis. *Computer Networks*, 75:491–503.

KELabTeam: A Statistical Approach on Figurative Language Sentiment Analysis in Twitter

Hoang Long Nguyen, Trung Duc Nguyen and Dosam Hwang
Department of Computer Engineering
Yeungnam University, Korea
{longnh238, duc.nguyentrung, dosamhwang}@gmail.com

Jason J. Jung*
Department of Computer Engineering
Chung-Ang University, Korea
j2jung@gmail.com

Abstract

In this paper, we propose a new statistical method for sentiment analysis of figurative language within short texts collected from Twitter (called tweets) as a part of SemEval-2015 Task 11. Particularly, the proposed model focuses on classifying the tweets into three categories (i.e., sarcastic, ironic, and metaphorical tweet) by extracting two main features (i.e., term features and emotion patterns). Our experiments have been conducted with two datasets, which are Trial set (1000 tweets) and Test set (4000 tweets). Performance is evaluated by cosine similarity to gold annotations. Using this evaluation methodology, the proposed method achieves 0.74 on the Trial set. On the Test set, we achieve 0.90 on sarcastic tweets and 0.89 on ironic tweets.

1 Introduction

Sentiment analysis in computer science is a difficult task which aims to identify the emotion from a given data source. The goal of sentiment analysis is to dissect a given document and determine whether its opinion represent positive, negative, or neutral. There have been many studies (which use lexicon-based methods and machine learning-based methods) to extract and identify the sentiment (Medhat et al., 2014). In case of figurative language, the task becomes more challenging because the document can have secondary or extended meanings. Hence, exactly finding the truth meaning of figurative language is an interesting problem for researchers due to its importance.

*Corresponding author

The first work that we want to mention here is contributed by Reyes and Rosso (2013a). The authors captured ironic sentences from low-level to high-level of irony according to three conceptual layers and their eight textual features. With customer reviews on Amazon, Reyes and Rosso (2012a) contributed an approach for distinguishing irony and non-irony based on six models. Also focusing on detecting irony, Hao and Veale (2010) classifies irony and non-irony by analyzing the large quantity of simile forms with 9-steps sequence. By considering short texts with case-study is Twitter, Reyes et al. (2013b) introduced a model to detect verbal irony by combining four types of conceptual features and their dimensions. Focusing on comprehending metaphor, Shutova et al. (2010) used unsupervised methods to find the associate from a small set of metaphorical expressions by verb and noun clustering processing to detect similarity structure of metaphor. Finally, Reyes et al. (2012b) analyzed humor and irony by adding more features to express the favorable and unfavorable ironic contexts using the theory of textual.

These above studies tried to solve the problem by focusing on lexical level. Therefore, the goal of our research is to find a new way to identify figurative meaning. In this work, we focus on analyzing three types of figurative languages (i.e., sarcasm, irony, and metaphor) on tweets collected from Twitter. With FLASA Model (Figurative Language Analysis using Statistical Approach) to detect multiple types of figurative language, we believe that this is a general model to solve the problem and easy-extending for characterizing other types.

2 System Description

The Training set includes 8000 tweets collected from Twitter. All the tweets are presented in English with three main types of tweets: sarcasm, irony, and metaphor with the respective ratio: 5000 sarcastic tweets, 1000 ironic tweets and 2000 metaphorical tweets.

$$Z = \{< t, s > \mid s \in [-5, 5]\} \quad (1)$$

where Z is a set of tweets in the Training set; t is a tweet, and s is the score of that tweet.

Tweets are extracted into the set of terms. All the tweets are pre-processed by: i) considering in lower-case mode, ii) removing unnecessary information such as: the tagged persons, pronouns, iii) formalizing words (e.g., remove redundancy characters which repeat more than three times, and correct the typos). The hash-tags and symbol in the tweets are kept because of the sentiment expressing property. The set of terms which is extracted from Z:

$$T_Z = \bigcup_{i=1}^{n} t_i = \bigcup_{i=1}^{n} \{w_j \mid w_j \in t_i\}_{j=1}^{m} \quad (2)$$

where T_Z is a set of terms that are extracted from Z; n is the number of tweets in the Training set; w_j is a term; and m is the number of terms that are extracted from Z.

2.1 FLASA Model

FLASA Model includes two main modules which are: i) Content-based Approach Module, and ii) Emotion Pattern-based Approach Module. The final score of a tweet is calculated by using the following formula:

$$S = \alpha \times SC + \beta \times SE \quad (3)$$

where S is the final score of a tweet; SC is the score that is calculated by Content-based Approach module; SE is the score that is calculated by Emotion Pattern-based Approach Module; and α, and β are coefficients identified based on the training error score of the classification model of each approach, with $\alpha + \beta = 1$.

2.1.1 Content-based Approach Module

Content-based approach module evaluate the sentiment of a tweet based on the co-occurrence of terms which are extracted from a tweet using the Training set. This method basically use statistics on the Training set to predict the score of a tweet.

With a tweet t_k that is needed to be annotated. First, it is extracted into set of terms:

$$T_k = \bigcup \{w_i \mid w_i \in t_k\}_{i=1}^{m_k} \quad (4)$$

where T_k is the set of terms extracted from tweet t_k; w_i is a term belongs to tweet t_k; and m_k is the number of terms which are extracted from tweet t_k.

From T_k, we build all the possible combinations from the set of terms to consider all the possible co-occurrence of terms because terms can express different meaning when they appear together. With this step, we can achieve all these aspects: i) all the meaning of the tweet t_k when terms co-exist, and ii) some main terms that affect the score of the tweet t_k. We can consider each of combination is a cluster which can respective as a feature vector:

$$C_k = \left\{ (\delta_k)_{i=1}^{\gamma_k} \middle| \gamma_k = \sum_{j=1}^{m_k} \binom{m_k}{j} \right\} \quad (5)$$

where C_k is the set of all possible clusters extract from the given tweet; δ_k is a cluster, each cluster can be represented as a feature vector; and γ_k is the number of all combinations which are created from terms in T_k.

Each cluster in C_k is represented as a feature vector, with the dimension equals with the number of terms in T_k. From the set of tweets Z in the Training set, we cluster every tweet into the set of cluster C_k. A tweet is assigned into a cluster in the case: i) the distance between a vector to a cluster is minimum comparing to its distance to other clusters, and ii) the distance has to smaller than a defined threshold. This has a significant meaning in expressing the co-occurrence of terms in a tweet. The distance between a tweet and a cluster is calculated by using the following formula:

$$dis(A, B) = 1 - \frac{A^T B}{|A||B|} \quad (6)$$

where $dis(A, B)$ is the distance between a term and a cluster.

Each cluster has a cluster coefficient which is calculated from the number of feature terms of a cluster. If a cluster has more terms, its coefficient will

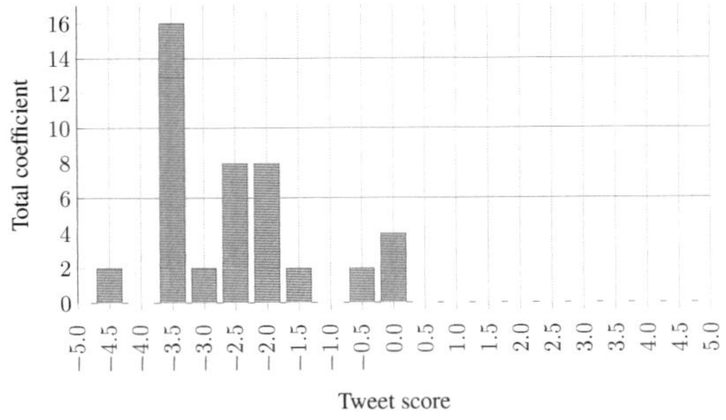

Figure 1: Histogram of score distribution.

be higher. The cluster coefficient can expresses how important it affects the final score of a tweet. Then, from tweets in clusters with their scores and coefficient, the histogram is built to represent the distribution of score in the Training set. Finally, the score of a tweet is annotated by selecting the peak of the histogram.

Example 1. We have 3 clusters: cluster $\{A, B, C\}$: includes 3 tweets ($< t_1, -2.5 >$; $< t_2, -3.5 >$; $< t_3, -3.5 >$); cluster $\{B, C\}$: includes 3 tweets ($< t_4, 0.0 >$; $< t_5, -2.0 >$; $< t_6, -2.0 >$); cluster $\{C\}$: includes 4 tweets ($< t_7, -4.5 >$; $< t_8, -3.0 >$; $< t_9, -0.5 >$; $< t_{10}, -1.5 >$). Figure 1 expresses the above data as histogram. In this case, the score of tweet which is calculated by Content-based Approach Module is -3.5.

2.1.2 Emotion Pattern-based Approach Module

The Emotion Pattern-based Approach Module determine the score of a given tweet based on the emotion change pattern in the content. This approach consists in calculating the sentiment score for each term, then construct the emotion distribution pattern using the termss score in the tweet corresponding to its occurrence positions.

Each term has a score which is calculated based on tweets in the Training set. By finding the score of term and the pattern of tweet, we can understand about how important a term contributes to the final score of a tweet, and about the sentiment degree of a term, whether it's positive, negative, or neutral. The score of a tweet is decided by the pattern of terms in a sentence. Our goal is try to find the real score of a term. In the Traning set, a term belongs to many tweets, and in each tweet, it represents a different score. Assuming that all the tweets have equatable meaning, the score of a term is calculated by the following formula:

$$S_w = \frac{\sum_{i=1}^{l} S_{w_i}}{l} \tag{7}$$

where S_w is the score of a term; and l is the number of tweets which contain this term.

From the set of tweets Z and the set of terms T, we can find the distribution of a term by using the score of tweets which contain it. The peak of histogram is the point at that a term has highest distribution with a score. At the beginning (i^0 step), each term has the score which is selected from the peak of its respective histogram. Then, the score in the step $i + 1$ is calculated by using the formula:

$$S_w^i = \frac{S_w^{i-1} * P(S_t|w)}{\sum_{j=1}^{n}(S_{w_j}^{i-1} * P(S_t|w_j))} * S_t \tag{8}$$

where S_w^i is the score of a term at step i_{th}; S_t is the score of tweet that contains this term; and $P(S_t|w)$ is the probability that a term has the score with given tweet score.

This step is conducted repeatably until the score of term at step i^{th} greater than the score of term at step $(i-1)^{th}$ a value of defined epsilon, with epsilon is extremely small.

With each tweet in the Training set, it is extracted into the list of terms and then create a pattern based on its term scores as we mentioned above. Due to the different of the number of terms in a tweet, the signal of pattern is needed to be scaled by using an interpolation function. The pattern is scaled to the maximum possible terms that a tweet in the Training set contain in order to be able to map all the tweets into vectors with same dimension.

Example 2. We have a tweet: *@SamySamson wow you're soooo funny #sarcasm it actually hurts a bunch!*. From this tweet, we have list of terms and their scores: ($< wow, -0.2057831 >$; $< soo, -0.1552674 >$; $< funny, -0.19274 >$; $< \#sarcasm, -2.34994 >$; $< actually, -0.03287 >$; $< hurts, -0.16091 >$; $< bunch, -0.02096 >$). Figure 2 expresses the pattern of the above data after the term scores are scaled down by the size of largest terms in a tweet found in the Training set. Here, the maximum number of terms that a tweet contains in the Training set is 24.

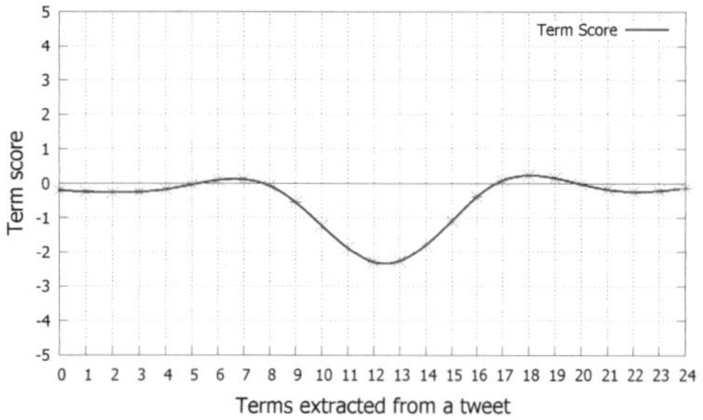

Figure 2: Sequential pattern of tweet term scores after length normalization.

Using the set of patterns from the Training set, we construct a vector space representation whereby each dimension signifies a match to one of the extracted patterns. We then train a decision tree based classifier to predict from these vectors the integer sentiment labels $[-5..5]$ of the corresponding tweets. And that is the score which is annotated by using Emotion Pattern-based Approach Module.

3 Experimental results

The test data comprises 4000 tweets with both figurative and non-figurative tweets with 70% of them are sarcasm, irony, or metaphor; and 30% of the data are other. We evaluate the test with: $i)$ Content-based Approach Module, $ii)$ Emotion Pattern-based Approach Module, and $iii)$ Combined Module.

FLASA Model works well with figurative tweets. Using cosine similarity to gold annotations to evaluate the system, the highest performance that we got is 0.90 with irony type, and the next is sarcastic type with 0.89. With metaphor type, we achieve 0.34 with annotated tweets. About non-figurative tweets, the performance is still low due to the tweets in the Training set. The root cause is that there are no non-figurative tweets in the Training set. If we add more non-figurative tweets to the Training set in order to learn, the result will be improved. Fig. 3 shows the performance that we got from testing our approach on the Test set.

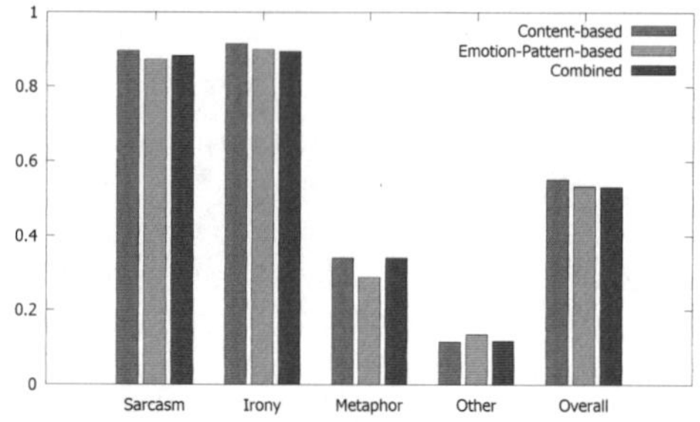

Figure 3: The performance of FLASA Model on Test set using cosine similarity.

4 Conclusion

In this paper, we proposed a new approach for analyzing the sentiment of figurative language basedon the statistics with two main approaches: content and emotional pattern. By combining all these features, we enhanced the performance of our algorithm. However, the result of FLASA Model is affected by these following reasons:

$i)$ Almost all the tweets in the Training set are sarcastic tweets, and irony tweets. Due to this reason, the performance on metaphor tweets, and non-figurative tweets are still low.

$ii)$ Is this work, we only consider unigram model when calculating the score for terms in Emotion Pattern-based Approach. This leads to the miss-expressing meaning of terms if they are co-showing an specific sense in a phrase.

$iii)$ Our training data has a little noise because some tweets are written in an unstandardized way(e.g. abbreviation word, and repeated word).

In the next work, we will improve the performance by increasing the number of tweets in the Training set, especially the metaphor tweets, and non-figurative tweets. Bigram or trigram model will be used to clearly comprehend the sentiment of a tweet. Moreover, we will add more heuristic to completely formalize tweets. Finally, we will extend FLASA Model to analyze the data from the other social network, such as Facebook, Instagram, Flick, and Google Plus also.

Acknowledgment

This work was supported by the National Research Foundation of Korea (NRF) grant funded by the Korea government (MSIP) (NRF-2014R1A2A2A05007154). Also, this research was supported by the MSIP (Ministry of Science, ICT & Future Planning), Korea, under the ITRC (Information Technology Research Cetner) support program (NIPA-2014-H0301-14-1044) supervised by the NIPA (National ICT Industry Promotion Agency).

References

Hao, Y., & Veale, T. 2010. *An Ironic Fist in a Velvet Glove: Creative Mis-Representation in the Construction of Ironic Similes.* Minds and Machines, 20(4), 635-650.

Kaur, A., & Gupta, V. 2013. *A Survey on Sentiment Analysis and Opinion Mining Techniques.* Ain Journal of Emerging Technologies in Web Intelligence, 5(4), 367-371.

Kumon-Nakamura, S., Glucksberg, S., & Brown, M. 1995. *How about Another Piece of Pie: The Allusional Pretense Theory of Discourse Irony.* Journal of Experimental Psychology General, 124(1), 3-21.

Medhat, W., Hassan, A., & Korashy, H. 2014. *Sentiment Analysis Algorithms and Applications: A Survey.* Ain Shams Engineering Journal, 5(4), 1093-1113.

Reyes, A., & Rosso, P. 2013a. *On the Difficulty of Automatically Detecting Irony: Beyond a Simple Case of Negation.* Knowledge and Information Systems, 40(3), 595-614.

Reyes, A., Rosso, P., & Veale, T. 2013b. *A Multidimensional Approach for Detecting Irony in Twitter.* Languages Resources and Evaluation, 47(1), 239-268.

Reyes, A., & Rosso, P. 2012a. *Making Objective Decisions from Subjective Data: Detecting Irony in Customers Reviews.* Journal on Decision Support Systems, 53(4), 754-760.

Reyes, A., Rosso, P., & Buscaldi, D. 2012b. *From Humor Recognition to Irony Detection: The Figurative Language of Social Media.* Data & Knowledge Engineering, 74(0), 1-12.

Shutova, E., Sun, L., & Korhonen, A. 2010. *Metaphor Identification Using Verb and Noun Clustering.* Proceedings of the 23rd International Conference on Computational Linguistics (COLING 2010), Beijing, China, August 23-27, pp. 1002-1010.

LT3: Sentiment Analysis of Figurative Tweets: piece of cake #NotReally

Cynthia Van Hee, Els Lefever and Véronique hoste
LT[3], Language and Translation Technology Team
Department of Translation, Interpreting and Communication – Ghent University
Groot-Brittanniëlaan 45, 9000 Ghent, Belgium
Firstname.Lastname@UGent.be

Abstract

This paper describes our contribution to the SemEval-2015 Task 11 on sentiment analysis of figurative language in Twitter. We considered two approaches, classification and regression, to provide fine-grained sentiment scores for a set of tweets that are rich in sarcasm, irony and metaphor. To this end, we combined a variety of standard lexical and syntactic features with specific features for capturing figurative content. All experiments were done using supervised learning with LIBSVM. For both runs, our system ranked fourth among fifteen submissions.

1 Introduction

Handling figurative language is currently one of the most challenging tasks in NLP. Figurative language is often characterized by linguistic devices such as sarcasm, irony, metaphors, and humour. Their meaning goes beyond the literal meaning and is therefore often hard to capture, even for humans. However, as an increasing part of our daily communication takes place on social media (e.g. Twitter, Facebook), which are prone to figurative language use, there is an urgent need for automatic systems that recognize and understand figurative online content. This is especially the case in the field of sentiment analysis where the presence of figurative language in subjective text can significantly undermine the classification accuracy.

Understanding figurative language often requires world knowledge, which cannot easily be accessed by machines. Moreover, figurative language rapidly evolves due to changes in vocabulary and language, which makes it difficult to train machine learning algorithms. Nevertheless, the identification of non-literal uses of language has attracted a fair amount of research interest recently. Veale (2012) investigated the relation between irony and our stereotypical knowledge of a domain and showed how the insight in stereotypical norms helps to recognize and understand ironic utterances. Reyes et al. (2013) built an irony model for Twitter for which they relied on a set of textual features for capturing ironic tweets. Their model obtained promising results concerning recall (84%). In what relates to the detection of metaphors, Turney et al. (2011) introduced an algorithm for distinguishing between metaphorical and literal word usages based on the degree of abstractness of a word's context. More recent work by Tsvetkov et al. (2014) presents a cross-lingual model based on lexical semantic word features for metaphor detection in English, Spanish, Farsi and Russian.

To date, most studies on figurative language use have focussed on the detection of linguistic devices such as sarcasm, irony and metaphor. By contrast, only a few studies have investigated how these devices affect sentiment analysis. Indeed, as stated by Maynard (2014), it is not sufficient to determine whether a text contains sarcasm or not. Instead, we need to measure its impact on sentiment analysis if we want to improve the state-of-the-art in sentiment analysis systems.

In this paper we describe our contribution to the SemEval-2015 shared task: *Sentiment Analysis of Figurative Language in Twitter* (Ghosh et al., 2015).

Our objective is to provide fine-grained sentiment scores for a set of tweets that are rich in sarcasm, irony and metaphor. The datasets for training, development and testing were provided by the task organizers. The training dataset contains 8,000 tweets (5,000 sarcastic, 1,000 ironic and 2,000 metaphorical) labeled with a sentiment score between -5 and 5. This training set was provided with both integer and real-valued sentiment scores. The trial and test sets were comparable to the training corpus and contain 1,000[1] and 4,000 labeled instances, respectively. All experiments were done using LIBSVM (Chang and Lin, 2011).

We submitted two runs for the competition. To this end, we built two models based on supervised learning: 1) a classification-based (C-SVC) and 2) a regression-based approach (epsilon-SVR). For both models, we implemented a number of word-based, lexical, sentiment and syntactic features in combination with specific features for capturing figurative content such as sarcasm. Evaluation was done by calculating the cosine similarity distance between the predicted and the gold-standard sentiment labels.

The remainder of this paper is structured as follows: Section 2 presents our system description whereas Section 2.2 gives an overview of the features we implemented. The experimental setup is described in Section 3, followed by our results in Section 4. Finally, we draw conclusions in Section 5 where we also suggest some directions for future research.

2 System Description

The main purpose of this paper was to develop a system for the fine-grained sentiment classification of figurative tweets. We tackled this problem by using classification and regression approaches and provided each instance with a sentiment score between -5 and 5. In addition to more standard NLP features (bags-of-words, PoS-tags, etc.), we implemented a number of features for capturing the figurative character of the tweets. In this section, we outline our sentiment analysis pipeline and describe the linguistic preprocessing and feature extraction.

[1]As some tweets were made inaccessible by their creators, we were able to download only 914 of them

2.1 Linguistic Preprocessing

All tweets were tokenized and PoS-tagged using the Carnegie Mellon University Twitter Part-of-Speech-Tagger (Gimpel et al., 2011). Lemmatization was done using the LT3 LeTs Preprocess Toolkit (Van de Kauter et al., 2013). We used a caseless parsing model of the Stanford parser (de Marneffe et al., 2006) for a dependency representation of the messages. As a final step, we tagged all named entities using the Twitter NLP tools for Named Entity Recognition (Ritter et al., 2011).

2.2 Features

As a first step, we implemented a set of features that have shown to perform well for sentiment classification in previous research (Van Hee et al., 2014). These include word-based features (e.g. bag-of-words), lexical features (e.g. character flooding), sentiment features (e.g. an overall sentiment score per tweet, based on existing sentiment lexicons), and syntactic features (e.g. dependency relation features)[2]. To provide some abstraction, we also added PoS n-gram features to the set of bag-of-words features.

Nevertheless, as a substantial part of the data we are confronted with is of a figurative nature, we implemented a series of additional features for capturing potential clues, for example of sarcasm, in the tweets[3].

Contrast – Binary feature indicating whether a contrastive sentiment (i.e. at least one positive and one negative sentiment word) is contained by the instance.

Interjection Count – Numeric feature indicating how many interjections are contained by an instance. This value is normalized by dividing it by the number of tokens in the instance. As stated by (Carvalho et al., 2009), interjections may be potential clues for irony detection.

Sarcasm Hashtag – Binary feature indicating whether an instance contains a hashtag that may indicate the presence of sarcasm. To this end, a list of

[2]For a detailed description of these features we refer to Van Hee et al. (2014).

[3]A number of these features (i.e. *contradiction*, *sudden change*, and *temporal imbalance*) are inspired by Reyes et al. (2013).

$\approx$ 100 sarcasm-related hashtags was extracted from the training data.

Punctuation Mark Count – Normalized numeric feature indicating the number of punctuation marks that are contained by an instance.

Emoticon count – Normalized numeric feature indicating the number of emoticons that are contained by an instance.

Contradiction – Binary feature that indicates whether an instance contains a linguistic contradiction marker (i.e. words like *nonetheless*, *yet*, *however*).

Sudden Change – Binary feature that indicates whether an instance contains a linguistic marker of a sudden change in the narrative of the tweet (i.e. words like *suddenly*, *out of the blue*).

Temporal Imbalance – Binary feature indicating the presence of a temporal imbalance (i.e. both present and past tenses are used) in the narrative of a message.

Polysemy – Normalized numeric feature indicating how many polyseme words are contained by an instance. As polyseme are considered those words that have more than seven different meanings according to WordNet[4], which may be an indication of metaphorical language.

3 Experimental Setup

As the training instances were provided with both integer and real-valued sentiment scores, we used two different approaches to the fine-grained sentiment labeling. Firstly, we implemented a classification approach where each tweet had to be given a sentiment label on an eleven-point scale ranging from -5 to 5. Secondly, we used regression to predict a real-valued sentiment score for each tweet, which could be any numeric value between -5 and 5.

Two feature sets were used throughout the experiments: firstly, we included a number of word-based, lexical, sentiment and syntactic features (we refer to these as the *sentiment* feature set). Secondly, we implemented an additional set of features for capturing possibly figurative content such as irony and metaphors. These features are referred to as the *figurative* feature set.

[4]Fellbaum, C. (1998)

Using 5-fold cross-validation on the training data, we performed a grid search to find the optimal cost and gamma parameters for both classification (c = 0.03, g = 0.008) and regression (c = 8, g = 0.063). For regression, an optimal epsilon value of p = 0.5 was determined.

As a first approach to evaluating our features, we used a subset of the trial data[5]. Secondly, we (randomly) split the data into 90% for training and 10% for testing. We calculated a baseline using the majority class label -3 (see Table 1). Tables 2 and 3 present the results on the training and trial data that were obtained throughout the experiments both for classification and for regression.

Evaluation Set	Cosine Similarity
Trial data	0.59
10% training set	0.80
Averaged baseline	**0.70**

Table 1: Majority class baseline.

Evaluation Set	feature set	Cosine Similarity
Trial data	sentiment	0.72
	figurative	0.74
10% training set	sentiment	0.82
	figurative	0.83

Table 2: Experimental results for classification (after a parameter grid search).

Evaluation Set	feature set	Cosine Similarity
Trial data	sentiment	0.75
	figurative	0.74
10% training set	sentiment	0.85
	figurative	0.84

Table 3: Experimental results for regression (after a parameter grid search).

As the table shows, adding figurative language specific features proves to be beneficial for classification. For regression, by contrast, adding more features does not improve the results on the training and trial data. However, both approaches clearly outperform the baseline.

[5]We only considered the tweets that were not included by the training data.

4 Competition Results

We submitted two runs for this task. For our first run, we implemented a classification approach whereas we used regression for the second run. As the official test data also contains a substantial part of regular Twitter data, we included both the standard sentiment feature set and the figurative feature set.

Our competition results can be found in Tables 4 and 5.

	Overall	Sarcasm	Irony	Metaphor	Other
Cosine Similarity	**0.66** (4/15)	0.89	0.90	0.44	0.35
MSE	**3.40** (4/15)	1.29	1.22	5.67	5.44

Table 4: Competition results for classification.

	Overall	Sarcasm	Irony	Metaphor	Other
Cosine Similarity	**0.65** (4/15)	0.87	0.86	0.36	0.36
MSE	**2.91** (4/15)	1.29	1.08	4.79	4.50

Table 5: Competition results for regression.

As shown in tables 4 and 5, our system achieved an overall cosine similarity score of 0.66 and 0.65 for the classification-based and regression-based approaches respectively and ranked fourth among fifteen submissions for both runs. When considering the competition results per category, we see that our system performs particularly well on the sarcasm and irony classes. For the latter, our classification performance (cosine similarity = 0.90) corresponds with that of the best reported system.

5 Conclusions and Future Work

We experimented with two experimental setups to compare the performance of a sentiment classifier using 1) more standard sentiment features and 2) features that may capture sarcastic content. The results of our experiments show that adding features that are specific to figurative language improves the performance of our classification approach. However, it does not improve the performance for regression.

An error analysis revealed that our system's performance benefits from the information provided by sentiment lexicon features. Given the high distribution of the negative class labels in this corpus, some positive instances are incorrectly assigned a negative class label:

- *Im not about that life though lol, Im literally a natural woman and I am proud of it :)* **(-3)**

Another remark that should be made is that some of our irony-specific features are possibly too coarse-grained. The contrast feature for instance, was sometimes activated even though the tweet under investigation was meant rather literally than sarcastically:

- *RT @laurenwalter: underwater walking was* ***pretty bloody amazing****! literally wanted to stay under there! was such an experience!! loved it!!*

The contrast feature was activated for this tweet since *bloody* was identified as a negative sentiment word whereas *pretty* and *amazing* are positive sentiment words. This problem may be solved by only considering the head of the adjectival phrase (*amazing*) as a sentiment word.

In this paper, we developed a sentiment analysis pipeline that takes irony and sarcasm clues into account to provide a fine-grained sentiment score for tweets. In future research, it would be interesting to implement a cascaded approach where 1) the output of a sarcasm detection system is used as a feature for a sentiment classifier or 2) a sarcasm detection system is used as a post-processing step where the sentiment label given by a regular sentiment classifier is flipped if the utterance is meant sarcastically.

Moreover, we will search for better features for modeling sarcasm in tweets and we aim to rebalance the data to approximate a realistic distribution of sarcastic messages in a random stream of Twitter messages.

To improve sentiment classification of metaphorical tweets, a classifier might benefit from word sense disambiguation and knowledge about stereotypes and commonly used similes.

Finally, we aim to perform feature selection since abounding bag-of-words features often suffer from overfitting. This way, they may introduce noise and hence decrease the classification accuracy.

References

Paula Carvalho, Luís Sarmento, Mário J. Silva, and Eugénio de Oliveira. 2009. Clues for detecting irony in user-generated contents: Oh...!! it's "so easy" ;-). In *Proceedings of the 1st International CIKM Workshop on Topic-sentiment Analysis for Mass Opinion*, TSA '09, pages 53–56, New York, NY, USA.

Chih-Chung Chang and Chih-Jen Lin. 2011. LIBSVM: A library for support vector machines. *ACM Transactions on Intelligent Systems and Technology*, 2:27:1–27:27.

Marie-Catherine de Marneffe, Bill MacCartney, and Christopher D. Manning. 2006. Generating Typed Dependency Parses from Phrase Structure Parses. In *Proc. of LREC'06*, pages 449–454, Genoa, Italy.

Christiane Fellbaum. 1998. *WordNet: An Electronic Lexical Database*.

A. Ghosh, Guofu Li, Tony Veale, Paolo Rosso, Ekaterina Shutova, Antonio Reyes, and John Barnden. 2015. Semeval-2015 task 11: Sentiment analysis of figurative language in Twitter. In *Proceedings of the International Workshop on Semantic Evaluation (SemEval-2015)*, Denver, Colorado, USA.

Kevin Gimpel, Nathan Schneider, Brendan O'Connor, Dipanjan Das, Daniel Mills, Jacob Eisenstein, Michael Heilman, Dani Yogatama, Jeffrey Flanigan, and Noah A. Smith. 2011. Part-of-speech tagging for Twitter: Annotation, features, and experiments. In *Proceedings of the 49th Annual Meeting of the Association for Computational Linguistics: Human Language Technologies: Short Papers - Volume 2*, HLT '11, pages 42–47, Stroudsburg, PA, USA.

Diana Maynard and Mark Greenwood. 2014. Who cares about sarcastic tweets? investigating the impact of sarcasm on sentiment analysis. In *Proceedings of the Ninth International Conference on Language Resources and Evaluation (LREC'14)*, Reykjavik, Iceland.

Antonio Reyes, Paolo Rosso, and Tony Veale. 2013. A multidimensional approach for detecting irony in Twitter. *Language Resources and Evaluation*, pages 238–269.

Alan Ritter, Sam Clark, Mausam, and Oren Etzioni. 2011. Named entity recognition in tweets: An experimental study. In *Proceedings of the Conference on Empirical Methods in Natural Language Processing*, EMNLP '11, pages 1524–1534, Stroudsburg, PA, USA.

Yulia Tsvetkov, Leonid Boytsov, Anatole Gershman, Eric Nyberg, and Chris Dyer. 2014. Metaphor detection with cross-lingual model transfer. *ACL 2014*, pages 248–258.

Peter D. Turney, Yair Neuman, Dan Assaf, and Yohai Cohen. 2011. Literal and metaphorical sense identification through concrete and abstract context. In *Proceedings of the Conference on Empirical Methods in Natural Language Processing*, EMNLP '11, pages 680–690, Stroudsburg, PA, USA.

Marjan Van de Kauter, Geert Coorman, Els Lefever, Bart Desmet, Lieve Macken, and Véronique Hoste. 2013. LeTs Preprocess: the multilingual LT3 linguistic preprocessing toolkit. *Computational Linguistics in the Netherlands Journal*, 3:103–120.

Cynthia Van Hee, Marjan Van de Kauter, Orphée De Clercq, Els Lefever, and Véronique Hoste. 2014. LT3: Sentiment classification in user-generated content using a rich feature set. In *Proceedings of the 8th International Workshop on Semantic Evaluation (SemEval 2014)*, pages 406–410, Dublin, Ireland.

Tony Veale. 2012. Detecting and generating ironic comparisons: An application of creative information retrieval. In *AAAI Fall Symposium: Artificial Intelligence of Humor*, volume FS-12-02 of *AAAI Technical Report*.

PRHLT: Combination of Deep Autoencoders with Classification and Regression Techniques for SemEval-2015 Task 11

Parth Gupta
PRHLT Research Center
Universitat Politècnica de València
Camino de Vera, s/n
46022 Valencia, SPAIN
pgupta@dsic.upv.es

Jon Ander Gómez
PRHLT Research Center
Universitat Politècnica de València
Camino de Vera, s/n
46022 Valencia, SPAIN
jon@dsic.upv.es

Abstract

This paper presents the system we developed for Task 11 of SemEval 2015. Our system had two stages: The first one was based on deep autoencoders for extracting features to compactly represent tweets. The next stage consisted of a classifier or a regression function for estimating the polarity value assigned to a given tweet. We tested several techniques in order to choose the ones with the highest accuracy. Finally, three regression techniques revealed as the best ones for assigning the polarity value to tweets. We presented six runs corresponding to three regression different techniques in combination with two variants of the autoencoder, one with input as bags of words and another with input as bags of character 3-grams.

1 Introduction

Sentiment Analysis from texts is a growing field of research due to its social and economic relevance. Task 11 of SemEval-2015 (Semantic Evaluation Exercises) was proposed to the research community in order to foster the development of systems and techniques for Sentiment Analysis (Ghosh et al., 2015).

We faced this challenging task with a system based on deep autoencoders in combination with classification and regression techniques. We used deep autoencoders to extract features from tweets by means of two ways of splitting text: i) words and ii) character 3-grams. The training of autoencoders was unsupervised. The extracted features (10) and a few manually added features (5) were used for training classifiers or regression functions to estimate the tweet's polarity value.

The rest of the paper is organized as follows. Section 2 describes the proposed system. Section 3 presents the obtained results on the test set. Finally, conclusions are discussed in Section 4.

2 System Description

Our system consists of two stages: (1) Dimensionality reduction by means of deep autoencoders. (2) Polarity value assignment by using different classification and regression techniques.

The text of tweets was preprocessed before being used as input to the autoencoders. The autoencoders take as input a representation of each tweet. Two different representations were used: bags of words and bags of character 3-grams. In both cases the output of an autoencoder was a vector of 10 real values. Optionally we added other features in order to improve the polarity assignment, these additional features are binary features indicating whether some symbols or hash tags appear in the tweet. The idea behind adding these extra features is to set a context for learning under their influence. The different subsets of used features are described in subsection 2.3. The step of assigning a polarity value to a given tweet was carried out by a classifier or a regression function. Several techniques for classification and regression were tested. Table 2 shows the relation of the used techniques.

2.1 Tweets Preprocessing

As mentioned above, the input for the autoencoders was prepared from two different ways of splitting

Pattern or regular expression	New text
"#"	" #"
"@"	" @"
"&"	" & "
"<"	"<"
">"	">"
"&.*;"	" HTML "
"\\u0092"	"'"
"[0-9]+:[0-9]+[Aa][Mm]"	" H "
"[0-9]+:[0-9]+"	" H "
"[0-9]+[Aa][Mm]"	" H "
"http[s]*://[a-zA-Z0-9\\./-_]+"	""
"http[s]*:/+"	""
"http"	""
"@[_a-zA-Z0-9]+"	""
" : "	" "
" [0-9\\.-:]+ "	" N "
"[\\u00ff-\\uffff]+"	" A "
"!!!+"	"!3+"
"\\?\\?\\?+"	"?3+"
"\\.\\.\\.+"	"?.+"
"\\p{Punct}{3,}"	" P "
"> >"	">"
"< <"	"<"
">+"	">"
"<+"	">"
"-+"	"-"
" +"	" "
" "	"_"
"_+"	"_"

Table 1: Substitution rules used for normalizing the text of tweets. The double quotes are used here as delimiters, like in Java for String literals, they are not part of the pattern. Rules are presented in the same format they were used as arguments for the method `replaceAll()` of class `String` of Java. Rules were applied in the same order they appear in this table.

the text of tweets. Before the splitting step, a cleaning process was carried out by applying a set of substitutions. The goal was to normalize the text before generating the bags of words or character 3-grams.

Table 1 shows the rules used for carrying out such substitutions. These rules were extracted by us after analyzing the text of tweets corresponding to the training set. The order in that these rules were applied was relevant to the final result. The desired effects were the following:

- Removing URLs from the text of tweets. We assumed URLs were not relevant for guessing the polarity.
- User identifiers were also removed.
- Emoticons and possible animations were also reduced to a capital `A`. We were interested in knowing whether they appear or not.
- Sequences of repeated symbols or punctuation signs were reduced to one instance or a sequence to indicate the repetition.
- Numbers or dates were reduced to a capital letter indicating their appearance.
- Some symbols were forced to be preceded by a white space in order to facilitate the posterior splitting into words.
- Sequences of several white spaces were reduced to one white space and all white spaces were converted to underscores.

After the normalizing step, the splitting step was carried out in order to prepare the input for deep autoencoders. Two splitting ways were applied, one for separating words using white spaces (or underscores) and another one using character sequences of size 3 (character 3-grams).

In the case a tweet was represented as a bag of words, all the words found in the training set were used. A special entry for out-of-vocabulary words was introduced into the word table for generating the bags of words. We considered tokens as words those including only letters from the Latin alphabet. Numbers or other symbols were not included.

In the case of representing tweets as bags of character 3-grams, only those that appeared three or more times in the training set were used. The remaining ones were considered as out-of-vocabulary. A special entry for out-of-vocabulary 3-grams was introduced into the 3-grams table for generating the bags of 3-grams.

2.2 Deep Autoencoders

Autoencoders provide an unsupervised way to learn low-dimensional embeddings of the data. Such representation can be used for discriminative tasks. We used a deep autoencoder to extract such features. The fundamental block of our autoencoder was the restricted Boltzman machine (RBM). We used the contrastive-divergence algorithm for pretraining the autoencoder followed by the fine-tuning to minimize the reconstruction error shown in Eq. 1 (Hinton and Salakhutdinov, 2006).

$$J = \|X - X'\|^2 \tag{1}$$

where, X is the original vector and X' is its reconstruction.

The architecture[1] of the autoencoder was $|X|$-200-100-100-10 and the sigmoid function was used to add non-linearity to the hidden layers except for the final layer which was linear. We used replicated softmax to model count data in the visible layer of the autoencoder (Hinton and Salakhutdinov, 2009).

2.3 Classification and Regression Techniques

Different classification and regression techniques were tested in order to figure out which ones were the more appropriated for estimating the polarity of tweets. This checking process was carried out with the training set. We used the Scikit-Learn toolkit (Pedregosa et al., 2011) for all the tested techniques.

Given the output of each autoencoder we used three different sets of features:

1. Just the vectors of 10 real values obtained from autoencoders. 10 features.
2. Same 10 features as above plus five binary features indicating whether some hash tags or symbols were present in the tweet. The additional five binary features corresponded to the presence of three hash tags `#irony`, `#sarcasm`, `#not`, and whether the tweet contains quotes or emoticons. In total 15 features.
3. Same 15 features as for the second set plus additional binary features for indicating whether any of the hash tags found in the training set was present in the tweet. In total 3580 (10+5+3565) features.

Table 2 shows the list of all classification and regression techniques used in the second stage of our system. All techniques are used from the Scikit-Learn toolkit (Pedregosa et al., 2011). For training each classifier or regression function we used the same input data, i.e. the feature vectors representing each tweet from the training set and its polarity.

The output of classifiers is the integer value of the polarity, but in the case of regression functions the output value is truncated to the nearest integer.

[1]We did not notice any difference in performance empirically with other configurations with a general caution that much larger number of parameters model might lead to over-fitting.

The different classification and regression techniques used in the second stage were configured with the default values for their hyperparameters (Pedregosa et al., 2011). Some variations of hyperparameters were tested, but no further improvements were observed. Our purpose was to check which techniques were more suitable.

A more exhaustive search in order to find optimal combinations of hyperparameters for each technique would be an interesting extension of this work.

3 Results

Tables 2 and 3 show the results obtained with the test set. The whole training set was used for training all the tested techniques. It could be observed that the best results were obtained by the Ensemble of Extremely Randomized Trees (or Extra-Trees) used for regression (Geurts et al., 2006). Other ensemble techniques presented similar results. Focusing our attention on Table 3 and comparing with the results shown in Table 2, it could be observed as two variants of SVMs get results similar to the best ones, but no significant improvements were observed when using the set of 3580 features.

4 Conclusions

We developed a system for participating in Task 11 of SemEval-2015 which consisted of two stages. In the first stage stage we used deep autoencoders for obtaining a compact representation of tweets. We tried three sets of features that were used as input for different classification and regression techniques.

Results obtained in average from the 10-fold cross-validation we carried out with the training set revealed that the three most appropriated techniques were three ensembles: Extremely Randomized Trees, Random Forest and Bagging of Decision Trees. The regression setting of these techniques performed better than that of classification.

The fact that the techniques which obtained the best results are purely non-parametric and have no weights for approximating the output value, tell us that the obtained compact representation of tweets by means of deep autoencoders needs more analysis. An effort in exploring more configurations of autoencoders will help us to obtain better compact representations, which we plan to do in future. We

Classification or Regression Technique	Cosine Similarity			
	3-grams 10	words 10	3-grams 15	words 15
Automatic Relevance Determination Regressor	0.469	0.451	0.462	0.525
Bayesian Ridge Linear Regressor	0.552	0.562	0.609	0.618
Elastic Net Regressor	0.544	0.557	0.541	0.557
Ensemble AdaBoost Regressor Exponential	0.311	0.332	0.377	0.351
Ensemble AdaBoost Regressor Linear	0.540	0.556	0.554	0.587
Ensemble AdaBoost Regressor Squared	0.199	0.213	0.314	0.212
Ensemble Bagging Regressor with Decision Trees	0.558	0.549	0.593	0.587
Ensemble of Extra Trees Classifier	0.549	0.542	0.549	0.537
Ensemble of Extra Trees Regressor	0.565	0.557	**0.623**	0.610
Ensemble of Random Forests Classifier	0.535	0.542	0.536	0.541
Ensemble of Random Forests Regressor	0.554	0.555	0.592	0.610
KNN Classifier with inverse distance weights	0.497	0.497	0.501	0.495
KNN Classifier with uniform weights	0.507	0.526	0.517	0.518
LARS Lasso Linear Regressor	0.546	0.546	0.546	0.546
Lasso Linear Regressor	0.545	0.557	0.545	0.557
Logistic Regression (Classifier)	0.556	0.542	0.545	0.541
Perceptron Classifier	0.469	0.451	0.462	0.525
Passive Aggresive Regressor	0.561	0.378	0.564	0.384
RANSAC Regressor	0.507	0.532	0.547	0.592
Ridge Linear Regressor	0.552	0.563	0.608	0.620
SVM Linear Classifier	0.555	0.539	0.552	0.545
SVM Linear Regressor	0.551	0.552	0.583	0.570
SVM Polynomial Classifier	0.545	0.539	0.540	0.550
SVM Polynomial Regressor	0.587	0.560	0.599	0.610
SVM RBF Classifier	0.541	0.542	0.541	0.538
SVM RBF Regressor	0.593	0.562	0.604	0.560

Table 2: Results of all the tested techniques for the two kind of inputs used for the deep autoencoder: 3-grams and words, and for feature sets with 10 and 15 features.

Classification or Regression Technique	Cosine Similarity	
	3-grams 3580 features	words 3580 features
Bayesian Ridge Linear Regressor	0.605	0.621
Ensemble Bagging Regressor with Decision Trees	0.595	0.605
Ensemble of Extra Trees Regressor	**0.626**	0.596
Ensemble of Random Forests Regressor	0.593	0.616
Ridge Linear Regressor	0.596	0.615
SVM Linear Regressor	0.598	0.593
SVM RBF Regressor	0.610	0.566

Table 3: Results of some of the tested techniques for the two kind of inputs used for the deep autoencoder: 3-grams and words, and for the feature set with 3580 features.

also plan to use the tweet polarity information during the fine-tuning stage of training as an additional supervised component.

Acknowledgments

The research work of the first author is supported by the FPI grant from UPV.

References

Pierre Geurts, Damien Ernst and Louis Wehenkel. 2006. Extremely Randomized Trees. *Machine Learning* (ISSN 0885-6125) vol. 63, no. 1, pp. 2–42. Kluwer Academic Publishers, 2006

Aniruddha Ghosh, Guofu Li, Tony Veale, Paolo Rosso, Ekaterina Shutova, Antonio Reyes and John Barnden. 2015. SemEval-2015 Task 11: Sentiment Analysis of Figurative Language in Twitter. In Proc. *Int. Workshop on Semantic Evaluation (SemEval-2015)*, Co-located with NAACL and *SEM, Denver, Colorado, US, June 4-5, 2015

Geoffrey Hinton and Ruslan Salakhutdinov. 2006. Reducing the Dimensionality of Data with Neural Networks. *Science* vol. 313, no. 5786, pp. 504–507, 2006

Fabian Pedregosa, Gael Varoquaux, Alexandre Gramfort, Vincent Michel, Bertrand Thirion, Olivier Grisel, Mathieu Blondel, Peter Prettenhofer, Ron Weiss, Vincent Dubourg, Jake Vanderplas, Alexandre Passos, David Cournapeau, Matthieu Brucher, Matthieu Perrot and Edouard Duchesnay. 2011. Scikit-learn: Machine Learning in Python, In *Journal of Machine Learning Research*, JMLR vol. 12, pp. 2825–2830, 2011

Geoffrey Hinton and Ruslan Salakhutdinov. 2009. Replicated Softmax: an Undirected Topic Model. In *Advances in Neural Information Processing Systems*, pp. 1607–1614, 2009

ValenTo: Sentiment Analysis of Figurative Language Tweets with Irony and Sarcasm*

Delia Irazú Hernández Farías
Universitat Politècnica de València
Pattern Recognition and Human Language Technology
dhernandez1@dsic.upv.es

Emilio Sulis, Viviana Patti, Giancarlo Ruffo, Cristina Bosco
University of Turin
Dipartimento di Informatica
{sulis,patti,ruffo,bosco}@di.unito.it

Abstract

This paper describes the system used by the ValenTo team in the Task 11, Sentiment Analysis of Figurative Language in Twitter, at SemEval 2015. Our system used a regression model and additional external resources to assign polarity values. A distinctive feature of our approach is that we used not only word-sentiment lexicons providing polarity annotations, but also novel resources for dealing with emotions and psycholinguistic information. These are important aspects to tackle in figurative language such as irony and sarcasm, which were represented in the dataset. The system also exploited novel and standard structural features of tweets. Considering the different kinds of figurative language in the dataset our submission obtained good results in recognizing sentiment polarity in both ironic and sarcastic tweets.

1 Introduction

Figurative language, which is extensively exploited in social media texts, is very challenging for both traditional NLP techniques and sentiment analysis, which has been defined as "the computational study of opinions, sentiments and emotions expressed in text" (Liu, 2010). There is a considerable amount of works related to sentiment analysis and opinion mining (Pang and Lee, 2008; Liu, 2010; Cambria et al., 2013). In particular, the linguistic analysis of social media (microblogging like Twitter especially) has become a relevant topic of research in different languages (Rosenthal et al., 2014; Basile et al., 2014) and several frameworks for detecting sentiments and opinions in social media have been developed for different application purposes.

In a sentiment analysis setting, the presence in a text of figurative language devices, such as for instance irony, can work as an unexpected polarity reverser, by undermining the accuracy of the systems (Bosco et al., 2013). Therefore, several efforts have been recently devoted to detect and tackle figurative language phenomena in social media, following a variety of computational approaches, mostly focussing on irony detection and sarcasm recognition (Davidov et al., 2010; González-Ibáñez et al., 2011; Riloff et al., 2013) as classification tasks. Buschmeier et al. present an analysis of features, previously applied in irony detection, in a dataset from a product reviews corpus from Amazon (Buschmeier et al., 2014). Veale and Hao present a linguistic approach to separate ironic from non-ironic expressions in figurative comparisons over a corpus of web-harvested similes (Veale and Hao, 2010). Concerning Twitter, the problem of irony detection is addressed in (Reyes et al., 2013), where a set of textual features is used to recognize irony at a linguistic level. In (Riloff et al., 2013) the focus is on identifying sarcastic tweets that express a positive sentiment towards a negative situation. A model to classify sarcastic tweets using a set of lexical features is presented in (Barbieri et al., 2014). Moreover, a recent analysis on the interplay between sarcasm detection and sentiment analysis is in (May-

* The National Council for Science and Technology (CONACyT-Mexico) has funded the research work of the first author (218109/313683 grant).

nard and Greenwood, 2014), where a set of rules has been proposed to improve the performance of the sentiment analysis in presence of sarcastic tweets.

In this paper we describe our participation to the *SemEval-2015 Task 11: Sentiment Analysis of Figurative Language in Twitter* (Ghosh et al., 2015). The task concerned with classification of tweets containing different kinds of figurative language, in particular irony, sarcasm and metaphors. ValenTo system used a linear regression model, exploiting novel and standard structural and lexical features of tweets. Considering the different kinds of figurative language in the Semeval dataset - sarcasm, irony and metaphors - our submission had good results in recognizing sentiment polarity in both ironic and sarcastic tweets, than in the other cases.

2 Our System

We propose a supervised approach that consists in assigning a polarity value to tweets by using a linear regression model constructed from an annotated dataset. In order to catch characteristics that allow us to measure the polarity value in each tweet, we considered a set of features described below.

2.1 Feature Description

2.1.1 Structural Features

Among the several structural characteristics of tweets, in our study we consider: the length of tweets in amount of words (*lengthWords*); the length of a tweet as the number of characters that composes the textual message (*lengthChar*); the frequency of commas, semicolons, colons, exclamation and question marks (*punctuation marks*); the frequency of some Part of Speech categories as nouns, adverbs, verbs and adjectives (*POS*); the frequency of uppercase letters in each tweet *upperFreq*; the frequency or presence of URL *urlFreq*; and the amount of emoticons used in order to express some kind of emotion, we consider both positive (*emotPosFreq*) and negative ones (*emotNegFreq*).

We also consider some features that belongs to tweets, like: the presence or absence of hashtags (*hashtagBinary*) and mentions (*mentionsBinary*); the amount of hashtags (*hashtagFreq*) and mentions (*mentionsFreq*) in each tweet; and if the tweet is a retweet (*isRetweet*). Finally, we decide to take into account a feature (*polReversal*) in order to reverse the polarity (positive to negative, and vice versa) if a tweet includes the hashtag #sarcasm or #not.

2.1.2 Lexical Resources

In order to take into account sentiments, emotions and psycholinguistic features, and to count their frequency, we use the following lexical resources:

AFINN: it is a dictionary of $2,477$ English manually labeled words collected by Nielsen (Nielsen, 2011). Polarity values varies from -5 up to $+5$ [1].

ANEW: the Affective Norms for English Words provides a set of emotional ratings for a large number of English words (Bradley and Lang, 1999). Each word in is rated from 1 to 9 in terms of the three dimensions of Valence, Arousal and Dominance.

DAL: the Dictionary of Affective Language developed by Whissell (Whissell, 2009) contains $8,742$ English words rated in a three-point scale[2]. Each word is rated into the dimensions of Pleasantness, Activation and Imagery.

HL: Hu–Liu's lexicon (Hu and Liu, 2004) includes about $6,800$ positive and negative words[3].

GI: General Inquirer (Stone and Hunt, 1963) contains categories and subcategories for content analysis with dictionaries based on the Lasswell and Harvard IV-4 [4].

SWN: SentiWordNet (Baccianella et al., 2010) is a lexical resource for opinion mining and consists in three sentiment scores: positive, negative and objective[5]. We take into account the first two categories.

SN: SenticNet is a semantic resource for concept-level sentiment analysis (Cambria et al., 2012). We take into account the values of each one of the five dimensions (*senticnetDimensions*) provided by the lexical resource: Pleasantness (Pl), Attention (At), Sensitivity (Sn) and Aptitude (Ap) and Polarity (Pol); and also the polarity value p obtained by using the formula (*senticnetFormula*) below based

[1] `https://github.com/abromberg/sentiment_analysis/blob/master/AFINN/AFINN-111.txt`

[2] `ftp://perceptmx.com/wdalman.pdf`

[3] `http://www.cs.uic.edu/~liub/FBS/`

[4] `http://www.wjh.harvard.edu/~inquirer/homecat.htm`.We are mostly interested in the positive and negative words.

[5] `http://sentiwordnet.isti.cnr.it/download.php`

on a combination of the first four dimensions:

$$p = \sum_{i=1}^{n} \frac{Pl(c_i) + |At(c_i)| - |Sn(c_i)| + Ap(c_i)}{3N}$$

where c_i is an input concept, N the total number of concepts which compose the tweet, and 3 a normalisation factor.

LIWC: Linguistic Inquiry and Word Counts dictionary[6] contains 127,149 words distributed in categories that can further be used to analyze psycholinguistic features in texts. We select two categories for positive and negative emotions: PosEmo (12,878) entries and NegEmo (15,115 entries).

NRC: in the NRC word-emotion association lexicon (Mohammad and Turney, 2013) each word is labeled according to the Plutchik's primary emotions.

3 Results

3.1 Task Description and Dataset

The goal of the Task 11 at SemEval 2015, is the following: *given a set of tweets rich w.r.t. the presence of such figurative devices, to determine for each message whether the user expressed positive, negative or neutral sentiment, and the sentiment degree.* To have a measure of the sentiment intensity expressed in the message, it was proposed a fine-grained 11-point sentiment polarity scale.

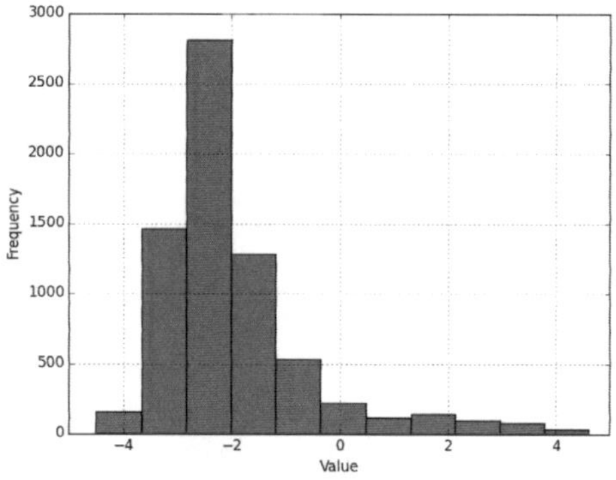

Figure 1: Frequency distribution of tweets by polarity intensity.

Two measures evaluated the similarity of the participant systems predictions to the manually annotated gold standard: Cosine Similarity (CS) and Mean Squared Error (MSE). The corpus available for training and trial consists of around $9,000$ figurative tweets with sentiment scores ranging from -5 to $+5$. Because of the perishability of Twitter data, some of them cannot be recovered by the published list of tweet identifiers; finally, we could rely on a corpus of $7,390$ messages considering both training and trial datasets. With respect to the polarity, the whole distribution is positively skewed (Fig. 1). The median value is very negative (-2.3) and the average of the tweets polarity is -2.

Table 1: Criteria for assigning classes.

3c-approach		4c-approach	
Original	**New**	**Original**	**New**
pv>0	pos	*pv* > 0	pos
pv<0	neg	-2.5 > *pv* <= 0	nsn
pv=0	neu	-3.5 > *pv* <= -2.5	neg
		pv <= -3.5	vn

3.2 ValenTo System

As a first step, we decided to address the problem as a classification task. We experimented three approaches, each featured by a different amount of considered classes; in the first one (**3c-approach**) we used just three classes: *positive (pos)*, *negative (neg)* and *neutral (neu)*; in the second one (**4c-approach**) we used four classes: *positive*, *negative*, *not so negative (nsn)* and *very negative (vn)*; and in the third one (**11c-approach**) we used the original values included in the corpus, i.e. eleven classes from -5 to $+5$. For the first two approaches we changed the polarity values (*pv*) in each one of the tweets contained in the dataset according to the criteria summarized in Table 1. Based on polarity value distribution shown in Fig. 1, we separated the classes in different ranges that cover all the possible values. A small set of widely classification algorithms was used: Naive Bayes (NB), Decision Tree (DT) and Support Vector Machine (SVM)[7]. We performed classification experiments using only the training set (i.e. 6,928 tweets); a ten fold-cross-validation criterium was applied. Table 2 presents results obtained in F-measure terms.

[6] http://www.liwc.net

[7] We used Weka toolkit's version available at http://www.cs.waikato.ac.nz/ml/weka/downloading.html

Table 2: Classification experiments: results.

Approach	NB	DT	SVM
3c-approach	0.829	0.804	0.790
4c-approach	0.458	0.440	0.462
11c-approach	0.324	0.311	0.302

As expected, from our classification results, the performance in terms of F-Measure drops while the number of classes increase. We decided to apply a different approach: Regression.

In order to build a regression model able to assign polarity values, we decided to merge both training and trial datasets (*fullTrainingSet* composed by 7,390 tweets). We used the Linear Regression Algorithm in Weka.
First, from the whole *fullTrainingSet* corpus we randomly extracted a set for training, containing the 70% of the tweets, and a set for the test, with the remaining 30%, obtaining *Subset-1*. We repeated the procedure two times more and we obtained *Subset-2* and *Subset-3*.Second, we made up 11 different combinations of features ***ft-conf[1-11]***. Each one contains a subset of the features described in Sec. 2.1. We built the features combination according to a preliminary analysis with respect to frequency distribution. Then, we applied our regression model for each *Subset* and ***ft-conf***. In order to evaluate the performance of our model, we used the script to obtain the cosine similarity measure provided by the organizers. Table 3 shows the results of these experiments for what concerns ***ft-conf2*** configuration, the one we selected for constructing the final model submitted to SemEval-Task 11 (due to lack of space, not have been included all results obtained). ***ft-conf2*** contains the following features:

lengthChar, punctuation marks, POS, upperFreq, urlFreq, emotPosFreq, emotNegFreq, hashtagBinary, mentionsBinary, hashtagFreq, mentionsFreq, isRetweet, polReversal, AFINN, ANEW, DAL, HL,GI, SWN, senticnetDimensions, senticnetFormula, LIWC, NRC

Table 3: Regression experiments: results.

Features	Subset-1	Subset-2	Subset-3
ft-conf2	0.8218	0.8161	0.8199

In order to measure the relevance of each feature used in our model, we applied the RELIEF algorithm[8]. The best ranked features are those related to emotional words (*NRC*) and polarity lexicons (*AFINN* and *HL*).

3.3 Official Results

We ranked 6th out of 15 teams in the SemEval-2015 Task 11 (Ghosh et al., 2015)[9]. ValenTo achieved the score of **0.634** using the CS measure, and a score of **2.999** using the MSE measure, while the best team achieved the score of **0.758** for CS, and a score of **2.117** for MSE.

Our results in terms of *irony* and *sarcasm* seem to be close to the best ones in each category (See Table 4).

Table 4: Official ValenTo and best results in each category of figurative type.

Category	CS		MSE	
	ValenTo	*Best*	ValenTo	*Best*
Overall	0.634	*0.758*	2.999	*2.117*
Sarcasm	**0.895**	***0.904***	**1.004**	***0.934***
Irony	**0.901**	***0.918***	**0.777**	***0.671***
Metaphor	0.393	*0.655*	4.730	*3.155*
Other	0.202	*0.612*	5.315	*3.411*

4 Conclusions

We described our participation at SemEval-2015 Task 11. A distinctive feature of our approach is that we used not only word-sentiment lexicons but also novel resources for dealing with emotions and psycholinguistic information. Based on both features analysis and evaluation results, we can draw a first insight about the importance of using such high-level information about affective value of the words in a tweet to tackle with figurative language such irony and sarcasm. As future work, the use of additional features for addressing figurative language under other perspectives (e.g. metaphor) will be explored.

[8] ReliefFAttributeEval version included in Weka (Robnik-Sikonja and Kononenko, 1997).

[9] `http://alt.qcri.org/semeval2015/task11/index.php?id=task-results-and-initial-analysis-1`, Table1.

References

Stefano Baccianella, Andrea Esuli, and Fabrizio Sebastiani. 2010. Sentiwordnet 3.0: An enhanced lexical resource for sentiment analysis and opinion mining. In *Proceedings of the Seventh International Conference on Language Resources and Evaluation (LREC'10)*.

Francesco Barbieri, Horacio Saggion, and Francesco Ronzano, 2014. *Proceedings of the 5th Workshop on Computational Approaches to Subjectivity, Sentiment and Social Media Analysis*, chapter Modelling Sarcasm in Twitter, a Novel Approach, pages 50–58.

Valerio Basile, Andrea Bolioli, Malvina Nissim, Viviana Patti, and Paolo Rosso. 2014. Overview of the Evalita 2014 SENTIment POLarity Classification Task. In *Proceedings of the 4th evaluation campaign of Natural Language Processing and Speech tools for Italian (EVALITA'14)*, pages 50–57.

Cristina Bosco, Viviana Patti, and Andrea Bolioli. 2013. Developing corpora for sentiment analysis: The case of irony and senti-tut. *IEEE Intelligent Systems*, 28(2):55–63.

Margaret Bradley and Peter Lang. 1999. Affective norms for english words (ANEW): Instruction manual and affective ratings. Technical report, Citeseer.

Konstantin Buschmeier, Philipp Cimiano, and Roman Klinger. 2014. An impact analysis of features in a classification approach to irony detection in product reviews. In *Proceedings of the 5th Workshop on Computational Approaches to Subjectivity, Sentiment and Social Media Analysis*, pages 42–49.

Erik Cambria, Catherine Havasi, and Amir Hussain. 2012. Senticnet 2: A semantic and affective resource for opinion mining and sentiment analysis. In *AAAI FLAIRS Conference*, pages 202–207.

Erick Cambria, B. Schuller, Yunqing Xia, and C. Havasi. 2013. New avenues in opinion mining and sentiment analysis. *Intelligent Systems, IEEE*, 28(2):15–21, March.

Dmitry Davidov, Oren Tsur, and Ari Rappoport. 2010. Semi-supervised recognition of sarcastic sentences in twitter and amazon. In *Proceedings of the Fourteenth Conference on Computational Natural Language Learning*, CoNLL '10, pages 107–116.

A. Ghosh, G. Li, T. Veale, P. Rosso, E. Shutova, A. Reyes, and J. Barnden. 2015. Semeval-2015 task 11: Sentiment analysis of figurative language in twitter. In *Proc. Int. Workshop on Semantic Evaluation (SemEval-2015), Co-located with NAACL and *SEM*.

Roberto González-Ibáñez, Smaranda Muresan, and Nina Wacholder. 2011. Identifying sarcasm in twitter: A closer look. In *Proceedings of the 49th Annual Meeting of the Association for Computational Linguistics: Human Language Technologies: Short Papers - Volume 2*, HLT '11, pages 581–586.

Minqing Hu and Bing Liu. 2004. Mining and summarizing customer reviews. In *Proceedings of the Tenth ACM SIGKDD International Conference on Knowledge Discovery and Data Mining*, KDD '04, pages 168–177.

Bing Liu. 2010. Sentiment analysis and subjectivity. In *Handbook of Natural Language Processing*.

Diana Maynard and Mark Greenwood. 2014. Who cares about sarcastic tweets? investigating the impact of sarcasm on sentiment analysis. In *Proceedings of the Ninth International Conference on Language Resources and Evaluation (LREC-2014)*.

Saif M. Mohammad and Peter D. Turney. 2013. Crowdsourcing a word–emotion association lexicon. *Computational Intelligence*, 29(3):436–465.

Finn Årup Nielsen. 2011. A new ANEW: evaluation of a word list for sentiment analysis in microblogs.

Bo Pang and Lillian Lee. 2008. Opinion mining and sentiment analysis. *Foundations and Trends in Information Retrieval*, 2(12):1–135.

Antonio Reyes, Paolo Rosso, and Tony Veale. 2013. A multidimensional approach for detecting irony in twitter. *Language Resources and Evaluation*, 47(1):239–268.

Ellen Riloff, Ashequl Qadir, Prafulla Surve, Lalindra De Silva, Nathan Gilbert, and Ruihong Huang. 2013. Sarcasm as contrast between a positive sentiment and negative situation. In *Proceedings of the EMNLP: Conference on Empirical Methods in Natural Language Processing*, pages 704–714.

Marko Robnik-Sikonja and Igor Kononenko. 1997. An adaptation of relief for attribute estimation in regression. In *Fourteenth International Conference on Machine Learning*, pages 296–304.

Sara Rosenthal, Alan Ritter, Preslav Nakov, and Veselin Stoyanov. 2014. Semeval-2014 task 9: Sentiment analysis in twitter. In *Proceedings of the 8th International Workshop on Semantic Evaluation (SemEval 2014)*, pages 73–80, August.

Philip J. Stone and Earl B. Hunt. 1963. A computer approach to content analysis: Studies using the general inquirer system. In *Proceedings of the May 21-23, 1963*, AFIPS '63 (Spring), pages 241–256.

Tony Veale and Yanfen Hao. 2010. Detecting ironic intent in creative comparisons. In *ECAI*, volume 215, pages 765–770.

Cynthia Whissell. 2009. Using the revised dictionary of affect in language to quantify the emotional undertones of samples of natural languages. In *Psychological Reports*.

CPH: Sentiment analysis of Figurative Language on Twitter #easypeasy #not

Sarah McGillion **Héctor Martínez Alonso** **Barbara Plank**
University of Copenhagen, Njalsgade 140, 2300 Copenhagen S, Denmark
zhg159@alumni.ku.dk, alonso@hum.ku.dk, bplank@cst.dk

Abstract

This paper describes the details of our system submitted to the SemEval 2015 shared task on sentiment analysis of figurative language on Twitter. We tackle the problem as regression task and combine several base systems using stacked generalization (Wolpert, 1992). An initial analysis revealed that the data is heavily biased, and a general sentiment analysis system (GSA) performs poorly on it. However, GSA proved helpful on the test data, which contains an estimated 25% non-figurative tweets. Our best system, a stacking system with backoff to GSA, ranked 4th on the final test data (Cosine 0.661, MSE 3.404).[1]

1 Introduction

Sentiment analysis (SA) is the task of determining the sentiment of a given piece of text. The amplitude of user-generated content produced every day raises the importance of accurate automatic sentiment analysis, for applications ranging from, e.g., reputation analysis (Amigó et al., 2013) to election results prediction (Tjong Kim Sang and Bos, 2012). However, figurative language is pervasive in user-generated content, and figures of speech like irony, sarcasm and metaphors impose relevant challenges for a sentiment analysis system usually trained on literal meanings. For instance, consider the following example:[2] *@CIA We hear you're looking for sentiment analysis to detect sarcasm in Tweets. That'll be easy! #SLA2014 #irony*. Irony or sarcasm does not result always in the exact opposite sentiment and therefore it is not as simple as just inverting the scores from a general SA system. Only few studies have attempted SA on figurative language so far (Reyes and Rosso, 2012; Reyes et al., 2013).

The prediction of a fine-grained sentiment score (between -5 and 5) for a tweet poses a series of challenges. First of all, accurate language technology on tweets is hard due to *sample bias*, i.e., collections of tweets are inherently biased towards the particular time (or way, cf. §2) they were collected (Eisenstein, 2013; Hovy et al., 2014). Secondly, the notion of figurativeness (or its complementary notion of literality) does not have a strong definition, let alone do irony, sarcasm, or satire. As pointed out by Reyes and Rosso (2012), "there is not a clear distinction about the boundaries among these terms". Yet alone attaching a fine-grained score is far from straightforward. In fact, the gold standard consists of the average score assigned by humans through crowdsourcing reflecting an uncertainty in ground truth.

2 Data Analysis

The goal of the initial data exploration was to investigate the amount of non-figurativeness in the train and trial data. Our analysis revealed that 99% of the training data could be classified using a simple heuristic: a regular expression decision list, hereafter called Tweet Label System (TLS), to split the training data into different key-phrase subgroups. The system searches for the expression in a tweet and then assigns a label in a cascade fashion following the order in Table 2, which lists the 14 possible label types (plus NONE), their associated expressions along with the support for each category

[1] After submission time we discovered a bug in ST2, which means that the results on the official website are of the GSA and not of the stacking system with backoff.

[2] From the training data, label: -1.24; GSA prediction: +5.

in the training data. Table 1 shows that only a small fraction of the train and trial data could not be associated to a subgroup and it can be seen that the final test data was estimated to have a very different distribution with 25% of tweets presumably containing literal language use.

Dataset	Train	Trial	Test
Instances	7988	920	4000
% Non-figurative	1%	7%	25%

Table 1: Retrieved instances in each data set and estimated amount of non-figurativeness.

Since there are obvious subgroups in the data, our hypothesis is that this fact can be used to construct a more informed baseline. In fact (§ 4.1), simply predicting the mean per subgroup pushed the constant mean baseline performance considerably (from 0.73 to 0.81 Cosine, compared to random 0.59).

Figure 1 plots predicted scores (ridge model, §3.1) of three subgroups against the gold scores on the trial data. It can be seen that certain subgroups have similar behaviour, 'sarcasm' has a generally negative cloud and the model performs well in predicting these values, while other groups such as 'SoToSpeak' have more intra-group variance.

Label	Expression	Support	Label	Expression	Support
Sarcasm	#sarcas	2139	SoToSpeak	so to speak	135
Irony	#iron(y ic)	1444	Proverbial	proverbial	22
Not	#not	3601	JustKidding	#justkidding	-
Literally	literally	344	Not2	not	29
Virtually	virtually	8	about	about	8
YeahRight	#yeahright	47	Oh	oh	3
OhYouMust	Oh.*you	2	NONE	-	92
asXas	as .* as	83			

Table 2: Tweet Label Type and Expression.

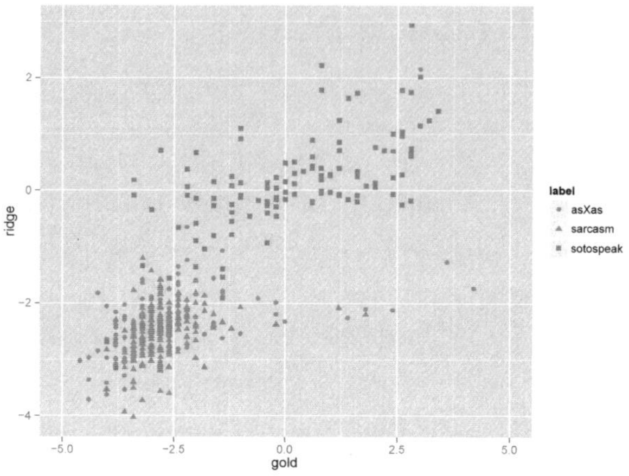

Figure 1: Label Plots for RR predictions.

The Effect of a General Sentiment System

The data for this task is very different from data that most lexicon-based or general sentiment-analysis models fare best on. In fact, running a general sentiment classifier (GSA) described in Elming et al. (2014) on the trial data showed that its predictions are actually slightly anti-correlated with the gold standard scores for the Tweets in this task (cosine similarity score of -0.08 and MSE of 18.62). We exploited these anti-correlated results as features for our stacking systems (cf. § 3.2). Figure 2 shows the distributions of the gold scores and GSA predictions for the trial data. It shows that the gold distribution is skewed with regards to the number of negative instances to positives, while the GSA predicts more positive sentiment.

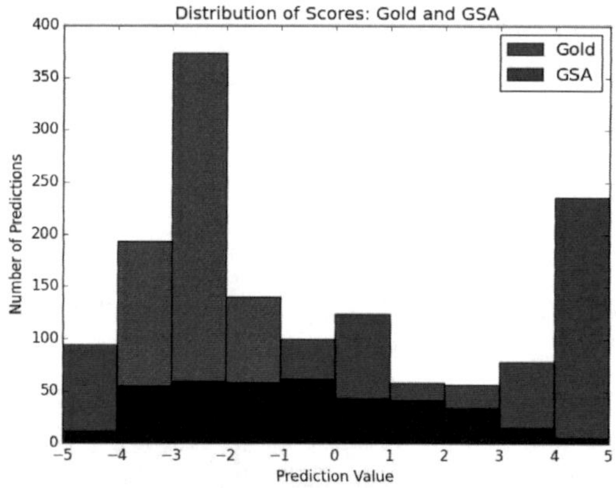

Figure 2: Distribution of Gold Scores and GSA Predictions for Trial Data.

3 System Description

We approach the task (Ghosh et al., 2015) as a regression task (cf. §4.4), combining several systems using stacking (§ 3.2), and relying on features without POS, lemma or explicit use of lexicons, cf. § 3.3.

3.1 Single Systems

Ridge Regression (RR) A standard supervised ridge regression model with default parameters.[3]

PCA_GMM Ridge Regression (GMM) A ridge regression model trained on the output of unsupervised induced features, i.e., a Gaussian Mixture Models (GMM) trained on PCA of word n-grams. PCA was used to reduce the dimensionality to 100, and GMM under the assumption that the data was sampled from different distributions of figurative language, k Gaussians were assumed (here k = 12).

Embeddings with Bayesian Ridge (EMBD) A Bayesian Ridge Regressor learner with default parameters trained on only word embeddings. A corpus was build from the training data and an in-house Tweet collection sampled with the expressions from the TLS. This resulted in a total of 3.7 million tweets and 67 million tokens. For details on how the word embeddings were built see §3.3.

3.2 Ensembles

We developed two stacking systems (Wolpert, 1992), *Stacking System 1* (ST1) and *Stacking System 2: Stacking with Backoff* (ST2). The systems used for these are shown in Table 3 and the Meta Learner used for both stacking systems is Linear Regression.

The systems used in ST1 and ST2 are not the only differences between the two. ST2 uses the TLS to identify the subgroup that each tweet belongs to. For any tweet with the NONE subgrouping, the system would back off to the predictions from the GSA. We built ST2 as a system that is not limited to sentiment analysis for a small subsection of language, the phenomenon of figurative language, but is applicable in situations covering many types of tweets including those in which literal language is used.

Single System / Stacking System	ST1	ST2
RR	X	X
GMM	X	
EMBD		X
GSA	X	X

Table 3: Systems in Ensemble Setups.

[3] http://scikit-learn.org/

3.3 Features

This section describe the features we used for the models in §3.1. Table 4 indicates the type of features used for the single models. Punctuation was kept as its own lexical item and we found removing stopwords and normalizing usernames to '@USER' increased performance and as such the preprocessing methods are the same across the models. Features were set on the trial data.

1. **Word N-Grams** Systems use different n-grams as features. In RR counts of 1 and 5 word grams, in GMM binary presence of 1,2, and 3 word grams.
2. **Uppercase Words** Counts of the numbers of word in a Tweet with all uppercase letters.
3. **Punctuation** Contiguous sequences of question, exclamation, and question and exclamation marks.
4. **TLS Label** The subgrouping label from TLS.
5. **Word Embeddings** Parameters for word embeddings:[4] 100 dimensions, 5 minimum occurrences for a type to be included in the model, 5 word context window and 10-example negative sampling. Each tweet was represented by 100 features that represented the average of all the embeddings of the content words in the tweet.

Features/Systems	RR	GMM	EMBD
Word N-grams	X	X	
Uppercase	X		
Punctuations	X		
TLS Label	X		
Word Embeddings			X

Table 4: Features used in Single Models.

4 Results

4.1 Constant Baselines & Single Systems

We implemented the Mean, Mode, Median, Random and TSL (§2) baseline systems. TSL is the hardest baseline, and RR is the only system that beats it.

4.2 Results Stacking Systems

The performance of the stacking systems on the trial data can be seen below in Table 6. ST2 did not perform well on the trial data although a reason for this

[4] https://code.google.com/p/word2vec/

System	Cosine	MSE
TLS	**0.81**	**2.34**
Mean	0.73	3.13
Mode	0.73	3.13
Median	0.73	3.31
Random	0.59	5.17
RR	**0.88**	**1.60**
GMM	0.79	2.55
EMB	0.78	2.64

Table 5: Baseline and Single Systems On Trial Data.

is that only 7% of the trial data was found as not belonging to a known figurative type of tweet.

System	Cosine	MSE
ST1	0.86	1.88
ST2	0.79	2.57

Table 6: Stacking Model Results on Trial Data.

4.3 Final Results

Three models were submitted for final evaluation on the test data. The three models were RR, ST1, and ST2. For the final results we scaled back values outside the range [-5,5] to the nearest whole number in range. Tables 7 and 8 show the results for our systems on the final dataset and the performance of the overall winning system for the task (CLAC) . Table 7 shows the overall cosine similarity and MSE for the systems on the test data and Table 8 shows the breakdown of the cosine similarity for the systems on the different parts of language. It is interesting to note that the performance of ST2 on the 'Other' type of language is identical as the performance for CLAC, this is also the best cosine similarity score 'Other' out of all submissions.

System	Test Cosine	Test MSE
RR	0.625	3.079
ST1	0.623	**3.078**
ST2	**0.661**	3.404
CLAC	<u>0.758</u>	<u>2.117</u>

Table 7: Submission System Test Results.[5]

System	Overall	Sarcasm	Irony	Metaphor	Other
RR	0.625	0.897	0.886	0.325	0.218
ST1	0.623	<u>**0.900**</u>	**0.903**	0.308	0.226
ST2	**0.661**	0.875	0.872	**0.453**	<u>**0.584**</u>
CLAC	<u>0.758</u>	0.892	<u>0.904</u>	<u>0.655</u>	<u>0.584</u>

Table 8: Cosine Test Results Breakdown.

4.4 The Case for Regression

Regression is less usual in NLP than classification. However for this data, it is desirable to use regression, because it incorporates the ordered relation between the labels, instead of treating them as orthogonal. It also keeps the decimal precision in the target variable when training, which is relevant when the target variable is the result of an average between several annotations. We ran classification experiments for this task but found that the best classification system's[6] performance (Cosine 0.82, MSE 2.51) is still far from the RR model (0.88,1.60).

5 Conclusions

We tested three systems for their abilities to analyse sentiment on figurative language from Twitter. Our experiments showed that a general SA system trained on literal Twitter language was highly anti-correlated with gold scores for figurative tweets. We found that for certain figurative types, sarcasm and irony, our system's predictions for these phenomena faired well. Our system did not explicitly use a lexicon to define the sentiment of a tweet, but instead used machine learning and strictly corpus-based features (no POS or lemma) to place us 4th in the task. More effort may be needed to discriminate metaphorical from literal tweets to build a more robust system, although, even for humans the sentiment of tweets is hard to judge. This can be seen from the data where a number of tweets were repeated, but did not always share the same gold score.

[5]The numbers in bold indicate the best performance among our systems, underlined indicates the best performance between any of our systems and the winning system.

[6]Decision Tree with 7 classes and using the minimum score for instances in the classes in the training data to convert for class labels to scores.

References

Enrique Amigó, Jorge Carrillo De Albornoz, Irina Chugur, Adolfo Corujo, Julio Gonzalo, Tamara Martín, Edgar Meij, Maarten De Rijke, and Damiano Spina. 2013. Overview of replab 2013: Evaluating online reputation monitoring systems. In *Information Access Evaluation. Multilinguality, Multimodality, and Visualization*, pages 333–352. Springer.

Jacob Eisenstein. 2013. What to do about bad language on the internet. In *NAACL*.

Jakob Elming, Barbara Plank, and Dirk Hovy. 2014. Robust cross-domain sentiment analysis for low-resource languages. In *Proceedings of the 5th Workshop on Computational Approaches to Subjectivity, Sentiment and Social Media Analysis*.

A. Ghosh, G. Li, T. Veale, P. Rosso, E. Shutova, A. Reyes, and J. Barnden. 2015. Semeval-2015 task 11: Sentiment analysis of figurative language in twitter. In *Int. Workshop on Semantic Evaluation (SemEval-2015)*.

Dirk Hovy, Barbara Plank, and Anders Søgaard. 2014. When POS datasets don't add up: Combatting sample bias. In *LREC*.

Antonio Reyes and Paolo Rosso. 2012. Making objective decisions from subjective data: Detecting irony in customer reviews. *Decision Support Systems*, 53(4):754–760.

Antonio Reyes, Paolo Rosso, and Tony Veale. 2013. A multidimensional approach for detecting irony in twitter. *Language Resources and Evaluation*, 47(1):239–268.

Erik Tjong Kim Sang and Johan Bos. 2012. Predicting the 2011 dutch senate election results with twitter. In *Proceedings of the Workshop on Semantic Analysis in Social Media*.

David H Wolpert. 1992. Stacked generalization. *Neural networks*, 5(2):241–259.

UPF-taln: SemEval 2015 Tasks 10 and 11
Sentiment Analysis of Literal and Figurative Language in Twitter *

Francesco Barbieri, Francesco Ronzano, Horacio Saggion
Universitat Pompeu Fabra, Barcelona, Spain
name.surname@upf.edu

Abstract

In this paper, we describe the approach used by the UPF-taln team for tasks 10 and 11 of SemEval 2015 that respectively focused on "Sentiment Analysis in Twitter" and "Sentiment Analysis of Figurative Language in Twitter". Our approach achieved satisfactory results in the figurative language analysis task, obtaining the second best result. In task 10, our approach obtained acceptable performances. We experimented with both word-based features and domain-independent intrinsic word features. We exploited two machine learning methods: the supervised algorithm Support Vector Machines for task 10, and Random-Sub-Space with M5P as base algorithm for task 11.

1 Motivation

During the last decade the study and characterisation of sentiments and emotions in on-line user-generated content has attracted more and more interest. Since 2013 several tasks dealing with Sentiment Analysis have been organised in the context of SemEval. These tasks have been mainly focused on the analysis of short texts like SMS or tweets. In this paper we describe the approach adopted by UPF-taln team for tasks 10 and 11 of SemEval 2015, both dealing with the analysis of English tweets. Task 10 concerned "Sentiment Analysis in Twitter" and included different subtasks. We participated in the subtask B, named "Sentiment Polarity Classification". Given a message, we were asked to classify whether the message was of positive, negative, or neutral sentiment. In Task 11 the participants were asked to determine the polarity score (between -5 to +5) of tweets rich in metaphor and irony. Our model reaches satisfactory results in the figurative language task 11, however it has suboptimal performance in task 10.

We exploited an extended version of the tweet classification features and approach described in (Barbieri and Saggion, 2014). In particular, we experimented the use of intrinsic word features, characterising each word in a tweet to try to model and thus automatically determine its polarity. Thanks to intrinsic word features, we aimed to detect two aspects of tweets: the style used (e.g. register used, frequent or rare words, positive or negative words, etc.) and the unexpectedness in the use of words, particularly important for figurative language. We also exploited textual features (like word occurrences, bigrams, skipgrams or other word patterns) in order to capture the way words are used in positive and negative tweets. As machine learning approach we choose the supervised method Support Vector Machines (Platt, 1999) for task 10 and the regression algorithm Random-Sub-Space (Ho, 1998) with M5P (Quinlan, 2014) as base algorithm for task 11.

In Section 2 and 3 we describe the dataset used and the tools we employed to process the tweets. In Section 4 we introduce the features we built our model on. In Section 5 we discuss the performance of our model in SemEval 2015 and in Section 6 we

*The research described in this paper is partially funded by the Spanish fellowship RYC-2009-04291, the SKATER-TALN_UPF project (TIN2012-38584-C06-03), and the EU project Dr. Inventor (n. 611383).

conclude with a recap of our approach and suggestions for further research.

2 Dataset

In order to train our systems we used in each task only the dataset provided by the organisers. For task 10 we were able to retrieve 9689 tweets, tagged as positive, negative and neutral (Rosenthal et al., 2015). For task 11 the dataset was a collection of 8000 figurative tweets annotated with sentiment scores from -5 to +5 (Li et al., 2015).

3 Text Analysis and Tools

In order to deal with the noisy text of Twitter we made use of the GATE application TwitIE (Bontcheva et al., 2013) where we modified the normaliser, adding new abbreviations, new slang words, removing URLs and changing the normalisation rules. Besides the tweet normalisation we also employed TwitIE for tokenisation, Part of Speech tagging and lemmatisation. We also used WordNet (Miller, 1995) to extract synonyms and synsets. We employed two sentiment lexicons, SentiWordNet3.0 (Baccianella et al., 2010) and the NRC Hashtag Sentiment Lexicon (Mohammad et al., 2013) and two emotion lexicons NRC Hashtag Emotion Lexicon (Mohammad, 2012) and Depeche Mood (Staiano and Guerini, 2014). As frequency data for determining how often a word is used in English, we relied on the American National Corpus (Ide and Suderman, 2004); we also exploited the VU Amsterdam Metaphors Corpus (Steen et al., 2010) to find out how often a word is used in metaphors. Finally, the machine learning tool we used was Weka (Hall et al., 2009).

4 Our Method

We employed different machine learning methods for the two tasks. In task 10, as the classes were only three (positive, negative and neutral) we opted for a supervised learning method, and from our experiments with several classifiers, Support Vector Machines resulted to be the best one. On the other hand, in task 11 tweets were classified as belonging to one of 11 polarity classes associated with values ranging from -5 to 5, hence a regression approach was more suitable. The regression method employed was Random-Sub-Space with M5P as base algorithm. We also tried different mixed techniques, like using a supervised method to classify positive (0 to 5) and negative (-5 to 0), then a regression method (over the two subsets) but with no luck: pure regression methods fitted better task 11.

In both tasks we characterised each tweet using nine groups of related features all describing both intrinsic aspects of the words and word patterns. These groups of features are the following:

- Sentiments and Emotional Lexicons
- Frequency
- Lemma-Based
- Ambiguity
- Synonyms
- Adjective / Adverb Intensity
- Characters
- Part of Speech
- Bad Words

4.1 Sentiments and Emotional Lexicons

Using sentiment lexicons in Sentiment Analysis has been a common and rewarding practice (Mohammad et al., 2013; Kiritchenko et al., 2014). The characterisation of the sentiment associated to words in tweets is important for two reasons: to detect the *global sentiment* (e.g. if tweets contain mainly positive or negative terms) and, in the case of figurative language, to capture *unexpectedness* created by a negative word in a positive context and viceversa. Using the two sentiment lexicons and two emotional lexicons mentioned in Section 3, we computed the *number of positive / negative words*, the *sum of the intensities of the positive / negative scores of words*, the *mean of positive / negative score of words*, the *greatest positive / negative score*, the *gap between the greatest positive / negative score and the positive / negative mean*. These features are computed including all the words of each tweet. We also determined these features by considering separately Nouns, Verbs, Adjectives, and Adverbs (we calculate the features by considering only words characterised by a specific Part of Speech).

4.2 Frequency

To design the Frequency feature we used two frequency corpora: the American National Corpus and the VU Amsterdam Metaphors Corpus. From these corpora we extracted three features: *rarest word frequency* (frequency of the rarest word included in the tweet), *frequency mean* (word frequency arithmetic average) and *frequency gap* (the difference between the two previous features). As previously done, we computed these features by considering only Nouns, Verbs, Adjectives, and Adverbs.

4.3 Lemma-Based

We designed this group of features to detect common word-patterns in positive and negative tweets. The lemma-based features are three: *lemma+pos* (the combination of each lemma and its Part of Speech in the tweet), *bigrams* (combination of two lemmas in a sequence) and *skip one gram*, combination of two lemmas with distance one (two lemmas separated by one lemma).

4.4 Ambiguity

Ambiguity is modelled with WordNet. Our hypothesis is that if a word has many meanings (synset associated) it is more likely to be used in an ambiguous way. For each tweet we calculated the *maximum number of synsets* associated to a single word, the *mean synset number* of all the words, and the *synset gap*—the difference between the two previous features. We determine the value of these features by including all the words of a tweet as well as by considering only Nouns, Verbs, Adjectives or Adverbs.

4.5 Synonyms

We carried out an analysis of the choice of synonyms as follows: for each word in the tweet we retrieve its list of synonyms, then we computed, across all the words of the tweet: the *greatest / lowest number of synonyms* with frequency higher than the one present in the tweet, the *mean number of synonyms* with frequency greater / lower than the frequency of the related word present in the tweet. We determine also the greatest / lowest number of synonyms and the mean number of synonyms of the words with frequency greater / lower than the one present in the the tweet (*gap* feature). We computed the set of Synonyms features by considering both all the words and also restricting the calculation to words with the Part of Speech tags as above.

4.6 Adjective / Adverb Intensity

Using the Potts (2011) intensity scores of Adjectives and Adverbs, we calculated three features: the *most intense* adjective/adverb and the *intensity mean* of the adjective/adverb of the tweet.

4.7 Characters

We also wanted to capture the punctuation style of the author of a tweet. Punctuation and type of characters used are very important in social networks: a full stop at the end of a subjective message may change the polarity of the message. Each feature is a count of specific punctuation marks, including: ".", "#", "!", "?", "$", "%", "&", "+", "-", "=", "/". Moreover we count as well number of *uppercase* and *lowercase* character.

4.8 Part of Speech

The features included in the Part of Speech group are designed to capture the structure of positive and negative tweets. The features of this group are eight and each one of them counts the number of occurrences of words characterised by a certain Part of Speech. The eight Part of Speech considered are *Verbs*, *Nouns*, *Adjectives*, *Adverbs*, *Interjections*, *Determiners*, *Pronouns*, and *Appositions*.

4.9 Bad Words

Since Twitter messages often include *bad words*[1], we count them as they may be used more often in negative messages.

5 Experiments and Results

In this section we present our results in the two tasks (see Table 1 and Table 2). We only report final results (mean of Precision, Recall and F-Measure of each class), for more details please refer to the task 10 and task 11 papers (Rosenthal et al., 2015; Li et al., 2015).

[1] We enriched with more variants this list: https://github.com/shutterstock/List-of-Dirty-Naughty-Obscene-and-Otherwise-Bad-Words

5.1 Task 10-B

Given a message, classify whether the message is of positive, negative, or neutral sentiment. Our model scores at position 27th out of 40 groups. Systems were evaluated with the mean of the F-measures of Positive, Negative and Neutral classes. Our score is 9 points less than the best system. A considerable number of tweets in the test set were considered sarcastic tweets complicating the sentiment analysis task. With this test subset our system improves its performances globally scoring at the 11th position. See Table 1 for the results in each test set. The features that perform better are from the group Sentiments and Emotion Lexicons, that achieve information gain scores of 0.133. Even if less influent, the Frequency group obtains a score of 0.09. The other group of features are not very important for this task, and the information gain scores are less than 0.3.

	F-Measure	Rank
Twitter 2014	65.05	27th
Sarcasm	50.93	11th
Twitter 2013	66.15	17th
SMS 2013	57.84	31st
LiveJournal 2014	64.5	31st

Table 1: Task 10 results. For each test set we report F-Measure and ranking comparing to other systems.

5.2 Task 11

Given a set of tweets that are rich in metaphor and irony, the goal is to determine whether the user has expressed a positive, negative or neutral sentiment in each, and the degree to which this sentiment has been communicated.

A vector space model was used to evaluate the similarity of the predictions of each participating system to the human-annotated gold standard. The list of expected gold-standard sentiment scores was used to construct a normalised gold-standard vector, while a comparable vector will be constructed from the predictions of a participating system. The cosine distance between vectors was then used as a measure of how well the participating system estimates the gold-standard sentiment scores for the whole of the test set (Li et al., 2015).

In this task our model ranked second out of 15 participants. We obtained a cosine similarity of 0.710 and a Mean Squared Error (MSE) of 2.458. The best system cosine and MSE scores were respectively 0.758 and 2.117. In Table 2 the reader can find all the results.

In Table 3 we show experiments to analyse the contribution of each type of feature to the final results. The most important contribution is given by the Sentiment lexicons NRC and SentiWordNet (see Section 4.1). Also the Synonyms feature is important with a cosine similarity of 0.564. The feature that was less influent to the final classification was Intensity of Adjectives and Adverbs.

	MSE	Cosine
Overall	2.458	0.711
Sarcasm	0.934	0.903
Irony	1.041	0.873
Metaphor	4.186	0.520
Other	3.772	0.486

Table 2: Task 11 results measured by the Cosine Similarity and the Mean Square Error over the test set (Overall) and for its subsets: sarcasm, irony, metaphor and other (non-figurative tweets).

Feature	Cosine Similarity
NRC H. Sentiment	0.578
SentiWordNet	0.562
Synonyms	0.564
Characters	0.550
Part of Speech	0.550
Depeche Mood	0.550
Lemma-Based	0.547
NRC H. Emotion	0.547
Bad Words	0.547
Frequency	0.546
Ambiguity	0.546
Intensity	0.544

Table 3: Task 11 contribution of each group of feature. The best feature group was Sentiment, in particular the features computed with the NRC Hashtag Sentiment Lexicon, see Section 4.1.

6 Conclusions

In this paper we have described our participation to the SemEval task 10 and 11. Besides the word-based features, we experimented the use of intrinsic word features to characterise positive and negative tweets. In task 10 our system obtains average performances leaving room for important improvements to our approach. Our system obtains very good results in task 11, ranking second out of 15 participating teams. The difference in performance in the two tasks was expected since our model is the adaption to sentiment analysis of a model for irony (Barbieri and Saggion, 2014) and sarcasm (Barbieri et al., 2014) detection in Twitter, thus it fits better the figurative language identification task. Yet, both models can be improved and we are planning to add new features (vector space models and distributional semantics among others) and experiment new machine learning techniques (e.g. cascade classifiers for task 10 or different regression algorithms for task 11).

References

Stefano Baccianella, Andrea Esuli, and Fabrizio Sebastiani. 2010. Sentiwordnet 3.0: An enhanced lexical resource for sentiment analysis and opinion mining. In *LREC*, volume 10, pages 2200–2204.

Francesco Barbieri and Horacio Saggion. 2014. Modelling Irony in Twitter. In *Proceedings of the Student Research Workshop at the 14th Conference of the European Chapter of the Association for Computational Linguistics*, Gothenburg, Sweden, April.

Francesco Barbieri, Horacio Saggion, and Ronzano Francesco. 2014. Modelling sarcasm in twitter, a novel approach. *ACL Workshop on Sentiment Analysis: WASSA*.

Kalina Bontcheva, Leon Derczynski, Adam Funk, Mark A. Greenwood, Diana Maynard, and Niraj Aswani. 2013. TwitIE: An Open-Source Information Extraction Pipeline for Microblog Text. In *Proceedings of Recent Advances in Natural Language Processing Conferemce*.

Mark Hall, Eibe Frank, Geoffrey Holmes, Bernhard Pfahringer, Peter Reutemann, and Ian H Witten. 2009. The WEKA data mining software: an update. *ACM SIGKDD explorations newsletter*, 11(1):10–18.

Tin Kam Ho. 1998. The random subspace method for constructing decision forests. *Pattern Analysis and Machine Intelligence, IEEE Transactions on*, 20(8):832–844.

Nancy Ide and Keith Suderman. 2004. The American National Corpus First Release. In *Proceedings of the Language Resources and Evaluation Conference*.

Svetlana Kiritchenko, Xiaodan Zhu, Colin Cherry, and Saif Mohammad. 2014. NRC-Canada-2014: Detecting Aspects and Sentiment in Customer Reviews. In *Proceedings of the 8th International Workshop on Semantic Evaluation (SemEval 2014)*, Dublin, Ireland, August.

Guofu Li, Aniruddha Ghosh, Tony Veale, Paolo Rosso, Ekaterina Shutova, Antonio Reyes, and John Barnden. 2015. Task 11: Sentiment Analysis of Figurative Language in Twitter. Denver, Colorado, USA, June, 4-5.

George A Miller. 1995. WordNet: a lexical database for English. *Communications of the ACM*, 38(11):39–41.

Saif Mohammad, Svetlana Kiritchenko, and Xiaodan Zhu. 2013. NRC-Canada: Building the State-of-the-Art in Sentiment Analysis of Tweets. In *Proceedings of the seventh international workshop on Semantic Evaluation Exercises (SemEval-2013)*, Atlanta, Georgia, USA, June.

Saif Mohammad. 2012. #Emotional Tweets. In **SEM 2012: The First Joint Conference on Lexical and Computational Semantics – Volume 1: Proceedings of the main conference and the shared task, and Volume 2: Proceedings of the Sixth International Workshop on Semantic Evaluation (SemEval 2012)*, Montréal, Canada, 7-8 June.

John Platt. 1999. Fast Training of Support Vector Machines Using Sequential Minimal Optimization. *Advances in kernel methodssupport vector learning*, 3.

Christopher Potts. 2011. Developing adjective scales from user-supplied textual metadata. *NSF Workshop on Restructuring Adjectives in WordNet. Arlington, VA.*

J Ross Quinlan. 2014. *C4. 5: programs for machine learning*. Elsevier.

Sara Rosenthal, Preslav Nakov, Svetlana Kiritchenko, Saif M Mohammad, Alan Ritter, and Veselin Stoyanov. 2015. Semeval-2015 task 10: Sentiment analysis in twitter. In *Proceedings of the 9th International Workshop on Semantic Evaluation*, SemEval '2015, Denver, Colorado, USA, June.

Jacopo Staiano and Marco Guerini. 2014. DepecheMood: a Lexicon for Emotion Analysis from Crowd-Annotated News. In *52nd Annual Meeting of the Association for Computational Linguistics (Short Papers)*, page 427433, Baltimore, Maryland, USA,, June.

Gerard J Steen, Aletta G Dorst, J Berenike Herrmann, Anna Kaal, Tina Krennmayr, and Trijntje Pasma. 2010. *A method for linguistic metaphor identification: From MIP to MIPVU*, volume 14. John Benjamins Publishing.

DsUniPi: An SVM-based Approach for Sentiment Analysis of Figurative Language on Twitter

Maria Karanasou
Dept. of Digital Systems
University of Piraeus
Greece
karanasou@gmail.com

Christos Doulkeridis
Dept. of Digital Systems
University of Piraeus
Greece
cdoulk@unipi.gr

Maria Halkidi
Dept. of Digital Systems
University of Piraeus
Greece
mhalk@unipi.gr

Abstract

The DsUniPi team participated in the SemEval 2015 Task#11: Sentiment Analysis of Figurative Language in Twitter. The proposed approach employs syntactical and morphological features, which indicate sentiment polarity in both figurative and non-figurative tweets. These features were combined with others that indicate presence of figurative language in order to predict a fine-grained sentiment score. The method is supervised and makes use of structured knowledge resources, such as SentiWordNet sentiment lexicon for assigning sentiment score to words and WordNet for calculating word similarity. We have experimented with different classification algorithms (Naïve Bayes, Decision trees, and SVM), and the best results were achieved by an SVM classifier with linear kernel.

1 Introduction

Sentiment analysis on figurative speech is a challenging task that becomes even more difficult on short social-media related text. Tweet text can be rich in irony that is either stated with hashtags explicitly (such as #irony) or implied. Identifying the underlying sentiment of such text is challenging due to its restricted size and features such as use of abbreviations and slang. Consequently, assigning positive or negative polarity is quite a difficult task. The actual meaning can be very different than what is stated, since, for example, in ironic language what is said can be the opposite of what it is meant. To address this challenge, we propose a system for sentiment analysis of figurative language, which relies on feature selection and trains a classifier to predict the label of a tweet. Given a labelled trial set, the objective of the system is to correctly determine how positive, negative or neutral a tweet is considered to be on a scale of [-5, 5].

2 Related Work

Tweets have unique characteristics compared to other text corpora, such as emoticons, abbreviations, and hashtags. Use of emoticons is considered a reasonably effective way to conveying emotion (Derks et al. 2008, Thelwall et al.). Go et al. (2009) show that machine learning algorithms achieve accuracy above 80% when trained with emoticon data. It is also indicated that the use of hashtags and presence of intensifiers, such as capitalization and punctuation, can affect sentiment identification (Kouloumpis et al., 2010). According to Agarwal et al. (2011) such features can add value to a classifier, but only marginally. Additionally, natural language related features, such as part-of-speech tagging and use of lexicon resources, can significantly contribute to detecting the sentiment of a tweet. Moreover, features that combine the prior polarity of words and their parts-of-speech tags are considered most useful.

The problem of sentiment analysis on figurative language has been addressed in many ways. Researchers have investigated the use of lexical and syntactic features in order to identify figurative language and classify the conveyed sentiment. The complexity of such a task is high, especially given the fact that irony and sarcasm are frequently mixed. Sarcasm is usually used for putting down the target of the comment and is somewhat easier to detect. Irony works as a negation, and it can be conveyed through a positive context, which makes it difficult to understand the actual meaning of a tweet (Reyes et al. 2012, Veale et al. 2010). Davidov et al. (2010) examined hashtags that indicated sarcasm to identify if such labelled tweets can be a reliable source of sarcasm. They concluded that user-labelled sarcastic tweets can be noisy and constitute the hardest form of sarcasm. Riloff et al. (2013) identify sarcasm that arises from the contrast between a positive sentiment referring to a negative situation. Reyes et al. (2012) involved in their work features that make use of contextual imbalance, natural language concepts, syntactical and morphological aspects of a tweet. Many studies exploit the use of contextual imbalance detection through calculation of semantic similarity among the words. This is achieved using lexical resources, such as WordNet or Whisel's dictionary, and the goal is to identify features like emotional content, polarity of words and pleasantness, adverbs implying negation or expressing timing. Shutova et al. (2010) have deployed an unsupervised method to identify metaphor using synonymy information from WordNet. Reyes et al. (2013) argue that other features such as punctuation marks, emoticons, quotes, and capitalized words, n-grams and skip-grams are also useful to the sentiment analysis process. Moreover, patterns such as "As * As *" or "about as * as *" have been shown to be useful in detecting ironic similes (Veale et al. 2010).

3 Approach

The proposed system consists of two main modules: (a) the preprocessing, and (b) the classification module. Each tweet t was submitted to preprocessing, in order to remove useless information and extract the desired/targeted features f. The result of the preprocessing of a given tweet t consists of a *feature dictionary* (*fd*) that stores the values calculated for each feature. In the classification part, the feature dictionaries are converted to vectors and the result matrix is converted to a term-frequency matrix. The aforementioned process is the same for trial and test data and the tf matrices are used by a classifier for training and prediction. We tested different classifiers, including Naïve Bayes, Decision trees, and SVM, in order to study their performance and select the best-performing.

3.1 Preprocessing

Each tweet is given as input to the preprocessing module, in order to transform it to a feature-value dictionary representation:

$$fd_t = \{f1{:}v1,\ \ldots,\ fn{:}vn\} \tag{1}$$

The preprocessing includes cleaning, which starts with the removal of non-ascii characters and is followed by the detection of certain features. Feature detection takes place before the actual cleaning of the text in order to avoid loss of information, such as punctuation, urls and emoticons. This process checks if a tweet contains question marks or exclamation marks, capitalized words, urls, negations, laughing, retweet, emoticons and hashtags. The last two are categorized concerning the sentiment they may convey. We manually categorized the top20 emoticons and some minor variations (http://datagenetics.com/blog/october52012) as positive or negative, whereas hashtags are categorized as positive, negative or neutral. Hashtag categorization makes use of SentiWordNet score (*swnScore*) and the result is a representation of all the hashtags present in a tweet.

In the hashtag categorization process, if a hashtag *ht* is spelled correctly, its swnScore is retrieved. Otherwise, spellchecking (Kelly) is tried once and if it fails then the hashtag is categorized as neutral. The result depends on the number of positive, negative, neutral hashtags in *HTt* as follows:

$$HTEm_t = \begin{cases} HT\_pos, & c(htPos) > c(htNeg) > 0 \\ HT\_neu, & c(htPos) = c(htNeg) = 0 \\ HT\_neg, & c(htNeg) \geq c(htPos) > 0 \end{cases} \tag{2}$$

where *c(htPos)*, *c(htNeg)* denote the count of positive and negative hashtags in a tweet t respectively.

Motivated by the "*As * as **" pattern and after studying the data set, we further identify in the feature selection process the presence of patterns such as "*Don't you**", "*Oh so*?*" and "*As * As **". Cleaning proceeds with punctuation, stop-words, urls, emoticons, hashtags and references removal. Additionally, multiple consecutive letters in a word are reduced to two. Finally, spellchecking is performed to words that have been identified as misspelled in order to deduce the correct word. After cleaning, the process continues with part of speech

(POS) tagging. POS-tagging is performed with the use of a custom model (Derczynski et al., 2013) and simplified tags (NN, VB, ADJ, RB). Words that belong to the same part of speech are used in semantic text similarity calculation sim_t. For this feature, different similarity measures (Resnik's, Lin's, and Wu & Palmer's) provided by nltk are used (Pedersen et al., 2008). The value sim_t is calculated as the maximum similarity score of every combination of two words and their synonyms.

$$sim_t = \frac{\sum sim_V + \sum sim_N + \sum sim_A + \sum sim_R}{c(V)+c(N)+c(A)+c(R)} \qquad (3)$$

$$sim_A = \begin{bmatrix} max\big(sim(A_i, A_{i+1})\big), & \dots \\ max\big(sim(A_{n-1}, A_n)\big) & \end{bmatrix} \qquad (4)$$

where V, N, A, and R denote the sets that contain the total words that have been identified as verbs, nouns, adjectives and adverbs respectively, while $max(sim(A_i, A_{i+1}))$ is the maximum similarity between the processed words and their n synonyms.

Finally, the SentiWordNet score for each word in a tweet is calculated (Baccianella et al., 2010), ignoring words that have fewer than two letters. If the score of a word cannot be determined, then we calculate the SentiWordNet score of the stemmed word. Given that the word wi occurs j times in the SentiWordNet corpus, the total score of wi is given by

$$swnScore_{wi} = \frac{\sum_{k=1}^{j} 1 + wScore(i,k)_p - wScore(i,k)_n}{j} \qquad (5)$$

where $wScore(i, k)_p$ and $wScore(i, k)_n$ is the k-th positive (PosScore) and negative (NegScore) score respectively of wi in SentiWordNet. The index i of each word was used in an attempt to correlate each word's position with the calculated sentiment.

Moreover, the total score of a tweet t is calculated as the average of SentiWordNet scores of the words in t.

The result is a dictionary with feature names as keys and values that indicate feature existence. Table 1 depicts the set of features considered by our system, together with the domain of values that they take.

3.2 Classification

For the classification process, the feature dictionaries fd_t of each data set were processed by a vectorizer to produce a vector array (http://scikit-learn.org/stable/modules/generated/sklearn.feature_extraction.DictVectorizer.html). From the vector array, a term-frequency matrix is calculated (with the use of a TfidfTransformer and the parameter "use_idf" set to False: http://scikit-learn.org/stable/modules/generated/sklearn.feature_extraction.text.TfidfTransformer.html) and is given as input for training to the chosen classifier. This frequency matrix is used to make predictions about the test set.

Feature	Value
Oh so* (*)	True/ False
Don't you*(*)	True/ False
As*As*(*)	True/ False
Question mark(*)	True/ False
Exclamation - mark(*)	True/ False
Capitals(*)	True/ False
Reference(*)	True/ False
RT	True/ False
Negations(*)	True/ False
URL	True/ False
HT_pos(*)	True/ False
HT_neg(*)	True/ False
HT_neu(*)	True/ False
Emoticon Pos(*)	True/ False
Emoticon Neg(*)	True/ False
POS-tags(*)	"NN", "VB", "ADJ","RB"
$swnScore_{wi}$(*)	"positive", "somewhat positive", "neutral", "negative" "somewhat negative"
swnScoreTotal	"positive", "somewhat positive", "neutral", "negative" "somewhat negative"
sim_t (Resnik*)	Decimal score

Table 1: Calculated features with their value.

4 Experiments and Results

The SemEval data set consists of 9000 tweets that are rich in figurative language and stemmed from user-generated tags, such as "#sarcasm" and "#irony". There is a 90-10 split for trial and test data. We retrieved 8529 tweets in total, 7606 from the trial set and 923 from the test set. Out of these data sets, positive tweets in total are 8,2%, negative tweets are 85,2% and neutral 6,6%.

4.1 Experiments

We experimented by incrementally adding features, and trying different classifiers. The results of the features that seem to contribute most were used to make the prediction with which the system participated in the task and are the ones marked with (*) in Table 1. It is also worthwhile mentioning that, after trials, discretization was applied to $swnScore_{wi}$ as follows:

$$swnScore_{wi} = \begin{cases} positive, & (> 1.2) \\ somewhat\ positive, & (> 0.05 \le 1.2) \\ neutral, & (\le 0.05 \ge 0.95) \\ somewhat\ negative, & (< 0.95 \ge 0.2) \\ negative, & (< 0.2) \end{cases} \quad (6)$$

4.2 Final Results

We evaluate the performance of our approach measuring the cosine similarity between the output of our system and the given scores for the test data set. Other measures such as accuracy, precision and recall are also used in our study.

The most useful features are pos-tags and SentiWordNet score. Semantic similarity (Resnik measure) and hashtags also seem to contribute and the rest of the selected features contribute marginally. These results are coherent with sentiment analysis literature where prior polarity along with POS-tagging seem to add most value to a classifier, and other features like emoticons add up only marginally (Agarwal et al., 2011, Kouloumpis et al., 2010).

Table 2 shows the evaluation results (cosine similarity and accuracy) of our system for both initial and final data set. We can observe that Linear SVM (default parameters: http://scikit-learn.org/stable/modules/generated/sklearn.svm.LinearSVC.html) achieves the best performance with respect to tweets classification. For the final submission, the total of the test and trial sets were used as input for the learning process of the classifier and only one run was submitted. The analysis of the results of the final submission, presented in Table 3, suggests that predictions on ironic and sarcastic tweets are more accurate than tweets that contain metaphor those that do not contain figurative language.

Classifiers	**Decision Tree**		**Naïve Bayes**		**Linear SVM**	
trials/ final	**t**	**f**	**t**	**f**	**t**	**f**
Cosine	0.68	0.45	0.70	0.55	0.78	0.60
Accuracy	0.31	0.21	0.33	0.23	0.38	0.29

Table 2: The results of the classifiers used on the initial test data set (t) and the final (f), with the selected features of the final submission.

	Cosine Similarity	**MSE**
Overall	0.601	3.925
Sarcasm	**0.87**	**1.499**
Irony	**0.839**	**1.656**
Metaphor	0.359	7.106
Other	0.271	5.744
Rank	10	10

Table 3: The final results by category.

5 Conclusion

The proposed system combines structured knowledge sources along with common tweet and figurative text features. A supervised learning approach is followed, having as goal to classify tweets containing irony and metaphors. The system ranked 10th (out of 15) based on both the cosine similarity measure and MSE. Among ironic, sarcastic, metaphoric and others, the best results were achieved in tweets containing irony and sarcasm. The most useful features for learning are pos-tags, Senti-WordNet score, text semantic similarity and hashtags. Our study shows that the performance of our system could be improved by adding features related to metaphor and considering better use of hashtags in the classification process. Besides, the use of non-figurative tweets in learning can significantly contribute to classify tweets that do not contain figurative language.

Acknowledgements

The work of C. Doulkeridis and M. Halkidi has been co-financed by ESF and Greek national funds through the Operational Program "Education and Lifelong Learning" of the National Strategic Reference Framework (NSRF) - Research Funding Program: Aristeia II, Project: ROADRUNNER.

References

Antonio Reyes, Paolo Rosso, Davide Buscaldi (2012). From Humor Recognition to Irony Detection: The Figurative Language of Social Media. Data & Knowledge Engineering 74:1-12.

Yanfen Hao, Tony Veale (2010). An Ironic Fist in a Velvet Glove: Creative Mis-Representation in the Construction of Ironic Similes. Minds and Machines 20(4):635–650.

Antonio Reyes, Paolo Rosso, Tony Veale (2013). A Multidimensional Approach for Detecting Irony in Twitter. Languages Resources and Evaluation 47(1): 239-268.

Ellen Riloff, Ashequl Qadir, Prafulla Surve, Lalindra De Silva, Nathan Gilbert, Ruihong Huang. Sarcasm as Contrast between a Positive Sentiment and Negative Situation. In Proceedings of the 2013 Conference on Empirical Methods in Natural Language Processing (EMNLP 2013).

Dmitry Davidov, Oren Tsur, and Ari Rappoport (2010). Semi-supervised recognition of sarcastic sentences in twitter and amazon. In Proceedings of the Fourteenth Conference on Computational Natural Language Learning, CoNLL 2010.

Aniruddha Ghosh, Guofu Li, Tony Veale, Paolo Rosso, Ekaterina Shutova, Antonio Reyes, John Barnden (2015). SemEval-2015 Task 11: Sentiment Analysis of Figurative Language in Twitter. In: Proc. Int. Workshop on Semantic Evaluation (SemEval-2015), Co-located with NAACL and *SEM, Denver, Colorado, US, June 4-5, 2015.

Ekaterina Shutova, Lin Sun and Anna Korhonen (2010). Metaphor Identification Using Verb and Noun Clustering. In: Proceedings of the 23rd International Conference on Computational Linguistics.

Alec Go, Richa Bhayani, and Lei Huang (2009). Twitter sentiment classification using distant supervision. In: Proceeding LSM '11 Proceedings of the Workshop on Languages in Social Media Pages 30-38.

Daantje Derks, Arjan E. R. Bos, and Jasper von Grumbkow (2007). Emoticons and online message interpretation. Social Science Computer Review, 26(3), 379-388.

Mike Thelwall, Kevan Buckley, Georgios Paltoglou, and Di Cai, Arvid Kappas (2010). Sentiment Strength Detection in Short Informal Text. Journal of the American Society for Information Science and Technology Volume 61, Issue 12, pages 2544–2558, December 2010

Efthymios Kouloumpis, Theresa Wilson, and Johanna Moore (2011). Twitter sentiment analysis: The Good the Bad and the OMG! In: Lada A. Adamic, Ricardo A. Baeza-Yates, and Scott Counts, editors, Proceedings of the Fifth International Conference on Weblogs and Social Media, ICWSM' 11, pages 538–541, Barcelona, Spain.

Apoorv Agarwal, Boyi Xie, Ilia Vovsha, Owen Rambow, Rebecca Passonneau (2011). Sentiment Analysis of Twitter Data. In: LSM'11 Proceedings of the Workshop on Languages in Social Media Pages 30-38.

Leon Derczynski, Alan Ritter, Sam Clark, and Kalina Bontcheva (2013). Twitter Part-of-Speech Tagging for All: Overcoming Sparse and Noisy Data. In: Proceedings of the International Conference on Recent Advances in Natural Language Processing, ACL.

Stefano Baccianella, Andrea Esuli, and Fabrizio Sebastiani (2010). SentiWordNet 3.0: An enhanced lexical resource for sentiment analysis and opinion mining. In: Proceedings of the 7th Conference on Language Resources and Evaluation (LREC 2010), Valletta, MT, 2010, pp. 2200-2204.

Christiane Fellbaum (1998, ed.) WordNet: An Electronic Lexical Database. Cambridge, MA.

Ted Pedersen, Siddharth Patwardhan, and Jason Michelizzi. (2004). Wordnet::similarity - measuring the relatedness of concepts. In: Demonstration papers at HLT-NAACL, pages 38-42.

Fabian Pedregosa et al. (2011). Scikit-learn: Machine Learning in Python. In Journal of Machine Learning Research 12, pp. 2825-2830.

Steven Bird, Ewan Klein, and Edward Loper (2009), Natural Language Processing with Python, O'Reilly Media.

Ryan Kelly, https://pythonhosted.org/pyenchant/, v. 1.6.5.

V3: Unsupervised Aspect Based Sentiment Analysis for SemEval-2015 Task 12

Aitor García-Pablos, Montse Cuadros
Vicomtech-IK4 research center
Mikeletegi 57
San Sebastian, Spain
{agarciap,mcuadros}@vicomtech.org

German Rigau
IXA Group
Euskal Herriko Unibertsitatea,
San Sebastian, Spain
german.rigau@ehu.es

Abstract

This paper presents our participation in SemEval-2015 task 12 (Aspect Based Sentiment Analysis). We participated employing only unsupervised or weakly-supervised approaches. Our attempt is based on requiring the minimum annotated or hand-crafted content, and avoids training a model using the provided training set. We use a continuous word representations (Word2Vec) to leverage in-domain semantic similarities of words for many of the involved subtasks.

1 Introduction

The continuous growing of textual content on the Internet has motivated an important research on finding automatic ways of processing and exploiting this valuable source of information. That is one of the reasons why sentiment analysis has become a very active research field during the last decade (Pang and Lee, 2008; Liu et al., 2012; Zhang and Liu, 2014). Sentiment analysis aims to detect and classify the polarity of sentiments expressed in a text. The granularity of this classification goes from the overall polarity of full documents to paragraphs, sentences or, as in Aspect Based Sentiment Analysis (ABSA), the sentiment about precise aspects being opinionated (Hu and Liu, 2004) (Popescu and Etzioni, 2005) (Wu et al., 2009) (Zhang et al. , 2010).

In this paper we describe our participation in SemEval-2015 task 12[1] (Pontiki et al., 2015), which is about ABSA. We have participated in all subtasks employing unsupervised or weakly supervised approaches.

The rest of the paper is structured as follows. Section 2 introduces the SemEval-2015 task 12 competition and provided datasets, and a brief introduction about how we have approached the different slots. Sections 3, 4 and 5 describe more in detail the employed techniques. Section 6 shows the results of the evaluation, and finally section 7 summarizes the conclusions.

2 Our approach

SemEval2015 task 12 was about ABSA. The task was divided into 3 slots. Slot 1 was about classifying review sentences into *entity-attribute* pairs, being the entity a main aspect of the reviewed item (e.g. food, drinks, location) and the attribute a particular facet of that aspect (e.g. food-quality, food-price, etc.). Slot 1 runs on two domains, restaurants and laptops. Slot 2 was about detecting explicit mentions to aspect-terms that are being reviewed (e.g. service in "The service was attentive"). Slot 2 runs only on restaurants domain. Slot 3 was about detecting the polarity/sentiment for the given gold entity-attribute pairs in sentences (see slot 1). Slot 3 was meant for restaurants and laptops domain, plus an additional hidden domain (i.e. revealed in the last moment and with no training data available) which resulted to be about hotels.

Two training datasets were provided. The first dataset contains 254 annotated reviews about restaurants (a total of 1315 sentences). The second dataset contains 277 annotated reviews about laptops (a total of 1,739 sentences). The annotation consists of

[1] http://alt.qcri.org/semeval2015/task12/

quintuples of aspect-term, entity-attribute, polarity, and starting and ending position of the aspect-term. When there is no explicit aspect-term mentioned *"null"* is employed to fill the gap. Only the restaurants dataset contains aspect-term annotation.

Our aim is to apply only unsupervised or minimally supervised techniques. We have applied different unsupervised approaches to the different slot tasks avoiding the use of the provided datasets to train a supervised system. We have used them only to evaluate and tune the performance of the employed techniques. For some of the employed techniques we have also used big unlabeled datasets. In particular, for the domain of restaurants we have employed a subset of 100k restaurant reviews from Yelp dataset[2]. We name this corpus as Yelp-restaurants. For laptops domain we have used a subset about 100k reviews from a big dataset of Amazon electronic device reviews [3] (retaining only the ones that contain the word laptop). We name this corpus as Amazon-laptops.

3 Aspect term extraction

SemEval2015 Task 12 slot 2 was about detecting mentions to explicit aspect terms, but only for restaurant domain (i.e. other slots run for restaurants and laptop domains).

For aspect term extraction our aim is to bootstrap a list of candidate domain aspect terms and use it to annotate the reviews of the same domain. We have implemented a system inspired in the method described at (Liu et al., 2014). In this work the authors employ what they call a graph co-ranking approach. They model aspect-terms (AT) and opinion-words (OW) as graph nodes, and then they generate three different sub-graphs defining different types of relations (what they call semantic-relations and opinion-relations) between the nodes. Finally they rank the nodes using a combined random walk on the three sub-graphs to obtain a list of reliable aspect-term candidates. Due to space limitations we cannot explain all the details here. Please, refer to the original article for more in detail explanation.

Based on some of these ideas we have implemented a system that aims to rank aspect-terms modeling them as a graph. From our datasets (i.e. Yelp-restaurants and Amazon-laptops) we have taken nouns as aspect term candidates, and adjectives as opinion word candidates, filtering out those words that appear less than 5 times. These are the nodes to build our graph. Then we have computed our own definition of semantic relations and opinion relations to build sub-graphs as follows:

- Opinion relations (AT-OW edges): we have computed how many times each AT has some syntactical dependency relation with each OW, from a certain set of dependency relations (i.e. direct object, adjectival modifier, attribute of a copulative verb). The result of this count is used as the weight of the edges between AT and OW nodes.

- Semantic relations (AT-AT and OW-OW edges): we have computed a continuous word representation of the datasets employing Word2Vec[4] (Mikolov et al., 2013) (with the following parameters: skip-grams, vector size of 200, context window of 5, hierarchical softmax). Then we have used the cosine similarity between word vectors as the weight of the semantic relation edges.

Once we have built the graph with the different type of nodes and different type of weighted edges, we execute a PageRank (Brin and Page, 1998) (alpha parameter set to 0.15) to score and rank the nodes. With the obtained score we generate an ordered list of aspect terms. We have done this only for restaurants since it was the only domain requested in the task 12 slot 2. Example of some of the higher scored words for restaurant domain are: *food, service, place, restaurant, portion, atmosphere, experience, dish, meal, burger*.

The obtained aspect term list is then cropped to retain only the top N ranked words, and this cropped word list is used to annotate the given sentences performing a simple lemma matching.

[2] http://www.yelp.com/dataset_challenge

[3] http://snap.stanford.edu/data/web-Amazon.html

[4] We have employed the implementation in Apache Spark MLlib library https://spark.apache.org/mllib/

3.1 Multiword handling

Handling multiword terms is important in an ABSA system (e.g. it is not the same to detect just memory than flash memory and/or RAM memory, etc.). Multiword terms affect also to some opinion expressions like top notch. Finally, multiword terms arise from usual collocations of single terms, so they vary between domains.

In order to bootstrap a list of candidate multiword terms for each given domain, we have employed again our own Yelp-restaurants and Amazon-laptops datasets. We have computed Log-Likelihood Ratio (LLR) of n-grams (with n¡=3) to detect the more salient word collocations keeping the top K candidates (i.e. the ones with higher confidence of being a true multiword).

Examples of obtained multiwords for restaurants: *happy hour, onion ring, ice cream, spring roll, live music.*

Examples of obtained multiwords for laptops: *tech support, power supply, customer service, operating system, battery life.*

We have used this list in a pre-processing step to merge individual words into a single token when they match a multiword in the list.

4 Entity-attribute detection

The definition of entity-attribute detection in slot 1 states the difference between entities (coarse grained aspects that are being reviewed, e.g. food, drinks) and attributes (particular facet that is being actually reviewed, e.g. price, quality). This subtask runs both for restaurant and laptop domain. Due to the big amount of possible combinations and the consequent overlapping of some of them, this subtask becomes very difficult for an unsupervised system. In order to employ a weakly-supervised approach we have faced this subtask defining some representative seed words for each possible entity (e.g. food: chicken, salad, rice) and attribute (e.g. price: expensive, cheap). Then we reused the Word2Vec model for each domain to compute the similarity between sentence words and the seed words. When the accumulated similarity with some entity and attribute seed words is salient enough, we annotate the sentence with that entity-attribute pair. If the similarity is low, or is equally distributed among a every candidate entity, we leave the sentence unlabeled.

Word	Polarity Score	Polarity label
delicious	0.424	positive
tasty	0.439	positive
inexpensive	0.341	positive
slow	-0.182	negative
arrogant	-0.254	negative
mediocre	-0.051	negative

Table 1: Examples of polarity values obtained from the restaurants polarity lexicon.

5 Polarity detection

For polarity detection we have developed a polarity lexicon reusing the generated Word2Vec model for each domain. The intuition we have followed is that a polarity word in a domain should be more "similar" to a set of "very positive" words than to a set of "very negative" words, and vice versa.

We have employed the in-domain generated Word2Vec models because the polarity of words may vary between domains and we want to capture the polarity for each particular domain.

Let POS be a domain-independent positive word (e.g. excellent) and NEG a domain-independent negative word (e.g. horrible). Let W be the set of words we want to know the polarity. Let sim be the similarity between words (computed using the Word2Vec model for the domain). Then for each $w \in W$ we calculate its polarity using (1).

$$\text{polarity}(w) = \text{sim}(w, POS) - \text{sim}(w, NEG) \quad (1)$$

We obtain $polarity(w) > 0$ if the word is more similar to POS than to NEG and vice versa. This gives us a continuous value from very positive to very negative, but we have simplified it to a binary labeling: "positive" for any word w with $polarity(w) >= 0$ and "negative" if $polarity(w) < 0$.

In the table 1 we can see some examples of words, their punctuation in the positive-negative axis, and the assigned polarity label.

With these sentiment lexicons for each of the domains we have performed the annotation of the sentences. We have faced the annotation as a simple polarity count process. For each sentence we counted the polarity of the words regarding our in-domain

Slot 2 systems	Restaurants F-score
Baseline	0.48
V3 (ours)	0.45
Best	0.70
Average	0.52

Table 2: Results on the restaurant reviews for slot 2.

lexicons and labeled the provided gold quintuples with the most frequent polarity. We have taken into account the negation words (e.g. not) present in the sentence in order to reverse the polarity of the words within a certain window (one token before and two tokens after the current word).

6 Experiments and results

We have participated in SemEval-2015 Task 12 slot 1 (entity-attribute detection), slot 2 (aspect-term detection) and slot 3 (polarity detection). In general the task definition is more challenging than in SemEval-2014 ABSA competition[5] as the average results of all participants indicate. The participation number is also lower and varies between of subtasks and domains (15 participants for restaurants slot 1, 9 for laptops slot 1, 21 for restaurants slot 2, and an average of 14 for slot 3 in the three available domains). As far as we know, we are the only team that has faced the competition using unsupervised approaches. As expected, the supervised systems obtain better results in general than our unsupervised one.

Slot 2 (detecting explicit aspect terms) was only available for restaurants. After performing the steps described in section 3, we employed the top 500 bootstrapped terms to annotate the provided set of reviews using a simple lemma matching. The results are shown in table 2, together with the official results of the supervised baseline, the best performing system, and the average of all participants.

Slot 1 (detecting entity-attribute pairs in sentences) was available both for restaurants and laptops. We employed the described manual bag of words plus Word2Vec approach. The results are quite modest as it can be appreciated in table 3.

Slot 3 (polarity annotation) was available both for restaurants and laptops, plus and additional hidden domain. This hidden domain, which was about hotels, was revealed in the last moment and no training data was provided. For this hidden domain we had no time to develop its own sentiment lexicon so we employed the one from restaurants domain. The results for all domains are shown in table 4.

[5]http://alt.qcri.org/semeval2014/task4/

Slot 1 systems	Restaur. F-score	Laptops F-score
Baseline	0.51	0.46
V3 (ours)	0.41	0.25
Best	0.62	0.50
Average	0.53	0.45

Table 3: Results on the restaurant and laptops reviews for entity-attribute detection (SemEval-2015 task 12 slot 1).

Slot 3 accuracy	Restaurants	Laptops	Hotels
Baseline	0.635	0.699	0.716
V3 (ours)	0.694	0.683	0.710
Best	0.786	0.793	0.805
Average	0.713	0.713	0.712

Table 4: Results on the restaurant, laptops and hotels for slot 3.

7 Conclusions

In this paper we have described our participation in SemEval-2015 task 12 (ABSA). We have approached all subtasks from an unsupervised or weakly-supervised point of view. To our opinion this year the tasks were more challenging than in the previous SemEval ABSA edition. We have explored different ways of approaching the challenges without requiring a manually labeled train set. We have made an intensive use of continuous word representations (e.g. Word2Vec) to exploit semantic similarities between words and despite the low results we have found some promising ideas. In the future we will explore how to improve the developed systems and how to combine with other unsupervised or semi-supervised techniques to achieve competitive results.

Acknowledgments

This work has been partially funded by SKaTer[6] (TIN2012-38584-C06-02), NewsReader[7] (ICT-316404) and Vicomtech-IK4.

[6]http://nlp.lsi.upc.edu/skater/
[7]http://www.newsreader-project.eu

References

Brin, Sergey and Page, Lawrence 1998. The anatomy of a large-scale hypertextual Web search engine *Computer networks and ISDN systems*

Hu, Minqing and Liu, Bing 2004. Mining opinion features in customer reviews *AAAI*

Bo Pang and Lillian Lee 2008. Opinion mining and sentiment analysis *Foundations and trends in information retrieval,*

Tomas Mikolov, Kai Chen, Greg Corrado, and Jeffrey Dean 2013. Efficient Estimation of Word Representations in Vector Space *Proceedings of Workshop at ICLR*

Liu, Kang and Xu, Liheng and Zhao, Jun 2014. Extracting Opinion Targets and Opinion Words from Online Reviews with Graph Co-ranking *Proceedings of the 52nd Annual Meeting of the Association for Computational Linguistics*

Bing Liu 2012. Sentiment analysis and opinion mining *Synthesis Lectures on Human Language Technologies*

Maria Pontiki, Dimitrios Galanis, Haris Papageogiou, Suresh Manandhar, and Ion Androutsopoulos 2015. SemEval-2015 Task 12: Aspect Based Sentiment Analysis *Proceedings of the 9th International Workshop on Semantic Evaluation (SemEval 2015), Denver, Colorado*

Popescu, AM and Etzioni, Oren 2005. Extracting product features and opinions from reviews *Natural language processing and text mining*

Wu, Yuanbin and Zhang, Qi and Huang, Xuanjing and Wu, Lide 2009. Phrase dependency parsing for opinion mining *Proceedings of the 2009 Conference on Empirical Methods in Natural Language Processing: Volume 3*

Zhang, L and Liu, Bing and Lim, SH and O'Brien-Strain, E 2010. Extracting and ranking product features in opinion documents *Proceedings of the 23rd International Conference on Computational Linguistics*

Zhang, Lei and Liu, Bing 2014. Aspect and Entity Extraction for Opinion Mining *Data Mining and Knowledge Discovery for Big Data*

LT3: Applying Hybrid Terminology Extraction to Aspect-Based Sentiment Analysis

Orphée De Clercq, Marjan Van de Kauter, Els Lefever and Véronique Hoste
LT^3, Language and Translation Technology Team
Department of Translation, Interpreting and Communication – Ghent University
Groot-Brittanniëlaan 45, 9000 Ghent, Belgium
Firstname.Lastname@UGent.be

Abstract

The LT3 system perceives ABSA as a task consisting of three main subtasks, which have to be tackled incrementally, namely aspect term extraction, classification and polarity classification. For the first two steps, we see that employing a hybrid terminology extraction system leads to promising results, especially when it comes to recall. For the polarity classification, we show that it is possible to gain satisfying accuracies, even on out-of-domain data, with a basic model employing only lexical information.

1 Introduction

There exists a large interest in sentiment analysis of user-generated content. Until recently, the main research focus has been on discovering the overall polarity of a certain text or phrase. A noticeable shift has occurred to consider a more fine-grained approach, known as aspect-based sentiment analysis (ABSA). For this task the goal is to automatically identify the aspects of given target entities and the sentiment expressed towards each of them. In this paper, we present the LT3 system that participated in this year's SemEval 2015 ABSA task. Though the focus was on the same domains (restaurants and laptops) as last year's task (Pontiki et al., 2014), it differed in two ways. This time, entire reviews were to be annotated and for one subtask the systems were confronted with an out-of-domain test set, unknown to the participants.

The task ran in two phases. In the first phase (Phase A), the participants were given two test sets (one for the laptops and one for the restaurants domain). The restaurant sentences were to be annotated with automatically identified <*target, aspect category*> tuples, the laptop sentences only with the identified aspect categories. In the second phase (Phase B), the gold annotations for the above two datasets, as well as for a hidden domain, were given and the participants had to return the corresponding polarities (positive, negative, neutral). For more information we refer to Pontiki et al. (2015).

We tackled the problem by dividing the ABSA task into three incremental subtasks: (i) aspect term extraction, (ii) aspect term classification and (iii) aspect term polarity estimation (Pavlopoulos and Androutsopoulos, 2014). The first two are at the basis of Phase A, whereas the final one constitutes Phase B. For the first step, viz. extracting terms (or *targets*), we wanted to test our in-house hybrid terminology extraction system (Section 2). Next, we performed a multiclass classification task relying on a feature space containing both lexical and semantic information to aggregate the previously identified terms into the domain-specific and predefined aspects (or *aspect categories*) (Section 3). Finally, we performed polarity classification by deriving both general and domain-specific lexical features from the reviews (Section 4). We finish with conclusions and prospects for future work (Section 5).

2 Aspect Term Extraction

Before starting with any sort of classification, it is essential to know which entities or concepts are present in the reviews. According to Wright (1997), these "words that are assigned to concepts used in the special languages that occur in subject-field or domain-related texts" are called terms. Translated to the current challenge, we are thus looking for words or terms specific to a specific domain or interest, such as the restaurant domain.

In order to detect these terms, we tested our in-house terminology extraction system TExSIS (Macken et al., 2013), which is a hybrid system combining linguistic and statistical information. For the linguistic analysis, TExSIS relies on tokenized, Part-of-Speech tagged, lemmatized and chunked data using the LeTs Preprocess toolkit (Van de Kauter et al., 2013), which is incorporated in the architecture. Subsequently, all words and chunks matching certain Part-of-Speech patterns (i.e. nouns and noun phrases) were considered as candidate terms. In order to determine the specificity of and cohesion between these candidate terms, we combine several statistical filters to represent the termhood and unithood of the candidate terms (Kageura and Umino, 1996). To this purpose, we employed Log-likelihood (Rayson and Garside, 2000), C-value (Frantzi et al., 2000) and termhood (Vintar, 2010). All these statistical filters were calculated using the Web 1T 5-gram corpus (Brants and Franz, 2006) as a reference corpus.

After a manual inspection of the first output for the training data, we formulated some filtering heuristics. We filter out terms consisting of more than six words, terms that refer to location names or that contain sentiment words. Locations are found using the Stanford CoreNLP toolkit (Manning et al., 2014) and for the sentiment words, we filter those terms occurring in one of the following sentiment lexicons: AFINN (Nielsen, 2011), General Inquirer (Stone et al., 1966), NRC Emotion (Mohammad and Turney, 2010; Mohammad and Yang, 2011), MPQA (Wilson et al., 2005) and Bing Liu (Hu and Liu, 2004).

The terms that resulted from this filtered TExSIS output, supplemented with those terms that were annotated in the training data but not recognized by our terminology extraction system, were all considered as candidate terms. Finally, this list of candidate targets was further extended by also including coreferential links as null terms. Coreference resolution of each individual review was performed with the Stanford multi-pass sieve coreference resolution system (Lee et al., 2011). We should also point out that we only allowed terms to be identified in the test data when a sentence contains a subjective opinion. This was done by running it through the above-mentioned sentiment lexicons.

3 Phase A

Given a list of possible candidate terms, the next step consists in aggregating these terms to broader aspect categories. As our main focus was on combining aspect term extraction with classification and since no targets were annotated for the laptops, we decided to focus on the restaurants domain. The organizers provided the participants with training data consisting of 254 annotated restaurant reviews. The task was then to assign each identified term to a correct aspect category.

For the classification task, we relied on a rich feature space for each of the candidate targets and performed classification into the domain-specific categories. Whereas the annotations allow for a two-step classification procedure by first classifying the main categories and afterwards the subcategories, we chose to perform the joint classification as this yielded better results in our exploratory experiments.

3.1 Feature Extraction

For all candidate terms present in our data sets we derived a number of lexical and semantic features. For those candidate targets that have been recognized as anaphors (see Section 2), these features were derived based on the corresponding antecedent.

First of all, we derived bag-of-words token unigram features of the sentence in which a term occurs in order to represent some of the lexical information present in each of the categories.

The main part of our feature vectors, however, was made up of semantic features, which should enable us to classify our aspect terms into the predefined categories. These semantic features consist of:

1. **WordNet features**: for each main category, a value is derived indicating the number of (unique) terms annotated as aspect terms from that category in the training data that (1) co-occur in the

synset of the candidate term or (2) which are a hyponym/hypernym of a term in the synset. In case the candidate term is a multi-word term whose full term is not found, this value is calculated for all nouns in the multi-word term and the resulting sum is divided by the number of nouns.

2. **Cluster features**: using the implementation of the Brown hierarchical word clustering algorithm (Brown et al., 1992) by Liang (2005), we derived clusters from the Yelp dataset[1]. Then, we derived for each main category a value indicating the number of (unique) terms annotated as aspect terms from that category in the training data that co-occur with the candidate term in the same cluster. Since clusters can only contain single words, we calculate this value for all the nouns in a multi-word term and take the mean of the resulting sum.

3. **Linked Open Data (LOD) features**: using DBpedia (Lehmann et al., 2013), we included binary values indicating whether a candidate term occurs in one of the following DBpedia categories: *Foods*, *Cuisine*, *Alcoholic_beverages*, *Non-alcoholic_beverages*, *Atmosphere*, *People_in_food_and_agriculture_occupations* or *Food_services_occupations*. These features were automatically derived using the RapidMiner Linked Open Data Extension (Paulheim et al., 2014).

4. **Training data features**: number of annotations in the training data for each of the main categories. We filtered out candidate terms for which all of these feature values are "0", but decided to keep proper nouns and proper noun phrases.

3.2 Classification and Results

For all our experiments, we used LIBSVM (Chang and Lin, 2001). In order to tune our system, we split the training data into a train (90%) and test fold (10%) and ran various rounds of experiments, after which we manually analyzed the output. Based on this analysis, we were able to derive some post-processing heuristics to rule out some of the low-hanging fruit (i.e. misclassification which could be ruled out univocally). To do so, we built a dictionary containing all targets annotated in the training data, together with their associated category label(s). In case our classifier assigns a main category to a target term that is never associated with the respective target in the training dictionary, we overrule the classification output and replace it by the (most frequent) category-subcategory label that is associated with this target in the training dictionary.

[1] https://www.yelp.com/academic_dataset

The results of our system on the final test set and rank are presented in Table 1, where Slot 1 refers to the aspect category classification and Slot 2 to the task of finding the correct opinion target expressions (or terms).

Slot	Precision	Recall	F-score	Rank
Slot 1	51.54	56.00	53.68	8/15
Slot 2	36.47	79.34	49.97	13/21
Slot 1,2	29.44	44.73	35.51	6/13

Table 1: Results of the LT3 system on Phase A

For the design of our system we wanted to focus most on the combination of Slot 1 and 2, i.e. finding the target terms and being able to classify them in the correct category. This is the most difficult task of all three, hence the lower F-scores in general (Pontiki et al., 2015). Though there is much room for improvement for our system, we do observe that our rank increases for this more difficult task. Our precision scores are rather low, but we obtain the best recall scores for Slot 2 and Slot 1,2. For Slot 1,2 we are able to find 378 of the 845 possible targets, resulting in the best recall score of all participating systems (e.g. 44.73 compared to a recall score of 41.73 obtained by the winning team).

This leads us to conclude that there's quite some room for improvement for the aggregation phase. Normally, the similarity between terms is first computed after which some sort of clustering is performed

4 Phase B

In recent years, sentiment analysis has been a popular research strand. An example is last year's SemEval task 9 Sentiment Analysis in Twitter, which drew over 45 participants. The competition revealed that the best systems use supervised machine learning techniques and rely much on lexical features in the form of n-grams and sentiment lexicons (Rosenthal et al., 2014). For Phase B, in which we had all gold standard terms and aspect categories available, we decided to extend our LT3 system with another classification round where we classify every aspect as positive, negative or neutral. All features are derived from the sentence in which the terms were found and we participated in all three domains.

4.1 Feature Extraction

We implemented a number of lexical features. First of all, we derived bag-of-words token unigram features. Then, we also generated features using two of the more well-known sentiment lexicons: General Inquirer (Stone et al., 1966) and Bing Liu (Hu and Liu, 2004) and a manually constructed list of negation cues based on the training data of SemEval-2014 task 9 (Van Hee et al., 2014). Moreover, for both the restaurants and laptops domain we created a list of all the domain-specific positive, negative and neutral words based on the training data. For the hotels we were not able to compile such a list.

Finally, we also included PMI features based on three domain-specific datasets. PMI (pointwise mutual information) values indicate the association of a word with positive and negative sentiment: the higher the PMI score, the stronger the word-sentiment association. We calculated this for each unigram based on the word-sentiment associations found in the respective training dataset. PMI values were calculated as follows:

$$PMI(w) = PMI(w, positive) - PMI(w, negative) \quad (1)$$

As the equation shows, the association score of a word with negative sentiment is subtracted from the word's association score with positive sentiment. For the restaurants domain we relied on the Yelp dataset (cfr. Section 3.1), for the laptops domain on a subset of the Amazon electronics dataset (McAuley and Leskovec, 2013), and for the hidden – hotel – domain we worked with reviews collected from TripAdvisor (Wang et al., 2011). All datasets were filtered by only including reviews with strong subjective ratings (e.g. we preferred a 5 star rating for positive reviews over one of 3 stars).

4.2 Classification and Results

We again used LIBSVM as our learner. For the restaurants and laptops domain, we used the respective training data sets. For the hidden (hotel) domain, we only used the restaurants training data since we assumed hotels to be more similar to restaurants than they are to laptops. The results of our system are presented in Table 2.

Domain	Accuracy	Rank
Restaurants	75.03	4/15
Laptops	73.76	5/13
Hotels	80.53	2/11

Table 2: Result of the LT3 system on Phase B

Our results show that using only lexical features already results in quite satisfying accuracy scores for all three domains. Considering the hotels dataset, we can conclude that having training data available from a very similar domain does already result in a satisfying accuracy (our system has the second best score on the hidden domain). In the future, we will investigate the performance gain when also including domain-specific training data.

5 Conclusions and Future Work

We presented the LT3 system, which is able to tackle the aspect-based sentiment analysis task incrementally by first deriving candidate terms, after which these are classified into various categories and polarities. Applying a hybrid terminology extraction system to the first phase seems to be a promising approach. Our experiments revealed that we are able to receive high recall for the task of deriving targets and aspect categories using a variety of lexical and semantic features. When it comes to the polarity estimation, we see that a classifier mostly relying on lexical information achieves a satisfying performance, even on out-of-domain data.

Based on our results, we see different directions for follow-up research. For the term extraction, we will focus on more powerful filtering techniques. With respect to term aggregation, we will explore new techniques of clustering our list of candidate terms in different manners. Furthemore, we will explore in future experiments to which extent deeper syntactic, semantic and discourse modelling leads to better polarity classification. Since the TExSIS system was developed as a multilingual framework (Macken et al., 2013), we are currently translating the LT3 system so that it can handle Dutch reviews.

References

Thorsten Brants and Alex Franz. 2006. Web 1T 5-gram Version 1 LDC2006T13. Web Download.

Peter F. Brown, Peter V. deSouza, Robert L. Mercer, Vincent J. Della Pietra, and Jenifer C. Lai. 1992. Class-based n-gram models of natural language. *Computational Linguistics*, 18:467–479.

Chih-Chung Chang and Chih-Jen Lin, 2001. *LIBSVM: a library for support vector machines.*

Katerina Frantzi, Sophia Ananiadou, and Hideki Mima. 2000. Automatic recognition of multi-word terms: the C-value/NC-value method. *International Journal on Digital Libraries*, 3(2):115–130.

Minqing Hu and Bing Liu. 2004. Mining and summarizing customer reviews. In *Proceedings of the tenth ACM SIGKDD international conference on Knowledge discovery and data mining, KDD04*, pages 168–177, New York, NY. ACM.

Kyo Kageura and Bin Umino. 1996. Methods of automatic term recognition. A review. *Terminology*, 3(2):259–289.

Heeyoung Lee, Yves Peirsman, Angel Chang, Nathanael Chambers, Mihai Surdeanu, and Dan Jurafsky. 2011. Stanford's multi-pass sieve coreference resolution system at the conll-2011 shared task. In *Proceedings of the CoNLL-2011 Shared Task.*

Jens Lehmann, Robert Isele, Max Jakob, Anja Jentzsch, Dimitris Kontokostas, Pablo N. Mendes, Sebastian Hellmann, Mohamed Morsey, Patrick van Kleef, Soren Auer, and Christian Bizer. 2013. DBpedia – A Large-scale, Multilingual Knowledge Base Extracted from Wikipedia. *Semantic Web Journal.*

Percy Liang. 2005. Semi-supervised learning for natural language. In *MASTERS THESIS, MIT.*

Lieve Macken, Els Lefever, and Véronique Hoste. 2013. TExSIS: Bilingual Terminology Extraction from Parallel Corpora Using Chunk-based Alignment. *Terminology*, 19(1):1–30.

Christopher D. Manning, Mihai Surdeanu, John Bauer, Jenny Finkel, Steven J. Bethard, and David McClosky. 2014. The Stanford CoreNLP natural language processing toolkit. In *Proceedings of 52nd Annual Meeting of the Association for Computational Linguistics: System Demonstrations.*

Julian McAuley and Jure Leskovec. 2013. Hidden factors and hidden topics: Understanding rating dimensions with review text. In *Proceedings of the 7th ACM Conference on Recommender Systems*, RecSys '13, pages 165–172.

Saif Mohammad and Peter Turney. 2010. Emotions Evoked by Common Words and Phrases: Using Mechanical Turk to Create an Emotion Lexicon. In *Proceedings of the NAACL-HLT 2010 Workshop on Computational Approaches to Analysis and Generation of Emotion in Text*, LA, California.

Saif Mohammad and Tony Yang. 2011. Tracking Sentiment in Mail: How Genders Differ on Emotional Axes. In *Proceedings of the 2nd Workshop on Computational Approaches to Subjectivity and Sentiment Analysis (WASSA 2011)*, pages 70–79, Portland, Oregon. ACL.

Finn Nielsen. 2011. A new anew: Evaluation of a word list for sentiment analysis in microblogs. In *Proceedings of the ESWC2011 Workshop on Making Sense of Microposts: Big things come in small packages.*

Heiko Paulheim, Petar Ristoski, Evgeny Mitichkin, and Christian Bizer. 2014. Data mining with background knowledge from the web. In *Proceedings of the 5th RapidMiner World.*

John Pavlopoulos and Ion Androutsopoulos. 2014. Aspect term extraction for sentiment analysis: New datasets, new evaluation measures and an improved unsupervised method. In *Proceedings of the 5th Workshop on Language Analysis for Social Media (LASM)@ EACL.*

Maria Pontiki, Dimitris Galanis, John Pavlopoulos, Harris Papageorgiou, Ion Androutsopoulos, and Suresh Manandhar. 2014. Semeval-2014 task 4: Aspect based sentiment analysis. In *Proceedings of the 8th International Workshop on Semantic Evaluation (SemEval 2014)*, pages 27–35, Dublin, Ireland, August. Association for Computational Linguistics and Dublin City University.

Maria Pontiki, Dimitris Galanis, Harris Papageorgiou, Suresh Manandhar, and Ion Androutsopoulos. 2015. Semeval-2015 task 12: Aspect based sentiment analysis. In *Proceedings of the 9th International Workshop on Semantic Evaluation (SemEval 2015)*, Denver, Colorado.

Paul Rayson and Roger Garside. 2000. Comparing corpora using frequency profiling. In *Proceedings of the workshop on Comparing corpora, 38th annual meeting of the Association for Computational Linguistics*, pages 1–6, Hong Kong, China.

Sara Rosenthal, Alan Ritter, Preslav Nakov, and Veselin Stoyanov. 2014. Semeval-2014 task 9: Sentiment analysis in twitter. In *Proceedings of the 8th International Workshop on Semantic Evaluation (SemEval 2014)*, pages 73–80, Dublin, Ireland, August. Association for Computational Linguistics and Dublin City University.

Philip J. Stone, Dexter C. Dunphy, Marshall S. Smith, and Daniel M. Ogilvie. 1966. The General Inquirer: A Computer Approach to Content Analysis. *MIT Press.*

Marjan Van de Kauter, Geert Coorman, Els Lefever, Bart Desmet, Lieve Macken, and Véronique Hoste. 2013.

LeTs Preprocess: The multilingual LT3 linguistic preprocessing toolkit. *Computational Linguistics in the Netherlands Journal*, 3:103–120.

Cynthia Van Hee, Marjan Van de Kauter, Orphee De Clercq, Els Lefever, and Veronique Hoste. 2014. Lt3: Sentiment classification in user-generated content using a rich feature set. In *Proceedings of the 8th International Workshop on Semantic Evaluation (SemEval 2014)*, pages 406–410, Dublin, Ireland, August. Association for Computational Linguistics and Dublin City University.

Špela Vintar. 2010. Bilingual term recognition revisited: The bag-of-equivalents term alignment approach and its evaluation. *Terminology*, 16:141–158.

Hongning Wang, Yue Lu, and ChengXiang Zhai. 2011. Latent aspect rating analysis without aspect keyword supervision. In *Proceedings of the 17th ACM SIGKDD International Conference on Knowledge Discovery and Data Mining*, KDD '11, pages 618–626.

Theresa Wilson, Janyce Wiebe, and Paul Hoffmann. 2005. Recognizing contextual polarity in phrase-level sentiment analysis. In *Proceedings of the conference on Human Language Technology and Empirical Methods in Natural Language Processing, HLT05*, pages 347–354, Stroudsburg, PA. ACL.

Sue Ellen Wright. 1997. Term selection: the initial phase of terminology management. In Sue Ellen Wright and Gerhard Budin, editors, *Handbook of terminology management*, pages 13–23. John Benjamins, Amsterdam.

UFRGS: Identifying Categories and Targets in Customer Reviews

Anderson Kauer
Institute of Informatics – UFRGS
Porto Alegre – RS – Brazil
aukauer@inf.ufrgs.br

Viviane P. Moreira
Institute of Informatics – UFRGS
Porto Alegre – RS – Brazil
viviane@inf.ufrgs.br

Abstract

This paper reports on our participation in SemEval-2015 Task 12, which was devoted to Aspect-Based Sentiment Analysis. Participants were required to identify the category (entity and attribute), the opinion target, and the polarity of customer reviews. The system we built relies on classification algorithms to identify aspect categories and on a set of rules to identify the opinion target. We propose a two-phase classification approach for category identification and use a simple method for polarity detection. Our results outperform the baseline in many cases, which means our system could be used as an alternative for aspect classification.

1 Introduction

Aspect Based Sentiment Analysis aims at discovering the opinions or sentiments expressed by a user on the different aspects of a given entity (Hu and Liu, 2004; Liu, 2012). Recently, a number of methods and techniques have been developed to tackle this task and some of them rely on syntactic dependencies to locate the opinion target (Kim and Hovy, 2004; Qiu et al., 2011; Liu et al., 2013). A syntactic parser takes a natural language sentence as input and outputs the relationships between the words in the sentence. Figure 1 shows the dependency tree for the sentence "The phone has a good screen." and the grammatical relations of each token (det, subj, mod, obj). We explore using grammatical relations to help identify the opinion targets.

In this paper, we describe a system which took part on SemEval-2015, and the way it was applied to category and polarity classification. Our system participated in all subtasks from Task 12 (Aspect Based Sentiment Analysis). For more details on this task, please refer to Pontiki et al. (2015). Our system combines classification algorithms, coreference resolution tools, and a syntactic parser. One of our goals was to minimize the use of external resources.

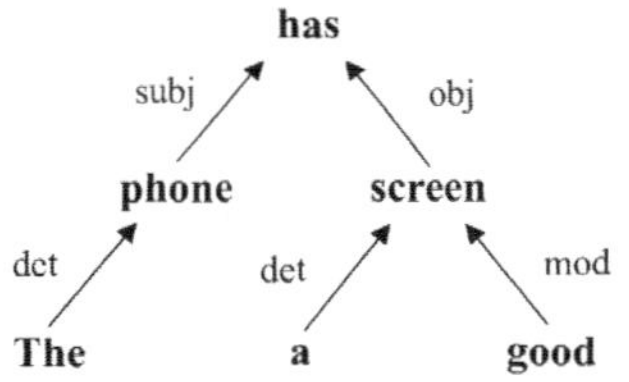

Figure 1: Example of a dependency tree (Liu et al., 2013).

The remainder of this paper is organized as follows: Our system is described in Section 2. Section 3 reports on the evaluation results. Finally, section 4 concludes the paper.

2 Description of the System

In this section, we describe the different components of the system.

2.1 Pre-processing

A distinctive characteristic of Web content is the high prevalence of noise. This directly impacts the quality of the results generated by a syntactic parser. In our system, we used the StanfordNLP Core toolkit (Manning et al., 2014).

The training sentences provided by the organizers were sometimes composed by more than one sentence. Thus, before submitting them to the parser, a cleaning step based on regular expressions was performed. In this step, we replaced all punctuation marks by commas and removed non-alphabetic characters.

Then, the standard pre-processing tools available from the StanfordNLP Core were applied (tokenization, sentence splitting, part-of-speech tagging, morphological analysis, syntactic parsing, coreference resolution, and sentiment analysis).

2.2 Aspect Category Identification

We treated the problem of identifying aspect categories as a classification task. Thus, we made use of the classifiers available from Weka (Hall et al., 2009) to build models based on the training data. In Task 12, categories are formed by a pair Entity#Attribute. The organizers have provided a list of possible entities and, for each entity, a list of attributes.

For each entity, we built a binary classifier where each instance contains the lemmas on the sentence and coreference lemmas to the previous sentences. The class indicates whether the instance belongs to the entity (*i.e.*, *positive* means that the instance belongs to the entity and *negative* means it does not belong to the entity). For each entity, the features were selected using the *InfoGainAttributeEval* with *Ranker* as a search method (available from Weka). The threshold set up to Ranker was 0, which means that the words selected by the method must contribute to identify the class.

We used two approaches to classify the sentences. In the first approach, *one-phase classification*, for each entity dataset we trained six classifiers using *all* the sentences. These six classifiers (namely IBk, ThresholdSelector, BayesianLogisticRegression, Logistic, MultiClassClassifier, and SMO) were the top performers on our experiments on the training data. We will refer to those as *Category classifiers*, as they will be used to actually determine the class. Since the classifiers for each category are independent, it is possible that a sentence is predicted as belonging to more than one category.

Classifiers were also built for each attribute belonging to that entity using *only* the sentences containing the entity. We call these *Attribute classifiers*, as they will be used to generate features for the *Category classifiers*.

In the two-phase approach (Figure 2), first we train n *Attribute classifiers* using all sentences but the current. In the experiments reported in Section 3, we used twenty *Attribute classifiers* (n=20). Then, the outputs from each of the n *Attribute classifiers* were used as features for the *Category classifiers* (second phase). This phase requires significant processing time since a new dataset is created for each instance and the models have to be updated. This method assumes that the features in each instance contain "what the others tell about it" using different prediction models.

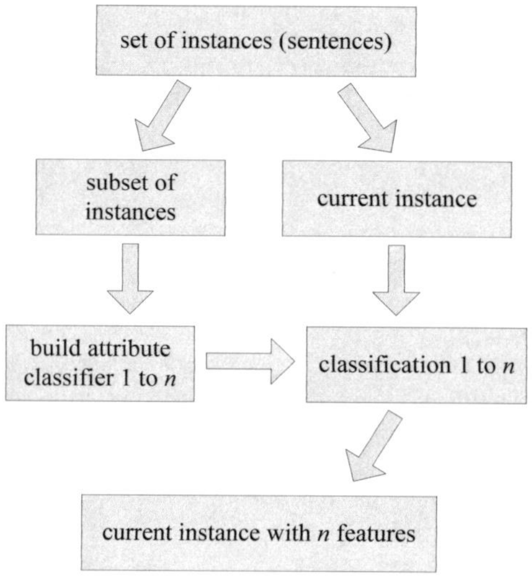

Figure 2: Two-phase classification pipeline.

To classify a new unseen instance, first it needs to be processed so that its lemmas and coreferences are identified. Then, word frequencies are selected and the n *Attribute classifiers* generate the values of the features for the second phase.

The final predicted class is the top scoring (*i.e.*, with the highest sum of scores) obtained from the results of the six *Category classifiers*. Although this has not happened in our experiments, a tie between the scores of the positive and negative classes is possible. In such a case, the sentence will be assigned to the positive class (*i.e.*, as belonging to the category).

2.3 Opinion Target Identification

The opinion target is detected after the category has been identified. For each pair Entity#Attribute discovered in the sentence, the candidate words are selected in order of information gain for that category. The words from attribute classification are concatenated with the words for entity classification. The assumption is that the words from attribute classification are more significant than the words from entity classification (which are more generic).

We select the word pairs which are directly associated (on the dependency tree) by a grammatical relation such as *adjectival modifier*, *noun compound modifier*, and *nominal subject*. We consider the opinion targets to be nouns/noun phrases as this has been widely adopted in the related literature (Hu and Liu, 2004; Qiu et al., 2011; Liu et al., 2013). Thus, the potential POS tags for targets are NN (singular nouns) and NNS (plural nouns). In order to identify incorrect targets, we rely on a list of 5k words assembled by Qian (2013). This exceptions list contains words with little or no meaning and that normally are not an aspect. The main target is the first candidate noun which is not in such a list.

If no nouns are found among the candidates, we find the nouns in the same sentence that are indirectly related to the candidate words (*i.e.* by transitivity), then we select the first noun. When still no nouns are found, then the opinion is set to *NULL* (it does not exist in the sentence). Target expressions are obtained using *noun compound modifier* (nn) associations.

A current limitation is that we do not identify multiple target expressions for the same category. We assume that for each category found, there is only one target in the sentence. However, since a sentence may be assigned to several categories, in these cases, more than one target may be identified and returned.

2.4 Sentiment Polarity Attribution

For this subtask, we used a simple approach that assigns the polarity of the target as the general polarity of the sentence. Stanford NLP Core provides sentiment analysis based on a compositional model over trees using deep learning (Socher et al., 2013). The nodes of a binarized tree of each sentence are assigned a sentiment score.

We opted for this approach to minimize the external resources in the our system, such as sentiment lexicons or reviews collected from other sources. The underlying model for Stanford NLP Core Sentiment Analysis was built on a corpus consisting of 11,855 sentences extracted from movie reviews. We have made no attempt to change the model to adapt to our reviews and used it as is to determine the polarity of the sentences. Our contribution in this phase was just the benchmarking of an existing tool.

3 Evaluation

We experimented with all three datasets from Task 12, namely Restaurants (Res), Laptops (Lap), and Hidden (Hid) for which the domain was unknown. Details on the datasets are in Pontiki et al. (2015).

The evaluation occurs in two phases. In the first phase, participating systems were evaluated on category detection for Restaurants and Laptops. Additionally, identifying opinion target and the pair $(category, target)$ was requested for the Restaurants domain. In the second phase, the systems were evaluated on polarity detection on all three domains.

3.1 Opinion Category and Target Detection

When evaluating opinion category and target detection (first phase), three measures were taken into account: precision, recall, and F1. For both category and target detection, the baseline methodologies are presented in Pontiki et al. (2015). Table 1 shows the results obtained using our approach compared to the baseline for aspect category detection, whereas Table 2 outlines the results regarding aspect target detection. The results for the pair $(category, target)$ are presented in Table 3.

Table 1: Opinion Category detection.

Domain	Method	P	R	F1
Res	2Phase	0.6556	0.4323	0.5210
Res	1Phase	0.6835	0.4181	0.5188
Res	Baseline			0.5133
Res	1Phase-coref	0.6821	0.4180	0.5184
Res	2Phase-coref	0.6509	0.4090	0.5023
Lap	Baseline			0.4631
Lap	1Phase	0.5066	0.4040	0.4495
Lap	2Phase	0.4773	0.4209	0.4473
Lap	1Phase-coref	0.4834	0.4462	0.4640
Lap	2Phase-coref	0.4689	0.4388	0.4534

The system outperforms the baseline on both approaches for the Restaurants domain. In this domain, the two-phase approach was superior to the one-phase approach. For the laptop domain, however, we scored lower than the baseline. We attribute that to the increased difficulty the coreference resolution step had when processing the review texts in this domain because of the large number of out of vocabulary words (CPU, HD, RAM, etc). Table 1 shows that the results improve when the coreference resolution step is not performed. Nevertheless, for the Restaurant domain, it brought improvements.

Table 2: Opinion Target detection.

Domain	Method	P	R	F1
Res	2Phase	0.5656	0.4373	0.4932
Res	1Phase	0.5764	0.4244	0.4888
Res	Baseline			0.4807
Res	2Phase-exc.	0.5632	0.4354	0.4911
Res	1Phase-exc.	0.5739	0.4225	0.4867

Considering the results for opinion target detection, both versions of our system outperformed the baseline. The two-phase classification achieved better recall in both category and target detection, but worse precision compared to one-phase classification.

We ran some additional experiments to evaluate the use of the exceptions list during target identification. These runs in which the exceptions list were not used are labelled 1Phase-exc and 2Phase-exc in Table 2. The results show that using such a list did not impact the results.

Table 3: Opinion Category and Target pair detection.

Domain	Method	P	R	F1
Res	2Phase	0.4852	0.2722	0.3487
Res	Baseline			0.3444
Res	1Phase	0.4521	0.2734	0.3407
Res	1Phase-coref	0.4694	0.2639	0.3378
Res	2Phase-coref	0.4496	0.2591	0.3288

As for the results for the pair $(category, target)$ the two-phase classification outperforms both the baseline and the one-phase classification. The gain in terms of precision is three percentage points, while recall was slightly reduced. The best configuration was using coreference resolution and the exceptions list.

3.2 Opinion Polarity Detection

Table 4 shows the results in terms of accuracy on opinion polarity. Here, the methodology for the baseline is similar to the ones used for aspect category detection (also described in Pontiki et al. (2015)). In this subtask, we submitted only the results for the one-phase classification.

Table 4: Opinion Polarity detection.

Domain	Method	Accuracy
Res	1Phase	0.7172
Res	Baseline	0.5373
Lap	1Phase	0.6733
Lap	Baseline	0.5701
Hid	Baseline	0.7168
Hid	1Phase	0.6578

The Stanford Core Toolkit uses a model trained on movie reviews, and this was not the same domain of the datasets in the task. Still, the classification results outperformed the baseline on Restaurants and Laptops. However, for the Hidden domain, we scored lower than the baseline.

3.3 Error Analysis

The results obtained with our system are ranked between the 5th (out of 15) and the 14th (out of 22) places. A case by case analysis was performed to identify the most frequent causes of errors. In the task of aspect category classification, the choice of the threshold used during feature selection by the Ranker (0) may have negatively impacted the results. Nevertheless, some feature selection method is necessary since the use of all the words as features greatly increases the processing time.

We used words selected by their Information Gain as seeds to identify the target expression. In our experiments, in many cases, the target was next to the words selected by this strategy. This happens because the $positive$ class had fewer instances than the $negative$ class, and the Information Gain tends to select words that characterize the least frequent class. However, most classification errors happened because this strategy failed to identify infrequent words that corresponded to the expected categories. One possible alternative to mitigate this problem could be the use of synonyms.

The method we used for polarity detection considered the entire sentence. The limitation here is that many sentences contain more than one opinion, which may not convey the same polarity. This could be solved by identifying the context (*i.e.*, a region around the target) and limit the polarity attribution to that region.

4 Conclusion

This paper reports on the experiments that we conducted while taking part on SemEval-2015 Task 12. We showed that classification algorithms, coreference resolution tools, and a syntactic parser may be combined in a category/target detection system.We employed a two-phase approach to classify instances. Our results show that this approach can be an alternative to classify sentences without using lexicons, improving recall with a small decay in precision. As future work, we plan to improve the coreference resolution of review texts so as to further improve recall.

Acknowledgments

This work has been partially funded by CNPq-Brazil project 478979/2012-6. Anderson Kauer receives a scholarship from CNPq-Brazil. We would like to thank the anonymous reviewers for their helpful suggestions and comments.

References

Mark Hall, Eibe Frank, Geoffrey Holmes, Bernhard Pfahringer, Peter Reutemann, and Ian H. Witten. 2009. The WEKA data mining software: an update. *SIGKDD Explor. Newsl.*, 11(1):10–18, November.

Minqing Hu and Bing Liu. 2004. Mining and summarizing customer reviews. In *Proceedings of the Tenth ACM SIGKDD International Conference on Knowledge Discovery and Data Mining*, pages 168–177, New York, NY, USA. ACM.

Soo-Min Kim and Eduard Hovy. 2004. Determining the sentiment of opinions. In *Proceedings of the 20th International Conference on Computational Linguistics*, Stroudsburg, PA, USA. Association for Computational Linguistics.

Qian Liu, Zhiqiang Gao, Bing Liu, and Yuanlin Zhang. 2013. A logic programming approach to aspect extraction in opinion mining. In *Web Intelligence (WI) and Intelligent Agent Technologies (IAT), 2013 IEEE/WIC/ACM International Joint Conferences on*, volume 1, pages 276–283, Nov.

Bing Liu. 2012. Sentiment analysis and opinion mining. *Synthesis Lectures on Human Language Technologies*, 5(1):1–167.

Christopher D. Manning, Mihai Surdeanu, John Bauer, Jenny Finkel, Steven J. Bethard, and David McClosky. 2014. The Stanford CoreNLP natural language processing toolkit. In *Proceedings of 52nd Annual Meeting of the Association for Computational Linguistics: System Demonstrations*, pages 55–60, Baltimore, Maryland. Association for Computational Linguistics.

Maria Pontiki, Dimitrios Galanis, Haris Papageogiou, Suresh Manandhar, and Ion Androutsopoulos. 2015. Semeval-2015 task 12: Aspect based sentiment analysis. In *Proceedings of the 9th International Workshop on Semantic Evaluation (SemEval 2015)*, Denver, Colorado.

Guang Qiu, Bing Liu, Jiajun Bu, and Chun Chen. 2011. Opinion word expansion and target extraction through double propagation. *Computational Linguistics*, 37(1):9–27.

Richard Socher, Alex Perelygin, Jean Y Wu, Jason Chuang, Christopher D Manning, Andrew Y Ng, and Christopher Potts. 2013. Recursive deep models for semantic compositionality over a sentiment treebank. In *Proceedings of the Conference on Empirical Methods in Natural Language Processing (EMNLP)*, pages 1631–1642.

SINAI: Syntactic approach for Aspect Based Sentiment Analysis

Salud M. Jiménez-Zafra, Eugenio Martínez-Cámara,
M. Teresa Martín-Valdivia, L. Alfonso Ureña-López
SINAI Research Group
University of Jaén
E-23071, Jaén (Spain)
{sjzafra, emcamara, maite, laurena}@ujaen.es

Abstract

This paper describes the participation of the SINAI research group in the task Aspect Based Sentiment Analysis of SemEval Workshop 2015 Edition. We propose a syntactic approach for identifying the words that modify each aspect, with the aim of classifying the sentiment expressed towards each attribute of an entity.

1 Introduction

Opinion Mining (OM), also known as Sentiment Analysis (SA), is the discipline that focuses on the computational treatment of opinion, sentiment and subjectivity in texts (Pang and Lee, 2008). Currently, OM is a trendy task in the field of Natural Language Processing, due mainly to the fact of the proliferation of user-generated content and the interest in the knowledge of the opinion of people by consumers and businesses.

Most of the systems developed up to now carry out opinion analysis at document level ((Pang et al., 2002), (Turney, 2002)) or at sentence level ((Wilson et al., 2005), (Yu and Hatzivassiloglou, 2003)), that is, they determine the overall sentiment expressed by the reviewer about the topic, product, person... of study. However, the fact that the overall sentiment of a product is positive does not mean that the author thinks that all the aspects of the product are positives, or the fact that is negative does not involve that everything about the product is bad. For this reason, users and companies are not satisfied with knowing the overall sentiment of a product or service, they seek a more detailed knowledge. Consequently, to achieve a higher level of detail, part of the scientific community related to this area is working on SA at aspect level ((Quan and Ren, 2014), (Marcheggiani et al., 2014), (Lu et al., 2011), (Thet et al., 2010)) and even, there is a competition on this topic that began to conduct last year (Pontiki et al., 2014) in the International Workshop on Semantic Evaluation 2014 (SemEval 2014).

This year, the 2015 edition of SemEval has also proposed a task for SA at aspect level. The SemEval-2015 Aspect Based Sentiment Analysis task is a continuation of SemEval-2014 Task 4 (Pontiki et al., 2014). The aim of this task is to identify the attributes of an entity that are being reviewed and the sentiment expressed for each one. It is divided into three slots. The first one is focused on the identification of every entity E and attribute A pair (E#A) towards which an opinion is expressed in the given text. Slot 2 proposes to determine the expression used in the text to refer to the reviewed entity, that is, the Opinion Target Expression (OTE). Finally, Slot 3 has as goal to classify the sentiment expressed over each category (E#A pair) as positive, negative or neutral. We have participated in the slot related to sentiment polarity (Slot 3).

Due to the fact that OM is a domain-dependent task, the organization proposes the three slots in different domains, two known (restaurants and laptops) and one unknown until the evaluation (hotels). A wider description of the task and the dataset used can be found in the task description paper (Pontiki et al., 2015).

The rest of the paper is organized as follows. Section 2 describes the system developed and the resources that we have used. To sum up, the results reached and an analysis of the same are shown in Section 3.

2 System description - Slot 3

As we have mentioned above, we have taken part in the Slot 3. The aim of this slot is to identify the polarity of each category or each <category, OTE> pair on which an opinion is expressed in a given review. This task has been carried out on two known domains an one unknown domain. For each of the known domains, restaurants and laptops, the organization has provided a dataset for training, whereas for the unknown domain any information has been given until the test set has been released. Therefore, we have used a supervised method for restaurants and laptops domains and we have developed an unsupervised method for the unknown domain.

2.1 Slot 3 - Restaurant domain ABSA

The training data related to restaurants domain contains 254 reviews. Each review is composed of different sentences annotated with opinion tuples. Each opinion tuple has information about the Opinion Target Expression (OTE), the Entity and Attribute pair (E#A category) towards the opinion is expressed, the polarity (positive, negative or neutral) and the position of the OTE in the text (from - to).

Using this information we have developed different experiments for polarity prediction. In all of them an SVM classifier of type C-SVC with linear kernel and the default configuration has been trained, and a 10-fold-cross validation model has been used for the assessment (Table 1).

The features that have provided the best results in the training and that we have used for our participation in this slot are the following. For each <category, OTE, polarity> tuple of the training data, we have used as label the polarity value and as features the words that modify the OTE, their PoS tag, their syntactic relation and their polarity using three lexicons (taking into account negation): SentiWordNet (Baccianella et al., 2010), MPQA (Wilson et al., 2005) and eBLR (enriched version of Bing Liu Lexicon (Hu and Liu, 2004) adapted to restaurant domain). Below, we describe briefly how this information has been obtained. Thereby, each <category, OTE> tuple of the test data is classified using its features vector and the trained SVM model.

Exp.	Type	Accuracy	Features
Exp_1	U	75.57%	Modifying words, PoS, syntactic relation, polarity (SentiWordNet, MPQA, BinLiu)
Exp_2	U	75.88%	Modifying words, PoS, syntactic relation, polarity (SentiWordNet, MPQA, BinLiu) taking into account negation
Exp_3	U	75.67%	Modifying words, PoS, syntactic relation, polarity (SentiWordNet, MPQA, eBLR)
Exp_4	**U**	**75.94%**	Modifying words, PoS, syntactic relation, polarity (SentiWordNet, MPQA, eBLR) taking into account negation

Table 1: Experiments restaurants training data (U = Unconstrained, C = Constrained).

2.1.1 Features

Words that modify the OTE

We call words that modify an OTE those words that specifically have been used in the review to discuss about the OTE. In order to determine what these words are, we use the Stanford Dependencies Parser[1]. This parser was designed to provide a simple description of the grammatical relationships that can appear in a sentence and it can be easily understood and effectively used by people without linguistic expertise who want to extract textual relations (De Marneffe and Manning, 2008). It represents all sentence relationships uniformly as typed depen-

[1] http://nlp.stanford.edu/software/lex-parser.shtml

dency relations. In this experiment, we have considered the main relationships for expressing opinion about a noun or nominal expression: using an adjectival modifier ("amod"), an active or passive verb ("nsub", "nsubjpass"), a noun compound modifier ("nn") or a dependency relation with another word ("dep"). In this way, for each OTE of a review, we use these relationships to extract all the words that modify the aspect of the entity that has been reviewed and we use them as features. If there is no word related to the aspect using these relationships, the previous word to the OTE and the following four words will be used.

Pos Tag

In addition, for each of the words that modify an aspect we get their particular Part of Speech Tag (noun, verb, adjective...).

Syntactic relations

As it has been mentioned above, the syntactic relation of each modifying word with the OTE has also been used as feature.

Polarity

The last feature of our SVM classifier is the polarity of each modifying word according to three lexicons: SentiWordNet, MPQA and eBLR. In addition, it has been used the fixed window method for the treatment of negation. Then, if any of the preceding or following 3 words is a negative particle ("not", "n't", "no", "never"...), the modifying word polarity will be reversed (positive —> negative, negative —> positive, neutral —> neutral).

SentiWordNet is a lexical resource that assigns to each synset of WordNet[2] (Miller, 1995) three sentiment scores (positivity, negativity and objectivity) that describe how positive, negative and objective the terms contained in the synset are.

MPQA is a subjectivity lexicon formed by over 8000 subjectivity clues. For each word, it has information about its prior polarity, its part of speech tag and its grade of subjectivity (strong or weak).

Finally, eBLR is an enriched version of Bing Liu Lexicon that we explain below. As is well-known in the SA research community, the semantic orientation of a word is domain-dependent. Therefore, we decided to generate a list of opinion words for the restaurant domain, taking as baseline the Bing Liu Lexicon and using the training data for restaurant domain supplied by the organization. For this, we have employed a corpus-based approach following the methodology of (Molina-González et al., 2013) that consists of the use of a sentiment labeled corpus in order to select the most frequent positive and negative words. A word is added to the list of opinion positive words if it only appears in positive reviews and its frequency exceeds a certain threshold. The same process is followed for negative words. In the case of words that appear in both positive and negative reviews, a word is considered as opinion positive/negative word if the frequency of occurrence in positive/negative reviews exceeds the frequency of occurrence in negative/positive reviews in a certain threshold.

2.2 Slot 3 - Laptops domain ABSA

The training data for laptops domain contains 277 reviews. Each review has different sentences annotated at aspect level with the Entity and Attribute pair (E#A category) towards each opinion is expressed and the polarity (positive, negative or neutral). In this case no information about the OTE is provided and thus, we have followed a different approach to that used in the restaurant domain. We have also developed different experiments with an SVM classifier of type C-SVC with linear kernel and the default configuration, and we have also used a 10-fold-cross validation model for the assessment but with different features (Table 2).

Exp.	Type	Accuracy	Features
Exp_1	**C**	**75.08%**	Unigrams, PoS
Exp_2	U	73.76%	Unigrams, total positive words (Bin Liu), total negative words (Bin Liu)
Exp_3	**U**	**79.64%**	Unigrams, total positive words (eBLL), total negative words (eBLL)

Table 2: Experiments laptops training data (U = Unconstrained, C = Constrained).

[2] Wordnet is an English lexical database which groups words according to their meaning.

For this domain we have submitted two runs, one constrained (using only the provided training data) and another unconstrained (using additional resources for training). These experiments are those that have provided better results with the training data and we have used them for our participation in this domain.

- SINAI_B_Lap_1 (Exp_1 - constrained). For each <category(E#A pair), polarity> tuple of the training data we have used as label the polarity and as features the entity and the specific attribute of this entity about someone is reviewing, and all the words of the sentence with their pertinent Part of Speech Tag.
- SINAI_B_Lap_2 (Exp_3 - unconstrained). In this case, the features that we have selected for each <category (E#A pair), polarity> tuple of the training data are the entity and the attribute about someone is reviewing, all the words of the sentence and the number of positive and negative opinion words according to eBLL. eBLL is an enriched version of Bing Liu Lexicon for laptops domain. It has been built using the training data supplied by the organization for laptops domain, in the same way that eBLR Lexicon.

Thus, given a category of the test data, it is classified using its features vector and the trained SVM model.

2.3 Slot 3 - Out of domain ABSA

For the last domain, the organization has not provided any information until the test set has been released. We only knew that we had to assign a polarity value for each <OTE, category> tuple present in the test data. In this case we have followed an unsupervised approach that we present below.

In order to classify the sentiment expressed about each OTE is important to determine the words that have been used in the review to discuss about the aspect. For this, we have employed the Stanford Dependencies Parser and the main relationships for expressing opinion about a noun or nominal expression: "amod", "nsubj", "nsubjpass", "nn", "dep" (they are explained in Subsection 2.1). In this way, for each OTE of a review, we use these relationships to extract all the words that modify it and we use them to determine the sentiment expressed about the OTE. If there is no word related to the aspect using these relationships, the previous word to the aspect and the following four words will be used. We calculate the polarity of each OTE through a voting system based on three classifiers: Bing Liu Lexicon, SentiWordNet and MPQA. To do this we determine, with each of the classifiers individually, the polarity of an OTE using the words that modify it. Thus, according to Bing Liu Lexicon, we count the number of positive (pw) and negative words (nw) that modify the OTE and tag it following the equation 1. On the other hand, we use MPQA as classifier following the same approach but in this case we take into account the PoS of the modifying words in order to get their polarity. At last, we employ SentiWordNet also following the approach of comparing the number of positive and negative words but as this lexicon assigns three sentiment scores to each synset, we calculate the polarity of each modifying word using the Denecke method (Denecke, 2008), that is, we calculate the average of the positivity, negativity and objectivity scores of all the synsets of the word with the same PoS and assign the word the polarity of the highest average.

$$pol(OTE) = \begin{cases} positive & \text{if } (pw > nw) \\ negative & \text{if } (pw < nw) \\ neutral & \text{if } (pw = nw) \end{cases} \quad (1)$$

Therefore, an OTE is positive/negative if there are at least two classifiers that tag it as positive/negative and neutral in another case. It may happen that an OTE is affected by negation, so if any of the preceding or following 3 words is a negative particle ("not", "n't", "no", "never"...), the OTE polarity will be reversed (positive —> negative, negative —> positive, neutral —> neutral).

3 Analysis of results

This section shows the results reached in the evaluation of the task using the system described in Section 2. Table 3 presents the official results of our submissions. We also include the results of the best team and the average of all participants for comparision.

A clear difference between the results obtained by our team and the average may be seen in Table 3.

Furthermore, the results in restaurants and laptops domain are worse than those achieved in the training phase (Table 1 and Table 2). Therefore, we have calculated the confusion matrix related to each experiment for a deeper analysis (Table 4, Table 5, Table 6 and Table 7).

	Accuracy		
	SINAI	Avg.	Best team
Restaurants	0.6071 (U)	0.7119	0.7870 (U)
Laptops	0.6586 (C) 0.5184 (U)	0.7093	0.7935 (U)
Hotels	0.6372 (U)	0.7079	0.8053 (U)

Table 3: Results test data (U = Unconstrained, C = Constrained).

	Restaurants			
	Pred. pos.	Pred. neu.	Pred. neg.	Recall
Real pos.	446	0	8	0.9824
Real neu.	43	0	2	0
Real neg.	276	3	67	0.1936
Precision	0.583	0	0.8701	

Table 4: Confusion matrix restaurants submission.

	Laptops (C)			
	Pred. pos.	Pred. neu.	Pred. neg.	Recall
Real pos.	491	0	50	0.9076
Real neu.	51	0	28	0
Real neg.	195	0	134	0.4073
Precision	0.6662	0	0.6321	

Table 5: Confusion matrix laptops constraint submission.

	Laptops (U)			
	Pred. pos.	Pred. neu.	Pred. neg.	Recall
Real pos.	391	0	150	0.7227
Real neu.	63	0	16	0
Real neg.	228	0	101	0.3070
Precision	0.5733	0	0.3783	

Table 6: Confusion matrix laptops unconstraint submission.

	Hotels			
	Pred. pos.	Pred. neu.	Pred. neg.	Recall
Real pos.	181	56	6	0.7449
Real neu.	5	6	1	0.5
Real neg.	15	40	29	0.3452
Precision	0.9005	0.0588	0.8056	

Table 7: Confusion matrix hotels submission.

	Restaurants	Laptops
Positive opinions	1198	1103
Neutral opinions	53	106
Negative opinions	403	765

Table 8: Opinions in training data per class.

If we observe Table 4, Table 5 and Table 6, we can see that, in restaurants and laptops domains, the system has failed mainly in the classification of negative and neutral opinions. It has classified most of them as positive. We think that one of the reasons may be that the training data for restaurants and laptops domains is unbalanced (Table 8). For restaurants, the number of positive opinions is almost three times the number of negative opinions. Another possible reason, in restaurants domain, is that we have only taken into account the scope (words that modify the OTE) and not the whole context (all words present in the review). In future works, we will do experiments balancing the datasets in order to test how the system works. Furthermore, we will take into account the whole context in restaurants domain to see if that improves the system.

Regarding the unsupervised system, that has been

tested with hotels domain, there are also differences with respect to the mean accuracy of all teams (Table 3). This is a first approach that can be improved with the consideration of other relationships to determine which words modify the OTE and with a treatment of negation more exhaustive. In future works we will consider these possible improvements.

Acknowledgments

This work has been partially supported by a grant from the Fondo Europeo de Desarrollo Regional (FEDER), ATTOS project (TIN2012-38536-C03-0) from the Spanish Government, AORESCU project (P11-TIC-7684 MO) from the regional government of Junta de Andalucía and CEATIC-2013-01 project from the University of Jaén.

References

Stefano Baccianella, Andrea Esuli, and Fabrizio Sebastiani. 2010. Sentiwordnet 3.0: An enhanced lexical resource for sentiment analysis and opinion mining. In *LREC*, volume 10, pages 2200–2204.

Marie-Catherine De Marneffe and Christopher D Manning. 2008. Stanford typed dependencies manual.

Kerstin Denecke. 2008. Using sentiwordnet for multilingual sentiment analysis. In *Data Engineering Workshop, 2008. ICDEW 2008. IEEE 24th International Conference on*, pages 507–512. IEEE.

Minqing Hu and Bing Liu. 2004. Mining and summarizing customer reviews. In *Proceedings of the tenth ACM SIGKDD international conference on Knowledge discovery and data mining*, pages 168–177. ACM.

Bin Lu, Myle Ott, Claire Cardie, and Benjamin K Tsou. 2011. Multi-aspect sentiment analysis with topic models. In *Data Mining Workshops (ICDMW), 2011 IEEE 11th International Conference on*, pages 81–88. IEEE.

Diego Marcheggiani, Oscar Täckström, Andrea Esuli, and Fabrizio Sebastiani. 2014. Hierarchical multi-label conditional random fields for aspect-oriented opinion mining. In *Advances in Information Retrieval*, pages 273–285. Springer.

George A Miller. 1995. Wordnet: a lexical database for english. *Communications of the ACM*, 38(11):39–41.

M Dolores Molina-González, Eugenio Martínez-Cámara, María-Teresa Martín-Valdivia, and José M Perea-Ortega. 2013. Semantic orientation for polarity classification in spanish reviews. *Expert Systems with Applications*, 40(18):7250–7257.

Bo Pang and Lillian Lee. 2008. Opinion mining and sentiment analysis. *Found. Trends Inf. Retr.*, 2(1-2):1–135, January.

Bo Pang, Lillian Lee, and Shivakumar Vaithyanathan. 2002. Thumbs up?: Sentiment classification using machine learning techniques. In *Proceedings of the ACL-02 Conference on Empirical Methods in Natural Language Processing - Volume 10*, EMNLP '02, pages 79–86, Stroudsburg, PA, USA.

Maria Pontiki, Haris Papageorgiou, Dimitrios Galanis, Ion Androutsopoulos, John Pavlopoulos, and Suresh Manandhar. 2014. Semeval-2014 task 4: Aspect based sentiment analysis. In *Proceedings of the 8th International Workshop on Semantic Evaluation (SemEval 2014)*, pages 27–35.

Maria Pontiki, Dimitrios Galanis, Harris Papageorgiou, Suresh Manandhar, and Ion Androutsopoulos. 2015. Semeval-2015 task 12: Aspect based sentiment analysis. In *Proceedings of the 9th International Workshop on Semantic Evaluation (SemEval 2015), Denver, Colorado*.

Changqin Quan and Fuji Ren. 2014. Unsupervised product feature extraction for feature-oriented opinion determination. *Information Sciences*, 272:16–28.

Tun Thura Thet, Jin-Cheon Na, and Christopher SG Khoo. 2010. Aspect-based sentiment analysis of movie reviews on discussion boards. *Journal of Information Science*, page 0165551510388123.

Peter D. Turney. 2002. Thumbs up or thumbs down?: Semantic orientation applied to unsupervised classification of reviews. In *Proceedings of the 40th Annual Meeting on Association for Computational Linguistics*, ACL '02, pages 417–424, Stroudsburg, PA, USA.

Theresa Wilson, Janyce Wiebe, and Paul Hoffmann. 2005. Recognizing contextual polarity in phrase-level sentiment analysis. In *Proceedings of the Conference on Human Language Technology and Empirical Methods in Natural Language Processing*, HLT '05, pages 347–354, Stroudsburg, PA, USA.

Hong Yu and Vasileios Hatzivassiloglou. 2003. Towards answering opinion questions: Separating facts from opinions and identifying the polarity of opinion sentences. In *Proceedings of the 2003 Conference on Empirical Methods in Natural Language Processing*, EMNLP '03, pages 129–136, Stroudsburg, PA, USA.

ECNU: Extracting Effective Features from Multiple Sequential Sentences for Target-dependent Sentiment Analysis in Reviews

Zhihua Zhang, Man Lan*
Shanghai Key Laboratory of Multidimensional Information Processing
Department of Computer Science and Technology,
East China Normal University, Shanghai 200241, P. R. China
51131201039@ecnu.cn, mlan@cs.ecnu.edu.cn*

Abstract

This paper describes our systems submitted to the target-dependent sentiment polarity classification subtask in aspect based sentiment analysis (ABSA) task (i.e., Task 12) in SemEval 2015. To settle this problem, we extracted several effective features from three sequential sentences, including sentiment lexicon, linguistic and domain specific features. Then we employed these features to construct classifiers using supervised classification algorithm. In laptop domain, our systems ranked $2nd$ out of 6 constrained submissions and $2nd$ out of 7 unconstrained submissions. In restaurant domain, the rankings are $5th$ out of 6 and $2nd$ out of 8 respectively.

1 Introduction

Reviews express opinions of customers towards various aspects of a product or service. Mining customer reviews (i.e., opinion mining) has emerged as an interesting new research direction in recent years. Since sentiment expressed in reviews usually adheres to specific categories or target terms, it is much meaningful to identify the sentiment target and its orientation, which helps users gain precise sentiment insights on specific sentiment target.

Unlike most existing sentiment analysis methods which try to detect the polarity of a sentence or a review, the aspect based sentiment analysis task (ASBA) shared as task 12 in SemEval 2015 is aiming at addressing the category- or target- dependent sentiment analysis in reviews. There are two types of subtasks organized in ASBA. The first aspect detection subtask is to identify the sentiment adherent from reviews, i.e., the category (i.e., entity-attribute (E-A) pair) or opinion target expression (*OTE*) in reviews. In most cases, the customers may not explicitly indicate the entity and attribute words in reviews but the opinion target expression is a segment of review. For example, in a given review: *"The pizza is overpriced and soggy."*, *target="pizza"*, *category="FOOD-QUALITY"*. Its category label *FOOD-QUALITY* does not exist in reviews, while its *OTE* word *"pizza"* is explicitly present in reviews. The second sentiment polarity classification subtask is to assign a polarity label (i.e., positive, negative or neutral) for every E-A pair or *OTE* identified from the given reviews. We participated the second type subtask, i.e., performing sentiment polarity classification on reviews. There are two domains in this sentiment analysis subtask, i.e, laptop and restaurant. In laptop domain, only E-A pairs are annotated and provided in reviews while in restaurant domain, both E-A pairs and *OTE* are provided. Comparing with laptop reviews, the restaurant reviews provide the annotated surface words adhering to sentiment. Therefore we speculate that the performance in restaurant domain would be much better than that of laptop domain.

The study of aspect based sentiment analysis focuses on discovering the opinions or sentiments expressed by a customer on different categories or aspects (Liu, 2012). In recent years, it has drawn a lot of attentions. For example, (Branavan et al., 2009; He et al., 2012; Mei et al., 2007) used topic or category information. (Lin and He, 2009; Jo and Oh, 2011) presented LDA-based models, which incorporate aspect and sentiment analysis together to model sentiments towards different aspects. (Hu and Liu, 2004; Ding et al., 2008) adopted lexicon-based approaches to detect the sentiment on different aspects. In addition, (Boiy and Moens, 2009; Jiang et al., 2011) explored the work to determine whether the reviews contain the aspect information. Unlike the above study, (Xiang et al., 2014) split the data into multiple subsets based on category distributions and then built seperate classifier for each category.

Following previous work (Brun et al., 2014; Brychcín et al., 2014; Castellucci et al., 2014; Kiritchenko et al., 2014), a rich set of features are adopted in this work: linguistic features (e.g., *n-grams*, grammatical relationship, *POS*, negations), sentiment lexicon features (e.g., MPQA, General Inquirer, SentiWordNet, etc) and domain specific features (e.g., in-domain word list, punctuation, etc). We also performed a series of experiments to compare supervised machine learning algorithms with different parameters and to choose effective feature subsets for performance of classification.

The rest of this paper is structured as follows. In Section 2, we describe our system in details, including preprocessing, feature engineering, evaluation metrics, etc. Section 3 reports data sets, experiments and result discussion. Finally, Section 4 concludes our work.

2 System Description

2.1 Motivation

Unlike tweets with word length limitation, a review usually consists of several sentences and one single sentence may contain mixed opinions towards different targets. However, based on our observation and statistics on the data provided by SemEval 2015 Task 12, we find that most reviews (about 70%) have consistent opinion in their sentences, even though these sentences contain different category descriptions. Furthermore, although the E-A pair annotation is provided for each sentence, it is usually inferred by human being based on common knowledge from review rather than a single sentence. That is, the E-A pair information is supposed to be induced from contextual sentences rather than a single sentence alone. On the other hand, since one sentence may contain more than one category (i.e. E-A pair), this sentence alone may not provide enough information for every E-A pair. In consideration of above described reasons, we use multiple sentences rather than one single sentence to extract features for sentiment analysis. In this work, we used three sequential sentences, that is, for one given sentence, we combined its preceding and subsequent sentence with this current sentence together to perform sentiment analysis.

As we mentioned, one sentence may contain more than one E-A pair. As a result, for each E-A pair, not all words in this sentence or review are quite relevant and we need to select out only relevant words from three sequential sentences in terms of the corresponding E-A pair. Unlike the *OTE* words which already exist in reviews, most E-A pairs are not present in the sentence. Thus, for each E-A pair, we first extracted target words having top *tfidf* scores from three sequential sentences and then chose the relevant words from parse tree. Specifically, in laptop domain, the sentences contain only E-A pairs, so we selected two words having the highest *tfidf* scores from three sequential sentences in terms of corresponding E-A pair as its target words. Inspired by (Kiritchenko et al., 2014), for each target word in E-A pair, we selected the words from parse tree with distance $d =< 2$ as relevant words in terms of this E-A pair. After that, for all words in target words, we combined all their relevant words as pending words to extract features for sentiment analysis. While in restaurant domain since the sentences contain both E-A pair and opinion target expressions (*OTE*), we only combined the words in *OTE* with two words mentioned before as target words and chose their relevant words as pending words.

For each domain, each participant can submit two runs: (1) *constrained:* only the provided data can be used; (2) *unconstrained:* any additional resources can be used. In this task, we adopted 7 sentiment lexicons as external resources. Thus, the only difference of our two systems lies in the sentiment lexicon score features. For both systems, we extracted many traditional types of features to build classifiers for classification.

2.2 Data Preprocessing

Four preprocessing operations were performed. We first removed the XML tags from data and then transformed the abbreviations to their normal forms, i.e., "*don't*" to "*do not*". We used *Stanford Parser tools*[1] for tokenization, POS tagging and parsing. Finally, the WordNet-based Lemmatizer implemented in NLTK[2] was adopted to lemmatize words to their base forms with the aid of their POS tags.

2.3 Feature Engineering

In this work, we used three types of features: sentiment lexicon features, linguistic features and domain-specific features. All features were extracted from pending words as described above.

Sentiment Lexicon Features: Given pending words, we first converted them into lowercase and then calculated five feature values for each sentiment lexicon: (1) the ratio of positive words to pending words, (2) the ratio of negative words to pending words, (3) the maximum sentiment score, (4) the minimum sentiment score[3], (5) the sum of sentiment scores. If the pending word does not exist in one sentiment lexicon, its corresponding score is set to zero. The following 8 sentiment lexicons are used in our systems. Specifically, the first lexicon is employed to build constrained system and others 7 lexicons for unconstrained system.

- *Constrained PMI*: To build constrained system, we generated two domain-specific sentiment lexicons from the given training data respectively (i.e., laptop and restaurant). Given a term *w*, this PMI-based score is calculated from labeled reviews as below:

  $$score(w) = PMI(w, pos) - PMI(w, neg)$$

  where *PMI* stands for pointwise mutual information.

- *Bing Liu opinion lexicon*[4]: This sentiment lexicon contains two annotated words lists: positive (about $2,000$) and negative(about $4,800$).

- *General Inquirer lexicon*[5]: The General Inquirer lexicon tries to classify English words along several dimensions, including sentiment polarity and we selected about $1,500$ positive words and $2,000$ negative words.

- *IMDB*[6]: This lexicon is generated from a large data set from IMDB which contains $25,000$ positive and $25,000$ negative movie reviews and the PMI-based sentiment score of each word is calculated as above.

- *MPQA*[7]: MPQA contains about $8,000$ subjective words with 6 types of label: strong/weak positive, strong/weak negative, both (having positive and negative sentiment) and neutral. Then we transformed these above nominal labels to $1, 0.5, -1, -0.5, 0, 0$ respectively.

- *SentiWordNet*[8]: The sentiment scores of each item in SentiWordNet is represented as a tuple i.e., positivity and negativity.We use the difference between positive and negative score as its sentiment score. When locating the corresponding item, we retrieved the word lemma and selected the first term in searched results according to its POS tag.

- *NRC Hashtag Sentiment Lexicon*[9]: (Mohammad et al., 2013) collected two tweet sets containing hashtags and used the sentiment of its hashtags as the sentiment label for each tweet. In this experiment, we used both unigrams and bigrams sentiment lexicons.

- *NRC Sentiment140 Lexicon*[10]: This lexicon is generated from a collection of 1.6 million tweets with positive or negative emoticons and contains about $62,000$ unigrams, $677,000$ bigrams and $480,000$ non-contiguous pairs. We used unigrams and bigrams.

Linguistic Features

- *Word n-grams:* We converted all pending words into lowercase and removed low frequency terms (≤ 5). After that, we extracted word-level unigram and bigrams.

[1] http://nlp.stanford.edu/software/lex-parser.shtml

[2] http://nltk.org

[3] We convert the sentiment scores in all sentiment lexicons to the range of $[-1, 1]$, where "-" denotes negative sentiment.

[4] http://www.cs.uic.edu/liub/FBS/sentiment-analysis.html#lexicon

[5] http://www.wjh.harvard.edu/inquirer/homecat.htm

[6] http://anthology.aclweb.org//S/S13/S13-2.pdf#page=444

[7] http://mpqa.cs.pitt.edu/

[8] http://sentiwordnet.isti.cnr.it/

[9] http://www.umiacs.umd.edu/saif/WebDocs/NRC-Hashtag-Sentiment-Lexicon-v0.1.zip

[10] http://help.sentiment140.com/for-students/

- *POS Features:* (Pak and Paroubek, 2010) found that subjective texts often contain more adjectives or adverbs and less nouns than objective texts. Therefore, the POS tags are important features for sentiment analysis. We recorded the number of nouns (the corresponding POS tags are *NN, NNP, NNS and NNPS*), verbs (*VB, VBD, VBG, VBN, VBP and VBZ*), adjectives (*JJ, JJR and JJS*) and adverbs (*RB, RBR and RBS*) in pending words.

- *Grammatical Relationship:* The grammatical relationship usually expresses the role of words in phrase and contains certain semantic information (Zhao et al., 2014). We obtained dependency information from parse tree and the grammatical information is denoted as a tuple, e.g., *amod(surprises, great)*, where *amod* represents the dependency relationship between *surprises* and *great* (here *great* is a modifier). We presented two types of features: the relationship with the first word in tuple as *Rel1* and with the second word as *Rel2*. The size of each feature set is approximately 150.

- *Negation Features:* We collected 29 negations from Internet and designed this binary feature to record if there is negation in pending words.

Domain Specifical Features

- *In-domain word list*: For different domains, the words indicative of viewpoints are quite different. For example, *useful, fast, excellent* represent positive opinion in laptop domain and *delicious, cheap, beautiful* stand for positive opinion in restaurant domain. Therefore, we manually built two in-domain word lists from training instances indicative of positive and negative for both domains respectively. This feature records the number of in-domain words in pending words.

- *Punctuation*: Exclamation (!) and question (?) signs often indicate emotions (i.e., surprise, shock, interrogative, etc.) of users. Thus this feature counts the number of exclamations and questions in pending words.

- *All-caps*: This feature is the number of uppercase words in pending words.

2.4 Evaluation Measures

To evaluate the performance of different systems, the official evaluation measure *accuracy* is adopted.

3 Experiment

3.1 Datasets

The organizers provided two XML format documents regarding *laptop* and *restaurant* domain. In laptop, the {*E-A, P*} (i.e., {*EntityAttribute, Polarity*}) annotations are assigned at the sentence level taking the context of the whole review into account. In restaurant, it is a quadruple, i.e., {*E-A, OTE, P*}, where *OTE* stands for opinion target expression. In laptop, 22 entities (e.g., *LAPTOP, DISPLAY, CPU*, etc.) and 9 attributes (e.g., *PORTABILITY, PRICE, CONNECTIVITY*, etc.) are tagged while the restaurant data contains 6 entities (e.g., *SERVICE, RESTAURANT, FOOD*, etc.) and 5 attributes (i.e., *PRICES, QUALITY, STYLE_OPTIONS*, etc.). Table 1 shows the statistics of the data sets used in our experiments. Specifically, in restaurant, the opinions are adhered to *OTEs* and if the target does not exist explicitly, the *OTE* is tagged as *NULL*.

Dataset	Reviews	Sentences	Positive	Negative	Neutral	All
Laptop:						
train	277	1,739	1,103	765	106	1,974
test	173	725	541	329	79	949
Restaurant:						
train	254	1,315	1,198	403	53	1,654
test	96	663	454	346	45	845

Table 1: Statistics of training and test dataset in laptop and restaurant domains. *Positive, Negative, Neural* and *All* stand for the number of corresponding instances.

3.2 Experiments on Training data

To address this task, we adopted similar methods for both laptop and restaurant domains, i.e, employing rich features to build classifiers and adopting *Constrained PMI* features as sentiment lexicon feature for constrained systems while other sentiment lexicons for unconstrained systems. The 5-fold cross validation was performed for system development.

Table 2 shows the results of feature selection experiments for unconstrained and constrained systems in restaurant and laptop domains.

From Table 2, it is interesting to find: (1) SentiLexi features are the most effective feature type-

Restaurant				Laptop			
Constrained		Unconstrained		Constrained		Unconstrained	
Feature	**Accuracy**	**Feature**	**Accuracy**	**Feature**	**Accuracy**	**Feature**	**Accuracy**
ConPMI	79.80	SentiLexi	82.82	ConPMI	80.09	SentiLexi	81.21
+bigram	80.77(+0.97)	+Domain	83.49(+0.67)	+Domain	80.49(+0.40)	+bigram	82.02(+0.81)
+Negation	81.07(+0.30)	+Negation	84.28(+0.77)	+Negation	81.30(+0.81)	+rel2	83.54(+1.52)
+rel2	81.25(+0.18)	+rel1	**84.52**(+0.24)	+rel2	**81.71**(+0.41)	+rel1	83.94(+0.40)
+Domain	**81.43**(+0.18)	+rel2	84.34(-0.18)	+POS	81.25(-0.46)	+Negation	**84.19**(+0.25)
+rel1	81.07(-0.36)	+bigram	84.03(-0.31)	+unigram	81.00(-0.25)	+unigram	84.04(-0.15)
+POS	80.89(-0.18)	+POS	83.67(-0.36)	+rel1	79.53(-0.47)	+Domain	83.99(-0.05)
+unigram	78.71(-2.18)	+unigram	81.63(-2.04)	+bigram	79.38(-0.15)	+POS	82.77(-0.78)

Table 2: Results of feature selection experiments for restaurant and laptop domains on training datasets. The numbers in the brackets are the performance increments compared with the previous results. *ConPMI* stands for *Constrained PMI* features while *SentiLexi* is other external sentiment lexicons features.

s to detect the polarity regardless of constrained or unconstrained. (2) *POS* features are not quite effective in all systems. The possible reasons may be that *POS* aims at identifying the subjective instances from objective ones and it has no discriminating power for the type of sentiment polarity. (3) The *unigram* features are not as effective as expected because most words are already present in *rel1* or *rel2* feature. (4) The performances in laptop and restaurant domain are comparable, which is inconsistent with our previous speculation (i.e., the result of restaurant domain performs better than that of laptop domain since both A-E pair and *OTE* are provided in restaurant). We do a deep analysis and find that the top two words with *tfidf* score usually include the *OTE* words in restaurant domain. This also confirmed that this target words selection method is effective for laptop domain.

Besides, in our preliminary experiments for both domains, we examined the SVM classifiers with various parameters implemented in scikit-learn tools[11]. Finally we employed the configurations listed in Table 3 for test data.

Domain	**Constrained**	**Unconstrained**
Restaurant	SVM,kernel=linear,c=0.1	SVM,kernel=linear,c=0.5
Laptop	SVM,kernel=linear,c=0.1	SVM,kernle=linear,c=1

Table 3: System configurations for the constrained and unconstrained runs in two domains.

3.3 Results and Discussion

Using the optimum feature set shown in Table 2 and configurations described in Table 3, we trained separate models for each domain and evaluated them against the SemEval-2015 Task 12 test set.

Table 4 presents the results of our systems and top-ranked systems on test data provided by organizer for laptop and restaurant domain. In laptop domain, our systems ranked 2nd out of 6 constrained submissions and 2nd out of 7 unconstrained submissions while in restaurant domain, the rankings are 5th/6 and 2nd/8 respectively.

The results in Table 4 shows that in both domains our unconstrained systems performed comparable to the best results. It indicated that using the external sentiment lexicons as additional resources makes great contribution although the majority of these external sentiment lexicons are out of domain, e.g., NRC lexicons are generated from tweets and IMDB is about movie reviews. On the other hand, the constrained system which calculated the PMI score for each word from training data only, would involve a lot of noise due to (1) no sufficient training instances and (2) without consideration of the relationship between word sentiment and its opinion adherent.

TeamID	**Restaurant**		**Laptop**	
	Con	Uncon	Con	Uncon
ECNU	69.82(5)	78.11(2)	74.50(2)	78.29(2)
lsislif	75.50(1)	-	77.87(1)	-
sentiue	-	78.70(1)	-	79.35(1)

Table 4: Performance of our systems and the top-ranked system for laptop and restaurant domains in terms of *Accuracy(%)* on test datasets. *Con* stands for *constrained* and *Uncon* represents *unconstrained*. The numbers in the brackets are the rankings on corresponding submissions.

[11]http://scikit-learn.org/stable/

4 Conclusion

In this paper, we examined several feature types, i.e., surface text, syntax feature, sentiment lexicon feature, etc, to detect sentiment polarity towards category or opinion target expression in reviews. Moreover, we extracted features from three sequential sentences in consideration of the characteristic of review. Our systems perform better than majority of submissions (e.g., rank 2nd out of 7 and 2nd out of 8 on unconstrained submissions in laptop and restaurant domains respectively). For the future work, we would like to construct domain-specific sentiment lexicons and present more effective in-domain features to settle this problem.

5 Acknowledgments

This research is supported by grants from Science and Technology Commission of Shanghai Municipality under research grant no. (14DZ2260800 and 15ZR1410700) and Shanghai Collaborative Innovation Center of Trustworthy Software for Internet of Things (ZF1213).

References

Erik Boiy and Marie-Francine Moens. 2009. A machine learning approach to sentiment analysis in multilingual web texts. *Information retrieval*, 12(5):526–558.

SRK Branavan, Harr Chen, Jacob Eisenstein, and Regina Barzilay. 2009. Learning document-level semantic properties from free-text annotations. *Journal of Artificial Intelligence Research*, 34(2):569.

Caroline Brun, Diana Nicoleta Popa, and Claude Roux. 2014. XRCE: Hybrid classification for aspect-based sentiment analysis. *SemEval 2014*, page 838.

Tomáš Brychcín, Michal Konkol, and Josef Steinberger. 2014. UWB: Machine learning approach to aspect-based sentiment analysis. *SemEval 2014*, page 817.

Giuseppe Castellucci, Simone Filice, Danilo Croce, and Roberto Basili. 2014. UNITOR: Aspect based sentiment analysis with structured learning. *SemEval 2014*, page 761.

Xiaowen Ding, Bing Liu, and Philip S Yu. 2008. A holistic lexicon-based approach to opinion mining. In *Proceedings of the 2008 International Conference on Web Search and Data Mining*, pages 231–240.

Yulan He, Chenghua Lin, Wei Gao, and Kam-Fai Wong. 2012. Tracking sentiment and topic dynamics from social media. In *Sixth International AAAI Conference on Weblogs and Social Media*.

Minqing Hu and Bing Liu. 2004. Mining and summarizing customer reviews. In *Proceedings of the tenth ACM SIGKDD international conference on Knowledge discovery and data mining*, pages 168–177.

Long Jiang, Mo Yu, Ming Zhou, Xiaohua Liu, and Tiejun Zhao. 2011. Target-dependent Twitter sentiment classification. In *Proceedings of the 49th Annual Meeting of the ACL: Human Language Technologies-Volume 1*, pages 151–160.

Yohan Jo and Alice H Oh. 2011. Aspect and sentiment unification model for online review analysis. In *Proceedings of the 4th ACM international conference on Web search and data mining*, pages 815–824.

Svetlana Kiritchenko, Xiaodan Zhu, Colin Cherry, and Saif M Mohammad. 2014. NRC-Canada-2014: Detecting aspects and sentiment in customer reviews. *SemEval 2014*, page 437.

Chenghua Lin and Yulan He. 2009. Joint sentiment/topic model for sentiment analysis. In *Proceedings of the 18th ACM conference on Information and knowledge management*, pages 375–384.

Bing Liu. 2012. Sentiment analysis and opinion mining: synthesis lectures on human language technologies. *Morgan & Claypool Publishers*.

Qiaozhu Mei, Xu Ling, Matthew Wondra, Hang Su, and ChengXiang Zhai. 2007. Topic sentiment mixture: modeling facets and opinions in weblogs. In *Proceedings of the 16th international conference on WWW*, pages 171–180.

Saif Mohammad, Svetlana Kiritchenko, and Xiaodan Zhu. 2013. NRC-Canada: Building the state-of-the-art in sentiment analysis of tweets. In *Second Joint Conference on Lexical and Computational Semantics (*SEM), Volume 2: Proceedings of the Seventh International Workshop on Semantic Evaluation (SemEval 2013)*, pages 321–327, Atlanta, Georgia, USA, June.

Alexander Pak and Patrick Paroubek. 2010. Twitter as a corpus for sentiment analysis and opinion mining. In *LREC*, pages 1320–1326.

Bing Xiang, Liang Zhou, and Thomson Reuters. 2014. Improving Twitter sentiment analysis with topic-based mixture modeling and semi-supervised training. In *Proceedings of the 52nd Annual Meeting of the ACL (Short Papers)*, pages 434–439.

Jiang Zhao, Tian Tian Zhu, and Man Lan. 2014. ECNU: One stone two birds: Ensemble of heterogenous measures for semantic relatedness and textual entailment. *SemEval 2014*, page 271.

UMDuluth-CS8761-12: A Novel Machine Learning Approach for Aspect Based Sentiment Analysis

Akshay Reddy Koppula, Ranga Reddy Pallelra, Ravikanth Repaka, Venkata Subhash Movva
Department of Computer Science
University of Minnesota Duluth
320 Heller Hall
1114 Kirby Drive
Duluth, MN 55812-2496, USA
{koppu001, palle015, repak003, movva002}@d.umn.edu

Abstract

This paper provides a detailed description of the approach of our system for the Aspect-Based Sentiment Analysis task of SemEval-2015. The task is to identify the Aspect Category (Entity and Attribute pair), Opinion Target and Sentiment of the reviews. For the In-domain subtask that is provided with the training data, the system is developed using a supervised technique Support Vector Machine and for the Out-of-domain subtask for which the training data is not provided, it is implemented based on the sentiment score of the vocabulary. For In-domain subtask, our system is developed specifically for restaurant data.

1 Introduction

With the increase in usage of internet, most of the users record their experiences of a particular product or item in the form of online reviews. Users might express their opinion about many different aspects of an item in a review.

While most of existing systems try to extract the overall polarity of a sentence, Semeval 2015 conducted a task on Aspect-Based Sentiment Analysis and the requirement was to extract entities (e.g., Food, Price, Service for Restaurant data), attributes(e.g., Quality, Style) for each sentence and then to determine the polarity for each entity-attribute pair.

The fajitas were delicious, but expensive.

In the above example, there are two opinions.The first opinion has FOOD#QUALITY as the entity-attribute pair with positive polarity and second has FOOD#PRICES with negative polarity. The target for both these opinions is fajitas. Since there are two opinions with two different polarities, it is useful to identify entities, attributes and targets for each sentence.

Our system tries a new approach of trying to split the sentence to find out more than one opinion in a sentence. Initially, all the unnecessary words are removed and then sentences are split in a way such that each split sentence has an opinion. These split sentences are given to a classifier for identifying entities and attributes. Later, these entities are used to extract opinion targets. Polarity is found using a classifier and voting mechanisms.

The rest of the paper is structured as follows: Section 2 presents the description of SemEval-Task Aspect-Based Sentiment Analysis. Section 3 presents the description of our system. Section 4 discusses the results of our system and analyze them. Section 5 presents a conclusion to the paper.

2 SemEval Task Description

The SemEval Task is divided into two subtasks.

2.1 Subtask 1

Following are the slots in the Subtask 1

2.1.1 Slot 1 - Aspect Category (Entity and Attribute)

It specifies the category of the domain to which the review refers. Aspect Category contains the Entity#Attribute pair of the review.

Entity is the aspect of the domain for which an opinion is expressed in the given review. Attribute is the quality or feature the review refers to and this is dependent on the Entity.

Great for a romantic evening, but over-priced. {Entity#Attribute} ->{Ambience#General, Restaurant#Prices}

2.1.2 Slot 2 - Opinion Target Expression

Opinion target is the target word in the review on which an opinion is expressed.

The Shrimp was awesome, but over-priced. {Entity#Attribute, Target} ->{Food#Quality, "Shrimp"}, {Food#Prices, "Shrimp"}

2.1.3 Slot 3 - Sentiment Polarity

Every Entity#Attribute pair obtained from sentence should be assigned a polarity of either positive, negative, or neutral depending on the sentiment expressed by the user.

2.2 Subtask 2

The task is to find out the polarity for each entity, attribute pair of the review which will be provided in the test data. No training data is provided for this task.

Further details of the task description are provided in (SemEval, 2015).

3 System Description

This system has been developed specifically for Restaurant data for subtask 1 and it is constrained for subtask1, unconstrained for subtask2.

The different stages in which the system proceeds are described in respective subsections. Most of them use an SVM classifier for predictions. This classifier is described extensively in subsection 3.9.

3.1 Subjectivity Classification

There are two types of sentences: Subjective and Objective. Subjective sentences are based on personal opinions. Objective sentences are factual and observable. Linear SVM classifier is used to categorize the subjective and objective sentences.

Training: Training sentences that have opinions are given a constant value and that do not have opinions are given another constant value. Using this binary classification model, a Linear SVM classifier is trained using unigram Bag of words feature for the given training dataset.

Testing: The trained Linear SVM classifier is used in predicting the test sentences with subjective information.

Only these predicted subjective test sentences are considered for further processing.

3.2 Clean the Sentence

The main functionality of this module is to remove unnecessary words and modify the sentence in a way that helps in splitting of the sentence in next stage. Specifically, clean the sentence to remove the articles (a, an, and the) and append ',' before 'but', 'at', and 'with' words. This addition of ',' will help to split the sentence in the next processing stage. A ',' is prepended to 'at' if it is preceded by an adjective and to 'with' if any adjective exists in any of the three previous words. These rules are extracted by observing the training data.

The food is great and they have a good selection of wines at reasonable prices.

In the above example, 'at' will be prepended with ',' and 'a' will be removed.

3.3 Split the Sentence

Each sentence may contatin multiple opinions and we believe that divison of sentence into subsentences will help in making these predictions better. Observations from the training data led to the understanding that ',' and 'and' are used frequently to express multiple opinions in one sentence and hence these tokens are used to divide the sentence. Some words like 'at', 'but', 'with' are also being used to express multiple opinions and as ',' has been appended in the previous stage this helps in splitting these sentences also properly.

Below are some examples on this splitting

The food is great and they have a good selection of wines, at reasonable prices.

Split sentences: 1) The food is great 2) they have a good selection of wines 3) wines at reasonable prices

Thalia is a beautiful restaurant, with beautiful people serving you, but the food doesn't quite match up

Split sentences: 1) Thalia is a beautiful restaurant 2) with beautiful people serving you 3) but the food doesn't quite match up

If a split sentence has an adjective but does not have a noun, then the noun(s) in the previous split sentence will be appended to current split sentence.

Similarly, if the split sentence has a noun but does not have an adjective, then the adjective from the previous split sentence will be appended to current split sentence.

We love food, drinks, and atmosphere

Split sentences: 1) we love the food 2) love drinks 3) love atmosphere

In contrast, if a split sentence does not have both noun and adjective then append this split sentence to the previous split sentence.

3.4 Identify Entities

In this section, we use the output from the split sentences. Since there can be multiple split sentences and entities, each split sentence has to be matched with it's corresponding entity. For Example:

Pizza is delicious, ambience is bad.

This example has two different entities: Food, Ambience. After splitting the sentences, assigning an entity to its respective part of sentence is important:

Pizza is delicious- Food

ambience is bad - Ambience

To assign each split sentence with it's respective entity, Wordnet is used. Find the similarities between the words in each split sentence and each entity using wordnet. For each entity, assign a split sentence to which the most similar word for that entity belongs to.

After each split sentence has been assigned to it's respective entity, the words from that split sentence whose parts of speech are among nouns, verbs, adjectives or adverbs are extracted and given as input to SVM. Use the linear SVM model as described in subsection 3.9 to predict the entity.

3.5 Identify Attributes

All the nouns, verbs, adjectives, adverbs for each particular attribute are extracted from the training data. Each attribute along with their respective extracted words are given as input to the SVM Classifier. Use the linear SVM model as described in subsection 3.9 to predict the entity.

Apart from this process some predefined lexicons from the training data are extracted manually. For example, if there are words like money or price in the sentence then it is likely that the sentence is talking about the attribute price. Words like these will, in almost all of the cases, belong to attribute 'price', these were extracted manually from training data as only a few of them were present. Upon the encounter of such words in the test data, the attribute associated with them is assigned. If none of these predefined words are encountered, then SVM classifier is used as described above.

3.6 Extract Opinion Targets

In order to extract opinion targets, The following procedure is applied for finding targets where the entities extracted in previous section are among 'Food', 'Restaurant', 'Drinks', 'Location'.

Training: Targets are found out based on Entities and most of them are nouns with a few being adjectives. Each entity has some nouns that will not be the targets. For example, a noun such as 'food' will not be the target for the 'restaurant' entity. In the training data, for each entity, identify all the nouns, adjectives that are not targets. Also, identify the target words for each entity. All these extracted words are used for finding the targets in a test sentence.

Testing: If a given test sentence has one of target words extracted in training, return that target. If not, remove all the non-targets in the sentence that were extracted from training. After this removal, if there are no more nouns in the sentence, then return the target as NULL. If more nouns exist in the sentence, then return the largest substring of the consecutive nouns and adjectives. If the entity is restaurant then return the proper noun as the target if it is preceded with 'at' or 'to'.

For Entities (Ambience and Service): For sentences that has Ambience and Service as the identified entities, a different approach is employed to extract opinion targets: A vocabulary of targets is constructed from the training data and is given as input to a classifier along with the corresponding sentences and their labels. This classifier is described in subsection 3.9

3.7 Sentiment Polarity

From the given sentence, all noun(s), adjective(s), adverb(s), and verb(s) are extracted and given as input to the classifier to predict the polarity as either positive, negative or neutral. Usually classifiers can have multiple parameters. So, using the grid search method from Scikit Learn package, different parameters such as unigrams, bigrams and trigrams are tested and it was observed that trigrams resulted in better performance of the classifier. Hence trigrams are used whenever needed.

Two different techniques are tried for the classification of the given training data:

1. All unique tri-grams in the training sentences are identified and TF-IDF values are calculated for these trigrams. Count Vectorizer and TF-IDF transformer from 'Scikit Learn' package are used to extract the BoW features from the sentences.

2. Categorical Probability Proportion Difference (CPPD) (CPPD, 2012)

When compared to CPPD, BoW features resulted in higher accuracy. But, CPPD model might work good for other domains. To predict the polarity for test sentences, voting (Brill et al., 2001) among classifiers is used. The classifiers used in the voting procedure are Naive Bayes, Linear SVC, and Logistic Regression.

By experimentation it is observed that Naive Bayes has a good "negative recall" when compared to voting. This experiment was helpful in deciding the polarity of a sentence. If Naive Bayes predicts negative, then the polarity for that sentence is assigned as negative, else it is assigned as the value predicted from voting.

3.8 Out-of-Domain

In the out-of-domain subtask, no training data or knowledge about the domain would be provided or used to predict the polarity of the given test sentence.

The steps taken in this task are:

1. Splitting of the test sentence into sub sentences is done based on the number of opinions it has. From the split sentences, words with parts of speech tag as noun, verb, adjective, or adverb are extracted.

2. Polarity is predicted using two tools Sentiwordnet and Pattern. The nearest opinion word (adjective, adverb, or verb) to the target word is identified and polarity is found out for this word and is set as the polarity for the sentence. If this word does not have polarity, then the average polarity score for the remaining opinion words in the sentence is calculated and is set as the polarity for the sentence. Apart from these two predictions, Pattern tool is also used to predict the polarity for the complete sentence.

3. Voting is applied to these three predictions and the output of this would be the final polarity for the sentence.

3.9 Linear SVM Model

The steps involved in training the Linear SVM classifier for our system are described below:

Features are extracted using unigram Bag of words (BoW), Tf-Idf, Univariate feature selection model (Scikitlearn, 2011). An optimized regularization parameter (C value) is also used.

Train the Classifier: With the help of all the above mentioned parameters, the classifier is trained for the given training dataset. Linear SVM model with BoW as features is trained using the multi-class classification method for the given training dataset.

Predict the Label: The Linear SVM classifier predicts the output label for each test sentence by using the C value identified in the Cross-validation step.

4 Results and Analysis

Our system was trained on 1314 review sentences and tested on 685 review sentences for sub task 1. Evaluations are done for slot 1, slot 2, slot 1 and slot 2, slot 3, and subtask 2. The results for each of them are provided in the tables. Each table has the scores of the best team, our system and the SemEval baseline. Table1 provides the results for slot 1 in which our system is ranked 2nd among all the constrained systems participated in the task and is ranked 3rd among all the participating systems. As our system for subtask 1 is constrained, all our scores are compared only with the best constrained system. For subtask 2, the best score among all systems is considered.

As evident from the results, extraction of opinion targets can be attributed to the failure of both slot 2 and slot 1 & slot 2. We suspect that the reason behind this could be our concentration on finding those

Team	F1-Score
Best	61.94
UMDuluth-CS8761-12	57.20
Baseline	51.32

Table 1: Slot 1.

Team	F1-Score
Best	66.91
UMDuluth-CS8761-12	50.36
Baseline	48.06

Table 2: Slot 2.

Team	F1-Score
Best	42.72
UMDuluth-CS8761-12	32.60
Baseline	34.44

Table 4: Slot 1 and Slot 2.

Team	Accuracy
Best	75.50
UMDuluth-CS8761-12	71.12
Baseline	63.55

Table 5: Slot 3.

words that are non-targets rather than on trying to find words that should be targets. If a noun is not a target in one sentence, it doesnt mean that it cannot be a target in any sentence having similar entity.

5 Conclusion

Overall, our system performed well especially in slot 1 and slot 3. Identifying the number of opinions that each sentence might express is an important step to be taken, which we have achieved by splitting the sentence so that each split sentence can express an opinion. Applying supervised machine learning techniques on these split sentences resulted in a much better predictions compared to the complete sentences.

Acknowledgments

We would like to take this opportunity to thank our professor Dr. Ted Pedersen for encouraging us to participate in this task and for his guidance and advice.

References

Pedregosa, F. and Varoquaux, G. and Gramfort, A. and Michel, V. and Thirion, B. and Grisel, O. and Blondel, M. and Prettenhofer, P. and Weiss, R. and Dubourg, V. and Vanderplas, J. and Passos, A. and Cournapeau, D. and Brucher, M. and Perrot, M. and Duchesnay, E. Scikit-learn: Machine Learning in Python. *Journal of Machine Learning Research*, 122825–2830, 2011.

Hu, Minqing and Liu, Bing Mining and summarizing customer reviews. *Proceedings of the tenth ACM SIGKDD international conference on Knowledge discovery and data mining*, ACM 168–177,2004

Maria Pontiki, Dimitrios Galanis, Haris Papageogiou, Suresh Manandhar, and Ion Androutsopoulos. 2015. *SemEval-2015 Task 12: Aspect Based Sentiment Analysis* In Proceedings of the 9th International Workshop on Semantic Evaluation (SemEval 2015), Denver, Colorado.

Agarwal, Basant, and Namita Mittal. 2015. *Categorical probability proportion difference (CPPD): A feature selection method for sentiment classification.* Proceedings of the 2nd Workshop on Sentiment Analysis where AI meets Psychology (SAAIP 2012), COLING. 2012.

Tan, Songbo, Xueqi Cheng, Yuefen Wang, and Hongbo Xu. *Adapting Naive Bayes to Domain Adaptation for Sentiment Analysis.* ECIR, LNCS 5478, pp. 337–349, 2009.

Moghaddam, Samaneh, and Martin Ester. *Opinion digger: an unsupervised opinion miner from unstructured product reviews* Proceedings of the 19th CIKM, pp. 1825–1828, Toronto, ON, 2010.

Glorot, Xavier, Antoine Bordes, and Yoshua Bengio *Domain Adaptation for Large-Scale Sentiment Classification: A Deep Learning Approach.* ICML, 2011.

Team	Accuracy
Best	85.84
UMDuluth-CS8761-12	71.38
Baseline	71.68

Table 3: Subtask 2.

Banko, Michele, and Eric Brill *Scaling to very very large corpora for natural language disambiguation.* Proceedings of the 39th Annual Meeting on Association for Computational Linguistics, 2001.

EliXa: A modular and flexible ABSA platform

Iñaki San Vicente, Xabier Saralegi
Elhuyar Foundation
Osinalde industrialdea 3
Usurbil, 20170, Spain
{i.sanvicente,x.saralegi}@elhuyar.com

Rodrigo Agerri
IXA NLP Group
University of the Basque Country (UPV/EHU)
Donostia-San Sebastián
rodrigo.agerri@ehu.eus

Abstract

This paper presents a supervised Aspect Based Sentiment Analysis (ABSA) system. Our aim is to develop a modular platform which allows to easily conduct experiments by replacing the modules or adding new features. We obtain the best result in the Opinion Target Extraction (OTE) task (slot 2) using an off-the-shelf sequence labeler. The target polarity classification (slot 3) is addressed by means of a multiclass SVM algorithm which includes lexical based features such as the polarity values obtained from domain and open polarity lexicons. The system obtains accuracies of 0.70 and 0.73 for the restaurant and laptop domain respectively, and performs second best in the out-of-domain hotel, achieving an accuracy of 0.80.

1 Introduction

Nowadays Sentiment Analysis is proving very useful for tasks such as decision making and market analysis. The ever increasing interest is also shown in the number of related shared tasks organized: TASS (Villena-Román et al., 2012; Villena-Román et al., 2014), SemEval (Nakov et al., 2013; Pontiki et al., 2014; Rosenthal et al., 2014), or the SemSA Challenge at ESWC2014[1]. Research has also been evolving towards specific opinion elements such as entities or properties of a certain opinion target, which is also known as ABSA. The Semeval 2015 ABSA shared task aims at covering the most common problems in an ABSA task: detecting the specific topics an opinion refers to (slot1); extracting the opinion targets (slot2), combining the topic and target identification (slot1&2) and, finally, computing the polarity of the identified word/targets (slot3). Participants were allowed to send one constrained (no external resources allowed) and one unconstrained run for each subtask. We participated in the slot2 and slot3 subtasks.

Our main is to develop an ABSA system to be used in the future for further experimentation. Thus, rather than focusing on tuning the different modules our main goal is to develop a platform to facilitate future experimentation. The EliXa system consists of three independent supervised modules based on the IXA pipes tools (Agerri et al., 2014) and Weka (Hall et al., 2009). Next section describes the external resources used in the unconstrained systems. Sections 3 and 4 describe the systems developed for each subtask and briefly discuss the obtained results.

2 External Resources

Several polarity Lexicons and various corpora were used for the unconstrained versions of our systems. To facilitate reproducibility of results, every resource listed here is publicly available.

2.1 Corpora

For the restaurant domain we used the Yelp Dataset Challenge dataset[2]. Following (Kiritchenko et al., 2014), we manually filtered out categories not corresponding to food related businesses (173 out of 720

[1] http://challenges.2014.eswc-conferences.org/index.php/SemSA

[2] http://www.yelp.com/dataset_challenge

were finally selected). A total of 997,721 reviews (117.1M tokens) comprise what we henceforth call the *Yelp food corpus* (C_{Yelp}).

For the laptop domain we leveraged a corpus composed of Amazon reviews of electronic devices (Jo and Oh, 2011). Although only 17,53% of the reviews belong to laptop products, early experiments showed the advantage of using the full corpus for both slot 2 and slot 3 subtasks. The *Amazon electronics corpus* (C_{Amazon}) consists of 24,259 reviews (4.4M tokens). Finally, the English Wikipedia was also used to induce word clusters using word2vec (Mikolov et al., 2013).

2.2 Polarity Lexicons

We generated two types of polarity lexicons to represent polarity in the slot3 subtasks: general purpose and domain specific polarity lexicons.

A general purpose polarity lexicon L_{gen} was built by combining four well known polarity lexicons: SentiWordnet SWN (Baccianella et al., 2010), General Inquirer GI (Stone et al., 1966), Opinion Finder OF (Wilson et al., 2005) and Liu's sentiment lexicon Liu (Hu and Liu, 2004). When a lemma occurs in several lexicons, its polarity is solved according to the following priority order: $Liu > OF > GI > SWN$. The order was set based on the results of (San Vicente et al., 2014). All polarity weights were normalized to a $[-1, 1]$ interval. Polarity categories were mapped to weights for GI ($neg_{+} \rightarrow -0.8$; $neg \rightarrow$-0.6; $neg_{-} \rightarrow$-0.2; $pos_{-} \rightarrow$0.2; $pos \rightarrow$0.6; $pos_{+} \rightarrow$0.8), Liu and OF ($neg \rightarrow$-0.7; $pos \rightarrow$0.7 for both). In addition, a restricted lexicon L_{genres} including only the strongest polarity words was derived from L_{gen} by applying a threshold of $\pm$0.6.

Domain	Polarity Lexicon	Total
General	L_{gen}	42,218
General	L_{genres}	12,398
Electronic devices	L_{Amazon}	4,511
Food	L_{Yelp}	4,691

Table 1: Statistics of the polarity lexicons.

Domain specific polarity lexicons L_{Yelp} and L_{Amazon} were automatically extracted from C_{Yelp} and C_{Amazon} reviews corpora. Reviews are rated in a $[1..5]$ interval, being 1 the most negative and 5 the most positive. Using the Log-likelihood ratio (LLR) (Dunning, 1993) we obtained the ranking of the words which occur more with negative and positive reviews respectively. We considered reviews with 1 and 2 rating as negative and those with 4 and 5 ratings as positive. LLR scores were normalized to a $[-1, 1]$ interval and included in L_{Yelp} and L_{Amazon} lexicons as polarity weights.

3 Slot2 Subtask: Opinion Target Extraction

The Opinion Target Extraction task (OTE) is addressed as a sequence labeling problem. We use the *ixa-pipe-nerc* Named Entity Recognition system[3] (Agerri et al., 2014) off-the-shelf to train our OTE models; the system learns supervised models via the Perceptron algorithm as described by (Collins, 2002). *ixa-pipe-nerc* uses the Apache OpenNLP project implementation of the Perceptron algorithm[4] customized with its own features. Specifically, *ixa-pipe-nerc* implements basic non-linguistic local features and on top of those a combination of word class representation features partially inspired by (Turian et al., 2010). The word representation features use large amounts of unlabeled data. The result is a quite simple but competitive system which obtains the best constrained and unconstrained results and the first and third best overall results.

The local features implemented are: current token and token shape (digits, lowercase, punctuation, etc.) in a 2 range window, previous prediction, beginning of sentence, 4 characters in prefix and suffix, bigrams and trigrams (token and shape). On top of them we induce three types of word representations:

- Brown (Brown et al., 1992) clusters, taking the 4th, 8th, 12th and 20th node in the path. We induced 1000 clusters on the Yelp reviews dataset described in section 2.1 using the tool implemented by Liang[5].

- Clark (Clark, 2003) clusters, using the standard configuration to induce 200 clusters on the Yelp reviews dataset and 100 clusters on the food portion of the Yelp reviews dataset.

[3] https://github.com/ixa-ehu/ixa-pipe-nerc
[4] http://opennlp.apache.org/
[5] https://github.com/percyliang/brown-cluster

- Word2vec (Mikolov et al., 2013) clusters, based on K-means applied over the extracted word vectors using the skip-gram algorithm[6]; 400 clusters were induced using the Wikipedia.

The implementation of the clustering features looks for the cluster class of the incoming token in one or more of the clustering lexicons induced following the three methods listed above. If found, then we add the class as a feature. The Brown clusters only apply to the token related features, which are duplicated. We chose the best combination of features using 5-fold cross validation, obtaining 73.03 F1 score with local features (e.g. constrained mode) and 77.12 adding the word clustering features, namely, in unconstrained mode. These two configurations were used to process the test set in this task. Table 2 lists the official results for the first 4 systems in the task.

System (type)	Precision	Recall	F1 score
Baseline	55.42	43.4	48.68
EliXa (u)	68.93	71.22	**70.05**
NLANGP (u)	70.53	64.02	67.12
EliXa (c)	67.23	66.61	66.91
IHS-RD-Belarus (c)	67.58	59.23	63.13

Table 2: Results obtained on the slot2 evaluation on restaurant data.

The results show that leveraging unlabeled text is helpful in the OTE task, obtaining an increase of 7 points in recall. It is also worth mentioning that our constrained system (using non-linguistic local features) performs very closely to the second best overall system by the NLANGP team (unconstrained). Finally, we would like to point out to the overall low results in this task (for example, compared to the 2014 edition), due to the very small and difficult training set (e.g., containing many short samples such as "Tasty Dog!") which made it extremely hard to learn good models for this task. The OTE models will be made freely available in the *ixa-pipe-nerc* website in time for SemEval 2015.

4 Slot3 Subtask: Sentiment Polarity

The EliXa system implements a single multiclass SVM classifier. We use the SMO implementation provided by the Weka library (Hall et al., 2009). All the classifiers built over the training data were evaluated via 10-fold cross validation. The complexity parameter was optimized as ($C = 1.0$). Many configurations were tested in this experiments, but in the following we only will describe the final setting.

4.1 Baseline

The very first features we introduced in our classifier were token ngrams. Initial experiments showed that lemma ngrams (lgrams) performed better than raw form ngrams. One feature per lgram is added to the vector representation, and lemma frequency is stored. With respect to the ngram size used, we tested up to 4-gram features and improvement was achieved in laptop domain but only when not combined with other features.

4.2 PoS

PoS tag and lemma information, obtained using the IXA pipes tools (Agerri et al., 2014), were also included as features. One feature per PoS tag was added again storing the number of occurrences of a tag in the sentence. These features slightly improve over the baseline only in the restaurant domain.

4.3 Window

Given that a sentence may contain multiple opinions, we define a window span around a given opinion target (5 words before and 5 words after). When the target of an opinion is null the whole sentence is taken as span. Only the restaurant and hotel domains contained gold target annotations so we did not use this feature in the laptop domain.

4.4 Polarity Lexicons

The positive and negative scores we extracted as features from both general purpose and domain specific lexicons. Both scores are calculated as the sum of every positive/negative score in the corresponding lexicon divided by the number of words in the sentence. Features obtained from the general lexicons provide a slight improvement. L_{genres} is better for restaurant domain, while L_{gen} is better for laptops. Domain specific lexicons L_{Amazon} and L_{Yelp} also help as shown by tables 3 and 4.

[6]https://code.google.com/p/word2vec/

4.5 Word Clusters

Word2vec clustering features combine best with the rest as shown by table 3. These features only were useful for the restaurant domain, perhaps due to the small size of the laptops domain data.

4.6 Feature combinations

Every feature, when used in isolation, only marginally improves the baseline. Some of them, such as the E&A features (using the gold information from the slot1 subtask) for the laptop domain, only help when combined with others. Best performance is achieved when several features are combined. As shown by tables 4 and 5, improvement over the baseline ranges between 2,8% and 1,9% in the laptop and restaurant domains respectively.

Classifier	Acc Rest
Baseline (organizers)	78.8
Baseline	
1lgram	80.11
2lgram	79.3
$1lgram + E\&A$	79.8
$1lgram(w5)$	80.41
$1lgram + PoS$	80.59 (c)
Lexicons	
$1lgram + L_{gen}$	80.6
$1lgram + L_{genres}$	81
$1lgram + L_{Yelp}$	80.9
Combinations	
$1lgram(w5) + w2v(C_{Yelp}) + L_{genres} + L_{Yelp} + PoS$	82.34 (u)

Table 3: Slot3 ablation experiments for restaurants. (c) and (u) refer to constrained and unconstrained tracks.

4.7 Results

Table 5 shows the result achieved by our sentiment polarity classifier. Although for both restaurant and laptops domains we obtain results over the baseline both performance are modest.

In contrast, for the out of domain track, which was evaluated on hotel reviews our system obtains the third highest score. Because of the similarity of the domains, we straightforwardly applied our restaurant domain models. The good results of the constrained system could mean that the feature combination used may be robust across domains. With respect to the unconstrained system, we suspect that such a good performance is achieved due to the fact that word cluster information was very adequate for the hotel domain, because C_{yelp} contains a 10.55% of hotel reviews.

Classifier	Acc Lapt
Baseline (organizers)	78.3
Baseline	
1lgram	79.33
2lgram	79.7
$1lgram + clusters(w2v)$	79.23
$1lgram + E\&A$	79.23
$1lgram + PoS$	78.88
Lexicons	
$1lgram + L_{gen}$	79.2
$1lgram + L_{genres}$	79
$1lgram + L_{Amazon}$	79.7
Combinations	
$1lgram + PoS + E\&A$	79.99 (c)
$2lgram + PoS + E\&A$	78.27
$1lgram + L_{genres} + L_{Amazon} + PoS + E\&A$	80.85 (u)

Table 4: Slot3 ablation experiments for laptops; (c) and (u) refer to constrained and unconstrained tracks.

System	Rest.	Lapt.	Hotel
Baseline	63.55	69.97	71.68 (majority)
Sentiue	**78.70 (1)**	**79.35 (1)**	71.68 (4)
Isislif	75.50 (3)	77.87 (3)	**85.84 (1)**
EliXa (u)	70.06(10)	72.92 (7)	79.65 (3)
EliXa (c)	67.34 (14)	71.55 (9)	74.93 (5)

Table 5: Results obtained on the slot3 evaluation on restaurant data; ranking in brackets.

5 Conclusions

We have presented a modular and supervised ABSA platform developed to facilitate future experimentation in the field. We submitted runs corresponding to the slot2 and slot3 subtasks, obtaining competitive results. In particular, we obtained the best results in slot2 (OTE) and for slot3 we obtain 3rd best result in the out-of-domain track, which is nice for a supervised system. Finally, a system for topic detection (slot1) is currently under development.

6 Acknowledgments

This work has been supported by the following projects: ADi project (Etortek grant No. IE-14-382), NewsReader (FP7-ICT 2011-8-316404), SKaTer (TIN2012-38584-C06-02) and Tacardi (TIN2012-38523-C02-01).

References

Rodrigo Agerri, Josu Bermudez, and German Rigau. 2014. Ixa pipeline: Efficient and ready to use multilingual nlp tools. In *Proceedings of the 9th Language Resources and Evaluation Conference (LREC2014)*, pages 26–31, Reykjavik, Iceland, May.

S. Baccianella, A. Esuli, and F. Sebastiani. 2010. SentiWordNet 3.0: An enhanced lexical resource for sentiment analysis and opinion mining. In *Seventh conference on International Language Resources and Evaluation (LREC-2010), Malta.*, volume 25.

Peter F Brown, Peter V Desouza, Robert L Mercer, Vincent J Della Pietra, and Jenifer C Lai. 1992. Class-based n-gram models of natural language. *Computational linguistics*, 18(4):467–479.

Alexander Clark. 2003. Combining distributional and morphological information for part of speech induction. In *Proceedings of the tenth conference on European chapter of the Association for Computational Linguistics-Volume 1*, pages 59–66.

Michael Collins. 2002. Discriminative training methods for hidden markov models: Theory and experiments with perceptron algorithms. In *Proceedings of the ACL-02 conference on Empirical methods in natural language processing-Volume 10*, pages 1–8.

Ted Dunning. 1993. Accurate methods for the statistics of surprise and coincidence. *Computacional Linguistics*, 19(1):61–74, March.

Mark Hall, Eibe Frank, Geoffrey Holmes, Bernhard Pfahringer, Peter Reutemann, and Ian H. Witten. 2009. The WEKA data mining software: an update. *SIGKDD Explor. Newsl.*, 11(1):10–18, november.

M. Hu and B. Liu. 2004. Mining and summarizing customer reviews. In *Proceedings of the tenth ACM SIGKDD international conference on Knowledge discovery and data mining*, pages 168–177.

Yohan Jo and Alice H. Oh. 2011. Aspect and sentiment unification model for online review analysis. In *Proceedings of the fourth ACM international conference on Web search and data mining*, WSDM '11, pages 815–824, New York, NY, USA. ACM.

Svetlana Kiritchenko, Xiaodan Zhu, Colin Cherry, and Saif Mohammad. 2014. NRC-canada-2014: Detecting aspects and sentiment in customer reviews. In *Proceedings of the 8th International Workshop on Semantic Evaluation (SemEval 2014)*, pages 437–442, Dublin, Ireland, August.

Tomas Mikolov, Ilya Sutskever, Kai Chen, Greg S Corrado, and Jeff Dean. 2013. Distributed representations of words and phrases and their compositionality. In *Advances in Neural Information Processing Systems*, pages 3111–3119.

Preslav Nakov, Sara Rosenthal, Zornitsa Kozareva, Veselin Stoyanov, Alan Ritter, and Theresa Wilson. 2013. SemEval-2013 task 2: Sentiment analysis in twitter. In *Proceedings of the Seventh International Workshop on Semantic Evaluation (SemEval 2013)*, pages 312–320, Atlanta, Georgia, USA, June.

Maria Pontiki, Dimitrios Galanis, John Pavlopoulos, Harris Papageorgiou, Ion Androutsopoulos, and Suresh Manandhar. 2014. Semeval-2014 task 4: Aspect based sentiment analysis. In *Proceedings of the International Workshop on Semantic Evaluation (SemEval)*.

Sara Rosenthal, Preslav Nakov, Alan Ritter, and Veselin Stoyanov. 2014. Semeval-2014 task 9: Sentiment analysis in twitter. In *Proceedings of the 8th International Workshop on Semantic Evaluation, SemEval*, volume 14.

Iñaki San Vicente, Rodrigo Agerri, and German Rigau. 2014. Simple, robust and (almost) unsupervised generation of polarity lexicons for multiple languages. In *Proceedings of the 14th Conference of the European Chapter of the Association for Computational Linguistics, EACL2014*, pages 88–97, Gothenburg, Sweden.

P. Stone, D. Dunphy, M. Smith, and D. Ogilvie. 1966. *The General Inquirer: A Computer Approach to Content Analysis.* Cambridge (MA): MIT Press.

Joseph Turian, Lev-Arie Ratinov, and Yoshua Bengio. 2010. Word representations: A simple and general method for semi-supervised learning. In *Proceedings of the 48th Annual Meeting of the Association for Computational Linguistics*, pages 384–394, Uppsala, Sweden, July.

Julio Villena-Román, Sara Lana-Serrano, Eugenio Martínez-Cámara, and José Carlos González-Cristóbal. 2012. Tass-workshop on sentiment analysis at sepln. *Procesamiento del Lenguaje Natural*, 50:37–44.

Julio Villena-Román, Janine García-Morera, Sara Lana-Serrano, and José Carlos González-Cristóbal. 2014. Tass 2013 - a second step in reputation analysis in spanish. *Procesamiento del Lenguaje Natural*, 52(0).

Theresa Wilson, Janyce Wiebe, and Paul Hoffmann. 2005. Recognizing contextual polarity in phrase-level sentiment analysis. In *Proceedings of the conference on Human Language Technology and Empirical Methods in Natural Language Processing*, page 347–354.

Lsislif: CRF and Logistic Regression for Opinion Target Extraction and Sentiment Polarity Analysis

Hussam Hamdan
Aix-Marseille University
hussam.hamdan@lsis.org

Patrice Bellot
Aix-Marseille University
patrice.bellot@lsis.org

Frederic Bechet
Aix-Marseille University
frederic.bechet@lif.univ-mrs.fr

Abstract

This paper describes our contribution in Opinion Target Extraction OTE and Sentiment Polarity sub tasks of SemEval 2015 ABSA task. A CRF model with IOB notation has been adopted for OTE with several groups of features including syntactic, lexical, semantic, sentiment lexicon features. Our submission for OTE is ranked fifth over twenty submissions. A Logistic Regression model with a weighting schema of positive and negative labels have been used for sentiment polarity; several groups of features (lexical, syntactic, semantic, lexicon and Z score) are extracted. Our submission for Sentiment Polarity is ranked third over ten submissions on the restaurant data set, third over thirteen on the laptops data set, but the first over eleven on the hotel data set that is out-of-domain set.

1 Introduction

Sentiment Analysis (SA) has become more and more interesting since the year 2000, many techniques in Natural Language Processing have been used to understand the expressed sentiment on an entity.

Many levels of granularity have been also distinguished: Document Level SA considers the whole document is about an entity and classifies whether the expressed sentiment is positive, negative or neutral; Sentence Level SA determines the sentiment of each sentence, some papers have focused on Clause Level SA, but they are still not enough; Entity or Aspect-Based SA performs finer-grained analysis in which all entities and their aspects should be extracted and the sentiment towards them should also be determined.

Aspect-Based SA task consists of several subproblems, the document is about many entities which could be for example a restaurant, a laptop, a printer. Users may refer to an entity by different writings, but normally there are not a lot of variations to indicate the same entity, each entity has many aspects which could be its parts or attributes. Some aspects could be another entity such as screen of laptop, but most work did not take this case into account. Therefore, we could define the opinion by the quintuple (Liu, 2012) (e_i, a_{ij}, s_{ijkl}, h_k, t_l) where e_i is the entity i, a_{ij} are the aspects of the entity i, s_{ijkl} is the expressed sentiment on the aspect at the time t_l, h_k the holder which created the document or the text. This definition does not take into account that the entity has aspects that could have also other aspects which leads to an aspect hierarchy, in order to avoid this information loss, few work has handled this issue, they proposed to represent the aspect as a tree of aspect terms.

In this paper, we focus on Opinion Target Extraction (OTE) and Sentiment Polarity towards a target or a category. The description of each subtask is provided by ABSA organizers (Pontiki et al., 2015). For OTE or aspect term extraction, a CRF model is proposed with IOB annotation and several groups of features including syntactic, lexical, semantic, sentiment lexicon features. For aspect term polarity detection, a logistic regression classifier is trained with weighting schema for positive and negative labels and several groups of features are extracted including lexical, syntactic, semantic, lexicon and Z score features.

The rest of this paper is organized as follows. Section 2 outlines existing work in aspect extraction and polarity detection. Section 3 describes our system for aspect term extraction. Aspect term polarity detection is presented in Section 4. Section 6 shows the conclusion and the future work.

2 Related Work

Aspect-Based Sentiment Analysis consists of several sub tasks. Some papers have proposed different methods for aspect detection and sentiment polarity analysis, others have proposed joint models in order to obtain the aspect and their sentiments from the same model, these models are generally unsupervised or semi-supervised.

The earliest work on aspect detection from online reviews presented by Hu and Liu (Hu and Liu, 2004) that used association rule mining based on Apriori algorithm to extract frequent noun phrases as product features, for polarity detection they used two seed sets of 30 positive and negative adjectives, then WordNet has been used to find and add the synonyms of the seed words. Infrequent features had been processed by finding the noun related to an opinionated word.

Opinion Digger (Moghaddam and Ester, 2010) also used Apriori algorithm to extract the frequent aspects. KNN algorithm is applied to estimate the aspect rating scaling from 1 to 5 stands for (Excellent, Good, Average, Poor, Terrible).

Supervised methods uses normally the CRF or HMM models. Jin and Ho (Jin and Ho, 2009) applied a lexicalized HMM model to extract aspects using the words and their part-of-speech tags in order to learn a model, then unsupervised algorithm for determining the aspect sentiment using the nearest opinion word to the aspect and taking into account the polarity reversal words (such as not). A CRF model was used by Jakob and Gurevych (Jakob and Gurevych, 2010) with the following features: tokens, POS tags, syntactic dependency (if the aspect has a relation with the opinionated word), word distance (the distance between the word in the closest noun phrase and the opinionated word), and opinion sentences (each token in the sentence containing an opinionated expression is labeled by this feature), the input of this method is also the opinionated expressions, they use these expressions for predicting the aspect sentiment using the dependency parsing for retrieving the pair aspect-expression from the training set. A CRF model is also used by (Hamdan et al., 2014b) with lexical and POS features.

Unsupervised methods based on LDA (Latent Dirichlet allocation) have been proposed. Brody and Elhadad (Brody and Elhadad, 2010) used LDA to figure ou the aspects, determined the number of topics by applying a clustering method, then they used a similar method proposed by Hatzivassiloglou and McKeown (Hatzivassiloglou and McKeown, 1997) to extract the conjunctive adjectives, but not the disjunctive due to the specificity of the domain, seed sets were used and assigned scores, these scores were propagated using propagation method through the aspect-sentiment graph building from the pairs of aspect and related adjectives. Lin and He (Lin et al., 2012) proposed Joint model of Sentiment and Topic (JST) which extends the state-of-the-art topic model (LDA) by adding a sentiment layer, this model is fully unsupervised and it can detect sentiment and topic simultaneously. Wei and Gulla (Wei and Gulla, 2010) modeled the hierarchical relation between product aspects. They defined Sentiment Ontology Tree (SOT) to formulate the knowledge of hierarchical relationships among product attributes and tackled the problem of sentiment analysis as a hierarchical classification problem. Unsupervised hierarchical aspect Sentiment model (HASM) was proposed by Kim et al (Kim et al., 3 07) to discover a hierarchical structure of aspect-based sentiments from unlabeled online reviews.

Aspect term polarity detection can be seen as a sentence level sentiment analysis. Therefore, many papers can be mentioned. Supervised methods have been widely exploited for this purpose, a classification algorithms with a wise feature extraction could achieve good results (Mohammad et al., 2013) (Hamdan et al., 2015a) (Hamdan et al., 4 29).

3 Opinion Target Expression (OTE)

An opinion target expression (OTE) is an expression used in the given text to refer to an aspect or

an aspect term related to the reviewed entity. The objective of OTE slot is to extract all opinion target expressions in a restaurant review, OTE could be a word or multiple words. For this purpose, we have used CRF (Conditional Random Field) which have proved its performance in information extraction. We choose the IOB notation for representing each sentence in the review. Therefore, we distinguish the terms at the Beginning, the Inside and the Outside of OTE. For example, for this review *"But the staff was so horrible to us."* Where *staff* is OTE, the target of each word will be:
But:O the:O staff:B was:O so:O horrible:O to:O us:O.
We extract for each single word the following features for the word itself and the 2 and 3 previous and subsequent words, respectively.
-word lemma using WordNet.
-word POS using NLTK parser.
-word shape: the shape of each character in the word (capital letter, small letter, digit, punctuation, other symbol)
-word type: the type of the word (uppercase, digit, symbol, combination)
-Named entity: the IOB annotation for the named entity extracted from the review using Senna (Collobert, 2011).
-chunk: the chunk of the word (NP, VP, PP) extracted using Senna.
-polarity: the sum of word polarity score calculated using Bing Liu Lexicon (Hu and Liu, 2004) and MPQA subjectivity Lexicon (Wilson et al., 2005).
-Prefixes (all prefixes having length between one to four).
-Suffixes (all suffixes having length between one to four).
-Stop word: if the word is a stop word or not.
-if the initial letter is uppercase, if all letters are uppercase, All letters lowercase, All letters digit, Contains a uppercase letter, Contains a lowercase letter, Contains a digit, Contains a alphabet letter, Contains a symbol.
We also extract the value of each two successive features in the the range -2,2 (the previous and subsequent two words of actual word) for the following features:
word surface, word POS, word chunk, word shape, word type.
Finally, we extract the value of each three successive features in the the range -1,1 for the two features: word POS and word lemma.

3.1 Experiments

The data set is extracted from restaurant reviews, provided by SemEval 2015 ABSA organizers (Pontiki et al., 2015). Table 1 shows the training and testing data sets statistics of restaurant reviews, where each review is composed of several sentences and each sentence may contain several OTE. CRFsuite tool is used for this experiment with lbfgs algorithm. This tool is fast in training and tagging (Okazaki, 2007).

Data	Reviews	Sentences	OTE
Train	254	1315	1654
Test	96	685	845

Table 1. Training and testing data sets for restaurant OTE slot.

Our submission is ranked fifth with the F1 score over twenty submissions with gain of 14% over the baseline provided by the organizers. This baseline uses the training reviews to create for each category *c* a list of targets to which it is linked to. Then, given a test sentence *s* and a category *c*, the baseline finds the first occurrence in s of each target encountered in *c*s list. Table 2 shows our system and the baseline results.

Experiment	Recall	Precision	F1 Score
Our System	0.55	0.72	0.62
Baseline	-	-	0.48

Table 2. The results of OTE slot.

4 Sentiment Polarity

For a given set of aspect terms within a sentence, we determine whether the polarity of each aspect term is positive, negative, neutral. For example, the system should extract the polarity of `fajitas` and *salads* in the following sentence: *"I hated their fajitas, but their salads were great"*, fajitas: negative and salads: positive.

This sub-task can be seen as sentence level or phrase level sentiment Analysis. At the first step, we detect the context of the aspect term or OTE,

the context is the aspect term itself and all the surrounding terms enclosed between two separators like (,, ;, !), if another aspect term is also enclosed by these separators we consider it as a separator instead, and we do not take the terms after it or before it (according to its direction to the current aspect term). If the sentence has only an aspect term the separators will be the beginning and the end of the sentence.
For example, for this review *"It took half an hour to get our check, which was perfect since we could sit, have drinks and talk!"* where we have two aspect terms *drinks* and *check*, the context of *check* will be *"It took half an hour to get our check"* and the context of *drinks* will be *"have drinks and talk!"*. Another example, *"All the money went into the interior decoration, none of it went to the chefs."*. The context for interior decoration will be *"All the money went into the interior decoration"* and the context for *chefs* will be *"none of it went to the chefs"*.
At the second step, we should determine the polarity, which could be positive, negative, neutral. We propose to use a logistic regression classifier with weighting schema of positive and negative labels with the following features:

- Word n-grams Features

Unigrams and bigrams are extracted for each word in the context without any stemming or stop-word removing, all terms with occurrence less than 3 are removed from the feature space.

- Sentiment Lexicon-based Features

The system extracts four features from the manual constructed lexicons (Bing Liu Lexicon (Hu and Liu, 2004) and MPQA subjectivity Lexicon (Wilson et al., 2005)) and six features from the automatic ones (NRC Hashtag Sentiment Lexicon (Mohammad, 6 07), Sentiment140 Lexicon (Mohammad et al., 2013), and SentiWordNet (Baccianella et al., 2010)). For each context the number of positive words, the number of negative ones, the number of positive words divided by the number of negative ones and the polarity of the last word are extracted from manual constructed lexicons. In addition to the sum of the positive scores and the sum of the negative scores from the automatic constructed lexicons.

- Negation Features

The rule-based algorithm presented in Christopher Potts Sentiment Symposium Tutorial is implemented. This algorithm appends a negation suffix to all words that appear within a negation scope which is determined by the negation key and a certain punctuation. All these words are added to the feature space.

4- Z score Features

Z score can distinguish the importance of each term in each class, their performances have been proved (Hamdan et al., 2014a). We assume as in the mentioned work that the term frequencies are following the multi-nomial distribution. Thus, Z score can be seen as a standardization of the term frequency using multi-nomial distribution. We compute the Z score for each term ti in a class C_j (t_{ij}) by calculating its term relative frequency tfr_{ij} in a particular class C_j, as well as the mean $(mean_i)$ which is the term probability over the whole corpus multiplied by n_j the number of terms in the class C_j, and standard deviation (sd_i) of term ti according to the underlying corpus (see Eq.1). We tested different threshold for choosing the words which have higher Z score, we found 3 is the best one for restaurant data and 4 for laptop data.

$$Zscore(ti) = \frac{tfr_{ij} - mean_i}{sd_i} \tag{1}$$

Thus, we added the number of words having Z score higher than 3,4 in each class positive,negative and neutral, the two classes which have the maximum number and minimum numbers of words having Z score higher than the threshold. These 5 features have been added to the feature space.

- Brown Cluster Features

Each word in the text is mapped to its cluster in Brown clusters, 1000 features are added to feature space where each feature represents the number of words in the text mapped to each cluster. The 1000 clusters is provided in Twitter Word Clusters of CMU ARK group which were constructed from approximately 56 million tweets.

- Category Feature

We also added the category of each OTE as a feature to the feature space.

4.1 Experiments

In addition to the restaurant data set presented in tabel 1, two other data sets statistics are presented in table 3 (Laptops data which consists of training and testing data sets while the Hotel test set is out of domain set that was provided to test our model on new domain without having training data).

We trained a L1-regularized Logistic regression classifier implemented in LIBLINEAR, which has given good results in several papers (Hamdan et al., 2015b) (Hamdan et al., 2015a). The classifier is trained on the training data set using the previous features with the three polarities (positive, negative, and neutral) as labels. A weighting schema is adapted for each class, we use the weighting option -wi which enables a use of different cost parameter C for different classes. Since the training data is unbalanced, this weighting schema adjusts the probability of each label. Thus, we tuned the classifier in adjusting the cost parameter C of Logistic Regression, weight w_{pos} of positive class and weight w_{neg} of negative class.

We used the 1/10 of training data set for tuning the three parameters in the two data sets (Restaurant, Laptop), all combinations of C in range 0.1 to to 4 by step 0.1, w_{pos} in range 1 to 8 by step 0.1, w_{neg} in range 1 to 8 by step 0.1 are tested. The combination C=0.3, textitwpos=1.2, w_{neg}=1.9 have been chosen for the restaurant set and C=0.2 w_{pos}=2.1 w_{neg}=1.9 for the laptops set.

Data	Reviews	Sentences	OTE
Train Lap	277	1739	1973
Test Lap	173	761	949
Test hotel	30	266	339

Table 3. Data set statistics for Hotel and Laptops Reviews.

Table 4 shows the results of our system on the three data sets. It should note that we use the trained classifier on restaurant data set for predicting the polarity in the Hotel test set the out-of-domain set. Our system outperforms the baseline over the three data set. The gain is of 11.95%, 7.9%, 14.16% in restaurant, laptop, hotel reviews respectively. The baseline of Hotels is the majority baseline while the other baselines are provide by the organizers which use a trained SVM on the BOW features and the category name feature in each data set. Our system is ranked third over ten submissions in the restaurant data set, third over thirteen in the laptops set, and the first over eleven in the hotel set.

Experiment	Correct	All	Accuracy
Restaurant			
Our system	638	845	75.5
Baseline	537	845	63.55
Laptops			
Our system	739	949	77.87
Baseline	664	949	69.97
Hotels			
Our system	291	339	85.84
Baseline	243	339	71.68

Table 4. Results of sentiment polarity in Restaurant, laptops, hotels reviews.

5 Conclusion and future work

We have built two systems for opinion target extraction of restaurant data set, and sentiment polarity analysis for three data sets (restaurant and laptops) and one out-of-domain set (hotel). We have used supervised tagger for OTE, trained a CRF model with several features. A Logistic regression classifier is used for sentiment polarity where we adopted a weighting schema in each domain and applied the same classifier and weighting schema trained on restaurant set on the Hotel test set. In future work, we will focus on using parsing tree for determining the context of OTE instead of the syntactic method. And play with other types of features for the two subtasks OTE and Sentiment Polarity.

References

Baccianella, S., Esuli, A., and Sebastiani, F. (2010). SentiWordNet 3.0: An enhanced lexical resource for sentiment analysis and opinion mining. In *in Proc. of LREC*.

Brody, S. and Elhadad, N. (2010). An unsupervised aspect-sentiment model for online reviews. In *Human Language Technologies: The 2010 Annual Conference of the North American Chapter of the Association for Computational Linguistics*, HLT '10, pages 804–812. Association for Computational Linguistics.

Collobert, R. (2011). Deep learning for efficient discriminative parsing. In Gordon, G. J. and Dunson, D. B., editors, *Proceedings of the Fourteenth International Conference on Artificial Intelligence and Statistics (AISTATS-11)*, volume 15, pages 224–232. Journal of Machine Learning Research - Workshop and Conference Proceedings.

Hamdan, H., Bechet, F., and Bellot, P. (2013-04-29). Experiments with DBpedia, WordNet and SentiWordNet as resources for sentiment analysis in micro-blogging. In *International Workshop on Semantic Evaluation SemEval-2013 (NAACL Workshop)*.

Hamdan, H., Bellot, P., and Bechet, F. (2014a). The impact of z_score on twitter sentiment analysis. In *In Proceedings of the Eighth International Workshop on Semantic Evaluation (SemEval 2014)*, page 636.

Hamdan, H., Bellot, P., and Bechet, F. (2014b). Supervised methods for aspect-based sentiment analysis. In *In Proceedings of the Eighth International Workshop on Semantic Evaluation (SemEval 2014)*.

Hamdan, H., Bellot, P., and Bechet, F. (2015a). lsislif: Feature extraction and label weighting for sentiment analysis in twitter. In *In Proceedings of the 9th International Workshop on Semantic Evaluation (SemEval 2015)*.

Hamdan, H., Bellot, P., and Bechet, F. (2015b). Sentiment lexicon-based features for sentiment analysis in short text. In *In Proceeding of the 16th International Conference on Intelligent Text Processing and Computational Linguistics*.

Hatzivassiloglou, V. and McKeown, K. R. (1997). Predicting the semantic orientation of adjectives. In *Proceedings of the Eighth Conference on European Chapter of the Association for Computational Linguistics*, EACL '97, pages 174–181. Association for Computational Linguistics.

Hu, M. and Liu, B. (2004). Mining and summarizing customer reviews. In *Proceedings of the Tenth ACM SIGKDD International Conference on Knowledge Discovery and Data Mining*, KDD '04, pages 168–177. ACM.

Jakob, N. and Gurevych, I. (2010). Extracting opinion targets in a single- and cross-domain setting with conditional random fields. In *Proceedings of the 2010 Conference on Empirical Methods in Natural Language Processing*, EMNLP '10, pages 1035–1045. Association for Computational Linguistics.

Jin, W. and Ho, H. H. (2009). A novel lexicalized HMM-based learning framework for web opinion mining-NOTE FROM ACM: A joint ACM conference committee has determined that the authors of this article violated ACM's publication policy on simultaneous submissions. therefore ACM has shut off access to this paper. In *Proceedings of the 26th Annual International Conference on Machine Learning*, ICML '09, pages 465–472. ACM.

Kim, S., Zhang, J., Chen, Z., Oh, A., and Liu, S. (2013-07). A hierarchical aspect-sentiment model for online reviews. In *Proceedings of The Twenty-Seventh AAAI Conference on Artificial Intelligence (AAAI-13)*. AAAI.

Lin, C., He, Y., Everson, R., and Ruger, S. (2012). Weakly supervised joint sentiment-topic detection from text. 24(6):1134–1145.

Liu, B. (2012). *Sentiment Analysis and Opinion Mining*. Synthesis Lectures on Human Language Technologies. Morgan & Claypool Publishers.

Moghaddam, S. and Ester, M. (2010). Opinion digger: An unsupervised opinion miner from unstructured product reviews. In *Proceedings of the 19th ACM International Conference on Information and Knowledge Management*, CIKM '10, pages 1825–1828. ACM.

Mohammad, S. (2012-06-07). #emotional tweets. In **SEM 2012: The First Joint Conference on Lexical and Computational Semantics Volume 1: Proceedings of the main conference and the shared task, and Volume 2: Proceedings of the Sixth International Workshop on Semantic Evaluation (SemEval 2012)*, pages 246–255. Association for Computational Linguistics.

Mohammad, S. M., Kiritchenko, S., and Zhu, X. (2013). NRCCanada: Building the state-of-the-art in sentiment analysis of tweets. In *In Proceedings of the International Workshop on Semantic Evaluation, SemEval 13*.

Okazaki, N. (2007). *CRFsuite: a fast implementation of Conditional Random Fields (CRFs)*.

Pontiki, M., Galanis, D., Papageogiou, H., Manandhar, S., and Androutsopoulos, I. (2015). SemEval-2015 task 12: Aspect based sentiment analysis. In *In Proceedings of the 9th International Workshop on Semantic Evaluation (SemEval 2015)*.

Wei, W. and Gulla, J. A. (2010). Sentiment learning on product reviews via sentiment ontology tree. In *In Proceedings of the 48th Annual Meeting of the ACL*, pages 404–413. ACL.

Wilson, T., Hoffmann, P., Somasundaran, S., Kessler, J., Wiebe, J., Choi, Y., Cardie, C., Riloff, E., and Patwardhan, S. (2005). OpinionFinder: A system for subjectivity analysis. In *Proceedings of HLT/EMNLP on Interactive Demonstrations*, HLT-Demo '05, pages 34–35. Association for Computational Linguistics.

SIEL: Aspect Based Sentiment Analysis in Reviews

Satarupa Guha, Aditya Joshi, Vasudeva Varma
Search and Information Extraction Lab
International Institute of Information Technology, Hyderabad
Gachibowli, Hyderabad, Telengana, India
{satarupa.guha,aditya.joshi}@research.iiit.ac.in
vv@iiit.ac.in

Abstract

Following the footsteps of SemEval-2014 Task 4 (Pontiki et al., 2014), SemEval-2015 too had a task dedicated to aspect-level sentiment analysis (Pontiki et al., 2015), which saw participation from over 25 teams. In Aspect-based Sentiment Analysis, the aim is to identify the aspects of entities and the sentiment expressed for each aspect. In this paper, we present a detailed description of our system, that stood 4th in Aspect Category subtask (slot 1), 7th in Opinion Target Expression subtask (slot 2) and 8th in Sentiment Polarity subtask (slot 3) on the Restaurant datasets.

1 Introduction

When a review or a social media post talks about a product or service, the user might want to discuss multiple aspects or sub-topics related to the product or service being discussed. For example, in a restaurant review, while the customer might have good things to say about the food quality offered at a restaurant, she might be disappointed with the service offered to her, and she might think the decor needs to be revamped. So a general sentiment analyzer that determines the overall sentiment towards the product or service might not be able to capture the full essence of the review. Hence the need for Aspect-based Sentiment Analysis, for better and more fine-grained analysis of user feedback, which would enable service providers and product manufacturers to identify those business aspects that needs improvement. Specifically, SemEval-2015 Task 12 expects systems to automatically determine the aspect categories present in the data and the sentiment expressed towards each of those categories, given a customer review. For the Aspect Category (Entity and Attribute) Detection subtask, one has to identify every entity E and attribute A pair E#A towards which an opinion is expressed in the given text. E and A should be chosen from predefined inventories of Entity types and Attribute labels per domain. Each E#A pair together defines an aspect category of the given text. The E#A inventories for the restaurants domain has been shown in Table 1.

For the Opinion Target Expression (OTE) identification subtask (Slot 2), we need to identify an expression used in the given text that refers to the reviewed entity E of a pair E#A. The OTE is defined by its starting and ending offsets in the given text. The OTE slot takes the value "NULL" when there is no explicit mention of the opinion entity or no mention at all.

For Sentiment Polarity Detection task, each identified E#A pair of the given text has to be assigned a polarity - positive, negative, or neutral.

2 Related Work

The Aspect Category Detection task can be thought of as similar to document classification task, which has a huge trove of excellent literature. Specifically delving into classification of reviews, (Kiritchenko et al., 2014) showed state-of-art performance, using interesting linguistic and lexicon features. (Castellucci et al., 2014) used simple bag of words based features, generalized using distributional vectors learnt from external data. (Brychcín et al., 2014) employed MaxEnt classifiers using additional features like word clusters learnt using various methods like LDA.

(Hu and Liu, 2004b) initiated works on aspect identification in product reviews using an association rule based system. In his book (Liu, 2012) specifies four methods for aspect extraction, namely, frequent phrases, opinion and target relations, supervised learning and topic models. (Jakob and Gurevych, 2010) highlighted the use of Conditional Random Fields to extract the aspect terms and phrases and demonstrated a significant improvement in the F-Measure compared to then state-of-the-art by (Zhuang et al., 2006), which used a supervised approach to extract feature-opinion pairs. There are some approaches that utilize NLP semantics to extract aspect terms. Bhattacharyya (Mukherjee and Bhattacharyya, 2012) created a system to discover dependency parsing rules to extract opinion expressions. Many new works use hybrid approaches combining both NLP as well as statistical methods to create improved systems. In SemEval 2014, (Kiritchenko et al., 2014) used an in-house entity tagging system to find labels for Outside Term (O) and Aspect Term (T). (Toh and Wang, 2014) used tagging approach with more linguistic features and extra resources like Wordnet and word clusters.

The task of Sentiment Analysis has been enriched with some of the seminal works like (Pang and Lee, 2004) and (Wilson et al., 2005), and has reached new heights with recent publications from (Socher et al., 2013) which combines grammatical cues with deep learning. (Carrascosa, 2014) presented innovative techniques of ensemble learning for the task of Sentiment Analysis, which we too have adopted in concept. (Bakliwal et al., 2012) presents a simple sentiment scoring function which uses prior information to classify and weight various sentiment bearing words/phrases in tweets. However, none of these works are crafted to handle Aspect based Sentiment Analysis and it is not trivial to adapt them for this task. Similar to the task at hand are works done by (Mcauley et al., 2012) and (Lakkaraju et al., 2011), both of whom mined great benefits from the topic modelling paradigm. (Mohammad et al., 2013) achieved the best performance in Aspect Category Polarity Detection task in SemEval 2014 using various innovative linguistic features and publicly available sentiment lexica and two automatically compiled polarity lexica. (Brun et al., 2014) used information from its syntactic parser, BoW features, and an out-of-domain sentiment lexicon to train an SVM model.

Entities
RESTAURANT, FOOD, DRINKS, SERVICE, AMBIENCE, LOCATION
Attributes
GENERAL, PRICES, QUALITY, STYLE_OPTIONS, MISCELLANEOUS

Table 1: Entities and Attributes in Restaurants dataset.

We have experimented with the techniques and features from these previous works and have also added some of our own.

3 Subtask 1: Aspect Category Detection

The Aspect Category Detection task involves identifying every entity E and attribute A pair E#A towards which an opinion is expressed in the given review.

We take a supervised classification approach where we use C one-vs-all Random Forest Classifiers, for each of the C {entity,attribute} pairs or aspect categories in the training data, with basic bag of words based approach. We have also tried other features that we explain shortly, but surprisingly the bag of words approach yielded us the best performance. As a part of the pre-processing procedure, we did the following:

- Removed stop words, except pronouns, because we observed that the category SERVICE#GENERAL can easily be distinguished from other categories by using pronouns as cues
- Stemmed all words
- Removed punctuation
- Normalized all numbers by replacing them by zeros, with the motivation that the exact figures do not hold any semantic meaning and are not of importance to us.

Following is the list of features we experimented with:

- *Unigrams* — For each word in a review, we mark its corresponding position True if it is present in the vocabulary.

- *Presence of number* — We check if a review sample contains numbers or not, with the motivation reviews talking about the PRICES attribute are more likely to have numbers in them.

- *Presence of word in Food and Drinks list* [1] — The motivation behind using this feature is, sentences talking about say, FOOD#PRICES and DRINKS#PRICES are likely to use similar words like "cheap", "expensive", "value for money", "dollars", etc., but we need to be able to distinguish between the two (FOOD and DRINKS). Hence we use look-up lists for food and drinks with the hope that the customers would explicitly use names of food and drinks items in reviews, wherever applicable.

- *WordNet synsets* — WordNet is a large lexical database of English. In Wordnet, synonyms or words that denote the same concept and are interchangeable in many contexts, are grouped into unordered sets called synsets. Word forms with several distinct meanings are represented in as many distinct synsets, and hence this feature is useful for capturing semantic information. For each word we find its corresponding synset and use it as a feature for our classifier in a bag of words fashion.

- *TF-IDF* — Instead of using binary values to denote absence or presence of a word in the sentence, we put its corresponding TF-IDF score pre-computed from the train data. Normally for document classification tasks, TF-IDF performs better than n-grams because the former rightly penalizes common words that are not helpful in distinguishing one topic from the other. Although our Aspect Detection task is very similar to document classification task, this feature did not help much, probably because of the small size of the data set.

- *Word2Vec* — The Word2Vec is an efficient implementation of skip-gram and continuous bag of words architectures that takes a text corpus as input and produces the word vectors of its constituent words as output. We trained Word2Vec on a corpus comprising Yelp Restaurant reviews data, SemEval 2014 data, SemEval 2015 train data. Let the vector dimension to be D. For each word in a review sentence, we get a vector representation of dimension D. We take an average over all words and end up with a single D-dimensional vector. We experiment with the value of D, which is essentially an optimization over time required to train, and the performance and finally set it to be 30. However, vectors averaged over all words in a sentence are not very good representations for the sentence, which is possibly why this feature did not add much value to our system.

For train and test data were pre-processed and their features extracted in the same way. As for the Random Forest Classifier, we used 50 decision tree estimators using Gini index criterion and at each step we consider only S features when looking for the best split, where S is the square root of the total number of features.

We had also tried hierarchical 2-level classification, i.e. first classifying a review sentence into one of the entities and then classifying them further into one of the pre-defined attributes. However, this 2-level classification technique, with the same set of features mentioned above, yielded poorer performance. So we decided to not make any distinction between entities and attributes, and consider an entity-attribute pair together as an aspect category.

This task required us to categorize reviews into very fine-grained and inter-related categories, with hierarchical dependencies among themselves. This might have been one of the reasons why many of the popular features used for regular document classification did not perform as good as they promised to. Another challenge was the small number of training examples, as compared to the large number of categories to be classified into, which was not the case in any of the previous works to the best of our knowledge.

[1] Food list compiled from http://eatingatoz.com/food-list/ and Drinks list compiled manually

4 Subtask 2: Opinion Target Expression

Given a review sentence, the aim of this task is to find the Opinion Target Expressions (OTE), that is, the particular attribute of the entity the user expresses his/her sentiment about. Aspects may either be explicitly explained in the review as in the sentence "The service was really quick and I loved the fajitas." Here "service" and "fajita "are explicit aspects. In a sentence like "Don't go. Really horrible", the user didn't use any individual term but still gives an impression of her sentiment. In such cases, the slot takes the value "NULL". Our system uses a sequence labelling approach to tackle this problem by the use of Conditional Random Fields. The tagger from Mallet toolkit, is trained to identify three possible tags, namely BEG and INT for beginning and intermediate target words and OTH for other words.

Our features are as follows:-

- *Word* — The lowercase form of the word itself
- *POS* — Part of speech tag of the word
- *Dependency* — We use two kinds of dependency features — the dependency label on incoming edge on the word, and the first dependency label on outgoing edge. This proved to be a very important feature.
- *Capitalization* — If the first character of the word is in capital, mark it as capital.
- *Punctuation* — If the word contains any non-alphanumeric character, we mark it as punctuation.
- *Seed* — The word is marked as a seed if it was present in the seed-list created by collecting all the OTEs in the training data, splitting them by word and removing all the stop words.
- *Brown Cluster* — Brown Cluster ID is obtained by first training Brown Clustering on the same corpus we described for Word2Vec features in Subtask 1. Brown clustering is a form of hierarchical clustering of words based on the context in which they occur. The intuition behind the method is that a class-based language model where probabilities of words are based on the clusters of previous words, can overcome the data sparsity problem inherent in language modeling. From brown clustering, for each word in the corpus we get the cluster ID to which it has been assigned. We generate 100 clusters.
- *Presence in Expanded List* — We curated an expanded seed list from the original seed list explained above. We utilized WiBi, which is a taxonomy of Wikipedia pages and categories. We traversed the WiBi Page graph and collected the pages located next to the words (if present) in the seed list. The new list was again split by spaces and punctuation, and stop words were removed. This feature is marked if the term is present in the expanded list.
- *Stop Word* — This feature is marked if the current term is a stop word in English language.
- *Seed Stem* — This feature contains the stemmed form of the original word as obtained from Porter Stemmer.

5 Subtask 3: Sentiment Polarity Classification

In this subtask, the input consists of a review sentence and the set of aspect categories it belongs to. The expected output is a polarity label for each of the associated aspect categories. We have first extracted Bag of Words and Wordnet Synset features from both train and test data. Then we run a variety of classifiers (like Stochastic Gradient Descent, SVM, Adaboost) multiple times and store the confidence scores obtained from decision functions of each of these classifiers. Finally we build a linear SVM classifier that uses the scores obtained from the classifiers in the 1st level as features, along with 15 other hand-crafted lexicon features as explained in Section 5.2. This is also known as stacking, a form of ensemble learning. It is essentially stacking of classifiers inside a classifier. Stacking typically yields performance better than any single one of the trained models, and this is what we wanted to leverage. However, since we need polarity labels per aspect category, we need to identify the segments in the sentence that deals with each of the categories and then treat those segments as individual samples for polarity detection. For example, if there are three aspect categories associated with a sentence, we want to break it down into 3 {sentence,category} pairs:

$$sent1, \{cat1, cat2, cat3\} \rightarrow$$
$$\{sent1, cat2\}, \{sent2, cat2\}, \{sent3, cat3\}$$

For each {sentence, category} pair, we find a word in the sentence that is the best representative of the category, which we call as centroid. Then we take a window of n words surrounding the centroid and consider that window to be the segment of interest for that category. So in this example sentence, we need to have three centroids and hence three segments, not necessarily disjoint:

$$\{sent1, cat1\}, \{sent1, cat2\}, \{sent1, cat3\} \rightarrow$$
$$\{seg1, cat1\}, \{seg2, cat2\}, \{seg3, cat3\}$$

We experimented with the window size, and decided upon using a window size of 3 words to the left and to the right of the centroid. It is interesting to note that among sentences that have more than one category, the average length of a review sentence is 15 words in train data and 17 words in test data.

After we get these segments, we extract the following features from these segments for polarity detection:

- *Bag of Words*
- *Grapheme Stretching* i.e. words with repeated characters. For example, words like "Tooooo goooood" indicates strong subjectivity and therefore is less likely to belong to Neutral class.
- *Presence of exclamation* also signals subjectivity, usually positivity.
- *Presence of wh-words and conditional words* like why, what,if, etc. Observation tells us that such presence are mostly characteristic of sentences with negative polarity.
- *Wordnet Synsets*, as explained before

While bag of words features include statistical information, WordNet synsets help incorporate semantic information. These two complementary features help us in making the maximal discrimination among the target classes.

5.1 Extracting Centroid for a {Sentence, Category} Pair

We automatically generate a set of seed words for each of the aspect categories by the following technique: From the train data, we consider all sentences labelled with a single category as a single document. As a result, for 13 possible categories in the train data, we have 13 documents. Now for each document (corresponding to each category), we compute the TF-IDF scores of all the words and consider words having TF-IDF greater than a certain threshold as seed words for that category. We ascertain the optimal value of the threshold to be 0.2 through experimentation. We generate a co-occurrence matrix of words from three datasets SemEval 2015 train data, SemEval 2014 train and test data. Typically, it is considered that two words co-occur if they are present as bigram in the corpus. However, we define co-occurrence as occurring in the same review sentence, rather than occurring as a bigram as it is less likely to find repetition of co-occurring bigrams in a smaller corpus. This co-occurrence matrix stores the frequency of co-occurrence of two words in the corpus. For N words in the vocabulary, we have a $N \times N$ co-occurrence matrix. Given a {sentence, category} pair, for each word in the review sentence, we find the Point wise Mutual Information (P.M.I.) between that word and each word in the seed list of the assigned category and take their average for that word. We do the same for all words in the sentence. The word in the sentence having the maximum average P.M.I. score is defined as the centroid for the {sentence, category} pair. P.M.I is defined as the ratio of the probability of occurrence of two words together in the corpus to the product of the probabilities of occurrence of the two words independently in the corpus. We derive the co-occurrence frequencies from the co-occurrence matrix we built in the previous step.

5.2 Ensemble Learning – Stacking Classifiers

After feature extraction, we train 3 kinds of classifiers — Linear Support Vector Machines, Stochastic Gradient Descent and Adaboost, for each of the features — Bag of words and Wordnet Synsets. We repeat the process K times where $K \in \mathbb{Z}$. We have experimentally chosen K to be 30 — it is actually a trade off between the time taken to train the model and the performance improvements. As we increased K over 30, the improvement in performance started to diminish. For each test sample, we obtain 3 scores (corresponding to three classes — positive, negative, neutral) from the decision function of each classifier. We use these confidence scores as features along with 15 other hand-crafted lexicon features for a linear Support Vector Machine classifier. We employ features such as number of positive tokens, number of negative tokens, total positive sentiment score, total negative sentiment score, sum of sentiment scores, maximum sentiment score, etc. from Sentiwordnet (Baccianella et al., 2010), Bing Liu's opinion lexicon (Hu and Liu, 2004a), MPQA subjectivity lexicon (Wilson et al., 2005), NRC Emotion Association lexicon (Mohammad and Turney, 2013), Sentiment140 lexicon (Go et al., 2009), and NRC Hashtag Lexicon (Mohammad and Kiritchenko, 2014).

For the final linear SVM classifier, we experimentally ascertain the optimal value of the parameter C to be 0.024. The linear SVM classifiers, in the first level of stacking, had a default value of 1.0 for parameter C. We did not have enough time to tune them, as we had many classifiers inside the main SVM classifier. The Ada Boost Classifier uses 100 decision tree estimators and a default learning rate of 1. We have used Scikit Learn for building all the classifiers. Although we employ several classiers, the time taken is negligible. This is because the different classifiers in the first stage of stacking can be trained in parallel quite easily.

6 Results

We submitted unconstrained systems for the Restaurants dataset. We did not run our system for other domains mainly due to lack of time during the competition. Table 2 shows our final F1-scores obtained on SemEval official test data, for each of the three slots. Tables 3, 4 and 5 presents the results of ablation experiments carried out for slots 1, 2 and 3 respectively. We show the effect of varying the size of the context window surrounding the centroid, on F1-score in Figure 1. Finally Table 6 compares our ensemble system with a baseline system trained on a single linear SVM with only lexicon features.

Subtask	Our Score	Best Score	Rank
Slot 1	0.57	0.62	4
Slot 2	0.53	0.70	7
Slot 3	0.71	0.78	8

Table 2: Official Results for SemEval 2015.

Feature	Precision	Recall	F1
Unigrams	0.64	0.51	0.57
Unigrams+Bigrams	0.51	0.45	0.48
Unigrams+WordNet syn	0.53	0.48	0.50
Unigrams+Word2Vec	0.52	0.46	0.49
TF-IDF	0.47	0.42	0.44

Table 3: Experiment with Features for Slot 1.

Feature	Precision	Recall	F1
All	0.51	0.55	0.52
All - (Seed+Expanded Seed)	0.52	0.55	0.53 [2]
POS+Dep.+Punct.+Brown	0.35	0.54	0.43
POS+Dep.+Punct.+Stopwords	0.64	0.53	0.58 [3]
POS+Dep.	0.62	0.51	0.57

Table 4: Ablation Experiment for Slot 2.

Feature	Accuracy
All (BoW + WordNet syn)	0.71
All - BoW	0.68
All - WordNet syn	0.70

Table 5: Ablation Experiment for Slot 3.

System	Accuracy
Linear SVM with only lexicon	0.68
Our system	0.71

Table 6: Slot 3: Comparison of our ensemble learning technique with a baseline system trained on a single LinearSVM with only lexicon features.

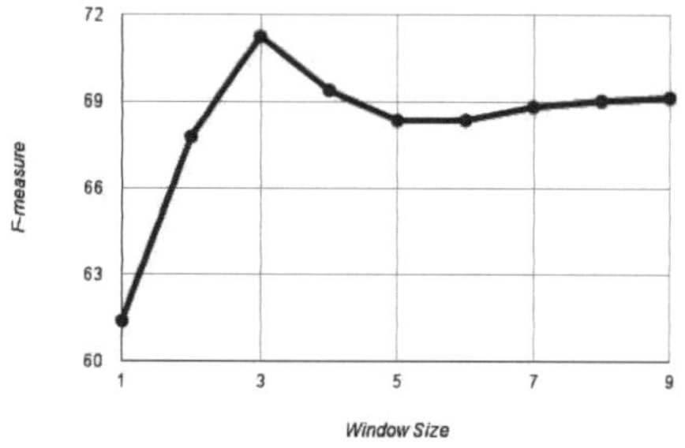

Figure 1: Variation of F1 score with context window size.

[2]Submitted system

[3]This result was obtained during ablation experiment post-competition

7 Conclusion

This paper describes the system submitted by team SIEL for SemEval 2015 Task 12. For all the three subtasks, our system performs quite well, ranking between 4th and 8th. We experimented with Ensemble Learning technique for slot 3, which we want to explore and improve further. In future, we would like to work on adapting our system to other domains as well.

Acknowledgements

We sincerely thank Samik Datta and Mohit Kumar for all the fruitful discussions and encouragement, Riddhiman Dasgupta for insights on Ensemble Learning and Mark Franco-Salvador for guiding us with Wibi.

References

Stefano Baccianella, Andrea Esuli, and Fabrizio Sebastiani. 2010. Sentiwordnet 3.0: An enhanced lexical resource for sentiment analysis and opinion mining. In *in Proc. of LREC*.

Akshat Bakliwal, Piyush Arora, Senthil Madhappan, Nikhil Kapre, Mukesh Singh, and Vasudeva Varma. 2012. Mining sentiments from tweets. In *Proceedings of the 3rd Workshop in Computational Approaches to Subjectivity and Sentiment Analysis*, WASSA '12, pages 11–18, Stroudsburg, PA, USA.

Caroline Brun, Nicoleta Diana Popa, and Claude Roux. 2014. Xrce: Hybrid classification for aspect-based sentiment analysis. In *Proceedings of the 8th International Workshop on Semantic Evaluation (SemEval 2014)*, pages 838–842.

Tomáš Brychcín, Michal Konkol, and Josef Steinberger. 2014. Uwb: Machine learning approach to aspect-based sentiment analysis. In *Proceedings of the 8th International Workshop on Semantic Evaluation (SemEval 2014)*, pages 817–822.

Rafael Carrascosa. 2014. An entry to kaggle's 'sentiment analysis on movie reviews' competition.

Giuseppe Castellucci, Simone Filice, Danilo Croce, and Roberto Basili. 2014. Unitor: Aspect based sentiment analysis with structured learning. In *Proceedings of the 8th International Workshop on Semantic Evaluation (SemEval 2014)*, pages 761–767, Dublin, Ireland, August.

Ingo Feinerer and Kurt Hornik, 2014. *wordnet: WordNet Interface*. R package version 0.1-10.

Jenny Rose Finkel, Trond Grenager, and Christopher Manning. 2005. Incorporating non-local information into information extraction systems by gibbs sampling. In *In ACL*, pages 363–370.

Alec Go, Richa Bhayani, and Lei Huang. 2009. Twitter sentiment classification using distant supervision. *Processing*, pages 1–6.

Minqing Hu and Bing Liu. 2004a. Mining and summarizing customer reviews. In *Proceedings of the Tenth ACM SIGKDD International Conference on Knowledge Discovery and Data Mining*, KDD '04, pages 168–177, New York, NY, USA.

Minqing Hu and Bing Liu. 2004b. Mining opinion features in customer reviews. In *Proceedings of the 19th National Conference on Artifical Intelligence*, AAAI'04, pages 755–760.

Niklas Jakob and Iryna Gurevych. 2010. Extracting opinion targets in a single- and cross-domain setting with conditional random fields. In *Proceedings of the 2010 Conference on Empirical Methods in Natural Language Processing*, EMNLP '10, pages 1035–1045, Stroudsburg, PA, USA.

Svetlana Kiritchenko, Xiaodan Zhu, Colin Cherry, and Saif Mohammad. 2014. Nrc-canada-2014: Detecting aspects and sentiment in customer reviews. In *Proceedings of the 8th International Workshop on Semantic Evaluation (SemEval 2014)*, pages 437–442.

Himabindu Lakkaraju, Chiranjib Bhattacharyya, Indrajit Bhattacharya, and Srujana Merugu, 2011. *Exploiting Coherence for the Simultaneous Discovery of Latent Facets and associated Sentiments*, chapter 43, pages 498–509.

Bing Liu. 2012. *Sentiment Analysis and Opinion Mining*. Synthesis Lectures on Human Language Technologies.

Bing Liu. May 2012. *Sentiment Analysis and Opinion Mining (Introduction and Survey)*.

Edward Loper and Steven Bird. 2002. Nltk: The natural language toolkit. In *In Proceedings of the ACL Workshop on Effective Tools and Methodologies for Teaching Natural Language Processing and Computational Linguistics. Philadelphia: Association for Computational Linguistics*.

Julian Mcauley, Jure Leskovec, and Dan Jurafsky. 2012. Pale lagerthe pale lager model.

Tomas Mikolov, Kai Chen, Greg Corrado, and Jeffrey Dean. 2013. Efficient estimation of word representations in vector space. *CoRR*, abs/1301.3781.

Saif M. Mohammad and Svetlana Kiritchenko. 2014. Using hashtags to capture fine emotion categories from tweets. *Computational Intelligence*, pages n/a–n/a.

Saif M. Mohammad and Peter D. Turney. 2013. Crowdsourcing a word-emotion association lexicon. 29(3):436–465.

Saif M. Mohammad, Svetlana Kiritchenko, and Xiaodan Zhu. 2013. Nrc-canada: Building the state-of-the-art in sentiment analysis of tweets. *CoRR*, abs/1308.6242.

Subhabrata Mukherjee and Pushpak Bhattacharyya. 2012. Feature specific sentiment analysis for product reviews. In Alexander Gelbukh, editor, *Computational Linguistics and Intelligent Text Processing*, volume 7181 of *Lecture Notes in Computer Science*, pages 475–487.

Bo Pang and Lillian Lee. 2004. A sentimental education: Sentiment analysis using subjectivity summarization based on minimum cuts. In *Proceedings of the 42Nd Annual Meeting on Association for Computational Linguistics*, ACL '04, Stroudsburg, PA, USA.

F. Pedregosa, G. Varoquaux, A. Gramfort, V. Michel, B. Thirion, O. Grisel, M. Blondel, P. Prettenhofer, R. Weiss, V. Dubourg, J. Vanderplas, A. Passos, D. Cournapeau, M. Brucher, M. Perrot, and E. Duchesnay. 2011. Scikit-learn: Machine learning in Python. *Journal of Machine Learning Research*, 12:2825–2830.

Maria Pontiki, Dimitris Galanis, John Pavlopoulos, Harris Papageorgiou, Ion Androutsopoulos, and Suresh Manandhar. 2014. Semeval-2014 task 4: Aspect based sentiment analysis. In *Proceedings of the 8th International Workshop on Semantic Evaluation (SemEval 2014)*, pages 27–35, Dublin, Ireland, August.

Maria Pontiki, Dimitris Galanis, John Pavlopoulos, Harris Papageorgiou, Suresh Manandhar, and Ion Androutsopoulos. 2015. Semeval-2015 task 12: Aspect based sentiment analysis. In *Proceedings of the 9th International Workshop on Semantic Evaluation (SemEval 2015)*, Denver, Colorado.

Radim Řehůřek and Petr Sojka. 2010. Software Framework for Topic Modelling with Large Corpora. In *Proceedings of the LREC 2010 Workshop on New Challenges for NLP Frameworks*, pages 45–50, Valletta, Malta, May.

Sara Rosenthal, Alan Ritter, Preslav Nakov, and Veselin Stoyanov. 2014. Semeval-2014 task 9: Sentiment analysis in twitter. In *Proceedings of the 8th International Workshop on Semantic Evaluation (SemEval 2014)*, pages 73–80, Dublin, Ireland, August.

Richard Socher, Alex Perelygin, Jean Y. Wu, Jason Chuang, Christopher D. Manning, Andrew Y. Ng, and Christopher Potts. 2013. Recursive deep models for semantic compositionality over a sentiment treebank.

Zhiqiang Toh and Wenting Wang. 2014. Dlirec: Aspect term extraction and term polarity classification system. In *Proceedings of the 8th International Workshop on Semantic Evaluation (SemEval 2014)*, pages 235–240, Dublin, Ireland, August.

Joachim Wagner, Piyush Arora, Santiago Cortes, Utsab Barman, Dasha Bogdanova, Jennifer Foster, and Lamia Tounsi. 2014. Dcu: Aspect-based polarity classification for semeval task 4. In *Proceedings of the 8th International Workshop on Semantic Evaluation (SemEval 2014)*, pages 223–229, Dublin, Ireland, August.

Theresa Wilson, Janyce Wiebe, and Paul Hoffmann. 2005. Recognizing contextual polarity in phrase-level sentiment analysis. In *Proceedings of the Conference on Human Language Technology and Empirical Methods in Natural Language Processing*, HLT '05, pages 347–354, Stroudsburg, PA, USA.

Li Zhuang, Feng Jing, and Xiao-Yan Zhu. 2006. Movie review mining and summarization. In *Proceedings of the 15th ACM International Conference on Information and Knowledge Management*, CIKM '06, pages 43–50, New York, NY, USA.

Sentiue: Target and Aspect based Sentiment Analysis in SemEval-2015 Task 12

José Saias
DI - ECT - Universidade de Évora
Rua Romão Ramalho, 59
7000-671 Évora, Portugal
jsaias@uevora.pt

Abstract

This paper describes our participation in SemEval-2015 Task 12, and the opinion mining system sentiue. The general idea is that systems must determine the polarity of the sentiment expressed about a certain aspect of a target entity. For slot 1, entity and attribute category detection, our system applies a supervised machine learning classifier, for each label, followed by a selection based on the probability of the entity/attribute pair, on that domain. The target expression detection, for slot 2, is achieved by using a catalog of known targets for each entity type, complemented with named entity recognition. In the opinion sentiment slot, we used a 3 class polarity classifier, having BoW, lemmas, bigrams after verbs, presence of polarized terms, and punctuation based features. Working in unconstrained mode, our results for slot 1 were assessed with precision between 57% and 63%, and recall varying between 42% and 47%. In sentiment polarity, sentiue's result accuracy was approximately 79%, reaching the best score in 2 of the 3 domains.

1 Introduction

Social networks and other online platforms are an important communication mechanism in current lifestyle. These platforms aggregate user-generated content, such as opinions that people write and publish freely on the Web, and are now valued for market research and trend analysis. Natural language processing (NLP) helps to automatically extract information from these written opinions.

This paper describes a participation in SemEval-2015 Task 12[1], Aspect Based Sentiment Analysis (Pontiki et al., 2015), with the sentiue system, from Universidade de Évora. In previous editions of SemEval, we participated in Sentiment Analysis (SA) tasks, but in terms of overall polarity, over Twitter messages (Rosenthal et al., 2014), not being aspect oriented. The general idea for this challenge, is that, for a text, the system must determine the polarity of the sentiment expressed about a certain aspect of a particular target entity. Our sentiue system is an evolution from our previous work (Saias and Fernandes, 2013; Saias, 2014), for target oriented SA.

Task 12 was run in two phases. In phase A systems are tested for aspect detection with one slot to aspect category, and a second slot for the opinion target expression on the text. Test data includes review texts for two domains: restaurants and laptops. In phase B, aspect category is provided, and systems must assign a polarity (positive, negative, or neutral) for each opinion. In this phase, systems received also texts from a third domain, hotels, for which no sentiment training data was given.

We used a supervised machine learning classifier combined with a probability based selection process, for entity and attribute category detection, on slot 1. Target expression detection was performed with an entity catalog, filled with known targets for each entity type, and named entity recognition (NER). For the sentiment polarity slot, we used a a supervised machine learning classifier, having bag-of-words (BoW), lemmas, bigrams after verbs, and

[1] http://alt.qcri.org/semeval2015/task12/

punctuation based features, along with sentiment lexicon based features. The detailed procedure is explained in section 3.

2 Related Work

Many SA related publications, originating both in industry and in academia, have appeared, and it is notorious the growing interest by companies. Popular scientific forums and events include activities and workshops on this area, such as RepLab (Amigó et al., 2014) at CLEF[2], for online reputation, or ABSA and Twitter SA tasks in SemEval.

In last year's edition of this SemEval task (Pontiki et al., 2014), there were 26 systems participating in the polarity subtask. The two systems with better polarity classification accuracy were from NRC-Canada and DCU teams. NRC-Canada system (Kiritchenko et al., 2014) was trained with the data provided in the task, and complemented with lexicons generated from other corpora of customer reviews, to help feature extraction in machine learning. Stanford CoreNLP was used to tokenize, POS tagging, and dependency parse trees. They address polarity classification with a linear SVM classifier, with features for: the target, and its surrounding words; POS based features; dependency tree based features; unigrams and bigrams; lexicon based features. The DCU system (Wagner et al., 2014) also uses SVM for aspect and for polarity classification, combining bag-of-n-gram features with rule-based features. N-grams (with size from 1 to 5) in a window around the aspect term, are used as features, as well as features derived from a sentiment lexicon. The rule-based approach to predict the polarity of an aspect term, generated features considering all words score and their distance to the aspect term.

3 Method

Our participation involved the adaptation of our previous real-time system, for text overall sentiment classification, into a target oriented SA system. The next subsections explain how the system works, for each part of Task 12 challenge.

[2]http://clef2014.clef-initiative.eu/

3.1 Aspect Entity and Attribute

The first annotation task focuses on aspect category. This category is an **entity** and **attribute** pair, each chosen from an inventory with possible values, in each domain, for entity types and attributes. Since the possible category types are known and limited, we decided to use a classifier for each entity type (e.g. *food, laptop*) and for each attribute label (e.g. *price, quality*). Our approach comprises two stages. The first processes each review sentence assigning to it zero, one, or more entity types and attribute labels. The second stage chooses and combines identified entities and attributes, forming the aspect annotation. Analyzing the training data, we found that in the same sentence, there may be opinions on various types of entity (e.g. CPU, battery) or attributes. Thus, we have chosen to train a classifier for each entity type, and a classifier for each attribute label. We set a supervised machine learning text classifier, using MALLET (McCallum, 2002), a Java-based tool for NLP, with machine learning applications to text. For the purpose of this stage, it was necessary to prepare the training data for each binary classifier, that would determine whether a sentence contains an opinion on its tag (entity type or attribute label). The train process was the same for all tags, entity type or attribute label, of each domain. We created a dataset where each instance is a sentence text, and its class is *tag*, if the sentence had at least one opinion with that tag, or *no_tag* otherwise. Text preprocessing includes tokenization, POS tagging and lemmatization, all performed with Stanford CoreNLP (Toutanova et al., 2003; Manning et al., 2014) tool. The classifier algorithm was Maximum Entropy[3], and the classifier model features were text words and lemmas.

Second stage starts with each sentence annotated with a set and tags, some for entity type and some for attribute label. When a sentence has no annotations, the system assumes that there is no opinion. In case of 1 tag on entity type and 1 tag in the attribute label, then it is the trivial case where the junction of the two results in the aspect annotation. For sentences with 1 tag on entity type and 0 tags for the attribute, our system searches for the most frequent aspect annotation, within the sentence domain, that

[3]MALLET class: cc.mallet.classify.MaxEnt

includes that entity type. The equivalent is applied in the case of 0 tags to entity and 1 tag for the attribute label. If both sides have one or more tags, the system applies a cycle, where each loop iteration forms the more frequent pair (entity,attribute) in that domain, and removes these two tags from the sentence tag set. This is repeated until the first, entity or attribute side, exhausts the tags provided by the previous stage classifier. And if some tags are left, on the opposite side of the pair, the system applies, for each, the same process already explained for case 0-1 or 1-0.

3.2 Opinion Target Expression

At this point, sentences are already marked as having (or not) opinions on certain aspect category. For each opinion on restaurants domain, the system needed to identify the entity mention on the sentence text, referred to as the opinion target expression (OTE). We collected the opinion targets for each entity type, from the training data, forming a catalog. If any of the targets already known (e.g. restaurant name, or meal) appears in the sentence text, next to a verb or adjective, it is chosen as the OTE. If this does not lead to any OTE candidate, our system applies named entity recognition, looking for references to organization and location entities, using Stanford NER tool (Finkel et al., 2005; Manning et al., 2014). Having found one OTE, through the catalog or by NER, its text and position are marked in slot 2. If no mention is found, OTE slot is filled with the NULL value.

3.3 Sentiment Polarity

Phase B was held in a subsequent period, and the input given to the systems is a little different, having the correct annotations on the aspect category, in restaurants, laptops and hotels domains. For each opinion, the participating systems must assign a sentiment polarity (positive, negative or neutral), considering the opinion aspect.

For training, there were 1654 opinions on restaurants domain, and 1974 more opinions about laptops, all annotated for polarity. No sentiment training data was given for hotels domain. Considering the available data, and the objective of this phase, we used a supervised machine learning classifier to predict each opinion polarity. Instead of multiple classifiers, such as implemented for slot 1, we prepared a single classifier, thought, as before, for text but tuned with a different model, so that it can choose between positive, negative or neutral polarity.

Sentences without opinion are not considered in the training, because here the polarity is associated with opinions. Further, a single sentence may have several opinions about different aspects, and each may have a different and independent polarity. To train the classifier, for each opinion we created a polarity data instance, containing the sentence text, its domain, its aspect entity and attribute, OTE (if available, in restaurants), and the opinion polarity to be learned. As before, MALLET was used with a Maximum Entropy classifier. The sentence text preprocessing was the same we did for aspect category classification. The features to represent each instance were:

- BoW with a feature for each token text;
- lemmas for verbs and adjectives;
- bigram after verb (lemmatized);
- presence of negation terms;
- bigram after negation term;
- presence of exclamation/question mark;
- presence of polarized terms (positive or negative), according to each sentiment lexicon;
- whether there are polarized terms before exclamation mark and question mark;
- bigram before, and after, any polarized term;
- polarity inversion, by negation detection before some polarized term;
- presence of polarized terms in the last 5 tokens;
- a feature for the domain, and two features for the entity type and the attribute label.

To see whether a term is polarized, each token text is verified in each sentiment lexicon. These polarity support resources are AFINN lexicon (Nielsen, 2011), Bing Liu's opinion lexicon (Liu et al., 2005) and MPQA subjectivity clues (Wiebe et al., 2005).

Domain	Precision	Recall	F-measure
restaurants	0,633	0,472	0,541
laptops	0,577	0,441	0,500

Table 1: sentiue's evaluation on aspect category.

Domain	Precision	Recall	F-measure
restaurants	0,488	0,336	0,398

Table 2: sentiue's evaluation on target detection.

After some experimentation, we decided to use a single full train, joining the instances of restaurants and laptops as a whole training set. The resulting model was used to classify the opinion polarity for the three domains.

Because we used sentiment lexicons, our system operates in unconstrained mode. These additional resources served as support for features extraction. No supplementary training texts were used. In our development testing, we obtained an 80% accuracy for polarity. After this, the result is written in XML format for submission.

4 Results

The phase A test data had 685 sentences on restaurants domain and 761 on laptops domain. With the method described above, the sentiue system extracted 596 opinion categories for restaurants domain and 751 other for laptops domain.

Table 1 shows the evaluation for slot 1. Among the 15 submissions evaluated in the first domain, the best system F-score value was 0,627, while our result F-score was 0,541. For laptops aspect category, sentiue's scores were lower, but improving in the comparison with other systems, achieving the second best F-measure, out of 9 evaluated submissions. The evaluation of our result in opinion target expression in given in Table 2. This was a poor result, when compared with the 0,524 average F-measure of the 21 submissions for this slot.

In phase B systems had to fill the slot 3, with sentiment polarity to 845 opinions on restaurants domain, 949 opinions on laptops domain, and 339 opinions on hotels domain.

On Table 3 we find our system's result accuracy, in the two trained domains plus the untrained hotels domain. In this slot we got the most satisfactory result, with the best accuracy in restaurants and laptops, and an above average score, in the hotels domain. The detailed evaluation is shown in Table 4, with values for precision, recall and f-measure, per domain and polarity class.

Domain	Accuracy
restaurants	0,787
laptops	0,793
hotels	0,788

Table 3: sentiue accuracy on sentiment polarity.

Domain,Polarity	Precision	Recall	F-measure
restaurants, positive	0,767	0,914	0,834
restaurants, negative	0,825	0,708	0,762
restaurants, neutral	0,714	0,111	0,192
laptops, positive	0,831	0,891	0,860
laptops, negative	0,766	0,787	0,777
laptops, neutral	0,387	0,152	0,218
hotels, positive	0,887	0,840	0,863
hotels, negative	0,608	0,738	0,667
hotels, neutral	0,143	0,083	0,105

Table 4: sentiue's SA evaluation per domain.

5 Conclusions

By participating in this SemEval edition, we sought to develop our previous work, in order to achieve SA results focused on the opinion targets.

Our results were poor for OTE detection, but we think it will be easy to correct the implementation problems for that part. As example, while checking if a sentence contained a known target, from the catalog, the system did not require whole words to be matched, and this led to some misidentification of word substrings as target.

Our result was more satisfactory for slot 1, with a F-measure slightly above average between the 15 evaluated submissions for restaurants domain, and 4.5% better than submissions average for laptops domain. The distribution of opinions for each aspect category is not uniform. For example, for attribute label classification, we already know that QUALITY and GENERAL have much more instances than other labels. This analysis inspired our approach in the second stage, explained in section 3.1. To improve this part, we think to introduce a cascade classifier.

After the classification obtained in the current first stage, other machine learning classifier will decide how to pair entity+attribute, based on the wording of the sentence. Another future work idea is to use more corpora for training the aspect classifiers, as other systems (Kiritchenko et al., 2014) have tried.

In phase B `sentiue` achieved good results. This, perhaps, is justified by our previous experience in overall SA. Many of the polarity classifier features are inherited from our former system. SemEval challenge is always a motivation to test our system and an opportunity to learn from other participants.

Acknowledgments

We would like to thank to LabInterop project, for providing the infrastructure for the developed system. LabInterop is funded by *Programa Operacional Regional do Alentejo* (INALENTEJO).

References

Enrique Amigó, Jorge Carrillo-de-Albornoz, Irina Chugur, Adolfo Corujo, Julio Gonzalo, Edgar Meij, Maarten de Rijke, Damiano Spina. 2014. Overview of RepLab 2014: Author Profiling and Reputation Dimensions for Online Reputation Management. In Information Access Evaluation. Multilinguality, Multimodality, and Interaction. Lecture Notes in Computer Science, Volume 8685, 2014, pp 307-322.

Jenny Rose Finkel, Trond Grenager, and Christopher Manning. 2005. Incorporating Non-local Information into Information Extraction Systems by Gibbs Sampling. Proceedings of the 43nd Annual Meeting of the Association for Computational Linguistics (ACL 2005), pp. 363-370.

Svetlana Kiritchenko, Xiaodan Zhu, Colin Cherry, and Saif M. Mohammad. 2014. NRC-Canada-2014: Detecting Aspects and Sentiment in Customer Reviews. Proceedings of the 8th International Workshop on Semantic Evaluation (SemEval 2014). p. 437–442. Dublin, Ireland, August 2014.

Bing Liu, Minqing Hu and Junsheng Cheng. 2005. *Opinion Observer: Analyzing and Comparing Opinions on the Web*. In Proceedings of the 14th International World Wide Web conference (WWW-2005). Chiba, Japan.

Manning, Christopher D., Surdeanu, Mihai, Bauer, John, Finkel, Jenny, Bethard, Steven J., and McClosky, David. 2014. The Stanford CoreNLP Natural Language Processing Toolkit. In Proceedings of 52nd Annual Meeting of the Association for Computational Linguistics: System Demonstrations, pp. 55-60.

Andrew Kachites McCallum. 2002. MALLET: A Machine Learning for Language Toolkit.

Finn Årup Nielsen. 2011. *A New ANEW: Evaluation of a Word List for Sentiment Analysis in Microblogs*. In Proceedings, 1st Workshop on Making Sense of Microposts (#MSM2011): Big things come in small packages. pp: 93-98. Greece.

Maria Pontiki, D. Galanis, J. Pavlopoulos, H. Papageorgiou, I. Androutsopoulos, S. Manandhar. SemEval-2014 Task 4: Aspect Based Sentiment Analysis. Proceedings of the 8th SemEval, 2014. Dublin, Ireland.

Maria Pontiki, Dimitrios Galanis, Haris Papageogiou, Suresh Manandhar, and Ion Androutsopoulos. 2015. SemEval-2015 Task 12: Aspect Based Sentiment Analysis. In Proceedings of the 9th International Workshop on Semantic Evaluation (SemEval 2015), Denver, Colorado.

Sara Rosenthal, Alan Ritter, Veselin Stoyanov, and Preslav Nakov. 2014. SemEval-2014 Task 9: Sentiment Analysis in Twitter. In Proceedings of the Eighth International Workshop on Semantic Evaluation (SemEval'14). August 23-24, 2014, Dublin, Ireland.

José Saias and Hilário Fernandes. 2013. Senti.ue-en: An approach for informally written short texts in SemEval-2013 Sentiment Analysis task. In *Second Joint Conference on Lexical and Computational Semantics (*SEM), Volume 2: Proceedings of the Seventh International Workshop on Semantic Evaluation (SemEval 2013)*, pages 508–512, Atlanta, Georgia, USA.

José Saias. Senti.ue: Tweet overall sentiment classification approach for SemEval-2014 task 9. In *Proceedings of the 8th International Workshop on Semantic Evaluation (SemEval 2014)*, pages 546–550, Dublin, Ireland, August 2014. ISBN 978-1-941643-24-2.

Kristina Toutanova, Dan Klein, Christopher Manning, and Yoram Singer. 2003. Feature-Rich Part-of-Speech Tagging with a Cyclic Dependency Network. In Proceedings of HLT-NAACL 2003, pp. 252-259.

Joachim Wagner, Piyush Arora, Santiago Cortes, Utsab Barman, Dasha Bogdanova, Jennifer Foster and Lamia Tounsi. 2014. DCU: Aspect-based Polarity Classification for SemEval Task 4. Proceedings of the 8th International Workshop on Semantic Evaluation (SemEval 2014). p. 223–229. Dublin, Ireland, August 2014.

Janyce Wiebe, Theresa Wilson, and Claire Cardie. 2005. Annotating expressions of opinions and emotions in language. Language Resources and Evaluation, 39:165–210.

TJUdeM: A Combination Classifier for Aspect Category Detection and Sentiment Polarity Classification

Zhifei Zhang and **Jian-Yun Nie**
Dept. of Comp. Sci. and Oper. Res.
University of Montreal
Quebec H3C 3J7, Canada
{zhanzhif, nie}@iro.umontreal.ca

Hongling Wang
Dept. of Comp. Sci. and Tech.
Soochow University
Suzhou 215006, China
hlwang@suda.edu.cn

Abstract

This paper describes the system we submitted to In-domain ABSA subtask of SemEval 2015 shared task on aspect-based sentiment analysis that includes aspect category detection and sentiment polarity classification. For the aspect category detection, we combined an SVM classifier with implicit aspect indicators. For the sentiment polarity classification, we combined an SVM classifier with a lexicon-based polarity classifier. Our system outperforms the baselines on both the laptop and restaurant domains and ranks above average on the laptop domain.

1 Introduction

Sentiment analysis aims at identifying people's opinions, sentiments, attitudes, and emotions towards entities and their attributes (Liu, 2012), which has a wide range of applications on user-generated content, e.g., reviews, blogs, and tweets.

Most previous work in sentiment analysis mainly attempted to identify the overall polarity of a given text or text span (Pang and Lee, 2008; Wilson et al., 2009; Zhang et al., 2009). The document-level or sentence-level sentiment classification is often insufficient for applications. Each document may talk about different entities, or express different opinions about different aspects of the entity even if the document concerns a single entity. Therefore, we need to discover the aspects of entities and determine the sentiment polarity on each entity aspect. This task is called aspect-based sentiment analysis or feature-based opinion mining (Hu and Liu, 2004).

The aspect-based sentiment analysis (ABSA) task (Task 12) (Pontiki et al., 2015) in SemEval 2015 is a continuation of SemEval 2014 Task 4 (Pontiki et al., 2014). The ABSA task consists of two subtasks: In-domain ABSA and Out-domain ABSA. We participated in the former subtask that aims to identify the aspect category (i.e., an entity and attribute pair) and the sentiment polarity given a review text about a laptop or a restaurant.

Each entity and attribute pair is an aspect category chosen from the predefined inventories of entity types and attribute labels per domain. For the aspect category detection, an SVM classifier with the bag-of-words features can be used, and this approach is used as our baseline method. However, if a token implying an aspect, e.g., "overpriced", is not taken as a feature, the SVM classifier cannot correctly identify its corresponding category. Therefore, we enhance the results from the SVM classifier by using implicit aspect indicators (Cruz-Garcia et al., 2014). For the sentiment polarity classification, an SVM classifier with the bag-of-words features plus the category feature is trained and this is used as our baseline. However, again, if a sentiment word does not appear in the training data, the SVM classifier cannot predict its polarity. Therefore, we combined the SVM classifier and a lexicon-based polarity classifier (Taboada et al., 2011).

The remainder of this paper is organized as follows. In Section 2, we describe our approach to the aspect category detection. In Section 3, our approach to the sentiment polarity classification is presented. Experimental results are shown in Section 4. Section 5 provides the conclusion.

2 Aspect Category Detection

The aspect category detection task is to identify the specific entities and their attributes about the laptop or restaurant reviews. We use an SVM classifier enhanced by implicit aspect indicators. The process of the whole system is illustrated in Figure 1. We will describe the details in the following subsections.

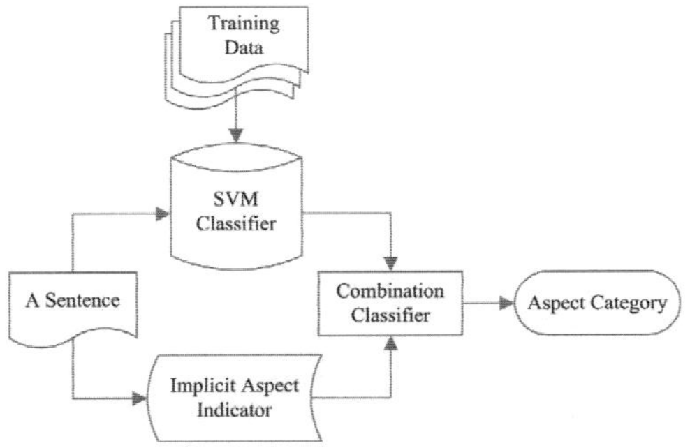

Figure 1: System flowchart for aspect category detection.

2.1 SVM Classifier

The SVM classifier uses words as features to determine the aspect categories. We use the LIBSVM package (Chang and Lin, 2011) to implement an SVM classifier. The "-t" option is set to 0 for linear kernel, and the "-b" option is set to 1 for probability estimates. The top n frequent tokens in the training data are used as the bag-of-words features. We set $n = 1000$ as the number of bag-of-words features.

An aspect category (C) is an entity (E) and attribute (A) pair, i.e., $C = E\#A$. For instance,

I received prompt service with a s-mile.$\rightarrow${Service#General}

It would cost too much to repair it.$\rightarrow${Support#Price}

For a test sentence s, the LIBSVM package can predict the probability of assigning each category $E\#A$ to s. The category should be assigned to s only if its probability is higher than a predefined threshold t. We set t to 0.2 for the restaurant reviews and to 0.12 for the laptop reviews. It's easy to see that our SVM classifier is configured in accordance with the SVM baseline system provided by the task organizers (Pontiki et al., 2015).

$$Aspect_{svm}(s) = \{E\#A|Prob(E\#A) > t\} \quad (1)$$

2.2 Implicit Aspect Indicator

If the tokens implying aspects are beyond bag-of-words features, the SVM classifier is unable to predict it. For example,

It was totally overpriced- fish and chips was about $15.

Both "overpriced" and "$15" in the above sentence are associated with the "price" aspect. These tokens are considered as the implicit aspect indicators.

The different methods can be used to identify the implicit aspect indicators (Cruz-Garcia et al., 2014). In our case, we do it manually by setting a set of indicators for several aspects (see Table 1). The list of words associated with the "price" aspect includes "cost", "overpriced", "expensive", etc. The list for the "quality" aspect includes "feels", "durable", "taste", etc.

Implicit Aspect	Word List	Size
Price	expensive, overpriced, cheap, discount, cost, ······	16
Quality	feels, durable, overcooked, taste, breaks, ······	50
Performance	improves, stable, crashed, performs, powerful, ······	40
Design	lightweight, heavy, elegant, fit, looks, ······	27
Usability	access, store, typing, flexible, upgrade, ······	62

Table 1: Implicit aspect indicator.

In addition, an expression of the amount of money is strongly related to the "price" aspect. To identify these expressions, we use the following regular expression: "\s$\d+(\.\d+)?\s".

If the word W indicates the implicit aspect A', the aspects determined by implicit aspect indicators are denoted as follows:

$$Aspect_{iai}(s) = \{A'|W \in s\} \quad (2)$$

2.3 Combination Classifier

We find the SVM classifier often obtains the category like "E|General" which means that a general opinion is expressed and it is not specific to a particular aspect. On the other hand, for the same case, the implicit aspect indicators may suggest other specific aspect categories (e.g., "price"). This case occurs when the words corresponding to the implicit aspect indicators are not included in the features used by SVM. It is in this case that it is the most useful to combine the two classifiers.

Our combination is done as follows: if the "General" category is suggested by the SVM classifier, then we replace it by the categories identified through the implicit aspect indicators. Otherwise, the categories given by the SVM classifier remain unchanged. The method is described in the following algorithm.

Algorithm 1 A combination classifier for aspect category detection.

Input: $Aspect_{svm}(s)$ and $Aspect_{iai}(s)$ for a test sentence s
Output: $Aspect(s)$
if $Aspect_{iai}(s) = \emptyset$ **then**
  return $Aspect_{svm}(s)$
end if
$Aspect(s) = \emptyset$
for all $E\#A \in Aspect_{svm}(s)$ **do**
  if A is 'General' **then**
    for all $A' \in Aspect_{iai}(s)$ **do**
      $Aspect(s) = Aspect(s) \cup \{E\#A'\}$
    end for
  else
    $Aspect(s) = Aspect(s) \cup \{E\#A\}$
  end if
end for
return $Aspect(s)$

3 Sentiment Polarity Classification

The sentiment polarity classification task is to assign a polarity from a set {*positive*, *negative*, *neutral*} to each identified aspect category of a sentence. We use a similar method as for the previous task. The processes of the system are illustrated in Figure 2 that includes three parts: an SVM classifier, a lexicon-based polarity classifier, and their combination classifier.

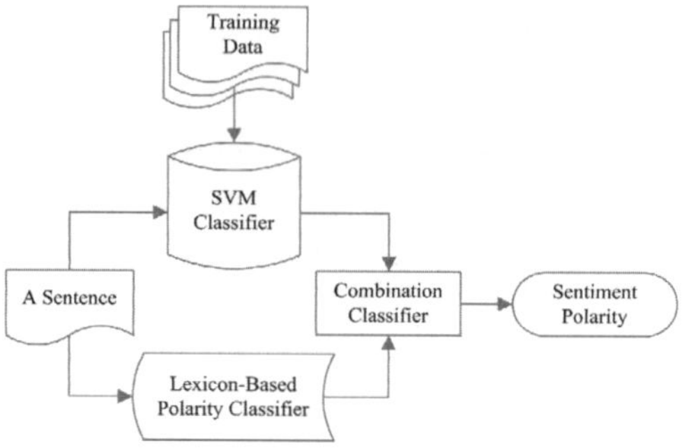

Figure 2: System flowchart for sentiment polarity classification.

3.1 SVM Classifier

We also use the LIBSVM package (Chang and Lin, 2011) to implement an SVM classifier with linear kernel. Again, n ($n = 1000$) bag-of-words features are extracted from the training data. In addition, a feature that indicates the aspect category is used. Our SVM configurations are also the same with that of the SVM baseline system (Pontiki et al., 2015).

The SVM classifier can predict a polarity (*positive*, *negative*, or *neutral*) for each aspect category C within a test sentence s. We represent three polarity labels with three respective numbers.

$$Polarity_{svm}(s, C) \in \{1, -1, 0\} \quad (3)$$

3.2 Lexicon-Based Polarity Classifier

If the sentiment words are beyond the bag-of-words features, the SVM classifier assigns the neutral polarity, and what's worse, it assigns the reverse polarity if the sentence contains negation words (Zhu et al., 2014), like "not" and "no". In fact, the lexicon-based methods can also be effective in sentiment classification (Taboada et al., 2011). We therefore adopt a simple lexicon-based method in our system.

The sentiment lexicons, such as Bing Liu's Opinion Lexicon (Hu and Liu, 2004) and MPQA Subjectivity Lexicon (Wilson et al., 2009), are used to generate our sentiment word list. We denote all positive words and negative words by POS and NEG respectively.

We use the Stanford Parser package (Klein and Manning, 2003) for POS tagging and parsing. The typed dependency "$neg(X, Y)$" shows that one sentence contains a negation Y modifying X, and "$root(ROOT, X)$" shows that X is a core word.

Assume that one sentiment word X is in a test sentence s and $X \in POS \cup NEG$, if $X \in POS$, then $Polarity(X) = 1$, otherwise $Polarity(X) = -1$. The polarity for the aspect category is determined by,

$$Polarity_{lex}(s, C) = \begin{cases} -Polarity(X) & \exists neg(X, Y) \\ -Polarity(X) & \exists neg(Z, Y) \\ & \wedge root(ROOT, Z) \\ Polarity(X) & otherwise \end{cases} \tag{4}$$

where $Y \in s$ is a negation word, and $Z \in s$ but $Z \notin POS \cup NEG$.

The following examples are corresponding to three circumstances in the above equation:

*Overpriced and **not** tasty* $\{neg(tasty, not)\}$

*Our experience did **not** ever get any better* $\{neg(get, not), root(ROOT, get)\}$

Overpriced and not tasty $\{root(ROOT, overpriced)\}$

3.3 Combination Classifier

If none of the sentiment words in the lexicon appear in a sentence, the lexicon-based polarity classifier is helpless, but the SVM classifier could still determine a reasonable polarity (Pang et al., 2002).

We propose a classifier combining the SVM classifier and the lexicon-based polarity classifier. It works as follows: If there is disagreement between the polarity of SVM classifier and the lexicon, we will rely on the polarity based on the lexicon if the latter is not neutral (0). Otherwise, we take the polarity of the SVM classifier.

Algorithm 2 A combination classifier for sentiment polarity classification.

Input: $Polarity_{svm}(s, C)$ and $Polarity_{lex}(s, C)$ for an aspect category C of a test sentence s
Output: $Polarity(s, C)$

```
if Polarity_svm(s, C) = Polarity_lex(s, C) then
    Polarity(s, C) = Polarity_svm(s, C)
else if Polarity_lex(s, C) = 0 then
    Polarity(s, C) = Polarity_svm(s, C)
else
    Polarity(s, C) = Polarity_lex(s, C)
end if
return Polarity(s, C)
```

4 Experiments

4.1 Data Sets

The training and test data is described in Table 2.

Domain			Training	Test
Laptop	Sentence		1739	761
	Category	Positive	1103	541
		Negative	765	329
		Neutral	106	79
		Total	1974	949
Restaurant	Sentence		1315	685
	Category	Positive	1198	454
		Negative	403	346
		Neutral	53	45
		Total	1654	845

Table 2: Data sets.

The laptop training data, consisting of 1739 sentences, includes 1974 aspect category instances. The laptop test data, consisting of 761 sentences, includes 949 aspect category instances. The restaurant training data, consisting of 1315 sentences, includes 1654 aspect category instances. The restaurant test data, consisting of 685 sentences, includes 845 aspect category instances.

There are 22 entity labels and 9 attribute labels on the laptop domain, and there are 6 entity labels and 5 attribute labels on the restaurant domain.

4.2 Experimental Results

Aspect category detection Table 3 lists the results of our system for the aspect category detection.

	Laptop	Restaurant
SVM Baseline	0.4631	0.5133
Top	0.5086	0.6268
Average	0.4548	0.5383
Our System	0.4649	0.5245

Table 3: F-score comparison for aspect category detection.

Our system clearly outperforms the SVM baseline on both two domains. This indicates that the implicit aspect indicators can further improve the performance. Our system ranks above average on the laptop domain. But our system is far from the top system. This is possibly due to the simple features used by the SVM classifier. Globally, our method is comparable to the average performance of all the participating systems.

Sentiment polarity classification Table 4 lists the results of our system for the sentiment polarity classification. The majority baseline is obtained by majority voting in all the participating results.

	Laptop	Restaurant
SVM Baseline	0.6997	0.6355
Majority Baseline	0.5701	0.5373
Top	0.7935	0.7870
Average	0.7131	0.7132
Our System	0.7323	0.6888

Table 4: F-score comparison for sentiment polarity classification.

The performance of our system is obviously better than two baselines on both two domains, but fails to reach the average on the restaurant domain. The conclusion of this experiment is that the lexicon-based method is helpful to sentiment classification when it is combined with a baseline method. As for the task of aspect category detection, a possible reason lies in the simple bag-of-words features we used. With more sophisticated features, one can likely improve the performance of the baseline methods, and as a result, the combination method.

Comparing the results on the two domains, we observe that our system produced lower performance than average for the restaurant reviews, but higher performance for the laptop reviews. A possible reason can be the lexicon we defined for the two domains. The Opinion Lexicon is originally designed for the customer reviews about 5 digit products, which is more related to the laptop domain.

5 Conclusions

In this task, we proposed a combination classifier for the aspect category detection which combines an SVM classifier with implicit aspect indicators, and a combination classifier for the sentiment polarity classification which combines an SVM classifier with a lexicon-based polarity classifier. Our system ranks above average on the laptop domain and outperforms the baselines, but is still lower than the average for the restaurant domain. Our experiments show that implicit aspect indicators and polarity lexicon are both useful in these tasks. For the future work, more and better features will be examined to help to improve the classification performance.

Acknowledgments

We are really grateful to the organizers and reviewers for this interesting task and their helpful suggestions and comments. This research is supported by the Quebec-China Postdoctoral Scholarship (File No. 188040).

References

Chih-Chung Chang and Chih-Jen Lin. 2011. LIBSVM: A library for support vector machines. *ACM Transactions on Intelligent Systems and Technology*, 2(3):27:1–27:27.

Ivan Omar Cruz-Garcia, Alexander Gelbukh, and Grigori Sidorov. 2014. Implicit aspect indicator extraction for aspect-based opinion mining.

Minqing Hu and Bing Liu. 2004. Mining and summarizing customer reviews. In *Proceedings of KDD*, pages 168–177, New York, NY, USA.

Dan Klein and Christopher D. Manning. 2003. Accurate unlexicalized parsing. In *Proceedings of ACL*, pages 423–430, Sapporo, Japan.

Bing Liu. 2012. Sentiment analysis and opinion mining. *Synthesis Lectures on Human Language Technologies*, 5(1):1–167.

Bo Pang and Lillian Lee. 2008. Opinion mining and sentiment analysis. *Foundations and Trends in Information Retrieval*, 2(1-2):1–135.

Bo Pang, Lillian Lee, and Shivakumar Vaithyanathan. 2002. Thumbs up? Sentiment classification using machine learning techniques. In *Proceedings of EMNLP*, pages 79–86, Philadelphia, PA, USA.

Maria Pontiki, Haris Papageorgiou, Dimitrios Galanis, Ion Androutsopoulos, John Pavlopoulos, and Suresh Manandhar. 2014. SemEval-2014 Task 4: Aspect based sentiment analysis. In *Proceedings of SemEval*, pages 27–35, Dublin, Ireland.

Maria Pontiki, Dimitrios Galanis, Haris Papageogiou, Suresh Manandhar, and Ion Androutsopoulos. 2015. SemEval-2015 Task 12: Aspect based sentiment analysis. In *Proceedings of SemEval*, Denver, CO, USA.

Maite Taboada, Julian Brooke, Milan Tofiloski, Kimberly Voll, and Manfred Stede. 2011. Lexicon-based methods for sentiment analysis. *Computational Linguistics*, 37(2):267–307.

Theresa Wilson, Janyce Wiebe, and Paul Hoffmann. 2009. Recognizing contextual polarity: An exploration of features for phrase-level sentiment analysis. *Computational Linguistics*, 35(3):399–433.

Changli Zhang, Daniel Zeng, Jiexun Li, Fei-Yue Wang, and Wanli Zuo. 2009. Sentiment analysis of Chinese documents: From sentence to document level. *Journal of the American Society for Information Science and Technology*, 60(12):2474–2487.

Xiaodan Zhu, Hongyu Guo, Saif Mohammad, and Svetlana Kiritchenko. 2014. An empirical study on the effect of negation words on sentiment. In *Proceedings of ACL*, pages 304–313, Baltimore, MD, USA.

SemEval-2015 Task 4: TimeLine: Cross-Document Event Ordering

Anne-Lyse Minard[1], **Manuela Speranza**[1], **Eneko Agirre**[2], **Itziar Aldabe**[2], **Marieke van Erp**[3], **Bernardo Magnini**[1], **German Rigau**[2], **Rubén Urizar**[2]
[1] Fondazione Bruno Kessler, Trento, Italy
[2] The University of the Basque Country (UPV/EHU), Spain
[3] VU University Amsterdam, the Netherlands
{minard,manspera,magnini}@fbk.eu, marieke.van.erp@vu.nl
{itziar.aldabe,e.agirre,german.rigau,ruben.urizar}@ehu.eus

Abstract

This paper describes the outcomes of the TimeLine task (Cross-Document Event Ordering), that was organised within the Time and Space track of SemEval-2015. Given a set of documents and a set of target entities, the task consisted of building a timeline for each entity, by detecting, anchoring in time and ordering the events involving that entity. The TimeLine task goes a step further than previous evaluation challenges by requiring participant systems to perform both event coreference and temporal relation extraction across documents. Four teams submitted the output of their systems to the four proposed subtracks for a total of 13 runs, the best of which obtained an F_1-score of 7.85 in the main track (timeline creation from raw text).

1 Introduction

In any domain, it is important that professionals have access to high quality knowledge for taking well-informed decisions. As daily tasks of information professionals revolve around reconstructing a chain of previous events, an insightful way of presenting information to them is by means of timelines. The aim of the Cross-Document Event Ordering task is to build timelines from English news articles. To provide focus to the timeline creation, the task is presented as an ordering task in which events involving a particular target entity are to be ordered chronologically. The task focuses on cross-document event coreference resolution and cross-document temporal relation extraction.

The latter has been the topic of the three previous TempEval tasks within the SemEval challenges:

- TempEval-1 (2007): Temporal Relation Identification (Verhagen et al., 2009)
- TempEval-2 (2010): Evaluating Events, Time Expressions, and Temporal Relations (Verhagen et al., 2010)
- TempEval-3 (2013): Temporal Annotation (UzZaman et al., 2013)

Additionally, it has also been the focus of the 6th i2b2 NLP Challenge for clinical records (Sun et al., 2013). The cross-document aspect, however, has not often been explored. One example is the work described in (Ji et al., 2009) using the ACE 2005 training corpora. Here the authors link pre-defined events involving the same centroid entities (i.e. entities frequently participating in events) on a timeline. Nominal coreference resolution has been the topic of SemEval 2010 Task on Coreference Resolution in Multiple Languages (Recasens et al., 2010). TimeLine is a pilot task that goes beyond the above-mentioned evaluation exercises by addressing coreference resolution for events and temporal relation extraction at a cross document level.

This task was motivated by work done in the NewsReader project[1]. The goal of the NewsReader project is to reconstruct story lines across news articles in order to provide policy and decision makers with an overview of what happened, to whom, when, and where. Thus, the NewsReader project aims to present end-users with cross-document storylines. Timelines are intermediate event represen-

[1] http://www.newsreader-project.eu

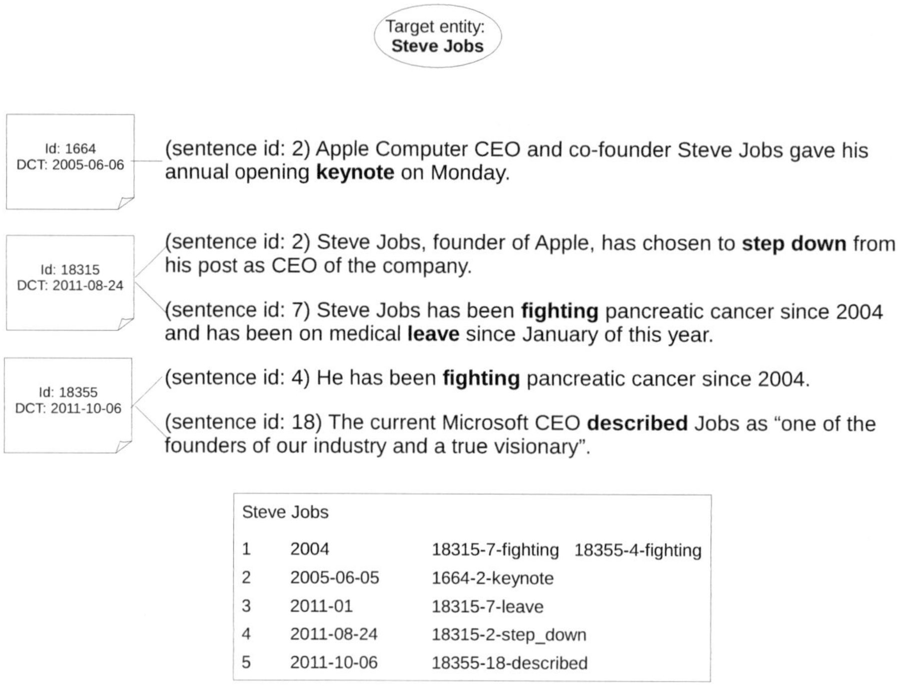

Figure 1: Example of a timeline for the target entity "Steve Jobs" built from five sentences coming from three documents.

tations towards this goal.

The remainder of this paper is organised as follows. In Section 2, we introduce the task. In Section 3, we describe the data annotation protocol. In Section 4, we present the characteristics of our dataset and gold standard timelines. In Section 5, we describe our evaluation methodology, followed by the description of participant systems in Section 6 and the results obtained by the participants to the task in Section 7. Lessons learnt and limitations of our setup are discussed in Section 8.

2 Task Description

Given a set of documents and a set of target entities, the task consists of building a timeline related to each entity, i.e. detecting, anchoring in time, and ordering the events in which the target entity is involved (Minard et al., 2014b). We base our notion of event on TimeML, according to which an *event* is a cover term for situations that happen or occur, including predicates describing states or circumstances in which something obtains or holds true (Pustejovsky et al., 2003).

As input data, we provide a set of documents and a set of target entities; only entities involved in more than two events across at least two different documents are considered as candidates target entities. We also propose two different tracks on the basis of the data used as input: **Track A**, for which we provided only the raw text sources (main track), and **Track B**, for which we also made gold event mentions available.

The expected output, both for Track A and B, is one timeline for each target entity. A timeline for a specific target entity consists of the ordered list of the events in which that entity participates. Events in a timeline are anchored in time through the time anchor attribute; however, for both Track A and B, we also propose a subtrack in which the events do not need to be associated to a time anchor.

In Figure 1 we show an example of a timeline for the target entity *Steve Jobs* built using five sentences extracted from three documents. In bold we represent the events that form the timeline.

In order to perform the task, participants are required to resolve entity coreference, as timelines should contain events involving all coreferring textual mentions of the target entities (including pronominal mentions). For example, in Figure 1, the event *fighting* involving the target entity *Steve Jobs* mentioned as *he* is included in the timeline together with other events also referring to *Steve Jobs*.

The dataset released for this task is composed of 120 Wikinews[2] articles and 44 target entities. 30 documents and 6 target entities (each associated to a timeline) are provided as trial data, while the evaluation dataset consist of 90 documents and 38 target entities (each associated to a timeline).

3 Data Annotation

We manually selected a set of target entities that appeared in at least two different documents and were involved in more than two events.

The target entities are restricted to type PERSON (single persons or sets of people), ORGANISATION (corporations, agencies, and other groups of people defined by an established organisational structure), PRODUCT (anything that might satisfy a want or need, including facilities, food, products, services, etc.), and FINANCIAL (the entities belonging to the financial domain that are not included in one of the other entity types).

Some examples of target entities are *Steve Jobs* (PERSON), *Apple Inc.* (ORGANISATION), *Airbus A380* (PRODUCT), and *Nasdaq* (FINANCIAL).

The annotation procedure for the creation of gold standard timelines for the target entities required one person month. It consisted of four steps, as described below.

Entity annotation. All occurrences of the target entities in the four corpora were marked following (Tonelli et al., 2014). Cross-document co-reference was annotated according to the NewsReader cross-document annotation guidelines (Speranza and Minard, 2014). For this task, we used CROMER[3] (Girardi et al., 2014), a tool designed specifically for cross-document annotation.

[2]`http://en.wikinews.org.`

[3]`https://hlt.fbk.eu/technologies/cromer`

Event and time anchor annotation. Using CROMER, the corpora were annotated with events following the NewsReader cross-document annotation guidelines (Speranza and Minard, 2014). The annotation of events as defined in (Tonelli et al., 2014) was restricted by limiting the annotation to events that could be placed on a timeline. Thus, we did not annotate adjectival events, cognitive events, counter-factual events (which certainly did not happen), uncertain events (which might or might not have happened) and grammatical events[4]. For example, the events *gave*, *chosen* and *been (on medical leave)* in Figure 1 are excluded from the timeline as they are grammatical events.

Furthermore, timelines only contain events in which target entities explicitly participate in a *has_participant* relation as defined in (Tonelli et al., 2014), with the semantic role ARG0 (i.e. agent) or ARG1 (i.e. patient), as defined in the PropBank Guidelines (Bonial et al., 2010). In the example in Figure 1 we have an explicit *has_participant* relation between the entity *Steve Jobs* and the event *fighting* with semantic role ARG0, and one with semantic role ARG1 between *Steve Jobs* and *described*.

Based on TimeML (Pustejovsky et al., 2003), a time anchor corresponds to a TIMEX3 of type DATE; the time anchor attribute of an event takes as value the point in time when the event occurred (in the case of punctual events) or began (in the case of durative events). Its format follows the ISO-8601 standard: YYYY-MM-DD (i.e. Year, Month, and Day).

The finest granularity for time anchor values is DAY; other granularities admitted are MONTH and YEAR (references to months are specified as YYYY-MM and references to years are expressed as YYYY). The place-holder character, X, is used for unfilled positions in the value of a component. Thus, an event happened some day (not specified in the text) in July 2010 (for example, *resigned* in *The company's CEO met his employees one morning last July*) has time anchor 2010-07-XX (granu-

[4]Grammatical events are verbs or nouns that are semantically dependent on a governing content verb/noun. Typical examples of grammatical events are copula verbs, light verbs followed by a nominal event, aspectual verbs and nouns, verbs and nouns expressing causal and motivational relations, and verbs and nouns expressing occurrence.

larity DAY), while an event happened in the same month but with a granularity lower than day (for example in *Apple received criticism last month for the placement of the antenna on iPhone 4*), has time anchor 2010-07. Similarly, XXXX-XX-XX is used when the time anchor is completely unknown and the granularity is DAY, while XXXX-XX and XXXX are used when the time anchor is unknown and the granularity is MONTH and YEAR respectively (Minard et al., 2014a).

Automatic creation of timelines. We represent timelines in a simple tab format. On each line, we first have a cardinal number indicating the position of an event in the timeline, then the value of the anchor time attribute for the same event, and finally the event itself, which is represented as follows: document identifier, sentence number and textual extent of the event. For example, the event *18315-7-leave* in Figure 1 (occurring in sentence 7 of document 18315) occupies position *4* in the timeline and is anchored to *2011-01*.

In the case of event coreference, in the third column, there is a list of coreferring events separated by tabs instead of a single event (see the coreferring events *18315-7-fighting* and *18355-4-fighting* at position 1 in the example in Figure 1).

If two events have the same value for the anchor time attribute, they are placed in the same position (i.e. the same number in the first column), but on different lines.

The automatic created timelines are produced by a script that orders events in a timeline on the basis of the time anchors (all events with the same time anchor are simultaneous and all events with unknown time anchor are at position 0).

Manual revision of the timelines. The manual revision consists of ordering events with the same time anchor or with unknown time anchor taking into consideration textual information that goes beyond the defining of time anchor (Minard et al., 2014a).

For example both *founded* and *closed* in *The firm was founded in 2010 and closed before the end of the year* have anchor time 2010; nonetheless, based on textual information, it is possible to order them (the firm first was founded and then closed). When it is not possible to order events based either on the time anchor or on textual information, annotators leave them at the same position on the timeline. The same holds for events with anchor time XXXX-XX-XX; if annotators have no textual information that can help ordering them, they leave them at position 0; otherwise they place them on the timeline.

Inter-annotator agreement Three annotators have annotated a corpus starting from one target entity, i.e. they have annotated entity coreferences refering to the target entity and the events in which this entity participates. The corpus used is the trial corpus about *Apple Inc.* and the target entity *iPhone 4*. We compute the inter-annotator agreement using the Dice's coefficient (Dice, 1945). For the annotation of entity and event mentions, the agreement is respectively 0.81 and 0.66, and for entity coreferences of 0.84.

4 Task Dataset

The dataset used for this task is composed of articles from Wikinews, a collection of multilingual online news articles written collaboratively in a wiki-like manner. The reason for choosing Wikinews as a source is its creative commons license allowing us to freely release this dataset to the research community. For this task, we selected Wikinews articles around four topics:

- Apple Inc. (trial corpus);
- Airbus and Boeing (corpus 1);
- General Motors, Chrysler and Ford (corpus 2);
- Stock Market (corpus 3).

The trial data consists of one corpus of 30 documents and gold standard timelines for six target entities. The other three corpora, each consisting of 30 documents (about 30,000 tokens each) were used as the evaluation dataset.

As reported in Table 1, the total number of target entities in the evaluation dataset amounts to 38, but for the evaluation we used 37 timelines instead as one of the timelines contained no events.

The trial data contains one target entity of type ORGANISATION, one of type PERSON and 4 of type PRODUCT. The distribution of target entity types in the evaluation dataset is the following: 18 of type ORGANISATION, 10 of type FINANCIAL, 7 of type PERSON and 3 of type PRODUCT.

	Trial corpus	Evaluation dataset			
	Apple Inc.	Airbus	GM	Stock	Total
# documents	30	30	30	30	90
# sentences	464	446	430	459	1,335
# tokens	10,373	9,909	10,058	9,916	29,893
# events	187	343	308	264	915
# event chains	168	244	234	210	688
# target entities	6	13	12	13	38
# timelines	6	13	11	13	37
# events / timeline	31.2	26.4	25.7	20.3	24.1
# event chains / timeline	28	18.8	19.5	16.2	18.1
# docs / timeline	5.8	6.2	5.7	9.1	6.9

Table 1: Quantitative data about the dataset.

The three evaluation corpora are very similar in terms of size. It is interesting to notice, however, that the timelines created from the Stock Market corpus have peculiar features as they contain a lower average number of events with respect to those created from the other corpora. On the other hand, on average, Stock Market timelines contain events from a higher number of different documents, i.e. 9.1, versus 6.2 for Airbus and 5.7 for GM.

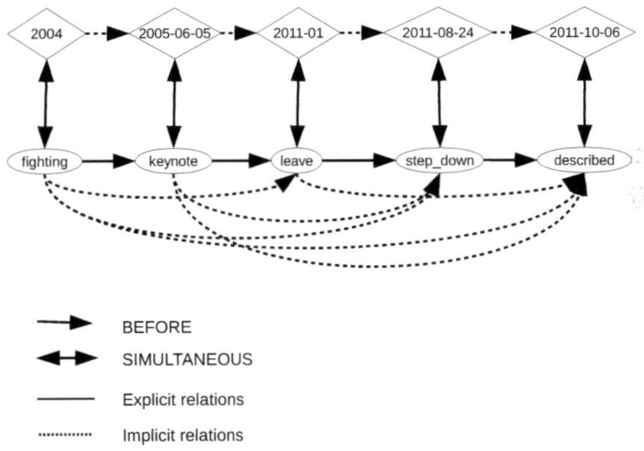

Figure 2: Explicit and implicit relations resulting from the timeline of Figure 1.

5 Evaluation Methodology

The evaluation methodology of this task is based on the evaluation metric used for TempEval-3 (UzZaman et al., 2013) to evaluate relations in terms of recall, precision and F_1-score. The metric captures the temporal awareness of an annotation (UzZaman and Allen, 2011).

> Temporal awareness is defined as the performance of an annotation as identifying and categorizing temporal relations, which implies the correct recognition and classification of the temporal entities involved in the relations.
>
> We calculate the Precision by checking the number of reduced system relations that can be verified from the reference annotation temporal closure graph, out of number of temporal relations in the reduced system relations. Similarly, we calculate the Recall by checking the number of reduced reference annotation relations that can be verified from the system output's temporal closure graph, out of number of temporal relations in the reduced reference annotation. (UzZaman et al., 2013)

Before evaluating temporal awareness, each timeline needs to be transformed into a set of temporal relations. Figure 2 shows the explicit relations resulting from the timeline of Figure 1 as well as the implicit relations captured by the temporal graph. In order to convert each timeline, we defined the following transformation steps:

1. Each time anchor is represented as a TIMEX3.
2. Each event is related to one TIMEX3 with the SIMULTANEOUS relation type.

3. If one event happens before another one, a BEFORE relation type is created between both events.
4. If one event happens at the same time as another one, a SIMULTANEOUS relation type is created between both events.

Note that the evaluation of subtracks (ordering only), requires steps 3 and 4 alone.

For this first pilot on timelines, we decided to simplify the representation of durative events in the timelines by anchoring them in time considering their starting point. For this reason we represent relations between each event and its time anchor with the SIMULTANEOUS relation type (instead of other possibilities like BEGUN_BY or INCLUDES).

Events placed at the beginning of the timeline at position 0, i.e. events that were not ordered, are not considered in the evaluation. The official scores are based on the micro-average of the individual F_1-scores for each timeline, i.e. the scores are averaged over the events of the timelines of each corpus. The micro-average precision and recall values are also provided.

6 Participant Systems

29 teams signed up for the evaluation task, 8 teams downloaded the evaluation dataset and only 4 teams submitted results. A total of 13 unique runs were submitted: 3 for Track A (for which the participants worked on the raw texts), 2 for SubTrack A, 4 for Track B (for which the event mentions were provided) and 4 for SubTrack B.

The WHUNLP team processed the texts with Stanford CoreNLP. They applied a rule-based approach to extract target entities and their predicates, and perform temporal reasoning.

The SPINOZAVU[5] system is based on the pipeline developed in the NewsReader project and on the TIPSem tool. The tools are used for pre-processing, dependency parsing, semantic role labelling, event detection, temporal expression normalisation, coreference resolution and temporal relations extraction.

The GPLSIUA team also used a pipeline approach, employing the OpeNER language analysis toolchain, the Semantic Role Labeller from SENNA and the TIPSem tool for temporal processing. In addition, in order to detect event coreferences, they used the topic modelling algorithm of MALLET.

The HEIDELTOUL team used the HeidelTime tool for time expression recognition and normalisation and Stanford CoreNLP for coreference resolution. Afterwards, they used a cosine similarity matching function and a distance measure to select sentences relevant for a target entity and their events.

Three teams, SPINOZAVU, GPLSIUA and HEIDELTOUL, participated in the subtracks. They all submitted the same timelines both for the Tracks and the SubTracks, simply removing time anchors.

7 Evaluation Results

The official results are presented in Table 2. For each corpus we present the micro F_1-score and in the last three columns the micro precision, micro recall and micro F_1-score overall the three corpora. In the main track, Track A, WHUNLP_1 was the best run and achieved an F_1 of 7.28%. In Track B, GPLSIUA_1 obtained the best scores with an F_1 of 25.36%.

The subtracks were proposed in order to evaluate systems that do not perform time normalisation or event anchoring in time but focus on temporal relations between events. In the end, the events ordering of the runs submitted to the subtracks was the same as those submitted to the main tracks. In SubTrack A the best results are obtained with the run 1 of SPINOZAVU team, achieving an F_1-score of 1.69%. In SubTrack B, the best system is the same as in Track B, GPLSIUA_1, with an F_1-score of 23.15%.

We evaluate the selection of the relevant events involving a target entity using the classic evaluation metrics: recall, precision and F_1-score. All events are taken into account independently of their ordering in timelines; events placed at position 0 are also evaluated. The number of true positives and F_1-scores obtained on each corpus as well as the micro-average F_1-scores are presented in Table 3. In Table 3 we also provide the evaluation of time anchors assignment in terms of accurracy. For each timeline, the accurracy is computed by dividing the number of matching events/time anchors by the number of

[5] The members of the SPINOZAVU team involved in the NewsReader project were not involved in any annotation work or discussions around the organisation of the TimeLine task.

Track	Team run	Airbus F_1	GM F_1	Stock F_1	Total P	Total R	Total F_1
Track A	WHUNLP_1	8.31	6.01	6.86	14.10	4.90	**7.28**
	WHUNLP_1 [6]	*9.42*	*5.97*	*7.26*	*14.59*	*5.37*	***7.85***
	SPINOZAVU-RUN-1	4.07	5.31	0.42	7.95	1.96	3.15
	SPINOZAVU-RUN-2	2.67	0.62	0.00	8.16	0.56	1.05
SubTrackA	SPINOZAVU-RUN-1	1.20	1.70	2.08	6.70	0.97	**1.69**
	SPINOZAVU-RUN-2	0.00	0.92	0.00	13.04	0.14	0.27
TrackB	GPLSIUA_1	22.35	19.28	33.59	21.73	30.46	**25.36**
	GPLSIUA_2	20.47	16.17	29.90	20.08	26.00	22.66
	HEIDELTOUL_2	16.50	10.94	25.89	13.58	28.23	18.34
	HEIDELTOUL_1	19.62	7.25	20.37	20.11	14.76	17.03
SubTrackB	GPLSIUA_1	18.35	20.48	32.08	18.90	29.85	**23.15**
	GPLSIUA_2	15.93	14.44	27.48	16.19	23.52	19.18
	HEIDELTOUL_2	13.24	15.88	21.99	12.18	26.41	16.67
	HEIDELTOUL_1	12.23	14.78	16.11	19.58	11.42	14.42

Table 2: Official results of the TimeLine task of the four participating teams[7] presented per subcorpus and over the whole dataset. (**Track A**: *timelines with time anchors from raw text;* **SubTrack A**: *timelines without time anchors from raw text;* **Track B**: *timelines with time anchors from texts annotated with events;* **SubTrack B**: *timelines without time anchors from texts annotated with events.)*

	Airbus			GM			Stock			Total		
	Events		TA	Events		TA	Events		TA	Events		TA
Team runs	TP	F_1	Acc	TP	F_1	Acc	TP	F_1	Acc	TP	F_1	Acc
WHUNLP	120	34.53	42.50	120	34.33	34.17	91	42.52	17.58	331	**36.33**	**32.63**
SPINOZAVU_1	46	17.59	23.91	61	22.93	36.07	57	30.24	0.00	164	22.91	20.12
SPINOZAVU_2	30	13.16	26.67	50	21.69	30.00	45	26.55	0.00	125	19.90	18.40
GPLSIUA_1	240	59.33	36.67	234	67.73	24.34	190	72.80	43.16	664	**65.68**	**34.17**
GPLSIUA_2	197	53.53	32.49	188	57.58	22.87	152	59.14	41.45	537	56.44	31.66
HEIDELTOUL_1	172	50.44	38.95	119	49.90	10.92	98	46.34	47.96	389	49.18	32.65
HEIDELTOUL_2	250	45.83	37.60	182	54.98	16.48	178	55.02	48.31	610	50.83	**34.43**

Table 3: Evaluation of the selection of events in which a target entity is involved and of time anchors assignment; *TP*: number of correctly identified events; F_1: micro-average F_1-score for the selection of events; *Acc*: accurracy in assignment of time anchors.

correctly identified events (TP in the table).

The results obtained in SubTracks, when evaluating only events ordering, are mainly lower than in Tracks, except on the "GM" corpus. For example the HEIDELTOUL_1 system achieved an F_1-score of 17.03% overall the 3 corpora in Track B and 14.42% in SubTrack B. But on "GM" corpus, the HEIDELTOUL_1 system obtained an F_1-score twice as high as in Track B, obtaining an F_1-score of 14.78% (vs. 7.25% in Track B). In evaluating the time anchors assignment (see Table 3), we observed that HEIDELTOUL and GPLSIUA systems performed better on the "Airbus" and "Stock" corpora than on "GM". This explains in part the better performance of their systems on the "GM" corpus when evaluating only events ordering (SubTrack B) than when evaluating both time anchors assignment and events ordering

[6]We found an error in the format of some event ids and reprocessed the evaluation on a corrected version of the timelines.

[7]HEIDELTOUL_1 and HEIDELTOUL_2 are shorthand for HEIDELTOUL_NONTOLMATCHPRUNE and HEIDELTOUL_TOLMATCHPRUNE respectively.

(Track B). Furthermore, the task of time expression extraction and normalisation has been the topic of different shared tasks and the obtained results are high with an F_1-score of 90.30 for time expression detection and of 77.61 for normalisation (results obtained by HeidelTime (Strötgen et al., 2013) at TempEval-3). However, the performance of temporal relation extraction systems is quite low with an F_1-score of 36.26 obtained by ClearTK-2 (Bethard, 2013), the best system at TempEval-3 on Task C.

Observing the results by corpus in Table 2, we notice that, except for Track A, the best results are obtained on the "Stock Market" corpus. One of the reasons is that in the timelines related to this corpus all events were ordered (only one event was placed at position 0), while in "Airbus" and "GM" corpora less than 70% of the events were ordered.

In the "GM" corpus, one timeline was empty ("General Motors creditors"), i.e. the corpus does not contain any event that have this target entity as Arg0 or Arg1, therefore this timeline was removed from the evaluation. We observed that SPINOZAVU systems in Track A and GPLSIUA systems in Track B correctly returned an empty timeline, while WHUNLP created a timeline with 3 events in Track A and HEIDELTOUL_1 and HEIDELTOUL_2 produced a timeline containing respectively 32 and 78 events for this target entity in Track B.

Track B was proposed as a simplified task given that annotated texts with events were distributed to participants. Unfortunately no results from the same system run on both Tracks A and B were submitted, therefore, at the moment, we cannot evaluate the impact of pre-annotation of events.

8 Conclusion

The TimeLine task is the first task focusing on cross-document ordering of events. For this task, we have defined guidelines for cross-document annotation and for timeline creation, as well as annotated trial and evaluation datasets. The results submitted by four teams show much room for improvement. Obviously, timeline creation is a very challenging task which deserves more attention in future research.

Additionally, during the organisation of this task, many issues arose that provide interesting avenues of future research into timeline creation. Our three main issues concern durative versus punctual events, events without explicit time anchors and the relation between target entities and events. Below, we detail each of these questions.

Anchoring events in time. The ordering of an event in a timeline is based on the time when the event occurred. However, many events are durative events that have a starting point and/or an ending point. For the task, we decided to order durative events according to their starting points. We are investigating whether a new timeline format can be defined to represent the durative aspect of these events.

Events without explicit textual time anchor. We made the choice to include them in the timelines but not to evaluate them (events at position 0). The difficulty is to identify cases in which an event cannot be ordered in order to give instruction to annotators and systems. When ordering an event, should we take into consideration the information contained inside one document or inside one corpus, or could (should) we consider also background knowledge?

The relation between target entities and events. We chose to select events in which one target entity is explicitly involved in a participant relation. Amongst others, this rule excludes events involving a group of which a target entity is member. For example the event *received* in *The two companies have received $13.4 billion* (in which *the two companies* refers to General Motors and Chrysler) does not appear either in the "General Motors" timeline or in the "Chrysler" timeline. Considering also implicit *has_participant* relations would take the timeline task into the domain of complex entity relationships, but could possibly be interesting if considered in combination with taxonomy induction tasks.

With this TimeLine task, we aimed to take a step forward in the current state-of-the-art in cross-document coreference and temporal relation extraction. As organisers, we needed to come up with new ways of annotating and representing data. For the participating teams, the task meant that they needed to combine cutting-edge NLP technologies. This pilot task has shown us that the goal of automatic timeline extraction from raw text is challenging, but it has given us many more insights into what is possible, and what issues still need to be addressed.

Acknowledgments

This research was funded by the European Union's 7th Framework Programme via the NewsReader (ICT-316404) project.

References

Steven Bethard. 2013. ClearTK-TimeML: A minimalist approach to TempEval 2013. In *Proceedings of the Seventh International Workshop on Semantic Evaluation*, SemEval '13, pages 10–14, Atlanta, Georgia, USA, June.

Claire Bonial, Olga Babko-Malaya, Jinho D. Choi, Jena Hwang, and Martha Palmer. 2010. Propbank annotation guidelines, December. `http://www.ldc.upenn.edu/Catalog/docs/LDC2011T03/propbank/english-propbank.pdf`.

Lee Raymond Dice. 1945. Measures of the amount of ecologic association between species. *Ecology*, 26(3):297–302, July.

Christian Girardi, Manuela Speranza, Rachele Sprugnoli, and Sara Tonelli. 2014. CROMER: a Tool for Cross-Document Event and Entity Coreference. In *Proceedings of the Ninth International Conference on Language Resources and Evaluation (LREC'14)*, Reykjavik, Iceland, may.

Heng Ji, Ralph Grishman, Zheng Chen, and Prashant Gupta. 2009. Cross-document event extraction and tracking: Task, evaluation, techniques and challenges. In *RANLP*, pages 166–172.

Anne-Lyse Minard, Alessandro Marchetti, Manuela Speranza, Bernardo Magnini, Marieke van Erp, Itziar Aldabe, Rubén Urizar, Eneko Agirre, and German Rigau. 2014a. TimeLine: Cross-Document Event Ordering. SemEval 2015 - Task 4. Annotation Guidelines. Technical Report NWR2014-11, Fondazione Bruno Kessler. `http://www.newsreader-project.eu/files/2014/12/NWR-2014-111.pdf`.

Anne-Lyse Minard, Manuela Speranza, Bernardo Magnini, Marieke van Erp, Itziar Aldabe, Rubén Urizar, Eneko Agirre, and German Rigau. 2014b. TimeLine: Cross-Document Event Ordering. SemEval 2015 - Task 4. Technical Report NWR2014-10, Fondazione Bruno Kessler. `http://www.newsreader-project.eu/files/2013/01/SemEvaltaskdescription.pdf`.

James Pustejovsky, José Castaño, Robert Ingria, Roser Saurí, Robert Gaizauskas, Andrea Setzer, and Graham Katz. 2003. TimeML: robust specification of event and temporal expressions in text. In *Fifth International Workshop on Computational Semantics (IWCS-5)*, pages 1–11.

Marta Recasens, Lluís Màrquez, Emili Sapena, M. Antònia Martí, Mariona Taulé, Véronique Hoste, Massimo Poesio, and Yannick Versley. 2010. SemEval-2010 Task 1: Coreference Resolution in Multiple Languages. In *Proceedings of the 5th International Workshop on Semantic Evaluation*, SemEval '10, pages 1–8, Stroudsburg, PA, USA.

Manuela Speranza and Anne-Lyse Minard. 2014. NewsReader Cross-Document Annotation Guidelines. Technical Report NWR2014-9, Fondazione Bruno Kessler. `http://www.newsreader-project.eu/files/2015/01/NWR-2014-9.pdf`.

Jannik Strötgen, Julian Zell, and Michael Gertz. 2013. Heideltime: Tuning english and developing spanish resources for tempeval-3. In *Proceedings of the Seventh International Workshop on Semantic Evaluation*, SemEval '13, pages 15–19, Atlanta, Georgia, USA.

Weiyi Sun, Anna Rumshisky, and Ozlem Uzuner. 2013. Evaluating temporal relations in clinical text: 2012 i2b2 Challenge. *Journal of the American Medical Informatics Association*, 20(5):806–813, September.

Sara Tonelli, Rachele Sprugnoli, Manuela Speranza, and Anne-Lyse Minard. 2014. NewsReader Guidelines for Annotation at Document Level. Technical Report NWR2014-2-2, Fondazione Bruno Kessler. `http://www.newsreader-project.eu/files/2014/12/NWR-2014-2-2.pdf`.

Naushad UzZaman and James Allen. 2011. Temporal evaluation. In *Proceedings of the 49th Annual Meeting of the Association for Computational Linguistics: Human Language Technologies*, pages 351–356, Portland, Oregon, USA.

Naushad UzZaman, Hector Llorens, Leon Derczynski, James Allen, Marc Verhagen, and James Pustejovsky. 2013. SemEval-2013 Task 1: TempEval-3: Evaluating Time Expressions, Events, and Temporal Relations. In *Proceedings of the Seventh International Workshop on Semantic Evaluation*, SemEval '13, pages 1–9, Atlanta, Georgia, USA.

Marc Verhagen, Robert J. Gaizauskas, Frank Schilder, Mark Hepple, Jessica Moszkowicz, and James Pustejovsky. 2009. The TempEval challenge: identifying temporal relations in text. *Language Resources and Evaluation*, 43(2):161–179.

Marc Verhagen, Roser Saurí, Tommaso Caselli, and James Pustejovsky. 2010. SemEval-2010 Task 13: TempEval-2. In *Proceedings of the 5th International Workshop on Semantic Evaluation*, SemEval '10, pages 57–62, Stroudsburg, PA, USA.

SPINOZA_VU: An NLP Pipeline for Cross Document TimeLines

Tommaso Caselli **Antske Fokkens** **Roser Morante** **Piek Vossen**
Computational Lexicology & Terminology Lab (CLTL)
VU Amsterdam, De Boelelaan 1105
1081 HV Amsterdam Nederland
{t.caselli}{antske.fokkens}{r.morantevallejo}{p.t.j.m.vossen}@vu.nl

Abstract

This paper describes the system SPINOZA_VU developed for the SemEval 2015 Task 4: Cross Document TimeLines. The system integrates output from the NewsReader Natural Language Processing pipeline and is designed following an entity based model. The poor performance of the submitted runs are mainly a consequence of error propagation. Nevertheless, the error analysis has shown that the interpretation module behind the system performs correctly. An out of competition version of the system has fixed some errors and obtained competitive results. Therefore, we consider the system an important step towards a more complex task such as storyline extraction.

1 Introduction

This paper reports on a system (SPINOZA_VU) for timeline extraction developed at the CLTL Lab of the VU Amsterdam in the context of the SemEval 2015 Task 4: Cross Document TimeLines. In this task, a timeline is defined as a set of chronologically anchored and ordered events extracted from a corpus spanning over a (large) period of time with respect to a target entity.

Cross-document timeline extraction benefits from previous works and evaluation campaigns in Temporal Processing, such as the TempEval evaluation campaigns (Verhagen et al., 2007; Verhagen et al., 2010; UzZaman et al., 2013) and aims at promoting research in temporal processing by tackling the following issues: cross-document and cross-temporal event detection and ordering; event coreference (in-document and cross-document); and entity-based temporal processing.

The SPINOZA_VU system is based on the NewsReader (NWR) NLP pipeline (Agerri et al., 2013; Beloki et al., 2014), which has been developed within the context of the NWR project[1] and provides multi-layer annotations over raw texts from tokenization up to temporal relations. The goal of the NWR project is to build structured event indexes from large volumes of news data addressing the same research issues as the task. Within this framework, we are developing a storyline module which aims at providing more structured representation of events and their relations. Timeline extraction from raw text qualifies as the first component of this new module. This is why we participated in Track A and Subtrack A of the task, timeline extraction from raw text. Participating in Track B would require a full re-engineering of the NWR pipeline and of our system.

The remainder of the paper is structured as follows: Section 2 provides an overview of the model implemented in the two versions of our system. Section 3 presents the results and error analysis, and Section 4 puts forward some conclusions.

2 From Model to System

Timeline extraction involves a number of independent though highly connected subtasks, the most relevant ones being: entity resolution, event detection, event-participant linking, coreference resolu-

[1] http://www.newsreader-project.eu

tion, factuality profiling, and temporal relation processing (ordering and anchoring).

We designed a system that addresses these subtasks, first at document level, and then, at cross-document level. We diverted from the general NWR approach and adopted an entity based model and representation rather than an event based one in order to fit the task. This means that we used entities as hub of information for timelines. Using an entity driven representation allows us to better model the following aspects:

- **Event co-participation**: the data collected with this method facilitates the analysis of the interactions between the participants involved in an event individually;
- **Event relations**: in an entity based representation, event mentions with more than one entity as their participants will be repeated in the final representation (both at in-document at cross-document levels); such a representation can be further used to explore and discover additional event relations[2];
- **Event coreference**: we assume that two event mentions (either in the same document or in different documents) are coreferential if they share the same participant set (i.e., entities) and occur at the same time and place (Chen et al., 2011; Cybulska and Vossen, 2013);
- **Temporal relations**: temporal relation processing can benefit from an entity driven approach as sequences of events sharing the same entities (i.e., co-participant events) can be assumed to stand in precedence relation (Chambers and Jurafsky, 2009; Chambers and Jurafsky, 2010).

2.1 The SPINOZA_VU System

The NWR pipeline which forms the basis of the SPINOZA_VU system consists of 15 modules carrying out various NLP tasks and outputs the results in NLP Annotation Format (Fokkens et al., 2014), a layered standoff representation format. Two versions of the system have been developed, namely:

- **SPINOZA_VU_1** uses the output of a state of the art system, TIPSem (Llorens et al., 2010), for event detection and temporal relations;
- **SPINOZA_VU_2** is entirely based on data from the NWR pipeline including the temporal (TLINKs) and causal relation (CLINKs) layers.

The final output is based on a dedicated rule-based module, the TimeLine (TML) module. We will describe in the following paragraphs how each subtask has been tackled with respect to each version of the system.

Entity identification Entity identification relies on the entity detection and disambiguation layer (NERD) of the NWR pipeline. Each detected entity is associated with a URI (a unique identifier), either from DBpedia or a specifically created one based on the strings describing the entity. We extracted the entities by merging information from the NERD layer with that from the semantic role labelling (SRL) layer. We retained only those entity mentions which fulfil the argument positions of proto-agent (Arg0) or proto-patient (Arg1) in the SRL layer.

Event detection and classification The SPINOZA_VU_1 event module is based on TIPSem, which provides TimeML compliant data. We developed post processing rules to convert the TimeML event classes (OCCURRENCE, STATE, I_ACTION, I_STATE, ASPECTUAL, REPORTING and PERCEPTION) to specific FrameNet frames (e.g., *Communication*, *Being_in_operation*, *Body_movement*) and/or Event Situation Ontology (ESO) types (Segers et al., 2015) (e.g., *contextual*), which correspond to the event types specified in the task guidelines. For instance, not all mentions of TimeML I_STATE, I_ACTION, OCCURRENCE and STATE events can enter a timeline. The alignment with FrameNet and ESO is made by combining the data from the Word Sense Disambiguation (WSD) layer of the pipeline with Predicate Matrix (version 1.1) (Lacalle et al., 2014).

As for the SPINOZA_VU_2, we have used the NWR SRL layer to identify and retain the eligible events. In this case the access to the Predicate Matrix is not necessary as each predicate in the SRL layer is also associated with corresponding FrameNet frames and ESO types. Only the pred-

[2] We are referring to a broader set of relations that we labeled as "bridging relations" among events which involve co-participation, primary and secondary causal relations, temporal relations, and entailment relations.

icates matching specific FrameNet frames and/or ESO types were retained as candidate events.

Factuality The factuality filter consists of a collection of rules in order to determine whether an event is within the scope of a factuality marker negating an event or indicating that it is uncertain, in which case the event is excluded from the set of eligible events. Factuality markers are different types of modality and negation cues (adverbs, adjectives, prepositions, modal auxiliaries, pronouns and determiners). For instance, if a verb has a dependency relation of type `AM-MOD` with a modal auxiliary is excluded from the candidate event in the timeline.

Coreference relations Two levels of coreference need to be addressed: in-document and cross-document. As for the former, both versions of the system rely on the coreference layer (COREF layer) of the pipeline. Concerning the cross-document level, two strategies have been implemented:

- Cross-document entity mentions are identified using the URI links associated with entity mentions; all entity mentions from different documents sharing the same URIs are associated with the same entity instance;
- Cross-document event coreference is obtained during a post-processing step of the timeline creation following the assumption that two event mentions denote the same event instance (i.e., they co-refer) if they share the same participants, time of occurrence and (possibly) location. Entity-based timelines are used as a basis to identify instances of cross-document event coreferential expressions.

Temporal Relations For the SPINOZA_VU_1 version, we used the Temporal Relations from TIPSem (TLINKs), including temporal expression detection and normalization. For the SPINOZA_VU_2 version, we used the TLINK and CLINK layers of the NWR pipeline. As for the CLINK layer, we converted all causal relations into temporal ones, with the value `BEFORE`. For both versions of the system we maximized temporal anchoring by recovering the beginning or end point of temporal expressions of type `DURATION` and resolving all TLINKs between a temporal expression and a target event except "`IS_INCLUDED`" relations into an anchoring relation.

TimeLine Extraction The TimeLine Extraction (TML) module[3] harmonizes and orders cross-document temporal relations (anchoring and ordering). It provides a method for selecting the initial (relevant) temporal relations (namely, all anchoring relations) and enhance an updating mechanism of information so that additional temporal relations (both anchoring and ordering relations) can be inferred. Timelines are first created at a document level and subsequently merged. The cross-document timeline model is event-based and aims at building a global timeline between all events and temporal expressions regardless of the target entities. This approach allows us to also make use of temporal information provided by events that are not part of the final timelines. Finally, the target entities for the timelines are extracted using two strategies: i) a perfect match between the target entities and the DBpedia URIs, and ii) the Levenshtein distance (Levenshtein, 1966) between the target entities and the URIs. For this latter strategy, an empirical threshold was set to maximize precision on the basis of the trial data.

3 Results and Error Analysis

In Table 1 we report the results of both versions of the system for Track A - Main. We also include the results of the best performing system and out of competition results of a new version of the system (OC_SPINOZA_VU), which obtained competitive results with respect the best system, WHUNLP_1.

System Version	Corpus 1	Corpus 2	Corpus 3	Overall
SPINOZA_VU_1	4.07	5.31	0.42	3.15
SPINOZA_VU_2	2.67	0.62	0.00	1.05
OC_SPINOZA_VU	7.50	6.64	6.59	7.12
Best system WHUNLP_1	8.31	6.01	6.86	7.28

Table 1: System Results (micro F1 score) for the SemEval 2015 Task 4 Task A - Main Track.

The OC_SPINOZA_VU system is based on SPINOZA_VU_2, and the main differences concern temporal relations identification at in-document and cross-document level, and entity extraction. In particular, we assume that: if a temporal expression

[3]https://github.com/antske/BiographyNet/tree/master/TimeLineExtraction

occurs in the same sentence of an event, the temporal expression is the event's temporal anchor; if no temporal expression occurs in the same sentence, we check if there are any temporal expressions in the two previous sentences or, if any, in the one following it. The event is then anchor to the closest temporal expression identified. Finally, if no temporal expression can be found in this sentence window, no temporal anchor is assigned to the event. As for event ordering, we have used the order of appearance of the event in the document to establish precedence relations. The final timeline is obtained by ordering cross-document event with a modified version of the TML module based on time anchors only. Entity extraction is extended by adding pure substring match.

Table 2 reports the results of the submitted systems and of the out of competition one. No other results are reported for Track A - Subtask A because only our system participated. The null results of the out of competition system are due to the modified version of the TML module.

System Version	Corpus 1	Corpus 2	Corpus 3	Overall
SPINOZA_VU_1	1.20	1.70	2.08	1.69
SPINOZA_VU_2	0.00	0.92	0.00	0.27
OC_SPINOZA_VU	0.00	0.00	0.00	0.00

Table 2: System Results (micro F1 score) for the SemEval 2015 Task 4 Task A - Subtrack.

Overall, the results of the submitted system are not satisfying. Out of 37 entity based timelines, the system produced results only for 31 of them. Three sources of errors occur in both versions of our system. Error analysis yields the following explanations:

Event detection We analyzed both entity-based event detection (all events associated with each target entity) and global event detection (all events regardless of the target entities). On entity-based event detection, SPINOZA_VU_1 scores an average F1 score on the 31 detected entities of 23.58 (38.7 precision and 17.35 for recall), whereas SPINOZA_VU_2 scores an average F1 of 20.46 (47.83 precision and 13.32 recall). As for global event detection, both versions of the system present a high recall and low precision pattern, although with substantial differences in terms of results. In particular, SPINOZA_VU_1 has an average recall of 44.96 and an average precision of 25.5, while SPINOZA_VU_2 has an average recall of 77.03 and an average precision of 14.86;

Entity detection This layer is strictly connected to the event detection layer. The lower results are mainly due to the output of the COREF and SRL layers. Missing coreference chains (e.g. "the aircraft" not connected to a target entity like "Airbus A380")) and wrong spans of event arguments negatively impacts on the extraction of candidate events for the timeline;

Event ordering and anchoring The difference in performance between the submitted system and OC_SPINOZA_VU clearly indicates that there is room for improvement concerning the amount of temporal relations (anchoring and ordering ones) which are extracted. Furthermore, the difference in performance between the Main track and the Subtrack suggests that the main issues concern event ordering rather than their detection or anchoring.

4 Conclusions and Future Work

In this paper we presented the SPINOZA_VU system for timeline extraction system in the context of the SemEval 2015 Task 4: Cross Document TimeLines. The low ranking show not only that the task is very complex, but also that there is room for improving the system, as the results of the OC_SPINOZA_VU system show. The low performance is mainly a consequence of a combination of cascading errors and missing data from the different modules of the system, namely event detection, temporal relation extraction and entity detection. However, on the positive side, the theoretical model that has guided the development of the system can be further extended to address more complex tasks on top of the timeline extraction, such as storyline extraction.

Acknowledgments

Our thanks to the anonymous reviewers for their suggestions and comments. This work has been supported by EU NewsReader Project (FP7-ICT-2011-8 grant 316404), the NWO Spinoza Prize project Understanding Language by Machines (sub-track 3) and the BiographyNet project (Nr. 660.011.308), funded by the Netherlands eScience Center.

References

Rodrigo Agerri, Itziar Aldabe, Zuhaitz Beloki, Egoitz Laparra, Maddalen Lopez de Lacalle, German Rigau, Aitor Soroa, Antske Fokkens, Ruben Izquierdo, Marieke van Erp, Piek Vossen, Christian Girardi, and Anne-Lyse Minard. 2013. Event detection, version 2. NewsReader Deliverable 4.2.2.

Zuhaitz Beloki, German Rigau, Aitor Soroa, Antske Fokkens, Piek Vossen, Marco Rospocher, Francesco Corcoglioniti, Roldano Cattoni, Thomas Ploeger, and Willem Robert van Hage. 2014. System design. NewsReader Deliverable 2.1.

Nathanael Chambers and Dan Jurafsky. 2009. Unsupervised Learning of Narrative Schemas and their Participants. In *Proceedings of the Joint Conference of the 47th Annual Meeting of the ACL and the 4th International Joint Conference on Natural Language Processing of the AFNLP*, pages 602–610, Suntec, Singapore, August.

Nathanael Chambers and Dan Jurafsky. 2010. A Database of Narrative Schemas. In *Proceedings of the Seventh Conference on International Language Resources and Evaluation (LREC'10)*, Valletta, Malta, May.

Bin Chen, Jian Su, Sinno Jialin Pan, and Chew Lim Tan. 2011. A Unified Event Coreference Resolution by Integrating Multiple Resolvers. In *Proceedings of the 5th International Joint Conference on Natural Language Processing*, pages 102–110, Chiang Mai, Thailand.

Agata Cybulska and Piek Vossen. 2013. Semantic relations between events and their time, locations and participants for event coreference resolution. In *Proceedings of Recent Advances in Natural Language Processing (RANLP-2013)*, pages 156–163.

Antske Fokkens, Aitor Soroa, Zuhaitz Beloki, Niels Ockeloen, German Rigau, Willem Robert van Hage, and Piek Vossen. 2014. NAF and GAF: Linking linguistic annotations. In *Proceedings 10th Joint ISO-ACL SIGSEM Workshop on Interoperable Semantic Annotation*, pages 9–16.

Maddalen Lopez De Lacalle, Egoitz Laparra, and German Rigau. 2014. Predicate Matrix: extending SemLink through WordNet mappings. In *Proceedings of the Ninth International Conference on Language Resources and Evaluation (LREC'14)*, Reykjavik, Iceland, May.

Vladimir I. Levenshtein. 1966. Binary codes capable of correcting deletions, insertions and reversals. In *Soviet physics doklady*, volume 10, pages 707–710.

Hector Llorens, Estela Saquete, and Borja Navarro. 2010. TIPSem (English and Spanish): Evaluating CRFs and Semantic Roles in TempEval-2. In *Proceedings of the 5th International Workshop on Semantic Evaluation*, pages 284–291.

Roxane Segers, Piek Vossen, Marco Rospocher, Luciano Serafini, Egoitz Laparra, and German Rigau. 2015. ESO: A Frame Based Ontology for Events and Implied Situations. In *Proceedings of Maplex2015*.

Naushad UzZaman, Hector Llorens, James Allen, Leon Derczynski, Marc Verhagen, and James Pustejovsky. 2013. SemEval-2013 Task 1: TempEval-3: Evaluating time expressions, events, and temporal relations. In *Proceedings of the 7th International Workshop on Seman- tic Evaluation*, pages 1–9.

Marc Verhagen, Robert Gaizauskas, Frank Schilder, Mark Hepple, Graham Katz, and James Pustejovsky. 2007. SemEval-2007 Task 15: TempEval Temporal Relation Identification. In *Proceedings of the 4th International Workshop on Semantic Evaluation*, pages 75–80, June.

Marc Verhagen, Roser Saurí, Tommaso Caselli, and James Pustejovsky. 2010. SemEval-2010 Task 13: TempEval-2. In *Proceedings of the 5th International Workshop on Semantic Evaluation*, pages 57–62, Uppsala, Sweden.

SemEval-2015 Task 5: QA TEMPEVAL - Evaluating Temporal Information Understanding with Question Answering

Hector Llorens[♣], **Nathanael Chambers**[◇], **Naushad UzZaman**[♣],
Nasrin Mostafazadeh[⋈], **James Allen**[⋈], **James Pustejovsky**[♠]
[♣] Nuance Communications, USA
[◇] United States Naval Academy, USA
[⋈] University of Rochester, USA
[♠] Brandeis University, USA
hector.llorens@nuance.com, nchamber@usna.edu

Abstract

QA TempEval shifts the goal of previous TempEvals away from an intrinsic evaluation methodology toward a more extrinsic goal of question answering. This evaluation requires systems to capture temporal information relevant to perform an end-user task, as opposed to corpus-based evaluation where all temporal information is equally important. Evaluation results show that the best automated TimeML annotations reach over 30% recall on questions with 'yes' answer and about 50% on easier questions with 'no' answers. Features that helped achieve better results are event coreference and a time expression reasoner.

1 Introduction

QA TempEval is a follow up of the TempEval series in SemEval: TempEval-1 (Verhagen et al., 2007), TempEval-2 (Verhagen et al., 2010), and TempEval-3 (UzZaman et al., 2013). TempEval focuses on evaluating systems that extract temporal expressions (timexes), events, and temporal relations as defined in the TimeML standard (Pustejovsky et al., 2003) (timeml.org). QA TempEval is unique in its focus on evaluating temporal information that directly address a QA task. TimeML was originally developed to support research in complex temporal QA within the field of artificial intelligence (AI). However, despite its original goal, the complexity of temporal QA has caused most research on automatic TimeML systems to focus on a more straightforward temporal information extraction (IE) task. QA TempEval still requires systems to extract temporal relations just like previous TempEvals, however, the QA evaluation is solely based on how well the relations answer questions about the documents. It is no longer about annotation accuracy, but rather the accuracy for targeted questions.

Not only does QA represent a more natural way to evaluate temporal information understanding (UzZaman et al., 2012), but also annotating documents with question sets requires much less expertise and effort for humans than corpus-based evaluation which requires full manual annotation of temporal information. In QA TempEval a document does not require the markup of all the temporal entities and relations, but rather a markup of a few key relations central to the text. Although the evaluation schema changes in QA TempEval, the task for participating systems remains the same: extracting temporal information from plain text documents.

Here we re-use TempEval-3 task ABC, where systems are required to perform end-to-end TimeML annotation from plain text, including the complete set of temporal relations (Allen, 1983). However, unlike TempEval-3, there are no subtasks focusing on specific elements (such as an event extraction evaluation). Also, instead of IE performance measurement for evaluation, a QA performance (on a set of human-created temporal questions on documents) is used to rank systems. The participating systems are supposed to annotate temporal entities relations across the document, and the relations are used to build a larger knowledge base of temporal links to obtain answers to the temporal questions.

In QA TempEval, annotators are not required to tag and order all events, but instead ask questions about temporal relations that are relevant or interesting to the document, hence this evaluation better captures the understanding of the most important temporal information in a document. Annotators are not limited to relations between entities appearing in the same or consecutive sentences, i.e., they can ask any question that comes naturally to a reader's mind, e.g., "did the election happen (e3) before the president gave (e27) the speech". Finally, QA TempEval is unique in expanding beyond the news genre and including Wikipedia articles and blog posts. In the upcoming sections we will discuss details of the conducted task and evaluation methodology.

2 Task Description

The task for participant systems is equivalent to TempEval-3 task ABC, see Figure 1. Systems must annotate temporal expressions, events, and temporal relations between them[1]. The input to participants is a set of unannotated text documents in TempEval-3 format. Participating systems are required to annotate the plain documents following the TimeML scheme, divided into two types of elements:

- **Temporal entities**: These include **events** (EVENT tag, "came", "attack") and temporal expressions (**timexes**, TIMEX3 tag, e.g., "yesterday", "8 p.m.") as well as their attributes like event class, timex type, and normalized values.
- **Temporal relations**: A temporal relation (tlink, TLINK tag) describes a pair of entities and the temporal relation between them. The TimeML relations map to the 13 Allen interval relations. The included relations are: SIMULTANEOUS (and IDENTITY), BEFORE, AFTER, IBEFORE, IAFTER, IS_INCLUDED, INCLUDES (and DURING), BEGINS, BEGUN_BY, ENDS, and ENDED_BY. Since the TimeML DURING does not have a clear mapping, we map it to SIMULTANEOUS for simplicity. The following illustrates how the expression "6:00 pm" BEGINS the state of being "in the gym".

  (1) John was <u>in the gym</u> between <u>6:00 p.m</u> and 7:00 p.m.

Each system's annotations represent its temporal knowledge of the documents. These annotations are

[1]http://alt.qcri.org/semeval2015/task5

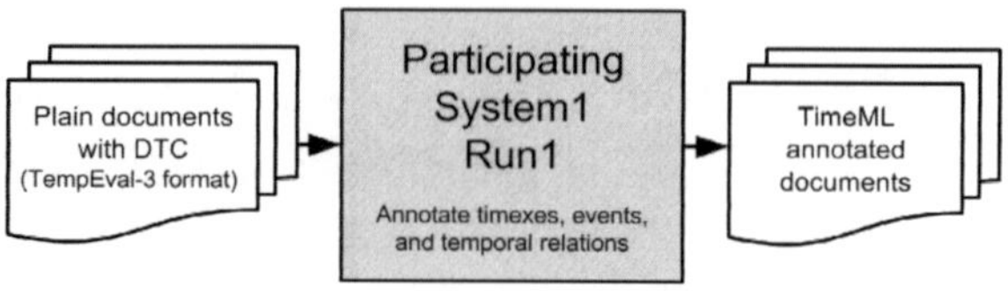

Figure 1: Task - Equivalent to TempEval-3 task ABC

then used as input to a temporal QA system (UzZaman et al., 2012) that will answer questions on behalf of the systems, and the accuracy of their answers is compared across systems.

3 QA Evaluation Methodology

The main difference between QA TempEval and earlier TempEval editions is that the systems are not scored regarding how similar their annotation to a human annotated key is, but how useful is their TimeML annotation to answer human annotated temporal questions. There are different kinds of temporal questions that could be answered given a TimeML annotation of a document. However, this first QA TempEval focuses on yes/no questions in the following format:

```
IS <entityA> <RELATION> <entityB> ?
(e.g., is event-A before event-B ?)
```

This makes it easier for human annotators to create accurate question sets with their answers. Other types of questions such as list-based make it more difficult and arguable in edge cases (e.g., list events between event-A and event-B). Questions about events not included in the document are not possible, but theoretically one could ask about any time reference. Due to the difficulty of mapping external time references to a specific time expression in the document, these types of questions are not included in the evaluation.

The questions can involve any of the thirteen relations described above. Two relations not in the set of thirteen, OVERLAPS and OVERLAPPED_BY, cannot be explicitly annotated in TimeML, but they could happen implicitly (i.e., be inferred from other relations) if needed by an application.

The evaluation process is illustrated in Figure 2. After the testing period, the participants send their TimeML annotations of the test documents. Organizers evaluate the TimeML annotations of all the participating systems with a set of questions. The

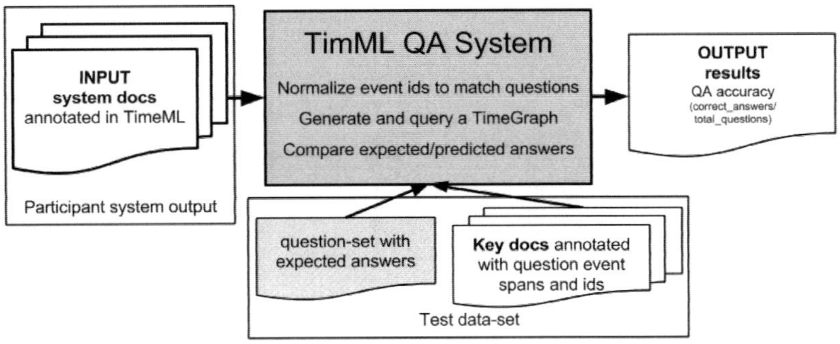

Figure 2: QA based on participant annotations

systems are scored comparing the expected answers provided by human annotators against the predicted answers obtained from the system's TimeML annotations.

Given a system's TimeML annotated documents, the process consists of three main steps:

- **ID Normalization**: Entities are referenced by TimeML tag ids (e.g., eid23). The yes/no questions must contain two entities with IDs (e.g., "is event[eid23] after event[eid99] ?"). The entities of the question are annotated in the corresponding key document. However, systems may provide different ids to the same entities. Therefore, we align the system annotation IDs with the question IDs that are annotated in the key docs using the TempEval-3 normalization tool[2].

- **Timegraph Generation**: The normalized TimeML docs are used to build a graph of time points representing the temporal relations of the events and timexes identified by each system. Here we use Timegraph (Gerevini et al., 1993) for computing temporal closure as proposed by Miller and Schubert (1990). The Timegraph is first initialized by adding the TimeML explicit relations. Then the Timegraph's reasoning mechanism infers implicit relations through rules such as transitivity. For example, if eventA BEFORE eventB and eventB BEFORE eventC, then the implicit relation eventA BEFORE eventC can be inferred. Timegraph expands a system's TimeML annotations and can answer both explicit and implicit Allen temporal relation questions, including OVERLAPS.

- **Question Processing**: Answering questions requires temporal information understanding and reasoning. Note that asking 'IS <entity1> <relation> <entity2>?' is not only asking if there is that explicit tlink between them, but also, if it is not, if that relation can be inferred from other tlinks implicitly. Unlike corpus based evaluation, the system gets credit if its annotations provide the correct answer regardless of whether it annotates other irrelevant information or not. In order to answer the questions about TimeML entities (based on time intervals) using Timegraph, we convert the queries to point-based queries. For answering yes/no questions, we check the necessary point relations in Timegraph to verify an interval relation. For example, to answer the question "*is event1* AFTER *event2*", our system verifies whether start(event1) > end(event2); if it is verified then the answer is true (YES), if it conflicts with the Timegraph then it is false (NO), otherwise it is UNKNOWN.

4 QA Scoring

For each question we compare the obtained answer from the Timegraph (created with system annotations) and the expected answer (human annotated). The scoring is based on the following Algorithm 1. With this we calculate the following measures:

- **Precision (P)** $= \frac{num\_correct}{num\_answered}$
- **Recall (R)** $= \frac{num\_correct}{num\_questions}$

[2]https://github.com/hllorens/timeml-normalizer

```
num_questions=0
num_answered=0
num_correct=0
foreach question q ∈ questionset do
    num_questions += 1
    if predicted_ans[q] != unknown
    or key_ans[q] == unknown then
        num_answered += 1
        if predicted_ans[q] == key_ans[q] then
            num_correct += 1
```

Algorithm 1: QA Scoring

- **F-measure (F1)** $= \frac{2*P*R}{P+R}$

We use Recall (QA accuracy) as the main metric and F1 is used in case of draw.

5 Datasets

In QA TempEval, the creation of datasets does not require the manual annotation of all TimeML elements in source docs. The annotation task in QA TempEval only requires reading the doc, making temporal questions, providing the correct answers, and identifying entities included in the questions by bounding them in the text and designating an ID. The format of the question sets is as follows:

```
<question-num>|<source-doc>|
<question-with-ids>|<NL-question>|
<answer>|[opt-extra-info]
```

Following is an example question and its corresponding annotated document:

```
3|APW.tml|IS ei21 AFTER ei19|
Was he cited after becoming general?|yes

APW.tml (KEY)
Farkas <event eid="e19">became</event>
a general. He was
<event eid="e21">cited</event>...

APW.tml (system annotation, full-TimeML)
Farkas <event eid="e15"...>became</event>
a general. He was
<event eid="e24"...>cited</event>...
<tlink eventID=e15 relatedToEventID=e24
relType=before />
```

5.1 Training Data

TimeML training data consists of TempEval-3 annotated data: TimeBank, AQUAINT (TBAQ, TempEval-3 training), and TE-3 Platinum (TempEval-3 testing). Furthermore, a question-set in the format explained earlier is provided to the participants for training purposes. It consists of 79 Yes/No questions and answers about TimeBank documents (UzZaman et al., 2012). Participants can easily extend the question-set by designing new questions over TimeML corpora.

5.2 Test Data

The test dataset comprises three domains:

- News articles (Wikinews, WSJ, NYT): This covers the traditional TempEval domain used in all the previous editions.
- Wikipedia[3] articles (history, biographical): This covers documents about people or history, which are rich in temporal entities.
- Informal blog posts (narrative): We hand selected blog entries from the Blog Authorship Corpus (Schler et al., 2006). They are in narrative nature, such as the ones describing personal events as opposed to entries with opinions and political commentary.

For each of these domains, human experts select the documents, create the set of questions together with the correct answer, and annotate the corresponding entities of the questions in the key documents. The resulting question-set is then peer-reviewed by the human experts. Table 1 depicts statistics of the test dataset. In this table, the column *dist-* shows the number of questions about entities that are in the same or consecutive sentences while *dist+* refers to questions about non-consecutive (more distant) entities.

	docs	**words**	**quest**	**yes**	**no**	**dist-**	**dist+**
news	10	6920	99	93	6	40	59
wiki	10	14842	130	117	13	58	72
blogs	8	2053	65	65	0	30	35
total	28	23815	294	275	19	128	166

Table 1: Test Data

Annotators were asked to create positive (yes) questions unless a negative (no) question came naturally. This is due to the fact that we can automatically generate negative questions from positive questions, but not the other way around. Note that the number of questions about distant entities is considerable. TimeML training data and thus systems tend to only annotate temporal relations about less

[3] http://en.wikipedia.org

distant entities. Therefore, to answer distant questions the necessary implicit relations must be obtainable from the annotated explicit relations.

5.3 Development Time Cost

One of the claims of QA evaluation of temporal text understanding (UzZaman et al., 2012) is that the time cost of creating question sets in QA schema is lower than the one for fully annotating a document with TimeML elements and attributes. Both tasks involve reading the document. However, question-set creation only requires designing yes/no questions paired with answers and annotating the corresponding entities in the document, while full TimeML annotation needs identifying all entities, their attributes, and large set of relations among them. There is not any rigorous information available about the time it takes to perform these different annotation tasks. Comparison is difficult since many factors play a role in timing (e.g., human annotators skills, dedicated software help). In order to provide an approximate comparison, following we present information regarding some real experiences:

- Question Set annotation (about 10 questions per document, without dedicated software help): QA TempEval consists of 28 docs (23,815 words), i.e., about 850 words per document. Human annotators reported that the annotation task from raw text took them 30min-2h per document, i.e., 15min-1h for 360 words.

- TimeML all-elements and attributes annotation (with dedicated software help): Annotators of the Spanish TimeBank spent a year to complete the annotation working 3h/day, approximately 3h per document or 360 words. We don't have available to us similar data for the English TimeBank's creation.

- Other experiences regarding full TimeML annotation such as correcting a pre-annotated document by a system took about 2-3h per document. TLINK annotation reportedly took about 1.5h per document.

We do not aim to provide an exact quantification or comparison; however, based on the information we have available, creating a QA test set takes considerably less time than full TimeML annotation. TimeML annotated documents can also be used for training and evaluating temporal extraction systems, whereas TempQA annotated documents can be used only for evaluation. Given that we have enough annotated data, TempQA helps to easily create more data to evaluate temporal systems in new domains.

6 Participating Systems

Nine approaches addressing automatic TimeML annotation for English were presented in the QA TempEval evaluation, divided into two groups:

Regular participants, optimized for task:

- **HITSZ-ICRC**[4]. rule-based timex module, SVM (liblinear) for event and relation detection and classification
- **hlt-fbk-ev1-trel1**. SVM, separated event detection and classification, without event co-reference
- **hlt-fbk-ev1-trel2**. SVM, separated event detection and classification, with event coref
- **hlt-fbk-ev2-trel1**. SVM, all predicates are events and classification decides, without event co-reference
- **hlt-fbk-ev2-trel2**. SVM, all predicates are events and classification decides, with event co-reference

Off-the-Shelf Systems, not optimized on task:

- **CAEVO**[5] (Chambers et al., 2014). Cascading classifiers that add temporal links with transitive expansion. A wide range of rule-based and supervised classifiers are included
- **ClearTK**[6] (Bethard, 2013) A pipeline of machine-learning classification models, each of which have simple morphosyntactic annotation pipeline as feature set
- **TIPSemB** (Llorens et al., 2010) CRF-SVM model with morphosyntactic features
- **TIPSem** (Llorens et al., 2010) TIPSemB + lexical (WordNet) and combinational (PropBank roles) semantic features

[4]Annotations Submitted 1-day after the deadline
[5]Off-the-shelf system: the author was co-organizer
[6]Off-the-shelf system: trained and tested by organizers

7 Time Expression Reasoner (TREFL)

As an extra evaluation, task organizers added a new run for each system augmented with a post-processing step. The goal is to analyze how a general time expression reasoner could improve results. The TREFL component is straightforward: resolve all time expressions, and add temporal relations between the time expressions when the relation is unambiguous based on their resolved times.

We define a "timex reference" as a temporal expression consisting of a date or time (e.g., "Jan 12, 1999", "tomorrow") that is normalized to a Gregorian calendar interval (e.g., 1999-01-12, 2015-06-06). These are perfectly suited for ordering in time. In addition, finding timex references and obtaining their normalized values are tasks in which automatic systems perform with over 90% accuracy. Thus, given a system normalized-values, we can automatically produce timex-timex reference relations or links (**TREFL**) that represent a temporal relation backbone (base Timegraph) with high accuracy. This backbone can then assist the much more difficult event-event and event-timex links that are later predicted by system classifiers. Any relations predicted by a classifier can be discarded if they are inconsistent with this TREFL backbone.

For example, if a system TimeML annotation contains three timexes **t1** (1999), **t2** (1998-01-15), and **t3** (1999-08), a minimal set of relations can be deterministically extracted as *t2* BEFORE *t1* and *t3* IS_INCLUDED *t1*. The corresponding Timegraph is:

t2 < t1_start < t3_start < t3_end < t1_end

To automatically obtain such minimal set of relations from the system timex-values, the TREFL component orders them by date and granularity using SIMULTANEOUS, BEFORE, BEGINS, IS_INCLUDED, or ENDS relations. More complicated cases have not been included in this evaluation for simplicity.

The only drawback or risk of this strategy is that some of the system timex-values could be incorrect, but previous work suggests these errors are less numerous than those occurring in later event-event relation extraction. Our hypothesis is that (i) many systems do not include a strategy like this, and (ii) even taking into account the drawback of this strategy most systems would benefit from using it, reaching a higher performance. The evaluation compares original systems with their TREFL-augmented variant that discarded system relations in conflict with its TREFL Timegraph.

8 Evaluation

The objective of this evaluation is to measure and compare QA performance of TimeML annotations of participating and off-the-shelf systems. Participants were given the documents of the previously defined test set (TE3-input format). They were asked to annotate them with their systems within a 5-day period. Organizers evaluated the submitted annotations using the test question-sets. Result tables include Precision (P), Recall (R), F-measure (F1), percentage of the answered questions (awd%) and number of correct answers (corr). As mentioned earlier, Recall is the main measure for ranking systems. The percentage of the questions which are answered by the system provides a coverage metric, measuring a system's ability to provide more complete set of annotation on entities and relations.

8.1 Results without TREFL

Table 2 shows the combined results over all three genres in the test set, comprising 294 test questions.

	Measures			Questions	
System	P	R	F1	awd%	corr
HITSZ-ICRC	.54	.06	.12	.12	19
hlt-fbk-ev1-trel1	**.57**	.17	.26	.30	50
hlt-fbk-ev1-trel2	.47	.23	.31	.50	69
hlt-fbk-ev2-trel1	.55	.17	.26	.32	51
hlt-fbk-ev2-trel2	.49	**.30**	**.37**	**.62**	**89**
ClearTK	.59	.06	.11	.10	17
CAEVO	.56	**.17**	**.26**	**.31**	**51**
TIPSemB	.47	.13	.20	.28	38
TIPSem	**.60**	.15	.24	.26	45

Table 2: QA Results over all domains.

The participant system hlt-fbk-ev2-trel2 system (.30 R) outperformed all the others by a significant margin. CAEVO performed best among the off-the-shelf systems, but behind the winning participant recall by 13% absolute. The awd% of the hlt-fbk-ev2-trel2 system doubles the one by the best off-the-shelf system, CAEVO. Interstingly, CAEVO and the two hlt-fbk *trel1* systems performed approximately the same. The *trel2* versions included event coreference.

Table 3 shows three result tables from the three genres: news, wiki, and blogs. The best overall sys-

News Genre Results

System	P	R	F1	awd%	corr
	Measures			Questions	
HITSZ-ICRC	.47	.08	.14	.17	8
hlt-fbk-ev1-trel1	**.59**	.17	.27	.29	17
hlt-fbk-ev1-trel2	.43	.23	.30	.55	23
hlt-fbk-ev2-trel1	.56	.20	.30	.36	20
hlt-fbk-ev2-trel2	.43	**.29**	**.35**	**.69**	**29**
ClearTK	**.60**	.06	.11	.10	6
CAEVO	.59	**.17**	**.27**	.29	**17**
TIPSemB	.50	.16	.24	**.32**	16
TIPSem	.52	.11	.18	.21	11

Wiki Genre Results

System	P	R	F1	awd%	corr
	Measures			Questions	
HITSZ-ICRC	**.83**	.08	.14	.09	10
hlt-fbk-ev1-trel1	.55	.16	.25	.29	21
hlt-fbk-ev1-trel2	.52	.26	.35	.50	34
hlt-fbk-ev2-trel1	.58	.17	.26	.29	22
hlt-fbk-ev2-trel2	.62	**.36**	**.46**	**.58**	**47**
ClearTK	.60	.05	.09	.08	6
CAEVO	.59	.17	.26	**.28**	22
TIPSemB	.52	.13	.21	.25	17
TIPSem	**.74**	**.19**	**.30**	.26	**25**

Blogs Genre Results

System	P	R	F1	awd%	corr
	Measures			Questions	
HITSZ-ICRC	.17	.02	.03	.09	1
hlt-fbk-ev1-trel1	**.57**	.18	.28	.32	12
hlt-fbk-ev1-trel2	.43	.18	**.26**	.43	12
hlt-fbk-ev2-trel1	.47	.14	.21	.29	9
hlt-fbk-ev2-trel2	.34	**.20**	.25	**.58**	**13**
ClearTK	**.56**	.08	.14	.14	5
CAEVO	.48	**.18**	**.27**	**.38**	**12**
TIPSemB	.31	.08	.12	.25	5
TIPSem	.45	.14	.21	.31	9

Table 3: QA Results broken down by genre, based on 99 News, 130 Wiki, and 65 Blog questions.

tem, hlt-fbk-ev2-trel2, maintained its top position.

The main difference in genre results appears to be the smaller blog corpus where the leading hlt-fbk-ev2-trel2 participant and CAEVO performed similarly, .20 and .18 R respectively. The hlt-fbk system exhibited similar behavior as the other genres showing a high coverage, as demonstrated by awd% metric. However, it simply guessed incorrectly much more often (precision dropped to the 30's).

We make note that the ClearTK off-the-shelf system's lower performance is because it was used without modification from its TempEval-3 submission. ClearTK was TempEval-3 best system, partly due to its optimization to the task where it maximized precision and not recall. It likely would perform better if optimized to this new QA task.

8.2 Results with TREFL

Table 4 shows the results for systems augmented with TREFL (explained in Section 7).

System	P	R	F1	awd%	corr
	Measures			Questions	
HITSZ-ICRC	.58	.09	.15	.15	25
hlt-fbk-ev1-trel1	**.62**	.28	.38	.45	81
hlt-fbk-ev1-trel2	.55	.31	**.40**	.57	92
hlt-fbk-ev2-trel1	.61	.29	.39	.48	86
hlt-fbk-ev2-trel2	.51	**.34**	**.40**	**.67**	**99**
ClearTK (TREFL not applied because of its TLINK format)					
CAEVO	.60	.21	.32	.36	63
TIPSemB	.64	.24	.35	.37	70
TIPSem	**.68**	**.27**	**.38**	**.40**	**79**

Table 4: QA Results **augmented with TREFL**

Recall went up on all systems (by 49% relative on average), but the degree of improvement varied. Recall of the top system (hlt-fbk-ev2-trel2) improved 4% absolute (13% relative). The largest gain was with TIPSem which improved from .15 to .27, becoming the top off-the-shelf system. TREFL is mainly focused on improving recall which explains the differences. The best system had higher recall already, so TREFL had less contribution. TIPSem had lower recall, so it sees the greatest gain. TREFL did not penalize TIPSem precision as much as it did for other systems. That made TIPSem obtain the top F1 in wiki and blogs domains.

By genre, on average TREFL improved systems' *relative* recall by 60% (news), 48% (wiki), and 47% (news).

In news and wiki, hlt-fbk-ev2-trel2+terfl was the system answering correctly more questions about distant entities (22 news, 20 wiki), while for blogs it was TIPSem (9).

We also found that hlt-fbk-ev2-trel2+terfl answers more questions that no other system is capable of answering (4 news, 11 wiki, 5 blogs), demonstrating that it has some features that others system lack. One of the distinguishing features of this system, required to answer some of the testset questions, is event co-reference (clustering) which could be responsible for this good result.

Analyzing the questions answered correctly after the TREFL augmentation, in both the news and wiki domains, we found that around 35% of the questions were not answered by any system because they didn't find a temporal entity in the question (either an event or time expression, or both). This is mostly because no system found one of the entities in the question. In the blog genre, 50% of errors were due to missing entities, and blogs/news were 75%. These missing entity errors exist in both the original system submissions and this TREFL augmentation. The remaining unanswered questions were simply due to sparsity in relation annotation. The relation needed to answer the question is neither annotated nor do transitive inferences exist.

8.3 Results with TREFL (no-questions)

As mentioned earlier the evaluation is mainly focused on positive questions (with *yes* answer) since annotating them provides more information and negative questions can be automatically generated from them. Moreover, in general, answering positive questions is more challenging, e.g., asking IS e1 BEFORE e2 requires a system to guess the single correct relation if the correct answer is *yes*; However, if the correct answer is *no*, there are 12 possible correct relations (all but BEFORE).

In order to have more insight into this issue, we automatically obtained negative questions by asking about the opposite[7] relation with "no" as the expected answer. For example, IS e1 BEFORE e2 (yes) becomes IS e1 AFTER e2 (no). The aim of this evaluation is to analyze system performance in determining if a relation is not correct. In this easier test, participating and off-the-shelf systems obtain better results going over .50 R in the news domain. The best obtained recalls are .52 in news, .39 in wiki, and .42 in blogs, as compared to .38, .36 and .22 obtained for *yes*-questions in the main test.

It is interesting to see that in this negative alternative, systems were better in blogs than in wiki, unlike in the positive test. Likewise the positive variant, the addition of trefl has improved results, but the improvements is smaller in this case.

[7]SIMULTANEOUS has no opposite and IAFTER was used.

9 Conclusions and Future Work

QA evaluation task attempts to measure how far we are on temporal information understanding applied to temporal QA (an extrinsic task) instead of only TimeML annotation accuracy. One of the benefits of QA evaluation is that test set creation time and human expertise required is considerably less than in TimeML annotation. QA TempEval also included Wikipedia and blog domains, in addition to the regular news domain, for the first time. Evaluation results suggest that we are still far from systems that more deeply understand temporal aspects of natural language and can answer temporal questions. The best overall recall was 30% (34% with TREFL). This top result is higher than best off-the-shelf system 17% (27% with TREFL).

The main findings include:

- The only system using event co-reference obtained the best results, so adding event coref may help other systems.
- Adding TREFL improved the QA recall of all systems, ranging from 3% to 12% absolute (13% to 80% relative).
- Training data is news, but the best system performed well on Wikipedia. Some off-the-shelf systems even performed better on Wikipedia/blogs than on the news domain.
- Human annotators annotated as many questions about close entities as distant entities. In the same line, automated systems were capable of answering correctly approximately the same amount of questions of each type.

As future work we aim to extend the analysis of the results presented in this paper. On the one hand, by explaining TREFL technique and its effects in more detail. On the other hand, by finding out what features made some systems unique being the only ones capable of answering certain questions correctly. The question-sets[8], tools and results[9] have been released for future research.

Acknowledgments

We want to thank participant Paramita Mirza for her collaboration on reviewing and correcting the test data, and also Marc Verhagen and Roser Sauri for their help on approximating the time-cost of human TimeML annotation.

[8]http://bitbucket.org/hector_llorens/qa-tempeval-test-data
[9]http://alt.qcri.org/semeval2015/task5/

References

James F. Allen. 1983. Maintaining knowledge about temporal intervals. *Communications of ACM*, 26(11):832–843.

Steven Bethard. 2013. Cleartk-timeml: A minimalist approach to tempeval 2013. In *Second Joint Conference on Lexical and Computational Semantics (*SEM), Volume 2: Proceedings of the Seventh International Workshop on Semantic Evaluation (SemEval 2013)*, pages 10–14.

Nathanael Chambers, Taylor Cassidy, Bill McDowell, and Steven Bethard. 2014. Dense event ordering with a multi-pass architecture. *Transactions of the Association for Computational Linguistics*, 2(10):273–284.

Alfonso Gerevini, Lenhart Schubert, and Stephanie Schaeffer. 1993. Temporal reasoning in Timegraph I–II. *SIGART Bulletin*, 4(3):21–25.

Hector Llorens, Estela Saquete, and Borja Navarro. 2010. TIPSem (English and Spanish): Evaluating CRFs and Semantic Roles in TempEval-2. In *Proceedings of SemEval-5*, pages 284–291.

Stephanie Miller and Lenhart Schubert. 1990. Time revisited. In *Computational Intelligence*, volume 26, pages 108–118.

James Pustejovsky, José M. Castaño, Robert Ingria, Roser Saurí, Robert Gaizauskas, Andrea Setzer, and Graham Katz. 2003. TimeML: Robust Specification of Event and Timexes in Text. In *IWCS-5*.

Jonathan Schler, Moshe Koppel, Shlomo Argamon, and James W. Pennebaker. 2006. Effects of age and gender on blogging. In *AAAI Spring Symposium: Computational Approaches to Analyzing Weblogs*, pages 199–205.

Naushad UzZaman, Hector Llorens, and James Allen. 2012. Evaluating temporal information understanding with temporal question answering. In *Proceedings of IEEE International Conference on Semantic Computing*.

Naushad UzZaman, Hector Llorens, Leon Derczynski, James Allen, Marc Verhagen, and James Pustejovsky. 2013. Semeval-2013 task 1: Tempeval-3: Evaluating time expressions, events, and temporal relations. In *2nd Joint Conference on Lexical and Computational Semantics (*SEM), Vol 2: Proceedings of the Seventh International Workshop on Semantic Evaluation (SemEval 2013)*, pages 1–9, Atlanta, Georgia, USA, June.

Marc Verhagen, Robert Gaizauskas, Mark Hepple, Frank Schilder, Graham Katz, and James Pustejovsky. 2007. Semeval-2007 task 15: Tempeval temporal relation identification. In *Proceedings of the 4th International Workshop on Semantic Evaluations*, pages 75–80, Prague.

Marc Verhagen, Roser Saurí, Tommaso Caselli, and James Pustejovsky. 2010. Semeval-2010 task 13: Tempeval-2. In *Proceedings of SemEval-5*, pages 57–62.

HLT-FBK: a Complete Temporal Processing System for QA TempEval

Paramita Mirza
FBK, Trento, Italy
University of Trento
paramita@fbk.eu

Anne-Lyse Minard
FBK, Trento, Italy
minard@fbk.eu

Abstract

The HLT-FBK system is a suite of SVMs-based classification models for extracting time expressions, events and temporal relations, each with a set of features obtained with the NewsReader NLP pipeline. HLT-FBK's best system runs ranked 1st in all three domains, with a recall of 0.30 over all domains. Our attempts on increasing recall by considering all SRL predicates as events as well as utilizing event co-reference information in extracting temporal links result in significant improvements.

1 Introduction

QA TempEval is a continuation of the TempEval task series (Verhagen et al., 2007; Verhagen et al., 2010; UzZaman et al., 2013), which shifts its evaluation methodology from temporal information extraction accuracy to temporal question-answering (QA) accuracy. However, the main task is the same as its predecessor tasks, which is to automatically annotate texts with temporal information following TimeML specification (Pustejovsky et al., 2003a).

This paper describes the HLT-FBK system submitted to QA TempEval. The system decomposes the task into three sub-tasks, i.e. temporal expression (timex) extraction, event extraction and temporal relation extraction. Each sub-task is formulated as a supervised classification problem using SVMs-based classifiers, which make use of the information acquired from the NewsReader[1] NLP pipeline.

[1]http://www.newsreader-project.eu

2 Data, Resources and Tools

The training data set is the TimeML annotated data released by the task organizers, which includes *TBAQ-cleaned* and *TE3-Platinum* corpora reused from the TempEval-3 task (UzZaman et al., 2013). We extended the training corpus for the timex extraction system with the TempEval-3 *silver* corpus.

The test data are 30 plain texts of *News*, *Wikipedia* and *Blogs* domains (10 documents each). For evaluating the system, 294 temporal-based questions and the test data annotated with entities relevant for the questions are used.

The resources used by the system to extract some features are **lists of temporal signals** extracted from the TimeBank corpus (Pustejovsky et al., 2003b) and a **list of nominalizations** extracted from the SPECIALIST Lexicon[2] distributed by the U.S. National Library of Medicine, which contains commonly occurring English words in addition to biomedical terms, with syntactic and morphological information. We extracted all nouns resulting from a nominalization. Other features come from the annotation of the **addDiscourse** tool (Pitler and Nenkova, 2009), which identifies discourse connectives and assigns them to one of the four semantic classes: *Temporal*, *Expansion*, *Contingency* and *Comparison*.

The **MorphoPro** module, part of the TextPro tool suite[3], is used to get the morphological analysis of each token in a text. The time expression nor-

[2]http://www.nlm.nih.gov/research/umls/new_users/online_learning/LEX_001.html

[3]http://textpro.fbk.eu/

malization sub-task is carried out by **TimeNorm**[4] (Bethard, 2013), a library for converting natural language expressions of dates and times into their normalized form.

The HLT-FBK system is a suite of classification models that have been built and applied using **YamCha**[5] (Kudo and Matsumoto, 2003), a text chunker using the Support Vector Machines (SVMs) algorithm. It supports the dynamic features that are decided dynamically during the classification, multi-class classification using either *one-vs-rest* or *one-vs-one* strategies, and *polynomial kernels*.

3 The End-to-end System

3.1 Pre-processing: NewsReader Pipeline

The data pre-processing was done using the NLP pipeline developed for the NewsReader project. The pipeline includes, amongst others, tokenization, part-of-speech tagging, constituency parser, dependency parser, named entity recognition, semantic role labeling (SRL) and event co-reference.[6]

3.2 Timex Extraction System

The task of recognizing the extent of a timex, as well as determining the timex type (i.e. DATE, TIME, DURATION and SET), is taken as a text chunking task. Since the timex extent can be a multi-token expression, we employ the IOB2 tagging to annotate the data, so each token will be classified into 9 classes: B-DATE, I-DATE, B-TIME, I-TIME, B-DURATION, I-DURATION, B-SET, I-SET and O (for other).

The classifier is built with *one-vs-one* strategy for multi-class classification. The features used to represent a token are token's text, lemma, part-of-speech (PoS) tag, chunk, named entity type (if any), and whether a token matches regular expression patterns for a time unit, part of a day, name of days, name of months, duration (e.g. *1h3'*), etc. In addition, all mentioned features for the preceding 4 and following 4 tokens, and the preceding 4 labels tagged by the classifier, are also included in the feature set.

For timex normalization, we decided to use TimeNorm. For English, it is shown to be the best performing system for most evaluation corpora (Llorens et al., 2012). We added pre- and post-processing rules in order to obtain the best normalized form.

3.3 Event Extraction System

Event detection is taken as a text chunking task, in which tokens have to be classified into two classes: EVENT (i.e. the token is included in an event extent) or O (for other). Then events are classified into one of the 7 TimeML classes (i.e. REPORTING, PERCEPTION, ASPECTUAL, I_ACTION, I_STATE, STATE and OCCURRENCE).

The classification models are built with *one-vs-rest* strategy for multi-class classification. For both event extent identification and event classification tasks we use various features to represent each token. The classic features are token's lemma, PoS tag, and entity type (if the token is part of a named entity or a time expression). Other features that are more specific for the task include: verb's tense and polarity[7], whether the token is annotated as predicate by the SRL module, whether it is part of an event co-reference chain and whether it is in the nominalization list. In addition, all mentioned features for the preceding 4 and following 4 tokens, and the preceding 4 labels tagged by the classifier, are also considered as features.

Specifically for event classification, additional features are used: token's chunk, whether the token is part of a temporal discourse connective, whether a verb is the main verb of the sentence (*root* verb), the predicate for which the token is part of a participant and its semantic role (e.g. Arg0, Arg1), and finally whether the token is in an event extent (annotated in the previous step).

We submitted two different runs:

- **Run 1** (*ev1*) Two classifiers are used as described above.
- **Run 2** (*ev2*) We consider all predicates identified by the SRL module as events. We then used a classifier to determine the class of each event.

[4]http://github.com/bethard/timenorm

[5]http://chasen.org/~taku/software/yamcha/

[6]More information about the NewsReader pipeline, as well as a demo, are available on the project website http://www.newsreader-project.eu/results/.

[7]The tense, aspect and polarity attributes of events, as defined in TimeML, are obtained through manually written rules based on the morphological analysis produced by MorphoPro.

3.4 Temporal Relation Extraction System

The temporal relation extraction system extracts temporal relations (TLINKs) holding between two events or between an event and a time expression. We consider all combinations of event/event and event/timex pairs within the same sentence (in a forward manner[8]), and pairs of main events (*root* verbs) of consecutive sentences, as candidate temporal links.

Given an ordered pair of entities (e_1, e_2), either event/event or event/timex pair, the classifier has to assign a label, i.e one of the 13 TimeML temporal relation types. However, we simplified the considered temporal relation types to better fit the QA TempEval task description and to deal with the unbalanced training data as follows: *(i)* IDENTITY and DURING are mapped to SIMULTANEOUS; *(ii)* IBEFORE/IAFTER are mapped to BEFORE/AFTER;[9] and *(iii)* INCLUDES, BEGINS and ENDS are converted to their inverse counterparts (IS_INCLUDED, BEGUN_BY and ENDED_BY, resp.) by exchanging the order of entities in the pair. In the end, we only consider 6 temporal relation types (i.e. SIMULTANEOUS, BEFORE, AFTER, IS_INCLUDED, BEGUN_BY and ENDED_BY).

The classification models for event/event and event/timex pairs are built with *one-vs-one* strategy for multi-class classification. The overall approach is largely inspired by an existing work for classifing temporal relations (Mirza and Tonelli, 2014). The implemented features are as follows:

String and grammatical features. Tokens, lemmas, PoS tags and chunks of e_1 and e_2, along with a binary feature indicating whether e_1 and e_2 in an event/event pair have the same PoS tags.

Textual context. Sentence distance (e.g. 0 if e_1 and e_2 are in the same sentence) and entity distance inside a sentence (i.e. the number of entities occurring between e_1 and e_2).

Entity attributes. Event attributes (*class*, *tense*, *aspect* and *polarity*) taken from the output of the event extraction module, and the timex attribute (*type*) obtained from the timex extraction module of e_1 and e_2; a binary feature to represent whether the timex in an event/timex pair is the document creation time; and four binary features to represent whether e_1 and e_2 in an event/event pair have the same event attributes or not. We also include as features the PoS chain of VP chunks containing events (e.g. VHZ-VBN-VVG for *has been [raining]*$_{e_1}$, VM-VVB for *would [send]*$_{e_2}$), which captures tense and aspect, as well as modality information of the event.

Dependency information. Dependency path existing between e_1 and e_2, and binary features indicating whether e_1/e_2 is the *root* verb.

Temporal signals. Tokens of temporal signals occurring around e_1 and e_2 and their positions with respect to e_1 and e_2 (i.e. *before/after* e_1, *before/after* e_2, or at the beginning of the sentence).

Temporal discourse connectives. We take into account discourse connectives belonging to the *Temporal* class, acquired from the *addDiscourse* tool. Similar to temporal signals, tokens of connectives occurring in the textual context of e_1 and e_2, and their position with respect to e_1 and e_2, are used as features. These features are only relevant for event/event pairs.

There are two variations of system submitted:

- **Run 1** (*trel1*) We incorporate pre-processing rules based on timex pattern matching (e.g. *from...to...*, *between...and...*), to recognize event/timex pairs of BEGUN_BY and ENDED_BY types, which are not well represented in the training corpus.
- **Run 2** (*trel2*) Similar as Run 1, however, we also incorporate the event co-reference information obtained from the NewsReader pipeline. Whenever two events co-refer, the event/event pair is excluded from the classifier, and automatically labelled SIMULTANEOUS.

4 Results

We submitted 4 system runs, i.e. the combinations of 2 system runs for event extraction (*ev1* and *ev2*) and 2 system runs for temporal relation extraction (*trel1* and *trel2*). Table 1 shows HLT-FBK system results in terms of coverage, precision, recall and F1-score for the three considered domains; recall is the main evaluation metric used to rank the systems.

[8]For example, for a sentence "...ev_1...tmx_1...ev_2...", the candidate pairs are (ev_1, tmx_1), (ev_1, ev_3) and (ev_2, tmx_1).

[9]Because event pairs of IBEFORE/IAFTER types are too scarce as training examples, and they are by definition specific types of BEFORE/AFTER.

	News				Wikipedia				Blogs				All domains
	Cov	P	R	F1	Cov	P	R	F1	Cov	P	R	F1	R
ev1-trel1	0.29	0.59	0.17	0.27	0.29	0.55	0.16	0.25	0.32	0.57	0.18	0.28	0.17
ev1-trel2	0.55	0.43	0.23	0.30	0.50	0.52	0.26	0.35	0.43	0.43	0.18	0.26	0.23
ev2-trel1	0.36	0.56	0.20	0.30	0.29	0.58	0.17	0.26	0.29	0.47	0.14	0.21	0.17
ev2-trel2	0.69	0.43	**0.29**	0.35	0.58	0.62	**0.36**	0.46	0.58	0.34	**0.20**	0.25	**0.30**

Table 1: HLT-FBK system results in terms of coverage (Cov), precision (P), recall (R) and F1-score (F1).

	News					Wikipedia					Blogs				
		Answered		Unknown			Answered		Unknown			Answered		Unknown	
	Q	Cor	Inc	Ent	Rel	Q	Cor	Inc	Ent	Rel	Q	Cor	Inc	Ent	Rel
ev2-trel1	99	20	16	17	46	130	22	16	48	44	65	9	10	22	24
ev2-trel2	99	29	39	16	15	130	47	29	48	6	65	13	25	22	5

Table 2: HLT-FBK system results in terms of number of answered questions, correctly (Cor) and incorrectly (Inc), and unanswered questions because of unknown entities (Ent) and unknown relations (Rel).

	News		Wikipedia		Blogs	
	ev	tx	ev	tx	ev	tx
ev1	0.72	0.83	0.81	0.59	0.68	0.35
ev2	0.80	0.83	0.84	0.54	0.70	0.35

Table 3: HLT-FBK system results in terms of recall on identifying events (ev) and timexes (tx) with strict match.

The best results are achieved with the combination of *ev2* and *trel2*, which significantly outperformed other participating systems and reported off-the-shelf systems (not optimized for the task), i.e. *CAEVO* with 0.17 and 0.18 recall scores on News and Blogs respectively, and *TIPSem* with 0.19 recall on Wikipedia.

Table 2 compares *trel1* and *trel2* runs, in terms of the number of answered questions (correctly and incorrectly) and unanswered questions (due to unknown entities and non-established/unknown relations). Meanwhile, Table 3 compares *ev1* and *ev2* in terms of recall scores on identifying EVENT and TIMEX3 tags, with the annotated test data as the gold standard.[10] Both results give more insight on the question answering-based evaluation.

5 Discussion

The timex extraction system performs well on News texts, but not on texts from Wikipedia and Blogs (see Table 3). Our error analysis shows that many time expressions in Wikipedia texts are not represented in the training corpus (e.g. *4th millennium BCE*).

Considering all SRL predicates as events (*ev2*) improves the recall on identifying relevant events (see Table 3), but lowers the precision on answering the questions (except for Wikipedia, in which the precision is also improved, see Table 1). In this task, the focus is on the recall and as expected the best results are obtained by the system with the best recall (*ev2*).

For temporal relation extraction, using event co-reference information (*trel2*) reduces the number of unknown relations (Rel) down by 77% in average for all domains (see Table 2). Hence, the recall scores increase significantly as shown in Table 1, especially for the Wikipedia domain with almost 20% improvement.

Our attempts on improving the overall performance by increasing the recall (*ev2* and *trel2* runs) work well on News and Wikipedia, shown by improving F1-scores. This unfortunately does not hold for Blogs, since the precision is greatly compromised while the recall is only slightly improved.

In general, the system performs best on News and Wikipedia texts, but not so well on informal Blogs texts. This difference can be due to the fact that our systems, as well as most of the pipeline's modules, are trained using the corpus of formal news texts. Moreover, Blogs texts contain orthographic errors, a lot of punctuation signs, etc. and their pre-processing with the pipeline do not run well.

[10] The gold standard only contains the annotated entities relevant for answering the set of questions. For this reason, we computed only the recall.

Acknowledgments

The research leading to this paper was partially supported by the European Union's 7th Framework Programme via the NewsReader Project (ICT-316404).

References

Steven Bethard. 2013. A Synchronous Context Free Grammar for Time Normalization. In *Proceedings of the 2013 Conference on Empirical Methods in Natural Language Processing*, pages 821–826, Seattle, Washington, USA.

Taku Kudo and Yuji Matsumoto. 2003. Fast Methods for Kernel-based Text Analysis. In *Proceedings of the 41st Annual Meeting on Association for Computational Linguistics - Volume 1*, ACL '03, pages 24–31, Stroudsburg, PA, USA.

Hector Llorens, Leon Derczynski, Robert Gaizauskas, and Estela Saquete. 2012. TIMEN: An Open Temporal Expression Normalisation Resource. In *Proceedings of the Eight International Conference on Language Resources and Evaluation (LREC'12)*, pages 3044–3051, Istanbul, Turkey.

Paramita Mirza and Sara Tonelli. 2014. Classifying Temporal Relations with Simple Features. In *Proceedings of the 14th Conference of the European Chapter of the Association for Computational Linguistics*, pages 308–317, Gothenburg, Sweden.

Emily Pitler and Ani Nenkova. 2009. Using Syntax to Disambiguate Explicit Discourse Connectives in Text. In *Proceedings of the ACL-IJCNLP 2009 Conference Short Papers*, ACLShort '09, pages 13–16, Stroudsburg, PA, USA.

James Pustejovsky, José Castaño, Robert Ingria, Roser Saurí, Robert Gaizauskas, Andrea Setzer, and Graham Katz. 2003a. TimeML: Robust Specification of Event and Temporal Expressions in Text. In *Proceedings of the Fifth International Workshop on Computational Semantics (IWCS-5)*.

James Pustejovsky, Patrick Hanks, Roser Saurí, Andrew See, Robert Gaizauskas, Andrea Setzer, Dragomir Radev, Beth Sundheim, David Day, Lisa Ferro, and Marcia Lazo. 2003b. The TIMEBANK Corpus. In *Proceedings of Corpus Linguistics 2003*, pages 647–656, Lancaster, March.

Naushad UzZaman, Hector Llorens, Leon Derczynski, James Allen, Marc Verhagen, and James Pustejovsky. 2013. SemEval-2013 Task 1: TempEval-3: Evaluating Time Expressions, Events, and Temporal Relations. In *Proceedings of the Seventh International Workshop on Semantic Evaluation*, SemEval '13, pages 1–9, Atlanta, Georgia, USA.

Marc Verhagen, Robert Gaizauskas, Frank Schilder, Mark Hepple, Graham Katz, and James Pustejovsky. 2007. SemEval-2007 Task 15: TempEval Temporal Relation Identification. In *Proceedings of the Fourth International Workshop on Semantic Evaluations (SemEval-2007)*, pages 75–80.

Marc Verhagen, Roser Sauri, Tommaso Caselli, and James Pustejovsky. 2010. SemEval-2010 Task 13: TempEval-2. In *Proceedings of the 5th International Workshop on Semantic Evaluation*, pages 57–62.

SemEval-2015 Task 6: Clinical TempEval

Steven Bethard
University of Alabama at Birmingham
Birmingham, AL 35294, USA
bethard@cis.uab.edu

Leon Derczynski
University of Sheffield
Sheffield, S1 4DP, UK
leon@dcs.shef.ac.uk

Guergana Savova
Harvard Medical School
Boston, MA 02115, USA
Guergana.Savova@childrens.harvard.edu

James Pustejovsky, Marc Verhagen
Brandeis University
Waltham, MA 02453, USA
jamesp@cs.brandeis.edu
marc@cs.brandeis.edu

Abstract

Clinical TempEval 2015 brought the temporal information extraction tasks of past TempEval campaigns to the clinical domain. Nine sub-tasks were included, covering problems in time expression identification, event expression identification and temporal relation identification. Participant systems were trained and evaluated on a corpus of clinical notes and pathology reports from the Mayo Clinic, annotated with an extension of TimeML for the clinical domain. Three teams submitted a total of 13 system runs, with the best systems achieving near-human performance on identifying events and times, but with a large performance gap still remaining for temporal relations.

1 Introduction

The TempEval shared tasks have, since 2007, provided a focus for research on temporal information extraction (Verhagen et al., 2007; Verhagen et al., 2010; UzZaman et al., 2013). Participant systems compete to identify critical components of the timeline of a text, including time expressions, event expressions and temporal relations. However, the TempEval campaigns to date have focused primarily on in-document timelines derived from news articles.

Clinical TempEval brings these temporal information extraction tasks to the clinical domain, using clinical notes and pathology reports from the Mayo Clinic. This follows recent interest in temporal information extraction for the clinical domain, e.g., the i2b2 2012 shared task (Sun et al., 2013), and broadens our understanding of the language of time beyond newswire expressions and structure.

Clinical TempEval focuses on discrete, well-defined tasks which allow rapid, reliable and repeatable evaluation. Participating systems are expected to take as input raw text such as:

> April 23, 2014: The patient did not have any postoperative bleeding so we will resume chemotherapy with a larger bolus on Friday even if there is slight nausea.

And output annotations over the text that capture the following kinds of information:

- *April 23, 2014*: TIMEX3
  - TYPE=DATE
- *postoperative*: TIMEX3
  - TYPE=PREPOSTEXP
  - CONTAINS
- *bleeding*: EVENT
  - POLARITY=NEG
  - BEFORE document creation time
- *resume*: EVENT
  - TYPE=ASPECTUAL
  - AFTER document creation time
- *chemotherapy*: EVENT
  - AFTER document creation time
- *bolus*: EVENT
  - AFTER document creation time
- *Friday*: TIMEX3
  - TYPE=DATE
  - CONTAINS
- *nausea*: EVENT
  - DEGREE=LITTLE
  - MODALITY=HYPOTHETICAL
  - AFTER document creation time

That is, the systems should identify the time expressions, event expressions, attributes of those expressions, and temporal relations between them.

2 Data

The Clinical TempEval corpus was based on a set of 600 clinical notes and pathology reports from cancer patients at the Mayo Clinic. These notes were manually de-identified by the Mayo Clinic to replace names, locations, etc. with generic placeholders, but time expressions were not altered. The notes were then manually annotated by the THYME project (`thyme.healthnlp.org`) using an extension of ISO-TimeML for the annotation of times, events and temporal relations in clinical notes (Styler et al., 2014b). This extension includes additions such as new time expression types (e.g., PREPOSTEXP for expressions like *postoperative*), new EVENT attributes (e.g., DEGREE=LITTLE for expressions like *slight nausea*), and an increased focus on temporal relations of type CONTAINS (a.k.a. INCLUDES).

The annotation procedure was as follows:

1. Annotators identified time and event expressions, along with their attributes
2. Adjudicators revised and finalized the time and event expressions and their attributes
3. Annotators identified temporal relations between pairs of events and events and times
4. Adjudicators revised and finalized the temporal relations

More details on the corpus annotation process are documented in a separate article (Styler et al., 2014a).

Because the data contained incompletely de-identified clinical data (the time expressions were retained), participants were required to sign a data use agreement with the Mayo Clinic to obtain the raw text of the clinical notes and pathology reports.[1] The event, time and temporal relation annotations were distributed separately from the text, in an open source repository[2] using the Anafora standoff format (Chen and Styler, 2013).

	Train	Dev
Documents	293	147
EVENTs	38890	20974
TIMEX3s	3833	2078
TLINKs with TYPE=CONTAINS	11176	6173

Table 1: Number of documents, event expressions, time expressions and narrative container relations in the training and development portions of the THYME data. (Dev is the Clinical TempEval 2015 test set.)

The corpus was split into three portions: Train (50%), Dev (25%) and Test (25%). For Clinical TempEval 2015, the Train portion was used for training and the Dev portion was used for testing. The Test portion was not distributed, and was reserved as a test set for a future iteration of the shared task. Table 1 shows the number of documents, event expressions (EVENT annotations), time expressions (TIMEX3 annotations) and narrative container relations (TLINK annotations with TYPE=CONTAINS attributes) in the Train and Dev portions of the corpus.

3 Tasks

A total of nine tasks were included, grouped into three categories:

- Identifying time expressions (TIMEX3 annotations in the THYME corpus) consisting of the following components[3]:
  - The spans (character offsets) of the expression in the text
  - Class: DATE, TIME, DURATION, QUANTIFIER, PREPOSTEXP or SET
- Identifying event expressions (EVENT annotations in the THYME corpus) consisting of the following components:
  - The spans (character offsets) of the expression in the text
  - Contextual Modality: ACTUAL, HYPOTHETICAL, HEDGED or GENERIC
  - Degree: MOST, LITTLE or N/A
  - Polarity: POS or NEG
  - Type: ASPECTUAL, EVIDENTIAL or N/A

[1] The details of this process are described at `http://thyme.healthnlp.org/`

[2] `https://github.com/stylerw/thymedata`

[3] Normalized time values (e.g. 2015-02-05) were originally planned, but annotation was not completed in time.

- Identifying temporal relations between events and times, focusing on the following types:
  - Relations between events and the document creation time (BEFORE, OVERLAP, BEFORE-OVERLAP or AFTER), represented by DOCTIMEREL annotations in the THYME corpus
  - Narrative container relations (Pustejovsky and Stubbs, 2011) between events and/or times, represented by TLINK annotations with TYPE=CONTAINS in the THYME corpus

The evaluation was run in two phases:

1. Systems were given access only to the raw text, and were asked to identify time expressions, event expressions and temporal relations
2. Systems were given access to the raw text and the manual event and time annotations, and were asked to identify only temporal relations

4 Evaluation Metrics

All of the tasks were evaluated using the standard metrics of precision (P), recall (R) and F_1:

$$P = \frac{|S \cap H|}{|S|}$$

$$R = \frac{|S \cap H|}{|H|}$$

$$F_1 = \frac{2 \cdot P \cdot R}{P + R}$$

where S is the set of items predicted by the system and H is the set of items manually annotated by the humans. Applying these metrics to the tasks only requires a definition of what is considered an "item" for each task.

- For evaluating the spans of event expressions or time expressions, items were tuples of (begin, end) character offsets. Thus, systems only received credit for identifying events and times with exactly the same character offsets as the manually annotated ones.
- For evaluating the attributes of event expressions or time expressions – Class, Contextual Modality, Degree, Polarity and Type – items were tuples of (begin, end, value) where begin and end are character offsets and value is the value that was given to the relevant attribute. Thus, systems only received credit for an event (or time) attribute if they both found an event (or time) with the correct character offsets and then assigned the correct value for that attribute.
- For relations between events and the document creation time, items were tuples of (begin, end, value), just as if it were an event attribute. Thus, systems only received credit if they found a correct event and assigned the correct relation (BEFORE, OVERLAP, BEFORE-OVERLAP or AFTER) between that event and the document creation time. Note that in the second phase of the evaluation, when manual event annotations were given as input, precision, recall and F_1 are all equivalent to standard accuracy.
- For narrative container relations, items were tuples of ((begin$_1$, end$_1$), (begin$_2$, end$_2$)), where the begins and ends corresponded to the character offsets of the events or times participating in the relation. Thus, systems only received credit for a narrative container relation if they found both events/times and correctly assigned a CONTAINS relation between them.

For attributes, an additional metric measures how accurately a system predicts the attribute values on just those events or times that the system predicted. The goal here is to allow a comparison across systems for assigning attribute values, even when different systems produce very different numbers of events and times. This is calculated by dividing the F_1 on the attribute by the F_1 on identifying the spans:

$$A = \frac{\text{attribute } F_1}{\text{span } F_1}$$

For the narrative container relations, additional metrics were included that took into account *temporal closure*, where additional relations can be deterministically inferred from other relations (e.g., A CON-

TAINS B and B CONTAINS C, so A CONTAINS C):

$$P_{\text{closure}} = \frac{|S \cap \text{closure}(H)|}{|S|}$$

$$R_{\text{closure}} = \frac{|\text{closure}(S) \cap H|}{|H|}$$

$$F_{\text{closure}} = \frac{2 \cdot P_{\text{closure}} \cdot R_{\text{closure}}}{P_{\text{closure}} + R_{\text{closure}}}$$

These measures take the approach of prior work (UzZaman and Allen, 2011) and TempEval 2013 (UzZaman et al., 2013), following the intuition that precision should measure the fraction of system-predicted relations that can be verified from the human annotations (either the original human annotations or annotations inferred from those through closure), and that recall should measure the fraction of human-annotated relations that can be verified from the system output (either the original system predictions or predictions inferred from those through closure).

5 Baseline Systems

Two rule-based systems were used as baselines to compare the participating systems against.

memorize For all tasks but the narrative container task, a memorization-based baseline was used.

To train the model, all phrases annotated as either events or times in the training data were collected. All exact character matches for these phrases in the training data were then examined, and only phrases that were annotated as events or times greater than 50% of the time were retained. For each phrase, the most frequently annotated type (event or time) and attribute values for instances of that phrase were determined.

To predict with the model, the raw text of the test data was searched for all exact character matches of any of the memorized phrases, preferring longer phrases when multiple matches overlapped. Wherever a phrase match was found, an event or time with the memorized (most frequent) attribute values was predicted.

closest For the narrative container task, a proximity-based baseline was used. Each time expression was predicted to be a narrative container, containing only the closest event expression to it in the text.

6 Participating Systems

Three research teams submitted a total of 13 runs:

BluLab The team from Stockholm University and University of Utah participated in all tasks, using supervised classifiers with features generated by the Apache clinical Text Analysis and Knowledge Extraction System (cTAKES)[4]. Their runs differed in whether and how many rules were used to constrain the search for narrative container relations.

KPSCMI The team from Kaiser Permanente Southern California participated in the time expression tasks. Their runs compared an extended version of the rule-based HeidelTime[5] system (run 1) with systems based on supervised classifiers (run 2-3).

UFPRSheffield The team from Universidade Federal do Paraná and University of Sheffield participated in the time expression tasks. Their runs compared in-house rule-based systems (the Hynx runs) to systems based on supervised classifiers (the SVM runs).

7 Human Agreement

We also give two types of human agreement on the task, measured with the same evaluation metrics as the systems:

ann-ann Inter-annotator agreement between the two independent human annotators who annotated each document. This is the most commonly reported type of agreement, and often considered to be an upper bound on system performance.

adj-ann Inter-annotator agreement between the adjudicator and the two independent annotators. This is usually a better bound on system performance in adjudicated corpora, since the models are trained on the adjudicated data, not on the individual annotator data.

[4] https://ctakes.apache.org

[5] https://code.google.com/p/heideltime/

Team	span			span + class			
	P	R	F1	P	R	F1	A
Baseline: memorize	0.743	0.372	0.496	0.723	0.362	0.483	0.974
BluLab: run 1-3	**0.797**	0.664	**0.725**	**0.778**	0.652	**0.709**	0.819
KPSCMI: run 1	0.272	0.782	0.404	0.223	0.642	0.331	0.948
KPSCMI: run 2	0.705	0.683	0.694	0.668	0.648	0.658	0.948
KPSCMI: run 3	0.693	0.706	0.699	0.657	0.669	0.663	0.973
UFPRSheffield-SVM: run 1	0.732	0.661	0.695	0.712	0.643	0.676	0.977
UFPRSheffield-SVM: run 2	0.741	0.655	0.695	0.723	0.640	0.679	0.950
UFPRSheffield-Hynx: run 1	0.479	0.747	0.584	0.455	0.709	0.555	0.952
UFPRSheffield-Hynx: run 2	0.494	0.770	0.602	0.470	0.733	0.573	0.951
UFPRSheffield-Hynx: run 3	0.311	0.794	0.447	0.296	0.756	0.425	0.951
UFPRSheffield-Hynx: run 4	0.311	**0.795**	0.447	0.296	**0.756**	0.425	0.952
UFPRSheffield-Hynx: run 5	0.411	**0.795**	0.542	0.391	**0.756**	0.516	**0.978**
Agreement: ann-ann	-	-	0.690	-	-	0.644	0.933
Agreement: adj-ann	-	-	0.774	-	-	0.747	0.965

Table 2: System performance and annotator agreement on TIMEX3 tasks: identifying the time expression's span (character offsets) and class (DATE, TIME, DURATION, QUANTIFIER, PREPOSTEXP or SET). The best system score from each column is in bold. The three BluLab runs are combined because they all have identical performance (since they only differ in their approach to narrative container relations).

Precision and recall are not reported in these scenarios since they depend on the arbitrary choice of one annotator as the "human" (H) and the other as the "system" (S).

Note that since temporal relations between events and the document creation time were annotated at the same time as the events themselves, agreement for this task is only reported in phase 1 of the evaluation. Similarly, since narrative container relations were only annotated after events and times had been adjudicated, agreement for this task is only reported in phase 2 of the evaluation.

8 Evaluation Results

8.1 Time Expressions

Table 2 shows results on the time expression tasks. The BluLab system achieved the best F_1 at identifying time expressions, 0.725. The other machine learning systems (KPSCMI run 2-3 and UFPRSheffield-SVM run 1-2) achieved F_1 in the 0.690-0.700 range. The rule-based systems (KPSCMI run 1 and UFPRSheffield-Hynx run 1-5) all achieved higher recall than the machine learning systems, but at substantial costs to precision. All systems outperformed the memorization baseline in terms of recall, and all machine-learning systems outperformed it in terms of F_1, but only the BluLab system outperformed the baseline in terms of precision.

The BluLab system also achieved the best F_1 for predicting the classes of time expressions, though this is primarily due to achieving a higher F_1 at identifying time expressions in the first place. UFPRSheffield-Hynx run 5 achieved the best accuracy on predicting classes for the time expressions it found, 0.978, though on this metric it only outperformed the memorization baseline by 0.004.

Across the time expression tasks, systems did not quite achieve performance at the level of human agreement. For the spans of time expressions, the top system achieved 0.725 $F1$, compared to 0.774 adjudicator-annotator F_1, though almost half of the systems exceeded the lower annotator-annotator F_1 of 0.690. For the classes of time expressions, the story was similar for F_1, though several models exceeded the adjudicator-annotator accuracy of 0.965 on just the time expressions predicted by the system.

8.2 Event Expressions

Table 3 shows results on the event expression tasks. The BluLab system outperformed the memorization baseline on almost every metric on every task. The

Team	span			span + modality				span + degree			
	P	R	F1	P	R	F1	A	P	R	F1	A
Baseline: memorize	0.876	0.810	0.842	0.810	0.749	0.778	0.924	0.871	0.806	0.838	**0.995**
BluLab: run 1-3	**0.887**	**0.864**	**0.875**	**0.834**	**0.813**	**0.824**	**0.942**	**0.882**	**0.859**	**0.870**	0.994
Agreement: ann-ann	-	-	0.819	-	-	0.779	0.951	-	-	0.815	0.995
Agreement: adj-ann	-	-	0.880	-	-	0.855	0.972	-	-	0.877	0.997

Team	span + polarity				span + type			
	P	R	F1	A	P	R	F1	A
Baseline: memorize	0.800	0.740	0.769	0.913	**0.846**	0.783	0.813	**0.966**
BluLab: run 1-3	**0.868**	**0.846**	**0.857**	**0.979**	0.834	**0.812**	**0.823**	0.941
Agreement: ann-ann	-	-	0.798	0.974	-	-	0.773	0.944
Agreement: adj-ann	-	-	0.869	0.988	-	-	0.853	0.969

Table 3: System performance and annotator agreement on EVENT tasks: identifying the event expression's span (character offsets), contextual modality (ACTUAL, HYPOTHETICAL, HEDGED or GENERIC), degree (MOST, LITTLE or N/A), polarity (POS or NEG) and type (ASPECTUAL, EVIDENTIAL or N/A). The best system score from each column is in bold.

one exception was the semantic type of the event, where the memorization baseline had a better precision and also a better accuracy on the classes of the events that it identified.

The BluLab system got close to the level of adjudicator-annotator agreement on identifying the spans of event expressions (0.875 vs. 0.880 F_1), identifying the degree of events (0.870 vs. 0.877 F_1), and identifying the polarity of events (0.857 vs. 0.869 F_1), and it generally met or exceeded the lower annotator-annotator agreement on these tasks. There is a larger gap (3+ points of F_1) between the system performance and adjudicator-annotator agreement for event modality and event type, though only a small gap (<1 point of F_1) for the lower annotator-annotator agreement on these tasks.

8.3 Temporal Relations

Table 4 shows performance on the temporal relation tasks. In detecting the relations between events and the document creation time, the BluLab system substantially outperformed the memorization baseline, achieving F_1 of 0.702 on system-predicted events (phase 1) and F_1 of 0.791 on manually annotated events (phase 2). In identifying narrative container relations, the best BluLab system (run 2) outperformed the proximity-based baseline when using system-predicted events (F_{closure} of 0.123 vs. 0.106) but not when using manually annotated events (F_{closure} of 0.181 vs. 0.260). Across both phase 1 and phase 2 for narrative container relations, the top BluLab system always had the best recall, while the baseline system always had the best precision.

Annotator agreement was higher than system performance on all temporal relation tasks. For relations between events and the document creation time, adjudicator-annotator agreement was 0.761 F_1, compared to the best system's 0.702 F_1, though this system did exceed the lower annotator-annotator agreement of 0.628 F_1. For narrative container relations using manually annotated EVENTs and TIMEX3s, the gap was much greater, with adjudicator-annotator agreement at 0.672 F_{closure}, and the top system (the baseline system) at 0.260 F_{closure}. Even the lower annotator-annotator agreement of 0.475 F_{closure} was much higher than the system performance.

9 Discussion

The results of Clinical TempEval 2015 suggest that a small number of temporal information extraction tasks are solved by current state-of-the-art systems, but for the majority of tasks, there is still room for improvement. Identifying events, their degrees and their polarities were the easiest tasks for the participants, with the best systems achieving within about 0.01 of human agreement on the tasks. Systems for identifying event modality and event type were not far behind, achieving within about 0.03 of human agree-

	To document time			Narrative containers					
				Without closure			With closure		
	P	R	F1	P	R	F1	P	R	F1
Phase 1: systems are given only the raw text									
Baseline: memorize	0.600	0.555	0.577	-	-	-	-	-	-
Baseline: closest	-	-	-	**0.368**	0.061	**0.104**	**0.400**	0.061	0.106
BluLab: run 1	**0.712**	**0.693**	**0.702**	0.085	0.080	0.082	0.100	0.099	0.100
BluLab: run 2	**0.712**	**0.693**	**0.702**	0.080	**0.142**	0.102	0.094	**0.179**	**0.123**
BluLab: run 3	**0.712**	**0.693**	**0.702**	0.084	0.086	0.085	0.090	0.103	0.096
Agreement: ann-ann	-	-	0.628	-	-	-	-	-	-
Agreement: adj-ann	-	-	0.761	-	-	-	-	-	-
Phase 2: systems are given manually annotated EVENTs and TIMEX3s									
Baseline: memorize	-	-	0.608	-	-	-	-	-	-
Baseline: closest	-	-	-	**0.514**	0.170	0.255	**0.554**	0.170	**0.260**
BluLab: run 1	-	-	**0.791**	0.100	0.104	0.102	0.117	0.128	0.123
BluLab: run 2	-	-	**0.791**	0.109	**0.210**	0.143	0.140	**0.254**	0.181
BluLab: run 3	-	-	**0.791**	0.119	0.137	0.128	0.150	0.155	0.153
Agreement: ann-ann	-	-	-	-	-	0.449	-	-	0.475
Agreement: adj-ann	-	-	-	-	-	0.655	-	-	0.672

Table 4: System performance and annotator agreement on temporal relation tasks: identifying relations between events and the document creation time (DocTimeRel), and identifying narrative container relations (Contains). The best system score from each column is in bold.

ment. Time expressions and relations to the document creation time were at the next level of difficulty, with a gap of about 0.05 from human agreement.

Identifying narrative container relations was by far the most difficult task, with the best systems down by more than 0.40 from human agreement. In absolute terms, performance on narrative container relations was also quite low, with system F_{closure} scores in the 0.10-0.12 range on system-generated events and times, and in the 0.12-0.26 range on manually-annotated events and times. For comparison, in TempEval 2013, which used newswire data, F_{closure} scores were in the 0.24-0.36 range on system-generated events and times and in the 0.35-0.56 range on manually-annotated events and times (UzZaman et al., 2013). One major difference between the corpora is that the narrative container relations in the clinical domain often span many sentences, while almost all of the relations in TempEval 2013 were either within the same sentence or across adjacent sentences. Most past research systems have also focused on identifying within-sentence and adjacent-sentence relations. This focus on local relations might explain the poor performance on the more distant relations in the THYME corpus. But further investigation is needed to better understand the challenge here.

In almost all tasks, the submitted systems substantially outperformed the baselines. The one exception to this was the narrative containers task. The baseline there – which simply predicted that each time expression contained the nearest event expression to it in the text – achieved 4 times the precision of the best submitted system and consequently achieved the best F_1 by a large margin. This suggests that future systems may want to incorporate better measures of proximity that can capture some of what the baseline is finding.

While machine learning methods were overall the most successful, for time expression identification, the submitted rule-based systems achieved the best recall. This is counter to the usual assumption that rule-based systems will be more precise, and that machine learning systems will sacrifice precision to increase recall. The difference is likely that the rule-based systems were aiming for good coverage, trying to find all potential time expressions, but had too few constraints to discard such phrases in inappropriate contexts. The baseline system is suggestive of this possibility: it has a constraint to only memorize phrases that corresponded with time expressions more than 50% of the time, and it has high precision (0.743) and low recall (0.372) as is typically expected of a rule-based system, but if the constraint is removed, it has low precision (0.126) and high recall (0.521) like the participant rule-based systems.

Clinical TempEval was the first TempEval exercise to use narrative containers, a significant shift from prior exercises. Annotator agreement in the dataset is moderate, but needs to be further improved. Similar agreement scores were found when annotating temporal relations in prior corpora (for TempEval or using TimeML), although these typically involved the application of more complex temporal relation ontologies. The narrative container approach is comparatively simple. The low annotator-adjudicator scores (i.e. below 0.90, a score generally recognized to indicate a production-quality resource) suggests that annotation is difficult independent of the number of potential temporal relation types. Difficulty may lie in the comprehension and reification of the potentially complex temporal structures described in natural language text. Nevertheless, systems did well on the DCT task, achieving high scores – similar to the pattern seen in Task D of TempEval-2, which had a comparable scoring metric.

Though the results of Clinical TempEval 2015 are encouraging, they were limited somewhat by the small number of participants in the task. There are two likely reasons for this. First, there were many different sub-tasks for Clinical TempEval, meaning that to compete in all sub-tasks, a large number of sub-systems had to be developed in a limited amount of time (six months or less). This relatively high barrier for entry meant that of the 15 research groups that managed to sign a data use agreement and obtain the data before the competition, only 3 submitted systems to compete. Second, the data use agreement process was time consuming, and more than 10 research groups who began the data use agreement process were unable to complete it before the evaluation.

In future iterations of Clinical TempEval, we expect these issues to be reduced. The next Clinical TempEval will use the current Train and Dev data as the training set, and as these data are already available, this leaves research teams with a year or more to develop systems. Furthermore, arrangements with the Mayo Clinic have been made to further expedite the data use agreement process, which should significantly reduce the wait time for new participants.

Acknowledgements

This work was partially supported by funding from R01LM010090 (THYME) from the National Library of Medicine and from the European Union's Seventh Framework Programme (grant No. 611233, PHEME).

References

Wei-Te Chen and Will Styler. 2013. Anafora: A web-based general purpose annotation tool. In *Proceedings of the 2013 NAACL HLT Demonstration Session*, pages 14–19, Atlanta, Georgia, June.

James Pustejovsky and Amber Stubbs. 2011. Increasing informativeness in temporal annotation. In *Proceedings of the 5th Linguistic Annotation Workshop*, pages 152–160, Portland, Oregon, USA, June.

William F. Styler, IV, Steven Bethard, Sean Finan, Martha Palmer, Sameer Pradhan, Piet de Groen, Brad Erickson, Timothy Miller, Chen Lin, Guergana Savova, and James Pustejovsky. 2014a. Temporal annotation in the clinical domain. *Transactions of the Association for Computational Linguistics*, 2:143–154.

William F. Styler, IV, Guergana Savova, Martha Palmer, James Pustejovsky, Tim O'Gorman, and Piet C. de Groen. 2014b. THYME annotation guidelines, 2.

Weiyi Sun, Anna Rumshisky, and Ozlem Uzuner. 2013. Evaluating temporal relations in clinical text: 2012 i2b2 challenge. *Journal of the American Medical Informatics Association*, 20(5):806–813.

Naushad UzZaman and James Allen. 2011. Temporal evaluation. In *Proceedings of the 49th Annual Meeting of the Association for Computational Linguistics: Human Language Technologies*, pages 351–356, Portland, Oregon, USA, June.

Naushad UzZaman, Hector Llorens, Leon Derczynski, James Allen, Marc Verhagen, and James Pustejovsky. 2013. SemEval-2013 Task 1: TempEval-3: Evaluating Time Expressions, Events, and Temporal Relations. In *Second Joint Conference on Lexical and Computational Semantics (*SEM), Volume 2: Proceedings of the Seventh International Workshop on Semantic Evaluation (SemEval 2013)*, pages 1–9, Atlanta, Georgia, USA, June.

Marc Verhagen, Robert Gaizauskas, Frank Schilder, Mark Hepple, Graham Katz, and James Pustejovsky. 2007. SemEval-2007 Task 15: TempEval Temporal Relation

Identification. In *Proceedings of the Fourth International Workshop on Semantic Evaluations (SemEval-2007)*, pages 75–80, Prague, Czech Republic, June.

Marc Verhagen, Roser Sauri, Tommaso Caselli, and James Pustejovsky. 2010. SemEval-2010 Task 13: TempEval-2. In *Proceedings of the 5th International Workshop on Semantic Evaluation*, pages 57–62, Uppsala, Sweden, July.

BluLab: Temporal Information Extraction for the 2015 Clinical TempEval Challenge

Sumithra Velupillai[1,2], Danielle L Mowery[2], Samir Abdelrahman[2], Lee Christensen[2] and Wendy W Chapman[2]
[1]Dept. of Computer and Systems Sciences (DSV)
Stockholm University, Sweden
[2]Department of Biomedical Informatics
University of Utah, Salt Lake City
sumithra@dsv.su.se, {firstname.lastname}@utah.edu

Abstract

The 2015 Clinical TempEval Challenge addressed the problem of temporal reasoning in the clinical domain by providing an annotated corpus of pathology and clinical notes related to colon cancer patients. The challenge consisted of six subtasks: TIMEX3 and event span detection, TIMEX3 and event attribute classification, document relation time and narrative container relation classification. Our BluLab team participated in all six subtasks. For the TIMEX3 and event subtasks, we developed a ClearTK support vector machine pipeline using mainly simple lexical features along with information from rule-based systems. For the relation subtasks, we employed a conditional random fields classification approach, with input from a rule-based system for the narrative container relation subtask. Our team ranked first for all TIMEX3 and event subtasks, as well as for the document relation subtask.

1 Introduction

Temporal information extraction plays a crucial role in improved information access, in particular for creating timelines and detailed question answering. Several previous natural language processing (NLP) research community challenges have dealt with temporal reasoning in the newswire domain (Verhagen et al., 2010; UzZaman et al., 2013) and the clinical domain (Sun et al., 2013).

The 2015 Clinical TempEval challenge (Bethard et al., 2015) addressed temporal reasoning subtasks similar to these previous efforts by providing a new benchmark corpus in the clinical domain with annotated pathology and clinical notes from colon cancer patients. The corpus is annotated with a modified version of the TimeML schema (Pustejovsky et al., 2010), where adaptations specific to this domain have been developed (Styler et al., 2014).

For successful temporal modelling, three core concepts need to be defined: **temporal expressions (TIMEX3)**, *denoting time references like dates*; **events (EVENT)**, *denoting salient occurrences*; and **temporal relations (TLINK)** *denoting order (e.g. before, after) between an event and/or TIMEX3.*

As part of the 2012 i2b2/VA Challenge, the best performing systems for classification of TIMEX3 (F1: 0.66), EVENTS (F1: 0.92), their attributes (average accuracy: 0.86) and TLINKS (F1: 0.69) applied regular expressions as well as machine learning approaches such as conditional random fields (CRF) and support vector machines (SVM) (Sun et al., 2013). For the 2013/2014 CLEF/ShARe Challenges, the best approaches for strict information extraction (F1: detection and accuracy: normalization) of TIMEXs (0.287 F1 and 0.354 accuracy), disease/disorder EVENTS (0.750 F1 and 0.589 accuracy), and EVENT attributes (0.676 F1 and 0.868 accuracy) leveraged the Apache cTAKES (Savova et al., 2010) framework, Begin-Inside-Outside (BIO) tagging, and CRF and SVM for (Pradhan et al., 2015; Mowery et al., 2014).

The 2015 Clinical TempEval consisted of six subtasks related to these core concepts: TIMEX3 span (TS) and attribute (TA) classification, EVENT span (ES) and attribute (EA) classification, document creation time (DR) and narrative container (CR) relations. Our team participated in all six subtasks, with the aim of benchmarking existing tools and methods on this corpus for further development of semantic processing of clinical notes. In this paper, we describe our system, its results, and an error analysis for each of the challenge subtasks.

2 Methods

We received 293 training reports for system development and 147 testing reports for blind system evaluation. For all subtasks, we extracted morphological (lemma), lexical (tokens), and syntactic (part-of-speech) features encoded from cTAKES. In the following sections, we enumerate additional subtask-specific features from various NLP systems used to train supervised learning (combined with rule-based in some cases) approaches for each subtask.

2.1 TIMEX3, EVENTS, and their Attributes

A UIMA pipeline using ClearTK (Bethard et al., 2014) was built for the subtasks TS, TA, ES and EA, using SVM classifiers (Liblinear) with parameters (C-value) set manually using a grid search. For TS, a separate classifier was built for each TA type using simple lexical features (the token itself in full and without its ending (2 characters), part-of-speech tag, numeric type, capital type, lower case, surrounding tokens) and gazetteer information based partly on an adapted version of HeidelTime (Strötgen and Gertz, 2013). Each token was classified as either B (Begin), I (Inside) or O (Outside) using the ClearTK BIO-chunking representation. Slightly different context window sizes and gazetteer information were employed for each TA value. For ES, one classifier was built for classifying tokens using the same BIO-chunking representation, employing similar lexical features and a context window size of ± 2, as well as a chunk type feature, followed by separate classifiers for each EA value. The values for TA and EA can be found in Table 1.

For EA, we used lexical features (similar to those used for TS and ES) along with new features from the pyConText system (Chapman et al., 2011). For each non-default EA, we evaluated the predictiveness of each cue from the pyConText linguistic knowledge base on the training set to determine its association. For example, the "denies" predicts **polarity**: NEG. We eliminated cues that were not relevant for the task e.g., **experiencer**. We then conducted an error analysis on the training data for missed cues and added them to the existing knowledge base for final evaluation. These cues were provided to the SVM model in addition to section information and previous EA assignments for each ES. For TA and EA, we used adapted versions of pyConText and HeidelTime as baselines.

Attribute	Potential Values
TA: **type**	*DATE, TIME, DURATION, QUANTIFIER, PREPOSTEXP or SET
EA: **modality**	*ACTUAL, HEDGED, HYPOTHETICAL or GENERIC
EA: **degree**	*N/A, MOST or LITTLE
EA: **polarity**	*POS or NEG
EA: **type**	*N/A, ASPECTUAL or EVIDENTIAL

Table 1: Possible values for TIMEX3 attributes (TA) and event attributes (EA). *default majority value.

2.2 DocTimeRel and Contains Relations

The challenge relation classification task consisted of two subtasks: DocTimeRel (DR) and narrative container relation (CR). For DR, the task was defined to identify 4 classes: before, after, overlap, and before/overlap which describe the relation between the event mentioned in the document and the related document time. For CR, the task was defined for the contains class to recognize whether one event/time mention in the document contains or is contained by another.

We used token-level features for each sentence. We parsed the cTAKES output to extract the following features: a binary feature indicating if the token is the first token in the sentence, the token lemma and normalization forms, its type of token (word/punctuation/symbol/number/contraction) and if it was tagged as any of the following semantic types by cTAKES: medical, procedure, anatomical site, sign/symptom, disease/disorder, and concept. We also added a feature indicating whether the token was part of an event mention, a time mention, or none of these, extracted from the predictions (phase 1 in the challenge) or the gold annotations (phase 2).

We used CRF++[1] for the DR task using the aforementioned features along with a window of ± 5 tokens for each feature as contextual features. For the CR task, we aimed at integrating machine learning (ML) and rule-based techniques as a potential solution. The search space was limited to three event or time mentions in ascending sequential order from the text to classify CR between two mentions. We used CRF++ again for the machine learning part, with the same token features as for DR. If two adjacent mentions were located in separate sentences, we merged the sentences to one.

For the rule-based part, we used the Moonstone system. Moonstone is a language processing tool which uses both a semantic grammar, and a rule engine which can take as input (among other things) the output of its grammatical parser (Christensen and Chapman, 2015). We situated Moonstone in a UIMA pipeline, along with the ClearTK predictions for TS, TA, ES, and EA, to recognize potential instances of the contains relation, using two rules which can be paraphrased in English as follows:

- If a DATE annotation initiates a sentence, and an EVENT annotation occurs anywhere in the following three sentences, with no intervening DATE mention, then infer a CR between the two.
- If two EVENT annotations appear within a sentence, and one appears commonly as the first argument in the training annotations denoting the contains relation, and the second commonly appears as the second contains argument in the training annotations, then infer a CR between the two.

Finally, to integrate both techniques, we conducted three runs. The first run (V1) was based entirely on the ML solution. In the second run (V2), we added the mentions extracted from the Moonstone rules to the V1 search space. In the third run (V3), we started with the mentions extracted from the Moonstone rules as an initial search space, then, we added pairs randomly from the first run such that each mention had maximum 3 nearest mentions including those of the Moonstone rules (if any).

[1]http://crfpp.googlecode.com/svn/trunk/doc/index.html, accessed Jan. 26 2015

Subtask	**P**	**R**	**F1**
TS	0.788	0.669	0.724
TS (b)	0.549	0.654	0.597
TA: **type**	0.772	0.658	0.710
TA (b): **type**	0.549	0.654	0.597
ES (*)	0.886	0.867	0.876
EA: **modality**	0.883	0.872	0.877
EA (b):**modality**	0.744	0.734	0.739
EA: **degree**	0.946	0.933	0.940
EA (b): **degree**	0.854	0.842	0.848
EA: **polarity**	0.931	0.919	0.925
EA (b): **polarity**	0.930	0.917	0.923
EA: **type**	0.894	0.883	0.888
EA (b): **type**	0.814	0.803	0.809

Table 2: Training set results for TIMEX3 span (TS), and attributes (TA), event span (ES), and attributes (EA). (b) = baseline. (*) For ES, no rule-based method was used as baseline, only different feature settings in ClearTK.

Subtask	**P**	**R**	**F1**
TS	0.797	0.664	0.725
TA: **type**	0.778	0.652	0.709
ES	0.887	0.864	0.875
EA: **modality**	0.834	0.813	0.824
EA: **degree**	0.882	0.859	0.870
EA: **polarity**	0.868	0.846	0.857
EA: **type**	0.834	0.812	0.823

Table 3: Test set results for TIMEX3 spans (TS), attributes (TA), event spans (ES), and attributes (EA).

3 Results

We present results on the training data and the final results on the test set for all challenge subtasks.

In Table 2, results on the training data for the TIMEX3 (TS, TA) and EVENT (ES, EA) tasks are shown, for the final ClearTK models that were used for system submission, as well as baseline results using adapted versions of pyConText and HeidelTime. The ClearTK modules resulted in improved performance for all subtasks. Final results on the test set are shown in Table 3.

For the relation subtasks DocTimeRel (DR) and narrative containers (CR), results on the training data are shown in Tables 4 and 5. For testing, two phases were provided in the challenge: one where

Subtask	P	R	F1
DR: **before**	0.814	0.801	0.807
DR: **overlap**	0.836	0.818	0.827
DR: **before-overlap**	0.745	0.736	0.740
DR: **after**	0.808	0.796	0.802
Overall	0.801	0.788	0.794

Table 4: Results for all relation types (before, overlap, before-overlap, after) for Document relation time (DR) on the training data.

Subtask	P	R	F1
CR: V1	0.118	0.124	0.121
CR: V2	0.142	0.266	0.185
CR: V3	0.160	0.176	0.168

Table 5: Results for the Contains relation (CR) on the training data. V# indicates the run.

only plain text was given (#1), and one where gold TIMEX3 and event annotations were given (#2). For CR, final results were calculated with or without closure. In Table 6 final results on the two relation tasks are shown.

Phase	Subtask	P	R	F1
1	DR	0.712	0.693	0.702
	CR V1	0.100	0.099	0.100
	CR V2	0.094	0.179	0.123
	CR V3	0.090	0.103	0.096
2	DR	-	-	0.791
	CR V1	0.117	0.128	0.123
	CR V2	0.140	0.254	0.181
	CR V3	0.150	0.155	0.153

Table 6: Results for DocTimeRel (DR) and narrative container relations (CR) on the test set. During Phase 1, only text was provided, while in Phase 2 manual EVENT and TIMEX3 annotations were provided. V# indicates the run. Results for CR are reported with closure.

4 Discussion

Our team had the highest F1 on all TIMEX3, EVENT and DR subtasks in the 2015 Clinical TempEval challenge. Similar to other best performing systems in previous temporal modelling challenges, we applied CRF, SVM, and rule-based approaches, using mostly simple features.

We observed moderate recall for TS which can be attributed to missing words ("perioperative") and span errors (e.g. "early July" (gold) vs. "early July apparently" (system)). TA values with very few training examples (e.g. **type**: TIME) were difficult for both approaches, with the exception of PREPOSTEXP, which resulted in high F1 on the training data. For ES, spanning issues were not the source for errors as much as for TS. Most errors were due to previously unseen words or contexts. For different EA types, rare classes were problematic, e.g. **degree**: LITTLE and MOST, but also distinguishing subtle differences between **modality**: GENERIC, HEDGED, and HYPOTHETICAL values.

In the DR subtask, we achieved high precision, recall, and F1 using simple cTAKES features. Careful analysis of our outputs revealed that some events have similar features with different relation classes. Moreover, in some cases, the **before-overlap** class was mistakenly recognized as **before** or **overlap** which degraded the overall recognition performance.

In the CR task, our second run (V2) performed best overall, indicating that a combination of machine learning and rule-based approaches is useful for this task. The main limitation of our approach is to use exhaustive (blind) search to extract possible pair relations. This results in many false positives and decreases the overall performance. Also, Moonstone rules are still under development, and will be further analyzed to increase accuracy.

Our aim was to benchmark existing tools and methods on this corpus. Adaptations of rule-based systems such as pyConText and HeidelTime proved insufficient on their own for the event and TIMEX3 subtasks compared to machine-learning based approaches, but were useful as feature input. Simple lexical features and cTAKES outputs were useful for the SVM and CRF classification approaches on the different subtasks. The narrative container relation is a very challenging task, requiring further feature engineering and analysis. We plan to further investigate and develop solutions where machine learning and rule-based approaches are combined, and to evaluate performance on other similar corpora.

Acknowledgments

The authors wish to thank the Mayo clinic and the 2015 Clinical TempEval challenge organizers for providing access to the clinical corpus. This work was partially funded by Swedish Research Council (350-2012-6658) and NLM R01 LM010964.

References

Steven Bethard, Philip Ogren, and Lee Becker. 2014. ClearTK 2.0: Design Patterns for Machine Learning in UIMA. In *Proceedings of the Ninth International Conference on Language Resources and Evaluation (LREC'14)*, pages 3289–3293, Reykjavik, Iceland, May.

Steven Bethard, Leon Derczynski, James Pustejovsky, and Marc Verhagen. 2015. Semeval-2015 task 6: Clinical tempeval. In *Proceedings of the 9th International Workshop on Semantic Evaluation (SemEval 2015)*.

Brian E Chapman, Sean Lee, Hyunseok P Kang, and Wendy W Chapman. 2011. Document-level classification of CT pulmonary angiography reports based on an extension of the ConText algorithm. *J Biomed Inform*, 44(5):728–737.

Lee Christensen and Wendy W. Chapman. 2015. Moonstone. Manuscript in preparation.

Danielle Mowery, Sumithra Velupillai, Brett R. South, Lee Christensen, David Martinez, Liadh Kelly, Lorraine Goeuriot, Noemie Elhadad, Sameer Pradhad, Guergana Savova, and Wendy W. Chapman. 2014. Task 2: ShARe/CLEF eHealth Evaluation Lab 2014. In *CEUR Workshop Proceedings on CLEF 2014*, volume 1180, pages 31–42.

Sameer Pradhan, Noemie Elhadad, Brett R South, David Martinez, Lee Christensen, Amy Vogel, Hanna Suominen, Wendy W Chapman, and Guergana Savova. 2015. Evaluating the State of the Art in Disorder Recognition and Normalization of the Clinical Narrative. *J Am Med Inform Assoc.*, 22:143–154.

James Pustejovsky, Kiyong Lee, Harry Bunt, and Laurent Romary. 2010. ISO-TimeML: An International Standard for Semantic Annotation. In *Proceedings of the Seventh International Conference on Language Resources and Evaluation (LREC'10)*, pages 394–397, Valletta, Malta, May.

Guergana K Savova, James J Masanz, Phillip V Ogren, Jiaping Zheng, Sunghwan Sohn, Karin C Kipper-Schuler, and Christopher G Chute. 2010. Mayo clinical Text Analysis and Knowledge Extraction System (cTAKES): architecture, component evaluation and applications. *J Am Med Inform Assoc.*, 17(5):507–513.

Jannik Strötgen and Michael Gertz. 2013. Multilingual and Cross-domain Temporal Tagging. *Language Resources and Evaluation*, 47(2):269–298.

William IV Styler, Steven Bethard, Sean Finan, Martha Palmer, Sameer Pradhan, Piet de Groen, Brad Erickson, Timothy Miller, Chen Lin, Guergana Savova, and James Pustejovsky. 2014. Temporal Annotation in the Clinical Domain. *Transactions of the Association for Computational Linguistics*, 2:143–154.

Weiyi Sun, Anna Rumshisky, and Özlem Uzuner. 2013. Evaluating temporal relations in clinical text: 2012 i2b2 Challenge. *JAMIA*, 20(5):806–813.

Naushad UzZaman, Hector Llorens, Leon Derczynski, James Allen, Marc Verhagen, and James Pustejovsky. 2013. SemEval-2013 Task 1: TempEval-3: Evaluating Time Expressions, Events, and Temporal Relations. In *Second Joint Conference on Lexical and Computational Semantics (*SEM), Volume 2: Proceedings of the Seventh International Workshop on Semantic Evaluation (SemEval 2013)*, pages 1–9, Atlanta, Georgia, USA, June.

Marc Verhagen, Roser Saurí, Tommaso Caselli, and James Pustejovsky. 2010. SemEval-2010 Task 13: TempEval-2. In *Proceedings of the 5th International Workshop on Semantic Evaluation*, SemEval '10, pages 57–62, Stroudsburg, PA, USA.

GPLSIUA: Combining Temporal Information and Topic Modeling for Cross-Document Event Ordering

Borja Navarro-Colorado and Estela Saquete
Natural Language Processing Group
University of Alicante
Alicante, Spain
borja@dlsi.ua.es, stela@dlsi.ua.es

Abstract

Building unified timelines from a collection of written news articles requires cross-document event coreference resolution and temporal relation extraction. In this paper we present an approach event coreference resolution according to: a) similar temporal information, and b) similar semantic arguments. Temporal information is detected using an automatic temporal information system (TIPSem), while semantic information is represented by means of LDA Topic Modeling. The evaluation of our approach shows that it obtains the highest Micro-average F-score results in the SemEval-2015 Task 4: "TimeLine: Cross-Document Event Ordering" (25.36% for TrackB, 23.15% for SubtrackB), with an improvement of up to 6% in comparison to the other systems. However, our experiment also showed some drawbacks in the Topic Modeling approach that degrades performance of the system.

1 Introduction

Since access to knowledge is crucial in any domain, connecting and time-ordering the information extracted from different documents is a very important task. The goal of this paper is therefore to build ordered timelines for a set of events related to a target entity. In doing so, our approach is dealing with two problems: a) cross-document event coreference resolution and b) cross-document temporal relation extraction.

In order to arrange event mentions in a timeline it is necessary to know which event mentions co-refer to the same event or fact and occur at the same moment. Our approach attempts to formalize the idea that two or more event mentions co-refer if they have not only temporal compatibility (the events occur at the same time) but also semantic compatibility (the event mentions refers to the same facts, location, entities, etc.).

Of a set of event mentions in one or more texts, our proposal groups together the event mentions that (i) have the same or a similar temporal reference, (ii) have the same or a similar event head word, and (iii) whose main arguments refer to the same or similar topics. In order to evaluate the system, we have participated in the SemEval-2015 Task 4 "TimeLine: Cross-Document Event Ordering".

In the following sections we will present the theoretical background to our approach (section 2) and the main technical aspects (sections 3 and 4). Then we will present the results obtained (section 5) and some conclusions.

2 Background

Two or more event mentions co-refer when they refer to the same real fact or event. Two events can denote the same fact whereas the linguistic mentions have a different syntax structure, different words, or even a different meaning. Whatever the case may be, both event mentions must be semantically related.

An event mention is formed of an event head (usually a verb or a deverbal noun) that is related to a semantic structure (linguistically represented as an argument structure with an agent, patient, theme, instrument, etc., that is, the semantic roles) in which there are some event participants (entities) and which is located in place and time (Levin and Rappaport-Hovav, 2005; Hovav et al., 2010). The meaning of an event mention is therefore not only the meaning of the event head, but also the compositional meaning of all the components and their relations: head, participants, time, place, etc.

In order to detect this semantic relation between event mentions, previous papers have isolated the main components of the event structure. For instance, Cybulska and Vossen (2013) apply an event model based on four components: location, time, participant and action. Moreover, with regard to temporal information, only explicit temporal expressions that appears in the text are considered, but no temporal information is inferred by navigating temporal links. Bejan and Harabagiu (2014) use a rich set of linguistic features to model the event structure, including lexical features such as head word and lemmas, class features such as PoS or event class, semantic features such as WordNet sense or semantic roles frames, etc. They use an unsupervised approach based on a non-parametrical Bayesian model.

3 Our Approach

In our approach we represent each event mention as a head word (the event tag in the TimeML (Saurí et al., 2006) annotation scheme) related to a temporal expression (implicit or explicit), a set of entities (0 or more), and a set of topics that represents what the event mention is referring to. This paper is focused on temporal information processing and topic-based semantic representation.

3.1 Temporal Information Processing

The TimeML (Saurí et al., 2006) annotation scheme has now been adopted as a standard by a large number of researchers in the field of temporal information annotation. It represents not only events and temporal expressions, but also links (Pustejovsky et al., 2003)

A manual annotation of event mentions and the DCT of texts have been considered as an input of the system, and an automatic system has been used to perform the annotation with temporal expressions and temporal links in order to be able to establish a complete timeline of the input texts. If a plain text is considered, systems such TIPSem (Temporal Information Processing using Semantics) (Llorens et al., 2013; Llorens et al., 2012)[1] are able to automatically annotate all the temporal expressions (TIMEX3), events (EVENT) and links between them.

Once the temporal links have been established, all the specific temporal information for each event is inferred by means of temporal links navigation. This information allows us to determine temporal compatibility between all the events considered.

3.2 Topic-based Semantic Representation

The meaning of each event structure has been represented by using Topic Modeling (Blei, 2012) on a reference corpus. Topic modeling is a family of algorithms that automatically discover topics from a collection of documents. More specifically, we apply the Latent Dirichlet Allocation (LDA) (Blei et al., 2003), which follows a bottom up approach. Each word is assigned to a topic according to the co-ocurrence words in the context (document) and the topics assigned to this word in other documents. In formal terms, a topic is a distribution on a fixed vocabulary.

We have applied the LDA to the WikiNews corpus.[2] Each topic in this corpus is represented using the twenty most prominent words.

4 Architecture of the System

Our approach to build timelines from written news in English implies event coreference resolution by applying three cluster processes in sequential order: a temporal cluster, a lemma cluster, and a topic cluster. It combines various resources:

- Named entity recognition, using OpeNER web services.[3]
- TimeML automatic annotation of texts using TipSEM system (Llorens et al., 2010).
- The NLTK[4] verb lemmatizer based on WordNet (Fellbaum, 1998).
- The SENNA (Collobert et al., 2011) Semantic Roles Labeling.

[1] http://gplsi.dlsi.ua.es/demos/TIMEE/

[2] https://dumps.wikimedia.org/enwikinews/

[3] http://www.opener-project.eu/webservices/

[4] http://www.nltk.org/

- The LDA Topic Modeling algorithm, using MALLET (McCallum, 2002).

4.1 Target Entity Filtering

If the target entity filtering is to be performed then it is first necessary to resolve the named entity recognition and coreference resolution. This is done by integrating the external OpeNER web services into our proposal. More specifically, the components applied in our proposal are the NER component,[5] which identifies the names of people, cities, and museums, and classifies them in a semantic class (PERSON, LOCATION, etc.) and the coreference resolution component,[6] whose objective is to identify all those words that refers to the same object or entity.

Only those events that are part of sentences containing the target entity or a coreference entity of the target will be selected for the final timeline.

4.2 Temporal Clustering Approach

A plain text was considered and we use the TIPSem system to automatically annotate all the temporal expressions (TIMEX3), events (EVENT) and links between them. The TLINKS annotated in the text are used in order to extract the time context of each event and make it possible to infer both time at which each event occurs and the temporal ordering between the events in the text. Moreover, if we are able to determine the time of the event, we will be able to determine temporal compatibility between events, even when they are contained in different documents, thus signifying that cross-document event coreference resolution is also possible.

In this first step, all the events from the different documents that occurring on the same date will therefore be part of the same cluster. The clusters are positioned in ascending ordered based on the date assigned.

4.3 Semantic Clustering Based on Lemmas

Once all the events that share temporal information and the target entity have been grouped together, we apply a simple clustering based on head word lemmas. This lemma-based clustering groups together all event mentions with the same head word lemma, the same temporal information and the same target entity. We therefore assume that all these event mentions corefer to the same event. This is our Run 1 at the competition.

4.4 Semantic Clustering Based on Topics

The problem of the lemma-based cluster is that it does not take into account the argument structure of the event. This last clustering therefore attempts to solve this problem by extracting the semantic roles from each event and representing their meaning by using topics on a reference corpus. This approach has three steps:

1. Using SENNA (Collobert et al., 2011) as Semantic Roles Labeling, we have detected roles A0 and A1.[7] which are related to the event mention head word. For each role we extract only the nouns.
2. We have extracted 500 topics from WikiNews using Topic Modeling with MALLET. All these topics are used as a knowledge base. We will use only the most representative words for each topic (the twenty words with the greatest weight) and the weights that they have in each topic.
3. Finally, we have created an event-topic matrix. Each event (raws) is represented by a vector. The values of the vector are the addition of weights of each argument noun in each topic (columns).

For example, if the nouns in arguments A0 and A1 are "users, problems, phones", we represent their meanings according to the topics t_n assigned to them by applying LDA to WikiNews ($user = t_0, t_3, t_5$, $problems = t_0, t_2$, $phones = t_5, t_6$, etc). Then, the event e of this sentence is represented by a n-dimensional vector in which n is the amount of topics (500) and whoses values are the addition of weight of each noun in each topic T_n.

In order to group together similar event mentions, we have applied a k-means clustering algorithm to these event vectors.[8] The distance metric used has

[5] http://opener.olery.com/ner

[6] http://opener.olery.com/coreference

[7] In order to represent Semantic Roles, SENNA uses the tag set proposed by Proposition Bank Project (http://verbs.colorado.edu/~mpalmer/projects/ace.html) A0 and A1 represent the main roles related to each verb.

[8] Note that it has been applied only to the events previously clustered following the lema-based approach (Run 1).

been Euclidean Distance. The number of cluster has been adjusted to two.[9] Therefore, each cluster with the same head word lemma, the same temporal information and the same target entity is then reclustered according to the similarity of the main topics of its arguments. This cluster corresponds to our Run 2 at the competition.

5 Evaluation Results

SemEval-2015 Task 4 consists on building timelines from written news in English in which a target entity is involved. The input data provided by the organizers is therefore a set of documents and a set of target entities related to those documents. Two different tracks are proposed in the task, along with their subtracks:

- Track A: This consists of using raw texts as input and obtaining full timelines. Subtrack A has the same input data, but the output will be the timeLines of only ordered events (no assignment of time anchors).
- Track B: This consists of using texts with manual annotation of events mentions as input data. Subtrack B has the same input data but the output will be timeLines of only ordered events.

In the Semeval-2015 Task 4 competition we have participated in Track B and Subtrack B. The results for the Micro-average F-score measure obtained by our approach in the competition are shown in Table 1.

TRACK	Corpus1	Corpus2	Corpus3	Total
TrackB-R1	22.35	19.28	33.59	**25.36**
TrackB-R2	20.47	16.17	29.90	**22.66**
SubTrackB-R1	18.35	20.48	32.08	**23.15**
SubTrackB-R2	15.93	14.44	27.48	**19.18**

Table 1: Results for GPLSIUA Approach.

Although the Micro-FScore results are not very high, the results obtained by our approach are the highest in all of the corpus evaluated by the organizers. Our approach obtained an improvement of 7% compared with the other participant in Track B and a 6.48% in Subtrack B.

[9]We have used PyCluster tool: `https://pypi.python.org/pypi/Pycluster`

6 Conclusions

The results show that our approach is suitable for the task in hand. On the one hand, temporal information is automatically extracted with a temporal information processing system which makes it possible to infer and determine the time at which each event has occurred. On the other hand, the semantic similarity based on the verb is sufficient to group together coreferent events.

The basic method (Run 1), consisting of searching for similar verb lemma, eventually proved to be the best. We have therefore carried out an in-depth analysis of the results obtained for Run 2 and have observed three main drawbacks in the Topic Modeling approach:

- The K-means algorithm forces us to fix the number of clusters beforehand, and this has been fixed at 2. However, there is often only one correct cluster. Another approach without a fixed number of topics will improve the approach. Bejan and Harabagiu (2014), for example, suggest inferring this value from data.
- The representativity of each event mention depends directly on the amount of topics extracted from the reference corpus. Many topics will produce excessive granularity, and few topics will be unrepresentative. We have set the number of topics at 500, but it is necessary to study whether another amount of topics will improve the results.
- This approach depends excessively on the representativity of the reference corpus. We believe using larger corpora should improve the results.

As Future work, we plan to use other similarity measures and clustering algorithms in an attempt to solve the problem of previously fixed number of clusters. We also plan to evaluate using different Topic Modeling configurations.

Acknowledgments

We would like to thank the anonymous reviewers for their helpful suggestions and comments. Paper partially supported by the following projects: ATTOS (TIN2012-38536-C03-03), LEGOLANG-UAGE (TIN2012-31224), SAM (FP7-611312), FIRST (FP7-287607) DIIM2.0 (PROMETEOII/2014/001)

References

Cosmin Adrian Bejan and Sanda Harabagiu. 2014. Unsupervised Event Coreference Resolution. *Computational Linguistics*, 40(2):311–347.

David M Blei, Andrew Y Ng, and Michael I Jordan. 2003. Latent Dirichlet Allocation. *Journal of Machine Learning Research*, 3:993–1022.

David M Blei. 2012. Probabilistic Topic Models. *Communications of the ACM*, 55(4):77–84.

Ronan Collobert, Jason Weston, Léon Bottou, Michael Karlenand Koray Kavukcuoglu, and Pavel Kuksa. 2011. Natural Language Processing (Almost) from Scratch. *Journal of Machine Learning Research*, pages 41–71.

Agata Cybulska and Piek Vossen. 2013. Semantic relations between events and their time, locations and participants for event coreference resolution. In *RANLP*.

Christiane Fellbaum. 1998. *WordNet: An Electronic Lexical Database (Language, Speech, and Communication)*. MIT Press.

Malka Rappaport Hovav, Edit Doron, and Ivy Sichel. 2010. *Lexical Semantics, Syntax, and Event Structure*. Oxford University Press, Oxford.

Beth Levin and Malka Rappaport-Hovav. 2005. *Argument realization*. Cambridge University Press, Cambridge.

Hector Llorens, Estela Saquete, and Borja Navarro-Colorado. 2010. TIPSem (English and Spanish): Evaluating CRFs and Semantic Roles in TempEval-2. In *Proceedings of the 5th International Workshop on Semantic Evaluation*.

Hector Llorens, Estela Saquete, and Borja Navarro-Colorado. 2012. Automatic System for Identifying and Categorizing Temporal Relations in Natural Language. *International Journal of Intelligent Systems*, 27(7):680–703.

Hector Llorens, Estela Saquete, and Borja Navarro-Colorado. 2013. Applying Semantic Knowledge to the Automatic Processing of Temporal Expressions and Events in Natural Language. *Information Processing & Management*, 49(1):179–197.

Andrew Kachites McCallum. 2002. Mallet: A machine learning for language toolkit. http://mallet.cs.umass.edu.

James Pustejovsky, José M. Castaño, Robert Ingria, Roser Saurí, Robert Gaizauskas, Andrea Setzer, and Graham Katz. 2003. TimeML: Robust Specification of Event and Temporal Expressions in Text. In *IWCS-5*.

Roser Saurí, Jessica Littman, Robert Knippen, Robert Gaizauskas, Andrea Setzer, and James Pustejovsky, 2006. *TimeML Annotation Guidelines 1.2.1 (http://www.timeml.org/)*.

HeidelToul: A Baseline Approach for Cross-document Event Ordering

Bilel Moulahi[1,3*] and **Jannik Strötgen**[2] and **Michael Gertz**[2] and **Lynda Tamine**[1]
[1] IRIT, University of Toulouse Paul Sabatier, France
[2] Institute of Computer Science, Heidelberg University, Germany
[3] Faculty of Science of Tunis, University of Tunis El-Manar, Tunisia
{bilel.moulahi,lynda.lechani}@irit.fr
{stroetgen,gertz}@informatik.uni-heidelberg.de

Abstract

In this paper, we give an overview of our participation in the timeline generation task of SemEval-2015 (task 4, TimeLine: Cross-Document Event Ordering). The main goals of this new track are, given a collection of news articles and a so-called target entity, to determine events that are relevant for the entity, to resolve event coreferences, and to order the events chronologically. We addressed the sub-tasks, in which event mentions were provided, i.e., no additional event extraction was required. For this, we developed an ad-hoc approach based on a temporal tagger and a coreference resolution tool for entities. After determining relevant sentences, relevant events are extracted and anchored on a timeline. The evaluation conducted on three collections of news articles shows that our approach – despite its simplicity – achieves reasonable results and opens several promising issues for future work.

1 Introduction

Due to the tremendous amount of documents being constantly published on the Internet, there is a need for more enhanced search facilities to retrieve relevant information. Consider, for example, a user looking for information about the "Golden Globe Awards". It might be possible that the user's information need is about the recent "72nd edition". However, it is also reasonable to assume that the user would appreciate relevant information about previous editions. Thus, presenting search results for time- and event-sensitive information needs in the form of a complete and updatable timeline would be a promising approach. While this issue is tackled by some applications, early techniques required manual effort (Shahar and Musen, 1992) and recent approaches rely on heavily structured information such as Google's entity-related search results, which are based on Google's knowledge graph (Singhal, 2012). However, instead of listing only structured knowledge on a timeline, e.g., winners of the 71st Golden Globes in our example, search results would become much more valuable when adding temporally anchored event information extracted from text documents (e.g., recent updates about the event).

In the SemEval task 4,[1] the goal is to detect all events in a document collection that are relevant for a target entity, and to anchor these events on a timeline. Thus, events are to be sorted chronologically, and, if possible, specific dates are to be assigned to the events. As in previous SemEval tasks addressing temporal relation extraction, namely in the TempEval series (see, e.g., Verhagen et al., 2010), the TimeML event definition is used. However, a special focus is now put on the cross-document aspect, i.e., on cross-document event coreference resolution and cross-document temporal relation extraction. While the document collection contains news articles, target entities can be persons, organizations, products, or financial entities.

The organizers offered the task in two tracks. While the final goals of timeline construction are

*The work was done during an internship at Heidelberg University.

[1] http://alt.qcri.org/semeval2015/task4/

identical in both tracks, systems addressing track A had to extract event mentions, while event annotations were provided to participants of track B. Furthermore, both tracks were evaluated with and without assigning explicit temporal information to the events. Since we participated in track B, the main challenges for our approach were to

- filter events relevant for the target entities,
- assign date information to relevant events,
- determine cross-document event coreferences,
- and to construct a timeline for each entity.

In the following section, we describe our approach and give an example for cross-document event ordering. In Section 3, we present and analyze the official evaluation results. Finally, we discuss open issues for future research in the context of cross-document timeline construction.

2 Cross-document Event Ordering

Given a set of documents and a set of target entities, the task is to build an event timeline for each entity. Documents are provided with annotated sentences, which may contain several event annotations.

2.1 System Architecture

We implemented an ad-hoc approach for both the retrieval and the anchoring of relevant events. Figure 1 illustrates the general architecture of our approach. Our system is based on five main components:

- ***Matching***: In this step, we identify sentences in the document collection, in which parts of the target entity name occur. Furthermore, we use the cosine similarity matching function with a threshold to not select sentences that contain too few parts of the entity name. The result of this step is a list of sentences with event candidates for the timeline of the target entity.

- ***Coreference resolution***: To avoid extracting event candidates only from sentences in which parts of the entity name occur explicitly, we apply entity coreference resolution using the Stanford CoreNLP tool (Lee et al., 2013; Manning et al., 2014). Thus, sentences, in which other terms, e.g., pronouns, are used to refer to the target entity, can be added to the list of sentences with event candidates.

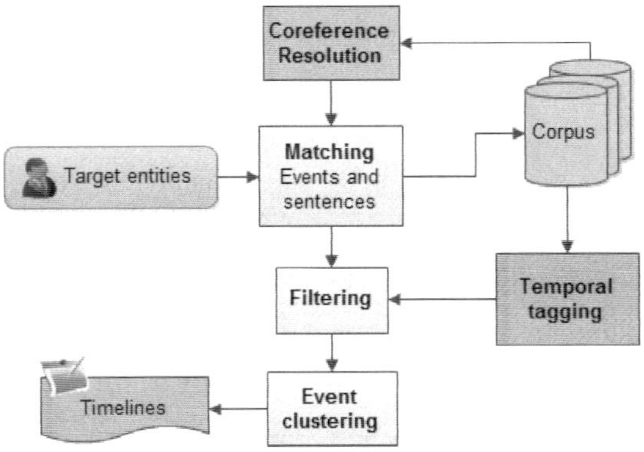

Figure 1: General architecture of our approach.

- ***Temporal tagging***: To extract and normalize temporal expressions, HeidelTime (Strötgen and Gertz, 2013) is applied. If a temporal expression cooccurs with an event candidate in a sentence, the event is anchored at the respective point in time. If no expressions are detected in a sentence, we use the document creation time as anchor date for respective events.

- ***Filtering***: Since the first steps result in many event candidates, we aim to filter out non relevant events to improve the precision of our approach. Using a threshold for the token distance between the event and the closest term referring to the target entity, we prune events for which it is unlikly that the entity is involved.

- ***Cross-document event clustering***: Finally, all events anchored at the same point in time with identical covered text are clustered.

We apply several filtering techniques in order to prune non relevant sentences and events. These thresholds were tuned using the trial data provided by the organizers. Since the performance of our system depends on these parameters, we submitted two runs with different configurations:

- *HeidelToul_NonTolMatchPrune*: The first run uses a non-tolerant pruning setting with low values for the thresholds and distances.

- *HeidelToul_TolMatchPrune*: The second run performs a more tolerant pruning of events and sentences using quite high thresholds.

	anchor date	event	rel
1	1994	8983-13-flight	1
2	2000-02	4764-6-received	0
2	2000-02	4764-6-announced	1
3	2004-11-24	1173-6-negotiations	0
...	...	...	...
9	2008	8983-14-development	0
9	2008	8983-14-scheduled	0

Table 1: Timeline excerpt returned for *Boeing 777*. Events are either relevant (1) or not (0).

Evaluation results are discussed in Section 3.

2.2 Timeline Construction Example

Table 1 shows some events of the timeline constructed by our system for the entity *Boeing 777*. The listed events are extracted from the document parts depicted in Figure 2. Events mentioned in the timeline are surrounded by boxes, and (parts of) the entity mentions are underlined. In the following, we explain the timeline and the reasons for incorrectly returned and anchored events.

The first column of the timeline refers to the rank of the events, the second contains the dates in which events are anchored, and the third corresponds to the events that are detected as relevant for the target entity. Each event of the timeline is represented by the document *id* and sentence *id* from which it was extracted, and the covered text of the event mention. For instance, our system correctly determines the event *flight* as chronologically first relevant event (rank 1) occurring in 1994. It was extracted from sentence *13* of document *8983* (c.f. Figure 2c).

If two events are simultaneous, they can be associated with the same rank, as the second and third event. If a systems fails to extract the anchor dates of relevant events, these should be returned at rank 0 and are ignored in the evaluation.

Using the excerpts in Figure 2, we explain why events in Table 1 have been selected as relevant for *Boeing 777*. All sentences contain only substrings of the target entity name, i.e., the full entity name never occurs. For instance, sentence 13 of document 8983 contains the string *777* while sentence 14 contains the string *Boeing*. As explained above, we used substring matching with a threshold and coreference resolution to increase the number of potentially relevant events. While for many target entities, it is important to not require a full entity name (e.g., for persons), the term *Boeing* in the three document excerpts never refers to *Boeing 777*, resulting in some non-relevant events in our timeline. Note, however, that relying on strict entity matching, no event could be extracted from the sentences shown in Figure 2, and that some events considered as not relevant in the gold standard are at least debatable, e.g., *received*: Although our anchor date is incorrect (it should be the document creation time of the article due to *so far*), the event is relevant for the target entity since *Boeing 777* is the subject of the orders.

```
<s id="6">The original
    <EVENT eid="e134">negotiations</EVENT>
     with Boeing were over a no-bid
    contract .
</s>
```

(a) Doc. #1173: Internal emails expose Boeing . . .

```
<s id="6">So far , Boeing has
    <EVENT eid="e131">received</EVENT>
    five orders from two customers for
    the 777-200LR since it was
    <EVENT eid="e88">announced</EVENT> in
    February 2000 .
</s>
```

(b) Doc. #4764: Boeing unveils long-range 777.

```
<s id="13">The first
    <EVENT eid="e126">flight</EVENT> of
    the 777 was in 1994 .
</s>
<s id="14">The Boeing 787 , or Dreamliner
, is a mid-sized passenger airliner
currently under
    <EVENT eid="e85">development</EVENT>
    by Boeing Commercial Airplanes and
    <EVENT eid="e132">scheduled</EVENT>
    to enter service in 2008 .
</s>
```

(c) Doc. #8983: Boeing secures $11bn of aircraft deals.

Figure 2: Three document excerpts with sentences containing events returned for entity *Boeing 777*.

3 Experimental Results and Discussion

The evaluation data consists of 3 sets of 30 documents from Wikinews annotated with event men-

track	run	MICRO-FSCORE corpus 1	corpus 2	corpus 3	overall	details (overall) precision	recall
TrackB	GPLSIUA_1	22.35	19.28	33.59	25.36	21.73	30.46
TrackB	GPLSIUA_2	20.47	16.17	29.90	22.66	20.08	26.00
TrackB	HeidelToul_NTMP[2]	19.62	7.25	20.37	17.03	20.11	14.76
TrackB	HeidelToul_TMP[3]	16.50	10.94	25.89	18.34	13.58	28.22
SubTrackB	GPLSIUA_1	18.35	20.48	32.08	23.15	18.90	29.85
SubTrackB	GPLSIUA_2	15.93	14.44	27.48	19.18	16.19	23.52
SubTrackB	HeidelToul_NTMP	12.23	14.78	16.11	14.42	19.58	11.42
SubTrackB	HeidelToul_TMP	13.24	15.88	21.99	16.67	12.18	26.41

Table 2: Official results of participating groups in SemEval 2015 task 4. [2]NonTolMatchPrune: non tolerant matching and pruning setting; [3]TolMatchPrune: tolerant matching and pruning setting (cf. Section 2.1).

tions and a total of 38 target entities. Our system ranked second among only two participating groups.

While there have been a total of four teams participating in the task, only two participated in (sub)track B. Participants of (sub)track A additionally performed event extraction so that a comparison between results of all four participants is not possible. Thus, in Table 2, we only present the results of the two teams that addressed (sub)track B.

Table 2 (left) reports the results by means of Micro-FSCORE obtained by our runs and that of the other participating group. As shown, our system is outperformed by the system "GPLSIUA" for both settings. The performance difference is most significant for corpus 2, especially within TrackB. However, we notice that our tolerant setting gives better overall results than the non tolerant one. These improvements are less significant for corpora 1 and 2 than for corpus 3.

To get a deep understanding of the results, we report in Table 2 (right) the overall precision and recall values for our system configurations and that of the other participating group. Our non tolerant setting is slightly outperformed by the run "GPLSIUA_1" in terms of precision for trackB. However, it relatively enhances the other runs within the SubTrackB. This can be explained by the important number of relevant retrieved events due to the high values of distances and thresholds used to prune the events. In contrast, in terms of recall, our tolerant setting performs better than the non tolerant one in both subtracks. Actually, this is not surprising given that the filtering techniques are not strict.

Interestingly, an in-depth analysis of the nature of the target entities and the types of temporal expressions in the documents for which our system fails to provide good timeline, may help to improve the overall performance of our system in the future. For instance, for the target entities "Boeing 777" and "Airbus A380" in corpus 1, we obtained the lowest values in terms of MicroFSCORE among all target entities. Clearly, this is due to the partial matching technique we used, which results in the extraction of many events related to other entities (e.g., "Boeing 787" instead of "Boeing 777"; cf. Table 1 and Figure 2). Moreover, all events that do not cooccur with a temporal expression in the same sentence are anchored at the document creation time by our system. This hurts the performance of our system in particular for TrackB, because many of those events are placed at rank 0 in the gold standard.

4 Conclusions

In this paper, we presented an overview of our participation in the timeline generation task of SemEval-2015. We proposed a baseline approach for the extraction and anchoring of events. Our system is evaluated using three corpora of news articles and shows reasonable results.

Interesting future work to improve our approach could include a fine tuning of the matching function as well as the filtering parameters used to prune non relevant events. In addition, more sophisticated entity disambiguation could further improve the performance of our system.

Acknowledgments

We thank the task organizers for their guidance and prompt support in all organizational matters.

References

Heeyoung Lee, Angel Chang, Yves Peirsman, Nathanael Chambers, Mihai Surdeanu, and Dan Jurafsky. 2013. Deterministic Coreference Resolution Based on Entity-centric, Precision-ranked Rules. *Computational Linguistics*, 39(4):885–916, December.

Christopher D. Manning, Mihai Surdeanu, John Bauer, Jenny Finkel, Steven J. Bethard, and David McClosky. 2014. The Stanford CoreNLP Natural Language Processing Toolkit. In *Proceedings of 52nd Annual Meeting of the Association for Computational Linguistics: System Demonstrations*, pages 55–60.

Yuval Shahar and Mark A. Musen. 1992. A Temporal-Abstraction System for Patient Monitoring. In *Proceedings of the Annual Symposium on Computer Application in Medical Care*, pages 121–127.

Amit Singhal. 2012. Introducing the Knowledge Graph: Things, not Strings". *Official Google Blog*, May.

Jannik Strötgen and Michael Gertz. 2013. Multilingual and Cross-domain Temporal Tagging. *Language Resources and Evaluation*, 47(2):269–298.

Marc Verhagen, Roser Saurí, Tommaso Caselli, and James Pustejovsky. 2010. SemEval-2010 Task 13: TempEval-2. In *Proceedings of the 5th International Workshop on Semantic Evaluation (SemEval '10)*, pages 57–62.

HITSZ-ICRC: An Integration Approach for QA TempEval Challenge

Yongshuai Hou, Cong Tan, Qingcai Chen and Xiaolong Wang
Department of Computer Science and Technology
Harbin Institute of Technology Shenzhen Graduate School
HIT Campus, The University Town of Shenzhen, Shenzhen, 518055, China
{yongshuai.hou, viptancong, qingcai.chen}@gmail.com
wangxl@insun.hit.edu.cn

Abstract

This paper presents the HITSZ-ICRC system designed for the QA TempEval challenge in SemEval-2015. The system used an integration approach to annotate temporal information by merging temporal annotation results from different temporal annotators. TIPSemB, ClearTK and TARSQI were used as temporal annotators to get candidate temporal annotation results. Evaluation demonstrated that our system was effective for improving the performance of temporal information annotation, and achieved recalls of 0.18, 0.26 and 0.19 on Blog, News and Wikipedeia test sets.

1 Introduction

The QA TempEval (Llorens et al., 2015) in SemEval-2015 is a temporal information annotation challenge, which is a follow-up task after TempEval-1 (Verhagen et al., 2007), TempEval-2 (Verhagen et al., 2010) and TempEval-3(UzZaman et al., 2013). QA TempEval task is similar to the task ABC in TempEval-3, requires participant system (1) extracting and normalizing temporal expressions, (2) extracting events and (3) identifying temporal relations on plain documents. Temporal information annotation should follow TimeML scheme (Pustejovsky et al., 2003a). Difference between QA TempEval task and task ABC in TempEval-3 is evaluation method: in all previous TempEval tasks, annotated result was evaluated by the temporal information annotation accuracy based on manually annotated test corpus; in QA TempEval, annotated result was evaluated by temporal question-answering(QA) accuracy in the given temporal QA system (UzZaman et al., 2012) based on temporal knowledge produced from participant's annotation.

Temporal annotation is useful in information retrieval, QA, natural language understanding and so on. A lot of researches have been attracted on this topic in the past years. Many methods were proposed and many toolkits were implemented for temporal information annotation.

TIMEN (Llorens et al., 2012a) is a community-driven tool using rule-based method based on knowledge base to solve the temporal expression normalization problem. TARSQI Toolkit (Verhagen and Pustejovsky, 2008) is a modular system for automatic temporal information annotation. The toolkit can extract temporal expressions, events and recognize temporal relations by its different components. Llorens et al. (2010) used CRF models based on semantic information to annotate temporal information according to TimeML scheme, and their TIPSem system got outstanding performance results in TempEval-2. Steve (2013) piped machine-learning models in his ClearTK system to annotate temporal information using a small set of features. His system got best performance for temporal relation identification in TempEval-3. The TIMEN toolkit was integrated into the ClearTK system for temporal expression normalization. Llorens et al. (2012b) proposed an automatic method to improve the correctness of each individual annotation by merging different annotation results with different strategies.

This paper described the method HITSZ-ICRC system used for QA TempEval challenge. This was first time for HITSZ-ICRC team to do the temporal annotation task. An integration approach was chosen to get improved annotation result on currently available temporal annotation toolkits for QA TempEval task. Annotation results from those toolkits were merged using a temporal annotation merging method (Llorens et al., 2012b).

The remainder of this paper is structured as follows: Section 2 describes the system modules used for temporal information annotation. Section 3 introduces the data sets and toolkits used, explains and analysis the evaluation results. Section 4 concludes the paper.

2 Integration Approach for Temporal Information Annotation

QA TempEval task required participant system to annotate temporal expressions, events and temporal relations following TimeML scheme.

Many toolkits are available for temporal information annotation, such as TARSQI (Verhagen and Pustejovsky, 2008), ClearTK (Bethard, 2013) TIPSemB (Llorens et al., 2010) and so on. Each toolkit can be used as a temporal annotator to get candidate annotation result.

But annotation results from current toolkits cannot be used for QA TempEval directly because some annotations do not in the TimeML format. For example, time expression normalization values in some results are in independent format, such as "*20140804AF*", should be as "2014-08-04TAF"; some time expressions are not normalized and are set to "*default_norm*" or no value; some toolkits change source text content after annotating temporal information, such as changing adjacent spaces to single space. So an annotation corrector module is necessary to correct candidate annotation results.

Automatic method proposed by Llorens et al. (2012b) was employed to merge annotation results from different annotators. The method used weighted voting techniques to merge temporal annotations. Weight for each candidate result and threshold for choosing final annotation were variable. Element in merged result should get weight above the threshold. Based on different weight and threshold settings, merged results can satisfy different requirements: such as high recall, high precision and balanced precision and recall.

Annotation toolkits and the results merging method were used to get final annotation result. Steps to get final result are as follows:

Step1: re-training models with train dataset for temporal annotator;

Step2: annotating temporal information on test data using each annotator;

Step3: correcting annotation results from all annotators using temporal annotation corrector;

Step4: integrating all candidate annotation results to get final temporal annotation result using temporal result merger.

The temporal information annotation process of our system is shown in figure 1.

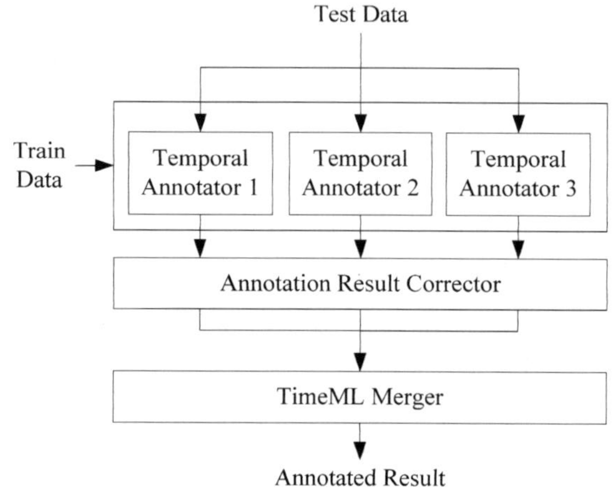

Figure 1. Temporal annotation process.

Annotation module used three temporal annotators here. The function of this module is for getting candidate temporal annotation results using different annotators.

Corrector module corrects all annotated results following TimeML scheme. Its functions include: (1) changing format of temporal expression values to TimeML format; (2) normalizing temporal expressions which have no value; (3) removing temporal expression tags which cannot be normalized, and removing the related temporal links at same time; (4) removing temporal entity tags with class labels not in TimeML label set and removing the related temporal links; (5) removing temporal links with class labels not in TimeML label set; (6) correcting the text content to source text.

The TimeML merger module used the temporal annotation merging method to merge annotation results. The F1 value for different annotators evaluated on develop data was used as voting weights. For QA TempEval task, high recall annotation result will be more effective, so high recall settings for the merging method were chosen. Different weight and threshold setting strategies were tried, which include: (1) Best F1 prior voting: the annotation chose as final result should be annotated by the best F1 annotator or at least two annotators; (2) Better F1 prior voting: the annotation chose as final result should be annotated by at least one annotator except the worst F1 annotator; (3) Union: the annotation chose as final result should be annotated by at least one annotator.

3 Results Evaluation

3.1 Dataset and toolkits

Train dataset provided for QA TempEval task is the same dataset in TempEval-3, includes TBAQ-cleaned dataset and TE3-Platinum (UzZaman et al., 2013) dataset. TBAQ-cleaned contains cleaned and improved AQUAINT and TimeBank corpus (Pustejovsky et al., 2003b). The TE3-Platinum is the evaluation corpus for TempEval-3 manually annotated by organizers. All the datasets are annotated in TimeML format.

The test dataset was in TempEval-3 format, and includes 28 plain text documents in Blog (8 documents), News (Wikinews, NYT, WSJ) (10 documents) and Wikipedia (10 documents).

Results evaluation was based on 294 temporal questions, 65 questions for Blog documents, 99 for News and 130 for Wikipedia. The question set was created by human experts based on the test documents. Annotated result was evaluated by the temporal QA system (UzZaman et al., 2012) using the question set.

The three annotation toolkits TARSQI, ClearTK and TIPSemB were used as temporal annotators. Default models in the toolkits were used for TARSQI and TIPSemB. Models in ClearTK were re-trained with the training data. In merging step, the temporal annotation merging toolkit (Llorens et al., 2012b) was used to get the final result.

3.2 Measures

Answers' precision (*P*), recall (*R*), and F1 value (*F1*) of the temporal QA system are used to evaluate annotation results. Recall is used as the main metric to sort results and F1 is used as secondary metric.

P, *R* and *F1* are calculated as:

$$P = \frac{num\_correct}{num\_answered} \quad (1)$$

$$R = \frac{num\_correct}{num\_questions} \quad (2)$$

$$F1 = \frac{2 \times P \times R}{P + R} \quad (3)$$

where *num_correct* is the number of questions correctly answered by the temporal QA system based on temporal knowledge produced from participant's annotation result; *num_answered* is the number of questions answered by the temporal QA system based on participant's annotation result; *num_questions* is the number of test questions used in the temporal QA system.

3.3 Evaluation results with QA TempEval

Giving a test document, firstly it was annotated by three temporal annotators separately, including ClearTK, TIPSemB and TARSQI; then the annotated results were corrected to follow TimeML scheme by corrector module and were used as candidate results; finally, the three candidate results were merged using three different strategies. The models in ClearTK toolkit were trained with TBAQ-cleaned dataset.

Six results from different annotators and merging strategies were compared, including three results annotated by different annotators and three results annotated by different merging strategies. For the system had not been finished before submission deadline, only the result of TARSQI was submitted to QA TempEval challenge.

The evaluation results for the six temporal annotation results are shown in table 1, 2 and 3 in domain Blog, News and Wikipedia separately. *awd%* is the percentage of the answered questions and *corr* is the number of correct answers.

Run *TARSQI*, *TIPSemB* and *ClearTK* is the result annotated by corresponding temporal annotator. Run *BSTF_VOTE*, *BTRF_VOTE* and *RES_UNION* is the result produced with different merging strategies.

F1 value of each annotator result was used as its weight in merging step. *BSTF_VOTE* is the result merging with best F1 prior voting strategy. *BTRF_VOTE* is the result with better F1 prior voting strategy. R*ES_UNION* is the result with union strategy.

Results in table 1, 2 and 3 shows that performance of all merged results are better than results annotated by single annotator in each test domain. It means integration approach is effective for improving temporal information annotation performance. The union strategy performs best in all the six run results in all domains. So merging results from all annotators with union strategy is an effective way to get better annotation results based on QA TempEval evaluation method.

Run	Measures			Questions	
	P	R	F1	awd%	corr
TARSQI	0.17	0.02	0.03	0.09	1
TIPSemB	0.37	0.11	0.17	0.29	7
ClearTK	**0.55**	0.09	0.16	0.17	6
BSTF_VOTE	0.34	0.17	0.23	0.49	11
BTRF_VOTE	0.30	0.15	0.20	0.51	10
RES_UNION	0.36	**0.18**	**0.24**	**0.51**	**12**

Table 1. Evaluation results on Blog test data.

Run	Measures			Questions	
	P	R	F1	awd%	corr
TARSQI	0.47	0.08	0.14	0.17	8
TIPSemB	**0.55**	0.18	0.27	0.33	18
ClearTK	0.53	0.08	0.14	0.15	8
BSTF_VOTE	0.51	0.24	0.33	0.47	24
BTRF_VOTE	0.49	0.23	0.32	0.47	23
RES_UNION	0.51	**0.26**	**0.35**	**0.52**	**26**

Table 2. Evaluation results on News test data.

Run	Measures			Questions	
	P	R	F1	awd%	corr
TARSQI	**0.83**	0.08	0.14	0.09	10
TIPSemB	0.41	0.11	0.17	0.26	14
ClearTK	0.57	0.06	0.11	0.11	8
BSTF_VOTE	0.48	0.18	0.26	**0.37**	23
BTRF_VOTE	0.48	0.18	0.26	**0.37**	23
RES_UNION	0.54	**0.19**	**0.28**	0.35	**25**

Table 3. Evaluation results on Wikipedia test data.

Evaluation results show that annotation results from different annotators could be used to improve temporal information annotation performance by results merging. The precision of all merging results cannot achieve to the highest, and are lower than some annotator results. It means that the merging step merged wrong annotation into final result. The merging strategies tried in our experiments were more effective on improving the recall of temporal information annotation, which increased the chance that the temporal question could be answered, but were useless for question answering precision. So balancing the precision and recall is necessary for improving the performance of annotation results merging. Improving performance of single annotator also is important job for getting better final annotation result. We have tried the integration approach using results of the top 3 best performance systems in QA TempEval challenge(Llorens et al., 2015), and the result still can be improved.

4 Conclusions

We used an integration approach to annotate temporal information in HISZ-ICRC system for QA TempEval challenge. Annotation results from different annotators were merged using automatic merging method with different strategies. Evaluation results showed that the integration approach for temporal information annotation can effectively improve annotation performance than single annotator. Union strategy performed best in all strategies we tried.

We used same weight for temporal expression, event and temporal relation merging. But performance of different annotation modules is different in an annotator. We will try different weight setting for temporal expression, event and temporal relation annotation merging in future work. And the precision and recall have not been tried as merging weight in our experiment, which also will be tried in future work.

Acknowledgments

The authors thank Hector Llorens and Naushad UzZaman for sharing the TIPSemB and the temporal annotation merging toolkit, and thank the anonymous reviewers for their insightful comments.

This work was supported in part by the National Natural Science Foundation of China (61272383 and 61173075), the Strategic Emerging Industry Development Special Funds of Shenzhen (ZDSY20120613125401420 and JCYJ20120613151940045) and the Key Basic Research Foundation of Shenzhen (JC201005260118A).

References

Hector Llorens, Naushad UzZaman, and James Allen. 2012b. Merging Temporal Annotations. In *2012 19th International Symposium on Temporal Representation and Reasoning (TIME)*, pages 107–113, Leicester, UK, 12-14 September.

Hector Llorens, Estela Saquete, and Borja Navarro. 2010. TIPSem (English and Spanish): Evaluating CRFs and Semantic Roles in TempEval-2. In *Proceedings of the 5th International Workshop on Semantic Evaluation*, pages 284–291, Uppsala, Sweden, 15-16 July

Hector Llorens, Leon Derczynski, Robert J Gaizauskas, and Estela Saquete. 2012a. TIMEN: An Open Temporal Expression Normalisation Resource. In *Proceedings of the Eight International Conference on Language Resources and Evaluation (LREC'12)*, pages 3044–3051, Istanbul, Turkey, May.

Hector Llorens, Nate Chambers, Naushad UzZaman, Nasrin Mostafazadeh, James Allen, and James Pustejovsky. 2015. SemEval-2015 Task 5: QA TEMPEVAL - Evaluating Temporal Information Understanding with QA. In *Proceedings of the 9th International Workshop on Semantic Evaluation (SemEval 2015)*, Denver, Colorado, USA.

James Pustejovsky, José M Castano, Robert Ingria, Roser Sauri, Robert J Gaizauskas, Andrea Setzer, Graham Katz, and Dragomir R Radev. 2003a. TimeML: Robust Specification of Event and Temporal Expressions in Text. *New directions in question answering*, 3:28–34.

James Pustejovsky, Patrick Hanks, Roser Sauri, Andrew See, Robert Gaizauskas, Andrea Setzer, Dragomir Radev, Beth Sundheim, David Day, Lisa Ferro, and others. 2003b. The timebank corpus. In *Corpus linguistics*, 2003:40.

Marc Verhagen and James Pustejovsky. 2008. Temporal Processing with the TARSQI Toolkit. In *22nd International Conference on Computational Linguistics: Demonstration Papers*, pages 189–192, Manchester, August.

Marc Verhagen, Robert Gaizauskas, Frank Schilder, Mark Hepple, Graham Katz, and James Pustejovsky. 2007. SemEval-2007 Task 15: TempEval Temporal Relation Identification. In *Proceedings of the Fourth International Workshop on Semantic Evaluations (SemEval-2007)*, pages 75–80, Prague, Czech Republic, June.

Marc Verhagen, Roser Sauri, Tommaso Caselli, and James Pustejovsky. 2010. SemEval-2010 Task 13: TempEval-2. In *Proceedings of the 5th International Workshop on Semantic Evaluation*, pages 57–62, Uppsala, Sweden, 15-16 July.

Naushad UzZaman, Hector Llorens, and James Allen. 2012. Evaluating Temporal Information Understanding with Temporal Question Answering. In *2012 IEEE Sixth International Conference on Semantic Computing (ICSC)*, pages 79–82.

Naushad UzZaman, Hector Llorens, Leon Derczynski, James Allen, Marc Verhagen, and James Pustejovsky. 2013. SemEval-2013 Task 1: TempEval-3: Evaluating Time Expressions, Events, and Temporal Relations. In *Second Joint Conference on Lexical and Computational Semantics (*SEM), Volume 2: Proceedings of the Seventh International Workshop on Semantic Evaluation (SemEval 2013)*, pages 1–9, Atlanta, Georgia, USA, 14-15 June.

Steven Bethard. 2013. ClearTK-TimeML: A minimalist approach to TempEval 2013. In *Second Joint Conference on Lexical and Computational Semantics (*SEM), Volume 2: Proceedings of the Seventh International Workshop on Semantic Evaluation (SemEval 2013)*, pages 10–14, Atlanta, Georgia, USA, 14-15 June.

UFPRSheffield: Contrasting Rule-based and Support Vector Machine Approaches to Time Expression Identification in Clinical TempEval

Hegler Tissot
Federal University of Parana
Cel. Franc. H. dos Santos, 100
Curitiba, PR 81531-980, Brazil
hctissot@inf.ufpr.br

Genevieve Gorrell
The University of Sheffield
211 Portobello
Sheffield, S1 4DP, UK
g.gorrell@shef.ac.uk

Angus Roberts
The University of Sheffield
211 Portobello
Sheffield, S1 4DP, UK
angus.roberts@shef.ac.uk

Leon Derczynski
The University of Sheffield
211 Portobello
Sheffield, S1 4DP, UK
leon.derczynski@shef.ac.uk

Marcos Didonet Del Fabro
Federal University of Parana
Cel. Franc. H. dos Santos, 100
Curitiba, PR 81531-980, Brazil
marcos.ddf@inf.ufpr.br

Abstract

We present two approaches to time expression identification, as entered in to SemEval-2015 Task 6, Clinical TempEval. The first is a comprehensive rule-based approach that favoured recall, and which achieved the best recall for time expression identification in Clinical TempEval. The second is an SVM-based system built using readily available components, which was able to achieve a competitive F1 in a short development time. We discuss how the two approaches perform relative to each other, and how characteristics of the corpus affect the suitability of different approaches and their outcomes.

1 Introduction

SemEval-2015 Task 6, Clinical TempEval (Bethard et al., 2015), was a temporal information extraction task over the clinical domain. The combined University of Sheffield/Federal University of Parana team focused on identification of spans and features for time expressions (TIMEX3), based on specific annotation guidelines (TS and TA subtasks).

For time expressions, participants identified expression spans within the text and their corresponding classes: DATE, TIME, DURATION, QUANTIFIER, PREPOSTEXP or SET.[1] Participating systems had to annotate timexes according to the guidelines for the annotation of times, events and temporal relations in clinical notes – THYME Annotation Guidelines (Styler et al., 2014) – which is an extension of ISO TimeML (Pustejovsky et al., 2010) developed by the THYME project.[2] Further, ISO TimeML extends two other guidelines: a) TimeML Annotation Guidelines (Sauri et al., 2006), and b) TIDES 2005 Standard for the Annotation of Temporal Expressions (Ferro et al., 2005). Clinical TempEval temporal expression results[3] were given in terms of Precision, Recall and F1-score for identifying spans and classes of temporal expressions.

For Clinical TempEval two datasets were provided. The first was a training dataset comprising 293 documents with a total number 3818 annotated time expressions. The second dataset comprised 150 documents with 2078 timexes. This was used for evaluation and was then made available to participants, after evaluations were completed. Annotations identified the span and class of each timex. Table 1 shows the number of annotated timex by class in each dataset.

We present a rule-based and a SVM-based approach to time expression identification, and we discuss how they perform relative to each other, and how characteristics of the corpus affect outcomes and the suitability of the two approaches.

[1] There was no time normalisation task in Clinical TempEval

[2] http://thyme.healthnlp.org/ (accessed 27 Mar. 2015)

[3] http://alt.qcri.org/semeval2015/task6/index.php?id=results (accessed 27 Mar. 2015)

Class	Training	Evaluation
DATE	2583	1422
TIME	117	59
DURATION	433	200
SET	218	116
QUANTIFIER	162	109
PREPOSTEXP	305	172
Total	**3818**	**2078**

Table 1: Time expressions per dataset.

2 HINX: A Rule-Based Approach

HINX is a rule-based system developed using GATE[4] (Cunningham et al., 2011). It executes a hierarchical set of rules and scripts in an information extraction pipeline that can be split into the 3 modules: 1) text pre-processing; 2) timex identification; and 3) timex normalisation, which are described below. These modules identify and normalise temporal concepts, starting from finding basic tokens, then grouping such tokens into more complex expressions, and finally normalising their features. An additional step was included to produce the output files in the desired format.

2.1 Text Pre-processing

This module is used to pre-process the documents and identify the document creation time (DCT).

HINX used GATE's ANNIE (Cunningham et al., 2011) – a rule-based system that was not specifically adapted to clinical domain – to provide tokenization, sentence splitting and part of speech (POS) tagging. We used the Unicode Alternate Tokenizer provided by GATE to split the text into very simple tokens such as numbers, punctuation and words. The Sentence Splitter identifies sentence boundaries, making it possible to avoid creating a timex that connects tokens from different sentences or paragraphs. POS Tagging produces a part-of-speech tag as an annotation on each word or symbol, which is useful in cases such as identifying whether the word "may" is being used as a verb or as a noun (the month).

We use rules written in JAPE, GATE's pattern matching language, to identify the DCT annotation reference within the "[meta]" tag at the beginning of each document. The DCT value was split into different features to be stored at the document level – year, month, day, hour, minute, and second.

[4] `http://gate.ac.uk` (accessed 27 Mar. 2015)

2.2 Timex Identification

This module uses a set of hierarchical JAPE rules to combine 15 kinds of basic temporal tokens into more complex expressions, as described in the sequence of steps given below:

- **Numbers**: A set of rules is used to identify numbers that are written in a numeric or a non-numeric format, as numbers as words (e.g. "two and a half").
- **Temporal tokens**: Every word that can be used to identify temporal concepts is annotated as a basic temporal token - e.g. temporal granularities; periods of the day; names of months; days of the week; season names; words that represent past, present and future references; and words that can give an imprecise sense to a temporal expression (e.g. the word "few" in "the last few days"). Additionally, as a requirement for Clinical TempEval, we included specific rules to identify those words that corresponded to a timex of class PREPOSTEXP (e.g. "postoperative" and "pre-surgical").
- **Basic expressions**: A set of rules identifies the basic temporal expressions, including explicit dates and times in different formats (e.g. "2014", "15th of November", "12:30"), durations (e.g. "24 hours", "the last 3 months"), quantifiers, and isolated temporal tokens that can be normalised.
- **Complex expressions**: Complex expressions are formed by connecting two basic expressions or a basic expression with a temporal token. These represent information corresponding to ranges of values (e.g. "from July to August this year"), full timestamps (e.g. "Mar-03-2010 09:54:31"), referenced points in time (e.g. "last month"), and precise pre/post-operative periods (e.g. "two days postoperative").
- **SETs**: Temporal expressions denoting a SET (number of times and frequency, or just frequency) are identified by this specific set of rules (e.g. "twice-a-day", "three times every month", "99/minute", "every morning").
- **Imprecise expressions**: These expressions comprise language-specific structures used to refer to imprecise periods of time, including im-

precise expressions defined with boundaries (e.g. "around 9-11 pm yesterday"), imprecise values of a given temporal granularity (e.g. "a few days ago", "the coming months"), precise and imprecise references (e.g. "that same month", "the end of last year", "the following days"), imprecise sets (e.g. "2 to 4 times a day"), and vague expressions (e.g. "some time earlier", "a long time ago").

2.3 Timex Normalisation

As the above identification process is run, the basic temporal tokens are combined to produce more complex annotations. Annotation features on these complex annotations are used to store specific time values, for use by the normalisation process. Such features comprise explicit values like "year=2004", references to the document creation time/DCT (e.g. "month=(DCT.month)+1" for the expression "in the following month", and "day=(DCT.day)-3" in "three days ago"), and a direct reference to the last mentioned timex in the previous sentences (e.g. "year=LAST.year" for the timex "April" in "In February 2002,... Then, in April,...").

The normalisation process uses these features to calculate corresponding final values. It also captures a set of other characteristics, including the precision of an expression, and whether or not it represents a boundary period of time. This last one is used to split the DURATION timexes into two different DATE expressions, as explicitly defined in the THYME Annotation Guidelines (e.g. "between November/2012 and March/2013").

3 Using an SVM-Based Approach

GATE provides an integration of LibSVM (Chang and Lin, 2011) technology with some modifications enabling effective rapid prototyping for the task of locating and classifying named entities. This was used to quickly achieve competitive results. An initial system was created in a few hours, and although a couple of days were spent trying parameter and feature variants, the initial results could not be improved. No development effort was required, the system being used as "off the shelf" software.

State of the art machine learning approaches to timex recognition often use sequence labeling (e.g. CRF) to find timex bounds (UzZaman et al., 2013), then a use separate instance-based classification step (e.g. with SVM) to classify them (Sun et al., 2013). Our approach uses SVM to implement separate named entity recognizers for each class, then makes a final selection for each span based on probability. GATE's LibSVM integration incorporates the uneven margins parameter (UM) (Li et al., 2009), which has been shown to improve results on imbalanced datasets especially for smaller corpora. In positioning the hyperplane further from the (smaller) positive set, we compensate for a tendency in smaller corpora for the larger (negative) class to push away the separator in a way that it doesn't tend to do when sufficient positive examples exist for them to populate their space more thoroughly, as this default behaviour can result in poor generalization and a conservative model. Since NLP tasks such as NER often do involve imbalanced datasets, this inclusion, as well as robust default implementation choices for NLP tasks, make it easy to get a respectable result quickly using GATE's SVM/UM, as our entry demonstrates. The feature set used is:

- String and part of speech of the current token plus the preceding and ensuing five.
- If a date has been detected for this span using the Date Normalizer rule-based date detection and normalization resource in GATE, then the type of date in this location is included as a feature. The mere presence of such a date annotation may be the most important aspect of this feature. Note that this Date Normalizer was not used in HINX, which used a custom solution.
- As above, but using the "complete" feature on the date, to indicate whether the date present in this location is a fully qualified date. This may be of value as an indicator of the quality of the rule-based date annotation.

A probabilistic polynomial SVM is used, of order 3. Probabilistic SVMs allow us to apply confidence thresholds later, so we may: 1) tune to the imbalanced dataset and task constraints, 2) use the "one vs. rest" method for transforming the multiclass problem to a set of binary problems, and 3) select the final class for the time expression. In the "one vs. rest" approach, one classifier is created for each class, allowing it to be separated from all others, and the class with the

SVM	Threshold	P	R	F1
Linear	0.2	0.68	0.59	0.63
Linear	0.4	0.76	0.55	0.64
Poly (3)	0.2	0.64	0.61	0.63
Poly (3)	0.25	0.69	0.61	**0.65**
Inc. hinx feats	0.25	0.72	0.54	0.62

Table 2: SVM tuning results.

	Span			Class		
Submission	P	R	F1	P	R	F1
HINX-1	0.479	0.747	0.584	0.455	0.709	0.555
HINX-2	0.494	0.770	0.602	0.470	0.733	0.573
HINX-3	0.311	0.794	0.447	0.296	**0.756**	0.425
HINX-4	0.311	**0.795**	0.447	0.296	**0.756**	0.425
HINX-5	0.411	**0.795**	0.542	0.391	**0.756**	0.516
SVM-1	0.732	0.661	0.695	0.712	0.643	0.676
SVM-2	0.741	0.655	0.695	0.723	0.640	0.679

Table 3: Final Clinical TempEval results.

highest confidence score is chosen. A UM of 0.4 is selected based on previous work (Li et al., 2005).

Two classifiers are trained for each class; one to identify the start of the entity and another to identify the end. This information is then post-processed into entity spans first by removing orphaned start or end tags and secondly by filtering out entities with lengths (in number of words) that did not appear in the training data. Finally, where multiple annotations overlap, a confidence score is used to select the strongest candidate. A separate confidence score is also used to remove weak entities.

Table 2 shows negligible difference between a linear and polynomial SVM (degree 3). A confidence threshold of 0.25 was selected empirically. Task training data was split 50:50 to form training and test sets to produce these figures. An additional experiment involved including the output from the HINX rule-based system as features for the SVM. This did not improve the outcome.

4 Results and Discussion

We submitted 5 runs using the HINX system and 2 runs using our SVM approach to Clinical TempEval. Results of both systems are shown in Table 3. For completeness, both SVM runs submitted are included. However the only difference between the two is that SVM-2 included the full training set, whereas SVM-1 included only the half reserved for testing at development time, and submitted as a backup for its quality of being a tested model. As expected, including more training data leads to a slightly superior result, and the fact that the improvement is small suggests the training set is adequate in size.

The HINX runs shown in Table 3 correspond to the following variants: 1) using preposition "at" as part of the timex span; 2) disregarding timexes of class QUANTIFIER; 3) using full measures span for QUANTIFIERs (e.g. "20 mg"); 4) considering measure tokens as non-markable expressions; and 5) disregarding QUANTIFIERs that represent measures. The timex type QUANTIFIER was targeted in different submitted runs as it was not clear how these expressions were annotated when comparing the training corpus to the annotation guidelines.

The HINX system had the best Recall over all Clinical TempEval systems in both subtasks. The low precision of the rule-based system was, however, a surprise, and led us to examine the training and test corpora in detail. While we would expect to see inconsistencies in any manually created corpus, we found a surprising number of repeated inconsistencies between the guidelines and the corpora for certain very regular and unambiguous temporal language constructs. These included: a) timex span and class inconsistencies, b) non-markable expressions that were annotated as timexes, c) many occurrences of SET expressions that were not manually annotated in the corpus, and d) inconsistencies in the set of manually annotated QUANTIFIERs. Had these inconsistencies not been present in the gold standard, HINX would have attained a precision between 0.85 and 0.90 (Tissot et al., 2015).

We suggest that inconsistent data such as this will tend to lower the precision of rule-based systems. To illustrate this, we ran HeidelTime (Strötgen et al., 2013) on this year's dataset and found that precision and recall were low (0.44; 0.49) despite this being a demonstrably successful system in TempEval-3. Similarly low results can be observed from ClearTK-TimeML (0.593; 0.428), used to evaluate the THYME Corpus (Styler et al., 2014). Systems were run "as-is", unadapted to the clinical domain. Styler et al. (2014) suggest that clinical narratives introduce new challenges for temporal information extraction systems, and performance degrades when moving to this domain. However, they do not consider how far performance can be impaired by inconsistencies in the annotated corpus.

The appearance of a superior result by our machine learning system, which is agnostic about what information it uses to replicate the annotators' assertions, is therefore not to be taken at face value. A machine learning system may have learned regularities in an annotation style, rather than having learned to accurately find time expressions. This is an example of data bias (Hovy et al., 2014). Machine learning systems have a flexibility and power in finding non-obvious cues to more subtle patterns, which makes them successful in linguistically complex tasks, but also gives them a deceptive appearance of success where the irregularity in a task comes not from its inherent complexity but from flaws in the dataset.

Acknowledgments

We would like to thank the Mayo Clinic for permission to use the THYME corpus, and CAPES,[5] which is partially financing this work. This work also received funding from the European Union's Seventh Framework Programme (grant No. 611233,PHEME). AR, GG and LD are part funded by the National Institute for Health Research (NIHR) Biomedical Research Centre and Dementia Biomedical Research Unit at South London and Maudsley NHS Foundation Trust and King's College London.

References

Steven Bethard, Leon Derczynski, James Pustejovsky, and Marc Verhagen. 2015. SemEval-2015 Task 6: Clinical TempEval. In *Proceedings of the 9th International Workshop on Semantic Evaluation*.

Chih-Chung Chang and Chih-Jen Lin. 2011. LIBSVM: a library for support vector machines. *ACM Transactions on Intelligent Systems and Technology*, 2(3).

Hamish Cunningham, Diana Maynard, Kalina Bontcheva, Valentin Tablan, Niraj Aswani, Ian Roberts, Genevieve Gorrell, Adam Funk, Angus Roberts, Danica Damljanovic, Thomas Heitz, Mark A. Greenwood, Horacio Saggion, Johann Petrak, Yaoyong Li, and Wim Peters. 2011. *Text Processing with GATE (Version 6)*.

Lisa Ferro, Laurie Gerber, Inderjeet Mani, Beth Sundheim, and George Wilson. 2005. TIDES 2005 Standard for the Annotation of Temporal Expressions. Technical report, MITRE Corp.

Dirk Hovy, Barbara Plank, and Anders Søgaard. 2014. When POS data sets don't add up: Combatting sample bias. In *Proc. LREC*, LREC.

Yaoyong Li, Kalina Bontcheva, and Hamish Cunningham. 2005. SVM Based Learning System For Information Extraction. In Joab Winkler, Mahesan Niranjan, and Neil Lawerence, editors, *Deterministic and Statistical Methods in Machine Learning: First International Workshop, 7–10 September, 2004*, volume 3635 of *Lecture Notes in Computer Science*, pages 319–339, Sheffield, UK.

Yaoyong Li, Kalina Bontcheva, and Hamish Cunningham. 2009. Adapting SVM for Data Sparseness and Imbalance: A Case Study on Information Extraction. *Natural Language Engineering*, 15(2):241–271.

James Pustejovsky, Kiyong Lee, Harry Bunt, and Laurent Romary. 2010. ISO-TimeML: An international standard for semantic annotation. In *Proceedings of the 7th International Conference on Language Resources and Evaluation (LREC'10)*.

Roser Sauri, Jessica Littman, Robert Gaizauskas, Andrea Setzer, and James Pustejovsky. 2006. TimeML Annotation Guidelines, v1.2.1.

Jannik Strötgen, Julian Zell, and Michael Gertz. 2013. HeidelTime: Tuning English and Developing Spanish Resources for TempEval-3. In *Proceedings of the 7h International Workshop on Semantic Evaluation (SemEval 2013)*, pages 15–19.

William Styler, Steven Bethard, Sean Finan, Martha Palmer, Sameer Pradhan, Piet de Groen, Brad Erickson, Timothy Miller, Chen Lin, Guergana Savova, and James Pustejovsky. 2014. Temporal Annotation in the Clinical Domain. *Transactions of the Association for Computational Linguistics*, 2:143–154.

Weiyi Sun, Anna Rumshisky, and Ozlem Uzuner. 2013. Evaluating temporal relations in clinical text: 2012 i2b2 challenge. *Journal of the American Medical Informatics Association*, 20(5):806–813.

Hegler Tissot, Angus Roberts, Leon Derczynski, Genevieve Gorrell, and Marcos Didonet Del Fabro. 2015. Analysis of temporal expressions annotated in clinical notes. In *Proceedings of 11th Joint ACL-ISO Workshop on Interoperable Semantic Annotation*, pages 93–102, London, UK.

Naushad UzZaman, Hector Llorens, Leon Derczynski, Marc Verhagen, James F. Allen, and James Pustejovsky. 2013. SemEval-2013 Task 1: TempEval-3: Evaluating Time Expressions, Events, and Temporal Relations. In *Proceedings of the 7th International Workshop on Semantic Evaluations*.

[5] `http://www.iie.org/en/programs/capes` (accessed 27 Mar. 2015)

IXAGroupEHUDiac: A Multiple Approach System towards the Diachronic Evaluation of Texts

Haritz Salaberri[†], **Iker Salaberri**[‡], **Olatz Arregi**[†], **Beñat Zapirain**[†]
†*IXA* Group - Faculty of Computer Sciences, ‡Faculty of Arts
University of the Basque Country, Spain
firstname.lastname@ehu.eus

Abstract

This paper presents our contribution to the SemEval-2015 Task 7. The task was subdivided into three subtasks that consisted of automatically identifying the time period when a piece of news was written (1,2) as well as automatically determining whether a specific phrase in a sentence is relevant or not for a given period of time (3). Our system tackles the resolution of all three subtasks. With this purpose in mind multiple approaches are undertaken that use resources such as Wikipedia or Google NGrams. Final results are obtained by combining the output from all approaches. The texts used for the task are written in English and range from the years 1700 to 2000.

1 Introduction

According to Mihalcea and Nastase (2012) current applications within human language technology work with languages as if they were constant. However, changes in language are taking place constantly, for example: new meanings for old words are coined; metaphoric and metonymic uses become so ingrained that they are considered literal from one specific point in time on; new words are constantly being created.

These changes in language are what in part has motivated the task addressed by our system. In fact, subtasks (1) and (2) tackle the problem of computationally identifying the time period in which a piece of news was written. This is undertaken based on, among other things, the changes that take place in language over time. The difference between subtasks (1) and (2) is that the texts in subtask (1) contain clear references to time anchors. This means that e.g. historical events, relevant people, commercial products etc. are mentioned in the text that are specific to the period of time in which the texts were written. Subtask (3), on the other hand, consists of determining whether a phrase within a clause is specific or not to the period of time in which the text was written. The training corpus for this subtask is made up of the texts from other subtasks. As a consequence our system will be able to use information on both time anchors and language changes in order to generate the results for subtask (3).

This paper is organized as follows: section 2 presents the resources available to the diachronic evaluation of texts; section 3, on the other hand, shortly reviews the relevant literature on this matter. Section 4 makes a description of the developed system; results are then described in section 5 and, finally, our conclusions are given in section 6.

2 Resources

To the extent of our knowledge, there exist two main resources as of today for computationally addressing the diachronic evaluation of texts as defined in task 7: Google NGrams and Wikipedia. The former holds statistics on word usage on Google Books, a textual corpus consisting of books written in English and printed between 1505 and 2008. Google NGrams can be used to map language changes to specific time periods. The latter requires no presentation as it is a well-known resource; it can be used to establish the period a time anchor belongs to.

3 Related Work

To the best of our knowledge several techniques have been previously used to computationally address language-change. We consider it important to note that the motivation to study the language-change phenomena differs from one work to another: Some of the techniques make use of it in order to establish the period of time in which a text was produced (Jong et al., 2005; Dalli and Wilks, 2006), which is our main concern; others, on the other hand, use the phenomena in order to study topics such as the changes that have taken place in culture (Juola, 2013; Michel et al., 2011).

Some of the techniques used so far to address the task of temporal classification are based on language models built from texts belonging to a same period of time. This way the task of temporally classifying texts consists basically of identifying the model that best fits the text that wants to be classified. Some of the systems that follow this approach are Kumar (2011) and Wang et al. (2012).

Another relevant class of models for temporal classification is based on the idea that the change of word meaning and word usage over time can help determine the period of time in which a text was written. Normally the resource used by the systems that are based on this approach is Google NGrams (see section 2). Some example models that use this approach are presented in Mihalcea and Nastase (2012) and Popescu and Strapparava (2013).

Other systems that can be brought up in this section make use of stylistic and readability features (Štajner and Zampieri, 2013), neural nets (Kim et al., 2014) and lexical features (Dalli and Wilks, 2006).

From the approaches here presented we decided to implement our system using, among others, the change of word usage and word meaning over time approach (see subsection 4.1.3) and the lexical and stylistic features approach (see subsection 4.1.4) as we believe both to have reported good performance in previous works (Mihalcea and Nastase, 2012; Štajner and Zampieri, 2013; Dalli and Wilks, 2006). Although we think that the approach to epoch delimitation based on using language models can also come up with good results, we have not used it as we believe that the training set is too limited for this approach to be effective.

4 System Description

The way in which our system deals with temporal text classification (subtasks (1) and (2)) is described under subsection 4.1. The way in which our system deals with recognizing time-specific phrases (subtask (3)), on the other hand, is presented under subsection 4.2.

4.1 Temporal Text Classification

Four different approaches are undertaken in order to automatically determine the period of time in which a piece of news was written: the first approach consists of searching for the mentioned time period within the text. The second approach, on the other hand, consists of searching for named entities present in the text and then establishing the period of time by linking these to Wikipedia. The third approach uses Google NGrams and, to conclude, the fourth approach consists of using linguistic features that are significant with respect to language change in combination with machine learning.

4.1.1 Year Entity Detection

The present approach was implemented based on the observation made upon the training texts, in the development of which we have realized that the period of time that corresponds to a text is present within the text. This approach is characterized by a very high precision and a very low recall as only 10% of the training texts contain a period of time and in 85% of the cases these are the ones that correspond to texts. In order to establish the time period, year entities are detected by our system using the Apache OpenNLP name finder tool Baldridge (2005).

It is considered here that this approach is strongly dependent on the domain; in fact, if historical texts (or texts that in general describe past events) were to be diachronically evaluated, the precision would drop and recall would improve considerably.

4.1.2 Wikipedia Entity Linking

For the second approach our system detects named entities that correspond to persons and organizations within the texts; the Apache OpenNLP name finder tool and the pre-trained models for this type of entities are used. After named entities are recognized, these are searched for in Wikipedia; if a named entity can be found, then year entities are detected in the corresponding entry: with this purpose in mind the OpenNLP name finder tool is used and tuned as in 4.1.1. Finally, an average of all years (which stem from the Wikipedia entries that correspond to the named entities in the text) is calculated for every text and the time period that corresponds to the average assigned. The workflow for this approach can be seen in figure 1:

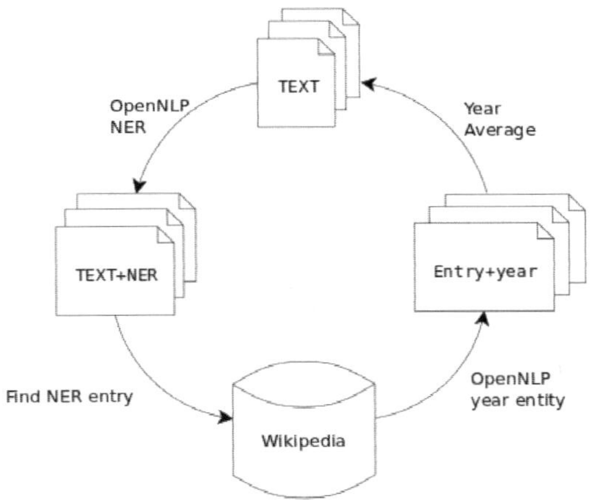

Figure 1: Wikipedia Entity Linking.

Different scenarios are possible concerning this approach: some texts do not contain named entities and some others have many of them, and sometimes entities are not detected or can not be found in Wikipedia. For these reasons not all texts are assigned a time period by this approach[1].

4.1.3 Google NGrams

The Google NGrams 1-gram corpus is used for the third approach. We consider all nouns (proper and common) within the texts to be of interest as we consider these to be the kind of words that change most across time and as a result provide the highest amount of information on the time in which a piece of news was written. In order to identify these nouns the ClearNLP PoS tagger and lemmatizer is used Choi and Palmer (2012). The system computes for each noun the percentage of occurrences that that noun has in a year with respect to the sum of words available for that year (normalization). The amount of published data in Google Books is not the same for all years; in fact, it grows exponentially from the second half of the 20th century on. For this reason the percentage of occurrences with respect to the sum of words needs to be calculated, rather than simply using the amount of occurrences.

When percentages for all nouns in a text are calculated, the year that corresponds to the highest percentage is associated to each noun. Then, the average value for these years is calculated. If the year associated to a noun differs in 40 or more years from the average value, our system considers this noun to be period-specific. Consequently, the time period that includes this year is assigned to the text. Period-specific nouns are determined locally within a given text since the same noun might be period-specific in one text but not in another.

If there is more than one noun that is considered to be period-specific, the average value of the years that correspond to these nouns is used. If there are no detected period-specific nouns, on the other hand, the average value calculated for all nouns is used.

4.1.4 Language Change

The fourth approach used by our system consists of using linguistic features (patterns or tendencies) that are significant regarding language change in combination with machine learning. For this purpose the different diachronic or language-change tendencies that are observable in the training data have been studied. These tendencies include both linguistic and extra-linguistic factors, and they affect different areas of grammar such as orthography, lexicon, semantics, morphology or syntax. Some examples can be seen in figure 2.

The patterns resulting from the study are classified into six different fifty-year periods ranging from the years 1700 to 2000 as we consider these to be the finest grain period patterns can be classified into. Said patterns are used as features for the learning algorithm; some examples include: the loss of subjunctive mood in subordinate clauses, the arisal of *do so*-verbal substitution and the extinction of postpositions and of various inflectional morphemes. In spite of the richness of extracted linguistic change patterns, this approach has proved in any case to be

[1]Our approach does not handle cases where more than one Wikipedia pages match a name.

ORTHOGRAPHY

- Until about 1720 reflexive pronouns and their possessors are written separately instead of together:
  ...she fancies her self in a Wood... (1707-1713)
- About 1895 the contraction Messr. is replaced by Mr. for 'mister' or 'messieur':
  ...from Messrs. Chatto & Windus... (1894-1900)
  ...Mr. Balfour appears in the strange capacity... (1904-1910)

LEXICON

- Use of the archaic locative adverb 'thither' in the sense of 'in this direction, here'. 1720 at the latest:
  ...the reinforcements sent thither from Milan and Spain... (1698-1704)
- Loss of the word guineas for pounds, around 1900:
  ...lowest price 130 guineas... (1814-1820)
  ...just pays a couple of pounds... (1970-1976)

SEMANTICS

- Use of the verb 'fit' in the sense of 'walk, move' instead of 'to suit', until around 1715:
  ...as I fate under the Shadow of it... (1706-1712)
- The verb 'to wit' is used in the sense of 'to know' in a phossilized expression. These verb and expression are no longer used nowadays.
  ...That afterwards, to wit, on the twenty seventh day... (1715-1717)

MORPHOLOGY

- Fossilized trace of 2nd person singular marker in verbal morphology: (you) Could'st instead of you could, 1710 at the latest.
  ...Jerusalem! Could'st thou but know... (1699-1705)
- Citicization of the pronoun 'it' to the conjugated copula 'is' into 'tis'. Until about 1720, although frozen uses could exist even today.
  ...Tis such an Entertaiment... (1707-1713)

SYNTAX

- Complete loss of the non-do-auxiliary pattern of the do-auxiliary in negative clauses, emphatic constructions, and yes/no questions, approximate date 1730. This implies loss of the pattern of the negative particle following the finite verb..
  ...and I hear of I know not how... (1709-1715)

Figure 2: Some of the language-change patterns used by our system.

much less effective when compared to the other approaches.

The classifier used by the approach here described is a standard multi-class *Support Vector Machine* classifier implemented using the *SVM-multiclass* package in Joachims (1999). The decision of using a standard SVM learning algorithm comes from our experience on classification tasks with such a large number of classes.

4.1.5 Final Decision

In order to ultimately determine the period of time in which a text was written the system follows a procedure that takes into account the precision given by each approach (since the systems seeks maximum precision). We consider the year entity detection approach to be the one with the highest precision, followed by the Wikipedia entity linking, the Google NGrams and the language-change approaches. The present procedure establishes that the period of time yielded by the approach with the maximum precision that is available must be set to the text. It must be kept in mind that both the year entity detection and the Wikipedia entity linking approaches have a low recall as only some of the texts are assigned a period of time by these approaches.

Subtask \ Grain	Coarse		Medium		Fine	
	Precision	Score	Precision	Score	Precision	Score
1	0.0902	0.5575	0.0413	0.3672	0.0225	0.187
2	0.0987	0.6225	0.0677	0.428	0.0377	0.2618
3	0.5739					

Table 1: Official results reported for our system for all three subtasks.

4.2 Recognizing Time-Specific Phrases

We consider that determining whether the phrases within a sentence are particularly relevant or not for the period of time in which the sentence was written can be viewed as a two-step procedure: first, markable phrases need to be detected, and then it must be decided whether these phrases are indicative features for the period of time or not. Our system performs just the classification step since the markable phrases are provided by the task organizers. This is achieved by making use of the period-specific words identified in the Google NGrams approach described in 4.1.3. Our system marks the set of consecutive words that start and end with period-specific words as a relevant phrase for the period of time in which the text was written. This procedure is followed if there is no punctuation mark between the words and the distance is not greater than four words.

The decision to consider phrases that have a maximum of four words is based upon observation. We consider this to be the appropriate number of words in order not to miss too many relevant phrases. The system can be easily tuned for phrases with a greater or a smaller number of words.

5 Results

Table 1 contains the official results reported for our system. In order to evaluate subtasks (1) and (2) three configurations are considered: a fine-graded evaluation were periods of time span two years in subtask (1) and six years in subtask (2); a medium-graded evaluation were periods of time span six years for subtask (1) and twelve years for subtask (2) and a coarse-graded evaluation were periods of time span twelve years in subtask (1) and twenty years in subtask (2).

There is no fine-, medium- or coarse-graded evaluation for subtask (3). Certain phrases from a piece of news are selected by the task organizers and marked as *yes* or *no* by our system according to their relevance for the period of time when the news was produced (the period of time is also provided by the organizers). The score for this subtask is computed by counting the number of times our system has correctly marked the phrases.

As far as we know the only works that bear a slight resemblance to what is proposed in the temporal text classification subtasks (subtasks (1) and (2)) are Mihalcea and Nastase (2012) and Popescu and Strapparava (2013), in which computational approaches to temporal classification of words are presented. We consider that our results cannot be even loosely compared to the results in the cited papers as there is too little resemblance between temporal text classification and temporal word classification. We are not aware of any work that performs recognition of time-specific phrases (subtasks (3)).

As can be observed in table 1, the scores for subtask (2) are higher than the scores reported for subtask (1); however, we find that establishing the period of time when a piece of news was written is more complicated for the texts in subtask (1) as it mainly depends on a correct exploitation of time anchors. For this reason, we understand that the performance of our system is higher in subtask (1) than in subtask (2). Finally, we believe that the score obtained for the third subtask (0.5739) can be understood as an indicator of high performance as the difficulty of the subtask is, in our opinion, higher than that of other subtasks.

6 Conclusions and Future Works

In this paper we have presented our system for the diachronic evaluation of English texts, which has taken part in the SemEval-2015 task 7. Our system has been the only participant system that has reported results for the three subtasks that comprehended the task. We believe that many issues still need to be reviewed.

We intend to improve the overall performance of the system in the near future by trying out new techniques that we have not been able to implement due to time limitations.

Acknowledgments

Haritz Salaberri holds a PhD grant from the University of the Basque Country (UPV/EHU)(*IXA* Group, Research Group of type A (2010-2015)(IT34410)). In addition, this work has been supported by the FP7 *NewsReader* project (Grant No. 316404).

References

Jason Baldridge. 2005. The opennlp project. *URL: http://opennlp. apache. org/index. html,(accessed 2 February 2012).*

Jinho D. Choi and Martha Palmer. 2012. Fast and robust part-of-speech tagging using dynamic model selection. In *Proceedings of the 50th Annual Meeting of the Association for Computational Linguistics: Short Papers-Volume 2*, pages 363–367. Association for Computational Linguistics.

Angelo Dalli and Yorick Wilks. 2006. Automatic dating of documents and temporal text classification. In *Proceedings of the Workshop on Annotating and Reasoning about Time and Events*, pages 17–22. Association for Computational Linguistics.

Thorsten Joachims. 1999. Making large scale SVM learning practical. *Universität Dortmund.*

F. de Jong, Henning Rode, Djoerd Hiemstra. 2005. Temporal language models for the disclosure of historical text. *Royal Netherlands Academy of Arts and Sciences.*

Patrick Juola. 2013. Using the Google N-Gram corpus to measure cultural complexity. In *Literary and linguistic computing 28(4)*, pages 668–675. Association for Computational Linguistics.

Yoon Kim, Yi-I Chiu, Kentaro Hanaki, Darshan Hegde, Slav Petrov. 2014. Temporal analysis of language through neural language models. *arXiv preprint arXiv:1405.3515.*

Abhimanu Kumar, Matthew Lease, Jason Baldridge. 2011. Supervised language modeling for temporal resolution of texts. In *Proceedings of the 20th ACM international conference on Information and knowledge management*, pages 2069–2072. Association for Computational Linguistics.

Jean-Baptiste Michel, Yuan Kui Shen, Aviva Presser Aiden, Adrian Veres, Matthew K. Gray, Joseph P. Pickett, Dale Hoiberg, Dan Clancy, Peter Norvig, Jon Orwant and others. 2011. Quantitative analysis of culture using millions of digitized books. *Science*, 331(6014):176–182.

Rada Mihalcea and Vivi Nastase. 2012. Word epoch disambiguation: Finding how words change over time. In *Proceedings of the 50th Annual Meeting of the Association for Computational Linguistics: Short Papers-Volume 2*, pages 259–263. Association for Computational Linguistics.

Octavian Popescu and Carlo Strapparava. 2013. Behind the times: Detecting epoch changes using large corpora. In *Proc. of IJCNLP.*

Octavian Popescu and Carlo Strapparava. 2014. Time corpora: Epochs, opinions and changes. *Knowledge-Based Systems.*

Sanja Štajner and Marcos Zampieri. 2013. Stylistic changes for temporal text classification. *Text, Speech, and Dialogue*, pages 519–526. Springer.

Chong Wang, David Blei, David Heckerman. 2012. Continuous time dynamic topic models. *arXiv preprint arXiv:1206.3298.*

USAAR-CHRONOS: Crawling the Web for Temporal Annotations

Liling Tan and Noam Ordan
Universität des Saarlandes
Campus A2.2, Saarbrücken, Germany
alvations@gmail.com, noam.ordan@uni-saarland.de

Abstract

This paper describes the USAAR-CHRONOS participation in the Diachronic Text Evaluation task of SemEval-2015 to identify the time period of historical text snippets. We adapt a web crawler to retrieve the original source of the text snippets and determine the publication year of the retrieved texts from their URLs. We report a precision score of >90% in identifying the text epoch. Additionally, by crawling and cleaning the website that hosts the source of the text snippets, we present Daikon, a corpus that can be used for future work on epoch identification from a diachronic perspective.

1 Introduction

"*Time changes all things: there is no reason why language should escape this universal law*" (De Saussure, 1959). Traditionally, there are two ways to collect linguistic data to explore how words change over time, viz. (i) the 'armchair' method and (ii) the 'tape-recorder' method (Aitchison, 2001). In the first, the linguist cross-examines numerous documents from bygone years and in the latter, the linguist goes around recording language and studies the changes as they happen.

With the ingress of historical data provided by Google (Michel et al. 2011), the 'armchair' method goes into warp speed as computational linguists explore the different facets of lexical changes in English (Mihalcea and Nastase, 2012; Popescu and Strapparava, 2013; Niculae et al., 2014).

This paper presents the Saarland University (USAAR-CHRONOS) participation in the Diachronic Text Evaluation task in SemEval-2015. We participated in Subtask 1 that requires participants to identify the year of publication for texts with clear reference to time anchors (i.e. explicit references to famous persons or events).

1.1 Task Definition

In Subtask 1 of the Diachronic Text Evaluation participants are required to identify the epoch (i.e. time period) of a text snippet with clear reference to certain famous persons or events. The text snippets may not necessarily contain temporal information such as year or date but it has clear reference to a historical event that can be identified from external knowledge bases. For instance, given the following text, participants are required to identify its epoch:

"*Dictator Saddam Hussein ordered his troops to march into Kuwait. After the invasion is condemned by the UN Security Council, the US has forged a coalition with allies. Today American troops are sent to Saudi Arabia in Operation Desert Shield, protecting Saudi Arabia from possible attack.*"

The text has clear temporal evidence with reference to a historical figure ("*Saddam Hussein*"), a notable organization ("*UN Security Council*") and a factual event ("*Operation Desert Shield*"). Historically, we know that Saddam Hussein lived between 1937 to 2006, that the UN Security Council has existed since 1946 and that Operation Desert Shield (i.e. the Gulf War) occurred between 1990-1991. Given the specific chronic deicticity ("*today*") that indicates that the text is published during the Gulf

War, we can conceive that the text snippet should be dated 1990-1991.

For each text snippet, different epoch choices are provided at three granularity levels; fine, medium and coarse graded epochs, and they are assigned the time periods of 3, 6 and 12 years, respectively. For the given example above, the correct epochs are 1990-1992, 1988-1993 and 1985-1995 for the three granularity levels respectively.

2 Related Work

Michel et al. (2011) launch the field of *culturonomics* to study changes in human culture through language change; for this, they release ngrams taken from millions of digitized books; they show, for example, that censorship and suppression can be determined by comparing the frequencies of proper names in multilingual ngrams in this dataset.

Mihalcea and Nastase (2012) explore word sense disambiguation over time using snippets from Google Books; they add a semantic dimension on top of lexical frequency to conduct word epoch disambiguation based on the fact that words change their neighbors throughout time.

The Google Ngram corpus has spawned several related studies. To create a sense pool, Yu et al. (2007) extract pairs of ngrams and filter them with an appropriate statistical test using their frequencies, where the resulting sense pool is manually verified. Interestingly, their experiments conflate the ngrams across time, yet it is unclear whether the resulting sense pool contains ngrams across different epochs. Juola (2013) uses the bigrams from the Google Books Ngram dataset to measure changes in the Kolmogorov complexity of American culture at ten-year intervals between 1900 and 2000. Related to this, Štajner and Zampieri (2013) show, for Portuguese, that lexical richness, average word length and lexical density increase over a span of 400 years.

Topic models are also applied to study topical changes across epochs (e.g. (Blei and Lafferty, 2007; Wijaya and Yeniterzi, 2011)). Related to epoch identification, Wang and McCallum (2006) develop time-specific topic models to a time stamp prediction task.

With the renaissance of neural nets, recent studies are using deep neural language models to detect diachronic lexical changes from several text types ranging from published books (Kim et al., 2014) to Twitter microblogs and Amazon movie reviews (Kulkarni et al., 2014).

3 Approach

We take a different approach compared to previous studies that treat epoch identification as a classification task. We see it as an information retrieval task where we want to know whether we can get the temporal information of the text snippets from the Internet.

In the age where there is a contest (known as "Googlewhack") for finding one-hit results on Google since they are so rare , it is clear that a great deal of the information we are looking for is just "out there" for us to search. It is recommended to use machine learning classifiers for cases where test data is supposedly unknown, but more often than not it can be known by those who know how to retrieve, clean and harvest systematically.

Prior to the days of Google and search engines, historians and librarians[1] had to cross-reference history books and newspaper archives to identify the text epoch. The Internet is vast and infinite. Given the advent of Wikipedia and Google, epoch identification can be as simple as searching "*When was Operation Desert Shield?*" on Google[2] (see Figure 1).

Figure 1: Google Result for "*When was Operation Desert Shield?*".

Tan et al. (2014a) develop a Web Translation Memory (`WebTM`) crawler capable of harvesting parallel texts from the web given an initial seed corpus, similar to the BootCaT system (Baroni and Bernardini, 2004). They adapt `WebTM` such that it attempts to find occurrences of the text snippets from the web. This is akin to developing a dedicated

[1]With the exception of the polymath librarian, Flynn Carsen

[2]See http://goo.gl/VD2Xtx

search- and crawl-system for the purpose of knowledge extraction.

Surprisingly, the source of the all the text snippets of Subtask 1 is found on `http://freepages.genealogy.rootsweb.ancestry.com/~dutillieul` and `http://archive.spectator.co.uk/`. Moreover, these webpages contain dates in their URL, so we extract the publication year with regex pattern matching. Since the task requires an epoch (time period) instead of a discrete publication year, we perform some minor integer manipulation to fit the publication year to the expected epoch[3].

4 Results

Out of the 267 text snippets, our system correctly identifies 243, 248, 252 epochs for the fine, medium and coarse epoch granularities.

	Fine	Medium	Coarse
AMBRA	0.0374	0.0711	0.0749
IXA-EHUDIAC	0.0225	0.0413	0.0902
USAAR-CHRONOS	**0.9288**	**0.9101**	**0.9438**

Table 1: Precision scores on Subtask 1.

Table 1 presents the precision scores of the participating teams in subtask 1. Our system scores best on all three granularity levels.

Figure 2 shows a heatmap of the fine graded epochal (6 years interval) differences between the outputs and the gold standard[4]. The warm colors indicate higher values within the interval. Looking at the orange region of the heatmap, the other systems were way off in the epoch identification where respectively, AMBRA and IXA-EHUDIAC have 195 and 186 predictions that are 54 years off from the gold standards. We have a total of 24 predictions different from the gold standard and 9 out 24 were 6 years off from the gold standards.

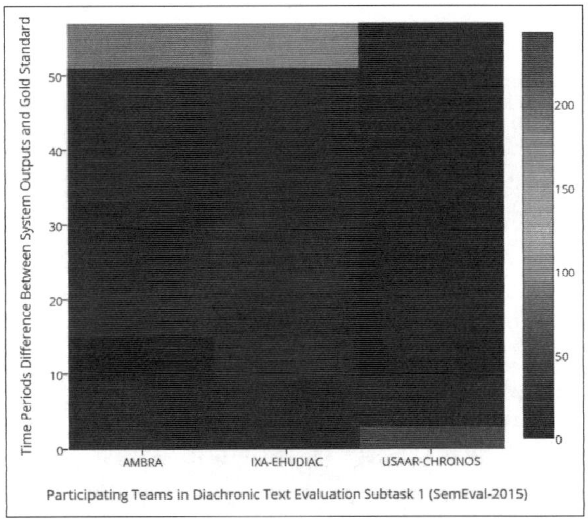

Figure 2: Fine Graded Epoch Differential between Systems outputs and Gold Standards (warmer colors indicates higher values).

5 Discussion

We have manually checked our epoch predictions and the years encoded in the URL to check whether they correspond to the date of the source articles. Some of our predictions are dated older than the gold standards and vice versa.

For instance, the following text refers to the *Battle of Salamanca* on 22 July 1812 and the text snippet is from a battle report written on 16 August 1812 and published on 24 August 1812 in the *Salisbury and Winchester Journal*; the gold annotation records the epoch as 1813-1815 whereas our system reports 1810-1812.

"*On Thursday last, the 69th Annual Conference of the people called Methodists, was concluded. It had been held by adjournment in Leeds from the 27th ult. About 309 Itinerant Preachers were present from various parts of the United Kingdom, who gave very gratifying accounts of the success with which their ministry have been crowned.*"

In this case, the gold standard source is clearly a different source and the assumption that there are hard boundaries in epoch identification should be relaxed. One should consider different granularity levels of the epochs involved when evaluating the system's accuracy.

Relating to the historian and librarian anecdote, the discrepancy in dates from different sources shows that cross-referencing temporal annotations from various sources should be considered in future diachronic studies and temporal analyses.

[3]Details on http://goo.gl/TcZ9z0

[4]An interactive version of the heatmap can be viewed on https://plot.ly/ alvations/21/epochs-differential/

6 Daikon Corpus

After the SemEval task, we crawled the full articles from `http://archive.spectator.co.uk/`, cleaned the corpus and annotated it with the exact publication date of the article, its title and the URL from which it was retrieved. The Daikon Corpus is made up of articles from the British Spectator news magazine from year 828 to 2008.

The Daikon corpus can be used for future diachronic studies and epoch identification tasks; it provides a complementary dataset to the gold standard provided by task. The corpus is saved in JSON format. An excerpt from the corpus looks like this:


```
{
  "url": "http://archive.spectator.co.uk/article/25th-
september-1999/37/death-has-no-dominion",
  "date": "24 Sep 1999",
  "title": "ego and I",
  "body": [
    "The English are not very suicidal, they are just
not good at it",
    "IN THE 18th century, suicide was regard- ed,
particularly by the French, as an English disease. 'The
English destroy themselves most unaccountably,' wrote
Montesquieu, and Voltaire was told that during an East
wind the English hanged themselves by the dozen. True or
not, the chaussure is now on the other foot. The suicide
rate for men in England and Wales is about 10 per
100,000 inhabitants, com- pared with 30 in
France.", ...],
}
```


Figure 3: An Excerpt from the Daikon Corpus.

Each item in the body list is a paragraph embedded within the `<p>...</p>` tags of the webpage. The corpus contains 24,280 articles with 19 million tokens; the token count is calculated by summing the number of whitespaces plus 1 for each paragraph.

To clean the corpus, the encodings are converted to Unicode (UTF8) and XML escape tokens are converted to its Unicode counterparts automatically[5]. However, the current version still contains minor tokenization errors such as the hyphenation error seen in Figure 3. Probably, a character language model could be developed to identify lexical items bounded by the r'\w+- \w+' regex.

7 Conclusion

In this paper, we have described our submission to the Diachronic Text Evaluation for SemEval-2015. We have adapted a web crawler to search for the source of the text snippets used for the evaluation and achieved the highest precision score. Additionally, we have crawled and cleaned the source articles of the snippets and produced the `Daikon` corpus that can be used for future research in diachronic/temporal analysis and epoch identification.

[5]The cleaning tool used is a compilation of web cleaning scripts (Emerson et al., 2014; Tan et al., 2014b; Tan and Bond, 2011)

Acknowledgements

The research leading to these results has received funding from the People Programme (Marie Curie Actions) of the European Union's Seventh Framework Programme FP7/2007-2013/ under REA grant agreement n ° 317471. In addition, we received support from Deutsche Forschungsgemeinschaft (DFG) through grants from the Cluster of Excellence – Multimodal Computing and Interaction (EXC-MMCI) and SFB 1102. We thank Elke Teich for her encouraging input.

References

Jean Aitchison. 2001. *Language Change: Progress or Decay?* Cambridge University Press.

Marco Baroni and Silvia Bernardini. 2004. BootCaT: Bootstrapping Corpora and Terms from the Web. In *Proceedings of the Fourth International Conference on Language Resources and Evaluation (LREC'04)*.

David M Blei and John D Lafferty. 2007. A Correlated Topic Model of Science. *The Annals of Applied Statistics*, pages 17–35.

Ferdinand De Saussure. 1959. *Course in General Linguistics*. New York:McGrawHill.

Guy Emerson, Liling Tan, Susanne Fertmann, Alexis Palmer, and Michaela Regneri. 2014. SeedLing: Building and Using a Seed corpus for the Human Language Project. In *Proceedings of the 2014 Workshop on the Use of Computational Methods in the Study of Endangered Languages*, pages 77–85, Baltimore, Maryland, USA, June.

Patrick Juola. 2013. Using the Google N-Gram corpus to Measure Cultural Complexity. *Literary and linguistic computing*, 28(4):668–675.

Yoon Kim, Yi-I Chiu, Kentaro Hanaki, Darshan Hegde, and Slav Petrov. 2014. Temporal Analysis of Language through Neural Language Models. *arXiv preprint arXiv:1405.3515*.

Vivek Kulkarni, Rami Al-Rfou, Bryan Perozzi, and Steven Skiena. 2014. Statistically Significant Detection of Linguistic Change. *CoRR*, abs/1411.3315.

Jean-Baptiste Michel, Yuan Kui Shen, Aviva Presser Aiden, Adrian Veres, Matthew K Gray, Joseph P Pickett, Dale Hoiberg, Dan Clancy, Peter Norvig, Jon Orwant, et al. 2011. Quantitative Analysis of Culture using Millions of Digitized Books. *science*, 331(6014):176–182.

Rada Mihalcea and Vivi Nastase. 2012. Word Epoch Disambiguation: Finding how Words Change over Time. In *Proceedings of the 50th Annual Meeting of the Association for Computational Linguistics: Short Papers-Volume 2*, pages 259–263.

Vlad Niculae, Marcos Zampieri, Liviu P. Dinu, and Alina Maria Ciobanu. 2014. Temporal Text Ranking and Automatic Dating of Texts. In *Proceedings of the 14th Conference of the European Chapter of the Association for Computational Linguistics (EACL 2014)*.

Octavian Popescu and Carlo Strapparava. 2013. Behind the Times: Detecting Epoch Changes using Large Corpora. In *Proceedings of 6th International Joint Conference on Natural Language Processing (IJCNLP)*.

Sanja Štajner and Marcos Zampieri. 2013. Stylistic Changes for Temporal Text Classification. In *Proceedings of the 16th International Conference on Text Speech and Dialogue (TSD2013), Lecture Notes in Artificial Intelligence (LNAI)*, pages 519–526, Pilsen, Czech Republic. Springer.

Liling Tan and Francis Bond. 2011. Building and Annotating the Linguistically Diverse NTU-MC (NTU-Multilingual Corpus). In *Proceedings of the 25th Pacific Asia Conference on Language, Information and Computation*, pages 362–371, Singapore.

Liling Tan, Anne Schumann, Jose Martinez, and Francis Bond. 2014a. Sensible: L2 Translation Assistance by Emulating the Manual Post-Editing Process. In *Proceedings of the 8th International Workshop on Semantic Evaluation (SemEval 2014)*, pages 541–545, Dublin, Ireland.

Liling Tan, Marcos Zampieri, Nikola Ljubešic, and Jörg Tiedemann. 2014b. Merging Comparable Data Sources for the Discrimination of Similar Languages: The DSL Corpus Collection. In *Proceedings of The 7th Workshop on Building and Using Comparable Corpora (BUCC)*.

Xuerui Wang and Andrew McCallum. 2006. Topics over Time: A Non-Markov Continuous-Time Model of Topical Trends. In *Proceedings of the 12th ACM SIGKDD international conference on Knowledge discovery and data mining*, pages 424–433.

Derry Tanti Wijaya and Reyyan Yeniterzi. 2011. Understanding Semantic Change of Words over Centuries. In *Proceedings of the 2011 international workshop on DETecting and Exploiting Cultural diversiTy on the social web*, pages 35–40.

Liang-Chih Yu, Chung-Hsien Wu, Andrew Philpot, and EH Hovy. 2007. OntoNotes: Sense Pool Verification using Google N-gram and Statistical Tests. In *Proceedings of the OntoLex Workshop at the 6th International Semantic Web Conference (ISWC 2007)*.

AMBRA: A Ranking Approach to Temporal Text Classification

Marcos Zampieri[1,2], Alina Maria Ciobanu[3], Vlad Niculae[4], Liviu P. Dinu[3]
Saarland University, Germany[1]
German Research Center for Artificial Intelligence (DFKI), Germany[2]
Center for Computational Linguistics, University of Bucharest, Romania[3]
Deptartment of Computer Science, Cornell University, USA[4]
marcos.zampieri@uni-saarland.de; alina.ciobanu@my.fmi.unibuc.ro;
vn66@cornell.edu; ldinu@fmi.unibuc.ro;

Abstract

This paper describes the AMBRA system, entered in the SemEval-2015 Task 7: 'Diachronic Text Evaluation' subtasks one and two, which consist of predicting the date when a text was originally written. The task is valuable for applications in digital humanities, information systems, and historical linguistics. The novelty of this shared task consists of incorporating label uncertainty by assigning an interval within which the document was written, rather than assigning a clear time marker to each training document. To deal with non-linear effects and variable degrees of uncertainty, we reduce the problem to pairwise comparisons of the form *is Document A older than Document B?*, and propose a non-parametric way to transform the ordinal output into time intervals.

1 Introduction

Temporal text classification consists of learning to automatically predict the publication date of documents, by using the information contained in their textual content. The task finds uses in fields as varied as digital humanities, where many texts have are unidentified or controversial publication dates, information retrieval (Dakka et al., 2012), where temporal constraints can improve relevance, and historical linguistics, where the interpretation of the learned models can confirm and reveal insights.

From a technical point of view, the task is usually tackled either as regression or, more commonly, as a single-label multi-class problem, with classes defined as time intervals such as months, years, decades or centuries. The regression approach assumes that precise timestamps are uniformly available for each document, which is suitable for cases of social media documents (Preotiuc-Pietro, 2014), but less suitable for documents surrounded by more uncertainty. Multi-class classification, on the other hand, suffers from a coarseness tradeoff: using coarser classes is less informative, and using finer classes reduces the number of training instances in each class, making the problem more difficult. Furthermore, with a multi-class formulation, the temporal relationship between classes is lost.

The 'Diachronic Text Evaluation' subtasks one and two from SemEval-2015 are formulated similarly to a multi-class problem, where each document is assigned to an interval such as 1976-1982. To accommodate such labels, we propose an approach based on pairwise comparisons. We train a classifier to learn which document out of a pair is older and which is newer. If two documents come from overlapping intervals, then their order cannot be determined with certainty, so the pair is not used in training. We use the property of linear models to extend a set of pairwise decisions into a ranking of test documents (Joachims, 2006).

While previous work uses a regression-based method to map the ranking back to actual timestamps, we propose a novel non-parametric method to choose the most likely interval. In light of this, our system is named AMBRA (Anachronism Modeling by Ranking). Our implementation is available under a permissive open-source license.[1]

[1] https://github.com/vene/ambra

2 Related Work

An important class of models for temporal classification employs prototype-based classification methods, using probabilistic language models and distances in distribution space to classify documents to the time period with the most similar language (de Jong et al., 2005; Kumar et al., 2011). Kanhabua and Nørvåg (2009) use temporal language models to assign timestamps to unlabeled documents.

An extension of such models for continuous time is proposed by Wang et al. (2008), who use Brownian motion as a model for topic change over time. This approach is simpler and faster than the discrete time version, but it cannot be directly applied to documents with different degrees of label uncertainty, such as interval labels.

Dalli and Wilks (2006) train a classifier to date texts within a time span of nine years. The method uses lexical features and it is aided by words whose frequencies increase at some point in time, most notably named entities. Abe and Tsumoto (2010) propose similarity metrics to categorise texts based on keywords calculated by indexes such as *tf-idf*. Garcia-Fernandez et al. (2011) explore different NLP techniques on a digitized collection of French texts published between 1801 and 1944. Style-related markers and features, including readability features, have been shown to reveal temporal information in English as well as Portuguese (Stamou, 2005; Štajner and Zampieri, 2013).

An intersecting research direction combines diatopic (regional) and diachronic variation for French journalistic texts (Grouin et al., 2010) and for the Dutch Folktale Database, which includes texts from different dialects and varieties of Dutch, as well as historical texts (Trieschnigg et al., 2012).

More recently, Ciobanu et al. (2013) propose supervised classification with unigram features with χ^2 feature selection on a collection of historical Romanian texts, noting that the informative features are words having changed form over time. Niculae et al. (2014) circumvent the limitations of supervised classification by posing the problem as ordinal regression with a learning-to-rank approach. They evaluate their method on datasets in English, Portuguese and Romanian. The superior flexibility of the ranking approach makes it a better fit for the problem formulation of the 'Diachronic Text Evaluation' task, motivating us to base our implementation on it.

A different, but related, problem is to model and understand how words usage and meaning change over time. Wijaya and Yeniterzi (2011) use the Google NGram corpus aiming to identify clusters of topics surrounding the word over time. Mihalcea and Nastase (2012) split the Google Books corpus into three wide epochs and introduce the task of *word epoch disambiguation*. Turning this problem around, Popescu and Strapparava (2013) use a similar approach to statistically characterize epochs by lexical and emotion features.

3 Methods

The 'Diachronic Text Evaluation' shared task consists of three subtasks (Popescu and Strapparava, 2015): classification of documents containing explicit references to time-specific persons or events (**T1**), classification of documents with time-specific language use (**T2**), and recognition of time-specific expressions (**T3**). The AMBRA system participated in T1 and T2.

3.1 Corpus

The training data released for the shared task consists of 323 documents for T1 and 4,202 documents for T2. Each document has a paragraph containing, on average, 71 tokens, along with a tag indicating when each text was written/published. The publication date of texts is indicated by time intervals at all three granularity levels: *fine-*, *medium-* and *coarse-grained* (e.g. `<textM yes="1695-1707">` for a text written between the years 1695 and 1707 in the medium-grained representation).

The shared task mentions no limitation regarding the use of external corpora. Nevertheless, to avoid thematic bias, we use only the corpora provided by the organizers under the assumption that the test and training sets are sampled from the same distribution.

The released test set consists of 267 instances for T1 and 1,041 instances for T2.

3.2 Algorithm and Features

We use a ranking approach by pairwise comparisons, previously proposed for temporal text modeling by Niculae et al. (2014) .

Learning. The model learns a linear function $g(x) = w \cdot x$ to preserve the temporal ordering of the texts, i.e. if document[2] x_i predates document x_j, which we will henceforth denote as $x_i \prec x_j$, then $g(x_i) < g(x_j)$. This step can be understood as *learning to rank* texts from older to newer. By making pairwise comparisons, the problem can be reduced to binary classification using a linear model.

A dataset annotated with intervals has the form $\mathcal{D} = \{(x, [y^{\text{first}}, y^{\text{last}})]\}$ where $y^{\text{first}} < y^{\text{last}}$ are the years between which document x was written. Document x_i can be said to predate document x_j only if its interval predates the other without overlap:

$$x_i \prec x_j \iff y_i^{\text{last}} < y_j^{\text{first}}.$$

This allows us to construct a dataset consisting only of correctly-ordered pairs:

$$\mathcal{D}_p = \{(x_i, x_j) : x_i \prec x_j\}.$$

This reduces to linear binary classification:

$$w \cdot x_i < w \cdot x_j \iff w \cdot (x_i - x_j) < 0.$$

We form a balanced training set by flipping the order of half of the pairs in D_p at random.

Prediction. Niculae et al. (2014), following Pedregosa et al. (2012), fit a monotonic function mapping from years to the space spanned by the learned linear model. In contrast, to better deal with the interval formulation, we propose a non-parametric memory-based approach. After training, we store:

$$D_{\text{scores}} = \{(z = w \cdot x, [y^{\text{first}}, y^{\text{last}}]\}.$$

When queried about when a previously unseen document x was written, we compute $z = w \cdot x$ and search for the k closest entries in D_{scores}, which we denote D^z_{scores}. For each candidate interval for the test document $[y^{\text{first}}, y^{\text{last}}]$ we compute its average distance to the intervals of the k nearest training documents $[y_i^{\text{first}}, y_i^{\text{last}}] \in D^z_{\text{scores}}$ where:

$$\text{dist}\,(y_a, y_b) = \left| \frac{y_a^{\text{last}} + y_a^{\text{first}}}{2} - \frac{y_b^{\text{last}} + y_b^{\text{first}}}{2} \right|.$$

[2]We overload x_i to refer to the document itself as well as its representation as a feature vector.

The predicted interval is the one minimizing the average distance:

$$\hat{y} = \arg\min_{y \in \mathcal{Y}} \frac{1}{k} \sum_{y_i \in D^z_{\text{scores}}} \text{dist}(y, y_i).$$

Importantly, this approach allows for even more flexibility in interval labels than needed for the 'Diachronic Text Evaluation' task. While in the task all intervals (at a given granularity level) have the same size, our method can deal with intervals of various sizes,[3] half-lines $[-\infty, a]$ or $[a, \infty]$ for expressing only a lower or only an upper bound on the time of writing of a document, and even degenerate intervals $[a, a]$ for when the time is known exactly.

Features. AMBRA uses four types of features:

- Length meta-features (number of sentences, types, tokens);
- Stylistic (Average Word Length, Average Sentence Length, Lexical Density, Lexical Richness);[4]
- Grammatical (part-of-speech tag n-grams);
- Lexical (token n-grams).

We use χ^2 feature selection with classes defined as the $[50 \cdot n, 50 \cdot (n+1)]$ interval that overlaps the most with the true one. This coarse approach to feature selection has been shown to work well for temporal classification (Niculae et al., 2014).

4 Results

We perform 5-fold cross-validation over the training set to estimate the task-specific score. We fix the number of neighbours used for prediction to $k = 10$ after cross-validation using only number of tokens as feature. The model parameter space consists of the logistic regression's regularization parameter C, the minimum and maximum frequency thresholds for pruning too rare and too common features, n-gram range for tokens and for part-of-speech tags, and the number of features to keep after feature selection. We choose the best configuration after many

[3]In our implementation, we set $\text{dist}(y_a, y_b)$ to 0 if the smaller interval is fully contained in the wider one.

[4]Lexical Density = unique tokens / total tokens; Lexical Richness = unique lemmas / total tokens.

		Task 1				Task 2			
Model	**Features**	**Fine**	**Medium**	**Coarse**	**MAE**	**Fine**	**Medium**	**Coarse**	**MAE**
Random	—	0.09	0.21	0.44	73.16	0.30	0.43	0.59	80.58
Ridge	lengths+style	0.15	0.32	0.52	67.94	0.33	0.59	0.77	54.77
AMBRA	lengths+style	0.12	0.26	0.48	74.67	0.38	0.58	0.75	57.00
AMBRA	full	0.17	0.38	0.55	63.24	0.60	0.77	0.87	31.74

Table 1: Evaluation of AMBRA and the baselines on the test data. We report the task-specific score (between 0 and 1, higher is better) for the three levels of granularity, as well as the mean absolute error (*MAE*, lower is better) for the fine level of granularity.

iterations of randomized search. We compare our ranking model to a ridge regression baseline, employing the document length meta-features and using the middle of the time intervals as target values. We also evaluate a random baseline where one of the candidate intervals is chosen with uniform probability. For evaluation, we use the task-specific metric defined by the organizers (Popescu and Strapparava, 2015), based on the number of interval divisions between the prediction and the right answer. For context, we also report the mean absolute error obtained by taking the center of the intervals as a point estimate of the year. Table 1 shows the performance of AMBRA and the baseline systems on the test documents. On T1, the full AMBRA system is the only to beat the random baseline in all metrics (95% confidence). On T2, where more data is available, AMBRA with length and style features outperforms ridge regression at fine granularity (95% confidence), and the full AMBRA system outperforms all others in all metrics (99% confidence).[5]

4.1 Most Informative Features

To better understand the performance of our method we analyze the most informative features selected by our best models. We use identical feature sets for both tasks, and while there are some common patterns, we observe important differences in the feature rankings, confirming that T1 and T2 are different enough in nature to warrant separate modeling.

Among the features useful for both tasks we find the length of a document in sentences highly predictive, with newer texts being longer. Also, the linguistic structure *determiner + singular proper noun* is predictive of older texts, while *adjective + singular noun* is predictive of newer texts. The decrease in use of the contraction *'d* is captured in both cases. From the lexical features, the word *letters* indicates older texts, corresponding to the decreasing use of mail as telecommunication became mainstream.

Words useful for T1 are more topic- and time-specific ones, such as *army*, *emperor*, *troops*, while the T2 model, possibly enabled by the larger amount of data, proves capable of detecting diachronic spelling variation (*publick* and *public* are both selected, with opposite signs), outdated words (*upon*), and more subtle stylistic changes such as the decrease in use of the Oxford comma (a comma followed by a conjunction at the end of a list).

5 Conclusion and Future Work

We propose a ranking-based method to handle interval prediction and account for uncertainty in temporal text classification. Our approach proved competitive in the Semeval-2015 'Diachronic Text Evaluation' subtasks one and two. The features we used are simplistic but effective. We expect performance to improve by including linguistic and etymology expertise in the feature engineering and selection process, as well as by including world knowledge through named entities and linked data.

Our model allows for arbitrary interval labels, which is more expressive and more realistic than the task formulation. We plan to refine collections of historical texts and tighten the annotation intervals wherever possible. Our implementation can be made more scalable by following the random sampling methodology of Sculley (2009).

[5] All significance results are based on 10000 boostrap iterations with bias correction.

Acknowledgments

The authors are thankful to Fabian Pedregosa for valuable discussion, to the anonymous reviewers for their helpful and constructive comments, and to the organizers for preparing and running the shared task. Liviu P. Dinu was supported by UEFISCDI, PNII-ID-PCE-2011-3-0959.

References

Hidenao Abe and Shusaku Tsumoto. 2010. Text categorization with considering temporal patterns of term usages. In *Proceedings of ICDM Workshops*.

Alina Maria Ciobanu, Liviu P. Dinu, Anca Dinu, and Vlad Niculae. 2013. Temporal classification for historical Romanian texts. In *Proceedings of LaTeCH*.

Wisam Dakka, Luis Gravano, and Panagiotis G. Ipeirotis. 2012. Answering general time-sensitive queries. *IEEE Transactions on Knowledge and Data Engineering*, 24(2):220–235.

Angelo Dalli and Yorick Wilks. 2006. Automatic dating of documents and temporal text classification. In *Proceedings of ARTE*, Sidney, Australia.

Franciska de Jong, Henning Rode, and Djoerd Hiemstra. 2005. Temporal language models for the disclosure of historical text. In *Proceedings of AHC*.

Anne Garcia-Fernandez, Anne-Laure Ligozat, Marco Dinarelli, and Delphine Bernhard. 2011. When was it written? Automatically determining publication dates. In *Proceedings of SPIRE*.

Cyril Grouin, Dominic Forest, Lyne Da Sylva, Patrick Paroubek, and Pierre Zweigenbaum. 2010. Présentation et résultats du défi fouille de texte DEFT2010 où et quand un article de presse a-t-il été écrit? *Actes du sixième DÉfi Fouille de Textes*.

Thorsten Joachims. 2006. Training linear SVMs in linear time. In *Proceedings of KDD*.

Nattya Kanhabua and Kjetil Nørvåg. 2009. Using temporal language models for document dating. In *Proceedings of ECML/PKDD*.

Abhimanu Kumar, Matthew Lease, and Jason Baldridge. 2011. Supervised language modelling for temporal resolution of texts. In *Proceedings of CIKM*.

Rada Mihalcea and Vivi Nastase. 2012. Word epoch disambiguation: Finding how words change over time. In *Proceedings of ACL*.

Vlad Niculae, Marcos Zampieri, Liviu P. Dinu, and Alina Ciobanu. 2014. Temporal text ranking and automatic dating of texts. In *Proceedings of EACL*.

Fabian Pedregosa, Elodie Cauvet, Gael Varoquaux, Christophe Pallier, Bertrang Thirion, and Alexandre Gramfort. 2012. Learning to rank from medical imaging data. *CoRR*, abs/1207.3598.

Octavian Popescu and Carlo Strapparava. 2013. Behind the times: Detecting epoch changes using large corpora. In *Proceedings of IJCNLP*.

Octavian Popescu and Carlo Strapparava. 2015. Semeval-2015 task 7: Diachronic text evaluation. In *Proceedings of SemEval*.

Daniel Preotiuc-Pietro. 2014. *Temporal models of streaming social media data*. Ph.D. thesis, University of Sheffield.

D. Sculley. 2009. Large scale learning to rank. In *NIPS Workshop on Advances in Ranking*, pages 1–6.

Sanja Štajner and Marcos Zampieri. 2013. Stylistic changes for temporal text classification. In *Proceedings of TSD*.

Constantina Stamou. 2005. *Dating Victorians: An experimental approach to stylochronometry*. Ph.D. thesis, University of Bedfordshire.

Dolf Trieschnigg, Djoerd Hiemstra, Mariet Theune, Franciska de Jong, and Theo Meder. 2012. An exploration of language identification techniques for the dutch folktale database. In *Proceedings of LREC2012*.

Chong Wang, David Blei, and Heckerman David. 2008. Continuous time dynamic topic models. In *Proceedings of UAI*.

Derry Tanti Wijaya and Reyyan Yeniterzi. 2011. Understanding semantic change of words over centuries. In *Proceedings of the Workshop on Detecting and Exploiting Cultural Diversity on the Social Web (DETECT)*.

IXAGroupEHUSpaceEval: (*X-Space*) A WordNet-based approach towards the Automatic Recognition of Spatial Information following the ISO-Space Annotation Scheme

Haritz Salaberri, Olatz Arregi, Beñat Zapirain
IXA Group, Faculty of Computer Sciences
University of the Basque Country (UPV-EHU)
Manuel Lardizabal pasealekua, 1 - 20018 Donostia-San Sebastián
{haritz.salaverri, olatz.arregi, benat.zapirain}@ehu.eus

Abstract

This paper presents *X-Space*, a system that follows the ISO-Space annotation scheme in order to capture spatial information as well as our contribution to the SemEval-2015 task 8 (SpaceEval). Our system is the only participant system that reported results for all three evaluation configurations in SpaceEval.

1 Introduction

Nowadays the need for algorithms that have the ability to reason spatially over texts are in growing demand within applications concerning human language processing and in navigation services. Well-studied topics in computational linguistics such as named entity recognition and question answering, for example, will presumably experience important progress through such algorithms. Navigation systems, on the other hand, will gain the ability to interpret indications given by users beyond the "string matching" methods used at present (Wu et al., 2010). In order for such systems to reason spatially, however, they require the enrichment of textual data with the annotation of spatial information in language (Pustejovsky et al., 2013). As of today there have been several attempts at capturing spatial information (annotation schemes): SpatialML (Mani et al., 2008), Spatial Role Labeling (Kordjamshidi et al., 2010) and ISO-Space (Pustejovsky et al., 2011). *X-Space* follows the ISO-Space specification.

Section 2 describes the system architecture and section 3 presents the results and discusses them. Finally, our conclusions are given in section 4.

2 System architecture

X-Space uses a four-stage pipeline: first texts are preprocessed; second candidates to be spatial elements and signals are selected by generating word lists from the texts; then, spatial elements and signals are identified from the candidate lists and their attributes set according to type. Finally, spatial relations are established between the previously identified and the attributes that correspond to these relations are set.

2.1 Preprocessing and Candidate Selection

As an initial step texts that are inputted into *X-Space* are syntactically and semantically parsed (SRL), and named entities as well as coreference chains are identified. These annotations are used in the later stages as features for machine learning.

The parsing of syntactic and semantic dependencies is achieved with the *ClearNLP* semantic role labeler (Choi and Palmer, 2012); for the recognition of named entities, on the other hand, the *Apache OpenNLP* name finder tool is used (Baldridge, 2005). Chains of coreference are identified using the *Standford CoreNLP* coreference resolution system (Manning et al., 2014).

After the preprocessing of input texts is performed the words that compose these texts are used to form candidate lists by taking words one-by-one, two-by-two, three-by-three and four-by-four. We assume that spatial elements and signals with more than four words are highly improbable to occur. For this reason only candidates with up to four words are considered.

2.2 Spatial Elements and Signals

Five different spatial elements are distinguished: places and paths which designate a region of space (locations); spatial entities, words of motion and non-motion events. These do not designate a region of space but are allowed to be coerced into behaving like a region of space, so that they may participate in the same kinds of relationships as regions of space (Pustejovsky and Yocum, 2013).

In order to identify places, paths and words of motion we have used WordNet as well as several other resources such as PropBank and the Predicate Matrix (de Lacalle et al., 2014) in combination with a binary *Support Vector Machine classifier* implemented using the *SVM-light* package (Joachims, 1999). For spatial entities and non-motion events, on the other hand, an approach without WordNet is used for reasons that are discussed in 2.2.2.

2.2.1 The WordNet approach

The WordNet approach is used to identify words of motion, paths and places within the lists of candidates. This approach is based on the idea that within the hierarchical organization of WordNet a domain, as for example the path domain, can be defined as a set of subtrees by properly identifying the root of these subtrees. According to (Feizabadi and Padó, 2012) the challenge is to find a set of nodes whose subtrees cover as much as possible of the desired domain while avoiding overgeneration.

Root nodes We consider these nodes to be the ones that best fulfill these conditions after manually examining WordNet (v3.0): for the motion domain we have considered nodes "move, locomote, travel, go" (01835496-V) and "to be" (02604760-V); for the place domain, on the other hand, we have considered nodes "topographic point, place spot" (08664443-N), "place, property" (08513718-N), "position, place" (08621598-N), "location" (00027167-N), "state, nation, country, land, commonwealth, *res publica*, body politic" (08168978-N), "country, state, land" (08544813-N), "country, rural area" (08644722-N) and "area, country" (08497294-N). Finally, for the path domain we have considered nodes "path" (03899328-N), "path, route, itinerary" (08616311-N), "path, track, course" (09387222-N) and "way" (04564698-N).

Domain definition After the place and path domains are defined by capturing the corresponding sets of subtrees, the domains are completed by adding the places and paths in the training set that are not covered by the subtrees. In total 5,572 places and 664 paths form the final domains. For motion words, however, most of them being verbs, sense needs to be disambiguated; as a matter of fact many verbs have motion as well as non-motion senses. *X-Space* uses the Predicate Matrix (v1.1) in order to map the WordNet synset IDs that correspond to the subtrees rooted in the nodes that have been considered for the motion domain (01835496-V and 02604760-V) with their corresponding PropBank sense. The Predicate Matrix is a lexical resource resulting from the integration of multiple sources of predicate information, including FrameNet, VerbNet, PropBank and WordNet. 511 senses form the words of motion domain used by our system.

Identification process When domains are defined *X-Space* iterates over the list of candidates in search for places and paths. Words of motion, on the contrary, are only looked for in the one-by-one candidate list as we consider that only these can be words of motion. For the identification of words of motion the disambiguation of senses is used which is performed in the semantic dependency parsing in the preprocessing stage. This way only the candidates labeled with a sense present in the words of motion domain will be identified as such.

Avoiding overgeneration We observed that too many candidates were identified using just the straightforward procedure, where candidates are looked for in the domains. In order to avoid this over-generation we attached a machine-learning module to the identification process. The classifier used is a binary classifier based on *Support Vector Machines*, and once the identification of places, paths and words of motion within the identification process is completed, the classifier decides whether an identified element is or not correctly identified. The following is the list of the features used:

- CAND_Lex, CAND_Lemma, CAND_PoS: Lexical form, lemma and PoS category tag of the candidate.

- CAND_DepRel: Dependency relation between the candidate and its head.

- PRED_Roleset: Roleset ID of the predicate on which the candidate semantically depends.

- PREVW_Lex, PREVW_PoS: Lexical form and PoS category tag of the word previous to the candidate.

- PREVW_DepRel: Dependency relation between the word previous to the candidate and its head.

- NEXTW_Lex, NEXTW_PoS: Lexical form and PoS category tag of the word next to the candidate.

- NEXTW_DepRel: Dependency relation between the word next to the candidate and its head.

X-Space uses this classifier (same set of features, same implementation) several times throughout the entire process of annotating input texts with spatial information. The reason not to perform a thorough feature selection process whenever machine learning needs to be used throughout the annotation conducted by *X-Space* lies in the time limitations we encountered due to the extent of the SpaceEval task. The values taken by the training parameters are shown next:

- Trade-Off: The trade-off between training error and margin is computed through the $avg(x * x)^{-1}$ formula.

- Bias: A biased hyperplane is used.

- Cost-Factor: The cost-factor, by which training errors on positive examples outweigh errors on negative examples is 1.

- Kernel: The type of kernel function used is linear.

2.2.2 Other approaches

This section describes the approaches used to identify non-motion events, spatial entities and signals from the candidates lists. The reason why the WordNet approach is not used on non-motion events is that we could not accurately determine a set of nodes whose subtrees cover the desired domain properly. For spatial entities, on the other hand, we believe that using the WordNet approach is not correct given the heterogeneous nature of these spatial elements. We also believe that the same reason applies not to use WordNet in the identification of spatial and motion signals. All three use a classifier like the one in section 2.2.1 as a final step to avoid overgeneration.

Non-motion events In order to identify non-motion events our system first generates a list with the PropBank senses taken by the non-motion events in the training set. Then *X-Space* iterates over the one-by-one candidate list (as we consider that only these can be ISO-Space non-motion events) and checks whether a candidate is labeled with one of these senses or not. With this aim in mind the disambiguation of senses is used that has been performed in the preprocessing.

Spatial entities For the identification of spatial entities the semantic role labels have been used that were given by the semantic dependency parser to predicate arguments. We believe spatial entities to be viewable as arguments of a predicate which is a word of motion or a word that expresses a non-motion event. Arguments that correspond to these kind of predicates are in the majority of cases located in space and participate in ISO-Space link tags. These, therefore, can be understood as spatial entities. In order to identify spatial entities *X-Space* iterates over the lists of candidates and searches for arguments of words that have been previously marked as of motion or as expressing a non-motion event.

Signals For the purpose of identifying signals two lists are formed based on the signal annotations in the training set. One list holds the signals that are exclusively of motion (e.g., into, from) and another list holds the signals that can only be of space (e.g., within, without). Then *X-Space* iterates over the one-by-one and two-by-two candidate lists. As we observed in the training set, only signals with up to two words occurred. In the iteration process candidates are looked for in both lists; if a candidate can be found in the spatial signals list, it is assigned the spatial signal tag; on the other hand, if the candidate is present in the motion signals list this is marked as a motion signal. Many signals, however, overlap, meaning that they can be of motion and space (e.g., by, over). In order to capture these signals the candidate lists are searched for prepositions and function words.

2.2.3 Attribute identification

The ISO-Space annotation language specifies several attributes for spatial elements as well as for signals. The classifier in section 2.2.1 is used to give values to these attributes. When an attribute can take more than two values, however, a version of the classifier that has been extended from binary to multiclass is used. This is achieved with the *SVM-multiclass* package. Several attributes are specified. However, not all attributes are given values: in fact many of them are never annotated in the training set, and for this reason *X-Space* does not annotate them either.

2.3 Spatial Relation Links

When the spatial elements and the signals within the input texts as well as their corresponding attributes are identified *X-Space* tries to detect the spatial relations that lay between them. The SpaceEval task addresses the detection of three types of relations: movement (MoveLink), qualitative (QSLink) and orientational (OLink).

2.3.1 Link identification

In order to identify the spatial relation links, *X-Space* follows what is stated in (Pustejovsky and Yocum, 2013). For movement relations that typically involve motion-event triggers (words of motion), motion signals, and motion-event participants a link is created for each identified word of motion. For qualitative relations, on the other hand, which normally involve spatial signals and spatial elements and are used to capture topological relationships, a link of this type is created for each spatial signal with an identified TOPOLOGICAL or DIR_TOP `semantic_type`. Finally, an orientational link is introduced for every spatial signal with a DIRECTIONAL `semantic_type`; this kind of link describes non-topological relationships between spatial signals and spatial elements.

2.3.2 Attribute identification

There are several attributes specified by the ISO-Space annotation scheme for the MoveLink, QSLink and OLink relations. Nonetheless, not all these attributes are viewed, and, consequently, identified by *X-Space* following the same procedure. In fact, the system distinguishes three types of attributes: triggers, which are the spatial elements or signals that trigger the creation of links, roles, which are the spatial elements involved in these relations and common attributes, which indicate other characteristics of the links.

Triggers Triggers are directly established for all three kinds of links based on the link identification process.

Roles We believe that attributes `source`, `goal`, `mover` and `landmark` within a MoveLink relation can be seen as arguments of the trigger, which is usually a verbal predicate (word of motion). For a QSLink or OLink relation, on the other hand, we think that attributes `trajector` and `landmark` can be seen as arguments of the predicate that dominates the trigger, which is usually a preposition (spatial signal). The idea behind these attributes is based on the Spatial Role Labeling annotation schema described in (Kordjamshidi et al., 2010). According to this scheme there are indicators that can be spatial (spatial signals) or of motion (words of motion) that introduce spatial relations. These spatial relations take arguments with roles `trajector` and `landmark`. For this reason, in order to identify attributes `source`, `goal`, `mover` and `landmark` of MoveLinks, *X-Space* looks for arguments of the triggers using the semantic dependency parsing carried out in the preprocessing. Then it establishes which PropBank argument (A0, A1, A2, etc.) corresponds to which attribute (spatial role) using a multiclass classifier

	Precision		Recall		F_1		Accuracy	
	Baseline	*X-Space*	Baseline	*X-Space*	Baseline	*X-Space*	Baseline	*X-Space*
1-a	0.55	0.81	0.52	0.72	0.53	0.76	0.75	0.88
1-b	0.55	0.75	0.51	0.72	0.53	0.74	0.86	0.9
1-c	0.1	0.18	0.02	0.15	0.04	0.16	0.05	0.3
1-d	0.5	0.54	0.5	0.51	0.5	0.53	0.5	0.55
1-e	0.05	0.06	0.02	0.05	0.02	0.05	0.06	0.25
2-a	0.27	0.26	0.28	0.33	0.27	0.29	0.76	0.63
2-b	0.79	0.55	0.58	0.51	0.67	0.53	0.9	0.89
2-c	0.19	0.06	0.2	0.08	0.19	0.07	0.66	0.46
3-a	0.86	0.63	0.84	0.51	0.85	0.56	0.98	0.89
3-b	0.26	0.07	0.26	0.09	0.26	0.08	0.79	0.48

Table 1: Official results reported for *X-Space* plus the results of one baseline system provided by the task organizers (overall results).

like the one in section 2.2.1. The procedure for QSLinks and OLinks is the same but arguments are searched for the predicate that dominates the trigger and not for the trigger itself.

Common attributes We have named common attributes all attributes taken by spatial relations that do not indicate a spatial role or a trigger. *X-Space* once again uses the classifier on 2.2.1 in order to give values to these attributes.

3 Results

The SpaceEval task considers three separate evaluation configurations: (1) only unannotated text is given as an input; (2) manually annotated spatial element extents (no attributes) are given; (3) manually annotated spatial element extents and their attributes are given.

The subtasks that are evaluated for each configuration are: (1-a) identifying spans of spatial elements, (1-b) classifying spatial elements according to type, (1-c) identifying attributes for spatial elements according to type, (1-d) identifying MoveLink, QSLink and OLink relations and (1-e) identifying attributes for spatial relations; (2-a) classifying spatial elements and identifying their attributes according to type, (2-b) identifying MoveLink, QSLink and OLink relations and (2-c) identifying attributes for spatial relations; (3-a) identifying MoveLink, QSLink and OLink relations and (3-b) identifying attributes for spatial relations.

Table 1 shows the results obtained by *X-Space* in every configuration and subtask and compares them with the results of one baseline system provided by the task organizers. As can be noted our results improve the ones in the baseline for 1-a, 1-b, 1-c, 1-d, 1-e and 2-a. On the other hand, our results are worse for 2-b, 2-c, 3-a and 3-b. From the three systems that participated in the SpaceEval task ours was the only one that presented results for all evaluation configurations and all subtasks. We believe that in general the results for our system are good.

4 Conclusion and Future Works

In this paper *X-Space*, our contribution to the SemEval-2015 Task 8, is presented. We consider that many things still remain to be improved. For instance, the problem of annotating non-consuming location tags could be addressed.

In the future, we intend to adapt our system to other languages. This adaptation will bring the opportunity to see how *X-Space* adapts to languages of different natures.

Acknowledgments

Haritz Salaberri holds a PhD grant from the University of the Basque Country (UPV/EHU). In addition, this work has been supported by the FP7 *News-Reader* project (Grant No. 316404) and *IXA* Group, research group of type A (2010-2015)(IT34410).

References

Jason Baldridge. 2005. The opennlp project. *URL: http://opennlp. apache. org/index. html,(accessed 2 February 2012).*

Jinho D. Choi and Martha Palmer. 2012. Optimization of natural language processing components for robustness and scalability.

Maialen. L. de Lacalle, Egoitz Laparra, and German Rigau. 2014. Predicate matrix: extending semlink through wordnet mappings. In *Proceedings of the 9th conference on International Language Resources and Evaluation (LREC'14).*

Parvin Sadat Feizabadi and Sebastian Padó. 2012. Automatic identification of motion verbs in wordnet and framenet. In *Empirical Methods in Natural Language Processing*, page 70.

Thorsten Joachims. 1999. Making large scale svm learning practical.

Parisa Kordjamshidi, Marie-Francine Moens and Martijn van Otterlo. 2010. Spatial role labeling: Task definition and annotation scheme. In *Proceedings of the Seventh conference on International Language Resources and Evaluation (LREC'10)*, pages 413–420.

Inderjeet Mani, Janet Hitzeman, Justin Richer, Dave Harris, Rob Quimby and Ben Wellner. 2008. Spatialml: Annotation scheme, corpora, and tools. In *LREC*.

Christopher D. Manning, Mihai Surdeanu, John Bauer, Jenny Finkel, Steven J. Bethard and David McClosky. 2014. The Stanford CoreNLP natural language processing toolkit. In *Proceedings of 52nd Annual Meeting of the Association for Computational Linguistics: System Demonstrations*, pages 55–60, Baltimore, Maryland. Association for Computational Linguistics.

James Pustejovsky, Jessica Moszkowicz and Marc Verhagen. 2013. A linguistically grounded annotation language for spatial information.

James Pustejovsky, Jessica Moszkowicz and Marc Verhagen. 2011. Iso-space: The annotation of spatial information in language. In *Proceedings of the Sixth Joint ISO-ACL SIGSEM Workshop on Interoperable Semantic Annotation*, pages 1–9.

James Pustejovsky and Zachary Yocum. 2013. Capturing motion in iso-spacebank. In *Workshop on Interoperable Semantic Annotation*, page 25.

Yunhui Wu, Stephan Winter, John A. Bateman, Anthony G. Cohn and James Pustejovsky. 2010. Interpreting place descriptions for navigation services. In *Dagstuhl Seminar on Spatial Representation and Reasoning in Language: Ontologies and Logics of Space, Schloss Dagstuhl, Germany.*

UTD: Ensemble-Based Spatial Relation Extraction

Jennifer D'Souza and **Vincent Ng**
Human Language Technology Research Institute
University of Texas at Dallas
Richardson, TX 75083-0688
{jld082000,vince}@hlt.utdallas.edu

Abstract

SpaceEval (SemEval 2015 Task 8), which concerns spatial information extraction, builds on the spatial role identification tasks introduced in SemEval 2012 and used in SemEval 2013. Among the host of subtasks presented in SpaceEval, we participated in subtask 3a, which focuses solely on spatial relation extraction. To address the complexity of a MOVELINK, we decompose it into smaller relations so that the roles involved in each relation can be extracted in a joint fashion without losing computational tractability. Our system was ranked first in the official evaluation, achieving an overall spatial relation extraction F-score of 84.5%.

1 Introduction

SpaceEval[1] was organized as a shared task for the semantic evaluation of spatial information extraction (IE) systems. The goals of the shared task include identifying and classifying particular constructions in natural language for expressing spatial information that are conveyed through the spatial concepts of locations, entities participating in spatial relations, paths, topological relations, direction and orientation, motion, etc. It presents a wide spectrum of spatial IE related subtasks for interested participants to choose from, building on the two previous years shared tasks on the same topic (Kordjamshidi et al., 2012; Kolomiyets et al., 2013).

Our goal in this paper is to describe the version of our spatial relation extraction system that participated in subtask 3a of SpaceEval. Systems participating in this subtask assume as input the *spatial elements* in a text document. For example, in the sentence *The flower is in the vase*$_1$ *and the vase*$_2$ *is on the table*, the set of spatial elements {*flower*, *in*, *vase*$_1$, *vase*$_2$, *on*, *table*} are given and subsequently used as candidates for predicting spatial relations. Leveraging the successes of a joint role-labeling approach to spatial relation extraction involving stationary objects, we employ it to extract so-called MOVELINKs, which are spatial relations defined over objects in motion. In particular, we discuss the adaptations needed to handle the complexity of MOVELINKs. Experiments on the SpaceEval corpus demonstrate the effectiveness of our ensemble-based approach to spatial relation extraction. Among the three teams participating in subtask 3a, our team was ranked first in the official evaluation, achieving an overall F-score of 84.5%.

The rest of the paper is organized as follows. We first give a brief overview of the subtask 3a of SpaceEval and the corpus (Section 2). After that, we describes related work (Section 3). Finally, we present our approach (Section 4), evaluation results (Section 5), and conclusions (Section 6).

2 The SpaceEval Task

2.1 Subtask 3a: Task Description

Subtask 3a focuses solely on spatial relation extraction using a specified set of spatial elements for a given sentence. Specifically, given an n-tuple of participating entities, the goal is to (1) determine whether the entities in the n-tuple form a spatial re-

[1]http://alt.qcri.org/semeval2015/task8/

lation, and if so, (2) classify the roles of each participating entity in the relation.

2.2 Training Corpus

To facilitate system development, 59 travel narratives are marked up with seven types of spatial elements (Table 1) and three types of spatial relations (Table 2), following the ISO-Space (Pustejovsky et al., 2013) annotation specifications, and provided as training data. Note that a *spatial-signal* entity has a semantic-type attribute expressing the type of the relation it triggered. Its semantic-type can be topological, directional, or both.[2]

What is missing in Table 2 about spatial relations is that each entity participating in a relation has a *role*. In QSLINKs and OLINKs, an element can participate as a $trajector$ (i.e., object of interest), $landmark$ (i.e., the grounding location), or $trigger$ (i.e., the relation indicator). Thus the QSLINK and OLINK examples shown in Table 2, are actually represented as the triplet (flower$_{trajector}$, vase$_{landmark}$, in$_{trigger}$). While QSLINK and OLINK relations can have only three fixed participants, a MOVELINK relation has two fixed participants and up to six optional participants to capture more precisely the relational information expressed in the sentence. The two mandatory MOVELINK participants are a $mover$ (i.e., object in motion), and a $trigger$ (i.e., verb denoting motion). The six optional MOVELINK participants are: $source$, $midpoint$, $goal$, $path$, and $landmark$, express different aspects of the $mover$ in space, whereas a $motion\text{-}signal$ connects the spatial aspect to the $mover$.

Note that all spatial relations are *intra-sentential.* In other words, all spatial elements participating in a relation must appear in the same sentence.

3 Related Work

Recall from Section 2 that spatial relation extraction is composed of two subtasks, *role labeling* and *relation classification* of spatial elements. Prior systems have adopted either a *pipeline* approach or a *joint* approach to these subtasks. Given an n-tuple of distinct spatial elements in a sentence, a pipeline spatial relation extraction system first assigns a role to each spatial element and then uses a binary classifier to determine whether the elements form a spatial relation or not (Kordjamshidi et al., 2011; Bastianelli et al., 2013; Kordjamshidi and Moens, 2014).

One weakness of pipeline approaches is that errors in role labeling can propagate to the relation classification component. To address this problem, *joint* approaches were investigated (Roberts and Harabagiu, 2012; Roberts et al., 2013). Given an n-tuple of distinct spatial elements in a sentence with an assignment of roles to each element, a joint spatial relation extraction system uses a binary classifier to determine whether these elements form a spatial relation with the roles correctly assigned to all participating elements. In other words, the classifier will label the n-tuple as TRUE if and only if (1) the elements in the n-tuple form a relation and (2) their roles in the relation are correct.

We conclude this section by noting that virtually all existing systems were developed on datasets that adopted different or simpler representations of spatial information than SpaceEval's ISO-Space (2013) representation (Mani et al., 2010; Kordjamshidi et al., 2010; Kordjamshidi et al., 2012; Kolomiyets et al., 2013). In other words, none of these systems were designed to identify MOVELINKs.

4 Our Approach

To avoid the error propagation problem, we perform *joint* role labeling and relation extraction. Unlike previous work, where a single classifier was trained, we employ an ensemble of eight classifiers. Creating the eight classifiers permits (1) separating the treatment of MOVELINKs from QSLINKs and OLINKs; and (2) simplifying MOVELINK extraction.

We separate MOVELINKs from QSLINKs and OLINKs for two reasons. First, MOVELINKs involve objects in motion, whereas the other two link types involve stationary objects. Second, MOVELINKs are more complicated than the other two link types: while QSLINKs and OLINKs have three fixed participants, $trajector$, $landmark$ and $trigger$, MOVELINKs can have up to eight participants, including two mandatory participants (i.e., $mover$ and $trigger$) and six optional participants (i.e., $source$, $midpoint$, $goal$, $path$, $landmark$,

[2] In the ISO-Space scheme (Pustejovsky et al., 2013), different spatial entities have different attributes. We omit their description here owing to space limitations.

place (e.g., Rome)	*path* (e.g., road)	*spatial-entity* (e.g., car)	*non-motion* event (e.g., is "serving")	*motion* event (e.g., arrived)	*motion-signal* (e.g., by car)	*spatial-signal* (e.g., north of)

Table 1: Seven types of spatial elements in SpaceEval.

Relation	**Description**	**Total**
QSLINK	Exists between stationary spatial elements with a regional connection. E.g., in *The flower is in the vase*, the region of the *vase* has an internal connection with the region of the *flower* and hence they are in a QSLINK.	968
OLINK	Exists between stationary spatial elements expressing their relative or absolute orientations. E.g., in *The flower is in the vase*, the *flower* and the *vase* also have an OLINK relation conveying that the *flower* is oriented inside the *vase*.	244
MOVELINK	Exists between spatial elements in motion. E.g., the sentence *He biked from Cambridge to Maine* has a MOVELINK between mover *He*, motion verb *biked*, source of motion *Cambridge*, and goal of motion *Maine*.	803

Table 2: Three spatial relation types in SpaceEval. The "Total" column shows the number of instances annotated with the corresponding relation in the training data.

and *motion-signal*). Given the complexity of a MOVELINK, we decompose a MOVELINK into a set of simpler relations that are to be identified by an ensemble of classifiers.

In the rest of this section, we describe how we train and test our ensemble.

4.1 Training the Ensemble

We employ one classifier for identifying QSLINK and OLINK relations (Section 4.1.1) and seven classifiers for identifying MOVELINK relations (Section 4.1.2).

4.1.1 The LINK Classifier

We collapse QSLINKs and OLINKs to a single relation type, LINK, identifying these two types of links using the LINK classifier. To understand why we can do this, first note that in QSLINKs and OLINKs, the *trigger* has to be a *spatial-signal* element having a semantic-type attribute. If its semantic-type is topological, it triggers a QSLINK; if it is directional, it triggers an OLINK; and if it is both it triggers both relation types. Hence, if a LINK is identified by our classifier, we can simply use the semantic-type value of the relation's *trigger* element to automatically determine whether the relation is a QSLINK an OLINK, or both.

We create training instances for training a LINK classifier as follows. Following the joint approach described above, we create one training instance for each possible role labeling of each triplet of distinct spatial elements in each sentence in a training document. The role labels assigned to the spatial elements in each triplet are subject to the following constraints: (1) each triplet contains a *trajector*, a *landmark*, and a *trigger*; (2) neither the *trajector* nor the *landmark* are of type *spatial-signal* or *motion-signal*; and (3) the *trigger* is a *spatial-signal*.[3] Note that these role constraints are derived from the data annotation scheme. It is worth noting that while we enforce such global role constraints when creating training instances, Kordjamshidi and Moens (2014) enforce them at inference time using Integer Linear Programming.

A training instance is labeled as TRUE if and only if the elements in the triplet form a relation and their roles in the relation are correct. As an example, for the QSLINK and OLINK sentence in Table 2, exactly one positive instance, LINK($\text{flower}_{trajector}$, $\text{vase}_{landmark}$, $\text{in}_{trigger}$), will be created.

Each instance is represented using the 31 features shown in Table 3. These features are modeled after those employed by state-of-the-art spatial rela-

[3]LINKs can have at most one *implicit* spatial element. For example, the sentence *The balloon went up* has LINK($\text{balloon}_{trajector}$,$\text{on}_{trigger}$) with an implicit *landmark*. To account for LINKs with implicit *trajector*, *landmark*, or *trigger* participants, we generate three additional triplets from each LINK triplet, one for each participant having the value IMPLICIT.

1. **Lexical** (6 features)
    1. concatenated lemma strings of e_1, e_2, and e_3
    2. concatenated word strings of e_1, e_2, and e_3
    3. lexical pattern created from e_1, e_2, and e_3 based on their order in the text (e.g., $Trajector\_is\_Trigger\_Landmark$)
    4. words between the spatial elements
    5. e_3's words
    6. whether e_2's phrase was seen in role r_3 in the training data
2. **Grammatical** (5 features)
    1. dependency paths from e_1 to e_3 to e_2 obtained using the Stanford Dependency Parser (de Marneffe et al., 2006)
    2. dependency paths from e_1 to e_2
    3. dependency paths from e_3 to e_2
    4. paths from e_3 to e_2 concatenated with e_3's string
    5. whether e_1 is a prepositional object of a preposition of an element posited in role r_3 in any other relation
3. **Semantic** (9 features)
    1. WordNet (Miller, 1995) hypernyms and synsets of e_1/e_2
    2. semantic role labels of $e_1/e_2/e_3$ obtained using SENNA (Collobert et al., 2011)
    3. General Inquirer (Stone et al., 1966) categories shared by e_1 and e_2
    4. VerbNet (Kipper et al., 2000) classes shared by e_1 and e_2
4. **Positional** (2 features)
    1. order of participants in text (e.g., r_2-r_1-r_3)
    2. whether the order is r_3-r_2-r_1
5. **Distance** (3 features)
    1. distance in tokens between e_1 and e_3 and that between e_2 and e_3
    2. using a bin of 5 tokens, the concatenated binned distance between (e_1,e_2), (e_1,e_3), and (e_2,e_3)
6. **Entity attributes** (3 features)
    1. spatial entity type of $e_1/e_2/e_3$
7. **Entity roles** (3 features)
    1. predicted spatial roles of $e_1/e_2/e_3$ obtained using our in-house relation role labeler

Table 3: 31 features for spatial relation extraction. Each training instance corresponds to a triplet (e_1,e_2,e_3), where e_1, e_2, and e_3 are spatial elements of types t_1, t_2, and t_3, with participating roles r_1, r_2, and r_3, respectively.

tion extraction systems. Recall that these systems were developed on datasets that adopted different or simpler representations of spatial information than SpaceEval's ISO-Space (2013) representation (Mani et al., 2010; Kordjamshidi et al., 2010; Kordjamshidi et al., 2012; Kolomiyets et al., 2013). Hence, these 31 features have not been used to train classifiers for extracting MOVELINKs.

We train the LINK classifier using the SVM learning algorithm as implemented in the SVM^{light} software package (Joachims, 1999). To optimize classifier performance, we tune two parameters, the regularization parameter C (which establishes the balance between generalizing and overfitting the classifier model to the training data) and the cost-factor parameter J (which outweights training errors on positive examples compared to the negative examples), to maximize F-score on development data.

4.1.2 The Seven MOVELINK Classifiers

If we adopted the aforementioned joint method as is for extracting MOVELINKs, each instance would correspond to an octuple of the form: MOVELINK($trigger_i$, $mover_j$, $source_k$, $mid\text{-}point_m$, $goal_n$, $landmark_o$, $path_p$, $motion\text{-}signal_r$), where each participant in the octuple is either a distinct spatial element with a role or the NULL element (if it is not present in the relation). However, generating role permutations for octuples from all spatial elements in a sentence is computationally infeasible. In order to address this tractability problem, we simplify MOVELINK extraction as follows. First, we decompose the MOVELINK octuple into seven smaller tuples including one pair and six triplets. The seven tuples are: (i) ($trigger_i$, $mover_j$); (ii) ($trigger_i$, $mover_j$, $source_k$); (iii) ($trigger_i$, $mover_j$, $mid\text{-}point_m$); (iv) ($trigger_i$, $mover_j$, $goal_n$); (v) ($trigger_i$, $mover_j$, $landmark_o$); (vi) ($trigger_i$, $mover_j$, $path_p$); (vii) ($trigger_i$, $mover_j$, $motion\text{-}signal_r$). Then, we create seven separate classifiers for identifying the seven MOVELINK tuples, respectively.

Using this decomposition for MOVELINK instances, we can generate instances for each classifier using the aforementioned joint approach as is. For instance, to train classifier (i), we generate candidate pairs of the form ($trigger_i$, $mover_j$), where $trigger_i$ and $mover_j$ are spatial elements proposed as a candidate *trigger* and *mover*, respectively. Positive training instances are those ($trigger_i$, $mover_j$) pairs annotated with a relation in the training data, while the rest of the candidate pairs are negative training instances. The instances for training the remaining six classifiers are generated similarly.

As in the LINK classifier, we enforce global role constraints when creating training instances for the MOVELINK classifiers. Specifically, the roles assigned to the spatial elements in each training instance of each of the MOVELINK classifiers are subject to the following constraints: (1) the *trigger* has type *motion*; (2) the *mover* has type *place*, *path*, *spatial-entity* or *non-motion* event; (3) the *source*, the *goal*, and the *landmark* can be NULL or has type *place*, *path*, *spatial-entity*, or *non-motion* event; (4) the *mid-point* can be NULL or has type *place*, *path*, or *spatial-entity*; (5) the *path* can be NULL or has type *path*; and (6) the *motion-signal* can be NULL or has type *motion-signal*.

Our way of decomposing the octuple along roles can be justified as follows. Since the shared task evaluates MOVELINKs only based on its mandatory *trigger* and *mover* participants, we have a classifier for classifying this core aspect of a motion relation. The next six classifiers, (ii) to (vii), aim to improve the core MOVELINK extraction by exploiting the stronger contextual dependencies with each of its unique spatial aspects namely the *source*, the *mid-point*, the *goal*, the *landmark*, the *path*, and the *motion-signal*.

As an example, for the MOVELINK sentence in Table 2, we will create three positive instances: ($\text{He}_{trigger}$, biked_{mover}) for classifier (i), ($\text{He}_{trigger}$, biked_{mover}, $\text{Cambridge}_{source}$) for classifier (ii), and ($\text{He}_{trigger}$, biked_{mover}, Maine_{goal}) for classifier (iv).

We represent each training instance using the 31 features shown in Table 3, and train each of the MOVELINK classifiers using SVM^{light}, with the C and J values tuned on development data.

4.2 Testing the Ensemble

After training, we apply the resulting classifiers to classify the test instances, which are created in the same manner as the training instances. As noted before, the LINK spatial relations extracted from a test document by the LINK classifier are further qualified as QSLINK, OLINK, or both based on the semantic-type attribute value of its *trigger* participant. The MOVELINK relations are extracted from a test document by combining the outputs from the seven MOVELINK classifiers. We explore three different ways of combining the outputs. The first way is simply to combine the outputs from all seven classifiers. However, combining outputs in this way could produce erroneous MOVELINK results, because it could result in a spatial element being classified with more than one role in the same relation since the classifications are made independently. To address this problem, we adopt a second way of combining the seven classifier outputs to generate MOVELINKs. Our second approach resolves multiple role classifications for the same element in a relation by se-

	QSLINK						OLINK						MOVELINK						OVERALL		
	False			True			False			True			False			True					
	R	P	F	R	P	F	R	P	F	R	P	F	R	P	F	R	P	F	R	P	F
Training Data	99.5	99.4	99.5	46.9	48.9	47.9	100	99.4	99.7	50.3	100	66.9	91.3	99.8	95.3	84.8	61.5	71.3	78.8	84.8	80.1
Test Data	99.6	99.3	99.4	55.3	68	61	99.9	99.9	99.9	67.9	76	71.7	98.3	97.3	97.8	72.7	81.6	76.9	82.3	87	84.5

Table 4: Results for spatial relation extraction using gold spatial elements.

lecting the role that was predicted with highest confidence by the SVM. Our third approach addresses this problem, alternatively, by using a predetermined precedence of roles, decided based on training data statistics of roles' frequency, and selecting the role that appears more frequently in the training data than the other classified roles. Evaluations of the respective outputs produced by adopting each of these three ways showed that they all achieved a very similar level of performance.

5 Evaluation

In this section, we evaluate our ensemble approach to spatial relation extraction.

5.1 Experimental Setup

Dataset. We use the 59 travel narratives released as the SpaceEval challenge training data for system training and development. For testing, we use the 16 travel narratives released as the SpaceEval challenge test data.

Evaluation metrics. Evaluation results are obtained using the official SpaceEval challenge scoring program. Results are expressed in terms of recall (R), precision (P), and F-score (F). When computing recall and precision, true positives for QSLINKs and OLINKs are those extracted $(trajector, landmark, trigger)$ triplets that match with those in the gold data. True positives for MOVELINKs are those extracted $(trigger, mover)$ pairs found in the gold data.[4]

Parameter tuning. As mentioned in the previous section, we tune the C and J parameters on development data when training each SVM classifier. More specifically, during system training and development, we perform five-fold cross validation. In each fold experiment, we use three folds for training, one fold for development, and one fold for testing.

Since joint tuning of these two parameters are computationally expensive, we tune them as follows. We first tune C by setting the J parameter to the default value in SVM^{light}. After finding the C parameter that maximizes F-score on the development set, we fix C and tune J to maximize F-score on the development set.[5]

5.2 Results and Discussion

Table 4 shows the spatial relation extraction results using gold spatial elements of our classifier ensemble from the official SpaceEval scoring program.

The first row shows results from five-fold cross validation on the training data. In each fold experiment, we first tune the learning parameters of each classifier as described in Section 5.1, and then retrain the classifier on all four folds using the learned parameters before applying it to the test fold. The results reported are averaged over the five test folds. The second row results are obtained from evaluation on the official test data. Here, we train each classifier on all of the training data. The learning parameters of each classifier are tuned based on cross validation on the training data. Specifically, we select the parameters that give the best averaged F-score over the five development folds described in Section 5.1.

The column-wise results in the table show performance on extracting the QSLINK, OLINK, and MOVELINK spatial relations types, respectively, and overall. The results under column "False" for each relation type show performance in rejecting the relation candidates that are not actual relations in the gold data. And the results under column "True" for

[4]During system development, we observed that $(trigger, mover)$ extraction can be improved by exploiting its stronger dependencies with the optional MOVELINK participants. Therefore, we have classifiers (ii) to (vii) in our ensemble for extracting $(trigger, mover)$ pairs missed by classifier (i).

[5]For parameter tuning, C is chosen from the set $\{0.01, 0.05, 0.1, 0.5, 1.0, 10.0, 50.0, 100.0\}$ and J is chosen from the set $\{0.01, 0.05, 0.1, 0.5, 1.0, 2.0, 4.0, 6.0\}$.

	R	P	F
Training Data	60.7	70.1	62
Test Data	65.3	75.2	69.9

Table 5: Overall results for spatial relation extraction of "True" relations using gold spatial elements.

each relation type show performance in extracting relation candidates that are actual relations in the gold data.

From Table 4, we see that on both the training and test data, performance on rejecting the False relation candidates is close to 100%. However, performance on extracting the True relations is relatively much lower. In decreasing order of performance, our approach is most effective on extracting MOVELINKs, followed by OLINKs, and then QSLINKs. Thus the relation types on which our approach performs poorly can direct our future efforts in improving performance on this task. We see close to 80% overall relation extraction F-score of our system on both training and test data. This high performance is mainly owing to the high performance of our approach in rejecting the False relation candidates. To better reflect the overall performance of our approach, we show in Table 5 our overall results in extracting True relation types using only the results in "True" columns of Table 4 for the three relation types. From these results, we see that our system performance is in the range of 65-70% F-score on extracting the "True" spatial relations in both datasets. Thus we see that there is still more scope for improvement of our system in order to make it practically usable for spatial relation extraction.

6 Conclusion

We employed an ensemble approach to spatial relation extraction. To address the complexity of a MOVELINK, we decomposed it into smaller relations so that the roles involved in each relation could be extracted in a joint fashion without losing computational tractability. When evaluated on the SpaceEval official test data for subtask 3a, our approach was ranked first, achieving an F-score of 84.5%.

Acknowledgments

We would like to thank the SpaceEval organizers for creating the corpus and organizing the shared task. We would also like to thank Daniel Cer and the anonymous reviewers for their helpful suggestions and comments.

References

Emanuele Bastianelli, Danilo Croce, Daniele Nardi, and Roberto Basili. 2013. Unitor-HMM-TK: Structured kernel-based learning for spatial role labeling. In *Proceedings of SemEval 2013*, pages 573–579.

Ronan Collobert, Jason Weston, Léon Bottou, Michael Karlen, Koray Kavukcuoglu, and Pavel Kuksa. 2011. Natural language processing (almost) from scratch. *Journal of Machine Learning Research*, 12:2493–2537.

Marie-Catherine de Marneffe, Bill MacCartney, and Christopher D. Manning. 2006. Generating typed dependency parses from phrase structure parses. In *Proceedings of the 5th International Conference on Language Resources and Evaluation*, pages 449–454.

Thorsten Joachims. 1999. Making large-scale SVM learning practical. In *Advances in Kernel Methods - Support Vector Learning*, pages 44–56. MIT Press.

Karin Kipper, Hoa Trang Dang, and Martha Palmer. 2000. Class-based construction of a verb lexicon. In *Proceedings of the Seventeenth National Conference on Artificial Intelligence and the Twelfth Conference on Innovative Applications of Artificial Intelligence*, pages 691–696.

Oleksandr Kolomiyets, Parisa Kordjamshidi, Steven Bethard, and Marie-Francine Moens. 2013. SemEval-2013 Task 3: Spatial role labeling. In *Proceedings of SemEval 2013*, pages 255–266.

Parisa Kordjamshidi and Marie-Francine Moens. 2014. Global machine learning for spatial ontology population. *Web Semantics: Science, Services and Agents on the World Wide Web*.

Parisa Kordjamshidi, Marie-Francine Moens, and Martijn van Otterlo. 2010. Spatial role labeling: Task definition and annotation scheme. In *Proceedings of 7th International Conference on Language Resources and Evaluation*, pages 413–420.

Parisa Kordjamshidi, Martijn Van Otterlo, and Marie-Francine Moens. 2011. Spatial role labeling: Towards extraction of spatial relations from natural language. *ACM Transactions on Speech and Language Processing*, 8(3):4.

Parisa Kordjamshidi, Steven Bethard, and Marie-Francine Moens. 2012. SemEval-2012 task 3: Spatial role labeling. In *Proceedings of SemEval 2012*, pages 365–373.

Inderjeet Mani, Christy Doran, Dave Harris, Janet Hitzeman, Rob Quimby, Justin Richer, Ben Wellner, Scott Mardis, and Seamus Clancy. 2010. SpatialML: annotation scheme, resources, and evaluation. *Language Resources and Evaluation*, 44(3):263–280.

George A. Miller. 1995. WordNet: a lexical database for English. *Communications of the ACM*, 38(11):39–41.

James Pustejovsky, Jessica Moszkowicz, and Marc Verhagen. 2013. A linguistically grounded annotation language for spatial information. *ATALA: Association pour la Traitment Automatique des Langues*, 53(2):87–113.

Kirk Roberts and Sanda M. Harabagiu. 2012. UTD-SpRL: A joint approach to spatial role labeling. In *Proceedings of SemEval 2012*, pages 419–424.

Kirk Roberts, Michael A. Skinner, and Sanda M. Harabagiu. 2013. Recognizing spatial containment relations between event mentions. In *Proceedings of the 10th International Conference on Computational Semantics*.

Philip J. Stone, Dexter C. Dunphy, and Marshall S. Smith. 1966. *General Inquirer: A Computer Approach to Content Analysis*. The MIT Press.

SemEval 2015, Task 7: Diachronic Text Evaluation

Octavian Popescu
IBM Research
Yorktown, NY 10598, USA
o.popescu@us.ibm.com

Carlo Strapparava
FBK
Povo, TN 38123, Italy
strappa@fbk.eu

Abstract

In this paper we describe a novel task, namely the Diachronic Text Evaluation task. A corpus of snippets which contain relevant information for the time when the text was created is extracted from a large collection of newspapers published between 1700 and 2010. The task, subdivided in three subtasks, requires the automatic system to identify the time interval when the piece of news was written. The subtasks concern specific type of information that might be available in news. The intervals come in three grades: fine, medium and coarse according to their length. The systems participating in the tasks have proved that this a doable task with very interesting possible continuations.

1 Introduction

Language changes over the time, even over relatively small periods. For example, as the main intent of publishing newspapers is to disseminate information to the population of a whole country, there is an objective pressure to impose a standard and to smooth over the dialectical differences. However, since the late 1600s, each generation has read pieces of news containing new words, borrowed or invented, exhibiting new drifts in the meanings of old words, printed with different spelling etc.

The examples (1), (2), (3) and (4) below exhibit a series of features which are useful to pin point the year when the respective piece of news was created. Well known global events, sense superseding, specific spelling and new vocabulary entry words are all time relevant features. At a deeper level of analysis, time is revealed also by the mentions of named entities, such as *Security Council*, the topic and the linguistic genre are also relevant features.

1. Dictator Saddam Hussein ordered his troops to march into Kuwait. After the invasion is condemned by the UN Security Council, the US has forged a coalition with allies. Today American troops are sent to Saudi Arabia in Operation Desert Shield, protecting Saudi Arabia from possible attack. **circa 1990**

2. We have cabled the English house from which we get it and expect a reply to-morrow. **circa 1900**

3. Occasional selfies are acceptable, but uploading a new picture of yourself every day is not necessary. **circa 2014**

4. ...The House of Samuel Sandbroke was brokt and several Pistols discharged ... Her Majesty, for the better Discovery of the Offenders, is pleased to promise Her most Gracious Pardon for the said Crime. **circa 1705**

While for humans it is relatively easy to notice the language differences between two texts, and even to be accurate in determining the period when a piece of news was written, for computational systems this task is challenging. On the other hand, with the availability of large time-tagged corpora, a computational system can perform various analyses and extract correlations that are impossible for humans to know beforehand or acquire through manual inspection of the information scattered over huge collections of texts.

We propose to tackle the task of automatically identifying the time period when a piece of news was written. We provide a corpus of fragments of pieces of news, for both training and testing. The interesting question is whether it is possible to automatically determine the period when a text was written. To this end, we have devised a SemEval 2015 task, called *Diachronic Text Evaluation*, hence DTE task. For this task, all aspects of language change may be taken into account and systems of various levels of analysis can be developed. The systems could benefit for a training corpus and are evaluated against a gold standard.

Organizing a diachronic task has proven to be a difficult one and we made decisions regarding what type of pieces of news are selected, what type of information they contain and how the evaluation could be carried out. In a nutshell, we have selected pieces of news of variable length ranging from ten to a couple of hundred words, and we have made a differentiation between pieces of news that mention famous named entities and those which do not. Our definition of famous is associated with the possibility of finding information about the respective named entities in external resources, such as Wikipedia. Consequently, we proposed two subtasks according to the difference above. For both tasks, the system has to guess the correct time interval in which the text was created. The intervals come in three types: fine, medium and coarse, according to their length. The third and last subtasks regard the phrases that carry time information and the systems only have to decide if a certain phrase in a given context is time relevant, and not to assign a precise time interval to the text.

The systems could use any type of algorithm to analyze the text and find the time relevant information. In fact, the main goal of the task was to identify fragments of text which by themselves, or in conjunction with a publicly available external resource, are time relevant. As such, the task is a systematic investigation into the actual capacity of NLP to combine both textual and meta-textual information in order to place a piece of text into a larger, temporal, context.

To the best of our knowledge, the present task is one of the very first systematic investigation in diachronic corpora with a focus on the textual and meta-textual features that are time relevant. We believe that systems for finding diachronic information for pieces of text are very interesting from both theoretical and practical point of view. Socio and historical linguistics are both based on the analyses of specific linguistics variability in a certain epoch, location, social class etc. The statistical methods are able to discover correlations and linguistic provable evidence of language change at all levels: morphological, syntactical, semantic and discourse. It would be physically impossible for a human, or a team of humans for what it matters, to analyze and corroborate the data from hundreds of gigabytes of data and find all the relevant differences. Looking at the distribution of words across timeline, salient periods, with statistically non-random behavior, can be automatically inferred (Popescu and Strapparava, 2013). The structure of such periods, or epochs, are by far more complex than what it could be manually performed. From a practical point of view, diachronic systems have a wide range of applications from emergent fields such as computational forensics, computational journalism to more traditional tasks, such as discourse similarity, sense shifting, readability and narrative frameworks, etc.

The paper is organized as follow: in the next section we review the relevant literature. In Section 3 we present the main motivation for the DTE task and the three subtasks with their specific corpora. In Section 4 we present the data format and the evaluation method together with a simple baseline. In Section 5 we discuss the main properties of the submitted systems and their results. The paper ends with a substantial section on conclusion and main future research direction in DTE.

2 Related Work

The availability of large time annotated corpora like Google N-gram open the perspective of a new field of the research which focuses on the distribution of the linguistics elements in certain periods. (Popescu and Strapparava, 2014; Popescu and Strapparava, 2013) showed how such corpora can be used to infer transition periods between epoch with specific characteristics. A ground breaking paper, (Niculae et al., 2014) focuses on historical documents in three languages, English, Portuguese and Romanian. The paper shows how statistical method can be used to predict the date when the documents have been created. The similarity of the ideas in the present task and their paper, although developed in completely autonomy, prove that there is indeed a major interest in building diachronic systems and that the time is high for this task. We believe that there is a lot to do in this emergent field.

3 Task Description

In this section we present the main motivations for a diachronic task and in particular, we focus on how these motivations have influenced the choice in the present task. Let us start from the example (1)-(4) presented in Section 1.

We can observe that the choice of words, the morphology and word particular meaning, are an important part of time detection. Words like *brokt*, *selfie*, spellings like *to-morrow* or a sense like the one of the verb *cable* in (2) are used only within a certain period. Also, the topics are time specific and the reader may not even need to consult other sources in order to realize that an *American war in Saudi Arabia* and *Her Majesty pardon for a domestic incident* cannot possibly happen in the same period, as much as *telegraphing* and *uploading selfies* cannot either. Any of these clues seems to be a strong clue, but it would have been difficult to consider them before seeing this particular set of sentences. Intuitively, if one would read another set of sentences, some other clues, equally strong, are found. It makes sense to ask ourselves: How many such clues exist? Can such clues be systematically found and consistently organized? A human investigation of large corpora is hopeless, as billions of sentences must be inspected.

3.1 From News Corpora to Diachronic Data and Tasks

To answer this question we may want to link the linguistic information to the timeline. A big quantity of data, chronologically ordered, allows accurate statistical statements regarding the covariance between the frequencies of two or more terms over a certain period of time. By discovering significant statistical changes in word usage behavior, it is possible to define epoch boundaries. Inside these epochs the news are written in a rather uniform way. However, small changes as well as reference to famous historical events may lead to the formation of sub epochs.

Clearly, the mentioning of specific historical events makes it much easier for a diachronic system. The system must be able to consult an external resource such as Wikipedia, in order to assign a time stamp to the extracted entities. However, an extra analysis is required in order to make sure that the text does not refer to the respective historical event as past experience. On the other hand, surface features, such as spelling, reference to institutions that are specific to a epoch, or the usage of words in specific context, can be used to infer a time interval within which the text was written. Generally, this interval is much larger when compared to the time stamp assigned to the historical events and unless the system is provided with a crystal globe, no more accurate predictions can be made. It becomes clear that one needs to differentiate between the two types of information discussed above. And, also, that different precision is to be expected between these two subtasks. Let us call subtask 1 the diachronic task which considers pieces of news in which specific historical events, named entities etc. are clearly mentioned and let us call subtask 2 the diachronic task in which such information is missing, but in which there is enough surface information to assign a time interval, at least for a human. We present and discuss below a few typical examples for each of the subtasks mentioned here.

Task 1

5. At the Court at St.James's, the 29th Day of March, and1744 Present, the King's most excellent Majesty in Council. His Majesty's Declaration of War against the French King.

6. The Troubles which broke out in Germany on Account of the Succession of the late Emperor Charles the Sixth, having been begun, and carried on, by the Instigation, Assistance, and Support of the French King

7. By 1971 about one-third of Edison's electric output will be generated with nuclear capacity,

8. 1935 Ford V-8 Tudor Sedan Only an year old. not a flaw in it anywhere.

In example (5) the date is clearly indicated and the phrase *war against the French King* anchors the text very precisely in time. The mention of *the late Emperor Charles the Sixth* in example (6) pinpoints the time very precisely. The epoch is indicated in example (7) as *nuclear capacity* cannot possible happen before mid sixties. The last example, (8), requires a subtraction of the dates expressed via temporal phrase, *1935* and *one year old* respectively. To sum up, task 1 requires systems to work with temporal expressions, name entity recognition and external resources, such as Wikipedia.

Task 2

9. By Letters from the Frontiers there is Advice, that the French Intendant has given Orders for tracing out a Camp near Givet for 10000 Men;

10. Receipts at Chicago to-day. Wheats 206 cars; corn fill; oats, 181 cars. Estimated receipts to-morrow. Wheat, 400 cars; corn, 85 cars; oats, 235 cars; hogs, 16,000 head.

11. There is a theory evolved by a French scientist to the effect that tho human. race is diminishing In size and will finally become microscopic and vanish into thin air. He says that statistics from the days of the giants to the present time prove that man is getting smaller and shorter and more diminutive live in every way.

12. Red Blankets $1.98 a pair. White Blankets 69c a pair.Bed Comforts 69c each. Heavy Knit Skirts 69c each.

Advice was used at the beginning of the 18th century for military information. The fact that the event takes place in Europe, *Givet*, and what is a small amount of troops for modern times is mentioned, plus the whole linguistics register of the text determines clearly the date of the text in Example (9). As displayed in example (10), the spelling, *to-day* and *to-morrow* is a characteristics of the period between 19th and 20th century, and the quantity involved shows that indeed the time stamp is about that time. The scientific language used in example (11), especially the term *statistics* shows that the text cannot be produced earlier than the second half of the 19th century, yet the mentioning of *days of giants* shows clearly that the science was not yet fully evolved and it was still tributary to an ecclesiastical view of the world. Thus, the text must have been produced around the last quarter of 18th century. The prices specified in example (12) are clearly related to an epoch when the American dollar had a very high value, but yet, it has to be close enough to the modern times in order for an advertisement to the *bed comforts* to be made.

The examples above, which are prototypical for task 2, show that in order to identify correctly the time interval a system must corroborate different types of information, among which an important role play the linguistics register and the details specific to each epoch. In fact, there are few NLP systems, if any, which are able to identify and cluster accordingly to these features. This is why our main effort was directed to provide a good coverage of diachronic corpus especially for task 2, see next section. As we worked on compiling the data for task 2 it becomes clear that a different accuracy is to be expected between task 1 and task 2, and consequently, different types of intervals must be provided for the two subtasks.

The focus of subtask number three is on individual phrases in context. There are certain phrases that are time specific. In fact we can distinguish two categories of such phrases: (i) phrases that have been used preponderantly in a certain epoch and (ii) phrases that have a specific meaning within a certain epoch. For the first type, it is sufficient to recognize them, while for the second, a deeper analysis is necessary and the context in which they are used is relevant. A system able to deal with the challenges posed by task 1 and, especially task 2, must be able to correctly make the distinction between phrases, which carry temporal value and those which do not.

Task 3

13. According to Advices from Germany, a Rupture between the *Courts of Dresden and Berlin* is at Hand

14. The Regiments of Guelderland, and another belonging to this *Republick*, which were accused to not charging the Enemy

15. *corporal punishment*

16. his *artillery* retreat so that he constantly marched under the *grapeshot*

For the contiguous phrases marked with italic format in the examples (13)-(15), a system must be able to decide whether, in the provided context, there is temporal information attached to them. The context is crucial, because, out of context, the temporal value may be cancelled. In a sentence, more than a phrase can be proposed. Roughly, all the features discussed above for task 1 and task 2 are present in the examples of task 3. From this point of view, task 3 can be viewed as a classical feature selection task.

3.2 News Corpus and Data Statistics

Instead of considering whole pieces of news, we focused on individual parts of text that may carry relevant time information. The data proposed for training and test is made out of snippets of text of variable length. Typically a snippet will have between tens to a couple of hundred of words.

We used a series of journals available in electronic format from extracting the data. Most of the electronic archive do not make available newspapers that are older than the beginning of 19th century. However, we wanted to cover the whole period between 1,700 to 2,010. A second detail to consider is the diversity of the sources. Most of the archives are linked to one journal, which restricts the scope of the news to one location and one community. Another aspect that we want to consider for our data is to be hard to find it by searching the web. That will kind of prohibiting a simple system that only does string match to correctly solve the task. A system that find the whole piece of news and its publishing date on the web , may produce good results for task 1 , but would fail to do so for task 2 and task 3.
In order to cope with this restriction we subscribed to several web newspaper archives. The influence of each of these sources in our data set is specified in Table 1.

Source	*address*	*Data task coverage*
NPA	newspaper.achive.com	75%
SPR	archive.spectator.co.uk	12%
BDY	www.bodley.ox.ac.uk/ilej/	10%
OTHER		3%

Table 1: Data Sources.

The separation of the data into trial, training and test is presented in table 2. The data for task1 is not very rich. This is because the learning methodology for task 1 is pretty clear, so we are mainly interested in having a statistical sufficient pool for drawing accurate conclusions after the evaluation of the task. For task 2 the methodology is still a matter of research we want to provide as much data as possible in order for machine learning systems to be able to learn both the surface and meta-textual features. For task 3, there is no need for training. A phrase is or it is not time relevant, and each case must be treated separately.

data	*task 1*	*task 2*	*task 3*
trial	17	87	7
training	167	5, 436	NA
test	267	1, 041	108
total	451	6, 568	115

Table 2: Data size.

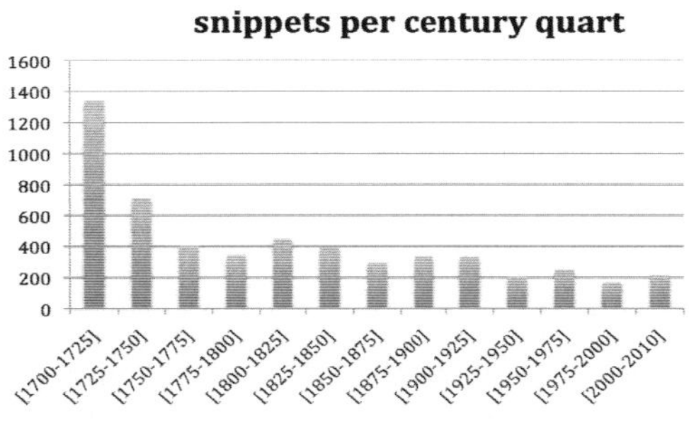

Figure 1: Task 2 distribution.

The snippets cover the last three centuries. However, the number of snippets per year may vary. In Figure 1 we plot the distribution of the number of snippets for each time interval of 25 years for task 2. With the notable difference of the first 50 years of the 18th century, each quarter of the century is covered by a number between 200 to 400 snippets, which men an average between 4 to 8 snippets per year. The first two quarters of the 18th centuries are substantially better covered: 1, 343 and 780 snippets respectively. The explanation for this skewness is two fold: (1) the data for the beginning of the 18th century is much more difficult to acquire than the rest of the data. Basically the text exists only as pdf and the OCRss are not trained to work on this kind of text. Therefore, it is really hard to get a good corpus for the beginning of 18th century, but, as this is in fact our goal, we pursued into acquiring the snippets for this period with priority. (2) the data at the beginning of the 18th century is the one which has a rich variation of linguistic constructions, and the present corpus can be used further for different analyses. We note here, that from the point of view of lexical variability, the 19th century is very rich and there is a huge jump from the previous century in the size of vocabulary.

In this section we have defined the broad scope of the DTE task, we have reviewed the main characteristics of the subtasks, and we have shown to what type of information must be extracted and managed by a diachronic system. In the next section we present the details of task organization - the format of data, the input and expected output and the evaluation procedure.

4 Task Organization

4.1 Data Format

As this task is the first of its genre, it is hard to know priorly how accurate a system can be in determining epochs and sub epochs from a news corpus. On the basis of our previous experience (Popescu and Strapparava, 2014; Popescu and Strapparava, 2013), we have reasons to believe that separation into epochs is not linear: the epochs tend to change much faster in modern times. However, the topics seemed to be much better differentiate a couple of hundred of years ago than in the modern times. All in all, it seems that a 50 years time interval is something that could be inferred without carrying out a special analysis for both tasks T1 and T2. Thus, in order to be able to judge justly the contribution to each system, a shorter time interval should be taken into account. We have decided to consider an interval centered around the year in which the news was actually produced and to have three types of intervals: fine, medium and coarse. The three intervals are included one in another, and for all three there is an equal number of years to the left and to the right of the actual date. This condition creates intervals with even number of years. We considered the intervals for task T1 and T2 as presented in Table 3.

accuracy	*task1*	*task2*
fine	2	6
medium	6	12
coarse	12	20

Table 3: Time intervals.

The system has to choose the correct time period, e.g. 1700-1720, ..., 1900-1920, ..., from the given set of contiguous intervals which cover the whole period considered, i.e. from 1700 to 2014. In both subtasks 1 and 2 the explicit choice of intervals is available. Only one interval is correct for each level of accuracy. In the training data each snippet has an unique ID, followed by three lines, one for each level of precision and each containing the set of intervals with the specific length. Only one interval is marked with *yes* in training, while in test all are marked with *no*. At the evaluation time, the system performances are compared against the gold standard.

4.2 Evaluation and baseline

The results on each snippet can be evaluated individually. The system has to specify the chosen interval, and if this is the same as the one specified in the gold standard, then the answer is correct, otherwise not. However, the distance from the chosen interval and the correct interval is relevant. Between two systems that have exactly the same number of strictly correct answers, it is preferable to work with the one that has the minimal error average. Keeping in mind these ideas we implemented an evaluation script, which takes into account the distance between the chosen and the gold standard interval. The score is normalized to [0,1) interval. The correct answer is marked with a zero loss and a ten or more interval difference is marked with 0.99 loss. According to the number of intervals off, a loss is computed between 0 and 1, see Table 4. The final score is 1- loss. The evaluation script also outputs the number of years by which the system was off and their distributions, that is, the distribution of loss function from 0 to 9.

We have considered a simple baseline, that is random choice. Another candidate is to always choose the median interval, like 1850, for example. However, both options are bad, and the number of 9 or more intervals off is very large, these baselines tend to have a very high loss function. Their behavior is not actually very different one another. That is why we choose officially to have just one baseline, namely random choice. This choice is supported by the following reason: the median produces every time the same output, while the random choice is different. Averaging over several runs of the random choice we have a much better approximation of what are the baseline performances.

intervals off	*loss*	*intervals off*	*loss*
0	0	5	.5
1	.1	6	.6
2	.15	7	.8
3	.2	8	.9
4	.4	≥ 9	.99

Table 4: Loss as function of off intervals.

5 Submitted Runs and Results

There were 7 teams that expressed their interest in the task, but in the end there were only four teams which successfully submitted the results. The number of submitted runs was less, though, as not all the teams participated in all the tasks. In fact there is only one team that participated in all three tasks, namely **IXA**. As such, we are glad to acknowledge them as the winner of the tasks, if the average over the all three task is made.

We are going to present the team by including their own description of their systems. More details can be found in their system paper, submitted to the SemEval 2015. Then we present their results and discuss the performances of their system individually.

5.1 Systems

A short description of the system follows:

I **AMBRA**

Our approach is based on the learning-to-rank framework using pairwise comparisons, previously proposed for temporal text modelling by (Niculae et al., 2014). We train a classifier to learn which document out of a pair is older and which is newer. If two documents come from overlapping intervals, then their order cannot be determined with certainty, so the pair is not used in training. We use the property of linear models to extend a set of pairwise decisions into a ranking of test documents (Joachims, 1998). In light of this, our system is named AMBRA (Anachronism Modelling by Ranking). We used four types of features: document length meta-features, stylistic, grammatical, and lexical features. The four stylistic features used were previously proposed by (Stajner and Zampieri, 2013): Average Word Length (AWL), Average Sentence Length (ASL), Lexical Density (LD) and Lexical Richness (LR).

II **IXA**

Four different approaches are undertaken in order to automatically determine the period of time in which a piece of news was written: the first approach consists of searching for the mentioned time period within the text. The second approach, on the other hand, consists of searching for named entities present in the text and then establishing the period of time by linking these to Wikipedia. The third approach uses Google NGrams and, to conclude, the fourth approach consists of using linguistic features that are significant with respect to language change in combination with machine learning.

III **UCD**

We approach the task of dating a text (subtask 2) as a stylistic classification problem. For each level of granularity (6-year, 12-year, and 20-year), we train a multi-class SVM classifier using a set of stylistic features extracted from the texts. These features include frequency counts of character, word, and POS-tag n-grams, and syntactic phrase-structure rule occurrences. We also incorporate date estimates of syntactic nodes from the Google syntactic n-grams database. Our submission is a classifier incorporating all of these features and trained on the task training data. We find that of the stylistic features, character n-grams are the most informative. The Google syntactic n-gram dates, while weak predictors on their own, are also among the most informative features in our combined classifier.

IV **USAAR**

We built a crawler to crawl the text snippets in the task and also we found that the webpages retrieved were dated. We use those dates as answers to the task evaluation. We then crawl the two webpages fully and then clean the website to produce a corpus of diachronic texts for future use (in total 24,280 articles).

5.2 Evaluation

The results are presented in Table 5. The *acc* column lists the score of the system, computed as described in Section 4.2, and the *P* shows how many times the system was perfectly accurate, that is, it found the exact interval. The fine grade seems to be a problem for the big majority of the systems. The only system which reports very high value, USAAR, is

System	*Task 1*						*Task 2*						*Task 3*
	F		M		C		F		M		C		
	acc	*P*	*acc*	*P*	*acc*	*P*	*acc*	*P*	*acc*	*P*	*acc*	*P*	*acc*
AMBRA	.167	.037	.367	.071	.554	.074	.605	.143	.767	.143	.868	.292	NA
IXA	.187	.02	.375	.041	.557	.090	0.261	.037	.428	.067	0.622	.098	.573
UCD	NA	NA	NA	NA	NA	NA	0.759	.463	.846	.472	0.910	0.542	.551
USAAR	.953	.910	.972	.928	.981	.943	NA	NA	NA	NA	NA	NA	NA
baseL	.107	.112	.174	.187	.377	.037	.224	0	.391	0	.524	0	.237

Table 5: DTE results.

based on web crawling, thus is not a generalizable method. In fact, the team participated only in task 1. The medium grade seems to be doable, all systems scoring better than the baseline. For the coarse grade the systems outperform the baseline by several tens of percent and obtain very good results, with accuracy between 0.868-0.91. These results confirm the fact that the task is doable and a 20 years interval is appropriate for DTE. We hope these results can be further improved in the future.

The results for task 3 show that this task is indeed difficult, and even if the baseline has been overcome with a great margin, the results show that the system could be improved further. We plot the distribution of errors for the system which participated in task 2, see Figure 2. Interestingly, AMBRA and UCD have very similar distributional curves, with the exception of perfect guess. The IXA system has a more regular shape and its errors seem to be evenly distributed with a big exception for the maximum error category. Maybe an interpolation between these three methods could lead to a better overall result.

To conclude, we are glad we received different systems which produce good and very good results. These initial ideas represent a valuable pool from which further work can be developed in the future.

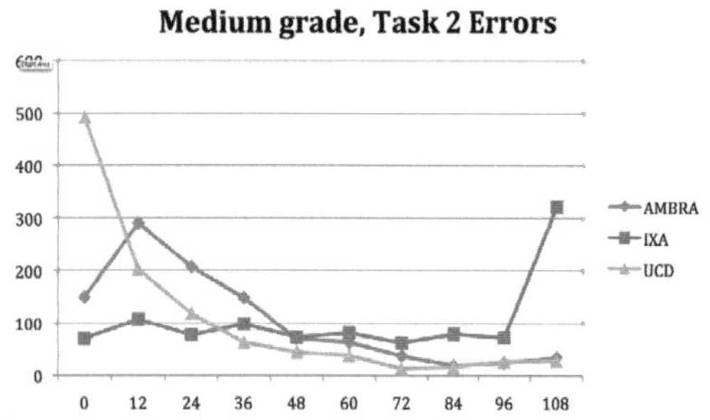

Figure 2: Task 2 medium error distribution.

6 Conclusion and Further Research

In this paper we described the Diachronic Text Evaluation task. We explain the main motivation for this task and we presented what the main issues behind the diachronic task are and how these issues have influenced our decisions. We presented the sources and the distribution of snippets in task data. A short paragraph description for each of the participating systems is provided, and we carried out a global evaluation. Finally we have provided an analysis of errors for task 2.

We think that there are some very interesting directions we would like to investigate further. The first one is to consolidate the actual corpus. This a necessary step in order to build a solid basis for further experiments and developments. We would like to improve the quality and quantity of training text for allowing search of changes at all linguistics level. We would like to work more in revealing the connection between diachronic evaluation and epoch discovery.

Another direction of research is a systematic study of the textual and meta-textual features that are relevant for the DTE task and what their individual contributions to the over all accuracy is. Besides the overt temporal features we need to identify, the linguistics register, the topics and the discourse features - from grammar to pragmatics must be taken into account. We believe that DTE is a very good indicator on the performance of machine learning systems for the meta-textual feature management.

Last, but not least, we would like to bridge the gap between different old and emergent fields, such as sociology, socio-historic linguistics and social computational analysis, computational journalism and forensic linguistics respectively. We think that NLP systems are able to tackle the difficult issues posed by this research.

References

Thorsten Joachims. 1998. Text categorization with Support Vector Machines: learning with many relevant features. In *Proceedings of the European Conference on Machine Learning*, pages 137–142.

Vlad Niculae, Marcos Zampieri, Liviu Dinu, and Alina Ciobanu. 2014. Temporal text ranking and automatic dating of texts. In *Proceedings of EACL 2014*, Gothenburg, Sweden.

Octavian Popescu and Carlo Strapparava. 2013. *Behind the Times*: Detecting epoch changes using large corpora. In *Proceedings of the* 6th *International Joint Conference on Natural Language Processing (IJCNLP-2013)*, Nagoya, Japan, October.

Octavian Popescu and Carlo Strapparava. 2014. Time corpora: Epochs, opinions and changes. *Knowledge-Based Systems*, 69:3—13, October.

Sanja Stajner and Marcos Zampieri. 2013. Stylistic changes for temporal text classification. In *Proceedings of the 16th International Conference on Text, Speech and Dialogue (TSD2013)*.

UCD : Diachronic Text Classification with Character, Word, and Syntactic N-grams

Terrence Szymanski
Insight Centre for Data Analytics
School of Computer Science and Informatics
University College Dublin, Ireland
terrence.szymanski@ucd.ie

Gerard Lynch
Centre for Applied Data Analytics Research
University College Dublin, Ireland
gerard.lynch.@ucd.ie

Abstract

We present our submission to SemEval-2015 Task 7: Diachronic Text Evaluation, in which we approach the task of assigning a date to a text as a multi-class classification problem. We extract n-gram features from the text at the letter, word, and syntactic level, and use these to train a classifier on date-labeled training data. We also incorporate date probabilities of syntactic features as estimated from a very large external corpus of books. Our system achieved the highest performance of all systems on subtask 2: identifying texts by specific time language use.

1 Introduction

This paper describes our submission to the SemEval-2015 Task 7, "Diachronic Text Evaluation" (Popescu and Strapparava, 2015). The aim of this shared task is to evaluate approaches toward diachronic text analysis of a corpus of English-language news articles from The Spectator[1] archive, originally published between 1700 and 2014.

We solely address subtask 2: "texts with specific time language usage." The goal of this subtask is to infer the composition date of a text based on implicit clues in language of the text, as opposed to overt mentions of datable named entities or events. This task has inherent utility, for example, for historians dating texts in an archive with no external datable properties. However, it is equally interesting as an investigation into methods for quantifying changes in language and writing style over a period of centuries.

We approach this task in a similar manner as previous work on stylistic text classification (Argamon-Engelson et al., 1998) in that we aim to model stylistic, rather than topical, features of the text. From each text we extract a variety of character, lexical, and syntactic features, as described in section 3. We also use a set of syntactic features whose frequencies over time have been estimated from a very large corpus of books (Goldberg and Orwant, 2013). While many of these features have previously been used for stylistic analysis, our approach is not to model *style* per se. Many types of variation may be captured indirectly by our features: the spelling, typography, lexicon, and grammar of English have changed markedly over the past centuries, as has the genre of news writing. We consider any time-correlated variation to be useful for dating.

2 Data

We used the two training sets of texts provided by the challenge organizers for subtask 2. After removing errors (repeated items, items containing no text, items with invalid dates), our training set consisted of 4130 items. Each item contains the text of a snippet of news, typically consisting of a few sentences (the average length of a text is 70 words), and three year-range labels: one for each of the Fine (6-year), Medium (12-year) and Coarse (20-year) granularities specified in the task.

The given labels are not well-suited for classification, since the set of labels used for one text is not necessarily the same as the set of labels used for an-

[1] http://www.spectator.co.uk/.

other text. For example, here are the labels provided for two texts in the training set:

```
<text id="378rn324911597">
<textF yes="1698-1704" no="1705-1711" ...
<textM yes="1695-1707" no="1708-1720" ...
<textC yes="1691-1711" no="1712-1732" ...

<text id="74gi329732114">
<textF yes="1699-1705" no="1706-1712" ...
<textM yes="1696-1708" no="1709-1721" ...
<textC yes="1692-1712" no="1713-1733" ...
```

These two texts are very close in date, yet have completely different (and incomparable) year ranges. Therefore, we create our own non-overlapping year-range classes at 6-, 12-, 20-, and 50-year levels. We assume that the true date of a text is the midpoint of the "yes" year ranges and assign a non-overlapping class appropriately. All of our training, cross-evaluation, and prediction is done using these non-overlapping classes. To make predictions for our official submission, we predict whichever given year range has the greatest overlap with our predicted class.

The training data is unevenly distributed over the possible range of years from 1700 to 2014. Just three years (1717, 1817, and 1897) account for 11% (444 of 4130) of the training instances, while 48% (150 of 314) of the years in the possible range are unattested in the training data. Overall, there is a general bias towards earlier years in the time range. We do not attempt to control for this bias in the data, since we assume that the test data will be drawn from a similar distribution. While the uneven distribution may artificially boost the accuracy of our classifiers, the baseline classifier captures this effect.

3 Features for Classification

We extract four types of features from each text: character n-grams (`Char`), part-of-speech tag n-grams (`POS`), word n-grams (`Word`) and syntactic phrase-structure rule occurrences (`Syn`). We refer to the combined feature set as `CPWS`. (Stamou, 2008) surveys diachronic classification of literary text and finds that parts of speech, character frequencies, and function word frequencies are all used in chronologically dating text composition. Part-of-speech and word n-grams have been used for stylistic text classification (Argamon-Engelson et al., 1998), and syntactic phrase-structure rules have successfully been used as stylometric features for detecting deceptive writing in online reviews (Feng et al., 2012). We have not included document-level stylistic features (e.g. average sentence length, average word length, lexical richness, lexical density, and readability measures) although they have been used successfully for diachronic stylistic analysis (Štajner and Zampien, 2013), and could be incorporated in our classification approach. However, our n-gram features may capture features such as sentence length by proxy (e.g. in the frequency of periods).

Character n-grams are an expressive feature set which can capture variation on the morphological level (word stems), syntactic level (gaps between words and punctuation) and also word-level frequency fluctuations (prepositions and conjunctions). Character bigrams were used previously on Latin text by (Frontini et al., 2008) to date the Donation of Constantine, a study which did not verify the work as a forgery but did place it in the correct stylistically implied period.[2] Additionally, character n-grams are used in stylometric tasks such as authorship attribution (Keselj et al., 2003) and detection of *translationese* (Popescu, 2011).

All n-gram features were extracted for $n \in \{1, 2, 3\}$ using an in-house Java concordancer. Punctuation and spacing was not modified during this process, although case information was discarded. No stop words were removed. Raw frequency counts of the features were used in the process, and those features with less than 20 occurrences in the entire corpus were discarded. Texts were parsed with the Stanford parser,[3] and the 250 most-frequent syntactic rules in the training set were used as features. The dependency parse was also produced and used as described below.

3.1 Google Syntactic N-grams

As an external source of data, we used the Google Books Syntactic N-Grams (GSN) database (Goldberg and Orwant, 2013). Due to the size of the datasets and time limitations, we focused solely on the *nodes* collection of the *Eng-1M* corpus, a sample of 1 million English-language books dating from 1520 to 2008. Each data point in the *nodes* collec-

[2] Verification of forgery was based on false information contained in the text, rather than stylistic idiosyncracy.

[3] http://nlp.stanford.edu/software/lex-parser.shtml

tion is a POS-tagged word and the label of the syntactic dependency between that word and its head, which gives a sense of the word's syntactic function in a given sentence. For each node, the total number of occurrences in each year is provided.

Because the GSN database is particularly sparse for years prior to 1800, we smoothed all node counts by averaging over the five nearest years with nonzero counts. Then the smoothed counts are normalized within each year to estimate the probability of a node in a given year.

We use a Naive Bayes classifier ($\texttt{Google}_{nb}$) to predict the most likely year for a given text, represented as a set of nodes extracted from the dependency parse. We also produce a GSN feature set consisting of 308 features (one for each year in the range 1700-2008), whose values are based on the total log probability of the text in that year, normalized to the interval [0,1] for each text. The normalization controls for text length and allows comparison between texts. These features are then used in the combined `CPWS+G` classifier.

3.2 Feature Informativeness

When all features are combined, the GSN features are the most predictive. In order to assess the effectiveness of the other features and also to reduce the feature set for classification, we performed attribute selection using the Weka data mining software (Hall et al., 2009). Table 1 shows the top-ranked `CPWS` features using the the 50-year class labels, using Weka's information gain attribute evaluation with 10-fold cross-validation.

Rank	Attribute	Type	Rank	Attribute	Type
1	NN	`P-1`	10.9	t	`C-1`
2	i	`C-1`	11.7	l	`C-1`
3.5	␣	`C-1`	13.3	o	`C-1`
3.9	. → .	`S`	13.8	.	`W-1`
5	ROOT → S	`S`	15.7	[' d]	`C-2`
5.8	a	`C-1`	15.9	[␣ .]	`C-2`
7.3	e	`C-1`	16.3	r	`C-1`
8.1	.	`C-1`	18.6	[JJ NN]	`P-2`
8.5	n	`C-1`	19.3	JJ	`P-1`
10.7	s	`C-1`	19.8	c	`C-1`

Table 1: Top 20 `CPWS` features using Information Gain

The rankings show that the character n-gram features were particularly expressive in capturing temporal variation, yet it can be difficult to assign a linguistic motivation to them. Because our feature counts are not normalized by text length, many of these features may simply be redundantly capturing an overall length effect.

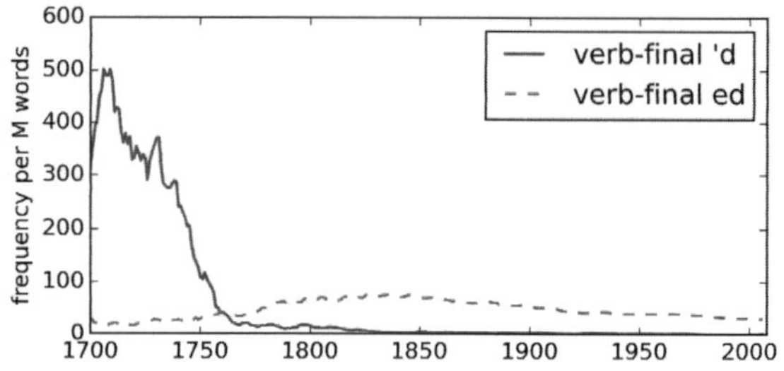

Figure 1: Changing frequencies of verb endings in the Google Books English corpus, 1700-2000.

However, some meaningful features can clearly be recognized, such as [' d], refering to the 18th century abbreviation of *-ed* as a past participle verb ending in English. The frequency of verb-final *'d* in the POS-tagged Google N-grams dataset (Lin et al., 2012), shown in Figure 1, illustrates how use of this linguistic feature has declined over time.

Another highly informative feature is the character bigram [␣ .]. In some texts, punctuation has been separated from the neighboring words with a space, possibly due to OCR errors on older texts.

4 Classification and Evaluation

We employ attribute selection as above in all of our cross-validation experiments and our official submission. Table 2 illustrates how SVM classification accuracy varies with feature set size. The value of 4000 features was chosen to maximize accuracy while minimizing running time, and was used to produce all of the results described in this paper.

$\|F\|$	6-Year	12-Year	20-Year	50-Year
4000	**37.61**	**39.30**	52.07	**67.74**
2000	35.75	37.61	50.77	67.59
1000	32.55	37.26	51.24	67.53
500	33.09	38.62	**52.22**	65.94
200	33.77	35.28	50.41	64.07
100	31.87	33.62	47.10	60.32
50	29.57	31.82	44.91	57.07

Table 2: Effect of feature set size ($|F|$) on classification accuracy. (`Char+POS+Google` features)

Assigning a date to a text is not a typical classification problem, because the classes are not independent of one another. We experimented with SVM regression, but this produced lower accuracy than the SVM classifier. Ordinal classification is a method that may be used when classes exhibit a natural order, as in this task. We performed some experiments with the Weka implementation of ordinal regression (Frank and Hall, 2001) using a SVM base classifier, but these produced lower accuracy than the standard SVM classifier. Therefore, we used a standard multi-class SVM classifier for all of our evaluations and predictions.

System	6-Year	12-Year	20-Year	50-Year
Baseline	10.4	12.6	20.5	36.6
$\texttt{Google}_{nb}$	10.9	18.7	31.7	52.4
Char	36.1	38.4	47.9	64.5
POS	24.6	26.8	36.3	53.6
Word	26.1	29.6	37.2	54.6
Syn	23.4	26.3	38.5	54.6
CPWS	36.9	40.1	50.7	67.8
CPWS+G	**41.5**	**45.9**	**55.3**	**73.3**

Table 3: Classification accuracy of various feature sets, using 10-fold cross-validiation on the training data set.

Table 3 lists the cross-validation classification accuracy for our various models. The baseline classifier looks only at the class labels and chooses the most frequent class. The $\texttt{Google}_{nb}$ classifier is a Naive Bayes classifier using only the GSN probabilities and assuming a uniform prior over years. This represents a classifier with no domain knowledge of the text genre or date range distribution.

The remaining rows show the results for SVM classifiers trained independently on each of the four stylistic feature sets. While each feature type outperforms the baseline, the character n-gram features are clearly the single most effective feature type. The combination of all four features together (CPWS) outperforms any single feature set individually, and this represents the maximal performance we achieve using solely the training data provided by the task organizers.

The final row shows the performance of a SVM classifier using all of our stylistic features plus features derived from the GSN probabilities. This achieves the highest accuracy and this is the system we submitted to the task.

Table 4 shows the official results of the CPWS+G classifier, trained on the full training set and evaluated on a test set of 1041 texts whose true dates were unknown to us. The accuracy values are in line with our cross-validation scores. The score is a weighted classification metric that rewards predictions that are not fully correct but are near the correct date. The third row lists the mean deviation of our predictions from the true date. By all three measures, our system was the top performing submission to this subtask.

	Fine (6-year)	Medium (12-year)	Coarse (20-year)
Accuracy	46.3	47.3	54.3
Score	0.7592	0.8466	0.9104
Avg. Years Off	14	19	19

Table 4: Official results on the SemEval test data.

Our 73.3% accuracy on the 50-year class may be loosely compared to (Mihalcea and Nastase, 2012), who achieve 62% classification accuracy dating words in context to 50-year epochs. Their task, word epoch disambiguation, is comparable but different: they classify words, not texts, using local context features and a targeted set of 165 words.

5 Conclusion

We have shown that a stylistic classification approach is capable of accurately predicting the date when a text from the sample category was written. Additionally, our approach is straightforward to implement and can function well using only a moderate sized sample of training data, although its accuracy can be improved by incorporating features trained from a large external corpus.

We cast a wide net in order to produce a large feature set and allow the classifier to select whichever features most improved the classification accuracy. While this produces good classification results, it remains difficult to interpret the linguistic or stylistic significance of the most-predictive features. It is also unknown how the results would differ on other data sets in different languages, genres, or time periods. In addition to the features we have explored, there are a number of others, such as sentence length, capitalization, and lexical richness measures which might be considered in future work.

Acknowledgments

This work is supported by Science Foundation Ireland through the Insight Centre for Data Analytics under grant number SFI/12/RC/2289 and Enterprise Ireland through the Centre for Applied Data Analytics Research under grant number TC 2013 0013.

Thanks to Mark Keane for his feedback and suggestions, particularly on the use of syntactic features for dating. Thanks also to the Insight Centre Future of News discussion group for their feedback on a presentation of an early version of this work.

References

Shlomo Argamon-Engelson, Moshe Koppel, and Galit Avneri. 1998. Style-based text categorization: What newspaper am I reading? Technical report, AAAI.

Song Feng, Ritwik Banerjee, and Yejin Choi. 2012. Syntactic stylometry for deception detection. In *Proceedings of ACL 2012: Short Papers*, pages 171–175.

Eibe Frank and Mark Hall. 2001. A simple approach to ordinal classification. Technical report, University of Waikato.

Francesca Frontini, Gerard Lynch, and Carl Vogel. 2008. Revisiting the 'Donation of Constantine'. In *Proceedings of AISB 2008*, pages 1–9.

Yoav Goldberg and Jon Orwant. 2013. A dataset of syntactic-ngrams over time from a very large corpus of English books. In *Proceedings of *SEM 2013*, pages 241–247.

Mark Hall, Eibe Frank, Geoffrey Holmes, Bernhard Pfahringer, Peter Reutemann, and Ian H. Witten. 2009. The WEKA data mining software: An update. *SIGKDD Explorations*, 11(1).

Vlado Keselj, Fuchun Peng, Nick Cercone, and Calvin Thomas. 2003. N-gram-based author profiles for authorship attribution. In *Proceedings of PACLING 2003*, pages 255–264.

Yuri Lin, Jean-Baptiste Michel, Erez Lieberman Aiden, Jon Orwant, Will Brockman, and Slav Petrov. 2012. Syntactic annotations for the Google Books ngram corpus. In *Proceedings of the ACL 2012 System Demonstrations*, pages 169–174.

Rada Mihalcea and Vivi Nastase. 2012. Word epoch disambiguation: Finding how words change over time. In *Proceedings of ACL 2012*.

Octavian Popescu and Carlo Strapparava. 2015. Semeval-2015 task 7: Diachronic text evaluation. In *Proceedings of SemEval 2015*.

Marius Popescu. 2011. Studying translationese at the character level. In *Proceedings of RANLP 2011*, pages 634–639.

Sanja Štajner and Marcos Zampien. 2013. Stylistic changes for temporal text classification. In *Proceedings of TSD 2013*, pages 519–526.

Constantina Stamou. 2008. Stylochronometry: Stylistic development, sequence of composition, and relative dating. *Literary and Linguistic Computing*, 23(2):181–199.

SemEval-2015 Task 8: SpaceEval

James Pustejovsky[(1)], **Parisa Kordjamshidi**[(2,3)], **Marie-Francine Moens**[(2)],
Aaron Levine[(1)], **Seth Dworman**[(1)], **Zachary Yocum**[(1)]
[(1)]Brandeis University, Waltham, MA
[(2)]Katholieke Universiteit Leuven, Belgium
[(3)]University of Illinois, Urbana/Champaign, IL
{jamesp,zyocum,aclevine,sdworman}@brandeis.edu,
Sien.Moens@cs.kuleuven.be, kordjam@illinois.edu

Abstract

Human languages exhibit a variety of strategies for communicating spatial information, including toponyms, spatial nominals, locations that are described in relation to other locations, and movements along paths. SpaceEval is a combined information extraction and classification task with the goal of identifying and categorizing such spatial information. In this paper, we describe the SpaceEval task, annotation schema, and corpora, and evaluate the performance of several supervised and semi-supervised machine learning systems developed with the goal of automating this task.

1 Introduction

SpaceEval builds on the Spatial Role Labeling (SpRL) task introduced in SemEval 2012 (Kordjamshidi et al., 2012) and used in SemEval 2013 (Kolomiyets et al., 2013). The base annotation scheme of the previous tasks was introduced in (Kordjamshidi et al., 2010), with empirical practices in (Kordjamshidi et al., 2011; Kordjamshidi and Moens, 2015). While those previous tasks are similar in their goal, SpacEval adopts the annotation specification from ISOspace (Pustejovsky et al., 2011a; Moszkowicz and Pustejovsky, 2010; ISO/TC 37/SC 4/WG 2, 2014), a new standard for capturing spatial information. The SpRL in SemEval 2012 had a focus on the main roles of *trajectors*, *landmarks*, *spatial indicators*, and the links between these roles which form *spatial relations*. The formal semantics of the relations were considered at a course-grained level, consisting of three types: directional, regional (topological), and distal. The related annotated data, CLEF IAPR TC-12 Image Benchmark (Grubinger et al., 2006), contained mostly static spatial relations. In SemEval 2013, the SpRL task was extended to the recognition of *motion indicators* and *paths*, which are applied to the more dynamic spatial relations. Accordingly, the data set was expanded and the text from the Degree Confluence Project (Jarrett, 2013) webpages were annotated.

SpaceEval extends the task in several dimensions, first by enriching the granularity of the semantics in both static and dynamic spatial configurations, and secondly by broadening the variety of annotated data and the domains considered. In SpaceEval the concept of *place* is distinguished from the concept of *spatial entity* as a fundamental typing distinction. That is, the roles of trajector (figure) and landmark (ground) are roles that are assigned to spatial entities and places when occurring in spatial relations. Places, however, are inherently typed as such, and remain places, regardless of what spatial roles they may occupy. Obviously, an individual may assume multiple role assignments, and in both ISOspace and SpRL this is assumed to be the case. However, because SpRL focuses on role assignment, it does not introduce the general concept of spatial entity.

There are other differences in the relational schemas of SpRL and SpaceEval which can be easily mapped to each other. For example, in SpRL the general concept of *spatial relation* is defined and the semantics of the relationship (e.g., directional, regional) is added as an attribute of the relation while in SpceEval these semantics introduce new types of relations (e.g., QSLINK and OLINK). In addition to the variations in relational schemas, there are some additional extensions in the SpaceEval annotation. These include augmenting the main elements with more fine-grained attributes. These attributes, in turn, impact the way the spatial semantics are interpreted. For example, the spatial entities are described with their *dimensionality*, *form*, etc. SpaceEval, also strongly highlights the concepts involved in dynamic spatial relations by introducing *movelink* relations and *motion* tags for annotating motion verbs or nominal motion events and their category from the perspective of spatial semantics. These fine-grained annotations of all the relevant concepts that contribute to grasping spatial semantics makes this scheme and the accompanying corpus unique. The details of the task, including the annotation schema, evaluation configurations, breakdown of the sub-tasks, data set, participant systems, and evaluation results are described in the rest of the paper.

2 The Task

The goals of SpaceEval include identifying and classifying items from an inventory of spatial concepts:

- Places: toponyms, geographic and geopolitical regions, locations.
- Spatial Entities: entities participating in spatial relations.
- Paths: routes, lines, turns, arcs.
- Topological relations: *in*, *connected*, *disconnected*.
- Orientational relations: *North*, *left*, *down*, *behind*.
- Object properties: intrinsic orientation, dimensionality.
- Frames of reference: absolute, intrinsic, relative.
- Motion: tracking objects through space over time.

Participants were offered three test configurations for this task.

Configuration 1 Only unannotated test data was provided.

Configuration 2 Manually annotated spatial elements, without attributes, were provided.

Configuration 3 Manually annotated spatial elements, with attributes, were provided.

The SpacEval task is broken down into the following sub-tasks:

Spatial Elements (SE)

a. Identify spans of spatial elements including locations, paths, events and other spatial entities.

b. Classify spatial elements according to type: PATH (road, river, highway), PLACE (mountain, village), MOTION (walk, fly), NONMOTION_EVENT (sit, read), SPATIAL_ENTITY (any entity in a spatial relation).

c. Identify their attributes according to type.

Spatial Signal Identification (SS)

a. Identify spans of spatial signals (in, on, above).

b. Identify their attributes.

Motion Signal Identification (MI)

a. Identify spans of path-of-motion and manner-of-motion signals (arrive, leave, drive, walk).

b. Identify their attributes.

Motion Relation Identification (MoveLink)

a. Identify relations between motion-event triggers, motion signals, and motion-event participants (source, goal, landmark, path).

b. Identify their attributes.

Spatial Configuration Identification (QSLink)

a. Identify qualitative spatial relations between spatial signals and spatial elements (connected, unconnected, part-of, etc.).

b. Identify their attributes.

Spatial Orientation Identification (OLink)

a. Identify orientational relations between spatial signals and spatial elements (above, under, in front of, etc.).

b. Identify their attributes.

3 The SpaceBank Corpus

The data for this task are comprised of annotated textual descriptions of spatial entities, places, paths, motions, localized non-motion events, and spatial relations. The data set selected for this task, a subset of the SpaceBank corpus first described in (Pustejovsky and Yocum, 2013), consists of submissions retrieved from the Degree Confluence Project (DCP) (Jarrett, 2013), Berlitz Travel Guides retrieved from the American National Corpus (ANC) (Reppen et al., 2005), and entries retrieved from a travel weblog, Ride for Climate (RFC) (Kroosma, 2012). The DCP documents are the same set as those annotated with Spatial Role Labeling (SpRL) for SemEval-2013 Task 3 (Kolomiyets et al., 2013), however, for this task, the DCP texts were re-annotated according to ISO-Space.

3.1 Annotation Schema

The annotation of spatial information in text involves at least the following: a PLACE tag (for locations and regions participating in spatial relations); a PATH tag (for paths and boundaries between regions); a SPATIAL_ENTITY tag (for spatial objects whose location changes over time); link tags (for topological relations, direction and orientation, frames of reference, and motion event participants); and signal tags (for spatial prepositions)[1]. ISO-Space has been designed to capture both spatial and spatio-temporal information as expressed in natural language texts (Pustejovsky et al., 2012). We have followed a strict methodology of specification development, as adopted by ISO TC37/SC4 and outlined in (Bunt, 2010) and (Ide and Romary, 2004), and as implemented with the development of ISO-TimeML (Pustejovsky et al., 2005) and others in the family of SemAF standards.

SpaceEval's three link tags are as follows:

1. MOVELINK – for movement relations;
2. OLINK – orientation relations;
3. QSLINK – qualitative spatial relations;

QSLINKs are used in ISO-Space to capture topological relationships between tagged elements. The `relType` attribute values come from an extension to the RCC8 set of relations that was first used by SpatialML (Mani et al., 2010). The possible RCC8+ values include the RCC8 values (Randell et al., 1992), in addition to IN, a disjunction of TPP and NTPP.

Orientation links describe non-topological relationships. A SPATIAL_SIGNAL with a DIRECTIONAL `semantic_type` triggers such a link. In contrast to topological spatial relations, OLINK relations are built around a specific frame of reference type and a reference point. The `referencePt` value depends on the `frame_type` of the link. The ABSOLUTE frame type stipulates that the `referencePt` is a cardinal direction. For INTRINSIC OLINKs, the `referencePt` is the same identifier that is given in the `landmark` attribute. For OLINKs with a RELATIVE frame of reference, the identifier for the viewer should be provided as to the `referencePt`.

The following samples from the RFC and ANC sub-corpora have been annotated with a subset of ISO-Space for the SpaceEval task[2]:

1. [**Arriving**$_{m1}$] [**in**$_{ms1}$] the [**town of Juanjui**$_{pl1}$], near the [**park**$_{pl2}$], [**I**$_{se1}$] learned that my map had lied to me.

```
<MOTION id=m1 extent=''Arriving''
motion_type=PATH motion_class=REACH
motion_sense=LITERAL>
<MOTION_SIGNAL id=ms1 extent=''in''
motion_signal_type=PATH>
<PLACE id=pl1 extent=''town of
Juanjui'' form=NAM countable=TRUE
dimensionality=AREA>
<PLACE id=pl2 extent=''park'' form=NAM
countable=TRUE dimensionality=AREA>
<SPATIAL_ENTITY id=se1 extent=''I''
form=NOM countable=TRUE
dimensionality=VOLUME>
<MOVELINK id=mvl1 trigger=m1
goal=pl1 mover=se1 goal_reached=TRUE
motion_signalID=ms1>
```

2. Just [**south of**$_{s1}$] [**Ginza**$_{pl3}$] itself, as [**you**$_{se2}$] [**walk**$_{m2}$] [**toward**$_{ms2}$] the [**bay**$_{pl4}$], you see [**on**$_{s2}$] your [**left**$_{pl5}$] the red [**lanterns**$_{se4}$] and long [**banners**$_{se5}$] of the [**Kabuki-za**$_{pl6}$]...

```
<SPATIAL_SIGNAL id=s1 extent=''south
of'' semantic_type=DIRECTIONAL>
<PLACE id=pl3 extent=''Ginza''
form=NAM countable=TRUE
dimensionality=AREA>
<SPATIAL_ENTITY id=se2 extent=''you''
form=NOM countable=TRUE
dimensionality=VOLUME>
<MOTION id=m2 extent=''walk''
motion_type=COMPOUND
motion_class=REACH
motion_sense=LITERAL>
<MOTION_SIGNAL id=ms2
extent=''toward''
motion_signal_type=PATH>
<PLACE id=pl4 extent=''bay'' form=NAM
countable=TRUE dimensionality=AREA>
<PLACE id=pl5 extent=''left'' form=NAM
countable=TRUE dimensionality=AREA>
<SPATIAL_ENTITY id=se4
```

[1]For more information, cf. (Pustejovsky et al., 2012).

[2]The MEASURE and MLINK tags were not a part of this task.

```
extent=''lanterns'' form=NAM
countable=TRUE dimensionality=VOLUME>
<SPATIAL_ENTITY id=se5
extent=''banners'' form=NAM
countable=TRUE mod=''long''
dimensionality=VOLUME>
<PLACE id=pl6 extent=''Kabuki-za''
form=NAM countable=TRUE
dimensionality=VOLUME>
<OLINK id=ol1 trajector=m2
landmark=pl3 trigger=s1
frame_type=ABSOLUTE referencePt=SOUTH
projective=FALSE>
<MOVELINK id=mvl2 trigger=m2
mover=se2 goal=pl4 goal_reached=NO
motion_signalID=ms2>
<QSLINK id=qsl1 trigger=s2
trajector=se5 landmark=pl5 relType=IN>
<QSLINK id=qsl2 trigger=s2
trajector=se6 landmark=pl5 relType=IN>
```

Since SpaceEval is building on the SpRL shared tasks, we opted to retain the `trajector` and `landmark` attributes for labeling the participants in QSLINK and OLINK relations. This is a deviation from the ISO-Space (Pustejovsky et al., 2011b) standard, which specifies `figure` and `ground` labels based on cognitive-semantic categories explored in the semantics of motion and location by Leonard Talmy (Talmy, 1978; Talmy, 2000) and others. ISO-Space adopted the `figure/ground` terminology to identify the potentially asymmetric roles played by participants within spatial relations. For MOVELINKs, however, we distinguish the notion of a `figure/trajector` with the ISO-Space `mover` attribute label.

3.2 Corpus Statistics

Table 1 includes corpus statistics broken down into the ANC, DCP, and RFC sub-corpora in addition to the train:test partition (~3:1). The counts of document, sentence, and lexical tokens are tabulated as well as counts of each annotation tag type.

	Sub-corpus			Partition		
	ANC	**DCP**	**RFC**	**Train**	**Test**	**Total**
words	1577	7673	21048	24150	6148	30298
sents	61	369	821	1001	250	1251
docs	3	22	44	55	14	69
pl	148	691	1250	1661	428	2089
se	34	461	1175	1347	323	1670
qsl	69	348	693	886	224	1110
mvl	15	345	614	779	195	974
m	16	330	588	751	183	934
s	39	216	550	653	152	805
ms	17	260	365	508	134	642
p	19	246	278	415	128	543
e	14	66	301	321	60	381
ol	14	82	191	225	62	287

pl=PLACE; se=SPATIAL_ENTITY; qsl=QSLINK; mvl=MOVELINK; m=MOTION; s=SPATIAL_SIGNAL; ms=MOTION_SIGNAL; p=PATH; e=NONMOTION_EVENT; ol=OLINK

Table 1: Corpus Statistics

3.3 Annotation and Adjudication

All annotations for this task were of English language texts and all annotations were created and adjudicated by native English speakers. Due to dependencies of link tag elements on extent tag elements, the annotation and adjudication tasks were broken down into the following phases:

Phase 1 Extent tag span and attribute annotation.

Phase 2 Extent tag adjudication.

Phase 3 Link tag argument and attribute annotation.

Phase 4 Link tag adjudication.

Phases 2 and 4 produced gold standards from annotations in the preceding annotation phases. This annotation strategy ensured that the intermediate gold standard extent tag set was adjudicated before any link tag annotations were performed.

The annotation and adjudication effort was conducted at Brandeis University using Multi-document Annotation Environment (MAE) and Multi-annotator Adjudication Interface (MAI) (Stubbs, 2011). We used MAE to perform each phase of the annotation procedure and MAI to adjudicate and produce gold standard standoff annotations in XML format. In addition to the ISO-Space annotation tags and attributes, as a post-process, we also provided sentence and lexical tokenization as a separate standoff annotation layer in the XML data for the training and test sets.

Each document was covered by a minimum of three annotators for each annotation phase (though not necessarily the same annotators per phase). As such, we report inter-annotator agreement (IAA) as a mean Fleiss's κ coefficient for all extent tag types annotated in Phase 1, and individual kappa scores for each of the three link tag types annotated in

Phase 3 in Table 2. The scores for extent tags and MOVELINK indicate high agreement, however link tag annotation was less consistent for the remaining link tags. Though the OLINK and QSLINK tag agreement is better than chance, it is not high. We believe the lower agreement for these link tags reflects the complexity of the annotation task.

Extent Tags	Link Tags		
All Types	MOVELINK	OLINK	QSLINK
0.85	0.91	0.39	0.33

Table 2: Overall Fleiss's κ Scores

4 Evaluation

Participant systems were evaluated for each enumerated configuration as follows:

1 a. SE.a precision, recall, and F1.
   b. SE.b precision, recall, and F1 for each type, and an overall precision, recall, and F1.
   c. SE.c precision, recall, and F1 for each attribute, and an overall precision, recall, and F1.
   d. MoveLink.a, QSLink.a, OLink.a precision, recall, and F1.
   e. MoveLink.b, QSLink.b, OLink.b precision, recall, and F1 for each attribute, and an overall precision, recall, and F1.

2 a. SE.b and SE.c precision, recall, and F1 for each type and its attributes, and an overall precision, recall, and F1.
   b. MoveLink.a, QSLink.a, OLink.a precision, recall, and F1.
   c. MoveLink.b, QSLink.b, OLink.b precision, recall, and F1 for each attribute, and an overall precision, recall, and F1.

3 a. MoveLink.a, QSLink.a, OLink.a precision, recall, and F1.
   b. MoveLink.b, QSLink.b, OLink.b precision, recall, and F1 for each attribute, and an overall precision, recall, and F1.

5 Submissions and Results

In this section we evaluate results from runs of five systems. Three systems were submitted by outside groups including Honda Research Institute Japan (HRIJP-CRF-VW), Ixa Group in the University of the Basque Country (IXA), and University of Texas, Dallas (UTD)[3]. We also present results for two systems developed internally at Brandeis University: a suite of logistic regression classifiers with minimal feature engineering intended as a performance baseline covering all sub-tasks in addition to a CRF system with more advanced features, but limited to subtasks 1a and 1b for Configuration 1.

BASELINE A suite of logistic regression models using Scikit-learn (Pedregosa et al., 2011) with simple bag-of-words and n-gram features.[4]

BRANDEIS-CRF A system using a conditional random field (CRF) model (Okazaki, 2007) with features including Stanford POS and NER tags (Toutanova et al., 2003) (Finkel et al., 2005) in combination with Sparser (McDonald, 1996) tags.[5]

HRIJP-CRF-VW A system using a CRF model using CoreNLP, (Manning et al., 2014), CRFSuite (Okazaki, 2007) and Vowpal Wabbit (Langford et al., 2007) with lemmatization, POS, NER, GloVe word vector (Pennington et al., 2014) and dependency parse features.

IXA *X-Space*: A system using a binary support vector machine model from SVM-light (Joachims, 1999) and a pipeline architecture using ClearNLP (Choi and Adviser-Palmer, 2012), OpenNLP (OpenNLP, 2014), and leveraging computational linguistic resources including WordNet (Fellbaum, 1998), PropBank (Palmer et al., 2003) and the Predicate Matrix (de la Calle et al., 2014).

UTD A suite of 13 classifiers for classifying spatial roles and relations including classifiers for stationary spatial relations and their participants in addition to classification of participants of motion events and their attributes.

[3]UTD submitted three runs, however, after evaluating all the data, all three runs achieved similar scores; the results reported here are for their third and final submitted run.

[4]These baseline classifiers were developed at Brandeis University by Aaron Levine and Zachary Yocum. Cf. Section 5.1 for full description.

[5]This system was developed at Brandeis University by Seth Dworman. Cf. Section 5.2 for full description.

5.1 Baseline

Our baseline classification system (BASELINE) consists of a suite of 47 classifiers built from Scikit-learn's (Pedregosa et al., 2011) `sklearn.linear_model` logistic regression package. The system builds a collection of extent objects from the annotation and lexical tokenizations provided in the SpaceEval XML distribution data. Each extent instance has attributes for further feature and label extraction: the target chunk used to form the extent instance; any annotation tag associated with the chunk; lists of all surrounding tokens in the sentence, split between tokens preceding the target and those following, and a pointer to the original annotation XML for the purposes of global feature extraction and generating new XML tags based on the eventual model predictions.

Some extent attributes are optional, depending on the sub-task. E.g., in sub-task 1a, no attributes are required since this sub-task is a simple classification task. For link tags, extent objects are instantiated using the text chunks associated with the extent tags that serve as the link trigger. After pre-processing, the system has a complete collection of extent instances for the corpus.

Subsequent to pre-processing, the extent data are further processed for label and feature extraction. The label and feature extractors were hand-tweaked for each sub-task:

- For extent tag identification, the label extractor checks if a given token occurs at the end of a chunk, and the feature extractors include capitalization and POS tags.
- For classifying extent tag types, the feature extractors include the target chunk string, POS tag, and a seven-token context window (bounded by the sentence) centered on the target token.
- For extent tag attribute classification, the only feature extracted was the text of the chunk associated with the target tag.
- For link tag identification, a heuristic system was developed to select candidate extent tags for the trigger argument. The remaining arguments in the relation were identified by their distance and direction from the trigger. Feature extractors for this process included the text of the trigger chunk, a count of the tags in local context (the same sentence) before and after the trigger, and the types of the extent tags that occur in the context.
- For open-class link tag attributes, feature extractors included the count of extent tags before and after the trigger tag in the sentence. For closed-class link tag attributes feature extractors were limited to the text of the trigger chunk and the trigger tag type.[6]
- For link tag arguments that take an `IDREF` as a value, a unique label function was created that extracts the offsets of the candidate extent tags in the same sentence as the trigger.

The label and feature vectors were maintained using the `DictVectorizer` from Scikit-learn's `feature_extraction` module. To train the system, the vectors were used to fit the model to the training data. For decoding, the tag labels and attributes from the test data were discarded and the remaining feature vectors were transformed into a hypothesis index based on the model, which was translated to a final value using a codebook. The hypotheses were then written out to XML in accordance to the task DTD.

5.2 Brandeis CRF

In addition to the BASELINE system, we also developed a more advanced pipeline (BRANDEIS-CRF) to automate the SpaceEval sub-tasks 1a and 1b using a linear-chain conditional random field model using lexical, part-of-speech (POS), named-entity-recognition (NER), and semantic labels. We report overall F1 measures of 0.83 and 0.77 for tasks 1a and 1b, respectively, which are comparable to other top results (cf. Section 5.3). Our implementation used the CRFSuite (Okazaki, 2007) open source package, which facilitated rapid training and model inspection. The hypotheses were written out to XML in accordance to the task DTD.

We used a small set of 9 core features, augmented with bigram contexts, resulting in a total of 27 features. These features consist of lexical, syntactic, and semantic information, many of which have

[6] We experimented with additional features for attribute classification, such as counting tags and their types in the local context of the trigger, however additional features all resulted in performance decreases.

been applied successfully in a variety of information extraction tasks (Fei Huang et al., 2014), such as named entity recognition (Vilain et al., 2009b) or coreference resolution (Fernandes et al., 2014). The complete set of features are outlined in Table 3.

Type	Id	Value
Lexical	word[-1,0,1]	string
	isupper[-1,0,1]	binary
	wordlen[-1,0,1]	ternary[7]
Syntactic	pos[-1,0,1]	POS tag
Semantic	ner[-1,0,1]	NER tag
Sparser	CATEGORY[-1,0,1]	Sparser category
	FORM[-1,0,1]	Sparser form
	LCATEGORY[-1,0,1]	Sparser category
	LFORM[-1,0,1]	Sparser form

Table 3: BRANDEIS-CRF Features

For part-of-speech (POS) and named entity (NE) tags, we used the Stanford Log-linear Part-of-Speech Tagger (Toutanova et al., 2003) and the Stanford Named Entity Recognizer (Finkel et al., 2005). Additionally, we made use of Sparser (McDonald, 1996), a rule-based natural language parser in order to provide rich semantic features. Sparser parses unstructured text in cycles, where a variety of handwritten rules apply given the applications of previous rules or the current parse of the text. After parsing, Sparser provides a set of edges, which provide both semantic and syntactic information. For our purposes, we used the `CATEGORY` and `FORM` attributes of the resulting edges. Table 4 shows that the Sparser features can be informative for this task, as five of the top ten positive weights are from Sparser. As a disclaimer, we acknowledge that model weights are not always sufficient for determining the most informative features (Vilain et al., 2009a).

However, there were several problems using Sparser. One issue is that Sparser performs its own internal tokenization and chunking, as it expects unstructured text as input, i.e. a string. To align the already tokenized sentences with a Sparser parse, we used a matching algorithm that aligned a token with its corresponding Sparser edge. A second problem was that Sparser frequently fails on inputs, and the points of failure can be difficult to identify due to the interaction of its various phases and context based rules. Thus, we were not able to get `CATEGORY` and `FORM` for all tokens. As a remedy, we included *local* forms of these Sparser features (prefixed with *L*), which were collected by inputting tokens by themselves to Sparser. This suggests that word lists could be very informative for this task.

[7]Token character length is ≤ 5, $(5..10]$, or > 10.

Weight	Feature	State
3.45	LCATEGORY=PATH-TYPE	p
2.95	LCATEGORY=REGION-TYPE	pl
2.66	word=(	∅
2.66	LCATEGORY=BE	∅
2.47	word=)	∅
2.33	word=near	me
2.28	word=border	p
2.21	LCATEGORY=TIME-UNIT	∅
2.17	LCATEGORY=NEAR	me
2.16	pos=PRP	se

p=PATH; pl=PLACE; me=MEASURE; se=SPATIAL_ENTITY

Table 4: Top Ten Positive Feature Weights

5.3 Evaluation Results

Table 5 shows mean precision (P), recall (R), F1, and accuracy (ACC) scores for each group for each evaluation configuration and sub-task that was attempted. The overall precision and recall measures we report are the arithmetic means of the precision and recall for each tag label or attribute in the corresponding sub-task. The overall, macro-average F1 measures we report are the harmonic mean of the overall P and R. Accuracy is computed as the number of correctly classified labels or attributes divided by the total number of labels or attributes in the gold standard. Overall accuracy and F1 are plotted in Appendix A.

Not all groups attempted all of the evaluation configurations[8]. The HRIJP-CRF-VW system was evaluated only for Configuration 1 tasks 1a, 1b, 1d, and 1e (not 1c), and Configuration 3 sub-tasks 3a and 3b. HRIJP-CRF-VW was not evaluated for Configuration 2 since those sub-tasks were not attempted. The UTD submission only covered Configuration 3, thus was only evaluated for sub-tasks 3a and 3b.

[8]The IXA system was the only one to complete all evaluation configurations.

System	Task		P	R	F1	ACC
BASELINE	1	a	0.55	0.52	0.53	0.75
		b	0.55	0.51	0.53	0.86
		c	0.10	0.02	0.04	0.05
		d	0.50	0.50	0.50	0.50
		e	0.05	0.02	0.02	0.06
	2	a	0.27	0.28	0.27	0.76
		b	0.79	0.58	0.67	0.90
		c	0.19	0.20	0.19	0.66
	3	a	0.86	0.84	0.85	0.98
		b	0.26	0.26	0.26	0.79
BRANDEIS-CRF	1	a	0.85	0.80	0.83	0.89
		b	0.78	0.76	0.77	0.92
HRIJP-CRF-VW	1	a	0.84	0.83	0.83	0.89
		b	0.77	0.76	0.76	0.91
		d	0.56	0.51	0.53	0.57
		e	0.03	0.04	0.03	0.25
	3	a	0.78	0.57	0.66	0.86
		b	0.05	0.06	0.05	0.48
IXA	1	a	0.81	0.72	0.76	0.88
		b	0.75	0.72	0.74	0.90
		c	0.18	0.15	0.16	0.30
		d	0.54	0.51	0.53	0.55
		e	0.06	0.05	0.05	0.25
	2	a	0.26	0.33	0.29	0.63
		b	0.55	0.51	0.53	0.89
		c	0.06	0.08	0.07	0.46
	3	a	0.63	0.51	0.56	0.89
		b	0.07	0.09	0.08	0.48
UTD	3	a	0.87	0.82	0.85	0.98
		b	0.05	0.09	0.07	0.51

Table 5: Overall Performance

6 Conclusion

It is clear from the participating system results that recognizing spatial entities as a sub-task is a fairly well-understood area, with reasonable performance. All systems using CRF models for recognizing places, paths, motion and non-motion events, and spatial entities performed well. Furthermore, MOVELINK recognition results were extremely promising, due to the general tendency for movement to be accompanied by recognizable clues. The overall poor performance for recognition of spatial relations between entities, on the other hand (QSLINKS and OLINKS) indicates that these are difficult relational identification tasks, reflected in the lower IAA scores for these relations as well.

For the next SpaceEval evaluation, we believe that a more focused task, possibly embedded within an application, would lower the barrier to entry in the competition. It would also permit us to use an extrinsic evaluation for performance of the systems. We also hope to release the SpaceBank corpus through LDC later this year. This would enable the community to become more familiar with the dataset and specification.

Acknowledgements

This research was supported by grants from NSF's IIS-1017765 and NGA's NURI HM1582-08-1-0018. We would like to acknowledge all the annotators and adjudicators who have contributed to the SpaceBank annotation effort, including Adam Berger, Alexander Elias, Alison Marqusee, April Dobkin, Benjamin Beaudett, Eric Benzschawel, Heather Friedman, Katie Glanbock, Keelan Armstrong, Kenyon Branan, Kiera Sarill, Lauren Weber, Martha Schwarz, Meital Singer, Rebecca Loewenstein-Harting, Sean Bethard, and Stephanie Grinley.

References

Harry Bunt. 2010. A methodology for designing semantic annotation languages exploiting syntactic-semantic iso-morphisms. In *Proceedings of ICGL 2010, Second International Conference on Global Interoperability for Language Resources*.

Jinho D Choi and Martha Adviser-Palmer. 2012. Optimization of natural language processing components for robustness and scalability.

Maddalen López de la Calle, Egoitz Laparra, and German Rigau. 2014. First steps towards a predicate matrix. In *Proceedings of the Global WordNet Conference (GWC 2014), Tartu, Estonia, January. GWA*.

Arun Ahuja Fei Huang, Doug Downey, Yi Yang, Yuhong Guo, and Alexander Yates. 2014. Learning representations for weakly supervised natural language processing tasks. *Computational Linguistics*, 40:1(85-120).

Christiane Fellbaum, editor. 1998. *Wordnet: an electronic lexical database*. MIT Press.

Eraldo Rezende Fernandes, Cícero Nogueira dos Santos, and Ruy Luiz Milidiú. 2014. Latent trees for coreference resolution. *Computational Linguistics*, 40:4(801-835).

Jenny Rose Finkel, Trond Grenager, and Christopher Manning. 2005. Incorporating non-local information into information extraction systems by gibbs sampling. In *Proceedings of the 43rd Annual Meeting on Association for Computational Linguistics*, pages 363–370. Association for Computational Linguistics.

Michael Grubinger, Paul Clough, Henning Müller, and Thomas Deselaers. 2006. The IAPR benchmark: A new evaluation resource for visual information systems. In *Int. Conf. on Language Resources and Evaluation, LREC'06*.

Nancy Ide and Laurent Romary. 2004. International standard for a linguistic annotation framework. *Natural Language Engineering*, 10(3-4):211–225.

Kiyong Lee ISO/TC 37/SC 4/WG 2, Project leaders: James Pustejovsky. 2014. Iso 24617-7:2014 language resource management - part 7: Spatial information (isospace). ISO/TC 37/SC 4/WG 2.

Alex Jarrett. 2013. The degree confluence project. *Retrieved August, 2013, http://www.confluence.org*.

Thorsten Joachims. 1999. Svmlight: Support vector machine. *SVM-Light Support Vector Machine http://svmlight. joachims. org/, University of Dortmund*, 19(4).

Oleksandr Kolomiyets, Parisa Kordjamshidi, Steven Bethard, and Marie-Francine Moens. 2013. Semeval-2013 task 3: Spatial role labeling. In *Second joint conference on lexical and computational semantics (* SEM), Volume 2: Proceedings of the seventh international workshop on semantic evaluation (SemEval 2013)*, pages 255–266.

Parisa Kordjamshidi and Marie-Francine Moens. 2015. Global machine learning for spatial ontology population. *Web Semantics: Science, Services and Agents on the World Wide Web*, 30(0):3 – 21. Semantic Search.

Parisa Kordjamshidi, Marie-Francine Moens, and Martijn van Otterlo. 2010. Spatial role labeling: task definition and annotation scheme. In *Proceedings of LREC 2010 - The sevent international conference on langauge resources and evaluation*.

Parisa Kordjamshidi, Martijn van Otterlo, and Marie-Francine Moens. 2011. Spatial role labeling: towards extraction of spatial relations from natural language. *ACM - Transactions on Speech and Language Processing*, 8:1–36.

Parisa Kordjamshidi, Steven Bethard, and Marie-Francine Moens. 2012. Semeval-2012 task 3: Spatial role labeling. In *Proceedings of the First Joint Conference on Lexical and Computational Semantics-Volume 1: Proceedings of the main conference and the shared task, and Volume 2: Proceedings of the Sixth International Workshop on Semantic Evaluation*, pages 365–373. Association for Computational Linguistics.

David Kroosma. 2012. Ride for climate. *Retrieved September, 2012, http://rideforclimate.com/blog/*.

John Langford, L Li, and A Strehl. 2007. Vowpal wabbit. *URL https://github.com/JohnLangford/vowpal_wabbit/wiki*.

Inderjeet Mani, Christy Doran, Dave Harris, Janet Hitzeman, Rob Quimby, Justin Richer, Ben Wellner, Scott Mardis, and Seamus Clancy. 2010. Spatialml: annotation scheme, resources, and evaluation. *Language Resources and Evaluation*, 44(3):263–280, September.

Christopher D. Manning, Mihai Surdeanu, John Bauer, Jenny Finkel, Steven J. Bethard, and David McClosky. 2014. The Stanford CoreNLP natural language processing toolkit. In *Proceedings of 52nd Annual Meeting of the Association for Computational Linguistics: System Demonstrations*, pages 55–60.

David McDonald. 1996. Internal and external evidence in the identification and semantic categorization of proper names. *Corpus processing for lexical acquisition*, pages 21–39.

Jessica L. Moszkowicz and James Pustejovsky. 2010. Iso-space: towards a spatial annotation framework for natural language. *Processing Romanian in Multilingual, Interoperational and Scalable Environments*.

Naoaki Okazaki. 2007. Crfsuite: a fast implementation of conditional random fields (crfs).

Apache OpenNLP. 2014. Apache software foundation. *URL http://opennlp. apache. org*.

Martha Palmer, Dan Gildea, and Paul Kingsbury. 2003. The proposition bank: an annotated corpus of semantic roles. *Computational Linguistics*.

Fabian Pedregosa, Gaël Varoquaux, Alexandre Gramfort, Vincent Michel, Bertrand Thirion, Olivier Grisel, Mathieu Blondel, Peter Prettenhofer, Ron Weiss, Vincent Dubourg, et al. 2011. Scikit-learn: Machine learning in python. *The Journal of Machine Learning Research*, 12:2825–2830.

Jeffrey Pennington, Richard Socher, and Christopher D Manning. 2014. Glove: Global vectors for word representation. *Proceedings of the Empiricial Methods in Natural Language Processing (EMNLP 2014)*, 12.

James Pustejovsky and Zachary Yocum. 2013. Capturing motion in iso-spacebank. In *Workshop on Interoperable Semantic Annotation*, page 25.

James Pustejovsky, Robert Knippen, Jessica Littman, and Roser Saurí. 2005. Temporal and event information in natural language text. *Language Resources and Evaluation*, 39:123–164, May.

James Pustejovsky, Jessica L. Moszkowicz, and Marc Verhagen. 2011a. Iso-space: the annotation of spatial information in language. In *Proceedings of ISA-6: ACL-ISO International Workshop on Semantic Annotation*, Oxford, England, January.

James Pustejovsky, Jessica L. Moszkowicz, and Marc Verhagen. 2011b. Iso-space: The annotation of spatial information in language. In *Proceedings of ISA-6: ACL-ISO International Workshop on Semantic Annotation*, Oxford, England, January.

James Pustejovsky, Jessica Moszkowicz, and Marc Verhagen. 2012. A linguistically grounded annotation language for spatial information. *TAL*, 53(2).

David Randell, Zhan Cui, and Anthony Cohn. 1992. A spatial logic based on regions and connections. In Morgan Kaufmann, editor, *Proceedings of the 3rd Internation Conference on Knowledge Representation and REasoning*, pages 165–176, San Mateo.

Randi Reppen, Nancy Ide, and Keith Suderman. 2005. American national corpus (anc). *Linguistic Data Consortium, Philadelphia. Second release.*

Amber Stubbs. 2011. Mae and mai: Lightweight annotation and adjudication tools. In *Proceedings of the 5th Linguistic Annotation Workshop*, pages 129–133. Association for Computational Linguistics.

Kristina Toutanova, Dan Klein, Christopher D Manning, and Yoram Singer. 2003. Feature-rich part-of-speech tagging with a cyclic dependency network. In *Proceedings of the 2003 Conference of the North American Chapter of the Association for Computational Linguistics on Human Language Technology-Volume 1*, pages 173–180. Association for Computational Linguistics.

Marc Vilain, Jonathan Huggins, and Ben Wellner, 2009a. *Proceedings of the Thirteenth Conference on Computational Natural Language Learning (CoNLL-2009)*, chapter A simple feature-copying approach for long-distance dependencies, pages 192–200. Association for Computational Linguistics.

Marc Vilain, Jonathan Huggins, and Ben Wellner. 2009b. Sources of performance in crf transfer training: a business name-tagging case study. In *Proceedings of the International Conference RANLP-2009*, pages 465–470. Association for Computational Linguistics.

A. Performance Plots

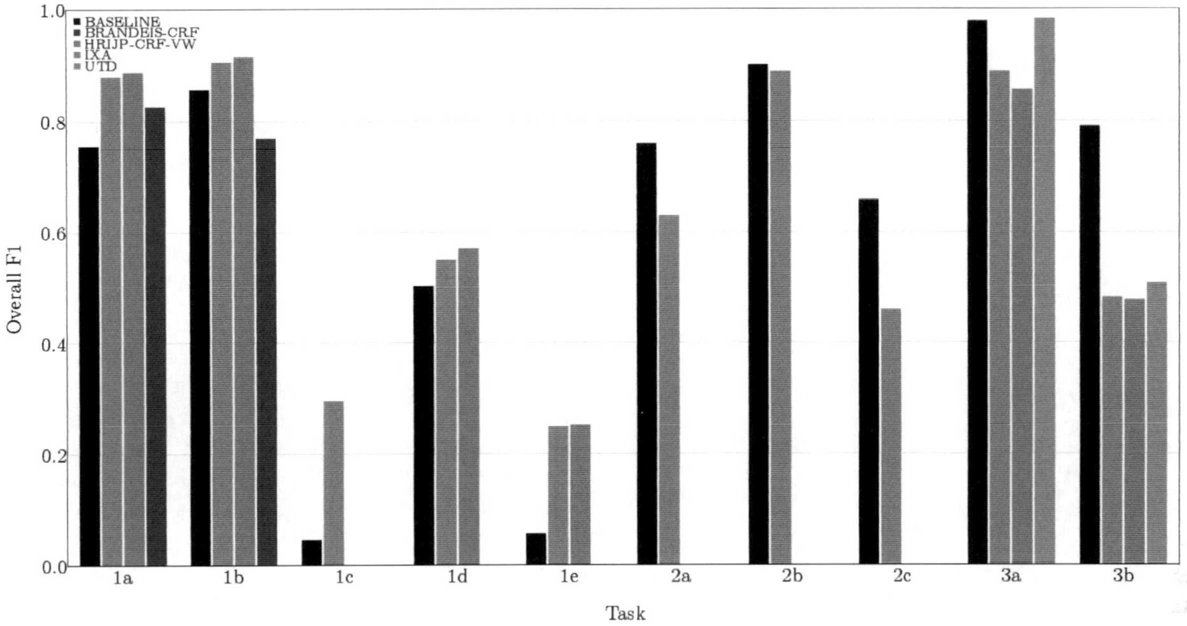

Figure 1: Overall Accuracy for All Sub-tasks

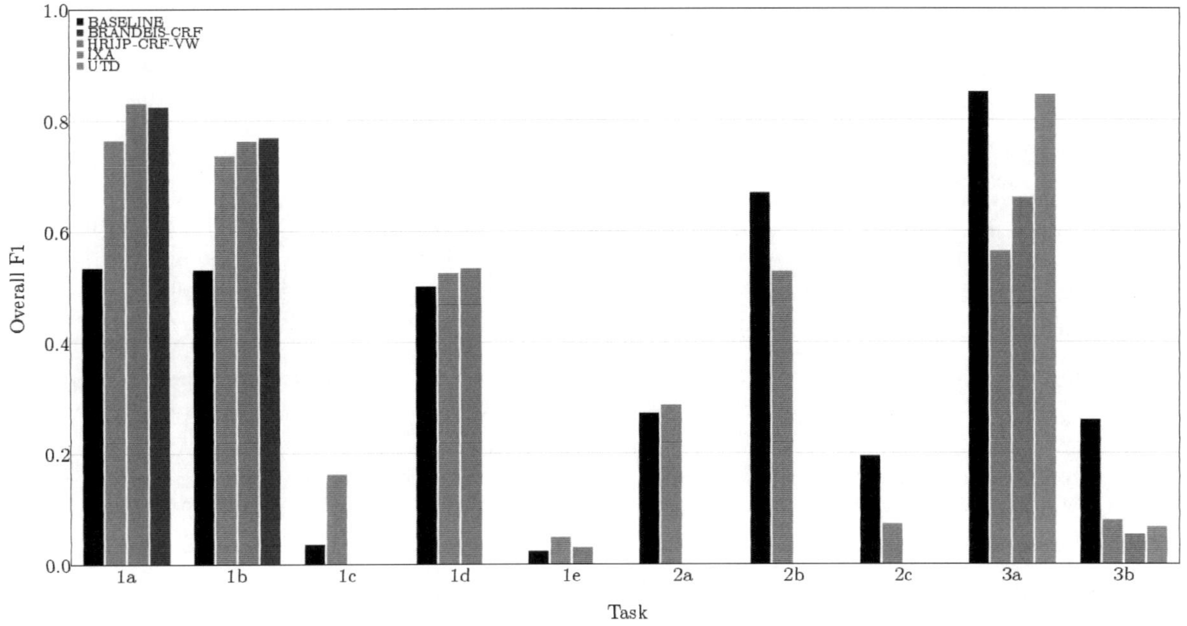

Figure 2: Overall F1 for All Sub-tasks

SpRL-CWW: Spatial Relation Classification with Independent Multi-class Models

Eric Nichols
Honda Research Institute Japan Co., Ltd.
e.nichols@jp.honda-ri.com

Fadi Botros
University of Calgary
fnmbotro@ucalgary.ca

Abstract

In this paper we describe the SpRL-CWW entry into SemEval 2015: Task 8 SpaceEval. It detects spatial and motion relations as defined by the ISO-Space specifications in two phases: (1) it detects spatial elements and spatial/motion signals with a Conditional Random Field model that uses a combination of distributed word representations and lexico-syntactic features; (2) given relation candidate tuples, it simultaneously detects relation types and labels the spatial roles of participating elements by using a combination of syntactic and semantic features in independent multi-class classification models for each relation type. In evaluation on the shared task data, our system performed particularly well on detection of elements and relations in unannotated data.

1 Introduction

Understanding human language about location and motion is important for many applications including robotics, navigation systems, and wearable computing. Shared tasks dedicated to the problem of representing and detecting spatial and motion relations have been organized for SemEval 2012 (Kordjamshidi et al., 2012), 2013 (Kolomiyets et al., 2013), and 2015. In this paper we present SpRL-CWW, our entry to SemEval 2015 Task 8: SpaceEval, and present extended evaluation of our system to investigate the impact of the task annotations and system configurations on task performance.

2 SpaceEval Task Definition

Kordjamshidi et al. (2011) proposed the task of Spatial Role Labeling (SpRL) to detect spatial and motion relations in text. SpRL was modeled after semantic role labeling (see (Fillmore et al., 2003; Màrquez et al., 2008)), with spatial indicators instead of predicates signaling the presence of relations, and spatial roles instead of semantic roles.

A canonical example of a spatial relation from (Kordjamshidi et al., 2011) is:

(1) *Give me the [grey book]$_{TR}$ [on]$_{SP}$ the [large table]$_{LM}$.*

The spatial indicator (SP) *on* indicates that there is a *spatial* relation between the trajector (TR; primary object of spatial focus) and the landmark (LM; secondary object of spatial focus). SpRL was formalized as a task of classifying tuples of $< w_{SP}, w_{TR}, w_{LM} >$ as spatial relations or not.

The SpRL task was reformulated and reintroduced in SpaceEval[1] using the ISO-Space annotation specifications (Pustejovsky et al., 2012). The biggest change was the decoupling of the semantic *type* and *role* of spatial relation arguments. A taxonomy of Spatial Element (SE) types was introduced to describe the meaning of arguments independent of their participation in relations, and spatial roles were treated as instance-specific annotations on spatial and motion relations.

The SE types introduced are: SPATIAL_ENTITY, PATH, PLACE, MOTION, NON_MOTION_EVENT, and MEASURE. Two types were also introduced to represent expressions that indicated the presence of relations: SPATIAL_SIGNAL and MOTION.

Spatial and motion relations were redefined as:

- MOVELINK: motion relation
- QSLINK: qualitative spatial relation
- OLINK: spatial orientation relation

[1] http://alt.qcri.org/semeval2015/task8/

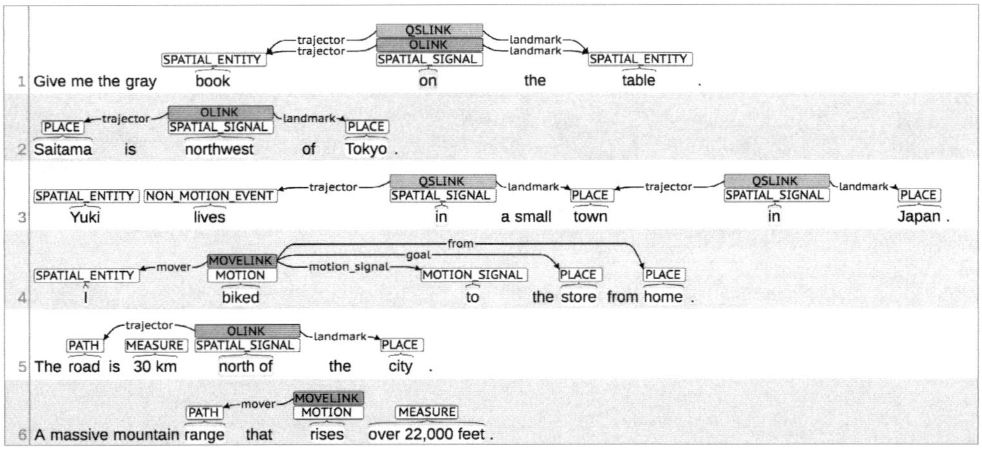

Figure 1: Example relations from the SpaceEval shared task. Only annotations that are targets are shown.

1. Only Unannotated Text is Provided

- a. `SE`: precision, recall, and F1
- b. `SE`: precision, recall, and F1 for each type, and an overall precision, recall, and F1 precision, recall, and F1
- d. `MOVELINK`, `QSLINK`, `OLINK`: precision, recall, and F1
- e. `MOVELINK`, `QSLINK`, `OLINK`: precision, recall, and F1 for each attribute, and an overall precision, recall, and F1

3. Spatial Elements, their Types, and their Attributes are Provided

- a. `MOVELINK`, `QSLINK`, `OLINK`: precision, recall, and F1
- b. `MOVELINK`, `QSLINK`, `OLINK`: precision, recall, and F1 for each attribute, and an overall precision, recall, and F1

Figure 2: SpaceEval task configurations participated in by `SpRL-CWW`.

Examples of SpaceEval annotations are given in Figure 1. The training data for SpaceEval consists of portions of the corpora from past SemEval SpRL tasks as well as a new dataset consisting of passages from guidebooks. Following the schema described in this section, a total of 6,782 spatial elements and signals comprising 2,186 relations were annotated.

We participated in the task configurations given in Figure 2, as defined by the official SpaceEval task description.

3 Related Research

`KUL-SKIP-CHAIN-CRF` (Kordjamshidi et al., 2011) was a skip-chain CRF-based sequential labeling model. It used a combination of lexico-syntactic information and semantic role information and used *preposition templates* to represent long distance dependencies. It was used as a baseline system in the SemEval 2012 and 2013 SpRL tasks.

`UTD-SpRL` (Roberts and Harabagiu, 2012) was an entry into the SemEval 2012 SpRL task that adopted a joint relation detection and role labeling approach with the motivation that roles in spatial relations were dependent on each other. The approach used heuristics to gather spatial relation candidate tuples. A hand-crafted dictionary was used to detect `SPATIAL_INDICATOR` candidates, and noun phrase heads were treated as `TRAJECTOR` and `LANDMARK` candidates. A model for relation classification and role labeling was then trained with libLINEAR using POS, lemma, and dependency-path-based features, with feature selection used to prune away ineffective features.

`UNITOR-HMM-TK` (Bastianelli et al., 2013) was an entry into the SemEval 2013 SpRL task. It used a pipeline approach with three sub-tasks: (1) spatial indicator detection, (2) spatial role[2] classification and (3) spatial relation identification.

Spatial indicators and roles were detected with sequential labeling using SVM^{hmm} with detected indicators used as features for spatial role labeling. In addition, shallow grammatical features in the form of POS n-grams were used in place of richer syntactic information in order to avoid overfitting. The model also used PMI-score based word space representations as described in (Sahlgren, 2006).

`UNITOR-HMM-TK`'s approach to spatial relation identification avoided feature engineering by employing an SVM model with a smoothed partial tree

[2]Referred to as *spatial annotations* in the paper.

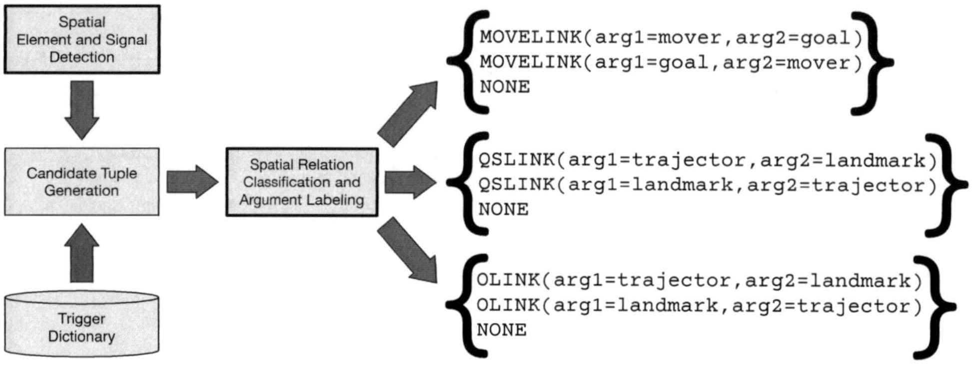

Figure 3: The SpRL-CWW system architecture. Spatial elements and signals are detected, from which relation candidate tuples are generated, and then relations with their arguments labeled are identified by a separate classifier for each relation type. The red arrow indicates special trigger dictionary processing that is only carried out for SpaceEval tasks 1d and 1e, and for Setting F of the relation classification task extended evaluation in Table 3.

EF.1 Raw string in a 5-word window
(i.e. *Saitama is northwest of Tokyo*)

EF.2 Lemma in a 5-word window
(i.e. *Saitama be northwest of Tokyo*)

EF.3 POS in a 5-word window
(i.e. NNP VBZ RB IN NNP)

EF.4 Named Entity in a 5-word window
(i.e. LOC NONE NONE NONE LOC)

EF.5 Lemma concatenated with the POS in a 3-word window
(i.e *be*::VBZ *northwest*::RB *of*::IN)

EF.6 Named Entity concatenated with the POS in a 3-word window
(i.e NONE::VBZ NONE::RB NONE ::IN)

EF.7 Direct dependency on the head of the sentence if present
(i.e. *advmod*)

EF.8 Direct dependency on the head of the sentence concatenated with the lemma of the head
(i.e. *advmod::be*)

EF.9 300-dimension GloVe word vector

EF.10 POS bigrams for a 5-word window
(i.e. NNP_VBZ VBZ_RB RB_IN IN_NNP)

EF.11 Raw string n-grams for 3-word window
(i.e. *is_northwest northwest_of*)

Figure 4: Features for spatial element/signal detection for the sentence *"Saitama is northwest of Tokyo."*

kernel over modified dependency trees to capture syntactic information.

More recent work on spatial relation identification includes (Kordjamshidi and Moens, 2014).

4 Spatial Element and Signal Detection

4.1 Approach

SpRL-CWW uses a feature-rich CRF model to jointly label spatial elements and spatial/motion signals. Previous approaches (Kordjamshidi et al., 2011; Bastianelli et al., 2013) proposed a two-step sequential labeling method for this task. In the first step, they label spatial signals[3] since they indicate the presence of a relation, which spatial roles depend on. In the second step, they label all the other spatial roles in the sentence using the extracted signals as features. However, any errors made in the first step will deteriorate the performance of the second. Furthermore, for SpaceEval 2015 the spatial element annotations are less likely to depend on the presence of a relation and can be detected independently. Thus, our system avoids the performance degradation associated with pipeline approaches by combining the two steps.

SpRL-CWW's CRF model labels each word in a sentence with one of the labels described in Section 2, or with NONE. In line with UNITOR-HMM-TK (Bastianelli et al., 2013), shallow lexico-syntactic features are applied instead of the full syntax of the sentence to avoid over-fitting the training data. We use word vectors trained on Web-scale corpora for a fine-grained lexical representation.

An example of our feature representation for the sentence *"Saitama is northwest of Tokyo."* is given in Figure 4.

4.2 Evaluation

4.2.1 Setup

Sentences were processed with Stanford CoreNLP (Manning et al., 2014) for POS tagging, lemmatiza-

[3]Also known as *spatial indicators*.

Task	Overall Precision	Overall Recall	Overall F1	Mean F1	Overall Accuracy
1a	0.84	0.83	0.83	0.83	0.89
1b	0.77	0.76	0.76	0.76	0.91
1d	0.56	0.51	0.53	0.40	0.57
1e	0.03	0.04	0.03	0.03	0.25
3a	0.78	0.57	0.66	0.57	0.86
3b	0.05	0.06	0.05	0.05	0.48

Table 1: Official SpaceEval submission results.

	Training 5-fold cross validation			Test		
Label	P	R	F1	P	R	F1
MEASURE	0.889	0.707	0.788	0.869	0.726	0.791
MOTION	0.823	0.700	0.756	0.808	0.733	0.769
MOTION_SIGNAL	0.766	0.600	0.673	0.801	0.772	0.786
NON_MOTION_EVENT	0.663	0.371	0.476	0.688	0.478	0.564
PATH	0.815	0.614	0.701	0.759	0.519	0.617
PLACE	0.802	0.777	0.789	0.742	0.752	0.747
SPATIAL_ENTITY	0.793	0.653	0.716	0.858	0.763	0.808
SPATIAL_SIGNAL	0.750	0.603	0.668	0.740	0.681	0.709
OVERALL	**0.795**	**0.674**	**0.730**	**0.785**	**0.712**	**0.746**

Table 2: Spatial Element/Signal detection results on training data and test data. Results are reproduced independently of official evaluation.

tion, NER, and dependency parsing. The word representations are publicly-available 300-dimension GloVe[4] word vectors trained on 42 billion tokens of Web data (Pennington et al., 2014). The model was trained using CRFsuite (Okazaki, 2007) with L-BFGS using L2 regularization with $\lambda_2 = 1 * 10^{-5}$.

4.2.2 Datasets

We evaluated our system on the SpaceEval training data as described in Section 2, and additionally on the SpaceEval Task 3 test data, which was distributed with gold labeled Spatial Elements, Indicators, and Motions. The test data consisted of 16 files with 317 sentences and 1,609 spatial roles.

4.2.3 Results

Official task results for spatial element/signal identification (Task 1a) and classification (Task 1b) are shown in Table 1.

We performed more detailed evaluation using 5-fold cross validation on the training data and on the released gold test data. Our results are presented in Table 2. These results and have an f1-score that is slightly lower than the official reported result.[5]Evaluation over the test data produced a slightly higher f1-score than on the training data. We theorize that this is due to cross-fold validation using a smaller dataset for its model.

[4]`http://www-nlp.stanford.edu/projects/glove/`

[5]As the official evaluation data and scripts have not been fully released at the time of writing, it is not possible to determine the cause of the discrepancy in f1-scores. Comparison between strict and "relaxed" matching as used in prior SemEval SpRL tasks did not account for the difference.

Features representing the extracted trigger:

RF.1 Raw string
RF.2 Lemma
RF.3 POS
RF.4 RF.2 concatenated with RF.3

Features representing each of the two arguments:

RF.5 Raw string
RF.6 Lemma
RF.7 POS
RF.8 RF.6 concatenated with RF.7
RF.9 Spatial element type (i.e Place, Path, etc.)
RF.10 RF.9 of each argument concatenated together
RF.11 RF.10 concatenated with RF.2
RF.12 Direction of the argument with the respect to the extracted trigger (i.e left/right)
RF.13 RF.12 of each argument concatenated together
RF.14 RF.13 concatenated with RF.2
RF.15 Boolean value representing whether there are other spatial elements in between the argument and the extracted trigger
RF.16 RF.15 of each argument concatenated together
RF.17 Dependency path between the argument and the extracted trigger (i.e. $\uparrow$ *conj* $\downarrow$ *dep* $\downarrow$ *nsubj*)
RF.18 RF.17 of each argument concatenated together
RF.19 Dependency path between the two arguments
RF.20 Length of the dependency path between the argument and the extracted trigger
RF.21 Bag-of-words of tokens in between the argument and the extracted trigger
RF.22 Number of tokens in between the argument and the extracted trigger
RF.23 RF.22 of each argument added together
RF.24 Boolean value representing whether either of the arguments are null values

Features representing the spatial elements that are directly to the left and to the right of the trigger:

RF.25 Raw string
RF.26 Lemma
RF.27 POS
RF.28 RF.26 concatenated with RF.27
RF.29 Number of tokens in between the spatial element and the extracted trigger

Figure 5: Features for joint spatial relation classification and role labeling. Underlined features are withheld from quadratic feature Settings D and E of Table 3.

5 Spatial Relation Classification and Argument Labeling

5.1 Approach

To identify spatial relations, the `SpRL-CWW` system determines which spatial elements and signals, can be combined to form valid spatial relations. Since the type of a relation (`MOVELINK`, `QSLINK`, or `OLINK`) is dependent upon its arguments, our method, inspired by `UTD-SpRL` (Roberts and Harabagiu, 2012), jointly classifies spatial relations and labels participating arguments in one classification step. We aim to simplify our model and improve learning by only

Setting	Regularization	Features	SEs	Triggers	P	R	F1
A	no	all	gold	gold	0.560	0.500	0.527
B	yes	all	gold	gold	0.599	0.496	0.544
C	yes	-SE types	gold	gold	0.597	0.430	0.500
D	yes	all + semantic types	gold	gold	0.636	**0.501**	**0.561**
E	yes	pre-quadratic	gold	gold	0.575	0.411	0.480
F	yes	quadratic	gold	gold	**0.762**	0.345	0.463
G	yes	all	predicted	dictionary	0.423	0.427	0.425
H	yes	all	predicted	predicted	0.382	0.364	0.372

Table 3: Settings for extended relation detection evaluation over the SpaceEval 2015 training data. All evaluation is conducted with 5-fold cross validation, the full RE feature set from Figure 5, gold standard SEs, and gold standard triggers. The overall precision, recall, and f1-scores are reported for each setting with the highest performing in bold. Setting A was used for our official submission. Where indicated, L2 regularization was performed with $\lambda_2 = 1 * 10^{-14}$.

considering relations that contain a trigger and by labeling only the following attributes which correspond to primary spatial and motion roles:

- `MOVELINK`: trigger, mover, goal
- `QSLINK` and `OLINK`: trigger, trajector, landmark

5.1.1 Candidate Trigger Extraction

First, candidate triggers are extracted from each sentence. The model we presented for detecting signals in Section 4.1 has a high f1-score but low precision. Because we want to prioritize recall for generating candidate tuples, when classifying relations on unannotated text, dictionaries of triggers automatically compiled from the training data are used to extract potential triggers from sentences. These dictionaries are used in Task 1d and 1e in Figure 2. In Task 3, where gold spatial roles are provided, `MOTION`s are used as potential `MOVELINK` triggers, `SPATIAL_SIGNAL`s are used as potential `QSLINK` and `OLINK` triggers. Evaluation of the trigger dictionaries shows that they have much higher recall than CRF models[6]. Additional relation classification evaluation in Table 3 show that the dictionaries (Setting F) achieve an f1-score improvement of 0.055 over the CRF models (Setting G).

5.1.2 Candidate Tuple Generation

All possible candidate relations in a sentence are then generated using the extracted triggers and the spatial elements in the sentence. A candidate tuple consists of an extracted trigger and two other spatial elements: arg1 and arg2. Since some relations, such as the one represented in Figure 1 Example 6, can have undefined arguments, tuples with undefined arguments are also generated. For Example 4 in Figure 1, the following candidate tuples will be generated for `MOVELINK` classification:

- < **trigger**:*biked*, **arg1**:*I*, **arg2**:*store* >
- < **trigger**:*biked*, **arg1**:*I*, **arg2**:*home* >
- < **trigger**:*biked*, **arg1**:*I*, **arg2**:$\emptyset$ >
- < **trigger**:*biked*, **arg1**:*home*, **arg2**:*store* >
- < **trigger**:*biked*, **arg1**:*home*, **arg2**:$\emptyset$ >
- < **trigger**:*biked*, **arg1**:*store*, **arg2**:$\emptyset$ >

Each tuple is represented by three main groups of features outlined in Figure 5. A one-against-all multi-class classifier is then applied to classify each candidate relation tuple into one of three possible classes. Three independent classifiers are trained, one for each spatial relation type, using Vowpal Wabbit (Agarwal et al., 2011). The classes used by the `MOVELINK` classifier are:

Class 1 - `REL(arg1=mover,arg2=goal)`
Class 2 - `REL(arg1=goal,arg2=mover)`
Class 3 - `NONE`

The classes used by the `QSLINK` and `OLINK` classifiers are:

Class 1 - `REL(arg1=trajector,arg2=landmark)`
Class 2 - `REL(arg1=landmark,arg2=trajector)`
Class 3 - `NONE`

5.2 Evaluation

5.2.1 Setup

Once again, Stanford CoreNLP was used for POS tagging, lemmatization and dependency parsing. The classification models were trained with Vowpal Wabbit's one-against-all multi-class classifier using its online stochastic gradient descent implementation with all the default settings.

[6] In particular, recall for `SPATIAL_SIGNALS` increases from 0.603 to 0.936 and `MOTION` recall increases from 0.700 to 0.812 on the SpaceEval test data.

Relation Type	P	R	F1
QSLINK	0.661	0.538	0.594
MOVELINK	0.571	0.451	0.504
OLINK	0.691	0.517	0.591
OVERALL	0.636	0.501	0.561

Table 4: `SpRL-CWW`'s relation classification results for the highest-performing Setting D.

5.2.2 Datasets

We evaluated our system on the trial and training data that was released for SpaceEval, with the exception of 9 files that didn't have spatial relations annotated. Since our system focuses on relations with a trigger, we filtered out the relations that contained no trigger. The resulting dataset of 1,801 relations was used for training and evaluation.

5.2.3 Results

Official task results for relation classification are shown in Table 1. Task 1d results use the SEs that were detected in the previous step (Task 1b). Task 3a results are for relation classification using gold spatial elements and signals.

6 Discussion

Participation in SpaceEval raised several questions which we attempt to answer by conducting extended evaluation of our system on the SpaceEval training data using 5-fold cross validation[7]. The settings and results are summarized in Table 3.

Which features were effective?

The feature ablation results in Table 5 show the three features with the largest contribution to SE and SI classification. They verify the contribution of word vectors trained on Web-scale data and support Bastianelli's et al. (2013)'s claim that shallow grammatical information is essential.

Does the fine-grained SpaceEval annotation scheme help or hinder?

In order to explore this, we compare the top performing setting with SE type-related features (Setting B) to a setting with them removed (Setting C). Absence of these features decrease the f1-score by 0.044, providing evidence that fine-grained SE types help relation classification, though the relation and spatial role taxonomy requires consideration.

[7]Partitions were made by taking a stratified split of the document set when ordered by decreasing size.

Features	P	R	F1	ΔF1
all	**0.795**	**0.674**	**0.730**	-
-EF.1	0.807	0.604	0.691	-0.039
-EF.9	0.808	0.602	0.690	-0.040
-EF.10	0.761	0.600	0.671	-0.059

Table 5: The three spatial element classification features with the largest delta in feature ablation.

Furthermore, each gold Spatial Signal that was provided for Task 3 had one of three possible semantic types; *DIRECTIONAL*, *TOPOLOGICAL* or *DIR_TOP* (both). Instead of using all Spatial Signals as candidate triggers for QSLINKs and OLINKs, we only considered TOPOLOGICAL Spatial Signals as candidate triggers for QSLINK and DIRECTIONAL Spatial Signals as candidate triggers for OLINK. This setting (Setting D) achieved the highest f1-score and recall, demonstrating the importance of Spatial Signal semantic types in relation classification. Full relation classification results for Setting D are summarized in Table 4.[8]

Is less (or no) feature engineering feasible?

We attempt this by automatically generating features using Vowpal Wabbit's quadratic feature generation. We disable all features underlined in Figure 5) and instruct VW to automatically construct features by generating all possible feature combinations. Settings E and F compare the base feature set before and after quadratic features are added. While quadratic features achieve a lower f1-score, they have the highest precision of all settings, suggesting feature generation may be useful for increasing precision of relation classification, but the low f1-score of Setting F indicates care is needed in selecting the base feature set. We are exploring feature engineering reduction further with a phrase vector-based model inspired by (Hermann et al., 2014).

7 Conclusion

In this paper we presented the `SpRL-CWW` entry to SpaceEval 2015: Task 8. Official evaluation showed that it performed especially well on unannotated data. Extended evaluation verified the contribution of Web-scale word vectors, trigger dictionaries, and SE type information; and automatic feature generation showed promise. For future work, we plan to explore phrase vector-based approaches to SpRL.

[8]We thank an anonymous reviewer for the suggestion to use Spatial Signal semantic types.

Acknowledgments

This research was supported by Honda Research Institute Japan, Co., Ltd. We also thank the anonymous reviewers for their many fruitful suggestions.

References

Alekh Agarwal, Olivier Chapelle, Miroslav Dudík, and John Langford. 2011. A reliable effective terascale linear learning system. *CoRR*, abs/1110.4198.

Emanuele Bastianelli, Danilo Croce, Roberto Basili, and Daniele Nardi. 2013. UNITOR-HMM-TK: Structured kernel-based learning for spatial role labeling. *Proceedings of the Seventh International Workshop on Semantic Evaluation (SemEval 2013)*.

Charles J. Fillmore, Christopher R. Johnson, and Miriam R.L. Petruck. 2003. Background to FrameNet. *International Journal of Lexicography*, 16.3:235–250.

Karl Moritz Hermann, Dipanjan Das, Jason Weston, and Kuzman Ganchev. 2014. Semantic frame identification with distributed word representations. In *Proceedings of ACL*, June.

Oleksandr Kolomiyets, Parisa Kordjamshidi, Steven Bethard, and Marie-Francine Moens. 2013. SemEval-2013 task 3: Spatial role labeling. In *Second Joint Conference on Lexical and Computational Semantics (*SEM), Volume 2: Proceedings of the Seventh International Workshop on Semantic Evaluation (SemEval 2013), Second joint conference on lexical and computational semantics, Atlanta, USA, 14-15 June 2013*, pages 255–266.

Parisa Kordjamshidi and Marie-Francine Moens. 2014. Global machine learning for spatial ontology population. *Web Semantics: Science, Services and Agents on the World Wide Web*.

Parisa Kordjamshidi, Martijn Van Otterlo, and Marie-Francine Moens. 2011. Spatial role labeling: Towards extraction of spatial relations from natural language. *ACM Transactions on Speech and Language Processing (TSLP)*, 8(3):4.

Parisa Kordjamshidi, Steven Bethard, and Marie-Francine Moens. 2012. SemEval-2012 task 3: Spatial role labeling. In **SEM 2012: The First Joint Conference on Lexical and Computational Semantics – Volume 1: Proceedings of the Main Conference and the Shared Task, and Volume 2: Proceedings of the Sixth International Workshop on Semantic Evaluation (SemEval 2012), SemEval-2012*, pages 365–373, June.

Christopher D. Manning, Mihai Surdeanu, John Bauer, Jenny Finkel, Steven J. Bethard, and David McClosky. 2014. The Stanford CoreNLP natural language processing toolkit. In *Proceedings of 52nd Annual Meeting of the Association for Computational Linguistics: System Demonstrations*, pages 55–60.

Lluís Màrquez, Xavier Carreras, Kenneth C Litkowski, and Suzanne Stevenson. 2008. Semantic role labeling: an introduction to the special issue. *Computational Linguistics*, 34(2):145–159.

Naoaki Okazaki. 2007. CRFsuite: a fast implementation of conditional random fields (CRFs). `http://www.chokkan.org/software/crfsuite/`.

Jeffrey Pennington, Richard Socher, and Christopher Manning. 2014. Glove: Global vectors for word representation. In *Proceedings of the 2014 Conference on Empirical Methods in Natural Language Processing (EMNLP)*, pages 1532–1543, Doha, Qatar, October.

James Pustejovsky, Jessica Moszkowicz, and Marc Verhagen. 2012. A linguistically grounded annotation language for spatial information. *TAL*, 53(2).

Kirk Roberts and Sanda Harabagiu. 2012. UTD-SpRL: A joint approach to spatial role labeling. In **SEM 2012: The First Joint Conference on Lexical and Computational Semantics – Volume 1: Proceedings of the main conference and the shared task, and Volume 2: Proceedings of the Sixth International Workshop on Semantic Evaluation (SemEval 2012)*, pages 419–424.

Magnus Sahlgren. 2006. *The Word-Space Model*. Ph.D. thesis, University of Stockholm (Sweden).

SemEval-2015 Task 17: Taxonomy Extraction Evaluation (TExEval)

Georgeta Bordea, Paul Buitelaar
Insight
Centre for Data Analytics
National University of Ireland, Galway
name.surname@insight-centre.org

Stefano Faralli, Roberto Navigli
Dipartimento di Informatica
Sapienza University of Rome
Italy
surname@di.uniroma1.it

Abstract

This paper describes the first shared task on Taxonomy Extraction Evaluation organised as part of SemEval-2015. Participants were asked to find hypernym-hyponym relations between given terms. For each of the four selected target domains the participants were provided with two lists of domain-specific terms: a WordNet collection of terms and a well-known terminology extracted from an online publicly available taxonomy. A total of 45 taxonomies submitted by 6 participating teams were evaluated using standard structural measures, the structural similarity with a gold standard taxonomy, and through manual quality assessment of sampled novel relations.

1 Introduction

SemEval-2015 Task 17 is concerned with the automatic extraction of hierarchical relations from text and subsequent taxonomy construction. A taxonomy is a hierarchy of concepts that expresses parent-child or broader-narrower relationships. Because of their many applications in search, retrieval, website navigation, and records management, taxonomies are valuable resources for libraries, publishing companies, online databases, and e-commerce companies. Taxonomies are most often manually created resources that are expensive to construct and maintain, and therefore there is a need for automatic methods for taxonomy enrichment and construction. Recently, the task of taxonomy learning from text, also called taxonomy induction, has received an increased interest in the natural language processing community, as taxonomical information is a valuable input to many semantically intensive tasks including inference, question answering (Harabagiu et al., 2003) and textual entailment (Geffet and Dagan, 2005).

Taxonomy learning can be divided into three main subtasks: term extraction, relation discovery, and taxonomy construction. *Term extraction* is a relatively well-known task, hence we decided to abstract from this stage and provide a common ground for the next steps by making available the list of terms beforehand. Most approaches for *relation discovery* from text rely on lexico-syntactic patterns (Hearst, 1992; Kozareva et al., 2008), co-occurrence information (Sanderson and Croft, 1999), substring inclusion (Nevill-Manning et al., 1999), or exploit semantic relations provided in textual definitions (Navigli and Velardi, 2010). Any asymmetrical relation that indicates subordination between two terms can be considered, but here the focus is mainly on hyponym-hypernym relations. Depending on the approach selected, the task may or may not require large amounts of text to extract relations between terms, therefore no corpus is provided as part of the shared dataset.

This stage usually produces a large number of noisy, inconsistent relations, that assign multiple parents to a node and that contain cycles, i.e., sequences of vertices that start and end at the same vertex. Hence, the third stage of taxonomy learning, *taxonomy construction*, focuses on the overall structure of the resulting graph and aims to organise terms into a hierarchical structure, more specifically a directed acyclic graph (Kozareva and Hovy,

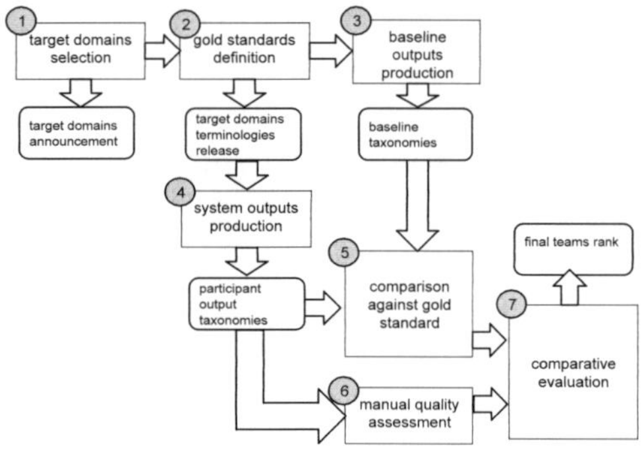

Figure 1: The task workflow.

2010; Navigli et al., 2011; Wang et al., 2013). To address the inherent complexity of evaluating taxonomy quality, several methods have been considered in the past including manual evaluation by domain experts, structural evaluation, and automatic evaluation against a gold standard (Velardi et al., 2012). In this task, all these existing evaluation approaches are considered, using a voting scheme to aggregate the results for the final ranking of the systems. We introduce four new domains that have not previously been considered for this task, covering general knowledge domains such as food and equipment and technical domains such as chemicals and science. For each domain, we provide a gold standard taxonomy gathered exclusively from WordNet (Fellbaum, 2005), as well as a gold standard taxonomy that combines terms and relations gathered from other domain-specific sources.

2 Task workflow

In this section we present the task workflow, the considered dataset, and the evaluation method used in this task.

Competition setup: In order to provide a common ground to all the competing teams, we applied the task workflow described in Figure 1, as follows: 1) select and announce a set of target domains (see Section 2.1 for more details); 2) define and collect gold standard taxonomies that will be used for evaluation and extract and release the set of terms that they cover; 3) select and produce baseline taxonomies using naive baselines to be compared against the team outputs in the competition.

Competition and evaluation flow: As described in Figure 1, the next steps of the workflow concern the participation of the competing teams and the evaluation of the resulting outputs as follows: 4) in this stage participants produce and submit the output taxonomies. For each domain, test data consists of a list of domain terms that participants have to structure into a taxonomy, with the possibility of adding further intermediate terms. Each system will return a list of pairs (term, hypernym). In this way, taxonomy learning is limited to finding relations between pairs of terms and organising them into a hierarchical structure. Participants are encouraged to consider polyhierarchies when organising terms. In this setting, nodes can have more than one parent and the final structure of the taxonomy is not necessarily a tree; 5) compare system outputs (4) and baseline taxonomies (3) with taxonomies produced as gold standards (2); 6) manually annotate a sample of system outputs to estimate the quality of hypernym-hyponym relationships that are not in the gold standards; 7) create a combined rank of the teams based on the individual rank that each team reached on different aspects of the evaluation.

Table 1: Structural measures of Combined and WordNet gold standard taxonomies.

		Combined taxonomies		WordNet taxonomies	
Domain	**Root concept**	**|V|**	**|E|**	**|V|**	**|E|**
Chemicals	chemical	17584	24817	1351	1387
Equipment	equipment	612	615	475	485
Food	food	1156	1587	1486	1533
Science	science	452	465	429	441

2.1 Data

We selected four target domains with a rich, deep, hierarchical structure (i.e. Chemicals, Equipment, Food and Science) with four root concepts (i.e. chemical, equipment, food and science, respectively). Then, for each domain we produced two kinds of gold standard taxonomies.

WordNet taxonomy Concepts and relationships in the WordNet hypernym-hyponym hierarchy rooted on the corresponding root concept.

Combined taxonomy Domain-specific terms and relations from well-known, publicly available, taxonomies other than WordNet: CheBI[1] for Chemicals, "The Google product taxonomy"[2] for Foods, the "Material Handling Equipment"[3] taxonomy for Equipment, and the "Taxonomy of Fields and their Subfields"[4] for Science. Hypernym-hyponym relationships were also gathered from a general purpose resource, the Wikipedia Bitaxonomy (WiBi) (Flati et al., 2014), using a semi-automatic approach. For each domain we first manually identified domain sub-hierarchies from WiBi (W); Second we automatically searched for the terms of W in common with the corresponding gold standard G. For each common term t we added in G the taxonomy rooted on t from W.

Table 1 shows the resulting number of vertices $|V|$, i.e., the number of terms given to the participants, and the number of edges $|E|$ of the produced gold standard taxonomies for the four target domains. Finally, test data consists of eight lists of domain concepts, for which participants were asked to output a set of hypernym-hyponym relationships.

2.2 Evaluation method

Let $S = (V_S, E_S)$ be an output taxonomy produced by a system for a given domain, where V_S includes the set of domain concepts initially provided by the task organisers and E_S is the set of taxonomy edges extracted by the system. To broadly analyze the quality of the produced set of hypernymy relationships E_S, these results are benchmarked against two naive baselines, described in Section 2.2.1, using the following evaluation approaches: i) analyse the graph structure and check if the produced taxonomy is a Directed Acyclic Graph (DAG); ii) compare the edges E_S, against the set of relations from each type of gold standard; iii) manually validate a sample of novel relationships produced by the system that are not contained in the gold standard.

The final ranking of the systems takes into consideration these three types of evaluation by aggregating the achieved ranks using a voting scheme. First, the output taxonomies are ranked on the basis of the average performance obtained for each evaluated aspect and for each domain. The resulting ranks are simply summed up, favouring systems at the top of the ranked list and penalising systems at the lower end.

2.2.1 Baselines

The main purpose of introducing the baselines described in this section is to check the performance of a system that relies mainly on the fact that the root of the domain is known and implements simple string-based approaches. In this task, the following two naive approaches for taxonomy construction are implemented and used for benchmarking systems:

Baseline 1 Simply connect all the nodes to the root concept: $B_1 = (V_{B_1}, E_{B_1})$ where $E_{B_1} = \{(root, a), a \in V_{B_1} \setminus \{root\}\}$;

Baseline 2 A basic string inclusion approach that covers relations between compound terms such as *(science, network science)*: $B_2 = (V_{B_2}, E_{B_2})$ where $E_{B_2} = \{(a, b)$, b starts with a or ends with a and $|b| > |a|\}$, and where a is a term and b is a compound term that includes a as a substring.

Both approaches require only the root of the taxonomy and the list of terms and do not require any external corpora or other structured information.

2.2.2 Structural analysis

The main goal of the structural evaluation of a taxonomy is to quantify the size of the taxonomy under investigation in terms of nodes and edges. A second objective is to evaluate whether the overall structure connects all the nodes in the graph with the root and whether it is consistent with the semantics of the ISA relation. Hierarchical relations are generally inconsistent with the presence of cycles. Also, we highlight the number of nodes located on higher levels of a taxonomy, called intermediate nodes. These nodes are considered more important than leaves, to favour taxonomies with a deep, rich structure.

Based on these considerations, structural evaluation is performed by computing the cardinality of $|V_S|$ and $|E_S|$. A topological sorting-based algorithm (Kahn, 1962) is used to establish if the taxonomy S contains simple directed cycles (self loop included). We then use an approach based on the Tarjan algorithm (Tarjan, 1972) to calculate the number

[1]http://www.ebi.ac.uk/chebi/init.do
[2]http://www.google.com/basepages/producttype/taxonomy.en-US.txt
[3]http://www.ise.ncsu.edu/kay/mhetax/index.htm
[4]http://sites.nationalacademies.org/PGA/Resdoc/PGA_044522

of connected components in S. Finally, we compute the number of intermediate nodes as the number of nodes $|V_S| - |L_S|$ where L_S is the set of leaf nodes in S. A leaf node is a node with out-degree = 0.

2.2.3 Comparison against Gold Standard

Previous datasets for evaluating taxonomy extraction (Kozareva et al., 2008) mainly rely on WordNet to gather gold standards from several general knowledge domains, such as animals, plants, and vehicles. The datasets proposed in (Velardi et al., 2013) enrich this experimental setting by including two specialized domains, Virus and Artificial Intelligence, that have low coverage in WordNet. A limitation of these datasets is that currently there is no gold standard taxonomy for these domains, therefore only a manual evaluation is possible. The dataset introduced here, instead, covers four new domains, providing two separate gold standards for each domain: one collected from WordNet, a general purpose resource, and a second one that combines relations from domain-specific resources and from a collaborative resource, Wikipedia, for a higher coverage of the domain. This dataset allows us to investigate how a system performs when taxonomising frequently used terms in comparison with more specialised, rarely used terms.

Given a gold standard taxonomy $G = (V_G, E_G)$, the comparison between a target taxonomy and a gold standard taxonomy is quantified using the following measures:

- common nodes: $|V_S \cap V_G|$
- vertex coverage: $|V_S \cap V_G|/|V_G|$
- number of common edges: $|E_S \cap E_G|$
- edge coverage: $|E_S \cap E_G|/|E_G|$
- ratio of novel edges: $(|E_S| - |E_S \cap E_G|)/|E_G|$
- edge precision: $P = |E_S \cap E_G|/|E_S|$
- edge recall: $R = |E_S \cap E_G|/|E_G|$
- F-score: $F = 2(P * R)/(P + R)$

Additionally, we consider the Cumulative Fowlkes&Mallows (Cumulative F&M) measure (Velardi et al., 2013): the value $B_{S,G}$ between 0.0 and 1.0 which measures level by level how well a target taxonomy S clusters similar nodes compared to a gold standard taxonomy G. $B_{S,G}$ is calculated as follows: let k be the maximum depth of both S and G, and H_{ij} a cut of the hierarchy, where $i \in \{0, ..., k\}$ is the cut level and $j \in \{G, S\}$ selects the clustering of interest. Then, for each cut i, the two hierarchies can be seen as two flat clusterings C_{iS} and C_{iG} of the n concepts. When $i = 0$ the cut is a single cluster incorporating all the objects, and when $i = k$ we obtain n singleton clusters. Now let: n_{11} be the number of object pairs that are in the same cluster in both C_{iS} and C_{iG}; n_{00} be the number of object pairs that are in different clusters in both C_{iS} and C_{iG}; n_{10} be the number of object pairs that are in the same cluster in C_{iS} but not in C_{iG}; n_{01} be the number of object pairs that are in the same cluster in C_{iG} but not in C_{iS}.

The generalized Fowlkes&Mallows measure of cluster similarity for the cut i ($i \in \{0, ..., k\}$), as reformulated in (Wagner and Wagner, 2007), is defined as:

$$B^i_{S,G} = \frac{n^i_{11}}{\sqrt{(n^i_{11} + n^i_{10}) \cdot (n^i_{11} + n^i_{01})}}. \quad (1)$$

And the cumulative Fowlkes&Mallows Measure:

$$B_{S,G} = \frac{\sum_{i=0}^{k-1} \frac{i+1}{k} B^i_{S,G}}{\sum_{i=0}^{k-1} \frac{i+1}{k}} = \frac{\sum_{i=0}^{k-1} \frac{i+1}{k} B^i_{S,G}}{\frac{k+1}{2}}. \quad (2)$$

2.2.4 Manual quality assessments

The gold standard taxonomies are not complete, therefore it is possible for systems to identify correct relations that are not covered by the gold standard. Normally these relations are considered incorrect using a simple comparison with the gold standard taxonomy. For this reason we manually evaluate a subset of new relations proposed by each system to estimate the number of relations in E_S that do not belong to E_G. A random sample is extracted from all the taxonomies submitted by the participants and then manually annotated to compute the precision P as: $|correctISA|/|sample|$. A total of 100 term pairs were evaluated by three different annotators for each system and each domain, for a total of 800 pairs per system.

The chemical domain is not considered for this evaluation because it requires a considerable amount of domain knowledge and we did not have access to experts in the chemical domain. Two of the authors of this paper independently annotated each sample relation, while the third assessment was done by a group of five annotators who have a background in Computational Linguistics, with the exception of one annotator who focused on the food domain. Annotators were provided with a list of term pairs organised by domain and were asked if the relation was a correct ISA relation, if the relation and the terms were domain specific, and if the relation was too generic. In our evaluation, a relation is considered correct only if it is a correct hypernym-hyponym relation, if it is relevant for the given domain and not over-generic. Take for example the following edges from the food domain: *(linguine, pasta)* and *(lemon, food)*. Both edges are correct ISA relations and are domain specific, but the second edge is over-generic because lemons are also fruits. The agreement for identifying correct edges is measured using the Fleiss kappa statistic and is overall substantial (Fleiss kappa 0.65). The easiest domain is Food (Fleiss kappa 0.69), followed by Equipment (Fleiss kappa 0.63). Not surprisingly, the Science domain is the most challenging (Fleiss kappa 0.60), as this is a rapidly changing domain and there is in general less consensus about the relations between fields.

3 Submitted runs

Overall, 6 teams participated in the task. Participants were allowed to submit two runs for each of the four domains, one for each type of gold standard, for a total of 8 different runs. Most teams submitted a run for each domain and type of gold standard, with the exception of the LT3 team, which did not submit a system for the Chemical domain and the QASSIT team, which submitted only one run for the WordNet Chemical taxonomy. Next, we will provide a short description of each approach in alphabetical order, discussing corpora collection and the approaches adopted for relation discovery and taxonomy construction.

INRIASAC (supervised) *Corpus:* Wikipedia search using terms; *Relation discovery:* substring inclusion, lexico-syntactic patterns, co-occurrence information based on sentences and documents; *Taxonomy construction:* none.

LT3 (unsupervised) *Corpus:* web corpus constructed using BootCat (Baroni and Bernardini, 2004) using the provided terms as seed terms; *Relation discovery:* lexico-syntactic patterns, morphological structure of compound terms, WordNet lookup (Lefever et al., 2014); *Taxonomy construction:* none.

ntnu (unsupervised) *Corpus:* Wikipedia and WordNet definitions; *Relation discovery:* hypernym extraction from definitions, WordNet lookup, Wikipedia categories, similarity between keywords; *Taxonomy construction:* none.

QASIT (semi-supervised) *Corpus:* Wikipedia, DBpedia; *Relation discovery:* lexico-syntactic patterns, co-occurrence information; *Taxonomy construction:* Learning Pretopological Spaces (LPS) method that learns a Parameterized Space by using an evolutionary strategy.

TALN-UPF (semi-supervised) *Corpus:* Wikipedia definitions retrieved using BabelNet (Navigli and Ponzetto, 2012); *Relation discovery:* based on (Navigli and Velardi, 2010), CRF model trained with the WCL dataset, linguistic rules added to traverse the dependency tree, missing nodes connected to root; *Taxonomy construction:* none.

USAAR (semi-supervised) *Corpus:* Wikipedia documents; *Relation discovery:* lexico-syntactic patterns, co-occurrence information used to construct a vector space model using the word2vec tool;[5] *Taxonomy construction:* none.

4 Results

Table 2 presents the results of the structural analysis (see Section 2.2.2) for all the system outputs and for the two baselines. Only 20 out of 45 submitted taxonomies consist of one weakly connected component (c.c. = 1), and 18 out of 45 are directed acyclic graphs (Cycles=N). Overall, only 10 taxonomies comply with the ideal structural requirements of a taxonomy and are directed acyclic graphs consisting of one connected component. 6 of these were submitted by the only system that addressed the taxonomy construction subtask, QASSIT. Table 3 shows the average edge precision, recall and F-score of the six systems compared to the baselines (see Sections 2.2.3 and 2.2.4). LT3 outperforms the other systems on all the measures. It is worth noting that our string-based baseline (B_2) achieves the

[5] https://code.google.com/p/word2vec/

Table 2: Structural analysis of the submitted taxonomies and of the baseline taxonomies, including the number of: nodes ($|V|$), edges ($|E|$), connected components (c.c.), and intermediate nodes (i.n.).

Combined gold standard taxonomies

		INRIASAC	LT3	ntnu	QASSIT	TALN-UPF	USAAR	B_1	B_2
Chemicals	**|V|**	12432	n.a.	1114	n.a.	17584	13785	17584	10120
	|E|	28444		1563		17606	30392	17583	12672
	c.c.	293		116		**1**	302	**1**	991
	Cycles	Y		**N**		**N**	Y	**N**	**N**
	i.n.	5808		1052		34	13766	1	10117
Equipment	**|V|**	520	260	251	610	612	337	612	248
	|E|	1168	282	247	614	665	548	611	244
	c.c.	6	10	35	**1**	**1**	28	**1**	17
	Cycles	**N**	Y	**N**	**N**	Y	Y	**N**	**N**
	i.n.	164	174	251	70	20	320	1	229
Food	**|V|**	1518	819	834	1550	1549	1118	1549	636
	|E|	4363	1632	1227	1560	1569	2692	1548	627
	c.c.	2	6	27	**1**	**1**	23	**1**	47
	Cycles	Y	**N**	Y	Y	**N**	Y	**N**	**N**
	i.n.	397	159	810	72	18	1105	1	631
Science	**|V|**	417	187	338	453	1280	355	452	232
	|E|	1164	441	386	511	1623	952	451	214
	c.c.	3	8	23	**1**	**1**	14	**1**	28
	Cycles	**N**	Y	**N**	**N**	Y	Y	**N**	**N**
	i.n.	151	88	329	80	422	261	1	207

WordNet gold standard taxonomies

		INRIASAC	LT3	ntnu	QASSIT	TALN-UPF	USAAR	B_1	B_2
Chemicals	**|V|**	1913	n.a.	1475	1351	1347	1173	1351	820
	|E|	4611		1855	1380	1451	3107	1350	808
	c.c.	2		28	**1**	**1**	31	**1**	129
	Cycles	Y		Y	**N**	Y	Y	**N**	**N**
	i.n.	1262		1272	56	63	920	1	819
Equipment	**|V|**	468	462	1081	476	2574	354	475	232
	|E|	1369	1452	1333	490	3370	547	474	188
	c.c.	**1**	**1**	12	**1**	**1**	43	**1**	46
	Cycles	Y	Y	Y	**N**	Y	Y	**N**	**N**
	i.n.	371	142	1036	65	1025	339	1	213
Food	**|V|**	1458	1471	1843	1487	1486	1200	1486	826
	|E|	4238	6913	2760	1539	1548	3465	1485	812
	c.c.	2	**1**	35	**1**	**1**	23	**1**	79
	Cycles	**N**	Y	Y	**N**	**N**	Y	**N**	**N**
	i.n.	478	374	1386	60	53	1189	1	813
Science	**|V|**	366	370	524	371	370	307	370	217
	|E|	1102	1573	681	436	393	892	369	174
	c.c.	**1**	**1**	11	**1**	**1**	8	**1**	48
	Cycles	Y	Y	**N**	**N**	**N**	Y	**N**	**N**
	i.n.	135	114	505	74	25	255	1	208

highest precision, which leads to high F-score, second only to the best system. This is an indication that the test dataset can be improved by removing relations that do not require more sophisticated approaches. The first baseline (B_1) is not competitive, because the gold standard taxonomies are specifically selected to have a rich, deep structure. A large number of novel relations produced by the USAAR system are too generic because they apply a similar strategy. The results of the manual analysis of previously unknown edges are shown in the last line of Table 3. Again, LT3 and INRIASAC systems take the lead. The ntnu system discovers the largest number of novel edges compared to other systems on the WordNet Science taxonomy. In this case, LT3 discovers a larger number of new edges than other participants on Combined taxonomies. In Table 4 we report the Cumulative F&M measure (see Section 2.2.3) for the 45 systems and for the 16 baseline taxonomies. Results are grouped on the basis of the source of the gold standard, that is, combined taxonomies and WordNet taxonomies. LT3 outperforms the other systems on all three submitted WordNet taxonomies by a wide margin (there is no submission for the Chemicals domain), but for the combined taxonomies the INRIASAC system holds the

Table 3: Average Precision, Recall and F-score of ISA relationships across gold standards and Average Precision of novel relations based on human judgement.

	INRIASAC	LT3	ntnu	QASSIT	TALN-UPF	USAAR	B_1	B_2
	Comparison against gold standards							
Average Precision	0.1725	0.3612	0.1754	0.1564	0.0720	0.2015	0.0226	**0.5432**
Average Recall	0.4279	**0.6307**	0.2756	0.1589	0.1165	0.3139	0.0212	0.2413
Average F-score	0.2427	**0.3886**	0.2076	0.1575	0.0799	0.2377	0.0219	0.3326
	Manual evaluation							
Average Precision	0.4800	**0.5967**	0.4200	0.3533	0.2467	0.1017	-	-

Table 4: Cumulative Fowlkes&Mallows measure for 45 system runs and for 16 baselines.

	INRIASAC	LT3	ntnu	QASSIT	TALN-UPF	USAAR	B_1	B_2
	Combined gold standard taxonomies							
Chemicals	**0.2353**	n.a	0.0009	n.a	0.2225	0.00001	0.2281	0.0
Equipment	**0.4905**	0.1137	0.0000	0.4881	0.4482	0.0000	0.3970	0.0012
Food	**0.4522**	0.2163	0.0076	0.3405	0.3267	0.0037	0.3162	0.0007
Science	**0.4706**	0.3303	0.0088	0.5232	0.2202	0.2249	0.4214	0.0108
	WordNet gold standard taxonomies							
Chemicals	0.0084	n.a	0.0719	**0.3947**	0.2787	0.2103	0.2683	0.0
Equipment	0.0700	**0.6892**	0.0935	0.3637	0.0901	0.0015	0.2969	0.0007
Food	0.4804	**0.5899**	0.2673	0.3153	0.3091	0.0036	0.2933	0.0022
Science	0.4153	**0.5391**	0.0158	0.2921	0.2126	0.1721	0.1963	0.0016

lead. This difference is explained by the fact that LT3 makes use of a WordNet lookup of hypernym-hyponym relations, which is similar to the method used to collect the WordNet gold standard. More detailed statistics and charts are available on the task website[6]. Finally, in order to obtain an overall rank of the system outputs we first assigned a penalty score (from 1 to 6) for six cue aspects of the evaluation: presence of Cycles, Cumulative F&M measure, number of Intermediate Nodes, F-score from Gold Standard Evaluation, number of Submitted Domains and estimated precision from Manual Evaluation. Then, the total number of penalty points was computed and, following the inverse order of the total penalty scores, we finally ranked the teams (see Table 5).

At the end of the evaluation it emerged that the INRIASAC team had outperformed the other teams in the production of taxonomies for the selected target domains. Although the LT3 team achieved better performance for quantitative approaches (precision, F-score, Cumulative F&M), it was penalised in the final ranking because the constructed taxonomies were generally smaller than the taxonomies produced by INRIASAC, the LT3 team did not submit a taxonomy for Chemicals, and they submitted a larger number of taxonomies with cycles.

[6] http://alt.qcri.org/semeval2015/task17/index.php?id=evaluation

Table 5: Overall ranking of submitted systems: INRIASAC (INR), LT3, ntnu, QASSIT (QA), TALN-UPF (TA), USAAR (US).

	INR	**LT3**	**ntnu**	**QA**	**TA**	**US**
Cycles	3	4	2	1	3	4
Cumulative F&M	2	1	6	3	4	5
Intermediate Nodes	2	5	3	6	4	1
Gold Standard Evaluation	2	1	4	5	6	3
Submitted Domains	1	3	1	2	1	1
Manual Evaluation	2	1	4	5	6	3
Total	12	15	20	22	24	17
Final Ranking	1	2	4	5	6	3

5 Discussion

A main limitation of this shared task is that participants were allowed to use the same resources as those used to create the gold standards, and were able to apply simple lookups to retrieve the relations. No recall was computed on the basis of the manual evaluation because of the relatively small number of evaluated relations. A possible solution for this problem would be to use result pooling from all the systems to estimate recall. But this solu-

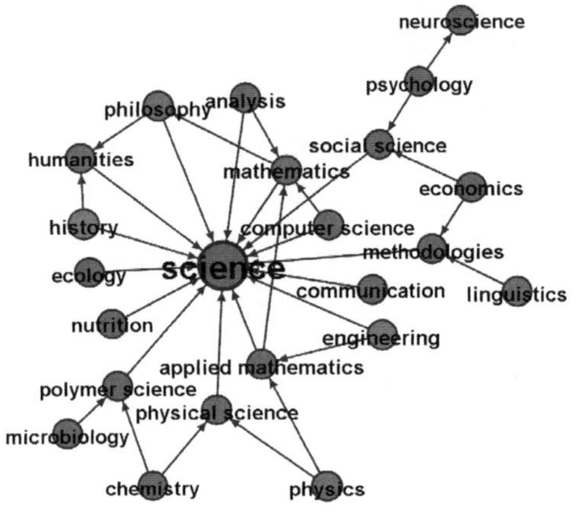

Figure 2: Intermediate nodes of the QASSIT taxonomy on Science.

Figure 3: Intermediate nodes of the gold standard taxonomy on Science.

tion would be more appropriate when there was a larger number of systems. Most participants decided not to address the taxonomy construction subtask, focusing mainly on relation discovery. This could be because the subtask is less well-known and more recently introduced, but also because existing approaches for taxonomy construction are complex and difficult to reimplement. None of the systems was able to address this subtask for the combined Chemicals taxonomy, which is the largest in our dataset. This points to the computational limits of existing algorithms for taxonomy construction. The choice of corpora shows a trend towards using Wikipedia-based corpora instead of web-based corpora (Hovy et al., 2013). Only one participant team relied on web-based corpora. Another lesson that can be drawn from this shared task is that lexico-syntactic patterns, known to have high precision but low recall, can benefit from co-occurrence based approaches, even if these tend to be less reliable. A visualisation of the top levels of the taxonomy constructed by the QASSIT system is presented in Figure 2. The relative size of the nodes within a graph is proportional to the degree of the node. Compared to the gold standard taxonomy for the same domain presented in Figure 3, the QASSIT taxonomy connects a larger number of leaves directly to the Science root, introducing a large number of over-generic relations. There are three times more relations between intermediate nodes and the root node than in the gold standard taxonomy. The QASSIT hierarchy is more shallow than the gold standard, and contains a smaller number of intermediate nodes.

6 Conclusion

This paper provides an overview of the SemEval 2015 task on Taxonomy Extraction. The task aimed to foster research in hierarchical relation extraction from text and taxonomy construction. We constructed and released benchmark datasets for four domains (chemicals, equipment, foods, science). The task attracted 45 submissions from six teams that were automatically evaluated against gold standards collected from WordNet, as well as other well known sources. This evaluation was complemented by a structural analysis of the submitted taxonomies and a manual evaluation of previously unknown edges. Most systems focused on the relation extraction subtask, with the exception of the QASSIT team who addressed the taxonomy construction subtask as well. In future, the datasets can be improved by removing relations that can be identified through string-based inclusion.

Acknowledgements

This work was funded in part by a research grant from Science Foundation Ireland (SFI) under Grant Number SFI/12/RC/2289 (INSIGHT) and also by the MultiJEDI ERC Starting Grant No. 259234 (http://multijedi.org/).

References

Marco Baroni and Silvia Bernardini. 2004. Bootcat: Bootstrapping corpora and terms from the web. In *4th Edition of Language Resources and Evaluation Conference (LREC2004)*.

Christiane Fellbaum. 2005. Wordnet and wordnets. In Keith Brown, editor, *Encyclopedia of Language and Linguistics*, pages 665–670, Oxford.

Tiziano Flati, Daniele Vannella, Tommaso Pasini, and Roberto Navigli. 2014. Two Is Bigger (and Better) Than One: the Wikipedia Bitaxonomy Project. In *Proceedings of the 52nd Annual Meeting of the Association for Computational Linguistics (ACL 2014)*, pages 945–955, Baltimore, Maryland.

Maayan Geffet and Ido Dagan. 2005. The distributional inclusion hypotheses and lexical entailment. In *Proceedings of the 43rd Annual Meeting on Association for Computational Linguistics*, ACL '05, pages 107–114, Stroudsburg, PA, USA.

Sanda M. Harabagiu, Steven J. Maiorano, and Marius Pasca. 2003. Open-domain textual question answering techniques. *Natural Language Engineering*, 9(3):231–267.

Marti A. Hearst. 1992. Automatic acquisition of hyponyms from large text corpora. In *In Proceedings of the 14th International Conference on Computational Linguistics*, pages 539–545.

Eduard H. Hovy, Roberto Navigli, and Simone Paolo Ponzetto. 2013. Collaboratively built semi-structured content and Artificial Intelligence: The story so far. *Artificial Intelligence*, 194:2–27.

Arthur B. Kahn. 1962. Topological sorting of large networks. *Commun. ACM*, 5(11):558–562.

Zornitsa Kozareva and Eduard Hovy. 2010. A semi-supervised method to learn and construct taxonomies using the web. In *Proceedings of the 2010 Conference on Empirical Methods in Natural Language Processing*, EMNLP '10, pages 1110–1118, Stroudsburg, PA, USA.

Zornitsa Kozareva, Ellen Riloff, and Eduard H Hovy. 2008. Semantic class learning from the web with hyponym pattern linkage graphs. In *Proceedings of the 46th Annual Meeting of the Association for Computational Linguistics*, volume 8, pages 1048–1056. Citeseer.

Els Lefever, Marjan Van de Kauter, and Véronique Hoste. 2014. Hypoterm: Detection of hypernym relations between domain-specific terms in dutch and english. *Terminology*, 20(2):250–278.

Roberto Navigli and Simone Paolo Ponzetto. 2012. BabelNet: The automatic construction, evaluation and application of a wide-coverage multilingual semantic network. *Artificial Intelligence*, 193:217–250.

Roberto Navigli and Paola Velardi. 2010. Learning word-class lattices for definition and hypernym extraction. In *Proceedings of the 48th Annual Meeting of the Association for Computational Linguistics*, pages 1318–1327, Uppsala, Sweden, July.

Roberto Navigli, Paola Velardi, and Stefano Faralli. 2011. A graph-based algorithm for inducing lexical taxonomies from scratch. In *Proceedings of the 22nd International Joint Conference on Artificial Intelligence*, pages 1872–1877, Barcelona, Spain.

Craig Nevill-Manning, Ian Witten, and Gordon W. Paynter. 1999. Lexically-generated subject hierarchies for browsing large collections. *International Journal on Digital Libraries*, 2:111–123.

Mark Sanderson and Bruce Croft. 1999. Deriving concept hierarchies from text. In *In Proceedings of the 22nd annual international ACM SIGIR conference on Research and Development in Information Retrieval*, pages 206–213.

Robert Tarjan. 1972. Depth-first search and linear graph algorithms. *SIAM Journal on Computing*, 1:146–160.

Paola Velardi, Roberto Navigli, Stefano Faralli, and Juana Maria Ruiz-Martinez. 2012. A new method for evaluating automatically learned terminological taxonomies. In *Proceedings of the Eight International Conference on Language Resources and Evaluation (LREC'12)*, Istanbul, Turkey.

Paola Velardi, Stefano Faralli, and Roberto Navigli. 2013. OntoLearn Reloaded: A Graph-Based Algorithm for Taxonomy Induction. *Computational Linguistics*, 39(3):665–707.

Silke Wagner and Dorothea Wagner. 2007. Comparing clusterings an overview. Technical Report 2006-04, Faculty of Informatics, Universität Karlsruhe (TH).

Zhichun Wang, Juanzi Li, and Jie Tang. 2013. Boosting cross-lingual knowledge linking via concept annotation. In *Proceedings of the Twenty-Third International Joint Conference on Artificial Intelligence*, IJCAI '13, pages 2733–2739.

INRIASAC: Simple Hypernym Extraction Methods

Gregory Grefenstette
Inria
1 rue Honoré d'Estienne d'Orves
91120 Palaiseau, France
Gregory.grefenstette@inria.fr

Abstract

For information retrieval, it is useful to classify documents using a hierarchy of terms from a domain. One problem is that, for many domains, hierarchies of terms are not available. The task 17 of SemEval 2015 addresses the problem of structuring a set of terms from a given domain into a taxonomy without manual intervention. Here we present some simple taxonomy structuring techniques, such as term overlap and document and sentence co-occurrence in large quantities of text (English Wikipedia) to produce hypernym pairs for the eight domain lists supplied by the task organizers. Our submission ranked first in this 2015 benchmark, which suggests that overly complicated methods might need to be adapted to individual domains. We describe our generic techniques and present an initial evaluation of results.

1 Introduction

This paper describes two simple hypernym extraction methods, given a list of domain terms and a large amount of text divided into documents. Task 17 of the 2015 Semeval campaign (Bordea *et al.*, 2015) consists in structuring a flat list of pre-identified domain terms into a list of hypernym pairs. Task organizers provide two lists of terms for each of four domains: *equipment, food, chemical, science*, one extracted from WordNet and one from an unknown source. Participants in the task were allowed to use any resource (except existing taxonomies) to automatically transform the lists of terms into lists of pairs of terms, the first term being a hyponym of the more general second term. For example, if the words `airship` and `blimp` were included in the lists of terms for a domain, the system was expected to return lines such as:

```
blimp      airship
```

The task organizers provided training data from the domains of Artificial Intelligence, vehicles and plants, different from the test domains. The training data consisted in term lists (for plants), and term lists and lists of hypernyms (for AI and for vehicles). We examined these files to get an understanding of the task but did not exploit them.

We used the English text of Wikipedia (downloaded from http://dumps.wikimedia.org on August 13, 2014) as our only resource for discovering these relations. We extracted only the text of each article, ignoring titles, section headings, categories, infoboxes, or other meta-information present in the article. We recognized task terms in these articles and gathered statistics on document and sentence co-occurrence between domain terms, as well as term frequency. To recognize hypernyms, we used term inclusion (explained in section 3.1 below) and co-occurrence statistics (see section 3.2) to decide whether two terms were possibly in a hypernym relation, and document frequency to chose which term was the hypernym. Our submission ranked first in the SemEval 2015 task 17 benchmark.

2 Domain Lists

Participants were provided with the eight lists of domain terms, each containing between 370 and 1555 terms. Some terms examples:

chemical: agarose, nickel sulfate heptahydrate, aminoglycan, pinoquercetin, …
equipment: storage equipment, strapping, traveling microscope, minneapolis-moline, …
food: sauce gribiche, botifarra, phitti, food colouring, bean, limequat, kalach, …
science: biological and physical, history of religions of eastern origins, linguistic anthropology, religion, semantics…
WN_chemical: abo antibodies, acaricide, acaroid resin, acceptor, acetal, acetaldehyde…
WN_equipment: acoustic modem, aerator, air search radar, amplifier, anti submarine rocket, apishamore, apparatus, …
WN_food: absinth, acidophilus milk, adobo, agar, aioli, alcohol, ale, alfalfa, allemande, allergy diet, …
WN_science: abnormal psychology, acoustics, aerology, aeromechanics, aeronautics, …

Terms consisted of one to nine words. Some terms were very short and ambiguous (only two or three characters: `ga, os, tu, ada, aji, ...`) and some very long (e.g., `udp-n-acetyl-alpha-d-muramoyl-l-alanyl-gamma-d-glutamyl-l-lysyl-d-alanyl-d-alanine, korea advanced institute of science and technology satellite 4`). It is specified that the taxonomies produced during the task should be rooted on `chemical` for the two chemical domain lists, on `equipment` for the equipment lists, on `food` for the food lists, and on `science` for the science lists, even though the term `chemical` was absent from the WN_chemical domain list. Participants were allowed to add additional nodes, i.e. terms, in the hierarchy as they consider appropriate. We did not add any new terms, except for `chemical` in the WN_chemical list.

2.1 Preprocessing the resource

Our only resource for discovering hypernym relations was the English Wikipedia. Starting from the wiki-latest-pages-articles.xml, we extracted all the text between <text> markers, and marked off document boundaries using <title> markers. No other information (infoboxes, categories, etc.) was kept. The text was then tokenized and output as one sentence per line. The first English Wikipedia sentence extracted looked like this: `' Anarchism ' is a political philosophy that advocates stateless societies often defined as self-governed voluntary institutions , but that several authors have defined as more specific institutions based on non-hierarchical free associations .` We applied Porter stemming (Willet, 2006) and replaced stopwords (Buckley *et al.,* 1995) by underscores. The first sentence then becomes: `anarch _ _ _ polit philosophi _ advoc stateless societi _ defin _ self-govern voluntari institut _ _ _ sever author _ defin _ _ specif institut base _ non-hierarch free associ`

We applied the same Porter stemming and stopword removal to the task-supplied domain terms. So the *science* term list, for example, becomes

```
0 electro-mechan system
1 biolog _ physic
2 histori _ religion _ eastern origin
3 linguist anthropolog
4 metaphys
```

We retained both Porter-stemmed versions of the Wikipedia sentences and domain terms as well as the original unstemmed versions for the treatment described below.

3 Extracting Hypernyms

In order to extract hypernyms, we used the following features: (i) presence of terms in the same sentence, (ii) presence in the same document (iii) term frequency (iv) document frequency, and (v) subsequences.

3.1 Subterms

In addition to domain lists supplied for the Semeval task, we were supplied with training data. One file in this training data, ontolearn_AX.taxo, gives ground truth for the training file ontolearn_AX.terms, and contains:

```
source code    < code
theory of inheritance < theory
```

From these validated examples, we concluded that an 'easy' way to find hypernyms is to check whether one term is a suffix of the other (e.g., `communications satellite` as a type of `satellite`), or whether one term B is the prefix of another term B A C where A is any two-letter word (e.g. `helmet of coţofeneşti` as a type of `helmet; caterpillar d9` as a type of `caterpillar`). We chose two letters for the second term to cover English prepositions such as *of, in, by*, ... This heuristic was unexpectedly productive in the chemical domain where many hypernym pairs were similar to: `ginsenoside mc` as a type of `ginsenoside` (see Table 1). But our prefix matching using second words of length two missed hypernyms such as `fortimicin b` as a type of `fortimicin` or `ginsenoside c-y` as a type of `ginsenoside`. Obviously chemical terms should have their own heuristics for subterm matching.

Other examples of errors, false positives, caused by these heuristics are `licorice` as a type of `rice` or `surface to air missile system` as a type of `surface`.

3.2 Sentence and Document Co-occurrence Statistics

For other domain terms (which could include the hypernyms found by the suffix and prefix heuristics), we use the statistics of document presence, and of co-occurrence of terms in sentences to predict hypernym relations. Let D_{porter}(term) be the document frequency of a Porter-stemmed term in the stemmed version of Wikipedia. Since Wikipedia article boundaries were stored, we considered each Wikipedia article as a new document. Let $SentCooc_{porter}(term_i, term_j)$ be the number of times that the Porter-stemmed versions of $term_i$ and $term_j$ appear in the same sentence in the stemmed English Wikipedia. Given two terms, $term_i$ and $term_j$, if $term_i$ is appears in more documents than $term_j$, then $term_i$ is a candidate hypernym for $term_j$.

$$CandHypenym(term_i) = \{ term_j : SentCooc_{porter}(term_i, term_j) > 0 \ \&\& \ D_{porter}(term_j) > D_{porter}(term_i) \}$$

This heuristically derived set is meant to capture the intuition that general terms are more widely distributed than more specific terms (e.g., `dog` appears in more Wikipedia articles than `poodle`).

Domain	*suffix*	*prefix*	*cooc*	*Total hypernyms produced*
WN_chemical	750	10	3766	4001
WN_equipment	171	3	1338	1369
WN_food	616	25	4121	4238
WN_science	174	0	1070	1102
chemical	10780	91	19322	28443
equipment	241	17	1126	1168
food	471	33	4277	4363
science	193	17	1130	1164

Table 1. Number of prefix and suffix hypernyms produced, compared to the total number of hypernyms returned for each domain.

Next, we define the best hyperym candidate for $term_i$ as being the term $term_k$ that appears in the most documents (from Wikipedia in this case):

$$BestHypernym(term_i) = term_k \text{ such that } \forall\ term_j \in CandHypernym(term_i) : D_{porter}(term_k) \geq D_{porter}(term_j)$$

Next, we remove this term $term_k$ from CandHypernym($term_i$) and repeat the heuristic twice, retaining, then, the three candidate hypernyms appearing in the most documents for each term not found by using the prefix or suffix heuristics.

3.2.1 Co-occurrence Example

Consider the following example. In the domain file science.terms there is the term `biblical studies`. The Porter-stemmed version of this term `biblic studi` appears in 887 documents. Considering all the other terms in science.terms, we find that `biblic studi` appears 215 times in the same sentence as the stemmed version of theology (`theologi`), 111 times in the same sentences as stemmed history (`histori`), 50 times with religion, 43 times with music, and 42 times with science (`scienc`).

```
215 887 21977      biblic studi       theologi
111 887 383927     biblic studi       histori
50  887 64044      biblic studi       religion
43  887 412791     biblic studi       music
```

We decided to keep the top three for simplicity, so this term contributed three bolded lines above to our submitted science.taxo file.

3.3 Other Attempts at Finding Relations

We tried a number of other methods to find hypernyms, none of which gave results that looked good from a cursory glance. We implemented a method to recognize sentences containing Hearst patterns (list from (Cimiano *et al.*, 2005)) involving the domain terms. For example, `tape` is in *equipment*, and were able to find stemmed sentences of the form A, B and other C … such as `todai , sticki note , 3m #tape# @, and other@ #tape# ar exampl of psa ( pressure-sensit adhes )` from which we should have been able to extract relations such as `3m tape` is a type of `tape`, and `sticky note` is a type of `tape`. But we would have had to the parse the sentence, and been willing to add new terms (which was permitted by the organizers) to the derived hypernym lists but we did not want to make that processing investment yet. We also tried to discover the *basic vocabulary* (Kit, 2002) of each domain without success.

4 Evaluation

Each participant in Task 17 of SemEval 2015 was allowed to submit one run for each of the 8 domains (see Table 1 for the names of the domains, and the number of hypernym pairs we submitted. Suffix and prefix subterms account for 10% to 36% of the hypernyms we produced. The cooccurence technique produced the most hypernym candidates). The task organizers evaluated the submissions of the six participating teams, using automated and manual methods, and published their evaluation three weeks after the submission deadline. Our team placed first in the official ranking of the six teams.

Domain	*suffix*	*prefix*	*cooc*	*union*	*gold to find*
WN_chemical	377	5	574	644	1387
WN_equipment	119	0	168	184	485
WN_food	371	2	681	726	1533
WN_science	119	0	230	240	441
chemical	2019	9	715	2407	24817
equipment	184	1	286	305	615
food	279	1	807	822	1587
science	121	7	193	209	465

Table 2. Number of gold standard relations to find in the last column. Columns 2, 3 and 4 are the number of gold standard relations found by each technique. "union" is the union of columns 2, 3 and 4. Since the cooccurrence technique can find relations that have been found by the suffix and prefix techniques.

Domain	*suffix*	*prefix*	*cooc*	*union*	*gold to find*
WN_chemical	26%	0.3%	40%	46%	1387
WN_equipment	24%	0%	34%	38%	485
WN_food	23%	0.1%	43%	47%	1533
WN_science	26%	0%	51%	54%	441
chemical	8%	0.03%	3%	10%	24817
equipment	30%	0.02%	47%	50%	615
food	18%	0.06%	51%	52%	1587
science	26%	1.8%	42%	45%	465

Table 3. Percentage of correct answers found by each method.

The evaluation criteria, which were not published before the submission, combined the presences of cycles in the hypernyms submitted, the Fowlkes & Mallows measure of the overlap between the submitted hierarchy and the gold standard hierarchy, the F-score ranking, the number of domains submitted (not all teams returned results for all domains), and a manual precision ranking (for hypernyms not present in the gold standard). The gold standards used by the task organizers came from published taxonomies, or from subtrees of WordNet (prefixed as WN_ above). A quick evaluation of how well our simple hypernym extraction techniques fared on each gold standard is shown in Table 2.

As Table 3 shows, most of the correct answers found come from the sentence and document cooccurrence method described in section 3.2.

5 Conclusion

Even though training data was provided for this taxonomy creation task, we did not exploit it in this our first participation in Semeval. We implemented some simple frequency-based cooccurrence statistics, and substring inclusion heuristics to propose a set of hypernyms. We did not implement any graph algorithms (cycle detection, branch deletion) that would be useful to build a true hierarchy. Future plans involve examining and eliminating cycles generated by this method. Since we only used wikipedia as a resource, the method depends on the given terms being present in Wikipedia, which was not always the case, especially in the chemical domain. In future work, we will also examine using web documents, in lieu of or to supplement Wikipedia.

Acknowledgments

This research is partially funded by a research grant from INRIA, and the Paris-Saclay Institut de la Société Numérique funded by the IDEX Paris-Saclay, ANR-11-IDEX-0003-02.

References

Georgeta Bordea, Paul Buitelaar, Stefano Faralli, and Roberto Navigli. 2015. Semeval-2015 task 17: Taxonomy Extraction Evaluation. *Proceedings of the 9th International Workshop on Semantic Evaluation*. Association for Computational Linguistics

Chris Buckley, Gerard Salton, James Allan, and Amit Singhal. 1995. Automatic query expansion using SMART: TREC3. *Proceedings of the 3rd Text REtrieval Conference (TREC-3)*. NIST Special Publication 500–226. National Institute of Standards and Technology (NIST), Gaithersburg, MD, pp: 69–80.

Philipp Cimiano, Aleksander Pivk, Lars Schmidt-Thieme, and Steffen Staab. 2005. Learning taxonomic relations from heterogeneous sources of evidence. *Ontology Learning from Text: Methods, evaluation and applications*. IoS Press.

Chunyu Kit. 2002. Corpus tools for retrieving and deriving termhood evidence. *Proceedings of the 5th East Asia Forum of Terminology*, pp. 69-80.

Peter Willett. 2006. The Porter stemming algorithm: then and now. *Program* 40(3): 219-223

SemEval 2015 Task 18: Broad-Coverage Semantic Dependency Parsing

Stephan Oepen♣♠, Marco Kuhlmann♡, Yusuke Miyao◇, Daniel Zeman°, Silvie Cinková°, Dan Flickinger•, Jan Hajič°, and Zdeňka Urešová°

♣ University of Oslo, Department of Informatics

♠ Potsdam University, Department of Linguistics

♡ Linköping University, Department of Computer and Information Science

◇ National Institute of Informatics, Tokyo

° Charles University in Prague, Faculty of Mathematics and Physics, Institute of Formal and Applied Linguistics

• Stanford University, Center for the Study of Language and Information

sdp-organizers@emmtee.net

Abstract

Task 18 at SemEval 2015 defines *Broad-Coverage Semantic Dependency Parsing* (SDP) as the problem of recovering sentence-internal predicate–argument relationships for *all content words*, i.e. the semantic structure constituting the relational core of sentence meaning. In this task description, we position the problem in comparison to other language analysis sub-tasks, introduce and compare the semantic dependency target representations used, and summarize the task setup, participating systems, and main results.

1 Background and Motivation

Syntactic dependency parsing has seen great advances in the past decade, but tree-oriented parsers are ill-suited for producing meaning representations, i.e. moving from the analysis of grammatical structure to sentence semantics. Even if syntactic parsing arguably can be limited to tree structures, this is not the case in semantic analysis, where a node will often be the argument of multiple predicates (i.e. have more than one incoming arc), and it will often be desirable to leave nodes corresponding to semantically vacuous word classes unattached (with no incoming arcs). Thus, Task 18 at SemEval 2015, *Broad-Coverage Semantic Dependency Parsing* (SDP 2015),[1] seeks to stimulate the parsing community to move towards more general graph processing, to thus enable a more direct analysis of *Who did What to Whom?*

Extending the very similar predecessor task SDP 2014 (Oepen et al., 2014), we make use of three distinct, parallel semantic annotations over the same common texts, viz. the venerable Wall Street Journal (WSJ) and Brown segments of the Penn Treebank (PTB; Marcus et al., 1993) for English, as well as comparable resources for Chinese and Czech. Figure 1 below shows example target representations, bi-lexical semantic dependency graphs in all cases, for the WSJ sentence:

(1) A similar technique is almost impossible to apply to other crops, such as cotton, soybeans, and rice.

Semantically, *technique* arguably is dependent on the determiner (the quantificational locus), the modifier *similar*, and the predicate *apply*. Conversely, the predicative copula, infinitival *to*, and the vacuous preposition marking the deep object of *apply* can be argued to not have a semantic contribution of their own. Besides calling for node re-entrancies and partial connectivity, semantic dependency graphs may also exhibit higher degrees of non-projectivity than is typical of syntactic dependency trees.

Besides its relation to syntactic dependency parsing, the task also has some overlap with Semantic Role Labeling (SRL; Gildea & Jurafsky, 2002).[2] However, we require parsers to identify 'full-

[1] See http://alt.qcri.org/semeval2015/task18/ for further technical details, information on how to obtain the data, and official results.

[2] In much previous SRL work, target representations typically draw on resources like PropBank and NomBank (Palmer et al., 2005; Meyers et al., 2004), which are limited to argument identification and labeling for verbal and nominal predicates. A plethora of semantic phenomena—for example negation

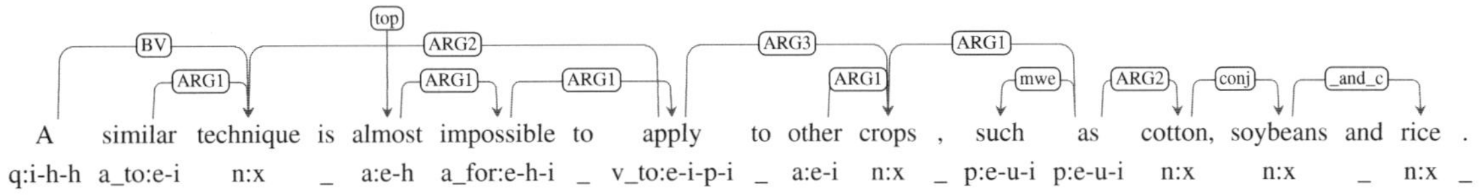

(a) DELPH-IN Minimal Recursion Semantics–derived bi-lexical dependencies (DM).

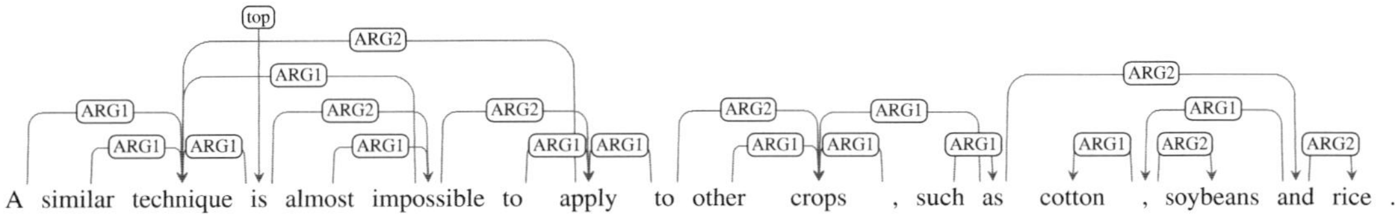

(b) Enju Predicate–Argument Structures (PAS).

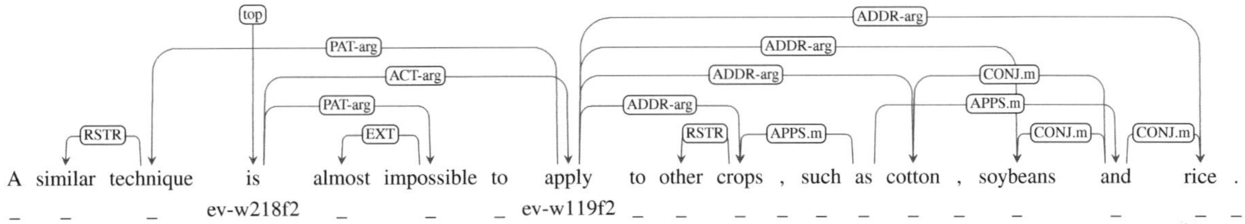

(c) Parts of the tectogrammatical layer of the Prague Czech-English Dependency Treebank (PSD).

Figure 1: Sample semantic dependency graphs for Example (1).

sentence' semantic dependencies, i.e. compute a representation that integrates *all* content words in one structure. Finally, a third related area of much interest is often dubbed 'semantic parsing', which Kate and Wong (2010) define as "the task of mapping natural language sentences into complete formal meaning representations which a computer can execute for some domain-specific application." In contrast to much work in this tradition, our SDP target representations aim to be task- and domain-independent.

2 Target Representations

We use three distinct target representations for semantic dependencies. As is evident in our running example (Figure 1), showing what are called the DM, PAS, and PSD semantic dependencies, there are contentful differences among these annotations, and there is of course not one obvious (or even objective) truth. Advancing in-depth comparison of representations and underlying design decisions, in fact, is among the motivations for the SDP task series. Please see Oepen et al. (2014) and Miyao et al. (2014) for additional background.

DM: DELPH-IN MRS-Derived Bi-Lexical Dependencies These semantic dependency graphs originate in a manual re-annotation, dubbed DeepBank, of Sections 00–21 of the WSJ Corpus and of selected parts of the Brown Corpus with syntactico-semantic analyses of the LinGO English Resource Grammar (Flickinger, 2000; Flickinger et al., 2012). For this target representation, top nodes designate the highest-scoping (non-quantifier) predicate in the graph, e.g. the (scopal) adverb *almost* in Figure 1.[3]

PAS: Enju Predicate–Argument Structures The Enju Treebank and parser[4] are derived from the automatic HPSG-style annotation of the PTB (Miyao, 2006). Our PAS semantic dependency graphs are extracted from the Enju Treebank, without contentful conversion, and from the application of the same basic techniques to the Penn Chinese Treebank (CTB;

and other scopal embedding, comparatives, possessives, various types of modification, and even conjunction—often remain unanalyzed in SRL. Thus, its target representations are partial to a degree that can prohibit semantic downstream processing, for example inference-based techniques.

[3]However, non-scopal adverbs act as mere intersective modifiers, e.g. in a structure like *Abrams sang loudly*, the adverb is a predicate in DM, but the main verb nevertheless is the top node.

[4]See http://kmcs.nii.ac.jp/enju/.

Xue et al., 2005). Top nodes in this representation denote semantic heads.

PSD: Prague Semantic Dependencies The Prague Czech-English Dependency Treebank (PCEDT; Hajič et al., 2012)[5] is a set of parallel dependency trees over the WSJ texts from the PTB, and their Czech translations. Our PSD bi-lexical dependencies have been extracted from what is called the *tectogrammatical* annotation layer (t-trees). Top nodes are derived from t-tree roots; i.e. they mostly correspond to main verbs. In case of coordinate clauses, there are multiple top nodes per sentence.

3 Data Format

The SDP target representations can be characterized as labeled, directed graphs. Nodes are labeled with five pieces of information: word *form*, *lemma*, *part of speech*, a Boolean flag indicating whether the node represents a *top* predicate, and optional *frame* (or sense) information—for example the distinction between causative vs. inchoative predicates like *increase*. Edges are labeled with semantic relations that hold between source and target.

All data provided for the task uses a column-based file format that extends the format of the SDP 2014 task by a new `frame` column (thus making it a little more SRL-like). More details about the file format are available at the task website.

4 Data Sets

All three target representations for English are annotations of the same text, Sections 00–21 of the WSJ Corpus, as well as of a balanced sample of twenty files from the Brown Corpus (Francis & Kučera, 1982). For this task, we have synchronized these resources at the sentence and tokenization levels and excluded from the SDP 2015 training and testing data any sentences for which (a) one or more of the treebanks lacked a gold-standard analysis; (b) a one-to-one alignment of tokens could not be established across all three representations; or (c) at least one of the graphs was cyclic. Of the 43,746 sentences in these 22 first sections of WSJ text, DeepBank lacks analyses for some 11%, and the Enju Treebank has gaps for a little more than four percent.[6] Finally, 139 of the WSJ graphs obtained through the above conversions were cyclic. In total, we were left with 35,657 sentences (or 802,717 tokens; eight percent more than for SDP 2014[7]) as training data (Sections 00–20), 1,410 in-domain testing sentences (31,948 tokens) from WSJ Section 21, and 1,849 out-of-domain testing sentences (31,583 tokens) from the Brown Corpus.

Besides the additions of out-of-domain test data and frame (or sense) identifiers for English, another extension beyond the SDP 2014 task concerns the inclusion of additional languages, albeit only for select target representations. Our training data included an additional 31,113 Chinese sentences (649,036 tokens), taken from Release 7.0 of the CTB, for the PAS target representation, and 42,076 Czech sentences (985,302 tokens), drawing on the translations of the WSJ Corpus in PCEDT 2.0, for the PSD target representation. Additional out-of-domain Czech test data was drawn from the Prague Dependency Treebank 3.0 (PDT; Bejček et al., 2013). For these additional languages, the task comprised 1,670 sentences (38,397 tokens) of in-domain Chinese test data, and 1,670 sentences (38397 tokens) and 5,226 sentences (87,927 tokens) of in- and out-of-domain Czech data, respectively.

Quantitative Comparison As a first attempt at contrasting our three target representations, Table 1 shows some high-level statistics of the graphs comprising the training and testing data.[8] In terms of distinctions drawn in dependency labels (1), there are clear differences between the representations, with PSD appearing linguistically most fine-

[5]See `http://ufal.mff.cuni.cz/pcedt2.0/`.

[6]Additionally, some 500 sentences show tokenization mismatches, most owing to DeepBank correcting PTB idiosyncrasies like ⟨`G.m.b`, `H.`⟩, ⟨`S.p`, `A.`⟩, and ⟨`U.S.`, `.`⟩, and introducing a few new ones (Fares et al., 2013).

[7]In comparison to the SDP 2014 data, our DM graphs were extracted from a newer, improved release of DeepBank (Version 1.1), and its conversion to bi-lexical dependencies was moderately revised to provide more systematic analyses of contracted negated auxiliaries and comparatives. At the same time, the extraction of PSD graphs from the PCEDT t-trees was refined to include edges representing grammatical coreference, e.g. re-entrancies introduced by control verbs.

[8]These statistics are obtained using the 'official' SDP toolkit. Our notions of singletons, roots, re-entrancies, and projectivity follow common graph terminology, but see Oepen et al. (2014) for formal definitions.

		EN i-d			CS i-d	ZH i-d	EN o-o-d			CS o-o-d
		DM	PAS	PSD	PSD	PAS	DM	PAS	PSD	PSD
(1)	**# labels**	59	42	91	61	32	47	41	74	64
(2)	**% singletons**	22.97	4.38	35.76	28.91	0.11	25.40	5.84	39.11	29.04
(3)	**edge density**	0.96	1.02	1.01	1.03	0.98	0.95	1.02	0.99	1.00
(4)	**$\%_g$ trees**	2.30	1.22	42.19	37.66	3.49	9.68	2.38	51.43	51.49
(5)	**$\%_g$ noncrossing**	69.03	59.57	64.58	63.22	67.61	74.58	65.28	74.26	72.41
(6)	**$\%_g$ projective**	2.91	1.64	41.92	38.32	12.89	8.82	3.46	54.35	53.02
(7)	**$\%_g$ fragmented**	6.55	0.23	0.69	1.17	15.22	4.71	0.65	1.73	3.50
(8)	**$\%_n$ reentrancies**	27.44	29.36	11.42	11.80	24.96	26.14	29.36	11.46	11.44
(9)	**$\%_g$ topless**	0.31	0.02	–	0.04	6.92	1.41	–	–	0.02
(10)	**# top nodes**	0.9969	0.9998	1.1276	1.2242	0.9308	0.9859	1.0000	1.2645	1.2771
(11)	**$\%_n$ non-top roots**	44.91	55.98	4.35	4.73	46.65	39.89	50.93	5.27	5.31
(12)	**# frames**	297	–	5426	–	–	172	–	1208	–
(13)	**$\%_n$ frames**	13.52	–	16.77	–	–	15.79	–	19.50	–
(14)	**average treewidth**	1.30	1.72	1.61	1.66	1.35	1.31	1.69	1.50	1.49
(15)	**maximum treewidth**	3	3	7	6	3	3	3	5	5

Table 1: Contrastive high-level graph statistics across target representations, languages, and domains.

grained, and PAS showing the smallest label inventory. Unattached singleton nodes (2) in our setup correspond to tokens analyzed as semantically vacuous, which (as seen in Figure 1) include most punctuation marks in PSD and DM, but not PAS. Furthermore, PSD (unlike the other two) analyzes some high-frequency determiners as semantically vacuous. Conversely, PAS on average has more edges per (non-singleton) nodes than the other two (3), which likely reflects its approach to the analysis of functional words (see below).

Judging from both the percentage of actual trees (4), the proportions of noncrossing graphs (5), projective graphs (6), and the proportions of reentrant nodes (8), PSD is more 'tree-oriented' than the other two, which at least in part reflects its approach to the analysis of modifiers and determiners (again, see below). We view the small percentages of graphs without at least one top node (9) and of graphs with at least two non-singleton components that are not interconnected (7) as tentative indicators of general well-formedness. Intuitively, there should always be a 'top' predicate, and the whole graph should 'hang together'. Only DM exhibits non-trivial (if small) degrees of topless and fragmented graphs, which may indicate imperfections in DeepBank annotations or room for improvement in the conversion from full logical forms to bi-lexical dependencies, but possibly also exceptions to our intuitions about semantic dependency graphs.

	Directed			**Undirected**		
	DM	PAS	PSD	DM	PAS	PSD
DM	–	.6425	.2612	–	.6719	.5675
PAS	.6688	–	.2963	.6993	–	.5490
PSD	.2636	.2963	–	.5743	.5630	–

Table 2: Pairwise F_1 similarities, including punctuation (upper right diagonals) or not (lower left).

Frame or sense distinctions are a new property in SDP 2015 and currently are only available for the English DM and PSD data. Table 1 reveals a stark difference in granularity: DM limits itself to argument structure distinctions that are grammaticized, e.g. causative vs. inchoative contrasts or differences in the arity or coarse semantic typing of argument frames; PSD, on the other hand, draws on the much richer sense inventory of the EngValLex database (Cinková, 2006). Accordingly, the two target representations represent quite different challenges for the predicate disambiguation sub-task of SDP 2015.

Finally, in Table 2 we seek to quantify pairwise structural similarity between the three representations in terms of unlabeled dependency F_1 (dubbed UF in Section 5 below). We provide four variants of this metric, (a) taking into account the directionality of edges or not and (b) including edges involving punctuation marks or not. On this view, DM and PAS are structurally much closer to each other than either of the two is to PSD, even more so when discarding punctuation. While relaxing the comparison to ignore edge directionality also increases similarity scores for this pair, the effect is much more pronounced when comparing either to PSD. This suggests that directionality of semantic dependencies is a major source of diversion between DM and PAS on the one hand, and PSD on the other hand.

Linguistic Comparison Among other aspects, Ivanova et al. (2012) categorize a range of syntactic and semantic dependency annotation schemes according to the role that functional elements take. In Figure 1 and the discussion of Table 1 above, we already observed that PAS differs from the other representations in integrating into the graph auxiliaries, the infinitival marker, the case-marking preposition introducing the argument of *apply* (*to*), and most punctuation marks;[9] while these (and other functional elements, e.g. complementizers) are analyzed as semantically vacuous in DM and PSD, they function as predicates in PAS, though do not always serve as 'local' top nodes (i.e. the semantic head of the corresponding sub-graph): For example, the infinitival marker in Figure 1 takes the verb as its argument, but the 'upstairs' predicate *impossible* links directly to the verb, rather than to the infinitival marker as an intermediate.

At the same time, DM and PAS pattern alike in their approach to modifiers, e.g. attributive adjectives, adverbs, and prepositional phrases. Unlike in PSD (or common syntactic dependency schemes), these are analyzed as semantic predicates and, thus, contribute to higher degrees of node reentrancy and non-top (structural) roots. Roughly the same holds for determiners, but here our PSD projection of Prague tectogrammatical trees onto bi-lexical dependencies leaves 'vanilla' articles (like *a* and *the*) as singleton nodes.

The analysis of coordination is distinct in the three representations, as also evident in Figure 1. By design, DM opts for what is often called the Mel'čukian analysis of coordinate structures (Mel'čuk, 1988), with a chain of dependencies rooted at the first conjunct (which is thus considered the head, 'standing in' for the structure at large); in the DM approach, coordinating conjunctions are not integrated with the graph but rather contribute different types of dependencies. In PAS, the final coordinating conjunction is the head of the structure and each coordinating conjunction (or intervening punctuation mark that acts like one) is a two-place predicate, taking left and right conjuncts as its arguments. Conversely, in PSD the last coordinating conjunction takes all conjuncts as its arguments (in case there is no overt conjunction, a punctuation mark is used instead); additional conjunctions or punctuation marks are not connected to the graph.[10]

A linguistic difference between our representations that highlights variable granularities of analysis and, relatedly, diverging views on the scope of the problem can be observed in Figure 2. Much noun phrase–internal structure is not made explicit in the PTB, and the Enju Treebank from which our PAS representation derives predates the bracketing work of Vadas and Curran (2007). In the four-way nominal compounding example of Figure 2, thus, PAS arrives at a strictly left-branching tree, and there is no attempt at interpreting semantic roles among the members of the compound either; PSD, on the other hand, annotates both the *actual* compound-internal bracketing and the assignment of roles, e.g. making *stock* the `PAT`(ient) of *investment*. In this spirit, the PSD annotations could be directly paraphrased along the lines of *plans by employees for investment in stocks*. In a middle position between the other two, DM disambiguates the bracketing but, by design, merely assigns an underspecified, construction-specific dependency type; its `compound` dependency, then, is to be interpreted as the most general type of dependency that can hold between the elements of this construction (i.e. to a first approximation either an argument role or a relation parallel to a preposition, as in the above paraphrase). The DM and PSD annotations of this specific example happen to diverge in their bracketing decisions, where the DM analysis corresponds to *[...] investments in stock for employees*, i.e. grouping

[9] In all formats, punctuation marks like dashes, colons, and sometimes commas can be contentful, i.e. at times occur as both predicates, arguments, and top nodes.

[10] As detailed by Miyao et al. (2014), individual conjuncts can be (and usually are) arguments of other predicates, whereas the topmost conjunction only has incoming edges in nested coordinate structures. Similarly, a 'shared' modifier of the coordinate structure as a whole would take as its argument the local top node of the coordination in DM or PAS (i.e. the first conjunct or final conjunction, respectively), whereas it would depend as an argument on all conjuncts in PSD.

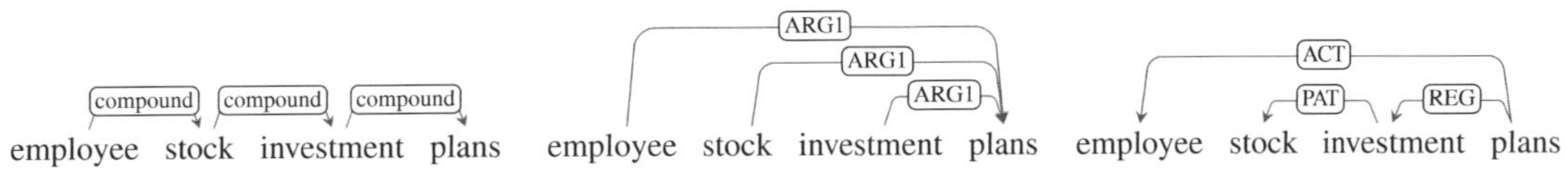

Figure 2: Analysis of nominal compounding in DM, PAS, and PSD, respectively .

the concept *employee stock* (in contrast to 'common stock').

Without context and expert knowledge, these decisions are hard to call, and indeed there has been much previous work seeking to identify and annotate the relations that hold between members of a nominal compound (see Nakov, 2013, for a recent overview). To what degree the bracketing and role disambiguation in this example are determined by the linguistic signal (rather than by context and world knowledge, say) can be debated, and thus the observed differences among our representations in this example relate to the classic contrast between 'sentence' (or 'conventional') meaning, on the one hand, and 'speaker' (or 'occasion') meaning, on the other hand (Quine, 1960; Grice, 1968; Bender et al., 2015). In turn, we acknowledge different plausible points of view about which level of semantic representation should be the target representation for data-driven *parsing* (i.e. structural analysis guided by the grammatical system), and which refinements like the above could be construed as part of a subsequent task of *interpretation*.

5 Task Setup

English training data for the task, providing all columns in the file format sketched in Section 3 above, together with a first version of the SDP toolkit—including graph input, basic statistics, and scoring—were released to candidate participants in early August 2014. In mid-November, cross-lingual training data, a minor update to the English data, and optional syntactic 'companion' analyses (see below) were provided. Anytime between mid-December 2014 and mid-January 2015, participants could request an input-only version of the test data, with just columns (1) to (4) pre-filled; participants then had six days to run their systems on these inputs, fill in columns (5), (6), (7), and upwards, and submit their results (from up to two different runs) for scoring. Upon completion of the testing phase, we have shared the gold-standard test data, official scores, and system results for all submissions with participants and are currently preparing all data for general release through the Linguistic Data Consortium.

Evaluation Systems participating in the task were evaluated based on the accuracy with which they can produce semantic dependency graphs for previously unseen text, measured relative to the gold-standard testing data. For comparability with SDP 2014, the primary measures for this evaluation were labeled and unlabeled precision and recall with respect to predicted dependencies (predicate–role–argument triples) and labeled and unlabeled exact match with respect to complete graphs. In both contexts, identification of the top node(s) of a graph was considered as the identification of additional, 'virtual' dependencies from an artificial root node (at position 0). Below we abbreviate these metrics as (a) labeled precision, recall, and F_1: LP, LR, LF; (b) unlabeled precision, recall, and F_1: UP, UR, UF; and (c) labeled and unlabeled exact match: LM, UM.

The 'official' ranking of participating systems is determined based on the arithmetic mean of the labeled dependency F_1 scores (i.e. the geometric mean of labeled precision and labeled recall) on the three target representations (DM, PAS, and PSD). Thus, to be competitive in the overall ranking, a system had to submit semantic dependencies for all three target representations.

In addition to these metrics, we apply two additional metrics that aim to capture fragments of semantics that are 'larger' than individual dependencies but 'smaller' than the semantic dependency graph for the complete sentence, viz. what we call (a) *complete predications* and (b) *semantic frames*. A complete predication is comprised of the set of all core arguments to one predicate, which for the DM and PAS target representations corresponds to all outgoing dependency edges, and for the PSD target representation to only those outgoing dependencies marked by an '`-arg`' suffix on the edge label. Pushing the units of evaluation one step further towards inter-

		DM				PAS				PSD			
	$\overline{\text{LF}}$	LF	LP	LR	FF	LF	LP	LR	PF	LF	LP	LR	FF
Turku✧	86.81	88.29	89.52	87.09	58.39	95.58	95.94	95.21	87.99	76.57	78.24	74.97	56.85
Lisbon*	86.23	89.44	90.52	88.39	00.20	91.67	92.45	90.90	84.18	77.58	79.88	75.41	00.06
Peking	*85.33*	*89.09*	90.93	87.32	63.08	*91.26*	92.90	89.67	79.08	75.66	78.60	72.93	49.95
Lisbon	85.15	88.21	89.84	86.64	00.15	90.88	91.87	89.92	81.74	*76.36*	78.62	74.23	00.03
Riga	84.00	87.90	88.57	87.24	58.12	90.75	91.50	90.02	80.03	73.34	75.25	71.52	52.54
Turku*	83.47	86.17	87.80	84.60	54.67	90.62	91.38	89.87	80.60	73.63	76.10	71.32	53.20
Minsk	80.74	84.13	86.28	82.09	54.24	85.24	87.28	83.28	64.66	72.84	74.65	71.13	51.63
In-House*	61.61	92.80	92.85	92.75	83.79	92.03	92.07	91.99	87.24	–	–	–	–

		DM				PAS				PSD			
	$\overline{\text{LF}}$	LF	LP	LR	FF	LF	LP	LR	PF	LF	LP	LR	FF
Turku✧	83.50	82.11	84.26	80.07	42.89	92.92	93.52	92.33	83.80	75.47	77.77	73.31	42.37
Lisbon*	82.53	83.77	85.79	81.84	00.35	87.63	88.88	86.41	80.19	76.18	80.12	72.61	02.25
Lisbon	*81.15*	81.75	84.81	78.90	00.27	86.88	88.52	85.30	78.47	*74.82*	78.68	71.31	02.09
Peking	80.78	*81.84*	84.29	79.53	47.49	*87.23*	89.47	85.10	74.75	73.28	77.36	69.61	34.28
Riga	79.23	80.69	81.69	79.72	41.88	86.63	87.56	85.72	76.26	70.37	73.23	67.71	40.76
Turku*	78.85	79.01	81.54	76.63	39.15	85.95	86.95	84.98	76.38	71.59	74.92	68.55	38.75
Minsk	75.79	77.24	80.24	74.46	42.18	80.44	83.07	77.96	62.00	69.68	72.26	67.27	41.25
In-House*	59.24	89.69	89.80	89.58	76.39	88.03	88.10	87.96	81.69	–	–	–	–

Table 3: Results of the gold track (marked ✧), open track (marked *) and closed track (unmarked) submissions for the English in-domain (top) and out-of-domain (bottom) data. For each system, the second column ($\overline{\text{LF}}$) indicates the averaged LF score across all representations, used to rank the systems. The best *closed track* scores are highlighted in italices.

	LF	LP	LR	PF
Peking	*83.43*	84.75	82.15	66.09
Riga	82.47	83.12	81.84	66.05
Lisbon	82.02	83.81	80.31	66.05
Turku*	79.64	80.81	78.51	62.04
Minsk	77.68	79.27	76.15	58.23

	LF	LP	LR	PF
Lisbon	*79.33*	83.52	75.54	55.91
Peking	78.45	83.61	73.89	55.36
Riga	75.34	78.77	72.19	50.90
Turku*	75.30	77.53	73.20	54.26

	LF	LP	LR	PF
Peking	*64.37*	69.41	60.02	48.82
Turku*	63.70	65.11	62.35	51.04
Lisbon	63.50	67.94	59.61	43.10
Riga	61.32	64.50	58.44	44.34

Table 4: Results of the open (Turku) and closed (other teams) tracks for the Chinese in-domain (left) and Czech in- (center) and out-of-domain (right) data. The systems are ranked according to their LF scores.

pretation, a semantic frame is comprised of a complete predication combined with the frame (or sense) identifier of its predicate. Both complete-predicate and semantic-frame evaluation are restricted to predicates corresponding to verbal parts of speech (as determined by the gold-standard part of speech), and semantic frames are further restricted to those target representations for which frame or sense information is available in our data (English DM and PSD). As with the other metrics, we score precision, recall, and F_1, which we abbreviate as PP, PR, and PF for complete predications, and FP, FR, and FF for semantic frames.

Closed vs. Open vs. Gold Tracks Much like in 2014, the task distinguished a *closed* track and an *open* track, where systems in the closed track could only be trained on the gold-standard semantic dependencies distributed for the task. Systems in the open track, on the other hand, could use additional resources, such as a syntactic parser, for example—provided that they make sure to not use any tools or resources that encompass knowledge of the gold-standard syntactic or semantic analyses of the SDP 2015 test data.[11] To simplify participation in the open track, the organizers prepared ready-to-use 'companion' syntactic analyses, sentence- and token-aligned to the SDP data, in the form of Stanford Basic syntactic dependencies (de Marneffe et al., 2006) produced by the parser of Bohnet and Nivre (2012).

Finally, to more directly gauge the the contributions of syntactic structure on the semantic dependency parsing problem, an idealized *gold* track was introduced in SDP 2015. For this track, gold-standard syntactic companion files were provided in a varity of formats, viz. (a) Stanford Basic dependencies, derived from the PTB, (b) HPSG syntactic dependencies in the form called DM by Ivanova et al. (2012), derived from DeepBank, and (c) HPSG syntactic dependencies derived from the Enju Treebank.

6 Submissions and Results

From almost 40 teams who had registered for the task, twelve teams obtained the test data, and test runs were submitted for six systems—including one 'inofficial' submission by a sub-set of the task organizers (Miyao et al., 2014). Each team submitted up to two test runs per track. In total, there were seven runs submitted to the English closed track, five to the open track and two to the gold track; seven runs were submitted to the Chinese closed track, two to the open track; and five runs submitted to the Czech closed track, two to the open track. One team submitted only to the open and gold tracks, three teams submitted only to the closed track, one team submitted to open and closed tracks in English but only to the closed tracks in the other two languages. The main results are summarized and ranked in Tables 3 and 4. The ranking is based on the average $\overline{\text{LF}}$ score across all three target representations. Besides LF, LP and LR we also indicate the F_1 score of prediction of semantic frames (FF), or, where frame (or sense) identifiers are not available, of complete predications (PF). In cases where a team submitted two runs to a track, only the highest-ranked score is included in the table.

In the English closed track, the average LF scores across target representations range from 85.33 to 80.74. Comparing the results for different target representations, the average LF scores across systems are 89.13 for PAS, 87.09 for DM, and 74.24 for PSD. The scores for semantic frames show a much larger variation across representations and systems.[12]

The Lisbon team is the only one that submitted to both the open and the closed tracks; with the additional resources allowed in the open track, they were able to improve over all closed-track submissions. Similarly, the perfect Stanford dependencies in the gold track helped the Turku team a lot in PAS and somewhat in DM and PSD; interestingly, they did not obtain the best results in the latter two representations, but their cross-representation average was still the best. The In-House system is ranked low because its submission was incomplete (no of-the-shelf parser for PSD being available); however, for DM and PAS they yielded the best open-track scores.

We see very similar trends for the out-of-domain data, though the scores are a few points lower.

Chinese PAS seems to be more difficult than English (cross-system average LF being 81.05, as opposed to English 90.07). The Czech and English in-domain data are actually parallel translations and the Czech PSD average LF is slightly higher (77.11, as opposed to English 74.90). The Turku open-track system shined in the Czech out-of-domain data, presumably because the additional dependency parser they used was trained on data from the target domain.

7 Overview of Approaches

Table 5 shows a summary of the tracks in which each submitted system participated, and Table 6 shows an overview of approaches and additionally used resources. All the teams except In-House submitted results for cross-lingual data (Czech and Chinese). Teams except Lisbon also tackled with predicate disambiguation. Only Turku participated in the Gold track.

The submitted teams explored a variety of approaches. Riga and Peking relied on the graph-to-tree transformation of Du et al. (2014) as a basis. This method converts semantic dependency graphs into tree structures. Training data of semantic dependency

[11] This restriction implies that typical off-the-shelf syntactic parsers have to be re-trained, as many data-driven parsers for English include WSJ Section 21 in their default training data.

[12] Please see the task web page at the address indicated above for full labeled and unlabeled scores.

Team	Closed	Open	Cross-Lingual	Predicate Disambiguation	Gold
In-House		✓		✓	
Lisbon	✓	✓	✓		
Minsk	✓		✓	✓	
Peking	✓		✓	✓	
Riga	✓		✓	✓	
Turku		✓	✓	✓	✓

Table 5: Summary of tracks in which submitted systems participated

Team	Approach	Resources
In-House	grammar-based parsing (Miyao et al., 2014)	ERG & Enju
Lisbon	graph parsing with dual decomposition (Martins & Almeida, 2014)	companion
Minsk	transition-based dependency graph parsing in the spirit of Titov et al. (2009)	—
Peking	(Du et al., 2014) extended with weighted tree approximation, parser ensemble	—
Riga	(Du et al., 2014)'s graph-to-tree transformation, Mate, C6.0, parser ensemble	—
Turku	sequence labeling for argument detection for each predicate, SVM classifiers for top node recognition and sense prediction	companion

Table 6: Overview of approaches and additional resources used (if any).

graphs are converted into tree structures, and well-established parsing methods for tree structures are applied to converted structures. In run-time, the tree parser is applied, and predicted trees are converted back into graph structures. Labels of tree edges encode additional information to recover original graph structures. This idea was applied in Du et al. (2014) and contributed to their best-performing system in the 2014 SDP task.

In addition to applying the Mate parser to the tree-transformed data of Du et al. (2014), Riga developed a high-precision but low-recall semantic parser. This method applies a decision tree classifier (C6.0) to edge detection. C6.0 learns patterns of semantic dependencies, which means it outputs highly reliable prediction when a learned pattern applies, while in most cases it cannot produce any predictions. These two types of parsers are finally combined by parser ensemble. They also applied C6.0 to frame (or sense) label prediction for DM and PSD. Graph parsing and frame prediction are performed independently.

Peking proposed a novel method for graph-to-tree transformation, namely weighted tree approximation. The intuition behind this method is that the core part of graph-to-tree transformation is the extraction of an essential tree-forming subset of edges from semantic dependency graphs, but it is not trivial to determine a reasonable subset. Therefore, the idea of weighted tree approximation is to define an edge score to quantify importance of each edge, and extract tree-forming edges that maximizes the sum of edge scores globally. After defining edge scores, tree-forming edges with optimal scores can be extracted by applying decoding methods like maximum spanning tree and the Eisner algorithm. They applied this method as well as the previous method proposed in Du et al. (2014) with several variations on encoding edge labels, finally obtaining nine tree parsers. In the final submission, outputs from these parsers are combined by the parser ensemble technique. For predicate disambiguation, they independently applied a sequence labeling technique.

Turku took a completely different approach. They consider each predicate separately, and apply sequence labeling for each predicate individually, to recognize arguments of the target predicate. That is, the task is reduced to assign each word an argument tag (e.g. ARG1) or a negative 'pseudo-'label indicating it is not an argument of the target predicate. Outputs from sequence labeling for each predicate are combined to derive final semantic dependencies. Top node recognition and frame label prediction are performed separately. Turku is the only team who participated in the Gold track; they used gold syntactic dependencies as features for sequence labeling.

Lisbon and In-House applied their parsers from

SDP 2014 without substantive changes. The Lisbon parser (*TurboSemanticParser*) computes globally optimal semantic dependencies using rich second order features on semantic dependencies, such as siblings and grand parents. This optimization is impractical in general, but they achieve tractable parsing time by applying dual decomposition. In-House uses deep parsers with specifically developed linguistically motivated grammars, namely the LinGO English Resource Grammar and the Enju grammar. As described in Section 2, these same grammars were used for deriving the training and test data sets of this task, i.e. these components of the In-House ensemble exclusively support the DM and PAS target representations, respectively.

Peking and Lisbon tend to attain high scores in their participated tracks in LF. Riga ranked third in LF in the closed tracks (both in-domain and out-of-domain), while it achieved higher scores than others in FF. This might be due to high-precision rules obtained by their model, although this does not apply in the cross-lingual track. The Turku results in the gold track achieved considerably higher scores, which indicate that better syntactic parsing will help improve semantic dependency parsing.[13] It is difficult to describe a tendency in the out-of-domain track; all the systems scree three to five points lower scores than the in-domain track, indicating that domain variation is still a significant challenge in semantic dependency parsing.

8 Conclusion

We have described the motivation, design, and outcomes of the SDP 2015 task on semantic dependency parsing, i.e. retrieving bi-lexical predicate–argument relations between all content words within an English sentence. We have converted to a common format three existing annotations (DM, PAS, and PSD) over the same text and have put this to use in training and testing data-driven semantic dependency parsers. In contrast to SDP 2014 the task was extended by cross-domain testing and evaluation at the level of 'complete' predications and semantic frame (or sense) disambiguation. Furthermore, we provided comparable annotations of Czech and Chinese texts to enable cross-linguistic comparison. To start further probing of the role of syntax in the recovery of predicate–argument relations, we added a third (idealized) 'gold' track, where syntactic dependencies are provided directly from available syntactic annotations of the underlying treebanks.

[13]The SDP 2014 and 2015 task setups, however, somewhat artificially constrain the possible contributions of syntactic analysis, as all training and testing data (even in the closed track) includes high-quality parts of speech and lemmata.

Acknowledgements

We are grateful to Angelina Ivanova for help in DM data preparation and contrastive analysis, to Željko Agić and Bernd Bohnet for consultation and assistance in preparing our companion parses, to the Linguistic Data Consortium (LDC) for support in distributing the SDP data to participants, as well as to Emily M. Bender and two anonymous reviewers for feedback on an earlier version of this manuscript. We warmly thank the general SemEval 2015 chairs, Preslav Nakov and Torsten Zesch, for always being role-model organizers, equipped with an outstanding balance of structure, flexibility, and community spirit. Data preparation was supported through the ABEL high-performance computing facilities at the University of Oslo, and we acknowledge the Scientific Computing staff at UiO, the Norwegian Metacenter for Computational Science, and the Norwegian taxpayers. Part of the work was supported by the grants 15-10472S, GP13-03351P and 15-20031S of the Czech Science Foundation, and by the infrastructural funding by the Ministry of Education, Youth and Sports of the Czech Republic (LM2010013).

References

Bejček, E., Hajičová, E., Hajič, J., Jínová, P., Kettnerová, V., Kolářová, V., ... Zikánová, Š. (2013). *Prague dependency treebank 3.0.* Retrieved from http://hdl.handle.net/11858/00-097C-0000-0023-1AAF-3

Bender, E. M., Flickinger, D., Oepen, S., Packard, W., & Copestake, A. (2015). Layers of interpretation. On grammar and compositionality. In *Proceedings of the 11th International Conference on Computational Semantics.* London, UK.

Bohnet, B., & Nivre, J. (2012). A transition-based system for joint part-of-speech tagging and labeled non-projective dependency parsing. In *Proceedings of the 2012 Joint Conference on Empirical Methods in Natural Language Processing and Conference on Natural Language Learning* (p. 1455 – 1465). Jeju Island, Korea.

Cinková, S. (2006). From PropBank to EngValLex. Adapting the PropBank lexicon to the valency theory of the Functional Generative Description. In *Proceedings of the 5th International Conference on Language Resources and Evaluation.* Genoa, Italy.

de Marneffe, M.-C., MacCartney, B., & Manning, C. D. (2006). Generating typed dependency parses from phrase structure parses. In *Proceedings of the 5th International Conference on Language Resources and Evaluation* (p. 449 – 454). Genoa, Italy.

Du, Y., Zhang, F., Sun, W., & Wan, X. (2014). Peking: Profiling syntactic tree parsing techniques for semantic graph parsing. In *Proceedings of the 8th international workshop on semantic evaluation (semeval 2014).*

Fares, M., Oepen, S., & Zhang, Y. (2013). Machine learning for high-quality tokenization. Replicating variable tokenization schemes. In *Computational linguistics and intelligent text processing* (p. 231 – 244). Springer.

Flickinger, D. (2000). On building a more efficient grammar by exploiting types. *Natural Language Engineering, 6 (1),* 15 – 28.

Flickinger, D., Zhang, Y., & Kordoni, V. (2012). DeepBank. A dynamically annotated treebank of the Wall Street Journal. In *Proceedings of the 11th International Workshop on Treebanks and Linguistic Theories* (p. 85 – 96). Lisbon, Portugal: Edições Colibri.

Francis, W. N., & Kučera, H. (1982). *Frequency analysis of English usage. Lexicon and grammar.* New York, USA: Houghton Mifflin.

Gildea, D., & Jurafsky, D. (2002). Automatic labeling of semantic roles. *Computational Linguistics, 28,* 245 – 288.

Grice, H. P. (1968). Utterer's meaning, sentence-meaning, and word-meaning. *Foundations of Language, 4*(3), 225 – 242.

Hajič, J., Hajičová, E., Panevová, J., Sgall, P., Bojar, O., Cinková, S., ... Žabokrtský, Z. (2012). Announcing Prague Czech-English Dependency Treebank 2.0. In *Proceedings of the 8th International Conference on Language Resources and Evaluation* (p. 3153 – 3160). Istanbul, Turkey.

Ivanova, A., Oepen, S., Øvrelid, L., & Flickinger, D. (2012). Who did what to whom? A contrastive study of syntacto-semantic dependencies. In *Proceedings of the Sixth Linguistic Annotation Workshop* (p. 2 – 11). Jeju, Republic of Korea.

Kate, R. J., & Wong, Y. W. (2010). Semantic parsing. The task, the state of the art and the future. In *Tutorial abstracts of the 20th Meeting of the Association for Computational Linguistics* (p. 6). Uppsala, Sweden.

Marcus, M., Santorini, B., & Marcinkiewicz, M. A. (1993). Building a large annotated corpora of English. The Penn Treebank. *Computational Linguistics, 19,* 313 – 330.

Martins, A. F. T., & Almeida, M. S. C. (2014). Priberam: A turbo semantic parser with second order features. In *In proceedings of the 8th international workshop on semantic evaluation (semeval 2014).*

Mel'čuk, I. (1988). *Dependency syntax. Theory and practice.* Albany, NY, USA: SUNY Press.

Meyers, A., Reeves, R., Macleod, C., Szekely, R., Zielinska, V., Young, B., & Grishman, R. (2004). Annotating noun argument structure for NomBank. In *Proceedings of the 4th International Conference on Language Resources and Evaluation* (p. 803 – 806). Lisbon, Portugal.

Miyao, Y. (2006). *From linguistic theory to syntactic analysis. Corpus-oriented grammar development and feature forest model.* Unpublished doctoral dissertation, University of Tokyo, Tokyo, Japan.

Miyao, Y., Oepen, S., & Zeman, D. (2014). In-House. An ensemble of pre-existing off-the-shelf parsers. In *Proceedings of the 8th International Workshop on Semantic*

Evaluation (p. 63 – 72). Dublin, Ireland.

Nakov, P. (2013). On the interpretation of noun compounds: Syntax, semantics, and entailment. *Natural Language Engineering*, *19*(3), 291 – 330.

Oepen, S., Kuhlmann, M., Miyao, Y., Zeman, D., Flickinger, D., Hajič, J., ... Zhang, Y. (2014). SemEval 2014 Task 8. Broad-coverage semantic dependency parsing. In *Proceedings of the 8th International Workshop on Semantic Evaluation.* Dublin, Ireland.

Palmer, M., Gildea, D., & Kingsbury, P. (2005). The Proposition Bank. A corpus annotated with semantic roles. *Computational Linguistics*, *31*(1), 71 – 106.

Quine, W. V. O. (1960). *Word and object.* Cambridge, MA, USA: MIT Press.

Titov, I., Henderson, J., Merlo, P., & Musillo, G. (2009). Online graph planarisation for synchronous parsing of semantic and syntactic dependencies. In *Proceedings of the 21st International Joint Conference on Artificial Intelligence.* Pasadena, CA, USA.

Vadas, D., & Curran, J. (2007). Adding Noun Phrase Structure to the Penn Treebank. In *Proceedings of the 45th Meeting of the Association for Computational Linguistics* (p. 240 – 247). Prague, Czech Republic.

Xue, N., Xia, F., Chiou, F.-D., & Palmer, M. (2005). The Penn Chinese TreeBank. Phrase structure annotation of a large corpus. *Natural Language Engineering*, *11*, 207 – 238.

Peking: Building Semantic Dependency Graphs with a Hybrid Parser

Yantao Du, Fan Zhang, Xun Zhang, Weiwei Sun* and **Xiaojun Wan**
Institute of Computer Science and Technology, Peking University
The MOE Key Laboratory of Computational Linguistics, Peking University
`{duyantao,zhangxunah,ws,wanxiaojun}@pku.edu.cn`
`zhangf717@gmail.com`

Abstract

This paper is a description of our system for SemEval-2015 Task 18: Broad-Coverage Semantic Dependency Parsing. We implement a hybrid parser which benefits from both transition-based and graph-based parsing approaches. In particular, the tree approximation method is explored to take advantage of well-studied tree parsing techniques. Evaluation on multilingual data sets demonstrates that considerably good semantic analysis can be automatically built by applying state-of-the-art data-driven parsing techniques.

1 Introduction

Dependency grammar is a long-standing tradition that determines syntacto-semantic structures on the basis of word-to-word connections. It names a family of approaches to linguistic analysis that all share a commitment to typed relations between ordered pairs of words. Partially due to the powerful expressiveness of bi-lexical dependency structures, the corresponding parsing problem has been widely studied especially in the last decade. The majority of these studies, however, only focus on tree-structured representations. Beyond tree-shaped structures, SemEval-2014 Task 8 (Oepen et al., 2014) seeked to stimulate the dependency parsing community to move towards more general graph processing. Quite a number of teams all over the world participated in this shared task, which suggests a growing community interest in parsing into graph-shaped dependency representations.

SemEval-2015 Task 18 is a subsequent task of SemEval-2014 Task 8. Following several well-established syntactic theories, this task proposes using graphs to represent semantics and provides high-quality annotations for three typologically different languages. We have developed a system, dubbed DZSW14 (Du et al., 2014) for the task last year. The system employed a hybrid architecture which benefits from both transition-based and graph-based parsing approaches. Evaluation on multiple English data sets provided by SemEval-2014 indicated that DZSW14 is able to obtain high-quality parsing results. Following the key idea to employ heterogeneous models to enhance hybrid parsing, we extend DZSW14 by developing more tree approximation models, namely the weighted tree approximation models. Evaluation on multilingual data sets provided by this year's task confirms the effectiveness of the techniques we have studied.

In this paper, we first give an introduction of the architecture of the baseline system DZSW14. Then we demonstrate the weighted tree approximation models. Finally we show the experiment results on SemEval-2015 Task 18. The tree approximation system can be downloaded at `http://www.icst.pku.edu.cn/lcwm/grass`.

2 Baseline System: DZSW14

Our system is based on the system we constructed for SemEval-2014 Task 8. In this section we present a brief overview of its architecture. Refer to (Du et al., 2014) for more information.

Inspired by the research on discriminative dependency tree parsing, DZSW14 employed a hybrid parsing architecture. DZSW14 explored two

*Email correspondence.

kinds of heterogeneous approaches: transition-based and tree approximation approaches. The transition-based model use transitions on configurations to obtain graph parses, while the tree approximation model transform graphs into trees for training and test. To further combine the complementary prediction power, DZWS14 applied a voting-based ensemble method.

2.1 Transition-Based Models

Transition-based models consist of transitions and configurations that can be manipulated by the transitions. The configurations generally encode the information of the current parsing state, especially including partial parsing results, and the transitions can be applied to a configuration, turning it into a new one. When the system reaches any acceptable configuration, a coherent semantic graph is also successfully built. The key to the success of building transition-based parsers is to train good classifiers to approximate transition oracles. DZSW14 implements 5 different transition systems for graph parsing. Experiments from last year's evaluation suggest that this method can be applied to build considerably good parsers for more general linguistic graphs.

2.2 Tree Approximation Models

The core of tree approximation is transformations between graphs and trees. At the training time, we convert the dependency graphs from the training data into dependency trees, and train second-order arc-factored models[1] (Bohnet, 2010). At the test phase, we parse sentences using this tree parser, and convert the output trees back into semantic graphs. In DZSW14, We develop several different methods to convert a semantic graph into a tree. The main idea is to apply graph traversal algorithms to convert a directed graph to a directed tree. During the traversal, we may lose or modify some dependency relations in order to make a tree.

2.3 Experience from DZSW14

From a lot of experiments on DZSW14, we learned several lessons as follows.

- Overall, the tree approximation models perform better than the transition-based models.
- The outputs of the different models exhibit significant diversity.
- The model ensemble is quite effective, resulting in a boost in performance.

This motivates us to explore more heterogeneous tree approximation models for this year's evaluation.

3 Weighted Tree Approximation Models

In our system for SemEval-2015, we develop more tree approximation models for model ensemble. We call the graph-to-tree conversions in DZSW14 unweighted conversions since every edge in the graph are treated equally. In this section, we demonstrate weighted conversions which assign weights for different edges.

3.1 Weighted Conversion

Given a graph $G = \langle V, E \rangle$, the edge selection in the unweighted conversion is locally decided by its current traversal state. In the weighted conversion, we take the importance of different edges into account and try to globally improve the integrity with respect to the losing edges. For example, in the top of Figure 1, the undirected edges (Ward, was), (Ward, relieved), (was, relieved) form a cycle. Only two edges can be kept by the converted tree T. It allows us to decide which edges to keep according to the sum of the weights of them.

Let $x \rightarrow_t y$ denote edges in the tree, and $x \rightarrow_g y$ edges in the graph. We assign each possible edge $x \rightarrow_t y$ a heuristic value $\omega(x, y)$, and intend to obtain a tree with maximum weight . More formally, the result $T^{\max} = (V, E_t^{\max})$ contains the maximum sum of values of edges:

$$T^{\max} = \arg\max_{T=(V,E_t)} \sum_{(x,y)\in E_t} \omega(x, y)$$

3.2 Weight

We define weight $\omega(x, y)$ as follows, where I is the indicator function:

- $\omega(x, y) = A(x, y) + B(x, y) + C(x, y)$: The weight is separate into 3 parts.

[1]The mate parser (`code.google.com/p/mate-tools/`) is used.

- $A(x, y) = I_{x \to y \in E \vee y \to x \in E}(x, y) \times a$: a is the weight for the existing edge on graph ignoring direction.

- $B(x, y) = I_{x \to y \in E}(x, y) \times b$: b is the weight for the directed edge in the graph.

- $C(x, y) = n - |x - y|$: This is to value the importance of edges where n is the length of sentence. We consider edges linking closer words more important because they are generally easier to be predicted.

- $a \gg b \gg n$ or $a > b \times n > n \times n$: First the transformed tree should contain the original edges in G as many as possible. Then we need to consider the quantity of edges with correct direction in G. And the distance between nodes in the sentence is in the last place.

3.3 Decoding

After the edges are weighted, the core decoding task for graph transformation can be solved by maximum spanning tree (MST) algorithms, where the search space $\mathcal{T}$ consists of all projective and non-projective dependency trees. To transform a graph to a projective tree, we use Eisner's algorithm, and for non-projective, we use Chu-Liu-Edmonds algorithm.

3.4 Adding Labels

Now we get the MST $T^{\max}(V, E_t^{\max})$. For each $(x, y) \in E_t^{\max}$, we assign a new label to (x, y) as follows,

Case 1: $x \to_g y$, add the original label in $G(V, E)$ to the new edge $x \to_t y$;

Case 2: $y \to_g x$, add the original label with symbol $\tilde{\text{R}}$ to $x \to_t y$;

Case 3: $x \to_g y \wedge y \to_g x$, add label as Case 1;

Case 4: $x \nrightarrow_g y \wedge y \nrightarrow x$, add label *None* to the edge $x \to_t y$.

To improve the coverage of original edges, a variant model with modified labels in trees to help encode more edges in graphs.Suppose that $x \to y$ is a lost edge which is not on the new dependency tree but is on the original dependency graph. The statistic shows the structure of a majority of lost edges are in one of three different types:

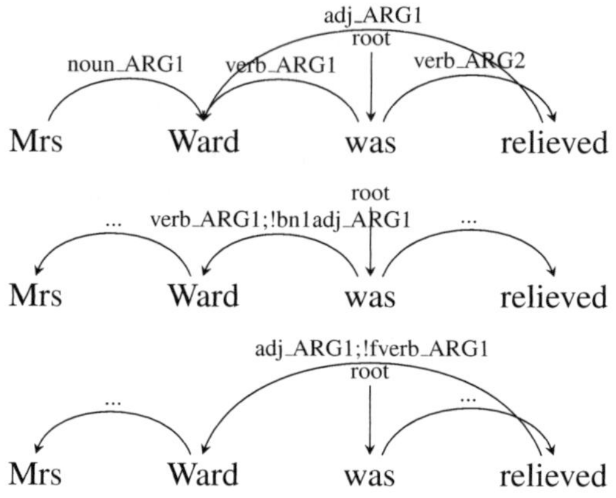

Figure 1: One dependency graph and two possible dependency trees after converting.

1. The nodes are siblings.
2. One is the grandparent of the other.
3. One is the great-grandparent of the other.

The conversions can be enhanced by adding more symbols to labels to indicate lost edges if they are of the three types above. The method is to append semicolon (;) and exclamation mark (!) to some degree and then add new label with information of lost edge directly. If $x \to_g y$ is not in the converted tree and its structure is of one of aforementioned types, we change the label connecting node y and its parent node with assumption that y is not higher than x in the dependency tree.

- x is great-grandparent node of y: New label is the label of $x \to_g y$ following the symbol 'g'.

- x is grandparent node of y: New label is the label of $x \to_g y$ following the symbol 'f'.

- x and y are siblings: Let z be the two nodes' parent. We sort all the z's children by the order of position in the sentence And we use an integer P to indicate the position. If the two siblings are on the same side of z, P will be the distance of the two siblings' positions in the sorted children sequence and extra symbol will be 'y'. If the two siblings are on the different sides of z, extra symbol will be 'n' and P will be x's rank in the same side's nodes in the sorted children sequence. New label is the symbol 'b' with extra symbol followed and the label of $x \rightarrow_g y$.

If node y is higher than x in the dependency tree, we would add symbol $\tilde{\mathrm{R}}$ to indicate the additional edge is reversed. Figure 1 is an example of a converted tree.

4 Model Ensemble

We select 9 tree approximation models from DZSW14, and propose 4 new weighted models ({projective, non-projective} $\times$ {original, label-modification-variant}). Together with the transition models, we have to combine the outputs of them into one. We use a simple voter to combine the outputs just like in DZSW14. For each pair of words of a sentence, we count the number of the models that give positive predictions. If the number is greater than a threshold, we put this arc to the final graph, and label the arc with the most common label of what the models give.

Furthermore, we find that the performance of the tree approximation models are better than the transition based models, so we assign weights for individual models too. Then instead of just counting, we sum the weights of the models that give positive predictions. The tree approximation models are assigned higher weights.

5 Sense Labeling

In this task, two representations DM and PSD of English require to label the words additional sense label. We develop a sequence labeler for this requirement. The sequence labeler is based on a second-order linear-chain global linear model and utilize the perceptron algorithm for parameter estimation. To accelerate processing, we apply a Viterbi decoder but constrain it with beam search. In particular, the number of cells in the dynamic programming table for each word is bounded by a fixed beam size. This decoder can be also viewed as a beam decoder with state-merging.

The representation DM can be labeled directly. However due to the large amount of different senses in representation PSD, it is difficult to label senses without preprocessing. We finally decide to filter out the rare senses that have a frequency lower than 10, substituting "unknown" for them.

Algorithm	DM_{en}	PAS_{en}	PSD_{en}	PAS_{cs}	PSD_{cz}
PROJ	4.24	6.31	8.89	9.36	3.56
NON-PROJ	2.31	6.16	8.42	9.04	2.81
PROJ′	2.30	1.85	2.73	3.26	2.21
NON-PROJ′	0.60	1.62	2.33	3.07	1.55

Table 1: Edge loss of conversion algorithms (%).

Domain	Format	LP	LR	LF	LM
id	DM_{en}	0.9093	0.8732	0.8909	0.2702
	PAS_{en}	0.9290	0.8967	0.9126	0.3028
	PSD_{en}	0.7860	0.7293	0.7566	0.0872
	PAS_{cs}	0.8191	0.7434	0.7794	0.1144
	PSD_{cz}	0.8475	0.8215	0.8343	0.2809
ood	DM_{en}	0.8429	0.7953	0.8184	0.2499
	PAS_{en}	0.8947	0.8510	0.8723	0.3012
	PSD_{en}	0.7736	0.6961	0.7328	0.1790
	PAS_{cs}	0.6941	0.6002	0.6437	0.1146

Table 2: Final results of the ensembled model.

6 Experiments

We participated in the closed track. The tree approximation algorithms may cause some edge loss, and the statistics for the weighted conversions are shown in Table 1. We can see that all the algorithms cause edge loss, and edge loss of the variants is much lower. In addition, non-projective tree conversions cause less loss compared to projective tree conversions. Edge loss may result in a lower recall and higher precision, but we can tune the final results during model ensemble.

The final results given by the organizers are shown in Table 2. Here we only give the labeled score.

7 Conclusion

Based on our previous system DZSW14, we developed a hybrid system for SemEval-2015 Task 18. Our new system extends DZSW14 by providing several more tree approximation models. The final result shows that our system as well as our new models are effective.

Acknowledgement

The work was supported by NSFC (61300064, 61170166 and 61331011) and National High-Tech R&D Program (2012AA011101).

References

Bernd Bohnet. 2010. Top accuracy and fast dependency parsing is not a contradiction. In *Proceedings of the 23rd International Conference on Computational Linguistics (Coling 2010)*, pages 89–97, Beijing, China, August. Coling 2010 Organizing Committee.

Yantao Du, Fan Zhang, Weiwei Sun, and Xiaojun Wan. 2014. Peking: Profiling syntactic tree parsing techniques for semantic graph parsing. In *Proceedings of the 8th International Workshop on Semantic Evaluation (SemEval 2014)*.

Stephan Oepen, Marco Kuhlmann, Yusuke Miyao, Daniel Zeman, Dan Flickinger, Jan Hajič, Angelina Ivanova, and Yi Zhang. 2014. SemEval 2014 Task 8: Broad-coverage semantic dependency parsing. In *Proceedings of the 8th International Workshop on Semantic Evaluation*, Dublin, Ireland.

USAAR-WLV: Hypernym Generation with Deep Neural Nets

Liling Tan, Rohit Gupta$^{\alpha}$ and Josef van Genabith$^{\beta}$
Universität des Saarlandes / Campus A2.2, Saarbrücken, Germany
University of Wolverhampton$^{\alpha}$ / Wulfruna Street, Wolverhampton, UK
Deutsches Forschungszentrum für Knstliche Intelligenz$^{\beta}$ /
Stuhlsatzenhausweg, Saarbrücken, Germany
alvations@gmail.com, r.gupta@wlv.ac.uk,
josef.van_genabith@dfki.de

Abstract

This paper describes the USAAR-WLV taxonomy induction system that participated in the Taxonomy Extraction Evaluation task of SemEval-2015. We extend prior work on using vector space word embedding models for hypernym-hyponym extraction by simplifying the means to extract a projection matrix that transforms any hyponym to its hypernym. This is done by making use of function words, which are usually overlooked in vector space approaches to NLP. Our system performs best in the chemical domain and has achieved competitive results in the overall evaluations.

1 Introduction

Traditionally, broad-coverage semantic taxonomies such as CYC (Lenat, 1995) and WordNet ontology (Miller, 1995) have been manually created with much effort and yet they suffer from coverage sparsity. This motivated the move towards unsupervised approaches to extract structured relational knowledge from texts (Lin and Pantel, 2001; Snow et al., 2006; Velardi et al., 2013).[1]

Previous work in taxonomy extraction focused on rule-based, clustering and graph-based approaches. Although vector space approaches are popular in current NLP researches, ontology induction studies have yet to catch on the frenzy. Fu et al. (2014) proposed a vector space approach to hypernym-hyponym identification using word embeddings that trains a projection matrix[2] that converts a hyponym vector to its hypernym. However, their approach requires an existing hypernym-hyponym pairs for training before discovering new pairs.

Our system submitted to the SemEval-2015 taxonomy building task is most similar to the approach by Fu et al. (2014) in using word embeddings projections to identify hypernym-hyponym pairs. As opposed to previous method our method does not requires prior taxonomical knowledge.

Instead of training a projection matrix, we capitalize on the fact that hypernym-hyponym pair often occurs in a sentence with an *'is a'* phrase, e.g. *"The goldfish (Carassius auratus auratus) is a freshwater fish"*.[3] Intuitively, if we single-tokenize the *'is a'* phrase prior to training a vector space, we can make use of the vector that represents the phrase in capturing a hypernym-hyponym pair as such the multiplication of v(`goldfish`) and v(`is-a`) will be similar to the cross product v(`fish`) (v(`goldfish`) $\times v$(`is-a`) $\approx v$(`fish`)).

There is little or no previous work that manipulates non-content word vectors in vector space models studies for natural language processing. Often, non-content words[4] were implicitly incorporated into the vector space models by means of syntactic frames (Sarmento et al., 2009) or syntactic parses (Thater et al., 2010).

Our main contribution for ontological induction

[1]For the rest of the paper, *taxonomy* and *ontology* will be used interchangeably to refer to a hierarchically structure that organizes a list of concepts.

[2]In this case, the projection matrix is a vector space feature function.

[3]From http://en.wikipedia.org/wiki/Goldfish.

[4]Words that are not noun (entities/arguments), verbs (predicates), adjectives or adverbs (adjuncts).

using vector space models are primarily (i) the use of non-content word vectors and (ii) simplifying a previously complex process of learning a hypernym-hyponym transition matrix. The implementation of our ontological induction approach is open-sourced and available on our GitHub repository.[5]

1.1 Task Definition

Similar to Fountain and Lapata (2012), the SemEval-2015 Taxonomy Extraction Evaluation (TaxEval) task addresses taxonomy learning without the term discovery step, i.e. the terms for which to create the taxonomy are given (Bordea et al., 2015). The focus is on creating the hypernym-hyponym relations.

In the TaxEval task, taxonomies are evaluated through comparison with gold standard taxonomies. There is no training corpus provided by the organisers of the task and the participating systems are to generate hyper-hyponyms pairs using a list of terms from four different domains, viz. chemicals, equipment, food and science.

The gold standards used in evaluation are the *ChEBI ontology* for the chemical domain (Degtyarenko et al., 2008), the *Material Handling Equipment taxonomy*[6] for the equipment domain, the Go*ogle product taxonomy*[7] for the food domain and the *Taxonomy of Fields and their Different Sub-fields*[8] for the science domain. In addition, all four domains are also evaluated against the sub-hierarchies from the WordNet ontology that subsumes the Suggested Upper Merged Ontology (Pease et al., 2002).

2 Related Work

There are a variety of methods used in taxonomy induction. They can be broadly categorized as (i) pattern/rule based, (ii) clustering based, (iii) graph based and (iv) vector space approaches.

[5]https://github.com/alvations/USAAR-SemEval-2015/tree/master/task17-USAAR-WLV

[6]http://www.ise.ncsu.edu/kay/mhetax/index.htm

[7]http://www.google.com/basepages/producttype/taxonomy.en-US.txt

[8]http://sites.nationalacademies.org/PGA/Resdoc/PGA_044522

2.1 Pattern/Rule Based Approaches

Hearst (1992) first introduced ontology learning by exploiting lexico-syntactic patterns that explicitly links a hypernym to its hyponym, e.g. "*X and other Ys*" and "*Ys such as X*". These patterns could be manually constructed (Berland and Charniak, 1999; Kozareva et al., 2008) or automatically bootstrapped (Girju, 2003).

These methods rely on surface-level patterns and incorrect items are frequently extracted because of parsing errors, polysemy, idiomatic expressions, etc.

2.2 Clustering Approaches

Clustering based approaches are mostly used to discover hypernym (is-a) and synonym (is-like) relations. For instance, to induce synonyms, Lin (1998) clustered words based on the amount of information needed to state the commonality between two words.[9]

Contrary to most bottom-up clustering approaches for taxonomy induction (Caraballo, 2001; Lin, 1998), Pantel and Ravichandran (2004) introduced a top-down approach, assigning the hypernyms to clusters using co-occurrence statistics and then pruning the cluster by recalculating the pairwise similarity between every hyponym pair within the cluster.

2.3 Graph-based Approaches

In graph theory (Biggs et al., 1976), similar ideas are conceived with a different jargon. In graph notation, ***nodes/vertices*** form the atom units of the graph and nodes are connected by directed ***edges***. A *graph*, unlike an ontology, regards the hierarchical structure of a taxonomy as a by-product of the individual pairs of *nodes* connected by a directed *edges*. In this regard, a single *root* node is not guaranteed and to produce a tree-like structure.

Disregarding the overall hierarchical structure, the crux of graph induction focuses on the different techniques of edge weighting between individual node pairs and graph pruning or edge collapsing (Kozareva and Hovy, 2010; Navigli et al., 2011; Fountain and Lapata, 2012; Tuan et al., 2014).

[9]Commonly known as Lin information content measure.

2.4 Vector Space Approaches

Semantic knowledge can be thought of as a two-dimensional vector space where each word is represented as a point and semantic association is indicated by word proximity. The vector space representation for each word is constructed from the distribution of words across context, such that words with similar meaning are found close to each other in the space (Mitchell and Lapata, 2010; Tan, 2013).

Although vector space models have been used widely in other NLP tasks, ontology/taxonomy inducing using vector space models has not been popular. It is only since the recent advancement in neural nets and word embeddings that vector space models are gaining ground for ontology induction and relation extraction (Saxe et al., 2013; Khashabi, 2013).

3 Methodology

This section provides a brief overview of our system's approach to taxonomy induction. The full system is released as open-source and contains documentation with additional implementation details.[10]

3.1 Projecting a Hyponym to its Hypernym with Transition Matrix

Fu et al. (2014) discovered that hypernym-hyponyms pairs have similar semantic properties as the linguistics regularities discussed in Mikolov et al. (2013b). For instance: v`(shrimp)`-v`(prawn)` $\approx$ v`(fish)`-v`(goldfish)`.

Intuitively, the assumption is that all words can be projected to their hypernyms based on a transition matrix. That is, given a word x and its hypernym y, a transition matrix Φ exists such that $y = \Phi x$, e.g. v`(goldfish)` $= \Phi \times v$`(fish)`.

Fu et al. proposed two projection approaches to identify hypernym-hyponym pairs, (i) uniform linear projection where Φ is the same for all words and Φ is learnt by minimizing the mean squared error of $||\Phi x\text{-}y||$ across all word-pairs (i.e. a domain independent Φ) and (ii) piecewise linear projection that learns a separate projection for different word clusters (i.e. a domain dependent Φ, where a taxonomy's domain is bounded by its terms' cluster(s)). In both projections, hypernym-hyponym pairs are required to train the transition matrix Φ.

3.2 Inducing a Hypernym with *is-a* Vector

Instead of learning a supervised transition matrix Φ, we propose a simpler unsupervised approach where we learn a vector for the phrase "*is-a*". We single-tokenize the adjacent "is" and "a" tokens and learn the word embeddings with *is-a* forming part of the vocabulary in the input matrix.

Effectively, we hypothesize that Φ can be replaced by the "*is-a*" vector. To achieve the piecewise projection effects of Φ, we trained a different deep neural net model for each TaxEval domain and assume that the "*is-a*" scales automatically across domains. For instance, the multiplication of the v`(tiramisu)` and the $v(\texttt{is-a}_{food})$ vectors yields a proxy vector and we consider the top ten word vectors that are most similar to this proxy vector as the possible hypernyms, i.e. $v(\texttt{tiramisu}) \times v(\texttt{is-a}_{food}) \approx v(\texttt{cake})$.

4 Experimental Setup

4.1 Training Data

There is no specified training corpus released for the SemEval-2015 TaxEval task. To produce a domain specific corpus for each of the given domains in the task, we used the Wikipedia dump and preprocessed it using WikiExtractor[11] and then extracted documents that contain the terms for each domain individually.

We trained a skip-gram model phrasal word2vec neural net (Mikolov et al., 2013a) using gensim (Řehůřek and Sojka, 2010). The neural nets were trained for 100 epochs with a window size of 5 for all words in the corpus.[12]

4.2 Evaluation Metrics

For the TaxEval task, the multi-faceted evaluation scheme presented in Navigli (2013) was adopted to compare the overall structure of the taxonomy against a gold standard, with an approach used for comparing hierarchical clusters. The multi-faceted

[10] https://github.com/alvations/USAAR-SemEval-2015/blob/master/task17-USAAR-WLV/README.md

[11] We use the same Wikipedia dump to text extraction process from the SeedLing - Human Language Project (Emerson et al., 2014).

[12] i.e. words with minimum count of 1; other parameters set for the neural nets can be found on our GitHub repository.

	|V|	|E|	#c.c	cycles	#VC	%VC	#EC	%EC	:NE
Chemical	13785	30392	302	YES	13784	**0.7838**	2427	0.0977	1.1268
Equipment	337	548	28	YES	336	0.549	227	0.3691	0.5219
Food	1118	2692	23	YES	948	0.6092	428	0.2696	1.4265
Science	355	952	14	YES	354	0.7831	173	**0.3720**	1.6752
WN Chemical	1173	3107	31	YES	1172	**0.8675**	532	**0.3835**	1.8566
WN Equipment	354	547	43	YES	353	0.7431	149	0.3072	0.8206
WN Food	1200	3465	23	YES	1199	0.8068	549	0.3581	1.9021
WN Science	307	892	8	YES	306	0.7132	156	0.3537	1.6689

Table 1: Structural Measures and Comparison against Gold Standards for `USAAR-WLV`. The labels of the columns refer to no. of distinct vertices and edges in induced taxonomy (|**V**| and |**E**|), no. of connected components (**#c.c**), whether the taxonomy is a Directed Acyclic Graph (**cycles**), vertex and edge coverage, i.e. proportion of gold standard vertices and edges covered by system (**%VC** and **%EC**), no. of vertices and edges in common with gold standard (**#VC** and **#EC**) and ratio of novel edges (**:NE**).

	INRIASAC	LT3	NTNU	QASSIT	TALN-UPF	USAAR-WLV
Avg. F&M	0.3270	**0.4130**	0.0580	0.3880	0.2630	0.0770
Avg. Precision	0.1721	**0.3612**	0.1754	0.1563	0.0720	0.2014
Avg. Recall	0.4279	**0.6307**	0.2756	0.1588	0.1165	0.3139
Avg. F-Score	0.2427	**0.3886**	0.2075	0.1575	0.0798	0.2377
Avg. Precision of NE	0.4800	**0.5960**	0.3530	0.2470	0.1020	0.4200

Table 2: Averaged F&M Measure, Precision, Recall, F-score for All Systems Outputs when Compared to Gold Standard and Manually Evaluated Average Precision of Novel Edges.

evaluation scheme evaluates (i) the structural measures of the induced taxonomy (left columns of Table 1), (ii) the comparison against gold standard taxonomy (right columns of Table 1 and leftmost column of Table 2) and (iii) manual evaluation of novel edges precision (last row of Table 2).

Regarding the two types of automatic evaluation measures, the structural measures provides a gauge of the system's coverage and the ontology structural integrity, i.e. "tree-likeness" of the ontology produced by the hypernym-hyponym pairs, and the comparison against the gold standards gives an objective measure of the "human-likeness" of the system in producing a taxonomy that is similar to the manually-crafted taxonomy.

5 Results

Table 1 presents the evaluation scores for our system in the TaxEval task, the %VC and %EC scores summarize the performance of the system in replicating the gold standard taxonomies.

In terms of vertex coverage, our system performs best in the chemical and WordNet chemical domain. Regarding edge coverage, our system achieves highest coverage for the science domain and WordNet chemical domain. Having high edge and vertex coverage significantly lowers false positive rate when evaluating hypernym-hyponyms pairs with precision, recall and F-score.

We also note that the wikipedia corpus extracted that we used to induce the vectors lacks coverage for the food domain. In the other domains, we discovered all terms in the wikipedia corpus plus the domains' root hypernym (i.e. |**V**| = **#VC** + 1).

Table 2 presents the comparative results between the participating teams in the TaxEval task averaged over all domains. We performed reasonable well as compared to the other systems in all measures. While our system's F&M measure is low, it is only representative of the clusters we have induced as compared to the gold standard. To improve our F&M measure, we could reduce the number of redundant novel edges by pruning our system outputs and achieve comparable results to the other teams given our relatively precision of novel edges.

A detailed evaluation on the results for the individual domains is presented on Bordea et al. (2015).

6 Conclusion

In this paper, we have described our submissions to the Taxonomy Evaluation task for SemEval-2015. We have simplified a previously complex process of inducing a hypernym-hyponym ontology from a neural net by using the word vector for the non-content word text pattern, "is a".

Our system achieved modest results when compared against other participating teams. Given the simple approach to hypernym-hyponym relations, it is possible that future research can apply the method to other non-content words vectors to induce other relations between entities. The implementation of our system is released as open-source.

Acknowledgements

The research leading to these results has received funding from the People Programme (Marie Curie Actions) of the European Union's Seventh Framework Programme FP7/2007-2013/ under REA grant agreement no 317471. We would like to thank the Daniel Cer and other anonymous reviewers for their helpful suggestions and comments.

References

Matthew Berland and Eugene Charniak. 1999. Finding Parts in Very Large Corpora. In *Proceedings of the 37th annual meeting of the Association for Computational Linguistics on Computational Linguistics*, pages 57–64.

Norman Biggs, E. Keith Lloyd, and Robin J. Wilson. 1976. *Graph theory 1736-1936*. Clarendon Press.

Georgeta Bordea, Paul Buitelaar, Stefano Faralli, and Roberto Navigli. 2015. Semeval-2015 task 17: Taxonomy Extraction Evaluation. In *Proceedings of the 9th International Workshop on Semantic Evaluation*.

Sharon Ann Caraballo. 2001. *Automatic Construction of a Hypernym-labeled Noun Hierarchy from Text*. Ph.D. thesis, Providence, RI, USA. AAI3006696.

Kirill Degtyarenko, Paula De Matos, Marcus Ennis, Janna Hastings, Martin Zbinden, Alan Mcnaught, Rafael Alcántara, Michael Darsow, Mickaël Guedj, and Michael Ashburner. 2008. ChEBI: A Database and Ontology for Chemical Entities of Biological Interest. *Nucleic acids research*, 36(suppl 1):D344–D350.

Guy Emerson, Liling Tan, Susanne Fertmann, Alexis Palmer, and Michaela Regneri. 2014. SeedLing: Building and Using a Seed corpus for the Human Language Project. In *Proceedings of the 2014 Workshop on the Use of Computational Methods in the Study of Endangered Languages*, pages 77–85.

Trevor Fountain and Mirella Lapata. 2012. Taxonomy Induction using Hierarchical Random Graphs. In *Proceedings of the 2012 Conference of the North American Chapter of the Association for Computational Linguistics: Human Language Technologies*, pages 466–476.

Ruiji Fu, Jiang Guo, Bing Qin, Wanxiang Che, Haifeng Wang, and Ting Liu. 2014. Learning Semantic Hierarchies via Word Embeddings. In *Proceedings of the 52nd Annual Meeting of the Association for Computational Linguistics (Volume 1: Long Papers)*, pages 1199–1209.

Roxana Girju. 2003. Automatic Detection of Causal Relations for Question Answering. In *Proceedings of the ACL 2003 workshop on Multilingual summarization and question answering-Volume 12*, pages 76–83.

Marti A Hearst. 1992. Automatic Acquisition of Hyponyms from Large Text Corpora. In *Proceedings of the 14th conference on Computational linguistics-Volume 2*, pages 539–545.

Daniel Khashabi. 2013. On the Recursive Neural Networks for Relation Extraction and Entity Recognition. Technical report.

Zornitsa Kozareva and Eduard Hovy. 2010. A Semi-Supervised Method to Learn and Construct Taxonomies using the Web. In *Proceedings of the 2010 Conference on Empirical Methods in Natural Language Processing*, pages 1110–1118.

Zornitsa Kozareva, Ellen Riloff, and Eduard Hovy. 2008. Semantic Class Learning from the Web with Hyponym Pattern Linkage Graphs. In *Proceedings of ACL-08: HLT*, pages 1048–1056, Columbus, Ohio, June.

Douglas B Lenat. 1995. CYC: A Large-Scale Investment in Knowledge Infrastructure. *Communications of the ACM*, 38(11):33–38.

Dekang Lin and Patrick Pantel. 2001. Discovery of Inference Rules for Question-Answering. *Natural Language Engineering*, 7(04):343–360.

Dekang Lin. 1998. Automatic Retrieval and Clustering of Similar Words. In *Proceedings of the 17th international conference on Computational linguistics-Volume 2*, pages 768–774.

Tomas Mikolov, Kai Chen, Greg Corrado, and Jeffrey Dean. 2013a. Efficient estimation of word representations in vector space. *arXiv preprint arXiv:1301.3781*.

Tomas Mikolov, Wen-tau Yih, and Geoffrey Zweig. 2013b. Linguistic Regularities in Continuous Space Word Representations. In *Proceedings of the 2013*

Conference of the North American Chapter of the Association for Computational Linguistics: Human Language Technologies, pages 746–751.

George A Miller. 1995. WordNet: A Lexical Database for English. *Communications of the ACM*, 38(11):39–41.

Jeff Mitchell and Mirella Lapata. 2010. Composition in Distributional Models of Semantics. *Cognitive Science*, 34(8):1388–1439.

Roberto Navigli, Paola Velardi, and Stefano Faralli. 2011. A Graph-Based Algorithm for Inducing Lexical Taxonomies from Scratch. In *IJCAI 2011, Proceedings of the 22nd International Joint Conference on Artificial Intelligence, Barcelona, Catalonia, Spain, July 16-22, 2011*, pages 1872–1877.

Patrick Pantel and Deepak Ravichandran. 2004. Automatically Labeling Semantic Classes. In *Proceedings of the Human Language Technology Conference of the North American Chapter of the Association for Computational Linguistics: HLT-NAACL 2004*.

Adam Pease, Ian Niles, and John Li. 2002. The Suggested Upper Merged Ontology: A Large Ontology for the Semantic Web and its Applications. In *Working Notes of the AAAI-2002 Workshop on Ontologies and the SemanticWeb*, Edmonton, Canada.

Radim Řehůřek and Petr Sojka. 2010. Software Framework for Topic Modelling with Large Corpora. In *Proceedings of the LREC 2010 Workshop on New Challenges for NLP Frameworks*, pages 45–50, Valletta, Malta, May. ELRA.

Luís Sarmento, Paula Carvalho, and Eugénio Oliveira. 2009. Exploring the Vector Space Model for Finding Verb Synonyms in Portuguese. In *Proceedings of the International Conference RANLP-2009*, pages 393–398.

Andrew M. Saxe, James L. McClelland, and Surya Ganguli. 2013. Learning Hierarchical Category Structure in Deep Neural Networks. pages 1271–1276.

Rion Snow, Daniel Jurafsky, and Andrew Y Ng. 2006. Semantic Taxonomy Induction from Heterogenous Evidence. In *Proceedings of the 21st International Conference on Computational Linguistics and the 44th annual meeting of the Association for Computational Linguistics*, pages 801–808.

Liling Tan. 2013. Examining crosslingual word sense disambiguation. Master's thesis, Nanyang Technological University. pages 17-21.

Stefan Thater, Hagen Fürstenau, and Manfred Pinkal. 2010. Contextualizing Semantic Representations using Syntactically Enriched Vector Models. In *Proceedings of the 48th Annual Meeting of the Association for Computational Linguistics*, pages 948–957.

Luu Anh Tuan, Jung-jae Kim, and Kiong See Ng. 2014. Taxonomy construction using syntactic contextual evidence. In *Proceedings of the 2014 Conference on Empirical Methods in Natural Language Processing (EMNLP)*, pages 810–819.

Paola Velardi, Stefano Faralli, and Roberto Navigli. 2013. OntoLearn Reloaded: A Graph-based Algorithm for Taxonomy Induction. *Computational Linguistics*, 39(3):665–707.

NTNU: An Unsupervised Knowledge Approach for Taxonomy Extraction

Bamfa Ceesay
Department of Computer Science and Information Engineering
National Taiwan Normal University
No. 88, Tingz Chou Road, Section 4,
Taipei 116, Taiwan, R.O.C.
bmfceesay@csie.ntnu.edu.tw

Wen Juan Hou
Department of Computer Science and Information Engineering
National Taiwan Normal University
No. 88, Tingz Chou Road, Section 4,
Taipei 116, Taiwan, R.O.C.
emilyhou@csie.ntnu.edu.tw

Abstract

Taxonomy structures are important tools in the science of classification of things or concepts, including the principles that underlie such classification. This paper presents an approach to the problem of taxonomy construction from texts focusing on the hyponym-hypernym relation between two terms. Given a set of terms in a particular domain, the approach in this study uses Wikipedia and WordNet as knowledge sources and applies the information extraction methods to analyze and establish the hyponym-hypernym relationship between two terms. Our system is ranked fourth among the participating systems in SemEval-2015 task 17.

1 Introduction

Taxonomies are essential tools for many Natural Language Processing (NLP) applications and the backbone of many structured knowledge resources. Taxonomies specific to a domain are becoming indispensable to a growing number of applications (Velardi *et al*., 2013). Several state-of-the-art approaches already exist to extract taxonomies to characterize the domains of interest from the corpus using the information extraction techniques. Recently, attention has been devoted to inducing the taxonomy from a set of keyword phrases instead of from a text corpus (Liu *et al*., 2012). Such approaches enrich the set of keyword phrases by aggregating search results for each keyword phrase into a text corpus to overcome the lack of explicit relationships between keyword phrases from which the taxonomy can be induced.

This approach faces a key challenge of extracting explicit relationships among keyword phrases. However, semantic relatedness between concepts in a domain is an important clue to extracting their taxonomy relationships. An important contribution in relation to this is reported by Gabrilovich *et al*. (2007) that present an explicit semantic analysis using the natural concepts and propose a uniform method of computing relatedness of both individual concept and arbitrarily long text fragments. Lexical databases such as WordNet (Miller, 1995) encode relations between words such as synonymy and hypernymy. Quite a few metrics have been defined that compute relatedness using various properties of the underlying graph structures of these resources. The obvious drawback of this approach is that the creation of lexical resources requires the lexicographic expertise as well as a lot of time and effort, and consequently such resources cover only a small fragment of the language lexicon. Specifically, such the resources contain few proper names, neologisms, slang, and domain-specific technical terms. Furthermore, these resources have strong lexical orientation and mainly contain information about individual words but little world knowledge in general.

With the advent of new information sources, many new methods and ideas are developed for the large scale information extraction taking advantages of huge amounts of unstructured available resources. Barbu and Poesio (2009) propose a novel method for acquisition of knowledge for taxonomies of concepts from the raw Wikipedia text. Their approach uses the learning process to derive concept hierarchies from WordNet and maps them to Wikipedia pages for extraction of appropriate knowledge. Most state-of-the-art approaches for the domain-specific taxonomy induction use the text corpus as its input and some information extraction methods to extract ontological relationships from the text corpus, and finally apply the relationships to build the taxonomy. Other automatic approaches to taxonomy construction from texts include a statistical method to compare the syntactic context of terms for taxonomic relations identification (Tuan *et al.*, 2014).

There have been a number of handcrafted, well-structured taxonomies publicly available online, including WordNet (Miller, 1995). However, such taxonomies are also not perfect since human experts are liable to miss some relevant terms.

In this study, we consider the challenging problem of deriving taxonomies of a set of concepts under a specific domain of interest. Consider for illustration, the domain *vehicle* containing concepts such as *car*, *bicycle*, *Toyota*, *automobile*, *bus*, *Toyota_cambire*, *cruiser* and *Motorcycle*. Establishing hyponym-hypernym relationships among concepts is a difficult task if no other information is provided. We propose an approach to the taxonomy extraction task in SemEval-2015 (Bordea *et al.*, 2015) with the following contributions:

- To derive the statistical information about individual concepts in a given domain, the study uses WordNet and Wikipedia to find the definition for the concept.
- Using the definitions of concepts, the statistical information derived from these definitions is used to determine concept relationships and to represent the concepts in a domain with a Bayesian Rose Tree (BRT).
- The study finally extracts taxonomies for domain concepts using the BRT tree and WordNet type binary relations.

Bayesian hierarchical clustering algorithm (BRT) is used to cluster concepts having hyponym-hypernym relationships (Blundell *et al.*, 2012). Figure 1 presents our level approach to constructing the taxonomy for the domain concepts.

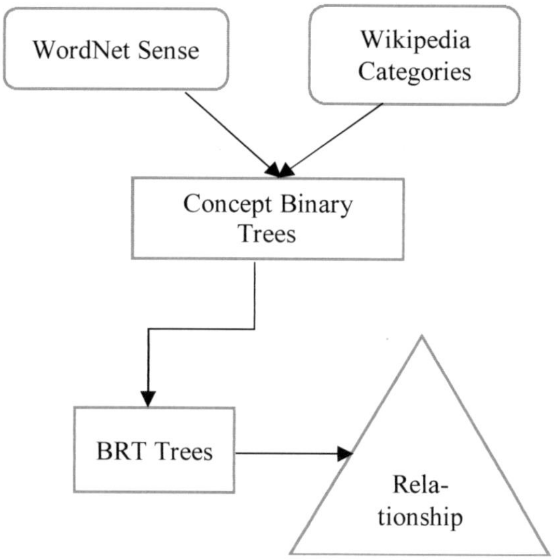

Figure 1. Approach to Taxonomy Extraction.

In Figure 1, resources WordNet and Wikipedia are first used to help the extraction of the definitions of the concepts. Then, information extracted from WordNet sense and Wikipedia categories are utilized to build the concept binary trees. With the concept binary trees, the system can construct the BRT tree and furthermore generate the relationships in the taxonomy for the concepts. Details in each step are described in the following sections.

2 Concept Definition and Bayesian Ross Tree

Definitions for describing concepts can be extracted from a variety of sources: dictionaries, databases, corpora, web directories and others. Wikipedia and WordNet have drawn attentions on derivation of concepts for taxonomy construction (Barbu and Poesio, 2009; Song *et al.*, 2011) and the syntactic conceptual taxonomy (Tuan *et al.* 2014).

In this study, to generate definitions for concepts and map concepts and keywords in definitions to a BRT tree for taxonomy extraction, we follow the steps below:

- First, given a concept, we use WordNet and Wikipedia to derive its definitions. In addition, the related WordNet synset and Wikipedia category are extracted for the taxonomy induction.
- Using the Wikipedia categories that describe the corresponding concept article, the WordNet sense, and the WordNet hyponym tree from the first step, the study uses a binary tree to represent each concept in the given domain. The left node represents the set of terms considered to be hypernyms and the right node represents the set of terms considered to be hyponyms.

Applying the above steps, the binary tree representation of concepts in the given domain is used to construct the BRT tree for the taxonomy construction. One example of the BRT tree is shown in Figure 2 as below.

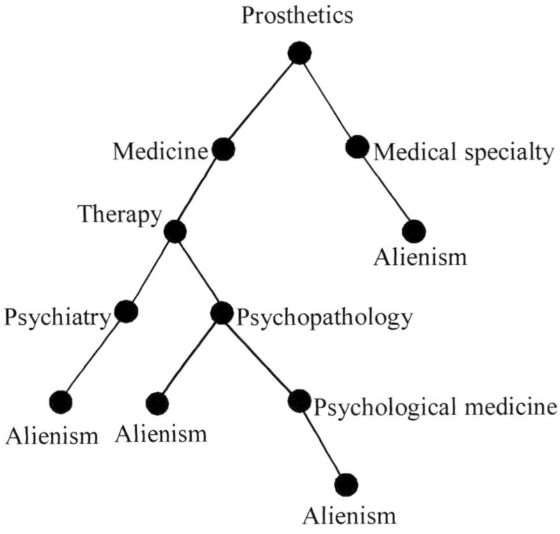

Figure 2. BRT Tree for a Term "Alienism," in Science Domain.

Figure 2 illustrates the concept of BRT tree for a domain term, "*alienism*." Each node represents a hypernym of the child node. For example, "psychiatry" is the hypernym of "alienism," and "therapy" is the hypernym of "psychiatry" and "psychopathology" respectively.

3 Concept Binary Tree Construction

This study defines a set of concepts derived from the Wikipedia category structure, a set of terms in the WordNet hypernym sense, *whyp*, and a set of terms in the WordNet hyponym, *whypo*, for a given concept in the domain.[1] For the set of terms in the Wikipedia category, a syntax-based method is employed by referencing the research of Tuan *et al.* (2014) to derive the taxonomy structure for the category terms. In our case of study, *is_a* relationship is an identification of the hypernym and hyponym relationship between terms in the category set. That is, "**X** *is_a* **Y**" is translated as "**X** is a hyponym of **Y**." However, this only shows a relationship among terms in the category set. To identify the hypernym-hyponym relationship between the domain concept and the terms in the category, the study uses the semantic relatedness approach proposed in the research of Wu *et al.* (2009). Finally, set operations are used to collect hypernyms and hyponyms and we use these features to construct a binary tree with the domain concept as the root, if no category term is a hypernym of domain concept. If there exists a category term that is a hypernym of the domain concept, the term becomes the root. For a given concept in the domain, a set of hypernym, *hyper*, and a set of hyponym, *hypo* are defined. After deriving the category taxonomy, *wt*, for Wikipedia categories, the following operations are defined:

$$hyper = whyper \cap wt.hypernym \quad \textbf{(1)}$$

$$hypo = whypo \cap wt.hyponym \quad \textbf{(2)}$$

[1]Wikipedia can be downloaded at *http://downlaod.wikimedia.org*. This study uses the English Wikipedia database dump

where *wt.hypernym* represents all hypernym terms connected to the category taxonomy *wt* and *wt.hyponym* represents all hyponym terms connected to the category taxonomy *wt*.

The multiple binary trees are used to construct BRT trees for the taxonomy extraction. However, it is worth to note that a cascading binary tree can be used instead of a BRT tree. For efficiency and computational purposes, a BRT tree is used, since a concept hypernym (parent node) can have more than two hyponyms (child node). The objective is to find relatedness between root concepts and the assigned parent node to the root concept of the binary tree. Figure 3 shows an illustration presenting concepts in our example domain in Section 3.

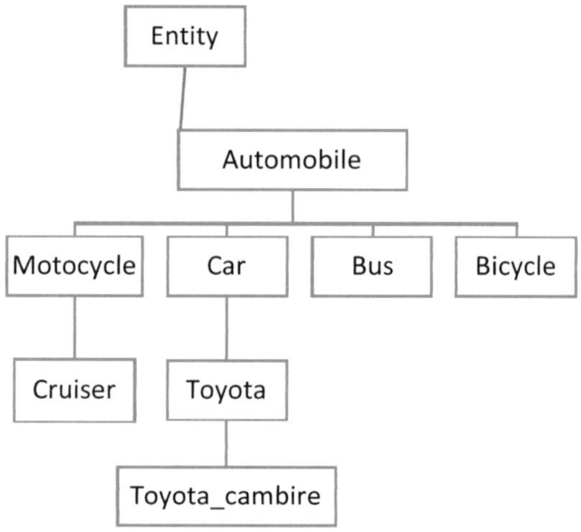

Figure 3. An Illustration of Concept Representation.

4 Extraction of Taxonomy Relationships

To extract the hypernym-hyponym relation between concepts, our approach uses the taxonomy de-scribed in Section 3. The concepts from the given domain are replaced by their concept IDs to distinguish them from the rest of the concepts in the BRT tree. The root of the BRT tree is an empty node, label entity. We use the Breath First Traversal algorithm to extract concepts and their corresponding hyponyms from the BRT tree.[2]

For a given concept in the BRT tree, we consider the concepts in the immediate child nodes, and extract the corresponding hypernyms and the hyponyms. Consequently, we can build the relationships of hypernyms and hyponyms for the concept.

5 Evaluation Matrix and Result

Our system is ranked fourth among the comparative evaluation final ranking of the task participant.[3] The table below shows the performance of participants' system based on average precision (Avg. P), recall (Avg. R), and average F-score measure (Avg. F) for the taxonomy extraction.

Participant	Rank	Avg. P	Avg. R	Avg. F
INRIASAC	1	0.1721	0.4279	0.2427
LT3	2	0.3612	0.6307	0.3886
ntnu	**4**	**0.1754**	**0.2756**	**0.2075**
QASSIT	5	0.1563	0.1588	0.1575
TALNUPF	6	0.0720	0.1165	0.0798
USAARWLV	3	0.2014	0.3139	0.2377

Table 1. Comparative evaluation results for SemEval-2015 Task 17, showing our system result in bold letters.

The evaluation tool measures a system-generated taxonomy against the gold standard taxonomy by comparing the following items:[4]

- The overall structure of the taxonomy against a gold standard, with an approach used for comparing hierarchical clusters.
- Structural measures.
- Manual quality assessment of novel edges.

In comparison against the gold standard data, the system's average performance under certain domain terms (chemical (CH), equipment (EQ), food and science (SC) domains) with respect to vertices in common, edge coverage and ratio of novel edges are shown in the table below.

[2]BFT is efficient in traversing a tree level by level and from left to right *http://en.wikipedia.org/wikiTree_traversal*

[3] http://alt.qcri.org/semeval2015/task17/index.php?id=evaluation

[4] http://alt.qcri.org/semeval2015/task17/index.php?id=evaluation

Features	CH	EQ	Food	SC
Vertices in coverage	0.3149	0.3144	0.3165	0.4390
Edge coverage	0.2803	0.2331	0.2603	0.3287
Ratio of Novel edges	0.4198	1.3419	1.0264	0.8584

Table 2. System's comparison against gold standard data.

In the table, the feature "vertices in coverage" represent the ratio of number of vertices in common with the gold standard taxonomy to the number of the gold standard vertices. The feature "edge coverage" is the fraction of number of edges in common with the gold standard over the number of edges in the gold standard. The ration of the product of the number of taxonomy edges and the number of edges in common with the gold standard to the number of gold standard edges is represented by "Ratio of Novel edges" in the result in Table 2.

From Table 2, it can be observed that, the system has the best and the worst performance in taxonomies for the science and equipment domains respectively. The bases of these differences in the system's performance are its precision for individual domain against its gold standard. For instance, from 452 vertices for the gold standard science domain from the taxonomy of fields and their subfields, the system was able to extract 338 vertices. Furthermore, the system's cumulative measure of the similarity against the gold standard is affected by the precision rate. For instance, in the worst performance for the gold standard domain of material handling equipment combined with IS-A relations from WiBi (Flati *et al.*, 2014), our system has a precision of 1.61% as shown in the evaluation result[5] while SC has good results in edge and vertex retrieval due to the good cumulative results.

6 Conclusion

In this paper, we present an approach for the unsupervised knowledge extraction for taxonomies of concepts using WordNet and Wikipedia as the sources of information. We first induce the construction of binary tree structures for each term in the domain using the extracted hypernym and hyponym. From the set of binary trees, we attempt to construct a BRT tree for the taxonomy extraction.

We regard this work as initial, as there is some improvement space to be made as well as many related areas to look into. First, in any future work we will investigate what better evaluation framework we can propose for the system. Second, we would like to give more attention to optimize the system result to a more formalized taxonomy. Third, we would like to include more concepts of relatedness extraction to obtain the stronger features.

Acknowledgements. Research of this paper was partially supported by Ministry of Science and Technology, Taiwan, under the contract MOST 103-2221-E-003-014.

References

Barbu, Eduard and Poesio, Massimo. (2009). Unsupervised Knowledge Extraction for Taxonomies of Concepts from Wikipedia. *RANLP-2009*, pp. 28-32. Borovets, Bulgaria.

Blundell, Charles, Teh, Yee Whye, and Heller, Katherine A. (2012). Bayesian Rose Trees. *DBLP, abs/1203.3468*.

Bordea, Georgeta, Buitelaar, Paul, Faralli, Stefano, and Navigli, Roberto. (2015). Semeval-2015 task 17: Taxonomy Extraction Evaluation (TExEval). *Proceedings of the 9th International Workshop on Semantic Evaluation.*

Flati, Tiziano, Vannella, Daniele, Pasini, Tommaso, and Navigli Roberto. (2014). Two Is Bigger (and Better) Than One: the Wikipedia Bitaxonomy Project. *ACL 2014*, Baltimore, Maryland, USA June 22-27, 2014.

Gabrilovich, Evgeniy and Markovitch, Shaul. (2007). Computing Semantic Relatedness Using Wikipedia-based Explicit Semantic Analysis. *IJCAI-07*, pp. 1606-1611.

Liu, Xueqing, Song, Yangqiu, Liu, Shixia, and Wang, Haixun. (2012). Automatic Taxonomy Construction from Keywords. *ACM.*

Miller, George A. (1995). WordNet: A Lexical Database for English. *Communications of the ACM*, 38(11), 39-41.

[5] http://alt.qcri.org/semeval2015/task17/index.php?id=evaluation

Song, Yangqiu, Wang, Haixun, Wang, Zhongyuan, Li, Hongsong, and Chen, Weizhu. (2011). Short Text Conceptualization Using a Probabilistic Knowledgebase. *Proceedings of the Twenty-Second international joint conference on Artificial Intelligence*, Vol. 3, pp. 2330-2336, AAAI Press

Tuan, Luu Anh, Kim, Jung-jae, and Kiong, Ng See. (2014). Taxonomy Construction Using Syntactic Contextual Evidence. *EMNLP-2104*, pp. 810-819.

Velardi, Paola, Faralli, Stefano, and Navigli Roberto. (2013). OntoLearn Reloaded: A Graph-Based Algorithm for Taxonomy Induction. *Computational Linguistics*, 39(3), 665-707.

Wu, Fang, Lu, Zhao, Yan, Yu, and Gu, Junzhong. (2009). Measuring Taxonomic Relationships in Ontologies Using Lexical Semantic Relatedness. *ICADIWT'09. Second International Conference on the. IEEE, 2009*, pp. 784-789.

LT3: A Multi-modular Approach to Automatic Taxonomy Construction

Els Lefever
LT^3, Language and Translation Technology Team
Department of Translation, Interpreting and Communication – Ghent University
Groot-Brittanniëlaan 45, 9000 Ghent, Belgium
els.lefever@UGent.be

Abstract

This paper describes our contribution to the SemEval-2015 task 17 on "Taxonomy Extraction Evaluation". We propose a hypernym detection system combining three modules: a lexico-syntactic pattern matcher, a morpho-syntactic analyzer and a module retrieving hypernym relations from structured lexical resources. Our system ranked first in the competition when considering the gold standard and manual evaluation, and second in the overall ranking. In addition, the experimental results show that all modules contribute to finding hypernym relations between terms.

1 Introduction

Because of globalization and rapid technological evolution, it is no longer feasible to manually create and manage taxonomies for the large variety of scientific and technological (sub)domains. In addition to domain-specific terminology, also companies desire to build their own mono- or bilingual taxonomies containing the relevant sector- and company-specific terminology. This clear need for automatisation has encouraged researchers to investigate how terminological and semantically structured resources such as taxonomies or ontologies can be automatically constructed from text (Biemann, 2005).

Different approaches have been proposed to automatically detect hierarchical relations between terms: pattern-based approaches (Hearst, 1992; Pantel and Ravichandran, 2004), statistical and machine learning techniques (Ritter et al., 2009), distributional approaches (Caraballo, 1999; van der Plas and Bouma, 2005; Lenci and Benotto, 2012), morpho-syntactic approaches (Tjong Kim Sang et al., 2011) and word class latices (Navigli and Velardi, 2010).

The SemEval-2015 "Taxonomy Extraction Evaluation" Task (Bordea et al., 2015) is concerned with automatically finding relations between pairs of terms and organizing them in a hierarchical structure. In this way, the task assumes that a list of domain specific terms is already available in order to focus on the relation detection between these terms.

To tackle this SemEval taxonomy learning task, we propose a multi-modular approach that combines lexico-syntactic, morphological and external structured lexical information. We will describe our hypernym detection system in Section 2. The results of the evaluation are presented in Section 3, while Section 4 concludes this paper.

2 System Description

Our hypernym detection system contains three main components: a lexico-syntactic pattern-based approach, a morpho-syntactic analyzer and a module retrieving hypernym relations from a structured lexical resource. Each module takes as input a domain specific term list.

2.1 Pattern-based Approach

The first module that automatically detects hypernym relations is a lexico-syntactic pattern-based approach, based on Hearst (1992). These patterns are implemented as a list of regular expressions containing lexicalized expressions (e.g. *like*), as well as isolated Part-of-Speech tags (e.g. noun) and chunk tags, which represent different Part-of-Speech sequences (e.g. noun phrase (NP) = determiner + adjective + noun, adjective + noun, etc.). An example of these manually defined patterns is "NP {, NP}* {,} or/and other NP",[1] as in "*green beans, carrots, peas and other vegetables*", which results in four hypernym pairs, being (*vegetables, green beans*), (*vegetables, carrots*), (*vegetables, peas*) and (*vegetables, onions*).

Domain specific corpus. As this module aims to find hypernym relations by detecting terms occurring in specific lexico-syntactic constructions, we first needed to compile a domain specific corpus containing these terms. To compile the corpus, we used the the BootCaT toolkit (Baroni and Bernardini, 2004), which can be used to build a specialized web-based corpus starting from a list of seed terms. We considered the different term lists for task 17 as the "seed terms" to build the domain specific corpora, by allowing 10 queries per seed term. Due to technical reasons (the Bing search engine that is used by BootCat only allows 5000 queries per user account), we only compiled corpora for three domains, being *equipment, food and science*. As a post-processing step, we removed all sentences containing (1) only URL links or (2) no domain specific term, resulting in three corpora containing about 12 million tokens for the *food* domain, 6 million tokens for the *equipment* domain and 27 million tokens for the *science* domain.

Linguistic preprocessing. We performed a number of linguistic preprocessing steps in order to enrich the original web-based corpus: (1) tokenisation, (2) Part-of-Speech Tagging, (3) Lemmatisation and (4) Chunking. All linguistic preprocessing was per performed by means of the LeTs Preprocess toolkit (Van de Kauter et al., 2013).

Lexico-syntactic pattern matching. The resulting linguistically preprocessed corpus is the input for the pattern-based module. Example 1 shows a sentence matching the pattern:

{*other*}* *NP such as NP* {, *NP*}* {*(and-or) NP*}*

[1] Curly brackets indicate optional parts of the pattern.

resulting in the two hypernym pairs (*cranberry products, tablets*) and (*cranberry products, capsules*). As can be seen in example 1, the lexicalised parts of the patterns (*other* and *such as* in this case) are not considered for the generation of the hyponym–hypernym tuples.

(1)
```
other other JJ B-NP
cranberry cranberry NN I-NP
products product NNS I-NP
such such JJ B-AP
as as IN I-AP
tablets tablet NNS B-NP
and and CC O
capsules capsule NNS B-NP
```

We optimized the pattern-based model presented by (Lefever et al., 2014) in different ways. The efficiency of the module was improved by only considering noun phrases containing a maximum of 6 consecutive nouns and by ignoring named entities. This appeared to be necessary as the web-based corpus contains a lot of lists and enumerations, causing problems for the recursive way the regular expressions are built. Precision, on the other hand, was improved by ignoring tuples containing both terms as hypernym and hyponym (e.g. hand truck – truck and truck – hand truck) and by only considering patterns that revealed to obtain high precision in previous research (Lefever et al., 2014).

Finally, the output of the pattern-based module is filtered by only considering tuples where both terms (either lemma or full form) occur in the term list of the considered domain.

2.2 Morpho-syntactic Analyzer

Our second hypernym detection module applies a morpho-syntactic approach where the morphological structure of compound terms is used to extract a hypernym-hyponym relation from this term. This approach is inspired by the head-modifier principle (Sparck Jones, 1979) stating that in a compound noun, the linear arrangement of the compound parts expresses the kind of information being conveyed, the head referring to the more general semantic category, whereas the modifiers restrict the sense of the compound term. This way, the complete compound term can be considered as a hyponym of the head term. We implemented rules for three different syntactic hypernym-hyponym relations in compounds:

1. **Single-word terms**: *If term T0 is a suffix string of term T1, T0 is considered to be a hypernym of T1.* Examples of hypernym pairs detected within single-word terms are (*sachertorte, torte*), (*candlepin, pin*) and (*psycholinguistics, linguistics*).

2. **Multiword terms**: *If term T0 is the head term of term T1, T0 is considered to be a hypernym of T1.* It is important to mention that we also allow multiple possible hypernyms in case different terms occur as suffixes of the compound term, e.g. *phu quoc fish sauce* is the hyponym of both *sauce* and *fish sauce*. As the head of a nominal phrase appears at the right edge of a multiword NP in English, the last constituent of the NP is regarded as the head of the compound, and thus as the hypernym of the complete term, as is the case in the generated hypernym pair (*béarnaise sauce, sauce*).

3. **Complex prepositional phrases**: *If term T0 is the first part of a term T1 containing a noun phrase + preposition + noun phrase, T0 is considered to be a hypernym of T1.* In the case of a prepositional compound phrase, the head is situated at the left edge of the compound term. Examples of such hypernym pairs are (*sociology of culture, sociology*) and (*soup all'imperatrice, soup*)

In addition, we added some restrictions to these general rules in order to improve the precision of the module. First, we set a threshold of minimum three characters for the detection of valid hypernyms. An example of invalid hypernyms filtered out this way is *tu* that could be detected as a hypernym of *pesarattu*, both terms occurring in the food term list. Second, we noticed that food terms (etc. dishes) are often loan words from other languages. Therefor we added a list of foreign adjectival affixes (e.g. french affix *al/ale*) that should not be considered as a hypernym of the compound term. This way we prevent for instance *ale* to be detected as the hypernym of *chicken provencale* or *café royale*.

2.3 Structured Lexical Resources: WordNet

The third hypernym detection module retrieves information from an external lexical resource, being WordNet in this case. This module looks up the synsets in WordNet for all domain-specific terms and retrieves all hypernyms appearing in the full hierarchical path of these synsets. Hypernym tuples containing identical terms were removed. Examples of hyponym-hypernym pairs retrieved from WordNet are (*semantics, science*) and (*semantics, linguistics*).

2.4 Combined System

To generate the final list of hypernym relations, we combined the output of all three modules and removed all doubles from the hyponym–hypernym pair list.

3 Results

The resulting taxonomies are evaluated through comparison with gold standard relations collected from existing domain specific ontologies and WordNet. In addition, expert evaluation has been performed on the hypernym relations submitted by the participants. The system organizers calculated precision, recall and F-score as well as a cumulative Fowlkes & Mallows measure, which is inspired by clustering evaluation and takes into account the hierarchical structure of the gold standard taxonomy and the taxonomy that is produced by the system.

In addition, a number of structural measures were calculated such as the number of distinct vertices and edges, the number of connected components and intermediate nodes to evaluate whether the taxonomy connects all nodes with the root. From this evaluation it was clear that our taxonomy contains cycles, which is conflicting with correct hierarchical relations. For more detailed information about the gold standards and evaluation metrics, we refer to (Bordea et al., 2015). Table 1 lists the averaged Precision, Recall, F-measure and Fowlkes & Mallows scores for all participating systems, while Table 2 lists the individual scores for the three domains in which we participated. The very high recall scores for the *WN* data sets can be explained by the fact that our system also contains a module that retrieves hypernym relations from WordNet.[2]

[2]We included a WordNet module, since originally only BabelNet was specified as the gold standard for the task. At evaluation time, however, WordNet was also used to evaluate the taxonomies.

	INRIASAC	LT3	ntnu	QASSIT	TALN-UPF	USAAR-WLV
Precision	0.1721	0.3612	0.1754	0.1563	0.0720	0.2014
Recall	0.4279	0.6307	0.2756	0.1588	0.1165	0.3139
F-score	0.2427	0.3886	0.2075	0.1575	0.0798	0.2377
Fowlkes & Mallows	0.3278	0.4130	0.0582	0.3882	0.2635	0.0770

Table 1: Comparative evaluation of all participating systems considering the average Precision, Recall, F-measure and Cumulative Fowlkes & Mallows measure scores.

Test set	Precision	Recall	F-Score	F&M
Equipment	0.7021	0.3219	0.4414	0.1137
Food	0.2892	0.2974	0.2932	0.2163
Science	0.4013	0.3806	0.3907	0.3303
WN_Equipment	0.3168	0.9484	0.4749	0.6892
WN_Food	0.2155	0.9719	0.3528	0.5899
WN_Science	0.2422	0.8639	0.3783	0.5391

Table 2: Precision, Recall, F-measure and Cumulative Fowlkes & Mallows measure scores for all test sets.

As we wanted to gain more insights in the contribution of the different modules, we also calculated precision and recall per module for the different term lists. The results per module and for the combined system are shown in Table 3.

		Morpho-syntactic Module	Pattern-based Module	Word-Net Module	full system
WN_Equip	P	0.696	0.143	0.320	0.317
	R	0.245	0.008	0.932	0.948
Equipment	P	0.791	0.214	0.310	0.702
	R	0.307	0.005	0.021	0.322
WN_Food	P	0.613	0.204	0.230	0.216
	R	0.242	0.091	0.958	0.972
Food	P	0.602	0.191	0.219	0.289
	R	0.176	0.059	0.134	0.297
WN_Science	P	0.696	0.215	0.778	0.242
	R	0.270	0.063	0.857	0.864
Science	P	0.641	0.292	0.277	0.401
	R	0.273	0.045	0.144	0.381

Table 3: Precision (P) and recall (R) from relation overlap scores per hypernym detection module per domain.

We notice that the WordNet module indeed achieves very high recall for the *WN* test sets, but that the recall for the more technical term lists is much lower (with only 0.021 for the *Equipment* data set). The recall achieved by the pattern-based module is also very modest, with scores ranging from 0.005 (*Equipment*) to 0.063 (*WN_Science*). The Morpho-syntactic Module, on the other hand, contributes in a consistent way to the recall for all term lists. Finally, table 3 also shows that the obtained recall by the system that combines all different modules consistently beats the recall of the individual modules for all test sets. With regard to precision, we observe that the morpho-syntactic approach obtains very good results for all the different test domains, resulting in system precision scores that outperform all participating systems.

A qualitative analysis of the output revealed shortcomings of the different hypernym detection modules. As discussed above, the *morpho-syntactic* module achieves good recall. The downside is that the module clearly over generates. Examples of invalid hypernym pairs are for instance (*pineapple juice, apple juice*), (*hot and sour soup, sour soup*) and (*ice cream, cream*). Although WordNet is a manually verified taxonomy, we also discovered invalid hypernym pairs in the output of the WordNet module. For the *food* domain, for instance, we discovered that all beverages have "food" as an inherited hypernym, resulting in hypernym pairs such as (*pineapple juice, food*) and (*absinth, food*).

4 Conclusion

To tackle the SemEval "Taxonomy Extraction Evaluation" task, we proposed a hypernym detection system combining a lexico-syntactic pattern matcher, a morpho-syntactic analyzer and a module retrieving hypernym relations from WordNet and showed promising results for the different test domains. Analyzing the recall per hypernym detection module revealed that all modules contribute to the final hyponym–hypernym list generated by the combined system.
In future work, we would like to improve the recall of the system by adding additional hypernym detection modules (e.g. a distributional model built on the basis of the domain corpora). We will also add a dedicated module to construct the taxonomy based on the hierarchical relations in order to remove the cycles from the resulting taxonomy.

References

Marco Baroni and Silvia Bernardini. 2004. BootCaT: Bootstrapping Corpora and Terms from the Web. In *In Proceedings of LREC 2004*, pages 1313–1316.

Chris Biemann. 2005. Ontology Learning from Text: A Survey of Methods. *LDV Forum*, 20(2):75–93.

Georgeta Bordea, Paul Buitelaar, Stefano Faralli, and Roberto Navigli. 2015. Semeval-2015 task 17: Taxonomy extraction evaluation (texeval). In *Proceedings of the 9th International Workshop on Semantic Evaluation*.

Sharon A. Caraballo. 1999. Automatic acquisition of a hypernym-labeled noun hierarchy from text. In *Proceedings of ACL-99*, pages 120–126, Baltimore, MD.

Marti Hearst. 1992. Automatic Acquisition of Hyponyms from Large Text Corpora. In *Proceedings of the International Conference on Computational Linguistics*, pages 539–545.

Els Lefever, Marjan Van de Kauter, and Véronique Hoste. 2014. HypoTerm: detection of hypernym relations between domain-specific terms in Dutch and English. *Terminology*, 20(2):250–278.

Alessandro Lenci and Giulia Benotto. 2012. Identifying hypernyms in distributional semantic spaces. In *Proceedings of the first Joint conference on Lexical and Computational Semantics (*SEM)*, pages 75–79, Montréal, Canada.

Roberto Navigli and Paola Velardi. 2010. Learning Word-Class Lattices for Definition and Hypernym Extraction. In *Proceedings of the 48th Annual Meeting of the Association for Computational Linguistics*, pages 1318–1327, Uppsala, Sweden.

Patrick Pantel and Deepak Ravichandran. 2004. Automatically labeling semantic classes. In *Proceedings of HLT/NAACL-04*, pages 321–328, Boston, MA.

Alan Ritter, Stephen Soderland, and Oren Etzioni. 2009. What is this, anyway: Automatic hypernym discovery. In *Proceedings of Association for Advancement of Artificial Intelligence Spring Symposium on Learning by Reading and Learning to Read*, pages 88–93.

Karen Sparck Jones. 1979. Experiments in relevance weighting of search terms. *Information Processing and Management*, 15:133–144.

Erik Tjong Kim Sang, Katja Hofmann, and Maarten De Rijke. 2011. Extraction of hypernymy information from text. In A. Van den Bosch and G. Bouma, editors, *Interactive multi-modal question-answering*, Series: Theory and Applications of Natural Language Processing, pages 223–245.

Marjan Van de Kauter, Geert Coorman, Els Lefever, Bart Desmet, Lieve Macken, and Véronique Hoste. 2013. LeTs Preprocess: the Multilingual LT3 Linguistic Preprocessing Toolkit. *Computational Linguistics in the Netherlands Journal*.

Lonneke van der Plas and Gosse Bouma. 2005. Automatic acquisition of lexico-semantic knowledge for question answering. In *Proceedings of the IJCNLP Workshop on Ontologies and Lexical Resources*, Jeju Island, Korea.

TALN-UPF: Taxonomy Learning Exploiting CRF-Based Hypernym Extraction on Encyclopedic Definitions

Luis Espinosa-Anke and **Horacio Saggion** and **Francesco Ronzano**
Tractament Automàtic del Llenguatge Natural (TALN)
Department of Information and Communication Technologies
Universitat Pompeu Fabra
Carrer Tànger, 122-140
08018 Barcelona, Spain
{luis.espinosa, horacio.saggion, francesco.ronzano}@upf.edu

Abstract

This paper describes the system submitted by the TALN-UPF team to SEMEVAL Task 17 (Taxonomy Extraction Evaluation). We present a method for automatically learning a taxonomy from a flat terminology, which benefits from a definition corpus obtained by querying the BabelNet semantic network. Then, we combine a machine-learning algorithm for term-hypernym extraction with linguistically-motivated heuristics for hypernym decomposition. Our approach performs well in terms of vertex coverage and newly added vertices, while it shows room for improvement in terms of graph topology, edge coverage and precision of novel edges.

1 Introduction

Learning semantic relations out of flat terminologies is an appealing task due to its potential application in tasks like Question Answering (Cui et al., 2005; Boella et al., 2014), automatic glossary construction (Muresan and Klavans, 2002), Ontology Learning (Navigli et al., 2011) or Textual Entailment (Roller et al., 2014). Today, in the context of massive web-enabled data, hypernym (is-a) relations are the focus of much research, as they constitute the backbone of ontologies (Navigli et al., 2011). However, one challenge remains open in the automatic construction of knowledge bases that exploit this type of relation. It is unfeasible to have up-to-date semantic resources for each domain, as they are limited in scope and domain, and their manual construction is knowledge intensive and time consuming (Fu et al., 2014).

Given this rationale, Task 17 (Bordea et al., 2015) in the SEMEVAL 2015 set of shared tasks focuses on Taxonomy Extraction Evaluation, i.e. the construction of a taxonomy out of a flat set of terms belonging to one of the four domains of choice (food, chemical, equipment and science). These terms have to be hierarchically organized, and new terms are allowed to be included in the taxonomy. As for evaluation, for each domain, two taxonomies were used as gold standard: One created by domain experts; and one derived from the WordNet taxonomy rooted at the domain node, e.g. food[1]. Finally, evaluation is carried out from two standpoints: (1) The taxonomy topology and the rate of replicated nodes and edges are taken into account when compared to a gold standard taxonomy; and (2) Human experts validated as correct or incorrect a subset of the newly added edges.

In this paper we describe our contribution to this shared task. Our approach relies on a set of definitional sentences for each term, from which term→hypernym relations are extracted using a machine-learning classifier. In a second step, linguistically-motivated rules are applied in order to (1) extract a hypernym candidate when the confidence of the classifier was below a threshold, and (2) decompose multiword hypernyms in more general concepts (e.g. from *coca-cola→carbonated soft drink* to *carbonated soft drink→soft drink* and *soft drink→drink*).

[1] For our domain notation we simply use the name of the domain for manually constructed taxonomies (e.g. "food"), and add the prefix *wn_* for the WordNet taxonomies (e.g. "wn_food").

The remainder of the paper is structured as follows: Section 3 describes the modules of our approach, Section 4 presents and discusses the evaluation procedure as well as results, and finally Section 5 analyzes the performance of our system as well as the difficulties encountered, and suggests potential avenues for future work.

2 Background

Generally, taxonomy learning from text has been carried out either following rule-based or distributional approaches. In terms of rule-based methods reported in the literature, (Hearst, 1992) introduced lexico-syntactic patterns, which were exploited in subsequent work (Berland and Charniak, 1999; Kozareva et al., 2008; Widdows and Dorow, 2002; Girju et al., 2003). Distributional approaches, on the other hand, have become increasingly popular due to the availability of large corpora. Systems aimed at extracting hypernym relations from text have exploited hybrid patterns as word-class lattices (Navigli and Velardi, 2010), syntactic relations as features for an SVM classifier (Boella et al., 2014) or word-embedding-based semantic projections (Fu et al., 2014; Roller et al., 2014). Inspired by the reported success in the latter methods, we opted for combining syntactic patterns with machine learning to extract hypernyms from domain sentences.

3 Method

This section describes the main modules that constitute our taxonomy learning system.

3.1 Definition corpus compilation

We benefit from BabelNet, a very large multilingual semantic network that combines, among other resources, Wikipedia and WordNet (Navigli and Ponzetto, 2010). We get a set of BabelNet synsets associated to each term and for each synset, we extract its definition. In this step we assume that a term's definition appears in the first sentence of its Wikipedia article, which is a regular practice in the literature (see (Navigli and Velardi, 2010) or (Boella et al., 2014)). This step allowed us to compile a domain corpus of definitional knowledge, and thus maximizing the number of relevant terms definitions. However, noise is also introduced in our corpus. For example, given the term *botifarra* (a Catalan type of sausage), we add two definitions to our corpus:

Relevant: Botifarra is a type of sausage and one of the most important dishes of the Catalan cuisine.

Noisy: Botifarra is a point trick-taking card game for four players in fixed partnerships played in Catalonia.

3.2 Hypernym Extraction

Given a set of definitional text fragments where the definiendum[2] term is known, i.e. can be extracted from the url of the Wikipedia page, our goal is to tag the tokens of the definition that correspond to one or more hypernyms. To this end, we train a Conditional Random Fields (Lafferty et al., 2001) classifier[3] with the WCL Dataset (Navigli and Velardi, 2010). We argue that CRFs are a valid approach for sequential classification, and particularly for this task, due to their potential to capture prior and posterior token features on the current iteration. The WCL dataset includes near 2000 definitional sentences with terms and hypernyms manually annotated. We preprocess and parse the WCL dataset with a dependency parser (Bohnet, 2010), and then train our classifier with the following set of features.

surface: A word's surface form.

lemma: The lemma of the word.

pos: The word's part-of-speech.

head_id: The id of the word to which the current token depends in a dependency syntactic tree.

deprel: Syntactic function of the current word in relation to its head.

def—nodef: Whether the current token appears before or after the first verb of the sentence.

[2]The classic components lexicographic *genus-et-differentia* definition are (1) Definiendum (concept being defined); (2) genus (hypernym or immediate superordinate that describes the definiendum); and (3) definiens or cluster of words that differentiate a definiendum from others of its kind.

[3]https://code.google.com/p/crfpp/

term—noterm: Whether the token is part of the definiendum term or not.

Our CRF classifier learns the above word-level features in a word window of $[-2, 2]$. The prediction the classifier must learn follows the classic BIO format, i.e. whether a word is at the beginning of a hypernym phrase, inside or outside. We evaluate this hypernym extraction module on the WCL dataset (Navigli and Velardi, 2010) performing 10-fold cross-validation. It achieves and F-score of 79.86, outperforming existing state-of-the-art systems described in the literature (Navigli and Velardi, 2010; Boella et al., 2014).

Despite the good performance of this module, we observe two potential drawbacks in terms of its fitness for the taxonomy learning task. Firstly, we aim at recovering hypernym candidates even in cases in which they are predicted with low confidence at the classification step. We build on the assumption that all encyclopedic definitions are very likely to include a hypernym, and hypothesize that it will help increasing recall while keeping precision at a reasonable rate. Secondly, when a multiword hypernym is retrieved by our module, it might not match exactly a term from the seed terminology (e.g. *original_term→soft drink*, and *retrieved_term→carbonated soft drink*). Therefore, we aim at decomposing it by dropping one modifier at a time and creating new arcs recursively. These two steps are described in more detail in the following subsection.

Post-classification Heuristic

Our recall-enhancing strategy consists in a post-classification heuristic inspired by Flati et al. (2014): (1) We exploit the tree-like dependency structure of a parsed sentence in order to find the most likely token to be the head of a hypernymic phrase. We look for definitions where no hypernym was identified. Then, we find the node with the *Predicative Complement* (PRD) syntactic function. If such node is not a *stop-hypernym* (such as *type*, *class*, *family* or *kind*), we consider it a valid head of a hypernymic-phrase[4]. Then, we collect all its noun and adjective children with the syntactic function *Modifier of Nominal* (NMOD). If, however, such node is a stop-hypernym, we go down the syntactic tree one level and look for a direct *Preposition* node with syntactic function NMOD. Then, we extract this preposition's adjective and noun children if they have the syntactic function *Modifier of Prepositional* (PMOD).

For example, consider the following sentence: "Whisky or whiskey is a type of distilled alcoholic beverage made from fermented grain mash". Here, *type* is the Predicative Complement node but it is an uninformative word for describing the term *whisky*. Therefore, our algorithm goes one level down the syntactic tree and identifies the token *beverage* as the direct child of the preposition and therefore extracts this token as hypernym.

3.3 Hypernym Decomposition

This step is aimed at generating deeper paths from a term and its hypernym by recursively decomposing a candidate hypernym. For example, consider the previous example's *term→hypernym* relation if the hypernym's modifiers are taken into account: *whisky→distilled alcoholic beverage*. Our objective is to generate the following set of relations: *distilled alcoholic beverage→alcoholic beverage* and *alcoholic beverage→beverage*. In this way, we improve the taxonomy since, in taxonomy learning, longer hypernymy paths should be preferred (Navigli et al., 2011), and we enable other potential *distilled alcoholic beverages* to be connected with *alcoholic beverage* rather than the more generic term *beverage*.

We achieve this by performing a similar algorithm as in the post-classification heuristic, i.e. exploiting head and modifier relations in a dependency tree.

3.4 Graph Generation

At this stage, we have a dataset of *term→hypernym* pairs, and from here populating the taxonomy is a trivial task. For each pair, if neither *term* nor *hypernym* exist in the graph, add both nodes and connect them. If *term* exists in the graph, only add the *hypernym* and connect the existing *term* node with it. If on the contrary, only the *hypernym* is found in the graph, connect the term to the existing hypernym node. Finally, we go back to the initial flat terminology and, if no path is found between a term node and the root node, add a direct edge between them. This last step guarantees that the taxonomy will preserve

[4]The full list of stop-hypernyms is available at www.wibitaxonomy.org

	chem	wn_chem	equip	wn_equip	food	wn_food	sci	wn_sci
VC	1	0.997	1	1	0.8695	1	0.9977	0.8624
EC	0.0004	0.093	0.1577	0.0453	0.0359	0.0782	0.0172	0.1111
RNE	0.7089	0.9531	0.9235	6.903	0.9527	0.9315	3.4731	0.78
F&M	0.2225	0.2787	0.4482	0.0901	0.3267	0.3091	0.2202	0.2126
Cycles	no	yes	yes	yes	no	yes	yes	no
Precision	0.0006	0.0889	0.1458	0.0287	0.0363	0.0775	0.0733	0.1246
Recall	0.0004	0.093	0.1577	0.2	0.0359	0.0782	0.2559	0.1111
F-Score	0.0005	0.0909	0.1515	0.0503	0.0361	0.0778	0.1139	0.1175

Table 1: Summary of the results obtained with our approach in the structural evaluation in terms of vertex coverage (VC), edge coverage (EC), ratio of novel edges (RNE), cumulative Fowlkes and Mallows Measure (F&M), whether the taxonomy contains cycles (Cycles), and Precision, Recall and F-Score against gold standard taxonomies.

the vast majority of the initial terms (if not all, as can be seen in Table 1).

4 Evaluation

Evaluation is carried out considering the structural properties of the taxonomy, as well as its quality when compared to gold-standard (see Table 1). These gold taxonomies can be either the subgraphs rooted at one relevant WordNet term (chemical, food, equipment or science), or taxonomies manually crafted by domain experts.

These results suggest that the approach described in this paper can be safely followed to construct a taxonomy from a flat terminology as input, provided major issues like domain-specificity or WSD are addressed. Our approach strongly depends of available definitions of terms in Wikipedia, which was not the case in very specific domains (such as the *chemical* terminology). On the other hand, however, the hypernym extraction pass worked well and thus we are encouraged to work in this direction, stressing the importance of an appropriate domain dataset from which definitional knowledge can be extracted.

In order to compare the system and reference taxonomies, the evaluation consists in computing node and edge coverage by taking into account the number of nodes and edges in common and the sizes of the taxonomies. In addition, the results of a structural metric are also provided, such metric being the Fowlkes&Mallows measure (Fowlkes and Mallows, 1983), a method for comparing hierarchical clusters. The results show poor performance of our system in inferring relations among concepts at deeper levels in the taxonomy. One of the reasons this might be due to is the fact that the lexicalization of a term does not necessarily have to be exact between a BabelNet synset and an associated Wikipedia definition.

Regarding the manual evaluation of the quality of newly acquired edges, our system is unsurprisingly weak (P=10.2%)[5] due to the inherent term ambiguity which makes our system retrieve noisy definitions at each step. We hypothesize that our results might be higher in the chemical domain, since terminology would be less prone to be polysemous. However, this domain was not considered for this evaluation measure. These negative results together with the good performance of the hypernym-extraction module stress the need to retrieve valid domain specific definitional sentences for our approach to work well.

5 Conclusions and Discussion

We have described a system designed for constructing a taxonomy from a flat list of terms. It is based on a module that queries BabelNet for Wikipedia definitions in order to obtain definitional knowledge

[5]Full results for all systems are reported in http://alt.qcri.org/semeval2015/task17/index.php?id=evaluation.

for each term. Then, a machine-learning algorithm is trained with a manually annotated dataset with hypernym relations in definitional sentences, and applied to our definition dataset. Different post-classification heuristics are afterwards incorporated to the pipeline with a two-fold objective: (1) Extract a candidate hypernym in cases where the classifier lacked the confidence to tag one or more tokens as possible hypernyms, and (2) Decompose candidate hypernyms exploiting the syntactic relation between their head and its modifiers in a syntactic dependency tree. Finally, with a set of *term→hypernym* pairs we populate a domain taxonomy by connecting terms and hypernyms, and finally by fixing disconnected nodes from the root.

We have demonstrated that our approach has very high vertex coverage, and on the other hand is flawed in capturing deep taxonomic relations among entities. The hypernym extraction module achieves state-of-the-art performance and due to the simplicity of the features used is open for improvements, either by incorporating semantic similarity among tokens, frequencies in domain corpora, or a token's position in the syntactic tree.

We observe a clear room for improvement in the domain corpus compilation part, and for the future we are investigating the potential of the Wikipedia Categories Graph in order to gather domain definitions from pages that are in recurrent categories in the BabelNet synset list.

Acknowledgments

We would like to express our gratitude to the anonymous reviewers for their helpful comments. This work is partially funded by the SKATER project, TIN2012-38584-C06-03, Ministerio de Economía y Competitividad, Secretaría de Estado de Investigación, Desarrollo e Innovación, España; and project Dr. Inventor (FP7-ICT-2013.8.1 611383).

References

Matthew Berland and Eugene Charniak. 1999. Finding parts in very large corpora. In *Proceedings of the 37th annual meeting of the Association for Computational Linguistics on Computational Linguistics*, pages 57–64. Association for Computational Linguistics.

Guido Boella, Luigi Di Caro, Alice Ruggeri, and Livio Robaldo. 2014. Learning from syntax generalizations for automatic semantic annotation. *Journal of Intelligent Information Systems*, pages 1–16.

Bernd Bohnet. 2010. Very high accuracy and fast dependency parsing is not a contradiction. In *Proceedings of the 23rd International Conference on Computational Linguistics*, COLING '10, pages 89–97, Stroudsburg, PA, USA. Association for Computational Linguistics.

Georgeta Bordea, Paul Buitelaar, Stefano Faralli, and Roberto Navigli. 2015. Semeval-2015 task 17: Taxonomy extraction evaluation (texeval). In *Proceedings of the 9th International Workshop on Semantic Evaluation*. Association for Computational Linguistics.

Hang Cui, Min-Yen Kan, and Tat-Seng Chua. 2005. Generic soft pattern models for definitional question answering. In *Proceedings of the 28th annual international ACM SIGIR conference on Research and development in information retrieval*, pages 384–391. ACM.

Edward B. Fowlkes and Colin L. Mallows. 1983. A method for comparing two hierarchical clusterings. *Journal of the American statistical association*, 78(383):553–569.

Ruiji Fu, Jiang Guo, Bing Qin, Wanxiang Che, Haifeng Wang, and Ting Liu. 2014. Learning semantic hierarchies via word embeddings. In *Proceedings of the 52th Annual Meeting of the Association for Computational Linguistics: Long Papers*, volume 1.

Roxana Girju, Adriana Badulescu, and Dan Moldovan. 2003. Learning semantic constraints for the automatic discovery of part-whole relations. In *Proceedings of the 2003 Conference of the North American Chapter of the Association for Computational Linguistics on Human Language Technology-Volume 1*, pages 1–8. Association for Computational Linguistics.

Marti A. Hearst. 1992. Automatic acquisition of hyponyms from large text corpora. In *Proceedings of the 14th conference on Computational linguistics-Volume 2*, pages 539–545. Association for Computational Linguistics.

Zornitsa Kozareva, Ellen Riloff, and Eduard H. Hovy. 2008. Semantic class learning from the web with hyponym pattern linkage graphs. In *ACL*, volume 8, pages 1048–1056. Citeseer.

John D. Lafferty, Andrew McCallum, and Fernando C. N. Pereira. 2001. Conditional Random Fields: Probabilistic Models for Segmenting and Labeling Sequence Data. In *Proceedings of the Eighteenth International Conference on Machine Learning*, ICML '01, pages 282–289, San Francisco, CA, USA. Morgan Kaufmann Publishers Inc.

A Muresan and Judith Klavans. 2002. A method for automatically building and evaluating dictionary resources. In *Proceedings of the Language Resources and Evaluation Conference (LREC*.

Roberto Navigli and Simone Paolo Ponzetto. 2010. Babelnet: Building a very large multilingual semantic network. In *Proceedings of the 48th annual meeting of the association for computational linguistics*, pages 216–225. Association for Computational Linguistics.

Roberto Navigli and Paola Velardi. 2010. Learning word-class lattices for definition and hypernym extraction. In *Proceedings of the 48th Annual Meeting of the Association for Computational Linguistics*, ACL '10, pages 1318–1327, Stroudsburg, PA, USA. Association for Computational Linguistics.

Roberto Navigli, Paola Velardi, and Stefano Faralli. 2011. A graph-based algorithm for inducing lexical taxonomies from scratch. In *IJCAI*, pages 1872–1877.

Stephen Roller, Katrin Erk, and Gemma Boleda. 2014. Inclusive yet selective: Supervised distributional hypernymy detection. In *Proceedings of the Twenty Fifth International Conference on Computational Linguistics (COLING-14), Dublin, Ireland*.

Dominic Widdows and Beate Dorow. 2002. A graph model for unsupervised lexical acquisition. In *Proceedings of the 19th international conference on Computational linguistics-Volume 1*, pages 1–7. Association for Computational Linguistics.

QASSIT: A Pretopological Framework for the Automatic Construction of Lexical Taxonomies from Raw Texts

Guillaume Cleuziou[1], **Davide Buscaldi**[2], **Gael Dias**[3] **Vincent Levorato**[4], **Christine Largeron**[5]
[1] LIFO - University of Orléans, France
[2] LIPN - University of Paris 13, France
[3] GREYC - University of Caen-Basse Normandie, France
[4] IRISE - CESI Orléans, France
[5] LHC - University of Saint-Etienne, France
cleuziou@univ-orleans.fr, davide.buscaldi@lipn.univ-paris13.fr
gael.dias@unicaen.fr, vlevorato@cesi.fr
christine.largeron@univ-st-etienne.fr

Abstract

This paper presents our participation to the SemEval Task-17, related to "Taxonomy Extraction Evaluation" (Bordea et al., 2015). We propose a new methodology for semi-supervised and auto-supervised acquisition of lexical taxonomies from raw texts. Our approach is based on the theory of pretopology which offers a powerful formalism to model subsumption relations and transforms a list of terms into a structured term space by combining different discriminant criteria. In order to reach a good pretopological space, we define the Learning Pretopological Spaces method that learns a parameterized space by using an evolutionary strategy.

1 Introduction

Lexical Taxonomies (LTs) play an essential role in Information Retrieval (IR) and Natural Language Processing (NLP). By coding the semantic relations between terminological concepts, LTs can enrich the reasoning capabilities of applications in IR and NLP. However, the globalized development of semantic resources is largely limited by the efforts required for their construction (Kozareva and Hovy, 2010). As a consequence, instead of manually creating LTs, many research studies have emerged to automatically learn such structures (Buitelaar et al., 2005; Biemann, 2005; Cimiano et al., 2009; Kozareva and Hovy, 2010; Velardi et al., 2013).

The two main stages for the automatic construction of LTs are Term Extraction and Term Structuring. The proposed approach is focused on the second stage, thus matching with the aim of the SemEval task, by inducing LTs from pre-existing lists of terms (provided by the organizers).

As starting point, we consider the work from (Cleuziou et al., 2011) which introduced new statistically-based criteria (e.g. Nearest-Neighbor-like relations) and combined them using the theory of pretopology (Brissaud, 1975). This formalism offers a new framework to model the subsumption relation at the term set level rather than considering (binary) subsumption relations only between pairs of terms. Based on the concepts of (pseudo-)closure and closed subsets the authors transform the list of terms into a semantic space. A structuring algorithm based on the work of Largeron and Bonevay (2002) is then applied to transform the semantic space of terms into a LT i.e. an acyclic directed (non-triangular) graph.

This theory should allow to combine both associative- and pattern-based methods within a virtuous multi-criteria structuring process. To achieve this objective, we consider pretopology on the multi-criteria analysis point of view, where criteria are statistical indices and linguistic patterns retrieved from a corpus. In particular, we define the concept of *Parameterized pretopological space* (P-space), where parameters express the confidence that exists over each criterion. As such, LT induction can be viewed as learning the set of parameters (confidences), which best (1) approximates the expected LT structure and (2) verifies a given number of linguistic patterns constraints.

In order to learn the parameters, we define a new *Learning Pretopological Spaces* (LPS) method and use an evolutionary strategy which leads to induce a LT from an "optimized" P-space.

In the remaining of this paper, we first introduce the new concept of P-Space in Section 2. Then, we present the general LPS learning process in Section 3. Finally, we describe in Section 4 the use of the LPS paradigm in the particular context of the SemEval Task-17 and discuss the obtained results.

2 Pretopology and P-Spaces

Pretopology is a theory introduced by Brissaud (1975) that generalizes both Topology and Graph theories. This formalism, as reviewed by (Belmandt, 2011) is commonly used to model complex propagation phenomena thanks to a pseudo-closure operator, recently employed in (Cleuziou et al., 2011) for LT acquisition.

Let us consider a non-empty set E, and its powerset $\mathcal{P}(E)$. A (V-type) pretopological space is noted (E, a), where $a(.)$ is a pseudo-closure function ($\mathcal{P}(E) \rightarrow \mathcal{P}(E)$) such that :

i) $a(\emptyset) = \emptyset$,

ii) $\forall A \in \mathcal{P}(E), A \subseteq a(A)$,

iii) $\forall A, B \in \mathcal{P}(E), A \subseteq B \Rightarrow a(A) \subseteq a(B)$.

It is crucial to notice that $a(.)$ is not necessarily idempotent unlike in Topology (where $a(a(A)) = a(A)$). So, the pseudo-closure behaves as an expansion operator that enlarges any non-empty subset $A \subset E$. As a consequence, successive applications of $a(.)$ on A lead to a fix-point, called *closed subset* and noted F_A (or $F(A)$). At this stage, the reader has to consider E as a set of unstructured terms and the pseudo-closure operator $a(.)$ modeling the propagation of the term domination (or subsumption) relation.

Let us also define the notions of *elementary closed subset* ($F_{\{x\}}$) that refers to the closure of a singleton that is maximal if $\nexists y,\ F_{\{x\}} \subset F_{\{y\}}$. In the scope of LT acquisition, these concepts will be used to model the domination/subsumption inheritance between terms, $F_{\{x\}}$ referring to a set of terms dominated by a term x that has no dominator when $F_{\{x\}}$ is maximal.

In order to perform the expansion process, we define a *P-Space* as a V-type pretopological space with a parameterized pseudo-closure function $a(.)$ defined for any $A \in \mathcal{P}(E)$ by

$$a(A) = \{x \in E \mid \sum_{N_k \in \mathcal{N}} w_k.\mathbb{1}_{N_k(x) \cap A \neq \emptyset} \geq w_0\} \quad (1)$$

with $\mathcal{N}$ a family of neighborhoods over E and such that $w_0 > 0$, $\sum_{k=1}^{K} w_k \geq w_0$ and $\forall k \neq 0,\ w_k \geq 0$.

Here, a neighborhood can be viewed as a statistical indice or a linguistic pattern retrieved from a corpus which identifies a subsumption relation between terms. In particular, each parameter w_k in (1) quantifies a kind of reliability on the kth neighborhood and w_0 represents a global required confidence to expand the subset A. Thus, a subset A will be expanded to an element x only if the sum of the confidences on the criteria in agreement with the expansion exceeds the global required confidence w_0. The P-Space concept thus offers a wide range of neighborhood combinations by considering the set of any monotonic linear threshold functions.

Given a V-type pretopological space, (Largeron and Bonnevay, 2002) proposed an algorithm that structures the set E into a DAG (Directly Acyclic Graph).

3 Learning P-Spaces process (LPS)

We propose a learning pretopological spaces framework (LPS), illustrated in Figure 1. Considering a partial knowledge S providing a true partial structuring on E, LPS aims to find a P-Space - namely a function as in (1) and more concretely a set of parameters $\mathbf{w}$ - inducing a good structuring according to a fitness function defined by :

$$Score(\mathbf{w}, S) = F_{Measure}(\mathbf{w}, S) \times I_{structure}(\mathbf{w}) \quad (2)$$

with F and I, two terms quantifying respectively the satisfactions about :

(1) the constraints implied by the partial knowledge S and

(2) the expected structural properties of the output : a taxonomy-like structuring in the specific LT acquisition context.

The score (2) is used to guide the exploration of the space of solutions through a learning strategy based on a Genetic Algorithm (GA).

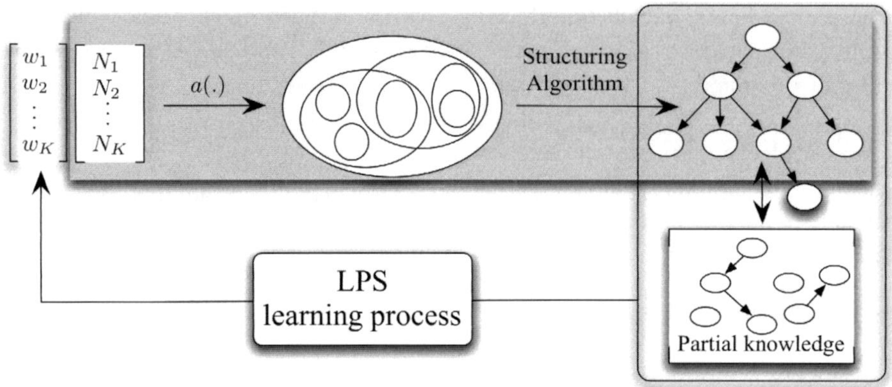

Figure 1: The LPS process uses partial knowledge on the expected structure in order to improve the parameterization of the pseudo-closure operator.

4 LPS for the SemEval Task 17

Let us recall that, in addition to the list of terms E to structure, the LPS system requires as input : a family of neighborhoods $\mathcal{N}$ over E and a partial knowledge S.

Three kinds of associative criteria served as basis neighborhoods :

N_{kSand} corresponds to the subsumption relation modeled by Sanderson and Croft (1999) : $y \in N_{kSand}(x)$ iff $P(y|x) \approx \frac{hits(x,y)}{hits(x)} \geq \sigma_k \wedge P(y|x) > P(x|y)$.

N_{kNP} associates to each term x its k Nearest Parents in the sense of $P(y|x)$: $y \in N_{kNP}(x)$ iff $P(y|x)$ is one of the k best $\{P(z|x)\}_{z \in E}$.

N_{kNC} associates to each term x its k Nearest Children: $y \in N_{kNC}(x)$ iff $P(y|x)$ is one of the k best $\{P(y|z)\}_{z \in E}$.

All criteria depend of the parameter k that controls the number of selected relations. In particular, we adjust the thresholds σ_k in such a way that N_{kSand} selects as many relations as the two other criteria for a same value of k (i.e. $k.|E|$ relations). So, each type of criterion provides several effective criteria depending of the parameter k. We considered three different values for k ($\{1 \dots 3\}$) leading to nine neighborhood, plus the partial knowledge (that can also serve as a neighborhood).

The english subpart of wikipedia.org has been used as corpus for frequency counts extraction. For each pair of terms (x, y), we retrieve the number of wikipedia pages where both terms occur ($hits(x, y)$) in the corresponding sub-domain of wikipedia. Subdomains are artificially identified by introducing the root term of the taxonomy into the wikipedia query. For example, $hits(memory, politics)$ is retrieved with the following query ["memory" AND "politics" AND "science"] as *memory* and *politics* are two terms contained into the *wn_science* list of terms to structure.

The partial knowledge has been obtained by first extracting a list of candidate subsumption pairs observing linguistic patterns into a corpus and then by manually correcting the candidate list and/or adding new pairs of subsumptions with the aim to reach at least two hundreds subsumption relations into S. The 10 linguistic patterns used, from (Kozareva and Hovy, 2010; Snow et al., 2004), are the following : {*X are Y that - X is a Y that - X is an Y that - Y such as X - Y including X - Y like X - X and other Y - X or other Y - such Y as X - Y, specially X*}

For any pairs of terms (x, y) from the list E, each pattern is tested on en.wikipedia.org and each time a pattern is observed between x and y, an edge $x \rightarrow y$ (x subsumes y) is added to S (after manual validation). A quantitative summary of the partial knowledge construction for each considered domain is reported in Table 1.

The LPS process has been applied on the four first lists of terms : *wn_science*, *science*, *wn_equipment* and *equipment* of limited sizes (less than 1,000).

Table 1: Quantitative summary of semi-automatic acquisition of the partial knowledges S.

List of terms	Nb. terms	Nb. candidate pairs	Nb. selected pairs	Nb. added pairs	Size of S
WN_Science	370	341	272	0	272
Science	462	347	230	0	230
WN_Equipment	475	296	162	133	295
Equipment	612	83	38	169	207
WN_Food	1485	2130	200	52	252
Food	1555	1630	144	83	227
WN_Chemical	1350	1908	227	0	227
Chemical	17,584		*not processed*		

GA was parameterized so that it iterates crossings and mutations on a population of 200 P-Spaces and finally selected the one maximizing the score (2). For example, on the *science* list, the P-Space acquired induces a LT reaching a score of 0.948, with a matching of 0.98 with S (the F term) and a structuring term (I) of 0.97. The underlying parameters $\mathbf{w}$ can be interpreted as a logical propagation rule combining neighborhoods from the given family $\mathcal{N}$; the obtained rule is

$$\begin{gathered} \delta_S(x) \vee (\delta_{N_{1NS}}(x) \wedge \delta_{N_{2NF}}(x)) \\ \vee(\delta_{N_{3NS}}(x) \wedge \delta_{N_{1NF}}(x) \wedge \delta_{N_{1Sand}}(x)) \\ \vee(\delta_{N_{3NS}}(x) \wedge \delta_{N_{2NF}}(x)) \end{gathered} \quad (3)$$

formalizing the extension of a subset A to an element x when either :

- the neighborhood $N_S(x)$ intersects A (*i.e.* x is dominated by a term $y \in A$ according to the partial knowledge S) or,
- both neighborhoods $N_{1NS}(x)$ and $N_{2NF}(x)$ intersect A or,
- neighborhoods $N_{3NS}(x)$ and $N_{1NF}(x)$ and $N_{1Sand}(x)$ intersect A or,
- neighborhoods $N_{3NS}(x)$ and $N_{2NF}(x)$ intersect A.

The final external evaluation (comparison against the gold standard) revealed that the LT induced by the previous P-Space obtains the best score (0.523) using the cumulative Fowlkes&Mallows measure (Fowlkes and Mallows, 1983).

Due to time limitations, learning P-Spaces with LPS was not possible for the domains *wn_food*, *food* and *wn_chemical*. For these domains, we computed the neighborhoods and rather than *learning* a combination rule fitting to the dataset, we tested the four combination rules acquired from the four previous domains, computed their ability to induce a good LT (by computing the score (2)) and finally we kept the best one. Table 2 finally summarizes the results obtained by the team QASSIT and its relative positioning into the task.

Table 2: Results obtained on the 8 domains in terms of fitness and gold standard evaluation ; symbol * indicates domains for which a learning stage has been performed.

Domains	internal score (2)	F&M measure	Best F&M	rank
WN_Science*	0.97	0.29	0.54	3/6
Science*	0.95	0.52	0.52	1/6
WN_Equip.*	0.63	0.36	0.69	2/6
Equipment*	0.34	0.49	0.49	2/6
WN_Food	0.56	0.32	0.59	3/6
Food	0.73	0.34	0.45	2/6
WN_Chemical	0.54	0.39	0.39	1/6
Chemical		*not processed*		

5 Conclusion

The automatic evaluation against the gold standards has been then completed by a manual analysis that revealed lower comparative results for the seven taxonomies acquired with the LPS approach. But the main lesson to learn from this second type of evaluation is the high discrepancy between the taxonomies obtained with a learning stage (at least 0.20 of F-measure each time) and the the ones obtained by reusing combination rules (less than 0.10 each time). These results encourages future research toward the scalability of the LPS learning process and various improvements in terms of statistical neighborhoods enhancement and linguistic patterns selection.

References

Z.T. Belmandt. 2011. *Basics of pretopology*. Hermann.

Chris Biemann. 2005. Ontology learning from text: a survey of methods. *LDV-Forum*, 20(2):75–93.

Georgeta Bordea, Paul Buitelaar, Stefano Faralli, and Roberto Navigli. 2015. Semeval-2015 task 17: Taxonomy extraction evaluation. In *Proceedings of the 9th International Workshop on Semantic Evaluation*.

Marcel Brissaud. 1975. Les espaces prétopologiques. *Compte-rendu de l'Académie des Sciences*, 280(A).

Paul Buitelaar, Philipp Cimiano, and Bernardo Magnini, editors. 2005. *Ontology Learning from Text: Methods, Evaluation and Applications*, volume 123 of *Frontiers in Artificial Intelligence and Applications*. IOS Press.

Philipp Cimiano, Alexander Mädche, Stephen Staab, and Johanna Völker. 2009. Ontology learning. In *Handbook of Ontologies*, pages 245–267. Springer Verlag.

Guillaume Cleuziou, Davide Buscaldi, Vincent Levorato, and Gaël Dias. 2011. A pretopological framework for the automatic construction of lexical-semantic structures from texts. In *Proceedings of the 20th ACM International Conference on Information and Knowledge Management (CIKM)*, pages 2453–2456.

Edward B. Fowlkes and Colin L. Mallows. 1983. A method for comparing two hierarchical clusterings. *Journal of the American Statistical Association*, 78(383):553–569.

Zornitsa Kozareva and Eduard Hovy. 2010. A semi-supervised method to learn and construct taxonomies using the web. In *Proceedings of the Conference on Empirical Methods in Natural Language Processing (EMNLP)*, pages 1110–1118.

Christine Largeron and Stéphane Bonnevay. 2002. A pretopological approach for structural analysis. *Information Sciences*, 144:169–185, July.

Mark Sanderson and Bruce Croft. 1999. Deriving concept hierarchies from text. In *Proceedings of the 22nd Annual International ACM SIGIR Conference on Research and Development in Information Retrieval (SIGIR)*, pages 206–213.

Rion Snow, Daniel Jurafsky, and Andrew Y Ng. 2004. Learning syntactic patterns for automatic hypernym discovery. *Advances in Neural Information Processing Systems 17*.

Paola Velardi, Stefano Faralli, and Roberto Navigli. 2013. Ontolearn reloaded: A graph-based algorithm for taxonomy induction. *Computational Linguistics*, 39(3):665–707.

Riga: from FrameNet to Semantic Frames with C6.0 Rules

Guntis Barzdins, Peteris Paikens, Didzis Gosko
University of Latvia, IMCS
Rainis Blvd. 29, Riga, LV-1459, Latvia
{guntis.barzdins,peteris.paikens,didzis.gosko}@lumii.lv

Abstract

For the purposes of SemEval-2015 Task-18 on the semantic dependency parsing we combined the best-performing closed track approach from the SemEval-2014 competition with state-of-the-art techniques for FrameNet semantic parsing. In the closed track our system ranked third for the semantic graph accuracy and first for exact labeled match of complete semantic graphs. These results can be attributed to the high accuracy of the C6.0 rule-based sense labeler adapted from the FrameNet parser. To handle large SemEval training data the C6.0 algorithm was extended to provide multi-class classification and to use fast greedy search without significant accuracy loss compared to exhaustive search. A method for improved FrameNet parsing using semantic graphs is proposed.

1 Introduction

The trend of natural language processing in recent years is shifting towards multilingual natural language understanding based on full-text shallow semantic parsing (e.g., Banarescu et al., 2013). Despite various formalisms proposed, these approaches are characterized by direct extraction of a bi-lexical semantic graph rather than a bi-lexical dependency tree from the surface form of the sentence.

Following the best practice for semantic parsing established already by the SemEval-2014 Task 8 (Oepen et al., 2014) we modified the best-performing closed-track system there (Du et al., 2014) by removing some less essential components while adding a new component of our own. The newly added component is the C6.0 rule-based classifier (Barzdins et al., 2014) used both for graph parsing and for sense labeling. Sense labeling is a novelty of SemEval-2015 Task 18 and was not present in the previous year competition. Semantic frame is comprised of a complete predication combined with the sense identifier of its predicate as shown in Figure 1. Semantic frames are similar to FrameNet (Fillmore et al., 2003) frames, except that FrameNet argument labels are sense-specific – this mismatch can be resolved by feeding the semantic graph (instead of dependency tree) through the regular FrameNet parser.

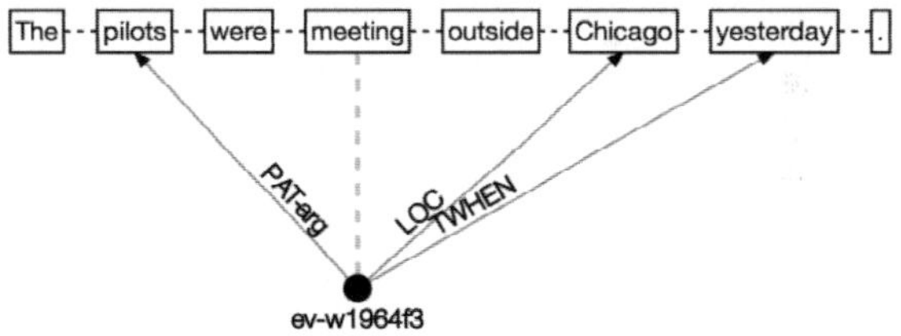

Figure 1. Semantic frame from the PSD corpus.

We participated only in the closed track. Despite ranking third for the semantic graph accuracy, our system ranked first for exact labeled match of complete semantic graphs, and close second for semantic frame accuracy.

2 Baseline Architecture

For semantic graph parsing we started by implementing a straight-forward baseline architecture described on the SemEval-2015 Task-18 evaluation page by the task organizers. The baseline architecture consists of two components: reduction of the SDP graphs to trees and training the Mate-tools dependency parser (Bohnet, 2010) to produce such trees from the unparsed text. Instead of a destructive reduction of the SDP graphs to trees, we implemented a fully reversible depth-first transformation from the last year best-performing system (Du et al., 2014). This simple approach immediately produced competitive graph parsing results (Table 1) in line with the best-performing systems from the last year.

	in domain			out of domain		
	LP	LR	LF	LP	LR	LF
en.dm	87.34	87.05	87.19	79.95	79.42	79.68
en.pas	90.47	90.03	90.25	85.98	85.48	85.73
en.psd	72.81	71.05	71.92	70.34	67.55	68.92
cs.psd	74.44	71.56	72.97	60.19	57.43	58.78
cz.pas	82.15	81.74	81.94	-	-	-

Table 1. Baseline architecture labeled scores.

For sense labeling in *en.dm* and *en.psd* representations (a new task not present in the previous SemEval-2014 competition) we reused a technique from prior work on FrameNet labeling (Barzdins et al., 2014) based on C6.0 classifier[1]. For this task the C6.0 classifier was modified (see Section 3) to directly produce the multi-class output. By using as the features values from the *form, lemma, POS* columns for the previous, current, and next word, this approach gave good results on the development set: 93.86% accuracy for *en.psd* representation and 94.50% accuracy for *en.dm* representation. We did not try to improve it any further and the same baseline approach was used also for producing senses in the final submitted parses.

In the submitted parses we carried out the graph parsing and sense labeling completely independently, naively combining both annotations afterwards. Later experiments have shown that using graph parsing results as additional features for sense labeling would improve sense accuracy by approximately 0.2%.

3 Sense Labeling with C6.0 Rules

C6.0 rule-based classification algorithm (Barzdins et al., 2014) was inspired by the popular C4.5 decision-tree classification algorithm (Quinlan, 1993) and has been used in the state-of-the-art FrameNet parser.

To accommodate the large training data sets provided in SemEval competition we extended the original C6.0 algorithm with support for the multi-class classification and with the fast greedy search as a replacement for the exhaustive search in the original C6.0 version.

Given *k* training examples of the form:

$$(a_{11}, a_{12}, a_{13}, \ldots a_{1n}, class_1)$$
$$(a_{21}, a_{22}, a_{23}, \ldots a_{2n}, class_2)$$
$$\ldots$$
$$(a_{k1}, a_{k2}, a_{k3}, \ldots a_{kn}, class_k)$$

where features a_{ij} and $class_i$ are arbitrary character strings, C6.0 classifier builds a list of rules (illustrated in Figure 2) for predicting the class of unseen examples. The left side of the rule is a pattern where any feature position may contain a specific character string to be matched or an unspecified value denoted by "_".

	lemma	POS		Predicted sense	*p*	*n*	*Laplace ratio*
if(	the,	DT	*)then*	q:i-h-h	*227*	*0*	*0.996*
if(	_,	CD	*)then*	card:i-i-c	*147*	*9*	*0.937*
if(	_,	DT	*)then*	q:i-h-h	*336*	*31*	*0.913*
if(	trade,	_	*)then*	n_of:x-i	*13*	*1*	*0.875*

Figure 2. Classification rules generated by C6.0. Rule quality is estimated by the Laplace ratio based on positive *p* and negative *n* matching training examples.

The greedy search algorithm for building a multi-class classifier can be described as follows.

Training data is converted to a pool of classifier training examples. Each training example is considered positive for the class it belongs to, and negative for any other class. A candidate rule is matched against all positive and negative training examples relative to its class. The count of matched positive and negative training examples allows to calculate rule's Laplace ratio $(p+1)/(p+n+2)$, where p is the number of matching positive training examples and n is the number of matching negative training examples. The rules with higher Laplace ratio are better.

For each training example a set of rules correctly classifying this training example is generated by incrementally adding to the left side of the rule feature values from this training example. Fast greedy search one-by-one adds the features in such

[1] Available at http://c60.ailab.lv

order that the resulting rule has the highest possible Laplace ratio in every feature adding iteration. This is contrary to the original C6.0 exhaustive search strategy which tried all feature relaxation combinations instead. The greedy approach eliminates exponential complexity of C6.0 with respect to feature count and when tested, yielded as good results as the exhaustive search on SemEval data.

All generated rules (regardless of the class they predict) are sorted by the highest Laplace ratio. The resulting list of rules is a multi-class classifier which can be considered consisting of multiple binary classifiers (individual rules). For unseen examples the class is assigned by the matching rule with the highest Laplace ratio.

Fig. 2 shows some classification rules for predicting the sense column value in *en.dm* training dataset from two features. The actual production classifier for sense labeling uses more features (listed in Section 2) and generates several thousand rules.

4 Semantic Graph Parsing

We tried three approaches described below to improve the graph parsing results above the baseline.

4.1 Peking and MateTools Graph Parser

The primary approach chosen for semantic graph parsing is to implement a fully reversible transformation between the semantic graph and a tree representation that encodes the extra information in edge labels. It allows training a dependency parser (Bohnet, 2010) on the labeled tree data, and using it to parse text to structures that can be converted back to a semantic graph.

For reversible graph to tree transformation we have implemented the depth-first search transformation and the auxiliary label system used by last year's best-performing Peking system (Du et al, 2014). The auxiliary labels encode:

- A separator to indicate multiple original edges encoded in this label;
- Ancestor-number indicating that in the original graph, an edge with this label is drawn from the dependent to the n-th ancestor instead of the direct parent of this tree edge;
- A reverse-edge symbol to indicate edges that have reversed direction compared to the original graph.

For the multi-root sentences that appear in some of the datasets, we choose the first root (according to word order in sentence) as the main tree root, and iteratively link all the other sentence fragments to the nearest node in the accumulated tree according to the number of words between them; in case of ties preferring the leftmost node. When creating the transformed tree, we also used special labels to distinguish the secondary root nodes of other fragments, so that the transformation is reversible for graphs with multiple root nodes.

After parsing, a tree may contain labels that are invalid according to the principles of this transformation – i.e., a reference to the grandparent of a node that does not have one. In this case, we draw an edge with the appropriate label to the closest possible node.

In this approach the cyclic graph structures are transformed to the different tree branch topologies depending on the traversal order. Traversal order thus affects the likelihood of the parser to correctly reconstruct these cyclic graph structures. To improve cyclic graph structure reconstruction we developed multiple parser variations for ensemble voting based on the following traversal orders for each node:

- Linear distance of linked words, starting with the closest words and preferring the left node in case of ties;
- Frequency of the edge labels, prioritizing the most frequent labels;

In addition, we also applied the same transformations for sentences with reversed word order to provide further variation. The resulting parsers have comparable accuracy, but produce different mistakes, making them useful for ensemble voting. Simple ensemble voting improves graph parsing accuracy over the baseline (Table 2).

	in domain			out of domain		
	LP	LR	LF	LP	LR	LF
en.dm	88.63	87.12	87.87	81.75	79.61	80.67
en.pas	91.46	90.01	90.73	87.55	85.71	86.62
en.psd	75.25	71.29	73.22	73.28	67.52	70.28
cs.psd	78.66	71.73	75.04	64.27	57.72	60.82
cz.pas	83.10	81.85	82.47	-	-	-

Table 2. Ensemble method labeled scores.

4.2 C6.0 Rule Based Graph Parser

We also applied our C6.0 rule-based classifier (described in Section 3) for semantic graph parsing through exact dependency phrase matching. Due to low recall rate it provided only a tiny positive boost to the final ensemble voting result (Table 4) despite the high precision of the rules method (Table 3). Here we considered only edges of length up to 4 and C6.0 rules with Laplace ratio above 90%. Due to low recall we signaled "abstain" vote for the edges not covered by these rules.

	in domain			out of domain		
	LP	LR	LF	LP	LR	LF
en.dm	92.80	33.47	49.20	91.84	19.78	32.56
en.pas	92.94	35.53	51.40	92.58	28.07	43.08
en.psd	88.34	18.76	30.94	86.70	11.34	20.05
cs.psd	95.29	16.70	28.42	80.46	8.13	14.77
cz.pas	90.97	22.91	36.60	-	-	-

Table 3. Labeled scores for the rules method.

4.3 Other parsing approaches

Experiments with transition based parsers (MaltParser/MaltOptimizer) showed approximately 2% lower accuracy than Mate-tools on the same transformed tree data. This is consistent with findings made by others during the earlier SemEval-2014 Task-8. We chose not to use those parsers for the final submission.

5 Final Results

We submitted two runs but report results only for run-1, because run-2 was discovered to include a corrupted Mate-tools dataset.

Our final semantic graph and semantic frames parsing results are shown in Tables 4 and 5. Semantic frames results measure overall sense labeling and graph parsing accuracy, which is the novelty of this year SemEval task.

	in domain			out of domain		
	LP	LR	LF	LP	LR	LF
en.dm	88.57	87.24	87.90	81.69	79.72	80.69
en.pas	91.50	90.02	90.75	87.56	85.72	86.63
en.psd	75.25	71.52	73.34	73.23	67.71	70.37
cs.psd	78.66	71.84	75.10	64.29	57.83	60.89
cz.pas	83.12	81.84	82.47	-	-	-

Table 4. Labeled scores for the submitted result.

	in domain			out of domain		
	FP	FR	FF	FP	FR	FF
en.dm	58.45	57.79	58.12	42.62	41.17	41.88
en.psd	52.48	52.59	52.54	40.60	40.93	40.76

Table 5. Semantic frame scores for the submitted result.

Table 6 shows ranking of averaged SemEval scoring metrics for the best runs of the systems participating in the closed task. Although we ranked third for the semantic graph (labeled dependencies) metric, our system ranked close second for semantic frame accuracy, and first for labeled exact match of the complete semantic dependency graphs. These results suggest that the C6.0 rule accuracy for sense labeling and for exact match semantic graph parsing was able to compensate for slightly lower overall graph parsing accuracy.

System	LF	LM	PF	SF	FF
Peking	**80.51**	21.14	62.64	69.45	**48.70**
Lisbon	80.42	20.05	**63.59**	--	--
Riga	78.68	**21.84**	61.29	73.76	48.33
Minsk	78.18	15.04	56.40	**79.40**	47.32

Table 6. Ranking of scores averaged over all available datasets for the best runs of the systems in the closed track: labeled dependencies (LF), labeled exact match of the complete semantic dependency graphs (LM), complete predications (PF), sense identification (SF), semantic-frames (FF).

6 Conclusions

Variations of Peking depth-first reversible graph-to-tree conversion algorithm in combination with state-of-the-art dependency parser is still a competitive graph parsing approach.

C6.0 rule-based classifier provides competitive sense labeling accuracy and some improvement also for graph parsing accuracy.

An ensemble method with "abstain" voting option for joining outputs of various graph parsing approaches boosts the results by ironing out the weaknesses of individual parsers. Required computational resources are the main limitation here.

Acknowledgments

This work was supported by the Latvian National research program SOPHIS under grant agreement Nr.10-4/VPP-4/11. We thank Lauma Pretkalniņa for the experiments with transition-based parsers.

References

Laura Banarescu, Claire Bonial, Shu Cai, Madalina Georgescu, Kira Griffitt, Ulf Hermjakob, Kevin Knight, Philipp Koehn, Martha Palmer, and Nathan Schneider. 2013. Abstract Meaning Representation for Sembanking. In: *Proc. Linguistic Annotation Workshop (SIGANN-2013)*, pp. 178-186.

Guntis Barzdins, Didzis Gosko, Laura Rituma, and Peteris Paikens. 2014. Using C5.0 and Exhaustive Search for Boosting Frame-Semantic Parsing Accuracy. In: *Proceedings of the 9th Language Resources and Evaluation Conference (LREC),* pp. 4476-4482.

Bernd Bohnet. 2010. Very High Accuracy and Fast Dependency Parsing is not a Contradiction. *The 23rd International Conference on Computational Linguistics (COLING 2010)*, pp. 89-97.

Charles J. Fillmore, Christopher R. Johnson, and Miriam R.L. Petruck. 2003. Background to FrameNet. *International Journal of Lexicography,* 16, pp. 235-250.

John R. Quinlan. 1993. C4.5: Programs for Machine Learning. *Morgan Kaufmann Publishers.* 302 p.

Stephan Oepen, Marco Kuhlmann, Yusuke Miyao, Daniel Zeman, Dan Flickinger, Jan Hajic, Angelina Ivanova, and Yi Zhang. 2014. SemEval 2014 Task 8: Broad-Coverage Semantic Dependency Parsing. *Proceedings of the 8th In-ternational Workshop on Semantic Evaluation (SemEval-2014)*, pp. 63-72.

Yantao Du, Fan Zhang, Weiwei Sun, and Xiaojun Wan. 2014. Peking: Profiling Syntactic Tree Parsing Techniques for Se-mantic Graph Parsing. *Proceedings of the 8th In-ternational Workshop on Semantic Evaluation (SemEval-2014)*, pp. 459-464.

Turku: Semantic Dependency Parsing as a Sequence Classification

Jenna Kanerva[1,2], **Juhani Luotolahti**[1], **Filip Ginter**[1]
[1] Department of Information Technology, University of Turku, Finland
[2] University of Turku Graduate School (UTUGS), Turku, Finland
jmnybl,mjluot,figint@utu.fi

Abstract

This paper presents the University of Turku entry to the SemEval-2015 task on Broad-Coverage Semantic Dependency Parsing. The system uses an existing transition-based parser as a sequence classifier to jointly predict all arguments of one candidate predicate at a time. Compared to our 2014 entry, the 2015 system gains about 3pp in terms of F-score for a fraction of the development time. Depending on the subtask, the difference between our entry and the winning system ranges between 1 and 5pp.

1 Introduction

The SemEval-2015 task on Broad-Coverage Semantic Dependency Parsing is a continuation to the semantic parsing shared task organized for the first time in 2014. The objective of the shared task is to produce a rich semantic analysis for a given sentence in three distinct annotation formats. In contrast to the 2014 task, this year predicate disambiguation and two additional languages are included: Czech data from the Prague Czech–English Dependency Treebank (Hajič et al., 2012) and Chinese data from the Penn Chinese Treebank (Xue et al., 2005). For English and Czech also out-of-domain test data is provided in order to test the generalization ability of the systems.

The semantic parsing task includes three different tracks. In the closed track the systems must be trained using only the official training data, whereas in the open track all additional sources of information are allowed. Together with the training data the organizers provided also syntactic dependency parses produced in the Stanford Dependencies scheme (De Marneffe and Manning, 2008) with the dependency parser of Bohnet and Nivre (2012). In addition to the closed and open tracks, also a gold track is included, where gold standard dependency parses are given for both training and test data.

This paper describes our system used to take part in the open and gold tracks of the shared task. The system is a sequence classifier built on top of an existing dependency parser. The main idea behind the implementation is to turn the task of predicting all arguments for a single predicate to a sequence classification problem, but still process each predicate independently. Predicting one predicate at a time feels very natural when working with data annotated in PropBank style (Palmer et al., 2005), and since our main objective is to develop an SRL system optimized for Finnish PropBank (Haverinen et al., 2013), we did not want to merely follow the main methods from last year. Our system also requires syntactic analyses of the data, which is why we participated only on the tasks which allow their use (open and gold tracks). The system will be described in detail in Section 3.

2 Related Work

The main approaches in the 2014 semantic dependency parsing task (Oepen et al., 2014) relied on the methods developed in the context of syntactic parsing, and existing state-of-the-art dependency parsers were widely used. Systems using dependency parsers are mainly based on graph-to-tree transformations (Koller, 2014; Schluter et al., 2014), parsers able to produce directed acyclic graphs (Ribeyre et al., 2014; Kuhlmann, 2014), or a combination of these two (Du et al., 2014). The winner system of the 2014 open track is based on the graph-based dependency parser able to produce full non-projective graphs (Martins and Almeida, 2014).

The system we used to participate in the same task last year was a pipeline of three different support vector machine classifiers trained separately for dependency detection, role assignment and top node prediction, where each governor–dependent pair was classified individually without any global view of the semantic structures (Kanerva et al., 2014a). A similar approach with the exception of using a structured support vector machine and therefore gaining a bit more of a global view to the problem was introduced by Jeffrey et al. (2014).

3 System Architecture

The main approach is based on the recent progress on syntactic dependency parsing, yet taking a completely different approach than the mainstream graph-to-tree transformation methods and DAG parsers discussed in Section 2. Our main focus is to process each predicate independently (i.e. other predicates and their arguments do not affect the decision), but when assigning arguments for one predicate, keep a global view of arguments already predicted for this particular predicate.

The system is built on top of the open-source Turku transition-based dependency parser[1] to obtain the full functionality of such a parser and to be able to freely modify it to fit to the needs of our approach. The Turku Dependency Parser is an implementation of the parser of Bohnet and Kuhn (2012), with full functionality of that parser, including e.g. online learning implemented with the generalized perceptron (Collins, 2002), beam search and graph-based completion features, and the full feature representation taken from the Bohnet and Nivre (2012).

3.1 Data Processing

Before training the parser, the data is processed to meet the requirements of the standard, off-the-shelf dependency parsers. As the arguments are predicted separately for each predicate, semantic graphs can be subtracted into several smaller units where each subgraph preserves the semantic arguments of one particular predicate. This means that each sentence is turned into as many pseudotrees as there are tokens in the sentence, where each token in turns acts as a candidate predicate and preserves only its own arguments and all other relations are dropped from this particular pseudotree. These pseudotrees are finalized by attaching all other tokens to the candidate predicate with an empty relation type *NOTARG*, which at the same time causes the candidate predicate to be the root token of the tree. Since the data does not include self-loops or multiple arguments between the same governor and dependent pair, this transformation can be made without losing any information. These pseudotrees created from one sentence can again be merged into a one semantic graph by just preserving the real semantic relations and leaving out the empty *NOTARG* relations.

As will be explained later, syntactic parses are a major source of features. For English, the syntactic parses are obtained from the companion and gold data provided by the organizers. Since for Czech and Chinese no companion data was available, the Czech syntactic representation is obtained using the MaltParser (Nivre et al., 2007) trained on the training section of the Prague Dependency Treebank (Hajič et al., 2000) and the Chinese analysis is acquired using DuDuPlus, a graph-based dependency parser (Chen et al., 2009) with a model trained on the training section of the Chinese Treebank (Xue et al., 2005).

3.2 Transition System

Since the structure of the input trees is completely flat (i.e. all words are attached to the sentence root, which is the predicate under inspection) the transition system of the parser can be simplified substantially. For every token other than the root, only the relation type must be predicted (using the *NOTARG* relation for tokens which are not arguments of this particular predicate). Thus, the transition system is modified to keep the root token always in the parsing stack, and one by one taking the next token from the queue, predicting its relation type and reducing it from the stack in a single operation.

Since the simplified transition system requires that the root token is in the stack already when the

[1] `https://github.com/jmnybl/Turku-Dependency-Parser`

parsing starts, the order of the tokens in the parsing queue must be manipulated. Manipulating the parsing queue also changes the order in which the predictions are made and since the parser is beam searched and the system has an ability to recover from a wrong prediction made earlier on, the different order of predictions may affect the final sequence of predictions. Two different approaches are tested. First and by far the simplest method is to use the normal linear order of the tokens and just remove the sentence root from the queue (run 1 in the official results). Second method is to reorder the tokens based on the syntactic distance, where the tokens closest to sentence root in the syntactic tree are first in the queue (and thus their relations are also predicted first) (run 2 in the official results). The idea behind this is to assume that tokens which are most likely to be arguments of the predicate are close to it in the syntactic representation and therefore predicted first. Official results showed that the first method performed better and therefore all numbers reported in this paper are based on the first run.

3.3 Feature Generation

The basic features used are based on the standard features of dependency parsers. However, few modifications to the parser feature representation were made. The function of the graph-based completion features is to model the partial structures of the tree already built at any given point. Since in the simplified transition system all tokens are forced to be dependents of the sentence root, taking into account all created relations would not distinguish semantically meaningful tokens from all other tokens (as is in the case of syntactic parsing where only real syntactic dependents are attached to any given token). Thus, tokens attached with the empty relation *NOTARG* are discarded and the graph-based completion features are created only from the real semantic relations.

Additional features are created from the syntactic structure of the sentence. The most important feature extracted from the syntactic tree is the path between the predicate and the potential argument. Two variations of the syntactic path are used; the dependency types and the part-of-speech tags between the two tokens. If the distance of the tokens is smaller than seven dependencies, full paths are used as features, otherwise only the beginning and the end of the path are used. Finally, from each aforementioned path all dependency type and part-of-speech tag trigrams are created.

	P	R	F	UF
Open in-domain				
DM	87.80	84.60	86.17	88.07
PAS	91.38	89.87	90.62	91.91
PSD	76.10	71.32	73.63	86.44
Overall	85.09	81.93	83.47	88.81
Open out-of-domain				
DM	81.54	76.63	79.01	81.68
PAS	86.95	84.98	85.95	87.83
PSD	74.92	68.55	71.59	86.54
Overall	81.14	76.72	78.85	85.35

Table 1: English open track (in-domain & out-of-domain) results in terms of precision (P), recall (R), labeled F-score (F) and unlabeled F-score (UF).

3.4 Top Node and Sense Prediction

Prediction of top nodes and predicate senses are implemented as separate steps and carried out after the argument prediction. The top nodes are predicted in the same manner as in our 2014 system (Kanerva et al., 2014a), where a support vector classifier is trained to classify individual tokens.

Predicate senses are predicted with the approach introduced by Kanerva and Ginter (2014), where vector space representations of tokens are used to calculate an average vector to represent each individual sense. Then for each predicate the sense is assigned by calculating a vector to represent this particular predicate and taking the sense which maximizes the cosine similarity of the predicate vector and the sense vector.

4 Results

The final system performance is shown in Table 1. The overall labeled F-score in the English in-domain data is 83.47%. When compared to our overall score in the 2014 shared task (overall labeled F-score 80.49%) a clear improvement of 3pp can be seen. This reflects the fact that predicting all arguments for a single predicate as a sequence is better than predicting them independently. The same behavior can be seen also from the methods using pure syntactic dependency parsing techniques, which have been shown to achieve the current state-of-the-art perfor-

	P	R	F	UF
Czech Open				
ID	77.53	73.20	75.30	83.03
OOD	65.11	62.35	63.70	83.10
Chinese Open				
ID	80.81	78.51	79.64	81.36

Table 2: Results for Czech and Chinese data in the open track. The Czech data is in PSD format and includes both in-domain (ID) and out-of-domain (OOD) test sets, whereas the Chinese data is in PAS format and has only in-domain test set.

	DM	PAS	PSD	Overall
Gold in-domain				
SD	88.29	**95.58**	**76.57**	86.81
DB	**93.88**	92.63	75.00	87.17
Overall-max				88.68
Gold out-of-domain				
SD	82.11	**92.92**	**75.47**	83.50
DB	**88.60**	88.93	73.43	83.65
Overall-max				85.66

Table 3: English gold track (in-domain & out-of-domain) results in terms of labeled F-score when using Stanford Dependencies (SD) and DeepBank (DB) style syntactic annotations.

mance. From out-of-domain scores we see that our system performs clearly better on in-domain data, the overall labeled F-score being 4.6pp lower when tested with out-of-domain data. Czech and Chinese open track scores are shown in Table 2.

We also provide evaluation on gold syntactic trees (gold track) using both Stanford Dependencies and DeepBank syntactic representations.[2] As can be seen from the gold track results (see Table 3) our system clearly benefits from gold-standard syntactic analyses. When comparing the performances of two syntactic representations on different formats, we can see that the optimal syntactic representation for DM format is DeepBank, whereas Stanford Dependencies fare better on PAS and PSD formats. When the best-performing syntactic representation is chosen for each format, the overall benefit on in-domain data is 5.2pp and 6.8pp on out-of-domain data compared to the open track results. Out-of-domain results improving more than in-domain results points out that better syntactic analyses help the system make more universal decisions.

[2]Unfortunately, Enju parses are not included since we could not overcome some of the problems they had in time.

The system is better at predicting relations between tokens close to each other. For example in the case of DM in-domain, relations between tokens next to each other are predicted at F-score of 92.04% while relations longer than 10 tokens at a rate of 65.11%. However, the gold syntactic analyses help predicting long relations. If we look only the relations which are ten or more tokens apart, the maximum improvement brought by gold standard syntax is 19pp for out-of-domain PAS and the minimum improvement is 6pp for in-domain DM.

5 Conclusions

Our entry in the shared task was based on an existing dependency parser, whose transition system we modified so as to essentially use the parser as a sequence classifier based on online learning and beam search. Compared to our last year's entry, the arguments of a single predicate are thus no longer predicted independently. This is accompanied by a notable gain in accuracy over the previous system which used similar features but predicted all arguments independently. From a technical point of view, basing the work on an existing parser was rather straightforward and the entire development was carried out over a period of less than two weeks.

Even though clearly better than our last year's system, the overall performance still leaves room for improvement. One possible direction would be to carry out a proper feature selection and improve the underlying machine learning algorithm of the parser to, for example, incorporate regularization. As the parser generates a large number of features optimized for syntactic parsing, it is likely that many of these are irrelevant and potentially harmful for the online-trained linear classifier.

Finally, we will evaluate the system on the Finnish PropBank data, and intend to apply it at scale to carry out SRL of the 3.2 billion token Finnish Internet Parsebank (Kanerva et al., 2014b).

Acknowledgments

This work was supported by the Emil Aaltonen Foundation and the Kone Foundation. Computational resources were provided by CSC – IT Center for Science. We would like to thank Dan Zeman for providing us the MaltParser model for Czech.

References

Bernd Bohnet and Jonas Kuhn. 2012. The best of both worlds: a graph-based completion model for transition-based parsers. In *Proceedings of the 13th Conference of the European Chapter of the Association for Computational Linguistics*, pages 77–87.

Bernd Bohnet and Joakim Nivre. 2012. A transition-based system for joint part-of-speech tagging and labeled non-projective dependency parsing. In *Proceedings of the 2012 Joint Conference on Empirical Methods in Natural Language Processing and Computational Natural Language Learning*, pages 1455–1465.

Wenliang Chen, Jun'ichi Kazama, Kiyotaka Uchimoto, and Kentaro Torisawa. 2009. Improving dependency parsing with subtrees from auto-parsed data. In *Proceedings of the 2009 Conference on Empirical Methods in Natural Language Processing: Volume 2 - Volume 2*, EMNLP '09, pages 570–579, Stroudsburg, PA, USA.

Michael Collins. 2002. Discriminative training methods for hidden markov models: Theory and experiments with perceptron algorithms. In *Proceedings of EMNLP'02*, pages 1–8.

Yantao Du, Fan Zhang, Weiwei Sun, and Xiaojun Wan. 2014. Peking: Profiling syntactic tree parsing techniques for semantic graph parsing. *SemEval 2014*, page 459.

Jan Hajič, Alena Böhmová, Eva Hajičová, and Barbora Vidová-Hladká. 2000. The Prague Dependency Treebank: A three-level annotation scenario. In *Treebanks: Building and Using Parsed Corpora*, pages 103–127.

Jan Hajič, Eva Hajičová, Jarmila Panevová, Petr Sgall, Silvie Cinková, Eva Fučíková, Marie Mikulová, Petr Pajas, Jan Popelka, Jiří Semecký, et al. 2012. Prague Czech-English Dependency Treebank 2.0.

Katri Haverinen, Veronika Laippala, Samuel Kohonen, Anna Missilä, Jenna Nyblom, Stina Ojala, Timo Viljanen, Tapio Salakoski, and Filip Ginter. 2013. Towards a dependency-based PropBank of general Finnish. In *Proceedings of the 19th Nordic Conference on Computational Linguistics (NoDaLiDa'13)*, pages 41–57.

Sam Thomson Brendan OConnor Jeffrey, Flanigan David Bamman, Jesse Dodge Swabha Swayamdipta Nathan Schneider, and Chris Dyer Noah A Smith. 2014. CMU: Arc-factored, discriminative semantic dependency parsing. *SemEval 2014*, page 176.

Jenna Kanerva and Filip Ginter. 2014. Post-hoc manipulations of vector space models with application to semantic role labeling. In *Proceedings of the 2nd Workshop on Continuous Vector Space Models and their Compositionality (CVSC) at EACL'14*, pages 1–10.

Jenna Kanerva, Juhani Luotolahti, and Filip Ginter. 2014a. Turku: Broad-coverage semantic parsing with rich features. In *Proceedings of the 8th International Workshop on Semantic Evaluation (SemEval 2014)*, pages 678–682.

Jenna Kanerva, Matti Luotolahti, Veronika Laippala, and Filip Ginter. 2014b. Syntactic n-gram collection from a large-scale corpus of Internet Finnish. In *Proceedings of the Sixth International Conference Baltic HLT 2014*, pages 184–191.

Alexander Koller. 2014. Potsdam: Semantic dependency parsing by bidirectional graph-tree transformations and syntactic parsing. *SemEval 2014*, page 465.

Marco Kuhlmann. 2014. Linköping: Cubic-time graph parsing with a simple scoring scheme. *SemEval 2014*, page 395.

Marie-Catherine De Marneffe and Christopher D Manning. 2008. The Stanford typed dependencies representation. In *Coling 2008: Proceedings of the workshop on Cross-Framework and Cross-Domain Parser Evaluation*, pages 1–8.

André FT Martins and Mariana SC Almeida. 2014. Priberam: A turbo semantic parser with second order features. *SemEval 2014*, page 471.

Joakim Nivre, Johan Hall, Jens Nilsson, Atanas Chanev, Gülsen Eryigit, Sandra Kübler, Svetoslav Marinov, and Erwin Marsi. 2007. MaltParser: A language-independent system for data-driven dependency parsing. *Natural Language Engineering*, 13(02):95–135.

Stephan Oepen, Marco Kuhlmann, Yusuke Miyao, Daniel Zeman, Dan Flickinger, Jan Hajic, Angelina Ivanova, and Yi Zhang. 2014. SemEval 2014 task 8: Broad-coverage semantic dependency parsing. In *Proceedings of the 8th International Workshop on Semantic Evaluation (SemEval 2014)*, pages 63–72.

Martha Palmer, Daniel Gildea, and Paul Kingsbury. 2005. The proposition bank: An annotated corpus of semantic roles. *Computational linguistics*, 31(1):71–106.

Corentin Ribeyre, Eric Villemonte de la Clergerie, and Djamé Seddah. 2014. Alpage: Transition-based semantic graph parsing with syntactic. *SemEval 2014*, page 97.

Natalie Schluter, Jakob Elming, Sigrid Klerke, Héctor Martınez Alonso, Dirk Hovy, Barbara Plank, Anders Johannsen, and Anders Søgaard. 2014. Copenhagen-Malmö: Tree approximations of semantic parsing problems. *SemEval 2014*, page 213.

Naiwen Xue, Fei Xia, Fu-Dong Chiou, and Marta Palmer. 2005. The Penn Chinese TreeBank: Phrase structure annotation of a large corpus. *Natural language engineering*, 11(02):207–238.

Lisbon: Evaluating TurboSemanticParser on Multiple Languages and Out-of-Domain Data

Mariana S. C. Almeida[*†] **André F. T. Martins**[*†]
[*]Priberam Labs, Alameda D. Afonso Henriques, 41, 2°, 1000-123 Lisboa, Portugal
[†]Instituto de Telecomunicações, Instituto Superior Técnico, 1049-001 Lisboa, Portugal
{atm,mla}@priberam.pt

Abstract

As part of the SemEval-2015 shared task on Broad-Coverage Semantic Dependency Parsing, we evaluate the performace of our last year's system (*TurboSemanticParser*) on multiple languages and out-of-domain data. Our system is characterized by a feature-rich linear model, that includes scores for first and second-order dependencies (arcs, siblings, grandparents and co-parents). For decoding this second-order model, we solve a linear relaxation of that problem using alternating directions dual decomposition (AD^3). The experiments have shown that, even though the parser's performance in Chinese and Czech attains around 80% (not too far from English performance), domain shift is a serious issue, suggesting domain adaptation as an interesting avenue for future research.

1 Introduction

The last years have witnessed a continuous progress in statistical multilingual models for syntax, thanks to shared tasks such as CoNLL 2006-7 (Buchholz and Marsi, 2006; Nivre et al., 2007) and, more recently, SPMRL 2013-14 (Seddah et al., 2013; Seddah et al., 2014). As a global trend, we observe that models that incorporate rich global features are typically more accurate, even if pruning is necessary or decoding needs to be approximate (McDonald et al., 2006; Koo and Collins, 2010; Bohnet and Nivre, 2012; Martins et al., 2009, 2013). The same rationale applies to **semantic dependency parsing**, also a structured prediction problem, but where the output variable is a **semantic graph**, rather than a syntactic tree. Indeed, the best performing systems in last year shared task on broad-coverage semantic dependency parsing follow this principle (Oepen et al., 2014). This year, a new challenge was put forth: how to handle multiple languages and out-of-domain data?

Our proposed parser (§2) is essentially the same that we submitted in the previous year to the same SemEval task (Martins and Almeida, 2014), where we scored top in the open challenge and second in the closed track. This year, we report results using new out-of-domain and multilingual data (namely, Czech and Chinese, in addition to English). For the English language, we participated in the closed and open tracks, using as additional resources the syntactic dependency annotations provided by the organizers. For Czech and Chinese, we only addressed the closed track, since no companion data were provided for these languages. We did not participate in the gold track that uses gold-standard syntactic annotations; and we did not address the prediction of predicate senses.

2 Semantic Parser

For this year's shared task, we re-run the semantic parser that we developed last year, which is fully desc1ribed in Martins and Almeida (2014), on the new datasets. Since this parser was designed to be multi-lingual, it was straightforward to apply it to the languages introduced this year (Chinese and Czech), as well as on the out-of-domain data.

We briefly describe our semantic parser (which we dub *TurboSemanticParser* and release as open-source software[1]), and refer the interested reader to

[1]http://labs.priberam.com/Resources/TurboSemanticParser

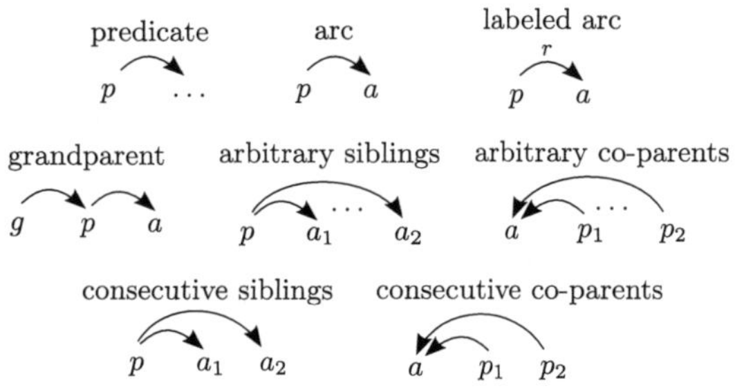

Figure 1: Parts considered by our semantic parser. The top row illustrate the *basic parts*, representing the event that a word is a predicate, or the existence of an arc between a predicate and an argument, eventually labeled with a semantic role. Our *second-order model* looks at some pairs of arcs: arcs bearing a grandparent relationship, arguments of the same predicate, predicates sharing the same argument, and consecutive versions of these two.

Martins and Almeida (2014) for further details.

The parser was built as an extension of a recent dependency parser, *TurboParser* (Martins et al., 2010, 2013), with the goal of performing semantic parsing using any of the three formalisms considered in the shared task (DM, PAS, and PSD). We have followed prior work in semantic role labeling (Toutanova et al., 2005; Johansson and Nugues, 2008; Das et al., 2012; Flanigan et al., 2014), by adding constraints and modeling interactions among arguments within the same frame; however, we went beyond such sibling interactions to consider more complex grandparent and co-parent structures, effectively correlating different predicates. The overall set of parts used by our parser is illustrated in Figure 1; note that by using only a subset of the parts (predicate, arc, labeled arc, and sibling parts), the semantic parser decodes each predicate frame independently from other predicates; it is the co-parent and grandparent parts that have the effect of creating inter-dependence among predicates; we will analyze the effect of these dependencies in the experimental section (§3).

For each part in our model (shown in Figure 1), we computed binary features based on various combination of lexical forms, lemmas, POS tags and syntactic dependency relations of words related to the corresponding predicates and arguments. Most of these features were taken from *TurboParser* (Martins et al., 2013), and others were inspired by the semantic parser of Johansson and Nugues (2008).

To tackle all the parts, we formulate parsing as a global optimization problem and solve a relaxation through AD^3 (Martins et al., 2011), a fast dual decomposition algorithm in which several simple local subproblems are solved iteratively. Through a rich set of features, we arrive at top accuracies at parsing speeds around 1,000 tokens per second. See Martins and Almeida (2014) for details on the model, features and decoding process that were used.

3 Experimental Results

All models were trained by running 10 epochs of max-loss MIRA with $C = 0.01$ (Crammer et al., 2006). The cost function takes into account mismatches between predicted and gold dependencies, with a cost c_P on labeled arcs incorrectly predicted (false positives) and a cost c_R on gold labeled arcs that were missed (false negatives). These values were set through cross-validation in the dev set, yielding $c_P = 0.4$ and $c_R = 0.6$ in all runs, except for the English PSD dataset in the closed track, for which $c_P = 0.3$ and $c_R = 0.7$.

As in the previous work, we speed up decoding by training a probabilistic unlabeled first-order pruner and discarding the arcs whose posterior probability is below 10^{-4}. This allows a significant reduction of the search space with a very small drop in recall.

Table 1 shows our final results in the test set, for a model trained in the train and development partitions. Note that we do not report scores for complete predications, since we did not predict predicate sense. Our system achieved the best final score in 3 out of the 4 tracks for the English language, and for the in-domain closed track in the Czech language. For the remaining 3 tracks we scored relatively close to the best system (Peking), which consists of an ensemble of various methods. For all languages, the runtimes are in par with last year's submission (around 1,000 tokens per second).

As expected, the scores obtained for out-of-domain data are significantly below those obtained with in-domain data. This degradation becomes particularly striking for Czech, with F_1-scores dropping more than 15%. This suggests that domain adaptation (Blitzer et al., 2006; Daumé III, 2007) is an interesting research avenue for future work. In ad-

	Our System							Peking
	UP	UR	UF	LP	LR	LF	Avg. LF	Avg. LF
Eng. DM, closed, id	91.13	87.88	89.48	89.84	86.64	88.21		
Eng. PAS, closed, id	93.12	91.14	92.12	91.87	89.92	90.88	85.15	**85.33**
Eng. PSD, closed, id	89.83	84.81	87.25	78.62	74.23	76.36		
Eng. DM, open, id	91.62	89.46	90.52	90.52	88.39	89.44		
Eng. PAS, open, id	93.50	91.93	92.71	92.45	90.90	91.67	**86.23**	–
Eng. PSD, open, id	91.27	86.16	88.64	79.88	75.41	77.58		
Eng. DM, closed, ood	86.78	80.74	83.65	84.81	78.90	81.75		
Eng. PAS, closed, ood	90.17	86.89	88.50	88.52	85.30	86.88	**81.15**	80.78
Eng. PSD, closed, ood	88.32	80.05	83.98	78.68	71.31	74.82		
Eng. DM, open, ood	87.56	83.52	85.49	85.79	81.84	83.77		
Eng. PAS, open, ood	90.42	87.91	89.15	88.88	86.41	87.63	**82.53**	–
Eng. PSD, open, ood	89.91	81.47	85.48	80.12	72.61	76.18		
Chi. PAS, closed, id	85.56	81.99	83.74	83.81	80.31	82.02	82.02	**83.43**
Cze. PSD, closed, id	90.15	81.55	85.63	83.52	75.54	79.33	**79.33**	78.45
Cze. PSD, closed, ood	86.58	75.97	80.93	67.93	59.61	63.50	63.50	**64.37**

Table 1: Final scores in the test data. For comparison, we show the scores of the Peking system – our best competitor.

dition, as found last year for English, the gap between labeled and unlabeled scores is much higher in the PSD formalism (for English and Czech) then it is for the DM and PAS formalism (for English and Chinese).

Finally, to assess the importance of the second order features, Table 2 reports experiments in the dev-set that progressively add several groups of features. We can see that second order features provide valuable information that improves the final scores. In particular, the higher-order features are extremely useful for Chinese and Czech, where we can observe gains of 1.5–2.0% over a sibling model that factors over predicates.

	UF	LF
Eng. DM, arc-factored	90.19	89.20
Eng. DM, arc-factored, pruned	90.13	89.16
+siblings	90.56	89.53
full system	91.21	90.12
Eng. PAS, arc-factored	92.42	91.52
Eng. PAS, arc-factored, pruned	92.44	91.54
+siblings	92.50	91.53
full system	92.98	91.98
Eng. PSD, arc-factored	87.54	79.69
Eng. PSD, arc-factored, pruned	87.47	79.73
+siblings	88.10	79.87
full system	89.82	80.08
Chi. PAS, arc-factored	81.10	79.49
Chi. PAS, arc-factored, pruned	81.06	79.43
+siblings	81.54	79.70
full system	83.48	81.62
Cze. PSD, arc-factored	84.27	79.77
Cze. PSD, arc-factored, pruned	83.96	79.39
+siblings	85.53	80.44
full system	87.90	81.82

Table 2: Unlabeled/labeled F_1 scores in the dev-set, progressively adding groups of features. English results are for the open track, while Czech and Chinese results are for the closed track.

4 Conclusions

Our system, which is inspired by prior work in syntactic parsing, implements a linear model with second-order features, being able to model interactions between siblings, grandparents and co-parents. We have shown empirically that, for all the three languages, second-order features that correlate multiple predicates have a strong impact in the final scores. However, there is a large drop in accuracy when moving to out-of-domain data.

Acknowledgements

We would like to thank the reviewers for their helpful comments. This work was partially supported by the EU/FEDER programme, QREN/POR Lisboa (Portugal), under the Intelligo project (contract 2012/24803), and by the FCT grants UID/EEA/50008/2013 and PTDC/EEI-SII/2312/2012.

References

John Blitzer, Ryan McDonald, and Fernando Pereira. 2006. Domain adaptation with structural correspondence learning. In *Proc. of Empirical Methods in Natural Language Processing (EMNLP)*, pages 120–128.

Bernd Bohnet and Joakim Nivre. 2012. A transition-based system for joint part-of-speech tagging and labeled non-projective dependency parsing. In *Proc. of the Empirical Methods in Natural Language Processing (EMNLP)*, pages 1455–1465.

Sabine Buchholz and Erwin Marsi. 2006. CoNLL-X shared task on multilingual dependency parsing. In *Proc. Int. Conf. on Natural Language Learning (CoNLL)*, pages 149–164.

Koby Crammer, Ofer Dekel, Joseph Keshet, Shai Shalev-Shwartz, and Yoram Singer. 2006. Online passive-aggressive algorithms. *Journal of Machine Learning Research*, 7:551–585.

Dipanjan Das, André F. T. Martins, and Noah A. Smith. 2012. An exact dual decomposition algorithm for shallow semantic parsing with constraints. In *Proc. of First Joint Conference on Lexical and Computational Semantics (*SEM 2012)*, pages 209–217.

Hall Daumé III. 2007. Frustratingly easy domain adaptation. In *Proc. of Annual Meeting of the Association for Computational Linguistics (ACL)*, pages 256–263.

Jeffrey Flanigan, Sam Thomson, Jaime Carbonell, Chris Dyer, and Noah A. Smith. 2014. A discriminative graph-based parser for the abstract meaning representation. In *Proc. of the Annual Meeting of the Association for Computational Linguistics*, pages 1426–1436.

Richard Johansson and Pierre Nugues. 2008. Dependency-based syntactic–semantic analysis with PropBank and NomBank. *Int. Conf. on Natural Language Learning (CoNLL)*, pages 183–187.

Terry Koo and Michael Collins. 2010. Efficient third-order dependency parsers. In *Proc. of Annual Meeting of the Association for Computational Linguistics (ACL)*, pages 1–11.

André F. T. Martins and Mariana S. C. Almeida. 2014. Priberam: A turbo semantic parser with second order features. In *Proc. of the 8th Int. Workshop on Semantic Evaluation (SemEval 2014)*, pages 471–476.

André F. T. Martins, Noah A. Smith, and Eric P. Xing. 2009. Concise integer linear programming formulations for dependency parsing. In *Proc. of Annual Meeting of the Association for Computational Linguistics (ACL)*, pages 342–350.

André F. T. Martins, Noah A. Smith, Eric P. Xing, Pedro M. Q. Aguiar, and Mário A. T. Figueiredo. 2010. Turbo parsers: Dependency parsing by approximate variational inference. In *Proc. of Empirical Methods for Natural Language Processing (EMNLP)*, pages 34–44.

André F. T. Martins, Noah A. Smith, Pedro M. Q. Aguiar, and Mário A. T. Figueiredo. 2011. Dual decomposition with many overlapping components. In *Proc. of Empirical Methods for Natural Language Processing (EMNLP)*, pages 238–249.

André F. T. Martins, Miguel B. Almeida, and Noah A. Smith. 2013. Turning on the turbo: Fast third-order non-projective turbo parsers. In *Proc. of the Annual Meeting of the Association for Computational Linguistics (ACL)*, pages 617–622.

Ryan McDonald, Kevin Lerman, and Fernando Pereira. 2006. Multilingual dependency analysis with a two-stage discriminative parser. In *Proc. of Int. Conf. on Natural Language Learning (CoNLL)*, pages 216–220.

Joakim Nivre, Johan Hall, Sandra Kübler, Ryan McDonald, Jens Nilsson, Sebastian Riedel, and Deniz Yuret. 2007. The CoNLL 2007 shared task on dependency parsing. In *Proc. of the CoNLL Shared Task Session of Empirical Methods for Natural Language Processing*, volume 7, pages 915–932.

Stephan Oepen, Marco Kuhlmann, Yusuke Miyao, Daniel Zeman, Dan Flickinger, Jan Hajič, Angelina Ivanova, and Yi Zhang. 2014. Semeval 2014 task 8: broad-coverage semantic dependency parsing. In *Proc. of the 8th Int. Workshop on Semantic Evaluation (SemEval 2014)*, pages 63–72.

Djamé Seddah, Reut Tsarfaty, Sandra Kübler, Marie Candito, Jinho D. Choi, Richárd Farkas, Jennifer Foster, Iakes Goenaga, Koldo Gojenola, Yoav Goldberg, et al. 2013. Overview of the SPMRL 2013 shared task: cross-framework evaluation of parsing morphologically rich languages. In *Proc. of the 4th Workshop on Statistical Parsing of Morphologically Rich Languages (SPMRL 2013)*, pages 146–182.

Djamé Seddah, Sandra Kübler, and Reut Tsarfaty. 2014. Introducing the SPMRL 2014 shared task on parsing morphologically-rich languages. In *Proc. of the 5th Workshop on Statistical Parsing of Morphologically Rich Languages (SPMRL 2014)*, pages 23–29.

Kristina Toutanova, Aria Haghighi, and Christopher D. Manning. 2005. Joint learning improves semantic role labeling. In *Proc. of the Annual Meeting of the Association for Computational Linguistics (ACL)*, pages 589–596.

Author Index

Association for Computational Linguistics
209 N. Eighth Street
Stroudsburg, Pennsylvania 18360

CURRAN ASSOCIATES INC
proceedings.com